PENGUIN REFERENCE BOOKS

THE PENGUIN
ENGLISH DICTIONARY

GEORGE NORMAN GARMONSWAY, M.A. (Cantab.),
F.S.A., F.R.HIST.S., became Professor of English
Language in the University of London, King's
College, in 1956, and was Professor Emeritus from
1965 until his death in February 1967. He was a
member of several learned societies, including the
Executive Committee of the English Association,
and on two occasions was a visiting professor of
English in American universities; in 1965–7 he was a
visiting professor in the University of Toronto. In
addition to papers and reviews in learned journals, he
published *An Early Norse Reader*, *Ælfric's Colloquy*, a
translation of *The Anglo-Saxon Chronicle*, *Canute
and his Empire* and *Beowulf and its Analogues* (written
in collaboration with Jacqueline Simpson, who
completed it after his death).

JACQUELINE SIMPSON, who worked with Professor
Garmonsway on *The Penguin English Dictionary* both
on the first edition and on the present revised and
enlarged edition, gained her B.A. and M.A. degrees in
the University of London, at Bedford College and
at King's College, and was awarded a D.Litt. of the
University of London in 1980. She is a member of
the Viking Society and the Folklore Society, and has
published articles and reviews, mainly on folklore
and Old Icelandic literature, in learned journals. Her
other publications include *The Northmen Talk*, *Everyday Life in the Viking Age*, *Icelandic Folktales and
Legends*, *Legends of Icelandic Magicians*, *The Folklore
of Sussex*, *The Folklore of the Welsh Border*, *The
Viking World* and *British Dragons*.

Twee. The last word this has been used on.

D0308338

THE PENGUIN
ENGLISH
DICTIONARY

COMPILED BY G. N. GARMONSWAY

WITH JACQUELINE SIMPSON

Third Edition

PENGUIN BOOKS

Penguin Books Ltd, Harmondsworth, Middlesex, England
Penguin Books, 40 West 23rd Street, New York, New York 10010, U.S.A.
Penguin Books Australia Ltd, Ringwood, Victoria, Australia
Penguin Books Canada Ltd, 2801 John Street, Markham, Ontario, Canada L3R 1B4
Penguin Books (N.Z.) Ltd, 182–190 Wairau Road, Auckland 10, New Zealand

—

First published August 1965
Reprinted September 1965
Second edition 1969
Reprinted 1971, 1972, 1973 (twice), 1974, 1975, 1976 (twice),
1977 (twice), 1978, 1979
Third edition 1979
Reprinted 1980, 1981, 1982 (twice), 1984

—

—

Printed and bound in Great Britain by
Cox & Wyman Ltd, Reading
Set in Monotype Imprint

TO
ROSALINDA

PREFACE TO THE FIRST EDITION

The aim of *The Penguin English Dictionary* is to capture and record *Modern English* and to present a selection of its vocabulary – i.e. the vocabulary in actual written and spoken use in the mid twentieth century. The emphasis in the selection of vocabulary has been away from archaisms and obsolete words towards the contemporary and colloquial, but a certain amount of the older vocabulary has been included so as to enable the reader to understand the writings of past centuries that do not demand specialized knowledge of obsolete forms and phrases.

As regards colloquialisms and slang, the aim has been to be as inclusive as possible. Such words form so important a part of current spoken English and of contemporary fiction that they must be represented as fully as possible in any dictionary that aims at recording the vocabulary of modern English. The distinction between colloquial and slang is necessarily arbitrary. Words and phrases which, though unsuitable for formal usage, are nevertheless in common use among a wide range of speakers and would be acceptable in a wide variety of social contexts are classified as colloquial; those which would be incomprehensible or unacceptable outside specific restricted groups (e.g. children, soldiers, jazz enthusiasts) are considered to be slang. The abbreviation (*coll*) implies that the word is more frequent in informal speech or writing, and that its use may be considered unsuitable in a serious context; the marking of a word as (*sl*) implies that its use is, *at present*, restricted to certain age-groups, or social or professional groups, and that it is unlikely to prove socially acceptable outside these groups. The marking of a word as (*vulg*) is a warning that it is considered highly offensive by most social groups.

Americanisms, too, have been included to an extent unusual in English dictionaries. Owing to the influence of the cinema, TV, journalism, etc., the influence of American vocabulary on English is widely diffused, and the foreign reader (and indeed the English reader too) frequently finds himself faced with Americanisms without necessarily realizing their origin or understanding their meaning. One can no longer attempt to impose nationalistic divisions on a language whose divergent branches are in such frequent and intimate contact. The indication (*US*) means that a word, or a particular meaning of a word, is not, *at present*, assimilated into British usage; words and phrases of American origin that have been assimilated are *not* so marked, even if their origin is remembered.

It should of course be remembered that the categories mentioned above are not intended to indicate final judgements, but merely to serve as guides to the feel or flavour that a word has for us today. The language grows from year to year, almost from month to month, both as regards new words and the development of new meanings in old words. The utmost effort has been made to do justice to this constant process of development, despite the realization that perfection in this matter is unobtainable. Information of any omissions will be gratefully received by the publishers.

The first definition given under a headword is, wherever possible, that of the most frequent *current* usage, not that which is oldest or which comes nearest to the language of origin of loan-words. After this, subsequent meanings are arranged in order of frequency of usage, the most specialized, obsolescent, or archaic meanings being put last and marked as such. The chief exceptions to this arrangement are certain terms that have both a scientific and a popular usage (e.g. *inferiority complex*), where, in the interests of accuracy, the scientific definition is sometimes given precedence over the loose popular usage. The symbol (~) is used to introduce derivatives of headwords. An abbreviation in brackets, for example (*chem*) or (*mus*). preceding a definition, introduces a specialized meaning of a word in the particular branch of knowledge indicated; for a list of such abbreviations, see pp. xiii–xiv.

Scientific and technical terms associated with obsolete theories have been reduced in number, but an effort has been made to include a wide range of those which are current and which occur most frequently without explanation in newspaper articles or broadcasts. For technical detail and expertise, readers are advised to consult other dictionaries in Penguin Reference Books as indicated by an appropriate abbreviation preceded by the symbol (>).

*

The editors are indebted to Mr W. S. Aitken, M.A., who devised and applied the pronunciation system which has been used.

St Catherine's Day
1964

G.N.G.
J.S.

PREFACE TO THE THIRD EDITION

I am grateful to all who offered additions or emendations for the improvement of this Dictionary, especially Mrs P. Garmonsway, Dr Hugh de Glanville, Professor Stuart E. Mann and F. H. Smith. Further suggestions will be gladly received.

1978

J.S.

PRONUNCIATION GUIDE

Although there is no attempt in this dictionary to give exact phonetic equivalents, the guide to pronunciation which is given for each word should offer a quick and practical indication of how it is normally pronounced. For this reason the usual accents, hyphens, and other diacritic marks, which can be so confusing to readers unfamiliar with the devices of phoneticians, have been avoided. Instead, a system of phonetic spelling is used which consists of letters and groups of letters the pronunciation of which is already familiar to the reader. No phonetic signs or symbols are used in this Dictionary other than the common letters of the alphabet, as can be seen from the table of symbols given on page xi. In addition, phonetic equivalents are given in the form of complete and undivided words, so that the pronunciation may be quickly and easily read off in a natural way,

e.g. jollification [jolifi*kay*shon]

The following notes taken in conjunction with the table on page xi should provide a sufficient explanation of the system of phonetic spelling used and how it works in practice:

1. After each headword in the dictionary its phonetic equivalent is given within square brackets, thus:

   easel [*ee*zel] *n* adjustable frame to support a blackboard or a picture.

   Phonetic equivalents are also given where necessary for variants, derivations, and irregular forms of headwords, thus:

   edifice [*ed*ifis] *n* a large building ∼ **edificial** [edi*fish*al] *adj*.

2. *Stressed syllables*

   In the phonetic equivalent which follows each word the stressed syllable is printed in italic type, thus:

   kerchief [*kur*cheef] *n* (*hist*) square piece of cloth folded and worn as head-covering by women; scarf.

   Only one stress is indicated for each word and no attempt is made to indicate secondary stress. In certain compound and polysyllabic words the position of the stress is sometimes determined by the position of the word within the sentence: in such cases only the most common form of pronunciation is given.

3. *Unstressed syllables*

   Although the pronunciation of unstressed syllables is almost impossible to represent without highly specialized phonetic symbols, the approximations given in this Dictionary should provide a useful guide. Many of these approximations, such as [-shon] for -tion and [-cher] for -ture, are used consistently throughout and will quickly become familiar. In general, unstressed syllables are represented as accurately as the system will allow, although in some cases the original spelling has been retained where it is not misleading, rather than introduce a more clumsy phonetic approximation. The following examples will show the extent to which phonetic equivalents have been attempted:

nation [*nay*shon] **picture** [*pik*cher] **envenom** [en*ven*om]
envious [*en*vi-us] **effulgence** [e*ful*jens] **gossamer** [*gos*amer]

4. *Words containing 'r'*

The two symbols [R] and [r] used in the pronunciation guide are intended to represent two distinct r-sounds of accepted English speech. [R] represents the consonantal sound which occurs initially and between vowels (as in 'rope' and 'curry'), whereas [r] represents the vocalic glide which may occur finally and between vowel and consonant (as in 'pure' and 'pair'). In some cases the latter symbol merely represents a modification of the normal vowel. It was considered useful, however, to represent these quite different r-sounds consistently throughout, and for this reason a separate section of the table on page xi is devoted to differentiating vowel syllables with a greater or less degree of r-quality. It is sufficient to remember that the letter groups used in that section of the table, such as [air] or [oor], are to be taken as single symbols representing a distinct English speech sound.

5. *Use of hyphens*

Hyphens are used to separate vowels that occur side by side in the phonetic spellings, when these are not intended to represent a single sound; and also to indicate when a single consonant represents two distinct sounds. Both principles are seen in:

jingoism [*jing*-go-izm]

They are also used to separate two distinct utterances of the same sound, e.g. at the end of one syllable and the beginning of the next; and to prevent possible confusion of adjacent consonants with a digraph.

disserve [dis-*surv*] **pothook** [*pot*-hook]

PRONUNCIATION TABLE

CONSONANTS

PENGUIN SYMBOL	USUAL PHONETIC	EXAMPLE	PENGUIN SYMBOL	USUAL PHONETIC	EXAMPLE
b	[b]	bit	R	[r]	rot
ch	[tʃ]	chin	r	[ɹ]	fear
d	[d]	dog			pure
f	[f]	fat	s	[s]	sit
g	[g]	got	sh	[ʃ]	she
h	[h]	hit	t	[t]	top
j	[dʒ]	jet	th	[θ]	thin
k	[k]	kill	TH	[ð]	this
l	[l]	lot	v	[v]	vat
m	[m]	mud	w	[w]	wit
n	[n]	not	wh	[hw]	whet
ng	[ŋ]	song	y	[j]	yet
nk	[ŋk]	lank	z	[z]	zeal
p	[p]	pin	zh	[ʒ]	vision

VOWELS

PENGUIN SYMBOL	USUAL PHONETIC	EXAMPLE	PENGUIN SYMBOL	USUAL PHONETIC	EXAMPLE
a	[æ]	cat	I	[ai]	die
a [unstressed]	[ə]	sofa	o	[ɔ]	got
aa	[a:]	spa	O	[ou]	tone
ay	[ei]	day	oi	[ɔi]	oil
aw	[ɔ:]	law	OO	[u:]	food
e	[ɛ]	get	oo	[u]	look
ee	[i:]	feet	ow	[au]	cow
ew	[ju:]	few	u	[ʌ]	cup
i	[i]	sit			

WORDS CONTAINING 'r'

PENGUIN SYMBOL	USUAL PHONETIC	EXAMPLE	PENGUIN SYMBOL	USUAL PHONETIC	EXAMPLE
aar	[a:ɹ]	hard	oor	[uəɹ]	tour, poor
air	[ɛəɹ]	pair	awr	[ɔ:ɹ]	lord, lore
eer	[iəɹ]	beer	ewr	[juəɹ]	pure
er	[əɹ]	enter	owr	[auəɹ]	power
ar	[aɹ]	artistic	ur	[ə:ɹ]	bird, urge
Ir	[aiəɹ]	fire			

xi

LIST OF ABBREVIATIONS

abbr	abbreviation	*eccles*	ecclesiastical	*Ir*	Irish
ac	acoustics	*econ*	economics	*iron*	ironical
adj	adjective	*eg*	for example	*Ital*	Italian
adv	adverb	*elect*	electricity		
aer	aeronautics	*emph*	emphasis,	*Jap*	Japanese
agr	agriculture		emphatic	*joc*	jocular(ly)
anat	anatomical	*eng*	engineering		
anthrop	anthropology	*ent*	entomology	*Lat*	Latin
antiq	antiquity	*esp*	especially	*lang*	language
ar	archaic	*euph*	euphemistic	*leg*	legal
arch	archaeology	*exc*	except	*lit*	literary
archi	architecture	*exclam*	exclamation	*liturg*	liturgical
art	article	*expl*	expletive	*log*	logic
arts	in the arts				
astrol	astrology	*fac*	facetious(ly)	*magn*	magnetism
astron	astronomy	*fem*	feminine	*masc*	masculine
attrib	attributive	*fig*	figurative(ly)	*math*	mathematics
Aust	Australian	*fr*	from	*mech*	mechanics
aux	auxiliary	*Fr*	French	*med*	medical
		freq	frequently	*met*	metaphysics
bibl	biblical	*fut*	future	*metal*	metallurgy
bioch	biochemistry			*meteor*	meteorology
biol	biology	*Gael*	Gaelic	*mil*	military
bot	botany	*gen*	genitive	*min*	mineralogy
bui	building	*geneal*	genealogy	*mot*	motoring
		gener	generally	*mus*	music
cap	capital letter	*geog*	geography	*myth*	mythology
carp	carpentry	*geol*	geology		
cer	ceramics	*geom*	geometry	*n*	noun
chem	chemistry	*ger*	gerund	*N*	North
cin	cinema	*Germ*	German	*nat*	natural history
class	classical	*Gk*	Greek	*naut*	nautical
coll	colloquial	*gramm*	grammar	*neg*	negative
collect	collective			*neut*	neuter
comm	commerce	*Heb*	Hebrew	*nom*	nominative
comp	comparative	*her*	heraldry	*Norw*	Norwegian
concr	concrete	*hist*	history, historical	*NT*	New Testament
conj	conjunction	*hort*	horticulture	*num*	numeral
cont	contemptuous			*numis*	numismatics
contr	contraction	*i*	intransitive		
corr	corruption of	*ie*	that is	*obs*	obsolete
		imp	imperative	*occ*	occasionally
Dan	Danish	*impers*	impersonal	*opp*	opposite
dat	dative	*incl*	including	*opt*	optics
def	definite	*ind*	indicative	*orig*	originally
dem	demonstrative	*indef*	indefinite	*orni*	ornithology
dial	dialect	*infin*	infinitive	*OT*	Old Testament
dim	diminutive	*inter*	interrogative		
		interj	interjection	*p/t*	past tense
					(preterite)

xiii

part	participle	*pres/part*	present participle	*surg*	surgery
pass	passive	*print*	printing	*Swed*	Swedish
path	pathology	*pron*	pronoun		
pej	pejorative	*pros*	prosody	*t*	transitive
pers	person	*psych*	psychology	*tel*	telegraphy
phil	philology			*theat*	of the theatre
philos	philosophy	*rad*	radio	*theol*	theology
phon	phonetics	*refl*	reflexive	*theos*	theosophy
phot	photography	*rel*	relative	*tr*	trade name and/or
phr	phrase	*rhet*	rhetoric(al)		registered trade-
phys	physics	*RC*	Roman Catholic		mark
physiol	physiology	*Rom*	Roman	*TV*	television
pl	plural	*Rus*	Russian	*typ*	typography
poet	poetic(al)	*S*	South	*US*	United States
pol	politics	*sci*	science	*usu*	usually
pol/ec	political economy	*Scots*	Scots, Scottish		
pop	popular(ly) but	*sculp*	sculpture	*v*	verb
	inaccurate(ly)	*sing*	singular	*v/aux*	auxiliary verb
Port	Portuguese	*sl*	slang	*v/i*	verb intransitive
pos	positive	*Sp*	Spanish	*v/t*	verb transitive
poss	possessive	*st*	statistics	*vet*	veterinary
p/part	past participle	*subj*	subjunctive	*vulg*	vulgar
pref	prefix	*suff*	suffix	*w*	with
prep	preposition	*superl*	superlative	*Wel*	Welsh
pres	present	*sur*	surveying	*zool*	zoology

*

References to other Penguin Dictionaries are made by the use of the following abbreviations

This dictionary includes some words that are or are asserted to be trade-names and/or registered trade-marks; they are indicated by the abbreviation (*tr*). In commercial usage such a word is capitalized, but in other writings the capital is often dropped once the word has been accepted into current English. Further, the trade-name, or trade-mark, proprietor may apply the capitalized word to different items made by him, and/or may disapprove of the word being applied to similar items made by others. Neither the use of the abbreviation (*tr*) nor the inclusion or omission of a capital is to be taken as making or implying any judgement on the legal status of the word in question.

A

a (1) [*ay*] the first letter of the English alphabet; (*mus*) the sixth note in the diatonic scale of C major; **A 1** (*US*, **A no. 1**) first-class, in perfect condition.

a (2), **an** [*a*, *an*] *indef art* one; *also used to express ratio*.

a- (1) *pref* engaged in doing.

a- (2) *pref* in, on, from, to, without *etc*.

aardvark [*aard*-vaark] *n* South African burrowing quadruped.

aardwolf [*aard*-woolf] *n* South African carnivorous quadruped akin to the hyena and civet.

Aaron's rod [airRonz-rod] *n* various plants with tall flowering stems, *esp* Golden Rod.

ab- *pref* off, from, away, away from.

ab- *pref* attached to names of practical electrical units to indicate corresponding electromagnetic unit > PDS.

aback [*abak*] *adv* backward; in the rear; (*of sail*) flattened against the mast by a head-wind > PDSa; **taken a.** (*fig*) surprised and disconcerted.

abacus [*abakus*] *n* calculating frame with balls sliding on wires; (*archi*) slab of stone which crowns the capital of a column.

abaft [*abaaft*] *adv* (*naut*) at or near the stern ~ **abaft** *prep* behind.

abandon [*aband*on] *v/t* and *refl* forsake; give up; depart from; yield oneself (to one's passions *etc*) ~ **abandon** *n* freedom from restraint.

abandoned [*aband*ond] *adj* forsaken; given up to evil influences; immoral, profligate.

abandonee [abandon*ee*] *n* underwriter who accepts the salvage of a wrecked vessel.

abandonment [*aband*onment] *n* act of abandoning.

abase [*abays*] *v/t* degrade, humiliate.

abasement [*abays*ment] *n* state of being abased; humiliation.

abash [*abash*] *v/t* cause to feel shy, disconcert.

abate [*abayt*] *v/t* and *i* lessen, reduce; grow less, weaken, become null and void; (*leg*) bring to an end ~ **abatable** *adj* capable of being abated.

abatement [*abayt*ment] *n* decrease, deduction; (*leg*) annulling, destruction; (*her*) a mark of dishonour in a coat of arms.

abattoir [*abat*waar] *n* (*Fr*) slaughter-house.

abb [*ab*] *n* yarn for the woof or weft in a web.

abba [*aba*] *n* father; title of a bishop in the Syriac and Coptic churches.

abbacy [*abesi*] *n* office, dignity, jurisdiction or tenure of an abbot.

abbatial [*abaysha*l] *adj* pertaining to an abbacy, abbot, or abbess.

abbé [*abay*] *n* title given to a French priest.

abbess [*abes*] *n* mother superior of a convent.

abbey [*abi*] *n* religious house of either men or women celibates, ruled over by an abbot or abbess; buildings housing such a community; church formerly part of an abbey; dwelling house converted from abbey buildings.

abbot [*abot*] *n* male superior or head of an abbey or monastery ~ **abbotship** *n* abbacy.

abbreviate [*abReevi*-ayt] *v/t* shorten ~ **abbreviator** *n*.

abbreviation [abreevi-*ay*shon] *n* shortening; a shortened form of a word or words; a contraction.

a b c [ay-bee-*see*] *n* the alphabet; a children's book with pictures of the alphabet; rudiments of a subject; a railway time-table with stations in alphabetical order.

abdicate [*abd*ikayt] *v/t* and *i* give up, renounce (office, dignity *etc*); resign sovereign power.

abdication [abdi*kay*shon] *n* act of abdicating.

abdomen [*abd*omen/abd*O*men] *n* belly, cavity of the body between the diaphragm and the pelvis > PDB.

abdominal [abd*o*minal] *adj* from or in the abdomen.

abduct [abd*ukt*] *v/t* take away illegally, kidnap.

abduction [abd*uk*shon] *n* act of abducting; (*log*) a syllogism with the minor premise merely probable.

abductor [abd*uk*ter] *n* one who abducts; (*anat*) a muscle which moves one part of the body away from another.

abeam [*abeem*] *adv* (*naut*) at right angles to the fore-and-aft line at the centre point of a vessel.

abed [*abed*] *adv* in bed, confined to bed.

abele [*abeel*/*ay*bel] *n* white poplar tree.

Aberdeen [aber*deen*] *n* variety of Scotch terrier.

aberrance [abe*R*ans] *n* a deviation; a moral lapse ~ **aberrancy** *n*.

aberrant [abe*R*ant] *adj* wandering from right path; (*biol*) with characteristics not in accordance with type; abnormal.

aberration [abe*Ray*shon] *n* deviation from the normal; moral or mental disorder; (*astron*) variation in the apparent position of a star or heavenly body, due to the motion of the observer with the Earth; (*opt*) failure of parallel rays of light to converge to a single point focus when passing through an optical system > PDP, PDS ~ **aberrational** *adj* eccentric.

abet (*pres/part* **abetting**, *p/t* and *p/part* **abetted**) [*abet*] *v/t* encourage, incite (*esp* to wrong-doing); instigate (a crime) ~ **abetment** *n*.

abettor, abetter [abet*er*] *n* one who abets (another's crime).

abeyance [abe*yens*] *n* temporary inactivity, suspension; **in a.** (*leg*) without a claimant ~ **abeyant** *adj* dormant.

abhor (*pres/part* **abhorring**, *p/t* **abhorred**) [ab*hawr*] *v/t* shrink from with disgust, loathe.

abhorrence [ab*ho*Rens] *n* act of abhorring; loathing, disgust.

abhorrent [ab*ho*Rent] *adj* repugnant, hateful; feeling abhorrence (of) ~ **abhorrently** *adv*.

abidance [ab*I*dens] *n* remaining, continuance; **a. by** conformity to.

abide (*p/t* and *p/part* **abode, abided**) [ab*I*d] *v/i* and *t* remain, stay, dwell; **a. by** hold to, remain faithful to; await; endure, stand up to; **I cannot a.** I cannot put up with.

abiding [ab*I*ding] *adj* permanent, enduring.

abigail [*abi*gayl] *n* (*obs coll*) lady's maid.

1

ability [abiliti] *n* power, capacity, proficiency.

abiogenesis [abI-ojenisis] *n* supposed production of living organisms from lifeless matter, spontaneous generation > PDB.

abiotic [abI-otik] *adj* without life or living organisms; inimical to life.

abject [abjekt] *adj* cast down, despairing; servile, despicable ~ **abject** *n* outcast, person of lowest condition ~ **abjectly** *adv*.

abjection [abjekshon] *n* degradation.

abjuration [abjewrRayshon] act of abjuring.

abjure [abjewr] *v/t* renounce on oath; recant an opinion; repudiate (a claim) on oath; **a. the realm** swear to leave the country for ever.

ablation [ablayshon] *n* removal, *esp* of part of the body through surgery; (*geol*) wearing away of rock by natural forces, of a glacier by melting.

ablative [ablativ] *adj* (*Lat gramm*) case used to express instrument, source, or cause; **a. absolute** construction of noun or pronoun and participle not dependent on any other word.

ablaut [ablowt] *n* (*phil*) variation of vowel-sounds, in relation to meaning, in forms of the same root; vowel-gradation.

ablaze [ablayz] *adv* on fire; (*fig*) aglow with dazzling brilliance; strongly excited.

able [ayb'l] *adj* being in a position to do something; competent, clever.

able-bodied [ayb'l-*bod*id] *adj* physically fit, robust; **a. seaman** one capable of all duties of seamanship and with special rating.

ablution [ablOOshon] *n* (*freq pl*) washing, cleansing (*esp* of person).

ably [aybli] *adv* cleverly, competently.

abnegate [abnigayt] *v/t* deny oneself, renounce; abjure ~ **abnegation** [abnigayshon] *n*.

abnormal [abnawrmal] *adj* departing from the type or standard unusual, peculiar > PDP ~ **abnormally** *adv*.

abnormality [abnawrmaliti] *n* deviation from standard, irregularity; thing or person deviating from a standard.

abnormity [abnawrmiti] *n* abnormality.

abo [abO] *n* and *adj* (*Aust coll*) aboriginal.

aboard [abawrd] *adv* into or on a ship; **all a.!** a warning of imminent departure; **close a., hard a.** alongside; **fall a.** collide with the side of a ship ~ **aboard** *prep* into or on (a ship).

abode (1) [abOd] *n* dwelling-place, residence.

abode (2) *p/t* of **abide**.

aboil [aboil] *adv* and *adj* boiling; (*fig*) bursting with passion.

abolish [abolish] *v/t* do away with, bring to an end ~ **abolishment** [abolishment] *n*.

abolition [abolishon] *n* act of bringing to an end, *esp* of a rule or law.

abolitionism [abolishonizm] *n* effort to secure abolition of unjust laws or customs, *esp* capital punishment or slavery ~ **abolitionist** *n* and *adj*.

A-bomb [ay-bom] *n* atomic bomb.

abominable [abominab'l] *adj* hateful, detestable ~ **abominableness** *n* ~ **abominably** *adv*.

abominate [abominayt] *v/t* loathe, detest.

abomination [abominayshon] *n* abhorrence, detestation; detestable thing; degrading practice.

aboriginal [aborijinal] *adj* belonging to a country from the most primitive time known; dwelling in a country before later colonists arrived ~ **aboriginal** *n* aborigine.

aborigine [aborijinee] *n* original inhabitant of a country; indigenous animal or plant.

abort [abawrt] *v/i* and *t* miscarry; cause a miscarriage to; (*biol*) undergo arrested development; (*fig*) come to nothing, fail; cancel prematurely because of accident or emergency.

abortion [abawrshon] *n* deliberate termination of pregnancy, act of causing a foetus to die or of removing an immature foetus; spontaneous miscarriage, *esp* of cattle; (*med*) delivery of foetus less than twenty-eight weeks old; (*biol*) arrest of development; (*fig*) failure of a project to develop; (*ar*) dwarf or misshapen person.

abortionist [abawrshonist] *n* person who deliberately terminates a pregnancy.

abortive [abawrtiv] *adj* (*of plans*) fruitless, coming to nothing ~ **abortive** *n* medicine to produce abortion ~ **abortively** *adv* ~ **abortiveness** *n*.

aboulia, abulia [abOOli-a] *n* (*path*) inability to make or to act on decisions.

abound [abownd] *v/i* be plentiful; **a. in** have plenty of ~ **abounding** *adj*.

about [abowt] *adv* on all sides; in every direction; approximately; hither and thither, to and fro, up and down; in the opposite direction; (*naut*) on the opposite tack; **to the right a.** right round to the opposite direction; **much a.** more or less; **turn and turn a.** alternately; **a. to do** on the point of doing; **is he a.?** is he close at hand?; **out and a.** recovered after illness; **up and a.** out of bed and stirring ~ **about** *prep* surrounding, all round; in the vicinity of; in attendance on; concerning, with reference to; not far from; all round, all over.

about-face [abowt-fays] *n* complete reversal of opinion, behaviour *etc*.

above [abuv] *adv* overhead, higher up; higher on printed page; earlier in book; higher in rank; in heaven; **over and a.** in addition ~ **above** *prep* on the top of, vertically over; higher up; in addition to; **a. oneself** conceited; elated ~ **above** *adj* preceding, previous; **the a. (words)** the statement just made.

aboveboard [abuvbawrd] *adv* and *adj* without concealment, fair, honourable.

abracadabra [abRakadabRa] *n* a spell, charm or magic word; an incantation; gibberish.

abradant [abRaydent] *n* substance for rubbing or grinding down surfaces.

abrade [abRayd] *v/t* wear down by rubbing; rub away from.

abranchiate [abRanki-it] *adj* (*zool*) without gills.

abrasion [abRayzhon] *n* act of wearing or rubbing away; grazed portion of skin.

abrasive [abRaysiv] *adj* causing abrasion; harsh, ruthless ~ **abrasive** *n* substance used for scratching, grinding, or polishing.

abreact [abRee-akt] *v/t* (*psych*) release by abreaction.

abreaction [abRi-akshon] *n* (*psych*) release of a repressed emotion by reliving in imagination the original experience.

abreast [abRest] *adv* side by side, on a level with; **a. of** (with) keeping up with, up to date.

abridge [abRij] *v/t* shorten, epitomize; lessen.

abridg(e)ment [ab*Rij*ment] *n* act of abridging; abridged version; summary, précis.

abroach [ab*ROch*] *adv* and *adj* (*of a cask*) pierced so as to let out the liquor; (*of ideas etc*) circulating freely, afoot.

abroad [ab*Rawd*] *adv* in or into foreign lands; over a wide space; widely; out in the open air; not in one's own house; wide of the truth.

abrogate [*ab*ROgayt] *v/t* repeal, annul ~ **abrogation** [abROg*ayshon*] *n*.

abrupt [ab*Rupt*] *adj* sudden, unexpected; hasty, brusque; disconnected; steep; (*geol*) cropping out suddenly; (*bot*) not tapering.

abruption [ab*Rup*shon] *n* breaking away of part of a mass.

abruptly [ab*Rupt*li] *adv* in an abrupt way.

abruptness [ab*Rupt*nis] *n* quality of being abrupt.

abscess [*abs*es] *n* a collection of pus formed within or upon the body.

abscind [abs*ind*] *v/t* cut off.

abscissa (*pl* **abscissae**) [abs*isa*] *n* horizontal line of reference in fixing the position of a point > PDP PDS.

abscission [abs*izhon*] *n* cutting off.

abscond [abs*kond*] *v/i* go away hurriedly into concealment, *gener* to evade the law.

absence [*abs*ens] *n* state of being away; duration of this state; lack, non-existence; **a. of mind** inattention due to concentration on other matters.

absent [*abs*ent] *adj* not present; absent-minded; not existing, lacking ~ **absent** [abs*ent*] *v/refl* stay away, not be present.

absentee [absent*ee*] *n* one who is not present; one who is continually absent from duty; landlord who does not live on his estate.

absenteeism [absent*ee*-izm] *n* state of being an absentee; habitual unjustified absence from work.

absent-minded [absent-*mIn*did] *adj* inattentive owing to concentration on other matters ~ **absent-mindedly** *adv* ~ **absent-mindedness** *n*.

absinth, absinthe [*abs*inth] *n* wormwood; liqueur distilled from wine mixed with wormwood.

absolute [*abs*olewt, *abs*oloot] *adj* complete, perfect; with unrestricted authority, despotic; not relative or measured by comparison with other things; unconditional; self-existent; **a. zero** lowest temperature theoretically possible, equal to $-273 \cdot 16^{\circ}$ C > PDS ~ **absolute** *n* that which exists in itself, without necessary relation to any other being > PDP; **decree a.** final stage in the granting of divorce.

absolutely [absolewt*li*/absoloot*li*] *adv* perfectly, without reservation.

absoluteness [*abs*olewtnes/*abs*olootnes] *n* state or quality of being absolute.

absolution [absol*ew*shon/absol*OO*shon] *n* forgiveness of sins declared by ecclesiastical authority; formula conveying this; forgiveness.

absolutism [*abs*olewtizm/*abs*olootizm] *n* (*pol*) the theory and practice of absolute government, despotism; (*theol*) the doctrine of predestination.

absolutist [*abs*olewtist/*abs*olootist] *n* one who favours absolute government; (*philos*) one who believes in the absolute identity of subject and object ~ **absolutist** *adj* practising or favouring absolute government, despotic.

absolve [abs*olv*/abz*olv*] *v/t* declare free from guilt, obligation, vow or oath, give absolution to.

absorb [abs*awrb*] *v/t* swallow up, incorporate; drink in; take in by chemical action; engross the attention of.

absorbable [abs*awrb*ab'l] *adj* capable of being absorbed ~ **absorbability** [absawrba*bili*ti] *n*.

absorbent [abs*awr*bent] *n* and *adj* (substance) which absorbs fluids.

absorbing [abs*awr*bing] *adj* swallowing, drinking in; (*fig*) engrossing, occupying the attention, very interesting ~ **absorbingly** *adv*.

absorption [abs*awrp*shon] *n* taking in, incorporation; engrossment (of the mind); sucking up (of fluids *etc*) > PDS; (*phys*, *rad*) loss of power.

absquatulate [absk*wo*tewlayt] *v/i* (*coll*) decamp, run away.

abstain [abst*ayn*] *v/i* refrain (from).

abstainer [abst*ayn*er] *n* one who does not take intoxicants.

abstemious [abst*eemi*-us] *adj* sparing in food, drink or pleasure; temperate, not self-indulgent.

abstention [abst*en*shon] *n* act of refraining, *esp* from voting; abstinence; self-denial.

abstinence [*abs*tinens] *n* self-restraint, *esp* in food and drink; **total a.** refraining from all intoxicants ~ **abstinency** [*abs*tinensi] *n*.

abstinent [*abs*tinent] *adj* temperate in bodily pleasures, abstemious ~ **abstinently** *adv*.

abstract [*abs*tRakt] *adj* not connected with matter or material objects; ideal, theoretical; (*arts*) not representing any material object > PDAA; producing non-representational art; **in the a.** without considering special examples ~ **abstract** *n* part containing in itself the properties of the whole, essence; summary; abstract painting or sculpture ~ **abstract** [abst*Rakt*] *v/t* take away, withdraw; make a summary of ; (*coll*) steal.

abstracted [abst*Rak*tid] *adj* drawn off, separated; absent-minded ~ **abstractedly** *adv* ~ **abstractedness** *n*.

abstraction [abst*Rak*shon] *n* taking away, removal, pilfering; act of considering a thing independently of its attributes; a state of mental seclusion; a figment of the mind; absent-mindedness > PDP; (*arts*) a design which is non-representational in purpose.

abstractive [abst*Rak*tiv] *adj* having the power of abstraction; epitomizing.

abstruse [abst*ROOs*] *adj* hidden; deep, hard to understand, recondite ~ **abstrusely** *adv* ~ **abstruseness** *n*.

absurd [abs*urd*] *adj* unreasonable, ridiculous; obviously false; meaningless ~ **absurd** *n* that which is irrational, *esp* as a subject for drama.

absurdity [abs*urd*iti] *n* folly; example of folly, foolish statement.

absurdly [abs*urd*li] *adv* in an absurd way.

abulia see **aboulia**.

abundance [ab*und*ens] *n* plentifulness, superfluity; wealth; (*phys*) concentration of a particular isotope in a mixture of isotopes > PDS.

abundant [ab*und*ent] *adj* plentiful, ample; wealthy (in) ~ **abundantly** *adv*.

abuse [ab*ewz*] *v/t* make a wrong use of; maltreat; take unfair advantage of; revile ~ **abuse** [ab*ews*] *n* misuse; evil custom, corrupt practice; reviling, vituperation.

abusive [a*bewsiv*] *adj* grossly insulting; misapplied ~ **abusively** *adv* ~ **abusiveness** *n*.

abut (*pres/part* abutting, *p/t* and *p/part* abutted) [a*but*] *v/i* (*of land*) border (on); **a. on** (*of building*) stand with its end against.

abutment [a*but*ment] *n* junction, meeting end to end; (*archi*) masonry built up to resist the pressure of an arch.

abutter [a*but*er] *n* that which abuts; (*leg*) owner of adjoining property.

abysm [a*bizm*] *n* (*poet*) abyss.

abysmal [a*bizm*al] *adj* immeasurably deep, unfathomable; (*coll*) very bad ~ **abysmally** *adv*.

abyss [a*bis*] *n* very deep place; chasm; infernal regions; primeval chaos; subterranean waters.

abyssal [a*bis*al] *adj* unfathomable; belonging to the lowest depths of the oceans > PDG.

acacia [a*kaysh*a] *n* genus of trees or shrubs of *Mimosa* tribe.

academe [a*kadeem*] *n* (*poet*) academy.

academic [a*kadem*ik] *adj* of or like an academy, learned society or university; purely theoretical, unpractical; scholarly; (*of art*) not experimental, conventional ~ **academic** *n* member of the teaching or research staff of a university; scholar ~ **academically** *adv*.

academicals [a*kadem*ikalz] *n* (*pl*) college or university robes.

academician [a*kadem*ish*an*] *n* member of an academic society, *esp* the Royal Academy.

academy [a*kadem*i] *n* learned society or institution devoted to the study of arts and sciences; teaching institution ranking between a school and university; **Royal A.** a British association of artists of established merit, *usu* conservative and non-experimental > PDAA.

acajou [a*kazhoo*] *n* cashew.

acaleph [a*kal*eef/a*kal*ef] *n* jellyfish.

acanth, acanthus [a*kanth*, a*kanthus*], *n* genus of herbaceous plants with prickly leaves; (*arts*) formalized pattern based on acanthus leaves.

acardiac [a*kaard*i-ak] *adj* (*physiol*) without a heart.

acarpous [a*kaarp*us] *adj* (*bot*) not producing fruit.

acaudate [a*kawd*ayt] *adj* tailless.

accede [ak*seed*] *v/i* agree, assent; **a. to** assent to; enter upon; join.

accelerate [ak*sele*Rayt] *v/t* and *i* increase the speed of; cause to happen earlier; go faster ~ **accelerated** *adj*.

acceleration [ak*sele*Rayshon] *n* increase of speed; rate of increase of speed per unit of time > PDS.

accelerative [ak*sele*Rativ] *adj* tending to increase speed.

accelerator [ak*sele*Rayter] *n* that which increases speed; contrivance for increasing the speed of a motor engine; (*chem*) catalyst; (*phys*) machine for producing a stream of very high energy subatomic particles > PDS.

accelerometer [ak*sele*Rom*iter*] *n* instrument for determining the acceleration of an aircraft.

accent [ak*sent*] *n* quality of voice of one belonging to a certain nation, locality or class; characteristic manner of speech; prominence given to one syllable of a word, either by stress or by musical pitch; mark placed over a vowel to denote this; mark used to show the quality of a vowel sound, diacritic; (*mus, pros*) recurrent stress which marks

rhythm ~ **accent** [ak*sent*] *v/t* stress, emphasize; mark, make outstanding.

accentual [ak*sent*ewal] *adj* of or by accent.

accentuate [ak*sent*ewayt] *v/t* pronounce with emphasis; mark with written accent; give prominence to, heighten ~ **accentuation** *n*.

accept [ak*sept*] *v/t* and *i* take willingly, consent to take, receive with favour; undertake (office); believe, admit, consent to, concede; (*leg*) take responsibility for; (*comm*) agree to pay.

acceptability [ak*septa*biliti] *n* quality of being acceptable.

acceptable [ak*sept*ab'l] *adj* worthy of acceptance, agreeable, welcome ~ **acceptably** *adv* ~ **acceptableness** *n*.

acceptance [ak*sept*ans] *n* approval, favourable reception; (*comm*) agreement to pay.

acceptation [ak*sept*ayshon] *n* approval; recognized meaning.

accepter [ak*sept*er] *n* one who accepts what is offered; **a. of persons** one who shows partiality on personal grounds.

acceptor [ak*sept*awr] *n* (*comm*) one who accepts a bill of exchange, promising to pay it when due; (*phys*) imperfection or impurity in a semiconductor which causes conduction by holes > PDEl.

access [ak*ses*] *n* approach, means of approach; right of entrance (to); sudden attack (of illness or passion); easy of **a.** approachable.

accessary [ak*ses*aRi] *n* and *adj* (person) assisting a criminal but not taking part in the crime itself; accessory.

accessibility [ak*ses*ibiliti] *n* state or quality of being accessible.

accessible [ak*ses*ib'l] *adj* approachable, easy to reach; attainable; **a. to** open to ᵗhe influence of, amenable to.

accession [ak*sesh*on] *n* approach; act of attaining to (office, dignity, condition); addition, acquisition; assent, backing; (*leg*) increase in value.

accessional [ak*sesh*onal] *adj* additional.

accessorial [ak*ses*awRi-al] *adj* auxiliary, supplementary.

accessory [ak*ses*eRi] *adj* contributory, helpful though subordinate; helpful to the main effect, person or plan; accessary ~ **accessory** *n* that which helps a main effect *etc*; subordinate but useful person or thing; (*leg*) accessary; (*pl*) minor items of clothing, equipment *etc*.

accidence [ak*sidens*] *n* that part of grammar which deals with the inflexions of words; first steps in any subject.

accident [ak*sident*] *n* chance occurrence, unforeseen event; mishap; disaster; (*log*) property of a substance which is not part of its essential nature.

accidental [aksi*dent*al] *adj* occurring by chance, unexpected, casual; incidental; (*log*) pertaining to logical accident, not essential ~ **accidental** *n* (*mus*) sharp or flat prefixed to a particular note > PDM ~ **accidentally** *adv*.

accident-prone [ak*sident*-pROn] *adj* liable to suffer accidents because of abnormal carelessness, anxiety *etc* ~ **accident-proneness** *n*.

accipiter [ak*sipiter*] *n* bird of prey; (*surg*) bandage over the nose resembling hawk's claw.

accipitrine [ak*sipitrIn*] *adj* rapacious, hawklike.

4

acclaim [aklaym] v/t greet with applause; proclaim with applause ~ **acclaim** n applause, shout of approval.

acclamation [aklamayshon] n applause, shout of approval ~ **acclamatory** [aklamatoRi] adj.

acclimate [aklImet] v/t and i acclimatize.

acclimatization [aklImatIzayshon] n process of acclimatizing or becoming acclimatized.

acclimatize [aklImetIz] v/t and i habituate, or become habituated, to a new climate or to new surroundings.

acclivity [akliviti] n upward slope.

accolade [akOlayd/akOlaad] n ceremony of conferring knighthood by laying a sword on the shoulder of the recipient; (fig) public approval and honour; mark or reward indicating this.

accommodate [akomOdayt] v/t adjust, adapt; bring to agreement; supply (with some requisite); supply with board and lodging, receive into one's house.

accommodating [akomOdayting] adj obliging, conciliatory.

accommodation [akomOdayshon] n adjustment; adaptation; settlement of a difference; house, rooms etc; board and lodging; loan of money; **a. road** road used only for a limited purpose.

accompaniment [akumpaniment] n anything attending on or added to another; (mus) subsidiary part or parts of a musical composition supporting the voice or solo instrument.

accompanist, accompanyist [akumpanist, akumpani-ist] n (mus) one who plays the accompaniment.

accompany [akumpani] v/t and i go along with, travel with; (mus) play the subsidiary part of a musical composition for a singer or solo player.

accomplice [akomplis] n partner in evil-doing.

accomplish [akomplish] v/t complete, carry out.

accomplishable [akomplishab'l] adj that can be carried out.

accomplished [akomplisht] adj highly skilled; versed in the social arts and graces, talented.

accomplishment [akomplishment] n fulfilment; achievement; talent, artistic skill; intellectual or cultural achievement.

accord [akawrd] v/i and t agree, come to a settlement; grant, vouchsafe ~ **accord** n agreement, consent; harmony; **with one a.** unanimously; **of one's own a.** freely, without solicitation.

accordance [akawrdans] n accord, agreement.

accordant [akawrdant] adj in conformity.

according [akawrding] adv agreeing with; **a. as** in so far as, to the extent that; **a. to** by the account of, on the authority of; agreeing with, conforming to.

accordingly [akawrdingli] adv therefore; in agreement with that.

accordion [akawrdi-on] n portable musical instrument consisting of keys and bellows > PDM; **a. pleating** series of narrow parallel pleats.

accordionist [akawrdi-onist] n one who plays the accordion.

accost [akost] v/t open conversation with, address; solicit with immoral intent.

accouchement [akooshmaw(ng)/akooshment/akowshment] n childbirth, confinement.

account [akownt] v/t and i give a reckoning, estimate; **a. for** explain, answer for; (sport) deal with, make an end of ~ **account** n reckoning; statement of money due; (pl) reckoning of money received and paid; detailed statement of handling of money in trust; explanation; importance, esteem; description, narration; **of some a.** held in esteem; **on a. of** because of; **to one's a.** to one's advantage; **last a.** the Judgement; **current a.** a running account with a bank, to which payments are made, and from which sums are withdrawn on demand; **on no a.** for no reason, not at all; **call to a.** demand an explanation from.

accountability [akowntabiliti] n quality of being accountable.

accountable [akowntab'l] adj responsible; explainable ~ **accountably** adv.

accountancy [akowntansi] n profession of an accountant.

accountant [akowntant] n one who inspects and audits accounts.

accoutre [akOOter] v/t dress, array, equip.

accoutrement [akOOtRement] n (usu pl) equipment; (mil) equipment other than arms and dress.

accredit [akRedit] v/t invest with credit, authority; vouch for, sanction; provide with credentials; **accredited milk** milk guaranteed to be of an approved standard of quality.

accrete [akReet] v/t and i grow together by adhesion; adhere; cause to unite (to) ~ **accrete** adj formed by accretion; (bot) grown together by adhesion.

accretion [akReeshon] n increase in size, esp by uniting separate parts; anything added in this way; (leg) increase of a legacy through the death of a co-legatee ~ **accretive** adj.

accrue [akROO] v/i come as normal profit or by natural right, esp as interest on capital.

acculturate [akultewRayt] v/t cause (persons) to adopt customs etc from a foreign culture ~ **acculturation** n.

accumulate [akewmewlayt] v/t and i heap up; amass; grow into a mass; increase in bulk or numbers.

accumulation [akewmewlayshon] n process of accumulating; accumulated mass.

accumulative [akewmewlativ] adj arising from the addition of many particulars; invested at compound interest; acquisitive, given to hoarding.

accumulator [akewmewlayter] n one who accumulates; apparatus for collecting and storing electricity.

accuracy [akewRisi] n quality of being accurate.

accurate [akewRit] adj exact, correct ~ **accurately** adv.

accursed [akursid] adj lying under a curse; detestable; doomed to perdition, ill-fated.

accurst [akurst] adj accursed.

accusable [akewzab'l] adj liable to the charge (of); culpable.

accusal [akewzal] n an accusation.

accusant [akewzant] n an accuser.

accusation [akewzayshon] n act of accusing; crime or offence of which one is accused, charge.

accusative [akewzativ] n and adj (gramm) (case) of the direct object of a transitive verb or of certain prepositions ~ **accusatively** adv.

accusatory [akewzatoRi] adj pertaining to an accuser; suggesting an accusation.

accuse [a*kewz*] *v/t* charge with wrong-doing, impute guilt to; **a. of** charge with the fault of.

accustom [a*kustom*] *v/t* and *refl* make familiar by use or habit; get used (to).

accustomed [a*kustom*d] *adj* usual, customary.

ace [*ays*] *n* face of dominoes, dice, cards, containing a single point; (*coll*) one who is extremely skilful in a sport, *esp* skilful fighter pilot or marksman; **within an a.** of within a hair's breadth of; **service a.** (*lawn tennis*) service which opponent cannot return; **a. point** first point on backgammon board ~ **ace** *adj* (*coll*) extremely expert and successful.

acentric [a*sentrik*] *adj* (*geom*) without a centre, not centred.

acephalous [a*sefalus*] *adj* without a head; (*pros*) wanting the first syllable of the line.

acerbate [a*serbayt*] *v/t* embitter, exasperate ~ **acerbate** [a*surbayt*] *adj* embittered.

acerbic [a*surbik*] *adj* bitter, sour.

acerbity [a*surbiti*] *n* sourness of taste; bitterness of speech.

aceric [a*seRik*] *adj* pertaining to the maple; **a. acid** acid found in the sap of maple.

acescent [a*sesent*] *adj* turning sour , slightly sour.

acetabulum [a*sitabewlum*] *n* (*anat*) cup-shaped organ.

acetate [a*sitayt*] *n* a salt or an ester of acetic acid; (*pop*) cellulose acetate in the form of rayon.

acetic [a*seetik/asetik*] *adj* sour, of the nature of vinegar; **a. acid** the organic acid contained in vinegar > PDS.

acetify [a*setifI*] *v/t* and *i* ferment, turn into vinegar; become sour.

acetone [a*sitOn*] *n* colourless inflammable liquid used as a solvent > PDS.

acetose [a*sitOs*] *adj* sour, tasting like vinegar.

acetous [a*situs*] *adj* sour, acetose; **a. fermentation** chemical reaction by which sugar or alcohol is changed into vinegar.

acetylene [a*setaleen*] *n* (*chem*) ethyne; a colourless poisonous inflammable gas, made by the action of water on calcium carbide > PDS.

ache [*ayk*] *v/i* feel continuous pain, physical or mental; feel overwhelming desire (for, to) ~ **ache** *n*.

achene [a*keen*] *n* dry, one-seeded fruit.

achieve [a*cheev*] *v/t* attain, gain, carry out by one's own efforts.

achievement [a*cheev*ment] *n* carrying out, accomplishment; successful action > PDP; (*her*) escutcheon, hatchment.

achromatic [akR*Omatik*] *adj* (*opt*) colourless, not decomposing white light > PDS; (*biol*) not absorbing colour from a fluid.

achromatism [akR*Omatizm*] *n* quality of being achromatic.

achromatopsy [akR*Omatopsi*] *n* colour-blindness > PDS.

acicula (*pl* **aciculae**) [a*sikewla*] *n* (*biol*) bristle, spike; (*chem*) sharp-pointed crystal.

aciculate [a*sikewlayt*] *adj* provided with aciculae; having scratch-like markings.

acid [a*sid*] *adj* sour to the taste, tart; (*fig*) sour, testy, sarcastic; (*chem*) having properties of an acid; **a. drop** sweet made with sugar and tartaric acid; **a. salt** an acid in which only a part of the hydrogen has been replaced by a metal > PDS ~

acid *n* sour-tasting substance; (*chem*) substance often corrosive which contains hydrogen which may be replaced by a metal to form a salt > PDS; (*sl*) LSD or other hallucinogenic drug; **a. test** test of gold by means of acid; (*fig*) crucial test.

acid-head [a*sid-hed*] *n* (*sl*) one who frequently takes LSD or other hallucinogens.

acidic [a*sidik*] *adj* (*chem*) having properties of an acid; acid-forming.

acidify [a*sidifI*] *v/t* make sour, acid; (*chem*) convert into an acid.

acidity [a*siditi*] *n* sharpness of flavour; acid state of stomach.

acidly [a*sidli*] *adv* sourly; sarcastically.

acidness [a*sidnis*] *n* quality of being acid.

acidosis [a*sidOsis*] *n* acid condition of the blood.

acidulate [a*sidewlayt*] *v/t* flavour with acid ~ **acidulated** *adj* (*fig*) caustic, testy.

acidulous [a*sidewlus*] *adj* slightly acid; sour-tempered.

acierage [*aysi-eRij*] *n* process of plating a metal with a layer of steel.

acinose [asin*Os*] *adj* consisting of acini; resembling a cluster of berries.

acinus (*pl* **acini**) [a*sinus*] *n* (*bot*) drupel; fruit composed of clustered drupels; (*anat*) blind end of the duct of a secreting gland.

ack-ack [ak–*ak*] *adj* (*mil coll*) anti-aircraft.

acknowledge [aknol*ij*] *v/t* recognize, own to be true; admit the claim of; show gratitude for; notify the receipt of.

acknowledg(e)ment [aknol*ij*ment] *n·* act of acknowledging; expression of thanks, appreciation *etc*; notification of receipt.

aclinic [a*klinik*] *adj* without inclination, not dipping; **a. line** line joining the points where the magnetic needle does not dip, magnetic equator.

acme [*akmi*] *n* culminating point, highest degree.

acne [*akni*] *n* skin disease in which the blocking of sebaceous glands causes small pustules.

acolyte [a*kolIt*] *n* (*eccles*) one who attends on the priest during a religious service; attendant, assistant.

aconite [a*konIt*] *n* (*bot*) genus of poisonous plants; wolf's bane; drug extracted from this.

acorn [*aykawrn*] *n* fruit of the oak-tree.

acorn-cup [*aykawrn-kup*] *n* cup-shaped envelope in which the acorn grows.

acotyledon [akoti*leedon*] *n* (*bot*) plant with no distinct seed-lobes; cryptogam.

acoustic [ak*OOstik/akowstik*] *adj* pertaining to hearing or audibility; of or by sound-waves; designed to absorb sounds.

acoustics [ak*OOstiks/akowstiks*] *n* (*pl*) science of sound; qualities of a building enabling sound to be heard clearly within it > PDM.

acquaint [a*kwaynt*] *v/t* inform of; **be acquainted with** have knowledge of, know personally.

acquaintance [a*kwaynt*ans] *n* state of being acquainted (with); person whom one knows slightly; **make the a. of** get to know.

acquainted [a*kwaynt*id] *adj* on friendly terms, but not intimate; **a. with** having knowledge of.

acquiesce [akwi-*es*] *v/i* agree without hesitation; accept submissively; give in; **a. in** agree to, abide by.

acquiescence [akwi-*esens*] *n* willing agreement.

acquire [ak*w*Ir] *v/t* obtain, gain.

acquired [ak*w*Ird] *adj* gained through one's own exertions, experience or environment; not spontaneous, not natural.

acquisition [akwi*zi*shon] *n* act of acquiring; something acquired; something the obtaining of which is an advantage.

acquisitive [ak*wizi*tiv] *adj* eager to acquire things, greedy ~ **acquisitively** *adv* ~ **acquisitiveness** *n*.

acquit [ak*wit*] *v/t* and *refl* declare innocent of a charge; discharge, pay (a debt, claim); discharge one's duty, play one's part.

acquittal [ak*wit*al] *n* act of acquitting; verdict declaring innocence.

acquittance [ak*wit*ans] *n* discharge from a debt, *esp* when given formally in writing.

acre [ay*ker*] *n* measure of land comprising 4,840 square yards; **God's A.** a churchyard.

acreage [ay*keRij*] *n* number of acres (of a piece of land).

acrid [ak*Rid*] *adj* bitter to the taste; pungent, stinging; (*fig*) ill-tempered, sarcastic ~ **acridly** *adv* ~ **acridness** *n*.

acriflavine [akri*flayveen*] *n* (*chem*) yellow granular solid used in dilute solution as an antiseptic.

acrimonious [akRim*Oni*-us] *adj* bitterly angry, resentful ~ **acrimoniously** *adv* ~ **acrimoniousness** *n*.

acrimony [ak*Rimoni*] *n* bitterness, asperity of temper.

acrita [ak*Rita*] *n* (*pl*) (*zool*) animals without a distinct nervous system.

acrobat [ak*RObat*] *n* entertainer performing gymnastic feats.

acrobatic [akR*Obatik*] *adj* of or like an acrobat; agile ~ **acrobatics** *n* (*pl*) acrobatic feats.

acronym [ak*RONim*] *n* word made up from the initial letters of an organization, group *etc*.

acrophobia [akR*OfObi*-a] *n* dread of heights.

acropolis [ak*Ropolis*] *n* fortress on a height above a city, *esp* in ancient Greece.

across [ak*Ros*] *adv* from one side to the other; on (to) the opposite side; crosswise ~ **across** *prep* on (to) the opposite side of; from side to side of; **a. country** in a straight line, without following the roads; **come a.** meet by accident; (*coll*) yield information sought, confess; **get, come, put a.** reach an audience effectively; **put it a.** get even with, impose upon.

acrostic [ak*Rostik*] *n* poem in which the initial letters of consecutive lines spell out a word or phrase; puzzle in which the aim is to guess a series of words which will similarly spell out other words ~ **acrostic** *adj*.

acrylic [ak*Rilik*] *adj* **a. acid** a pungent acid derived from alkenes; **a. fibre, a. plastic, a. resin** types of synthetic materials derived from this ~ **acrylics** *n* (*pl*) synthetic substances from acrylic acid.

act [akt] *n* action, deed; decree made by a legislative body; major division of a play; variety turn; **a. of God** action of natural forces in causing disaster; **a. of grace** formal pardon granted by Act of Parliament; **put on an a.** (*coll*) behave insincerely for the sake of effect ~ **act** *v/t* and *i* perform (a play); represent (a character in a play), simulate; do things, fulfil functions; behave; **a. a part** behave hypocritically.

actable [akt*ab'l*] *adj* (*theat*) easy to act; effective when acted.

acting [ak*ting*] *n* carrying out into action; performing of plays ~ **acting** *adj* carrying out duties for, holding temporary rank or position.

actinic [ak*tinik*] *adj* produced by chemical action of sunlight.

actinides [ak*tinideez*] *n* (*pl*) (*chem*) group of radioactive elements including actinium > PDS.

actinism [ak*tinizm*] *n* property of the sun's rays by which chemical changes are produced.

actinium [ak*tini*-um] *n* radioactive metallic element found in pitchblende.

actino-chemistry [aktinO-*kemistRi*] *n* study of chemical changes caused by the sun's rays.

actinograph [ak*tinOgraaf*] *n* instrument for recording the actinic power of light.

actinolite [ak*tinOlit*] *n* variety of hornblende.

actinometer [aktin*omiter*] *n* instrument for measuring the heating power of solar rays; instrument for measuring the actinic effect of rays of light.

action [ak*shon*] *n* process of doing, exertion of energy; deed; (*in drama*) succession of events represented; manner of bodily movement; mechanism; legal process, lawsuit; battle; (*phys*) product of work and time; (*coll*) vigorous activity; **man of a.** one who acts vigorously; one who enjoys an active life; **a. painting** form of abstract painting made by splashing or dribbling paint on canvas > PDAA; **a. stations** (*mil*) positions to be taken up in readiness for battle.

actionable [ak*shonab'l*] *adj* giving ground for an action at law.

activate [ak*tivayt*] *v/t* move to action; (*phys*) make radioactive; (*chem*) aerate (sewage).

activation [akti*vayshon*] *n* process of activating; state of being activated.

active [ak*tiv*] *adj* brisk, energetic, agile; not contemplative; not passive; **a. deposit** radioactive material deposited on surfaces > PDS; **on the a. list** among those, *esp* in the armed forces, who have not retired; **a. verb** one which has for subject the person or thing performing the action ~ **actively** *adv*.

activist [ak*tivist*] *n* and *adj* (person) taking a vigorous part in a political movement.

activity [ak*tiviti*] *n* briskness, nimbleness; diligence, state of being busy; that at which one is busy; (*phys*) rate at which a radioactive substance disintegrates; (*pl*) actions, doings.

actor [ak*ter*] *n* performer in a play for stage, film, or television; one who performs an action.

actress [ak*tRes*] *n* female actor.

actual [ak*tew-al*] *adj* rea , literal; existing at the present moment.

actuality [aktew-*aliti*] *n* reality; realistic description; event of current interest.

actualize [ak*tew-alIz*] *v/t* make actual; realize in action.

actually [ak*tew-ali*] *adv* really, in fact; at present, now.

actuary [ak*tew-aRi*] *n* expert adviser on insurance risks and premiums on life-insurances ~ **actuarial** [aktew-*airRi-al*] *adj*.

actuate [ak*tew-ayt*] *v/t* cause to act, motivate.

actuation [aktew-*ayshon*] *n* motivation; state of being actuated.

7

acuity [akew-iti] *n* sharpness, intensity > PDP.

aculeus (*pl* aculei) [akewli-us] *n* (*zool*) the sting of an insect; (*bot*) a prickle.

acumen [akewmen] *n* mental acuteness.

acuminate [akewminit] *adj* (*biol*) pointed ~ **acuminate** *v/t* sharpen, give point to.

acuminous [akewminus] *adj* acute, marked by acumen.

acunation [akewnayshon] *n* process or technique of coining money ~ **acunator** *n*.

acupuncture [akewpunkcher] *n* pricking with a needle, *esp* for remedial purposes.

acushla [akooshla] *adj* (*Ir*) darling.

acute [akewt] *adj* ending in a sharp point; keen-witted; (*of emotions*) keen, intense; (*of senses*) sharp; (*of disease*) severe and sudden; **a. angle** one less than a right angle; **a. accent** line (´) sloping over a letter to indicate its pronunciation.

acutely [akewtli] *adv* sharply, keenly ~ **acuteness** *n*.

ad [ad] *n* (*coll abbr*) advertisement.

adage [adij] *n* an old saying, a proverb.

adagio [adaaji-O] *adv* (*mus*) slowly ~ **adagio** *n* piece of music played in slow time.

Adam [adam] *n* name of the first man; **the old A.** unregenerate human nature; **A.'s ale** water; **A.'s apple** projection formed in the neck by the thyroid cartilage of the larynx.

adamant [adamant] *n* any extremely hard substance ~ **adamant** *adj* stubborn, unyielding ~ **adamantly** *adv*.

adamantine [ademantIn] *adj* extremely hard; inflexible.

adapt [adapt] *v/t* to fit, make suitable; alter so as to make fit.

adaptability [adaptabiliti] *n* quality of being adaptable.

adaptable [adaptab'l] *adj* that can be adapted; changing easily or willingly to suit different circumstances ~ **adaptably** *adv*.

adaptation [adaptayshon] *n* act or process of adapting; altered version; state of being adapted > PDB.

adapter, adaptor [adapter] *n* one who adapts; (*elect*) fitting enabling several plugs, or a plug of different type, to be used from one socket.

adaptometer [adaptomiter] *n* any instrument for measuring sensory adaptation > PDP.

add [ad] *v/t* and *i* join, unite; put (two or more numbers) into one sum; make an addition, cause an increase; go on to say; **a. up** (*coll*) make sense, give an understandable result.

addax [adaks] *n* North African antelope.

addendum (*pl* addenda) [adendum] *n* something to be added, *esp* to a printed book.

adder (1) [ader] *n* one who adds; an adding-machine.

adder (2) *n* venomous snake of the viper family, the only poisonous British snake; **a.'s tongue** fern with snake-like reproductive fronds.

addict [adikt] *n* one who is incapable of freeing himself of a harmful habit, *esp* of taking drugs; (*joc*) fan, enthusiast ~ **addict** [adikt] *v/t* and *refl* form an addiction to; be enslaved by or devoted to; be in the habit of.

addiction [adikshon] *n* (*med*) state in which a harmful drug has become physically necessary;

unbreakable harmful habit > PDP; (*coll*) intense fondness, constant habit.

addictive [adiktiv] *adj* (*of drug*) causing addiction.

additament [aditament] *n* something added.

addition [adishon] *n* action of adding; something added.

additional [adishonal] *adj* coming by way of addition, supplementary, extra.

additive [aditiv] *adj* to be added; tending to addition ~ **additive** *n* substance to be added to another for specified purpose.

addle [ad'l] *v/t* and *i* confuse, muddle, *esp* of the brain; (*of an egg*) become rotten.

addled [ad'ld] *adj* (*of eggs*) rotten; (*of the brain*) muddled.

address [adRes] *v/t* and *refl* speak to; apply oneself (to some activity); **a. a letter** write the name and residence of the recipient on it; **a. the ball** (*golf*) take aim by preliminary swings of the club ~ **address** *n* speech made to an audience; formal speech; manner of speaking; skill and tact in conversation; dexterity, adroitness; place to which a letter is directed; place where a person resides; **pay addresses to** woo, court.

addressee [adResee] *n* person to whom a letter is addressed.

adduce [adews] *v/t* bring forward as evidence or example; cite.

adductor [adukter] *n* (*physiol*) muscle drawing a part of the body inwards.

ademption [ademshon] *n* (*leg*) act of revoking a legacy or grant.

adenoid [adenoid] *adj* gland-like; adenoidal.

adenoidal [adenoidal] *adj* of the adenoids; speaking as if suffering from enlarged adenoids; gland-like.

adenoids [adenoidz] *n* (*pl*) gland-like growths at back of the nose and throat; (*pop*) enlarged or inflamed condition of these.

adenoma [adenOma] *n* overgrowth of glandular tissue.

adenose [adenOs] *adj* glandular.

adenous [adenoos] *adj* glandular.

adept [adept] *adj* proficient, expert ~ **adept** *n* one who is proficient in a subject.

adequacy [adikwisi] *n* state or quality of being adequate.

adequate [adikwit] *adj* sufficient, fully suitable; only just sufficient ~ **adequately** *adv*.

adhere [adheer] *v/i* stick, cleave (to); give allegiance (to); persevere in.

adherence [adheerRens] *n* act of adhering; loyal support, allegiance; perseverance.

adherent [adheerRent] *adj* sticking, clinging ~ **adherent** *n* follower or supporter.

adhesion [adheezhon] *n* act of adhering, condition of sticking to; force with which something sticks; (*surg*) reunion of parts which have been severed; (*path*) abnormal joining of parts to each other.

adhesive [adheesiv] *adj* sticky, tenacious ~ **adhesive** *n* substance used to stick things together ~ **adhesively** *adv* ~ **adhesiveness** *n*.

adiabatic [adi-abatik] *adj* (*phys*) without loss or gain of heat.

adiactinic [adi-aktinik] *adj* opaque to actinic rays.

adiantum [adi-antum] *n* maidenhair fern.

adieu [adew] *interj* and *n* farewell, goodbye.

8

adipocere [adipOseer] *n* fatty waxy substance generated in dead bodies buried in moist places.

adipose [adipOs] *adj* fatty; **a. tissue** connective tissue in animal body, containing the fat.

adiposity [adipositi] *n* fattiness; fatness.

adit [adit] *n* entrance, approach; (*mining*) horizontal tunnel into a mine.

adjacent [ajaysent] *adj* contiguous, lying near ~ **adjacently** *adv*.

adjectival [ajektIval] *adj* of, as or like an adjective ~ **adjectivally** *adv*.

adjective [ajektiv] *n* word used with a noun to qualify, describe or define it.

adjoin [ajoin] *v/t* be contiguous to; add, append.

adjoining [ajoining] *adj* adjacent, neighbouring.

adjourn [ajurn] *v/t* and *i* postpone; discontinue (a meeting) till a later date or indefinite time; (*coll*) break off work; go elsewhere.

adjournment [ajurnment] *n* act of adjourning; duration of interruption of meeting *etc*.

adjudge [ajuj] *v/t* give a judicial decision on; award, grant judicially; sentence (to a penalty).

adjudicate [ajOOdikayt] *v/t* and *i* act as judge, give a judicial decision; award judicially.

adjudication [ajOOdikayshon] *n* act of adjudicating, judgement.

adjudicator [ajOOdikayter] *n* judge.

adjunct [ajunkt] *adj* added, connected; subordinate ~ **adjunct** *n* one who or that which is added on; associate, subordinate; quality increasing value; (*gramm*) word(s) amplifying part of a sentence.

adjunctive [ajunktiv] *adj* forming an adjunct.

adjuration [ajewrRayshon] *n*, solemn appeal, *esp* made to a person upon oath.

adjuratory [ajewrRaytoRi] *adj* containing a solemn appeal.

adjure [ajewr] *v/t* make a solemn appeal to; urge solemnly; charge on oath.

adjust [ajust] *v/t* and *i* settle, put in order; regulate, make fit for use, alter slightly; modify one's attitude to suit one's circumstances or environment.

adjustable [ajustab'l] *adj* that can be adjusted.

adjuster [ajuster] *n* one who adjusts.

adjustment [ajustment] *n* arrangement, settlement; act of adjusting; way in which something is adjusted; adaptation of attitudes or feelings.

adjutancy [ajootansi] *n* office or rank of an adjutant.

adjutant [ajootant] *n* (*mil*) officer whose duty is to assist superior officers in administrative duties; **a. bird** large Indian stork.

ad lib. [ad-*lib*] *adv* (*Lat*) freely, as much as one wishes ~ **ad lib.** *v/i* and *t* (*theat coll*) freely improvise (speech *etc*) ~ **ad-lib** *adj* (*coll*) improvised, spontaneous.

adman (*pl* **admen**) [adman] *n* (*coll*) one who composes commercial advertisements.

admass [admas] *n* section of public easily influenced by advertisements, publicity *etc*.

admin [admin]. *adj* (*coll abbr*) administrative, administration.

administer [administer] *v/t* control the business affairs of, manage the finances of; dispense; give; organize; (*leg*) manage as executor or trustee; offer to receive (an oath).

administration [administRayshon] *n* act of administering; management of a business, estate, public affairs; government; the Government or one of its Ministries.

administrative [administRativ] *adj* executive, concerned with management.

administrator [administRayter] *n* one who administers; trustee.

admirable [admiRab'l] *adj* worthy of respect; excellent; deserving admiration ~ **admirably** *adv*.

admiral [admiRal] *n* naval officer of highest rank commanding a fleet or squadron; (*ent*) species of butterfly.

admiralty [admiRalti] *n* office of an admiral; board of commissioners which superintends the navy; building where this board transacts business.

admiration [admiRayshon] *n* pleasurable surprise; high esteem; object producing such feelings.

admirative [admiRativ] *adj* feeling or expressing admiration.

admire [admIr] *v/t* regard as remarkably fine, esteem; look on with pleasure.

admirer [admIrRer] *n* one who admires.

admissibility [admisibiliti] *n* quality of being admissible.

admissible [admisib'l] *adj* that can be allowed or considered; entitled to be admitted (to); (*leg*) allowable as judicial evidence ~ **admissibly** *adv*.

admission [admishon] *n* permission to enter; price paid for this; act of admitting; acknowledgement, confession.

admissive [admisiv] *adj* tending to admit.

admit (*pres/part* **admitting**, *p/t* and *p/part* **admitted**) [admit] *v/t* allow to enter; be means of entering; have capacity or room for; acknowledge, confess, allow, concede.

admittance [admitans] *n* permission to enter; action of giving entrance; (*elect*) reciprocal of impedance > PDEI.

admittedly [admitidli] *adv* by general agreement.

admix [admiks] *v/t* mix together; add as an ingredient.

admixture [admikstcher] *n* act of mixing; ingredient added to a mixture; mixture.

admonish [admonish] *v/t* give warning advice to, exhort, remind (of a duty).

admonition [admonishon] *n* warning, exhortation.

admonitory [admonitoRi] *adj* that admonishes.

adnominal [adnominal] *adj* adjectival.

adnoun [adnown] *n* qualifier of a noun, adjective.

ado [adOO] *n* doing, action; fuss, bustle; difficulty, trouble; **without more a.** immediately, without preliminaries; **with much a.** with difficulty.

adobe [adObi] *n* sun-dried clay building block; house made of these.

adolescence [adOlesens] *n* youth, period between childhood and manhood or womanhood.

adolescent [adOlesent] *adj* in the period of adolescence ~ **adolescent** *n* young person.

Adonis [adOnis] *n* strikingly handsome young man.

adopt [adopt] *v/t* receive as one's own the child of other parents; take over and use as one's own; give formal approval to; choose.

adoption [adopshon] *n* act of adopting; choosing.

adorable [adawRab'l] *adj* worthy of devoted love; very lovely or attractive; worthy of worship ~ **adorably** *adv*.

adoration [adoRayshon] *n* act of worshipping; feeling of deep love.

adore [adawr] *v/t* worship as God; venerate, idolize; love devotedly; (*coll*) like very much.

adorer [adawRer] *n* worshipper; ardent lover.

adorn [adawrn] *v/t* ornament, beautify; be an ornament to; add importance, attractiveness to.

adornment [adawrnment] *n* act of adorning; ornament, decoration.

adown [adown] *adv* and *prep* (*poet*) down.

adrenal [adReenal] *adj* near the kidney; **a. gland** gland secreting adrenalin > PDB.

adrenalin [adRenalin] *n* hormone secreted by the adrenal glands under stress of anger, fear *etc* and promoting violent activity > PDB, PDS.

adrift [adRift] *adv* drifting with wind and tide; not properly secured, unfastened.

adroit [adRoit] *adj* skilful, dexterous, quick in emergency ~ **adroitly** *adv* ~ **adroitness** *n*.

adsorb [adsawrb] *v/t* take in a gas, liquid, or dissolved substance by concentration on a surface.

adsorbate [adsawrbayt] *n* substance which is adsorbed.

adsorption [adsawrpshon] *n* concentration of a substance on a surface > PDS.

adulation [adewlayshon] *n* excessive praise, slavish flattery ~ **adulatory** *adj*.

adult [adult] *adj* grown up, having reached maturity ~ **adult** *n* full-grown mature person, animal or plant; person intellectually and emotionally mature; person legally of age.

adulterate [adulteRayt] *v/t* spoil by admixture of inferior material (*esp* of food-stuffs) ~ **adulterate** *adj* made by adulteration; guilty of adultery; of adulterous origin; spurious.

adulteration [adulteRayshon] *n* act of adulterating food.

adulterer [adulteRer] *n* man who commits adultery.

adulteress [adulteRes] *n* woman who commits adultery.

adulterous [adulteRus] *adj* of or committing adultery ~ **adulterously** *adv*.

adultery [adulteRi] *n* sexual intercourse of two people of opposite sex, where one (or both) is married to someone else.

adumbrate [adumbRayt] *v/t* give a rough sketch of; foreshadow; forecast roughly.

adumbration [adumbRayshon] *n* act of adumbrating; rough or incomplete forecast.

adust [adust] *adj* scorched, parched.

advance [advaans] *v/t* and *i* move forward; fix an earlier time for; further (scheme, prospects *etc*); lend (money); put forward (proposal); go forward; make progress ~ **advance** *n* forward motion, progress; rise in price; payment beforehand, loan; (*pl*) offers of friendship or love; **in a.** in front, ahead in time.

advanced [advaanst] *adj* having progressed far; elderly; modern in ideas, opinions, behaviour; **a. guard** troops sent out in front of the main army.

advancement [advaansment] *n* progress, promotion.

advantage [advaantij] *n* superior position; fav-

ouring circumstance; benefit; (*tennis*) the point scored after deuce; **to take a. of** profit by, make use of; deceive, outwit; seduce ~ **advantage** *v/t* benefit; further.

advantageous [advantayjus] *adj* beneficial, helpful; profitable ~ **advantageously** *adv* ~ **advantageousness** *n*.

advent [advent] *n* coming, arrival, *esp* the coming of Christ; (*eccles*) four-week period preceding Christmas; **Second A.** the future coming of Christ in judgement.

Adventist [adventist] *n* member of a sect looking forward to a thousand-year period of Christ's reign on earth.

adventitious [adventishus] *adj* casual, coming by accident ~ **adventitiously** *adv* casually; by an addition from without.

adventure [advencher] *n* dangerous enterprise; a novel or exciting experience; commercial or financial speculation; **a. playground** playground where children devise their own games equipment out of waste materials ~ **adventure** *v/t* risk, set at stake; dare, incur risk.

adventurer [advencheRer] *n* one who takes risks, *esp* for social or financial gain; one who lives by his wits.

adventuresome [advenchersum] *adj* fond of adventures.

adventuress [advencheRes] *n* woman scheming to improve her position in society.

adventurous [advencheRus] *adj* daring, bold; fond of adventures; perilous, risky ~ **adventurously** *adv* ~ **adventurousness** *n*.

adverb [advurb] *n* (*gramm*) word which modifies a verb, adjective or another adverb.

adverbial [advurbi-al] *adj* of, as or like an adverb ~ **adverbially** *adv*.

adversary [adversaRi] *n* enemy, opponent.

adversative [advursativ] *adj* (*gramm*) expressing opposition or antithesis.

adverse [advurs] *adj* opposing, contrary, inimical; opposite in position ~ **adversely** *adv* in a hostile or prejudicial manner.

adversity [advursiti] *n* misfortune, calamity; state of distress.

advert (1) [advert] *n* (*coll abbr*) advertisement.

advert (2) [advurt] *v/i* turn one's attention (to); refer in speech (to).

advertence [advurtens] *n* attentiveness.

advertency [advurtensi] *n* attentiveness.

advertise [advertIz] *v/t* and *i* publicly make known the existence or merits of, *esp* in order to sell; give notice of, call attention to.

advertisement [advurtisment] *n* act of advertising; public announcement; notice of goods *etc* for sale displayed by newspaper, placard, cinema, or television; notification.

advertiser [advurtIzer] *n* one who advertises, *esp* commercially.

advice [advIs] *n* counsel, opinion on a question of action; (*esp* in *comm*) formal notice of action taken.

advisable [advIzab'l] *adj* that can be recommended; prudent, wise.

advise [advIz] *v/t* and *i* give advice to; inform; consult with.

advised [advIzd] *adj* deliberate, considered; **well**

a. (*fig*) prudent, wise ~ **advisedly** *adv* deliberately, intentionally.

advisement [adv*ɪz*ment] *n* consultation.

adviser [adv*ɪz*er] *n* one who gives advice.

advisory [adv*ɪz*oRi] *adj* empowered to give advice; imparting advice.

advocacy [*a*dvokasi] *n* function of an advocate; support by speaking in favour (of).

advocate [*a*dvokit] *n* one who supports another's cause, one who intercedes for another; public supporter of a proposal or theory; barrister; **Devil's A.** (*RC*) official whose function is to oppose suggested canonizations; (*fig*) one who argues on the wrong side for the sake of debate ~ **advocate** [*a*dvokayt] *v/t* uphold or recommend publicly.

advowson [advowz*on*] *n* (*eccles*) right of presentation to a benefice.

adynamia [adin*aym*i-a] *n* (*med*) lack of vital force, weakness due to illness.

adytum [*a*ditum] *n* innermost part of a classical temple.

adze [adz] *n* tool with curved blade set with cutting edge at right angles to handle.

aedile [eed*ɪ*l] *n* (*Rom hist*) magistrate in charge of buildings, roads *etc*.

aegis [eejis] *n* (*myth*) shield of Zeus or Athene; (*fig*) protection.

aegrotat [eegRotat] *n* (*in English universities*) certificate that a student was prevented by illness from taking certain of the papers in an examination.

aeolian [ee-*Ol*i-an] *adj* of the wind; **A. harp** musical instrument in the form of a box containing strings, which are played on by the wind.

aeon, eon [*ee*-on] *n* immeasurably long period of time.

aerate [*air*Rayt] *v/t* expose to action of air; charge (liquids) with carbonic acid gas or oxygen to make effervescent drinks; let fresh air into.

aeration [airRayshon] *n* process of aerating.

aerator [ayerRayter] *n* contrivance for forcing carbonic acid gas or oxygen into liquids.

aerial [*air*Ri-al] *adj* of, in or from the air; airy, ethereal; carried on overhead wires, cables *etc* ~ **aerial** *n* wires or rods supported high in the air to collect or transmit radio or television waves > PDS, PDEI ~ **aerially** *adv*.

aerie, aery, eyrie, eyry [*air*Ri, *eer*Ri] *n* nest of an eagle or other bird of prey; nest of any high-building bird; the brood in the nest; house built in a lofty and lonely position.

aerification [airRifik*ay*shon] *n* process of aerating or aerifying; process of changing into gas.

aeriform [ayerRif*aw*rm] *adj* gaseous; (*fig*) intangible.

aerify [ayerRif*ɪ*] *v/t* turn into vapour; aerate.

aerobatics [airROb*a*tiks] *n*(*pl*) display of daring and spectacular evolutions in an aircraft; stunt flying.

aerobic [airROb*ik*] *adj* pertaining to, or requiring, air or free oxygen.

aerodrome [*air*RodROm] *n* aircraft station with hangars, buildings, runways *etc*.

aerodynamics [airRodIn*a*miks] *n* (*pl*) the study of the behaviour of air in motion, of air resistance to bodies ~ **aerodynamic** *adj* pertaining to aerodynamics; causing minimum air-resistance or turbulence.

aerodyne [*air*ROdIn] *n* aircraft.

aeroengine [airRO-*enj*in] *n* engine for the propulsion of aircraft.

aerofoil [*air*ROfoil] *n* wing of aircraft shaped to produce lift at right angles to the direction of its motion.

aerograph [*air*ROgRaaf] *n* spray gun for paint.

aerography [air*Rog*Rafi] *n* description of the properties, dimensions *etc* of the atmosphere.

aerolite, aerolith [*air*Rolit, *air*Rolith] *n* (*geol*) meteorite composed almost wholly of silicates.

aerology [air*Rol*oji] *n* science which treats of the atmosphere.

aerometer [air*Rom*iter] *n* instrument for measuring the density of air and other gases.

aeronaut [*air*Ronawt] *n* one who pilots a balloon or aircraft.

aeronautics [airRon*aw*tiks] *n*(*pl*) science of navigating and manoeuvring aircraft and airships.

aerophobia [airRO*f*Obi-a] *n* irrational fear of travelling in aircraft.

aerophyte [*air*Rofit] *n* plant which grows on other plants, but obtains nourishment from the air.

aeroplane [*air*Roplayn] *n* aircraft.

aerosol [*air*Rosol] *n* suspension of small particles in gas; spray of such suspension; canister with spray nozzle containing such suspension.

aerospace [*air*ROspays] *n* the earth's atmosphere and the space beyond it.

aerostat [*air*Rostat] *n* aircraft lighter than air.

aerostatics [airRost*a*tiks] *n* (*pl*) science which treats of the equilibrium and pressure of air and gases, and of bodies in them; aeronautics.

aertex [*air*teks] *n* (*tr*) type of loosely woven cotton fabric used for underwear.

aery see **aerie**.

aesthete [*ee*stheet] *n* one who is particularly appreciative of artistic beauty.

aesthetic [ees*thet*ik] *adj* pertaining to appreciation of beauty, *esp* in art; keenly appreciating beauty ~ **aesthetically** *adv*.

aestheticism [ees*thet*isizm] *n* exaggerated devotion to artistic beauty.

aesthetics [ees*thet*iks] *n* (*pl*) study of beauty and ugliness; the philosophy of taste.

aestival, estival [ees*tɪv*al] *adj* of or in summer.

aestivate [*ee*stivayt] *v/i* (*zool*) spend the summer in a state of torpor.

aestivation [eestiv*ay*shon] *n* (*zool*) act of aestivating; (*bot*) arrangement of petals in a flower-bud before opening.

aether see **ether**.

aetiological [eeti-olo*j*ikal] *adj* of aetiology; explaining the origin.

aetiology [eeti-*ol*oji] *n* philosophy of causation; research into origins; (*med*) causes of disease.

afar [a*faar*] *adv* far away, at a distance; **from a.** from a distance.

affability [afab*ɪl*iti] *n* quality of being affable.

affable [a*fab*'l] *adj* pleasant of demeanour, courteous ~ **affably** *adv*.

affair [a*fair*] *n* business, concern, occupation; event, object; relationship of people in love with each other, *esp* as it develops over a period; illicit sexual relationship; **a. of honour** duel.

affect (1) [a*fekt*] *v/t* have a preference for, use, assume, adopt *etc* habitually: make a pretence of.

affect (2) v/t act upon, influence; move, stir (emotions); infect, attack (of disease).

affect (3) n (psych) feeling, emotion > PDP.

affectation [afektayshon] n artificial behaviour, pretence; display (of).

affected [afektid] adj pretended; artificial in manner; inclined, disposed; grieved, moved to sorrow; attacked, afflicted (with a disease etc) ~ **affectedly** adv ~ **affectedness** n.

affecting [afekting] adj moving, pathetic.

affection [afekshon] n love, fondness; mental state, emotion; (med) malady, complaint.

affectionate [afekshonit] adj loving, fond ~ **affectionately** adv ~ **affectionateness** n.

affective [afektiv] adj emotional > PDP.

afferent [aferent] adj (physiol) conducting inwards or towards > PDP.

affiance [afI-ans] v/t solemnly promise to marry.

affidavit [afidayvit] n statement made in writing, on oath, to be used as judicial proof.

affiliate [afili-ayt] v/t and i adopt as a member of a society, or as a branch of it; associate, connect; (leg) fix the paternity of a child (on).

affiliation [afili-ayshon] n adoption by a society of smaller ones as branches; establishing paternity of a child; assignment of a thing to its origin; **a. order** (leg) order compelling the father of a bastard child to contribute to its support.

affinal [afInal] adj related by affinity.

affined [afInd] adj related, connected.

affinity [afiniti] n relationship; similarity; harmonious relationship based on points of resemblance; mutual attraction; (biol, philol) similarity indicating derivation from a common source; (chem) tendency of certain elements to combine with certain others and form new compounds; (leg, eccles) relationship to one's wife's or husband's blood-relations.

affirm [afurm] v/t and i declare positively; make a formal declaration; declare to be true; (leg) ratify; (leg) declare solemnly but not by oath.

affirmation [afermayshon] n act of affirming; solemn statement made by one who has a conscientious objection to taking an oath.

affirmative [afurmativ] n and adj (word) asserting that a fact is so, answering 'yes'; **answer in the a.** answer 'yes'.

affix [afiks] v/t stick on, fasten, attach; add ~ **affix** [afiks] n something added, appendage; (gramm) syllable added to the beginning or end of a word in order to modify its meaning.

afflatus [aflaytus] n supernatural inspiration.

afflict [aflikt] v/t torment, cause pain or sorrow to.

afflicted [afliktid] adj oppressed; grievously troubled, esp with sickness.

affliction [aflikshon] n state of being afflicted; that which afflicts; trouble, distress, calamity.

affluence [afloo-ens] n wealth, prosperity; plenty, profusion.

affluent [afloo-ent] adj wealthy; flowing freely, profuse ~ **affluent** n tributary stream flowing into a larger one ~ **affluently** adv.

afflux [afluks] n a flow of fluid; increase.

afford [afawrd] v/t and i grant, bestow; yield naturally; be able and willing to pay for; be able to do, give etc without damage to oneself.

afforest [afoRest] v/t plant with trees to form a forest.

afforestation [afoRestayshon] n process of turning land into forest.

affranchise [afRanchIz] v/t free.

affray [afRay] n public brawl, riot.

affright [afRIt] n (poet) fright ~ **affright** v/t (poet) frighten.

affront [afRunt] v/t insult publicly; offend the pride of; face boldly ~ **affront** n open insult.

aficionado [afithi-onaadO/afisi-onaadO] n (Sp) enthusiast, connoisseur, esp of bull-fighting.

afield [afeeld] adv in the field; **far a.** a long way from home; (fig) astray, off the mark.

afire [afIr] adv and adj on fire.

aflame [aflaym] adv and adj blazing; filled with excitement.

afloat [aflOt] adv and adj floating on the water; at sea: covered with overflowing water; floating lightly in the air; (fig) current, in general circulation; (fig) out of debt.

afoot [afoot] adv and adj being planned or prepared, imminent; active, on the move; on foot.

afore [afawr] adv and prep (naut) in the fore-part of the ship; in front of.

afore- pref before, previously.

aforesaid [afawrsed] adj previously mentioned.

aforethought [afawrthawt] adj premeditated.

aforetime [afawrtIm] adv formerly.

afraid [afRayd] adj frightened; **I am a. that . . .** I am sorry to tell you that . . .

afreet, afrit, afrite [ayfReet] n evil demon in Muslim belief.

afresh [afResh] adv again, anew, with a fresh start.

Afrikaans [afRikaans] n South African Dutch.

Afrikaner [afRikaaner] n settler in South Africa of European, esp Dutch blood.

Afro [afRO] adj African, negro; (of hair) worn long and very frizzy.

aft [aaft] adv (naut) in or towards the stern.

after [aafter] adv in the rear, behind; subsequently ~ **after** prep and conj following; in pursuit of; after a period of; in view of; in imitation of; in spite of; about; next in importance to; **take a.** resemble; **a. all** when everything has been said and done; **a. you** I yield precedence to you; **a. you with I** wish to be next to use ~ **after** adj following, subsequent; (naut) of, at or near the stern.

after- pref subsequent, later; (naut) near the stern.

afterbirth [aafterburth] n placenta.

aftercare [aafterkair] n care and advice given to persons discharged from a hospital or prison etc.

afterdamp [aafterdamp] n poisonous mixture of gases left in a mine after an explosion of firedamp > PDS.

after-effect [aafter-efekt] n effect persisting long after its cause has ceased; secondary effect.

afterglow [aaftergIO] n radiance sometimes seen in the sky after sunset.

after-image [aafteRimij] n impression retained of a vivid sensation after the external stimulus has ceased > PDP.

afterlife [aafterlIf] n life after death; later period of life.

aftermath [aaftermaath] n unpleasant consequences of some catastrophe.

after-mentioned [aafter-menshond] adj to be mentioned later.

aftermost [*aa*ftermOst] *adj* (*naut*) nearest the stern, furthest aft.

afternoon [aafter*n*OOn] *n* period between midday and evening.

afters [*aa*fterz] *n* (*pl*) (*coll*) second or third course at a meal, following the main course.

aftertaste [*aa*ftertayst] *n* taste remaining in the mouth after food.

afterthought [*aa*fterthawt] *n* something thought of later.

afterwards [*aa*fterwerdz] *adv* at a later time.

Aga [*aa*ga] *n* (*hist*) title of military or civil rank in the Ottoman empire; form of polite address to men in certain Near Eastern countries; **A. Khan** hereditary title of the spiritual head of the Ismaelian sect of Islam.

again [a*gayn*/a*gen*] *adv* as before; back to its former position; once more, some other time; in addition, besides; in response; **as much a. twice as much; a. and a.** repeatedly.

against [a*gaynst*/a*genst*] *prep* into collision with; so as to be supported by; in the opposite direction to, counter to; opposed to; in anticipation of; **run (up)** a. meet by chance; **over a.** directly facing; **a. the grain** contrary to one's natural inclination.

agama [*a*gama] *n* species of Caribbean lizard.

agamic [a*gam*ik] *adj* (*biol*) without sexual union.

agamogenesis [agam*O*je*n*isis] *n* (*biol*) reproduction without sexual union.

agape (1) [a*gayp*] *adv* with gaping mouth; expectant; wondering.

agape (2) [a*gap*i] *n* love-feast of the early Christians, held in connexion with the Eucharist; spiritual love, charity.

agar-agar [aygaar-*ay*gaar] *n* gelatinous substance obtained from certain seaweeds > PDB, PDS.

agaric [*a*ga*R*ik] *n* species of fungi growing on trees; very light spongy stone.

agate [*a*get] *n* semi-precious stone, variegated kind of chalcedony; a burnishing tool.

agave [a*gayv*i/a*gayv*] *n* (*bot*) genus of plants including the American aloe.

age [*ayj*] *n* length of time a person or thing has existed; latter period of life; geological epoch; historical period; long period of time; (*pl*, *coll*) far too long; **come of a.** reach the age of full legal majority (formerly at 21, now at 18); **under a.** too young; **over a.** too old ~ **age** *v*/*i* and *t* grow old; cause to grow old; look or cause to look older; (*of metals*) grow weaker after prolonged stress.

age-bracket [*ayj*-b*R*akit] *n* period of life between two specified ages; persons of this age considered as a group.

aged [*ayj*id/*ayj*id] *adj* advanced in years, old; of the age of (so many years) ~ **aged** [*ayj*id] *n* (*pl*) old people.

age-group [*ayj*-g*R*OOp] *n* group of persons of the same age.

ageless [*ayj*les] *adj* never growing old; showing no signs of old age ~ **agelessness** *n*.

age-long [*ayj*long] *adj* lasting for a long period.

agency [*ayj*ensi] *n* means by which something is brought about; occupation, business or office of an agent.

agenda [a*jen*da] *n* programme of subjects to be discussed at a meeting.

agent [*ay*jent] *n* one who acts, or exerts power to bring something about; one who acts for another or manages another's business; intermediary; (*sci*) natural force acting upon matter; **a. provocateur** agent employed to trap suspects by inciting them to commit crime.

agential [a*jen*shal] *adj* pertaining to an agent or agency.

age-old [*ayj*-Old] *adj* very ancient.

agger [*aj*er] *n* (*arch*) rampart made by earth thrown from the ditch.

agglomerate [a*glome*Rayt] *v*/*t* and *i* gather together into a heap without method ~ **agglomerate** [a*glome*Rit] *n* agglomeration; (*min*) fragments of rock fused together by volcanic activity.

agglomeration [aglome*Ray*shon] *n* action of collecting in a mass; untidy heap of things.

agglutinant [a*glOO*tinant] *n* and *adj* (substance) which makes things stick together.

agglutinate [a*glOO*tinayt] *v*/*t* and *i* stick together; coalesce; join simple words together to form compound terms ~ **agglutinate** [a*glOO*tinit] *adj*.

agglutination [a*glOO*tina*y*shon] *n* act or process of agglutinating; state of being agglutinated.

agglutinin [a*glOO*tinin] *n* agent that causes agglutination.

aggrandize [a*gRand*Iz] *v*/*t* increase the power, wealth *etc* of; cause to appear greater ~ **aggrandizement** [a*gRand*izment] *n*.

aggravate [*ag*Ravayt] *v*/*t* increase, make worse; cause to appear graver; (*coll*) irritate, exasperate.

aggravating [*ag*Ravayting] *adj* making worse; (*coll*) annoying, exasperating ~ **aggravatingly** *adv*.

aggravation [agRa*vay*shon] *n* action of aggravating; act or circumstance that makes something more serious; (*coll*) annoyance.

aggregate [*ag*Rigit] *adj* made by collection of many separate units; total; unified; collective; (*leg*) composed of associated persons; (*geol*) made of separate minerals combined in one rock ~ **aggregate** *n* sum total; (*phys*) mass formed by the union of homogeneous particles; **in the a.** taken as a whole ~ **aggregate** [*ag*Rigayt] *v*/*t* gather together into one mass; amount to.

aggregation [agRi*gay*shon] *n* act of aggregating; aggregate.

aggregative [*ag*Rigativ] *adj* pertaining to aggregation; tending to aggregate.

aggress [a*gRes*] *v*/*i* attack first, begin a quarrel.

aggression [a*gRe*shon] *n* unprovoked attack; impulse to show hostility > PDP.

aggressive [a*gRes*iv] *adj* disposed to attack others, threatening; eager to quarrel; (*mil*) taking the offensive ~ **aggressively** *adv* ~ **aggressiveness** *n*.

aggressor [a*gRes*er] *n* one who makes the first attack, *esp* if unprovoked; State that declares war on or first attacks another.

aggrieved [a*gReev*d] *adj* having a feeling of injury, of being unfairly treated.

aggro [*ag*RO] *n* (*sl*) deliberate aggressive violence, *usu* by a gang or crowd; deliberately provocative act.

aghast [a*gaast*] *adj* horrified, dumbfounded.

agile [*aj*Il] *adj* nimble, quick in motion.

agility [a*jil*iti] *n* quality of being agile.

13

agio [*aji*-O] *n* percentage charged for exchanging one currency into another; agiotage.

agiotage [*aji*-Otij] *n* exchange business; speculation in stocks and shares.

agitate [*aji*tayt] *v/t* and *i* stir vigorously, wave, shake about; disturb, excite, worry; discuss; stir up unrest; draw public attention to a demand or protest.

agitated [*aji*tayted] *adj* disturbed; anxious, upset, overexcited ~ **agitatedly** *adv*.

agitation [aji*tay*shon] *n* state or quality of being agitated; public unrest in support of a demand or protest; restlessness; worry, mental disturbance.

agitato [aji*taat*O] *adv* (*mus*) in an agitated manner, restlessly.

agitator [*aji*tayter] *n* one who provokes political or industrial unrest; machine which stirs up pulp *etc*.

agit-prop [*aji*t-pRop] *n* of or for political unrest and propaganda, *esp* by Communists in non-Communist countries.

aglet, aiglet [*aglet, ay*glet] *n* metal tag of a lace; metal ornament on a fringe; gold braid or cord hanging from the shoulder in some uniforms.

agley [agl*I/ag*lay] *adv* (*Scots*) awry, badly.

aglimmer [*ag*limer] *adv* glimmering.

aglitter [*ag*liter] *adv* glittering.

aglow [ag*lO*] *adv* glowing with colour; flushed with excitement or exercise.

agnail [*ag*nayl] *n* torn skin at base of fingernail.

agnate [*ag*nayt] *n* kinsman on the father's side; one descended from the same male ancestor ~ **agnate** *adj*.

agnatic [ag*nat*ik] *adj* related on the father's side.

agnation [ag*nay*shon] *n* relationship through the male line.

agnostic [ag*nos*tik] *n* one who believes that nothing is or can be known concerning the existence of God or the truth of theological doctrines; one who claims that a specified point can be neither proved nor disproved ~ **agnostic** *adj*.

agnosticism [ag*nos*tisizm] *n* belief and outlook of an agnostic; scepticism.

Agnus Dei [agnus-*day*-ee] *n* prayer sung at Mass beginning with these words (= Lamb of God); (*her*) figure of a lamb bearing a banner charged with a cross.

ago [ag*O*] *adv* in the past.

agog [ag*og*] *adj* and *adv* in excited expectation.

à-go-go [a-gO-g*O*] *adv* (*Fr*) (*coll*) lavishly provided, galore.

agometer [ag*om*iter] *n* (*elect*) rheostat.

agonic [ag*on*ik] *adj* making no angle; **a. line** imaginary line on the earth's surface from which magnetic north and true north are in the same direction > PDG.

agonize [*agon*Iz] *v/i* and *refl* suffer agony; make desperate efforts.

agonizing [*agon*Izing] *adj* causing intense pain ~ **agonizingly** *adv*.

agony [*agon*i] *n* extreme suffering; pains of death; (*cap*) sufferings of Christ in Gethsemane; **a. column** advertisement column of newspaper containing appeals for missing relatives *etc*; **pile on the a.** (*coll*) exaggerate one's feelings.

agora [*ago*Ra] *n* (*Gk hist*) place of assembly, the market-place.

agoraphobia [agoRa*fO*bi-a] *n* morbid fear of open spaces and public places.

agouti [ag*OO*ti] *n* rodent found in West Indies and South America.

agraffe [ag*Raf*] *n* type of clasp or buckle.

agraphia [ag*Raf*i-a] *n* (*med*) inability to write, as a result of brain lesion.

agrarian [ag*Rair*Ri-an] *adj* of agricultural land; of land ownership; (*bot*) growing wild in the fields ~ **agrarian** *n* one in favour of redistribution of landed property.

agrarianism [ag*Rair*Ri-anizm] *n* policy advocating redistribution of ownership of land.

agree [ag*Ree*] *v/i* and *t* give consent, approve, accept; come to terms; hold the same views; live on good terms; correspond; (*gramm*) be in concord; approve the terms of; **a. with** suit the health of.

agreeable [ag*Ree*-ab'l] *adj* pleasant, delightful; **a. to** in conformity with; (*coll*) ready to agree to ~ **agreeably** *adv* ~ **agreeableness** *n*.

agreement [ag*Ree*ment] *n* mutual understanding, harmony; business arrangement, legal contract binding on the signatories; (*gramm*) concord.

agrestic [ag*Res*tik] *adj* rural, rustic; uncultured.

agricultural [agRi*kul*cheRal] *adj* of, by or used in agriculture.

agriculturalist [agRi*kul*cheRalist] *n* expert on agriculture; farmer.

agriculture [*ag*Rikulcher] *n* cultivation of the ground and management of stock, farming.

agrimony [*ag*Rimoni] *n* common wild plant with spike of small yellow flowers.

agrimotor [*ag*RimOter] *n* agricultural motor tractor.

agriology [agRi-*ol*oji] *n* study of the history and customs of primitive peoples ~ **agriologist** *n*.

agronomics [agRo*nom*iks] *n* (*pl*) science of the management of land, rural economy.

agronomist [ag*Ron*omist] *n* student of rural economy.

aground [ag*Round*] *adv* (*naut*) lodged in shallow water, stranded.

ague [*ay*gew] *n* periodic malarial fever, characterized by fits of shivering.

aguish [*ay*gew-ish] *adj* resembling ague; prone to attacks of ague; (*of climate*) causing ague.

ah [aa] *interj* expressing surprise, regret, longing *etc*.

aha [aahaa/ahaa] *interj* expressing triumph, mockery *etc*.

ahead [a*hed*] *adv* farther in front, in advance; straight in front of; moving forward or onward rapidly; headlong; **a. of** before; **get a.** succeed.

ahem [a*hem/hm*] *interj* slight cough used to attract attention, or to convey a warning.

ahimsa [a*him*sa] *n* (*Hindu*) doctrine that all life is sacred; total non-violence.

ahoy [a*hoi*] *interj* (*naut*) call used in hailing.

ahull [a*hul*] *adv* (*naut*) with sails furled and helm lashed on the lee-side.

aid [ayd] *v/t* help, assist, give support to ~ **aid** *n* help, assistance; person or thing giving help; subsidy, financial grant; exchequer loan; **first a.** simple medical treatment given in emergency; **in a. of** in support of, to help pay for; **legal a.** legal representation paid for from public funds for those who cannot pay fees.

aide [ayd] *n* confidential assistant, *esp* to a politician, governor, general *etc*.

aide-de-camp (*pl* **aides-de-camp**) [ayd-de-*kaa*(ng)] *n* (*mil*) officer who assists a general in military duties.

aiglet see aglet.

aigrette [*ayg*Ret/*ayg*Ret] *n* egret; plume of feathers or spray of gems worn on the head; (*astron*) rays of light seen at moon's edge during a solar eclipse.

aiguille [*ayg*wee] *n* sharp peak of rock.

ail [ayl] *v*/*t* (*ar*, *poet*) trouble, afflict.

aileron [*ayle*Ron] *n* hinged flap near the wing-tips of an aeroplane; (*archi*) ornamental scroll.

ailing [*ayling*] *adj* in poor health, frequently ill.

ailment [*ayl*ment] *n* sickness, indisposition.

aim [aym] *v*/*t* and *i* point or direct (blow, missile) towards target to be struck; direct one's course, make it one's object to reach; (*fig*) try; make (remarks) to influence someone; (*coll*) intend, plan; **a. high** be ambitious ~ **aim** *n* act of directing a weapon, missile or blow towards object to be hit; purpose, intention.

aimless [*aym*les] *adj* without definite purpose; trivial ~ **aimlessly** *adv* ~ **aimlessness** *n*.

ain't [aynt] (*dial* and *sl abbr*) are not; is not; am not; have not.

air [air] *n* gaseous substance surrounding the earth, atmosphere > PDS; sky; breeze; outward appearance, impression given; (*pl*) affected manner; (*mus*) melody > PDM; **in the a.** current vaguely as a rumour; not finally settled; **in the open a.** out of doors; **on the a.** in or making a broadcast; **hot a.** (*sl*) stupid talk; **give (someone) the a.** (*sl*) dismiss; **airs and graces** affected mannerisms; **give oneself airs** assume a superior manner; **tread on a.** (*coll*) be wildly happy ~ **air** *v*/*t* and *i* let air into, ventilate; free from damp by exposing to heat; express or discuss publicly; display publicly, show off; take out into the open air, exercise (animals) ~ **air** *adj* of, in or through the air, by or for aircraft.

airbase [*air*bays] *n* airfield used as a base of operations for military aircraft.

airbed [*air*bed] *n* mattress inflated with air.

air-bells [*air*-belz] *n* (*pl*) air bubbles formed during processing of photographs or making of glass.

air-bladder [*air*-blader] *n* swim-bladder of fishes; sac filled with air in seaweeds > PDB.

airborne [*air*bawrn] *adj* in the air; transported by air; **a. division** (*mil*) troops transported by air to a battle area and dropped by parachute or glider.

airbrake [*air*bRayk] *n* brake worked by compressed air.

airbrick [*air*bRik] *n* brick pierced with holes for ventilation.

air-brush [*air*-bRush] *n* atomizer for spraying paint.

air-bump [*air*-bump] *n* jerk caused by aircraft passing through an air-pocket.

airbus [*air*bus] *n* passenger aircraft flying on short routes.

aircell [*air*sel] *n* small cavity in animal or plant tissue containing air; airsac > PDB.

air-chamber [*air*-chaymber] *n* cavity in animal or plant filled with air; receptacle in a pump containing air.

Air Chief Marshal [air-cheef-*maar*shal] *n* officer of the R.A.F. ranking next below Marshal and above Air Marshal.

Air Commodore [air-*kom*odawrl *n* officer of the R.A.F. ranking next below Air Vice-Marshal.

air-condenser [*air*-kondenser] *n* instrument for condensing air.

airconditioned [airkon*dish*ond] *adj* automatically ventilated with air at regulated temperature and humidity.

airconditioning [airkon*dish*oning] *n* apparatus regulating temperature and humidity of air used in ventilation.

air-cooling [*air*-kooling] *n* reducing temperature by means of currents of air ~ **air-cooled** *adj*.

aircraft (*pl* **aircraft**) [*air*kRaaft] *n* a winged flying machine, heavier than air, and *usu* powered by an engine.

aircraft-carrier [*air*kRaaft-kaRi-er] *n* warship designed to carry naval aircraft with a flight-deck for taking off and landing.

aircraft(s)man [*air*kRaaft(s)man] *n* the lowest rank in the R.A.F.

aircrew [*air*kROO] *n* crew of an aircraft.

air-cushion [*air*-kooshon] *n* rubber cushion inflated with air.

airdrome [*air*dROm] *n* aerodrome.

Airedale [*air*dayl] *n* large rough-coated breed of terrier.

air-engine [*air*-enjin] *n* engine worked by heated air.

airer [*air*Rer] *n* frame on which clothes are aired or towels are dried.

airfield [*air*feeld] *n* level area of ground where aircraft take off and land.

air-filter [*air*-filter] *n* apparatus for removing dirt, germs *etc* from air.

airflow [*air*flO] *n* passage of air over surfaces or through passages.

air-flue [*air*-flOO] *n* channel for the passage of heated air.

airfoil [*air*foil] *n* aerofoil.

Air Force [*air*-fawrs] *n* branch of the armed forces concerned with attack or defence from the air.

airgun [*air*gun] *n* gun firing a shot by compressed air.

airhole [*air*hOl] *n* hole for air to pass through; hole made in ice of river *etc*; hole made by air bubbles in any material.

air-hostess [*air*-hOstes] *n* stewardess on airliner.

airily [*air*Rili] *adv* lightly, flippantly.

airiness [*air*Rinis] *n* state or quality of being airy; flippancy.

airing [*air*Ring] *n* drying of clothes *etc* by dry air or heat; excursion in open air; exercising of animals; public discussion; **a. cupboard** heated cupboard for drying clothes *etc*.

air-jacket [*air*-jaket] *n* inflatable jacket to support its wearer in the water.

airlane [*air*layn] *n* route regularly used by aircraft.

airless [*air*les] *adj* short of fresh air, stuffy.

airlift [*air*lift] *n* transport of equipment, supplies *etc* by aircraft.

airline [*air*lIn] *n* service of passenger aircraft; (*tel*) a line above ground.

airliner [*air*lIner] *n* a large passenger aircraft.

airlock [*air*lok] *n* bubble of air preventing flow of air or liquid in a pipe; airtight chamber between areas of different air pressure.

airmail [*air*mayl] *n* and *adj* (letters *etc*) carried by aircraft.

15

airman [*air*man] *n* one who flies an aircraft; (*R.A.F.*) man of any rank up to and including Warrant Officer.

Air Marshal [air-*maarsh*al] *n* officer in the R.A.F. ranking next below Air Chief Marshal.

air-passage [*air*-pasij] *n* (*bot*) air-filled cavity between the walls of neighbouring cells; accommodation in an airliner.

airplane [*air*playn] *n* aeroplane.

airplant [*air*plaant] *n* plant which grows upon a tree but derives its nourishment from the air.

air-pocket [*air*-poket] *n* local variation in air pressure or currents which causes an aircraft to drop suddenly in flight.

airport [*air*pawrt] *n* aerodrome used by international airlines.

air-power [*air*-powr] *n* a country's resources in military and transport aircraft.

air-pump [*air*-pump] *n* machine or apparatus for pumping air or gas; vacuum pump.

air-raid [*air*-Rayd] *n* attack by aircraft with bombs or missiles ~ **air-raid** *adj* of an air-raid; for protection from air-raids.

airsac [*air*sak] *n* (*orni*) aircell > PDB.

airscrew [*air*skROO] *n* propeller on an aircraft.

airshaft [*air*-shaaft] *n* shaft for ventilation.

airship [*air*ship] *n* large gas-filled dirigible balloon used for air transport.

airsickness [*air*siknes] *n* sickness caused by the motion of an aircraft in flight ~ **airsick** *adj*.

airspace [*air*spays] *n* volume of air in a room or building; air-filled cavity; air above a particular country or territory.

airstream [*air*stReem] *n* high altitude wind, airflow.

airstrip [*air*stRip] *n* long narrow runway.

airtight [*air*tIt] *adj* impenetrable to air.

air-to-air [*air*-too-air] *adj* fired by one aircraft to hit another.

airtrap [*air*tRap] *n* contrivance for preventing the escape of foul air from sewers.

Air Vice-Marshal [air-vIs-*maarsh*al] *n* officer in the R.A.F. ranking next below Air Marshal.

airway [*air*way] *n* passage or shaft carrying ventilating air-current; route of a service of aircraft.

airwoman [*air*wooman] *n* woman who flies an aircraft; (*W.R.A.F.*) woman of any rank up to and including Warrant Officer.

airworthy [*air*werTHi] *adj* (*of aircraft*) fit to fly ~ **airworthiness** *n*.

airy [*air*Ri] *adj* of, like or in the air; well ventilated, open to the fresh air; lofty, aerial; light, thin; immaterial; imaginary; flippant, casual.

airy-fairy [airRi-*fair*Ri] *adj* (*coll*) fanciful, whimsical; too delicate; too idealistic, impractical; vague.

aisle [*Il*] *n* part of a church parallel to nave and choir, and separated from them by pillars; passage between rows of seats in church or theatre; passage between display stands in supermarket.

ait [*ayt*] *n* small island, *esp* in a river, eyot.

aitchbone [*aych*bOn] *n* the rump bone; cut of beef from above this bone.

ajar [a*jaar*] *adv* (*of door or window*) slightly open.

akimbo [a*kimb*O] *adv* with hands on hips and elbows jutting sideways.

akin [a*kin*] *adv* related, of the same family; of the same type.

alabaster [*al*abaaster] *n* white translucent easily carved variety of gypsum ~ **alabaster** *adj* made of alabaster; very white.

alack [a*lak*] *interj* (*poet*) alas!

alacrity [a*lak*Riti] *n* cheerful willingness, briskness.

alalia [a*layli*-a] *n* (*med*) loss of power of speech.

alar [*aylar*] *adj* of or like a wing; axillary.

alarm [a*laarm*] *n* state of sudden fear; sound giving warning of approaching danger; bell rung by a clock to awaken sleepers; **alarms and excursions** (*joc*) fuss; petty quarrels ~ **alarm** *v/t* arouse to sense of danger; excite with sudden fear; perturb.

alarmbell [a*laarm*bel] *n* bell rung to warn of approaching danger.

alarmclock [a*laarm*klok] *n* clock which can be set to ring a bell at a certain hour.

alarm-gauge [a*laarm*-gayj] *n* device attached to a steam-engine to warn of excessive pressure.

alarm-gun [a*laarm*-gun] *n* gun fired to give notice of approaching danger.

alarming [a*laarm*ing] *adj* startling, terrifying ~ **alarmingly** [a*laarm*ingli] *adv*.

alarmist [a*laarm*ist] *n* one who raises unnecessary alarm; one who fears imaginary dangers ~ **alarmist** *adj* likely to cause alarm.

alarum [a*laa*Rum] *n* (*poet*) alarm; ringing mechanism attached to a clock or watch.

alas [a*laas*/a*las*] *interj* expressing grief or pity.

alate [*aylayt*] *adj* winged; having side appendages resembling wings.

alb [*alb*] *n* long white linen vestment.

albacore [*alb*akawr] *n* large species of tunny-fish.

albata [al*bayta*] *n* white metal resembling silver.

albatross [*alb*atRos] *n* name of a family of birds allied to the petrels, *esp* the Great Albatross, largest of seabirds.

albeit [awl*bee*-it] *conj* even though, although.

albert [*albert*] *n* man's watch-chain.

albescent [al*bes*ent] *adj* shading into white.

albinism [*alb*inizm] *n* deficiency of natural pigment of skin, hair *etc* > PDB.

albino [al*been*O] *n* person or animal lacking natural colouring in skin and hair.

albinotic [albi*not*ik] *adj* of albinism.

albite [*al*bIt] *n* white feldspar.

albuginea [albewj*ini*-a] *n* white fibrous substance of eyeball and other organs.

album [*al*bum] *n* blank book in which photographs, autographs, stamps *etc* are collected; long-playing record containing several items by the same performer(s).

albumen, albumin [*al*bewmin] *n* solution of protein in many animal tissues and fluids > PDB, PDS; egg white; (*bot*) substance surrounding the embryo in many seeds.

albumenize [al*bewm*inIz] *v/t* cover or coat with albumen.

albumin see **albumen**.

albuminoid [al*bewm*inoid] *adj* resembling albumen ~ **albuminoid** *n* one of class of complex proteins forming the framework of many animal tissues.

albuminous [al*bewm*inus] *adj* of, like or containing albumin.

alburnum [al*burn*um] *n* soft freshly formed wood.

alcazar [al*kaz*er/alkat*haar*] *n* Spanish palace or fortress.

alchemic [al*k*emik] *adj* of or by alchemy.
alchemist [*al*kemist] *n* one who practises alchemy.
alchemize [*al*kemIz] *v/t* change as by alchemy.
alchemy, alchymy [*al*kemi] *n* medieval semi-magical chemistry aiming at changing base metals into gold; (*fig*) mysterious or magical transformation.
alcohol [*al*kohol] *n* intoxicating product of fermentation in wine, beer, spirits *etc*; drink containing this; (*chem*) class of organic compounds derived from the hydrocarbons > PDS.
alcoholic [alko*h*olik] *adj* containing alcohol; of or like alcohol; caused by intoxication with alcohol; suffering from alcoholism ~ **alcoholic** *n* one addicted to alcoholic drinks > PDP; one suffering from disease caused by this.
alcoholism [*al*koholizm] *n* addiction to alcohol; habitual excessive drinking of alcohol; diseased condition caused by this.
Alcoran [alko*Raan*] *n* the Koran.
alcove [*al*kOv] *n* vaulted recess in wall of room; summerhouse, bower.
aldehyde [*al*dehId] *n* class of organic compounds intermediate between alcohols and acids; colourless liquid with a pungent fruity smell > PDS.
alder [*awl*der] *n* small water-loving tree.
alderman [*awl*derman] *n* one of the senior members of a borough or county council.
aldermanry [*awl*derman*Ri*] *n* office or rank of an alderman; district of a borough having its own alderman; ward.
Alderney [*awl*derni] *n* a breed of cattle.
ale [*ayl*] *n* fermented malt liquor flavoured with hops.
aleatory [*ay*lee-ato*Ri*] *adj* depending on the throw of dice; depending on chance.
alee [a*lee*] *adv* (*naut*) to leeward.
alegar [*ay*liger] *n* sour ale; malt vinegar.
alehouse [*ay*lhows] *n* public-house.
alembic [a*lem*bik] *n* apparatus formerly used in distilling.
alert [a*lurt*] *adj* vigilant; brisk, nimble ~ **alert** *n* signal to be ready for an attack; air-raid warning; **on the a.** on guard, wary; watchful ~ **alert** *v/t* rouse the attention of, put on guard, warn ~ **alertly** *adv* ~ **alertness** *n*.
aleurone [a*lewr*Ron] *n* albuminoid substance found in seeds of plants.
ale-vat [*ayl*-vat] *n* vat in which ale is brewed.
alevin [*al*evin] *n* young fish, *esp* salmon or trout.
Alexandrian [aleg*zaand*Ri-an] *adj* belonging to the school of Greek literature in Alexandria under the Ptolemies.
Alexandrine [aleg*zaand*RIn] *n* (*pros*) line of six feet and twelve syllables.
alexia [a*lek*si-a] *n* (*med*) word-blindness, inability to read resulting from cerebral lesion.
alexin [a*lek*sin] *n* (*biol*) type of proteid substances found in blood serum which destroy bacteria.
alexipharmic [aleksi*faar*mik] *n* and *adj* (substance) able to counteract poison.
alexiteric [aleksite*Rik*] *n* and *adj* alexipharmic.
alfa [*al*fa] *n* esparto grass.
alfalfa [al*fal*fa] *n* American lucerne.
alfresco [al*fResk*O] *adv* in the open air.
alga [*al*ga] *sing* of algae.
algae (*sing, rare,* **alga**) [*al*jee] *n* (*pl*) class of

aquatic or moisture-loving plants including seaweeds, vegetal plankton *etc* > PDB.
algal [*al*gal] *adj* of algae.
algebra [*al*jib*R*a] *n* branch of mathematics dealing with the properties of and relationships between quantities by means of general symbols.
algebraic [alji*bR*ay-ik] *adj* of or by algebra ~ **algebraical** *adj* ~ **algebraically** *adv*.
algebraist [alji*bR*ay-ist] *n* student of algebra.
algid [*al*jid] *adj* (*med*) cold; **a. cholera** Asiatic cholera.
algidity [al*jid*iti] *n* (*med*) coldness.
algoid [*al*goid] *adj* of or like algae.
algology [al*gol*oji] *n* scientific study of algae.
algometer [al*gom*iter] *n* instrument for measuring sensitivity to pain.
algorism [*al*go*R*izm] *n* Arabic system of numerals.
algorithm [*al*go*R*ithm] *n* (*math*) method of computation by pre-arranged steps designed to solve a specific type of problem.
algous [*al*gus] *adj* of or full of seaweeds.
algraphy [*al*g*R*afi] *n* process of printing from aluminium plates.
algum [*al*gum] *n* (*OT*) sandalwood tree.
alias [*ay*li-as] *adv* otherwise (called) ~ **alias** *n* an assumed name, false name.
alibi [*al*ibI] *n* (*leg*) plea that accused was elsewhere when the crime was committed; (*coll*) excuse.
alidade [*al*idayd] *n* instrument for measuring heights and distances.
alien [*ay*li-en] *adj* belonging to another country; foreign in origin or character; repugnant, opposed (to) ~ **alien** *n* foreigner, *esp* one living in one's own country and not naturalized.
alienable [*ay*li-enab'l] *adj* (*of property*) capable of being transferred to another owner.
alienage [*ay*li-enij] *n* (*leg*) state of being an alien.
alienate [*ay*li-enayt] *v/t* estrange, turn away the affection of; (*leg*) transfer to another owner.
alienation [ayli-e*nay*shon] *n* estrangement; transference of ownership; mental disorder; failure to recognize familiar persons or things > PDP; **a. effect** (*theat*) way of making an audience react intellectually, not emotionally, to a problem presented to them.
alienee [ayli-e*nee*] *n* one to whom property is transferred.
alienist [*ay*li-enist] *n* specialist in mental disorders, psychiatrist.
aliform [*al*ifawrm] *adj* wing-shaped.
alight (1) [a*lIt*] *v/i* get down from, dismount; end one's journey; come to rest from the air.
alight (2) *adj* on fire, flaming; lighted up.
align, aline [a*lIn*] *v/t* and *i* place in a line, bring into line; bring (sights of gun) into line (with target); fall into line; **a. oneself with** (*fig*) act in alliance with.
alignment, alinement [a*lIn*ment] *n* act of aligning; state of being arranged in a straight line; objects so arranged; (*fig*) alliance.
alike [a*lIk*] *adj* similar, resembling each other ~ **alike** *adv* similarly, to the same extent.
aliment [*al*iment] *n* nourishment, food; support; (*Scots leg*) alimony ~ **aliment** [*al*i*ment*] *v/t* feed.
alimentary [ali*men*ta*R*i] *adj* nutritious, concerned with nutrition; **a. canal** the system of organs in the body through which food passes.

17

alimentation [alimen*tay*shon] *n* process of supplying with food; support, maintenance.

alimony [*ali*moni] *n* maintenance, *esp* allowance which a husband may be ordered to pay to his wife after a divorce or legal separation.

aline, alinement see **align, alignment.**

aliphatic [ali*fatik*] *adj* (*chem*) pertaining to fat, fatty; (*of organic compounds*) containing open chains of carbon atoms > PDS.

aliquant [*ali*kwant] *adj* (*arith*) not being a factor of another number.

aliquot [*ali*kwot] *adj* (*arith*) being a factor of another number ~ **aliquot** *n* (*chem*) part of a whole.

alive [a*lIv*] *adv* and *adj* living; (*fig*) in full vigour, unforgotten; sensitive, readily responding; lively; alert, active; swarming with; charged with electric current; **look a.** make haste!

alizarin [a*liza*Rin] *n* a red dye > PDS.

alkalescent [alka*lesent*] *adj* tending to become alkaline; partially alkaline.

alkali [*alka*lI] *n* soluble product obtained from the ashes of marine plants, soda-ash; (*chem*) soluble hydroxide of a metal > PDS; substance which in solution turns litmus blue and neutralizes acids.

alkalify [*alka*lifI] *v/t* and *i* convert into an alkali; become alkaline.

alkalimetry [alka*limit*Ri] *n* process of measuring the amount of alkali in a solution.

alkaline [*alka*lIn] *adj* of or like an alkali.

alkalinity [alka*lini*ti] *n* quality of being alkaline.

alkalize [*alka*lIz] *v/t* and *i* turn into an alkali.

alkaloid [*alka*loid] *n* (*chem*) group of nitrogenous compounds of plant origin, *usu* poisonous or used in medicine > PDS.

alkaloidal [alka*loidal*] *adj* of alkaloids.

alkane [*al*kayn] *n* (*chem*) saturated aliphatic hydrocarbon.

alkanet [*al*kanet] *n* red dye obtained from the root of the bugloss plant.

alkene [*al*keen] *n* (*chem*) unsaturated aliphatic hydrocarbon containing one double bond.

alkine, alkyne [*al*kIn] *n* (*chem*) unsaturated aliphatic hydrocarbon containing one triple bond.

alkyne see **alkine.**

all [*awl*] *adj* whole extent or number, amount of; greatest possible amount of; **for good and a.** finally, for ever; **once for a.** finally, for the last time ~ **all** *n* everything; anything; everyone; one's whole property; (*pl*) all men; **after a.** nevertheless; **not at a.** not in any way; **in and a.** and everything connected therewith; **a. in a.** most precious object; **in a.** altogether; **at a.** in the least degree, in any way; **a. clear** signal that danger is past ~ **all** *adv* entirely, completely; **a. the (more)** so much the (more); **a. at once** suddenly; **a. but** almost; **a. in a.** on the whole, taken as a whole; **a. out** fully extended; **a. over** finished, done for; **a. right** satisfactory, well; **a. there** (*coll*) far from stupid, shrewd; **a. up with** (*coll*) ruined, done for.

all- *pref* consisting only of; of or for the whole of.

Allah [*ala*] *n* name of God used by Muslims.

allantois [a*lant*O-is] *n* membrane in the foetus of mammals, birds and reptiles > PDB.

allay [a*lay*] *v/t* calm, assuage, appease, alleviate; temper, diminish.

all-clear [awl-*kleer*] *n* signal that an air-raid or other danger is over.

allegation [ali*gay*shon] *n* statement or assertion, *esp* one not yet proved; accusation.

allege [a*lej*] *v/t* assert, state; bring forward as a plea ~ **alleged** [a*lejd*] *adj* asserted but not yet proved.

allegiance [a*lee*jans] *n* fealty, duty of a subject to the sovereign or the state; loyalty.

allegoric, allegorical [aligo*Rik*, aligo*Rik*al] *adj* of or expressed through allegory; symbolic ~ **allegorically** *adv.*

allegorist [*aligo*Rist] *n* one who composes allegories.

allegorize [a*ligo*RIz] *v/t* and *i* turn into an allegory; compose allegories.

allegory [*aligo*Ri] *n* story, poem, picture *etc* in which a spiritual or poetic meaning is conveyed by a system of symbols.

allegretto [alig*Ret*O] *n*, *adj* and *adv* (*mus*) (passage played) fairly fast, but slower than allegro.

allegro [a*leg*RO] *n*, *adj* and *adv* (*mus*) (passage played) in lively, quick time.

alleluia, hallelujah [(h)ali*lOO*ya] *interj* praise the Lord!

allemande [*al*maand] *n* (*mus*) movement in dance suites > PDM.

allergen [a*lur*jen] *n* (*med*) substance causing an allergy.

allergic [a*lur*jik] *adj* suffering from allergy to specified substance; **a. to** (*coll*) intensely disliking or repelled by.

allergy [a*ler*ji] *n* (*med*) condition of unusually high sensitivity to a substance, contact with which may produce unpleasant physical symptoms; (*coll*) intense dislike.

alleviate [a*lee*vi-ayt] *v/t* relieve (suffering).

alley (1) [*ali*] *n* walk in garden or park bordered by bushes or trees; narrow road between buildings; long narrow piece of ground for playing at skittles or bowls; **blind a.** road that is closed at the end; (*fig*) occupation or plan that will lead to nothing; **a. cat** stray cat; (*sl*) whore.

alley (2) see **ally** (2).

alleyway [*ali*way] *n* narrow road between buildings.

allfired [*awlf*Ird] *adj* and *adv* (*sl*) utter, utterly.

All Fools' Day [awl-*fOOlz*-day] *n* the 1st of April.

alliaceous [ali-*ay*shus] *adj* (*bot*) belonging to genus *Allium*, including garlic, onions and leeks; smelling like garlic and onions.

alliance [a*lI*-ans] *n* covenant of mutual friendship between States; union by marriage; relationship; agreement to act in concert for a particular aim.

allied [a*lId*/*al*Id] *adj* joined by treaty or covenant; related by blood; of the same type.

alligator [*ali*gayter] *n* American or Chinese reptile resembling the crocodile; **a. pear** avocado; **a. tortoise** large marsh tortoise.

all-in [*awl*-in] *adv* inclusive of everything ~ **all-in** *adj* (*coll*) exhausted; (*wrestling*) with no holds barred.

alliterate [a*lite*Rayt] *v/i* (*of words*) begin with the same sound, *esp* consonantal; write a series of words beginning with the same sound.

alliteration [a*lite*Ray*shon] *n* act or state of alliterating.

alliterative [a*lite*Rativ] *adj* using alliteration.

all-night [*awl*-nIt] *adj* lasting, available, open *etc* during the whole night.

allocate [a*l*Okayt] *v/t* apportion, allot.

allocation [a*l*Okayshon] *n* act of allocating; allotted portion, ration.

allochroic, allochrous [a*l*okRO-ik, a*l*okRO-us] *adj* (*med*) changeable in colour.

allocution [a*l*okewshon] *n* formal speech.

allodium [a*l*Odi-um] *n* land held in absolute ownership, without feudal obligations.

allogamy [a*l*ogami] *n* (*bot*) cross-fertilization.

allomerism [a*l*omeRizm] *n* (*chem*) similarity in the crystalline structure of substances of different chemical composition.

allomorph [a*l*omawrf] *n* (*min*) one of several crystalline forms having the same chemical composition.

allomorphic [a*l*omawrfik] *adj* of or as an allomorph.

allopathy [a*l*opathi] *n* (*med*) curing by remedies which produce effects opposite to those of the ailment.

allophane [a*l*ofayn] *n* (*min*) hydrated silicate of aluminium.

allophone [a*l*OfOn] *n* one of two or more sounds differing acoustically but whose difference is not heard by the speaker.

allot (*pres/part* **allotting**, *p/t* and *p/part* **allotted**) [a*lot*] *v/t* divide among several persons giving each his due share.

allotment [a*l*otment] *n* act of allotting; that which is allotted; allowances made from pay by members of the armed forces to dependants; small plot of ground let out for an individual to cultivate.

allotropic [a*l*otRopik] *adj* of allotropy.

allotropy [a*l*otRopi] *n* (*chem*) existence of a chemical element in two or more forms differing in physical properties but giving rise to identical chemical compounds.

all-out [*awl*-out] *adj* (*coll*) whole-hearted.

all-over [*awl*-Over] *adj* covering all parts.

allow [a*l*ow] *v/t* and ′ permit; admit, grant, concede; make a grant of; render possible.

allowable [a*l*owab'l] *adj* that can be allowed ~ **allowably** *adv*.

allowance [a*l*owans] *n* fixed quantity of money or other substance given regularly; deduction from a bill, rebate; share, portion; **make a. for** take into account as an extenuating circumstance.

allowed [a*l*owd] *adj* permitted; recognized as true, acknowledged.

alloy [a*l*oi] *n* combination of two or more metals > PDS; inferior metal mixed with one of greater value; standard of purity of gold or silver; (*fig*) that which detracts from value, pleasure *etc* ~ **alloy** [a*l*oi] *v/t* combine two or more metals; mix with baser metal; (*fig*) injure by introducing an inferior element.

all-round [*awl*-Rownd] *adj* equally good at many skills, non-specialized.

all-rounder [awl-*Rown*der] *n* (*coll*) one who is equally good at many sports or skills.

allsorts [*awl*sawrts] *n* (*pl*) mixture of sweets, *usu* containing liquorice.

allspice [*awl*spIs] *n* West Indian dried berry that combines the flavours of several spices.

all-star [*awl*-staar] *adj* acted only or mainly by star actors.

alltime [*awl*tIm] *adj* and *adv* (*coll*) greatest, most successful *etc* ever known.

allude [a*l*ewd] *v/i* refer lightly or briefly (to).

allure [a*l*ewr] *v/t* tempt by offering attractions, entice; charm ~ **allure** *n* charm, attractiveness; (*coll*) sex-appeal.

allurement [a*l*ewrment] *n* enticement, fascination, attraction.

alluring [a*l*ewrRing] *adj* tempting, enticing.

allusion [a*l*ewzhon] *n* passing reference; indirect, brief, or unclear reference.

allusive [a*l*ewsiv] *adj* containing an allusion ~ **allusively** *adv* ~ **allusiveness** *n*.

alluvial [a*l*OOvi-al] *adj* (*of soil*) washed away and deposited elsewhere by flowing water; composed of such soil > PDG ~ **alluvial** *n* gold-bearing alluvial soil.

alluvion [a*l*OOvi-on] *n* wash of sea on the shore; flood containing alluvial matter; matter deposited by a river; (*leg*) formation of new land by slow alluvial deposit, alluvium.

alluvium [a*l*OOvi-um] *n* deposit of earth, sand *etc* washed down by a river.

all-white [*awl*-wIt] *adj* excluding Negroes, Oriental races *etc*.

ally (I) (*p/t* and *p/part* **allied**) [a*l*I] *v/t* and *refl* join, unite for a special purpose; **allied to** connected with, having similar character ~ **ally** (*pl* **allies**) *n* one who cooperates with another; State leagued with another by agreement or treaty.

ally (2), **alley** [a*l*i] *n* large white marble used in playing marbles.

almacantar [almak*ant*er] *n* a small circle of the celestial sphere parallel to the horizon.

almanac [*awl*manak] *n* calendar giving times of sunrise and sunset, changes of the moon, anniversaries *etc*; similar work with prophecies of future events.

almandine [*al*mandIn] *n* violet garnet.

almighty [awl*mI*ti] *adj* all-powerful, omnipotent; (*coll*) huge; very violent; extreme, absolute; **the A.** God.

almond [*aam*ond] *n* tree related to the peach; edible kernel of the nut of this tree.

almond-eyed [*aam*ond-Id] *adj* having long narrow eyes of Eastern type.

almond-oil [*aam*ond-oil] *n* benzoic aldehyde, oil pressed from almond kernels.

almond-paste [*aam*ond-payst] *n* mixture of sugar, eggs and ground almonds.

almoner [*aam*oner/*al*moner] *n* official in a hospital who administers social service work for patients; official who distributes the alms of a religious institution.

almost [*awl*mOst] *adv* very nearly.

alms [aamz] *n* money given for charitable purposes, *esp* for the poor.

almsbox [*aamz*boks] *n* box in a church to receive donations for charitable purposes.

almsgiving [*aamz*giving] *n* giving of money for charity.

almshouse [*aamz*hows] *n* house endowed by charity where aged poor can be received.

almsman [*aamz*man] *n* man who is supported by alms.

aloe [alO] n genus of plants with spikes of flowers and bitter juice; (pl) (med) purgative drug obtained from the juice of aloes.

aloetic [aloetik] n and adj (medicine) containing aloes.

aloft [aloft] adv high up, high in the air; upwards; (naut) in the rigging, at the mast-head.

aloin [alO-in] n (chem) bitter purgative element in aloes.

alone [alOn] adv solely, only ~ **alone** adj solitary; unique; with no companion; **let a.** (v) not interfere with; (conj) far less, not to mention.

along [along] prep beside and in the same direction as ~ **along** adv forward; **all a.** all the time, continuously; **get a.** prosper (well or ill); **get a.!** (coll) be off with you; **a. with** together with.

alongshore [alongshawr] adv (naut) along by the shore, on the shore.

alongside [alongsId] adv and prep close to the side of, beside.

aloof [alOOf] adv at a distance; not joining in, not approving of; **stand a. from** show no sympathy with ~ **aloof** adj distant, haughty, reserved ~ **aloofly** adv ~ **aloofness** n.

alopecia [alopeesi-a] n (med) baldness.

aloud [alowd] adv with a loud voice, loudly; audibly, not in silence; **read a.** read to others.

alow [alO] adv (naut) below, downwards.

alp [alp] n single mountain peak; (pl, cap) mountain range between France and Italy.

alpaca [alpaka] n Peruvian quadruped akin to the llama, with long woolly hair; cloth made from this hair.

alpenhorn [alpenhawrn] n wooden trumpet used by Swiss shepherds.

alpenstock [alpenstok] n staff pointed with iron used in mountaineering.

alpha [alfa] n first letter of the Greek alphabet; first-class mark in an examination; (astron) chief star in a constellation; **A. and Omega** the beginning and the end; **a. particle** positively charged helium nucleus > PDS, PDEl; **a. rays** streams of fast-moving alpha particles > PDS; **a. rhythm** rhythm of electrical waves of the brain in a state of relaxation.

alphabet [alfabet] n set of letters used in any language; (fig) rudiments.

alphabetical [alfabetikal] adj in the order of the alphabet ~ **alphabetically** adv.

alphenic [alfenik] n white barley-sugar.

alphos [alfus] n non-contagious disorder of the skin resembling leprosy.

alpine [alpIn] adj of or found on the Alps.

already [awlRedi] adv by or before a specified or expected time; by now.

Alsatian [alsayshan] n breed of large fierce dog used by police, as watchdogs etc.

also [awlsO] adv in addition, besides.

also-ran [awlsO-Ran] n (coll) horse who does badly in a race; person who is a failure.

alt [alt] n (mus) first octave above the treble stave.

altar [awlter] n raised structure with a flat top, on which sacrifices are offered or the Christian Eucharist is celebrated; **lead to the a.** marry (a wife); **a. boy** acolyte.

altarcloth [awlterkloth] n white linen cloth placed on the altar frontal.

altarpiece [awlterpees] n painting or sculpture placed behind and above an altar; reredos.

altar-rails [awlter-Raylz] n (pl) rails separating the sanctuary from the rest of the chancel.

altarstone [awlterstOn] n slab forming the top of an altar.

alter [awlter] v/t and i change, make or become different.

alterable [awlteRab'l] adj that can be altered ~ **alterably** adv.

alterant [awlteRant] adj causing alteration ~ **alterant** n something which alters another.

alteration [awlteRayshon] n action of altering; state of being altered; change made.

altercate [awlterkayt] v/i quarrel fiercely.

altercation [awlterkayshon] n fierce quarrel or argument.

alter ego [alter-egO] n an inseparable friend who shares one's pursuits; confidential representative.

alternate [awlturnit] adj (of two things) following continuously one after the other; arranged alternately; (bot) growing along an axis, first on one side, then on the other; **a. generation** (biol) reproduction by two alternate methods > PDB.

alternate [awlternayt] v/i and t (of two things) follow each other by turns; cause (two things) to follow each other by turns; **alternating current** a flow of electricity which reverses its direction at regular intervals.

alternately [awlturnitli] adv first one then the other.

alternation [awlternayshon] n alternate occurrence.

alternative [awlturnativ] adj offering choice of two courses; **a. society** minority group pursuing moral and social aims markedly different from those of the majority ~ **alternative** n choice between two courses; either of the two courses which are open; choice between more than two courses ~ **alternatively** adv.

alternator [awlternayter] n (elect) dynamo producing alternating current.

although [awlTHO] conj though, even though.

altimeter [altimeeter] n aneroid barometer used in aircraft recording the height reached.

altitude [altitewd] n height; height above sea-level; (geom) length from apex to base of a triangle; (pl) high regions; (astron) angular height of a heavenly body above the horizon; (fig) eminence, distinguished position.

alto [altO] n (mus) highest male voice, countertenor; female voice of similar range, contralto; person with such a voice; music written for such a voice; **a. clef** the C clef when placed on the third line of the stave.

altogether [awltogeTHer] adv entirely, quite; on the whole; **the a.** (coll) the nude.

altruism [altRoo-izm] n consideration of the good of others before one's own; unselfishness.

altruist [altRoo-ist] n habitually unselfish person ~ **altruistic** [altRoo-istik] adj ~ **altruistically** adv.

alum [alum] n sulphate of aluminium used as an astringent and styptic > PDS.

alumina [alewmina] n aluminium oxide > PDS.

aluminium [alewmini-um] n white metal, very light and malleable, and resistant to oxidation > PDS.

aluminous [alewminus] adj of the nature of alum.
aluminum [alewminum] n (US) aluminium.
alumna (pl alumnae) [alumna] n woman graduate or former pupil of school or university.
alumnus (pl alumni) [alumnus] n graduate or former pupil of school or university.
alveolar [alvee-oler] adj pertaining to the sockets of teeth; (phon) pronounced by the tongue against the roots of the upper teeth.
alveolate [alvee-olayt] adj pitted with small cavities.
alveole [alvi-Ol] n alveolus.
alveolus (pl alveoli) [alvee-olus] n socket of a tooth; cell of a honeycomb; aircell of the lungs > PDB.
alvine [alvIn] adj pertaining to the abdomen.
always [awlwayz] adv at all times, continually.
alyssum [alisum] n (bot) genus of cruciferous plants with yellow or white flowers.
am [am] 1st pers sing pres ind of be.
amadou [amadOO] n tinder prepared from a species of fungus.
amah [aama] n China, Japan, S. India) wet-nurse; English child's Indian nurse.
amain [amayn] adv with full force, violently; at full speed; very greatly.
amalgam [amalgam] n mixture, blending of different elements; alloy of mercury.
amalgamate [amalgamayt] v/t and i blend to a unified whole; (comm, of companies) unite into one.
amalgamation [amalgamayshon] n act of combining into one unified whole; (comm) union of companies into one concern; (min) process of separating gold or silver from rock or sand by treatment with mercury > PDS.
amalgamator [amalgamayter] n (min) apparatus for the process of amalgamation.
amanitin [amanitin] n poisonous substance in certain fungi.
amanuensis [amanew-ensis] n secretary; copyist; literary assistant.
amaranth [amaRanth] n genus of plant with drooping purple flowers; a purple colour; imaginary fadeless flower.
amaranthine [amaRanthIn] adj purple; never fading, immortal.
amaryllis [amaRilis] n genus of bulbous plants which flower in autumn.
amass [amas] v/t collect together, accumulate for oneself.
amateur [amatur] n one who follows a sport or pursuit for love of it, and not for money; one whose mastery of a subject is only superficial; (sport) player receiving no salary or wages ~ **amateur** adj of, for or by amateurs.
amateurish [amaturRish] adj superficial, clumsy, lacking knowledge and practice ~ **amateurishly** adv ~ **amateurishness** n.
amative [amativ] adj inclined to loving, amorous.
amatol [amatol] n explosive mixture of trinitrotoluene (T.N.T.) and ammonium nitrate.
amatory [amatoRi] adj pertaining to love-making.
amaurosis [amoROsis] n (med) blindness caused by disease in the optic nerve.
amaze [amayz] v/t astound, fill with astonishment ~ **amaze** n (poet) amazement.
amazement [amayzment] n astonishment.

amazing [amayzing] adj causing astonishment, highly surprising or wonderful ~ **amazingly** adv.
amazon [amazon] n legendary Scythian female warrior; very strong athletic woman.
amazon-ant [amazon-ant] n species of red ant.
amazonian [amazOni-an] adj of or like an amazon.
ambassador [ambasader] n diplomat of high rank sent on a mission to a foreign country, or residing there as the representative of his sovereign or State; (fig) messenger.
ambassadorial [ambasadawrRi-al] adj of an ambassador.
ambassadress [ambasadRis] n female ambassador; ambassador's wife.
amber [amber] n yellow-brown fossil resin used for ornamental purposes; yellow cautionary light in traffic signals; (fig) signal of approaching danger ~ **amber** adj of amber, of amber colour.
ambergris [ambergRees] n grey or black waxy substance from the intestines of the sperm-whale, used in perfumery.
amberite [ambeRIt] n smokeless explosive.
ambi- pref both, on both sides, around.
ambidexter [ambidekster] n ambidextrous person; double-crosser.
ambidexterity [ambideksteRiti] n quality or state of being ambidextrous.
ambidextrous [ambidekstRus] adj able to use either hand equally well ~ **ambidextrously** adv.
ambience [ambi-ens] n environment.
ambient [ambi-ent] adj surrounding.
ambiguity [ambigew-iti] n capability of being understood in two or more ways; doubtful meaning; lack of clarity; ambiguous expression.
ambiguous [ambigew-us] adj that can mean two or more different things; vaguely expressed; obscure; equivocal ~ **ambiguously** adv ~ **ambiguousness** n.
ambit [ambit] n circumference, circuit, precincts; (fig) extent, sphere (of influence).
ambition [ambishon] n strong desire to achieve success; object of this desire.
ambitious [ambishus] adj eager for success, aspiring to high position; aiming at success in a difficult undertaking ~ **ambitiously** adv.
ambivalence [ambivalens] n coexistence of two opposite emotions, esp love and hate, towards the same object ~ **ambivalent** adj ~ **ambivalently** adv.
amble [amb'l] v/i (of horse) move at an easy pace; (of person) walk at an easy pace, stroll.
ambo [ambO] n pulpit or reading-desk in early Christian churches.
ambrosia [ambROzi-a] n (Gk myth) food of the gods; (fig) anything unimaginably delightful to taste or smell ~ **ambrosial** adj pertaining to the gods; exquisite in taste or smell.
ambrosian (1) [ambROzi-an] adj ambrosial.
ambrosian (2) adj pertaining to, instituted by St Ambrose.
ambry, aumbry [ambRi, awmbRi] n (eccles) cupboard near altar for sacred vessels etc.
ambulance [ambewlans] n vehicle for carrying sick people or victims of accidents to hospital; (mil) mobile field-hospital.
ambulant [ambewlant] adj moving, shifting about-

ambulatory-amount

ambulatory [ambewlatoRi] adj of, for or capable of walking ~ **ambulatory** n covered place for walking in; cloister; semicircular aisle round apse.

ambuscade [ambuskayd] n concealment of a body of troops lying in wait to surprise an enemy ~ **ambuscade** v/t and i conceal (troops) in ambush; lie in ambush.

ambush [amboosh] n ambuscade; act of lying in wait to attack an unprepared enemy or victim; place where such attackers hide ~ **ambush** v/t place (men) in ambush; lie in wait (for).

Ameer, Amir [ameer] n title of various Mohammedan rulers, esp of Afghanistan.

ameliorate [ameeli-oRayt] v/t and i make better; grow better.

amen [aamen/aymen] interj so be it!; so it is in truth; **say a.** to concur with, approve.

amenable [ameenab'l] adj submissive; responsive (to); answerable, responsible ~ **amenably** adv.

amend [amend] v/t and i make better, free from errors; improve one's character.

amendment [amendment] n removal of faults; reformation of character; improvement in health; alteration proposed in a bill before parliament; (leg) correction of an error in a bill or process.

amends [amendz] n (pl) reparation; **make a.** make restitution.

amenity [ameeniti] n that which is agreeable; pleasantness; (pl) convenient or agreeable features of a dwelling, estate, or district.

amentia [amenshi-a] n lack of intelligence > PDP.

amerce [amurs] v/t impose a fine on; fine.

amercement, amerciament [amursment, amursi-ament] n a fine.

American [ameRikan] adj belonging to the continent of America; belonging to the United States; **A. Beauty** type of rose; **A. cloth** type of oilcloth ~ **American** n inhabitant of America; citizen or language of the United States.

Americanism [ameRikanizm] n any peculiarity of idiom, accent, vocabulary etc characteristic of the United States.

Americanize [ameRikanIz] v/t make American in character.

americium [ameRiki-um] n (chem) a transuranic element > PDS.

Amerindian [ameRindi-an] n and adj (contr) American Indian.

amethyst [amithist] n mauve-coloured quartz used as a semi-precious gemstone.

amethystine [amithistIn] adj containing amethyst; amethyst-coloured.

amiability [aymi-abiliti] n quality of being amiable.

amiable [aymi-ab'l] adj pleasant of disposition; friendly, kindly ~ **amiably** adv.

amianthus [ami-anthus] n fine asbestos.

amicable [amikab'l] adj friendly, harmonious, peaceable ~ **amicably** adv.

amice (1) [amis] n square or oblong piece of fine linen worn over the shoulders under the alb.

amice (2) n fur hood worn by the religious orders.

amid [amid] prep (poet) amidst.

amidships [amidships] adv in the middle of the ship.

amidst [amidst] prep in the middle of; surrounded by, among.

amino-acid [aminO-asid] n one of various organic compounds forming basic constituents of living matter > PDB, PDS.

Amir see Ameer.

amiss [amis] adv wrongly, erroneously; **come a.** turn out contrary to one's wishes; **take a.** take offence at ~ **amiss** adj out of order, unsatisfactory.

amity [amiti] n friendship, friendly relationship.

ammeter [amiter] n instrument for the measurement in amperes of electric current > PDS.

ammo [amO] n (sl) ammunition.

ammonal [amonal] n high explosive formed from ammonium nitrate and powdered aluminium.

ammonia [amOni-a] n colourless, pungent, alkaline gas > PDS; **liquid a.** solution of ammonia in water.

ammoniac [amOni-ak] adj of the nature of ammonia; **sal a.** ammonium chloride, a hard white salt used medicinally.

ammoniacal [amonI-akal] adj of, like, or containing ammonia.

ammoniated [amOni-aytid] adj combined with ammonia.

ammonite [amonIt] n extinct genus of mollusc; fossil shell of this.

ammonium [amOni-um] n (chem) univalent radical derived from ammonia plus a hydrogen ion or atom > PDS.

ammunition [amewnishon] n bullet, shell, or other missile to be fired from a gun; (obs mil) stores ~ **ammunition** adj (obs mil) of regulation type.

amnesia [amneesi-a] n (path) loss of memory > PDP ~ **amnesic** [amneesik] adj.

amnesty [amnesti] n general pardon granted to political offenders or criminals ~ **amnesty** v/t.

amnion [amni-on] n (physiol) membrane enclosing the foetus before birth > PDB.

amniotic [amni-otik] adj of the amnion; **a. fluid** fluid in which an unborn foetus floats.

amoeba [ameeba] n (zool) unicellular organism without any constant form or organs > PDB.

amoebic [ameebik] adj of or caused by an amoeba.

amoeboid [ameeboid] adj of or like an amoeba.

amok see amuck.

among [amung] prep surrounded by; associated with; by the joint action of; in the general opinion of; between.

amongst [amungst] prep among.

amontillado [amontilaadO] n type of sherry.

amoral [amoRal] adj lacking moral sense, disregarding morality; outside the sphere of morals, non-moral.

amorist [amoRist] n one who delights in lovemaking; writer of amatory literature.

amorous [amoRus] adj showing or inclined to love, esp sexual love ~ **amorously** adv ~ **amorousness** n.

amorphous [amawrfus] adj shapeless; (min and chem) non-crystalline; (fig) unorganized, ill-constructed ~ **amorphousness** n.

amortization [amawrtizayshon] n repayment of borrowed capital together with the interest on it.

amortize [amawrtIz] v/t hand over (property) to a corporation in perpetuity; pay off (debt).

amount [amownt] v/i and t increase so as to reach, add up to; be tantamount to, mean as much as ~ **amount** n quantity; sum total; total significance.

22

amour [*amoor*] *n* love-affair, *gener* illicit.

amperage [*ampe*Rij] *n* strength of an electric current expressed in amperes.

ampere [*am*pair] *n* unit of electric current > PDS.

ampersand [*am*persand] *n* symbol [&] for 'and'.

amphetamines [amf*eet*aminz] *n* (*pl*) (*med*) group of drugs used as stimulants and to induce feelings of well-being or excitement.

amphibia [am*fibi*-a] *n* class of vertebrates which breathe either through gills or through lungs.

amphibian [am*fibi*-an] *adj* able to live or function either on land or in water; of amphibia ~ amphibian *n* member of the amphibia; amphibious aircraft, tank *etc*.

amphibious [am*fibi*-us] *adj* living both on land and in water; (*mil*) able to land or move either on land or water; attacking by both land and sea.

amphigamous [am*figa*mus] *adj* (*bot*) withou distinct sexual organs.

amphioxus [amfi-*oks*us] *n* (*zool*) lowest genus of fishes > PDB.

amphisbaena [amfis*beena*] *n* mythical serpent with a head at each end; (*zool*) worm-like genus of lizards.

amphitheatre [*am*fithee-ater] *n* building containing an oval space surrounded by seats rising in tiers; one of the galleries in a modern theatre.

amphora [*am*foRa] *n* two-handled earthenware vessel used for storing wine, oil *etc*.

amphoteric [amf*Oteer*Rik] *adj* (*chem*) able to act either as an acid or as a base > PDS.

ample [*amp*'l] *adj* quite large enough, spacious; abundant, unstinted.

amplifier [*ampl*ifi-er] *n* (*opt*) lens which increases the field of vision; (*elect*) device for increasing the strength of an electronic impulse.

amplification [amplifi*kay*shon] *n* act of amplifying; state of being amplified; degree to which something is amplified.

amplify [*ampl*ifi] *v/t* increase, enlarge, expand; make more important.

amplitude [*ampl*itewd] *n* size, dimensions; wide range; abundance; (*astron*) deviation from due east or due west in rising or setting; (*phys*) maximum value of a periodically varying quantity.

amply [*ampl*i] *adv* in an ample way; to an ample degree.

ampoule, ampule [*am*pool] *n* small glass vessel containing dose for a hypodermic injection.

ampulla [am*pula*] *n* small round two-handled wine bottle; (*med*) swelling at end of each semi-circular canal in the inner ear.

amputate [*am*pewtayt] *v/t* and *i* cut off, sever, *esp* by surgery ~ amputation [ampew*tay*shon] *n*.

amputee [ampew*tee*] *n* one who has had a limb amputated.

amuck, amok [*am*uk, *am*ok] *adv* run a. rush about madly causing injury or death; get out of control.

amulet [*am*ewlet] *n* a charm, something worn to protect one against misfortune, disease, witchcraft *etc*.

amuse [a*mewz*] *v/t* and *i* give pleasure to, entertain; cause pleasant mirth; occupy the mind agreeably.

amusement [a*mewz*ment] *n* state of being amused; pastime, recreation.

amusing [a*mewz*ing] *adj* causing pleasant laughter, entertaining ~ amusingly *adv*.

amygdalate [a*mig*dalayt] *adj* made of almonds ~ amygdalate *n* (*chem*) a salt of amygdalic acid.

amygdalic [a*mig*dalik] *adj* (*chem*) pertaining to or obtained from almonds.

amygdalin [a*mig*dalin] *n* (*chem*) a glucoside derived from the kernels of almonds.

amyl [*am*il] *n* starch; a. alcohol colourless liquid used as solvent > PDS.

amylaceous [ami*lay*shus] *adj* starchy.

amylase [*am*ilayz] *n* (*chem*) enzyme capable of splitting up starches > PDS.

amyloid [*am*iloid] *n* and *adj* (substance) akin to starch.

amylopectin [amil*Opek*tin] *n* (*chem*) insoluble component of starch > PDS.

amylose [*am*ilOz] *n* (*chem*) soluble component of starch > PDS.

an (1) [*an*] *indef art* form of a used before unaccented *h* and vowel sounds.

an (2) *conj* (*ar*) if.

an- *neg pref*, used before vowels.

ana- *pref* up, again.

Anabaptist [ana*bap*tist] *n* member of a sixteenth-century sect which practised the re-baptism of adults.

anabas [*an*abas] *n* genus of fishes which leave the water and climb trees.

anabatic [ana*batik*] *adj* (*of wind*) blowing inland to take the place of warmer air > PDG.

anabiotic [anabI-*otik*] *adj* apparently lifeless but capable of being revived ~ anabiotic *n* any agent used to effect such a restoration or revival.

anabolism [an*abo*lizm] *n* process of building up the complex organic substances in living tissues.

anabranch [*an*aBRaansh] *n* stream which turns out of a river and rejoins it lower down.

anacathartic [anaka*thaar*tik] *adj* causing vomiting or spitting.

anachronism [an*ak*Ronizm] *n* error in stating the date of an event; error in assigning a custom, device, form of speech *etc* to a period when it was not used; thing so misplaced.

anachronistic [anakRon*istik*] *adj* of or containing an anachronism.

anacoluthon (*pl* anacolutha) [anako*lewth*on] *n* lack of grammatical sequence, when a clause is left unfinished and another begun.

anaconda [ana*konda*] *n* large non-poisonous, constricting snake of South America.

anacrusis [anak*ROO*sis] *n* (*pros*) extra-metrical syllable at the beginning of a line.

anadem [*an*adem] *n* wreath for the head, garland.

anadromous [an*ad*Romus] *adj* (*zool*) (*of fish*) going up rivers from the sea to spawn.

anaemia [a*neemi*-a] *n* deficiency or poor quality of red corpuscles in blood.

anaemic [a*neemik*] *adj* of or suffering from anaemia; (*fig*) feeble, lifeless; pale.

anaerobe [*an*ay-eROb] *n* any bacterium which can live without oxygen.

anaerobic [anairR*Obik*] *adj* pertaining to, or capable of existing in, the absence of air or free oxygen.

anaesthesia [anis*theez*i-a] *n* loss, abolition, or lessening of sensitivity to stimuli.

23

anaesthetic [anis*thet*ik] *adj* lessening sensitivity to stimuli ~ **anaesthetic** *n* substance which produces abolition or lessening of sensitivity, used in surgical operations.

anaesthetist [a*nees*thetist] *n* one who administers anaesthetics to patients during surgery.

anaesthetize [a*nees*thetiz] *v/t* administer an anaesthetic to.

anaglyph [*anag*lif] *n* embossed ornament worked in low relief; (*phot*) stereoscopic picture > PDP.

anagogy, anagoge [anag*Oji*] *n* mystical interpretation; allegorical interpretation of the Scriptures ~ **anagogical** [anag*oji*kal] *adj*.

anagram [*anag*Ram] *n* rearrangement of letters in a word or phrase so as to make another word or phrase.

anal [*aynal*] *adj* of or near the anus; (*psych*) of or in a stage of infancy when pleasure is mostly concerned with defecation and the anus; **a. character** (*psych*) person tending to anal-eroticism; person obsessively neat, miserly, obstinate or self-disciplined.

anal-erotic [aynal-i*Rot*ik] *n* of or showing anal-eroticism.

anal-eroticism, anal-erotism [aynal-i*Rot*isizm, aynal-i*Rot*izm] *n* (*psych*) pleasure or sexual excitement caused by or symbolizing stimulation of the anus.

analect (*pl* **analecta**) [*anal*ekt] *n* collection of literary extracts or fragments.

analgesia [anal*jees*i-a] *n* (*med*) abolition of pain sensation.

analgesic [anal*jees*ik] *n* and *adj* (drug) which gives relief from pain.

analogical [anal*oji*kal] *adj* of, as or expressing an analogy ~ **analogically** *adv*.

analogize [anal*oji*z] *v/t* and *i* explain or reason by analogy ~ **analogist** *n* one who reasons by analogy.

analogous [an*al*ogus] *adj* similar in certain respects ~ **analogously** *adv*.

analogue [*anal*og] *n* something partially similar or corresponding to something else; **a. computer** calculating machine that operates by representing numerical magnitudes by such physical quantities as voltages.

analogy [an*al*oji] *n* likeness between two things in certain respects; something partially similar; (*log*) assumption that if things agree in some attributes, they will agree in others; (*philol*) influence on the form of one word by another having a resemblance to it.

analyse, analyze [*anal*Iz] *v/t* divide into component parts or elements; examine minutely; study the nature, function and effects of every part of; make a detailed description and criticism of; subject to psycho-analysis; (*gramm*) distinguish the main parts in (a sentence).

analysis (*pl* **analyses**) [an*al*isis] *n* process of analysing; result of analysing; tabular synopsis; psycho-analysis; decomposition of substances into their elements or constituent parts > PDS; (*math*) solution of problems by reduction to equations.

analyst [*anal*ist] *n* one skilled in chemical analysis; psycho-analyst.

analytic, analytical [anal*it*ik, anal*it*ikal] *adj* using analysis; (*philol*) expressing grammatical relations by separate words instead of by inflexions; (*geom*) using coordinates to define positions in space ~ **analytically** *adv*.

analytics [anal*it*iks] *n* use of analysis; that part of logic which treats of analysis.

anamnesis [anam*nee*sis] *n* recollection, *esp* of a previous existence of the soul; (*med*) patient's account of an illness.

anamorphosis [anamawrf*Os*is] *n* distorted image which will look normal if viewed from a certain angle or in a curved mirror; (*bot*) abnormal distortion of a plant; (*biol*) gradual evolutionary change in form.

anamorphous [anam*awr*fus] *adj* distorted; of abnormal development.

ananas [an*aan*as] *n* pineapple plant or fruit.

anandrous [an*and*Rus] *adj* (*bot*) without stamens.

anapaest [*an*apest] *n* (*pros*) foot consisting of two short syllables followed by a long one; two unstressed syllables followed by a stressed one; verse consisting of anapaests ~ **anapaestic** *adj*.

anaphrodisiac [anafR*Od*izi-ak] *n* and *adj* (drug) diminishing sexual appetite.

anaplasty [*an*aplasti] *n* (*surg*) repair of external injuries by use of adjacent healthy tissue.

anarch [*an*ark] *n* (*ar*) anarchist.

anarchic, anarchical [an*aar*kik, an*aar*kikal] *adj* pertaining to anarchy; lawless.

anarchism [*an*arkizm] *n* theory that society should do without any form of government.

anarchist [*an*arkist] *n* one who advocates or tries to bring about anarchy ~ **anarchist** *adj*.

anarchy [*an*arki] *n* absence of government; lawlessness causing political disorder; absence of order and discipline.

anasarca [anas*aar*ka] *n* diffused dropsy.

anastigmat [an*ast*igmat] *n* anastigmatic lens.

anastigmatic [anastig*mat*ik] *adj* (*of lens*) designed to correct astigmatism.

anastomosis [anast*omOs*is] *n* intercommunication between two sets of channels.

anathema [an*ath*ema] *n* (*eccles*) solemn curse of the church with excommunication; person or thing so cursed; curse, imprecation; person or thing heartily disliked.

anathematize [an*ath*ematIz] *v/t* curse; denounce.

anatomical [anat*om*ikal] *adj* pertaining to anatomy ~ **anatomically** *adv*.

anatomist [an*at*omist] *n* one skilled in dissection.

anatomize [an*at*omIz] *v/t* dissect; examine minutely and critically.

anatomy [an*at*omi] *n* dissection of bodies to study their structure; science of bodily structures; (*obs coll*) skeleton; (*fig*) detailed analysis.

ancestor [*an*sester] *n* one from whom a person is directly descended.

ancestral [an*sest*Ral] *adj* inherited from ancestors; of an ancestor.

ancestress [*an*sestRis] *n* female ancestor.

ancestry [*an*sestRi] *n* line of ancestors.

anchor [*an*ker] *n* heavy piece of iron with two curved arms used for mooring a ship to the sea-bottom > PDSa; (*fig*) something which gives the certainty of security; **cast a., come to a.** let go the anchor; **weigh a.** draw the anchor up ~ **anchor** *v/i* and *t* come to anchor; make (a ship) fast by letting go the anchor; (*fig*) fix firmly.

24

anchorage (1) [*ank*oRij] *n* state of being anchored; place suitable for this; point at which something is firmly fixed to framework *etc*; fee charged for anchoring in harbour.

anchorage (2) *n* dwelling of an anchoret or anchoress.

anchored [*ank*erd] *adj* held by the anchor; made secure.

anchoress, ancress [*ank*Res] *n* female anchoret.

anchoret, anchorite [*ank*oRit, *ank*oRIt] *n* religious recluse, hermit.

anchor-ground [*ank*er-gRownd] *n* place suitable for anchoring.

anchor-ice [*ank*er-Is] *n* ice clinging to the bottom of lakes and rivers.

anchorite see anchoret.

anchorman [*ank*erman] *n* (*TV*) chairman or linking commentator in a discussion programme; (*fig*) one who provides stability and continuity.

anchovy [*anch*Ovi/*anch*Ovi] *n* small fish of the herring family, eaten pickled and used to make piquant sauces and savouries.

anchylosis see ankylosis.

ancien régime [ongsi-ang Rayz*heem*] *n* (*Fr*) political and social system of France before the 1789 Revolution; (*fig*) outdated or reactionary system or outlook.

ancient [*ayn*shent] *adj* very old; having existed from early times; belonging to, living in or dealing with early times ~ **ancient** *n* one living in early times; (*pl*) members of ancient civilized nations, *esp* Greeks and Romans; (*ar*) old man; **A. of Days** biblical title of God.

ancillary [*ansi*laRi] *adj* subordinate, auxiliary.

anconeal [ank*Oni*-al] *adj* pertaining to the elbow.

and [*and*] *conj* together with; used as a link between parts of a sentence.

andante [an*danti*] *adv* (*mus*) moderately slowly ~ **andante** *n* movement in andante time > PDM.

andantino [andan*teen*O] *adv* between andante and allegretto; (*obs*) slower than andante.

andiron [*and*I-ern] *n* one of a pair of iron utensils which hold up the logs in the fire, firedog.

andro- *pref* man; male.

androecium [and*Rees*i-um] *n* stamens.

androgen [*and*Rojen] *n* any male sex hormone > PDB.

androgynous [and*Roj*inus] *adj* uniting male and female physical characteristics; hermaphrodite; (*bot*) having stamens and pistil in the same flower.

anear [a*neer*] *adv* (*poet*) nearly; near, not far.

anecdotal [anekd*O*tal] *adj* of, containing or telling anecdotes.

anecdote [*an*ekdOt] *n* short story with some striking point.

anechoic [ane*kO*-ik] *adj* having a low degree of reverberation.

anemograph [*anem*OgRaaf] *n* instrument for recording the direction and force of the wind.

anemometer [ani*mom*iter] *n* instrument for measuring the force of the wind > PDG.

anemone [a*nem*Oni] *n* (*bot*) genus of plants including the wind-flower; **sea a.** name of various actinoid zoophytes.

anent [a*nent*] *prep* regarding, concerning.

aneroid [*ani*Roid] *n* and *adj* (barometer) in which atmospheric pressure is measured by the displacement of the flexible lid of a metal box nearly exhausted of air > PDS.

aneurism [a*newr*izm] *n* (*path*) distention of an artery due to rupture of its tough fibrous coat.

anew [a*new*] *adv* again, afresh; in a different way.

anfractuous [an*fRakt*ew-us] *adj* winding; craggy.

angary [*ang*-gari] *n* seizure or destruction of the property of a neutral state by a belligerent for which an indemnity is paid.

angel [*ayn*jel] *n* spiritual being attendant on God, acting as his messenger; person resembling an angel in beauty or loving service; image or representation of an angel; old English gold coin bearing the figure of St Michael; (*sl*) financial backer of a stage production.

angel-fish [*ayn*j'l-fish] *n* fish of the shark family with wing-like pectoral fins.

angelic [an*jel*ik] *adj* of or like an angel; very good or beautiful.

angelica [an*jel*ika] *n* aromatic umbelliferous plant; candied root of this.

angelical [an*jel*ikal] *adj* angel-like ~ **angelically** *adv.*

angelolatry [aynje*lolat*Ri] *n* worship of angels.

angelology [aynje*loloj*i] *n* doctrine which treats of angels.

angelus [*anj*elus] *n* (*RC*) prayer to commemorate the Incarnation said in the early morning, at noon, and at sunset, when a bell is rung.

anger [*ang*-ger] *n* wrath, rage, passionate resentment ~ **anger** *v/t* cause to feel anger, incense.

angina [an*jIn*a] *n* (*path*) quinsy; **a. pectoris** sudden paroxysm with acute pain in the chest ~ **anginous** [an*jIn*us] *adj.*

angiology [anji-*oloj*i] *n* (*anat*) science dealing with the veins and arteries of the human body.

angle (1) [*ang*-g'l] *n* space between two intersecting lines or planes; (*geom*) inclination of two lines to each other, measured in degrees; corner; (*fig*) aspect, point of view ~ **angle** *v/t* (*coll*) distort so as to reveal a particular point of view.

angle (2) *v/i* fish with hook and line; (*fig*) use subtle means to attain an objective.

angler [*ang*-gler] *n* one who fishes with rod and line; (*zool*) fish which lures others by moving filaments attached to its head.

Angles [*ang*-g'lz] *n* (*pl*) Low German tribe which invaded Britain and settled in Northumbria, Mercia and East Anglia.

Anglian [*ang*-gli-an] *adj* of the Angles.

Anglican [*ang*-glikan] *n* and *adj* (member) of the Church of England or of an affiliated episcopal Church ~ **Anglicanism** *n.*

anglicism [*ang*-glisizm] *n* English idiom or phrase introduced into a foreign language.

anglicize [*ang*-glisiz] *v/t* make English (in speech, character, habits *etc*).

angling [*ang*-gling] *n* fishing with hook and line.

Anglo-American [ang-glO-ame*Rik*an] *n* an American of English origin ~ **Anglo-American** *adj* concerning the relations between England and America.

Anglo-Catholic [ang-glO-*kath*olik] *n* (member) of the High Church party of the Church of England.

Anglo-French [ang-glO-*fRensh*] *n* dialect of French current in medieval England ~ **Anglo-**

25

French *adj* pertaining to relations between England and France.

Anglo-Indian [ang-glO-*indi*-an] *adj* or *n* (of) English people born or living in India; (of) Indians of partly English descent.

Anglo-Irish [ang-glO-*Ir*Rish] *n* (*pl*) English resident in Ireland ~ **Anglo-Irish** *adj* pertaining to the inter-relations of English and Irish in Ireland.

anglomania [ang-glO*mayni*-a] *n* exaggerated admiration of England and English ways.

Anglo-Norman [ang-glO-*nawrm*an] *n* dialect of Norman-French as spoken in England in the Middle Ages.

anglophile [*ang*-glOfIl] *n* and *adj* (person) well-disposed to England and everything English.

anglophobe [*ang*-glOfOb] *n* and *adj* (person) hating England and everything English.

anglophobia [ang-glO*fo*bi-a] *n* fear or hatred of England and everything English.

Anglo-Saxon [ang-glO-*saks*on] *n* inhabitant of England before the Norman Conquest; language spoken by the Anglo-Saxons; person of English stock ~ **Anglo-Saxon** *adj*.

angola [ang-g*O*la] *n* angora.

angora [ang-*gaw*Ra] *n* fabric made from the wool of an Asiatic goat; long-haired variety of cat; variety of rabbit with fine white hair and pink eyes.

angostura, angustura [ang-gos*tewr*Ra] *n* bitter medicinal bark of a S. American tree; **a. bitters** flavouring for drinks.

angry [*ang*-gRi] *adj* showing anger, wrathful, enraged; looking threatening; inflamed, painful ~ **angrily** *adv*.

angst [*angst*] *n* (*Germ*) anxiety or pessimism caused by reflection on the situation of mankind.

anguiform [*ang*-gwifawrm] *adj* shaped like a snake.

anguilliform [ang-*gwili*fawrm] *adj* shaped like an eel.

anguish [*ang*-gwish] *n* extreme pain ~ **anguish** *v/t* distress with acute pain or grief.

angular [*ang*-gewler] *adj* sharp-cornered; pointed; with prominent bones; without curves; (*math*) measured in terms of the angle > PDS.

angularity [ang-gewl*aR*iti] *n* quality of being angular.

angulate [*ang*-gewlayt] *adj* having angles.

angustate [ang-*gust*ayt] *adj* narrowed.

anhelation [anhil*ay*shon] *n* shortness of breath.

anhydride [anh*I*dRId] *n* (*chem*) compound formed by removal of water from another compound.

anhydrous [anh*I*dRus] *adj* (*chem*) without water.

aniconic [an*I*k*on*ik] *adj* (*of idols and symbols*) not shaped into human or animal form.

anigh [an*I*] *adv* and *prep* (*poet*) near.

anil [*an*il] *n* indigo shrub; indigo dye.

aniline [*an*ilIn] *n* colourless oily liquid used in manufacture of dyes, drugs, and plastics > PDS ~ **aniline** *adj* derived from aniline.

anima [*an*ima] *n* soul, inner personality; (*psych*) feminine aspect of a man's personality > PDP.

animadversion [animadv*ur*shon] *n* observation, comment; hostile criticism, blame.

animadvert [animadv*urt*] *v/i* comment critically.

animal [*an*imal] *n* living creature possessing sensation and power of voluntary motion; non-human creature of this class; (*coll*) quadruped;

(*fig*) man of brutish type ~ **animal** *adj* of or like animals; physical, sensual; **a. magnetism** (*obs*) hypnotism; **a. spirits** natural high spirits.

animalcule (*pl* -la) [ani*mal*kewl] *n* microscopic animal ~ **animalcular** [ani*mal*kewler] *adj*.

animalism [*an*imalizm] *n* absence of spiritual feeling, sensuality; doctrine that man is a mere animal ~ **animalist** *adj*.

animality [ani*mal*iti] *n* qualities or behaviour typical of an animal.

animalize [*an*imalIz] *v/t* give animal life to; arouse the sensual nature of; brutalize.

animate [*an*imit] *adj* living, alive; lively ~ **animate** [*an*imayt] *v/t* give life to; enliven, add interest to; inspire, encourage.

animated [*an*imaytid] *adj* living; lively, spirited; **a. cartoon** film made from drawings photographed one at a time ~ **animatedly** *adv* in a lively manner.

animation [ani*may*shon] *n* vitality; vivacity, liveliness; (*cin*) process of preparing drawings to be photographed in cartoon making.

animatism [*an*imatizm] *n* primitive belief which attributes life to inanimate objects.

animator [*an*imayter] *n* one who animates; one who prepares drawings for animated cartoons.

animism [*an*imizm] *n* doctrine that the soul is the only cause of life; primitive belief that natural objects are inhabited by spirits; animatism; belief in the existence of the soul as distinct from the body ~ **animist** *n* and *adj*.

animistic [ani*mist*ik] *adj* of animism.

animosity [ani*mos*iti] *n* hatred, enmity.

animus [*an*imus] *n* bias; animosity; (*psych*) masculine aspect of a woman's personality.

anion [an*I*-on] *n* (*chem*) negatively charged ion > PDS.

anise [*an*is] *n* umbelliferous plant having aromatic seeds.

aniseed [*an*iseed] *n* seed of anise.

aniso- *pref* not symmetrical.

ankh [*ank*] *n* ancient Egyptian symbol of life, a T-cross surmounted by a loop.

ankle [*ank*'l] *n* joint connecting the foot with the leg; slender part of the leg below the calf.

anklet [*ank*lit] *n* fetter; ornamental chain worn on the ankle.

ankylosis [ank*I*l*O*sis] *n* (*med*) stiffening of the joints; union of bones ~ **ankylosed** *adj*.

anna [*an*a] *n* (*obs*) former coin worth one sixteenth of a rupee.

annal [*an*al] *n* entry for a particular year in a chronicle; (*pl*) record of events written year by year; historical records.

annalist [*an*alist] *n* one who writes annals.

anneal [a*neel*] *v/t* temper metals *etc* by very slow regulated cooling.

annelida [a*nel*ida] *n* (*zool*) ringed or segmented worms > PDB ~ **annelidan** *adj*.

annex [a*neks*] *v/t* add (smaller thing to a greater); take possession of by force; take over (small country) as colony, dependency *etc* ~ **annex, annexe** [a*neks*] *n* something added, appendix; room or building for additional accommodation.

annexation [aneks*ay*shon] *n* action of annexing.

annexure [a*nek*shOOr] *n* something annexed.

annihilate [a*nI*hilayt] *v/t* destroy completely; make null and void.

annihilation [anIhi*l*ayshon] *n* utter destruction; (*theol*) destruction of soul and body; **a. radiation** electromagnetic radiation produced when a particle and its anti-particle collide with mutual annihilation > PDS.

anniversary [aniv*u*rsaRi] *n* yearly return of a certain date; commemoration of an event on the yearly return of its date.

annotate [*an*Otayt] *v*/*t* and *i* add explanatory notes to, furnish with notes; make notes.

annotation [an*O*tayshon] *n* act of annotating; explanatory note.

announce [a*nowns*] *v*/*t* proclaim, make known; declare the presence or immediate arrival of.

announcement [a*nowns*ment] *n* proclamation, public notification; declaration, statement.

announcer [a*nowns*er] *n* one who announces; person who announces radio programmes and reads the news.

annoy [an*oi*] *v*/*t* and *i* trouble, harass, irritate.

annoyance [an*oi*-ans] *n* vexation, irritation; that which irritates or vexes.

annual [a*new*-al] *adj* occurring once a year; lasting a year and repeated every year ~ **annual** *n* publication appearing once a year, year-book; (*bot*) plant which lives for one year only; **hardy a.** (*fac*) event which recurs with tiresome monotony ~ **annually** *adv*.

annuitant [a*new*-itant] *n* person in receipt of an annuity.

annuity [a*new*-iti] *n* yearly grant of a fixed sum; investment in return for which the investor receives a fixed sum annually.

annul (*pres*/*part* **annulling**, *p*/*t* and *p*/*part* **annulled**) [a*nul*] *v*/*t* declare invalid; abolish; make void in law.

annular [a*new*ler] *adj* ring-like, ring-shaped; **a. eclipse** eclipse in which the moon's disc eclipses the whole of the sun except an outer ring.

annulary [a*new*laRi] *n* ring-finger.

annulate, annulated [a*new*layt, a*new*latid] *adj* marked with rings; consisting of rings.

annulation [a*new*l*a*yshon] *n* formation of rings; ring-like formation.

annulet [a*new*lit] *n* small ring.

annulment [a*nul*ment] *n* act of annulling; state of being annulled.

annuloid [a*new*loid] *adj* ring-like; (*zool*) with body divided into ring-like segments.

annulose [a*new*lOs] *adj* annuloid.

annunciation [anunsi-*a*yshon] *n* announcement, *esp* of the Incarnation made by the archangel Gabriel to the Virgin Mary; feast commemorating this (25 March).

annunciator [a*nun*si-ayter] *n* one who announces; signal board which indicates which bell button was pushed to ring a signal bell.

anode [a*n*Od] *n* (*elect*) positive electrode > PDS.

anodize [a*n*Odiz] *v*/*t* coat a metal with its oxide by electrolysis.

anodyne [a*n*Odin] *n* and *adj* (that) which relieves pain; (that) which is quite harmless.

anoesis [anO-*ee*sis] *n* (*psych*) primitive consciousness without objective reference.

anoetic [anO-*etik*] *adj* relating to consciousness in which there is sensation but no thought.

anoint [an*oint*] *v*/*t* apply oil to, *esp* in a religious ceremony; apply ointment to.

anomalistic [anoma*l*istik] *adj* anomalous; irregular; **a. year** (*astron*) time taken by the earth in passing from perihelion to perihelion.

anomalous [a*nom*alus] *adj* forming an exception to a rule, abnormal ~ **anomalously** *adv*.

anomaly [a*nom*ali] *n* deviation from law, irregularity; example of such irregularity; (*astron*) angular distance of a planet or satellite from its last perihelion or perigee.

anomia [an*Om*i-a] *n* (*psych*) difficulty in recalling names of things.

anomy [a*n*Omi] *n* lawlessness; belief that one is not bound to observe social or moral laws.

anon (1) [a*non*] *adv* presently, in a short time; again; **ever and a.** repeatedly at intervals.

anon (2) *adj* (*abbr*) anonymous.

anona [a*n*Ona] *n* (*bot*) genus of plants including the pineapple.

anonym [a*n*onim] *n* person whose name is not stated; pseudonym.

anonymity [anon*i*miti] *n* state of being anonymous.

anonymous [a*non*imus] *adj* (*of a writer*) not avowing his authorship; (*of writings*) bearing no author's name; (*fig*) lacking personality or individuality.

anopheles [a*n*Ofileez] *n* (*ent*) mosquito which conveys malaria.

anorak [a*n*eRak] *n* hooded water- and wind-proof jacket, windcheater.

anorexia [an*O*Reksi-a] *n* (*psych*) loss of appetite; **a. nervosa** obsessional refusal to eat.

anorthopia [anawr*th*Opi-a] *n* (*med*) distorted vision.

anosmia [a*nos*mi-a] *n* loss of the sense of smell.

another [a*nuT*Her] *adj* one more, one in addition; a different.

anoxaemia [anok*seem*i-a] *n* (*med*) lack of oxygen in bloodstream.

anoxia [a*nok*si-a] *n* (*med*) lack of oxygen in tissues.

anserine [a*n*seRin] *adj* pertaining to a goose; silly.

answer [a*an*ser] *n* words uttered in response to a question, call or challenge; reply to an argument; something done in retaliation; (*leg*) reply to a charge; (*math*) solution of a problem ~ **answer** *v*/*t* and *i* reply, respond; say or do in retaliation; take the responsibility (for); fulfil, come up to (expectations); reply to a charge, defend oneself; (*of a plan*) succeed; **a. back** (*coll*) give a cheeky answer; **a. to** correspond with, agree with.

answerable [a*an*siRab'l] *adj* responsible; proportional.

ant [ant] *n* small social insect of the Hymenopterous order.

ant- (1) *pref* ante-.

ant- (2) *pref* anti-.

antacid [ant*asid*] *n* and *adj* (substance) counteracting acidity, *esp* in stomach.

antagonism [ant*agonizm*] *n* active opposition; hostility; opposing force.

antagonist [ant*agonist*] *n* opponent ~ **antagonistic** [antagon*i*stik] *adj*.

antagonize [ant*agoniz*] *v*/*t* make hostile, drive into opposition; oppose actively.

antalkali [ant*a*lkali] *n* (*chem*) anything that neutralizes an alkali.

antaphrodisiac [antafro*d*izi-ak] *n* and *adj* (medicine or drug) counteracting sexual desire.

antarctic [antaarktik] *adj* pertaining to the south polar region ~ **antarctic** *n* the south polar region; **a. circle** line of latitude 66° 32′ south > PDG.

ant-bear [ant-bair] *n* the great ant-eater.

ante [anti] *n* (*gambling*) stake put up before the draw; money paid in advance; **raise the a.** procure money.

ante- *pref* before in time, place, order.

ant-eater [ant-eeter] *n* member of group of quadrupeds feeding upon ants.

antecede [antiseed] *v/t* precede.

antecedence [antiseedens] *n* priority in time; (*astron*) motion from east to west, retrograde motion; position more to the west.

antecedent [antiseedent] *adj* preceding, occurring before > PDG ~ **antecedent** *n* something occurring before; cause; (*gramm*) word(s) to which a pronoun refers; (*log*) conditional statement in a hypothetical proposition; (*math*) the first term of a ratio; (*pl*) details of a person's past history.

antechamber [antichaymber] *n* room used as entrance to more important one.

antedate [antidayt] *v/t* date earlier than the true date; precede in time; anticipate ~ **antedate** *n* date earlier than the true date.

antediluvian [antidiloOvi-an] *adj* existing before the Flood; (*cont*) quite out of date, antiquated.

antelope [antilOp] *n* genus of ruminant, graceful, deer-like animals.

antemeridian [antimeRidi-an] *adv* before noon.

antemetic [antimetik] *adj* checking vomiting.

antenatal [antinaytal] *adj* of or for pregnant women; existing or occurring before birth.

antenna (*pl* **antennae**) [antena] *n* horn or feeler on head of insect (usually in pairs) > PDB; (*rad*) aerial.

antennule [antenewl] *n* (*zool*) small antenna.

antenuptial [antinupshal] *adj* before marriage.

ante-orbital [anti-awrbital] *adj* (*physiol*) situated in front of the eyes.

antepenult [antipenult] *adj* last but two.

antepenultimate [antipenultimit] *adj* last but two.

anteposition [antipOzishon] *n* (*gramm*) reversal of normal word-order.

ante-post [anti-pOst] *adj* (*of betting*) before the numbers of the runners go up on the board.

anteprandial [antipRandi-al] *adj* preceding dinner.

anterior [anteerRi-er] *adj* earlier in time, prior; more to the front.

anteroom [antiROOm] *n* room forming an entrance to another room; waiting-room.

ant-fly [ant-flI] *n* winged ant, *esp* if used as bait.

ant-heap [ant-heep] *n* ant-hill.

anthelion (*pl* **anthelia**) [antheeli-on/ant-heeli-on *n* halo seen surrounding the shadow of an observer's head on a bank of clouds or mist.

anthelmintic [anthelmintik] *n* and *adj* (*med*) (remedy) of use against parasitic worms.

anthem [anthem] *n* piece of sacred music (*usu* four-part) sung in church; any dignified song of praise; **National A.** song used by any country as symbol of its national identity.

anther [anther] *n* (*bot*) terminal portion of a stamen containing pollen ~ **antheral** *adj*.

antheridium [antheRidi-um] *n* male sex organ of cryptogams.

ant-hill [ant-hil] *n* small mound of earth over an ants' nest.

anthologize [antholojIz] *v/t* include in an anthology.

anthologist [antholojist] *n* compiler of an anthology.

anthology [antholoji] *n* collection of short poems by various authors; collection of literary extracts.

anthracene [anthRaseen] *n* (*chem*) white crystalline hydrocarbon used as a dye.

anthracite [anthRasIt] *n* non-bituminous coal, hard and slow-burning.

anthracitic [anthRasitik] *adj* of or like anthracite.

anthrax [anthRaks] *n* malignant boil; infectious pustular disease in sheep and cattle producing fatal gastro-enteritis or pneumonia in man.

anthropo- *pref* of human beings.

anthropocentric [anthROposentRik] *adj* regarding man as the centre of the universe.

anthropogenic [anthROpojenik] *adj* caused by human actions; concerning the origin of man.

anthropogeny [anthROpojini] *n* study of the origin of man.

anthropoid [anthROpoid] *adj* (*of apes*) resembling human form; (*of men, coll*) like an ape ~ **anthropoid** *n* anthropoid ape.

anthropological [anthROpolojikal] *adj* of or by anthropology.

anthropologist [anthROpolojist] *n* student of anthropology.

anthropology [anthROpoloji] *n* science of the nature of man embracing his physiological aspects, his racial characteristics, and his social and religious development.

anthropometry [anthROpometRi] *n* measurement of the bodily form and proportions of different races, sexes, ages *etc* of human beings.

anthropomorphic [anthROpomawrfik] *adj* having human characteristics; attributing these to non-human beings or things.

anthropomorphism [anthROpomawrfizm] *n* attribution of human form and characteristics to gods or animals or inanimate things.

anthropomorphize [anthROpomawrfIz] *v/t* and *i* regard (non-human creatures) as having human characteristics.

anthropophagi [anthROpofagI] *n* (*pl*) cannibals.

anthropophagous [anthROpofagus] *adj* practising cannibalism.

anthropophagy [anthROpofagi] *n* cannibalism.

anthroposophy [anthRoposofi] *n* a religious movement aimed at increasing spiritual awareness.

anti- *pref* opposed to, opposite of; destroying, counteracting, acting as defence against.

anti [anti] *n* one who is opposed to (a plan, law *etc*).

anti-aircraft [anti-airkRaaft] *adj* used for defence against hostile aircraft.

antibiotic [antibI-otik] *n* and *adj* (*physiol*) (substance) produced by a living organism and capable of destroying bacteria or preventing their growth.

antibody [antibodi] *n* (*physiol*) a protein produced in the blood in response to an antigen as a natural antidote to infection.

antic [antik] *n* (*ar*) clown ~ **antic** *adj* like a buffoon, grotesque.

antichlor [*anti*klawr] *n* substance used to remove chlorine from materials after bleaching.

antichrist [*anti*kRIst] *n* opponent of Christ, *esp* one whom the early church expected to appear shortly before Doomsday.

antichristian [anti*k*Risti-an] *adj* opposed to Christianity.

anticipant [an*ti*sipant] *adj* operating in advance; expectant ~ **anticipant** *n* one who anticipates.

anticipate [an*ti*sipayt] *v/t* expect, *usu* with excitement or fear; forestall by acting earlier than was expected; put forward the time of; deal with, make use of, before the due time.

anticipation [antisi*p*ayshon] *n* act of anticipating; presentiment; (*mus*) moving to a note of the next chord before the chord is properly sounded.

anticipatory [antisi*p*aytoRi] *adj* that anticipates; done in advance; done too early.

anticlerical [anti*k*leRikal] *adj* opposed to the undue influence of the clergy, *esp* in politics ~ **anticlericalism** [anti*k*leRikalizm] *n*.

anticlimax [anti*k*lImaks] *n* (*rhet*) reverse of climax; the addition of a detail which, instead of heightening the effect, weakens it.

anticlinal [anti*k*lInal] *adj* (*geol*) forming the arch or crest of a fold in rock strata; (*bot*) (*of cell-walls*) situated approximately at right angles to the outer surface of the plant part.

anticline [*anti*klIn] *n* (*geol*) the arch or crest of a fold in rock strata.

anti-clockwise [anti-*k*lokwIz] *adj* and *adv* revolving in the opposite direction to hands of a clock.

anticoagulant [antikO-*a*gewlant] *n* and *adj* (substance) preventing clotting of blood.

antics [*anti*ks] *n* (*pl*) ridiculous behaviour.

anticyclone [anti*sik*lOn] *n* air condition in which atmospheric pressure is high, giving quiet and settled weather conditions > PDG.

anti-dazzle [anti-*daz*'l] *adj* (*mot*) designed to reduce glare (from motorcar headlights).

antidemocratic [antidem*Ok*Ratik] *adj* opposed to democratic rule.

antidotal [*anti*dOtal] *adj* of or as an antidote.

antidote [*anti*dOt] *n* medicine to counteract a poison; (*fig*) remedy.

antifreeze [anti*f*Reez] *n* ethylene glycol added to the water in a motorcar radiator to prevent freezing.

antigen [*anti*jen] *n* (*physiol*) substance capable of stimulating the formation of an antibody.

anti-gravity [anti-gRaviti] *adj* counteracting the effects of gravity.

anti-hero [*anti*-heerRO] *n* principal character in a play, novel *etc* who elicits sympathy or respect yet lacks conventionally admirable qualities.

antihistamine [anti*histam*In] *n* compound used to counteract allergic reactions.

antilogarithm [anti*loga*Rithm] *n* number which a logarithm represents.

antimacassar [antima*k*aser] *n* ornamental covering thrown over the back of a chair to protect it from hair-oil.

antimasque, -mask [*anti*maask] *n* grotesque interlude between the acts of a masque.

anti-matter [*anti*-mater] *n* matter composed of anti-particles > PDS.

antimony [*anti*moni] *n* brittle crystalline silvery-white metal > PGS.

anting [*anti*ng] *n* (*of birds*) rubbing insects or small objects against their feathers.

antinomian [antin*Omi*-an] *n* one who holds that the obligations of morality and natural law are superseded by Christianity.

antinomy [an*ti*nomi] *n* contradiction between laws; conflict of authority; contradiction between two logical conclusions.

anti-novel [*anti*-novel] *n* fictional prose work which discards conventional forms of structure and presentation.

anti-particle [anti-*paa*rtik'l] *n* elementary particle which annihilates a corresponding particle of the same mass but opposite charge or magnetic moment > PDS.

antipathic, antipathetical [antipa*thet*ik, antipa-*thet*ikal] *adj* having or inspiring a fixed aversion; opposed in character or nature.

antipathic [antipa*thik*] *adj* of a contrary character (to); (*med*) producing contrary symptoms.

antipathy [an*ti*pathi] *n* hostile feeling; fixed aversion; essential difference between two substances which prevents their uniting.

anti-personnel [anti-purson*el*] *adj* (*of bombs, etc*) designed to be used against persons, not against buildings, fortifications *etc*.

antiphlogistic [antiflO*jist*ik] *n* and *adj* (*med*) (substance) tending to reduce inflammation.

antiphon [*anti*fOn] *n* versicle sung by one side of a choir in response to one sung by the other; short piece of plainsong sung before and after a psalm or canticle.

antiphonal [an*ti*fOnal] *adj* of or like an antiphon; said or sung alternately ~ **antiphonal** *n* antiphonary ~ **antiphonally** *adv*.

antiphonary [an*ti*fonaRi] *n* collection of antiphons.

antiphony [an*ti*foni] *n* antiphonal singing; composition sung antiphonally.

antiphrasis [an*ti*fRasis] *n* (*rhet*) use of a word to imply the exact opposite of its normal meaning.

antipodal [an*ti*pOdal] *adj* of or at the antipodes.

antipodean [antipO*dee*-an] *adj* antipodal.

antipodes [an*ti*podeez] *n* (*pl*) places situated on opposite sides of the earth > PDG; (*fig*) complete opposite.

antipole [*anti*pOl] *n* opposite pole; direct opposite.

antipope [*anti*pOp] *n* a pope elected uncanonically.

anti-proton [anti-pROton] *n* (*phys*) particle equal in mass but opposite in electric charge to a proton.

antipyretic [antipI*Ret*ik] *n* and *adj* (*med*) (substance) used to lower the body temperature.

antiquarian [anti*kwair*Ri-an] *adj* pertaining to the study of antiquities ~ **antiquarian** *n* antiquary; a large size of drawing-paper.

antiquary [*anti*kwaRi] *n* student of antiquities; collector of antiques.

antiquated [*anti*kwaytid] *adj* obsolete; old-fashioned, out of date.

antique [an*teek*] *adj* ancient, belonging to the ancient world; old-fashioned ~ **antique** *n* piece of furniture, jewellery *etc* at least a hundred years old; (*coll*) old or old-fashioned person.

antiquity [an*ti*kwiti] *n* great age; remote period, *esp* classical period of Greece and Rome; (*pl*) buildings, objects *etc* of a remote historical period.

antirrhinum [anti*RI*num] *n* genus of plants popularly called snapdragon.

antiscorbutic [antiskawr*bewtik*] *n* and *adj* (medicine) of use against scurvy.

anti-semite [anti*semite*/anti*seemite*] *n* one hostile to the Jews; one who persecutes Jews.

anti-semitic [anti*semitik*] *adj* of or showing anti-semitism.

anti-semitism [anti*semitizm*] *n* hostility, prejudice or persecution against Jews.

antiseptic [anti*septik*] *n* and *adj* (substance) preventing the growth of bacteria.

antisocial [anti*sOshal*] *adj* contrary to the well-being of society or of one's fellow-men; selfish; violent, destructive; opposed to the principles governing organized society; unwilling to mix with society.

antistrophe [anti*stROfi*] *n* (*Gk drama*) return movement of chorus from left to right; lines sung during this movement; second stanza in a true Pindaric ode.

anti-tank [anti-*tank*] *adj* (*of gun*) used against tanks.

antithesis [an*tithisis*] *n* (*rhet*) the contrasting of two ideas by using words of opposite meaning in consecutive clauses or phrases; striking contrast; direct opposite.

antithetic, antithetical [anti*thetik*, anti*thetikal*] *adj* of antithesis; directly contrasted.

antitoxic [anti*toksik*] *adj* of an antitoxin.

antitoxin [anti*toksin*] *n* serum used to neutralize bacteria and viruses in the blood.

anti-trade [anti-*tRayd*] *adj* wind of the upper air in the regions of the trade winds but blowing in the reverse direction > PDG.

antitype [*antitIp*] *n* that which is represented by a type or symbol ~ **antitypical** [anti*tipikal*] *adj*.

antivenene [anti*veneen*] *n* antidote against snake-bite.

anti-vivisectionist [anti-vivi*sek*-shonist] *n* and *adj* (person) opposed to vivisection; (person) seeking to forbid the use of animals for medical research.

antler [*antler*] *n* branched horn of a stag ~ **antlered** [*antlerd*] *adj*.

ant-lion [*ant*-lI-on] *n* insect the larva of which preys on ants.

antonym [*antonim*] *n* word exactly opposite in meaning to another.

antrum [*antRum*] *n* (*physiol*) cavity in the body.

anura [a*newrRa*] (*zool*) the order of tailless amphibia such as frogs and toads.

anus [*aynus*] *n* (*anat*) lower opening of the alimentary canal.

anvil [*anvil*] *n* iron block on which a smith hammers metals.

anxiety [angz*I*-iti] *n* state of being anxious; that which makes one anxious.

anxious [*ankshus*] *adj* uneasy in mind, troubled about the future; eager, very desirous ~ **anxiously** *adv*.

any [*eni*] *adj* and *pron* every; of whatever sort; one, some of whatever kind; (*w neg*) none at all ~ **any** *adv* in any degree; **at a. rate, in a. case** whatever may happen.

anybody [*enibodi*] *pron* any person at all; some-

body; person of some importance; **a.'s guess** a matter of uncertainty.

anyhow [*enihow*] *adv* in any case, at least; haphazard, carelessly.

anyone [*eniwun*] *pron* anybody, any person taken at random.

anyplace [*eniplays*] *adj* (*US*) anywhere.

anything [*enithing*] *pron* any unspecified thing taken at random; **a. but** (*coll*) quite the contrary.

anywhere [*eniwhair*] *adv* in, into any place whatever.

anywise [*eniwIz*] *adv* (*ar*) in any manner.

Anzac [*anzak*] *n* member of the Australian and New Zealand Army Corps; **A. Day** 25 April 1915, when the Anzacs landed in Gallipoli.

aorist [*ay*-oRist] *n* (*Gk gramm*) past tense of a verb with no limitations in duration of time.

aorta [ay-*awrta*] *n* the great artery which carries the blood from the heart > PDB.

apace [a*pays*] *adv* quickly, with speed.

Apache [a*pachi*] *n* one of a warlike tribe of North American Indians; (*fig*) [a*paash*] member of a gang of roughs in Paris; ruffian.

apanage, appanage [a*panij*] *n* provision made for the younger children of kings, ruling princes *etc*; perquisite attached to an office; natural or customary attribute.

apart [a*paart*] *adv* some way away, to or at a distance; separately, independently; out of consideration; not being taken into account; **a. from** without taking into consideration.

apartheid [a*part*-hIt] *n* racial segregation in South Africa; (*fig*) rigid segregation of social groups.

apartment [a*paart*ment] *n* room in a house; (*US*) flat; (*pl*) set of furnished rooms, with no cooking facilities, let on hire; **a. house** house divided into rooms or flats for letting.

apathetic [apa*thetik*] *adj* of or showing apathy, lacking any emotion or energy ~ **apathetically** *adv*.

apathy [*apathi*] *n* lack of emotion, insensibility to passion; indifference; extreme listlessness.

ape [*ayp*] *n* monkey, *esp* one with no tail; (*fig*) one who imitates, a mimic ~ **ape** *v/t* imitate, *esp* pretentiously or mockingly.

apeak [a*peek*] *adv* and *adj* (*naut*) vertical.

ape-man [*ayp*-man] *n* human being with ape-like characteristics; hypothetical creature intermediate between apes and men; (*pop*) hominid.

aperient [a*peer*Ri-ent] *adj* and *n* laxative.

aperitif [a*peRitif*/apay*Reeteef*] *n* alcoholic drink taken before a meal as an appetizer.

aperitive [a*peRitiv*] *adj* aperient.

aperture [a*percher*] *n* hole, gap; opening admitting light to optical or photographic instruments.

apery [*aypeRi*] *n* colony of apes.

apetalous [a*petalus*] *adj* (*bot*) without petals.

apex (*pl* **apices**) [*aypeks*] *n* summit, tip; (*geom*) vertex of a triangle or cone.

aphasia [a*fayzi*-a] *n* (*path*) a disorder of the speech function owing to damage to the brain > PDP ~ **aphasiac** *adj*.

aphelion (*pl* **aphelia**) [a*feeli*-on] *n* (*astron*) point in planet's orbit farthest from the sun.

apheliotropism [afeeli-*ot*ROpizm] *n* property possessed by certain plants of turning away from the sun ~ **apheliotropic** [afeeli-ot*Ropik*] *adj*.

aphesis [afisis] n loss of a short unstressed vowel at the beginning of a word ~ **aphetic** [afetik] adj.

aphid [ayfid] n an aphis insect.

aphis (pl **aphides**) [afis/ayfis] n genus of small insects that suck plant juices > PDB.

aphonia, aphony [afOni-a, afoni] n (path) inability to utter sounds because of defect of vocal chords ~ **aphonic** [afonik] adj.

aphorism [afoRizm] n maxim or general principle expressed in a few words.

aphorist [afoRist] n composer of aphorisms.

aphoristic [afoRistik] adj of, like or containing aphorisms ~ **aphoristically** adv.

aphrodisiac [afROdizi-ak] n and adj (drug) exciting sexual activity

aphtha (pl **aphthae**) [aftha] n (path) disease of children gen called 'thrush'; (pl) white specks which are its symptoms.

aphyllous [afilus] adj (bot) without leaves.

apian [aypi-an] adj pertaining to bees.

apiarist [aypi-aRist] n bee-keeper.

apiary [aypi-aRi] n place where bees are kept.

apical [aypikal/apikal] adj pertaining to an apex.

apices [aypiseez] pl of apex.

apiculture [aypikulcher] n bee-keeping.

apiece [apees] adv to, by or for each article or each person.

aping [ayping] n mocking or pretentious imitation.

apish [aypish] adj resembling an ape; foolish as an ape; foolishly imitative.

aplanatic [aplanatik] adj (opt) free from aberration > PDS.

aplastic [aplastik] adj characterized by irregularity of organic structure.

aplomb [aplom] n self-possession, confidence.

apo- pref off, away; separate.

Apocalypse [apokalips] n (NT) book containing prophetic description of the end of the world.

apocalyptic [apokaliptik] adj of or like the Apocalypse; prophetic of vast disasters; like the end of the world.

apocarpous [apokaarpus] adj (bot) having distinct carpels.

apocope [apokOpi] n omission of the last syllable of a word.

Apocrypha [apokRifa] n books of the Old Testament not counted genuine by Jews or Protestants but accepted by Roman Catholics; gospels, epistles etc ascribed to various apostles but rejected by modern Christians as not genuine.

apocryphal [apokRifal] adj pertaining to the Apocrypha; of doubtful authenticity; false.

apodal [apOdal] adj (zool) footless; (of fish) without ventral fins.

apodeictic, apodictic [apodIktik, apodiktik] adj clearly established, incontrovertible.

apodosis [apodOsis] n (gramm) consequent clause in a conditional sentence, which expresses the result.

apogee [apOjee] n point where the moon, other earth satellite, or sun is farthest from the earth; highest point of a career etc.

apolitical [aypolitikal] adj not interested in political issues.

apologetic [apolojetik] adj expressing regret for a fault or mistake; conciliatory, deferential; setting forth a defence ~ **apologetically** adv.

apologetics [apolojetiks] n (pl) defensive method of argument, esp on behalf of a religion.

apologia [apolOji-a] n defence, vindication by argument.

apologist [apolojist] n one who defends an opinion by argument.

apologize [apolojIz] v/i express regret (for a fault or error).

apologue [apolog] n moral fable.

apology [apoloji] n statement of regret for a fault or error; poor substitute; (ar) apologia.

apophthegm [apOfthem] n moral maxim, short pithy saying.

apoplectic [apOplektik] adj of, like, suffering from or caused by apoplexy ~ **apoplectic** n one suffering from apoplexy.

apoplexy [apOpleksi] n seizure usually caused by the breaking of a blood-vessel in the brain, affecting sense and motion.

apostasy [apostasi] n rejection of former religious faith, principles or allegiance to any cause.

apostate [apostayt] n one who has renounced his faith or allegiance.

apostatize [apostatIz] v/i commit apostasy.

a posteriori [ay-posteRi-awRI] adv (reasoning) from effect to cause, inductively.

apostle [apos'l] n one of twelve men sent out by Jesus Christ to preach the gospel; one who first brings Christianity to a particular region; leader in a reform movement; a. spoons set of spoons with the knops in the form of figures of the Apostles.

apostolate [apostOlit] n position or authority of an apostle; missionary activity.

apostolic [apostolik] adj of or from the Apostles; A. See see of Rome.

apostrophe [apostROfi] n (rhet) act of making an exclamatory address to some person present or absent; (gramm) sign (') used to indicate the omission of one or more letters in a word; also to indicate the possessive case.

apostrophize [apostROfIz] v/t address with rhetorical apostrophe; insert grammatical apostrophe.

apothecary [apothikaRi] n druggist, pharmaceutical chemist.

apothegm [apOthem] n apophthegm.

apotheosis [apothi-Osis] n deification, raising of a mortal to the rank of a god; supreme glorification.

apotropaic [apOtROpay-ik] adj with the power to ward off evil influences or bad luck.

appal (pres/part **appalling**, p/t and p/part **appalled**) [apawl] v/t dismay, shock, terrify.

appalling [apawling] adj shocking, horrible ~ **appallingly** adv.

appanage see apanage.

apparatchik [apaRaatchik] n (Rus) Communist bureaucrat.

apparatus [apaRaytus] n instruments required to carry out any purpose, esp scientific investigation; appliances, machinery; (fig) any device or materials needed for achieving a practical effect or purpose.

apparel [apaRel] n clothing, dress; (eccles) embroidery on vestments ~ **apparel** (pres/part **apparelling**, p/t and p/part **apparelled**) v/t clothe.

apparent [apaRent/apairRent] adj seeming, not

31

necessarily real; obvious, plain; **heir a.** direct heir to a kingdom, estate *etc* ~ **apparently** *adv.*

apparition [apaRishon] *n* ghost; appearance, *esp* unexpected or sudden; (*astron*) reappearance of a heavenly body after occultation.

apparitor [apaRiter] *n* officer of a civil or ecclesiastic court.

appeal [apeel] *v/i* make an earnest request; ask for a favourable decision; refer to as supporting evidence; call upon a higher court of justice to reverse the judgement of a lower one; be attractive, seem pleasing or touching ~ **appeal** *n* earnest request; call to a recognized authority for a decision; call to a higher court to reverse the judgement of a lower one; attraction; power to move the feelings; **Court of A.** court which hears appeals from lower courts.

appealing [apeeling] *adj* moving, touching the feelings; attractive ~ **appealingly** *adv.*

appear [apeer] *v/i* become visible, come into view; be seen; come before the public as performer or actor; go before a tribunal *etc*; (*of book*) be published; be obvious, clear; seem, convey the impression.

appearance [apeerRans] *n* action of appearing; outward visible characteristics, look; something seen, *esp* if strange or deceptive; **keep up appearances** maintain a good outward show.

appease [apeez] *v/t* pacify, soothe the anger of, *esp* by satisfying demands; satisfy (hunger *etc*).

appeasement [apeezment] *n* act of appeasing; policy of soothing threatening enemies by satisfying their demands.

appellant [apelant] *n* and *adj* (*leg*) (one) who accuses; (one) who appeals to a higher court.

appellate [apelit] *adj* (*leg*) hearing appeals.

appellation [apelayshon] *n* name, designation.

appellative [apelativ] *n* (*gramm*) common noun.

appellee [apelee] *n* (*leg*) one who is accused.

appellor [apelawr/apelawr] *n* (*leg*) accuser.

append [apend] *v/t* attach, add as a minor element.

appendage [apendij] *n* something attached, hung on; addition to property, apanage.

appendices [apendiseez] *pl* of **appendix.**

appendicitis [apendisItis] *n* inflammation of the vermiform appendix.

appendix (*pl* **appendices, appendixes**) [apendiks] *n* something appended; subsidiary material added at the end of a book; **vermiform a.** small sac-like branch of gut at junction of large and small intestines.

apperceive [aperseev] *v/t* (*psych*) be conscious of perceiving.

apperception [apersepshon] *n* clear mental perception involving recognition or identification; reinforcement of a sensation by revival of kindred ideas > PDP.

appertain [apertayn] *v/i* belong as forming part of; belong as a right; be appropriate to.

appetence [apitens] *n* strong natural desire ~ **appetent** [apitent] *adj.*

appetite [apitIt] *n* eager desire for food; desire to satisfy a physical need; insistent impulse > PDP.

appetizer [apitIzer] *n* something taken to increase desire for food.

appetizing [apitIzing] *adj* causing desire, *esp* for food; looking wholesome and pleasant ~ **appetizingly** *adv.*

applaud [aplawd] *v/t* and *i* express approval (of), *esp* by clapping the hands.

applause [aplawz] *n* approval loudly expressed.

applausive [aplawsiv] *adj* applauding.

apple [ap'l] *n* common round fleshy red or yellow fruit of a rosaceous tree; **a. of discord** cause of dispute; **a. of one's eye** object of special affection.

apple-brandy [ap'l-bRandi] *n* spirit distilled from cider.

applecart [ap'lkaart] *n* cart carrying apples; **upset the a.** frustrate a person's plans.

apple-dumpling [ap'l-dumpling] *n* apple enclosed in pastry and cooked.

applejack [ap'l-jak] *n* (*US*) spirit liquor distilled from cider.

apple-pie [ap'l-pI] *n* pie made of apples baked under a crust; **a. bed** bed made for a joke with the sheets so turned that it cannot be entered; **a. order** perfectly neat arrangement.

appliance [aplI-ans] *n* act of applying; mechanical contrivance applied to obtain a result; apparatus, utensil; fire-engine.

applicable [aplikab'l] *adj* capable of being applied; having reference; appropriate.

applicant [aplikant] *n* one who applies for anything; candidate for a post.

application [aplikayshon] *n* act of applying; state of being applied; use, employment; testing of law or theory in actual practice; act of working diligently; request, *esp* in writing.

applicator [aplikayter] *n* any simple device for applying an ointment, glue *etc.*

applied [aplId] *adj* (*of a science*) practical as opposed to abstract.

appliqué [apleekay] *n* (*Fr*) piece of one material applied to another to form a design; act of so applying or sewing.

apply [aplI] *v/t* and *i* put beside, on or touching; make use of; use (a word) with reference (to); have a special bearing on, be relevant; make an application; offer oneself as a candidate; work zealously (at).

appoggiatura [apojatoorRa] *n* (*mus*) melodic ornament in which the principal note is delayed by a grace note introduced before it > PDM.

appoint [apoint] *v/t* elect, ordain to a position; fix, determine; assign; (*leg*) declare authoritatively the destination of specified property.

appointed [apointid] *adj* assigned; previously arranged or fixed; furnished, equipped.

appointment [apointment] *n* agreement fixing time and place of a meeting; election of a person to a position; position so obtained; (*leg*) act of declaring with authority the destination of certain property; (*pl*) equipment, furnishings.

apport [apawrt] *n* (*spiritualism*) supernormal transporting of objects from a distance into an enclosed space; object thus transported.

apportion [apawrshon] *v/t* and *i* assign as share; divide into proportionate shares ~ **apportionment** *n.*

apposite [apozit] *adj* apt, appropriate, suitable ~ **appositely** *adv* to the point.

apposition [apozIshon] *n* juxtaposition; (*gramm*) placing of a word, *esp* a noun, to amplify and parallel another.

appraisal [ap*Rayz*al] *n* evaluation; analysis of and judgement on a person, situation *etc*.

appraise [ap*Rayz*] *v/t* fix a price for, evaluate.

appreciable [ap*Ree*shi-ab'l] *adj* capable of being estimated or perceived; large enough to be noticed ~ **appreciably** *adv*.

appreciate [ap*Ree*shi-ayt] *v/t* and *i* realize the value or qualities of; esteem highly, be grateful for; perceive, realize; raise in value; rise in value.

appreciation [ap*Ree*shi-*ay*shon] *n* act of appreciating; account of the merits of a person or thing; ability to perceive qualities.

appreciative [ap*Ree*shi-ativ] *adj* grateful; perceptive; sensitive ~ **appreciatively** *adv*.

apprehend [ap*Rih*end] *v/t* grasp; arrest; perceive; understand; look forward to, *esp* with fear.

apprehension [ap*Rih*enshon] *n* fear of the future, anxiety; act of apprehending; ability to understand.

apprehensive [ap*Rih*ensiv] *adj* fearful of the future; discerning, intelligent.

apprentice [ap*Rent*is] *n* learner of a craft, who is bound to serve his employer for a set number of years in return for instruction ~ **apprentice** *v/t* bind as an apprentice ~ **apprenticeship** *n*.

apprise (1) [ap*RIz*] *v/t* inform, tell.

apprize, apprise (2) [ap*RIz*] *v/t* appraise.

appro [ap*RO*] *n* (*abbr*) approval, approbation.

approach [ap*ROch*] *v/t* and *i* move towards, come near to; be nearly equal; draw near; make advances to, offer to open negotiations with; attempt to influence ~ **approach** *n* act of coming near; means of access; (*golf*) shot which places the ball on the green; (*aer*) last stage of flight before landing; (*pl*) advances, offers to enter into personal relations.

approachable [ap*ROchab*'l] *adj* that can be approached; friendly, welcoming.

approbation [ap*Roba*yshon] *n* approval, formal declaration of agreement; praise; **on a.** (*of goods supplied*) to be returned if not to the satisfaction of the customer.

approbatory [ap*RO*bateRi/ap*RO*bayteRi] *adj* showing approval.

appropriate (1) [ap*ROPRi*-it] *adj* suitable to a particular person, thing or situation ~ **appropriately** *adv* ~ **appropriateness** *n*.

appropriate (2) [ap*ROPRi*-ayt] *v/t* take for oneself; assign possession of; (*eccles*) annex (a benefice); assign to a special purpose.

appropriation [ap*ROPRi*-*ay*shon] *n* act of appropriating.

approval [ap*ROO*val] *n* act of approving; **on a.** on approbation.

approve [ap*ROO*v] *v/t* and *i* think favourably of, commend; confirm authoritatively; (*refl*) show oneself by one's actions to be.

approved [ap*ROO*vd] *adj* proved by experience; sanctioned by authority; esteemed; **a. school** school provided by the State for juvenile delinquents.

approver [ap*ROO*ver] *n* informer; one who confesses a felony and turns Queen's evidence.

approximate [ap*Roks*imit] *adj* nearly accurate, almost exact ~ **approximate** [ap*Roks*imayt] *v/t* and *i* make or come very near ~ **approximately** *adv* almost, about, nearly.

approximation [ap*Roks*i*may*shon] *n* close approach.

appui [ap*wee*] *n* (*mil*) defensive support; **point of a.** fixed point on which troops wheel into line.

appurtenance [ap*urt*inans] *n* that which belongs to another thing; appendage, adjunct, accessory.

appurtenant [ap*urt*inant] *adj* belonging, pertaining (to); suitable.

après-ski [ap*Re*-ski] *adj* and *n* (*Fr*) (of or for) a period of relaxation after skiing.

apricot [*ayp*Rikot] *n* stone-fruit of orange colour; tree bearing it.

April [*ayp*Ril] *n* fourth month of the year; **A. fool** one who is deceived by a trick played on him on 1 April; **A. Fool's Day** 1 April.

a priori [ay-p*RI*-*aw*r*RI*] *adv* (*Lat*) (reasoning) from cause to effect; (*fig*) judging by appearances or probabilities, presumptively ~ **aprioristic** [aypRI-o*Ristik*] *adj*.

apron [*ayp*Ron] *n* garment worn in front of the body to protect the clothing; ceremonial garment resembling this; protective covering; projecting part of stage; paved area of an airfield near hangars.

apron-stage [*ayp*Ron-stayj] *n* part of the stage in some theatres which juts out into the pit.

apronstrings [*ayp*RonstRingz] *n* (*pl*) strings tied at the back of an apron; **tied to the a.** too much dependent on (a woman).

apropos [ap*Ro*p*O*] *adj* and *adv* (*Fr*) to the point; opportune(ly); with regard to, talking of.

apse [aps] *n* semi-circular recess at the east end of a church; (*astron*) apsis.

apsidal [*ap*sidal] *adj* of or like an apse or apsis.

apsis (*pl* **apsides**) [*ap*sis] *n* (*astron*) either of the two points in a planet's or satellite's course when its distance from the body it revolves round is least or greatest.

apt [apt] *adj* fit, suitable; ready to learn, intelligent; **a. to** inclined to, prone to.

apteral [*apt*eRal] *adj* (*archi*) having no columns along the sides; (*zool*) wingless.

apterous [*apt*eRus] *adj* (*zool*) wingless.

apteryx [*apt*eRiks] *n* New Zealand bird with only rudimentary wings and no tail.

aptitude [*apt*itewd] *n* fitness, suitability; natural capacity (for); intelligence.

aptly [*apt*li] *adv* in an apt way.

aptness [*apt*nis] *n* quality of being apt.

aqualung [*akw*alung] *n* diver's portable equipment providing a supply of compressed air.

aquamarine [*akw*ama*Reen*] *n* bluish-green transparent beryl; bluish-green colour.

aquanaut [*akw*anawt] *n* one who swims underwater with an aqualung.

aquaplane [*akw*aplayn] *n* board towed by a motorboat, on which one rides standing ~ **aquaplane** *v/i* ride on an aquaplane for sport.

aquarelle [akwa*Rel*] *n* painting in very transparent watercolours; (*print*) tinted printed plates.

aquarium [akw*air*Ri-um] *n* glass-sided tank containing fish and water animals; building containing a collection of such tanks.

Aquarius [akw*air*Ri-us] *n* (*astron*) a constellation, the Water-bearer, giving its name to the eleventh sign of the zodiac.

aquatic [akw*at*ik] *adj* living in the water; (of sports) taking place on or in the water.

aquatint [*ak*watint] *n* method of engraving on copper plate with nitric acid > PDAA; picture thus obtained.

aqua-vitae [aykwa-*vi*tee] *n* (*Lat*) alcohol; brandy.

aqueduct [*ak*widukt] *n* artificial channel or elevated structure for carrying a water-supply; structure for carrying a canal across a valley.

aqueous [*ay*kwi-us] *adj* of, like, in or containing water; **a. humour** transparent fluid between lens and cornea of the eye.

aquilegia [akwi*leeg*i-a] *n* columbine.

aquiline [*ak*wilIn] *adj* of or like an eagle; (*of nose*) thin and hooked.

Arab [*a*Rab] *n* member of a Semitic but non-Jewish race inhabiting various Middle Eastern countries; Arab horse; **street a.** (*obs coll*) neglected child who wanders in the street ~ **Arab** *adj*.

arabesque [aRa*besk*] *n* (*arts*) flowing linear decorative design; fanciful design of leaves and scrolls; (*mus*) brilliant instrumental piece; florid ornamentation; (*ballet*) pose of dancer on one leg with the other stretched horizontally backwards ~ **arabesque** *adj*.

Arabian [a*Ray*bi-an] *adj* belonging to Arabia; **A. bird** the phoenix.

Arabic [*a*Rabik] *adj* pertaining to Arabia or its language; **a. numerals** the numbers 1, 2, 3 *etc* ~ **Arabic** *n* language of the Arabs.

Arabist [*a*Rabist] *n* student of Arabic.

arable [*a*Rib'l] *adj* (*of land*) fit for ploughing.

arachnid [a*Rak*nid] *n* (*zool*) member of the genus including spiders, scorpions and mites.

arachnitis [aRak*nI*tis] *n* inflammation of the arachnoid membrane.

arachnoid [a*Rak*noid] *adj* (*bot*) covered with or formed of long delicate hairs ~ **arachnoid** *n* (*physiol*) the middle of the three membranes covering the brain and spinal cord.

araeometer, areometer [airRi-*omiter*] *n* instrument for measuring the specific gravity of fluids; hydrometer.

Aramaic [aRa*may*-ik] *adj* and *n* (of) the ancient Syriac and Chaldee languages.

arbalest [*aar*balest] *n* powerful crossbow with mechanical device for bending the bow.

arbiter [*aar*biter] *n* judge; arbitrator; one who has absolute control.

arbitrage [*aar*bitRij] *n* traffic in stocks and bills of exchange drawn on various places to profit from the difference of prices and rates in the various markets.

arbitral [*aar*bitRal] *adj* pertaining to arbitration.

arbitrament [aar*bit*Rament] *n* deciding of a dispute by an agreed authority.

arbitrary (1) [*aar*bitReRi] *adj* of uncontrolled power; despotic; impulsive, capricious; deciding or decided on inadequate grounds ~ **arbitrarily** *adv* ~ **arbitrariness** *n*.

arbitrary (2) *n* (*typ*) special character used to supplement those in the ordinary fount.

arbitrate [*aar*bitRayt] *v/t* and *i* mediate between opposing claims; settle a dispute by referring it to an umpire.

arbitration [aar*bit*Rayshon] *n* hearing and settlement of a dispute by an umpire acceptable to both disputants.

arbitrator [*aar*bitRayter] *n* one chosen by others to settle their disputes.

arbor [*aar*ber] *n* axle of wheel or drill.

arboraceous [aarbo*Ray*shus] *adj* wooded; tree-like.

arboreal [aar*baw*Ri-al] *adj* pertaining to trees; living in trees.

arboreous [aar*baw*Ri-us] *adj* wooded; living in trees.

arboretum [aarbo*Ree*tum] *n* botanical garden devoted to trees.

arboriculture [*aar*boRikulcher] *n* cultivation of trees ~ **arboriculturist** *n*.

arboriform [aarbo*Ri*fawrm] *adj* of tree-like shape.

arborist [*aar*boRist] *n* scientific cultivator of trees.

arborvirus [aarborv*I*tRus] *n* (*med*) virus borne by arthropod animals.

arbour [*aar*ber] *n* shelter made by training trees or climbing shrubs.

arbutus [*ar*bewtus] *n* genus of evergreens.

arc [*aar*k] *n* part of a curve; (*astron*) path of a heavenly body; (*elect*) highly luminous discharge produced when a current of electricity flows through a gap between two electrodes; **a. lamp** technical application of this to produce a very bright light; **a. welding** type of electric fusion welding > PDE.

arcade [aar*kayd*] *n* succession of arches supported by columns; covered avenue, covered walk lined by shops.

arcadian [aar*kay*di-an] *adj* pastoral, of or like an ideally happy innocent country life.

arcane [aar*kayn*] *adj* secret, mysterious, esoteric.

arcanum (*pl* **arcana**) [aar*kay*num] *n* mystery, hidden thing; secret remedy, elixir.

arch (1) [*aar*ch] *n* curved structure spanning a doorway, window-opening, piers of bridge *etc*; anything shaped like an arch; middle of the sole of the foot ~ **arch** *v/t* and *i* build an arch over; form into the shape of an arch; take the shape of an arch.

arch (2) *adj* chief, principal.

arch (3) *adj* coy, roguish, slily mischievous.

arch- *pref* chief, leading.

archaean [aar*kee*-an] *adj* belonging to the earliest geological period.

archaeological [aarki-o*loj*ikal] *adj* of archaeology.

archaeologist [aarki-o*loj*ist] *n* student of archaeology.

archaeology [aarki-o*loj*i] *n* scientific study of the cultural remains and monuments of the remote past; **industrial a.** study of types of machinery, factories *etc* no longer in use.

archaic [aar*kay*-ik] *adj* belonging to an early period, antiquated; (*of language*) no longer in common use.

archaism [*aar*kay-izm] *n* archaic word or phrase; deliberate use of this; quality of being archaic.

archaize [*aar*kay-Iz] *v/t* and *i* make archaic; use archaisms.

archangel [*aar*kaynjel] *n* angel of the second rank; kind of fancy pigeon.

archbishop [aarch*bish*op] *n* chief bishop of a province, a metropolitan.

archbishopric [aarch*bish*opRik] *n* see, jurisdiction, rank, office, of an archbishop.

archdeacon [aarch*dee*kon] *n* (*eccles*) administrative assistant of a bishop.

archdeaconry [aarch*dee*konRi] *n* jurisdiction, office or residence of an archdeacon.

34

archdiocese [aarch*dI*-osis] *n* see of an arch-bishop.

archduchess [aarch*duchi*s] *n* wife of an arch-duke; princess of the former Imperial House of Austria.

archduke [*aarch*dewk] *n* chief duke; prince of the former Imperial House of Austria ~ **archducal** [aarch*dewk*al] *adj*.

archegonium [aark*i*g*Oni*-um] *n* (*bot*) female sex organ of liverworts, mosses, ferns, and related plants > PDB.

arch-enemy [arch-*eni*mi] *n* chief enemy; Satan.

archer [*aarch*er] *n* one who shoots with bow and arrow; the ninth sign of the zodiac, Sagittarius.

archery [*aarch*eRi] *n* use of bow and arrow; (*coll*) company of archers.

archetypal [aark*itI*pal] *adj* of an archetype ~ **archetypally** *adv*.

archetype [*aark*it*I*p] *n* original model from which copies are made, prototype; perfectly typical specimen; most primitive type; (*psych*) concept, symbol *etc* assumed to be based on primitive experiences of all mankind; (*pop*) constantly recurring symbol *etc* in literature, art or myth.

arch-fiend [arch-*feend*] *n* chief of fiends; Satan.

archidiaconal [aark*i*dI-*ak*onal] *adj* pertaining to an archdeacon.

archiepiscopal [aarki-ip*isk*Opal] *adj* pertaining to an archbishop.

archil [*aarch*il/*aark*il] *n* name of various lichens which yield a violet dye; colour of this dye.

archimandrite [aark*imand*RIt] *n* superior of a Greek monastery or group of monasteries.

archipelago (*pl* -os, -oes) [aark*i*p*e*lagO] *n* sea containing many islands; large group of islands.

architect [*aark*itekt] *n* one who designs plans for buildings and oversees their construction; one who designs and carries out any comprehensive plan.

architectonic [aark*i*tek*to*nik] *adj* pertaining to architecture; constructive; (*met*) relating to the classification of knowledge ~ **architectonics** *n* (*pl*) science of architecture; (*met*) systematic arrangement of knowledge.

architectural [aark*i*tek*che*Ral] *adj* of architecture; harmoniously constructed, *esp* on a large scale ~ **architecturally** *adv*.

architecture [*aark*itekcher] *n* art and science of building construction; style, mode or design of thing built; (*fig*) construction, workmanship; large-scale planning.

architrave [*aark*itRayv] *n* (*archi*) lowest member of an entablature; moulded frame surrounding a door or window.

archival [aark*I*val] *adj* pertaining to archives.

archives [*aark*Ivz] *n* (*pl*) place where historical records and documents are kept; documents thus preserved.

archivist [*aark*Ivist] *n* keeper of archives.

archly [*aarch*li] *adv* in an arch way, coyly.

archness [*aarch*nes] *n* arch conduct, coyness.

archon [*aark*on] *n* one of the nine chief magistrates of ancient Athens; a ruler.

archway [*aarch*way] *n* covered passage; arched entrance to a castle or precinct.

arctic [*aark*tik] *adj* pertaining to the North Pole and regions round it; (*fig*) intensely cold; **a.**

circle parallel of latitude 66° 32' North > PDG.

ardency [*aard*ensi] *n* fieriness.

ardent [*aard*ent] *adj* burning, fiery; passionate, fervent; **a. spirits** inflammable spirits with a fiery taste ~ **ardently** *adv*.

ardour [*aard*er] *n* intensity of emotions, fervour.

arduous [*aard*ew-us] *adj* difficult to climb; difficult to accomplish; strenuous, laborious ~ **arduously** *adv* ~ **arduousness** *n*.

are (1) [*aar*] *n* metric unit of area, 1 square deka-metre, 100 square metres, 119·6 square yards.

are (2) *pres pl ind* of the verb be.

area [*air*Ri-a] *n* amount of surface contained between given limits; region, district; open space; sunk open-air court in front of a house giving access to the basement; district to which one's responsibilities or activities are limited; (*fig*) scope, extent.

areal [*air*Ri-al] *adj* of an area.

areca [a*Ri*ka] *n* East Indian palm-tree.

arena [a*Ree*na] *n* central sand-strewn part of a Roman amphitheatre or circus; (*fig*) sphere of conflict; sphere of any form of public action; **a. theatre** theatre where the audience sits right round the stage.

arenaceous [aRi*nay*shus] *adj* sandy.

aren't [*aarnt*] (*coll abbr*) are not; (*inter*) am not.

areography [aRi-*og*Rafi] *n* description of the physical features of the planet Mars.

areola [a*Ree*-ola] *n* coloured circle round the human nipple; red inflamed ring round a pustule; interstice in tissue.

areolar [a*Ree*-olar] *adj* full of interstices.

areolate [a*Ree*-olayt/*air*Ri-olayt] *adj* divided into small areas ~ **areolation** [a*Rio*l*a*yshon] *n*.

areometer see araeometer.

arete [a*Rayt*] *n* sharp ridge of a mountain.

argala [*aar*gala] *n* Indian adjutant bird.

argali [*aar*gali] *n* wild sheep of Asia.

argent [*aar*jent] *n* and *adj* (*her*, *poet*) silver.

argentan [*aar*jintan] *n* alloy of nickel, copper, and zinc; nickel silver.

argentic [aarj*en*tik] *adj* (*chem*) containing silver.

argentiferous [aarj*enti*fi*R*us] *adj* (*min*) silver-bearing.

argentine [*aar*jent*I*n] *adj* like or of silver, containing silver ~ **argentine** *n* silver; imitation silver; (*zool*) silvery substance on the scales of fish; genus of small fishes of the salmon family; (*bot*) silver-weed; (*min*) slate-spar.

argentite [*aar*jentIt] *n* natural silver sulphite.

argentous [ar*jen*tus] *adj* (*chem*) containing silver.

argil [*aar*jil] *n* potter's clay.

argillaceous [aarji*la*yshus] *adj* clayey.

argillite [*aar*jilIt] *n* (*min*) clay slate.

argle-bargle [aarg'l-*baarg*'l] *n* and *v*/*i* (*coll*) dispute, wrangle.

argol [*aar*gol] *n* tartar deposited from fermented wines > PDS.

argon [*aar*gon] *n* an inert gas > PDS.

argosy [*aar*gosi] *n* (*ar*) large merchant-vessel.

argot [*aar*gO] *n* thieves' slang; slang belonging to a class.

argue [*aar*gew] *v*/*t* and *i* debate, dispute; bring strong reason to prove; back (an opinion) by reasoning in favour of it.

arguify [*aar*gewfI] *v/i* (*coll*) argue angrily or persistently.

argument [*aar*gewment] *n* reason urged in support of a theory; discussion of a question, debate; angry discussion; summary, synopsis.

argumentation [aargewment*ay*shon] *n* process of reasoning; debate.

argumentative [aargew*ment*ativ] *adj* characterized by argument, logical; fond of arguing.

argus-eyed [*aar*gus-Id] *adj* extremely vigilant.

argy-bargy [aarji-*baar*ji] *n* and *v/i* (*coll*) dispute, argument.

aria [*aa*Ri-a] *n* air, melody; solo in an opera or oratorio > PDM.

Arian [*air*Ri-an] *n* and *adj* (heretic) denying that Jesus Christ was consubstantial with God the Father.

Arianism [*air*Ri-anism] *n* denial of Christ's consubstantiality with God.

arid [*a*Rid] *adj* dry, parched; lacking all spiritual fervour; uninteresting, lifeless.

aridity [a*Ri*diti] *n* state or quality of being arid.

aridly [*a*Ridli] *n* in an arid way.

ariel [*air*Ri-el] *n* gazelle found in W. Asia and Africa.

Aries [*air*Ri-eez] *n* (*astron*) the constellation of the Ram, first sign of the zodiac.

aright [a*RI*t] *adv* rightly, correctly.

arioso [ari-O*sO*] *adv* (*mus*) in a style halfway between recitative and aria > PDM.

arise (*p/t* **arose**, *p/part* **arisen**) [a*RI*z] *v/i* get up, rise up; come into existence, appear; derive origin (from); come into the public eye; present itself, come about; **a. out of** be a consequence of.

arisen [a*Ri*z'n] *p/part* of **arise**.

aristocracy [a*Ris*tok*R*asi] *n* members of the highest social class, *esp* those with hereditary titles; (*fig*) those outstanding in any sphere of activity; (*pol*) form of government vested in those most distinguished by birth or fortune.

aristocrat [*a*Rist*Ok*Rat] *n* member of the aristocracy.

aristocratic [a*Ris*t*Ok*Ratik] *adj* of, by, like or befitting an aristocrat; distinguished in style or manner ~ **aristocratically** *adv*.

Aristophanic [a*Ris*to*f*anik] *adj* of or like Aristophanes, the Greek comic dramatist.

Aristotelian [a*Ris*to*teel*i-an] *n* and *adj* (follower) of the Greek philosopher Aristotle.

aristotype [a*Ris*t*Ot*Ip] *n* (*phot*) printing process in which silver salts are used in collodion or gelatin.

arithmetic [a*Rith*mitik] *n* science of numbers; counting by figures.

arithmetical [a*Rith*metikal] *adj* pertaining to arithmetic; **a. progression** series of quantities in which each term differs from the preceding by a constant common difference > PDS ~ **arithmetically** *adv*.

arithmetician [a*Rith*mit*i*shan] *n* one skilled in arithmetic.

ark [*aar*k] *n* chest, coffer; **A. of the Covenant** coffer in which the Tables of the Law were kept in the Tabernacle; **Noah's A.** ship in which Noah and his family were saved from the Deluge; child's toy representing the ark with wooden figures of Noah, his family and the animals that went with him; **a. of refuge** place of safety.

arm (1) [*aar*m] *n* limb of the human body extend-

ing from the shoulder; fore limb of an animal; sleeve; part of chair *etc* on which the arm may rest; branch; inlet of sea; (*fig*) authority, executive power; **keep at arm's length** avoid being familiar with; **with open arms** with great cordiality; **child in arms** one that cannot yet walk.

arm (2) *n* a particular kind of weapon; a branch of the fighting services; (*pl*) offensive weapons of war; military profession; (*her*) armorial bearings; **up in arms** roused to indignant protest; **take up arms** go to war; **lay down arms** surrender; **arms race** competition between hostile nations in producing weapons ~ **arm** *v/t* and *i* furnish with arms; provide with the necessary equipment; be in possession (of some advantage); (*refl*) take up arms.

armada [aar*maa*da] *n* fleet of warships, *esp* that sent by Philip of Spain against England in 1588.

armadillo [aarma*dil*O] *n* small S. American animal with hard bony plates.

Armageddon [aarmage*do*n] *n* scene of the future great battle at the Day of Judgement; (*fig*) any great decisive or disastrous conflict.

armament [*aar*mament] *n* force ready for war; (*usu pl*) munitions of war; the great guns on a warship; process of equipping a force for war.

armature [*aar*matewr] *n* military equipment, *esp* defensive; defensive covering of plants or animals; piece of iron placed across the two poles of a magnet; (*elect*) rotating coil of a dynamo; any device inducing voltage by magnetism > PDEl.

armband [*aar*mband] *n* badge *etc* worn as band round the arm.

armchair [*aar*m*chair*] *n* chair with supports for the arms ~ **armchair** *adj* (*of critics etc*) offering theoretical advice without sharing the practical difficulties.

armed [*aar*md] *adj* furnished with weapons; (*fig*) provided, fortified.

armful [*aar*mfool] *n* as much as can be held in the arms; more than enough, a great quantity.

armhole [*aar*mhOl] *n* opening in a garment to which the sleeve is fitted.

armiger [*aar*mijer] *n* esquire; one entitled to heraldic arms.

armipotent [ar*mi*potent] *adj* powerful in arms, of great military strength.

armistice [*aar*mistis] *n* truce, suspension of hostilities; **A. Day** November 11, anniversary of the end of the First World War.

armlet [*aar*mlit] *n* band worn round upper arm.

armorial [ar*mawr*Ri-al] *adj* pertaining to heraldic arms ~ **armorial** *n* book of heraldic arms.

armour [*aar*mer] *n* defensive covering for the body in fighting; defensive metal plating of warships, tahks *etc*; (*coll*) armoured vehicles; (*biol*) protective covering of animals or plants; **coat a.** coat of arms ~ **armour** *v/t*.

armour-bearer [aarmer-*bair*Rer] *n* squire who carried a warrior's armour.

armoured [*aar*merd] *adj* furnished with, protected by, armour; **a. cable** electric cable fortified by metal casing > PDE; **a. car** vehicle fortified by armour-plate; **a. corps** military force equipped with armoured vehicles.

armourer [*aar*me*R*er] *n* maker of arms or armour; official in charge of arms in a ship or regiment;

technician who services the guns and bomb-dropping equipment of an aircraft.

armour-plate [aarmer-*playt*] *n* metal plating used as armour of ships, armoured vehicles *etc*.

armour-plated [aarmer-*play*tid] *adj* protected with armour-plate; (*fig*) callous.

armoury [*aarme*Ri] *n* place where weapons are stored and serviced; (*US*) place where weapons are manufactured.

armpit [*aarm*pit] *n* hollow under the arm where it joins the body.

army [*aarmi*] *n* body of men under a commander-in-chief, armed for land-fighting; organized body of people united by some special object; the military profession; vast crowd.

army-corps [*aarmi*-kawr] *n* main division of an army in the field.

army-list [*aarmi*-list] *n* official list of commissioned officers in the army.

arnica [*aarni*ka] *n* plant used as a tincture for bruises, sprains *etc*.

aroma [a*ROma*] *n* agreeable scent, *esp* spicy; (*fig*) characteristic quality or charm of something.

aromatic [a*ROmatik*] *n* and *adj* (substance) spicy in smell and taste; (*chem*) (*of organic compounds*) having an unsaturated ring structure, *esp* one derived from benzene > PDS.

aromatize [a*ROmatIz*] *v/t* make aromatic.

arose [a*ROz*] *p/t* of **arise**.

around [a*Rownd*] *adv* on every side, in every direction; nearby, in the district; in existence; approximately ~ **around** *prep* all round; on all sides of; (*coll*) towards; near; round about.

arousal [a*Rowz*al] *n* state of being sexually aroused.

arouse [a*Rowz*] *v/t* awaken from sleep: stir up from slothfulness; cause sexual excitement in.

arpeggio [ar*pe*ji-O] *n* (*mus*) notes of a chord played successively instead of simultaneously.

arquebus, arquebusier see **harquebus, harquebusier.**

arraign [a*Rayn*] *v/t* accuse, call to account before a tribunal; find fault with ~ **arraignment** [a*Rayn*ment] *n*.

arrange [a*Raynj*] *v/t* and *i* draw up in formation, set in order; prepare, plan beforehand; adjust, settle; come to an agreement; (*mus*) recast (a composition) for different instruments > PDM.

arrangement [a*Raynj*ment] *n* act of arranging; way that something is arranged, order, design; plan, preparation; that which has been arranged.

arrant [a*Rant*] *adj* notorious; complete.

arras [a*Ras*] *n* rich tapestry hung on walls

array [a*Ray*] *v/t* draw up in order, *esp* for battle; dress (for some special occasion), adorn; (*leg*) impanel ~ **array** *n* order, *esp* military; military force; imposing assemblage of people or things; (*poet*) dress, equipment; (*leg*) panel of jurors.

arrear [a*Reer*] *n* debt remaining unpaid; **in arrear(s)** behindhand in discharge of debts.

arrearage [a*Reer*Rij] *n* money still owing.

arrest [a*Rest*] *v/t* stop, hinder, retard; apprehend in the name of the law; catch attention of ~ **arrest** *n* act of stopping, check; (*leg*) act of seizing and detaining a person for alleged crime; **under a.** in custody; (*leg*) **a. of judgement** stay of legal proceedings after a verdict on the ground of error.

arresting [a*Resting*] *adj* attracting and holding the

attention; striking, surprising; vivid ~ **arrestingly** *adv*.

arrestor-hook [a*Rester*-hook] *n* a device for bringing an aircraft to a halt after landing.

arris [a*Ris*] *n* sharp ridge formed by the contact of two surfaces; raised edge between flutings.

arriswise [a*Risw*Iz] *adv* diagonally; forming a ridge.

arrival [a*RIv*al] *n* act of arriving; one who arrives.

arrive [a*RIv*] *v/i* come to a destination; come to pass, happen; (*coll*) attain success or public distinction; **a. at** reach.

arriviste [a*Reeveest*] *n* (*Fr*) an ambitious person.

arrogance [a*ROg*ans] *n* haughtiness, open display of pride.

arrogant [a*ROg*ant] *adj* haughty, overbearing ~ **arrogantly** *adv*.

arrogate [a*ROg*ayt] *v/t* claim and seize upon as a right but without justification; attribute unjustly.

arrogation [a*ROg*ayshon] *n* unjustified claim and seizure.

arrow [a*RO*] *n* missile shot from a bow, consisting of a slender shaft, feathered and barbed; object of this shape; **broad a.** mark of an arrow-head upon government stores and convicts' clothes.

arrowhead [a*ROhed*] *n* pointed end of an arrow.

arrow-headed [a*RO-hed*id] *adj* shaped like an arrowhead; cuneiform.

arrowroot [a*ROROOt*] *n* starchy food obtained from West Indian plants.

arse [*aars*] *n* (*vulg*) buttocks; (*of boats*) stern ~ **a. about, a. around** *v/i* (*vulg sl*) play the fool.

arse-hole [*aars*-hOl] *n* (*vulg*) anus.

arsenal [*aarsi*nal] *n* government depot where arms are made and stored.

arsenic [*aarsi*nik] *n* (*chem*) steel-grey brittle crystalline substance; poisonous oxide of this.

arsenical [aars*i*nikal] *adj* containing arsenic.

arsenious [aars*i*ni-us] *adj* containing arsenic.

arsis (*pl* **arses**) [*aars*is] *n* stressed syllable in English prosody.

arson [*aars*on] *n* act of wilfully and maliciously setting fire to property.

arsonist [*aars*onist] *n* person attempting or committing arson.

art (1) [*aart*] *n* skill resulting from study and practice; perfection of execution; process of creating something beautiful; painting, sculpture *etc*; any occupation or process requiring great skill and intelligence; rules for the exercise of a craft, profession *etc*; an acquired faculty, a knack; cunning trick; (*pl*) term for university courses other than those in science, medicine, theology, economics; **black a.** magic, sorcery; **fine arts** painting, sculpture, architecture *etc* ~ **art** *adj* designed for artistic effect; consciously artistic.

art (2) (*ar*) *2nd pers sing pres ind* of the verb **be**.

artefact, artifact [*aarti*fakt] *n* anything made by human workmanship.

arterial [ar*teer*Ri-al] *adj* of, in, or like an artery; **a. blood** blood flowing in arteries; **a. road** main road.

arterialize [ar*teer*Ri-alIz] *v/t* convert venous blood into arterial blood by exposing it to oxygen in the lungs ~ **arterialization** [arteerRi-al*Izay*shon] *n*.

arteriole [ar*teer*Ri-Ol] *n* small artery > PDB.

arteriosclerosis [arteerRi-oskleROsis] *n* degenerative changes in the walls of the arteries.

arteriotomy [arteerRi-otomi] *n* (*med*) cutting open or dissection of an artery.

artery [*aa*rteRi] *n* one of the tubes which carry the blood to all parts of the body > PDB; (*fig*) important channel of communication.

artesian [arteezi-an] *adj* (*of wells*) sunk to below the level of the source of water > PDG, PDE.

art-form [*aart*-fawrm] *n* any medium in which works of artistic merit can be produced.

artful [*aart*fool] *adj* clever; crafty; deceitful; skilfully constructed, ingenious; deceptive ~ **artfully** *adv* ~ **artfulness** *n*.

arthralgia [arth*R*alji-a] pain in a joint.

arthritic [arth*R*itik] *adj* of or suffering from arthritis.

arthritis [arth*R*Itis] *n* inflammation of the joints.

arthropoda [arth*R*opoda] *n* (*pl*) (*zool*) category of animals with jointed feet and external skeletons > PDB.

Arthurian [aar*thoor*Ri-an] *adj* pertaining to legends of King Arthur and his knights.

artichoke [*aa*rtichOk] *n* thistle-like plant cultivated as a vegetable; **Jerusalem a.** species of sunflower with edible roots.

article [*aa*rtik'l] *n* any particular thing, object or item; object for sale; (*leg*) distinct section of a document or contract; tenet of faith; essay in a periodical; (*gramm*) name for the adjectives 'the' and 'a'; **leading a.** principal essay in a newspaper representing editorial opinion ~ **article** *v/t* bind by contract of apprenticeship; bring charges, indict.

articular [art*i*kewlar] *adj* pertaining to or situated at a joint of the body.

articulate [art*i*kewlit] *adj* having joints; (*of sound*) divided into words and syllables; speaking clearly and distinctly; able to express oneself easily ~ **articulate** [art*i*kewlayt] *v/t* connect by joints; pronounce distinctly; express in words; construct in flexible sections (lorry *etc*).

articulation [art*i*kew*lay*shon] *n* jointing; joint; manner of speaking; clear enunciation; (*anat*) jointing of two bones; (*bot*) jointure or knot in stalk or root of a plant.

artifact see **artefact.**

artifice [*aa*rtifis] *n* contrivance; ingenious device (*gener* dishonest); work of skilled craft.

artificer [art*i*fiser] *n* one who follows a skilled handicraft; craftsman; (*naval*) engineer with the rank of petty officer; (*mil*) army mechanic.

artificial [aarti*fi*shal] *adj* made by human skill, not natural; made as substitute for a natural product; insincere, affected in manner, shallow; **a. insemination** artificial injection of semen into uterus > PDB; **a. respiration** any method of forcing air into lungs of suffocating person ~ **artificially** *adv*.

artificiality [aartifishi-*a*liti] *n* insincerity.

artillery [art*i*leRi] *n* large guns, cannon; branch of the army trained in their use; science of gunnery.

artilleryman [art*i*leRiman] *n* soldier trained to use artillery.

artily [*aa*rtili] *adv* in an arty way.

artiness [*aa*rtinis] *n* quality of being arty.

artisan [*aa*rtizan] *n* mechanic; craftsman.

artist [*aa*rtist] *n* one who practises any creative art, *esp* painting; one whose work shows artistic skill; performer in an entertainment.

artiste [art*eest*] *n* (*Fr*) professional performer on the music-hall stage, radio, television *etc*.

artistic [aart*i*stik] *adj* proficient in the fine arts; having a good critical appreciation of the arts; (*of objects*) made with art; beautiful, aesthetically pleasing ~ **artistically** *adv*.

artistry [*aa*rtistRi] *n* artistic skill.

artless [*aa*rtless] *adj* unskilful; making no attempt at artistic effect, crude; without artificiality or guile, sincere ~ **artlessly** *adv* ~ **artlessness** *n*.

Art Nouveau [aar-nOOvO] *adj* and *n* (*Fr*) (of or in) a decorative style employing plant forms and exotic linear motifs > PEnc.

art-silk [*aart*-silk] *n* rayon.

art-song [*aart*-song] *n* song composed by a musician with academic training, and disseminated through a written score, not by oral tradition.

arty [*aa*rti] *adj* (*coll*) affectedly artistic; aping the behaviour and eccentricities of artists.

arty-crafty [*aa*rti-k*R*aafti] *adj* (*coll*) practising handicrafts; wearing or using handmade articles, *esp* exclusively and ridiculously.

Aryan [*air*Ri-an] *n* primitive language from which European and Indian languages descend, Indo-European; speaker of this; (*pop*) fair-haired, blue-eyed, non-Jewish person; person of Germanic or Scandinavian descent ~ **Aryan** *adj*.

as (1) [*az*] *adv conj* and *rel pron* equal to; in the same proportion that; in the capacity of; at the time that; because, seeing that; for example; that, who, which; **a. long a.** provided that; **a. well** in addition; **a. good a.** equivalently to; **a. many a.** all who; **a. for, a. to** with regard to.

as (2) [*as*] *n* Roman copper coin.

asafoetida [asa*fe*tida] *n* an umbelliferous plant; gum produced from this having a strong smell of garlic.

asbestos [az*bes*tos] *n* mineral of fibrous texture used as a heat-insulating material and for fireproof fabrics > PDBl.

ascend [a*send*] *v/t* and *i* go up; climb up, mount; rise, slope upwards; (*mus*) rise in pitch; **a. the throne** become king.

ascendancy, ascendency [a*sen*densi] *n* power, dominating influence, control (over).

ascendant, -ent [a*sen*dent] *adj* superior, dominating; (*astron*) rising towards the zenith ~ **ascendant, -ent** *n* (*astrol*) sign of the zodiac just rising on the eastern horizon at a given time; **in the a.** (*fig*) increasing in importance.

ascension [a*sen*shon] *n* act of ascending; (*cap*) ascent of Jesus Christ to Heaven; **A. Day** sixth Thursday after Easter on which this is commemorated.

ascensional [a*sen*shonal] *adj* pertaining to ascension; **a. screw** helical propeller to give a lifting motion to an aircraft.

Ascensiontide [a*sen*shontId] *n* period of ten days between Ascension Day and Whitsun Eve.

ascent [a*sent*] *n* act of ascending; (*fig*) advancement; slope or way leading upwards; flight of steps.

ascertain [aser*tayn*] *v/t* find out by experiment or inquiry ~ **ascertainable** *adj* ~ **ascertainment** *n*.

ascetic [asetik] *n* and *adj* (person) practising severe self-denial in bodily pleasures ~ ascetical *adj* ~ ascetically *adv*.

asceticism [asetisizm] *n* systematic severe self-denial, extreme austerity.

ascorbic [askawrbik] *adj* counteracting scurvy; a. acid vitamin C; white crystalline solid which occurs in fruits and vegetables.

ascot [askot] *n* (*US*) man's broad necktie; man's scarf knotted at neck.

ascribable [askRĪbab'l] *adj* that can be ascribed.

ascribe [askRĪb] *v/t* assign, impute, attribute.

ascription [askRĪpshon] *n* attribution; formula or declaration that ascribes.

asdic [azdik] *n* device for the detection of submarines by echo-sounding.

asepsis [aysepsis/asepsis] *n* absence of septic matter in wounds; aseptic method in surgery.

aseptic [ayseptik/aseptik] *adj* free from bacteria; surgically clean.

asexual [ayseksewal/aseksewal] *adj* (*biol*) without sex or sexual organs ~ asexuality *n*.

ash (1) [ash] *n* a common forest tree; wood of this tree; mountain a. the rowan tree.

ash (2) *n* incombustible residue left after the complete burning of any substance; (*pl*) remains of a human body after cremation; the Ashes (*cricket*) fictitious trophy won or lost according to the result of the Test Matches between England and Australia; a. blonde woman with very fair hair; sit in sackcloth and ashes show deep penitence; turn to dust and ashes (*fig*) come to nothing, be destroyed.

ashamed [ashaymd] *adj* abashed, overcome with a sense of guilt; feeling or showing shame.

ashbin [ashbin] *n* receptacle for ashes and household refuse.

ashcan [ashkan] *n* ashbin, dustbin.

ashen (1) [ashen] *adj* made of ash-wood.

ashen (2) *adj* greyish, deadly pale.

Ashkenazi [ashkenaazi] *n* Jew from any part of Europe other than Spain or Portugal.

ashlar [ashler] *n* (*bui*) square-hewn stone; stone walls or facings finely dressed > PDE.

ashlaring [ashleRing] *n* (*bui*) ashlar masonry; (*carp*) vertical timbers in an attic to cut off the acute angle where the roof meets the floor.

ashore [ashawr] *adv* on shore; on to the shore.

ashpan [ashpan] *n* tray fitted under a grate into which the ashes fall.

ashpit [ashpit] *n* receptacle for ashes and rubbish.

ashram [ashRaam] *n* Hindu hermitage and teaching centre.

ashtray [ashtRay] *n* receptacle for smokers' tobacco-ash.

Ash Wednesday [ash-wenzday] *n* first day of Lent.

ashy [ashi] *adj* consisting of ashes; grey in colour.

Asian [ayshi-an] *adj* Asiatic ~ Asian *n* person belonging to one of the Asiatic races.

Asiatic [ayshi-atik] *adj* pertaining to Asia ~ Asiatic *n* native of Asia.

aside [asĪd] *adv* to one side; apart; to set a. (*leg*) declare of no authority, quash ~ aside *n* remark made so as to be inaudible to the general company; actor's remark conventionally supposed inaudible to others.

asinine [asinĪn] *adj* like an ass, stupid, silly.

ask [aask] *v/t* and *i* call for an answer to; make a request (for); invite; require; inquire (for); a. after inquire for information of; a. for request to see; a. for it (*sl*) behave so as to bring trouble on oneself; a. out invite to a meal, entertainment *etc*.

askance [askans] *adv* sideways, obliquely; look a. at view with mistrust.

askew [askew] *adv* crookedly, askance ~ askew *adj* (*archi*) standing oblique.

asking [aasking] *n* act of one who asks; for the a. simply by asking for it; that's a. (*coll*) I will not tell you.

aslant [aslaant] *adv* in a slanting direction.

asleep [asleep] *adv* sleeping; (*of a limb*) numbed through being kept in a cramped position; fall a. pass into a sleeping state; (*euph*) die.

aslope [aslOp] *adv* and *adj* sloping, leaning.

asp [asp] *n* (*zool*) small venomous serpent found in Egypt and Libya; (*poet*) any venomous serpent.

asparagus [aspaRagus] *n* plant whose shoots provide a choice vegetable.

aspect [aspekt] *n* direction in which a house or window faces; appearance; single element in a complex situation, idea *etc*; partial view of a problem *etc*; (*astrol*) relative positions of the heavenly bodies as seen at a given time; (*gramm*) verbal form marking distinctions of duration, continuity, completion *etc*; a. ratio (*television*) ratio between the width and height of an image.

aspen [aspen] *n* tree of the poplar family whose leaves continually quiver; wood of this tree.

asperge [aspurj] *v/t* sprinkle with holy water.

asperges [aspurjeez] *n* (*RC*) ceremony in which the altar, clergy, and people are sprinkled with holy water.

aspergillum [asperjil-um] *n* brush or sprinkling holy water.

asperity [aspeRiti] *n* roughness of surface; harshness of manner.

asperse [aspurs] *v/t* besprinkle; calumniate.

aspersion [aspurshon] *n* calumny, slanderous accusation; (*eccles*) sprinkling.

asphalt [asfalt] *n* black semi-solid sticky bituminous substance; substance made by adding sand, gravel *etc* to bitumen and used for paving roads *etc* > PDE ~ asphalt *v/t* cover with asphalt.

asphodel [asfOdel] *n* genus of plants resembling the lily; (*poet*) immortal flowers covering the Elysian fields.

asphyxia [asfiksi-a] *n* suffocation.

asphyxiate [asfiksi-ayt] *v/t* and *i* kill or die by deprivation of oxygen, suffocate ~ asphyxiation [asfiksi-ayshon] *n*.

aspic [aspik] *n* savoury meat-jelly.

aspidistra [aspidistRa] *n* indoor pot-plant once popular in living-rooms.

aspirant [aspIrRant/aspiRant] *n* and *adj* (person) striving for a higher position.

aspirate [aspiRit] *n* and *adj* (consonant) pronounced with a breathing ~ aspirate [aspiRayt] *v/t* sound with a breathing; draw out a gas or vapour from a vessel; (*med*) remove fluid from a cavity.

aspiration [aspiRayshon] *n* act of breathing; act of aspiring, lofty hope, ambition; act of aspirating; aspirated sound.

aspirator [aspiRayter] *n* apparatus for drawing a stream of liquid or gas through a tube.

aspire [aspIr] *v/i* have ambitious hopes or plans; strive towards a high goal; rise upwards.

aspirin [aspRin] *n* white crystalline compound of acetyl-salicylic acid, used as an analgesic.

aspiring [aspIrRing] *adj* rising upwards; ambitious.

asquint [askwint] *adv* (looking) out of the corners of the eyes, sidelong.

ass (1) [as] *n* quadruped related to the horse, but smaller, with large ears and tufted tail; (*fig*) foolish person; **make an a. of oneself** behave ridiculously.

ass (2) *n* (*vulg coll*) arse.

assagai, assegai [asagI] *n* wooden spear tipped with iron formerly used by African tribes.

assai [asI] *adv* (*mus*) very.

assail [asayl] *v/t* attack violently.

assailant [asaylant] *n* one who attacks by force; controversial opponent.

assassin [asasin] *n* one who murders, *esp* for political reasons.

assassinate [asasinayt] *v/t* kill by treacherous violence; kill for political reasons.

assassination [asasinayshon] *n* act of assassinating; **character a.** deliberate destruction of a person's good reputation.

assault [asawlt] *n* hostile attack; sudden onrush against a fortress or walled city; (*leg*) unlawful personal attack or threat of attack; **a. and battery** threats followed by blows; **a. craft** small vessels from which attacking troops land on beaches *etc* ~ **assault** *v/t* make an assault (on).

assay [asay] *n* test, trial, *esp* of metals, alloys and ores ~ **assay** *v/t* and *i* test, put to the proof, *esp* metals *etc*; attempt.

assegai see **assagai**.

assemblage [asemblij] *n* coming together of a number of people; crowd of people; fitting together of the parts of a machine.

assemble [asemb'l] *v/t* and *i* collect together; put together the parts of; come together, meet.

assembly [asembli] *n* meeting together; gathering of people for a special object; legislative council; assembling of parts; **a. line** process of assembling components into a final product, *esp* on a conveyor belt.

assent [asent] *v/i* agree (to a proposal, statement) ~ **assent** *n* agreement, concurrence; **with one a.** unanimously.

assentient [asenshi-ent] *adj* approving, agreeing.

assert [asurt] *v/t* declare to be true; maintain (a claim); **a. oneself** insist upon one's claims, push oneself forward aggressively.

assertion [asurshon] *n* act of asserting, declaration; that which is claimed to be true, right *etc*.

assertive [asurtiv] *adj* making aggressive claims or statements ~ **assertively** *adv* ~ **assertiveness** *n*.

assess [ases] *v/t* determine the amount or value of.

assessment [asesment] *n* act of assessing; valuation.

assessor [aseser] *n* one who sits with a judge or magistrate to give advice on technical matters; one who assesses taxes; one who values property.

asset [aset] *n* valuable possession; that which adds to the value of anything, advantage; (*pl*) property, *esp* that available to pay debts.

asset-stripping [aset-stRiping] *n* buying a company or concern solely to sell its assets, i.e. property, plant *etc*, where the realizable value of the assets is greater than the cost of all the shares.

asseverate [aseveRayt] *v/t* affirm solemnly, aver.

asseveration [aseveRayshon] *n* emphatic affirmation; oath.

assiduity [asidew-iti] *n* quality of being assiduous.

assiduous [asidew-us] *adj* constantly persevering; unremitting; eagerly attentive ~ **assiduously** *adv* ~ **assiduousness** *n*.

assign [asIn] *v/t* allot as a portion; make over to another; lay down, determine, fix; appoint, designate; ascribe ~ **assign** *n* (*leg*) one to whom a right or property is transferred.

assignation [asignayshon] *n* arrangement to meet, often for a secret and illicit purpose; love-tryst; apportionment; (*leg*) transference of a property.

assignee [asInee] *n* (*leg*) one deputed to act for another; one to whom a right or property is transferred.

assignment [asInment] *n* allotment; task, commission; attribution; (*leg*) transference of a right or property; document authorizing this.

assignor [asInawr] *n* (*leg*) one who assigns.

assimilable [asimilab'l] *adj* that can be assimilated.

assimilate [asimilayt] *v/t* and *i* cause to be similar; become like; digest (food); become digested; (*fig*) absorb thoroughly; understand fully; (*phon*) make a sound more closely resemble another sound in the same word.

assimilation [asimilayshon] *n* act of assimilating; state of being assimilated.

assist [asist] *v/t* and *i* help; give, lend money to; take part in, *esp* as subordinate helper; be present (at).

assistance [asistans] *n* help.

assistant [asistant] *n* subordinate helper, co-worker ~ **assistant** *adj* helpful, subordinate.

assize [asIz] *n* trial by a judge and jury; (*pl*) periodical sessions held by judges in provincial centres throughout England and Wales.

associate [asOshi-it] *n* comrade; partner; ally; subordinate member of an association who has not all the rights of full members ~ **associate** [asOshi-ayt] *v/t* and *i* join, combine, form an association; connect in one's mind; **a. with** be a frequent companion of; **a. oneself with** express agreement with ~ **associate** *adj* associated.

association [asOshi-ayshon/asOsi-ayshon] *n* act of combining together for a purpose; body of persons who have so combined; intimacy in daily pursuits; **a. of ideas** mental connexion between an object and the ideas related to it > PDP; **A. football** football played with eleven players a side and a round ball which only the goalkeeper may handle.

associationism [asOsi-ayshonizm/asOshi-ayshonizm] *n* (*psych*) theory that association of ideas is the fundamental principle of mental life > PDP.

assonance [asOnans] *n* (*pros*) similarity of words having the same vowel sound but different consonants, or different vowels but the same consonants ~ **assonant** [asOnant] *adj*.

assort [asawrt] v/t and i arrange into different sorts, group; put into the same group (with others); suit.

assorted [asawrtid] adj of different sorts mixed together.

assortment [asawrtment] n act of assorting, arranging; set of different varieties mixed together.

assuage [aswayj] v/t soothe, relieve.

assume [asewm] v/t and i take on, adopt; take upon oneself; pretend to possess, simulate; take for granted, accept as true without proof; be presumptuous.

assumed [asewmd] adj pretended, false; taken for granted ~ **assumedly** adv presumably.

assuming [asewming] conj if one accepts as true (that).

assumption [asumshon] n act of assuming; that which is assumed, supposition; (cap) reception into heaven in bodily form of the Virgin Mary; Church feast commemorating this, 15 August.

assumptive [asumtiv] adj taken for granted; inclined to take things for granted; arrogant.

assurance [ashoorRans] n formal promise, pledge; assertion made to inspire confidence; certainty, confidence; self-reliance; audacity; insurance.

assure [ashoor] v/t make safe (against risk); insure (life); make certain; assert or promise confidently; convince.

assured [ashoord] adj definitely promised, certain; feeling certain, confident; self-possessed; possessing an insurance ~ **assuredly** adv certainly.

astatic [astatik] adj unaffected by the earth's magnetism; (elect) producing no magnetic field > PDS.

aster [aster] n (bot) genus of composite flowers.

asterisk [asteRisk] n (typ) star-like symbol used to refer to a note at the foot of the page, to mark an omission or to mark a conjectural form of a word ~ **asterisk** v/t mark with an asterisk.

astern [asturn] adv (naut) at the stern; in the rear; towards the rear; stern foremost.

asteroid [asteRoid] n planetoid or minor planet revolving between the orbits of Mars and Jupiter ~ **asteroid** adj star-shaped.

asthenia [asthinI-a] n (path) weakness, debility.

asthenic [asthenik] adj weakening, depressive; (of human physique) with small trunk and long limbs > PDP.

asthma [asthma/asma] n .(med) a disease of respiration characterized by intermittent attacks of difficult breathing ~ **asthmatic** [asthmatik] adj and n.

astigmatic [astigmatik] adj of, suffering from, or counteracting, astigmatism.

astigmatism [astigmatizm] n a defect of vision caused by irregular curvature of the cornea; (opt) similar defect in a lens.

astir [astur] adv in a state of movement.

astonish [astonish] v/t take by surprise, amaze.

astonishing [astonishing] adj extremely surprising, very remarkable ~ **astonishingly** adv.

astonishment [astonishment] n great surprise.

astound [astownd] v/t overwhelm with astonishment ~ **astounding** adj.

astraddle [astRad'l] adv with the legs stretched across something, astride.

astragal [astRagal] n (anat) ball of the ankle-joint; (archi) small semicircular moulding.

astrakhan [astRakan] n curly-fleeced skin of very young lambs; kind of cloth imitating this.

astral [astRal] adj of or from the stars; **a. body** (theos) a shadow body or aura alleged to be visible to certain individuals.

astray [astRay] adv out of the right way, into error.

astride [astRId] adv and prep with a leg on each side (of).

astringency [astRinjensi] n astringent quality; harshness, austerity.

astringent [astRinjent] adj having the effect of contracting the tissues; stopping bleeding; (fig) harsh, severe.

astro- pref concerning the stars.

astro-fix [astRO-fiks] n (aer) process of determining position of aircraft or rocket by observing the stars.

astrolabe [astROlayb] n (astron) instrument used formerly for taking altitudes of the heavenly bodies.

astrologer [astRolojer] n one who professes to predict the future by observing the stars.

astrology [astRoloji] n system of predicting the future and casting horoscopes by observing positions of planets, moon and stars.

astronaut [astROnawt] n one who has travelled beyond earth's atmosphere in a rocket-propelled capsule; expert on space travel ~ **astronautics** n (pl) science of space travel.

astronavigation [astROnavigayshon] n (aer) navigation of aircraft or rocket by observing the stars.

astronomer [astRonomer] n one who studies astronomy.

astronomic, astronomical [astROnomik, astROnomikal] adj concerned with astronomy; (fig) enormously great ~ **astronomically** adv.

astronomy [astRonomi] n scientific study of the heavenly bodies.

astrophysics [astRofiziks] n branch of astronomy treating of the physical and chemical properties of the heavenly bodies.

astute [astewt] adj keen, sharp-witted; cunning ~ **astutely** adv ~ **astuteness** n.

asunder [asunder] adv apart; into separate parts.

asylum [asIlum] n sanctuary, place of refuge; hospital or institution for persons with mental disorders.

asymmetrical [asimetRikal] adj not constructed symmetrically ~ **asymmetrically** adv.

assymmetry [asimetRi] n lack of symmetry; nonsymmetrical arrangement.

asymptote [asimtOt] n (geom) line approaching a curve, but never reaching it short of infinity.

asyndeton [asinditon] n (rhet) a construction which omits the conjunctions.

asyntactic [asintaktik] adj loosely constructed, ungrammatical.

at [at] prep near, by, in, close to; at the house of; towards, against; for the price or rate of; at the time of, age of, occasion of; because of; **be a.** be engaged in; **hard a. it** hard at work; **a. once** immediately; **a. one** in agreement; **a. that** (coll) even so; then.

ataraxy [ataRaksi] n indifference to pain.

atavism [atavizm] n resemblance more to distant ancestors than to parents ~ **atavistic** [atavistik] adj.

ataxia [ataksi-a], **ataxy** [ataksi, ataksi] n (path) loss of control over bodily functions; **locomotor a.** loss of coordination of voluntary movements ~ **ataxic** adj.

ate [ayt] p/t of eat.

atelier [atelyay] n (Fr) artist's studio.

atheism [aythee-izm] n disbelief in the existence of a God ~ **atheist** [aythee-ist] n.

atheistic, atheistical [aythee-istik, aythee-istikal] adj of or supporting atheism ~ **atheistically** adv.

atheling [atheling] n (hist) an Anglo-Saxon prince.

Athenaeum [athinee-um] n temple of Athene at Athens; a literary or scientific society; building housing a library and reading-room for members.

athermic [athurmik/aythurmik] adj not conducting heat.

atheroma [atheROma] n (med) thickening of arteries by areas of lipids etc deposited on their walls.

athirst [athurst] adj thirsty; eagerly desirous (for).

athlete [athleet] n one skilled in physical exercises and strenuous games.

athletic [athletik] adj of physical exercises; strong, vigorous; requiring physical strength and skill ~ **athletically** adv.

athleticism [athletisizm] n special devotion to athletic exercises.

athletics [athletiks] n (pl) practice of athletic sports.

athwart [athwawrt] adv across, transversely; (naut) from side to side of a ship ~ **athwart** prep from side to side of; across the path of.

Atlantic [atlantik] adj pertaining to the ocean west of Africa and Europe; **A. states** those on the east coast of America ~ **Atlantic** n Atlantic Ocean.

atlas [atlas] n volume of maps; (anat) top vertebra of the spinal column, supporting the skull.

atman [aatman] n (Hindu) supreme principle of life; the absolute.

atmology [atmoloji] n (phys) the study of aqueous vapours.

atmolysis [atmolisis] n (phys) separation of a mixture of gases into their constituents.

atmometer [atmomiter] n instrument for measuring the rapidity of evaporation.

atmosphere [atmosfeer] n gaseous envelope surrounding any heavenly body, esp earth > PDG; air; (fig) feeling conveyed to one by one's environment, emotional impression; (phys) pressure of one kilogram to the square centimetre.

atmospheric [atmosfeRik] adj pertaining to the earth's atmosphere ~ **atmospherically** adv.

atmospherics [atmosfeRiks] n (pl) crackling sounds made in radio receivers due to electrical discharges in the atmosphere.

atoll [atol] n ring-shaped coral reef > PDG.

atom [atom] n smallest portion of an element which can take part in a chemical reaction > PDS; (fig) a very minute portion, a particle.

atom-bomb [atom-bom] n extremely powerful bomb depending on rapid release of atomic energy > PDS.

atomic [atomik] adj pertaining to atoms; of or

by use of nuclear fission to secure release of energy > PDS; of, by, or possessing atom-bombs; (sl) amazing, terrific; (philos) irreducible; **a. energy** energy released from an atomic nucleus at the expense of its mass; **a. number** the number of electrons rotating round the nucleus of the neutral atom of an element, or the number of protons in the nucleus; **a. pile** a nuclear reactor, a structure which continuously releases energy in a controlled manner from nuclear fission > PDS; **a. weight** weight of an atom of an element expressed on a scale in which the weight of the most abundant carbon isotope is taken as 12.

atomicity [atomisiti] n valency.

atomize [atomIz] v/t reduce (liquid) to small particles, to a fine spray ~ **atomizer** n.

atonal [atOnal] adj (mus) without conscious reference to any scale > PDM.

atonality [atOnaliti] n quality of being atonal.

atone [atOn] v/i make amends, expiate.

atonement [atOnment] n act of atoning, esp the act of Christ in expiating the sins of man.

atonic [atonik] adj (pros) unaccented; (path) lacking muscular tone.

atop [atop] adv and prep on the top (of).

atrabilious [atRabili-us] adj surly, morose.

atrocious [atROshus] adj savagely cruel, heinously wicked; (coll) shockingly bad ~ **atrociously** adv ~ **atrociousness** n.

atrocity [atRositi] n act of cruelty or brutality.

atrophic [atRofik] adj of atrophy.

atrophied [atRofid] adj withered, undeveloped, esp for lack of use or nourishment.

atrophy [atRofi] n wasting away of an organ or tissue of the body ~ **atrophy** v/t and i (cause to) waste away, esp for lack of use.

atropine [atROpIn] n poisonous alkaloid extracted from deadly nightshade.

atropism [atROpizm] n poisoning by atropine.

attaboy [ataboi] interj (US) expression of encouragement and admiration.

attach [atach] v/t and i fasten, join; adhere, stick; tie; appoint to with authority; win the affection of; affix; (fig) attribute; (reflex) join oneself to; (pass) become fond of; (leg) arrest or seize by legal authority.

attaché [atashay] n one on the staff of an ambassador or minister at foreign court.

attaché-case [atashay-kays] n small rectangular box-shaped case for carrying papers.

attachment [atachment] n action of attaching, the condition of being attached; fastening, tie; thing attached; bond of affection, devotion; (leg) arrest of person or seizure of his goods; writ authorizing this.

attack [atak] v/t try to harm; begin a fight; begin military operations against; bring hostile arguments against; take up (an enterprise) with vigour; seize upon, inflict harm on ~ **attack** n act of attacking; acts or words designed to injure; method of beginning; (mus) method of first sounding a note > PDM.

attain [atayn] v/t reach, arrive at.

attainable [ataynab'l] adj that can be attained.

attainder [ataynder] n (leg) forfeiture of estate and extinction of civil rights; **Bill of A.** Parliamentary bill for attainting anyone without trial.

attainment [ataynment] n act of attaining; thing attained, esp mental accomplishment.

attaint [ataynt] v/t convict of crime punishable by attainder; corrupt; soil, sully.

attar [atar] n fragrant oil distilled from flowers.

attemper [atemper] v/t modify by blending; soothe; assuage.

attempt [atemt] v/t and i make effort, endeavour; try to accomplish (difficult task), venture upon; try to take by force, attack ~ **attempt** n act of trying, effort; attack.

attend [atend] v/i and t pay attention; apply oneself (to); look after; follow closely as a consequence; accompany, wait upon; (of doctor) visit (patient); be present (at).

attendance [atendans] n act of attending; number of persons present (at a gathering); **dance a. on** wait upon assiduously.

attendant [atendant] adj accompanying, following ~ **attendant** n servant; follower; one who is present; one who is employed to serve, assist, guide or give information to visitors to a public building etc.

attention [atenshon] n consideration, earnest thought; special notice, careful observation; ceremonious politeness; (mil) cautionary word given before ordering a movement; **stand at (to) a.** (mil) stand motionless and erect.

attentive [atentiv] adj observant; listening carefully; careful to fulfil the wishes of; polite ~ **attentively** adv ~ **attentiveness** n.

attenuate [atenew-ayt] v/t and i make thin, slender; dilute, rarefy; (fig) diminish the force, value, amount of; become thin, grow less ~ **attenuate** adj slender, rarefied; (fig) refined.

attenuation [atenew-ayshon] n act of attenuating; that which attenuates; state of being attenuated: (phys) loss of power suffered by radiation as it passes through matter ~ **attenuator** device for reducing the power of an electric signal.

attest [atest] v/t and i testify, certify; witness (signature); be proof of, vouch for; put (person) on oath.

attestation [atestayshon] n act of bearing witness; evidence; formal confirmation, esp verification of a will by the signature of witnesses.

attested [atestid] adj (of cattle) certified to be free of disease.

attic (1) [atik] adj pertaining to Attica or to Athens; of pure classical style; **a. salt** delicate wit.

attic (2) n room with a sloping ceiling just below the roof; small garret.

atticism [atisizm] n characteristic style of Athenian Greek; elegant Greek; a well-turned phrase.

attire [atIr] n dress ~ **attire** v/t dress, array.

attitude [atitewd] n position of the body; mental disposition; opinion, judgement; policy; **strike an a.** throw oneself into a theatrical posture.

attitudinarian [atitewdinairRi-an] n person given to striking attitudes.

attitudinize [atitewdinIz] v/i strike an attitude, pose, behave affectedly.

atto- pref one million million millionth.

attorney [aturni] n (leg) one authorized to act for another in business or legal affairs; solicitor; **A. General** chief legal officer of the Crown; **power of a.** authorization to act for another.

attract [atRakt] v/t draw towards one; inspire affection for oneself in; entice, charm; (phys) draw by gravitation or other physical forces.

attraction [atRakshon] n act of attracting; force which attracts; anything which appeals widely and draws numbers of people to it; charm.

attractive [atRaktiv] adj having the quality of attracting; (fig) interesting, pleasing, alluring, charming ~ **attractively** adv ~ **attractiveness** n.

attribute [atRibewt] n any quality ascribed to a person; characteristic; object or symbol associated with a person or his office; (gramm) an essential and permanent quality of a thing; (gramm) adjective, adjectival phrase ~ **attribute** [atRibewt] v/t consider appropriate to; ascribe (a quality) to a person; explain as being caused by; assign (work) to author, date, or place.

attribution [atRibewshon] n act of attributing; authority granted to a minister, tribunal etc.

attributive [atRibewtiv] adj relating to an attribute; (gramm) denoting an attribute ~ **attributive** n thing attributed; (gramm) word denoting an attribute.

attrition [atRishon] n rubbing together, mutual friction; slow wearing away caused by this; (mil) tactic of exhausting an enemy before attacking decisively; (theol) sorrow for sin caused only by fear of punishment.

attune [atewn] v/t (mus) tune (an instrument); (fig) bring into accord.

atypical [atipik'l] adv deviating markedly from type.

aubade [Obad] n dawn-song, morning serenade.

aubergine [Oberzheen] n fruit of the egg-plant used as a vegetable.

aubrieta [awbReeta] n aubrietia.

aubrietia [awbReeshi-a] n spring-flowering dwarf perennial purple plant.

auburn [awbern] adj (of human hair) reddish brown; girl with hair of this colour.

auction [awkshon] n public sale of goods to the highest bidder; **Dutch a.** sale in which high prices are gradually lowered until someone buys; **a. bridge** variety of bridge with privileges for the player who undertakes to make the highest score ~ **auction** v/t sell by auction.

auctioneer [awkshoneer] n one who sells goods by auction.

auctorial [oktawrRial] adj pertaining to an author.

audacious [awdayshus] adj daring; intrepid; presumptuous, impudent ~ **audaciously** adv.

audacity [awdasiti] n quality of being audacious.

audibility [awdibiliti] n state or quality of being audible; degree of clarity with which something can be heard.

audible [awdib'l] adj able to be heard ~ **audibly** adv.

audience [awdi-ens] n act of hearing, judicial hearing; formal interview; assembly of persons listening to a play, concert, lecture, radio, or television etc.

audile [awdIl] adj involving hearing, capable of hearing ~ **audile** n person who relies mainly on auditory impressions.

audio- pref related to sound, or to hearing; of or at a frequency audible to human beings.

43

audio-video [awdi-O-*vidi*-O] *adj* combining sound transmission and television.

audiovisual [awdi-O*vize*wal] *adj* using simultaneously both seeing and hearing.

audit [*awd*it] *n* official examination of the accounts of a firm *etc* by an auditor; periodic settlement of accounts; **a. ale** specially strong ale ~ **audit** *v/t* and *i* examine accounts (of); carry out an audit.

audition [awd*ish*on] *n* act of hearing; power of hearing; preliminary trial given to an actor, entertainer *etc* applying for an engagement ~ **audition** *v/t* test (actor *etc*) by audition.

auditive [*awd*itiv] *adj* pertaining to hearing.

auditor [*awd*iter] *n* hearer, listener; learner, disciple; one who audits accounts.

auditorial [awdi*tawr*Ri-al] *adj* pertaining to an audit or an auditor.

auditorium [awdi*tawr*Ri-um] *n* part of a public hall or theatre in which the audience sits.

auditory [*awd*iteRi] *adj* of or by the sense of hearing ~ **auditory** *n* audience; auditorium.

augean [aw*jee*-an] *adj* horribly filthy.

auger [*awg*er] *n* steel drilling tool shaped like a corkscrew.

aught [*awt*] *n* anything whatever ~ **aught** *adv* in any respect, at all.

augment [awg*ment*] *v/t* and *i* increase in size or in amount ~ **augment** [*awg*ment] *n* (*gramm*) vowel prefixed to the past tenses of verbs in Sanskrit and Greek.

augmentation [awgmen*tay*shon] *n* act, process of increasing in size or amount; condition of being increased; (*her*) addition to a coat of arms, given as an honour; (*mus*) proportionate increase of the note values of a theme > PDM.

augmented [awg*ment*id] *adj* (*mus*) larger by a semitone.

augur [*awg*er] *n* (*Rom hist*) religious official whose duty was to foretell the future from omens ~ **augur** *v/t* and *i* predict, forebode; promise (well, ill).

augury [*awg*ewRi] *n* art of divination as practised by the Romans; presentiment; prediction.

August (1) [*awg*ust] *n* eighth month of the year.

august (2) [awg*ust*] dignified, majestic; noble, highly born ~ **augustly** *adv* ~ **augustness** *n*.

Augustan [og*ust*an] *adj* pertaining to the reign of Augustus Caesar and the Latin literature of that age; applied to the period of classicism in any literature.

Augustinian [awgust*ini*-an] *n* member of a religious order called after St Augustine.

auk [*awk*] *n* northern web-footed seabird.

aularian [aw*lair*Ri-an] *n* and *adj* (member) of a hall in an English university.

aumbry see **ambry**.

aunt [*aant*] *n* sister of one's father or mother; wife of one's uncle; **A. Sally** figure of a woman at fairs *etc* for competitors to throw at; (*fig*) object of general abuse.

auntie [*aant*i] *n* (*coll*) aunt.

au pair [O-*pair*] *n*, *adj* and *adv* (*Fr*) (person, *usu* foreign girl) undertaking housework *etc* in return for board and lodging and pocket money.

aura [*aw*Ra] *n* emotional impression made by person or place; an astral shadow body alleged to be visible to individuals of super-normal sensi-

bility; (*path*) subjective feelings preceding an attack of epilepsy.

aural (1) [*aw*Ral] *adj* pertaining to an aura.

aural (2) *adj* of or received through the ear.

aureate [*aw*Ri-it] *adj* gold-coloured, splendid.

aureola, aureole [aw*Ree*-ola, *aw*Ri-Ol] *n* halo; (*astron*) halo of light surrounding the sun during a total eclipse.

aureoled [*aw*Ri-Old] *adj* encircled with an aureole.

auric [*aw*Rik] *adj* of or pertaining to gold.

auricle [*aw*Rik'l] *n* external ear of animals; any lobed appendage; name of the two upper cavities of the heart.

auricula [aw*Rik*ewla] *n* (*bot*) species of primula.

auricular [aw*Rik*ewlar] *adj* pertaining to the ear; of, in, or shaped like an auricle; **a. confession** private confession to a priest.

auriculate [aw*Rik*ewlit] *adj* (*bot*) ear-shaped.

auriferous [aw*Rif*eRus] *adj* gold-bearing.

Aurignacian [oRiny*ay*shi-an] *adj* belonging to latest period of palaeolithic culture.

aurist [*aw*Rist] *n* an ear-specialist.

aurochs [*owr*Roks/*aw*Roks] *n* extinct species of wild ox; European bison.

Aurora [aw*Raw*Ra] *n* dawn, goddess of the dawn; **a. borealis** lights seen in the night sky in the north, with electric discharge > PDG, PDS.

auroral [aw*Raw*Ral] *adj* of the dawn; of the aurora borealis.

aurous [*aw*Rus] *adj* containing gold.

aurum [*aw*Rum] *n* gold.

auscultation [awskul*tay*shon] *n* (*med*) act of listening, *usu* with a stethoscope, to noises made by internal organs as a means of diagnosis.

auspice [*aw*spis] *n* favourable omen; (*pl*) patronage, favouring protection.

auspicious [aw*spish*us] *adj* of good omen, giving favourable promise; predicting success.

Aussie [*aw*si/*osi*] *n* (*coll*) Australian.

austere [aw*steer*] *adj* stern, severe; serious; self-disciplined, spartan; (*of style*) plain, sparing in ornament ~ **austerely** *adv* ~ **austereness** *n*.

austerity [aw*steR*iti] *n* quality of being austere; strict economizing, *esp* when imposed by the State ~ **austerity** *adj* of or conforming to standards of strict economy.

austral [*awst*Ral] *adj* belonging to the south.

Australasian [awst*Ra*layshi-an] *adj* pertaining to Australia and its adjoining islands ~ **Australasian** *n* native or colonist of Australasia.

Australian [awst*Ray*li-an] *n* and *adj* (native) of Australia.

autarchy (1) [*aw*tarki] *n* absolute sovereignty, despotism; self-government.

autarky, autarchy (2) *n* theory that a country should produce everything at home that she requires, and not depend on imports.

auteur [O*tur*] *n* (*Fr*, *cin*) creative film director.

authentic [aw*then*tik] *adj* really proceeding from its alleged source, genuine; of reliable truth ~ **authentically** *adv*.

authenticate [aw*then*tikayt] *v/t* make legally valid; establish the authenticity or truth of.

authentication [awthenti*kay*shon] *n* act of authenticating; proof of genuineness.

authenticity [awthen*tisi*ti] *n* genuineness; authoritativeness; actual truth.

author [*aw*ther] *n* originator, maker (of a theory, plan), writer of a book, article *etc*.

authoress [*aw*thoRes] *n* woman author.

authoritarian [awthoRi*tair*Ri-an] *n* and *adj* (supporter) of authoritarianism; tyrannic (person).

authoritarianism [awthoRi*tair*Ri-anizm] *n* imposition of decisions, opinions *etc* by those in power regardless of wishes of others; nondemocratic rule.

authoritative [aw*tho*Ritativ] *adj* asserting authority, peremptory; possessing authority; vouched for by authorities ~ **authoritatively** *adv*.

authority [aw*tho*Riti] *n* power to compel obedience; person or group of persons having such power; power of influence; authoritative pronouncement; one who can give an expert opinion; book or document giving trustworthy information and reliable opinions.

authorization [awthoRIz*ay*shon] *n* formal permission; delegation of authority.

authorize [*aw*thoRIz] *v/t* officially allow, approve; empower; (of things) justify; **Authorized Version** English translation of the Bible published in 1611.

authorship [*aw*thership] *n* profession of writing books; origin of a book; identity of its author.

autism [*aw*tizm] *n* (*psych*) inability to correlate impressions received through the senses; morbid lack of contact with reality, absorption in fantasy >PDP ~ **autistic** *adj*.

auto- *pref* automatic; by oneself, spontaneous; self-induced; of or for motocars.

autobahn [*aw*tObaan] *n* (*Germ*) arterial road for high-speed traffic only, motorway.

autobiographical [autObi-og*Raf*ikal] *adj* of autobiography; based on one's own experiences.

autobiography [awtObI-og*Raf*i] *n* writing of one's own life; life of a person written by himself.

autocade [*aw*tOkayd] *n* (*US*) ceremonial procession of motorcars.

autocephalous [awtO*se*falus] *adj* (*eccles*) independent of any governing authority.

autochthon (*pl* **autochthones**) [aw*tok*thon] *n* aboriginal inhabitant.

autochthonic [awtok*thon*ik], **autochthonous** [aw*tok*thonus] *adj* aboriginal.

autoclave [*aw*toklayv] *n* a pressure-cooker; (*med*) apparatus for sterilization by steam at high pressure.

autocracy [aw*tok*Rasi] *n* government by a single absolute ruler; absolute power in government.

autocrat [*aw*tOkrat] *n* absolute ruler; one who conducts affairs without reference to the wishes of others; dictatorial person.

autocratic [awtOk*Rat*ik] *adj* of or like an autocrat; dictatorial, overbearing ~ **autocratically** *adv*.

autocriticism [awtOk*rit*isizm] *n* criticism of oneself or one's own work.

autocue [*aw*tOkew] *n* (*TV*) concealed device from which a speaker can read his script.

autocycle [*aw*tOsIk'l] *n* pedal bicycle fitted with light auxiliary engine.

auto-da-fe (*pl* **autos-da-fe**) [awtO-da-*fay*] *n* the burning of a heretic by the Inquisition.

autodrome [*aw*tOdROm] *n* race-track for motor racing.

autoerotism [awtO-e*Rot*izm] *n* self-produced sexual excitement > PDP.

autogamy [aw*tog*ami] *n* (*bot*) self-fertilization.

autogenesis [awto*jen*isis] *n* spontaneous generation ~ **autogenetic** [awtojen*et*ik] *adj* reproducing spontaneously.

autogenic [awto*jen*ik] *adj* self-produced; caused by the reactions of the organisms themselves.

autogenous [aw*toj*enus] *adj* self-produced, produced in the same organism.

Autogiro [awtO*jI*RO] *n* (*tr*) trade name for certain gyroplanes; (*pop*) gyroplane.

autograph [*aw*tog*Raaf*] *n* person's own handwriting, *esp* a signature; author's original manuscript; **a. album** album in which to collect signatures of friends or celebrities ~ **autograph** *v/t* write one's signature (in).

autography [aw*tog*Rafi] *n* lithographic process by which a writing or drawing is reproduced.

autogravure [awtog*Rav*ewr] *n* process of photographic engraving; picture produced by this process.

autogyro see **Autogiro**.

auto-intoxication [autO-intoksi*kay*shon] *n* poisoning by toxins developed within one's own body.

autolysis [awt*Ol*sis] *n* (*bioch*) self-destruction of cells after death brought about by their own enzymes > PDB.

automat [*aw*tOmat] *n* slot-machine supplying food, cigarettes *etc* to customers.

automata [aw*tom*ata] *pl* of **automaton**.

automate [*aw*tOmayt] *v/t* and *i* operate (machinery) by automatic control; convert to automatic production.

automatic [awto*mat*ik] *n* self-loading pistol or revolver ~ **automatic** *adj* self-acting, going by itself; performed mechanically without human intervention; performed unconsciously, *esp* as a routine; occurring as inevitable result; caused by subconscious forces ~ **automatically** *adv*.

automation [awto*may*shon] *n* automatic control of production process or machine so that no workers are needed to operate it.

automatism [aw*tom*atizm] *n* mechanical or involuntary action; mechanical routine; power of independent action > PDP.

automaton (*pl* **automata**, **automatons**) [aw*tom*aton] *n* thing which moves of itself; machine or mechanical device which moves spontaneously; mechanical figure which moves and acts as if alive; human being acting mechanically.

automatous [aw*tom*atus] *adj* having power of spontaneous motion; acting mechanically.

automobile [awtom*Ob*il/awtOm*Obe*el] *n* motorcar.

automotive [awtOm*Ot*iv] *adj* self-propelling.

autonomic [awto*nom*ik] *adj* self-governing; (*biol*) functioning independently > PDB.

autonomist [aw*ton*omist] *n* advocate of autonomy.

autonomous [aw*ton*omus] *adj* self-governing.

autonomy [aw*ton*omi] *n* (*of a State*) right of self-government; self-governing community.

autopilot [*aw*tOpIlot] *n* automatic device controlling flight of an aircraft or rocket.

autoplasty [*aw*toplasti] *n* (*surg*) grafting of skin or tissue from other parts of a patient's body.

autopsy [*aw*topsi/awt*op*si] *n* (*med*) post-mortem examination by dissection.

autopsychosis [awtosIk*Os*is] *n* mental disorder in which all ideas are centred round self.

autoptical [awt*op*tikal] *adj* founded on personal observation.

autoradiograph [awtO*R*aydi-O*g*Raaf] *n* photograph obtained by exposing a plate to a specimen containing a radioisotope.

autoroute [awtO*r*Oot] *n* (*Fr*) motorway.

autostrada [awtO*st*Raada] *n* (*Ital*) motorway.

autosuggestion [awtOsu*j*eschon] *n* process by which one induces irrationally in oneself a conviction or a subjective sensation *etc* > PDP.

autotomy [awt*ot*omi] *n* (*zool*) casting off by an animal of a useless or injured part of its body.

autotoxication [awto-toksi*k*ayshon] *n* poisoning by a virus generated within the body.

autotoxin [awto-*tok*sin] *n* poisonous substance formed within the body.

autotrophic [awt*ot*R*o*fik] *adj* (*biol*) independent of outside sources for organic food materials > PDB.

autotype [*aw*totIp] *n* a facsimile; (*phot*) a process of photographic printing; a reproduction by this process ~ **autotypography** [awtoti*pog*Rafi] *n*.

autumn [*aw*tum] *n* third season of year, extending in the northern hemisphere from 21 September to 21 December; (*fig*) late middle age.

autumnal [awt*um*nal] *adj* of, like or in autumn.

auxanometer [awksa*nom*iter] *n* instrument for measuring the growth of plants.

auxiliary [awg*zil*i-aRi] *n* and *adj* (person or thing) giving assistance as a subordinate; (*gramm*) (verb) which helps to form the tenses and moods of other verbs; (*pl*) (*mil*) foreign or allied troops in the service of a nation at war.

auxins [*aw*ksins] *n* hormones which promote growth in plants > PDB.

avail [a*vay*l] *n* help, use, advantage ~ **avail** *v/i* and *t* be of assistance, help, advantage (to); **a. oneself** make use (of).

availability [avayla*bi*liti] *n* quality of being easy or possible to get.

available [a*vay*lab'l] *adj* obtainable, easy to get, within reach; (*leg*) valid ~ **availably** *adv*.

avalanche [*av*alaansh] *n* large mass of snow and ice sliding rapidly down a mountain side; (*fig*) sudden arrival in huge quantity.

avant-garde [avaant-*gaard*] *n* (*Fr*) innovators in literature or art; pioneers.

avanturine see **aventurine**.

avarice [*av*aRis] *n* excessive greed for wealth, covetousness.

avaricious [ava*Ri*shus] *adj* greedy for wealth; miserly; covetous ~ **avariciously** *adv* ~ **avariciousness** *n*.

avast [a*vaast*] *interj* (*naut*) stop! cease!

avatar [avat*aar*/avataar] *n* (*myth*) incarnation of a Hindu deity; manifestation, display; phase.

avaunt [a*vawnt*] *interj* (*ar*) begone!

ave [*aa*vi] *n* a prayer to the Virgin Mary, the Hail Mary ~ **ave** *interj* hail!

avenge [a*venj*] *v/t* take vengeance on behalf of (person); take vengeance on account of (injury).

aventail, aventayle [*av*entayl] *n* movable mouthpiece of a helmet.

aventurin(e), avanturin(e) [a*vent*ewRin] *n* pale brown glass with golden specks.

avenue [*av*enew] *n* roadway or approach to a house bordered by regular rows of trees; wide street in a town; (*fig*) way of approach; possibility of progress.

aver (*pres*/*part* averring, *p*/*t* averred) [a*vur*] *v/t* declare, assert; (*leg*) prove or justify (a plea).

average [*av*eRij] *n* the mean value of a group of unequal quantities which is obtained by adding them together and dividing by the number of quantities in the group; a rough estimate; common standard or rate ~ **average** *v/t* and *i* estimate the average of; amount to on the average; **a. out** work out so as to produce an average ~ **average** *adj* estimated by average; medium, ordinary.

averse [a*vurs*] *adj* opposed, disinclined, feeling repugnance ~ **aversely** *adv* ~ **averseness** *n*.

aversion [a*vur*shon] *n* strong feeling of dislike, repugnance; disinclination; person or thing disliked; **a. therapy** (*psych*) method of training someone to loathe something he had previously liked, by giving him emetics or electric shocks every time he sees or experiences it.

avert [a*vurt*] *v/t* turn away; prevent from happening, ward off.

avertable [a*vur*tab'l] *adj* that can be prevented.

avian [*ay*vi-an] *adj* pertaining to birds.

aviary [*ay*vi-aRi] *n* large cage for keeping birds.

aviate [*ay*vi-ayt] *v/t* and *i* fly an aircraft or travel in one.

aviation [ayvi-*ay*shon] *n* art or science of flying aircraft.

aviator [*ay*vi-*ay*ter] *n* pilot of an aircraft.

aviculture [*ay*vikulcher] *n* breeding of birds, bird-fancying ~ **aviculturist** [ayvi*kul*cherRist]

avid [*av*id] *adj* ardently desirous, greedy, eager.

avidity [a*vid*iti] *n* ardent eagerness.

avidly [*av*idli] *adv* in an avid way.

avifauna [*ay*vifawna] *n* the different varieties of birds in a district.

aviform [*ay*vifawrm] *adj* bird-like in shape.

avocado [aavO*kaad*O] *n* pear-shaped tropical fruit used as an hors d'œuvre or in salads.

avocation [avO*kay*shon] *n* employment, occupation; minor occupation, distraction.

avocet, avoset [*av*Oset] *n* bird of the snipe type.

avoid [a*void*] *v/t* keep away from, have nothing to do with; refrain from; escape from; (*leg*) quash, annul.

avoidance [a*void*ans] *n* act of avoiding, holding aloof; vacancy (of office or benefice).

avoirdupois [averdew*poiz*] *n* standard system of weights used in Great Britain for most goods until the 1970s; (*coll*) excessive weight, obesity.

avoset see **avocet**.

avouch [a*vowch*] *v/t* and *i* vouch for, guarantee; declare, affirm; acknowledge, confess.

avow [a*vow*] *v/t* assert; confess, admit; declare oneself; (*leg*) justify (an act done).

avowal [a*vow*-al] *n* frank admission.

avowed [a*vow*d] *adj* openly declared or admitted.

avulsion [a*vul*shon] *n* action of pulling off; forcible separation.

avuncular [a*vun*kewler] *adj* pertaining to an uncle; kind-hearted and cheerful.

await [a*wayt*] *v/t* wait for; be in store for, be reserved for.

awake (*p*/*t* awoke, *p*/*part* awoke, awoken or awaked) [a*wayk*] *v/t* and *i* rouse from sleep; stir up, excite; cease to sleep; (*fig*) become watchful or aware ~ **awake** *adj* in a waking state, not asleep; vigilant; **a. to** conscious of; **wide a.** fully roused; (*coll*) not easily duped.

awaken (*p/t* and *p/part* **awoken**) [awayken] *v/t* and *i* awake, arouse; become awake.

award [awawrd] *v/t* give as prize for merit; grant; impose (a fine) ~ **award** *n* payment or fine assigned by judge or arbitrator; prize or scholarship granted; judgement.

aware [awair] *adj* having knowledge, cognizant ~ **awareness** [awairness] *n*.

awash [awosh] *adj* level with the surface of the water; washing about, drifting with the waves.

away [away] *adv* to a distance, to another place, off, aside; absent; to nothing, to the end, till death; continuously, on; **fire a.** (*fig*) begin at once; **a. with you** go away; **work a.** go on working; **a. match** match not played on the home ground.

awe [aw] *n* reverential fear; **stand in a. of** feel deep reverence for ~ **awe** *v/t* strike with fear and dread; inspire with reverence.

aweary [aweerRi] *adj* (*poet*) tired.

aweather [aweTHer] *adv* (*naut*) towards the wind.

aweigh [away] *adv* (*naut*) with the anchor just clear of the ground.

awe-inspiring [aw-inspIrRing] *adj* causing feelings of awe.

awesome [awsum] *adj* inspiring awe, weird, mysterious ~ **awesomely** *adv* ~ **awesomeness** *n*.

awestruck [awstRuk] *adj* overwhelmed with awe.

awful [awfool] *adj* dreadful, terrible; (*coll*) very bad; (*ar*) awe-inspiring, majestic ~ **awfully** *adv* in an awful manner; (*coll*) very, extremely ~ **awfulness** *n*.

awhile [awIl] *adv* for a short time.

awkward [awkwerd] *adj* bungling, clumsy; embarrassed; (*of things*) inconvenient, embarrassing, hard to deal with; **a. customer** person who may be dangerous; **a. age** adolescence; **a. squad** recruits who do not know their drill ~ **awkwardly** *adv*.

awl [awl] *n* small tool for piercing holes.

awn [awn] *n* spiny growth from the ends of ears of oats, barley *etc* ~ **awned** *adj* with awns.

awning [awning] *n* canvas covering stretched so as to provide shelter from the sun; **a. deck** (*naut*) superstructure deck, the top deck.

awoke [awOk] *p/t* and *p/part* of **awake**.

awoken [awOken] *p/t* of **awaken**, *p/part* of **awake** or **awaken**.

awry [aRI] *adv* and *adj* crookedly, askew; improperly, wrongly; crooked, distorted.

ax [aks] *n* axe.

axe [aks] *n* tool for cutting and chopping wood, with a long wooden handle and heavy head with one sharp edge; **the a.** execution by beheading; drastic cutting down of public expenditure; **have an a. to grind** have an ulterior motive for one's actions ~ **axe** *v/t* dismiss or abolish to cut down expenses.

axe-helve [aks-helv] *n* wooden axe-handle.

axial [aksi-al] *adj* forming an axis; of an axis.

axially [aksi-ali] *adv* along an axis.

axil [aksil] *n* (*bot*) angle between the upper side of leaf and stem or between branch and trunk.

axile [aksIl] *adj* belonging to an axis; (*bot*) having the same direction as the axis of the seed.

axilla (*pl* **axillae**) [aksila] *n* armpit.

axillary [aksilaRi] *adj* of the armpit; of or on an axil.

axiom [aksi-om] *n* generally accepted principle or proposition; (*log* and *math*) self-evident proposition requiring no proof.

axiomatic, axiomatical [aksi-omatik, aksi-omatikal] *adj* of, like, or containing an axiom; self-evident ~ **axiomatically** *adv*.

axis [aksis] *n* imaginary line about which a given body or system rotates; (*geom*) line dividing a regular figure symmetrically; (*opt*) line from eye to object of sight; (*physiol*) central core of an organism or organ; **the A.** political collaboration of Fascist Germany, Italy and Japan.

axle [aks'l] *n* spindle upon which a wheel revolves; rounded ends of the axletree.

axlebox [aks'lbox] *n* box containing lubricant within which the ends of an axle revolve.

axlepin [aks'lpin] *n* bolt to fasten a cart to the axletree.

axletree [aks'ltRee] *n* fixed bar on rounded ends of which the wheels of a carriage revolve.

Axminster [aksminster] *n* kind of carpet.

axolotl [aksolot'l] *n* salamander-like amphibian found in Mexican lakes.

axon [akson] *n* long nerve fibre which carries impulses away from a neuron > PDB.

ay, aye (1) [ay] *adv* (*poet*) ever.

ay, aye (2) [I] *interj* yes.

ayah [I-a] *n* native Hindu nurse for European children.

aye-aye [I-I] *n* (*zool*) nocturnal squirrel-like animal found only in Madagascar.

ayes [Iz] *n* (*pl*) those in Parliament who vote for a motion; **the ayes have it** the motion is carried.

azalea [azayli-a] *n* genus of shrubby flowering plants allied to the rhododendron.

azimuth [azimuth] *n* any arc of the heavens from the zenith to the horizon; (*of a heavenly body*) the angle at the zenith between the meridian and the vertical circle through the heavenly body, measured by the arc intercepted by these two circles on the horizon > PDG.

azoic [azO-ik] *adj* having no trace of life; (*geol*) containing no organic remains.

azote [azOt] *n* Lavoisier's name for nitrogen.

Aztec [aztek] *n* member of the Indian tribe which founded the empire of Mexico.

azure [azher/ayzhewr] *n* blue, *esp* of the sky ~ **azure** *adj*.

azurine [azewrRIn/azewrRin] *adj* blue, pale blue ~ **azurine** *n* the blue roach; (*dyeing*) dark blue base obtained from aniline black.

azurite [azewrRIt] *n* natural blue copper carbonate.

azyme [azim] *n* cake of unleavened bread eaten at the Jewish Passover; (*pl*) the Jewish feast of unleavened bread ~ **azymous** *adj* unleavened.

B

b [*bee*] second letter of the English alphabet; (*mus*) seventh note in the scale of C major.

baa [*baa*] *v/i* to bleat ~ **baa** *n*.

Baal (*pl* **Baalim**) [*bayl*, *pl* *bayl*im] *n* chief god of the Phoenicians; (*fig*) false god or idol.

babacoote [*bab*akOOt] *n* species of lemur.

babble [*bab*'l] *v/i* and *t* talk indistinctly, foolishly, or incessantly; chatter, murmur (of birds, streams *etc*); let out (secrets) ~ **babble** *n* idle chatter; confused sounds ~ **babbler** *n*.

babe [*bayb*] *n* baby, small child; (*fig*) inexperienced person.

babel [*bayb*'l] *n* (*bibl*) tower in Shinar (Gen. xi) where God confused the speech of men; (*fig*) noisy confused assembly, uproar, din; meaningless mixture of sounds.

baboon [*bab*OOn] *n* large monkey with long snout and hairless buttocks ~ **baboonery** *n* colony of baboons.

babouche [*bab*OOsh] *n* oriental slipper.

babu, baboo [*baab*OO] *adj* and *n* (of or like) a pedantic and ornate style of English allegedly used by Indians.

babul [*bab*OOl] *n* thorny tree of the mimosa species; the gum-arabic tree.

baby [*bayb*i] *n* infant; childish person; something which is a small example of its kind; (*sl*) girlfriend, sweetheart; **hold the b.** (*sl*) be saddled with unwanted responsibility ~ **baby** *adj* of or for a baby; (*coll*) miniature, small; **b. grand** small grand piano ~ **baby** *v/t* (*coll*) treat as a baby.

baby-farmer [*bayb*i-faarmer] *n* woman who fosters babies for pay (*gener pej*).

babyhood [*bayb*ihood] *n* infancy.

babyish [*bayb*i-ish] *adj* like a baby.

Babylon [*babil*on] *n* (*hist*) capital of the empire of the Chaldees; (*fig*) rich, dissolute city; (*cont*) the Papacy ~ **Babylonian** [*babil*Oni-an] *adj* and *n*.

baby-minder [*bayb*i-mInder] *n* woman who is paid to look after small babies or small children in her home while their mothers are at work.

babysit [*bayb*isit] *v/i* act as a babysitter.

babysitter [*bayb*isiter] *n* one engaged to mind young children in the absence of their parents.

baby-snatcher [*bayb*i-snatcher] *n* one who kidnaps babies; (*coll*) one who has a love-affair with a much younger person.

baby-talk [*bayb*i-tawk] *n* distorted ungrammatical speech used by or to babies.

baccalaureate [bakal*aw*Ri-it] *n* university degree of Bachelor; first grade of French university examination taken while still at school.

baccarat, baccara [*bak*aRaa] *n* gambling card game.

bacchanal [*bak*anal] *adj* of or belonging to Bacchus; riotously drunk ~ **bacchanal** *n* worshipper of Bacchus; reveller; drunken orgy.

bacchanalia [bakan*ay*li-a] *n* (*pl*) festival to honour Bacchus; drunken orgy ~ **bacchanalian** *adj* and *n* drunken (reveller).

bacchant [*bak*ant] *n* devotee of Bacchus; drunken reveller ~ **bacchantic** [bak*ant*ik] *adj*.

bacchante [*bak*ant/bak*ant*i] *n* female devotee of Bacchus; female drunken reveller.

bacchic [*bak*ik] *adj* of Bacchus; in a drunken frenzy, jovial.

Bacchus [*bak*us] *n* (*myth*) the god of wine.

bacciform [*bak*sifawrm] *adj* shaped like a berry.

baccivorous [baks*iv*oRus] *adj* feeding on berries.

baccy [*bak*i] *n* (*coll*) tobacco.

bachelor [*bach*eler] *n* unmarried man; one who has taken the first degree of a university; (*hist*) apprentice knight in arms; **knight b.** (title of) one who has been knighted; **bachelor's buttons** (*bot*) various flowers of button-like shape; (*coll*) buttons fixed in place by a press stud.

bachelor-girl [*bach*eler-girl] *n* independent unmarried woman.

bachelorhood [*bach*elerhood] *n* state of being a bachelor.

bacillary [basil*a*Ri] *adj* of or like or comprising little rods; (*path*) pertaining to bacilli.

bacilliform [basil*i*fawrm] *adj* shaped like a rod.

bacillus (*pl* **bacilli**) [basil*us*] *n* rod-shaped microscopic organism.

back (1) [*bak*] *n* that part of the body near the spine extending from the shoulders to the base of the spine; upper surface of an animal's body; that part of a thing opposite to the front and away from an observer; (*of chair*) upright which supports the spine; (*of hand*) the knuckle side; (*of book*) the covers; (*of tool, knife*) the blunt edge; (*of ship*) the keel; (*of wave*) the upper surface; (*in football etc*) player in rear position; **break one's b.** strive earnestly; **break the b. of** finish the hardest part (of task); **put one's b. into anything** strive diligently at; **put someone's b. up** antagonize; **turn one's b. upon** abandon, ignore; **be on one's b.** be laid up ill; **at the b. of one's mind** forgotten for the moment; **behind one's b.** in an underhand way; **with one's b. to the wall** hard-pressed; **the Backs** lawns and grounds of certain Cambridge colleges overlooking the river ~ **back** *v/t* and *i* form the back of; cover the back of; make a back for; support either morally or materially; bet on a contestant's chance of winning; sign on the back of (document); make to go backwards; mount (horse); (*sport*) follow the lead of the pointer dog; move back; (*of winds*) change direction anti-clockwise; **b. up** support; **b. down, b. out of** withdraw from ~ **back** *adv* in the direction of the rear, away from the front; to a former state or position; away from the present in time, into the past; in time past, ago; at a distance; in return; in arrear; in state of restraint, checked; **b. and forth** to and fro; **answer b.** make an impertinent reply; **go b. on** betray (friends), break (promise), repudiate (principles); **pay someone b.** retaliate; **take b.** withdraw (offensive remark) ~ **back** (*superl* **backmost**) *adj* behind; remote, obscure; out of date; inferior; in arrear; **b. vowel** guttural vowel.

back (2) *n* trough, vat for brewing, dyeing.

backband [*bak*band] *n* leather strap passing over a horse's saddle to take the weight of the shafts.

backbench [*bak*bench] *n* any bench in the House of Commons occupied by members who are not Ministers or leading members of the Opposition ~ **backbench** *adj* ~ **backbencher** *n*.

backbite [*bak*bIt] *v/t* and *i* speak ill of; speak ill of others in their absence ~ **backbiter** *n*.

backboard [*bak*bawrd] *n* board placed at the back of anything (*eg* picture-frame); movable board at the back of a cart; board strapped across a person's back to improve his posture.

backboiler [*bak*boiler] *n* small tank built in behind an open fire to provide hot water.

backbone [*bak*bOn] *n* the spine; main part, chief support, axis of something; (*fig*) stability of character, purposefulness; **to the b.** entirely.

backchat [*bak*chat] *n* (*coll*) impertinent retort; (*theat*) comedians' patter.

backcloth [*bak*kloth] *n* the painted cloth hung at the back of the stage in a theatre.

back-comb [*bak*-kOm] *v/t* and *i* comb underlying hairs upwards towards scalp.

backdate [*bak*dayt] *v/t* make retrospective, cause (agreement *etc*) to apply from a past date.

backdoor [*bak*dawr] *adj* secret, underhand.

backdown [*bak*down] *n* (*coll*) surrender, retreat.

backdrop [*bak*dRop] *n* backcloth.

back-end [*bak*-end] *n* rear end; (*coll*) late autumn.

backer [*bak*er] *n* one who gives moral or material help; supporter; one who bets on a contestant's chance of winning.

backfire [*bak*fIr] *n* premature explosion in the cylinder of an internal combustion engine which tends to send it into reverse ~ **backfire** *v/i* (*mot*) emit a backfire; (*coll*) (of schemes) go wrong and so cause trouble for the schemer.

back-formation [*bak*-fawrmayshon] *n* (*phil*) invention of a root-word from one which might seem to derive from it but does not.

backgammon [*bak*gamon] *n* game played on a hinged board with draughtsmen and dice.

background [*bak*gRownd] *n* setting in a scene or picture *etc* behind the objects or people in the foreground; a less prominent position, obscurity; (*fig*) cultural climate; general knowledge; education, experience; (*phys*) level of constant natural radiation ~ **background** *adj* of or in the background; as subordinate accompaniment.

backhand [*bak*hand] *n* (*tennis etc*) stroke made with the racket well across the front of the body with the back of the hand facing front; handwriting sloping to the left ~ **backhand** *adj*.

backhanded [*bak*handid] *adj* with the back of the hand; sloping to the left; (*fig*) unfair; equivocal, doubtful (compliment).

backhander [*bak*hander] *n* blow with the back of the hand; reproof; extra glass of wine got by the bottle circulating the wrong way.

backing [*bak*ing] *n* action of supporting; act of moving back or putting back; action of providing with a back; material to form or cover the back of an object; mounting a horse; assistance, moral support; body of supporters.

backlash [*bak*lash] *n* excessive play between parts of a piece of machinery; (*fig*) hostile reaction aroused by a reform movement.

backlog [*bak*log] *n* (*comm*) accumulation of unfinished work or arrears of payment.

back-number [bak-*number*] *n* (*of periodical*) issue earlier than the current one; (*fig*) out-of-date thing or person.

backpedal [bak*pedal*] *v/i* rotate the pedals of a bicycle in the reverse direction; (*fig*) retreat, back down from.

back-projection [bak-pRO*jek*shon] *n* (*cin*) use of a previously photographed background.

backrest [*bak*Rest] *n* support at the back of a person or machine.

back room [*bak*-ROOm] *n* room at the back of a house; (*coll*) **back-room boy** expert engaged in research of a confidential nature.

back-seat [bak-*seet*] *n* seat at the rear of hall or vehicle; (*fig*) position of inferiority; **back-seat driver** (*fig*) one who persists in offering gratuitous advice.

backset [*bak*set] *n* a reverse, relapse ; countercurrent.

backsheet [*bak*sheet] *n* last page of newspaper.

backside [*bak*sId] *n* rear or back part; (*coll*) the buttocks.

backsight [*bak*sIt] *n* (*sur*) sight taken towards the last station passed; sight nearer the butt of a rifle.

back-slang [*bak*-slang] *n* words spelt backwards and pronounced accordingly.

backslide [bak*slId*] *v/i* relapse into sin; fall from grace ~ **backslider** *n* ~ **backsliding** *n*.

backstage [bak*stayj*] *n*, *adj* and *adv* (*theat*) behind the curtain; in wings or dressing-room.

backstairs [bak*stairz*] *n* (*pl*) staircase in a house leading from the servants' quarters ~ **backstairs** *adj* (*fig*) underhand, secret.

backstays [bak*stayz*] *n* (*pl*) (*naut*) wire stays running aft from the masthead as standing rigging.

backstitch [*bak*stich] *n* method of sewing in which the needle is inserted behind the thread and comes out in front of it.

backstroke [*bak*stROk] *n* a stroke used when swimming on the back.

backsword [*bak*sawrd] *n* one-edged sword; a single-stick used in fencing.

backtrack [*bak*tRak] *v/i* retrace one's steps, return to one's starting point; move backwards.

back-up [*bak*-up] *n* (*coll*) support, backing; something held in reserve for emergency use.

backward [*bak*werd] *adj* towards the rear; towards the past; returning; reversed; reluctant, shy; retarded in development; behind time, late ~ **backwardly** *adv* ~ **backwardness** *n*.

backward, backwards [bak*werd(z)] *adv* with the back foremost; towards one's rear, away from the front; (*of things*) back towards the starting point; in the reverse order; **know something b.** understand it perfectly.

backwardation [bakwaw*day*shon] *n* (*comm*) compensatory payment for late delivery of shares made by seller to buyer.

backwash [*bak*wosh] *n* the backward motion of a wave or of a current; broken water left behind a ship or oars; (*fig*) disturbance ~ **backwash** *v/t* run water (through a filter) in reverse direction.

backwater [*bak*wawter] *n* stagnant pool beside a river hardly affected by the main flow of the water; backwash; (*fig*) condition or place of intellectual stagnation.

backwoods [*bak*woodz] *n* (*pl*) uncleared forest land far from civilization ~ **backwoodsman** *n* settler in the backwoods; (*coll*) uncouth rustic; a peer who seldom attends the House of Lords.

bacon [*bay*kon] *n* back and sides of a pig cured by salting *etc*; **save one's b.** have a narrow escape.

Baconian [bay*k*Oni-an] *adj* and *n* (person) connected with, believing in, the theory that Bacon wrote Shakespeare's works.

bacteria [bak*teer*Ri-a] *n* (*pl*) microscopic organisms found in organic matter > PDB ~ **bacterial** *adj* belonging to, caused by, bacteria.

bactericide [bak*teer*Risid] *n* a substance that kills bacteria.

bacteriologist [bakteerRi-*olo*jist] *n* an expert in bacteriology.

bacteriology [bakteerRi-*olo*ji] *n* study of bacteria ~ **bacteriological** [bakteerRi-*olo*jikal] *adj*.

bacteriolysis [bakteeRi-*ol*isis] *n* destruction of bacteria by serum; use of bacteria in the disposal of sewage.

bacteriolytic [bakteerRi-*ol*itik] *adj* able to destroy bacteria by dissolving them.

bacteriophage [bak*teer*Ri-Ofayj] *n* type of virus requiring a bacterium in which to replicate; *abbr* phage.

bacterium (*pl* **bacteria**) [bak*teer*Ri-um] *n* a microscopic organism > PDB.

bad (*comp* **worse**, *superl* **worst**) [*bad*] *adj* defective, deficient, of little worth, inferior; incorrect; unfavourable; wicked, vicious, depraved; decayed, unsound; disagreeable, offensive; injurious; unwell, in pain; (*leg*) invalid; **b. blood** ill feeling; **with b. grace** unwillingly; **b. debts** irrecoverable debts; **b. form** (*sl*) lack of manners, incorrect behaviour; **b. egg, b. hat, b. lot** (*sl*) a disreputable character ~ **bad** *n* misfortune; deficit, loss; **go to the b.** become depraved.

baddie, baddy [*bad*i] *n* (*coll*) villainous personage, *esp* in a thriller.

baddish [*bad*ish] *adj* slightly bad.

bade [bayd/*bad*] *p/t* of **bid**.

badge [*baj*] *n* distinguishing mark or emblem worn to indicate position, office, or the membership of a society.

badger (1) [*baj*er] *n* grey nocturnal quadruped; brush made from its hair.

badger (2) *v/t* pester, tease; heckle by questions.

badinage [badin*aazh*] *n* (*Fr*) light banter, raillery.

badlands [*bad*landz] *n* (*pl*) (*US*) barren regions.

badly [*bad*li] *adv* faultily, imperfectly; hopelessly; unkindly, cruelly; (*coll*) strongly, very much.

badminton [*bad*minton] *n* game like lawn-tennis in which a shuttlecock is hit over a net with a racket; a claret drink.

baffle (1) [*baf*'l] *v/t* bewilder, perplex, frustrate.

baffle (2) *n* (*eng*) a plate used to direct the flow of air or liquid; shielding device, screen.

baffle-board [*baf*'l-bawrd] *n* large board on which a loudspeaker is mounted to increase its resonance.

baffling [*baf*ling] *adj* perplexing, puzzling.

bag [*bag*] *n* any flexible container which may be closed at the top; pouch; purse; diplomatic mail bag; amount killed on a hunting expedition; sac or pouch in an animal's body; (*sl*) ugly old woman; (*sl*) preoccupation; varying measure of quantity; (*pl coll*) trousers; (*pl coll*) plenty, many; **the whole b. of tricks** every device,

everything possible; **let the cat out of the b.** give away a secret unwittingly; **b. of bones** emaciated creature; **b. and baggage** with all one's belongings; **in the b.** as good as got ~ **bag** (*pres/part* **bagging**, *p/t* and *p/part* **bagged**) *v/t* and *i* put into a bag; (*sport*) kill game; (*coll*) steal, seize; bulge, hang loosely; **bags I!** (*sl*) I claim that!

bagasse [ba*gas*] *n* remains of sugar-cane left after extraction of sugar.

bagatelle [baga*tel*] *n* unimportant trifle; light piece of verse or music; game like billiards played with small metal balls and a cue; small pintable.

baggage [*bag*ij] *n* army equipment; luggage; (*coll*) pert young woman; prostitute.

bagging [*bag*ing] *n* material for bags.

baggy [*bag*i] *adj* inflated, puffy; sagging, hanging loosely ~ **bagginess** *n*.

bagman [*bag*man] *n* (*coll*) commercial traveller; (*Aust*) swagman, tramp.

bagnio [*ban*yO] *n* Oriental prison; brothel.

bagpipe [*bag*pIp] *n* (*mus*) instrument (chiefly played in Scotland) comprising a wind-bag and a set of reed pipes into which air is pressed.

bah [*baa*] an interjection expressing contempt.

bail (1) [*bayl*] *n* sum of money paid as security on behalf of a person which frees him temporarily from prison while awaiting trial; person who thus offers security for someone; **forfeit b.** fail to appear for trial; **go, stand b. for** stand surety for, (*fig*) guarantee ~ **bail** *v/t* free from custody by becoming security for; deliver goods in trust.

bail (2) *n* (*cricket*) one of the two small pieces of wood placed across the top of the stumps; bar separating horses in an open stable.

bail (3) *n* shallow scoop for bailing water from a boat ~ **bail** *v/t* and *i* throw water out of a boat with buckets, scoops *etc*.

bailee [bay*lee*] *n* (*leg*) one to whom goods are entrusted.

bailer [*bay*ler] *n* one who bails; scoop used for bailing.

bailey [*bay*li] *n* outer walls round a castle; enclosed courtyard; **Old Bailey** London's Central Criminal Court.

Bailey bridge [bayli-b*Ri*j] *n* kind of pontoon bridge designed for rapid erection.

bailie [*bay*li] *n* (*Scots*) an alderman.

bailiery [baylee-e*Ri*] *n* jurisdiction of a bailie.

bailiff [*bay*lif] *n* sheriff's officer; landowner's agent or steward.

bailiwick [*bay*liwik] *n* district, jurisdiction, of a bailie or bailiff; (*US*) proper sphere or function.

bailment [*bayl*ment] *n* (*leg*) delivery of goods by a bailor to a bailee under an agreement for their return when they are no longer required; the standing of bail for an accused person.

bailor [*bay*ler] *n* (*leg*) one who delivers goods to a bailee under an agreement of bailment.

bailsman [*bayl*zman] *n* (*leg*) one who stands bail for another.

bairn [*bairn*] *n* (*dial*) child.

bait (1) [*bayt*] *n* food, or an imitation of it, used to entice and catch fish or animals; fodder for horses; (*fig*) snare, temptation.

bait (2) *v/t* and *i* provide (hook *etc*) with bait; feed

(horses); worry and harass (animals) with dogs; (*fig*) allure; exasperate, tease ~ **bait** *n* (*sl*) rage.
baize [*bayz*] *n* coarse woollen material.
bake [*bayk*] *v/t* and *i* cook by dry heat in an oven or on a hot surface without direct exposure to fire; harden by heat; tan (a skin); be cooked, hardened by heat; **half baked** (*coll*) stupid; immature ~ **bake** *n* process of baking.
bakehouse [*bayk*hows] *n* building where baking is done.
Bakelite [*bayk*elIt] *n* (*tr*) a synthetic resin compound of phenol and formaldehyde.
baker [*bayk*er] *n* one who makes or sells bread; **baker's dozen** thirteen.
bakery [*bayk*eRi] *n* place where bread is baked and sold.
baking [*bayk*ing] *n* the making of bread, cakes *etc*; firing of earthenware; the bread baked at one time ~ **baking** *adj* excessively hot.
baking-powder [*bayk*ing-powder] *n* mixture containing cream of tartar and sodium bicarbonate which makes dough rise.
baksheesh, bakshish [*bak*sheesh] *n* money given as tip, gratuity; eastern begging cry.
balaclava [*bala*klaava] *n* close-fitting woollen covering for head and neck.
balalaika [*bala*lRka] *n* (*mus*) triangular-shaped guitar popular in Russia.
balance [*bal*ans] *n* apparatus for measuring weight, scales; counterpoise, weight balancing another; equilibrium, equipoise either physical or mental; harmony between parts of a whole, proportion; preponderating weight; difference between debit and credit; device regulating the speed of a timepiece; constellation of Libra; seventh sign of the zodiac; **b. of trade** difference in value between exports and imports; **strike a b.** work out the difference between debits and credits; **on b.** taking everything into account ~ **balance** *v/t* and *i* bring to, or keep in, or be in a state of equilibrium; weigh in the mind (one possibility *etc* against another); equal in weight, make up for; equalize in proper form the credit and debit sides of an account, make up (accounts); settle (account) by paying what is owed; become balanced; waver, hesitate.
balance-sheet [*bal*ans-sheet] *n* statement in tabular form of debits and credits.
balata [*bal*ata] *n* rubber latex from the bullet tree.
balcony [*bal*koni] *n* small balustraded platform projecting from an upper floor of a building; tier of seats in a theatre above the dress-circle.
bald [*bawld*] *adj* lacking hair on the head, hairless; bare, without vegetation; (*of style*) simple, monotonous, unadorned; undisguised; (*of animals*) marked with white ~ **baldly** *adv* ~ **baldness** *n*.
baldachin, baldaquin [*bal*dakin] *n* canopy of rich brocade; canopy above altar or throne.
balderdash [*bawl*derdash] *n* meaningless jumble of words, nonsense.
bald-headed [bawld-*hed*id] *adj* and *adv* without hair on the head; (*coll*) **go b. at** (*coll*) rush precipitately at without regard for the consequences.
balding [*bawld*ing] *adj* beginning to go bald.
baldric [*bawld*Rik] *n* belt hanging from the shoulder across the breast to the opposite hip and used for carrying a sword *etc*.

bale (1) [*bayl*] *n* evil, calamity, misery.
bale (2) *n* large bundle of goods; (*pl*) merchandise ~ **bale** *v/t* make into bales.
bale (3) *v/i* **b. out** make a descent from aircraft by parachute.
baleen [ba*leen*] *n* and *adj* whalebone.
bale-fire [*bayl*-fIr] *n* bonfire; signal-fire, beacon; (*hist*) funeral pyre.
baleful [*bayl*fool] *adj* harmful, injurious; malicious, sinister ~ **balefully** *adv*.
baler [*bayl*er] *n* machine for baling hay, scrap metal, *etc*.
baling-press [*bayl*ing-pRes] *n* compressor for scrap metal.
balk, baulk (1) [*bawk*] *n* ridge of earth left unploughed between furrows; large sawn or hewn beam of timber; area of a billiard table marked off by a white line behind which a player stands to begin the game; (*fig*) hindrance.
balk, baulk (2) *v/t* and *i* shirk, ignore; check, foil, thwart; disappoint; stop short, jib.
ball (1) [*bawl*] *n* spherical object (*esp* as used in games); (*cricket*) delivery of a ball by the bowler; missile fired from a weapon; (*fig*) a celestial body, the earth; (*pl vulg*) testicles; nonsense; **b. of foot** sole of the foot just below the big toe; (*cricket*) **no b.** ball bowled unfairly; **keep the b. rolling** prevent anything from flagging; **make a balls of** (*sl, vulg*) make a mess of, do badly; **on the b.** competent, alert ~ **ball** *v/t* and *i* form or make into a ball; clog or become clogged; **balled up** (*sl*) muddled, mixed up.
ball (2) *n* formal social assembly met to dance; **have oneself a b.** (*coll*) enjoy oneself greatly; **open the b.** start operations.
ballad [*bal*ad] *n* traditional poem of simple direct narrative told in short stanzas sometimes with a refrain; sentimental song > PDM.
ballade [ba*laad*] *n* poem of three stanzas of eight lines each, concluding with an envoy of four lines; musical composition of a romantic character.
ballad-monger [*bal*ad-munger] *n* maker or seller of ballads; (*cont*) an inferior poet.
balladry [*bal*adRi] *n* poetry in ballad style.
ballast (1) [*bal*ast] *n* weighty material carried in a ship's hold or a yacht's keel or in a balloon to provide stability; coarse stone or hard clinker or slag; unscreened gravel; (*fig*) that which makes for stability of character.
ballast (2) *v/t* provide with ballast; make steady.
ballbearing [bawl*bair*Ring] *n* (*eng*) one of a number of small metal balls used for lessening friction.
ballcock [*bawl*kok] *n* cistern valve or tap regulated by the rise and fall of a hollow floating ball.
ballerina (*pl* **ballerine, ballerinas**) [bale*Reen*a] *n* (*Ital*) female dancer who sustains the chief classical roles in a ballet company.
ballet [*bal*ay] *n* a theatrical entertainment of group and solo dancing ~ **balletic** [ba*let*ik] *adj*.
balletomane [balet*o*mayn] *n* a ballet lover ~ **balletomania** *n* enthusiasm for the ballet.
ballistic [ba*list*ik] *adj* relating to projectiles; **b. missile** missile which is not powered after launching and therefore has a parabolic flight path.
ballistics [ba*list*iks] *n* (*pl*) science of projectiles.
ballocks [*bal*oks] *n* (*pl*) (*vulg*) testicles; nonsense.
balloon [ba*lOOn*] *n* inflated sphere of skin or

plastic material; aircraft supported by a large envelope of gas lighter than air; device in strip cartoons of putting the dialogue inside balloon-shaped outlines; **b. barrage** defensive screen of balloons held in position by steel cables which obstruct attacking aircraft; **the b. goes up** (*coll*) the excitement or trouble begins; **b. tyre** auto-mobile tyre of low pressure ~ **balloon** *v/t* and *i* ascend in a balloon; swell out; kick a ball wildly into the air.

balloonist [ba*lOO*nist] *n* one who ascends in a balloon.

ballot (1) [ba*lot*] *n* ball, ticket, or card used in voting secretly; the method of voting secretly; votes so recorded ~ **ballot** *v/i* vote by ballot; **b. for** select, elect by secret vote.

ballot (2) *n* small bale between 70 and 120 lb.

ballot-box [ba*lot*-boks] *n* box into which the ballots are put by the voters.

ballot-rigging [ba*lot*-Riging] *n* falsification of results of ballot.

ballpoint [ba*wl*poynt] *n* pen with ball-shaped tip.

ballroom [ba*wl*rOOm] *n* large room for dancing ~ **ballroom** *adj* (*of dances*) stately.

balls-up [ba*wl*z-up] *n* (*vulg sl*) blunder, mistake; mess, confusion ~ **balls-up** *v/t*.

bally [ba*li*] *adj* (*coll euph*) bloody.

ballyhoo [bali*hOO*] *n* exaggerated advance publi-city; empty talk, nonsense.

balm [baam] *n* aromatic sap or resin which oozes from certain trees; tree which exudes balm; sweet-smelling oil or healing ointment; perfume; (*fig*) any substance which assuages physical or mental pain; (*hort*) various fragrant garden herbs.

balmy [baami] *adj* producing balm; fragrant, sweet-smelling; (*fig*) soothing; (*of weather, wind*) mild, fragrant; (*sl*) feeble-minded.

balneal [ba*lni*-al] *adj* relating to baths or bathing.

balneology [balni-*oloji*] *n* study of the beneficial effects of bathing in natural and medicinal waters.

balneotherapy [balni-othe*Rapi*] *n* (*med*) treatment of disease by baths and medicinal waters.

baloney [ba*lOni*] *n* (*sl*) nonsense.

balsa [ba*lsa*] *n* cork wood; raft or float.

balsam (1) [ba*wl*sam] *n* balm; (*med*) fragrant oily or resinous substance used for healing purposes; (*fig*) healing influence; (*chem*) compounds of volatile oils and resins, insoluble in water; a flowering plant ~ **balsamiferous** [bawlsam*ife*-Rus] *adj* producing balsam.

balsamic [bawl*samik*] *adj* containing balsam, soothing ~ **balsamic** *n* a soothing medicine.

baluster [ba*luster*] *n* short circular post or pillar; one of a number of posts supporting a handrail; (*pl*) banisters.

balustrade [balus*tRayd*] *n* a coping or handrail with its supporting posts or pillars ~ **balustrad-ed** *adj* ~ **balustrading** *n*.

bambino [bam*beenO*] *n* (*Ital*) baby boy; represen-tation of the infant Jesus.

bamboo [bam*bOO*] *n* an East Indian plant of the reed variety.

bamboozle [bam*bOOz*'l] *v/t* hoodwink, mislead.

ban [ban] *n* prohibition; denunciation; curse; excommunication ~ **ban** (*pres/part* **banning**, *p/t* **banned**) *v/t* proscribe, prohibit, forbid.

banal [ba*y*nal/ba*naal*] *adj* commonplace, trite, trivial ~ **banality** [ba*naliti*] *n*.

banana [ba*naana*] *n* type of tropical tree; its fruit which has an edible pulp.

band (1) [band] *n* thin flat strip of material used to tie or encircle something; neck-band, stripe, belt; (*pl*) pair of white linen strips fastened at the throat worn by clergymen, barristers *etc* with their robes; (*mech*) flat belt; (*archi*) continuous line of ornament round a wall or column; (*rad*) range of frequencies ~ **band** *v/t* and *i* put a band on; decorate with a band or stripe; fasten to-gether; form into a company, collect, unite.

band (2) *n* company of people with an aim in common; assemblage of persons; troop (of armed men); any combination of instruments for the performance of music > PDM.

bandage [ba*ndij*] *n* strip of lint or cloth for dress-ing wounds ~ **bandage** *v/t* tie with a bandage.

bandanna, bandana [ba*ndana*] *n* coloured silk handkerchief with yellow or white spots.

bandbox [ba*nd*boks] *n* box of cardboard or thin wood for light articles (*esp* hats).

bandeau (*pl* **bandeaux**) [ba*ndO*] *n* (*Fr*) ribbon for binding a woman's hair; band inside a hat.

banderilla [bande*Rilya*] *n* (*Sp*) barbed dart used in bull-fighting.

banderole, banderol [bande*ROl*] *n* narrow flag at the masthead, streamer; pennant attached to a lance; (*archi*) sculptured course with an inscrip-tion.

bandicoot [ba*ndikOOt*] *n* large destructive Indian rat; Australian insect-eating pouched animal.

bandit [ba*ndit*] *n* brigand, armed robber; **one-armed b.** slot-machine for gambling.

banditry [ba*nditRi*] *n* armed robbery by bandits.

bandmaster [ba*nd*maaster] *n* (*mus*) conductor.

bandog [ba*ndog*] *n* fierce chained dog; blood-hound, mastiff.

bandoleer, bandolier [bando*leer*] *n* shoulder-belt with small pockets for holding cartridges.

bandrol [ba*ndROl*] *n* banderole.

bandsaw [ba*nd*saw] *n* (*eng*) mechanical saw con-sisting of an endless steel band.

bandstand [ba*nd*stand] *n* platform on which a band of musicians performs in the open air.

bandwagon [ba*nd*wagon] *n* (*US*) wagon in which a band rides at the head of a procession; **climb on the b.** (*coll*) secure an important posi-tion by throwing in one's lot with a successful party.

bandy (1) [ba*ndi*] *v/t* and *i* toss, hit, or convey to and fro; exchange (blows *etc*); **b. words** wrangle; **have one's name bandied about** be talked about (*usu* unfavourably).

bandy (2) *n* a form of ice hockey; stick used in this game.

bandy (3) *adj* with legs curved outwards at the knees.

bandy-legged [ba*ndi*-legd] *adj* bowlegged.

bane [bayn] *n* cause of ruin or of distress, curse; poison; (*poet*) ruin, woe; (*vet*) sheep-rot.

baneful [ba*yn*fool] *adj* poisonous, destructive, in-jurious ~ **banefully** *adv*.

bang (1) [bang] *v/t* and *i* strike noisily, make a violent noise, thump; slam, shut noisily; thrash; come or bring into violent collision with; (*Stock Exchange*) depress (prices *etc*); (*sl*) copulate with

~ **bang** *n* sudden explosive noise; hard knock; drive, dash, go; sudden effectiveness or success ~ **bang** *adv* with a bang; precisely, exactly, directly; **b. on** right on.

bang (2) *n* hair cut square across the forehead ~ **bang** *v/t* cut (hair) short and square.

banger [*bang*er] *n* (*coll*) sausage; noisy old car; noisy firework; hearty kiss.

bangle [*bang*-g'l] *n* circular bracelet or anklet.

bang-on [*bang*-on] *adj* and *adv* (*coll*) directly on target; first-rate, very good.

bang-up [*bang*-up] *adj* and *adv* (*coll*) bang-on.

banian, banyan [*banyan*] *n* Hindu trader; loose flannel gown ,jacket, or shirt; Indian fig-tree.

banish [*banish*] *v/t* condemn person to leave his native land, exile; drive away, expel; dismiss from one's mind ~ **banishment** *n*.

banister, bannister [*banister*] *n* staircase rail; (*pl*) rail together with supporting railings.

banjo (*pl* **banjoes,** *US* **banjos**) [*banjO*] *n* (*mus*) instrument of the guitar variety, with five to nine strings, having a belly of parchment but no back > PDM ~ **banjoist** *n*.

banjulele [banjoo*layl*i] *n* (*mus*) stringed instrument of type between a banjo and a ukulele.

bank (1) [*bank*] *n* mound of earth, snow, sand *etc*; slope, hillside; raised shelf in the sea or on a river bed; mass of cloud; sloping margin of a stream; heightened road surface at difficult bends; tilt (of aircraft); (*mining*) coalface ~ **bank** *v/t* and *i* form a bank to; enclose within a bank; heap (up), become piled up; tilt (aircraft).

bank (2) *n* rowers' bench in a galley; tier of oars; bench or table; row of organ keys, typewriter keys, electrical switches, *etc*.

bank (3) *n* institution trading in money; premises where money is deposited or borrowed; (*fig*) store of objects kept in reserve till needed; pool in a game of chance; **b. rate** percentage at which the Bank of England discounts bills of exchange; **B. Holiday** day observed as a public holiday ~ **bank** *v/t* and *i* trade in money; deposit or keep money at a bank; keep the pool in a game of chance; **b. upon** count upon.

bankable [*bank*ab'l] *adj* such as would be accepted at a bank.

bankbill [*bank*bil] *n* bill of exchange drawn by one bank on another; banker's draft.

bankbook [*bank*book] *n* book issued to a customer containing a statement of his account at a bank; pass-book.

banker (1) [*bank*er] *n* one who directs the affairs of a bank; person holding the pool in a game of chance; gambling card game.

banker (2) horse trained to jump banks; vessel engaged in cod-fishing on the Bank of Newfoundland; mason's stone workbench.

banking [*bank*ing] *n* the keeping and management of a bank; the building of an embankment; heightened road surface at difficult bends; fishing on a sea bank; tilt of an aircraft when turning.

banking-house [*bank*ing-hows] *n* commercial firm engaged in banking.

banknote [*bank*nOt] *n* paper money.

bankrupt [*bank*Rupt] *n* (*leg*) insolvent person whose assets are administered under Bankruptcy Laws for the benefit of his creditors; (*pop*) person unable to pay his debts; one with no resources ~

bankrupt *adj* insolvent; (*fig*) lacking (in) ~ **bankrupt** *v/t* make bankrupt ~ **bankruptcy** *n*.

banksia [*bank*si-a] *n* (*bot*) Australian evergreen shrub.

banner [*ban*er] *n* flag attached to a pole and used as a standard; square or oblong cloth ornamented with symbolic designs and carried between two poles in processions; (*fig*) as a symbol of leadership, profession of faith, belief in a cause *etc*; **b. headline** prominent newspaper headline ~ **bannered** *adj* provided with banners.

banneret [*ban*eRet] *n* (*hist*) knight entitled to put vassals into the field under his own banner; one knighted for valour on the field of battle.

bannerette [bane*Ret*] *n* small banner.

bannerol [*ban*erOl] *n* banner borne at funerals of great men and placed over the tomb.

bannister see **banister**.

bannock [*ban*ok] *n* flat round oatmeal or barley cake baked quickly on a griddle or on the hearth.

banns [*banz*] *n* (*pl*) announcement in church of intended marriage made on three successive Sundays.

banquet [*bank*wet] *n* lavish feast; ceremonial dinner frequently with speeches ~ **banquet** *v/t* and *i* entertain at or participate in a banquet ~ **banqueter** *n* guest at a banquet.

banquette [*bank*et] *n* (*Fr*) (*mil*) the fire step of a trench; bridge footway above road level.

banshee [*ban*shee] *n* Irish female fairy whose wail is said to forebode a death in the family; (*coll*) air-raid siren.

bantam [*bant*am] *n* small variety of domestic fowl noted for its fighting spirit; (*fig*) small but pugnacious person; **b. weight** boxer whose weight is between eight stone and eight stone six pounds.

banter [*bant*er] *n* pleasant raillery, humorous jesting ~ **banter** *v/t* and *i* chaff, poke fun at; talk jocularly.

ban-the-bomb [*ban*-THe-bom] *adj* advocating nuclear disarmament.

banting [*bant*ing] *n* method of reducing weight by avoiding fats, starch, and sugar ~ **bant** *v/i* follow such a diet.

banyan see **banian**.

baobab [*bay*-obab] *n* African tree.

bap [*bap*] *n* (*Scots*) loaf with soft, thin crust.

baptism [*bap*tizm] *n* religious sacrament administered by sprinkling with or immersion in water to denote initiation into membership of the Christian Church; **b. of fire** (*fig*) soldier's first battle; severe ordeal.

baptismal [bap*tiz*mal] *adj* of baptism; **b. name** Christian name.

Baptist [*bap*tist] *n* one who believes that baptism should be by total immersion in water and be administered to adults and not to infants.

baptistery [*bap*tiste Ri] *n* part of a church where baptism takes place; receptacle in a Baptist chapel containing water for the baptism.

baptize [bap*tIz*] *v/t* administer the sacrament of baptism to, christen; (*fig*) give a name to.

bar (1) [*baar*] *n* long piece of rigid material often used as a barrier or as a fastening; slab (of metal), slab (of soap); narrow strip of light or colour; thin strip of metal below the clasp of a medal to signify that the decoration has been twice won; barrier; city gate; ridge of sand and rock fragments formed across mouth of river or harbour; wooden barrier in court at which the prisoner stands; place in court where the judges sit; railing in the House of Commons where persons are arraigned; (*fig*) tribunal (of public opinion); counter over which drinks are served; room in an inn where this is done; (*comm*) counter where only one class of goods is sold; (*her*) division of a shield between two parallel lines; **b. sinister** mark of illegitimacy; (*sci*) unit of atmospheric pressure; (*mus*) vertical line drawn across the stave; music between one such line and the next; (*fig*) hindrance, obstacle; (*leg*) **be called to, be at, go to, the B.** become a barrister ~ **bar** (*pres/part* **barring**, *p/t* and *p/part* **barred**) *v/t* fasten; confine, enclose; obstruct; exclude, prohibit (from); object to; mark with stripes; make into bars.

bar (2) *prep* except for, save; **b. none** without exception.

bar (3) *n* large Mediterranean fish.

barb (1) [*baarb*] *n* sharp point curving back below the tip of a fish-hook, arrow *etc*; tuft of hair; filaments on each side of the shaft of a feather; linen covering for the throat and chin worn by nuns; (*fig*) wounding jibe ~ **barb** *v/t* provide with a barb.

barb (2) *n* horse or pigeon from Barbary.

Barbadian [baar*baydi*-an] *n* and *adj* (native) of Barbados.

barbarian [baar*bairRi*-an] *n* savage or uncivilized person; uncultured person; (*hist*) foreigner (*eg* non-Greek; non-Roman; non-Christian) ~ **barbarian** *adj* foreign; uncivilized, savage.

barbaric [baar*baRik*] *adj* rough, primitive; uncultured in taste; cruel ~ **barbarically** *adv*.

barbarism [*baar*baRizm] *n* the opposite of civilization; condition of being uncivilized; brutality; (*lang*) word or expression not accepted as current in the language, or a foreign borrowing.

barbarity [baar*baRiti*] *n* inhuman cruelty.

barbarize [*baar*baRiz] *v/t* make barbarous; corrupt (speech, style).

barbarous [*baar*baRus] *adj* uncultured, savage, uncivilized; cruel; (*lang*) impure, not classical, unrefined, unpolished; harsh, noisy; foreign, outlandish ~ **barbarously** *adv*.

barbate [*baar*bayt] *adj* (*bot* and *zool*) provided with hairy tufts, bearded.

barbecue [*baar*bikew] *n* large framework or grid for smoking or broiling meat over a fire; animal roasted whole; open floor for drying coffee beans; open-air social occasion at which steaks are roasted over a charcoal fire ~ **barbecue** *v/t* broil on a grid or barbecue; roast whole.

barbed [*baarbd*] *adj* provided with a barb or barbs; (*fig*) malicious, wounding.

barbel [*baarb*'l] *n* freshwater fish of the carp family; filaments on certain fishes.

barbellate [*baar*belayt] *adj* (*bot*) with bristles.

barber [*baarb*er] *n* one who cuts hair and shaves and trims beards, hairdresser; **b.'s pole** pole painted with spiral stripes outside barber's shop.

barberry, berberry [*baarb*eRi, burbeRi] *n* (*bot*) kind of shrub with prickly shoots and yellow flowers; red, tart berry of this tree.

barbershop [*baar*bershop] *n* shop where a barber

works; (*US*) style of four-part unaccompanied singing in close harmony.

barbet [*baarbit*] *n* species of gaily-coloured birds; small poodle dog with curly hair.

barbette [baar*bet*] *n* (*mil*) gun platform.

barbican [*baar*bikan] *n* towered outpost on walls of castle or city; twin tower over gate or bridge.

barbitone [*baar*bitOn] *n* drug used for nervous insomnia; veronal.

barbiturates [baarbi*tyOO*Rayts] *n* (*pl*) (*chem*) class of organic compounds derived from barbituric acid, many of which have a powerful and dangerous soporific effect ~ **barbituric** [baarbi*tew*Rik] *adj*.

barbola [baar*bOla*] *n* ornamentation by plastic mouldings representing flowers, fruit *etc*.

barcarole, barcarolle [*baar*kaROl] *n* song of a Venetian boatman; music like this > PDM.

bard (1) [*baard*] *n* (*hist*) Celtic minstrel or poet; poet or singer; poet who has won acclaim at a Welsh Eisteddfod; **the B. of Avon** Shakespeare.

bard (2) *n* slice of bacon with which a fowl is covered before roasting ~ **bard** *v/t*.

bardic [*baard*ik] *adj* of or like a bard (1).

bardolatry [baar*dolat*Ri] *n* excessive admiration for Shakespeare.

bare (1) [*bair*] *adj* naked, bald, without the usual covering; uncovered, unprotected; unconcealed, undisguised; empty, meagre, unadorned, scantily furnished; just enough, mere.

bare (2) *v/t* uncover, strip; unsheathe; reveal.

bareback [*bair*bak] *adj* and *adv* without a saddle.

barefaced [*bair*fayst] *adj* with the face uncovered; (*fig*) undisguised, avowed; shameless, brazen.

barefoot [*bair*foot] *adj* and *adv* without shoes and stockings ~ **barefooted** *adj*.

bareheaded [*bair*hedid] *adj* without hat or cap.

barely [*bair*li] *adv* scantily, poorly; openly, plainly; only just, not quite, scarcely.

barfly [*baar*flI] *n* (*coll*) one who spends much time in public-house bars.

bargain [*baar*gin] *n* business agreement reached between two or more persons; what is so obtained; article bought cheaply; article on sale at a reduced price; **Dutch, wet b.** agreement sealed with a drink; **into the b.** over and above; besides, also ~ **bargain** *v/i* haggle over terms; **b. for** be prepared for.

bargainer [*baar*giner] *n* a haggler over prices.

bargainor [baargin*awr*] *n* (*leg*) the seller.

barge [*baarj*] *n* flat-bottomed freighter used on canals and rivers and for lading and discharging ships; large, oared vessel used on ceremonial occasions; boat of a warship used by the chief officers; college houseboat ~ **barge** *v/t* and *i* carry by barge; (*coll*) bump clumsily (into, against, about); intrude (into).

barge-board [*baarj*-bawrd] *n* (*archi*) sloping board built as decoration along a gable.

barge-couple [*baarj*-kup'l] *n* (*archi*) end pair of rafters when they oversail the gable.

barge-course [*baarj*-kawrs] *n* (*archi*) brick coping to a gable wall; course of bricks on edge laid across a wall as a coping; tiles next to the gable.

bargee [baar*jee*] *n* man who works on a barge; **swear like a b.** swear volubly and forcibly.

bargepole [*baarj*pOl] *n* long pole for pushing a

barge; **not touch with a b.** have nothing to do with, dislike intensely.

baric (1) [*bair*Rik] *adj* (*chem*) containing barium.

baric (2) [*ba*Rik] *adj* barometric.

baritone [*ba*RitOn] *n* male voice of range between bass and tenor; singer with such a voice; brass wind instrument ~ **baritone** *adj*.

barium [*bair*Ri-um] *n* (*chem*) silvery-white soft metal; **b. meal** barium sulphate swallowed to render digestive tract opaque to X-rays.

bark (1) [*baark*] *n* outer covering of the trunk and branches of a tree, used in tanning or dyeing; bark of the Cinchona tree which yields quinine ~ **bark** *v/t* treat with bark, tan; strip bark from; (*coll*) scrape skin off.

bark (2) *n* staccato cry made by dogs, wolves *etc*; report of a gun; (*coll*) cough ~ **bark** *v/i* and *t* utter a bark; speak sharply; (*of gun*) go off with a sharp report; (*coll*) cough noisily; **b. up the wrong tree** misdirect one's efforts, be mistaken.

bark (3) see **barque.**

barkbound [*baark*bownd] *n* (*hort*) backward in growth because of the tightness of the bark.

barker [*baar*ker] *n* plausible showman who harangues the crowd at a fair to induce them to walk up and see the show; a tout; (*coll*) pistol.

barley [*baar*li] *n* a hardy bearded cereal and its grain, grown for food and for making malt; **patent b.** grain ground into flour; **pearl b.** grain finely ground; **Scotch b.** grain without the husk.

barley-break [*baar*li-bRayk] *n* a chasing game.

barleycorn [*baar*likawrn] *n* barley; grain of barley; (*as a measure of length*) ⅓ inch; **John Barleycorn** personification of malt liquor.

barley-mow [*baar*li-mO] *n* stack of barley.

barley-sugar [*baar*li-shooger] *n* flavoured sweetmeat made from boiled sugar .

barley-water [*baar*li-wawter] *n* medicinal drink made by boiling pearl barley in water.

barm [*baarm*] *n* froth which forms on liquor as it ferments, used as yeast or leaven.

barmaid [*baar*mayd] *n* woman who serves behind the bar of a public-house or inn ~ **barman** *n*.

barmecide [*baar*mesId] *adj* (*fig*) unreal, illusory.

Bar-mitzvah [baar-*mitz*va] *n* (*Heb*) Jewish ceremony celebrating a boy's religious adulthood at thirteen.

barmy [*baar*mi] *adj* full of barm, frothy; (*sl*) witless, silly, insane.

barn [*baarn*] *n* building where hay, grain *etc* is stored; large, comfortless room or building; (*phys*) unit of area for measuring nuclear cross-sections > PDS.

barnacle (1) [*baar*nak'l] *n* (*usu pl*) pincer-like device applied to the nose of a restive horse to quieten it; (*coll*) spectacles.

barnacle (2) *n* marine animal which clings to rocks and ships' bottoms; (*fig*) person difficult to shake off; kind of wild goose; (*coll*) old sailor.

barndance [*baarn*daans] *n* rustic dance.

barndoor [baarn*dawr*] *n* large door of a barn; (*coll*) target too big to miss ~ **barndoor** *adj* (*of fowls*) crossbred on the farm.

barn-owl [*baarn*-owl] *n* the screech-owl.

barnstorming [baarn*stawr*ming] *n* touring rural areas giving theatrical performances or making political speeches ~ **barnstormer** *n* inferior actor.

barogram [*ba*RogRam] *n* graph traced by a barograph.

barograph [*ba*RogRaaf] *n* self-recording barometer.

barology [ba*Rol*oji] *n* science of weight.

barometer [ba*Rom*eter] *n* (*meteor*) instrument which registers changes in atmospheric pressure, used to forecast the weather and to measure height above sea-level > PDG; (*fig*) person or thing indicating changes in public opinion ~ **barometric(al)** [ba*Rom*etRik(al)] *adj* ~ **barometry** [ba*Rom*etRi] *n*.

baron [*ba*Ron] *n* lowest rank or hereditary title in the British peerage; a foreign title; powerful industrial magnate; (*hist*) landowner who held his fief from the king in return for undertaking military duties; **b. of beef** double sirloin of beef.

baronage [*ba*Ronij] *n* (*collect*) the nobility, the peerage; a list of the barons of the realm with information about them.

baroness [*ba*Rones] *n* wife of a baron; lady holding a baronial title in her own right.

baronet [*ba*Ronet] *n* lowest hereditary title (not included in the order of nobility) ranking next below a baron and above a knight ~ **baronet** *v/t* raise to the rank of baronet.

baronetage [*ba*Ronetij] *n* (*collect*) baronets; a list of baronets with information about them.

baronetcy [*ba*Ronetsi] *n* title and dignity of a baronet.

baronial [ba*ROn*i-al] *adj* pertaining to or befitting the rank of a baron; (*archi*) grandiose in style and construction; stately, sumptuous.

barony [*ba*Roni] *n* estate of a baron; rank or dignity of baron; (*Ir*) division of a county; (*Scots*) large estate or manor.

baroque [ba*Rok*] *n* the florid extravagant style prevalent in European art and architecture from about 1600 to 1760 ~ **baroque** *adj* irregularly shaped, grotesque, lavishly embellished.

baroscope [*ba*RoskOp] *n* kind of barometer.

barouche [ba*ROOsh*] *n* four-wheeled horse-drawn carriage with a collapsible half-hood.

barque, bark [*baark*] *n* a three-, four-, or five-masted sailing vessel, square-rigged, but with fore-and-aft sails on the mast farthest aft; (*poet*) boat.

barquentine, barkentine [*baark*enteen] *n* a three-, four-, or five-masted sailing vessel having square sails on the foremast only.

barrack (1) [*ba*Rak] *n* (*usu pl*) permanent buildings used as quarters for soldiers; (*fig*) bleak or rambling building ~ **barrack** *v/t* and *i*.

barrack (2) *v/t* and *i* (*sport*) applaud (player) derisively, jeer at ~ **barracking** *n* ironical applause; slow clapping.

barracoon [ba*Rak*OOn] *n* slave-pen.

barracuda, barracoota, barracouta [ba*Ra*kOOda, ba*Ra*kOOta] *n* voracious tropical sea-fish.

barrage [*ba*Raazh] *n* a low dam, gated across its entire width, placed across a river to raise its level; (*mil*) intense concentration of artillery fire over an area; **b. balloon** captive balloon forming part of a system of anti-aircraft defence.

barratry [*ba*RatRi] *n* (*leg*) offence of frequently exciting and stirring up quarrels and lawsuits;

traffic in preferments and offices; fraud or negligence by the captain or crew of a ship to the detriment of the owners ~ **barrator** *n* malicious litigant ~ **barratrous** *adj* maliciously litigious.

barrel [ba*R*el] *n* flat-ended cylindrical wooden vessel made of outwardly bulging staves hooped together, cask; varying measure of capacity; revolving cylinder forming part of some mechanism; hollow cylinder forming the trunk of something; tubular metal part of a gun through which the projectile is fired; belly and loins of a horse *etc*; **b. bulk** (*naut*) five cubic feet; **b. light** curved roof light; **b. vault** continuous plain arch of semicircular shape; **over a b.** (*sl*) helpless; **scrape the b.** gather up low-quality material; use the last of one's resources.

barrelled [ba*R*eld] *adj* put in barrel; shaped like barrel.

barrel-organ [ba*R*el-awrgan] *n* musical instrument which grinds out tunes when the handle is turned.

barren [ba*R*en] *adj* unproductive, sterile, incapable of bearing offspring; (*fig*) lacking in interest or ideas; unprofitable; **barren of** totally lacking in ~ **barren** *n* (*usu pl*) unproductive region ~ **barrenness** *n*.

barret [ba*R*et] *n* small flat cap, biretta.

barricade [ba*R*ikayd] *n* hastily improvised barrier or obstruction ~ **barricade** *v/t*.

barrier [ba*R*i-er] *n* obstruction or obstacle preventing access or halting advance; fence, palisade, boundary-line; (*fig*) hindrance, restriction, impediment; **b. cream** protective cream for skin.

barring [baar*R*ing] *prep* excluding.

barrister [ba*R*ister] *n* member of the legal profession who has been called to the Bar and has the right to plead as advocate in superior courts.

barrow (1) [ba*R*O] *n* (*arch*) burial mound, tumulus.

barrow (2) *n* light handcart with one or two wheels and two legs, lifted and pushed forwards by two hand-holds; the amount a barrow holds.

barrow-boy [ba*R*O-boi] *n* costermonger.

Bart. *abbreviation of* **Baronet.**

bartender [baartender] *n* barman.

barter [baarter] *v/t* and *i* exchange goods considered of equal value; (*fig*) exchange, part with for a negligible return, bargain away; trade by exchanging goods ~ **barter** *n* trade by the exchange of goods without the use of money.

bartizan [baartizan] *n* small overhanging turret for a sentry at the corner of a castle; pedestal for a flag post.

barton [baarton] *n* farmyard.

barycentric [ba*R*isent*R*ik] *adj* relating to the centre of gravity.

baryon [ba*R*i-on] *n* (*phys*) collective name for nucleons and hyperons > PDS.

baryphonia [ba*R*if*O*ni-a] *n* thick voice.

baryta [ba*R*eeta] *n* (*chem*) barium oxide.

barytes [ba*R*eeteez] *n* (*min*) natural barium sulphate, heavy spar ~ **barytic** [ba*R*itik] *adj* related to baryta or barium.

barytone [ba*R*iton] *n* (*Gk gramm*) word without acute accent on the final syllable; type of stringed instrument.

basal [baysal] *adj* at, relating to, constituting, the base; (*fig*) fundamental ~ **basally** *adv*.

basalt [basawlt/basawlt] *n* (*min*) dark-coloured

rock of volcanic origin ~ **basaltic** [basa*w*ltik] *adj*.

basanite [basanIt] *n* a basaltic rock.

bascule [baskewl] *n* (*eng*) apparatus actuated like a see-saw; **b. bridge** bridge hinged at the bank to allow ships to pass under it.

base (1) [bays] *n* bottom of anything acting as a support or foundation; main ingredient; (*fig*) fundamental principle, starting point; (*archi*) widening or moulding at the foot of a wall or column; (*chem*) substance which reacts with an acid to form a salt and water only; (*geom*) side on which a geometric figure stands; (*her*) lowest part of a shield; (*math*) the factor (*usu* the number 10) used to construct a series of logarithms; (*phys*) the part of a transistor which separates the emitter from the collector; (*mil*) headquarters behind the front line; naval or air force station; (*phil*) root of a word; (*sport*) starting or finishing points in a race; (*surveying*) a line accurately measured to serve as the starting length for the triangulations of a survey; **get to first b.** (*coll*) reach the first stage towards one's goal ~ **base** *v/t* place upon a foundation; (*fig*) establish securely; (*refl*) rely (upon).

base (2) *adj* of low birth; despicable, servile, inferior; debased, worthless, spurious; **b. metals** metals which corrode or oxidize.

baseball [baysbawl] *n* American national ball game similar to rounders.

base-born [bays-bawrn] *adj* of humble birth; illegitimate.

baseless [baysles] *adj* without foundation, not justified ~ **baselessness** *n*.

baseline [bayslIn] *n* (*sur*) measured line from which other distances are calculated; line at the base of anything.

basely [baysli] *adv* in base manner.

basement [baysment] *n* lowest living space of a house, usually below ground level.

baseness [baysnes] *n* wickedness of character.

bash [bash] *v/t* strike violently, beat ~ **bash** *n* a blow; **have a b.** (*coll*) make a vigorous attempt ~ **bashing** *n* (*coll*) a thrashing.

bashful [bashfool] *adj* shy, excessively modest, shamefaced ~ **bashfully** *adv* ~ **bashfulness** *n*.

bashi-bazouk [bashi-baz*OO*k] *n* Turkish irregular mercenary soldier notorious for his brutality.

basi- *pref* of, at, constituting, the base of.

basic [baysik] *adj* forming a base, fundamental; constituting a starting point for scales of pay, rations, hours of work *etc*; (*chem*) opposite to acidic; reacting with acids to form salts; (*of igneous rock*) containing less than 52% silica; (*metal*) special process in the manufacture of steel > PDE; **B. English** a simplified variety of English using a limited vocabulary of about 850 words; **b. slag** phosphates produced in manufacturing steel and used as fertilizer ~ **basically** *adv*.

basicity [basisiti] *n* (*chem*) an acid's capacity to combine with a base.

basil [bazil] *n* varieties of aromatic herb.

basilar [basilar] *adj* near or growing from the base.

basilica [basilika] *n* (*orig*) royal palace; (*hist*) oblong hall with aisles and an apse, used by the Romans for public administration and as a place of assembly; building of this type used as a

56

Christian church ~ **basilical** *adj* ~ **basilican** *adj*.

basilisk [*baz*ilisk] *n* fabulous deadly reptile, also called the cockatrice; small lizard with inflatable hollow crest ~ **basilisk** *adj* deadly, venomous.

basin [*bay*sin] *n* circular vessel broader at the top with curved sides; contents of a basin; hollow or trough in the earth's crust whether filled with water or not; circular valley; stretch of country drained by a river; bay or harbour enclosed by land; dock with flood-gates; (*geol*) region in which the layers of rock dip in all directions towards a central point.

basinet, basnet [*basi*net, *bas*net] *n* (*hist*) basin-shaped helmet sometimes with a visor.

basis (*pl* **bases**) [*bay*sis] *n* foundation, base; chief part; underlying principle on which something rests or is constructed.

bask [*baask*] *v/i* expose oneself to the warmth of the sun; take delight in.

basket [*baas*kit] *n* plaited wickerwork container; its contents; guard on a sword-stick; (*coll euph*) bastard; **pick of the b.** best of the lot.

basketball [*baas*kitbawl] *n* game in which a goal is scored when the ball is dropped through a kind of basket hung from a ten-foot pole.

basket-hilt [*baas*kit-hilt] *n* sword-hilt shaped like a basket or made of wickerwork.

basketry [*baas*kitRi] *n* basket making.

basket-stitch [*baas*kit-stich] *n* criss-cross stitch.

basket-work [*baas*kit-wurk] *n* wickerwork.

basking-shark [*baas*king-shaark] *n* largest species of shark; the sunfish or sailfish.

basnet see **basinet**.

bason [*bay*son] *n* bench used in processing felt for hat-making ~ **bason** *v/t* harden felt.

Basque [*baask*] *n* one of a race of people living in the Western Pyrenees; their language; prolongation of a bodice below the waist ~ **Basque** *adj* pertaining to the Basques.

bas-relief, bass-relief [bas-Re*leef*] *n* low relief; method of sculpturing in which the raised portions do not stand out with any prominence.

bass (1) [*bays*] *n* lowest part in a musical composition; low-toned male voice, singer, or musical instrument > PDM ~ **bass** *adj* descriptive of music of low pitch; low-sounding; **b. clef** the F clef which indicates the F below middle C.

bass (2) [*bas*] *n* fibre obtained from the inner bark of the linden tree and from the leaves of certain palms; mats, brooms, twine *etc* made from this.

bass (3) [*bas*] *n* (*zool*) common perch; sea perch.

bass-baritone [bays-*ba*RitOn] *n* bass voice or singer with the range of both bass and baritone.

basset (1) [*bas*et] *n* short-legged dog used to unearth badgers.

basset (2) *n* (*obs*) card game like Faro.

basset (3) *n* (*geol*) outcrop.

basset-horn [*bas*et-hawrn] *n* (*mus*) single reed woodwind instrument like the clarinet > PDM.

bassinet, bassinette [basi*net*] *n* hooded wickerwork basket used as a cradle or as a perambulator.

bassoon [bas*OOn*] *n* (*mus*) low-sounding double reed woodwind orchestral instrument > PDM ~ **bassoonist** *n*.

bass-relief see **bas-relief**.

basswood [*bas*wood] *n* timber from the American linden tree, called American whitewood.

bast [*bast*] *n* flexible fibrous material, raffia.

bastard [*bast*erd] *n* child born out of wedlock; (*vulg*) fellow, chap; thing; unpleasant or ill-tempered person ~ **bastard** *adj* illegitimate; (*fig*) spurious, false, abnormal in size or shape.

bastardize [*bast*erdIz] *v/t* pronounce or make illegitimate ~ **bastardization** *n*.

bastardy [*bast*erdi] *n* illegitimacy; **b. order an** order made by a magistrate for the support of an illegitimate child by its father.

baste (1) [*bayst*] *v/t* tack with long loose stitches.

baste (2) *v/t* moisten a roast while cooking with melted fat or gravy.

baste (3) *v/t* thrash, beat severely.

bastinado [basti*naad*O] *n* Eastern torture in which the soles of the feet are beaten; a stick ~ **bastinado** *v/t*.

bastion [*bast*i-on] *n* projecting strong-point of a fortification, usually four-sided.

bat (1) [*bat*] *n* quadruped with mouse-shaped body which flies about at night on membranous wings.

bat (2) *n* wooden implement used for striking the ball in cricket *etc*; cotton wadding in quilts, batting; layer of felt used in making hats; brick cut across; (*cer*) cast iron ledge in a decorating kiln; (*abbr*) batsman; (*sl*) smart blow; (*US sl*) frolic, spree; **off one's own b.** unaided; **carry one's b.** (*cricket*) be not out at the close of the innings ~ **bat** (*pres/part* **batting**, *p/t* and *p/part* **batted**) *v/t* and *i* beat; wield a bat; (*cricket*) go in to bat; blink; **not b. an eye** show no emotion.

batch [*bach*] *n* quantity of loaves at a single baking; one mixing of concrete, mortar *etc*; group or set of similar things or persons.

bate (1) [*bayt*] *v/t* and *i* lessen in force, diminish; **with bated breath** anxiously, expectantly.

bate (2) *n* fermenting alkaline solution used to make hides pliable; vat containing this.

bath [*baath*, *pl* baa*THz*] *n* large receptacle to contain water in which a person can immerse himself completely for washing purposes; immersion of the body in water, vapour *etc*; the water or other liquid used; (*usu pl*) building for bathing or taking medicinal baths; (*phot*) solution or its container used in developing; **Order of the B.** order of British knighthood; **B. bun** spiced fruit bun topped with sugar; **B. Oliver** unsweetened digestive biscuit ~ **bath** *v/t* and *i* give a bath to; take a bath.

bathchair [*baath*chair] *n* old-fashioned type of wheeled chair for invalids.

bathe [*bay*TH] *v/t* and *i* apply water to, soak; plunge oneself in sea, river *etc*; (*of rivers, sea*) flow past, wash; (*of light etc*) surround, envelop; take a bath ~ **bathe** *n* act of swimming or dipping oneself in water ~ **bather** *n*.

bathetic [bath*et*ik] *adj* characterized by bathos.

bathing [*bay*THing] *n* act, practice, or conditions, of entering the sea ~ **bathing** *adj* of or for bathing in the sea.

bathing-machine [*bay*THing-masheen] *n* hut set on wheels and drawn down into the sea.

bathos [*bay*thos] *n* (*rhet*) anticlimax, descent from the sublime to the ludicrous.

bathmat [*baath*mat] *n* floor mat used in bathroom.

bathroom [*baath*Room] *n* room containing fixed bath and other apparatus for washing; (*coll euph*) lavatory.

bathwater [*baath*wawter] *n* water in which one will bath or has bathed; **throw the baby out with the b.** lose something vital when getting rid of what is useless.

bathyscaphe [*bath*iskayf] *n* a strong, pressure-resisting sphere buoyed by a float entirely filled with petrol.

bathysphere [*bath*isfeer] *n* hollow sphere for deep-sea observation.

batik, battik [*bat*eek] *n* and *adj* (fabric) partly coated with wax and then dyed.

bating [*bay*ting] *prep* except.

batiste [*bat*eest] *n* (*Fr*) plain woven fabric of cotton or linen.

batman [*bat*man] *n* (*mil*) officer's servant.

baton [*bat*on] *n* staff of office; truncheon; (*mus*) wand used by conductor to beat time.

bats [*bats*] *adj* (*coll*) crazy, eccentric; **have b. in the belfry** be mad, eccentric.

batsman [*bats*man] *n* one who bats at cricket.

battalion [*bat*alyon] *n* (*mil*) large unit of an infantry regiment, comprising three or more companies.

battels [*bat*els] *n* (*pl*) bills for provisions obtained from an Oxford college buttery; college charges.

batten (1) [*bat*en] *n* length of square-sawn timber used for flooring, roofing *etc*; metal slat to secure hatchway covers and tarpaulins; wooden or plastic strip to stiffen a mainsail ~ **batten** *v/t* provide with battens; **b. down** secure hatchway covers *etc* with steel battens ~ **batten** *n* strip of wood solidly fixed to a wall *etc* as a base for plaster, joinery *etc*; act of fixing battens.

batten (2) *n* movable frame of a loom.

batten (3) *v/i* thrive, feed greedily (on), grow fat; (*fig*) prosper at someone else's expense.

batter (1) [*bat*er] *v/t* and *i* strike repeatedly with shattering blows; beat shapeless; **b. at** (door) hammer on; **battered baby** infant that has received multiple deliberate injuries from its parent(s); **battered wife** woman who has been repeatedly beaten up by her husband.

batter (2) *n* mixture of flour, butter, and eggs beaten up in milk; (*print*) damaged type.

batter (3) *n* inclination of a wall ~ **batter** *v/t* and *i* slope gently.

batter (4) *n* (*cricket*) batsman.

battering-ram [*bat*eRing-Ram] *n* military engine formerly used for demolishing walls.

battery [*bat*eRi] *n* (*leg*) unlawful attack on a person; (*mil*) assemblage of artillery and its emplacements; an artillery unit; a number of similar pieces of equipment grouped together; a series of boxes in which poultry are kept for fattening or intensive egg-laying; small pens confining cattle for fattening; (*elect*) number of primary or secondary cells arranged in series or parallel; box containing a group of cells to provide power.

batting [*bat*ing] *n* action of wielding a bat; cotton wadding in quilts.

battle [*bat*'l] *n* fight between large opposing forces; war, hostilities; (*fig*) conflict, contention; **b. royal** free fight; **trial by b.** (*hist*) legal decision of a dispute by single combat; **line of b.** troops, ships, drawn up in line of battle; **pitched b.** battle planned beforehand to be fought on an agreed field ~ **battle** *v/t* and *i* fight, struggle (with);

contend (against) ~ **battler** *n* fighter, plucky boxer.

battleaxe [*bat*'laks] *n* (*hist*) heavy axe used as weapon; (*coll*) fierce domineering middle-aged woman.

battle-cruiser [*bat*'l-kROOzer] *n* ship of war with heavy armament but speedier than a battleship.

battlecry [*bat*'lkRI] *n* shout to rally one's comrades in battle; (*fig*) slogan.

battledore [*bat*'ldawr] *n* bat used in the game of battledore and shuttlecock.

battledress [*bat*'ldRes] *n* (*mil*) uniform worn in battle, as opposed to regimentals.

battlefield [*bat*'lfeeld] *n* place where a battle is fought.

battlement [*bat*'lment] *n* (*archi*) parapet indented or crenellated at regular intervals ~ **battlemented** *adj* with battlements.

battleship [*bat*'lship] *n* largest ship of war with the heaviest armament; **pocket b.** small but powerful battleship.

battue [*bat*yOO] *n* beating the bushes and covers to drive game towards the sportsmen; the game so disturbed and shot; wholesale slaughter.

batty [*bat*i] *adj* (*coll*) mad, crazy.

bauble [*bawb*'l] *n* attractive article of little value,
• pretty trifle; (*hist*) jester's baton of office; (*fig*) emblem of the worthlessness of rank, riches *etc*.

baulk see **balk**.

bauxite [*bawk*sIt] *n* (*min*) ore from which aluminium is obtained.

bawbee [*bawb*ee] *n* (*Scots*) halfpenny.

bawd [*bawd*] *n* procurer or procuress, woman keeping a brothel; prostitute.

bawdily [*bawd*ili] *adv* in a bawdy manner ~ **bawdiness** *n*.

bawdry [*bawd*Ri] *n* bawdy language.

bawdy [*bawd*i] *n* and *adj* (language) referring frankly to sex, *usu* for humorous effect.

bawdy-house [*bawd*i-hows] *n* brothel.

bawl [*bawl*] *v/i* and *t* shout, bellow or sing with a harsh and rough voice ~ **bawl** *n* loud shout.

bay (1) [*bay*] *n* wide indentation into the land formed by the sea or by a lake; recess in a range of hills.

bay (2) *n* bay-tree, a species of laurel; (*pl*) garland of bay or laurel leaves worn by a hero or poet as a badge of honour; (*fig*) honours, fame.

bay (3) *n* recess in a wall between columns or buttresses; window placed at the projection of a wall beyond its general line; terminus for local trains at a railway station; ship's hospital; horse's stall.

bay (4) *n* deep continuous bark of a hunting dog; cry produced by a pack of hounds nearing a hunted animal; **at b.** compelled to turn and face pursuers; **keep at b.** ward off ~ **bay** *v/i* and *t* bark continuously; bark at; drive to bay with barking.

bay (5) *n* dam to retain water or to divert its course ~ **bay** *v/t* to dam.

bay (6) *adj* (*of horses*) of reddish-brown colour ~ **bay** *n* horse of this colour.

bayonet [*bay*-onet] *n* (*mil*) short steel blade for fixing to the muzzle of a rifle; **b. 'oint** connexion made by fitting two lugs into grooves and turning ~ **bayonet** *v/t* stab with a bayonet.

bayou [*bi*-ew] *n* marshy creek or offshoot to a river or lake > PDG.

bayrum [bay*Rum*] *n* a kind of hair lotion.

bazaar, bazar [ba*zaar*] *n* Eastern market; sale of work held to raise money for charitable purposes; large shop selling a great variety of fancy goods.

bazooka [baz*OOk*a] *n* (*mil*) anti-tank rocket-launcher.

bdellium [*deli*-um] *n* tree or shrub bearing myrrh-like balsam; balsam.

be (*pres ind* **am, art, is** *pl* **are**; *p/t* **was** *pl* **were**; *p/part* **been**) [*bee*] *v/i* exist; happen, occur; remain, stay, continue *etc*; *used as aux v in compound and passive tenses*; **been** (*coll*) paid a visit; **been and** (*coll*) *exclam of disapproval or of amazement* (*eg* now you've been and done it!).

**be - ** *pref used to form transitive verbs, verbs from adjectives and nouns, intensive verbs etc.*

beach [*beech*] *n* the shingle on the edge of a sea; land skirting a sea or lake, *esp* that part of the seashore lying between high and low water mark ∼ **beach** *v/t* cause to go ashore, drag up on a beach.

beachcomber [*beech*k*Omer*] *n* one who makes a living from what he finds on the beaches; idle vagrant; long curling wave.

beachhead [*beech*-hed] *n* (*mil*) area of enemy shore seized and held by invasion troops.

beach-la-mar [beech-la-*maar*] *n* pidgin English.

beacon [*beek*on] *n* fire lit on a hill-top to serve as a signal; light or radio transmitter to guide aircraft; (*in place-names*) conspicuous hill; lighthouse or prominent object as a warning of danger; **Belisha b.** flashing yellow globe on a pole to indicate a pedestrian crossing-place ∼ **beacon** *v/t* and *i* act as a beacon; warn, guide.

bead [*beed*] *n* one of a number of small balls pierced and strung and used for counting prayers or for ornament; (*pl*) necklace of these; drop of liquid, bubble; type of front sight on a gun; semicircular moulding; **tell one's beads** say prayers; **draw a b. on** aim at ∼ **bead** *v/t* and *i* provide with beads; thread together.

beading [*beed*ing] *n* semicircular moulding.

beadle, bedel(l) [*beed*'l] *n* (*orig*) parish constable; university officer who bears the mace in processions in front of the Vice-Chancellor; porter at a college lodge ∼ **beadledom** *n* officiousness.

bead-roll [*beed*-*ROl*] *n* list of names.

beadsman, bedesman [*beedz*man] *n* one who prays for another; one paid to pray for the souls of his benefactors; inmate of an almshouse.

beady [*beed*i] *adj* beadlike; (*of eyes*) small, round and bright ∼ **beadiness** *n*.

beagle [*beeg*'l] *n* small English dog to hunt hares ∼ **beagle** *v/i* hunt with beagles ∼ **beagling** *n*.

beak [*beek*] *n* sharp-pointed horny projection from the mouths of birds; horny front of the jaws of animals such as the turtle; beak-shaped projection; projection at the prow of ancient ships; (*sl*) hooked or pointed nose; (*sl*) judge, magistrate; (*sl*) schoolmaster ∼ **beaked** *adj* with a beak; pointed, hooked.

beaker [*beek*er] *n* drinking-cup; glass vessel used in scientific processes.

be-all [*bee*-awl] *n* **b. and end-all** supreme or exclusive consideration or aim.

beam [*beem*] *n* long, squared, horizontal piece of timber, steel, light alloy or concrete used in building to carry great weight; wooden cylinder in a loom; main timber part of a plough; horizontal bar of a balance from which the scales hang; greatest width of a ship; ray or stream of light; (*phys*) electromagnetic waves radiated in a particular direction; stream (of electrons); (*aer*) radio signal sent out to guide an aircraft on its course; (*fig*) radiant smile or look of pleasure; **port (starboard) b.** (*naut*) left (right) side of a ship; **on the b.** (*naut*) at right angles to the keel; **on her b. ends** (*naut*) (*of a ship*) lying far over on one side; **on one's b. ends**(*fig*) destitute; **broad in the b.** having a big backside ∼ **beam** *v/i* and *t*, shine, shed light; (*fig*) smile genially; (*rad*) direct a broadcast to a specific target; find by radiolocation.

beaming [*beem*ing] *adj* with an expression of radiant happiness; (*phys*) transmission of electromagnetic waves in a particular direction.

beamish [*beem*ish] *adj* radiant.

bean [*been*] *n* kidney-shaped seed carried in long pods by leguminous plants; plant bearing this seed; seed similar in shape borne by other plants; bean-shaped object; (*sl*) coin; **full of beans** in high spirits; **give (person) beans** punish, scold; **old b.** (*sl*) (*familiar form of address*) old boy.

beanfeast, beano [*been*-feest, *been*O] *n* (*coll*) dinner, feast, celebration, a jolly good time.

bear (1) [*bair*] *n* massive four-legged mammal with thick fur; (*fig*) massively built man; clumsy loutish person; (*Stock Exchange*) one who speculates hoping for a fall in prices when he can buy back stock which he sold at higher levels; **Great B. and Little B.** two constellations in the northern hemisphere ∼ **bear** *v/i* and *t* speculate for a fall in prices; produce a fall in prices.

bear (2) (*p/t* **bore**, *p/part* **born, borne**) *v/t* and *i* carry, transport; convey, remove, wear, have, exhibit; possess and use, wield; hold (office); cherish (feelings); allow, admit of; (*fig*) stand (test); endure, put up with; hold (up), support; be inscribed with; push, drive, apply weight to; press; lean, rest; refer to, be relevant to; force a way with effort in some direction, turn; extend or point in a certain direction; produce, give birth to; **b. a hand** assist; **b. away**, (*naut*) set course further off the wind; **b. down** overcome; **b. down upon** sail quickly towards; **b. off** move away; **b. out** confirm; **b. up** be of good heart; **b. up for** (*naut*) sail towards; **b. with** be patient with.

bearable [*bai*Rab'l] *adj* endurable.

bear-baiting [*bair*-bayting] *n* (*hist*) sport in which dogs attacked a chained bear.

beard [*beerd*] *n* hair growing on a man's cheeks and chin; tufts of hair on the face of some animals; (*bot*) bristly hair-like growth on grain; (*zool*) gills of the oyster; (*typ*) space between the foot of a letter and the bottom edge of the type-body ∼ **beard** *v/t* approach boldly, defy.

beardless [*beerd*les] *adj* lacking a beard, youthful.

bearer [*bair*Rer] *n* one who carries; one of those who carry the coffin at a funeral; one of those who walk beside the coffin over which is draped the pall; one of those who carry a litter or palanquin; Indian manservant; one who delivers a letter; one who presents a cheque payable on demand; (*bot*) tree which produces a good crop of fruit; **b. bonds**

stocks and bonds which do not have the owner's name upon them, and which can change hands without the formalities of a transfer.

beargarden [*bair*gaarden] *n* place where bears were baited; scene of tumult and disorder.

bearing [*bair*Ring] *n* behaviour, deportment; relevance, relation, aspect; suffering, endurance; (*math*) direction of a point from a fixed point, measured in degrees as a variation from North–South > PDS; (*pl*) relative position of surroundings; (*geog*) direction of a point in relation to the meridian > PDG; (*mech*) (*pl*) supports which hold a revolving shaft in its true position; (*archi*) support of a beam or the part of the beam which rests on its support; production of offspring; cropping of fruit; (*her*) a single device on a shield; **get (lose) one's bearings** find out (lose) one's relative position.

bearing-rein [*bair*Ring-rayn] *n* short rein passing from bit to saddle to keep a horse's head up.

bearish [*bair*Rish] *adj* like a bear; churlish, uncivil; (*Stock Exchange*) with prices showing a tendency to fall.

bearleader [*bair*leeder] *n* (*coll*) tutor or travelling-companion to a rich young man.

bearpit [*bair*pit] *n* sunken enclosure where bears are exhibited.

bearskin [*bair*skin] *n* skin of a bear; (*mil*) tall furry headgear worn by the Brigade of Guards.

beast [*beest*] *n* animal; quadruped (as distinct from birds, fishes *etc*); wild animal; (*pl*) farm stock, cattle; animal for riding or drawing loads; (*fig*) depraved human being; (*joc*) obstinate or unkind person.

beastly [*beest*li] *adj* disgusting, filthy; (*coll*) unpleasant ~ **beastly** *adv* (*with following adj*) exceedingly ~ **beastliness** *n*.

beat (1) (*p/t* beat, *p/part* beaten) [*beet*] *v/t* and *i* strike repeatedly; punish by blows; strike with force; crush, batter; hammer, forge; strike against, knock; force out of; assail; defeat, master; perplex; pulsate, throb; flap; stir up rapidly; **b. to windward** (*naut*) keep close hauled on a wind; **beating up** beating on alternate tacks; **b. the air** strive uselessly; **b. about the bush** evade the point at issue; **b. down** reduce the price by bargaining; **b. up** brutally maltreat; **b. a retreat, b. it** (*sl*) run away! ~ **beat** *adj* exhausted ~ **beat** *n* stroke or blow; regular succession of strokes and the sound thereby made; (*ac*) periodic increase and decrease in loudness which is heard when two notes of nearly the same frequency are sounded together > PDP; section of ground patrolled; (*mus*) motion of the hand to indicate rhythm; recurring emphasis in music or poetry; strongly rhythmic jazz or pop music.

beat (2) *adj* (*coll*) of or like beatniks.

beaten [*beet*en] *adj* struck with repeated blows, hammered out; defeated, exhausted; worn bare, well-worn; scoured for game.

beater [*beet*er] *n* one who beats; object used for beating, pounding, whisking things; man employed to drive game towards the sportsmen.

beatific [bee-*atif*ik] *adj* making blessed or supremely happy; **b. vision** immediate sight of God granted to the saints ~ **beatifical** *adj* ~ **beatifically** *adv*.

beatification [bee-atifi*kay*shon] *n* making blessed

or being blessed; (*R.C. Church*) act of the Pope declaring the first step towards canonization.

beatify [bee-*atif*I] *v/t* make or declare blessed; (*R.C. Church*) pronounce (a person) to be in enjoyment of heavenly bliss.

beating [*beet*ing] *n* punishment by blows; defeat; (*naut*) sailing close hauled on a wind; pulsation, throbbing ~ **beating** *adj* palpitating.

beatitude [bee-*atit*ewd] *n* state of supreme happiness; one of the sayings of Christ which characterize those who attain blessedness.

beatnik [*beet*nik] *n* defiantly unconventional young person of the 1950s who adopted strange modes of dress and held ultra-modern opinions.

beat-up [*beet*-up] *adj* (*coll*) worn out or damaged by constant hard use.

beau (*pl* beaux) [*bO*] *n* dandy, fop, lady's man; (*coll*) young girl's boy friend.

Beaujolais [*bO*zholay] *n* (*Fr*) a light red wine of Burgundy.

beau-monde [bO-*mond*] *n* (*Fr*) fashionable society.

Beaune [*bOn*] *n* (*Fr*) a red wine of Burgundy.

beaut [*bewt*] *n* (*Aust coll*) something beautiful or excellent.

beauteous [*bewt*i-us] *adj* (*poet*) beautiful.

beautician [bewti*shan*] *n* person who runs a beauty-parlour.

beautification [bewtifi*kay*shon] *n* adornment, embellishment.

beautiful [*bewt*ifool] *adj* possessing beauty; eminently satisfying to the senses or to the mind; pleasing, admirable ~ **beautiful** *n* beauty in any form; abstract beauty ~ **beautifully** *adv*.

beautify [*bewt*ifI] *v/t* adorn, make beautiful.

beauty [*bewt*i] *n* quality or combination of qualities giving aesthetic pleasure or moral satisfaction; beautiful woman; exceptionally good example of its kind; pleasing feature, fine trait, ornament; (*joc*) a term of affectionate address ~ **beauty** *adj* of or for beauty or beautifying.

beauty-parlour [*bewt*i-paarler] *n* establishment where women can receive treatment to increase their physical attractions.

beauty-queen [*bewt*i-kween] *n* girl voted the most attractive in a beauty contest.

beauty-sleep [*bewt*i-sleep] *n* sleep taken before midnight, thought to be especially beneficial.

beauty-spot [*bewt*ispot] *n* place of scenic beauty; small patch or spot placed on a lady's face to enhance its beauty.

beaver (1) [*beev*er] *n* amphibious broad-tailed rodent; fur of the beaver; hat made of beaver fur; thick woollen cloth; (*sl*) bearded person; **eager b.** (*coll*) person zealous for hard work.

beaver (2) *n* lower part of the face-guard of a visored helmet.

beaverboard [*beev*erbawrd] *n* type of chipwood board used for making partitions *etc*.

bebop [*bee*bop] *n* sophisticated jazz exploiting harmonic and rhythmic novelties.

becalm [be*kaam*] *v/t* and *i* to quiet, make calm, soothe; (*naut*) deprive (ship) of wind; become motionless.

because [be*kawz*] *conj* and *adv* for the reason that, inasmuch as, since; by reason (of), on account of (of).

bechamel [*be*shamel] *n* thick white sauce.

bêche-de-mer [baysh-de-*mai*R] *n* (*Fr*) the tre-pang; beach-la-mar.

beck (1) [*bek*] *n* a brook.

beck (2) *n* gesture, sign, nod; **at the b. and call of** ready to give instant obedience to ~ **beck** *v/t* and *i* beckon.

beckon [*bek*on] *v/t* and *i* attract someone's atten-tion by making a sign with the hand, finger, or head; make such a sign to a person.

becloud [be*klowd*] *v/t* cover with clouds; (*fig*) make obscure, darken.

become (*p/t* **became**, *p/part* **become**) [*bekum*] *v/i* and *t* come to be, develop into; acquire posi-tion of; suit, befit, look well on; **b. of** happen to.

becoming [be*kum*ing] *adj* befitting, suitable; (*of clothes etc*) attractive ~ **becomingly** *adv*.

bed [*bed*] *n* place to sleep or rest, *usu* article of furniture complete with mattress, sheets *etc*; animal's resting place; (*fig*) sexual relationship; marriage; plot of ground prepared for plants; bottom of a sea, lake, or river; layer of fresh mor-tar into which stones or bricks are to be placed; level surface or base on which something rests; **b. and board** lodging and food; **make the b.** rearrange the coverings after use; **get out of b. on the wrong side** be ill-tempered for the day; **b. of roses** easy position; **narrow b.** the grave; **take to (keep) one's b.** become ill; **lie in the b.** one has made accept the consequences of one's actions; **bring to b.** be delivered of a child ~ **bed** (*pres/part* **bedding**, *p/t* and *p/part* **bedded**) *v/t* and *i* place in a bed, provide with a bed; (*bui*) lay flat on a foundation; (*hort*) plant; (*coll*) have sexual relationship with.

bedabble [be*dab*'l] *v/t* splash, stain.

bedaub [be*dawb*] *v/t* smear; bedizen.

bedazzle [be*daz*'l] *v/t* completely confuse or blind the vision by the brilliance of something.

bedclothes [*bed*klOTHz] *n* (*pl*) sheets and blankets for a bed.

beddable [*bed*ab'l] *adj* sexually attractive or available.

bedding [*bed*ing] *n* mattress, sheets, pillows, coverlet used to make a bed; straw for animals; (*geol*) stratification; (*hort*) putting plants in beds.

bedeck [be*dek*] *v/t* adorn, cover with ornament.

bedeguar [*bed*egaar] *n* mossy gall on rose-bushes.

bedel [*beed*'l] *n* beadle at Oxford.

bedell [*beed*'l] *n* beadle at Cambridge.

bedesman see **beadsman**.

bedevil (*p/t* and *p/part* **bedevilled**) [be*dev*il] *v/t* upset completely, throw into confusion; exasper-ate; bewitch ~ **bedevilment** *n*.

bedew [be*dyOO*] *v/t* cover with dew, sprinkle.

bedfellow [*bed*felO] *n* sharer of a bed; (*fig*) associate.

bedight [be*dIt*] *adj* (*poet*) decorated, equipped.

bedim (*p/t* and *p/part* **bedimmed**) [be*dim*] *v/t* make dim, cloud, obscure.

bedizen [be*diz*en] *v/t* dress up gaudily.

bedlam [*bed*lam] *n* madhouse, lunatic asylum; (*fig*) scene of violent tumult.

bedlamite [*bed*lamIt] *n* and *adj* lunatic.

Bedlington [*bed*lington] *n* sporting terrier.

Bedouin [*bed*OO-in] *n* (*sing* and *pl*) desert Arab.

bedpan [*bed*pan] *n* chamber-pot for use in bed.

bedplate [*bed*playt] *n* cast-iron plate or steel frame on which a machine sits.

bedpost [*bed*pOst] *n* one of the four uprights of a bed to which the frame is fastened; **between you and me and the b.** confidentially.

bedraggle [be*drag*'l] *v/t* soil (dress) by trailing on dirty ground ~ **bedraggled** *adj* untidy, slovenly.

bedridden [*bed*Riden] *adj* confined to bed because of age or infirmity.

bedrock [*bed*Rok] *n* (*geol*) hard rock underlying gravel or loose surface soil; (*fig*) first principles, basic facts ~ **bedrock** *adj* fundamental.

bedroom [*bed*ROOm] *n* room furnished with a bed or beds ~ **bedroom** *adj* for use in a bedroom; (*fig*, *coll*) sexy.

bedside [*bed*sId] *n* place by the side of a bed, *esp* an invalid's; **good b. manner** (*fig*) (*of a doctor*) calm, reassuring bearing.

bed-sitter [bed-*sit*er] *n* (*coll*) bed-sitting-room.

bed-sitting-room [bed-*sit*ing-ROOm] *n* room serving both as a bedroom and a sitting-room.

bedsocks [*bed*soks] *n* (*pl*) woollen socks to be worn in bed.

bedsore [*bed*sawr] *n* sore on the skin developed by an invalid lying in bed.

bedspread [*bed*spred] *n* coverlet placed over the bedclothes during the daytime.

bedstead [*bed*sted] *n* frame of a bed.

bedstraw [*bed*straw] *n* popular name for certain plants of the genus *Galium*.

bedtime [*bed*tIm] *n* hour for going to bed.

bed-wet [bed-wet] *v/i* emit urine while in bed ~ **bed-wetter** *n* ~ **bed-wetting** *n*.

bed-worthy [bed-*wur*THi] *adj* (*coll*) sexually attractive.

bee [*bee*] *n* four-winged stinging insect which produces wax and collects honey; (*fig*) industrious person; social gathering for communal work or for entertainment; **have a b. in one's bonnet** be unreasonably obsessed with an idea.

Beeb [*beeb*] *n* (*coll abbr*) the B.B.C., i.e. British Broadcasting Corporation.

beech [*beech*] *n* forest tree having thin smooth bark and glossy oval leaves and bearing three-cornered nuts known as mast; the wood of this tree.

beechen [*beech*en] *adj* of, or relating to, the beech tree; made of beech wood.

beech-marten [*beech*-maarten] *n* bird with a white breast called the stone marten.

beechy [*beech*i] *adj* covered with beech trees.

beef (*pl* **beeves**) [*beef*] *n* the flesh of an ox, bull, or cow when killed; (*fig*) human flesh; muscular strength ~ **beef** *v/i* (*sl*) voice com-plaints.

Beefeater [*beef*eeter] *n* a Yeoman of the Guard; a Warder of the Tower of London; kind of African bird.

beefsteak [beef*stayk*] *n* thick slice of beef.

beef-tea [beef-*tee*] *n* juice of beef prepared as a nutritious drink for invalids.

beefwood [*beef*wood] *n* timber of an Australian tree so named from its reddish colour.

beefy [*beef*i] *adj* stolid, muscular.

beehive [*bee*hIv] *n* house or dome-shaped re-ceptacle provided for bees in which they store their honey; (*fig*) very busy place; (*of hairstyle*) resembling a dome-shaped beehive.

beeline [*bee*lIn] *n* direct line between two points.

Beelzebub [be-*elzebub*] *n* the prince of demons; the Devil, Satan.

been [*been*] *p/part* of **be**.

beep [*beep*] *n* short high-pitched sound or signal; (*sl*) small jeep.

beer [*beer*] *n* alcoholic drink made from fermented malt and flavoured with hops; **small b.** weak beer; (*fig*) thing of little value; unimportant person.

beerpull [*beer*pool] *n* lever of machine dispensing beer.

beery [*beRRi*] *adj* smelling or tasting of beer; slightly drunk.

beestings [*bee*stingz] *n* (*pl*) first milk of a cow after she has calved.

beeswax [*beez*waks] *n* wax from honey bees ~ **beeswax** *v/t* polish with beeswax.

beeswing [*beez*wing] *n* thin crust which forms on wine (*esp* port) bottled a long time.

beet [*beet*] *n* plant with a red root used as a vegetable; plant with a white root used for making sugar.

beetle (1) [*beet*'l] *n* heavy mallet or maul used for striking pegs, paving slabs *etc*.

beetle (2) *n* coleopterous insect which has a hard scaly covering to protect its wings; (*pop*) the blackbeetle, the cockroach.

beetle (3) *v/i* (*of cliffs, eyebrows*) project, overhang; **b. off** (*sl*) go away ~ **beetle** *adj* overhanging, bushy.

beetle-crusher [*beet*'l-kRusher] *n* (*sl*) large foot; large shoe.

beetling [*beet*ling] *adj* overhanging.

beetroot [*beet*ROOt] *n* edible red root of the beet.

beeves [*beevz*] *pl* of **beef**.

beezer [*beezer*] *n* (*sl*) nose; fellow.

befall (*p/t* **befell, befel,** *p/part* **befallen**) [be*fawl*] *v/i* and *t* pertain, be fitting; happen; happen to.

befit (*pres/part* **befitting,** *p/t* and *p/part* **befitted**) [be*fit*] *v/t* be fit for, suit; be seemly ~ **befitting** *adj* ~ **befittingly** *adv*.

befog (*pres/part* **befogging,** *p/t* and *p/part* **befogged**) [be*fog*] *v/t* surround by fog; (*fig*) obscure, make obscure; puzzle.

befool [be*fOOl*] *v/t* make a fool of, dupe.

before [be*fawr*] *adv* in front, ahead; on the front; earlier, beforehand, already, in the past ~ **before** *prep* ahead of, in front of; in the sight or presence of; earlier than; previous to; in advance of; compared with; in preference to, rather than ~ **before** *conj* previous to the time when; rather than, sooner than.

beforehand [be*fawr*hand] *adv* in advance, in readiness.

befoul [be*fowl*] *v/t* cover with dirt; (*fig*) cast aspersions on, slander.

befriend [be*fRend*] *v/t* help, be a friend to.

beg (*pres/part* **begging,** *p/t* and *p/part* **begged**) [*beg*] *v/t* and *i* ask for; solicit alms; ask as a favour; entreat, ask earnestly; (*of dog*) sit up expectantly with forepaws raised; **b. the question** take as true a point that is still disputed.

begad [be*gad*] *interj* by God.

began [be*gan*] *p/t* of **begin**.

beget (*pres/part* **begetting,** *p/t* **begot,** *p/part* **begotten**) [be*get*] *v/t* procreate; (*fig*) give rise to ~ **begetter** *n* one who begets.

beggar [*beg*ar] *n* one who lives by begging; person who is extremely poor; (*coll*) fellow, youngster ~ **beggar** *v/t* reduce to poverty, ruin; (*fig*) outdo, go beyond (description).

beggarly [*beg*arli] *adj* poor; valueless; mean, sordid ~ **beggarliness** *n* ~ **beggarly** *adv*.

beggar-my-neighbour [*beg*ar-mI-*nay*ber] *n* card game.

beggary [*beg*aRi] *n* extreme poverty.

begging [*beg*ing] *n* action of asking for alms *etc* ~ **begging** *adj* asking for something.

begin (*pres/part* **beginning,** *p/t* **began,** *p/part* **begun**) [be*gin*] *v/t* and *i* commence, start; be the first to do, bring into existence; come into being, arise; start to speak; **to b. with** in the first place.

beginner [be*gin*er] *n* novice, tyro.

beginning [be*gin*ing] *n* start, commencement; time at which anything begins; source, origin; first part; (*pl*) rudiments.

begird (*p/t* and *p/part* **begirt**) [be*gurd*] *v/t* gird around, encircle; bind.

begone [be*gon*] *interj* go away!

begonia [be*gOni*-a] *n* plant of tropical origin with brilliant foliage.

begot [be*got*] *p/t* of **beget**.

begrudge [be*gRuj*] *v/t* be reluctant; envy (someone) possession of (something); give unwillingly.

beguile [be*gIl*] *v/t* deceive, cheat; deprive of by trickery; charm, captivate; while away, divert attention pleasantly from ~ **beguiling** *adj* ~ **beguilingly** *adv*.

Beguine (1) [be*geen*] *n* member of a community of women who devote themselves to a religious life but take no vows.

beguine (2) *n* dance based on folk-tunes of the West Indies.

begum [*bee*gum] *n* Moslem lady of high rank.

begun [be*gun*] *p/part* of **begin**.

behalf [bi*haaf*] *n* **on b. of** in the name of, in the interest of, as the representative of.

behave [bi*hayv*] *v/i* and *refl* conduct oneself, act; conduct oneself well; (*of machinery*) function.

behaviour [bi*hayv*yer] *n* manner, bearing, deportment; conduct towards or treatment of others; response made in any particular situation > PDP; **b. pattern** recurrent series of acts.

behavioural [be*hayv*yeRal] *adj* relating to behaviour.

behaviourism [bi*hayv*yeRizm] *n* (*psych*) method of psychology which emphasizes objective study of actual responses > PDP ~ **behaviourist** *n* and *adj* ~ **behaviouristically** *adv*.

behaviouristics [be*hayv*yeRistiks] *n* (*pl*) the study of the reactions of living creatures to environment.

behead [bi*hed*] *v/t* cut the head from, decapitate.

beheld [bi*held*] *p/t* and *p/part* of **behold**.

behemoth [bi*hee*moth] *n* (*bibl*) gigantic animal.

behest [bi*hest*] *n* command.

behind [bi*hInd*] *adv* at the back; backwards; to the back; remaining; in the past; still to come; in arrear; following ~ **behind** *prep* after, following, inferior to; later than; in the rear of; in support of; beyond; **b. time** late; **b. the scenes** privately; **b. one's back** without one's knowledge, deceitfully ~ **behind** *n* (*coll*) buttocks.

behindhand [bi*hInd*hand] *adv* and *adj* late; backward; in arrears; old-fashioned.

behold (*p/t* and *p/part* **beheld**) [bi*hOld*] *v/t* and *i* see, look at; (*imp*) look! take notice! ~ **beholder** *n*.

beholden [bihOlden] *adj* under an obligation.

behove [bihOv] *v/impers* be incumbent upon; be required as a duty.

beige [*bayzh*] *n* any yarn or fabric in its natural or undyed state; yellowish grey colour.

be-in [*bee*-in] *n* a gathering of hippies.

being [*bee*-ing] *n* life, existence; that which exists; living creature; essential nature, essence; **human b.** member of mankind, person.

bel [*bel*] *n* (*ac*) unit of sound intensity equal to ten decibels.

belabour [bilayber] *v/t* beat soundly; (*fig*) assail with words.

belated [bilaytid] *adj* arriving late; coming too late, unduly postponed; overtaken by darkness.

belay [bilay] *v/t* (*naut*) make fast (rope) round a belaying pin or cleat; (*imp*) stop! cancel the order; **b. there** (*imp*) hold on and belay the rope!

belaying-pin [bilaying-pin] *n* (*naut*) metal pin to which a rope may be made fast.

bel canto [bel-kantO] *n* a lyrical style in singing as opposed to the declamatory.

belch [belch] *v/i* and *t* expel wind noisily from the stomach through the mouth; utter (curses, insults) in an offensive manner; (*of volcanoes, cannon etc*) throw out with force ~ **belch** *n*.

belcher [belcher] *n* coloured neckerchief.

beldam, beldame [beldam] *n* old woman, hag.

beleaguer [bileeger] *v/t* lay siege to, blockade.

belfry [belfRi] *n* space at the top of a church tower where bells are hung; bell tower separate from church; **have bats in the b.** be crazy, eccentric.

Belgian [beljan] *n* and *adj* (native) of Belgium.

Belial [beeli-al] *n* personification of evil; the Devil.

belie [bilI] *v/t* tell lies about, misrepresent; give a false impression of; fail to justify (hopes, expectations).

belief [bileef] *n* confidence or trust or faith (in); acceptance of something as true or real; religious doctrine, a creed; convinced opinion.

believable [bileevab'l] *adj* capable of being believed.

believe [bileev] *v/i* and *t* have trust or confidence (in), rely (on); accept truth of; accept as truthful; think, consider true; **make b.** pretend.

believer [bileever] *n* one who believes a religion.

belike [bilIk] *adv* perhaps, possibly.

Belisha beacon [beleesha-beekon] *n* post with an amber globe on the top signifying a pedestrian crossing-place in a street.

belittle [bilit'l] *v/t* make little of, disparage, depreciate ~ **belittlement** *n*.

bell (1) [bel] *n* hollow inverted cast metal cup with the lip curved outward which rings with musical vibration when struck by a clapper hanging within > PDM; anything shaped like a bell; (*naut*) (*pl*) strokes of a ship's bell indicating the half-hours of the watch; the half-hour period thus indicated; (*usu pl*) instrument of metal bars or tubes; **ring the b.** win the prize; **ring a b.** recall a memory; **sound as a b.** perfectly healthy or sound; **by b., book, and candle** (*eccles*) curse of excommunication ~ **bell** *v/t* and *i* provide with a bell; **b. the cat** undertake a dangerous enterprise on behalf of others.

bell (2) *n* cry made by a stag or by a buck at rutting time ~ **bell** *v/i* bellow.

belladonna [beladona] *n* (*bot*) deadly nightshade; (*med*) drug made from its root and leaves.

bell-bottomed [bel-botomd] *adj* (*of trousers*) very wide at the bottom of the leg.

bellboy [belboi] *n* page employed by hotel or club to escort guests, take messages *etc*.

bellbuoy [belboi] *n* buoy with a warning bell rung by the movement of the waves.

belle [bel] *n* (*Fr*) beautiful woman; the most attractive woman (of group *etc*).

belles-lettres [bel-letR] *n* (*pl*) (*Fr*) artistic and literary writings; light literature; the aesthetics of literature ~ **bellettrist** [bel-letRist] *n*.

bell-founder [bel-fownder] *n* one who casts large bells ~ **bell-foundry** *n* place where bells are cast.

bellhop [belhop] *n* (*US*) hotel page.

bellicose [belikOs] *adj* warlike, aggressive.

bellicosity [belikositi] *n* pugnacity.

bellied [belid] *adj* bulging; blown or puffed out.

belligerence [belijeRens] *n* eagerness for war, aggressiveness.

belligerent [belijeRent] *adj* waging war; (*fig*) aggressive ~ **belligerent** *n* person or nation at war.

bellman [belman] *n* town-crier; adult bellboy.

bellmetal [belmetal] *n* alloy of copper and tin.

bellow [belO] *v/t* roar like a bull; shout or sing with a loud deep voice, roar with pain; make a loud booming sound ~ **bellow** *n* ~ **bellowing** *n*.

bellows [belOz] *n* (*pl*) contrivance for supplying a strong blast of air.

bellpull [belpool] *n* rope or handle which when pulled makes a bell ring.

bellpunch [belpunch] *n* mechanical device which rings a bell whenever a bus conductor punches a ticket with it.

bellpush [belpoosh] *n* button which when pressed rings a bell.

bellringer [belRinger] *n* one who rings church bells or other kinds of bells ~ **bell-ringing** *n*.

bell-tent [bel-tent] *n* conical bell-shaped tent.

bell-wether [bel-weTHer] *n* leading sheep (carrying a bell round its neck) in a flock; (*fig*) leader.

belly [beli] *n* that part of the human body extending below the diaphragm to the thighs; stomach, abdomen; under part of animals; bulging part or surface of anything; front part of the sound box of a stringed instrument across which the strings are stretched; the interior or inside of anything; (*fig*) greed, gluttony; **b. tank** (*aer*) extra fuel tank carried by aircraft which can be jettisoned when empty ~ **belly** *v/i* swell out, bulge.

bellyache [beli-ayk] *v/i* (*sl*) grumble without good cause ~ **bellyaching** *n* grumbling.

belly-band [beli-band] *n* harness strap round the belly of a horse.

belly-button [beli-buton] *n* (*sl*) navel.

bellydance [belidaans] *n* erotic solo dance by a woman, with movements of belly and pelvis ~ **bellydancer** *n*.

bellyful [belifool] *n* as much of anything as one wants; (*coll*) more than enough.

bellying [beli-ing] *adj* swelling out.

bellyland [beliland] v/t (sl) crash-land an aircraft with landing gear retracted ~**bellylanding** n.

belong [bilong] v/i pertain to, be an attribute of, form part of; be the duty or concern of; be an inhabitant or native of; be the property of; fit in with, have its right place.

belongings [bilongingz] n (pl) a person's goods, property or (joc) family.

beloved [biluvd] adj dearly loved ~**beloved** [biluvid/biluvd] n one who is beloved; betrothed person, husband, wife.

below [bilO] adv lower down; later (in a book or on a page); on earth; in hell; (naut) beneath the deck; lower down a slope or down stream ~ **below** prep lower than; deeper than; underneath, beneath; inferior to; down stream from; too low to be influenced by.

belt [belt] n flat strip of leather or of other material worn round the person; girdle worn as a badge of distinction or of rank; corset, suspender-belt; area, zone, tract of land; (bui) simple string course; flexible strap; strap carrying the cartridges to feed a machine-gun; (mech) broad encircling strap serving to transmit motion from one wheel to another; **conveyor b.** endless belt of rubber-covered cotton duck used for carrying coal, gravel etc; **green b.** circle of undeveloped land surrounding a town or city; **hit below the b.** take unfair advantage; **tighten one's b.** reduce one's expenditure ~ **belt** v/t and i fasten with a belt; encircle with a belt; beat with a belt; (sl) rush, run; **b. up** (sl) be quiet, shut up; (coll) fasten a seat-belt.

Beltane [beltayn] n May Day spring festival in Celtic countries in pre-Christian times.

belted [beltid] adj having a belt; wearing a belt, esp that of knight or earl; marked by bands of colour; (coll) beaten with a belt.

belting [belting] n (collect) belts; material from which belts are made; (coll) a beating with a belt.

belvedere [belvedeer] n high turret or summer-house commanding a wide view.

bemedalled [bimedald] adj wearing medals.

bemoan [bimOn] v/t and i grieve for; lament.

bemuse [bimyOOz] v/t confuse utterly, stupefy, bewilder.

ben (1) [ben] adj (Scots dial) inner ~ **ben** prep in or towards the inner part ~ **ben** adv within ~ **ben** n inner room of a cottage.

ben (2) n (Gael) mountain-peak.

bench [bensh] n long seat; work table; thwart of boat; judge's seat in court; office of a judge; court of justice; (collect) judges or magistrates; seat holding occupants who sit in some official capacity; (collect) occupants of such a seat ~ **bench** v/t provide with benches; exhibit (dog) at a show.

bencher [bensher] n (leg) senior member of an Inn of Court.

bench-mark [bensh-maark] n surveyor's reference mark for determining further heights and distances.

bend [bend] n curve, anything not straight; curve of a road or river; (naut) any method of joining one rope to a loop in another; (her) parallel lines extending from the right of the upper part of a shield to the left of the lower; **b. sinister** (her) diagonal band from the left of the upper part of

a shield to the right of the lower as a sign of bastardy ~ **bend** (p/t and p/part bent) v/t and i make curved or angular (something rigid); cause to bow or incline; (fig) cause to submit or relent; deflect, turn from the straight; direct or turn (steps, eyes, ears etc) in a particular direction; bring into tension, tighten up, brace up; (refl) strain every nerve; (naut) make fast; become curved or angular in shape; incline the body, bow, stoop; (fig) yield, submit; incline in any direction from the straight; (sl) use dishonestly; **be bent on** be resolved on.

bended [bendid] adj bent; **on b. knee** kneeling; (fig) imploringly.

bender [bender] n pair of pliers; (coll) sixpenny piece; (coll) spree.

bends [bendz] n (pl) (coll) caisson disease.

beneath [bineeth] adv immediately below, underneath; below ~ **beneath** prep underneath; hidden by; below; unworthy of; subject to.

Benedick [benidik] n recently married man.

Benedictine [benidikteen] n and adj (monk) of order founded by St Benedict, black monk; liqueur made by these monks.

benediction [benidikshon] n a blessing; formal conferring of a blessing; expression of thanks; special service in the R.C. Church ~ **benedictional** n ~ **benedictionary** n book containing forms of benediction.

benedictory [benidikteRi] adj expressing a blessing.

Benedictus [benidiktus] n (Lat) the hymn of Zacharias (Luke i. 68) sung as a canticle; fifth movement in musical settings of the Mass.

benefaction [benifakshon] n good deed; gift of money for a charitable purpose; endowment, gift.

benefactor [benifakter] n one who helps others, patron; person giving financial aid to a cause or to an institution.

benefactory [benefakteRi] adj beneficial.

benefactress [benifaktRes] n female benefactor.

benefice [benifis] n a church living held by a vicar or rector ~ **beneficed** adj holding a benefice.

beneficence [benefisens] n doing good; kindly and generous acts.

beneficent [benefisent] adj doing good, charitable, generous ~ **beneficently** adv.

beneficial [benifishal] adj helpful, useful, producing good results, advantageous.

beneficiary [benifishaRi] n person who receives benefits, esp under a will or trust; holder of church living ~ **beneficiary** adj (of land) held from an overlord.

benefit [benifit] n advantage, good; financial gain; financial or other entitlements of a person paying insurance; performance in a theatre or a match in sport the proceeds of which are given over to a particular player as a token of esteem; (leg) privilege involving exemption from the normal jurisdiction of the courts ~ **benefit** v/t and i do good to; profit from.

Benelux [beniluks] n a customs union of Belgium, the Netherlands, and Luxembourg.

benevolence [benevolens] n generosity, love of humanity, inclination to do good; a kindness, a gift; (hist) forced loan levied by certain kings of England ~ **benevolent** adj doing good to others, charitable ~ **benevolently** adv.

Bengali [beng-*gawli*] *n* and *adj* (native, language) of Bengal; **B. light** firework signal.

benighted [bin*I*tid] *adj* overtaken by darkness; (*fig*) ignorant, backward.

benign [bin*I*n] *adj* kindly, gracious; gentle, mild; favourable, propitious; (*med*) not malignant.

benignant [bin*ig*nant] *adj* kind, benign ~ **benignity** *n*.

benison [*ben*ison] *n* (*ar*) blessing; benediction.

bent (1) [*bent*] *n* coarse reedy grass or rushes; land on which such grass grown, heath.

bent (2) *n* inclination of the mind, propensity, aptitude; **follow one's b.** pursue one's own interests; **to the top of one's b.** to the utmost.

bent (3) *p/t* and *p/part* of **bend** ~ **bent** *adj* curved, crooked; (*sl*) dishonest, stolen, bribed.

Benthamism [*bent*hamizm] *n* philosophy of Jeremy Bentham the guiding principle of which was 'the greatest happiness of the greatest number' ~ **Benthamite** *n*.

benthos [*bent*hos] *n* (*biol*) animals and plants living on the bottom of sea or lake.

bentwood [*bent*wood] *n* and *adj* (furniture) made from hard wood bent by steaming.

benumb [bin*um*] *v/t* make numb or powerless, deprive of feeling; (*fig*) paralyse.

Benzedrine [*benz*edReen] *n* (*tr*) a drug used as a nasal spray and as a nerve stimulant.

benzene [*benz*een] *n* (*chem*) C_6H_6; an aromatic hydrocarbon in the form of a colourless liquid obtained from coal-tar > PDS; (*comm*) benzol.

benzine [*benz*een] *n* (*chem*) inflammable liquid distilled from crude petroleum, used as solvent and in dry cleaning; (*comm*) benzoline, benzene.

benzoin [*benz*O-in] *n* fragrant resin got from a tree of E. Indies and used in medicine and perfumery.

benzol [*benz*ol] *n* benzene.

benzoline [*benz*oleen] *n* benzine.

beplaster [be*plaas*ter] *v/t* cover thickly.

bequeath [bik*weeth*] *v/t* leave (property or money) to a person by will; transmit to succeeding generations ~ **bequeathal** *n* act of bequeathing.

bequest [bek*west*] *n* act of bequeathing; legacy.

berate [be*Ray*t] *v/t* scold, chide angrily.

berberry see **barberry**.

berceuse [bursu(r)z] *n* (*mus*) cradle-song.

bereave [*p/t* and *p/part* **bereaved, bereft**] [bi*Reev*] *v/t* rob, deprive, *usu* of something nonmaterial; leave destitute or desolate; inflict the loss of a relative by death ~ **bereavement** *n*.

beret [be*Ray*] *n* (*Fr*) round flat cap without a peak.

berg [*burg*] *n* (*abbr*) iceberg.

bergamot (1) [*burg*amot] *n* tree of the citrus family; the oil or essence from the rind of this plant; kind of mint yielding an oil with similar scent; kind of tapestry.

bergamot (2) *n* a highly-flavoured, juicy pear.

bergschrund [*bairg*shroont] *n* gap or crevasse left round the upper rim of a glacier > PDG.

bergylt [*berg*ilt] *n* the Norwegian haddock.

berhyme [bi*RI*m] *v/t* write verses about.

beriberi [be*Rib*eRi] *n* (*path*) an endemic form of polyneuritis, prevalent *esp* in India, caused by deficiency of certain vitamins in the diet.

berk, burk [*burk*] *n* (*sl*) stupid person.

berkelium [bur*keel*i-um] *n* (*chem*) a transuranic element > PDS.

Berlin [ber*lin*] *n* old-fashioned four-wheeled carriage with a hooded seat behind; **B. black** black enamel paint; **B. blue** Prussian blue; **B. iron** soft variety of iron used in making small ornaments; **B. wool** coarse wool for knitting or embroidery.

Bernardine [*bair*naadeen] *n* and *adj* (monk) of the Cistercian order.

berry [be*Ri*] *n* (*pop*) any small juicy fruit without a stone; (*bot*) fruit in which seeds are contained throughout the pulp; a coffee bean; eggs in fish roe; lobster's eggs ~ **berry** *v/i* produce berries; go picking berries.

berserk [bur*zurk*] *adj* violently angry, frenzied ~ **berserk** [bur*surk*] *n* Norse warrior liable to wild fury in fighting.

berth [*burth*] *n* (*naut*) place where a ship lies when alongside wharf or at anchor; sleeping place on a ship, train *etc*; job, situation, appointment; **give a wide b.** to steer clear of ~ **berth** *v/t* and *i* moor (a ship) in position; furnish with a sleeping place; provide with a job.

bertha, berthe [*burt*ha, *burt*h] *n* broad collar at the top of a low-necked dress.

berthage [*burt*hij] *n* provision of berth for a ship.

berthing [*burt*hing] *n* (*of a ship*) act of putting in a berth; place where berthed; provision of sleeping accommodation; bulwark.

beryl [*be*Ril] *n* precious stone of transparent palegreen colour; (*min*) species including beryl, emerald, and aquamarine.

beryllium [be*Ril*i-um] *n* (*chem*) a name for the hard white metal glucinum, used for light, corrosion-resisting alloys.

beseech [*p/t* and *p/part* **besought**] [bi*seech*] *v/t* ask pleadingly for; entreat, petition humbly ~ **beseecher** *n* ~ **beseeching** *adj* ~ **beseechingly** *adv*.

beseem [bi*seem*] *v/t* suit, befit; be fitting ~ **beseeming** *adj* attractive ~ **beseemly** *adj*.

beset [*p/t* and *p/part* **beset**] [bi*set*] *v/t* encompass, hem in; invest, besiege (a place); assail (a person); set round (with adornments).

besetment [bi*set*ment] *n* whatever besets one.

besetting [bi*set*ing] *adj* to which one is habitually tempted.

beshrew [bish*ROO*] *v/t* invoke evil upon; **beshrew thee!** (*ar*) may evil befall thee!

beside [bi*sI*d] *prep* by the side of, by; compared with; irrelevant to, wide of; **b. oneself** overwrought.

besides [bi*sI*dz] *adv* in addition, moreover; otherwise, else ~ **besides** *prep* in addition to, other than; except.

besiege [bi*seej*] *v/t* lay siege to; (*fig*) crowd round; ply (with), demand eagerly, urge acceptance of ~ **besieger** *n*.

beslobber [bi*slob*er] *v/t* slaver over; caress in a slobbering manner.

besmear [bi*smeer*] *v/t* smear over, daub; (*fig*) calumniate.

besmirch [bi*smurch*] *v/t* soil, tarnish, make dirty.

besom [*beez*om/*bez*om] *n* broom made of a bunch of twigs tied round a handle; (*fig*) ugly old woman, witch.

besotted [bi*sot*ed] *adj* stupefied (with drink); infatuated; foolish.

besought [bi*sawt*] *p/t* and *p/part* of **beseech**.

bespangle [bispang-g'l] v/t cover with spangles.

bespatter [bispater] v/t splash (something) all over; (fig) besmirch, abuse.

bespeak (p/t **bespoke**, p/part **bespoke(n)**) [bispeek] v/t order in advance; arrange for beforehand; indicate, suggest; (poet) speak to.

bespoke [bispOk] adj made to special order.

besprent [bispRent] adj (poet) besprinkled (with); strewn about.

besprinkle [bispRink'l] v/t sprinkle or scatter over.

Bessemer [besemer] adj and n name of a process for making steel from cast iron > PDS.

best [best] adj (superl of **good**) of excellent quality; unequalled; most beneficial; most fitting; greatest, largest ~ **best** adv (superl of **well**) with all excellence; in the most advantageous way; in the most fitting manner; to the greatest extent~ **best** n the thing or the people of the highest quality; **make the b. of** it accept whatever advantage is to be gained; **b. man** friend who attends a bridegroom at a wedding; **have the b. of it** win, have the advantage; **for the b.** with good intentions; with most desirable outcome; **with the b.** as well as anybody; **at b.** making every allowance ~ **best** v/t get the better of, defeat.

bestead (p/t **besteaded**, p/part **bestead, bested**) [bisted] v/t and i (ar) help, benefit, assist, avail.

bested [bisted] adj beset; situated, circumstanced; **hard b.** hard-pressed.

bestial [besti-al] adj brutish; depraved, obscene, barbarous ~ **bestially** adv ~ **bestialize** v/t.

bestiality [besti-aliti] n brutal cruelty; disgusting behaviour, esp sexual; (leg) sexual act between a human being and an animal.

bestiary [besti-aRi] n medieval collection of animal stories describing their habits and characteristics to draw a moral.

bestir [bistur] v/refl exert oneself.

bestow [bistO] v/t confer (upon) as a gift, grant, give; put in a certain place, deposit; find room for ~ **bestower** n ~ **bestowment** n.

bestowal [bistO-al] n disposal; gift.

bestrew (p/part **bestrewed, bestrewn**) [bestROO] v/t strew (with); strew about; lie scattered over.

bestride (p/t **bestrode, bestrid**, p/part **bestridden, bestrid, bestrode**) [bistRId] v/t stand or sit over with legs astride; mount (a horse); stride across, extend across.

bestseller [bestseler] n a successful book which sells a very large number of copies.

bet [bet] n wagering of money or something of value upon the outcome of something uncertain; support of one's opinion against another's by backing it with money etc; money etc so staked ~ **bet** (pres/part **betting**, p/t and p/part **betted or bet**) v/t and i wager; **you b.** you may be sure.

beta [beeta] n the second letter of the Greek alphabet; used to denote the second thing in various numberings; **b. particle** (phys) electron or positron emitted by a radioactive nucleus > PDS; **b. rays** stream of fast-moving beta particles > PDS.

betake (p/t **betook**, p/part **betaken**) [bitayk] v/refl have recourse (to); make one's way, go, turn.

betatron [beetatRon] n (phys) apparatus for accelerating electrons to very high energies > PDS.

betel [beet'l] n plant leaf which is wrapped round areca-nut parings and used in India for chewing.

bête noire [bayt-nwaar] n (Fr) person or thing that one particularly dislikes or detests.

bethel [bethel] n holy place; Nonconformist chapel; seamen's church.

bethink (p/t and p/part **bethought**) [bithink] v/refl reflect, consider, recollect.

betide [bitId] v/t and i happen to; happen, befall.

betimes [bitImz] adv early; in good time, quickly.

betoken [bitOken] v/t portend, augur; signify, show, indicate.

betony [betoni] n (bot) plant with spiked purple flowers.

betook [bitook] p/t of **betake**.

betray [bitRay] v/t treacherously hand over to an enemy; be false or disloyal to (a trust or trusting person); disclose treacherously or inadvertently (a secret); mislead, deceive; show signs of.

betrayal [bitRay-al] n act of treachery.

betroth [bitROTH] v/t affiance, promise to marry; become engaged to be married.

betrothal [bitROTHal] n engagement of marriage.

betrothed [bitROTHd] adj fiancé, fiancée.

better (1) [beter] adj (comp of **good**) superior; more profitable; more suitable; larger, greater, more; improved in health, quite recovered; **b. half** (coll) wife ~ **better** adv (comp of **well**) in a superior way; **think b. of** change one's mind about, form a better opinion of; **b. off** in easier circumstances; **know b.** be more sensible; **he had b.** (do something) it would be to his advantage to; he ought to ~ **better** n (usu pl **betters**) person of higher social position, greater age, or merit etc; **get the b. of** defeat, prove superior to ~ **better** v/t and refl improve.

better (2), **bettor** [beter] n person who bets.

betterment [beterment] n improvement; increased value (of property).

betting [beting] n practice of making bets; way in which money is wagered.

bettor see **better** (2).

between [bitween] prep separating or connecting two objects; in the interval following one moment and preceding another ~ **between** adv in an intermediate position; in the interval; **betwixt and b.** (coll) neither one thing nor the other; **b. whiles** in the intervals.

betwixt [bitwikst] prep and adv between.

bevatron [beevatRon] n (phys) apparatus for accelerating protons to very high energies > PDS.

bevel [bevel] n surface (usu of glass or metal) meeting another surface of the same material at an angle which is not a right angle; oblique or sloping edge; joiner's or mason's tool for setting or marking out ~ **bevel** adj at an oblique angle, slanted ~ **bevel** (pres/part **bevelling**, p/t and p/part **bevelled**) v/t and i cut on the slant.

beverage [beveRij] n a drink, esp tea or soft drinks.

bevy [bevi] n assembly, company (esp of young ladies); (collect) group of quails, larks, or roes.

bewail [biwayl] v/t and i lament loudly over; mourn for, lament; make lament ~ **bewailment** n ~ **bewailingly** adv.

beware [biwair] v/t and i take care, be cautious (of).

bewilder [bi*wil*der] *v/t* puzzle, perplex ~ **be-wildering** *adj* ~ **bewilderingly** *adv.*

bewilderment [bi*wil*derment] *n* perplexity.

bewitch [bi*wich*] *v/t* influence by witchcraft or magic; (*fig*) charm, delight ~ **bewitched** *adj* ~ **bewitching** *adj* ~ **bewitchingly** *adv.*

bewray [bi*Ray*] *v/t* (*ar*) divulge, reveal.

bey [*bay*] *n* Turkish district governor; title of rank.

beyond [bi*yond*] *adv* on the farther side ~ **beyond** *prep* on or to or towards the farther side of, past; later than; more than, surpassing; in addition to, besides; (*with negative*) except; (*fig*) outside the range or scope of ~ **beyond** *n* remote place; the next world; the unknown beyond experience; **the back of b.** a very remote place.

bezant, byzant [*bezant*, bi*zant*] *n* (*numis*) gold or silver piece (first struck at Byzantium); (*her*) gold roundlet.

bezel [*bezel*] *n* the cutting edge of a chisel, plane iron or other cutting tool; oblique faces of a cut gem; groove and flange holding the glass in a watch or the stone of a jewel in the setting ~ **bezel** (*pres/part* **bezelling**, *p/t* and *p/part* **bez-elled**) *v/t* cut a sloping edge on, bevel.

bezique [be*zeek*] *n* card-game for two or four players in which none of the low cards from six downwards is used; the knave of diamonds and the queen of spades together.

bhang [*bang*] *n* Indian hemp; its leaves and stalks used as a narcotic or intoxicant; hashish.

bi- *pref* twice, doubly, having two, twofold, lasting for two, every two *etc*; (*chem*) indicating an acid salt of a dibasic acid.

biannual [bi-*anew*-al] *adj* twice a year.

bias [*bi*-as] *n* (*in the game of bowls*) the weight on one side of a bowl causing it to swerve; the oblique line in which it runs; impetus or influence causing this deviation; (*fig*) inclination, bent, leaning; prejudice; (*dressmaking*) a piece of material cut diagonally across the texture ~ **bias** *v/t* impart bias to; prejudice.

biased, biassed [*bi*-ast] *adj* prejudiced.

bib (1) [*bib*] *n* cloth worn by a child under the chin to protect the clothes at meals; top of an apron; **best b. and tucker** (*coll*) best clothes.

bib (2) *n* an edible fish, the whiting-pout.

bib (3) (*pres/part* **bibbing**, *p/t* and *p/part* **bibbed**) (*obs coll*) *v/t* and *i* drink, tipple ~ **bibber** *n* tippler.

bib (4), **bibcock** [*bib*kok] *n* (*bui*) the domestic tap.

bibelot [*beeb*lO] *n* (*Fr*) small trinket of artistic value; an unusually small book or edition.

Bible [*bi*b'l] *n* the Scriptures of the Old and New Testaments; a copy or an edition of them; (*fig*) authoritative or sacred book; **B. belt** (*US*) region where fanatically puritan Christians abound; **B. puncher** (*coll*) preacher who aggressively expounds Bible teaching.

biblical [*bib*likal] *adj* of or relating to the Bible ~ **biblically** *adv.*

biblio- *pref* relating to the Bible.

biblio- *pref* relating to books.

bibliographer [bibli-*og*Rafer] *n* person concerned with, skilled in, bibliography.

bibliography [bibli-*og*Rafi] *n* systematic study of the history of books (*eg* printing, publishing, authorship *etc*); list of books relating to a particular author or printer or subject *etc* ~ **biblio-**

graphic(al) [bibli-O*gRaf*ik(al)] *adj* ~ **bibliographically** *adv.*

bibliolatry [bibli-*ol*atRi] *n* exaggerated respect for the literal meaning of the words of the Bible.

bibliomancy [*bib*li-omansi] *n* prophecy or divination from verses of the Bible chosen at random.

bibliomania [bibli-o*mayni*-a] *n* excessive zeal for collecting books ~ **bibliomaniac** *n.*

bibliophile [*bib*li-ofIl] *n* book-lover, person fond of collecting books.

bibliopole [*bib*li-opOl] *n* dealer in (*esp rare*) books ~ **bibliopoly** [bibli*opoli*] *n* bookselling.

bibulous [*bib*ewlus] *adj* addicted to drink.

bicarbonate [bi*kaar*bonayt] *n* (*chem*) salt of carbonic acid in which only half the acidic hydrogen has been replaced by a metal.

bice [*bIs*] *n* dull blue; pigments used to produce dull shades of blue and green.

bicentenary [bIsen*teena*Ri] *n* two-hundredth anniversary ~ **bicentenary** *adj.*

bicentennial [bIsen*teni*-al] *adj* happening every two hundred years; lasting for two hundred years; (*US*) bicentenary.

bicephalous [bI*sefa*lus] *adj* having two heads.

biceps [*bIseps*] *n* muscle with two heads or origins, *esp* the flexor on front of upper arm.

bichloride [bI*klaw*RId] *n* (*chem*) compound in which two equivalents of chlorine are combined with a metal.

bichromate [bI*kRO*mayt] *n* (*chem*) salt containing two equivalents of chromic acid.

bicipital [bI*sipi*tal] *adj* of the biceps.

bicker [*biker*] *v/i* wrangle, squabble, quarrel; skirmish, fight; (*of stream*) babble ~ **bicker** *n* quarrel ~ **bickering** *n* wrangling, petty dispute.

bicorn [*bI*kawrn] *adj* having two horns.

bicornute [bIkawrny*OOt*] *adj* (*bot*) with two horn-like projections.

bicrural [bI*Roor*Ral] *adj* two-legged.

bicuspid [bI*kus*pid] *n* tooth with two cusps, human premolar tooth ~ **bicuspid** *adj.*

bicycle [*bI*sik'l] *n* vehicle with two wheels propelled by pedalling ~ **bicycle** *v/i* ride a bicycle.

bicyclist [*bI*siklist] *n* one who rides a bicycle.

bid (*p/t* **bade, bid**; *p/part* **bidden, bid**) [*bid*] *v/t* and *i* pray, beg; command, order, tell; say (goodbye, welcome *etc*); ask to come, invite; offer, make an offer at an auction sale; (*cards*) make a bid; **b. fair to** appear likely to ~ **bid** *n* offer of a price (for something); (*bridge*) declaration of the number of tricks a player hopes to make and in which suit; attempt, effort, appeal (to secure something).

biddable [*bida*b'l] *adj* docile, obedient.

bidder [*bider*] *n* one who bids at auction.

bidding [*biding*] *n* offers of prices at an auction sale; bids at the start of a game of bridge; order, command; invitation.

biddy [*bidi*] *n* (*coll*) unpleasant old woman, hag; (*sl*) girl, woman; **red b.** mixture of red wine and methylated spirits.

bide [*bId*] *v/t* and *i* tolerate, put up with; (*dial*) stay, wait.

bidet [*bee*day] *n* small raised tub on which one sits to wash oneself.

biennial [bI*eni*-al] *adj* happening every two years; lasting for only two years ~ **biennial** *n* (*bot*) plant that requires two years to complete its life-cycle from seed germination to seed production and death > PDB ~ **biennially** adv.

bier [beer] n movable stand on which a corpse or a coffin is taken for burial; (fig) tomb.

bifer [bɪfer] n (bot) plant which flowers or fruits twice a year ~ **biferous** [bɪfeRus] adj.

biff [bif] n (coll) sharp blow ~ **biff** v/t.

biffin [bifin] n red variety of cooking apple.

bifid [bɪfid] adj divided by a cleft into two parts.

bifocal [bɪfOkal] adj (of spectacles) with lenses having two sections of different focus for near and distant vision ~ **bifocals** n (pl) spectacles with lenses of this type.

bifoliate [bɪfOli-it] adj (bot) having two leaves.

bifurcate [bɪfurkayt] v/t and i divide into two branches, fork ~ **bifurcate** adj two-forked.

bifurcation [bifurkayshon] n forking into two branches; one or both branches; forking point.

big [big] adj large in size, bulk, mass, extent or capacity; loud in sound; (fig) important, noble, distinguished; proud, conceited; generous; (coll) elder; **B. Brother** all-powerful dictator; (fig) excessive government interference and control; **b. bug** (sl) important person; **talk b.** boast; **b. stick** show of force; **too b. for one's boots** conceited; **b. business** (freq cont) commerce on the grand scale; **b. noise, b. shot** (sl) person of importance.

bigamist [bigamist] n person guilty of bigamy.

bigamous [bigamus] adj living in bigamy; involving bigamy.

bigamy [bigami] n crime of marrying a second time while still legally married.

bigarreau, bigaroon [bigaRO/bigaRo, bigaROOn] n large white-heart cherry.

bigeminal [bɪjeminal] adj (med) in two pairs.

big-end [big-end] n (eng) the part of a connecting-rod that bears on a crankshaft.

bigg, big [big] n the four-rowed barley.

bighead [bighed] n (coll) conceited person.

bigheaded [bighedid] adj (coll) conceited.

bight [bɪt] n bend, curve; (geog) bend or curve of a coastline or of a river; shallow bay; loop of a rope.

bigot [bigot] n narrow-minded person whose belief in something is obstinate and intolerant ~ **bigoted** adj narrow-minded, prejudiced ~ **bigotry** n attitude of a bigot; act of a bigot.

bigwig [bigwig] n (coll) important person.

bijou [beezhOO] adj (Fr) small, elegant, perfect.

bijouterie [beezhOOteRi] n articles of jewellery.

bike [bɪk] n (coll abbr) bicycle; motorcycle ~ **bike** v/t to cycle.

bikini [bikeeni] n scanty two-piece swim-suit worn by women.

bilabial [bɪlaybi-al] n and adj (phon) sound articulated by both lips.

bilabiate [bɪlaybi-it] adj two-lipped.

bilateral [bɪlateRal] adj of or relating to two sides; (leg) affecting or relating to two parties ~ **bilaterally** adv on both sides.

bilberry [bilbeRi] n blue-black fruit from a small hardy shrub found on heaths, moors and in mountain woods; whortleberry, blaeberry.

bilbo (pl bilboes) [bilbO] n long iron bar with one end fastened to the floor and having sliding shackles for the ankles of prisoners.

bile [bɪl] n bitter yellowish-green fluid secreted by the liver to emulsify fats and assist excretion > PDB; disorder of the bile; (fig) anger, irritability; (hist) one of the four humours, choler.

bilge [bilj] n exterior and interior of ship's bottom; waste water, filth, and slime which collects in the bottom of a ship; belly of a cask; (coll) rubbish, nonsense ~ **bilge** v/t and i stave in the bottom of a ship; spring a leak in the bilge; bulge.

bilgewater [biljwawter] n (naut) foul water that collects in the bottom of a ship.

bilharzia [bilhaarzi-a] n tropical weakening disease caused by parasitic flat-worms in veins, whose eggs penetrate the liver or bladder; worm causing this.

bilharziasis [bilhaarzi-asis] n (path) chronic disease caused by parasitic flat-worm.

biliary [bilyaRi] adj of or relating to the bile; **b. fever** febrile infection of the blood in horses.

bilingual [bɪling-gwal] adj speaking two languages like a native; written in two languages.

bilious [bilyus] adj susceptible to or caused by disorder of the bile; (fig) irritable, peevish ~ **biliously** adv ~ **biliousness** n.

bilk [bilk] v/t defraud, avoid payment (of); elude, escape from; deceive, trick; (in cribbage) spoil one's opponent's score in his crib ~ **bilker** n.

bill (1) [bil] n slender or flat beak of some birds; narrow headland; (naut) point on the fluke of an anchor ~ **bill** v/i (of birds) rub beaks together; (fig) caress; **b. and coo** converse amorously.

bill (2) n (hist) weapon with a handle and curved blade; halberd; tool with a long curved blade used for lopping branches etc ~ **bill** v/t lop, hack.

bill (3) n a written document or statement; draft of proposed legislation submitted to the Houses of Parliament; (leg) written statement of a case; poster, advertisement; account rendered for goods or services; **b. of exchange** order to pay sum on given date; **b. of fare** menu; **b. of health** (naut) certificate testifying to the health of a ship's crew before a voyage; **b. of lading** (naut) official receipt given by a ship's captain for the cargo he carries; **b. of quantities** (bui) list of numbered items describing the quantity of work to be done on a civil engineering or building contract; **fill the b.** be up to the standard required; **foot the b.** pay all expenses.

bill (4) v/t announce by placards; plaster with posters ~ **billed** adj announced, scheduled; (of actor) advertised (to appear in a certain role).

billboard [bilbawrd] n notice-board, hoarding.

billet (1) [bilet] n (carp) piece of wood with three sides sawn and the fourth left round; (metal) intermediate product in the hot rolling or forging of steel or wrought iron; enrichment in Norman architecture consisting of short cylinders or square blocks in a hollow moulding; (pl) fox dung.

billet (2) n (mil) document requiring a householder to provide board and lodgings for a soldier; accommodation of this kind; (fig) employment, berth, job ~ **billet** v/t quarter in billets.

billet-doux [bilaydOO] n (Fr) love-letter.

billhook [bilhook] n heavy knife or small chopper with a hooked end used for lopping branches etc.

billiards [bilyaardz] n (pl) game played with ivory balls which are struck by cues on a smooth cloth-covered rectangular table with pockets and a cushioned edge.

billing [bi*ling*] *n* act of fondling or exchanging caresses after the fashion of doves.

Billingsgate [bi*lingzgayt*] *n* London fish-market; coarse, vituperative language.

billion [bi*lyon*]*n* a million millions; (*econ, sci* and *US*) a thousand millions.

billon [bi*lon*] *n* alloy of gold or of silver with a high proportion of base metal such as copper.

billow [bi*lO*] *n* large swelling sea-wave; (*poet*) wave, (*pl*) the sea; (*fig*) anything moving with a surging motion ~ **billow** *v/i* ~ **billowy** *adj*.

bill-poster, bill-sticker [*bil-pOster, bil-stiker*] *n* one who pastes up bills or placards.

billy [bi*li*] *n* (*Aust*) (*coll*) tin can used for cooking.

billycan [bi*likan*] *n* (*coll*) billy.

billycock [bi*likok*] *n* (*coll*) bowler hat.

billy-goat [*bili-gOt*] *n* male goat.

billy-o [bi*li-O*] *n* (*coll*) like b. very vigorously.

biltong [bi*ltong*] *n* strips of lean sun-dried meat.

bimetallic [bImeta*lik*] *adj* (*of currency*) based on or consisting of two metals; **b. strip** strip made of two adjacent metals with different coefficients of expansion.

bimetallism [bIme*talizm*] *n* (*econ*) monetary system in which the relative values of two metals, *eg* gold and silver, are fixed.

bimonthly [bImunth*li*] *adj* every two months; twice a month; every other month.

bin [*bin*] *n* container for bread, corn, meal, also for ore, coal, gravel, rubbish *etc*; rack in a wine-cellar for storing bottles of wine; wine from a particular bin; kind of basket used in hop-picking ~ **bin** (*p/t* binned) *v/t* store in a bin.

binary [bI*naRi*] *adj* dual, of or relating to a pair; (*math*) having two variables; **b. compound** (*chem* and *min*) compound of two elements only; **b. form** (*mus*) structure of a piece of music in which balance is obtained by a second phrase (or section) answering the first > PDM; **b. measure** (*mus*) with two beats to a bar; **b. notation** (*math*) number system with only two digits, usually o and ɪ > PDS; **b. system** (*astron*) two stars either revolving one round the other or both revolving round a common centre.

binate [bI*nayt*] *adj* (bot) arranged in pairs.

binaural [bina*wRal*] *adj* (*ac*) using two ears in-stead of one, adapted for use with both ears; (*rad*) relating to stereophonic reproduction of sound from records which have two sound channels in each groove.

bind (*p/t* and *p/part* bound) [bI*nd*] *v/t* and *i* tie, tie up, tie together; fasten; make prisoner, restrain; bandage; tie round; secure with a border of stout material; (*bookbinding*) fasten together the leaves of a book within a cover; make costive; (*fig*) ratify (bargain); (*refl*) pledge oneself to; (*leg*) to subject (person) to a specific legal obligation; stick together, cohere; **I'll be bound** I am certain; **bound up in** entirely en-grossed in ~ **bind** *n* anything used to bind; (*mus*) curved line joining two notes of the same pitch indicating that the first only is to be struck > PDM; twining stalk of a plant; measure of quantity of eels and salmon; hard clay between layers of coal; (*sl*) nuisance.

binder [bI*nder*] *n* person who binds; material used for binding; machine that binds; machine that cuts standing corn and ties it into sheaves;

(*bui*) cement, bitumen *etc* used for joining stones or sand together; building joist.

binding [bI*nding*] *n* that which binds; cover holding pages of a book; **bias b.** tape cut on the bias; **perfect b.** form of bookbinding holding single leaves by adhesive.

bindweed [bI*ndweed*] *n* (*bot*) convolvulus and similar climbing plants.

bine [*bin*] *n* (*bot*) climbing stem *esp* of the hop plant; (*bot*) pliant stem of a shrub.

binge [*binj*] *n* (*sl*) drinking bout, spree.

bingo [*bing-gO*] *n* gambling game played by cover-ing numbered squares on a card according to numbers drawn at random.

bingo-hall [*bing-gO-hawl*] *n* public hall where games of bingo are commercially organized.

binit [bi*nit*] *n* (*math*) a digit used in binary nota-tion.

binnacle [bina*k'l*] *n* (*naut*) box containing a com-pass on a ship's deck by the helm.

binocular [bino*kewlar*] *adj* using both eyes together ~ **binocular** *n* any optical instrument designed for the simultaneous use of both eyes.

binoculars [bino*kewlarz*] *n* (*pl*) field or opera glasses.

binomial [bInO*mi-al*] *adj* (*math*) consisting of two terms ~ **binomial** *n* expression consisting of the sum or difference of two terms; **b. theorem** formula which gives any power of a binomial without lengthy multiplication > PDS.

binominal [bIno*minal*] *adj* (bot and *zool*) possess-ing two names; **b. nomenclature** method of naming animals and plants scientifically by genus and species > PDB.

bint [*bint*] *n* (*sl*) girl.

bio- *pref* life; organic life; of biology.

bioblast [bI-O*blast*] *n* minute unit of protoplasm ranking between the molecule and the cell.

biochemistry [bI-O*kemi*stRi] *n* study of chemistry of living things.

biodegradable [bI-Odig*Rayd*ab'l] *adj* (*chem*) capable of being rotted by the natural action of bacteria.

biofeedback [bI-O*feed*bak] *n* method of acquiring control over normally involuntary bodily re-sponses to stimuli.

biogenesis [bI-O*jeni*sis] *n* origin and evolution of living forms ~ **biogenetic** [bI-Oje*netik*] *adj*.

biographer [bI-*og*Rafer] *n* one who writes the life story of a person.

biographic, biographical [bI-O*gRa*fik(al)] *adj* pertaining to biography.

biography [bI-*og*Rafi] *n* account of an individual's life; branch of literature dealing with the history of individual lives.

biologic, biological [bI-O*loj*ik(al)] *adj* pertaining to biology; **b. warfare** deliberate spreading of disease as a method of warfare.

biologist [bI-*ol*Ojist] *n* scientist engaged in the study of biology.

biology [bI-*ol*oji] *n* study of living organisms.

biomass [bI-O*mas*] *n* total weight of living organisms in a stated area.

biometrics [bI-O*met*Riks] *n* (*pl*) application of mathematical and statistical methods to the study of biology.

biometry [bI-*ome*tRi] *n* biometrics.

bionics [bɪ-*oniks*] *n* (*pl*) study of machines designed to behave like living beings.

bionomics [bɪ-O*nomiks*] *n* (*pl*) branch of biology which studies organisms in relation to their environment.

biophysics [bɪ-O*fiziks*] *n* (*pl*) application of the laws of physics to biological phenomena.

bioplasm [*bɪ*-O*plazm*] *n* living matter; protoplasm ~ **bioplasmic** [bɪ-O*plaz*mik] *adj*.

bioplast [*bɪ*-O*plast*] *n* a minute quantity of living protoplasm capable of reproducing itself ~ **bioplastic** [bɪ-O*plastik*] *adj*.

biopsy [*bɪ*-opsi] *n* (*med*) removal of tissues or cells from a living body for examination.

biosphere [*bɪ*-O*sfeer*] *n* regions of earth, sea and air inhabited by living organisms.

biostatics [bɪ-O*statiks*] *n* (*pl*) science of structure in relation to the function of organisms.

biosynthesis [bɪ-O*sinthesis*] *n* production of a chemical substance by a living organism.

biotic [bɪ-*otik*] *adj* relating to life and living organisms.

biotin [bɪ-*otin*] *n* vitamin of the B complex > PDS.

biotype [*bɪ*-O*tɪp*] *n* group of organisms having the same genetic characteristics > PDB.

bipartisan [bɪpaarti*zan*] *adj* agreed on by two political parties; of or representing members of two parties.

bipartite [bɪ*paar*tɪt] *adj* divided into two parts; shared by two parties; (*leg*) drawn up in two corresponding parts, one for each party.

biped [*bɪ*ped] *n* animal having two feet ~ **biped** *adj* having two feet ~ **bipedal** *adj*.

biplane [*bɪ*playn] *n* aeroplane with two sets of wings.

bipolar [bɪ*pOlar*] *adj* having two opposite extremities ~ **bipolarity** [bɪpO*la*Riti] *n*.

birch [*burch*] *n* (*bot*) hardy northern forest tree with smooth bark and slender branches; the wood of this tree; bundle of birch-twigs used for whipping, birch-rod; canoe of birch-bark ~ **birch** *v/t* flog with a birch ~ **birchen** *adj* made of birch.

bird [*burd*] *n* feathered biped; game bird; (*sl*) attractive girl; (*sl*) fellow; **b. of passage** migratory bird; (*fig*) wanderer; **a b. in the hand** a certainty; **get the b.** (*sl*) be hissed by an audience; get the sack; **birds of a feather** people of similar type; **kill two birds with one stone** achieve a double purpose; **little b.** secret source of information; **strictly for the birds** (*coll*) only for inexperienced fools.

birdcage [*burd*kayj] *n* cage for captive birds.

bird-eye see **bird's-eye**.

bird-fancier [*burd*-fansi-er] *n* bird dealer.

birdie [*burd*i] *n* (*golf*) holing out in one stroke less than par.

birdlime [*burd*lɪm] *n* sticky substance spread on twigs to catch birds ~ **birdlime** *v/t*.

birdlore [*burd*lawr] *n* facts and beliefs about birds.

bird-nesting [*burd*-nesting] *n* searching for the nests of birds.

bird's-eye, bird-eye [*burdz*-ɪ, *burd*-ɪ] *n* (*bot*) plants with bright round flowers; kind of fine-cut tobacco; (*timber*) figure formed by small pointed depressions ~ **bird's-eye** *adj* as seen from above;

marked as with bird's eyes, spotted; **b. view** panoramic view of the landscape; (*fig*) summary.

bird's-foot [*burdz*-foot] *n* (*bot*) varieties of vetch, fern, trefoil; **b. trefoil** yellow-flowered plant.

bird's-nest [*burdz*-nest] *n* nest of a bird; nest of kind of swallow, eaten by the Chinese; (*naut*) crow's nest; (*bot*) name given to certain plants with a nest-like cluster of roots.

birdwatcher [*bird*wocher] *n* one who studies birds in their natural habitats.

bireme [*bɪ*Reem] *n* galley with two banks of oars.

biretta [bi*Reta*] *n* square cap worn by clergy of the Roman Catholic Church.

Biro [*bɪ*RO] *n* (*tr*) ballpoint pen.

birth [*burth*] *n* process of being born; that which is born, offspring; childbirth; parentage, ancestry, descent; noble lineage; (*fig*) beginning.

birth-control [*burth*-kontROl] *n* any method of prevention of conception.

birthday [*burth*day] *n* day of one's birth; anniversary of that day; **in one's b. suit** naked; **B. honours** distinctions awarded on the Sovereign's birthday.

birthmark [*burth*maark] *n* mark on the body present from birth.

birthpangs [*burth*pangz] *n* (*pl*) painful muscular contractions during childbirth; (*fig*) unrest or social upheavals indicating the start of a new era or social order.

birthplace [*burth*plays] *n* place where one is born.

birthrate [*burth*Rayt] *n* proportion of births to the population of a country.

birthright [*burth*Rɪt] *n* that which belongs to one by virtue of one's birth; the rights and privileges of a first-born; inheritance, patrimony.

birthstone [*burth*stOn] *n* one of twelve gem-stones associated with Zodiacal signs and believed lucky for those born under the relevant sign.

bis [*bis*] *adv* occurring twice; (*mus*) to be repeated.

biscuit [*biskit*] *n* thin, flat, crisp cake, sweetened or unsweetened; (*cer*) any clay object that has been fired prior to glazing; unglazed pottery; light-brown colour; (*mil sl*) soldier's brown square mattress; **take the b.** (*sl*) be the best (or worst) at anything; do something outrageous.

bise [*beez*] *n* (*Fr*) dry northerly wind experienced in southern France and Switzerland.

bisect [bɪ*sekt*] *v/t* and *i* divide into two parts (usually equal), fork ~ **bisection** *n* division into two equal parts ~ **bisector** *n* line which bisects.

bisegment [bɪ*segment*] *n* one of two equal parts of a line.

bisexual [bɪ*seksew*-al] *adj* (*bot, biol*) having both male and female reproductive organs; (*psych*) equally attracted by both sexes.

bisexuality [bɪseksewa*liti*] *n* condition of having the characteristics of both sexes, or being attracted equally by members of both sexes.

bishop [*bisho*p] *n* (*eccles*) spiritual governor of a diocese next in rank below an archbishop; piece shaped like a mitre used in chess; a sweet drink; mulled and spiced port; (*ent*) ladybird.

bishopric [*bisho*pRik] *n* (*eccles*) diocese of a bishop; office of a bishop.

bisk, (*US***) bisque** [*bisk*] *n* a rich soup.

bismuth [*biz*muth] *n* (*chem*) crystalline metal used in alloys and medicinal compounds > PDS.

bison [*bɪ*son] *n* American buffalo; European wild ox.

bisque (1) [*bisk*] *n* (*tennis*) handicap allowance given to a player who takes one point without winning it at some stage in the game; (*golf*) extra stroke so allowed; (*croquet*) extra turn.

bisque (2) *n* any object of clay that has been fired prior to glazing, unglazed pottery, (*cer*) biscuit.

bisque (3) see **bisk**.

bissextile [*bisekstɪl*] *n* a leap-year ~ **bissextile** *adj* containing the extra day of a leap-year.

bister see **bistre**.

bistoury [*bistoRɪ*] *n* (*surg*) scalpel.

bistre, (*US*) **bister** [*bister*] *n* brown pigment made from soot; colour of this.

bistro [*beest*RO] *n* (*Fr*) small wine-shop or restaurant.

bit (1) [*bit*] *n* cutting edge of a tool; interchangeable cutting point used by a carpenter in a brace or electric drill, by a miner in a rock drill *etc* > PDE; jaws of pincers *etc*; metal mouthpiece of a horse's bridle; copper working head of a soldering iron ~ **bit** (*pres/part* **bitting**, *p/t* and *p/part* **bitted**) *v/t* put the bit into a horse's mouth, accustom to the bit; (*fig*) curb, restrain.

bit (2) *n* small piece or portion; mouthful of food, morsel; a short time; (*coll*) a jot, a whit; (*coll*) small coin; (*sl*) young woman; (*coll*) small part in film or play; (*sl*) role, attitude, course of action; (*computers*) unit of information; amount of information required to distinguish between two alternatives.

bit (3) *p/t* and archaic *p/part* of **bite**.

bitch [*bich*] *n* female of dog, fox, or wolf; (*coll*) lewd, immoral woman; spiteful, catty woman ~ **bitch** *v/t* and *i* (*coll*) behave treacherously or spitefully towards; spoil, mess up; grumble.

bitchy [*bichi*] *adj* sexually provoking, immoral; spiteful, mean.

bite (*p/t* **bit**, *p/part* **bitten**) [*bɪt*] *v/t* and *i* pierce or grip with the teeth, cut into; have the habit of biting; accept bait; (*fig*) be tempted by an offer, (*pass*) swindle; sting; suck blood; make to smart, nip, pinch with cold, (*fig*) wound feelings; grip, take hold; **b. the dust** fall to the ground, be defeated; **bitten with** (*coll*) enthusiastic about ~ **bite** *n* piece bitten off, mouthful of food; wound made by teeth; manner in which teeth meet; grip, hold; sting, pungency; seizure of or snap at the bait by the fish; (*print*) texture of the surface of paper causing it to take ink or other markings readily; **put the b. on** (*sl*) put pressure on, blackmail; borrow money from.

biting [*bɪt*ing] *adj* piercing, very cold; stinging, pungent, painfully sarcastic ~ **bitingly** *adv*.

bitter [*biter*] *adj* sour or acrid to the taste; (*fig*) painful, distressing; harsh, wounding, relentless; bitingly cold; **b. beer** strongly flavoured beer; **b. end** (*naut*) the end of a rope loose after belaying; (*fig*) the very end whatever the consequences.

bittern (1) [*bitern*] *n* long-legged wading bird.

bittern (2) *n* solution remaining after the crystallization of common salt from sea-water.

bitters [*biterz*] *n* (*pl*) liquors flavoured with bitter herbs *etc* to aid digestion or appetite.

bittersweet [*biter*sweet] *adj* sweet but with a bitter after-taste; (*fig*) agreeable but with an element of pain ~ **bittersweet** *n* kind of cider apple; woody nightshade.

bitts [*bits*] *n* (*pl*) (*naut*) stout vertical timbers or iron heads to which cable or mooring rope is passed or secured ~ **bitt** *v/t* fasten at or secure to the bitts.

bitty [*biti*] *adj* incomplete, disjointed, consisting only of bits.

bitumen [*bite*wmen] *n* (*min*) mineral pitch, asphalt; (*chem*) term covering numerous mixtures of hydrocarbons > PDS.

bituminiferous [*bitewminiferus*] *adj* yielding ʾbitumen.

bituminous [*bitewminus*] *adj* containing bitumen.

bivalent [*bɪvaylent/bivalent*] *adj* (*chem*) able to combine with or replace two hydrogen atoms; (*biol*) two homologous chromosomes present during meiosis > PDB.

bivalve [*bɪvalv*] *n* (*zool*) mollusc (*eg* oyster, mussel) with a shell in two parts hinged together; (*bot*) seed-vessel with two valves ~ **bivalve(d)** *adj* ~ **bivalvular** [*bɪvalvewlar*] *adj*.

bivouac [*bivoo*-ak] *n* (*mil*) camp pitched for the night in the open without tents ~ **bivouac** (*p/t* **bivouacked**) *v/i* camp out in the open.

bi-weekly [*bɪ-weekli*] *adj* fortnightly; twice in one week.

biz [*biz*] *n* (*sl*) business.

bizarre [*bizaar*] *adj* eccentric, odd, strange; grotesque, quaint.

blab (*pres/part* **blabbing**, *p/t* and *p/part* **blabbed**) [*blab*] *v/t* and *i* divulge indiscreetly; reveal secrets ~ **blabber** *n*.

black [*blak*] *adj* of the very darkest colour or approaching this; with a very dark skin, negroid; dark, sombre; dirty; (*of coffee*) without milk; (*of jokes*) macabre; illegal, illicit; boycotted by a trade union; malignant, deadly, sinister; wicked, infamous; gloomy, dismal; threatening, sullen, angry; **b. and blue** badly bruised; **B. and Tans** constabulary used against Irish Sinn Feiners in 1921; **b. art** magic, necromancy; **b. cap** cap worn by an English judge when passing sentence of death; warbler bird with black crown; **b. body** (*phys*) hypothetical perfect radiator or absorber of electromagnetic radiation; **b. box** flight recorder of aircraft; **b. eye** discoloured bruise around eye; **b. flag** pirate flag; **B. Friar** Dominican friar; **b. frost** hard rimeless frost; **b. hole** (*astron*) area of such intense gravity that no light or other radiation can escape it; **b. ice** thin colourless compacted ice on roads; **b. Maria** (*coll*) police van; **b. market** illegal dealing in rationed or scarce commodities or in controlled currencies; **b. marketeer** operator on the black market; **B. Mass** obscene travesty of the Mass; **B. Power** movement seeking political influence for Negroes in white countries, and stressing the achievements of Negro culture; **B. Rod** gentleman usher to the Lord Chamberlain and House of Lords; **in b. and white** written, printed; **in the b.** solvent, not in debt ~ **black** *n* the colour black, the darkest colour; black material, black clothes; (*fig*) mourning; coloured person, Negro; sooty smut or speck ~ **black** *v/t* and *i* blacken; polish with blacking or blacklead; (*coll*) put on a blacklist; boycott, refuse to have anything to do with; (*fig*) sully, defame; **b. out** obliterate; screen (lights) to prevent observation by enemy aircraft; suppress by censorship; jam a radio transmitter; suffer temporary loss of vision or consciousness.

blackamoor [*blak*amoor] *n* (*obs*) Negro.

blackball [*blak*bawl] *n* black wooden ball used to record an adverse vote in a ballot ~ **blackball** *v/t* vote against in this way; exclude, ostracize.

blackbeetle [blak*beet*'l] *n* cockroach.

blackberry [*blak*beRi] *n* the bramble and its fruit ~ **blackberrying** *n* the picking of blackberries.

blackbird [*blak*burd] *n* kind of European thrush.

blackbirding [*blak*burding] *n* commerce in kidnapped Negro slaves.

blackboard [*blak*bawrd] *n* wooden board painted black and used for writing upon with chalk.

blackcock [*blak*-kok] *n* male of the Black Grouse.

blackcurrant [blak-*ku*Rant] *n* (fruit of) shrub bearing edible black berries.

blackdamp [*blak*damp] *n* air containing carbon dioxide which causes suffocation in coal mines.

blacken [*blak*en] *v/t* and *i* make black; (*fig*) sully, defame; grow black, darken.

blackfish [*blak*fish] *n* name given to several kinds of fish, *esp* to salmon which have just spawned; small-toothed whale.

Blackfoot [*blak*foot] *n* (*US*) an Algonquin Indian of the Siksika tribe.

blackguard [*blag*ard] *n* scoundrel, rogue ~ **blackguard** *v/t* abuse with violent language ~ **blackguardism** *n* ~ **blackguardly** *adj* and *adv*.

blackhead [*blak*hed] *n* black pimple.

blacking [*blak*ing] *n* preparation for blackening and polishing boots and shoes.

blackjack [*blak*jak] *n* pirate flag; large drinking vessel; (*min*) sphalerite, blende; (*US*) leather-covered club with a weighted head and a pliant shaft; (*US*) vingt-et-un, pontoon.

blacklead [*blak*led] *n* plumbago, graphite; soft grey-black solid, used for blackening grates, in the making of pencils, as a lubricant *etc* ~ **blacklead** *v/t* polish with blacklead.

blackleg [*blak*leg] *n* workman prepared to work while his mates are on strike; person who lives by his wits, turf swindler ~ **blackleg** *v/t* and *i*.

blackletter [blak*let*er] *n* (*print*) typeface of thick black lines used by early printers, also called Gothic; **b. day** non-festive or inauspicious day.

blacklist [*blak*list] *n* confidential list of fraudulent and undesirable persons; list of delinquents who have incurred suspicion or punishment ~ **blacklist** *v/t* enter the name of a person on a blacklist.

blackmail [*blak*mayl] *n* payment extorted by intimidation to prevent the revelation of indiscretions; (*Scots hist*) protection money; (*fig*) unfair emotional pressure used in getting one's way ~ **blackmail** *v/t* ~ **blackmailer** *n*.

blackout [*blak*owt] *n* temporary amnesia; brief temporary loss of vision or consciousness; total failure of a town's electricity supply at night; sudden complete darkening of the stage in a theatre for dramatic effect; screening of all lights in wartime to prevent observation by enemy aircraft ~ **blackout** *v/t* and *i*.

blackplate [*blak*playt] *n* sheet steel which has no protective metal coating like tinplate.

black-pudding [blak-*pood*ing] *n* sausage made from pig's blood and suet.

blackrot [blak*Rot*] *n* fungus which attacks certain vegetables.

blackrust [blak*Rust*] *n* disease in cereal plants.

Blackshirt [*blak*shurt] *n* fascist.

blacksmith [*blak*smith] *n* worker in iron.

blackstrap [*blak*stRap] *n* cheap kind of port wine; rum and treacle beverage.

blackthorn [*blak*thawrn] *n* thorny white-flowering shrub bearing blue-black fruits called sloes; stick made from wood of this.

blackwater fever [blakwawter-*fee*ver] *n* a tropical disease, a complication of malaria.

bladder [*blad*er] *n* membranous sac in human and animal bodies filled with air or fluid > PDB; windbag for bagpipes; inflated bag in a football or used as a float in swimming; (*fig*) pretentious person, windbag ~ **bladdery** *adj* inflated.

bladder-kelp [*blad*er-kelp] *n* seaweed with airbladders on its fronds.

bladder-wort [*blad*er-wurt] *n* (*bot*) flowering water-plant kept afloat by small bladders.

bladder-wrack [*blad*er-rak] *n* bladder-kelp.

blade [*blayd*] *n* young, narrow leaf of grass or corn; (*bot*) broad part of a leaf; broad flattish part of an oar, paddle *etc*; cutting part of tool or weapon; (*poet*) sword; (*anat*) broad flattish bone; (*coll*) gay fellow, gallant; **in the b.** (*bot*) as yet without the ear ~ **bladed** *adj*.

blaeberry [*blay*beRi/*blee*beRi] bilberry or whortleberry.

blah [*blaa*] *n* (*sl*) pretentious nonsense, claptrap.

blain [*blayn*] *n* inflamed spot, pimple, blister; growth on the root of the tongue in cattle.

blamable [*blay*mab'l] *adj* culpable, deserving censure.

blame [*blaym*] *v/t* find fault with, censure; lay the blame on, accuse; **be to b.** deserve censure ~ **blame** *n* censure, reproof, reprimand; responsibility for mistake or misdeed, culpability ~ **blameful** *adj* culpable.

blameless [*blaym*les] *adj* free from blame, innocent, virtuous ~ **blamelessly** *adv* ~ **blamelessness** *n*.

blameworthy [*blaym*wurTHi] *adj* meriting blame, culpable ~ **blameworthiness** *n*.

blanch [*blaansh*] *v/t* and *i* make white, bleach; turn (plants) white by depriving them of light; (*cookery*) plunge briefly in boiling water; turn pale; **b. over** (*fig*) gloss over, whitewash (shortcomings).

blancmange [blo*monzh*] *n* opaque white jelly made in a mould with milk and cornflour.

bland [*bland*] *adj* ingratiatingly polite, suave; mild, gentle; non irritant; not highly flavoured ~ **blandly** *adv* ~ **blandness** *n*.

blandish [*bland*ish] *v/t* cajole, flatter, coax ~ **blandishment** *n* (*freq pl*) persuasive flattery (with ulterior motive).

blank [*blank*] *adj* unmarked, not written upon; empty; fruitless, abortive; entirely without interest; nonplussed; unrelieved; expressionless; sheer absolute; (*pros*) unrhymed; **b. cheque** signed cheque with amount to be filled in by the payee; (*fig*) complete freedom of action; **b. cartridge** one without a bullet ~ **blank** *n* unmarked space on a page; unsuccessful lottery ticket; piece of timber or metal cut to size and shape; domino without spots on one or both halves;

emptiness, void; (*fig*) vacancy of mind; **draw a b.** be unsuccessful ~ **blank** *v/t* screen from sight.

blanket [*blank*it] *n* thick fabric of woollen material used as a bed-covering *etc*; (*print*) material covering the impression surface on a rotary press; (*fig*) heavy layer of cloud or fog; **a wet b.** a killjoy ~ **blanket** *v/t* cover with a blanket or with fog or snow; toss in a blanket; (*naut*) take the wind of a vessel by passing close to windward of her ~ **blanket** *adj* covering all cases, all-embracing; indiscriminate.

blanketing [*blank*iting] *n* material for blankets; a tossing in a blanket.

blankety [*blank*eti] *adj* (*coll*) euphemistic expression replacing a swear-word, *similarly* **b. blank.**

blankly [*blank*li] *adv* without expression, vacantly; flatly, point-blank.

blanquette [blaan(*g*)*ket*] *n* (*Fr*) name of a highly-seasoned veal stew prepared with white sauce.

blare [*blair*] *n* loud vociferous blast like that of a trumpet ~ **blare** *v/t* and *i* bellow, utter loud noise.

blarney [*blaar*ni] *n* (*coll*) persuasive flattery ~ **blarney** *v/t* and *i* flatter, use persuasive flattery.

blasé [*blaa*zay] *adj* (*Fr*) satiated, bored, exhausted by pleasure.

blasphème [blas*feem*] *v/t* and *i* utter profane words about; curse, swear, utter abuse; revile, abuse ~ **blasphemer** *n*.

blasphemous [*blas*femus] *adj* uttering or containing profanities ~ **blasphemously** *adv*.

blasphemy [*blas*femi] *n* impious talk regarding God and sacred things, profanity; profane abuse, bad language.

blast [*blaast*] *n* strong gust of wind or current of air; sound of a trumpet or horn; ignition of an explosive charge; destructive wave of air produced by an explosion; (*min*) compressed air piped to the coal face; blight which attacks animals or plants; (*fig*) malignant influence; **in (at) full b.** working as hard as possible ~ **blast** *v/t* blow up with explosives, shatter; blight, wither; (*fig*) destroy, ruin, discredit; use profane language; (*expl*) **blast (it)!**

blasted [*blaast*id] *adj* blighted; (*euph*) damned.

blast-furnace [*blaast*-furnis] *n* furnace for the smelting of iron in which heated air is blown in at the bottom > PDS.

blasting [*blaast*ing] *n* breaking of rock by boring a hole and filling it with explosive which is detonated; blighting; (*mus*) blare of brass instruments; (*rad*) distortion produced by overloading the capacity of the set.

blasto- *pref* (*biol*) relating to the germ or bud > PDB.

blastoderm [*blast*Oderm] *n* (*biol*) superficial sheet of cells formed as a result of cleavage of a yolky egg > PDB.

blast-off [*blast*-of] *v/i* (*of rockets*) take off, begin to ascend ~ **blast-off** *n* launching of a rocket.

blastula [*blast*ula] *n* (*biol*) hollow ball of cells formed in the early embryonic development of animals > PDB.

blatant [*blay*tant] *adj* palpably obvious, flagrant; shameless ~ **blatancy** *n* ~ **blatantly** *adv*.

blather see **blether.**

blaze (1) [*blayz*] *n* burst of brilliant flame, fire; area of dazzling light or colour; bright light, brilliancy; **like blazes** vigorously; **to blazes!**

(*expl*) to the devil!; (*exclam*) **what the blazes!** ~ **blaze** *v/t* and *i* burst into flame; burn or shine brilliantly; **b. away** fire rapidly or wildly; (*fig*) work vigorously; **b. up** burst into flame; (*fig*) fire up in anger.

blaze (2) *n* white marking on face of horse or ox; white mark made by chipping the bark of a tree ~ **blaze** *v/t* mark (tree) by chipping bark; indicate, mark (trail, spot).

blaze (3) *v/t* proclaim; spread news far and wide.

blazer [*blay*zer] *n* sports jacket, often made in the colours of some club, school, or college, with a badge on the breast-pocket.

blazing [*blay*zing] *adj* burning fiercely; bright-coloured, dazzling; (*fig*) in a great rage; (*of an animal's scent*) very strong; (*fig*) rash.

blazon [*blay*zon] *n* (*her*) shield or coat of arms or banner with heraldic devices upon it; description or drawing of armorial bearings; (*fig*) enumeration of titles to fame ~ **blazon** *v/t* describe or depict armorial bearings; embellish; **b. abroad** proclaim widely.

blazonry [*blay*zonRi] *n* (*her*) description or representation of a coat of arms; (*fig*) colourful display.

bleach [*bleech*] *v/t* and *i* whiten by exposure to sun or by chemicals ~ **bleach** *n* any chemical used for bleaching ~ **bleacher** *n* person or thing that bleaches ~ **bleachery** *n* place where bleaching is done ~ **bleaching** *n*.

bleak (1) [*bleek*] *n* small river fish.

bleak (2) *adj* bare, windswept, cold; dreary, dismal ~ **bleakly** *adv* ~ **bleakness** *n*.

blear [*bleer*] *adj* watery, misty, obscure ~ **blear** *v/t* and *i* dim, make indistinct, blur; **b. the eyes** deceive, hoodwink ~ **bleary** *adj*.

bleat [*bleet*] *v/t* and *i* make the cry of a sheep; (*fig*) talk nonsense; keep on complaining ~ **bleat** *n* cry of sheep; (*fig*) a feeble whine or complaint.

bleb [*bleb*] *n* small blister; bubble of air.

bled [*bled*] *adj* (*of illustrations*) running to extreme margins.

bleed (*p/t* and *p/part* **bled**) [*bleed*] *v/i* and *t* lose blood; lose sap when cut; ooze forth; let blood from; draw sap from; (*fig*) extort money from; (*bookbinding*) overcut the margins and mutilate the printing; (*mot*) let out air trapped in braking system; **one's heart bleeds** (*fig*) one feels deeply sorry ~ **bleeder** *n* person subject to haemophilia; (*coll*) unpleasant fellow.

bleeding [*bleed*ing] *n* flow of blood; (*bot*) flow of sap from a cut stem; (*surg*) the letting of blood ~ **bleeding** *adj* (*fig*) full of pity; (*sl*) bloody.

bleep [*bleep*] *v/i* emit high-pitched sound or radio signal ~ **bleep** *n* ~ **bleeper** *n*.

blemish [*blem*ish] *v/t* mar, damage, lessen the perfection of; tarnish (reputation) ~ **blemish** *n* fault, flaw, disfigurement.

blench [*blensh*] *v/i* flinch, shy away, quail.

blend (*p/part* **blended, blent**) [*blend*] *v/t* and *i* mix together (*esp* to achieve a certain quality); mix well together; (*of colours*) shade imperceptibly into each other ~ **blend** *n* a mixture of different things or varieties to form a whole.

blende [*blend*] *n* (*min*) natural zinc sulphide.

Blenheim [*blen*im] *n* breed of spaniel; **B. orange pippin** apple of golden colour.

blent see **blend.**

blesbok [*bles*bok] *n* large South African antelope.
bless [*bles*] *v/t* consecrate by prayer or by making
a sacred gesture; worship as holy; adore, feel
gratitude towards; invoke divine favour on;
make happy or fortunate; be favoured with.
blessed, blest [*bles*id, *blest*] *adj* holy, consecrated;
enjoying heavenly bliss, beatified; happy, fortunate; giving joy and happiness; (*euph*) cursed ~
blessed, blest *n* (*collect*) souls in heaven ~
blessedness *n*.
blessing [*bles*ing] *n* prayer, benediction, invocation of divine favour; divine gift or favour;
benefit, advantage, cause for gratitude; (*euph*)
curse (*eg* stepmother's b.); **b. in disguise** something unexpectedly beneficial.
blest see **blessed.**
blether, blather [*bleTH*er, *blaTH*er] *n* foolish talk
~ **blether, blather** *v/i.*
bletherskite [*bleTH*erskit] *n* (*coll*) foolish talk.
blew [*blOO*] *p/t* of **blow.**
blewet, blewit [*blOO*-it] *n* an edible fungus.
blight [*blit*] *n* disease which withers plants;
insect, fungus *etc* causing plant disease; (*fig*)
malignant influence; deterioration of buildings
through neglect, *esp* when due to uncertainty
about future planning; ~ **blight** *v/t* affect with
blight, wither up; (*fig*) shatter (hopes).
blighter [*blit*er] *n* (*sl*) fellow; contemptible cad.
Blighty [*blit*i] *n* (*mil sl*) England; **a B.** one
wound severe enough for a casualty to be sent
to England.
blimey [*blim*i] *interj* (*sl*) exclamation of surprise.
blimp [*blimp*] *n* small non-rigid airship; (*coll*)
pompous ultra-conservative nationalist.
blind (1) [*blind*] *adj* without sight or with impaired
vision; (*fig*) without appreciation or judgement;
acting without proper knowledge or foresight;
dark, obscure, admitting no light; closed at
one end; walled up; (*aer*) navigating solely by
instruments; **b. drunk** (*coll*) completely drunk; **b.
spot** point on retina insensible to light; (*fig*) lack
of discernment; **turn a b. eye** to pretend not to
notice ~ **blind** *v/t* and *i* make blind; (*fig*) deceive; (*refl*) refuse to notice or understand; (*sl*)
drive heedlessly ~ **blind** *n* window shade on
roller; (*fig*) deception, pretext; (*sl*) drinking
spree; **the b. blind** persons; **Venetian b.** window
screen with horizontal slats which may be turned
to admit or exclude light.
blind (2) *v/i* (*sl euph*) use the word 'bloody'; **eff
and b.** (*sl*) swear coarsely.
blind-alley [*blind-ali*] *n* road closed at one end;
(*fig*) job with no prospects ~ **blind-alley** *adj*
with no prospects of promotion.
blindfold [*blind*fOld] *v/t* cover the eyes with a
bandage ~ **blindfold** *adj* and *adv* with eyes
bandaged; (*fig*) without forethought.
blinding [*blind*ing] *adj* dazzling.
blindly [*blind*li] *adv* without seeing; (*fig*) recklessly, without deliberation; in ignorance.
blind-man's-buff [*blind-manz-buf*] *n* game in
which a blindfolded player tries to catch and
identify one of those not blindfolded.
blindness [*blind*nes] *n* condition of being blind;
(*fig*) ignorance; folly.
blind-side [*blind-sid*] *n* unguarded side; weak spot.
blindworm [*blind*wurm] *n* the slow-worm.
blink [*blink*] *v/t* and *i* move the eyelids quickly up

and down, wink; glance; shine fitfully, twinkle;
ignore, close eyes to; send (tears) away by blinking ~ **blink** *n* temporary gleam of light; glance,
glimpse, twinkle; **on the b.** (*elect*) functioning
irregularly; about to fail.
blinker [*blink*er] *n* intermittently flashing light;
(*pl*) leather eye-shields to prevent a horse seeing
sideways.
blinkered [*blink*erd] *adj* (*fig*) unaware of new
ideas, narrow-minded; insensitive to surroundings or circumstances.
blinking [*blink*ing] *adj* (*expl*) confounded.
blip [*blip*] *n* bleep, short high-pitched sound;
bloop; image on radar screen.
bliss [*blis*] *n* supreme happiness, perfect felicity,
perfect joy of heaven; source of delight ~ **blissful** *adj* ~ **blissfully** *adv.*
blister [*blist*er] *n* small swelling or vesicle on the
skin filled with serum; similar swelling on a
metal or painted surface; (*med*) application to
raise a blister; (*coll*) unpleasant fellow ~ **blister**
v/t and *i* raise a blister; come out in blisters; (*fig*)
wither with scorn or bitter sarcasm.
blithe [*blITH*] *adj* (*usu poet*) gay, lively, joyful,
happy ~ **blithesome** *adj* ~ **blithely** *adv.*
blithering [*blithe*Ring] *adj* (*coll cont*) drivelling;
(*as an intensive*) absolute, utter; contemptible.
blitz [*blits*] *n* (*Germ*) 'lightning-war'; sudden
attack, *esp* from the air; (*coll*) energetic burst of
work; **have a b. on** (*coll*) work energetically at
clearing up or getting rid of ~ **blitz** *v/t* ~
blitzed *adj.*
blizzard [*bliz*ard] *n* storm of powdery snow driven
along by a high wind > PDG.
bloat (1) [*blOt*] *v/t* and *i* cure (herrings) by salting
and smoking over an oak fire.
bloat (2) *v/t* and *i* blow out, inflate.
bloated [*blOt*id] *adj* swollen with gluttony or with
pride; overgrown; pampered.
bloater [*blOt*er] *n* smoked and salted herring.
blob [*blob*] *n* small drop of liquid, sticky stuff, or
paint; (*coll cricket*) score of no runs.
bloc [*blok*] *n* combination of political parties
formed to support or oppose a government; any
combination formed to foster a particular interest.
block [*blok*] *n* tree-stump, log of wood, lump
of rock; wooden chopping bench; piece of wood
on which those condemned to be beheaded laid
their necks; frame holding the pulley(s) of lifting
tackle; letter-press printing plate; mould for
shaping hats; an obstruction; (*psych*) temporary
inability to think creatively or clearly; masonry
laid in mortar; hardwood floor block; (*pl*) child's
building bricks; large quantity (of seats, shares
etc); row of buildings not detached; large building
containing several flats or offices; writing pad;
(*cricket*) mark made on crease directly in front of
wicket; (*fig*) dull stupid person; **b. letters** plain
capital letters; **b. plan** small scale plan showing
the broad outlines of existing buildings or a
project; **b. grant** subsidy which is fixed and non-
recurrent; **b. section** length of track on a railway
between signals; **b. tin** commercially pure tin ~
block *v/t* obstruct, shut up or in, blockade;
(*cricket*) stop (ball with bat); shape on a block;
cut out into blocks; prevent or attempt to prevent; restrict use or expenditure of (currency or

other asset); **b. out** sketch out roughly (scheme, plan); obstruct (view).

blockade [blo*kayd*] *n* complete or partial closure of a harbour or place by hostile forces to prevent any contact with the outside world; (*fig*) obstruction; **raise the b.** end or relieve a blockade; **run the b.** evade the blockading forces; **paper b.** blockade declared to exist but not made effective ~ **blockade** *v/t*.

blockage [blo*kij*] *n* state of being obstructed or stopped up; mass of material preventing passage through a tube, pipe, canal *etc*; obstruction.

blockbuster [blo*kbuster*] *n* (*coll*) large type of bomb capable of destroying a block of buildings; something massive and powerful.

blockhead [blo*khed*] *n* (*cont*) stupid person.

blockhouse [blo*khows*] *n* (*mil*) small concrete shelter used as observation point; house built of squared logs.

blockish [blo*kish*] *adj* dull, stupid, obstinate.

bloke [blO*k*] *n* (*coll*) chap, fellow.

blonde, blond [blond] *n* and *adj* (person, *usu* woman) having fair hair and complexion; **dumb b.** (*coll*) pretty but very stupid fair-haired girl.

blood [blud] *n* red fluid circulating in the veins or arteries; bloodshed, manslaughter, death; guilt of murder; (*fig*) temper, passion, mettle; kinship, lineage; noble birth, good family; (*sl*) lurid highly sensational story; (*coll*) man about town, dandy; **bad b.** ill feeling; **blue b.** noble birth; **first b.** initial advantage; **in cold b.** deliberately; **b. and iron** ruthless use of force; **flesh and b.** near relatives; human nature; **b. bank** place where blood is kept ready for transfusion; **b. count** process of finding the number of corpuscles in a specified quantity of blood; **b. feud** lasting and deadly enmity between families; **b. orange** orange having red juice; **b. pressure** (*coll*) hypertension; **b. sports** hunting and killing of animals; **one's b. is up** one's anger is aroused; **make one's b. boil** arouse one's indignation ~ **blood** *v/t* draw blood, bleed; give a hound its first smell or taste of blood; smear (novice at hunting) with blood; (*fig*) initiate.

bloodbath [blu*dbaath*] *n* a massacre, purge.

blood-brother [blud-BRU*THer*] *n* one who swears to treat another as his brother, and confirms this by mingling their bloods.

bloodcurdling [blu*dkurdling*] *adj* horrifying.

blood-donor [blud-dO*ner*] *n* person who gives his blood for transfusion.

blooded [blu*did*] *adj* ceremonially smeared with blood; given the first taste of blood; (*of animals*) of pure or superior breed or stock.

blood-group [blud-grOo*p*] *n* (*med*) one of the four types of blood; classification of people according to these types > PDB.

blood-guilty [blud-gi*lti*] *adj* responsible for bloodshed or murder ~ **blood-guiltiness** *n*.

blood-heat [blud-hee*t*] *n* normal temperature of human blood, 98·4° F (37° C).

bloodhound [blu*dhownd*] *n* large dog used for tracking; (*fig*) sleuth, detective.

bloodily [blu*dili*] *adv* in a bloody way.

bloodiness [blu*dinis*] *n* state or quality of being bloody.

bloodless [blu*dles*] *adj* without blood; pallid; without involving bloodshed ~ **bloodlessly** *adv*.

bloodletting [blu*dleting*] *n* (*surg*) phlebotomy, drawing off blood from a vein; bloodshed.

bloodlust [blu*dlust*] *n* desire for bloodshed.

blood-money [blud-mu*ni*] *n* compensation paid to next of kin for slaughter of a relative; reward for information leading to someone's death.

blood-poisoning [blud-po*izoning*] *n* (*med*) condition in which the blood is infected by septic matter.

blood-pudding [blud-po*oding*] *n* black pudding.

blood-red [blud-Red] *adj* of the colour of blood.

blood-relation [blud-Ri*layshon*] *n* person related by birth.

bloodshed [blu*dshed*] *n* the spilling of blood by violent attack, slaughter.

bloodshot [blu*dshot*] *adj* tinged with blood.

bloodsports [blu*dspawrts*] *n* (*pl*) sports such as hunting, involving bloodshed.

bloodstain [blu*dstayn*] *n* mark or discoloration made by blood ~ **bloodstained** *adj* smeared or marked with blood; (*fig*) guilty of murder.

bloodstock [blu*dstok*] *n* (*of animals*) thoroughbred stock.

bloodstone [blu*dstOn*] *n* a deep-green precious stone flecked with red; a variety of chalcedony.

bloodstream [blu*dstReem*] *n* blood circulating in a body.

blood-sucker [blud-su*ker*] *n* the leech; (*fig*) person who extorts money ~ **blood-sucking** *n* and *adj*.

bloodthirsty [blu*dthursti*] *adj* eager to shed blood ~ **bloodthirstiness** *n*.

blood-transfusion [blud-transfewz*hon*] *n* transference of blood from one person to another.

blood-vessel [blud-ve*sel*] *n* vein or artery or capillary through which the blood circulates.

bloodworm [blu*dwurm*] *n* small bright-red worm used as bait by anglers; (*ent*) blood-coloured larva of kind of crane-fly.

bloodwort [blu*dwurt*] *n* (*bot*) name of various plants having red roots or red leaves.

bloody [blu*di*] *adj* of the nature or colour of blood; stained with blood; bloodthirsty; (*sl*) bad, unpleasant; *used as intensive or expletive* ~ **bloody** *v/t* make bloody.

bloody mary [bludi-mai*rRi*] *n* cocktail of vodka, tomato juice, seasoning, lemon juice *etc*.

bloody-minded [bludi-mI*ndid*] *adj* cruel; (*sl*) unhelpful, obstructive ~ **bloody-mindedness** *n*.

bloom (1) [blOo*m*] *n* blossom of a flowering plant; prime of life, highest development, perfection; rosy glow of health in the cheeks, delicate beauty; fine powdery deposit on some freshly-picked fruits; thin film which forms on old glossy paint, varnish coatings *etc* ~ **bloom** *v/i* flower; (*fig*) flourish.

bloom (2) *n* a half-finished, rolled or forged piece of steel or wrought iron.

bloomer [blOo*mer*] *n* (*coll*) a mistake, blunder.

bloomers [blOo*merz*] *n* women's long baggy knickers; (*orig*) loose, gathered trousers for women.

blooming [blOo*ming*] *n* condition of being in bloom; (*eng*) process of reducing cast iron into malleable iron ~ **blooming** *adj* in flower, in blossom; in radiant health; (*fig*) flourishing; (*coll*) confounded, wretched, bloody.

bloop [blOo*p*] *n* brief sound on tape-recording or sound-track where words have been cut out.

blossom [blo*som*] *n* flower *esp* that preceding fruit;

(*collect*) mass of flowers on a fruit tree ~ **blossom** *v/i* bloom; **b. forth, out** (*fig*) achieve success or prominence unexpectedly.

blot [*blot*] *n* ink spot, stain; (*fig*) disgrace, fault ~ **blot** (*p/t* and *p/part* **blotted**) *v/t* make ink spots on paper; dry (ink) with blotting paper; smudge (writing); (*fig*) sully; **b. out** obscure, obliterate.

blotch [*bloch*] *n* spot or discoloured mark on the skin; dab of colour, ink *etc* ~ **blotch** *v/t* mar with blotches, blur ~ **blotchy** *adj* marked with blotches.

blotter [*bloter*] *n* anything used to dry ink-marks; a wad of blotting-paper; an implement with blotting-paper on the bottom.

blotting-paper [*bloting-payper*] *n* absorbent paper used for drying up ink.

blotto [*blotO*] *adj* (*sl*) drunk.

blouse [*blowz*] *n* light upper outer garment.

blow (1) (*p/t* **blew**, *p/part* **blown**) [*blO*] *v/i* and *t* produce gust of wind or current of air; breathe hard, pant; (*of whale*) spout out water; (*of instrument*) make a sound; (*of electric fuse*) melt and break the circuit; emit current of air from the lungs; drive air through, into, or upon an object; drive, or carry by a current of air; cause to breathe heavily; (*of a fly*) deposit eggs; (*of nose*) clear; (*coll*) reveal (secrets); (*coll*) squander; **b. the gaff** let out secrets; **b. hot and cold** approve and disapprove alternately; **b. in** appear unexpectedly; **b. the lid off** expose a state of affairs; **b. over** pass off; **b. off steam** (*coll*) give vent to feelings; **b. one's top** (*coll*) lose one's temper violently; **b. one's mind** (*coll*) induce hallucinations by drugs, send into ecstasy; **b. one's own trumpet** boast; **b. up** inflate; explode; destroy with explosives; (*coll*) enlarge a picture; **b. it!** (*expl*) confound it!; **be blowed** (*sl*) be damned ~ **blow** *n* blast of wind; forcible expulsion of breath through the nose or mouth; breath of fresh air; egg deposited by a fly; (*min*) sudden rush of gas into a mine.

blow (2) *n* violent stroke from a fist, weapon *etc*; (*fig*) sudden misfortune, severe shock or setback; (*pl*) hostilities; **at one b.** all at once; **come to blows** begin to fight.

blow (3) *v/i* burst into flower, be in bloom.

blowcock [*blOkok*] *n* tap on a boiler for blowing off steam.

blower [*blO-er*] *n* metal plate used to create a current of air in a grate; blast-pipe in a furnace; a whale; (*mech coll*) supercharger; (*min*) a crack which discharges firedamp; an auxiliary fan or ventilation pipe to get fresh air into a dead end; (*sl*) telephone; loudspeaker system.

blowfly [*blOfli*] *n* (*pop*) fly which deposits its eggs in dead flesh.

blow-hole [*blO-hOl*] *n* whale's nostril; vent for escape of steam, foul air, or gas; (*pl*) gas-filled cavities in solid metals; hole in the ice.

blowlamp [*blOlamp*] *n* paraffin lamp which gives off a powerful flame for melting solder or burning off paint.

blow-out [*blO-owt*] *n* (*coll*) hearty meal; tyreburst; (*elect*) melting of a fuse.

blowpipe [*blOpIp*] *n* tube used by savage tribes for propelling poisoned darts; tube for blowing through to increase heat of a flame; tube used for blowing molten glass into shape.

blow-up [*blO-up*] *n* (*phot coll*) enlargement of a picture; explosion; (*coll*) quarrel, row.

blowzy [*blowzi*] *adj* untidy, sluttish, slatternly.

blub (*pres/part* **blubbing**, *p/t* **blubbed**) [*blub*] *v/i* (*coll*) shed tears.

blubber (1) [*bluber*] *n* whale-fat ~ **blubbery** *adj*.

blubber (2) *adj* (*of lips*) swollen.

blubber (3) *v/i* and *t* cry, weep; utter sobbingly; wet and distort the face with copious weeping.

bluchers [*blOOcherz*] *n* (*pl*) short boots.

bludgeon [*blujon*] *n* stick with heavy head used as weapon ~ **bludgeon** *v/t* beat with bludgeon; (*fig*) bully, persuade by constant pressure.

blue [*blOO*] *n* a primary colour, the hue of the unclouded sky; pigment of this colour; preparation used in washing clothes; player who has represented his university in a sporting contest between Oxford and Cambridge, also the distinction or colours awarded for this; (*fig*) the sky, the sea ~ **blue** *adj* blue in colour; (*fig*) miserable; (*coll*) Tory; (*sl*) obscene; **b. baby** infant suffering from congenital cyanosis; **b. chip** sound equity share; **b. funk** (*coll*) extreme fear; **once in a b. moon** very rarely; **B. Peter** blue flag with white square centre hoisted on ship before sailing; **b. riband** (*naut*) the open ocean; distinction for the fastest Atlantic crossing; (*fig*) highest honour; **b. ribbon** Order of the Garter; any high distinction; **true b. faithful**, loyal ~ **blue** *v/t* treat clothes with blue; (*coll*) squander.

bluebeard [*blOObeerd*] *n* folktale villain who murdered his wives; man who has had many wives.

bluebell [*blOObel*] *n* the wild hyacinth; (*Scots and northern dial*) the harebell.

bluebird [*blOOburd*] *n* (*US*) small bird with sky-blue back and reddish throat; (*fig*) bringer of happiness.

blue-bonnet [*blOO-bonit*] *n* (*Scots*) round blue woollen flat cap; blue-bonneted soldier.

blue-book [*blOO-book*] *n* report or document of Parliament or of the Privy Council published in a blue paper cover.

bluebottle [*blOObot'l*] *n* blow-fly, large bluish fly; (*coll*) policeman; (*bot*) blue cornflower.

bluecap [*blOOkap*] *n* (*orni*) blue titmouse; bluebonnet; (*dial*) salmon in first year of growth.

bluecoat boy [*blOOkOt-boi*] *n* schoolboy of Christ's Hospital who wears a long-skirted coat.

blue-collar [*blOO-kolar*] *adj* doing manual or industrial work.

blue-eyed [*blOO-Id*] *adj* (*sl*) favourite, darling.

bluegrass [*blOOgRaas*] *n* type of American folk music.

bluegum [*blOOgum*] *n* eucalyptus tree.

blueing [*blOO-ing*] *n* increasing the apparent whiteness of clothes or paint by adding a trace of blue; (*eng*) imparting a blue oxide film to polished steel; extravagant spending of money.

bluejacket [*blOOjakit*] *n* naval seaman.

blue-pencil [*blOO-pensil*] *v/t* score through, delete; censor ~ **blue-pencilled** *adj*.

blueprint [*blOOpRint*] *n* technical drawing or diagram made with white lines on blue paper > PDS; (*fig*) detailed plan.

blue-rinsed [*blOO-rinst*] *adj* having had one's grey hair dyed blue.

blues [*blOOz*] *n* (*pl*) sad, haunting kind of Negro

music, dance of this kind; (*fig*) fit of despondency;
The B. Royal Horse Guards.
bluestocking [*blOO*stoking] *n* learned, pedantic
woman.
bluey [*blOO*-i] *adj* and *adv* more or less blue.
bluff (1) [*bluf*] *adj* broad and steep; (*fig*) good-
naturedly blunt and frank ~ **bluff** *n* headland
formed by steep slopes bordering a river or lake.
bluff (2) *v/t* and *i* disguise one's true intentions;
(*poker*) deceive opponent as to the strength of
one's hand ~ **bluff** *n* calculated deception to
conceal motives or the true state of affairs; **call
one's b.** (*poker*) expose player who has been
overcalling his hand; (*fig*) challenge a person to
make good his statements.
bluffer [*bluf*er] *n* person who hoodwinks others.
bluffly [*bluf*li] *adv* bluntly ~ **bluffness** *n* steepness; well-meant bluntness.
bluish [*blOO*ish] *adj* tinged with blue.
blunder [*blund*er] *v/t* and *i* stumble over or
against; make a stupidly careless mistake; mismanage (affairs); **b. upon** come upon by chance
~ **blunder** *n* mistake, error; ill-judged speech
or action ~ **blunderer** *n* stupid, tactless person.
blunderbuss [*blund*erbus] *n* (*hist*) short large-bore
gun capable of firing many slugs at short range;
clumsy person.
blundering [*blund*eRing] *adj* clumsy, tactless.
blunt [*blunt*] *adj* lacking point or sharpness of
edge; (*of mind*) insensitive, dull; (*of speech*) curt,
abrupt, outspoken ~ **blunt** *n* thick short needle
with strong point ~ **blunt** *v/t* lessen the sharpness
of, dull; (*fig*) (*of feelings, sensibilities*) make less
sensitive or acute ~ **bluntly** *adv* outspokenly,
curtly, without sparing feelings ~ **bluntness** *n.*
blur [*blur*] *n* smear, blot, or blemish; vague outline
or appearance ~ **blur** (*pres/part* **blurring**; *p/t*
and *p/part* **blurred**) *v/t* and *i* smear, smudge,
make vague or indistinct.
blurb [*blurb*] *n* publisher's laudatory description
of a book; any advertisement with lavish praise.
blurt [*blurt*] *v/t* utter something suddenly and without thought; **b. out** reveal (secrets).
blush [*blush*] *v/i* turn red in the face from some
emotion; (*fig*) be ashamed ~ **blush** *n* reddening
of face caused by some emotion; pink or rosy
colour; glow of light or colour; **at the first b.** at
the first glance.
blushing [*blush*ing] *adj* covered with blushes;
(*fig*) modest ~ **blushing** *n* becoming red in the
face; milky opalescence in a lacquer ~ **blushing-
ly** *adv.*
bluster [*blust*er] *v/i* (*of winds and waves*) blow or
storm violently; (*fig*) talk in menacing fashion,
hector ~ **bluster** *n* boisterous noise; (*fig*) empty
boasts or menaces ~ **blusterer** *n* truculent person ~ **blustering** *adj* ~ **blustery** *adj* windy.
bo [*bO*] *exclam* (*uttered to surprise or startle*); **can't
say b. to a goose** be very timid.
boa [*bO*-a] *n* kind of large South American non-
poisonous snake which coils itself round its prey;
woman's fur or feather wrap worn round the
throat.
boa-constrictor [bO-a-kon*stRik*ter] *n* kind of boa
found in Brazil; (*pop*) any large snake which
crushes its victims to death.
Boanerges [bO-a*nur*jeez] *n* fiery preacher or orator with a powerful voice.

boar [*bawr*] *n* male pig not castrated; its flesh.
board (1) [*bawrd*] *n* long thin rectangular plank of
wood (over 4″ wide and under 2″ thick); panel of
wood or other material for the display of notices
or for playing games on; blackboard; thick stiff
compressed paper, boxboard; (*bookbinding*)
strong pasteboard used as a book-cover; (*pl*) the
stage; **across the b.** including all categories,
making no exceptions ~ **board** *v/t* provide or
cover with boards.
board (2) *n* provision of daily meals for a fixed
price; table prepared for a meal; group of officials
with functions of administration and management; **above b.** openly, fairly; **sweep the b.**
win everything in a contest ~ **board** *v/t* and *i*
provide with, or be supplied with, daily meals.
board (3) *n* (*naut*) the side of a ship; **on b.** aboard
ship; **go by the b.** (*of masts*) be swept away; (*fig*)
fail utterly; be neglected ~ **board** *v/t* go on
board, come alongside to attack; enter a public
vehicle; (*fig*) accost; (*naut*) tack.
boarder [*bawrd*er] *n* person who is provided with
meals and lodging in someone's house in return
for fixed regular payment, *esp* pupil who eats and
sleeps at school during term; one who boards an
enemy ship.
boarding [*bawrd*ing] *n* (*carp*) boards closely laid
over rafters or studs to act as a surface for fixing
tiles, slates, insulation *etc.*
boarding-house [*bawrd*ing-hows] *n* house catering
for boarders.
boarding-out [*bawrd*ing-owt] *n* taking of regular
meals away from home; placing of neglected
children in families where they are cared for.
boarding-school [*bawrd*ing-skOOl] *n* school at
which pupils lodge and have meals during
term.
boardroom [*bawrd*Room] *n* room where a board
of officials or administrators meets.
Board-school [*bawrd*-skOOl] *n* (*hist*) school
managed by one of the school boards set up by
the Elementary Education Act of 1870.
board-wages [bawrd-*way*jiz] *n* (*pl*) money allowed
to servants in lieu of food.
boart see **bort.**
boast [*bOst*] *n* proud ostentatious assertion; self-
glorification; thing one is proud of ~ **boast** *v/t*
and *i* praise oneself, brag; be proud possessor of.
boaster [*bOst*er] *n* (*bui*) mason's chisel struck by a
mallet in dressing a stone surface ~ **boasting** *n*
surfacing of a stone by strokes of a boaster.
boastful [*bOst*fool] *adj* given to boasting, full
of boasts ~ **boastfully** *adv* ~ **boastfulness** *n.*
boasting [*bOst*ing] *n* the making of boasts ~
boasting *adj* full of boasts ~ **boastingly** *adv.*
boat [*bOt*] *n* small deckless rowing or sailing-
vessel; fishing-vessel; small steamer; (*occ*) ocean
liner; dish shaped like a boat; **be in the same b.**
share the same predicament; **burn one's boats**
commit oneself irretrievably to a course of action
~ **boat** *v/i* go in a boat (for pleasure).
boatbill [*bOt*bil] *n* bird of the heron family native
to South America.
boat-drill [*bOt*-dRil] *n* practice by crew and passengers on how to launch and man the lifeboats.
boater [*bOt*er] *n* (*coll*) hard straw hat with a low
crown once the popular wear in summer.

boatfly [bOtflI] n water-insect which swims on its back using its legs as paddles; water-bug.

boatful [bOtfool] n number of persons a boat can hold.

boathook [bOthook] n long stave with a hook at one end for fending off or holding a boat alongside.

boathouse [bOthows] n shed near water used for housing boats.

boating [bOting] n rowing or sailing boats.

boatman [bOtman] n one who hires out or sails boats.

boat-race [bOt-Rays] n race between rowing-boats, esp the annual contest between the Oxford and Cambridge crews rowed on the Thames.

boatswain [bOs'n] n (naut) officer responsible for the supervision and maintenance of a ship's boats, sails, rigging etc.

boat-train [bOt-tRayn] n railway train scheduled to connect with a ship's arrival or departure.

bob (1) [bob] n docked tail of horse; bunch of hair, bobbed hair, short curl; weight on a pendulum or on a plumb-line; bunch or knot of ribbons; knob-like object; bunch of lob-worms used for eel-bait; (poet) short line ending a stanza or followed by group of longer lines called the wheel; (dial) cluster ~ **bob** (pres/part **bobbing**, p/t and p/part **bobbed**) v/t and i dock (horse's tail); cut (woman's hair) short and level above the shoulders; fish (for eels) using a bob.

bob (2) (pres/part **bobbing**, p/t and p/part **bobbed**) v/i move jerkily up and down; dance; curtsy ~ **bob** n a jerky motion; curtsy; (Scots) a dance.

bob (3) (pres/part **bobbing**, p/t and p/part **bobbed**) v/t tap, strike lightly; cause to tap (against etc) ~ **bob** n light blow, tap.

bob (4) n (bell-ringing) name given to certain permutations or 'changes' in ringing bells in a continuously changing order.

bob (5) n (sl) shilling; (decimal coinage) fivepenny piece.

bob (6) n one of the runners on which a sleigh or bobsled is mounted; (abbr) bobsleigh.

bobbed [bobd] adj (of women's hair) cut short.

bobbery [bobeRi] n rumpus, noisy disturbance ~ **bobbery** adj noisy, excitable; **b. pack** heterogeneous pack of dogs for hunting.

bobbin [bobin] n small cylinder of wood or other material round which thread, yarn, or wire is wound; spool, reel; kind of fine cord or braid; knob of wood attached to a string for raising a door-latch.

bobbinet [bobinet] n machine-made lace.

bobbish [bobish] adj (coll and dial) lively, in fine fettle ~ **bobbishly** adv.

bobble [bob'l] n small woolly ball.

bobby [bobi] n (coll) policeman.

bobby-dazzler [bobi-dazler] n (coll) something which is flashy and ostentatious in appearance.

bobby-pin [bobi-pin] n type of hairpin.

bobbysoxer [bobisokser] n (coll) adolescent girl; teenager.

bobcat [bobkat] n (US) lynx or wildcat.

bobolink [bobOlink] n North American song-bird; the reedbird.

bobsled, bobsleigh [bobsled, bobslay] n a sled or sleigh mounted on runners for tobogganing.

bobstay [bobstay] n (naut) rope to the bowsprit to counteract the upward strain of the fore stays.

bobtail [bobtayl] n docked tail; horse or dog with docked tail; **rag-tag and b.** mob, rabble ~ **bobtail** adj ~ **bobtailed** adj; **b. coat** (US) coat shorter than usual.

bob-white [bob-wIt] n North American quail.

bob-wig [bob-wig] n wig with short curls.

bocasin [bokasin] n a fine buckram.

boche [bosh] n and adj (sl pej) (a) German.

bock [bok] n strong dark German beer.

bocking [boking] n coarse woollen baize material.

bod [bod] n (coll) person, fellow.

bode [bOd] v/t and i (of things) indicate, promise, portend (well or ill).

bodega [bodeega] n wine-shop.

bodice [bodis] n tight-fitting upper part of women's dress to waist; (obs) type of vest.

bodied [bodid] adj having a body, embodied.

bodiless [bodiles] adj having no body, unsubstantial; lacking the body or trunk.

bodily [bodili] adv in the flesh, in person; (fig) all together, as a whole ~ **bodily** adj of or relating to the body, physical.

bodkin [bodkin] n blunt needle with large eye for threading tape or piercing holes; (hist) ornate stiletto-like pin once worn by ladies in their hair; (coll) person squeezed between two others.

body [bodi] n physical structure or frame of living creatures; trunk without head and limbs; corpse; main part; part of a vehicle which accommodates passengers or load; bodice; a material object; collection of people with a common purpose; group of soldiers; legally constituted group of officials; collection (of information, laws); (of materials etc) quality, strength, consistency, viscosity; (coll) a person, human being; (theol) the sacramental bread; **b. politic** the State; **heavenly bodies** sun, moon, and planets ~ **body** v/t provide with a body, embody; **b. forth** typify.

bodyblow [bodIblO] n heavy blow to the body in boxing; (fig) serious setback or disappointment.

body-builder [bodi-bilder] n one who builds the bodies of vehicles; a nourishing food; apparatus for developing muscles by exercise; person who develops the muscles of his body.

body-colour [bodi-kuler] n (painting) pigment that has consistency and hiding power in contrast to a transparent wash or tint; a colour mixed with white and so rendered opaque.

bodyguard [bodigaard] n escort to ensure a person's safety.

bodyline [bodilIn] n (cricket) (of bowling) aimed at the batsman's person to intimidate him.

body-servant [bodi-survant] n valet.

body-snatcher [bodi-snacher] n (hist) one who disinterred and sold corpses for dissection.

body-stocking [bodi-stoking] n very close-fitting garment, usu flesh-coloured, worn as underclothing or by dancers etc.

bodywork [bodiwerk] n material and construction of vehicle bodies.

Boer [bO-er] n inhabitant of South Africa of Dutch descent.

boffin [bofin] n (sl) scientist in the armed forces engaged in research; any scientist.

Bofors [bOferz] n (mil) quick-firing anti-aircraft gun.

bog [*bog*] *n* area of marshy, spongy ground; morass > PDG; (*vulg*) latrine ~ **bog** (*pres/part* **bogging,** *p/t* and *p/part* **bogged**) *v/t* and *i* sink or be trapped in a bog.

bogey (1) [*bOg*i] *n* (*golf*) score for a hole or for the course which a good player should achieve.

bogey (2), **bogy, bogie** (*pl* **bogeys, bogies**) *n* goblin, frightening spectre, the devil; (*fig*) bugbear, imaginary terror; (*coll*) piece of dried snot.

bogey (3) see **bogie** (2).

boggle [*bog*'l] *v/i* shrink from, be alarmed (at); hesitate, raise scruples about; bungle ~ **boggler** *n* person who is hesitant, a stickler.

boggy [*bog*i] *adj* marshy, swampy.

bogie (1) see **bogey** (2).

bogie (2), **bogy, bogey** [*bOg*i] *n* undercarriage with two or more pairs of wheels pivoted beneath the front of a railway-engine or beneath the ends of a railway-carriage; railway platelayers' trolly.

bogle [*bOg*'l] *n* spectre, goblin, bogey; bugbear; scarecrow.

bog-oak [*bog*-Ok] *n* black oak wood as preserved in peat.

bogspavin [*bog*spavin] *n* tumour on the inside of the hock of a horse.

bogtrotter [*bog*tRoter] *n* (*cont*) Irishman.

bogus [*bOg*us] *adj* sham, not genuine, counterfeit.

bogy see **bogey** (2), **bogie** (2).

bohea [*bOhee*] *n* variety of black China tea.

Bohemian [*bOheem*i-an] *adj* gipsy; happy-go-lucky artist; person leading unconventional life ~ **Bohemian** *adj*.

boil (1) [*boil*] *n* inflamed swelling on the skin full of pus.

boil (2) *v/i* and *t* bubble up when heated, be agitated; reach boiling point; be cooked by boiling; (*fig*) be inflamed with rage; (*coll*) feel hot; heat to boiling-point; cook (eggs *etc*) or wash (clothes) by boiling in water; **b. down** reduce by boiling; (*fig*) shorten ~ **boil** *n* boiling-point.

boiled [*boild*] *adj* cooked by boiling; boiling hot; **b. shirt** (*coll*) dress shirt with starched front.

boiler [*boil*er] *n* container in which liquid is boiled; (*eng*) plant for raising steam > PDE; copper in which clothes are boiled; water tank heated by kitchen fire; fowl more suitable for boiling than roasting; person who boils.

boilersuit [*boil*ersewt] *n* denim (or similar) one-piece suit for rough work, overalls.

boiling [*boil*ing] *n* process of making liquids boil or of cooking by boiling; what is boiled in one process; **the whole b.** (*coll*) the whole lot, everyone ~ **boiling** *adj* bubbling under the influence of heat; (*fig*) intensely (hot); emotionally agitated.

boiling-point [*boil*ing-point] *n* temperature at which a liquid is freely converted into vapour > PDS; (*fig*) high pitch of excitement.

boisterous [*boiste*Rus] *adj* rough, violent; noisily exuberant ~ **boisterously** *adv*.

boko [*bOk*O] *n* (*sl*) nose.

bolas [*bOl*as] *n* (*pl*) South American missile of two or more balls tied by a length of cord.

bold [*bOld*] *adj* brave, daring; displaying vigour or originality; visibly striking; forward, impudent, presumptuous; (*of coast-line*) rising sheer; **be (make) so b. as to** presume to.

bold-face [*bOld*-fays] *n* (*typ*) letters made with thick bold strokes ~ **bold-faced** *adj* impudent, (*typ*) having thick bold strokes.

boldly [*bOld*li] *adv* in a bold way.

boldness [*bOld*nis] *n* quality of being bold.

bole (1) [*bOl*] *n* tree trunk; object of cylindrical shape.

bole (2) *n* kinds of fine clay, generally of reddish colour; pigment material laid as a ground for gold leaf.

bolero [*bolair*RO] *n* (*Sp*) lively Spanish dance > PDM; music for this; woman's short jacket with or without sleeves

bolide [*bOl*id] *n* large meteor; fireball.

bolivar [*bolee*vaar] *n* silver coin of Venezuela.

boll (1) [*bOl*] *n* pod of flax or cotton.

boll (2) *n* measure of capacity or weight.

bollard [*bol*aard] *n* cast iron post on a quay to which vessels are moored; short post in a roadway to protect a kerb, wall or street island, or to indicate a traffic diversion.

bollocks [*bol*oks] *n* (*pl, vulg*) testicles; nonsense.

bolometer [*bol*omiter] *n* sensitive instrument for measuring weak heat radiations; a device for measuring current or power > PDEl.

boloney [*bolOn*i] *n* (*US sl*) nonsense, bosh.

Bolshevik [*bol*shivik] *n* member of the radical faction of the Russian Social-Democratic party which seized power in Russia in 1917; (*pop*) a Communist or extreme radical; person with revolutionary or disruptive ideas ~ **Bolshevik** *adj*.

Bolshevism [*bol*shivizm] *n* Communism > PDPol.

Bolshevist [*bol*shivist] *n* and *adj* Bolshevik.

Bolshie, bolshy [*bol*shi] *n* and *adj* (*coll*) Bolshevik; person with disruptive ideas or a rebellious attitude; person difficult to control.

bolster [*bOl*ster] *n* long under-pillow on a bed; (*bui*) supporting or strengthening part; bricklayer's chisel ~ **bolster** *v/t* support; **b. up** prop up, countenance ~ **bolstering** *n* support.

bolt (1) [*bOlt*] *n* sliding rod fitting into a staple and fastening a door; sliding part of a lock; cylindrical bar which is screwed at one end for a nut, and forged with a square or hexagonal head at the other; thunderbolt, lightning flash with noise of thunder; roll of fabric; bundle of osiers; (*hist*) arrow of crossbow; sliding bar which locks the breech of a rifle; sudden start or run, dash; **b. from the blue** complete surprise; **shoot one's b.** make a last attempt.

bolt (2) *v/i* and *t* dash away out of control, run away, dart off; (*of plants*) grow too many leaves; gulp down without chewing; fasten with a bolt.

bolt (3), **boult** *v/t* sift; (*fig*) inquire into.

bolt (4) *adv* **b. upright** erect in posture.

bolthead [*bOlt*hed] *n* (*chem*) kind of long-necked flask used for distilling.

bolthole [*bOlt*hOl] *n* hole into which an animal runs for safety; (*fig*) place of safety.

bolting [*bOlt*ing] *n* act of fastening with bolts; act of gulping down food; darting away, flight; **b. iron** narrow chisel for mortising drawer locks.

bolt-rope [*bOlt*-ROp] *n* (*naut*) rope sewn round the edge of a sail to prevent tearing or fraying.

bolus (*pl* **boluses**) [*bOl*us] *n* (*med*) lump of half-chewed food; (*ar*) large pill.

bomb [*bom*] *n* metal container filled with explosive or incendiary material, or with gas or smoke.

which will explode either on impact or by the operation of a time mechanism; **go like a b.** (*coll*) be a great success; **make a b.** (*coll*) make a lot of money ~ **bomb** *v/t* attack with bombs; **b. out** drive from home or building by reason of bomb damage; **b. up** load (aircraft) with bombs.

bombard (1) [bom*baard*] *v/t* (*mil*) attack continuously with shells; (*fig*) direct or hurl (series of questions) at (someone); (*phys*) direct stream of high-speed particles at ~ **bombardment** *n*.

bombard (2) [bom*baard*] *n* (*hist*) crude form of cannon; (*mus*) instrument like a bassoon.

bombardier [bomber*deer*] *n* (*mil*) corporal in the artillery; bomb-aimer (in a bomber).

bombardon, bombardone [bom*baard*on] *n* (*mus*) one of two types of brass tuba; reed organ stop.

bombasine, (*US*) **bombazine** [bom*bazeen*] *n* lightweight fabric of silk warp and woof used chiefly for mourning.

bombast [*bom*bast] *n* pompous verbiage ~ **bombastic** [bom*bastik*] *adj*.

Bombay duck [*bom*bay-duk] *n* small fish found in S. Asiatic waters and used to flavour curry.

bombazine see **bombasine**.

bomb-bay [*bom*-bay] *n* (*mil*) part of aircraft where bombs are carried.

bomb-disposal [bom-disp*Ozal*] *n* removal and detonation of unexploded bombs.

bombe [*bawmb*] *n* (*Fr*) sweet or savoury made in a cone-shaped mould.

bomber [*bom*er] *n* aircraft designed for carrying and dropping bombs; person who throws bombs.

bombic [*bom*bik] *adj* of or relating to the silkworm; **b. acid** (*chem*) acid from the silkworm.

bomb-proof [*bom*-pROOf] *adj* affording complete protection against exploding bombs.

bombshell [*bom*shel] *n* explosive shell or bomb; (*fig*) shattering surprise.

bombsight [*bom*sIt] *n* precision optical instrument for aiming bombs carried by aircraft.

bombsite [*bom*sIt] *n* area in a town or city devastated by air-raids.

bona fide [bOna-*fId*i] *adj* and *adv* (*Lat*) genuine; genuinely.

bona fides [bOna-*fId*eez] *n* (*Lat*) good faith.

bonanza [bon*anza*] *n* (*min*) richest part of an ore deposit; (*fig*) lucky opportunity to get rich; boom.

bonbon [*bon*bon] *n* (*Fr*) a sugar confection, a sweet.

bond [*bond*] *n* that which binds or restrains; tie, link; (*chem*) link holding atoms together in a molecule; (*plastics*) adhesion, interface strength; fetter; binding agreement between two or more parties; agreement given to pay or repay a sum of money; debenture; method of laying bricks or stones in a wall to a recognized pattern to ensure strength; arrangement of slates or tiles; superior type of writing paper; official custody of goods until payment of customs duty ~ **bond** *v/t* bind (bricks *etc*) together; to finance by the issue of bonds; hold (goods) until payment of duty ~ **bond** *adj* in slavery, not free.

bondage [*bond*ij] *n* servitude, slavery; restraint.

bonded [*bond*id] *adj* (*of goods*) deposited in a warehouse until the duty is paid; **b. warehouse** store in which such goods are kept.

bonder [*bond*er] *n* owner of merchandise in bond; (*bui*) a bond stone or brick.

bondholder [*bond*hOlder] *n* holder of a bond.

bonding [*bond*ing] *n* (*bui*) strengthening by means of bonders; (*plastics*) gluing wood or metal surfaces together by the use of synthetic resin cements; (*elect*) short conductor > PDE.

bondmaid [*bond*mayd] *n* female slave.

bondman [*bond*man] *n* serf, slave.

bondslave [*bond*slayv] *n* person who is a slave.

bondsman [*bondz*man] *n* slave; one who stands surety.

bond(s)woman [*bond*(z)wooman] *n* female slave.

bondwashing [*bond*woshing] *n* illegal operation in gilt-edged stock by which income is turned to capital gains to evade tax.

bone [bOn] *n* each of the separate parts of a skeleton and the substance of which each is made > PDB; same, with meat on it; strip of stiff material in corsets *etc*; (*pl*) the body, a corpse; dice; castanets; **skin and b.** extreme emaciation; **have a b. to pick** have a complaint to take up; **bred in the b.** deep-rooted; **b. of contention** cause of strife; **to the b.** (frozen) to the core; **to the b.** (cut costs) to the minimum; **make no bones** have no hesitation ~ **bone** *v/t* remove the bones from; (*sl*) steal; **b. up on** (*sl*) study.

bone-ash [bOn-ash] *n* ash obtained by heating bones in air; calcium phosphate.

bone-black [bOn-blak] *n* black pigment of pure carbon made from charred bones.

bone-china [bOn-*chI*na] *n* (*cer*) chinaware of great strength and delicacy.

boned [bOnd] *adj* with the bones removed; (*clothing*) with stiffeners put in.

bone-dry [bOn-*drI*] *adj* completely dry.

bone-dust [bOn-dust] *n* crushed bones used for manure.

bonehead [bOnhed] *n* (*sl*) blockhead, stupid person ~ **boneheaded** *adj* (*sl*) stupid.

bone-idle [bOn-*Id*'l] *adj* extremely lazy.

boneless [bOnles] *adj* without bones; (*fig*) lacking strength of character.

bonemeal [bOnmeel] *n* fertilizer made of crushed bones.

bonesetter [bOnseter] *n* osteopath who sets fractured or dislocated bones.

boneshaker [bOnshayker] *n* bicycle without rubber tyres; vehicle almost falling to pieces.

bonespavin [bOnspavin] *n* (*vet*) growth of bone on inside of horse's hock.

bonfire [bonfIr] *n* large fire in the open air either for burning rubbish or for festive celebrations.

bongo [bong-gO] *n* large African antelope; one of a pair of small drums used in Cuban music.

bonhomie [bonomee] *n* (*Fr*) joviality, kindliness.

boniness [bOnines] *n* quality of being bony.

boning [bOning] *n* process of judging the straightness of a line or surface by looking along a line of rods, *etc*; removing bones from meat or fish; inserting stiffeners in garment.

bonito [bon*eet*O] *n* the striped tunny.

bonkers [bonkerz] *adj* (*coll*) mad.

bon mot (*pl* bons mots) [bawn(g)-mO] *n* (*Fr*) witty remark.

bonnet [bonit] *n* woman's outdoor brimless headdress tied beneath the chin; (*Scots*) man's brimless cap; (*bui*) roof over a bay window; cowl on a vent stack or chimney; engine-cover of motorcar; cover on miner's safety lamp; (*naut*) extra canvas fixed at the bottom of a sail; (sl) accomplice, decoy ~ **bonnet** v/t put a bonnet on (someone); pull (someone's) hat down over his brow ~ **bonneted** adj.

bonny [boni] adj comely, pretty, good-looking ~ **bonnily** adv ~ **bonniness** n.

bonsai [bonsI] n (Jap) artificially dwarfed tree or pot-plant; method of cultivating and displaying these.

bonus [bOnus] n additional payment beyond what is due or expected; gratuity to workmen; extra dividend; unexpected extra advantage.

bony [bOni] adj of or relating to bone(s); hard, thin; full of bones; large-boned.

bonze [bonz] n Buddhist priest of Japan or China.

boo [bOO] (interj) exclamation of contempt or disapproval or to frighten away an animal ~ **boo** v/i and t express disapproval by boos; hoot at (person).

boob [bOOb] n (sl) simpleton, dunce; blunder, mistake; breast ~ **boob** v/i (sl) make a big mistake.

booby [bOObi] n dull stupid person, dunce; (orni) species of gannet.

boobyhatch [bOObihach] n (naut) covered entrance or sliding top over stairs leading below.

boobyprize [bOObipRIz] n consolation prize given to the one who has the lowest score.

boobytrap [bOObitRap] n object rigged up for a practical joke so that it will fall on the head of some unsuspecting person or trip him up; (mil) some apparently harmless object that will detonate an explosive charge if disturbed.

boodle [bOOd'l] n (sl) crowd, lot; counterfeit money, money used in graft, money in general; a card-game.

boogie-woogie [bOOgi-wOOgi] n (coll) style of playing swing music characterized by free variations over a persistent bass rhythm.

book [book] n set of blank, printed or written sheets of paper bound together along one edge and enclosed within protective covers to form a volume; a treatise or literary work; subdivision of a poem, novel, or treatise; words of an opera; (cap) Bible; small booklet (containing tickets, stamps etc); (pop) magazine; (coll) list of criminal charges against an accused person; list of bets laid on a race; first six tricks in whist; (fig) anything that instructs (eg **b. of** Nature); (pl) a firm's accounts; **in one's good (bad) books** regarded with favour (disfavour); **bring to b.** call to account; **go by the b.** obey the rules; **take a' leaf out of someone's b.** copy or imitate him; **suit one's b.** please, be agreeable to ~ **book** v/t enter in a book; reserve (seat, place etc); buy ticket; make an entry that goods are not yet paid for; engage (guest, speaker) in advance; (of police, wardens etc) record the name of (someone who has broken a law or regulation).

bookable [bookab'l] adj (of seats etc) able to be reserved.

bookbinder [bookbInder] n binder of books ~ **bookbindery** n place where books are bound.

bookbinding [bookbInding] n art of binding books; example of the art.

bookcase [book-kays] n set of shelves for books.

book-debt [book-det] n amount debited to a person's account in a ledger.

booked [bookt] adj reserved, bespoken; scheduled; engaged to do something; **b. up** with no seats left available; unable to make further appointments.

bookends [bookendz] n (pl) pair of heavy ornamental props for a short row of books.

bookie [booki] n (coll) bookmaker.

booking [booking] n the entering in a book; anything so entered; a reservation (of seats, rooms, tickets etc).

booking-clerk [booking-klaark] n clerk who issues tickets for travel or makes seating reservations.

booking-office [booking-ofis] n place where one obtains tickets for travel or the theatre etc; ticket-office.

bookish [bookish] adj studious; derived from books; more interested in books than life ~ **bookishness** n ~ **bookishly** adv.

book-keeper [book-keeper] n person who keeps a record of the financial transactions of a firm or other organization.

book-keeping [book-keeping] n art or system of keeping business or public accounts.

bookland [bookland] n (hist) an estate secured to its holder by a royal charter or 'book'.

book-learning [book-lurning] n knowledge in general; knowledge entirely derived from books as distinct from personal experience.

booklet [booklet] n small book, pamphlet.

bookmaker [book-mayker] n person whose occupation is the taking and placing of bets.

bookman [bookman] n scholar; literary man.

bookmark [bookmaark] n anything placed between the pages of a book to mark a place.

book-oath [book-Oth] n oath sworn on the Bible.

bookplate [bookplayt] n decorative label inside the cover of a book to indicate the owner.

book-post [book-pOst] n service whereby books and papers may be sent by post at special rates.

bookseller [bookseler] n person whose trade is selling books ~ **bookselling** n.

bookshop [bookshop] n shop where books are sold.

bookstall [bookstawl] n stall where books, periodicals, and newspapers are sold.

bookstore [bookstawr] n bookseller's shop.

book-token [book-tOken] n gift voucher enabling holder to buy books to the value indicated.

bookwork [bookwurk] n (math) the study of theorems as opposed to problems based on them.

bookworm [bookwurm] n maggot which destroys books; (fig) person with a passion for reading.

boom (1) [bOOm] n barrier of logs or chains to obstruct passage of ships; long spar to extend foot of a sail; beam used in lifting tackle; jib of crane; long movable arm for swinging a microphone or camera into position.

boom (2) v/i and t make a low resounding noise; display sudden activity; rise rapidly into notice or prosperity; advance sharply in price as the result of speculation; boost by a vigorous advertisement campaign ~ **boom** n low resounding noise; strong increase in business activity; rapid rise in prices; sudden and often artificial inflation in the value of a commodity, land, stocks and shares etc.

boomer [bOOmer] n large male kangaroo.

boomerang [bOOmeRang] n curved hardwood missile with sharp outer edge which can be thrown so as to return to starting-point; (fig)

boon-borough

argument or suggestion that recoils on its originator ~ **boomerang** v/i (fig) recoil.

boon (1) [bOOn] n blessing, thing to be thankful for; (ar) favour, request.

boon (2) adj **b. companion** favourite comrade, esp in merry-making.

boor [boor] n peasant; (fig) coarse, clumsy person.

boorish [boorRish] adj coarse, ill-mannered ~ **boorishly** adv ~ **boorishness** n.

boost [bOOst] v/t hoist, increase; increase the popularity or saleability of anything by advertisement etc; promote the interests or increase the reputation of a person by publicity, commendation etc ~ **boost** n (coll) a help forward, a push; helpful publicity, praise.

booster [bOOster] n any auxiliary device supplying extra power or effectiveness; (of rockets) device giving extra thrust in launching; (med) supplementary injection; (elect) device for raising voltage.

boot (1) [bOOt] n leather footwear extending above the ankle; compartment for luggage in a motorcar; **get the b.** be dismissed; **b. and saddle** trumpet call for the cavalry to mount; **bet one's boots** be quite sure about ~ **boot** v/t kick; **b. out** (coll) dismiss, eject.

boot (2) n advantage, profit; **to b.** in addition ~ **boot** v/i (impers) avail, profit.

bootblack [bOOtblak] n one whose job is to clean boots and shoes.

booted [bOOtid] adj wearing boots; **b. and spurred** equipped for a journey.

bootee [bOOtee] n a half-boot or high shoe for women; baby's boot or shoe of knitted wool.

booth [bOOTH] n shed or canvas-covered stall at market or fair; kiosk containing a public telephone; **polling b.** building or temporary erection where electors vote at elections.

bootjack [bOOtjak] n device for pulling off boots.

bootlace [bOOtlays] n thong for fastening up front of boot.

bootleg [bOOtleg] v/t and i (US sl) carry (liquor) illicitly on one's person; sell, make, import (liquor) illegally; traffic illegally, smuggle.

bootlegger [bOOtleger] n (US sl) one who traffics illicitly in liquor ~ **bootlegging** n.

bootless [bOOtles] adj fruitless, of no avail ~ **bootlessly** adv ~ **bootlessness** n.

bootlicker [bOOtliker] n sycophant, toady.

boots [bOOts] n hotel servant who cleans the boots and does odd jobs.

boot-tree [bOOt-tRee] n metal or wooden last inserted into boots and shoes to stretch and keep them in good shape.

booty [bOOti] n plunder, spoils; loot captured in war or stolen by thieves.

booze [bOOz] v/i (coll) drink hard, tipple ~ **booze** n alcoholic drink; drinking-bout.

boozed [bOOzd] adj (coll) drunk.

boozer [bOOzer] n (coll) drunkard; public house; bar.

boozy [bOOzi] adj (coll) rather drunk, fuddled.

bop [bop] n and adj (abbr) bebop.

bo-peep [bO-peep] n nursery game of hide and seek.

bora [bawRa] n cold dry north-east wind of the Upper Adriatic > PDG.

boracic [boRasik] adj (chem) of or relating to borax; **b. acid** obsolescent term for boric acid.

borage [buRij] n (bot) plant with hairy stem and bright blue flowers, frequently used to flavour a claret cup etc.

borate [bawRayt] n (chem) a salt of boric acid.

borax [bawRaks] n (chem) sodium tetraborate decahydrate, a white soluble salt prepared from boric acid or from borates.

Bordeaux [bawrdO] n wine from the district round Bordeaux; claret.

Bordeaux mixture [bawrdO-mikscher] n (hort) preparation of copper sulphate and lime used as a fungicide spray.

border [bawrder] n edge, side, margin, boundary, frontier; narrow strip of ground forming an edging plot usually planted with flowers; edging to a piece of material; **The B.** boundary between England and Scotland and the country adjacent ~ **border** v/t provide with a border; **b. on** be adjacent to; (fig) resemble closely, verge on.

borderer [bawrdeRer] n one who lives on the frontiers of a country.

borderland [bawrderland] n area near a frontier between two countries.

borderline [bawrderlIn] n frontier between two countries or districts; line of division between two categories or classes > PDP ~ **borderline** adj doubtful, indeterminate; verging on, but not to be included in, a particular category; **b. case** person verging on madness.

bore (1) [bawr] v/t and i pierce with rotating tool; make a hole in or through; hollow out uniformly; (horse-racing) push aside, obstruct; make a hole; push one's way forward ~ **bore** n hollow interior, or internal diameter, of a tube, pipe, or gun-barrel; a borehole > PDE.

bore (2) n tedious person or occupation; a nuisance ~ **bore** v/t weary with dull conversation.

bore (3) n high tidal-wave peculiar to some estuaries > PDG.

bore (4) p/t of bear.

boreal [bawRi-al] adj northern; relating to the north or the north wind.

borecole [bawrkOl] n kind of cabbage, kale.

boredom [bawrdom] n tedium; state of being bored.

borehole [bawrhOl] n hole driven into the ground to reach water, oil etc.

borer [bawRer] n tool or person that drills holes; insect that bores through wood.

boric [boRik] adj (chem) of or relating to boron; **b. acid** formerly called boracic acid, a white crystalline soluble solid used as a mild antiseptic and in various industries > PDS.

boring [bawRing] adj causing boredom; dull, tedious ~ **boringly** adv.

born [bawrn] adj brought forth as offspring; (of qualities) innate; natural, perfect.

borne [bawrn] p/part of bear.

boron [bawRon] n (chem) a non-metallic element present in borax and boracic acid.

borough [buRu] n town or city; **municipal b.** town granted special privileges by royal charter and having a mayor and corporation; **parliamentary b.** town with one or more parliamentary representatives; **The B.** Southwark in London; **pocket b.** (hist) one controlled by a person with power to return the member he desired;

rotten b. (*hist*) one where the constituency had become practically non-existent.

borrow [*bo*RO] *v/t* and *i* receive (something) temporarily on loan; make use of; adopt (loan-word); get a loan of money.

borrower [*bo*RO-er] *n* one who borrows.

borsch, bortsch [*bawrsh*] *n* (*Rus*) variously compounded Russian beetroot soup.

Borstal [*bawr*stal] *adj* name given to system of imprisonment for reforming young criminals; **B. boy** youth who has been sent to a Borstal prison.

bort, boart [*bawrt*] *n* crystalline diamond which is only valuable as a cutting agent.

bortsch see **borsch**.

borzoi [*bawr*zoi] *n* Russian wolf-hound.

boscage, boskage [*bosk*ij] *n* thicket; grove of trees.

bosh [*bosh*] *n* and *exclam* nonsense.

bosk, bosket, bosquet [*bosk, bosk*it] *n* plantation of small trees; thicket.

boskage see **boscage**.

bosky [*bosk*i] *adj* covered with underwood or bushes, bushy.

bosom [*booz*um] *n* human breast, *esp* of a woman; part of dress covering the breast; (*fig*) surface of the ground, sea, or lake; (*fig*) loving protection, embrace; inmost thoughts, feelings, heart; **b. of one's family** intimacy of the family circle ~ **bosom** *adj* familiar, intimate ~ **bosom** *v/t* to carry or conceal in the bosom.

boson [*bo*son] *n* (*phys*) type of elementary particle, the numbers of which may not be conserved during interactions > PDS.

bosquet see **bosk**.

boss (1) [*bos*] *n* knob-shaped piece of decoration *esp* the knob in the centre of a shield; (*archi*) decorative moulding where ribs cross in a vaulted roof; boxwood cone for opening lead pipes ~ **boss** *v/t* emboss; provide with bosses.

boss (2) *n* (*coll*) employer, foreman, master; (*US*) professional politician in charge of a political organization ~ **boss** *v/t* manage, be in authority over; (*coll*) be inclined to dictate ~ **boss** *adj* (*sl*) very fine, wonderful.

boss (3) *v/t* (*sl*) bungle, make a bad shot at.

boss-eyed [*bos*-Id] *adj* (*coll*) having a squint, cross-eyed; (*fig*) crooked, one-sided.

boss-shot [*bos*-shot] *n* bad shot, bungling attempt.

bossy [*bos*i] *adj* domineering.

Boston [*boston*] *n* card game resembling whist; **B. two-step** waltz-like dance.

bo'sun [*bO*sun] *n* boatswain.

bot, bott (1) [*bot*] *n* parasitic maggot which infests the skin and intestines of horses, sheep, and cattle; **the botts** (*vet*) disease or swelling caused by the botfly.

bot, bott (2) *n* (*coll abbr*) bottom, buttocks.

botanic, botanical [*bo*tanik, *bo*tanikal] *adj* relating to the science of botany ~ **botanically** *adv*.

botanist [*botanist*] *n* student of botany.

botanize [*botan*Iz] *v/i* and *t* search for plants to study; examine (plants) botanically ~ **botanizer** *n* one who seeks and studies plants.

botany (1) [*botani*] *n* scientific study of plants.

botany (2) *n* any fine grade of worsted fabric; fine Australian wool.

botargo [*bo*taargO] *n* relish prepared from the roe of tunny or mullet.

botch [*boch*] *v/t* and *i* repair clumsily; bungle;

put together unskilfully ~ **botch** *n* flaw, blemish; badly-finished work; a worthless opal.

botcher [*boch*er] *n* a young salmon, a grilse.

botchy [*boch*i] *adj* clumsily done.

botfly [*bot*flI] *n* fly whose larva is a parasite of horses, sheep *etc*.

both [*bOth*] *adj* and *pron* the two; the one and the other ~ **both** *adv* at the same time; **both . . . and** not only . . . but also.

bother [*boTH*er] *v/t* and *i* annoy, cause trouble, pester, perplex; worry oneself, take trouble; **b. (it)!** (*exclam*) confound it! ~ **bother** *n* trouble, fuss, disturbance, worry.

botheration [*boTH*e*Ray*shon] *n* annoyance, irritation; (*exclam*) confound it!

bothersome [*boTH*ersum] *adj* causing trouble.

bothy, bothie [*bothi*] *n* (*Scots*) small hut.

bo-tree [*bO*tRee] *n* large Indian fig-tree like the banyan, the pipal.

bott see **bot**.

bottle (1) [*bot*'l] *n* narrow-necked container (*usu* of glass) for holding liquid; its contents; glass receptacle from which infants take milk; (*fig*) alcoholic drink; drinking-habit ~ **bottle** *v/t* put into bottles; **b. up** (*fig*) suppress, conceal.

bottle (2) *n* bundle of hay or straw.

bottled [*bot*'ld] *adj* kept in bottles; stored up, concentrated; (*coll*) drunk, soused.

bottleglass [*bot*'lglaas] *n* coarse dark-green glass.

bottlegreen [*bot*'lgReen] *adj* and *n* dark green.

bottle-holder [*bot*'l-hOlder] *n* boxer's second; (*fig*) supporter.

bottleneck [*bot*'lnek] *n* narrow part of road *etc* obstructing flow of traffic; one particular operation in a manufacturing process that holds up the flow of production.

bottlenose [*bot*'lnOz] *n* whale of the dolphin family.

bottlenosed [*bot*'lnOzd] *adj* with a swollen, red nose.

bottle-party [*bot*'l-paarti] *n* party to which each guest brings a bottle of liquor.

bottlewasher [*bot*'lwosher] *n* general drudge; **head cook and b.** general factotum.

bottom [*botom*] *n* lowest or deepest part, base, foot; seat of chair; bed of sea, lake, or river; keel of ship, (*fig*) the ship itself; lowest place (at table, in class *etc*); hollow or valley; most inaccessible point of bay or coastline; (*min*) lowest workings in a mine; (*mot*) lowest gear; (*coll*) buttocks; (*fig*) foundation, basis; (*obs*) staying power, stamina; **touch b.** run aground; (*fig*) get no worse; **be at the b. of** be the cause of; **get to the b. of** investigate thoroughly ~ **bottom** *v/t* and *i* put a bottom to; (*of prices*) reach lowest level; (*fig*) understand fully, fathom ~ **bottom** *adj* lowest, last; **bet one's b. dollar** stake all; **b. drawer** (*fig*) a woman's store of clothes, household linen *etc* for use after marriage.

bottoming [*botoming*] *n* stones laid for a foundation in the building of a road; (*railroad*) ballast in a permanent way.

bottomless [*botomles*] *adj* of great depth; (*fig*) unfathomable, inexhaustible; unjustifiable.

bottommost [*botom*-mOst] *adj superl* lowest.

bottomry [*botom*Ri] *n* (*leg*) nautical contract involving borrowing on the security of a vessel or her cargo.

botulism [*bot*ewlizm] *n* food-poisoning from tinned foods.

boudoir [*bOO*dwaar] *n* (*Fr*) lady's private apartment.

Bougainvillaea, Bougainvillia, Bougainvillea, Bouganvilia [bOOgan*vil*i-a] *n* tropical climbing shrub.

bough [*bow*] *n* large branch of tree.

bought [*bawt*] *p/t* and *p/part* of **buy.**

bougie [*bOO*zhee] *n* wax candle; (*med*) flexible surgical instrument for probing passages of the body.

bouillabaisse [bOO*ya*bays] *n* (*Fr*) thick fish soup.

bouillon [*bOO*yon(g)] *n* (*Fr*) thin soup, broth.

boulder [*bOl*der] *n* large rounded stone; (*geol*) weather-worn mass of stone foreign to the district in which it is found; **b. clay** unstratified glacial deposit of clay containing stones of various sizes; **b. period** the Ice Age, Pleistocene period.

boule see **buhl.**

boulevard [*bOOl*vaard] *n* (*Fr*) broad avenue flanked by trees; broad main road.

boult see **bolt (3).**

boulter, bulter [*bOl*ter] *n* long stout fishing-line with many hooks attached.

bounce (1) [*bowns*] *v/t* and *i* hit and rebound springily as a ball; make bounce; cause to be reflected; rush or burst unceremoniously (into, out of); bluster, swagger; deceive a person into doing something rash; (*of cheque*) (*sl*) be returned as worthless; (*sl*) eject forcibly, dismiss summarily; **b. about** jump up and down, play roughly ~ **bounce** *n* act of rebounding, the rebound; elasticity, spring; (*fig*) swagger, impudence; vigour, vitality.

bounce (2) *n* a name of the dogfish.

bounceable [*bowns*ab'l] *adj* capable of being bounced.

bouncer [*bown*ser] *n* bully, cocksure liar; barefaced lie; anything of unusually large size; man employed at hotel *etc* to eject undesirables.

bouncing [*bown*sing] *adj* that which bounces; (*fig*) healthy and well-developed; lusty, vigorous.

bouncy [*bown*si] *adj* resilient; (*fig*) exuberant and self-confident in manner.

bound (1) [*bownd*] *n* boundary of area of land; (*pl*) area limited by certain restrictions; (*fig*) limit, restriction; **out of bounds** forbidden territory ~ **bound** *v/t* and *i* limit, be boundary of.

bound (2) *v/t* spring upward or forward, bounce ~ **bound** *n* springy movement up or forward; quickened heart-beat.

bound (3) *adj* prepared, ready, purposing to go, making or heading (for); **homeward b.** starting for home.

bound (4) *adj* (*used with infin*) compelled, obliged, certain.

boundary [*bownd*aRi] *n* that which marks the extreme limits of anything, frontier; (*cricket*) stroke worth four or six runs which sends the ball beyond the limits of the field.

bounden [*bownd*en] *adj* (*ar*) obliged (to), indebted; **b. duty** duty to which one is morally bound.

bounder [*bownd*er] *n* (*coll*) ill-bred man with plenty of noisy self-confidence.

boundless [*bownd*les] *adj* without limit ~ **boundlessly** *adv* ~ **boundlessness** *n*.

bounteous [*bownt*i-us] *adj* full of goodness, beneficent; liberal, generous; ample, plentiful ~ **bounteously** *adv* ~ **bounteousness** *n*.

bountiful [*bownt*ifool] *adj* generous; yielding abundantly, plentiful; **lady b.** upper-class woman who helps the poor, *esp* if patronizing or domineering ~ **bountifully** *adv* ~ **bountifulness** *n*.

bounty [*bownt*i] *n* generosity, liberality; a gift, gratuity; sum of money given as an inducement.

bouquet [boo*kay*] *n* bunch of flowers, nosegay; aroma of wine; (*fig*) praise, compliments.

Bourbon [*ber*bon] *n* (*US*) whisky made from Indian corn and rye.

bourdon [*boor*don] *n* bass stop in an organ or harmonium; the drone of a bagpipe.

bourgeois (1) [*boor*zhwa] *n* (*Fr*) member of the middle class, *esp* one engaged in trade; person of limited and conventional ideas; capitalist ~ **bourgeois** *adj* of or like the middle class.

bourgeois (2) [ber*jois*] *n* (*typ*) a nine point type, eight and a half lines to the inch.

bourgeoisie [boorzhwa*zee*] *n* (*Fr*) the middle class.

bourn, bourne (1) [*bawrn*] *n* small stream.

bourn, bourne (2) *n* (*poet*) destination ; (*ar*) limit.

bourrée [*boor*Ray] *n* (*Fr*) lively Spanish or French dance like a gavotte; music composed for this.

bourse [*boors*] *n* (*Fr*) foreign money-market.

bout [*bowt*] *n* period, spell of work (illness, exercise, drinking *etc*) ; contest, fight, single round in a boxing match.

boutique [bOO*teek*] *n* (*Fr*) small shop specializing in fashionable clothes and accessories.

bouzouki [bOOz*OO*ki] *n* Greek type of mandolin.

bovate [*bO*vayt] *n* (*hist*) a measure of land, equivalent to about 20 acres.

bovine [*bO*vIn] *adj* like an ox; (*fig*) dull, sluggish, stupid.

Bovril [*bov*Ril] *n* (*tr*) a kind of meat extract.

bovver [*bov*er] *n* (*sl*) 'bother', i.e. gang-fighting, assaults, or hooliganism; **b. boots** heavy boots worn for kicking in fights.

bow (1) [*bO*] *n* weapon for shooting arrows consisting of a long thin piece of flexible wood or metal bent into an arc by a string stretched tightly from end to end which when pulled back and released propels the arrow; (*mus*) pliable wooden rod with horsehairs stretched between the two ends for playing on stringed instruments of the violin type > PDM; looped knot; ribbon or necktie *etc* tied with a looped knot; (*poet*) rainbow; **draw the long b.** (*coll*) exaggerate; **have many strings to one's b.** have many talents; not be limited to one expedient or course of action ~ **bow** *v/t* and *i* (*mus*) use the bow; curve strongly, arch.

bow (2) [*bow*] *v/i* and *t* lower the head or bend the body as a gesture of greeting, assent, respect, or submission *etc*; submit, yield; usher (person) in or out with bows; lower, bend downwards; make stoop, burden, crush down ~ **bow** *n* bending of the head or body; **make one's b.** appear; retire.

bow (3) *n* (*naut*) fore-end of a ship (*freq pl*); (*rowing*) oarsman nearest the bow.

bow-backed [*bO*-bakt] *adj* hump-backed; with back arched.

Bow bells [bO-*belz*] *n* (*pl*) the bells of the church of St Mary-le-Bow in Cheapside; **within the sound of Bow bells** in the City of London.

bow-compass [*bO*-kumpas] *n* pair of compasses with jointed legs which may be bent inwards; (*freq*) compasses for drawing small circles.

bowdlerize [*bowdl*eRIz] *v*/*t* expurgate (a book) by removing or altering what is considered indelicate or coarse ~ **bowdlerization** *n*.

bowel [*bow*il] *n* (*pl*) the intestines; (*fig*) recesses of the earth, mountain *etc*; emotions; **bowels of mercy** compassionate feelings.

bower (1) [*bow*er] *n* arbour, shady spot formed by trees or by trellised plants; (*poet*) lady's bedroom; rustic cottage.

bower (2) *n* (*naut*) anchor; **b. anchor** main anchor of a vessel.

bower (3) *n* name of each of the two highest cards in game of euchre.

bowerbird [*bower*burd] *n* name of several Australian birds of the starling family.

Bowery (1) [*bowe*Ri] *n* (*US*) district in New York City noted for its cheap theatres, beer halls *etc*.

bowery (2) *adj* leafy, shady.

bow-hand [*bO*-hand] *n* hand holding the bow (the *right* for the violin, the *left* in archery).

bowie-knife [*bO*-i-nIf] *n* (*US*) heavy sheath knife having a strong single-edged blade from nine to fifteen inches long, originally made by frontier blacksmiths from old files *etc*.

bowing [*bO*-ing] *n* (*mus*) the manner in which the bow is employed by a string player; the particular way in which a passage is to be played > PDM.

bowl (1) [*bOl*] *n* semi-rounded vessel for holding liquids; basin, drinking vessel; contents of bowl; bowl-shaped part of anything.

bowl (2) *n* hard wood ball constructed to run with a bias used in the game of bowls; wooden ball used in the game of skittles ~ **bowl** *v*/*t* and *i* roll (hoop, bowl); (*cricket*) deliver ball to the batsman; dismiss (batsman) with a ball that breaks his wicket; (*bowls*) play the game of bowls; **b. along** travel rapidly (in wheeled vehicle); **b. out** (*cricket*) dismiss batsman by breaking his wicket; (*fig*) defeat, frustrate; **b. over** knock over; (*fig*) nonplus, worst, disconcert.

bowleg [*bO*leg] *n* leg which curves outwards in the shape of a bow; malformation of this nature ~ **bowlegged** *adj* bandy.

bowler (1) [*bO*ler] *n* (*bowls*) one of the players; (*cricket*) player who delivers the ball to the batsman.

bowler (2) *n* stiff felt hat with roundish crown and rolled brim; billycock.

bowlful [*bOl*fool] *n* amount in a bowl when full.

bowline [*bO*lin] *n* (*naut*) knot used to tie a loop or bight in a rope; a bridle used on a square sail bent to a lower yard > PDSa.

bowling [*bO*ling] *n* (*cricket*) action of delivering a ball to the batsman; style or manner in which this is done; playing at bowls or skittles.

bowling-alley [*bO*ling-ali] *n* long narrow enclosure with raised sides down which the balls are thrown in the game of skittles.

bowling-crease [*bO*ling-kRees] *n* (*cricket*) mark from behind which the bowler delivers the ball.

bowling-green [*bO*ling-gReen] *n* level lawn of close smooth turf upon which the game of bowls is played.

bowls [*bOlz*] *n* a game played with biased wooden balls on a bowling-green; (*US*) skittles, tenpins.

bowman [*bO*man] *n* (*hist*) soldier armed with bow; archer.

bow-net [*bO*-net] *n* wicker basket used for trapping lobsters *etc*.

bow-saw [*bO*-saw] *n* saw with a removable blade held in a wooden frame which is tightened by twisting a string, and used for cutting curves.

bowser [*bow*zer] *n* hose for fuelling car, aircraft *etc* with petrol; petrol tanker.

bowshot [*bO*shot] *n* distance an arrow can be sent by a bow.

bowsprit [*bO*spRit] *n* (*naut*) large spar projecting from the bow of a sailing vessel to which the headsails are secured.

bowstring [*bO*stRing] *n* string of a bow; cord used for strangling in the old Turkish method of execution ~ **bowstring** *v*/*t* strangle with a bow-string.

bowstring-bridge [*bO*stRing-bRij] *n* (*eng*) arched bridge with a horizontal tie-beam.

bow-window [*bO*-windO] *n* curved window built to project from the wall of a house, bay-window; (*sl*) big paunch ~ **bow-windowed** *adj* having bow-windows; (*sl*) big-bellied.

bow-wow [*bow*-wow] *n* (imitative of) a dog's bark; child's word for dog; **the big b. strain** grandiloquent tone or style of speech.

box (1) [*boks*] *n* container or chest of rigid material, usually with a lid; contents of a box, a boxful; driver's seat on a coach; private compartment with seats in a theatre; horse's stall in stable or truck; small country lodge; part of the court where members of the jury sit; enclosed stand where a witness gives evidence; hut or shelter; protective case over various pieces of mechanism; axle-box; piston of a pump; (*print*) cell of a type-case; space enclosed between lines; (*sl*) coffin; **the b.** (*coll*) television set; **b. car** closed railway truck; **b. drain** (*bui*) a drain of rectangular section; **b. girder** (*bui*) girder of rectangular section; **b. sextant** compact sextant in a small metal box; **in the same b.** in the same predicament ~ **box** *v*/*t* put into or fit with a box; cut a cavity in the trunk of a tree to collect the sap; (*leg*) lodge (document) in a law court; **b. in, b. up** enclose in a box, confine in an uncomfortably restricted space; **b. the compass** (*naut*) name all the consecutive points or quarter points; (*fig*) finish up where one began; **b. off** (*naut*) pay off from a wind that has shifted ahead; **b. about** (*naut*) cruise up and down; **b. up** (*sl*) bungle.

box (2) *n* smart blow on the ears ~ **box** *v*/*t* and *i* deliver slap on the ears; fight with the fists wearing padded gloves; **b. clever** use one's brains.

box (3) *n* (*bot*) small evergreen tree or shrub; box-tree; wood of this.

box-barrage [*boks*-baRaazh] *n* (*mil*) anti-aircraft barrage in which the shells explode in a box-like area.

boxboard [*boks*bawrd] *n* thick compressed paper used in the manufacture of cartons.

boxcalf [*boks*kaaf] *n* (*tr*) calfskin tanned with chrome salts and rolled in such a way as to leave square markings on the grain.

boxcloth [*boks*kloth] *n* stout closely-woven cloth.

boxer [*boks*er] *n* person skilled in fighting with his fists; professional pugilist; (*hist*) member of a Chinese secret society with extreme nationalist aims; brown smooth-haired dog of the bulldog type.

boxhaul [*boks*hawl] *v/t* (*naut*) veer ship quickly round on her keel > PDSa.

boxing [*boks*ing] *n* the art of fighting with the fists; pugilism; (*bui*) recess at the side of a window into which a shutter is folded away; ballast between railway sleepers.

Boxing-day [*boks*ing-day] *n* first weekday after Christmas Day, on which Christmas-boxes are traditionally given.

box-kite [*boks*-kIt] *n* box-shaped kite used as toy or for meteorological research.

box-office [*boks*-ofis] *n* office at a theatre *etc* where seats may be booked and tickets obtained; (*fig*) attractiveness of play *etc* to general public.

box-pleat [*boks*-pleet] *n* flattened and pressed double fold in a cloth ~ **box-pleated** *adj*.

boxroom [*boks*Room] *n* small room used for storage.

box-spanner [*boks*-spaner] *n* tubular spanner shaped to fit a nut and turned by a tommy bar.

box-tree [*boks*-tRee] *n* evergreen tree or shrub.

box-up [*boks*-up] *n* (*sl*) confusion resulting from mismanagement.

boxwood [*boks*wood] *n* wood of the box-tree; the box-tree.

boxy [*boksi*] *adj* small and enclosed.

boy [*boi*] *n* male child; (*freq*) young man; member of a group of men of similar tastes or habits; (*joc* and *cont*) fellow; native servant; (*sl*) heroin; **b. friend** (*coll*) girl's sweetheart, male lover; **B. Scout** (*obs*) member of the Scout organization.

boyar, boyard [bo*yaar*, *boi*-ard] *n* (*Rus hist*) man of aristocratic rank.

boycott [*boi*kot] *v/t* combine together against a person by breaking off all relations with him; ostracize; (*comm*) refuse to do business with ~ **boycott** *n* ~ **boycotting** *n*.

boyhood [*boi*hood] *n* period of life of a male child after babyhood, up to puberty.

boyish [*boi*-ish] *adj* like a boy; high-spirited; amateurish, puerile ~ **boyishly** *adv* ~ **boyishness** *n*.

bra [bRaa] *n* (*coll*) brassière.

braccate [*bRa*kayt] *adj* (*orni*) with legs entirely covered by feathers.

brace [bRays] *n* anything which supports, strengthens, or provides rigidity; (*bui*) strut or stay to give stability to a structure; thong to tighten the skins of a drum; (*pl*) shoulder straps to hold trousers up; (*carp*) tool that holds and rotates a drilling bit; (*of dogs, game, pistols*) a couple or pair; (*print*) bracket shaped thus { } to link together two or more words or staves of music; (*naut*) rope attached to yard for trimming sail ~ **brace** *v/t* support, strengthen, render firm; plant (feet) firm; tighten; (*of climate*) freshen, invigorate; (*refl*) summon up one's resolution to face something; (*pass*) feel encouraged, invigorated; **b. up** pull oneself together; take a drink or bracer for this purpose.

bracelet [*bRays*lit] *n* circular ornament worn on the wrist or arm; (*pl coll*) handcuffs.

bracer (1) [*bRay*ser] *n* anything which binds *etc*, brace; (*coll*) drink to brace one up, pick-me-up.

bracer (2) *n* wrist-guard worn in fencing and in archery; (*hist*) part of armour protecting the arm.

brach [bRach] *n* (*ar*) bitch hound.

brachial [*bRa*ki-al/*bRa*yki-al] *adj* like an arm; pertaining to the arm > PDB.

brachiate [*bRa*ki-ayt/*bRa*yki-it] *adj* (*bot*) with pairs of branches at right angles to the stem.

brachy- *pref* short.

brachycephalic [bRakisi*fa*lik] *adj* short-headed; (*eth*) (*of skulls*) broad in proportion to length; (*of races*) exhibiting this characteristic.

bracken [bRaken] *n* kind of coarse fern; (*freq collect*) mass of growing fern.

bracket [*bRa*kit] *n* angled support for shelf *etc*; (*archi*) projecting support; ornamental metal pipe projecting from wall and supporting lamp or burner; small shelf; support for the trunnion of a gun-carriage; (*print*) mark for enclosing words or figures; (*coll*) group classified together ~ **bracket** *v/t* enclose in brackets, join by brackets; (*coll*) associate, show connexion between; classify in the same category; (*gunnery*) to drop one shot beyond the target and another short of it to obtain the range.

brackish [*bRa*kish] *adj* tasting salty.

bract [bRakt] *n* (*bot*) small leaf with relatively undeveloped blade.

bracteate [*bRa*kti-it] *n* (*arch*) thin gold or silver medallion with repoussé designs ~ **bracteate** *adj* (*bot*) possessing bracts; (*arch*) made of thin beaten metal.

brad [bRad] *n* (*carp*) nail with a square head projecting on one edge only, used for fixing floorboards ~ **brad** (*pres/part* **bradding**, *p/t* and *p/part* **bradded**) *v/t* secure with brads.

bradawl [*bRa*dawl] *n* short awl with a narrow chisel point for making holes for nails and screws.

Bradshaw [*bRad*shaw] *n* former railway timetable of all the passenger services in Great Britain.

brae [bRay] *n* (*Scots*) steep bank of river-valley; slope, hill-side.

brag [bRag] *n* boast; boaster; card game like poker ~ **brag** (*pres/part* **bragging**, *p/t* and *p/part* **bragged**) *v/i*.

braggadocio [bRaga*dOshi*-O] *n* boastful talk.

braggart [*bRa*gart] *adj* and *n* boastful (person).

Brahmin, Brahman [*bRaa*min, *bRaa*man] *n* member of the highest (priestly) Hindu caste; (*fig*) elitist intellectual ~ **Brahminical** [bRaa*mini*kal] *adj*.

braid [bRayd] *v/t* intertwine strands, weave; plait (hair); fasten (hair) with ribbon; ornament with braid ~ **braid** *n* plait of hair; band of woven material for trimming; narrow strip of ornamental fabric or thread, *esp* one with gold or silver wire ~ **braiding** *n* embroidery.

Braille [bRayl] *n* system of printing in raised letters which enables the blind to read by touch.

brain [bRayn] *n* central nervous system within the skull; (*freq pl*) the soft cerebral substance enclosed by the skull; (*fig*) the mind, intellect, imagination; (*coll*) very intelligent person; **have something on the b.** be obsessed by an idea; **the brains of the family** the most intelligent member; **pick someone's brains** obtain information from another instead of studying oneself ~ **brain** *v/t* knock out the brains of.

brainchild [*braynch*Ild] *n* something one has invented, planned or thought up.

brain-drain [*brayn*-dRayn] *n* emigration of scientists, intellectuals, technicians and professional people to seek higher paid posts.

brain-fag [*brayn*-fag] *n* nervous exhaustion.

brainfever [*brayn*feever] *n* inflammation of the brain.

brainless [*brayn*lis] *adj* very stupid.

brainpan [*brayn*pan] *n* the skull.

brainsick [*brayn*sik] *adj* disordered in mind, frantic ~ **brainsickness** *n*.

brainstorm [*brayn*stawrm] *n* sudden outburst of crazy behaviour or wild ideas.

Brains Trust, Brain Trust [*brayn*(z) tRust] *n* (*US*) group of intellectuals acting in advisory capacity to the President; body of advisory experts; (*coll*) group of celebrities chosen to entertain an audience by answering questions on topics of general interest.

brainwash [*brayn*wosh] *v/t* clear the mind of established ideas and loyalties by indoctrination under duress and persistent psychological pressure ~ **brainwashing** *n*.

brainwave [*brayn*wayv] *n* (*coll*) sudden bright idea or inspiration; (*med*) electric impulse in the brain.

brainy [*brayn*i] *adj* (*coll*) clever, intelligent.

braise [*brayz*] *v/t* stew in closed pan.

brake (1) [*brayk*] *n* device for reducing the motion of any mechanism or the speed of a vehicle ~ **brake** *v/t* and *i* apply brakes; slow up.

brake (2), **break** *n* large open wagonette with four wheels; car that can carry either passengers or goods, estate car.

brake (3) *n* bracken; clump of brushwood.

brake (4) *n* toothed implement for beating hemp or flax; machine for kneading dough; (*agr*) heavy type of harrow for breaking clods; device for peeling off willow-bark ~ **brake** *v/t* crush hemp or flax by beating; break up with harrow.

brakesman [*brayks*man] *n* man in charge of a brake; man working the winding-apparatus at pit-head; (*US*) railroad employee who assists the conductor of a train.

brake-van [*brayk*-van] *n* railway van which has a brake.

bramble [*bramb*'l] *n* thorny shrub; blackberry-bush; the wild blackberry ~ **brambly** *adj*.

brambling [*bramb*ling] *n* (*orni*) the mountain finch.

bran [*bran*] *n* the husk of grain separated from the flour after grinding and used as coarse meal.

branch [*braanch*] *n* limb of tree (smaller than a bough); any kind of offshoot, subdivision, or extension, *eg* a language deriving from another, part of a race or of a family; local business office with headquarters elsewhere; division of a subject, science *etc*; **root and b.** thoroughly ~ **branch** *v/i* put forth branches; separate into branches; (*of river, road*) fork; **b. off** turn away in a new direction; **b. out** expand.

branchia, branchiae [*brank*i-a, *brank*i-ee] *n* (*pl*) gills in fishes ~ **branchial** *adj* resembling gills ~ **branchiate** *adj* having gills.

brand [*brand*] *n* burning or burnt piece of wood; mark left by hot iron; mark of ownership; trademark; particular make of goods; kind of blight on leaves; (*fig*) mark of infamy, stigma; (*poet*) torch; (*hist*) sword ~ **brand** *v/t* burn with a hot iron; place mark of ownership upon; mark as a sign of quality; (*fig*) denounce; (*fig*) imprint indelibly on one's memory ~ **branded** *adj* marked with a brand.

brandied [*brand*id] *adj* soaked in brandy; flavoured with brandy.

brand-image [*brand*-*im*aj] *n* ideas and assumptions held by potential customers about a particular make of goods.

brandish [*brand*ish] *v/t* flourish, wave about threateningly or ostentatiously.

brandling [*brand*ling] *n* red worm used for fish-bait.

brand-new [*brand*-*new*] *adj* completely new.

brandreth [*brand*Reth] *n* wooden framework on which stands a hayrick or barrel; fence around a well.

brandy [*brand*i] *n* strong alcoholic spirit distilled from wine or grapes.

brandyball [*brand*ibawl] *n* round sweetmeat the colour of brandy.

brandy-pawnee [*brand*i-pawnee] *n* (*Anglo-Indian*) brandy and water.

brandysnap [*brand*isnap] *n* crisp kind of gingerbread made up into folded rolls.

branks [*branks*] *n* (*hist*) iron framework with a metal gag to muzzle scolds; the mumps.

branpie, brantub [*bran*pI, *bran*tub] *n* tub filled with bran into which children dip their hands for hidden prizes.

brant [*brant*] *n* smallest species of wild goose.

brash (1) [*brash*] *n* rubble; brittle timber; hedge-clippings.

brash (2) *n* acid belch; **water b.** belching of acid liquid from the stomach.

brash (3) *adj* reckless, rash; bumptious, impudent, coarse; tactless; (*of colour*) bold ~ **brashly** *adv*.

brashy [*brash*i] *adj* crumbly, brittle.

brass [*braas*] *n* an alloy of zinc and copper; memorial tablet incised with an effigy *etc* set in pavement or wall of church; (*mus*) the trumpets, horns, tubas, trombones *etc* in an orchestra; (*sl*) high-ranking officers of the armed forces; (*fig*) impudence, effrontery; (*coll*) money ~ **brass** *adj* made of brass; **b. tacks** fundamentals; **a b. farthing** one little bit; **part b. rags** (*coll*) quarrel.

brassage [*bras*ij] *n* charge made by a mint to cover the cost of coining.

brassard [*bras*saard] *n* arm-badge, armlet; (*hist*) armour worn on the upper arm.

brass-band [*braas*-band] *n* ensemble of musicians performing on percussion and brass wind instruments > PDM.

brasserie [*bras*eRi] *n* (*Fr*) restaurant or saloon providing beer and food.

brass-hat [*braas*-hat] *n* (*coll*) high-ranking officer in the armed forces.

brassie, brassy [*braas*i] *n* golf club with brass-shod head; the wrasse fish.

brassière [*bras*i-air] *n* woman's strong close-fitting underbodice for supporting the breasts.

brassy (1) [*braas*i] *adj* made of or like brass; pitiless, shameless; strident; ostentatious ~ **brassily** *adv* ~ **brassiness** *n*.

brassy (2) see **brassie**.

brat [*brat*] *n* (*cont*) child.

brattice [bRatis] n (min) screen of wood or cloth to divert air currents into or away from places where gas collects ~ **bratticing** n (archi) ornamental work along a cornice or coping of a building.

bravado [bRavaadO] n showy display of courage, bold defiant attitude.

brave [bRayv] adj fearless, courageous; (lit) fine, handsome, gay, making a good display ~ **brave** n (US) Red Indian warrior; (ar) hired ruffian ~ **brave** v/t defy, face courageously ~ **bravely** adv ~ **braveness** n.

bravery [bRayveRi] n courage, boldness; ostentation; showy clothes.

bravo (1) [bRaavO] exclam well done!

bravo (2) (pl **bravoes**) n a desperado; hired ruffian.

bravura [bRavoorRa] n brilliance of performance, dash; (mus) passage calling for brilliant execution.

braw [bRaw] adj (Scots) splendidly-dressed; first-rate, excellent.

brawl [bRawl] v/i and t quarrel noisily, create a disturbance; (of stream) flow noisily; utter noisily ~ **brawl** n uproar, row.

brawler [bRawler] n one who brawls.

brawling [bRawling] adj noisy, quarrelsome.

brawn [bRawn] n meat cooked, seasoned and pressed into a mould; (fig) muscle, muscular strength.

brawny [bRawni] adj physically strong, well-developed ~ **brawniness** n.

bray (1) [bRay] n the cry of an ass; noise of a trumpet; (fig) noisy protests ~ **bray** v/i make a strident noise.

bray (2) v/t crush small, pound in a mortar.

braze [bRayz] v/t join together two pieces of metal with a film of copper zinc alloy between the red hot contact surfaces; solder.

brazen [bRayzen] adj made from brass, like brass, giving out a sound like that of a brass instrument; (fig) quite shameless ~ **brazen** v/t **b. a thing out** attempt to vindicate oneself by adopting an impudent and defiant manner.

brazen-faced [bRayzen-fayst] adj shameless, impudent ~ **brazen-facedly** adv.

brazenly [bRayzenli] adv shamelessly.

brazier (1) [bRayzher] n craftsman in brass.

brazier (2) n perforated iron basket for holding burning coal or coke.

Brazil-nut [bRazil-nut] n large three-sided nut from Brazil.

brazilwood [bRazilwood] n hard reddish wood yielding red and orange dyes.

breach [bReech] n breaking, violation, infraction (of obligation, promise etc); estrangement; rent or gap in wall made by assault or gunfire; (coll abbr) breach of promise; **b. of the peace** (leg) public disturbance, riot ~ **breach** v/t make a breach; break through.

bread [bRed] n kneaded moistened flour leavened with yeast and baked in an oven; food generally; sacramental bread; (fig) livelihood; (sl) money.

breadbasket [bRedbaaskit] n basket for bread; (sl) the stomach; bomb which bursts with shrapnel-like effect.

breadfruit [bRedfROOt] n fruit growing in the Pacific Islands which tastes like bread when baked.

breadknife [bRednIf] n large knife for cutting loaves.

breadline [bRedlIn] n (US) queue of poor or unemployed waiting for food or relief; **on the b.** on relief.

breadstuffs [bRed-stufs] n (pl) grain, cereals for making bread.

breadth [bRedth] n extent from side to side, width; (fig) broad-mindedness, liberality of attitude; distance, scope, dimension; (painting) subordination of detail, colour etc to the general effect.

breadthways [bRedthwayz] adv from side to side.

breadthwise [bRedthwIz] adv from side to side.

breadwinner [bRedwiner] n person who supports a family by his or her earnings.

break (1) (p/t **broke**, p/part **broken**) [bRayk] v/t and i divide or separate violently into parts, smash, fracture; split, burst; disrupt; separate, part; escape from by force or in haste; escape from restraint; reveal (news etc) tactfully; decipher (a code); surpass (a record); (mil) throw or fall into disorder; destroy, incapacitate, overpower; ruin financially; fail to observe (a promise); curb, tame; (of health) deteriorate; (of light, day etc) start to appear; pierce through, penetrate, disturb, interrupt; suspend temporarily, stop; (of voice) change at adolescence or under stress of emotion; (of ball) deviate or cause to deviate suddenly; (prices) fall suddenly or sharply; (coll, of news) become publicly known; **b. camp** move elsewhere; **b. cover** come into the open; **b. down** demolish; decompose; divide into categories, analyse; **b. even** gain and lose equally; **b. in** interrupt; wear (shoes) until comfortable; **b. into** burgle; (coll) get into some occupation or into high society; get something published for the first time; **b. in upon** intrude, interrupt; **b. the ice** overcome initial shyness; **b. off** interrupt, stop abruptly; discontinue; **b. open** with some force; **b. out** escape from restraint; (of infection) make sudden appearance; **b. out into** suffer the eruption of (boils) on the skin; **b. up** disperse; **b. with** discontinue; quarrel with; **b. wind** fart, belch ~ **break** n breakage, fracture; gap; interruption; rest period; (jazz) short instrumental solo; (cricket) change in direction of the ball as it pitches; (billiards) succession of scoring strokes; score thus obtained; escape from prison; (sl) piece of good (or bad) luck; opportunity; (sl) fair or equal chance.

break (2) see **brake** (2).

breakable [bRaykab'l] adj easily broken.

breakage [bRaykij] n act of breaking; objects broken; loss or damage caused by breaking.

breakaway [bRaykaway] n act of breaking away; (football) sudden rush forward; (boxing) separation of the fighters after a clinch; (athletics) premature start to a race ~ **breakaway** adj (of group etc) formed by splitting off from larger group.

breakdown [bRaykdown] n stoppage, mechanical failure; collapse (of negotiations etc); collapse of physical or mental health; division into categories or processes; statistical analysis; (chem, med) decomposition; **b. gang** workmen sent to clear the permanent way after a railway accident; **b. van** van with special equipment for dealing with mechanical breakdowns.

breaker [bRayker] n one who breaks; large seawave breaking into foam as it rolls towards the shore; (*naut*) small cask; (*min*) machine for crushing rock or stone.

breakfast [bRekfast] *n* first meal of the day ~ **breakfast** *v/i* and *t* eat breakfast; give (breakfast) to.

break-in [bRayk-in] *n* forcible and illegal entry into premises, *esp* for burglary.

breaking [bRayking] *n* (*phon*) the diphthongization in Old English of certain front vowels.

breakneck [bRayknek] *adj* (*of speed*) headlong, dangerously fast.

break-out [bRayk-owt] *n* escape from prison.

breakthrough [bRaykthROO] *n* penetration in force through and beyond an enemy's line; (*fig*) sudden rise in prices or values; sensational and important advance in scientific knowledge; discovery or event that removes a longstanding obstacle to progress.

break-up [bRayk-up] *n* disintegration; dispersal, *esp* of school at end of term; b. value value of assets on the liquidation of a business concern.

breakwater [bRaykwawter] *n* stone structure to protect a harbour from the force of the waves.

bream [bReem] *n* yellowish fresh-water carp; spiny-finned salt-water fish.

breast [bRest] *n* bosom, chest; milk-secreting organ of women; (*fig*) the heart; (*min*) working coal-face in a colliery; (*of chimney*) projection into room which contains the flue and hearth of fireplace; **make a clean b. of** make a full confession ~ **breast** *v/t* face with resolution; struggle with, oppose; ascend over top of (hill, waves *etc*).

breast-feeding [bRest-feeding] *n* process of feeding babies on human milk from the mother's or wet-nurse's breast ~ **breast-fed** *adj*.

breast-high [bRest-hI] *adj* and *adv* reaching to the height of the breast.

breastplate [bRestplayt] *n* square embroidered fabric worn on breast of Jewish high priest; defensive medieval armour for the front of the body.

breastsummer, bressummer [bResumer] *n* (*archi*) beam or lintel spanning a wall or window and carrying the weight of the superstructure.

breastwood [bRestwood] *n* (*collect*) (*hort*) young shoots on espaliers or on fruit trees trained against a wall.

breastwork [bRestwurk] *n* (*mil*) low parapet of earth; (*naut*) rails and stanchions placed across the deck.

breath [bReth] *n* air taken in and expelled by the lungs; single act of breathing; respiration, (*fig*) life; whiff, puff (of air, wind); facility in breathing; (*phon*) voiceless breathing out; **draw b.** breathe, be alive; **take b.** pause to rest; **take one's b. away** startle, surprise one.

breathable [bReeTHab'l] *adj* able to be breathed.

breathalyzer [bRethalIzer] *n* chemical device for detecting traces of alcohol in the breath.

breathe [bReeTH] *v/i* and *t* inhale and exhale air with the lungs, respire; be alive, exist; (*fig*) of wind, blow gently; utter softly, whisper; (*fig*) infuse (into); exhibit, express; allow to rest; blow (wind instrument); **b. freely** recover from fear; **b. again** experience relief.

breather [bReeTHer] *n* exercise in the open-air; brief interval for rest.

breathing [bReeTHing] *n* inhaling and exhaling air with the lungs, respiration; gentle motion of the air; (*phon*) aspiration; (*Gk*) mark to indicate aspiration or its absence.

breathing-space [bReeTHing-spays] *n* time to breathe, pause.

breathless [bRethles] *adj* gasping for breath, out of breath; holding the breath under stress of some emotion; unruffled by the wind; lifeless ~ **breathlessly** *adv* ~ **breathlessness** *n*.

breathtaking [bRethtayking] *adj* astonishing; superb, thrilling.

breathy [bRethi] *adj* (*of the singing voice*) thin in tone, lacking resonance ~ **breathiness** *n*.

breccia [bRecha/bReshya] *n* (*geol*) rock consisting of angular fragments cemented together in a matrix.

bred [bRed] *adj* reared, properly trained; of good breed.

breech (*pl* **breeches**) [bReech, *pl* bRichiz] *n* buttock, thigh; rear of gun-barrel, part of gun which opens for loading; (*pl*) garments covering legs and lower part of body; (*coll*) trousers; garment buttoned below the knees worn for riding ~ **breech** [bRich] *v/t* put (boy) into trousers for the first time.

breechblock [bReechblok] *n* movable block of steel closing the breech of a gun.

breeches-buoy [bReechiz-boi] *n* lifebuoy fitted with canvas breeches to hold a person.

breeching [bReeching] *n* strap passing round carthorse's hind-quarters for pushing backwards; (*hist*) rope lashing gun to ship's side.

breechloader [bReechlOder] *n* gun loaded at the breech, not through muzzle ~ **breechloading** *adj*.

breed (*p/t* and *p/part* **bred**) [bReed] *v/t* and *i* bear, produce (offspring); reproduce itself; organize the begetting of, raise, rear; engender, give rise to; (*fig*) arise, spring forth, originate ~ **breed** *n* stock, race, lineage; kind, species; good breeding.

breeder [bReeder] *n* (*phys*) apparatus which produces more radioactive material than is put into it.

breeding [bReeding] *n* act or process of reproduction; nurture, good manners and behaviour; education; (*phys*) production of radioactive material at a rate higher than the consumption of the parent element.

breeks [bReeks] *n* (*pl*) (*Scots*) trousers.

breeze (1) [bReez] *n* a wind varying from light to strong; (*coll*) sharp quarrel, altercation ~ **breeze** *v/i*; **b. in** (*coll*) enter briskly or casually.

breeze (2) *n* small cinders, small coke; **b. block** precast building block of clinker concrete used for building partitions or external walls.

breezy [bReezi] *adj* exposed to breezes; fresh, airy; (*fig*) convivial, jolly, lively ~ **breezily** *adv* ~ **breeziness** *n*.

Bren gun [bRen-gun] *n* (*mil*) light machine-gun.

brent, brent-goose [bRent (gOOs)] *n* brant.

bressummer see **breastsummer**.

brethren [bReTHRen] *ar pl* of **brother**.

Breton [bReton] *n* and *adj* (a native, the Celtic language) of Brittany.

breve [bReev] *n* (*print*) mark (˘) over a vowel to indicate it is short; (*mus*) note equivalent to two semibreves > PDM.

brevet [bRevit] *n* document conferring a privilege, *esp* (*mil*) that conferring promotion on an officer without extra pay ~ **brevet** *adj* holding rank by brevet ~ **brevet** *v/t* confer rank by brevet.

breviary [bRevi-aRi] *n* book used in the Roman Catholic Church containing priest's daily office.

brevier [bReveer] *n* (*print*) small type about eight point, nine and a half lines to the inch.

brevity [bReviti] *n* quality in writing and speech of being brief and to the point.

brew [bROO] *v/t* and *i* make ale or beer from malt and hops; make (tea); mix (punch); (*fig*) contrive (disaster, mischief); be in preparation, be imminent ~ **brew** *n* the drink brewed.

brewage [bROO-ij] *n* a brewing, process of brewing.

brewer [bROO-er] *n* one whose trade is brewing.

brewery [bROO-eRi] *n* factory where brewing is carried on.

brewing [bROO-ing] *n* process of brewing; one particular brew.

brewster [bROOster] *n* a brewer; **B. Sessions**, sittings of magistrates at which licences to sell alcoholic liquor are issued or renewed.

briar (1), **brier** (1) [bRI-er] *n* a wood (*Erica arborea*) native to S. France and Corsica; pipe made from this wood.

briar (2), **brier** (2) *n* the wild rose; any thorny bush or shrub; a thorn; (*fig*) (*pl*) vexations, difficulties.

bribable [bRIbab'l] *adj* open to bribes.

bribe [bRIb] *n* reward offered to a person to influence his judgement and to induce him to act contrary to what is just and right ~ **bribe** *v/t* influence by bribery.

bribery [bRIbeRi] *n* act, practice of offering or accepting bribes.

bric-à-brac, bricabrac [bRik-a-bRak] *n* (*Fr*) old-fashioned ornaments, curios, furniture *etc* of little intrinsic or artistic value.

brick [bRik] *n* burnt clay used for building; block (*usu* rectangular and of standard size) of this material; any block of other substance with similar shape; light red colour; (*coll*) an estimable person, decent fellow; **drop a b.** be indiscreet and tactless ~ **brick** *adj* made of brick ~ **brick** *v/t*; **b. in, b. up** close with brickwork.

brickbat [bRikbat] *n* piece of brick, usually one used as missile; hostile or critical remark.

brickfield [bRikfeeld] *n* factory where bricks are made.

brick-kiln [bRik-kiln/bRik-kil] *n* furnace in which bricks are burnt.

bricklayer [bRiklay-er] *n* tradesman who builds and repairs brickwork ~ **bricklaying** *n*.

brick-nogging [bRik-noging] *n* brickwork between the studs of a framed wooden partition or building frame.

brickwork [bRikwurk] *n* bricks built into a wall or structure; art of bonding bricks effectively.

brickyard [bRikyaard] *n* factory where bricks are made and burnt, usually near a clay pit.

bricole [bRik'l] *n* (*hist*) medieval catapult for besieging towns; (*real tennis*) a stroke off the side wall; (*billiards*) a shot made off the cushion.

bridal [bRIdal] *n* (*poet*) a wedding, wedding feast ~ **bridal** *adj* of or relating to a bride or a wedding.

bride (1) [bRId] *n* a woman about to be married or just married.

bride (2) *n* delicate network connecting the patterns in lace; bonnet-string.

bridegroom [bRIdgROOm] *n* a man about to be married or just married.

bridesmaid [bRIdzmayd] *n* girl or unmarried woman attending the bride at a wedding.

bridge (1) [bRij] *n* structure carrying a road or railway over a river, gap, or canal > PDE; (*naut*) a raised deck amidships; (*mus*) wooden strut over which the strings of a stringed instrument are stretched > PDM; the upper bony ridge of the nose; (*dentistry*) false tooth or teeth supported by adjacent teeth; (*billiards*) a rest for the cue; **b. roll** small plain, oval bun ~ **bridge** *v/t* erect a bridge; span; (*fig*) overcome; fill in.

bridge (2) *n* card game like whist.

bridgehead [bRijhed] *n* (*mil*) fortified position dominating and protecting the end of a bridge; position established by a landing-force in enemy territory from which further advances may be launched.

bridge-train [bRij-tRayn] *n* (*mil*) company of engineers equipped for bridge-building.

bridging [bRijing] *n* (*carp*) strutting.

bridle [bRId'l] *n* head-gear of a horse by which the rider controls it; (*naut*) a mooring cable; (*fig*) restraint, curb ~ **bridle** *v/t* and *i* put a bridle on (a horse); (*fig*) curb, restrain; draw oneself up in anger or disdain.

bridle-hand [bRId'l-hand] *n* the hand that holds the horse's reins, the left.

bridlepath [bRId'lpaath] *n* path wide enough to ride or lead a horse, but too narrow for vehicles.

bridlerein [bRId'lRayn] *n* leather strap attached to horse's bit.

bridleway [bRId'lway] *n* bridlepath.

bridoon [bRidOOn] *n* snaffle and rein of a bridle.

Brie [bRee] *n* (*Fr*) kind of cream cheese.

brief (1) [bReef] *n* (*leg*) summary of facts and legal points in a case compiled by solicitor for barrister; papal letter on disciplinary matters; **take a b.** (*leg*) accept a case; **hold a b. for** (*leg*) be retained as counsel for; (*fig*) argue in favour of; **watching b.** (*leg*) barrister's function in observing a case on behalf of a client interested but not directly concerned ~ **brief** *v/t* (*leg*) instruct, retain, employ (barrister); give detailed instructions.

brief (2) *adj* short, concise; short-lived; (*of manner*) abrupt; **in b.** in short; to sum up.

briefcase [bReefkays] *n* flat case suitable for carrying documents.

briefing [bReefing] *n* detailed orders, plan or information given to those about to begin some course of action.

briefless [bReefles] *adj* without a brief; (*of barrister*) without clients, unsuccessful.

briefly [bReefli] *adv* in brief, shortly.

briefness [bReefnes] *n* quality of being brief.

briefs [bReefs] *n* (*pl*) (*coll*) very short knickers.

brier see **briar**.

brig [bRig] *n* a two-masted sailing vessel having square sails on both masts and a gaff mainsail; naval or military prison.

brigade [bRigayd] *n* military unit smaller than a division; a band of persons forming an organization with a special purpose ~ **brigade** *v/t* form into brigades.

brigade-major [bRigayd-mayjor] *n* (*mil*) the orderly adjutant or staff officer of a brigade.

brigadier [bRigadeer] *n* (*mil*) the commander of

a brigade, in rank below a major-general but above a colonel.

brigand [bRIgand] *n* bandit who lives by robbery and kidnapping persons for ransom.

brigandage [bRIgandij] *n* highway-robbery.

brigandine, brigantine (1) [bRIgandeen, bRIganteen] *n* (*hist*) coat of mail.

brigantine (2) *n* a two-masted sailing vessel with square sails on the foremast only > PDSa.

bright [bRIt] *adj* not dull, shining, characterized by much light; of intense colour, vivid; vivacious, animated; hopeful, encouraging; splendid, distinguished; (*coll*) clever ~ **bright** *adv*.

brighten [bRIten] *v/t* and *i* make bright; become bright.

brightly [bRItli] *adv* in a bright way.

brightness [bRItnes] *n* quality of being bright.

Bright's disease [bRIts-dizeez] *n* (*path*) disease of the kidneys.

brill [bRil] *n* a flatfish like the turbot.

brilliance [bRilyans] *n* dazzling brightness; keen intelligence ~ **brilliancy** *n* brilliance.

brilliant (1) [bRilyant] *adj* sparkling, dazzling, scintillating; of keen intellect ~ **brilliantly** *adv*.

brilliant (2) *n* a diamond of the finest cut and brilliance; smallest size of printing type.

brilliantine [bRilyanteen] *n* preparation for fixing and giving a gloss to the hair.

brim [bRim] *n* lip or rim of a vessel, cup *etc*; edge or verge of a steep descent; projecting rim below the crown of a hat; shore of river, lake, or sea ~ **brim** (*pres/part* **brimming**, *p/t* and *p/part* **brimmed**) *v/i* be full to the brim; **b. over** overflow.

brimful [bRimfool] *adj* full to the top; (*fig*) very full.

brimmer [bRimer] *n* a drinking vessel filled to overflowing.

brimming [bRiming] *adj* overflowing.

brimstone [bRimstOn] *n* (*pop*) sulphur; (*bibl*) fuel of hell-fire.

brindle, brindled [bRind'l, bRind'ld] *adj* of streaky brownish colour.

brine [bRIn] *n* water saturated with salt; sea-water; (*poet*) salt tears.

bring (*p/t* and *p/part* **brought**) [bRing] *v/t* fetch, cause to come; carry; conduct; attract; persuade; fetch (price); (*leg*) start (action), prefer (charge *etc*); **b. about** cause to happen; **b. back** remind one of; **b. down** shoot down: reduce (price); **b. forward** carry figures from one page to the next; **b. off** (*coll*) carry to a successful issue (deal *etc*); **b. on** cause; **b. out** introduce (young lady into society); emphasize; publish; **b. over** convert; **b. round** restore from illness or a faint; persuade, change the views of; **b. to** (*naut*) check the way of a ship; come to a stop; restore to consciousness; **b. up** raise, educate; vomit; raise (matter) for consideration; (*leg*) indict; (*naut*) stop; anchor, moor, or secure to a buoy.

brink [bRink] *n* extreme edge or verge of a steep descent; place where steep ground meets river or lake; (*fig*) verge (of ruin *etc*).

brinkmanship [bRinkmanship] *n* art and practice of pursuing a dangerous policy to the limit of safety.

briny [bRIni] *adj* salty ~ **briny** *n* (*coll*) the sea.

brio [bRee-O] *n* (*Ital*) vivacity, liveliness.

brioche [bRee-osh] *n* (*Fr*) light roll or pastry made in circular shape.

briony see **bryony**.

briquette, briquet [bRiket] *n* brick-shaped block of compressed coal-dust.

brisk [bRisk] *adj* quick-moving, lively, abrupt in manner; (*of liquors*) sparkling, the reverse of flat; (*of weather*) keen, exhilarating ~ **brisk** *v/t* and *i* enliven; become brisk ~ **briskly** *adv* ~ **briskness** *n*.

brisket [bRiskit] *n* the breast of an animal; the part of the breast nearest the ribs cut as a joint.

brisling, bristling [bRizling] *n* small sardine-like fish of the herring family.

bristle [bRis'l] *n* short, stiff hair on the back of the hog and wild boar; any short prickly hair; hairs in a brush ~ **bristle** *v/i* (*of animals*) raise bristles in anger or fear; (*fig*) display indignation, show fight; (*fig, of problems etc*) be beset (with difficulties); (*fig*) show a group of projecting points.

bristling see **brisling**.

bristly [bRisli] *adj* prickly; unshaven.

Bristol-board [bRistol-bawrd] *n* good cardboard white on both sides. used by artists.

Bristol diamond [bRistol-dIamond] *n* (*min*) rock crystal found near Bristol.

Bristol-fashion [bRistol-fashon] *adj* (*naut*) attaining perfection in appearance and efficiency.

Britannia metal [bRitanya-metal] *n* silver-like alloy of tin with some antimony and copper.

Britannic [bRitanik] *adj* of Britain, British.

British [bRitish] *adj* of or relating to Great Britain and its inhabitants; relating to the Celtic ancient Britons; **B. thermal unit** quantity of heat required to raise the temperature of 1 lb. of water 1° F (*abbr* B.T.U.); **B. warm** short military overcoat ~ **British** *n* (*pl*) British people.

Britisher [bRitisher] *n* (*US*) a British subject.

Briton [bRiton] *n* native of Great Britain; one of the early Celtic inhabitants of Britain.

brittle [bRit'l] *adj* fragile, easily broken ~ **brittleness** *n* state of being brittle.

broach [bROch] *n* tapered hand tool for making holes; awl, boring bit; mason's pointed chisel; spit for roasting; pin inside a lock; a squinch arch; **b. spire** octagonal spire carried on a square tower which has no parapets ~ **broach** *v/t* bore a hole in a cask to draw the liquor, tap; (*naut*) bring (ship) broadside to the wind and sea > PDSa; (*fig*) introduce; raise (topic *etc*).

broad [bRawd] *adj* large across, of great amplitude across; roomy, extensive; principal, main; obvious, definite; full (daylight); (*of dialect*) strongly marked; general, with wide application; indelicate, coarse; tolerant, liberal; **as b. as it's long** the same either way; **The Broads** (*pl*) extensive stretches of river water in Norfolk; **b. bean** common garden variety of bean ~ **broad** *n* that which is broad; (*US*) (*sl*) woman, *esp* if immoral.

broadcast (*p/t* and *p/part* **broadcast**) [bRawdkaast] *v/t* and *i* transmit by radio or television; speak or perform in a radio or TV programme ~ **broadcast** *adj* (*of seed*) widely scattered; (*fig*) widespread; widely disseminated; (*rad*) transmitted by radio or television ~ **broadcast** *n* speech, music *etc* transmitted by radio or television.

broadcaster [bRawdkaaster] *n* one who broadcasts, an announcer ~ **broadcasting** *n* and. *adj*.

broadcloth [*bRawd*kloth] *n* fine, plain, woollen black cloth; cloth of double width.

broaden [*bRaw*den] *v/t* and *i* widen; become broader.

broadloom [*bRawd*lOOm] *adj* (*of* carpets) woven in a width of at least 54 inches.

broadly [*bRawd*li] *adv* widely; generally, approximately.

broadminded [bRawd*mInd*id] *adj* tolerant.

broadsheet [*bRawd*sheet] *n* large sheet of paper printed on one side only; a ballad or tract so printed and sold in the streets.

broadside [*bRawd*sId] *n* a broadsheet; (*naut*) side of a ship above the waterline between bow and quarter; (*nav*) simultaneous discharge of all guns on one side of a warship at the same target; (*fig*) opinions forcibly expressed ~ **broadside** *adv* with the side fully in view; **b. on** (to) (*naut*) sideways on to.

broadsword [*bRawd*sawrd] *n* broad-bladed sword.

broadtail [*bRawd*tayl] *n* fur resembling Persian lamb or astrakhan.

broadways, broadwise [*bRawd*wayz, *bRawd*wIz] *adv* along the breadth, laterally.

Brobdingnagian [bRobding*nag*i-an] *adj* huge.

brocade [bRo*kayd*] *n* heavy silk fabric with elaborate raised patterns in gold and silver thread ~ **brocade** *v/t* and *i* ornament (material) with thread; do elaborate stitching.

brocatelle [bRoka*tel*] *n* kind of imitation brocade; **b. marble** fine grade of marble quarried in the French Pyrenees.

broccoli [*bRok*oli] *n* hardy kind of cauliflower.

broché [bRo*shay*] *adj* woven with embossed pattern ~ **broché** *n* fabric thus woven.

brochure [bRo*shoor*] *n* a booklet, stitched but not bound; pamphlet, *esp* of advertisements.

brock [bRok] *n* badger.

brocket [*bRok*it] *n* a stag in its second year.

brogue (1) [bROg] *n* strong shoe designed for country wear.

brogue (2) *n* broad accent, *esp* that of the English-speaking Irish.

broider [*bRoi*der] *v/t* (*ar*) embroider ~ **broidery** *n*.

broil (1) [bRoil] *v/t* and *i* prepare (meat) by cooking over fire (on grill *etc*), grill; subject to great heat; be extremely hot.

broil (2) *n* quarrel, noisy dispute; commotion.

broiler [*bRoi*ler] *n* one who cooks by broiling; a gridiron; fowl suitable for broiling; smallish chicken reared in a concrete henhouse, and not a free-range bird; (*coll*) a very hot day; quarrelsome person; **b. grower** table poultry producer; **b. house** sunless henhouse where broilers are reared.

broke [bROk] *adj* (*coll*) bankrupt, penniless, ruined.

broken [*bRO*ken] *adj* fractured, in pieces; uneven; (*of* speech) imperfect; (*of* water) choppy; (*of* weather) unsettled; (*fig*) exhausted; reduced to obedience, tamed; humbled, contrite; ruined; routed; (*phon*) diphthongized; **b. home** home from which one parent is absent through divorce, desertion *etc*.

broken-down [bROken-*down*] *adj* worn out, infirm; dilapidated.

broken-hearted [bROken-*haar*tid] *adj* grief-stricken; inconsolable.

brokenly [*bRO*kenli] *adv* spasmodically, jerkily.

broken-winded [bROken-*wind*id] *adj* (*of* horses) incapacitated by a disease of the lungs which causes laboured irregular breathing.

broker [*bRO*ker] *n* an agent or middleman who does business for a client in return for payment on a commission basis; a stockbroker who buys and sells stocks and shares; licensed appraiser and seller of goods distrained for rent; dealer in second-hand goods.

brokerage [*bRO*keRij] *n* a broker's commission for services rendered; business of a broker.

broking [*bRO*king] *n* business of a broker.

brolly [*bRo*li] *n* (*sl*) umbrella.

bromate [*bRO*mayt] *n* (*chem*) a salt of bromic acid.

bromic [*bRO*mik] *adj* (*chem*) containing bromine.

bromide [*bRO*mId] *n* (*chem*) a compound of bromine; a sedative (potassium bromide); (*fig*) conventional truism, trite remark ~ **bromidic** [bRO*mid*ik] *adj* addicted to bromides; (*fig*) dull.

bromine [*bRO*mIn] *n* (*chem*) poisonous dark red fuming liquid with an irritating smell > PDS.

bromism [*bRO*mizm] *n* (*path*) condition resulting from overdoses of potassium bromide.

bronchial [*bRong*ki-al] *n* (*anat*) pertaining to or affecting the tubes of the windpipe and lungs.

bronchitis [bRong*kI*tis] *n* (*med*) inflammation of the bronchial tubes ~ **bronchitic** [bRong*kit*ik] *adj*.

broncho-, bronch- *pref* of or relating to the bronchial tubes.

broncho-pneumonia [bRongko-newm*O*ni-a] *n* (*med*) inflammation of the lungs.

bronchotomy [bRong*kot*omi] *n* surgical cutting of the windpipe.

bronchus [*bRong*kus] (*pl* **bronchi** [*bRong*kI]) *n* (*anat*) a branch of the windpipe.

bronco [*bRong*kO] *n* (*US*) small, wiry, half-wild horse of the western plains.

bronco-buster [*bRong*kO-buster] *n* (*US*) (*coll*) one who breaks in broncos; a cowboy.

brontosaurus [bRonto*saw*Rus] *n* huge prehistoric reptile.

bronze [bRonz] *n* brownish alloy mainly of copper and tin; work of art made of bronze; brownish colour of bronze; **B. Age** (*arch*) prehistoric period in which bronze was largely used for making weapons and tools ~ **bronze** *v/t* and *i* make to look like bronze; become the colour of bronze ~ **bronze** *adj*.

brooch [bROch] *n* ornament of metal, jewels *etc* mounted on a pin and worn on a dress or coat.

brood [bROOd] *n* family of young birds hatched at one time; the young children of one mother; (*usu* cont) family, offspring; (*coll*) thoughtful mood ~ **brood** *v/i* sit on eggs to hatch them; hover over with outstretched wings; (*fig*) think deeply, ponder over moodily ~ **brooding** *adj* sitting on eggs; (*fig*) anxiously pondering.

brood-mare [*bROOd*-mair] *n* mare kept for breeding purposes.

broody [*bROO*di] *adj* (*of* hen) wishing to sit on its eggs; (*fig*) depressed, moody.

brook (1) [bROok] *n* small stream, rivulet.

brook (2) *v/t* put up with, bear, tolerate.

brooklet [*bROok*let] *n* small brook.

brooklime [*bRook*lIm] *n* (*bot*) the commonest waterside speedwell.

92

broom [bROOm] *n* (*bot*) shrub with yellow flowers common in sandy places and on heaths; besom or brush for sweeping; **new b.** person newly-appointed to a post and displaying excessive zeal.

broomrape [bROOmRayp] *n* (*bot*) weed found on roots of broom and similar plants.

broomstick [bROOmstik] *n* handle of a broom.

broomtail [bROOmtayl] *n* (*US*) pony having a short bushy tail.

brose [bROz] *n* (*Scots*) porridge.

broth [bRoth] *n* thin soup made from a boiling of meat and vegetables; (*biol*) liquid used as a culture medium for growing cells, bacteria *etc.*

brothel [bRothel] *n* bawdy-house; house for prostitution.

brother (*pl* **brothers, brethren**) [bRuTHer] *n* male with the same parents as another person; fellow-member of a trade, order, profession, guild *etc* (*pl* brethren); fellow-member of a religious order; comrade, associate; **b. german** full brother; **b. uterine** having the same mother only.

brotherhood [bRuTHerhood] *n* fraternal relationship; fraternity, association with common interests, guild; (*collect*) members of such an association; fellowship.

brother-in-law [bRuTHer-in-law] *n* brother of one's husband or wife; a sister's husband.

brotherly [bRuTHerli] *adj* like a brother; affectionate, kind ∼ **brotherliness** *n.*

brougham [bROOm/bROO-am] *n* four-wheeled closed carriage for two or four drawn by one horse.

brought [bRawt] *p/t* and *p/part* of **bring.**

brouhaha [bROOhaha] *n* (*coll*) uproar, fuss.

brow [bRow] *n* the arch above each eye; the hair growing there; part of the forehead above each eye; the forehead; edge of a steep cliff or hill; top of a rise in a road; (*min*) top of the shaft.

browbeat (*p/t* browbeat, *p/part* **browbeaten**) [bRowbeet] *v/t* intimidate with words or looks, bully ∼ **browbeater** *n.*

brown [bRown] *n* colour produced by mixing red, yellow, and black ∼ **brown** *adj* dusky-skinned, sun-tanned ∼ **brown** *v/t* and *i* make brown; roast brown; become brown in colour; **browned off** (*sl*) thoroughly disgruntled; **do b.** swindle; **b. study** deep thought.

brown-coal [bRown-kOl] *n* (*min*) lignite.

brownie [bRowni] *n* good-natured fairy or goblin; junior Guide; (*phot tr*) kind of camera.

Browning (1) [bRowning] *n* (*tr*) type of automatic pistol, rifle or machine-gun.

browning (2) *n* preparation for colouring gravy.

brownish [bRownish] *adj* slightly brown.

browse [bRowz] *v/i* feed on grass and shoots of trees *etc*, graze; (*fig*) read at random for pleasure.

brucellosis [brOOselOsis] *n* disease causing contagious abortion in cattle; a type of fever in men.

Bruin [bROO-in] *n* personification of the brown bear; its name in fairy-tales and animal stories.

bruise [bROOz] *v/t* and *i* discolour the skin by a blow without breaking it, contuse; grind or beat small, crush; show the effects of a blow ∼ **bruise** *n* injury from a blow ∼ **bruiser** *n* (*sl*) pugilist.

bruit [bROOt] *v/t* spread a rumour or report.

brumal [bROOmal] *adj* wintry.

brume [bROOm] *n* (*Fr*) fog; mist.

brumous [bROOmus] *adj* wintry; foggy.

brunch [bRunch] *n* a substantial meal taken at midday in place of breakfast and lunch.

brunette [bROOnet] *n* woman with a brown complexion and dark hair ∼ **brunette** *adj* brown-complexioned; dark-haired.

brunt [bRunt] *n* main impact; violence of an attack; heaviest stress.

brush [bRush] *n* utensil made of tufts of bristles, hairs *etc* fixed into a piece of wood with a handle, and used for sweeping, applying paint *etc*; tail of fox; (*elect*) conductor to make electrical contact between a fixed and a moving surface; discharge of electricity from sharp points on a conductor > PDS; thicket of small trees and shrubs, undergrowth, scrub; brief but lively encounter with an opponent, skirmish; **b. work** painting ∼ **brush** *v/t* and *i* use a brush upon, clean, polish; touch lightly in passing; **b. aside** ignore, dismiss summarily; **b. away, b. off** remove with a quick movement; dismiss curtly; **b. up** smarten, renovate; (*fig*) get back one's proficiency in.

brush-off [bRush-of] *n* (*sl*) curt refusal or dismissal.

brushwood [bRushwood] *n* undergrowth, scrub; tree- and hedge-cuttings.

brushy [bRushi] *adj* like a brush, bushy; thick with scrub.

brusque [bRoosk/bRusk] *adj* abrupt in manner, curt ∼ **brusquely** *adv* ∼ **brusqueness** *n.*

brussels sprouts [bRuselz-spRowts] *n* (*pl*) vegetables shaped like tiny cabbages which sprout in clusters from a stalk.

brutal [bROOtal] *adj* characteristic of a brute; cruel, rough, coarse, savage.

brutalism [bROOtalizm] *n* (*art*) deliberate harshness or crudeness in design ∼ **brutalist** *n* and *adj.*

brutality [bROOtaliti] *n* savage cruelty, savagery.

brutalize [bROOtaliz] *v/t* make brutal; treat with brutality; degrade.

brutally [bROOtali] *adv* cruelly, savagely.

brute [bROOt] *n* lower animal, beast; coarse, cruel, inhuman person; (*coll*) selfish or ill-tempered person ∼ **brute** *adj* brutish, purely physical; stupid; crude; **b. force** sheer physical strength.

brutish [bROOtish] *adj* like a brute; coarse, unfeeling, stupid, uncultured ∼ **brutishly** *adv.*

bruxism [bRuksizm] *n* (*med*) involuntary grinding of teeth, *esp* while sleeping.

bryology [bRI-oloji] *n* branch of botany dealing with mosses ∼ **bryologist** *n* an expert on mosses.

bryony, briony [bRI-oni] *n* (*bot*) kind of climbing plant.

bryozoa (*sing* **bryozoon**) [bRI-ozO-a] *n* (*pl*) (*zool*) lowest class of molluscs; (*sing*) animal belonging to this class.

Brythonic [bRithonik] *adj* pertaining to the Celts who lived in Brittany, Wales, and in southern Britain in early times.

bub [bub] *n* (*sl*) woman's breast.

bubal, bubale [bewbal] *n* kind of North African antelope.

bubble [bub'l] *n* globular or hemispherical film of liquid filled with air or gas; small pocket of air or gas in a liquid or solid; (*fig*) anything unsound or speculative; **b. bath** bath whose water has been rendered foamy by detergent liquid or crystals; **b. car** miniature motorcar with transparent rounded roof; **b. chamber** (*phys*) apparatus for making the tracks of ionizing particles visible as a row of bubbles in a super-heated liquid ~ **bubble** *v/i* form bubbles, effervesce; rise in bubbles, boil; flow making the sound of bubbles bursting continuously, gurgle.

bubble-and-squeak [bub'l-and-*skweek*] *n* minced meat and vegetables fried together.

bubble-gum [*bub*'l-gum] *n* chewing-gum that can be blown into large bubbles.

bubbly [*bub*li] *adj* full of bubbles ~ **bubbly** *n* (*sl*) champagne.

bubo (*pl* **buboes**) [*bew*bO] *n* (*med*) glandular swelling in armpit or groin ~ **bubonic** [bew*bon*ik] *adj* characterized by appearance of buboes; **b. plague** the plague, the Black Death.

buccal [*buk*al] *adj* of or relating to the cheek.

buccaneer [buka*neer*] *n* (*hist*) pirate infesting the Caribbean about 1700; sea-rover, privateer ~ **buccaneer** *v/i* live the life of a buccaneer.

buccinal [*buk*sinal] *adj* trumpet-like in shape or sound > PDM.

buccinator [*buk*sinayter] *n* (*anat*) thin flat muscle of the cheek.

Buchmanite [*buk*manIt] *n* member of the religious society, founded by Frank Buchman, known as Oxford Group or Moral Rearmament.

buck [*buk*] *n* male of certain animals (deer, hare, rabbit, antelope, reindeer, chamois); (*fig*) fop, dandy; a counter used in poker; (*US*) (*coll*) dollar; **pass the b.** (*sl*) shift responsibility to another ~ **buck** *v/t* and *i* (*of horses etc*) make a sudden leap upwards in an effort to throw the rider; object to, oppose; swagger, talk big; **b. up** (*fig*) make haste, exert onself; take confidence, cheer up.

bucked [*bukt*] *adj* (*coll*) pleased, encouraged.

bucket [*buk*it] *n* vessel with arched handle for holding water *etc*; **b. elevator** endless chain of buckets on a dredger > PDE; **b. seat** car or airplane seat for one person; **kick the b.** (*sl*) die ~ **bucket** *v/t* and *i* ride (horse) hard; (*rowing*) swing forward too quickly after a stroke; be tossed (about).

bucketful [*buk*itfool] *n* as much as a bucket will hold.

bucketshop [*buk*itshop] *n* office of stockbrokers not members of the Stock Exchange dealing largely in speculative and worthless shares.

buckhorn [*buk*hawrn] *n* hard material of a buck's horn sometimes used for knife handles.

buckhound [*buk*hownd] *n* breed of hound for hunting stags.

buckish [*buk*ish] *adj* like a buck-goat (smelly, lustful *etc*); foppish.

buckjump [*buk*jump] *n* sudden leap upwards of an unbroken horse ~ **buckjumper** *n* untamed or vicious horse.

buckle [*buk*'l] *n* device with hinged prong or prongs for fastening the two ends of a strap together; on shoes *etc* often ornamental ~ **buckle** *v/t* and *i* fasten with a buckle; bend out of shape under pressure, crumple; **b. to** set to work in earnest, start work.

buckled [*buk*'ld] *adj* (*of shoes*) fastened with buckles; (*of wheels, struts etc*) bent out of shape.

buckler [*buk*ler] *n* small round shield to parry blows or thrusts; (*fig*) defence, protector; (*zool*) hard protective casing of some animals.

bucko (*pl* **buckoes**) [*buk*O] *n* (*naut sl*) domineering fellow ~ **bucko** *adj* boastful, blustering.

buckra [*buk*Ra] *n* (*US*) white man, boss, master.

buckram [*buk*Ram] *n* durable cotton or linen cloth used to make linings and to bind books.

buckshee [*buk*shee] *adj* (*sl*) free, without charge ~ **buckshee** *n* (*sl*) extra rations; anything obtained without payment.

buckshot [*buk*shot] *n* large-sized shot used for game-hunting.

buckskin [*buk*skin] *n* leather prepared from the skin of the buck; (*pl*) breeches made of this ~ **buckskin** *adj*.

buckthorn [*buk*thawrn] *n* thorny shrub with berries which yield pigment and which are also strongly purgative.

bucktooth [*buk*tOOth] *n* projecting tooth.

buckwheat [*buk*weet] *n* a cereal plant, the seeds of which are used as food for horses, cattle, and poultry; (*US*) meal, flour, or batter made from buckwheat; a buckwheat cake.

bucolic [bew*kol*ik] *adj* of or relating to shepherds, pastoral; of the countryside, rural ~ **bucolics** *n* (*pl*) poems about country life, pastorals.

bud (1) [*bud*] *n* (*bot*) compact, undeveloped shoot, consisting of a short stem bearing crowded, overlapping, immature leaves; partly-opened flower or blossom; **nip in the b.** (*fig*) put an end to (plan, idea *etc*) in its early stages ~ **bud** (*pres/part* **budding**, *p/t* and *p/part* **budded**) *v/t* and *i* graft (a bud) on to another plant; put forth buds, start growing.

bud (2) see **buddy.**

Buddhism [*bood*izm] *n* Asiatic religion founded by Siddartha Gautama, called the Buddha, The Enlightened, The Awakened.

Buddhist [*bood*ist] *n* and *adj* (follower) of Buddhism.

Buddhistic [bood*is*tik] *adj* pertaining to Buddhists and Buddhism.

budding [*bud*ing] *n* sprouting of buds; operation of inserting a bud from one tree under the bark of another ~ **budding** *adj* putting forth buds; (*fig*) showing great promise.

buddleia [*bud*lee-a] *n* (*bot*) shrub which bears clusters of yellow or violet flowers.

buddy, bud [*bud*i, *bud*] *n* (*US coll*) pal, brother.

budge [*buj*] *v/t* and *i* move slightly, give way.

budgerigar [*buj*eRigaar] *n* Australian love-bird, green parakeet.

budget [*buj*it] *n* annual estimate of the national revenue and expenditure; similar estimate made by public body or private person ~ **budget** *v/i* prepare a budget; estimate cost and make provision for it; **b. for** allow for, take into consideration when estimating expenses.

budgetary [*buj*itaRi] *adj* of a budget.

budgie [*buj*i] *n* (*coll dim*) budgerigar.

buff [*buf*] *n* leather made from the hide of buffalo or ox; (*fig*) (*coll*) bare skin; (*coll*) enthusiastic admirer, devotee; (*eng*) high-speed disc used for polishing metals; colour of buff leather, a pale brownish yellow ~ **buff** *v/t* polish or grind down.

buffalo (*pl* **buffaloes**) [*buf*ulO] *n* wild ox; (*pop*) North American bison.

buffer (1) [*buf*er] *n* one of two spring-loaded steel pads fitted to the front and rear of railway rolling-stock to absorb the shock of collision; hydraulic buffers mounted on a structure at the end of the permanent way at a railway terminus; anything which reduces impact or preserves stability; **b. solution** (*chem*) solution whose acidity or alkalinity is practically unchanged by dilution; **b. stop** a railway sleeper bolted across the rails to take the impact of wagons moving into it; **b. state** small country or state which by its position between two greater powers lessens the risk of hostilities between them.

buffer (2) *n* (*coll*) fellow; old man.

buffet (1) [*buf*it] *n* blow struck with the hand; (*fig*) misfortune, calamity ~ **buffet** *v/t* and *i* strike with the hand; contend, struggle (with).

buffet (2) [*boo*fay] *n* refreshment bar; place, table, where light refreshments are served.

buffet (3) [*buf*it] sideboard; china cupboard.

buffeting [*buf*iting] *n* succession of blows; violence (of the weather).

buffoon [bu*fOOn*] *n* (*cont*) clown, jester, knock-about comedian, wag ~ **buffoonery** *n*.

bug [bug] *n* verminous, blood-sucking insect found in dirty houses and furniture; (*coll*) a mild virus infection; (*coll* and *US*) any insect; (*coll*) hidden microphone; light vehicle consisting only of essential functional parts; (*sl*) mechanical snag or fault; obsessional enthusiasm; fan, enthusiast; (*aer sl*) lem; **big b.** (*coll*) (*freq iron*) important person ~ **bug** (*pres/part* **bugging**, *p/t* and *p/part* **bugged**) *v/t* (*coll*) install hidden microphones in (room etc) for spying; (*sl*) annoy.

bugbear [*bug*bair] *n* (*orig*) hobgoblin in the shape of bear; anything which inspires fear or dislike.

bugger [*bug*er] *n* man having anal intercourse with man or animal, sodomite; (*vulg*) term of abuse for a man or animal ~ **bugger** *v/t* commit sodomy with; (*sl*) spoil, ruin; damn; **b. off** (*sl*) go away; **b. up** (*sl*) make a mess of, spoil.

buggery [*bug*eRi] *n* sodomy.

buggy (1) [*bug*i] *adj* infested with bugs.

buggy (2) *n* light four-wheeled vehicle drawn by one horse and having a collapsible top.

bugle (1) [*bewg*'l] *n* (*bot*) plant of the genus *Ajuga* with a leafy spike of powder-blue flowers.

bugle (2) *n* wind instrument of brass or copper similar to the trumpet used for military calls > PDM ~ **bugle** *v/i* and *t*.

bugle (3) *n* bead of glass or jet, sewn on to a woman's dress for ornament.

bugler [*bewg*ler] *n* one who sounds a bugle.

bugloss [*bew*glos] *n* (*bot*) either of two plants akin to borage.

buhl, boule [bOOl] *n* style of fine inlay work, with complicated figures of brass, gold, or bronze set as ornaments into surfaces of ebony, ivory, or tortoise-shell.

build (*p/t* and *p/part* **built**) [bild] *v/t* and *i* fit together, construct, erect; be occupied in building; establish, develop gradually; give stability to, strengthen, improve; **b. on** rely upon; **b. up** strengthen, increase; block up, wall up; (*fig*) magnify the importance of a person or event by favourable publicity ~ **build** *n* shape, design, cut; proportions of the human body; application of adequate pigment in painting ~ **builder** *n*.

building [*bild*ing] *n* work of a builder; what is built, edifice; **b. society** society lending money

to enable persons to build or buy houses, and accepting money for investment.

build-up [*bild*-up] *n* (*coll*) gradual increase, steady accumulation; advance preparation (for an attack, effect *etc*); advance publicity.

built [bilt] *adj* constructed, erected; **be b. that way** (*of person*) be so constituted or disposed.

built-in [*bilt*-in] *adj* (*of cupboards etc*) erected as permanent fixtures; included as a standard feature in design of a machine *etc*; (*fig*) essential, forming a basic part; inescapable; instinctive.

built-up [*bilt*-up] *adj* (*of an area*) completely covered with buildings; built of different sections joined together.

bulb [bulb] *n* enlarged bud at the base of the stem of certain plants such as the daffodil; spherical expansion in a glass tube; electric lamp; pneumatic rubber device on syringes *etc* ~ **bulbed** *adj* having a bulb, round.

bulbiferous [bul*bif*eRus] *adj* bearing bulbs.

bulbil, bulbel [*bul*bil] *n* small bulb at the side of an old one.

bulbous [*bul*bus] *adj* bulb-shaped; with bulb-like roots; round; swollen.

bulbul [*bool*bool] *n* Persian song-bird.

bulge [bulj] *n* irregular outward swelling; (*mil*) projecting sector of an army's front line; temporary increase in volume or numbers ~ **bulge** *v/t* and *i* make stick out; swell outwards.

bulger [*bul*jer] *n* (*golf*) brassy or driver with convex face.

bulging [*bul*jing] *adj* swelling, full to overflowing.

bulimia [bew*limi*-a] *n* (*path*) morbid hunger.

bulk [bulk] *n* great size (of mass, volume, body *etc*); the main part; (*naut*) cargo in the hold of a ship; **in b.** not pre-packed, loose; in large quantities; **b. buying** purchasing the whole of a manufacturer's output of a particular article ~ **bulk** *v/t* and *i* put several consignments of goods together for transport; (*of cargo*) ascertain the bulk of; seem important, loom large.

bulkhead [*bulk*hed] *n* (*naut*) partition within a ship's hull or superstructure.

bulky [*bul*ki] *adj* taking up a lot of space, unwieldy.

bull (1) [bool] *n* uncastrated male of ox and other bovine animals; male of other large animals such as the elephant, whale *etc*; speculator who has gambled on a rise in the prices of stocks and shares; the constellation Taurus; the second sign of the zodiac; bull's eye; (*sl*) policeman; (*mil sl*) cleaning and smartening up, 'spit and polish'; (*sl*) humbug, claptrap; **take the b. by the horns** face a difficult situation without shrinking; **b. in a china shop** one who is clumsy in a confined space, or tactless in a delicate situation ~ **bull** *v/t* and *i* try to raise prices of (stocks); gamble for a rise (in price); (*sl*) talk humbug or nonsense (to) ~ **bull** *adj* (*of market*) rising.

bull (2) *n* a statement made ludicrous by some inconsistency or contradiction which it contains; a blunder in speech or conduct.

bull (3) *n* edict issued by the Pope.

bullace [*bool*as] *n* wild plum.

bullate [*bool*ayt] *adj* (*bot*) puckered.

bull-baiting [*bool*-bayting] *n* (*hist*) sport of baiting a bull with dogs.

bullcalf [*bool*kaaf] *n* male calf.

bulldog [booldog] *n* thickset English breed of dog famed for its obstinate courage; (*coll*) attendant of a proctor at Oxford and Cambridge.

bulldoze [booldOz] *v/t* intimidate by violence or threats; demolish with a bulldozer.

ulldozer [booldOzer] *n* powerful machine of a caterpillar tractor type for levelling rough ground and removing obstacles.

buller [booler] *n* (*coll*) proctor's 'bulldog'.

bullet [boolit] *n* pellet of lead or a slender, tapered, metal bar, fired from rifle or revolver.

bullet-head [boolit-hed] *n* (*US*) obstinate person ~ **bullet-headed** *adj* having a small, round head.

bulletin [boolitin] *n* brief public announcement; official statement about the progress of an eminent invalid; broadcast account of the news.

bulletproof [boolitpROOf] *adj* reinforced against impact of bullets.

bullfight [boolfIt] *n* spectacle in arena where a bull is goaded into attacking and finally killed.

bullfighter [boolfIter] *n* man skilled in bullfights.

bullfinch (1) [boolfinch] *n* song-bird with a strong rounded beak and fine plumage.

bullfinch (2) *n* tall, quickset hedge with a ditch.

bullfrog [boolfRog] *n* species of large frog.

bullhead [boolhed] *n* small freshwater fish with a large head; (*fig*) blockhead, fool.

bullheaded [boolhedid] *adj* with a large or broad head; rash, blundering.

bullion (1) [boolyon] *n* gold and silver in bulk, not in the form of coins or manufactured articles; the gold and silver content of coins and such articles.

bullion (2) *n* fringe or lace with gold or silver threads.

bullish [boolish] *adj* (*Stock Exchange*) speculating for, conducive to, a rise in prices.

bullnecked [boolnekt] *adj* with a short thick neck.

bullnose [boolnOs] *n* (*bui*) brick with a rounded corner.

bullock [boolok] *n* young or gelded bull.

bull-point [bool-*point*] *n* (*coll*) point of advantage; where one scores over one's opponent.

bullpup [boolpup] *n* bulldog puppy.

bullring [boolRing] *n* arena for bullfighting.

bullroarer [boolRawrRer] *n* powerful type of wooden rattle.

bullseye [boolzI] *n* centre of a target, or a shot hitting it; round, peppermint-flavoured sweet; small circular or oval window.

bullshit [boolshit] *n* (*vulg sl*) nonsense, humbug.

bull-terrier [bool-*te*Ri-er] *n* breed of dog between bulldog and terrier.

bulltrout [booltROwt] *n* large trout with thick, short head resembling a small salmon.

bully [booli] *n* one who persecutes the weak; blustering ruffian; (*hockey*) putting the ball into play by crossing sticks three times ~ **bully** (*pres* **bullies**, *p/t* **bullied**), *v/t* tyrannize over, scold and torment; treat cruelly; **b. off** (*hockey*) cross sticks three times to start play ~ **bully** *adj* (*sl*) first-rate ~ **bully!** *interj* well done! hurrah!

bully beef, bully [booli-*beef*, booli] *n* soldiers' term for tinned corned beef.

bully-boy [booli-boi] *n* young ruffian.

bulrush [boolRush] *n* (*bot*) kind of tall sedge.

bulter see **boulter**.

bulwark [boolwark] *n* earthwork, rampart; mole, breakwater; (*naut*) side of vessel above deck-level; (*fig*) strong defence, protector ~ **bulwark** *v/t* defend, protect, shelter.

bum (1) [bum] *n* (*coll abbr*) bumbailiff.

bum (2) *n* (*coll*) the buttocks.

bum (3) *v/i* and *t* (*US sl*) sponge; get by sponging; **b. around** wander about while living by begging or by casual labour ~ **bum** *n* (*US sl*) habitual loafer, vagrant ~ **bum** *adj* (*US sl*) bad, useless, unpleasant.

bumbailiff [bumbaylif] *n* (*cont*) sheriff's officer; bailiff who distrains debtors, serves writs *etc.*

bumble [bumb'l] *v/i* buzz, drone; talk vaguely; behave clumsily, blunder.

bumblebee [bumb'lbee] *n* large wild bee with a loud buzz.

bumbledom [bumb'ldom] *n* the pompous manner and fussy officiousness of some minor officials.

bumble-puppy [bumb'l-pupi] *n* game in which a tennis ball strung from a post is hit alternately in opposite directions by the rackets of two players; (*joc*) whist or other game played more for fun than as test of skill.

bumbo [bumbO] *n* a drink made with rum or gin mixed with sugar, nutmeg, and water.

bumboat [bumbOt] *n* (*naut*) small flat-bottomed boat ferrying provisions to ships lying off shore.

bumf, bumph [bumf] *n* (*vulg*) toilet paper; (*pej sl*) paper, official forms and documents; trashy magazines or novels *etc.*

bummalo [bumalO] *n* small Indian fish, the Bombay duck.

bummaree [bumaRee] *n* dealer or middleman in Billingsgate fish-market; self-employed licensed meat porter.

bump [bump] *n* blow or thud made by a knock or collision; unevenness on a road surface; jolt given to vehicle or aircraft; swelling caused by a blow; protuberance on the skull, and the propensity it is thought to indicate; (*boat-racing*) the touching of the stern of one boat by the prow of the next ~ **bump** *v/t* and *i* strike heavily, knock, thump; (*boat-racing*) overtake and touch; (*cricket*) make (a ball) rise abruptly after pitching; come with a jolt (against); jolt along a rough road in a vehicle; (*cricket*) rise abruptly after pitching; **b. off** (*sl*) murder; **b. up** increase sharply ~ **bump** *adv* with a thud.

bumper [bumper] *n* glass or tankard full to the brim; fender at the front and rear of a motor vehicle; (*cricket*) a ball pitched short to fly menacingly past the batsman's head ~ **bumper** *adj* big, full, abundant.

bumph see **bumf**.

bumpiness [bumpines] *n* unevenness of surface.

bumpkin [bumpkin] *n* a yokel from the country, a rustic; (*naut*) small boom ~ **bumpkinish** *adj.*

bumptious [bumpshus] *adj* self-assertive, conceited ~ **bumptiously** *adv* ~ **bumptiousness ss** *n.*

bumpy [bumpi] *adj* full of bumps, uneven; causing bumps, jolting, rough.

bun [bun] *n* small, round, sweet cake; knot of hair at the nape of a woman's neck; **take the b.** (*sl*) be best (or worst) in anything; behave in an irritating or ridiculous fashion.

buna [bOOna] *n* synthetic rubber > PDS.

bunch [*bunch*] *n* group or cluster of things of the same sort growing together or fastened together; company of people; (*sl*) mob, gang ~ **bunch** *v/t* and *i* form into a bunch; cluster together ~ **bunchy** *adj* forming a bunch; growing in bunches.

bunco [*bunk*O] *v/t* (*US sl*) swindle, *esp* at cards.

buncombe see **bunkum**.

bundle [*bund'l*] *n* collection of things gathered together; package, parcel; (*sl*) large sum of money ~ **bundle** *v/t* and *i* put away in an untidy heap; **b. up** tie up; **b. out, off, away** get rid of in a hurry; **b. out** make an unceremonious departure with all one's belongings.

bung [*bung*] *n* plug of wood or cork for the hole in a cask ~ **bung** *v/t* stop the hole in a cask with a bung; (*coll*) hurl, thrust; **bunged up** stopped up by foreign matter; (*of eyes*) swollen.

bungaloid [*bung*-galoid] *adj* of, with the appearance of, bungalows; **b. growth** area of haphazard building development.

bungalow [*bung*-galO] *n* one-storeyed house.

bunghole [*bung*-hOl] *n* hole in a cask for filling it.

bungle [*bung*-g'l] *v/t* and *i* spoil by clumsiness, botch; act clumsily ~ **bungle** *n* clumsy piece of work; mistake, muddle ~ **bungler** *n* one who bungles, unskilled craftsman; inexpert administrator.

bunion [*bunyon*] *n* inflamed swelling on the foot, usually on the large joint of the big toe.

bunk (1) [*bunk*] *n* sleeping berth in ship's cabin or on a train; one of two or more beds placed one above the other; **do a b.** (*sl*) run away, disappear ~ **bunk** *v/i* lie down on one's bunk, go to bed; (*sl*) make off, run away.

bunk (2) *n* (*sl abbr*) bunkum, nonsense.

bunker [*bunk*er] *n* large storage container for coal, ore, or stone; sandy hollow or other obstruction on a golf course; (*fig*) obstacle; (*mil*) strong-point; dug-out strongly roofed, hide-out ~ **bunker** *v/t* and *i* fill bunkers of (ship) with coal; put (coal) into the bunkers; (*of ship*) take in a supply of coal.

bunkered [*bunk*erd] *adj* (*golf*) impeded by a bunker or other obstruction; (*fig*) obstructed.

bunkum, buncombe [*bunk*um] *n* humbug, claptrap, calculated to impress or impose on people.

bunny [*buni*] *n* child's name for a rabbit; (*coll*) nightclub waitress or dancing partner wearing few clothes, with mock rabbit's tail and ears.

bunsen burner [bunsen-*bur*ner] *n* jet which burns air with gas to obtain greater heat.

bunt (1) [*bunt*] *n* sagging or bulging part of a net or sail ~ **bunt** *v/t* and *i* (*naut*) haul up middle of (sail) when furling; (*of a sail*) belly out.

bunt (2) *n* parasitic fungoid which attacks wheat and turns the grain black.

bunt (3) *n* (*aer*) manoeuvre of half an outside loop followed by a half roll; (*baseball*) blocking of a pitched ball ~ **bunt** *v/i* and *t* butt, push; (*aer*) execute a bunt; (*baseball*) block ball with the bat.

bunting (1) [*bunting*] *n* brightly-coloured coarse worsted cloth used for flags, streamers, and pennants; a flag, flags.

bunting (2) *n* common name for various small birds such as the finch, yellow-hammer.

bunyip [*bunyip*] *n* fabulous animal supposed to inhabit Australia.

buoy [*boi*] *n* floating metal sphere or cylinder (sometimes with bell attached) moored to mark

the presence of dangerous reefs and shoals, or to indicate a navigable channel ~ **buoy** *v/t* and *i* mark with buoy(s); keep afloat; (*fig*) sustain; raise.

buoyage [*boi*-ij] *n* system of buoys; the provision or positioning of buoys.

buoyancy [*boi*-ansi] *n* ability to keep afloat; (*phys*) upward pressure exerted on a body immersed in a fluid; (*fig*) lightheartedness, power of recovery; (*stocks and shares*) tendency to rise (in price).

buoyant [*boi*-ant] *adj* floating, able to surface if submerged; (*fig*) lighthearted, irrepressible; tending to rise (in price) ~ **buoyantly** *adv*.

bur (1), **burr** [*bur*] *n* plant's seed-vessel which clings very readily to clothing; husk of chestnut; curly natural markings on furniture; rough edge left on metal by a cutting tool, or on a moulding by a press; kind of dentist's drill; (*pl*) bricks which have fused together in the kiln; (*fig*) anything that clings like a bur; person difficult to shake off ~ **burr** *v/t* make a rough edge on (metal).

bur (2), **burr** *n* pronunciation of *r* with a trill made by the uvula, as in some Northumberland dialects ~ **bur, burr** (*pres/part* burring, *p/t* and *p/part* burred) *v/i* speak with a bur; speak indistinctly.

burble [*burb*'l] *v/i* flow with a bubbling sound, gurgle; (*fig*) mutter on ~ **burble** *n* continuous muttering.

burbot [*bur*bot] *n* freshwater fish like an eel.

burden (1), **burthen** [*bur*den, *bur*THen] *n* load carried, a load; (*naut*) carrying capacity of a ship (in tons); (*fig*) something wearisome or heavy to carry or endure; **beast of b.** animal for carrying loads; **b. of proof** responsibility of proving ~ **burden, burthen** *v/t* load, impose a burden upon; oppress.

burden (2), **burthen** *n* chorus of a song; chief topic, theme.

burdensome [*bur*densum] *adj* heavy to bear, oppressive ~ **burdensomeness** *n*.

burdock [*bur*dok] *n* weed with prickly flowers and large dock-like leaves.

bureau (*pl* **bureaux**) [*bew*rO/*bew*rO] *n* office, agency, specialized business or department; writing desk with drawers and a movable flap for writing on; (*US*) chest of drawers.

bureaucracy [*bew*ROk*Rasi*] *n* government by state officials from a central department or office; undue multiplication of, and concentration of power in, departments; body of officials.

bureaucrat [*bew*ROk*Rat*] *n* official whose executive duties are performed in or from an office; state official with an undue respect for the strict interpretation of the rules and procedure of his department.

bureaucratic [*bew*RO*kRatik*] *adj* slavishly following all the petty details of departmental procedure; characteristic of bureaucracy.

burette [*bew*Ret] *n* graduated glass tube with a ground-glass tap, for measuring the volume of liquid run out from it.

burg [*burg*] *n* (*US coll*) town, city.

burgage [*burg*ij] *n* (*hist*) tenure of land from an overlord for a yearly rent.

burgee [*bur*jee] *n* (*naut*) small three-cornered pennant flown from a yacht.

burgeon [*bur*jon] *v/i* begin to grow, put forth buds.

burgess [bur̄jis] n citizen, dweller in borough having full municipal rights ~ **burgess-ship** n the freedom of a borough.

burgh [buRu] n (*Scots*) town having charter.

burgher [bur̄ger] n inhabitant of a borough; a citizen (*usu* of Dutch and German towns).

burglar [burglar] n person who commits burglary.

burglarious [burglairi-us] adj pertaining to, addicted to, constituting the crime of, burglary ~ **burglariously** adv after the manner of, in such a manner as to constitute, burglary.

burglarize [burglaRIz] v/t (*US*) rifle by burglary.

burglary [burglaRi] n forcible entry into a house after dark with intent to steal.

burgle [burg'l] v/t and i break into a building in order to steal; commit burglary.

burgomaster [burgomaaster] n mayor of Dutch or Flemish town.

burgonet [burgonet] n (*hist*) steel cap or visored helmet.

Burgundy [burgundi] n wine made in Burgundy.

burial [beRi-al] n interment; funeral.

burial-ground [beRi-al-gRownd] n cemetery.

burial-mound [beRi-al-mownd] n tumulus, barrow.

burin [bewRin] n sharp tool used in engraving; the engraver's style or artistry.

burinist [bewRinist] n an engraver.

burk see **berk**.

burke [burk] v/t murder by smothering; kill secretly and get rid of; (*fig*) hush up, suppress quietly.

burl [burl] n a lump in cloth; a wart on trunk of tree ~ **burl** v/t dress (cloth) by removing burls.

burlap [burlap] n coarse cloth used for sacking made from jute or hemp; curtain material.

burlesque [burlesk] n mocking imitation, parody of a serious literary or dramatic work; kind of revue ~ **burlesque** adj exciting laughter by caricature ~ **burlesque** v/t make ridiculous by caricature; to parody, travesty.

burly [burli] adj of stout and sturdy build; robust.

burn (1) [burn] n (*dial*) small stream, brook.

burn (2) n a mark, or some bodily hurt, caused by fire, heat, or a corrosive; (*sl*) cigarette; (*aer*) act of firing a spacecraft's rockets; **slow b.** (*coll*) state of silent fury.

burn (3) (*p/t* and *p/part* **burnt, burned**) v/t and i destroy or injure by fire, heat, or a corrosive; scorch; put to death by burning; consume to obtain heat or light; cut metal with a gas flame; be on fire; give light, shine; undergo nuclear fission or fusion; (*fig*) feel hot; be inflamed (with passion, hatred *etc*); **b. down** reduce to ashes; **b. one's fingers** suffer damage or loss through meddling or rashness; **b. up** (*sl*) get very angry.

burner [burner] n jet, wick *etc* where gas burns to provide heat or light.

burnet [burnit] n (*bot*) salad **b.** and great **b.**, plants with purple-tinged flowers.

burning [burning] adj on fire; being scorched by fire; raging (thirst); (*fig*) vehement, ardent; much discussed; **b. bush** name of various shrubs which give off highly volatile oil; **b. glass** lens which concentrates the sun's rays to a point of intense heat ~ **burning** n a conflagration; a fire.

burnish [burnish] v/t and i polish by friction; make smooth and shiny; take a polish (well, badly) ~ **burnish** n polish, gloss ~ **burnisher** n.

burnous [burnOOs] n hooded Arab cloak.

burnt, burned [burnt] adj affected, damaged, or hurt by fire; coloured deep yellowish, or matt, brown; **b. lime** quicklime; **b. offering** sacrifice offered up to a deity by burning it with fire; **b. sacrifice** burnt offering; **b. sienna** orange-red pigment.

burp [burp] v/i and t (*coll*) belch; pat (baby) to make him belch ~ **burp** n (*coll*) belch.

burr see **bur**.

burro [booRo] n small donkey, *esp* as pack-animal.

burrow [buRO] n hole made in the ground for a dwelling-place by rabbits, foxes *etc* ~ **burrow** v/t make a burrow; dig a passage underground; (*fig*) delve deeply ~ **burrower** n one who burrows.

bursar [bursar] n university student or school pupil holding a bursary or grant; college treasurer ~ **bursarship** n status or office of a bursar.

bursary [bursaRi] n grant of money made to support a student at a school or university; bursar's rooms in a college.

burst (*p/t* and *p/part* **burst**) [burst] v/t and i break open; shatter in pieces; rend, split; break (into pieces) under tension; explode; fly open suddenly, open out; break; (*fig*) be well endowed (with); appear suddenly; **b. out** exclaim ~ **burst** n act of bursting; a splitting apart; an explosion; sudden outbreak (of applause *etc*); brief strenuous effort, spurt; (*coll*) succession of shots from an automatic gun.

burthen see **burden**.

burton [burton] n (*naut*) type of tackle > PDSa; a kind of beer brewed at Burton-on-Trent; **gone for a b.** (*sl*) dead, disappeared.

bury (*p/t* and *p/part* **buried**) [beRi] v/t put anything into the earth, cover with soil to hide; inter with funeral rites; hide away; engross (oneself in); (*fig*) forget (quarrels); **b. the hatchet** become reconciled.

bus (*pl* **buses**, *US* **busses**) [bus] n omnibus; (*coll*) motor vehicle, aircraft; **miss the b.** miss a favourable opportunity ~ **bus** v/i and t go by bus; (*US*) transport by bus, *esp* to another district.

busby [buzbi] n (*mil*) tall fur cap worn on parade by certain British regiments.

bush (1) [boosh] n shrub with several branches growing from the root; thicket of shrubs; untouched forest region with dense undergrowth; wild uncultivated region (not necessarily wooded); (*hist*) branch or bunch of ivy hung outside a tavern; **b. telegraph** system of rapid communication over long distances by drum-beat, smoke signals *etc*; (*fig*) mysteriously rapid spreading of information; **good wine needs no b.** good quality needs no advertisement; **beat about the b.** evade the point at issue ~ **bush** v/i be bushy, grow thickly ~ **bush** adj working, living or used in wild regions; crude, rough; untrained, unqualified.

bush (2) n (*eng*) cylindrical sleeve of metal which forms a bearing surface for a rotating shaft ~ **bush** v/t provide with a bush.

bushbuck [booshbuk] n an African antelope.

bush-cat [boosh-kat] n South African tiger-cat.

bushed [boosht] adj (*coll*) exhausted; (*Aust*) lost in the bush.

bushel [booshel] n measure of capacity containing eight gallons; **hide one's light under a b.** be unduly modest about one's capabilities.

bush-harrow [*boosh*-haRO] *n* (*agr*) heavy barred frame with bushes or branches interwoven and used for covering seed or for harrowing grass-land ~ **bush-harrow** *v/t*.

bushido [*bOOsh*eedO] *n* chivalrous code of conduct observed by the Japanese military caste.

Bushman [*boosh*man] *n* member of primitive South African tribe; (*no cap*) (*Aust*) one who lives or travels in the bush.

bushranger [*boosh*Raynjer] *n* (*Aust*) bandit (*orig* escaped convict) living in the bush and committing robbery under arms ~ **bush-ranging** *n*.

bushwhacker [*boosh*waker] *n* (*Aust*) lumberjack; (*US*) dweller in the backwoods, frontiersman; guerrilla soldier or bandit.

bushy [*boosh*i] *adj* covered, overgrown with bushes; covered with long hairs ~ **bushiness** *n*.

busily [*bizi*li] *adv* in a busy manner, eagerly, actively; laboriously; (*pej*) inquisitively, officiously.

business [*biz*nis] *n* trade, profession, regular employment; commercial transactions; commercial undertaking, shop, office *etc*; responsibility or duty; (*used vaguely*) affair, concern, matter; (*theat*) what the performers do on the stage in addition to speaking their lines.

businesslike [*biz*nislik] *adj* methodical, systematic, efficient, practical.

businessman [*biz*nisman] *n* one whose occupation is in commerce or finance.

busing, bussing [*bus*ing] *n* transport by bus; (*US*) integration of schools by transporting Negro children to schools in white areas and vice versa.

busk (1) [*busk*] *n* strip of steel or whalebone in a corset to stiffen it.

busk (2) *v/t* get ready; attire oneself; hurry.

busker [*busk*er] *n* itinerant musician or actor.

buskin [*busk*in] *n* half-boot or high shoe with thick soles worn by actors in Athenian tragedy; (*fig*) tragedy; the tragic style; woman's low, laced shoe ~ **buskined** *adj* wearing buskins; (*fig*) tragic, dignified, lofty.

busky [*busk*i] *adj* (*poet*) bosky, wooded.

busload [*bus*lOd] *n* as many passengers as a bus is carrying or can carry.

busman [*bus*man] *n* driver or conductor of a bus; **busman's holiday** holiday spent in one's usual occupation.

buss [*bus*] *n* (*ar*) a loud and playful kiss ~ **buss** *v/t*.

bussing see **busing**.

bus-stop [*bus*-stop] *n* place where a bus stops to pick up and set down passengers.

bust (1) [*bust*] *n* representation in sculpture of a person's head and shoulders; the front of the human body between the waist and neck; a woman's bosom; measurement of this.

bust (2) *v/t* and *i* (*sl*) burst, break; (*sl*) catch red-handed; arrest; sack, demote; ruin ~ **bust** *adj* (*sl*) broken; bankrupt, penniless ~ **bust** *n* (*sl*) drinking-bout, spree; police raid; (*US*) bankruptcy.

bustard [*bust*ard] *n* European bird, akin to the crane and plover.

bustle (1) [*bus*'l] *v/t* and *i* rouse, hustle; **b. about** hurry busily round, bestir oneself ~ **bustle** *n* fuss, commotion.

bustle (2) *n* wire frame or padding worn on the buttocks to puff out a skirt.

bustling [*bus*ling] *n* activity; going and coming.

bust-up [*bust*-up] *n* (*sl*) violent quarrel.

busy [*biz*i] *adj* fully or actively engaged in some occupation; full of stir and activity; (*pej*) officious, inquisitive, fussy; (*arts*) overcrowded with detail; (*of telephone*) engaged; **get b.** go into action, become active ~ **busy** *v/t* keep active (with, about *etc*), occupy (oneself) ~ **busy** *n* (*sl*) detective.

busybody [*biz*ibodi] *n* meddlesome or officious person.

busyness [*biz*ines] *n* state of being busy.

but [*but*] *prep* with the exception of, except, without ~ **but** *conj* except that, unless, than, only ~ **but** *adv* only, not more than, without ~ **but** *neg rel pron* who . . . not.

butadiene [bewta*dI*-een] *n* highly inflammable gas used in the manufacture of synthetic rubber.

butane [*bew*tayn] *n* gas of the paraffin series.

butch [*booch*] *n* (*sl*) lesbian woman who adopts semi-masculine clothes and behaviour; active male homosexual; tough, aggressive man ~ **butch** *adj* aggressively displaying masculinity; (*of hair styles*) very short.

butcher [*booch*er] *n* person whose business is to kill animals for food; one whose trade is selling meat; (*fig*) indiscriminate or brutal murderer; artificial salmon-fly used by anglers ~ **butcher** *v/t* kill (animals) for food; slaughter (people) mercilessly.

butcher-bird [*booch*er-burd] *n* large shrike.

butchery [*booch*eRi] *n* place where animals are slaughtered; the trade of a butcher; massacre, wanton slaughter.

butler [*but*ler] *n* chief manservant of a household who has charge of the plate and wines.

butt (1) [*but*] *n* the thick end (of weapon, tool *etc*).

butt (2) *n* large cask for wine or beer; barrel; measure of 108 gallons.

butt (3) *n* target for archery practice; mound of earth behind the targets on a shooting-range; position behind a bank of earth or low stone wall from which grouse are shot; (*fig*) object of ridicule or abuse

butt (4) *n* violent push or thrust given by the head of an animal ~ **butt** *v/t* and *i* strike, push, thrust violently with the head or the horns; run into; (*bui*) meet without overlapping; **b. on, out** project; **b. in** intrude, intervene.

butte [*bewt*] *n* (*US*) conspicuous isolated hill or peak rising abruptly from the plains.

butt-end [*but*-end] *n* remnant; thick end.

butter [*but*er] *n* fatty product made from cream by churning; similar foodstuffs made from vegetable fats; (*fig*) flattery ~ **butter** *v/t* cover or spread with butter; **b. up** flatter.

butterbean [*but*erbeen] *n* large dried haricot bean.

butterbur [*but*erbur] *n* (*bot*) plant with large rhubarb-like leaves and pinkish-purple flowers rich in nectar.

buttercup [*but*erkup] *n* kind of crowfoot with yellow cup-shaped flowers.

butter-fingered [*but*er-fing-gerd] *adj* apt to drop things (*esp* a ball) ~ **butter-fingers** *n* person who often drops things.

butterfly [*but*erflI] *n* insect with knobbed antennae and four wings, usually of brilliant variegated colour; (*fig*) vain, gaudily-dressed person; one who is changeable and shallow ~ **butterfly** *adj* giddy, frivolous; **b. bomb** bomb which opens wings and drops slowly like a parachute; **b. nut** (*eng*) a nut with wings to enable it to be turned easily by thumb and fingers.

buttering [*bu*tering] *n* (*bui*) the spreading of mortar on a vertical face of a brick before laying; (*coll*) a dose of flattery.

butteris [*bu*teRis] *n* sharp knife used by farriers to pare a horse's hoof.

butter-knife [*bu*ter-nIf] *n* blunt-edged knife for cutting butter.

buttermilk [*bu*termilk] *n* liquid remaining after butter has been churned from cream.

butter-muslin [*bu*ter-muzlin] *n* thin cloth of loose weave used to wrap butter in bulk.

butternut [*bu*ternut] *n* (*US*) sweet oily nut of the white walnut tree; (*hist*) name for a Confederate soldier in the Civil War.

butterscotch [*bu*terskoch] *n* kind of toffee.

butterwort [*bu*terwurt] *n* (*bot*) a marsh plant with leaves which secrete a sticky fluid to catch insects.

buttery [*bu*teRi] *n* (*at Oxford and Cambridge*) part of a college kitchen from which students are supplied with provisions.

buttery-hatch [*bu*teRi-hatch] *n* half-door over which provisions are served from the buttery.

buttock [*bu*tok] *n* one of the two cheeks of the posterior; (*pl*) posterior, rump; a manoeuvre in wrestling ~ **buttock** *v/t* throw by using buttock.

button [*bu*ton] *n* disc or knob sewn on garments for fastening one part to another by passing through a buttonhole; similar object worn as a badge or emblem or for ornament; undeveloped mushroom; any knob or button-shaped object; small piece of wood secured loosely by a screw to keep a door shut ~ **button** *v/t* and *i* fasten with button(s).

buttonhole [*bu*tonhOl] *n* small slit in a garment through which a button is passed; flower or small nosegay worn on the lapel of a coat ~ **buttonhole** *v/t* and *i* sew buttonholes; (*fig*) hold a person in conversation against his will.

buttonhook [*bu*tonhook] *n* hook for fastening up boot buttons.

buttons [*bu*tonz] *n* (*coll*) uniformed page-boy.

button-stick [*bu*ton-stik] *n* (*mil*) U-shaped appliance for polishing metal buttons without soiling the uniform beneath.

button-through [*bu*ton-thROO] *adj* (*of dress*) fastened with buttons from neck to hem.

buttress [*bu*tRis] *n* structure built against wall as support; (*fig*) support, prop ~ **buttress** *v/t* support with a buttress; (*fig*) reinforce (argument).

butts [*bu*ts] *n* (*pl*) the archery-ground; rifle-range.

butty [*bu*ti] *n* (*coll*) pal, mate; piece of bread and butter for sandwiches.

butyric [*bew*tiRik] *adj* made of, pertaining to, butter; **b. acid** thick acid liquid of rancid odour.

buxom [*bu*ksom] *adj* (*of women*) attractively plump, comely ~ **buxomness** *n*.

buy (*p/t* and *p/part* **bought**) [*bI*] *v/t* purchase, acquire by giving an equivalent value, usually in money; (*sl*) agree with, accept; (*fig*) **b. dear** acquire (*eg* experience) by sacrifice; **b. in** repurchase for the owner, *esp* at an auction when the bidding is low; **b. it** (*coll*) get hurt or killed;

I'll **b. it** (*sl*) I'll believe or accept it; **b. off** pay (someone) to relinquish a claim *etc*; **b. out** pay (someone) to surrender interest in some concern; **b. over** bribe; **b. up** purchase to acquire control of or to take over ~ **buy** *n* (*coll*) a purchase, *esp* a bargain; **a good b.** something well worth buying.

buyable [*bI*-ab'l] *adj* able to be bought.

buyer [*bI*-er] *n* one who buys; person employed by a large store who is responsible for the selection and purchase of goods from the wholesalers.

buzz [*bu*z] *v/t* and *i* make the humming noise of a bee *etc*; whisper; spread (news) abroad by whispering; move quickly (after); to signal by means of a buzzer; (*aer*) fly alarmingly close to; **b. about** move busily from place to place; **b. off** (*coll*) go away ~ **buzz** *n* hum of a bee *etc*; confused sounds of a number of people in conversation; (*coll*) phone call; **b. bomb** German rocket V1, (*coll*) flying bomb; **b. saw** circular saw.

buzzard [*bu*zard] *n* bird of the falcon family; (*euph*) bastard; (*coll*) objectionable fellow.

buzzer [*bu*zer] *n* steam-whistle or hooter to summon people to work in a factory; (*elect*) vibrating reed which makes a buzzing sound when the current flows.

by (1) [*bI*] *prep* close to, through, across, past; through the work, means, or agency of; (*of time*) at, in, during, not later than; with the authority or help of (*esp* with oaths); to the number or amount of ~ **by** *adv* near, at hand; aside; so as to pass; **b. the b.** in passing, by the way; **b. and large** on the whole; **b. and b.** soon.

by (2), **bye** *n* something not of main importance, something incidental; (*cricket*) run scored when the ball passes the batsman without touching him and is neither a wide nor a no-ball; (*games*) team or player who is left without an opponent when competitors are being paired for the next round of a competition; **leg b.** (*cricket*) run scored when the ball touches the batsman's body.

by- (3), **bye-** *pref* of less importance, minor, secondary, subsidiary; secret, indirect.

byblow [*bI*blO] *n* a side-blow; illegitimate child.

bye see by (2).

by-election [*bI*-ilekshon] *n* election to Parliament held not during a General Election.

bygone [*bI*gon] *adj* former, past ~ **bygone** *n* an incident which happened in the past; (*pl*, *coll*) obsolete domestic or agricultural implements, ornaments *etc*; **let bygones be bygones** forgive and forget.

bylaw [*bI*law] *n* a regulation made by a local authority, town council, corporation *etc*.

bylina (*pl* **byliny**) [*bu*leena] *n* old Russian oral narrative poem or folk-song.

by-line [*bI*-lIn] *n* (*journalism*) indication of the author's name accompanying an article or report.

byname [*bI*naym] *n* a sobriquet; nickname.

bypass [*bI*paas] *n* road built for fast traffic to pass by, and not through, a town; a smaller pipe to allow the free passage of gas, oil *etc* when the main supply is shut off; electrical shunt ~ **bypass** *v/t* avoid.

bypath [*bI*paath] *n* a side or secluded path.

byplay [*bI*play] *n* subsidiary or secondary action, often in dumb show, taking place during the main action of a play.

byproduct [*b*ɪpRodukt] *n* something produced in the process of manufacturing another article; secondary effect.

byre [*b*ɪr] *n* cowshed.

Byronic [bɪRonik] *adj* typical of the poet Byron or of his work; world-weary, cynical *etc*.

byssinosis [bisin*O*sis] *n* (*med*) chronic bronchial disease caused by inhaling cotton dust over a long period.

byssus [*bi*sus] *n* fine linen used in ancient times.

bystander [*b*ɪstander] *n* onlooker, spectator.

byway [*b*ɪway] *n* side road; (*fig*) (*of a subject*) an aspect of less importance.

byword [*b*ɪwurd] *n* something widely known and discussed; notorious instance.

Byzantine [biz*ant*ɪn/bɪz*ant*ɪn] *adj* of or relating to medieval Byzantium and its art and culture; (*fig*) intricate, subtle; rigidly hierarchical.

C

c [see] third letter of the English alphabet; (mus) key-note of the scale of C major (or minor); (Roman numeral) 100.

cab [kab] n vehicle plying for hire; driver's compartment in a train or lorry.

cabal [kabal] n secret intrigue, gener political; small group of persons engaged in it ~ **cabal** (pres/part **caballing**, p/t and p/part **caballed**) v/i intrigue, plot.

cabala, cabbala [kabala] n Jewish oral tradition of mystical interpretation of the Old Testament; any esoteric doctrine.

cabaret [kabaRay] n small drinking-house in France; restaurant where an entertainment or floor-show is provided while dinner or supper is served; the floor-show itself.

cabbage (1) [kabij] n table vegetable with globular head or heart of unexpanded leaves; (fig) stupid, unimaginative person; **c. white** large white butterfly; **c. rose** large coarse double pink rose.

cabbage (2) n cloth clippings which a tailor keeps for himself after making a garment ~ **cabbage** v/i pilfer, purloin.

cabbage-tree [kabij-tRee] n palm tree whose leaves are eaten as a vegetable.

cabbala see cabala.

cabby [kabi] n (coll) the driver of a cab.

caber [kayber] n (Scots) trunk of a tree, with its branches lopped, tossed by contestants in Highland games as a trial of strength.

cabin [kabin] n small roughly-built dwelling; room in a ship, aircraft or spacecraft; foreman's hut on a building site; railway signal-box; **c. class** second class accommodation on passenger ship.

cabin-boy [kabin-boi] n lad who waits on passengers or officers on board ship.

cabinet [kabinet] n piece of furniture with shelves or drawers in which to store or display jewels, china etc; piece of furniture containing a radio or television set; standard size of photographic print (6″ × 4″); (cap) principal ministers of the government; **C. Minister** head of a government department and a member of the Cabinet; **shadow c.** leading members of the opposition who will take charge of government departments when returned to power; **c. pudding** steamed pudding made of bread and butter, milk, eggs, dried fruit, and sugar.

cabinet-maker [kabinet-mayker] n joiner who makes high-class furniture.

cable [kayb'l] n strong thick rope of hemp or woven steel wire; (naut) rope or chain to which a ship's anchor is attached; measure of depth about 100 fathoms; (elect) insulated conductors for submarine telegraphic cables or for conveying electric power overhead or underground; (tel) a message sent by cable; (archi) moulding resembling a rope ~ **cable** v/t and i send (a message) or communicate by submarine telegraphy.

cablecar [kayb'lkaar] n tramcar drawn by a cable operated by a stationary engine.

cablegram [kayb'lgRam] n message sent by cable.

cable-laid [kayb'l-layd] adj (of a wire rope) having the twist of the rope opposite to the twist of the strands.

cablese [kaybleez] n (coll) jargon of words contracted and joined to reduce the cost of cabling.

cable-ship [kayb'l-ship] n ship equipped to lay submarine cables.

cable-stitch [kayb'l-stich] n a twisted rope-like stitch in knitting or embroidery.

cableway [kayb'lway] n (eng) device for transporting materials from a carriage which runs on a heavy steel rope between two towers > PDE.

cabling [kaybling] n (elect) a collection of cables.

cabman [kabman] n man who drives a cab for hire.

cabochon [kaboshon] n ornamental stone with rounded top.

caboodle [kabOOd'l] n (coll) **the whole c.** the whole lot.

caboose [kabOOs] n (naut) kitchen or galley on deck for cooking; oven for cooking in the open; (US) van attached to the rear of freight trains.

cabotage [kabOtij] n (naut) coastal navigation; trade carried on by ships which coast from port to port; restriction of transport within a country to its own shipping and aircraft.

cabrank [kabRank] n parking place in a street where taxicabs stand for hire.

cabriole [kabRi-Ol] n double-curved chair or table leg; (ballet) a step in which the dancer springs upwards.

cabriolet [kabRi-Olay] n light covered two-wheeled carriage drawn by one horse.

cabstand [kabstand] n a cabrank.

ca'canny [kaw-kani] (ie call canny) v/i proceed carefully, go slow ~ **ca'canny** n workers' policy of 'go-slow' to reduce output; 'working to rule'.

cacao [kakay-O/kakaa-O] n tropical American tree from the seeds of which cocoa and chocolate are made; seed of this tree.

cachalot [kashalot/kashalO] n genus of whales, including the sperm whale.

cache [kash] n hiding-place for stores, arms, treasure etc; what is hidden in a cache; (zool) store of food collected by some animals for the winter ~ **cache** v/t hide, store in a cache.

cachet [kashay] n distinguishing mark or sign of authenticity or superiority; (med) a capsule.

cachination [kakinayshon] n loud harsh laugh.

cachou [kashOO] n (Fr) lozenge eaten to sweeten the breath; any small scented sweet.

cack-handed [kak-handid] adj (dial) left-handed; (coll) clumsy, awkward.

cackle [kak'l] n noise made by hen after laying; foolish chatter; short raucous laugh ~ **cackle** v/i.

caco- pref evil, unpleasant, bad.

cacodemon, cacodaemon [kakOdeemon] n malignant spirit or person.

cacodyl, kakodyl [kakOdil] n highly inflammable colourless liquid of nauseous smell > PDS.

102

cacophonous [ka*kof*onus] *adj* very discordant.

cacophony [ka*kof*Oni] *n* unpleasing discordant sound or speech.

cacotopia [KaKo*t*Opi-a] *n* imaginary community where everything is evil or unpleasant.

cactus (*pl* cactuses or cacti) [*kak*tus] *n* (*bot*) genus of plants with thick fleshy stems armed with prickles.

cad [*kad*] *n* ill-bred fellow of mean behaviour.

cadastral [ka*daast*Ral] *adj* pertaining to a register or survey of landed property.

cadaver [ka*day*ver/ka*dav*er] *n* a corpse.

cadaveric [ka*dav*eRik] *adj* of a corpse.

cadaverous [ka*dav*eRus] *adj* looking like a corpse; deadly pale; gaunt, haggard.

caddice see caddis.

caddie see caddy (1).

caddis, caddice (1) [*kad*is] *n* coarse cheap serge.

caddis, caddice (2) *n* larva of the mayfly.

caddish [*kad*ish] *adj* characteristic of a cad.

caddy (1), caddie [*kad*i] *n* attendant who carries a golfer's clubs.

caddy (2) *n* small box for holding tea.

cadence [*kayd*ens] *n* rhythm; rise and fall of the voice, intonation; (*mus*) sequence of chords at the end of a musical phrase > PDM.

cadency [*kayd*ensi] *n* cadence; descent from a younger member of a family.

cadet [*kad*et] *n* a younger son; student in military college; boy who receives military training as a member of a school group or boys' club.

cadge [*kaj*] *v*/*t* and *i* beg; get by begging ~ cadger *n* one who sponges on other people.

cadi, kadi [*kaad*i/*kayd*i] *n* magistrate of a town or village in Turkey, Persia, Arabia.

cadmium [*kad*mi-um] *n* soft silvery-white metal resembling tin, used to make fusible alloys and for electroplating; c. yellow vivid yellow pigment, a sulphide of cadmium.

cadre [*kaad*er/*kayd*er] *n* a framework; (*mil*) the officers and men forming the permanent nucleus of a regiment or battalion; (*pl*) group of Communist party workers; (*coll*) grade, rank.

caduceus [ka*dews*i-us] *n* wand carried by ancient Greek or Roman herald, *esp* wand of Hermes.

caducity [ka*dews*iti] *n* state of being caducous.

caducous [ka*dews*us] *adj* (*bot*) tending to fall very early, deciduous; perishable, transitory.

caecum [*seek*um] *n* first part of the colon.

Caesarean, Caesarian [si*zair*Ri-an] *adj* pertaining to Caesar; (*surg*) c. operation, c. section delivery of a child by cutting abdomen.

caesium [*seez*i-um] *n* silvery-white metal resembling sodium in its properties > PDS.

caesura [si*zewr*Ra/si*sewr*Ra] *n* (*pros*) pause about the middle of a metrical line.

café [*kaf*ay] *n* coffee-house; restaurant where light meals and refreshments are served.

cafeteria [kafi*teer*Ri-a] *n* restaurant where customers serve themselves as they pass a counter.

caff [*kaf*/*kayf*] *n* (*sl*) café.

caffeic [ka*fee*-ik] *adj* pertaining to coffee or caffeine.

caffeine [*kaf*een] *n* organic compound found in tea-leaves and coffee-beans > PDS.

caftan, kaftan [*kaf*taan/*kaf*tan] *n* long tunic-like Turkish garment; long, loose dress of similar shape.

cafuffle see kerfuffle.

cage [*kayj*] *n* structure for keeping birds or wild animals behind wires or iron bars; (*fig*) anything which imprisons; (*mining*) structure hung by a rope in which men, materials and minerals travel up or down a vertical shaft ~ cage *v*/*t* confine in a cage; imprison.

cagey, cagy [*kayj*i] *adj* (*coll*) unwilling to be frank or to commit oneself, cautious ~ cagily *adv* ~ caginess *n*.

cahoot [ka*hOOt*] *n* (*US sl*) share; partnership; in cahoots in secret agreement.

caiman see cayman.

cainozoic, kainozoic [kIn*Oz*O-ik/kayn*Oz*O-ik] *adj* (*geol*) belonging to the third (tertiary) geological period > PDG.

caique [ka-*eek*] *n* light rowing-boat used on the Bosphorus; Levantine sailing-ship.

cairn [*kairn*] *n* heap of stones, *esp* when raised as a landmark or memorial; small shaggy-coated breed of Scots terrier.

cairngorm [*kairng*awrm] *n* yellow or wine-coloured precious stone found in Scotland.

caisson [*kay*son] *n* (*mil*) ammunition chest or wagon; (*eng*) cylindrical or rectangular structure for keeping water or soft ground from flowing into an excavation; water-tight air container used in refloating sunken vessels; floating structure placed across the entrance to a lock or dry dock to keep the water out; (*bui*) deeply recessed panel in a ceiling or dome; box-like mould to receive cement; c. disease paralysis or pains in the joints caused by working in compressed air.

caitiff [*kayt*if] *adj* and *n* (typical of) a coward.

cajole [ka*jOl*] *v*/*t* coax (someone) with flattery to do what one wants; deceive (someone) by specious promises ~ cajolery *n* persuasion b ﹐ flattery *etc*.

cake [*kayk*] *n* a baked piece of sweet and flavoured dough with fruit, fillings *etc*; dried, compressed, or flattened piece; cakes and ale fun and merry-making; take the c. (*joc*) surpass everything; a piece of c. (*coll*) something very pleasant and easy; you cannot have your c. and eat it if you choose one alternative you cannot have the other ~ cake *v*/*t* and *i* harden into a cake-like mass.

cakewalk [*kayk*wawk] *n* strutting dance of American Negro origin.

calabar-bean [kala*baar*-been] *n* poisonous seed of an African plant.

calabash [*kala*bash] *n* gourd, *esp* of a S. American tree; dried gourd; musical instrument made from this.

calaboose [kala*bOOs*] *n* a prison, jail.

calamine [*kala*meen/*kalam*In/*kala*min] *n* natural zinc carbonate.

calamitous [ka*lam*itus] *adj* disastrous, causing distress ~ calamitously *adv*.

calamity [ka*lam*iti] *n* a disaster causing havoc and misery; sudden misfortune.

calamus [*kala*mus] *n* reed; reed-pipe; genus of palms used to make rattan canes.

calash [ka*lash*] *n* light low carriage with movable hood.

calc- *pref* lime, chalk.

calcar (1) [*kalka*ar] *n* small furnace.

calcar (2) *n* (*bot*) hollow spur at base of petal.

calcareous [kal*kair*Ri-us] *adj* made of or containing lime.

calcavella [kalka*vela*] *n* Portuguese sweet wine.

calcedony see **chalcedony**.

calceolaria [kalsi-O*lair*Ri-a] *n* (*bot*) garden flower which has some likeness to a slipper.

calces [*kals*eez] *pl* of **calx**.

calciferol [kal*sif*erol] *n* vitamin D$_2$ > PDS.

calciferous [kal*sif*eRus] *adj* containing or producing lime.

calcification [kalsifi*kay*shon] *n* hardening by the action of lime salts; (*med*) stiffening of the joints through lime deposits in tissue.

calcify [*kals*ifI] *v/t* and *i* become or make hard through lime deposits.

calcimine [*kals*imeen] *n* white or tinted wash for distempering walls and ceilings.

calcination [kalsi*nay*shon] *n* strong heating; conversion of metals into oxides by heating in air.

calcine [kals*In*] *v/t* and *i* reduce to quicklime by burning; burn to ashes.

calcite [*kals*It] *n* (*min*) calc-spar, natural crystalline calcium carbonate.

calcium [*kals*i-um] *n* a chemical element, the metallic basis of lime > PDS.

calc-spar [*kalk*-spaar] *n* calcite.

calculable [*kalk*ewlab'l] *adj* capable of being calculated ~ **calculability** [kalkewla*bili*ti] *n*.

calculate [*kalk*ewlayt] *v/t* and *i* reckon or compute by mathematics; think out accurately ~ **calculated** *adj* planned, thought out, adapted; of a kind likely (to); cold-blooded, deliberate.

calculating [*kalk*ewlayting] *adj* that calculates; shrewd, cautious; scheming; **c. machine** device that performs arithmetical calculations mechanically.

calculation [kalkew*lay*shon] *n* act or result of calculating; estimate of probability; forecast; shrewd, selfish or coldblooded planning.

calculator [*kalk*ewlayter] *n* one who calculates; calculating machine.

calculus (1) (*pl* **calculi**) [*kalk*ewlus] *n* (*med*) stony concretion forming in certain organs.

calculus (2) *n* (*math*) branch of mathematics dealing with variable quantities.

caldron see **cauldron**.

Caledonian [kalid*On*i-an] *n* and *adj* (native) of Scotland.

calefactory [kali*fakt*eRi] *adj* producing heat.

calendar [*kal*ender] *n* a system by which time is divided into fixed periods > PDG; set of tables which number and name the days of each month of the year; list of days in the year of especial interest to members of a particular group *etc*; index of a collection of documents; list of cases for trial before a criminal court; **c. month** a month reckoned from any day to the day of the same number in the following month ~ **calendar** *v/t* record in a calendar; index documents.

calender [*kal*ender] *n* machine for pressing and smoothing cloth and paper between rollers.

calends, kalends [*kal*endz] *n* (*pl*) the first day of every month in the Roman calendar; **Greek c.** date or occasion which never comes.

calendula [kal*end*ewla] *n* marigold.

calf (1) (*pl* **calves**) [*kaaf*] *n* a young cow or bull; a young buffalo, seal, whale *etc*; a stupid, callow youth; calfskin with a smooth finish; **c.**

love immature romantic love of an adolescent for one of the opposite sex.

calf (2) (*pl* **calves**) *n* curved muscular part of the back of the leg below the knee.

calfdozer [*kaaf*dOzer] *n* (*eng*) a small bulldozer.

calfskin [*kaaf*skin] *n* the hide of a calf.

calibrate [*kal*ibRayt] *v/t* determine the calibre of; check the graduations of an instrument, machine, piece of artillery *etc*.

calibration [kali*bRay*shon] *n* the graduation of an instrument to enable measurements to be made with it > PDS; testing fire-power of artillery.

calibre [*kal*iber] *n* internal diameter or bore of a tube, *esp* of a gun; (*fig*) degree of importance, mental capacity, moral quality.

calices [*kal*iseez] *pl* of **calix**.

calico [*kal*ikO] *n* cotton cloth; **c. printing** process by which cotton cloth is decorated with coloured patterns.

calif see **caliph**.

californium [kali*fawr*ni-um] *n* (*chem*) a transuranic element > PDS.

calipash [*kal*ipash] *n* green gelatinous substance found beneath a turtle's upper shell.

calipee [*kal*ipee] *n* yellow gelatinous substance found above a turtle's lower shell.

caliper see **calliper**.

caliph, calif [*kal*if/*kay*lif] *n* title once given in Mohammedan countries to the chief ruler.

caliphate [*kal*ifayt] *n* rank, dignity, office of a caliph; the reign of a caliph.

calisthenics see **callisthenics**.

calix (*pl* **calices**) [*kal*iks] *n* (*biol*) cup-like cavity in an organ of the body.

calk (1) [*kawk*] *n* sharpened plate of iron on a shoe to prevent slipping on ice; a calkin ~ **calk** *v/t*.

calk (2) [*kawk*/*kalk*] *v/t* copy a design by a transfer from coloured chalk on the back of it.

calk (3) see **caulk**.

calkin [*kawk*in/*kalk*in] *n* turned-down ends of a horseshoe sharpened to prevent slipping.

call [*kawl*] *v/t* and *i* cry out, shout; give a name to; pay a short visit; (*of tradespeople*) pay regular visits; summon, demand presence of; rouse from sleep; (*at cards*) bid or make a demand; consider to be; make a telephone call; summon (a meeting); order (a halt); **c. to account** reprove, rebuke; **c. attention to** point out; **c. the banns** publish banns of marriage; **c. to the bar**, admit as a barrister; **c. over the coals** blame (a subordinate) for some fault; **c. it a day** decide that one has done enough for the day; **c. to mind** recollect; **c. names** abuse, vilify; **c. into play** bring into action; **c. in question** cast doubt upon; **c. for** demand; **c. forth** elicit; **c. in** (*of money*) withdraw from circulation; (*of debts, mortgages*) demand repayment of; **c. off** give up (an undertaking); **c. out** challenge to a duel; summon (soldiers) to preserve order; **c. over** read aloud (list of names) to detect absentees; **c. up** summon to join branch of Forces; ring up on the telephone ~ **call** *n* cry, shout; cry of a bird; a ring on the telephone, a request to be connected to another subscriber, a conversation over the telephone; summons to an office (*esp* in the church); inward conviction urging one to a particular duty; a need to defecate or urinate; short formal visit; visit by tradesman on his round;

(*cards*) a bid; player's right or turn to make a bid; (*theat*) summons from audience by applause to a performer to reappear; notice requiring performers to come to a rehearsal; (*Stock Exchange*) notice to a buyer of stock that payment of another instalment of the purchase price is due; loan of money which can be withdrawn at any time; right exercisable by a company to demand payment, in whole or in part, of the balance on 'partly paid' shares; c. option right to buy at an agreed future date a stock or share at an agreed price; at c., on c. immediately available; within c. nearby, within hearing; have no c. to have no need to.

callbox [*kawl*boks] *n* public telephone booth.

callboy [*kawl*boi] *n* (*theat*) boy who calls the actors to be ready to appear on stage.

caller (1) [*kawl*er] *n* one who pays a short visit; one who makes a telephone call; one who calls out the steps in country-dancing.

caller (2) [*kal*er] *adj* (*dial*) fresh; c. herring fresh herrings; (*of weather*) cool and fresh.

callgirl [*kawl*gurl] *n* prostitute who makes appointments with clients by telephone.

calligraphist [*kalig*Rafist] *n* one skilled in fine handwriting.

calligraphy [*kalig*Rafi] *n* art of elegant handwriting, penmanship.

calling [*kawl*ing] *n* occupation, business, profession; summoning (of a meeting) ; strong inward impulse to a duty.

calliope [*kal*I-Opi] *n* an organ consisting of steam-whistles played from a keyboard.

calliper, caliper [*kal*iper] *n* (*med*) metal splint supporting a leg; (*pl*) instrument for measuring the distance between two points, especially on a curved surface.

callisthenics, calisthenics [kalis*then*iks] *n* (*pl*) exercises developing bodily strength and grace.

callnote [*kawl*nOt] *n* cry of a bird to its mate.

callosity [kal*os*iti] *n* unnatural hardness of skin.

callous [*kal*us] *adj* (*of skin*) hardened either naturally or through friction; (*fig*) unfeeling, brutal ~ **callously** *adv* unfeelingly.

callousness [*kal*usnes] *n* lack of feeling.

callow [*kal*O] *adj* unfledged; (*fig*) inexperienced.

call-up [*kawl*-up] *n* conscription.

callus [*kal*us] *n* (*zool*) hardened and thickened part of skin; material which makes initial union of fractured bone; (*bot*) superficial tissue developing in wounded plants.

calm [*kaam*] *n* stillness, rest, tranquillity of mind or of the elements ~ calm *adj* devoid of wind, tranquil; not agitated, under control. leisurely; (*coll*) too easy-going, impudent, presuming ~ **calm** *v/t* and *i* render calm, become calm; pacify, soothe; c. down become calm.

calmative [*kaam*ativ] *adj* and *n* (*med*) sedative.

calmia see kalmia.

calmly [*kaam*li] *adv* quietly; coolly, casually.

calmness [*kaam*nis] *n* quality of being calm.

calomel [*kal*Omel] *n* (*med*) mercurous chloride, formerly used as purgative.

calorescence [kalo*Res*ens] *n* (*phys*) conversion of light radiations into heat > PDS.

caloric [kal*O*Rik] *adj* of heat.

caloricity [kalo*Ris*iti] *n* (*biol*) capability of developing and maintaining bodily heat.

calorie [*kal*oRi] *n* unit of quantity of heat, the amount of heat required to raise the temperature of one gramme of water one degree centigrade; (*pop*) large calorie; large c. unit of one thousand calories, used in quoting the energy value of foods.

calorific [kalo*Rif*ik] *adj* heat-producing; pertaining to heat; c. value (*of fuel*) quantity of heat produced by complete combustion of a given weight of fuel > PDS; (*of food*) energy-giving value.

calorifier [kalo*Rif*I-er] *n* water tank in which water is heated by a submerged coil of heating pipes circulating hot water or steam.

calorimeter [kalo*Rim*iter] *n* instrument for measuring quantities of heat evolved, absorbed, or transferred > PDS.

calotte [kal*ot*] *n* skull-cap worn by Roman Catholic ecclesiastics; (*archi*) domed ceiling.

calque [kalk] *n* imitation in one language of an idiom of another.

caltrop [*kal*tRop] *n* (*mil*) spiked iron ball used against cavalry horses; (*bot*) flower with spiky head.

calumet [*kal*ewmet] *n* ceremonial pipe used by North American Indians.

calumniate [ka*lum*ni-ayt] *v/t* spread malicious reports concerning, malign; accuse falsely and maliciously ~ **calumniation** [kalumni-*ay*shon] *n* ~ **calumniator** [ka*lum*ni-ayter] *n* ~ **calumniatory** [ka*lum*ni-ayte*Ri*] *adj*.

calumnious [ka*lum*ni-us] *adj* defamatory, slanderous; (*of person*) given to calumny.

calumny [*kal*umni] *n* slanderous statement, malicious misrepresentation, false accusation.

calvary [*kal*vaRi] *n* place of the Crucifixion; life-size representation of the Crucifixion erected in the open air; (*archi*) a cross-surmounted chapel.

calve [kaav] *v/i* and *t* give birth to a calf; (*of glacier, iceberg*) throw off a mass of ice.

calves [kaavz] *pl* of calf.

Calvinism [*kal*vinizm] *n* theological doctrines of John Calvin (1509–64) ~ **Calvinist** [*kal*vinist] *n* ~ **Calvinistic** [kalvin*is*tik] *adj*.

calx (*pl* calces) [kalks] *n* powder left when a metal or mineral has been strongly heated.

calypso [ka*lip*sO] *n* type of ballad popular in the West Indies, improvised and topical.

calyx (*pl* calyces) [*kal*iks/*kayl*iks, *kal*iseez] *n* (*bot*) outermost part of a flower, consisting of sepals.

cam [kam] *n* (*mech*) a non-circular wheel.

camaraderie [kamaRad*eRee*] *n* loyalty and good comradeship among associates.

camber [*kam*ber] *n* convex curvature on a road, girder, ship's deck *etc*; upward slope on a road surface towards the edge of a curve; curvature of the wing sections of an aircraft ~ **camber** *v/t* and *i* give camber to; have camber.

cambist [*kam*bist] *n* dealer in bills of exchange.

cambium [*kam*bi-um] *n* (*bot*) soft woody tissue.

Cambrian [*kam*bRi-an] *adj* pertaining to Wales; name of group of Palaeozoic rocks.

cambric [*kaym*bRik] *n* fine cloth, originally made of linen only, but now usually of cotton.

came [kaym] *p/t* of come.

camel [*kam*el] *n* large ruminant with humped back, domesticated as beast of burden in the Middle East and North Africa; (*eng*) large hollow steel float; colour akin to fawn; **c. corps** troop of soldiers mounted on camels.

camelback [*kam*elbak] *n* second-grade rubber used for retreading tyres.

camelhair [*kam*elhair] *n* hair of the camel; fine hair used to make artists' brushes.

camellia [kam*eli*-a/kam*eeli*-a] *n* oriental evergreen shrub with red or white double rose-like flowers.

Camembert [*kam*embair] *n* a French variety of cheese, soft, rich, and with a strong smell.

cameo [*kam*i-O] *n* piece of ornamental jewellery carved in relief on contrasting background; (*fig*) polished character-sketch; **c. ware** (*cer*) pottery with figures in relief of a different colour.

camera [*kam*eRa] *n* (*phot*) light-proof box at one end of which is a lens that opens and throws an image of the object at which it is pointed upon a sensitive plate or film placed at the back of the box > PDS; (*television*) the part of a television system in which optical images are converted into electrical signals > PDEl; **c. lucida** (*opt*) prismatic device to facilitate the drawing of an image seen in a microscope; **c. obscura** (*opt*) a dark room in which images of outside objects are thrown on a screen from a long-focus convex lens; **in c.** (*leg*) in private, not in open court.

camiknicks, camiknickers [*kam*iniks, *kam*inikerz] *n* (*pl*) woman's garment combining camisole and knickers.

camion [*kam*i-on] *n* low wagon, dray; motor truck, large lorry.

camisole [*kam*isOl] *n* woman's cotton or linen under-bodice.

camomile, chamomile [*kam*OmIl] *n* strong-scented plant with flower resembling a daisy; **c. tea** infusion of camomile flowers.

camouflage [*kam*ooflaazh] *n* (*mil*) concealment from the enemy of troops, artillery, stores *etc* by means of paint, branches of trees, smoke-screens *etc*; subterfuge of making something appear different ~ **camouflage** *v/t* disguise, conceal.

camp (1) [*kamp*] *n* place where troops are housed temporarily in tents; place of training for troops; temporary shelter for hunters, gipsies *etc*; (*fig*) army life, military service; faction, party ~ **camp** *v/i* dwell in a tent, pitch a camp; **c. out** sleep in the open in a tent.

camp (2) *adj* (*coll*) self-consciously dramatic, affected; effeminate; too ornate or dainty; dandified; once considered beautiful or valid but now thought ridiculously sentimental or old-fashioned; displaying obvious bad taste in a spirit of mocking irony ~ **camp** *v/i* (*theat sl*) **c. it up** over-act, behave melodramatically, seek to draw attention to oneself.

campaign [*kam*payn] *n* series of actions designed to achieve a particular aim, *esp* a political or military success ~ **campaign** *v/i* conduct, or serve in, a campaign ~ **campaigner** *n* one who takes an active part in a (political) campaign; veteran soldier.

campanile [kam*pan*eeli/*kam*panIl] *n* a lofty bell tower detached from surrounding buildings.

campanology [kam*pan*oloji] *n* art or technique of making or ringing bells.

campanula [kam*pan*ewla] *n* (*bot*) kinds of plants with flowers shaped like bells.

campanulate [kam*pan*ewlit] *adj* bell-shaped.

campbed [*kamp*bed] *n* narrow bed made to fold up flat.

campchair [*kamp*chair] *n* folding chair for out-of-doors.

camper [*kamp*er] *n* one who sleeps in the open in a tent.

camp-follower [kamp-*folO*-er] *n* a civilian, male or female, *esp* a prostitute, who follows, or lives near an army camp.

camphor [*kam*fer] *n* white crystalline substance with a characteristic smell > PDS.

camphorated [*kam*foRayted] *adj* impregnated with camphor.

camphoric [kam*fo*Rik] *adj* related to or containing camphor.

camping [*kam*ping] *n* the act of living in camp or under canvas.

campion [*kam*pi-on] *n* (*bot*) name of red- or white-flowered lychnis, related to pink.

campstool [*kamp*stOOl] *n* folding seat of canvas on a wooden frame, usually without a back.

campus [*kam*pus] *n* grounds of a university, college, or (*in US*) school.

camshaft [*kam*shaaft] *n* (*mot*) shaft on which cams are fixed to operate the valves of the engine.

can (1) [*kan*] *n* tin vessel for holding liquid; air-tight tin containing meat, fruit *etc* for preservation; **carry the c.** (*sl*) take the blame; **in the c.** recorded on film ~ **can** (*pres/part* canning, *p/t* and *p/part* canned) *v/t* preserve (meat *etc*) in a properly sealed can or tin; (*rad sl*) record, transcribe; **c. do** (*coll*) yes, that is possible; **c. it** (*sl*) stop that (foolish) talk.

can (2) (*p/t* could) *v/aux* be able to, allow oneself to, be allowed to.

canal [ka*nal*] *n* channel dug or built up to carry water for navigation, water power, irrigation *etc*; (*physiol*) passage or duct in a living body; **c. rays** (*phys*) beams of positive ions which have passed through canals in the cathode of a discharge tube. > PDS.

canalization [kanalIzayshon] *n* dividing of a river into reaches separated by dams and weirs > PDE; (*surg*) method of draining wounds; (*fig*) act of guiding efforts *etc* into particular directions.

canalize [*kan*alIz] *v/t* provide with canals; make (river) into a canal; form a duct (in); (*surg*) drain; (*med*) become unblocked; (*fig*) provide outlet for; direct into particular channels.

canapé [*kan*apay] *n* (*Fr*) toast or bread with savoury topping.

canard [ka*naard*/ka*naar*] *n* false report, hoax.

canary [ka*nair*Ri] *n* bright yellow song-bird kept as cage-bird; sweet wine from the Canary Islands ~ **canary** *adj* bright yellow.

canary-creeper [ka*nair*Ri-k*Reep*er] *n* bright yellow trailing plant.

canary-grass [ka*nair*Ri-g*Raas*] *n* grass which yields seed used as food for canaries.

canasta [ka*nas*ta] *n* a card-game, a variety of gin rummy.

canaster [ka*nas*ter] *n* kind of coarse-cut tobacco.

can-can [*kan*-kan] *n* spirited high-kicking dance which originated in French dance halls.

cancel [*kan*sel] *v/t* and *i* cross out, delete; wipe out, annul (debt, arrangement *etc*); counter-balance, make up for; (*math*) strike out figures in reducing fractions to their lowest terms; remove equal quantities from the opposite sides of an equation; (*print*) suppress page which has already been set up, and replace it with another.

cancellation [kanse*lay*shon] *n* act of cancelling, fact of being cancelled; countermanding of booked seats in aircraft, rooms in hotels *etc*.

cancer [kan*ser*] *n* (*path*) malignant growth in the body; (*fig*) insidious spreading evil in an individual or the community; (*cap*) (*astron*) constellation of the Crab, fourth sign of the zodiac; **Tropic of C.** the northern tropic, the parallel of latitude 23½° N > PDG.

cancerous [kan*se*Rus] *adj* of, like, or suffering from cancer.

cancroid [kank*Roid*/kank*RO*-id] *adj* like a crab; resembling cancer.

candela [kan*de*la] *n* unit of luminous intensity > PDS.

candelabrum (*pl* **candelabra**), **candelabra** (*pl* **candelabras**) [kandi*la*brum] *n* large branched candlestick; chandelier.

candid [kan*did*] *adj* frank, sincere, outspoken; **c. camera** an easily concealed miniature camera used to photograph people unawares ~ **candid** *n* an unposed photograph ~ **candidly** *adv*.

candescent [kan*de*sent] *adj* glowing with white heat; dazzling ~ **candescence** [kan*de*sens] *n*.

candidacy [kan*di*dasi] *n* candidature.

candidate [kan*di*dayt] *n* one who applies to be chosen for an office, position, *esp* for seat in House of Commons or other elected body; one who presents himself for an examination.

candidature [kan*di*dachoor] *n* position or status of a candidate; act of offering oneself as candidate.

candied [kan*di*d] *adj* coated with sugar; turned partly or wholly into sugar; (*fig*) flattering.

candle [kan*d*'l] *n* slender cylinder of wax, tallow *etc*, enclosing a wick of cotton or flax which burns to give light; **not fit to hold a c.** to greatly inferior to; **the game is not worth the c.** the result is not worth the penalty or expense it entails; **burn the c. at both ends** work early and late; overdo things.

candlelight [kan*d*'l-lIt] *n* light given by candles.

candlepower [kan*d*'l-power] *n* luminous intensity of a source of light in a given direction expressed in terms of candelas > PDS.

candlestick [kan*d*'lstik] *n* portable stand for holding a candle.

candletree [kan*d*'ltRee] *n* the wax-myrtle shrub.

candlewick [kan*d*'lwik] *n* wick of a candle ~ **candlewick** *adj* (*of a bedspread*) with a raised ornamental tufted pattern.

candour [kan*d*er] *n* sincerity, frankness.

candy [kan*di*] *n* crystallized sugar, made by boiling and evaporating, sugar-candy; (*US*) any sort of sweetmeat ~ **candy** *v/t* and *i* conserve by boiling in sugar; become encrusted with sugar.

candyfloss [kan*di*flos] *n* mass of fine candy threads wound round a stick; (*fig*) something attractive but insubstantial.

candystripe [kan*di*stRIp] *n* pattern of alternate white and coloured stripes.

candytuft [kan*di*tuft] *n* plant with white, pink, or purple tufts of flowers.

cane [kay*n*] *n* hollow, pointed, woody stem of

certain plants; stem of slender palms; stem of raspberry, loganberry *etc*; length of cane used as walking-stick; a walking-stick; rod with which schoolmasters whip boys; split cane made suitable for seating chairs; **c. sugar** sucrose, saccharose obtained from the sugar-cane > PDS ~ **cane** *v/t* punish with a cane; use strips of split cane to make or repair a chair.

canine [kan*In*] *adj* of or like a dog; **c. tooth** (*in human beings*) one of four pointed teeth between the incisors and premolars ~ **canine** *n*.

caning [kay*ning*] *n* action of punishing with a cane.

canister [kan*i*ster] *n* a container generally of tin for keeping tea or coffee; **c. shot** early type of shrapnel shell.

canker [kan*ker*] *n* ulcerous sore; gangrene; disease in trees which destroys wood; any insect pest destroying buds and leaves of plants; (*fig*) anything which corrupts morally ~ **canker** *v/t* and *i* infect or destroy by canker; suffer from canker ~ **cankered** *adj* (*fig*) soured, spiteful.

canker-worm [kan*ker*-werm] *n* caterpillar which destroys buds and leaves.

cannabis [kan*abis*] *n* preparation of Indian hemp smoked as an intoxicant drug; hashish, marijuana.

canned [kan*d*] *adj* (*of food*) preserved in tins; (*coll, of music*) recorded; (*coll*) intoxicated by drink or drugs.

canner [kan*er*] *n* one who cans foodstuffs.

cannery [kan*e*Ri] *n* factory where foodstuffs are canned.

cannibal [kan*ibal*] *n* human being who eats human flesh; animal that preys on its own kind.

cannibalism [kan*ibalizm*] *n* practice of eating one's own kind; (*fig*) barbarous cruelty.

cannibalize [kan*ibalIz*] *v/t* (*mech*) dismantle (a machine) to provide spare parts.

can(n)ikin [kan*ikin*] *n* small can; drinking-vessel.

cannily [kan*ili*] *adv* (*coll*) cautiously, prudently, comfortably.

canniness [kan*inis*] *n* quality of being canny.

canning [kan*ing*] *n* process or business of preserving foodstuffs in sealed food containers.

cannon (1) (*pl* **cannons, cannon**) [kan*on*] *n* large gun; mounted piece of ordnance; **c. fodder** soldiers callously sent to their deaths.

cannon (2) *n* (*billiards*) stroke in which player directs his ball so that it may rebound from one ball and strike the other ~ **cannon** *v/i* (*billiards*) make a cannon; **c. into** come into collision with.

cannonade [kan*onayd*] *n* continuous discharge of artillery ~ **cannonade** *v/t* and *i*.

cannonball [kan*onbawl*] *n* heavy iron ball discharged from a cannon.

cannon-bit, canon-bit [kan*on-bit*] *n* smooth round bit for a horse.

cannon-bone [kan*on-bOn*] *n* bone in a horse's leg from hock to fetlock.

cannonshot [kan*onshot*] *n* cannonballs or shells fired from a cannon; distance a cannon can fire.

cannot [kan*ot*] *contraction* = can not.

canny [kan*i*] *adj* and *adv* (*coll*) cautious, careful, wary, shrewd; frugal; **to ca' c.** (*ie* **to call c.**) proceed carefully, be cautious; 'go slow' at work.

canoe [kan*OO*] *n* light boat propelled by paddling ~ **canoe** *v/i* paddle, carry in, sail in, a canoe.

canoeist [kanOO-ist] *n* one who paddles a canoe.

canon (I) [kanon] *n* (*eccles*) established law of the Church; body of sacred writings accepted by the Church as genuine; general principle governing the treatment of a subject; standard of judgement; the genuine authenticated writings of an author; (*mus*) composition based on strict imitation of one part by a following part > PDM; **c. law** body of ecclesiastical law; **c. of the Mass** second part of the Mass containing the Consecration.

canon (2) *n* member of the chapter of a cathedral or collegiate church.

cañon see **canyon**.

canonical [kanonikal] *adj* in conformity with ecclesiastical law; orthodox, standard; **c. hours** seven times of day for official prayers.

canonicals [kanonikalz] *n* (*pl*) robes and vestments appropriate to any particular ecclesiastical or academic status.

canonicate [kanonikit] *n* (*eccles*) the office of a canon; canonry.

canonicity [kanonisiti] *n* inclusion in the canon; authenticity.

canonist [kanonist] *n* one expert in canon law.

canonistic [kanonistik] *adj* pertaining to a canonist or to canon law.

canonization [kanonIzayshon] *n* (*RC*) official declaration that a person was a saint while alive and is now in heaven; ceremony at which this is proclaimed.

canonize [kanonIz] *v/t* officially declare to have been a saint; approve by religious authority.

canonry [kanonRi] *n* office of a canon.

canoodle [kanOOd'l] *v/t* and *i* (*sl*) caress, cuddle.

can-opener [kan-Opener] *n* tool for opening metal containers of preserved foodstuffs.

canopic [kanOpik] *adj* **c. jar** (*arch*) jar used by ancient Egyptians for embalmed human entrails.

canopy [kanopi] *n* a covering fixed or suspended above a throne, bed, or carried ceremonially over persons or sacred objects; (*archi*) roof-like projection; (*aer*) the extended fabric of a parachute; plastic cockpit cover ~ **canopy** *v/t* cover overhead with a canopy.

canst [kanst] (*ar*) 2nd pers sing pres of **can** (3).

cant (I) [kant] *n* slanting, sloping surface; toss which overturns; sudden movement which causes tilting ~ **cant** *v/t* and *i* tilt, turn over.

cant (2) *n* slang used by thieves; jargon of a particular class of people; hypocritical talk, *esp* in speaking of religion ~ **cant** *v/i* use any peculiar jargon; speak hypocritically.

can't [kaant] (*coll abbr*) cannot.

Cantab [kantab] *n* and *adj* (member) of Cambridge University.

cantabile [kantaabilay] *adj* (*mus*) in smooth singing style.

cantaloup(e) [kantaloop] *n* kind of melon.

cantankerous [kantankeRus] *adj* quarrelsome.

cantata [kantaata] *n* a dramatic sacred or secular choral composition shorter than an oratorio.

cantatrice [kantatRees] *n* professional female singer.

canted [kanted] *adj* tilted, sloping; (*bui*) splayed, bevelled, off-square; **c. wall** wall joining another at an angle.

canteen [kanteen] *n* food shop or refreshment counter in camps, barracks, factories *etc*; soldier's mess-tin or water-bottle; case of cutlery.

canter [kanter] *n* easy gallop; **preliminary c.** trial trip; **win in a c.** win easily ~ **canter** *v/t* and *i*.

canterbury [kanterberi] *n* piece of furniture with divisions for holding music *etc*.

Canterbury bell [kanterberi-bel] *n* flowering plant with large bell-shaped flowers.

canticle [kantik'l] *n* hymn taken from Scriptures.

cantilever [kantileever] *n* (*archi*) beam or girder securely fixed at one end but hanging freely at the other > PDE; **c. bridge** bridge with suspended central portion resting on cantilever arms > PDE.

canting [kanting] *adj* whining, hypocritical.

canto [kantO] *n* one of the main divisions of a long poem; (*mus*) the soprano voice; the upper melody in a concert piece; **c. fermo** (*mus*) melody adapted for contrapuntal treatment > PDM.

canton [kanton/kanton] *n* subdivision of a country; one of the states of the Swiss republic; (*her*) small square rectangle in the upper corner of a shield or flag ~ **canton** *v/t* divide (land) into portions; provide (soldiers) with quarters.

cantonment [kantonment/kantOOnment] *n* place set aside for quartering troops.

cantor [kanter] *n* a soloist or the leader of the singing in a synagogue or church; the precentor of a cathedral.

cantorial [kantawRi-al] *adj* pertaining to the precentor's or northern side of a choir.

cantrip [kantRip] *n* (*Scots*) witch's spell; magic trick.

canvas [kanvas] *n* strong coarse cloth made of hemp or flax; **under c.** in tents; (*of ship*) with sails spread ~ **canvas** *adj* made of canvas.

canvasback [kanvasbak] *n* North American species of wild duck.

canvass [kanvas] *v/t* and *i* discuss, scrutinize fully; solicit votes before an election; ask for custom, orders *etc* ~ **canvass** *n* act of canvassing.

canyon, cañon [kanyon] *n* long gorge bounded by steep slopes > PDG.

canzonet [kanzonet] *n* (*mus*) short song of the folk-song type.

caoutchouc [ka-OOchOO] *n* raw rubber.

cap [kap] *n* brimless cloth head-covering; woman's lace or muslin indoor head-dress; cap denoting that wearer has been chosen as member of a special team or crew; cap-like cover on the end of various objects; paper percussion case; **black c.** cap worn by judge in passing sentence of death; **c. and bells** head-gear of professional jester; **with c. in hand** humbly asking a favour; **set one's c. at** (*of woman*) do everything possible to attract the attentions of (a man) ~ **cap** (*pres/part* **capping**, *p/t* and *p/part* **capped**) *v/t* put cap on the head of; confer University degree on; award (player) his cap; cover top of, protect end of; (*fig*) surpass, excel, beat; (*of anecdote etc*) follow it up with a better one.

capability [kaypabiliti] *n* quality of being capable; capacity for action; (*pl*) condition, faculty capable of development.

capable [kaypab'l] *adj* possessed of ability, competent; **c. of** able or fit to receive and be affected by; open to, susceptible; able to perform; wicked enough for ~ **capably** *adv* in a capable manner.

capacious [kap*ay*shus] *adj* roomy, spacious ~ **capaciously** *adv* ~ **capaciousness** *n*.

capacitance [kap*a*sitans] *n* (*elect*) electrical capacity; property enabling a capacitor to store electric charge; the extent of this measured in farads > PDS.

capacitate [kap*a*sitayt] *v/t* make capable (for); make legally eligible or competent.

capacitor [kap*a*sitawr] *n* (*elect*) assembly of conductors and insulators for storing electric charge > PDEl.

capacity [kap*a*siti] *n* power of receiving, containing or absorbing; mental ability and grasp; capability, talent; volume, cubic content; position, character; (*elect*) capacitance; output of a piece of electrical apparatus > PDS.

cap-à-pie [kapa*pee*] *adv* (armed) from head to foot.

caparison [kap*a*Rison] *n* ornamental cloth covering for a horse; ornaments ~ **caparison** *v/t* deck out, provide with trappings.

cape (1) [kayp] *n* short sleeveless cloak hanging over the shoulders.

cape (2) *n* promontory jutting into the sea; The C. Cape of Good Hope; Cape Colony; **C. Dutch** the Dutch spoken in S. Africa.

caper (1) [kayper] *n* South European shrub; pickled flower-bud of this; pickled seed vessel of the nasturtium.

caper (2) a frisky jump, leap; (*coll*) occupation, business; racket, illegal activity; (*pl*) silly pranks, irresponsible behaviour; **cut capers** frolic and jump around; (*fig*) play foolish pranks ~ **caper** *v/i* leap about.

capercailye, capercailzie [kaper*kayl*yi, kaper *kayl*zi] *n* the wood-grouse.

capibara see **capybara**.

capillaceous [kapi*lay*shus] *adj* of or like hair.

capillarity [kapi*la*Riti] *n* (*phys*) power or property of exerting capillary attraction or repulsion.

capillary [kap*i*laRi] *n* a minute hairbreadth blood-vessel > PDB ~ **capillary** *adj* consisting of hair; pertaining to hair; hair-like; **c. tube** tube of minute diameter; very fine blood-vessel; **c. attraction** surface activity of a capillary tube which causes a liquid to rise or fall > PDS.

capilliform [kap*i*lifawrm] *adj* (*bot*) hair-shaped.

capital (1) [kap*i*tal] *n* (*archi*) the head of a column or pillar.

capital (2) *adj* punishable by death; involving the death-penalty; important, weighty; (*of error*) having grave results; (*coll*) excellent; **c. letter** upper case letter as used to begin sentences and proper names; **c. ship** battleship ~ **capital** *n* capital letter; chief town of a country; stock of a company with which it starts business; accumulated wealth; (*pol*) capitalists and employers; **c. distribution** a tax-free dividend paid by a company from profits other than those earned by normal trading; **c. goods** plant, machinery, rolling stock *etc* manufactured for use in further production.

capitalism [kap*i*talizm] *n* possession of capital; economic system based on the private ownership of land or wealth.

capitalist [kap*i*talist] *n* one who has accumulated

wealth and makes it available for business enterprises ~ **capitalist** *adj* of capitalism or capitalists.

capitalization [kapital*ı*zayshon] *n* act of capitalizing; **c. issue** issue of shares by a company to existing shareholders for which a cash payment is not required.

capitalize [kap*i*tal*ı*z] *v/t* convert to capital; convert into an equivalent capital sum; make profit out of, turn to account; spell with capital letter; **c. on** turn to advantage.

capitally [kap*i*tali] *adv* in an excellent manner, admirably.

capitation [kapi*tay*shon] *n* levying of a tax on each person, poll-tax; **c. grant** grant made to an institution at rate of so much per head.

Capitol [kap*i*tol] *n* citadel on a hill, *esp* Temple of Jupiter at Rome; (*US*) building in which Congress meets at Washington.

Capitolian [kapit*Oli*-an], **Capitoline** [kap*it*Ol*ı*n] *adj* of the Capitol in Rome.

capitular [kap*i*tewlar] *adj* of cathedral chapter.

capitulate [kap*i*tewlayt] *v/i* surrender on agreed terms; yield, surrender.

capitulation [kapitewl*ay*shon] *n* act of capitulating; terms of surrender; summary of chief points.

capoc see **kapok**.

capon [kaypon] *n* castrated domestic fowl.

cappuccino [kapew*cheen*O] *n* (*Ital*) milky coffee, *esp* when topped with foam.

capriccio [kap*Rich*i-O] *n* (*mus*) piece of music whimsical in character and free in form > PDM.

caprice [kap*Rees*] *n* whim, sudden turn of fancy; (*mus*) capriccio.

capricious [kap*Rish*us] *adj* governed by caprice rather than judgement ~ **capriciously** *adv* ~ **capriciousness** *n*.

Capricorn [kap*Ri*kawrn] *n* (*astron*) constellation of the He-Goat, tenth sign of the zodiac; **Tropic of C.** the southern tropic, the parallel of latitude $23\frac{1}{2}°$ S > PDG.

caproic [kap*RO*-ik] *adj* like a goat; **c. acid** an acid found in butter.

capsicum [kap*si*kum] *n* genus of tropical plants from which cayenne pepper is made.

capsize [kaps*ız*] *v/t* and *i* (*of boats, carts etc*) overturn, upset.

capstan [kap*s*tan] *n* a hand-operated or small power-driven winch > PDSa, PDE.

capstone [kap*s*tOn] *n* coping-stone; (*arch*) horizontal stone of a cromlech.

capsular [kap*s*ewler] *adj* of or in a capsule.

capsule [kap*s*ewl] *n* (*med*) gelatine envelope containing a dose of medicine; metal or plastic closure for the neck of a bottle; (*bot*) seed-vessel; (*aer*) that part of a spaceship in which an astronaut is placed; detachable self-contained unit in a spaceship; (*anat*) membrane sac ~ **capsule** *adj* compressed, compact, brief.

captain [kap*t*in] *n* naval or military commander; officer between the rank of commander and rear-admiral in the navy and between lieutenant and major in the army; officer in command of a man-of-war; master of a merchant-ship; pilot of a civil aircraft; officer in command of a fire-brigade; (*games*) leader of a team or side; (*in industry*) leader, magnate ~ **captain** *v/t* be captain of, lead, command.

captaincy [kap*t*insi] *n* rank and status of a captain.

caption [*kap*shon] *n* printed heading of a chapter, page, table, section *etc*; title or heading of a story, newspaper article, film scene; title, description, or legend, printed below an illustration.

captious [*kap*shus] *adj* fault-finding, carping ~ **captiously** *adv* ~ **captiousness** *n*.

captivate [*kap*tivayt] *v/t* fascinate, enchant ~ **captivating** *adj* ~ **captivation** *n*.

captive [*kap*tiv] *n* one who has been captured, prisoner ~ **captive** *adj* taken prisoner, kept in confinement; unable to escape unwanted information; c. **balloon** balloon secured by a cable from the ground.

captivity [*kap*tiviti] *n* condition of being captive.

captor [*kap*ter] *n* one who captures a prisoner.

capture [*kap*tewr] *n* taking by force; booty so taken; (*phys*) process by which atom or nucleus acquires an additional particle; process by which a star, planet *etc* draws an object permanently into its gravitational field ~ **capture** *v/t* catch, take prisoner, seize.

Capuchin [*kap*ewchin] *n* member of order of Franciscan friars who wear a brown habit with pointed cowl; c. **monkey** South American monkey with black hair resembling a cowl; c. **pigeon** pigeon with crested head.

capybara, capibara [kapi*baa*Ra] *n* (*zool*) large semi-aquatic South American rodent.

car [*kaar*] *n* passenger vehicle driven by a petrol engine; railway carriage; tramcar; part of airship for crew, passengers *etc*; (*ar*) wheeled vehicle, chariot.

carabineer [kaRabi*neer*] *n* mounted soldier armed with a carbine.

carack see **carrack**.

caracole [*ka*Rak*O*l] *n* (*horseriding*) a half turn; a succession of wheels to left and right; (*bui*) spiral staircase ~ **caracole** *v/t* and *i* make (horse) wheel; execute a turn or series of turns.

caracul [*ka*Rak*OO*l] *n* a broadtail sheep from Bokhara; curled, glossy, black coat of this.

carafe [ka*Raaf*] *n* type of bottle for wine or water.

caramel [*ka*Ramel] *n* burnt sugar, used for flavouring and colouring; a sweetmeat.

carapace [*ka*Rapays] *n* upper shell of tortoises and crabs.

carat [*ka*Rat] *n* measure of weight of diamonds and other gems; measure of fineness of gold.

caravan [*ka*Ravan/kaRa*van*] *n* covered vehicle housing holiday-makers, gipsies, travelling showmen *etc*; company of travellers journeying across deserts; (*US*) a train of wagons or string of pack-mules.

caravanner [*ka*Ra*van*er] *n* person travelling or living in a caravan.

caravanserai [*ka*Ra*van*seRay] *n* inn in the East with spacious courtyard where caravans put up.

caraway [*ka*Raway] *n* plant with aromatic seeds used for flavouring.

carbide [*kaar*bId] *n* (*chem*) binary compound of carbon; loose term for calcium carbide.

carbine, carabine [*kaar*bIn, *ka*RabIn] *n* short firearm used by mounted troops.

carbohydrate [kaarb*Oh*IdRayt] *n* an organic compound composed of carbon, hydrogen, and oxygen only > PDS; (*pl*) (*coll*) starchy foods.

carbolic [kar*bol*ik] *adj* derived from carbon;

c. **acid** phenol, a white crystalline solid used as disinfectant and in the manufacture of plastics and dyes > PDS.

carbon [*kaar*bon] *n* non-metallic element occurring as diamond, graphite, and charcoal > PDS; piece of carbon-paper; copy from this; (*elect*) carbon electrode of an electric arc lamp; c. **dating** method of dating prehistoric objects by decay of radioactive carbon isotopes; c. **dioxide** colourless gas with faint tingling smell and taste > PDS ~ **carbon** *v/t* and *i* coat or become coated with carbon.

carbonaceous [kaarbo*nays*hus] *adj* consisting of or containing carbon.

carbonado [kaarbo*nay*dO] *n* black, discoloured or impure variety of diamond used for drills.

carbonari [kaarb*O*naa*Ri*] *n* (*pl*) members of an Italian 19th-century republican secret society.

carbonate [*kaar*bonit] *n* a salt of carbonic acid.

carbonated [*kaar*bonaytid] *adj* aerated, saturated with carbon dioxide under pressure.

carbon-copy [*kaar*bon-kopi] *n* copy made with carbon-paper; (*fig*) exact copy, replica.

carbonic [kar*bon*ik] *adj* pertaining to, got from carbon; c. **acid** weak acid formed when carbon dioxide is dissolved in water; carbon dioxide > PDS.

carboniferous [kaarbo*nife*Rus] *adj* (*geol*) containing coal; relating to that part of the palaeozoic era when coal was extensively formed > PDG.

carbonize [*kaar*bonIz] *v/t* turn into carbon ~ **carbonization** [kaarbonIzayshon] *n*.

carbon-paper [*kaar*bon-payper] *n* paper coated on one side with carbon black used for the duplication of typescript or writing.

carbonyls [*kaar*bonilz] *n* (*pl*) compounds of metals with carbon monoxide.

carborundum [kaarbo*Rund*um] *n* silicon carbide, a hard crystalline solid used for grinding and as a refractory material > PDE.

carboy [*kaar*boi] *n* large globular coloured glass jar, enclosed in basket-work.

carbuncle [*kaar*bunk'l] *n* gem of deep red colour, *esp* a garnet or ruby; inflamed boil or tumour; red pimple on the nose.

carburetted [kaarbew*Ret*id] *adj* combined with carbon; charged with carbon.

carburettor, carburetter [kaarbew*Ret*er] *n* device in the internal combustion engine for mixing air with petrol vapour preliminary to explosion.

carburize [*kaar*bewRIz] *v/t* combine with carbon.

carcanet [*kaar*kanet] *n* (*ar*) ornamental jewelled collar.

carcass, carcase [*kaar*kas] *n* dead body of animal; trunk of dead animal after head, limbs, and offal have been removed by a butcher; (*cont*) body of human being; shell of building, ship *etc*.

carcinogen [*kaar*sin*O*jen] *n* substance causing cancer ~ **carcinogenic** *adj*.

carcinology [kaarsin*ol*oji] *n* part of zoology dealing with crabs and other crustaceans.

carcinoma [kaarsin*Om*a] *n* (*med*) form of cancer.

card (1) [*kaard*] *n* implement used for disentangling and cleaning wool or cotton for spinning ~ **card** *v/t* prepare (wool *etc*) with a card.

card (2) *n* piece of stiffened paper; postcard; card printed with person's name and address, or carrying a greeting; (*bridge, whist, etc*) one of fifty-two playing cards; advertisement; floating face of compass; (*coll*) eccentric person; **on the cards** probable, likely; **put one's cards on the table** abandon secrecy, reveal one's resources; **show one's cards** disclose one's intentions; **house of cards** project with no chance of success.

cardamom [*kaar*damom] *n* an aromatic spice.

cardan [*kaar*dan] *adj* (*eng*) **c. joint** universal joint; **c. shaft** shaft with a cardan joint at one or both ends.

cardboard [*kaard*bawrd] *n* flat sheet of strong pasteboard ~ **cardboard** *adj* (*fig*) unreal, appearing stronger than it is; stiff, unnatural.

cardiac [*kaar*di-ak] *adj* (*anat*) pertaining to the heart or to the upper part of the stomach.

cardigan [*kaar*digan] *n* knitted woollen jacket.

cardinal (1) [*kaar*dinal] *adj* on which other things depend or hinge, fundamental; chief; deep scarlet; **c. numbers** the numbers 1, 2, 3 *etc*; **c. points** the four points of the compass; **c. virtues** justice, prudence, temperance, and fortitude.

cardinal (2) *n* one of the senior ecclesiastical princes of the Roman Catholic Church.

card-index [kaard-*index*] *n* index in which each entry is on separate card ~ **card-index** *v/t*.

carding-machine [*kaard*ing-masheen] *n* machine for combing and cleaning cotton fibres *etc*.

cardiograph [*kaar*di-Ograaf] *n* instrument which records heart beats.

cardiography [kaardi-*og*Rafi] *n* the recording of heart action.

cardiology [kaardi-*oloji*] *n* scientific study and treatment of the heart.

cardiovascular [kaardi-Ova*skewlar*] *adj* relating to heart and blood-vessels.

carditis [kard*It*is] *n* inflammation of muscular substance of the heart.

cardoon [kaard*OOn*] *n* globe artichoke.

cardsharper [*kaards*haarper] *n* professional cheater at card games.

card-table [*kaard*-tab'l] *n* small table covered with green baize for card-playing.

care [*kair*] *n* trouble, anxiety; object causing anxiety; heedfulness, pains; attention, caution; charge, responsibility; safe-keeping; upkeep, maintenance; **in c.** under official guardianship; **c. of** (*written c/o*) (*in addressing letter*) living at the address of; **take c.** be prudent, do not run into danger ~ **care** *v/i* feel strongly; **not c.** have no interest, be indifferent; **c. for** feel affection for; look after.

careen [ka*Reen*] *v/t* and *i* (*naut*) turn (ship) on her side for repairs or caulking; heel over ~ **careenage** *n* careening a ship; place for, or cost of, this.

career [ka*Reer*] *n* course and progress of a person's life; profession, business or long-term occupation offering progressive increase of achievement; swift motion, impetus ~ **career** *v/i* move at full speed, rush wildly ~ **career** *adj* of, as or having a career.

careerist [ka*Reer*Rist] *n* one whose overriding aim is personal success in a profession or business.

carefree [*kair*Free] *adj* free from anxiety.

careful [*kair*fool] *adj* painstaking, attentive; cautious ~ **carefully** *adv*.

careless [*kair*les] *adj* unconcerned; inattentive, negligent ~ **carelessly** *adv*.

caress [ka*Res*] *n* gesture of affection ~ **caress** *v/t* stroke affectionately; embrace; touch gently; soothe, flatter.

caressing [ka*Res*ing] *adj* expressive of affection, soothing ~ **caressingly** *adv*.

caret [*ka*Ret] *n* a mark (∧) used in proof correction to indicate an omission.

caretaker [*kair*tayker] *n* person employed to look after school buildings, block of flats, public buildings *etc*, or to look after a house in the absence of its owner; **c. government** an administration temporarily holding office until a new government can be appointed.

carfax [*kaar*faks] *n* place where four roads meet, *esp* in the centre of a town.

car-ferry [*kaar*-fe*Ri*] *n* ship or aircraft service ferrying motorcars.

cargo [*kaarg*O] *n* goods carried by a ship, freight.

Carib [*ka*Rib] *n* one of the native race found in the West Indian islands.

caribou, cariboo [ka*Rib*OO] *n* North American reindeer.

caricatural [ka*Rik*atewr*Ral] *adj* of or like a caricature.

caricature [ka*Rik*atewr] *n* drawing or imitation of an individual exaggerating his characteristics with comic effect; grotesque or ludicrous exaggeration; any ugly or debased likeness ~ **caricature** *v/t*.

caricaturist [ka*Rik*atewr*Rist] *n* one who makes caricatures, *esp* in drawings.

caries [*kair*Ri-eez] *n* decay of the bones or teeth.

carillon [*ka*Rilyon] *n* set of bells hung in a tower, which can be played from a keyboard; tune played on bells; small musical instrument or part of organ imitating peal of bells > PDM.

carious [*kair*Ri-us] *adj* affected with caries; decayed, rotten.

carking [*kaar*king] *adj* worrying, harassing.

carless [*kaar*les] *adj* having no motorcar; containing no motorcars.

carline [*kaar*lin] *n* type of thistle; (*Scots*) (*cont*) old woman.

Carlovingian [kaarlO*vinj*i-an] *adj* belonging to dynasty of French kings founded by Charlemagne.

carman [*kaar*man] *n* man who drives van or lorry carrying goods.

Carmelite [*kaar*melIt] *n* member of order of enclosed contemplative nuns.

carminative [kaar*min*ativ/*kaar*minaytiv] *n* and *adj* (medicine) relieving flatulence.

carmine [*kaar*min] *n* crimson pigment obtained from cochineal ~ **carmine** *adj*.

carnage [*kaar*nij] *n* slaughter, massacre.

carnal [*kaar*nal] *adj* fleshly; sensual, sexual; worldly, unspiritual; **c. knowledge** of sexual intercourse with ~ **carnality** [kar*nal*iti] *n* fleshly appetite, lust ~ **carnally** *adv*.

carnation [kar*nay*shon] *n* bright, rosy, pink colour; deeper red colour of carnation flower; a cultivated variety of the clove-pink ~ **carnation** *adj* rosepink.

carnelian see **cornelian**.

carnival [*kaar*nival] *n* popular festivities and revelry before Lent; any occasion of revelry; organized festivities and celebrations.

carnivora [kar*niv*oRa] *n* (*pl*) (*zool*) flesh-eating mammals.

carnivore [*kaar*nivawr] *n* flesh-eating mammal or plant.

carnivorous [kaar*niv*awRus] *adj* flesh-eating.

carob [*ka*Rob] *n* tree of the senna family and its fruit; the locust-tree and the locusts it bears.

carol [*ka*Rol] *n* joyous religious song, *esp* one dealing with the birth of Christ; (*poet*) song of birds ~ **carol** (*pres/part* **carolling**, *p/t* and *p/part* **carolled**) *v/i* and *t* sing joyously; celebrate in song.

Carolingian [kaRo*linj*i-an] *adj* Carlovingian.

carotid [ka*Rot*id] *n* (*anat*) one of the two chief arteries in the neck ~ **carotid** *adj*.

carotin, carotine [*ka*Rotin, *ka*Roteen] *n* a yellow pigment present in carrots *etc* > PDS.

carousal [ka*Rowz*al] *n* merry drinking-bout.

carouse [ka*Rowz*] *n* carousal ~ **carouse** *v/i* drink freely and make merry ~ **carouser** *n*.

carousel [*ka*Roosel] *n* a roundabout, merry-go-round; a circular conveyor-belt.

carp (1) [*kaarp*] *n* a freshwater fish.

carp (2) *v/i* find fault sharply and unreasonably.

carpal [*kaar*pal] *adj* (*anat*) of the wrist > PDB.

car-park [*kaar*-paark] *n* open space or building reserved for the parking of motorcars.

carpel [*kaar*pel] *n* (*bot*) division of the seed vessel; a simple pistil ~ **carpellary** [*kaar*pelaRi] *adj*.

carpenter [*kaar*penter] *n* man who makes wood frames, floors, stairs *etc* in building construction; man who makes useful objects from wood ~ **carpenter** *v/t* and *i* work or make as a carpenter.

carpentry [*kaar*pentRi] *n* craft of cutting timber to make structural frameworks; craft of making useful objects of wood.

carpet [*kaar*pet] *n* a textile covering for floor and stairs of heavy woven foundation; covering (*eg* of leaves) evenly spread over the ground; **on the c. under consideration**; (*coll*) being reprimanded ~ **carpet** *v/t* cover with or as with a carpet; (*coll*) reprimand.

carpetbag [*kaar*petbag] *n* bag made of carpet material.

carpet-bedding [*kaar*pet-beding] *n* (*hort*) planting of a garden bed with low-growing brightly coloured plants in a carpet-like pattern.

carpeting [*kaar*peting] *n* carpet material.

carpet-slippers [*kaar*pet-slipers] *n* (*pl*) slippers with uppers of woollen cloth.

carping [*kaar*ping] *adj* harshly critical, captious, fault-finding.

carpo- *pref* of fruit.

carport [*kaar*pawrt] *n* open-fronted shelter for a motorcar.

carpus [*kaar*pus] *n* (*anat*) the wrist.

carrack, carack [*ka*Rak] *n* (*hist*) armed merchantman formerly used by Spaniards and Portuguese.

carrageen, carragheen [*ka*Rageen] *n* kind of seaweed from which an edible jelly is extracted.

carrel [*ka*Rel] *n* reserved alcove in a library.

carriage [*ka*Rij] *n* act of carrying, conveyance; cost of carrying; bearing, deportment; wheeled vehicle carrying people; vehicle unit of railway train; private vehicle with two horses; movable framework on which gun is mounted; part of typewriter which carries and moves the paper;

c. forward cost of transit to be paid by recipient; **c. paid** cost of transit paid by sender.

carriageway [*ka*Rijway] *n* that part of a road which carries vehicles.

carrier [*ka*Ri-er] *n* one who carries goods and parcels for payment and delivers them to the addressees; person or animal that carries and passes on germs or genetic characteristics without himself showing their effects; carrier-pigeon; contrivance affixed to car or bicycle for carrying parcels, luggage *etc*; paper or plastic bag for carrying shopping purchases; (*chem*) type of catalyst > PDS; (*elect*) mobile electron or hole which carries the charge in a semiconductor; **c. wave** continuous electro-magnetic wave motion emitted by a radio transmitter.

carrier-bag [*ka*Ri-er-bag] *n* strong paper or plastic bag with hand-grips for carrying parcels *etc*.

carrier-pigeon [*ka*Ri-er-pijn] *n* breed of pigeon with strong homing instinct, used to carry messages.

carrion [*ka*Ri-on] *n* dead and rotting flesh ~ **carrion** *adj* feeding on, or like, carrion.

carrot [*ka*Rot] *n* plant with large orange-red tapering root, cultivated as vegetable; (*fig*) promised reward; inducement; (*pl*) (*coll*) redhaired person ~ **carroty** *adj* reddish.

carry [*ka*Ri] *v/t* and *i* take from one place to another in one's hands or by one's own effort; convey in vehicle; bear (message, news *etc*); lead by force, conduct, escort; (*math*) transfer number from one column to the next on the left; (*of wind, water*) bear along with it; (*of drain, channel*) provide passage for; extend, continue (a work to a certain distance); seize by military attack; obtain by one's own efforts; (*of voice etc*) reach to a certain distance; be pregnant with; support, bear weight of, sustain; hold (body, limbs) in a certain position; **be carried away** become profoundly stirred by an emotional experience; (*refl*) comport oneself; **c. forward** transfer (item) to next column or page; **c. off** win (prize); (*of disease*) remove from life; **c. it off well** manage a difficult situation with ease and assurance; **c. on** continue on the same lines; (*coll*) behave conspicuously and in bad taste; flirt; **c. out** continue to the end, fulfil; **c. over** (*Stock Exchange*) hold over (payment) until the next settling day; **c. through** bring safely through difficulties; **c. all before one** overcome all obstacles with ease; **c. the day** win the conflict; **c. weight** have influence ~ **carry** *n* (*mil*) position of rifle or sword when held vertically in front of the right shoulder; (*of shell, ball*) distance of flight.

carry-all [*ka*Ri-awl] *n* capacious bag.

carrycot [*ka*Rikot] *n* light cot with handles but no legs, for carrying a baby.

carry-on [*ka*Ri-on] *n* (*coll*) fuss, silly excitement.

carryings-on [kaRi-ingz-*on*] *n* (*pl*) (*coll*) silly frivolous behaviour.

carrying-trade [*ka*Ri-ing-tRayd] *n* transport of goods *esp* by water.

carry-over [kaRi-*Ov*er] *n* (*Stock Exchange*) arrangement whereby the settlement of securities bought or sold for one account is deferred until the next; business, work *etc* left to be dealt with at some future date; something remaining from a previous period.

carsick [*kaar*sik] *adj* suffering from nausea and vomiting when riding in cars ~ **carsickness** *n*.

cart [*kaart*] *n* strong springless farm vehicle with two wheels; lighter vehicle used by tradesman; **put the c. before the horse** reverse the natural order of things; **in the c.** (*coll*) in an awkward position, in trouble ~ **cart** *v/t* and *i* carry in a cart; carry with difficulty or unwillingly.

cartage [*kaart*ij] *n* process or price of carting.

carte (1) [*kaart*] *n* bill of fare, menu; **à la c.** selected from separate items on the menu.

carte (2), **quarte** *n* position in fencing.

carte-blanche [kaart-*blaansh*] *n* blank sheet of paper given to person on which to write his own conditions; full power of action, *esp* in expenditure.

cartel [*kaart*el] *n* agreement between manufacturers regulating output and prices, syndicate; challenge to a duel; written agreement relating to exchange of prisoners.

cartelize [*kaart*elIz] *v/t* and *i* combine to form a cartel.

Cartesian [kart*eezi*-an/kart*eezhi*-an] *n* and *adj* (follower) of Descartes.

carthorse [*kart*hawrs] *n* strong thick-set horse for heavy work.

Carthusian [kart*hewzi*-an/kart*hewzhi*-an] *n* member of an order of monks with very severe rule; pupil of Charterhouse School ~ **Carthusian** *adj*.

cartilage [*kaart*ilij] *n* strong elastic tissue, gristle.

cartilaginous [kaartil*aj*inus] *adj* of the nature of cartilage.

cartographer [kart*og*Rafer] *n* one who draws maps ~ **cartography** [kart*og*Rafi] *n*.

cartomancy [*kaart*Omansi] *n* fortune-telling from playing-cards.

carton [*kaart*on] *n* small container made of light cardboard; cardboard box; white disc in the centre of a target; shot which strikes this.

cartonnage [*kaart*onij] *n* (*arch*) Egyptian mummy-case.

cartoon [kart*OO*n] *n* full-scale drawing for a fresco, mosaic, or mural painting *etc*; humorous drawing in a newspaper offering satirical commentary on current events; (*cin*) film made from drawings not from life ~ **cartoon** *v/t* and *i* ridicule by means of a cartoon.

cartoonist [kaart*OO*nist] *n* one who draws humorous cartoons.

cartouche [kart*OO*sh] *n* design or tablet enclosing an inscription; decoration for the title page of a book.

cartridge [*kaart*Rij] *n* case containing a charge of explosive; (*for small arms*) cartridge and bullet in one, a ball-cartridge; (*phot*) spool of film in lightproof case; removable capsule in a record-player pickup; cassette; **blank c.** cartridge containing no shot.

cartridge-paper [*kaart*Rij-payper] *n* strong paper used for cartridge-cases; hard opaque white drawing paper used for pencil or ink drawing.

cart-track [*kaart*-tRAk] *n* rough unmetalled road.

cartulary, chartulary [*kaart*ewlaRi] *n* collection of charters and grants of land.

cartwheel [*kaart*weel] *n* wheel of a cart; (*coll*) a sideways somersault; (*US*) (*coll*) a silver dollar.

caruncle [ka*Runk*'l] *n* fleshy outgrowth, as on the head of certain birds.

carve [*kaarv*] *v/t* and *i* cut and fashion wood, stone, marble *etc* into a particular form; cut up meat or poultry at table for the company; (*sl*) slash, cut; (*fig*) make for oneself by vigorous or ruthless efforts; **c. up** cut into pieces; share out; (*sl*) swindle.

carvel-built [*kaar*vil-bilt] *adj* (*naut*) built with the planks meeting flush at the seams.

carving [*kaar*ving] *n* work of one who carves; piece of carved work.

carving-knife [*kaar*ving-nIf] *n* strong long-bladed knife for carving meat.

caryatid (*pl* **caryatides**) [ka*Ri*-*at*id, ka*Ri*-*at*ideez] *n* (*Gk archi*) draped female figure serving as a column to support an entablature.

cascade [kask*ayd*] *n* small waterfall or series of falls; (*elect*) series of devices so connected that each operates the next > PDS ~ **cascade** *adj* arranged so that the effect of each stage in a multiple process is multiplied in subsequent stages ~ **cascade** *v/i* fall in lavish streams.

cascara [kask*aa*Ra] *n* (*med*) laxative obtained from the bark of the Californian buckthorn.

case (1) [*kays*] *n* example, instance; condition, plight; (*leg*) suit brought into court, suit which has been decided; sum of arguments brought forward by one of the parties; (*med*) instance of a disease, person having a particular disease; person whose social, legal, or medical problems are being studied or treated; (*gramm*) a variation in the form of a noun, pronoun, or adjective indicating the relation in which it stands to other words in a sentence; the grammatical relation in which a noun, pronoun, or adjective stands to other words in a sentence; **c. history** (*med*) account of relevant factors in patient's past; **in c.** in the event that, on the chance that; **in c. of** in the event of; **put the c. that** suppose, assume that; **in any c.** at all events, whatever happens; **in that c.** if that is so, if that happens.

case (2) *n* movable receptacle fitted to enclose something; outer protecting part of something; (*print*) compositor's box containing sorted type; **lower c.** (*print*) small letters; **upper c.** capital letters ~ **case** *v/t* enclose in a case; cover with protective material.

casebook [*kays*book] *n* record kept by doctor, detective *etc* of cases dealt with.

caseharden [*kays*haarden] *v/t* harden the surface of steel or timber > PDE; (*fig*) harden in disposition, render callous or insensitive.

casein [*kay*see-in] *n* (*chem*) main protein of milk, obtained by curdling > PDS.

case-law [*kays*-law] *n* (*leg*) law based upon the precedent of judgements given in previous cases.

caseload [*kays*lOd] *n* total number of cases being dealt with by a doctor, social worker *etc* at one time.

casemate [*kays*mayt] *n* (*mil*) fortified gun emplacement.

casement [*kays*ment/*kayz*ment] *n* (*bui*) window hung by one vertical edge to open like a door; **c. cloth** cotton cloth used for window curtains.

caseous [*kays*i-us] *adj* like cheese.

case-shot [*kays*-shot] *n* canister shot, shrapnel.

casework [*kays*wurk] *n* the care of individuals with medical or social problems.

cash (1) [*kash*] *n* ready money, coin and banknotes; (*coll*) money in any form; **c. down** im-

mediate payment to be made; **c. on delivery**
(C.O.D.) payment to be made to person delivering goods ~ **cash** *v/t* give or receive cash in exchange for cheque *etc*; **c. in on** profit by.
cash (2) (*pl* **cash**) *n* a small coin used in the East Indies and China.
cashable [*kash*ab'l] *adj* that may be cashed.
cashbook [*kash*book] *n* book in which ready money transactions are entered.
cashew [*kash*OO] *n* large tropical tree bearing a kidney-shaped fruit; **c. nut** fruit of this.
cashier (1) [ka*sheer*] *n* member of the staff of a bank or mercantile firm who is in charge of the payments and receipts; shop attendant who takes the customers' money but does not serve goods.
cashier (2) *v/t* dismiss from employment; (*mil*) dismiss from the service with ignominy.
cashmere [*kash*meer/kash*meer*] *n* fine material made from the soft hair of certain goats.
cashoo see **catechu**.
cash-register [*kash*-Rejister] *n* a till which automatically records sums of money put into it.
casing [*kay*sing] *n* protective covering; (*bui*) a timber lining round a wooden stair; frame enclosing the sash-weights of a window; a door frame; outer rubber covering of an automobile tyre.
casino [ka*seen*O] *n* public place with facilities for gambling.
cask [*kaask*] *n* cylindrical wooden vessel with flat ends, used principally for liquids; kind of barrel; variable measure of capacity.
casket [*kaas*kit] *n* small box of fine workmanship for jewellery and trinkets; (*US*) coffin.
casque [*kaask*] *n* (*ar*) helmet.
cassation [ka*say*shon] *n* (*leg*) annulment.
cassava, cassada [ka*saa*va, ka*saa*da] *n* tropical plant with tuberous roots; flour obtained from its roots; bread made from this flour.
casserole [*kas*eROl] *n* heat-resisting baking dish with a lid in which food is stewed or braised; a stew; bordering of rice round a curry; mould of rice or mashed potato in which meat is served.
cassette [ka*set*] *n* small container holding magnetic tape for recording and reproducing sound; similar container holding videotape for transmission on a television screen; light-proof container for film-spool or X-ray film.
cassia [*kas*i-a] *n* inferior variety of cinnamon; (*bot*) genus of tropical plants including senna.
cassiterite [ka*site*Rit] *n* natural tin oxide.
cassock [*kas*ok] *n* long black vestment worn by clergy, choristers, and other church officials.
cassowary [*kas*OwaiRi] *n* bird like an ostrich.
cast (*p/t* and *p/part* **cast**) [*kaast*] *v/t* and *i* hurl; throw down, throw off; let down (anchor); turn (eyes); reject; discard, shed; add up, calculate; (*trees, animals*) drop (leaves, young) prematurely; (*eng*) mould (metal *etc*); (*theat*) allot parts to actors; (*leg*) defeat (in lawsuit); (*dial*) discard clothing; throw a fishing-line; (*eng*) form into a shape; **c. about** search this way and that; consider; (*naut*) change course; **c. off** abandon, disown; (*knitting*) remove last row of stitches from needles; let loose (dogs); let fly (hawks); **c. on** (*knitting*) make the first row of stitches on needle; **c. up** calculate ~ **cast** *n* act of throwing, a throw; the distance thrown; something shed or

rejected; skin of snake; small heap of earth thrown up by worms; (*theat*) the actors in a play; figure or model made by running material into a mould; impression taken from person or thing; tinge of colour added to the prevailing hue; characteristic quality of a person's appearance, character, or bent of mind; squint; (*hunting*) spreading out of hounds in search of the scent ~ **cast** *adj* formed by moulding metal; **c. iron** impure, brittle iron formed in blast furnaces and poured into a mould; **c. steel** steel not rolled or forged since casting > PDE.
castanets [kastan*ets*] *n* percussion instrument of two hollowed-out pieces of hard wood or ivory rhythmically clicked together by the fingers ⁊ PDM.
castaway [*kaas*taway] *n* one cast adrift at sea or shipwrecked; (*fig*) an outcast from society.
caste [*kaast*] *n* one of the hereditary social divisions among Hindus; any exclusive social group or class; **to lose c.** to forfeit one's right to social privileges and lose the respect of one's associates.
castellated [*kas*telaytid] *adj* built to look like a castle; having battlements, turrets *etc*; (*of district*) rich in castles; **c. beam** (*eng*) type of steel beam > PDE.
castellation [kaste*lay*shon] *n* the building of castles; the addition of battlements to a building; a battlement.
caster (1) [*kaas*ter] *n* one who casts metal; one who takes plaster casts.
caster (2), **castor** (1) [*kaas*ter] *n* bottle or other container with a perforated closure for sprinkling sugar, pepper *etc*; small wheel on a swivel fixed to each leg of a piece of furniture so that it may turn easily on the floor; **c. action** (*mot*) mechanism which provides a self-centring action for the front wheels of an automobile; **c. sugar** sugar finely ground; s fted sugar.
castigate [*kas*tigayt] *v/t* chastise, punish or rebuke severely; correct, emend (literary work).
castigation [kasti*gay*shon] *n* severe punishment.
castile soap [kasteel-*sOp*] *n* hard soap made with olive oil and soda.
casting [*kaas*ting] *n* act of throwing; operation of placing molten metals or phenolic resins into moulds in which they solidify; the object so shaped; act of choosing actors for a play or film.
casting-vote [*kaas*ting-vOt] *n* decisive vote given by the chairman of a meeting when the votes on each side are equal.
castiron [*kaast*I-ern] *adj* made of cast iron; (*fig*) inflexible; insensible to fatigue; unshakable.
castle [*kaas*'l] *n* massive building situated and fortified for defence; an imposing mansion; stronghold; piece in chess made like a castle, also called **rook**; **c. in the air, c. in Spain** day-dream, visionary hopes and plans ~ **castle** *v/i* (*in chess*) move king two squares towards castle and move castle to further side of king ~ **castled** *adj* with castles; castellated.
cast-off [*kaast*-of] *n* something discarded as useless; (*typ*) calculation of printed space required for a certain amount of copy ~ **cast-off** *adj* thrown aside, discarded.
castor (1) see **caster** (2).

castor (2) [*kaaster*] *n* the beaver; pungent oily substance obtained from the beaver.

castor-oil [kaaster-*oil*] *n* oil obtained from seeds of the plant *Ricinus communis*, used as laxative.

castrate [kas*tRayt*] *v/t* remove the testicles of, emasculate; remove objectionable passages from (book), expurgate ~ **castration** [kas*tRayshon*] *n*.

castrato (*pl* **castrati**) [kas*RaatO*, *pl* kas*tRaatee*] *n* male singer castrated in boyhood to allow the development of a powerful voice in soprano or contralto range > PDM.

casual [*kazhewl/kazewl*] *adj* accidental, happening by chance; leaving things to chance, careless; showing lack of interest; brief and superficial; (*of clothes*) informal, to be worn for sport, holidays *etc*; **c. labourer** one without fixed employment, who takes odd jobs; **c. ward** workhouse ward for vagrants ~ **casual** *n* casual labourer; (*pl*) informal clothes; low-heeled shoes ~ **casually** *adv*.

casualty [*kazhewlti/kazewlti*] *n* victim of a serious or fatal accident; (*pl*) soldiers wounded or killed in battle; **c. list** list of those killed or hurt in battle or in an accident; **c. ward** hospital ward for those injured in accidents.

casuarina [kazewa*Reena*] *n* Australian species of trees with leafless branches.

casuist [*kazew-ist/kazhew-ist*] *n* one skilled in casuistry; a quibbler ~ **casuistic** *adj*.

casuistry [*kazew-istRi/kazhew-istRi*] *n* the application of ethical rules and principles to special cases where conflicting obligations arise; equivocal or specious reasoning.

casus belli [kayzus-*belI*] *n* action justifying declaration of war; (*fig*) ground for a quarrel.

cat [*kat*] *n* domesticated carnivorous quadruped; (*zool*) any animal of the genus *Felis*, as lion, tiger; (*fig*) spiteful woman; (*abbr*) hepcat; a musician who plays swing music; (*sl*) person; (*hist*) movable penthouse used by besiegers when approaching a fortification; piece of wood tapering at both ends used in game of tip-cat; the game itself; (*naut*) cathead; (*abbr*) cat-o'-nine-tails; **a c. may look at a king** even the lowest have some rights; **enough to make a c. laugh** exceptionally funny; **see which way the c. jumps** see what course events are taking; **cat's whiskers, cat's pyjamas** (*sl*) something wonderful ~ **cat** (*pres/part* **catting** *p/t* and *p/part* **catted**) *v/t* and *i* (*naut*) raise (the anchor) to the cathead; (*coll*) vomit.

cata-, cat-, cath- *pref* down from, down to, in opposition to, throughout, completely *etc*.

catabolism [kat*abolizm*] *n* (*biol*) the breaking down by living things of complex organic molecules, with liberation of energy.

catachresis [katak*Reesis*] *n* misuse of words, malapropism ~ **catachrestic** [katak*Restik/katakRees*-tik] *adj*.

cataclastic [katak*lastik*] *adj* (*geol*) formed by violent crushing.

cataclysm [*kat*aklizm] *n* overwhelming flood; violent upheaval; political or social catastrophic change ~ **cataclysmal** [katak*liz*mal] *adj* ~ **cataclysmic** [katak*liz*mik] *adj*.

catacomb [*kat*akOm] *n* underground cemetery with interconnecting galleries for burials.

catafalque [*kat*afalk] *n* platform erected in church for a coffin to rest on.

catalase [*kat*alays] *n* enzyme capable of breaking down hydrogen peroxide into water and oxygen.

catalepsy [*kat*alepsi] *n* (*med*) state associated with mental or nervous disorder, or with hypnosis, where the patient maintains his limbs in any position in which they are placed ~ **cataleptic** [katal*eptik*] *n* and *adj*.

catalo [*kat*alO] *n* (*US*) a hybrid or cross between the American buffalo and domestic cattle.

catalogue [*kat*alog] *n* classified list of goods in shop or offered in a sale; **c. raisonné** a classified list with descriptions of the items ~ **catalogue** *v/t* make a list of; insert in a catalogue.

catalpa [katal*pa*] *n* (*bot*) ornamental tree with large white trumpet-shaped flowers.

catalysis [katal*isis*] *n* (*chem*) alteration of the rate at which a chemical reaction proceeds by the introduction of a catalyst.

catalyst [*kat*alist] *n* (*chem*) an agent which helps forward a chemical reaction without itself suffering any chemical change > PDS.

catalytic [katal*itik*] *n* (*med*) a remedy which by promoting nutrition leads to a patient's recovery ~ **catalytic(al)** *adj* acting by catalysis.

catalyse [*kat*alIz] *v/t* (*chem*) break down, decompose.

catamaran [katama*Ran/katama*Ran] *n* raft made by lashing logs together; (*naut*) sailing vessel with twin hulls; (*coll*) quarrelsome woman.

catamenia [katam*eeni*-a] *n* menstrual discharge.

catamite [*kat*amIt] *n* man or boy submitting to sodomy.

catamount, catamountain [*kat*amownt, kata-*mownt*in] *n* wild animal of the cat family; lynx.

cataplasm [*kat*aplazm] *n* (*med*) a poultice.

cataplexy [*kat*apleksi] *n* a condition of immobility shown in some animals as a result of fear or shock or as a defensive reaction.

catapult [*kat*apult] *n* former military engine for throwing stones and darts; contrivance of forked stick with prongs joined by elastic for shooting small stones; device for launching aircraft from the deck of a ship ~ **catapult** *v/t* and *i* throw by catapult; (*fig*) place suddenly in unexpected situation.

cataract [*kat*aRakt] *n* precipitous waterfall; violent storm of rain; (*fig*) flood (of eloquence); (*path*) disease of the eye in which the crystalline lens becomes opaque.

catarrh [kat*aar*] *n* inflammation of mucous membrane; a cold accompanied by discharge of mucus from nose and throat ~ **catarrhal** [kat*aarRal*] *adj* of, like, or suffering from catarrh.

catastrophe [kat*astRofi*] *n* sudden widespread disaster; geological upheaval; great misfortune; (*theat*) final decisive event in a tragedy.

catastrophic [katastRofik] *adj* like or as a catastrophe, disastrous ~ **catastrophically** *adv*.

catatonia [katat*Oni*-a] *n* (*psych*) state of inertness and muscular rigidity, *usu* in schizophrenia ~ **catatonic** [katat*onik*] *n* and *adj* (person) suffering from catatonia.

catawba [kat*awba*] *n* a light-red American grape, light-coloured wine made from catawbas.

cat-bird [*kat*-burd] *n* (*US*) kind of thrush.

115

catboat [*kat*bOt] *n* (*naut*) sailing boat with one sail and mast placed forward.

cat-burglar [kat-*burgler*] *n* thief who enters a building by daring feats of climbing.

catcall [*kat*kawl] *n* derisive hoot or whistle made to show disapproval at the theatre or public gathering; a whistle with a shrill screaming sound once used for this purpose.

catch (*p/t* and *p/part* **caught**) [*kach*] *v/t* and *t* capture; deceive, entrap; take by surprise; seize and hold; be in time for (train, the post); become entangled; seize (something flying through the air); be infected by (a disease); manage to see, hear, understand; arrest attention of, captivate; **c. on** (*coll*) become popular; grasp meaning; **c. out** (*cricket*) put batsman out by catching ball straight from his bat; (*coll*) show to be at fault; **c. up** overtake; **c. it** be reprimanded, punished; **c. one's breath** draw in one's breath suddenly; **c. me doing that** (*coll*) I have no intention of doing that ~ **catch** *n* act of catching; haul of fish; contrivance for securing door, window *etc*; concealed trick in an apparently advantageous offer; (*mus*) a round for three or more voices > PDM; (*coll*) person matrimonially desirable on account of wealth or position.

catchall [*kach*awl] *n* and *adj* (container) into which anything can be put; (*fig*) a law or regulation which seems to forbid all sorts of loosely-defined actions.

catch-crop [*kach*-kROp] *n* crop sown between two regular crops on land which would otherwise have remained fallow.

catcher [*kach*er] *n* one who catches.

catchily [*kach*ili] *adv* in a catchy way.

catchiness [*kach*inis] *n* quality of being catchy.

catching [*kach*ing] *adj* (*of diseases*) infectious; attractive, appealing; easily imitated, *esp* unconsciously.

catchment [*kach*ment] *n* drainage; **c. area** area drained by a watercourse or providing water for a reservoir; area from which pupils, patients *etc* are sent to a central school, hospital *etc*.

catchpenny [*kach*peni] *adj* worthless, but got up attractively to sell.

catchpole, catchpoll [*kach*pOl] *n* sheriff's officer, *esp* warrant officer who arrests for debt.

catchword [*kach*werd] *n* (*print*) first word of a page printed at the foot of the preceding page; word or phrase caught up and made temporarily popular, slogan; actor's cue.

catchy [*kach*i] *adj* attractive; difficult, tricky; (*of tunes*) easy to pick up and remember.

catechetic, catechetical [katiketik, katiketikal] *adj* consisting of questions and answers.

catechism [*kat*ikizm] *n* instruction in the form of question and answer, *esp* in religious doctrine; manual of religious instruction in dialogue form.

catechist [*kat*ikist] *n* one who instructs by questioning; a teacher of catechumens ~ **catechistic(al)** *adj* ~ **catechistically** *adv*.

catechize [*kat*ikIz] *v/t* teach by means of question and answer; teach the catechism to; examine by probing questions.

catechu, cashoo [*kat*ishoo/*kat*ichoo, *ka*shoo] *n* name of several astringent substances obtained from bark and wood of various eastern trees.

catechumen [kati*kew*men] *n* convert under instruction before baptism; novice, beginner.

categorical [katigoRikal] *adj* unconditional, without qualification, absolute; explicit, direct; (*log*) pertaining to the categories ~ **categorically** *adv* absolutely, positively, unconditionally.

categorize [*kat*igoRIz] *v/t* place in a category.

category [*kat*igoRi] *n* a class or group in which each member has a characteristic common to all the rest; (*philos*) one of the fundamental classes to which objects of knowledge can be assigned.

catenary [ka*teen*aRi] *n* (*geom*) curve formed by a chain or string hanging from two fixed points.

catenoid [*kat*inoid] *n* (*math*) surface formed by the revolution of catenary about its axis.

cater [*kay*ter] *v/i* provide food or amusement; **c. for** supply what will suit the tastes of.

caterer [*kay*teRer] *n* one who provides and prepares meals for restaurants, large parties *etc*.

catering [*kay*teRing] *n* act of providing meals in large quantities; business of a caterer.

caterpillar [*kat*erpiler] *n* larva of a butterfly, moth and certain insects; endless chain of plates used instead of wheels by tractors, tanks *etc*; **c. wheel** large wheel with divided tyre tread.

caterwaul [*kat*erwawl] *v/i* utter loud discordant cry; sing with voice resembling that of cat; quarrel like cats ~ **caterwaul** *n*.

cates [*kay*ts] *n* (*pl*) choice food, delicacies.

cat-eyed [*kat*-Id] *adj* able to see in the dark.

catfall [*kat*fawl] *n* (*naut*) rope or chain to hoist the anchor to the cathead.

catfish [*kat*fish] *n* fish like a whiting with large mouth and whiskers like a cat.

catgut [*kat*gut] *n* dried and twisted intestines of animals used as strings of musical instruments, tennis-rackets *etc*.

catharsis [ka*thaar*sis] *n* (*med*) purging, evacuation of the bowels; (*lit*) purging of the emotions through feelings excited by tragic drama; (*psych*) the freeing of repressed emotion; abreaction > PDP.

cathartic [ka*thaar*tik] *n* a purgative medicine ~ **cathartic(al)** *adj* purgative, cleansing, purifying.

cathartin [ka*thaar*tin] *n* purgative substance extracted from senna.

cathead [*kat*-hed] *n* (*naut*) beam projecting from the bows of a ship for weighing anchor.

cathedra [ka*theed*Ra/*kath*edRa] *n* bishop's throne; the episcopal see; **ex c.** declared with authority.

cathedral [ka*theed*Ral] *n* chief church in a diocese, containing the bishop's throne ~ **cathedral** *adj* containing, belonging to, ranking as, a cathedral.

Catherine-wheel [*kath*eRin-weel] *n* firework which rotates while burning; sideways somersault, cartwheel; (*bui*) a rose-window.

catheter [*kath*iter] *n* (*surg*) tube which can pass into the bladder and draw off urine.

cathetometer [kathi*tom*iter] *n* instrument for measuring minute vertical distances.

cathode [*kath*Od] *n* (*elect*) negative electrode; negatively charged conductor in electrolysis and in vacuum tubes; **c. rays** stream of electrons emitted from the negatively charged electrode or cathode when an electric discharge takes place in a vacuum tube > PDS; **c. ray oscilloscope** instrument which allows electrical changes to be observed on a cathode ray tube; **c. ray tube**

vacuum tube allowing the movements of a beam of cathode rays to be observed on a luminescent screen which forms one end of the tube > PDEI.

catholic [*katholik*] *adj* universal, of general interest; liberal, broad-minded; **C. Church** the whole body of Christians; the early Christian Church; any Church claiming continuity with this; the Roman Catholic Church ~ **Catholic** *n* a Roman Catholic; a Christian who stresses the value of sacraments and ritual.

Catholicism [*katholisizm*] *n* faith, doctrine, and liturgical usages of early and medieval Christianity, or of Roman Catholicism.

catholicity [*katholisiti*] *n* universality; comprehensiveness; unity with Catholic, *esp* Roman Catholic, doctrine, beliefs *etc*.

cation [*katI*-on] *n* positively charged ion > PDS.

catkin [*katkin*] *n* flower of the willow, hazel *etc* which hangs down like the tail of a tiny cat.

catmint [*katmint*] *n* (*bot*) plant with a strong smell.

catnap [*katnap*] *n* short light sleep.

catnip [*katnip*] *n* catmint.

cat-o'nine-tails [kat-OnIn-taylz] *n* whip with nine knotted lashes used to punish prisoners.

catoptric [*katoptRik*] *adj* relating to the reflection of light ~ **catoptrics** *n* (*pl*) branch of optics dealing with reflection phenomena.

catscradle [katskrayd'l] *n* game played with loop of string twisted round the fingers into various geometrical patterns and transferred from the fingers of one player to those of another.

catseye [*katsI*] *n* semi-precious stone of chalcedonic quartz; stud on a motor road which reflects the light.

catspaw [*katspaw*] *n* person duped by another into performing a difficult or dangerous action with no profit to himself; (*naut*) sailor's knot; light wind.

cat-suit [*kat*-sewt] *n* woman's one-piece trousersuit.

catsup see **ketchup**.

cat's-whisker [kats-*wisker*] *n* fine adjustable wire in a crystal wireless set.

cattily [*katili*] *adv* spitefully.

cattiness [*katinis*] *n* spitefulness.

cattish [*katish*] *adj* catlike; (*fig*) spiteful.

cattle [*kat'l*] *n* (*pl*) bovine farm animals such as oxen, bulls, cows; (*pej*) human beings, wretches.

catty [*kati*] *adj* catlike; (*fig*) spiteful.

catwalk [*katwawk*] *n* narrow platform running high up along the side of a building.

Caucasian [kawkayshi-an] *n* member of the white races of mankind; Indo-European ~ **Caucasian** *adj*.

caucus [*kawkus*] *n* small group in a political party or administrative body powerful enough to control and influence policy.

caudal [*kawdal*] *adj* of, on, near, or like a tail.

caudate [*kawdayt*] *adj* having a tail.

caudle [*kawd'l*] *n* a hot drink for invalids made of fine gruel mixed with sugar, wine or brandy, lemon peel, and nutmeg.

caught [*kawt*] *p/t* and *p/part* of **catch**.

caul [*kawl*] *n* membrane sometimes found covering the head of a child at birth.

cauldron, caldron [*kawldRon*] *n* large pot for boiling.

cauliflower [*koliflowr*] *n* cultivated variety of cabbage with a large white centre.

caulk, calk [*kawk*] *v/t* make a seam or joint airtight or watertight by filling it with tow, oakum, and pitch ~ **caulking, calking** *n*.

causal [*kawzal*] *adj* relating to a cause; of nature of cause and effect; acting as cause; (*gramm*) expressing a cause ~ **causal** *n* (*gramm*) word introducing a sentence expressing a cause.

causality [*kawzaliti*] *n* state of being a cause; operation or relation of cause and effect.

causation [*kawzayshon*] *n* action of causing; relation of cause and effect.

causative [*kawzativ*] *adj* producing an effect.

cause [*kawz*] *n* that which produces an effect; motive for action; (*leg*) subject about which one goes to law; object for which one contends; **c. célèbre** famous lawsuit; **good c.** a worthwhile voluntary scheme to help people in need; **make common c.** take joint action ~ **cause** *v/t* bring about, produce, be cause of.

causerie [kOze*Ree*] *n* informal discussion.

causeway, causey [*kawzway/kawzi, kawzi/kawsay*] *n* raised road over marshy place; raised footpath; (*Scots*) road surfaced with setts.

caustic [*kawstik*] *n* a solid which is corrosive towards organic matter ~ **caustic** *adj* corrosive, destructive of living tissue; (*fig*) sarcastic, biting; (*phys*) curve formed by the reflection of light from a curved surface > PDS; **c. potash** potassium hydroxide; **c. soda** sodium hydroxide.

caustically [*kawstikali*] *adv* sarcastically, with biting wit.

cauter [*kawter*] *n* branding-iron; (*med*) instrument for cauterizing.

cauterize [*kawteRIz*] *v/t* burn with a caustic or cautery; (*fig*) render (conscience) insensible ~ **cauterization** [kawteRIza*yshon*] *n*.

cautery [*kawteRi*] *n* heated metal instrument for cauterizing; operation of cauterizing.

caution [*kawshon*] *n* prudence, act of taking care; warning to be heedful; (*mil*) preliminary instruction before word of command; (*sl*) person who creates laughter by droll behaviour; **c. money** money deposited as security for good conduct ~ **caution** *v/t* advise (person) to be prudent or to observe the law.

cautionary [*kawshonaRi*] *adj* conveying advice or a warning.

cautious [*kawshus*] *adj* careful, wary ~ **cautiously** *adv* ~ **cautiousness** *n*.

cavalcade [kaval*kayd*] *n* company of riders; ceremonial procession; pageant.

cavalier [kaval*eer*] *n* horseman; knight; courtly gentleman, *esp* follower of Charles I; gentleman escorting a lady or dancing with her ~ **cavalier** *adj* careless, free and easy; supercilious, disdainful ~ **cavalierly** *adv*.

cavalry [*kavalRi*] *n* (*mil*) troops who fight on horseback.

cave (1) [*kayv*] *n* a hollow space worn out of a rock or cliff > PDG; small group seceding from a political party ~ **cave** *v/i* (*obs*) hollow out; **c. in** fall in, collapse; (*coll*) submit suddenly.

cave (2) [*kayvi*] *interj* (*school sl*) look out! beware!

caveat [*kayvi*-at] *n* a warning; (*leg*) notice given to suspend proceedings temporarily.

caveator [*kayvi*-aytawr] *n* one who enters a caveat.

cave-man [*kayv*-man] *n* prehistoric man living in caves; man of violent impulses and passions.

cavendish [*kav*endish] *n* cake of strong tobacco which has been sweetened with molasses.

cavern [*kav*ern] *n* a cave.

cavernous [*kav*ernus] *adj* abounding in caverns; hollowed out; hollow-sounding.

caviar, caviare [*kav*i-aar, *kav*yaar] *n* the salted roe of the sturgeon eaten as an appetizer; (*fig*) that which is appreciated only by a person of cultivated taste.

cavil (*pres/part* **cavilling**, *p/t* and *p/part* **cavilled**) [*kav*il] *v/i* raise trivial objections, quibble; find fault without good reason ~ **cavil** *n*.

cavity [*kav*iti] *n* a hole; **c. block** (*bui*) precast concrete block; **c. wall** hollow wall > PDE.

cavort [kav*awrt*] *v/i* (*coll*) prance about, frisk.

cavortings [kav*awr*tingz] *n* (*pl*) undignified conduct.

cavy [*kayv*i] *n* a small rodent, guinea-pig.

caw [*kaw*] *n* croaking cry of rook or crow ~ **caw** *v/i*.

cay [*kay/kee*] *n* sandbank; low island of sand or coral.

cayenne [kay-*en*/kī-*en*] *n* hot red pepper made from capsicums.

cayman, caiman [*kay*man] *n* alligator.

cease [*sees*] *v/i* and *t* come to an end; desist (from); discontinue, stop; **c. fire** (*mil*) command to stop firing and end hostilities ~ **cease** *n* without c. continuously, incessantly.

cease-fire [*sees*-fīr] *n* (*mil*) agreement to cease fighting, truce; order imposing this.

cecity [*sees*iti] *n* blindness, physical or mental.

cedar [*seed*er] *n* a coniferous evergreen tree yielding timber yellowish in colour and of fine uniform texture ~ **cedared** *adj* planted with cedars.

cede [*seed*] *v/t* give up, surrender; admit, allow (point in argument).

cedilla [si*dil*a] *n* mark (ȷ) placed in French and Portuguese under *c* preceding *a*, *o*, or *u* to denote that it has the soft sound of *s*.

ceiling [*seel*ing] *n* plastered upper surface of a room concealing the rafters or floor-boards above; (*aer*) extreme height to which a particular aircraft will climb; uppermost limit of prices, wages *etc*; **hit the c.** (*coll*) get very angry.

celadon [*sel*adon] *n* a pale shade of green; (*cer*) a light-green glazed ware.

celandine [*sel*andīn] *n* name of two plants with yellow or white star-like flowers.

celanese [selan*eez*] *n* (*tr*) type of artificial silk.

celebrant [*sel*iбRant] *n* priest who consecrates the Eucharist.

celebrate [*sel*iбRayt] *v/t* and *i* perform (solemn function); consecrate the Eucharist; observe solemnly, commemorate (a festival, anniversary); extol; (*coll*) have a gay time.

celebrated [*sel*iбRaytid] *adj* well-known, famous.

celebration [seliбRay*shon*] *n* act of celebrating; festival, commemoration ceremony.

celebrity [si*leb*Riti] *n* a well-known, famous person; a public figure; fame.

celeriac [si*leR*i-ak] *n* variety of celery, cultivated for its turnip-shaped root.

celerity [si*leR*iti] *n* swiftness, rapidity.

celery [*sel*eRi] *n* a vegetable with long white edible stalks.

celesta [si*lest*a] *n* (*mus*) keyboard instrument in which a bell-like sound is produced by hammers striking upon metal bars > PDM.

celeste [si*lest*] *n* (*mus*) name of an organ stop with two pipes to each note > PDM.

celestial [si*lest*i-al] *adj* belonging to the sky or heavens; divine, heavenly.

celestine [se*lest*In] *n* (*min*) strontium sulphate.

celibacy [*sel*ibasi] *n* the unmarried state, single life, *esp* of a person under a vow.

celibatarian [seliba*taiR*i-an] *n* and *adj* (person) favouring or practising celibacy.

celibate [*sel*ibayt] *n* and *adj* (person) choosing the unmarried state; vowed to a single life.

cell [*sel*] *n* one-roomed dwelling inhabited by hermit; small room in prison, monastery, or convent for single occupant; group of persons forming basic unit in a secret political organization; compartment in honeycomb; (*elect*) device for producing a current of electricity by chemical action > PDS; (*biol*) the structural unit of which living organisms are built > PDB.

cellar [*sel*er] *n* a storage room of which more than half is below ground-level; wine-cellar; **a good c.** plenty of choice wine.

cellarage [*sel*eRij] *n* cellars of a house; storage accommodation in a cellar; charge made for this.

cellarer [*sel*eReR] *n* officer in conventual house or other institution who is in charge of the cellar and provisions ~ **cellaress** *n*.

cellaret [*sel*eRet] *n* cabinet in dining-room for keeping wine and spirits.

celliform [*sel*ifawrm] *adj* cell-shaped.

cellist [*chel*ist] *n* person who plays the violoncello.

cello [*chel*O] *n* violoncello.

Cellophane [*sel*Ofayn] *n* (*tr*) type of transparent foil used for packaging.

cellular [*sel*ewlar] *adj* containing or consisting of cells, porous; of open texture.

cellulate, cellulated [*sel*ewlayt, *sel*ewlayted] *adj* composed of cells.

cellule [*sel*ewl] *n* a small cell; a tiny room.

celluloid [*sel*ewloid] *n* a tough, inflammable nitro-cellulose plastics material; photographic film made of this; (*fig*) the cinema ~ **celluloid** *adj*.

cellulose [*sel*ewlOs] *n* structural tissue which forms the cell-walls of plants; one of the raw materials used in plastics and obtained from plant cells ~ **cellulose** *v/t* apply a nitrocellulose lacquer (to an article) ~ **cellulose** *adj*.

cell-wall [*sel*-wawl] *n* comparatively rigid protoplasmic layer limiting a plant cell > PDB.

Celt (1), **Kelt** [*kelt/selt*, *kelt*] *n* member of one of the peoples speaking Welsh, Breton, Erse, Gaelic, Manx, or of their prehistoric forerunners.

celt (2) [*selt*] *n* (*arch*) prehistoric axe-head.

Celtic [*keltik/seltik*] *n* any language of the Celts ~ **Celtic** *adj* pertaining to the Celts.

celticism [*kelt*isizm/*selt*isizm] *n* a custom or idiom peculiar to the Celts.

cembalo [*chemb*alO] *n* harpsichord; the continuo part of a concerted composition > PDM.

cement [si*ment*] *n* (*bui*) a powder made by heating a mixture of limestone and clay, which after mixing with water sets to a hard mass; (*geol*) the bond or matrix between the particles in a rock; liquid glue; plastic material for filling teeth; (*anat*) bone-like substance which makes a thin covering to the root of a tooth; (*fig*) a binding force ∼ **cement** *v/t* cover, or stick, with cement; join together; (*fig*) unite firmly, make more secure.

cementation [simen*tay*shon] *n* (*eng*) process of injecting a cement mixture into foundations and walls of buildings.

cementite [si*ment*It] *n* (*metal*) iron carbide; hard, brittle compound responsible for the brittleness of cast iron.

cement-mixer [siment-mikser] *n* revolving drum in which ingredients for cement are mixed.

cemetery [*semet*Ri] *n* consecrated ground, other than a churchyard, set apart for burials.

cenobite, coenobite [*seen*ObIt] *n* a member of a religious community living in a convent or monastery with others of the order.

cenotaph [*sen*Otaaf] *n* tomb or monument raised as a memorial to one who is buried elsewhere; the national monument in Whitehall, London, to the British soldiers who fell in the two World Wars.

cense [sens] *v/t* burn incense in front of.

censer [*sen*ser] *n* vessel in which incense is burnt.

censor [*sen*ser] *n* official authorized to ban publications, plays, films *etc* which contain material of an immoral or seditious nature; (*in wartime*) official who examines private correspondence and newspapers to stop information reaching the enemy; (*psych*) a selective agency which prevents repressed impulses, memories, and ideas from coming into consciousness; (*hist*) Roman magistrate ∼ **censor** *v/t* subject to censorship; delete, suppress.

censorial [sen*saw*Ri-al] *adj* of a censor; censorious.

censorious [sen*saw*Ri-us] *adj* severely critical; given to fault-finding.

censorship [*sen*sership] *n* action of a censor; office, powers, duties of a censor.

censurable [*sen*sewRab'l] *adj* culpable, blamable ∼ **censurably** [*sen*sewRabli] *adv*.

censure [*sen*sewr/*sen*shoor] *n* blame, disapproval, adverse criticism ∼ **censure** *v/t* blame, reprimand, criticize.

census [*sen*sus] *n* official count of the population.

cent [sent] *n* (*US*) one-hundredth part of a dollar; coin of that value; **per c.** rate by the hundred; **hundred per c.** (*coll*) completely, whole-heartedly.

cental [*sen*tal] *n* a weight of 100 lb. avoirdupois.

centaur [*sen*tawr] *n* (*Gr myth*) fabulous creature half man and half horse.

centenarian [sentin*air*Ri-an] *n* and *adj* (person) who has reached the age of a hundred years.

centenary [sen*teen*aRi] *n* hundredth anniversary of some event ∼ **centenary** *adj*.

centennial [sen*ten*i-al] *adj* having lived or lasted for a hundred years; occurring once every hundred years.

centering, centring [*sent*eRing, *sent*Ring] *n* placing in the centre; (*bui*) temporary wooden frame on which a dome or arch is built.

centesimal [sen*tes*imal] *adj* reckoning by hundredths; calculated according to percentage ∼ **centesimal** *n* a hundredth part.

centigrade [*sen*tigRayd] *adj* having a hundred equal gradations; **c. thermometer** that in which freezing point is 0° and boiling point 100°.

centigramme [*sen*tigRam] *n* one-hundredth part of a gramme.

centilitre [*sen*ti*leeter*] *n* one-hundredth part of a litre.

centillion [sen*tilyon*] *n* the number obtained when a million is multiplied by itself one hundred times.

centime [*son*teem] *n* one-hundredth of a franc.

centimetre [*sen*timeeter] *n* one-hundredth part of a metre.

centipede [*sen*tipeed] *n* crawling wingless insect with a very large number of feet.

central [*sen*tRal] *adj* at or near the centre; chief, most important; accessible; holding a midway position between two opposing parties; **c. heating** heating of a building by a system of pipes carrying hot water, air, or steam.

centralism [*sen*tRalizm] *n* policy or system of centralizing ∼ **centralist** [*sen*tRalist] *n* and *adj* (advocate) of centralization.

centrality [sen*tRal*iti] *n* state of being central.

centralization [sentRali*zay*shon] *n* process of centralizing.

centralize [*sen*tRalIz] *v/i* and *t* come together at a centre; bring to a centre; concentrate administrative powers under a central authority.

centrally [*sen*tRali] *adv* in the centre.

centre [*sen*ter] *n* middle point; (*geom*) point equidistant from every point on the circumference of a circle or surface of sphere; axis about which a body revolves; most vital part of an organization, movement *etc*; group of buildings or town area where a particular activity is concentrated; central portion of a chocolate sweet; part of a target between the bull's-eye and the outer; (*sport*) player-in the middle of a line; (*pol*) party holding moderate views; **c. of attraction** something or someone rousing general interest; **c. of gravity** point in a body at which it will balance if supported > PDS ∼ **centre** *v/t* and *i* place on or in the centre; (*fig*) concentrate (hopes, affections); be concentrated together, converge ∼ **centre** *adj* middle, central.

centrebit [*sen*terbit] *n* wood-boring tool for drilling with a brace.

centreboard [*sen*terbawrd] *n* (*naut*) keel which can be raised or lowered.

centrepiece [*sen*terpees] *n* ornament in the centre of a table, ceiling *etc*; something prominent or important.

centric [*sen*tRik] *adj* at the centre, central; (*physiol*) pertaining to a nerve-centre ∼ **centrically** *adv*.

centricity [sen*tRis*iti] *n* centrality.

centrifugal [sen*tRif*ewgal] *adj* tending to move away from the centre; **c. force** (*phys*) the outward force acting on a body rotating in a circle round a central point > PDS.

centrifuge [*sen*tRifewj] *n* (*mech*) a rapidly rotating machine used to separate small solid particles distributed in a liquid.

centring [*sen*tRing] *n* moving towards the centre.

centripetal [sen*tRip*ital] *adj* tending towards the centre; **c. force** force drawing a body to a centre.

centrism [*sen*tRizm] *n* (*pol*) adoption of a middle position between extreme views ∼ **centrist** *n* and *adj*.

centro- *pref* centre, central, centrally.

centuple [*sen*tewp'l] *adj* a hundredfold ~ **centuple** *v/t* multiply by a hundred.

centurion [sen*tewr*Ri-on] *n* (*hist*) Roman officer in command of a hundred men.

century [*sen*cheRi] *n* period of one hundred years; one of the hundred-year periods reckoned forward and backward from the assumed date of the birth of Christ; (*cricket*) a hundred runs made by a batsman in one innings; (*hist*) company of infantry in the Roman army.

cephal(o)- *pref* head.

cephalic [si*fal*ik] *adj* pertaining to the head; situated in the head; **c. index** ratio of the breadth to the length of a skull.

cephalopod [*sef*alOpod] *n* mollusc with tentacles on its head, as octopus, cuttlefish, squid *etc*.

ceraceous [se*Ray*shus] *adj* resembling wax, waxy.

ceramic, keramic [se*Ram*ik, ke*Ram*ik] *adj* relating to the making and ornamentation of pottery ~ **ceramics** *n* (*pl*) art of making pottery; (*bui*) bricks, terra cotta, glazed tiles *etc*.

cerate [*seer*Rayt] *n* ointment or paste made of white wax softened with oil ~ **cerated** *adj* coated with wax.

cere [*seer*] *n* (*orni*) wax-like skin at base of beak.

cereal [*seer*Ri-al] *adj* producing grain used for food ~ **cereal** *n* (*gen pl*) grass producing seed used for food; breakfast dish made from a cereal.

cerealin [*seer*Ri-alin] *n* (*chem*) nitrogenous substance found in bran.

cerebellar [se*Ri*beler] *adj* of the cerebellum.

cerebellum [se*Ri*belum] *n* (*anat*) 'little brain', hinder and smaller part of the brain > PDB.

cerebral [se*Ri*bRal] *adj* pertaining to the brain; intellectual.

cerebration [se*Ri*bRayshon] *n* physiological activity in the brain; (*coll*) hard thinking.

cerebro-spinal [se*Ri*bRo-*spI*nal] *adj* (*anat*) relating to the central nervous system; **c. meningitis** inflammation of the brain and spinal cord.

cerebrum [se*Ri*bRum] *n* the main division of the brain in vertebrates > PDB, PDP.

cerecloth [*seer*kloth] *n* wax-coated shroud.

cerements [*seer*ments] *n* (*pl*) grave-clothes.

ceremonial [se*Rim*Oni-al] *adj* marked by ceremony; formal ~ **ceremonial** *n* prescribed ceremony, a ritual; (*RC*) book prescribing the ordering of ceremonies ~ **ceremonially** *adv*.

ceremonious [se*Rim*Oni-us] *adj* accompanied by ceremonies; according to customary formalities; behaving with elaborate politeness ~ **ceremoniously** *adv* ~ **ceremoniousness** *n*.

ceremony [*se*Rimuni] *n* act or rite performed with customary solemnity; formal polite behaviour; **stand (up)on c.** insist upon customary formalities; **Master of Ceremonies** person who directs proceedings on a formal occasion.

cereous [*seer*Ri-us] *adj* waxen, waxy.

ceresin [*se*Reseen] *n* hard brittle paraffin wax.

ceriph see **serif**.

cerise [se*Rees*] *n* and *adj* cherry-red.

cerium [*seer*Ri-um] *n* a steel-grey soft metal used in the manufacture of lighter flints *etc* > PDS.

cermet [*ser*met] *n* heat-resisting alloy of sintered metal and a ceramic substance.

cerography [si*Rog*Rafi] *n* any variety of painting or engraving on wax.

ceroplastic [seerR*Oplas*tik] *adj* pertaining to

modelling in wax ~ **ceroplastics** *n* (*pl*) art of modelling in wax; waxworks.

cert [*surt*] *n* (*sl*) a certainty; (*sl*) a certificate; **dead c.** an absolute certainty; a racehorse certain to win.

certain [*sur*tin] *adj* fixed, definite; sure to happen; accurate; unerring, reliable; sure, having no doubt; of some amount, degree *etc*, though small; unspecified, not named; **for c.** assuredly; **make c. of** assure oneself of obtaining; **a c. age** middle age.

certainly [*sur*tenli] *adv* beyond all doubt, unquestionably; by all means.

certainty [*sur*tenti] *n* quality of having certain knowledge, assurance, conviction, confidence; quality of being certain to happen; security; **moral c.** certainty so absolute that we are morally justified in accepting it; **for (to) a c.** beyond the possibility of doubt.

certes [*sur*teez/*sur*tiz] *adv* (*ar*) certainly, truly.

certifiable [surti*fI*-ab'l] *adj* that can be certified; (*coll*) obviously insane ~ **certifiably** *adv*.

certificate [ser*tif*ikit] *n* document in which a fact (*eg* a person's status, success in an examination, ownership of a company's shares *etc*) is formally attested; **bankrupt's c.** document certifying that a bankrupt is legally discharged and can set up again in business ~ **certificate** [ser*tif*ikayt] *v/t* grant a certificate to.

certify [*sur*tifI] *v/t* guarantee as certain; attest by formal certificate; give formal information to; authoritatively declare insane.

certitude [*sur*titewd] *n* state of feeling certain.

cerulean [si*ROO*li-an] *adj* deep blue, sky-blue.

cerumen [si*ROO*min] *n* waxy secretion in the ear.

cervical [*sur*vikal/*ser*veekal] *adj* of the cervix; **c. smear** test to detect cancer of the narrow end of the womb.

cervine [*sur*vIn] *adj* of, or like, a deer or stag.

cervix [*sur*viks] *n* narrow part of an organ, *esp* the womb; neck.

cess [*ses*] *n* assessment, tax, rate; (*bui*) waterproofed box at the end of roof gutters; (*bui*) a cesspit.

cessation [se*say*shon] *n* ceasing, pause, stop.

cession [*se*shon] *n* (*leg*) act of giving up to another property to which one has a right; surrender by debtor of all his effects to his creditors.

cesspit, cesspool [*ses*pit, *ses*pOOl] *n* tank of brick or concrete, usually underground, for collecting sewage > PDE.

cestoid [*ses*toid] *n* tapeworm.

cetacean [si*tay*shan] *n* whale, dolphin, porpoise *etc* ~ **cetacean** *adj* relating to the cetaceans.

cetaceous [si*tay*shus] *adj* of or like a cetacean.

cetane [*see*tayn] *n* (*chem*) colourless liquid found in mineral oil; **c. number, c. rating** measure of the ignition quality of a diesel fuel oil.

ceteosaur(us) [*see*ti-osawr(us)] *n* gigantic fossil lizard, found in the oolite and chalk.

cetic [*see*tik] *adj* of the whale; obtained from spermaceti.

cetin [*see*tin] *n* white crystalline fatty substance.

Chablis [*shab*lee] *n* a white wine.

chaconne [sha*kon*] *n* a stately Spanish dance; the music for this dance in three-four time > PDM.

chafe [*chayf*] *v/t* and *i* rub with hands in order to warm; rub so as to injure or disfigure surface of irritate, rub against; (*fig*) become irritated or peevish ~ **chafe** *n* friction; sore caused by friction; (*fig*) state of irritation.

chaff [*chaf/chaaf*] *n* husks of grain separated by threshing; cut hay and straw used for fodder; (*bot*) bracts of grass-flowers; (*coll*) light good-humoured banter; (*fig*) worthless rubbish ~ **chaff** *v/t* tease, banter.

chaffer [*chafer*] *v/i* bargain, haggle over price ~ **chaffer** *n* bargaining.

chaffinch [*chafinch*] *n* common British bird.

chaffy [*chafi/chaafi*] *adv* full of husks; resembling husks; (*fig*) light, worthless; full of fun.

chafing-dish [*chayfing-dish*] *n* portable stove; vessel with a spirit-lamp beneath it for heating or cooking food at table.

chagrin [*shagRin/shagReen*] *n* annoyance, vexation, disappointment ~ **chagrin** *v/t* cause vexation to; wound feelings of.

chain [*chayn*] *n* series of metal links each passing through the next; bond, fetter; line of mountains; surveyor's measuring line of 100 steel links, 66 ft in length > PDE; (*fig*) series of connected events, facts *etc*; (*chem*) series of atoms linked together; a number of stores, theatres *etc* owned and operated by one person or company ~ **chain** *v/t* fasten with a chain; keep in captivity with a chain or fetter; obstruct with a chain.

chainbelt [*chayn*belt] *n* endless chain passing over cogged wheels to transmit motion.

chainbridge [*chayn*bRij] *n* suspension bridge supported by chains hanging between piers.

chain-coupling [*chayn*-kupling] *n* connecting chain between railway carriages.

chaindrive [*chaynd*Riv] *n* (*eng*) method of transmitting power from one shaft to another by means of an endless chain.

chaingang [*chayng*ang] *n* a number of convicts chained together, or wearing chains, while working.

chain-letter [chayn-*leter*] *n* letter in which each recipient is asked to transmit copies of it to others.

chainmail [*chayn*mayl] *n* body armour made of interwoven rings.

chain-pump [*chayn*-pump] *n* machine for raising water by buckets on an endless chain.

chain-reaction [chayn-Ree-*ak*shon] *n* (*sci*) a chemical or atomic process, yielding energy or products which in turn promote a continuous series of processes of the same kind; (*fig*) series of rapidly developing consequences.

chainshot [*chayn*shot] *n* two cannonballs connected by a chain.

chainsmoker [*chayn*smOker] *n* one who smokes cigarettes in unbroken succession.

chainstitch [*chayn*stich] *n* (*sewing*) one of a series of stitches resembling the links of a chain.

chain-store [*chayn*-stawr] *n* one of a series of shops belonging to one firm usually selling the same class of goods.

chair [*chair*] *n* seat for one person, with four legs and a back; cast iron support bolted to a railway sleeper > PDE; (*fig*) seat of authority, status, dignity, leadership; chairmanship of a meeting; leadership of a University department; (*US*) the electric chair for the execution of criminals ~ **chair** *v/t* carry a person aloft in triumph after some notable achievement; serve as chairman of.

chairlift [*chair*lift] *n* series of chairs fixed to a moving overhead cable by which skiers *etc* are transported up a mountain.

chairman [*chair*man] *n* person who presides over a meeting; principal director of a commercial firm, bank *etc*; (*obs*) sedan or bathchair attendant.

chairmanship [*chair*manship] *n* office of chairman.

chairperson [*chair*purs'n] *n* (*freq joc*) person who presides over a meeting.

chairwoman [*chair*woman] *n* woman who presides over a meeting.

chaise [*shayz*] *n* light one-horsed carriage.

chaise-longue [shayz-*lOng*] *n* long couch, sofa.

chalcedony, calcedony [kal*sedoni*] *n* semi-precious kind of quartz, transparent or milky.

chalcolithic [kalko*lith*ik] *adj* (*arch*) using both bronze and stone implements.

chalcopyrite [kalko*pIr*Rit] *n* a yellowish mineral, the most important source of copper > PDG.

chalet [*shalay*] *n* wooden hut on Swiss Alps; house with overhanging steep roof; small bungalow.

chalice [*chalis*] *n* (*eccles*) cup used in celebration of the Eucharist; (*poet*) drinking-cup; (*bot*) cup-shaped blossom ~ **chaliced** *adj* contained in a cup; (*bot*) having a cup-like flower.

chalk [*chawk*] *n* soft white limestone; (*geol*) the upper strata of the Cretaceous system; crayon in white or colour for writing on a blackboard or for drawing; mark made with chalk to indicate score in a game *etc*; **not to know c. from cheese** (*coll*) not to be able to distinguish between things obviously different; **better by a long c.** better by far ~ **chalk** *v/t* mark or draw with a chalk; rub with chalk; **c. up** record (score in a game).

chalkiness [*chawk*inis] *n* quality of being chalky.

chalkpit [*chawk*pit] *n* pit from which chalk is dug.

chalky [*chawk*i] *adj* of, like, containing, or covered with chalk.

challenge [*chal*enj] *n* invitation or summons to engage in a contest, duel *etc*; provocation, a calling in question to prove one's ability, skill *etc*; summons to justify one's presence, *esp* demand of a sentry for the password; (*leg*) exception taken to a juror ~ **challenge** *v/t* invite or summon to a contest *etc*, defy, dare; call in question; claim (admiration, attention) ~ **challenger** *n*.

challenging [*chal*enjing] *adj* provoking disagreement or competition, acting as a challenge ~ **challengingly** *adv*.

chalybeate [ka*libi*-it] *n* and *adj* (natural waters) containing iron salts in solution.

chalybite [*kalib*It] *n* (*min*) natural ferrous carbonate.

cham [*kam/cham*] *n* (*obs*) khan.

chamber [*chaym*ber] *n* small private room; bedroom; hall set apart for meetings of a judicial or legislative body; enclosed space, cavity; compartment in a firearm which holds the charge; chamberpot ~ **chamber** *v/t* and *i* hollow out; reside in a chamber.

chamberlain [*chaym*berlin] *n* (*hist*) attendant on king or noble, who waited on him in his bedroom; officer in charge of the household of a king or noble; **Lord C. of the Household** one of the superintendents of the Royal Household, and formerly licenser of plays.

chambermaid [*chay*bermayd] *n* female servant at hotel or inn who attends to the bedrooms.

chamber-music [*chay*mber-mewzik] *n* music suitable for private room or small hall > PDM.

chamberpot [*chay*mberpot] *n* vessel in bedroom for urine and slops.

chambers [*chaym*berz] *n* (*pl*) rooms in house set apart for single occupant; rooms in Inns of Court occupied by lawyers; private room of a judge where he hears cases of lesser importance.

Chambertin [*shaam*bairtan] *n* a Burgundy wine.

chameleon [ka*meeli*-on] *n* genus of lizards that can change their skin colour according to their surroundings; symbol of inconstancy; fickle person ~ **chameleon** *adj* changeable.

chamfer [*cham*fer] *n* a right angle corner or bevel cut off symmetrically, that is at 45° ~ **chamfer** *v/t* cut a chamfer in, or bevel.

chammy-leather [*shami*-leTHer] *n* chamois leather; soft cleaning-cloth imitating this.

chamois [*sham*waa] *n* goat-shaped antelope inhabiting lofty mountain ranges ~ **chamois** [*shami*] *n* soft leather of chamois skin, used for polishing.

chamomile see **camomile.**

champ (1) [*champ*] *v/t* and *i* (*of a horse*) munch (fodder) noisily; make action or noise of chewing; keep biting upon (*eg* a bit).

champ (2) *n* (*coll abbr*) champion.

champagne [sham*payn*] *n* an effervescent French wine; c. brandy best brandy of the cognac class.

champaign [*cham*payn] *n* wide expanse of open flattish country.

champers [*sham*perz] *n* (*coll*) champagne.

champion [*cham*pi-on] *n* one who upholds or fights for a cause, belief, person *etc*; one who is unbeaten in any trial of strength or skill; animal or object winning first prize in a show ~ **champion** *adj* surpassing all in good or bad qualities; (*coll*) first-rate ~ **champion** *adv* (*coll*) in a first-rate manner ~ **champion** *v/t* defend, as a champion; stand up for; uphold (cause).

championship [*cham*pi-onship] *n* position or status of the winner of a series of eliminating contests; the contest or series of contests held to find a champion; defence, advocacy; leadership.

chance [*chaans*] *n* course of events; fortuitous occurrence; luck, fortune; opportunity; possibility; probability; risk; **on the (off) c.** acting on the (remote) possibility; **the main c.** chance of making personal profit; **take one's c.** trust to luck ~ **chance** *adj* accidental, fortuitous ~ **chance** *v/t* and *i* happen, come to pass; happen to find, meet *etc*; (*coll*) risk, dare; **c. one's arm** do something risky, risk a failure; **c. upon** find or meet unexpectedly.

chancel [*chaan*sel] *n* the eastern part of a church where the clergy and choir sit.

chancellery, chancellory [*chaan*seleRi] *n* dignity or position of a chancellor; his department with its officials; the building in which it is situated; the offices of an embassy or consulate.

chancellor [*chaan*seler] *n* the title of various high officials; **Lord High C.** the chief judge who also presides over the House of Lords; **C. of the Exchequer** the chief finance minister; (*of university*) its titular head; **c. of a diocese** a bishop's legal adviser ~ **chancellorship** *n*.

chancel-screen [*chaan*sel-skReen] *n* openwork screen of wood or stone dividing the chancel from the main body of a church.

chancery [*chaan*seRi] *n* (*leg*) a division of the High Court of Justice, presided over by the Lord Chancellor; **in c.** in litigation in a court of chancery.

chanciness [*chaan*sinis] *n* quality of being chancy.

chancre [*shan*ker] *n* (*med*) venereal ulcer ~ **chancrous** *adj* ulcerous.

chancy [*chaan*si] *adj* (*coll*) uncertain, risky.

chandelier [shandi*leer*] *n* ornamental branched fitting hanging from a ceiling for holding a number of lights.

chandler [*chaand*ler] *n* one who makes or sells candles; **ships' c.** dealer in stores and provisions for ships ~ **chandlery** *n* place where candles are kept; goods sold by a chandler.

change [*chaynj*] *n* act of substituting one thing for another; alteration in composition; variety; a holiday in different surroundings; (*collect*) coins of small value; coins of lower value given in exchange for one of higher value or for a note; money given when a purchase is paid for by coin above its value; (*cap*) place where merchants meet to do business; sequence in which a peal of bells is rung > PDM; **c. of life** ceasing of menstruation; **ring the changes** repeat (process) with every conceivable variation; **get no c. out of a person** fail to get information from, or advantage over, him ~ **change** *v/t* and *i* replace one thing by another; alter, make different; exchange; give coins of smaller denomination for coin or note; become different; be in a state of transition; take off one's clothes and replace them with others; put a clean nappy on (a baby); go from one train to another in the course of a journey; **c. over** transfer to or adopt a new method, system *etc*; **c. up (down)** (*mot*) change to a higher (lower) gear.

changeability [chaynja*biliti*] *n* quality of being changeable; fickleness.

changeable [*chaynj*ab'l] *adj* liable to change; fickle, variable ~ **changeableness** *n* ~ **changeably** *adv*.

changeful [*chaynj*fool] *adj* constantly changing, inconstant, fickle ~ **changefully** *adv* ~ **changefulness** *n*.

changeless [*chaynj*les] *adj* unchanging.

changeling [*chaynj*ling] *n* child substituted for another in infancy, *esp* one supposed to be left by fairies.

change-over [*chaynj*-Over] *n* alteration from one working system to another; radical change.

channel [*chan*el] *n* river bed; the deep navigable part of a bay or harbour; narrow stretch of sea between two land masses and connecting two seas; a groove cut in a surface; tube or duct through which anything passes; (*rad, television*) band of frequencies of sufficient width for transmission; (*fig*) means of communication ~ **channel** (*pres/part* **channelling**, *p/t* and *p/part* **channelled**) *v/t* form channels in; groove, flute; provide with a channel; guide or supply through a channel.

chant [*chaant*] *n* song; type of harmonized melody used for psalm-singing; psalm or canticle;

monotonous song ~ **chant** v/t and i sing a song; intone; recite verse; celebrate in song.

chanty, shanty [shanti] n sailors' work-song.

chantry [chaantRi] n endowment for the saying of a daily requiem; chapel where this was said.

chaos [kay-os] n (myth) primeval formless abyss out of which the universe was made; state of confusion and disorder.

chaotic [kay-otik] adj in a state of chaos, confused ~ **chaotically** adv.

chap (1) [chap] n (usu pl) jaw.

chap (2) n (coll) man, boy, fellow.

chap (3) (pres/part **chapping**, p/t and p/part **chapped**) v/t and i cause (skin) to form cracks; (of skin) split, become rough ~ **chap** n a skin-crack.

chapbook [chapbook] n small book of popular ballads, tales etc sold by chapmen.

chape [chayp] n metal tip of a scabbard.

chapel [chapel] n place of worship having no parish attached to it; compartment in cathedral or large church with separate altar and dedication; place of Christian worship for Nonconformists; place set aside for worship in palace, nobleman's house, college etc; (at university) chapel service; attendance at it; (typ) an association of journeymen in a printing-office; **c. of ease** chapel built for parishioners living a long way from their parish church.

chapel-goer [chapel-gO-er] n a Nonconformist.

chapelry [chapelRi] n district attached to a chapel.

chaperon [shaperOn] n married or elderly lady who accompanies a young girl where men are present ~ **chaperon** v/t act as chaperon to.

chapfallen, chopfallen [chapfawlen] adj having the lower jaw drooping; dejected, crestfallen.

chapiter [chapiter] n (archi) capital of a column.

chaplain [chaplin] n clergyman appointed to minister to the armed forces, to members of a university, hospital, factory etc, or to minister in the chapel of a sovereign, nobleman, college, school etc.

chaplaincy [chaplinsi] n office of a chaplain.

chaplet [chaplet] n wreath of flowers or precious stones for the head; rosary.

chapman [chapman] n itinerant dealer, pedlar.

chapped [chapt] adj (of skin) cut by cold and frost.

chapter [chapter] n one of the main sections of a book or treatise; principal topic or subject; episode; Act of Parliament; decretal epistle; governing body of a cathedral or collegiate church; assembly held by such a body; assembly of monks or nuns; (US) branch of a college fraternity; **c. of accidents** series of disasters; **c. and verse** exact authority for a statement.

chapter-house [chapter-hows] n meeting-place of a chapter; (US) clubhouse of a college fraternity.

char (1) [chaar] n (zool) small kind of trout.

char (2) n (coll) tea.

char (3) (pres/part **charring**, p/t and p/part **charred**) v/i do housework for payment by the hour or day ~ **char** n (coll abbr) charwoman.

char (4) (pres/part **charring**, p/t and p/part **charred**) v/t and i burn, render black, reduce to charcoal; burn slightly.

charabanc [shaRabang] n large public conveyance for pleasure-trips; motor coach.

character [kaRakter] n sum of qualities distinguishing an individual; description of these; reputation; testimonial; person of distinctive character; (coll) eccentric person; part in a play; person depicted in a novel; role, guise; symbol representing a sound or group of sounds; symbol that can be read or stored by a computer; style of handwriting or printing; **c. actor** actor who specializes in playing humorous or eccentric parts; **c. assassination** deliberate destruction of a person's reputation; **in c.** appropriate(ly) ~ **character** v/t describe character of; mark, stamp.

characterful [kaRakterfool] adj having a strong character; clearly expressing character.

characteristic [kaRakteRistik] n distinguishing trait or feature; (math) the integral or whole-number part of a logarithm ~ **characteristic** adj typical ~ **characteristically** adv.

characterization [kaRakteRIzayshon] n act of characterizing, esp portrayal of character in a play, novel etc.

characterize [kaRakteRIz] v/t describe character of; distinguish.

characterless [kaRakterles] adj without character or individuality; without a testimonial.

charade [shaRaad] n party game where a word has to be guessed from dramatizations; (fig) false or hypocritical display.

charcoal [chaarkOl] n name for numerous varieties of carbon, made by heating vegetable or animal substances with exclusion of air; dark grey colour; **c. burner** man who burns wood to make charcoal.

charge [chaarj] n quantity of powder, or of powder and shot, with which firearm is loaded for one discharge; quantity of anything which a receptacle is constructed to contain; quantity of electricity contained in, or on, a substance; quantity of electricity in a battery or condenser; burden, responsibility; price asked for a thing or for service rendered; payment due on property; custody, superintendence; person or thing committed to the care of anyone; district under care of clergyman; order, injunction; admonition given by judge to jury; accusation, esp that upon which prisoner is tried; violent rush to attack; (her) device or bearing on shield; (mil) trumpet call to the attack; (sl) dose of a drug; (sl) thrill, excitement; **curate in c.** curate responsible for district chapel; **in c. of** responsible for; **in the c. of** in the care of; **give in c.** hand over to custody of police ~ **charge** v/t and i put into (receptacle) as much as it should contain; load (firearm); restore the accumulation of electricity in (battery or condenser); place responsibility on; give order, instruction to; accuse; make liable, saddle with liability; claim as due (for goods supplied); rush violently against; (her) put charge on (shield).

chargeable [chaarjab'l] adj liable to a charge or payment; proper to be charged (to an account); (of persons) liable to become an expense (to others); liable to be accused.

chargé d'affaires [shaarzhay-dafair] n representative of country at capital of less important state, to which no ambassador is sent; deputy for ambassador during his absence.

charge-hand [*chaarj*-hand] *n* workman in charge of a piece of work; foreman.

charger (1) [*chaar*jer] *n* large flat dish.

charger (2) *n* horse of a military officer.

charge-sheet [*chaarj*-sheet] *n* paper kept at police station containing names of all persons brought in and charges against them.

charily [*chair*Rili] *adv* cautiously, with restraint.

chariness [*chair*ines] *n* quality of being chary.

chariot [*cha*Ri-ot] *n* (*hist*) two-wheeled vehicle used in warfare and for races; (*poet*) triumphal car ~ **chariot** *v/t* and *i*.

charioteer [chaRi-o*teer*] *n* driver of chariot.

charisma [kaRi*z*ma] *n* (*theol*) a spiritual gift; an ability to inspire great trust and devotion, supreme gift for leadership; high artistic genius.

charismatic [kaRiz*matik*] *adj* like, or possessing, charisma; **c. movement** (*theol*) modern Christian movement seeking miraculous powers of healing, exorcism, glossolalia *etc*.

charitable [*cha*Ritab'l] *adj* generous; liberal to the poor; slow to think evil of others; (*of institution*) concerned with relief of poor ~ **charitableness** *n* ~ **charitably** *adv*.

charity [*cha*Riti] *n* Christian love; disposition to think well of others; liberality to the poor; institution or trust for relief of poverty, sickness *etc*; **cold as c.** unfeeling, perfunctory ~ **charity** *adj* given as charity; supported by charity.

charivari [shaaRiva*a*Ri] *n* mock serenade of discordant noises; babel of noise; satirical journal.

charlady [*chaar*laydi] *n* (*joc*) charwoman.

charlatan [*shaar*latan] *n* one pretending to exceptional powers which he does not possess, *esp* in medicine; an impostor or quack.

charlatanism [*shaar*latanizm] *n* quackery.

charlatanry [*shaar*latanRi] *n* quackery.

Charleston [*chaar*lzton] *n* dance in which the knees touch and the heels are lifted alternately.

charlie, charley [*chaar*li] *n* (*coll*) utter fool.

charlock [*chaar*lok] *n* wild mustard plant.

charlotte [*shaar*lot] *n* pudding of stewed apple or other fruit mixed with breadcrumbs and baked; **c. russe** pudding made of sponge cakes filled with whipped cream.

charm [*chaarm*] *n* any words supposed to have magic power when recited; something worn on the person as a talisman; quality of exercising fascination; any attractive feature in person or thing; small ornament worn on a bracelet or chain; **like a c.** perfectly ~ **charm** *v/t* enchant, bewitch; assuage, calm; cause pleasure.

charmer [*chaar*mer] *n* one who charms; fascinating person, *esp* attractive woman; one who tames snakes; one who performs magic cures.

charming [*chaar*ming] *adj* delightful, attractive, fascinating ~ **charmingly** *adv*.

charnel [*chaar*nel] *n* charnel-house.

charnel-house [*chaar*nel-hows] *n* vault or place in which bones of the dead are piled.

chart [*chaart*] *n* map *esp* one to facilitate navigation; plan, graph ~ **chart** *v/t* make a chart of.

charter [*chaar*ter] *n* document granting a privilege or recognizing a right; document incorporating a borough, university, or company; (*of aircraft*) hired under contract for a particular journey ~ **charter** *v/t* hire (ship, vehicle); grant a charter to, license.

chartered [*chaar*terd] *adj* founded or protected by charter; licensed, privileged; (*fig*) acting as if privileged; (*of aircraft etc*) hired for a particular journey, not for regular service; **c. accountant** accountant who holds an official qualification.

charter-party [*chaar*ter-paarti] *n* (*comm*) agreement made between ship-owner and merchant for use of ship and safe delivery of cargo.

charthouse, chartroom [*chaart*hows, *chaart*ROOm] *n* room in ship where charts and navigating instruments are kept.

Chartism [*chaar*tizm] *n* early nineteenth-century democratic movement among working classes ~ **Chartist** [*chaar*tist] *n* and *adj*.

chartreuse [shaartRu(r)z] *n* liqueur made by Carthusian monks; pale apple-green colour.

chartulary see **cartulary**.

charwoman [*chaar*wooman] *n* woman who does housework for payment by the hour or day.

chary [*chair*Ri] *adj* cautious; frugal, sparing.

chase (1) [*chays*] *v/t* and *i* pursue in order to seize; hunt; drive away; (*fig*) drive out, dispel; **c. off** rush off (after something) ~ **chase** *n* act of pursuing; that which is pursued; open country where game is bred and hunted.

chase (2) *n* barrel of gun; (*bui*) groove in wall or floor for pipes, cables, *etc*; (*typ*) metal frame holding composed type.

chase (3) *v/t* ornament (metal) with embossed or engraved work.

chaser [*chay*ser] *n* one who chases; (*naut*) gun at bow or stern; (*eng*) a lathe tool for cutting threads on screws; (*cin*) a second-rate film; (*coll*) drink (*usu* one less potent) immediately following another; (*bui*) clerk employed on a building site to check arrival on time of materials and plant.

chasing [*chay*sing] *n* technique of embossing or engraving on metal; the design engraved.

chasm [*kazm*] *n* large fissure in earth's surface; narrow space between two precipices; (*fig*) break or breach of relations due to difference of character, opinions *etc*; gap, void, hiatus.

chassé [*sha*say] *n* dancing step in which one foot appears to 'chase' the other.

chassis [*sha*si] *n* base-frame of motor vehicle, radio set *etc* on which other components are mounted; window sash; (*fig, coll*) body.

chaste [*chayst*] *adj* sexually pure, continent; virtuous, decent (of speech); (*fig*) refined, restrained in style ~ **chastely** *adv*.

chasten [*chay*sn] *v/t* correct by punishment, discipline; subdue, calm; refine.

chastening [*chay*sning] *n* disciplinary correction ~ **chastening** *adj* punishing, correcting; purifying, refining, subduing.

chastise [chast*Iz*] *v/t* punish, *usu* by beating ~ **chastisement** [*chasti*zment] *n*.

chastity [*chasti*ti] *n* sexual purity, continence; virginity, celibacy; (*of style*) purity and refinement; **c. belt** (*hist*) device to prevent woman from having sexual intercourse.

chasuble [*cha*zewb'l] *n* sleeveless vestment worn over the alb by priest celebrating Mass.

chat (1) [*chat*] *n* friendly and casual conversation; an informal lecture ~ **chat** (*pres/part* **chatting**, *p/t* and *p/part* **chatted**) *v/i* talk in a friendly or casual way; **c. up** (*coll*) flatter, persuade or amuse by friendly talk.

chat (2) *n* name applied to several birds.

chat (3) *n* (*sl*) louse.

château (*pl* **châteaux**) [*shat*O] *n*(*Fr*) castle or great country house in France.

chatelaine [*shatelayn*] *n* mistress of large country house; hostess; lady's ornamental girdle from which various small articles hang.

chattel [*chatel*] *n* movable possession; (*occ*) slave: **goods and chattels** personal property.

chatter [*chater*] *v/i* talk rapidly about trifling matters; (*of teeth*) click together through cold or fright; (*of birds*) twitter; (*of monkeys*) gibber, make sounds resembling the human voice; (*mech*) vibrate ~ **chatter** *n*.

chatterbox [*chaterboks*] *n* talkative person.

chatty [*chati*] *adj* talkative; talking in a friendly informal way ~ **chattily** *adv* ~ **chattiness** *n*.

chauffeur [*shOfer*] *n* man who drives his employer's motorcar.

chautauqua [*shatawkwa*] *n* (*US*) summer school for educational and religious purposes.

chauvinism [*shOvinizm*] *n* aggressive or unquestioning belief in the superiority of one's own nation, sex or group ~ **chauvinist** *n* one who aggressively asserts the superiority of his country; **male c.** (*coll*) man who asserts or instinctively assumes that men are superior to women ~ **chauvinistic** [shOvinistik] *adj*.

cheap [*cheep*] *adj* inexpensive, worth more than its price; (*of tradesman*) charging low prices; (*of goods*) of poor quality; (*of person*) lightly esteemed, common; (*fig*) easily obtained; low, disparaging (opinion); (*of money*) obtainable at a low rate of interest; **dirt c.** remarkably cheap; **on the c.** cheaply ~ **cheap** *adv* at a low price; with little trouble, easily.

cheapen [*cheepen*] *v/t* and *i* make or become cheap; cut down price; make cheap; (*fig*) bring into contempt, lower the dignity of; vilify.

cheapjack [*cheepjak*] *adj* shoddy, of bad quality ~ **cheapjack** *n* (*ar*) pedlar of cheap goods.

cheaply [*cheepli*] *adv* at a low price; in a cheap way.

cheapness [*cheepnis*] *n* quality of being cheap.

cheat [*cheet*] *v/t* and *i* swindle, deceive, trick; escape from; practise deceit; obtain an unfair advantage ~ **cheat** *n* one who cheats; swindler.

check [*chek*] *n* sudden stop or slowing down in progress caused by opposition; obstruction, setback, rebuff; control or supervision to ensure accuracy, efficiency, progress *etc*; a count, test, verification (of calculation, survey *etc*); cloakroom ticket; restaurant bill; (*chess*) move which exposes the king to capture, and the situation thus produced; (*interj*) call to opponent announcing this; pattern of squares; fabric of this pattern ~ **check** *adj* patterned like a chessboard ~ **check** *v/t* and *i* stop, retard, delay progress; verify, test; inspect; (*chess*) make move which threatens opponent's king; come to a halt; (*coll*) reprimand; indicate by marking, tick; **c. in** (**out**) register one's arrival (departure); **c. up** (**on**) verify; confirm by test or inspection.

check-book see **cheque-book**.

checker (1) [*cheker*] *n* one who checks.

checker (2) *n* piece used in the game of draughts; **Chinese checkers** game resembling halma.

checker (3) see **chequer**.

check-list [*chek*-list] *n* reference list of names or items to be verified.

checkmate [*chek*mayt] *n* (*chess*) position where the king is in check and cannot move out, thus concluding the game; (*fig*) complete defeat or frustration ~ **checkmate** *v/t* (*chess*) put opponent's king out of action; (*fig*) thwart, circumvent.

check-out [*chek*-owt] *n* counter by the exit of a supermarket where customers show and pay for goods they have chosen.

checkpoint [*chek*point] *n* spot where traffic is halted for inspection, or where competitors in a race check in.

check-rein [*chek*-Rayn] *n* rein joining rein of one horse to the bit of the other; strap which prevents a horse from lowering its head.

check-up [*chek*-up] *n* detailed investigation or scrutiny (of accounts, statement *etc*); medical examination ~ **check-up** *v/t* examine closely, count up, compare.

checkweighman [chekwayman] *n* weighman representing the miners at a colliery > PDE.

cheek [*cheek*] *n* side of face below eye; (*coll*) impudence; impertinence of speech to a superior; (*coll*) buttock; **c. by jowl** in close companionship ~ **cheek** *v/t* (*coll*) speak impertinently to.

cheekbone [*cheek*bOn] *n* bone in the upper part of the cheek.

cheeky [*cheeki*] *adj* (*coll*) impudent ~ **cheekily** *adv* ~ **cheekiness** *n*.

cheep [*cheep*] *n* shrill note of young bird; squeak of mouse ~ **cheep** *v/i* and *t* utter a cheep; say (something) in a shrill voice ~ **cheeper** *n* partridge- or grouse-chick.

cheer [*cheer*] *n* state of mind; gaiety, cheerfulness, animation; rich fare, food and drink; encouragement, comfort, solace; shout of applause; **of good c.** cheerful, courageous; **make good c.** feast and make merry ~ **cheer** *v/t* and *i* encourage, make happier; enliven; acclaim with cheers; **c. up!** don't be depressed.

cheerful [*cheer*fool] *adj* happy, in good spirits; gladdening, inspiriting ~ **cheerfully** *adv* ~ **cheerfulness** *n*.

cheerily [*cheer*Rili] *adv* cheerfully, merrily.

cheeriness [*cheer*Rinis] *n* quality of being cheerful or cheery.

cheering [*cheer*Ring] *n* sound of cheers; prolonged applause ~ **cheering** *adj* heartening, encouraging.

cheerio [cheerRi-O] *interj* (*coll*) goodbye.

cheerleader [*cheer*leeder] *n* one who leads the cheering, *esp* at college athletic events.

cheerless [*cheer*les] *adj* dull, dreary, depressed, gloomy ~ **cheerlessness** *n*.

cheers [*cheerz*] *interj* (*coll*) an expression of good wishes in drinking a health.

cheery [*cheer*Ri] *adj* lively, cheerful, genial; too obviously cheerful, vulgarly hearty.

cheese (1) [*cheez*] *n* curd of milk pressed into a solid mass; **green c.** newly-made cheese; **c. straw** strip of pastry flavoured with cheese.

cheese (2) *v/t* (*sl*) **c. it** stop, desist.

cheesecake [*cheez*kayk] *n* tart filled with mixture of flavoured and sweetened curds; (*sl*) photography or photograph emphasizing sex appeal.

cheesecloth [*cheez*kloth] *n* cotton fabric in which

125

curds are pressed; thin plain cotton fabric for clothes.

cheesed [*cheezd*] *adj* (*sl*) thoroughly bored, depressed, or disgruntled (*also* c. off).

cheeseparing [*cheez*pairRing] *n* rind of cheese cut thinly off; (*fig*) miserliness, stinginess ~ **cheeseparing** *adj* niggardly, stingy on a small scale.

cheesy [*cheez*i] *adj* resembling cheese

cheetah [*cheeta*] *n* small type of leopard.

chef [*shef*] *n* chief male cook in hotel or restaurant.

chef-d'œuvre (*pl* chefs-d'œuvre) [shay-*durv*R] *n* (*Fr*) a masterpiece.

cheiroptera [kIrR*opt*eRa] *n* (*pl*) bats.

Cheka [*cheka*a] *n* Soviet secret police 1917–22.

chela (*pl* chelae) [*keel*a] *n* (*zool*) claw-like pincer.

chelate [*chel*ayt] *n* (*chem*) heterocyclic compound containing a central metal ion ~ **chelate** *v/i* form such a compound.

chelation [*chel*ayshon] *n* (*chem*) formation of a chelate > PDS.

chelonia [kel*Oni*-a] *n* (*pl*) tortoises and turtles.

chemical [*kemi*kal] *adj* relating to, made in, chemistry; **c. engineer** one who designs, operates, or manufactures chemical plant or machinery ~ **chemical** *n* substance used in chemistry, or made by a chemical process ~ **chemically** *adv*.

chemiluminescence [kemilOO*mines*ens] *n* (*chem*) the production of light at low temperatures during a chemical reaction.

chemin-de-fer [sheman(g)-de-*fair*] *n* (*Fr*) kind of baccarat.

chemise [she*meez*] *n* woman's undergarment, vest; (*bui*) a wall which revets an earth bank.

chemist [*kemi*st] *n* one working on chemical research; one licensed to sell medicinal drugs.

chemistry [*kemi*stRi] *n* the science of the composition of substances, and of their effects upon one another.

chemotherapy [kem*Othe*Rapi] *n* treatment of psychiatric disorders by drugs; treatment of cancer or infections by chemical substances.

chemurgy [*kem*urji] *n* (*chem*) application of chemistry to agriculture or to the use of organic raw materials.

chenille [she*neel*] *n* a fabric with surface composed of rows of fuzzy cord or fur.

cheque [*chek*] *n* written order directing a bank or banker to pay money as therein stated; stamped printed form supplied to customer of a bank for this purpose; **blank c.** cheque on which the sum to be paid is not yet written; (*fig*) authorization to act as one thinks best.

cheque-book, check-book [*chek*-book] *n* book of blank cheques with counterfoils.

chequer, checker [*chek*er] *n* pattern of squares; checker (2) ~ **chequer, checker** *v/t* cover with a check pattern; divide into squares; diversify; interrupt the uniformity of; **chequered career** a life with frequent ups and downs.

cherish [*che*Rish] *v/t* foster tenderly, *esp* young children, treat with affectionate care; nurture in one's heart (a desire, ambition).

cheroot [she*ROOt*] *n* small cigar cut square at each end.

cherry [*che*Ri] *n* popular small stone-fruit of many shades of red; tree bearing it ~ **cherry** *adj* cherry red in colour.

cherry-brandy [che*Rib*Randi] *n* a sweet liqueur in which Morello cherries have been steeped.

cherrypie [che*Rip*I] *n* the purple heliotrope; tart made with cherries.

chert [*churt*] *n* (*min*) a natural form of silica resembling flint ~ **cherty** [*churt*i] *adj*.

cherub (*pl* cherubs, (*eccles*) cherubim) [*che*Rub] *n* type of angel *freq* depicted as child's head with wings; young and beautiful child.

cherubic [che*ROOb*ik] *adj* like a cherub; (*of children*) plump, pretty, and healthy-looking; very well behaved.

chervil [*chur*vil] *n* aromatic garden herb.

chesil [*che*zil] *n* gravel, shingle.

chess [*ches*] *n* game of skill played by two people on chequered board with thirty-two pieces.

chessboard [*ches*bawrd] *n* board for chess marked in sixty-four squares of alternate black and white.

chessmen [*ches*men] *n* (*pl*) the thirty-two pieces used in chess.

chest [*chest*] *n* large box; place where money of an institution is kept, treasury; (*anat*) front upper part of human body containing heart and lungs; **c. of drawers** piece of furniture with drawers; **c. of tea** 108 lb. of tea.

chesterfield [*chest*erfeeld] *n* kind of overcoat; long sofa with two upholstered ends.

chestnut [*chest*nut] *n* edible nut of the chestnut tree; inedible nut of the horse-chestnut tree; trees bearing these; deep reddish-brown colour; horse of that colour; (*coll*) old and well-worn joke ~ **chestnut** *adj* reddish-brown.

chesty [*chest*i] *adj* liable to bronchitis.

cheval-de-frise [she*val*-de-f*reez*] *n* spiked iron or wood bars fixed over a wall or fence.

cheval-glass [she*val*-glaas] *n* full-length mirror hung on an upright frame so that it can be tilted.

chevalier [sheva*leer*] *n* member of certain orders of knighthood; a gallant.

chevin [*che*vin] *n* the chub.

chevron [*shev*Ron] *n* V-shaped piece of cloth worn on sleeve to indicate rank; (*archi*) deeply-cut V-shaped moulding ~ **chevroned** *adj*.

chevrotain, chevrotin [*shev*Rotayn, shev*Rot*in] *n* small species of musk deer found in S.E. Asia.

chevvy, chevy [*chiv*i] *v/t* chivy.

chew [*chOO*] *v/t* and *i* masticate, grind with the teeth; **c. over** (*coll*) discuss; ponder, turn over in the mind; **c. the cud** (*fig*) reflect; **c. the rag** (*sl*) grumble ~ **chew** *n* act of chewing.

chewing-gum [*chOO*-ing-gum] *n* a preparation of vegetable or resin, *esp* chicle, sweetened and flavoured, used for chewing.

Chian [*kI*-an] *n* type of Greek wine.

Chianti [ki-*anti*] *n* a dry Italian wine.

chiaroscuro [ki-aaR*oskoor*RO] *n* the proper division and distribution of light and shade in a picture; (*lit*) the use of contrast.

chiasma (*pl* chiasmata) [kI-*az*ma, kI-*az*mata] *n* an interchange at corresponding points between homologous chromosomes > PDB.

chibuk [*chi*buk] *n* long-stemmed Turkish tobacco pipe.

chic [*shik/sheek*] *n* good style; elegance ~ **chic** *adj* smartly dressed, stylish, in good taste.

chicane [shi*kayn*] *n* verbal trickery, quibbling;

(*mot*) artificial twists on a racetrack ~ **chicane** *v/t* and *i* cheat; make use of chicane, quibble over, cavil at.

chicanery [shi*kayne*Ri] *n* verbal trickery; sharp practice.

chichi [*shee*shi] *adj* (*coll*) fussily dainty or ornamental.

chick [*chik*] *n* young bird just hatched; chicken; (*sl*) girl.

chicken [*chik*en] *n* young domestic fowl; its flesh; young inexperienced person; (*sl*) coward **no c.** no longer young ~ **chicken** *adj* (*sl*) cowardly ~ **chicken** *v/i* **c. out** back out through fear.

chickenfeed [*chik*enfeed] *n* food for chickens; (*fig coll*) something of very little value.

chicken-hearted [chiken-*haart*id] *adj* timorous.

chickenpox [*chik*enpoks] *n* mild contagious disease, chiefly affecting children, which shows in a skin rash.

chickenrun [*chik*enRun] *n* area fenced off with wire netting for hens to be kept in.

chickenwire [*chik*enwIr] *n* light wire netting.

chickweed [*chik*weed] *n* small weed with white flowers liked by birds.

chicle [*chik*li] *n* the chief ingredient of chewing gum, obtained from the latex of the sapodilla.

chicly [*shik*li/*sheek*li] *adv* smartly, fashionably.

chicory [*chik*eRi] *n* a vegetable or salad plant; ground root of this, added to coffee.

chide (*p/t* **chid, chided;** *p/part* **chidden, chided**) [*chid*] *v/t* and *i* scold, reprove, rebuke.

chiding [*chId*ing] *n* a scolding ~ **chidingly** *adv*.

chief [*cheef*] *n* head of a body of men, organization, party *etc*; ruler of clan or tribe; one's superior in office; (*coll*) boss; (*her*) upper third of a shield ~ **chief** *adj* principal, highest in authority; greatest.

chiefly [*cheef*li] *adv* especially, above all; mainly.

chieftain [*cheef*tan] *n* ruler of a clan, primitive people, band of robbers ~ **chieftaincy** *n* ~ **chieftainship** *n*.

chiffchaff [*chif*chaf] *n* one of the warblers.

chiffon [*shi*fon] *n* gauze-like fabric.

chiffonier [shifo*neer*] *n* a sideboard.

chignon [*sheen*yong] *n* coil of hair.

chigoe [*chig*O] *n* tropical flea that burrows under the skin.

chihuahua [chi*waa*wa] *n* Mexican breed of small dogs.

chilblain [*chil*blayn] *n* painful and irritable sore on the feet, hands, ears, caused by exposure to cold or by bad circulation.

child (*pl* **children**) [*chIld*] *n* baby; young person below age of puberty; inexperienced person; naïve or foolish person; offspring; (*fig*) follower, disciple; one whose character, outlook *etc* is the product of a specified origin or environment.

childbearing [*chIld*bairRing] *n* act of bringing forth a child.

childbed [*chIld*bed] *n* state of woman in labour.

childbirth [*chIld*burth] *n* act of bringing forth a child.

childhood [*chIld*hood] *n* period of life up to puberty; **second c.** extreme old age, dotage.

childish [*chIld*ish] *adj* like a child; proper to a child; (*of adult*) foolish, naïve, ridiculous ~ **childishly** *adv* ~ **childishness** *n*.

childless [*chIld*les] *adj* having no child or children; having no descendants.

childlike [*chIld*lIk] *adj* characteristic of a child; (*of adult*) innocent, ingenuous, frank.

childminder [*chIld*mInder] *n* one who looks after a child while its mother is absent, *esp* at work.

childproof [*chIld*pROOf] *adj* that cannot be damaged, operated, opened *etc* by a child.

children [*child*Ren] *pl* of **child**.

child's-play [*chIld*z-play] *n* an extremely easy task.

chili see **chilli**.

chiliastic [chili-*astik*] *adj* of or believing in a golden age of future perfection.

chill [*chil*] *n* sensation of cold; coldness affecting the body, *gener* suddenly and preceding illness; lack of friendliness in manner; depressing influence ~ **chill** *v/t* and *i* make or become cold; strike cold into; accelerate cooling (of molten metal) by contact with the surface of a cold metal mould; keep (food) cold to preserve it ~ **chill** *adj* cold to the touch; (*fig*) frigid, austere, dismal.

chilled [*child*] *adj* made cold; made ill with cold; (*of meat*) kept at a moderately low temperature; **c. cast iron** iron cast in a metal mould to harden the surface of the casting > PDE.

chilli, chili [*chil*i] *n* dried pod of red pepper used as a condiment.

chillily [*chil*ili] *adv* in a chilly way.

chilliness [*chil*inis] *n* quality of being chilly.

chillness [*chil*nis] *n* quality of being chill.

chilly [*chil*i] *adj* slightly but unpleasantly cold; easily feeling cold; (*fig*) austere; unwelcoming.

chime [*chIm*] *n* resonant note made by bell or striking clock; (*freq pl*) sequence of sounds made by bells, striking clock, musical instrument; a bell or set of bells; melody, harmony ~ **chime** *v/i* and *t* ring out musically; (*fig*) agree, harmonize; ring chimes on (set of bells); indicate (hour of day) by chiming; **c. in** break into a conversation.

chimera [kI*meer*Ra] *n* (*class myth*) fabulous monster with a lion's head, goat's body, and serpent's tail; (*fig*) a wild fancy; an imagined horror; (*biol*) organism whose tissues are of two or more genetically different kinds.

chimerical [ki*me*Rikal] *adj* imaginary, fanciful, indulging in fantasies ~ **chimerically** *adv*.

chimney [*chim*ni] *n* flue by which smoke escapes from fireplace; part of this which rises from roof; tall erection carrying away smoke from factory furnace; open-ended glass cylinder fitting over flame of lamp; vent of volcano; cleft in vertical cliff by which it can be scaled.

chimney-breast [*chim*ni-bRest] *n* the chimney wall which projects into the room and contains the fireplace and flues.

chimney-corner [*chim*ni-kawrner] *n* recess under chimney with seats on either side of fire.

chimneypiece [*chim*nipees] *n* ornamental structure round and above fire-opening; mantelpiece.

chimneypot [*chim*nipot] *n* cylindrical pipe of earthenware or metal fixed on top of chimney to prevent its smoking; (*coll*) top-hat.

chimneystack [*chim*nistak] *n* brickwork containing several flues and projecting above a roof.

chimneysweep [*chim*nisweep] *n* one whose trade is to remove soot from chimneys.

127

chimp [*chimp*] *n* (*abbr*) chimpanzee.

chimpanzee [chimpan*zee*] *n* genus of African apes, most like man of all the anthropoids.

chin [*chin*] *n* part of face below lower lip.

china [*chi*na] *n* porcelain, first made in China; crockery in general ~ **china** *adj*.

chinaclay [*chi*naklay] *n* fine white potter's clay, kaolin > PDS.

Chinaman [*chi*naman] *n* native of China.

china-orange [*chi*na-O*ri*nj] *n* the sweet orange.

Chinatown [*chi*natown] *n* Chinese quarter of a city.

chinaware [*chi*nawair] *n* articles made of china.

chinchilla [chin*chi*la] *n* small rodent peculiar to S. America, with fine soft grey fur; fur of this.

chin-chin [chin-*chin*] *n* (*coll*) a greeting before drinking.

chine (1) [*chin*] *n* deep, narrow ravine.

chine (2) *n* backbone of animal; joint of meat consisting of backbone with adjoining flesh; ridge of a rock or ice formation ~ **chine** *v/t* cut along or across the backbone; slit or cut up.

Chinese (*pl* **Chinese**) [chi*neez*] *n* a native of China; person of Chinese descent; the language of China ~ **Chinese** [chi*neez*] *adj* pertaining to China or the Chinese; **C. lantern** collapsible lantern of coloured paper; **C. white** zinc oxide.

chink (1) [*chink*] *n* crack, cleft, crevice; slit between boards.

chink (2) *n* sound of coins or glasses striking together ~ **chink** *v/t* and *i* make or cause to make this kind of sound.

chink (3) *n* (*sl*) money.

Chink (4) *n* (*sl*, *pej*) a Chinese.

chinless [*chin*les] *adj* having a malformed receding chin; **c. wonder** (*coll*) upper-class fool.

chinstrap [*chin*stRap] *n* strap of military or police helmet held against wearer's chin.

chintz (*pl* **chintzes**) [*chints*] *n* cotton cloth printed with bright-coloured patterns.

chinwag [*chin*wag] *n* (*sl*) conversation, chat.

chip [*chip*] *n* small strip or splinter of wood; broken-off fragment; jagged crack, *esp* in glass or pottery; strip or slice of fried potato; counter used in games of chance; small square unit used for storage of information in microelectronic circuits; chip-basket; **c. off the old block** one taking after his father or ancestors; **pass in one's chips** to die; **have a c. on one's shoulder** be aggressive and embittered; feel quarrelsome; bear a grudge ~ **chip** (*pres/part* **chipping**, *p/t* and *p/part* **chipped**) *v/t* and *i* cut or knock small pieces out of; make potatoes into fried chips; (*of young birds*) crack (egg-shell); be liable to be chipped; (*sl*) poke fun at; **c. in** intervene abruptly in a conversation; contribute money; join with others in an enterprise.

chip-basket [chip-*baa*skit] *n* light basket of plaited strips of wood.

chipboard [*chip*bawrd] *n* a resin-bonded building-board made from sawdust and waste wood.

chip-carving [chip*kaa*rving] *n* type of relief decoration consisting of numerous incisions.

chipmunk [*chip*munk] *n* small, striped, squirrel-like American rodent.

chipolata [chipO*laa*ta] *n* type of slim spicy sausage.

Chippendale [*chip*endayl] *adj* applied to furniture made by Thomas Chippendale (1718–79).

chipper [*chip*er] *adj* (*US coll*) perky, cheerful.

chippings [*chip*ingz] *n* (*pl*) small rough pieces of stone used for resurfacing roads.

chippy [*chip*i] *adj* (*sl*) dry, uninteresting; off colour, not feeling at one's best ~ **chippy** *n* (*sl*) carpenter.

chip-shop [*chip*-shop] *n* shop selling fried fish and chips.

chip-shot [*chip*-shot] *n* (*golf*) short lofted approach-shot on to the putting-green.

Chi-rho [*kI-RO*] *n* monogram (☧) of the first two letters in Greek spelling of Christos.

chiro- *pref* hand.

chiromancy [*kI*Romansi] *n* attempt to foretell an individual's future from lines on the hand.

chiropodist [ki*Ro*podist] *n* one who treats corns, bunions, and other similar foot-troubles.

chiropractic [*kI*ROp*Rak*tik] *n* method of healing based upon manipulation of spinal joints ~ **chiropractor** *n* one who practises chiropractic.

chirp [*churp*] *v/t* and *i* make the short, shrill sounds of a bird or insect; make sound imitative of this ~ **chirp** *n* note or cry of a bird.

chirpy [*chur*pi] *adj* (*coll*) cheerful.

chirr [*chur*] *v/i* make the continuous monotonous sound of a grasshopper or cricket ~ **chirr** *n*.

chirrup [*chi*Rup] *n* a lively, cheerful sound ~ **chirrup** *v/i* utter a series of chirps, twitter; make a clicking sound to a horse ~ **chirrupy** *adj* (*coll*) lively, chatty.

chirurgeon [kI*Rur*jon] *n* (*ar*) surgeon.

chisel [*chi*zel] *n* steel tool the end of which is bevelled to a cutting edge ~ **chisel** (*pres/part* **chiselling**, *p/t* and *p/part* **chiselled**) *v/t* cut, shape with a chisel; (*sl*) cheat, swindle.

chiselled [*chi*zeld] *adj* cut or shaped with a chisel; clear-cut, having sharp outlines.

chiseller [*chi*zeler] *n* (*sl*) a cheat.

chit (1) [*chit*] *n* small child; (*cont*) pert young girl.

chit (2) *n* letter or note; certificate, memorandum.

chit-chat [*chit*-chat] *n* gossip.

chitin [*kI*tin] *n* (*zool*) substance forming covering of crustacea and some insects > PDB.

chiton [*kI*ton] *n* tunic worn in ancient Greece; (*zool*) genus of molluscs resembling limpets.

chitterlings [*chi*terlingz] *n* (*pl*) smaller intestines of pigs used for food

chiv [*chiv*] *n* (*sl*) knife; razor.

chivalric [*shiv*alRik] *adj* of chivalry, chivalrous.

chivalrous [*shiv*alRus] *adj* protecting the weak and oppressed; gallant, brave; courteous and protective, *esp* to women; of chivalry or knighthood ~ **chivalrously** *adv* ~ **chivalrousness** *n*.

chivalry [*shiv*alRi] *n* knightly system of feudal times with its rules for behaviour; gallant and courteous character marking the knight; (*collect*) noble and gallant gentlemen; **age of c.** period in which such behaviour flourished; **flower of c.** finest exponent of knightly behaviour or of martial prowess.

chive [*chiv*] *n* small plant of onion tribe, leaves of which are used for flavouring.

chivvy, chivy [*chiv*i] *v/t* (*coll*) drive along from place to place, force to keep moving; pester by constant demands or reminders; nag ~ **chivvy**, **chivy** *n* boys' game of prisoners' base.

chizz [*chiz*] *n* and *v/t* (*sl*) swindle.

chloral [*klaw*Ral] *n* (*chem*) pungent-smelling, colourless oily liquid obtained from chlorine by action of alcohol; (*pop*) the white crystalline solid, chloral hydrate > PDS.

chlorate [*klaw*Rayt] *n* (*chem*) a salt of chloric acid.

chloric [*klaw*Rik] *adj* of or from chlorine; **c. acid** powerful bleaching and oxidizing agent.

chloride [*klaw*Rid] *n* (*chem*) compound of chlorine with another element; name for various bleaching and disinfecting agents.

chlorinate [*klaw*Rinayt] *v/t* treat (drinking water, swimming baths *etc*) with chlorine.

chlorination [klaw*Rinayshon] *n* disinfection of water with chlorine > PDE.

chlorine [*klaw*Reen] *n* poisonous greenish-yellow gas with a choking irritating smell, used in the manufacture of bleaching powder, disinfectants *etc* > PDS.

chlorites [*klaw*Rits] *n* (*min*) group of minerals which consist of hydrated silicates of aluminium, iron, and magnesium.

chloroform [*klo*Rofawrm] *n* volatile colourless heavy liquid with a powerful sweet smell formerly used as an anaesthetic ∼ **chloroform** *v/t* administer chloroform to; render insensible by chloroform.

chlorophyll [*klo*ROfil] *n* (*bot*) green pigment contained in the leaves of green plants > PDB; deodorant preparation containing this.

chloroprene [*klo*ROpReen] *n* (*chem*) colourless liquid used in making synthetic rubber.

chlorosis [klo*ROsis] *n* (*med*) former name for anaemia in young girls; (*bot*) absence of green pigment in plants.

chlorotic [klo*Rotik] *adj* of or suffering from chlorosis.

choc [*chok*] *n* (*coll abbr*) chocolate.

chock [*chok*] *n* wooden block or thick wedge used to scotch wheels, barrels *etc*.

chock-a-block [chok-a-*blok*] *adj* and *adv* (*naut*) (*of tackle*) when the two blocks touch; (*fig*) crowded closely together.

chock-full [chok-*fool*] *adj* as full as possible.

chocolate [*choko*lit] *n* sweetmeat made from or coated with a paste of sweetened and flavoured crushed seeds of cacao-tree; drink made from this by boiling it in milk; the colour dark brown; **c. cream** flavoured creamy mixture with coating of chocolate ∼ **chocolate** *adj* dark brown; made of or coated with chocolate.

choctaw [*chok*taw] *n* fancy figure in ice skating.

choice [*chois*] *n* act of taking which one prefers out of two or more alternatives; thing selected; variety to choose from; **Hobson's c.** no alternative ∼ **choice** *adj* carefully chosen; of high excellence; discriminating in choosing ∼ **choicely** *adv* with care in choosing, carefully ∼ **choiceness** *n* condition of being choice.

choir [*kwIr*] *n* part of church east of the nave and west of the sanctuary, where singers are placed; singers who lead music in church; company of singers who perform in public; each of nine Orders of angels; (*abbr*) choir organ; **c. organ** lowest of the manuals in an organ, with soft stops suitable for accompanying a choir; **c. screen** screen between nave and choir ∼ **choir** *v/t* and *i* sing (songs) in chorus; sing together in chorus.

choirboy [*kwIr*boi] *n* boy singer in a church choir.

choke [*chOk*] *v/t* and *i* suffocate by compressing throat or by blocking the windpipe; smother, stifle for lack of air or light; stop, obstruct; lose power of speech through strong emotion; (*coll*) disappoint; infuriate; **c. down** swallow, stifle; **c. off** get rid of (a person) by discouragement; **c. up** block up ∼ **choke** *n* action and sound of choking; (*mot*) butterfly valve in a carburettor which reduces the air supply; (*rad*) inductance coil to suppress alternating currents; narrowed part of a gun; (*sl*) prison.

choke-bore [*chOk*-bawr] *n* gun with bore which narrows towards the muzzle.

choked [*chOkt*] *adj* (*coll*) disappointed, annoyed.

choke-damp [*chOk*-damp] *n* (*mining*) atmosphere depleted of oxygen.

choker [*chOk*er] *n* (*coll*) tight scarf, necklace or neck-band; clerical collar; stand-up collar.

chokey, choky [*chOk*i] *n* (*sl*) prison.

choky [*chOk*i] *adj* making one choke; having a choking feeling (from emotion).

chol-, chole- *pref* bile.

choler [*koler*] *n* anger; (*ar*) one of the four humours.

cholera [*kole*Ra] *n* a dysenteric disease, often very severe, leading to rapid dehydration.

choleraic [kole*Ray*-ik] *adj* (*of dysentery*) resembling cholera but due to some other cause.

choleric [*kole*Rik] *adj* hot-tempered, irascible.

cholesterol [*koleste*Rol] *sn* white waxy substance present in human tissue and blood > PDS.

choline [*kOl*in] *n* (*bioch*) organic base found in some fats and egg yolk, constituent of vitamin B complex > PDB.

choose (*p/t* chose, *p/part* chosen) [*chOOz*] *v/t* and *i* select from two or more alternatives; make a choice; (*with infin*) decide, determine, think fit; **cannot c.** but have no alternative but to; **pick and c.** select after careful scrutiny.

choosy [*chOOz*i] *adj* difficult to please, fussy.

chop (1) (*pres/part* chopping, *p/t* and *p/part* chopped) [*chop*] *v/t* and *i* cut by striking with a sharp instrument; cut into pieces, mince; (*cricket, tennis*) undercut (ball) with short sharp stroke; **c. down** fell; **c. off** sever; **c. up** cut into pieces ∼ **chop** *n* act of chopping; piece of mutton or pork containing part of rib; (*cricket, tennis*) undercut stroke; (*boxing*) short sharp blow from above; (*carp*) wooden movable outer plate of a bench of a bench vice; **get the c.** (*coll*) be dismissed; be killed.

chop (2) (*pres/part* chopping, *p/t* and *p/part* chopped) *v/t* and *i* (*of wind*) change direction suddenly; **c. logic** bandy arguments; **c. and change** keep altering.

chop (3) *n* (*gener pl*) jaw.

chop (4) *n* (*India, China*) seal, official stamp; passport; **first c.** of first quality, first rate.

chop-chop [*chop*-chop] *adv* (*sl*) quickly.

chopfallen see **chapfallen.**

chop-house [*chop*-hows] *n* restaurant where grilled chops and steaks are a speciality.

chopine, chopin [ch*Opeen*, *chop*in] *n* kind of shoe raised by a thick sole.

chopper [*choper*] *n* one who chops; axe; (*sl*) helicopter; type of modified motorcycle with vertical handlebars and large rear wheel; **get the c.** (*sl*) be killed.

choppily [*chop*ili] *adv* in a choppy way.

choppiness [*chop*inis] *n* quality of being choppy.

chopping [*chop*ing] *n* (*of waves*) abrupt motion; **c. and changing** variation, altering ~ **chopping** *adj* jerky, abrupt; choppy.

choppy [*chop*i] *adj* (*of wind*) veering about; (*of sea*) covered with short rough waves.

chopstick [*chop*stik] *n* one of two small sticks used by some Orientals instead of table-fork.

chop-suey [chop-*sOO*-i] *n* Chinese dish of meat, rice, and onions fried in sesame or peanut oil.

choral [*kaw*Ral] *adj* relating to a choir or chorus; written or arranged for a choir; sung by a choir; **full c. service** a church service in which versicles and responses as well as canticles and anthem are sung by the choir; **c. speaking** art of reciting poetry *etc* by several persons together.

chorale [ko*Raal*] *n* traditional German metrical hymn-tune for congregational use.

chorally [*kawr*Rali] *adv* by a choir or chorus.

chord [*kawrd*] *n* string of a musical instrument; (*anat*) string-like structure; (*mus*) simultaneous combination of notes; (*geom*) straight line joining two points on a curve; (*bui*) boom or flange of girder; **strike a c.** (*fig*) call up (emotion, memory) in the mind.

chore [*chawr*] *n* small domestic task; odd job; dull work; (*pl*) housework.

chorea [ko*Ree*-a] *n* neurological disorder characterized by jerky, spasmodic movements > PDP.

choreographer [koRi-*og*Rafer] *n* composer or author of the dances and steps of a ballet.

choreographic [koRi-*og*Rafik] *adj* of choreography.

choreography [koRi-*og*Rafi] *n* art of dance notation; art of dance or ballet composition.

choric [*ko*Rik] *adj* of or like a chorus in drama.

chorine [*kawr*Reen] *n* chorus-girl.

chorion [*kawr*Ri-on] *n* (*anat*) outer membrane enveloping the unborn child.

chorister [*ko*Rister] *n* member of choir, choirboy.

choroid [*kaw*Roid] *adj* (*of membrane*) enveloping an organ ~ **choroid** *n* membrane lining eye-ball.

chorology [ko*Ro*loji] *n* scientific study of geographical distribution of living organisms.

chortle [*chawrt*'l] *v/i* chuckle joyfully or triumphantly ~ **chortle** *n*.

chorus (*pl* **choruses**) [*kaw*Rus] *n* (*in drama*) actor or group of actors or singers who comment on the action but take no part in it; words spoken by these; group of singers who perform choral parts in oratorio, opera, musical comedy; troupe of dancing girls in musical comedy or revue; refrain of song, *esp* for several singers; part-song; any simultaneous sounds sung or spoken ~ **chorus** *v/t* and *i* sing or speak simultaneously.

chorus-girl [*kaw*Rus-gurl] *n* girl who sings and dances in the chorus of a musical comedy or revue.

chose (1) [*chOz*] *p/t* of **choose**.

chose (2) [*shOz*] *n* (*leg*) property; **c. in action** money due on a bond recoverable by legal action.

chosen [*chOz*en] *adj* selected; elect, chosen by God; **the C. People** the Jews ~ **chosen** *p/part* of **choose**.

chough [*chuf*] *n* red-legged, red-beaked crow.

chow [*chow*] *n* dog of Chinese breed with curled tail and black tongue; (*sl*) food of any kind; **c.**

mein Chinese dish of fried noodles and meat or vegetables.

chowchow [*chow*chow] *n* mixed pickles; chow.

chowder [*chow*der] *n* (*US*) stew or thick soup composed of game, fish, or clams, together with salt pork, onions, potatoes, crackers, milk *etc*.

chrism [*kRizm*] *n* consecrated oil used as unguent in certain sacraments of the Christian Church.

chrisom [*kRiz*um] *n* chrism; white cloth laid on child at baptism; christening robe; baby's shroud; **c. child** child dying within a month of its baptism; child less than a month old.

Christ [*kRIst*] *n* the Messiah, God's Anointed; title given to Jesus as fulfilling Messianic prophecy.

Christadelphian [kRistadelfi-an] *n* member of a religious sect founded in America in 1833.

christen [*kRis*'n] *v/t* baptize; administer baptism; (*pass*) receive (name) in baptism; give (name) to; perform ceremony of name-giving over (ship).

Christendom [*kRis*'ndum] *n* whole body of Christians; countries in which Christianity is professed.

christening [*kRis*'ning] *n* sacrament of baptism.

Christian [*kRis*tyan] *n* baptized believer in Christ; (*coll*) one who lives a good life and is always ready to help others ~ **Christian** *adj* baptized and believing in the faith taught by Christ; pertaining to Christ or Christianity; unselfish, charitable; willing to forgive; **C. era** period extending from birth of Christ; **C. name** name given in baptism; **C. Science** name of religious system based on theory that pain and evil are illusions to be healed through prayer.

Christianity [kRisti-*an*iti] *n* the Christian faith; Christian beliefs and character.

christianize [*kRis*tyanIz] *v/t* convert to Christianity; make Christian in character ~ **christianization** [kRistyanIzayshon] *n*.

Christlike [*kRIst*lIk] *adj* resembling Christ in character.

Christmas [*kRis*mas] *n* festival of birth of Christ, 25 December; the few days preceding and following it; **C. card** ornamental card of greeting sent to friends and relatives at Christmas; **father C.** legendary figure who is supposed to bring presents to children at Christmas; **C. rose** black hellebore, flowering at Christmas-time.

Christmas-box [*kRis*mas-boks] *n* gift of money given to tradesmen or servants at Christmas.

Christmastide, Christmas-time [*kRis*mastId, *kRis*mas-tIm] *n* season of Christmas.

Christmas-tree [*kRis*mas-tRee] *n* small fir-tree decorated with candles and ornaments, and bearing Christmas presents for the family.

Christology [kRis*tol*oji] *n* part of theology which deals with the doctrine concerning Christ.

chroma-, chromat-, chromato- *pref* colour.

chromate [*kRO*mayt] *n* (*chem*) a salt of chromic acid.

chromatic [kRO*mat*ik] *adj* pertaining to colour; (*mus*) pertaining to intervals outside the diatonic (major or minor) scale; (*of scale*) ascending or descending by semitones > PDM; **c. aberration** (*phot*) defect in lens which causes it to break up white light into colours.

chromatics [kRO*mat*iks] *n* (*opt*) the science of colours; (*mus*) chromatic notes.

chromatid [*kRO*matid] *n* (*biol*) one of the two strands of a chromosome before they separate.

chromatin [*kROmatin*] *n* (*biol*) a constituent of chromosomes > PDB.

chromato- see **chroma-**.

chromatography [*kROmatog*Rafi] *n* (*chem*) method of analysing liquid mixtures by selective adsorption in a column of inert material (**column c.**) or on filter paper (**paper c.**); **gas c.** analogous process for analysing volatile liquids > PDS.

chromatophore [*kRO*matofawr] *n* (*physiol*) a pigment-cell of plants and animals.

chrome [*kROm*] *n* yellow pigment obtained from lead chromate; chromium-plated metal; **c. steel** alloy of steel and chromium.

chromic [*kROmik*] *adj* pertaining to chromium; containing chromium.

chromite [*kROmIt*] *n* chrome iron ore > PDS.

chromium [*kROmi-um*] *n* (*chem*) hard white metal resembling iron > PDS; metal plated with chromium; **c. plating** protective finish consisting of an electroplated surface of chromium > PDS.

chromo- *pref* colour.

chromolithography [kROmolit*hog*Rafi] *n* art of printing in colours from stone.

chromosome [*kROmosOm*] *n* (*biol*) minute thread-shaped body a specific number of which exist in the nuclei of all living cells and carry the genetic code > PDB.

chromosphere [*kROmOsfeer*] *n* (*astron*) gaseous envelope surrounding the sun's photosphere.

chronic [*kROnik*] *adj* (*of disease*) long-continued, inveterate; (*sl*) very bad, objectionable ∼ **chronically** *adv*.

chronicity [kROnisiti] *n* (*med*) chronic state of disease.

chronicle [*kROnik'l*] *n* historical record of events in order of time; simple historical narrative ∼ **chronicle** *v/t* record the history of, *esp* in order of time ∼ **chronicler** *n*.

chrono- *pref* time. ·

chronograph [*kROnog*Raaf] *n* instrument for the accurate measurement of time intervals > PDP.

chronography [kROn*og*Rafi] *n* chronological arrangement of historical events.

chronologer [kROnolojer] *n* chronologist.

chronological [kROnolo*ji*kal] *adj* in order of time; of chronology ∼ **chronologically** *adv*.

chronologist [kROnol*oj*ist] *n* expert on chronology.

chronology [kROnol*oj*i] *n* science of assigning dates to events; order of succession of events.

chronometer [kROnom*i*ter] *n* accurate clock, *esp* one used in navigation.

chronometry [kROnom*e*tRi] *n* scientific measurement of time.

chronopher [kROnofer] *n* apparatus for automatically broadcasting time signals.

chronoscope [*kROnoskOp*] *n* instrument for measuring accurately short intervals of time.

chrys-, chryso- *pref* gold; of golden colour.

chrysalid [*kRisalid*] *n* a chrysalis ∼ **chrysalid** *adj* pertaining to a chrysalis.

chrysalis (*pl* **chrysalides, chrysalises**) [*kRisalis*] *n* (*ent*) sheath enclosing a pupa; pupa, insect larva in torpid stage of development > PDB.

chrysanthemum [kRis*an*thimum] *n* cultivated plant with large composite flowers blooming in autumn.

chryselephantine [kRiselif*ant*In] *adj* of gold and ivory, as used on some ancient Greek statues.

chrysoberyl [*kRis*obeRil] *n* yellowish-green gem, an aluminate of beryllium.

chrysolite [*kRis*olIt] *n* olivine in the form of pale yellow stones used as gems.

chrysoprase [*kRis*opRayz] *n* apple-green variety of chalcedony.

chthonian, chthonic [*thOni-*an, *thoni*k] *adj* pertaining to the gods of the underworld.

chub [*chub*] *n* river fish of carp family.

chubb [*chub*] *n* (*tr*) patent lock difficult to pick.

chubby [*chubi*] *adj* round-faced with plump cheeks ∼ **chubbiness** *n*.

chuck (1) [*chuk*] *n* noise made by driver encouraging horse, or person calling fowls ∼ **chuck** *v/i* make this sound.

chuck (2) *v/t* give an affectionate pat under the chin; (*coll*) throw; give up, abandon; **c. it** stop doing that; **c. out** eject forcibly; throw out (bill, motion); **c. up** give up (contest) ∼ **chuck** *n* light, affectionate tap under the chin; act of throwing; **give the c. to** (*sl*) get rid of; dismiss; break off relationship with.

chuck (3) *n* word of endearment.

chuck (4) *n* rotating part on a lathe for holding the work, or on a drill for holding the drilling bit.

chuck (5) *n* (*sl*) food.

chucker-out [chuker-*owt*] *n* (*coll*) man employed to eject disorderly persons from meeting, public-house *etc*.

chuckle [*chuk'l*] *v/i* laugh very quietly; gloat ∼ **chuckle** *n* a suppressed laugh.

chuckle-head [*chuk'l*-hed] *n* (*coll*) blockhead, stupid fellow ∼ **chuckle-headed** *adj*.

chuckling [*chuk*ling] *n* a succession of chuckles.

chuffed [*chuft*] *adj* (*sl*) delighted; displeased.

chug [*chug*] *n* repeated dull or muffled sound (of engine or automobile) ∼ **chug** (*pres/part* **chugging**, *p/t* and *p/part* **chugged**) *v/i* move with a puffing noise.

chukka, chukker [*chuk*er] *n* each of the periods into which a game of polo is divided.

chum [*chum*] *n* (*coll*) close friend ∼ **chum** (*pres/part* **chumming**, *p/t* and *p/part* **chummed**) *v/i* share lodgings; **c. up with** make friends with.

chummy [*chumi*] *adj* (*coll*) friendly, sociable ∼ **chummily** *adv* ∼ **chumminess** *n*.

chump [*chump*] *n* short, thick block of wood; thick end; (*coll*) fool; (*sl*) head; **c. chop** cut from the thick end of a loin of mutton; **off one's c.** (*sl*) crazy, mad.

chunk [*chunk*] *n* thick piece cut off something.

chunky [*chunk*i] *adj* forming thick lumps or knots; short and stout ∼ **chunkily** *adv* ∼ **chunkiness** *n*.

chunnel [*chun*el] *n* (*coll abbr*) proposed Channel Tunnel between England and France.

chunter [*chunt*er] *v/i* (*coll*) chatter, mumble.

church [*church*] *n* building set apart for Christian worship; members of a specified branch of Christianity; Christians collectively; the clergy; **enter the C.** become a clergyman or priest; **Established C.** form of Christianity officially supported by a State; the Church of England ∼ **church** *v/t* bring (woman) for churching.

churchgoer [*church*gO-er] *n* one who regularly goes to church.

churching [*church*ing] *n* service of thanksgiving for a woman after safe childbirth.

churchman [*church*man] *n* male member of the Established Church.

church-register [church-*Re*jister] *n* record of births, marriages, and deaths occurring in the parish

churchwarden [*church*wawden] *n* one of two lay officers elected yearly to assist the incumbent; (*coll*) long clay pipe.

churchwoman [*church*wooman] *n* woman member of the Established Church.

church-work [*church*-wurk] *n* any work done by lay-people for the church.

churchy [*church*i] *adj* (*coll*) obtrusively devoted to the Church and opposed to Nonconformity; excessively pious or addicted to church-work.

churchyard [*church*yaard] *n* burial-ground surrounding the church; **c. cough** cough which seems symptom of fatal disease.

churl [*churl*] *n* (*hist*) Anglo-Saxon peasant; ill-mannered person; skinflint, miser.

churlish [*churl*ish] *adj* showing boorish ill manners; surly, bad-tempered; miserly, mean ~ **churlishly** *adv* ~ **churlishness** *n*.

churn [*churn*] *n* vessel in which butter is made by shaking milk or cream; large milk-can ~ **churn** *v/t* and *i* agitate (cream) in a churn; (*fig*) agitate (a liquid) violently; seethe; proceed by violent agitation; **c. out** produce copiously and mechanically ~ **churning** *n*.

chute (1) [*shOOt*] *n* rapid channel of water in river; channel made to conduct water from higher to lower level; channel or slope down which anything is shot to reach a lower level; slope for tobogganing; **water c.** (*at fun fairs*) inclined track down which a boat slides into a pool.

chute (2) *n* (*coll abbr*) parachute.

chutney [*chut*ni] *n* hot pickle or relish made of fruits, acids, sugar, and spice.

chutzpah [*choot*spa] *n* (*coll*) bold cheek, shamelessness.

chyle [*kIl*] *n* lymph containing globules of emulsified fat.

chyme [*kIm*] *n* the partially digested food after leaving the stomach.

ciborium [sibaw*Ri*-um] *n* lidded chalice for the reservation of the Eucharist.

cicada (*pl* **cicadae**) [*sikaa*da] *n* the tree cricket.

cicala (*pl* **cicale**) [*sikaa*la] *n* the grasshopper.

cicatrice [*sik*atRis] *n* scar of a healed wound; scar on bark of tree; (*bot*) scar on stem of plant where leaf or flower-stalk has fallen away.

cicatricle [*sik*atRik'l] *n* (*biol*) white germinating spot on the surface of egg-yolk; (*bot*) cicatrice.

cicatrix (*pl* **cicatrices**) [*sik*atRiks] *n* cicatrice.

cicatrize [*sik*atRIz] *v/t* and *i* heal (wound) by the formation of new skin or a cicatrice.

cicely [*sis*ili] *n* name of several umbelliferous plants.

cicerone (*pl* **ciceroni**) [chiche*RO*ni] *n* guide who explains to visitors the history of the place or articles he is showing.

Ciceronian [sise*RO*ni-an] *n* and *adj* (imitator) of the style of Cicero's prose.

cider [*sId*er] *n* fermented drink made from apples.

cider-cup [*sId*er-kup] *n* summer drink made from sweetened cider with various flavourings.

ciderkin [*sId*erkin] *n* inferior quality of cider.

cider-press [*sId*er-pRes] *n* machine for pulping apples to make cider.

ci-devant [see-de*vaan*(g)] *adj* (*Fr*) former, late.

cigar [si*gaar*] *n* cylindrical solid roll of tobacco-leaves for smoking.

cigar-cutter [si*gaar*-kuter] *n* implement for cutting tips off cigars.

cigarette [siga*Ret*] *n* paper tube containing finely-cut tobacco for smoking.

cigarette-case [siga*Ret*-kays] *n* flat ornamental case for carrying cigarettes.

cigarette-end [siga*Ret*-end] *n* cigarette-stub.

cigarette-holder [siga*Ret*-hOlder] *n* tube in which a cigarette can be held in the mouth.

cigarette-paper [siga*Ret*-payper] *n* thin paper in which tobacco is rolled to make cigarettes.

cigarette-stub [siga*Ret*-stub] *n* unsmoked portion of a cigarette.

cigar-shaped [si*gaar*-shaypt] *adj* shaped like cylinder but tapering towards the ends.

cilia [*sili*-a] *n* (*pl*) eyelashes; hairs resembling these on margins of leaves and wings of some insects; (*physiol*) hair-like structures projecting from surface of cells > PDB.

ciliary [*sili*-aRi] *adj* pertaining to certain structures in the eyeball; pertaining to cilia.

ciliate [*sili*-ayt] *adj* provided with cilia.

cilium [*sili*-um] *sing of* cilia.

Cimmerian [si*meer*Ri-an] *adj* intensely dark.

cinch [*sinch*] *n* (*US*) a strong girth for a saddle; (*fig*) a dead certainty; something very easy ~ **cinch** *v/t* and *i* (*US*) fix (a saddle) by a girth; girth tightly; (*fig*) get (person) into a tight place; (*sl*) make sure or certain.

cinchona [sink*O*na] *n* S. American tree whose bark produces quinine; drug prepared from this.

cinchonine, cinchonidine [*sink*oneen, sink*oni*deen] *n* two alkaloids obtained from the cinchona bark, used to reduce fever.

cincture [*sink*cher] *n* enclosure, compass; girdle, waist-belt; border; (*archi*) small convex moulding around shaft of column ~ **cincture** *v/t* gird, encircle.

cinder [*sind*er] *n* residue of burnt-out coal.

Cinderella [sinde*Rel*a] *n* despised woman or girl whose beauty and merits are not recognized; (*fig*) that which has long been neglected.

cinderpath [*sind*erpaath] *n* footpath or running track laid with small cinders.

cinder-sifter [*sind*er-sifter] *n* sieve for separating cinders from ashes.

cindertrack [*sind*ertRak] *n* cinderpath.

cindery [*sind*eRi] *adj* of nature of cinder; full of cinders.

cine- *pref* of or by a cinematograph.

cinéast(e) [*sin*ay-ast] *n* (*Fr*) maker of artistic films; person who judges films by artistic standards.

cine-camera [sini-*kame*Ra] *n* camera for taking motion pictures using cine-film.

cine-film [*sini*-film] *n* film smaller in width than standard and wound on a spool.

cinema [*sin*ima] *n* art of making or acting in motion pictures; building where motion pictures are shown.

cinema-organ [*sin*ima-awrgan] *n* organ incorporating freak stops to produce novel effects.

cinemascope [*sin*imaskOp] *n* method of motion picture projection upon a wide screen.

cinematic [sinimatik] *adj* of or like the cinema.

cinematograph [sinimatogRaf] *n* apparatus for recording movement by a rapid succession of photographs; apparatus for projecting these on to a screen.

cinematography [sinimatogRafi] *n* art of making motion pictures by cinematograph.

cinemicrography [sinimIkRugRafi] *n* photographic recording of changes under a microscope.

cine-projector [sinipROjekter] *n* machine which projects a motion picture upon a screen.

cinerama [siniRaama] *n* method of motion picture projection upon a wide concave screen.

cineraria [sineRairRi-a] *n* genus of S. African plants with bright flowers.

cinerarium [sineRairRi-um] *n* place for depositing ashes of dead after cremation.

cinerary [sineRaRi] *adj* pertaining to ashes; **c. urn** sepulchral urn to preserve the ashes of the cremated dead.

cinereous [sineerRi-us] *adj* ash-coloured.

Cingalese see **Singhalese**.

cingle [sing-g'l] *n* belt, girdle; girth for horse.

cinnabar [sinabaar] *n* (*min*) natural mercuric sulphide > PDS.

cinnamon [sinamon] *n* spice made from the bark of an East Indian species of laurel; the tree itself; the colour of cinnamon, yellowish brown.

cinque [sink] *n* five; five at dice or cards; **C. Ports** five ports on the English Channel.

cinquecento [chinkwaychentO] *n* the sixteenth century, *esp* in Italian art and literature.

cinquefoil [sinkfoil] *n* plant with five-lobed leaves; (*archi*) circle enclosing five cusps.

cinquepace [sinkapays] *n* lively dance, galliard.

cipher [sIfer] *n* figure o representing zero in Arabic numeration; any Arabic numeral; (*fig*) person of no importance; secret way of writing; anything written in secret writing; monogram; organ-note which continues to sound after key has been released ~ **cipher** *v/t* and *i* work elementary sums in arithmetic; write in secret language; (*of organ-note*) continue to sound after key has been released ~ **ciphering** [sIfeRing] *n*.

cipher-key [sIfer-kee] *n* key with which to translate ciphered writing.

circ, cirque [surk] *n* prehistoric stone circle.

circa [surka] *adv* and *prep* about, round about, around.

circle [surk'l] *n* (*geom*) plane figure contained by a line, the circumference, which is everywhere equidistant from a fixed point, the centre; anything or number of things forming a ring; one of the galleries in a theatre; number of people sharing the same interests and associating together; a series ending where it begins and repeating itself; recurring succession of events, cycle; (*fig*) range, reach, area of influence; **vicious c.** argument which begs the question; succession of events aggravating each other; **square the c.** attempt the impossible; **great c.** circle on the earth's surface whose plane passes through its centre ~ **circle** *v/t* and *i* surround with a circle; revolve around; go round in a circle; wheel, swing round.

circlet [surklit] *n* small circle; ornamental ring or headband.

circling [surkling] *n* and *adj* (act of) moving round and round.

circs [surks] *n* (*pl*) (*sl*) circumstances.

circuit [surkit] *n* distance round, circumference; journey round a particular series of stopping-places; regular route or course; road built for motor-racing; district through which a judge travels; barristers practising on a circuit; division of the Methodist Church comprising a number of small congregations served by itinerant ministers; (*elect*) the complete path travelled by an electric current; group of theatres or cinemas associated under a common control ~ **circuit** *v/t* and *i* go round; move in a circuit.

circuitous [serkew-itus] *adj* roundabout, devious ~ **circuitously** *adv*.

circuitry [surkitRi] *n* plan, or components, of an electric circuit.

circuity [serkew-iti] *n* quality of being indirect; an indirect process.

circular [surkewler] *adj* circle-shaped; describing a circle; **c. letter** one of which copies are sent to a number of people; **c. note** letter of credit for travellers that can be cashed at various places; **c. tour** one ending at the place from which it started ~ **circular** *n* notice, advertisement, letter *etc* copies of which are sent to many people; **road** encircling a town.

circularity [serkewlaRiti] *n* quality of being circular.

circularize [surkewlaRIz] *v/t* send circulars to.

circularly [surkewlarli] *adv* so as to form a circle.

circulate [surkewlayt] *v/i* and *t* go or send round, pass round; move freely, go from place to place; .(*math*) recur.

circulating [surkewlayting] *adj* moving round or causing circulation; **c. decimal** recurring decimal; **c. library** one in which books are lent out to subscribers.

circulation [serkewlayshon] *n* movement round, *esp* of blood round the arteries and veins; process of passing round, distribution; (*of newspapers etc*) number of copies sold; continual flow of water, air, sap *etc* so that it returns to its starting point.

circulatory [serkewlayteRi] *adj* of, by, or for circulation.

circum- *pref* round.

circumambient [serkumambi-ent] *adj* surrounding; encompassing.

circumambulate [serkumambewlayt] *v/t* and *i* walk round; approach a subject indirectly ~ **circumambulation** [serkumambewlayshon] *n*.

circumcise [surkumsIz] *v/t* cut off or partially trim away the foreskin of; (*fig*) purify.

circumcision [serkumsizhon] *n* act of circumcising; state of being circumcised.

circumference [surkumfeRens] *n* (*geom*) bounding line of circle or any other closed curve; boundary enclosing anything ~ **circumferential** [serkumfeRenshal] *adj*.

circumflex [surkumfleks] *n* accent used in Greek and French indicated by ^.

circumfluent [serkumfloo-ent] *adj* flowing round.

circumjacent [serkumjaysent] *adj* lying all round.

circumlittoral [serkumlitoRal] *adj* bordering the shore.

circumlocution [serkumlokewshon] *n* roundabout manner of speech, use of several words to express one or two ~ **circumlocutory** [serkumlo*k*ewto*R*i] *adj*.

circumlunar [serkuml*OO*nar] *adj* revolving or flying round the moon.

circumnavigate [serkum*n*avigayt] *v/t* sail round.

circumnavigation [serkumnavi*g*ayshon] *n* act of sailing round; voyage round the whole earth.

circumnavigator [serkum*n*avigayter] *n* one who sails round the earth.

circumpolar [serkum*p*Oler] *adj* around either terrestrial or celestial pole; (*of stars*) which never dip below the horizon.

circumscribe [*s*urkumsk*R*ib] *v/t* draw a line round; encircle; lay down limits of; constrain within narrow limits.

circumscription [serkum*sk*Ripshon] *n* act of bounding, limiting; state of being restricted; inscription round coin, seal *etc*.

circumscriptive [serkum*sk*Riptiv] *adj* limited in space.

circumsolar [serkum*s*Oler] *adj* revolving round, situated near, the sun.

circumspect [*s*urkumspekt] *adj* cautious, watchful; (*of action*) well-considered ~ **circumspectly** *adv*.

circumspection [serkum*sp*ekshon] *n* caution, prudence; cautious behaviour.

circumstance [*s*urkumstans] *n* incident, event, fact, detail; (*pl*) attendant details, external conditions, *esp* means, financial position; formality, pomp, attendant ceremony ~ **circumstanced** *adj* placed in a certain position, situated.

circumstantial [serkum*stan*shal] *adj* fully detailed; relating to but not essential, incidental; **c. evidence** evidence based only on attendant circumstances ~ **circumstantially** *adv* in detail; indirectly, inferentially.

circumstantiality [serkumstanshi-*al*iti] *n* quality of being circumstantial.

circumstantiate [serkum*stan*shi-ayt] *v/t* support with details.

circumvent [serkum*v*ent] *v/t* get the better of, overreach, outwit, frustrate; evade by cunning.

circumvention [serkum*v*enshon] *n* act of outwitting or evading.

circumvolution [serkumvo*lew*shon] *n* rolling round, rotation; coil; rolled fold.

circus [*s*urkus] *n* round or oval arena surrounded by tiers of seats; entertainment consisting of performing animals, acrobatic and equestrian feats, clowns *etc*; open circular area in town where several roads converge.

cirque [*s*urk] *n* amphitheatre; (*geog*) extensive rounded hollow > PDG; prehistoric stone circle.

cirrhosis [si*R*Osis] *n* (*path*) a fibrous disease of the liver ~ **cirrhotic** [si*R*otik] *adj*.

cirri-, cirro- *pref* curl-like tuft, fringe, filament.

cirri [*s*i*R*i] *pl* of **cirrus**.

cirriped, cirripede [*s*i*R*iped, *s*i*R*ipeed] *n* (*zool*) class of marine animals including barnacles > PDB.

cirro-cumulus (*pl* -cumuli) [si*R*o-*kew*mewlus] *n* type of high cloud consisting of small flakes or globular masses, in groups or lines.

cirrose [*s*i*R*Os] *adj* (*bot, zool*) having appendages like a curl; resembling a curl.

cirro-stratus (*pl* -strati) [si*R*O-*st*Raatus] *n* uniform, thin, milky veil of high cloud.

cirrous [*s*i*R*us] *adj* cirrose.

cirrus (*pl* cirri) [*s*i*R*us] *n* (*meteor*) type of high cloud consisting of detached pieces resembling curls of hair; (*bot*) curling tendril; (*zool*) filamentary appendage > PDB.

cis- *pref* on this side of.

cisalpine [sis*al*pin] *adj* on this side of the Alps *ie* on the Italian side.

cissy, sissy [*s*isi] *n* (*sl*) effeminate youth or man.

cist [sist] *n* (*arch*) prehistoric burial chamber.

Cistercian [sistu*r*shi-an] *adj* belonging to monastic order founded at Cîteaux in 1098 ~ **Cistercian** *n* member of this order.

cistern [*s*istern] *n* artificial reservoir or tank; flushing cistern above a water-closet fitment; fluid-containing sac or cavity in an organism.

cistus [*s*istus] *n* (*bot*) rock-rose.

citadel [*s*itadel] *n* fortress protecting or dominating a city.

citation [sI*t*ayshon] *n* reference, quotation; (*leg*) summons to appear in a court of law; (*mil*) mention in an official despatch.

cite [sIt] *v/t* quote as an authority; allege as precedent; refer to; (*leg*) summon to appear in a court of law.

cithara [*s*it*h*aRa] *n* musical instrument of ancient Greece > PDM.

cithern, cittern [*s*ithern, *s*itern] *n* obsolete plucked wire-stringed instrument > PDM.

citified [*s*itifId] *adj* accustomed to or conformed to the fashion or ways of a city or the City.

citizen [*s*itizen] *n* dweller in a city; burgess of a city; subject of a State; **c. of the world** a cosmopolitan.

citizenry [*s*itizenRi] *n* citizens collectively.

citizenship [*s*itizenship] *n* state of being a citizen; rights and duties of a citizen.

citrate [*s*itRit] *n* (*chem*) a salt of citric acid.

citric [*s*itRik] *adj* (*chem*) obtained from the citron and other citrus fruits; **c. acid** the free acid in lemons and other sour fruits.

citrin [*s*itRin] *n* vitamin P, found in lemon juice.

citrine [*s*itReen] *adj* lemon-coloured ~ **citrine** *n* yellow variety of quartz.

citron [*s*itRon] *n* fruit akin to lemon, but larger and less acid; tree bearing this fruit; pale yellow.

citronella [sitRo*n*ela] *n* fragrant grass which yields an oil used in perfumery; the oil itself.

citrous [*s*itRus] *adj* of the citrus fruits.

citrus [*s*itRus] *n* genus of trees including citron, lemon, lime, orange, grapefruit ~ **citrus** *adj*.

cittern see **cithern**.

city [siti] *n* town of size and standing, *esp* one with a cathedral and with a royal charter; **the C.** that part of London within the ancient boundaries; business interests congregated in it; **C. man** one engaged in finance in the City.

cityscape [*s*itiskayp] *n* city scenery, visual effect produced by a city.

citywards [*s*itiwerdz] *adv* towards the city.

civet [*s*ivit] *n* genus of small carnivora which yield a secretion used in perfumery, civet-cat; the secretion itself.

civic [*s*ivik] *adj* pertaining to citizens or citizenship; pertaining to city or municipality; **c. centre** group of buildings containing the administrative headquarters of a municipality and its various welfare centres *etc.*

civics [síviks] *n* the science of citizenship; the science of civil administration.

civil [sívil] *adj* of or pertaining to the individual citizen or community of citizens; relating to the non-military members or activities of a community; considerate, polite, respectful; **c. case** action at law concerned with the settlement of private differences between members of a community and not with criminal offences; **c. defence** wartime civilian organization responsible for air-raid precautions and the safety of the civilian population; **c. disobedience** group refusal to pay taxes or obey laws on political grounds; **c. law** system of laws concerning the rights and obligations of individuals, as distinguished from criminal law; **c. list** annual grant by Parliament for maintenance of the Royal household *etc*; **c. rights** legal and constitutional rights of citizens; **C. Service** the administrative departments of the State as distinct from the armed forces; **c. war** war between citizens of the same State.

civilian [sívilyan] *n* one who is not a member of the armed forces ~ **civilian** *adj* relating to all non-military life and activities.

civility [síviliti] *n* polite behaviour, courtesy; **act** of politeness; (*pl*) polite conversation.

civilization [sívilzáyshon] *n* social, moral, and intellectual attainments of a particular society; (*arch*) highly organized society, *usu* literate and urban; state of not being primitive or savage.

civilize [síviltz] *v/t* bring from state of savagery into civilization; refine in manners.

civilly [sívili] *adv* with reference to civil matters; politely, courteously.

civvies [síviz] *n* (*pl*) (*coll*) civilian clothes.

civvy, civy [sívi] *adj* (*coll*) civilian; **c. street** civilian life.

clack [klak] *n* sound as of two pieces of wood striking together; clatter of human voices; (*mech*) a feed-check valve ~ **clack** *v/t* and *i* make a sharp flat sound; chatter away noisily.

clad (1) [klad] *adj* clothed.

clad (2) (*pres/past* **cladding**, *p/t* and *p/part* **cladded**) *v/t* cover (outside walls of building) with decorative or protective plates ~ **cladding** *n*.

claim [klaym] *n* demand for something as one's due; right, title (to a thing); right to make demands (on person); (*mining*) piece of land claimed by a prospector > PDE ~ **claim** *v/t* demand as one's right; (*leg*) ask for (damages); profess (to have); contend, maintain; assert one's ownership of; call for, require (attention *etc*); put in a claim.

claimant [kláymant] *n* (*leg*) one who brings an action in law; one who makes a claim.

clairvoyance [klairvói-ans] *n* faculty of seeing, by abnormal mental power, events taking place at a distance ~ **clairvoyant** *adj* and *n*.

clam [klam] *n* edible shellfish; (*fig*) a silent uncommunicative person ~ **clam** (*pres/part* **clamming**, *p/t* and *p/part* **clammed**) *v/i* **c. up** (*coll*) become resolutely silent.

clamant [kláymant/klámant] *adj* noisy, vociferous; urgent, pressing, calling for action.

clamber [klamber] *v/i* climb with difficulty, scramble up ~ **clamber** *n* a rough steep climb.

clammy [klámi] *adj* damp, cold, and sticky ~ **clammily** *adv* ~ **clamminess** *n*.

clamorous [klámoRus] *adj* noisy, vociferous; (*fig*) urgently claiming attention ~ **clamorously** *adv* ~ **clamorousness** *n*.

clamour [klámer] *n* noise, outcry, *esp* of opposition or complaint; cries of animals; noise of storm ~ **clamour** *v/t* and *i*.

clamp (1) [klamp] *n* metal or wood fastening for holding things firmly together; rivet used in mending broken china; tool for squeezing together wood parts during gluing, cramp ~ **clamp** *v/t* hold together or fasten with a clamp; (*fig*) seize or press firmly; **c. down on** suppress, put a stop to; suppress news of.

clamp (2) *n* stack of dried bricks burnt over flues built up from burnt bricks; mound of potatoes or mangolds covered with earth for keeping in winter ~ **clamp** *v/t* pile up in a clamp.

clamp (3) *n* heavy stamping tread with the feet ~ **clamp** *v/i* and *t* tread heavily.

clamp-down [klamp-down] *n* suppression; deliberate abrupt cessation of news *etc.*

clamper [klamper] *n* one who fixes clamps; piece of iron with prongs, fitted on sole of boot to prevent slipping on ice; (*pl*) pincers.

clan [klan] *n* number of families holding together and claiming descent from a common ancestor, *esp* in Scottish Highlands; tribal group; (*fig*) group of people united by some common interest; clique, set ~ **clan** (*pres/part* **clanning**, *p/t* and *p/part* **clanned**) *v/i* join (together).

clandestine [klandestín] *adj* secret, surreptitious ~ **clandestinely** *adv.*

clang [klang] *n* loud metallic resonant sound, *esp* of large bell; harsh cry of certain bird; (*ac*) sound when a note and its overtones are heard together > PDP ~ **clang** *v/t* and *i* ~ **clanger** *n* (*coll*) unfortunate remark or mistake.

clank [klank] *n* abrupt sound, duller than a clang, as of heavy pieces of metal striking ~ **clank** *v/t* and *i.*

clannish [klánish] *adj* pertaining to a clan; sticking closely together and resenting the intrusion of strangers, cliquish ~ **clannishly** *adv* ~ **clannishness** *n.*

clansman [klánzman] *n* member of a clan.

clap (1) [klap] *n* abrupt noise of two hard flat surfaces brought sharply together; noise of applause by striking together the palms of the hands; explosive burst of thunder; a friendly slap; lower mandible of hawk; tongue of bell, clapper ~ **clap** (*pres/part* **clapping**, *p/t* and *p/part* **clapped**) *v/t* and *i* strike together; flap (wings); applaud by hand claps; strike lightly with the hand by way of encouragement, approval; put or place promptly in position; put (into prison) summarily; **c. eyes on** see, catch sight of.

clap (2) *n* (*vulg*) gonorrhoea.

clapboard [klapbawrd] *n* (*US*) weather-boarding.

clap-net [klap-net] *n* net used by fowlers and entomologists, which can be closed by pulling a string.

clapped [klapt] *adj* (*vulg*) infected with gonorrhoea; **c. out** (*sl*) worn out, worthless.

clapper [*klap*er] *n* person or thing that claps; tongue of bell; rattle for scaring birds; (*coll*) tongue; (*dial*) rough bridge of planks or slabs.

clapper-board [*klap*er-bawrd] *n* (*cin*) device for giving sharp rapping noise as signal for synchronizing picture and sound.

claptrap [*klap*trap] *n* empty, plausible nonsense.

claque [*klak*] *n* group of people hired to applaud at a theatrical performance or public meeting.

clarabella [klaRa*bel*a] *n* name of an organ stop.

clarendon [*kla*Rendon] *n* (*typ*) name of a bold-faced type.

claret [*kla*Ret] *n* red wine of Bordeaux; rich red colour ~ **claret** *adj* rich red in colour.

claret-cup [*kla*Retkup] *n* drink made of iced claret sweetened and flavoured, mixed with soda water.

clarification [klaRifi*kay*shon] *n* process of clarifying, state of being clarified.

clarify [*kla*Rifi] *v/t* and *i* make clear, free from impurities, make transparent; make intelligible or plain; become clear, be more readily understandable.

clarinet [*kla*Rinet] *n* woodwind instrument with single reed and normally a wooden body; reed organ stop of 8-foot pitch > PDM.

clarion [*kla*Ri-on] *n* small trumpet of narrow bore with a clear tone; 4-foot organ stop of similar tone; shrill rousing call ~ **clarion** *adj* clear, ringing; (*fig*) inspiring, inspiriting.

clarionet [klaRi-o*net*] *n* clarinet.

clarity [*kla*Riti] *n* clearness, transparency; lucidity, clearness of style.

clarkia [*klaar*ki-a] *n* (*bot*) herbaceous garden annual with brightly coloured flowers.

clary [*klair*Ri] *n* a pot-herb.

clash [*klash*] *n* noisy metallic sound of objects in collision; (*fig*) warlike encounter; conflict (of opinions) ~ **clash** *v/t* and *i* strike together noisily; come into conflict; be incompatible (with); (*of events*) happen at the same time and so interfere with each other; (*of colours*) look ugly when near one another.

clasp [*klaasp*] *n* fastening of two interlocking pieces, used to hold together parts of garment, belt *etc*; action of holding, embrace; grasp (of hand with hand) ~ **clasp** *v/t* fasten with a clasp; embrace; grasp (another's hand).

claspknife [*klaasp*nIf] *n* knife the blade of which folds into the handle.

claspnail [*klaasp*nayl] *n* a cut nail of square section with two points in the head.

class [*klaas*] *n* kind, sort, division; a grouping together of a number of persons and things having common attributes; grade of society as classified by birth, wealth, or occupations; category of organisms intermediate between phylum and order; group of students following the same course of instruction; course of instruction in a subject; division of examination candidates according to merit; distinction based on the quality or comfort of accommodation on a train, ship, or aircraft; distinction, high quality ~ **class** *adj* relating to class or a class; high-class ~ **class** *v/t* place in a class, classify.

class-conscious [*klaas*-konshus] *adj* acutely aware of belonging to a particular social class; feeling hostility to the other social classes ~ **class-consciousness** *n*.

class-distinction [*klaas*-distinkshon] *n* awareness and preservation of differences between social classes; criterion by which social classes are distinguished.

classic [*klas*ik] *adj* of recognized merit; approved as a model, standard; restrained, balanced, austere; noted, famous; (*occ*) classical ~ **classic** *n* work of art, music, or literature distinguished for universality and lasting merit; the author of such a work; ancient Greek or Latin author; Greek and Latin scholar; one who follows classical rules and models; (*pl*) the Greek and Latin languages; (*coll*) anything that is a lasting model of excellence in its kind; anything of austere beauty.

classical [*klas*ikal] *adj* pertaining to, expert in, founded on, the language, literature, thought and civilization of ancient Greece and Rome; in accordance with accepted tastes and traditions; of recognized merit, critically satisfying; restrained, balanced, austere; (*of music, coll*) in any of the major styles of serious European music; not being light, popular, jazz, or folk music; **c. physics** physics prior to the quantum theory or the theory of relativity.

classicality [klasi*kal*iti] *n* quality of being classical.

classically [*klas*ikali] *adv* in a classical way; as a classic.

classicism [*klas*isizm] *n* (*gramm*) idiom or construction from Latin or Greek introduced into another language; classical scholarship; adherence to classical principles and taste in art and literature.

classicist [*klas*isist] *n* follower of classical models; upholder of Greek and Latin as school subjects.

classifiable [klasifi-ab'l] *adj* that can be classified.

classification [klasifi*kay*shon] *n* act or method of classifying; division or class to which something is assigned.

classificatory [klasifi*kay*teRi] *adj* that classifies.

classified [*klas*ifId] *adj* arranged in groups or categories; (*mil, pol*) of the highest secrecy for reasons of national security, top secret.

classify [*klas*ifI] *v/t* arrange into groups and categories according to a particular method; assign to a particular type, class, or group; (*mil, pol*) class as top secret.

classily [*klaas*ili] *adv* (*coll*) in a classy way.

classiness [*klaas*inis] *n* (*coll*) quality of being classy.

classis [*klas*is] *n* (*US*) class in college or school.

classless [*klaas*lis] *adj* free from class-distinctions; acceptable to any social class.

class-list [*klaas*-list] *n* official University list of the names of examination candidates arranged in classes according to merit.

classman [*klaas*man] *n* Oxford man whose name appears in a class-list (contrasted with *passman*).

classroom [*klaas*Room] *n* school room where a number of pupils are taught together.

class-war [*klaas*-wawr] *n* hostility between one social class and another, *esp* between workers and employers, landowners *etc*.

classy [*klaas*i] *adj* (*coll*) stylish in appearance and manner; upper-class, aristocratic.

clastic [*klas*tik] *adj* (*geol*) consisting of broken pieces of older rocks.

clatter [*klat*er] *n* harsh din made by the repeated knocking or rattling together of hard objects;

confused babble of talk and laughter ~ **clatter**
v/t and *i* make a clatter, cause to clatter.

clausal [*klawz*al] *adj* of a clause.

clause [*klawz*] *n* (*gramm*) group of words (not a complete sentence) containing a single finite verb; (*leg*) proviso in an agreement.

claustrophobia [klawstRofObi-a] *n* (*psych*) morbid dread of confined spaces ~ **claustrophobic** *adj* suffering from claustrophobia; inducing feelings of claustrophobia, narrow, enclosed.

claustrum [*klawst*Rum] *n* (*anat*) thin layer of grey substance in the cerebral hemispheres.

clave [*klayv*] *ar p/t* of cleave.

clavecin [*klav*isin] *n* harpsichord > PDM.

clavichord [*klav*ikawrd] *n* early type of piano having strings hit by metal tangents > PDM.

clavicle [*klav*ik'l] *n* (*anat*) the collarbone.

clavier [*klav*i-er/*klav*eer] *n* (*mus*) keyboard; manual of organ; piano > PDM.

claviform [*klav*ifawrm] *adj* club-shaped.

claw [*klaw*] *n* horny nail on feet of birds and some beasts; pincer of crabs and lobsters; (*carp*) bar with split end for drawing nails; (*bot*) narrow base of petal securing it to plant ~ **claw** *v/t* and *i* tear or clutch with claws; (*fig*) snatch at; (*naut*) bear to windward from a lee shore ~ **clawed** *adj* having claws; scratched.

claw-back [*klaw*-bak] *n* tax that takes back part of sum granted as allowance *etc*.

claw-hammer [*klaw*-hamer] *n* hammer with one split, claw-shaped peen for drawing nails.

clay [*klay*] *n* sticky earth composed mainly of aluminium silicate and becoming plastic when mixed with water, forming material of bricks and earthenware > PDS; earth thought of as the covering of the dead; (*fig*) human flesh, *esp* of a corpse ~ **clay** *v/t* mix or cover with clay.

clayey [*klay*-i] *adj* clay-like, sticky; containing clay; smeared with clay; (*fig*) mortal.

claymore [*klay*mawr] *n* two-edged broadsword.

clay-pigeon [klay-*pij*in] *n* clay disc fired from a trap, representing a bird in shooting competition.

clay-pipe [*klay*-pIp] *n* tobacco pipe made of clay.

cleading [*klee*ding] *n* (*eng*) close timber sheeting of a lock gate or cofferdam; lagging.

clean [*kleen*] *adj* free from dirt, just washed; not having dirty habits; non-septic; unwritten on; (*print*) (of *proofs*, *revises*) with few errors, pulled after matter has been corrected; without jagged edges; (*phys*) producing little radioactive fall-out; (*fig*) not bawdy or obscene, pure; shapely; dexterous, adroit, unobstructed, complete; **come in** (*coll*) make a full confession ~ **clean** *adv* completely, exactly ~ **clean** *v/t* free from dirt, scrub, brush, polish; **c. out** remove dust and dirt from; (*coll*) leave penniless; drive out, eject; **c. up** make tidy; finish off arrears of work; (*coll*) eradicate crime and corruption ~ **clean** *n* process of cleaning.

cleancut [*kleen*kut] *adj* sharply defined; (*fig*) clear, definite (plan, scheme).

cleaner [*kleen*er] *n* person or substance that cleans; one who cleans offices, railway carriages *etc*.

clean-handed [*kleen*-handid] *adj* free from reproach or blame, upright.

cleaning [*klee*ning] *adj* used for making things clean ~ **cleaning** *n* process of making clean.

cleanlily [*klen*lili] *adv* in a cleanly manner.

clean-limbed [*kleen*-limd] *adj* well-proportioned in body.

clean-living [kleen-*living*] *adj* chaste.

cleanly [*klen*li] *adj* habitually clean in habits and person; chaste ~ **cleanly** *adv* in a clean manner, chastely; exactly, neatly.

cleanness [*kleen*-nes] *n* state of being clean.

clean-out [*kleen*-owt] *n* act of cleaning a room, house *etc*; act of getting rid of unwanted things.

cleanse [*klenz*] *v/t* remove dirt or impurity from ~ **cleanser** *n*.

clean-shaven [kleen-*shayven*] *adj* having no beard or moustache.

cleansing [*klen*zing] *n* process of making clean ~ **cleansing** *adj* able to cleanse, making clean.

clean-up [*kleen*-up] *n* act of cleaning oneself or any object; process of putting an end to crime or corruption.

clear [*kleer*] *adj* transparent, bright; free from cloud *etc*; fresh-coloured (complexion); easily seen, distinct; keen, discerning, lucid; resonant, ringing, distinctly heard; easy to understand, obvious; not in cipher; innocent; unobstructed, unimpeded; without deduction, net; entire (day, year *etc*); **in the c.** free from suspicion; **out of debt**; **c. days** time to be reckoned exclusive of the first and last ~ **clear** *adv* completely, without impediment ~ **clear** *v/t* make clear, clarify; free from obstructions, hindrances; disentangle; surmount; get rid of; declare innocent, free from suspicion; make as net gain; get cash for (cheque); *v/i* become clear, bright or limpid; (*naut*) discharge harbour dues; **c. away** remove what is left after a meal; **c. off** get rid of (arrears of work) by dealing with; (*coll*) get out, go quickly away; **c. out** remove obstruction (in drain *etc*); go away abruptly; **c. up** (of *weather*) become fine; make tidy; solve (mystery), elucidate.

clearage [*kleer*Rij] *n* act of clearing; a clearance.

clearance [*kleer*Rans] *n* act of clearing, *esp* of land by cutting down trees; space so made; approval; permission to approach or have access; (*comm*) passing of cheque or bill through Clearing House; (*mech*) space between a moving object and a stationary one, *esp* that between a vehicle and a wall or tunnel; certificate that a ship has been cleared at the Custom House; **c. sale** sale to get rid of surplus stock; **make a c.** of tidy up and destroy where possible.

clearcole [*kleer*kOl] *n* diluted glue size containing whiting applied to ceilings and walls.

clearcut [*kleer*kut] *adj* sharply defined.

clear-eyed [*kleer*-Id] *adj* having clear sight; bright-eyed.

clear-headed [kleer-*hed*id] *adj* sharp-witted, intelligent; not fuddled by drink or drugs.

clearing [*kleer*Ring] *n* act of making or becoming clear; land cleared for cultivation, *esp* in forest.

clearing-house [*kleer*Ring-hows] *n* (*comm*) central office through which bankers pass the bills and cheques they hold on other banks; (*fig*) central organization through which documents or applicants must pass to be sorted.

clearing-station [*kleer*Ring-stayshon] *n* (*mil*) field hospital where the wounded receive first-aid treatment before being sent to the base.

clearly [*kleer*li] *adv* in a clear manner; distinctly.

clearness [*kleer*nes] *n* quality of being clear.

clearsighted [kleers*i*tid] *adj* having good sight; perceptive; foreseeing clearly.

clearstarch [*kleer*staarch] *v/t* stiffen (linen) with colourless starch.

clearway [*kleer*way] *n* road on which the stopping of vehicles is forbidden.

cleat [*kleet*] *n* wedge; (*naut*) piece of wood or iron bolted on to part of a ship to prevent something from slipping, to fasten a rope or to give foothold on a gangway; batten; nail on sole of boot or shoe; (*pl*) the planes along which coal breaks most easily ∼ **cleat** *v/t* secure to, or by, a cleat; provide with cleats.

cleavage [*kleev*ij] *n* division, break, caused by cutting or splitting; (*geol*) splitting of a rock under pressure into thin sheets or slabs > PDG; (*chem*) manner of breaking of a crystalline substance; (*biol*) cell-division, segmentation > PDB; (*fig*) splitting up of parties, communities *etc* through differences of opinion; cleft between a woman's breasts, *esp* when visible above a low-cut dress.

cleave (1) (*p/t* **clove, cleft, cleaved,** (*ar*) **clave**; *p/part* **cloven, clove, cleft, cleaved**) [*kleev*] *v/t* and *i* hew apart, split; cut a way through.

cleave (2) (*p/t* **cleaved,** (*ar*) **clave**; *p/part* **cleaved**) *v/i* cling, adhere; continue faithful.

cleaver [*kleev*er] *n* butcher's chopper.

cleavers [*kleev*erz] *n* rough hedgerow weed also called goosegrass.

cleek [*kleek*] *n* iron hook; iron-headed golf club.

clef [*klef*] *n* (*mus*) sign placed at the beginning of each line of music to fix the location of a particular note on the staff > PDM.

cleft (1) [*kleft*] *n* crack, fissure, *esp* in rock; one of the divisions of animal's foot; split made in tree to receive a graft ∼ **cleft** *adj* split apart, divided.

cleft (2) *p/t* and *p/part* of **cleave** (1).

cleft-graft [*kleft*-gRaaft] *v/t* (*hort*) insert graft in cleft of tree.

cleft-palate [kleft-*pal*at] *n* abnormal gap from front to back in the roof of the mouth.

cleg [*kleg*] *n* horse-fly.

cleistogamic [kl*i*sto*gam*ik] *adj* (*bot*) applied to flower which does not open and is self-fertilized.

clem (*pres/part* **clemming,** *p/t* and *p/part* **clemmed**) [*klem*] *v/t* and *i* (*dial*) starve.

clematis [*klem*atis/kli*may*tis] *n* genus of climbing shrubs with showy flowers.

clemency [*klem*ensi] *n* gentleness, leniency.

clement [*klem*ent] *adj* gentle, merciful; (*of weather*) mild, calm ∼ **clemently** *adv*.

clench [*klench*] *v/t* and *i* grip firmly; close (fingers, fist, or teeth) tightly; fix securely, make fast (nail or bolt) by hammering back the end after it has been driven through; rivet; conclude definitely (bargain or argument).

clepsydra (*pl* **clepsydras**) [*klep*sidRa] *n* device for measuring time by the controlled flow of liquid through an aperture.

clerestory [*kleer*stawRi] *n* (*archi*) upper part of nave wall, containing row of windows.

clergy [*klur*ji] *n* body of ordained men conducting the services of any Christian Church; (*hist*) **benefit of c.** former privilege of the clergy and others able to read to be tried by an ecclesiastical court if accused of felony.

clergyman [*klur*jiman] *n* ordained minister of a Christian (*esp* Anglican) Church.

cleric [*kle*Rik] *n* clergyman.

clerical [*kle*Rikal] *adj* pertaining to a clergyman; pertaining to a clerk in an office.

clericalism [*kle*Rikalizm] *n* rule of the clergy and support for it; undue influence of the clergy.

clerihew [*kle*RihyOO] *n* four-lined verse of a comic and biographical character.

clerk [*klaark*, (*US*) *klurk*] *n* person employed in office or bank to file letters, keep records *etc*; term applied to various legal, governmental, municipal officials; man in Holy Orders; minor parish official; (*ar*) learned man, scholar ∼ **clerk** *v/i* (*coll*) work as a clerk.

clever [*klev*er] *adj* intelligent, quick to learn; ingenious, adroit, dexterous; (*pej*) impressive but superficial ∼ **cleverish** *adj* fairly clever.

cleverly [*klev*erli] *adv* in a clever manner.

cleverness [*klev*ernis] *n* quality of being clever.

clevis [*klev*is] *n* a U-shaped iron shackle.

clew [*klOO*] *n* ball of yarn or thread; (*naut*) lower corner of a square sail; loop at corner of a sail; cords supporting a hammock ∼ **clew** *v/t* wind into a ball; (*naut*) haul (sail) up to the yard-arm for furling; finish off a job.

cliché [*klee*shay] *n* stereotyped, hackneyed expression; (*typ*) a stereo or electro block; **c. ridden** full of clichés.

click [*klik*] *n* sharp sound like piece of metal snapping into position ∼ **click** *v/t* and *i* make a click; fasten or bring together with a click; (*coll*) succeed in attracting someone's favour, friendship or love; make good sense; (*sl*) become pregnant; **c. for** (*mil*) be detailed for, come in for.

click-beetle [*klik*-beet'l] *n* type of small beetle.

clicker [*klik*er] *n* (*print*) foreman compositor.

client [*kli*-ent] *n* one who employs another professionally as adviser or agent; customer of a tradesman.

clientele [klee-on*tel*] *n* (*collect*) clients, customers.

cliff [*klif*] *n* perpendicular face of rock, *esp* on seashore or in river-valley.

cliff-hanger [*klif*-hanger] *n* (*coll*) serial story in which each episode ends at a moment of danger and suspense ∼ **cliff-hanging** *adj*.

climacteric [kl*i*makteRik/kl*i*makte*Rik*] *n* critical phase, period of change, *esp* in living organisms; menopause; **grand c.** the sixty-third year of life.

climactic [kl*i*mak*tik*] *adj* forming a climax.

climate [*kli*mit] *n* general weather conditions of a region; region where certain weather conditions prevail; (*fig*) general trend of opinions, beliefs, in a community or nation.

climatic [kl*i*mat*ik*] *adj* pertaining to climate; **c. region** one of the main areas into which the earth is divided according to climate > PDG.

climatology [kl*i*mato*loj*i] *n* study of climate.

climax [*kli*maks] *n* final and culminating point in a series of events; (*rhet*) arrangement of a series of statements so that each is more impressive than the preceding; (*euph*) orgasm ∼ **climax** *v/t* and *i* be the climax (*of*); (*euph*) attain orgasm.

climb [*kli*m] *v/t* and *i* ascend something steep; get to the top of, scale; rise in the sky; (*of plants*) creep up by their tendrils or twining stems *etc*; (*fig*) work one's way up, *esp* in social scale; **c. down** abandon the position one has taken up, abate one's pretensions ~ **climb** *n* act of climbing; height to be climbed.

climbable [*klI*mab'l] *adj* capable of being climbed.

climb-down [*klI*m-down] *n* humiliating withdrawal or retraction.

climber [*klI*mer] *n* one who climbs; one who climbs in the social scale; (*bot*) climbing plant.

climbing [*klI*ming] *adj* that climbs; (*of plants*) supported by clinging tendrils or twining stems *etc* ~ **climbing** *n* act of one who climbs.

clime [*klI*m] *n* (*poet*) region, climate.

clinch [*klinch*] *v/t* and *i* fix securely, make fast, rivet, clench; (*boxing*) fall into a clinch; (*fig*) finally settle an argument or business deal ~ **clinch** *n* firm grip; close embrace; manoeuvre in boxing where one of the boxers holds his opponent round the body; a clenched nail or bolt.

clincher [*klinsh*er] *n* (*coll*) argument which cannot be answered.

cling (*p/t* and *p/part* **clung**) [*kling*] *v/i* stick fast, adhere; hold on to by embracing or entwining; remain attached to; keep near; (*fig*) remain constant to, persist in; be highly unwilling to give up or go away; fit closely to the body.

clinging [*kling*ing] *adj* that clings; adhering closely; (*fig*) emotionally possessive or dependent ~ **clingingly** *adv*.

clingy [*kling*i] *adj* (*coll*) that clings; fitting very closely.

clinic [*klini*k] *n* (*med*) institution for the diagnosis and treatment of various medical and psychological disorders; session at which patients with specified illnesses are seen; teaching of medicine and surgery to students in hospitals by practical demonstration.

clinical [*klini*kal] *adj* pertaining to a clinic; (*fig*) showing calm scientific attitude to illness; (*med*) of or for direct examination and treatment of a patient; (*coll*) bare, bleak, functional; **c. thermometer** instrument for measuring bodily temperature ~ **clinically** *adv*.

clinician [*klini*shan] *n* doctor working in a clinic; medical specialist.

clink (1) [*klink*] *n* sharp sound as of glasses striking together ~ **clink** *v/t* and *i* make a clink.

clink (2) *n* (*sl*) prison, prison-cell.

clink (3) *n* (*eng*) pointed steel bar used for breaking up road surfaces > PDE.

clinker [*klink*er] *n* sintered or fused ash from furnaces; (*sl*) first-class specimen.

clinker-built [*klink*er-bilt] *adj* (*of boats*) having external planks which overlap.

clinometer [klI*nom*iter] *n* (*surveying*) hand-held instrument for sighting down or up inclined planes to measure the angle of dip.

clint [*klint*] *n* flinty or projecting rock.

clip (1) [*klip*] (*pres/part* **clipping**; *p/t* and *p/part* **clipped**) *v/t* and *i* fasten or be gripped by a clip; (*ar*) embrace ~ **clip** *n* device for holding things together, *esp* papers; metal container for cartridges; brooch; short excerpt from a film.

clip (2) (*pres/part* **clipping**; *p/t* and *p/part* **clipped**) *v/t* and *i* cut (hair); shear (sheep); trim (lawn, hedge); punch (coin); pare edges of (coin); drop parts of (words) in hurried speech; hit smartly; (*sl*) move or run quickly; **c. the wings of** render powerless ~ **clip** *n* act of clipping off;

that which is clipped off; season's wool crop; smart blow; (*sl*) rapid pace.

clipboard [*klip*bawrd] *n* small board holding papers for writing notes while standing.

clipjoint [*klip*joint] *n* nightclub or restaurant charging very high prices and cheating customers.

clipper [*klip*er] *n* sheep-shearer; coin-clipper; fast-sailing ship; airliner; fast horse; (*sl*) first-rate person or thing; (*pl*) small shears or cutters.

clippie [*klip*i] *n* (*coll*) bus conductress.

clipping [*klip*ing] *n* small piece trimmed off; cutting from a newspaper.

clique [*kleek*] *n* exclusive set of persons, coterie.

cliquey, cliquy [*kleek*i] *adj* cliquish.

cliquish [*kleek*ish] *adj* tending to form a clique, excluding all but a few persons ~ **cliquishly** *adv* ~ **cliquishness** *n*.

clitoris (*pl* **clitorides**) [*klite*Ris] *n* (*anat*) rudimentary organ in females analogous to penis.

cloaca (*pl* **cloacae**) [klO-*ayk*a] *n* underground drain, sewer; terminal part of gut > PDB.

cloacal [klO-*ayk*al] *adj* of a sewer or sewage; of excrement.

cloak [*klOk*] *n* loose sleeveless outer garment worn by both sexes; (*fig*) something assumed to disguise one's real aim or feelings; **c. and dagger** melodramatic, in the manner of tales of espionage ~ **cloak** *v/t* cover with a cloak; (*fig*) disguise.

cloakroom [*klOk*Room] *n* room at theatre *etc* where coats and wraps may be left; office at railway station where luggage may be deposited; lavatory.

clobber (1) [*klob*er] *n* black paste used by cobblers; (*sl*) one's belongings, clothes *etc*.

clobber (2) *v/t* (*sl*) arrest; thrash, attack; ruin.

cloche [*klosh*] *n* plastic or glass protection for plants; woman's close-fitting brimless hat.

clock (1) [*klok*] *n* instrument other than chronometer or watch for telling the time of day ~ **clock** *v/t* and *i* time (runner) in race; record (a speed or time); (*sl*) hit; **c. in, on, out, off** record the time of arrival or departure from work on an automatic timekeeper.

clock (2) *n* ornamental pattern worked on side of stocking ~ **clocked** *adj* ornamented with clocks.

clock-golf [klok-*golf*] *n* name of a putting game on greens arranged in a circle.

clockwatcher [*klok*wocher] *n* (*coll*) one who ceases work as soon as permissible.

clockwise [*klok*wIz] *adv* (moving) in the same direction as the hands of a clock are seen to move.

clockwork [*klok*wurk] *n* mechanism like that of a clock; **like c.** perfectly regularly, without interruption.

clod [*klod*] *n* lump of earth or clay; (*fig*) fool.

clodhopper [*klod*hoper] *n* country bumpkin; awkward person.

clog [*klog*] *n* heavy wooden-soled shoe; lump of wood tied to leg of beast to hamper movement; (*fig*) encumbrance, impediment ~ **clog** (*pres/part* **clogging**; *p/t* and *p/part* **clogged**) *v/t* and *i* fetter with clog; encumber, hamper; become hampered or obstructed; block up with semi-solid matter.

clog-dance [*klog*-daans] *n* tap dance in wooden-soled shoes.

cloisonné [kloi*z*onay/klwa*z*onay] *adj* (*arch*) with

small cells fixed to a metal background and filled with vitreous enamel pastes.

cloister [*klois*ter] *n* covered arcade built against wall of cathedral or monastic buildings, generally running round a quadrangle; monastery, nunnery ~ **cloister** *v/t* confine in a monastic house; (*refl*) shut oneself up in retirement.

cloistered [*klois*terd] *adj* provided with a cloister; shut up in a cloister; secluded, sheltered.

cloistral [*klois*tRal] *adj* monastic; dwelling in a cloister, belonging to a monastic order; living a solitary life.

clonal [*klOn*al] *adj* (*biol*) of a clone.

clone [*klOn*] *n* (*biol*) group of plants produced from single ancestor by cuttings or grafting; descendants produced by asexual multiplication of cells from a single animal ~ **clone** *v/t*.

clop [*klop*] *n* noise of horse's hoofs.

close (1) [*klOs*] *adj* near at hand, near together; nearly equal; firm in texture; compact; intimate; (*fig*) difficult to obtain, scarce; stingy, niggardly; uncommunicative, reticent; well-guarded; restricted, not open to all; sultry, stuffy; careful, thorough; **c. call, c. shave** narrow escape; **c. season** one in which the hunting of certain game is prohibited; **c. timbering** planks placed touching each other against the ground; **c. vowel** one pronounced with tongue near palate ~ **close** *n* enclosure; quadrangle enclosed by buildings; precincts of cathedral containing houses of dean and chapter; alley leading from street to an inner courtyard ~ **close** *adv* very near; tightly, so as to leave no spaces.

close (2) [*klOz*] *v/t* and *i* shut; forbid public access to; finish, bring to an end; come to an end; (*elect*) make (circuit) complete by uniting its parts; come close; come to close quarters (with); agree (with); make bargain (with); **c. in** approach from all round; **c. up** close completely; **c. down** come or bring to an end, wind up ~ **close** *n* termination, end; (*mus*) end of a phrase.

closed [*klOzd*] *adj* shut; confined to a few people; limited by certain conditions; **c. shop** factory or workshop in which only trade-union members are employed; **c. syllable** one ending in a consonant; **c. circuit** television service transmitted by wire to a limited number of receivers.

closedown [*klOz*down] *n* stoppage of work by the closing down of a factory; end of a broadcast; permanent closing of any enterprise.

close-fisted [klOs-*fistid*] *adj* mean, stingy.

close-hauled [klOs-*hawld*] *adj* (*naut*) having sheets braced up tight so as to sail close to wind.

closely [*klOs*li] *adv* in a close manner.

closeness [*klOs*nes] *n* condition of being close; oppressiveness; intimacy; niggardliness.

close-quarters [klOs-*kwawrterz*] *n* (*pl*) close contact with the enemy; narrow, restricted space; **come to c. with** come to grips with.

close-reefed [klOs-*Reeft*] *adj* (*naut*) with all the reefs of (ship or sail) taken in.

close-stool [*klOz*-stOOl] *n* chamberpot enclosed in stool or chair.

closet [*klozit*] *n* small private room; closed storage cupboard or recess; water-closet, privy; **c. drama** play or dramatic poem written to be read and not performed.

closeted [*klozitid*] *adj* holding a private conversation in a room apart.

close-up [*klOs*-up] *n* (*cin*) cinema shot taken much nearer than usual; detailed view.

closing [*klOzing*] *n* way in which or device by which a thing is closed; act of one who closes; end, termination.

closing-time [*klOzing*-tIm] *n* hour at which public-houses or shops close.

closure [*klOzher*] *n* act of closing; termination; closing of debate in House of Commons by vote of the members; (*eng*) metal or plastic cap for a bottle or food container ~ **closure** *v/t* apply the closure to (debate, speaker).

clot [*klot*] *n* lump, *esp* of earth; partly liquid lump formed from curdled liquid; (*of blood*) the part which thickens and separates from the serum; (*sl*) idiot, fool ~ **clot** (*pres/part* **clotting**, *p/t* and *p/part* **clotted**) *v/t* and *i* form into lumps.

cloth [*kloth*] *n* fabric woven from various materials; woollen fabric to be made into clothing; rectangular piece of fabric for covering, cleaning, or wiping; (*theat*) painted fabric drops used as scenery *etc*; closely-woven material used in bookbinding; **the c.** the clergy ~ **cloth** *adj*.

clothe (*p/t* and *p/part* **clothed, clad**) [*klOTH*] *v/t* provide with clothes; dress; (*fig*) cover as with clothes; conceal as with a cloak; endue; endow; express.

clothes [*klOTHz*] *n* (*pl*) wearing apparel; bedcoverings; **in plain c.** out of uniform.

clothes-basket [*klOTHz*-baaskit] *n* basket in which clothes are sent to and from the wash.

clothes-brush [*klOTHz*-bRush] *n* brush for freeing clothes from dust and mud.

clothes-horse [*klOTHz*-hawrs] *n* wooden framework for drying or airing clothes.

clothesline [*klOTHz*lIn] *n* cord stretched out on which clothes are hung out to dry.

clothes-moth [*klOTHz*-moth] *n* small moth the larva of which is very destructive to woollen materials and fur.

clothespeg [*klOTHz*peg] *n* clip made of forked wood for attaching clothes to a line.

clothes-press [*klOTHz*-pRes] *n* cupboard for storing clothes; device for pressing clothes.

clothes-sense [*klOTHz*-sens] *n* good taste in choice of one's clothes.

clothier [*klOTHi*-er] *n* one who sells men's clothing.

clothing [*klOTHing*] *n* wearing apparel in general.

clothyard [*kloth*yaard] *n* measure of length formerly used for cloth; length of arrow used with the long bow.

clotted [*klotid*] *adj* coagulated, thickened; (*of hair*) with locks stuck together.

clottish [*klotish*] *adj* (*sl*) very silly.

cloud [*klowd*] *n* mass of watery condensed vapour floating high in the air; mass of dust or smoke in the air; (*fig*) flock of birds or insects; a multitude, a crowd; anything that causes mental gloom; yarn made by twisting together two threads of different colours; **under a c.** looked on with suspicion; **have one's head in the clouds** ignore everyday matters and live in a world of fantasy ~ **cloud** *v/t* and *i* cast shadow on, sully (reputation); cover with clouds; cover with condensation; become gloomy or overcast.

cloudberry [*klowd*beRi] *n* moorland plant with yellow fruit.

cloudburst [*klowd*burst] *n* sudden torrential rain-storm.

cloud-capt, -capped [*klowd*-kapt] *adj* (*of mountain*) having clouds about its summit; lofty.

cloudchamber [*klowd*chaymber] *n* (*phys*) apparatus used to study the tracks of ionizing radiations > PDS.

cloud-cuckoo-land [klowd-*kook*OO-land] *n* fanciful or ideal place.

clouded [*klowd*id] *adj* covered with clouds, obscured; marked with stripes, spots, or veins of colour; (*fig*) gloomy, anxious, ill-tempered.

cloudily [*klowd*ili] *adv* in a cloudy way.

cloudiness [*klowd*inis] *n* quality of being cloudy.

cloudless [*klowd*les] *adj* free from clouds, clear, untroubled.

cloudlet [*klowd*let] *n* little cloud.

cloud-rack [*klowd*-Rak] *n* broken drifting clouds.

cloudy [*klowd*i] *adj* overcast, dull, full of clouds; not transparent; marked with stripes, spots, or veins of colour; (*fig*) obscure, vague.

clough [*kluf*] *n* steep-sided valley.

clout [*klowt*] *n* rag of cloth; dishcloth; (*coll*) any article of clothing; (*coll*) heavy blow with the hand or bat; (*archery*) the mark shot at; (*coll*) influence, authority ~ **clout** *v/t* (*coll*) to strike with a clout, hit; patch or mend.

clout-nail [*klowt*-nayl] *n* short galvanized nail with large, round, flat head.

clove (1) [*kl*Ov] *n* small bulb which has budded off from larger one, as in garlic.

clove (2) *n* dried flower-bud of an aromatic plant used as a spice.

clove (3) *p/t* of **cleave** (1).

clove-gillyflower [klOv-*jili*flowr] *n* species of pink scented like clove.

clovehitch [*kl*Ovhich] *n* (*naut*) knot in rope passing round spar.

cloven (1) [*kl*Oven] *p/part* of **cleave** (1).

cloven (2) [*kl*Oven] *adj* split to a certain depth, bifurcate; **c. hoof** divided hoof of ruminant quadrupeds, ascribed to the devil; (*fig*) sign of diabolic wickedness.

clove-pink [klOv-*pink*] *n* clove-gillyflower.

clover [*kl*Over] *n* small plant with three-lobed leaves; **be in c.** enjoy every luxury.

cloverleaf [*kl*Overleef] *n* system of road construction in which one highway crosses another on a higher level.

clown [*klown*] *n* the fool or buffoon in pantomime or circus; person of coarse manners or fond of horseplay; (*ar*) peasant, rustic; jester ~ **clown** *v/i* act the fool ~ **clownery** *n*.

clowning [*klown*ing] *n* deliberately ridiculous behaviour.

clownish [*klown*ish] *adj* boorish, clumsy ~ **clownishly** *adv*.

cloy [*kloi*] *v/t* satiate, weary, *esp* with excess.

club [*klub*] *n* thick stick knobbed at end, which can be used as weapon; stick used to play golf; one of the four suits of playing-cards, represented by black trefoil; association of people with common interest (political, athletic *etc*) who meet periodically; building used for this purpose ~ **club** (*pres/part* **clubbing**; *p/t* and *p/part* **clubbed**) *v/t*

and *i* strike with a club; join together in a club; contribute jointly.

clubbable [*klub*ab'l] *adj* sociable, likely to be popular in a club.

clubbed [*klubd*] *adj* shaped like a club, thickened at the end; struck by a club.

clubfoot [*klub*foot] *n* distortion of the foot, which gives it a lumpy appearance ~ **clubfooted** *adj*.

clubhaul [*klub*hawl] *v/t* (*naut*) put (vessel) on the other tack by emergency methods > PDSa.

clubhouse [*klub*hows] *n* house in grounds of athletic club where members can get refreshments, change clothes *etc*.

clubland [*klub*land] *n* district in the West End of London where the principal clubs are situated.

clubman [*klub*man] *n* member of a club; man about town.

clubmoss [*klub*mos] *n* (*bot*) kind of moss with club-like spore-cases.

clubroom [*klub*Room] *n* room hired by club to meet in.

cluck [*kluk*] *n* sound made by hen calling chickens, or when she is broody ~ **cluck** *v/i*.

clue [*kl*OO] *n* anything which serves to point the way out of difficulties, contributes to the solving of a mystery *etc*; **not have a c.** be completely at a loss to understand, know nothing about.

clued [*kl*OOd] *adj* having been shown a clue; **c. up, well c. up** (*coll*) well informed.

clueless [*kl*OOlis] *adj* (*coll*) utterly helpless, stupid, ignorant.

clump [*klump*] *n* shapeless mass of material; number of trees or plants planted together in cluster; stout extra sole on shoe; sound of heavy footfalls; (*coll*) heavy knock, clout ~ **clump** *v/t* and *i* tread with heavy footfalls; group together in a mass; (*coll*) strike, punch.

clumsy [*klumz*i] *adj* awkward in movements; awkwardly made; inelegant ~ **clumsily** *adv* ~ **clumsiness** *n*.

clung [*klung*] *p/t* and *p/part* of **cling**.

cluster [*kluster*] *n* number of people or things grouped together; number of fruits or flowers growing together, *esp* grapes ~ **cluster** *v/i*.

clustered [*kluster*d] *adj* gathered in clusters; **c. column** (*archi*) column encircled by more slender columns.

clutch (1) [*kluch*] *v/t* and *i* seize eagerly or grasp tightly with hands or claws; grasp tightly ~ **clutch** *n* a snatch, grasp, or grip; (*mech*) device for connecting and disconnecting a driving and a driven part of a mechanism, *esp* one permitting gradual engagement; pedal controlling this.

clutch (2) *n* brood of chickens; number of eggs laid by a bird at one time; (*fig*) cluster, bunch ~ **clutch** *v/t* hatch (chickens).

clutter [*kluter*] *n* confused mass, untidy collection ~ **clutter** *v/t* crowd (a place) with disorderly mass of things, litter.

clyster [*klister*] *n* an enema.

co- *pref* together, in common, jointly, equally, mutually.

coach [*k*Och] *n* formerly, large type of carriage or horse-drawn passenger vehicle; railway carriage, which may be divided into compartments; public motor vehicle for long runs; single-deck bus; tutor preparing candidate for examination; one who trains competitors for athletic contests ~

coach v/t and i travel by coach; prepare (pupil) for examination; train (team or person) for contest.

coachbuilder [kOchbilder] n craftsman who makes the bodies of motor vehicles.

coachbuilt [kOchbilt] adj (mot) with the bodywork specially built on a wooden framework.

coach-house [kOch-hows] n outhouse for carriages.

coaching [kOching] n special tuition or training to prepare candidate for examination or athlete for contest; act of travelling in or driving a horse-drawn coach.

coachload [kOchlOd] n persons travelling by coach; as many persons as a coach can carry.

coachman [kOchman] n driver of horse-drawn coach; artificial fly used in trout-fishing.

coach-office [kOch-ofis] n office where places are booked for a coach.

coach-party [kOch-paarti] n group of persons travelling by motor coach.

coachwork [kOchwerk] n the material and craftsmanship of vehicle bodies.

coaction [kO-akshon] n interaction of organisms.

coadjutant [kO-ajootant] adj assisting, helping ~ **coadjutant** n helper.

coadjutor [kO-ajooter] n helper, esp cleric appointed as assistant and successor to a bishop.

coagulant [kO-agewlant] n agent bringing about coagulation.

coagulate [kO-agewlayt] v/t and i thicken into semi-solid mass, curdle ~ **coagulation** [kO-agewlayshon] n ~ **coagulative** adj.

coaita [kO-Ita] n S. American spider-monkey.

coal [kOl] n hard black mineral consisting of carbonized vegetable matter, mined from the earth; (pl) coal in pieces suitable for the domestic fire; **carry coals to Newcastle** do something superfluous; **haul over the coals** reprimand for failure in duty; **heap coals of fire on a person's head** ostentatiously return good for evil ~ **coal** v/t and i (of ship) take in supply of coal; supply (ship) with coal; convert into charcoal.

coalbed [kOlbed] n stratum of coal.

coalblack [kOlblak] adj absolutely black.

coal-bunker [kOl-bungker] n space in ship or railway engine for storing coal.

coal-cellar [kOl-seler] n cellar or shed where coal is stored.

coaler [kOler] n man employed in coaling; ship supplying others with coal.

coalesce [kO-ales] v/i grow or come together, fuse or blend into one mass; (fig) unite ~ **coalescence** n ~ **coalescent** adj.

coalface [kOlfays] n that part of a coalseam from which coal is being cut.

coalfield [kOlfeeld] n region in which coal is mined; a seam of coal.

coalgas [kOlgas] n fuel gas manufactured by the destructive distillation of coal > PDS.

coal-heaver [kOl-heever] n labourer employed to shovel or carry coal.

coalhole [kOlhOl] n small coal-cellar; hole in pavement, covered by lid, down which coal is shot into a cellar.

coalhouse [kOlhows] n shed for storage of coal.

coaling [kOling] n act of supplying with coal; the filling of a ship's bunkers.

Coalite [kOlIt] n trade name for a smokeless fuel obtained from coal.

coalition [kO-alishon] n joining together, union; temporary alliance of two or more parties, esp in politics ~ **coalitionist** adj and n.

coal-measures [kOl-mezhers] n (geol) coal-bearing strata.

coalmine [kOlmIn] n underground workings from which coal is dug ~ **coalminer** n a worker in a coalmine.

coalpit [kOlpit] n a colliery.

coal-screen [kOl-skReen] n mechanical sieve for grading coal.

coal-scuttle [kOl-skut'l] n bucket in which coal is carried and kept in room.

coalseam [kOlseem] n thick layer of coal.

coaltar [kOltaar] n thick black oily liquid obtained in coalgas manufacture > PDS.

coaltit [kOltit] n (orni) type of titmouse.

coaly [kOli] adj like or containing coal; very black ~ **coaly** n (coll) coal-heaver.

coaming [kOming] n (naut) raised border round hatches and scuttles of a ship, to keep water out.

coarse [kawrs] adj harsh, rough; not finely made; (of grain etc) having large particles; (of screws) having the threads widely spaced; (fig) ill-mannered, vulgar; (of jokes etc) indecent.

coarse-grained [kawrs-gRaynd] adj having coarse texture; (fig) vulgar, rough.

coarsely [kawrsli] adv in a coarse way.

coarsen [kawrsen] v/t and i make or become coarse.

coarseness [kawrsnis] n quality of being coarse.

coast [kOst] n stretch of land bordering the sea or a large tract of water; **the c. is clear** there is no danger or obstacle ~ **coast** v/t and i sail along the coast of; skirt round the edge of; ride downhill on bicycle without pedalling; drive motor vehicle downhill out of gear, freewheel; (coll) move effortlessly, win easily.

coastal [kOstal] adj relating to, near, at, the coast.

coaster [kOster] n vessel engaged in trading along the coast; tray for sliding decanters of wine around a table; small mat for a glass.

coastguard [kOstgaard] n one of a body of men stationed along the coast to keep a look-out for passing vessels etc.

coasting [kOsting] adj keeping near or trading along the coast; freewheeling.

coastline [kOstlIn] n outline of the coast seen from the sea.

coastwise [kOstwIz] adj and adv following the coast.

coat [kOt] n sleeved outer garment descending below waist and fastened in front; fur, wool etc covering animal; outer layer of anything; (bui) single layer of plaster, paint etc applied to a surface; (anat) membrane enclosing an organ; **c. of arms** shield bearing heraldic devices; **cut one's c. according to one's cloth** live within one's means ~ **coat** v/t cover with a layer.

coat-armour [kOt-aarmer] n (her) coat of arms.

coatee [kOtee] n short close-fitting coat.

coat-hanger [kOt-hanger] n curved piece of wood etc with a hook, on which clothes are hung.

coati [kO-aati] n small South American racoon-like animal with long flexible snout.

coating [*kOt*ing] *n* layer of paint *etc*; material for coats.

coat-tails [*kOt*-taylz] *n* (*pl*) divided tapering skirts of man's dress coat.

coat-trailing [*kOt*-tRayling] *n* provocative behaviour.

coax [*kOks*] *v*/*t* persuade or obtain by tenderness, flattery *etc*; wheedle ~ **coaxer** *n*.

coaxial [kO-*ak*si-al] *adj* (*math*) having the same axis; **c. cable** (*tel*) cable with a central conductor surrounded by an insulated outer conductor.

coaxing [*kOks*ing] *adj* tenderly persuasive or entreating ~ **coaxingly** *adv*.

cob [*kob*] *n* small lump of ore or coal; an unburnt brick with straw binder; smallish thick-set horse; spike of maize; the male swan; greater black-backed gull; cobnut ~ **cob** (*pres/part* **cobbing**, *p/t* and *p/part* **cobbed**) *v*/*t* (*coll*) fling; beat, thwack.

cobalamine [*kO*balamIn] *n* (*bioch*) vitamin B₁₂; vitamin containing cobalt > PDB.

cobalt [*kO*bawlt] *n* hard silvery-white magnetic metal resembling iron > PDS; **c. blue** pigment obtained from this ~ **cobaltic** [kobaw*l*tik] *adj*.

cobber [*kob*er] *n* (*Aust coll*) mate, pal, friend.

cobble (1) [*kob*'l] *n* small rounded stone, used to pave streets; (*pl*) coal in small lumps ~ **cobble** *v*/*t* pave with cobbles.

cobble (2) *v*/*t* mend roughly; mend and patch shoes ~ **cobble** *n* a clumsily done job of sewing, mending *etc*.

cobbler [*kob*ler] *n* a repairer of boots and shoes; a clumsy workman; (*US*) iced drink flavoured with lemon and sweetened; **cobbler's punch** hot spiced beer.

cobblestone [*kob*'lstOn] *n* rounded stone used in paving.

cobbly [*kob*li] *adj* paved with cobbles; uneven.

co-belligerent [kO-be*lij*eRent] *adj* and *n* (relating to) a wartime ally of a nation.

coble [*kOb*'l/*kob*'l] *n* flat-bottomed rowing-boat.

cob-loaf [*kob*-lOf] *n* small rounded loaf not baked in a tin.

cobnut [*kob*nut] *n* variety of hazel-nut.

cobra [*kOb*Ra/*kob*Ra] *n* venomous Asiatic and African snake with erectile hood.

coburg [*kO*burg] *n* thin fabric of worsted with cotton or silk; variety of white loaf.

cobweb [*kob*web] *n* spider's web; single thread of this; (*fig*) anything flimsy or gauzy; **blow the cobwebs away** refresh oneself (mentally) ~ **cobwebbed** *adj* ~ **cobwebby** *adj*.

coca [*kO*ka] *n* South American shrub, leaves of which act as stimulant.

Coca-Cola [kOka-*kO*la] *n* (*tr*) proprietary name for a carbonated soft drink.

cocaine [kO*kayn*] *n* alkaline product obtained from the coca shrub, used as a local anaesthetic or taken as a drug.

cocainism [kO*kayn*Izm] *n* addiction to cocaine as drug; morbid condition caused by this ~ **cocainist** *n* cocaine addict.

cocainization [kO*kayn*Izayshon] *n* treatment with cocaine; state of being drugged with cocaine.

cocainize [kO*kayn*Iz] *v*/*t* drug with cocaine.

coccus (*pl* **cocci**) [*kok*us, *koks*I/*kok*I] *n* spherical kind of bacterium; (*bot*) carpel of ripe compound fruit.

coccyx [*kok*siks] *n* (*anat*) the bone at the base of the spine ~ **coccygeal** [koks*ij*i-al] *adj*.

cochin [*koch*in] *n* breed of domestic fowl.

cochineal [kochi*neel*] *n* insect of Mexico and Central America; red dye made from its dried body.

cochlea (*pl* **cochleae**) [*kok*li-a] *n* (*anat*) spiral cavity of internal ear ~ **cochlear** *adj*.

cock (1) [*kok*] *n* male of the domestic fowl or other birds; tap regulating flow of water in pipe; hammer of gun; weather-vane; pointer of balance; gnomon of a sundial; rapid movement; upward tilt; (*fig*) swaggering fellow; (*coll*) fellow; (*vulg*) penis; nonsense; **c. of the walk** unchallenged leader, swaggering fellow; **go off at half c.** begin prematurely and ineffectively ~ **cock** *v*/*i* and *t* lift rapidly or jauntily; turn upwards; set at a sharp angle; draw back the hammer of.

cock (2) *n* heap of hay, manure *etc* ~ **cock** *v*/*t* heap up in a cock.

cockade [ko*kayd*] *n* ornamental rosette, or badge of office or party, worn at the side of a hat.

cock-a-hoop [kok-a-*hOOp*] *adj* and *adv* exultant(ly).

Cockaigne, Cockayne [ko*kayn*] *n* imaginary land of idleness and plenty; (*joc*) London.

cock-a-leeky see **cocky-leeky.**

cockalorum [koka*law*Rum] *n* (*coll*) small but conceited man.

cockatiel [koka*teel*] *n* Australian cockatoo.

cockatoo [koka*tOO*] *n* crested parrot.

cockatrice [*kok*atRis] *n* fabulous serpent hatched from a cock's egg, basilisk.

cockboat [*kok*bOt] *n* small boat towed behind a ship.

cockchafer [*kok*chayfer] *n* type of large beetle.

cockcrow [*kok*-kRO] *n* early dawn.

cocked [*kokt*] *adj* turned up, erect; ready for firing; **c. hat** three-cornered hat with upturned brim; hat with pointed crown; **knock into a c. hat** damage beyond recognition.

cocker (1) [*kok*er] *n* breed of spaniel.

cocker (2) *v*/*t* pamper, coddle.

cockerel [*kok*eRel] *n* a young cock.

cockeyed [kok*Id*] *adj* (*coll*) squinting; (*sl*) crooked; inaccurate; inferior; crazy; drunk.

cock-fighting [kok-*fIt*ing] *n* sport of setting gamecocks to fight each other.

cockily [*kok*ili] *adv* in a cocky way.

cockiness [*kok*inis] *adj* pertness, conceit.

cocking [*kok*ing] *n* cock-fighting.

cockle (1) [*kok*'l] *n* purple flower among corn.

cockle (2) *n* edible shellfish; small shallow boat; **warm the cockles of one's heart** invigorate, cheer up.

cockle (3) *v*/*t* and *i* pucker up, wrinkle.

cockleshell [*kok*'lshel] *n* one of the shells of a cockle; the badge of a pilgrim; a frail boat.

cockloft [*kok*loft] *n* the space above the highest ceiling and below the roof.

Cockney [*kok*ni] *n* person born within the sound of Bow Bells, a Londoner; the London dialect ~ **Cockney** *adj* pertaining to, characteristic of, a Cockney; belonging to London.

cockneyism [*kok*ni-izm] *n* Cockney dialect or expression.

cockpit [*kok*pit] *n* small arena for cock-fighting; space occupied by the pilot of an aircraft or the driver of a racing car; (*fig*) scene of frequent battles; (*naut*) space on lower deck.

cockroach [*kok*ROch] *n* large brown nocturnal insect infesting houses.

cockscomb [*kok*skOm] *n* fleshy red crest on a cock's head; jester's cap; showy garden flower.

cockshot [*kok*shot] *n* (*coll*) a throw at an object for amusement; anything set up to be thrown at.

cockshy [*kok*shI] *n* a cockshot.

cock-sparrow [kok-spaRO] *n* male of the sparrow; (*fig*) conceited little man.

cocksure [kok*shoor*] *adj* conceitedly self-confident.

cocktail [*kok*tayl] *n* short well-mixed drink of spirits and various flavourings, *usu* shaken and iced; an appetizer of fruit or tomato juice; a dish of mixed fruits, shellfish *etc*; horse with docked tail; racehorse not quite thoroughbred; **Molotov c.** bomb formed by a bottle full of petrol.

cock-teaser [kok-teezer] *n* (*vulg*) woman who enjoys rousing sexual desire in men but refuses to satisfy them.

cock-up [kok-up] *n* (*typ*) a superior letter or number, as *r* in M^r; (*sl*) mess, blunder.

cocky [*kok*i] *adj* (*coll*) conceited, bumptious.

cocky-leeky [koki*leek*i] *n* (*Scots*) soup made from a fowl boiled with leeks.

coco [*k*Ok*O*] *n* tropical palm-tree which bears the coconut.

cocoa [*k*Ok*O*] *n* powder from the seeds of the cacao-tree; drink made from this.

cocoa-bean [*k*Ok*O*-been] *n* cacao seed.

coconut, cocoanut [*k*Ok*O*nut] *n* large edible nut of a tropical palm; (*coll*) head; **c. butter** a butter substitute made from flesh of coconut; **c. matting** matting made from fibres of coconut husks.

cocoon [kok*O*On] *n* silky protective envelope spun by many insect larvae before they become pupae; anti-corrosive protective coating ~ **cocoon** *v/t* wrap up in a close protective covering.

cocotte [k*O*kot] *n* prostitute.

cod (1) [*kod*] *n* large edible sea-fish.

cod (2) (*pres/part* **codding**, *p/t* and *p/part* **codded**) *v/t* (*sl*) hoax, make a fool of ~ **cod** *n* and *adj* (as) a hoax, joke or parody.

coda [*k*Oda] *n* (*mus*) independent concluding passage at the end of a composition > PDM.

coddle (1) [*kod*'l] *v/t* boil gently, simmer.

coddle (2) *v/t* treat as an invalid, pamper.

code [*k*Od] *n* authoritative collection of laws; established social customs; system of special symbols for transmitting messages rapidly or secretly; system of symbols for use in electronic computers > PDEl ~ **code** *v/i* translate (message) into the symbols of a code.

codeine [*k*Odeen] *n* mild alkaloid narcotic made from opium.

codex (*pl* **codices**) [*k*Odeks, *k*Odiseez] *n* ancient manuscript.

codfish [*kod*fish] *n* the cod.

codger [*ko*jer] *n* (*coll*) eccentric elderly man.

codicil [*ko*disil] *n* (*leg*) later addition to a will.

codification [kOdifik*ay*shon] *n* act of codifying; systematic presentation.

codify [*k*OdifI] *v/t* put into systematic form.

coding [*k*Oding] *n* process of translating into code; assigning of a code-number or letter; (*pop*) code-number.

codling (1) [*kod*ling] *n* young cod.

codling (2), **codlin** [*kod*ling, *kod*lin] *n* kind of cooking-apple; unripe or inferior apple.

cod-liver-oil [kod-liver-*oil*] *n* nutritive oil obtained from the liver of cod.

codpiece [*kod*pees] *n* (*hist*) pouch for the genitals in men's tight breeches; leather shield for the genitals.

co-ed [k*O*-ed] *n* and *adj* (*coll abbr*) (school) where boys and girls are educated together.

co-education [kO-edew*kay*shon] *n* the education of boys and girls together ~ **co-educational** *adj*.

coefficient [kO-i*fi*shent] *n* that which combines with something else to produce a result; (*math*) a number or other known factor written in front of an algebraic expression; (*phys*) factor or multiplier which measures some specified property of a given substance > PDS ~ **coefficient** *adj* cooperating, combining.

coelacanth [*seel*akanth] *n* primitive type of fish of the Indian Ocean.

coeliac [*seel*i-ak] *adj* abdominal.

coemption [kO-*emp*shon] *n* cornering the market in a particular commodity.

coenobite see **cenobite**.

coenzyme [kO-*enz*Im] *n* (*bioch*) substance which plays an essential part in some reactions catalysed by enzymes > PDB.

coequal [kO-*eek*wal] *n* one who is the equal of another ~ **coequal** *adj* of the same rank *etc*.

coerce [kO-*urs*] *v/t* compel by force, constrain.

coercion [kO-*ur*shon] *n* act of coercing.

coercive [kO-*ur*siv] *adj* having the power to or tending to coerce ~ **coercively** *adv*.

coessential [kO-i*sen*shal] *adj* being equally essential; (*theol*) having one and the same substance or being.

coeternal [kO-i*tur*nal] *adj* equally eternal.

coeval [kO-*eev*al] *adj* of the same age, period, or duration ~ **coeval** *n* a contemporary.

coexist [kO-eg*zist*] *v/i* exist at the same time or together; exist side by side without strife.

coexistence [kO-eg*zis*tens] *n* act or state of coexisting; **peaceful c.** simultaneous existence of two incompatible political systems without attacking each other ~ **coexistent** *adj*.

coextend [kO-eks*tend*] *v/i* extend equally in time or space.

coextension [kO-eks*ten*shon] *n* state of extending equally.

coextensive [kO-eks*ten*siv] *adj* of equal extent.

coffee [*kof*i] *n* shrub producing berries with hard aromatic seeds; the seeds roasted and ground; drink made from this; a light brown colour; **black c.** strong coffee served without milk.

coffeebar [*kof*ibaar] *n* establishment serving coffee and light refreshments.

coffee-bean [*kof*i-been] *n* seed of coffee berry.

coffee-break [*kof*i-bRayk] *n* short mid-morning interval at work, when refreshment is taken.

coffee-grounds [*kof*i-gROwndz] *n* (*pl*) dregs of coffee.

coffee-house [*kof*i-hows] *n* establishment where coffee and other refreshments are sold.

coffeemill [*kof*imil] *n* machine for grinding coffeebeans.

coffeepot [*kof*ipot] *n* vessel in which coffee is brewed or served.

coffee-stall [*kof*i-stawl] *n* movable street stall at which coffee and light refreshments are served.

coffee-table [*kof*i-tab'l] *n* small low table; **c. book** (*coll*) large book with lavish illustrations.

coffer [*kof*er] *n* strong box, *esp* one for holding valuables; (*pl*) pecuniary resources, funds; (*bui*) recessed panel in a ceiling; (*hydraulics*) a caisson or watertight box; a canal lock chamber.

cofferdam [*kof*erdam] *n* (*eng*) temporary wall built to exclude water from any site ordinarily submerged or waterlogged > PDE.

coffin [*kof*in] *n* box in which a corpse is buried; anything resembling this; **c. block** (*print*) brass-fitted frame holding electrotype or stereotype plates; **c. bone** soft bone in a horse's hoof; **c. nail** (*sl*) a cigarette ~ **coffin** *v/t* place in a coffin; entomb.

coffle [*kof*'l] *n* gang of men, or string of beasts, fastened together.

cog (1) [*kog*] *n* one of a series of tooth-like projections on the rim of a wheel; (*carp*) a tenon.

cog (2) (*pres/part* **cogging,** *p/t* and *p/part* **cogged**) *v/t* and *i* (*sl*) cheat (*esp* at dice).

cogency [*kO*jensi] *n* quality of being cogent.

cogent [*kO*jent] *adj* compelling, urgent; forcible (logically) ~ **cogently** *adv*.

cogitate [*koj*itayt] *v/i* and *t* think, reflect, meditate; plan, devise.

cogitation [kojit*ay*shon] *n* deep thought.

cogitative [*koj*itaytiv] *adj* capable of thinking; thinking deeply.

cognac [*kOn*yak] *n* best quality French brandy.

cognate [*kog*nayt] *n* and *adj* (*phil*) (word) derived from same primitive form as, and corresponding in form to, a word in another language; (*leg*) (person) descending from same ancestor as another.

cognition [kog*nish*on] *n* faculty of knowing and perceiving > PDP ~ **cognitive** [*kog*nitiv] *adj*.

cognizance [*kog*nizans/*kon*izans] *n* awareness, knowledge > PDP; (*her*) distinctive badge, coat of arms *etc*; (*leg*) the hearing and trial of a case in court; right of trying a case; admission of a fact alleged; **take c. of** take notice of.

cognizant [*kog*nizant/*kon*izant] *adj* aware of.

cognize [kogn*I*z] *v/t* become aware of, perceive.

cognomen [kogn*O*men] *n* family name, surname; nickname ~ **cognominal** [kogn*om*inal] *adj*.

cognoscente (*pl* **cognoscenti**) [konyOsh*en*ti] *n* well-informed person, expert, connoisseur.

cognoscible [kogn*os*ib'l] *adj* capable of being known.

cognovit [kogn*O*vit] *n* (*leg*) acknowledgement by defendant that plaintiff is in the right.

cogwheel [*kog*weel] *n* wheel fitted with cogs.

cohabit [kO*hab*it] *v/i* live together as husband and wife, *gen* used of persons not married ~ **cohabitation** [kOhabit*ay*shon] *n*.

cohabitee [kOhabit*ee*] *n* man or woman who cohabits.

coheir [kO-*air*] *n* joint heir.

coheiress [kO-*air*Res] *n* joint heiress.

cohere [kO*heer*] *v/i* remain united, stick together (as parts of one mass); (*fig*) be logically consistent.

coherence, coherency [kO*heer*Rens, kO*heer*Rensi] *n* state or quality of being coherent.

coherent [kO*heer*Rent] *adj* sticking together; (*fig*) logically consistent, well knit; clear and intelligible; (*phys*) (of a beam of electromagnetic radiation) having all its waves in phase.

coherer [kO*heer*Rer] *n* (*rad*) an early form of detector of electromagnetic waves.

cohesion [kO*hee*zhon] *n* holding together; (*phys*) force holding a solid or liquid together owing to attraction between the molecules; (*fig*) interdependence, unity.

cohesive [kO*hee*ziv] *adj* bringing about cohesion, inclined to cohere.

cohort [*kO*hawrt] *n* tenth part of a Roman legion; body of troops; (*bot*) a group of related families; (*stat*) group of persons born the same year.

coif [*koif*] *n* close-fitting headdress; skull-cap.

coiffeur [kwaa*fur*] *n* hairdresser.

coiffure [kwaa*fewr*] *n* hairstyle, headdress.

coign [*koin*] *n* corner, cornerstone (see **quoin**); **c. of vantage** position giving a good view.

coil (1) [*koil*] *n* series of spiral loops or rings; single loop or ring; (*elect*) loops of wire carrying a current ~ **coil** *v/t* and *i* twist into spiral loops; move in spirals.

coil (2) *n* (*ar*) noise, turmoil.

coin [*koin*] *n* piece of metal officially stamped and used as currency; cash; die used in minting ~ **coin** *v/t* stamp (metal) into money, mint; (*fig*) invent (new word or phrase); **c. money** (*coll*) grow rich, prosper.

coinage [*koin*ij] *n* act of coining; coins of a particular place or period, the currency; right of coining; (*fig*) act of inventing a new word or phrase; word or phrase so invented.

coinbox [*koin*boks] *n* receptacle for coins in an automatic coin-operated machine; coin-operated telephone.

coincide [kO-ins*I*d] *v/i* occupy the same space; occur at the same time; be equivalent to; be in agreement; accidentally occur together.

coincidence [kO-*in*sidens] *n* fact of coinciding; exact agreement; accidental concurrence of events which might seem related but are not.

coincident [kO-*in*sident] *adj* coinciding ~ **coincidently** *adv*.

coincidental [kOinsid*en*tal] *adj* by coincidence; accidentally resembling exactly or occurring simultaneously ~ **coincidentally** *adv*.

coiner [*koin*er] *n* one who coins, *esp* counterfeit money; an inventor, originator.

coir [*koir*] *n* coconut fibre for matting, ropes *etc*.

coital [kO-*it*al] *adj* relating to coition.

coition [kO-*ish*on] *n* act of inserting the penis in the vagina and ejaculating semen into it.

coitus [kO-*it*us] *n* (*Lat*) coition; **c. interruptus** act of coition deliberately interrupted to prevent ejaculation of semen into the vagina.

coke (1) [*kOk*] *n* solid fuel obtained as a residue in the manufacture of coalgas > PDS ~ **coke** *v/t* convert into coke.

coke (2) *n* (*sl*) cocaine; (*abbr*) Coca-Cola.

cokernut [*kO*kernut] *n* (*coll*) coconut.

cokey [*kO*ki] *n* (*sl*) a cocaine addict.

col [*kol*] *n* high pass between mountain peaks.

col- *pref* together.

cola, kola [*k*Ola] *n* West African tree; **c. nut** seed of this tree used as a tonic.

colander, cullender [*kul*inder] *n* a strainer.

colcannon [kolk*anon*] *n* (*Ir*) boiled potatoes and cabbage, *usu* fried in butter.

colchicine [*kol*kisin] *n* alkaloid obtained from colchicum (meadow saffron).

colchicum [*kol*chikum] *n* autumn crocus, meadow saffron.

cold [*k*Old] *adj* low in temperature, lacking heat; feeling chilled; (*fig*) unemotional, distant, frigid, unfriendly; gloomy, depressing; (*of colours*) lacking warmth or brilliance, greyish, bluish; (*of trail*) faint, hard to follow; (*coll*) unconscious; dead; (*in games*) far from the object sought; **in c. blood** with cool deliberation, callously; **c. comfort** poor consolation; **have c. feet** (*coll*) be afraid; **it leaves me c.** it fails to interest me; **c. sweat** sweat of fear; **c. war** state of tension and hostility stopping short of armed conflict; **throw c. water on** discourage ~ **cold** *n* low temperature, lack of heat; sensation caused by lack or loss of heat; acute nasal inflammation caused by virus; **catch c.** become ill with a cold; **out in the c.** neglected, avoided.

coldblooded [kOld*blud*id] *adj* (*of fish, reptiles*) having blood of temperature less than surrounding air or water; sensitive to cold; (*fig*) with unnatural lack of feeling, callous, cruel ~ **coldbloodedly** *adv* ~ **coldbloodedness** *n*.

cold-chisel [kOld-*chiz*el] *n* chisel for cutting soft metals when cold.

cold-cream [kOld-*k*Reem] *n* soothing ointment for skin.

cold-frame [kOld-*f*Raym] *n* protective box for growing plants, unheated but covered by glass.

cold-front [kOld-*f*Runt] *n* (*meteor*) boundary between an advancing mass of cold air and a mass of warm air > PDG.

cold-hammer [kOld-*ham*er] *v/t* hammer (metal) when cold.

cold-hearted [kOld-*haar*tid] *adj* unfeeling, unsympathetic ~ **cold-heartedly** *adv*.

coldish [kOld*ish*] *adj* chilly, rather cold.

coldly [*k*Old*li*] *adv* in a cold way.

coldness [*k*Old*n*is] *n* state or quality of being cold.

cold-short [kOld-shawrt] *adj* (*metal*) brittle when cold.

cold-shoulder [kOld-*shOl*der] *n* studied indifference or rebuff, snub ~ **cold-shoulder** *v/t*.

cold-storage [kOld-*staw*Rij] *n* the preservation of food in refrigerating chambers; **put in c.** (*fig*) postpone indefinitely.

cold-wave [kOld-wayv] *n* (*meteor*) fall of temperature after a depression > PDS; permanent wave in which hair is set by chemicals.

cole [kOl] *n* kinds of cabbage; rape, sea-kale.

coleoptera [koli-*opt*eRa] *n* (*pl*) (*zool*) order of insects comprising beetles and weevils > PDB.

coleseed [*k*Olseed] *n* seed from which rape or sweet oil is obtained; plant producing this seed.

coleslaw [*k*Olslaw] *n* a salad of sliced or shredded raw cabbage.

colewort [*k*Olwurt] *n* cabbage without a heart.

colibri [*k*olibRi] *n* a humming-bird.

colic [*k*olik] *n* attack of severe griping pains in bowels ~ **colic** *adj* pertaining to the colon or to

colic ~ **colicky** *adj* having, resembling, or causing colic.

colitis [kol*It*is] *n* (*med*) inflammation of the colon.

collaborate [kol*abo*Rayt] *v/i* work in conjunction with another; produce work jointly (*esp* literary work); assist and cooperate w.th an enemy occupier of one's country.

collaboration [kolabo*Ray*shon] *n* act of collaborating.

collaborationist [kolabo*Ray*shonist] *n* one who collaborates with an enemy of his country.

collaborator [kol*abo*Rayter] *n* one who collaborates, *esp* on literary work; collaborationist.

collage [kol*aaj*] *n* a picture built up wholly or partly from pieces of paper, cloth, or other material stuck on to the canvas or other ground.

collagen [*kol*ajen] *n* gelatinous substance in bone and cartilage.

collapse [kol*aps*] *v/i* fall down, fall to pieces, crumble away; abruptly lose strength, courage *etc*; (*med*) be physically or emotionally prostrated; fail utterly ~ **collapse** *n* act of collapsing; state of prostration or exhaustion.

collapsible [kol*aps*ib'l] *adj* capable of being folded up.

collar [*kol*er] *n* part of garment fitting round neck; separate band of material attached to neck of shirt; flap of material at neck of blouse, dress *etc*; close-fitting necklace or ornamental band; chain worn as insignia; leather band round dog's neck; part of harness round horse's neck; (*mech*) connecting or strengthening band or ring; (*zool*) markings round neck; (*bot*) junction of root and stem ~ **collar** *v/t* put a collar on to; seize by collar; (*coll*) grab, tackle; (*coll*) appropriate; master ~ **collared** *adj*.

collarbone [*kol*erbOn] *n* frontal bone linking ribcage to shoulder joint.

collaret, collarette [kole*Ret*] *n* small collar; piece of lace or fur worn round the neck.

collate [kol*ayt*] *v/t* compare (texts *etc*) critically in detail; (*print*) arrange sheets of a book in proper sequence; examine book for missing pages; appoint (clergyman) to benefice.

collateral [kol*ate*Ral] *adj* side by side, parallel, descended from a common ancestor but in a different line; subordinate, secondary; additional; **c. security** security for a loan in addition to the principal security ~ **collateral** *n* a collateral relation; collateral security ~ **collaterally** *adv* ~ **collateralness** *n*.

collation [kol*ay*shon] *n* process or result of collating; a light meal which has taken little preparation

collator [kol*ay*ter] *n* one who collates.

colleague [*kol*eeg] *n* fellow-worker, professional associate.

collect (1) [*kol*ekt] *n* short prayer appointed to be read in church on specified occasions.

collect (2) [kol*ekt*] *v/t* and *i* gather together, accumulate; gather (rare objects *etc*) as a hobby; obtain or solicit (money, *usu* for specified purpose); (*coll*) fetch, call for; (*refl*) regain control of one's feelings or thoughts ~ **collectable** *adj*.

collected [kol*ekt*id] *adj* gathered together; self-possessed, calm; (*of literary works*) gathered into one book or set of books ~ **collectedly** *adv* ~ **collectedness** *n*.

collection [kole*k*shon] *n* act or process of collecting, *esp* of money for a religious or charitable purpose; sum so collected; assemblage of objects gathered and preserved; official emptying of post-boxes; (*pl*) college terminal examination.

collective [kole*k*tiv] *adj* considered as a whole; relating or belonging to all members of a group; **c. bargaining** negotiation about wages *etc* between employer and trade-union; **c. farm** farm made up of the holdings of a number of individual farmers and worked on a cooperative basis under state control; **c. noun** (*gramm*) noun singular in form but denoting a number of individuals; **c. security** a system by which the security and territorial integrity of each country are guaranteed by all countries > PDPol; **c. unconscious** (*psych*) part of the unconscious mind derived from ancestral, not personal, experiences ~ **collectively** *adv*.

collectivism [kole*k*tivizm] *n* any economic or political system based on cooperation and central planning > PDPol ~ **collectivist** *n* and *adj* (adherent) of collectivism.

collectivization [kolektiv*i*zayshon] *n* transference of farms to collective ownership; process of forming a collectivist economy.

collector [kole*k*ter] *n* one who, or that which collects; official who gathers in passengers' tickets; gatherer of money due; formerly the chief administrator of an Indian district; (*phys*) electrode in a transistor which collects the charge carriers > PDEl.

colleen [kole*en*] *n* (*Ir*) a girl.

college [ko*lij*] *n* self-governing educational unit within a university; senior or specialized educational establishment; buildings in which a college is housed; self-governing association of persons; **electoral c.** body of electors to a specified office; **c. pudding** pudding made of dried fruit, suet, and flour ~ **colleger** *n* member of college.

collegial [kole*ej*i-al] *adj* constituted as, belonging to, a college; belonging to a society of scholars.

collegiality [kole*ej*i-*al*iti] *n* (*RC*) joint responsibility of bishops and Pope in Church government.

collegian [kole*ej*i-an] *n* member of a college.

collegiate [kole*ej*i-it] *adj* constituted as a college; **c. church** one with a chapter but no see.

collet [ko*lit*] *n* band or ring; circular flange.

collide [ko*lid*] *v/i* strike violently against, crash into; (*fig*) be in conflict with.

collie [ko*li*] *n* long-haired Scottish sheepdog.

collier [ko*li*-er] *n* coalminer; ship for carrying coal; dealer in coal.

colliery [ko*li*-eRi] *n* a coalmine with its surface buildings.

collimate [ko*li*mayt] *v/t* make parallel; (*of a telescope*) line up accurately.

collimator [ko*li*maytor] *n* small fixed telescope for aligning a larger instrument; part of an optical system which transmits a parallel beam of light; device for limiting a beam of radiation to required dimensions.

collision [ko*li*zhon] *n* act of colliding; violent impact between moving vehicles; (*fig*) hostile encounter; **c. course** course certain to cause a collision.

collocate [ko*lo*kayt] *v/t* place side by side; arrange.

collocation [kolo*k*ayshon] *n* a placing side by side; normal or customary arrangement (*esp* of words); effect produced by this.

collodion [ko*lo*di-on] *n* solution of cellulose nitrate in a mixture of alcohol and ether ~ **collodionize** *v/t* treat with collodion.

collogue [ko*lo*g] *v/i* confer confidentially.

colloid [ko*lo*id] *n* (*chem*) substance present in solution whose molecules group together to form solute particles which are unable to pass through a semi-permeable membrane > PDS ~ **colloidal** *adj*.

collop [ko*lo*p] *n* piece, slice (*esp* of meat).

colloquial [ko*lo*kwi-al] *adj* used in informal speech, characteristic of everyday conversation ~ **colloquially** *adv* ~ **colloquialism** *n* colloquial word or expression.

colloquium [ko*lo*kwi-um] *n* conference to discuss a scholarly subject.

colloquy [ko*lo*kwi] *n* formal conversation; conference; literary work in dialogue form.

collotype [ko*lo*tIp] *n* (*print*) a gelatine-process plate.

collude [ko*lewd*] *v/i* act in collusion.

collusion [ko*lewzh*on] *n* secret cooperation for a dishonest purpose.

collusive [ko*lewsiv*] *adj* in collusion ~ **collusively** *adj* ~ **collusiveness** *n*.

collywobbles [ko*li*wob'lz] *n* (*pl*) (*coll*) stomach-ache; looseness of bowels.

colocynth [ko*lo*sinth] *n* the bitter-apple, a plant of the gourd family; purgative made from this.

Cologne [ko*lO*n] *n* fragrant liquid made of alcohol and various oils.

colon (1) [*k*Olon] *n* major part of large intestine.

colon (2) *n* (*gramm*) the punctuation mark (:).

colonel [*k*urnel] *n* officer in command of a regiment; military rank immediately below that of brigadier ~ **colonelcy** *n* office, rank, or commission of colonel.

colonial [ko*lO*ni-al] *n* and *adj* (inhabitant) of a colony.

colonialism [ko*lO*ni-alizm] *n* a characteristic of colonial life, speech *etc*; a colonial system, *esp* the habitual acquisition and exploitation of colonies for the benefit of the mother-country ~ **colonialist** *n* and *adj* (supporter) of a colonial system.

colonially [ko*lO*ni-ali] *adv* as a colony.

colonist [ko*lo*nist] *n* one who colonizes; pioneer settler in a colony.

colonization [kolon*i*zayshon] *n* process of colonizing.

colonize [ko*lo*nIz] *v/t* and *i* take possession of a relatively undeveloped country and settle one's surplus population there; go to live in a colony ~ **colonizer** *n*.

colonnade [kolo*nayd*] *n* a row of columns at regular intervals; avenue of trees.

colony [ko*lo*ni] *n* semi-independent settlement of emigrants and their descendants, *usu* in relatively undeveloped areas distant from their fatherland; area thus settled; body of settlers; group of aliens in a community, *esp* those preserving their own national characteristics; quarter where such aliens live; (*biol*) group of related organisms.

colophon [ko*lo*fon] *n* (*typ*) the imprint (*usu* tailpiece) of a book.

colophony [ko*lo*foni] *n* rosin.

Colorado beetle [kolo*Raad*O-*beet*'l] *n* a beetle the larva of which is destructive to the potato.

coloration [kule*Ray*shon] *n* colouring; arrangement of colours.

coloratura [koloRa*toor*Ra] *n* (*mus*) florid style of vocal music or its performance > PDM.

colorific [kule*Rif*ik] *adj* producing, connected with, colour; highly coloured.

colorimeter [kule*Rim*iter] *n* instrument for comparing intensities of colour.

colossal [ko*los*al] *adj* gigantic; (*coll*) incredible; remarkably great or fine ~ **colossally** *adv*.

colossus [ko*los*us] *n* huge statue; (*fig*) person of unusual size or strength.

colostomy [ko*los*tomi] *n* (*surg*) artificial anal opening made in the colon.

colostrum [ko*los*tRum] *n* the first milk secreted after parturition.

colotomy [ko*lo*tomi] *n* (*surg*) incision in the colon.

colour [*kuler*] *n* effect of light of varying wavelengths on the human eye; chromatic hue, tint, pigment; variously tinted pigments and their use in painting; pigmentation of human skin, complexion; pigmentation of non-white peoples; (*fig*) outward appearance, semblance; (*fig*) false show, pretext, cloak; (*fig*) vividness of personality, zest; (*mus*) timbre, difference in tone; (*lit*) atmosphere, vivid imagery; (*pl*) coloured badge as mark of party, school *etc*; coloured shirt worn by jockey to indicate owner of horse; (*pl*) flag of ship or regiment; (*pl*) (*fig*) party, opinions; **change c.** grow pale or red; **get one's colours** (*sport*) get into team, crew *etc*; **join the colours** enlist; **local c.** vivid and authentic detail (in literary work); **off c.** unwell; **with flying colours** triumphantly ~ **colour** *v/t* and *i* paint, stain, dye; (*fig*) distort, exaggerate; influence deeply; become coloured; flush; (*of fruit*) show ripeness ~ **colour** *adj* of or in colour; pertaining to coloured peoples or their relationship with white peoples.

colourable [*kule*Rab'l] *adj* plausible, specious ~ **colourableness** *n* ~ **colourably** *adv*.

colour-bar [*kuler*-baar] *n* discrimination against persons with coloured skins, *esp* Negroes.

colourblind [*kuler*blInd] *adj* unable to distinguish colours > PDP ~ **colourblindness** *n*.

colour-company [*kuler*-kumpani] *n* (*mil*) company carrying the flag of a battalion.

coloured [*kuler*d] *adj* having a colour or colours; belonging to a dark-skinned group, *esp* Negro; having both Negro and white parents or ancestors; (*fig*) distorted; influenced.

colourful [*kuler*ful] *adj* brightly coloured; (*fig*) vivid, gay ~ **colourfully** *adv* ~ **colourfulness** *n*.

colouring [*kule*Ring] *n* substance applied to give colour; the manner or effect of its application; complexion; (*fig*) aspect, appearance.

colourist [*kule*Rist] *n* one skilled in the artistic use of colour ~ **colouristic** *adj*.

colourless [*kuler*les] *adj* without colour; pale (of complexion); (*fig*) dull, insipid, drab ~ **colourlessly** *adv*.

colourman [*kuler*man] *n* one who sells paints.

colour-sergeant [*kuler*-saarjant] *n* senior sergeant of a colour-company.

colourtype [*kuler*tIp] *n* printing process for reproducing paintings *etc* by three-colour blocks.

colporteur [*kol*pawrter] *n* hawker of books.

colt (1) [*kOlt*] *n* young horse; inexperienced youth; professional cricketer in his first season.

colt (2) *n* early American type of revolver.

colter see **coulter**.

coltish [*kOlt*ish] *adj* frisky, high-spirited; inexperienced ~ **coltishly** *adv* ~ **coltishness** *n*.

coltsfoot [*kOlts*foot] *n* plant with yellow flowers, the leaves of which are used medicinally.

columbarium [kolum*bair*Ri-um] *n* a dovecot; a place for cremation urns; (*bui*) hole in wall for the end of a beam.

columbine [*ko*lumbIn] *n* a herbaceous, perennial plant.

column [*kolum*] *n* (*archi*) pillar, tall shaft or support > PDE; any tall, slender, upright mass; vertical division of page of print; regular feature article in newspaper; set of figures grouped in short lines; (*mil*) formation of troops so that there are more in depth than in breadth; **dodge the c.** (*coll*) shirk, evade duty.

columnar [ko*lum*ner] *adj* shaped like a column.

columned [*kolum*d] *adj* having columns.

columnist [*kolum*ist] *n* writer regularly contributing an article of special interest to a paper or magazine.

colza [*kol*za] *n* rape-seed; rape-oil.

coma (1) [*kO*ma] *n* (*med*) state of deep unconsciousness, caused by injury or disease.

coma (2) *n* (*astron*) nebulous envelope round nucleus of comet; (*bot*) tuft of silky hairs.

comatose [*kO*matOs] *adj* in a state of coma; drowsy, lethargic.

comb [*kOm*] *n* toothed instrument for unravelling and adjusting the hair, or holding it in place; similar instrument for dressing wool, flax *etc*; crest of a cock; group of wax cells built by bees or wasps ~ **comb** *v/t* and *i* separate, adjust, or cleanse (hair, wool *etc*) with a comb; (*fig*) search minutely and systematically; **c. out** disentangle; select carefully.

combat [*kombat/kumbat*] *n* fight, battle ~ **combat** (*pres/part* **combating**, *p/t* and *p/part* **combated**) [kum*bat*] *v/t* and *i* fight against, oppose; fight, struggle.

combatant [*kombatant/kumbatant*] *n* and *adj* (person) taking active part in fighting.

combative [*kombativ/kumbativ*] *adj* pugnacious ~ **combatively** *adv* ~ **combativeness** *n*.

combe see **coomb**.

comber (1) [*kOmer*] *n* one who combs; machine for combing wool *etc*; long curling wave breaking on beach.

comber (2) *n* sea-perch; variety of wrasse.

combinable [kom*bIn*ab'l] *adj* capable of combining, or of being combined.

combination [kombi*nay*shon] *n* act or process of joining together; state of being joined; league, alliance, partnership; (*math*) selection of a specified number of different objects from some larger specified number > PDS; series of movements required to open the lock of a safe; (*pl*) one-piece under-garment combining vest and drawers; **motor-cycle c.** motor-cycle with side-car; **c. room** Fellows' common-room at Cambridge University ~ **combinational** *adj*.

combinative [*kombinativ*] *adj* connected with, occurring as a result of, combination.

combine [*kombIn*] *n* alliance of persons or trading companies to further their joint interests; mechanical harvester which reaps, threshes, and bags the corn ~ **combine** [*kumbIn*] *v/t* and *i* cause to unite, join together; come together, mix, coalesce; **combined operations** (*mil*) operations in which land, sea, and air forces act under a single command ~ **combiner** *n*.

combings [*kOmings*] *n* (*pl*) hair brought out by a comb.

combo [*kombO*] *n* (*sl*) small group of jazz or pop musicians.

combustibility [*kombustibiliti*] *n* quality of being combustible.

combustible [*kombustib'l*] *adj* liable to catch fire; (*fig*) excitable ~ **combustible** *n* inflammable material ~ **combustibly** *adv* ~ **combustibleness** *n*.

combustion [*kombustshon*] *n* process of burning; bursting into flame.

come (*p/t* came, *p /pt* come) [*kum*] *v/i* approach, move towards; arrive, appear; happen; be derived from; be caused by; become; (*coll*) play the part of; (*vulg*) experience orgasm; **c. !** (*exclam*) expressing annoyance, reproof *etc*; **c. about** happen; (*naut*) change tack; **c. across** meet or find by chance; (*sl*) hand over; lend; **c. along** hurry, make haste; **c. at** reach; attack; **c. away** break off; **c. back** return; (*sl*) retort; **c. between** cause estrangement, separate; **c. by** obtain; **c. clean** (*sl*) confess; **c. down** lose wealth, social position *etc*; be handed down; descend; (*coll*) pay, subscribe; **c. down on** blame, scold; **c. down with** fall ill of; **c. forward** offer help, services *etc*; volunteer; **c. in** enter; arrive; become fashionable; **c. in for** (*coll*) get; incur; **c. into** inherit; **c. off** succeed; happen, take place; become unfastened or detached; **c. off it!** (*coll exclam*) stop pretending!; **c. on** make progress; advance; meet or find by chance; (*of pain*) begin; (*theat*) make an entrance; **c. on!** (*exclam*) hurry up!; please!; **c. out** be revealed, become known, be published; make one's first appearance in society; go on strike; **c. out with** blurt out; **c. over** feel (impulse, illness *etc*); convey one's meaning, produce an impression; **c. round** recover; be reconciled; (*coll*) cajole, wheedle; (*coll*) visit informally; **c. through** survive; make an impression; succeed; **c. to** regain consciousness; amount to; (*naut*) come to a standstill; **c. to oneself** recover self-control or consciousness; **c. under** be included under; be under authority of; **c. up** arise; be mentioned; appear above ground; come to university or capital; **c. up to** equal; **c. up with** catch up, draw level; produce (an idea); **c. upon** find or meet by chance.

come-at-able [kum-*at*-ab'l] *adj* accessible.

comeback [*kumbak*] *n* (*coll*) return to former position after retirement or failure; (*coll*) retort.

comedian [*komeedi*-an] *n* entertainer who tells jokes, sings comic songs *etc*; actor in comic parts or in comedies; (*fig*) one who tries to amuse; (*pej*) ridiculous person; one who plays the fool.

comedienne [komeedi-*en*] *n* female comedian.

comedown [*kum*down] *n* change for the worse, humiliation.

comedy [*komidi*] *n* amusing play, in which humour springs from character and situation rather than farcical events; branch of drama comprising such plays; similarly gay or amusing incident in real life.

come-hither [kum-*hiTHer*] *adj* (*coll*) deliberately alluring.

comely [*kumli*] *adj* of agreeable appearance ~ **comeliness** *n*.

comestible [ku*mestib'l*] *adj* edible ~ **comestible** *n* (*usu pl*) food.

comet [*komit*] *n* heavenly body consisting of a hazy gaseous cloud containing a brighter nucleus and a fainter tail ~ **cometary** *adj*.

come-uppance [kum-*upens*] *n* (*coll*) well-deserved defeat or downfall.

comfit [*kumfit*] *n* a sweetmeat.

comfort [*kumfert*] *n* consolation, encouragement (in grief, fear *etc*); person or thing that consoles or encourages; freedom from pain, well-being; freedom from want, pleasant conditions of life, prosperity; (*pl*) things which bring bodily ease; **c. station** (*US*) public lavatory ~ **comfort** *v/t* console, encourage.

comfortable [*kumfertab'l*] *adj* affording comfort; enjoying comfort; having sufficient (money) for one's needs ~ **comfortably** *adv*.

comforter [*kumferter*] *n* one who or that which comforts; the Holy Spirit; long woollen scarf; quilted bed-cover; baby's dummy, teat; **Job's c.** one who professes to console, but actually discourages.

comfortless [*kumfertles*] *adj* devoid of physical comfort, dreary, cheerless; inconsolable.

comfrey [*kumfRi*] *n* plant of the borage family.

comfy [*kumfi*] *adj* (*coll*) comfortable.

comic [*komik*] *adj* causing laughter; intended to amuse; pertaining to comedy ~ **comic** *n* (*coll*) variety comedian; paper consisting mainly of strip-cartoon serials.

comical [*komikal*] *adj* humorous; provoking laughter; ludicrous ~ **comically** *adv*.

comicality [komi*kaliti*] *n* quality of being comic.

comic-strip [komik-*stRip*] *n* humorous serial cartoon in newspaper.

Cominform [*kominfawrm*] *n* the Communist Information Bureau.

coming [*kuming*] *adj* approaching; future; showing promise; likely to become important ~ **coming** *n* approach; arrival; **Second C.** Christ's return at the end of the world.

Comintern [*kominturn*] *n* the Communist International, dissolved in 1943.

comity [*komiti*] *n* courtesy, civility; **c. of nations** nations on friendly terms with each other.

comma [*koma*] *n* punctuation mark (,) indicating the slightest degree of separation between words, phrases, or clauses; (*mus*) an enharmonic interval; **inverted commas** punctuation marks (' ') or (" ") enclosing quoted words.

command [*komaand*] *v/t* and *i* have authority over; order, bid; compel; control; (*mil*) dominate a position; (*fig*) overlook from a height; be sold for; have leadership or supreme power ~ **com-**

mand *n* authority, rule; control; order given; (*mil*) body of men, or area, under one's authority; dominating position; area dominated or held; subsection of Royal Air Force; **High C.** general staff of army; **c. performance** theatrical performance given by royal command.

commandant [koman*dant*] *n* commanding officer, *esp* military governor of fortress or town.

commandeer [koman*deer*] *v/t* seize for military use; (*coll*) take for one's own use.

commander [ko*maan*der] *n* one holding authority; officer in command of military force; officer in Royal Navy between ranks of lieutenant-commander and captain.

commanding [ko*maan*ding] *adj* possessing control; impressive, dignified; giving an extensive view ~ **commandingly** *adv*.

commandment [ko*maand*ment] *n* order, command, decree; **Ten Commandments** (*OT*) laws proclaimed by Moses on Mount Sinai.

commando [ko*maand*O] *n* (*mil*) military raiding force; member of such a force.

commemorate [ko*mem*eRayt] *v/t* call to remembrance, *esp* by some solemn ceremony or memorial; honour the memory of.

commemoration [komeme*Ray*shon] *n* act of commemorating; ceremony or function to honour the memory of some person or event ~ **commemorative** [ko*mem*eRativ] *adj*.

commence [ko*mens*] *v/t* and *i* begin, start.

commencement [ko*mens*ment] *n* beginning.

commend [ko*mend*] *v/t* praise; recommend; entrust (to the protection of); (*refl*) make favourable impression.

commendable [ko*mend*ab'l] *adj* praiseworthy ~ **commendably** *adv*.

commendation [komen*day*shon] *n* praise.

commendatory [ko*mend*atoRi] *adj* expressing praise.

commensurable [ko*mens*heRab'l] *adj* measurable by the same standard; (*of numbers*) having a common factor ~ **commensurability** [komenshe*Ra*biliti] *n* ~ **commensurably** *adv*.

commensurate [ko*mens*heRit] *adj* of equal extent or magnitude; proportionate; in accordance.

comment [*kom*ent] *n* brief expression of opinion, remark; explanatory editorial note on a text ~ **comment** *v/i*.

commentary [*kom*entaRi] *n* collection of critical comments on a text; **running c.** uninterrupted series of remarks describing an event as it is occurring.

commentate [*kom*entayt] *v/t* and *i* make comments on; (*rad*) give a running commentary on ~ **commentation** [komen*tay*shon] *n*.

commentator [*kom*entayter] *n* one who commentates, *esp* a broadcaster of a running commentary.

commerce [*kom*ers] *n* interchange of goods; trading; dealings in general, intercourse; **Chamber of C.** organization to promote and regulate trade in a district.

commercial [ko*mur*shal] *adj* relating to trade or business; organized for profit; designed for, used in trade; supported by fees charged to advertisers; **c. traveller** agent sent by wholesale manufacturer to obtain orders from retailers or from con-

sumers ~ **commercial** *n* (*coll*) television advertisement; commercial traveller.

commercialism [ko*mur*shalizm] *n* exclusive preoccupation with financial profit; business idiom or practice ~ **commercialist** *n*.

commercialize [ko*mur*shalIz] *v/t* put on a business basis; put on the market; make a mere matter of profit.

commercially [ko*mur*shali] *adv* in a commercial way.

commie [*kom*i] *n* and *adj* (*coll abbr*) communist.

commination [komi*nay*shon] *n* threatening, *esp* with Divine vengeance ~ **comminatory** *adj*.

commingle [ko*ming*g'l] *v/t* and *i* mix together.

comminute [*kom*inewt] *v/t* crush to splinters.

commiserate [ko*mize*Rayt] *v/t* and *i* express sympathy, condole with, pity ~ **commiseration** [komize*Ray*shon] *n* ~ **commiserative** *adj*.

commissar [komi*saar*] *n* Soviet state official.

commissariat [komi*sairR*i-at] *n* (*mil*) department responsible for supply of food; food-supply; department of Soviet civil service.

commissary [*kom*isaRi] *n* delegate, deputy; (*US*) supply store; canteen.

commission [ko*mish*on] *n* act of committing; warrant conferring authority, *esp* on officer of armed forces; body of persons empowered to hold an inquiry and issue a report; piece of work entrusted to or requested from someone; authority to act as agent, *esp* in trade; percentage taken in payment for so acting; **c. agent** bookmaker; **in c.** (*naut*) ready for sea; (*of office etc*) delegated to ~ **commission** *v/t* grant or delegate authority to; appoint as one's representative; give an order to or for; (*naut*) authorize officer to prepare ship for sea ~ **commissional** *adj*.

commissionaire [komishon*air*] *n* uniformed doorkeeper of hotel, shop, offices *etc*.

commission-day [ko*mish*on-day] *n* opening day of assizes.

commissioned [ko*mish*ond] *adj* authorized; (*mil*) (*of officer*) holding a commission.

commissioner [ko*mish*oner] *n* one appointed by commission; member of a commission; former high official of Indian Civil Service; local governor of certain colonies; **High C.** chief representative in England of a self-governing British Dominion.

commissure [*kom*isewr] *n* (*anat*) juncture.

commit (*pres/part* **committing**, *p/t* and *p/part* **committed**) [ko*mit*] *v/t* perform, perpetrate (a bad action); entrust, hand over; give into charge of, consign; (*leg*) send to prison; send for trial to higher court; (*refl*) pledge, bind oneself.

commitment [ko*mit*ment] *n* act of committing; undertaking to which one is bound; total devotion to a religious, moral, political or social cause or doctrine; financial obligation, liability; responsibility; court order consigning person to prison.

committal [ko*mit*al] *n* act of committing; act of placing a corpse in a grave or crematory oven.

committed [ko*mit*ed] *adj* dedicated, showing moral or social commitment.

committee [ko*mit*ee] *n* group of persons appointed to consider and report on specific questions referred to them; governing body of club.

committee-man [ko*mit*ee-man] *n* a member of a committee; one addicted to committees.

committee-room [komitee-Room] *n* room in which a committee meets.

commixture [komikscher] *n* act of mixing; state of being mixed; solution or compound formed by mixing.

commode [komOd] *n* chamberpot enclosed in chair-like frame; movable washstand; chest of drawers.

commodious [komOdi-us] *adj* roomy, spacious ~ **commodiously** *adv* ~ **commodiousness** *n*.

commodity [komoditi] *n* article of commerce, merchandise; (*pl*) (*econ*) agricultural products and minerals.

commodore [komodawr] *n* (*naut*) officer in command, ranking between captain and rear-admiral; senior captain in merchant-fleet; president of yacht club; R.A.F. officer ranking between Group Captain and Air Vice-Marshal.

common [komun] *adj* shared by two or more; accessible to, related to, performed by or characteristic of all members of a group; public; widespread, usual, plentiful; average, ordinary; lowclass, vulgar; badly made, shoddy; in bad taste; (*math*) standing in same relationship to two or more quantities; **c. ground** facts, views *etc* shared by both parties in a dispute; **c. law** body of unwritten laws; **c. noun** (*gramm*) name applicable to any member of a group; **c. pleas** civil actions at law; **c. room** living-room shared at a school or college; **c. sense** practical intelligence, sagacity ~ **common** *n* unenclosed tract of land open to the public.

commonage [komonij] *n* right of pasturing animals on common land.

commonalty, commonality [komonalti, komunaliti] *n* the common people, ordinary citizens.

commoner [komoner] *n* one of the common people; one without hereditary rank; Oxford undergraduate without a college grant; one who has rights in common lands.

commonly [komonli] *adv* usually.

commonness [komon-nes] *n* quality of being common; vulgarity, low-class manners *etc*.

commonplace [komonplays] *n* a trite remark, truism, platitude ~ **commonplace** *adj* ordinary, usual, trite ~ **commonplaceness** *n*.

commonplace-book [komonplays-book] *n* notebook for quotations, passages of interest *etc*.

commons [komunz] *n* (*pl*) the common people, below the nobles in rank; the commonalty; members of the House of Commons; allowance of food, rations; **short c.** insufficient food.

commonweal [komonweel] *n* general good of the community; whole body of the people.

commonwealth [komonwelth] *n* whole body of people comprising a democratic state; protectorate under Cromwell; Federated States of Australia; (*cap*) group of self-governing territories formerly British colonies or dominions > PDPol.

commotion [komOshon] *n* agitation, disturbance; tumult, uprising.

communal [komewnal] *adj* owned in common; public; relating to a community or commune.

communalism [komewnalizm] *n* system of government in which power is delegated to local communes ~ **communalist** *n* and *adj*.

communally [komewnali] *adv* in a communal way.

commune (1) [komewn] *n* group of people living together and sharing resources while pursuing a common moral or social aim; (*in France*) territorial division governed by mayor and municipal council; revolutionary government of Paris in 1792 and 1871.

commune (2) [komewn] *v/i* talk intimately with; meditate, have spiritual contact with; (*US*) receive Holy Communion.

communicable [komewnikab'l] *adj* capable of being imparted, shared, or transmitted ~ **communicability** [komewnikabiliti] *n* ~ **communicably** *adv*.

communicant [komewnikant] *n* one who receives Holy Communion; one who gives information ~ **communicant** *adj* communicating, linking.

communicate [komewnikayt] *v/t* and *i* impart, transmit; give or exchange messages, information *etc*; be connected with, open into; receive Holy Communion.

communication [komewnikayshon] *n* transmission, imparting; giving of information, messages *etc*; message, written information; means of communicating; (*pl*) system of transmitting messages; (*pl*) (*mil*) all means of contact between an army and its base; **c. cord** cord in railway carriage by which a passenger can stop the train in an emergency; **c. satellite** artificial earth satellite used for relaying radio or television signals round the earth's curved surface.

communicative [komewnikativ] *adj* ready or eager to communicate ~ **communicativeness** *n*.

communicator [komewnikaytor] *n* person or thing that communicates ~ **communicatory** *adj*.

communion [komewnyon] *n* fellowship, intimate relationship; mutual relationship based on shared beliefs, *esp* religious doctrines; organized and homogeneous religious group; (Holy) **C.** celebration of the Eucharist; receiving of the Eucharist.

communiqué [komewnikay] *n* an official report or bulletin.

communism [komewnizm] *n* theory that all property should be vested in the community, each individual receiving according to his needs and working according to his capacity; revolutionary movement seeking to establish the dictatorship of the proletariat; the governmental system of the Soviet Union and other states that follow the teachings of Karl Marx; (*coll*) sympathy with the policies of these states > PDPol ~ **communist** *n* and *adj*.

communistic [komewnistik] *adj* of, like, or sympathizing with communism.

community [komewniti] *n* society of people linked together by common conditions of life, beliefs *etc* or organized under one authority; (*bot, zool*) a group of plants or animals growing together in natural conditions and found inhabiting a restricted area; all members of a State, the public; group of nations having purposes or interests in common; ownership in common; **c. singing** singing in which all present join.

communization [komewnIzayshon] *n* process of communizing; state of being communized.

151

communize [*kom*ewnIz] *v/t* transfer to public ownership; convert to communism; impose communist government on.

commutable [*kom*ewtab'l] *adj* capable of being commuted ~ **commutability** [komewt*abi*liti] *n*.

commutate [*kom*ewtayt] *v/t* (*elect*) commute.

commutation [komewt*ay*shon] *n* act of commuting ~ **commutative** [*kom*ewtativ] *adj*.

commutator [*kom*ewtayter] *n* device for altering or reversing the direction of an electric current.

commute [*kom*ewt] *v/t* and *i* exchange, substitute; change; (*leg*) reduce a sentence; (*elect*) regulate direction of current; (*coll*) travel daily to and from work by train, bus or car.

commuter [*kom*ewter] *n* (*coll*) one who travels daily to work, *esp* season-ticket holder; **c. belt** area round a city from which commuters travel to it.

comose [*kO*mOs] *adj* (*bot*) hairy.

compact (1) [*kom*pakt] *n* bargain, agreement.

compact (2) [kom*pakt*] *adj* fitting into small space; dense; tightly packed; (*fig*) concise, terse ~ **compact** *v/t* compress, join closely together.

compact (3) [*kom*pakt] *n* small case for face-powder.

compacted [kom*pak*tid] *adj* compressed, caked together.

compaction [kom*pak*shon] *n* compressing (of soil *etc*) into a hard, dense mass.

compactly [kom*pakt*li] *adv* so as to fit in a small space.

compactness [kom*pakt*nis] *n* quality of being compact.

companion (1) [kom*pan*yun] *n* associate, friend; fellow-traveller; cheerful, friendly person; person hired to relieve the loneliness of another; member of lowest grade of order of knighthood; instructive book, guide; one object in a pair ~ **companion** *adj* matching, forming a pair ~ **companion** *v/t* be a companion to, accompany.

companion (2) *n* (*naut*) framing or skylight on quarter-deck; hood covering stairway; **c. hatch** opening leading from deck to cabins below; **c. ladder** ladder to quarter eck; staircase from deck to cabin; **c. way** staircase to cabin.

companionable [kom*pan*yunab'l] *adj* sociable, easy to get on with ~ **companionably** *adv* ~ **companionableness** *n*.

companionship [kom*pan*yunshup] *n* friendly company, fellowship; body of companions; (*print*) group of compositors working together.

company [*kum*pani] *n* group of persons in friendly association; (*coll*) guests, visitors; companionship, fellowship; qualities which make one a pleasing companion; group of business associates; ship's crew; actors working under one management; (*mil*) subdivision of a battalion; **good** (**poor**) **c.** a pleasant (dull) companion; **keep c. with** associate habitually with; **part c.** separate, disagree.

comparable [*kom*paRab'l] *adj* capable of being compared; similar; worthy of comparison ~ **comparably** *adv*.

comparative [kom*pa*Rativ] *adj* based on, or involving, comparison; relative; moderate; **c. degree** (*gramm*) the form of an adjective or adverb expressing a higher degree of the quality denoted by the positive ~ **comparatively** *adv*.

compare [kom*pair*] *v/t* and *i* examine similarities and differences between two or more objects; declare (an object) to be like another; (*gramm*) (of *adj* or *adv*) give the degrees of comparison of; resemble; be worthy of comparison ~ **compare** *n* (*rare*) comparison.

comparison [kom*pa*Rison] *n* act of comparing; possibility of comparison; degree of similarity; an expression or simile which compares two or more things; **degrees of c.** (*gramm*) positive, comparative, and superlative forms.

compartment [kom*paart*ment] *n* subdivision partitioned off from the whole; sub-section of railway carriage.

compartmentalize [kompaart*mental*iz] *v/t* divide into sections; separate rigidly.

compass [*kum*pas] *n* instrument to find direction by a magnetized needle pointing to the magnetic north > PDS; instrument with two hinged legs, used for drawing circles or taking measurements (also *pl*); circumference, boundary; (*fig*) range, scope, limit; (*mus*) range of voice or instrument > PDM ~ **compass** *v/t* go round, surround, enclose; scheme for, plot; achieve, attain.

compassing [*kum*pasing] *adj* surrounding; achieving.

compassion [kom*pa*shon] *n* sympathy, pity.

compassionate [kom*pa*shonit] *adj* feeling pity; showing mercy; granted without legal obligation, for motives of compassion ~ **compassionate** [kom*pa*shonayt] *v/t* take pity on ~ **compassionately** *adv* ~ **compassionateness** *n*.

compass-plane [*kum*pas-playn] *n* (*carp*) a metal plane with an adjustable curved underside.

compass-saw [*kum*pas-saw] *n* tapered hand saw.

compass-window [*kum*pas-windO] *n* circular bay window.

compatibility [kompatib*i*liti] *n* state or quality of being compatible; (*med, biol*) capacity of tissue, blood *etc* to be introduced into a living body without causing destructive reaction; (*TV*) capacity to be received in both colour and monochrome; (*ac*) capacity to be received both stereophonically and monophonically.

compatible [kom*pat*ib'l] *adj* capable of existing together; consistent, in agreement with; suitable; able to live happily with (a person) ~ **compatibly** *adv*.

compatriot [kom*pat*Ri-ot] *n* fellow-countryman.

compeer [kom*peer*/*kom*peer] *n* one of equal rank.

compel (*pres/part* **compelling**, *p/t* and *p/part* **compelled**) [kom*pel*] *v/t* and *i* make (person) do something; bring about by force; enforce respect or attention ~ **compelling** *adj* irresistible.

compendious [kom*pend*i-us] *adj* comprehensive and concise ~ **compendiously** *adv* ~ **compendiousness** *n*.

compendium (*pl* **compendiums, compendia**) [kom*pend*i-um] *n* comprehensive summary.

compensate [*kom*pensayt] *v/t* and *i* make amends for loss or injury, *esp* by money payment; make up for, counterbalance; (*mech*) counteract a variation; (*psych*) disguise defect by exaggerating some other characteristic.

compensation [kompens*ay*shon] *n* act of compensating; sum given to make up for injury *etc*; (*psych*) mechanism whereby a defect is disguised by exaggerating some other characteristic > PDP ~ **compensational** *adj* as compensation.

compensative [kom*p*ensativ] *adj* compensatory.

compensatory [kom*p*ensateRi] *adj* designed to compensate; that compensates.

compère [*kom*pair] *n* person introducing the turns in a variety show ~ compère *v/t* and *i*.

compete [kom*p*eet] *v/i* pit oneself against others to gain some end; take part (in contest); rival, challenge comparison with.

competence [*kom*pitens] *n* ability, efficiency; money or means for one's livelihood; (*leg*) legal capacity.

competency [*kom*pitensi] *n* competence.

competent [*kom*pitent] *adj* efficient, capable; properly qualified; (*leg*) legally qualified; with authority to act; (*of witness, evidence*) admissible ~ competently *adv*.

competition [kompi*ti*shon] *n* act of competing, rivalry; contest for a prize; test of skill.

competitive [kom*p*etitiv] *adj* based on, by means of, competition ~ competitively *adv*.

competitor [kom*p*etiter] *n* one who competes.

compilation [kompi*lay*shon] *n* act or process of compiling; book composed of material gathered from others.

compile [kom*p*Il] *v/t* put together (literary work) out of materials from various sources; (*cricket*) score (many runs).

complacence [kom*play*sens] *n* complacency.

complacency [kom*play*sensi] *n* unruffled self-satisfaction.

complacent [kom*play*sent] *adj* self-satisfied.

complain [kom*p*layn] *v/i* express discontent or pain, find fault, grumble; state a grievance, make a formal accusation; (*rare*) make mournful sounds.

complainant [kom*p*laynant] *n* (*leg*) plaintiff.

complaint [kom*p*lavnt] *n* expression of grief or discontent, fault-finding; cause of discontent, grievance; illness; (*leg*) formal accusation.

complaisance [kompli*zans*/kum*p*layzans] *n* readiness to fall in with others' wishes, easy-going nature; courtesy.

complaisant [*kom*plizant/kum*p*layzant] *adj* ready to fall in with the wishes of others, obliging.

complement [*kom*pliment] *n* that which completes; number required to complete a company, crew *etc*; each of two parts which complete each other; (*math*) angle added to another to make 90°; (*mus*) interval added to another to make an octave; (*gramm*) word or words added to predicate to complete the sense ~ complement *v/t* make complete ~ complemental [kompli*men*tal] *adj*.

complementary [kompli*men*taRi] *adj* completing, making up a whole; c. angles (*math*) angles together totalling 90°; c. colours pairs of colours which when combined give the effect of white.

complete [kom*p*leet] *adj* entire, whole; brought to an end, brought to perfection; (*coll*) perfect, absolute, utter ~ complete *v/t* bring to an end, finish; make whole or perfect ~ completely *adv* ~ completeness *n*.

completion [kom*p*leeshon] *n* act or process of making complete; condition of being completed; fulfilment, accomplishment.

complex [*kom*pleks] *adj* consisting of several closely connected parts; complicated, intricate; involved; (*fig*) hard to understand; c. sentence (*gramm*) sentence containing one or more subordinate clauses; c. number (*math*) number con-

sisting of real numbers combined with the square root of − 1 > PDS ~ complex *n* a complexity; a whole made of many closely connected parts; group of associated buildings; (*psych*) group of repressed ideas or emotions in conflict with others already accepted > PDP; group of associated ideas; (*coll*) neurotic or obsessional feeling ~ complexly *adv*.

complexion [kom*plek*shon] *n* natural colouring of the face; (*fig*) appearance, outlook ~ complexional *adj*.

complexity [kom*plek*siti] *n* state of being complex or complicated; intricacy.

compliance [kom*p*lI-ans] *n* disposition to give in to others; act of yielding; in c. with in obedience to ~ compliancy *n* complaisance.

compliant [kom*p*lI-ant] *adj* yielding, complying, submissive ~ compliantly *adv*.

complicate [*kom*plikayt] *v/t* make more difficult, intricate, or complex ~ complicate *adj* (*biol*, *bot*) folded lengthwise.

complicated [*kom*plikaytid] *adj* intricate, complex, difficult.

complication [kompli*kay*shon] *n* state of being complicated, intricacy, tangle; act of complicating; that which complicates, difficulty; (*med*) fresh element or symptom arising during illness and rendering treatment more difficult.

complicity [kom*p*lisiti] *n* state of being an accomplice in some wrongful action.

compliment [kom*p*liment] *n* expression of admiration, praise; polite action; (*pl*) polite or formal greeting, expression of good wishes ~ compliment [kom*p*liment] *v/t*.

complimentary [kompli*men*taRi] *adj* full of praise, flattering; given as an expression of regard; free of charge.

compline [*kom*plin] *n* (*eccles*) last service of the day.

comply [kom*p*lI] *v/i* act in accordance (with request *etc*), give way, yield.

compo [*kom*pO] *n* (*bui*) cement-lime mortar.

component [kom*p*Onent] *adj* forming part of a whole, constituent ~ component *n* one part in the composition of a whole; single part of a machine, *esp* of a car.

comport [kom*p*awrt] *v/refl* and *i* behave, conduct oneself; be consistent; be appropriate.

compose [kom*p*Oz] *v/t* and *i* constitute, form, make up; settle, reconcile; create an original work (in literature or music); plan out, design (a picture); (*print*) set up (copy) in type; set up (type); restore to calmness; arrange in suitable position or order, re-adjust ~ composed *adj* formed by composing; calm, tranquil ~ composedly *adv* ~ composedness *n*.

composer [kom*p*Ozer] *n* one who composes music.

composing-frame [kom*p*Ozing-fRaym] *n* (*print*) frame holding type-cases.

composing-stick [kom*p*Ozing-stik] *n* (*print*) tray of adjustable width in which type is set up in lines.

composite [*kom*pozit] *adj* made up of various distinct parts; (*bot*) having flower head composed of many clustered florets; (*math*) divisible into two or more numbers other than one; (*phot*) formed by superimposed images; (*archi*) blending various styles ~ composite *n* thing made up of distinct

composition–concave

parts; (*bot*) composite flower; **c. board** plywood or hardboard with an insulating sheet.

composition [kompo*zishon*] *n* act of putting together or combining; act of composing (literary work or music); piece of music composed; essay, *esp* if written as school exercise; arrangement of elements in painting; compound of substances; (*fig*) character; (*leg*) agreement to come to terms, settlement; partial settlement of debts; compromise; (*print*) setting-up of type.

compositor [kompo*ziter*] *n* (*print*) skilled craftsman who sets up type.

compost [*kompost*] *n* a fertilizing mixture of leaf mould, soil and manure *etc* ~ **compost** *v/t*.

composure [kompo*zher*] *n* calmness; unruffled demeanour.

compote [*kompOt*] *n* stewed fruit in syrup.

compound (1) [kompo*wnd*] *v/t* and *i* put together various parts to form a composite whole, make a mixture; make more difficult, worsen, aggravate; multiply, increase; (*chem*) unite elements into a substance; settle by agreement or compromise; settle by payment of a lump sum; make partial payment (of debts); (*leg*) forbear to prosecute, in return for money ~ **compound** [*kom*pownd] *adj* made of various parts; **c. fracture** (*surg*) broken bone exposed through a flesh wound; **c. householder** householder whose rates are included in the rent; **c. interest** interest on interest accruing from capital; **c. quantity** (*math*) quantity made up of simple quantities connected by a mathematical sign; **c. sentence** sentence made of two or more coordinate main clauses; **c. word** word made up of two or more words ~ **compound** *n* anything composed of distinct parts; (*chem*) substance consisting of chemically united elements > PDS.

compound (2) [*kom*pownd] *n* enclosed space round building.

compounder [kompo*wnder*] *n* one who compounds for a debt; one who compounds a felony or offence.

comprehend [kompR*ihend*] *v/t* understand; contain, include.

comprehensible [kompR*ihens*ib'l] *adj* capable of being understood ~ **comprehensibility** [kompR*ihensibiliti*] *n* ~ **comprehensibly** *adv*.

comprehension [kompR*ihenshon*] *n* mental grasp, understanding; inclusion; exercise designed to test pupil's understanding of written English.

comprehensive [kompR*ihensiv*] *adj* including a great deal, wide in scope; **c. school** large school providing all types of secondary education ~ **comprehensively** *adv* ~ **comprehensiveness** *n*.

compress [kompR*es*] *v/t* put pressure on, squeeze together; crush into smaller space; concentrate ~ **compress** [*kom*pRes] *n* (*surg*) soft pad to maintain pressure upon an artery *etc*; wet bandage applied to inflamed area.

compressed [kompR*est*] *adj* pressed closely together, flattened; reduced in size or volume; (*fig*) terse, concise.

compressible [kompR*esib*'l] *adj* that can be compressed ~ **compressibility** [kompR*esibiliti*] *n*.

compression [kompR*eshon*] *n* act of compressing;

state of being compressed; (*fig*) conciseness, concentration; (*mot*) efficiency of piston rings in holding gas while compressed; **c. ratio** (*mot*) ratio of volume of cylinder to volume of its gases after compression.

compressive [kompR*esiv*] *adj* that compresses.

compressor [kompR*eser*] *n* anything used to compress; (*eng*) pump for raising the pressure of a gas.

comprise [kompR*Iz*] *v/t* contain, consist of.

compromise [*kom*pRomIz] *n* settlement of dispute by concessions on both sides; middle course between incompatible claims ~ **compromise** *v/i* and *t* reach settlement by mutual concessions; take middle course; lay open to danger or suspicion; (*refl*) endanger one's reputation.

comptometer [kompto*miter*] *n* calculating machine.

comptroller [kon*tROler*] *n* (*ar*) controller.

compulsion [kompu*lshon*] *n* act of compelling, coercion; (*psych*) force driving a person to perform an act without, or against, his conscious will > PDP.

compulsive [kompu*lsiv*] *adj* compelling; done under compulsion, *esp* of obsessions ~ **compulsively** *adv* ~ **compulsiveness** *n*.

compulsory [kompu*lsoRi*] *adj* obligatory; coercive, compelling ~ **compulsorily** *adv*.

compunction [kompu*nkshon*] *n* pricking of conscience, contrition; hesitation, scruple; regret for an act; impulse towards mercy.

compurgation [kompurg*ayshon*] *n* vindication; (*leg hist*) procedure of clearing a man from a charge by the oaths of a number of his neighbours that he was innocent.

computable [kompe*wtab*'l] *adj* capable of being reckoned.

computation [kompewt*ayshon*] *n* process or result of reckoning.

compute [kompe*wt*] *v/t* and *i* reckon, calculate.

computer [kompe*wter*] *n* machine which 'memorizes', sifts, analyses and correlates data, and produces selective information as required > PDEl; one of various simple calculating instruments.

computerize [kompe*wteRIze*] *v/t* calculate or regulate by electronic computer; equip with a computer; prepare for handling by a computer.

comrade [*kom*Rid/*kom*Rayd] *n* friend, companion; mode of address used by Communists; (*coll*) a Communist ~ **comradely** *adj* and *adv*.

comradeship [*kom*Ridship] *n* friendship.

con (1) (*pres/part* **conning**, *p/t* and *p/part* **conned**) [*kon*] *v/t* examine carefully, learn by heart.

con (2) (*pres/part* **conning**, *p/t* and *p/part* **conned**) *v/t* (*naut*) direct course of (a ship).

con (3) *n* (*abbr*) (*sl*) confidence; **c. man** confidence trickster, swindler ~ **con** (*pres/part* **conning**, *p/t* and *p/part* **conned**) *v/t* (*sl*) swindle by winning victim's confidence.

con- *pref* with, together.

conation [kOn*ayshon*] *n* (*philos*) faculty of striving and desiring; (*psych*) mental activity > PDP.

conative [*kOnativ*] *adj* of or by conation.

concatenate [konk*atinayt*] *v/t* link together.

concatenation [konkatin*ayshon*] *n* linked series.

concave [*konk*ayv] *adj* hollowed, curving inwards ∼ **concave** n a curving inwards ∼ **concavely** adv.

concavity [kon*k*aviti] n concave surface; hollow place; inside surface of sphere or vault.

conceal [kon*seel*] v/t hide, keep secret.

concealment [kon*seel*ment] n act of concealment: state of being concealed; a hiding-place.

concede [kon*seed*] v/t and i grant, admit; yield without dispute.

conceit [kon*seet*] n over-high opinion of oneself, vanity; ingenious or quaint figure of speech.

conceited [kon*seetid*] adj holding exaggerated opinion of one's own qualities and importance ∼ **conceitedly** adv.

conceivable [kon*seev*ab'l] adj that can be imagined, possible ∼ **conceivability** n ∼ **conceivableness** n ∼ **conceivably** adv.

conceive [kon*seev*] v/t and i become pregnant with; form in the womb; form in the mind, devise, think out; imagine, suppose.

concentrate [*kon*sentRayt] v/t and i bring together at one centre, cause to converge to one point; bring all one's thought to bear (on); (chem) increase strength of (solution, liquid) by evaporation; (mining) reduce amount of gangue in an ore ∼ **concentrate** n and adj (product) produced by concentrating.

concentration [konsent*R*ayshon] n act of concentrating; state of being concentrated; fixed or intense attention; (chem) amount of substance present in a given space or in a solvent; **c. camp** prison camp for military or political prisoners.

concentric [kon*sent*Rik] adj having the same centre ∼ **concentrically** adv.

concept [*kon*sept] n an abstract or general idea.

conception [kon*sep*shon] n act of conceiving; thing conceived; (physiol) the fertilization of the ovum and the beginning of the growth of the embryo in the womb; imagination, mental creativeness; idea, notion > PDP; plan; **Immaculate C.** doctrine that the Virgin Mary was conceived free from original sin.

conceptive [kon*sep*tiv] adj capable of conceiving.

conceptual [kon*sep*choo-al] adj pertaining to conception or to concepts.

conceptualize [kon*sep*choo-alIz] v/t form concept of.

concern [kon*surn*] v/t relate to, be connected with; be important to, affect; (refl) take interest in, take trouble; (pass) be anxious; be involved in ∼ **concern** n that which affects one; affair, business; responsibility; care, anxiety; a commercial firm.

concerned [kon*surnd*] adj interested, involved; anxious, showing concern.

concerning [kon*surn*ing] prep with relation to, with regard to, about.

concert [*kon*sert] n (mus) entertainment by several players or singers > PDM; concord, agreement; harmony, unison ∼ **concert** [kon*surt*] v/t agree on, plan jointly.

concertante [koncher*tan*tay] n (mus) composition for solo instrument(s) and orchestra > PDM.

concerted [kon*surtid*] adj pre-arranged jointly; (mus) arranged in parts.

concert-grand [*kon*sert-gRand] n large grand piano suitable for public concerts.

concertina [konser*teen*a] n (mus) manual wind instrument consi stingof expanding bellows with hexagonal ends each having studs for the fingers > PDM; (mil) collapsible wire entanglement.

concerto (pl concertos) [kon*chairt*O] n (mus) composition for solo instrument(s) and orchestra > PDM.

concert-pitch [*kon*sert-pich] n (mus) a tuning to a pitch rather higher than usual, used at concerts for brilliancy and effect; (fig) in prime condition.

concession [kon*sesh*on] n act of conceding, yielding, acknowledging; thing conceded; grant of land, trading rights etc.

concessionaire [konsesho*nair*] n holder of official concession.

concessionary [kon*sesh*onaRi] adj by way of a concession ∼ **concessionary** n a concessionaire.

concessive [kon*ses*iv] adj relating to or expressing concession.

conch [konk] n large spiral univalve shell; such a shell used as trumpet; (archi) dome over semi-circular apse; concha.

concha [*konk*a] n a marine shell, conch; (anat) central cavity of the outer ear.

conchologist [kon*k*olojist] n one who studies shells and shellfish; collector of shells.

conchology [kon*k*oloji] n the study of shells or shellfish.

conchy see **conshy.**

concierge [kon*si*-airzh] n janitor; caretaker.

conciliar [kon*sili*-er] adj pertaining to an ecclesiastical council.

conciliate [kon*sili*-ayt] v/t overcome hostility of, placate; (ar) reconcile.

conciliation [konsili-*ay*shon] n act of conciliating; settlement of labour disputes by negotiation; adjustment of differences.

conciliatory [kon*sili*-ateRi] adj trying to overcome hostility or win favour; showing good will, friendly; seeking conciliation.

concise [kon*sIs*] adj clear and brief, to the point, terse ∼ **concisely** adv ∼ **conciseness** n.

concision [kon*sizh*on] n conciseness.

conclave [*kon*-klayv] n (RC) assembly of cardinals met to elect a Pope; (fig) secret discussion.

conclude [kon-*klOOd*] v/t and i finish, bring or come to an end; effect, settle, arrange; draw an inference, arrive at an opinion.

concluding [kon-*klOOd*ing] adj completing, final.

conclusion [kon-*klOO*zhon] n end; termination; final outcome or result; (log) third proposition in a syllogism; final arranging (of treaty etc); **a foregone c.** inevitable outcome; **try conclusions with** pit oneself against.

conclusive [kon*klOO*siv] adj decisive, convincing, final ∼ **conclusively** adv.

concoct [kon-*kokt*] v/t prepare by mixing ingredients; (fig) invent, make up.

concoction [kon-*kok*shon] n a mixture; something made up; unpleasant food, medicine etc.

concomitant [kon-*kom*itant] adj and n accompanying (circumstance) ∼ **concomitantly** adv.

concord [*kon*-kawrd] n agreement, peaceful relationship; (gramm) agreement in person, number, gender and case; (mus) chord which seems harmonically at rest > PDM.

concordance [kon-*kawrd*ans] n agreement; index

of the principal words in a book or used by an author with references and contexts.

concordant [kon-*kawrd*ant] *adj* agreeing, harmonious, consistent ~ **concordantly** *adv*.

concordat [kon-*kawrd*at] *n* (*RC*) formal agreement between Pope and State > PDPol.

concourse [*kon*kawrs] *n* a running or gathering together; crowd of people; broad open space within a building or among buildings.

concrescence [kon-*kRes*ens] *n* (*biol*) a union, a growing together > PDB.

concrete [*kon*kReet] *adj* actual, material, real; formed of matter; specific; (*gramm*) denoting a material object, not abstract; (*bui*) made from concrete; **c. music** composition formed of distortions of recorded sounds > PDM; **c. poetry** poetry using visual typographical devices ~ **concrete** *n* mixture of water, sand, stone and cement, used in building > PDE; **reinforced c.** this mixture strengthened with steel rods or mesh ~ **concrete** [*kon*kReet] *v/t* and *i* form into a mass; become solid; cover with concrete ~ **concretely** *adv* ~ **concreteness** *n*.

concretion [kon-*kRee*shon] *n* growing together into mass; mass so formed; (*med*) stone in the bodily organs ~ **concretional** *adj*.

concretize [*kon*-kRetIz] *v/t* make real or specific; give definite form to.

concubinage [kon-*kew*binij] *n* cohabiting of man and woman not legally married.

concubine [*kon*-kewbIn] *n* woman cohabiting with a man without marriage.

concupiscence [kon-*kew*pisens] *n* lust, sexual desire ~ **concupiscent** *adj*.

concur (*pres*/*part* **concurring**, *p*/*t* and *p*/*part* **concurred**) [kon-*kur*] *v/i* agree, *esp* in opinion; cooperate; meet at one point; coincide ~ **concurrence** *n*.

concurrent [kon-*ku*Rent] *adj* occurring at the same time; agreeing, acting together; converging to a point ~ **concurrent** *n* a concurrent circumstance; a contributory cause ~ **concurrently** *adv* at the same time.

concuss [kon-*kus*] *v/t* strike or shake violently; injure (brain) by concussion; knock out.

concussion [kon-*kush*on] *n* (*med*) injury caused to brain by heavy blow; violent impact or shaking ~ **concussive** *adj*.

concyclic [kon*sI*klik] *adj* (*geom*) lying on the circumference of a circle.

condemn [kon*dem*] *v/t* (*leg*) declare guilty, pass sentence on; blame severely, censure; declare unfit for use; order (building *etc*) to be destroyed; **condemned cell** prison cell for persons sentenced to death ~ **condemnable** *adj*.

condemnation [kondem*nay*shon] *n* act of condemning; state of being condemned; reason for condemning ~ **condemnatory** *adj*.

condensate [*kon*densayt] *n* (*chem*) a product of condensation.

condensation [konden*say*shon] *n* act of condensing; change of vapour into liquid; moisture condensed on to a surface.

condense [kon*dens*] *v/t* and *i* make more dense, compress; become dense; (*chem*) change from vapour to liquid; (*opt*) concentrate, focus; (*elect*) increase or intensify (charge); (*fig*) compress into

few words; **condensed milk** thickened and sweetened evaporated milk.

condenser [kon*dens*er] *n* one who or that which condenses; (*chem*) apparatus in which vapour is reduced to liquid; (*elect*) apparatus for holding static electricity, capacitor; (*opt*) lens used to converge rays of light > PDS.

condescend [kondi*send*] *v/i* deliberately act in a manner below one's station; behave with patronizing kindness; act unworthily, stoop to ~ **condescending** *adj* ~ **condescendingly** *adv*.

condescension [kondi*sen*shon] *n* conscious display of affability to inferiors; a patronizing air.

condign [kon*dIn*] *adj* fitting, deserved ~ **condignly** [kond*In*li] *adv*.

condiment [*kon*diment] *n* strong seasoning.

condition [kon*dish*on] *n* something stipulated, proviso; necessary or determining factor; state of being; state of health or repair; social position; (*pl*) external circumstances, environment; **on c.** provided that ~ **condition** *v/t* stipulate, make conditions; determine; bring into a healthy or required state; purify; (*psych*) cause to acquire determined reflexes in response to certain stimuli; (*coll*) train to accept unquestioningly a previously unwelcome situation or idea.

conditional [kon*dish*onal] *adj* depending on, containing, a condition; provisional, qualified; (*gramm*) expressing a condition ~ **conditionality** [kondishon*ali*ti] *n* ~ **conditionally** *adv*.

conditioned [kon*dish*ond] *adj* subject to conditions; taught to adopt certain beliefs, habits, attitudes *etc*; (*of air*) purified and cooled; **c. reflex** (*psych*) reflex acquired in response to repeated stimuli; **well c.** in good condition.

conditioner [kon*dish*oner] *n* substance which improves healthiness; apparatus which purifies air.

conditioning [kon*dish*oning] *n* (*psych*) extensive modification of responses by acquired reflexes > PDP, PDB.

condole [kon*dOl*] *v/i* express sympathy (with).

condolence [kon*dOl*ens] *n* expression of sympathy with another in sorrow.

condom [*kon*dom] *n* thin rubber sheath for the penis, used as a contraceptive or to prevent venereal infection.

condominium [kond*Omi*ni-um] *n* the common rule of a territory by two or more countries; (*US*) set of luxury apartments with shared amenities such as swimming-pool and sports facilities.

condone [kon*dOn*] *v/t* forgive, overlook (*esp* adultery) ~ **condonation** [kond*Ona*yshon] *n*.

condor [*kon*dawr] *n* large S. American vulture.

condottiere (*pl* **condottieri**) [kondoty*air*Ri] *n* leader of troop of mercenaries.

conduce [kon*dews*] *v/i* tend to produce ~ **conducive** *adj* ~ **conduciveness** *n*.

conduct [*kon*dukt] *n* management, guidance; behaviour; **safe c.** guarantee of safe passage through enemy's territory ~ **conduct** [kon*dukt*] *v/t* direct, manage; guide, lead; (*mus*) direct performers by movements of baton and hand; (*phys*) transmit; (*refl*) behave; **conducted tour** tour of a building, town *etc* with a guide to point out interesting features.

conductance [kon*duk*tans] *n* (*elect*) degree of conductivity, conducting power > PDS.

conductible [kond*u*ktib'l] *adj* (*phys*) capable of conducting or being conducted ∼ **conductibility** [konduktib*i*liti] *n*.

conduction [kond*u*kshon] *n* act of conducting; (*phys*) transmission of heat in a substance by the interaction of molecules; (*physiol*) passage of an excitation through a cell or tissue > PDS, PDB.

conductive [kond*u*ktiv] *adj* able to conduct (heat, electricity *etc*) ∼ **conductivity** [kondukt*i*viti] *n*.

conductor [kond*u*kter] *n* leader, guide; controller of orchestra or choir; official who collects fares on public transport vehicles; channel; (*phys*) substance or body capable of conducting heat, electricity *etc* ∼ **conductorship** *n*.

conductress [kond*u*ktRes] *n* female conductor.

conduit [k*u*ndit/k*o*ndit] *n* channel or pipe for flowing water; encasement for electric cables.

condyle [k*o*ndil] *n* (*anat*) rounded end of bone.

cone [k*O*n] *n* (*math*) solid figure traced by a straight line passing through a fixed point, the vertex, and moving along a fixed circle > PDS; solid body tapering to a point from a circular base; anything resembling this shape; scaly fruit of pine and fir trees; volcanic peak; signal hoisted as warning of storm; edible container for ice-cream.

coney see cony.

confab [k*o*nfab] *n* (*coll*) confabulation.

confabulation [konfabewl*a*yshon] *n* private friendly discussion.

confection [konf*e*kshon] *n* putting together, making up; sweet, small fancy cake *etc*; elaborate stylish article of dress ∼ **confection** *v*/*t*.

confectionary [konf*e*kshoneRi] *n* sweetmeat; place where sweetmeats are made ∼ **confectionary** *adj* of the nature of a confection or sweetmeat.

confectioner [konf*e*kshoner] *n* maker of, or dealer in, sweetmeats, pastries, cakes *etc*.

confectionery [konf*e*kshoneRi] *n* things made by a confectioner; business of a confectioner.

confederacy [konf*e*deRasi] *n* league of States or bodies of men for mutual help and joint action; confederation; conspiracy.

confederate [konf*e*deRit] *adj* allied, leagued; **C. States of America** the eleven Southern States which seceded from the Union 1860–65 ∼ **confederate** *n* ally; member of a confederacy; fellow-conspirator, associate in crime ∼ **confederate** [konf*e*deRayt] *v*/*t* and *i* bring or come into alliance.

confederation [konfedeR*a*yshon] *n* confederacy > PDPol; act of confederating.

confer (*pres*/*part* **conferring**, *p*/*t* and *p*/*part* **conferred**) [konf*u*r] *v*/*t* and *i* bestow; discuss, consult together ∼ **conferrable** *adj*.

conferee [konfeR*ee*] *n* person with whom one confers; person on whom something is conferred.

conference [k*o*nfeRens] *n* meeting for discussion and exchange of views.

conferment [konf*u*rment] *n* act of bestowing.

conferring [konf*u*Rring] *n* bestowal; discussion, consultation.

confess [konf*e*s] *v*/*t* and *i* admit, acknowledge (fault); (*eccles*) declare sins to a priest to obtain absolution; hear confession of; (*ar*) formally declare one's faith in.

confessedly [konf*e*sidli] *adv* admittedly.

confession [konf*e*shon] *n* act of confessing; acknowledgement, admission of guilt; (*eccles*)

declaration of sins to a priest who absolves them; communal declaration of guilt; declaration of faith or creed; religious sect or denomination.

confessional [konf*e*shonal] *n* (*eccles*) enclosed or curtained place where a priest hears confessions; book of penitential prayers ∼ **confessional** *adj*.

confessor [konf*e*ser] *n* (*eccles*) one who openly declares his religion in face of persecution; priest who hears confessions.

confetti [konf*e*ti] *n* (*pl*) little pieces of coloured paper thrown at weddings or carnivals.

confidant (*fem* **confidante**) [konfid*a*nt] *n* person to whom one tells one's intimate thoughts.

confide [konf*I*d] *v*/*t* and *i* entrust to; tell as a secret; **c. in** tell one's secrets to; have trust in.

confidence [k*o*nfidens] *n* trust, reliance; lack of fear, assurance; self-reliance; something told as a secret; a private communication; **in c.** as a secret; **c. trick** swindle worked by winning the victim's trust.

confident [k*o*nfident] *adj* assured, certain; self-reliant; cocksure ∼ **confidently** *adv*.

confidential [konfid*e*nshal] *adj* told as secret, private; entrusted with secrets; easily imparting confidences ∼ **confidentially** *adv*.

confidentiality [konfidenshi-*a*liti] *n* quality of being told as a secret; privacy.

confiding [konf*I*ding] *adj* trustful ∼ **confidingly** *adv*.

configuration [konfigewR*a*yshon] *n* shape, outline, contour; (*astron*) relative position of planets; (*chem*) arrangement of atoms in a molecule; (*geog*) horizontal outline and elevation of an area > PDG.

confinable [konf*I*nab'l] *adj* that can be limited.

confine [konf*I*n] *v*/*t* keep within limits, restrict, restrain; imprison; keep in; (*pass*) be about to give birth to a child.

confinement [konf*I*nment] *n* imprisonment; restriction of freedom; period of labour pains and childbirth.

confines [k*o*nfInz] *n* (*pl*) boundaries, frontiers; (*fig*) limits, borders.

confirm [konf*u*rm] *v*/*t* strengthen, establish; ratify, make valid; corroborate, verify; (*eccles*) administer confirmation to ∼ **confirmable** *adj*.

confirmation [konferm*a*yshon] *n* act of confirming; state of being confirmed; ratification; strengthening; that which confirms, corroboration; (*eccles*) rite performed by bishop whereby candidate becomes complete member of church.

confirmative [konf*u*rmativ] *adj* tending to confirm, strengthen, corroborate ∼ **confirmatively** *adv*.

confirmatory [konf*u*rmateRi] *adj* confirmative.

confirmed [konf*u*rmd] *adj* habitual, long-established; inveterate; chronic.

confiscable [konf*i*skab'l] *adj* liable to confiscation.

confiscate [k*o*nfiskayt] *v*/*t* seize by legal authority; take away as penalty; appropriate without compensation ∼ **confiscate** *adj* (*leg*) confiscated.

confiscation [konfisk*a*yshon] *n* act of confiscating; appropriation of property without compensation.

confiteor [konf*i*ti-awr] *n* (*RC*) prayer of confession of sins.

157

conflagration [konflagRayshon] *n* large destructive fire.

conflate [konflayt] *v/t* (*in a text*) put together variant readings so as to form a composite text ~ **conflation** [konflayshon] *n*.

conflict [konflikt] *n* struggle; battle; strong disagreement; (*psych*) clash between contradictory impulses or wishes ~ **conflict** [konflikt] *v/i* clash, be incompatible, be opposed.

confluence [konfloo-ens] *n* a flowing together; place where two streams meet; (*fig*) large gathering, crowd.

confluent [konfloo-ent] *adj* flowing together, joining ~ **confluent** *n* a stream which flows into another.

conflux [konfluks] *n* confluence.

conform [konfawrm] *v/t* and *i* make similar to; adapt; be of the same form; adapt one's behaviour to that of others, obey prevalent customs; (*eccles hist*) comply with the usages of the Established Church.

conformable [konfawrmab'l] *adj* similar in form or behaviour; compliant, submissive; (*geol*) in parallel strata ~ **conformability** [konfawrmabiliti] *n* ~ **conformably** *adv*.

conformation [konfawrmayshon] *n* structure, arrangement of parts.

conformist [konfawrmist] *n* and *adj* (of or like) one who complies with prevalent ideas, usages *etc*.

conformity [konfawrmiti] *n* outward likeness; agreement; compliance; (*eccles*) adherence to the usages of the Established Church.

confound [konfownd] *v/t* mix up, confuse; throw into confusion, dismay; overthrow; **c. it!** (*coll exclam*) drat!, bother it!

confounded [konfowndid] *adj* confused, abashed; (*coll*) wretched, annoying ~ **confoundedly** *adv* (*coll*) extremely, very.

confraternity [konfRaturniti] *n* a brotherhood or guild.

confront [konfRunt] *v/t* face boldly or threateningly; bring face to face, cause to meet ~ **confrontation** [konfRuntayshon] *n*.

Confucian [konfewshan] *n* and *adj* (follower) of the Chinese ethical teacher Confucius.

confuse [konfewz] *v/t* bewilder, throw into disorder; fail to see difference between, mix up; embarrass ~ **confusable** *adj*.

confused [konfewzd] *adj* muddled; bewildered; embarrassed ~ **confusedly** *adv*.

confusion [konfewzhon] *n* state of being confused; act of confusing.

confutation [konfewtayshon] *n* act of confuting.

confute [konfewt] *v/t* convict of error through argument; disprove ~ **confutable** *adj*.

conga [kong-ga] *n* dance in which dancers form winding line; **c. drum** type of drum played with the hands.

congé [kawnzhay] *n* (*Fr*) abrupt dismissal; formal leave-taking.

congeal [konjeel] *v/t* and *i* freeze; stiffen, clot.

congelation [konjelayshon] *n* frozen state; process of freezing; formation of stalactites; coagulation.

congener [konjener] *n* person or thing nearly related or similar to another.

congeneric [konjeneRik] *adj* akin.

congenial [konjeeni-al] *adj* similar in tastes, temperament *etc*; suited, agreeable ~ **congeniality** [konjeeni-aliti] *n* ~ **congenially** *adv*.

congenital [konjenital] *adj* (*med*) present at birth, born with; (*fig*) inborn; life-long ~ **congenitally** *adv*.

conger [kong-ger] *n* large salt-water eel.

congeries [konjeRi-eez] *n* heap, pile.

congest [konjest] *v/t* and *i* pack densely, crowd together; overcrowd; impede the flow of; (*med*) (*of blood*) accumulate abnormally.

congestion [konjeschon] *n* state of being congested; state of being overcrowded, *esp* by traffic.

conglomerate [kon-glomeRayt] *v/t* and *i* gather into mass ~ **conglomerate** [kon-glomeRit] *n* heaped up mass; (*geol*) rock composed of pebbles cemented together by sandy matrix.

conglomeration [kon-glomeRayshon] *n* collection of things gathered together in a mass.

congratulate [kon-gRatewlayt] *v/t* express one's joy to (a person) on his success, good fortune *etc*; wish joy to.

congratulation [kon-gRatewlayshon] *n* act of congratulating; (*pl*) expression of pleasure in congratulating ~ **congratulatory** *adj*.

congregate [kong-gRigayt] *v/i* and *t* collect together, assemble, gather.

congregation [kong-gRigayshon] *n* assembly, *esp* of persons in church; body of regular worshippers; senior members of a university; (*RC*) committee of cardinals; religious community or brotherhood ~ **congregational** *adj*.

congregationalism [kong-gRigayshonalizm] *n* system of Nonconformist church organization in which each congregation is self-governing ~ **congregationalist** *n*.

congress [kong-gRes] *n* formal assembly or conference; legislative body of various republics, *esp* of the United States and of India > PDPol; (*coll*) sexual intercourse ~ **congressional** [kong-gReshonal] *adj*.

congressman [kong-gResman] *n* (*US*) member of Congress.

congruence [kong-gROO-ens] *n* agreement; (*math*) relation between two numbers which give same remainder when divided by a third number ~ **congruency** *n* ~ **congruent** *adj* in agreement, exactly corresponding, suitable; (*geom*) (*of figures*) such as being laid one upon another will exactly meet and cover one another.

congruity [kong-gROO-iti] *n* condition of being congruous.

congruous [kong-gRoo-us] *adj* suitable, conformable, consistent ~ **congruously** *adv* ~ **congruousness** *n*.

conic [konik] *adj* in the shape of a cone; relating to cones and their properties; **c. sections** curves obtained by the intersection of a plane with a cone ~ **conical** *adj* ~ **conically** *adv*.

conics [koniks] *n* (*pl*) (*math*) theory of conic sections.

conifer [kOnifer] *n* (*bot*) cone-bearing tree.

coniferous [kOnifeRus] *adj* cone-bearing.

coniform [kOnifawrm] *adj* cone-shaped.

conjectural [konjekcheRal] *adj* reached by conjecture ~ **conjecturally** *adv*.

conjecture [konjekcher] *n* surmise, inference based on evidence insufficient for proof, *esp* suggested emendation in a text ~ **conjecture** *v/t* and *i* guess, think likely.

conjoin [kon*join*] *v/t* and *i* join together, combine.

conjoint [kon*joint*] *adj* united, associated ~ **conjointly** *adv*.

conjugal [*kon*joogal] *adj* pertaining to marriage.

conjugate (1) [*kon*joogayt] *v/t* and *i* (*gramm*) enumerate all inflexional forms of (a verb); possess inflexions.

conjugate (2) [*kon*joogit] *adj* joined in pairs.

conjugation [konjoogayshon] *n* (*gramm*) scheme of all inflectional forms of a verb; a class of verbs with similar inflectional forms; (*biol*) union of two similar cells > PDB ~ **conjugational** *adj*.

conjunct [kon*junkt*] *adj* joined ~ **conjunctly** *adv*.

conjunction [kon*junk*shon] *n* act of joining together; state of being joined; association, union; (*gramm*) uninflected word joining sentences or parts of sentences; combination, coincidence; (*astron*) nearness to each other of two heavenly bodies > PDS ~ **conjunctional** *adj*.

conjunctiva [konjunkt*Iv*a] *n* mucous membrane lining eyelids ~ **conjunctival** *adj*.

conjunctive [kon*junk*tiv] *adj* connective, uniting; (*gramm*) serving to join words or sentences.

conjunctivitis [konjunktiv*It*is] *n* inflammation of the mucous membrane of the eyelids.

conjuncture [kon*junk*cher] *n* combination of circumstances; important occasion; crisis.

conjuration [konjoor*Ray*shon] *n* solemn invocation; incantation; (*ar*) conspiracy.

conjure (1) [kon*joor*] *v/t* appeal solemnly to.

conjure (2) [*kun*jer] *v/i* perform tricks by sleight-of-hand; **c. up** cause to appear; (*fig*) evoke mental picture of; **name to c. with** influential name.

conjurer, conjuror [*kun*jeRer] *n* one who performs tricks by sleight-of-hand.

conjuring [*kun*jeRing] *n* art or act of performing tricks by sleight-of-hand ~ **conjuring** *adj* produced by sleight-of-hand.

conk (1) [*konk*] *n* (*sl*) nose; (*coll*) blow, *esp* on nose.

conk (2) *v/i* (*coll*) fire badly; **c. out** (*of motor*) fail, stall ~ **conked** *adj* stopped, stalled.

conker [*konker*] *n* (*coll*) horse-chestnut; (*pl*) game played with these.

connate [*konayt*] *adj* (*of qualities*) inborn.

connect [kon*ekt*] *v/t* and *i* join together, link; show relationship between; associate; follow logically; (*of trains*) be so timed that passengers can transfer from one to the other; **c. with** (*sl*) hit.

connected [kon*ek*tid] *adj* joined; related by family; coherent; associated ~ **connectedly** *adv* ~ **connectedness** *n*.

connecting-rod [kon*ek*ting-Rod] *n* (*eng*) rod connecting the crank to the piston.

connection see **connexion**.

connective [kon*ek*tiv] *adj* joining, linking; **c. tissue** (*anat*) tissue binding organs together.

connexion, connection [kon*ek*shon] *n* act of joining together; state of being joined; relationship, association; union; sexual intimacy; circle of acquaintances, clients, customers *etc*; influential friend; relative; religious group; connecting tube, rod *etc*; train *etc* timed to meet passengers arriving by another; (*elect*) circuit; (*tel*) line of communication ~ **connexional** *adj*.

conning [*kon*ing] *n* (*nau*) directing the helm; **c.**

tower *n* armour-plated observation tower in a warship or submarine.

conniption [kon*ip*shon] *n* hysterical fit of rage, fear or excitement.

connivance [kon*Iv*ans] *n* act of conniving.

connive [kon*Iv*] *v/i* **c. at** pretend to be unaware of, aid and abet (wrong-doing).

connoisseur [kone*sur*] *n* an expert on art or matters of taste ~ **connoisseurship** *n*.

connotation [konOt*a*yshon] *n* implication; associations and emotional overtones of a word; (*log*) all that is implied by a word or term.

connote [kon*Ot*] *v/t* imply, suggest; imply in addition to main meaning; (*coll*) mean.

connubial [kone*wb*i-al] *adj* pertaining to marriage.

conoid [*kOn*oid] *n* (*geom*) solid formed by the revolution of a conic section about its axis; (*anat*) pineal gland.

conquer [*konker*] *v/t* and *i* overpower; win by war, subjugate; be victorious; overcome, win.

conqueror [*konke*Rer] *n* one who conquers; **the C.** William I, King of England.

conquest [*konk*west] *n* act of conquering; that which is conquered; (*coll*) person whose affections one has won; **the C.** (*hist*) Norman conquest of England in 1066.

conquistador [kon*kis*tadawr] *n* one of the Spanish conquerors of Mexico and Peru.

consanguineous [konsang-*gwin*i-us] *adj* related by blood.

consanguinity [konsang-*gwin*iti] *n* blood relationship.

conscience [*kon*shens] *n* an individual's system of accepted moral principles; the subjective sense of right and wrong, *esp* as applied to a particular act > PDP; **c. clause** (*leg*) one allowing for possible moral scruples, *esp* in religious or educational matters; **in all c.** (*coll*) surely, by reasonable standards; **c. money** money paid to set one's conscience at rest; anonymous payment of tax *etc* previously evaded ~ **conscienceless** *adj*.

conscience-smitten [*kon*shens-smiten] *adj* remorseful.

conscientious [konshi-*en*shus] *adj* loyal to conscience, scrupulous; having a strong sense of duty; **c. objector** one who refuses military service because he considers fighting immoral ~ **conscientiously** *adv* ~ **conscientiousness** *n*.

conscious [*kon*shus] *adj* able to feel, perceive and think; in full possession of one's senses; knowing, aware; self-conscious, embarrassed; intentional ~ **consciously** *adv* ~ **consciousness** *n*.

conscript [kon*skRipt*] *v/t* enrol compulsorily in armed forces, call up for military service ~ **conscript** [*kon*skRipt] *adj* and *n* conscripted (man).

conscription [kon*skRip*shon] *n* compulsory enrolment for military service.

consecrate [*kon*sikRayt] *v/t* set apart for service of God; dedicate, devote; ordain (bishop); (*fig*) make venerable ~ **consecrate, consecrated** *adjs*.

consecration [konsikR*a*yshon] *n* act or ceremony of consecrating; state of being consecrated.

consecution [konsik*ew*shon] *n* regular succession.

consecutive [kon*sek*ewtiv] *adj* following in regular or unbroken order; (*gramm*) expressing consequence or result; **c. chords** (*mus*) harmonic

intervals of like kind succeeding one another >
PDM ~ **consecutively** *adv* ~ **consecutiveness** *n*.
consensus [kon*sensus*] *n* general agreement.
consent [kon*sent*] *v/i* agree (to proposal or request) ~ **consent** *n* agreement, assent; **age of c.**
(*leg*) age at which consent to marriage or sexual
intercourse is valid in law; **with one c.** unanimously ~ **consentingly** *adv* with consent.
consentient [kon*senshent*] *adj* agreeing.
consequence [*konsikwens*] *n* result; logical conclusion; importance, value.
consequent [*konsikwent*] *adj* following as result
following by logical argument ~ **consequent** *n*
result; (*log*) second part of conditional proposition.
consequential [konsi*kwen*shal] *adj* following as a
consequence; claiming undue importance,
pompous ~ **consequentially** *adv* ~ **consequentialness** *n*.
consequently [*kon*sikwentli] *adv* as a result;
therefore.
conservancy [kon*survansi*] *n* body of officials appointed to control and protect rivers and forests;
care of rivers and forests.
conservation [konser*vay*shon] *n* act of conserving; preservation, *esp* of the environment or of
natural resources; conservancy; **c. of energy**
(*phys*) the principle that energy cannot be created
or destroyed > PDS ~ **conservational** *adj*.
conservationist [konser*vay*shonist] *n* and *adj*
(person) seeking to preserve unspoilt countryside,
wildlife, old buildings *etc*.
conservatism [kon*survatizm*] *n* desire to keep
established customs *etc*; opposition to change;
(*pol*) principles of the Conservative Party.
conservative [kon*survativ*] *adj* wishing to keep
existing conditions unchanged; disliking violent
change; cautious, moderate; (*of estimates*) deliberately low; **C. Party** (*pol*) moderately rightwing British political party > PDPol ~ **conservative** *n* person of conservative mentality;
(*cap*) member of Conservative Party.
conservatoire [kon*survatwaar*] *n* school of
musical training > PDM.
conservator [*kon*servayter, kon*survater*] *n* protector; custodian.
conservatory [kon*survatoRi*] *n* ornamental glass
house for delicate flowering plants; school of
music, art, or drama.
conserve [kon*survl*] *v/t* preserve from injury, keep
safe; keep unchanged; keep unused ~ **conserve**
n candied fruit; jam ~ **conserver** *n*.
conshy, conshie, conchy [*kon*shi] *n* (*coll abbr*)
conscientious objector.
consider [kon*sider*] *v/t* and *i* think over, ponder,
reflect on; take account of, allow for; esteem,
respect; be of opinion; maintain.
considerable [kon*side*Rab'l] *adj* worthy of consideration, important; rather large ~ **considerably** *adv*.
considerate [kon*side*Rit] *adj* thoughtful for other
people's feelings ~ **considerately** *adv* ~ **considerateness** *n*.
consideration [konside*Ray*shon] *n* act of considering; careful thought, reflection; fact to be
taken into account; payment, reward; thoughtful
care for others.

considered [kon*siderd*] *adj* carefully reflected on;
esteemed.
considering [kon*side*Ring] *prep* with regard to,
making allowance for; (*coll*) taking everything
into account.
consign [kon*sIn*] *v/t* and *i* hand over, deliver to
another; entrust; (*comm*) send (goods) to be delivered ~ **consignable** *adj* ~ **consignation**
[konsig*nay*shon] *n*.
consignee [konsi*nee*] *n* person to whom goods are
consigned.
consigner see consignor.
consignment [kon*sInment*] *n* act of handing over;
quantity of goods consigned to a trader.
consignor, consigner [konsI*nawr*, konsI*ner*] *n*
one who consigns goods.
consist [kon*sist*] *v/i* **c. in** comprise, be essentially
based on; **c. of** be made up of, be composed
from; **c. with** be in keeping with.
consistence, consistency [kon*sistens*, kon*sistensi*] *n* state of being consistent; degree of density,
firmness; fidelity to convictions, unchanging
character, reliability; logical compatibility.
consistent [kon*sistent*] *adj* in accordance, logically compatible; unchanging, uniform; fixed;
regular ~ **consistently** *adv*.
consistory [kon*sistoRi*] *n* (*eccles*) tribunal, council.
consolable [kon*solab'l*] *adj* capable of being consoled or comforted.
consolation [konso*lay*shon] *n* act of comforting
those in grief; source of comfort; **c. prize** one
given to runner-up.
consolatory [kon*solatoRi*] *adj* bringing comfort.
console (1) [kon*sOl*] *v/t* comfort, lessen grief
of.
console (2) [*kons*Ol] *n* (*archi*) ornamental bracket;
(*mus*) the part of an organ operated by the player
cabinet radio set of radiogram or record-player
switchboard, panel of controls.
consolidate [kon*solidayt*] *v/t* and *i* make solid;
make strong, establish firmly; combine into one
large unit; become solid.
consolidated [kon*solidaytid*] *adj* combined; **c.
fund** fund for payment of interest on the national
debt.
consolidation [konsoli*day*shon] *n* act of consolidating; gradual compression of a cohesive soil.
consols [*kon*solz] *n* (*pl*) (*abbr*) consolidated annuities *ie* British Government securities.
consommé [kon*somay*] *n* clear meat soup.
consonance [*kon*sonans] *n* agreement; pleasing
combination of sounds; (*mus*) concord ~ **consonancy** *n*.
consonant (1) [*kon*sonant] *adj* in agreement, in
harmony ~ **consonantly** *adv*.
consonant (2) *n* (*phon*) sound in speech produced
by partial or complete stoppage of the breath;
letter or symbol representing such a sound ~
consonantal [konso*nan*tal] *adj*.
consort (1) [*kon*sawrt] *n* husband or wife, spouse,
esp of reigning monarch; ship sailing in company
with another.
consort (2) [kon*sawrt*] *v/i* associate with, be companion of; be in harmony with.
consortium [kon*sawrti*-um] *n* alliance, association,
esp of commercial or financial organizations.
conspectus [kon*spektus*] *n* survey; synopsis.
conspicuous [kon*spikew*-us] *adj* plainly visible,

catching 'he eye; noticeable, outstanding ~ **conspicuously** *adv* ~ **conspicuousness** *n*.

conspiracy [konsp*i*Rasi] *n* act of conspiring, plot; secret and usually illegal agreement; **c. of silence** agreement to keep silent, to hush up some topic.

conspirator [konsp*i*Rater] *n* member of a conspiracy ~ **conspiratorial** [konspiRat*aw*Ri-al] *adj*.

conspire [konsp*i*r] *v/i* plot together; combine, cooperate se cretly (*usu* for unlawful purpose).

constable [*kun*stab'l] *n* policeman; (*hist*) chief officer of King's household; commander-in-chief; **chief c.** head of police in city or county; **special c.** civilian acting as constable in time of emergency; **outrun the c.** get into debt.

constabulary [kon*stabe*wlaRi] *n* police force in a town or district ~ **constabulary** *adj* relating to, consisting of, constables.

constancy [*kon*stansi] *n* steadfastness, fidelity; unchangingness, stability.

constant '*kon*stant] *adj* unchanging, faithful; frequent, persistent; invariable, fixed ~ **constant** *n* (*math*) any quantity which does not vary ~ **constantly** *adv* continually; very frequently; faithfully.

constellation [konste*lay*shon] *n* stars forming an apparent group when viewed from earth; gathering of distinguished persons; (*astrol*) grouping of the stars and planets at a person's birth; (*psych*) group of related thoughts.

consternation [konster*nay*shon] *n* dismay.

constipate [*kon*stipayt] *v/t* (*med*) cause sluggish or irregular functioning of bowels.

constipation [konsti*pay*shon] *n* sluggishness of the bowels.

constituency [konstitew-ensi] *n* (*pol*) electorate or area of a parliamentary division.

constituent [konst*i*tew-ent] *adj* forming part, component; (*pol*) entitled to elect; entitled to make a constitution ~ **constituent** *n* component part; (*pol*) elector in parliamentary constituency.

constitute [*kon*stitewt] *v/t* establish, set up; appoint; be legally regarded as; make up, compose.

constitution [konsti*tew*shon] *n* act of constituting; structure; state of health of a person's body; temperament, disposition > PDP; (*pol*) principles of government; organization of a state; (*hist*) decree.

constitutional [konsti*tew*shonal] *adj* determined by physical or mental constitution; related to, in agreement with, the constitution of a State; **c. ruler** ruler whose power is restricted by the constitution of a State ~ **constitutional** *n* regular walk for the sake of health.

constitutionalism [konsti*tew*shonalizm] *n* principles of, or belief in, constitutional government ~ **constitutionalist** *n*.

constitutionally [konsti*tew*shonali] *adv* in accordance with the constitution; naturally. ·

constitutive [*kon*stitewtiv] *adj* having power to constitute; constituent.

constrain [konst*Rayn*] *v/t* force, compel; keep within bounds; restrict.

constrained [konst*Raynd*] *adj* embarrassed, awkward; cramped ~ **constrainedly** *adv*.

constraint [konst*Raynt*] *n* compulsion, force; restriction of liberty; embarrassment.

constrict [konst*Rikt*] *v/t* compress, squeeze; cause to contract; (*fig*) restrict, inhibit.

constriction [konst*Rik*shon] *n* drawing together, tightness; sensation of tightness, *esp* in the chest.

constrictor [konst*Rik*ter] *n* (*anat*) muscle which contracts or compresses a bodily organ; (*zool*) snake which crushes its prey in its coils.

constringent [konst*Rin*jent] *adj* causing contraction or constriction.

construct [konst*Rukt*] *v/t* build up, make by putting together; (*geom*) draw ~ **construct** [*kon*stRukt] *n* anything built up or put together; larger unit made up of smaller ones; (*psych*) a concept.

construction [konst*Ruk*shon] *n* act or manner of constructing; thing constructed; (*geom*) drawing of lines to solve a problem; explanation, interpretation; (*gramm*) syntactic arrangement of words in sentence ~ **constructional** *adj*.

constructive [konst*Ruk*tiv] *adj* able or helping to construct; helpful, formative, bringing improvement; structural; inferred; not directly expressed ~ **constructively** *adv* ~ **constructiveness** *n*.

constructivism [konst*Ruk*tivizm] *n* art movement characterized by massive geometrical and abstract forms > PDAA.

constructor [konst*Ruk*ter] *n* one who constructs, builder.

construe [konst*ROO*] *v/t* and *i* (*gramm*) analyse construction of sentence; translate literally; (*fig*) interpret; perform syntactic analysis.

consubstantial [konsubst*an*shal] *adj* having the same nature or essence ~ **consubstantiality** *n*.

consubstantiation [konsubstanshi-*ay*shon] *n* (*theol*) doctrine of the simultaneous presence of the body and blood of Christ together with the bread and wine in the Eucharist.

consul [*kon*sul] *n* agent appointed by a State to live in a foreign land and protect its nationals and commercial interests there; (*hist*) one of two chief magistrates of Rome ~ **consular** [*kon*sewlar] *adj*.

consulate [*kon*sewlit] *n* office or rank of consul; consul's official residence or headquarters.

consulship [*kon*sulship] *n* office, or term of office, of a consul.

consult [kon*sult*] *v/t* and *i* ask advice or information of; refer to (book); take into consideration; take counsel; confer.

consultant [kon*sul*tant] *n* specialist called in to give advice; person who consults another.

consultation [konsul*tay*shon] *n* act of consulting; conference; meeting for giving or taking of advice.

consultative [kon*sul*tativ] *adj* advisory.

consulting [kon*sul*ting] *adj* capable of giving expert or specialist advice; **c. room** room where doctor interviews patients, or lawyer interviews clients.

consumable [kon*sew*mab'l] *adj* capable of being burnt up or eaten.

consume [kon*sewm*] *v/t* and *i* destroy by fire; spend, waste; use up; eat up, drink up; (*fig*) preoccupy excessively, obsess; **c. away** waste away.

consumer [kon*sew*mer] *n* user of an article; one who buys and uses goods; **c. goods** (*econ*) goods produced to be used in daily life; **c. durables** long-lasting domestic equipment; **c. research** research by associations of consumers into the quality of goods offered for sale, or by manufacturers into the opinions and wishes of consumers.

consummate (1) [kon*sum*it] *adj* perfect, complete ~ **consummately** *adv*.

consummate (2) [*kon*sumayt] *v/t* bring to perfection; complete, *esp* complete (marriage) by sexual intercourse ~ **consummation** [konsu*may*shon] *n*.

consumption [kon*sump*shon] *n* act of consuming; quantity consumed; (*econ*) use of goods; amount of goods used; (*obs med*) tuberculosis of lungs.

consumptive [kon*sump*tiv] *n* and *adj* (person) suffering from tuberculosis of lungs.

contact [*kon*takt] *n* state of touching; close association, meeting; communication; (*elect*) the touching or sufficient proximity of two conductors for current to pass from one to the other; (*math*) meeting of two curves or surfaces; (*coll*) person one can get in touch with, acquaintance; **c. lens** corrective optical lens resting directly on eyeball; **c. print** (*phot*) a print made with the negative in contact with paper sensitive to light ~ **contact** *v/t* get in touch with.

contact-breaker [*kon*takt-bRayker] *n* device for repeatedly breaking and making an electric circuit.

contagion [kon*tay*jon] *n* communication of disease by contact; disease so communicated; (*fig*) harmful influence.

contagious [kon*tay*jus] *adj* communicated by contact; spreading, or capable of spreading, an infection; (*fig*) easily communicated, catching ~ **contagiously** *adv* ~ **contagiousness** *n*.

contain [kon*tayn*] *v/t* hold, enclose; have as component, comprise; have space or capacity for; keep within limits; (*math*) be divisible by; (*geom*) bound, enclose; (*mil*) prevent movement of; keep within limits; (*refl*) restrain oneself, be self-controlled ~ **containable** *adj*.

container [kon*tay*ner] *n* one who, or that which, contains; box, carton, sealed tinplate can; large metal box of standardized size for transporting goods in bulk by lorry or ship; **c. ship** ship designed to receive cargo in containers.

containerize [kon*tay*neRIz] *v/t* and *i* pack into standardized containers for bulk transport; adopt the use of large standardized containers ~ **containerization** [kontayneRIz*ay*shon] *n*.

containment [kon*tayn*ment] *n* act or process of restraining or enclosing; (*phys*) process of preventing plasma from contacting containing walls in a controlled thermonuclear reaction.

contaminant [kon*tam*inant] *n* and *adj* (substance) which contaminates.

contaminate [kon*tam*inayt] *v/t* pollute, make impure or poisonous by contact with noxious matter, *esp* poison-gas or radioactivity; (*fig*) corrupt, exert evil influence on.

contamination [kontamin*ay*shon] *n* act of contaminating; state of being contaminated; that which contaminates; corruption of texts by influence of variant versions.

contango [kon*tang*-gO] *n* (*Stock Exchange*) an arrangement whereby the settlement of securities bought or sold for one account is deferred or carried over until the next; interest paid for this.

contemn [kon*tem*] *v/t* (*ar*) despise.

contemplate [*kon*templayt] *v/t* and *i* look intently at, gaze at, watch; think deeply about, meditate; intend; expect.

contemplation [kontem*play*shon] *n* act of contemplating; deep meditation; act of suppressing normal mental activity in order to commune with God; concentrated attention.

contemplative [kon*templ*ativ] *adj* given to contemplation or meditation; meditative, thoughtful; **c. order** (*eccles*) religious order whose members spend their time mainly in meditation and prayer ~ **contemplative** *n* a person devoted to religious meditation ~ **contemplatively** *adv*.

contemporaneous [kontempoRay*ni-us*] *adj* existing or happening at the same time.

contemporary [kon*tempo*RaRi] *adj* existing or happening at the same period; existing or happening at the present time; equal in age; (*coll*) up to date, in the most modern style ~ **contemporary** *n* one who, or that which, is contemporary.

contempt [kon*tempt*] *n* act of despising, scorn; state of being scorned; **c. of court** disregard for, or disobedience to, a court of law.

contemptibility [kontempti*bil*iti] *n* quality of being contemptible.

contemptible [kon*tempt*ib'l] *adj* worthy of scorn, despicable ~ **contemptibly** *adv*.

contemptuous [kon*tempt*ew-us] *adj* scornful ~ **contemptuously** *adv* ~ **contemptuousness** *n*.

contend [kon*tend*] *v/i* struggle, compete; argue; dispute; assert, affirm; face, oppose.

content (1) [*kon*tent] *n* that which is contained; amount contained; meaning, gist, essential significance; (*pl*) that which is contained; chief topics of a book; list of such topics.

content (2) [kon*tent*] *adj* satisfied, pleased, willing ~ **content** *n* satisfaction, state of being content ~ **content** *v/t* satisfy; (*refl*) be satisfied, accept as sufficient ~ **contented** *adj* ~ **contentedly** *adv*.

contention [kon*ten*shon] *n* strife, dispute; argument; point maintained or argued; **bone of c.** subject of dispute.

contentious [kon*ten*shus] *adj* quarrelsome; leading to strife, controversial ~ **contentiously** *adv* ~ **contentiousness** *n*.

contentment [kon*tent*ment] *n* act of contenting; state of content.

contents see **content** (1).

conterminous [kon*tur*minus] *adj* having common boundary, adjacent; with two ends meeting; equally extensive (in time, range, sense *etc*).

contest [kon*test*] *v/t* fight for, struggle to gain; (*leg*) try to disprove or invalidate; (*pol*) stand for election against another candidate; argue against, call in question ~ **contest** [*kon*test] *n* fight, struggle; competition.

contestant [kon*test*ant] *n* one who contests.

contestation [kontes*tay*shon] *n* act of contesting.

context [*kon*tekst] *n* general setting (of remark, experience *etc*), surrounding and connected circumstances; passages which immediately precede or follow a given extract from a written work; (*coll*) the extract (rather than its setting).

contextual [kon*tek*stew-al] *adj* arising from the context ~ **contextually** *adv*.

contiguity [konti*gew*-iti] *n* state of being contiguous.

contiguous [kon*ti*gew-us] *adj* in contact, touching; adjoining; near ~ **contiguously** *adv*.

continence, continency [*kon*tinens, *kon*tinensi] *n* self-restraint, moderation, *esp* as regards sexual intercourse; chastity.

continent (1) [*kon*tinent] *adj* practising continence, chaste; able to control one's urine and faeces.

continent (2) *n* large unbroken mass of land > PDG; the mainland of Europe.

continental [kontin*en*tal] *adj* pertaining to a continent; pertaining to, characteristic of, the mainland of Europe; **c. drift** (*geog*) gradual movement of continents across earth's surface; **c. shelf** (*geog*) gentle slope of the sea bed bordering on continents > PDG ~ **continental** *n* inhabitant of the European mainland.

contingency [kon*tin*jensi] *n* possibility of happening; something which may or may not happen; chance occurrence; event depending on another; (*stat*) probability of an association between two facts, occurrences *etc* > PDP.

contingent [kon*tin*jent] *adj* possibly occurring; dependent, conditional; uncertain; (*leg*) dependent on possible occurrences ~ **contingent** *n* allotted share; (*mil*) quota of troops, ships *etc*; group of persons forming part of larger group ~ **contingently** *adv*.

continual [kon*ti*new-al] *adj* frequently repeated, persistent; unceasing, uninterrupted ~ **continually** *adv*.

continuance [kon*ti*new-ans] *n* act or quality of continuing; (*leg*) adjournment, stay.

continuation [kontinew-*ay*shon] *n* act of continuing; state of being continued; that which continues something else; extension, prolongation; resumption; further instalment; **c. classes** further classes for those who have left school.

continuative [kon*ti*newativ] *adj* as continuation.

continuator [kon*ti*new-ayter] *n* one who adds to a literary work.

continue [kon*ti*new] *v/t* and *i* keep on, prolong; carry onward, extend; resume (discourse); retain (in office); go on without interruption; extend; endure, last; remain, abide, stay; go on speaking; go on doing something.

continued [kon*ti*newd] *adj* unceasing, uninterrupted; extended; resumed.

continuing [kon*ti*newing] *adj* abiding, lasting.

continuity [kontinew-*iti*] *n* quality or state of being continuous; connectedness; logical connexion; (*rad*, *TV*) script of programme; series of linking comments *etc*; **c. girl** (*cin*) one who ensures the consistency of detail in a film by keeping a record of each scene as it is shot.

continuo [kon*ti*new-O] *n* (*mus*) type of bass-line accompaniment for keyboard instrument > PDM.

continuous [kon*ti*new-us] *adj* without break or interruption; unceasing ~ **continuously** *adv*.

continuum (*pl* **continua**) [kon*ti*new-um] *n* continuous series of component parts passing into one another > PDS.

contort [kon*tawrt*] *v/t* twist out of shape, distort ~ **contortion** *n* ~ **contortive** *adj*.

contortionist [kon*tawr*shonist] *n* acrobat who twists his body into unnatural positions.

contour [*kon*toor] *n* outline > PDAA; (*geog*) line drawn on map to join all places at the same height above sea-level > PDG; **c. line** (*geog*) contour; **c. map** map showing contours of given area, **c. ploughing** method of ploughing with furrows at very gentle slopes > PDE ~ **contour** *v/t* indicate contours of.

contra- *pref* against; (*mus*) lower in pitch.

contra [*kon*tRa] *prep* and *adv* against, in opposition to; to the contrary ~ **contra** *n* the contrary or opposite; an argument against.

contraband [*kon*tRaband] *n* smuggling; smuggled goods; **c. of war** anything which must not be supplied to belligerents by neutrals in time of war ~ **contraband** *adj* ~ **contrabandist** *n* smuggler.

contrabass [*kon*tRabays] *n* (*mus*) double-bass, largest instrument of violin-class > PDM.

contraception [kontRa*sep*shon] *n* prevention of conception by drug or mechanical device.

contraceptive [kontRa*sep*tiv] *n* and *adj* (device or drug) preventing conception.

contract (1) [*kon*tRakt] *n* solemn and binding agreement, bond; promise, undertaking; bargain, compact; marriage; betrothal; business agreement on work to be done, rates to be paid *etc*; document embodying an agreement; **c. bridge** (*cards*) form of bridge in which only tricks undertaken to be won can be scored ~ **contract** [kon*tRakt*] *v/t* and *i* arrange by contract, bind oneself to; betroth oneself; enter into a contract; **c. in, c. out** bind oneself to take part in, or not to take part in.

contract (2) [kon*tRakt*] *v/t* and *i* draw together, make or become smaller or tighter, shorten; wrinkle (forehead); shrink; acquire (habit); incur (liability); catch (disease); (*gramm*) abridge, shorten by elision ~ **contracted** *adj* ~ **contractedly** *adv*.

contractible [kon*tRak*tib'l] *adj* capable of being contracted ~ **contractibility** [kontRakti*bili*ti] *n*.

contractile [kon*tRak*tIl] *adj* capable of contracting; causing contraction ~ **contractility** [kontRak*ti*liti] *n* power of contracting, *esp* of muscle.

contracting [kon*tRak*ting] *adj* entering into a contract; shrinking, narrowing.

contraction [kon*tRak*shon] *n* act of contracting; that which is contracted; (*gramm*) shortened form of word ~ **contractive** *adj*.

contractor [kon*tRak*ter] *n* one who contracts to supply goods or services at fixed price; muscle which causes contraction.

contractual [kon*tRak*tew-al] *adj* (*leg*) of the nature of a contract ~ **contractually** *adv*.

contracture [kon*tRak*cher] *n* (*med*) persistent contraction and rigidity in muscles or joints.

contradict [kontRa*dikt*] *v/t* deny emphatically; assert the opposite of; be inconsistent with; (*coll*) argue, squabble ~ **contradictable** *adj*.

contradiction [kontRa*dik*shon] *n* act of contradicting, denial; that which contradicts; state of being contradictory, inconsistency; **c. in terms** statement which contradicts itself.

contradictory [kontRa*dik*toRi] *adj* tending to contradict, incompatible, inconsistent; (*coll*) deliberately opposing one's wishes ~ **contradictory** *n* contradicting assertion ~ **contradictorily** *adv*.

contradistinction [kontRadis*tink*shon] *n* distinction by contrast.

contradistinguish [kontRadis*ting*wish] *v/t* distinguish between things by contrasting them.

contrail [*kon*Rayl] *n* vapour trail of jet aircraft.

contra-indicate [kontRa-*in*dikayt] *v/t* (*med*) make (the proposed treatment) inadvisable ~ **contra-indication** [kontRa-indi*kay*shon] *n* symptom or state that makes usual treatment inadvisable.

contralto [kon*Ral*tO] *n* (*mus*) lower-pitched type of female voice; woman with such voice > PDM ~ **contralto** *adj*.

contraption [kon*Rap*shon] *n* (*coll*) clumsy machine, gadget *etc*.

contrapuntal [kontRa*pun*tal] *adj* (*mus*) relating to counterpoint.

contrapuntist [kontRa*pun*tist] *n* composer skilled in counterpoint.

contrariety [kontRa*RI*-eti] *n* opposition; inconsistency; setback, hindrance.

contrarily [*kon*tRaRili/kon*tRair*Rili] *adv* in a contrary manner; on the contrary; (*coll*) perversely.

contrariness [*kon*tRaRines/kon*tRair*Rines] *n* (*coll*) opposition for its own sake, perverseness.

contrariwise [*kon*tRaRiwIZ] *adv* on the contrary; in the opposite direction.

contrary [*kon*tRaRi] *adj* opposed to, against; contradictory; opposite in direction; unfavourable ~ **contrary** *n* exact opposite; (*log*) opposite terms or contradictory propositions; **on the c.** far from it, not at all; **to the c.** to the opposite effect ~ **contrary** [kon*tRair*Ri] *adj* fond of opposing or contradicting; perverse, obstinate; raising difficulties for their own sake.

contrast [kon*tRaast*] *v/t* and *i* point out differences between; cause dissimilarity to appear clearly; appear strongly dissimilar; stand out clearly ~ **contrast** [*kon*tRaast] *n* act of contrasting; marked dissimilarity; person or thing contrasting with another; unfavourable comparison; degree of variation between light and shade.

contra-suggestible [kontRa-su*jesti*b'l] *adj* likely to react to suggestions by doing or thinking the opposite.

contravene [kontRa*veen*] *v/t* violate, disobey (law); contradict ~ **contravention** [kontRa*ven*shon] *n*.

contretemps [*kon*tRataw(m)] *n* (*Fr*) unlucky or embarrassing accident.

contribute [kon*tRi*bewt] *v/t* and *i* give, *esp* money or help; supply, furnish; help to cause, share in producing; write (articles *etc*) for the press.

contribution [kontRi*bew*shon] *n* act of contributing; object or amount contributed.

contributor [kon*tRi*bewter] *n* one who contributes.

contributory [kon*tRi*bewteRi] *adj* sharing in, being a partial cause of; pertaining to, financed by contributions ~ **contributory** *n* a contributor.

contrite [*kon*tRIt] *adj* repentant, feeling sorrow for sin ~ **contritely** *adv* ~ **contriteness** *n*.

contrition [kon*tRish*on] *n* remorse for sin.

contrivance [kon*tRI*vans] *n* act of contriving; thing contrived; clever scheme; device.

contrive [kon*tRIv*] *v/t* bring about cleverly; devise, plan; invent; manage.

control (*pres/part* **controlling**, *p/t* and *p/part* **controlled**) [kon*tROl*] *v/t* restrain, guide, hold in

check; regulate; check (accounts); verify by reference to accepted standard ~ **control** *n* authority, guidance; restraint, check; checkpoint; means taken to validate experimental results > PDS; management of a machine; accepted standard for verifying results; (*spiritualism*) spirit guiding a medium; (*pl*) instruments guiding machine; regulations on trade *etc*.

controller [kon*tROl*er] *n* one who controls; official supervising expenditure; device regulating movement of machine.

controversial [kontRo*vur*shal] *adj* causing argument; fond of arguing ~ **controversially** *adv*.

controversialist [kontRo*vur*shalist] *n* one skilled in controversy.

controversy [*kon*tRovursi/kon*tRov*ursi] *n* heated argument, dispute.

controvert [*kon*tRovurt] *v/t* dispute, contest; contradict, oppose.

controvertible [kontRo*vur*tib'l] *adj* able to be controverted ~ **controvertibly** *adv*.

contumacious [kontew*may*shus] *adj* disobedient, rebellious; (*leg*) wilfully disobedient to order of court ~ **contumaciously** *adv*.

contumacy [*kon*tewmasi] *n* wilful disobedience.

contumelious [kontew*meeli*-us] *adj* scornful.

contumely [*kon*tewmli/kon*tew*meli] *n* scornful or insulting behaviour or language; humiliating treatment, disgrace.

contuse [kon*tewz*] *v/t* bruise without breaking the skin ~ **contusion** [kon*tew*zhon] *n* a bruise.

conundrum [ko*nun*dRum] *n* a riddle whose answer involves a pun; puzzling question.

conurbation [koner*bay*shon] *n* group of adjacent towns which have merged into a continuous built-up area.

convalesce [konva*les*] *v/t* recover from illness, regain health and strength ~ **convalescence** *n*.

convalescent [konva*les*ent] *n* and *adj* (person) recovering from illness ; **c. home** nursing home for convalescent patients.

convection [kon*vek*shon] *n* transference of heat through a liquid or gas by the actual movement of the fluid or gas > PDS ~ **convective** *adj* conveying; of the nature of convection.

convector [kon*vek*ter] *n* heating apparatus circulating warm air.

convenances [*kawn*venaansiz] *n* (*pl*) accepted social usages.

convene [kon*veen*] *v/t* and *i* call together, summon to meeting; gather, assemble.

convenience [kon*veen*yens] *n* quality of being convenient; that which is convenient; suitableness, usefulness; comfort; advantage ; any useful object, *esp* domestic appliance; (*euph*) lavatory; **at one's c.** where and when it suits one; **make a c. of** take advantage of, impose upon; **c. food** precooked food sold ready, or almost ready, for eating.

convenient [kon*veen*yent] *adj* suitable, well adapted for use *etc*; suiting one's comfort; (*coll*) easily accessible, near ~ **conveniently** *adv*.

convent [*kon*vent] *n* community (*gen* of women) living under a religious rule; building in which they live.

conventicle [kon*ven*tik'l] *n* (*hist*) illegal religious meeting of Dissenters; small Nonconformist chapel.

convention [konvenshon] *n* formal assembly convened to discuss or legislate; formal agreement, pact; accepted social standard of behaviour (normally in minor matters); custom, usage.

conventional [konvenshonal] *adj* established by social convention; in accordance with accepted artificial standards of conduct or taste; rigidly bound by convention, conformist; artificial; (*mil*) not atomic ~ **conventionally** *adv*.

conventionality [konvenshonaliti] *n* adherence to conventional standards.

conventionalize [konvenshonalIz] *v/t* make conventional; (*arts*) depict by customary symbol.

conventionary [konvenshonaRi] *adj* by solemn agreement, under terms of a convention.

conventual [konventew-al] *n* and *adj* (member) of a convent.

converge [konvurj] *v/t* and *i* bring to a point; come together and meet at a point; (*math*) (*of series*) approximate towards a definite sum the more terms are taken; (*zool*) become similar through influence of environment ~ **convergence** *n* ~ **convergent** *adj*.

conversable [konvursab'l] *adj* pleasant in conversation, easy to talk to.

conversant [konvursant/konvursant] *adj* knowing well, familiar; experienced ~ **conversance** *n*.

conversation [konversayshon] *n* friendly, social talk; informal discussion; **make c.** talk merely to avoid a silence; **c. piece** informal painting of a group of human figures > PDAA.

conversational [konversayshonal] *adj* ready to talk; lively in conversation; appropriate to conversation, colloquial, fluent, informal ~ **conversationalist** *n* fluent and interesting talker.

conversazione [konversatsi-Oni] *n* social gathering, *esp* for discussion of learned or cultural topics; evening reception given by learned society, college *etc*.

converse (1) [konvurs] *v/i* talk, have conversation with ~ **converse** [konvers] *n* conversation; friendly relationship.

converse (2) [konvers] *adj* and *n* opposite, contrary, transposed (statement *etc*) ~ **conversely** [konvursli] *adv*.

conversion [konvurshon] *n* act of converting; state of being converted; complete change of beliefs, opinions *etc*, *esp* in religion > PDP; spiritual awakening; alteration from one state or form to another; (*leg*) appropriation of another's property to one's own use; (*phys*) transformation of fertile material into fissile material in a nuclear reactor > PDS; **c. table** a tabular arrangement for converting weights, measures or currencies from one system to another.

convert [konvurt]*v/t* transform, change; alter into something else, adapt to new use; change the beliefs or opinions of; induce to accept different religion; rouse religious feelings in, awaken spiritually; (*leg*) appropriate another's property to one's own use; (*Stock Exchange*) change Convertible Loan Stock into Ordinary Shares; (*econ*) change a sum in one currency into the equivalent in another; (*Rugby football*) kick a goal from (a try) ~ **convert** [konvert] *n* one who has been converted, *esp* to a different religion.

converter [konvurter] *n* one who, that which, converts; (*eng*) furnace used in steel manu-

facture; (*elect*) dynamo for changing current to another form; (*phys*) nuclear reactor which produces fissile material by conversion of fertile material.

convertible [konvurtib'l] *adj* capable of being converted; (*econ*) (*of currency*) capable of being exchanged ~ **convertible** *n* automobile whose top can be folded back ~ **convertibility** [konvertibiliti] *n* ~ **convertibly** *adv*.

convex [konveks] *adj* curving outwards; **c. lens** (*opt*) one thicker at the centre than at the edges ~ **convexed** *adj* made convex ~ **convexly** *adv*.

convexity [konveksiti] *n* convex curve.

convey [konvay] *v/t* carry, take from, one place to another; transmit; (*fig*) impart, make known; (*leg*) make over (property) by deed ~ **conveyable** *adj*.

conveyance [konvay-ans] *n* act of conveying; vehicle; (*leg*) transfer of real property or title; document effecting this.

conveyancer [konvay-anser] *n* (*leg*) lawyer who draws up deeds for the conveyance of property.

conveyancing [konvay-ansing] *n* (*leg*) the drawing up of deeds for the conveyance of property.

conveyer, conveyor [konvay-er] *n* one who, that which, conveys; apparatus for moving goods; **c. belt** continuous moving belt for moving goods.

convict [konvikt] *v/t* find guilty of crime by legal trial; (*fig*) prove guilty of sin, fault *etc*; cause to feel guilty ~ **convict** [konvikt] *n* person found guilty by law; person serving sentence of imprisonment ~ **convicted** [konvikted] *adj*.

conviction [konvikshon] *n* act of convicting; fact of being convicted; state of being convinced; belief without any tincture of doubt, complete certainty; deep-rooted opinion; **carry c.** sound convincing.

convince [konvins] *v/t* bring certainty to the mind of, compel belief by demonstration or evidence; persuade, arouse belief in ~ **convincible** *adj* open to conviction.

convincing [konvinsing] *adj* causing conviction, compelling belief ~ **convincingly** *adv* ~ **convincingness** *n*.

convivial [konvivi-al] *adj* festive; sociable, jovial, fond of merry-making; (*coll*) slightly drunk ~ **conviviality** [konvivi-aliti] *n*.

convocation [konvokayshon] *n* act of calling together; formal assembly called together for a particular purpose; legislative body or body of registered graduates of certain universities; (*eccles*) synod ~ **convocational** *adj*.

convoke [konvOk] *v/t* summon to assemble.

convolute [konvolewt] *adj* (*biol*) coiled

convoluted [konvolewtid] *adj* twisting; tangled.

convolution [konvolewshon] *n* act of twisting together; state of being coiled; fold, coil, twist.

convolvulus (*pl* **convolvuluses**) [konvolvewlus] *n* genus of twining plants, including bindweed.

convoy [konvoi] *v/t* accompany and protect, escort; (*naut*) (*of warship*) escort non-combatant ships in wartime ~ **convoy** *n* (*naut*) fleet of merchant ships travelling under escort of warships; warships escorting other ships; (*coll*) group of vehicles travelling in company.

convulse [konvuls] *v/t* agitate violently; disturb

deeply; cause violent muscular spasms in; distort (features) by strong emotion.

convulsion [kon*vul*shon] *n* violent agitation; disturbance, upheaval; (*med*) violent and extensive muscular spasm caused by processes in nervous system; (*pl*) fit marked by succession of spasms, twitchings *etc*; (*coll*) uncontrolled gestures or grimaces caused by emotion.

convulsive [kon*vul*siv] *adj* of nature of, affected with, causing, convulsions.

cony, coney [*kO*ni] *n* the rabbit; fur made from rabbit skins; (*OT*) the hyrax.

coo (*p/t* and *p/part* **cooed**) [*kOO*] *v/i* (*of pigeons and doves*) make soft murmuring sound; (*of babies*) murmur softly and happily; talk gently or caressingly; **bill and c.** (*coll*) talk softly with kisses and caresses ∼ **coo** *n* sound made by pigeons or doves; any similar sound; **c.!** (*coll*) exclamation of surprise or disbelief.

cooee [*kOO*-ee] *interj* cry used to attract attention or as signal.

cook [*kook*] *v/t* and *i* prepare food for eating by subjecting it to heat; undergo this preparation; (*fig*) subject to great heat; (*coll*) falsify, fake; **c. one's goose** spoil one's plans, frustrate, ruin; **c. up** (*coll*) invent falsely, fake ∼ **cook** *n* one who cooks; servant employed to cook.

cook-book [*kook*-book] *n* (*coll*) book of recipes.

cooker [*kook*er] *n* stove or other apparatus for cooking; fruit meant to be cooked.

cookery [*kook*eRi] *n* art and practice of cooking.

cook-general [kook-*jene*Ral] *n* servant doing both cooking and general housework.

cookhouse [*kook*hows] *n* outdoor kitchen; camp kitchen.

cookie [*kook*i] *n* small flat sweetened cake or biscuit; (*sl*) girl; person; bomb.

cooking [*kook*ing] *adj* that cooks; suitable for cooking.

cook-out [*kook*-owt] *n* (*coll*) barbecue.

cook-shop [*kook*-shop] *n* shop where cooked food is sold; eating-house.

cool [*kOOl*] *adj* moderately or pleasantly cold, not too warm; (*fig*) calm, level-headed; not passionate; lacking friendliness; casual, impudent; (*coll*) sophisticated, smart; (*jazz*) not crudely rhythmical, subtle and relaxed; (*coll*) no less than ∼ **cool** *n* coolness; that which is cool; (*coll*) self-control, calmness; **keep one's c.** (*coll*) remain calm and good-tempered ∼ **cool** *v/t* and *i* make or become cool; (*of feelings*) become less ardent, affectionate, or violent; **c. it** (*sl*) calm down; **c. one's heels** be forced to wait.

coolant [*kOOl*ent] *n* (*eng*) liquid used to cool engines, the cutting edges of tools *etc*.

cooler [*kOOl*er] *n* anything that makes cool; vessel in which anything is made or kept cool; (*sl*) prison.

cool-headed [kOOl-*hed*id] *adj* calm, unflustered.

coolie [*kOOl*i] *n* Indian or Chinese hired labourer.

coolly [*kOOl*-li] *adv* in a cool manner.

coolness [*kOOl*nes] *n* state of being cool; calmness, lack of excitement; lack of friendliness; slight estrangement; calm assurance.

coolth [*kOOl*th] *n* (*coll*) coolness.

coomb, combe [*kOOm*] *n* narrow valley.

coon [*kOOn*] *n* racoon; (*coll*) Negro; sly, shrewd fellow; **a gone c.** (*coll*) someone in hopeless position.

coop [*kOOp*] *n* wooden cage for hens; wicker basket for catching fish; (*sl*) prison ∼ **coop** *v/t* put or keep in a coop; **c. in, c. up** confine in narrow space or cramping conditions.

co-op [*kO*-op] *n* (*coll*) co-operative society or shop.

cooper [*kOO*per] *n* maker and repairer of casks, barrels, tubs *etc* ∼ **cooper** *v/t*.

cooperage [*kOO*p Rij] *n* work or workshop of a cooper; price charged by cooper.

cooperate [kO-*ope*Rayt] *v/i* work together for common aim, help one another.

cooperation [kO-opeRayshon] *n* act of co-operating; association of number of persons in trading or industry, the profits being shared among the members ∼ **cooperator** [kO-*op*eRayter] *n*.

cooperative [kO-*ope*Rativ] *adj* working together with others to the same end; willing to work with others; (*of trading association*) sharing profits among members ∼ **cooperative** *n* profit-sharing business concern, shop *etc* ∼ **cooperatively** *adv*.

co-opt [kO-*opt*] *v/t* add (person) to committee *etc* by vote of existing members ∼ **co-option** *n*.

coordinate (1) [kO-*awrd*init] *adj* equal in rank or importance ∼ **coordinate** *n* that which is co-ordinate; (*math*) any one of a system of magnitudes used to determine the position of a point > PDS ∼ **coordinately** *adv*

coordinate (2) [kO-*awrd*inayt] *v/t* arrange in correct relationship or order; adjust (parts of a whole) so that they will work efficiently together.

coordination [kO-awrdin*ay*shon] *n* act of arranging in correct relationship or order; condition of working together efficiently and harmoniously.

coot [*kOOt*] *n* type of water-bird; (*coll*) fool.

cootie [*kOO*ti] *n* (*sl*) louse.

cop (1) [*kop*] *n* ball of thread wound on a spindle; mound; hillock.

cop (2) (*pres/part* **copping**, *p/t* and *p/part* **copped**) *v/t*.(*sl*) catch in the act; arrest; **c. it** be punished, get into trouble; **c. out** (*sl*) avoid, evade (a duty); fail to take (an opportunity) ∼ **cop** *n* (*sl*) a catching or being. caught; policeman; **no great c.** not worth having, valueless.

copaiba, copaiva [ko*pI*ba, ko*pI*va] *n* type of aromatic medicinal resin.

copal [*kO*pal] *n* type of resin for varnish.

copartner [kO-*paart*ner] *n* fellow-partner, associate; employee having share in profits of firm.

cope (1) [*kOp*] *n* (*eccles*) long vestment in form of cloak ∼ **cope** *v/t* dress in a cope; (*archi*) put a coping on.

cope (2) *v/t* and *i* manage successfully; **c. with** deal successfully with (a difficulty); handle efficiently.

copeck [*kO*pek] *n* Russian copper coin, a hundredth part of a rouble.

coper [*kOp*er] *n* horse-dealer.

Copernican [ko*pur*nikan] *adj* (*astron*) pertaining to Copernicus; **C. theory** theory that planets, including the earth, move round sun.

copestone [*kOp*stOn] *n* (*bui*) layer of concrete used as a foundation for a rubble wall.

copier [*kop*i-er] *n* one who copies; imitator.

co-pilot [kO-*pI*lot] *n* assistant pilot.

coping [*kO*ping] *n* top protective course of a wall.
coping-stone [*kO*ping-stOn] *n* one of the stones in a coping; (*fig*) climax, final touch.
copious [*kO*pi-us] *adj* abundant, plentiful; profuse ~ **copiously** *adv* ~ **copiousness** *n*.
cop-out [*kop*-owt] *n* (*coll*) cowardly escape or evasion; person who refuses responsibility.
copper (1) [*kop*er] *n* a reddish metal, malleable, ductile and a good conductor > PDS; penny, halfpenny or (*obs*) farthing; reddish-brown colour; vessel for boiling clothes in ~ **copper** *v*/*t* cover with copper ~ **copper** *adj* of or like copper.
copper (2) *n* (*sl*) policeman.
copperas [*kop*eRas] *n* ferrous sulphate.
copper-beech [*kop*er-beech] *n* beech-tree with copper-coloured leaves.
copper-bottomed [koper-*bot*omd] *adj* (*naut*) having bottom plated with copper; sea-worthy; (*fig*) thoroughly safe; genuine, authentic.
copperhead [*kop*erhed] *n* poisonous North American snake.
copperize [*kop*erIz] *v*/*t* impregnate with copper.
copperplate [*kop*erplayt] *n* plate of copper engraved for printing; print made from this; neat regular handwriting.
coppersmith [*kop*ersmith] *n* worker in copper.
coppery [*kop*eRi] *adj* of or like copper.
coppice [*kop*is] *n* wood of small trees, cut periodically ~ **coppicing** *n* the cutting down of trees periodically so that new shoots may grow.
copra [*kop*Ra] *n* dried kernel of coconut.
coprolite [*kop*RolIt] *n* fossilized dung.
coprophilia [kopRo*fili*-a] *n* (*psych*) interest in or liking for faeces.
copse [*kop*s] *n* coppice.
Copt [*kopt*] *n* a Christian Egyptian ~ **Coptic** *n* and *adj* (language) of the Copts.
copula (*pl* **copulae**) [*kop*ewla] *n* (*gramm*) word which connects subject and predicate.
copulate [*kop*ewlayt] *v*/*i* unite in sexual intercourse.
copulation [kopew*lay*shon] *n* uniting, joining together; the sexual act, coition ~ **copulatory** *adj*.
copulative [*kop*ewlativ] *adj* relating to copulation; (*gramm*) acting as a copula.
copy [*kop*i] *n* imitation, reproduction; transcript; one of series of examples of book, document *etc*; manuscript material ready for printing; text of an advertisement; suitable subject for journalist or writer; model to be copied; (*leg*) record of admission of tenants to copyhold tenure of land ~ **copy** *v*/*t* and *i* reproduce by imitation, transcribe, imitate.
copybook [*kop*ibook] *n* book with specimens of handwriting for children to imitate; exercise book; **blot one's c.** spoil one's record ~ **copybook** *adj* trite; exemplary, perfect.
copycat [*kop*ikat] *n* (*coll*) person who imitates others slavishly or annoyingly; child who copies another's work.
copyhold [*kop*ihOld] *n* (*leg*) tenure of land at the will of the lord of the manor; estate held thus.
copying-pencil [*kop*i-ing-pensil] *n* indelible pencil.
copyist [*kop*i-ist] *n* one who makes written copies, transcriber; imitator.
copyline [*kop*ilIn] *n* advertising slogan.
copyright [*kop*iRIt] *n* exclusive right of an author,

artist *etc* to reproduce his own works during a certain period fixed by law ~ **copyright** *adj* ~ **copyright** *v*/*t* protect by securing copyright for.
copy-typist [*kop*i-tIpist] *n* typist who knows no shorthand.
copywriter [*kop*iRIter] *n* one who writes the text of advertisements.
coquet, coquette (*pres*/*part* **coquetting,** *p*/*t* and *p*/*part* **coquetted**) [kO*ket*] *v*/*i* (*of a woman*) try to attract a man's admiration, flirt; (*fig*) consider briefly and superficially.
coquetry [*kO*kitRi] *n* flirtatious behaviour.
coquette [kO*ket*] *n* woman who seeks admiration, flirt ~ **coquettish** *adj* ~ **coquettishly** *adv*.
cor [*kawr*] *interj* (*sl*) exclamation of surprise.
coracle [*koRak*'l] *n* small boat made of wickerwork covered with hide or tarpaulin.
coral [*koRal*] *n* hard substance formed of skeletons of various marine polyps; polyp capable of forming this > PDG; ornament made from this; shade of red or pink ~ **coral** *adj*.
coralline [*koRal*In] *adj* made of coral; shaped or coloured like coral ~ **coralline** *n* seaweed or animal resembling coral.
corallite [*koRal*It] *n* (*zool*) skeleton of a single coral polyp; fossilized coral.
coral-reef [koRal-*Reef*] *n* chain of rocks at or near surface of sea, built up by coral polyps > PDG.
cor anglais [kawr-ong-*glay*] *n* (*mus*) woodwind instrument one-fifth below the oboe > PDM.
coranto [koRant*O*] *n* type of lively dance.
corban [*kawr*ban] *n* (*OT*) offering given to God.
corbel [*kawr*bel] *n* (*archi*) stone bracket jutting from a wall face as support for some structural feature; short beam placed lengthwise under girder *etc* ~ **corbel** (*pres*/*part* **corbelling,** *p*/*t* and *p*/*part* **corbelled**) *v*/*t* support by a corbel; provide with corbels.
corbie [*kawr*bi] *n* (*Scots*) crow or raven.
cord [*kawrd*] *n* thick string or thin rope; (*anat*) structure resembling cord; unit of measurement for timber; corduroy ~ **cord** *v*/*t* tie with cord.
cordage [*kawr*dij] *n* ropes or cords, *esp* rigging.
cordate [*kawr*dayt] *adj* (*bot*) heart-shaped.
corded [*kawr*did] *adj* tied up with cords; made of cords; (*of cloth etc*) ribbed.
cordial [*kawr*di-al] *adj* hearty, friendly; heartfelt; (*med*) reviving, stimulating ~ **cordial** *n* medicine to stimulate the heart; warming, reviving drink ~ **cordially** *adv*.
cordiality [kawrdi-*ali*ti] *n* hearty feeling, friendliness.
cordillera [kawrdily*air*Ra] *n* ridge in group of mountain ranges > PDG.
cordite [*kawr*dIt] *n* explosive prepared from nitrocellulose and nitroglycerine.
cordon [*kawr*don] *n* ribbon worn as insignia of an order; (*hort*) fruit-tree pruned back to a single stem; (*archi*) course of stone jutting from wall; (*mil*) chain of military posts isolating an area; line of persons preventing access to some place or person; **c. bleu** first-class cook ~ **cordon** *v*/*t* surround with a cordon of military posts; **c. off** isolate (an area) with a cordon of guards, police *etc*.
corduroy [*kawr*deRoi] *n* thick cotton fabric ribbed and with velvety pile; (*pl*) trousers made of this;

road made of tree trunks laid across swampy ground ~ **corduroy** *adj*.

cordwainer [*kawrd*wayner] *n* (*ar*) shoemaker.

core [*kawr*] *n* central part, innermost part; hard central part of certain fruits; (*founding*) piece inserted into a mould to provide a hole or cavity; (*elect*) central soft iron bar in induction coil; (*min*) cylinder of rock, soil *etc* cut out by boring; column of sediment extracted from bed of sea or lake; **hard c.** (*fig*) persons impossible to reform or convince; of or for the most callous or vicious type; **soft c.** (*fig*) comparatively mild or inoffensive ~ **core** *v/t* take core out of (fruit).

corelation, corelative see **correlation, corelative.**

co-religionist [kO-Ri*lij*onist] *n* member of the same religion.

coreopsis [koRi-*opsis*] *n* (*bot*) genus of plant with bright yellow aster-like flowers.

corer [*kaw*Rer] *n* implement for removing fruit-cores; (*min*) drill for extracting cores of rock *etc*.

co-respondent [kO-Ri*spond*ent] *n* (*leg*) person charged with adultery with the petitioner's spouse in a divorce suit.

corf (*pl* **corves**) [*kawrf*] *n* basket formerly used for hoisting coal; small truck or wagon used in mines; floating basket or cage for keeping fish.

corgi [*kawr*gi] *n* breed of small Welsh dogs.

coriander [koRi-*ander*] *n* umbelliferous plant the seeds of which are used as flavouring.

Corinthian [koRinthi-an] *adj* of Corinth; **C. column** (*archi*) ornate type of Greek column.

corium [*kaw*Ri-um] *n* (*anat*) main part of the skin.

cork [*hawrk*] *n* bark of the cork-tree; piece of this cut to form a stopper ~ **cork** *v/t* close with a cork; (*fig*) keep in check; blacken with burnt cork.

corkage [*kawr*kij] *n* charge made by innkeeper for serving wine not provided by the house; corking or uncorking of bottles.

corked [*kawrkt*] *adj* closed by a cork; (*of wine*) tasting of cork; (*sl*) very drunk.

corker [*kawr*ker] *n* (*coll*) something which puts a stop to a discussion or a course of action; daring lie; a striking or eccentric personality.

corking [*kawrk*ing] *adj* (*coll*) large, outstanding, excellent.

corkscrew [*kawrk*skROO] *n* instrument of spirally twisted steel, for drawing corks from bottles ~ **corkscrew** *adj* twisting, spiralling ~ **corkscrew** *v/t* and *i* move in spiral course, twist.

cork-tree [*kawrk*-tRee] *n* type of evergreen oak.

corky [*kawr*ki] *adj* made of cork; like a cork; tasting of cork; (*sl*) lively, perky.

corm [*kawrm*] *n* (*bot*) fleshy underground stem.

cormorant [*kawr*moRant] *n* large voracious seabird; (*fig*) greedy person.

corn (1) [*kawrn*] *n* seeds of cereals, grain; any plant producing grain; wheat; oats; (*US*) maize; (*coll*) anything trite, old-fashioned, or sentimental ~ **corn** *v/t* and *i* swell into grains; sow with corn; feed oats *etc* to animals.

corn (2) *n* hardened and painful skin usually on the foot; **tread on a person's corns** offend his feelings.

corn (3) *v/t* preserve by pickling and salting.

cornbrash [*kawrn*bRash] *n* coarse chalky soil.

corn-chandler [*kawrn*-chaandler] *n* retail dealer in corn.

corncob [*kawrn*kob] *n* central spike on which grains of maize grow; pipe made from this.

corncrake [*kawrn*kRayk] *n* type of bird with piercing harsh cry.

corn-dolly [*kawrn*-doli] *n* figure made from plaited wheat, oats or barley.

cornea (*pl* **corneae**) [*kawr*ni-a] *n* (*anat*) transparent membrane protecting front of eyeball.

corned beef [kawrnd-*beef*] *n* pickled salted beef.

cornel [*kawr*nel] *n* genus of hard-wooded trees.

cornelian, carnelian [kawr*neel*yan] *n* a semiprecious stone, a variety of reddish chalcedony.

corneous [*kawr*ni-us] *adj* horn-like, horny.

corner [*kawr*ner] *n* place where two lines, sides, or surfaces meet; enclosed angle; junction of two streets; secluded or hidden spot; region of the earth; (*comm*) monopolizing purchase of some article, in order to re-sell profitably; (*Association football*) free kick from corner of field; **drive into a c.** trap, put in awkward situation; **round the c.** very near, almost in sight; **tight c.** difficult or dangerous situation; **turn the c.** begin to recover after difficulty or illness ~ **corner** *v/t* and *i* put or drive into a corner; trap, force into awkward situation; (*comm*) buy up all stocks of; (*mot*) turn a corner.

corner-boy [*kawr*ner-boi] *n* (*coll*) loafer.

cornered [*kawr*nerd] *adj* having corners; (*fig*) trapped, caught.

corner-kick [*kawr*ner-kik] *n* (*Association football*) free kick from the corner-flag.

cornerstone [*kawr*nerstOn] *n* (*archi*) stone at the corner of a building where two walls meet; foundation stone; (*fig*) indispensable part, basis.

cornerwise [*kawr*nerwIZ] *adv* diagonally; with the corner in front.

cornet [*kawr*nit] *n* (*mus*) brass wind-instrument with three valves > PDM; player of this instrument in orchestra; name of organ-stop; cone-shaped paper wrapping; cone-shaped ice-cream wafer; stiff white head-dress formerly worn by Sisters of Charity.

corn-exchange [*kawrn*-ikschaynj] *n* building where corn-merchants do business.

cornfactor [*kawrn*fakter] *n* corn-merchant.

corn-fed [*kawrn*-fed] *adj* fed on maize or corn; (*coll*) plump, healthy-looking; (*sl*) trite, old-fashioned.

cornfield [*kawrn*feeld] *n* field where corn (in US, maize) is grown.

cornflakes [*kawrn*flayks] *n* (*tr*) a cereal dish prepared from roasted maize.

cornflour [*kawrn*flowr] *n* finely ground flour of maize, rice *etc*.

cornflower [*kawrn*flowr] *n* (*bot*) blue-flowered plant growing wild in cornfields; similar garden plant with blue, white and pink flowers.

cornice [*kawr*nis] *n* (*archi*) the crowning overhang of an entablature; (*bui*) projecting course of masonry at top of building; moulding covering junction between wall and ceiling; decorative pelmet; overhanging snow at edge of precipice.

cornily [*kawr*nili] *adv* (*sl*) in a corny way.

corniness [*kawr*ninis] *n* (*sl*) quality of being corny.

Cornish [*kawr*nish] *n* and *adj* (ancient language) of Cornwall.

cornland [*kawrn*land] *n* land growing corn; land suitable for corn (in US, maize).

cornucopia [kawrnew*kOp*i-a] *n* (*myth*) the horn of plenty; (*arts*) representation of a goat's horn overflowing with flowers, fruit, and corn.

cornuted [kawr*newt*id] *adj* having horns.

corny [*kawr*ni] *adj* producing or made from corn; (*sl*) hackneyed, old-fashioned, over-sentimental.

corolla [ko*Ro*la] *n* (*bot*) whorl of petals contained by sepals or calyx.

corollary [ko*Role*Ri] *n* (*log*, *geom*) inference following directly from a proposition already proved.

corona [ko*RO*na] *n* (*astron*) fringe of light round sun seen in total eclipse; circle of light round sun or moon > PDG; (*eccles*) circular hanging chandelier; (*anat*) upper surface of tooth or skull; (*archi*) a vertical part of cornice; (*elect*) luminous discharge from a conductor at high potential; long, blunt-ended cigar.

coronach [ko*Ro*nak] *n* (*Scots*) bagpipe dirge.

coronal (1) [ko*Ro*nal] *n* circlet of gold, jewels *etc* for the head; garland for the head.

coronal (2) *adj* pertaining to the corona; **c. suture** junction between frontal and parietal bones.

coronary [ko*Rene*Ri] *adj* like a crown; (*anat*) relating to the arteries supplying blood to the heart; **c. thrombosis** formation of a clot in a coronary artery ~ **coronary** *n* heart attack caused by coronary thrombosis and infarction.

coronation [ko*Ro*nayshon] *n* act or ceremony of crowning a sovereign or sovereign's consort.

coroner [ko*Ro*ner] *n* (*leg*) officer of county or borough appointed to hold inquiry into cause of any violent or mysterious death, or into ownership of treasure-trove.

coronet [ko*Ro*nit] *n* small crown worn by princes or peers; gold or jewelled band for head; garland for head ~ **coroneted** *adj*.

corozo [ko*ROz*O] *n* South American tree.

corporal (1) [*kawr*po*Ral*] *adj* of the human body; **c. punishment** whipping or flogging.

corporal (2) *n* (*eccles*) linen cloth spread on the altar during Mass.

corporal (3) *n* non-commissioned military officer ranking below sergeant; (*naut*) petty officer under master-at-arms.

corporalcy [*kawr*po*Ral*si] *n* rank of a corporal.

corporality [kawrpo*Ral*iti] *n* state of existing in bodily form; material existence.

corporally [*kawr*po*Ral*i] *adv* in bodily form.

corporate [*kawr*po*Rit*] *adj* pertaining to, forming a corporation; joint; **c. state** system of government based on trade and professional corporations > PDPol ~ **corporately** *adv*.

corporation [kawrpo*Ray*shon] *n* (*leg*) group of persons considered as a single unit; elected body carrying on civic business; (*US*) joint-stock company; (*coll*) large protruding stomach ~ **corporative** [*kawr*po*Rativ*] *adj*.

corporeal [kawr*pawR*i-al] *adj* bodily, physical, material; (*leg*) consisting of tangible objects.

corporeality [kawrpawR*i*-aliti] *n* corporeity.

corporealize [kawr*pawR*i-alIz] *v/i* materialize.

corporeally [kawr*pawR*i-ali] *adv* in bodily form.

corporeity [kawrpaw*Ree*-iti] *n* physical existence.

corposant [*kawr*pOzant] *n* flame-like electrical discharge sometimes seen on ship during storm.

corps (*pl* corps) [*kawr*] *n* (*mil*) largest tactical unit; department or branch of army; organized and trained group; **c. de ballet** (*Fr*) dancers in ballet not classed as soloists; **c. diplomatique** (*Fr*) persons attached to embassies or legations.

corpse [*kawrps*] *n* dead body of human being.

corpse-candle [*kawrps*-kand'l] *n* will-o'-the-wisp, *esp* in churchyards; tall candle by a bier.

corpulence [*kawr*pewlens] *n* stoutness of body, obesity ~ **corpulency** *n* ~ **corpulent** *adj*.

corpus (*pl* corpora) [*kawr*pus] *n* all extant writings of given type, age *etc*; principal, capital; (*anat*) main part of an organ; **C. Christi** (*eccles*) feast day in honour of the Eucharist.

corpuscle, corpuscule [*kawr*pus'l/*kawr*pus'l, *kawr*pus*kewl*] *n* a particle of matter; (*biol*) a protoplasmic cell, *esp* one floating in the blood.

corpuscular [*kawr*pus*kewl*er] *adj* of corpuscles; **c. theory** theory that light consists of minute particles in rapid motion > PDS.

corral [ko*Ral*] *n* pen for horses or cattle or for capturing wild animals; defensive enclosure formed of wagons *etc* ~ **corral** (*pres/part* corralling, *p/t* and *p/part* corralled) *v/t* enclose in a corral; (*sl*) seize possession of.

correct [ko*Rekt*] *v/t* put right, remove errors or defects from; blame or punish for faults of character; adjust, bring into conformity with accepted standard; neutralize, cure ~ **correct** *adj* right, accurate; conforming to accepted standards; seemly, suitable.

correction [ko*Rek*shon] *n* act of correcting; alteration made in correcting; punishment; **house of c.** reformatory, prison ~ **correctional** *adj*.

correctitude [ko*Rekt*itewd] *n* correctness of behaviour.

corrective [ko*Rekt*iv] *n* and *adj* (something) tending to correct.

correctly [ko*Rekt*li] *adv* in a correct way.

correctness [ko*Rekt*nis] *n* quality of being correct.

corrector [ko*Rek*ter] *n* one who, or that which, corrects; (*print*) proof-reader.

correlate [ko*Ri*layt] *v/i* and *t* be mutually related; bring into relation with; show relationship between ~ **correlate** *n* either of two mutually related things, *esp* if each implies the other.

correlation [ko*Ri*layshon] *n* mutual relation of two or more things; act or process of showing the existence of a relation between things.

correlative [ko*Rel*ativ] *adj* mutually related; (*phys*) mutually convertible; (*gram*) (*of pairs of words*) corresponding and habitually used together (*eg either . . . or*) ~ **correlative** *n* correlative thing, force, or word ~ **correlatively** *adv*.

correligionist see co·religionist.

correspond [ko*Ris*pond] *v/i* agree with, be in accordance with; be similar or equivalent to; regularly write letters to.

correspondence [ko*Ris*pondens] *n* agreement, accordance; equivalence; analogy; communication by letters; collection of letters; **c. column** part of newspaper reserved for letters from readers; **c. course** course of postal tuition.

correspondency [ko*Ris*pondensi] *n* similarity, analogy; equivalence.

correspondent [ko*Ris*pondent] *n* one who writes letters to another; one who writes regular articles for newspaper or magazine, *esp* one reporting from abroad; (*comm*) person or firm having regular business relations with another; **foreign c.** journalist specializing in reporting from abroad; (*comm*) clerk dealing with firm's foreign letters ~ **correspondent** *adj* similarly related, agreeing, equivalent.

corresponding [koRis*pond*ing] *adj* similarly related, agreeing, equivalent; keeping in touch by letters ~ **correspondingly** *adv*.

corrida [koReeda] *n* (*Sp*) bull-fight.

corridor [koRider] *n* long passage into which many doors open; passage in railway coach into which compartments open; route to which aircraft are restricted; (*pol*) strip of territory independent of State through which it passes; **c. train** one composed of coaches with corridors.

corrie [koRi] *n* (*Scots*) steep hollow on a hillside.

corrigendum (*pl* **corrigenda**) [koRi*jend*um] *n* note of error in a printed book; (*pl*) list of corrections to be made.

corrigible [koRijib'l] *adj* capable of being corrected; submitting to correction.

corroborant [koRoboRant] *adj* and *n* invigorating (medicine); corroborative (fact).

corroborate [koRoboRayt] *v/t* confirm, strengthen by fresh evidence ~ **corroboration** [koRoboRayshon] *n* act of corroborating; evidence which corroborates ~ **corroborative** [koRoboRativ] *adj* ~ **corroboratory** [koRoboRayteRi] *adj*.

corroboree [koRoboRee] *n* festive dance of Australian aborigines; (*coll*) celebration, spree.

corrode [koROd] *v/t* and *i* gradually destroy, *esp* by chemical action; wear, waste away, grow rusty; (*fig*) torment, prey upon ~ **corrodent** *n* and *adj* (substance) which corrodes ~ **corrodible** *adj* corrosible.

corrosible [koROzib'l] *adj* capable of corrosion.

corrosion [koROzhon] *n* act or process of corroding; (*chem*) surface chemical action, especially on metals, by moisture, air, or chemicals.

corrosive [koROsiv] *adj* corroding; (*med*) caustic; (*fig*) destructive, fretting, wearing; **c. sublimate** mercuric chloride > PDS ~ **corrosive** *n* substance which corrodes ~ **corrosively** *adv* ~ **corrosiveness** *n*.

corrugate [koRoogayt] *v/t* and *i* wrinkle up; contract into rounded folds ~ **corrugated** *adj* formed into ridges or folds; **c. iron** steel sheet corrugated and galvanized on both sides.

corrugation [koRoogayshon] *n* ridge or fold of a corrugated surface.

corrupt [koRupt] *adj* putrid, rotten, infected; morally evil, vicious; willing to take bribes; decaying; (*of languages*) mixed; (*of texts*) untrue to original, incorrect ~ **corrupt** *v/t* and *i* render corrupt, deprave; bribe; (*of texts*) falsify; become corrupt; putrefy ~ **corrupter** *n*.

corruptible [koRuptib'l] *adj* subject to decay; bribable; mortal ~ **corruptibly** *adv*.

corruption [koRupshon] *n* act of corrupting; state of being corrupt; that which corrupts; depravity; bribery; decay ~ **corruptive** *adj*.

corruptly [koRuptli] *adv* in a corrupt way.

corruptness [koRuptnis] *n* state or quality of being corrupt.

corsage [kawrsaazh/kawrsaazh/kawrsij] *n* bodice of a dress; posy worn at the waist or bodice.

corsair [kawrsair] *n* pirate; pirate ship.

corse [kawrs] *n* (*poet*) corpse.

corset [kawrsit] *n* close-fitting undergarment worn to improve the shape of the figure ~ **corseted** *adj* ~ **corseting** *n*.

corsetry [kawrsitRi] *n* art of making or fitting corsets; corsets in general.

corslet, corselet [kawrslit] *n* sleeveless close-fitting body-armour; flexible corset; (*ent*) thorax.

cortège [kawrtayzh] *n* train of attendants; ceremonial procession, *esp* funeral procession.

cortex (*pl* **cortices**) [kawrteks, kawrtiseez] *n* (*bot*) bark of tree; (*anat*) outer layer, *esp* of brain.

cortical [kawrtikal] *adj* (*bot*) pertaining to cortex; (*anat, zool*) forming outer part of body or organ; (*med*) of or in the brain cortex.

cortisone [kawrtizOn] *n* (*med*) a steroid hormone used as a powerful anti-inflammatory drug.

corundum [koRundum] *n* natural aluminium oxide, used as an abrasive.

coruscate [koRuskayt] *v/i* sparkle, glitter.

coruscation [koRuskayshon] *n* sudden flash.

corvette [kawrvet] *n* fast naval escort vessel.

corvine [kawrvIn] *adj* pertaining to raven or crow.

corymb [koRimb] *n* (*bot*) flat cluster of flowers.

coryza [koRIza] *n* (*med*) nasal catarrh.

cos (1) [kos] *n* long-leaved lettuce.

cos (2) abbreviation of **cosine**.

'cos [koz] *abbr* (*coll*) because.

cosecant (*abbr* **cosec**) [kOseekant] *n* (*geom*) secant of the complement of an angle.

coseismal [kosIzmal] *n* (*geog*) line or area where earthquake shocks are equally and simultaneously felt ~ **coseismal** *adj* ~ **coseismic** *adj*.

cosh [kosh] *n* (*coll*) small weighted bludgeon ~ **cosh** *v/t* strike with a cosh; render unconscious.

cosher [kosher] *v/t* pamper, coddle.

co-signatory [kO-signatoRi] *n* and *adj* (one) who signs jointly with others.

cosily [kOzili] *adv* in a cosy way, comfortably.

cosine (*abbr* **cos**) [kOsIn] *n* (*geom*) sine of the complement of an angle.

cosiness [kOzinis] *n* state of being cosy.

cosmetic [kosmetik] *n* preparation for beautifying skin, complexion, or hair ~ **cosmetic** *adj* increasing beauty; **c. surgery** surgery to remedy defects in or damage to one's appearance.

cosmetician [kosmetishen] *n* one who makes, sells, or applies cosmetics.

cosmic [kozmic] *adj* pertaining to whole universe; of outer space; grandiose, vast; harmonious; **c. dust** small particles of matter distributed throughout space; **c. philosophy** theory of evolution of universe; **c. rays** very energetic radiation reaching earth from outer space > PDS ~ **cosmical** *adj* > **cosmically** *adv*.

cosmo- *pref* the universe.

cosmogony [kozmogoni] *n* origin of the universe; theory of the origin and early history of the universe ~ **cosmogonic** [kozmOgonik] *adj*.

cosmography [kozmogRafi] *n* description of the universe; science of the constitution of the universe ~ **cosmographer** *n* ~ **cosmographic(al)** [kozmOgRafik(al)] *adj*.

cosmology [kozmoloji] *n* study of the universe as a system; branch of metaphysics regarding the universe as an ordered whole ~ **cosmological** [kozmolojikal] *adj* ~ **cosmologist** *n*.

cosmonaut [kozmOnawt] *n* astronaut.

cosmopolitan [kozmo*politan*] *adj* living or found in all parts of world; belonging to whole world; free from national prejudice; widely-travelled ~ **cosmopolitan** *n* person feeling himself at home anywhere ~ **cosmopolitanism** *n*.

cosmopolite [kozmo*polit*] *n* a cosmopolitan.

cosmopolitical [kozmopo*litikal*] *adj* of international politics.

cosmos (1) [*kozmos*] *n* universe, as an ordered system; (*fig*) harmonious system.

cosmos (2) *n* (*bot*) group of composite flowers.

cosmotron [*kozmot*Ron] *n* (*phys*) machine for accelerating protons.

Cossack [*kosak*] *n* member of tribe of horsemen in southern Russia ~ **Cossack** *adj*.

cosset [*kosit*] *v/t* pet, pamper.

cost [*kost*] *n* price of purchase; expense of production; (*fig*) expenditure (of energy, time *etc*) in achieving an object; suff ing, loss; (*pl*) expenses of lawsuit; **at all costs** whatever may happen; **c. of living** average cost of necessities of life; **c. price** seller's own outlay; **to one's c.** to one's detriment; **cost-plus contract** one in which a contractor is paid for his work according to the cost of materials and labour, plus a fixed percentage fee ~ **cost** (*p/t* and *p/part* **cost**) *v/t* cause expenditure of; (*fig*) involve the loss of, cause pain *etc*; (*comm*) estimate expense of producing.

costal [*kostal*] *adj* (*anat*) of the ribs.

co-star (*pres/part* **co-starring**, *p/t* and *p/part* **co-starred**) [kO-*staar*] *v/i* and *t* have parts of equal prominence in play or film; (*of film*) include two or more star actors.

costard [*kosterd*] *n* kind of large apple.

costate(d) [*kostayt*(id)] *adj* (*bot*, *zool*) having ribs.

costean [*kosteen*] *v/i* (*min*) search for lodes by sinking pits or trenching at right-angles to presumed outcrop; clear by controlled rush of water > PDE.

cost-effective [*kost*-ifektiv] *adj* producing a result that justifies the outlay.

cosfer [*koster*] *n* a costermonger.

costermonger [*kostermung*-ger] *n* man who sells fruit and vegetables from a barrow.

costing [*kosting*] *n* (*bui etc*) process of calculating the cost of doing a unit of work.

costive [*kostiv*] *adj* constipated; causing constipation; (*fig*) sluggish.

costly [*kostli*] *adj* expensive, dear; sumptuous ~ **costliness** *n*.

costume [*kostewm*] *n* style of clothing, *esp* if characteristic of given period or place; period or fantastic clothing worn by actors in play; woman's two-piece dress or suit; appearance of an animal proper to a particular season; **c. ball** fancy-dress ball; **c. jewellery** items of adornment made from metals, stones *etc* of little or no value ~ **costume** *v/t* provide costumes for ~ **costumer** *n* maker or seller of period costumes.

costumier [kos*tewmi*-er] *n* one who makes or sells costumes; dressmaker.

cosy [kOzi] *adj* warm, comfortable ~ **cosy** *n* covering to keep teapot or egg-cup warm.

cot (1) [*kot*] *n* (*poet*) humble cottage; hut.

cot (2) *n* child's bed; bed in hospital; light bed-stead; (*naut*) bed suspended from beams of a ship for officers and the sick; (*med*) sheath, stall.

cotangent (*abbr* cot) [kO*tanjent*] *n* (*geom*) tangent of complement of an angle.

cot-case [*kot*-kays] *n* (*coll*) patient too ill to walk.

cote [*kOt*] *n* shelter for domestic animals or birds.

cotenant [kO*tenent*] *n* joint tenant.

coterie [*kOteRee*] *n* clique, small exclusive group with similar views, tastes *etc*.

co-terminous [kO-*turminus*] *adj* conterminous.

cothurnus (*pl* **cothurni**) [kO*thurnus*] *n* thick-soled boot worn by actors in Greek tragedy.

co-tidal [kO-*tidal*] *adj* having high tide at the same time; **c. line** line on map linking places where high tide occurs simultaneously

cotillion [ko*tilyon*] *n* elaborate dance with frequent changes of partner; music for this dance.

cotoneaster [kotOni-*aster*] *n* genus of small trees and shrubs with bright berries.

cotta [*kota*] *n* (*eccles*) short surplice.

cottage [*kotij*] *n* small dwelling-house, *esp* in the country; (*sl*) public lavatory; **c. cheese** type of soft white cheese; **c. industry** industrial work done at home; **c. loaf** loaf formed of two rounded lumps; **c. piano** small upright piano; **c. pie** minced meat covered with mashed potatoes and baked ~ **cottage** *v/i* (*sl*, *of homosexuals*) solicit in public lavatories ~ **cottager** *n* one who lives in a cottage.

cottar, cotter (1) [*koter*] *n* (*Scots*) man occupying cottage on farm in exchange for work; cottager.

cotter (2) *n* wedge or bolt to tighten machinery and hold it together; **c. pin** split pin the ends of which are bent outwards after it has been inserted into a slot ~ **cotter** *v/t*.

cottier [*koti*-er] *n* a cottager.

cotton [*kot*'n] *n* plant producing downy seed-hairs; thread made from these hairs; cloth woven from cotton thread ~ **cotton** *adj* ~ **cotton** *v/i* (*fig*) like, be favourably impressed by; **c. on to** take a liking to; understand and accept (an idea); **c. up** to make friends with.

cottoncake [*kot*'nkayk] *n* mass of compressed and oil-free cotton-seed used as cattle food.

cottongrass [*kot*'ngRaas] *n* species of sedge bearing heads with long silky hairs.

cottonpress [*kot*'npRes] *n* machine for pressing cotton into bales.

cottontail [*kot*'ntayl] *n* (*US*) rabbit.

cotton-waste [*kot*'n-wayst] *n* refuse from manufacture of cotton, used for cleaning machinery.

cottonwood [*kot*'nwood] *n* (*US*) species of poplar.

cottonwool [*kot*'nwool] *n* fluffy mass of clean cotton hairs used for dressing wounds, wiping off ointments, *etc*; **wrap in c.** (*coll*) pamper, spoil.

cottony [*kot*'ni] *adj* resembling cotton, covered with soft down.

cotyledon [koti*leedon*] *n* (*bot*) leaf forming part of embryo of seeds > PDB ~ **cotyledonous** *adj*.

couch (1) [*kowch*] *n* long padded seat, sofa; (*poet*) bed; resting-place; first coat of paint, size *etc*; frame ~ **couch** *v/t* and *i* lay down, lower as if in rest; lie down, recline; crouch; lie in wait; express in words or writing; hold (lance) ready.

couch (2) *n* couch-grass.

couchant [*kowchant*] *adj* (*her*) lying down.

couch-grass [*kooch*-gRaas/*kowch*-gRaas] *n* species of grass with long creeping roots.

couching [kowching] n (sewing) laying down of threads held by single transverse stitches.

cougar [kOOgaar] n large feline quadruped, puma.

cough [kof] v/i drive air explosively and noisily from lungs to relieve irritation; do this repeatedly or habitually; **c. up** expel by coughing; (coll) reveal or pay up unwillingly ~ **cough** n noisy, violent expulsion of air from lungs; disease or inflammation of lungs or throat causing this.

cough-drop [kof-dRop] n lozenge taken to alleviate a cough; (sl) person hard to outwit.

could [kood] p/t of **can** (3).

couldn't [koodent] (abbr) could not.

couldst [koodst] (ar) 2nd pers sing p/t of **can** (3).

coulisse [kOOlees] n (carp) a timber grooved for a frame to slide in it; (pl) wings in a theatre.

coulomb [kOOlom] n (elect) quantity of electricity transferred by one ampere in one second.

coulter, colter [kOlter] n the front vertical blade of a plough in front of the share.

coumarin [kOOmaRin] n crystalline substance obtained from the tonka bean or other plants, used as an anti-coagulant.

coumarone [kOOmaROn] n (chem) benzofuran; organic compound used in paints and varnishes.

council [kownsil] n assembly called together for deliberative or executive purposes; persons elected to carry on local government, or to run the business of parish, society etc; (fig) discussion of plan of action; **Privy C.** persons appointed to advise Sovereign; **C. of War** emergency conference of generals in the field.

council-chamber [kownsil-chaymber] n room where council meets.

council-house [kownsil-hows] n dwelling-house built by a local authority.

councillor [kownsiler] n member of a council.

council-school [kownsil-skOOl] n school financed by a local authority.

counsel [kownsel] n advice, guidance; consultation; legal adviser, advocate, barrister; group of barristers or advocates acting in lawsuit or trial; **keep one's own c.** keep one's thoughts secret; **King's (Queen's) C.** barrister appointed as Counsel to the Crown; **c. of perfection** excellent but impracticable advice ~ **counsel** (pres/part **counselling**, p/t and p/part **counselled**) v/t advise; recommend, urge adoption of.

counsellor [kownseler] n adviser; person trained to advise others on personal problems; counsel, barrister; diplomat ranking immediately below minister ~ **counsellorship** n.

count (1) [kownt] v/t and i repeat numerals in order up to and including specified numeral; reckon total number of; calculate; include in calculations; be included in calculations; be of value or importance; esteem, consider important; (phys) apply a Geiger counter to detect radioactivity; **c. down** count backwards, esp in reckoning time; **c. for** be considered as; **c. in** include; **c. on** rely on; **c. out** adjourn for lack of a quorum; (boxing) declare boxer to be loser when he fails to rise within ten seconds; **c. out** (coll) exclude, omit ~ **count** n act of reckoning; total; (boxing) process of counting out; (leg) each separate charge in an indictment; (spinning) number of hanks of cotton to a pound; **on all counts** in every

respect; **take no c. of** disregard; **take the c.** (boxing) be counted out.

count (2) n European title of nobility corresponding to English title of Earl.

countdown [kowntdown] n process of counting backwards to zero in timing the firing of a missile.

countenance [kowntinans] n expression of face; favour, encouragement; patronage; **keep one's c.** prevent one's emotions from appearing; **lose c.** lose composure, show grief or embarrassment; **out of c.** disconcerted ~ **countenance** v/t approve, encourage; permit, tolerate.

counter (1) [kownter] n one who or that which counts, computer; small disc used to count score in card-games; imitation coin; any small disc; **Geiger c.** instrument for measuring radioactivity > PDE; **c. word** term of praise or blame weakened by indiscriminate use.

counter (2) n table in bank or shop across which money is counted out or goods sold; **under the c.** surreptitiously, illegally.

counter (3) part of horse's breast between shoulders and under neck; (naut) curved part of stern of ship; depressed part of face of printing type, coin or medal; stiff leather at heel of boot.

counter (4) adj and adv opposite, contrary, in opposition to ~ **counter** v/t and i reply to an attack, make a countermove; (boxing) strike a blow while parrying ~ **counter** n (boxing) blow dealt to parry that of opponent; (fencing) circular parry.

counter- pref opposite; retaliating; neutralizing.

counteract [kownteRakt] v/t neutralize the effects of, check, hinder, mitigate ~ **counteraction** n.

counterattack [kownteRatak] v/t (mil) attack in reply to enemy advance; (fig) retort aggressively ~ **counterattack** n.

counter-attraction [kownter-atRakshon] n attraction competing with another.

counterbalance [kownterbalans] n weight balancing another; (fig) opposing force or influence of equal strength ~ **counterbalance** v/t weigh against or oppose with an equal weight or power; compensate for.

counterblast [kownterblaast] n violent denunciation, aggressive retort.

countercharge [kownterchaarj] n (leg) charge brought by accused against accuser.

countercheck [kownterchek] n check arresting the course of something; double confirmatory check ~ **countercheck** v/t.

counterclaim [kownterklaym] n (leg) claim set up by defendant against plaintiff.

counter-clockwise [kownter-klokwIz] adv and adj anti-clockwise.

counter-die [kownter-dI] n upper stamp of die.

counter-espionage [kownter-espi-onaazh] n system of spying to defeat enemy spies.

counterfeit [kownterfitl] adj made in imitation with intent to deceive; forged; spurious ~ **counterfeit** n skilful and dishonest imitation; forgery; impostor, cheat ~ **counterfeit** v/t.

counterfoil [kownterfoil] n the counterpart of a bank-cheque, postal order, receipt etc retained by issuer as a record.

counter-irritant [kownter-iRitant] n (med) irritant applied to skin to relieve more deep-seated inflammation ~ **counter-irritation** n.

counter-jumper [*kown*ter-jumper] *n* (*coll cont*) shop-assistant.

countermand [kownter*maand*] *v/t* revoke, cancel (an order) ~ **countermand** *n* annullation.

countermarch [*kown*termaarch] *v/i* march in opposite direction to previous march; change relative order of soldiers during march.

countermark [*kown*termaark] *n* additional mark put on goods for extra security; hallmark added by Goldsmiths' Company.

countermine [*kown*term*I*n] *n* (*mil* and *naut*) mine to destroy enemy's mine; (*fig*) plot to defeat another plot ~ **countermine** *v/t* and *i*.

countermove [*kown*term*OO*v] *n* move in opposition to another.

counter-offensive [kownter-o*fen*siv] *n* (*mil*) attack by those previously on the defensive.

counterpane [*kown*terpayn] *n* bedspread.

counterpart [*kown*terpaart] *n* part corresponding or complementary to another; person or thing similar to another in function; duplicate, copy.

counterphobia [kownter*f*Obi-a] *n* (*psych*) denial or sublimation of inner fears by symbolic experience of them or by hostile projections of them onto others ~ **counterphobic** *adj* ~ **counterphobe** *n*.

counterplea [*kown*terplee] *n* (*leg*) answer to a plea.

counterplot [*kown*terplot] *n* plot to defeat another plot; subsidiary plot of a play.

counterpoint [*kown*terpoint] *n* (*mus*) simultaneous and harmonious combination of two or more melodies > PDM.

counterpoise [*kown*terpoiz] *n* weight which balances another weight; equilibrium; (*fig*) influence *etc* neutralizing another; (*rad*) insulated wiring beneath an aerial ~ **counterpoise** *v/t* and *i* counterbalance; act as a counterbalance.

counter-productive [kownter-pR*Odu*ktiv] *adj* having a result opposite to that intended.

counter-revolution [kownter-R*evol*OOshon] *n* revolution designed to reverse effect of a previous revolution ~ **counter-revolutionary** *adj* and *n*.

countersign (1) [*kown*ters*I*n] *n* password in answer to sentry's challenge; secret sign given in reply.

countersign (2) *v/t* sign (document) already signed by someone else; (*fig*) ratify, confirm.

countersink (*p/t* **countersank**, *p/part* **countersunk**) [*kown*tersink] *v/t* bevel the edge of a hole until screw, bolt *etc* can be sunk flush with surface; sink (screw *etc*) in such a hole ~ **countersink** *n* drill or bit for countersinking; degree to which hole is bevelled.

counter-suggestible see **contra-suggestible**.

counter-tenor [*kown*ter-tener] *n* (*mus*) male alto voice; part written for such a voice > PDM.

countess [*kown*tis] *n* wife or widow of earl; wife, widow, or daughter of count.

counting-house [*kown*ting-hows] *n* business office where accounts are kept.

countless [*kown*tles] *adj* innumerable.

count-out [kownt-*owt*] *n* premature adjournment of assembly for lack of quorum.

countrified [*kunt*Rif*I*d] *adj* fond of country life; resembling country people in manner, outlook *etc*; rustic, rural.

country [*kunt*Ri] *n* land with well-marked boundaries, with distinctive name and inhabited by one nation; inhabitants of such a land; one's native land; district sparsely built over and free from industry, rural area; area considered as possessing given physical characteristics or as suitable for given sport *etc*; (*fig*) range of knowledge, ideas *etc*; (*cricket*) outfield; **c. club** sporting or social club owning land in country district; **c. cousin** person bewildered by, or naïvely admiring, town life; **go to the c.** hold general election; **God's own c.** (*US*) America; **c. and western** type of popular American folk music ~ **country** *adj* rural, rustic.

country-dance [kuntRi-*daans*] *n* dance for several couples arranged in rows or circles.

countryman [*kunt*Riman] *n* man from one's native land; man living and working in the country.

country-seat [*kunt*Ri-seet] *n* residence of wealthy rural landowner.

countryside [*kunt*Risid] *n* rural area.

countrywide [kuntRiw*I*d] *adj* extending through a whole country or nation.

countrywoman [*kunt*Riwoman] *n* woman from one's native land; woman living in country.

county [*kown*ti] *n* administrative division of a state, a shire; people of a county; landed gentry of a county; **c. borough** borough administratively independent; **c. council** elected body running business of a county; **c. court** local civil court chiefly for recovering small debts; **c. town** administrative centre of a county ~ **county** *adj* pertaining to a county or to landed gentry; (*coll*) upper-class; socially exclusive.

coup [k*OO*] *n* (*Fr*) sudden action, sudden change of government by force; successful stroke, deal, or stratagem; **c. de grâce** death blow, finishing stroke; **c. de théâtre** startling development, *esp* in a drama; **coup d'état** sudden overthrow of a government by force.

coupé [k*OO*pay] *n* closed two-seater motorcar or carriage; closed two-door motorcar; end compartment of railway carriage with one row of seats only.

couple [*kup*'l] *n* pair, two similar persons or things closely associated or linked; husband and wife; engaged pair; two dancing partners; pair of sexual partners; (*phys*) two equal and opposite parallel forces acting on a body; (*bui*) a pair of rafters in roof; leash for two hounds ~ **couple** *v/t* and *i* fasten together, link; connect; associate (two ideas *etc*); copulate, mate.

coupler [*kup*ler] *n* he who, that which, couples; any device for linking two parts of machinery.

couplet [*kup*lit] *n* pair of rhyming lines of verse.

coupling [*kup*ling] *n* act of joining together; that which joins or connects; device for joining parts of machinery: link connecting railway carriages; (*elect*) device for connecting two circuits; (*biol*) copulation, mating.

coupon [k*OO*pon] *n* detachable portion of ticket, document *etc*; detachable section of bond, entitling holder to claim interest; ticket to be exchanged for goods *etc*; ration ticket; entry form for football pools, newspaper competitions *etc*.

courage [*ku*Rij] *n* power of facing danger, pain *etc* without fear, bravery.

courageous [ku*Ray*jus] *adj* brave, fearless ~ **courageously** *adv* ~ **courageousness** *n*.

courgette [koorz*het*] *n* small vegetable marrow.

courier [*koo*Ri-er] *n* express messenger, despatch-rider; person employed to make all arrangements for a conducted foreign tour.

course [*kaws*] *n* continuous onward movement, progress, trend; passage of time; sequence of related events; direction of movement; natural development; path along which something moves, channel; (*fig*) mode of action, regular procedure; area of land prepared for races, sport *etc*; route to be followed by competitors in a race; connected series of lessons; part of meal served at one time; (*archi*) unbroken horizontal layer of bricks, stone *etc* along surface of building; race between two greyhounds pursuing a hare; (*pl*) (*naut*) sails on lowest yards; (*bell-ringing*) complete set of changes; (*pl*) period of menstrual bleeding; **in due c.** at proper time; **of c.** naturally; **a matter of c.** natural, to be expected ∼ **course** *v/t* and *i* hunt, pursue; hunt with greyhounds by sight; move swiftly, run freely.

courser [*kaws*er] *n* one who pursues sport of coursing; dog used for coursing; swift horse.

coursing [*kaws*ing] *n* hunting by sight, *esp* of hares by greyhounds.

court [*kawt*] *n* roofless space enclosed by walls or buildings; paved yard surrounded by houses; large house or block of flats; enclosed place marked out for certain ball games; residence of sovereign; household and retinue of sovereign; formal gathering held by sovereign; place where trials, judicial inquiries *etc* are held; the judges, magistrates *etc* assembled to administer justice; homage, behaviour designed to win favour, amorous attentions; **c. circular** daily bulletin of activities of royal court; **put oneself out of c.** forfeit right to consideration ∼ **court** *v/t* seek the favour of, endeavour to please by constant attentions; woo; (*fig*) act in such a way as to deserve, run the risk of.

court-card [*kawt*-kaard] *n* king, queen, or knave in a pack of playing-cards.

court-dress [*kawt*-dRes] *n* formal clothes worn by those attending a royal court.

courteous [*kurti*-us] *adj* polite, gracious, showing courtesy ∼ **courteously** *adv*.

courtesan [*kawt*izan] *n* prostitute.

courtesy [*kurt*isi] *n* politeness compounded of good breeding, considerateness, and dignity; courteous action; favour; **by c.** as a favour, not by legal right; **c. title** title customarily given but of no legal value.

court-fool [*kawt*-fOOl] *n* (*hist*) official jester at royal court.

court-guide [*kawt*-gId] *n* directory of persons presented at court and of those living in upper-class district.

court-hand [*kawt*-hand] *n* form of handwriting formerly used in legal documents.

courthouse [*kawt*hows] *n* building in which courts of law are held.

courtier [*kawt*i-er] *n* person frequenting a royal court; person with ingratiating manner, flatterer.

courting [*kawt*ing] *n* process or period of wooing before marriage ∼ **courting** *adj*.

courtly [*kawt*li] *adj* having polished manners, dignified ∼ **courtliness** *n*.

court-martial (*pl* **courts-martial**) [kawt-*maar*-sha*l] *n* (*mil*) trial of soldier, sailor, or airman by his officers for offences against military law; tribunal of officers empowered to conduct this; **drumhead c.** summary court-martial in time of war ∼ **court-martial** (*pres/part* **court-martialling**, *p/t* and *p/part* **court-martialled**) *v/t*.

court-plaster [*kawt*-plaaster] *n* type of sticking-plaster for small cuts.

courtship [*kawt*ship] *n* courting.

courtyard [*kawt*yaard] *n* large paved space surrounded by walls or buildings.

cousin [*kuz*'n] *n* name given to certain blood-relatives; **first c., c. german** child of one's uncle or aunt; **first c. once removed** one's parent's first cousin; child of one's first cousin; **second c.** child of one's parent's first cousin ∼ **cousinly** *adj* ∼ **cousinship** *n*.

couth [*kOOth*] *adj* (*coll*) having good manners.

couture [*kOO*tewr] *adj* and *n* (*Fr*) (*of*) fashionable designing of clothes.

couturier [kOO*tewr*Ri-ay] *n* (*Fr*) dress-designer.

couvade [koovaad] *n* (*Fr*) custom among some primitive races in which a man takes to his bed while his wife is in childbirth.

covalent [kO*vay*lent] *adj* (*of a chemical bond*) consisting of two shared electrons; **c. crystal** one in which the atoms are held in their lattice by covalent bonds > PDS.

cove (1) [*kOv*] *n* small bay, inlet; steep ravine in mountain-side; sheltered spot among hills; (*archi*) concave moulding where wall joins ceiling ∼ **cove** *v/t* (*archi*) arch over, mould concavely.

cove (2) *n* (*sl*) fellow, chap.

coven [*kuv*'n] *n* gathering of witches.

covenant [*kuv*enant] *n* solemn mutual agreement or undertaking; (*leg*) contract containing undertaking, *esp* to pay specified annual sum to charity; (*OT*) promise of God to Jews ∼ **covenant** *v/t* and *i* promise by covenant; make a covenant.

covenanter [*kuv*enanter] *n* one who enters into a covenant; (*Scots*) adherent of the Solemn League and Covenant in 1643, or the National Covenant in 1638.

Coventry [*kov*entRi/*kuv*entRi] *n* **send to C.** punish by refusing to speak to or have dealings with.

cover [*kuv*er] *v/t* place or spread one thing completely over another; extend over, lie upon, be abundant on surface of; place a protection in front of, shield; (*mil*) stand, or march, directly behind; conceal; protect financially; protect by insurance; be sufficient for (an expense); go over (a certain distance), travel; (*fig*) be adequate to meet, take into account; (*fig*) deal with, treat of, survey; (*fig*) overcome, overwhelm; (*journalism*) report on; aim a firearm at; (*refl*) protect oneself; acquire; (*of male animals*) mate with; (*of hens*) incubate; **c. in** fill in (a hole); **c. over** cover completely; **c. up** cover completely, wrap; (*boxing*) protect oneself by defensive posture; (*coll*) conceal, disguise; **remain covered** keep hat on ∼ **cover** *n* anything that protects or hides by covering; wrapping; lid; bookbinding; case; hiding-place, shelter, protection; (*mil*) protecting escort; table-utensils laid out for use; (*comm*) money deposited against possible loss through falling prices; (*cricket*) cover-point; (*journalism*) report; stamped envelope that has passed through the post; **break c.** come out of hiding; **c. girl** girl whose picture appears on outer page of magazine; **take c.** hide or protect oneself; **under c. of** concealed, protected by; under pretence of.

coverage [kuveRij] n series or group of press reports; risks covered by insurance policy; section of public accessible through specified means of communication; range, inclusiveness.

coverall [kuveRawl] adj all-inclusive ~ **coverall** n long outer garment.

cover-charge [kuver-chaarj] n restaurant charge for service in addition to the cost of the meal.

covered-way [kuverd-way] n roofed passage with open sides between buildings.

covering [kuveRing] n anything which covers or protects; sheath ~ **covering** adj enclosing, protecting; **c. letter** letter accompanying and explaining a document.

coverlet, coverlid [kuverlit] n bedspread.

cover-point [kuver-point] n (cricket) position beyond point to the left of bowler; fielder in this position.

covert (1) [kuvert] adj disguised, secret.

covert (2) [kuvert] n hiding-place; place which shelters game; small feather covering base of quill; **draw a c.** search undergrowth etc for game.

covert-coat [kuvert-kOt] n short light overcoat.

covertly [kuvertli] adv in secret.

covertness [kuvertnis] n quality of being covert.

coverture [kuvercher] n anything which covers; disguise; (leg) status of married woman.

covert-way [kuvert-way] n (fortification) protected passage on a counterscarp.

cover-up [kuver-up] n (coll) plan, statement etc, that helps a wrong-doer to avoid detection.

covet [kuvit] v/t and i desire eagerly to possess, esp property of another; hanker after.

covetous [kuvitus] adj eagerly desirous (of); avaricious, greedy ~ **covetously** adv ~ **covetousness** n.

covey [kuvi] n brood of partridges; (joc) group.

coving [kOving] n (archi) arched part of roof or ceiling; curved sides of fireplace.

cow (1) [kow] n female of any bovine animal; female of domestic ox; female of certain other large animals; (sl) ugly and bad-tempered woman; **a fair c.** (Aust) highly objectionable person or thing; **till the cows come home** for ever.

cow (2) v/t subdue by violence or threats.

coward [kowerd] n one who lacks courage, one excessively or easily frightened ~ **coward** adj.

cowardice [kowerdis] n lack of courage.

cowardly [kowerdli] adj and adv like a coward.

cowbane [kowbayn] n water hemlock.

cowboy [kowboi] n (US) cattle herdsman on ranch, usually mounted.

cowcatcher [kowkacher] n (US) metal frame fixed to front of railway engine to remove obstructions.

cower [kowr] v/i crouch down in fear, cringe.

cow-heel [kow-heel] n stewed foot of cow or ox.

cowherd [kowhurd] n one who looks after cows.

cowhide [kowhId] n leather made from hide of cow; whip made from this.

cowhouse [kowhows] n shed for cows.

cowl [kowl] n hood of a monk's garment; hood-shaped covering for chimney-pot, to improve draught; hood-shaped ventilator on deck of large ship; wire cage at top of locomotive funnel ~ **cowl** v/t cover with a cowl.

cowlick [kowlik] n tuft of hair on forehead which will not lie flat; curling lock flattened against brow or cheek.

cowling [kowling] n (aer) casing round an aero-engine.

cowman [kowman] n cowherd; ranch-owner.

co-worker [kO-wurker] n one who works with another.

cow-parsley [kow-paarsli] n wild chervil.

cow-parsnip [kow-paarsnip] n wild parsnip.

cowpat [kowpat] n lump of cow's dung.

cowpox [kowpoks] n disease in which small pustules appear on cows' udders.

cowpuncher [kowpuncher] n (US coll) cowboy.

cowrie [kowRi] n small shell used as money in parts of Africa and Asia.

cowslip [kowslip] n wild flowering plant of primrose family.

cox [koks] n one who steers a racing-boat ~ **cox** v/t and i.

coxa (pl **coxae**) [koksa] n (anat) hip-joint; (zool) basal segment of insect's leg ~ **coxal** adj.

coxcomb [kokskOm] n foolish dandy, conceited swaggering fop; (ar) jester's cap.

coxswain [kokswayn/koks'n] n sailor in charge of a boat and its crew; helmsman.

coy [koi] adj (of girl) pretending shyness in flirtation; (ar) shy ~ **coyly** adv ~ **coyness** n.

coyote [kI-Ot/kI-Oti] n N. American prairie wolf.

coypu [koipOO] n large furry water-rat.

coz [kuz] n (ar) (abbr) cousin.

cozen [kuz'n] v/t and i cheat, defraud; deceive ~ **cozenage** n ~ **cozener** n.

crab (1) [kRab] n eight-legged broad-bodied shellfish with pincers; crab-louse; moving hoist of crane > PDE; (astron) a constellation of the zodiac; **catch a c.** (rowing) lose balance through thrusting oar too deeply ~ **crab** (pres/part **crabbing**, p/t and p/part **crabbed**) v/i fish for crabs; move sideways; (aer) head into crosswind in order to counteract drift.

crab (2) n wild apple; cultivated sour apple; (fig) sour-tempered grumbler ~ **crab** v/i and t (pres/part **crabbing**, p/t and p/part **crabbed**) (coll) complain; find fault with; spoil, ruin.

crab-apple [kRab-ap'l] n crab (2).

crabbed [kRabid] adj sour-tempered, bitter; cramped, hard to read or understand ~ **crabbedly** adv ~ **crabbedness** n.

crabby [kRabi] adj crabbed; ill-natured.

crab-louse (pl **crab-lice**) [kRab-lows] n species of body louse infesting the pubic hair.

crab-pot [kRab-pot] n wicker trap for crabs.

crabwise [kRabwIz] adv and adj (moving) sideways or backwards.

crack [kRak] n sudden sharp noise; sharp blow; slight split in brittle substance; long narrow opening, slit; (coll) attempt, endeavour; (coll) witty or sarcastic remark; **c. of dawn** daybreak; **c. of doom** Last Judgement ~ **crack** adj (coll) first-rate, expert ~ **crack** v/t and i break by pressure or by sharp blow; cause a fissure or slight split to appear in; split open suddenly, open out into fissure; (of voice) become hoarse, become lower in pitch (esp at puberty); break down (petroleum) by distillation or pressure > PDS; make a loud sharp noise; cause (whip, gun etc) to make such a noise; (coll) hurry; (coll) hit sharply; (*coll*) tell (a joke); **be cracked** (*coll*) be slightly crazy; **get cracking** (*coll*) start working or moving briskly; **c. a crib** (*sl*) burgle a house; **c. down on** (*coll*) reprimand, deal strictly with; **c. on** give a spurt of speed; **c. up** (*coll*) praise enthusiastically; show signs of age, illness *etc*, go to pieces.

crack-brained [kRak-bRaynd] *adj* crazy.

crackdown [kRakdown] *n* strong action to suppress social evils, discontent *etc*.

cracked [kRakt] *adj* partially broken without falling apart; full of cracks; (*of voice*) harsh, dissonant; (*coll*) slightly mad.

cracker [kRaker] *n* firework which explodes with series of loud cracks; small roll of coloured paper containing small trinket, paper hat *etc*, exploding when pulled apart; thin flaky biscuit; (*US*) any biscuit; (*pl*) implement for cracking nuts.

crackerjack [kRakerjak] *n* and *adj* (*coll*) (person or thing) remarkably fine.

crackers [kRakerz] *adj* (*coll*) mad, crazy.

cracking (1) [kRaking] *n* (*chem*) pyrolysis, the decomposition of a chemical substance by heat.

cracking (2) *adj* (*coll*) very fast.

crackjaw [kRakjaw] *adj* (*coll*) unpronounceable.

crackle [kRak'l] *n* series of faint crackling sounds; kind of china or glassware ornamented with network of small cracks ∼ **crackle** *v/i* emit series of faint rapid cracks.

crackling [kRakling] *n* crisp rind of roast pork; network of fine cracks on china, glassware *etc*; series of light cracking sounds.

cracknel [kRaknel] *n* light, crisp, puffy biscuit.

crackpot [kRakpot] *n* and *adj* (*coll*) crazy (person).

cracksman [kRaksman] *n* (*sl*) burglar.

crack-up [kRak-up] *n* (*coll*) disintegration, total breakdown; crash; a nervous breakdown.

cradle [kRayd'l] *n* baby's bed, sometimes on rockers; (*fig*) infancy, earliest stages, place of origin; anything resembling a cradle; supporting framework; (*med*) framework to protect injured limb from pressure of bedclothes; framework hanging from pulleys used by men working on face of building; (*min*) rocking trough ∼ **cradle** *v/t* and *i* rock (child) in cradle; hold tenderly; lull to rest; bring up from infancy; (*min*) wash (gold) in cradle ∼ **cradling** *n* (*archi*) framework of wood; timber fixed round steel beams as a ground for lathing.

cradle-snatcher [kRaydl-snacher] *n* (*coll*) one who marries or has a love-affair with someone much younger.

craft [kRaaft] *n* cunning, guile; skill, dexterity; occupation or trade needing high manual skill; members of such trade organized into collective body; manual art; a boat, aircraft or spacecraft (*pl* craft).

craftily [kRaaftili] *adv* cunningly, deceitfully ∼ **craftiness** *n*.

craftsman [kRaaftsman] *n* skilled manual worker; artist practising one of the manual arts.

craftsmanship [kRaaftsmanship] *n* high skill shown in making some object.

crafty [kRaafti] *adj* cunning, deceitful.

crag [kRag] *n* rough steep rock or point of rock.

craggy [kRagi] *adj* having or like a crag.

cragsman [kRagzman] *n* expert rock-climber.

crake [kRayk] *n* corncrake.

cram (*pres/part* **cramming**, *p/t* and *p/part* **crammed**) [kRam] *v/t* and *i* fill tightly, force into small space; overfeed (poultry) to fatten; eat greedily; (*fig*) coach (pupil) hastily and intensively; study intensively for an examination; (*coll*) tell a lie ∼ **cram** *n* information learnt by cramming; (*coll*) lie.

crambo [kRambO] *n* game in which one player gives a word to which others seek a rhyme; **dumb c.** charade in which a rhyming clue is given.

cramfull [kRamfool] *adv* full to overflowing.

crammer [kRamer] *n* one who fattens poultry; apparatus for fattening poultry; one who crams pupils for examination.

cramp (1) [kRamp] *n* involuntary painful contraction of muscles ∼ **cramp** *v/t* affect with cramp; fasten with a cramp, clamp together; (*fig*) confine in narrow space; hamper, restrict.

cramp (2) *n* tool for squeezing together wood parts during gluing; (*bui*) a cramp-iron; (*bui*) metal strap fixed to a door frame > PDBl.

cramped [kRampt] *adj* restricted in space; (*fig*) narrow; (*of handwriting*) badly formed.

cramp-iron [kRamp-I-ern] *n* (*bui*) metal U-shaped bar to hold ashlars to each other or to a beam.

crampon [kRampon] *n* (*bui*) two curved levers to grip and raise a block of stone; (*pl*) iron spikes on a climber's boots.

cran [kRan] *n* measure for herrings, 37½ gallons.

cranage [kRaynij] *n* the right of using a crane; dues paid for use of crane.

cranberry [kRanberi] *n* small red berry of dwarf shrub, used in cookery.

crane [kRayn] *n* tall wading-bird with long legs and neck; machine for raising and moving heavy weights, consisting of vertical post and jib; moving platform for a camera ∼ **crane** *v/t* and *i* stretch out one's neck.

cranefly [kRaynfll] *n* daddy-long-legs.

cranesbill [kRaynzbil] *n* wild geranium.

cranial [kRayni-al] *adj* pertaining to the skull; **c. index** ratio of breadth of skull to length.

craniology [kRayni-oloji] *n* study of the skull.

craniometry [kRayni-omitRi] *n* science of measurement of skulls.

craniotomy [kRayni-otomi] *n* (*surg*) cutting open of the skull.

cranium (*pl* **crania**) [kRayni-um] *n* the skull.

crank [kRank] *n* (*eng*) a bar with a right-angle bend which gives a leverage in turning; (*fig*) eccentricity of word or thought; (*coll*) person with odd fads, eccentric person ∼ **crank** *adj* unsteady, tottering, liable to capsize ∼ **crank** *v/t* bend into form of crank; furnish with a crank; set in motion by means of a crank; **c. up** start up car-engine by hand.

crankily [kRankili] *adv* in a cranky way ∼ **crankiness** *n*.

crankpin [kRankpin] *n* (*eng*) the cylindrical piece which forms the handle of a crank.

crankshaft [kRankshaft] *n* (*eng*) a shaft turning or driven by, a crank.

cranky [kRanki] *adj* unsteady; out of order; (*coll*) eccentric, full of odd ideas; bad-tempered.

crannied [kRanid] *adj* having crannies.

crannog [kRanug] n (arch) ancient Celtic lake-dwelling.

cranny [kRani] n chink, small hole.

crap (pres/part crapping, p/t and p/part crapped) [krap] v/i (vulg) defecate ~ crap n (vulg) dung; (sl) nonsense, rubbish.

crape [kRayp] n thin cloth with wrinkled surface, crêpe; black band worn as mourning; c. paper soft paper with wrinkled surface ~ crapy adj.

craps [kRaps] n (US) gambling game with two dice ~ crapshooter [kRapshOOter] n one who plays craps.

crapulence [kRapewlens] n drunkenness, debauchery; sickness caused by this ~ crapulent adj ~ crapulous adj.

crash (1) [kRash] v/i and t fall violently and noisily; damage or destroy through fall or collision; collide violently; (of aircraft) fall heavily to the ground; (fig) collapse, fail hopelessly; deliberately cause car, aircraft etc to crash; (coll) gatecrash ~ crash n loud noise caused by fall or impact; sudden accidental fall of aircraft; violent collision of moving vehicles; (fig) collapse, ruin ~ crash adj done or made rapidly or vigorously, esp in emergency; abrupt; urgent; for use in emergencies.

crash (2) n coarse linen used as towelling.

crash-dive [kRash-dIv] n sudden dive of a submarine or aircraft ~ crash-dive v/i.

crash-helmet [kRash-helmit] n protective padded helmet worn by aviators, motorcyclists etc.

crashing [kRashing] n noise of a crash ~ crashing adj that crashes; (coll) complete, utter.

crash-land [kRash-land] v/t (aer) make a forced landing; land violently or dangerously ~ crash-landing n.

crasis [kRaysis] n (gramm) combining of adjacent vowels of two syllables into one.

crass [kRas] adj coarse, gross; extremely dull, stupid; (coll) absolute, utter ~ crassly adv grossly, completely ~ crassness n.

cratch [kRach] n rack for fodder; wooden grating.

crate [kRayt] n packing-case of open slats or wickerwork; (coll) decrepit aircraft or car ~ crate v/t pack in a crate.

crater [kRayter] n hole in ground caused by explosion; funnel-shaped hollow at top of volcano > PDG; large hollow on surface of moon ~ cratered adj pitted with craters.

cravat [kRavat] n broad, loosely knotted necktie ~ cravatted adj wearing a cravat.

crave [kRayv] v/t ask earnestly; long for.

craven [kRayv'n] n coward; cry c. give in ~ craven adj cowardly.

craving [kRayving] n desire, longing; intense yearning ~ craving adj ~ cravingly adv.

craw [kRaw] n crop of a bird.

crawfish see crayfish.

crawl (1) [kRawl] v/i move on hands and knees; advance slowly and with difficulty; advance by creeping or wriggling; (fig) abase oneself, come humbly; be full of, or covered with, crawling creatures; (of skin) tickle ~ crawl n act of crawling; slow pace; (swimming) type of stroke in which head is kept low; (sl) a peripatetic drinking tour of the local public-houses.

crawl (2) n enclosure in shallow water for fish.

crawler [kRawler] n he who, that which, crawls;

(fig) lazy person; abject flatterer; (pl) infant's overall garment.

crawling [kRawling] adj moving very slowly or abjectly; swarming with crawling creatures; (coll) covered with, full of.

crawly [kRawli] adj (coll) having the sensation of insects crawling over the skin.

crayfish, crawfish [kRayfish, kRawfish] n edible crustacean resembling small lobster.

crayon [kRay-on] n thin stick of charcoal, waxy pencil, or coloured chalk; drawing done with this; carbon point in electric arc-lamp ~ crayon v/t draw with crayons.

craze [kRayz] v/t and i drive mad; become mad; (cer) cause cracking of glaze ~ craze n irrational enthusiasm, passing popular fashion; exaggerated fondness ~ crazed adj insane, excited; (cer) marked with surface cracks.

crazing [kRayzing] n forming of small cracks.

crazy [kRayzi] adj mad, wild; (coll) wildly enthusiastic; rickety, shaky; (sl) exciting, admirable; c. pavement, c. paving ornamental pavement of irregularly shaped slabs ~ crazily adv ~ craziness n.

creak [kReek] n a grating, squeaking sound ~ creak v/t and i ~ creaky adj.

cream [kReem] n oily element rising to surface of standing milk; sauce, dressing, flavoured filling etc containing or resembling this; oily cosmetic ointment or hair fixative; yellowish white colour; (fig) best part; cold c. type of cosmetic ointment; c. of tartar potassium hydrogen tartrate ~ cream v/t and i take cream from; (fig) take best part of; form into cream; foam, froth; add cream to, cook with cream; cover with ointment.

cream-cake [kReem-kayk] n cake filled with a creamy mixture.

cream-cheese [kReem-cheez] n soft cheese made of unskimmed milk and cream.

creamer [kReemer] n instrument for separating cream from milk; jug for cream.

creamery [kReemeRi] n place where milk is prepared for consumption and bottled; place where butter and cheese are made; shop where dairy produce is sold.

creamy [kReemi] adj containing cream; resembling cream in consistency or colour.

crease (1) [kRees] n line or ridge on material caused by folding and pressure; long straight ridge down leg of trousers; (cricket) line marking position of bowler or batsman ~ crease v/t and i cause ridges and wrinkles to appear in; press into a crease; become wrinkled; (sl) stun; exhaust; amuse intensely.

crease (2) see creese.

create [kRee-ayt] v/t make out of nothing, bestow existence on; cause, bring about; produce or make something new or original; confer new rank etc on; (theat) be the first to act (a certain part); v/i (coll) make a fuss.

creation [kRee-ayshon] n act or process of creating; thing created; universe; original invention, production etc; (coll) strikingly fashionable garment.

creationism [kRee-ayshonizm] n (theol) doctrine that all matter was created by God from nothing; doctrine that all living species were simultaneously created by God ~ creationist n.

creative [kRee-*aytiv*] *adj* having power to create; related to process of creation; constructive, original, producing an essentially new product; produced by original intellectual or artistic effort ~ **creatively** *adv* ~ **creativeness** *n*.

creativity [kRee-*aytiv*iti] creative power or faculty; ability to create.

creator [kRee-*ayter*] *n* one who creates; God.

creature [*kRee*echer] *n* living being; servile dependant, tool; (*ar*) anything created; **c. comforts** material comforts; **the c.** (*coll*) whisky.

crèche [*kResh*] *n* day nursery for infants whose mothers are at work; (*obs*) foundling hospital.

credal [*kRee*dal] *adj* of or as a creed.

credence [*kRee*dens] *n* belief, acceptance as true; **letter of c.** letter of recommendation, credentials.

credentials [kRi*den*shalz] *n* (*pl*) document testifying to bearer's trustworthiness, competence *etc*.

credible [*kRed*ib'l] *adj* that can be believed, deserving belief ~ **credibly** *adv*.

credibility [kRedi*bil*iti] *n* quality of being credible, ability to command belief; **c. gap** discrepancy between a claim or statement and the truth; failure of a government or person to win belief and trust from others because of previous lies.

credit [*kRed*it] *n* belief, trust; trustworthiness, good reputation; that which gives honour; person or act of which one may be proud; due praise, acknowledgement of merit; acknowledgement by name of persons whose work has contributed to a film, play, programme *etc*; (*comm*) confidence in a person's promise or ability to pay at future date; reputation of solvency, honesty *etc*; sum in person's bank account; (*book-keeping*) side where incoming sums are entered; (*coll*) examination grade higher than pass-mark but below distinction; (*US*) broadcast advertisement; **c. card** card enabling the holder to obtain goods, services *etc* which are charged to his bank account or his account with the company issuing the card; **letter of c.** banker's letter authorizing payment to holder; **c. titles** list shown at start of film, naming specialists concerned in its production; **do c. to** bring honour to ~ **credit** *v/t* believe, trust; attribute, ascribe to; acknowledge indebtedness to; enter on credit side.

creditable [*kRed*itab'l] *adj* bringing credit to, adding to honour of ~ **creditably** *adv*.

creditor [*kRed*iter] *n* one to whom money is owed; (*book-keeping*) credit side of account.

credo [*kReed*O/*kRayd*O] *n* creed, *esp* Apostles' Creed; musical setting of the Nicene Creed.

credulity [kRe*dew*liti] *n* exaggerated facility in believing on slight evidence; foolish trust.

credulous [*kRed*ewlus] *adj* too ready to believe without sufficient evidence ~ **credulously** *adv*.

creed [*kReed*] *n* formulated system of religious beliefs; summary of essential Christian dogmas; set of principles.

creek [*kReek*] *n* narrow coastal inlet; small tributary river; **up the c.** (*sl*) in trouble.

creel [*kReel*] *n* fisherman's wicker basket.

creep (*p/t* **creeping,** *p/t* and *p/part* **crept**) [*kReep*] *v/i* move stealthily with body near ground, crawl; move slowly or silently; (*bot*) grow along ground or wall; (*fig*) advance imperceptibly; cringe, flatter; (*of skin*) tickle, as if insects were creeping over it; (*fig*) shudder, squirm with fear, horror *etc*; (*naut*) drag with creeper; (*eng*) become slowly deformed or lengthened under stress > PDE; (*phys*) form crystals by evaporation along sides of vessel ~ **creep** *n* (*eng*) slow deformation or lengthening under stress > PDE; (*mining*) rising of floor of gallery through weight of rock above, pucking; (*geol*) slow movement of loose rock or earth; opening in hedge, bank *etc* for animals to pass through; (*sl*) sneak thief; spy, snooper; despicable unpleasant or boring person; **the (cold) creeps** shuddering feeling of fear, horror *etc*.

creeper [*kRee*per] *n* one who or that which creeps; bird which runs along tree-trunks; plant which climbs walls by tendrils or suckers; plant growing along ground; hooked grapnel, drag; spiked plate on climbing boots; conveyor-belt; (*coll*) one who fawns; (*pl, sl*) rubber-soled shoes.

creepily [*kRee*pili] *adv* in a creepy way ~ **creepiness** *n*.

creeping [*kRee*ping] *adj* moving slowly, crawling; growing along the ground; **c. barrage** (*mil*) barrage which slowly advances; **c. Jesus** (*coll*) pious hypocrite; sly, cowardly or servile person; **c. paralysis** (*med*) locomotor ataxia ~ **creeping** *n*.

creepy [*kRee*pi] *adj* horrifying, eerie; feeling fear or horror.

creepy-crawly [*kRee*pi-kRawli] *n* (*coll*) insect, worm *etc* ~ **creepy-crawly** *adj* horrifying.

creese, crease, kris [*kRees*] *n* Malay dagger.

cremate [kRi*mayt*] *v/t* burn (corpse) to ashes; burn up (rubbish *etc*) ~ **cremation** *n*.

cremator [kRi*mayter*] *n* one who cremates; furnace for cremating corpses; rubbish incinerator.

crematorium [kRema*taw*Ri-um] *n* building where corpses are cremated; refuse destructor.

crematory [*kRe*mateRi] *adj* pertaining to cremation ~ **crematory** *n* a crematorium.

crème de menthe [kRem-der-*mont*] *n* green liqueur flavoured with peppermint.

crenate, crenated [*kRe*nayt, *kRe*naytid] *adj* (*bot*) notched or scalloped.

crenellated, crenelate [*kRe*nilaytid, *kRe*nilayt] *adj* (*archi*) having battlements ~ **crenellation** [kReni*lay*shon] *n*.

creole [*kRee*-Ol] *n* person of European ancestry born in West Indies or parts of South America; coloured or halfcaste person from these regions ~ **creole** *adj*.

creosote [*kRee*-osOt] *n* colourless oily liquid containing cresol and phenol > PDS.

crêpe [*kRayp*] *n* crape; crape-like fabric; thin pancake; **c. de Chine** crape-like silk fabric; **c. paper** soft crinkled paper; **c. rubber** rubber in corrugated sheets; **c. shoes** shoes soled with this rubber.

crepitate [*kRe*pitayt] *v/i* crackle, creak, rattle.

crept [*kRept*] *p/t* and *p/part* of **creep**.

crepuscular [kRe*pus*kewlar] *adj* of, like, twilight; dim; (*zool*) active only at twilight or before dawn.

crepy [*kRay*pi] *adj* like crêpe; covered with fine wrinkles.

crescendo [kRi*shend*O] *n* (*mus*) increase in loudness; passage showing such increase; (*fig*) growing intensity, rise towards climax ~ **crescendo** *adj* and *adv*.

crescent (1) [*kRes*'nt] *n* shape of waxing or waning moon during first or last quarter; a half-moon, anything curved in this shape; national emblem of various Muslim countries; symbol of Muslim power and religion; row of houses built in form of arc; small crescent-shaped roll of bread ~ **crescent** *adj* shaped like waxing or waning moon; growing.

cresol [*kReesol*] *n* caustic fluid from coal-tar.

cress [*kRes*] *n* name of various edible cruciferous plants.

cresset [*kResit*] *n* iron basket containing fuel and hung up as torch or beacon.

crest [*kRest*] *n* ridge or tuft on the head of bird or animal; topmost point or ridge; (*anat*) ridge on bone; maned ridge of neck of horse; plume or device on helmet; (*poet*) helmet; (*her*) distinctive device above shield on coat of arms, or used on seals *etc* ~ **crest** *v/t* and *i* reach top of; adorn with a crest ~ **crested** *adj*.

crestfallen [*kRestfawlen*] *adj* humiliated, abashed.

cretaceous [*kRitayshus*] *adj* chalky; (*geol*) belonging to last Mesozoic period.

cretin [*kRetin*] *n* person suffering from stunted growth and idiocy through deficiency of thyroid gland > PDP; (*coll*) complete fool ~ **cretinism** *n* ~ **cretinous** *adj*.

creton [*kReeton*] *n* a potted meat delicacy.

cretonne [*kReton*] *n* strong unglazed cotton cloth printed with coloured pattern.

crevasse [*kRevas*] *n* deep crack in glacier > PDG.

crevice [*kRevis*] *n* small fissure, cleft.

crew (1) [*kROO*] *n* personnel of a ship (excluding captain and sometimes officers); persons manning an aircraft or spacecraft; rowing team *gen* of eight; gang of workmen; (*coll*) group of people, gang ~ **crew** *v/i* and *t* act as crew (for).

crew (2) *p/t* of **crow**.

crewcut [*kROOkut*] *n* a closely cropped style of haircut.

crewel [*kROO*-il] *n* thin worsted yarn.

crewman [*kROO*man] *n* member of a crew.

crib [*kRib*] *n* manger, fodder-rack; group of statues representing Christ's Nativity in the stable; (*ar*) stall for oxen; child's cot; small room or house; (*mining*) framework shoring up sides of shaft; cards discarded to dealer at cribbage; (*coll*) close translation; plagiarism; (*sl*) house to be burgled ~ **crib** (*pres/part* **cribbing**, *p/t* and *p/part* **cribbed**) *v/t* and (*coll*) make use of another's work, plagiarize; translate by copying from crib; cheat in examination; pilfer.

cribbage [*kRibij*] *n* card-game for two, three, or four players; **c. board** scoring board used in cribbage.

cribber [*kRiber*] *n* one who cribs or uses a crib.

cribbing [*kRibing*] *n* act of one who cribs; timbering of mine-shaft > PDE.

crick [*kRik*] *n* painful spasmodic stiffening of neck or back muscles ~ **crick** *v/t* cause a crick in.

cricket (1) [*kRikit*] *n* small brown insect which makes shrill harsh noise by rubbing its wings.

cricket (2) *n* outdoor game played with ball, bats and wickets by two teams of eleven players; **not c.** (*coll*) unfair, not according to accepted code.

cricketer [*kRikiter*] *n* one who plays cricket.

cried [*kRid*] *p/t* and *p/part* of **cry**.

crier [*kRI*-er] *n* one who cries; usher in court of justice; official who makes public announcements.

crikey [*kRIki*] *interj* (*coll*) exclamation of astonishment.

crime [*kRIm*] *n* grave offence punishable by law; serious wrongdoing; (*fig*) sin; (*coll*) very foolish deed; **c. passionel** (*Fr*) murder motivated by sexual jealousy; **c. sheet** (*mil*) list of offenders against military law and of charges against them ~ **crime** *v/t* (*mil*) charge with or convict of a military offence.

criminal [*kRiminal*] *adj* amounting to a crime; concerned with crime; guilty of a crime; wicked; **c. conversation** (*leg*) adultery ~ **criminal** *n* person guilty of a crime; habitual law-breaker ~ **criminally** *adv*.

criminality [kriminaliti] *n* quality of being criminal.

criminate [*kRiminayt*] *v/t* accuse of a crime.

criminology [kriminoloji] *n* study of crime and criminals ~ **criminological** [kriminolojikal] *adj* ~ **criminologist** *n*.

crimp (1) [*kRimp*] *n* agent who decoys men as crew for undermanned ship; one who cheats sailors ~ **crimp** *v/t* and *i*.

crimp (2) *v/t* press into tiny folds; curl (hair); gash (fish) to make it firm when cooked ~ **crimp** *n* small tight fold; (*coll*) obstacle, restraint ~ **crimp** *adj* crisp, brittle.

crimping-iron [*kRimp*ing-I-ern] *n* instrument for curling hair, or for crimping fabric.

crimplene [*kRimpleen*] *n* (*tr*) trade name for a polyester fabric woven from crimped fibre.

crimpy [*kRimpi*] *adj* frizzy, waved.

crimson [*kRimz*'n] *n* deep, slightly purplish red ~ **crimson** *adj* ~ **crimson** *v/t* and *i* make or become crimson; (*fig*) blush.

cringe [*kRinj*] *v/i* shrink back in fear, cower; behave with cowardly servility, fawn upon ~ **cringing** *adj* ~ **cringingly** *adv*.

cringle [*kRing*'l] *n* ring or loop on sail's edge.

crinkle [*kRink*'l] *v/t* and *i* wrinkle, shrink up ~ **crinkle** *n* ~ **crinkly** *adj*.

crinoid [*kRinoid*] *n* lily-shaped sea-urchin.

crinoline [kRinoleen/kRinolin] *n* framework covered with stiff fabric worn to distend or support a skirt; torpedo-net protecting warship.

cripes [*kRips*] *interj* (*vulg*) Christ.

cripple [*kRip*'l] *n* maimed or disabled person, *esp* one with maimed legs ~ **cripple** *v/t* maim, disable; (*fig*) injure, impair, gravely handicap.

crisis (*pl* **crises**) [*kRIsis*, *kRIseez*] *n* decisive moment; (*med*) turning-point of disease; (*fig*) moment of acute danger or difficulty.

crisp [*kRisp*] *adj* firm and dry, brittle; curled, frizzy, wrinkled; (*fig*) sharp, clear-cut, brisk; (*of air*) bracing, cold and dry; (*of style*) incisive ~ **crisp** *n* thin hard wafer of fried potato ~ **crisp** *v/t* and *i* make or become crisp; curl tightly.

crispy [*kRispi*] *adj* crisp; frizzy.

crisscross [*kRiskRos*] *n* intersecting lines; network of lines ~ **crisscross** *adj* and *adv* crosswise; marked with, moving in, intersecting lines ~ **crisscross** *v/t* and *i*.

criterion (*pl* **criteria**) [kRIteerRi-on, kRIteerRi-a] *n* standard of judgement, test.

crith [*kRith*] *n* (*phys*) unit of weight of gases.

critic [kʀitik] n expert judge of literary or artistic merit; professional reviewer of books, drama *etc*; one expert in study of manuscripts and texts; severe judge, fault-finder.

critical [kʀitikal] adj relating to, indicating a crisis; dangerous, causing anxiety, crucial; pertaining to criticism or a critic; expressing sound judgement, discriminating; (*of an edition*) containing textual criticism; judging harshly, finding fault; (*phys, math*) indicating point of transition > PDS, PDE; (*bot, zool*) differing only slightly; **c. mass** (*phys*) minimum weight of fissile material required to sustain a chain reaction; **c. path** quickest or most efficient course of action in carrying out a complex undertaking; **c. temperature** temperature above which a gas cannot be liquefied by pressure alone ~ **critically** adv.

criticism [kʀitisizm] n art or process of judging merits of artistic or literary work; analysis or review of such work; principles guiding critic's method; expression of unfavourable opinion, pointing-out of faults; **textual c.** scientific analysis and investigation of manuscript texts; **the New C.** method of close analysis of language, imagery, thought and emotion in a literary work.

criticize [kʀitisIz] v/t pass judgement on, estimate aesthetic merits of; point out defects of, find fault with ~ **criticizable** adj ~ **criticizer** n.

critique [kʀiteek] n critical discussion, essay, or review; art of criticism.

critter, crittur [kʀiter] n (*coll*) creature.

croak [kʀOk] v/i utter low-pitched harsh cry (*esp* of raven or frog); speak with hoarse voice; (*fig*) talk gloomily, grumble; (*sl*) die; (*sl*) kill ~ **croak** n.

croaker [kʀOker] n animal that croaks; person with harsh voice or loud cough; grumbler, dismal pessimist ~ **croaking** adj and n.

croaky [kʀOki] adj that croaks; harsh.

crochet [kʀOshay] n kind of knitting done with one hooked needle; hook used for this ~ **crochet** v/t and i.

crock [kʀok] n earthenware pot; broken piece of earthenware; old broken-down horse; (*coll*) old, worn-out, or useless person; cripple; old motorcar ~ **crock** v/t and i (*coll*) **c. up** become a crock; lose health or strength; injure, damage.

crockery [kʀokeʀi] n domestic utensils of earthenware or china; (*coll*) any china objects.

crocket [kʀokit] n (*archi*) leaf-like ornament on gable, spire *etc* ~ **crocketed** adj.

crocky [kʀOki] adj (*coll*) broken-down.

crocodile [kʀokodIl] n large amphibious reptile with strong jaws and long tail; skin of this; (*coll*) group of schoolchildren walking two by two; (*fig*) person showing hypocritical grief; **c. tears** insincere grief ~ **crocodilian** [kʀokodili-an] adj.

crocus [kʀOkus] n spring-flowering plant with yellow, white, or purple flowers; similar autumnal flower; orange-yellow colour, saffron.

croft [kʀoft] n small enclosed piece of arable or pasture land, *gen* adjoining house; small farm > PDG ~ **crofter** n one who owns or works a croft.

croissant [kʀwason(g)] n small crescent-shaped roll of bread.

Cro-Magnon [kʀO-manyon(g)] adj of a prehistoric European race of the late palaeolithic age.

cromlech [kʀomlek] n prehistoric structure consisting of a large flat stone resting on upright ones; circle of standing stones round a mound.

crone [kʀOn] n withered old woman.

crony [kʀOni] n close companion, old friend.

crook [kʀook] n long stick with hooked end; shepherd's staff; crozier; hook; sharp curve; (*coll*) criminal, thief, swindler; (*mus*) detachable section of tube of brass instruments governing pitch ~ **crook** v/t and i bend sharply ~ **crook** adj (*coll*) dishonest; (*Aust*) ill; bad; unpleasant; out of order; bad-tempered.

crooked [kʀookid] adj bent, twisted, winding; deformed; (*fig*) illicit, dishonest ~ **crookedly** adv ~ **crookedness** n.

croon [kʀOOn] v/t and i sing in soft sentimental tones, *esp* through microphone; (*ar*) hum, sing gently ~ **crooner** n ~ **crooning** n and adj.

crop [kʀop] n produce of cultivated land; season's yield of cultivated plants; (*fig*) a lot of things together; pouch in gullet of birds, craw; handle of whip; short whip with leather loop at end; (*geol, mining*) outcrop; whole tanned hide; short haircut; earmark on animal made by clipping; **neck and c.** entirely ~ **crop** (*pres/part* **cropping**, *p/t* and *p/part* **cropped**) v/t and i cut short, cut off, lop; bite off, nibble tops of; trim margin of (book); sow, plant (with crops); produce a crop; **c. out, c. up** (*geol, mining*) appear at surface; **c. up** (*coll*) appear unexpectedly, arise.

crop-eared [kʀop-eerd] adj having had ears cut off; with short hair showing ears.

cropper [kʀoper] n he who, that which, crops; plant yielding a crop; pouter pigeon; tool for cutting steel bars; small platen printing machine; (*coll*) heavy fall; **come a c.** (*coll*) fall heavily; fail, meet misfortune or ruin.

croquet [kʀOkay] n lawn-game in which balls are struck by mallets through hoops ~ **croquet** v/t and i strike opponent's ball and one's own.

croquette [kʀOket] n rissole of minced meat or fish or potato seasoned and fried crisp.

crore [kʀawr] n (*Anglo-Indian*) ten million rupees.

crosier, crozier [kʀOzhi-er] n bishop's staff.

cross [kʀos] n (*hist*) upright post with intersecting beam, to which criminals were fastened to die; that on which Christ died; (*fig*) suffering, affliction; representation of a cross as symbol of Christianity, a religious monument *etc*; ornament, badge, or medal shaped like a cross; mark or design made by intersecting lines; intermixture of breeds; hybrid, mongrel; **on the c.** diagonally; (*sl*) dishonestly; **sign of the C.** ritual gesture of touching forehead, breast and shoulders in outline of cross; **take the c.** become a crusader; **take up one's c.** bear sufferings with devout patience ~ **cross** v/t and i make sign of Cross over or on; place across or crosswise; lie across; intersect; draw line or lines across; pass from one side to the other of; extend from side to side; meet and pass; oppose, thwart; interbreed; (*sl*) cheat, betray; **c. a cheque** draw two lines across it so that it can only be paid through bank; **c. off, c. out** cancel, delete by drawing lines through; **c. oneself** make sign of Cross; **c. one's fingers** fold one finger over another to bring good luck; **c. one's heart** make sign of Cross over heart as proof of truth-telling; **c. one's mind** (*impers*) come suddenly or briefly into one's thoughts; **c. the path of** meet, thwart; **c. the palm of** pay money to ~ **cross** *adj* placed across, lying transversely; intersecting; passing from side to side; irritated, angry, bad-tempered; opposite, contrary.

cross- *pref* crossing; across, transverse; opposing.

cross-banded [kRos-*band*id] *adj* (*carp*) covered with wood veneer with crosswise grain.

crossbar [*kRos*baar] *n* horizontal bar across or between uprights.

crossbeam [*kRos*beem] *n* a transverse beam.

cross-bearings [kRos-*bair*Ringz] *n* (*pl*) bearings of two known points taken to determine a third.

crossbench [*kRos*bench] *n* a bench in Parliament, on which independent members sit.

crossbill (1) [*kRos*bil] *n* bird whose mandibles cross each other when bill is closed.

crossbill (2) *n* (*leg*) bill filed in Chancery by defendant against plaintiff or co-defendant in same suit; (*comm*) bill of exchange given in consideration of another bill.

crossbones [*kRos*bOnz] *n* representation of crossed human thighbones, generally below skull, as symbol of death or piracy.

crossbow [*kRos*bO] *n* medieval weapon consisting of bow fixed across a grooved stock.

crossbred [*kRos*bRed] *adj* and *n* mongrel, hybrid.

crossbreed (*p*/*t* and *p*/*part* **crossbred**) [*kRos*bReed] *v*/*t* and *i* breed from animals or plants of different species or varieties ~ **crossbreed** *n* hybrid.

cross-channel [kRos-*chan*el] *adj* that crosses the English Channel.

cross-check [*kRos*-chek] *v*/*t* and *i* to check from a different standpoint, recheck.

cross-country [kRos-*kunt*Ri] *adj* and *adv* advancing across fields *etc*, not by roads.

crosscut [*kRos*kut] *n* transverse cut; path connecting parallel roads ~ **crosscut** *adj* having crosscuts; used for making transverse cuts; **c. chisel** chisel of rectangular section with cutting edge at steep angle; **c. file** file with two intersecting rows of cuts; **c. saw** large saw for tree-felling *etc*, worked by two men, one at each end ~ **crosscut** (*pres*/*part* **crosscutting**, *p*/*t* and *p*/*part* **crosscut**) *v*/*t* cut from side to side.

crosse [kRos] *n* long-handled pouched racket used in playing lacrosse.

cross-examine [kRos-igz*amin*] *v*/*t* (*leg*) question witness who has already given evidence for opposing side; (*coll*) question closely or harshly ~ **cross-examination** [kRosigzamin*ay*shon] *n*.

cross-eyed [*kRos*-Id] *adj* squinting.

cross-fertilize [kRos-*furt*ilIz] *v*/*t* (*bot*) fertilize with pollen from another plant ~ **cross-fertilization** [kRos-furtilIz*ay*shon] *n*.

crossfire [*kRos*fIr] *n* (*mil*) lines of fire converging from two or more directions.

cross-grained [kRos-*gRaynd*] *adj* (*of timber*) having fibres which do not run parallel with the length of the piece of wood; (*fig*) stubborn, cantankerous.

crosshatch [*kRos*hach] *v*/*t* and *i* mark or shade (drawings) by crossing close lines > PDAA.

crosshead [*kRos*-hed] *n* (*mech*) steel block at end of piston-rod > PDE; rod or beam across top of

mechanism; (*print*) heading across page or column; sub-heading.

crossing [*kRos*ing] *n* act of passing across; sea-passage; place where roads *etc* cross each other; place where one may cross road *etc*; cross-breeding; act of marking or making a cross; **level c.** intersection of road and railway, *gen* controlled by gates; **pedestrian c.** track marked across road, on which pedestrians have right of way over traffic; **zebra c.** pedestrian crossing marked by broad white bands.

crosslegged [kRos*legd*] *adj* sitting with ankles crossed and knees wide apart; sitting with one leg across the other.

cross-linkage [kRos-*linkij*] *n* (*chem*) the joining of polymer molecules to each other by valency bonds > PDS.

crossly [*kRos*li] *adv* adversely; irritably, ill-temperedly ~ **crossness** [*kRos*nes] *n*.

crossover [*kRos*Over] *n* woman's wrap or bodice crossing in front; road passing over another road; (*biol*) passing of gene or factor from one chromosome to another.

crosspatch [*kRos*pach] *n* cross, peevish person.

crosspiece [*kRos*pees] *n* piece of anything lying across some other piece.

crossply [*kRos*plI] *adj* (*of tyres*) made up of layers whose cords cross at right angles.

cross-pollination [kRos-polin*ay*shon] *n* (*bot*) cross-fertilization.

cross-purpose [kRos-*pur*pos] *n* conflicting purpose; **be at cross-purposes** be in conflict through misunderstanding of each other's aim.

cross-question [kRos-*kwe*schon] *v*/*t* and *i* cross-examine.

cross-reference [kRos-*Refe*Rens] *n* reference from one part of a book to another.

crossroad [*kRos*ROd] *n* road that crosses another; minor road joining two main roads; (*pl used as sing*) place where roads cross; (*fig*) moment of decision.

cross-section [*kRos*-sekshon] *n* shape of any body cut transversely to its length; drawing of this; (*phys*) effective area which atom presents to incident beam of particles > PDS; (*fig*) representative sample ~ **cross-sectional** *adj*.

cross-stitch [*kRos*-stich] *n* pair of stitches crossing diagonally; embroidery composed of these.

crosstalk [*kRos*tawk] *n* (*coll*) repartee, argument; rapid dialogue of two comedians.

crosstie [*kRos*tI] *n* transverse connecting-piece; (*US*) railway sleeper.

crosstrees [*kRos*tReez] *n* (*pl*) (*naut*) horizontal timbers fixed to masthead.

crossways [*kRos*wayz] *adv* crosswise.

crosswise [*kRos*wIz] *adv* in the form of a cross; across, athwart.

crossword [*kRos*wurd] *n* puzzle consisting of squares to be filled up with letters forming words in either direction, according to clues provided.

crotch [kRoch] *n* forked stick; fork of tree or branch; place where legs fork from body.

crotchet [*kRoch*it] *n* (*mus*) note having half time-value of minim; symbol of this; (*typ*) square bracket; (*coll*) obstinate idea, odd whim.

crotchety [*kRoch*iti] *adj* (*coll*) obstinate and full of odd ideas ~ **crotchetiness** *n*.

crouch [kRowch] *v*/*i* stoop low with limbs drawn

181

together; (*of animals*) lie close to ground; (*fig*) cringe ~ **crouch** *n* crouching posture.

croup (1), **croupe** [*kROOp*] *n* rump of horse *etc*.

croup (2) *n* (*med*) inflammation of larynx, with hard cough and noisy difficult breathing.

croupier [*kROOpi-er*] *n* person who presides at gaming-table; vice-chairman at public dinner.

croupy [*kROOpi*] *adj* like or suffering from croup (2).

croûton [*kROOton*] *n* crisp piece of toast or fried bread served in soup.

crow (1) [*kRO*] *n* large black bird of genus *Corvus*; crowbar; **as the c. flies** in a straight line.

crow (2) (*p/t* **crowed** *or* **crew,** latter used only of bird; *p/part* **crowed**) *v/i* (*of cock*) utter characteristic loud shrill cry; (*of baby*) utter cry of joy; (*fig*) express triumph, exult at success ~ **crow** *n* cry of cock; joyful cry of baby.

crowbar [*kRObaar*] *n* iron bar used as lever.

crowd (1) [*kRowd*] *n* large number of people massed together; large audience, mass of spectators; large number of things close together; (*coll*) group, set, clique; **c. of sail** (*naut*) many sails simultaneously hoisted ~ **crowd** *v/i* and *t* gather in large numbers; press forward in large numbers; thrust into small space, fill too full; (*US coll*) hurry, hustle; push; **c. out** exclude for lack of space or time; **c. on sail** (*naut*) hoist all sails possible.

crowd (2) *n* obsolete Celtic stringed instrument.

crowded [*kRowdid*] *adj* filled by a crowd; too full.

crowfoot [*kROfoot*] *n* name for various plants, *esp* buttercups; (*elect*) type of electrode; (*mil*) caltrôp.

crown [*kRown*] *n* wreath or garland worn on head as sign of honour, victory *etc*; gold and jewelled head-dress worn as sign of royalty; sovereignty, royal office or power; king; supreme power in monarchy; representation of royal crown; coin worth five shillings; size of paper, 15×20 in.; summit, top part, *esp* of rounded object; top of head; head; top of hat; centre of cambered road; (*archi*) highest part of arch; top part or artificial top of tooth; (*naut*) end of shank of anchor; (*fig*) highest achievement, moment of perfection; (*coll, mil*) sergeant-major ~ **crown** *adj* pertaining to, belonging to, bestowed by royal authority; **C. Agents** independent office acting as British business agents for foreign administrations; **C. Colony** colony governed directly from Colonial Office; **C. law** criminal law; **c. prince** heir to throne ~ **crown** *v/t* place crown on head of; make king, invest with royal power; honour, reward; adorn splendidly; cover head or summit of; (*fig*) complete successfully; put finishing touch to; (*dentistry*) put artificial top on tooth; (*sl*) hit on head.

crown-court [*kRown-kawrt*] *n* (*leg*) assize court for criminal cases.

crowned [*kRownd*] *adj* decorated with, invested with a crown; tufted, crested; having a crown.

crowning [*kRowning*] *n* coronation; completion; top of arch ~ **crowning** *adj* completing; highest, perfect.

crown-piece [kRown-*pees*] *n* coin worth five shillings, *i.e.* twenty-five new pence.

crown-wheel [*kRown*-weel] *n* gear-wheel with cogs at right angles to its plane.

crown-witness [kRown-*wit*nes] *n* (*leg*) witness for the Crown in a criminal case.

crowsfeet [*kROzfeet*] *n* (*pl*) (*coll*) small wrinkles at the outer corners of the eyes.

crowsnest [*kROznest*] *n* look-out platform at a ship's masthead; (*coll*) attic room.

crozier see **crosier.**

crucial [*kROOshi-al*] *adj* marking a crisis; decisive, severe; difficult but essential (argument *etc*).

crucible [*kROOsib'l*] *n* vessel of heat-resisting material used for high-temperature chemical reactions; (*metal*) hollow at bottom of a furnace; (*fig*) severe test; **c. steel** high-grade steel.

cruciferous [kROO*sif*eRus] *adj* (*bot*) having four petals arranged cross-shape.

crucifix [*kROOsifiks*] *n* carved figure of Christ on the Cross.

crucifixion [kROOsi*fik*shon] *n* act of crucifying; death of Christ on the Cross; representation of this.

cruciform [*kROOsi-fawrm*] *adj* cross-shaped.

crucify [*kROOsifI*] *v/t* put to death by nailing or binding to a cross; (*fig*) subdue (desires *etc*) by asceticism; torment, torture; criticize harshly ~ **crucifying** *adj*.

cruck [*kRuk*] *n* one of several curved timbers used as framework for a house.

crud [*kRud*] *n* (*sl*) dirt; rubbish; dirty or unpleasant person; disease ~ **cruddy** *adj*.

crude [*kROOd*] *adj* raw, in a natural state, not prepared for use; (*fig*) immature, badly planned; harsh, gaudy; coarse, vulgar; blunt, outspoken; unrefined, unpolished; **c. oil** natural mineral oil ~ **crudely** *adv* ~ **crudeness** *n* ~ **crudity** *n.*

cruel [*kROO-el*] *adj* intending to cause pain; enjoying sufferings of others; unkind, hard-hearted; designed to cause pain; painful, distressing ~ **cruel** *adv* (*coll*) very harshly, badly ~ **cruelly** *adv.*

cruelty [*kROO-elti*] *n* quality of being cruel; cruel behaviour.

cruet [*kRoo-it*] *n* small container for condiments; group of these in stand; (*eccles*) vessel holding wine and water used in the Eucharist.

cruise [*kROOz*] *v/i* sail about on leisurely trip; sail in various directions on patrol; (*of taxi*) drive slowly looking out for a fare; (*mot*) travel at a good steady pace ~ **cruise** *n.*

cruiser [*kROOzer*] *n* lightly-armoured fast warship; yacht or ship designed for pleasure trips; (*coll*) aircraft; spaceship; (*boxing*) light heavy-weight.

crumb [*kRum*] *n* small particle of bread or cake; soft inner part of loaf; (*fig*) tiny portion, scrap; **crumbs!** (*coll*) exclamation of surprise.

crumble [*kRumb'l*] *v/t* and *i* break into crumbs or small fragments; fall to pieces, disintegrate ~ **crumble** *n* type of pudding or soft cake.

crumbly [*kRumbli*] *adj* easily crumbled.

crumby [*kRumi*] *adj* of, like, or full of crumbs; lousy, dirty; shoddy; bad.

crummy [*kRumi*] *adj* (*sl*) inferior, worthless.

crump [*kRump*] *n* sound of heavy explosion; (*sl*) heavy explosive shell ~ **crump** *v/i* and *t* explode with heavy noise; hit hard.

crumpet [*kRumpit*] *n* thin spongy unsweetened cake, usually toasted; (*sl*) head, brain; (*sl*) sexually attractive and easy-going girl.

crumple [kRump'l] v/t and i crush roughly into creases; become creased; crush into ball; (fig) reduce to helplessness; collapse under pressure.

crunch [kRunch] v/t and chew up noisily; crush, grind or trample noisily ~ crunch n act or noise of crunching; the c. (sl) moment of crisis; decisive encounter; showdown.

crunchy [kRunchi] adj brittle, producing crunching noise when eaten or trampled.

crupper [kRuper] n hind quarters of a horse; strap from back of saddle under horse's tail.

crural [kRoorRal] adj (anat) pertaining to the leg.

crusade [kRoosayd] n (hist) military expedition to free Holy Land from Mohammedan rule; war for religious purpose; (fig) zealous campaign against some social evil or abuse ~ crusade v/i ~ crusader n.

cruse [kROOz] n small jar for liquid.

crush [kRush] v/t and i compress violently, squash, squeeze out of shape; pulverize; crumple; force into small space; (fig) suppress forcibly; disconcert, overwhelm; become compressed; become crumpled ~ crush n act of crushing; tightly packed mass, dense crowd; (coll) crowded party; (coll) infatuation; object of infatuation.

crush-barrier [kRush-baRi-er] n steel barrier to control dense crowds.

crushing [kRushing] adj overwhelming, disconcerting, unnerving ~ crushingly adv.

crust [kRust] n hard outer part of loaf of bread; dry hard piece of bread; outer covering of pie; any hard outer shell, layer, or covering; scab; (geol) outer portion of earth's mass; film deposited by wine inside bottle; (sl) impertinence, boldness; upper c. (coll) upper class, aristocracy ~ crust v/t and i cover with crust; form crust.

crustacea [kRustaysh-a] n (pl) (zool) class of animals, nearly all aquatic, with jointed legs and hard shells ~ crustacean adj and n.

crustaceous [kRustavshus] adj like or relating to crust or shell; (zool) belonging to crustacea.

crusted [kRustid] adj having a crust; (of wine) having deposited a crust; (fig) old, venerable.

crusty [kRusti] adj like crust; having much crust; (fig) surly, easily angered ~ crustily adv ~ crustiness n.

crutch [kRuch] n staff for lame person with crosspiece at top to go under armpit; (fig) support, help; any forked support, prop etc crotch, fork of human body; elbow c. metal staff with handgrip and curving band supporting the upper arm.

crux [kRuks] n problem or passage difficult to explain, puzzle; important or essential point.

cry (pl cries) [kRI] n characteristic call of animal or bird; loud vocal sound, gen expressing emotion; call, shout; act of weeping; prayer, entreaty; slogan, catchphrase; shout of streethawkers etc; pack of hounds; a far c. a long way; in full c. (of hounds) yelping while pursuing quarry; (fig) pursuing hotly; hue and c. pursuit; public anger, protestations etc; great c. and little wool much ado about nothing; within c. within earshot ~ cry (p/t and p/part cried) v/t and i utter a cry; utter loudly, call out, shout; weep; announce, hawk by calling out; c. down belittle; c. for beg for; beg with tears; c. for the moon ask the impossible; c. off withdraw from (an

arrangement), decline, refuse; c. quits declare dispute ended on equal terms; c. up praise loudly.

crybaby [kRIbaybi] n child who weeps for little or no reason.

crying [kRI-ing] adj that cries; (fig) demanding redress, notorious ~ crying n.

cryogen [kRI-Ojen] n substance for producing a low temperature; freezing mixture.

cryogenics [kRI-Ojeniks] n (pl) study of materials and phenomena close to the absolute zero of temperature.

cryophorus [kRI-oferus] n apparatus to demonstrate the cooling effect of evaporation.

cryostat [kRI-Ostat] n vessel in which a specified low temperature can be maintained.

cryotherapy [kRI-OtheRapi] n medical treatment involving reduction of body temperature.

crypt [kRipt] n underground vault, esp chapel or burying-place beneath church.

cryptanalysis [kRiptanalisis] n art of deciphering a code ~ cryptanalist n.

cryptic, cryptical [kRiptik, kRiptikal] adj secret, mysterious; (zool) concealing ~ cryptically adv.

crypto- pref hidden, secret.

crypto-communist [kRipto-komewnist] n secret member of, or sympathizer with, a Communist movement.

cryptogam [kRiptogam] n (bot) plant propagating by spores.

cryptogram [kRiptogRam] n anything written in code.

cryptographer [kRiptogRafer] n one skilled in writing codes or in decoding.

cryptology [kRiptoloji] n the study of codes and ciphers.

crystal [kRistal] n (chem, min) substance solidified in definite geometrical form; structure resembling crystal in form; (min) variety of transparent quartz; ball of this, or of glass, used in fortunetelling; fine brilliant glass; (fig) anything transparent; (rad) crystalline substance conducting current in one direction only; c. set simple wireless set using crystal to rectify incoming waves ~ crystal adj made of crystal; like crystal; clear, transparent; (rad) using a crystal.

crystal-gazing [kRistal-gayzing] n method of foreseeing future by looking into a crystal ball; (fig) fanciful or unscientific attempt to predict future conditions.

crystalline [kRistalIn] adj made of or like crystal; clear, transparent; (chem) having structure of crystal; c. lens (anat) transparent body behind the iris, which focuses rays of light.

crystallize [kRistalIz] v/t and i form into crystals; become crystalline in structure; coat with crystals of sugar; (fig) give definite form to; take definite shape ~ crystallization [kRistalIzayshon] n.

crystallography [kRistalogRafi] n study of geometrical form of crystals ~ crystallographer n.

crystalloid [kRistaloid] adj crystal-like ~ crystalloid n substance able to pass through a semipermeable membrane when in solution.

crystallose [kRistalOz] n sodium salt of saccharin.

cub [kub] n young of fox bear, lion etc; (fig) rough-mannered uncouth boy; junior member of Scouts; (coll) lad, youth; inexperienced beginner ~ cub (pres/part cubbing, p/t and p/part cubbed) v/i give birth to cubs; hunt fox-cubs.

cubage [*kewbij*] *n* cubic content of a solid; determination of this.

cubature [*kewbacher*] *n* determination of the cubic content of a solid.

cubbing [*kubing*] *n* hunting of foxcubs.

cubbyhole [*kubihOl*] *n* very small room.

cube [*kewb*] *n* (*geom*) regular solid figure with six square faces; anything shaped like this; (*math*) product obtained by multiplying a quantity by itself twice; **c. root** (*math*) number producing a given cube when multiplied by itself twice ~ **cube** *v/t* (*math*) calculate the cube of.

cubeb [*kewbeb*] *n* aromatic berry from East Indies.

cubic [*kewbik*] *adj* of shape of cube; of three spatial dimensions; (*math*) relating to calculation of cubes; **c. centimetre** metric unit of volume, one-thousandth of a litre ~ **cubically** *adv*.

cubicle [*kewbik'l*] *n* small enclosed compartment in larger room.

cubism [*kewbizm*] *n* abstract style of painting which attempts to reduce natural forms to their fundamental geometric shapes > PDAA ~ **cubist** [*kewbist*] *n* and *adj*.

cubit [*kewbit*] *n* (*ar*) measure of length, about 18 to 22 in.; (*anat*) the elbow ~ **cubital** *adj*.

cuboid [*kewboid*] *n* six-sided rectangular solid figure ~ **cuboid** *adj* ~ **cuboidal** *adj*.

cucking-stool [*kuking-stOOl*] *n* (*hist*) chair to which petty rogues, scolding women *etc* were tied and exhibited or ducked.

cuckold [*kukold*] *n* man whose wife commits adultery ~ **cuckold** *v/t* make a husband a cuckold ~ **cuckoldry** *n* adultery.

cuckoo [*kookOO*] *n* migratory bird called after its note; cry of this bird; (*coll*) fool; **c. in the nest** harmful intruder ~ **cuckoo** *adj* (*coll*) mad.

cuckoo-clock [*kookOO-klok*] *n* clock which marks the hour by call and movement of a toy cuckoo.

cuckoo flower [*kookOO-flowr*] *n* wild orchis.

cuckoopint [*kookOOpint*] *n* wild arum.

cuckoospit [*kookOOspit*] *n* frothy secretion deposited by certain insects on stems and leaves.

cucumber [*kewkumber*] *n* fruit of plant of gourd family eaten in salads or as vegetable; this plant; **cool as a c.** very self-possessed.

cucurbit [*kewkurbit*] *n* gourd.

cud [*kud*] *n* food which ruminating animal brings up into its mouth from its first stomach to chew at leisure; **chew the c.** (*fig*) reflect.

cuddle [*kud'l*] *v/t* and *i* embrace warmly, hug; **c. up** lie close together; curl up ~ **cuddle** *n*.

cuddlesome [*kud'lsum*] *adj* (*coll*) cuddly.

cuddly [*kudli*] *adj* (*coll*) suitable for cuddling, inspiring the wish to cuddle.

cuddy (1) [*kudi*] *n* (*naut*) cabin where officers have meals; cook's galley; small cabin.

cuddy (2) *n* (*Scots*) donkey.

cudgel [*kujel*] *n* short heavy stick used as weapon; **take up the cudgels (for)** defend strongly ~ **cudgel** (*pres/part* **cudgelling**, *p/t* and *p/part* **cudgelled**) *v/t* beat with a cudgel; **c. one's brains** think hard.

cue (1) [*kew*] *n* (*theat*) words, action *etc* serving as signal to actor to enter or speak; (*biol*) stimulus, signal; (*mus*) indication of re-entry after rest; (*fig*) hint, lead ~ **cue** *v/t*.

cue (2) *n* long tapering rod with which ball is struck in billiards; (*hist*) short pigtail.

cuff (1) [*kuf*] *n* wrist end of sleeve; wristband of shirt; (*US*) trouser turn-up; (*pl*) (*coll*) handcuffs; **off the c.** (*coll*) impromptu.

cuff (2) *n* blow with fist or hand ~ **cuff** *v/t*.

cufflink [*kuflink*] *n* two ornamental metal discs joined by short link, used to fasten cuff of shirt.

cuirass [*kwiRas*] *n* piece of body-armour.

cuirassier [*kwiRaseer*] *n* cavalryman wearing a cuirass.

cuisine [*kwizeen*] *n* (*Fr*) style or quality of cookery.

cul-de-sac [*kul-de-sak*] *n* blind alley, street, or passage open at one end only; (*fig*) situation without outlet, inescapable position.

culex [*kewleks*] *n* (*ent*) genus of insects including some mosquitoes and gnats.

culinary [*kulineRi*] *adj* pertaining to the kitchen or cookery; suitable for cooking.

cull [*kul*] *v/t* pick out, select; pick (flowers); kill a specified percentage of (a herd or population of animals) ~ **cull** *n* something selected; something rejected.

cullender see **colander**.

cully [*kuli*] *n* (*sl*) fellow, pal.

culm (1) [*kulm*] *n* coal-dust; slack of anthracite; (*geol*) deposit of shale or sandstone.

culm (2) *n* (*bot*) jointed stalk of grass.

culminant [*kulminant*] *adj* at highest point.

culminate [*kulminayt*] *v/i* reach highest point, greatest development *etc*; (*astron*) reach zenith ~ **culmination** [*kulminayshon*] *n*.

culottes [*kewlots*] *n* (*pl*) (*Fr*) knee-length divided skirt; knee-breeches.

culpability [*kulpabiliti*] *n* guilt, state of deserving blame ~ **culpable** [*kulpab'l*] *adj* blameworthy.

culprit [*kulpRit*] *n* guilty person; (*leg*) prisoner accused of crime.

cult [*kult*] *n* religious worship expressed in customs, ritual and ceremonies; devotion, homage; enthusiastic admiration; popular fashion craze.

cultism [*kultizm*] *n* the practice of a religious cult or fashionable craze ~ **cultist** *n* and *adj*.

cultivable [*kultivab'l*] *adj* that can be tilled.

cultivate [*kultivayt*] *v/t* prepare (land) for growing crops; grow, raise; (*fig*) improve, develop; give special attention to ~ **cultivatable** *adj*.

cultivated [*kultivaytid*] *adj* brought under cultivation; (*fig*) educated, refined, cultured.

cultivation [kultivayshon] *n* art of cultivating; state of being cultivated; (*fig*) culture.

cultivator [*kultivayter*] *n* one who or that which cultivates; machine for tilling the land.

cultural [*kulcheRal*] *adj* pertaining to culture; pertaining to a particular civilization or culture; **c. revolution** Chinese Communist movement (1966–9) enforcing the doctrines of Mao Tse-tung ~ **culturally** *adv*.

culture [*kulcher*] *n* cultivation; commercial growing or breeding; artificial rearing of bacteria, micro-organisms *etc*; organisms so produced; (*fig*) improvement of mental faculties; refined taste or judgement, high intellectual and aesthetic development; state of intellectual, artistic and social development of a group > PDP; type and degree of civilization; (*arch*) social group characterized by a specified level of material achievement ~ **culture** *v/t* grow or rear artificially or commercially.

cultured [*kulcherd*] *adj* showing artistic or intellectual qualities and good taste; artificially grown or reared.

cultus [*kul*tus] *n* religious cult.

culver [*kul*ver] *n* wood-pigeon.

culverin [*kul*veRin] *n* long slender cannon.

culvert [*kul*vert] *n* large pipe or channel carrying stream of water underground.

cumber [*kum*ber] *v/t* burden ~ **cumber** *n*.

cumbersome [*kum*bersum] *adj* unwieldy, heavy and inconvenient ~ **cumbersomely** *adv*.

cumbrous [*kum*bRus] *adj* cumbersome ~ **cumbrously** *adv* ~ **cumbrousness** *n*.

cumin [*ku*min] *n* plant with carminative seeds.

cummerbund [*ku*merbund] *n* sash round waist.

cumquat [*kum*kwot] *n* small Japanese orange.

cumulate [*kew*mewlayt] *v/t* and *i* heap up.

cumulation [kewmewl*ay*shon] *n* accumulation.

cumulative [*kew*mewlativ] *adj* growing by successive additions; **c. vote** system in which voter has as many votes as there are candidates, and can apportion them as he likes; **c. preference shares** (*comm*) shares entitling holder to receive arrears of interest before other shareholders receive current interest ~ **cumulatively** *adv*.

cumulo-nimbus [kewmewlO-*nim*bus] *n* heavy dark thunderstorm cloud of great depth > PDG.

cumulus [*kew*mewlus] *n* pile, accumulation; domed cloud with flat base > PDG.

cuneiform [*kew*ni-ifawrm] *adj* and *n* (of or in) wedge-shaped lettering used in ancient Babylon and Assyria.

cunnilingus [kunil*ing*-gus] *n* stimulation of the vulva with the lips or tongue; one who practises this.

cunning [*ku*ning] *n* artfulness, slyness, clever deceit; skill ~ **cunning** *adj* artful, sly; subtle; skilful, ingenious; (*US*) pretty, attractive ~ **cunningly** *adv*.

cunt [*kunt*] *n* (*vulg*) female sexual organ, vagina; woman considered solely as a sexual partner; (*of a man, vulg pej*) complete fool.

cup [*kup*] *n* small drinking vessel with handle; ornamental vessel given as prize; (*eccles*) chalice; liquid contained in a cup; drink made by mixing wine with other ingredients; (*fig*) allotted share, fate; any object shaped like cup; (*anat*) socket of bone; (*bot*) calyx; **in one's cups** in drunken state; **one's c. of tea** (*coll*) what one likes, what suits one best ~ **cup** (*pres/part* **cupping**, *p/t* and *p/part* **cupped**) *v/t* and *i* form into shape of cup; (*surg, obs*) draw blood to skin by applying glass cup to create partial vacuum.

cup-bearer [*kup*-bairRer] *n* official wine-server.

cupboard [*ku*berd] *n* set of shelves enclosed by doors, for storing objects; **c. love** display of love assumed for selfish motives.

cupful [*kup*ful] *n* as much as a cup can hold.

cupidity [kew*pid*iti] *n* avarice.

cupola [*kew*pola] *n* (*archi*) small dome of roof; revolving gun-turret on warship; vertical cylindrical furnace for melting pig iron.

cuppa [*ku*per] *n* (*coll*) cup of tea.

cupreous [*kew*pRi-us] *adj* of or like copper.

cupric [*kew*pRik] *adj* (*chem*) containing bivalent copper.

cuprite [*kew*pRIt] *n* (*chem*) red oxide of copper.

cupronickel [kewpROn*ik*'l] *n* alloy of copper and nickel used in coinage.

cuprous [*kew*pRus] *adj* (*chem*) containing univalent copper.

cup-tie [*kup*-tI] *n* football match in a knock-out competition for prize of a cup.

cur [*kur*] *n* mongrel dog; snappy bad-tempered dog; (*fig*) cowardly, ill-bred or surly man.

curaçao [kewrRas*O*] *n* orange-flavoured liqueur.

curacy [*kew*Rasi] *n* post or office of a curate.

curare [kOO*Raa*Ri/kewr*Raa*Ri] *n* strong poison extracted from bark of certain S. American trees.

curassow [*kew*RasO] *n* large bird of South and Central America.

curate [*kew*Rit] *n* assistant clergyman to incumbent of parish; **c.'s egg** something partly good and partly bad.

curative [*kew*Rativ] *adj* healing, remedial.

curator [kew*Ray*ter] *n* official in charge of museum, library *etc*; (*Scots leg*) guardian of minor or lunatic ~ **curatorship** *n*.

curb [*kurb*] *n* restraining chain or strap passing under horse's jaw and fastened to bit; (*fig*) check, restraint; border, edging rim; edging of long stones along pavement (*usu* spelt *kerb*) ~ **curb** *v/t* restrain, check, control.

curcuma [*kur*kewma] *n* plant whose root is used in curry powder.

curd [*kurd*] *n* thick substance which separates from milk when mixed with acid ~ **curd** *v/t* and *i* form into curd ~ **curdy** *adj*.

curdle [*kurd*'l] *v/t* and *i* form into curd; thicken, coagulate; **c. the blood** (*fig*) terrify.

cure [*kewr*] *n* (*med*) that which restores to health, remedy; course of remedial treatment; fact of being healed; (*fig*) remedy; (*eccles*) spiritual charge, priestly office ~ **cure** *v/t* heal, provide a remedy for; put right; preserve (food) by salting, pickling *etc*; prepare (tobacco) for smoking; vulcanize (rubber); harden (plastics).

curé [*kew*Ray] *n* (*Fr*) parish priest in France.

curer [*kewr*Rer] *n* one who cures, *esp* food or tobacco.

curettage [kew*Ret*ij] *n* (*med*) act of scraping with a curette.

curette [kew*Ret*] *n* (*surg*) small instrument ending in a loop with a sharp edge ~ **curette** *v/t* and *i* scrape with curette.

curfew [*kur*few] *n* regulation requiring all persons to be indoors by a fixed hour or during a fixed period; (*hist*) bell rung at evening as signal to put out lights and fires.

curia [*kewr*Ri-a] *n* (*hist*) medieval judicial council or king's court of justice; Papal court.

curie [*kewr*Ri] *n* measure of activity of radioactive substance; the amount of an insotope that decays at a rate of 3.7×10^{10} disintegrations per second.

curio (*pl* **curios**) [*kewr*Ri-O] *n* object valuable through its rarity, age, or beauty.

curiosa [kewrRi-*Oza*] *n* (*pl*) pornographic or erotic objects or books; rare or curious items.

curiosity [kewrRi-*ositi*] *n* desire to know or learn; inquisitive interest; strange, interesting, or rare object; a curio.

curious [*kewr*Ri-us] *adj* eager to know or learn; inquisitive; rare; surprising; strange, odd; (*euph*) pornographic ~ **curiously** *adv*.

curium [*kewr*Ri-um] *n* (*chem*) a transuranic element > PDS.

curl [*kurl*] *n* lock of twisted hair, ringlet; lock of hair curving upwards; spiral; anything similar in shape; (*pl*) curly hair ~ **curl** *v/t* and *i* twist into a curl or curls; curve upwards; roll up at edges; move in twisting curves; ripple; play at curling; **c. up** lie with limbs drawn close to body; (*fig*) collapse; shrink in horror; overwhelm.

curler [*kurler*] *n* clip, roller *etc* for curling hair.

curlew [*kurlew*] *n* wading bird with long slender bill; inland bird with short bill, whimbrel.

curlicue [*kurlikew*] *n* elaborate twisting design.

curliness [*kurlinis*] *n* quality of being curly.

curling (1) [*kurling*] *adj* that curls, curly; used for curling (hair *etc*); **c. irons, c. tongs** instruments heated and applied to hair to curl it.

curling (2) *n* Scottish game played by sliding flat heavy stones over ice towards a mark.

curlpaper [*kurl*payper] *n* soft paper in which hair is twisted up to produce ringlets.

curly [*kurli*] *adj* curling, strongly curved; with curling hair; rippling.

curmudgeon [kurmujon] *n* gloomy, bad-tempered man ~ **curmudgeonly** *adj*.

currach, curragh [*ku*Rak/*ku*Ra] *n* coracle.

currant [*ku*Rant] *n* dried small seedless grape; fruit of several species of cultivated shrubs.

currency [*ku*Rensi] *n* state of being current; particular type of money in use in a State; total amount of money in circulation; prevalence, general acceptance.

current [*ku*Rent] *adj* in general use; in present use; present, up-to-date; (*of money*) in circulation; generally known, accepted *etc*; **c. account** (*banking*) money which can be drawn out for immediate use; **pass c.** be generally accepted ~ **current** *n* flow, stream, continuous movement of air, water, or electricity; (*fig*) course, onward movement; trend ~ **currently** *adv* commonly, generally; nowadays, at present.

curricle [*ku*Rik'l] *n* light open two-wheeled carriage drawn by two horses.

curriculum [ku*Ri*kewlum] *n* prescribed course of study, training *etc*.

currish [*kur*Rish] *adj* like a cur; mean-spirited, quarrelsome ~ **currishly** *adv* ~ **currishness** *n*.

curry (1) [*ku*Ri] *n* dish of stewed meat or fish in hotly flavoured sauce ~ **curry** *v/t* season with curry-powder, make into a curry.

curry (2) *v/t* rub down (horse) with a comb; dress (tanned leather); **c. favour** seek favour by flattery *etc*.

currycomb [*ku*RikOm] *n* metal comb for currying horses ~ **currycomb** *v/t*.

curry-powder [*ku*Ri-powder] *n* compound of turmeric and various strong spices.

curse [*kurs*] *n* words calling down God's anger or supernatural evil on a person; the calling down of misfortune, death *etc*; (*eccles*) excommunication, formal censure; blasphemous expression of anger, profane oath; source of misfortune or evil; nuisance; (*coll*) menses; **c. of Scotland** the nine of diamonds ~ **curse** *v/t* and *i* call down God's anger, evil, misfortune *etc* upon; swear (at); utter oaths or blasphemies; complain of resentfully; afflict, torment; excommunicate.

cursed, curst [*kurst*] *adj* hateful, deserving a curse; afflicted by a curse; (*coll*) wretched, annoying; obstinate, bad-tempered ~ **cursedly** *adv* ~ **cursedness** *n*.

cursive [*kursiv*] *n* handwriting in which letters are formed and linked without raising the pen ~ **cursive** *adj* flowing.

cursor [*kurser*] *n* transparent slider used in slide-rules.

cursory [*kurse*Ri] *adj* hasty and superficial ~ **cursorily** *adv* ~ **cursoriness** *n*.

curst see **cursed**.

curt [*kurt*] *adj* rudely brief, abrupt.

curtail [kert*ayl*] *v/t* cut short, shorten, abridge; deprive, diminish ~ **curtailment** *n*.

curtain [*kurtin*] *n* long piece of hanging cloth which can be drawn to screen window, door, bed *etc*, or to divide one part of room from another; sheet of heavy material dividing stage from auditorium; act of lowering this; curtain-call; anything which screens, protects, or divides; **draw a c. over** (*fig*) say no more about, conceal; **c. of fire** (*mil*) artillery barrage; **iron c.** frontiers dividing Communist from non-Communist States of Europe; (*fig*) lack of freedom of ideas and movement into and out of Communist States; **lift the c.** (*fig*) reveal; **c. wall** (*archi*) façade of a framed building ~ **curtain** *v/t* cover with a curtain; **c. off** shut off, divide by a curtain.

curtain-call [*kurtin*-kawl] *n* (*theat*) applause recalling performer after end of play *etc*.

curtain-raiser [*kurtin*-Rayzer] *n* (*theat*) short play performed before principal play.

curtal-axe [*kurtal*-aks] *n* (*hist*) cutlass.

curtilage [*kurtilij*] *n* (*leg*) enclosed land attached to a house.

curtly [*kurtli*] *adv* with rude brevity.

curtness [*kurtnis*] *n* quality of being curt.

curtsy, curtsey [*kurtsi*] *n* woman's gesture of respect, consisting of bending the knees and inclining the head and shoulders ~ **curtsy, curtsey** *v/i* make a curtsy.

curvaceous [kurv*ayshus*] *adj* (*coll*) (*of a woman*) having a well-developed figure.

curvature [*kurv*acher] *n* act of curving; fact or manner of being curved; amount of curve; (*med*) abnormal curve.

curve [*kurv*] *n* rounded bend, line of which no part is straight; curved part of anything ~ **curve** *v/t* and *i* bend into a curve, form a curve.

curvet [kurv*et*] *n* leap of horse which raises forelegs and springs off hind-legs while fore-legs are still in air ~ **curvet** (*pres/part* **curvetting**, *p/t* and *p/part* **curvetted**) *v/i* perform a curvet.

curvilineal, curvilinear [kurvi*li*ni-al, kurvi*li*ni-er] *adj* formed of curved lines.

cuscus [kooskoos] *n* genus of tree-living marsupials.

cusec [*kew*sek] *n* (*eng*) unit of flow, one cubic foot per second.

cushat [kooshat] *n* wood pigeon.

cushion [kooshon] *n* fabric bag filled with some soft yielding stuff, used to lean against or sit or kneel on; any resilient support or shock-absorber; lining round inner side of billiard table ~ **cushion** *v/t* provide with cushions; protect with padding; (*fig*) protect from hardship or sudden change; provide a shock-absorber for.

cushy [kooshi] *adj* (*coll*) easy, safe, profitable.

cusp [*kusp*] *n* (*geom*) point formed by two curves meeting; point of a tooth; (*archi*) ornamental feature projecting from inner curve of a Gothic arch;

(*astron*) horn of new moon ~ **cuspate** *adj* ~ **cusped** *adj*.

cuspidor [*kus*pidawr] *n* spittoon.

cuss [*kus*] *n* (*coll*) curse; fellow, chap ~ **cuss** *v/t* and *i* (*coll*) curse.

cussed [*kus*id] *adj* (*coll*) obstinate, troublesome ~ **cussedly** *adv* ~ **cussedness** *n*.

custard [*kus*terd] *n* boiled or baked mixture of eggs and sweetened milk; **c. pie** pie containing custard; (*fig*) slapstick farce; **c. powder** powder mixed with milk to make custard.

custard-apple [*kus*terd-ap'l] *n* pulpy fruit of East and West Indies.

custodian [kust*Odi*-an] *n* guardian, keeper, caretaker.

custody [*kus*todi] *n* safe-keeping, guardianship; legal detention; **take into c.** arrest.

custom [*kus*tom] *n* usual practice, habit; (*leg*) established usage; regular patronage of shop or trader; (*pl*) duties levied on exports or imports; building where travellers' luggage is inspected for dutiable goods; civil servants engaged in levying such duties; **customs union** agreement by several States on common tariff policy.

customary [*kus*tomeRi] *adj* usual, habitual; (*leg*) established by custom ~ **customarily** *adv* usually, commonly ~ **customariness** *n*.

custom-built [*kus*tom-bilt] *adj* built to customer's specifications.

customer [*kus*tomer] *n* one who buys at a shop; (*coll*) fellow.

custom-house [*kus*tom-hows] *n* office at which customs revenue is collected; building where vessels are cleared, or where travellers' luggage is inspected.

custom-made [*kus*tom-mayd] *n* (*comm*) made to order following customer's specifications.

cut (*pres/part* **cutting,** *p/t* and *p/part* **cut**) [*kut*] *v/t* and *i* make incision in; gash, wound, or divide into pieces with sharp instrument; shape by hacking or splitting; carve into shape; engrave; chisel; shape (gem) into facets; mow, reap; pass through or across; remove (flowers *etc*) from stalk by use of sharp instrument; shape cloth for clothes; shorten by clipping off the ends, trim; abridge; delete, omit; reduce in amount, price *etc*; castrate; strike sharply; (*fig*) cause sharp sorrow to *etc*; (*cricket*) strike with chopping motion; (*tennis, billiards*) hit edge of ball; (*of tooth*) appear through gum; perform brisk movement; (*sl*) run away; (*coll*) ignore, pretend not to know (a person); avoid, absent oneself from; (*sl*) stop, desist from; (*cin*) stop shooting a scene; change abruptly to a different shot; edit; (*rad*) make a sound recording; (*cards*) divide pack at random; expose card by removing part of pack; (*geom*) intersect; **c. back** prune back to main stem; (*coll*) return on one's tracks; **c. both ways** produce two opposite effects; **c. corners** take risks for the sake of simplicity or speed; **c. a dash** make showy impression; **c. down** fell; kill; reduce; **c. fine** (*coll*) leave very small margin (of time, money *etc*); **c. in** interrupt; (*mot*) overtake regardless of oncoming traffic; (*cards, dancing*) take another's place; **c. loose** sever connexion with; behave wildly; **c. no ice** make no difference, have no effect; **c. off** discontinue supply of; interrupt (telephone conversation); **be c. off** die suddenly,

esp when young; **c. off with a shilling** disinherit; **c. out** cut shaped pieces of paper, material *etc* from whole piece; switch off, disconnect; (*of a motor*) stop; (*coll*) oust, gain advantage over (a rival); **be c. out for** be naturally well suited for; **c. it out** stop it ; **c. and run** (*coll*) run away; **c. up** cut into small pieces; criticize harshly; cause grief to, distress; **c. up rough** become threatening or angry; **c. up well** (*coll*) die rich ~ **cut** *adj* divided, engraved, shaped by cutting; severed; reduced; castrated; sliced or shredded; **c. and dried** (*coll*) prepared beforehand, readymade, stereotyped ~ **cut** *n* act of cutting; smart blow, slash; mark or wound made by cutting; slice or piece removed by cutting; style in which something has been cut; abridgement, curtailment, reduction; passage deleted; (*cin*) abrupt transition; canal; (*sl*) share; **a c. above** superior to; **a short c.** more direct route or means of access.

cutaneous [kewt*ayni*-us] *adj* (*med*) of the skin.

cutaway [*kut*away] *n* tail-coat curving sharply back from the waist.

cutback [*kut*bak] *n* (*cin*) repetition of previous shots; (*econ*) cutting of expenses, retrenchment.

cute [*kewt*] *adj* (*coll*) sharp, quick-witted; (*US*) charming, quaint ~ **cutely** *adv* ~ **cuteness** *n*.

cuticle [*kew*tik'l] *n* outer layer of epidermis > PDB; hard skin at base of fingernails.

cutie [*kew*ti] *n* (*coll*) pretty girl.

cutis [*kew*tis] *n* skin..

cutlass [*kut*las] *n* short sword with wide blade.

cutler [*kut*ler] *n* one who mends, makes or sells knives.

cutlery [*kut*leRi] *n* knives and other sharp-edged instruments; implements used in eating; business of a cutler.

cutlet [*kut*lit] *n* small piece of meat cut from bone.

cut-off [*kut*-of] *n* device to interrupt flow of liquid; construction below ground level to reduce water seepage; device preventing cartridges of magazine rifle from passing into the breech; device which shuts off steam from an engine cylinder.

cut-out [*kut*-owt] *n* (*elect*) fuse or circuit breaker; (*mot*) device to free exhaust gases; figure cut out of wood or paper; portion deleted from play *etc*.

cut-price [*kut*pRis] *adj* reduced in price, cheap.

cutpurse [*kut*purs] *n* (*ar*) thief.

cut-rate [*kut*-Rayt] *adj* at much reduced price.

cutter [*kut*er] *n* one who or that which cuts; one who cuts out cloth for clothes; (*naut*) small boat used by warships; small vessel having a bowsprit, with deep keel; (*Canada, US*) small sleigh.

cut-throat [*kut*-thROt] *adj* murderous; merciless, unscrupulous; (*cards*) for three players ~ **cut-throat** *n* murderer, fierce ruffian.

cutting [*kut*ing] *n* act of cutting; that which is cut off; slip cut off from plant and replanted; excerpt cut out from newspaper *etc*; excavation for canal, railway, road, or pipeline; price reduction ~ **cutting** *adj* that cuts; sharp-edged; (*of wind*) keen, piercing; (*fig*) bitter, sarcastic, intended to cause pain.

cuttlebone [*kut*'lbOn] *n* internal shell of cuttlefish.

cuttlefish [*kut*'lfish] *n* marine mollusc with tentacles, that squirts out inky fluid when attacked.

cutty [*kuti*] *adj* (*Scots*) very short.

cutwater [*kut*wawter] *n* forward edge of ship's prow; streamlined head of a bridge pier.

cwm [*kOOm*] *n* (*Welsh*) valley, *esp* with steep sides; bowl-shaped hollow.

cyanamide [sɪ-*anam*ɪd] *n* an artificial fertilizer.

cyanic [sɪ-*anik*] *adj* containing cyanogen.

cyanide [*sɪ*-anɪd] *n* (*chem*) salt of hydrocyanic acid, prussic acid > PDS ~ **cyanide** *v/t* (*min*) extract (gold or silver) from ore by dissolving in sodium cyanide; harden (steel) by contact with molten cyanides > PDE, PDS.

cyanogen [sɪ-*anojin*] *n* a poisonous gas > PDS.

cyanose [sɪ-an*Oz*] *v/i* (*med*) turn blue.

cyanosis [sɪ-an*Osis*] *n* (*med*) blueness of lips and skin due to lack of oxygen in the blood.

cybernetics [sɪburn*etiks*] *n* (*pl*, used as *sing*) study of communication mechanisms in electronic calculating machines and the human brain.

cyclamate [*sɪk*lamayt] *n* one of several artificial sweetening substances derived from petrochemicals.

cyclamen [*sɪk*lamin] *n* genus of plants of the primrose family with fleshy root-stocks.

cycle [*sɪk*'l] *n* series of events recurring as a whole at regular intervals; time needed for such a series to return to original state; (*fig*) great length of time; group of poems, songs *etc* connected with some central theme or person; (*elect*) series of regularly recurrent changes in an electric current; (*coll*) bicycle ~ **cycle** *v/i* pass through a cycle; recur in cycles; (*coll*) ride a bicycle.

cycle-car [*sɪk*'l-kaar] *n* type of light motorcar, *gen* three-wheeled.

cycle-clips [*sɪk*'l-klips] *n* (*pl*) clips holding a cyclist's trousers close to his ankles.

cyclic [*sɪk*lik] *adj* pertaining to, recurring in, a cycle; belonging to cycle of poems; (*math*) capable of being inscribed in a circle; (*chem*) containing a closed ring structure ~ **cyclical** *adj* ~ **cyclically** *adv*.

cycling [*sɪk*ling] *n* act of riding a bicycle ~ **cycling** *adj* for use in bicycling.

cyclist [*sɪk*list] *n* one who rides a bicycle.

cyclo- *pref* circular.

cycloid [*sɪk*loid] *adj* approximately circular; circular ~ **cycloid** *n* (*math*) figure traced by point on circumference of circle which rolls along straight line ~ **cycloidal** [sɪk*loid*al] *adj*.

cyclometer [sɪk*lomiter*] *n* device attached to wheel of vehicle to register distance travelled; instrument for measuring circular arcs.

cyclone [*sɪk*l*On*] *n* (*meteor*) region of low atmospheric pressure surrounded by rotating winds > PDG; tornado, whirlwind; (*min*) cone-shaped air-cleaner ~ **cyclonic** [sɪk*lonik*] *adj*.

cyclopean [sɪk*lopee*-an] *adj* gigantic; (*archi*) composed of large and irregular blocks of stone.

cyclops [*sɪk*lops] *n* (*Gk myth*) one-eyed giant.

cyclorama [sɪk*loRaama*] *n* a landscape panorama extended circularly so that the spectator is surrounded by it; (*cin*, *tele*) curved scenic backcloth.

cyclostyle [*sɪk*lost*ɪl*] *n* duplicator printing from stencil ~ **cyclostyle** *v/t*.

cyclotron [*sɪk*l*Otron*] *n* (*phys*) apparatus for increasing energies of charged particles > PDS.

cygnet [*signit*] *n* young swan.

cylinder [*silinder*] *n* (*geom*) solid figure traced out by rectangle rotating round one side as axis; any object of this shape; (*eng*) cylindrical chamber in which piston works; hollow metal roller ~ **cylindrical** [silind*Rik*al] *adj*.

cylindroid [*silind*Roid] *n* figure resembling a cylinder, *esp* one with elliptical base.

cyma [*sɪma*] *n* (*archi*) moulding formed of a concave and convex curve.

cymbal [*simbal*] *n* (*mus*) percussion instrument consisting of thin metal plate > PDM.

cymbalo [*simbalO*] *n* (*mus*) type of dulcimer.

cyme [*sɪm*] *n* (*bot*) manner of blossoming where main single-flowered stem throws out lateral flowering branches which also throw out branches.

cymograph [*sɪmograaf*] *n* revolving cylinder bearing paper on which graphs can be traced.

Cymric [*kimRik*] *adj* Welsh.

cynic [*sinik*] *n* person tending to interpret motives, character *etc* unfavourably; person sceptical of human goodness; one who constantly mocks.

cynical [*sinikal*] *adj* of or like a cynic; believing the worst of people; mocking at or disbelieving in good motives ~ **cynically** *adv*.

cynicism [*sinisizm*] *n* quality of being a cynic; mocking disregard for or doubt of good motives.

cynosure [*sinoshoor*] *n* centre of attention.

cypher see **cipher**.

cypress [*sɪpRes*] *n* genus of dark, evergreen, coniferous tree.

Cypriot [*sipRi*-ot] *n* and *adj* (inhabitant or language) of Cyprus.

cyrillic [siRil*ik*] *adj* and *n* (pertaining to) the Slavonic alphabet.

cyst [*sist*] *n* (*med*) abnormal sac containing fluid.

cystic [*sistik*] *adj* of the bladder or gall-bladder; (*of swellings*) containing fluid.

cystitis [sist*ɪtis*] *n* inflammation of the bladder.

cystotomy [sist*otomi*] *n* (*surg*) cutting into bladder or gall-bladder.

cytochrome [*sɪtokR*Om] *n* (*biol*) respiratory pigment containing iron > PDB.

cytogenous [sɪt*ojenus*] *adj* producing cells.

cytology [sɪt*oloji*] *n* (*biol*) study of living cells ~ **cytologist** *n*.

cytolysis [sɪt*olɪsis*] *n* dissolution of cells by destruction of their surface membranes > PDB.

cytoplasm [*sɪtoplazm*] *n* protoplasm surrounding nucleus of a cell.

czar, tsar, tzar [*zaar*] *n* title of former emperors of Russia; (*fig*) tyrant.

czardas [*zaar*das] *n* national dance of Hungary.

czarevitch, tsarevich, tzarevich [*zaar*ivich] *n* eldest son of reigning czar.

czarina, tsarina, tzarina [zaa*Reena*] *n* title of former empress of Russia.

D

d [*dee*] fourth letter of the English alphabet; (*mus*) second note in the scale of C major; (*Rom num*) 500; (*abbr*) old penny; one twelfth of a shilling; **D.J.** (*coll*) disk jockey; dinner jacket.

dab (1) [*dab*] *n* a light tap or blow; small amount of a soft substance dropped on a surface; (*pl*) (*coll*) fingerprints ~ **dab** (*pres/part* **dabbing**, *p/t* and *p/part* **dabbed**) *v/t* touch lightly, put on with a light touch.

dab (2) *n* small flatfish.

dab (3) *adj* (*coll*) highly skilful, expert.

dabber [*daber*] *n* that which dabs; (*print*) pad for inking type; (*bui*) brush for applying spirit varnish.

dabble [*dab*'l] *v/t* and *i* wet by splashing or dipping in water; move feet or hands in shallow water; occupy oneself in a trifling way (with some pursuit) ~ **dabbler** *n*.

dabchick [*dabchik*] *n* small freshwater bird.

da capo [daa-*kaap*O] *phr* (*Ital*) (*mus*) repeat from the beginning.

dace [*days*] *n* small freshwater fish.

dacha [*daacha*] *n* (*Rus*) country house for summer use.

dachshund [*dak*shoond/*dash*hund] *n* (*Ger*) breed of dog with long body and short legs.

dacoit [da*koit*] *n* (*in India and Burma*) one of a gang of armed robbers ~ **dacoity** *n* robbery with violence.

Dacron [*dak*Ron] *n* trade-name for a polyester textile fibre.

dactyl [*dak*til] *n* (*pros*) foot consisting of one long syllable followed by two short, or of one stressed syllable followed by two unstressed ~ **dactylic** [dak*ti*lik] *adj*.

dactylitis [daktil*I*tis] *n* inflammation of a finger or toe.

dactylogram [*dak*tilogRam] *n* a fingerprint.

dactylology [daktil*olo*ji] *n* art of communication by means of signs with hands and fingers.

dactyloscopy [daktil*oskopi*] *n* identification by fingerprints.

dad [*dad*] *n* (*coll*) father.

dada [*da*da] *n* (*coll*) father.

dadaism [*da*da-izm] *n* an anti-rational movement in painting, sculpture, and literature which began in Zurich in 1916 ~ **dadaist** *n* and *adj*.

daddy [*dadi*] *n* (*coll*) father.

daddy-long-legs [dadi-*long*-legz] *n* popular name for the cranefly.

dado [*dayd*O] *n* (*archi*) portion of a pedestal between its base and cornice; (*bui*) border or panelling over the lower half of the walls of a room above the skirting; strip of patterned wallpaper just below picture-rail ~ **dadoed** *adi*.

daedal [*deedal*/*day*dal] *adj* skilful; skilfully made, intricate ~ **daedalian, daedalean** [deed*ay*li-an] *adj* intricate, maze-like.

daemon [*deem*on/*day*mon/*dI*mon] *n* (*Gk*) guardian deity or spirit.

daffodii [*daf*odil] *n* yellow spring flower of the genus *Narcissus*; pale yellow colour ~ **daffodil** *adj*.

daffy [*dafi*] *adj* (*sl*) daft.

daft [*daaft*] *adj* foolish, weak-minded, mad.

dagga [*dag*a] *n* S. African name for marijuana.

dagger [*dag*er] *n* weapon with short double-edged blade for thrusting; (*print*) mark of reference formed like a dagger (†) or a double dagger (‡); **at daggers drawn** at bitter enmity; **look (speak) daggers** look (speak) with hatred.

daggle [*dag*'l] *v/t* trail in wet grass or mud.

dago [*dayg*O] *n* (*pej*) person of Spanish, Portuguese, or Italian origin; Spanish or Italian language.

daguerreotype [da*ger*ROtIp] *n* an early photographic process.

dahlia [*day*li-a] *n* popular garden flower with large blossoms.

Dail Eireann [doil-*air*Ran] *n* the lower chamber of parliament in the Irish Republic.

daily [*day*li] *adj* occurring, done, produced every day ~ **daily** *n* newspaper appearing every weekday; non-resident maidservant; **d. dozen** physical exercises done every day ~ **daily** *adv* every day, day by day.

dainty [*day*nti] *n* food pleasing to the palate, a delicacy ~ **dainty** *adj* pleasing to the palate; pretty, elegant, tastefully made; fastidious (especially as regards food) ~ **daintily** *adv* ~ **daintiness** *n*.

daiquiri [dIk*I*Ri/*dak*eRi] *n* iced alcoholic drink consisting of rum, lime-juice, and sugar.

dairy [*dair*Ri] *n* place in which milk and cream are kept and made into butter and cheese; shop in which milk and its products are sold ~ **dairy** *adj* made in a dairy.

dairy-cattle [*dair*Ri-kat'l] *n* cattle bred for milking, not for beef.

dairy-farm [*dair*Rifaarm] *n* farm specializing in milk and its products.

dairying [*dair*Ri-ing] *n* management of a dairy.

dairymaid [*dair*Rimayd] *n* woman employed in a dairy.

dairyman [*dair*Riman] *n* man managing or employed in a dairy.

dais [*day*-is] *n* raised platform at one end of a hall for a throne or seats of honour.

daisied [*day*zid] *adj* covered with daisies.

daisy [*day*zi] *n* popular name of *Bellis perennis*, a white flower with yellow centre; (*sl*) something or someone first-rate or charming.

daisychain [*day*zichayn] *n* garland of daisies linked together by their own stems.

dakota [da*kO*ta] *n* type of aircraft chiefly used for troop transport.

Dalai Lama [dalI-*laama*] *n* chief Lama (Buddhist priest) of Tibet.

dale [*day*l] *n* valley.

dalek [*daa*lek] *n* an imaginary type of destructive robot in TV fiction.

dalesman [*day*lzman] *n* one who lives in a valley (*esp* in the North of England).

189

dalliance [*dal*i-ens] *n* trifling, frivolity; amorous or wanton behaviour.

dally [*dal*i] *v/i* waste time, delay, dawdle; play; **d. with** (*fig*) consider, entertain (scheme, idea).

Dalmatian [dal*may*shun] *n* type of dog, white with black spots, originally bred in Dalmatia ~ **Dalmatian** *adj* of or from Dalmatia.

dalmatic [dal*mat*ik] *n* (*eccles*) vestment worn by deacons and bishops at High Mass; robe worn by kings and emperors at their coronation.

daltonism [*dawl*tonizm] *n* colour-blindness.

dam (1) [*dam*] *n* wall to hold back water > PDE; body of water so obstructed ~ **dam** (*pres*/*part* **damming,** *p*/*t* and *p*/*part* **dammed**) *v/t* obstruct with a dam.

dam (2) *n* female parent (*usu* of animals).

damage [*dam*ij] *n* injury, harm; (*coll*) cost; **stand the d.** pay a bill for others; (*pl*) (*leg*) money claimed or paid in compensation for injury or loss ~ **damage** *v/t* and *i* injure; be easily liable to injury ~ **damageable** *adj*.

damascene [*dam*aseen] *v/t* ornament metal with patterns inlaid in gold or silver; ornament steel with wavy lines; pattern-weld ~ **damascene** *adj* of or pertaining to Damascus.

damask [*dam*ask] *n* reversible fabric of silk or linen woven with wavy patterns on its surfaces; the colour of a damask rose; steel ornamented with designs made, or like that made, in Damascus ~ **damask** *adj* made of damask; rose-coloured; **d. rose** rose introduced from Damascus; **d. plum** damson ~ **damask** *v/t* adorn with damascene patterns.

dam-buster [*dam*-buster] *n* (*mil*) type of large powerful aerial bomb.

dame [*daym*] *n* legal title of wife of baronet or knight, or of woman who has received an order of knighthood (used with Christian name); (*theat*) farcical female character in pantomime, played by male actor; (*obs*) mistress of small school for young children; (*US*) (*coll*) woman.

damfool [dam*fOOl*] *adj* foolish, stupid ~ **damfoolishness** *n*.

dammar [*dam*aar] *n* a natural resin used in many varnishes.

damn [*dam*] *v/t* condemn judicially, or by expressing disapproval; condemn to eternal punishment; swear at ~ **damn** *interj* oath expressing anger ~ **damn** *adj* (*sl*) damned ~ **damn** *n* (an oath); **not care a d.** not care at all.

damnable [*dam*nab'l] *adj* extremely wicked ~ **damnably** *adv*.

damnation [dam*nay*shon] *n* state of being condemned to eternal punishment; (*interj*) damn.

damnatory [*dam*natoRi/dam*nay*toRi] *adj* conveying sentence of condemnation.

damned [*damd*] *adj* condemned; consigned to hell, accursed; (*expl*) confounded; **do one's damnedest** do all one can.

damnification [damnifi*kay*shon] *n* (*leg*) act of injuring; state of being injured.

damnify [*dam*nifI] *v/t* (*leg*) cause injury or loss to.

damning [*dam*ing] *adj* causing condemnation or ruin.

damosel [*dam*ozel] *n* (*ar*) damsel, maid, virgin.

damp [*damp*] *n* moisture in the air; condensation on surfaces; (*mining*) undesirable gases > PDE; (*fig*) dejection, discouragement ~ **damp** *adj*

moist ~ **damp** *v/t* moisten; dull, deaden; reduce or eliminate any vibration or oscillation; (*mus*) stop vibration of a string; (*fig*) discourage, depress; slow the combustion of a fire; **d. off** *v/i* (*of flowers etc*) rot from excess of moisture.

dampcourse [*damp*kawrs] *n* (*bui*) horizontal layer of impervious material laid in a wall just above ground level to prevent the damp from rising.

dampen [*dam*pen] *v/t* make damp; (*fig*) depress.

damper [*damp*er] *n* person or thing that damps; (*fig*) something which has a depressing effect; pad for wetting stamps; device for stopping vibration in the strings of a piano; movable plate across a flue of stove to regulate the draught.

damping [*damp*ing] *n* decrease in the amplitude of an oscillation or wave motion with time.

dampish [*damp*ish] *adj* slightly damp.

damply [*damp*li] *adv* in a damp way.

dampness [*damp*nis] *n* condition of being damp, humidity.

damp-proof [*damp*-pROOf] *adj* impervious to damp ~ **damp-proofing** *n* (*bui*) providing a building with a horizontal or vertical damp course.

damsel [*dam*zel] *n* young girl, maiden.

damson [*dam*zon] *n* small purple plum; tree bearing this plum.

damson-cheese [damzon-*cheez*] *n* damson preserve of firm consistency.

dance [*daans*] *n* rhythmical sequence of steps, accompanied by music; social gathering for the purpose of dancing; **lead a person a d.** tantalize, put difficulties in someone's way; **D. of Death** medieval allegorical representation of Death leading all classes of persons to the grave; **St Vitus's D.** nervous disorder causing jerkings of the limbs ~ **dance** *v/t* and *i* perform (a dance); move to music in rhythmical steps; **d. attendance upon** wait upon assiduously; be kept waiting by; **d. to (someone's) piping** obey his wishes.

danceband [*daans*band] *n* orchestra which performs for dances.

dancer [*daan*ser] *n* one who dances; a professional dancer.

dancing [*daan*sing] *n* art and practice of the dance.

dandelion [*dand*il1-on] *n* common plant with yellow flowers and deeply indented leaves.

dander [*dand*er] *n* anger, temper; (*pl*) fragments of dead skin, fur, scales *etc*.

dandiacal [dand*I*-akal] *adj* dandified.

Dandie Dinmont [dandi-*din*mont] *n* breed of Scotch terrier.

dandify [*dand*ifI] *v/t* make to appear like a dandy, dress like a dandy ~ **dandified** *adj*.

dandle [*dand*'l] *v/t* dance (a child) up and down in the arms or on the knee.

dandruff [*dand*Ruf] *n* dead skin scaling off in the hair, scurf.

dandy (1) [*dand*i] *n* man who devotes extravagant attention to fashionable dress, a fop ~ **dandy** *adj* fashionably dressed, smart; (*coll*) first-rate.

dandy (2) *n* (*naut*) kind of sloop or cutter.

dandybrush [*dand*ibRush] *n* stiff brush used for grooming horses.

dandyism [*dand*i-izm] *n* quality of being a dandy; behaviour or outlook of a dandy.

Dane [dayn] *n* native of Denmark; **great D.** powerful, short-haired breed of dog.

danegeld [*dayn*geld] *n* (*hist*) a heavy tax first raised in the tenth century in order to buy off the Danish invaders; (*fig*) money paid or concessions made to appease one who threatens.

Danelaw [*dayn*law] *n* (*hist*) that part of England before the Conquest where Danish custom and law was observed – Northumbria and the Midlands.

danger [*dayn*jer] *n* exposure to risk of death or injury, peril; cause of peril, menace; (*of signal*) **at d.** in a position giving warning of danger.

danger-money [*dayn*jer-muni] *n* extra payment given for a dangerous task.

dangerous [*dayn*jerus] *adj* hazardous, unsafe, risky; likely to cause injury ~ **dangerously** *adv.*

dangle [dangg'l] *v/t* and *i* cause to swing loosely; swing loosely; (*fig*) display as an enticement; **d. after** hang round (person, as an admirer).

Danish [*dayn*ish] *adj* belonging to Denmark ~ **Danish** *n* language of Denmark.

dank [dank] *adj* unpleasantly damp ~ **dankness** *n* ~ **dankish** *adj.*

danseuse [daansu(r)z] *n* (*Fr*) woman professional dancer.

daphne [*daf*ni] *n* kind of flowering shrub.

dapper [*dap*er] *adj* (*of men*) neat and smart in dress and bearing; brisk in movement.

dapple [*dap*'l] *v/t* mark with spots on a background of different colour or shade ~ **dappled** *adj* variegated with spots.

dapple-grey [*dap*'l-grAy] *n* and *adj* (horse) of grey dappled with darker spots.

darbies [*daar*biz] *n* (*pl*) (*sl*) handcuffs.

dare (*p/t* **dared, durst,** *p/part* **dared**) [dair] *v/i* and *t* have courage for, venture to do; challenge, defy (person to do something); **I d. say** (*freq ironically*) I think it likely; very likely ~ **dare** *n* (*coll*) a challenge to some risky act; deed done in reply to a challenge.

daredevil [*dair*dev'l] *adj* and *n* (typical of) a person of reckless courage.

daring [*dair*Ring] *n* courage, audacity ~ **daring** *adj* brave, bold, adventurous, audacious.

dark [daark] *adj* without light; (*of hair or complexion*) black or deep brown; (*of any colour*) a deep shade; (*fig*) gloomy; secret, mysterious; evil, wicked; **d. horse** competitor whose capabilities and chances of success are not known; **D. Blues** Oxford men or Harrow schoolboys; **D. Ages** earliest part of the medieval period in Europe; **D. Continent** Africa; **d. glasses** spectacles with dark tinted lenses ~ **dark** *n* absence of light, darkness; (*fig*) ignorance, secrecy.

darken [*daar*ken] *v/t* and *i* make dark or darker; shut out light from; (*of colour*) give a deeper tone to; (*fig*) cloud, perplex; make foul, sully; cast a gloom upon; become dark or darker.

darkish [*daar*kish] *adj* rather dark in colour.

darkling [*daar*kling] *adj* growing dark, gloomy, dim ~ **darkling** *adv* in the dark.

darkly [*daar*kli] *adv* in a dark manner; gloomily; mysteriously, obscurely; (*ar*) indistinctly, imperfectly; maliciously.

darkness [*daar*knes] *n* absence of light; night; blindness; (*fig*) ignorance wickedness, obscurity.

darksome [*daar*ksum] *adj* (*poet*) dark, dismal.

darky, darkey [*daar*ki] *n* (*coll*) a Negro.

darling [*daar*ling] *n* one dearly loved ~ **darling** *adj* dearly loved; (*coll*) sweet, charming; (*of hopes*) greatly desired.

darn (1) [*daarn*] *v/t* repair a fabric by filling the hole with interwoven threads ~ **darn** *n* a repair so made ~ **darner** *n* needle or device for darning.

darn (2) *v/t* (*expl, euph*) damn ~ **darnation** [daar*nay*shon] *n* ~ **darned** *adj.*

darnel [*daar*nel] *n* a grass growing as a weed among corn.

darning [*daar*ning] *n* process of mending a hole with a darn; clothes to be darned; **d. needle** large-eyed needle for darning.

dart [daart] *n* pointed missile; weighted and feathered spike thrown at a target in the game of darts; sting (of animal); swift movement forward; short tapering seam in a fabric ~ **dart** *v/t* and *i* shoot out, send forth quickly; move swiftly forward; fly swiftly through the air.

dartboard [*daart*bawrd] *n* wooden board, marked out with a circle cut into segments, at which players throw darts.

darts [daarts] *n* game in which players compete in throwing small feathered darts at a dartboard.

Darwinian [daar*win*i-an] *adj* pertaining to Charles Darwin and his theory of the evolution of species ~ **Darwinian** *n* follower of Charles Darwin ~ **Darwinism** [*daar*winizm] *n.*

dash [dash] *v/t* and *i* hurl with violence; splash; rush furiously or hastily; (*fig*) discourage, abash; (*expl, euph*) damn; **d. off** produce hastily ~ **dash** *n* sudden rush; splash; small admixture; short horizontal line (—) to mark a pause or parenthesis; a Morse code signal; (*mot abbr*) dashboard; (*fig*) energy, vigorous action; show, ostentation; **cut a d.** make a brilliant impression, appear important.

dashboard [*dash*bawrd] *n* instrument panel in front of the driver of a motor vehicle.

dasher [*dash*er] *n* the agitator in a churn; (*coll*) a smart fellow.

dashing [*dash*ing] *adj* bold, spirited, showy.

dashpot [*dash*pot] *n* mechanical damping device consisting of a piston and cylinder > PDS.

dastard [*das*taard] *n* contemptible coward ~ **dastardly** *adj* cowardly, brutal.

data [*day*ta] *n* (*pl*) group of known, given, or ascertained facts, from which inferences or a conclusion can be drawn, or on which a discussion is based; symbols or characters on which computers operate; series of electrical impulses, magnetic tapes, punched cards *etc* by which these are recorded or transmitted; **d. bank** place where factual records and files are stored; **d. processing** automatic classification, analysis or calculation of data.

datable [*day*tab'l] *adj* capable of being dated.

datal [*day*tal] *adj* chronological; containing the date of a document.

date (1) [dayt] *n* unit in a classification of days used to indicate the time of an event, *usu* day of month, month, and year; indication on document, coin *etc* of its day or year of issue; (*coll*) appointment for a certain time; person with whom an appointment is made ~ **date** *v/t* and *i* affix the date to (a letter *etc*); assign a date to; take origin (from a certain time); (*coll*) make an appointment to meet (*usu* of a young man inviting a girl); bear evidence of its date or one's age, become unfashionable; **out of d.** old-fashioned; **up to d.** modern, with all the latest improvements.

date (2) *n* fruit of the date-palm.

dated [*dayt*id] *adj* (*coll*) obviously belonging to a past period, old-fashioned.

dateless [*dayt*lis] *adj* that cannot be dated; immemorial; endless.

dateline [*dayt*lin] *n* meridian 180° from Greenwich, east and west of which the date differs; a line, or part of one, giving the date of issue of a newspaper, or the date and place of origin of a dispatch, letter *etc*.

date-palm [*dayt*paam] *n* palm tree which produces the date fruit.

date-stamp [*dayt*-stamp] *n* adjustable stamp for printing date of cancellation, delivery, issue *etc*; mark made by this ~ **date-stamp** *v/t*.

dative [*dayt*iv] *adj* (*gramm*) name of the case denoting the indirect object of a verb; (*chem*) (of a covalent bond) having both electrons donated by one atom; coordinate ~ **datival** [dayt*I*val] *adj* relating to the dative.

datum (*pl* **data**) [*dayt*um] *n* a fact, known, given or ascertained, from which inferences may be drawn; (*surveying*) any level taken as a reference point for levelling.

daub [*dawb*] *v/t* and *i* smear with a sticky substance; (*bui*) coat with a layer of plaster or clay, to rough-cast; (*painting*) lay on colour roughly and crudely ~ **daub** *n* material for daubing walls; a crude inartistic painting ~ **dauber, daubster** *n* unskilful painter.

daughter [*dawt*er] *n* female child; female descendant; (*fig*) woman considered as intellectually or spiritually the offspring of some person or movement.

daughter-in-law [*dawt*eR-in-law] *n* son's wife.

daughterly [*dawt*erli] *adj* characteristic of a good daughter, filial.

daunt [*dawnt*] *v/t* inspire with fear or dismay; intimidate, abash, cow; discourage, dishearten.

dauntless [*dawnt*les] *adj* courageous.

dauphin [*dO*fan(g)] *n* (*hist*) title of the eldest son of the King of France.

davenport [*dav*'npawrt] *n* pedestal desk with sloping top; (*US*) large upholstered sofa.

davit [*dav*it] *n* one of pair of uprights which suspend a ship's boat and lower it over the side; crane in bows for hoisting the anchor.

davy [*dayv*i] *n* miner's safety lamp, invented by Sir Humphry Davy.

Davy Jones [dayvi-*jO*nz] *n* (*naut*) the malignant spirit of the sea, the Devil; **Davy Jones's locker** the sea as the graveyard of those drowned.

daw [*daw*] *n* the jackdaw.

dawdle [*dawd*'l] *v/i* idle, loiter, be sluggish in doing anything; **d. away** (one's time) waste ~ **dawdler** *n*.

dawn [*dawn*] *n* daybreak; (*fig*) a beginning ~ **dawn** *v/i* begin to grow light; (*fig*) begin to develop; **d. upon** become evident to ~ **dawning** *n* the dawn; (*fig*) beginning, birth.

day [*day*] *n* period between sunrise and sunset; daylight; period from midnight to midnight;

hours of work; a specified or appointed day; (*usu pl*) period, epoch; **d. by d.** daily; **one of these days** some day soon; **Last D.** Judgement Day; **win the d.** gain the victory; **days of grace** extra days allowed for payment; **call it a d.** leave off doing something; **name the d.** fix date of marriage; **pass the time of d.** exchange greetings ~ **day** *adj* during the day; for one day only.

daybed [*day*bed] *n* sofa or couch; hospital bed for day patients.

day-blindness [*day*-bl*I*ndnes] *n* condition of vision in which the individual sees better in dim light > PDP.

day-boarder [*day*-bawrder] *n* child who has lunch at school, but goes home to sleep.

daybook [*day*book] *n* (*comm*) book for recording transactions day by day.

dayboy [*day*boi] *n* boy who attends school daily, while living at home.

daybreak [*day*bRayk] *n* dawn.

daydream [*day*dReem] *n* reverie in which the mind wanders aimlessly among pleasant imagery ~ **daydream** *v/i* ~ **daydreamer** *n*.

daygirl [*day*gurl] *n* girl who attends school daily.

day-labour [*day*-layber] *n* work, *gener* manual, paid for by the day ~ **day-labourer** *n* workman paid by the day.

daylight [*day*lit] *n* light coming from the sun; **see d.** begin to understand a matter.

daylight-saving [*day*lit-sayving] *n* plan for saving daylight by putting the clock forward during the summer months.

daylong [*day*long] *adj* lasting all day.

day-nursery [*day*-nurseRi] *n* place where young children can be left during mother's absence.

day-release [*day*-Rilees] *adj* **d. course** educational or training course for employees held during working hours.

day-school [*day*skOOl] *n* school which children attend while living at home.

dayshift [*day*shift] *n* period of working during all or part of daylight hours in factories, mines *etc*; gang of workers working during this time.

dayspring [*day*spRing] *n* (*poet*) dawn.

daystar [*day*staar] *n* the morning star.

daytime [*day*tim] *n* time of daylight.

day-to-day [day-too-*day*] *adj* and *adv* of or for every day; continuous(ly), normal(ly); without variation, boring(ly).

daze [*dayz*] *v/t* stupefy and confuse the faculties ~ **daze** *n* dazed state ~ **dazedly** *adv*.

dazzle [*daz*'l] *v/t* and *i* confuse the vision of; be partially blinded by a glaring light; (*fig*) be bewildered or overwhelmed ~ **dazzle** *n* glaring light; light reflected from wet surfaces.

D-day [*dee*-day] *n* (*mil*) code name for the day fixed for launching a major offensive, *esp* the day (6 June 1944) on which British and American forces invaded Normandy.

de- *pref* down, away, off; thoroughly; also expressing deficiency, deprivation, completeness, negation.

deacon [*deek*'n] *n* (*eccles*) church official helping the priest; (*in the Anglican and Roman churches*) cleric in orders next below a priest; (*in the Presbyterian, Baptist, and Congregational churches*) layman appointed to attend principally to the secular affairs of the church ~ **deaconess** *n*

192

churchwoman with duties similar to those of a deacon ~ **deaconry, deaconship** n office or status of a deacon.

dead [*ded*] *adj* no longer living, deprived of life, having never lived; resembling death; insensible, numbed, lifeless; obsolete, no longer effective;(*coll*) absolute, complete; (*of colour*) dull, neutral; (*of sound*) dull, lacking in resonance; (*sport*) no longer in play; (*of a language*) no longer spoken; (*elect*) not electrically charged; (*bui*) bricked in (of door *etc*); **d. end** terminus or cul-de-sac; **d. from the neck up** (*sl*) devoid of intelligence; **d. ground** (*mil*) ground hidden from view; **d. heat** result of a race in which two or more contestants reach the winning-post simultaneously; **d. letter** undelivered or unclaimed letter; obsolete law; **d. march** funeral march; **d. men** (*coll*) empty bottles; **d. reckoning** (*naut*) fixing a ship's position without the aid of the stars; **d. set** determined attack; (*coll*) persistent attempt to gain someone's affection; **d. shot** excellent marksman ~ **dead** n (*pl*) those who have died; **the d. of night** the middle of the night ~ **dead** *adv* thoroughly.

dead-alive, dead-and-alive [ded-al*I*v, ded-and-al*I*v] *adj* lethargic; depressing, dreary; (*of place*) where nothing interesting ever happens.

deadbeat [ded*beet*] **adj** completely exhausted; (*mech*) oscillating without a recoil ~ **deadbeat** n (US) a loafer, sponger.

dead-centre [ded-*senter*] n (*eng*) position of a crank when it is in straight line with the connecting-rod; exact centre.

deaden [ded*en*] *v/t* benumb, blunt, muffle; dull the brilliancy of.

dead-end [ded-*end*] *adj* leading nowhere; **d. job** job offering no chance of promotion; **d. kid** street urchin, juvenile delinquent.

deadening [ded*ening*] n (*bui*) material used to soundproof floors or walls.

deadhead [ded*hed*] n person admitted free to a theatrical performance; a feeble, ineffectual person; faded flower-head.

deadlight [ded*lIt*] n (*naut*) storm-shutter over port-hole; thick pane of glass let into deck; skylight which cannot be opened.

deadline [ded*lIn*] n time by which some task has to be completed.

deadliness [ded*lines*] n quality of being deadly.

deadlock [ded*lok*] n position in which it is impossible to act; standstill ~ **deadlocked** *adj*.

deadly [ded*li*] *adj* likely or certain to cause death; like death; poisonous; fatal; implacable; (*coll*) boring ~ **deadly** *adv* as if dead; (*coll*) extremely.

deadly-nightshade [dedli-*nItt*shayd] n popular name for the poisonous plant *Atropa belladonna*.

dead-man's handle [dedmanz-*hand*'l] n device on an electrically driven vehicle, which cuts off the power and applies the brakes if the operator releases his hold.

deadness [ded*nis*] n state of being dead; lack of animation, colour, interest *etc*.

deadnettle [ded*net*'l] n plant of genus *Lamium* with leaves like a nettle, but stingless.

deadpan [ded*pan*] *adj* (*of face*) without expression, blank ~ **deadpan** n face without expression.

dead-point [ded-*point*] n dead-centre.

dead-weight [ded-*wayt*] n heavy, inert mass of anything; useless encumbrance.

dead-wood [ded-*wood*] n fallen trees or branches; (*fig*) anything useless or obstructive.

deaf [*def*] *adj* unable to hear; with defective hearing; (*fig*) unwilling to give attention ~ **deaf** n (*pl*) people who are deaf.

deaf-aid [def-*ayd*] n electrical device to assist hearing.

deafen [def*en*] *v/t* make deaf; drown by a louder noise.

deaf-mute [def-*mewt*] n one who is both deaf and dumb.

deafness [def*nis*] n inability to hear.

deal (1) (*p/t* and *p/part* dealt) [*deel*] *v/t* and *i* distribute, hand out; deliver (blow); distribute playing cards to the players; (*Stock Exchange*) carry out a transaction or bargain; **d. in** trade in (articles); **d. with** have to do with, argue about, discuss; handle, settle, manage (affairs); trade or do business with, shop at; (*of persons*) behave towards; **d. by** behave towards ~ **deal** n quantity, amount; business transaction or bargain; (*Stock Exchange*) purchase or sale of shares; (*cards*) act of dealing; a hand of cards; **big d.** (*coll*) iron exclam of applause.

deal (2) [*deel*] n redwood; piece of square sawn softwood timber 2 to 4 in. thick and 9 to 11 in. wide ~ **deal** *adj* made of deal.

dealer [deel*er*] n one engaged in buying and selling; trader, merchant; (*Stock Exchange*) a jobber; player whose turn it is to deal out the cards.

dealing [deel*ing*] n behaviour towards others; (*pl*) buying and selling, commerce, trade.

dealt [*delt*] *p/t* and *p/part* of deal (1).

dean [*deen*] n (*eccles*) head of the chapter or body of canons in a cathedral or collegiate church; head of a faculty in a university or university college; **rural d.** priest with jurisdiction over a group of parishes.

deanery [deen*eRi*] n office of a dean; group of parishes over which a rural dean presides; official residence of a dean.

deanship [deen*ship*] n office, status, or tenure of a dean.

dear [*deer*] *adj* beloved; valuable, costly, in excess of the normal price; used as a form of address in beginning a letter ~ **dear** n dear one, lovable person ~ **dear** *adv* at too high a price ~ **dear** *interj* expressing surprise, distress *etc* ~ **dearly** *adv* affectionately; at great cost ~ **dearness** n quality of being dear.

dearth [*durth*] n scarcity (*esp* of food), famine.

deary, dearie [deer*Ri*] n (*coll*) little dear, darling.

death [*deth*] n cessation of life; end of life; state of being dead; manner of dying; cause of death; **civil d.** loss of civil rights; **at death's door in** extreme danger of death; **in at the d.** present when the fox is killed by the hounds; (*fig*) present at the final phase (of an enterprise, series of events); **Black D.** (*hist*) plague of the fourteenth century; **d. duties** tax levied on the estate of a person at death; **d. wish** (*psych*) conscious or unconscious attraction towards the idea of one's own death; urge to self-destruction.

death-adder [deth-*ader*] n venomous Australian snake.

deathbed [deth*bed*] n bed on which a person

dies; (*fig*) last illness ~ **deathbed** *adj* felt or expressed just before death.

deathblow [*deth*blO] *n* action or shock which destroys life or hope.

death-knell [*deth*-nel] *n* sound of a bell at a death or funeral.

deathless [*deth*les] *adj* not liable to death, immortal.

deathlike [*deth*lIk] *adj* resembling death.

deathly [*deth*li] *adj* like death ~ **deathly** *adv* in a deathly manner.

deathmask [*deth*maask] *n* plaster cast taken of a person's face after death.

deathrate [*deth*Rayt] *n* proportion of deaths to the population.

death-rattle [*deth*-Rat'l] *n* sound heard in the throat of a dying person.

death's-head [*deths*-hed] *n* a human skull; representation of a skull as an emblem of death; **d. moth** species of hawk-moth with skull-like markings.

death-toll [*deth*-tOl] *n* number of people killed (in an accident *etc*).

death-trap [*deth*-tRap] *n* place or structure concealing unseen danger.

death-warrant [*deth*-woRant] *n* official document authorizing the execution of a condemned person; (*fig*) something which makes one's doom inevitable.

deathwatch [*deth*woch] *n* a grub which burrows deeply into structural timber and makes a ticking noise popularly thought to foretell death.

deb [*deb*] *n* (*coll*) debutante.

debacle, débâcle [day*baak*'l] *n* breaking up of ice in a river; (*geol*) sudden rush of water, breaking through barriers and carrying with it masses of debris; (*fig*) overwhelming disaster, disorderly retreat; collapse.

debag (*p/t* and *p/part* debagged) [di*bag*] *v/t* (*sl*) forcibly remove the trousers from.

debar (*pres/part* debarring, *p/t* and *p/part* debarred) [di*baar*] *v/t* exclude; prevent.

debark [dee*baark*] *v/t* and *i* put or go ashore.

debase [di*bays*] *v/t* lower in value or dignity, adulterate (*esp* of coinage) ~ **debased** *adj*.

debatable [di*bayt*ab'l] *adj* admitting of discussion, open to question; **d. land** ground to which two parties lay claim.

debate [di*bayt*] *n* formal and public discussion of a motion by a succession of speakers; argument, controversy ~ **debate** *v/t* and *i* discuss thoroughly, argue; (*fig*) reflect, deliberate ~ **debater** *n*.

debauch [di*bawch*] *v/t* lead away from virtue or morality, corrupt; seduce from chastity ~ **debauch** *n* occasion of excessive indulgence in drinking and sensual pleasure, orgy.

debauchee [diba*wchee*] *n* one given to dissipation and sensual pleasure.

debauchery [di*bawch*eRi] *n* habitual immorality.

debenture [di*ben*cher] *n* certificate that a sum of money is owing to a specified person.

debilitate [di*bil*itayt] *v/t* make weak ~ **debilitating** *adj* tending to make weak ~ **debilitation** [dibilit*ay*shon] *n*.

debility [di*bil*iti] *n* weakness, generally physical.

debit [*deb*it] *n* (*comm*) entry in account recording sum of money owing; the left-hand side of a ledger where such entries are made ~ **debit** *v/t* charge (an account) with a debt.

debonair [debon*air*] *adj* affable, cheerful, sprightly of manner.

debouch [di*bowch*/di*bOOsh*] *v/i* (*of troops*) march into the open from cover or from a confined place; (*of river reaching its mouth*) widen out ~ **debouchment** *n* act of debouching; rivermouth.

debrief [dee*bReef*] *v/t* question (a returning airman, soldier *etc*) about the mission he has returned from ~ **debriefing** *n*.

debris [*deb*Ree/*day*bRee] *n* fragments left after some act of destruction; accumulation of wreckage or rubbish; (*geol*) pieces of rock accumulated at the base of a mountain or cliff.

debt [*det*] *n* something owed to another; liability, obligation; **in d.** owing money; **bad d.** debt which will not be paid; **d. of honour** one not legally recoverable.

debtor [*deter*] *n* one in debt to another person.

debug (*pres/part* debugging, *p/t* and *p/part* debugged) [dee*bug*] *v/t* remove lice from; remove faults from (machinery); cure snags in (process).

debunk [dee*bunk*] *v/t* (*coll*) divest of humbug, sentimentality, glamour; expose the sham pretensions of.

début, debut [*day*bew] *n* first public appearance of an actor, actress, or musician; entrance of a girl into society; beginning, start.

debutante [*deb*ewtont] *n* girl making her début in society.

dec-, deca- *pref* ten, tenfold.

decade [*dek*ayd/*dek*ayd] *n* group of ten; period of ten years; division of the Rosary comprising ten *Ave Marias*, one *Pater Noster* and one *Gloria Patri*; division of a literary work containing ten parts ~ **decadal** *adj* having a period of ten years.

decadence [*dek*adens] *n* process of deterioration; decline in moral quality; cultural demoralization.

decadent [*dek*adent] *adj* in a state of decadence; seeking artificial refinements of sensibility; aesthetically or morally corrupted.

decaffeinate [dee*kaf*eenayt] *v/t* remove or reduce caffeine in (coffee).

decagon [*dek*agon] *n* (*geom*) ten-sided plane figure ~ **decagonal** [dek*ag*onal] *adj* having ten sides.

decagram, decagramme [*dek*agRam] *n* weight of ten grammes.

decahedron [deka*heed*Ron] *n* (*geom*) solid figure with ten faces ~ **decahedral** *adj*.

decal [*dee*kal] *n* sticker or transfer for display on cars.

decalcify [dee*kals*ifI] *v/t* deprive of lime salts.

decalitre [*dek*aleeter] *n* measure of ten litres.

Decalogue [*dek*alog] *n* the Ten Commandments.

decametre [*dek*ameeter] *n* length of ten metres.

decamp [di*kamp*] *v/i* break up a camp; depart hastily, run away, abscond.

decanal [di*kayn*al] *adj* belonging to the office of a dean; relating to south side of choir of a cathedral, where the Dean sits.

decant [di*kant*] *v/t* pour a liquid gently from one vessel to another without disturbing the sediment; pour wine from a bottle into a decanter; (*coll*) eject abruptly, tip out, turn out.

decantation [deekan*tay*shon] *n* act of decanting.

decanter [di*kanter*] *n* ornamental glass vessel with stopper in which wine or whisky is served.

decapitate [di*kapi*tayt] *v/t* cut off the head of ~ **decapitation** [dikapi*tay*shon] *n*.

decapod (*pl* **decapoda**) [*deka*pod] *n* (*zool*) crustacean having ten feet ~ **decapod** *adj*.

decarbonize [dee*kaar*bonIz] *v/t* deprive of carbon; remove solid carbon deposited on the pistons and cylinder head of an internal-combustion engine.

decasyllabic [dekasi*labi*k] *n* and *adj* (*pros*) (line of verse) containing ten syllables.

decay [di*kay*] *v/i* deteriorate, rot, decompose, disintegrate through age; grow weak; decline from prosperity; (*phys*) transform into different nuclei or particles through gradual decrease of radioactivity ~ **decay** *n* decomposition, disintegration, rotting; gradual weakening, decline~ **decayed** *adj*.

decease [di*sees*] *n* death ~ **decease** *v/i* die.

deceased [di*seest*] *adj* dead ~ **deceased** *n* (*leg*) dead person.

deceit [di*seet*] *n* wilful giving of a false impression, cheating, guile; quality of deceitfulness.

deceitful [di*seet*ful] *adj* giving a false impression, misleading; given to deceiving ~ **deceitfully** *adv* ~ **deceitfulness** *n*.

deceivable [di*seev*ab'l] *adj* able to be deceived.

deceive [di*seev*] *v/t* and *i* mislead wilfully, delude, cheat; delude oneself; be mistaken; practise deceit.

decelerate [dee*sele*Rayt] *v/t* and *i* reduce the speed of; move more slowly ~ **deceleration** [deesele*Ray*shon] *n*.

December [di*sem*ber] *n* twelfth month of the year.

decency [*dee*sensi] *n* propriety of behaviour, decorum; (*coll*) good manners; (*coll*) goodness.

decennial [de*sen*ial] *adj* of or pertaining to a period of ten years; happening every ten years.

decent [*dee*sent] *adj* becoming, seemly, respectable; not immodest or indelicate; (*coll*) good enough, passable; kind, generous; agreeable ~ **decently** in a decent manner; (*coll*) generously.

decentralize [dee*sent*RalIz] *v/t* remove (government, authority *etc*) from a single centre and distribute it ~ **decentralization** [deesentRalIza*y*shon] *n*.

deception [di*sep*shon] *n* the act of deceiving; the state of being deceived; that which deceives; illusion, trickery, fraud.

deceptive [di*sep*tiv] *adj* liable to deceive, designed to mislead; misleading ~ **deceptively** *adv* ~ **deceptiveness** *n*.

deci- *pref* one tenth.

decibel [*desi*bel] *n* unit used to express the loudness of sounds > PDS.

decide [di*sId*] *v/t* and *i* give judgement in, settle, determine; make up one's mind ~ **decidable** *adj* capable of being settled.

decided [di*sId*id] *adj* definite, undoubted; resolute ~ **decidedly** *adv*.

decider [di*sI*der] *n* extra race or game to decide a tie.

deciduous [di*side*wus] *n* falling off at stated periods; (*bot*) shedding its leaves annually.

decigramme [*desi*gRam] *n* one tenth of a gramme.

decilitre [*desi*leeter] *n* one tenth of a litre.

decillion [di*sil*yon] *n* (*math*) a million raised to the tenth power.

decimal [*desi*mal] *adj* based on the number ten; expressed or calculated in tens or multiples of ten; **d. fraction** fraction in which the denominator (not expressed) is a power of ten; **d. point** dot placed between the unit figure and the numerator; **d. system** standard numerical system based on the number ten ~ **decimal** *n* (*math*) a decimal fraction; **recurring d.** decimal fraction in which the last figure or succession of figures repeats indefinitely.

decimalize [*desi*malIz] *v/t* express as decimal or in terms of decimal system ~ **decimalization** *n*.

decimally [*desi*mali] *adv* by means of decimals.

decimate [*desi*mayt] *v/t* put to death one man in every ten of (a group); destroy large numbers of ~ **decimation** [desi*may*shon] *n*.

decimetre [*desi*meeter] *n* one tenth of a metre.

decipher [di*sI*fer] *v/t* turn from a cipher into ordinary writing, decode; make out the meaning of ~ **decipherable** *adj*.

decision [di*sizh*on] *n* final judgement, settlement; (*leg*) authoritative ruling or verdict of a judge; determination, firmness of character.

decisive [di*sI*siv] *adj* having the power of deciding, conclusive; showing decision, firm ~ **decisively** *adv* ~ **decisiveness** *n*.

deck (1) [*dek*] *n* platform forming the floor of a horizontal division of a ship, bus *etc*; horizontal section formed by such a division; floor carrying-surface of bridge; any floor or platform; pack of cards; **clear the decks** prepare for action ~ **deck** *adj* of or on a ship's deck.

deck (2) *v/t* adorn, array, decorate; cover (a ship) with a deck.

deckchair [*dek*chair] *n* portable folding-chair with a canvas back and seat.

decker [*dek*er] *n* ship or omnibus possessing (a certain number of) decks.

decking [*dek*ing] *n* adornment, embellishment; a flat roof or a quay, jetty or bridge floor, generally a floor with no roof over.

deckle [*dek*'l] *n* (*paper-making*) wooden frame for hand mould; **d. strap** device in a paper-making machine which determines the width of the sheet.

deckle-edge [dek'l-*ej*] *n* uncut, feathery edge of hand-made paper formed by the deckle ~ **deckle-edged** *adj* with a feathery edge.

deck-tennis [dek-*teni*s] *n* tennis as played on board ship.

declaim [di*klaym*] *v/t* and *i* speak or recite rhetorically and dramatically; make a set speech as an exercise in oratory; **d. against** protest against ~ **declaimer** *n*.

declamation [dekla*may*shon] *n* act of declaiming; technique of correct enunciation of the words in vocal music; a dramatic and emotional speech ~ **declamatory** [de*klam*ateRi] *adj*.

declarable [di*klair*Rab'l] *adj* to be declared on passing through Customs, dutiable.

declaration [dekla*Ray*shon] *n* act of declaring; that which is declared; the document, instrument, or public act embodying this; (*leg*) affirmation before a magistrate; statement of a claim; formal announcement (of love, war, peace *etc*).

declarative [di*kla*Rativ] *adj* having the nature of a declaration; explanatory ~ **declaratively** *adv*.

declaratory [diklaRateRi] *adj* making a declaration, explanatory, affirmatory.

declare [diklair] *v/t* and *i* proclaim, announce formally; assert; state before Customs officer to be in one's possession; (*cricket*) close an innings before ten wickets have fallen; (*bridge*) name the trump suit, or announce that there are to be 'no trumps'; (*racing*) withdraw from race; **d. for side** with; **d. oneself** announce oneself to be; **well, I d.** (*coll*) an exclamation of surprise.

declared [diklaird] *adj* openly avowed, not secret ~ **declaredly** *adv* professedly, avowedly.

déclassé [dayklasay] *adj* having lost caste or social standing; belonging to no one social class.

declassify [deeklasifI] *v/t* (*mil, pol*) release (information) previously classified as secret.

declension [diklenshon] *n* a falling away from a standard, deterioration; (*gramm*) variation of form of noun, pronoun, or adjective according to its case; class of nouns, pronouns, or adjectives having the same case endings.

declinable [diklInab'l] *adj* (*gramm*) capable of declension.

declination [deklinayshon] *n* a downward slope; deviation; (*astron*) angular distance of a heavenly body from the celestial equator; (*elect*) angular variation of the magnetic needle from true north at any point.

decline [diklIn] *v/t* and *i* slope down; droop; (*fig*) draw to an end; lessen in strength, qualities, value *etc*, deteriorate; turn aside from (an argument); refuse (an invitation); (*chess*) refuse to take a piece or pawn offered; (*gramm*) give the inflected forms of (a *n, adj*, or *pron*) ~ **decline** *n* gradual lessening of strength, quality, vigour *etc*; a period of deterioration; (*obs*) wasting disease, *esp* tuberculosis of the lungs; (*astron*) journey of a heavenly body to the horizon; **on the d.** in process of lessening, deteriorating.

declinometer [deklinomiter] *n* (*elect eng*) instrument for measuring the variation of the magnetic needle.

declivitous [diklivitus] *adj* steep.

declivity [dikliviti] *n* downward slope (of ground).

declutch [deekluch] *v/i* disengage the clutch of a motor vehicle preparatory to changing gear.

decoct [dikokt] *v/t* boil down so as to concentrate ~ **decoction** [dikokshon] *n* action of decocting; extract produced by boiling.

decode [deekOd] *v/t* translate from code.

decoder [deekOder] *n* person who translates coded messages; automatic device to restore scrambled telephone messages.

decoke [deekOk] *v/t* (*coll*) decarbonize.

decollate [dikolayt/dekolayt] *v/t* behead; break off the point of a spiral shell ~ **decollation** [deekolayshon] *n* beheading, *esp* of John the Baptist.

décolletage [daykoltaazh] *n* low-cut dress; the wearing of a low-necked dress.

décolleté (*fem* **décolletée**) [daykoltay] *adj* wearing a low-necked dress; low-necked.

decolonization [deekolonIzayshon] *n* acquisition (or granting) of independence by (or to) former colonies.

decolor, decolour [deekuler] *v/t* deprive of colour, bleach ~ **decolorant** *n* substance that removes colour.

decolorize, decolourize [deekuleRIz] *v/t* and deprive of colour; lose colour.

decompose [deekompOz] *v/t* and *i* separate into its constituent parts; decay, rot.

decomposite [deekompozit] *adj* formed by adding an element to something already composite.

decomposition [deekompozishon] *n* process of disintegration, decay; (*chem*) breaking up of a chemical compound.

decompound [deekompownd] *v/t* decompose; combine into a new compound something already compounded ~ **decompound** *n* and *adj*.

decompress [deekompRes] *v/t* reduce pressure; release gradually from excessive pressure ~ **decompression** *n* (*med*) any operation to relieve abnormal pressure; (*eng*) gradual release of air pressure on tunnel workers, divers *etc* in returning to the surface; **d. sickness** formation of nitrogen bubbles in the blood due to sudden lessening of pressure.

deconsecrate [deekonsikRayt] *v/t* secularize.

decontaminate [deekontaminayt] *v/t* cleanse from harmful substances, *esp* poison-gases, radio-activity *etc* ~ **decontamination** [deekontaminayshon] *n*.

decontrol (*p/t* and *p/part* **decontrolled**) [deekontROl] *v/t* release from control (*esp* State control); (*of a road*) abolish the speed limit for vehicular traffic ~ **decontrolled** *adj*.

décor [*daykawr*] *n* scenery and furnishings of a theatre stage; artistically planned furnishings.

decorate [*deke*Rayt] *v/t* adorn, embellish; renovate with wallpaper and paint; invest with a badge of honour or order ~ **decorated** (*archi*) describing a style of English Gothic during the fourteenth century.

decoration [deke*Ra*yshon] *n* action of decorating; ornament; medal *etc* worn as honour; (*pl*) flags *etc* put up on occasions of public rejoicing.

decorative [*deke*Rativ] *adj* ornamental.

decorator [*deke*Rayter] *n* one whose business is papering and painting houses.

decorous [*deko*Rus] *adj* showing good manners and dignity ~ **decorously** *adv*.

decorum [dikav*o*Rum] *n* conformity to social standards of behaviour and conduct; dignified behaviour in public.

decoy [*deeko*i] *n* tame bird or animal trained to lure wild ones into a trap; artificial bird or animal used as a lure; (*fig*) human being used similarly; place into which game is lured for trapping ~ **decoy** *v/t*.

decoy-duck [*deeko*i-duk] *n* duck trained to ensnare wild ducks; (*fig*) person who decoys others.

decrease [dikRees] *v/t* and *i* cause to grow less; grow gradually less, diminish ~ **decrease** [*deek*Rees] *n* process of lessening; the amount by which a thing is lessened ~ **decreasingly** *adv*.

decree [dikRee] *n* edict, law, or official decision of an authority; (*eccles*) judgement of a church council; (*leg*) judgement of the Court of Admiralty, Probate, and Divorce; **d. nisi** order for divorce, provided no cause to the contrary is shown within three months ~ **decree** *v/t* and *i* command or pronounce by decree.

decrement [*dek*Riment] *n* amount lost through decrease.

decremeter [dek*Re*meeter] *n* (*rad*) instrument for measuring dampening of oscillation.

decrepit [dik*Re*pit] *adj* worn out with age ~ decrepitude *n*.

decrepitation [deek*Re*pit*ay*shon] *n* (*chem*) breaking of certain crystals on heating; *esp* due to expansion of water in the crystals.

decrescendo [deek*Ri*shend*O*] *n* (*mus*) gradual decrease in volume of tone; passage played in this manner.

decretal [dik*Re*etal] *n* (*eccles*) decree of a Pope; (*pl*) collection of such decrees, forming part of canon law ~ decretal *adj* containing, pertaining to, a decree.

decretist [dik*Re*etist] *n* expert on canon law.

decrial [dik*Ri*-al] *n* act of decrying, disparagement.

decrier [dik*Ri*-er] *n* one who decries.

decrustation [deek*Ru*st*ay*shon] *n* removal of a crust.

decry [dik*Ri*] *v/t* disparage, cry down.

decuple [dek*e*wp'l] *adj* tenfold ~ decuple *v/t* multiply by ten.

decussate [deek*u*sayt] *v/t* cross or intersect.

dedicate [*de*dikayt] *v/t* devote solemnly (to God or sacred purpose) ; set aside for a special purpose; inscribe (a book) to a person.

dedicated [*de*dikaytid] *adj* whole-heartedly devoted to an art, vocation, career, system of beliefs *etc*.

dedicatee [dedikay*tee*] *n* person to whom something is dedicated.

dedication [dedi*kay*shon] *n* act of dedicating; fact of being dedicated; dedicatory inscription (in book *etc*); commemoration of the dedicating of a religious building ~ dedicative *adj* ~ dedicatory [dedikayte*Ri*] *adj*.

deduce [di*dews*] *v/t* infer by reasoning from given facts ~ deducible *adj*.

deduct [di*duk*t] *v/t* subtract, take away ~ deductible, deductable *adj*.

deduction [di*duk*shon] *n* (*math*) process of subtracting; amount subtracted; (*log*) inference from given facts.

deductive [di*duk*tiv] *adj* (*log*) using deduction; d. reasoning reasoning from the general to the particular.

deed [*deed*] *n* thing consciously done, action; feat; (*leg*) sealed document stating terms of contract, settlement *etc*, or title to property.

deed-poll [*deed*-pOl] *n* deed executed by one party only.

dee-jay, D.J. [*dee*-jay] *n* (*coll*) disk jockey; (*coll abbr*) dinner jacket.

deem [*deem*] *v/t* and *i* suppose, believe.

deep [*deep*] *adj* extending far downwards, inwards, or across; extending to a specified distance down or in; serious, intense; hard to understand; (*of colour*) dark, rich; (*of sound*) low-pitched; (*coll*) cunning, sly; d. in absorbed by; in d. water in difficulties; go off the d. end lose control, become angry or excited ~ deep *n* that which is deep; deep water, the ocean; the unfathomable regions of the universe; (*fig*) depths of consciousness ~ deep *adv*.

deep-dyed [*deep*-dId] *adj* (*fig*) deeply stained (with guilt).

deepen [*deep*en] *v/t* and *i* make deeper, intensify; become deeper.

deep-freeze [*deep*-f*Reez*] *n* refrigerator to keep

food for a long period at very low temperatures ~ deep-freeze *v/t* ~ deep-frozen *adj*.

deep-fry [*deep*-f*RI*] *v/t* fry by plunging into hot fat.

deep-laid [*deep*-layd] *adj* craftily planned.

deeply [*deep*li] *adv* to a great depth; profoundly, intensely, thoroughly.

deerooted [*deep*ROOtid] *adj* firmly fixed, hard to remove.

deepsea [*deep*see] *adj* in the deeper levels of the sea; far out from land.

deepseated [*deep*seetid] *adj* far beneath the surface; hard to remove.

deer (*pl* deer) [*deer*] *n* four-footed animal with deciduous antlers of family *Cervidae*.

deerhound [*deer*hownd] *n* large, shaggy dog used for hunting deer.

deer-lick [*deer*-lik] *n* damp area of salty earth, licked by deer.

deermouse [*deer*mows] *n* (*US*) white-footed mouse.

deer-park [*deer*-paark] *n* enclosure where deer are preserved.

deerskin [*deer*skin] *n* hide of the deer; soft leather made from this.

deerstalker [*deer*stawker] *n* hunter who stalks deer to shoot them; low-crowned close-fitting hat with ear-flaps ~ deerstalking *n*.

deface [di*fays*] *v/t* spoil the appearance of, disfigure; make illegible ~ defacement *n*.

de facto [day-*fak*to] *adj* and *adv* (*Lat*) actually existing, though not by legal right.

defalcate [*dee*falkayt] *v/t* misappropriate property held on trust ~ defalcation [deefal*kay*shon] *n* embezzlement; amount embezzled.

defamation [defamayshon] *n* calumny, slander.

defamatory [di*fama*te*Ri*] *adj* slanderous.

defame [di*faym*] *v/t* speak evil of, calumniate, attack the reputation of.

defatted [*dee*fated] *adj* deprived of or lacking fat or fats.

default [di*fawlt*] *n* failure to act or appear when required, *esp* in a court of law; failure to pay money when due, judgement by d. (*leg*) judgement for plaintiff when defendant fails to appear; in d. of in the absence of, for lack of ~ default *v/t* and *i* (*leg*) adjudge (person) to be a defaulter; fail to fulfil an obligation, *esp* financial; (*leg*) fail to appear in court when required ~ defaulter *n* one who defaults; (*mil*) soldier guilty of an offence.

defeat [di*feet*] *v/t* conquer, overcome; bring to nothing, destroy; (*leg*) render null and void ~ defeat *n* act of defeating, conquest, overthrow; destruction, frustration.

defeatism [di*fee*tizm] *n* expectation or acceptance of defeat in war; pessimism, facile discouragement ~ defeatist *n* and *adj*.

defeature [di*fee*cher] *v/t* make unrecognizable.

defecate [*dee*feekayt] *v/t* and *i* empty the bowels ~ defecation [deefeek*ay*shon] *n*.

defect [di*fekt*/*dee*fekt] *n* failure to come up to the normal, or an agreed, standard; deficiency, imperfection, fault, error ~ defect [*dee*fekt] *v/i* desert one's duty or one's country.

defection [di*fek*shon] *n* desertion from duty or allegiance; backsliding, apostasy.

defective [di*fek*tiv] *n* and *adj* (one) having a defect

or defects, faulty, incomplete; (word) lacking some of the usual parts or forms; (person) mentally subnormal.

defence [difens] *n* protection against attack; (*pl*) (*mil*) fortifications; (*leg*) the case of a defendant in reply to charges made by the prosecution; **d. area** area where civilian movements are restricted by military authority; **d. mechanism** (*psych*) involuntary or unconscious measures adopted by an individual to protect himself against painful emotion > PDP.

defenceless [difensles] *adj* without defence, open to attack, helpless ~ **defencelessly** *adv* ~ **defencelessness** *n*.

defend [difend] *v/t* protect against attack, guard; argue in favour of, support, justify; (*leg*) oppose (an action); appear as counsel for (the accused).

defendant [difendant] *n* (*leg*) one accused or sued in court of law.

defenestrate [deefenestRayt] *v/t* throw out of a window ~ **defenestration** [deefenestRayshon] *n*.

defensible [difensib'l] *adj* capable of being defended; justifiable ~ **defensibility** [difensibiliti] *n*.

defensive [difensiv] *adj* protective; adapted for defence rather than offence ~ **defensive** *n* position of defence; **be on the d.** defend oneself without attacking ~ **defensively** *adv*.

defer (1) (*p/t* and *p/part* **deferred**) [difur] *v/t* and *i* put off, postpone, procrastinate.

defer (2) (*p/t* and *p/part* **deferred**) *v/i* submit to another's wish or judgement; yield to authority.

deference [defeRens] *n* compliance with the advice of a superior; respect, regard, consideration.

deferent [defeRent] *adj* (*anat*) (*of ducts*) conveying away fluids.

deferential [defeRensh'l] *adj* showing deference ~ **deferentially** *adv*.

deferment [difurment] *n* delay, postponement.

deferred [difurd] *adj* postponed, delayed; not due for immediate payment or delivery; (*of stocks and shares*) not ranking for dividend until after the ordinary, preference and other dividends have been met; **d. annuity** annuity payable after a certain period of time or at death; **d. payment** payment by instalments.

defiance [difI-ans] *n* act of defying; a challenge; open disobedience; **in d. of** in open opposition to, in spite of; **set at d.** act without regard for.

defiant [difI-ant] *adj* showing defiance, openly and insolently disobedient ~ **defiantly** *adv*.

deficiency [difishensi] *n* lack, shortage; amount by which a thing falls short; **d. disease** one caused by lack of vitamins or other essential food factors in the diet.

deficient [difishent] *adj* insufficient, falling short, defective; **mentally d.** of subnormal intelligence, imbecile.

deficit [defisit] *n* shortage; the amount short; excess of liabilities over assets, or of expenditure over income.

defile (1) [difIl] *v/t* make filthy, pollute; (*fig*) sully the purity of, corrupt, desecrate ~ **defilement** *n* ~ **defiler** *n*.

defile (2) *v/i* march in file.

defile (3) [deefIl] *n* narrow valley or gorge.

definable [difInab'l] *adj* capable of being defined ~ **definably** *adv* in a definable manner.

define [difIn] *v/t* mark limits of, show clearly the outlines of; describe in exact terms, give the precise meaning of.

definite [definit] *adj* having exact and well-defined limits; clear, precise, unambiguous; (*coll*) certain; **d. article** (*gramm*) the demonstrative adjective *the*; **past d.** (*gramm*) simple past tense ~ **definitely** *adv* in a definite manner; clearly, without doubt; (*coll*) certainly ~ **definiteness** *n*.

definition [definishon] *n* act of defining; process of being defined; exact description of the nature of a thing; brief explanation of the meaning of a word or phrase; (*opt*) capacity of a lens to form a sharp image; (*phot*) clarity of image; (*rad*) precise and clear reproduction of sound and picture.

definitive [difinitiv] *adj* decisive, conclusive, final; complete and authoritative ~ **definitively** *adv* ~ **definitiveness** *n*.

definitude [difinitewd] *n* precision, definiteness.

deflagration [deflagRayshon] *n* (*chem*) sudden combustion.

deflate [diflayt] *v/t* and *i* let the air out of; reduce (an inflated currency); pursue a policy of deflation; (*fig*) lessen conceit or self-confidence of.

deflation [diflayshon] *n* act or result of deflating; (*econ*) a decrease in the numbers of claims on goods and services without a corresponding decrease in the volume of these goods and services ~ **deflationary** *adj* producing or tending to produce deflation.

deflect [diflekt] *v/t* and *i* turn aside, deviate, change course ~ **deflective** *adj*.

deflection, deflexion [diflekshon] *n* act of deflecting; state or process of being deflected.

deflector [diflekter] *n* device to cause deflection.

defloration [deeflawRayshon] *n* act of deflowering.

deflower [diflowr] *v/t* deprive a woman of her virginity; ravish; strip of flowers; (*fig*) rob of its beauty or excellence.

defluent [deefloo-ent] *n* and *adj* (that) which flows down.

defoliant [deefOli-ant] *n* and *adj* (chemical) that kills leaves of trees and other plants.

defoliate [difOli-ayt] *v/t* strip of leaves ~ **defoliation** [difOli-ayshon] *n*.

deforest [deefoRist] *v/t* clear of trees ~ **deforestation** [deefoRistayshon] *n*.

deform [difawrm] *v/t* spoil the shape of, disfigure; make ugly or unsightly ~ **deformation** [deefawrmayshon] *n* alteration of form or shape.

deformed [difawrmd] *adj* having part of the body abnormally shaped; being misshapen.

deformity [difawrmiti] *n* marked deviation from the normal due to faulty development, accident, or disease; misshapen part of the body; defect of mind or personality; ugliness.

defraud [difRawd] *v/t* deprive (a person) by fraud (of his right), cheat, swindle.

defray [difRay] *v/t* pay the cost of ~ **defrayal** *n* ~ **defrayment** *n*.

defreeze (*p/t* **defroze**, *p/part* **defrozen**) [deefReez] *v/t* cause (frozen food) to thaw; remove ice from.

defrock [dee*frok*] *v/t* unfrock, deprive of ecclesiastical status.

defrost [dee*frost*] *v/t* remove frost or ice from; unfreeze (frozen food).

deft [*deft*] *adj* neat, handy, skilful ∼ **deftly** *adv* ∼ **deftness** *n.*

defunct [di*funkt*] *adj* dead, deceased ∼ **defunct** *n* dead person.

defuse [dee*fewz*] *v/t* remove fuse from (a bomb); (*fig*) render harmless, reduce urgency or tension (in).

defy (*p/t* and *p/part* **defied**) [di*fI*] *v/t* challenge; resist stubbornly; disobey openly, flout; (*of things*) resist, baffle, frustrate.

degauss [dee*gows*] *v/t* demagnetize a magnetic substance > PDS ∼ **degaussing** *n.*

degeneracy [di*jene*Rasi] *n* marked lowering of the level of social behaviour, or conduct, or mental functions, either congenital or acquired.

degenerate [di*jene*Rayt] *v/i* fall away from a former high standard, decline in character or qualities, deteriorate; become depraved ∼ **degenerate** [di*jene*Rat] *adj* having become of lower type; degraded, defective, depraved ∼ **degenerate** *n* person of lower mental, moral or physical type than standard.

degeneration [di*jene*Rayshon] *n* state of being degenerate; (*biol*) progressive lowering of the efficiency of an organ or organs.

degradation [degRa*day*shon] *n* act of degrading; state of being degraded; condition of misery and squalor; (*geol*) process of erosion; (*chem*) conversion of a complex molecule into simpler fragments.

degrade [di*gRayd*] *v/t* and *i* reduce in status, honour, or rank; reduce in quality, value, moral character *etc*; corrupt; humiliate, dishonour; degenerate; (*chem*) split (molecule) into simpler fragments.

degrading [di*gRay*ding] *adj* that degrades; humiliating.

degree [di*gRee*] *n* stage or position in any series or scale; relative intensity or amount; rank; step in direct line of descent; rank granted by university as mark of proficiency or as an honour; (*geom*) unit of measurement of angles or arcs, one 360th of a circle; (*phys*) unit of temperature difference; (*math*) the sum of the exponents of the variables in an expression; (*gramm*) stage in comparison of *adj* or *adv*; **to a d.** considerably; **by degrees** gradually; **third d.** interrogation with violence or torture.

degression [di*gRe*shon] *n* gradual decrease in rate of taxation on incomes below a certain amount ∼ **degressive** [di*gRe*siv] *adj.*

dehisce [dee*his*] *v/i* (*bot*) gape, burst open ∼ **dehiscence** [dee*hi*sens] *n* ∼ **dehiscent** *adj.*

dehumanize [dee*hew*manIz] *v/t* deprive of human qualities.

dehydrate [dee*hI*dRayt] *v/t* and *i* (*chem*) remove water from; lose water ∼ **dehydration** [dee-hI*dRay*shon] *n* elimination of water > PDB.

de-ice [dee-*Is*] *v/t* prevent the formation of ice; dislodge ice when formed ∼ **de-icer** *n* device for dislodging or dissolving ice.

deicide [*dee*-isId] *n* killing of a god; one who kills a god; one who destroys belief in God.

deiform [*dee*-ifawrm] *adj* having the form of a god; godlike, holy.

deify [*dee*-ifI] *v/t* exalt to the position of a god; make a god of; regard as a god ∼ **deification** [dee-ifi*Ray*shon] *n.*

deign [*dayn*] *v/i* and *t* vouchsafe, condescend.

deism [*dee*-izm] *n* belief in existence of God but not in revealed religion ∼ **deist** *n* ∼ **deistic** [dee*istik*] *adj* ∼ **deistical** *adj.*

deity [*dee*-iti] *n* divine nature, godhood; a god or goddess; **the D.** God.

déjà vu [*dayzha-vew*] *n* (*Fr*) strong but mistaken feeling that one has formerly experienced the same circumstances as those one now perceives.

deject [di*jekt*] *v/t* cast down, depress ∼ **dejected** *adj* ∼ **dejectedly** *adv.*

dejection [di*jek*shon] *n* depression of spirits.

de jure [day-*joor*Ray] *adj* and *adv* (*Lat*) rightful; by right, according to law.

deka- *pref* ten times.

dekko [*dek*O] *n* and *v/i* (*coll*) (a) look, (a) glance.

delaine [di*layn*] *n* a light plain-weave dress fabric.

delate [di*layt*] *v/t* (*leg*) accuse, inform against; report (offence) ∼ **delator** *n* ∼ **delation** *n.*

delay [di*lay*] *v/t* and *i* postpone, keep waiting, retard; linger ∼ **delay** *n* action of delaying; procrastination; period of waiting.

dele [*dee*li] *v/t imp* (*typ*) delete, remove.

delectable [di*lek*tab'l] *adj* delightful, pleasant, enjoyable ∼ **delectably** *adv.*

delectation [deelek*tay*shon] *n* enjoyment.

delegacy [*deli*gasi] *n* committee or body of delegates; system of representation by delegates.

delegate [*deli*git] *n* one sent as representative of a group ∼ **delegate** [*deli*gayt] *v/t* send or elect as representative; hand over to another as deputy.

delegation [deli*gay*shon] *n* action of delegating; body of delegates.

delete [di*leet*] *v/t* erase, cross out, remove ∼ **deletion** [di*lee*shon] *n* act of erasing; passage erased.

deleterious [deli*teer*Ri-us] *adj* harmful, noxious.

delf, delft [*delf, delft*] *n* glazed earthenware.

deliberate [di*libe*Rit] *adj* intentional, purposeful, studied; slow in deciding; ponderous in manner ∼ **deliberate** [di*libe*Rayt] *v/t* and *i* think over carefully, study closely; discuss ∼ **deliberately** *adv* ∼ **deliberateness** *n.*

deliberation [di*libe*Rayshon] *n* act of deliberating, careful consideration; debate; slowness and carefulness in movement, speech *etc.*

deliberative [di*libe*Rativ] *adj* appointed for deliberation; characterized by deliberation.

delicacy [*deli*kasi] *n* fineness, gracefulness; tasty food; perceptiveness, tact; modesty; sensitivity.

delicate [*deli*kit] *adj* pleasing; finely made, dainty; (*of colours*) pale; tender, frail, easily injured; perceptive, refined, tactful.

delicatessen [delika*tes*en] *n* (*pl*) cooked savoury foods, relishes and delicacies; (*sing*) shop selling such foods.

delicious [di*lish*us] *adj* most agreeable to the palate; giving intense pleasure to the senses; charming, delightful; amusing, entertaining.

delight [di*lIt*] *n* intense pleasure; that which is a source of pleasure ∼ **delight** *v/t* and *i* give, or take, great pleasure ∼ **delightful** *adj* giving delight ∼ **delightfully** *adv.*

delimit [dee*limit*] *v/t* fix the boundaries of; take off a specific restriction ~ **delimitation** [dee-limit*ay*shon] *n*.

delineate [di*lini*-ayt] *v/t* trace the outline of, sketch; describe ~ **delineation** [dilini-*ay*shon] *n*.

delinquency [di*link*wensi] *n* failure in duty; fault, misdeed; petty law-breaking, *esp* by the young.

delinquent [di*link*went] *n* a young offender against the law; one who neglects a duty ~ **delinquent** *adj* failing in duty; breaking the law.

deliquesce [deli*kwes*] *v/i* become liquid or melt by absorption of moisture from the air ~ **deliquescence** *n*.

deliquescent [deli*kwes*ent] *adj* (*chem*) becoming liquid on exposure to air; (*bot*) branching so that the main stem becomes lost among the branches; (*fig*) fading away, disintegrating.

delirious [di*liRi*-us] *adj* suffering from delirium, light-headed; frantically excited (*esp* with joy).

delirium [di*liRi*-um] *n* state of disturbed consciousness, with incoherent speech, hallucinations and excitement; frenzy, wild emotion; **d. tremens** delirium caused by chronic alcoholism.

deliver [di*liver*] *v/t* set free, rescue; hand over, distribute (letters); utter (a speech); aim, strike (blow); (*cricket*) bowl (ball); assist at childbirth; **be delivered of** give birth to.

deliverance [di*live*Rans] *n* liberation, rescue; formal utterance.

deliverer [di*live*Rer] *n* a liberator, rescuer.

delivery [di*live*Ri] *n* act of delivering; the handing over or conveyance of letters or goods; (*leg*) transfer of deed; style of speaking or singing; (*cricket*) ball bowled, or bowler's action in bowling; childbirth; (*mech*) volume of air or water delivered per minute or per second by a compressor ˌr pump.

dell [*del*] *n* small wooded valley.

delouse [dee*lowz*] *v/t* remove lice from.

delphic [*del*fik] *adj* pertaining to the oracle of Delphi; obscure, ambiguous.

delphinium [del*fini*-um] *n* genus of plants including the larkspur; deep blue colour.

delta [*del*ta] *n* fourth letter of Greek alphabet; fan-shaped alluvial tract formed at the mouth of a river > PDG; **d. connexion** (*elect*) method of connexion used in three-phase equipment; **d. metal** alloy of copper and zinc with small amounts of iron and other metals; **d. rays** electrons moving at relatively low speeds > PDS; **d. wing** broad backswept triangular wing of aircraft.

deltoid [*del*toid] *adj* triangular; of the nature of a river delta; **d. muscle** (*anat*) large shoulder muscle which lifts the arm.

delude [di*lewd*/di*lOOd*] *v/t* deceive, mislead.

deluge [*delewj*] *n* great flood of water; heavy rain; (*fig*) overwhelming rush; **the D.** Noah's flood ~ **deluge** *v/t* inundate; (*fig*) overwhelm.

delusion [di*lewz*hon/di*lOO*zhon] *n* act of deluding; mistaken impression or belief; false opinion or belief fixed in the mind by disease or madness ~ **delusive** *adj* ~ **delusory** *adj*.

de luxe [di-*looks*] *adj* (*of things*) sumptuous, elegant; of a superior type or model.

delve [*delv*] *v/t* and *i* dig with a spade; (*fig*) carry out exhaustive research (into a subject); (*of road etc*) make sudden dip.

demagnetize [dee*magnet*iz] *v/t* reduce the degree of magnetization; obliterate a previous recording on magnetic tape.

demagogic, demagogical [dema*gog*ik, demagog-ikal] *adj* characteristic of a demagogue.

demagogue [*dema*gog] *n* political agitator who plays on passions and prejudices of the masses; leader of masses against upper classes or minority groups.

demand [di*maand*] *n* claim that must be met; pressing request or claim; call for a commodity by consumers; **in great d.** much sought after; **payable on d.** payable on presentation; **d. deposit** deposit which can be withdrawn without notice ~ **demand** *v/t* claim as a right; ask for urgently or with authority; require, need.

demarcate [dee*maar*kayt] *v/t* mark out, delimit.

demarcation [deemaar*kay*shon] *n* act of establishing limits, *esp* of work allotted to different workmen.

demarche, démarche [day*maarsh*] *n* diplomatic representations made to a foreign government; course of action (*esp* one involving a change of policy).

demean (1) [di*meen*] *v/refl* behave (oneself).

demean (2) *v/t* and *refl* degrade (oneself).

demeanour [di*meener*] *n* behaviour; bearing.

demented [di*ment*id] *adj* driven mad.

dementia [di*menshi*-a] *n* (*psych*) madness marked by failure or loss of mental powers, feeble-mindedness; **d. praecox** schizophrenia > PDP.

demerara [deme*Rair*Ra] *n* a kind of brown sugar.

demerit [dee*meRit*] *n* blamable conduct; lack of merit; fault, defect ~ **demeritorious** [deemeRi-*taw*Ri-us] *adj*.

demersal [dee*mursal*] *adj* (*zool*) found near the sea-bottom.

demesne [di*mayn*/di*meen*] *n* estate surrounding a house and kept by the owner for his own use.

demi- *pref* half, partial.

demigod [*demi*god] *n* son of a god and a mortal; deified hero; (*fig*) outstanding person.

demijohn [*demi*jon] *n* large narrow-necked bottle with bulging sides enclosed in a wicker case.

demilitarize [dee*milite*Riz] *v/t* free from military control.

demi-monde [demi-*mawnd*] *n* class of women of doubtful reputation and dubious social standing.

demise [dim*Iz*] *n* death; (*leg*) transfer of an estate by will; **d. of the Crown** transfer of sovereignty by death or abdication ~ **demise** *v/t* (*leg*) convey or transfer by will or lease; convey or transfer a dignity or title.

demission [di*mish*on] *n* resignation, abdication.

demister [dee*mister*] *n* apparatus or substance for removing condensation from windscreens *etc*.

demiurge [*demi*-urj] *n* (*philos*) Platonic name for the Creator; superhuman being subordinate to the Creator.

demo [*dem*O] *n* (*coll abbr*) public demonstration of political or social protest.

demob (*pres/part* **demobbing,** *p/t* and *p/part* **demobbed**) [dee*mob*] *v/t* (*coll*) demobilize ~ **demob** *n* (*coll*) demobilization.

demobilize [dee*mObil*Iz] *v/t* disband armed forces; discharge (person) from the armed forces ~ **demobilization** [deemObil*Iz*ayshon] *n*.

democracy [di*mok*Rasi] *n* government by the

people; government by majority vote; community so governed; equality of rights, opportunities *etc*; absence of class feeling; the working classes.

democrat [*dem*OkRat] *n* supporter of democracy; (*US*) member of Democratic party.

democratic [demOk*Rat*ik] *adj* of the nature of democracy; believing in the rights of the people ~ **democratically** *adv*.

demode, démodé [daym*O*day] *adj* out of fashion.

demodulation [deemodew*lay*shon] *n* (*rad*) separation of a signal wave from the carrier.

demographer [dimog*Ra*fer] *n* one who studies population statistics.

demography [dimog*Ra*fi] *n* the study of population statistics ~ **demographic** [demOg*Ra*fik] *adj*.

demolish [di*mol*ish] *v/t* destroy, pull down; make an end of; (*coll*) eat up ~ **demolition** [demo*lish*on] *n* destruction, *esp* of a building.

demon [*dee*mon] *n* devil, evil spirit; diabolical man; person of remarkable energy or skill.

demonetize [deemun*i*tIz] *v/t* deprive (silver or gold) of its currency value, withdraw from use as currency ~ **demonetization** [deemunitIz*ay*shon] *n*.

demoniac [dim*O*ni-ak] *adj* pertaining to a demon; devilish; frenzied ~ **demoniac** *n* person possessed by a demon.

demoniacal [deemon*I*-akal] *adj* devilish, fiendish; possessed by a demon.

demonic [di*mon*ik] *adj* inspired by, under the influence of, a demon.

demonism [*dee*monizm] *n* belief in demons ~ **demonist** *n* believer in demons.

demonolatry [deemon*ol*atRi] *n* worship of demons.

demonology [deemon*ol*oji] *n* study of the belief in demons ~ **demonologist** *n*.

demonstrable [di*mon*stRab'l/*dem*onstRab'l] *adj* capable of being shown or proved ~ **demonstrability** [dimonstRa*bil*iti] *n* ~ **demonstrably** *adv*.

demonstrate [*dem*onstRayt] *v/t* and *i* explain or prove by reasoning, evidence, or experiment; show the working of; show (feelings) openly; show by public manifestation; make a show of military strength.

demonstration [demonst*Ray*shon] *n* act of demonstrating; practical lesson, illustration, proof; exhibition of method; expression of public feeling by processions, mass-meetings *etc*; (*anat*) exhibiting of parts dissected; (*mil*) show of military strength.

demonstrationist [demonst*Ray*shonist] *n* one who takes part in a public demonstration.

demonstrative [di*mon*stRativ] *adj* showing clearly or conclusively; expressing (feelings) openly; (*gramm*) pointing out.

demonstrator [*dem*onstRayter] *n* person joining in public demonstration; one who teaches or exhibits by demonstration; practical assistant to science professor.

demoralize [di*mo*RalIz] *v/t* pervert morally; weaken the resolution, lower the morale of ~ **demoralization** [dimoRalIz*ay*shon] *n*.

demos [*dem*os] *n* the common people, the masses.

demote [dee*mO*t] *v/t* reduce to lower rank or position ~ **demotion** [dee*mO*shon] *n*.

demotic [di*mot*ik] *adj* of the people, common;

earthy, vigorous, unsophisticated; in a simplified form of ancient Egyptian writing.

demount [dee*mownt*] *v/t* (*eng*) remove from a mounting.

demur (*pres/part* **demurring**, *p/t* and *p/part* **demurred**) [di*mur*] *v/i* hesitate; raise objections, make difficulties; (*leg*) put in a demurrer ~ **demur** *n* hesitation; objection.

demure [di*mewr*] *adj* sedate; affectedly modest, coy ~ **demurely** *adv* ~ **demureness** *n*.

demurrage [di*mu*Rij] *n* undue delaying of a ship, freight-truck, *etc*; compensation for this; charge made by transport companies for goods not removed after a reasonable time; Bank of England charge for changing bullion into notes or gold.

demurrer [di*mur*Rer] *n* (*leg*) objection against the legal effectiveness, though not against the facts, of an opponent's claim; person who demurs.

demy [di*mI*] *n* name of a certain size of paper (printing $17\frac{1}{2} \times 22\frac{1}{2}$; writing $15\frac{1}{2} \times 20$); scholar of Magdalen College, Oxford ~ **demyship** *n* scholarship at Magdalen College, Oxford.

demystify [dee*mist*ifI] *v/t* clarify, remove irrational or mysterious beliefs (about).

demythologize [deemi*thol*ojiz] *v/t* express (religious ideas) without using symbolical or figurative language.

den [*den*] *n* lair of a wild beast; cage for captive animal; cavern; hiding place of thieves; (*fig*) small private room; small squalid room.

denary [*dee*naRi] *adj* having ten as the basis of reckoning; decimal.

denationalize [dee*nash*onalIz] *v/t* deprive of national status or rights; restore to private ownership (industries which have been acquired by the State).

denaturalize [dee*nache*RalIz] *v/t* make unnatural; deprive of the rights of a citizen.

denature [dee*nay*cher] *v/t* adulterate or make unsuitable for consumption; destroy the essential natural qualities of; (*chem*) alter the structure of a soluble protein so that it becomes insoluble; (*phys*) add an isotope to a fissile material to make it unsuitable for use in nuclear weapons.

dendriform [*dend*Rifawrm] *adj* shaped like a tree.

dendrite [*dend*RIt] *n* stone or mineral with branching marks; branching structure of crystals; branching filaments which carry impulses into a neuron ~ **dendritic** [dend*Ri*tik] *adj*.

dendroid [*dend*Roid] *adj* shaped or marked like a tree.

dendrology [dend*Rol*oji] *n* study of trees.

dene [*deen*] *n* deep wooded valley of a small stream near the sea.

dengue [*deng*-gay/*deng*-gi] *n* (*med*) tropical fever with rash and pain in joints.

denial [din*I*-al] *n* act of denying; contradiction; disavowal; refusal ~ **deniable** *adj*.

denier (1) [di*neer*/*den*i-er] *n* small French coin; unit of weight to indicate the fineness of silk and nylon yarn.

denier (2) [den*I*-er] *n* one who denies.

denigrate [*den*igRayt] *v/t* speak ill of, sneer at ~ **denigration** [denig*Ray*shon] *n*.

denim [*den*im] *n* coarse cotton cloth; (*pl*) trousers or overall made of this.

denizen [*den*izen] *n* inhabitant; foreigner admitted to certain rights of citizenship, naturalized alien; naturalized plant, animal *etc* ~ **denizen** *v/t* admit to the rights of an inhabitant.

denominate [di*nom*inayt] *v/t* name, call, designate.

denomination [dinomi*nay*shon] *n* action of naming; group of individuals called by the same name, *esp* a religious body; unit of measure (of money, weights, numbers *etc*).

denominational [dinomi*nay*shonal] *adj* connected with a particular religious body, sectarian ~ **denominationalism** *n* exclusive adherence to denominational principles.

denominative [di*nom*inativ] *adj* giving a name; (*gramm*) derived from a noun.

denominator [di*nom*inayter] *n* giver of a name; (*arith*) the number below line in a vulgar fraction; **common d.** (*fig*) that which all members of a group have in common.

denotation [deen*Ot*ayshon] *n* act of denoting; that by which something is denoted, name, designation, symbol; the meaning of a word or term; (*log*) range of the application of a term in contrast to ideas suggested by it.

denote [din*Ot*] *v/t* mark out, indicate; stand as a symbol for, mean ~ **denotative** *adj*.

denouement, dénouement [dayn*OO*mo(ng)] *n* final unravelling of plot in a story.

denounce [di*nowns*] *v/t* accuse, inform against; condemn strongly or publicly; repudiate (treaty).

dense [dens] *adj* closely packed together; crowded; thick; (*phot*) opaque; impenetrable; (*fig*) stupid, crass ~ **densely** *adv*.

density [*dens*iti] *n* thickness; dullness; ratio of units to an area; (*phys*) ratio of mass to unit volume.

dent [dent] *n* small hollow on a surface caused by pressure or a blow ~ **dent** *v/t* make a dent in.

dental [*dent*al] *adj* pertaining to teeth; concerned with dentistry; (*phon*) pronounced with tip of tongue against front upper teeth; **d. floss** strong thread for removing particles from between teeth ~ **dental** *n* dental consonant.

dentary [*dent*aRi] *adj* dental ~ **dentary** *n* membrane bone in the lower jaw of many vertebrates.

dentate [*dent*ayt] *adj* notched, with tooth-like projections ~ **dentation** [den*tay*shon] *n*.

denticle [*dent*ik'l] *n* small tooth; tooth-like projection; (*zool*) tooth-like scale.

dentiform [*dent*ifawrm] *adj* tooth-shaped.

dentifrice [*dent*ifRis] *n* preparation for cleaning teeth.

dentil [*dent*il] *n* (*archi*) one of the small square blocks or teeth protruding from the lower part of a cornice ~ **dentilated** *adj* formed like teeth.

dentine [*dent*een] *n* hard elastic substance which forms the body of teeth and denticles.

dentist [*dent*ist] *n* one who treats or extracts diseased teeth and fits artificial teeth.

dentistry [*dent*istRi] *n* treatment by a dentist.

dentition [den*tish*on] *n* the number, arrangement, and kind of teeth; the formation and growth of teeth, teething; a set of teeth.

denture [*dench*er] *n* set of false teeth.

denudation [deenew*day*shon] *n* (*geol*) exposure of underlying rocks, through the action of water or air > PDG.

denude [di*newd*] *v/t* make bare, strip; deprive.

denumerant [di*newm*eRant] *n* number expressing how many solutions a given system of equations admits of.

denunciation [dinunsi-*ay*shon] *n* act of denouncing ~ **denunciator** *n*.

deny [din*I*] *v/t* declare (a statement) untrue, contradict; reject, disown, repudiate; refuse; **d. oneself** abstain from things desired ~ **deniable** *adj*.

deodar [*dee*-Odaar] *n* Himalayan cedar.

deodorant [dee-O*de*Rant] *n* and *adj* (substance) which destroys or lessens offensive smells.

deodorize [dee-O*de*Riz] *v/t* remove or counteract the smell of ~ **deodorization** [dee-OdeRIz*ay*shon] *n* ~ **deodorizer** *n*.

deoxidize [dee-*oks*idIz] *v/t* remove oxygen from; reduce from the state of an oxide.

deoxygenate [dee-*oks*ijenayt] *v/t* deoxidize; deprive of free oxygen.

depart [di*paart*] *v/i* go away, leave; die; (*of trains*) start; deviate, turn away from ~ **departed** *adj* vanished ~ **departed** *n* dead person; (*pl*) the dead.

department [di*paart*ment] *n* separate part within an organization; branch, subdivision; field of activity, particular concern; administrative district in France; **d. store** large shop selling many types of goods.

departmental [deepaart*ment*al] *adj* of or as an administrative subdivision.

departmentalism [deepaart*ment*alizm] *n* strict adherence to bureaucratic methods of administration; red tape.

departure [di*paar*cher] *n* going away, starting out; starting on new course of action; (*naut*) ship's position at start of voyage; distance sailed east or west of a given meridian; **d. platform** platform from which trains start.

depend [di*pend*] *v/i* (*ar*) to hang, be suspended; **d. on** be contingent on; rely on, trust; need support or help from; (*leg*) await settlement; **d. on it** you can be certain; **that depends** perhaps.

dependable [di*pend*ab'l] *adj* reliable ~ **dependability** [dipenda*bil*iti] *n*.

dependant, dependent [di*pend*ant] *n* person dependent on another for support; servant, subordinate.

dependence [di*pend*ens] *n* state of being dependent; subordination; contingency; reliance.

dependency [di*pend*ensi] *n* state of subordination; territory controlled by another country.

dependent [di*pend*ent] *adj* subordinate; contingent (on); obliged to rely (on); hanging down; **d. variable** (*math*) one whose variation depends on that of another variable; **d. clause** (*gramm*) subordinate clause.

depending [di*pend*ing] *adj* hanging down; contingent, dependent; (*leg*) awaiting settlement, pending.

depersonalize [dee*pur*sonalIz] *v/t* and *i* deprive of personality; (*psych*) lose one's feeling of the reality of one's own personality ~ **depersonalization** *n*.

depict [di*pikt*] *v/t* portray; describe vividly; represent ~ **depiction** *n*.

depilatory [di*pil*atoRi] *n* and *adj* (preparation) able to remove superfluous hair.

deplenish [di*plen*ish] *v/t* remove contents from.

deplete [di*pleet*] *v/t* reduce fullness of; exhaust; empty out ~ **depletion** [di*plee*shon] *n.*

deplorable [di*plaw*Rab'l] *adj* lamentable, wretched, regrettable.

deplore [di*plawr*] *v/t* lament, deeply regret; disapprove of ~ **deplored** *adj.*

deploy [di*ploi*] *v/t* and *i* (*mil*) spread out into open formation; (*fig*) make full use of ~ **deployment** *n.*

depolarize [dee*p*OlaRIZ] *v/t* (*elect*) prevent electrical polarization; (*fig*) upset (convictions).

depone [di*pOn*] *v/t* (*leg*) declare upon oath.

deponent (1) [di*pOn*ent] *n* and *adj* (*gramm*) (verb) passive or middle in form, but active in meaning.

deponent (2) *n* (*leg*) one who gives evidence under oath or gives written testimony for use in court.

depopulate [dee*pop*ewlayt] *v/t* and *i* reduce or drive out the population of (an area); become less populous ~ **depopulation** [deepopewl*ay*shon] *n.*

deport [di*pawrt*] *v/t* banish, expel; send (undesirable alien) back to his own country; carry off by force to another country.

deportation [deepawrt*ay*shon] *n* expulsion from a country; forcible removal of populations.

deportee [deepawr*tee*] *n* one who is or has been deported.

deportment [di*pawrt*ment] *n* bearing, behaviour.

depose [di*pOz*] *v/t* and *i* dethrone, remove from office; (*leg*) give evidence upon oath, testify.

deposit [di*poz*it] *n* something stowed away for safe keeping; money put into a banking account; money given as a pledge or part payment; (*geol*) sedimentary layer or a mineral vein or lode; sediment; place where things are stored ~ **deposit** *v/t* put or lay down; put away for safe-keeping; put in a bank; give as pledge or part payment; (*geol*) leave sediment, precipitate solid matter.

depositary [di*poz*iteRi] *n* person to whom something is committed for safe keeping; depository; **authorized d.** agency or bank authorized to hold foreign stocks on behalf of the owners.

deposition [deepo*zish*on] *n* laying or taking down; removal from throne or from office; removal of Christ's body from the Cross, or representation of this; (*leg*) testimony; (*geol*) laying down of solid material by some natural agency > PDG.

depositor [di*pos*iter] *n* one who pays deposits into a bank.

depository [di*poz*iteRi] *n* place where things are put for safe keeping; storehouse.

depot [dep*O*] *n* storehouse, *esp* military; (*mil*) headquarters or recruiting station of a regiment; garage for buses; (*US*) [dee*p*O] railway station.

deprave [di*p*Rayv] *v/t* make morally evil, pervert, corrupt ~ **depravation** [depRav*ay*shon] *n* corruption, depravity.

depravity [di*p*Raviti] *n* moral corruption; (*theol*) innate human sinfulness.

deprecate [*dep*Rikayt] *v/t* express disapproval of.

deprecatory [*dep*RikayteRi] *adj* disapproving; apologetic.

depreciate [di*p*Reeshi-ayt] *v/t* and *i* lower the value or price of; disparage, belittle; fall in value.

depreciation [dipReeshi-*ay*shon] *n* reduction in value, *esp* of property through wear and tear; allowance made for this in valuations *etc*; (*fig*) disparagement, underestimation.

depredate [*dep*Ridayt] *v/t* plunder, lay waste ~ **depredation** *n* ~ **depredatory** *adj.*

depress [di*p*Res] *v/t* press down, lower; make gloomy, sadden; weaken; lessen in value or price; (*mus*) lower in pitch.

depressant [di*p*Resant] *n* (*med*) a sedative.

depressed [di*p*Rest] *adj* pressed down, flattened; dejected, dispirited; underprivileged; **d. area** region of persistent unemployment and poverty.

depressing [di*p*Resing] *adj* causing sadness or gloom.

depression [di*p*Reshon] *n* lowering; (*psych*) persistent unhappiness and loss of energy; low place, hollow; (*econ*) period of reduced activity, slump; (*meteor*) lowering of atmospheric pressure; centre of minimum pressure > PDG; (*astron*) angular distance of star below horizon.

depressive [di*p*Resiv] *n* and *adj* (person) suffering from mental depression > PDP.

depressor [di*p*Reser] *n* (*med*) muscle which lowers or depresses any structure; nerve which checks the activity of an organ; reagent which checks metabolism; surgical instrument for pressing down some part.

deprivation [depRiv*ay*shon] *n* act of depriving; (*eccles*) removal from a benefice, dismissal from office; sense of loss; bereavement.

deprive [di*p*RIv] *v/t* take away from; debar from possession (of); (*eccles*) remove from a benefice or office ~ **deprived** *adj* lacking normal benefits or advantages.

depth [*depth*] *n* distance from top downwards or from surface inwards; deepness; intensity, profundity, strength; (*mus*) lowness of pitch; (*mil*) distance from front to rear of body of troops; middle (of night, winter); **the depth(s)** lowest point, most remote part of, most intense degree of; **out of one's d.** in water too deep to touch bottom; (*fig*) faced with something past one's abilities or understanding; **in d.** (*mil*) covering a wide area behind the front line; (*fig*) thoroughly, intensely; **d. psychology** analysis of the content of the unconscious; explanation of behaviour or experience based on this > PDP.

depth-charge [*depth*-chaarj] *n* explosive charge used against submarines set to detonate at a certain depth.

depth-gauge [*depth*-gayj] *n* instrument to measure depth.

deputation [depew*tay*shon] *n* appointment to act in another's place; body of persons sent as representatives.

depute [di*pewt*] *v/t* send or appoint as representative; hand over to a representative; delegate.

deputize [*dep*ewtIz] *v/t* and *i* appoint as a deputy; act as a deputy.

deputy [*dep*ewti] *n* one appointed to act for another; one sent on a deputation.

deracinate [deeRasinayt] *v/t* uproot, eradicate.

derail [di*Rayl*] *v/t* and *i* leave the rails; cause to leave the rails ~ **derailment** *n.*

derange [di*Raynj*] *v/t* throw into confusion, disorganize, disturb; drive mad ~ **derangement** *n* mental disorder.

derate [dee*Rayt*] *v/t* charge less rates (upon).

deration [dee*Rash*on] *v/t* free (commodity) from the restrictions of a rationing system, take off the ration.

Derby [*daar*bi] *n* horse race run annually at Epsom; (*US*) [*dur*bi] stiff felt hat; **Crown D.** kind of china first made at Derby.

derelict [*deRi*likt] *adj* deserted, abandoned; neglected, falling in ruins; worthless; remiss, neglectful of duty ~ **derelict** *n* abandoned and drifting ship; deserted property; a broken-down tramp; land exposed by the receding sea.

dereliction [deRi*lik*shon] *n* act of forsaking; condition of being abandoned; retreat of sea from the land; neglect of duty, remissness.

derequisition [deeRekwi*zi*shon] *v/t* restore (commandeered property *etc*) to its normal use.

deride [di*Rid*] *v/t* laugh to scorn, ridicule; express contempt for; hold of little account.

derision [di*Ri*zhon] *n* act of deriding, ridicule, mockery, contempt; state of being derided.

derisive [di*Ri*siv] *adj* expressing ridicule, mocking; ridiculous, petty ~ **derisively** *adv*.

derisory [di*Ri*seRi] *adj* inviting or worthy only of derision; too insignificant or futile for serious consideration.

derivate [*de*Rivayt] *n* and *adj* (thing) derived.

derivation [deRi*vay*shon] *n* act of deriving; thing derived; source, origin; etymology (of words); (*phil*) process of tracing a word back to its earliest form; deviation of bullet from a rifled gun.

derivative [di*Ri*vativ] *adj* derived from something else; secondary ~ **derivative** *n* that which is derived from something else; (*chem*) substance prepared from some other substance; (*phil*) word derived from another word; (*math*) derived function ~ **derivatively** *adv*.

derive [di*Riv*] *v/t* and *i* obtain or receive (from); take origin (from), be formed (from); trace the origin of, *esp* a word.

derm, derma [*durm, dur*ma] *n* (*anat*) layer of skin lying below the epidermis ~ **dermal** *adj*.

dermatitis [durma*ti*tis] *n* inflammation of the skin.

dermatology [durma*to*loji] *n* study of the skin and its diseases ~ **dermatologist** *n*.

dermis [*dur*mis] *n* derma > PDB.

derogate [*de*Rogayt] *v/i* take away, remove (a merit, good quality); lessen, detract; do something which injures one's position or reputation ~ **derogation** [deRo*gay*shon] *n* disparagement, detraction; deterioration.

derogatory [di*Ro*gatoRi] *adj* tending to lessen or discredit; disparaging, disrespectful.

derrick [*de*Rik] *n* a lifting device; a stationary crane employing hoisting tackle rigged at the end of a boom or lifting jib; square latticed tower of timber or steel above an oil-well > PDE.

derring-do [deRing-*dOO*] *n* (*ar*) knightly courage; brave deed.

derringer [*de*Rinjer] *n* (*US*) short pistol of large calibre for use at close quarters.

derris [*de*Ris] *n* tropical plant of the pea family, from the root of which insecticidal preparations are made.

derv [*derv*] *n* fuel oil for diesel engines.

dervish [*dur*vish] *n* member of an Islamic ascetic religious order practising ecstatic dancing.

desalination [deesali*nay*shon] *n* process of converting salt water to fresh; loss or removal of salt.

descale [dee*skayl*] *v/t* (*eng*) remove deposit from inside boilers or water pipes; remove oxide from metal surfaces by immersion in an acid bath.

descant [*des*kant] *n* (*mus*) additional part sung or improvised above a given melody; the soprano part; harmonized musical composition; comment, criticism; (*poet*) song, *esp* of birds ~ **descant** *v/i* (*mus*) sing or play a descant; comment on, enlarge (upon topic).

descend [di*send*] *v/t* and *i* go down (stairs *etc*); go downwards into; move downwards; slope downwards; sink; come from (a source), be derived; pass by inheritance; be transmitted; (*astron*) move southwards; (*mus*) go down the scale; **d. upon** attack or visit unexpectedly; **d. to** lower oneself, stoop to.

descendant [di*sen*dant] *n* issue, offspring.

descent [di*sent*] *n* going down, a fall from a higher to a lower position, downward motion, decline; downward slope or stairway; sudden attack; ancestry; hereditary transmission.

describe [di*skRib*] *v/t* give detailed account of; delineate (by words or drawing); (*geom*) trace the form of, mark out.

descried [di*skRid*] *adj* observed, seen, noticed.

description [di*skRip*shon] *n* act or process of describing; detailed account; sort, kind, class, variety ~ **descriptive** *adj*.

descry [di*skRi*] *v/t* catch sight of, see far off.

desecrate [*desi*kRayt] *v/t* damage the beauty of; spoil the holiness of, profane ~ **desecration** [desi*kRay*shon] *n*.

desegregate [dee*seg*Rigayt] *v/t* abolish racial segregation in ~ **desegregation** *n*.

desensitize [dee*sen*sitIz] *v/t* (*med*) render less sensitive to an irritant, stimulus, allergen *etc*; (*phot*) render less sensitive to light ~ **desensitization** *n*.

desert (1) [*de*zert] *n* uninhabited region, wilderness; large barren tract > PDG; **d. rat** British soldier who fought in N. Africa 1941–2 ~ **desert** *adj* uninhabited, lonely, barren.

desert (2) [di*zurt*] *n* what is deserved; merit.

desert (3) [di*zurt*] *v/t* and *i* abandon, forsake; (*mil*) abandon a post or leave the service without permission.

deserter [di*zur*ter] *n* soldier or sailor who deserts.

desertion [di*zur*shon] *n* act of deserting; state of being deserted.

deserve [di*zurv*] *v/t* and *i* have a right to; merit, be worthy of.

deservedly [di*zur*vedli] *adv* justly.

deserving [di*zur*ving] *adj* having merit, worthy (of praise, blame *etc*) ~ **deservingly** *adv*.

desex [dee*seks*] *v/t* castrate; spay; remove sexual characteristics of.

desexualize [dee*sek*sew-alIz] *v/t* deprive of sexual characteristics; castrate.

deshabille see **dishabille**.

desiccant [*desi*kent] *n* and *adj* (substance) absorbing moisture.

desiccate [*desi*kayt] *v/t* and *i* dry completely ~ **desiccation** [desi*kay*shon] *n* removal of moisture.

desiccator [*desi*kayter] *n* apparatus for removing moisture from a substance.

desideratum (*pl* **desiderata**) [dizide*Raa*tum] *n* a thing lacking and required.

design [di*zin*] *n* plan, project; purpose, end aimed at; evil or sinister intention; working plan;

draft; basic pattern; (*painting*) arrangement of colour, light, or line; (*mus*) artistic intention embodied in a composition; **by d.** deliberately ~ **design** *v/t* and *i* plan, contrive; intend; set apart for; invent a pattern for; construct designs.

designate [*de*zignayt] *v/t* point out, indicate; specify; name; appoint to an office ~ **designate** *adj* appointed to an office but not yet installed.

designation [dezignayshon] *n* act of designating; state of being designated, nominated, appointed; a distinctive name, description, or title.

designed [dizInd] *adj* planned, intended ~ **designedly** [dizInidli] *adv* intentionally.

designer [dizIner] *n* one who makes artistic designs, patterns, or plans of construction > PDE; a crafty, scheming person.

designing [dizIning] *n* art of making designs and patterns ~ **designing** *adj* crafty, scheming.

desirable [dizIrRab'l] *adj* worthy to be desired; attractive, pleasant.

desire [dizIr] *v/t* wish, long for ardently, yearn for; express a wish, request ~ **desire** *n* longing; sexual appetite, lust; wish, request; thing desired.

desirous [dizIrRus] *adj* wishful, ambitious.

desist [dizist] *v/i* stop, leave off, cease.

desk [*desk*] *n* piece of furniture for purposes of reading and writing, either resting on a table or itself standing on the floor, generally fitted with drawers and compartments; music-stand.

desolate [*de*solit] *adj* uninhabited, deserted; cheerless, forlorn ~ **desolate** [*de*solayt] *v/t* depopulate, lay waste; make wretched or forlorn.

despair [dis*pair*] *n* loss of hope, hopelessness; thing which or person who causes hopelessness ~ **despair** *v/i* lose, be without, hope.

despatch see **dispatch**.

desperado [despeRaadO] *n* reckless, violent ruffian.

desperate [*de*speRit] *adj* reckless, driven to extremity, stopping at nothing; with little room for hope, hopeless; beyond hope of recovery; (*of acts*) resorted to in the last extremity; (*coll*) extremely bad, very great ~ **desperately** *adv*.

desperation [despeRayshon] *n* condition of despair, state of being desperate; recklessness; (*coll*) state of irritation and anger.

despicable [*de*spikab'l/dis*pik*ab'l] *adj* contemptible, mean ~ **despicably** *adv*.

despise [dispIz] *v/t* look down on, feel contempt for ~ **despisingly** *adv*.

despite (1) [dispIt] *n* spite, malice; contempt; (*ar*) injury; **in d. of** in spite of, notwithstanding.

despite (2) *prep* notwithstanding, in spite of.

despoil [dispoil] *v/t* strip of belongings, rob, plunder ~ **despoliation** [dispOli-*ay*shon] *n*.

despond [dis*pond*] *v/i* lose heart, become dejected.

despondency [dis*pond*ensi] *n* dejection.

despondent [dis*pond*ent] *adj* dejected, depressed ~ **despondently** *adv*.

desponding [dis*pond*ing] *adj* despondent ~ **despondingly** *adv*.

despot [*de*spot] *n* one who rules with absolute power and authority; tyrant, oppressor.

despotic [dis*potik*] *adj* having absolute power, tyrannical ~ **despotically** *adv*.

despotism [*de*spotizm] *n* rule by a despot; state ruled by a despot; tyranny.

dessert [dizurt] *n* a course of fruit and confections at the end of a meal; sweet dish, pudding.

dessert-spoon [di*zurt*-spOOn] *n* spoon intermediate in size between a tablespoon and teaspoon ~ **dessert-spoonful** *n*.

destination [destin*ay*shon] *n* place towards which a person or thing is travelling or has been sent.

destine [*de*stin] *v/t* determine the future of, preordain, predestinate; set apart for a particular end, doom, intend; **destined for** intended for; bound for.

destiny [*de*stini] *n* a power determining events, Fate; that which is fated to happen.

destitute [*de*stitewt] *adj* lacking, in need (of); in utter poverty ~ **destitution** [desti*tew*shon] *n* utter poverty.

destroy [distRoi] *v/t* break to pieces, demolish; spoil completely; kill; do away with.

destroyer [distRoi-er] *n* person or thing that destroys; small fast warship armed with torpedoes and depth-charges.

destruct [distrukt] *v/t* (*aer*) detonate (rocket, missile) in flight; destroy.

destructibility [distRukti*bi*liti] *n* quality of being destructible.

destructible [dis*tRuk*tib'l] *adj* able to be destroyed.

destruction [dis*tRuk*shon] *n* act of destroying; state of being destroyed; ruin; that which destroys.

destructive [dis*tRuk*tiv] *adj* causing destruction; (*of criticism etc*) merely negative, not constructive ~ **destructive** *n* a destructive agent or force ~ **destructively** *adv*.

destructor [dis*tRuk*tor] *n* furnace for destroying refuse.

desuetude [*de*sweetewd] *n* state of disuse; discontinuance.

desultory [*de*sulteRi] *adj* disconnected; unmethodical, casual.

detach [ditach] *v/t* disconnect, unfasten; (*mil* and *naval*) separate from main body and send on special mission.

detached [ditacht] *adj* disconnected; standing apart; aloof, impartial; free from personal involvement.

detachment [ditachment] *n* separation; aloofness, unconcern, disinterestedness; (*mil*) party separated from main body for special duty.

detail [*dee*tayl] *n* small subordinate part of any whole; an item or particular; insignificant circumstance; minor decoration in building, picture *etc*; treatment of this; (*mil*) party told off for special duty; **in d.** item by item; thoroughly; **d. drawing** large-scale working drawing > PDE ~ **detail** *v/t* make a minute report of; enumerate or mention item by item; (*mil*) tell off for special duty ~ **detailed** *adj* described item by item, minute; given in detail, circumstantial.

detain [ditayn] *v/t* prevent (person) from going on, keep waiting, hinder; withhold, retain possession of; (*leg*) retain in custody, *esp* without trial.

detainee [deetaynee] *n* one held in custody; prisoner without trial.

detainer [di*tayn*er] *n* (*leg*) unlawful withholding

of what belongs to another; process by which a prisoner in custody may be held pending further charges.

detect [ditekt] v/t and i discover, find out; notice; act as detective.

detection [ditekshon] n process of detecting, esp crimes.

detective [ditektiv] adj pertaining to detection; **d. story** popular form of novel dealing with crime and its detection ~ **detective** n police officer or private operator who investigates crimes.

detectophone [ditektofOn] n apparatus for tapping telephone conversations.

detector [ditekter] n person or thing that detects; (rad) demodulator, frequency changer; high-frequency rectifier > PDS.

detent [ditent] n checking device in a machine; catch which regulates the striking of a clock.

detente, détente [daytaant] n relaxation of political tension between two countries.

detention [ditenshon] n keeping in custody, esp without trial; keeping in after hours as a school punishment; withholding what is due; enforced delay; **d. barrack** military prison.

deter [ditur] v/t prevent (person) from acting by fear of the consequences; discourage, restrain.

detergent [diturjent] n a cleaning agent > PDS; any synthetic substance other than soap used for household cleaning ~ **detergent** adj cleansing.

deteriorate [diteeRi-oRayt] v/t and i make or become worse; depreciate; degenerate ~ **deterioration** [diteeRi-oRayshon] n.

determent [diturment] n act of deterring; that which deters.

determinable [diturminab'l] adj capable of being determined, settled, or ascertained; (leg) terminable.

determinant [diturminant] adj having the power of determining, limiting, defining ~ **determinant** n (math) form of notation used for representing certain algebraic functions.

determinate [diturminit] adj having clearly defined limits; definite, limited, fixed; conclusive; (math) having a limited number of solutions.

determination [diturminayshon] n fixed purpose; resoluteness; decision, judicial or otherwise; delimitation; conclusion reached by investigation; (leg) cessation of an estate or interest.

determinative [diturminaytiv] adj and n deciding, defining (factor).

determine [diturmin] v/t and i settle conclusively, decide; come to a decision, resolve; set limits to, fix; ascertain, calculate; be cause of, be decisive factor in; decide the course of; (leg) end.

determined [diturmind] adj firm, resolute.

determinism [diturminizm] n theory that man has no free will, but that his actions are controlled by external causes ~ **determinist** n.

deterrence [diteRens] n act of deterring; that which deters.

deterrent [diteRent] n and adj (something) that deters, esp an atomic bomb or nuclear weapon.

detest [ditest] v/t hate deeply, abhor.

detestable [ditestab'l] adj hateful, abominable ~ **detestably** adv.

detestation [deetestayshon] n hatred, extreme dislike; object of hatred.

dethrone [deethROn] v/t remove from throne, depose; (fig) destroy the power or influence of.

detinning [deetining] n recovery of metallic tin from scrap tinplate by the action of chlorine.

detonate [detonayt] v/t and i cause to explode; explode violently and noisily ~ **detonating** adj that detonates; explosive, containing explosive; **d. fuse** one used in blasting > PDE.

detonation [detonayshon] n extremely rapid and powerful explosion; noise of this; (mot) spontaneous combustion of petrol gas.

detonator [detonaytor] n a contrivance which sets off an explosion > PDE; fog-signal which explodes on a railway track.

detour [daytoor/deetoor] n deviation from direct road; alternative route ~ **detour** v/i.

detract [ditRakt] v/t take away a part (from) or diminish (the reputation, estimation etc of a person or thing) ~ **detractor** n.

detraction [ditRakshon] n act of detracting; depreciation; disparagement, calumny ~ **detractive** adj tending to detract.

detrain [deetRayn] v/t and i set down (esp troops) from a railway train; alight from train.

detribalize [deetRIbalIz] v/t destroy a person's links with his tribe; destroy the tribal structure or customs of (a society).

detriment [detRiment] n damage; that which causes loss or damage.

detrimental [detRimental] adj causing damage, loss, injury; harmful ~ **detrimentally** adv.

detrited [ditRItid] adj worn down, formed by detrition.

detrition [ditRishon] n act of wearing away by rubbing.

detritus [ditRItus] n broken or crumbling fragments; (geol) material worn away from rock surfaces.

detrude [ditROOd] v/t force down; thrust out.

detumescence [deetewmesens] n (med) subsidence of swelling.

deuce [dews] n the die or playing card with two spots; score of forty-all at tennis; (coll) the devil.

deuced [dewsid/dewst] adj and adv (coll) confounded(ly), extreme(ly).

deut-, deuto- pref (chem) second in order; (biol) second.

deuter-, deutero- pref second, secondary.

deuterium [dewteeRi-um] n (chem) heavy hydrogen, the hydrogen isotope of atomic mass 2 > PDS.

deuteron [dewteRon] n (chem) the nucleus of the deuterium atom.

Deuteronomy [dewteRonomi] n fifth book of the Bible, containing second book of Mosaic law.

deuto- see **deut-**.

deutoplasm [dewtoplazm] n (biol) yolk or food material in the cytoplasm of ovum or other cell.

deva [dayva] n (Hindu myth) god, good spirit; (Zoroastrianism) evil spirit.

devaluate [deevalew-ayt] v/t reduce the value of (esp currency) ~ **devaluation** [deevalewayshon] n.

devalue [deevalew] v/t devaluate.

devastate [devastayt] v/t destroy wholly or **to a** large extent, ruin; cause great damage to.

devastating [devastayting] adj that destroys or

damages greatly; (coll) very effective as argument or mockery, unanswerable ~ **devastatingly** adv.

devastation [devas*tay*shon] n act of devastating; state of having been devastated; area laid waste or greatly damaged.

develop [di*vel*op] v/t and i unfold, bring out latent powers of; expand, strengthen, spread; grow, evolve; become more mature; show by degrees; explain more fully, elaborate; exploit the potentialities (of a site) by building, mining etc; (phot) make visible images on a negative by the use of chemicals.

developer [di*vel*oper] n chemical used in developing photographic negatives; one who exploits a site by building on it; apparatus for strengthening muscles.

development [di*vel*opment] n act, process, or result of developing; state of being developed; growth, expansion, evolution; fact or circumstance just arisen or come to light; (mus) that section of a movement between the initial statement of themes and their final recapitulation wherein they are expanded, modified, combined etc; **d. area** district to which new industries are directed in order to mitigate unemployment there.

deviance, deviancy [*dee*vi-ans, *dee*vi-ansi] n deviation from normality ~ **deviant** n and adj (person) deviating from normal behaviour or standards.

deviate [*dee*vi-ayt] v/i turn aside.

deviation [deevi-*ay*shon] n a turning aside, divergence, deflection; variation from some line, norm, or standard of reference; (math) variation from the mean in a series > PDP; (naut) deflection of a compass needle from the true north.

deviationist [deevi-*ay*shonist] n one who departs from strict party ideology, esp of communism.

device [di*vIs*] n plan, expedient, trick; mechanical contrivance; artistic design; (her) emblematic design borne by a person or family; motto; **leave (person) to his own devices** leave alone to follow his inclination.

devil [*dev*il] n chief spirit of evil, Satan; demon, wicked man; rogue; lively, mischievous person; unlucky wretch; source of trouble, anything difficult; junior counsel working without fee for his leader; hack writer; highly seasoned food, esp grilled; (coll) fighting spirit; (meteor) small whirlwind; sandspout; **printer's d.** errand boy in a printer's office; **d.'s advocate** (RC) official who argues against a canonization; one who argues to the contrary for the sake of debate; one whose support does more harm than good; **the d.** (coll) exclamation of surprise or anger; intensifying phrase; **go to the d.** be ruined; (exclam, v/imp) go away; **play the d.** with ruin, injure; **d. a bit not at all; d. to pay** unpleasant consequences to face; **between the d. and the deep sea** faced with two equally unpleasant alternatives; **d.'s Bible** playing cards; **raise the d.** make a din; **blue devils** low spirits, depression; **d.'s tattoo** rapid drumming of fingers or feet ~ **devil** (pres/part **devilling**, p/t and p/part **devilled**) v/t and i cook by grilling with hot condiments; do hack work for another; (bui) scratch plaster to prepare a rough surface for the next coat.

devil-fish [*dev*il-fish] n gigantic ray; octopus.

devilish [*dev*ilish] adj like a devil, diabolical ~ **devilish** adv (coll) extremely ~ **devilishly** adv in a devilish manner; (coll) excessively.

devil-may-care [*dev*il-may-kair] adj reckless; happy-go-lucky.

devilment [*dev*ilment] n action befitting a devil; mischievous prank.

devilry, deviltry [*dev*ilRi, *dev*iltRi] n black magic, diabolical art and practices; extreme wickedness or cruelty; reckless mischief or daring.

devious [*dee*vi-us] adj winding, roundabout; off the main path, remote; crooked; (fig) deceitful ~ **deviously** adv.

devisable [di*vIz*ab'l] adj (leg) that can be bequeathed; contrivable.

devise [di*vIz*] v/t plan, contrive, invent; (leg) bequeath (real property) by will ~ **devise** n (leg) gift of real property by will; clause in will effecting such gift; property so given.

devitalize [dee*vItal*Iz] v/t deprive of life; destroy the vigour of ~ **devitalization** [deevItalI*zay*shon] n.

devocalize [dee*vO*kalIz] v/t (phon) make (a voiced sound) voiceless.

devoid [di*void*] adj empty, destitute (of), without.

devolution [deevo*lew*shon] n handing down, transference (of authority, property etc); the granting of partial self-government to a region within a State; delegation; (biol) degeneration.

devolutionist [deevo*lew*shonist] n and adj (person) advocating partial regional self-government.

devolve [di*volv*] v/t and i transfer, delegate (duties etc); fall as a duty or responsibility, pass to; (leg) pass by transmission or succession.

Devonian [div*Oni*-an] adj belonging to Devonshire; (geol) designating the system of rocks lying below the Carboniferous and above the Silurian > PDG.

devote [di*vOt*] v/t set apart, dedicate; apply (oneself) wholeheartedly or exclusively (to).

devoted [di*vOt*id] adj given up (to); fond (of), deeply attached (to); loyal, faithful.

devotee [dev*O*tee] n one zealously devoted; enthusiast, zealot.

devotion [div*O*shon] n state of being devoted; piety, devoutness; (pl) prayers; deep tenderness, unselfish solicitude; conscientious application; enthusiastic addiction.

devour [di*vour*] v/t eat ravenously; consume, ravage; (fig) read with eager interest, absorb mentally; look at intently.

devout [di*vowt*] adj pious; reverential; earnest, sincere ~ **devoutly** adv ~ **devoutness** n.

dew [dew] n liquid produced by condensation of water vapour in the air; (fig) anything refreshing, pure, or falling gently like dew; moisture forming in drops, tears, sweat; **mountain d.** whisky ~ **dew** v/t and i moisten, bedew; fall as dew.

dewclaw [*dew*klaw] n useless inner claw on the feet of dogs and deer.

dewdrop [*dew*dRop] n drop of dew.

dewlap [*dew*lap] n fold of loose skin hanging from throat of cattle; loose skin on human throat.

dew-point [*dew*-point] n temperature at which dew begins to form > PDS.

dewpond [*dew*pond] n shallow artificial pond on downland fed by water condensation.

dewy [*dewi*] *adj* wet with dew;(*fig*) fresh, soft; refreshing; glistening.

dewy-eyed [*dewi*-Id] *adj* foolishly trustful or idealistic.

dexedrine [*deks*idReen/*deks*idRIn] *n* trade-name of a drug used as a nasal spray or nerve-stimulant.

dexio- *pref* on or towards the right.

dexter [*deks*ter] *adj* on the right-hand side; (*her*) on the spectator's left.

dexterity [*deks*teRiti] *n* manipulative skill; adroitness and skill in bodily movements; mental agility; using the right hand rather than the left.

dexterous, dextrous [*deks*teRus] *adj* skilful of hand; agile of movement; adroit, clever, deft; right-handed ∼ **dexterously, dextrously** *adv*.

dextral [*deks*tRal] *adj* on the right; turning to the right; right-handed ∼ **dextrality** *n*.

dextran, dextrone [*deks*tRan, *deks*tROn] *n* (*chem*) synthetic blood plasma.

dextrin [*deks*tRin] *n* (*chem*) gummy substance obtained from starch, used as a thickening agent.

dextro- *pref* towards the right.

dextrorotary [*deks*tROROtaRi] *adj* (*chem*) rotating to the right, *esp* the plane of polarization of light by certain crystals.

dextrorse [*deks*tRawrs] *adj* (*bot*, *zool*) twisting to the right.

dextrose [*deks*tROz] *n* (*chem*) form of glucose; granular sugar; purified grape-sugar.

dextrous see **dexterous**.

dharma [*daar*ma] *n* (*Buddhism*) natural law governing physical and mental phenomena; Buddhist teaching; upright conduct; all experienced events; (*Hinduism*) obedience to caste rules.

dhole [*dOl*] *n* Indian wild dog.

dhoti [*dOt*i] *n* nether garment of male Hindu.

dhow [*dow*] *n* single-masted Arab coasting vessel.

di- (1) *pref* expressing separation.

di- (2) *pref* double, twofold, twice, two.

dia-, di- (3) *pref* through the agency of, by means of; through, throughout; across; between; apart.

diabase [*dI*-abays] *n* (*min*) crystalline granular rock, variety of greenstone.

diabetes [*dI*-abeeteez/*dI*-abeetis] *n* (*med*) disease characterized by excessive production of sugar and abnormal discharge of urine.

diabetic [*dI*-abeetik/*dI*-abetik] *adj* (*med*) pertaining to, suffering from, diabetes ∼ **diabetic** *n* person suffering from diabetes.

diabetogenic [di-abeetojenik] *adj* causing diabetes.

diablerie [dee-aableRee] *n* (*Fr*) dealings with the devil, sorcery; devil-lore.

diabolic, diabolical [dI-abolik, dI-abolikal] *adj* pertaining to, proceeding from, the devil; fiendlike, wicked; (*coll*) very bad, difficult, unpleasant *etc* ∼ **diabolically** *adv*.

diabolism [dI-abolizm] *n* worship of the devil; witchcraft; fiendish conduct ∼ **diabolist** *n*.

diabolo [dI-abolO] *n* game played with two sticks connected by a string on which a reel is spun and jerked into the air.

diachronic [dI-akRonik] *adj* pertaining to results of the passage of time and historical development.

diaconal [dI-akonal] *adj* pertaining to a deacon.

diaconate [dI-akonayt] *n* office of deacon; period of tenure of a deacon's office; deacons.

diacritic [dI-akRitik] *adj* serving to distinguish,

distinctive; (*gramm*) (*of certain signs*) used to distinguish sounds or values of the same letter ∼ **diacritic** *n* a diacritic sign ∼ **diacritical** *adj*.

diadem [*dI*-adem] *n* arch rising from the rim of a crown; jewelled fillet worn by Eastern rulers; a crown; sovereignty; **d. spider** common garden spider ∼ **diademed** *adj* wearing a diadem.

diaeresis [dI-eerisis/dI-airisis/dI-erReesis] *n* separation of two adjacent vowels: sign (¨) over the second of two vowels to show that they are to be sounded separately.

diagnose [dI-agnOz] *v/t* (*med*) determine the nature of (disease) from observing symptoms or from results of tests.

diagnosis (*pl* **diagnoses**) [dI-agnOsis] *n* (*med*) identification of a disease from examining its symptoms; opinion or decision reached by such examination; (*bot*, *biol*) formal description of characteristics.

diagnostic [dI-agnostik] *adj* (*med*) pertaining to diagnosis; of value in diagnosis, characteristic ∼ **diagnostic** *n* symptom; diagnosis; (*pl*) study of symptoms ∼ **diagnosticate** *v/t* and *i* diagnose.

diagnostician [dI-agnostishan] *n* (*med*) specialist in making diagnoses.

diagometer [dI-agomiter] *n* (*elect*) instrument for measuring electro-conductive power.

diagonal [dI-agonal] *adj* (*geom*) joining the intersections of two pairs of sides of a rectilinear figure, slanting from corner to corner; oblique; marked by oblique lines ∼ **diagonal** *n* diagonal line or plane; twilled cloth ∼ **diagonally** *adv*.

diagram [*dI*-agRam] *n* (*geom*) drawing illustrating a proposition; explanatory plan or sketch; graphic representation of statistics *etc*.

diagrammatic [dI-agRamatik] *adj* of, by, or like a diagram ∼ **diagrammatical** *adj* ∼ **diagrammatically** *adv*.

diagrammatize [dI-agRamatiz] *v/t* express by a diagram.

diagraph [*dI*-agRaaf] *n* instrument for drawing projections of objects, or for enlarging maps, drawings *etc*.

dial [*dI*-al] *n* face of watch or clock; graduated face of any indicator, gauge, meter, or compass; (*rad*) turning mechanism and indicator; (*sur*) colliery surveyor's tripod-mounted compass; rotating disk on a telephone, used in making automatic connexion; sundial; (*sl*) human face ∼ **dial** (*pres/part* **dialling**; *p/t* and *p/part* **dialled**) *v/t* and *i* call a telephone number by automatic connexion; (*rad*) tune in; measure or survey with a dial: show on a dial.

dialect [*dI*-alekt] *n* form of speech characteristic of a district or of a defined group of speakers; form of speech varying from a recognized standard ∼ **dialectal** [dI-alektal] *adj* ∼ **dialectally** [dI-alektali] *adv*.

dialectic [dI-alektik] *n* (*freq* **dialectics**) investigation of truth by discussion; logical disputation; (*philos*) method of logic based on the statement and resolution of contraries.

dialectical [dI-alektikal] *adj*; **d. materialism** Marxist philosophic materialism > PDPol ∼ **dialectically** [dI-alektikali] *adv*.

dialectician [dI-alektishon] *n* expert in dialectics.

dialling [*dI*-aling] *n* the making or using of dials; (*sur*) making a compass traverse with a miner's dial; making a call on automatic telephone; **d. tone** sound heard on automatic telephone to show that caller can proceed to dial.

dialogue [*dɪ*-alog] *n* conversation; written work in form of conversation; passages of conversation in plays, novels *etc*; preliminary exchange of views between parties seeking eventual agreement ~ **dialogue** *v/t* and *i* carry on conversation; express in dialogue form.

dialysis (*pl* **dialyses**) [dɪ-a*lisis*] *n* (*chem*) separation of colloids in solution by selective diffusion through a semi-permeable membrane > PDS; (*med*) cleansing of blood by this process.

dialytic [dɪa*litik*] *adj* of or by dialysis.

diamagnetism [dɪ-a*magnetizm*] *n* (*phys*) a weak form of magnetism > PDS ~ **diamagnetic** [dɪ-a*magnetik*] *adj*.

diamanté [dee-a-*montay*] *m* material made to sparkle by use of powdered glass or paste brilliants.

diameter [dɪ-a*meter*] *n* (*geom*) straight line passing through centre of a circle, and bounded by the circumference; length of such a line; thickness of circular object; unit of measurement of magnifying power of a lens.

diametric, diametrical [dɪ-a*met*Rik,dɪ-a*met*Rikal] *adj* of or along a diameter; directly opposite; (of opposition) complete, absolute ~ **diametrically** *adv*.

diamond [*dɪ*-amond] *n* a crystalline form of carbon > PDE; piece of this substance used as gem or as cutting tool; (*geom*) rhombus drawn erect; playing-card marked with red lozenges, (*pl*) suit of such cards; (*baseball*) area marked by the four bases; (*print*) second smallest size of type; **d. anniversary, d. jubilee** sixtieth anniversary; **black d.** coal; **d. cut d.** clash between two people of equal cunning or ruthlessness; **d. drill** boring tool armed with diamonds; **rough d.** (*fig*) person of fine character but unpolished manners; **d. wedding** sixtieth anniversary of marriage ~ **diamond** *adj* made of, set with, diamonds; lozenge-shaped ~ **diamond** *v/t* adorn with diamonds ~ **diamonded** *adj* furnished with diamonds.

diamond-point [*dɪ*-amond-point] *n* tool tipped with diamond, used in engraving; (*pl*) oblique intersection of two sets of railway-lines.

diandrous [dɪ-*and*Rus] *adj* (*bot*) having two stamens; (*zool*) mating with two males.

Dianetics [dɪ-a*netiks*] *n* (*tr*) a system that attempts to remove harmful effects of images in the memory, and claims to cure psychosomatic illnesses.

dianthus [dɪ-a*nthus*] *n* genus of flowering plants including pinks and carnations.

diapason [dɪ-a*payzon*] *n* (*mus*) range, compass of voice or instrument; music written in harmony; standard of pitch; instrument for determining pitch; (*fig*) rich, swelling sound; **open d., stopped d.** the two main stops of an organ.

diaper [*dɪ*-aper] *n* linen or cotton fabric with diamond pattern; baby's napkin; diamond-shaped pattern used as decoration for walls *etc*; (*her*) similar pattern covering shield ~ **diaper** *adj* ~ **diaper** *v/t* decorate with diamond patterns.

diaphanous [dɪ-*af*anus] *adj* transparent.

diaphragm [*dɪ*-af*Ram*] *n* the muscular separation between thorax and abdomen; midriff; dividing membrane or partition; device for controlling the transmission of light; vibrating cone or plate producing sound-waves; stiffening plate in a bridge between main girders; brass fitting in a surveying telescope which carries the reticule; instrument to measure flow of water in pipes; woman's contraceptive cap ~ **diaphragmal** [dɪ-af*Rag*mal] *adj* ~ **diaphragmatic** [dɪ-af*Rag*matik] *adj*.

diarchy [dɪ-aarki] *n* government shared by two powers ~ **diarchal** [dɪ-*aark*al] *adj* ~ **diarchic** [dɪ-*aark*ik] *adj*.

diarist [dɪ-a*Rist*] *n* one who writes a diary.

diarrhoea [dɪ-a*Ree*-a] *n* excessively frequent and loose evacuation of bowels.

diary [*dɪ*-a*Ri*] *n* daily record of events, *esp* those directly concerning the writer; book prepared for use as a diary.

Diaspora [dɪ-a*spo*Ra] *n* (*hist*) dispersion of Jews after Babylonian captivity or after Roman destruction of Jerusalem; Jews living outside Israel.

diaspore [*dɪ*-aspawr] *n* hydrated aluminium oxide.

diastase [dɪ-a*stays*] *n* (*chem*) enzyme contained in malt which converts starch into maltose during brewing ~ **diastatic** [dɪ-a*statik*] *adj*.

diastole [dɪ-a*stoli*] *n* (*med*) the dilation phase of heart action, alternating with systole ~ **diastolic** [dɪ-a*stolik*] *adj*.

diastyle [*dɪ*-astɪl] *n* and *adj* (*archi*) (colonnade) having the intervals between the columns equal to three diameters of the columns.

diathermal [dɪ-a*thur*mal] *adj* able to transmit heat radiation.

diathermy [dɪ-a*thur*mi] *n* medical treatment by heating body tissues with a high-frequency electric field.

diathesis [dɪ-a*this*is] *n* constitutional predisposition to a particular disease or defect.

diatom [*dɪ*-atom] *n* type of unicellular algae with siliceous shells.

diatomaceous [dɪ-a*to*mayshus] *adj* consisting of, or containing, diatoms or their remains; **d. earth** kieselguhr, siliceous deposit formed from diatom shells used as an abrasive and in filtration; **d. ooze** ooze formed from diatoms.

diatomic [dɪ-a*tomik*] *adj* (*chem*) consisting of two atoms in a molecule.

diatomite [dɪ-a*tom*ɪt] *n* diatomaceous earth.

diatonic [dɪ-a*tonik*] *adj* (*mus*) of or in a regular major. or minor scale without chromatic intervals > PDM ~ **diatonically** *adv*.

diatribe [*dɪ*-atRɪb] *n* bitter attack in speech or writing, abusive criticism ~ **diatribist** *n*.

dibasic [dɪ*baysik*] *adj* (*chem*) (*of an acid*) giving rise to two series of salts, normal and acid salts.

dibber [*dib*er] *n* instrument for dibbling, a dibble.

dibble [*dib*'l] *n* instrument used to make holes in the ground for planting ~ **dibble** *v/t* and *i* plant, sow with a dibble; use a dibble.

dibranchiate [dib*Ranki*-ayt] *n* and *adj* (*zool*) (cephalopod) having two gills.

dibs [*dibz*] *n* (*pl*) children's game; knuckle-bones or pebbles used in the game; counters used in card games; (*sl*) money.

dice [*dɪs*] *n* (*pl*) (*sing* die) cubes marked on each side with a different number of spots (one to six), used in games of chance; gambling game played with dice; small cubes of meat or vegetables ~ **dice** *v/i* and *t* play at dice; lose by gambling with dice; mark with chequered pattern; cut into small cubes; (*sl*) take great risks, *esp* in driving.

dicebox [*dIs*boks] *n* box in which dice are shaken.

dicephalous [*dIs*efalus] *adj* having two heads.

dicey [*dIs*i] *adj* (*coll*) risky, tricky, dangerous.

dichotomize [*dIkot*Om*Iz*] *v/t* and *i* divide into two parts.

dichotomous [*dIkot*Omus] *adj* divided or dividing in two ~ **dichotomously** *adv*.

dichotomy [*dIkot*Omi] *n* division into two parts, *esp* if strongly contrasted; (*log*) classification into two classes, on basis of presence or absence of a certain characteristic, or by paired opposites; (*bot*, *biol*) branching.

dichromatic [*dIk*ROmatik] *adj* showing two colours; (*biol*) having two varieties of coloration; (*opt*) able to perceive only two bands of colour in the spectrum ~ **dichromatism** [*dIk*ROmatizm] *n* partial colour blindness.

dichromic [*dIk*ROmik] *adj* showing one colour when looked at and another when looked through; (*opt*) dichromatic.

dicing [*dIs*ing] *n* dice-play; way of ornamenting leather in squares or diamonds.

dick (1) [*dik*] *n* (*coll*) man, fellow; (*sl*) detective; (*sl*) penis; (*coll*) fool.

dick (2) *n* (*sl*) declaration; **take one's d.** take an oath.

dickens [*dik*inz] *interj* (*sl*) the deuce, the devil.

dicker [*dik*er] *v/i* haggle, bargain; hesitate ~ **dickering** *n* bargaining.

dickey, dicky (1) [*dik*i] *n* driver's seat in a horse-drawn carriage; small folding seat at the back of motorcar or carriage; (*sl*) false shirt front.

dicky (2) *n* child's word for a bird.

dicky (3) *adj* (*sl*) unsteady, shaky; not in good health; financially unsound.

dicotyledon [*dIk*oti*leed*on] *n* (*bot*) plant having two cotyledons or seed-leaves.

dicta see **dictum**.

dictaphone [*dikt*afOn] *n* trade-name for a machine that records and reproduces spoken words.

dictate [*dik*tayt] *v/t* and *i* speak or read aloud something for another to write down verbatim; command, give order; arbitrarily impose one's will ~ **dictate** [*dik*tayt] *n* authoritative command.

dictation [*dik*tayshon] *n* act of dictating; passage dictated.

dictator [*dik*taytor] *n* absolute ruler, despot; person with absolute power; domineering person; (*hist*) Roman magistrate given absolute powers in times of emergency; one who dictates (letters *etc*).

dictatorial [*dikt*ataw*R*i-al] *adj* like a dictator; imperious, overbearing, self-assertive ~ **dictatorially** *adv*.

dictatorship [*dik*taytorship] *n* office of a dictator; period of a dictator's office; absolute authority; **d. of the proletariat** (*Marxism*) period in which supreme power is taken by representatives of the working class before the establishment of a classless society.

dictatory [*dik*tayte*R*i] *adj* dictatorial.

dictatrix [*dik*tayt*R*iks] *n* female dictator.

dictature [*dik*taytewr] *n* dictatorship.

diction [*dik*shon] *n* choice of words; manner of speaking, elocution; **poetic d.** use of words and phrases peculiar to poetry.

dictionary [*dik*shona*R*i] *n* lexicon, book listing the words of a language alphabetically and giving their meanings, pronunciations *etc*; alphabetical list of the words of one language with their equivalents in another; list of words used in connexion with some special subject, with explanations.

dictograph [*dikt*ogRaaf] *n* trade-name for a sound-recording instrument.

dictum (*pl* **dicta**) [*dik*tum] *n* saying, maxim, formal or authoritative pronouncement; (*leg*) expression of opinion by a judge not having legal validity.

did [*did*] *p/t* of **do** (1).

didactic [*did*aktik] *adj* intended to instruct or edify; giving unwanted instruction, pedantic ~ **didactically** *adv* ~ **didacticism** *n* ~ **didactics** *n* (*pl*) art or science of teaching.

diddle [*did*'l] *v/t* (*coll*) cheat, swindle ~ **diddler** *n*.

diddums [*did*umz] *interj* term of pity or endearment addressed to young children.

didikoi, didikye [*did*ikoi, *did*ik*I*] *n* vagrant who is not a gipsy.

didn't [*did*n't] (*abbr*) did not.

dido [*dId*O] *n* (*US coll*) prank, trick.

didymate, didymated [*did*imit, *did*imaytid] *adj* (*zool*, *bot*) in pairs, twin ~ **didymous** *adj*.

didymium [*did*imi-um] *n* a rare metal.

die (1) (*pres/part* **dying**) [*dI*] *v/i* cease to live, expire; cease, end; wither; grow weaker, fade away; suffer anguish; pine, wish greatly; **d. away** grow weaker; **d. back** (*bot*) wither from the top downwards to the stem or root; **d. down** grow less, subside; **d. hard** cling to life; remain persistently; **d. off** die one by one; **d. out** become extinct; **d. in one's boots**, **d. in harness** die while still at work; **d. on one** die while in one's care; become useless, lifeless or boring to one; **d. the death** suffer death as punishment.

die (2) (*pl* **dice**, **dies**) [*dI*, *dIs*, *dIz*] *n* (with *pl* **dice**) small cube marked with figures one to six, thrown in games of chance; **no dice** (*coll*) certainly not, quite impossible; **the d.** is cast an irrevocable step has been taken; (with *pl* **dies**) engraved metal block used in stamping; tool for cutting screw threads; mould for casting metal; (*archi*) the dado of a pedestal; enlarged ends of a baluster ~ **die** *v/t* stamp or mould with a die.

die-away [*dI*-away] *adj* languishing, affected.

dieb [*deeb*] *n* a North African jackal.

die-casting [*dI*-kaasting] *n* process of casting metal alloys in moulds under pressure; the casting so made.

diehard [*dI*haard] *n* one who resists to the last; rabid opponent of change or innovation; obstinate politician *etc* ~ **diehard** *adj* extreme; irreconcilably obstinate or conservative.

dielectric [*dI*-i*lekt*Rik] *adj* and *n* insulating, non-conductive (substance); **d. heating** heating of an insulating material by a high-frequency electric field.

diene [*dI*-een] *n* (*chem*) unsaturated hydrocarbon containing two double-bonds.

diesel [*deez*el] *n* internal-combustion engine that

210

burns oil > PDE; locomotive powered by this; **d. oil** grade of light oil for diesel engines.

diesel-electric [deezel-ilektRik] *adj* equipped with a diesel-operated electric generator.

dieselize [deezelIz] *v/t* and *i* convert to use of diesel oil; adopt diesel locomotives ∼ **dieselization** *n*.

die-sinker [dI-sinker] *n* engraver of dies.

diesis (*pl* **dieses**) [dI-isis] *n* (*print*) the double dagger sign (‡).

die-stock [dI-stok] *n* (*eng*) a hand screw-cutting tool.

diet (1) [dI-et] *n* prescribed course of food, devised for medical reasons or as a punishment; customary food ∼ **diet** *v/t* and *i* prescribe a diet; follow a diet, *esp* in order to lose weight.

diet (2) [dI-et] *n* conference for national or international business, *esp* regular meeting of the estates of a realm or confederation.

dietal [dI-ital] *adj* of a diet (2).

dietarian [dI-etairRi-an] *n* one who strictly follows a diet.

dietary [dI-etaRi] *n* prescribed course of diet; daily allowance of food ∼ **dietary** *adj*.

dietetic, dietetical [dI-etetik, dI-etetikal] *adj* pertaining to a diet (1).

dietetics [dI-etetiks] *n* (*pl*) study of food needed for health ∼ **dietetist** *n* dietician.

dietitian, dietician [dI-etishan] *n* an authority on diet.

differ [difer] *v/i* be unlike; hold opposite opinions, disagree; quarrel; **agree to d.** cease to argue though neither party is convinced.

difference [difeRens] *n* dissimilarity; disagreement; alteration; point in which things differ; (*math*) remainder left after subtracting one sum from another; dispute, quarrel; (*her*) addition to coat of arms to distinguish a younger branch from the main line of a family; **split the d.** compromise.

different [difeRent] *adj* unlike, dissimilar; various; distinct; altered; (*coll*) unusual, striking.

differentia (*pl* **differentiae**) [difeRenshi-a] *n* (*log*) distinguishing mark, characteristic.

differential (1) [difeRenshal] *n* (*math*) infinitesimal difference between two consecutive values of a variable; amount of difference between rates of pay or of charges; (*elect*) one of two coils producing opposite polarities; (*eng*) a differential gear.

differential (2) *adj* having, showing, causing, or making use of a difference; (*math*) relating to infinitesimal differences; **d. calculus** branch of mathematics dealing with variable quantities and their rates of change; **d. coefficient** (*math*) measurement of the rate of change of a function relative to its variable; **d. condenser** (*rad*) condenser using the difference in capacity between sets of fixed and moving plates; **d. equation** (*math*) equation involving differentials or differential coefficients; **d. gear** arrangement of toothed gear wheels connecting two axles so that they can rotate at different speeds; **d. motion** (*eng*) movement in which the velocity of the driven part is equal to the difference of the velocities of two parts connected to it; **d. pulley block** lifting tackle consisting of an endless chain threaded over two wheels of slightly different

diameters; **d. thermometer** thermometer with two linked bulbs, used to measure differences in temperature ∼ **differentially** *adv*.

differentiate [difeRenshi-ayt] *v/t* and *i* constitute a difference between; render unlike; recognize differences between, distinguish, discriminate; (*math*) operation of obtaining the differential coefficient; develop characteristic differences ∼ **differentiation** [difeRenshi-ayshon] *n*.

differently [difeRentli] *adv* in a different way.

differing [difeRing] *adj* disagreeing in opinion or statement.

difficult [difikult] *adj* not easy, hard to perform; obscure, involved; hard to get on with, troublesome, stubborn.

difficulty [difikulti] *n* quality of being hard to do or understand, troublesomeness; that which is hard to do or overcome; obstacle, objection; **in difficulties** in trouble, *esp* financial; **make difficulties** raise objections.

diffidence [difidens] *n* lack of self-confidence; shyness; self-effacement ∼ **diffident** *adj* ∼ **diffidently** *adv*.

diffluence [diflOO-ens] *n* readiness to become fluid; degree of fluidity ∼ **diffluent** *adj*.

diffract [difRakt] *v/t* cause to undergo diffraction; to break into pieces.

diffraction [difRakshon] *n* (*opt*) formation of patterns of light and dark bands, or coloured bands, near the edges of a beam of light when it is allowed to fall upon a screen after passing through an aperture or past the edge of an opaque obstacle; (*rad*) curvature of electromagnetic waves round obstacles; (*ac*) alteration in the direction of a soundwave; **d. grating** device used to disperse a beam of light into its constituent wavelengths to produce its spectrum > PDS ∼ **diffractive** *adj*.

diffuse [difewz] *v/t* and *i* pour in every direction, spread widely, scatter; radiate in all directions; (*phys*) mingle by diffusion ∼ **diffuse** [difews] *adj* widely or thinly spread; not localized or sharply defined; verbose, long-winded.

diffused [difewzd] *adj* spread widely; **d. lighting** illumination giving an even light distribution without glare ∼ **diffusedly** *adv* ∼ **diffusedness** *n*.

diffusely [difewsli] *adv* in a diffuse way.

diffuser [difewzer] *n* (*ac*) wedge or cone in front of an open-diaphragm loudspeaker; (*eng*) the gradually increasing cross-section at the outlet of a centrifugal pump > PDE; (*eng*) device through which air is blown to aerate sewage.

diffusible [difewzib'l] *adj* capable of being diffused ∼ **diffusibility** [difewzibiliti] *n*.

diffusion [difewzhon] *n* state of being diffused; spreading abroad, dissemination; verbosity; (*phys*) movement and intermingling of the molecules of gases; scattering or alteration of direction of light rays > PDS.

diffusive [difewsiv] *adj* capable of diffusing; being dispersed widely; verbose ∼ **diffusively** *adv*.

dig (*pres/part* **digging**, *p/t* and *p/part* **dug**) [dig] *v/t* and *i* turn over or remove earth; form (hole, tunnel *etc*) by digging; excavate; unearth, extract by digging; (*fig*) discover by careful enquiry; thrust sharply, prod; (*sl*) taunt, jeer; (*sl*) understand, grasp, be aware of the implications; enjoy, like; (*sl*) take notice of, *esp* listen carefully to;

(*sl*) work hard; (*sl*) lodge; **d. in** mix into the earth by digging; dig trenches or foxholes; establish one's position firmly; **d. into** (*coll*) work hard at; **d. out, d. up** discover, find ~ **dig** *n* act of digging; (*arch*) excavatory expedition; sharp prod, nudge; (*coll*) sarcastic remark, taunt; (*pl*) (*coll*) lodgings.

digenesis [dɪ*j*enesis] *n* (*zool*) reproduction by different processes in alternate generations, one sexual and one asexual ~ **digenetic** [dɪ*j*en*e*tik] *adj*.

digest (1) [di*j*est/dɪ*j*est] *v/t* and *i* convert food in the stomach and intestines for assimilation into the system; undergo digestion; arrange in systematic form, classify; summarize; absorb mentally, think over; (*fig*) accept, bear without resentment; (*chem*) dissolve by heat and solvents.

digest (2) [dɪ*j*est] *n* classified summary of some branch of knowledge; magazine containing condensed versions of popular books.

digestedly [di*j*estidli] *adv* methodically, regularly.

digester [di*j*ester] *n* one who compiles a digest; strong closed vessel in which substances may be softened by boiling.

digestible [di*j*estib'l] *adj* capable of being digested ~ **digestibility** [di*j*esti*bi*liti] ~ **digestibly** *adv*.

digestion [di*j*eschon] *n* breakdown and assimilation of complex foodstuffs into the system; ability to digest food thoroughly; boiling in a digester; (*sewage*) biochemical decomposition of organic matter.

digestive [dɪ*j*estiv] *adj* pertaining to digestion; helping or encouraging digestion; easily digested ~ **digestive** *n* (*med*) preparation which helps digestion; (*surg*) application to clear wounds of pus ~ **digestively** *adv*.

diggable [*dig*ab'l] *adj* capable of being dug.

digger [*dig*er] *n* person or animal that digs; gold-miner; (*sl*) an Australian or New Zealander; (*sl*) one who shares possessions communally; (*eng*) mechanical excavator; burrowing wasp.

diggings [*dig*ingz] *n* (*pl*) gold-field; (*coll*) lodgings.

dight [dɪt] *adj* (*poet*) adorned, equipped.

digit [*dij*it] *n* a single figure or numeral; finger, toe; (*astron*) twelfth part of apparent diameter of the sun or moon.

digital [*dij*ital] *adj* pertaining to the fingers, or to digits; **d. computer** calculating machine that operates by representing numbers as digits in the decimal or some other system ~ **digital** *n* finger; (*mus*) key struck by the finger.

digitalin [diji*t*aylin] *n* (*chem*) substance extracted from foxglove leaves.

digitalis [diji*t*aylis] *n* (*bot*) genus of plants including foxglove; powder of dried foxglove leaves; (*med*) drug extracted from these leaves, or made synthetically.

digitate [*dij*itayt] *adj* (*zool*) having parts arranged like fingers on a hand; (*bot*) dividing into lobes.

diglot [*dɪ*glot] *n* and *adj* (person) speaking two languages; (book) in two languages.

dignified [*dig*nifɪd] *adj* stately, majestic.

dignify [*dig*nifɪ] *v/t* confer dignity upon; ennoble; give dignity to.

dignitary [*dig*nitaRi] *n* person holding high office, *esp* in the church.

dignity [*dig*niti] *n* sense of superiority; loftiness of

manner, stateliness; excellence, worthiness; high office, rank, title; dignitary; (*astrol*) position of heightened influence of a planet.

digraph [*dɪ*gRaf] *n* group of two letters expressing a single sound.

digress [dɪgRes] *v/i* turn aside from one's path; (*fig*) deviate from the main subject.

digression [dɪgReshon] *n* act of digressing; passage which is not strictly relevant ~ **digressional** *adj* ~ **digressive** *adj*.

digs [*dig*z] *n* (*pl*) (*coll*) lodgings.

dihedral [dɪ*heed*Ral] *adj* (*math*) having two plane faces; formed by two intersecting planes; **d. angle** angle between two planes; angle of tilt of aircraft wings.

dik-dik [*dik*dik] *n* type of small African antelope.

dike, dyke (1) [*dɪk*] *n* channel dug to contain water, ditch; high bank or causeway to prevent flooding; barrier; (*mining*) fault in coal-seam; (*geol*) mass of igneous rock found in fissures of rock strata; (*sl*) lavatory ~ **dike** *v/t* make dikes; enclose or protect with dikes ~ **diking** *n* ~ **diker** *n*.

dike, dyke (2) [*dɪk*] *n* (*sl*, *pej*) lesbian.

dike-reeve [*dɪk*-Reev] *n* officer in charge of drains, sluices, and sea-banks in the fens.

diktat [*dik*tat] *n* (*Germ*) dictatorial decree.

dilapidate [di*lap*idayt] *v/i* and *t* fall, or allow to fall, into ruin and disrepair; spoil by neglect; squander ~ **dilapidated** *adj* fallen into disrepair; untidy, shabby, neglected.

dilapidation [dilapi*day*shon] *n* disrepair; process of becoming or causing to become dilapidated; (*leg*) damage done to premises during period of tenancy; sum charged against tenant to make good such damage; wearing away of rocks by natural causes; debris resulting from this process ~ **dilapidator** *n*.

dilatable [dɪ*lay*tab'l] *adj* capable of expansion ~ **dilatability** [dɪlayta*bi*liti] *n*.

dilatancy [dɪ*lay*tansi] *n* property of expanding.

dilatant [dɪ*lay*tant] *adj* expanding ~ **dilatant** *n* substance capable of expansion; (*surg*) instrument to widen an opening.

dilatation [dɪlata*y*shon] *n* action of dilating; condition of being dilated; expansion; diffuse treatment in speech or writing ~ **dilatative** *adj*.

dilate [dɪ*lay*t] *v/t* and *i* make larger, expand, widen; become larger, swell; write or speak at great length ~ **dilated** *adj* expanded and flattened.

dilation [dɪ*lay*shon] *n* (*phys*) dilatation; change in volume ~ **dilative** *adj*.

dilatometer [dɪlato*m*iter] *n* apparatus for measuring volume changes of substances.

dilator [dɪ*lay*ter] *n* person or thing that dilates; (*surg*) instrument to widen an opening or canal; (*anat*) muscle that dilates or expands a structure.

dilatory [*dil*ateRi] *adj* causing delay; tardy, slow ~ **dilatorily** *adv* ~ **dilatoriness** *n*.

dildo [*dild*O] *n* artificial penis.

dilemma [dɪ*lem*a/di*lem*a] *n* situation offering only two alternative and mutually exclusive courses of action, both presenting difficulties; quandary, perplexing situation; (*log*) argument forcing a choice of two equally unfavourable alternatives; **on the horns of a d.** faced with such a choice.

dilettante (*pl* **dilettanti**) [dili*tanti*] *n* one who has a superficial or casual interest in the fine arts, dabbler ~ **dilettantish** *adj* ~ **dilettantism** *n*.

diligence (1) [*dili*jens] *n* (*hist*) large public stage-coach.

diligence (2) *n* steady effort, perseverance.

diligent [*dili*jent] *adj* industrious; painstaking ~ **diligently** *adv*.

dill [*dil*] *n* umbelliferous plant with oily aromatic seeds; seeds of this plant; **d. pickle** cucumber pickle flavoured with dill; **d. water** medicinal preparation made from dill.

dilly-dally [*dili*-dali] *v/i* waste time in vacillation; act with indecision; dawdle.

diluent [*dilew*-ent] *n* substance used for thinning out a fluid.

dilute [di*lewt*] *v/t* weaken, thin down a fluid by adding other fluid; water down; use unskilled labour for work usually done by skilled workmen; (*fig*) lessen the effect of ~ **dilute** *adj* diluted.

dilutee [dilew*tee*] *n* unskilled worker introduced into a skilled occupation.

diluter [di*lewter*] *n* that which dilutes.

dilution [di*lewshon*] *n* action of diluting; thing in dilute state.

diluvial [di*lOOvi*-al] *adj* pertaining to a deluge, *esp* the Flood in Genesis; caused by a flood; **d. theory** (*geol*) that which explained certain geological phenomena as due to a general deluge; pertaining to the drift-formation or Glacial Drift ~ **diluvialist** *n* believer in the diluvial theory ~ **diluvian** *adj*.

diluvium [di*lOOvi*-um] *n* (*geol*) deposit formed by a flood or glacier.

dim [*dim*] *adj* fairly dark; shadowy, indistinct; tarnished; not clearly seen or heard; not seeing clearly; (*coll*) stupid; (*coll*) colourless, undistinguished (of persons) ~ **dim** (*pres/part* **dimming**, *p/t* and *p/part* **dimmed**) *v/t* and *i* make dim; become dim.

dime [*dim*] *n* (*US*) silver coin worth ten cents; **d. novel** cheap sensational novel.

dimension [di*menshon*] *n* measurement in length, breadth, or thickness; size, extent; scope, importance; aspect; (*algebra*) number of factors in a term; **fourth d.** hypothetical fourth form of measurement; time considered in relation to space > PDS; (*coll*) mysterious region or state beyond space and time ~ **dimensional** *adj*.

dimer [*dimer*] *n* substance composed of molecules each of which consists of two molecules of a monomer.

dimerous [*dimeRus*] *adj* consisting of two parts.

dimidiate [di*midi*-it] *adj* divided into halves; (*bot*, *biol*) having only one half fully developed, lopsided ~ **dimidiate** [di*midi*-ayt] *v/t* divide into halves; reduce by half ~ **dimidiation** [dimidi-*ayshon*] *n*.

diminish [di*minish*] *v/t* and *i* make smaller; become smaller; (*mus*) reduce by a semitone > PDM ~ **diminishable** *adj* ~ **diminished** *adj*.

diminuendo [diminew-*endO*] *n* (*mus*) gradual decrease of loudness; passage played thus; sign (>) indicating this > PDM.

diminution [dimi*newshon*] *n* act of diminishing, state of being diminished, lessening; (*mus*) proportionate decrease of the time values of the notes of a theme.

diminutive [di*minewtiv*] *adj* exceedingly small; (*gramm*) expressing diminution or smallness ~ **diminutive** *n* (*gramm*) word formed from another by the use of a suffix expressing smallness ~ **diminutively** [di*minewtivli*] *adv* ~ **diminutiveness** *n*.

dimissory [di*miseRi*/di*miseRi*] *adj* giving leave to depart; (*eccles*) giving leave to move to another diocese.

dimity [*dimiti*] *n* cotton fabric with raised pattern.

dimly [*dimli*] *adv* in a dim manner, obscurely.

dimmer [*dimer*] *n* device to dim stage lights or car headlamps.

dimness [*dimnes*] *n* state of being dim.

dimorphic [di*maurfik*] *adj* existing in two forms; (*chem*) capable of crystallizing in two different forms; (*zool*) existing in two distinct types within one species; showing marked differences between male and female ~ **dimorphism** *n* existence of a substance in two different crystalline forms ~ **dimorphous** *adj*.

dimple [*dimp'l*] *n* small natural hollow in the flesh; shallow hollow in earth or water ~ **dimple** *v/t* and *i* make dimples in; break into dimples ~ **dimpled** *adj* ~ **dimply** *adj*.

dimwit [*dimwit*] *n* (*sl*) fool, imbecile ~ **dimwitted** [dim*witid*] *adj*.

din [*din*] *n* loud confused noise, continuous clamour ~ **din** (*pres/part* **dinning**, *p/t* and *p/part* **dinned**) *v/i* and *t* make a din; repeat persistently or loudly.

dinar [dee*naar*] *n* Eastern gold coin; name of unit of currency in certain Arab countries and in Yugoslavia.

dine [*din*] *v/i* and *t* eat dinner; give a dinner to, entertain at dinner; (*of a room*) accommodate for dinner; **d. out** dine away from home; (*sl*) go without dinner; **d. out on** use (an anecdote *etc*) to entertain one's fellow-guests.

diner [*diner*] *n* one who dines; railway dining-car.

diner-out [*diner*-owt] *n* person who frequently goes to dinner-parties.

ding [*ding*] *v/i* and *t* make a ringing sound; repeat constantly ~ **ding** *n* sound of a bell.

ding-dong [*ding*-dong] *n* sound of bells continually ringing, or of two bells ringing alternately; lively argument ~ **ding-dong** *adj* equally balanced; each side having the advantage in turn; well-fought.

dinge [*dinj*] *v/t* (*coll*) knock a dent in.

dinghy [*ding*-gi] *n* small ship's boat; small pleasure boat; inflatable rubber boat.

dinginess [*dinj*iness] *n* state of being dingy.

dinging [*dinging*] *n* (*bui*) single coat of rough plaster on walls.

dingle [*ding'l*] *n* deep dell, narrow wooded valley.

dingle-dangle [*ding'l*-dang'l] *adj* and *adv* hanging loosely.

dingo [*ding-gO*] *n* Australian wild dog.

dingy [*dinji*] *adj* dull-looking, shabby; disreputable.

dining-car [*dining*-kaar] *n* railway carriage equipped to serve meals to passengers.

dining-hall [*dining*-hawl] *n* large room where dinner and other meals are eaten.

dining-room [*dining*-ROOm] *n* room in which dinner and other meals are eaten.

dining-table–dipper

dining-table [*dī*ning-tayb'l] *n* table on which meals are served.

dinkum [*dink*um] *adj* (*Aust sl*) genuine, honest.

dinky [*dinki*] *adj* (*coll*) neat, dainty.

dinner [*diner*] *n* chief meal of the day; formal banquet; **d. dress** formal long-skirted dress; **d. jacket** black dress coat without tails; **d. mat** tablemat; **d. time** usual time for dining; **d. wagon** wheel trolley for collecting plates *etc* used at dinner; sideboard with two tiers.

dinosaur [*dī*nosawr] *n* huge extinct reptile of the Mesozoic epoch ~ **dinosaurian** [dī*no*sawri-an] *adj*.

dinothere, dinotherium [*dī*notheer, dī*no*theeri-um] *n* huge extinct elephant-like mammal.

dint [*dint*] *n* dent, impression on a hard surface; **by d. of** by force of ~ **dint** *v/t* make dints in, dent; drive in with force.

diocesan [dī-*osi*zan] *adj* pertaining to a diocese ~ **diocesan** *n* a bishop.

diocese (*pl* **diocese**) [*dī*-osis, *pl* dī-oseez] *n* area under a bishop's jurisdiction.

diode [*dī*-Od] *n* thermionic valve containing two electrodes, anode and cathode.

diodone [*dī*-odOn] *n* (*med*) complex preparation containing iodine, used for contrast radiography.

dioecious [dī-*ee*shus] *adj* (*bot*) having male and female flowers on separate plants; (*zool*) unisexual, producing male and female gametes in separate animals.

Dionysiac, Dionysian [dī-*oni*zi-ak, dī-*oni*zi-an] *adj* pertaining to the Greek wine-god Dionysus or to his worship; orgiastic.

diopside [dī-*ops*Id] *n* (*min*) calcium magnesium silicate, a type of pyroxene.

diopsis [dī-*ops*is] *n* (*zool*) insect whose eyes grow on stalks.

dioptase [dī-*op*tays] *n* an emerald green silicate of copper.

diopter [dī-*op*ter] *n* ancient form of theodolite; index arm of a graduated circle; (*opt*) a dioptre ~ **dioptral** *adj*.

dioptre [dī-*op*ter] *n* (*opt*) unit of power of a lens.

dioptric [dī-*opt*Rik] *n* unit of power of a lens, dioptre; (*pl*) branch of optics which deals with the refraction of light ~ **dioptrical** *adj* pertaining to refraction, refractive; dioptral; helping the sight by the use of refracting lenses.

diorama [dī-*o*Raama] *n* views of scenery painted on translucent cloth, viewed through an opening, and animated by lighting effects; building where they are exhibited ~ **dioramic** [dī-*o*Ramik] *adj*.

diorite [*dī*-oRIt] *n* a coarse-grained igneous rock.

dioxide [dī-*oks*Id] *n* (*chem*) oxide formed by two equivalents of oxygen and one of metal.

dip (*pres/part* **dipping**, *p/t* and *p/part* **dipped**) [*dip*] *v/t* and *i* plunge rapidly into liquid and withdraw immediately; move rapidly down and up again; sink or drop suddenly; clean, dye, coat, or make by plunging into liquid; slope down; (*geol*) slope down at an angle to the horizontal; **d. into** study casually and superficially; read random passages of; **d. into one's pockets** spend much money ~ **dip** *n* action of dipping or being dipped; short, rapid plunge; liquid into which something is dipped for cleaning, dyeing *etc*; savoury dressing into which biscuits are dipped; downward slope; shallow hollow; candle made by dipping; (*cricket*) a hit at the bowling; (*coll*) short swim; (*geol*) angle of maximum slope of beds of rock measured from the horizontal; (*magn*) inclination of magnetic needle from the horizontal; (*sur*) apparent depression of the horizon when seen from above sea-level; **lucky d. tub** containing hidden prizes of varying worth, to be drawn by dipping one's hand in the tub.

dipartite [dī*paart*It] *adj* divided into various parts.

diphase [*dī*fayz] *adj* (*elect*) having two alternating currents whose phases differ by 90 electric degrees ~ **diphasic** [dī*fay*zik] *adj* (*zool*) periodically changing two states or appearances.

diphtheria [dif*thee*Ri-a] *n* grave infectious disease of the membranes of the throat and air-passages ~ **diphtherial** [dif*thee*Ri-al] *adj*.

diphthong [*dif*thong] *n* combination of two vowel sounds pronounced in one syllable; (*print*) the characters æ, œ, used for single sounds ~ **diphthongal** [dif*thong*-gal] *adj*.

diphthongization [difthong-gīz*ay*shon] *n* changing of a simple vowel into a diphthong ~ **diphthongize** *v/t* and *i*.

diplegia [dī*plee*ji-a] *n* (*med*) paralysis of similar parts on both sides of the body.

diplodocus [dī*plod*okus] *n* type of extinct herbivorous dinosaur.

diplogen [*dip*lojen] *n* form of hydrogen twice as heavy as normal form; deuterium.

diploid [*dip*loid] *n* and *adj* (*biol*) (cell) having its chromosomes in pairs > PDB.

diploma [dip*lO*ma] *n* state paper; charter; certificate granting some honour or privilege; educational certificate attesting the recipient's proficiency.

diplomacy [dip*lO*masi] *n* management of international relations; tactful skill in dealing with other people.

diplomat [*dip*lomat] *n* one engaged in international diplomacy; one skilful in dealing with others, tactful person.

diplomatic [diplO*mat*ik] *adj* pertaining to international diplomacy; skilful and tactful in handling people; relating to the study of ancient texts; presenting an exact transliteration; **d. corps** body of diplomats accredited to a state; **d. service** service at embassies abroad; **d. text** exact, unemended copy ~ **diplomatically** *adv*.

diplomatics [diplo*ma*tiks] *n* (*pl*) science of interpreting ancient documents and establishing their authenticity, date *etc*.

diplomatist [dip*lO*matist] *n* diplomat.

dip-needle [*dip*-need'l] *n* (*magn*) a magnetic needle with a horizontal pivot which allows the needle to swing only in a vertical plane; inclinometer > PDE.

dipnoan [*dip*nO-an] *n* and *adj* (fish) having both gills and lungs ~ **dipnoi** [dip*nO*-ee] *n* (*pl*) group of such fish.

dipolar [dī*pOl*ar] *adj* having two magnetic poles ~ **dipolarize** [dī*pO*laRIz] *v/t* magnetize.

dipole [*dī*pOl] *n* two equal point electric charges or magnetic poles of opposite sign, separated by a small distance > PDS; type of radio aerial.

dipper [*dip*er] *n* person who dips; implement for dipping, *esp* a ladle; bird which dips or dives; (*coll*) one who believes in baptism by immersion;

apparatus for raising or lowering the headlamp beam of a motor vehicle: (*eng*) bucket of a mechanical shovel; switchback at a fair; (*coll*) pickpocket.

dipping-needle [*dip*ing-need'l] *n* a dip-needle.

dippy [*dipi*] *adj* (*sl*) insane, crazy.

dipso [*dip*sO] *n* and *adj* (*coll abbr*) dipsomaniac.

dipsomania [dips*omayni*-a] *n* (*med*) morbid and insatiable craving for alcohol ~ **dipsomaniac** *n*.

dipstick [*dip*stik] *n* measuring rod inserted in a tank or sump to determine the depth of oil.

dipswitch [*dip*swich] *n* switch for dipping a car's headlights.

diptera [*dip*teRa] *n* (*pl*) (*ent*) order of two-winged insects ~ **dipteran** *adj*.

dipteral [*dip*teRal] *adj* (*archi*) having a double peristyle; (*bot*, *ent*) two-winged.

dipterous [*dip*teRus] *adj* (*ent*) having two wings; (*bot*) having two wing-like appendages.

diptych [*dip*tik] *n* painting or pair of paintings on two hinged panels.

dipus [*dI*pus] *n* (*zool*) the jerboa.

dire [dIr] *adj* terrible, disastrous.

direct [di*Rekt*/dI*Rekt*] *adj* straight, undeviating, uninterrupted; frank, unhesitating, plain; immediate; complete, absolute; (*geneal*) in uninterrupted line of descent; without intermediary; (*astron*) onward, from west to east; (*gramm*) in a speaker's exact words; (*mus*) with both hands moving in the same direction on the keyboard; (*mus*) not inverted; **d. action** use of strikes, demonstrations *etc* in industrial disputes; **d. current** (*elect*) one that flows in one direction only; **d. heating,** the heating of a room by a heat source within it; **d. hit** the dropping of a bomb on its exact target; **d. labour** employment of building labour by a client or his agent directly, without the mediation of a contractor; **d. line** descent from father to son; **d. method** the teaching of a foreign language by continual use of it, avoiding translation or explanation in the mother-tongue; **d. object** (*gramm*) word indicating that which receives the action of a transitive verb; **d. tax** tax levied on income or revenue ~ **direct** *adv* straight, not going round about ~ **direct** *v/t* and *i* give orders or directions; guide the movements of, control, manage, supervise; turn or point towards, focus, aim; tell or show (someone) the way; intend for, address to; address (letters *etc*); plan and supervise the performance of a play or film.

direction [di*Rek*shon/dI*Rek*shon] *n* act of directing; guiding, management; command; (*pl*) instructions for using, preparing *etc*; information on what to do; address on a letter *etc*; course taken by moving body; point towards which or from which movement goes; way something points, is facing; line of development; body of directors; work of a theatrical director; **in the d. of** towards; **d. of labour** compulsory transfer of workers from one district or occupation to another; **d. finder** (*rad*) instrument for finding the direction of incoming radio signals.

directional [di*Rek*shonal] *adj* relating to direction; (*rad*) giving the direction from which a radio message comes; **d. aerial** aerial which transmits or receives radio waves more clearly from one direction than from others ~ **directional** *n* (*rad*)

a signal giving the direction from which the message comes.

directive [di*Rek*tiv/dI*Rek*tiv] *adj* giving orders; indicating direction ~ **directive** *n* general instruction or order issued to subordinates.

directly [di*Rek*tli] *adv* immediately, at once; shortly, very soon; without an intervening medium; completely, precisely ~ **directly** *conj* as soon as.

directness [di*Rek*tnes/dI*Rek*tnes] *n* quality or state of being direct; frankness, bluntness of speech.

directoire [deeRektwaar] *adj* in the style of the period of the French Directory (1795–9).

director [di*Rek*ter/dI*Rek*ter] *n* one who directs; manager, member of board which manages a company; spiritual adviser; person who supervises the production of a play or film; (*mech*) part of a machine or instrument which guides the motion.

directorate [di*Rek*teRayt/dI*Rek*teRayt] *n* board of directors; the office of director; official order or instruction.

directorial [diRekt*awRi*-al/dIRekt*awRi*-al] *adj* of a director or directorate; containing directions.

directorship [di*Rek*tership/dI*Rek*tership] *n* the office of a company director.

directory [di*Rek*teRi] *n* book of directions; book listing the inhabitants of a locality or members of a profession, and their addresses; list of telephone subscribers and their numbers; list of streets in a locality; (*eccles*) book of directions for worship; (*hist*) governing body of France 1795–9 ~ **directory** *adj* instructing, guiding.

directress [di*Rek*tRes/dI*Rek*tRes] *n* female director.

directrix [di*Rek*tRiks/dI*Rek*tRiks] *n* female director; (*geom*) fixed line that guides the drawing of a curve.

direful [*dIr*fool] *adj* terrible, disastrous.

direly [*dIr*li] *adv* disastrously.

direness [*dIr*nis] *n* quality of being dire.

dirge [durj] *n* a lament for the dead, funeral hymn; mournful tune.

dirigible [di*Ri*jib'l] *n* and *adj* (balloon or airship) capable of being steered.

diriment [*dI*Riment] *adj* (*leg*) rendering null and void; **d. impediment** one that nullifies a marriage from the beginning.

dirk [durk] *n* short dagger, *esp* as used by Highlanders ~ **dirk** *v/t* stab with a dirk.

dirndl [*dur*nd'l] *n* (*Ger*) full skirt; full-skirted dress with tight bodice.

dirt [durt] *n* filth, mud, earth, dust; anything worthless, rubbish; obscenity, pornography; (*coll*) malicious gossip; **d. cheap** ridiculously cheap; **do d. to** (*sl*) cheat, play a mean trick on; **eat d.** accept an insult; **throw d. at** abuse; talk scandal about; **yellow d.** (*sl*) gold; **d. bed** (*geol*) layer of ancient vegetable mould.

dirtily [*dur*tili] *adv* in a dirty manner.

dirtiness [*dur*tinis] *n* state of being dirty.

dirt-track [*durt*-tRak] *n* track of cinders and brick-dust for motor-cycle and flat racing.

dirty [*dur*ti] *adj* soiled, filthy; obscene, indecent; mean, despicable; dingy, dull; (*coll*) lustful, lecherous; (*of weather*) wet and stormy; **d. look** (*coll*) angry or threatening look; **d. money** money earned by base or immoral means; bonus to labourers working in difficult or unusual conditions; **do the d. on** (*coll*) play an unfair trick on ~ **dirty** *v/t* and *i* make or become dirty; soil; tarnish.

dis- *pref* expressing before a verb reversal of the action of the simple verb; before a noun separation, dividing; before an adjective negation.

disability [disa*bili*ti] *n* state of being disabled; something that disables; loss or impairment of a bodily function.

disable [dis*ayb*'l] *v/t* make unfit, incapacitate; injure, maim; (*leg*) make legally incapable ~ **disabled** *adj* crippled ~ **disablement** *n* a physical disability.

disabuse [disa*bewz*] *v/t* reveal the truth to, undeceive.

disaccord [disa*kawrd*] *n* lack of harmony; disagreement ~ **disaccord** *v/i* disagree.

disaccredit [disak*Redit*] *v/t* cancel the credentials of; cause to be no longer authorized.

disadvantage [disadv*aanti*j] *n* lack of advantage, unfavourable situation; loss, injury ~ **disadvantage** *v/t*; deprive of normal advantages; act to the detriment of; treat unfavourably ~ **disadvantageous** [disadvan*tay*jus] *adj*.

disaffect [disa*fekt*] *v/t* alienate the loyalty or affection of, raise discontent in ~ **disaffected** *adj* discontented, disloyal (to authority) ~ **disaffectedness** *n* ~ **disaffection** *n*.

disafforest, disforest [disa*fo*Rist, dis*fo*Rist] *v/t* to clear of trees; to free from operation of forest laws and reduce to status of ordinary land.

disagree [disag*Ree*] *v/i* be different; differ in opinion; dissent; quarrel; **d. with** not to suit, upset, make ill.

disagreeable [disag*Ree*-ab'l] *adj* unpleasant, distasteful; bad-tempered ~ **disagreeableness** *n* ~ **disagreeably** *adv*.

disagreement [disag*Ree*ment] *n* refusal to agree; difference of opinion; dispute, quarrel; discrepancy.

disallow [disa*low*] *v/t* refuse to allow; prohibit; refuse to admit (into the mind); reject as illegal ~ **disallowance** *n* rejection.

disappear [disa*peer*] *v/i* go out of sight, vanish; pass from existence; pass out of use ~ **disappearance** *n*.

disappoint [disa*point*] *v/t* fail to come up to expectations of; fail to fulfil promise to; thwart, foil ~ **disappointed** *adj* with one's hopes or expectations not realized; balked in one's desires ~ **disappointment** *n* state or feeling of being disappointed; person or thing that disappoints.

disapprobation [disap*RObay*shon] *n* disapproval ~ **disapprobative** [disap*RO*baytiv] *adj* ~ **disapprobatory** [disap*RO*baytoRi] *adj*.

disapproval [disap*ROO*val] *n* unfavourable opinion, refusal to approve, condemnation.

disapprove [disap*ROO*v] *v/t* and *i* have unfavourable opinion (of); refuse to approve, condemn ~ **disapprovingly** *adv* showing disapproval.

disarm [dis*aarm*] *v/t* and *i* deprive of weapons or of defence; render harmless; (*fig*) conciliate, allay the suspicions of; lay down arms; reduce or abandon armaments.

disarmament [dis*aarm*ament] *n* reduction and limitation of a nation's armed forces and military equipment; state of being disarmed.

disarmer [dis*aarm*er] *n* one who advocates disarmament; **nuclear d.** one who wishes his own country to renounce the making and use of nuclear weapons.

disarming [dis*aarm*ing] *adj* removing anger or suspicion, mollifying ~ **disarmingly** *adv*.

disarrange [disa*Raynj*] *v/t* put into disorder, upset ~ **disarrangement** *n* disorder, confusion.

disarray [disa*Ray*] *v/t* put to confusion, throw into disorder; disrobe, undress ~ **disarray** *n* disorder, confusion.

disarticulation [disaartikew*lay*shon] *n* (*surg*) amputation of a bone through a joint.

disassimilate [disasi*mi*layt] *v/t* (*physiol*) transform by catabolism ~ **disassimilation** [disasimi*lay*shon] *n*.

disassociate [disas*Oshi*-ayt] *v/t* put an end to or repudiate a connexion of any kind, dissociate ~ **disassociation** [disasOshi-*ay*shon] *n*.

disaster [diz*aas*ter] *n* calamity, great misfortune ~ **disastrous** *adj* ~ **disastrously** *adv*.

disavow [disa*vow*] *v/t* refuse to acknowledge, repudiate, disclaim ~ **disavowal** *n* repudiation.

disband [dis*band*] *v/t* and *i* break up (an organized group); scatter, disperse; release from military service; (*mil*) break ranks ~ **disbandment** *n*.

disbar [*pres*/*part* **disbarring**, *p/t* and *p/part* **disbarred**] [dis*baar*] *v/t* (*leg*) expel (a barrister) from the Bar ~ **disbarment** *n*.

disbelief [disbi*leef*] *n* refusal to believe; belief that a statement is false; lack of belief ~ **disbelieve** *v/t* and *i* ~ **disbeliever** *n*.

disbud [dis*bud*] *v/t* remove buds from.

disburden [dis*burd*en] *v/t* relieve of a burden; get rid of, unload.

disburse [dis*burs*] *v/t* and *i* pay out (money).

disc, disk [disk] *n* round, flat, thin object; circular surface; apparent shape of sun or full moon; gramophone or phonograph record; (*anat, zool*) any flattened circular structure, *esp* of fibrocartilage between vertebrae; (*bot*) centre of composite flowers; **d. coupling** method of coupling rods by discs on their adjoining rods; **d. harrow** harrow with revolving sharp discs; **d. jockey** compère of a radio programme of popular recorded music; **slipped d.** displacement of a vertebral cartilage; **d. wheel** solid metal wheel without spokes.

discal [*disk*al] *adj* like, or pertaining to, a disc.

discalced [dis*kalst*] *adj* barefooted.

discard [dis*kaard*] *v/t* and *i* throw away; reject from a hand at cards; throw away a card which is not a trump when unable to follow suit; (*of garment*) take off, cease to wear; reject, cast off ~ **discard** *n* act of discarding; card thrown out from the hand; something discarded, waste.

discern [dis*urn*] *v/t* distinguish, see clearly (with senses or in mind) ~ **discernible** *adj* that can be clearly seen ~ **discernibly** *adv*.

discerning [dis*urn*ing] *adj* of keen discrimination; having insight, shrewd ~ **discerningly** *adv*.

discernment [dis*urn*ment] *n* power to perceive clearly, shrewdness.

discharge [dis*chaarj*] *v/t* and *i* relieve of, release from; unload; dismiss from office or service; release from custody; acquit; release from obligations; fire, shoot; send forth, emit; pay;

perform (duties); (*elect*) rid battery *etc* of electric charge; (*leg*) relieve of liabilities; (*archi*) relieve pressure by distribution of weight; remove dye from cloth ~ **discharge** [*dis*chaarj/*dis*chaarj] *n* act of discharging; state of being discharged; order or certificate of release or dismissal; acquittal, release; exemption; that which is emitted; (*med*) pus from a sore; (*eng*) rate of flow; (*elect*) neutralization or loss of electric charge.

disciple [dis*ip*'l] *n* follower, pupil, *esp* one of the original followers of Jesus Christ; (*pl*) an American branch of the Baptists ~ **discipleship** *n*.

disciplinable [*dis*iplinab'l] *adj* that can or should be subjected to discipline.

disciplinal [disipl*i*nal] *adj* relating to discipline.

disciplinarian [disiplin*ai*Ri-an] *n* one who enforces strict discipline ~ **disciplinarian** *adj* relating to discipline.

disciplinary [*dis*iplinaRi] *adj* pertaining to or involving discipline; corrective.

discipline [*dis*iplin] *n* maintenance of order and obedience among pupils, subordinates *etc*; acceptance of authority; system of training in obedience, orderliness, efficiency; branch of knowledge systematically studied; corrective punishment; (*eccles*) system of rules and punishments; penance; scourge used in penances ~ **discipline** *v/t* enforce discipline, control, train.

discipular [dis*ip*ewlar] *adj* relating to a disciple.

disclaim [dis*klaym*] *v/t* disown, repudiate, refuse to acknowledge; give up; (*leg*) renounce claim to.

disclaimer [dis*klaym*er] *n* disavowal of claims; denial; (*leg*) repudiation or renunciation of claim, right, or title.

disclose [dis*klOz*] *v/t* reveal, show; uncover; make known ~ **disclosure** [dis*klOz*her] *n*.

discobolus [dis*kob*olus] *n* a discus-thrower.

discography [dis*kog*Rafi] *n* list of recordings made by a musical performer, or issued by a musical composer.

discoid, discoidal [*dis*koid, dis*koi*dal] *adj* flat and circular.

discoloration, discolouration [diskule*Ray*shon] *n* deprivation or loss of colour; discoloured area.

discolour [dis*kul*er] *v/t* and *i* change or spoil the colour of, stain; lose colour, be tarnished ~ **discoloured** *adj* ~ **discolourment** *n*.

discolouration see **discoloration**.

discomfit [dis*kum*fit] *v/t* defeat in battle; throw into confusion; disconcert ~ **discomfiture** [dis*kum*ficher] *n*.

discomfort [dis*kum*fert] *n* lack of comfort, uneasiness; distress, inconvenience, hardship; anything causing lack of comfort ~ **discomfort** *v/t* cause discomfort to.

discommode [disko*mOd*] *v/t* inconvenience, disturb, annoy.

discommodity [disko*mod*iti] *n* inconvenience; (*ecom*) anything without utility.

discompose [diskom*pOz*] *v/t* disturb the calmness of, ruffle ~ **discomposure** [diskom*pO*zher] *n* agitation, embarrassment.

disconcert [diskon*surt*] *v/t* disturb self-possession of; embarrass, abash; throw into confusion, frustrate ~ **disconcertingly** *adv*.

disconnect [disko*nekt*] *v/t* sever connexion between, separate ~ **disconnected** *adj* separated;

not properly coordinated, disjointed, incoherent ~ **disconnectedly** *adv* ~ **disconnexion, disconnection** *n*.

disconsolate [diskon*sol*it] *adj* inconsolable, wretched, unhappy ~ **disconsolately** *adv*.

discontent [diskon*tent*] *n* dissatisfaction ~ **discontent** *adj* dissatisfied ~ **discontent** *v/t* fail to satisfy, make dissatisfied ~ **discontented** *adj* ~ **discontentedly** *adv* ~ **discontentment** *n*.

discontiguous [diskon*tig*ew-us] *adj* not touching.

discontinuance [diskon*tine*wans] *n* a ceasing or being stopped; interruption.

discontinue [diskon*tine*w] *v/t* and *i* put an end to, break off, give up; cease, come to an end; interrupt ~ **discontinuation** [diskontineway-shon] *n*.

discontinuity [diskontine*w*-iti] *n* lack of continuity, broken sequence; gap, interruption.

discontinuous [diskon*tine*w-us] *adj* intermittent, without continuity.

discophile [*disk*Ofil] *n* and *adj* (person) who collects gramophone records.

discord [*dis*kawrd] *n* lack of harmony; disagreement, dissension, conflict; harsh, confused noise; (*mus*) combination of dissonant notes > PDM.

discordance, discordancy [dis*kawr*dans, dis*kawr*dansi] *n* disagreement, cause of contention; dissonance, harshness of sound; clash ~ **discordant** *adj*.

discotheque [*disk*Otek] *n* place where young people dance to recorded music or to pop groups.

discount [*dis*kownt] *n* sum deducted from a debt or price if payment is made promptly or in cash, or as a special concession; interest deducted from bill of exchange when bought before it is due; rate of interest charged when discounting a bill, note *etc*; **at a d.** below face value; of little value or importance ~ **discount** [dis*kownt*] *v/t* pay or receive in advance the value of (a bill, note, *etc*), making a deduction for interest; deduct from, reduce the value of; make allowance for exaggeration or prejudice; take something into consideration beforehand; set aside, disregard ~ **discountable** *adj*.

discount-broker [*dis*kownt-bROker] *n* one who cashes bills of exchange or lends money at a discount on securities.

discourage [dis*ku*Rij] *v/t* deprive of courage, dishearten; disapprove of, advise against; try to prevent ~ **discouragement** *n* act of discouraging; state of being discouraged; depression, loss of hope ~ **discouraging** *adj*.

discourse [*dis*kawrs] *n* formal speech, address, sermon; written treatise; conversation ~ **discourse** [dis*kawrs*] *v/t* and *i* speak or write at length and learnedly; talk, converse.

discourteous [dis*kurt*i-us] *adj* lacking politeness, rude, ill-mannered ~ **discourteously** *adv* ~ **discourteousness** *n*.

discourtesy [dis*kurt*esi] *n* lack of courtesy, incivility; a discourteous act.

discover [dis*kuv*er] *v/t* find out for the first time; learn the existence of; make famous, publicize; make fashionable; (*ar*) reveal, disclose ~ **discoverable** *adj* capable of being discovered ~ **discoverer** *n* one who makes a discovery.

discovery [dis*kuv*eRi] *n* act of discovering; thing discovered; (*leg*) compulsory disclosure by party to an action of facts or documents on which he relies.

discredit [dis*kRed*it] *n* loss of reputation, dishonour, loss of standing; that which causes dishonour *etc*; disbelief, doubt ∼ **discredit** *v/t* damage the reputation of, cast a slur on; disbelieve, doubt strongly ∼ **discreditable** *adj* shameful, unworthy; disgraceful.

discreet [dis*kReet*] *adj* prudent, circumspect, cautious in speech ∼ **discreetly** *adv*.

discrepance, discrepancy [dis*kRep*ans, dis*kRep*ansi] *n* lack of agreement, inconsistency, difference; that which is inconsistent or causes inconsistency ∼ **discrepant** *adj* not agreeing, inconsistent.

discrete [dis*kReet*] *adj* separate, discontinuous; (*med, bot*) remaining separate, not running together ∼ **discreteness** *n*.

discretion [dis*kResh*on] *n* caution in word and deed, prudence, good judgement; freedom or authority to decide and choose; **at the d. of** in accordance with the judgement of; **surrender at d.** surrender unconditionally; **years of d.** age at which a person is thought capable of making his own decisions ∼ **discretional** *adj*.

discretionary [dis*kResh*oneRi] *adj* to be used as one thinks best; not earmarked, not restricted.

discretive [dis*kReet*iv] *adj* expressing a difference or distinction.

discriminate [dis*kRim*inayt] *v/t* and *i* make a difference, differentiate; observe a difference, distinguish; treat differently, show unfair preference for or hostility against ∼ **discriminate** [dis*kRim*init] *adj* showing or marked by discrimination ∼ **discriminately** *adv*.

discriminating [dis*kRim*inayting] *adj* discerning, able to perceive fine distinctions, perceptive; (*of tariff, duty*) varying in amount.

discrimination [dis*kRim*in*ay*shon] *n* perception of difference; ability to perceive slight differences; unfair difference in legal, social, or economic treatment of persons of a particular race, religion, social group *etc*; subtle accuracy of moral or aesthetic judgement.

discriminatory [dis*kRim*inateRi] *adj* showing discrimination, *esp* unfairly.

disculpate [dis*kul*payt] *v/t* free from blame.

discursive [dis*kur*siv] *n* dealing with a wide range of subjects and rambling from one topic to another ∼ **discursiveness** *n* ∼ **discursory** *adj*.

discursus [dis*kur*sus] *n* reasoned discussion or exposition.

discus [*dis*kus] *n* heavy disk, thrown in contests of strength and skill.

discuss [dis*kus*] *v/t* argue the case for and against; talk or write about in detail; (*coll*) eat or drink.

discussion [dis*kus*hon] *n* act of talking or writing systematically, reasoned argument.

disdain [dis*dayn*] *v/t* look down on, despise, scorn; think it beneath one, be too proud (to do something) ∼ **disdain** *n* scorn, contempt, haughty indifference ∼ **disdainful** *adj*.

disease [di*zeez*] *n* malady, specific destructive process or disorder in an organism; grave illness of body or mind; (*fig*) destructive or abnormal state of affairs, disorder ∼ **diseased** *adj*.

disembark [disem*baark*] *v/t* and *i* put or go

ashore from a vessel, land ∼ **disembarkation** [disembaar*kay*shon] *n* ∼ **disembarkment** *n*.

disembarrass [disem*ba*Ras] *v/t* free from an annoyance, trouble, burden; disentangle (from).

disembody [disem*bod*i] *v/t* separate from the body; (*mil*) discharge, disband ∼ **disembodiment** *n* act of disembodying; state of separation from the body.

disembogue [disem*bOg*] *v/t* and *i* (*of river*) discharge (its waters) at its mouth; flow, empty itself.

disembowel [disem*bow*-il] *v/t* remove entrails of; lay bare the entrails ∼ **disembowelled** *adj*.

disenchant [disen*chaant*] *v/t* set free from a spell or charm; destroy the illusions of ∼ **disenchantment** *n* disillusionment.

disencumber [disen*kum*ber] *v/t* relieve of a burden; free from an encumbrance.

disendow [disen*dow*] *v/t* deprive of endowment.

disenfranchise [disen*fRanch*Iz] *v/t* disfranchise.

disengage [disen*gayj*] *v/t* and *i* loosen, free, detach; free oneself; (*fencing*) pass the point of one's sword to the opposite side of one's opponent's; (*mil*) voluntarily withdraw troops from battle; break off an action ∼ **disengagement** *n*.

disengaged [disen*gayjd*] *adj* without engagements, free, at leisure; uncommitted.

disentail [disen*tayl*] *v/t* (*leg*) set free from entail.

disentangle [disen*tang*-g'l] *v/t* and *i* clear from entanglement, disengage; extricate; unravel, straighten out ∼ **disentanglement** *n*.

disentitle [disen*tIt*'l] *v/t* deprive of title or right.

disentomb [disen*tOOm*] *v/t* take out from a grave; (*fig*) unearth.

disentrain [disen*tRayn*] *v/t* and *i* (*mil*) put out or get out of a train.

disequilibrium [disekwi*lib*Ri-um] *n* absence of equilibrium, instability.

disestablish [dises*tab*lish] *v/t* deprive (a church) of its official connexion with and support by the State ∼ **disestablishment** *n*.

disesteem [dises*teem*] *v/t* hold in low estimation, think lightly of ∼ **disesteem** *n* disfavour, disrepute ∼ **disestimation** [disesti*may*shon] *n*.

diseur. (*fem*) **diseuse** [deezur, deezu(r)z] *n* entertainer who specializes in monologues.

disfavour [dis*fay*ver] *n* disapproval, dislike; displeasure; lack or loss of favour ∼ **disfavour** *v/t* disapprove of, dislike.

disfeature [dis*feech*er] *v/t* spoil the features of, disfigure.

disfiguration [disfigew*Ray*shon] *n* action of disfiguring; state of being disfigured; that which disfigures, blemish.

disfigure [dis*fig*er] *v/t* injure the appearance or beauty of, deface, mar ∼ **disfigurement** *n*.

disforest see **disafforest**.

disfranchise [dis*fRanch*Iz] *v/t* deprive of civic rights; deprive of the right to vote ∼ **disfranchisement** *n*.

disgorge [dis*gawrj*] *v/t* and *i* eject from the throat; give back unjust gains; (*of river*) disembogue ∼ **disgorgement** *n* ∼ **disgorger** *n* device for extracting a hook from a fish's throat.

disgrace [dis*gRays*] *n* loss of favour, *usu* because of bad conduct; public dishonour, downfall; state of being out of favour; that which is or should be a cause of shame ∼ **disgrace** *v/t* bring

218

shame on, be a discredit to; dismiss from favour; humiliate.

disgraceful [disgRaysfool] *adj* discreditable, shameful ~ **disgracefully** *adv*.

disgruntled [disgRunt'ld] *adj* dissatisfied, discontented, out of humour.

disguise [disgIz] *v/t* change the usual appearance of, make unrecognizable (in order to deceive); hide the true nature of, mask, dissimulate ~ **disguise** *n* clothing *etc* worn to conceal identity; deceptive appearance; act of disguising; state of being disguised ~ **disguisedly** *adv* ~ **disguisement** *n* ~ **disguiser** *n* person or thing that disguises.

disgust [disgust] *n* loathing, violent aversion and distaste ~ **disgust** *v/t* fill with loathing, sicken; be highly disagreeable to ~ **disgustedly** *adv*.

disgusting [disgusting] *adj* causing disgust, repulsive; objectionable, reprehensible ~ **disgustingly** *adv*.

dish [dish] *n* shallow vessel with a rim or raised sides for holding food; the food served in this; a specific kind of food, or food cooked in a particular way; any object shaped like a dish; a hollow; (*sl*) attractive person ~ **dish** *v/t* put or serve in a dish; shape like a dish, hollow out; (*coll*) upset, spoil, thwart; **d. out** serve food (*usu* to many persons); (*coll*) distribute, share out; **d. up** bring food to table; (*coll*) present attractively.

dishabilitate [dis-habilitayt] *v/t* disqualify.

dishabille, deshabille [disabeel] *n* state of being partially undressed; loose informal garment, untidy dress.

dishabituate [dis-habitew-ayt] *v/t* cause one to give up or break a habit, custom *etc*.

dishcloth [dishkloth] *n* cloth used for washing or wiping dishes.

dishclout [dishklowt] *n* dishcloth; (*sl*) dirty, slovenly woman.

dishcover [dishkuver] *n* metal or earthenware cover placed over a dish to keep its contents hot.

dishearten [dis-haarten] *v/t* deprive of courage. make despondent, depress ~ **disheartening** *adj*.

dished [disht] *adj* concave; (*bui*) domed, vaulted; (*eng*) farther apart at top than at bottom (of parallel wheels); concave; (*coll*) outmanoeuvred, defeated, ruined.

dishevelled [dishev'ld] *adj* (*of hair*) ruffled and hanging loosely; (*of person*) generally untidy ~ **dishevelment** *n*.

dishful [dishfool] *n* as much as a dish holds.

dishmat [dishmat] *n* small mat to prevent the heat of a dish from marking a table.

dishonest [disonist] *adj* lacking honesty; fraudulent; deceitful, insincere ~ **dishonesty** *n*.

dishonour [disoner] *n* disgrace, ignominy; source of shame; disrespect, indignity ~ **dishonour** *v/t* bring shame or discredit on; violate the chastity of; treat disrespectfully, insult; (*comm*) refuse to pay or accept (cheque *etc*); refuse to pay (debts); refuse to keep (promises).

dishonourable [disoneRab'l] *adj* disgraceful, despicable ~ **dishonourableness** *n* ~ **dishonourably** *adv*.

dishwasher [dishwosher] *n* person or machine that washes kitchen utensils and crockery; the pied wagtail.

dishwater [dishwawter] *n* water in which greasy dishes *etc* have been washed; **dull as d.** very dull.

dishy [dishi] *adj* (*sl*) attractive, having sex appeal.

disillusion [disilewzhon] *n* loss of illusion(s); act of removing illusions ~ **disillusion** *v/t* remove the illusions of, open the eyes of, undeceive ~ **disillusionize** *v/t* ~ **disillusionment** *n*.

disincentive [disinsentiv] *n* and *adj* (factor, consideration) which discourages action, deterrent.

disinclination [disinklinayshon] *n* unwillingness, reluctance.

disincline [disin-klIn] *v/t* and *i* make or become unwilling or reluctant ~ **disinclined** *adj*.

disinfect [disinfekt] *v/t* cleanse of infection; remove harmful germs *etc* from; sterilize.

disinfectant [disinfektant] *n* and *adj* (substance) which renders harmless or destroys germs *etc*.

disinfection [disinfekshon] *n* process of disinfecting.

disinfector [disinfektor] *n* apparatus for spreading or spraying disinfectant.

disinfest [disinfest] *v/t* rid of vermin, *esp* rats or lice ~ **disinfestation** [disinfestayshon] *n*.

disinflation [disinflayshon] *n* (*econ*) reduction of inflation ~ **disinflationary** *adj*.

disingenuous [disinjenew-us] *adj* not straightforward, insincere ~ **disingenuously** *adv* ~ **disingenuousness** *n*.

disinherit [disinheRit] *v/t* deprive of inheritance, reject as one's heir ~ **disinheritance** *n*.

disintegrate [disintigRayt] *v/t* and *i* break into fragments or parts; destroy cohesion of; fall to pieces, crumble; (*phys*) (*of an atom or nucleus*) emit particles or photons > PDS; (*fig*) show mental or moral collapse ~ **disintegration** [disintigRayshon] *n*.

disintegrator [disintigRaytor] *n* person or thing that causes disintegration; machine for crushing or pulverizing.

disinter (*pres/part* **disinterring**, *p/t* and *p/part* **disinterred**) [disintur] *v/t* take out of the grave, exhume; dig up; (*fig*) bring to light, reveal ~ **disinterment** *n*.

disinterest [disinteRest] *n* (*pop*) lack of interest, bored detachment; (*obs*) absence of selfish motives; impartiality, fairness.

disinterested [disintRestid] *adj* free from self-seeking; impartial; (*pop*) not interested, bored ~ **disinterestedly** *adv* ~ **disinterestedness** *n*.

disjoin [disjoin] *v/t* and *i* separate, disunite, detach.

disjoint [disjoint] *v/t* take to pieces at the joints, dismember; dislocate; destroy the unity or right order of ~ **disjointed** *adj* incoherent, disconnected; dismembered; ~ **disjointedly** *adv*.

disjunction [disjunkshon] *n* separation, severance.

disjunctive [disjunktiv] *adj* causing separation; (*gramm*) indicating contrast, linking alternatives; (*log*) presenting alternatives ~ **disjunctive** *n* (*gramm*) disjunctive conjunction; (*log*) a disjunctive proposition ~ **disjunctively** *adv*.

disk see **disc**.

dislike [dislIk] *v/t* not like, feel aversion to ~ **dislike** *n* feeling of aversion or mild hostility; that which one dislikes.

dislimn [dislim] *v/t* and *i* efface; be effaced, melt away.

dislocate [dislOkayt] *v/t* put out of place; put out

of joint; (*fig*) disorganize, upset the arrangements of, confuse ~ **dislocation** [dislO*kay*shon] *n*.

dislodge [dis*loj*] *v/t* remove from place of rest; remove by force; drive out ~ **dislodgement** *n*.

disloyal [dis*loi*-al] *adj* lacking loyalty, treacherous; unfaithful ~ **disloyally** *adv* ~ **disloyalty** *n*.

dismal [*diz*mal] *adj* gloomy, depressing, cheerless ~ **dismally** *adv*.

dismantle [dis*mant*'l] *v/t* strip of essential equipment or parts; (*naut*) remove sails and rigging; (*mil*) remove defences of; take to pieces; put out of action by removal of parts.

dismast [dis*maast*] *v/t* deprive (ship) of masts, carry away the masts of (a ship).

dismay [dis*may*] *v/t* fill with alarm, daunt, terrify ~ **dismay** *n* apprehension, alarm, consternation ~ **dismayedness** *n*.

dismember [dis*member*] *v/t* cut away the limbs of; tear limb from limb; divide up; (*fig*) partition (a country) ~ **dismemberment** *n*.

dismiss [dis*mis*] *v/t* send away, allow to go, disperse; discharge, discharge from office or employment; cease to consider; (*leg*) refuse further hearing to; (*mil*) (*imp*) word of command for soldiers to fall out of ranks.

dismissal [dis*misal*] *n* act of dismissing; notification of this.

dismissive [dis*misiv*] *adj* expressing dismissal or disregard; contemptuous.

dismissory [dis*mis*eRi] *adj* notifying dismissal.

dismount [dis*mownt*] *v/i* and ' alight (from bicycle, horse *etc*); unhorse; remove from its mounting.

disnatured [dis*naycherd*] *adj* unnatural, devoid of natural affection.

disobedience [disO*beedi*-ens] *n* failure or refusal to obey, rebelliousness.

disobedient [disO*beedi*-ent] *adj* failing, refusing to obey, guilty of disobedience.

disobey [disO*bay*] *v/t* and *i* refuse to obey; wilfully disregard.

disoblige [diso*bltj*] *v/t* disregard the wishes of; offend, pain; inconvenience ~ **disobliging** *adj* churlish, unhelpful ~ **disobligingly** *adv*.

disorder [dis*awrder*] *n* lack of order, confusion; tumult; breach of public order, riot; ailment, illness ~ **disorder** *v/t* disarrange, upset, confuse; upset the health of ~ **disordered** *adj*.

disorderly [dis*awrderli*] *adj* without proper order; riotous, unruly; (*leg*) violating public order or peace; **d. conduct** minor offence against public peace, order *etc*; **d. house** brothel; gambling house ~ **disorderly** *adv* ~ **disorderliness** *n*.

disorganization [disawrgan*Iza*yshon] *n* lack of order or system, confusion, disorder; act of throwing into confusion *etc*.

disorganize [dis*awrgan*Iz] *v/t* throw into confusion; upset the orderly working of ~ **disorganizer** *n*.

disorientate [dis*awr*Ri-en*tayt*] *v/t* confuse the sense of direction of; cause disorientation in; (*fig*) perplex ~ **disorientation** [disawrRi-en*tay*shon] *n* loss of sense of direction; (*psych*) state of mind in which times, places, persons are confused > PDP.

disoriented [disawrRi-en*tid*] *adj* confused about who one is, or about places and times.

disown [dis*On*] *v/t* disclaim responsibility for, repudiate, cast off ~ **disownment** *n*.

disparage [dis*paRij*] *v/t* bring discredit on; speak slightingly of, belittle ~ **disparagement** *n*.

disparate [*dispa*Rayt] *adj* essentially different, incapable of being compared, unequal ~ **disparity** [dis*pa*Riti] *n* inequality, unlikeness, incongruity.

dispassionate [dis*pash*onit] *adj* without emotion or bias.

dispatch, despatch [dis*pach*] *v/t* send off or out; send off promptly; kill; get through, finish quickly or promptly; (*coll*) eat up quickly ~ **dispatch, despatch** *n* a sending off or out; promptness, speed; that which is sent; official report or message; report sent to newspaper; killing, execution; **d. box, case** case for carrying documents; **d. rider** (*mil*) messenger on motorcycle carrying dispatches.

dispel (*pres*/*part* **dispelling**, *p*/*t* and *p*/*part* **dispelled**) [dis*pel*] *v/t* disperse, scatter, drive away, cause to vanish.

dispensable [dis*pens*ab'l] *adj* that can be omitted or done without; (*eccles*) admitting of dispensation, not universally binding ~ **dispensability** [dispensa*bili*ti] *n* ~ **dispensableness** *n*.

dispensary [dis*pens*eRi] *n* place where medicines are made up and handed out; a clinic.

dispensation [dispens*ay*shon] *n* giving out, distribution; that which is distributed; (*eccles, leg*) exemption or relaxation of a law as concession to an individual or group; (*eccles*) divine decree; ordering by providence; religious system.

dispensatory [dis*pens*ateRi] *n* book on the preparation and use of medicines ~ **dispensatory** *adj* able to grant dispensations.

dispense [dis*pens*] *v/t* and *i* distribute; administer, deal out; (*med*) make up (prescriptions); grant exemption from general rule; **d. with** do without, do away with.

dispenser [dis*pens*er] *n* one who dispenses medicines; slot-machine which supplies a measure of food, drink *etc*.

dispeople [dis*peep*'l] *v/t* deprive (a country) wholly or partially of inhabitants.

dispersal [dis*purs*al] *n* a dispersing or being dispersed; (*biol*) the spread of organisms to new areas.

disperse [dis*purs*] *v/t* and *i* scatter, put to flight, cause to disappear; spread widely, distribute; (*opt*) break up (light) into rays; move away in different directions ~ **dispersed** *adj*.

dispersion [dis*pur*shon] *n* a scattering or being scattered; (*opt*) the breaking-up of light into its component rays > PDS; **the D.** Diaspora.

dispersive [dis*pur*siv] *adj* tending to disperse, causing dispersion.

dispirit [di*spi*Rit] *v/t* deprive of spirit, deject, depress ~ **dispirited** *adj* ~ **dispiritedly** *adv*.

displace [dis*plays*] *v/t* move out of place; deprive of office; take the place of ~ **displaceable** *adj* ~ **displaced** *adj* removed from its place; **d. person** refugee left homeless in a foreign country.

displacement [dis*plays*ment] *n* removal from position; state of being removed; amount whereby a thing has moved; (*phys*) volume or weight of liquid or gas displaced by a body; (*geol*) fault; (*psych*) transference of an emotion to an inappropriate object; replacement of one dream-symbol by a more obscure one > PDP; **d. theory** (*geol*) theory that the continents once formed a single mass > PDG.

display [dis*play*] *v/t* and *i* exhibit, spread out; show to advantage, show off; reveal, make obvious; (*print*) print in conspicuous type; (*biol*) engage in display ∼ **display** *n* exhibition, show; things shown or spread out; manifestation, revelation; exaggerated manifestation, parade, ostentation; (*biol*) pattern of behaviour used as visual communication, *esp* in courtship; (*print*) passages conspicuously printed; arrangement of page.

displease [dis*pleez*] *v/t* and *i* cause dissatisfaction; offend, annoy ∼ **displeasing** *adj* ∼ **displeasingness** *n*.

displeasure [dis*plezh*er] *n* dissatisfaction, annoyance, anger.

disport [dis*pawrt*] *v/i* and *refl* play, gambol, amuse oneself.

disposable [dis*pOz*ab'l] *adj* capable of being disposed of; designed to be thrown away after being used once; not committed to any particular use.

disposal [dis*pOz*al] *n* act of disposing, dealing, making over; selling; arrangement in a particular order; freedom or power to dispose of; **at one's d.** to be used as one wishes.

dispose [dis*pOz*] *v/t* and *i* set in order, arrange; settle, make arrangements, regulate; make willing, influence, incline; make liable; prepare; have authority to arrange or settle; **d. of** deal with, settle; get rid of; sell, give away; (*coll*) eat.

disposed [dis*pOzd*] *adj* inclined, tending, liable.

disposition [dispo*zish*on] *n* arrangement; ordering, management; (*leg*) bestowal or conveyance by will or deed; temperament, usual frame of mind > PDP; inclination, tendency ∼ **dispositional** *adj* relating to disposition ∼ **dispositioned** *adj* inclined by temperament.

dispossess [dispo*zes*] *v/t* put out of possession; dislodge, oust ∼ **dispossession** *n* ∼ **dispossessor** *n*.

dispraise [dis*prayz*] *v/t* deny praise to, disparage, blame, censure ∼ **dispraise** *n*.

disproof [dis*prOOf*] *n* refutation; that which refutes.

disproportion [dis*prOpawr*shon] *n* lack of proper proportion; disparity ∼ **disproportion** *v/t* cause to be out of proportion.

disproportional [dis*prOpawr*shonal] *adj* disproportionate ∼ **disproportionally** *adv*.

disproportionate [dis*prOpawr*shonit] *adj* out of proper proportion; excessive ∼ **disproportionately** *adv*.

disprove [dis*prOOv*] *v/t* prove not to be true, refute ∼ **disprovable** *adj* that can be disproved ∼ **disproval** *n* disproof, refutation.

disputable [*dis*pewtab'l/dis*pewt*ab'l] *adj* that can be disputed, debatable, open to doubt ∼ **disputableness** *n* ∼ **disputably** *adv*.

disputant [*dis*pewtant] *n* and *adj* (person) engaged in debate or argument.

disputation [dispew*tay*shon] *n* argument, debate; formal argument following the conventions of medieval debates.

disputatious [dispew*tay*shus] *adj* argumentative,

fond of debate, contentious ∼ **disputatiously** *adv* ∼ **disputative** [dis*pewt*ativ] *adj*.

dispute [dis*pewt*] *v/t* and *i* discuss, argue, debate; quarrel; call in question, contest, doubt; oppose; strive to win ∼ **dispute** *n* argument, debate; controversy; quarrel; **beyond d.** settled, not open to doubt or question; **in d.** under discussion, questionable ∼ **disputed** *adj*.

disqualification [diskwolifi*kay*shon] *n* a disqualifying or being disqualified; that which disqualifies.

disqualify [dis*kwolif*I] *v/t* deprive of qualification; declare or make ineligible, debar; incapacitate; withdraw legal permission to drive motor vehicle.

disquiet [dis*kwI*-et] *v/t* disturb, make uneasy or anxious ∼ **disquiet** *n* restlessness, uneasiness, anxiety; social or political unrest.

disquieting [dis*kwI*-eting] *adj* causing disquiet, disturbing ∼ **disquietingly** *adv*.

disquietude [dis*kwI*-itewd] *n* anxiety, uneasiness.

disquisition [diskwi*zish*on] *n* systematic investigation of a subject; treatise setting forth its results; lengthy discussion or discourse.

disregard [disRi*gaard*] *v/t* pay no attention to, ignore; treat casually, slight, neglect ∼ **disregard** *n* ∼ **disregardful** *adj*.

disrepair [disRi*pair*] *n* dilapidation (of building) due to neglect.

disreputable [disRe*pewt*ab'l] *adj* not respectable; discreditable ∼ **disreputably** *adv*.

disrepute [disRi*pewt*] *n* ill repute, discredit.

disrespect [disRi*spekt*] *n* lack of respect, rudeness.

disrespectful [disRi*spekt*fool] *adj* rude, discourteous ∼ **disrespectfully** *adv*.

disrobe [disR*Ob*] *v/t* and *i* undress; take off official robes.

disrupt [disR*upt*] *v/t* and *i* break or burst apart; split up; throw into complete confusion.

disruption [disR*up*shon] *n* breaking up; violent dissolution ∼ **disruptive** *adj* causing disruption.

diss [*dis*] *n* fibre used in making cordage.

dissatisfaction [dis-satis*fak*shon] *n* state of not being satisfied, displeasure; discontent; cause of displeasure or discontent ∼ **dissatisfactory** *adj*.

dissatisfied [dis-*satis*fId] *adj* discontented; not satisfied (with), displeased (with).

dissatisfy [dis-*satis*fI] *v/t* fail to satisfy, disappoint, cause discontent in.

dissect [di*sekt*] *v/t* divide into pieces; (*anat, bot*) cut up in order to examine; (*fig*) criticize in detail ∼ **dissecting** *adj* used in dissection.

dissected [di*sekt*id] *adj* divided into pieces; (*of map*) divided and mounted on linen; (*bot*) segmented, having many lobes; (*geog*) divided by numerous valleys or ravines > PDG.

dissection [di*sek*shon] *n* act of dissecting; detailed analysis; animal, plant *etc* dissected ∼ **dissective** *adj* ∼ **dissector** *n* person or instrument that dissects.

disseise [di*seez*] *v/t* wrongfully dispossess (person) of estates; (*fig*) deprive, oust ∼ **disseisin** *n*.

dissemble (1) [di*semb*'l] *v/t* and *i* conceal under false appearance, disguise (feelings *etc*); behave hypocritically ∼ **dissembler** *n*.

dissemble (2) *v/t* take to pieces.

disseminate [di*semi*nayt] *v/t* scatter as seed; (*fig*) spread abroad; (*med*) spread all through an organ, or through the whole body ~ **dissemination** [disemi*nay*shon] *n* ~ **disseminative** *adj*.

dissension [di*sen*shon] *n* difference of opinion, lack of unity, discord, quarrel.

dissent [di*sent*] *v/i* withhold assent; disagree; hold religious views differing from those of the Established Church ~ **dissent** *n* disagreement, difference of opinion; religious nonconformity.

Dissenter [di*sent*er] *n* a Nonconformist, one belonging to a religious body not in conformity with the established churches of England or Scotland.

dissentient [di*sen*shent] *adj* differing in opinion; dissenting from the opinion of the majority ~ **dissentient** *n*.

dissenting [di*sent*ing] *adj* relating to religious dissent, nonconformist; disagreeing.

dissertation [diser*tay*shon] *n* discourse or treatise on a particular subject, *esp* one written as a requirement for a university degree.

disserve [dis-*surv*] *v/t* do an ill turn to, injure.

disservice [dis-*surv*is] *n* ill turn, injury ~ **disserviceable** *adj*.

dissever [di*sev*er] *v/t* and *i* cut apart, divide, separate; go asunder ~ **disseverance** *n*.

dissidence [*dis*idens] *n* difference of opinion, disagreement.

dissident [*dis*ident] *adj* disagreeing, of a different opinion ~ **dissident** *n* one who disagrees, *esp* with the ideology of his country.

dissimilar [di*sim*iler] *adj* unlike, not resembling ~ **dissimilarity** [disimila*ri*ti] *n* unlikeness; a point of difference.

dissimilate [di*sim*ilayt] *v/t* and *i* make unlike; become unlike.

dissimilation [disimi*lay*shon] *n* a making or becoming unlike; (*phil*) alteration of one of two similar adjacent sounds making them unlike.

dissimulate [di*sim*ewlayt] *v/t* and *i* conceal the true nature of, dissemble ~ **dissimulator** *n* person who dissimulates.

dissimulation [disimew*lay*shon] *n* act of dissimulating.

dissipate [*dis*ipayt] *v/t* and *i* drive away, dispel; waste (resources) by extravagance, squander, waste frivolously; disappear, melt away; engage in dissolute pleasures ~ **dissipative** *adj*.

dissipated [*dis*ipaytid] *adj* scattered, dispelled, squandered; dissolute, debauched.

dissipation [disi*pay*shon] *n* act of dissipating; dispersion, diffusion; wasteful expenditure, extravagance; loose and frivolous pursuits; intemperance, debauchery.

dissociable [dis-*sO*shab'l] *adj* unsociable; separable.

dissocial [dis-*sO*shal] *adj* unsociable ~ **dissocialize** *v/t* make unsociable.

dissociate [dis-*sO*shi-ayt] *v/t* and *refl* separate, disunite, sever association with; repudiate connexion or association with; think of as separate; part ~ **dissociative** *adj*.

dissociation [dis-sOshi-*ay*shon] *n* a dissociating or being dissociated, separation; (*chem*) reversible breaking down of a molecule into its simpler components > PDS; (*psych*) development of a group of mental activities into an independent centre of consciousness; a mild degree of split personality > PDP.

dissolubility [disolewbi*li*ti] *n* the property of being dissoluble.

dissoluble [di*sol*ewb'l/*dis*olewb'l] *adj* capable of being separated, untied, or disconnected.

dissolute [*dis*olewt] *adj* licentious, debauched, profligate ~ **dissolutely** *adv* ~ **dissoluteness** *n*.

dissolution [diso*lew*shon] *n* separation into parts, disintegration; (*fig*) death; dissolving in liquid; undoing of a bond or alliance; termination of an assembly or constituted body.

dissolvable [di*zol*vab'l] *adj* capable of being dissolved.

dissolve [di*zolv*] *v/t* and *i* disintegrate; liquefy, melt away; undo, bring to an end; disappear; cause to disappear; (*cin*) fade one shot into another ~ **dissolve** *n* (*cin*) a fading-in or fading-out.

dissolvent [di*zolv*ent] *n* and *adj* (substance) capable of dissolving other substances.

dissonance [*dis*onans] *n* (*mus*) discord, inharmonious sound; (*fig*) incompatibility, disagreement.

dissonant [*dis*onant] *adj* discordant, unmelodious; disagreeing, at variance.

dissuade [di*swayd*] *v/t* advise (a person) against; persuade against.

dissuasion [di*sway*zhon] *n* act of dissuading; advice against something ~ **dissuasive** *adj* tending to, intended to, dissuade ~ **dissuasively** *adv*.

dissyllabic, dissyllable see **disyllabic, disyllable**.

dissymmetry [dis-*sim*etRi] *n* absence of symmetry; symmetry in reverse.

distaff [*dis*taaf] *n* stick on which wool or flax is wound to be spun by hand; **d. line** female descent; **d. side** the female branch of a family.

distal [*dis*tal] *adj* (*biol*) widely spaced; at the outer end; away from the point of attachment of a limb or part of body.

distance [*dis*tans] *n* space between two objects; amount of intervening space or time, remoteness; far-off place or point; remote time; coolness of manner, aloofness; (*mil*) space between men in rank, or between ranks; (*mus*) interval between two tones; (*painting*) representation of the relative positions of objects, *esp* in landscape; **at a d.**, **in the d.** far-off, remote; **keep at a d.** treat with aloofness, be cool towards; **keep one's d.** remain aloof, keep away from ~ **distance** *v/t* put or keep far away; leave behind, outstrip; (*painting*) give the effect of space.

distant [*dis*tant] *adj* separated (by specified interval); far apart (in space, time, or relationship); aloof, cold; slight; **d. signal** railway signal giving a preliminary indication of the setting of the home signal ~ **distantly** *adv* remotely, widely apart; not intimately, coldly.

distaste [dis*tayst*] *n* dislike, aversion ~ **distasteful** *adj* unpleasant, disagreeable ~ **distastefully** *adv* ~ **distastefulness** *n*.

distemper (1) [dis*temp*er] *n* contagious catarrhal disease of young dogs; (*ar*) physical or mental disorder; (*fig*) turmoil, discontent ~ **distemper** *v/t* (*ar*) disorder, upset the health of.

distemper (2) *n* heavily pigmented matt paint which can be thinned with water; method of painting or decorating using this ~ **distemper** *v/t* paint with distemper.

distempered [dis*tem*perd] *adj* diseased in body or mind; (*fig*) ill-humoured, discontented; painted with distemper.

distend [dis*tend*] *v/t* and *i* stretch out, inflate.

distensible [dis*ten*sib'l] *adj* capable of being distended.

distension, distention [dis*ten*shon] *n* act of distending; state of being distended.

distich [*dis*tik] *n* (*pros*) couple of lines in poetry detachable from context.

distil (*pres/part* **distilling**, *pret* and *p/part* **distilled**) [dis*til*] *v/t* and *i* cause to fall in drops; evaporate a liquid and condense it again; extract or refine by this method; manufacture (whisky, scent) by this process; (*fig*) extract the essence, capture the spirit of; fall in minute drops, exude.

distillate [*dis*tilayt] *n* product of distilling.

distillation [distil*ay*shon] *n* process of distilling; product of distilling; (*fig*) essence; **destructive d.** distillation of compounds at high temperatures, to break them down; **fractional d.** gradual distillation of a compound so that its constituent parts may be collected separately according to their boiling points ~ **distillatory** *adj*.

distiller [dis*til*er] *n* one who distils, *esp* alcoholic spirits.

distillery [dis*til*eRi] *n* place where distilling of spirits is carried on.

distilling [dis*til*ing] *n* process of extracting or purifying a liquid by distillation.

distinct [dis*tinkt*] *adj* separate, individual; clearly perceptible, unmistakable.

distinction [dis*tink*shon] *n* action of keeping distinct; difference; distinguishing mark, characteristic; mark of special honour; honourable preeminence; refinement, good social manner.

distinctive [dis*tink*tiv] *adj* characteristic, distinguishing ~ **distinctively** *adv* in a distinct way ~ **distinctiveness** *n*.

distinctly [dis*tinkt*li] *adv* in a distinct manner; clearly, unmistakably; definitely, plainly.

distinctness [dis*tinkt*nis] *n* quality or state of being distinct, clarity.

distingué [dis*tang*-gay] *adj* (*Fr*) of distinguished appearance and manner.

distinguish [dis*ting*-gwish] *v/t* and *i* perceive or mark the difference between; characterize; perceive distinctly; (*refl*) make oneself prominent, become eminent ~ **distinguishable** *adj* ~ **distinguishably** *adv* ~ **distinguished** *adj* eminent; having an air of distinction.

distort [dis*tawrt*] *v/t* twist or press out of shape; (*fig*) give false impression of, misrepresent.

distortion [dis*tawr*shon] *n* act of distorting, twisting, misrepresenting; state of being distorted; degree to which a thing is distorted; misrepresentation, travesty; (*rad*) change of wave-form of signal during transmission or reception; lack of clarity in sound caused by this; (*psych*) alteration of elements in dreams to disguise their significance > PDP.

distract [dis*tRakt*] *v/t* turn (the attention) in a different direction, divert; prevent concentration; perplex, bewilder; drive mad.

distracted [dis*tRak*tid] *adj* perplexed, harassed; frantic, mad ~ **distractedly** *adv*.

distraction [dis*tRak*shon] *n* act of distracting; state of being distracted; that which distracts, cause of confusion or lack of attention; diversion, amusement; bewilderment, agitation; madness.

distrain [dis*tRayn*] *v/i* (*leg*) seize a person's goods as security for or payment of a debt ~ **distrainable** *adj* ~ **distrainee** *n* debtor whose goods have been seized ~ **distrainer, distrainor** *n* creditor who seizes goods.

distraint [dis*tRaynt*] *n* (*leg*) seizure of a debtor's possessions.

distraught [dis*tRawt*] *adj* extremely agitated or harassed, driven mad.

distress [dis*tRes*] *n* acute grief, anxiety, or suffering; state of danger, peril; cause of grief or anxiety; extreme want or poverty; physical exhaustion; (*leg*) right of distraint; the property distrained; **d. committee** committee set up to help those in extreme want, or victims of a disaster; **in d.** (*naut*) in danger, needing help; **d. gun** gun fired by ship in distress to summon help; **d. rocket** rocket sent up in similar circumstances ~ **distress** *v/t* cause grief, anxiety, or suffering to, afflict; (*leg*) distrain.

distressed [dis*tRest*] *adj* suffering distress; troubled; exhausted; in great poverty; **d. area** industrial district in which there is acute unemployment and poverty.

distressful [dis*tRes*fool] *adj* distressing, painful; in great distress ~ **distressfully** *adv*.

distressing [dis*tRes*ing] *adj* causing distress; pitiful ~ **distressingly** *adv*.

distributable [dis*tRib*ewtab'l] *adj* available for distribution.

distributary [dis*tRib*ewteRi] *n* branch or outlet which leaves a main river and does not rejoin it > PDG ~ **distributary** *adj* that distributes or is distributed.

distribute [dis*tRib*ewt] *v/t* and *i* share out among a number of people; spread out over a space, disperse; deal out; deliver to a number of people; classify; (*print*) break up type that has been used for printing and put back each letter and space into its proper compartment in the cases; (*log*) use term in its fullest and most inclusive meaning.

distributer see **distributor**.

distribution [dis*tRib*ewshon] *n* act of distributing, apportionment; that which is distributed, share; manner in which anything is distributed; (*pol/ec*) the distributing of commodities to consumers; the sharing of profits among producers; (*bot, zool*) geographical occurrence of a species; (*stat*) representation by a table or graphically of the frequency of occurrence of scores or measurements; **d. map** map showing the places or areas where specified objects or characteristics have been found.

distributism [dis*tRib*ewtizm] *n* theory that possession of personal property should be vested in as many individuals as possible ~ **distributist** *n* and *adj*.

distributive [dis*tRib*ewtiv] *adj* concerned with distribution; (*pol*) of distributism; (*log, gramm*) referring to each individual of a class separately ~ **distributive** *n* (*gramm*) a distributive pronoun or adjective ~ **distributively** *adv*.

distributor, distributer [dist*Ri*bewter] *n* person or thing that distributes; (*mot*) part of the ignition system which distributes electric current to the sparking plugs in the correct order.

district [dist*Ri*ct] *n* region, particular locality, quarter; division of a country, county, or parish for administrative purposes; **D. Commissioner** magistrate or government official with semi-judicial authority in a British Crown Colony; **d. heating** system of heating flats or houses in one part of a town from a central store of heat; **d. nurse** nurse who visits patients in their homes in a particular district; **d. visitor** churchworker assisting a clergyman in an area of his parish ~ **district** *v/t* divide into districts.

distrust [dist*Rust*] *n* want of trust or confidence, suspicion ~ **distrust** *v/t* have no trust or confidence in, suspect, doubt ~ **distrustful** *adj* ~ **distrustfully** *adv*.

disturb [dist*urb*] *v/t* alter the position or normal condition of; break up the quiet and tranquillity of (a person *etc*); interfere with the settled course or operation of; make uneasy, alarm, trouble, perplex; (*refl*) inconvenience oneself (by moving *etc*) ~ **disturber** *n*.

disturbance [dist*urb*ans] *n* act of disturbing; state of being disturbed; that which disturbs; commotion, disorder, tumult; breach of the peace; anxiety; (*leg*) interference with another's rights.

disturbed [dist*urb'd*] *adj* moved or altered; inconvenienced; agitated, troubled; emotionally unstable; mentally abnormal.

disturbing [dist*urb*ing] *adj* disquieting, unsettling; alarming.

distyle [dist*i*l/d*i*st*i*l] *n* porch with two columns.

disunion [dise*w*ni-on] *n* breaking of union, severance; want of union, dissension.

disunite [dise*w*n*i*t] *v/t* and *i* make or become separate; break the union or bond between; break or lose unity.

disunity [dise*w*niti] *n* lack of unity.

disuse [dise*w*z] *v/t* cease to use ~ **disuse** [dise*w*s] *n* state or fact of not being used; lack of use; discontinuation.

disyllabic, dissyllabic [disil*a*bik] *adj* having two syllables.

disyllable, dissyllable [dis*i*lab'l] *n* word, or metrical foot, of two syllables.

ditch [dich] *n* long narrow trench used in defence works; channel for drainage or irrigation; border of a bowling-green; (*Air Force coll*) English Channel or North Sea; **die in the last d.** defend position to the last ~ **ditch** *v/t* and *i* make or repair ditches; surround or border with a ditch; (*coll*) drive into a ditch; (*US*) derail; (*coll*) throw away, abandon, desert; make a forced landing in the sea ~ **ditcher** *n* one who makes and repairs ditches.

ditchwater [dich*w*awter] *n* stagnant water; **dull as d.** very dull and boring; **clear as d.** obscure.

dither [d*i*THer] *v/i* (*coll*) tremble, quiver; be agitated and nervous; hesitate nervously ~ **dither** *n* (*coll*) trembling, nervousness, agitation; **all of a d.** nervous, bewildered, hesitant.

dithyramb [dith*i*Ramb] *n* Greek hymn in honour of Dionysus; Bacchanalian song; prose or verse passage in highly emotional style ~ **dithyrambic** [dithi*Ram*bik] *adj*.

ditone [d*i*ton] *n* (*mus*) a major third > PDM.

ditto (*abbr* **do**) [d*i*tO] *n* the aforesaid, the same; **say d. to** agree with; (*pl*) **ditto(e)s** (*sl*) suit entirely made of the same cloth; **d. mark** mark (,,) used in lists to show that the word or figure above is to be considered as repeated.

dittography [dit*og*Rafi] *n* unintentional writing of same letter(s) or word twice.

ditty [dit*i*] *n* short song; simple lyric poem.

ditty-bag, ditty-box [dit*i*bag, dit*i*boks] *n* receptacle in which sailors keep small personal articles.

diuresis [dI-ew*Ree*sis] *n* (*med*) increased secretion of urine.

diuretic [dI-ew*Re*tik] *n* and *adj* (*med*) (substance) promoting the secretion of urine.

diurnal [dI-*urn*al] *adj* daily, happening every day; belonging to the daytime; (*zool*) active in daytime; (*ent*) living for one day only ~ **diurnal** *n* (*eccles*) service-book containing the offices for the day ~ **diurnally** *adv* daily, every day.

diva [*dee*va] *n* leading woman singer, prima donna.

divagate [d*i*vagayt] *v/i* wander about; digress, stray from the point ~ **divagation** [dIva*gay*shon] *n*.

divalent [dIv*ay*lent] *adj* (*chem*) having a valency of two, combining with two radicals, bivalent.

divan [div*an*] *n* a low armless and backless couch, fitted with cushions; low bed resembling such a couch; oriental state council; oriental council-hall; room open to the air on one side; smoking-room; café; tobacconist's shop; anthology of oriental lyric verse.

dive [dIv] *v/i* plunge head first into water; sink suddenly underwater; descend underwater in a diving suit; swoop down, descend steeply (through air); plunge one's hand into; dart down into; disappear suddenly; (*fig*) immerse oneself deeply (in study, book) ~ **dive** *n* a plunge head first into water; sudden submersion; sharp descent, swoop; (*coll*) drinking-place, gambling-den, cheap restaurant, *esp* one in a cellar or basement.

dive-bomb [d*i*v-bom] *v/t* and *i* release bombs over a target while diving steeply down towards it ~ **dive-bomber** *n* aircraft designed to attack in this way ~ **dive-bombing** *n*.

diver [d*i*ver] *n* one who dives; one who is lowered with a special breathing apparatus for work under water; name for several diving-birds.

diverge [dIv*urj*] *v/i* go in different directions, branch off; vary from a norm, deviate.

divergence, divergency [dIv*urj*ens(i)] *n* act of diverging; amount by which a thing diverges ~ **divergent** *adj* diverging; (*psych*) able to supply many different answers or suggestions.

divers [d*i*verz] *adj* various, several.

diverse [dIv*urs*/d*i*vurs] *adj* different, dissimilar ~ **diversely** *adv*.

diversifiable [dIvursif*i*-ab'l] *adj* capable of being diversified.

diversification [dIvursifik*ay*shon] *n* act of diversifying; state of being diversified; variety.

diversiform [dIv*ur*sifawrm] *adj* of various shapes.

diversify [dIv*ur*sifI] *v/t* make different, give variety to; (*comm*) invest in varied products or enterprises.

diversion [dIv*ur*shon] *n* a turning aside or away;

alternative route when a road is closed to traffic; (*mil*) manoeuvre to distract an enemy's attention; relaxation, recreation, amusement ~ **diversionary** *adj*.

diversity [dɪvʊrsiti] *n* marked difference; variety.

divert [dɪvʊrt] *v/t* turn aside (a thing) from its path or original purpose; distract the attention of, amuse.

divertimento (*pl* **divertimenti**) [divurtimento] *n* (*mus*) short, light composition in several movements > PDM.

diverting [dɪvʊrting] *adj* amusing, entertaining.

divertissement [diverteesmon(g)] *n* entertainment; short ballet, *usu* between the acts of a longer piece; divertimento > PDM.

divest [dɪvest/dɪvest] *v/t* and *refl* strip, remove; deprive of, dispossess; (*leg*) take away, alienate (property vested in a person) ~ **divestible** *adj*.

divestiture, divesture [dɪvesticher, dɪvescher] *n* act of divesting.

divi see **divvy**.

dividable [divɪdab'l] *adj* that can be divided.

divide [divɪd] *v/t* and *i* separate into parts, split, break apart; separate into classes; cause disagreement among; place or keep a partition between; share out, distribute, become separated, part, branch out; share; vote on a motion; ask that a vote be taken; (*math*) find out the number of times one number is contained in another; be contained an exact number of times in a number; (*eng*) mark divisions or gradations in ~ **divide** *n* dividing ridge, watershed > PDG.

divided [divɪdid] *adj* separated or marked out into parts; parted, at variance, disunited; distributed among a number.

dividend [divɪdend] *n* (*math*) number or quantity to be divided by another; portion of a limited company's profits paid out to shareholders; creditors' share of a bankrupt's estate; discount paid out to members of a cooperative society; **d. cover** actual profit as compared with that part of it paid out in dividend; **d. warrant** order to pay such a sum.

dividers [divɪderz] *n* (*pl*) pair of compasses with metal points for measuring and setting off small distances.

dividual [divɪdewal] *adj* separate, distinct; separable; shared out ~ **dividually** *adv* separately.

divination [divinayshon] *n* foretelling the future, or revealing the hidden, by magical, mystical, or supernormal means; inspired guesswork ~ **divinatory** *adj*.

divine [divɪn] *adj* pertaining to God or a god; godlike; religious, sacred; (*coll*) glorious, splendid, remarkably good or pleasant ~ **divine** *n* theologian; (*coll*) priest, clergyman ~ **divine** *v/t* and *i* practise divination, prophesy; discover by intuition, guess ~ **divinely** *adv* ~ **divineness** *n*.

diviner [divɪner] *n* one who divines, soothsayer; dowser, one who finds hidden water, metal, oil *etc* by means of a divining-rod.

diving-bell [dɪving-bel] bell-shaped steel chamber in which men may work under water.

diving-board [dɪving-bawrd] *n* plank projecting at some height over swimming-pool or other body of water, from which one can dive.

diving-dress [dɪving-dRes] *n* heavy waterproof

garment with helmet and tubes bearing air-supply, used by divers remaining under water.

divining-rod [divɪning-Rod] *n* forked twig which quivers and bends when held by a dowser over hidden metals or underground water *etc*.

divinity [diviniti] *n* property of being divine; a divine being, a god or deity; divine virtue or power; study of theology; **d. calf** dark-brown calfskin for bookbinding.

divisible [divizib'l] *adj* capable of division; (*math*) capable of being divided exactly ~ **divisibility** [divizibiliti] *n* ~ **divisibly** *adv*.

division [divizhon] *n* act of dividing; state of being divided; that which divides, partition, boundary; distribution, sharing-out; disagreement, discord; separated sub-unit, section, department, class; (*hort*) propagation of plants by separating and replanting sections of root; (*math*) process of finding how many times one number is contained in another; separation of members of an assembly into groups in order to vote; (*mil*) section of troops under one commander, about 10,000 to 15,000 men; (*naval*) group of ships under one commander; **d. bell** bell in House of Commons to summon Members to vote in a division; **d. sign** (*math*) sign ($\div$) indicating that the preceding number is to be divided by the following one ~ **divisional** *adj* ~ **divisionary** *adj*.

divisionism [divizhonizm] *n* (*art*) juxtaposition of touches of contrasted pure colours ~ **divisionist** *n* and *adj*.

divisive [divɪsiv] *adj* causing or showing division; causing disagreement or conflict; able to make divisions.

divisor [divɪzer] *n* (*math*) number or quantity by which another (the dividend) is to be divided.

divorce [divawrs] *n* legal dissolution of marriage; (*fig*) separation, disunion ~ **divorce** *v/t* and *i* dissolve legally the marriage between; obtain a divorce from; (*fig*) separate, repudiate.

divorcee [divawrsee] *n* divorced person.

divorcement [divawrsment] *n* act or process of divorcing, state of being divorced.

divot, divet [divet] *n* piece of turf; (*golf*) piece of turf sliced off by the club in a bad shot.

divulge [divulj/dɪvuli] *v/t* reveal, make known (a secret *etc*) ~ **divulgement** *n* ~ **divulgence** *n*.

divvy, divi [divi] *n* (*coll*) share or portion, *esp* dividend paid to members of a cooperative society ~ **divvy** *v/t* and *i* (*coll*) share out.

dixie [diksi] *n* iron pot used by soldiers for tea and stew.

dizzy [dizi] *adj* giddy, suffering from vertigo; bewildered; causing giddiness; (*coll*) foolish; amazing, extreme ~ **dizzy** *v/t* make giddy or confused ~ **dizzily** *adv* ~ **dizziness** *n* ~ **dizzying** *adj*.

djellaba [*je*laba] *n* hooded cloak with wide sleeves.

djinn see **jinn**.

do (1) (*p/t* **did**, *p/part* **done**) [dOO] *v/t*, *i* and *aux* perform, carry out; work at, study; translate; travel, go (a distance at a certain speed); ruin; cause, bring about; deal with, work on, attend to; cook; bestow, offer; act (play or role); suit, be sufficient for, meet the needs of; (*coll*) cheat, trick; visit as a sightseer; serve (term in prison); entertain; *v/i* act, behave; perform deeds; get on, prosper (well or ill); suffice; *v/aux* used to emphasize, to form interrogative and negative sentences, to avoid repetition of main verb, to form inversions; **d. away with** get rid of, destroy, kill; **d. by** treat, act towards; **d. down** get the better of; **d. for** (coll) destroy, ruin, kill; do domestic work for; **d. in** (sl) kill; (coll) exhaust; **d. in the eye** (sl) swindle; **make d.** manage with what is available; **d. out** clean out; **d. out of** cheat of, deprive of by a trick; **d. over** (coll) redecorate; clean or paint superficially; **d. to death** kill; (fig, coll) do too often, make trite; **d. up** wrap or tie up; redecorate; repair; (coll) dress; (sl) attack, beat up; (coll) exhaust; **d. with** endure, tolerate; **I could d. with** I need, I would like to have; **have to d. with** be concerned with or related to, have dealings with; **d. without** dispense with, forgo; **nothing doing** (coll) certainly not ~ **do** n (coll) social gathering, large party, festivity; trick, swindle; affair, happening, state of affairs; (pl) share; **fair dos (doos)!** share fairly.

do (2), **doh** [dO] (mus) the first note or tonic of the scale in tonic sol-fa; the note C.

do (3) abbr of ditto.

dobbin [dobin] n pet name for a farm-horse.

Doberman Pinscher [dOberman pinsher] n breed of short-haired, long-legged dog.

doc [dok] n (coll abbr) doctor.

doch-an-doris [dokh-an-doRis] n parting drink, stirrup-cup.

docile [dOsIl] adj tractable, manageable; willing to obey and learn ~ **docilely** adv.

docility [dOsiliti] n quality of being docile.

dock (1) [dok] n name of one of several large-leaved plants of the genus Rumex.

dock (2) n thick fleshy part of an animal's tail; piece of harness covering stump of horse's tail ~ **dock** v/t cut short (esp horse's tail); curtail, cut down; deduct part of.

dock (3) n basin for shipping which is cut off from the tides by dock gates (except for tidal docks); landing pier, wharf; **dry** or **graving d.** a dock from which water is pumped out; **floating d.** a steel floating structure which sinks itself beneath a vessel and then raises it out of the water > PDE; **tidal d.** a dock which has no gates; **wet d.** a dock in a tidal estuary in which the water is kept at high-tide level ~ **dock** v/t and i enter or cause to enter a dock; (of spacecraft) link up while in orbit.

dock (4) n enclosure in a criminal court in which the prisoner stands at his trial.

dockage [dokij] n dock accommodation; charges made for berthing a ship; deduction.

docker [doker] n dock labourer.

docket [dokit] n memorandum attached to a document summarizing its contents; (leg) register of legal judgements; abstract of the contents of a letter-patent; list of cases for trial; label on package describing contents with delivery instructions; warrant certifying payment of customs duty etc ~ **docket** v/t make a summary of; enter on a docket; fix a docket to.

dockyard [dokyaard] n series of docks where ships are built or repaired.

doctor [dokter] n physician or surgeon; (hist, eccles) learned man, esp theologian or philosopher; holder of the highest degree in any university

faculty; fish of the genus Acanthurus; type of artificial fly for angling; (naut) ship's cook ~ **doctor** v/t treat, give medicine to; repair; adulterate; give drugs to; alter fraudulently, falsify, tamper with.

doctoral [doktoRal] adj pertaining to a doctorate or doctor ~ **doctorally** adv.

doctorate [dokteRayt/doktoRat] n the degree of a doctor.

doctorship [doktership] n doctorate; scholarship; great learning; medical skill.

doctrinaire [doktRinair] n and adj (person) determined to apply a theory regardless of its practicability or consequences ~ **doctrinairianism** n.

doctrinal [doktRinal] adj pertaining to doctrine ~ **doctrinally** adv.

doctrine [doktRin] n body of teachings or principles; accepted belief, tenet, dogma.

doctrinism [doktRinizm] n adherence to a particular doctrine ~ **doctrinist** n.

document [dokewment] n something written which gives information on facts ~ **document** [dokewment] v/t support or furnish with written evidence; provide (a ship) with its papers ~ **documental** [dokewmental] adj.

documentary [dokewmentaRi] adj in the form of a document, written ~ **documentary** n factual report or film or broadcast.

documentation [dokewmentayshon] n provision of documentary evidence and authorities; verisimilitude in their use.

dodder (1) [doder] n leafless parasitic plant.

dodder (2) v/i move unsteadily, totter; be mentally feeble or vague ~ **doddery** adj.

dodeca- pref twelve.

dodecagon [dOdekagon] n polygon with twelve sides.

dodecahedron [dOdekaheedRon] n solid figure with twelve faces ~ **dodecahedral** adj.

dodecasyllable [dOdekasilab'l] n a line of verse of twelve syllables.

dodge [doj] v/t and i avoid or elude by sharp twisting movements; move quickly aside; evade or avoid by trickery; shirk; quibble ~ **dodge** n (coll) trick; dodging movement; shrewd plan; clever contrivance.

dodger [dojer] n shifty, dishonest person; shirker; (naut) sheltering screen on ship's bridge.

dodgy [doji] adj artful; (sl) difficult; insecure.

dodo [dOdO] n extinct bird, related to the pigeon but larger than a turkey, with useless wings; (coll) old-fashioned or stupid person; **dead as the d.**

doe [dO] n female of fallow deer; also used for female of rabbit and other animals.

doer [dOO-er] n one who does things, not a mere talker; (of plants, domestic animals) **a good (bad) d.** one that thrives well (or ill).

does [duz] third pers sing pres ind of **do** (1).

doeskin [dOskin] n leather made from skin of a female deer; soft, smooth woollen fabric.

doesn't [duznt] abbr does not.

doff [dof] v/t take off (headgear or clothing); lay aside, get rid of.

dog [dog] n animal of the genus Canis, esp one of the domesticated varieties; male of this genus; (pej) mean, worthless, or cowardly man; (coll) boy or man, esp lively, gay fellow; (pl) support for fire-irons or logs; mechanical device for holding or grappling; (*astron*) either of two constellations near Orion; **the dogs** (*coll*) greyhound racing; **every d. has his day** everyone has some luck one day; **die like a d.** die disgracefully, miserably; **d. eat d.** ruthless rivalry; **go to the dogs** go to ruin, degenerate; **a hair of the d. that bit you** drink taken to take off the effects of drunkenness; **hot d.** (*US*) sandwich of hot sausage meat; **lame d.** helpless, unfortunate person; **lead a d.'s life** be continually harassed and unhappy; **let sleeping dogs lie** leave things as they are for fear of stirring up trouble; **like a d.'s dinner** (*sl*) (dressed) flashily; **d. in the manger** one who will neither enjoy a thing himself nor let others enjoy it; **put on d.** show off ~ **dog** (*pres/part* **dogging**, *p/t* and *p/part* **dogged**) *v/t* follow closely or constantly.

dogate [*dOgayt*] *n* office of doge of Venice.

dogcart [*dogkaart*] *n* small cart drawn by dogs; high two-wheeled carriage with two seats back to back and a space between.

dogcollar [*dogkoler*] *n* collar for dog; (*coll*) clergyman's collar fastening at the back.

dogdays [*dogdayz*] *n* hottest period of the year.

doge [*dOj*] *n* (*hist*) chief magistrate in Venice or Genoa.

dog-eared [*dog-eerd*] *adj* (*of a book, paper etc*) having the corners of the leaves turned down.

dog-fancier [*dog-fansi-er*] *n* connoisseur of dogs; breeder or seller of dogs.

dogfight [*dogfIt*] *n* fray or mêlée, *esp* between fighter planes.

dogfish [*dogfish*] *n* species of small shark.

dog-fox [*dog-foks*] *n* male fox.

dogged [*dogid*] *adj* obstinate; tenacious, determined ~ **doggedly** *adv* ~ **doggedness** *n*.

dogger [*doger*] *n* two-masted Dutch fishing-boat.

doggerel [*dogeRel*] *n* comic verse of irregular metre; bad verse ~ **doggerel** *adj* (*of verse*) trivial, inferior.

doggie, doggy [*dogi*] *n* pet name for a dog; (*naval sl*) officer who assists an admiral in his duties.

dogginess [*dogines*] *n* resemblance to a dog; fondness for dogs.

doggo [*dogO*] *adv* (*coll*) in hiding, in such a way as to escape attention.

doggone [*dogon*] *adj* (*abbr, sl*) God-damned; confounded, wretched.

doggy [*dogi*] *adj* like, or of, a dog; (*coll*) fond of dogs; (*coll*) smart, stylish.

dog-hole [*dog-hOl*] *n* (*sl*) mean disgusting dwelling.

doghouse [*doghows*] *n* kennel; **in the d.** (*sl*) in disgrace.

dog-latin [*dog-latin*] *n* incorrect, barbarous, colloquial Latin.

dogma [*dogma*] *n* theory or doctrine asserted on authority without supporting evidence.

dogmatic, dogmatical [*dogmatik, dogmatikal*] *adj* as dogma; stating opinions arrogantly or without proof, assertive ~ **dogmatically** *adv*.

dogmatism [*dogmatizm*] *n* emphatic assertion of opinion without proof; (*philos*) system based wholly on reasoning without empirical observation ~ **dogmatist** *n*.

dogmatize [*dogmatIz*] *v/i* and *t* speak authoritatively without offering proof; formulate as a dogma ~ **dogmatizer** *n*.

do-gooder [*doo-gOOder*] *n* (*coll, cont*) zealous but impractical reformer or benefactor.

dogpaddle [*dogpad'l*] *n* elementary inefficient stroke in swimming ~ **dogpaddle** *v/i*.

dogrose [*dogROz*] *n* the wild rose.

dogsbody [*dogzbodi*] *n* (*sl*) underling, drudge.

dogskin [*dogskin*] *n* skin of a dog; type of soft leather made of dog's or sheep's skin.

dogstar [*dogstaar*] *n* Sirius, the brightest fixed star.

dog-tired [*dog-tIrd*] *adj* tired out.

dogtooth [*dogtOOth*] *n* a canine tooth; (*archi*) Early English moulding of radiating leaves resembling a dog's teeth; **d. spar** (*min*) calcite crystals sharply pointed like canine teeth; **d. violet** plant with spotted leaves and purple flowers.

dogtrot [*dogtRot*] *n* an easy trot.

dogviolet [*dogvI-Olet*] *n* scentless wild violet.

dogwatch [*dogwoch*] *n* (*naut*) one of the two short watches between 4 and 8 p.m.

dogwood [*dogwood*] *n* the wild cornel tree.

doh see do (2).

doily, doyley [*doili*] *n* small ornamental piece of linen or paper placed on or under plates.

doings [*dOO-ingz*] *n* (*pl*) activities, deeds, behaviour; (*sl*) a thrashing, scolding; anything that is needed; trimmings.

doit [*doit*] *n* small coin or sum; a trifle.

doited [*doitid*] *adj* (*Scots*) foolish, senile.

dolce [*dolchi*] *adv* (*mus*) sweetly, softly, smoothly; **d. vita** luxurious, pleasure-seeking life.

doldrums [*doldRumz*] *n* (*pl*) region near the equator where ships are often becalmed; (*fig*) low spirits, listlessness, depression.

dole (1) [*dOl*] *n* food or money given in charity; unemployment relief; **on the d** out of work and living on unemployment relief ~ **dole, d. out** *v/t* distribute in small amounts, give sparingly.

dole (2) *n* (*ar*) grief, lamentation, mourning.

doleful [*dOlfool*] *adj* sad, melancholy ~ **dolefully** *adv* ~ **dolefulness** *n*.

dolerite [*doleRIt*] *n* (*geol*) coarse basalt.

doll [*dol*] *n* child's toy representing a human or animal figure; (*coll*) pretty but empty-headed girl or woman; (*sl*) any girl or young woman ~ **doll** *v/t* and *refl* **d. up** dress (oneself) very smartly.

dollar [*doler*] *n* standard unit of coinage in the U.S.A., Canada *etc*; the coin or its equivalent; (*sl*) five shillings; **d. gap** an adverse balance between a country's receipts from, and its payments to, the group of countries which pay, and can command settlement of debts, in dollars.

dollop [*dolop*] *n* (*coll*) large shapeless lump; blob.

dolly [*doli*] *n* pet name for a doll; wooden implement for beating clothes in laundering; block of hardwood to receive the shock of a pile hammer > PDE; tool for holding a rivet while it is shaped > PDE; low truck or wheeled frame; (*cin, television*) mobile platform for camera; **d. bag** soft handbag closed by drawstrings; **d. shop** inferior pawn-shop; marine dealer's store; **d. tub** large tub for washing mineral ore ~ **dolly** *v/i* work with a dolly; **d. in, d. out** move camera forward or backward while photographing ~ **dolly** *adj* (*games*) slow, easy (catch or shot).

dolly-bird [*dol*i-burd] *n* (*coll*) pretty, young but silly girl.

dolman [*dol*man] *n* loose jacket with large hanging sleeves; long Turkish robe, open in front; hussar's jacket worn like a cape; **d. sleeve** sleeve tapering from wide armhole to narrow cuff.

dolmen [*dol*men] *n* cromlech, prehistoric stone chamber made by upright stones supporting a horizontal one.

dolomite [*dolo*mIt] *n* (*min*) pearl spar, found in vast amounts, comprising whole mountain ranges.

dolorous [*dole*Rus] *adj* sad, mournful; causing grief or pain ~ **dolorously** *adv*.

dolose [do*lOs*] *adj* (*leg*) with criminal intent.

dolour [*dole*r] *n* grief, sorrow.

dolphin [*dol*fin] *n* cetacean resembling a porpoise; (*pop*) the fish dorado; (*astron*) a northern constellation; type of buoy or mooring spar.

dolt [*dOl*t] *n* stupid person ~ **doltish** *adj* ~ **doltishness** *n*.

Dom [*dom*] *n* title of nobility in Portuguese speaking countries; title of certain monks.

domain [dO*mayn*] *n* estate, lands held in possession; district under control; (*fig*) sphere of influence ~ **domanial** *adj*.

dome [*dOm*] *n* a convex curved roof, cupola > PDAA; anything shaped like a dome; (*poet*) stately building, palace; (*coll*) head; **d. light a** roof light glazed with glass ~ **dome** *v/t* and *i* cover with a dome; rise in the form of a dome.

domelike [*dOm*lIk] *adj* high and rounded.

domesday [*dOO*mzday] *n* doomsday; **D. Book** record made in 1086 of the lands of England with their ownership, extent and value.

domestic [dO*mestik*] *adj* belonging to the home; attached or devoted to home; of or for the running of a household; (*of animals*) dependent on man; pertaining to, or made in, one's own country ~ **domestic** *n* household servant ~ **domestically** *adv*.

domesticate [dO*mesti*kayt] *v/t* tame (an animal) and accustom it to live with human beings; accustom (a person) to household duties ~ **domestication** [domesti*kay*shon] *n*.

domesticated [do*mesti*kaytid] *adj* adapted to, or content with, home life and its duties.

domesticity [dO*mesti*sitiI] *n* home life; love of home occupations; (*pl*) domestic affairs.

domicile [*domi*sIl] *n* usual dwelling-place, home, abode; (*leg*) permanent residence; (*comm*) place at which a bill of exchange is made payable ~ **domicile** *v/t* and *i* establish in a permanent home; (*comm*) make (a bill of exchange) payable in a certain place; make one's home, dwell.

domiciliary [domi*sili*-aRi] *adj* pertaining to a dwelling-place.

domiciliate [domi*sili*-ayt] *v/t* and *i* establish in a permanent home ~ **domiciliation** [domisili-*ay*shon] *n*.

dominance, dominancy [*domi*nans, *domi*nansi] *n* prevailing influence, authority, control.

dominant [*domi*nant] *adj* ruling, prevailing, most influential; in a commanding position; (*mus*) relating to the dominant or fifth note above the tonic; **d. character** (*biol*) genetic characteristic in an organism which will appear even if an opposite characteristic is also present ~ **dominant** *n*

(*mus*) fifth note above the tonic > PDM; (*psych*) emotion or complex which governs a person's behaviour.

dominate [*domi*nayt] *v/t* and *i* have the mastery of, have control of; prevail; rise high above, tower over.

domination [domi*nay*shon] *n* exercise of supreme power; (*pl*) fourth rank of angels.

dominative [*domi*nativ] *adj* ruling, imperious.

dominator [*domi*nayter] *n* ruler, ruling influence.

domineer [domi*neer*] *v/i* exercise authority haughtily or overbearingly; bully; behave arrogantly, overbearingly ~ **domineering** *adj*.

dominical [do*mini*kal] *adj* (*eccles*) pertaining to the Lord, or to Sunday; **d. day** Sunday; **d. letter** letter of alphabet used to denote the Sundays in a particular year on a church calendar; **d. year** the year as numbered from birth of Christ.

Dominican [do*mini*kan] *n* and *adj* (friar or nun) belonging to the religious order founded by St Dominic.

dominie [*domi*ni] *n* (*Scots*) schoolmaster.

dominion [do*mini*-on] *n* sovereign authority; territory subject to a ruler; title of the self-governing territories of the British Commonwealth.

domino [*domi*nO] *n* loose hooded robe, with mask, worn at masquerades as disguise; mask covering eyes only; person wearing such a robe or mask; small oblong piece of wood, plastic, or bone divided in halves each of which is either marked with from one to six dots or left blank; (*pl*) game played with twenty-eight such pieces; **it's d. with** (*coll*) there is no hope for; **d. theory** (*pol*) theory that a political change in one country will cause similar change in its neighbours.

Don (1) [*don*] *n* Spanish title; a Spaniard; fellow or tutor of a college; master at Winchester; **D. Juan** a seducer, rake, libertine; **D. Quixote** chivalrous idealist, defender of lost causes.

don (2) [*don*] *n* (*pres/part* **donning**, *p/t* and *p/part* **donned**) *v/t* put on (a garment).

dona, donah [*dO*na] *n* (*sl*) girl, sweetheart.

donate [dO*nayt*] *v/t* give (*esp* to a good cause).

donation [do*nay*shon] *n* act of giving; gift (*esp* to a good cause); (*leg*) contract whereby something is freely transferred into the ownership of another.

donator [do*nay*tor] *n* one who gives, donor.

donatory [*donate*Ri] *n* one who receives a gift.

done [*dun*] (*p/t* and *p/part* of **do**) *adj* brought to an end, completed; cooked sufficiently; worn out, used up; (*coll*) tired out; (*sl*) cheated, tricked; **not d.** against social custom, bad form; **the d. thing** the (socially) correct thing to do; **d. for** ruined; dying; **d. in, d. up** tired out; **d. up** finished; ruined; wearing excessive make-up; **have d. with** give up, finish ~ **done** *interj* agreed, settled.

donee [dO*nee*] *n* one who receives a gift.

donjon [*don*jon/*dun*jon] *n* castle tower or keep.

donkey [*donki*] *n* the ass; (*fig*) stupid person, fool; **d. jacket** thick jacket with leather shoulders; **d. work** (*coll*) hard, unspectacular work; **d.'s years** (*sl*) a long time.

donkey-engine [*donki*-enjin] *n* small auxiliary steam-engine.

donna [*dona*] *n* lady, title of courtesy for Italian and sometimes Spanish or Portuguese lady; **prima d.** principal woman singer in an opera.

donnish [*don*ish] *adj* like a college don; pedantic.

donor [*dOn*er] *n* giver, *esp* one who gives his blood for transfusion or an organ for transplantation; one who gives semen for artificial insemination; (*phys*) imperfection in a semiconductor which causes electron conduction.

don't [*dOnt*] *v/i* (*abbr*) do not ~ **don't** *n* (*coll*) prohibition.

doo-da, doodah [*dOO*da] *n* (*sl*) state of excitement or bewilderment; **all of a d.** flustered.

doodle (1) [*dOO*d'l] *n* (*coll*) silly fellow, noodle.

doodle (2) *v/i* scribble or draw aimlessly or unconsciously ~ **doodle** *n* mark or design made by doodling.

doodlebug [*dOO*d'lbug] *n* (*coll*) a flying bomb.

doom [*dOOm*] *n* (*ar*) formal judgement; condemnation; fate, destiny; ruin, death; **crack of d.** end of the world, Last Judgement ~ **doom** *v/t* condemn, pass sentence on; destine (to an evil fate).

doomsday [*dOOmz*day] *n* the Day of Judgement.

doomster [*dOOm*ster] *n* (*coll*) one who warns of vast future calamities.

doomwatch [*dOOm*woch] *n* (*coll*) the study of possible major threats to environmental and ecological balance.

door [*dawr*] *n* hinged, revolving, or sliding barrier which closes an entrance; entrance having a door in it, doorway; (*fig*) means of approach, access, opportunity; **answer the d.** go to open the door to a caller; **lie at the d. of** be attributable to; **next d. (in)** the next house; **next d. to** very nearly, almost; **out of doors** outside, in the open; **show a person the d.** ask or order someone to leave the house; **d. to d.** from one house to the next, calling at every house.

doorbell [*dawr*bel] *n* bell inside a house, connected to the outer door and rung from outside.

doorframe [*dawr*fRaym] *n* the surround to a door opening, usually rebated.

doorkeeper [*dawr*keeper] *n* janitor, one who guards an entrance.

doorman [*dawr*man] *n* attendant at the entrance of hotel or public building, hall-porter.

doormat [*dawr*mat] *n* mat before a door on which to wipe one's shoes; (*coll*) person who meekly accepts bullying, ill-treatment *etc*.

door-money [*dawr*-muni] *n* payment made on entering a place of entertainment.

doornail [*dawr*nayl] *n* large-headed nail with which doors were formerly studded; **dead as a d.** thoroughly, undoubtedly dead.

doorplate [*dawr*playt] *n* metal plate on outer door of a house showing occupant's name *etc*.

doorpost [*dawr*pOst] *n* a vertical in a doorframe.

doorstep [*dawr*step] *n* step upwards between ground-level and threshold; (*sl*) thick slice of bread.

doorstrip [*dawr*stRip] *n* strip of metal, rubber, felt, plastic *etc* fixed under or round a door to exclude draughts.

doorway [*dawr*way] *n* an opening closed by a door; (*fig*) means of access.

dope [*dOp*] *n* (*coll*) drug, *esp* narcotic, harmful or addictive; drug given to racehorses or greyhounds; (*coll*) secret or advance information; any one of various preparations for which a more accurate name is not immediately available; quick-drying cellulose lacquer used for tighten-

ing and protecting the fabric of aircraft, or for coating textiles or leather; (*phot*) developer; (*sl*) motor spirit; (*US sl*) one who takes drugs; fool; **d. fiend** drug addict; **d. merchant, d. pedlar** one who illegally sells addictive drugs ~ **dope** *v/t* and *i* treat with dope; (*coll*) give drugs to; (*fig*) smoothe; dupe, deceive; be a drug addict; (*phys*) add an impurity to a semiconductor to achieve a particular characteristic; **d. out** (*sl*) find out ~ **doper** *n*.

dopa [*dO*pa] (*med*) crystalline amino-acid used in treating Parkinson's disease.

dopey, dopy [*dO*pi] *adj* (*coll*) under the influence of drugs; slow-witted; half-asleep.

doppelgänger [*dopel*ganger] *n* apparition of a person not yet dead; a double, a fetch.

Doppler [*dop*ler] *n* (*phys*) **d. effect** change of observed frequency of light waves, sound waves *etc* caused by relative movement of source or observer.

dorado [*do*Raad*O*] *n* a brightly coloured sea-fish often called a dolphin; a southern constellation.

Dorian [*daw*Ri-an] *n* and *adj* (inhabitant) of Doris, district of ancient Greece; **d. mode** (*mus*) scale represented by the white keys of the piano beginning on D.

Doric [*do*Rik] *adj* Dorian; (*of dialect or manners*) plain, rustic; **D. order** (*archi*) oldest, strongest, and simplest of the three Greek orders of architecture > PDAA.

dormancy [*dawr*mansi] *n* dormant state.

dormant [*dawr*mant] *adj* sleeping; inactive, not in use, at rest; (*biol*) torpid, completely inactive, hibernating; (*bot*) inactive, not vegetating; (*of a title*) in abeyance; (*her*) in a sleeping posture, with head on paws.

dormer [*dawr*mer] *n* (*hist*) bedroom; vertical window coming through a sloping roof.

dormitory [*dawr*miteRi] *n* large sleeping apartment, sometimes divided into cubicles; **d. suburb** suburb whose inhabitants are absent all day at work in a nearby city.

dormouse (*pl* **dormice**) [*dawr*mows] *n* small hibernating rodent akin to squirrel.

dormy [*dawr*mi] *adj* (*golf*) leading by as many holes as there are left to play.

dorothy-bag [*do*Rothi-bag] *n* small soft pouch with drawstrings, carried from the wrist.

dorsal (1) [*dawr*sal] *adj* pertaining to, near, or on the back; ridge-shaped ~ **dorsally** *adv* on, at, towards, or from, the back.

dorsal (2), **dorsel** see **dossal**.

dorsi-, dorso- *pref* back.

dorsum [*dawr*sum] *n* (*anat*) the back; upper or outer part or surface.

dory (1) [*dawr*Ri] *n* edible sea-fish of golden colour.

dory (2) *n* small flat-bottomed ship's boat used by fishing-vessels.

dosage [*dO*sij] *n* giving of medicine or radiation in doses; amount of a single dose.

dose [*dOs*] *n* amount of medicine, X-rays or other radiation to be taken at any one time; amount of something regularly given, *esp* something unpleasant; flavouring or strengthening ingredient added to wine *etc*; bout (of illness); (*sl*) a venereal infection ~ **dose** *v/t* and *i* give or take medicine in doses; measure a dose of.

doss [dos] n (sl) bed in a cheap lodging-house; a sleep ~ **doss** v/i sleep, esp in a doss-house; **d. down** arrange a makeshift bed.

dossal, dossel, dorsal (2), **dorsel** [dosal] n (eccles) drapery behind altar or (formerly) round the chancel; ornamental upholstery behind a chair, throne etc; back of a high-backed upholstered chair.

dosser [doser] n one who sleeps at doss-houses.

doss-house [dos-hows] n cheap lodging-house.

dossier [dosi-ay] n collection of documents concerned with some individual person or matter.

dossil [dosil] n plug of lint for a wound; folded bandage used as compress; (print) wad of cloth for cleaning ink off a plate.

dost [dust] ar 2nd pers sing pres/ind of **do**.

dot (1) [dot] n small round mark made by pen, pencil, or brush; anything resembling a dot in size or appearance; small round spot; speck; (gramm) point indicating abbreviation or full stop; point used over i and j; (math) decimal point; (mus) point placed after note or rest which increases its length by half; staccato mark; (Morse code) symbol of short sound; **off one's d.** (sl) crazy; **on the d.** (coll) at the exact time or place; **in the year d.** (coll) very long ago ~ **dot** (p/part dotting, p/t and p/part dotted) v/t mark with a dot; form with dots; place a dot over or after; fill or cover with anything resembling dots; scatter haphazardly; (sl) hit, punch; **d. and carry one** (coll) walk with a limp; **d. one's i's** be very scrupulous or meticulous; **the dotted line** course of action marked out for one; **sign on the dotted line** agree fully or formally, agree blindly.

dot (2) [dot] n (Fr) woman's marriage portion, dowry.

dotage [dOtij] n feebleness of mind due to old age, second childhood; foolish or blind love.

dotard [dOterd] n weak foolish old man.

dote [dOt] v/i be weak-minded or foolish through old age; love blindly or excessively; **d. on be** infatuated by ~ **doter** n.

doth [duth] ar third pers sing pres/ind of **do**.

doting [dOting] adj infatuated, foolishly fond; senile; (bot) decaying through age ~ **dotingly** adv.

dottiness [dotines] n (coll) silliness craziness.

dottle, dottel [dot'l] n plug of tobacco left in pipe after smoking.

dotty [doti] adj (coll) silly, crazy; marked with dots.

double [dub'l] adj twice as much; as much again; having two layers, folded in two; in pairs, twofold, having two similar parts; designed for two users; serving two purposes; having two meanings, ambiguous; underhand, two-faced, deceptive; (bot) having more than one set of petals; (mus) pitched an octave lower ~ **double** adv twice over; twofold; two at a time, in pairs ~ **double** n twice a quantity, number, or size; thing or person exactly like another; doppelgänger; (theat) substitute, stand-in; actor taking two parts in one play; running pace about twice normal walking pace; sharp turn, return on one's own tracks; trick; (cards) twofold increase in points or stakes decided on by a player; hand justifying such an increase; (racing) bet on two horses in different races, the stake and winnings from the first being re-wagered on the second; (darts) a hit between the two outer circles of the board; (dominoes) piece with same number of pips on each half; (tennis) two successive faults when serving; (pl) game of tennis with two players on each side, foursome; **at the d.** at a run, quickly ~ **double** v/t and i multiply by two, increase twofold; fold in two; turn or twist sharply, turn back in one's tracks; duplicate, repeat exactly; be exactly like, be a replica of; (theat) act two parts in one play; act as substitute; (mus) duplicate a melody in an upper or lower octave; (naut) sail completely round; (mil) proceed at twice walking pace; (cards) increase points and penalties possible to the opponent; (billiards) cause ball to rebound from cushions before entering the pocket; **d. back** return on one's tracks; fold over; **d. up** bend or cause to bend in two; collapse with pain, crumple up; clench (fist); share a room or bed; (betting) continue to double the stake until a win.

double-acting [dub'l-akting] adj (eng) reciprocating, acting in two directions > PDE.

double-agent [dub'l-ayjent] n spy who appears to work for one of two countries while really serving the other.

double-banked [dub'l-bankt] adj (naut) carrying guns on two decks; having two men to an oar, or two opposite oars to a thwart; (mot) driving or parking two vehicles abreast.

double-barrelled [dub'l-baReld] adj (of gun) having two barrels; (fig) serving two purposes, having two effects, ambiguous; (of surname) hyphenated.

doublebass [dub'lbays] n largest instrument of the violin class > PDM.

double-bond [dub'l-bond] n (chem) two valency bonds linking two atoms in an unsaturated compound.

double-breasted [dub'l-bRestid] adj (of jacket etc) cut so that the fronts are, or seem to be, capable of being buttoned on either side.

double-chin [dub'l-chin] n fold of loose flesh below chin.

doublecross [dub'lkRos] v/t (coll) betray, cheat, act treacherously towards ~ **double-cross** n.

double-dealer [dub'l-deeler] n one who says one thing and does another, deceiver ~ **double-dealing** n duplicity.

double-decker [dub'l-deker] n bus with seats on top; biplane; any structure with seating accommodation on two levels.

double-declutch [dub'l-deekluch] v/i (mot) momentarily release clutch-pedal and press accelerator while in neutral to facilitate engagement of lower gear.

double-dutch [dub'l-duch] n (coll) gibberish.

double-dyed [dub'l-dId] adj twice dyed; (fig) deeply stained with evil, thoroughly wicked.

double-edged [dub'l-ejd] adj with two cutting-edges; (fig) capable of opposite applications.

double-entry [dub'l-entRi] n system of bookkeeping in which each transaction is entered both as debit and as credit.

double-exposure [dub'l-ekspOzher] n (phot) the

taking of two superimposed images on one negative; photograph so obtained.

double-faced [dub'l-*fayst*] *adj* having two faces; (*fig*) insincere, hypocritical.

double-feature [dub'l-*feecher*] *n* (*cin*) programme in which two full-length films are shown.

double-hung [dub'l-*hung*] *adj* (*of window*) having its sashes hung with weights and lines.

double-jointed [dub'l-*joint*id] *adj* having joints which can bend at abnormal angles; unusually supple.

double-lock [dub'l-*lok*] *v/t* lock by two turns of a key; make thoroughly secure.

doubleness [*dub*'lnis] *n* state or quality of being double; duplicity.

double-park [dub'l-*paark*] *v/t* park alongside a car already parked by a kerb.

double-quick [dub'l-*kwik*] *adj* and *adv* very quick, at the double.

double-stop [*dub*'l-stop] *v/i* (*mus*) produce chords on a violin by playing on two or more strings at once.

doublet [*dub*let] *n* (*hist*) man's close-fitting upper garment; one of a pair of similar objects; (*phil*) one of two words of the same origin but different in sense and spelling; (*pl*) throw of two dice showing same number on both.

doubletake [dub'l*tayk*] *n* (*theat*) the expressing of a delayed reaction to an ambiguous remark, unexpected situation *etc*.

doubletalk [dub'l*tawk*] *n* words which seem meaningful but are not; empty or ambiguous phrases (*esp* political slogans *etc*).

doublethink [dub'l*think*] *n* faculty of believing in two contradictory ideas simultaneously.

double-throw [dub'l-*thRO*] *adj* (*elect*) (*of switches*) capable of engaging with two alternative sets of fixed contacts.

double-tongued [dub'l-*tungd*] *adj* deceitful, backbiting.

double-tonguing [dub'l-*tung*ing] *n* (*mus*) method of playing staccato notes on a wind instrument by using the front and rear of the tongue alternately.

doubling [*dub*ling] *n* multiplication by two; act of darting back, dodging; a plait or fold; lining of robes of state; (*bui*) a double eaves course.

doubloon [dub*lOOn*] *n* (*hist*) Spanish gold coin.

doublure [*dub*lyoor] *n* (*Fr*) ornamental lining inside a book-cover.

doubly [*dub*li] *adv* in two ways, twice over.

doubt [*dowt*] *n* uncertainty, indecision; lack of belief or conviction; misgiving; **beyond d., out of d., without d.** certain; **in d.** not certain, in dispute; **no d.** certain; probable; **give the benefit of the d.** assume person's innocence when guilt is not fully proved ~ **doubt** *v/t* and *i* be uncertain, be inclined to disbelieve; be unconvinced or sceptical; distrust, feel suspicious of; **doubting Thomas** a sceptic ~ **doubtable** *adj* ~ **doubter** *n*.

doubtful [*dowt*fool] *adj* uncertain, undecided, hesitating; not proved, not clear, ambiguous; causing uncertainty or suspicion; disreputable, of bad reputation ~ **doubtfully** *adv* ~ **doubtfulness** *n*.

doubtless [*dowt*les] *adv* unquestionably; probably ~ **doubtless** *adj* (*poet*) fearless, unhesitating.

douceur [dOO*sur*] *n* (*Fr*) bribe; gratuity, tip.

douche [*dOOsh*] *n* jet of liquid directed on to or into the body; shower-bath; device for applying a douche; **cold d.** (*coll*) disagreeable surprise, sudden cause of discouragement ~ **douche** *v/t* and *i*.

dough [*dO*] *n* paste of flour, liquid *etc* for baking into bread or pastry; (*sl*) money.

doughboy [*dO*boi] *n* boiled dumpling; (*US sl*) American infantryman.

doughnut [*dO*nut] *n* small, sweet, deep-fried cake.

doughty [*dow*ti] *adj* (*poet* or *joc*) brave, formidable ~ **doughtily** *adv* ~ **doughtiness** *n*.

doughy [*dO*-i] *adj* like dough in appearance or texture; (*coll*) (*of complexion*) pale, pasty.

dour [*door*] *adj* (*Scots*) stern, obstinate, gloomy, forbidding ~ **dourly** *adv* ~ **dourness** *n*.

douse, dowse (1) [*dows*] *v/t* drench with water; (*naut*) pull down (sail) hurriedly; (*coll*) put out (a light).

dove [*duv*] *n* bird of pigeon family; (*fig*) the Holy Spirit; symbol of peace or innocence; darling; (*coll*) one who urges that a war be limited or ended.

dove-colour [*duv*-kuler] pinkish-grey.

dovecot [*duv*kot] *n* raised hutch with nesting-boxes for pigeons.

dovekie [*duv*ki] *n* the black guillemot.

dovelike [*duv*līk] *adj* innocent, tender.

dovetail [*duv*tayl] *n* (*carp*) joint with interlocking tenons, shaped like a pigeon's tail > PDE ~ **dovetail** *v/t* and *i* fit together by dovetail joints; (*fig*) fit closely together, be easily linked up.

dowager [*dow*-ajer] *n* prefix assumed by widow of man of title, to distinguish her from ! ie wife of his heir; (*coll*) stately or wealthy elde: y woman.

dowdily [*dow*dili] *adv* shabbily ~ **dowdiness** *n*.

dowdy [*dow*di] *n* and *adj* (woman) shabbily or unfashionably dressed ~ **dowdyish** *adj*.

dowel [*dow*el] *n* headless pin or peg holding together two pieces of wood or stone > PDE ~ **dowel** *v/t* fasten with dowels ~ **dowelling** *n*.

dowel-screw [*dow*el-skROO] *n* a wood screw threaded at each end.

dower [*dow*er] *n* portion of her husband's estate granted to his widow for life; money brought by wife to husband at marriage, dowry; gift from husband to wife; talent, natural gift; **d. house** house reserved for widow from husband's estate ~ **dower** *v/t* give a dower or dowry to; endow.

dowlas [*dow*las] *n* strong calico.

down (1) [*down*] *n* first feathers of young birds; under-feathers of fowls; any soft hairy substance.

down (2) *n* tract of open, treeless, hilly land; **the Downs** the chalk hills of southern England; the sea off the east coast of Kent.

down (3) *adv* from higher to lower position, amount, size, quality, or intensity; in low position, on the ground; from earlier to later period; away from central or important place; below surface, horizon, or normal level; in cash, as immediate payment; in writing, on record; **d. at heel** shabby, poor; dejected; **d. and out** penniless, destitute; **d. in the mouth** looking unhappy; **d. on** angry with or hostile to; **d. on one's luck** in difficulties, needing money; **d. to the**

ground thoroughly; **d. under** (*coll*) in Australia or New Zealand; **d. with!** destroy, get rid of ~ **down** *adj* descending; on the ground; dejected; (*of trains etc*) travelling away from the chief terminus, *esp* from London ~ **down** *prep* from higher to lower position on or in; outwards from, away from; from earlier to later time in; along; **d. wind** in the direction the wind is blowing ~ **down** *v/t* (*coll*) bring, put, throw, or knock down; defeat; **d. tools** stop working, go on strike ~ **down** *n* reversal of fortune; (*coll*) dislike, grudge.

down (4) *n* **D.'s syndrome** a congenital chromosome defect causing mental deficiency (formerly called 'mongolism')

downbeat [*down*beet] *n* (*mus*) first beat of bar ~ **downbeat** *adj* (*coll*) undramatic, casual, cool; pessimistic, gloomy.

downcast (1) [*down*kaast] *n* shaft bringing fresh air into mine; (*geol*) depression of strata on one side of a fault.

downcast (2) *adj* dejected, discouraged; (*of eyes*) directed downwards.

downdraught [*down*dRaaft] *n* descending current of air.

downfall [*down*fawl] *n* fall from power or prosperity; ruin, collapse; heavy fall of rain ~ **downfallen** *adj* ruined, decrepit.

downgrade [*down*gRayd] *n* downward slope; tendency to deteriorate; **on the d.** declining, waning, deteriorating ~ **downgrade** [downgRayd] *v/t* demote, place in inferior position or job.

downhearted [down*haart*id] *adj* dispirited, discouraged.

downhill [*down*hil/down*hil*] *adv* towards the bottom of a hill, downwards; **go d.** (*fig*) deteriorate; lose health, prosperity, or standing ~ **downhill** *adj* going or sloping down ~ **downhill** *n* downward slope of a hill, declivity.

downiness [*down*ines] *n* condition of being downy.

downland [*down*land] *n* hilly pasture land; temperate grasslands of Australia.

downlead [*down*leed] *n* (*rad*) conductor linking the aerial to receiver or transmitter.

downline [*down*lin] *n* railway line for trains travelling away from the main terminus.

downpipe [*down*pip] *n* (*bui*) rainwater pipe from roof-gutters to drain.

downpour [*down*pawr] *n* heavy continuous rain.

downright [*down*Rit] *adj* bluntly straightforward, frank; utter, unmistakable, thorough ~ **downright** *adv* utterly, thoroughly ~ **downrightly** *adv* bluntly, frankly ~ **downrightness** *n*.

downrush [*down*Rush] *n* sudden rush or flow downwards.

downstairs [downst..irz] *adv* and *adj* to a lower floor; on a lower floor ~ **downstairs** *n* lower floor, ground floor.

downstream [*down*stReem] *adv* and *adj* in the direction that the stream is flowing; on the lower reaches of the stream.

downthrow [*down*thRO] *n* (*geol*) downward displacement of strata by a fault, downcast (1).

downtown [*down*town] *adv*, *adj* and *n* (towards, into, in, or of) the main business section of a town.

down-train [*down*-tRain] *n* train travelling away from the main terminus.

downtrodden [*down*tRoden] *adj* trampled down; (*fig*) oppressed.

downturn [*down*turn] *n* fall in output, prices *etc*; slump.

downward, downwards [*down*ward, *down*wardz] *adv* and *adj* towards or in a lower position, towards a later date; descending; leading to ruin.

downwash [*down*wosh] *n* (*aer*) air thrust downwards by wing *etc* of aircraft in flight.

downy [*down*i] *adj* covered with down; soft and fluffy; (*sl*) sharp, knowing; resembling downland.

dowry [*dowr*Ri] *n* property brought by woman to husband at marriage; (*fig*) natural gift, talent.

dowse (1) [*dows*] see **douse.**

dowse (2) *v/i* search for water or ore deposits by the feeling of a branch or pendulum held in the hand ~ **dowser** *n* one who dowses.

dowsing-rod [*dows*ing-Rod] *n* branch used in dowsing.

doxological [doksOlojikal] *adj* relating to, or contained in, a doxology.

doxology [doksoloji] *n* (*eccles*) hymn of praise to God, *esp* the *Gloria Patri* or the *Gloria in excelsis*.

doxy [*dok*si] *n* (*sl*) hussy; beggarly and immoral woman.

doyen [*dway*an(g)/*doi*yen] *n* the senior member of a group, society, profession *etc*.

doyley see **doily.**

doze [*dOz*] *v/i* sleep lightly in snatches; be half-asleep ~ **doze** *n*.

dozen [*duzen*] *n* set of twelve; (*pl*) (*coll*) very many; **baker's d.** thirteen; **daily d.** physical exercise to be performed daily; **a round d.** a full dozen; **talk nineteen to the d.** (*coll*) talk fast and without stopping ~ **dozenth** *adj* twelfth.

doziness [*dOz*ines] *n* state of being half-asleep, drowsiness ~ **dozy** *adj* drowsy.

drab (1) [*dRab*] *n* slattern; prostitute.

drab (2) *adj* of dull fawn or mud colour; dull, monotonous, dingy ~ **drab** *n* coarse woollen cloth of yellowish-brown colour.

drabble [*dRab*'l] *v/t* and *i* make wet or dirty; trail along through mire; fish with a drail ~ **drabbling** *n* method of fishing with a drail.

drably [*dRab*li] *adv* dingily, dully.

drabness [*dRab*nis] *n* quality of being drab.

drabs see **dribs.**

drachm [*dRam*] *n* dram; (*fig*) very small quantity; (hist) drachma.

drachma (*pl* **drachmae, drachmas**) [*dRak*ma] *n* (hist) chief silver coin of the ancient Greeks; ancient Greek unit of weight; modern Greek copper coin; drachm.

draconian [dRak*Oni*-an] *adj* (*of laws etc*) harsh, inhuman.

draff [*dRaf*] *n* refuse of malt after brewing, dregs, swill; (*fig*) something worthless ~ **draffish** *adj* ~ **draffy** *adj*.

draft [*dRaaft*] *n* act of drawing; that which is drawn; (*mil*) body of men detailed for special duty; (*US*) selective conscription; body of persons conscripted; preliminary sketch, rough drawing or first copy; written order for payment of money; (*masonry*) smooth margin or strip worked on a stone face; (*moulding*) taper given to sides of a die or pattern; (*textiles*) attenuation of thread in spinning ~ **draft** *v/t* (*mil*) select men for special duty; (*US*) to conscript; persuade (someone) to be candidate for office; make preliminary sketch of, plan out, make rough first copy of.

draftee [dRaaftee] *n* (*US*) a conscript.

draft-horse see **draught-horse**.

draft-ox see **draught-ox**.

draftsman see **draughtsman**.

drag (*pres/part* **dragging**, *p/t* and *p/part* **dragged**) [dRag] *v/t* and *i* pull slowly or with effort; trail along ground or other surface; search (stretch of water) with grappling-irons, nets *etc*, dredge; break up soil with harrow; pass by slowly; lag behind; (*mus*) fail to keep time; grow tedious; **d. anchor** (*naut*) trail loosened anchor over sea-bottom; **d. in** (*coll*) bring in (a topic, remark *etc*) unnecessarily or in forced way; **d. on** continue too long, be tedious; **d. up** bring up (children) carelessly or roughly; **d. one's feet** (*coll*) act with deliberate slowness ~ **drag** *n* that which is pulled along a surface; heavy harrow; heavy sledge; type of large horse-drawn coach; apparatus for drawing up objects from under water; strong-smelling substance drawn over ground to distract hounds from quarry; brake on wheel; (*fig*) hindrance, obstruction; (*aer*) resistance of air to aeroplane in flight; loss of speed due to this; (*billiards*) method of reducing ball's speed by spinning it; (*coll*) a pull on a cigarette or pipe; (*coll*) something boring; (*coll*) women's clothing when worn by men; (*US coll*) personal influence, pull; (*sl*) motorcar.

draggle [dRag'l] *v/t* and *i* trail along the ground; make dirty by trailing through mud; lag behind, straggle ~ **draggle-tail** *n* a slovenly woman.

drag-hunt [dRag-hunt] *n* hunt in which hounds follow a drag.

dragline [dRaglin] *n* dragrope.

dragnet [dRagnet] *n* net dragged through water to catch fish; one dragged along ground to catch game; (*coll*) coordination of efforts for rounding up suspected criminals.

dragoman (*pl* **dragomans**) [dRagoman] *n* guide-interpreter for travellers in the East.

dragon [dRagon] *n* mythical reptile usually winged and breathing out fire; (*coll*) fierce person, *esp* severe old woman; type of short carbine or musket; (*zool*) type of lizard with wing-like membranes on which it glides; (*bibl*) name of various monsters; (*mil*) strong armoured tractor.

dragonfly [dRagonfli] *n* brightly coloured insect with long slender body and four transparent wings.

dragonish [dRagonish] *adj* like a dragon; fierce.

dragoon [dRagOOn] *n* (*hist*) mounted infantryman armed with short musket; soldier belonging to certain regiments of cavalry; ferocious person ~ **dragoon** *v/t* subdue by armed force; harass, persecute; enforce by harshness.

drag-racing [dRag-Raysing] *n* (*mot*) race to test acceleration of cars.

dragrope [dRagROp] *n* rope for hauling; rope hung from balloon to slow it down or moor it.

dragsman [dRagzman] *n* one who drives a drag, coachman; (*sl*) thief who steals from moving vehicles, *esp* trains.

drail [dRayl] *n* weighted fish-hook and line.

drain [dRayn] *v/t* and *i* draw away (liquid) gradually, *gen* through pipes, trenches *etc*; draw off liquid from, empty completely; drink up the contents of; (*fig*) exhaust, use up gradually; flow away gradually; provide drains for; **d. to the dregs** drink up to the last drop; (*fig*) experience to the full ~ **drain** *n* pipe or artificial channel to carry away sewage, excess water *etc*; (*surg*) tube to draw off discharge from abscess or wound; (*fig*) continual demand (on strength or resources), cause of exhaustion; small quantity of liquid, a drink; (*pl*) dregs; **go down the d.** (*coll*) be wasted, lost; **laugh like a d.** laugh loudly and vulgarly.

drainage [dRaynij] *n* act or method of draining; system of drains; that which is drained off, sewage; (*geol*) removal of superfluous water by river system; **d. basin** the area so drained.

drainer [dRayner] *n* container in which things are put to drain, colander; draining-board; person who lays drainpipes *etc*.

draining-board [dRayning-bawrd] *n* sloping grooved surface beside a sink on which wet crockery is placed to dry off.

drainpipe [dRainpip] *n* pipe below ground to remove sewage, waste water, or rainwater > PDE; (*pl*) (*sl*) trousers of very narrow cut.

drake (1) [dRayk] *n* male of the duck.

drake (2) *n* (*ar*) dragon; (*hist*) viking warship; type of small cannon; (*angling*) type of mayfly used as bait.

dram [dRam] *n* (*avoirdupois weight*) one-sixteenth of an ounce; (*apothecaries' weight*) one-eighth of an ounce; small drink of liquor.

drama [dRaama] *n* composition depicting a story through dialogue and action, for stage, radio, or television performance; stage play; group of plays considered collectively; theatrical profession or art; exciting, vivid, or emotionally stirring story or series of actions; quality of being dramatic.

dramatic [dRamatik] *adj* pertaining to, in the form of, a drama; like a drama; thrilling, vivid; tense, filled with emotion ~ **dramatical** *adj* ~ **dramatically** *adv*.

dramatics [dRamatiks] *n* (*pl*) art of acting or producing plays; (*coll*) display of exaggerated emotion.

dramatis personae [dRamatis-pursOni] *n* (*pl*) (*Lat*) the characters in a play; a list of these.

dramatist [dRamatist] *n* writer of plays.

dramatization [dRamatizayshon] *n* process of putting into form of drama; that which is dramatized; dramatized version (of novel *etc*).

dramatize [dRamatiz] *v/t* put into form of drama, turn (novel *etc*) into play or film; describe dramatically; consider or present with exaggerated emotion, give too much importance to.

dramaturge, dramaturgist [dRamaturj, dRamaturjist] *n* playwright, dramatist.

drambuie [dRambyOO-i] *n* (*tr*) type of Scottish whisky liqueur.

dram-drinker [dRam-dRinker] *n* habitual drinker of alcoholic spirits.

drank [drank] *p/t* of **drink**.

drape [dRayp] *v/t* and *i* cover with loosely hanging fabric; arrange (material) in graceful folds; **d. oneself** (*coll*) take up a casual but graceful attitude ∼ **drape** *n* manner in which loose cloth hangs; (*pl*) hangings, drapery; (*US*) curtains.

draper [dRayper] *n* dealer in cloth and clothing.

drapery [dRayperi] *n* a draper's business, wares, or shop; hangings; loose clothing arranged in folds; (*sculp, painting*) artistic arrangement or rendering of such clothing or hangings.

drastic [dRastik] *adj* having a powerful effect; violent, harshly effective, thorough ∼ **drastically** *adv*.

drat [dRat] *interj* and *v/t* (*coll*) bother, confound.

dratted [dRatid] *adj* (*coll*) wretched, infuriating.

draught [dRaaft] *n* action of drawing, pulling; quantity drawn; act of drinking; amount of a drink swallowed without stopping; dose of medicine; (*naut*) depth of water displaced by a ship, displacement; current of air indoors, up a chimney or through a boiler furnace; preparatory sketch; name of a piece in game of draughts; (*pl*) game resembling simple form of chess, played by two persons on a chessboard; **on d.** sold from the cask; **black d.** purgative medicine composed of senna; **feel the d.** (*coll*) be harmed by unfavourable conditions.

draught-board [dRaaft-bawrd] *n* board used in the game of draughts.

draught-horse, draft-horse [dRaaft-hawrs] *n* strong horse used for pulling loads.

draughtily [dRaaftili] *adv* in a draughty way.

draughtiness [dRaaftinis] *n* quality of being draughty.

draught-ox, draft-ox [dRaaft-ox] *n* ox used for pulling heavy loads.

draughtsman, draftsman [dRaaftsman] *n* one who makes drawings and plans for buildings, machines *etc*; one who draws up documents, *esp* legal and parliamentary; piece for playing draughts ∼ **draughtsmanship** *n* skill in drawing.

draughty [dRaafti] *adj* exposed to, full of, currents of air.

Dravidian [dRavidi-an] *n* and *adj* (member, language) of non-Aryan aboriginal race in India.

draw (*p/t* drew, *p/part* drawn) [dRaw] *v/t* and *i* cause to move towards oneself, pull or drag towards oneself; pull, drag, haul (in any direction); pull steadily out, **extract**; disembowel; pull (weapon) from sheath; extract (liquid) from, cause to flow; obtain (money); (*fig*) form (an opinion), deduce; obtain in a lottery; attract, allure; (*coll*) be an attraction, attract attention; elicit, bring about, cause; (*coll*) elicit information from; (*coll*) tease; take in (breath), cause air to flow; make lines or figures with pencil *etc*; make a linear representation, sketch, or diagram of; describe; make tense; extend; shape or flatten (metal) by beating or stamping; come, move; approach; contract; (*cards*) get (a card) from the pack; end a game without advantage to either side; obtain in a lottery; pick out at random; (*hunting*) drive quarry from its lair; track by scent; search (an area) for game; make a stronger infusion of tea by letting it stand; (*naut*) displace (a given depth of water); **d. back** move backwards, retreat, shrink (from an action); **d. a blank** find or obtain nothing, be disappointed; **d. down** incur, bring on oneself; **d. in** approach; (*of days*) grow shorter; **d. the line** show scruple, decline; **d. the long-bow** exaggerate, boast, lie;

d. it mild refrain from exaggeration; **d. on** approach; draw a weapon against; **d. out** lengthen, stretch; prolong; encourage someone to talk; **d. round** gather round; **d. the teeth of** make harmless; **d. up** arrange in order, *esp* in military formation; set out (a document) in due form; come to a halt; **d. oneself up** stand or sit more straight, *esp* as a sign of indignation *etc* ∼ **draw** *n* process of pulling or being pulled; the drawing out of one card from a pack or of one lot in a lottery; raffle, lottery; game which neither side wins, tie, stalemate; that which attracts, *esp* a popular entertainment; **quick on the d.** quick in drawing a weapon from its holster.

drawback [dRawbak] *n* disadvantage; refund.

drawbridge [dRawbRij] *n* bridge which can be raised and lowered at one end, or moved bodily to allow vessels to pass.

drawee [dRawee] *n* person who is to pay out on a money order, bill of exchange *etc*.

drawer [dRawer] *n* one who, that which draws; sliding lidless container set into a framework from which it can be pulled out; person drawing a cheque, money order *etc*; person drawing out drinks, tapster; (*pl*) undergarment for lower part of body and upper part of legs; **chest of drawers** piece of furniture consisting of several drawers in a framework.

drawing [dRaw-ing] *n* art of making pictures with pencil or pen and ink; picture thus made; (*metal*) process of extending and tapering.

drawing-board [dRaw-ing-bawrd] *n* board to which paper is fastened while making a drawing.

drawing-paper [dRaw-ing-payper] *n* paper suitable for drawing on.

drawing-pin [dRaw-ing-pin] *n* short pin with large flat head.

drawing-room [dRaw-ing-ROOm] *n* room set aside for formal entertainment of guests; parlour, main sitting-room; court reception at which ladies are presented.

drawl [dRawl] *v/i* and *t* speak in a slow affected manner ∼ **drawl** *n* ∼ **drawling** *adj* and *n*.

drawn [dRawn] *adj* (*p/part* of draw) (*of weapon*) unsheathed, bare; (*of game*) without victory to either side; (*of appearance*) haggard, weary, tense; disembowelled.

drawnet [dRawnet] *n* net for catching large birds.

drawn-threadwork [dRawn-thRedwurk] *n* embroidery on linen from which threads have been pulled out.

drawstring [dRawstRing] *n* string passed through a hem to close an opening by gathering the material.

draw-well [dRaw-wel] *n* well from which water is obtained by lowering a bucket into it.

dray (1) [dRay] *n* low cart without sides used for heavy loads.

dray (2) see **drey**.

drayhorse [dRayhawrs] *n* strong cart-horse.

drayman [dRayman] *n* one who drives a dray.

drayplough [dRayplow] *n* plough for heavy soils.

dread [dRed] *v/t* fear greatly; anticipate with fear or loathing; feel awe of ∼ **dread** *n* anxious fear, terror; apprehension, anxiety ∼ **dread** *adj* causing fear or awe ∼ **dreadable** *adj*.

dreadful [dRedfool] *adj* terrible, awe-inspiring; (*coll*) bad, unpleasant, tiresome; **penny d.** cheap sensational story, magazine *etc* ~ **dreadfully** *adv* terribly, terrifyingly; *(coll)* very.

dreadnought [dRednawt] *n* type of heavily armoured powerful battleship; type of thick woollen cloth; coat made of such cloth.

dream [dReem] *n* series of images or thoughts passing through the mind during sleep; fantasy, fanciful train of thought, daydream; reverie, state of abstraction; improbable hope, ambition; ideal way of life; remote political or social goal; pleasing but impractical plan; anything too pleasing to seem real ~ **dream** (*p/t* and *p/part* **dreamed, dreamt**) *v/i* and *t* have dreams or daydreams; see or experience in a dream; cherish wild hopes or impractical schemes; imagine, fancy; **d. up** *(coll)* invent, devise, imagine ~ **dream** *adj* of or in dreams; imaginary; *(coll)* ideal, perfect.

dreamer [dReemer] *n* one who dreams; unpractical person; idealist.

dreamily [dReemili] *adv* in a dreamy manner ~ **dreaminess** *n*.

dreamland [dReemland] *n* place imagined in dreams; sleep; *(fig)* fantastically beautiful place.

dreamless [dReemles] *adj (of sleep)* heavy, undisturbed by dreams ~ **dreamlessly** *adv*.

dreamlike [dReemlik] *adj* like a dream, fantastic, unreal, vague.

dreamt [dRemt] *p/t* and *p/part* of **dream**.

dreamy [dReemi] *adj* given to daydreams, inattentive, absent-minded; like a dream, vague, unreal; soothing, quiet, peaceful; *(sl)* lovely.

drear [dReer] *adj (ar)* gloomy, melancholy, dreary.

dreary [dReerRi] *adj* melancholy, sad, gloomy; depressing, boring ~ **drearily** *adv* ~ **dreariness** *n* ~ **drearisome** *adj*.

dredge (1) [dRej] *n* type of net for gathering objects from bottom of sea, river *etc*; vessel, equipped for underwater excavation or for mining alluvial deposits of tin *etc* > PDE ~ **dredge** *v/t* and *i* ~ **dredger** (1) vessel equipped for dredging.

dredge (2) *v/t (cookery)* sprinkle with flour, salt, sugar *etc* ~ **dredger** (2) *n* container with holes in lid for sprinkling.

dree [dRee] *v/t (ar)* endure.

dregs [dRegz] *n (pl)* sediment, *esp* of wine; lees, grounds; *(fig)* anything worthless; worthless people, criminals, paupers.

drench [dRench] *v/t* make thoroughly wet, soak, saturate; make (an animal) drink, *esp* medicine ~ **drench** *n* large dose of medicine, *esp* if given to animal; thorough wetting ~ **drencher** *n* funnel for giving medicine to an animal; *(coll)* heavy shower.

Dresden [dRezden] *adj* and *n* (of or like) a variety of porcelain or fine china.

dress [dRes] *v/t* and *i* put clothes on; make or provide clothes for; choose or wear clothes; adorn, arrange elegantly, decorate; arrange (troops) in straight lines; prepare for use; make smooth; *(carp)* plane and sandpaper timber; *(bui)* cut stones to final shape; clean and draw (a fowl); season (food); cultivate, manure (soil); apply medicaments to (a wound); **d. down** rub down (a horse); *(coll)* beat, scold; **d. up** wear formal or elaborate clothes; wear fancy dress ~ **dress** *n* clothing, apparel; woman's one-piece skirted

outer garment; formal clothes; **d. circle** first tier of seats in theatre; **d. coat** man's black coat with tails, for formal wear; **evening d.** conventional clothes worn for formal occasions in the evening; **full d.** formal uniform; **morning d.** conventional clothes for formal occasions during the day; **d. rehearsal** final rehearsal of play in full costume; **d. suit** man's formal suit for evening wear.

dressage [dResaazh] *n* training of a horse in obedience and deportment.

dresser (1) [dReser] *n* one who dresses another, *esp* actor's personal assistant; one who arranges goods in shop windows; surgeon's assistant; tool for shaping or smoothing wood or stone; hardwood tool shaped for beating lead.

dresser (2) *n* kitchen sideboard with shelves and drawers; *(US)* dressing-table.

dressing [dResing] *n* the process of clothing, decorating or preparing for use; sauce, seasoning; medicine and bandages for wounds; *(hort)* manure, mulches *etc*; beating lead to shape; *(mining)* the operations of ore concentration; *(bui)* masonry or mouldings round windows or the corners of buildings of better quality than the remainder of the facing brick or stone; starch used to stiffen linen in weaving.

dressing-case [dResing-kays] *n* box of toilet requisites for travelling.

dressing-down [dResing-down] *n (coll)* scolding, reprimand; thrashing.

dressing-gown [dResing-gown] *n* loose garment worn over night attire.

dressing-room [dResing-ROOm] *n* small room in which to dress or undress.

dressing-table [dResing-tayb'l] *n* low table with mirrors and toilet utensils.

dressmaker [dResmayker] *n* one who makes women's dresses ~ **dressmaking** *n*.

dressy [dResi] *adj* fond of smart or elaborate clothes; elegant, stylish, fashionable.

drew [dROO] *p/t* of **draw**.

drey, dray (2) [dRay] *n* squirrel's nest.

dribble [dRib'l] *v/i* and *t* flow or cause to flow in drips or trickles; let saliva trickle from the mouth; *(football, hockey etc)* take the ball across the field by series of quick light kicks or strokes ~ **dribble** *n* ~ **dribbler** *n*.

driblet [dRiblit] *n* small quantity.

dribs and dabs [dRibz-and-dRabz] *n (pl)* small amounts.

dried [dRId] *p/t* and *p/part* of **dry**.

drier (1) [dRI-er] *n* that which makes dry; any apparatus for drying by heat, warm air *etc*; substance used to accelerate the drying of oil paints.

drier (2) *adj comp* of **dry** *adj* ~ **driest** *adj superl* of **dry** *adj*.

drift [dRift] *n* condition of being driven along by an external force; slow surface movements of sea or sand caused by wind; deviation of ship or aircraft caused by currents or wind; *(linguistics)* consistent change in the pattern of a language in the course of time; tendency, trend; purpose, general meaning; mass of smoke, rain *etc* driven by wind; floating matter carried by currents; bank of snow or sand piled up by wind; *(geol)* deposit carried by wind, ice, *etc*; *(mining)* horizontal tunnel in an ore body following a vein; tunnel through stone; *(S. Africa)* large river ford

~ **drift** v/t and i cause to float, drive, in particular direction; cause to become heaped up; be carried along by currents or wind, float; be piled up in heaps by the wind; move aimlessly or without volition, let oneself be guided by exterior forces; (*coll*) stroll, wander.

driftage [dRiftij] n (*naut*) deviation from course due to currents or wind; wreckage, seaweed etc thrown ashore by the tide.

drift-anchor [dRift-anker] n anchor to keep ship's head to the wind, drag-anchor.

drift-bolt [dRift-bOlt] n tapered steel bar for aligning rivet holes or for expanding tubes > PDE.

drifter [dRifter] n one who, or that which, drifts; boat equipped with driftnets; person without aim in life.

drift-ice [dRift-Is] n detached pieces of ice carried out to sea by currents > PDG.

driftnet [dRiftnet] n floating fishing-net allowed to drift with the tide.

drift-sail [dRift-sayl] n sail dropped in the sea to check the course of a ship in a storm.

driftsand [dRiftsand] n sand driven or piled up by the wind.

driftway [dRiftway] n (*mining*) a drift; (*naut*) course of drifting ship; lane or road along which cattle are driven.

driftwood [dRiftwood] n wood washed ashore by the sea or floating in a river.

drill (1) [dRil] n tool or apparatus for boring holes by revolving a cutting point; **d. feed** mechanism for pushing a drilling tool into a hole; speed at which this is done ~ **drill** v/t and i bore by means of a drill; **d. a hole in** (*coll*) shoot.

drill (2) n physical exercises performed by a group of people, esp military exercises or manoeuvres; process of training by repeated exercises; rigorous teaching; (*coll*) correct way of doing something ~ **drill** v/t and i perform or cause to perform physical or military exercises; train rigorously.

drill (3) n narrow furrow in which seeds are planted; machine for making and sowing these furrows; row of seeds so planted ~ **drill** v/t sow seed in furrows; make furrows in field.

drill (4) n a twilled linen or cotton material.

drill (5) n type of small West African baboon.

drill-bow [dRil-bO] n instrument for spinning a drill with a cord.

drill-harrow [dRil-haRO] n machine for weeding between drills or rows.

drill-sergeant [dRil-saarjant] n sergeant who trains and drills soldiers.

drily see dryly.

drink (p/t drank, p/part drunk) [dRink] v/t and i swallow (liquid); swallow the liquid contents of; absorb; (*fig*) accept eagerly; take alcoholic liquor, esp habitually or excessively; **d. in** eagerly absorb, take in; **d. off** swallow down the whole contents at once; **d. to** drink a toast to; **d. like a fish** be a drunkard; **d. up** finish one's drink, esp hurriedly ~ **drink** n liquid swallowed, beverage, esp alcoholic; amount of liquid drunk; (*sl*) the sea.

drinkable [dRinkab'l] adj fit for drinking.

drinker [dRinker] n one who habitually drinks, esp alcoholic liquors.

drinking [dRinking] n act of one who drinks ~ **drinking** adj.

drinking-bout [dRinking-bowt] n session of hard drinking of alcoholic liquors.

drinking-fountain [dRinking-fowntin] n ornamental structure for providing jets of drinking water in public places.

drinking-horn [dRinking-hawrn] n hollowed horn to contain liquor.

drinking-song [dRinking-song] n song usually in praise of liquor.

drinking-water [dRinking-wawter] n water fit to drink.

drink-offering [dRink-ofeRing] n libation; wine, oil, or blood offered to a god.

drip [dRip] n liquid falling in drops; sound made by repeated fall of drops; (*bui*) an undercut edge of a cornice etc; (*sl*) weak, insipid person ~ **drip** (*pres/part* dripping, p/t and p/part dripped) v/i and t fall or cause to fall in drops; **dripping wet** thoroughly wet, soaked.

drip-dry [dRip-dRI] adj (*of fabric*) which is hung up to dry and needs neither wringing nor ironing ~ **drip-dry** v/t and i.

dripfeed [dRipfeed] v/t feed (patient) with liquids by a tube inserted in the stomach.

dripping [dRiping] n the falling of liquid in drops; fat collected from roasting meat.

dripping-pan [dRiping-pan] n shallow pan in which meat is roasted.

dripstone [dRipstOn] n (*archi*) moulding over door or window openings.

drip-tip [dRip-tip] n (*bot*) elongated tip of leaf.

drive (p/t drove, p/part driven) [dRIv] v/t and i force into movement; compel, thrust, or urge onward; set in motion by blow or stroke; impel, propel; advance violently or strongly; set in motion and control (a vehicle); go or convey in a vehicle; (*hunting*) chase (game) out of cover; search (an area) for game; (*fig*) compel, force; urge; carry through energetically; (*cricket etc*) propel the ball by a vigorous stroke; **d. at**, intend; **d. home** force right in; (*fig*) impress thoroughly on someone's mind; **let d.** aim (a blow) ~ **drive** n forcible blow or stroke; strong impulse, urge or need impelling a person or animal to activity; vigorous movement; energy, force of character, persistence, enterprise; intensive campaign; pleasure-trip in a vehicle; means by which mechanical power is transmitted to a machine; private road leading to a house; broad path through woods; the chasing of game towards hunters.

drive-in [dRIv-in] n and adj (restaurant, bank etc) at which customers are served without having to leave their cars; (*US*) open air cinema where patrons park their cars on inclined ramps and sit in them to watch the film.

drivel [dRivel] (*pres/part* drivelling, p/t and p/part drivelled) v/i let saliva flow from the mouth; talk childishly or stupidly ~ **drivel** n stupid talk, nonsense.

driven [dRiven] p/part of drive.

driver [dRIver] n one who, or that which, drives; one who controls a vehicle or machine; one who exacts hard work from subordinates; that which sets something else in motion; wooden golf-club to drive ball from tee; type of ant which travels in large bands.

driveway [dRɪvway] n (US) private road or track to a house or garage; scenic motorway.

driving [dRɪvɪng] n the setting in motion and controlling of a vehicle; (golf) the striking of the ball from the tee ~ **driving** adj transmitting movement or force; moving violently.

driving-licence [dRɪvɪng-lɪsens] n permit allowing one to drive a motor vehicle on the public highway.

driving-test [dRɪvɪng-test] n test of competence in driving a motor vehicle.

driving-wheel [dRɪvɪng-wheel] n (eng) wheel which transmits power or motion to other parts of a machine; steering wheel.

drizzle [dRɪz'l] n very fine rain ~ **drizzle** v/i ~ **drizzly** adj inclined to drizzle.

drogue [dROg] n sea-anchor; canvas sleeve used as drift-anchor by sea-planes; board on harpoon-line to hamper the whale's speed; device to check speed of falling bomb.

droit [dRoit] n (leg) moral and legal right, due..

droll [dROl] adj quaintly comic, facetious; queer, odd ~ **droll** n buffoon, comic person.

drollery [dROleRi] n anything laughable, quaint, etc; waggishness, buffoonery; comic story etc.

drome [dROm] n (coll) aerodrome.

dromedary [dRomidaRi] n riding-camel; one-humped Arabian camel.

dromond [dRomond] n large medieval ship-of-war.

drone [dROn] n male honey-bee; (fig) idler, useless loafer; (aer) robot plane guided by remote control; deep humming or buzzing sound; (mus) bass voice in part-song; bass pipe of bagpipe; bagpipe; dull, monotonous manner of speech ~ **drone** v/i and t produce a deep humming sound; talk dully or monotonously; idle away (time).

drool [dROOl] v/i and t let saliva trickle from the mouth, drivel; talk foolishly, talk nonsense; gloat lasciviously over ~ **drool** n drivel, foolish talk.

droop [dROOp] v/i and t hang limply down, sink, sag; (fig) grow weak, listless, or weary ~ **droop** n process or condition of drooping ~ **drooping** adj.

drop [dRop] n globule of liquid about to fall; minute quantity of liquid; any small globular object; pendant; small round sweet; distance between upper and lower level; vertical fall; distance of vertical fall; sudden fall, lowering, or decrease; descent by parachute; steep part of a channel or pipe; any contraption designed to fall; trap-door or hinged platform (esp of gallows); stage curtain; (football) dropkick; **at the d. of a hat** at once; **a d. in the ocean** insignificant amount ~ **drop** (pres/part **dropping**; p/t and p/part **dropped**) v/i and t fall or let fall in drops; fall vertically; fall, sink down; become lower or less; come to an end, lapse; pass gradually (into a condition); let fall from the hand, release hold of; lower; omit; set down (from vehicle); (coll) abandon; (of animals) give birth to; say or write casually; put an end to, dismiss; (sl) lose, part with (money); (football) score (a goal) by a drop-kick; (naut) float downstream or with tide; **d. behind** lag behind, be outdistanced; **d. a brick** (coll) make a tactless blunder; **d. down on** scold, blame, accuse; **d. in** visit casually or unexpectedly; **d. it!** stop that!; **let d.** say casually; **d. off** fall asleep; diminish, decline; **d. out** (coll) opt out, refuse to share conventional way of life; **d. out of**

disappear from, cease to take part in; **d. to** (sl) realize, understand.

drop-curtain [dRop-kurtin] n theatre curtain lowered or raised by pulleys.

drop-forging [dRop-fawrjing] n the process of shaping metal parts by forging between two dies, one fixed to a hammer and the other to an anvil.

drophead [dRophed] n soft roofing of car that can be rolled or folded back.

dropkick [dRopkik] n (Rugby football) kick made by dropping ball and kicking it as soon as it leaves the ground ~ **dropkick** v/i.

dropleaf [dRopleef] n hinged flap of a table-top ~ **dropleaf** adj.

droplet [dRoplet] n small drop.

drop-out [dRop-owt] n (sl) one who rejects or is rejected by society; one who refuses a materialistic way of life; one who abandons a course of study.

dropper [dRoper] n one who, that which, drops; instrument for releasing liquid in drops.

dropping [dRoping] n act of letting fall; that which falls; (pl) dung of animals.

dropscene [dRopseen] n drop-curtain.

dropscone [dRopskon/dRopskOn] n scone cooked on a griddle.

dropshot [dRopshot] n shot made by letting drops of molten metal fall into water; (tennis) stroke which causes the ball to drop abruptly after clearing the net.

dropsical [dRopsikal] adj suffering from dropsy; of, or like, dropsy.

dropsied [dRopsid] adj suffering from dropsy.

dropsy [dRopsi] n (med) unnatural collection of fluid in the cavities or tissues of the body.

drosera [dRoseRa] n (bot) genus of insectivorous plants, the sundew.

droshky [droshki] n light open four-wheeled carriage formerly used in Russia.

dross [dRos] n scum of melting metals; small, bad quality coal; waste matter, refuse; (fig) anything worthless; (coll) money ~ **drossy** adj.

drought, drouth [dRowt, dRowth/dROOth] n dryness, lack of rain; long period without rain; thirst ~ **droughty, drouthy** adj.

drove (1) [dROv] n flock of animals driven along; (Fen District) road along which animals are driven; channel for drainage or irrigation; broad chisel for dressing stone ~ **drove** v/t and i drive cattle; be a drover.

drove (2) p/t of **drive** (1).

drover [dROver] n one who drives cattle to market.

drown [dRown] v/i and t die, or kill, by suffocating in water; cover (land) with water, flood; (fig) overwhelm; muffle (sound), render inaudible ~ **drowning** adj and n.

drowse [dRowz] v/i and t be half-asleep; make sleepy; pass (time) away in sleepy state ~ **drowse** n.

drowsy [dRowzi] adj sleepy; inducing sleep; (fig) lethargic ~ **drowsily** adv ~ **drowsiness** n.

drub (pres/part **drubbing**, p/t and p/part **drubbed**) [dRub] v/t and i beat, thrash; abuse violently ~ **drubbing** n.

drudge [dRuj] n ill-treated, over-worked servant; person employed in heavy or monotonous tasks ~ **drudge** v/i.

drudgery [dRujeRi] n hard monotonous work.

drug–dubbin

drug [drʌg] *n* chemical substance used in medicine, *esp* narcotic, hallucinogenic, or stimulant; harmful substance causing addiction or psychological dependence; **d. addiction** pathological craving for habitual doses of a drug; **d. on the market** unsaleable goods ~ **drug** (*pres/part* **drugging,** *p/t* and *p/part* **drugged**) *v/t* and *i* add a (*usu* harmful) drug to (food *etc*); administer a drug (*esp* narcotic) to; habitually take harmful or excessive doses of a drug.

drugget [drʌgit] *n* coarse woollen floor-covering.

druggist [drʌgist] *n* pharmaceutical chemist.

drugstore [drʌgstawr] *n* (*US*) store which sells soft drinks, cosmetics, magazines and medicines.

druid [drOO-id] *n* (*hist*) priest of the ancient Celts; officer of Welsh Eisteddfod ~ **druidess** *n* ~ **druidic(al)** [drOO-idik(al)] *adj* ~ **druidism** *n*.

drum [drʌm] *n* (*mus*) percussion instrument having a skin stretched across a hollow space and struck with padded stick or hand > PDM; any hollow cylindrical object; cylinder on which cables are wound; cylindrical packing-case; (*anat*) membrane between outer and inner ear; (*archi*) circular wall supporting dome or cupola; round stone block which forms part of a stone column ~ **drum** (*pres/part* **drumming,** *p/t* and *p/part* **drummed**) *v/t* and *i* play on a drum; produce sound by repeated rapid thumping or tapping; tap rapidly with fingers or feet; **d. into** teach by constant repetition; **d. out** expel (from army); **d. up** summon, try to gather.

drumfire [drʌmfIr] *n* heavy sustained gunfire concentrated on one target.

drumhead [drʌmhed] *n* skin stretched across the opening of a drum; **d. courtmartial** emergency courtmartial held on field of battle.

drumlin [drʌmlin] *n* elongated hill or ridge formed by glacial pressure > PDG.

drum-major [drʌm-mayjer] *n* (*mil*) sergeant in command of regimental band ~ **drum-majorette** *n* (*US*) girl who marches in front of band in parades *etc*.

drummer [drʌmer] *n* one who beats the drum in a band; (*US*) commercial traveller.

drumstick [drʌmstik] *n* stick for beating drum; (*coll*) lower part of leg of cooked chicken.

drunk [drʌnk] *adj* (*p/part* of **drink**) intoxicated by alcohol; (*fig*) exalted by strong emotion ~ **drunk** *n* intoxicated person, *esp* if charged by police; (*coll*) drinking spree.

drunkard [drʌnkerd] *n* person habitually drunk, alcohol addict.

drunken [drʌnken] *adj* drunk, intoxicated; habitually drunk, addicted to drink; caused by intoxication; (*fig*) leaning or sloping at precarious angle ~ **drunkenly** *adv* ~ **drunkenness** *n*.

drupaceous [drOOpayshus] *adj* of a drupe.

drupe [drOOp] *n* (*bot*) fruit consisting of fleshy pulp round a kernel.

drupel, drupelet [drOOpel, drOOplet] *n* (*bot*) little drupe in compound fruit.

dry [drI] *adj* without moisture; without rain, having low rainfall; producing no moisture; (*coll*) thirsty; (*US*) (*of places*) where alcoholic liquor is forbidden; (*fig*) stiff, unemotional; rousing no emotion or interest, dull; (*of humour*) quiet but keen; (*of wine*) not sweet; (*of bread*) unbuttered;

d. battery, d. cell type of electric battery or cell containing no free liquid; **d. farming** method of farming without irrigation in area of low rainfall > PDG; **d. goods** textiles; **d. land** earth (as opposed to sea); **d. measure** system of measure by bulk; **d. rot** timber decay caused by dampness > PDBl; **d. spell** period of low rainfall; **d. valley** valley from which the water of its stream has disappeared > PDG; **d. wall** wall built without mortar; **d. work** work causing thirst ~ **dry** (*p/t* and *p/part* **dried**) *v/t* and *i* remove moisture from; become dry, lose moisture; **d. out** break an alcoholic's or drug-addict's addiction by a course of medical treatment; **d. up** cease to produce water, milk *etc*; become completely dry; (*coll*) forget what one meant to say; cease speaking.

dryad [drI-ad] *n* (*myth*) wood-nymph.

dryasdust [drI-azdust] *n* pedantic scholar ~ **dryasdust** *adj* dull.

dryclean [drIkleen] *v/t* clean (clothes *etc*) with chemical solvents, not water.

dry-dock [drI-dok] *n* dock which can be emptied of water.

dryer see **drier**.

dry-eyed [drI-Id] *adj* not weeping, tearless.

dryfly [drIflI] *n* artificial fly used in fishing~ **dryfly** *adj* using a dryfly.

dry-ice [drI-Is] *n* solid carbon dioxide.

dryish [drI-ish] *adj* fairly dry.

dryly, drily [drIli] *adv* without emotion, coldly; with dry humour.

drynurse [drInurs] *n* one who takes charge of a baby, but does not suckle it; (*fig*) devoted helper ~ **drynurse** *v/t* attend assiduously.

dryplate [drIplayt] *n* (*phot*) plate whose film need not be wet with solution before exposure.

drypoint [drIpoint] *n* needle for copper-plate engraving without use of acid; engraving produced this way ~ **drypoint** *v/i*.

drysalter [drIsawlter] *n* dealer in salted or preserved foods *etc* ~ **drysaltery** [drIsawlteRi] *n*.

dryshod [drIshod] *adj* and *adv* without wetting the shoes or feet.

dual [dew-al] *adj* twofold, double; relating to the number two; having two forms, parts *etc*; (*gramm*) (form of word) denoting two persons or things; **d. carriageway** road designed for two streams of traffic in each direction.

dualism [dew-alizm] *n* (*philos*) a metaphysical theory of reality, as consisting of two independent substances, mind and body, or matter and spirit; (*theol*) doctrine that the universe is ruled by two equal powers, one good and one evil ~ **dualist** *n* ~ **dualistic** [dew-alistik] *adj*.

duality [dew-aliti] *n* state of being dual.

dualize [dew-alIz] *v/t* make dual; regard as dual.

dual-purpose [dew-al-purpus] *adj* adapted, intended, to serve two purposes.

dub (*pres/part* **dubbing,** *p/t* and *p/part* **dubbed**) [dub] *v/t* confer knighthood on; confer (title, nickname *etc*) upon; (*cin*) provide new synchronized soundtrack in different language from the original; re-record soundtrack, *esp* with insertions *etc*; (*bui*) fill in hollows of; rub, dress (leather *etc*) with grease; **d. up** (*coll*) pay up ~ **dub** *n* (*cin*) dialogue *etc* inserted by dubbing.

dubbin, dubbing [dubin] *n* preparation of grease for softening and waterproofing leather.

238

dubiety [dew*bı*-eti] *n* doubt, hesitation.

dubious [*dew*bi-us] *adj* doubting, hesitating, uncertain; causing doubt; untrustworthy, disreputable; ambiguous ~ **dubiously** *adv* ~ **dubiousness** *n*.

ducal [*dew*kal] *adj* of or like a duke.

ducat [*du*kat] *n* medieval gold or silver coin.

Duce [*dOO*chay] *n* (*Ital*) leader; title assumed by Mussolini.

duchess [*du*ches] *n* wife or widow of duke; female holder of duchy; (*sl*) woman of imposing presence; size of notepaper, 5¾ × 8¾ in; (*bui*) size of slate, 12 × 24 in.

duchy [*du*chi] *n* territory ruled by a duke.

duck (1) [*du*k] *n* genus of web-footed, short-legged, broad-beaked water-birds; female of this species; flesh of this bird; (*coll*) lovable person; (*mil coll*) amphibious motor vehicle; (*cricket*) a score of nought; act of ducking; **Bombay d.** type of dried fish; **ducks and drakes** game of making flat stone ricochet from water; **play ducks and drakes with one's money** squander money; **lame d.** person in trouble, helpless person; **like water off a duck's back** without making the least impression; **like a d. takes to water** naturally, easily; **like a dying d. in a thunderstorm** forlorn, helpless ~ **duck** *v/i* and *t* suddenly lower one's head or body, stoop abruptly; dive suddenly; thrust suddenly into water, *esp* as punishment or joke; (*coll*) back out (of); avoid, evade, dodge.

duck (2) *n* coarse linen or cotton cloth; (*pl*) trousers made of this.

duck (3) *n* (*coll*) amphibious landing-craft.

duckbill [*du*kbil] *n* the platypus, an Australian egg-laying mammal with webbed feet and a beak like a duck's; variety of red wheat.

duckboard [*du*kbawrd] *n* board with laths nailed across it at intervals, used to make a pathway.

ducker [*du*ker] *n* a diving bird, *esp* the dabchick.

ducking [*du*king] *n* a thorough wetting.

ducking-stool [*du*king-stOOl] *n* chair at the end of a long pole in which minor offenders were tied and plunged into water.

duckling [*du*kling] *n* a young duck.

ducks [*du*ks] *n* (*coll*) darling, dear.

duck's-egg [*du*ks-eg] *n* a shade of greenish blue; (*cricket*) a score of nought.

duckshot [*du*kshot] *n* ammunition used for shooting wild duck.

duckweed [*du*kweed] *n* small plant growing on the surface of still water.

ducky [*du*ki] *n* and *adj* (*coll*) darling, dear; lovely.

duct [*du*kt] *n* tube for conveying liquid; metal flue for ventilation; underground pipe conveying wires or cables; (*anat*) channel conveying secretions.

ductile [*du*ktıl] *adj* (*of metal*) capable of being drawn out into wire; (*fig*) tractable, easily influenced ~ **ductility** *n* (*mech*) property of a metal to undergo deformation when cold.

ductless [*du*ktles] *adj* having no duct; **d. gland** an endocrine gland.

dud [*du*d] *n* (*coll*) shell or bomb which fails to explode; anything which fails to work; bad coin or note; useless person ~ **dud** *adj* useless, defective, bad.

dude [*dewd*] *n* (*US sl*) dandy, fop; **d. ranch** (*US*)

a ranch which provides entertainment in riding, cowpunching etc for paying guests.

dudgeon [*du*jon] *n* feeling of being offended, sullen resentment.

duds [*du*dz] *n* (*pl*) (*sl*) clothes.

due [*dew*] *adj* (*of money*) requiring to be paid, legally owing; required by justice, fair; fitting, proper, deserved; expected or promised (for a certain time); **d. to** caused by, because of ~ **due** *adv* (*with terms of direction*) exactly ~ **due** *n* sum to be paid; legal toll, levy, *etc*; consideration *etc* required by fairness; **give the devil his d.** be fair to one's enemy or to a person of bad character.

duel [*dew*-el] *n* combat between two persons held according to formal rules; (*fig*) contest between two well-matched opponents ~ **duel** (*pres/part* **duelling**, *p/t* and *p/part* **duelled**) *v/i* ~ **dueller** *n* ~ **duelling** *n* and *adj* ~ **duellist** *n*.

duenna [dew-*en*a] *n* elderly lady who takes charge of girls in a Spanish family; chaperon.

duet [dew-*et*] *n* (*mus*) piece of music performed by two people > PDM ~ **duettist** [dew-*et*ist] *n*.

duff (1) [*du*f] *n* boiled suet pudding; coal dust.

duff (2) *v/t* (*coll*) strike (a ball) clumsily; spoil, muff, bungle; (*sl*) recondition or alter the appearance of old or stolen goods; fake, cheat.

duffer [*du*fer] *n* stupid, slow, clumsy person.

duffle, duffel [*du*f'l] *n* coarse woollen cloth with thick nap; (*US*) camper's clothes and equipment; **d. bag** type of cloth kit-bag; **d. coat** short overcoat or jacket of duffle cloth, *gen* with hood.

dug (1) [*du*g] *n* teat of female mammal.

dug (2) *p/t* and *p/part* of **dig**.

dugong [*doo*gong] *n* seacow, manatee.

dugout [*du*gowt] *n* canoe made from hollowed log; underground shelter against shells, bombs *etc*; (*sl*) retired officer *etc* recalled to service.

duiker [*dı*ker] *n* a small antelope; a cormorant.

duke [*dew*k] *n* holder of the highest hereditary rank of the English peerage; size of notepaper, 7 × 10½ in; (*pl*) (*sl*) fists.

dukedom [*dew*kdum] *n* territory, jurisdiction, dignity, of a duke.

dulcet [*du*lsit] *adj* melodious, pleasing, sweet.

dulcify [*du*lsifı] *v/t* sweeten; mollify, appease.

dulcimer [*du*lsimer] *n* (*mus*) instrument with strings stretched over a soundboard and struck by hammers; (*US*) type of zither > PDM.

dull [*du*l] *adj* slow-witted, stupid; without keen perception; blunted; lacking clarity and vividness; dim, tarnished; muffled; overcast; lacking interest, boring; inactive; depressed, bored ~ **dull** *v/t* and *i* render stupid, dim, *etc*; blunt; lessen the effect of; become dull.

dullard [*du*lard] *n* stupid person.

dullness [*du*lnis] *n* quality of being dull.

dully [*du*li] *adv* in a dull way.

dulse [*du*ls] *n* type of edible seaweed.

duly [*dew*li] *adv* fitly, properly; punctually.

dumb [*du*m] *adj* without the power of speech; (*of animals*) incapable by nature of speech; unable to speak through shock, surprise *etc*; reticent, silent; (*coll*) incapable of expressing ideas, stupid; inarticulate; **d. blonde** pretty but stupid girl; **d. dog** taciturn person; **d. show** part of a play represented by action without speech; gestures expressing meaning without words.

dumb-bell [*dum*-bel] *n* bar with heavy knob at each end, swung for exercise; (*sl*) a fool.

dumbfound [dum*found*] *v/t* strike dumb with astonishment, confound.

dumbly [*dum*li] *adv* without speaking.

dumbness [*dum*nis] *n* quality of being dumb.

dumb-waiter [*dum*-wayter] *n* movable table from which food is served; revolving tray or set of shelves holding dishes; food service lift.

dumdum [*dum*dum] *n* soft-nosed bullet which expands on impact.

dummy [*dum*i] *n* sham object imitating and replacing a real one; model of a human being; imitation object used in advertising; (*theat*) actor without a speaking part; (*coll*) silent, stupid person; rubber teat for babies to suck; (*bridge*) player whose hand is exposed on the table and played by his partner; **double d.** game of whist played by two people with the two dummy hands exposed; **tailor's d.** (*sl*) showy worthless person; **d. run** testing a machine *etc* by reproducing the conditions in which it will be used.

dump [dump] *v/t* and *i* put down roughly or casually; unload, tip out (*esp* refuse); (*coll*) get rid of; (*comm*) get rid of quantities of surplus goods by selling at a low price on a foreign market ~ **dump** *n* pile of refuse; place where refuse may be deposited; (*mil*) large depot of ammunition or stores; (*coll*) dirty, ugly, or unpleasant place.

dumper [*dum*per] *n* (*eng*) vehicle for transporting and tipping out soil *etc*; (*mining*) man who fills coal-trains > PDE.

dumpiness [*dum*pines] *n* state of being dumpy.

dumpling [*dum*pling] *n* small lump of boiled suet dough; **apple d.** apple baked in pastry; (*eng*) heap of soil left in the middle of an open excavation > PDE; (*coll*) short thick-set person.

dumps [dumps] *n* (*pl*) dejection, low spirits.

dumpty [*dum*ti] *n* large upholstered cushion used as seat, pouffe.

dumpy [*dum*i] *adj* short and thick-set ~ **dumpy** *n* short-legged hen; short-handled umbrella; high hassock; **d. level** a levelling instrument > PDE.

dun (1) [dun] *adj* and *n* dull grey-brown (colour); horse of this colour; type of artificial fishing-fly.

dun (2) *n* agent employed to collect debts; insistent creditor; demand for payment ~ **dun** (*pres/part* dunning, *p/t* and *p/part* dunned) *v/t* persistently demand payment of debt.

dunce [duns] *n* pupil slow to learn, dullard.

dunderhead [*dun*derhed] *n* blockhead, obstinate fool ~ **dunderheaded** *adj*.

dundreary [dund*Reer*Ri] *n* (*usu pl*) long side whiskers worn without a beard.

dune [dewn] *n* hill or ridge of wind-driven sand.

dung [dung] *n* excrement, manure ~ **dung** *v/t* and *i* spread manure on (soil); drop excrement.

dungaree [*dung*-gaRee] *n* coarse Indian calico; (*pl*) overalls or trousers made of this material.

dungeon [*dun*jon] *n* underground prison-cell (*hist*) central tower of a castle, donjon.

dungfork [*dung*fawrk] *n* long-handled fork for lifting and spreading manure.

dunghill [*dung*hil] *n* heap of manure or refuse; **d. cock** barndoor cock, not bred for fighting.

dungy [*dung*i] *adj* of the nature of, smeared with, dung.

dunk [dunk] *v/t* dip (bread *etc*) into one's drink or soup; (*phot*) dip film into solution.

dunlin [*dun*lin] *n* (*orni*) red-backed sandpiper.

dunnage [*dun*ij] *n* brushwood, mats *etc* stowed round ship's cargo to protect it.

dunning [*dun*ing] *n* persistent demands for payment of debt.

dunno [dun*O*] *abbr* (*coll*) (I) don't know.

dunt [dunt] *n* hard thump; blow of vertical current of air against aircraft; (*cer*) crack in hot pottery caused by a cold draught.

duo- (1) *pref* two.

duo (2) [*dew*-O] *n* a musical composition for two instruments; (*music hall*) pair of variety artistes.

duodecennial [dew-Odeseni-al] *adj* occurring every twelve years.

duodecimal [dew-O*desi*mal] *adj* reckoned in twelves; of twelve or twelfths ~ **duodecimals** *n* (*pl*) system of reckoning by twelves, cross-multiplication.

duodecimo [dew-O*desi*mO] *n* book, or size of book, in which each sheet is folded into twelve leaves.

duodenal [dew-O*dee*nal] *adj* (*med*) of, or in, the duodenum.

duodenary [dew-O*dee*naRi] *adj* in twelves.

duodenum [dew-O*dee*num] *n* (*med*) first portion of small intestine below the stomach.

duologue [*dew*-olog] *n* conversation between two persons; dramatic piece spoken by two actors.

duotone [*dew*-OtOn] *adj* of or in two shades of colour ~ **duotone** *n* process for making prints by using two half-tone plates with the screen set at two different angles.

dupable [*dew*pab'l] *adj* easily deceived, gullible.

dupe [dewp] *v/t* deceive by trickery, cheat ~ **dupe** *n* person easily deceived or cheated.

duple [*dew*p'l] *n* and *adj* double; (*mus*) (rhythm) having an even number of beats to the bar > PDM; (*math*) (ratio) of two to one.

duplet [*dew*plet] *n* (*chem*) a pair of electrons shared between two atoms, forming a single bond.

duplex [*dew*pleks] *adj* (*elect, eng etc*) double, two-fold, having two parts ~ **duplex** *n* (*US*) house so divided that it can be occupied by two families.

duplicate [*dew*plikit] *adj* doubled, being an exact copy of something ~ **duplicate** *n* exact copy or reproduction, a replica ~ **duplicate** [*dew*plikayt] *v/t* make an exact copy of; make copies on a duplicator; repeat (an action).

duplication [dewpli*kay*shon] *n* exact reproduction or repetition.

duplicator [*dew*plikayter] *n* machine for making copies from a stencilled original.

duplicity [dew*plisi*ti] *n* deceit, hypocrisy, double-dealing.

durable [*dewr*Rab'l] *adj* long-lasting; withstanding hard wear ~ **durables** *n* (*pl*) goods made for prolonged use ~ **durability** [dewrRa*bili*ti] *n* ~ **durably** *adv*.

duralumin [dewr*Ra*lewmin] *n* light hard aluminium alloy > PDS, PDE.

dura mater [dewrRa-*maa*ter/dOORa-*may*ter] *n* (*Lat*) tough membrane surrounding the brain and spinal cord.

duramen [dewRaymen] *n* (*bot*) the hard central core of a tree-stem.

durance [dewRrans] *n* imprisonment.

duration [dewRayshon] *n* the period of time something lasts; **for the d.** until the end of the war, for a very long time indeed.

durbar [durbar] *n* Indian ruler's court; state levee of Indian prince or British viceroy.

duress [dewRes] *n* imprisonment; compulsion, constraint; (*leg*) constraint by threats of violence.

during [dewrRing] *prep* throughout the continuance of; in the course of.

durst [durst] *ar p/t* of **dare**.

durum [dewRum] *n* a species of wheat with hard seeds.

dusk [dusk] *n* the darker part of twilight or of dawn; gloom, shade ∼ **dusk** *adj* (*poet*) dim, shadowy ∼ **dusk** *v/t* and *i* (*poet*) make, become, look, dim or shadowy.

dusky [duski] *adj* dim, shadowy; dark in colour, swarthy ∼ **duskily** *adv* ∼ **duskiness** *n*.

dust [dust] *n* dry powdery particles of matter; small particles (of gold *etc*); mouldering corpse; (*sl*) money; **bite the d.** fall wounded or slain; **kick up a d.** (*coll*) cause a disturbance, make a fuss; **lick the d.** grovel; **shake the d. off one's feet** depart in scorn not to return; **throw d. in the eyes of** mislead, deceive ∼ **dust** *v/t* and *i* remove dust from; sprinkle powder on; (*of bird*) bathe in dust; **d. (a person's) jacket for him** (*coll*) thrash him.

dustbin [dustbin] *n* container for household refuse.

dustbowl [dustbOl] *n* region which suffers from severe drought and dust storms.

dustcart [dustkaart] *n* cart in which refuse is collected from dustbins.

dustcover [dustkuver] *n* removable protective paper cover around a new book; removable cloth cover to protect chairs *etc*.

dustdevil [dustdevil] *n* moving wind-whirled column of dust or sand > PDG.

duster [duster] *n* cloth for wiping away dust; sprinkler for sugar, pepper *etc*.

dustily [dustili] *adv* in a dusty way.

dustiness [dustines] *n* condition of being dusty.

dusting [dusting] *n* act of removing dust; act of sprinkling powder; (*coll*) a thrashing.

dust-jacket [dust-jakit] *n* protective paper cover around a new book.

dustman [dustman] *n* one employed to collect household refuse; (*coll*) sleep (personified).

dustpan [dustpan] *n* half-covered shovel into which dust is swept.

dustproof [dustpROOf] *adj* excluding, impervious to, protecting from, dust.

dustsheet [dustsheet] *n* sheet or similar large cloth spread over furniture to protect it from dust.

dust-shot [dust-shot] *n* the smallest size of shot.

dust-up [dust-up] *n* (*coll*) commotion, row, fight.

dusty [dusti] *adj* covered with dust; powdery; of the colour of dust; **not so d.** (*sl*) not too bad, fairly good.

dutch (1) [duch] *n* (*sl*) wife.

Dutch (2) *n* and *adj* (people or language) of the Netherlands; **D. cap** woman's cap with triangular flaps folded back at each side; **D. courage** false courage inspired by drink; **double D.** (*coll*) gibberish, incomprehensible talk; **talk (to a person) like a D. uncle** (*coll*) lecture severely; **go D.** (*coll*) pay for oneself; **D. treat** (*coll*) one at which each person pays his share.

Dutchman [duchman] *n* inhabitant of the Netherlands; Dutch ship.

duteous [dewti-us] *adj* obedient to authority, respectful ∼ **duteously** *adv* ∼ **duteousness** *n*.

dutiable [dewti-ab'l] *adj* liable to customs or other legal duty.

dutiful [dewtifool] *adj* showing due respect, obedience; conscientious ∼ **dutifully** *adv* ∼ **dutifulness** *n*.

duty [dewti] *n* what one is legally or morally bound to do, obligation; task obligatory upon some post or rank; proper expression of homage or respect; indirect tax levied on certain imports, exports, transfers of property *etc*; (*mech*) ratio of work done to fuel consumption; **do d. for** act as substitute for; **on d.** performing, or liable to be called on to perform, the duties of one's post; **d. officer** (*mil*) officer on duty at certain period.

duty-free [dewti-fRee] *adj* not liable to customs duty or other tax.

duty-stamp [dewti-stamp] *n* stamp recording payment of duty.

duvet [doovay] *n* (*Fr*) large warm quilt used instead of blankets.

dwarf [dwaawrf] *n* person, animal, or plant considerably below average size; (*myth*) small goblin ∼ **dwarf** *adj* below average size; belonging to small variety; **d. star** star of low luminosity; ∼ **dwarf** *v/t* cause to appear small, overshadow, render insignificant; stunt the growth of.

dwarfish [dwaawrfish] *adj* stunted, too small.

dwell (*p/t* and *p/part* **dwelt**) [dwel] *v/i* live, reside, remain; **d. on** ponder over; speak at length about; linger over ∼ **dwell** *n* regular pause in movement of a machine ∼ **dweller** *n* inhabitant.

dwelling [dweling] *n* place of residence, abode.

dwindle [dwind'l] *v/i* become smaller, waste away; lose importance.

dyad [dI-ad] *n* pair, couple; (*chem*) element having a valency of two > PDS; (*biol*) a bivalent chromosome; (*mus*) chord composed of two tones ∼ **dyadic** [dI-adik] *adj*.

Dyak [dI-ak] *n* member of aboriginal race of Borneo.

dybbuk [dibuk] *n* (*Heb*) evil ghost possessing a human being.

dye [dI] *n* substance used for colouring; colour so obtained ∼ **dye** (*pres/part* **dyeing**; *p/t* and *p/part* **dyed**) *v/t* and *i* give colour to, tint; change the colour of with a dye; receive colour by dyeing.

dyeing [dI-ing] *n* process of fixing colours firmly to a fabric; the business of a dyer.

dyer [dI-er] *n* one whose trade is dyeing.

dyestuffs [dIstufs] *n* (*pl*) substances used in dyeing.

dyeworks [dIwurks] *n* factory where dyeing is done.

dying [dI-ing] *adj* at point of death; near its end; fading, withering away; languishing.

dyke see **dike**.

dynamic [dInamik] *adj* having or producing force or energy; pertaining to force in motion; having energy of character, forceful, vigorous; (*med*) functional; (*philos*) pertaining to dynamism; d.

psychology one emphasizing motives and drives > PDP ~ **dynamic** *n* an energizing or motive force.

dynamical [dɪn*amikal*] *adj* relating to dynamics; (*theol*) (*of inspiration*) endowing with divine power ~ **dynamically** *adv*.

dynamics [dɪn*amiks*] *n* (*pl*) the mathematical and physical study of the behaviour of bodies under the action of forces which produce changes of motion in them.

dynamism [dɪn*amizm*] *n* doctrine which seeks to explain all phenomena by some immanent force or energy.

dynamite [dɪn*amɪt*] *n* explosive consisting of nitroglycerine absorbed in kieselguhr; (*coll*) anything potentially dangerous ~ **dynamite** *v/t* blow up with dynamite ~ **dynamiter** *n* one who uses dynamite, *esp* a criminal or terrorist.

dynamo [dɪn*amO*] *n* machine for converting mechanical energy into electrical energy > PDS; **human d.** extremely energetic person.

dynamometer [dɪn*amomiter*] *n* any instrument designed for the measurement of power.

dynast [d*in*ast/d*ɪn*ast] *n* hereditary ruler.

dynastic [d*in*astik/d*ɪn*astik] *adj* relating to, connected with, a dynasty or dynasties ~ **dynastical** *adj* ~ **dynastically** *adv*.

dynasty [d*in*asti] *n* line of hereditary rulers.

dyne [d*ɪn*] *n* a unit of force; the force which acting for one second on one gramme will impart to it an acceleration of one centimetre per second per second.

dys- *pref* bad, hard, difficult, defective.

dysentery [d*is*enteRi] *n* inflammation of the mucous membrane and glands of the large intestine ~ **dysenteric** *adj*.

dysfunction [dis*funk*shon] *n* abnormal or impaired functioning (of a bodily organ).

dysgenic [dis*j*enik] *adj* (*biol*) causing degeneration in a stock or race.

dyslexia [dis*lek*si-a] *n* (*psych*) pathological inability to spell, word-blindness ~ **dyslexic** *n* and *adj* (person) suffering from dyslexia.

dyspepsia [dis*pe*psi-a] *n* indigestion.

dyspeptic [dis*pe*ptik] *adj* suffering from dyspepsia; (*fig*) gloomy, morbid ~ **dyspeptic** *n* person suffering from dyspepsia.

dysprosium [dis*p*ROsi-um] *n* (*chem*) rare lanthanide element > PDS.

dystopia [dist*O*pi-a] *n* an imaginary community or place of maximum evil or unpleasantness.

dystrophy [dist*R*ofi] *n* (*med*) wasting away of muscles *etc*.

dysuria [dis*ewr*Ri-a] *n* (*med*) difficulty in passing urine.

E

e (1) [*ee*] fifth letter of the English alphabet; (*mus*) third note in scale of C major.

e- (2) *pref* out, out of, from *etc*.

each [*eech*] *pron* and *adj* every one (of two or more) considered separately.

eager [*eeger*] *adj* ardently wishing, impatient; keen, zealous; **e. beaver** (*coll*) one who volunteers for extra work ~ **eagerly** *adv* ~ **eagerness** *n*.

eagle [*eeg'l*] *n* large bird of prey; (*hist*) Roman military standard surmounted by an eagle; national symbol of United States; church reading-desk shaped like eagle with outstretched wings.

eagle-eyed [*eeg'l-Id*] *adj* keen-sighted.

eagle-owl [*eeg'l-owl*] *n* large European owl.

eaglet [*eeglit*] *n* young eagle.

eagre [*ayger/eeger/Iger*] *n* tidal wave in estuary or river, a bore.

ear (1) [*eer*] *n* the organ of hearing, *esp* the external part of this; sense or power of hearing; (*fig*) ability to distinguish sounds; (*fig*) favourable attention; **be all ears** listen very attentively; **play it by e.** act as circumstances dictate, follow no pre-arranged plan; **set by the ears** cause to disagree; **up to the ears** (*coll*) very deeply ~ **eared** *adj* having ears.

ear (2) *n* spike or head of corn ~ **ear** *v/i* sprout into ears.

eardrops [*eerdRops*] *n* (*pl*) pendant earrings; medicine to be dropped into the ear.

eardrum [*eerdRum*] *n* (*anat*) tympanum, membrane in inner ear which responds to sound vibrations.

earful [*eerfool*] *n* (*coll*) as much information, talk *etc* as one wishes to hear; an outburst of scolding or gossip.

earing [*eerRing*] *n* (*naut*) rope for fastening corner of sail to yard.

earl [*url*] *n* English nobleman ranking between a marquis and a viscount; **E. Marshal** president of the College of Heralds, hereditary title of the Dukes of Norfolk with the duty of arranging ceremonial occasions.

earldom [*urldom*] *n* rank, title, or territorial possessions of an earl.

early [*urli*] *adj* near beginning of specified period; in advance of specified or usual time; forward, advanced; **e. bird** (*coll*) one who gets up early in the morning; one who arrives early ~ **early** *adv* soon, in good time; at or near the beginning, among the first; prematurely ~ **earliness** *n*.

early-warning [*urli-wawrning*] *adj* (*of radar*) giving the earliest possible indication of the approach of enemy aircraft or missiles.

earmark [*eermaark*] *n* identifying mark on the ear of a sheep; any distinguishing mark ~ **earmark** *v/t* mark with an earmark; set aside for specific purpose.

earn [*urn*] *v/t* gain by work or service; deserve.

earnest (1) [*urnist*] *n* pledge, guarantee of future payment; first instalment of payment; (*fig*) foretaste.

earnest (2) *adj* serious, sincere; determined, steadfast ~ **earnest** *n* seriousness, sincerity; **in e.** not joking ~ **earnestly** *adv* ~ **earnestness** *n*.

earnings [*urningz*] *n* (*pl*) that which is earned, wages; reward.

earphone [*eerfOn*] *n* radio or telephone receiver worn over or in the ears; type of hearing aid.

ear-piercing (1) [*eer-peersing*] *adj* shrill.

ear-piercing (2) *n* process of drilling hole through ear-lobe for insertion of earring.

earplug [*eerplug*] *n* padding worn in the ear to exclude noise, wind, water *etc*.

earring [*eerRing*] *n* ornament worn at lobe of ear.

earshot [*eershot*] *n* distance within which sound, *esp* of voice, may be heard.

ear-splitting [*eer*-spliting] *adj* very loud.

earth [*urth*] *n* planet inhabited by man, third planet of solar system > PDG; solid surface of this planet, dry land; soil, dry ground; (*fig*) vast sum of money; lair of burrowing animal, *esp* fox; (*elect*) connexion of conductor to ground; (*chem*) certain type of oxide; **come back to e.** emerge from day-dreaming; **down to e.** realistic; **go to e.** go into hiding; **move heaven and e.** make great efforts; **run to e.** pursue (fox) to its burrow; (*fig*) track down, discover after search ~ **earth** *v/t* cover with earth; (*elect*) put end of conducting wire into ground.

earthborn [*urth*bawrn] *adj* born from the earth; human, mortal.

earthbound [*urth*bownd] *adj* unable to detach oneself from this earth; worldly, unspiritual, prosaic; moving towards the earth.

earth-closet [*urth*-klozit] *n* privy in which earth is used as an absorbent.

earthen [*urth*en] *adj* made of earth or clay.

earthenware [*urth*enwair] *n* coarse or domestic pottery.

earth-house [*urth*-hows] *n* ancient Celtic underground storehouse and refuge.

earthly [*urth*li] *adj* relating to the earth; belonging to this world, non-spiritual, materialistic; **not an e.** (*sl*) not a chance; **no e. use** no use at all ~ **earthliness** *n*.

earthly-minded [*urth*li-*mI*ndid] *adj* worldly, materialistic.

earthnut [*urth*nut] *n* pignut; peanut.

earthquake [*urth*kwayk] *n* violent tremor of the earth's crust which originates naturally and below the surface > PDG.

earth-shaking [*urth*-shayking] *adj* sensational.

earthshine [*urth*shIn] *n* (*astron*) sunlight reflected from earth's surface.

earthward, earthwards [*urth*ward, *urth*wardz] *adj* towards the earth.

earthwire [*urth*wIr] *n* (*elect*) wire connecting conductor to earth.

earthwork [*urth*wurk] *n* (*eng*) any digging or

artificial raising of the ground; (*mil*) a fortification, rampart.

earthworm [*urth*wurm] *n* common worm, living in soil.

earthy [*urth*i] *adj* of the nature of earth; having an admixture of earth; unrefined, gross.

ear-trumpet [*eer*-tRumpit] *n* tube placed at the ear to aid hearing.

earwax [*eer*waks] *n* waxy substance secreted by glands of ear.

earwig [*eer*wig] *n* insect with horny wing-cases and forceps on its tail.

ease [*eez*] *n* absence of pain, constraint or exertion; comfort; relaxation; tranquillity; absence of difficulty; **at e.** comfortable; unembarrassed; (*mil*) with legs apart and hands behind back; **with e.** easily ∼ **ease** *v/t* relieve from pain, constraint etc; loosen; comfort; facilitate; **e. off** (*naut*) slacken (rope) gradually; **e. off, e. up** (*coll*) relax gradually; diminish gradually.

easeful [*eez*fool] *adj* (*poet*) quiet, peaceful.

easel [*eez*el] *n* adjustable frame to support a blackboard or a picture.

easement [*eez*ment] *n* that which gives ease; (*leg*) right or privilege to use something not one's own.

easily [*eez*ili] *adv* in an easy way.

easiness [*eez*inis] *n* quality of being easy.

east [*eest*] *n* point of compass 90 degrees to the right of north; part of horizon where sun rises; eastern end or part of anything; (*cap*) countries in eastern part of globe; Communist countries ∼ **east** *adj* in the east; from the east ∼ **east** *adv* towards the east.

Easter [*eest*er] *n* annual festival commemorating Christ's resurrection; **E. dues, E. offerings** money given by congregation to clergy at Easter; **E. duty** (*RC*) obligatory confession and communion at Easter; **E. egg** coloured egg or egg-shaped chocolate, sweet *etc*, given as present at Easter.

easterly [*eest*erli] *adj* in or from or towards the east ∼ **easterly** *adv*.

eastern [*eest*ern] *adj* facing eastward; pertaining to the East, Oriental.

easternmost [*eest*ernmOst] *adj* most easterly.

Eastertide [*eest*ertId] *n* the week after Easter Sunday; period between Easter and Pentecost.

easting [*eest*ing] *n* (*naut*) distance eastward.

eastward, eastwards [*eest*ward, *eest*wardz] *adv* towards the east.

easy [*eez*i] *adj* not difficult, simple; comfortable; relaxed; loose-fitting; slack, loosened; tolerant, not strict; calm, tranquil; wealthy; casual; (*of style*) fluent; (*comm*) not in great demand; (*coll*) easily obtained, persuaded, enjoyed *etc*; ∼ **easy** *adv* (*coll*) without exertion; at ease; **e. does it!** (*coll*) go gently! take your time! **go e. with** use sparingly or cautiously; **honours e.** honours evenly divided.

easychair [*eez*ichair] *n* padded armchair.

easy-going [*eez*i-gOing] *adj* indolent; tolerant; casual.

eat (*p/t* ate, *p/part* eaten) [*eet*] *v/t* and *i* take in (food) through the mouth; consume; wear away, corrode; (*of audience*) appreciate (a play); (*coll*) consume extravagantly; (*sl*) worry; irritate; **e. away** consume gradually; wear away; **e. in** have a meal at home; **e. into** consume; penetrate

chemically; corrode; **e one's heart out** brood over grief or anxiety; **e. one's terms** study for the Bar; **e. one's words** recant; **e. out** have a meal away from home; **e. up** consume entirely.

eatable [*eet*ab'l] *adj* fit to be eaten ∼ **eatables** *n* (*pl*) anything fit for food.

eater [*eet*er] *n* one who or that which eats; an eating apple.

eating [*eet*ing] *adj* suitable to be eaten raw.

eating-house [*eet*ing-hows] *n* cheap restaurant.

eats [*eets*] *n* (*pl*) (*sl*) food.

eau-de-Cologne [O-de-ko*lOn*] *n* perfumed toilet-water.

eau-de-Nil [O-de-*neel*] *n* dull-green colour.

eau-de-vie [O-de-*vee*] *n* brandy or whisky.

eaves [*eevz*] *n* (*pl*) lower overhanging part of a sloping roof.

eavesdrop (*pres/part* **eavesdropping**, *p/t* and *p/part* **eavesdropped**) [*eevz*dRop] *v/i* deliberately listen to private conversation ∼ **eavesdropper** *n*.

ebb [*eb*] *n* the receding of the tide; (*fig*) decline, diminution ∼ **ebb** *v/i* recede, flow back; (*fig*) decline.

ebb-tide [*eb*-tId] *n* the receding tide.

ebon [*ebon*] *adj* (*poet*) of or like ebony; black.

ebonist [*ebon*ist] *n* worker in ebony.

ebonite [*ebon*It] *n* vulcanite > PDS.

ebonize [*ebon*Iz] *v/t* stain (wood) black.

ebony [*eboni*] *n* kind of hard, dark wood; blackness ∼ **ebony** *adj* made of ebony; quite black.

ebullience, ebulliency [*ibul*i-ens, *ibul*i-ensi] *n* act of boiling over; enthusiasm, high spirits ∼ **ebullient** *adj*.

ebullition [*ebul*ishon] *n* act of boiling or bubbling; (*fig*) sudden outburst.

eburnean [*ibur*ni-an] *adj* like ivory.

ec- *pref* out of, from.

écarté [ay*kaar*tay] *n* (*Fr*) a game of cards for two.

ecbolic [ek*bol*ik] *n* and *adj* (*med*) (drug) causing abortion.

Ecce Homo [eksi-*hOmO*] *n* (*Lat*) a representation of Christ crowned with thorns.

eccentric [eks*ent*Rik] *adj* odd, unconventional, slightly mad; (*geom*) not having the same centre; deviating from the centre ∼ **eccentric** *n* odd, unconventional or crazy person; (*mech*) device for converting rotatory motion into to-and-fro motion ∼ **eccentrically** *adv*.

eccentricity [eksent*Ris*iti] *n* state or quality of being eccentric.

ecchymosis [ekim*Osis*] *n* (*med*) discoloration caused by bruising.

ecclesia [ik*leez*i-a] *n* (*hist*) assembly of free citizens in ancient Athens; (*eccles*) a church; religious assembly.

Ecclesiastes [ikleezi-*asteez*] *n* the twenty-first book of the Old Testament.

ecclesiastic [ikleezi-*astik*] *adj* pertaining to the Church or clergy ∼ **ecclesiastic** *n* clergyman ∼ **ecclesiastical** *adj* ∼ **ecclesiastically** *adv*.

Ecclesiasticus [ikleezi-*astikus*] *n* apocryphal book of the Old Testament.

ecclesiology [ikleezi-*oloji*] *n* study of Church history and organization; study of Church architecture, decoration *etc* ∼ **ecclesiological** [ikleezio*loji*kal] *adj* ∼ **ecclesiologist** *n*.

eccrinology [ekRinoloji] n (physiol) study of secretions and excretions.

ecdysis (pl ecdyses) [ekdisis] n sloughing off of skin > PDB.

echelon [eshelon] n (mil) arrangement of troops, ships etc in step-like series; (fig) rank, grade; (phys) type of spectroscopic grating > PDS.

echidna [ekidna] n (zool) spiny Australian ant-eater.

echinate [ekinit] adj (bot, zool) having prickles or spikes, bristly.

echinus (pl echini) [ikīnus] n (zool) sea-urchin; (bot) prickly plant-head; (archi) type of rounded moulding.

echo [ekO] n sound heard after being reflected from solid obstacle; radar wave reflected from an object; visual representation of this; (fig) repetition; imitation; imitator; e. sounder instrument for determining depth of water > PDE ~ echo v/t and i reverberate; repeat; imitate.

echoic [ekO-ik] adj onomatopoeic ~ echoism n onomatopoeia.

echolocation [ekOlOkayshon] n location of objects by reflecting soundwaves or ultrasonic signals from them.

éclair [ayklair] n finger-shaped cake containing cream and coated with icing etc.

eclampsia [eklampsi-a] n epileptic fit; convulsive attack in pregnancy.

éclat [ayklaa] n brilliancy; applause, acclamation.

eclectic [eklektik] adj not exclusive, selecting what seems good from the views or teachings of others ~ eclectic n philosopher who selects from the doctrines of others; person whose opinions are a composite of those of others ~ eclectically adv.

eclecticism [eklektisizm] n formation of a body of views or teachings or of a work of art etc by combining views, methods etc from several sources.

eclipse [iklips] n total or partial darkening of a heavenly body caused by another passing between it and the observer > PDG; (fig) loss of brightness, obscurity, extinction ~ eclipse v/t and i obscure the light of (sun, moon etc) by eclipse; (fig) deprive of glory etc; surpass, outshine; become eclipsed.

ecliptic [ikliptik] n (astron) sun's apparent path in sky relative to stars > PDS, PDG ~ ecliptic adj pertaining to the ecliptic or to an eclipse.

eclogue [eklog] n short pastoral poem.

ecological [eekolojikal] adj of ecology.

ecologist [eekolojist] n one who studies ecology.

ecology, oecology [eekoloji] n study of relations of living organisms to their environment.

economic [eekonomik] adj relating to economics; concerned with industry or commerce; frugal; cheap.

economical [eekonomikal] adj related to or guided by economy; cheap; frugal, thrifty ~ economically adv.

economics [eekonomiks] n (pl) scientific study of production and distribution of wealth.

economist [eekonomist] n student of economics; one who economizes.

economize [ikonomIz] v/t and i cut down (expenses); live thriftily.

economy [ikonomi] n careful management of money, thrift; art of managing a household efficiently; efficiency, avoidance of waste of effort etc; principles of arrangement of any organized operative system; political e. economics.

ecosystem [eekOsistum] n (biol) group of mutually dependent plant and animal species together with the environment affecting them or affected by them.

ecotype [eekOtIp] n (biol) subspecies adapted to a particular environment.

ecru [ekROO] adj of the colour of unbleached linen.

ecstasy [ekstasi] n rapture, trance; intense delight, exaltation, enthusiasm > PDP.

ecstatic [ekstatik] adj of or like an ecstasy; showing intense delight ~ ecstatically [ekstatikali] adv.

ecto- pref outside.

ectoblast [ektOblaast] n (biol) outer membrane of a cell.

ectoderm [ektOdurm] n outer layer of animal embryo > PDB.

ectomorph [ektOmawrf] n person of lean build.

ectoplasm [ektOplazm] n outer layer of cytoplasm > PDB; (spiritualism) viscous substance supposedly emanating from a medium.

ectype [ektIp] n copy, reproduction; (archi) cast embossed or in relief.

ectypography [ektipogRafi] n method of etching with lines in relief upon the plate.

ecumenical, oecumenical [eekewmenikal] adj of the whole Christian world or Church; universal, world-wide; relating to unity among Christian Churches.

ecumenism [eekewmenizm] n movement seeking to bring unity among Christian Churches.

eczema [eksima] n (med) disease of skin, with inflammation and scaling.

edacious [idayshus] adj greedy, voracious ~ edaciously adv ~ edaciousness n ~ edacity n.

Edam [eedam] n kind of Dutch cheese.

Edda [eda] n medieval Icelandic compilation of mythological and legendary poems; medieval Icelandic prose work on versification and myth.

Eddaic, Eddic [eda-ik, edik] adj of the Edda.

eddish [edish] n crop of grass that grows after mowing; stubble field.

eddy [edi] n small whirlpool; circular movement of air, dust etc; e. current (elect) current induced in the iron core of an electromagnet and other electrical equipment ~ eddy v/i ~ eddying adj.

edelweiss [aydelvIs] n Alpine plant found at high altitudes.

edema, edematous see oedema, oedematous.

Eden [eeden] n (OT) garden in which Adam and Eve were placed at their creation, earthly Paradise; region of perfect happiness ~ Edenic [eedenik] adj.

edentate [identayt] adj (zool) having no front teeth; having no teeth ~ edentated adj.

edge [ej] n sharp side, cutting side; outer extremity, border, rim; margin; brink; (fig) keenness; on e. (fig) irritable, over-sensitive or over-excited; have the e. on have a slight advantage over; set the teeth on e. set up an unpleasant tingling in the teeth; (fig) irritate ~ edge v/t and i sharpen; give a border to; be a border or rim; (cricket) deflect (ball) with edge of bat; e. away move away cautiously sideways; e. into enter cautiously sideways, insinuate; **e. out** gradually remove.

edgebone [*ej*bOn] *n* the aitchbone.

edge-tool [*ej*-tOOl] *n* tool with cutting edge.

edgeways, edgewise [*ej*wayz, *ej*wIz] *adv* with the edge turned up or forward; sideways.

edging [*ej*ing] *n* trimming on the edge of a garment; act of trimming; fringe; (*hort*) border of small plants.

edgy [*ej*i] *adj* with an edge; (*fig*) irritable, oversensitive; (*arts*) having no sharp outline.

edible [*edi*b'l] *adj* fit for food ~ **edibility** [edi*bi*liti] *n*.

edict [*ee*dikt] *n* authoritative command, decree ~ **edictal** [i*dik*tal] *adj*.

edification [edi*fi*kayshon] *n* act of edifying; state of being edified; that which edifies ~ **edificatory** *adj*.

edifice [*edi*fis] *n* a large building ~ **edificial** [edi*fish*al] *adj*.

edify [*edi*f1] *v/t* give moral or spiritual instruction or example to, uplift the mind of ~ **edifying** *adj* morally instructive, uplifting ~ **edifyingly** *adv*.

edile see **aedile**.

edit [*edi*t] *v/t* prepare for publication with critical apparatus; select, alter, censor for publication; be responsible for publication of; put together final version of (film) from scenes previously photographed.

edition [i*dish*on] *n* the form in which a book or newspaper is published; total number of copies published at one time; reprint of a text with critical apparatus; (*fig*) reproduction, copy.

editor [*edi*tor] *n* one who edits; one who directs the publication of a newspaper or periodical; person in charge of a special department of a newspaper *etc*.

editorial [edi*taw*Ri-al] *adj* relating to editors or editing ~ **editorial** *n* newspaper article explicitly giving editor's views, leading article ~ **editorially** *adv*.

editorship [*edi*torship] *n* position and business of an editor.

editress [*edi*tRes] *n* woman editor.

educable [*edew*kab'l] *adj* able to be educated ~ **educability** [edewka*bi*liti] *n*.

educate [*edew*kayt] *v/t* bring up, train; teach, instruct; pay for the education of; develop, improve.

education [edew*kay*shon] *n* process of bringing up; systematic training and development of the moral and intellectual faculties; state of being educated; level of intellectual achievement ~ **educational** *adj* ~ **educationally** *adv*.

educationalist [edew*kay*shonalist] *n* one expert in educational methods.

educationist [edew*kay*shonist] *n* educationalist.

educative [*edew*kativ] *adj* that educates, instructive; of or for education.

educator [*edew*kaytor] *n* one who or that which educates.

educe [i*dews*] *v/t* bring or draw out; deduce, infer.

eduction [i*duk*shon] *n* deduction, inference.

edulcorate [i*dul*koRayt] *v/t* sweeten; purify; free from acids or salts by washing.

Edwardian [ed*wawr*di-an] *adj* relating to or characteristic of the reign of Edward VII.

eel [*eel*] *n* fish shaped like a snake.

eelbuck [*eel*buk] *n* basket trap for eels.

eelfare [*eel*fair] *n* young eels; passage of eels upstream.

eelgrass [*eel*gRaas] *n* a grasslike seaweed.

eelworm [*eel*wurm] *n* thread-like parasitic worm.

e'en (1) [*een*] *n* (*poet abbr*) even (1); evening.

e'en (2) *adv* (*poet abbr*) even (2).

e'er [*air*] *adv* (*poet abbr*) ever.

eerie, eery [*eer*Ri] *adj* causing fear; strange, uncanny ~ **eerily** *adv* ~ **eeriness** *n*.

eff [*ef*] *v/t* and *i* (*sl euph*) use the word 'fuck'; **e. and blind** (*sl*) swear coarsely ~ **effing** *adj*.

efface [i*fays*] *v/t* rub out, obliterate; (*refl*) make oneself inconspicuous, withdraw ~ **effaceable** *adj* ~ **effacement** *n*.

effect [i*fekt*] *n* result, consequence; impression produced on senses, feelings or mind; meaning, bearing; scientific phenomenon; (*pl*) goods, property; (*theat*) off-stage representation of sounds required in play *etc*; **in e.** in reality; **put into e.** make operative; **take e.** become operative; **to no e.** uselessly; **to this e.** in this sense; with this result ~ **effect** *v/t* cause, bring about ~ **effectible** *adj* practicable.

effective [i*fektiv*] *adj* capable of producing results; efficient; producing a striking impression; (*mil*) ready for active service ~ **effective** *n* (*mil*) soldier, unit *etc* ready for active service ~ **effectively** *adv* ~ **effectiveness** *n*.

effectual [i*fek*tew-al] *adj* producing a desired effect; capable of doing so; valid ~ **effectually** *adv* ~ **effectualness** *n*.

effectuate [i*fek*tew-ayt] *v/t* bring about, accomplish ~ **effectuation** [ifektew*ay*shon] *n*.

effeminacy [i*fem*inasi] *n* presence of feminine physical, emotional, or behavioural characteristics in a man; lack of virility, weakness of character; male passive homosexuality.

effeminate [i*fem*inat] *n* and *adj* (man) showing effeminacy ~ **effeminately** *adv*.

Effendi [e*fen*di] *n* Turkish title of respect.

efferent [*efe*Rent] *adj* (*anat*) leading away from, discharging > PDB.

effervesce [efer*ves*] *v/i* release gas vigorously as mass of bubbles, bubble up; (*fig*) show great excitement, be in high spirits.

effervescence [efer*ves*ens] *n* act or state of effervescing ~ **effervescent** *adj*.

effete [e*feet*] *adj* exhausted; lacking vigour; barren ~ **effetely** *adv* ~ **effeteness** *n*.

efficacious [efi*kay*shus] *adj* producing or capable of producing a desired effect ~ **efficaciously** *adv* ~ **efficaciousness** *n*.

efficacy [*efi*kasi] *n* power to produce a desired effect.

efficiency [i*fish*ensi] *n* competence, capability; (*mech*) ratio of work done to energy consumed > PDE; **e. expert** person employed to increase productivity in industry or business.

efficient [i*fish*ent] *adj* producing a desired result; competent; skilled ~ **efficiently** *adv*.

effigy [*efi*ji] *n* three-dimensional representation of a person.

effloresce [eflo*Res*] *v/i* blossom out, bloom; (*chem*) become powdery on the surface.

efflorescence [eflo*Res*ens] *n* the bursting into flower; the period of flowering; (*chem*) property of some crystalline salts of becoming powdery on the surface > PDS; skin rash ~ **efflorescent** *adj*.

effluence [*ef*loo-ens] *n* outflow.

effluent [*ef*loo-ent] *n* stream which flows out of another or from a lake; discharge of waste water from sewer, factory *etc* into stream; liquid sewage ~ **effluent** *adj* flowing out.

effluvial [*ef*lOOvi-al] *adj* relating to, or consisting of, effluvia.

effluvium (*pl* **effluvia**) [*ef*lOOvi-um] *n* smell, *esp* offensive smell; exhalation.

efflux [*ef*luks] *n* act of flowing out; that which flows out.

effort [*ef*et] *n* exertion of strength; struggle, strain; an endeavour, attempt; (*coll*) achievement.

effortless [*ef*etles] *adj* showing or making no effort; requiring no effort ~ **effortlessly** *adv* ~ **effortlessness** *n*.

effrontery [*ef*RunteRi] *n* impudence, audacity.

effulgence [*ef*uljens] *n* flood of brilliant light, radiance ~ **effulgent** *adj*.

effuse [*ef*ewz] *v/t* and *i* pour out; gush out; shed ~ **effuse** [*ef*ews] *adj* (*bot*) spreading.

effusion [*ef*ewzhon] *n* act of pouring out; that which is poured out; (*fig*) unrestrained expression in speech or writing; literary work written in a gushing style.

effusive [*ef*ewziv] *adj* showing unrestrained emotion; gushing, demonstrative ~ **effusively** *adv* ~ **effusiveness** *n*.

eft [*eft*] *n* a newt.

eftsoons [*eft*sOOnz] *adv* (*ar*) soon afterwards.

egad [*i*gad] *interj* (*ar*) by God.

egalitarian [*i*galitairRi-an] *n* and *adj* (person) believing in political or social equality ~ **egalitarianism** *n* egalitarian principles.

egality [*i*galiti] *n* equality.

egest [*i*jest] *v/t* excrete.

egestion [*i*jeschon] *n* excretion.

egg (1) [*eg*] *n* ovum of birds, fish, reptiles *etc*, consisting of embryo enclosed in protective membrane or shell; ovum of domestic hen, used as food; (*biol*) female reproductive cell; **bad e.** (*coll*) person of bad character; **good e.!** (*coll*) exclamation of approval.

egg (2) *v/t* urge, incite.

eggcup [*eg*kup] *n* small cup to hold a boiled egg at table.

egger [*eg*er] *n* popular name of various moths.

eggflip [*eg*flip] *n* drink made of eggs beaten up in milk, beer, or spirits, sweetened and spiced.

egghead [*eg*hed] *n* and *adj* (*sl*, *cont*) intellectual.

eggnog [*eg*nog] *n* eggflip.

eggplant [*eg*plaant] *n* the aubergine.

eggshell [*eg*shel] *n* shell which encloses bird's egg; **e. china** thin. translucent porcelain.

egg-timer [*eg*-tImer] *n* small sandglass for timing the boiling of an egg.

eggwhisk [*eg*whisk] *n* utensil for beating up eggs.

egis see **aegis**.

eglantine [*eg*lantIn] *n* the sweetbriar.

ego [*eeg*O/*eg*O] *n* consciousness aware of itself; an individual's experience or conception of himself; the self in contrast with outer objects; that part of the mind which is in touch with outer reality and in conscious control of inner impulses *etc* > PDP; (*coll*) conceit; selfishness.

egocentric [*eg*O-*sent*Rik] *adj* centred upon the ego; self-centred, selfish.

ego-ideal [*eg*O-*I*dee-al] *n* (*psych*) idealized picture of what one would like to be.

egoism [*eg*O-izm] *n* selfishness; self-centredness, egotism; (*philos*) theory that all morality and behaviour are ultimately based on self-interest ~ **egoist** *n* selfish or self-centred man; believer in theory of egoism.

egoistic [*eg*O-*ist*ik] *adj* pertaining to egoism; selfish ~ **egoistical** *adj* ~ **egoistically** *adv*.

egomania [*eg*Omayni-a] *n* extreme egotism ~ **egomaniac** *n*.

egotism [*eg*otizm] *n* habit of speaking too often of oneself; exaggerated sense of one's own importance; egoism ~ **egotist** *n* one who shows egotism.

egotistic [*eg*otistik] *adj* showing egotism; self-important ~ **egotistical** *adj* egotistic ~ **egotistically** *adv*.

ego-trip [*eeg*O-tRip] *n* (*coll*) outburst of self-important fantasy; period of totally self-centred activity.

egregious [*i*gReejus] *adj* extraordinarily bad, flagrant ~ **egregiously** *adv* ~ **egregiousness** *n*.

egress [*eeg*Res] *n* act of coming out or going out; exit, way out.

egression [*i*gReshon] *n* egress.

egret [*eeg*Rit] *n* lesser white heron; (*bot*) feathery tuft of seeds; aigrette.

Egyptian [*ij*ipshan] *n* native or inhabitant of Egypt; (*ar*) gipsy; large size of drawing-paper ~ **Egyptian** *aaj* relating to Egypt.

Egyptologist [eejip*tol*ojist] *n* expert in Egyptology.

Egyptology [eejip*tol*oji] *n* study of Egyptian antiquities.

eh [*ay*] *interj* expression of surprise, inquiry, or doubt.

eider [*I*der] *n* large Arctic sea-duck.

eiderdown [*I*derdown] *n* fine soft down of the eider-duck; quilt stuffed with this or with other soft, warm material.

eidetic [*I*detik] *adj* (*psych*) **e. image** extremely detailed and accurate visual image reproducing a past impression.

eidolon (*pl* **eidola**) [*I*dOlon] *n* image; phantom, apparition.

eight [*ayt*] *n* and *adj* cardinal number next above seven; symbol of this, 8; shape of this symbol; group, team *etc* of eight persons, *esp* rowing crew of eight persons; racing boat holding eight rowers; **figure of e.** movement tracing shape of an 8; **have one over the e.** (*sl*) get drunk; **piece of e.** Spanish coin.

eighteen [ay*teen*] *n* and *adj* eight more than ten; symbol of this, 18.

eighteenth [ay*teenth*] *n* and *adj* (that) which follows seventeen others in a series; (that) which is one of eighteen equal parts.

eighth [*aytth*] *n* and *adj* (that) which follows seven others in a series; (that) which is one of eight equal parts.

eightieth [*ayti*-eth] *n* and *adj* (that) which follows seventy-nine others in a series: (that) which is one of eighty equal parts.

eightsome [*ayt*sum] *n* Scottish reel for eight dancers.

eighty [*ayti*] *n* and *adj* eight times ten; the

eighties years from eighty to eighty-nine of a century or lifetime.

eikon see icon.

einsteinium [ɪnstɪ̄ni-um] *n* (*chem*) a transuranic element > PDS.

eirenic [ɪReenik] *adj* of peace-making.

eisteddfod [es-*teTH*vod] *n* (*Wel*) assembly of Welsh poets and musicians competing in poetry and music.

either [ɪ̄THer/ee̅THer] *adj* and *pron* one of two; each of two ~ **either** *adv* and *conj* introducing the first of two alternatives.

ejaculate [i*jak*ewlayt] *v/t* and *i* utter suddenly; exclaim; (*physiol*) emit semen; emit fluid abruptly.

ejaculation [ijakew*lay*shon] *n* sudden exclamation; (*physiol*) emission of fluid, *esp* semen; fluid emitted.

ejaculatory [i*jak*ewlaytoRi] *adj* that ejaculates; full of exclamations.

eject [i*jekt*] *v/t* discharge, thrust out; expel; dispossess; (*psych*) interpret (another's mind) by analogy with one's own mind > PDP ~ **eject** [*ee*jekt] *n* that which is inferred to exist in another's mind.

ejection [i*jek*shon] *n* act of ejecting.

ejectment [i*jekt*ment] *n* act of casting out; state of being ejected; (*leg*) action for recovery of possession of real estate or property.

ejector [i*jek*tor] *n* one who ejects or dispossesses another; apparatus which ejects; device ejecting cartridge from gun; **e. seat** device ejecting pilot from aircraft in emergency.

eke (1) [*eek*] *v/t* add to, increase; lengthen; **e. out** prolong, make to last; supplement.

eke (2) *adv* (*ar*) also.

elaborate [i*labo*Rit] *adj* complicated, intricate in detail; highly developed; highly ornamented ~ **elaborate** [i*labo*Rayt] *v/t* make more complicated, detailed or ornamented; take pains over; work out carefully ~ **elaborately** *adv*.

elaboration [ilabo*Ray*shon] *n* act of elaborating; adding of detail.

elaborative [i*labo*Rativ] *adj* that elaborates.

élan [ay*laan*(g)] *n* (*Fr*) impetuosity, dash; ardour.

eland [*ee*land] *n* large South African antelope.

elapse [i*laps*] *v/i* (*of time*) pass by.

elastance [i*las*tans] *n* (*elect*) reciprocal of capacitance.

elastic [i*las*tic] *adj* capable of resuming its original shape when no longer pulled or pushed; resilient, springy; (*fig*) easily adaptable; recovering easily from grief *etc*; **e. limit** the maximum stress that can be applied to a material without causing permanent deformation. ~ **elastic** *n* strip of material made springy by rubber woven into it; rubber band ~ **elastically** *adv*.

elasticated [i*las*tikayted] *adj* (*of fabric*) woven or stitched with rubber thread.

elasticity [elas*tis*iti] *n* quality of being elastic.

elastin [i*las*tin] *n* (*biol*) elastic fibrous protein found in connective tissues.

elastomer [i*las*tOmer] *n* natural or synthetic rubber-like material.

elate [i*layt*] *adj* (*ar*) in high spirits, exultant ~ **elate** *v/t* excite, exhilarate ~ **elated** *adj* ~ **elatedly** *adj*.

elater [e*lay*ter] *n* (*bot*) minute filament in certain plants which releases ripe spores > PDB; (*ent*) genus of beetles.

elation [i*lay*shon] *n* state of being elated; exaltation, proud delight; (*ar*) pride.

elbow [*el*bO] *n* joint between forearm and upper arm; any angular object resembling an elbow; **at one's e.** near by; **out at e.** shabby, impoverished; **rub elbows with** associate, mingle with ~ **elbow** *v/t* and *i* thrust with one's elbow; push oneself forward, *esp* through crowds; jostle.

elbow-grease [*el*bO-gRees] *n* vigorous, continuous rubbing; hard manual labour; (*sl*) sweat.

elbow-room [*el*bO-ROOm] *n* space to move, scope.

elder (1) [*el*der] *adj* older, senior; **e. statesman** politician no longer holding high office but still consulted on government decisions ~ **elder** *n* one who is older; person having authority by right of age or experience; ancestor; person having authority in early Christian Church; administrative member of Presbyterian Church.

elder (2) *n* a small tree which bears white flowers and dark berries.

elderberry [*el*derbeRi] *n* fruit of the elder.

elderly [*el*derli] *adj* approaching old age ~ **elderliness** *n*.

eldership [*el*dership] *n* office of elder in Presbyterian Church.

elder-wine [*el*der-wɪn] *n* wine made from elderberries.

eldest [*el*dest] *adj* oldest, first-born.

eldorado [eldoRaadO] *n* imaginary land of wealth.

eldritch [*el*dRich] *adj* (*Scots*) weird, uncanny.

elect [i*lekt*] *v/t* choose and appoint by vote; decide, choose (among various courses of action). ~ **elect** *adj* chosen, set apart; (*theol*) predestined for salvation; elected to office but not yet installed ~ **elect** *n* (*pl*) (*theol*) those predestined for salvation.

election [i*lek*shon] *n* act of electing, choice; selection of candidate to office by vote; state of being elected; (*theol*) predestination to salvation; **by-e.** parliamentary election in one constituency only; **General E.** parliamentary election in every constituency at once.

electioneer [ilekshon*eer*] *v/i* attempt to gain votes at an election, canvass ~ **electioneering** *adj* and *n*.

elective [i*lek*tiv] *adj* appointed by election; having power of election; optional; **e. affinity** (*chem*) tendency of substance to combine with certain substances in preference to others; (*fig*) instinctive preference or affection.

elector [i*lek*tor] *n* one entitled to vote in election; (*hist*) one of seven German princes entitled to elect the Emperor.

electoral [i*lek*toRal] *adj* relating to, or made up of, electors; **e. register** list of those entitled to vote.

electorate [i*lek*toRit] *n* body of electors.

Electra complex [i*lek*tRa *kom*pleks] *n* (*psych*) unconscious sexual attachment of a girl or woman to her father.

electric [i*lek*tRik] *adj* relating to, charged with electricity; worked by electricity; (*fig*) tense with emotion; **e. blue** bright metallic blue; **e. chair** (*US*) chair in which criminal is executed by electrocution; **e. eel** kind of South American fish capable of giving electric shock; **e. field** region near electric charge, within which force is exerted on charged particles; **e. motor** machine for converting electrical energy into mechanical energy; **e. ray** type of flatfish capable of giving electric shock; **e. shock** nervous disturbance caused by electric current passing through body ~ **electric** *n* non-conductive substance in which electricity can be generated by friction.

electrical [*ilekt*Rikal] *adj* relating to electricity; (*fig*) causing strong and sudden emotion ~ **electrically** *adv*.

electrician [elekt*Rish*an] *n* mechanic who maintains and repairs electric machinery; student of electricity.

electricity [elekt*Ris*iti] *n* general term for all phenomena associated with electrons and protons static or in motion > PDS; scientific study of these phenomena; supply of electric current.

electrifiable [ilekt*Rif*I-ab'l] *adj* that can be electrified.

electrification [ilekt*Rif*i*kay*shon] *n* state of being electrified; act of electrifying.

electrify [*ilekt*Rif*I] *v/t* charge with electricity; provide with electric power; (*fig*) startle, excite.

electro- *pref* of or by electricity.

electrocardiogram, electrocardiograph [ilekt*RO*kaardiO-gRam, -gRaaf] *n* (*med*) record of action currents in the heart.

electrochemistry [ilekt*RO*kemistRi] *n* study of processes involving the interconversion of electrical and chemical energy.

electro-convulsive [ilekt*RO*-konv*ul*siv] *adj* (*med*) inducing coma by electric shock; **e. therapy** treatment of mental disorders by such shocks.

electrocute [*ilekt*RO*kewt] *v/t* kill by electricity; execute (criminal) by electricity ~ **electrocution** [ilekt*RO*kew*shon] *n*.

electrode [*ilekt*RO*d] *n* conductor by which electricity enters or leaves an electrolyte, electric arc, or vacuum tube > PDS, PDE.

electro-dynamics [ilekt*RO*-d*I*n*amiks] *n* (*pl*) study of electric phenomena in action.

electroencephalogram [*ilekt*RO*-ensefalOgRam] *n* (*med*) record made of electric currents in the brain (*abbr* EEG).

electroform [*ilekt*RO*fawrm] *v/t* produce, or reproduce, metal articles by electrolytic deposition.

electrolier [elekt*RO*leer] *n* ornamental group of electric lights hanging from ceiling.

electrolysis [elekt*Ro*lisis] *n* chemical decomposition by an electric current > PDS, PDE.

electrolyte [*ilekt*ROl*It*] *n* liquid compound which carries and is decomposed by electric current.

electrolytic [ilekt*ROl*itik] *adj* of electrolysis.

electrolyse [*ilekt*ROl*iz] *v/t* decompose by electrolysis.

electromagnet [elekt*RO*magnit] *n* soft iron bar temporarily magnetized by passing electric current through wire coiled round it.

electromagnetic [ilekt*RO*mag*net*ik] *adj* relating to magnetism produced by an electric current; produced by an electromagnet; **e. radiation** waves of energy associated with electric and magnetic fields, resulting from the acceleration of an electric charge > PDS ~ **electromagnetics** *n* (*pl*) electromagnetism.

electromagnetism [ilekt*RO*magnetizm] *n* science

of the relations between magnetism and electric currents.

electrometer [elekt*Ro*miter] *n* instrument for measuring voltage differences > PDS, PDE.

electromotive [ilekt*RO*mOtiv] *adj* pertaining to a flow of electricity; **e. force** force tending to move electricity round a circuit; potential difference between the terminals of a source of electrical energy; **e. series** list of metals arranged in the order they will replace one another from their salts > PDS.

electromotor [ilekt*RO*mOter] *n* electric motor.

electron [*ilekt*Ron] *n* (*phys*) elementary particle of matter bearing negative electric charge; **e. microscope** high powered microscope using a beam of electrons instead of light > PDS.

electronegative [ilekt*RO*negativ] *adj* containing negative electricity; behaving as a negative ion; non-metallic > PDS.

electronic [ilekt*Ro*nik] *adj* relating to electrons; operated by means of electrons; **e. brain** (*coll*) calculating machine operated by thermionic valves; **e. music** music constructed by manipulating tape-recordings of sounds, electronically produced > PDM ~ **electronics** *n* (*pl*) science concerned with electric circuits in which the motion of electrons is controlled.

electron-volt [*ilekt*Ron-vOlt] *n* (*phys*) unit of energy equal to the work done on an electron when passing through a potential rise of 1 volt.

electrophoresis [ilekt*RO*fo*Ree*sis] *n* migration of colloidal particles in a suspension due to an electric field > PDS.

electroplate [*ilekt*ROplayt] *v/t* coat with layer of metal by means of electrolysis > PDS ~ **electroplate** *n* metal articles coated with other metal, *esp* silver.

electropositive [ilekt*RO*pozitiv] *adj* containing positive electricity; behaving as a positive ion.

electroscope [*ilekt*ROskOp] *n* instrument to detect presence and nature of an electric charge.

electrostatic [ilekt*RO*statik] *adj* pertaining to static electricity; **e. units** system of units based on the force of repulsion between two static charges > PDS.

electrostatics [ilekt*RO*statiks] *n* (*pl*) the study of static electricity.

electrotherapeutics [ilekt*RO*theRa*pew*tiks] n (*pl*) science of treatment of disease by electricity.

electrotherapy [ilekt*RO*theRapi] *n* treatment of disease by electricity.

electrotype (*abbr* **electro**) [*ilekt*ROtIp] *n* (*print*) hard-wearing printing plate made by the electrolytic deposition of a layer of metal on a previously prepared mould > PDS ~ **electrotype** *v/t* reproduce by electrotype.

electrovalent [ilekt*RO*valent] *adj* (*of a chemical bond*) formed by the transfer of an electron from one atom to another > PDS; **e. crystal** one in which the ions are held in place in their lattice by electrovalent bonds; ionic crystal > PDS.

electrum [*ilekt*Rum] *n* alloy of gold and silver; alloy of copper, nickel, and zinc; (*ar*) amber.

electuary [*ilekt*ew-aRi] *n* medicine compounded with honey or syrup.

eleemosynary [eli-eemo*zi*naRi] *adj* supported by alms; devoted to charity.

elegance, elegancy [*eli*gans, *eli*gansi] *n* state of being elegant.

elegant [*eli*gant] *adj* refined; tasteful; graceful; well-proportioned, harmonious ~ **elegantly** *adv.*

elegiac [elij*I*-ak] *adj* mournful, pertaining to elegy ~ **elegiacal** *adj* elegiac ~ **elegiacs** *n* (*pl*) elegiac verses; verses consisting of alternate hexameters and pentameters.

elegist [*eli*jist] *n* writer of elegies.

elegize [*eli*jIz] *v/t* and *i* write elegies (upon).

elegy [*eli*ji] *n* poem or song of lamentation; a dirge; sorrowful poem.

element [*eli*ment] *n* basic constituent; substance incapable of being analysed into any simpler form; (*chem*) substance consisting entirely of atoms having same atomic number; (*fig*) essential ingredient; small portion; (*elect*) electrode of primary or secondary cell; resistance wire or asbestos bar of electric heater; (*pl*) rudiments; (*pl*) atmospheric powers, storm, rain *etc*; (*pl*, *ar*) earth, air, fire, and water, considered as basic constituents of the world; **the Elements** (*eccles*) bread and wine of the Eucharist; **in one's e.** in one's favourite or usual surroundings, happy and at ease.

elemental [eli*ment*al] *adj* relating to elements; arising from first principles; simple ~ **elemental** *n* (*ar*) a spirit of air, earth, fire, or water; (*spiritualism*) non-human spirit producing physical effects ~ **elementally** *adv.*

elementary [eli*ment*aRi] *adj* simple; rudimentary; dealing with first principles; **e. particle** (*phys*) most simple constituent of matter > PDS; **e. school** former type of state school for children.

elemi [*eli*mi] *n* type of resin used in ointments and varnish.

elephant [*eli*fant] *n* largest mammal, with long trunk and two tusks; **white e.** (*fig*) costly and useless possession.

elephantiasis [elifant*I*-asis] *n* disease in which skin becomes hardened and limbs enlarged.

elephantine [eli*fant*In] *adj* relating to or like an elephant; huge, clumsy, heavy.

Eleusinian [elews*I*ni-an] *adj* pertaining to Eleusis in Attica; **E. mysteries** rites in worship of Demeter celebrated there.

elevate [*eli*vayt] *v/t* raise, lift up; promote in rank; improve in mind or morals; cheer ~ **elevated** *adj* exalted; lofty, noble; edifying; (*coll euph*) slightly drunk.

elevation [eli*vay*shon] *n* act of raising; state of being raised; promotion; high status, dignity; nobility in style, eloquence; state of emotional exaltation; (*archi*) scale plan of one side of building; (*sur*) altitude or level of a point; (*astron*) altitude above horizon; (*gunnery*) angle between axis of piece and line of sight; (*mus*) raising of pitch.

elevator [*eli*vaytor] *n* one who or that which raises or lifts; (*US*) a lift; conveyor which raises material or grain, hay *etc* to higher level; **grain storehouse.**

elevatory [eli*vay*toRi] *adj* capable of raising.

eleven [i*le*ven] *n* and *adj* cardinal number next above ten; symbol of this, 11; team of eleven players, *esp* cricket side.

eleven-plus [i*le*ven-plus] *n* selective examination

for pupils aged between eleven and twelve to assign them to different types of secondary school.

elevenses [i*le*venzis] *n* (*pl*) (*coll*) light midmorning snack.

eleventh [i*le*venth] *n* and *adj* (that) which follows ten others in a series; (that) which is one of eleven equal parts; **at the e. hour** at the last minute.

elf (*pl* **elves**) [elf] *n* (*myth*) supernatural being with magical powers, having human form but generally very small; malignant imp; fairy; (*fig*) small, slender child; mischievous child.

elfbolt [*elf*bOlt] *n* flint arrow-head.

elfin [*elf*in] *adj* of or like elves; tiny; dainty; mischievous.

elfish, elvish [*elf*ish, *elv*ish] *adj* of or like elves; magical; malevolent ~ **elfishly, elvishly** *adv* ~ **elfishness, elvishness** *n.*

elflock [*elf*lok] *n* tangled hair.

elicit [i*lis*it] *v/t* draw forth, bring to light.

elicitation [ilisi*tay*shon] *n* act of eliciting.

elide [i*lId*] *v/t* (*gramm*) omit (sound, syllable *etc*).

eligibility [eliji*bili*ti] *n* state of being eligible.

eligible [*eli*jib'l] *adj* worthy or qualified to be chosen; suitable ~ **eligibly** *adv.*

eliminable [i*li*minab'l] *adj* capable of being eliminated.

eliminant [i*li*minant] *n* and *adj* (*med*) (substance) purging harmful matter; (*math*) result of eliminating variables between homogeneous equations.

eliminate [i*li*minayt] *v/t* get rid of; (*joc coll*) kill; (*med*) purge away; set aside, cease to consider.

elimination [ilimi*nay*shon] *n* act of eliminating; state of being eliminated.

elision [i*li*zhon] *n* (*gramm*) act of eliding; state of being elided.

elite [ay*leet*] *n* select group of people; best part of anything; aristocratic or exclusive clique.

elitism [ay*leet*izm] *n* doctrine that education should seek to produce a social or intellectual elite; doctrine that an elite should receive social advantages ~ **elitist** *n* and *adj.*

elixir [i*lik*ser/ay*lik*seer] *n* (*med*) invigorating drink, strong cordial; tincture; (*ar*) substance believed capable of changing base metals into gold, or of prolonging life indefinitely.

Elizabethan [iliza*beet*han] *adj* relating to Queen Elizabeth I or to her times ~ **Elizabethan** *n* person living during reign of Queen Elizabeth I.

elk [elk] *n* (*zool*) largest species of deer, the moose; **e. hound** breed of hunting dog with shaggy coat.

ell [el] *n* measure of length, varying in different countries; **English e.** 1¼ yds.

ellipse [i*lips*] *n* an oval-shaped figure; (*geom*) closed plane figure formed by cutting all elements of a circular cone by a plane.

ellipsis (*pl* **ellipses**) [i*lip*sis] *n* (*gramm*) omission of word or words which would be logically necessary to the sentence construction, but whose absence does not obscure the meaning; (*print*) mark indicating omission.

ellipsoid [i*lip*soid] *n* (*geom*) solid figure traced out by an ellipse rotating about one of its axes.

elliptic [i*lip*tik] *adj* (*geom*) pertaining to, having the shape of an ellipse; (*gramm*) showing ellipsis, having omissions ~ **elliptical** [e*lip*tikal] *adj* elliptic ~ **elliptically** *adv.*

ellipticity [elip*tisi*ti] *n* quality of being elliptic.

elm [*elm*] *n* kind of deciduous tree; timber of this tree ~ **elmy** *adj* planted with elms.

elocution [elo*kew*shon] *n* manner of speaking; art of speaking clearly and with good pronunciation ~ **elocutionary** *adj*.

elocutionist [elo*kew*shonist] *n* expert in elocution.

elongate [*ee*long-gayt] *v/t* and *i* make longer, extend; stretch out, taper ~ **elongate** *adj* (*bot*) long and slender.

elongation [eelong-*gay*shon] *n* act of lengthening; prolongation, extension.

elope [i*lOp*] *v/i* run away secretly with a lover, *esp* in order to marry ~ **elopement** *n*.

eloquence [*e*lokwens] *n* power of speaking forcefully or persuasively.

eloquent [*e*lokwent] *adj* showing eloquence in speech or writing ~ **eloquently** *adv*.

else [els] *adv* in addition, besides; if not, otherwise; instead.

elsewhere [els*wair*] *adv* in or to another place.

elucidate [i*lew*sidayt] *v/t* clarify the meaning of, explain.

elucidation [ilewsi*day*shon] *n* act of making intelligible; explanation.

elucidatory [ilewsi*dayto*Ri] *adj* explanatory.

elude [i*lewd*] *v/t* escape, evade, dodge; baffle, escape (the mind).

elusion [i*lew*zhon] *n* act of eluding.

elusive [i*lew*siv] *adj* evasive; difficult to catch; difficult to understand or remember ~ **elusively** *adj* ~ **elusiveness** *n*.

elusory [i*lew*seRi] *adj* elusive.

elutriate [el*OO*tRi-ayt] *v/t* wash, separate, or size fine particles by suspending them in a current of air or water ~ **elutriator** *n*.

eluvial [i*lew*vi-al] *adj* of eluvium.

eluvium [e*lew*vi-um] *n* (*min*) residual soil; material which has disintegrated > PDE.

elvan [*el*van] *n* intrusive igneous rock.

elven [*el*ven] *adj* of or like an elf.

elver [*el*ver] *n* a young eel.

elves [*el*vz] *pl* of elf.

elvish see elfish.

Elysian [i*li*zi-an] *adj* of or like Elysium; delightful; glorious.

Elysium [i*li*zi-um] *n* (*Gk myth*) abode of heroes after death; place or state of perfect happiness.

em- (1) *pref* a form of *en-* used before *p*, *b*, *m*.

em (2) [em] *n* (*typ*) unit for measuring amount of printed matter in one line.

'em (3) [um] *pron* (*coll*) them.

emaciate [i*may*shi-ayt] *v/i* and *t* become excessively thin; cause to become thin ~ **emaciated** *adj*.

emaciation [imayshi-*ay*shon] *n* excessive thinness due to starvation.

emanate [*e*manayt] *v/i* come forth from, originate from.

emanation [ema*nay*shon] *n* act of emanating; that which emanates; effluvium; (*theol*) substance produced by God from His own essence; (*phys*) gaseous product of radioactive decay containing radon.

emanative [*e*manativ] *adj* of or by emanation.

emancipate [i*man*sipayt] *v/t* set free from legal, social, or moral restraints or disadvantages; set free from slavery ~ **emancipated** *adj* freed; (*coll*) uninhibited, unconventional.

emancipation [imansi*pay*shon] *n* act of setting free; freedom.

emancipator [i*man*sipayter] *n* one who sets others free.

emasculate [i*mas*kewlayt] *v/t* castrate; deprive of virility; (*fig*) weaken, deprive of vigour ~ **emasculate** *adj* castrated; effeminate; weak.

emasculation [imaskew*lay*shon] *n* act of emasculating; state of being emasculate ~ **emasculatory** *adj* weakening, tending to effeminize.

embalm [im*baam*] *v/t* preserve (corpse) from decay by removing viscera and impregnating with preservatives; (*fig*) cherish the memory of; fill with sweet scent ~ **embalming** *n* and *adj*.

embank [im*bank*] *v/t* enclose with a bank; build a bank for.

embankment [im*bank*ment] *n* ridge of earth or rock thrown up to carry a road, railway, canal *etc*, or to contain water.

embargo (*pl* **embargoes**) [em*baarg*O] *n* prohibition forbidding ships to enter or leave a port; prohibition of trade by government order; (*fig*) restraint, check ~ **embargo** (*p/t* and *p/part* **embargoed**) *v/t* lay embargo upon; requisition.

embark [im*baark*] *v/t* and *i* put on board a ship; go on board a ship; (*fig*) begin on, venture.

embarkation [embaar*kay*shon] *n* act of putting, or going, on board a ship; cargo.

embarrass [im*ba*Ras] *v/t* make shy or nervous, disconcert; perplex, hamper, obstruct; (*fig*) cause financial difficulty to ~ **embarrassing** *adj* ~ **embarrassingly** *adv*.

embarrassment [im*ba*Rasment] *n* act of embarrassing; that which embarrasses.

embassy [*em*basi] *n* official residence of an ambassador; ambassador's staff; position of ambassador; message or mission of ambassador; any duty, message *etc* undertaken by an agent.

embattle (1) [im*bat*'l] *v/t* arrange in order of battle ~ **embattled** *adj*.

embattle (2) *v/t* provide with battlements ~ **embattled** *adj*.

embay [im*bay*] *v/t* enclose in a bay; shut in, surround ~ **embayment** *n* bay; bay-like formation.

embed (*pres/part* **embedding**, *p/t* and *p/part* **embedded**) [im*bed*] *v/t* set firmly and deeply into surrounding material; (*fig*) fix unalterably.

embellish [im*bel*ish] *v/t* decorate, adorn; make beautiful; improve upon, touch up.

embellishment [im*bel*ishment] *n* act of embellishing; that which embellishes.

ember (1) [*em*ber] *n* (*usu pl*) glowing cinder.

ember (2) *n* (*orni*) the great northern diver.

ember-days [*em*ber-dayz] *n* (*pl*) (*eccles*) four groups of three days of penance and fasting.

ember-week [*em*ber-week] *n* week containing ember-days.

embezzle [im*bez*l] *v/t* make fraudulent use of money *etc* entrusted to one's charge ~ **embezzlement** *n* act of embezzling ~ **embezzler** *n*.

embitter [im*bit*er] *v/t* make bitter; aggravate; make worse.

emblazon [im*blay*zon] *v/t* paint or adorn with heraldic figures and devices; (*fig*) make glorious; praise, extol.

emblazonry [im*blay*zonRi] *n* blazonry.

251

emblem [*emblim*] *n* concrete symbol of abstract idea; sign, symbolic device.

emblematic [*embli*matik] *adj* of or as an emblem ~ **emblematically** *adv.*

emblemize *v/t* [*emblim*IZ] represent by an emblem.

embodiment [*imbod*iment] *n* act of embodying; state of being embodied; that which is embodied.

embody [*imbodi*] *v/t* give material form to; be an expression of; collect together; include.

embolden [*imbOlden*] *v/t* make bold.

embolism [*embolizm*] *n* (*med*) formation of an obstruction in a blood-vessel; regularization of calendar by insertion of days *etc.*

embolus [*embolus*] *n* (*med*) clot of blood obstructing a blood-vessel.

embonpoint [ongbong*pwang*] *n* (*Fr*) plumpness.

embosom [*imboozom*] *v/t* hold tightly to one's bosom, hug; (*fig*) enclose, shelter; cherish.

emboss [*imbos*] *v/t* (*metal*) adorn with designs in relief by hammering or pressing from behind ~ **embossed** *adj* ~ **embossment** *n* art of embossing; figure formed by embossing.

embouchure [embOO*shewr*] *n* mouth of river; (*mus*) mouthpiece of wind instrument; application of lips to mouthpiece.

embower [*imbow*-er] *v/t* place in, or cover with, a bower.

embrace [*imbRays*] *v/t* and *i* hug, hold tightly in one's arms; seize or accept eagerly; willingly make use of; include, comprise; perceive rapidly ~ **embrace** *n* a hug.

embraceable [*imbRays*ab'l] *adj* inviting an embrace.

embrangle [*imbRang-g'l*] *v/t* (*coll*) entangle; confuse.

embrasure [*imbRay*zher] *n* (*archi*) recess for window or door, *esp* one with inward splay; recessed opening in rampart *etc.*

embrocate [*embRokayt*] *v/t* (*med*) apply embrocation to.

embrocation [embRo*kay*shon] *n* lotion to be rubbed into affected part of body.

embroider [*imbRoider*] *v/t* decorate with needlework; (*fig*) embellish (story *etc*) with fanciful details.

embroidery [*imbRoide*Ri] *n* art of embroidering; embroidered material; (*fig*) embellishment.

embroil [*imbRoil*] *v/t* involve in discord or trouble; confuse ~ **embroilment** *n* act of embroiling; state of being embroiled; uproar; confusion.

embryo [*embRi-O*] *n* unborn animal in process of development from ovum; (*bot*) young plant developing within seed from ovum; (*fig*) any rudimentary, undeveloped object, idea *etc*; early stage of development ~ **embryo** *adj* not fully developed, rudimentary.

embryology [embRi-*oloji*] *n* study of the embryo.

embryonic [embRi-*onik*] *adj* of or like an embryo; undeveloped.

embus (*pres/part* **embussing**, *p/t* and *p/part* **embussed**) [*embus*] *v/t* and *i* (*mil*) put into or enter a motor vehicle.

emend [*imend*] *v/t* correct; improve (a text).

emendation [eemen*day*shon] *n* act of emending; alteration, correction (of text).

emendator [*eemen*daytor] *n* one who emends.

emendatory [ee*mend*ateRi] *adj* that emends.

emerald [*eme*Rald] *n* bright-green precious stone; vivid green colour; (*print*) small size of type ~ **emerald** *adj* set with emeralds; vivid green; **E. Isle** Ireland.

emeraldine [*emRald*In] *n* a dark-green dye.

emerge [*imurj*] *v/i* appear, come into view (from concealment *etc*); come out from; become known.

emergence [*imurj*ens] *n* act of emerging.

emergency [*imurj*ensi] *n* unexpected and dangerous situation requiring immediate action; (*sport*) reserve player to replace another in case of accident ~ **emergency** *adj* useful in, or designed for, an emergency.

emergent [*imurj*ent] *adj* emerging, arising (from); appearing for the first time; newly independent.

emeritus (*pl* **emeriti**) [*ime*Ritus] *adj* title of honour given to retired professor *etc* for outstanding achievement.

emersion [*imur*shon] *n* action of emerging; (*astron*) reappearance after eclipse.

emery [*eme*Ri] *n* mixture of corundum and iron oxide used as abrasive; **e. board** strip of cardboard coated with emery and used to file fingernails; **e. cloth, e. paper** cloth or paper coated with powdered emery and used for polishing; **e. wheel** wheel faced with emery used for polishing and grinding.

emetic [*imetik*] *n* and *adj* (medicine) which causes vomiting.

emetine [*emeteen*] *n* (*chem*) alkaloid used as an emetic and in the treatment of amoebic dysentery.

emiction [*emik*shon] *n* (*med*) act of discharging urine; urine discharged.

emigrant [*emig*Rant]· *n* one who emigrates or has emigrated ~ **emigrant** *adj.*

emigrate [*emig*Rayt] *v/i* leave one's own country to settle in another.

emigration [emig*Ray*shon] *n* act of emigrating; body of emigrants ~ **emigrational** *adj.*

emigratory [emig*Ray*teRi] *adj* relating to emigration; (*of birds*) migratory.

émigré [*emig*Ray] *n* (*Fr*) emigrant, *esp* political refugee from French or Russian Revolutions.

eminence, eminency [*emi*nens, *emi*nensi] *n* high level; high ground; (*fig*) high office; distinction; title given to cardinals.

eminent [*emi*nent] *adj* rising above others; high, prominent; famous, distinguished ~ **eminently** *adv* in the highest degree.

emir [*emeer*] *n* Muslim title of independent prince or chieftain; male descendant of Mohammed.

emissary [*emi*saRi] *n* messenger, agent.

emission [*imi*shon] *n* act of emitting; that which is emitted or discharged.

emissive [*imisiv*] *adj* capable of emitting.

emissivity [imi*siviti*] *n* power of emitting; tendency to emit; rate of emission; (*phys*) ratio of the emissive power of a body to that of a black body > PDS.

emit (*pres/part* **emitting**, *p/t* and *p/part* **emitted**) [*imit*] *v/t* cause to issue out, send forth, discharge; print and circulate (currency notes *etc*); issue (notes, bills *etc*).

emitter [*imiter*] *n* (*phys*) electrode in a transistor which emits the charge carriers > PDEl.

emmer [*emer*] *n* a species of wheat.

emmet [*emit*] *n* (*dial*) an ant.

252

emollient [imo*l*i-ent] *n* and *adj* (oily substance) tending to soothe and soften.

emolument [imo*l*ewment] *n* profit, gain; payment, salary.

emote [imO*t*] *v/i* (*coll*) give excessive or theatrical display of emotion.

emotion [imO*shon*] *n* strong feeling; excited and perturbed state of mind; passion > PDP.

emotional [imO*shonal*] *adj* pertaining to emotion; caused by an emotion; tending to rouse emotion; having easily roused feelings; expressive of emotion > PDP ~ **emotionally** *adv*.

emotionalism [imO*shonalizm*] *n* habitual encouragement of or appeal to emotion ~ **emotionalist** *n*.

emotionalize [imO*shonalIz*] *v/t* treat emotionally.

emotive [imO*tiv*] *adj* tending to excite emotion.

empanel (*pres/part* **empanelling**, *p/t* and *p/part* **empanelled**) [imp*anel*] *v/t* form a list of (jurors), enrol on a jury.

empathic [emp*athik*] *adj* of or having empathy.

empathy [emp*athi*] *n* (*psych*) power of losing one's sense of identity in contemplation of a work of art, person, or object > PDP; (*pop*) ability fully to understand and share another's feelings.

emperor [empe*Ror*] *n* ruler of an empire; kind of large butterfly; standard size of writing and drawing paper.

emphasis [emf*asis*] *n* stress; any method used to bring out the particular importance of one idea, statement, word *etc* relative to others; voluntary increase in vocal stress or heightening of pitch in speech; impressiveness; rhetorical vigour.

emphasize [emf*asIz*] *v/t* lay emphasis on, stress.

emphatic [emf*atik*] *adj* stressed, expressed with emphasis; forcible ~ **emphatically** *adv*.

emphysema [emf*iseema*] *n* (*med*) distention caused by air in interstices of connective tissues, *esp* of lungs.

empire [empIr] *n* large group of territories united by allegiance to one monarch; (*fig*) group of businesses *etc* controlled by one man; absolute control ~ **empire** *adj* pertaining to an empire; in the style fashionable during first French Empire.

empiric [emp*iRik*] *adj* based on experience, observation and experiment, rather than on theoretic principles ~ **empiric** *n* one who relies on empiric methods, *esp* in medicine; one who rejects orthodox medical theory; quack, charlatan.

empirical [emp*iRikal*] *adj* (*philos*) based on, verifiable by, observation and experiment; pertaining to empiricism; (*med*) empiric ~ **empirically** *adv*.

empiricism [emp*iRisizm*] *n* (*philos*) theory that experience is the only source of knowledge; (*psych*) theory that experience 'outweighs congenital factors in perceiving > PDP; dependence on empiric methods ~ **empiricist** *n* and *adj*.

emplacement [imp*laysment*] *n* position, place; (*mil*) prepared position for heavy gun.

employ [imp*loi*] *v/t* make use of (a person) to work for one, *usu* for wages; provide work for; use; occupy, spend (time) ~ **employ** *n* employment.

employable [imp*loi-ab'l*] *adj* able, fit to be employed ~ **employability** [imploi-a*bili*ti] *n*.

employee [imp*loi-ee*] *n* one who is employed by another and paid wages.

employer [imp*loi-er*] *n* one who employs others for wages; user.

employment [imp*loi*ment] *n* action of employing; state of being employed; work, occupation; **e. exchange** office for finding work for the unemployed and for payment of unemployment benefits.

emporium [emp*awrRi-um*] *n* large general shop; trading centre.

empower [impo*w*-er] *v/t* authorize; enable.

empress [emp*Res*] *n* wife of emperor; woman who rules an empire.

emptily [empt*ili*] *adv* in an empty way.

emptiness [empt*inis*] *n* state of being empty.

empty [empt*i*] *adj* containing nothing; lacking its usual or appropriate contents; (*fig*) meaningless, pointless; stupid; worthless; (*coll*) hungry ~ **empty** *v/t* and *i* make empty, remove contents of; become empty; (*refl*) discharge ~ **empty** (*pl* **empties**) *n* (*coll*) empty bottle, crate, or other container.

empty-handed [empti-*hand*id] *adj* bringing nothing; taking nothing away.

empty-headed [empti-*hed*id] *adj* silly.

empurple [imp*urp'l*] *v/t* tinge or dye with purple.

empyema [empI-*eema*] *n* (*med*) accumulation of pus in a cavity, *esp* in the chest.

empyreal [empI*Ree*-al] *adj* of or in the empyrean; pure, sublime; formed of fire.

empyrean [empI*Ree*-an] *n* highest heaven; region of celestial fire; sky.

emu [*ee*mew] *n* large Australian bird.

emulate [*eme*wlayt] *v/t* try to equal; imitate; rival.

emulation [emew*lay*shon] *n* act of emulating; desire to equal or surpass another; rivalry.

emulator [*eme*wlaytor] *n* one who emulates.

emulous [*eme*wlus] *adj* eager to imitate or surpass; eagerly seeking ~ **emulously** *adv* ~ **emulousness** *n*.

emulsification [imulsifi*kay*shon] *n* process of emulsifying.

emulsifier [imul*sif*I-er] *n* (*chem*) apparatus used for making emulsions; chemical agent used to form an emulsion.

emulsify [imul*sif*I] *v/t* change into an emulsion.

emulsion [imul*shon*] *n* relatively stable suspension of one liquid minutely dispersed in another in which it is not soluble; medical preparation in this form; (*phot*) mixture of silver salts suspended in collodion ~ **emulsive** *adj*.

en- *pref* in, into; put into; cause to become.

enable [inay*b'l*] *v/t* make able; give power or authority to; give means or opportunity to.

enabling [inay*bling*] *adj* (*leg*) rendering legal; giving new legal powers.

enact [in*akt*] *v/t* make into a law; decree; act the part of, perform, take place, do.

enactment [in*akt*ment] *n* act of passing bill into law; ordinance, statute.

enamel [in*amel*] *n* opaque substance similar to glass in composition, used to form hard glossy coating; smooth, glossy paint or varnish; outer coating of tooth ~ **enamel** *adj* coated with, made of, or like enamel ~ **enamel** (*pres/part* **enamelling**, *p/t* and *p/part* **enamelled**) *v/t* coat with enamel; decorate in bright colours ~ **enamelling** adj and n.

enamour [inamer] v/t inspire love in, attract strongly ~ **enamoured** adj in love, very fond of, attracted by.

en bloc [on(g)-blok] adv (Fr) as a whole group or mass; in general, as a whole.

encaenia [enseeni-a] n (pl) annual commemoration services or ceremonies.

encage [inkayj] v/t shut up in a cage; confine.

encamp [inkamp] v/i and t pitch tents; form a camp; settle (troops) in a camp.

encampment [inkampment] n action of making a camp; place where troops are encamped; camping site.

encapsulate [enkapsewlayt] v/t place in a capsule; present or express in brief or oversimplified form.

encase [inkays] v/t place in, or protect with, a case; enclose completely ~ **encasement** n.

encash [inkash] v/t turn into cash; receive ready money for (cheque etc).

encaustic [inkawstik] n technique of painting in which colours are fixed by heat > PDAA ~ **encaustic** adj formed or decorated by encaustic; **e. tile** tile decorated with designs burnt into it.

enceinte [aangsangt] n enclosure of fortifications ~ **enceinte** adj (Fr) pregnant.

encephalic [ensefalik] adj (med) pertaining to the brain.

encephalitis [ensefalItis] n (med) inflammation of the brain; **e. lethargica** sleepy sickness.

encephalogram [ensefalOgRam] n (med) record of electrical impulses emitted by the brain.

enchain [inchayn] v/t bind in chains; (fig) captivate.

enchant [inchaant] v/t bewitch, bind with a spell; (fig) charm, fascinate; delight ~ **enchanter** n one who enchants; magician.

enchanting [inchaanting] adj delightful, charming; very attractive ~ **enchantingly** adv.

enchantment [inchaantment] n act of enchanting, state of being enchanted; magic, spell, incantation; great attractiveness or beauty.

enchantress [inchaantRes] n fascinating woman; witch.

enchase [inchays] v/t set or frame in; engrave, emboss.

encircle [insurk'l] v/t surround, form circle round; move round about; pass right round.

encirclement [insurk'lment] n act of encircling; state of being encircled.

enclave [enklayv] n outlying territory belonging to one country and lying wholly within territory of another; district solely inhabited by people of one social, political or religious group and surrounded by hostile districts.

enclitic [inklitik] n and adj (gramm) (particle) forming unstressed suffix.

enclose, inclose [inklOz] v/t shut in; surround; place in envelope, wrapper etc; place (document) in same envelope with another; (of monks, nuns) isolate from contact with society.

enclosure [inklOzher] n act of enclosing; enclosed piece of ground; something enclosed (in a letter etc); that which encloses, fence.

encode [enkOd] v/t translate into a code, cipher, or electrical signal ~ **encoder** n.

encomiastic [enkOmi-astik] adj giving praise; flattering.

encomium (pl **encomiums**) [enkOmi-um] n ceremonious praise, panegyric.

encompass [enkumpas] v/t surround, encircle.

encore [onkawr] n demand by audience to performer to repeat part of performance or perform supplementary item; repetition or supplementary item performed in response, to applause ~ **encore** v/t and i demand an encore ~ **encore** [onkawr] interj once more!

encounter [inkownter] v/t meet; meet unexpectedly; meet in battle or hostility; be confronted by ~ **encounter** n meeting, esp unexpected or hostile; **e. group** (psych) type of group therapy in which people are encouraged to express openly to each other their thoughts and feelings.

encourage [inkuRij] v/t give courage to; inspire confidence in; urge onwards, incite to action; promote, support; help to develop or spread.

encouragement [inkuRijment] n act of giving courage or confidence; that which encourages; stimulus.

encouraging [inkuRijing] adj tending to encourage; inspiring confidence ~ **encouragingly** adv.

encroach [inkROch] v/i go beyond one's rights, abuse one's privileges; **e. on** intrude on, trespass on; usurp the rights of; gradually take possession of ~ **encroachment** n act of encroaching; territory, rights etc won by encroaching.

encrust, incrust [inkRust] v/t and i cover with a crust; stud thickly with; form a crust.

encumber [inkumber] v/t burden, weigh down; impede, obstruct.

encumbrance [inkumbRans] n that which encumbers, burden; a dependant; (leg) liability upon an estate.

encyclical, encyclic [insiklikal, insiklik] n Papal letter or message circulated to the whole Roman Catholic Church ~ **encyclical, encyclic** adj.

encyclopedia, encyclopaedia [ensIklopeedi-a] n book of classified information on all branches of knowledge, or on one specified branch ~ **encyclopedian, encyclopaedian** adj.

encyclopedic, encyclopaedic [ensIklopeedik] adj pertaining to, like, an encyclopedia; informative and wide-ranging in subject-matter ~ **encyclopedical, encyclopaedical** adj.

encyclopedist, encyclopaedist [ensIklopeedist] n compiler of an encyclopedia; compiler of French Encyclopedia shortly before French Revolution.

encyst [ensist] v/t and i enclose, or become enclosed, in a cyst.

end [end] n final extremity, last part, furthest limit; conclusion; cessation; (fig) death; aim, purpose; remnant; (sl) buttocks; (coll) intolerable person or thing; downfall; final fate; **bitter e.** unpleasant conclusion or outcome; **ends of the earth** remote or savage regions; **go off the deep e.** become unnecessarily excited, angry etc; **keep one's e. up** do one's share; hold one's own; **latter e.** old age; death; **at a loose e.** with nothing much to do; **make ends meet** live within one's income; live very economically; **no e.** (coll) extremely; **on e.** without stopping; upright; **e. play** strategy of play in last stages of game; **wrong e. of the stick** complete misunderstanding ~ end v/t and i finish, conclude; complete; spend the last part of; come to an end, cease; result (in).

endanger [indaynjer] v/t expose to danger.

endear [endeer] v/t make dear; cause to be loved.

endearing [endeerRing] adj attractive, causing affection ~ **endearingly** adv.

endearment [endeerment] n act of endearing; affection; caress; affectionate term of address.

endeavour [indever] v/i try hard, strive ~ **endeavour** n vigorous attempt, effort.

endemic [endemik]adj (med) peculiar to or prevalent in a specified area; (zool) indigenous ~ **endemically** adv.

endermic [endurmik] adj acting upon or penetrating beneath the skin.

endgame [endgaym] n strategy of final stages of game, esp of chess.

ending [ending] n conclusion; termination; death; (gramm) inflexional suffix.

endive [endiv] n species of chicory.

endless [endles] adj without end; infinite; perpetual, never ceasing; (coll) too long; e. chain chain with joined ends, revolving upon pulleys.

endlong [endlong] adv lengthwise; vertically.

endmost [endmOst] adj farthest away.

endo- pref inside, internal.

endocardium [endOkaardi-um] n (anat) membrane lining heart.

endocarp [endOkaarp] n (bot) inner layer of a seed-vessel.

endocrine [endOkrIn] n and adj (gland) producing hormones; (gland) secreting internally without duct; (secretion) produced by a ductless gland.

endoderm [endodurm] n (biol) germ layer of animal embryo; lining of alimentary canal; (bot) inner layer of cortex > PDB.

endogamy [endogami] n limitation of marriage to members within one group, community, or tribe.

endogenous [endojinus] adj (biol) growing or originating from within.

endomorph [endOmawrf] n person of soft, fleshy build.

endoplasm [endOplazm] n (biol) inner layer of protoplasm of cell > PDB.

endorphin [endawrfin] n (med) one of a class of pain-suppressing hormones in the brain.

endorse, indorse [indawrs] v/t sign one's name on back of (cheque etc); write on back of (document); (fig) confirm; approve of, support; record a motoring offence on (driving licence).

endorsee [indawrsee] n one in whose favour a cheque etc is endorsed.

endorsement, indorsement [indawrsment] n act of endorsing; signature etc written on back of document; (fig) confirmation, approval.

endosmosis [endosmOsis] n inward flow of liquids into cell through membrane, due to osmosis.

endosperm [endOsperm] n nutritive tissue round embryo of seed plants > PDB.

endospore [endOspawr] n endosperm.

endothermic [endOthurmik] adj (chem) accompanied by the absorption of heat.

endow [endow] v/t bestow property or money on; provide permanent financial support for; bestow (talents, natural qualities etc) on.

endowment [endowment] n act of endowing; property or revenue with which person or institution is endowed; natural capacity, inborn physical or mental quality: **e. policy** insurance policy whereby a fixed sum will be paid at certain date or at death, whichever is earlier.

endpapers [endpayperz] n (pl) blank flyleaves at the beginning and end of a book.

end-product [end-pRodukt] n final result of series of changes or processes.

end-stopped [end-stopt] adj (pros) having marked break in syntax coinciding with end of line.

endue [indew] v/t endow (with), bestow (on).

endurable [indewRab'l] adj bearable ~ **endurably** adv.

endurance [indewRans] n act or state of enduring; power to endure, fortitude.

endure [indewr] v/t and i bear bravely and patiently; bear without collapsing; undergo, suffer; tolerate; last, continue; stand firm.

enduring [indewrRing] adj long-lasting; everlasting ~ **enduringly** adv.

end-use [end-ews] n final use for which a product has been designed.

endways [endwayz] adv on end, upright; with its end pointing forwards.

endwise [endwIz] adv endways.

enema [enima] n injection of liquid into the rectum; apparatus for injecting this.

enemy [enimi] n one who shows hatred and hostility, foe; opponent, antagonist; nation at war with another; armed forces of such a nation; opposing force ~ **enemy** adj pertaining to an enemy.

energetic [enerjetik] adj full of energy, vigorous, active ~ **energetical** adj energetic ~ **energetically** adv.

energize [enerjIz] v/t and i stimulate; fill with energy; act energetically ~ **energizer** n.

energy [enerji] n power, force; capacity to act vigorously; vigour; (mech, phys) capacity for doing work > PDE, PDS.

enervate [enervayt] v/i deprive of strength, weaken ~ **enervation** [enervayshon] n.

enface [infays] v/t stamp or overprint (document, bond etc).

enfeeble [infeeb'l] v/t make feeble, weaken.

enfeoff [infeef] v/t (leg) invest (person) with the fief or fee of an estate ~ **enfeoffment** n act of enfeoffing; deed conveying lands in fee.

enfilade [enfilayd] v/t (mil) rake with fire from flanks ~ **enfilade** n enfilading fire.

enfold [infOld] v/t fold up; endorse; embrace.

enforce [infawrs] v/t compel by force or threats; make effective by force, compel the observance of (law etc); achieve by force; attempt by force.

enforceable [infawrsab'l] adj that can be enforced.

enforcement [infawrsment] n act of enforcing; compulsion; state of being enforced.

enfranchise [infRanchIz] v/t give the right to vote; set free from slavery; convert to freehold.

enfranchisement [infRanchizment] n act of enfranchising; state of being enfranchised.

engage [in-gayj] v/t and i bind by promise or contract; hire, take into employment; reserve; bind oneself, esp to marry; use, occupy; (mil) attack, begin combat with; (mech) interlock; pledge oneself, promise; **e. in** take part in.

engaged [in-*gayjd*] *adj* betrothed; promised; employed; occupied; in use, not available; committed to a political or philosophical cause.

engagement [in-*gayj*ment] *n* act of engaging; state of being engaged; betrothal; pledge; appointment to meet someone or do something at fixed time; obligation; military encounter; battle.

engaging [in-*gayj*ing] *adj* attractive, pleasant ∼ **engagingly** *adv*.

engender [in*jen*der] *v/t* give rise to cause; rouse; beget.

engine [*enj*in] *n* any machine to convert other sources of energy into mechanical energy, *esp* steam-engine; (*ar*) device; instrument of war ∼ **engine** *v/t* furnish with an engine.

engine-driver [*enj*in-d*Riv*er] *n* one who drives a locomotive.

engineer [enj*ineer*] *n* one whose profession is any form of engineering; one who designs, constructs, or supervises any engine or machine; one who organizes the building of public works, roads, bridges, *etc*; one in charge of engines, *esp* of ship; (*mil*) member of corps which builds fortifications, roads *etc* or organizes communications ∼ **engineer** *v/t* and *i* design and supervise the construction of; devise, contrive and carry out, *esp* dishonestly or secretly; act as engineer; (*fig*) organize, manipulate.

engineering [enj*ineer*Ring] *n* practical application of scientific knowledge in the design and construction of engines and machines *etc* (**mechanical e.**), roads, bridges and buildings (**civil e.**), electrical machines and communications (**electrical e.**), chemical plant and machinery (**chemical e.**), fortifications and communications (**military e.**); (*fig*) series of planned changes to a society, species *etc* designed to modify its basic characteristics; **genetic e.** modification of a species by planned breeding.

English [*ing*-glish] *n* and *adj* (people) of England; (language) of English people ∼ **English** *v/t* translate into English.

Englishism [*ing*-glishizm] *n* form of speech characteristic of English language as spoken in England.

engorge [in*gawrj*] *v/t* swallow greedily; fill to excess; (*med*) congest ∼ **engorgement** *n*.

engraft [in-g*Raaft*] *v/t* graft; (*fig*) implant.

engrain [in-g*Rayn*] *v/t* saturate, dye thoroughly; (*fig*) impart permanent habits of mind to ∼ **engrained** *adj* thorough, ineradicable.

engrave [in-g*Rayv*] *v/t* cut (lines, letters *etc*) into a hard surface; reproduce (picture *etc*) by taking impressions from a metal surface cut and inked; (*fig*) impress deeply, mark indelibly ∼ **engraver** *n* one who engraves.

engraving [in-g*Rayv*ing] *n* art of producing prints from an engraved metal plate; art of producing prints from an incised block of wood; print produced by such methods > PDAA.

engross [in-g*ROs*] *v/t* absorb whole attention of, exclusively occupy the mind of; (*leg*) copy in large writing; write out in formal manner.

engrossing [in-g*ROs*ing] *adj* absorbing, monopolizing one's attention.

engrossment [in-g*ROs*ment] *n* act of engrossing; state of being engrossed; (*leg*) document engrossed.

engulf [in-*gulf*] *v/t* swallow up.

enhance [in*haans*] *v/t* raise in importance; heighten, increase; exaggerate ∼ **enhancement** *n* that which enhances, state of being enhanced.

enharmonic [enhaar*monik*] *adj* and *n* (*mus*) (having) interval less than a semitone > PDM.

enigma [in*ig*ma] *n* mystery, puzzle, riddle; (*fig*) person or situation hard to understand.

enigmatic [enig*matik*] *adj* deliberately mysterious, puzzling; inexplicable ∼ **enigmatical** *adj* enigmatic ∼ **enigmatically** *adv*.

enjambment [en*jam*-ment] *n* (*pros*) unbroken syntactical continuation from end of one line to beginning of next.

enjoin [in*join*] *v/t* order, command, issue instructions.

enjoy [in*joi*] *v/t* take joy or pleasure in; have the use of, possess; (*ar*) possess sexually; **e. oneself** feel pleasure, joy *etc* in one's occupations or surroundings.

enjoyable [in*joi*-ab'l] *adj* giving, or capable of giving, pleasure ∼ **enjoyably** *adv*.

enjoyment [in*joi*ment] *n* act or state of enjoying; pleasure, joy; that which causes pleasure.

enkindle [in*kind*'l] *v/t* set on fire; (*fig*) inflame, rouse, excite.

enlace [in*lays*] *v/t* interlace, twine; enfold.

enlarge [in*laarj*] *v/t* and *i* make larger or more spacious, expand; become larger, grow; (*phot*) reproduce (print) on larger scale than negative; **e. upon** speak fully about, explain in detail.

enlargement [in*laarj*ment] *n* act of enlarging; that which has been made larger; addition; (*phot*) print made on larger scale than negative.

enlarger [in*laarj*er] *n* one who or that which enlarges.

enlighten [in*lit*en] *v/t* give knowledge or information to; free from ignorance, prejudice *etc*.

enlightened [in*lit*end] *adj* well-informed; not bound by prejudice, superstition *etc*.

enlightening [in*lit*ening] *adj* instructive.

enlightenment [in*lit*enment] *n* act of enlightening; state of being enlightened.

enlist [in*list*] *v/t* and *i* enrol for military service; obtain as active supporter or helper; volunteer for military service ∼ **enlistment** *n*.

enliven [in*liv*en] *v/t* give vigour or life to; make cheerful or gay ∼ **enlivenment** *n*.

en masse [ong-*mas*] *adv* (*Fr*) in a body; in general, as a whole.

enmesh [en*mesh*] *v/t* entangle; entrap ∼ **enmeshment** *n*.

enmity [*en*miti] *n* hostility; hatred, ill-will.

ennoble [in*Ob*'l] *v/t* make noble, raise to the rank of a peer; increase nobility of (character *etc*) ∼ **ennoblement** *n*.

ennui [aan*wee*] *n* (*Fr*) boredom.

enormity [in*awrm*iti] *n* outrageous wickedness; atrocious crimes; state of being enormous.

enormous [in*awrm*us] *adj* huge, vast, abnormally large ∼ **enormously** *adv* to a great extent, very much.

enosis [en*Os*is] *n* demand of Greek Cypriots for political union with Greece > PDPol.

enough [in*uf*] *adj* sufficient, neither too little nor too much ~ **enough** *n* sufficient quantity, as much as one wants ~ **enough** *adv* sufficiently; possibly; (*coll*) fairly well.

enounce [*inowns*] *v/t* pronounce; proclaim.

enow [*inow*] *adj* and *adv* (*ar, poet*) enough.

enprint [*enpRint*] *n* enlarged photographic print.

enquire, enquiry see **inquire, inquiry.**

enrage [*inRayj*] *v/t* provoke to rage.

enrapt [*inRapt*] *adj* in ecstatic joy.

enrapture [*inRapcher*] *v/t* fill with intense delight.

enregister [*inRejister*] *v/t* enter into a register; enrol; put on record.

enrich [*inRich*] *v/t* make rich; make more splendid or magnificent; (*of soil*) fertilize: increase food value of; (*phys*) increase the abundance of a particular isotope in a mixture of isotopes ~ **enrichment** *n* act of making or becoming richer; that which enriches.

enrobe [*enROb*] *v/t* invest or adorn with a robe.

enrol [*inROl*] (*pres/part* **enrolling,** *p/t* and *p/part,* **enrolled**) *v/t* place (a name) on a list, record, register; include as a member ~ **enrolment** *n.*

en route [*on(g)-Root*] *adv* (*Fr*) while travelling or being transported (to); on the way (to).

ensanguine [*ensang-gwin*] *v/t* stain with blood; redden.

ensconce [*inskons*] *v/t* place, settle in safety or comfortably.

ensemble [*onsomb'l*] *n* total effect; something composed of parts but regarded as a whole; (*mus*) item for several soloists in opera; group of performers; quality of teamwork in performance; (*coll*) several items of clothing designed to be worn together.

enshrine [*inshRIn*] *v/t* place in a shrine; revere ~ **enshrinement** *n.*

enshroud [*inshRowd*] *v/t* cover with a shroud; cover entirely; veil.

ensign [*ensIn/ensn*] *n* emblem of office, badge; national or regimental flag; (*US* navy) commissioned officer of lowest rank; (*mil*) obsolete rank equivalent to second lieutenant.

ensigncy [*ensInsi*] *n* rank of an ensign.

ensilage [*ensilij*] *n* preservation of green fodder in a pit; fodder thus preserved ~ **ensilage** *v/t* preserve in a silo.

ensile [*ensIl*] *v/t* preserve in a silo.

enslave [*inslayv*] *v/t* reduce to slavery; dominate entirely ~ **enslavement** *n.*

ensnare [*insnair*] *v/t* catch in a trap; (*fig*) catch or dominate by trickery; allure.

ensue [*insew*] *v/i* follow, result (from).

ensure [*inshoor*] *v/t* make certain; make safe; insure.

entablature [*intablatewr*] *n* (*archi*) that part of a structure above a column which includes cornice, frieze, and architrave.

entail [*intayl*] *v/t* have as inevitable consequence, necessarily involve; (*leg*) bequeath by entail ~ **entail** [*entayl*] *n* (*leg*) restriction of succession of landed estate to specified line of heirs; estate the inheritance of which is so limited.

entangle [*intang-g'l*] *v/t* twist together so that separation is difficult; catch in net-like obstacle; (*fig*) involve in difficulties, ensnare; obtain control over, entrap.

entanglement [*intang-g'lment*] *n* state of being entangled; (*mil*) interwoven barbed wire.

entelechy [*enteleKi*] *n* (*philos*) process by which a potentiality becomes actual.

entente [*ontont*] *n* (*Fr*) friendly understanding, *esp* between nations; **E. cordiale** friendly relations between Great Britain and France established in 1904.

enter [*enter*] *v/t* and *i* come or go in; penetrate; pierce; become a member of; put down in writing; enrol; come on to the stage; **e. for** register, enrol, as a competitor in; **e. into** be part of; take part in; comprehend, sympathize with; become a party to; **e. upon** begin, set out on; take possession of.

enteric [*enteRik*] *adj* pertaining to the intestines; **e. fever** typhoid fever.

enteritis [*enteRItis*] *n* inflammation of intestines.

enterprise [*enterpRIz*] *n* adventure, bold or difficult undertaking; business concern; capacity to take an initiative, adventurousness.

enterprising [*enterpRIzing*] *adj* adventurous, bold ~ **enterprisingly** *adv.*

entertain [*entertayn*] *v/t* and *i* amuse, provide pleasant diversion for; receive as guest; habitually offer hospitality, give parties *etc*; consider, bear in mind ~ **entertainer** *n.*

entertaining [*entertayning*] *adj* amusing ~ **entertainingly** *adv.*

entertainment [*entertaynment*] *n* act of entertaining; a reception or party; hospitality; (theatrical, musical *etc*) performance intended to interest or amuse; amusement.

enthalpy [*enthalpi*] *n* (*thermodynamics*) the internal energy of a substance or system plus the product of its pressure and volume.

enthral, enthrall (*pres/part* **enthralling,** *p/t* and *p/part* **enthralled**) [*inthRawl*] *v/t* hold the interest of, fascinate, absorb; (*ar*) enslave.

enthralling [*inthRawling*] *adj* fascinating.

enthrone [*inthROn*] *v/t* place on a throne; (*fig*) exalt; install as bishop.

enthuse [*inthewz*] *v/i* and *t* (*coll*) grow enthusiastic, express enthusiasm; cause enthusiasm in.

enthusiasm [*inthewzi-azm*] *n* intense admiration; great zeal; outward show of admiration, approval *etc*; something fervently admired or desired; religious fervour, exaltation ~ **enthusiast** *n.*

enthusiastic [*inthewzi-astik*] *adj* filled with enthusiasm; ardent, eager ~ **enthusiastically** *adv.*

entice [*intIs*] *v/t* tempt, allure, *esp* to evil; attract.

enticement [*intIsment*] *n* act of enticing; state of being enticed; that which entices.

enticing [*intIsing*] *adj* very attractive.

entire [*intIr*] *adj* whole, complete; unbroken; perfect; not gelded ~ **entire** *n* that which is unmixed; animal not gelded; blend of beer ~ **entirely** *adv* ~ **entireness** *n.*

entirety [*intIreti*] *n* state of being entire; completeness; the whole of something.

entitle [*intIt'l*] *v/t* give name or title to; give right or claim to ~ **entitlement** *n.*

entity [*entiti*] *n* (*philos*) anything that has real existence; existence as distinct from possession of attributes; (*coll*) thing, object.

ento- *pref* within, inner, inside.

entomb [*intOOm*] *v/t* bury in, or as if in, a tomb.

entomic [*entomik*] *adj* pertaining to insects.

entomological [ento*moloji*kal] *adj* of entomology.

entomologist [ento*moloji*st] *n* one who studies insects.

entomology [ento*moloji*] *n* scientific study of insects.

entophyte [*ent*OfIt] *n* vegetable parasite.

entourage [*ontoo*Raazh] *n* (*Fr*) surroundings, environment; retinue, attendants, associates.

entozoon (*pl* **entozoa**) [*ent*OzO-on] *n* (*biol*) parasitic animal living inside another animal.

entr'acte [*ont*Rakt] *n* (*Fr*) interval between acts of play or opera; music *etc* performed between acts.

entrails [*ent*Raylz] *n* (*pl*) internal organs, *esp* bowels; (*fig*) internal parts of anything.

entrain [int*Rayn*] *v/t* and *i* put into a train; board a train; carry along with, *esp* one fluid in a stream of another fluid.

entrammel (*pres/part* **entrammelling**, *p/t* and *p/part* **entrammelled**) [int*Ram*el] *v/t* entangle, hamper.

entrance (1) [*ent*Rans] *n* act of entering; right to be admitted; point of entry, way in, doorway; action of an actor on coming on the stage.

entrance (2) [int*Raans*] *v/t* put into a state of ecstasy, ravish with delight; enrapture.

entrancement [int*Raans*ment] *n* act of entrancing; state of being entranced; that which entrances.

entrancing [int*Raans*ing] *adj* charming, fascinating.

entrant [*ent*Rant] *n* one who enters; competitor, candidate.

entrap (*pres/part* **entrapping**, *p/t* and *p/part* **entrapped**) [int*Rap*] *v/t* catch in a trap; trick, deceive by cunning; trick (someone) into doing something.

entreat [int*Reet*] *v/t* beseech, implore ~ **entreating** *adj* ~ **entreatingly** *adv*.

entreaty [int*Reet*i] *n* earnest request, plea.

entrechat [*ont*Resha] *n* (*Fr*) high leap in which dancer crosses or strikes his feet together while descending.

entrée [*ont*Ray] *n* (*Fr*) right of entry; light dish served between fish and meat courses.

entremets [*ont*Remay] *n* (*Fr*) extra dish served between two main courses of a dinner.

entrench [int*Rensh*] *v/t* dig and occupy a trench; surround with trenches; (*fig*) establish (oneself) securely; strongly defend one's attitude, opinion *etc*; (*pol*) render (clause in law, *etc*) exceptionally difficult to repeal; ~ **entrenchment** *n*.

entrepot [*ont*Rep*O*] *n* (*Fr*) warehouse; place where goods are stored temporarily; place or district acting as intermediary centre of trade between foreign countries > PDG.

entrepreneur [*ont*Re-p*Renur*] *n* (*Fr*) a contractor; a promoter, *esp* of theatrical or musical performances; manager of a large commercial or industrial organization.

entresol [*ont*Resol] *n* (*Fr*) (*archi*) extra storey between ground and first floors.

entropy [*ent*Ropi] *n* (*thermodynamics*) ratio of amount of heat taken up to the absolute temperature at which the heat is absorbed > PDS; the measure of disorder in a thermodynamic system; (*astron*) measure of increasing disorganization of the universe.

entrust [int*Rust*] *v/t* give into a person's care; confide; charge with.

entry [*ent*Ry] *n* act of coming or going in; way in, doorway; act of noting down in a book; item noted down in a book; (*leg*) act of taking possession.

entwine [int*wIn*] *v/t* and *i* twist together, interlace.

enucleate [inew*k*li-ayt] *v/t* make clear, explain; (*surg*) extract (tumour *etc*) from its case, or eye from socket.

enumerate [inewme*Rayt*] *v/t* count, reckon up one by one; mention in order, go through a list of.

enumeration [inewme*Rayshon*] *n* act of reckoning up; detailed account; list.

enumerative [inewme*Rativ*] *adj* that enumerates.

enunciable [inunsi-ab'l] *adj* capable of being enunciated.

enunciate [inunsi-ayt] *v/t* state formally or carefully; utter distinctly.

enunciation [inunsi-*ayshon*] *n* act of enunciating; condition of being enunciated; manner of enunciating; (*geom*) formal statement of proposition.

enunciative [inunsi-ativ] *adj* that enunciates.

enure see **inure**.

enuresis [enew*Reesi*s] *n* (*med*) involuntary discharge of urine ~ **enuretic** *adj*.

envelop [inv*elop*] *v/t* surround completely; cover entirely; (*fig*) make obscure.

envelope [*env*elOp/*onv*'lOp] *n* cover in which a letter is placed; covering, wrapping; outer covering of gasbag of balloon or airship; (*bot*, *biol*) enclosing membrane or structure.

envelopment [env*elop*ment] *n* act of enveloping; state of being enveloped; wrapper, outer covering.

envenom [env*enom*] *v/t* poison; (*fig*) embitter, exasperate.

enviable [*env*i-ab'l] *adj* (*of thing*) most desirable; (*of person*) exciting envy ~ **enviably** *adv*.

envied [*env*id] *adj* that is the object of envy.

envious [*env*i-us] *adj* feeling envy; expressing envy ~ **enviously** *adv*.

environ [inv*I*-Ron] *v/t* be placed around.

environment [inv*I*Ronment] *n* act of surrounding; surroundings; external conditions in which a person or organism lives.

environmental [inv*I*Ron*ment*al] *adj* of, caused by, the environment.

environmentalist [inv*I*Ron*ment*alist] *n* one who wishes to protect a natural environment from pollution, *etc*; one who studies the environment; one who believes environment is the chief influence on animal or human development.

environs [inv*I*Ronz] *n* (*pl*) immediate neighbourhood, surrounding district; outskirts.

envisage [inv*izij*] *v/t* view mentally, visualize; consider as possible or desirable.

envoy (1) [*envoi*] *n* postscript to a poem or set of poems; concluding stanza of a ballade.

envoy (2) *n* a diplomatic representative; *esp* minister plenipotentiary; agent, messenger.

envy [*env*i] *n* vexation and ill-will roused by considering another's success, qualities *etc*; hostile longing to possess what is another's; object of such feelings ~ **envy** *v/t* regard with envy.

enwrap (*pres/part* **enwrapping**, *p/t* and *p/part* **enwrapped**) [in*Rap*] *v/t* wrap up completely, envelop.

enwreathe [inReeTH] v/t surround with a wreath; entwine.

enzyme [enzIm] n organic substances produced by living cells, which act as catalysts in chemical changes > PDB, PDS.

eo- pref very early, in the beginning.

eocene [ee-Oseen] adj (geol) belonging to earliest division of the Tertiary period.

eolith [ee-Olith] n flint tool of the earliest age.

eolithic [ee-Olithik] adj of or containing eoliths.

eon [ee-on] n vast period of time, aeon.

ep-, epi- pref on, upon, at; in addition etc.

epact [eepakt] n age of moon on first day of year; excess of solar over lunar year.

epaulet, epaulette [epawlet] n ornamental shoulder-piece of uniform.

epergne [aypairn] n large, branched centre-piece for a table for holding flowers or fruit.

ephedrin, ephedrine [efedRin] n (med) drug used in treatment of low blood-pressure and of hayfever.

ephemera (pl **ephemerae**) [ifeemeRa] n insect which lives for one day only; (fig) anything short-lived.

ephemeral [ifemeRal] adj lasting one day only, or only a few days; short-lived.

ephod [eefod] n sleeveless garment worn by Jewish priests.

epi- see **ep-**.

epic [epik] n long poem in elevated style narrating the adventures of a hero; (coll) long novel or film, esp one containing adventurous episodes ~ **epic** adj ~ **epical** adj ~ **epically** adv.

epicene [episeen] adj having characteristics of both sexes; indeterminate in style or character; (gramm) of common gender ~ **epicene** n epicene person.

epicentre [episenter] n area of land immediately above place of origin of earthquake > PDG.

epicure [epikewr] n one who has fastidious tastes in eating and drinking; one who is too fond of luxury and comfort.

epicurean [epikewrRee-an] n pertaining to an epicure; luxury-loving; (philos) maintaining that happiness is the highest good in life; pertaining to Epicurus ~ **epicurean** n epicure; follower of Epicurus.

epicureanism [epikewrRee-anizm] n (philos) doctrines of Epicurus; epicurism.

epicurism [epikewrRizm] n deliberate cultivation of tastes of an epicure; state of being an epicure.

epicycle [episIk'l] n small circle whose centre moves round the circumference of larger circle.

epicyclic [episIklik] adj of or in an epicycle.

epidemic [epidemik] n and adj (disease) rapidly spreading among many people in one area; (fig) (opinion, fashion etc) rapidly becoming wide-spread ~ **epidemical** adj ~ **epidemically** adv.

epidemiology [epideemi-oloji] n study of epidemics.

epidermal [epidurmal] adj epidermic.

epidermic [epidurmik] adj of, on, or in the epidermis.

epidermis [epidurmis] n (biol) outermost layer of cells, outer layer of skin >PDB.

epidiascope [epidI-askOp] n optical projector for throwing enlarged image of an opaque object or a transparency on a screen.

epiglottis [epiglotis] n (anat) leaf-like structure at the entrance to the larynx.

epigram [epigRam] n short poem with a witty or satirical ending; any pungent saying.

epigrammatic [epigRamatik] adj of, like, or using epigrams; pointed; concise ~ **epigrammatical** adv ~ **epigrammatically** adv.

epigrammatist [epigRamatist] n one who makes epigrams ~ **epigrammatize** v/t and i.

epigraph [epigRaaf] n carved inscription; quotation, motto etc at beginning of book or chapter.

epigraphic [epigRafik] adj of or as an epigraph.

epigraphist [epigRafist] n expert in epigraphy.

epigraphy [epigRafi] n study of ancient inscriptions.

epilepsy [epilepsi] n chronic nervous disorder characterized by fits or paroxysms with loss of consciousness and a succession of convulsions; falling sickness > PDP.

epileptic [epileptik] adj pertaining to epilepsy; suffering from epilepsy; convulsive ~ **epileptic** n one suffering from epilepsy ~ **epileptical** adj ~ **epileptically** adv.

epilogue [epilog] n short speech addressed to audience at the end of a play; conclusion of any literary work, radio or television programme.

Epiphany [ipifani] n manifestation of Christ to the Magi; festival on 6 January celebrating this; (fig) moment of manifestation of supernatural reality.

epiphyte [epifIt] n non-parasitic plant using another for support.

episcopacy [ipiskOpasi] n government of a church by bishops; body of bishops, episcopate.

episcopal [ipiskOpal] adj of or pertaining to a bishop or bishops; pertaining to episcopacy ~ **episcopally** adv.

episcopalian [ipiskOpayli-an] n member of an episcopal church; believer in episcopal government; member of Church of England ~ **episcopalian** adj.

episcopate [ipiskOpayt] n office or dignity of a bishop; bishopric; the whole body of bishops.

episode [episOd] n one of a series of events; subsidiary incident in a narrative; (mus) non-thematic part of a fugue; contrasting section in a rondo.

episodic [episodik] adj pertaining to an episode; like an episode; easily separable into episodes, disjointed ~ **episodical** adj ~ **episodically** adv.

epistemology [epistemoloji] n branch of metaphysics which deals with the nature and validity of knowledge.

epistle [ipis'l] n letter; a literary work in the form of a letter; apostolic letter included in New Testament; extract from any portion of Bible other than a gospel, appointed to be read during the Eucharist.

epistolary [ipistolaRi] adj of or pertaining to letter-writing or letters.

epitaph [epitaf] n inscription on tomb; memorial sentences.

epithalamium (pl **epithalamia**) [epithalaymi-um] n a marriage song or poem.

epithelium [epitheeli-um] n (biol) cellular tissue covering mucous membrane > PDB; (bot) thin epidermis lining the inner cavities of plants.

epithet [epithet] n a descriptive adjective or name ~ **epithetic** [epithetik] adj.

epitome [epitomi] n a single instance or item typical of a larger category; concentrated essence, embodiment; representation in miniature; summary.

epitomize [epitomIz] v/t make or be an epitome of.

epizoon (pl **epizoa**) [epizO-on] n (zool) external parasitic animal.

epoch [eepok] n period of time, era, esp one remarkable or distinctive.

epochal [epokal] adj of or marking an epoch.

epoch-making [eepok-mayking] adj marking the beginning of a new epoch; highly important.

epode [epOd] n (pros) last part of ode; poem in which short line follows a longer one.

eponym [eponim] n real or legendary person from whose name that of a tribe, family, place, poem etc is derived.

eponymous [eponimus] adj giving one's name to a group, place, poem etc.

epos [epos] n primitive oral epic.

epoxy [eepoksi] adj (chem) containing an oxygen atom in an organic ring compound; **e. resin** thermosetting plastic obtained by polymerization of an epoxy compound > PDS.

Epsom salts [epsum-sawltz] n (pl) magnesium sulphate, used as purgative.

equability [ekwabiliti] n state of being equable.

equable [ekwab'l] adj unvarying, uniform; tranquil, serene ~ **equably** adv.

equal [eekwal] adj identical in size, number, force etc; identical or closely similar in value, quality, rank etc; evenly balanced; calm, unruffled; **e. to** (fig) having the courage, strength, abilities etc needed for ~ **equal** n one having same rank, qualities, age etc as another ~ **equal** (pres/part **equalling**, p/t and p/part **equalled**) v/t be equal to; make equal; be as good as.

equalitarian [eekwolitairRi-an] n and adj egalitarian ~ **equalitarianism** n egalitarianism.

equality [eekwoliti] n condition of being equal.

equalization [eekwalIzayshon] n act of equalizing; state of being equalized.

equalize [eekwalIz] v/t and i make equal; (sport) reach a score equal to one's opponent's ~ **equalizer** n one who or that which equalizes.

equally [eekwali] adv to an equal degree; in equal shares.

equanimity [ekwenimiti/eekwanimiti] n composure, serenity; mental tranquillity.

equate [eekwayt] v/t treat as equal or equivalent.

equation [eekwayshon] n act of making equal or equating; state or process of being equalized or equated; (math) statement of equality between known and unknown qualities; (chem) symbolic representation of chemical reaction > PDS ~ **equational** adj ~ **equationally** adv.

equator [eekwayter] n imaginary circle on the surface of the earth, lying midway between the poles; **celestial e.** corresponding imaginary circle in celestial sphere > PDG.

equatorial [ekwatawRi-al] adj pertaining to the equator; near the equator.

equerry [ekweRi] n officer in personal attendance upon a royal personage; (ar) master of horse in royal household.

equestrian [ikwestRi-an] adj pertaining to horses or horse-riding; on horseback; skilled in horse-riding ~ **equestrian** n horseman; circus rider.

equestrienne [ikwestRi-en] n horsewoman, esp professional woman performer on horsèback.

equiangular [eekwi-ang-gewler] adj having all angles equal.

equidistance [eekwidistans] n equal distance.

equidistant [eekwidistant] adj equally distant.

equilateral [eekwilateRal] n and adj (geom) (figure) having all sides equal.

equilibrate [eekwilibRayt] v/t and i cause to balance; balance ~ **equilibration** [eekwilibRayshon] n state of balance; act of balancing.

equilibrist [eekwilibRist] n professional performer of balancing tricks.

equilibrium [eekwilibRi-um] n state of balance between opposing forces or effects; capacity of maintaining one's balance; sense of balance > PDP; (fig) equanimity; balance of power.

equine [ekwIn] adj of or like a horse.

equinoctial [ekwinokshal] adj pertaining to equinoxes.

equinox [ekwinoks] n time of year when the sun appears vertically overhead at noon at the equator > PDG.

equip (pres/part **equipping**, p/t and p/part **equipped**) [ikwip] v/t supply with necessities; supply with weapons; train.

equipage [ekwipij] n retinue of attendants; (ar) carriage with horses and attendants; a set of articles useful for some particular purpose.

equipment [ikwipment] n act of equipping; state of being equipped; collection of necessary weapons, tools, or other articles.

equipoise [ekwipoiz] n equality of force or weight, balance.

equipollence [eekwipolens] n equality of force or meaning ~ **equipollent** adj.

equiponderance [eekwiponderans] n equality of weight, equipoise ~ **equiponderant** adj.

equipotential [eekwipOtenshal] adj (phys) having equal power or potential at every point; (biol) having equal potentialities.

equitable [ekwitab'l] adj just; in accordance with equity ~ **equitably** adv.

equitant [ekwitant] adj (bot) overlapping.

equitation [ekwitayshon] n art of riding a horse.

equity [ekwiti] n justice, fairness; correction of law when too severe or defective; system of justice existing side'by side with and supplementing Common Law; **the e.** sum total of shares held in trust by a given company ~ **equities** n (pl) (Stock Exchange) Ordinary shares.

equivalence [ikwivalens] n state of being equivalent.

equivalent [ikwivalent] adj equal in value, amount etc; same in meaning; (chem) equal in combining weight > PDS ~ **equivalent** n that which is equivalent; **e. weight** (chem) combining weight relative to hydrogen; (for an element) atomic weight divided by valency > PDS ~ **equivalently** adv.

equivocal [ikwivokal] adj ambiguous, of uncertain meaning; deliberately misleading or vague; arousing doubt or suspicion; not clearly established ~ **equivocally** adv.

equivocate [ik*wiv*okayt] *v/i* use words ambiguously, *esp* in order to deceive; quibble, hedge.

equivocation [ikwivo*kay*shon] *n* act of equivocating; quibble.

equivocator [ik*wiv*okayter] *n* quibbler.

era [*eer*Ra] *n* historical period, epoch; system of dating which reckons from some particular event.

eradiate [i*Ray*di-ayt] *v/i and t* radiate.

eradicate [i*Rad*ikayt] *v/t* tear up by the roots; destroy, wipe out ∼ **eradication** [iRadi*kay*shon] *n* ∼ **eradicative** *adj*.

eradicator [i*Rad*ikayter] *n* one who or that which eradicates; chemical ink remover.

erase [i*Rayz*] *v/t* rub or scratch away (something written); remove (recorded sounds) from magnetic tape; (*fig*) destroy; (*sl*) kill ∼ **eraser** one who or that which erases, *esp* indiarubber.

erasion [i*Ray*zhon] *n* erasure.

Erastianism [e*Ras*ti-anizm] *n* theory that the State should be supreme in ecclesiastical matters.

erasure [i*Ray*zher] *n* act of erasing; mark left by erasing; word *etc* erased.

erbium [*urbi*-um] *n* (*chem*) rare lanthanide element > PDS.

ere [*air*] *prep* and *adv* (*ar*, *poet*) before.

erect [i*Rekt*] *adj* vertical, upright, raised straight up ∼ **erect** *adv* in vertical position ∼ **erect** *v/t* set upright; raise; build ∼ **erectly** *adv* ∼ **erectness** *n*.

erectile [i*Rekt*Il] *adj* capable of becoming erect; (*physiol*) becoming rigid from dilatation of bloodvessels.

erection [i*Rek*shon] *n* act of erecting; state of being erected; anything erected, building; dilatation and rigidity of penis.

erective [i*Rek*tiv] *adj* tending to make erect.

erector [i*Rek*ter] *n* one who or that which erects; engineer who assembles machine parts; (*anat*) muscle which erects an organ or part.

erelong [air*long*] *adv* (*ar*) before long, soon.

eremite [*e*RimIt] *n* (*ar*) hermit.

erewhile [air*wIl*] *adv* (*ar*) some while before.

erg [*urg*] *n* (*phys*) unit of work equal to a force of one dyne acting through a distance of one centimetre.

ergo [*urg*O] *adv* (*Lat*) (*usu fac*) therefore.

ergonomic [urgo*nomik*] *adj* designed for maximum functional efficiency.

ergonomics [urgo*nomiks*] *n* (*pl*) science of making the job fit the worker; study of men in their working environments ∼ **ergonomical** *adj*.

ergonomist [ur*gon*omist] *n* one who studies ergonomics.

ergosterol [ur*goste*Rol] *n* extract of ergot > PDS.

ergot [*urg*ot] *n* disease in cereals, *esp* in rye, caused by a fungus; this fungus; drug made from this > PDB.

ergotism [*urg*otizm] *n* (*med*) disease characterized by burning sensations and hallucinations, caused by eating ergot-infected cereals.

erica [*e*Rika] *n* genus of plants including heather, azaleas *etc*.

eristic [e*Ris*tik] *adj* of or liking controversy; trying to score points in argument.

erk [*urk*] *n* (*sl*) new recruit; lower-deck naval rating.

ermine [*urm*in] *n* the stoat; stoat's white winter fur; robes of judge or peer; (*fig*) office or functions of a judge.

erne [*urn*] *n* the sea-eagle.

erode [i*Rod*] *v/t* wear away by attrition; corrode.

erodent [i*ROd*ent] *adj* causing erosion.

erogenous [i*Roj*inus] *adj* sensitive to sexual stimulation.

erosion [i*Ro*zhon] *n* act of wearing away; state of being worn away; wearing away of land surface by natural forces > PDG ∼ **erosive** *adj*.

erotic [i*Rot*ik] *adj* of or concerned with sexual love; amorous ∼ **erotica** *n* (*pl*) erotic literature.

eroticism [i*Rot*isizm] *n* erotic temperament or outlook; sexual excitement > PDP.

erotogenic [iRotO*jen*ik] *adj* erogenous.

erotomania [iROtO*may*ni-a] *n* pathologically exaggerated eroticism.

err [*ur*] *v/i* make a mistake, be incorrect; commit sin.

errancy [*e*Ransi] *n* state of being in error.

errand [*e*Rand] *n* a commission, piece of business entrusted to a messenger; short journey with a message or with some definite purpose; **fool's e.** profitless undertaking.

errand-boy[*e*Rand-boi] *n* boy employed by shop or firm to deliver goods, carry messages *etc*.

errant [*e*Rant] *adj* wandering; roving, *esp* in search of adventure; (*fig*) sinful.

errantry [*e*RantRi] *n* way of life of knight-errant.

erratic [i*Rat*ik] *adj* having no fixed course; irregular, irresponsible; unpredictable in behaviour; **e. block** (*geol*) boulder transported from its source by glacier > PDG ∼ **erratic** *n* erratic person; erratic block ∼ **erratically** *adj*.

erratum (*pl* **errata**) [i*Raa*tum] *n* error in printing or writing.

erroneous [i*RO*ni-us] *adj* wrong; incorrect; mistaken ∼ **erroneously** *adv* ∼ **erroneousness** *n*.

error [*e*Rer] *n* deviation from accuracy or truth; mistake, sin; (*math*) difference between computed or estimated result and actual value.

ersatz [air*zats*] *adj* (*Germ*) artificial; used as substitute for superior or natural product.

Erse [*urs*] *n* Irish Gaelic; Scottish Gaelic.

erst [*urst*] *adv* (*ar*) once, formerly.

erstwhile [*urst*wIl] *adj* and *adv* (*ar*) former; formerly.

erubescence [eROO*be*sens] *n* act of reddening.

erubescent [eROO*be*sent] *adj* reddening; blushing.

eruct [i*Rukt*] *v/i* belch.

eructate [i*Ruk*tayt] *v/i* belch.

eructation [iRuk*tay*shon] *n* belch.

erudite [e*ROO*dIt] *adj* learned, scholarly ∼ **eruditely** *adv* ∼ **eruditeness** *n*.

erudition [eROO*di*shon] *n* learning, scholarship.

erupt [i*Rupt*] *v/i* burst forth; break through; (*of volcano*) emit lava or gasses.

eruption [i*Rup*shon] *n* act of bursting forth, *esp* of volcano; violent outbreak; (*med*) a rash.

eruptive [i*Rup*tiv] *adj* bursting forth; (*med*) accompanied by a rash.

erysipelas [e*Ri*sipilas] *n* (*med*) an acute inflammatory skin disease.

erythema [e*Ri*theema] *n* (*med*) abnormal redness of skin.

erythrocyte [e*Rith*ROsIt] *n* red blood corpuscle > PDS.

escalade [eska*layd*] v/t climb the walls of (fortress *etc*) with ladders.

escalate [eska*layt*] v/i increase by stages ~ **escalation** [eska*layshon*] n.

escalator [eska*layter*] n moving staircase with endless belt of steps.

escallop [eska*lop*] n scallop.

escapade [eska*payd*] n wild, adventurous prank; rash, unconventional action.

escape [eska*yp*] v/i and t break loose (from confinement), get free; flee to safety; issue out; avoid (danger *etc*), slip away from ~ **escape** n act of escaping; state or fact of having escaped; escapism; leakage, outward flow; pipe or valve through which steam *etc* issues out; (*bot*) cultivated plant found growing as wild ~ **escape** adj of or for escape; providing an escape from reality; allowing for the evasion of responsibility or a claim; **e. velocity** velocity required by projectile or space probe to escape from the Earth's gravitational field.

escapee [eskay*pee*] n one who has escaped.

escapement [eska*yp*ment] n balance wheel in clock or watch; mechanism controlling horizontal movement of typewriter carriage.

escapism [eska*yp*izm] n desire or tendency to avoid unpleasant realities by indulging in pleasant fantasies ~ **escapist** n and adj.

escapology [eskapo*loji*] n methods and technique of escaping from captivity.

escarpment [eskaarp*ment] n steep slope or inland cliff; ground cut steeply as fortification.

eschalot [esha*lot*] n shallot.

eschar [eskaar] n dry scab forming on burnt flesh.

eschatological [eskato*loj*ikal] adj of eschatology.

eschatology [eska*toloji*] n (*theol*) study of 'last things', death, judgement, heaven and hell; **realized e.** present religious acts or experiences corresponding to these.

escheat [es*cheet*] n (*leg*) reversion of property from tenant to owner, or to the Crown, when there are no heirs ~ **escheat** v/i and t revert to escheat; confiscate (property).

eschew [es*chOO*] v/t avoid; shun ~ **eschewal** n.

eschscholtzia [ishol*tsi-a*] n garden plant with deep yellow flowers, California poppy.

escort [es*kawrt*] v/t accompany as guard or protector; accompany as sign of courtesy, attend upon ~ **escort** [es*kawrt*] n person or persons escorting another; warship protecting unarmed ship.

escritoire [eskRit*waar*] n (*Fr*) writing desk.

escudo (*pl* escudos) [es*kOOdO*] n Spanish and Portuguese silver coin.

esculent [es*kewlent*] n and adj (something) edible.

escutcheon [es*kuchon*] n (*her*) shield bearing a coat of arms; part of a ship's stern bearing her name; keyhole plate; **blot on one's e.** stain on one's reputation.

Eskimo (*pl* Eskimos/Eskimoes) [es*kimO*] n member of a N. American Indian race inhabiting the extreme north of America and Greenland; their language; variety of dog bred by the Eskimos ~ **Eskimo** adj relating to the Eskimos; **E. roll** complete roll-over in covered kayak canoe.

eso- *pref* within.

esophagus see oesophagus.

esoteric [esOte*Rik*] adj intelligible to or intended for the initiated only; confidential, secret, mystical ~ **esoterical** adj ~ **esoterically** adv.

esotericism [esOte*Ri*-sizm] n the presence, in religious or philosophic systems, of concealed doctrines revealed only to initiates; (*fig*) deliberate cultivation of obscurity in art, literature *etc*.

espadrille [espad*Ril*] n sandal or light shoe with rope sole.

espalier [es*pali*-er] n trellis; a trained fruit-tree.

esparto [es*paart*O] n kind of coarse grass grown in Spain and Algeria, and made into paper, ropes *etc*.

especial [es*peshal*] adj special; particular ~ **especially** adv to a marked degree; in particular.

Esperantist [espe*Rant*ist] n one who uses Esperanto.

Esperanto [espe*Rant*O] n an artificial universal language.

espial [es*pI*-al] n act of espying.

espionage [es*pi*-onaazh] n spying; employment of spies.

esplanade [espla*nayd*] n level embankment, *esp* promenade by sea; open space between citadel and houses in fortress.

espousal [es*powzal*] n betrothal; marriage; (*fig*) adoption of a cause.

espouse [es*powz*] v/t marry; give in marriage; (*fig*) take up, support (a cause).

espresso [es*ResO*] n coffee made by forcing boiling water through ground coffee-beans under pressure; **e. bar** coffee-bar serving espresso coffee.

espy [es*pI*] v/t catch sight of, detect.

Esquire (*abbr* Esq.) [es*kwIr*] n title of respect added after a gentleman's name when addressing a letter; (*her*) gentleman entitled to bear arms; (*ar*) squire.

essay [es*ay*] n short informal prose composition; [es*ay*] attempt; effort ~ **essay** [es*ay*] v/t try, attempt; test.

essayist [es*ay*-ist] n one who writes essays.

essence [es*ens*] n fundamental or distinctive nature of a thing; (*philos*) that by which a thing exists; existence; indispensable characteristic; concentrated extract; spirituous liquid obtained by distillation; scent, perfume.

Essenes [es*eenz*] n (*pl*) puritanical and mystical sect of Jews appearing about second century B.C.

essential [is*enshal*] adj constituting or relating to the essence of a thing; indispensable; vitally important; characteristic; **e. oils** ethereal oils found in plants and flowers ~ **essential** n essential quality, condition or factor.

essentiality [isenshi-*aliti*] n quality of being essential.

essentially [is*enshali*] adv in essence; basically.

establish [es*tablish*] v/t give firm and permanent basis to; settle; set up; institute, found; install; prove the truth of, win acceptance for; convey basic facts about; link (Church) closely to State; enrol on permanent staff ~ **established** adj firmly instituted, permanent; settled; recognized by State.

establishment [es*tablish*ment] n act of establishing; state of being established; settlement; permanent civil or military force; business house; home, household; **the E. Church of England**; (*coll, pej*) ill-defined grouping of upper-class conservative persons and organizations wielding influence in background of public life.

estate [es*tayt*] *n* piece of property in land; state of life; condition; rank, class; subdivision of the body politic; (*leg*) possessions: **the fourth e.** (*coll*) the Press; **e. car** motorcar built or adapted to carry both passengers and goods; **e. duty** death duties; **personal e.** movable property; **real e.** landed property; **the Three Estates** Archbishops and Bishops, Peers, and Commons.

esteem [es*teem*] *v/t* respect, value highly; judge, consider ∼ **esteem** *n* respect, good opinion.

ester [*ester*] *n* (*chem*) organic compound formed by reaction of an acid with an alcohol > PDS.

esthete see **aesthete**.

esthetic see **aesthetic**.

estimable [*estimab'l*] *adj* worthy of respect ∼ **estimably** *adv*.

estimate [*estimayt*] *v/t* calculate value of, appraise; calculate roughly; form opinion of ∼ **estimate** [*estimat*] *n* approximate calculation of value, size, number *etc*; judgement, assessment; contractor's statement of approximate cost of undertaking certain work.

estimation [esti*mayshon*] *n* act of estimating; opinion, judgement; esteem.

estimative [*estimaytiv*] *adj* having power to estimate.

estrange [es*Raynj*] *v/t* destroy affection of or between, alienate ∼ **estrangement** *n* state of being estranged; decrease in affection.

estriol [*estRi*-ol] *n* a female sex hormone.

estrone [*estROn*] *n* a female sex hormone.

estuary [*eschoo*-eRi] *n* mouth of a river where the tide enters > PDG.

esurient [e*sewr*Ri-ent] *adj* hungry, voracious.

etcetera (*abbr* **etc**) [et*setRa*] *phr* and *n* (*Lat*) and the rest, and so on; (*pl*) sundries, minor additions.

etch [*ech*] *v/t* and *i* form (pictures) by engraving designs with acids on a metal plate, from which prints are then taken > PDAA ∼ **etcher** *n*.

etching [*eching*] *n* picture printed from an etched plate; art of an etcher; **e. ground** resinous coating on plate for etching; **e. needle** pointed steel tool for tracing lines through etching ground.

eternal [i*tur*nal] *adj* with no end or beginning; everlasting; timeless; unceasing; (*coll*) too frequent; **the E. God**; **E. City** Rome; **e. triangle** emotional problem arising from relationship between two men and a woman or two women and a man ∼ **eternalize** *v/t* render eternal; give immortal fame to ∼ **eternally** *adv*.

eternity [i*tur*niti] *n* state of being eternal; duration without end or beginning; state of timeless existence attained after death; the next world; **e. ring** ring set with small jewels right round it.

eternize [i*tur*nIz] *v/t* eternalize.

etesian [i*teez*han] *adj* annual; **e. winds** northerly winds prevailing in summer in the eastern Mediterranean > PDG.

ethane [*eethayn*] *n* (*chem*) colourless, odourless hydrocarbon gas > PDS.

ethanol [*eethanol*] *n* (*chem*) ethyl alcohol.

ether [*eether*] *n* (*chem*) powerful anaesthetic liquid; class of compounds containing an oxygen atom joining two organic groups > PDS; (*phys*) hypothetical medium formerly supposed to fill all space and support the propagation of electromagnetic radiation; (*ar*) upper air, clear sky.

ethereal [i*theer*Ri-al] *adj* light, airy; delicate; spiritual; (*chem*) volatile ∼ **ethereally** *adv*.

ethereality [itheerRi-*aliti*] *n* state of being ethereal.

etherealize [i*theer*Ri-alIz] *v/t* make ethereal, regard as ethereal; (*chem*) convert into ether, make volatile.

etherize [*eethe*RIz] *v/t* anaesthetize with ether.

ethic [*eth*ik] *n* system of morality ∼ **ethic** *adj* ethical.

ethical [*eth*ikal] *adj* moral; in accordance with a moral code; (*of medicines*) advertised only to doctors, not to the public ∼ **ethically** *adv*.

ethics [*eth*iks] *n* (*pl*) scientific study of morals; system of morality.

Ethiopian [eethi-*Op*i-an] *n* and *adj* (inhabitant or language) of Ethiopia, Abyssinian; (*ar*) Negro.

ethnic [*eth*nik] *adj* characteristic of a racial minority group in a population; preserving the culture, art or customs of such a group ∼ **ethnical** *adj* ethnic ∼ **ethnically** *adv*.

ethnographer [eth*nog*Rafer] *n* student of ethnography.

ethnographic [ethnog*Raf*ik] *adj* of ethnography.

ethnography [eth*nog*Rafi] *n* study of regional distribution and characteristics of races of men.

ethnological [ethno*loji*kal] *adj* of ethnology ∼ **ethnologically** *adv*.

ethnologist [eth*nolo*jist] *n* student of ethnology.

ethnology [eth*nolo*ji] *n* scientific study of human races, *esp* of cultures, customs *etc*.

ethology [i*tholo*ji] *n* (*biol*) study of the behaviour of animals in their natural environment; (*philos*) scientific study of growth of ethical systems; science of human character.

ethos [*eethos*] *n* predominant characteristics of a cul'ural community; ethics of a community.

eth [*eth*il] *n* (*chem*) the radical of common alcohol > PDS; anti-knock compound in motor fuel.

ethylene [*eth*ileen] *n* (*chem*) colourless inflammable gas with sweetish smell > PDS.

etiolate [*eeti*-Olayt] *v/t* (*bot*) make pale from lack of light > PDB; (*med*) make pale from malnutrition ∼ **etiolation** [eeti-O*lay*shon] *n*.

etiology [eti-*olo*ji] *n* study of causes, *esp* of disease.

etiquette [*etiket*] *n* conventional rules of polite behaviour ∼ **etiquettical** *adj*.

etna [*etna*] *n* (*tr*) type of small spirit stove.

Eton [*eeton*] *adj* connected with, characteristic of, Eton College; **E. coat, jacket** short black coat worn by boys; **E. collar** stiff, wide linen collar worn outside an Eton coat; **E. crop** woman's very short hair style.

Etonian [ee*tOn*i-an] *n* present or past member of Eton College.

etymological [etimo*loji*kal] *adj* of etymology.

etymologize [eti*molo*jIz] *v/i* study etymology; trace or suggest an etymology.

etymology [eti*molo*ji] *n* branch of philology concerned with origin and derivation of words; derivation (of a word).

etymon [*etimon*] *n* (*phil*) primitive word-form from which derivatives are formed.

eu- *pref* well, good, pleasant *etc*.

eucalyptus [yooka*lip*tus] *n* genus of Australasian

plants of the myrtle order; medicinal oil obtained from these.

Eucharist [*yook*aRist] *n* sacrament in which the worshipper is united to Christ by partaking of consecrated bread and wine; consecrated bread and wine given in this sacrament.

eucharistic [yookaRistik] *adj* of the Eucharist.

euchre [*yook*er] *n* a card game ~ **euchre** *v/t* get the better of (opponent) at this game; (*sl*) outwit.

Euclidean [yook*lid*i-an] *adj* pertaining to Euclid's geometry; three-dimensional.

eugenic [yoo*jen*ik] *adj* (*biol*) connected with improvement of a stock or race; promoting the breeding of healthy stock ~ **eugenically** *adv*.

eugenics [yoo*jen*iks] *n* (*pl*) (*biol*) study of possible improvement of human stock by encouraging breeding of those presumed to have desirable genes > PDB, PDP.

eugenist [*yoo*jenist] *n* student of, advocate of, eugenics.

eulogist [*yoo*lojist] *n* one who praises.

eulogistic [yoolo*jist*ik] *adj* full of praise ~ **eulogistically** *adv*.

eulogize [*yoo*lojIz] *v/t* praise, extol.

eulogy [*yoo*loji] *n* high praise; writing or speech praising a person or thing.

eunuch [*yoo*nuk] *n* castrated man.

eupeptic [yoo*pep*tik] *adj* having good digestion; easy to digest; (*fig*) cheerful, optimistic.

euphemism [*yoo*femizm] *n* substitution of mild or pleasant terms for those that are offensive or blunt; term so substituted ~ **euphemistic** [yoofe*mist*ik] *adj* ~ **euphemistically** *adv*.

euphemize [*yoo*femIz] *v/t* and *i* express by a euphemism; use euphemisms.

euphonic, euphonical [yoo*fon*ik, yoo*fon*ikal] *adj* euphonious.

euphonious [yoo*fO*ni-us] *adj* pleasing in sound ~ **euphoniously** *adv*.

euphonium [yoo*fO*ni-um] *n* a powerful bass brass wind instrument.

euphony [*yoo*foni] *n* pleasing sound; smooth, pleasant enunciation of sounds.

euphorbia [yoo*fawr*bi-a] *n* genus of plants which includes box, the spurges *etc*.

euphoria [yoo*fawr*Ri-a] *n* feeling of well-being; (*psych*) unfounded feelings of optimism, strength *etc*; (*coll*) mood of great cheerfulness ~ **euphoric** [yoo*fo*Rik] *adj*.

euphoriant [yoo*fawr*Ri-ant] *n* and *adj* (drug) inducing euphoria.

euphuism [*yoo*few-izm] *n* artificial, affected literary style, *esp* antithetical style fashionable in late sixteenth century ~ **euphuistic** [yoofew-*ist*ik] *adj* ~ **euphuistically** [yoofew-*ist*ikali] *adv*.

Eurasian [yoo*Ray*shan] *n* and *adj* (one) born of one Asiatic and one European parent.

eureka [yoo*Reek*a] *interj* (*Gk*) I have found it.

eurhythmics [yoo*Rith*miks] *n* (*pl*) study or art of rhythmical movement.

Euro- *pref* of Europe; of the European Common Market.

eurocrat [*yoor*Ok Rat] *n* bureaucrat in the administration of the European Common Market.

European [yoorO*pee*-an] *n* and *adj* (native) of Europe; (member, supporter) of the European Common Market.

europium [yoo*RO*pi-um] *n* (*chem*) rare lanthanide element > PDS.

Eurovision [yoo*RO*vizhon] *n* Western European television network.

Eustachian [yoo*stay*shan] *adj* E. tube (*anat*) small duct leading from ear-drum cavity to back of the mouth > PDB.

eutectic [ew*tek*tik] *adj* (*metal*) having the lowest freezing point > PDS.

euthanasia [yoothan*ayzi*-a] *n* painless death; practice of putting incurable invalids painlessly to death, *usu* at their request.

eutrophic [yoot*Ro*fik] *adj* (*biol*) (*of lakes etc*) depleted of oxygen by excessive algae and bacteria ~ **eutrophication** *n*.

evacuant [iv*ake*w-ant] *adj* and *n* emetic (drug); purgative (drug).

evacuate [iv*ake*w-ayt] *v/t* (*mil*) remove from dangerous area; withdraw troops from; (*med*) make empty; discharge contents of.

evacuation [ivakew-*ay*shon] *n* act or process of evacuating; withdrawal from an area; matter evacuated from bowels.

evacuative [iv*ake*w-ativ] *adj* purgative.

evacuee [ivakew-*ee*] *n* person who has been removed from a dangerous area in time of war.

evade [iv*ayd*] *v/t* get away from, escape; get round, dodge; avoid answering; shirk.

evaluate [iv*ale*w-ayt] *v/t* appraise, find value of.

evaluation [ivalew-*ay*shon] *n* appraisal.

evaluative [iv*ale*w-ativ] *adj* expressing an assessment of value.

evanesce [eevan*es*] *v/i* disappear, vanish.

evanescence [eevan*es*ens] *n* process or fact of vanishing; tendency to vanish rapidly.

evanescent [eevan*es*ent] *adj* transient; vanishing.

evangelic, evangelical [eevan*jel*ik, eevan*jel*ikal] *adj* of, pertaining to, based on, or found in the Gospels; belonging to Low Church party in Church of England; emphasizing doctrine of salvation by faith rather than sacramentalism ~ **evangelical** *n* one who holds evangelical views; Low Church Protestant ~ **evangelicalism** *n* ~ **evangelically** *adv*.

evangelism [iv*an*jelizm] *n* the spreading of the Gospel.

evangelist [iv*an*jelist] *n* one of the four writers of the Gospels; preacher of the Gospel; travelling preacher; preacher who holds religious meetings generally in the open air.

evangelization [ivanjelIz*ay*shon] *n* act of evangelizing.

evangelize [iv*an*jelIz] *v/i* and *t* preach the Gospel; convert to Christianity.

evaporate [iv*ape*Rayt] *v/t* and *i* turn into vapour; expel (moisture) by heating; become vapour; (*fig*) vanish; **evaporated milk** unsweetened milk thickened by evaporation.

evaporation [ivape*Ray*shon] *n* act of evaporating; state of being evaporated; that which is evaporated; expulsion of moisture by heating > PDG.

evaporative [iv*apo*Rativ] *adj* causing, promoting evaporation.

evaporator [iv*apo*Rayter] *n* one who or that which evaporates; apparatus for evaporating.

evasion [iv*ay*zhon] *n* act of escaping, avoiding, shirking; subterfuge; equivocation.

evasive [iv*ay*siv] *adj* not straightforward; intentionally ambiguous; avoiding the issue; avoiding attack, danger or trouble ~ **evasively** adv ~ **evasiveness** n.

eve [eev] n evening or day before church festival or important event; (ar) evening.

even (1) [eeven] n (ar) evening.

even (2) adj smooth, flat; parallel; equally balanced; in regular rhythm; exactly divisible by two; (fig) calm; unvarying, monotonous; **be (get) e. with** retaliate against; **break e.** (coll) show neither profit nor loss; **e. date** (comm) the same date; **e. money** (betting) return of double the stake ~ **even** v/t make even; **e. up** balance; **e. up on** retaliate against ~ **even** adv evenly; as much as; just as; as an emphatic particle expressing the most that can be expected; **e. if, e. though** in spite of the fact that ~ **evener** n one who or that which makes even.

even-handed [eeven-handid] adj impartial, fair.

evening [eevning] n time between sunset and total darkness; early part of night before bedtime; (fig) concluding part, decline; **e. clothes, e. dress** conventional clothes to be worn at social gatherings in evening; **e. star** planet Venus when seen soon after sunset.

evenly [eevenli] adv in an even way; calmly.

evenness [eeven-nis] n state or quality of being even.

evensong [eevensong] n (eccles) vespers; daily office of evening prayer.

event [ivent] n happening, occurrence; consequence; outcome; item in series of games or contests; **at all events** in any case; **in the e. of** in case of.

even-tempered [eeven-temperd] adj placid.

eventful [iventfool] adj full of incidents; momentous ~ **eventfully** adv.

eventide [eeventId] n and adj (poet) evening.

eventual [ivenchoo-al] adj happening as a consequence; in course of time; final ~ **eventually** adv.

eventuality [ivenchoo-aliti] n possible event which may occur as a consequence.

eventuate [ivenchoo-ayt] v/i happen; result.

ever [ever] adv at any time; in any degree; (ar) always; repeatedly; **e. and anon** (ar) from time to time; **for e.** eternally, unceasingly; **e. so much** (coll) very much; **e. so** (sl) very.

everglade [everglayd] n (US) swampy land.

evergreen [evergReen] n and adj (plant) which does not shed leaves in winter; (fig) (something) always vigorous.

everlasting [everlaasting] adj lasting always, endless; durable, long-lasting; repeated or lasting until it becomes tiresome ~ **everlastingly** adv.

evermore [evermawr] adv for ever, always.

evert [ivurt] v/t turn inside out or outwards.

every [evRi] adj each one of a number; all separately; **e. now and then** from time to time, occasionally; **e. other** each alternate.

everybody [evRibodi] n every person (with sing v).

everyday [evRiday] adj happening daily; usual.

everyone [evRiwun] n everybody (with sing v).

everything [evRithing] n all things; all; (coll) the main thing.

everyway [evRiway] adv in all ways.

everywhere [evRiwair] adv in all places.

evict [ivikt] v/t dispossess by law, expel (tenant) from property.

eviction [ivikshon] n act of evicting.

evidence [evidens] n testimony; (leg) witness's statement on oath in court; that which makes evident; that which provides proof or strong probability; witness; **circumstantial e.** (leg) indirect evidence showing only probability, not proof; **queen's (king's) e.** evidence from criminal against his accomplices; one who gives this ~ **evidence** v/t attest, prove by evidence.

evident [evident] adj visible; clear; obvious.

evidential [evidenshal] adj providing evidence ~ **evidentially** adv.

evidently [evidentli] adv obviously, clearly.

evil [eevil] adj morally bad, wicked; causing hardship or misfortune; **the e. eye** magical power of bringing misfortune by one's glance ~ **evil** n evil thing or act; misfortune.

evildoer [eevildOO-er] n one who does evil.

evilly [eevili] adv in an evil way.

evil-minded [eevil-mIndid] adj wicked; spiteful; salacious.

evilness [eevilnis] n quality of being evil.

evince [ivins] v/t show; demonstrate, prove.

evincible [ivinsib'l] adj that can be demonstrated ~ **evincibly** adv.

evincive [ivinsiv] adj giving proof.

eviscerate [iviseRayt] v/t disembowel; (fig) remove the essential character of.

evocation [evokayshon] n act of evoking; description etc tending to revive memories, past emotions etc ~ **evocative** [evokativ] adj.

evoke [ivOk] v/t call forth; summon up; call up from the past; elicit, provoke.

evolution [eevolewshon] n act or process of evolving, gradual development; progressive series of changes; (biol) cumulative change in characteristics of organisms, occurring through long series of generations > PDB, PDP; theory that this process accounts for origin of all extant organisms; (pl) (mil) manoeuvres; (fig) complicated series of movements ~ **evolutional** adj.

evolutionary [eevolewshonaRi] adj of or by evolution.

evolutionism [eevolewshonism] n belief in theory of biological evolution ~ **evolutionist** n.

evolve [ivolv] v/i and t develop gradually and naturally; develop from lower to higher state or form; work out, produce.

evulsion [ivulshon] n act of plucking out.

ewe [yOO] n female sheep; **e. lamb** (fig) that which one loves most.

ewer [yOO-er] n large water jug.

ex- pref from, down from, away from, out of, beyond; thoroughly; former etc.

ex [eks] n (coll) one's former husband or wife; (pl) expenses ~ **ex** v/t (coll) delete.

exacerbate [eksaserbayt] v/t make worse; provoke, irritate; embitter.

exacerbation [eksaserbayshon] n act of exacerbating; state of being exacerbated; that which exacerbates.

exact (1) [egzakt] adj precisely agreeing, strictly correct, accurate in detail; unambiguous, precise; having an exact mind, rigorous in method; **e. sciences** those which admit of absolute precision in their findings.

exact (2) *v/t* compel; demand, insist on; extort ~ **exactable** *adj* that can be exacted.

exacting [egza*k*ting] *adj* making severe or unreasonable demands.

exaction [egza*k*shon] *n* act of exacting; that which is exacted, tax, fee; oppressive demand, extortion.

exactitude [egza*k*titewd] *n* correctness, precision.

exactly [egza*k*tli] *adv* in an exact manner; precisely, completely; (*interj*) quite so!

exactor [egza*k*ter] *n* one who exacts.

exaggerate [egza*j*eRayt] *v/t* and *i* represent as greater than is true; intensify; give disproportionate importance to; overstate, over-emphasize; enlarge abnormally; use overstatements ~ **exaggeratedly** *adv*.

exaggeration [egza*j*eRayshon] *n* act of exaggerating; exaggerated remark, overstatement ~ **exaggerative** *adj* ~ **exaggerator** *n*.

exalt [egza*w*lt] *v/t* raise high; raise to high rank; praise highly, extol.

exaltation [egza*w*ltayshon] *n* act of exalting; state of being exalted; high elation; state of abnormal excitement; mystical rapture; (*astrol*) planet's position of greatest influence.

exalted [egza*w*ltid] *adj* in high position; noble; lofty; in state of exaltation.

exam [egza*m*] *n* (*coll abbr*) examination.

examinable [egza*m*inab'l] *adj* capable of being examined.

examination [egza*m*inayshon] *n* careful inquiry or search; inspection; investigation; formal testing of knowledge by question and answer; (*leg*) interrogation of witness by counsel.

examine [egza*m*in] *v/t* scrutinize, inspect carefully; inquire into, investigate; question; test (a person's knowledge) by questioning.

examinee [egza*m*inee] *n* one undergoing examination; candidate.

examiner [egza*m*iner] *n* one who examines; one who marks examination papers; one who interrogates a suspect or a witness.

example [egza*m*p'l] *n* instance which illustrates a rule or confirms a statement; pattern, precedent; precedent to be imitated; warning instance, deterrent; specimen; (*math*) problem, exercise; **for e.** as an illustration; **make an e.** punish as a warning to others; **without e.** unprecedented.

exanimate [eksa*n*imayt] *adj* dead; without animation.

exanthema (*pl* **exanthemata**) [eks-an*thee*ma] *η* (*med*) eruptive disease with feveı.

exarch [e*k*zaark] *n* (*Gk eccles*) title of primitive bishop; patriarchal legate; head of certain Orthodox Churches; (*hist*) viceroy of Byzantine emperor ~ **exarchate** [ek*z*aarkayt] *n* office of exarch.

exasperate [egza*a*speRayt] *v/t* annoy intensely, infuriate; aggravate, inflame.

exasperating [egza*a*speRayting] *adj* tending to exasperate, very annoying ~ **exasperatingly** *adv*.

exasperation [egzaaspe*R*ayshon] *n* act of exasperating; state of being exasperated; provocation; rage.

excavate [e*k*s-kavayt] *v/t* and *i* dig out; unearth, *esp* in archaeology; dig a pit; form by digging.

excavation [eks-ka*v*ayshon] *n* act of digging out; pit made by digging; site uncovered by archaeologists' digging.

excavator [e*k*s-kavayter] *n* one who or that which digs out; power-driven digging machine > PDE.

exceed [eks*eed*] *v/t* and *i* go beyond; excel, be greater than; go too far, be guilty of excess.

exceeding [eks*ee*ding] *adj* very great ~ **exceedingly** *adv* greatly; unusually.

excel (*pres/part* **excelling**, *p/t* and *p/part* **excelled**) [eks*el*] *v/t* and *i* surpass, be superior to; show unusual merit, be outstandingly good, clever *etc*.

excellence [e*k*selens] *n* superiority; outstanding goodness, skill, *etc*; great merit.

excellency [e*k*selensi] *n* title of honour given to ambassadors, viceroys, governors of colonies and their wives.

excellent [e*k*selent] *adj* surpassing others; of great value, merit *etc*; distinguished ~ **excellently** *adv*.

excelsior [eks*el*si-awr] *interj* (*Lat*) higher still.

except [eks*ept*] *v/t* and *i* exclude, leave out; **e. against** object, protest against ~ **except** *prep* omitting, apart from ~ **except** *conj* (*ar*) unless.

excepting [eks*e*pting] *prep* except.

exception [eks*e*pshon] *n* act of leaving out; that which is left out; that which does not conform to a rule; that which is different; **take e. to** object to; be offended by; find fault with.

exceptionable [eks*e*pshonab'l] *adj* liable to objection ~ **exceptionably** *adv*.

exceptional [eks*e*pshonal] *adj* unusual, rare ~ **exceptionally** *adv*.

exceptive [eks*e*ptiv] *adj* including or making an exception; captious; tending to take offence.

excerpt [e*k*serpt] *n* passage selected from a writing, play, film, musical work *etc* ~ **excerpt** [eks*urpt*] *v/t* select (passage) for quotation.

excerption [eks*ur*pshon] *n* act of excerpting.

excess [eks*es*] *n* that which goes beyond what is usual or necessary; lack of moderation, over-indulgence; (*usu pl*) an outrage; amount by which one amount or sum exceeds another ~ **excess** *adj* excessive; beyond what is allowed ~ **excess** *v/t* levy extra charge on, *esp* on luggage exceeding permitted weight.

excessive [eks*e*siv] *adj* beyond due measure; extravagant, immoderate; unreasonable ~ **excessively** *adv* ~ **excessiveness** *n*.

exchange [eks-*chaynj*] *v/t* and *i* give one thing in return, for another, barter; give in return for similar thing, interchange; leave one place, post *etc* to go to another; make an exchange; change currency of one country for its equivalent in that of another ~ **exchange** *n* act of exchanging; that which is given or received in exchange; place where city merchants, bankers and brokers meet to transact business; central telephone office of a district; foreign currency; method of exchanging debts or credits; method of settling accounts of bills, drafts *etc*; **e. force** (*phys*) force holding nucleons together in an atomic nucleus > PDS ~ **exchangeable** *adj* capable of being exchanged ~ **exchanger** *n* one who exchanges; money-changer.

exchequer [eks-*chek*er] *n* treasury; government department controlling matters of finance and revenue; **Chancellor of the E.** finance minister of the British Government.

excisable [eksɪzab'l] *adj* liable to excise dues.

excise (1) [eksɪz] *n* tax on certain articles made and consumed within a country; tax on licences to manufacture; branch of Inland Revenue dealing with collection of these taxes ∼ **excise** *v/t* impose excise duty on.

excise (2) [eksɪz] *v/t* cut out; cut away or off.

exciseman [eksɪzman] *n* collector of excise duties.

excision [eksizhon] *n* act of excising; removal by cutting; that which is cut out or off.

excitable [eksɪtab'l] *adj* easily excited; (*med*) capable of responding to stimulus ∼ **excitability** [eksɪtabɪliti] *n*.

excitant [eksitant/eksɪtant] *n* a stimulant.

excitation [eksitayshon] *n* act of exciting; state of excitement; response to stimulation.

excitative [eksɪtativ] *adj* tending to excite.

excitatory [eksɪtateRi] *adj* excitative.

excite [eksɪt] *v/t* rouse, stir up; set in motion; rouse the feelings of, agitate; (*biol*) stimulate, cause increased activity in; (*phys*) produce electric or magnetic field in; add energy to a nucleus, atom, or molecule to raise it above its ground state ∼ **excited** *adj* ∼ **excitedly** *adv*.

excitement [eksɪtment] *n* state of being excited; agitation; thrill; that which excites.

exciting [eksɪting] *adj* stimulating; thrilling ∼ **excitingly** *adv*.

exclaim [eks-klaym] *v/i* and *t* cry out suddenly, vigorously, or loudly; speak vehemently; **e. against** protest against; **e. at** express surprise at.

exclamation [eks-klamayshon] *n* expression of surprise or pain; outcry, clamour; (*gramm*) interjection; **e. mark, note of e.** punctuation mark (!) placed after written or printed exclamation.

exclamatory [eks-klamateRi] *adj* frequently using exclamations.

exclude [eks-klOOd] *v/t* shut out; thrust out; prevent from entering; disallow, debar (from), not include.

exclusion [eks-klOOzhon] *n* act of excluding; state of being excluded ∼ **exclusionary** *adj*.

exclusive [eks-klOOsiv] *adj* excluding others; reserved for a privileged small group; unapproachable, keeping others at a distance; snobbish; tending to monopolize one's time, too absorbing; sold by one firm only; appearing only in one newspaper, film *etc*; (*coll*) of unusually high quality; **e. of** not counting ∼ **exclusively** *adv* in an exclusive way; solely.

exclusiveness [eks-klOOsivnes] *n* quality of being exclusive; attitude of snobbish superiority.

excogitate [eks-kojitayt] *v/t* think out; devise.

excogitation [eks-kojitayshon] *n* careful thought.

excommunicate [eks-komewnikayt] *v/t* exclude by formal decree from privileges of membership of church, *esp* from receiving communion.

excommunication [eks-komewnikayshon] *n* act of excommunicating; state of being excommunicated.

excoriate [eks-kawrRi-ayt] *v/t* flay; graze; remove bark from; (*fig*) criticize severely.

excoriation [eks-koRi-ayshon] *n* flaying.

excrement [eks-kRiment] *n* waste matter from bowels, dung.

excremental [eks-kRimental] *adj* of dung.

excrementitious [eks-kRimentishus] *adj* excremental.

excrescence [eks-kResens] *n* natural outgrowth or projection; abnormal or useless outgrowth: (*fig*) ugly protuberance; unnecessary development.

excrescent [eks-kResent] *adj* growing unnaturally or uselessly; superfluous.

excreta [eks-kReeta] *n* (*pl*) excreted matter.

excrete [eks-kReet] *v/t* separate out and discharge (waste matter from body).

excretion [eks-kReeshon] *n* act of excreting; that which is excreted > PDB ∼ **excretive** *adj*.

excretory [eks-kReeteRi] *n* and *adj* (organ) serving to excrete.

excruciate [eks-kROOshi-ayt] *v/t* inflict severe pain upon; torture.

excruciating [eks-kROOshi-ayting] *adj* extremely painful, agonizing ∼ **excruciatingly** *adv*.

excruciation [eks-kROOshi-ayshon] *n* act of inflicting torture or pain; torture, extreme pain.

exculpate [eks-kulpayt] *v/t* free from blame or accusation; vindicate.

exculpation [eks-kulpayshon] *n* act of exculpating; state of being exculpated; that which exculpates ∼ **exculpatory** [eks-kulpateRi] *adj*.

excursion [eks-kurshon] *n* short journey, trip, *esp* for pleasure; digression; (*ar*, *mil*) sortie; **alarms and excursions** (*fig*) commotion; **e. train** train run for special trips at reduced rates.

excursionist [eks-kurshonist] *n* tripper.

excursive [eks-kursiv] *adj* desultory, digressive; going far afield ∼ **excursively** *adv* ∼ **excursiveness** *n*.

excursus (*pl* **excursuses**) [eks-kursus] *n* supplemental discussion of some point from the main body of a work.

excusable [eks-kewzab'l] *adj* pardonable ∼ **excusableness** *n* ∼ **excusably** *adv*.

excusatory [eks-kewzateRi] *adj* that excuses.

excuse [eks-kewz] *v/t* exonerate, try to clear from blame; set free from obligation or penalty; pardon, overlook; allow to leave; justify; (*refl*) apologize; attempt to justify one's conduct; ask permission to leave; **be excused** (*coll*) leave a classroom to go to the lavatory; **e. me** polite formula used to preface an interruption, protest, remark of disagreement *etc*, or to cover a breach of etiquette ∼ **excuse** [eks-kews] *n* extenuating plea; apology; justification; pretext.

ex-directory [eks-dɪRekteRi] *adj* not included in the telephone directory.

exeat [eksi-at] *n* (*Lat*) leave of absence.

execrable [eksikRab'l] *adj* detestable, hateful; (*coll*) very bad ∼ **execrably** *adv* in an execrable manner; (*coll*) very badly.

execrate [eksikRayt] *v/t* and *i* detest; express loathing (of); curse, utter curses.

execration [eksikRayshon] *n* act of execrating; loathing; act of cursing; curse; object execrated ∼ **execrative** *adj* ∼ **execratory** *adj*.

executant [egzekewtant] *n* performer; musician.

execute [eksikewt] *v/t* carry out; (*of artist, musician*) perform; inflict capital punishment upon; (*leg*) complete a legal instrument; fulfil provisions of will *etc*; put into effect.

execution [eksikewshon] *n* act of carrying out, performance; method of carrying out; skill in performance, exercise of technique; infliction of capital punishment; (*leg*) fulfilment of provisions of will *etc*; (*coll*) destructive action.

executioner [eksi*kew*shoner] *n* one who carries out capital punishment.

executive [egze*kew*tiv] *adj* carrying out, performing; of or for a high-ranking businessman or official ~ **executive** *n* person or body who carries into effect; administrative branch of government; official of a business organization having directive duties; high-standing official.

executor [egze*kew*ter] *n* (*leg*) person appointed by testator to carry out provisions in his will.

executorial [egzekewt*awr*Ri-al] *adj* of or as an executor.

executrix (*pl* **executrices**) [egze*kew*tRiks] *n* female executor

executry [egze*kew*tRi] *n* (*leg*) process of executing a will.

exegesis [eksi*jee*sis] *n* explanation, interpretation, *esp* of the Bible.

exegetic [eksi*jet*ik] *adj* explanatory; expository ~ **exegetical** *adj* exegetic ~ **exegetically** *adv*.

exegetics [eksi*jet*iks] *n* (*pl*) study of biblical interpretation.

exemplar [egz*emp*laar] *n* model to be copied; ideal pattern.

exemplary [egz*emp*laRi] *adj* serving as a model; deserving imitation; commendable; serving as a warning, deterrent; typical ~ **exemplarily** *adv*.

exemplification [egzemplifik*ay*shon] *n* illustrating by examples; that which serves as an illustration.

exemplify [egz*emp*lifI] *v/t* illustrate by examples, serve as an example of; (*leg*) take an attested copy of.

exemplum (*pl* **exempla**) [egz*emp*lum] *n* tale designed to point a moral, *esp* in medieval sermons *etc*.

exempt [egz*empt*] *v/t* release from duty or obligation ~ **exempt** *adj* exempted, not liable to ~ **exemptible** *adj* capable of being exempted.

exemption [egz*emp*shon] *n* act of exempting; immunity.

exequies [*eks*ikwiz] *n* (*pl*) funeral ceremonies.

exercise [*ek*sersIz] *n* act of using; practice; healthy physical exertion; repetition in learning; physical movement to be repeated to increase strength, health, skill *etc*; lesson, problem, or task designed to increase knowledge; (*mil*) manoeuvre; (*mus*) piece chiefly designed for practice in technique; (*eccles*) act of divine worship ~ **exercise** *v/t* and *i* make use of; exert; give exercise to; train; cause anxiety to, perplex; engage in physical activity, take exercise.

exert [egz*urt*] *v/t* put into action; make use of; (*refl*) make efforts, strive.

exertion [egz*ur*shon] *n* putting into action; vigorous activity; effort.

exeunt [*eks*i-unt] *v/i* (*Lat*) (*stage direction*) they leave.

exfoliate [eksf*Oli*-ayt] *v/i* (*geol*) flake off in thin layers > PDG; (*med*) come off in scales, peel.

exfoliation [eksf*Oli*-*ay*shon] *n* act of flaking or peeling.

ex-gratia [eks-g*Ray*shi-a] *adj* and *adv* (*Lat*) not obligatory; done, paid, given *etc* as a favour.

exhalation [eks-ha*lay*shon] *n* act of passing into vapour; that which is exhaled; vapour.

exhale [eks-*hayl*] *v/t* and *i* breathe out; give off (fumes *etc*) in vapour; be given off as vapour; cause or allow to evaporate; evaporate; (*fig*) vanish away.

exhaust [egz*awst*] *v/t* use up completely; drain out; tire out; deal with every part of (a subject) ~ **exhaust** *n* passage through which waste gas, steam *etc* is discharged from engine; gases, steam *etc* discharged; exhaust-pipe; **e. gas** gaseous products of combustion in internal combustion engine.

exhausted [egz*aws*ted] *adj* very tired; used up.

exhaustible [egz*aws*tib'l] *adj* capable of being exhausted.

exhausting [egz*aws*ting] *adj* extremely tiring.

exhaustion [egz*aws*chun] *n* state of being exhausted; act of exhausting; extreme fatigue.

exhaustive [egz*aws*tiv] *adj* tending to exhaust, comprehensive; thorough ~ **exhaustively** *adv* ~ **exhaustiveness** *n*.

exhaust-pipe [egz*awst*-pIp] *n* (*mot*) pipe through which spent gaseous products escape.

exhibit [egz*ib*it] *v/t* and *i* show; show signs of; display publicly; present (works of art, livestock *etc*) for public inspection ~ **exhibit** *n* anything publicly shown; (*leg*) document or object produced in court as material evidence.

exhibition [eksi*bish*on] *n* display of objects of art or manufacture *etc*; temporary display of art objects *etc* based on a central theme; maintenance grant awarded to student; **make an e. of oneself** (*coll*) show oneself in an unfavourable light.

exhibitioner [eksi*bish*oner] *n* student who holds a maintenance grant at school or university.

exhibitionism [eksi*bish*onizm] *n* extravagant behaviour intended to attract attention; (*psych*) pathological urge to exhibit publicly some part of the body normally clothed > PDP ~ **exhibitionist** *n* and *adj*.

exhibitor [egz*ib*iter] *n* one who exhibits in an exhibition.

exhilarate [egz*ile*Rayt] *v/t* make cheerful; invigorate ~ **exhilarating** *adj* ~ **exhilaratingly** *adv*.

exhilaration [egzile*Ray*shon] *n* state of being exhilarated; act of exhilarating; that which exhilarates.

exhort [egz*awrt*] *v/t* urge to good deeds; entreat; encourage; caution, admonish.

exhortation [egzawrt*ay*shon] *n* act of exhorting; words intended to exhort; admonition; incitement.

exhortator [egz*awr*tayter] *n* one who exhorts.

exhortatory [egz*awr*tatoRi] *adj* that exhorts.

exhorter [egz*awr*ter] *n* one who exhorts.

exhumation [eks-hewm*ay*shon] *n* act of disinterring.

exhume [eks-*hewm*] *v/t* dig up, *esp* from grave.

exigence, exigency [*eks*ijens, *eks*ijensi/eksi*jen*si] *n* state of being exigent; urgency; emergency; strong necessity.

exigent [*eks*ijent] *adj* urgent; exacting.

exigible [*eks*ijib'l] *adj* capable of being exacted.

exiguity [eksi*gew*-iti] *n* scantiness; smallness·

exiguous [egzigew-us] *adj* too small, scanty ~ **exiguousness** *n*.

exile [eksIl/egzIl] *n* one who is banished from his country; banishment; place to which one is banished ~ **exile** *v/t* banish.

exilian [egzili-an] *adj* pertaining to banishment, *esp* of Jews to Babylon.

exilic [egzilik] *adj* exilian.

exist [egzist] *v/i* be, have being, live; maintain an existence; be found, occur; (*coll*) live wretchedly.

existence [egzistens] *n* state of being; life; mode of existing ~ **existent** *adj* that exists.

existential [egzistenshal] *adj* pertaining to or having existence; pertaining to existentialism.

existentialism [egzistenshalizm] *n* (*philos*) any doctrine which maintains that the purpose of philosophy is the analysis and description of the individual's existence, regarded as the product of his own free and responsible choices, and as having no basis other than its own self-assertion; literary and intellectual movement derived from this doctrine ~ **existentialist** *adj* and *n*.

exit [eksit] *n* act of leaving a stage; (*fig*) departure, *esp* in noticeable manner; door through which one may leave a building, way out ~ **exit** *v/i* leave the stage; go away, go out; (*fig*) die.

exo- *pref* outside.

exodus [eksodus] *n* departure of many persons together, *esp* of Israelites from Egypt; (*cap*) the second book of the Old Testament.

ex officio [eks-ofishi-O] *adj* and *adv* (*Lat*) by virtue of office, officially.

exogamy [eksogami] *n* custom compelling a man to marry outside his own tribe ~ **exogamic** [eksogamik] *adj* ~ **exogamous** *adj*.

exogenous [eksojenus] *adj* originating outside an organism.

exon [ekson] *n* officer of the Yeomen of the Guard.

exonerate [egzoneRayt] *v/t* free or clear from blame; release from obligation.

exoneration [egzoneRayshon] *n* act of exonerating; that which exonerates.

exophthalmia [eksofthalmi-a] *n* (*path*) abnormal protrusion of the eyeballs ~ **exophthalmic** *adj*.

exorbitance [egzawrbitans] *n* quality of being exorbitant; extravagance, excess, *esp* in demands.

exorbitant [egzawrbitant] *adj* excessive; excessively demanding; far too expensive ~ **exorbitantly** *adv*.

exorcism [eksawrsizm] *n* act of exorcizing; expulsion ~ **exorcist** *n* one who exorcizes.

exorcize [eksawrsIz] *v/t* drive away (an evil spirit) by religious or magical means; expel, dispel ~ **exorcizer** *n* exorcist.

exordium (*pl* **exordiums**) [egzawrdi-um] *n* introductory part; beginning ~ **exordial** *adj*.

exoteric [eksOteRik] *adj* fit to be known by the uninitiated; suited to the general public; (*fig*) popular ~ **exoterical** *adj*.

exothermic [egzOthurmik] *adj* (*chem*) accompanied by the evolution of heat.

exotic [egzotik] *adj* foreign, not native; romantically foreign in appearance, customs *etc* ~ **exotic** *n* plant *etc* not of native origin; plant not fully naturalized.

expand [eks-pand] *v/t* and *i* make larger; spread out; extend; cause to develop; become larger; develop; spread; increase; (*fig*) become communicative; **expanded metal** metal mesh formed by widening slots in metal sheet > PDE.

expanse [eks-pans] *n* wide extent; unbroken area or surface.

expansible [eks-pansibl'l] *adj* that can be expanded.

expansile [eks-pansIl] *n* tending to expand.

expansion [eks-panshon] *n* act of expanding; state of being expanded; enlargement; extension; increase.

expansionism [eks-panshonizm] *n* policy of increasing territory of a state ~ **expansionist** *n* and *adj*.

expansive [eks-pansiv] *adj* capable of expanding or being expanded; communicative, unreserved ~ **expansively** *adv* ~ **expansiveness** *n*.

expatiate [eks-payshi-ayt] *v/i* speak or write at length ~ **expatiation** [eks-payshi-ayshon] *n* act of expatiating ~ **expatiative** *adj*.

expatriate [eks-paytRi-ayt] *v/t* banish from one's native country; (*refl*) give up one s nationality ~ **expatriate** *adj* and *n* expatriated (person); (person) living permanently abroad.

expatriation [eks-paytRi-ayshon] *n* banishment.

expect [eks-pekt] *v/t* look for as likely to happen, anticipate; (*coll*) think, suppose; consider as right or necessary; **be expecting** (*coll*) be pregnant.

expectancy [eks-pektansi] *n* hopeful and eager expectation; prospect of future possession.

expectant [eks-pektant] *adj* awaiting, *gener* hopefully or eagerly; **e. mother** pregnant woman ~ **expectantly** *adv*.

expectation [eks-pektayshon] *n* state or act of expecting; state of being expected; that which is expected; prospect; **e.** of life number of years one is likely to live, as computed by statistics.

expectorant [eks-pekteRant] *n* and *adj* (*med*) (substance) promoting expectoration.

expectorate [eks-pekteRayt] *v/t* and *i* cough up from the lungs; spit.

expectoration [eks-pekteRayshon] *n* spitting.

expedience, expediency [eks-peedi-ens, eks-peedi-ensi] *n* convenience; consideration of personal advantage, self-interest; suitability.

expedient [eks-peedi-ent] *adj* suitable, convenient; useful in attaining an aim, advantageous; politic ~ **expedient** *n* means to an end; method or device to accomplish something.

expedite [eks-pidIt] *v/t* accelerate, hasten; facilitate the progress of; (*comm*) despatch, post off.

expedition [eks-pidishon] *n* journey undertaken for special purpose, *esp* military or exploratory; persons engaged on an expedition; promptness, speed ~ **expeditionary** *adj*.

expeditious [eks-pidishus] *adj* speedy, active ~ **expeditiously** *adv* ~ **expeditiousness** *n*.

expel (*pres/part* **expelling**, *p/t* and *p/part* **expelled**) [eks-pel] *v/t* drive out by force; eject; force to leave in disgrace.

expellable [eks-pelab'l] *adj* that expels; deserving expulsion.

expellee [eks-pelee] *n* one who has been expelled.

expend [eks-pend] *v/t* spend; use up; employ.

expendable [eks-pendab'l] *adj* that can be expended; (*mil*) inessential, not to be defended or rescued at all costs; (*coll*) that can be spent, dismissed *etc* without serious loss; of little value.

expenditure [eks-*pend*icher] *n* act of spending; that which is expended; money spent.

expense [eks-*pens*] *n* that which is expended; cost; price paid; disbursement; **e. account** record of expenses incurred in course of business and to be refunded by employers or claimed against tax; **at the e. of** at the cost of injuring.

expensive [eks-*pens*iv] *adj* involving expenditure; costly; lavish ∼ **expensively** *adv* ∼ **expensiveness** *n*.

experience [eks-*peer*Ri-ens] *n* wisdom, skill, knowledge *etc* gained by personal practice, suffering, enjoyment or observation; process of acquiring such wisdom; event experienced, *esp* if rousing strong emotion; sum total of what one has observed, learnt, or undergone; ascertained result of series of experiments ∼ **experience** *v/t* have experience of; feel, undergo; suffer ∼ **experienced** *adj* grown skilful by experience.

experientialism [eks-peerRi-*ens*halizm] *n* (*philos*) doctrine that all knowledge is derived from experience ∼ **experientialist** *n*.

experiment [eks-*peR*iment] *n* test or observation for scientific purposes, under conditions controlled by the experimenter; test, attempt to verify theory or discover new facts; investigation by trial and error ∼ **experiment** *v/i* make experiments.

experimental [eks-peRi*ment*al] *adj* of, as, based on an experiment; not yet fully proved or tested; engaged in research by experiments; empirical.

experimentalism [eks-peRi*ment*alizm] *n* systematic reliance on experiments or on experience; empiricism ∼ **experimentalist** *n* one who practises experimentalism; scientific research worker ∼ **experimentalize** *v/i* perform experiments.

experimentally [eks-peRi*ment*ali] *adv* as an experiment.

experimenter [eks-*peR*imenter] *n* one who carries out experiments.

expert [*eks*-pert] *adj* having much experience or knowledge; highly skilled; dexterous; skilfully made or done ∼ **expert** *n* one who has special qualification, skill or knowledge.

expertise [eks-per*teez*] *n* expert knowledge.

expertly [*eks*-pertli] *adv* like an expert.

expertness [*eks*-pertnis] *n* quality of being expert.

expiable [*eks*-pi-ab'l] *adj* that can be expiated.

expiate [*eks*-pi-ayt] *v/t* atone for, make amends for; pay penalty of.

expiation [eks-pi-*ay*shon] *n* act of expiating, atonement; suffering *etc* undergone to expiate guilt.

expiatory [ekspi-*ay*teRi] *adj* tending to expiate.

expiration [eks-piRayshon/eks-pIRayshon] *n* act of breathing out; termination; end; death.

expiratory [eks-*pIr*RateRi] *adj* pertaining to breathing out.

expire [eks-*pIr*] *v/i* and *t* die; die out; come to an end; breathe out ∼ **expiring** *adj* dying; breathing out; spoken when dying.

expiry [eks-*pIr*Ri] *n* termination, end.

explain [eks-*playn*] *v/t* and *i* make clear or intelligible; illustrate the meaning of; account for;

give explanations; **e. away** diminish the importance of (a difficulty, fault *etc*) by explanations.

explanation [eks-plan*ay*shon] *n* act of explaining; statement designed to clarify an obscurity; justification, excuse; meaning; cause; process of clearing up mutual misunderstanding or dispute.

explanatory [eks-*plan*ateRi] *adj* providing an explanation ∼ **explanatorily** *adv* ∼ **explanatoriness** *n*.

expletive [eks-*pleet*iv] *n* exclamation; oath; (*gramm*) word inserted in sentence without materially affecting its meaning ∼ **expletive** *adj* serving to fill up; superfluous; exclamatory ∼ **expletively** *adv*.

expletory [eks-*pleet*eRi] *adj* expletive.

explicable [eks-*plik*ab'l] *adj* capable of being explained.

explicate [*eks*-plikayt] *v/t* unravel (a problem); explain; interpret, expound.

explication [eks-plik*ay*shon] *n* act or method of explicating ∼ **explicative** [eks-*plik*ativ] *adj* ∼ **explicatory** [eks-*plik*ateRi] *adj*.

explicit [eks-*plis*it] *adj* plainly stated; definite; outspoken ∼ **explicitly** *adv* ∼ **explicitness** *n*.

explode [eks-*plOd*] *v/i* and *t* burst violently and with a loud noise; cause to explode; (*fig*) refute, show to be false; suddenly yield to violent anger or to noisy laughter; increase suddenly and intensely; (*of models, plans etc*) represent each component separately ∼ **exploder** *n* one who or that which explodes; detonator; blasting machine.

exploit (1) [*eks*-ploit] *n* heroic deed.

exploit (2) [eks-*ploit*] *v/t* use unfairly or selfishly; make use of; make unfair profit from; develop the resources of.

exploitation [eks-ploit*ay*shon] *n* act of exploiting; state of being exploited; area of land, mine *etc* being exploited ∼ **exploitative** *adj*.

exploiter [eks-*ploit*er] *n* one who exploits.

exploration [eks-plawR*ay*shon] *n* investigation; research, inquiry; preliminary discussion; act of travelling to discover.

exploratory [eks-*plaw*RateRi] *adj* serving to explore; inquiring; discussing.

explore [eks-*plawr*] *v/t* and *i* search into; investigate, examine; travel over in order to discover; carry out exploration; (*surg*) probe.

explorer [eks-*plaw*Rer] *n* one who explores; (*surg*) instrument for examining wound or cavity; instrument for sounding depths; (*elect*) device to discover leakage in dynamo.

explosion [eks-*plO*zhon] *n* violent and rapid chemical reaction, *usu* with loud noise; destructive outburst; burst of rage, laughter *etc*; firing of gunpowder, dynamite, bombs *etc*; sudden large increase in numbers, *esp* of population.

explosive [eks-*plO*siv] *adj* liable to explode; hot-tempered; heard in sudden bursts; (*fig*) liable to cause sudden outbreaks of anger, hostility *etc*; tense and dangerous ∼ **explosive** *n* substance which explodes when fired or struck; (*phon*) type of stopped consonant ∼ **explosively** *adv* ∼ **explosiveness** *n*.

exponent [eks-*pO*nent] *n* one who or that which expounds or explains; (*math*) number indicating the power of a quantity > PDS.

exponential [eks-pO*nen*shal] *adj* (*math*) pertaining

to, involving exponents; (*fig*) multiplying more and more rapidly.

export [eks-*pawrt*] *v/t* send (goods) abroad as trade ~ **export** [eks-pawrt] *n* act of exporting; that which is exported, article or goods sent abroad > PDG ~ **export** *adj* of or for export.

exportable [eks-*pawr*tab'l] *adj* that can be exported.

exportation [eks-pawrt*ay*shon] *n* act of exporting.

exporter [eks-*pawr*ter] *n* one engaged in exporting goods.

exposal [eks-*pOz*al] *n* act of exposing; state of being exposed.

expose [eks-*pOz*] *v/t* uncover, lay bare; leave unprotected, endanger; disclose (a secret); unmask, make public; display; abandon (child) to hunger, cold, wild beasts *etc*; (*phot*) allow light to reach (film, plate *etc*).

exposé [eks-*pOz*ay] *n* (*Fr*) formal explanation; disclosure of something scandalous.

exposed [eks-*pOz*d] *adj* open; unprotected against weather; open to attack; revealed, unmasked ~ **exposedness** *n*.

exposition [eks-po*zish*on] *n* act of laying open; explanation; exposure; commentary; exhibition; (*RC*) service in which the host is displayed for worship.

expositive [eks-*po*zitiv] *adj* explanatory.

expositor [eks-*po*ziter] *n* one who expounds; interpreter.

expository [eks-*po*ziteRi] *adj* expositive.

expostulate [eks-*po*stewlayt] *v/i* remonstrate; reason earnestly, protest (against).

expostulation [eks-postew*lay*shon] *n* act of expostulating; remonstrance, protest ~ **expostulator** *n* one who expostulates ~ **expostulatory** *adj* expressing expostulation.

exposure [eks-*pOz*her] *n* act of exposing; act of exhibiting; state of being exposed; (*phot*) act of exposing; length of time film *etc* is exposed; (*archi*) position of building relative to points of compass, weather *etc*; **e. meter** photoelectric meter used to measure the amount of light required in a photographic exposure.

expound [eks-*pownd*] *v/t* explain; interpret.

express [eks-*pRes*] *v/t* make known (thought, feeling *etc*), communicate; represent, signify; (*med*) press out; (*refl*) make one's thoughts or feelings clear ~ **express** *adj* clearly stated, explicit; well-defined; designed for specific purpose; sent or travelling unusually fast ~ **express** *n* especially fast postal or train service; train which stops only at a few major stations ~ **express** *adv* unusually fast; by express post or train; expressly.

expressage [eks-*pRes*ij] *n* fee for article sent by express post.

expressible [eks-*pRes*ib'l] *adj* that can be expressed.

expression [eks-*pResh*on] *n* act of expressing; representation by words, symbols, or the arts; method, style or skill in expressing; utterance; idiom, phrase; manifestation of feeling; aspect of the face, *esp* as conveying feelings or temperament; vocal modulation; (*mus*) method of conveying emotion; phrasing; (*psych*) external sign indicating mental process > PDP ~ **expressional** *adj*.

expressionism [eks-*pResh*onizm] *n* (*arts*) use of

simplifications, exaggerations, and distortions to obtain strong emotional impact > PDAA; symbolic or distorted representation; stylization ~ **expressionist** *n* and *adj* ~ **expressionistic** [eks-presho*nist*ik] *adj*.

expressive [eks-*pRes*iv] *adj* showing clearly or vividly; significant; full of meaning ~ **expressively** *adv* ~ **expressiveness** *n*.

expressivity [ekspRes*iv*iti] *n* quality of being expressive.

expressly [eks-*pRes*li] *adv* plainly; directly; specially.

expropriate [eks-*pROp*Ri-ayt] *v/t* take from, deprive of (property) ~ **expropriation** [eks-pRO-pRi-*ay*shon] *n*.

expulsion [eks-*pul*shon] *n* action of expelling; state of being expelled.

expulsive [eks-*pul*siv] *adj* expelling.

expunction [eks-*punk*shon] *n* act of expunging; state of being expunged.

expunge [eks-*punj*] *v/t* erase; destroy.

expurgate [*eks*-purgayt] *v/t* remove offensive or obscene passages from (a book).

expurgation [eks-pur*gay*shon] *n* act of expurgating; state of being expurgated.

expurgator [*eks*-purgayter] *n* one who expurgates.

expurgatorial [eks-purga*taw*Ri-al] *adj* that expurgates.

expurgatory [eks-*pur*gateRi] *adj* that expurgates.

exquisite [*eks*-kwizit] *adj*. tasteful, refined; delicately beautiful; select; beautifully made, devised *etc*; acutely felt ~ **exquisite** *n* person of exaggerated refinement in taste, clothes *etc* ~ **exquisitely** *adv* ~ **exquisiteness** *n*.

exsanguine [eks*ang*-gwin] *adj* (*med*) anaemic.

exscind [*eks*sind] *v/t* cut out; destroy.

exserted [eks*urt*id] *adj* (*biol*) projecting.

ex-service [eks-*surv*is] *adj* having formerly served in the armed forces.

extant [eks-*tant*/*eks*-tant] *adj* still in existence.

extemporaneous [eks-tempe*Rayn*i-us] *adj* extemporary ~ **extemporaneously** *adv*.

extemporary [eks-*temp*eRaRi] *adj* done or made without preparation, unpremeditated; improvised ~ **extemporarily** *adv*.

extempore [eks-*temp*eRi] *adj* unprepared ~ **extempore** *adv* on the spur of the moment, without preparation.

extemporization [eks-tempeRi*zay*shon] *n* act of extemporizing; that which is extemporized.

extemporize [eks-*temp*eRIz] *v/t* and *i* do, make up, without preparation; improvise; (*mus*) perform according to spontaneous fancy; compose and perform simultaneously.

extend [eks-*tend*] *v/t* and *i* stretch or reach out; enlarge, expand; prolong; bestow, offer; last; be taxed to the utmost; (*refl*) use one's full strength or energy.

extended [eks-*tend*ed] *adj* fully stretched out or prolonged; **e. family** family group comprising uncles and aunts, grandparents, cousins *etc* as well as parents and children ~ **extendedly** *adv*.

extender [eks*tend*er] *n* substance added to paints, plastics, *etc* to modify their properties or reduce their cost.

extendible [eks-*tend*ib'l] *adj* extensible.

extensibility [eks-tensi*bil*iti] *n* quality of being extensible.

extensible [eks-*ten*sib'l] *adj* that can be extended.
extensile [eks-*tens*Il] *adj* extensile.
extension [eks-*ten*shon] *n* act of extending; state of being extended; amount extended, addition, enlargement; continuation, prolongation; extra telephone connected to same line as main telephone; **university e.** provision of instruction of university standard to persons not members of a university ~ **extensional** *adj*.
extensive [eks-*ten*siv] *adj* of great extent; spreading widely; comprehensive ~ **extensively** *adv* ~ **extensiveness** *n*.
extensor [eks-*ten*ser] *n* (*anat*) muscle serving to extend or straighten a limb.
extent [eks-*tent*] *n* degree to which a thing is extended; length; size; range, scope; degree; (*leg*) valuation of lands to be taxed; **writ of e.** (*leg*) writ authorizing seizure of debtor's person and property.
extenuate [eks-*tenew*-ayt] *v/t* and *i* lessen; reduce the guilt of, minimize ~ **extenuating** *adj*.
extenuation [eks-tenew-*ay*shon] *n* act of extenuating or palliating; palliation, excuse.
extenuator [eks-*tenew*-ayter] *n* one who extenuates ~ **extenuatory** *adj*.
exterior [eks-*teer*Ri-er] *adj* on the outside, external; outward ~ **exterior** *n* outer surface, part, or appearance; (*arts*) representation of outdoor scene; (*cin*) sequence shot out of doors.
exteriority [eks-teerRi-*o*Riti] *n* state or property of being exterior; external aspect.
exteriorize [eks-*teer*Ri-oRIz] *v/t* (*psych*) give external expression to; regard as external to oneself; (*surg*) bring (organ) out of abdomen.
exteriorly [eks-*teer*Ri-orli] *adv* on or from the exterior.
exterminate [eks-*turm*inayt] *v/t* kill all members of (a group); wipe out, destroy.
extermination [eks-turmi*nay*shon] *n* act of exterminating.
exterminator [eks-*turm*inayter] *n* one who or that which exterminates ~ **exterminatory** *adj*.
external [eks-*turn*al] *adj* outward, on the outside; visible; material; superficial, inessential; existing apart from one's own perception; (*theol*) consisting of physical acts, ceremonies *etc*; **e. evidence** evidence from independent sources; **e. policy** (*pol*) foreign policy ~ **external** *n* something external; (*pl*) outward aspect; inessential features.
externalize [eks-*turn*alIz] *v/t* give or attribute external existence to; express by outward signs ~ **externalization** [eks-turnalIz*ay*shon] *n*.
externally [eks-*turn*eli] *adv* on or from the outside.
exterritorial [eks-teRit*awr*Ri-al] *adj* not subject to the jurisdiction of the country in which one resides.
extinct [eks-*tinkt*] *adj* having come to an end; having died out; quenched, no longer alight; no longer active.
extinction [eks-*tink*shon] *n* act of extinguishing; state of being extinct; abolition; act of dying out.
extinguish [eks-*ting*-gwish] *v/t* put out, quench; put an end to; destroy ~ **extinguishable** *adj* ~ **extinguishment** *n*.
extinguisher [eks-*ting*-gwisher] *n* one who or that which extinguishes; apparatus containing chemicals to extinguish fires; hollow cap for putting out the light of a candle.

extirpate [*eks*-turpayt] *v/t* root out; destroy completely.
extirpation [eks-turp*ay*shon] *n* act of extirpating; state of being extirpated ~ **extirpator** *n* one who or that which extirpates.
extol (*pres/part* extolling, *p/t* and *p/part* extolled) [eks-*tOl*] *v/t* praise highly.
extort [eks-*tawrt*] *v/t* obtain by force or injustice; exact illegally.
extortion [eks-*tawr*shon] *n* act of extorting; illegal demand for money; act of charging excessive price.
extortionary [eks-*tawr*shonaRi] *adj* of or practising extortion.
extortionate [eks-*tawr*shonit] *adj* characterized by extortion; grossly excessive.
extra- *pref* outside, beyond the scope of.
extra [*eks*-tRa] *adj* additional, beyond what is usual or needed ~ **extra** *adv* additionally, specially ~ **extra** *n* something added; that for which additional charge is made; special edition of newspaper; (*cricket*) run scored otherwise than by stroke of bat; (*theat, cin*) one who acts very minor or non-speaking parts.
extract [eks-*tRakt*] *v/t* pull out; draw out by force or persuasion; select, excerpt; obtain; distil ~ **extract** [*eks*-tRakt] *n* that which is extracted; selected passage; concentrated substance obtained from another, *esp* by distillation.
extractable [eks-*tRak*tab'l] *adj* that can be extracted.
extraction [eks-*tRak*shon] *n* act of extracting; act of pulling out teeth; something extracted; lineage; place of origin ~ **extractive** *adj*.
extractor [eks-*tRak*ter] *n* one who or that which extracts; (*surg*) forceps for extracting.
extraditable [eks-tRad*I*tab'l] *adj* liable to extradition; rendering liable to extradition.
extradite [*eks*-tRadIt] *v/t* remove (a person) from territory of one State to that of another in which he is alleged to have committed a crime.
extradition [eks-tRa*dish*on] *n* act of extraditing > PDPol.
extrajudicial [eks-tRajOO*dish*al] *adj* outside normal course of legal procedure ~ **extrajudicially** *adv*.
extramarital [eks-tRama*Rit*al] *adj* (*of sexual relations*) with a partner to whom one is not married ~ **extramaritally** *adv*.
extramural [eks-tRa*mewr*Ral] *adj* outside the city walls; associated with, but not directly controlled by, a university.
extraneous [eks-*tRay*ni-us] *adj* external to, unrelated to; not essential ~ **extraneously** *adv* ~ **extraneousness** *n*.
extraordinary [eks-*tRawrd*ineRi] *adj* beyond what is common or ordinary; unusual; rare; surprising; peculiar; special; [eks-tRa-*awrd*ineRi] (*of ambassador or envoy*) employed on special service ~ **extraordinarily** *adv* ~ **extraordinariness** *n*.
extrapolate [eks-*tRap*olayt] *v/t* and *i* (*math*) fill in values or terms of a series on either side of the known values; continue a curve beyond the points for which data have been obtained; (*fig*) argue from known to unknown, infer.
extrapolation [eks-trapo*lay*shon] *n* act or process of extrapolating.

extrasensory [eks-tRasenseRi] *adj* beyond scope of normal perception, not perceivable by the senses.

extra-special [eks-tRa-*spesh*al] *adj* (*coll*) especially excellent.

extraterrestrial [eks-tRateRestRi-al] *n* and *adj* (living being) from outside the planet earth.

extraterritorial [eks-tRateRi*taw*Ri-al] *adj* exterritorial.

extravagance [eks-tRavagans] *n* state of exceeding reasonable limits, excess; excessive spending, wastefulness; flamboyant eccentricity.

extravagant [eks-tRavagant] *adj* showing extravagance; excessive, exaggerated; lavish, wasteful; flamboyant ~ **extravagantly** *adv*.

extravaganza [eks-tRavaganza] *n* (*theat*) wild burlesque or farce; spectacular show; (*mus*) irregular and fanciful composition; (*fig*) flight of fancy; wild behaviour or words.

extravasate [eks-tRavasayt] *v/t* (*med*) force (blood, lymph *etc*) out of its proper vessel ~ **extravasation** [eks-tRavasayshon] *n*.

extraversion see **extroversion**.

extravert see **extrovert**.

extreme [eks-tReem] *adj* furthest off; at outer limits; of the highest degree; last, final; uncompromising, unreasonable (in opinions *etc*); drastic, most severe; **e. penalty** capital punishment; **E. Unction** sacramental anointing of those in danger of death by sickness ~ **extreme** *n* furthest limit; highest degree; greatest intensity; **go to extremes** be incapable of moderation; **take severe measures** ~ **extremely** *adv* in an extreme degree; very much; very.

extremism [eks-tReemizm] *n* the holding of extreme views in politics or religion ~ **extremist** *n* and *adj* (person) holding extreme views.

extremity [eks-tRemiti] *n* utmost limit; farthest point; highest degree; state of very great danger or distress; end; (*pl*) hands and feet.

extricate [*eks*-tRikayt] *v/t* disentangle; free from difficulty, danger *etc*.

extrication [eks-tRi*kay*shon] *n* act or process of extricating.

extrinsic [eks-tRinsik] *adj* external; coming from outside; not inherent or essential ~ **extrinsical** *adj* ~ **extrinsically** *adv*.

extroversion, extraversion [eks-tROvurshon, eks-tRavurshon] *n* state of being an extrovert; state of being turned inside out; act or state of turning outwards.

extrovert, extravert [*eks*-tROvert, *eks*-tRavert] *n* (*psych*) one whose interests are directed outwards towards the outer world and other people rather than inwards to the thoughts and feelings of the self > PDP; person unable or unwilling to perform introspection; (*coll*) vigorous, non-intellectual personality.

extrude [eks-tROOd] *v/t* and *i* force out by pressure; shape (metal or plastics) into rods, tubes, or sections by forcing through a die > PDE; be extruded.

extrusion [eks-tROOzhon] *n* act of extruding; state of being extruded.

extrusive [eks-tROOsiv] *adj* tending to extrude; **e. rocks** (*geol*) rocks formed by solidification of magma above earth's surface > PDG.

exuberance, exuberancy [egzewbeRans, egzewbeRansi] *n* state of being exuberant.

exuberant [egzewbeRant] *adj* full of vitality, vigour or high spirits; growing luxuriantly; copious, abundant; over-abundant; over-ornate, flamboyant ~ **exuberantly** *adv*.

exudation [egzewdayshon] *n* act of exuding; exuded fluid.

exude [egzewd] *v/t* and *i* discharge through pores; give out slowly; ooze out.

exult [egzult] *v/i* rejoice greatly; triumph.

exultancy [egzultansi] *n* exultation.

exultant [egzultant] *adj* jubilant, triumphant ~ **exultantly** *adv*.

exultation [egzultayshon] *n* great joy; lively rejoicing; triumph.

exuviate [egzewvi-ayt] *v/t* and *i* cast off (skin).

ex voto [eks vOtO] *n* object donated to a shrine in gratitude for prayers answered.

eyas [*I*-as] *n* young hawk taken from nest.

eye [*I*] *n* receptor organ for light > PDB, PDP; visible part of this; iris of eye; power of seeing; power of observation; (*fig*) point of view; judgement, discrimination; oval dot or mark; small opening; thread-hole of needle; small metal loop on clothes; photo-electric cell; (*bot*) bud, shoot; spot on potato tuber where a bud will form; **all my e.** (*coll*) nonsense; **do in the e.** (*sl*) cheat; spoil; **easy on the e.** (*sl*) pleasant to look at; **glad e.** (*coll*) amorous glance; **have an e. for** be a good judge of; notice; **have an e. to** be on the watch for; **keep an e. on** watch; look after; **keep one's eyes open (skinned)** be very watchful; **make eyes at** look amorously at; **the mind's e.** imagination; **my e.!** (*sl*) exclamation of surprise; **open the eyes of** make (a person) aware, enlighten; **see e. to e. with** agree with; **see with half an e.** see easily; **sheep's eyes** amorous looks; **turn a blind e.** to ignore; **up to the eyes** in very busy with, overwhelmed with ~ **eye** *v/t* look at; stare at; glance frequently at.

eyeball [*I*bawl] *n* spheroidal body with optic nerve attached.

eyebath [*I*baath] *n* shaped glass vessel to hold liquid for bathing the eye.

eyebolt [*I*bOlt] *n* (*naut*) iron bar with hole at one end, fixed to ship's deck or side and used to fasten ropes to.

eyebright [*I*bRIt] *n* kind of small white flower.

eyebrow [*I*bRow] *n* ridge of bone above the eye-socket; row of hairs growing on this; **e. pencil** cosmetic pencil for tinting eyebrows.

eyecatching [*I*kaching] *adj* conspicuous, visually startling or attractive.

eyedrops [*I*dRops] *n* (*pl*) medicine for relief of irritation of the eye.

eye-filling [*I*-filing] *adj* (*coll*) looking attractive or striking.

eyeful [*I*fool] *n* as much as the eye can take in at a glance; (*coll*) one who or that which looks striking.

eyeglass [*I*glaas] *n* lens to help the sight; monocle; eyepiece; (*pl*) pair of lenses held by bar resting on the bridge of the nose.

eyehole [*I*hOl] *n* hole to look through; eyelet.

eyelash [*I*lash] *n* one of the hairs fringing the eyelids.

eyelet [*I*let] *n* small hole through which a lace,

273

cord, or rope can be passed; metal ring lining this hole.

eyelid [*I*lid] *n* one of two movable flaps of flesh covering the eyeball.

eyeliner [*I*lIner] *n* cosmetic applied in a line along the edge of the eyelid.

eye-opener [*I*-Opener] *n* (*coll*) surprising revelation; strong drink, *esp* if taken early in the day.

eyepiece [*I*pees] *n* (*in optical instrument*) lens nearest observer's eye > PDS.

eyeshadow [*I*shadO] *n* cosmetic paste for tinting eye-socket and eyelids.

eyeshot [*I*shot] *n* range of vision.

eyesight [*I*sIt] *n* power of vision; **range of vision**.

eyesore [*I*sawr] *n* something very ugly.

eyetooth [*I*tOOth] *n* canine tooth in upper jaw; **cut one's eyeteeth** grow up.

eyewash [*I*wosh] *n* lotion for the eyes; (*sl*) humbug; pretence; flattery.

eyewitness [*I*witnes] *n* one who has seen (a specified event).

eyot [*ay*-ot] *n* islet in lake or river.

eyrie [*air*Ri] *n* nest of bird of prey.

F

f [*ef*] sixth letter of the English alphabet; (*mus*) fourth note in scale of C major.

fa [*faa*] *n* (*mus*) fourth note in tonic sol-fa notation; fourth note in the scale of C major, F.

fab [*fab*] *adj* (*sl*) marvellous, fabulous.

fabaceous [*fab*ayshus] *adj* (*bot*) of the bean family; like a bean.

Fabian [*fa*ybi-an] *adj* using cautious delay to wear out an enemy; **F. Society** socialist society advocating change by non-revolutionary means ~ **Fabian** *n* member of the Fabian Society.

fable [*fa*yb'l] *n* short narrative conveying a moral, *esp* one whose characters are animals or objects; legend, myth; fantastic invention; falsehood; (*ar*) plot of play, epic *etc* ~ **fable** *v/t* and *i* invent; lie ~ **fabled** *adj* made famous in tales, legendary; invented.

fabliau [*fa*bli-O] *n* medieval French verse tale, usually humorous or coarse.

fabric [*fab*Rik] *n* structure, framework; cloth made of threads woven, knitted, or felted together; building; (*fig*) essential basis.

fabricate [*fab*Rikayt] *v/t* manufacture, construct, put together; state falsely, invent; forge (document) ~ **fabricator** *n*.

fabrication [fabRi*ka*yshon] *n* fictitious statement; a forgery.

fabulist [*fab*ewlist] *n* writer or teller of fables.

fabulous [*fab*ewlus] *adj* legendary, fictional; incredible; (*coll*) wonderful, excellent; vast, amazing ~ **fabulously** *adv* ~ **fabulousness** *n*.

façade [fa*saad*] *n* front of a building; (*fig*) false appearance.

face [*fays*] *n* front of head, countenance, visage; expression, look; grimace; boldness, impudence; appearance, outward aspect; outer, upper, or most important, surface; dial (of clock *etc*); (*fig*) prestige, self-respect; (*mining*) exposed surface (of coal *etc*), working-place; (*typ*) the printing surface of type; size or style of letter cast in type; **have the f. to** be bold or impudent enough to; **in the f. of** opposite to, opposed by; **fly in the f. of** defy, flout; **look (one) in the f.** confront; **lose f.** lose prestige, be humiliated; **make (pull) a f.** to grimace; **on the f. of it** judging by appearances; **pull (wear) a long f.** look sad or disapproving; **put a bold f. on it** act boldly despite difficulties; **save one's f.** avoid humiliation, preserve prestige; **set one's f. against** oppose; **show one's f.** appear; **to one's f. in** one's presence, openly; **f. to f.** confronting each other; **f. value** nominal or apparent value ~ **face** *v/t* and *i* stand looking towards, opposite to; be orientated towards; meet boldly, confront; oppose; be unafraid of, treat boldly; realize clearly and bravely; cover or dress the surface of; attach facings to; dress (stone *etc*); **f. the music** answer for one's actions; **f. out** override trouble by boldness or effrontery; **f. up to** confront, treat fearlessly; accept (unpleasant facts *etc*).

faceache [*fays*ayk] *n* neuralgia; (*sl*) gloomy or unpleasant-looking person.

facecloth [*fays*kloth] *n* cloth laid over the face of a corpse; small towel for washing the face; woollen cloth with smooth surface.

facecream [*fays*kReem] *n* cosmetic ointment to improve the skin of the face.

faced [*fayst*] *adj* having a face or facing; with the surface covered or rubbed down.

faceless [*fays*lis] *adj* having no face; with face hidden; (*fig*) remote and anonymous, impersonal.

facelift [*fays*lift] *n* operation to improve the appearance by tightening the skin of the face, removing wrinkles *etc*.

face-massage [*fays*-masaazh] *n* massage of facial muscles to improve the appearance.

facepack [*fays*pak] *n* cosmetic paste applied over the face and removed when dry.

facepowder [*fays*powder] *n* cosmetic powder applied to the face.

facer [*fays*er] *n* (*coll*) strong blow in the face; disconcerting difficulty, problem; playing card facing the wrong way in a pack.

face-saving [*fays*-sayving] *adj* designed to protect self-respect.

facet [*fas*et] *n* small surface of cut gem; (*ent*) single surface of insect's compound eye; single part; aspect ~ **faceted** *adj* having facets.

facetiae [fa*see*shi-ee] *n* (*pl*) humorous anecdotes; coarse or obscene books.

facetious [fa*see*shus] *adj* fond of joking, waggish; stupidly or inappropriately funny ~ **facetiously** *adv* ~ **facetiousness** *n*.

faceworker [*fays*wurker] *n* miner working at the face of a coal-seam.

facia see **fascia**.

facial [*fay*shal] *adj* of, relating to, the face ~ **facial** *n* massage and beauty-treatment of the face ~ **facially** *adv*.

facies [*fay*shi-eez] *n* (*anat*) face; (*geol*) general appearance of rocks and their contents; (*med*) appearance or expression of face.

facile [*fas*Il] *adj* easily done or won; easily persuaded, yielding; fluent, glib; hasty, superficial ~ **facileness** *n*.

facilitate [fa*sili*tayt] *v/t* make easy or easier; promote, help forward ~ **facilitation** [fasili*tay*shon] *n*.

facility [fa*sili*ti] *n* ease, absence of difficulty; aptitude, talent, dexterity; necessary equipment, accommodation *etc* required for a specified activity (*often pl*).

facing [*fay*sing] *n* outer layer, coating, or surface; decorative surface of wall; protective surface of dyke *etc* > PDE; (*pl*) collar and cuffs, *esp* in contrasting colour; trimmings, linings; (*mil*) turning movements in drill; **put person through his facings** test his proficiency.

facsimile [fak*sim*ili] *n* exact copy, accurate reproduction; transmission of still pictures *etc* by means of a radio link ~ **facsimile** *v/t*.

fact [*fakt*] *n* thing or event known to exist or to

have happened; something real or true, actual experience; **the f.** (*leg*) deed, crime; **in f., as a matter of f., in point of f.** in reality, actually; **the f. of the matter** the truth; **the facts of life** (*coll euph*) knowledge about human sexual behaviour; (*fig*) harsh, unwelcome truth.

fact-finding [*fakt*-fInding] *adj* set up to discover and establish facts.

faction [*fak*shon] *n* dissenting or troublesome minority, *esp* in political party; dissension, partisan strife.

factionary [*fak*shonaRi] *n* and *adj* (member) of a faction.

factious [*fak*shus] *adj* given to faction; causing dissension; seditious ~ **factiousness** *n*.

factitious [fak*tish*us] *adj* not natural or spontaneous; artificial, unreal, sham ~ **factitiously** *adv* ~ **factitiousness** *n*.

factitive [*fak*titiv] *adj* causative; **f. verb** (*gramm*) verb whose complement describes what the object has been called, or made into, or thought to be.

factor [*fak*ter] *n* a force, condition, or circumstance cooperating with others in bringing about a result; (*math*) one of the numbers which can be multiplied together to form a given product; man who does business for another on commission, agent, proxy; (*Scots*) estate manager; (*biol*) gene, determinant.

factorage [*fak*toRij] *n* commission payable to a factor, business of a factor.

factorial [fak*tawr*Ri-al] *adj* (*math*) pertaining to factors; **f. number** product of a number and all integers below it.

factorize [*fak*toRIz] *v/t* (*math*) analyse into factors.

factory [*fak*teRi] *n* building in which goods are manufactured; trading-post in foreign country; **F. Acts** Acts of Parliament controlling working conditions in factories; **f. farming** method of rearing animals in unnatural confinement to obtain maximum output and uniformity; **f. ship** ship on which catches of fish or whales are processed for food.

factotum [fakt*O*tum] *n* servant who has to do all kinds of work, general handyman.

factual [*fak*choo-al] *adj* pertaining to facts, actual, restricted to established facts.

factuality [fakchoo-*aliti*] *n* state of being factual.

factum [*fak*tum] *n* (*leg*) statement of facts, memorandum summarizing the facts of a case.

facture [*fak*cher] *n* process of making something; thing made.

facula (*pl* **faculae**) [*fak*ewla] *n* bright solar spot.

facultative [*fak*ultaytiv] *adj* permissive; optional; of a faculty; (*biol*) having the power of living under different conditions.

faculty [*fak*ulti] *n* special aptitude, capacity, ability; natural function of a bodily organ; one of the main divisions of knowledge composing university studies; the recognized teachers of one such division; (*leg, eccles*) authorization, dispensation; **the f.** (*coll*) doctors.

fad [*fad*] *n* whim, pet project, passing enthusiasm, craze; unreasonable but fixed notion.

faddist [*fad*ist] *n* one who has fads.

faddy [*fad*i] *adj* having fads ~ **faddiness** *n*.

fade [*fayd*] *v/i* and *t* lose or cause to lose strength, colour, or vividness; wither away, droop; become indistinct, die away, disappear gradually; (*rad*) lose volume of sound; **f. in, f. out** (*cin*) cause (a picture) to become gradually more, or less, distinct.

fadeless [*fayd*les] *adj* that cannot fade.

fade-out [*fayd*-owt] *n* gradual disappearance or dimming, *esp* of a filmed image.

fading [*fayd*ing] *n* process of losing colour, strength or vividness; degree to which something has faded ~ **fading** *adj*.

faecal, (*US*) **fecal** [*feek*al] *adj* of excrement.

faeces, (*US*) **feces** [*feeseez*] *n* (*pl*) excrement from the bowels; sediment, dregs.

faerie, faery [*fair*Ri] *n* power of fairies, enchantment; enchanted land, world of magic ~ **faerie** *adj* (*poet*) fairy-like; imaginary, fanciful.

faff [*faf*] *v/i* (*coll*) **f. about** dither, waver; be inefficient or feckless.

fag (*pres/part* **fagging**, *p/t* and *p/part* **fagged**) [*fag*] *v/t* and *i* make tired by work, exhaust; toil, work laboriously; fray, unravel; (*at public school*) employ as a fag; act as a fag ~ **fag** *n* (*at public school*) junior boy who has to do jobs for a senior; (*coll*) tiresome thing to have to do; (*coll*) cigarette; (*sl, pej*) male homosexual.

fag-end [*fag*-end] *n* last and worst part; remnant; cigarette-end.

fagged [*fagd*] *adj* tired out.

fagging [*fag*ing] *n* system of using boys as fags.

faggot, (*US*) **fagot** [*fag*ot] *n* bundle of sticks tied together; bundle of metal rods; savoury liver rissole; (*sl*) anything old or ugly; (*sl, pej*) male homosexual; **f. vote** (*hist*) vote obtained by the transfer to a person not otherwise qualified of sufficient property to qualify him as an elector ~ **faggot** *v/t* tie together.

Fahrenheit [*fa*RenhIt] *n* scale of temperature in which freezing-point of water is taken as 32° and its boiling-point 212°; thermometer marked according to this scale > PDS.

faience [fI-*yons*/faa-*yons*] *n* glazed terracotta.

fail [*fayl*] *v/i* and *t* be inadequate; be lacking, come to an end; break down; grow feeble, diminish, lose health or vigour; fall short; neglect, omit; be unsuccessful (*esp* in examination); become bankrupt; disappoint, let down, abandon; judge (a candidate) unsuccessful in examination ~ **fail** *n* failure; **without f. for** certain.

failing [*fayl*ing] *n* fault, imperfection, weakness ~ **failing** *prep* in default of, without.

faille [*fayl*/fIl] *n* soft, flat-ribbed fabric of silk, rayon, or cotton.

fail-safe [*fayl*-sayf] *n* so designed that a failure in any component causes the whole mechanism or system to remain inactive.

failure [*fayl*yer] *n* lack of success; unsuccessful person or thing; non-performance; omission, neglect; shortage, inadequacy; diminution, dwindling; breakdown (in supply); bankruptcy.

fain (1) [*fayn*] *adj* (*ar*) ready, willing, glad; **f. to** compelled to ~ **fain** *adv* gladly, with joy.

fain (2), **fains** *interj* (*school coll*) exclamation used in avoiding a request, claiming a truce, or refusing to join a game.

faint [*faynt*] *adj* weak, feeble; slight; lacking vigour, timid; vague, dim; dizzy, about to swoon;

sickly, oppressive; **ruled f.** (paper) marked with faint ruled lines ~ **faint** *n* swoon, temporary unconsciousness; **in a dead f.** completely unconscious ~ **faint** *v/i* lose consciousness, swoon; feel weak or giddy; grow weaker; lose heart.

faint-hearted [faynt-*haar*tid] *adj* timid, cowardly, easily discouraged ~ **faint-heartedly** *adv* ~ **faint-heartedness** *n*.

fainting [*faynting] *n* act of swooning.

faintish [*fayntish] *adj* somewhat faint.

faintly [*faynt*li] *adv* in a faint manner; slightly.

faintness [*fayntnes] *n* condition of being faint.

faints [*faynts] *n* (*pl*) impure spirit given off at the beginning and at the end of distillation.

fair (1) [*fair*] *n* periodical gathering for sale of goods, often with amusements, competitions, sideshows *etc*; charity bazaar; trade exhibition; **the day after the f. too late.**

fair (2) *adj* beautiful; clear, bright; sunny; light-coloured; blond; with fresh complexion; just, impartial, equitable; straightforward, honourable; (*fig*) pure, spotless; favourable, promising; plausible, specious; moderately good, not too bad; **f. copy** transcript free from corrections; **f. game** legitimate object of pursuit or attack; **f. play** equal conditions for all; **set f.** (*of barometer*) indicating spell of good weather; (*fig*) promising, encouraging; **the f. sex, the f. women**; **f. and square** straightforward, honourable, direct; **in a f. way** to likely to ~ **fair** *adv* justly, honourably; without cheating; politely, gently; directly; **bid f. to** seem likely to.

fair-faced [fair-*fayst*] *adj* beautiful; hypocritically charming.

fairground [*fair*Rownd] *n* open space where fairs are held.

fairily [*fair*Rili] *adv* in a fairylike manner.

fairing (1) [*fair*Ring] *n* gift bought at a fair.

fairing (2) [*fair*Ring] *n* streamlining; structure added to aircraft *etc* for this purpose.

Fair Isle [*fair*-Il] *adj* type of knitting design named after a Shetland island.

fairly [*fair*li] *adv* justly; tolerably, moderately, to some extent; completely, thoroughly.

fairminded [fair*mInd*ed] *adj* unbiased, just.

fairness [*fair*nes] *n* quality of being fair; justice, impartiality.

fairspoken [fairsp*Ok*en] *adj* polite, gracious; plausible, persuasive.

fairway [*fair*way] *n* navigation channel, regular course for ships; (*golf*) mown strip between tee and green.

fairweather [fair*weTH*er] *adj* only present when things go well, incapable of bearing trouble.

fairy [*fair*Ri] *n* small supernatural creature in human form and having magical powers; (*sl, pej*) male homosexual ~ **fairy** *adj* of, or like, a fairy; magical; beautiful, dainty, small; **f. cycle** child's miniature bicycle.

fairy-lamp, fairy-light [*fair*Ri-lamp, *fair*Ri-lIt] *n* small coloured lamp used as decoration.

fairyland [*fair*Riland] *n* the country of the fairies; enchanted or beautiful region; region of marvels.

fairylike [*fair*Rilik] *adj* like a fairy; ethereal, dainty.

fairy-ring [*fair*Ri-Ring] *n* circle of noticeably darker grass.

fairy-tale [*fair*Ri-tayl] *n* story about fairies; folk-tale about magical events *etc*; unlikely story, fantasy, lie.

faith [*fayth*] *n* reliance, trust, confidence; belief, *esp* in religious doctrines; acceptance of a belief without conclusive or logical evidence; system of religious beliefs; sincerity, honesty; word of honour, promise; **bad f.** intent to deceive; **in good f.** sincerely; **Punic f.** treachery.

faithful [*fayth*fool] *adj* loyal, conscientious, trustworthy; true to fact, accurate; **the f. true believers** ~ **faithfully** *adv* ~ **faithfulness** *n*.

faith-healing [*fayth*-heeling] *n* the curing of disorders by suggestion.

faithless [*fayth*les] *adj* sceptical, unbelieving; unreliable; fickle ~ **faithlessly** *adv* ~ **faithlessness** *n*.

fake [*fayk*] *v/t* make a sham imitation of, counterfeit; falsify, tamper with, touch up; (*theat*) improvise ~ **fake** *n* imitation, forgery, sham; (*coll*) insincere person, charlatan ~ **fake** *adj* ~ **faker** *n*.

fakir [fa*keer*] *n* Muslim or Hindu ascetic beggar.

Falange [faa*laan*khe] *n* the Spanish Fascist party ~ **Falangist** *adj* and *n* > PDPol.

falchion [*fawl*chon] *n* short curved broadsword.

falciform [*fals*ifawrm] *adj* shaped like a sickle.

falcon [*fawl*kon] *n* (*orni*) type of bird of prey; such a bird, *esp* the female, trained to hunt game; (*hist*) small cannon ~ **falconer** *n* one who breeds, trains, or hunts with, falcons.

falconet [*fawl*konet] *n* (*hist*) light cannon.

falconry [*fawl*konRi] *n* art of training hunting falcons.

falderal, folderol [falde*Ral*, folde*Rol*] *n* song refrain; a trifle, rubbish.

faldstool [*fawld*stOOl] *n* (*eccles*) folding-stool; armless chair used by a bishop when not in his own cathedral; movable kneeling-desk.

fall (*p/t* **fell**, *p/part* **fallen**) [*fawl*] *v/i* descend freely from high to low position, drop; come down, collapse, drop to the ground; subside; decrease, diminish, abate; hang down; yield, *esp* to temptation, commit sin; (*of women*) lose chastity; lose power or office; die in battle; occur, happen; pass into (a state); be spoken; be divided into; (*of the face*) show sudden disappointment; **f. about** (*sl*) laugh wildly; **f. away** desert; decrease; grown thin; **f. back** retreat; **f. back on** retreat to, turn to in need; **f. behind** be in the rear, be in arrears; **f. down (on)** (*coll*) make bad mistake, fail; **f. flat** fail, produce no effect; **f. foul of** (*naut*) collide with; quarrel with, antagonize; **f. for** be attracted by, fall in love with; be caught by (a trick); **f. in** collapse inwards; come to an end; (*mil*) get into line; **f. in with** happen to meet; agree, comply with; **f. off** decrease; (*naut*) not answer to the helm; **f. on** attack; be the duty of; **f. out** quarrel; happen, turn out; (*mil*) leave ranks; **f. over oneself** be very eager; **f. over backwards** make extreme efforts; **f. short** fail to reach, be inadequate; **f. through** come to nothing; **f. to** begin; attack; start eating; **f. under** be classified as ~ **fall** *n* act of falling, drop, collapse, sudden descent; lowering, lessening (in value *etc*); yielding, capitulation; yielding to temptation, sin; (*US*) autumn; amount of rain *etc* falling at one time; cascade, cataract; gradient; (*wrestling*) throw; bout; **the F. (of Man)** the sin of Adam; **free f.** unchecked descent; sport of leaping from an aircraft without opening parachute till last possible moment; (aer) movement of spacecraft caused by gravity alone; try a f. with pit oneself against.

fallacious [falayshus] adj based on false reasoning; deceptive, misleading ~ **fallaciousness** n.

fallacy [falasi] n mistaken opinion, wrong but prevalent notion; false reasoning, deceptive argument; error founded on false reasoning; (log) argument or conclusion which breaks the laws of logical proof.

fal-lal [fal-lal] n finery.

fallen [fawlen] adj sinful, degraded; f. **woman** prostitute; **the f.** (pl) those killed in battle.

fallguy [fawlgI] n (sl) one who is tricked into paying penalty for another's deed.

fallibility [falibiliti] n quality of being fallible.

fallible [falib'l] adj liable to err or deceive, unreliable ~ **fallibly** adv.

Fallopian [falOpi-an] adj F. **tubes** the oviducts in mammals.

fallout [fawlowt] n radioactive dust from nuclear detonation.

fallow (1) [falO] n and adj (land) ploughed and harrowed but left unsown; (fig) untrained, undeveloped; **lie f.** remain uncultivated ~ **fallow** v/t plough and harrow (land) without sowing it ~ **fallowness** n.

fallow (2) adj brownish-yellow.

fallow-deer [falO-deer] n species of small deer.

false [fawls] adj not true; incorrect, wrong, mistaken; untruthful, deceitful, treacherous; misleading, deceptive; counterfeit, sham; artificial; f. **bottom** (of box etc) one concealing a secret compartment; f. **position** a situation in which a person's motives and actions are liable to be misconstrued; f. **pretences** misrepresentations, deliberately deceptive appearances; f. **quantity** wrong vowel-length; f. **step** blunder ~ **false** adv play one f. deceive, betray.

false-hearted [fawls-haartid] adj disloyal, treacherous, fickle.

falsehood [fawlshood] n untruth, lie.

falsely [fawlsli] adv in a false way.

falseness [fawlsnis] n quality of being false.

falsetto [fawlsetO] n singing or speech produced by adult males in a register higher than their normal utterance > PDM; an unnaturally shrill voice ~ **falsetto** adj.

falsework [fawlswurk] n (bui) temporary framework, scaffolding.

falsies [fawlseez] n (pl) (sl) padded brassieres worn to enhance the bustline.

falsification [fawlsifikayshon] n fraudulent alteration, distortion (of facts).

falsify [fawlsifI] v/t forge or fraudulently alter document; misrepresent, distort; prove to be false, disappoint ~ **falsifiable** adj ~ **falsifier** n.

falsity [fawlsiti] n quality or condition of being false; false statement; dishonesty, treachery.

faltboat [fawltbOt/foltbOt] n (mil) collapsible kayak of rubberized sailcloth.

falter [fawlter] v/i move feebly or hesitatingly; totter, stumble; hesitate through fear; speak hesitantly or with broken voice; stammer ~ **faltering** adj and n.

fame [faym] n reputation; glory, celebrity, renown; (ar) report, rumour; **house of ill f.**

brothel ~ **famed** adj celebrated, well known; (ar) reported, believed.

familiar [familyer] adj in close friendship, intimate; private, domestic; excessively or presumptuously friendly, impudent, casual; well acquainted with (a subject), well versed in; usual, well known; f. **spirit** demon attending on witch or magician ~ **familiar** n attendant demon; close friend; (RC) official in household of Pope or Roman Catholic bishop.

familiarity [famili-aRiti] n close friendship, intimacy; cordiality; informality, presumption; acquaintance (with subject); (pl) caresses, liberties.

familiarize [famili-aRIz] v/t make familiar.

family [famili] n group of persons interrelated by blood and marriage; group of parents and children; children of same parents; group of objects having a common origin or having features in common; (bot, zool) subdivision of an order; group descended from common stock; (ar, hist) household, including dependants and servants; f. **man** man fond of domestic life; man with children; f. **tree** genealogical table; **in the f. way** (coll) pregnant ~ **family** adj of or for a family; suitable for a family.

famine [famin] n desperate shortage of food in a district; (fig) serious shortage or lack; starvation, hunger.

famish [famish] v/t and i starve; reduce or be reduced to extreme hunger; suffer from extreme cold; **be famished, be famishing** (coll) feel very hungry.

famous [faymus] adj renowned, well known; (coll) excellent, first-rate ~ **famously** adv (coll) very well, excellently.

famulus [famyoolus] n attendant, esp on magician or medieval scholar.

fan (1) [fan] n any device for causing air to flow in a given direction; small portable device for cooling the face by air-currents, usually shaped as the sector of a circle and capable of being folded; anything of similar shape; machine for winnowing chaff from grain; rotating instrument for ventilation; (mot) apparatus cooling radiator by air-currents; (naut) propeller; small sail on windmill to keep main sails across the wind; f. **vaulting** (archi) vaulting in which all the ribs have an identical curvature ~ **fan** (pres/part **fanning**, p/t and p/part **fanned**) v/t and i direct currents of air upon; spread out in shape of a fan; (of wind) blow gently; winnow; f. **the flame** increase excitement, anger, etc; f. **out** (mil) (of troops) spread out in the field.

fan (2) n (coll) ardent admirer, enthusiastic devotee; f. **club** association of admirers of an actor etc; f. **mail** letters written to a celebrity by admirers.

fanatic [fanatik/fanatik] n and adj (person) possessed by an excessive and irrational enthusiasm for, or devotion to, a theory, belief, line of action etc ~ **fanatical** adj ~ **fanatically** adv.

fanaticism [fanatisizm] n outlook of a fanatic.

fanbelt [fanbelt] n (mot) belt linking engine to cooling fan.

fancied [fansid] adj imaginary; preferred.

fancier [fansi-er] n person having special knowledge, esp of breeding animals; connoisseur.

fanciful [fansifool] adj indulging in fancies,

whimsical, faddy; fancy in design, odd, quaint; imaginary, non-existent ~ **fancifully** *adv* ~ **fancifulness** *n*.

fancy [*fan*si] *n* delusion, baseless belief or opinion; whim, capricious inclination; fondness, liking; faculty of forming mental images; an unsystematic, undirected form of aesthetic imagination; an idea or image so formed; **the f.** (*collect*) enthusiasts for some specific sport, *esp* boxing; **take a f.** to be drawn towards, like; **take (catch) the f.** of attract, please ~ **fancy** *adj* decorated, elaborate; fantastic, extravagant; expensive; imaginary; **f.** dog bred to special type; **f. dress** costume for masquerade, pageant *etc*; fantastic clothes; **f. goods** ornamental trifles, ribbons *etc*; **f. man** (*sl*) man living on a prostitute's earnings or his mistress's money; **f. woman** mistress; prostitute; **f. work** embroidery ~ **fancy** *v/t* imagine, picture to oneself; suppose, be inclined to think; believe without justification; have a liking for, be attracted by; **f. oneself** be conceited, have a good opinion of oneself.

fancy-free [*fan*si-fRee] *adj* not in love.

fandango [fan*dang*-gO] *n* a Spanish dance and its music > PDM.

fane [fayn] *n* (*poet*) a temple.

fanfare [*fan*fair] *n* (*mus*) short, brilliant series of notes on trumpets, bugles *etc*, used as salute > PDM.

fanfaronade [fanfaRo*nayd*] *n* brag, bluster.

fang [fang] *n* long pointed tooth, *esp* the canine tooth of dog or wolf; snake's poison-tooth; pronged root of a tooth; the tang of a tool; (*mining*) an airway > PDE ~ **fang** *v/t* prime (a pump) ~ **fanged** *adj*.

fanlight [*fan*lIt] *n* sash or window over a door.

fanny [*fan*i] *n* (*sl*) female pudenda; arse.

fanon, phanon [*fan*on] *n* (*RC*) striped cape worn by Pope at pontifical Mass; maniple.

fantail [*fan*tayl] *n* pigeon with fan-shaped tail; gas-burner with fan-shaped jet.

fan-tan [*fan*-tan] *n* a gambling game.

fantasia [fan*tay*zi-a] *n* (*mus*) free composition, not bound by set forms; medley of well-known tunes > PDM.

fantasize [*fan*tasIz] *v/i* indulge in fantasies, *esp* sexual.

fantast [*fan*tast] *n* a dreamer or visionary.

fantastic [fan*tas*tik] *adj* oddly elaborate, grotesque, exaggerated; capricious, eccentric; unbelievable, preposterous; (*coll*) excellent ~ **fantastical** *adj* ~ **fantasticalness** *n* ~ **fantastically** *adv*.

fantasticality [fantasti*kal*iti] *n* quality of being fantastic.

fantasticate [fan*tas*tikayt] *v/t* make elaborate or fanciful.

fantasy, phantasy [*fan*tasi] *n* non-realistic story, play *etc*; train of thought or of mental images indulged in to gratify one's wishes; fancy, whim; illusion, hallucination; (*mus*) a fantasia.

far [faar] *adv* at a distance, remote; to a great degree, very much; to a great distance; **f. and away** very much; **f. be it from me** I certainly would not; **go f.** (*fig*) be successful; **go f. towards** contribute much towards; **f. gone in an** advanced state ~ **far** *adj* distant, remote; **a f. cry** a long way; **few and f. between** rare; **the F.**

East countries of eastern Asia, *esp* China and Japan.

farad [*fa*Rad] *n* (*elect*) unit of capacitance, equal to one coulomb per volt > PDS.

faraday [*fa*Raday] *n* (*elect*) quantity of electricity used in electrolysis, equal to 96,490 coulombs > PDS.

faradic [fa*Rad*ik] *adj* **f. currents** (*med*) currents from an induction coil used for curative purposes.

faradization [faRadI*zay*shon] *n* application of medical electricity.

faraway [*faar*Raway] *adj* in the distance, remote; (*fig*) vague, dreamy.

farce (1) [faars] *n* dramatic work intended to provoke laughter; a boisterous low comedy; ridiculous and futile proceedings; absurd sham, mockery.

farce (2) *v/t* (*cookery*) stuff, season, spice ~ **farce** *n* force-meat.

farceur [faar*sur*] *n* a joker, wag.

farcical [*faar*sikal] *adj* like a farce, extravagantly comic; ridiculous, sham ~ **farcically** *adv*.

farcicality [faarsi*kal*iti] *n* ridiculousness.

farcing [*faar*sing] *n* (*cookery*) stuffing.

farcy [*faar*si] *n* a disease of horses akin to glanders.

fardel [*faar*del] *n* (*ar*) a bundle, burden.

fare [fair] *n* charge for conveyance of passenger; passenger who has paid to be transported; food ~ **fare** *v/i* travel, make one's way; get on; turn out (well or badly); prosper; feed.

farewell [fair*wel*] *interj* goodbye! ~ **farewell** *n* leave-taking, parting words.

far-fetched [faar-*fecht*] *adj* forced, unnatural, unlikely.

far-flung [faar-*flung*] *adj* extensive.

farina [fa*Reen*a] *n* flour or meal made from cereals, nuts *etc*; (*bot*) pollen; (*chem*) starch.

farinaceous [faRi*nay*shus] *adj* made from farina; mealy; containing much flour.

farinose [*fa*RinOs] *adj* mealy; sprinkled with floury powder; yielding farina.

farm [faarm] *n* land and buildings worked as a unit for agricultural or dairy purposes; main house on a farm; stretch of water used for breeding specified fish, molluscs *etc*; (*obs*) cheap establishment for unwanted children ~ **farm** *v/t* and *i* cultivate land, or use it for rearing cattle or sheep; undertake care of (persons) for fixed payment; take proceeds of, after paying fixed sum; **f. out** let out proceeds in return for a fixed sum; hire out ~ **farmable** *adj*.

farmer [*faar*mer] *n* one who farms; one who earns his living by cultivating land, breeding stock *etc*.

farmhand [*faarm*hand] *n* farm labourer.

farmhouse [*faarm*hows] *n* house on a farm.

farming [*faarm*ing] *n* occupations and business of a farmer; agriculture; the letting out to farm.

farmstead [*faarm*sted] *n* a farm.

farmyard [*faarm*yaard] *n* the enclosure around which the farm buildings stand.

faro [*fair*RO] *n* gambling card-game.

farouche [fa*ROOsh*] *adj* (*Fr*) awkward, shy, sullen.

far-out [*faar*-owt] *adj* remote, distant; (*sl*) up-to-date, experimental, eccentrically modern; excellent.

farraginous [fa*Raj*inus] *adj* of or as a medley.

farrago [fa*Ray*gO] *n* medley, hodge-podge.

far-reaching [faar-*Reech*ing] *adj* extensive; having important consequences.

farrier [*fa*Ri-er] *n* one who shoes horses; horse-doctor; non-commissioned officer in charge of the horses of a cavalry regiment ~ **farriery** *n* the trade of a farrier.

farrow [*fa*RO] *n* litter of pigs ~ **farrow** *v/t* give birth to (piglets); *v/i* (*of sow*) bring forth piglets.

far-sighted [faar-*si*tid] *adj* able to see distant objects more clearly than near ones; prudent, able to foresee distant consequences.

fart [*faart*] *n* (*vulg*) an escape of wind from the anus, *esp* if audible ~ **fart** *v/i*.

farther [*faar*THer] *adj* remoter, more distant; more advanced ~ **farther** *adv* to or at a greater distance ~ **farthermost** *adj*.

farthest [*faar*THest] *adj* most remote, most distant ~ **farthest** *adv* to, at, the greatest distance.

farthing [*faar*THing] *n* (*obs*) (coin worth) a quarter of an old penny.

farthingale [*faar*THing-gayl] *n* hooped petticoat.

fasces [*fa*seez] *n* (*pl*) (*hist*) bundle of rods round an axe carried before a magistrate in ancient Rome as symbol of authority; emblem of Italian Fascist Party.

fascia, facia [*fa*shi-a] *n* band, stripe; (*bui*) any long band or strip of wood, stone, or metal on the face of a building; part of shop-front over the window bearing proprietor's name; (*mot*) instrument-board of automobile; (*anat*) ensheathing band of connective tissue; (*zool*) broad band of colour.

fasciated [*fa*shi-aytid] *adj* (*bot*) (*of malformed stems*) growing into each other; marked with stripes ~ **fasciation** [fashi-*ay*shon] *n*.

fascicle, fascicule [*fa*sik'l, *fa*sikewl] *n* (*bot*) tuft, close cluster; one part of a book published by instalments.

fascinate [*fa*sinayt] *v/t* attract or influence irresistibly; charm, delight; render powerless by fixed stare, hypnotize ~ **fascinating** *adj*.

fascination [fasin*ay*shon] *n* act of fascinating; power to fascinate; charm, attractiveness.

fascinator [*fa*sinayter] *n* one who fascinates.

fascine [*fa*seen] *n* brushwood bundle > PDE; **f. dwelling** (*arch*) prehistoric lake-dwelling supported on fascines.

Fascism [*fa*shizm/*fa*sizm] *n* authoritarian and nationalistic right-wing political movement founded by Benito Mussolini in Italy in 1919; any extreme right-wing, anti-Communist, or racialist party, movement, or ideology; right-wing military dictatorship > PDPol ~ **Fascist** *n* and *adj*.

fash [*fash*] *v/t* (*dial*) annoy, vex; *v/i* and *refl* bother oneself, take trouble.

fashion [*fa*shon] *n* style, appearance; prevalent custom or taste, vogue, mode; latest or most admired style of clothes; method, way; **after a f. in a way**; not very well; **to some extent**; **in (the) f.** following current taste, smart ~ **fashion** *v/t* form, shape, make ~ **fashion** *adj* of or displaying fashions in clothes.

fashionable [*fa*shonab'l] *adj* in accord with prevailing taste, custom or vogue; smart, in good style; up-to-date; used by or characteristic of people in high society ~ **fashionably** *adv*.

fashion-plate [*fa*shon-playt] *n* picture showing latest styles in clothing; person dressed in the height of fashion.

fast (1) [*faast*] *v/i* abstain from all or certain kinds of food, *esp* as a religious observance; go without food (or drink) ~ **fast** *n* act of fasting; period or day appointed for fasting.

fast (2) *adj* firmly fixed, secure; firm, loyal; (*of colour*) non-fading; quick-moving, rapid; causing rapid movement; (*of clock*) showing time later than the actual; (*of people*) dissipated, immoral; **a f. one** (*coll*) an unfair trick; **play f. and loose** behave irresponsibly ~ **fast** *adv* firmly, fixedly; securely; quickly, rapidly; soundly (asleep); (*ar*) very near.

fast-day [*faast*-day] *n* day appointed for fasting.

fasten [*faa*sen] *v/t* and *i* make fast, firm, secure; fix, bind, close; become fastened, catch; **f. on** take firm hold of; single out (for criticism *etc*).

fastener [*faa*sener] *n* device for fastening things together.

fastening [*faa*sening] *n* anything that fastens.

fastidious [fast*i*di-us] *adj* hard to please, particular; sensitive, squeamish; discriminating ~ **fastidiously** *adv* ~ **fastidiousness** *n*.

fasting [*faa*sting] *n* act of person who fasts.

fastness [*faa*stnes] *n* stronghold, fortress; quality of being fast.

fat [*fat*] *n* greasy substance in animal bodies; similar substance in seeds *etc*; (*fig*) best part of anything; (*chem*) compound of glycerine with an acid; (*theat sl*) a good part; telling lines; (*print*) copy with void spaces; **the f. is in the fire** trouble is on the way; **live off the f. of the land** live in great comfort; **live on one's f.** live off one's reserves ~ **fat** *adj* having much fat; corpulent, plump; greasy, oily; thick, stumpy; (*of soil*) fertile; rich, profitable; (*coll*) stupid; (*theat coll*) giving opportunity for impressive acting; **a f. lot** (*coll*) a great deal (*usu ironic*), nothing at all; **cut up f.** (*sl*) die leaving much money ~ **fat** (*p/t* and *p/part* **fatted**) *v/t* and *i* fatten (beasts); grow fat.

fatal [*fay*tal] *adj* causing death or ruin; deadly; disastrous, destructive; caused by fate, destined.

fatalism [*fay*talizm] *n* belief that all events are predetermined by fate and so inevitable; resolute acceptance of one's fate; resignation.

fatalist [*fay*talist] *n* believer in fatalism.

fatalistic [fayta*li*stik] *adj* resigned to fate; believing in fatalism ~ **fatalistically** *adv*.

fatality [fat*a*liti] *n* death by accident, in war, or as a result of some disaster; misfortune fated to happen; inevitable course of destiny.

fatally [*fay*tali] *adv* so as to cause death.

fata Morgana [faata-mawr*gaa*na] *n* type of mirage in which object appears to be elongated vertically > PDG.

fate [*fayt*] *n* unalterable power determining events; destiny, necessity; that which is destined or certain to happen; one's lot, fortune; doom; death, destruction; **the Fates** (*myth*) three goddesses controlling human destiny.

fated [*fay*tid] *adj* destined, decreed by fate; doomed, *esp* to destruction.

fateful [*fay*tful] *adj* involving momentous consequences, decisive; ominous, irrevocable.

fathead [*fat*-hed] *n* (*coll*) fool ~ **fatheaded** *adj*.

father [*faa*THer] *n* male parent; progenitor, ancestor; (*fig*) guardian, protector; founder, originator; oldest member (of group); title of respect, *esp* for priests and religious leaders; **the F. God** as First Person of the Trinity; **Fathers of the Church** early Christian writers; **F. of the faithful** title of a Caliph; **the Holy F.** the Pope; **F. of lies** the Devil; **Pilgrim Fathers** emigrants who sailed to America on the *Mayflower* in 1620 ~ **father** *v/t* beget; act as father towards; protect; be originator of; acknowledge oneself as father of; admit or assume responsibility for; **f. on** ascribe paternity, authorship to; saddle with responsibility for.

father-figure [*faa*THer-figer] *n* (*psych*) older man whom one loves and respects as substitute for one's real father.

fatherhood [*faa*THerhood] *n* the relation of a father to a child, paternity.

father-in-law [*faa*THer-in-law] *n* father of one's wife or husband.

fatherland [*faa*THerland] *n* one's native country.

fatherless [*faa*THerles] *adj* having no father living; having an unidentified father; illegitimate.

fatherly [*faa*THerli] *adj* of or like a father; protective, kind ~ **fatherliness** *n*.

fathom [*fa*THom] *n* (*naut*, *mining*) a measure of depth, 6 ft; a measure for timber, 6 ft square in section, regardless of length ~ **fathom** *v/t* measure depth of, sound; (*fig*) understand.

fathomless [*fa*THomlis] *adj* impossible to fathom, very deep; (*fig*) incomprehensible.

fatigue [*fateeg*] *n* diminished efficiency or ability to carry on work because of previous expenditure of energy; exhaustion; (*mech*) deterioration of metal under repeated stresses > PDE; tiring task or occupation; (*mil*) non-military work done by soldiers ~ **fatigue** *v/t* make weary, tire; weaken (metal) by repeated stresses ~ **fatiguing** *adj*.

fatling [*fatling*] *n* young animal fattened for killing.

fatness [*fatnes*] *n* state or quality of being fat; greasiness; abundance, fertility.

fatted [*fatid*] *adj* fattened.

fatten [*faten*] *v/t* and *i* make fat, *esp* for slaughter; enrich (soil); grow fat.

fatty [*fati*] *adj* like fat, greasy; consisting of fat; having excessive fat; **f. acid** (*chem*) monobasic aliphatic acid > PDS ~ **fatty** *n* (*joc*) name for a fat person, *esp* a child.

fatuous [*fatyoo-us*] *adj* foolish, stupid, imbecile; futile ~ **fatuously** *adj* ~ **fatuousness** *n*.

faucal [*fawkal*] *adj* of the throat; (*phon*) guttural.

fauces [*fawseez*] *n* (*pl*) upper part of throat between palate and pharynx.

faucet [*fawset*] *n* tap for drawing liquid from a cask or pipe.

fault [*fawlt*] *n* defect, imperfection, blemish; failing (of character); offence, sin; responsibility for wrongdoing, culpability; error, mistake; (*geol*) fracture in the earth's crust displacing the rock strata > PDG; (*tennis*) ball wrongly placed in serving; (*hunting*) loss of scent; **at f.** defective, faulty; in the wrong; **find f. with** criticize, complain of, scold; **to a f.** excessively ~ **fault** *v/t* and *i* find fault with, blame; notice a mistake or defect in; (*tennis*) serve wrongly; (*geol*) displace strata; show a displacement of strata.

fault-finder [*fawlt*-finder] *n* one who habitually complains or criticizes ~ **fault-finding** *n*.

faultless [*fawlt*les] *adj* without fault, perfect ~ **faultlessly** *adv* ~ **faultlessness** *n*.

faulty [*fawlti*] *adj* with faults, defective, imperfect, inaccurate, unreliable ~ **faultily** *adv* ~ **faultiness** *n*.

faun [*fawn*] *n* (*Roman myth*) rural deity with horns, goats' feet, tail, and pointed ears; (*fig*) wild-looking but attractive young boy.

fauna [*fawna*] *n* the animal life of a region or geological period.

fauvism [*fOvizm*] *n* a modern style of painting using vivid colours ~ **fauvist(e)** *adj*.

faux pas [*fO-paa*] *n* (*Fr*) blunder, *esp* in etiquette; tactless remark or action.

favour [*fayver*] *n* goodwill, friendly regard; act of goodwill, an exceptional kindness; (*pl*) (*of women*) consent to intimacy; partiality, preference; something given or worn as a token of affection; rosette, badge; (*comm*) letter; **in f. of** in support of; (*comm*) to the advantage or account of ~ **favour** *v/t* show goodwill towards; treat with undue partiality, prefer; help, support; tend to promote, facilitate; (*coll*) resemble, *esp* by heredity ~ **favourer** *n*.

favourable [*fayve*Rab'l] *adj* well-disposed; advantageous, suitable; approving, promising, satisfactory ~ **favourably** *adv*.

favoured [*fayverd*] *adj* treated with favour; having exceptional advantages; fortunate.

favouring [*fayve*Ring] *adj* showing partiality to; propitious, favourable.

favourite [*fayve*Rit] *n* person or thing preferred above others; minion of a king *etc*; competitor generally expected to win ~ **favourite** *adj*.

favouritism [*fayve*Ritizm] *n* practice of showing unfair partiality towards favourites; partiality.

favus [*fayvus*] *n* skin disease of the scalp.

fawn (1) [*fawn*] *n* a deer less than a year old; a pale yellowish-brown colour ~ **fawn** *adj* pale yellowish-brown ~ **fawn** *v/t* and *i* give birth to (a fawn); bring forth young.

fawn (2) *v/i* (*of dogs etc*) show affection or joy by tail-wagging, licking, pawing *etc*; **f. on**, (**upon**) (*fig*) flatter, treat with servile deference, cringe before ~ **fawner** *n* ~ **fawning** *adj* ~ **fawningly** *adv*.

fay [*fay*] *n* (*poet*) a fairy.

faze [*fayz*] *v/t* (*sl*) upset, trouble.

fealty [*fee*-alti] *n* loyalty of a vassal to his feudal lord.

fear [*feer*] *n* distress caused by awareness of danger; dread, apprehension, terror; cowardice; anxiety, foreboding; risk or likelihood (of an unpleasant occurrence); respect mingled with dread, awe; **no f.!** (*coll*) certainly not! ~ **fear** *v/t* and *i* be afraid of, dread; revere, stand in awe of; anticipate anxiously; feel dread, anxiety, *etc*; **never f.** don't be anxious.

fearful [*feer*fool] *adj* filled with fear, afraid, timid; anxious; terrible, calamitous; (*coll*) annoying, very great ~ **fearfully** *adv* ~ **fearfulness** *n*.

fearless [*feer*les] *adj* without fear, courageous ~ **fearlessly** *adv* ~ **fearlessness** *n*.

fearsome [*feer*sum] *adj* causing fear, terrifying, horrible ~ **fearsomeness** *n*.

feasibility [feezi*biliti*] *n* practicability.

feasible [*feezib'l*] *adj* capable of being done;

possible, practicable; convenient; likely, probable ~ **feasibly** adv.

feast [feest] n religious day of rejoicing; joyful celebration; banquet, lavish meal; abundance of anything pleasant; pleasure, delight; **movable f.** (eccles) feast the date of which varies each year ~ **feast** v/t and i give a lavish meal to; give great pleasure to; take part in a banquet; eat sumptuously, regale oneself ~ **feaster** n ~ **feasting** n.

feast-day [feest-day] n religious festival; day of rejoicing, public holiday; joyful anniversary.

feat [feet] n remarkable act of bravery, strength, or skill ~ **feat** adj (ar) skilful, neat.

feather [feTHer] n quilled and barbed structure growing from bird's skin, plume; anything like a feather in shape or lightness; **birds of a f.** people of the same kind; **a f. in one's cap** something to be proud of; **in high f.** healthy, vigorous, in high spirits; **show the white f.** show cowardice ~ **feather** v/t and i adorn, furnish, line or trim with feathers; (rowing) turn the oar blade parallel to the water on return stroke; (aer) set propeller blades parallel to the direction of motion; (shooting) shoot feathers off (a bird) without killing it; **f. one's nest** grow rich, usually at someone else's expense.

feather-bed [feTHer-bed] n mattress stuffed with feathers; (fig) luxury; **f. industry** one sheltered and subsidized by the Government ~ **feather-bed** v/t pamper, shield from all hardship; limit work or output in order to avoid dismissing redundant workers.

feather-brained [feTHer-bRaynd] adj irresponsible, extremely silly.

feather-cut [feTHer-kut] n method of trimming hair into short upswept curls.

feathered [feTHerd] adj having feathers; shaped like a feather; **our f. friends** birds.

feathering [feTHeRing] n plumage; feather-like fringe; act of turning an oar blade parallel with the water on the return stroke; (mus) technique of using the bow in rapid violin passages; (archi) type of ornamental cusp.

feather-stitch [feTHer-stich] n ornamental zigzag embroidery.

featherweight [feTHerwayt] n boxer weighing no more than 9 st; jockey weighing no more than 4 st 7 lb; (fig) unimportant person or thing.

feathery [feTHeRi] adj covered with feathers; resembling feathers; very light.

featly [feetli] adv (ar) nimbly, gracefully.

feature [feecher] n part of face; noticeable or characteristic part; part designed to attract attention; prominent article or item (in newspaper, radio programme etc); **f. film** principal film in cinema programme; **f. programme** radio or TV programme about a factual topic ~ **feature** v/t characterize, mark distinctively; portray; (cin, theat) present, give prominence to, display the talents of, cast in leading part ~ **featured** adj.

feature-length [feecher-length] adj (cin) full-length.

featureless [feecherles] adj lacking distinctive features; dull, monotonous.

febrifuge [febRifewj] n and adj (medicine) reducing fever.

febrile [feebRil] adj caused by, pertaining to, fever; (fig) agitated, frenzied.

February [febROO-aRi] n second month of the year.

fecal, feces see faecal, faeces.

feckless [fekles] adj careless, reckless; inefficient, helpless ~ **fecklessness** n.

feculence [fekyewlens] n dirt, filth; filthiness; dregs ~ **feculent** adj.

fecund [feekund/fekund] adj fertile, prolific.

fecundate [feekundayt/fekundayt] v/t impregnate, make fruitful ~ **fecundation** [feekun-dayshon/fekundayshon] n.

fecundity [feekundity/fekundity] n power of a species to multiply rapidly; capacity to bear children.

fed [fed] p/t and p/part of feed; **f. up** (coll) bored, disgusted, tired (of).

fedayeen [fedayeen] n (pl) Arab guerrillas.

federal [fedeRal] adj relating to the policy by which States unite for external affairs but remain independent for internal affairs; (US) relating to central government as opposed to State government ~ **federally** adv.

federalism [fedeRalizm] n supporting federation ~ **federalist** n and adj.

federalize [fedeRaliz] v/t and i form into federation ~ **federalization** [fedeRalizayshon] n.

federate [fedeRayt] v/t and i unite for a common purpose; unite on a federal basis ~ **federate** [fedeRat] adj.

federation [fedeRayshon] n group of States forming a federal union > PDPol; a society or organization ~ **federative** [fedeRativ] adj.

fedora [fidawrRa] n (US) type of soft felt hat.

fee [fee] n payment for services of professional man, official, public body, school, college etc; entrance money for club, examination etc; feudal benefice, fief; inherited estate ~ **fee** v/t pay a fee to, hire.

feeble [feeb'l] adj weak, infirm; lacking resolution; hesitant, futile; dim, indistinct ~ **feebleness** n ~ **feeblish** adj ~ **feebly** adv.

feeble-minded [feeb'l-mIndid] adj of low intelligence; (psych) having an intelligence quotient between 50 and 70 > PDP ~ **feeble-mindedness** n.

feed (p/t and p/part fed) [feed] v/t and i give or administer food to; provide with food; serve as food for; supply with fuel, electric power, material etc; keep filled; (fig) keep active, gratify; take food, graze; **f. back** return part of output, signal, force etc to an earlier stage of the producing process, circuit etc. **f. on** eat habitually; **f. up** fatten ~ **feed** n act of taking or giving food (esp of animals); food, fodder; amount of food given at any one time; fuel or material supplied (to a machine); channel or mechanism conveying material to machine etc; charge of gun; rate of advance of drill, cutting tool etc; (theat) subordinate partner in comedy duo; **be off one's f.** have no appetite.

feedback [feedbak] n system in which the output of a process is coupled to the input, so that a rise in the output energy either causes a decrease in the input energy (**negative f.**) or reinforces it (**positive f.**); (fig) system by which information on the result of a process or activity modifies its further development.

feeder [*feed*er] *n* one that feeds; infant's feeding bottle; child's bib; tributary stream; secondary road; (*elect*) cable carrying current from power-stations to substations; device supplying material or fuel to machine; (*sport*) person throwing ball to striker.

feeding [*feed*ing] *adj* supplying food or material; (*of storm*) becoming increasingly violent; (*sl*) annoying.

feedpipe [*feed*pIp] *n* pipe supplying material to machines.

feel (*p/t* and *p/part* felt) [*feel*] *v/t* and *i* perceive, ascertain, become aware of by touch, test by hand, handle; grope; have a physical sensation of; experience; be emotionally aware of; be affected by, be sensitive to; appreciate; consider, be of opinion that; seem, produce the impression that; f. for sympathize with; f. like be inclined for; f. one's way grope; advance cautiously ~ **feel** *n* sense of touch; sensation, impression produced; sensitive appreciation or understanding.

feeler [*feel*er] *n* organ of touch, *esp* antenna of insects; tentative proposal or suggestion; put out a f. (*fig*) make a tentative proposal or suggestion.

feeling [*feel*ing] *n* sense of touch; act of touching; physical sensation; emotion, sensibility; sympathy, kindness; susceptibility; unfavourable opinion, annoyance; irrational conviction, intuition, premonition > PDP ~ **feeling** *adj* expressing or having strong emotion, sympathetic, sensitive ~ **feelingly** *adv*.

fee-simple [fee-*simp*'l] *n* absolute possession of inherited estate; freehold; inheritance not limited to particular class of heirs.

feet [*feet*] *pl* of foot.

feeze [*feez*] *v/t* screw in, twist in; (*coll*) disturb, alarm ~ **feeze** *n* (*coll*) agitation, fuss.

feign [*fayn*] *v/t* and *i* pretend, assume in order to deceive; dissimulate; (*rare*) invent, make up ~ **feigning** *n* and *adj*.

feint (1) [*faynt*] *n* sham attack intended to deceive; (*mil*) troop movement meant to deceive enemy ~ **feint** *v/i* pretend to attack.

feint (2) *adj* (*of lines on paper*) faint.

feldspar, felspar [*feld*spaar, *fel*spaar] *n* (*min*) group of rock-forming minerals consisting chiefly of alumino-silicates of potassium and sodium.

feldspathic [feld*spath*ik] *adj* consisting of, containing, feldspar.

felicitate [fe*lis*itayt] *v/t* congratulate.

felicitation [felisit*ay*shon] *n* congratulation.

felicitous [fe*lis*itus] *adj* happy, apt, appropriate ~ **felicitously** *adv*.

felicity [fe*lis*iti] *n* bliss, intense happiness; aptness, suitability (in style); apt remark.

felid [*feel*id] *n* member of the cat family.

feline [*feel*In] *adj* of, like, or pertaining to cats; spiteful; crafty ~ **feline** *n* member of cat family.

fell (1) [*fel*] *n* animal's hide with the hair still on it; thick tangled hair or wool.

fell (2) *n* rocky hill or mountain side.

fell (3) *adj* (*poet*) fierce, savage, cruel, ruthless.

fell (4) *v/t* cause to fall, strike down; cut down (trees).

fell (5) *v/t* stitch a seam to conceal raw edge of seam allowance ~ **fell** *n* a felled seam.

fell (6) *p/t* of fall.

fellah (*pl* **fellahin**) [*fel*a] *n* Egyptian peasant.

fellate [fe*layt*] *v/t* suck or lick the penis of.

fellatio [fe*laa*si-O] *n* (*Lat*) stimulation of the penis by the mouth.

fellator (*fem* **fellatrix**) [fe*layt*or, fe*layt*Riks] *n* one who practices fellatio.

feller (1) [*fel*er] *n* one who or that which fells trees; machine that fells seams.

feller (2) *n* (*coll*) fellow.

felloe, felly [*fel*O, *fel*i] *n* wheel rim.

fellow [*fel*O] *n* companion, comrade; partner, colleague; accomplice; (*coll*) man, boy, person; one of a pair; social equal, peer; member of governing body of a college; graduate research student receiving a grant from a university; member of certain learned or professional societies ~ **fellow** *adj* having similar background *etc*; in similar situation.

fellow-feeling [*fel*O-*feel*ing] *n* mutual understanding, sympathy.

fellowship [*fel*Oship] *n* a sharing of interest; companionship; society, company; the communion between members or branches of the same church; position of a fellow in a college, learned society *etc*; grant paid to a university graduate.

fellow-traveller [*fel*O-tRav*el*er] *n* travelling companion; (*fig*) one who accepts most Communist conclusions but is not, or denies he is, a Communist > PDPol.

felly (1) [*fel*i] *adv* (*poet*) fiercely, cruelly.

felly (2) *n* see **felloe**.

felon (1) [*fel*on] *n* one who has committed a felony, a criminal; a ruffian ~ **felon** *adj* (*poet*) cruel, wicked, base ~ **felonry** *n* felons in general.

felon (2) *n* a whitlow.

felonious [fe*lO*ni-us] *adj* (*leg*) concerning felony; done with criminal intent; wicked ~ **feloniously** *adv* ~ **feloniousness** *n*.

felony [*fel*oni] *n* (*leg*) a major crime.

felsite [*fel*sIt] *n* (*geol*) igneous rock consisting of feldspar and quartz ~ **felsitic** [fel*sit*ik] *adj*.

felspar see **feldspar**.

felstone [*fel*stOn] *n* (*geol*) felsite.

felt (1) [*fel*t] *n* a densely matted fabric of compressed wool, fur, or hair ~ **felt** *adj* made of felt ~ **felt** *v/t* and *i* make into felt; cover with felt; become tangled and matted.

felt (2) *p/t* and *p/part* of feel.

felting [*fel*ting] *n* felted cloth; the making of felt.

felucca [fe*luk*a] *n* small Mediterranean vessel with oars and sails.

female [*fee*mayl] *adj* of the sex which bears offspring; of, concerning, characteristic of women; consisting of women or girls; (*bot*) having pistils and no stamens; fruit-bearing; (*eng*) having hollowed part designed to receive an inserted part ~ **female** *n* female animal; (*cont, joc*) woman.

femineity [femin*ee*-iti] *n* womanliness; effeminacy.

feminine [*fem*inin] *adj* female; characteristic of, suitable for, like, women; (*gramm*) of the gender or form denoting females; f. ending (*pros*) ending in an unstressed syllable; f. rhyme rhyme formed by words with unstressed endings ~ **femininely** *adv* ~ **feminineness** *n*.

femininism [*femininizm*] *n* tendency towards effeminacy; (*gramm, pros*) feminine form or idiom.

femininity [femin*in*iti] *n* femineity.

feminism [*feminizm*] *n* social movement claiming political and economic equality of women with men ~ **feminist** *n* and *adj*.

feminize [*femin*Iz] *v/t* and *i* (*biol*) impart female characteristics to a male; acquire female characteristics; become effeminate > PDP ~ **feminization** [feminIz*ay*shon] *n*.

femme [*fam/fem*] *n* (*sl*) a lesbian of feminine appearance and outlook.

femoral [*femo*Ral] *adj* relating to the thigh.

femto- *pref* one thousand million millionth.

femur [*feemer*] *n* the thigh-bone; the thigh.

fen [*fen*] *n* low-lying marshy land.

fence [*fens*] *n* barrier enclosing an area, *esp* wooden railings; (*eng*) guard or guide on a machine; art of fighting with a rapier; (*sl*) receiver of stolen goods; **master of f.** skilled swordsman; (*fig*) clever debater; **sit on the f.** refuse to take sides ~ **fence** *v/t* and *i* enclose or protect with a fence; (*of horse*) leap a fence; fight with rapier; parry, ward off; (*fig*) evade an argument, quibble; (*sl*) receive stolen goods ~ **fenceless** *adj* ~ **fencer** *n* swordsman; horse that jumps fences.

fencing [*fensing*] *n* wooden barrier, railings; material for fences; art of sword-play; (*sl*) receiving of stolen goods.

fend [*fend*] *v/i* repel, keep off; shield; **f. for** provide for, support.

fender [*fender*] *n* metal guard to span open fireplace; surround to a hearth; rope mat or ball which protects a ship from impact; device on car or locomotive to push obstacles off its track; (*US, mot*) bumper.

fenestella [fenest*ela*] *n* (*archi*) small window; (*eccles*) small opening in an altar front through which relics can be seen; niche in the south wall of a chancel.

fenestral [fenest*Ral*] *n* window-opening covered with oiled paper or cloth instead of glass.

fenestrate [fenest*Rayt*] *adj* (*bot, zool*) perforated; (*ent*) having transparent spots ~ **fenestrated** *adj*.

fenestration [fenest*Ray*shon] *n* (*archi*) the arrangement of windows on a façade; (*bot, zool*) perforation; (*surg*) perforation of wall of inner ear.

Fenian [*feeni*-an] *n adj* (*hist*) (member) of Irish nationalist movement working for overthrow of English rule.

fennec [*fenek*] *n* small African long-eared fox.

fennel [*fenel*] *n* yellow umbelliferous plant used in cooking.

fenny [*feni*] *adj* marshy; found in fens.

fenugreek [*feny*oog*Reek*] *n* herb of bean family.

feod see **feud**.

feoff see **fief**.

feoffee [*fefee/fefee*] *n* one who receives a fief; trustee.

feoffment [*fef*ment/*fef*ment] *n* (*leg*) the giving of a fief or fee; fee given.

feoffor [*fef*awr/*fef*awr] *n* one making a feoffment.

feral (1) [*feerRal*] *adj* fatal; gloomy; funereal.

feral (2) *adj* wild, run wild, undomesticated; uncivilized, savage.

fer-de-lance [fair-di-*laans*] *n* large South American venomous snake.

feretory [*fe*Ret*oRi*] *n* shrine for relics; tomb; bier; that part of a church in which shrines were placed.

feria [*feer*Ri-a] *n* (*eccles*) week-day on which no feast occurs ~ **ferial** *adj* of or on a feria.

ferine [*feer*Rin] *adj* wild, untamed.

ferity [*fe*Riti] *n* state of being wild or savage.

ferment [*fur*ment] *n* yeast; substance causing fermentation; fermentation; (*fig*) agitation, tumult ~ **ferment** [fer*ment*] *v/t* and *i* cause or undergo fermentation; (*fig*) stir up, agitate.

fermentable [fer*ment*ab'l] *adj* capable of being fermented.

fermentation [ferment*ay*shon] *n* a process, characterized by effervescence, akin to that which occurs when yeast operates on sugar, converting it to alcohol and liberating carbon dioxide > PDS; (*fig*) extreme excitement or agitation.

fermentative [fer*ment*ativ] *adj* of, like, derived from, or likely to provoke fermentation.

fermion [*furmi*-on] *n* (*phys*) type of elementary particle, the numbers of which are always conserved during interactions > PDS.

fermium [*furmi*-um] *n* (*chem*) a transuranic element > PDS.

fern [*furn*] *n* plant with feathery fronds, reproducing by means of spores.

fernery [*furn*eRi] *n* place for the growing of ferns; mass of ferns.

fern-owl [*furn*-owl] *n* the nightjar.

fernseed [*furn*seed] *n* the spores of ferns.

ferny [*furni*] *adj* of, like, or containing ferns.

ferocious [fe*RO*shus] *adj* fierce, cruel ~ **ferociously** *adv* ~ **ferociousness** *n*.

ferocity [fe*Ros*iti] *n* quality of being fierce.

ferrate [*fe*Rayt] *n* (*chem*) a salt of ferric acid.

ferreous [*fe*Ri-us] *adj* like, of, made of, iron.

ferret (1) [*fe*Rit] *n* half-tamed variety of polecat, used for driving rats or rabbits from their holes ~ **ferret** *v/t* and *i* hunt with ferrets; (*fig*) search thoroughly; **f. out** discover by persistent search.

ferret (2) *n* kind of strong cotton tape.

ferrety [*fe*Riti] *adj* of or like a ferret.

ferriage [*fe*Ri-ij] *n* conveyance by, fare for, a ferry.

ferric [*fe*Rik] *adj* (*chem*) containing tervalent iron > PDS.

ferriferous [fe*Rif*eRus] *adj* producing iron.

ferrimagnetism [fe*Ri*magnetizm] *n* type of magnetism occurring in ferrites > PDS.

ferris-wheel [*fe*Ris-wheel] *n* large vertically revolving wheel at fairs, carrying passengers.

ferrite [*fe*Rit] *n* type of iron ore; type of ceramic material, consisting of iron oxide and other metallic oxides, with special magnetic properties; (*chem*) salt of hypothetical ferrous acid > PDS.

ferritin [*fe*Ritin] *n* (*bioch*) protein, found in the liver and spleen, which stores iron.

ferro-concrete [fe*RO*konkReet] *n* an obsolete term for reinforced concrete.

ferromagnetism [fe*RO*magnetizm] *n* strongest type of magnetism, occurring in iron, cobalt and nickel > PDS.

ferromanganese [fe*RO*mang-ganeez] *n* alloy of manganese (70%–80%) and iron.

ferrotype [*fe*ROtIp] *n* positive photograph on sensitized iron plate.

ferrous [*fe*Rus] *adj* pertaining to iron; (*chem*) denoting a compound of bivalent (divalent) iron.

ferruginous [feROOjinus] *adj* like, containing, iron or iron rust; red-brown, rust-coloured.

ferrule [feRool] *n* metal tip, ring, or band strengthening the end of a stick, tube, handle *etc*.

ferry [feRi] *n* system of transporting passengers or goods across a river or narrow stretch of water; boat, raft *etc* used for this; place of regular passage across water; regular transport service by air; (*leg*) right to operate a ferry and charge fees for its use; **f. pilot** one who flies an aircraft to its operational base ~ **ferry** *v/t* and *i* convey or cross by ferry.

ferryman [feRiman] *n* man operating a ferry.

fertile [furtIl] *adj* able to beget or bear children; abundantly productive; fruitful, prolific; fertilized; (*phys*) (*of an isotope*) one which can be transformed into fissile material by absorbing neutrons > PDS; (*fig*) rich; abundant ~ **fertilely** *adv* ~ **fertileness** *n*.

fertility [furtiliti] *n* state or quality of being fertile; number or rate of offspring born; **f. cult** religious ritual to increase or safeguard the fertility of crops, animals, and persons.

fertilization [furtilIzayshon] *n* act of fertilizing; state of being fertilized.

fertilize [furtilIz] *n* enrich (soil); (*biol*) make female reproductive cell fruitful by union with male cell; (*bot*) pollinate.

fertilizer [furtilIzer] *n* substance added to soil to increase its productivity.

fertle [furt'l] *v/i* use a metal-detector to seek buried objects, *esp.* as a hobby.

ferula [feROOla] *n* giant fennel; ferule.

ferule [feROOl] *n* schoolmaster's rod; ferula.

fervency [furvensi] *n* quality of being fervent.

fervent [furvent] *adj* burning, glowing; (*fig*) passionate, eager, intense ~ **fervently** *adv*.

fervid [furvid] *adj* passionate, intense ~ **fervidly** *adv* ~ **fervidness** *n*.

fervour, (*US*) **fervor** [furver] *n* intense feeling, zeal, ardour; great heat.

fescue [feskew] *n* small twig formerly used by a teacher as a pointer; type of meadow-grass.

fesse [fes] *n* (*her*) horizontal band comprising middle third of shield.

festal [festal] *adj* festive; of a feast; suitable to a great occasion; joyous ~ **festally** *adv*.

fester [fester] *v/i* and *t* become septic, suppurate; rot; cause to fester; (*fig*) become embittered, rankle ~ **fester** *n* ulcer; inflamed tumour.

festival [festival] *n* a feast, celebration; a day or period appointed for celebration, commemoration *etc*; series of musical, dramatic *etc* performances organized in one centre ~ **festival** *adj* of or befitting a feast; joyful, merry.

festive [festiv] *adj* suited to a feast; joyous, merry; convivial ~ **festively** *adv*.

festivity [festiviti] *n* feast; festival; (*freq pl*) merrymaking.

festoon [festOOn] *n* hanging chain or garland of paper, flowers, leaves *etc*; (*archi*) carving or moulding imitating this ~ **festoon** *v/t* adorn with festoons; form into a festoon ~ **festoonery** *n* series of festoons as decoration.

Festschrift [festshRift] *n* (*Germ*) collection of essays presented in honour of an eminent scholar.

fetal see **foetal.**

fetch (1) [fech] *v/t* and *i* go to get and bring back (an object or person); cause to come; induce, draw forth; strike (a blow); realize, bring in (money); (*coll*) charm, attract; **f. and carry** run errands; **f. away** (*naut*) cast off; **f. out** extract, bring out; **f. up at** (*naut* and *coll*) arrive at, stop at; **f. up** (*coll*) vomit ~ **fetch** *n* (*coll*) trick, dodge; **f. of wind** distance from the nearest coast in the direction of the wind > PDE.

fetch (2) *n* apparition or double of a living person; spectre.

fetching [feching] *adj* (*coll*) attractive.

fête [fayt] *n* (*Fr*) feast, festival; outdoor festivity, *esp* in aid of a charity; **f. champêtre** outdoor fête ~ **fête** *v/t* celebrate or honour by a fête.

fetial [feeshal] *adj* (*Rom Hist*) relating to priests who officiated at declaration of war or peace; ambassadorial; **f. law** (*leg*) international law on declaration of war and peace-treaties.

fetich see **fetish.**

fetid, foetid [feetid] *adj* stinking ~ **fetidly** *adv* ~ **fetidness** *n*.

fetidity [feetiditi] *n* stench.

fetish, fetich [fetish/feetish] *n* inanimate object worshipped or feared by savages for its magical powers and used as an amulet; object supposed to be inhabited by a spirit; (*fig*) anything exaggeratedly reverenced or loved; (*psych*) object rousing undue interest by its sexual associations.

fetishism [fetishizm/feetishizm] *n* (*psych*) pathological interest in objects associated with sex > PDP ~ **fetishist** *n* ~ **fetishistic** [fetishistik/feetishistik] *adj*.

fetlock [fetlok] *n* part of horse's leg just behind and above the hoof; tuft of hair growing there.

fetor, foetor [feeter] *n* stench.

fetter [feter] *n* chain for the feet, shackle; (*fig*) restraint, hindrance; captivity ~ **fetter** *v/t* shackle; (*fig*) confine, impede ~ **fetterer** *n*.

fetterlock [feterlok] *n* shackle for a horse.

fettle [fet'l] *n* condition, state; health; (*metal*) lining of furnace ~ **fettle** *v/t* put in order, put finishing touch to; (*metal*) line furnace with loose material ~ **fettler** *n* ~ **fettling** *n*.

fetus see **foetus.**

feud (1) [fewd] *n* prolonged and bitter hostility between two persons, families or clans ~ **feud** *v/i*.

feud (2), **feod** *n* a fief; land held in return for homage and service to an overlord.

feudal [fewdal] *adj* of or pertaining to land held as a feud (2); (*fig*) of or like an old-fashioned and rigid class-system; **f. system** medieval system of land tenure in exchange for services to overlord or king.

feudalism [fewdalizm] *n* feudal system.

feudalistic [fewdalistik] *adj* of or like feudalism.

feudality [fewdaliti] *n* feudal condition; feudal system.

feudalize [fewdalIz] *v/t* convert lands to feudal holdings, bring under the feudal system; reduce to vassalage ~ **feudalization** [fewdalIzayshon] *n*.

feudally [fewdali] *adv* in a feudal way.

feudatory [fewdateRi] *n* vassal holding land by feudal tenure ~ **feudatory** *adj*.

fever [feever] *n* any illness characterized by high temperature; (*fig*) intense nervous excitement; **f. heat** abnormally high body temperature; (*fig*) great intensity ~ **fevered** *adj* affected by fever; excited, overwrought.

feverfew [*feeverfew*] *n* plant of aster family.

feverish [*feeveRish*] *adj* showing symptoms of fever; having slight fever; like, caused by, fever; (*fig*) excited, restless; likely to cause fever ~ **feverishly** *adv* ~ **feverishness** *n*.

few [*few*] *adj* not many, a small number of; **every f.** days at intervals of a few days; **some f.** a fairly large number of ~ **few** *n* not many, a small number; the minority; **the F.** fighter pilots who took part in the Battle of Britain; **a good f., not a f.** a fairly large number.

fey [*fay*] *adj* fated to die, about to die; showing abnormal wild gaiety supposed to presage death; (*coll*) full of whimsical beliefs ~ **feyness** *n*.

fez [*fez*] *n* red flat-topped cap worn by men in some Muslim countries.

fiacre [fee-*aakR*] *n* (*Fr*) four-wheeled cab.

fiancé (*fem* **fiancée**) [fee-*aan*say] *n* man or woman engaged to be married.

fiasco [fee-*askO*] *n* an utter failure.

fiat [*fI*-at] *n* authorization; order, decree.

fib [*fib*] *n* petty, harmless lie ~ **fib** (*pres/part* **fibbing**, *p/t* and *p/part* **fibbed**) *v/i* ~ **fibber** *n*.

fibre [*fIber*] *n* a strand of nerve, muscle, or tissue; anything composed of fibre; raw material for textiles; (*fig*) character; **f. needle** gramophone needle made of bamboo ~ **fibred** *adj*.

fibreboard [*fIberbawrd*] *n* (*bui*) stiff board made from wood pulp, waste paper, or other fibrous material.

fibreglass [*fIberglaas*] *n* glass processed into filaments, used as insulating and constructional material.

fibriform [*fIbRifawrm*] *adj* like a fibre.

fibril [*fIbRil*] *n* a small thread-like fibre > PDP; a root-hair.

fibrillate [*fibRilayt*] *v/i* (*med*) move irregularly, twitch ~ **fibrillation** *n*.

fibrillose [*fIbRilOz*] *adj* of or containing fibrils.

fibrin [*fIbRin*] *n* insoluble protein found in coagulated blood and in vegetable tissue; gluten.

fibrinous [*fIbRinus*] *adj* of or containing fibrin.

fibroid [*fIbRoid*] *n* and *adj* (tumour) like fibre.

fibroin [*fIbRO*-in] *n* chief constituent of silk and cobweb.

fibrolite [*fIbROlIt*] *n* fibrous mineral containing aluminium.

fibrosis [*fIbROsis*] *n* (*med*) morbid growth of fibroid tissue.

fibrositis [*fIbROsItis*] *n* (*med*) inflammation of fibrous tissue, muscular rheumatism.

fibrous [*fIbRus*] *adj* composed or formed of fibres; fibre-like ~ **fibrousness** *n*.

fibster [*fibster*] *n* (*coll*) liar.

fibula [*fibyoola*] *n* (*med*) outer bone of leg, splint-bone; (*arch*) type of brooch ~ **fibular** *adj*.

fichu [*fishOO*] *n* piece of silk, lace *etc* draped round neck and shoulders.

fickle [*fik'l*] *adj* changeable, inconstant, unreliable ~ **fickleness** *n*.

fictile [*fiktIl*] *adj* that can be moulded; moulded; relating to pottery.

fiction [*fik*shon] *n* invented statement or story; literary work describing imaginary events, persons *etc*, *esp* novels or short stories; **legal f.** something assumed to be true for convenience; something known to be false but accepted as true ~ **fictional** *adj* ~ **fictionally** *adv*.

fictionist [*fik*shonist] *n* writer of fiction.

fictitious [fik*tish*us] *adj* invented, imaginary; not genuine, false; relating to a legal fiction ~ **fictitiously** *adv* ~ **fictitiousness** *n*.

fictive [*fiktiv*] *adj* invented; false; pertaining to fiction ~ **fictively** *adv*.

fid [*fid*] *n* (*naut*) wooden pin used in splicing a rope; pin to secure heel of topmast.

fiddle [*fid'l*] *n* (*coll*) violin; any instrument of the violin family; (*naut*) wooden frame to prevent objects from sliding off a table; (*sl*) minor illegal trading operation, a wangle; petty fraud; **as fit as a f.** very healthy; **play second f.** take subordinate place ~ **fiddle** *v/i* and *t* (*coll*) play violin; fidget, play aimlessly with; move restlessly; waste time; (*sl*) sell or buy illegally; contrive by illegal means, wangle.

fiddleback [*fid'l*bak] *n* type of chair-back shaped like a fiddle; mottled veneer on violin backs.

fiddledeedee [fid'l-*deedee*] *exclam* nonsense!

fiddle-faddle [*fid'l*-fad'l] *n* nonsense ~ **fiddle-faddle** *v/i* fuss over trifles.

fiddle-head [*fid'l*-hed] *n* (*naut*) ornamental scroll on ship's bow.

fiddler [*fidler*] *n* one who plays the fiddle; (*sl*) cheat, rogue; (*sl*) sixpence; a small crab.

fiddlestick [*fid'l*stik] *n* violin bow; (*coll*) a trifle ~ **fiddlesticks** *exclam* nonsense!

fiddling [*fidling*] *adj* petty, finicking, trivial; fussy.

fidelity [fi*deliti*/fI*deliti*] *n* faithfulness, loyalty; exactitude; close correspondence with an original; faithfulness in marriage; (*rad etc*) accuracy in reproducing sound.

fidget [*fijit*] *v/i* and *t* make frequent purposeless movements, move restlessly or nervously; irritate, disturb, get on the nerves of ~ **fidget** *n* person who fidgets; (*pl*) nervousness, restlessness ~ **fidgetiness** *n* ~ **fidgety** *adj*.

fiducial [fi*dew*shal] *adj* based on faith or trust; fiduciary; (*math*) assumed as standard of reference for calculation ~ **fiducially** *adv* honestly.

fiduciarily [fidewshi-*airRi*li] *adv* as trustee.

fiduciary [fi*dew*shaRi] *adj* concerning a trustee or trusteeship; held in trust; (*currency*) depending on public confidence ~ **fiduciary** *n* trustee.

fie [*fI*] *exclam* (*freq joc*) exclamation of disapproval or disgust.

fief, feoff [*feef*] *n* land held by feudal tenure.

field [*feeld*] *n* tract of unwooded land, *usu* enclosed and cultivated or used for pasture; tract of land producing coal, oil, minerals *etc*; open land on which games are played; scene of a battle; (*mil*) campaign, battle; wide expanse; plain background (of flag, coin *etc*); area of activity or observation; range; scope of study, province of knowledge; (*phys*) area over which force exerts influence; participants in sports, races *etc*; all competitors in a race except the favourite; (*cricket*) side which is not batting; **hold the f.** maintain one's position; **in the f.** (*sci*) in natural environment or circumstances, not in a laboratory; (*mil*) on active service; **take the f.** begin hostilities ~ **field** *v/t* and *i* (*cricket, baseball etc*) stop (ball) and return it to bowler; act as a fielder; put (team, army *etc*) into the field ~ **field** *adj*.

field-allowance [*feeld*-alow-ans] *n* (*mil*) extra pay for officers on active service.

field-ambulance [feeld-*am*bewlans] *n* (*mil*) medical unit to give emergency treatment on battlefield.

field-artillery [feeld-aar*tile*Ri] *n* (*mil*) light, mobile guns for use with infantry.

field-battery [*feeld*-bateRi] *n* group of field-guns.

fieldbook [*feeld*book] *n* surveyor's notebook recording measurements; naturalist's notebook.

fieldclub [*feeld*klub] *n* society for open-air nature study.

field-day [*feeld*-day] *n* (*mil*) review of field exercises and manoeuvres; (*fig*) day of large-scale activity, display, or celebration; an occasion of outstanding success; day spent on open-air nature study.

fielder [*feeld*er] *n* (*cricket, baseball etc*) one who fields.

field-events [*feeld*-ivents] *n* (*pl*) athletic sports excluding races.

fieldfare [*feeld*fair] *n* migratory bird akin to the thrush.

fieldglass [*feeld*glaas] *n* small binocular telescope.

field-gun [*feeld*-gun] *n* (*mil*) light mobile cannon.

field-hospital [*feeld*-hospital] *n* temporary hospital on or near battlefield.

field-ice [*feeld*-Is] *n* ice lying in large flat tracts.

field-magnet [*feeld*-magnet] *n* magnet which provides a magnetic field > PDS.

field-marshal [feeld-*maar*shal] *n* (*mil*) highest army rank.

field-mouse [*feeld*mows] *n* type of small wild mouse.

field-officer [*feeld*-ofiser] *n* (*mil*) officer above rank of captain and below that of general.

fieldsman [*feeld*z̄man] *n* (*cricket*) a fielder.

field-sports [*feeld*-spawrts] *n* (*pl*) open-air sports, *esp* hunting, shooting, or fishing; athletic sports excluding races.

fieldstone [*feeld*stOn] *n* any type of stone locally found in fields, *esp* when used for building.

fieldwork [*feeld*wurk] *n* scientific observation of natural phenomena in normal environment and conditions; investigation of social phenomena by observation, enquiries and interviews; (*mil*) temporary earthwork.

fiend [*feend*] *n* devil or evil spirit; person of excessive wickedness or cruelty; (*coll*) addict.

fiendish [*feend*ish] *adj* resembling a fiend; extremely cruel or wicked; very unpleasant ~ **fiendishly** *adv* ~ **fiendishness** *n*.

fierce [*feers*] *adj* savage, cruel; unrestrained, violent; intense, strong; (*sl*) very unpleasant ~ **fiercely** *adv* ~ **fierceness** *n*.

fiery [*fIr*Ri] *adj* like fire; bearing or containing fire; glowing, blazing; red; (*of horse*) mettlesome; (*fig*) eager, hasty, enthusiastic; quick-tempered; (*min*) liable to explode; (*med*) inflamed ~ **fierily** *adv* ~ **fieriness** *n*.

fiesta [fee-*esta*] *n* (*Sp*) festival.

fife [*fIf*] *n* small flute mainly used in military music > PDM; fife-player ~ **fife** *v/i* ~ **fifer** *n* a player on the fife.

fifteen [fif*teen*] *n* five more than ten; symbol of this 15; a Rugby football team; **the F.** Jacobite

rising of 1715 ~ **fifteen** *adj* ~ **fifteener** *n* (*pros*) line of fifteen syllables.

fifteenth [fif*teenth*] *adj* following fourteen others in a series; being one of fifteen equal parts ~ **fifteenth** *n* one fifteenth part; fifteenth object in a series; (*mus*) organ stop sounding two octaves above note played.

fifth [*fifth*] *adj* following four others in a series; being one of five equal parts; **f. column** persons within a country who are willing to assist its enemy > PDPol; **f. wheel** (*fig*) unnecessary object ~ **fifth** *n* one fifth part; fifth object in a series; (*mus*) interval reckoned as taking five steps in the scale > PDM; chord of two notes at this interval ~ **fifthly** *adv* in the fifth place.

fiftieth [*fif*ti-eth] *adj* following forty-nine others in a series; being one of fifty equal parts ~ **fiftieth** *n* one fiftieth part; fiftieth object in a series.

fifty [*fif*ti] *n* five times ten; group of fifty persons or things; **the fifties** sixth decade of century or of life ~ **fifty** *adj*.

fifty-fifty [*fif*ti-fifti] *adj* and *adv* equal, equally; **go f.** share equally.

fig (1) [*fig*] *n* soft, pear-shaped, pulpy fruit; tree bearing this fruit; thing of no value; gesture of contempt.

fig (2) *n* (*abbr*) figure.

fig (3) *n* elaborate dress; **in full f.** completely and showily dressed ~ **fig** (*pres/part* **figging**, *p/t* and *p/part* **figged**) *v/t* and *i* dress elaborately or showily; (*sl*) stimulate (horse) with drugs.

fight (*p/t* and *p/part* **fought**) [*fIt*] *v/t* and *i* seek to overcome by violence, strive against; oppose vigorously, struggle against; cause (cocks *etc*) to fight; engage in combat, struggle; (*mil, naut*) manoeuvre or control in battle; **f. down** repress, overcome; **f. off** struggle against, drive violently away; **f. it out** continue fighting till decision is reached; settle (dispute) by fighting; **f. shy of** avoid; **f. one's way** advance, succeed, by fighting ~ **fight** *n* act of fighting; contest, combat, battle; boxing match; conflict; (*coll*) party; ability, inclination for fighting; pugnacity; **free f.** confused, unregulated fight between many persons; **prize f.** boxing match; **show f.** prove one's readiness to fight; **stand-up f.** formal fight according to rules.

fighter [*fIt*er] *n* one who fights; combatant, soldier; boxer; one eager to fight, indomitable person; aeroplane designed to attack other aeroplanes.

fighting [*fIt*ing] *adj* able, eager to fight; trained or bred to fight; designed for combat; **f. chance** possibility of success after struggle.

figleaf [*fig*leef] *n* leaf of figtree; device to conceal sexual organs of statues; (*fig*) hypocritical concealment, flimsy disguise.

figment [*fig*ment] *n* something imagined or invented, fantasy.

figtree [*fig*tRee] *n* tree on which figs grow.

figuline [*fig*ewlIn] *n* pottery; potter's clay; statuette ~ **figuline** *adj*.

figurable [*fig*yoorRab'l] *adj* capable of assuming definite shape ~ **figurability** [figyooRa*bili*ti] *n*.

figural [*fig*yoorRal] *adj* of figures.

figurant (*fem* **figurante**) [*fig*yooRRant] *n* (*Fr*) ballet-dancer, *esp* in walking-on parts.

figuration [figyooRRayshon] *n* act of giving shape

or definite form to; form, shape, pattern; act of decorating with figures; (*mus*) type of florid counterpoint.

figurative [*figyoor*Rativ/*fige*Rativ] *adj* not literally true, metaphorical; symbolic; using many figures of speech; representing a human figure; pertaining to pictorial or plastic representation ~ **figuratively** *adv* ~ **figurativeness** *n*.

figure [*figer*] *n* outer shape, form; shape and proportions of human body; appearance; importance, important person; representation, imitation; statue; diagram; illustration, emblem, symbol; numerical symbol; sum of money; (*geom*) definitely constructed shape enclosed by lines or surfaces; (*log*) form of syllogism; (*gramm*) deviation from normal usage for sake of ornament or rhetorical effect; metaphorical or poetic phrase; (*arts*) decorative device or design; representation of the human form; (*mus*) short phrase, *esp* if repeated; (*dancing*) series of steps, subdivision of a dance; (*skating*) series of intricate movements; (*astrol*) horoscope; **f. of fun** person who looks ridiculous; **at a high (low) f.** dear (cheap) ~ **figure** *v/t* and *i* represent, depict; imagine; illustrate by diagrams; ornament, appear, be prominent in; (*US*) calculate, reckon; make sense; **f. out** calculate; think out, understand.

figured [*figerd*] *adj* ornamented with figures; containing figures of speech; **f. bass** (*mus*) continuo bass whose harmonies are indicated by figures written below bass-note > PDM.

figurehead [*figerhed*] *n* design or bust projecting from stem of ship; (*fig*) nominal leader with no real power.

figure-of-eight [*figer-ov-ayt*] *n* knot, pattern, or movement made in the shape of an eight.

figurine [*figyoor*Reen] *n* a statuette.

filagree see **filigree**.

filament [*filament*] *n* fine thread or fibre; incandescent wire in electric light bulb or wireless valve; (*bot*) stalk of stamen.

filamentary [*filament*eRi] *adj* of a filament.

filar [*fi*laar] *adj* of or relating to a thread; **f. microscope** one having threads stretched across the field of vision.

filaria (*pl* **filariae**) [*filair*Ri-a] *n* (*zool*) genus of parasitic worms infecting blood or tissues ~ **filarial** *adj* ~ **filarious** *adj*.

filariasis [*filair*Ri-asis] *n* (*path*) disease caused by filaria.

filature [*fila*choor] *n* reeling of silk from cocoons; device for doing this; place where this is done.

filbert [*fil*bert] *n* cultivated hazel nut or tree.

filch [*filch*] *v/t* and *i* steal, pilfer ~ **filcher** *n*.

file (1) [*fil*] *n* steel tool with rough surface for cutting through or smoothing metal; piece of stiff emery-paper or metal for smoothing finger nails; (*sl*) cunning person ~ **file** *v/t* smooth, reduce, or cut with a file; (*fig*) polish, perfect.

file (2) *n* stiff wire on which documents are threaded for keeping; box, folder *etc* in which documents are stored; collection of documents classified and kept for reference ~ **file** *v/t* place on or in a file; preserve among official documents.

file (3) *n* row of persons or objects one behind the other; vertical line of squares on chessboard; (*mil*) row of soldiers one behind another; **in f.** (*mil*) drawn up or marching one behind the other;

Indian f., single f. single line of men in file; **rank and f.** (*mil*) privates and corporals; (*fig*) ordinary people, those who are not leaders ~ **file** *v/i* and *t* march in file; pass by one by one; cause (soldiers) to march in files.

filemot [*filimot*] *n* and *adj* yellowish-brown.

filer [*fi*ler] *n* one who or that which files.

filet [*fee*lay] *n* type of square-meshed lace.

filial [*fili*-al] *adj* concerning a son or daughter; suitable to, expected from, son or daughter ~ **filially** *adv* ~ **filialness** *n*.

filiation [*fili-ay*shon] *n* state of being a son; descent; genealogical relationship; formation of new branches *etc* in an organization; (*leg*) determination of paternity of illegitimate child.

filibeg, philibeg [*fili*beg] *n* a kilt.

filibuster [*fili*buster] *n* pirate, adventurer; (*pol*) obstruction of passage of a bill by lengthy speech-making; one who attempts this ~ **filibuster** *v/i* ~ **filibustering** *n* > PDP ~ **filibusterism** *n*.

filicide [*filis*Id] *n* killing of son or daughter; one who does this.

filiform [*fili*fawrm] *adj* thread-like.

filigree, filagree [*filig*Ree, *fila*gRee] *n* delicate ornamental work in fine metal wire; (*fig*) frail, delicate structure.

filing [*fi*ling] *n* act of using a file; particle removed by use of file; act of storing a document on or in a file ~ **filing** *adj* that files; designed for storing documents *etc*; **f. clerk** clerk in charge of records.

filing-cabinet [*fi*ling-kabinet] *n* set of drawers designed for storing documents.

fill [*fil*] *v/t* and *i* put into (a container) as much as it can contain, make full; put large quantity into (a container); become full; occupy (a container) completely; pervade; occupy a post, office *etc*; appoint to a post *etc*; (*naut*) swell (of sails); cause to swell; supply abundantly; **f. the bill** (*coll*) be effective or sufficient; **f. in** complete (document *etc*) by insertion of necessary information; fill (a cavity) completely; **f. in for** temporarily take the place of; **f. (one) in (on)** (*coll*) give (one) detailed explanations (about); **f. out** expand, swell; grow fat; **f. up** fill completely or excessively; complete (document *etc*) by insertion of necessary information ~ **fill** *n* that which fills; as much as is needed; ample supply; (*arch*) material that fills up a pit, trench *etc*.

filler [*filler*] *n* one who or that which fills; tube or vessel used to fill another; opening through which something can be filled; (*eng*) fine mineral powder to stiffen road tars and bitumens; (*chem*) material added to plastics to vary their mechanical properties; (*bui*) paste put on surface after priming to fill up indentations.

fillet [*filit*] *n* narrow strip; thick slice of meat; boneless slice of fish cut lengthwise; head-band; (*print*) line stamped on book-cover; (*archi*) narrow band between two mouldings; narrow strip between flutings of column; (*her*) a horizontal division of a shield; (*pl*) loins of animal, *esp* horse ~ **fillet** *v/t* slice and remove bones of; bind or ornament with a fillet.

fill-in [*fil*-in] *n* and *adj* stopgap.

filling [*fi*ling] *n* material used to fill a cavity or to raise ground to higher level.

filling-station [*fil*ing-stayshon] *n* place where motorists can buy petrol.

fillip [*fil*ip] *n* snap of finger released from pressure of thumb; slight blow given in this way; stimulus, encouragement; mere trifle ~ **fillip** *v/t* and *i* strike or toss by a fillip; rouse, stimulate; snap the fingers.

fillister [*fil*ister] *n* (*joinery*) a rabbet cut in a glazing bar to receive glass and putty; an adjustable plane for rebating glazing bars.

filly [*fil*i]. *n* female foal, young mare; (*coll*) lively young girl.

film [*film*] *n* fine coating, thin layer; filament; (*phot*) flexible strip of sensitized material; reel of this on which cinema picture is photographed; motion-picture, item shown at cinema; art of making motion-pictures ~ **film** *v/t* and *i* cover or become covered with a film; photograph for cinematic reproduction; make, direct, or produce a motion-picture.

filmable [*film*ab'l] *adj* suitable for filming.

filmic [*film*ik] *adj* of or like a cinema film.

filmography [film*og*Rafi] *n* a list of films made by a particular director, or in which a particular actor appeared.

filmpack [*film*pak] *n* set of photographic films for daylight loading.

film-set [*film*-set] *n* furnishings, buildings *etc* used as background for scenes in a film.

film-star [*film*-staar] *n* well-known film actor or actress.

film-studio [*film*-stewdi-O] *n* permanent building in which motion-pictures are made.

film-test [*film*-test] *n* series of photographs taken to test person's suitability for acting in motion-pictures or for a particular part.

filmy [*film*i] *adj* forming a thin layer; covered with a film ~ **filmily** *adv* ~ **filminess** *n*.

filoselle [*fil*osel] *n* floss silk.

filter [*fil*ter] *n* device for separating solids or suspended particles from liquids > PDS; device for purifying water; apparatus for purifying air; any porous substance used in such devices; (*phot*) coloured plate allowing only selected colour or intensity of light to pass; (*rad*) circuit allowing only limited number of frequencies to pass; (*phys*) material excluding certain types of radiation or particles ~ **filter** *v/t* and *i* purify (liquid) by passing it through a filter; strain; pass through a filter, percolate; flow slowly; (*fig*) slowly become known; modify (light, sound *etc*) by passing through a filter; obtain by filtering; (*mot*) drive in specified direction independently of general flow of traffic.

filterable [*filte*Rab'l] *adj* that may be filtered; capable of passing through a filter.

filter-bed [*filter*-bed] *n* reservoir lined with sand, clinker *etc* through which water or sewage is filtered > PDE.

filter-paper [*filter*-payper] *n* (*chem*) porous paper used as a filter.

filter-tip [*filter*-tip] *n* cigarette with a filter at the mouth end ~ **filter-tipped** *adj*.

filth [*filth*] *n* that which defiles, dirt; (*fig*) corruption; obscenity.

filthy [*filth*i] *adj* foul, repellently dirty; obscene; low, mean; (*coll*) very unpleasant ~ **filthily** *adv* ~ **filthiness** *n*.

filtrate [*filt*Rayt] *n* clear liquid after being filtered ~ **filtrate** *v/t* filter ~ **filtration** [filt*Ray*shon] *n.*

fimbriated [*fimb*Ri-aytid] *adj* (*bot, zool*) fringed.

fin [*fin*] *n* flat projecting organ by which fish swim; similar organ in whales, seals *etc*; (*pl*) rubber flippers worn by persons swimming underwater; flat projection on tail of aircraft, airship, rocket or guided missile; (*sl*) the hand ~ **fin** *v/t* and *i* remove fins of; swim as a fish.

finable (1) [*fin*ab'l] *adj* liable to a fine.

finable (2) *adj* that can be purified, clarified, or refined.

finagle [fin*ayg*'l] *v/i* and *t* (*coll*) cheat; obtain by trickery; (*cards*) revoke ~ **finagler** *n.*

final [*fin*al] *adj* at the end, concluding, last; decisive, conclusive; **f. cause** ultimate cause, initiating cause; **f. clause** (*gramm*) clause expressing purpose ~ **final** *n* concluding object or event of a series; last of the day's editions of a newspaper; (*pl*) last and decisive game, race *etc* in a knock-out competition; university degree examination ~ **finally** *adv.*

finale [fin*aa*li] *n* conclusion, end; (*mus*) last movement; ensemble concluding act of opera; (*theat*) concluding number in an entertainment.

finalist [*fin*alist] *n* competitor in finals of a game, race *etc*; candidate at final examination.

finality [fin*al*iti] *n* quality of being final; conclusiveness, completeness; that which is final.

finalization [final*iz*ayshon] *n* act of finalizing.

finalize [*fin*aliz] *v/t* bring to final and definite form; settle, conclude.

finance [*fin*ans/*fin*ans] *n* science of managing money, *esp* public money; (*pl*) monies available to a nation, company or individual ~ **finance** *v/t* provide money or capital for.

financial [fin*an*shal/fin*an*shal] *adj* concerning money matters ~ **financially** *adv.*

financier [fin*an*si-er/fin*an*si-er] *n* one who provides capital for business; an expert in raising and administering public money.

finback [*fin*bak] *n* a rorqual.

finch [*finch*] *n* one of a class of small perching birds.

find (*p/t* and *p/part* **found**) [*find*] *v/t* and *i* discover after search; perceive what was unknown, hidden, or lost; learn by experience or study; obtain; provide; supply; (*leg*) judge, declare to be true; give verdict; **f. out** detect, discover, solve ~ **find** *n* something found; pleasing or useful discovery.

findable [*find*ab'l] *adj* that can be found.

finder [*find*er] *n.* one who or that which finds; (*phot*) external lens on camera, showing image of object to be photographed; small auxiliary telescope for locating object to be observed.

finding [*find*ing] *n* something found; (*leg*) verdict; result of inquiry.

fine (1) [*fin*] *n* (*leg*) sum of money paid as penalty for offence; sum paid at beginning or at transfer of a tenancy ~ **fine** *v/t* punish by a fine.

fine (2) *adj* in good condition, of good quality, excellent; thin; sharp, keen; delicate, skilfully made; minute; rarefied; pure; elegant; discriminating; subtle; elaborate, polished; pretentious, showy; (*of weather*) not raining; **f. arts** arts having aesthetic qualities rather than utilitarian; **one f. day** (*coll*) some time or other ~

fine adv (coll) very well; **cut it f.** leave a bare minimum or narrow margin (esp of time) ~ **fine** v/t and i refine, purify; become purer or more delicate; **f. down** make or become thinner or more delicate.

fine-draw [fin-dRaw] v/t sew together two edges of material so that the join or mending is invisible; draw (wire) out very thinly ~ **fine-drawn** adj invisibly mended; drawn out very thinly; (fig) subtly argued; over-ingenious.

finely [finli] adv in a fine way.

fineness [fin-nis] n quality of being fine.

finery (1) [fineRi] n elaborate clothes, jewels etc.

finery (2) n furnace for refining iron or for steel.

fine-spun [fin-spun] adj fragile, thin, delicate; (fig) over-subtle, over-elaborated.

finesse [fines] n tact, diplomatic skill, dexterity; artfulness; (cards) attempt to take a trick with a low card while holding a higher card of the same suit ~ **finesse** v/t and i.

finger [fing-ger] n one of five parts of end of hand; one of these other than the thumb; part of glove covering a finger; anything shaped like finger; pointer on clock-face or dial; long narrow piece; measure based on breadth or length of finger; **have a f. in** have a share in; **lay a f. on** touch, harm; **not lift a f.** do nothing; **put one's f. on** point out exactly, ascertain accurately; **put the f. on** (sl) inform against; **twist round one's little f.** dominate, influence ~ **finger** v/t touch, hold with fingers, handle; (mus) play (instrument) with fingers; play (note or series of notes) with particular finger or fingers; mark the fingering on a piece of music; (coll) pilfer; take or accept illegally.

finger-alphabet [fing-ger-alfabet] n series of positions of hands and fingers used as symbols for letters by the deaf and dumb.

fingerboard [fing-gerbawrd] n (mus) part of stringed instrument against which fingers press the strings; a keyboard.

fingerbowl [fing-gerbOl] n small bowl of water placed on table for rinsing fingers during a meal.

fingering (1) [fing-geRing] n fine woollen yarn.

fingering (2) n (mus) the use of the fingers in playing an instrument; indication on paper of which fingers are to be used for which notes > PDM.

fingernail [fing-gernayl] n thin horny growth at end of finger.

fingerplate [fing-gerplayt] n flat plate fixed near latch of a door to protect surface from fingermarks.

fingerpost [fing-gerpOst] n signpost at crossroads giving directions.

fingerprint [fing-gerpRint] n impression of the skin-pattern at the fingertip, used as means of identification ~ **fingerprint** v/t take fingerprints of.

fingerstall [fing-gerstawl] n protective sheath for finger.

fingertip [fing-gertip] n tip of finger; sheath protecting this; **have at one's fingertips** know thoroughly; have ready for use; **f. control** (of machine) with controls close at hand and easy to manipulate.

finial [fini-al] n (archi) ornamental feature placed at the base or apex of a gable, or on the top of a pinnacle.

finical [finikal] n fussy, over-particular; petty, trivial; too elaborate; full of petty detail ~ **finically** adv ~ **finicalness** n.

finicality [finikaliti] n quality of being finical.

finicking, finikin [finiking, finikin] adj finical.

finicky [finiki] adj finical.

fining [fining] n process of refining or purifying; (pl) preparation used for clarifying beer etc.

finis [finis] n the end, termination.

finish [finish] v/t complete, bring to an end; put an end to, destroy, kill; cease, come to an end; put final touches to, make perfect; **f. off** bring to an end; kill; **f. up** eat the whole of; conclude; end up ~ **finish** n last part, conclusion, end; completeness; perfection; that which completes or perfects; a final coat of paint or its appearance; **fight to a f.** fight till one combatant is thoroughly crushed ~ **finished** adj complete; perfect; accomplished.

finisher [finisher] n worker or machine carrying out last stage in manufacturing process; (coll) knock-out blow.

finishing [finishing] adj last; perfecting; **f. school** girls' school specializing in training for social life ~ **finishing** n completion; standard of workmanship.

finite [finit] adj bounded, having definite limits; of limited number or dimensions; (gramm) (of verb) having person, number and tense ~ **finitely** adv ~ **finiteness** n.

finitude [finitewd/finitewd] n finiteness.

fink [fink] n (US sl) despicable person, swine; informer, squealer; prig ~ **fink** v/t and i inform (against); squeal; **f. off** treacherously run away.

finnan [finan] n smoked haddock.

finner [finer] n whale with a dorsal fin, a rorqual.

Finnic [finik] n language of Finns; group of languages to which this belongs ~ **Finnic** adj pertaining to Finns or to their language.

Finnish [finish] n and adj (language) of the Finns.

finnoc [finok] n (Scots) white trout.

finny [fini] adj having fins; fin-like; of, teeming with, fish.

fino [feenO] n pale dry sherry.

fiord, fjord [fee-awrd] n long narrow steep-sided inlet into sea-coast > PDG.

fir [fur] n name of various coniferous trees; wood from these.

fircone [furkOn] n hard scaly fruit of a fir-tree.

fire [fir] n chemical action accompanied by light, heat, and flame; burning; destructive outbreak of burning; quantity of burning fuel; fever; discharge of firearms, (fig) strong feeling or imagination; energy; passion; light, glow; **between two fires** attacked from two sides at once; **catch f.** begin to burn; **go through f. and water** face the greatest perils; **hang f.** (of gun) be slow in going off; (coll) be slow, delay; **lay a f.** prepare fuel in fireplace; **on f.** burning; **open f.** begin to shoot; **play with f.** take unnecessary risks; **running f.** rapid gunfire; rapid series of questions, comments etc; **set f. to, set on f.** cause to burn; rouse feelings of, excite greatly; **set the Thames on f.** achieve some wonderful success; **under f.** (mil) exposed to enemy guns; (fig) attacked, criticized ~ **fire** v/t and i cause to burn, kindle;

290

supply fuel to; bake in kiln; dry by heat; shoot, discharge (guns *etc*); (*fig*) rouse, excite; (*fig*) utter rapidly or aggressively; (*coll*) dismiss (from post); (*cer*) react to heat; **f. away** (*coll*) begin, go ahead; **f. up** grow suddenly angry.

fire-alarm [*fɪr*Ralaarm] *n* signal to give warning of outbreak of fire.

firearm [*fɪr*Raarm] *n* weapon from which a missile is discharged by an explosive.

fireball [*fɪr*bawl] *n* large meteor.

firebomb [*fɪr*bom] *n* small bomb designed to set fire to houses *etc* in which it is left hidden.

firebox [*fɪr*boks] *n* place for fire in boiler *etc*.

firebrand [*fɪr*bRand] *n* flaming piece of wood; (*fig*) one eager to excite others to anger.

firebreak [*fɪr*bRayk] *n* strip of land cleared of trees *etc* to check advance of forest fire.

firebrick [*fɪr*bRik] *n* heat-resisting brick.

fire-brigade [*fɪr*-bRigayd] *n* body of men organized to combat fires.

firebug [*fɪr*bug] *n* firefly; (*sl*) arsonist.

fireclay [*fɪr*klay] *n* clay rich in silica and alumina, used in firebricks.

fire-control [*fɪr*-kontROl] *n* (*mil*) regulation of a battery's fire from some central point.

firedamp [*fɪr*damp] *n* explosive mixture of methane and air, formed in coal-mines.

firedog [*fɪr*dog] *n* iron support for logs on open hearth, andiron.

firedrill [*fɪr*dRil] *n* fire-brigade practice; organized practice of routine to be followed in case of fire.

fire-eater [*fɪr*Reeter] *n* entertainer who claims to swallow burning material; (*fig*) quarrelsome person.

fire-engine [*fɪr*Renjin] *n* vehicle carrying pumps, ladders *etc* for dealing with outbreaks of fire.

fire-escape [*fɪr*Riskayp] *n* metal staircase on exterior of building; extensible ladder or other device for rescue from burning building.

fire-extinguisher [*fɪr*Reksting-gwisher] *n* portable container of chemicals which can be sprayed on fire to extinguish it > PDS.

fire-fighter [*fɪr*-ftter] *n* voluntary auxiliary fireman to combat fires caused by enemy bombing.

firefly [*fɪr*flI] *n* insect emitting a phosphorescent glow.

fireguard [*fɪr*gaard] *n* wire screen round fireplace.

firehose [*fɪr*hOz] *n* large flexible tube for aiming a jet of water at a fire.

fire-insurance [*fɪr*RinshoorRans] *n* insurance against loss by fire.

fire-irons [*fɪr*RIrnz] *n* implements for tending a domestic fire.

fireless [*fɪr*les] *adj* without a fire; lacking fire.

firelight [*fɪr*lIt] *n* light cast by a fire.

firelighter [*fɪr*lIter] *n* piece of highly inflammable material for kindling fire.

firelock [*fɪr*lok] *n* obsolete musket whose priming was ignited by sparks.

fireman [*fɪr*man] *n* stoker; member of fire-brigade; (*min*) colliery official responsible for safety from fires.

fire-office [*fɪr*Rofis] *n* office of fire-insurance company.

fireplace [*fɪr*plays] *n* opening in a room for a fire, with a flue above.

fireplug [*fɪr*plug] *n* hydrant to which fire-hose can be connected.

fire-policy [*fɪr*-polisi] *n* insurance policy against loss by fire.

fireproof [*fɪr*pROOf] *adj* fire-resisting, non-inflammable.

fire-raiser [*fɪr*-Rayzer] *n* one who deliberately sets fire to buildings, arsonist ~ **fire-raising** *adj* and *n*.

firescreen [*fɪr*skReen] *n* screen to ward off the heat of a fire.

fireship [*fɪr*ship] *n* burning ship sent among enemy vessels to set fire to them.

fireside [*fɪr*sId] *n* part of room near fireplace; (*fig*) home-life, home.

firespotter [*fɪr*spoter] *n* a firewatcher.

fire-station [*fɪr*-stayshon] *n* headquarters of a fire-brigade.

firestone [*fɪr*stOn] *n* fireproof stone.

firewarden [*fɪr*wawrden] *n* official appointed to prevent or check forest fires; senior firewatcher.

firewatcher [*fɪr*wocher] *n* person posted to watch for fires caused by enemy bombing ~ **firewatching** *n*.

firewater [*fɪr*wawter] *n* (*coll*) strong, crude alcoholic drink.

firewood [*fɪr*wood] *n* wood for fuel, *esp* wood chopped small for lighting a fire.

firework [*fɪr*wurk] *n* small container holding explosive material which will flare, sparkle, go off with a bang *etc* when lit; (*pl*) a pyrotechnic display; (*fig*) display of anger.

firing [*fɪr*Ring] *n* action of setting on fire; baking, subjecting to treatment by great heat; discharge of guns; stoking; fuel; **f. line** (*mil*) area nearest to enemy positions; soldiers in that area; **f. party** soldiers detailed to shoot condemned man, or to fire salute at soldier's burial; **f. point** temperature at which a substance is liable to ignite or fuse; **f. squad** firing party.

firkin [*fur*kin] *n* small cask; a measure of capacity, about 9 gallons.

firm (1) [*furm*] *n* business company or partnership; name under which a company operates.

firm (2) *adj* not yielding easily to pressure, solid; fixed, stable; resolute, unwavering, stern; strong and steady; (*comm*) not depreciating, not fluctuating ~ **firm** *v/t* and *i* make or become firm ~ **firm** *adv*.

firmament [*furm*ament] *n* the sky.

firman [*furm*en] *n* an edict, decree.

firmly [*furm*li] *adv* in a firm way.

firmness [*furm*nis] *n* quality of being firm.

firry [*fur*Ri] *adj* of or containing fir-trees.

first [*furst*] *adj* earliest in order or time; foremost, chief; highest in rank or quality; original, primary; **f. thing** at earliest possible moment ~ **first** *n* the beginning; one who or that which is first; place in first class of examination or competition; one who has such a place; highest prize; (*mus*) part highest in pitch; leading part > PDM ~ **first** *adv* before anything else; for the first time; (*coll*) in preference, rather.

first-aid [furst-*ayd*] *n* immediate help to an injured person.

firstborn [*furst*bawn] *adj* and *n* eldest (child).

first-class [furst-*klaas*] *adj* belonging to highest

grade, best; excellent ~ **first-class** *adv* (*coll*) excellently.

first-floor [furst-*flawr*] *n* storey next above ground-floor; (*US*) ground-floor ~ **first-floor** *adj*.

first-foot [*furst*-foot] *n* first person to enter a house in the New Year.

first-fruits [*furst*-frOOts] *n* (*pl*) earliest products of harvest, *esp* if consecrated to God; earliest results.

firsthand [furst-*hand*] *adj* based on personal observation, obtained directly.

firstling [*furstling*] *n* first offspring of an animal; (*fig*) first result.

firstly [*furst*li] *adv* first.

first-night [furst-*nIt*] *n* first public performance of play *etc* ~ **first-nighter** *n* one who regularly attends opening performances.

firstrate [furst*Rayt*] *adj* of best quality; excellent ~ **firstrate** *adv* ~ **firstrate** *n* (*naut*) ship of largest and most powerful class.

firth [*furth*] *n* estuary; fjord.

fiscal [*fiskal*] *adj* pertaining to the public revenue; financial; **Procurator F.** (*Scots*) public prosecutor in minor cases ~ **fiscal** *n* public prosecutor ~ **fiscally** *adv*.

fish (1) (*pl* **fishes** or **fish**) [*fish*] *n* cold-blooded finned vertebrate, living in water and breathing by gills; any animal living in water; flesh of such animals used as food; (*coll*) fellow; **cry stinking f.** disparage oneself; **feed the fishes** (*coll*) be seasick; drown; **have other f. to fry** have other things to do; **f. out of water** person ill at ease in unsuitable surroundings; **pretty kettle of f.** (*coll*) muddle, trouble ~ **fish** *v/t* and *i* catch, or try to catch, fish; seek creatures or objects under water; **f. for** (*coll*) try to obtain by hinting or by leading questions; **f. in troubled waters** try to make profits from difficulties of others; **f. out** bring out from deep or inaccessible place; **f. up** pull up out of water; fish out ~ **fishable** *adj*.

fish (2) *n* flat piece of wood or metal used as strengthening or jointing plate; counter used in games ~ **fish** *v/t* join or strengthen with a fish.

fishball [*fish*bawl] *n* fried rissole of fish.

fishcake [*fish*kayk] *n* fishball.

fish-day [*fish*-day] *n* (*eccles*) abstinence day on which no meat may be eaten.

fisher [*fisher*] *n* fisherman; fishing-boat; animal that catches fish.

fisherman [*fisherman*] *n* man who catches fish for a living or as sport; fishing-boat.

fishery [*fish*eRi] *n* industry or business of catching fish; fishing ground; (*leg*) right to fish in certain waters.

fish-farming [*fish*-faarming] *n* controlled rearing of fish for food, *esp* in ponds or tanks.

fish-glue [*fish*-glOO] *n* glue made from bones and skin of fish boiled down.

fish-hawk [*fish*-hawk] *n* the osprey.

fish-hook [*fish*-hook] *n* barbed hook for catching fish.

fishily [*fish*ili] *adv* in a fishy way.

fishiness [*fish*inis] *n* quality of being fishy.

fishing [*fish*ing] *n* action or skill of catching fish; fishing-ground; right of catching fish in certain waters; stretch of water over which this right is held ~ **fishing** *adj* that fishes; designed for the catching of fish.

fish-kettle [*fish*-ket'l] *n* long oval saucepan.

fishknife [*fish*nIf] *n* blunt broad-bladed knife, for eating fish.

fish-ladder [*fish*-lader] *n* channel along which fish can travel past weir or dam.

fishmeal [*fish*meel] *n* powdered dried fish.

fishmonger [*fish*mung-ger] *n* one who sells fish.

fishnet [*fish*net] *adj* and *n* wide-meshed (fabric).

fishpaste [*fish*payst] *n* savoury sandwich spread made from fish or shellfish.

fishplate [*fish*playt] *n* steel plate joining rails of railway line > PDE.

fishpot [*fish*pot] *n* wicker trap for crabs, lobsters, eels *etc*.

fishslice [*fish*slIs] *n* utensil for lifting and turning fish when cooking; broad, blunt knife for serving fish at table.

fishtail [*fish*tayl] *adj* shaped like a fish's tail; **f. burner** gas-burner producing flat divided jet; **f. wind** wind continually shifting direction ~ **fishtail** *v/i* (*aer*) reduce speed of aircraft by swinging it or its tail from side to side.

fishwife [*fish*wIf] *n* woman who goes round selling fish; (*fig*) vulgar scolding woman.

fishy [*fish*i] *adj* like fish; full of fish; made from fish; (*fig*) (*of eyes*) dim, lustreless; (*coll*) dubious, dishonest, arousing suspicion.

fissile [*fis*Il] *adj* able to be split; inclined to split; capable of nuclear fission.

fissility [fis*ili*ti] *n* quality or state of being fissile.

fission [*fish*on] *n* splitting off, breaking up into parts; (*biol*) cellular division for reproduction > PDB; **nuclear f.** (*phys*) breaking up of heavy atoms into lighter atoms, with great release of energy > PDS ~ **fission** *v/i* (*phys*) break up into lighter atoms.

fissionable [*fish*onab'l] *adj* easily undergoing fission.

fissiparous [fisi*paR*us] *adj* (*biol*) reproducing by fission.

fissiped [*fis*iped] *adj* with separated toes.

fissure [*fish*er] *n* cleft, crack, narrow opening; (*anat*) narrow opening between lobes of an organ; crack in tissue or bone ~ **fissure** *v/t* and *i* split.

fist [*fist*] *n* clenched hand; (*coll*) hand; handwriting ~ **fist** *v/t* strike with fist, punch; (*naut*) grasp.

fistful [*fist*fool] *n* handful.

fistic [*fist*ik] *adj* (*coll*) concerned with boxing.

fisticuffs [*fist*ikufs] *n* (*pl*) fighting with the fists.

fistula [*fis*choola] *n* (*path*) narrow winding ulcer; abnormal opening caused by discharge from ulcer; (*ent*) pipe-like organ.

fistular [*fis*choolar] *adj* of or like a fistula; tubular, like a pipe.

fistulose [*fis*choolOz] *adj* fistular.

fit (1), **fytte** [*fit*] *n* (*ar*) section of long poem.

fit (2) *n* sudden sharp attack of some illness, spasm; (*pl*) convulsions; sudden bout; whim, mood; passing burst of energetic action; **by fits and starts** spasmodically; **throw a f.** (*coll*) become very angry or alarmed.

fit (3) (*pres/part* **fitting**, *p/t* and *p/part* **fitted**) *v/t* and *i* be of correct size and shape for; be well adjusted, adapted or suitable for; adjust, adapt; make suitable; supply with what is suitable; try on unfinished garment to see if adjustments are needed; **f. in** be well adapted to; **f. on** try on unfinished garment; **f. out** equip, furnish with supplies *etc*; **f. up** make ready, furnish, equip

~ **fit** *n* adjustment; way in which one thing fits another; that which fits ~ **fit** *adj* suitable, adjusted, appropriate; worthy; right, seemly; ready; in good health or condition.

fitch [*fich*] *n* the polecat; polecat's fur; small brush made of this.

fitchew [*fich*OO] *n* the polecat.

fitful [*fit*fool] *adj* irregular, spasmodic, capricious ~ **fitfully** *adv* ~ **fitfulness** *n*.

fitly [*fit*li] *adv* becomingly, appropriately.

fitment [*fit*ment] *n* built-in furniture; equipment accessory, detachable part of machine *etc*.

fitness [*fit*nes] *n* state or quality of being fit; good health.

fit-out [*fit*-owt] *n* (*coll*) equipment, outfit.

fitter [*fit*er] *n* one who or that which fits; tailor who fits and tries on clothes; skilled mechanic who can assemble machines or adjust their parts.

fitting [*fit*ing] *n* act of adjusting one thing to another; that which is adjusted; (*pl*) furnishings or equipment, *esp* fixtures in a building; detachable or accessory part of machine ~ **fitting** *adj* that fits; suitable; seemly ~ **fittingly** *adv* ~ **fittingness** *n*.

fit-up [*fit*-up] *n* (*theat*) makeshift stage scenery and properties; touring troupe using this.

five [*ftv*] *n* cardinal number next above four; symbol of this number, 5 ; group of five persons or things; card *etc* marked with five pips; score of five at a game; (*pl*) gloves, shoes *etc* of size five; ~ **five** *adj* one more than four.

fivefold [*ftv*fOld] *adj* five times as numerous; made up of five parts ~ **fivefold** *adv.*

fiver [*ftv*er] *n* (*coll*) five-pound note.

fives [*ftvz*] *n* ball-game played in walled court

fivescore [*ftv*skawr] *n* one hundred.

fix [*fiks*] *v/t* and *i* fasten, attach firmly, make secure; become fixed, congeal; decide on, settle; make permanent; ascertain; direct unwaveringly; gaze steadily at; concentrate; (*coll*) arrange, put in order; mend; prepare; (*coll*) render harmless or helpless; (*chem*) make stable or solid; (*phot*) render insensitive by washing in chemicals; (*sl*) arrange by bribery or trickery; (*sl*) get even with (a person); (*sl*) inject oneself with drugs; **f. on** decide on, choose; **f. up** arrange, organize; decide on, settle; (*coll*) make arrangements for; mend ~ **fix** *n* (*coll*) awkward situation; (*naut, aer*) position determined by bearings or radio; (*sl*) injection of drug ~ **fixable** *adj.*

fixate [*fiks*ayt] *v/t* and *i* make or become fixed; (*psych*) arrest (emotional development) at early stage ~ **fixated** *adj.*

fixation [*fiks*ayshon] *n* act of fixing; state of being fixed; focusing; (*bot, zool*) treatment of a specimen with a reagent preparatory to microscopic study > PDB; (*chem*) conversion of atmospheric nitrogen into nitrates for use as fertilizers > PDS; (*psych*) exclusive emotional attachment to one object or to early stage of development > PDP; (*coll*) obsession, fixed idea.

fixative [*fiks*ativ] *n* and *adj* (chemical substance) which fixes colour of drawing or photograph; (reagent) which fixes specimen for microscopic study; (gummy substance) which fixes hair in desired position.

fixed [*fikst*] *adj* unmoving; firmly attached; rigid; unalterable, stable, settled; (*chem*) non-volatile;

f. idea persistent or recurrent idea tending to dominate one's outlook, minor obsession > PDP; **f. star** true star (contrasted with planets, comets *etc*) ~ **fixedly** [*fiks*idli] *adv* ~ **fixedness** *n.*

fixer [*fiks*er] *n* one who or that which fixes; chemical which fixes photograph, dye *etc.*

fixing [*fiks*ing] *n* act of person or thing that fixes; (*phot*) rendering of sensitive film insensitive to exposure after developing > PDS; (*pl*) (*coll*) outfit; accessories, trimmings ~ **fixing** *adj* that fixes.

fixity [*fiks*iti] *n* state of being fixed.

fixture [*fiks*cher] *n* thing permanently attached to another; essential part (of apparatus *etc*); (*pl*) (*leg*) fittings attached to a building or land and legally constituting a part thereof; thing not easily moved; (*coll*) person long established in a place; permanent feature; sporting event to be held on date fixed in advance.

fizgig [*fiz*gig] *n* spluttering firework, squib; (*coll*) flirtatious girl; gadget.

fizz [*fiz*] *n* spluttering, hissing noise; effervescence; (*coll*) champagne; strongly effervescent drink ~ **fizz** *v/i* hiss; effervesce.

fizzer [*fiz*er] *n* that which fizzes; (*coll*) something first-rate; (*cricket*) a very fast ball.

fizzle [*fiz*'l] *v/i* fizz slightly; **f. out** peter out in weak splutterings; (*fig*) come to nothing, end lamely ~ **fizzle** *n* act of fizzling; (*coll*) abortive effort, fiasco.

fizzy [*fiz*i] *adj* that fizzes.

fjord see **fiord.**

flabbergast [*flab*ergaast] *v/t* (*coll*) astonish; disconcert.

flabby [*flab*i] *adj* hanging loose, limp; (*fig*) feeble, lacking energy ~ **flabbily** *adv* ~ **flabbiness** *n.*

flaccid [*flak*sid] *adj* flabby, limp; (*fig*) weak, without energy ~ **flaccidly** *adv* ~ **flaccidness** *n.*

flaccidity [*flaks*iditi] *n* limpness; weakness.

flag (1) [*flag*] *n* plant with blade-like leaf, *esp* iris; leaf of such a plant; type of coarse grass.

flag (2) *n* slab of stone, paving-stone; pavement of stone slabs; type of rock splitting easily into slabs ~ **flag** (*pres/part* **flagging,** *p/t* and *p/part* **flagged**) *v/t* pave with stone slabs.

flag (3) *n* (*pl*) (*orni*) the quill-feathers of a bird's wing; leg feathers of hawk, owl *etc.*

flag (4) *n* piece of cloth of distinctive colour or bearing distinctive emblem displayed from pole or halyard as signal, symbol, or decoration; (*naut*) admiral's ensign; flagship; slip of paper used as bookmarker; (*print*) corrector's mark indicating omission; attachment to taximeter showing whether taxi is engaged or not; **black f.** emblem of piracy or death; **green f.** signal of safety; **f. of convenience** foreign flag under which ships are registered to avoid taxes or other liabilities; **red f.** danger signal; symbol of Socialism, Communism, or revolution; **show the f.** (*coll*) put in an appearance; **strike the f.** lower a flag; (*fig*) surrender; **white f.** signal of truce or surrender; **yellow f.** signal of contagious disease; ~ **flag** (*pres/part* **flagging,** *p/t* and *p/part* **flagged**) *v/t* decorate with flags; signal by means of flag; **f. down** (*coll*) signal to car to stop.

flag (5) (*pres/part* **flagging,** *p/t* and *p/part*

293

flagged) *v/i* droop, hang limply; grow weak, diminish.

flag-day [*flag*-day] *n* day on which money is collected for charity by selling small paper flags or emblems to contributors.

flagellant [*flaj*elant] *n* one who whips himself or others for religious or erotic motives, *esp* member of medieval sect who practised public whipping ~ **flagellant** *adj*.

flagellate [*flaj*elayt] *v/t* scourge, whip.

flagellated [*flaj*elaytid] *adj* (*biol*) having a flagellum.

flagellation [flajel*ay*shon] *n* scourging.

flagelliform [flajel*ifa*wrm] *adj* (*biol*) shaped like a whiplash.

flagellum (*pl* **flagella**) [flaj*el*um] *n* (*biol*) long whip-like outgrowth of cell > PDB; (*bot*) runner, creeping shoot.

flageolet [*flaj*olet] *n* wind instrument of recorder type with six finger-holes > PDM.

flagging [*flag*ing] *n* pavement of flagstones; flag-stones.

flaggy [*flag*i] *adj* abounding in reeds or flags; having a large leaf; made of flagstones.

flagitious [flaj*ish*us] *adj* extremely wicked, criminal; vile, disgraceful ~ **flagitiously** *adv* ~ **flagitiousness** *n*.

flag-lieutenant [flag-left*en*ant] *n* admiral's aide.

flagman [*flag*man] *n* one who signals with flags.

flag-officer [*flag*-ofiser] *n* admiral, vice-admiral or rear-admiral.

flagon [*flag*on] *n* large vessel for serving wine; large wine bottle.

flagrance, flagrancy [*flayg*Rans, *flayg*Ransi] *n* quality of being flagrant.

flagrant [*flayg*Rant] *adj* scandalous, obviously evil, notorious ~ **flagrantly** *adv*.

flagship [*flag*ship] *n* ship carrying, and flying the flag of, the commander of the squadron.

flagstaff [*flag*staaf] *n* pole from which a flag is suspended.

flagstone [*flag*stOn] *n* large paving stone.

flagwagging [*flag*waging] *n* (*coll*) semaphore signalling; aggressively patriotic talk.

flail [*flayl*] *n* wooden implement for threshing corn by hand; **f. tank** (*mil*) tank fitted with revolving chains to detonate landmines ~ **flail** *v/t* thresh with a flail; beat.

flair [*flair*] *n* instinctive perception or discernment; natural aptitude, gift or bent.

flak [*flak*] *n* anti-aircraft guns or gunfire.

flake (1) [*flayk*] *n* storage or drying rack; workman's cradle slung over ship's side.

flake (2) *n* fleecy particle of snow; thin light layer or scale; carnation with striped flowers; **f. tobacco** thin layers of tobacco cut from compressed block ~ **flake** *v/t* and *i* split into flakes; fall in flakes; cover with flakes; mark with streaks; **f. out** (*coll*) become unconscious, fall asleep from exhaustion.

flake-white [*flayk*-wIt] *n* white pigment made from scales of white lead.

flaky [*flayk*i] *adj* made of or like flakes; splitting into flakes ~ **flakily** *adv* ~ **flakiness** *n*.

flam [*flam*] *n* a sham story; trick, deception; false flattery ~ **flam** *v/t* deceive, hoax.

flambeau (*pl* **flambeaux** or **flambeaus**) [*flam*bO] *n* large ceremonial torch.

flamboyance [flamb*oi*-ans] *n* showiness; exaggerated behaviour or speech ~ **flamboyant** *adj* showy, exaggerated; (*archi*) having flame-like tracery > PDA ~ **flamboyantly** *adv*.

flame [*flaym*] *n* glowing mass of gas rising from burning matter; fiery yellowish-red colour; fiery glow, vivid light; (*fig*) violent emotion, passion; intensity of thought, imagination *etc*; (*coll*) sweetheart ~ **flame** *v/i* emit flames, burn, blaze; glow brightly; be fiery red or yellow; blush violently; show violent excitement, anger *etc*.

flamen [*flay*men] *n* (*Rom hist*) priest dedicated to a particular god.

flamenco [flamenk*O*] *n* Spanish, particularly Andalusian, gipsy style of music and dance > PDM.

flame-thrower [*flaym*-thRO-er] *n* (*mil*) apparatus to project a burning stream of fuel oil at enemy positions.

flaming [*flaym*ing] *adj* emitting flames; hot; brilliant, brightly coloured; intense, passionate; (*coll*, *euph*) bloody ~ **flamingly** *adv*.

flamingo [flaming-g*O*] *n* aquatic bird with scarlet plumage, long legs and webbed feet.

flammable [*flam*ab'l] *adj* (*US* and *comm*) easily catching fire ~ **flammability** [flamab*ili*ti] *n*.

flamy [*flaym*i] *adj* of or like flame.

flan [*flan*] *n* round shallow open tart; disc of metal to be stamped as coin.

flanch [*flansh*] *n* a flange.

flâneur [flaan*ur*] *n* (*Fr*) idler, lounger.

flange [*flanj*] *n* projecting rim, disc, edge or rib on pipe, wheel, girder *etc* > PDE; tool for making flanges ~ **flange** *v/t* provide with a flange.

flank [*flank*] *n* fleshy part of side of animal or human being between ribs and hip; side of mountain, building *etc*; (*mil*, *naut*) side of armed force; **turn the f.** (*mil*) get round the side of ~ **flank** *v/t* and *i* (*mil*, *naut*) protect the flank of; attack the flank of; place troops at the flank of; be at the side of, stand beside.

flanker [*flank*er] *n* fortification protecting or menacing a flank; (*pl*) skirmishers defending flanks of marching army.

flannel [*flan*el] *n* loosely woven woollen material; piece of this used for rubbing *etc*; (*pl*) clothes made of flannel, *esp* sporting or casual trousers; (*sl*) nonsense; flattery ~ **flannel** *adj* made of flannel ~ **flannel** (*pres/part* **flannelling**, *p/t* and *p/part* **flannelled**) *v/t* rub with flannel ~ **flannelly** *adj*.

flannelette [flanel*et*] *n* cotton cloth resembling flannel.

flap (*pres/part* **flapping**, *p/t* and *p/part* **flapped**) [*flap*] *v/t* and *i* slap lightly; move quickly up and down; flutter loosely, *esp* with slight noise; hang down; (*coll*) get into a panic ~ **flap** *n* action or movement of flapping; noise made by flapping object; light blow from broad flexible object; hinged hanging part of table; piece of material attached over an opening and hanging so as to cover it; any broad flexible object partly attached and hanging loose; (*coll*) panic, nervousness.

flapdoodle [flapd*ood*'l] *n* nonsense.

flap-eared [*flap*-eerd] *adj* having broad drooping ears.

flapjack [*flap*jak] *n* large pancake; flat powder-compact.

flapper [*flap*er] *n* one who or that which flaps; fly-whisk; device for scaring birds; flipper; young wild duck or game-bird; (*obs coll*) young girl; (*sl*) hand.

flare [*flair*] *n* bright, unsteady blaze of light; vivid, briefly burning light used as signal, or by aircraft to illuminate target area; bright flame used as torch on airfields or roads in fog; (*coll*) outburst of anger; outward spread or curve, bulge ~ **flare** *v/i* burn brightly but unsteadily; emit brief dazzling light; (*of lamp etc*) burn up too high; spread outwards, swell; **f. up** blaze suddenly; (*fig*) grow suddenly and violently angry.

flarepath [*flair*paath] *n* illuminated landing strip of aerodrome.

flare-up [*flair*-up] *n* burst of flame, sudden blaze; (*fig*) sudden outbreak of anger, fighting *etc*.

flash [*flash*] *n* sudden brief bright ray of light; brief outburst of emotion; brief moment, instant; (*coll*) vulgar showiness; (*cin*) brief extract from film; brief announcement of news item, advertisement *etc*; distinguishing mark of cloth worn on uniform; rapid gush of water from weir; lake caused by subsidence; **in a f.** very rapidly; at once; **f. in the pan** something that begins brilliantly but soon fails ~ **flash** *v/t* and *i* emit a flash or series of flashes; light up, sparkle, gleam; pass rapidly by; (*fig*) pass suddenly through the mind, occur to one; show brilliance; signal by means of flashing lights; transmit by radio, telegraphy *etc*; direct sudden ray of light upon; (*fig*) direct (glance, smile *etc*) rapidly at; display rapidly and briefly; (*coll*) display showily, swagger; (*coll*) briefly display one's sexual organs ~ **flash** *adj* (*coll*) showy, smart; sham, forged; pertaining to the underworld.

flashback [*flash*bak] *n* (*cin*) sudden transition to earlier part of story; passage in novel describing events before main period of story.

flasher [*flash*er] *n* one who or that which flashes; automatic device to switch electric lamps on and off; boiler to raise heat of steam; (*coll*) one who indecently exposes his sexual organs.

flash-flood [*flash*-flud] *n* sudden localized flood.

flashgun [*flash*gun] *n* device to operate flashlight of camera.

flashily [*flash*ili] *adv* in a flashy way.

flashiness [*flash*inis] *n* quality of being flashy.

flashing [*flash*ing] *n* act of one who flashes; (*bui*) strips of metal or felt on roof areas to protect joints or projections against damp; method of brick burning to produce varied coloration.

flashlight [*flash*lìt] *n* light that flashes periodically; small electric torch; lamp used for signalling by flashes; dazzling momentary light used in taking photographs in darkness or dim light.

flashpoint [*flash*point] *n* lowest temperature at which a substance gives off sufficient vapour to ignite > PDS; (*fig*) place or moment at which violent trouble is likely to begin.

flashy [*flash*i] *adj* showy but worthless.

flask [*flaask*] *n* small flattened bottle for carrying spirits or wine in pocket; small narrow-necked bottle; (*ar*) container for carrying gunpowder.

flat [*flat*] *adj* level, having even surface, *gener* horizontal; only slightly raised or projecting; stretched along ground, prone, levelled; (*fig*)

dull, unvaried; depressed; (*comm*) inactive; (*mus*) lowered in pitch; one semitone below note indicated; (*painting*) uniform; not suggesting distance or depth; with little gloss or lustre; (*comm*) at fixed uniform rate; (*coll*) absolute, downright sheer, complete; (*of liquor*) no longer sparkling, stale; (*of tyre*) deflated; **f. race** race on level ground, without obstacles to be jumped; **f. spin** (*aer*) loss of control in flying; (*fig*) panic; **that's f.** (*coll*) that is final, plain, or certain ~ **flat** *adv* lying on ground, prone; (*mus*) below true pitch; (*coll*) entirely, directly; exactly; (*coll*) bluntly; definitely; **fall f.** fail to impress; **go f. out** (*coll*) move or act as fast as possible, strive with all one's energy ~ **flat** *n* that which is flat; flat side or part; suite of rooms on one floor arranged as self-contained dwelling; (*pl*) house divided into several such units; area of flat land, *esp* low-lying marshy land; level foreshore; shallow water, shoal; (*mus*) sign denoting lowering of pitch by a semitone; (*theat*) scenery mounted on frame and pushed on from wings; (*coll*) dupe, fool.

flatfish [*flat*fish] *n* any fish with both eyes on same side of head and broad flattened body.

flat-footed [flat-*foot*id] *n* having flat soles of feet, with little or no arch at instep; (*coll*) clumsy, stupid.

flat-iron [*flat*-ìrn] *n* implement for ironing clothes.

flatlet [*flat*let] *n* two- or three-roomed flat.

flatly [*flat*li] *adv* plainly, bluntly, decidedly; **in a** dull manner.

flatness [*flat*nis] *n* state or quality of being flat.

flat-rate [*flat*-Rayt] *adj* equal, the same in every case; not graduated or proportional.

flatten [*flat*en] *v/t* and *i* make flat; become flat; **f. out** flatten by spreading out; (*aer*) fly horizontally again after climbing or diving; (*fig*) crush, disconcert.

flatter [*flat*er] *v/t* and *i* praise insincerely; try to please by insincere praise; represent too favourably; please, gratify; (*refl*) congratulate oneself, feel agreeably certain ~ **flatterer** *n* ~ **flattering** *adj* and *n* ~ **flatteringly** *adv*.

flattery [*flat*eRi] *n* exaggerated or insincere praise.

flatting [*flat*ing] *n* act of pressing or beating flat; the resawing of timber parallel to one edge; paint with a dull non-glossy finish; **f. down** smoothing wood surfaces with glasspaper *etc*.

flattish [*flat*ish] *adj* somewhat flat.

flatulence, flatulency [*flat*ewlens, *flat*ewlensi] *n* accumulated gas in stomach or intestines; (*fig*) pretentiousness ~ **flatulent** *adj* suffering from flatulence; (*fig*) empty, vapid.

flatus [*flay*tus] *n* flatulence.

flaunt [*flawnt*] *v/t* and *i* wave proudly; display ostentatiously or offensively; make fine display, be magnificent ~ **flaunting** *adj* and *n* ~ **flauntingly** *adv*.

flautist [*flaw*tist] *n* flute-player.

flavin, flavine [*flay*vin, *flay*veen] *n* a yellow dye.

flavour [*flay*ver] *n* taste; flavouring; (*fig*) characteristic atmosphere, strong suggestion ~ **flavour** *v/t* give flavour to, season; (*fig*) give characteristic quality to; give zest to; suggest strongly.

flavouring [*flay*veRing] *n* substance used to add flavour to food; spice, essence *etc*.

flaw (1) [*flaw*] *n* crack; defect, fault, blemish; (*leg*)

imperfection invalidating a document ~ **flaw**
v/t break, crack.
flaw (2) *n* sudden squall.
flawless [*flaw*les] *adj* free from flaws, perfect ~
flawlessly *adv* ~ **flawlessness** *n*.
flax [*flaks*] *n* plant whose seeds produce linseed
oil, and whose fibres produce linen; fibre from
this plant.
flaxen [*flak*sen] *adj* of or like flax; pale yellow.
flax-lily [*flaks*-lili] *n* New Zealand lily-like plant
producing tough fibres.
flax-seed [*flaks*-seed] *n* linseed.
flay [*flay*] *v/t* strip off the skin or hide from; to
skin; beat severely; (*fig*) criticize savagely.
flea [*flee*] *n* small blood-sucking leaping insect;
small beetle resembling this; **f. in one's ear**
sharp rebuke.
fleabag [*flee*bag] *n* (*coll*) sleeping bag; hammock.
fleabane [*flee*bayn] *n* strong-smelling plant, said
to drive away fleas.
fleabite [*flee*bIt] *n* bite of flea; (*fig*) trifling discomfort.
fleabitten [*flee*biten] *adj* infested with fleas; (*of
horse*) having light coat flecked with reddish hair;
(*coll*) dingy, shabby.
fleam [*fleem*] *n* (*surg*) lancet, *esp* for opening veins.
fleapit [*flee*pit] *n* (*coll*) shabby, dirty room, building *etc*.
fleawort [*flee*wurt] *n* kind of plantain.
flèche [*flaysh*] *n* (*Fr*) (*archi*) a slender spire.
fleck [*flek*] *n* spot, speck; particle ~ **fleck** *v/t* to
spot, streak ~ **flecked** *adj*.
flection see **flexion.**
fled [*fled*] *p/t* and *p/part* of flee and of fly (3).
fledge [*flej*] *v/t* and *t* grow first crop of feathers;
rear (young bird); provide feathers for; **fully
fledged** able to fly; (*fig*) qualified, expert; adult.
fledgeling [*flej*ling] *n* young bird just fledged;
(*fig*) inexperienced young person.
flee (*p/t* and *p/part* fled) [*flee*] *v/t* and *i* run away
from, escape or try to escape by running; (*fig*)
avoid, shun; retreat hastily; vanish rapidly.
fleece [*flees*] *n* wool growing on sheep; mass of
freshly-shorn wool; soft woolly mass ~ **fleece**
v/t shear wool from; (*fig*) rob, swindle, plunder
by trickery or extortion.
fleecy [*flee*si] *adj* covered with fleece; resembling
fleece; soft, woolly; curly ~ **fleeciness** *n*.
fleer [*fleer*] *v/t* grin mockingly at; sneer, jeer.
fleet (1) [*fleet*] *n* number of warships under one
chief command; number of vessels engaged in the
same occupation; navy; (*coll*) group of vehicles
belonging to one owner; group of large vehicles
travelling together.
fleet (2) *adj* moving swiftly and lightly, rapid ~
fleet *v/i* and *t* move or pass swiftly and silently;
(*naut*) shift (rope, blocks *etc*).
fleet-footed [fleet-*foot*id] *adj* able to run very fast.
fleeting [*fleet*ing] *adj* rapid; passing away ~
fleetingly *adv*.
Fleming [*flem*ing] *n* native of Flanders.
Flemish [*flem*ish] *n* and *adj* (language or inhabitants) of Flanders.
flench, flense, flinch [*flensh, flenz, flinsh*] *v/t*
skin (a seal); strip blubber from (whale).
flesh [*flesh*] *n* soft tissue of body covering bones;
edible animal tissue, meat; soft pulp of fruit or
vegetable; (*arts*) surface of body; colour of this;

body, physical nature of man; (*fig*) sensuality,
physical cravings, lust; (*poet*) mankind; **in the f.**
alive; in bodily form; actually present; **one's
own f. and blood** one's relations; **proud f.**
granulated tissue forming over wound ~ **flesh**
v/t give portion of fresh-killed game to (hound or
hawk); thrust (sword) into flesh, *esp* for first time;
(*fig*) initiate into bloodshed; inure, harden.
flesh-coloured [*flesh*-kulerd] *adj* pale pink.
fleshed [*flesht*] *adj* plump, fleshy; hardened,
inured to bloodshed.
flesh-hook [*flesh*-hook] *n* hook used to hang meat,
or to remove it from the cooking-pot.
fleshiness [*flesh*ines] *n* plumpness.
fleshing [*flesh*ing] *n* inciting (hawk, hound) to the
chase by a taste of the game killed; (*pl*) flesh-
coloured tights.
fleshly [*flesh*li] *adj* pertaining to the body; carnal,
sensual ~ **fleshliness** *n*.
fleshpot [*flesh*pot] *n* pot for cooking meat; (*fig*)
luxury greatly wished for.
fleshy [*flesh*i] *adj* pertaining to, like, flesh; plump,
fat; bodily.
fletch [*flech*] *v/t* put feather on (an arrow) ~
fletcher *n* arrow-maker.
fleur-de-lis [flur-de-*lee*] *n* (*Fr*) heraldic lily.
flew [*flOO*] *p/t* of **fly** (2).
flews [*flOOz*] *n* (*pl*) hanging chaps of bloodhound.
flex (1) [*fleks*] *v/t* and *i* bend; (*geol*) (*of strata*)
fold.
flex (2) *n* cord or cable of insulated wire.
flexibility [fleks*i*biliti] *n* ability to bend.
flexible [*fleks*ib'l] *adj* capable of being bent;
supple; (*fig*) adaptable; compliant ~ **flexibly** *adv*.
flexile [*fleks*il] *adj* flexible.
flexion [*flek*shon] *n* act of bending; state of being
bent; degree to which something is bent; (*gramm*)
inflexion; fold; curve; modulation ~ **flexional** *adj*.
flexor [*flek*ser] *n* muscle which bends joint or limb
inwards.
flexuose [fleks-yOO-Os] *adj* (*bot*) winding.
flexuosity [fleks-yOO-ositi] *n* sinuosity.
flexuous [fleks-yOO-us] *adj* flexuose.
flexure [*flek*sher] *n* act of bending or curving;
bent part; state of being bent or curved.
flibbertigibbet [fliberti*jibit*] *n* flighty, restless,
irresponsible person.
flick [*flik*] *v/t* strike sharply and lightly, jerk, flip;
f. through rapidly turn pages of, read superficially ~ **flick** *n* sharp light blow, tap, snap;
rapid jerk; rapid, jerking twist or stroke.
flicker [*flik*er] *v/i* burn unsteadily; waver, quiver;
flutter ~ **flicker** *n* flickering movement; unsteady gleam, brief dart of flame.
flickering [*flik*eRing] *adj* burning unsteadily;
quivering.
flick-knife [*flik*-nIf] *n* knife whose blade springs
out when a button on the handle is pressed.
flicks [*fliks*] *n* (*pl*) (*coll*) cinema.
flier see **flyer.**
flight (1) [*flIt*] *n* act of flying; movement, passage,
or journey through air; (*fig*) swift passage, passing
away (of time *etc*); manner of flying; distance
flown; (*fig*) bold mental effort; number of creatures or objects flying together; unit or formation
of aeroplanes; flock of birds, *esp* migrating; volley
of arrows; series of stairs or terraces; (*archery*)
contest in distance shooting; arrow used for this;

in the first f. best, finest, first-class ~ **flight** *v/t*
and *i* shoot (birds flying in flock); put feather in
(arrow); fly or migrate in a flock; deliver (cricket
ball) of deceptive length and tantalizing trajectory.

flight (2) *n* act of running away, fleeing; **take f.**
flee; **put to f.** rout, defeat utterly.

flight-deck [*flīt*-dek] *n* (*naut*) level deck of aircraft-carrier, used as runway for aircraft.

flighted [*flītid*] *adj* (*of arrow*) feathered; (*of cricket
ball*) of deceptive length and tantalizing trajectory.

flightily [*flītili*] *adv* in flighty manner ~ **flighti-
ness** *n*.

flight-lieutenant [flīt-left*en*ant] *n* rank in Air
Force equivalent to captain in army.

flighty [*flīti*] *adj* frivolous, fickle, capricious.

flimsy [*flimzi*] *adj* light and thin; frail, slight,
weak ~ **flimsy** *n* (*coll*) thin paper; paper for
carbon copy; newspaper copy; (*sl*) banknote;
telegram ~ **flimsily** *adv* ~ **flimsiness** *n*.

flinch (1) [*flinsh*] *v/i* draw back in fear or pain.

flinch (2) see **flench.**

flinders [*flinderz*] *n* (*pl*) fragments, splinters.

fling (*p/t* and *p/part* **flung**) [*fling*] *v/t* and *i* throw
violently, hurl; move vigorously or impulsively;
(*of horse*) kick; **f. in one's teeth** reproach, taunt
with; **f. oneself into** (*fig*) take up enthusiastically or vigorously ~ **fling** *n* act of flinging;
sudden violent movement; (*fig*) sarcastic taunt,
jibe; (*coll*) bout of pleasure or dissipation; outburst of rage or other emotion; **Highland f.**
Scottish dance in which arms and legs are moved
rapidly and energetically.

flint [*flint*] *n* very hard natural variety of impure
silica; piece of this used to produce spark; prehistoric tool or weapon made of flint; piece of
hard alloy used to produce spark in automatic
lighter; (*fig*) hard-hearted person, miser; **skin a
f.** (*coll*) be very miserly ~ **flint** *adj* made of flint.

flintglass [*flint*glaas] *n* variety of brilliant glass
containing lead silicate.

flintlock [*flint*lok] *n* old type of gun where spark
is produced by striking flint against steel.

flinty [*flinti*] *adj* consisting of flint; full of flint-
stones; hard as flint; (*fig*) hard, unfeeling ~
flintily *adv* ~ **flintiness** *n*.

flip (1) [*flip*] *n* drink composed of hot milk, egg,
sugar and wine or spirits.

flip (2) (*pres/part* **flipping,** *p/t* and *p/part* **flipped**)
v/t and *i* flick, tap or toss smartly, *esp* by jerk of
thumb or fingernail; (*sl*) rouse, make enthusiastic;
f. through rapidly turn pages of, read superficially ~ **flip** *n* act of flipping; sharp tap or
stroke; recoil of gun-barrel; (*sl*) short flight in
aeroplane; **f. side** (*coll*) reverse side of a gramophone record, containing item(s) less popular than
the main side.

flip (3) *adj* (*sl*) mocking, flippant.

flip-flap [*flip*-flap] *adj* and *adv* with flapping
movement or noise.

flip-flops [*flip*-flops] *n* (*pl*) loose sandals held by a
single thong.

flippancy [*flip*ansi] *n* disrespect, frivolity; pertness ~ **flippant** *adj* ~ **flippantly** *adv*.

flipper [*flip*er] *n* limb of animal adapted for swimming; (*sl*) hand.

flipping [*fliping*] *adj* (*coll*) bad, unpleasant.

flirt [*flurt*] *v/i* and *t* play at courtship without

serious intentions, endeavour to attract the opposite sex; show superficial interest in, toy with; move
abruptly and jerkily; open and close (a fan) smartly
~ **flirt** *n* person (*esp* girl) who flirts with many
of the opposite sex, coquette; sudden jerk, flick.

flirtation [flurt*ay*shon] *n* act of flirting.

flirtatious [flurt*ay*shus] *adj* fond of flirting ~
flirtatiously *adv* ~ **flirtatiousness** *n*.

flirty [*flurti*] *adj* inclined to flirt.

flit (*pres/part* **flitting,** *p/t* and *p/part* **flitted**) [*flit*]
v/i fly or move about rapidly and quietly; move
to another house, *esp* by stealth ~ **flit** *n* act of flitting; stealthy change of dwelling-place.

flitch [*flich*] *n* side of bacon salted and cured;
steak of halibut ~ **flitch** *v/t* cut into flitches.

flite [*flīt*] *v/t* and *i* (*Scots*) quarrel, abuse, scold;
exchange jocular insults ~ **fliting** *n*.

flitter [*flīter*] *v/i* flutter.

flittermouse [*flīter*mows] *n* a bat.

flitting [*flīting*] *n* act of one who flits; stealthy
change of dwelling-place.

flivver [*flīver*] *n* (*sl*) cheap motorcar.

float [*flŌt*] *v/i* and *t* rest or drift on surface of
liquid; be suspended in liquid; glide through, be
carried along through the air; (*fig*) move aimlessly, drift; cause to float, set afloat; (*of liquid*)
bear on surface, buoy up; cover surface with
liquid; (*comm*) put in circulation, launch, set
going ~ **float** *n* that which floats; cork or quill on
fishing-line; mass of cork buoying up fishing-net;
raft; flat-bottomed boat; hollow floating ball
regulating water-level in cistern; device to regulate amount of petrol in carburettor; air-bladder
of a fish; shallow, low-floored cart; wheeled platform or lorry carrying a tableau in a pageant;
(*theat*) footlights; board on paddle-wheel;
wooden tool for smoothing plaster.

floatage [*flŌtij*] *n* act of floating; flotsam; part of
ship above water-line.

floatation, flotation [flŌt*ay*shon] *n* act of floating;
(*comm*) launching of a new company by an issuing house; study of floating bodies; (*metal*)
method of separating certain mixtures by the
tendency of their components to sink or float;
centre of f. centre of gravity of floating body.

floater [*flŌter*] *n* one who or that which floats;
(*coll*) security payable to bearer; (*sl*) blunder.

floating [*flŌting*] *adj* that floats, resting or drifting
on or near surface of liquid; (*fig*) changeable,
fluctuating; (*of cargo*) at sea; (*med*) displaced;
f. assets current, liquid assets; **f. bridge** bridge
of boats, of logs covered by planks *etc*; **f. dock**
steel floating structure with sides > PDE; **f.
kidney** kidney liable to abnormal displacement;
f. light buoy bearing light; lightship; **f. policy**
insurance policy the application of which is not at
first specified; **f. rib** one of the lower ribs not
attached to breastbone; **f. vote** that portion of the
electorate not committed to one party.

flocculate [*flok*ewlayt] *v/t* and *i* form flocculent
masses; aggregate ~ **flocculation** *n*.

floccule [*flok*ewl] *n* small portion of wool; flaky
substance in precipitate.

flocculence [*flok*ewlens] *n* woolliness; flakiness.

flocculent [*flok*ewlent] *adj* woolly, flaky, fluffy.

flock (1) [*flok*] *n* assemblage, crowd; number of
sheep or other domestic animals; assemblage of
gregarious birds; (*fig*) group of persons under

one leader; body of Christians; congregation ~
flock v/i crowd together, form a flock; assemble
in large numbers.

flock (2) n small tuft of wool; (pl) waste fibres
used to stuff furniture, beds etc; flaky precipitate; (coll) fluffy fibres of wool used to make flockpaper ~ **flock** v/t stuff or coat with flocks; give
rough surface to (glass) ~ **flocky** adj.

flockbed [flokbed] n bed stuffed with wool or
cotton waste.

flockpaper [flokpayper] n wallpaper dusted with
flock to give a textile effect.

floe [flO] n large sheet of floating ice.

flog (pres/part **flogging**, p/t and p/part **flogged**)
[flog] v/t and i beat with stick or whip, thrash;
urge on by beating; (cricket) hit hard; (coll)
sell or barter, esp illicitly; (of sails) flap noisily;
f. a dead horse waste one's efforts; **f.
the water** (fishing) cast fly repeatedly.

flogging [floging] n punishment by beating.

flong [flong] n paper for stereotyping.

flood [flud] n large body of water covering land
normally dry, inundation, deluge; rising tide;
copious outpouring of liquid, torrent; (fig) profuse flow, outburst; **the F. flood** described in
Genesis; **at the f.** (fig) at most favourable
moment ~ **flood** v/t and i cover with large
quantity of water, inundate; discharge much
water into or over; overflow; (of tide) rise; (fig)
overwhelm, fill excessively; (med) have uterine
haemorrhage.

floodgate [fludgayt] n adjustable sluice in a watercourse gate to control flood water.

flooding [fluding] n inundation; (mining) inrush
of water; (med) uterine haemorrhage.

floodlight [fludlIt] n powerful artificial light;
beam from such a light ~ **floodlight** (p/t and
p/part floodlighted or floodlit) v/t illuminate by
floodlights; (fig) reveal dramatically.

floodlighting [fludlIting] n illumination of the
outside of a building at night with powerful
searchlights from below.

floodtide [fludtId] n rising tide.

floor [flawr] n horizontal surface forming bottom
of room, passages, or building; main area of a
hall etc; storey, horizontal division of building;
level bottom (of sea etc); (comm) lower limit (of
prices); **take the f.** (coll) begin to dance; address
a meeting ~ **floor** v/t furnish with a floor; knock
to the ground; (coll) defeat, reduce to silence;
puzzle; (sl) answer correctly.

floorboard [flawrbawrd] n one of a set of planks
forming a wooden floor.

floorcloth [flawrkloth] n cloth for washing floors;
linoleum or other covering material for floors.

floorer [flawrRer] n (coll) question or remark that
cannot easily be answered.

flooring [flawrRing] n boards, tiles etc that form a
floor; decorative surface of a floor; act of knocking down, defeating, or silencing.

floorshow [flawrshO] n cabaret entertainment.

floorwalker [flawrwawker] n supervisor in a large
shop.

floosie, floozy [flOOzi] n (sl) prostitute.

flop (pres/part **flopping**, p/t and p/part **flopped**)
[flop] v/i and t move limply, heavily and clumsily;
fall clumsily or noisily; flap about; (coll) fail
utterly; (sl) sleep; throw down, let fall clumsily

and noisily ~ **flop** n act or noise of flopping;
(coll) utter failure, fiasco ~ **flop** adv.

flophouse [flophows] n disreputable lodging house.

floppy [flopi] adj limp, slack ~ **floppiness** n.

flora [flawRa] n plant population of particular
area; list of plant species > PDB.

floral [flawRal] adj pertaining to, adorned with
flowers or representations of flowers; pertaining
to floras ~ **florally** adv.

florescence [flawResens] n blossoming; period of
flowering; period of success or achievement.

florescent [flawResent] adj flowering.

floret [flawRit] n (bot) small separate flower within
head of composite flower; small flower.

floriated [flawRi-aytid] adj decorated with floral
ornament.

floribunda [floRibunda] n type of rose bearing
clusters of blossoms.

floriculturalist [flawRikulcheRalist] n one whose
trade is the cultivation of flowers.

floriculture [flawRikulcher] n cultivation of
flowering plants.

florid [floRid] adj elaborately ornamented; (of
complexion) ruddy, gaudy, showy ~ **floridity**
[floRiditi] n ~ **floridness** n ~ **floridly** adv.

floriferous [flawRifeRus] adj bearing flowers
abundantly.

florin [floRin] n British silver coin worth two
shillings (i.e. ten new pence); gold coin of
Edward III worth six shillings and eightpence.

florist [floRist] n person who grows flowers commercially; dealer in flowers.

floruit [flawrRoo-it] n period during which a writer
or artist was producing work.

floss [flos] n rough outer fibres of silkworm's
cocoon; silk spun from this; waxed silk thread
used for cleaning between the teeth ~ **flossy** adj.

flotation see floatation.

flotilla [flotila] n small fleet; fleet of small vessels.

flotsam [flotsam] n (leg) wreckage or goods found
floating on the sea.

flounce (1) [flowns] n sudden jerking movement,
esp of anger ~ **flounce** v/i move abruptly and
jerkily, esp in anger.

flounce (2) n ornamental strip of lace, silk etc,
gathered and sewn round edge of garment ~
flounce v/t trim with flounces.

flounder (1) [flownder] n small flatfish.

flounder (2) v/i struggle clumsily forward, esp
through mud or water; (fig) hesitate, make blund-
ers in speaking.

flour [flowr] n finely ground meal, esp of wheat;
very fine powder resembling this ~ **flour** v/t
cover with flour.

flourish [fluRish] v/i and t be healthy and vigorous, thrive; (fig) be active, produce one's works;
brandish, wave about; decorate with flowery
ornament; (mus) sound fanfare; improvise ornamentation ~ **flourish** n sweeping gesture;
brandishing; decorative sweeping pen-strokes;
elaborate ornamentation; (mus) fanfare; decorative figuration; florid extemporized passage.

flourishing [fluRishing] adj prosperous, well and
happy ~ **flourishingly** adv.

floury [flowrRi] adj covered with flour; of flour;
resembling flour.

flout [flowt] v/t and i mock at, insult, show scorn
of ~ **flout** n scornful jest, jibe.

flow [*flO*] *v/i* (*of liquids*) move along unceasingly and smoothly, gush, run freely; (*of blood*) circulate; (*fig*) move steadily, copiously, or smoothly; fall in loose graceful folds or curls; (*of tide*) rise; be poured out, issue ~ **flow** *n* act or manner of flowing; that which flows, stream; rising tide; (*fig*) steady copious supply or movement.

flower [*flowr*] *n* coloured head of plant consisting of petals; any plant producing these, except shrubs and trees; (*bot*) part of plant containing reproductive organs > PDB; state or period of blooming; representation of flower; (*fig*) rhetorical ornament; best part, finest specimen; prime of life; (*pl*) (*chem*) scum formed by fermentation; powdery deposit remaining after distillation; (*coll*) menstruation; **F. Children, F. People** (*coll*) hippies bedecked with flowers, bells and beads and preaching universal love; **F. Power** the ideals of Flower Children ~ **flower** *v/i* and *t* produce flowers, bloom; (*fig*) reach finest state of development; cause (plant) to flower; decorate with flowers.

flowerbed [*flowr*bed] *n* plot of earth containing flowering plants.

flowered [*flowrd*] *adj* decorated with pattern of flowers.

floweret [*flowr*Rit] *n* small flower.

floweriness [*flowr*Rinis] *n* quality of being flowery.

flowering [*flowr*Ring] *adj* bearing flowers; cultivated for its flowers.

flowerpiece [*flowr*pees] *n* painting of flowers.

flowerpot [*flowr*pot] *n* earthenware or plastic pot in which plants can be grown.

flower-show [*flowr*-shO] *n* competitive exhibition of flowers.

flowery [*flowr*Ri] *adj* full of flowers; like flowers; decorated with flowers; ornate, elaborate.

flowing [*flO*-ing] *adj* that flows; smoothly moving; smoothly curving; easy and copious, fluent; hanging in graceful folds ~ **flowingly** *adv*.

flown [*flOn*] *p/part* of **fly** (2).

flu [*flOO*] *n* (*coll*) influenza.

fluctuate [*fluk*choo-ayt] *v/i* move periodically up and down or backwards and forwards; vary, be unstable; (*fig*) hesitate; (*US*) cause to vary ~ **fluctuating** *adj*.

fluctuation [flukchoo-*ay*shon] *n* act of fluctuating; degree to which a thing fluctuates.

flue (1) [*flOO*] *n* pipe or duct conveying smoke or hot air; small chimney, branch of chimney; (*mus*) mouthpiece of an organ flue-pipe.

flue (2) *n* kind of fishing net.

flue (3) *n* light fluff or down.

flue (4) *v/i* and *t* (*bui*) be splayed; splay.

fluence [*flOO*-ens] *n* (*coll abbr*) influence, *esp* irrational or hypnotic.

fluency [*flOO*-ensi] *n* ready command of language, ease in speaking; graceful movement.

fluent [*flOO*-ent] *adj* speaking easily and well; moving gracefully ~ **fluent** *n* (*math*) a constantly varying quantity in fluxions ~ **fluently** *adv*.

flue-pipe [*flOO*-pip] *n* organ-pipe into which air is made to enter directly > PDM.

fluff [*fluf*] *n* light soft mass of down, dust, wool, or fur; first growth of beard; **bit of f.** (*sl*) girl ~ **fluff** *v/t* and *i* make fluffy, puff out; become fluffy; (*theat coll*) make mistakes through

faulty memory, stumble over lines; (*sl*) bungle, make mistakes in.

fluffy [*fluf*i] *adj* of or like fluff; covered with fluff; (*theat*) uncertain of one's lines ~ **fluffily** *adv* ~ **fluffiness** *n.'*

fluid [*flOO*-id] *adj* moving freely, flowing; (*fig*) mobile, easily changing ~ **fluid** *n* (*pop*) a liquid; (*chem*) a liquid or gas ~ **fluidic** *adj*.

fluidify [flOO-*id*ifi] *v/t* make fluid.

fluidity [flOO-*id*iti] *n* state of being fluid; (*phys*) reciprocal of viscosity.

fluidize [*flOO*-idiz] *v/t* make fluid.

fluke (1) [*flOOk*] *n* flounder or other flatfish; parasitic flatworm > PDB; variety of kidney potato.

fluke (2) *n* pointed triangular end on each arm of an anchor; barbed head of harpoon, lance, arrow *etc*; lobe of whale's tail.

fluke (3) *n* (*billiards etc*) lucky shot made by accident; (*coll*) unexpected piece of good luck ~ **fluke** *v/i* and *t* make a fluke; have unexpected luck; gain by a fluke.

fluky (1) [*flOO*ki] *adj* infested by parasitic flukes.

fluky (2) *adj* of or by unexpected good luck.

flume [*flOOm*] *n* artificial open channel used in sluicing or for water power; (*US*) narrow ravine cut out by a stream ~ **flume** *v/i* and *t* make a flume; convey by a flume.

flummery [*flume*Ri] *n* almond-flavoured blancmange; (*coll*) nonsense, humbug; flattery.

flummox [*flum*oks] *v/t* (*coll*) confound, disconcert, puzzle.

flump [*flump*] *v/i* and *t* (*coll*) fall with dull thud; throw down heavily ~ **flump** *n*.

flung [*flung*] *p/t* and *p/part* of **fling**.

flunk [*flunk*] *v/t* and *i* (*sl*) shirk; fail (examination); cause to fail.

flunkey [*flunk*i] *n* man-servant in livery; (*fig*) toady, servile flatterer.

fluor [*flOO*-er] *n* any mineral containing fluorine.

fluoresce [floo-e*Res*] *v/i* become fluorescent.

fluorescence [floo-e*Res*ens] *n* property of emitting light of different wavelength from that absorbed, so producing coloured luminosity > PDS.

fluorescent [floo-e*Res*ent] *adj* exhibiting fluorescence; **f. lamp** electric lamp consisting of cathode-ray tube coated with fluorescent material.

fluoridation [flOO-eRI*day*shon] *n* addition of fluorides to drinking water to prevent dental decay.

fluoride [*flOO*-eRId] *n* (*chem*) binary compound of fluorine.

fluorine [*flOO*-eReen] *n* (*chem*) pale yellowish-green gas resembling chlorine > PDS.

fluorite [*flOO*-eRIt] *n* fluorspar.

fluorocarbon [flOO-oRO*kaar*bon] *n* type of hydrocarbon in which hydrogen has been partially or totally replaced by fluorine, used in plastics, refrigerants, lubricants *etc*.

fluoroscope [floo-e*Rosk*Op] *n* instrument for examining internal structures by shadows cast by X-rays on a fluorescent screen.

fluorspar [*flOO*-erspaar] *n* natural calcium fluoride > PDS.

flurry [*flu*Ri] *n* sudden gust of wind; hurry and commotion; agitation of mind; death-throes of harpooned whale ~ **flurry** *v/t* bewilder, fluster.

flush (1) [*flush*] *v/t* and *i* drive (birds) from hiding place; (*of birds*) fly up suddenly ~ **flush** *n* flock of birds startled into flight; act of flushing birds.

flush (2) *v/i* and *t* flow suddenly and copiously; (*of blood*) rush to skin; blush, grow red; (*fig*) glow red; cleanse by rush of water, wash out; cause to blush, redden; (*fig*) exhilarate ~ **flush** *n* rush of water; rush of blood, blush; sudden growth; act of cleansing by flushing; mechanism for flushing drain *etc*; (*fig*) exhilaration, rush of emotion; height of vigour; abundance; sudden feeling of heat ~ **flushed** *adj* ~ **flushing** *n*.

flush (3) *adj* full to the brim, in full flow; forming one continuous surface, in same plane; even, level; (*coll*) having plenty of money; lavish; abundant; direct ~ **flush** *adv* on one level, in one plane ~ **flush** *v/t* make level.

flush (4) *n* (*cards*) hand containing only cards of same suit; run of same suit ~ **flush** *adj* consisting of cards of same suit.

fluster [*fluster*] *v/t* and *i* bewilder, make nervous; be nervous, get excited and agitated; be confused by drink ~ **fluster** *n* state of being flustered.

flute [*flOOt*] *n* (*mus*) wind-instrument without reeds, having blow-hole at side and holes stopped by fingers or keys; similar archaic instrument having blow-hole at end > PDM; flautist in orchestra; organ-stop resembling sound of flute; (*archi*) narrow vertical groove on column *etc*; similar groove in material *etc* ~ **flute** *v/t* and *i* play (tune) on flute; play flute; sing in flute-like tones; decorate with flutes ~ **fluted** *adj* decorated with flutes; flutelike, mellow.

flutiness [*flOOtinis*] *n* quality of being fluty.

fluting [*flOOting*] *n* act of playing a flute; shallow groove or series of grooves.

flutist [*flOOtist*] *n* player on a flute.

flutter [*fluter*] *v/i* and *t* move wings quickly or nervously; fly aimlessly to and fro; wave or flap quickly; vibrate, quiver; tremble; throb unevenly and faintly; be agitated; agitate, alarm ~ **flutter** *n* act of fluttering; agitation, nervousness; (*coll*) mild gamble or speculation; spree ~ **flutterer** *n*.

fluty [*flOOti*] *adj* having tone like that of a flute.

fluvial [*flOOvi-al*] *adj* of or living in rivers.

flux [*fluks*] *n* state of flowing, flow; continued change or movement; flowing in of tide; (*med*) excessive or abnormal discharge of fluid from body; (*phys*) rate of flow of fluid, radiation or particles; strength of a field of force per unit area; (*chem*) substance added to assist fusion > PDE ~ **flux** *v/t* and *i* cause to flow; flow; fuse (metals) by melting.

fluxion [*fluks*hon] *n* discharge of a liquid; (*med*) excessive flow of blood or fluid to a part of the body; (*math*) rate of increase of a variable quantity; (*pl*) Newtonian calculus.

fluxional [*fluks*honal] *adj* of or by fluxion.

fluxionary [*fluks*honaRi] *adj* variable.

fluxmeter [*fluks*meeter] *n* (*phys*) instrument for measuring magnetic flux > PDS.

fly (1) (*pl* **flies**) [*flI*] *n* two-winged insect; imitation of such insect fastened to angler's fish-hook as a lure; plant disease caused by insects; (*print*) person or device that removes printed sheets from press; **f. in the ointment** a drawback; **there are no flies on him** (*coll*) he is no fool ~ **fly** *adj* (*coll*) knowing, artful; nimble.

fly (2) (*p/t* **flew**, *p/part* **flown**) *v/i* and *t* move through the air by wings or mechanical power; be carried along by air; pass rapidly through air; hasten, rush; move violently and fast; flutter in the breeze; cause to fly; control (aircraft) in flight; display (flag) from pole; transport in aircraft; flee from; **f. at** (*fig*) attack violently; **f. high** (*coll*) be ambitious; **f. in the face of** defy; **f. into a rage** grow suddenly and violently angry; **let f.** hurl; hit out; abuse; **f. off the handle** (*coll*) lose one's temper; **f. out at** abuse violently ~ **fly** *n* act of flying, flight; distance flown; flap of cloth covering row of buttons; flap of canvas over entrance of tent; additional roof of tent; width of flag; part of flag farthest from pole; flywheel; hackney carriage; (*pl*) space above a stage to or from which scenery is hoisted or lowered by pulleys; sections of scenery thus raised and lowered; front opening of trousers.

fly (3) (*p/t* and *p/part* **fled**) *v/i* and *t* flee, escape hastily, run away.

flyaway [*flI*-away] *adj* (*of dress, hair*) loose, streaming; (*of person*) flighty.

flyblow [*flI*blO] *n* egg laid by fly in flesh of animal ~ **flyblow** *v/t* lay eggs in (meat); (*fig*) corrupt, taint ~ **flyblown** *adj* tainted by flyblow; (*fig*) corrupted, discredited.

flyboat [*flI*bOt] *n* swift canal barge.

fly-book [*flI*-book] *n* case holding angler's flies.

fly-by-night [*flI*-bI-nIt] *n* debtor who decamps by night; irresponsible person.

flycatcher [*flI*kacher] *n* one of several small birds that catch insects in flight; plant that catches and eats flies; trap for flies.

flyer, flier [*flI*r] *n* one who or that which flies.

fly-fishing [*flI*-fishing] *n* angling with natural or artificial flies on a fish-hook.

fly-half [*flI*-haaf] *n* (*Rugby football*) half-back positioned at some distance from the scrum.

flying [*flI*-ing] *adj* that flies; hasty, soon ended; temporary; moving rapidly; (*sport*) running or leaping at full speed; **f. column, squadron** body of troops equipped for rapid movement; **f. picket** group of workers coming from elsewhere to aid strikers by picketing; **f. saucer** unidentified disk-shaped object or light reported as moving at remarkable speed or height; **f. squad** body of police organized and equipped for rapid pursuit.

flying-boat [*flI*-ing-bOt] *n* (*aer*) seaplane with a fuselage which floats on water.

flying-bomb [*flI*-ing-bom] *n* small pilotless aircraft filled with explosives.

flying-bridge [*flI*-ing-bRij] *n* pontoon bridge or floating bridge.

flying-buttress [fII-ing-*but*Ris] *n* (*archi*) a buttress, its base not joined to the wall it supports.

flying-fish [fII-ing-*fish*] *n* tropical fish which can spring into the air and glide forward.

flying-fox [fII-ing-*foks*] *n* large fruit-eating bat.

flying-officer [fII-ing-*of*iser] *n* rank in R.A.F. below flight-lieutenant.

flyleaf [*flI*leef] *n* a blank leaf at beginning or end of a book; blank leaf of a circular.

flyman [*flI*man] *n* man who works in the flies of a theatre to shift scenes.

flyover [*flI*Over] *n* passage of one road or railway over or under another; bridge carrying such a road or railway.

flypaper [*fli*payper] *n* gummy or poisonous paper to trap flies.

flypast [*fli*paast] *n* ceremonial flight of aircraft over a given point.

flyposting [*fli*pOsting] *n* unauthorized posting of posters in public places.

flysheet [*fli*sheet] *n* a two- or four-page tract.

flytrap [*fli*tRap] *n* plant which traps and eats insects; trap for catching flies.

flyway [*fli*way] *n* migration route of birds.

flyweight [*fli*wayt] *n* boxer weighing eight stone or less.

flywheel [*fli*wheel] *n* heavy revolving wheel for regulating speed of machine.

foal [*fOl*] *n* young horse or ass ~ **foal** *v/t* and *i* give birth to a foal ~ **foaling** *n* act of giving birth to a foal.

foam [*fOm*] *n* froth, mass of small bubbles on surface of agitated or fermenting liquid; (*poet*) the sea; saliva; **f. rubber** porous elastic substance formed from latex ~ **foam** *v/i* form, produce, or emit foam; emit thick, profuse saliva or sweat; **f. at the mouth** (*fig*) be furiously angry.

foamy [*fOm*i] *adj* like, covered with, foam.

fob (1) [*fob*] *n* small pocket for a watch in the trouser waistband.

fob (2) (*pres/part* **fobbing**, *p/t* and *p/part* **fobbed**) *v/t* cheat; **f. off** delude or trick into accepting worthless articles, empty promises *etc*.

focal [*fOk*al] (*adj*) pertaining to a focus; **f. length** distance from the optical centre or pole to the principal focus of a lens or spherical mirror; **f. point** (*fig*) centre of activity or interest.

focalization [fOkalɪzayshon] *n* act of focusing.

focalize [*fOk*alɪz] *v/t* and *i* to focus.

focus (*pl* **foci** [*fOk*us, *pl* *fO*sɪ] *n* point at which converging rays meet; point from which diverging rays are considered to be directed; focal length; (*math*) one of the points from which the distances to any point of a given curve are linearly related; (*fig*) centre of intensity or activity; **in f.** (*phot*) adjusted to give clearly defined image; (*fig*) precise, not blurred ~ **focus** (*pres/part* **focusing**, *p/t* and *p/part* **focused**) *v/t* and *i* cause to converge; adjust so as to obtain clear image; converge; (*fig*) concentrate.

fodder [*fod*er] *n* dried food for cattle *etc* ~ **fodder** *v/t* supply fodder for.

foe [*fO*] *n* an enemy.

foehn, **föhn** [*furn*] *n* hot dry Alpine wind > PDG.

foeman (*pl* **foemen**) [*fO*man] *n* an enemy.

foetal [*feet*al] *adj* pertaining to a foetus.

foeticide [*feet*isɪd] *n* killing of foetus, abortion.

foetid, **foetor** see fetid, fetor.

foetus, **fetus** [*feet*us] *n* embryo in womb or egg after recognizable appearance of all the main features of fully developed animal > PDB.

fog (1) [*fog*] *n* dense mass of small water drops, smoke, or dust, in lower layers of the atmosphere > PDG; (*phot*) blur on negative or print; (*fig*) confusion, bewilderment ~ **fog** (*pres/part* **fogging**, *p/t* and *p/part* **fogged**) *v/t* and *i* envelop in fog; (*fig*) confuse, bewilder; become foggy; (*phot*) become blurred.

fog (2) *n* new growth of grass after mowing; long grass which has not been grazed.

fogbank [*fog*bank] *n* mass of fog resting on the sea.

fogbound [*fog*bownd] *adj* prevented from travelling by fog.

fogey, **fogy** (*pl* **fogies**) [*fO*gi] *n* old-fashioned, fussy, elderly person.

foggy [*fog*i] *adj* full of fog; (*fig*) vague, confused; (*phot*) blurred ~ **foggily** *adv* ~ **fogginess** *n*.

foghorn [*fog*hawrn] *n* loud hooter blown from ship or lighthouse as warning signal in fog.

fog-lamp [*fog*-lamp] *n* (*mot*) headlamp giving beam of light to penetrate fog.

fog-signal [*fog*-signal] *n* detonator placed on railway line as warning signal in fog.

fogy see fogey.

föhn see foehn.

foible [*foib*'l] *n* weak point, failing; point of vanity; idiosyncrasy; flexible part of swordblade.

foil (1) [*foil*] *n* very thin sheet of metal; coating of tin and quicksilver behind glass of mirror; (*fig*) that which enhances by contrast; (*archi*) small arc between cusps in Gothic tracery ~ **foil** *v/t* cover, back, or wrap with foil; adorn with foils.

foil (2) *n* light fencing sword, with button on end.

foil (3) *v/t* and *i* defeat, baffle, frustrate; (*hunting*) confuse (trail) by crossing and recrossing ~ **foil** *n* (*hunting*) trail of hunted animal.

foin [*foin*] *v/i* (*ar*) thrust, lunge.

foison [*foiz*on] *n* (*ar*) plentiful harvest.

foist [*foist*] *v/t* palm off, pass; introduce or insert unlawfully.

fold (1) [*fold*] *n* enclosure, pen for sheep; flock in a fold; (*fig*) congregation, denomination, the Church ~ **fold** *v/t* enclose (sheep) in pen; manure (land) by keeping sheep in folds on it.

fold (2) *v/t* and *i* double over part of (flexible object) against another part; bend back, double up; wrap round, envelop; embrace; clasp, join; twine (one's arms) across one's chest; be capable of folding; **f. up** make smaller by folding; (*coll*) collapse; fail ~ **fold** *n* bent or doubled part of flexible material; coil (of serpent); layer (of cloth); mark made by folding; hollow (in hill); winding of valley; (*geol*) bend in strata caused by movements of earth's crust > PDG.

folder [*fold*er] *n* one who or that which folds; container for loose papers; a folded circular.

folderol see falderal.

folding [*fold*ing] *adj* making a fold; capable of being folded; enclosing sheep in a fold; manure dropped in a fold; **f. door** door of two or more leaves hinged to each other for folding back.

fold-out [*fold*-owt] *n* large map, illustration *etc* bound into a book of smaller format, to be unfolded by reader.

foliaceous [fOli-*ay*shus] *adj* of or like a leaf; having leaves.

foliage [*fOl*i-ij] *n* leaves of plant; leaf-shaped ornamentation; **f. plant** one cultivated for its leaves and not for its flowers.

foliar [*fOl*i-er] *adj* of or like a leaf.

foliate [*fOl*i-ayt] *v/t* and *i* split into thin plates or leaves; decorate or coat with foil; decorate with leaf-like patterns; number leaves (not pages) of (a book) ~ **foliate** *adj* like a leaf; having leaves.

foliated [*fOl*i-aytid] *adj* coated with foil, silvered; (*min*) composed of layers; (*zool*) leaf-shaped;

(*archi*) decorated with leaf-work; (*mus*) with slurred grace notes.

foliation [fOli-*ay*shon] *n* bursting into leaf or being in leaf; process of beating metal into foil; (*min*) disposition of minerals in parallel layers in rock; (*archi*) tracery of cusps and foils; numbering of leaves of a book.

folio [*f*Oli-O] *n* sheet of paper folded once only; large size of paper; book made of such sheets; largest ordinary size of book; number of a page at top or bottom; two opposite pages of ledger used for both sides of account; (*leg*) unit of length of document, seventy-two or ninety words.

folk [*f*Ok] *n* people, persons; community; race, nation; class of people; primitive or peasant population; (*pl*) (*coll*) relations ∼ **folk** *adj* not learnt through formal education; traditional, orally transmitted; rustic; **f. museum** museum of tools and crafts, or of old houses *etc* restored and displayed with their contents.

folkdance [*f*Okdaans] *n* traditional popular dance; music for this.

folklore [*f*Oklawr] *n* traditional legends, beliefs, customs *etc* orally transmitted in a community; the scientific study of these.

folklorist [*f*OklawrRist] *n* student of folklore.

folk-rock [*f*OkRok] *n* music adapting folk melodies to rock rhythms.

folksong [*f*Oksong] *n* popular song transmitted by oral tradition > PDM.

folksy [*f*Oksy] *adj* (*coll*) of or like common people; rustic, simple; imitating rustic simplicity; friendly, sociable.

folktale [*f*Oktayl] *n* a popular story, *usu* told of unhistoric characters, and transmitted by oral tradition.

folkways [*f*Okwayz] *n* traditional and conventional forms of behaviour of a particular social group.

folkweave [*f*Okweev] *n* loosely woven fabric.

follicle [*f*olik'l] *n* (*anat*) small sac or lymphatic gland; (*bot*) vesicle distended with air; (*bot*) fruit with single carpel, opening on one side only; (*ent*) cocoon.

follicular [*f*olikewlar] *adj* of or like a follicle.

folliculate, folliculated [*f*olikewlayt, *f*olikew-laytid] *adj* having follicles.

follow [*f*olO] *v/t* and *i* go or come after; pursue; go in same direction as; come next in time or order; occur as logical consequence; engage in (a profession); imitate, be an adherent of; obey; understand clearly; watch or listen to carefully; take a keen interest in, study; **f. on** (*coll*) follow some time later; (*cricket*) have second innings directly after first; **f. out** pursue to conclusion; **f. suit** (*cards*) play card of suit which has been led; (*fig*) imitate; **f. through** (*golf*) continue stroke after hitting ball; (*billiards*) make ball continue in same direction after hitting another ball; **f. up** pursue, continue (inquiries *etc*) to the end; (*football*) keep close to player who has ball, to support him ∼ **follow** *n* act of following.

follower [*f*olO-er] *n* one who follows; disciple; retainer; (*obs coll*) wooer, *esp* of servant-girl.

following [*f*olO-ing] *adj* that follows; that is about to be mentioned ∼ **following** *n* group of supporters, adherents, or retainers; act of one who follows.

follow-my-leader [*f*olO-mI-*lee*der] *n* children's game in which players imitate actions of the leader.

follow-on [*f*olO-*on*] *n* (*cricket*) second innings immediately after the first.

follow-through [*f*olO-*th*ROO] *n* continuation of stroke after hitting ball; continuance of effort after a first success; (*billiards*) stroke that makes a ball continue on the same course after hitting another.

follow-up [*f*olO-*up*] *n* second stage of an action or effort; renewal or continuance of action; (*games*) act of supporting another player.

folly [*f*oli] *n* foolishness, rashness; foolish act, speech or behaviour; (*archi*) extravagant, fantastic building.

foment [fOment] *v/t* apply hot lotion or poultice to; (*fig*) encourage, stir up (trouble).

fomentation [fOmen*tay*shon] *n* act of fomenting; hot poultice or lotion; (*fig*) incitement.

fond [*f*ond] *adj* affectionate, loving; foolishly credulous or hopeful; doting; **be f. of** like; love; enjoy.

fondant [*f*ondant] *n* soft sweetmeat which melts in the mouth.

fondle [*f*ond'l] *v/t* caress.

fondly [*f*ondli] *adv* affectionately; credulously, foolishly ∼ **fondness** *n* affection, liking.

fondue [*f*ondew] *n* strong savoury sauce in which biscuits or bread are dipped; soufflé made with bread or biscuit crumbs.

font (1) [*f*ont] *n* basin for baptismal water; reservoir of oil-lamp; (*poet*) fountain, well.

font (2) see **fount** (2).

fontal [*f*ontal] *adj* pertaining to a source, original; baptismal.

fontanel, fontanelle [fontan*el*] *n* (*anat*) gap in skeletal covering of brain at birth > PDB.

food [*f*OOd] *n* nourishment for animal or plant; solid edible substance (not a drink); a processed or patent kind of food; (*fig*) that which sustains or stimulates thought, feelings *etc*; **f. chain** (*biol*) series of organisms each of which serves as food to the next; **f. poisoning** illness caused by bacteria or toxins in food; **f. value** nutritional value of a food.

foodstuff [*f*OOdstuf] *n* food, *esp* in bulk; anything used as food.

fool (1) [*f*OOl] *n* stupid person; imbecile; dupe; court jester, buffoon; **All Fools' Day** 1 April; **April f.** victim of joke or hoax on this day; **make a f. of** deceive, dupe, cause to appear ridiculous; **fool's (fools') paradise** happiness based on ignorance or self-deception; **play the f.** behave frivolously, joke, behave stupidly ∼ **fool** *v/t* and *i* deceive, dupe; cause to appear ridiculous; behave frivolously or stupidly; joke ∼ **fool** *adj* (*coll*) foolish.

fool (2) *n* dish of fruit pulped with custard or cream.

foolery [*f*OOleRi] *n* foolish behaviour or act.

foolhardy [*f*OOlhaardi] *adj* foolishly bold, rash; involving useless danger ∼ **foolhardily** *adv* ∼ **foolhardiness** *n*.

foolish [*f*OOlish] *adj* stupid, lacking good sense; rash; ridiculous; weak in mind ∼**foolishly** *adv* ∼ **foolishness** *n*.

foolproof [*f*OOlpROOf] *adj* (*coll*) simple enough for even fools to understand or use safely; infallible.

foolscap [*fOOl*skap] *n* size of writing paper, 17 × 13½ in.; cap of court jester; dunce's cap.

foot (*pl* **feet**) [*foot*] *n* end section of animal's leg, on which it stands or walks; anything resembling this; lowest part, base, bottom; part of sock or stocking covering foot; end of bed, grave *etc* where feet lie; (*mil*) infantry; lineal measure of 12 in. (*pl* **foot** or **feet**); unit of scansion of verse; measure of pitch > PDM; **at one's feet** at one's mercy; captivated; **cubic f.** volume equal to that of a cube with side of one sq. ft.; **drag one's feet** be slow to act; **fall on one's feet** have good luck; **find one's feet** learn to manage well, gain skill; **get (have) cold feet** withdraw from a projected action through fear or diffidence; **my f.!** (*coll*) nonsense!; **one f. in the grave** near death; **on f.** walking; **put one's f. down** act with decision or authority; (*mot*) accelerate; **put one's best f. forward** walk or run as fast as possible; do one's best; **put one's f. in it** (*coll*) make a blunder, act tactlessly; **set on f.** originate; **under f.** on the ground ~ **foot** *v/t* dance; walk; put new foot on (stocking); add up and note (total); (*coll*) kick; **f. the bill** (*coll*) pay.

footage [*foot*ij] *n* length measured in feet; (*mining*) payment by length of seam cut; (*cin*) length of film used.

football [*foot*bawl] *n* large inflated leather ball; game played with this ~ **footballer** *n*.

footboard [*foot*bawrd] *n* sloping board against which driver's feet rest; step along side of railway coach, car, or carriage; board at foot of bed.

footbridge [*foot*Rij] *n* bridge for pedestrians.

footed [*foot*id] *adj* having feet or a foot.

footer [*foot*er] *n* (*sl*) game of football.

footfall [*foot*fawl] *n* footstep; sound of footstep.

footfault [*foot*fawlt] *n* (*tennis*) service disallowed because of wrong position of server's feet ~ **footfault** *v/t* and *i* declare guilty of a footfault; commit a footfault.

Foot-Guards [*foot*-gaards] *n* (*pl*) the Grenadier, Coldstream, Scots, Irish, Welsh Guards.

foothill [*foot*hil] *n* smaller hill at foot of mountain or mountain range.

foothold [*foot*Old] *n* place where feet can be safely set in climbing; (*fig*) secure position.

footing [*foot*ing] *n* secure foothold; (*fig*) assured position; status; relationship; (*archi*) a widening of any structure at the base to improve stability.

footle [*fOOt*'l] *v/i* (*sl*) dawdle, potter about; talk or act foolishly ~ **footle** *n* nonsense, twaddle.

footlights [*foot*lIts] *n* (*pl*) row of lights along front of stage; (*fig*) theatrical profession.

footling [*fOOt*ling] *adj* (*coll*) stupid; insignificant, trivial; pettily fussy.

footloose [*foot*lOOs] *adj* free to go where one likes, free to do what one wants.

footman [*foot*man] *n* manservant in livery.

footmark [*foot*maark] *n* footprint.

footmuff [*foot*muf] *n* warmly lined bag for keeping feet warm.

footnote [*foot*nOt] *n* explanatory note inserted at foot of page, or at end of book or chapter ~ **footnote** *v/t* annotate with footnotes.

footpace [*foot*pays] *n* walking pace; raised area of floor; raised floor on which an altar stands.

footpad [*foot*pad] *n* highwayman who robs on foot.

footpath [*foot*paath] *n* path for pedestrians only.

footplate [*foot*playt] *n* platform in locomotive for the driver and fireman.

foot-pound [foot-*pownd*] *n* unit of work, work done in lifting 1 lb. through 1 ft.

footprint [*foot*pRint] *n* mark made by a foot.

foot-rot [*foot*-Rot] *n* contagious disease of feet in cattle and sheep.

footrule [foot-*ROOl*] *n* ruler 12 in. long.

footslog [*foot*slog] *v/i* (*sl*) tramp, march.

footsore [*foot*sawr] *adj* having pain in the feet from walking, wearied by walking.

footstalk [*foot*stawk] *n* (*bot*) petiole; peduncle; (*zool*) organ by which certain organisms attach themselves to rocks *etc*.

footstep [*foot*step] *n* step of a foot; mark left by a foot; sound of walking feet; **follow in the footsteps of** imitate.

footstool [*foot*stOOl] *n* low stool supporting feet of sitting person.

footway [*foot*way] *n* footpath.

footwear [*foot*wair] *n* shoes, boots *etc*.

footwork [*foot*wurk] *n* skilful use of feet in sport, dancing *etc*.

foozle [*fOOz*'l] *v/t* (*golf*) spoil (stroke) by clumsiness ~ **foozle** *n* bungling stroke; failure.

fop [*fop*] *n* dandy, man foolishly vain of his appearance, clothes *etc*.

foppery [*fop*eRi] *n* affectation, foolish vanity.

foppish [*fop*ish] *adj* of or like a fop, dandified ~ **foppishly** *adv* ~ **foppishness** *n*.

for [*fawr*] *prep* towards; to the benefit of; in favour of; suitable to; because of, on account of; for the sake of; in order to obtain, in hope of; in exchange for; during; through or over (a distance); considering (the circumstances); regarding, as concerns; as; **f. all that** in spite of all that; **be f. it** (*coll*) be about to get into trouble, *etc*; **f. good** permanently; **oh f.!** I wish that I had ~ **for** *conj* because, on account of the fact that.

forage [*fo*Rij] *n* food for horses and cattle; act of searching for provisions ~ **forage** *v/i* and *t* search for food; rummage about; plunder, pillage; obtain fodder for ~ **forager** *n* ~ **foraging** *n*.

forage-cap [*fo*Rij-kap] *n* undress cap for infantry.

foramen (*pl* **foramina**) [fo*Ray*men] *n* any small perforation; aperture through bone or membrane > PDB.

forasmuch [foRaz*much*] *conj* **f. as** because, considering that.

foray [*fo*Ray] *n* raid, plundering inroad ~ **foray** *v/t* and *i* raid, plunder; go out plundering.

forbad, forbade [fer*bad*/fer*bayd*] *p/t* of **forbid**.

forbear (1), **forebear** [*fawr*bair] *n* ancestor.

forbear (2) (*p/t* **forbore**, *p/part* **forborne**) [fawr*bair*] *v/t* and *i* refrain from; desist from, cease; check oneself.

forbearance [fawr*bair*Rans] *n* act of forbearing; patience; self-restraint; leniency.

forbearing [fawr*bair*Ring] *adj* showing forbearance.

forbid (*pres/part* **forbidding**, *p/t* **forbade**, *p/part* **forbidden**) [fer*bid*] *v/t* refuse to allow, prohibit; order not to do; prevent; refuse entry.

forbidden [fer*biden*] *adj* not allowed; **f. fruit** (*fig*) sinful or unlawful pleasure.

forbidding [fer*biding*] *adj* unfriendly in appear-

ance; grim, threatening; dangerous-looking ~
forbiddingly *adv* ~ **forbiddingness** *n*.

forbore [fawr*bawr*] *p/t* of **forbear** (2).

forborne [fawr*bawrn*] *p/part* of **forbear** (2).

forby, forbye [fawr*bI*] *prep* and *adv* (*Scots*) besides; near by; past.

force (1) [*fawrs*] *n* strength, power; violence; vigour, energy; validity, compulsory or operative power; (*phys*) external agency capable of altering state of rest or motion in a body; (*fig*) influence capable of acting on the mind; persuasive power; meaning, function; (*mil*) body of troops; police; persons organized for action; (*leg*) unlawful violence; **the F.** the police; **brute f.** physical violence; **in f.** operative; valid; in large numbers ~ **force** *v/t* overpower by physical violence; compel, constrain; break through or into by violence; rape; extort; overstrain; (*hort*) hasten the maturity of by artificial means; **f. the hand of** compel.

force (2) *n* a waterfall.

forced [*fawrst*] *adj* made, done under compulsion, not voluntary; artificially produced, unnatural; **f. march** very rapid emergency march ~ **forcedly** *adv*.

forceful [*fawrs*fool] *adj* powerful; impressive; vigorous ~ **forcefully** *adv* ~ **forcefulness** *n*.

force majeure [fawrs-ma*zhur*] *n* (*Fr*) (*leg*) irresistible force, compulsion.

forcemeat [*fawrs*meet] *n* meat minced and seasoned, used for stuffing.

forceps [*fawr*seps] *u* small pincers or tweezers; (*zool*) grasping organ resembling these.

force-pump [*fawrs*-pump] *n* pump which delivers liquid to level higher than the cylinder.

forcibility [fawrsi*bili*ti] *n* powerfulness.

forcible [*fawr*sib'l] *adj* done by force; possessing force, powerful; convincing ~ **forcibly** *adv*.

forcing [*fawr*sing] *n* action of person or thing that forces; process of bringing force to bear; (*hort*) hastening of growth of plant; (*fig*) artificial hastening of development.

forcite [*fawr*sIt] *n* variety of dynamite.

ford [*fawrd*] *n* shallow place where river or body of water can be crossed by wading ~ **ford** *v/t* cross by a ford, wade across ~ **fordable** *adj*.

fore (1) [*fawr*] *adv* and *adj* in front (of); before; (*naut*) nearest the bows; **f. and aft** (*naut*) from end to end; longitudinal ~ **fore** *n* front, forward part; **to the f.** prominent ~ **fore** *prep* (*ar*) before.

fore (2) *interj* (*golf*) warning call by player to those in the way.

fore- (3) *pref* in front; earlier in time, in advance.

forearm (1) [*fawr*Raarm] *n* part of arm between elbow and hand.

forearm (2) [fawr*Raarm*] *v/t* arm beforehand.

forebear see **forbear** (1).

forebode [fawr*bOd*] *v/t* foretell, prophesy; have presentiment of; be a portent of.

foreboding [fawr*bOd*ing] *adj* and *n* (being) a presentiment of evil ~ **forebodingly** *adv*.

forecast (*p/t* and *p/part* **forecast**) [*fawr*kaast] *v/t* estimate in advance; foretell, foresee ~ **forecast** [*fawr*kaast] *n* prediction of future events, *esp* of future weather; estimate ~ **forecaster** *n*.

forecastle [*fOks*'l] *n* (*naut*) short raised deck in

bows of vessel; forward part of warship; **crew's** quarters in merchant ship > PDSa.

foreclose [fawr*klOz*] *v/t* (*leg*) debar, exclude; prevent (mortgagor) from redeeming mortgaged property; settle beforehand; settle prematurely.

foreclosure [fawr*klO*zher] *n* act of foreclosing.

forecourt [*fawr*kawrt] *n* court in front of a building; outer court.

foredoom [fawr*dOOm*] *v/t* predestine; condemn beforehand.

forefather [*fawr*faaTHer] *n* ancestor.

forefinger [*fawr*fing-ger] *n* finger next to thumb.

forefoot [*fawr*foot] *n* front foot of quadruped; (*naut*) foremost part of keel.

forefront [*fawr*fRunt] *n* (*mil*) front rank; (*fig*) most important position.

foregift [*fawr*gift] *n* (*leg*) premium for lease.

forego (*p/t* **forewent**, *p/part* **foregone**) [fawr*gO*] *v/t* (*ar*) precede; forgo.

foregoing [*fawr*gO-ing] *adj* preceding; previously mentioned.

foregone [*fawr*gon] *adj* determined in advance, already settled; past; **f. conclusion** something already settled or arranged; something easy to foresee.

foreground [*fawr*gRound] *n* part of scene nearest to spectator, *esp* in picture; (*fig*) most prominent position.

forehand [*fawr*hand] *n* part of horse in front of rider; (*tennis*) right side of right-handed player, left side of left-handed player; range of strokes played on the right, or left, side ~ **forehand** *adj* (*tennis*) (stroke) played with palm of hand facing front.

forehanded [fawr*hand*id] *adj* (*US*) thrifty; looking ahead; timely.

forehead [*fo*Rid/*fawr*hed] *n* part of face between eyes and hair.

foreign [*fo*Rin] *adj* not belonging to, introduced from outside; strange, alien; different in nationality; pertaining to another nation; irrelevant; **f. affairs** policy of one country towards others.

foreigner [*fo*Riner] *n* person belonging to another country; an alien.

forejudge [fawr*juj*] *v/t* judge before knowing the facts ~ **forejudgement** *n*.

foreknow (*p/t* **foreknew**, *p/part* **foreknown**) [fawr*nO*] *v/t* know beforehand.

foreknowledge [fawr*noli*j] *n* previous knowledge.

forel, forrel [*fo*Ril] *n* kind of parchment for covering books.

foreland [*fawr*land] *n* promontory, headland; land along coastline.

foreleg [*fawr*leg] *n* front leg of quadruped.

forelock (1) [*fawr*lok] *n* linchpin ~ **forelock** *v/t*.

forelock (2) *n* lock of hair growing just above forehead; **take time by the f.** seize first opportunity.

foreman [*fawr*man] *n* skilled and experienced workman placed in charge of others; (*leg*) leader and spokesman of jury.

foremast [*fawr*maast] *n* (*naut*) mast nearest bows.

forementioned [fawr*men*shund] *adj* previously referred to.

foremost [*fawr*mOst] *adj* and *adv* farthest forward; first, most prominent, chief; **first and f.** first of all.

forename [*fawr*naym] *n* name by which an

individual is distinguished from others of the same surname; name preceding the surname.

forenoon [*fawr*nOOn] *n* morning.

forensic [fo*Ren*sik] *adj* pertaining to law-courts; **f. medicine** medical jurisprudence.

foreordain [fawr-awr*dayn*] *v/t* decree beforehand, predestinate ~ **fore-ordination** [fawr-awrdinay-shon] *n.*

forepart [*fawr*paart] *n* front part; first part.

foreplay [*fawr*play] *n* sexual stimulation preceding intercourse.

forequarter [*fawr*kwawrter] *n* front section of animal carcass, including one foreleg.

forerun (*p/t* foreran, *p/part* forerun) [fawr*Run*] *v/t* precede; herald, foreshadow ~ **forerunner** *n.*

foresail [*fawr*sayl/*fawrs*’l] *n* (*naut*) lowest square sail on foremast of ship, bark, or brig > PDSa.

foresee (*p/t* foresaw, *p/part* foreseen) [fawr*see*] *v/t* anticipate, know in advance ~ **foreseeing** *adj* prudent; knowing beforehand.

foreshadow [fawr*shad*O] *v/t* indicate in advance; represent or typify beforehand.

foresheet [*fawr*sheet] *n* (*naut*) rope attached to foresail; (*pl*) gratings in bow of open boat.

foreshore [*fawr*shawr] *n* part of shore between high and low water mark.

foreshorten [fawr*shawr*ten] *v/t* (*arts*) represent effects of perspective > PDAA ~ **foreshortening** *n.*

foreshow (*p/t* foreshowed, *p/part* foreshown) [fawr*shO*] *v/t* show beforehand, prefigure.

foresight [*fawr*sIt] *n* prudence, care for future; act of foreseeing; front-sight on muzzle of gun.

foresighted [fawr*sI*tid] *adj* prudent.

foreskin [*fawr*skin] *n* skin covering end of penis.

forest [fo*Rest*] *n* extensive area of land covered with trees; large unenclosed area of waste land; (*hist*) unenclosed royal hunting-ground; (*fig*) thick cluster of tree-like objects ~ **fores** *adj* pertaining to forests; found in forests ~ **forest** *v/t* plant with trees.

forestal [fo*Res*tal] *adj* pertaining to a forest.

forestall [fawr*stawl*] *v/t* get ahead of, anticipate; obstruct by prior action.

forester [fo*Res*ter] *n* officer in charge of a forest; man who works in a forest; man skilled in forestry.

forestry [fo*Res*tRi] *n* scientific care of forests.

foretaste [*fawr*tayst] *n* preliminary experience ~ **foretaste** [fawr*tayst*] *v/t.*

foretell (*p/t* and *p/part* foretold) [fawr*tel*] *v/t* predict, say beforehand what will happen.

forethought [*fawr*thawt] *n* previous consideration; thought for the future, prudence.

forethoughtful [fawr*thawt*fool] *adj* prudent.

foretime [*fawr*tIm] *n* old times, the past.

foretoken [*fawr*tOken] *n* bad omen, warning sign ~ **foretoken** [fawrt*Ok*en] *v/t* portend.

foretold [fawr*tOld*] *p/t* and *p/past* of foretell.

foretop [*fawr*top] *n* (*naut*) platform at top of foremast.

fore-topgallant [fawr-top*gal*ant] *n* (*naut*) mast above fore-topmast.

fore-topmast [fawr-*top*maast] *n* (*naut*) mast above foremast.

fore-topsail [fawr-*top*sail/*fawr*-tops’l] *n* sail on fore-topmast.

forever [faw*Rev*er/fe*Rev*er] *adv* always, endlessly.

forewarn [fawr*wawrn*] *v/t* warn in advance.

forewent [fawr*went*] *p/t* of forego or of forgo.

forewoman [*fawr*wooman] *n* female foreman.

foreword [*fawr*wurd] *n* preface.

forfeit [*fawr*fit] *n* anything lost as penalty in law or game; (*pl*) parlour game in which penalties are exacted ~ **forfeit** *adj* confiscated by law as penalty; liable to be confiscated or lost ~ **forfeit** *v/t* lose, be deprived of as penalty ~ **forfeitable** *adj* ~ **forfeiter** *n.*

forfeiture [*fawr*ficher] *n* act of forfeiting; thing forfeited.

forfend [fawr*fend*] *v/t* (*ar*) prevent, avert.

forgather [fawr*ga*THer] *v/i* assemble.

forgave [fawr*gayv*/fer*gayv*] *p/t* of forgive.

forge [*fawr*j] *n* furnace in which metal is softened before shaping; blacksmith’s workshop ~ **forge** *v/t* and *i* shape (hot metal) by pressing or hammering; produce by this process; (*fig*) form, invent painstakingly; imitate fraudulently, counterfeit; commit forgery; work as a blacksmith; **f. ahead** make slow but steady progress.

forger [*fawr*jer] *n* one who works at a forge; one who commits forgery, counterfeiter.

forgery [*fawr*jeRi] *n* (*leg*) fraudulent making or altering of document, signature, banknote *etc*; document or signature so made.

forget (*pres/part* forgetting, *p/t* forgot, *p/part* forgotten) [fawr*get*/fer*get*] *v/t* and *i* fail to remember, lose memory of; accidentally omit; leave behind accidentally; neglect; **f. oneself** behave in unseemly manner, lose dignity.

forgetful [fer*get*fool] *adj* liable to forget; neglectful ~ **forgetfully** *adv* ~ **forgetfulness** *n.*

forget-me-not [fawr*get*-mi-not] *n* small blue-flowered perennial or biennial plant.

forgive (*p/t* forgave, *p/part* forgiven) [fawr*giv*/fer*giv*] *v/t* and *i* pardon; overlook; remit (debt); cease to bear anger ~ **forgivable** *adj* ~ **forgiveness** *n.*

forgiving [fawr*giv*ing/fer*giv*ing] *adj* willing to forgive; habitually ready to forgive ~ **forgivingly** *adv* ~ **forgivingness** *n.*

forgo (*p/t* forwent, *p/part* forgone) [fawr*gO*] *v/t* refrain or abstain from, renounce.

forgot [fawr*got*/fer*got*] *p/t* and (*ar*) *p/part* of forget.

forgotten [fawr*got*en/fer*got*en] *p/part* of forget.

fork [*fawr*k] *n* implement with handle and two or more prongs; anything of similar shape; junction of two roads or rivers; junction of branch and trunk of tree; junction of legs and human trunk; supporting stake with forked ends; part of bicycle frame in which wheel is set; (*pl*) (*sl*) fingers ~ **fork** *v/ t* and *i* lift, dig or transfix with a fork; divide into two, bifurcate; cause to bifurcate; **f. in** dig in with fork; **f. out** (*coll*) pay out.

forked [*fawr*kt] *adj* shaped like a fork; divided into two prongs, points *etc.*

forkful [*fawr*kfool] *n* as much as may be carried on a fork.

forklift [*fawr*klift] *n* vehicle with movable prongs for raising loads from below.

forlorn [fawr*lawrn*] *adj* deserted, neglected, wretched; **f. hope** very faint hope; dangerous undertaking offering last chance of success ~ **forlornly** *adv* ~ **forlornness** *n.*

form [*fawr*m] *n* shape, outline, general appearance; body; type; particular kind; order, arrangement, structure; manner of presentation, style; established custom; etiquette, social behaviour; formula; document with blank spaces to be filled in with information; model; mould; (*bot, zool*) variant type > PDB; long bench; school class; (*philos*) essential character; (*theol*) essential words of sacrament; (*sport*) fitness; estimate of likely success; (*coll*) excellence, fine condition of mind or body; lair of hare; (*print*) forme; **good (bad)** f. socially (un)acceptable ~ **form** *v/t* and *i* shape; make, arrange, organize; train, develop; take shape, appear; act as, constitute; come into existence; (*mil*) draw up.

formal [*faw*rmal] *adj* according to prescribed form; conventional, ceremonial; stiff in manner; regular; having exterior appearance but no inner reality; (*philos*) essential; (*log*) concerning method of reasoning.

formaldehyde [fawr*m*aldihId] *n* (*chem*) soluble gas made by oxidation of methyl alcohol > PDS.

formalin [*faw*rmalin] *n* (*chem*) solution of formaldehyde used as disinfectant.

formalism [*faw*rmalizm] *n* careful adherence to external forms, without inner spiritual reality ~ **formalist** *n* and *adj* ~ **formalistic** *adj*.

formality [fawr*m*aliti] *n* accordance with legal form; conformity with established custom; something without real use or meaning; stiffness of manner.

formalize [*faw*rmalIz] *v/t* and *i* make formal, give definite shape to; act with formality ~ **formalization** [fawrmalIz*ay*shon] *n*.

formally [*faw*rmali] *adv* in formal manner.

format [*faw*rmat] *n* shape and size of book *etc*.

formate (1) [fawr*m*ayt] *v/i* (*aer*) fly in formation.

formate (2) *n* (*chem*) salt or ester of formic acid.

formation [fawr*m*ayshon] *n* act of forming; making, creation; way in which a thing is found; structure; (*mil, naut*) arrangement of troops or vessels; group of aircraft flying in fixed order; (*geol*) series of similar strata.

formative [*faw*rmativ] *n* and *adj* (that which is) capable of giving shape or causing development; (*gramm*) (element) helping to build up a word.

forme, form [*faw*rm] *n* (*print*) body of type secured in the frame called a chase.

former (1) [*faw*rmer] *n* one who or that which forms; creator; mould; frame for electrical coils.

former (2) *adj* earlier; first mentioned; belonging to previous period ~ **formerly** *adv* in past times.

formic [*faw*rmik] *adj* pertaining to ants; **f. acid** colourless, corrosive, fuming acid formerly obtained from ants > PDS.

formica [fawrm*I*ka] *n* (*tr*) type of laminated heat-resisting plastic.

formicary [*faw*rmikaRi] *n* ants' nest, ant-hill.

formication [fawrm*i*k*ay*shon] *n* (*med*) diffuse tingling sensation.

formidable [*faw*rmidab'l] *adj* terrifying; difficult, full of obstacles; huge ~ **formidableness** *n* ~ **formidably** *adv*.

formless [*faw*rmles] *adj* shapeless, without regular form ~ **formlessly** *adv* ~ **formlessness** *n*.

formula (*pl* **formulas/formulae**) [*faw*rmewla] *n* concise statement in words or symbols of general law, principle or relationship; prescribed set of words for use in particular circumstances; trite phrase; (*chem*) symbolic representation of molecule > PDS; (*math*) symbolic generalized statement; (*theol*) definition of dogma; (*med*) prescription.

formularize [*faw*rmewlaRIz] *v/t* express by a formula.

formulary [*faw*rmewlaRi] *n* collection of formulas; book containing set forms, *esp* for belief or ritual ~ **formulary** *adj* prescribed, ritual.

formulate [*faw*rmewlayt] *v/t* express in a formula; express precisely or authoritatively ~ **formulation** [fawrmewl*ay*shon] *n*.

formulism [*faw*rmewlizm] *n* excessive reliance on formulas ~ **formulist** *n* and *adj* ~ **formulistic** [fawrmewl*i*stik] *adj*.

formulize [*faw*rmewlIz] *v/t* express in a formula.

fornicate [*faw*rnikayt] *v/i* have sexual intercourse without marriage.

fornication [fawrnik*ay*shon] *n* sexual intercourse outside marriage ~ **fornicator** *n*.

fornicatress [*faw*rnikaytRis] *n* woman guilty of fornication.

forrader [*fo*Ruder] *adv* (*sl*) further forward.

forrard [*fo*Rud] *adv* and *n* (*naut*) (at) the bows.

forrel see **forel**.

forsake (*p/t* **forsook**, *p/part* **forsaken**) [fawr*sayk*] *v/t* renounce, give up; desert, abandon ~ **forsaken** *adj* deserted.

forsook [fawr*sook*] *p/t* of **forsake**.

forsooth [fawrs*OO*th/fers*OO*th] *adv* (*ar* or *joc*) indeed, in truth.

forswear (*p/t* **forswore**, *p/part* **forsworn**) [fawrs*wair*] *v/t* and *i* renounce solemnly; repudiate on oath; swear falsely; (*refl*) perjure oneself ~ **forsworn** [fawrs*waw*rn] *adj* perjured.

forsythia [fawrs*I*thi-a] *n* spring-flowering shrub with bright yellow four-petalled flowers.

fort [*faw*rt] *n* (*mil*) fortified place.

forte (1) [*faw*rt/*faw*rti] *n* quality in which one excels, strong point; upper part of sword blade.

forte (2) [*faw*rti] *adv* (*mus*) loudly.

forth [*faw*rth] *adv* forwards; onwards; **and so** f. and so on; **hold** f. speak lengthily.

forthcoming [fawrth*kum*ing] *adj* about to appear; available, at hand; (*fig*) friendly, sociable.

forthright [*faw*rthRit] *adj* straightforward, outspoken ~ **forthright** *adv* straightway.

forthwith [fawrth*wiTH*] *adv* immediately.

fortieth [*faw*rti-eth] *adj* following thirty-nine others in a series; being one of forty equal parts ~ **fortieth** *n* one-fortieth part; fortieth object in a series.

fortification [fawrtif*ik*ayshon] *n* (*mil*) act or science of fortifying; (*pl*) defensive works, walls, towers *etc*.

fortify (*p/t* and *p/part* **fortified**) [*faw*rtifI] *v/t* and *i* strengthen; encourage; corroborate; (*mil*) protect against attack by earthworks *etc*; raise earthworks; enrich (food) by adding vitamins *etc*; make liquor more potent by the addition of alcohol.

fortissimo [fawrt*isim*O] *adv* (*mus*) very loudly.

fortitude [*faw*rtitewd] *n* patient courage; strength of mind.

fortnight [*faw*rtnIt] *n* two weeks ~ **fortnightly** *adj* and *adv* once a fortnight.

fortress [*faw*rtRes] *n* military stronghold.

fortuitous [fawr*tew*-itus] *adj* due to chance, accidental ~ **fortuitously** *adv* ~ **fortuitousness** *n*.

fortuity [fawr*tew*-iti] *n* chance; accidental occurrence.

fortunate [*fawr*tewnit/*fawr*choonit] *adj* lucky; bringing luck ~ **fortunately** *adv* luckily; successfully.

fortune [*fawr*choon] *n* chance, luck; destiny, lot; wealth; success ~ **fortune** *v/i* (*ar*) happen by chance.

fortune-hunter [*fawr*choon-hunter] *n* one who seeks to acquire wealth, *esp* by marriage.

fortune-teller [*fawr*choon-teler] *n* one who professes to predict one's future.

forty [*fawr*ti] *n* and *adj* four times ten; group of forty persons or things; **the forties** years between forty and fifty of a century or a lifetime; **the Roaring Forties** stormy area of Atlantic between 40° and 50° north latitude; **f. winks** (*coll*) short daytime sleep.

forum [*fawr*Rum] *n* (*hist*) market-place of Roman city, used for legal or judicial business *etc*; (*fig*) tribunal; place or occasion for debate.

forward [*fawr*werd] *adj* situated in front; advancing; ahead; well advanced, precocious; ready, eager; presumptuous, pert; progressive; (*comm*) concerned with future transactions ~ **forward** *adv* towards the front, onwards; (*fig*) progressively; into prominence; (*naut*) [*fo*Rud] at or near the bows ~ **forward** *n* (*sport*) player in front line ~ **forward** *v/t* hasten progress of, help on; redirect (letter *etc*); transmit.

forward-looking [*fawr*werd-looking] *adj* progressive.

forwardness [*fawr*werdnis] *n* state of being well advanced; promptness, zeal; presumption.

forwards [*fawr*werdz] *adv* forward.

forwent [fawr*went*] *p/t* of forgo.

fossa (*pl* fossae) [*fos*a] *n* (*anat*) cavity, shallow pit.

fosse [*fos*] *n* ditch; moat; (*anat*) fossa.

fossick [*fos*ik] *v/i* (*coll*) hunt round, rummage; (*Aust sl*) search for gold overlooked by others.

fossil [*fos*il] *n* (*geol*) remains of organism preserved in rocks > PDB; (*fig*) old-fashioned person; outmoded idea *etc* ~ **fossil** *adj*; **f. fuel** fuel derived from fossils; coal, oil or natural gas.

fossilize [*fos*ilIz] *v/t* and *i* reduce to or become a fossil; (*fig*) become antiquated ~ **fossilization** [fosilIz*ayshon*] *n*.

fossorial [fos*awr*Ri-al] *adj* (*zool*) burrowing; adapted for digging.

foster [*foster*] *v/t* bring up or temporarily care for another's child, without adopting it; (*fig*) encourage; cherish, harbour.

fosterage [*foste*Rij] *n* rearing of another's child.

foster-brother [*foster*-bRuTHer] *n* boy brought up with another child of different parentage.

foster-child [*foster*-chIld] *n* one brought up by foster-parent.

foster-daughter [*foster*-dawter] *n* girl brought up by foster-parent.

foster-father [*foster*-faTHer] *n* man who brings up or looks after another's child.

fosterling [*fosterling*] *n* foster-child.

foster-mother [*foster*-muTHer] *n* woman who brings up or looks after another's child.

foster-sister [*foster*-sister] *n* girl brought up with another child of different parentage.

foster-son [*foster*-sun] *n* boy brought up by foster-parent.

fought [*fawt*] *p/t* and *p/part* of fight.

foul [*fowl*] *adj* very dirty, filthy; disgusting; clogged with dirt; (*fig*) abominable, wicked; obscene; (*of weather*) stormy; (*of ropes*) tangled, jammed; (*sport*) against the rules; unfair, unscrupulous; (*print*) full of errors, deletions *etc*; (*coll*) very bad; **fall f. of** (*naut*) collide with; (*coll*) come into conflict with; **f. play** murder; treacherous violence; (*sport*) breach of rules ~ **foul** *n* (*sport*) breach of rules, an irregular stroke, tackle *etc*; (*naut*) slight collision ~ **foul** *v/t* and *i* make dirty, defile; become dirty; clog, block; entangle; become entangled (with); collide with; (*sport*) break rules; play unfairly; **f. up** tangle up, jam; make a muddle or mess of.

foulard [*fOO*laard] *n* thin material of silk or rayon; scarf, necktie *etc* made from this.

foully [*fowl*-li] *adv* in a foul manner.

foul-mouthed [fowl-*mowT*Hd] *adj* habitually using obscene language.

foulness [*fowl*nis] *n* quality of being foul.

foumart [*fOO*maart] *n* the polecat.

found (1) [*fownd*] *v/t* establish, originate; begin to build; endow; base.

found (2) *v/t* make a metal casting.

found (3) *p/t* and *p/part* of **find** ~ **found** *adj* provided, equipped.

foundation [fownd*ay*shon] *n* act of founding; institution set up and endowed; base on which building is erected > PDE; underlying layer; support; (*fig*) basis, origin; **f. cream** film of cosmetic cream under facepowder *etc*; **f. garment** corset, *gener* with attached brassière; **f. stone** inscribed stone ceremonially laid to mark beginning of erection of a building.

foundationer [fownd*ay*shoner] *n* member of college or school who is supported by its endowed funds.

founder (1) [*fownd*er] *n* initiator; endower.

founder (2) *n* one who founds metal.

founder (3) *v/i* and *t* (*of horse*) collapse, fall lame; (*of ship*) fill with water and sink; (*fig*) collapse; cause to founder ~ **founder** *n* inflammation of horse's foot; rheumatism in horse's chest muscles.

foundling [*fownd*ling] *n* deserted infant.

foundress [*fownd*Res] *n* woman founder (1).

foundry [*fownd*Ri] *n* process of casting metal; works where metal castings are made.

fount (1) [*fownt*] *n* (*poet*) fountain; (*fig*) source.

fount (2), **font** *n* (*typ*) complete set of type of one particular face and size.

fountain [*fown*tin] *n* artificial jet or spout of water; ornamental structure from which water spouts or flows; jet of drinking water; reservoir of ink, oil *etc*; (*fig*) source; **soda f.** apparatus or bar supplying soft drinks.

fountainhead [*fown*tinhed] *n* source; origin.

fountain-pen [*fown*tin-pen] *n* pen containing reservoir of ink.

four [*fawr*] *n* and *adj* cardinal number next above three; symbol of this number, 4; group of four persons or things; card *etc* marked with four pips; age of four years; four o'clock; score of four at a game; (*pl*) gloves or shoes of size four; four-oared boat; (*pl*) race rowed with such boats;

(*pl mil*) marching formation four abreast; **on all
fours** on hands and knees; (*fig*) corresponding,
equivalent; **f. letter word** any of several short
words denoting sexual acts or organs or excretory
acts.

four-ale [*fawr*-ayl] *n* ale formerly sold at fourpence a quart; **f. bar** a public bar.

four-flusher [fawr-*flusher*] *n* (*sl*) deceiver, one
who bluffs.

fourfold [*fawr*fOld] *adj* made of four parts;
quadruple.

fourgon [*foorgon*] *n* a luggage-van.

four-handed [fawr-*hand*id] *adj* (*cards*) for four
players; (*mus*) for two players; (*zool*) capable of
using feet as equivalent to hands.

four-in-hand [*fawr*-in-hand] *n* carriage with
four horses driven by one man; kind of loose
flowing necktie.

fourpence [*fawr*pens] *n* sum of four pennies.

fourpenny [*fawr*p'ni] *adj* costing fourpence.

fourposter [fawr*pOster*] *n* bed with post at each
corner supporting frame for curtains.

fourpounder [fawr*pownder*] *n* gun throwing shot
weighing 4 lb.

fourscore [*fawr*skawr] *adj* (*ar*) eighty.

foursome [*fawr*sum] *n* game or dance with two
opposing pairs of partners.

foursquare [fawrs*kwair*] *adj* square; (*fig*) unyielding; firm; outspoken.

four-stroke [*fawr*-stROk] *adj* (*mot*, *of engine*) driven
by a single explosion to two revolutions.

fourteen [*fawr*teen] *n* and *adj* four more than ten;
symbol of this, 14.

fourteenth [fawr*teenth*] *n* and *adj* (that) which
follows thirteen others in a series; (that) which is
one of fourteen equal parts.

fourth [*fawr*th] *adj* following three others in a
series; being one of four equal parts; **f. dimension** time, considered as dimension in relation
to space > PDS; (*coll*) mysterious region or
state beyond normal space and time ~ **fourth**
n a quarter; fourth object in a series; (*mus*) interval reckoned as taking four steps in the scale;
chord of two notes at this interval > PDM;
the F. (*US*) Independence Day, 4 July ~
fourthly *adv* in fourth place.

fovea [*fO*vi-a] *n* (*anat*) pit, hollow; shallow pit
in retina > PDB.

fowl [*fowl*] *n* bird; domestic cock or hen; flesh of
birds as food ~ **fowl** *v/i* hunt birds ~ **fowler** *n*
one who shoots or snares wild birds ~ **fowling** *n*.

fowling-piece [*fowl*ing-pees] *n* light gun used
for shooting birds.

fowl-run [*fowl*-Run] *n* enclosed piece of ground
in which poultry are kept.

fox [*foks*] *n* animal of reddish colour with bushy
tail; fur of fox; (*fig*) crafty man; **f. and geese**
game played on squared board ~ **fox** *v/t* and *i*
deceive, dissemble, trick; puzzle; stain (paper)
yellowish-brown.

foxbrush [*foks*bRush] *n* bushy tail of fox.

fox-earth [*foks*-urth] *n* fox's burrow.

foxglove [*foks*gluv] *n* plant with long spike of
purple or white tubular flowers.

foxhole [*foks*hOl] *n* (*mil*) very short and narrow
trench.

foxhound [*foks*hownd] *n* type of hound used in
hunting foxes.

foxhunt [*foks*hunt] *n* pursuit of fox by riders and
hounds ~ **foxhunter** *n* ~ **foxhunting** *n* and
adj.

foxterrier [foks*teRi*-er] *n* kind of small terrier
formerly used for driving fox from cover.

foxtrot [*foks*tRot] *n* type of ballroom dance; music
for this; slow gait of horse.

foxy [*foks*i] *adj* crafty; reddish brown; strong-
smelling; (*of liquor*) sour.

foyer [*foi*-ay] *n* entrance hall or anteroom of
theatre; large hall or waiting-room.

frabjous [*fRab*jus] *adj* (*coll*) magnificent; joyous.

fracas [*fRak*aa] *n* disturbance, brawl.

fraction [*fRak*shon] *n* act of breaking; piece broken off; very small piece or amount; (*math*)
numerical quantity which is not an integer.

fractional [*fRak*shonal] *adj* pertaining to a fraction; incomplete, insignificant; **f. crystallization**
(*chem*) separation of mixture of dissolved substances by making use of their different solu-
bilities; **f. distillation** (*chem*) separation of mixture of liquids by making use of their different
boiling-points > PDS ~ **fractionally** *adv*.

fractionate [*fRak*shonayt] *v/t* (*chem*) separate
into constituents of differing properties.

fractionize [*fRak*shonIz] *v/t* and *i* separate into
fractions.

fractious [*fRak*shus] *adj* irritable, peevish.

fracture [*fRak*cher] *n* act of breaking, *esp* of a
bone; result of breaking ~ **fracture** *v/t* and *i*.

fragile [*fRaj*Il] *adj* brittle; easily destroyed; frail,
delicate.

fragility [fRa*jil*iti] *n* quality of being fragile.

fragment [*fRag*ment] *n* part broken off; incomplete portion of work of art ~ **fragmented**
[fRag*ment*id] *adj* broken into pieces.

fragmental [fRag*men*tal] *adj* fragmentary; **f.
deposits** (*geol*) rocks consisting of fragments of
other rocks or minerals.

fragmentary [fRag*men*taRi] *adj* incomplete, composed of fragments ~ **fragmentarily** *adv*,
~ **fragmentariness** *n*.

fragmentation [fRagmen*tay*shon] *n* separation
into fragments; **f. bomb** bomb that explodes into
small swiftly-moving fragments.

fragrance [*fRay*gRens] *n* sweet scent ~ **fragrant**
adj ~ **fragrantly** *adv*.

frail (1) [*fRayl*] *adj* fragile, liable to break; not
robust, weak; (*ar*) unchaste ~ **frailly** *adv*
~ **frailness** *n*.

frail (2) *n* rush basket in which figs and raisins are
packed; quantity contained in such a basket.

frailty [*fRayl*ti] *n* weakness; fault.

fraise [*fRayz*] *n* (*Fr*) (*mil*) outward-sloping palisade of barbed wire or pointed stakes.

frame [*fRaym*] *v/t* put together, construct;
express; pronounce; compose; adapt; surround
with a frame; act as frame or setting for; (*coll*)
fabricate evidence against, cause to appear guilty
~ **frame** *n* supporting structure; form, shape;
system; border surrounding picture *etc*; setting;
glass structure protecting seedlings *etc* from cold;
(*fig*) state of mind; (*cin*) one of series of small
pictures making up a film.

framed building [*fRaymd* bilding] *n* a structure
of which the framework carries all the loads
(instead of load-carrying walls) > PDBl.

framehouse [*fRaym*hows] *n* house of sawn timber

sheathed outside with weatherboards or shingles; half-timbered house.

framer [fRaymer] n one who frames.

frame-saw [fRaym-saw] n power saw held rigidly in a frame; (carp) heavy bow-saw.

frame-up [fRaym-up] n (coll) false charge; plot to discredit someone; swindle.

framework [fRaymwurk] n structure containing or supporting something; substructure; (fig) system, plan.

framing [fRayming] n act of constructing; that which serves as a frame.

franc [fRank] n French coin, monetary unit of France; corresponding coin and unit in Belgian and Swiss currency.

franchise [fRanchIz] n rights of citizenship, esp right of voting in elections; (leg) privilege, exemption; (insurance) a percentage below which the underwriter incurs no responsibility.

Franciscan [fRansiskan] n and adj (friar) of religious order of St Francis.

francium [fRanki-um] n (chem) rare radioactive element > PDS.

francolin [fRankOlin] n kind of partridge found in Asia and Africa.

francophile [fRankOfIl] n and adj (person) admiring all that is French.

francophobe [fRankOfOb] n and adj (person) having fear or hatred of the French.

franc-tireur [fRong-teeRur] n (Fr) member of irregular troops, guerrilla fighter.

frangible [fRanjibl] adj breakable.

frangipane [fRanjipaani] n perfume prepared from red jasmine; almond-flavoured pastry.

franglais [fRong-glay] n (Fr) modern style of French adopting many English words.

Frank (1) [fRank] n (hist) member of Germanic tribes which conquered Gaul in the sixth century; name given by Greeks and Moslems to West Europeans.

frank (2) n mark stamped on envelope recording payment of postage; (hist) signature exempting letter from postage; letter sent in this way ~ **frank** v/t set frank mark upon (envelope); (hist) exempt (letter) from postage, exempt from charges; arrange to pay expenses of (a person).

frank (3) adj straightforward, sincere; candid.

Frankenstein [fRankenstIn] n monster or invention beyond inventor's control.

frankfurter [fRankfurter] n small smoked sausage.

frankincense [fRankinsens] n aromatic gum resin used as incense.

Frankish [fRankish] adj of the Franks.

franklin [fRanklin] n (hist) small landowner.

frankly [fRankli] adv sincerely, openly.

frankness [fRanknis] n quality of being frank.

frantic [fRantik] adj wildly excited, distraught, greatly upset; (coll) terrible; hurried ~ **frantically** adv ~ **franticly** adv.

frappé [fRapay] adj iced, cooled ~ **frappé** n (Fr) dessert made of partly frozen fruit juice etc.

frass [fRas] n sawdust caused by woodworms.

fraternal [fRaturnal] adj brotherly; affectionate; (of twins) developed from separate ova, not identical ~ **fraternally** adv.

fraternity [fRaturniti] n brotherhood; brotherliness; body of men associated by religious vows;

any association of men with common object; (US) a male student association.

fraternize [fRaternIz] v/i be on friendly terms; (coll) be on terms of friendship or sexual relationship with member of enemy nation ~ **fraternization** [fRaternIzayshon] n.

fratricidal [fRatRisIdal] adj of or like fratricide.

fratricide [fRatRisId] n one who kills his brother or sister; murder of a brother or sister.

Frau [fRow] n German title for married woman.

fraud [fRawd] n deceitfulness; act of wilful dishonesty to gain advantage; dishonest stratagem; (coll) impostor, humbug, sham.

fraudulence [fRawdewlens] n quality of being fraudulent ~ **fraudulency** n.

fraudulent [fRawdewlent] adj acting with fraud; gained by fraud ~ **fraudulently** adv.

fraught [fRawt] adj laden with freight; (fig) full of; (coll) tense, harassed, agitated; causing agitation or distress.

Fräulein [fRoilIn] n German title of unmarried woman.

fray (1) [fRay] n brawl; fight, conflict.

fray (2) v/t and i wear away by friction, ravel out; (fig) exasperate.

frazil [fRazil] n slush ice; granular or spiky ice formed in rapids or other agitated water during long cold spells > PDG.

frazzle [fRaz'l] n shred, rag; **to a f.** very badly, utterly, thoroughly ~ **frazzle** v/t and i fray; wear out; exhaust.

freak [fReek] n abnormal form, monster; (coll) extraordinary person or thing; sudden change of mind, whim; capricious behaviour; (obs sl) drug addict; (coll) eccentric enthusiast; person who still pursues a hippy-like life-style ~ **freak** adj (coll) unusual, odd ~ **freak** v/i and t **f. out** undergo hallucinations etc caused by drugs; induce these in (a person); live or behave in an eccentric way.

freakish [fReekish] adj capricious; eccentric; extraordinary; grotesque ~ **freakishly** adv ~ **freakishness** n.

freak-out [fReek-owt] n (sl) drug-takers' party; enthusiastic gathering; painful experience of hallucinations under drugs.

freckle [fRek'l] n small brownish spot on skin, caused by sunlight; any small spot ~ **freckle** v/t and i mark with freckles; become marked with freckles ~ **freckled** adj ~ **freckly** adj.

free [fRee] adj unrestricted, not existing or acting under compulsion; not enslaved; not imprisoned; democratic; independent; costing nothing, obtainable without payment; exempt; not stiff, graceful; unrestrained, unconventional; unoccupied, available; lavish, generous; unconditional; irregular; not literal; not fastened; variable; (chem) uncombined; **F. Church** Scottish Presbyterian Church; Nonconformist Church; **f. fight** confused general fight; fight without rules; **f. hand** liberty to act at one's discretion; **f. house** public-house not dependent on one brewery; **make f. with** treat familiarly; use freely; **f. love** cohabitation without marriage; promiscuity; doctrine justifying this; **F. Trade** exemption of imports from customs duty; **f. verse** poetry not conforming to any traditional versification system; **f. wheel** wheel with gear in which driven member may freely outrun driving member; **f. will** power of human will to choose without external influence > PDP ~ **free** *adv* freely ~ **free** *v/t* set free; exempt; acquit; relieve (from obstacle, inconvenience *etc*).

free-and-easy [fRee-and-*eez*i] *adj* and *n* informal (gathering).

freeboard [*fRee*bawrd] *n* (*naut*) side of ship from waterline to deck or gunwale > PDE.

freebooter [*fRee*bOOter] *n* pirate, plunderer.

freeborn [*fRee*bawrn] *adj* not born in slavery.

freedman [*fRee*dman] *n* former slave who has been manumitted.

freedom [*fRee*dum] *n* state of being free, liberty; release from slavery, imprisonment *etc*; absence of restraint; exemption; frankness; excessive familiarity; permission to use or enjoy something belonging to another; **f. of the city** participation in privileges of a city; honorary grant of this; **f. of the seas** (*leg*) immunity of neutral shipping in wartime.

freehand [*fRee*hand] *adj* (*of drawing*) done without guiding instruments or other aids.

free-handed [fRee-*hand*id] *adj* generous.

free-hearted [fRee-*haart*id] *adj* frank; generous.

freehold [*fRee*hOld] *n* (*leg*) tenure of estate held in fee-simple, fee-tail, or for term of life; estate so held ~ **freeholder** *n* possessor of a freehold.

freelance [*fRee*laans] *n* and *adj* independent journalist, politician *etc* not attached to any particular paper, party, *etc* ~ **freelance** *v/i* write or work as a freelance.

freeliver [fRee*liv*er] *n* one who rejects moral restraints, *esp* about sex ~ **freeliving** *adj* and *n*.

freely [*fRee*li] *adv* in a free manner.

freeman [*fRee*man] *n* one who is free; one who possesses the freedom of a city.

freemartin [*fRee*maartin] *n* sterile and partially hermaphrodite cow > PDB.

Freemason [*free*mayson] *n* member of secret fraternity practising mutual benevolence; (*hist*) member of guild of masons.

freemasonry [fRee*may*sonRi] *n* principles and practices of Freemasons; (*fig*) instinctive understanding based on similar experience *etc*.

freerange [*fRee*Raynj] *adj* (*of poultry*) kept in a field, not in a battery or broiler house.

freesia [*fRee*zi-a] *n* South African plant of iris family.

freespoken [fRee*spO*ken] *adj* speaking plainly and without reserve.

freestone (1) [*fRee*stOn] *n* building stone which is fine grained and uniform enough to be worked in any direction.

freestone (2) variety of peach in which the stone parts easily from the flesh when ripe.

freethinker [fRee*think*er] *n* one who refuses to subordinate reason to authority in religious matters ~ **freethinking** *adj* and *n*.

freeway [*fRee*way] *n* (*US*) fast highway reserved for certain types of vehicle; motorway.

freewheel [fRee*weel*] *v/i* ride bicycle without moving pedals; allow car to coast downhill out of gear.

freewill [fRee*wil*] *adj* voluntary, spontaneous.

freeze (*p/t* froze, *p/part* frozen) [*fReez*] *v/t, i impers* change (liquid) to solid; kill by cold; chill; (*fig*) horrify; quell; immobilize; (*comm*)

make foreign-owned bank balances unrealizable; fix (prices *etc*) at a given level; be so cold that water turns to ice; be covered with ice; feel very cold; (*fig*) become rigid or motionless; **f. on to** seize and cling tightly to; **f. out** get rid of; **f. up** congeal, stiffen through cold ~ **freeze** *n* state of freezing; state of being frozen; period of frost; enforced stabilization of wages or prices.

freeze-dry [*fReez*-dRI] *v/t* dry a heat-sensitive substance by freezing and removing the frozen water under vacuum.

freezer [*fReez*er] *n* one who or that which freezes; refrigerated container or room for storing food in frozen state.

freeze-up [*fReez*-up] *n* (*coll*) long period of hard frost; immobility caused by cold.

freezing [*fReez*ing] *adj* that freezes; very cold; **f. mixture** mixture, *esp* of salt and ice, which produces considerable lowering of temperature > PDS; **f. point** temperature at which a liquid freezes at normal atmospheric pressure.

freight [*fRay*t] *n* load of goods for transport; ship's cargo; conveyance of goods by water, rail, or aircraft; hire of vessel for this; **f. train** goods train ~ **freight** *v/t* load (vessel); hire out (vessel) for transporting goods.

freightage [*fRay*tij] *n* freight; charge for transporting freight.

freighter [*fRay*ter] *n* one who charters and loads ship; one who receives and forwards goods; cargo ship.

French [*fRen*sh] *n* people or language of France ~ **French** *adj* pertaining to France or its people; **f. bean** haricot bean; kidney bean; **f. chalk** powdered talc used for marking cloth or removing grease; **f. grey** bluish grey; **f. horn** (*mus*) coiled brass wind instrument > PDM; **f. kiss** open-mouthed kiss with contact of tongues; **f. leave** absence without permission; **f. letter** condom; **f. window** glazed door to garden or balcony.

frenchify [*fRen*shifI] *v/t* make French in appearance or manner.

frenetic [fRe*net*ik] *adj* frenzied, frantic.

frenzied [*fRen*zid] *adj* mad, crazy, frantic; wildly enthusiastic ~ **frenziedly** *adv*.

frenzy [*fRen*zi] *n* violent emotional excitement; paroxysm of madness, rage, grief *etc*.

frequence [*fRee*kwens] *n* frequency.

frequency [*fRee*kwensi] *n* continual repetition; (*of pulse*) rapidity; (*phys*) number of vibrations (of wave) per second > PDS; (*st*) the number of observations having a value between two specified limits; **f. modulation** (*rad*) method of radio transmission in which the frequency of the carrier wave is modulated.

frequent (1) [*fRee*kwent] *adj* recurring at short intervals; often done, found, or experienced.

frequent (2) [fRi*kwent*] *v/t* visit habitually.

frequentation [fReekwen*tay*shon] *n* habitual visiting.

frequentative [fRee*kwen*tativ] *n* and *adj* (*gramm*) (form of verb) expressing repeated action.

frequented [fRi*kwent*id] *adj* often visited ~ **frequenter** *n* one who frequently visits a place.

frequently [*fRee*kwentli] *adv* often.

fresco [*fResk*O] *n* technique of painting with watercolour on plaster; painting or mural so executed > PDAA ~ **fresco** *v/t* paint in fresco.

fresh [*f*Resh] *adj* new; recently produced or made; not used; not worn out; pure, untainted; vigorous, lively; bracing; not faded; clean; inexperienced, new: (*of water*) not salt; (*of food*) not artificially preserved, tinned or frozen; not stale. (*of wind*) fairly strong; cool; (*coll*) slightly drunk; cheeky; inexperienced ~ **fresh** *n* a freshet; early part.

freshen [*f*Reshen] *v/i* and *t* become fresh; (*of wind*) increase in force; make brighter, make fresh, revive ~ **freshener** *n* one who, that which, freshens; refreshing drink.

fresher [*f*Resher] *n* (*coll*) first-year undergraduate

freshet [*f*Reshet] *n* clear stream; river flood caused by heavy rains or rapidly melting snow.

freshly [*f*Reshli] *adv* in a fresh way.

freshman [*f*Reshman] *n* male undergraduate in first year.

freshness [*f*Reshnis] *n* quality of being fresh.

freshwater [*f*Reshwawter] *adj* of or inhabiting fresh water; **f.** sailor inexperienced sailor.

fret (1) (*pres/part* **fretting**, *p/t* and *p/part* **fretted**) [*f*Ret] *v/t* and *i* erode; corrode; (*of wind*) ruffle; cause grief or worry to; grieve, feel anxiety, grief *etc*; complain querulously ~ **fret** *n* state of anxiety or grief; nervous agitation.

fret (2) *n* decorative pattern of horizontal and vertical straight lines; interlaced pattern, net; piece of wood cut into fine pattern; (*mus*) strip of wood on fingerboard of guitar *etc* > PDM ~ **fret** (*pres/part* **fretting**, *p/t* and *p/part* **fretted**) *v/t* decorate with fret pattern; carve, emboss; furnish (guitar) with frets.

fretful [*f*Retfool] *adj* discontented, complaining ~ **fretfully** *adv* ~ **fretfulness** *n*.

fretsaw [*f*Retsaw] *n* fine-toothed, narrow saw used for cutting wood into patterns.

fretwork [*f*Retwurk] *n* carved work in decorative patterns; woodwork with pattern cut by fine saw.

Freudian [*f*Roidi-an] *adj* relating to psychoanalysis; (*coll*) indirectly or subconsciously sexual; **F. slip** mistake in speaking or writing which reveals suppressed attitudes.

friability [*f*RI-abiliti] *n* quality of being friable.

friable [*f*RI-ab'l] *adj* liable to crumble; easily crumbled ~ **friableness** *n*.

friar [*f*RI-er] *n* member of a mendicant religious order; **friar's balsam** (*med*) tincture of benzoin.

friary [*f*RI-eRi] *n* convent of friars.

fribble [*f*Rib'l] *n* frivolous person, trifler; trifling occupation ~ **fribble** *v/i* waste one's time; squander foolishly.

fricassee [*f*Rikasee] *n* a white stew ~ **fricassee** *v/t*.

fricative [*f*Rikativ] *n* and *adj* (*phon*) (consonant) produced by expelling breath through small passage formed by tongue or lips.

friction [*f*Rikshon] *n* act of rubbing one thing against another; (*mech*) forces offering resistance to relative motion between surfaces in contact; (*fig*) antagonism, hostility ~ **frictional** *adj*.

Friday [*f*RIdi] *n* sixth day of the week; **Good F.** Friday before Easter, commemorating the Crucifixion; **girl F.** resourceful girl acting as personal secretary and assistant to businessman; **man F.** faithful servant, *esp* coloured.

fridge, frige [*f*Rij] *n* (*coll abbr*) refrigerator.

friend [*f*Rend] *n* person for whom one feels affection and whom one knows intimately; companion; helper, supporter; colleague, associate; acquaintance; **Society of Friends** Quakers.

friendly [*f*Rendli] *adj* like, characteristic of, a friend; kind, affectionate; gracious; favourable, helpful; **F. Society** mutual benefit insurance society ~ **friendlily** *adv* ~ **friendliness** *n*.

friendship [*f*Rendship] *n* relationship between friends; affection.

frieze (1) [*f*Reez/*f*Riz] *n* kind of coarse woollen cloth with nap.

frieze (2) *n* (*archi*) horizontal band between architrave and cornice; ornamental band, *esp* one just below ceiling or cornice.

frig (*pres/part* **frigging**, *p/t* and *p/part* **frigged**) [*f*Rig] *v/i* (*vulg sl*) masturbate; copulate.

frigate [*f*Rigit] *n* (*naut*) vessel smaller than destroyer; cruiser; fast sailing-ship smaller than ship of line.

frigate-bird [*f*Rigit-burd] *n* large predatory tropical seabird.

frige see **fridge**.

fright [*f*RIt] *n* sudden fear, alarm; (*coll*) ugly or ridiculous-looking person or thing.

frighten [*f*RIten] *v/t* terrify; alarm; **f. away, off** cause (someone) to flee through fear ~ **frightened** *adj*.

frightful [*f*RItfool] *adj* terrifying, alarming; (*coll*) shocking; very unpleasant ~ **frightfully** *adv* ~ **frightfulness** *n*.

frigid [*f*Rijid] *adj* extremely cold; (*fig*) lacking passion or affection; unemotional, unresponsive; lacking normal sexual desire; dull; **f. zone** regions within the polar circles > PDG.

frigidaire [*f*Rijidair] *n* (*tr*) refrigerator.

frigidity [*f*Rijiditi] *n* quality of being frigid.

frigorific [*f*RigeRifik] *adj* producing cold.

frill [*f*Ril] *n* loose ornamental flounced edging; ruffle; ornamental paper ruffle; (*fig*) useless adornment; (*pl*) superior or affected airs ~ **frill** *v/t* and *i* form into a frill; decorate with frills.

frilling [*f*Riling] *n* frill; act of putting frills on.

frilly [*f*Rili] *adj* having frills; like a frill.

fringe [*f*Rinj] *n* ornamental edging of tassels or hanging threads; border of short hair hanging over forehead; outer edge, most external part; (*fig*) initial stages of a subject ~ **fringe** *v/t* put a fringe on to; serve as fringe to ~ **fringe** *adj* beyond conventional limits, unorthodox; barely legal; **f. benefits** advantages, other than pay, gained from a job; **lunatic f.** group of extremists, fanatics, or irrational thinkers.

frippery [*f*RipeRi] *n* tawdry finery; showy knick-knacks; (*fig*) affected elegance, *esp* in literary style.

frisbee [*f*Rizbi] *n* concave disc thrown as game.

frisk [*f*Risk] *v/i* and *t* leap gaily, skip, gambol; whisk, wave briskly; (*sl*) search (someone) ~ **frisk** *n* brisk and lively movement; a frolic.

frisket [*f*Riskit] *n* (*print*) iron frame for holding paper in position while printing.

frisky [*f*Riski] *adj* playful, lively ~ **friskily** *adv* ~ **friskiness** *n*.

frit [*f*Rit] *n* finely ground sand, glass, and flint used for glazing bricks and other ceramic materials ~ **frit** (*pres/part* **fritting**, *p/t* and *p/part* **fritted**) *v/t* make into frit.

frith (1) [*f*Rith] *n* (*ar*) woodland; brushwood.

frith (2) *n* firth.

fritillary [fRitilleRi] *n* one of genus of speckled liliaceous flowers; one of genus of mottled-winged butterflies.

fritter (1) [fRiter] *n* slice of fruit or meat fried in batter.

fritter (2) *v/t* and *i* break into many small pieces; **f. away** (*fig*) waste; squander.

frivol (*pres/past* **frivolling**, *p/t* and *p/part* **frivolled**) [fRivol] *v/t* and *i* act frivolously; waste, squander.

frivolity [fRivoliti] *n* quality of being frivolous; frivolous behaviour.

frivolous [fRivolous] *adj* unimportant, useless; empty-headed, silly; superficial ~ **frivolously** *adv* ~ **frivolousness** *n*.

frizz (1) [fRiz] *v/t* and *i* curl or crisp (the hair); become curly or crisped into curls ~ **frizz** *n* crisped curl or curls; unmanageable mass of curls.

frizz (2) *v/i* sputter, sizzle (as bacon when fried).

frizzle (1) [fRiz'l] *v/t* and *i* curl the hair into tight curls; (*of hair*) crisped into tight curls.

frizzle (2) *v/t* and *i* sputter, fry briskly and thoroughly; (*fig*) be baked by the sun.

frizzy [fRizi] *adj* tightly curled.

fro [fRO] *adv* (*ar*) from; **to and f.** backwards and forwards, up and down.

frock [fRok] *n* long outer garment; woman's dress; monk's robe ~ **frock** *v/t* confer priesthood on; make a monk of; clothe in a frock.

frock-coat [fRok-kOt] *n* long coat for men, with skirts reaching almost to knees.

frog [fRog] *n* tailless amphibian animal; grooved plate at junction of railway lines > PDE; (*bui*) indentation on the face of a brick; horny pad on underside of horse's hoof; ornamental loop and button on clothes; attachment to belt supporting sword; (*coll*) Frenchman; **f. in the throat** (*coll*) hoarseness ~ **frogged** *adj* fastened by, ornamented with, loops of braid.

froghopper [fRoghoper] *n* small leaping insect that feeds on plant juices.

frogman [fRogman] *n* diver trained and equipped for underwater operations.

frogmarch [fRogmaarch] *n* method of carrying troublesome prisoner face downwards, by four men each holding a limb ~ **frogmarch** *v/t*.

frolic [fRolik] *n* merrymaking; gaiety; gay party or entertainment ~ **frolic** *adj* light-hearted ~ **frolic** (*pres/part* **frolicking**, *p/t* and *p/part* **frolicked**) *v/i* make merry, play.

frolicsome [fRoliksom] *adj* gay, merry, lively.

from [fRom] *prep* beginning at; out of; sent by; learnt, earned, derived *etc* by means of; not near to; unlike to; in imitation of; because of.

frond [fRond] *n* leaf-like organ bearing reproductive cells of certain plants; leaf; anything resembling a leaf.

frondescence [fRondesens] *n* process of coming into leaf; period when plant comes into leaf; foliage ~ **frondescent** *adj*.

front [fRunt] *n* foremost part; (*mil*) battle area; forward line; (*geog*) line of separation at earth's surface between cold and warm air masses > PDG; widespread political movement; promenade along sea; land adjoining stretch of water; position directly before a person; main façade of building; figurehead appointed to lend prestige to an organization; that which serves as a cover for illicit or illegal activities; (*theat*) auditorium; stiffened part of shirt; dickey; fringe of false hair; (*coll*) impudence; (*phon*) middle part of tongue; forward part of mouth; **come to the f.** become important; **put a bold f. on it** face boldly ~ **front** *adj* at, to, of, in, or on the front; first; prominent; (*phon*) uttered by middle of tongue; **F. Bench** one of two benches in House of Commons, occupied respectively by Ministers and by leading members of Opposition ~ **front** *v/t* and *i* face, stand opposite to; supply with a front; (*phon*) articulate further forward in mouth.

frontage [fRuntij] *n* length of a site in contact with a road; land between front of house and road; front of building ~ **frontager** *n* owner of such land.

frontal [fRuntal] *adj* in front; from the front; pertaining to the front; (*anat*) of the forehead ~ **frontal** *n* decorative drapery over front of altar; (*archi*) façade of building.

frontier [fRunteer] *n* boundary-line between two States; limit between settled and unexplored land; (*fig*) extreme limit ~ **frontier** *adj* of or on a frontier ~ **frontiersman** [fRunteerzman] *n* one who lives on a frontier.

frontispiece [fRuntispees] *n* illustration or ornamental design facing titlepage of book; (*archi*) principal façade.

frontlet [fRuntlet] *n* ornamental band worn on forehead; narrow embroidered strip hanging over altar frontal; front part of bird's head.

front-page [fRunt-payj] *adj* printed or fit to be printed on first page of newspaper; important, sensational.

frontward, frontwards [fRuntwerd, fRuntwerdz] *adv* towards the front, straight forward.

frost [fRost] *n* air temperature which causes water to freeze; particles of frozen moisture on earth's surface > PDG; (*fig*) coldness of manner; (*coll*) fiasco ~ **frost** *v/t* nip with frost; roughen surface of; cause to look like frost; quick-freeze (food).

frostbite [fRostbIt] *n* gangrenous injury to tissues through exposure to severe cold ~ **frostbite** *v/t* ~ **frostbitten** *adj*.

frosted [fRostid] *adj* covered with hoarfrost; (*of glass*) opaque and roughened; frostbitten.

frosting [fRosting] *n* (*bui*) translucent finely wrinkled finish in painting; opaque coating on glass; granulated icing for cake.

frosty [fRosti] *adj* ice-cold; (*of hair*) white; (*fig*) cold in manner ~ **frostily** *adv* ~ **frostiness** *n*.

froth [fRoth] *n* mass of small bubbles on agitated or fermenting liquid, foam; bubbles forming in saliva; (*fig*) shallowness, frivolity ~ **froth** *v/t* and *i* whisk into froth; emit froth, foam; (*fig*) talk frivolously.

frothy [fRothi] *adj* of, like, or covered with froth.

frottage [fRotaaj] *n* technique of making designs by rubbing rough surfaces across paint; picture produced thus.

frou-frou [fROO-fROO] *n* rustling of silk.

froward [fRO-erd] *adj* refractory, unreasonable ~ **frowardly** *adv* ~ **frowardness** *n*.

frown [fRown] *v/i* contract forehead and eyebrows; look angry or disapproving; (*fig*) appear unfavourable, threatening *etc*; **f. on** regard with disapproval ∼ **frown** *n* contraction of brows; look of anger, displeasure *etc* ∼ **frowning** *adj* ∼ **frowningly** *adv*.

frowst [*fROwst*] *n* hot, stuffy air in room; (*sl*) one who dislikes fresh air ∼ **frowst** *v/i* remain indoors in stuffy atmosphere.

frowsty [*fROwsti*] *adj* hot and airless, stuffy.

frowzy [*fROwzi*] *adj* stuffy, musty; unkempt, dirty-looking.

froze [*fROz*] *p/t* of **freeze**.

frozen [*fROzen*] *p/part* of **freeze**.

fructiferous [*fRuktifeRus*] *adj* yielding fruit.

fructification [*fRuktifikayshon*] *n* (*bot*) act of bearing fruit; act of making fruitful, fertilization; reproductive organs of plant.

fructify [*fRuktifI*] *v/i* and *t* bear fruit; make fruitful.

fructose [*fRuktOz*] *n* fruit sugar found in sweet ripe fruits, in the nectar of flowers, and in honey.

fructuous [*fRuktew-us*] *adj* fruitful; (*fig*) useful, profitable ∼ **fructuously** *adv* ∼ **fructuousness** *n*.

frugal [*fROOgal*] *adj* economical, thrifty; costing little ∼ **frugally** *adv*.

frugality [*fROOgaliti*] *n* thrift; cheapness.

fruit [*fROOt*] *n* (*bot*) ripened ovary of the flower, enclosing seeds; edible, pulpy, *usu* sweet seed-cases of various plants, eaten as dessert; any edible vegetable produce; (*fig*) offspring; result, outcome; reward; **f. machine** type of slot-machine used for gambling; **f. salad** dish of various fruits cut up and mixed ∼ **fruit** *v/i* bear fruit.

fruitarian [*fROOtairRi-an*] *n* one who lives on fruit.

fruitcake [*fROOtkayk*] *n* cake containing dried raisins or currants.

fruiter [*fROOter*] *n* tree that bears fruit; ship carrying fruit; fruit-grower.

fruiterer [*fROOteReR*] *n* fruit seller.

fruitful [*fROOtfool*] *adj* producing fruit; productive of offspring; prolific; remunerative, beneficial ∼ **fruitfully** *adv* ∼ **fruitfulness** *n*.

fruitily [*fROOtili*] *adv* in a fruity way.

fruitiness [*fROOtinis*] *n* quality of being fruity.

fruition [fROO-*ishon*] *n* pleasure arising from possessing or achieving something desired; enjoyment; fulfilment; achievement of maturity.

fruitless [*fROOtles*] *adj* bearing no fruit; (*fig*) producing no result; useless ∼ **fruitlessly** *adv* ∼ **fruitlessness** *n*.

fruity [*fROOti*] *adj* pertaining to, like, fruit; having taste of fruit; ripe; (*coll*) (*of voice*) rich, mellow; (*coll*) bawdy, scandalous.

frumentaceous [fROOmen*tayshus*] *adj* made of wheat; like wheat.

frumenty [*fROOmenti*] *n* wheat boiled in milk, sweetened and spiced.

frump [*fRump*] *n* dowdy, badly dressed woman ∼ **frumpish** *adj* ∼ **frumpy** *adj*.

frustrate [fRust*Rayt*] *v/t* prevent fulfilment of; render useless; foil, baffle.

frustration [fRust*Rayshon*] *n* state of being or feeling frustrated; act of frustrating.

frustum (*pl* frustums, frusta) [*fRustum*] *n* (*math*) any part of a solid figure cut off by a plane parallel to the base > PDS.

frutex [*fROOteks*] *n* (*bot*) woody-stemmed shrub.

fry (1) [*fRI*] *n* young fishes just spawned; the smaller kinds of fish and other animals; **small f.** unimportant persons; young children.

fry (2) *v/t* and *i* cook in fat in pan over fire ∼ **fry** *n* fried food; edible internal organs of animals.

fryer [*fRI*-er] *n* frying-pan; person who fries.

frying-pan [*fRI*-ing-pan] *n* shallow pan with long handle, in which food is fried.

fry-up [*fRI*-up] *n* (*coll*) mixture of foods fried together.

fubsy [*fubzi*] *adj* fat and stumpy.

fuchsia [*fewsha*] *n* genus of ornamental shrub with drooping red or purple flowers.

fuchsine [*fOOksin*] *n* kind of deep red dye.

fuck [*fuk*] *v/t* and *i* (*vulg*) (*of males*) have sexual intercourse (with); **f. up** (*sl*) spoil, mismanage ∼ **fuck** *n* act of sexual intercourse; sexual partner ∼ **fuck** *interj* oath expressing anger.

fucking [*fuking*] *adj* (*vulg expletive*) very bad or unpleasant; bloody, damned.

fucus (*pl* fuci, fucuses) [*fewkus*] *n* genus of seaweed.

fuddle [*fud*'l] *v/t* and *i* confuse the mind of, *esp* by drink; become stupid through drinking liquor ∼ **fuddle** *n* drunken stupidity.

fuddy-duddy [*fudi*-dudi] *n* fussy, old-fashioned person.

fudge [*fuj*] *n* soft sugary candy; made-up story; stop-press news; (*interj*) nonsense! ∼ **fudge** *v/t* fake, make up; put together clumsily.

fuehrer see **führer**.

fuel [*few*-el] *n* any substance used to produce heat by burning it; (*fig*) that which increases emotion *etc*; **f. cell** cell for producing electricity by oxidation of a fuel; **f. element** (*phys*) element of nuclear fuel for use in a reactor; **add f. to the flames** aggravate anger *etc* ∼ **fuel** (*pres/part* **fuelling**, *p/t* and *p/part* **fuelled**) *v/t* and *i* provide fuel for; stoke; obtain fuel.

fuelling [*few*-eling] *n* material used as fuel; act of providing with fuel.

fug [*fug*] *n* (*coll*) stuffy atmosphere; dust, fluff.

fugal [*fewgal*] *n* of, pertaining to, fugues.

fuggy [*fugi*] *adj* stuffy, airless.

fugitive [*fewjitiv*] *adj* fleeing, running away; swiftly passing away, transitory ∼ **fugitive** *n* one who flees or has fled from danger, captivity, oppression *etc*.

fugue [*fewg*] *n* (*mus*) type of contrapuntal composition for a given number of parts or 'voices' > PDM; (*psych*) disappearance associated with loss of memory > PDP.

fuguist [*fewgist*] *n* composer of fugues.

führer, fuehrer [*fewRer*] *n* (*Germ*) leader; title of Hitler; (*fig*) despot, autocratic leader.

fulcrum (*pl* fulcra) [*fulkRum*] *n* pivot about which a lever turns; (*fig*) means used to attain end.

fulfil (*pres/part* **fulfilling**, *p/t* and *p/part* **fulfilled**) [fool*fil*] *v/t* perform adequately; carry out; answer (purpose); comply with (conditions); (*refl*) develop and satisfy one's capacities.

fulfilment [fool*filment*] *n* act of fulfilling; that which fulfils, satisfaction.

fulgurating [*fulgewRayting*] *adj* like lightning; (*of pains*) darting through the body.

fulgurite [*fulgewRIt*] *n* (*min*) vitrified mass of sand produced by action of lightning.

full (1) [*fool*] *adj* containing all it can hold, filled to capacity; containing plenty of; crowded; well supplied with; (*of clothes*) large, roomy, flowing; at the maximum; complete; plump; resonant; overwhelmed by; preoccupied by; (*coll*) replete, having eaten enough; **f. age** adulthood; **f. dress** ceremonial dress; **f. face** showing the whole face; **in f. blast** very active; **in f. cry** in close pursuit of quarry; **f. of** preoccupied with; **f. stop** punctuation mark indicating end of sentence, or abbreviation; **f. up** absolutely full ~ **full** *n* utmost extent, degree, length *etc*; **in f.** completely; unabridged ~ **full** *adv* completely; directly; exactly; (*ar*) very ~ **full** *v/t* gather (material) in loose folds.

full (2) *v/t* cleanse and thicken (cloth).

full-blooded [fool-*blud*id] *adj* vigorous; virile; of unmixed race.

fullblown [fool*blOn*] *adj* (*of flowers*) fully opened; (*fig*) at the prime; complete.

full-bodied [fool-*bod*id] *adj* corpulent; richly flavoured.

full-bottomed [fool-*bot*omd] *adj* (*of ships*) having great capacity below water-line; **f. wig** one with large bottom.

fuller [*fool*er] *n* one who fulls cloth.

fuller's earth [foolerz-*urth*] *n* a variety of clay-like materials which absorb oil and grease, used in scouring textiles and in refining fats and oils.

full-fledged [fool-*flejd*] *adj* with all its feathers grown; (*fig*) fully qualified or established.

full-grown [fool*gROn*] *adj* having attained full size; mature, adult.

full-length [fool-*length*] *adj* fully stretched out; (*of portrait*) showing sitter's whole figure; unabridged; of standard length.

fullness [*fool*nes] *n* state of being full; abundance; full measure, amplitude; **in the f. of time** at the appointed time; eventually.

full-scale [*fool*-skayl] *adj* as complete, large or thorough as possible; not reduced in scale.

full-swing [fool-*swing*] *adj and adv* at highest pitch of activity.

full-time [fool*tIm*] *adj and adv* during all normal working hours; constant, unceasing ~ **full-timer** *n* one who works fulltime.

fully [*fool*i] *adv* in full measure, entirely; abundantly, amply; (*coll*) at least.

fully-fashioned [fooli-*fash*ond] *adj* (*of stockings*) seamed and shaped.

fulmar [*fool*mar] *n* seabird of the petrel family.

fulminant [*ful*minant] *adj* exploding; (*path*) developing suddenly.

fulminary [*ful*minaRi] *adj* (*path*) developing suddenly.

fulminate (1) [*ful*minayt] *n* compound of fulminic acid; **f. of mercury** mercuric isocyanate, causing detonation > PDS.

fulminate (2) *v/t and i* explode, detonate; (*fig*) denounce violently; (*med*) develop suddenly.

fulmination [fulmin*ay*shon] *n* loud explosion; (*fig*) violent denunciation ~ **fulminatory** [*ful*minayteRi] *adj*.

fulsome [*fool*sum] *adj* cloying, gushing ~ **fulsomely** *adv* ~ **fulsomeness** *n*.

fulvous [*ful*vus] *adj* tawny.

fumade [fewm*ayd*] *n* smoked pilchard.

fumarole [fewmaROl] *n* hole in earth's crust from which steam and gases are emitted.

fumatory [fewm*ate*Ri] *n* place set apart for fumigating purposes ~ **fumatory** *adj* pertaining to smoke or smoking.

fumble [*fumb*'l] *v/t and i* handle clumsily; grope; bungle ~ **fumbler** *n* ~ **fumbling** *adj* and *n*.

fume [*fewm*] *n* pungent smoke or vapour; strong smell; (*fig*) anger, agitation ~ **fume** *v/t and i* fumigate; darken by exposing to smoke; emit fumes; (*fig*) fret, be angry or agitated.

fumigate [*fewm*igayt] *v/t* disinfect or disinfest by applying smoke to ~ **fumigation** [fewmig*ay*shon] *n*.

fumigator [*fewm*igayter] *n* one who fumigates; apparatus for fumigating.

fumitory [*fewm*iteRi] *n* medicinal herb.

fumous [*fewm*us] *adj* smoky.

fumy [*fewm*i] *adj* full of fumes; smoky.

fun [*fun*] *n* amusement; playfulness, jollity; joking; source of amusement; **in f.** as a joke, not seriously; **like f.** (*sl*) not at all; very quickly; **make f. of, poke f. at** mock, tease, ridicule.

funambulist [fewn*am*bewlist] *n* tightrope walker.

function [*funk*shon] *n* natural activity, occupation or purpose; (*biol*) characteristic activity of part of organism in relation to the whole; duty; official task; public ceremony; (*coll*) large social gathering; (*math*) quantity so related to another that change in value of one produces change in value of other > PDS ~ **function** *v/i* fulfil one's purpose, allotted task *etc*; work.

functional [*funk*shonal] *adj* pertaining to functions; designed to fulfil a function; (*med*) affecting function, but not structure > PDP; (*archi*) designed solely with regard to practical use; having no ornamentation ~ **functionally** *adv*.

functionalism [*funk*shonalizm] *n* (*archi*) theory or practice of functional design.

functionary [*funk*shoneRi] *n* and *adj* official.

fund [*fund*] *n* accumulated stock; sum of money set apart for special purpose; (*pl*) government securities; cash resources, money ~ **fund** *v/t* provide fund for; invest in fund.

fundament [*fund*ament] *n* the buttocks; anus.

fundamental [fund*am*ental] *adj* basic, serving as foundation; primary, essential; important; **f. bass** (*mus*) lowest note of chord ~ **fundamental** *n* basic essential principle; (*mus*) primary note of harmonic series.

fundamentalism [fund*am*entalizm] *n* complete acceptance of literal truth of the Bible, *esp* of its accounts of the Creation ~ **fundamentalist** *n*.

fundamentally [fund*am*entali] *adv* basically, completely.

funded [*fund*id] *adj* made part of a permanent state debt bearing regular interest; invested in state securities.

funeral [*few*neRal] *n* ceremonial burial or cremation of the dead; procession taking corpse to cemetery; burial service ~ **funeral** *adj*.

funerary [*few*neRaRi] *adj* of or for a funeral.

funereal [fewn*eer*Ri-al] *adj* appropriate to a funeral; gloomy; deep black ~ **funereally** *adv*.

fun-fair [*fun*-fair] *n* fair with amusements, side-shows *etc*.

fungi [*fung*-gI/*funj*I] *pl.* of **fungus**.

fungible [*funj*ib'l] *adj* (*leg*) interchangeable.

fungicide [*fun*jisɪd] *n* substance for destroying fungi.

fungoid [*fung*-goid] *adj* of or like fungus.

fungous [*fung*-gus] *adj* pertaining to fungi; spongy; fast-growing.

fungus (*pl* **fungi** or **funguses**) [*fung*-gus] *n* (*bot*) one of large class of cryptogamous plants including toadstools, moulds, and lichens, lacking chlorophyll, and feeding on dead and living organic matter > PDB; (*med*) spongy growth.

funicular [few*ni*kewler] *adj* pertaining to ropes or fibres; worked by a rope; **f. railway** cable railway.

funk [*funk*] *n* (*sl*) fear, terror; a coward ~ **funk** *v/t* and *i* be afraid of; feel fear ~ **funky** *adj*.

funnel [*funel*] *n* Y-shaped vessel through which liquid or powder can be poured into a narrow-mouthed container; metal chimney or smoke-stack ~ **funnelled** *adj*.

funnily [*funili*] *adv* in an amusing manner; oddly; **f. enough** strange to say ~ **funniness** *n*.

funny [*funi*] *adj* amusing, comic; (*coll*) odd, queer; unexpected; underhand, mysterious, dishonest; slightly unwell; **f. business** fooling about; shady transaction or dealing.

funnybone [*funi*bOn] *n* sensitive bone of elbow.

fur [*fur*] *n* short, soft, close hair covering bodies of some animals; clothes, trimmings *etc* made from this; animals with such hair; insoluble gritty deposit in kettles, water-pipes *etc* > PDS; unhealthy coating on tongue; **make f. fly** quarrel violently ~ **fur** (*pres/part* **furring**, *p/t* and *p/part* **furred**) *v/t* and *i* trim, line, cover with fur; cover or become covered with deposit or coating; (*bui*) line (surface) with wood-strip and plasterwork.

furball [*fur*bawl] *n* mass of fur in an animal's stomach.

furbelow [*fur*belO] *n* flounce; showy trimmings.

furbish [*fur*bish] *v/t* remove rust from; brighten up, smarten.

furcate [*fur*kayt] *adj* forked, branched ~ **furcate** *v/t* and *i* divide into a fork.

furcation [fur*kay*shon] *n* division into a fork.

furfur (*pl* **furfures**) [*fur*fur] *n* dandruff, scurf.

furfuraceous [furfu*Ray*shus] *adj* scurfy, covered with dandruff; (*bot*) covered with bran-like scales.

furfural [*fur*furRal] *n* (*chem*) colourless, oily liquid used in the manufacture of thermosetting plastics.

furious [*few*Ri-us] *adj* raging; violent, wild, uncontrolled ~ **furiously** *adv* ~ **furiousness** *n*.

furl [*furl*] *v/t* roll up and bind securely.

furlong [*fur*long] *n* eighth of a mile, 220 yds.

furlough [*fur*lO] *n* leave of absence, *esp* to soldier or official.

furmety, furmenty see **frumenty**.

furnace [*fur*nis] *n* chamber of brick or metal in which great heat can be generated.

furnish [*fur*nish] *v/t* provide, supply; equip (house) with furniture and fittings ~ **furnisher** *n* one who furnishes or sells furniture.

furnishing [*fur*nishing] *n* act of equipping house with furniture; (*pl*) furniture, domestic equipment, fittings *etc*.

furniture [*fur*nicher] *n* movable household articles of equipment; necessary equipment, trappings, accessories.

furore [few*Raw*Ri/*few*Rawr] *n* wild outburst of enthusiasm; enthusiastic admiration.

furrier [*fu*Ri-er] *n* dresser of furs; dealer in furs.

furring [*fur*Ring] *n* fur trimming; state of being furred or encrusted; (*carp*) timber strips laid to level a surface; (*bui*) a wood-strip and plaster-work lining to a wall.

furrow [*fu*RO] *n* narrow trench cut by plough; groove, long rut; (*fig*) deep wrinkle ~ **furrow** *v/t* make furrows in.

furry [*fu*Ri] *adj* like fur; consisting of fur; made of fur; coated with fur.

further [*fur*THer] *adj* additional; more distant ~ **further** *adv* to greater distance, degree, or extent; besides, moreover ~ **further** *v/t* help forward, promote.

furtherance [*fur*THeRens] *n* assistance.

furthermore [*fur*THermawr] *adv* in addition, moreover.

furthermost [*fur*THermOst] *adj* most distant.

furthest [*fur*THest] *adj* most distant ~ **furthest** *adv* at or to the greatest distance or degree.

furtive [*fur*tiv] *adj* stealthy; sly, secretive ~ **furtively** *adv* ~ **furtiveness** *n*.

furuncle [*few*Runk'l] *n* (*med*) boil.

furuncular [few*Runk*ewlar] *adj* of or having boils.

furunculous [few*Runk*ewlus] *adj* furuncular.

fury [*few*Ri] *n* wild, violent anger; (*myth*) avenging goddess; (*fig*) fierce spiteful woman; **like f.** (*coll*) furiously, madly, very energetically.

furze [*furz*] *n* spiny evergreen shrub w th yellow flowers; gorse, whin ~ **furzy** *adj*.

fuscous [*fus*kus] *adj* dark in colour.

fuse (1) [*fewz*] *n* (*min*) train of black powder enclosed in a waterproof braided textile used for firing detonators > PDE; (*mil*) device to explode shell; (*elect*) small piece of wire in an electric circuit which melts when the current exceeds a certain strength.

fuse (2) *v/t* and *i* melt (metal); be melted, liquify; be liquified; melt and allow to solidify, blend; become blended; (*elect*) fail by blowing of fuse.

fusee [few*zee*] *n* conical pulley on wheel of watch or clock; bony tumour on horse's leg; match with large long-burning head.

fuselage [*few*zilaaj] *n* body of aeroplane.

fusel-oil [*few*zel-oil] *n* mixture of butyl and iso-amyl alcohols.

fusibility [fewzi*bili*ti] *n* quality of being fusible.

fusible [*fewzib*'l] *adj* capable of being melted, of low melting point.

fusilier [fewzi*leer*] *n* soldier belonging to regiment formerly bearing light muskets; rifleman.

fusillade [fewzi*layd*] *n* rapid continuous discharge of many firearms ~ **fusillade** *v/t* attack or kill by fusillade.

fusion [*few*zhon] *n* melting, melting together; a blend; coalition; (*psych*) combination of two or more stimuli into an unanalysed impression > PDP; **nuclear f.** (*phys*) thermonuclear reaction in which light nuclei join to form heavier nucleus > PDS.

fuss [*fus*] *n* nervous agitation and annoyance; unnecessary commotion, bustle; **make a f. (about)** complain angrily (about); show unnecessary worry (over); **make a f. of** treat with exaggerated care, tenderness *etc* ~ **fuss** *v/t* and *i* be in a fuss; make a fuss; worry, bother, irritate (person).

fusspot [*fus*pot] *n* (*coll*) very fussy person.

fussy [*fusi*] *adj* given to making a fuss; fussing about trifles; over-elegant ~ **fussily** *adv* ~ **fussiness** *n*.

fustian [*fusti-an*] *n* coarse twilled cloth, corduroy; (*fig*) bombast, pretentious language ~ **fustian** *adj* made of fustian; (*fig*) pretentious, bombastic.

fustic [*fustik*] *n* Mexican tree producing yellow dye; dye made from this.

fustigate [*fustigayt*] *v/t* (*joc*) thrash.

fusty [*fusti*] *adj* mouldy, smelling of dampness, (*fig*) old-fashioned ~ **fustily** *adv* ~ **fustiness** *n*.

futhorc [*fOOTHawrk*] *n* Runic alphabet.

futile [*fewtIl*] *adj* useless, without result; unimportant, petty ~ **futilely** *adv*.

futility [*fewtiliti*] *n* uselessness; useless act or thing.

future [*fewcher*] *adj* going to happen or exist later than present time; relating to life after death; (*gramm*) expressing time to come ~ **future** *n* time to come; events which will later occur; later career, fate, or life; (*pl*) (*comm*) goods bought at current price and not at price at time of delivery.

futureless [*fewcherles*] *adj* having nothing to look forward to.

futurism [*fewcherizm*] *n* belief in fulfilment of Bible prophecies; art movement devoted to dynamic study of figures in motion > PDAA; (*coll*) advanced, non-representational art ~ **futurist** *n* and *adj*.

futuristic [*fewcheRistik*] *adj* of futurism; (*coll*) of weirdly abstract appearance, eccentrically modern.

futurity [*fewtewRiti*] *n* the future.

futurology [*fewcheRoloji*] *n* the study of the world's probable future history by extrapolation from present trends.

fuzz [*fuz*] *n* tangled fluff; fluffy hair; (*sl*) police.

fuzzy [*fuzi*] *adj* fluffy; furry; blurred ~ **fuzziness** *n*.

fylfot [*filfot*] *n* the swastika.

G

g [*jee*] seventh letter of the English alphabet; (*mus*) fifth note in scale of C major; (*phys*) gravity; acceleration due to gravity; unit measuring this.

gab [*gab*] *n* talkativeness; (*sl*) mouth; **gift of the g.** facility of speech ~ **gab** (*pres/part* **gabbing**, *p/t* and *p/part* **gabbed**) *v/i* chatter, talk too much.

gabardine see **gaberdine**.

gabble [*gab'l*] *v/t* and *i* talk rapidly and indistinctly, jabber ~ **gabble** *n* quick, confused speech ~ **gabbler** *n*.

gaberdine, gabardine [*gab*erdeen] *n* thin woollen fabric, finely ribbed; rainproof coat made from this; (*hist*) long coat worn by Jews.

gabion [*gay*bi-on] *n* (*mil*) earth-filled wicker basket used as protection from rifle fire; (*eng*) small cellular cofferdam.

gable [*gayb'l*] *n* triangular piece of wall enclosed by ends of ridged roof; end wall of building, of which upper part is triangular; triangular decoration over window or door ~ **gable** *v/t* and *i* put a gable on; end in a gable ~ **gabled** *adj* having gables.

gaby [*gay*bi] *n* (*dial*) fool, simpleton.

gad (1) [*gad*] *n* (*obs sl*) God.

gad (2) (*pres/part* **gadding**, *p/t* and *p/part* **gadded**) *v/i* wander about restlessly, aimlessly, or in search of pleasure ~ **gad** *n* wandering; **on the g** (*of cattle*) restless; (*fig*) constantly moving from place to place.

gad (3) *n* goad; strikec bar > PDE.

gadabout [*gad*abowt] *n* restless pleasure-seeker.

gadfly [*gad*fl1] *n* fly which stings cattle; (*fig*) infuriating person.

gadget [*gaj*it] *n* small mechanical appliance or accessory.

gadgeteer [*gaji*teer] *n* one who invents or is interested in gadgets.

gadgetry [*gaj*itRi] *n* gadgets collectively.

gadolinium [*gad*Ol*ini*-um] *n* (*chem*) rare lanthanide element > PDS.

Gael [*gayl*] *n* Scottish or Irish Celt.

Gaelic [*gay*lik] *n* and *adj* (language) of the Gaels.

gaff (1) [*gaf*] *n* short-handled iron hook for landing fish; light fishing spear; (*naut*) spar for extending upper part of fore-and-aft sail ~ **gaff** *v/t* land (fish) with gaff.

gaff (2) *n* (*sl*) nonsense; **blow the g.** (*sl*) divulge a secret.

gaff (3) *n* (*sl*) low-class theatre or music-hall.

gaffe [*gaf*] *n* (*Fr*) error of tact, blunder.

gaffer [*gaf*er] *n* old countryman; old man; foreman.

gag [*gag*] *n* anything covering or filling person's mouth to force him to be silent; (*fig*) anything restraining free speech; (*surg*) device to keep patient's mouth open; (*theat*) unscripted remark; (*coll*) joke, funny story; (*sl*) hoax ~ **gag** (*pres/part* **gagging**, *p/t* and *p/part* **gagged**) *v/t* and *i* silence by means of a gag; prevent from speaking freely; silence by intimidation; interpolate gags; tell jokes; retch, be near to vomiting; choke.

gaga [*gaag*aa] *adj* (*sl*) crazy; senile.

gage (1) [*gayj*] *n* pledge, article offered as surety; challenge to fight; article offered as symbol of this ~ **gage** *v/t* pledge; stake.

gage (2) see **gauge**.

gage (3) *abbr* of **greengage**.

gaggle [*gag'l*] *n* flock of geese ~ **gaggle** *v/i* (*of geese*) cackle.

gagsman [*gag*zman] *n* one who devises jokes for a comedian.

gagster [*gag*ster] *n* one who devises or tells jokes.

gaiety [*gay*-iti] *n* cheerfulness, mirth; (*pl*) festivities, entertainments.

gaillardia [*gay*laardi-a] *n* composite flower with red and yellow petals.

gaily [*gay*li] *adv* in a gay manner.

gain [*gayn*] *v/t* and *i* earn; reach or obtain by effort or merit; win; obtain as profit or increase; improve; show profit; increase in speed; **g. ground** progress, spread, increase; **g. on** or **upon** move faster than, outdistance, catch up with; **g. time** obtain a delay ~ **gain** *n* profit; increase, addition; improvement; (*rad*) increase in signal power; ratio of output to input power in decibels > PDEl.

gain-control [*gayn*-contROl] *n* (*rad*) volume-control on receiving set.

gainful [*gayn*ful] *adj* bringing profit ~ **gainfully** *adv*.

gainings [*gayn*ings] *n* (*pl*) earnings; profits.

gainsay [*gayn*say] *v/t* contradict; deny; oppose.

gait [*gayt*] *n* manner of walking or running.

gaiter [*gay*ter] *n* cloth or leather covering for ankle, or for leg below knee ~ **gaiter** *v/t*.

gal [*gal*] *n* (*obs coll* or *joc*) girl.

gala [*gaala*/*gayla*] *n* festival ~ **gala** *adj* festive.

galactic [*gal*aktik] *adj* (*astron*) pertaining to a galaxy; (*med*) pertaining to milk.

galactin [*gal*aktin] *n* substance causing coagulation in milk; substance extracted from sap of a tropical American tree.

galantine [*gal*anteen] *n* loaf of white meat, boned, minced, boiled and served cold.

galaxy [*gal*aksi] *n* vast cluster of stars, of which solar system forms part; portion of this visible as irregular luminous band, Milky Way; similar cluster in distant regions of space, visible as nebula; (*fig*) group of distinguished persons.

gale (1) [*gayl*] *n* very violent wind > PDG; (*poet*) gentle breeze.

gale (2) *n* the bog-myrtle.

galeated [*gali*-aytid] *adj* helmet-shaped; wearing, or covered as with, a helmet.

galena [*gal*eena] *n* natural lead sulphide.

galingale [*gal*ing-gayl] *n* pungent root allied to ginger; kind of sedge.

galiot see **galliot**.

gall (1) [*gawl*] *n* bitter fluid secreted by liver into gallbladder, bile; gallbladder; (*fig*) bitterness; (*coll*) impudence.

gall (2) *n* painful swelling or pustule *esp* in horse; sore produced by friction; excrescence produced on trees by insect ~ **gall** *v/t* and *i* make sore, rub into a sore; (*fig*) irritate, annoy; become sore.

gallant [*ga*lant] *adj* brave, noble; chivalrous; fine-looking; [ga*lant*] attentive to women, politely amorous ~ **gallant** [*ga*lant/ga*lant*] *n* suitor; lover; man of fashion ~ **gallant** [*ga*lant/ga*lant*] *v/t* and *i* escort; flirt with; play the gallant ~ **gallantly** *adv*.

gallantry [*ga*lantRi] *n* bravery, chivalrousness; attentiveness to women, courtesy; a compliment; elegant and sophisticated flirtation.

gallbladder [*gawl*blader] *n* small bladder near liver, containing bile > PDB.

galleon [*gali*-on] *n* large sailing ship with high prow and stern formerly used by the Spaniards.

gallery [*gale*Ri] *n* raised platform or balcony projecting inwards from wall of room and supported by pillars; long, narrow, covered passageway, open on one side; long, narrow passage; (*mining*) roadway or tunnel; building for exhibitions of works of art; (*theat*) highest and cheapest floor of seats; audience occupying these seats; spectators; **play to the g.** seek applause by pleasing popular taste.

galley [*gali*] *n* (*hist*) ancient warship propelled by rowers; low single-decked ship propelled by rowers and sail; (*pl*) (*fig*) penal servitude; cook-house of ship; large rowing boat; (*print*) flat oblong tray for holding composed type; galley-proof.

galley-proof [*gali*-pROOf] *n* (*print*) a proof taken before the matter is made up into pages.

galley-slave [*gali*-slayv] *n* slave condemned to row on board a galley; (*fig*) drudge.

galliard [*gali*-aard] *n* (*ar*) lively type of dance.

Gallic (1) [*gali*k] *adj* pertaining to Gaul or the Gauls; pertaining to France or the French.

gallic (2) [*gawl*ik] *adj* pertaining to or obtained from galls on trees.

gallicism [*gali*sizm] *n* use of French words or idioms in another language.

gallicize [*gali*sIz] *v/t* make Gallic or French, frenchify.

gallimaufry [gali*maw*fRi] *n* hotchpotch.

gallinaceous [gali*nay*shus] *adj* of the family of birds which includes the domestic fowl, pheasant, partridge *etc*.

galling [*gaw*ling] *adj* chafing; (*fig*) irritating; bitter.

galliot (*US* **galiot**) [*gali*-ot] *n* (*naut*) small swift galley; Dutch cargo-boat or fishing-vessel.

gallipot [*gali*pot] *n* small jar to contain ointment.

gallium [*gali*-um] *n* (*chem*) silvery metal used in high temperature thermometers > PDS.

gallivant [gali*vant*] *v/i* gad about; flirt.

gallon [*ga*lun] *n* English measure of capacity, dry or liquid, equal to four quarts.

galloon [ga*lOOn*] *n* braid woven with gold and silver threads.

gallop [*ga*lop] *n* swiftest pace of quadruped, in which all feet are off the ground at once ~ **gallop** *v/t* and *i* ride at a gallop; cause (horse) to gallop; (*fig*) advance very rapidly; hurry.

galloway [*ga*lo-way] *n* breed of small, strong horses; Scottish breed of cattle.

gallows [*ga*lOz] *n* wooden structure with cross-bar on which criminals are hanged; anything resembling this; the punishment of hanging; **g. bird** one who deserves hanging, worthless ruffian; **g. tree** gallows.

gallowses [ga*lusiz*] *n* (*pl*) (*coll*) pair of braces.

gallstone [*gawl*stOn] *n* (*med*) concretion in gall-bladder.

Gallup-poll [*ga*lup-pOl] *n* (*tr*) method of assessing public opinion by questioning a representative cross-section of the population.

galluses [ga*lusiz*] *n* (*pl*, *coll*) braces for trousers.

galoot [ga*lOOt*] *n* (*sl*) fellow; clumsy fool.

galop [*ga*lop] *n* quick dance in two-four time; music for this ~ **galop** *v/i*.

galore [ga*lawr*] *adv* in plenty.

galosh, golosh [*ga*losh, go*losh*] *n* protective overshoe worn in wet weather.

galumph [ga*lumf*] *v/i* leap about clumsily but joyfully; express triumph by such movements.

galvanic [gal*va*nik] *adj* (*elect*) pertaining to, produced by, galvanism; (*fig*) convulsive; startling; wildly energetic ~ **galvanically** *adv*.

galvanism [*ga*lvanizm] *n* electricity produced by chemical action; treatment of diseases by electricity.

galvanize [ga*lvan*Iz] *v/t* subject to or stimulate by electric shock; cover with metal coating; (*fig*) startle; rouse to action ~ **galvanized** *adj* (*of iron*) coated with zinc to prevent rusting.

galvanometer [galva*no*miter] *n* apparatus for detecting, comparing, or measuring small electric currents > PDS.

gam (*pres/part* **gamming**, *p/t* and *p/part* **gammed**) [*gam*] *v/i* (*naut*) meet socially at sea, exchange visits from ship to ship; (*of whales*) congregate; (*fig*) exchange visits ~ **gam** *n* exchange of visits at sea; school of whales.

gambit [*gam*bit] *n* (*chess*) opening move, in which pawn is sacrificed for future advantage in position; (*fig*) initial move; cunning strategy, trick.

gamble [*gamb*'l] *v/i* and *t* play for money at games of chance; speculate financially; place (money) at stake; (*fig*) take a chance or risk ~ **gamble** *n* act of gambling; risky venture; that which depends on chance ~ **gambler** *n*.

gamboge [gam*bOOzh*] *n* a yellow pigment.

gambol (*pres/part* **gambolling**, *p/t* and *p/part* **gambolled**) [*gam*bol] *v/i* leap gaily about, frisk, skip ~ **gambol** *n*.

game (1) [*gaym*] *n* play, amusement, sport; organized play according to rules, *usu* competitive; sporting contest; single round of such contest; score needed to win such contest; scheme, *esp* to defeat another; trick, cunning device; joke; intention; undertaking; animal or bird that is hunted, quarry; edible flesh of such animals or birds; **fair g.** that which can be legitimately hunted or attacked; **make g. of** mock; **play the g.** act fairly and honourably; **the g. is up** everything has failed ~ **game** *v/i* gamble ~ **game** *adj* (*coll*) brave, spirited, willing.

game (2) *adj* crippled.

gamebird [*gaym*burd] *n* bird shot for sport.

gamecock [*gaym*kok] *n* a fighting cock.

gamekeeper [*gaym*keeper] *n* man employed to look after gamebirds *etc*.

game-laws [*gavm*-lawz] *n* (*pl*) laws relating to the preservation of gamebirds *etc*.

gamely [*gaym*li] *adv* bravely ~ **gameness** *n*.

game-reserve [*gaym*-Rizurv] *n* area of land set aside and protected for breeding animals or birds to be hunted.

gamesmanship [*gaymz*manship] *n* (*coll*) art of winning games by disconcerting one's opponent.

gamester [*gaym*ster] *n* a gambler.

gamete [*gameet*] *n* (*biol*) reproductive cell fusing with another to produce new individual > PDB.

gametic [*gametik*] *adj* of a gamete.

gametocyte [*gameet*Osit] *n* (*biol*) cell from which gametes are formed > PDB.

gamin (*fem* **gamine**) [*gam*an(g), *gam*een] *n* (*Fr*) street urchin, cheeky child.

gaming [*gaym*ing] *n* gambling.

gamma [*gama*] *n* third letter of Greek alphabet; **g. rays** (*phys*) very short electromagnetic waves produced by radioactive material > PDS.

gammer [*gamer*] *n* old woman.

gammon (1) [*gam*on] *n* lower end of flitch of bacon including hind leg; a cured ham ~ **gammon** *v/t* cure (bacon).

gammon (2) *n* (*coll*) nonsense, humbug, deceitful talk ~ **gammon** *v/t* and *i* (*coll*) humbug, hoax, deceive with lies; talk plausibly.

gammon (3) *n* method of victory at backgammon ~ **gammon** *v/t*.

gammy [*gami*] *adj* (*coll*) lame; crippled.

gamogenesis [gam*Oje*nisis] *n* reproduction through the union of two gametes.

gamp [*gamp*] *n* (*coll*) large umbrella.

gamut [*gamut*] *n* (*mus*) range, compass; scale; (*ar*) lowest note of scale > PDM.

gamy [*gaym*i] *adj* having the flavour of game, *esp* when high; (*coll*) spirited, plucky.

gander [*gander*] *n* male goose; simpleton; (*sl*) look.

gang (1) [*gang*] *n* group, band of associates; group of criminals working together; band of workmen; closely knit group of children or youths, *usu* hostile to other groups; group of similar machines automatically working together > PDE; set of tools to be used together ~ **gang** *v/i* (*coll*) associate, form a group; **g. up on** join together against.

gang (2) *v/i* (*Scots*) walk; go.

gang-bang [*gang*-bang] *n* (*sl*) copulation with one woman by several men successively.

ganger [*ganger*] *n* foreman of gang of labourers.

gangling [*gang*-gling] *adj* tall and thin, lanky.

ganglion (*pl* **ganglia**) [*gang*-gli-on] *n* (*med*) small solid mass of nervous tissue containing numerous cell-bodies > PDB; tumour in sheath of tendon; (*fig*) centre of various types of activity.

ganglionic [gang-gli-*onik*] *adj* of a ganglion.

gangplank [*gang*plank] *n* board used as ship's gangway.

gangrene [*gang*-gReen] *n* (*med*) extensive decay of part of living tissue, necrosis ~ **gangrene** *v/t* and *i* cause gangrene in; mortify, decay.

gangrenous [*gang*-gRinus] *adj* affected by gangrene.

gangster [*gang*ster] *n* armed professional criminal.

gangsterism [*gang*steRizm] *n* the way of life of gangsters.

gangue [*gang*] *n* valueless minerals in ore > PDE.

gangway [*gang*way] *n* road or passage; passage between rows of seats; movable bridge of planks from ship to wharf.

ganister [*gan*ister] *n* (*geol*) a hard stone.

gannet [*gan*it] *n* large seabird, the solan-goose.

ganoid [*gan*oid] *adj* (*of fish-scales*) like enamel; smooth and shining > PDB ~ **ganoid** *n* fish having ganoid scales.

gantry [*gant*Ri] *n* framework carrying travelling crane, heavy loads, or railway signals *etc* > PDE; wooden stand for barrels.

Ganymede [*gan*imeed] *n* (*fac*) waiter, pot-boy; boy kept for homosexual purposes; (*astron*) largest satellite of Jupiter.

gaol [*jayl*] *n* prison.

gaolbird [*jayl*burd] *n* habitual prisoner.

gaolbreak [*jayl*bRayk] *n* escape from prison.

gaoler [*jayl*er] *n* prison warder, keeper.

gaol-fever [*jayl*-feever] *n* typhus.

gap [*gap*] *n* opening, hole, empty space between two objects; interval; interruption.

gape [*gayp*] *v/i* open the mouth widely; yawn; look stupidly amazed; (*fig*) stand open; split apart, open into fissures; **g. at** stare in amazement at ~ **gape** *n* act of gaping; yawn; opening; (*pl*) disease of poultry; fit of yawning.

gap-toothed [*gap*-tOOtht] *adj* with teeth wide apart.

garage [*ga*Raaj/*ga*Rij] *n* building, either private or public, where motor vehicles can be left; petrol station where running repairs can be carried out ~ **garage** *v/t* put into a garage.

garb [*gaarb*] *n* style of dress, clothing ~ **garb** *v/t* and *refl* clothe.

garbage [*gaarb*ij] *n* refuse, rubbish, filth; **g. can** (*US*) dustbin.

garble [*gaarb*'l] *v/t* distort, misrepresent, *esp* by tendentious selection of facts.

garboard [*gaar*bawrd] *n* planks or plates next to ship's keel.

garden [*gaar*den] *n* plot of land for cultivation of flowers, plants *etc*; public park; **lead up the g. (path)** (*sl*) mislead ~ **garden** *adj* in, of, or for a garden ~ **garden** *v/i* cultivate a garden.

garden-city, garden-suburb [gaarden-*siti*, gaarden-*suburb*] *n* town or suburb laid out with gardens and open spaces.

gardener [*gaard*ener] *n* one fond of gardening; one employed to work in a garden.

gardenia [gaar*deeni*-a] *n* tropical shrub with fragrant white or yellow flowers; the flower of this shrub.

gardening [*gaard*ening] *n* the cultivation of a garden.

garefowl [*gair*fowl] *n* the great auk.

garfish [*gaar*fish] *n* slender sea-fish with long, spear-like snout.

gargantuan [gaar*gan*tew-an] *adj* very large.

gargle [*gaarg*'l] *v/i* and *t* wash or disinfect mouth and throat with liquid, while breathing out through the mouth ~ **gargle** *n* act of gargling; noise of gargling; medicated liquid used for gargling.

gargoyle [*gaarg*oil] *n* (*archi*) carved rainwater spout on roof.

garibaldi [ga*Ri*bawldi] *n* kind of shirt-like blouse; **g. biscuit** biscuit enclosing layer of currants.

garish [*gair*Rish] *adj* excessively bright, gaudy, showy ~ **garishly** *adv* ~ **garishness** *n*.

garland [*gaar*land] *n* wreath of flowers or leaves; representation of this; (*fig*) emblem of victory or merit ~ **garland** *v/t* crown with a garland.

garlic [*gaar*lik] *n* bulbous plant, whose bulb is used as seasoning.

garment [*gaar*ment] *n* article of clothing.

garn [*gaarn*] *interj* (*sl*) exclamation indicating disbelief.

garner [*gaar*ner] *n* granary; (*fig*) an anthology ~ **garner** *v/t* store up.

garnet [*gaar*nit] *n* type of dark-red gem; group of silicate minerals > PDS.

garnish [*gaar*nish] *v/t* decorate, adorn; add sauce, trimmings, relish *etc* to (food) ~ **garnish** *n* ornament, relish, sauce; accessories ~ **garnishing** *adj* and *n*.

garniture [*gaar*nicher] *n* ornamentation.

garotte see garrotte.

garret [*ga*Rit] *n* room immediately under roof of house, attic.

garrison [*ga*Rison] *n* troops guarding fortress or town ~ **garrison** *v/t* station troops in a place for its defence.

garrison-artillery [*ga*Rison-aar*tile*Ri] *n* heavy artillery for defence of fortifications.

garrotte, garotte [*ga*Rot] *v/t* strangle by cord twisted round neck, *esp* in order to rob victim ~ **garrotte, garotte** *n* throttling device used in Spain and Portugal for legal executions; act of strangling with a cord; cord so used.

garrulity [*ga*ROOliti] *n* quality of being garrulous.

garrulous [*ga*Roolus] *adj* loquacious, talkative about trivial matters ~ **garrulously** *adv* ~ **garrulousness** *n*.

garter [*gaar*ter] *n* elastic band round leg to keep up the stocking; **the G.** highest order of knighthood in Great Britain; badge of this order; membership of this order.

garth [*gaarth*] *n* enclosed space, yard, court, garden.

gas [*gas*] *n* substance consisting of molecules moving freely in space and occupying all available space > PDS; vapour; gas obtained from coal, used for heating and lighting; (*mil*) poisonous vapour, smoke *etc* used in warfare; kind of gas used as anaesthetic; (*mining*) methane, mixture of air and fire-damp: (*US*) petrol, gasoline; (*coll*) gossip, stupid talk; **natural g.** non-poisonous gas similar to coal-gas obtained from natural subterranean deposits; **step on the g.** (*coll*) accelerate; hurry ~ **gas** (*pres/part* **gassing**, *p/t* and *p/part* **gassed**) *v/t* and *i* kill or injure by fumes of coal-gas or poison-gas; (*coll*) chatter, talk stupidly and lengthily.

gasbag [*gas*bag] *n* bag for holding gas; (*coll*) talkative person.

gas-bracket [*gas*-bRakit] *n* gas pipe with burner projecting from a wall.

gas-burner [*gas*-burner] *n* jet from which coal-gas emerges and at which it can be lit.

gas-chamber [*gas*-chaymber] *n* airtight room in which animals or human beings are killed by poison-gas.

gas-cooker [*gas*-kooker] *n* stove for cooking by burning gas.

gaseity [gas*ee*-iti] *n* gaseousness.

gaseous [*gas*i-us/*gay*si-us] *adj* in form of gas; like gas ~ **gaseousness** *n*.

gasfire [*gas*fIr] *n* fire burning gas as fuel.

gas-fitter [*gas*-fiter] *n* workman who installs gas appliances.

gas-fittings [*gas*-fitingz] *n* (*pl*) pipes, jets *etc* for heating or lighting by gas.

gash [*gash*] *n* long, deep cut; open wound ~ **gash** *v/t* cut deeply.

gas-holder [*gas*-hOlder] *n* gasometer.

gasification [gasifi*kay*shon] *n* process of gasifying; state of being gasified.

gasify [*gas*ifI] *v/t* or *i* turn into gas.

gas-jet [*gas*-jet] *n* gas-burner.

gasket [*gas*kit] *n* (*mech*) asbestos sheet lined with copper for making gastight joints; jointing or packing material; sheet rubber jointing for pumps; (*naut*) rope or canvas band securing furled sail to yard.

gaslight [*gas*lIt] *n* light produced by burning gas.

gasmain [*gas*mayn] *n* large pipe carrying gas from gasworks.

gasman [*gas*man] *n* an official from the gasworks.

gas-mantle [*gas*-mant'l] *n* lace-like mesh fitted over gas-burner, becoming incandescent when gas is lit > PDS.

gasmask [*gas*maask] *n* breathing apparatus acting as filter against harmful gases > PDS.

gasmeter [*gas*meeter] *n* device for registering consumption of gas.

gasoline [*gas*oleen] *n* inflammable product of petroleum, used as fuel; (*US*) petrol.

gasometer [gas*om*iter] *n* large tank for storing gas; (*chem*) apparatus for containing or measuring gas.

gasp [*gaasp*] *v/t* and *i* breathe rapidly and with difficulty, fight for breath; catch the breath in fear or surprise; utter in gasps ~ **gasp** *n* a sudden catching of the breath; **at the last g.** at point of death; at the limit of one's strength.

gasper [*gaasp*er] *n* (*sl*) cheap cigarette.

gasping [*gaasp*ing] *adj* spasmodic, convulsive.

gas-ring [*gas*Ring] *n* hollow perforated metal ring for cooking with gas.

gas-stove [*gas*-stOv] *n* gas-cooker.

gassy [*gas*i] *adj* gaseous; full of gas; (*coll*) talkative.

gasteropod, gastropod [*gaste*Ropod] *n* (*zool*) member of a class of univalve molluscs such as snails, limpets *etc*.

gasteropoda, gastropoda [gaste*Ropo*da] *n* (*pl*) (*zool*) the mollusc class.

gastight [*gas*tIt] *adj* preventing the passage of gas.

gastric [*gas*tRik] *adj* of or in the stomach.

gastritis [gast*RI*tis] *n* inflammation of stomach.

gastronome, gastronomer [*gast*RonOm, gas*tRon*omer] *n* a judge of good eating.

gastronomic [gastRon*om*ik] *adj* of gastronomy.

gastronomy [gast*Ron*omi] *n* art and science of good eating; food connoisseurship.

gasworks [*gas*wurks] *n* (*pl*) place at which coal-gas is made.

gat [*gat*] *n* (*US sl*) revolver.

gate (1) [*gayt*] *n* hinged barrier and framework closing opening in wall, fence, *etc*, or placed across a road or path; structure controlling flow of water in canal, dock *etc*; gateway; number of persons in audience at sports event, exhibition *etc*; entrance money paid by these; (*mot*) H-shaped slots controlling forward and sideways movement of a gear-lever ~ **gate** *v/t* impose curfew on (student or schoolboy).

gate (2) *n* (*dial*) way, path.

gâteau [*gat*O] *n* (*Fr*) fancy cake.

gatecrash [*gayt*kRash] *v/t* and *i* (*coll*) attend a party uninvited ~ **gatecrasher** *n*.

gatehouse [*gayt*-hows] *n* building over or beside a gate.

gatekeeper [*gayt*keeper] *n* person in charge of a gate.

gate-legged [*gayt*-legd] *adj* (*of table*) having legs which fold back, so that flap of table-top can hang down.

gateman [*gayt*man] *n* gatekeeper.

gate-money [*gayt*-muni] *n* charge for admission to an entertainment.

gatepost [*gayt*pOst] *n* either of the two posts belonging to a gate.

gateway [*gayt*way] *n* opening in wall or fence, closed by a gate; (*fig*) means of approach.

gather [*ga*THer] *v/t* and *i* collect, assemble; muster; infer, conclude; learn; increase; come to a head; swell up with pus; (*sewing*) draw into small pleats with running stitch, pucker up; (*typ*) place printed sheets of a book in proper sequence ~ **gather** *n* small fold or pleat made by drawing thread through cloth.

gatherer [*ga*THerer] *n* one who or that which gathers.

gathering [*ga*THeRing] *n* act of collecting; number of people collected together; (*typ*) arrangement of the printed sheets of a book in proper sequence; inflamed purulent swelling.

gathers [*ga*THerz] *n* (*pl*) puckered pleats.

gatling [*gat*ling] *n* early type of machine gun.

gauche [*gOsh*] *adj* (*Fr*) clumsy, awkward, tactless.

gaucherie [*gO*sheRee] (*Fr*) clumsiness; tactlessness.

gaucho [*gowch*O] *n* a South American cowboy of mixed Spanish and Indian race.

gaud [*gawd*] *n* trinket, cheap finery.

gaudy (1) [*gaw*di] *n* feast, *esp* annual college dinner or reunion.

gaudy (2) *adj* showy, brilliant in colour ~ **gaudily** *adv* ~ **gaudiness** *n*.

gauge, gage [*gayj*] *n* a standard measure; diameter of gun-bore, tube, wire *etc*; distance between rails of railway track > PDG; instrument for measuring fluid pressure, force of wind, speed of current, rainfall *etc*; rod for measuring depth of liquid; device for testing size of tools, instruments *etc*; (*naut*) position of one vessel relative to another and to the wind; (*fig*) means of measuring or judging; extent, scope ~ **gauge** *v/t* measure by means of a gauge; measure accurately; (*fig*) estimate.

gauger [*gayj*er] *n* one who gauges; exciseman.

gauleiter [*gow*lIter] *n* (*Germ*) Nazi district governor; (*fig*) petty tyrant.

gault [*gawlt*] *n* (*geol*) beds of clay and marl, between upper and lower greensand.

gaunt [*gawnt*] *adj* very thin; angular; grim, desolate ~ **gauntly** *adv* ~ **gauntness** *n*.

gauntlet (1) [*gawnt*lit] *n* (*hist*) mailed glove; long glove covering wrist; **throw down the g.** issue a challenge; **take up the g.** accept a challenge.

gauntlet (2) *n* **run the g.** be compelled, as punishment, to run between two rows of men who strike the victim with rods; (*fig*) undergo continuous or repeated attack.

gauss [*gows*] *n* unit of magnetic induction > PDS.

gauze [*gawz*] *n* light-weight fabric of open texture ~ **gauzy** *adj*.

gave [*gayv*] *p/t* of give.

gavel [*ga*vel] *n* mallet used by chairman, auctioneer *etc* to call for attention.

gavotte [*ga*vot] *n* brisk, lively kind of dance; music for this > PDM.

gawk [*gawk*] *n* large, clumsy person ~ **gawky** *adj* clumsy, ungainly ~ **gawkiness** *n*.

gawp [*gawp*] *v/i* (*sl*) stare stupidly.

gay [*gay*] *adj* lively, cheerful, merry; bright in colour, showy; pleasure-loving; (*coll*) homosexual; **g. lib** (*coll*) militant movement to liberate homosexuals from legal or social penalties ~ **gayness** *n*.

gaze [*gayz*] *v/i* look steadily and intently ~ **gaze** *n* long, steady look.

gazebo [*ga*zeebO] *n* turret, summer-house, or balcony, with a wide open view.

gazelle [*ga*zel] *n* small kind of antelope.

gazette [*ga*zet] *n* official journal giving lists of public appointments and official announcements; official university journal; newspaper ~ **gazette** *v/t* publish in a gazette.

gazetteer [*ga*ziteer] *n* geographical dictionary.

gazump [*ga*zump] *v/i* and *t* increase the price demanded for a house after verbally agreeing to sell at lower price; deceive (one buyer) by accepting a better offer from another ~ **gazumper** *n* ~ **gazumping** *n*.

gear [*geer*] *n* tools, apparatus, equipment; harness; (*eng*) mechanism of moving parts to transmit or regulate motion; mechanism controlling relative speeds of driving part and driven part of machine; a gear ratio (first, second *etc*); (*sl*) clothes; **high g.** adjustment whereby driven part moves relatively slowly; **out of g.** disengaged from gearing mechanism; (*fig*) out of order, working badly; **g. to** connect with, make closely dependent on ~ **gear** *v/t* and *i* engage with gearing system, put into gear; harness, equip ~ **gear** *adj* (*sl*) very good, wonderful.

gearbox [*geer*boks] *n* case enclosing gearing mechanism.

gearing [*geer*Ring] *n* system of gears; (*comm*) relationship between the prior charges of a company and its Ordinary capital.

gearshift [*geer*shift] *n* device for engaging or disengaging gears.

gearwheel [*geer*wheel] *n* toothed wheel forming part of a gear.

gecko [*gek*O] *n* kind of small lizard.

gee [*jee*] *interj* exclamation used to urge on a horse; (*US*) exclamation of surprise.

gee-gee [*jee*-jee] *n* child's word for horse.

geese [*gees*] *pl* of goose.

gee-up [*jee*-up] *interj* exclamation to urge horse on.

geezer [*gee*zer] *n* (*sl*) fellow.

gehenna [*gi*hena] *n* place of torment by fire; Hell.

Geiger counter [*gI*ger-kownter] *n* instrument which detects ionizing radiations > PDS.

geisha [*gay*sha] *n* Japanese courtesan or nightclub hostess.

gel [*jel*] *n* (*chem*) colloidal solution which has set to a jelly > PDS ~ **gel** (*pres/part* **gelling**, *p/t* and *p/part* **gelled**) *v/i* set into a jelly.

gelatin, gelatine [*jel*atin, *jel*ateen] *n* brownish, jelly-like substance obtained by boiling animal cartilages and bones in water which on cooling sets to a solid gel > PDS.

gelatinate [jilatinayt] v/t and i make into gelatin; be made into gelatin.

gelatinization [jilatinIzayshon] n formation of jelly.

gelatinize [jilatinIz] v/t and i form into a jelly.

gelatinous [jilatinus] adj like gelatin; like jelly.

geld (1) [geld] n (hist) a general land-tax.

geld (2) v/t castrate, emasculate.

gelding [gelding] n castration; gelded animal, esp a horse.

gelid [jelid] adj frozen, icy cold ~ **gelidity** [jiliditi] n ~ **gelidly** adv ~ **gelidness** n.

gelignite [jelignIt] n highly explosive form of dynamite > PDS.

gelt [gelt] n (sl) money.

gem [jem] n jewel, precious stone; (fig) anything very valuable or highly prized ~ **gem** (pres/part **gemming**, p/t and p/part **gemmed**) v/t stud with gems.

geminate [jeminayt] v/t double; arrange in pairs; repeat ~ **geminate** adj (bot) in pairs, doubled.

gemination [jeminayshon] n doubling.

Gemini [jeminee] n (astron) constellation Castor and Pollux, the Twins; third sign of zodiac.

gemma (pl **gemmae**) [jema] n (bot) a leaf-bud; reproductive cell-group in mosses and liverworts, which separates from parent plant to become new plant; (zool) outgrowth from parent organism, separating to form new organism > PDB.

gemmate [jemayt] v/i reproduce itself by the budding-off of cell-groups ~ **gemmation** n.

gemmy [jemi] adj set with gems; like a gem.

gen [jen] n (sl) correct information, the truth ~ **gen** v/i **g. up** (sl) learn carefully or quickly.

gendarme [zhondarm] n (Fr) French soldier employed in police duties.

gendarmerie [zhondarmeRi] n (Fr) body of soldiers used as police.

gender [jender] n (gramm) classification of nouns into kinds, approximating to divisions of sex; (coll) sex.

gene [jeen] n (biol) carrier of a hereditary factor in chromosome; unit of inherited material > PDB.

genealogical [jeeni-alojikal] adj concerning or showing genealogy; **g. tree** diagram showing origin and development of family in form of branching tree ~ **genealogically** adv.

genealogist [jeeni-alojist] n one who studies genealogy.

genealogy [jeeni-aloji] n line of descent of person or family from earliest known ancestor; study of this; diagram representing this; line of development of animals, languages etc from earlier forms.

genera [jeneRa] pl of **genus**.

general [jeneRal] adj not limited to one part or section of a whole; concerning all, or almost all, members of a class; not specialized; widespread, common, usual; not specific or detailed; vague; (mil) above rank of colonel; **g. election** Parliamentary election held in every constituency simultaneously; **in g.** mostly; **g. meeting** meeting (of society etc) to which all members are invited ~ **general** n (mil) officer next in rank below field-marshal; (coll) any officer above rank of colonel; military commander; strategist; head of certain religious organizations; (coll) a maid undertaking most forms of housework.

generalissimo [jeneRalisimO] n supreme military commander.

generality [jeneRaliti] n quality of being general; large part, majority; general or vague statement.

generalization [jeneRalIzayshon] n act of generalizing; broad conclusion drawn from particular instances, general statement.

generalize [jeneRalIz] v/t and i form general conclusion from observations of specific instances; express in general terms; make popular or widespread.

generally [jeneRali] adv as a general rule, usually; in a general sense; widely, for the most part.

general-purpose [jeneRal-purpus] adj having many uses, not specialized.

generalship [jeneRalship] n (mil) rank of general; (fig) skill in military leadership; strategic ability; skill in organizing, authority.

generate [jeneRayt] v/t bring into existence, produce, cause; beget ~ **generating** adj producing; **g. station** (elect) power-house.

generation [jeneRayshon] n act of generating; one step in line of genealogical descent; all persons at same stage of descent from common ancestor; all persons of approximately same age-group; average period between birth of individual of a species and production of its offspring; period of about thirty years separating one human generation from the next; **g. gap** misunderstanding or intolerance between persons of different generations; **rising g.** young people.

generative [jeneRativ/jeneRaytiv] adj having power of generating.

generator [jeneRaytor] n one who generates; machinery for generating electricity, gas, etc.

generic [jineRik] adj pertaining to a genus or class; applicable to all members of a class ~ **generical** adj ~ **generically** adv.

generosity [jeneRositi] n quality of being generous; generous act.

generous [jeneRus] adj willing to give freely, open-handed; noble in nature, magnanimous; abundant; ample, large; (of wine) strong, full-bodied ~ **generously** adv.

genesis (pl **geneses**) [jenisis] n origin, beginning; (cap) first book of the Old Testament.

genet [jenit] n kind of civet-cat; its fur.

genetic [jinetik] adj of or by heredity; pertaining to origin and development; pertaining to genes; **g. code** code expressed in the molecular constitution of chromosomes by which inherited characteristics are transmitted; **g. engineering** systematic attempt to change hereditary features of a population by modifying or eliminating certain genes ~ **genetical** adj ~ **genetically** adv.

geneticist [jinetisist] n student of genetics.

genetics [jinetiks] n (pl) study of heredity.

geneva [jineeva] n gin.

genial [jeeni-al] adj cheerful, kindly, friendly; (of climate) mild ~ **genially** adv.

geniality [jeeni-aliti] n cheerfulness; friendliness.

genic [jenik] adj of or caused by genes; genetic.

genie (pl **genii**) [jeeni] n supernatural being, spirit.

genista [jenista] n genus of leguminous shrubs including broom.

322

genital [*ʃen*ital] *adj* relating to reproductive organs in animals ~ **genitals** *n* (*pl*) external organs of reproduction.

genetalia [jenitayli-a] *n* (*pl, Lat*) genitals.

genitival [jenit*ʃ*val] *adj* (*gramm*) belonging to the genitive case.

genitive [*ʃen*itiv] *n* and *adj* (*gramm*) (form) indicating possession, source, origin *etc*.

genius (*pl* **geniuses**) [*ʃeen*i-us] *n* exceptionally high artistic or intellectual ability; person having such ability; natural capacity, aptitude; prevalent tendency, characteristic trait; (*pl* **genii**) (*myth*) guardian spirit; (*fig*) person powerfully influencing another; **g. loci** (*myth*) spirit dwelling in a particular spot; (*fig*) characteristic atmosphere of a place.

genocide [*ʃen*Osid] *n* (*leg*) mass murder of a racial, national, or religious group.

genotype [*ʃen*Otip] *n* (*biol*) the genetic constitution of an organism > PDB.

genre [*zhon*(g)R] *n* (*Fr*) classification, grouping, category, *esp* of works of literature or art; a painting of everyday life and surroundings > PDAA.

gent [*ʃent*] *n* (*sl*) gentleman.

genteel [jen*teel*] *adj* exhibiting an unnatural degree of good manners; clumsily imitating upper-class ways; (*ar*) wellbred, elegant ~ **genteelly** *adv* ~ **genteelness** *n*.

gentian [*ʃen*shan] *n* genus of herbs with bright flowers and bitter roots; a vivid shade of blue; **g. bitter** (*med*) tonic extracted from gentian roots.

gentile [*ʃent*Il] *n* and *adj* (person) not of Jewish race.

gentility [jen*tʃ*liti] *n* upper-class manners and way of life; quality of being a gentleman; (*ar*) state of being well-born.

gentle (1) [*ʃent*'l] *adj* kind, tender-hearted, amiable; indulgent, tolerant; not violent, soft, mild; moderate; gradual; docile; (*ar*) born into the upper-class; wellbred; (*her*) entitled to bear arms.

gentle (2) *n* maggot used as bait by anglers.

gentlefolk [*ʃent*'lfOk] *n* people of upper or upper-middle class.

gentleman [*ʃent*'lman] *n* man of upper or upper-middle class; (*pop*) man; man showing good manners, chivalry, courtesy, and a sense of honour; (*leg*) man living on unearned income; (*her*) man entitled to bear arms, but not a nobleman; (*hist*) man of good birth attached to the court or to an aristocratic household; **g.'s agreement** agreement not legally binding, but the keeping of which is a matter of honour.

gentleman-at-arms [jent'lman-at-*aarmz*] *n* member of the royal bodyguard on state occasions.

gentlemanlike [*ʃent*'lmanlik] *adj* gentlemanly.

gentlemanly [*ʃent*'lmanli] *adj* characteristic of a gentleman.

gentleness [*ʃent*'lnes] *n* quality of being gentle.

gentlewoman [*ʃent*'lwooman] *n* woman of upper or upper-middle class; well-bred woman; (*hist*) woman who waited upon lady of high rank.

gently [*ʃent*li] *adv* in a gentle way.

gentry [*ʃent*Ri] *n* upper-class people not belonging to nobility; (*coll, fig*) class of people.

gents [*ʃent*s] *n* (*sing*) (*coll*) men's public lavatory.

genuflect [jenew*ʃflekt*] *v/i* bend one knee, as sign of reverence ~ **genuflexion, genuflection** *n*.

genuine [*ʃen*ew-in] *adj* from the original stock, pure-bred; real, true, authentic; sincere, not assumed ~ **genuinely** *adv* ~ **genuineness** *n*.

genus (*pl* **genera**) [*ʃeen*us, *ʃen*eRa] *n* (*biol*) group of similar species of organisms; kind, sort, class.

geo- *pref* of the earth.

geocentric [jee-osent*Rik*] *adj* having the earth as centre; reckoned from centre of earth ~ **geocentrical** *adj*.

geodesic [jee-o*dees*ik] *n* (*math*) shortest distance between two points on a spherical surface; arc of a great circle; **g. dome** faceted hemispherical structure formed by triangular or polygonal arrangements of struts ~ **geodesic** *adj*.

geodesy [jee-*odes*i] *n* scientific calculation of shape and size of the earth; surveying of very large portion of earth's surface > PDG.

geodetic [jee-o*det*ik] *adj* of geodesy.

geognosy [jee-*ognos*i] *n* study of the structure of the earth.

geographer [jee-*ograf*er] *n* student of geography.

geographic, geographical [jee-o*graf*ik, jee-o*graf*ikal] *adj* of geography; **g. mile** approximately 6,080 feet, one-sixtieth of a degree of latitude ~ **geographically** *adv*.

geography [jee-*ograf*i] *n* science that describes earth's surface, physical features, products, populations *etc* > PDG; (*fig*) arrangement in space, relative position, plan; book on geography.

geological [jee-o*loji*kal] *adj* of geology ~ **geologically** *adv*.

geologist [jee-*oloj*ist] *n* student of geology.

geologize [jee-*oloj*iz] *v/i* and *t* study geology; study the geology of.

geology [jee-*oloj*i] *n* science of composition, history, and structure of earth's crust > PDG.

geomagnetism [jee-o*magn*etizm] *n* magnetic properties of the earth; study of these ~ **geomagnetic** *adj*.

geometer [jee-*omi*ter] *n* student of geometry; (*ent*) looper moth and caterpillar.

geometric [jee-o*met*Rik] *adj* pertaining to geometry; resembling figures of geometry; regular, symmetrical; angular.

geometrical [jee-o*met*Rikal] *adj* geometric; **g. progression** (*math*) series of quantities in which each form is obtained by multiplying the preceding by some constant factor > PDS ~ **geometrically** *adv*.

geometrician [jee-ometRi*shan*] *n* student of geometry.

geometry [jee-*omit*Ri] *n* mathematical study of properties and relations of lines, surfaces, and solids in space.

geophysics [jee-o*fiz*i s] *n* (*pl*) study of physical processes of earth's structure > PDG.

geopolitics [jee-o*polit*iks] *n* (*pl*) study of the effect of a nation's geographic position upon its politics.

geoponic [jee-o*ponik*] *adj* of agriculture ~ **geoponics** *n* (*pl*) science of agriculture.

Geordie [*ʃaw*rdi] *n* (*coll*) native of Tyneside.

George [*ʃaw*rj] *n* man's name; jewelled figure of St George and the dragon, worn by Knights of the Garter as part of their insignia; **by G.** *exclam*.

georgette [jawr*ʃet*] *n* thin, transparent silk fabric.

Georgian [*ʃaw*rji-an] *adj* of the period of any of the Georges, Kings of England; of Georgia in the Caucasus; of Georgia in the United States; in the poetic style popular during reign of George V of England ~ **Georgian** *n* native of Georgia in the Caucasus, or of Georgia in the United States.

georgic [*jaw*rjik] *n* poem on rural life; title of one of Virgil's four poems on farming.

geotropism [jee-ot*Ro*pizm] *n* (*bot*) tendency in plant organs to grow towards (or away from) earth's centre.

geranium [je*Ray*ni-um] *n* kind of flowering plant with white, red, or blue flowers, and lobed leaves; crane's-bill; pelargonium.

gerbil [*jur*bil] *n* type of small desert rodent.

gerfalcon, jerfalcon [*jur*fawlkon] *n* large falcon of northern regions.

geriatric [jeRi-at*Rik*] *adj* (*med*) concerning old age; pertaining to the care of old people ~ **geriatrics** *n* (*pl*) (*med*) treatment and care of old people.

germ [*jurm*] *n* unicellular organism from which new individual can develop; microbe, *esp* one causing disease; (*fig*) source, origin, rudimentary form; **g. warfare** the use of bacteria as weapons ~ **germ** *v/i* (*fig*) develop.

German (1) [*jur*man] *n* and *adj* (native or language) of Germany; **g. measles** contagious disease resembling measles.

german (2) *adj* closely related; having same parents; having same grandparents.

germander [jer*man*der] *n* plant belonging to genus veronica, *esp* the speedwell.

germane [jer*mayn*] *adj* relevant, appropriate.

Germanic [jur*man*ik] *adj* pertaining to Germany or to the Germans; pertaining to the Teutonic peoples ~ **Germanic** *n* language of the Teutonic peoples, *esp* in its earliest form.

Germanism [*jur*manizm] *n* idiom derived from the German language; German characteristic or mode of thought; admiration for Germany and things German.

germanium [jur*mayn*i-um] *n* (*chem*) brittle white metal, used in transistors > PDS.

Germanize [*jur*manIz] *v/t* and *i* make German; become German; resemble the Germans.

German silver [jurman-*silver*] *n* alloy of copper, nickel, and zinc > PDS.

germ-cell [*jurm*-sel] *n* gamete.

germen [*jur*men] *n* (*bot*) ovary, seed-vessel.

germicidal [jermi*sId*al] *adj* that kills bacteria.

germicide [*jur*misId] *n* and *adj* (substance) which kills bacteria, *esp* those causing disease.

germinal [*jur*minal] *adj* of or like a germ-cell or germ; (*fig*) in earliest stage of development.

germinant [*jur*minant] *adj* germinating.

germinate [*jur*minayt] *v/i* and *t* begin to sprout; begin to develop; cause to sprout or develop.

germination [jurmi*nay*shon] *n* sprouting; earliest stage of plant growth.

germon [*jur*mun] *n* kind of tunny-fish.

germ-plasm [*jurm*-plazm] *n* (*biol*) type of protoplasm transmitted unchanged from generation to generation ~ PDB.

gerontology [je*Ron*toloji] *n* scientific study of old age and of ageing.

gerrymander [*je*Rimander] *n* a reorganization of electoral districts to gain some advantage in forthcoming election > PDPol; (*fig*) dishonest

trick ~ **gerrymander** *v/t* manipulate unfairly ~ **gerrymandering** *n*.

gerund [*je*Rund] *n* (*gramm*) verbal noun ~ **gerundial** [je*Rund*i-al] *adj*.

gerundive [je*Rund*iv] *n* (*gramm*) adjective formed from gerund.

gesso [*jes*O] *n* dense white ground of gypsum or plaster of Paris, for tempera painting > PDAA.

gest [*jest*] *n* (*ar*) brave exploit; tale of adventure.

gestalt [ge*shtalt*] *n* (*Germ*) form, pattern; (*psych*) type of psychology of perception > PDP.

Gestapo [ge*shtaap*O] *n* Nazi secret police; any secret or brutal police force > PDPol.

gestation [je*stay*shon] *n* pregnancy.

gestatory [je*stay*teRi] *adj* of pregnancy.

gesticulate [je*stik*ewlayt] *v/i* and *t* use movement of arms or body to emphasize or communicate; express thus; make excessive use of gesture.

gesticulation [jestikew*lay*shon] *n* act of gesticulating; gesture.

gesticulatory [je*stik*ewlatoRi] *adj* of, by, or using gesticulation.

gesture [*jes*cher] *n* movement of body or limbs to express meaning or emotion; action or behaviour expressive of feeling; something done for effect ~ **gesture** *v/t* and *i*.

get (*pres/part* **getting**, *p/t* and *p/part* **got**) [*get*] *v/t* and *i* obtain, acquire; receive; fetch; succeed in doing, achieve; catch (illness); cause to do; cause to be; persuade, contrive; become; be; come to be; reach; (*ar*) beget; (*coll*) communicate with; understand; notice; annoy; impress deeply; (*sl*) thrill; (*sl*) kill; arrest; **have got** own, have; **have got to** be obliged to; **g. about** be capable of walking; go visiting; travel widely; become widely known; **g. across** (*coll*) communicate clearly, make oneself understood; **g. ahead (of)** out-distance (competitors); excel; prosper; **g. along** go away; prosper; be fairly successful; manage; be on good terms; **g. along with you!** (*coll*) go away! nonsense!; stop it!; **g. around** get about; outwit; coax; circumvent; **g. at** reach; grasp; attack; (*coll*) bribe, influence unlawfully; tamper with; **be getting at** (*coll*) try to say; imply; taunt; **g. away (from)** escape; leave; avoid; **g. away with** succeed in doing undetected or unpunished; **g. away with you!** (*coll*) get along with you!; **g. back** return; recover; **g. back at** (*sl*) revenge oneself on; **g. one's own back** obtain revenge; **g. by** (*coll*) manage adequately but not easily; survive; pass; **g. cracking** (*coll*) begin work vigorously; **g. down** descend; dismount; **g. (one) down** (*coll*) depress; **g. down to** settle to work at; **g. hold of** grasp; understand; find, obtain; **g. home** reach home; (*fig*) reach its mark; **g. in** enter; be admitted; collect; be elected; **g. in with** (*coll*) associate with, become friendly with; **g. into** enter; put on; be involved in; **g. it** (*coll*) get into trouble, be punished; (*sl*) understand; **g. nowhere** achieve nothing; **g. off** dismount; come out of; come down from; escape; help to escape; save from punishment; take off; begin (race); **tell (one) where one gets off** put in one's place, scold; **g. off with** begin flirtation with; **g. on** mount; put on; make progress; succeed; go away; be on friendly terms; **be getting on** grow old; grow late; live, fare; **be getting on for** approach; **g. on to** get in touch with, *esp* by telephone; **g. on with** be friendly with; continue, progress; **g. out** extract; dismount; go away; work out; (*cricket*) be dismissed; **g. out of** go out from; alight from; avoid, escape; extract (information) from; **g. outside (of)** (*sl*) eat or drink; **g. over** recover from; surmount; communicate clearly; **g. past** pass; escape discovery; get by; **g. round** circumvent; surmount; coax, persuade; become widely known; circulate; **g. round to** find time or energy for; **g. there** (*coll*) succeed; **g. through** penetrate; come to the end of; spend; pass (examination); get by; **g. to** reach; **g. together** meet; assemble; collect; **g. up** climb, mount; rise from bed; stand up; study; dress elaborately, adorn; organize; **g. up to** be involved in (mischief *etc*), plan ~ **get** *n* (*of animals*) offspring; (*pej sl*) son or daughter, *esp* if bastard; fool.

get-at-able [get-*at*ab'l] *adj* accessible.

getaway [*get*away] *n* (*coll*) an escape; start of race.

getter [*get*er] *n* one who or that which gets; (*rad*) substance used for absorbing last traces of gases in attaining high vacuum > PDS.

get-together [get-togeTHer] *n* (*coll*) meeting; gathering, friendly assembly.

get-up [get-up] *n* (*coll*) style of dress; appearance (of book *etc*).

geum [*jee*-um] *n* garden perennial plant with red or yellow flower.

gewgaw [*gew*gaw] *n* gaudy trifle.

geyser [*gayzer*/*gIzer*] *n* hot spring which at times throws up jets of water and steam > PDG; [*freq geezer*] cylinder in which water is heated quickly by gas.

ghastly [*gaast*li] *adj* terrifying, hideous; death-like, pale; (*coll*) very bad ~ **ghastliness** *n*.

gherkin [*gur*kin] *n* small cucumber used for pickling.

ghetto [*get*O] *n* Jewish quarter of a city; town district to which a poor or unpopular minority group is confined.

ghost [*gOst*] *n* spirit of dead person appearing to the living, spectre, wraith; soul, spirit; pale, shadowy image; (*phys*) false line appearing in a line spectrum; false image appearing on radar screen; (*coll*) faint trace; slight chance; (*coll*) one who does literary or artistic work for another to pass off as his own; **give up the g.** die; **Holy G.** third person of Trinity; **g. town** town abandoned by its inhabitants ~ **ghost** *v/i* and *t* produce (literary or artistic work) for another to pass off as his own.

ghostly [*gOst*li] *adj* of or like a ghost; spiritual, holy; faint, insubstantial; **g. father** (*ar*) father confessor ~ **ghostliness** *n*.

ghost-word [*gOst*-wurd] *n* word formed by mis-understanding of a scribe or etymologist.

ghost-writer [*gOst*-RIter] *n* one who writes books, articles *etc* for another to pass off as his own.

ghoul [*gOOl*] *n* (*Oriental myth*) demon which feeds on corpses; human grave-robber; (*fig*) person delighting in morbid horrors ~ **ghoulish** *adj* ~ **ghoulishly** *adv*.

ghyll, gill [*gil*] *n* ravine, gully; brook.

giant [*jI*-ant] *n* mythical human being of enorm-ous size; abnormally large human being, animal,

or plant; (*fig*) exceptionally great man, genius ~ **giant** *adj* abnormally large; (*of star*) highly luminous.

giantess [*jI*-antes] *n* female giant.

giantism [*jI*-antizm] *n* pathological condition characterized by abnormal growth.

giaour [*jowr*] *n* Turkish name for non-Moslems, *esp* Christians.

gib (1) [*gib*] see jib (3).

gib (2) *n* tomcat; castrated cat.

gibber [*jib*er] *v/i* chatter quickly and incompre-hensibly.

gibberish [*jib*eRish] *n* rapid incoherent speech; meaningless words; language incomprehensible to the hearer.

gibbet [*jib*it] *n* gallows, *esp* one on which a corpse was displayed ~ **gibbet** *v/t* hang on gibbet; (*fig*) hold up to ridicule.

gibbon [*gib*on] *n* a long-armed ape.

gibbose see gibbous.

gibbosity [*gib*ositi] *n* a swelling, lump.

gibbous, gibbose [*gib*us, *gib*Os] *adj* bulging, convex; hump-backed; (*of moon or planets*) be-tween half and full.

gibe (1), **jibe** [*jIb*] *v/i* sneer, utter taunts; **g. at** mock, sneer at ~ **gibe, jibe** *n* ~ **gibingly** *adv*.

gibe (2) see gybe.

giblet [*jib*lit] *adj* made from giblets.

giblets [*jib*lits] *n* (*pl*) edible inner parts of fowl.

gibus [*jIb*us] *n* collapsible opera hat.

giddy [*gid*i] *adj* suffering from vertigo, dizzy, having sensation of whirling; (*fig*) frivolous; wildly gay ~ **giddily** *adv* ~ **giddiness** *n*.

gift [*gift*] *n* thing given; action of giving; power or right of giving; natural talent, aptitude; (*sl*) something extremely easy to obtain or under-stand; **g. coupon, g. voucher** voucher given with certain goods to be exchanged for some free object ~ **gift** *v/t* bestow on.

gifted [*gift*id] *adj* talented, naturally skilled in.

gift-horse [*gift*-hawrs] *n* horse given as a present; **look a g. in the mouth** criticize or question the value of a gift.

gift-wrap [*gift*-Rap] *v/t* wrap up in attractive paper, box *etc*.

gig (1) [*gig*] *n* light two-wheeled carriage; (*naut*) light, fast rowing boat; racing-boat similar to this.

gig (2) *n* (*theat sl*) single performance.

giga- *pref* one thousand million.

gigantic [*jI*gantik] *adj* enormous, huge.

gigantism [*jI*gantizm] *n* giantism.

giggle [*gig*'l] *v/i* utter bursts of high-pitched, convulsive laughter ~ **giggle** *n* shrill burst of laughter; (*coll*) anything silly or ridiculous; some-thing done just for fun, joke ~ **giggler** *n*.

gigolo [*jig*olO] *n* hired male dancing-partner; lover living at his mistress's expense.

gigot [*jig*ot/*jig*O] *n* leg of mutton; sleeve narrow below elbow, but puffed above.

gigue [*jeeg*] *n* (*mus*) lively old-fashioned dance; music for this; movement in a suite.

Gilbertian [*gilbur*shan] *adj* farcical, ludicrously nonsensical, in the style of W. S. Gilbert.

gild (*p/t* and *p/part* **gilded** or **gilt**) [*gild*] *v/t* cover with thin layer of gold; paint with gold-coloured paint; (*fig*) embellish; brighten; **g. the lily** spoil perfect beauty by embellishments; **g. the pill** make something unpleasant seem acceptable.

gilded [*gild*id] *adj* covered with thin layer of gold; golden in colour; **g. youth** rich, elegant, idle young men.

gilding [*gild*ing] *n* covering with a thin layer of metallic gold; gold or golden material used to gild an object.

gill (1) [*jil*] *n* quarter of a pint; vessel holding this amount.

gill (2) [*gil*] *n* organ by which a fish breathes > PDB; wattles of a fowl; flesh under chin and jaws of a man.

gill (3) see **ghyll**.

gillie [*gili*] *n* (*Scots*) outdoor manservant attendant on sportsmen in the Highlands.

gillion [*jili*-on] *n* and *adj* a thousand millions.

gillyflower [*jili*-flowr] *n* clove-scented pink; wallflower; scented stock.

gilt (1) [*gilt*] *n* gold leaf, gold paint *etc* used for gilding; (*fig*) lustre, superficial attractiveness.

gilt (2) *adj* gilded.

gilt (3) *n* young sow.

gilt-edged [gilt-*ejd*] *adj* with gilded edges; (*fig*) of the highest quality; **g. security** fixed-interest security, *usu* government stocks; safe investment.

gimbals [*jimb'lz/gimb'lz*] *n* (*pl*) a double concentric metal suspension fitting for supporting nautical instruments in horizontal position.

gimcrack [*jim*kRak] *n* showy but worthless article ~ **gimcrack** *adj*.

gimlet [*gim*lit] *n* small tool for boring holes.

gimlet-eyed [*gim*lit-Id] *adj* having sharp eyes.

gimme [*gimi*] *abbr* (*sl*) give me.

gimmick [*gimik*] *n* (*coll*) trick; secret device; characteristic of manner, dress, voice, presentation *etc* exploited to win publicity; gadget.

gimmickry [*gimi*kRi] *n* excessive use of gimmicks.

gimmicky [*gimiki*] *adj* of, like or using gimmicks.

gimp [*gimp*] *n* twisted and stiffened cord of silk *etc*, used as trimming for clothes.

gin (1) [*jin*] *n* alcoholic liquor distilled from grain or malt and flavoured with juniper berries.

gin (2) *n* mechanical contrivance; kind of crane; machine for separating cotton from seeds; trap, snare.

gin-fizz [jin-*fiz*] *n* drink made from gin, sodawater, and lemon.

ginger [*jin*jer] *n* aromatic tropical plant; pungent spice made from root of this; reddish-brown colour; (*coll*) energy, liveliness; **g. group** group of politicians *etc* working to activate more orthodox members of party ~ **ginger** *adj* bright red ~ **ginger** *v/t* flavour with ginger; stimulate (horse) with ginger; **g. up** (*coll*) make more lively, stir up, activate.

ginger-ale [jinjer-*ayl*] *n* aerated drink flavoured with ginger.

ginger-beer [jinjer-*beer*] *n* effervescent drink obtained by fermentation of sugar, ginger, and yeast.

gingerbread [*jin*jerbRed] *n* kind of cake, flavoured with treacle and ginger; **take the gilt off the g.** take away the attraction; disillusion, spoil.

gingerly [*jin*jerli] *adj* cautious ~ **gingerly** *adv*.

ginger-nut [*jin*jer-nut] *n* ginger biscuit.

ginger-pop [jinjer-*pop*] *n* (*coll*) ginger-beer.

gingery [*jin*jeRi] *n* flavoured with ginger; like ginger; reddish-brown; hot-tempered, irritable.

gingham [*ging*am] *n* kind of cotton cloth, often striped or checked.

gingivitis [jinjiv*I*tis] *n* (*med*) inflammation of the gums.

gingko [*gingk*O] *n* Japanese and Chinese tree with fan-shaped leaves and yellow fruit.

gink [*gink*] *n* (*US sl*) strange fellow.

ginseng [*jin*seng] *n* Asiatic and American plant with edible forked root, believed to be a panacea and an aphrodisiac.

gin-sling [*jin*-sling] *n* iced drink made of gin and flavourings.

gip see **gyp** (1).

gippo [*jip*O] *n* (*mil sl*) soup, stew, gravy.

gipsy, gypsy [*jip*si] *n* member of a wandering race of Indian origin; language of these, Romany; person of dark complexion; (*coll, pej*), person of roving or untidy habits ~ **gipsy, gypsy** *adj*.

giraffe [ji*Raaf*] *n* tall, large African ruminant.

girandole [*ji*RandOl] *n* branched chandelier; piece of jewellery in which central stone is surrounded by circle of smaller ones; rotating water-jet; rotating firework.

girasol, girasole [*ji*Rasol] *n* fiery-coloured opal.

gird (1) (*p/t* and *p/part* **girded, girt**) [*gurd*] *v/t* encircle (waist or hips) with belt; bind tightly; (*fig*) invest (with power *etc*); surround; **g. up one's loins** (*fig*) prepare for action, brace oneself.

gird (2) *v/i* **g.** at jeer at, mock.

girder [*gurd*er] *n* (*bui*) strong beam, *esp* of iron or steel.

girdle (1) [*gurd'l*] *n* belt or cord worn round waist; (*fig*) anything that encircles; (*coll*) light, boneless corset; (*bot*) ring round tree made by removing bark ~ **girdle** *v/t* surround, bind with a girdle.

girdle (2), **girdle-cake** see **griddle**.

girl [*gurl*] *n* female child; young unmarried woman; female employee or servant; (*coll*) sweetheart; (*sl*) cocaine; **old g.** (*coll*) past pupil of girls' school; elderly woman; **G. Guide** (*obs*) member of Guides organization.

girl-friend [*gurl*-fRend] *n* mistress; sweetheart; female friend.

girlhood [*gurl*hood] *n* period during which one is a girl.

girlie [*gurli*] *n* (*coll dim*) girl.

girlish [*gurl*ish] *adj* of or like a girl ~ **girlishly** *adv* ~ **girlishness** *n*.

giro [*ji*RO] *n* current account banking system available at Post Offices and run by a central organization.

girt [*gurt*] *p/t* and *p/part* of **gird**.

girth [*gurth*] *n* band round belly of horse, to secure saddle or load; waist or circumference measurement; corpulence.

gist [*jist*] *n* main points, essence (of argument *etc*).

git [*git*] *n* (*sl*) bastard, despicable person.

give (*p/t* **gave**, *p/part* **given**) [*giv*] *v/t* and *i* bestow, hand over to another without price or exchange; donate; confer; communicate to; allot, assign; pay; impose as penalty; produce; supply; yield to pressure, break down; bend; concede; perform, act, exhibit; produce, show; **g. and take** compromise, mutual concessions; **g. away** give as charity, sacrifice; reveal, *esp* accidentally; bestow (bride) on groom; **g. back** restore; retort; retreat; **g. best** to acknowledge superiority of; **g. chase** pursue; **g. forth** announce, proclaim; emit; **g. ground** retreat, yield; **g. in** yield, submit; hand over; **g. off** emit; **g. out** distribute; make known; come to an end; **g. over** cease; transfer; **g. place to** be succeeded by; **g. rise to** cause; **g. it to** (*coll*) scold, punish; **g. tongue** bark, cry; talk loudly; **g. up** abandon, renounce; cease; sacrifice; acknowledge defeat; regard as hopeless; **g. oneself up to** devote oneself to; abandon oneself to; **g. upon** look out over; **g. way** yield; **g. way to** abandon oneself to; **g. one's word** promise ~ **give** *n* pliancy, elasticity.

given [*given*] *adj* bestowed, donated; accepted as a basis for reasoning; **g. to** addicted to; **g. name** (*Scots* and *US*) Christian name.

giving [*giving*] *adj* that gives; generous; pliable ~ **giving** *n* act of one who gives.

gizzard [*gizard*] *n* second stomach of bird; (*coll*) throat; **stick in one's g.** be hard to accept.

glabrous [*glaybRus*] *adj* hairless, smooth.

glacé [*glasay*] *adj* glazed, shiny; iced, sugared.

glacial [*glaysi-al*] *adj* icy; pertaining to ice or glaciers; (*of acetic acid*) solid and crystalline.

glaciate [*glaysi-ayt*] *v/t* freeze; give frosted surface to; (*geol*) rub smooth by action of ice.

glaciation [glaysi-*ayshon*] *n* frost, *esp* extensive; ice-age.

glacier [*glasi-er*] *n* mass of ice moving slowly down valley towards sea > PDG.

glacis [*glasis*] *n* gentle slope.

glad [*glad*] *adj* happy, cheerful; willing; causing happiness, pleasant; **give the g. eye to** (*coll*) glance alluringly at; **g. hand** welcoming handshake; **g. rags** (*coll*) fine clothes; evening dress ~ **glad** (*pres/part* **gladding**, *p/t* and *p/part* **gladded**) *v/t* (*ar*) make glad.

gladden [*gladen*] *v/t* and *i* make glad; become glad.

glade [*glayd*] *n* open space among trees.

gladiator [*gladi-aytor*] *n* (*Rom hist*) one who fought in public spectacles.

gladiatorial [gladi-at*awRi-al*] *adj* of or like a gladiator.

gladiolus (*pl* **gladioli**) [gladi-*Ol*us] *n* cultivated plant with sword-shaped leaves and spikes of brilliant flowers.

gladly [*gladli*] *adv* in a glad way ~ **gladness** *n*.

gladsome [*gladsum*] *adj* (*ar*) cheerful, joyous.

Gladstone [*gladston*] *n* G. bag broadbased jointed leather bag for hand luggage.

glair [*glair*] *n* raw white of egg; any white viscous substance ~ **glair** *v/t* coat with glair.

glaive [*glayv*] *n* (*ar*) sword; halberd; lance.

glamorize [*glameRIz*] *v/t* glorify, make glamorous; extol by lavish publicity.

glamorous [*glameRus*] *adj* of or having glamour.

glamour [*glamer*] *n* alluring beauty, sex-appeal; romantic charm; (*ar*) magical power.

glance [*glaans*] *v/t* and *i* strike obliquely; flash, gleam; be deflected; look rapidly; **g. at** look hastily at; look sideways at; refer to briefly ~ **glance** *n* rapid look; oblique blow; brief reference ~ **glancing** *adj* ~ **glancingly** *adv*.

gland [*gland*] *n* organ whose main function is to build up secretions and discharge them into or out from the body > PDB; secretory organ in plants.

glandered [*glanderd*] *adj* suffering from glanders.

glanders [*glanderz*] *n* (*pl*) contagious disease of horses affecting nostrils and lungs.

glandular [*glande*wlar] *adj* pertaining to glands.

glandule [*glande*wl] *n* small gland; tumour.

glare [*glair*] *v/i* give out a dazzling light; look fiercely and angrily (at) ~ **glare** *n* intolerably bright light; angry look; (*fig*) obtrusive publicity.

glaring [*glair*Ring] *adj* dazzling; fierce; gaudy, conspicuous; obvious, flagrant (error) ~ **glaringly** *adv*.

glass [*glaas*] *n* hard transparent substance made by fusion of silicates of calcium, sodium, and other metals > PDS; drinking-vessel made of this; contents of such a vessel; mirror; optical lens; telescope; barometer; (*pl*) spectacles; binoculars ~ **glass** *adj* made of glass ~ **glass** *v/t* glaze.

glassblower [*glaas*blO-er] *n* one who shapes molten glass by blowing it.

glasscloth [*glaas*kloth] *n* cloth for polishing glass; material woven from glass thread.

glasscutter [*glaas*kuter] *n* one who cuts glass; tool for cutting glass ~ **glasscutting** *n*.

glassful [*glaas*fool] *n* as much as fills a drinking-glass.

glasshouse [*glaas*hows] *n* hothouse, greenhouse; (*sl*) military prison.

glassily [*glaas*ili] *adv* in a glassy way.

glassiness [*glaas*inis] *n* quality of being glassy.

glass-paper [*glaas*-payper] *n* abrasive paper made from powdered glass *etc* glued to paper.

glassware [*glaas*wair] *n* (*collect*) wine glasses, tumblers, dishes *etc* made of glass.

glass-wool [*glaas*-wool] *n* spun glass fibres used in filtration or for insulation or packing.

glassy [*glaas*i] *n* resembling glass; (*of water*) smooth, still; (*of the eye*) without expression.

Glaswegian [glas*weej*an] *n* and *adj* (inhabitant) of Glasgow.

Glauber's salt [*glawberz-sawlt*] *n* sodium sulphate; a purgative.

glaucoma [glawk*O*ma] *n* a disease of the eyeball.

glaucous [*glawk*us] *adj* greenish; (*bot*) covered with bloom.

glaze [*glayz*] *v/t* and *i* fit glass into; (*cer*) fire vitreous coating on to; become glassy; become expressionless ~ **glaze** *n* glass-like surface; (*cer*) vitreous coating on pottery; thin wash of varnish; transparent layer of oil paint applied over solid paint > PDAA; coating of jelly.

glazed [*glayzd*] *adj* fitted with glass windows; with a lustrous surface; coated with jelly.

glazer [*glayz*er] *n* a polisher by trade.

glazier [*glayzi-er*] *n* one who supplies or fits glass for window-panes, picture-frames *etc*.

glazing [*glayz*ing] *n* trade of a glazier; act of fitting window with glass; act of coating with glaze; substance used as glaze.

gleam [*gleem*] *n* beam or flash of light; light reflected from polished surface; (*fig*) flash of feeling or comprehension ~ **gleam** *v/i* flash ~ **gleaming** *adj*.

glean [*gleen*] *v/t* and *i* gather up stray ears of corn left by the reapers; gather up scraps; (*fig*) scrape together, pick up (information *etc*) ~ **gleaner** *n*.

gleanings [*gleen*ingz] *n* (*pl*) corn gleaned; scraps carefully gathered.

glebe [*gleeb*] *n* (*eccles*) land held by incumbent.

glee [*glee*] *n* joy, rejoicing, delight; (*mus*) unaccompanied part-song.

gleeful [*glee*fool] *adj* joyful, gay ~ **gleefully** *adv.*

gleeman [*glee*man] *n* (*ar*) minstrel.

gleet [*gleet*] *n* chronic discharge from bodily orifice.

glen [*glen*] *n* narrow mountain valley.

Glengarry [glen-*ga*Ri] *n* boat-shaped Scots Highland cap.

glib [*glib*] *adj* fluent, facile, plausible ~ **glibly** *adv* ~ **glibness** *n.*

glide [*glId*] *v/i* move along smoothly and continuously; slide; (*aer*) fly without mechanical propulsion, fly in a glider ~ **glide** *n* action or motion of gliding; (*phon*) sound produced in passing from one position of the organs of speech to another; (*cricket*) deflection of ball to legside.

glider [*glId*er] *n* (*aer*) aircraft without an engine.

gliding [*glId*ing] *adj* that glides ~ **gliding** *n* sport of flying in a glider.

glimmer [*glim*er] *v/i* shine faintly and fitfully, flicker ~ **glimmer** *n* faint, fitful light, gleam; (*fig*) faint sign of understanding or feeling ~ **glimmering** *adj* and *n.*

glimpse [*glimps*] *v/t* catch sight of briefly or intermittently ~ **glimpse** *n* brief, interrupted view.

glint [*glint*] *v/i* sparkle intermittently, flash ~ **glint** *n* a flash, gleam.

glissade [glisaad/glis*ayd*] *n* deliberate slide down a slope of snow or ice; sidelong glide in dancing ~ **glissade** *v/i.*

glissando [glisand*O*] *adj* and *adv* (*mus*) passing rapidly up or down the scale > PDM.

glisten [*glis*'n] *v/i* sparkle, glitter, twinkle ~ **glistening** *adj* ~ **glisteningly** *adv.*

glister [*glis*ter] *v/i* (*ar*) glitter ~ **glister** *n.*

glitch [*glich*] *n* (*sl*) sudden faulty working of machine, motor *etc.*

glitter [*glit*er] *v/i* shine brightly but intermittently, sparkle; (*fig*) make a splendid show ~ **glitter** *n* ~ **glittering** *n* and *adj.*

gloaming [*glO*ming] *n* (*Scots*) dusk, twilight.

gloat [*glOt*] *v/i* feel or show malicious pleasure; exult silently ~ **gloat** *n* act of gloating; gloating words or looks ~ **gloatingly** *adv.*

global [*glOb*al] *adj* world-wide; total, complete.

globe [*glOb*] *n* sphere; the earth; spherical model of the earth or of the heavens; spherical glass lampshade; spherical bowl; orb.

globe-trotter [*glOb*-tRoter] *n* insatiable sightseer who has travelled widely.

globose, globous [glob*Os*, glOb*us*] *adj* approximately spherical.

globular [*globe*wlar] *adj* spherical. **g. cluster** (*astron*) spherical cluster of stars.

globule [*globe*wl] *n* drop of liquid; blood corpuscle.

globulin [*globe*wlin] *n* a protein found in cells of animals and plants > PDS.

glockenspiel [*glok*enshpeel] *n* percussion instrument of tuned metal bars > PDM.

glomerate [*glome*Rat] *adj* gathered into a rounded mass.

gloom [*glOOm*] *n* darkness, obscurity; depression, melancholy.

gloomy [*glOO*mi] *adj* dismal, unlighted, dark; disheartening, pessimistic ~ **gloomily** *adv* ~ **gloominess** *n.*

Gloria [*glawr*Ri-a] *n* (*eccles*) doxology beginning with the word *Gloria*, 'glory'.

glorification [glawrRifik*ay*shon] *n* act of glorifying; state of being glorified; (*coll*) festivity, spree.

glorify [*glawr*Rif1] *v/t* worship, exalt; praise highly; make glorious; enrich, adorn; make to appear more imposing.

gloriole [*glawr*Ri-Ol] *n* halo.

glorious [*glawr*Ri-us] *adj* brilliant, splendid; bringing renown, famous; (*coll*) delightful; (*joc*) ecstatically drunk ~ **gloriously** *adv* ~ **gloriousness** *n.*

glory [*glawr*Ri] *n* splendour, magnificence; earthly pomp; celestial bliss; resplendent beauty; fame, renown; worship, praise; a halo ~ **glory** *v/i* rejoice in, exult; boast.

glory-hole [*glawr*Ri-hOl] *n* cupboard or small room where rubbish accumulates; (*naut*) steward's storeroom.

gloss (1) [*glos*] *n* interlinear or marginal translation of or commentary upon a text; (*fig*) excuse, favourable explanation ~ **gloss** *v/t* provide with a gloss; **g. over** extenuate, explain away.

gloss (2) *n* shiny surface; (*fig*) deceptive appearance ~ **gloss** *v/t* polish, make shiny.

glossarial [glos*air*Ri-al] *adj* pertaining to, like, a glossary.

glossary [*glosa*Ri] *n* explanatory list of difficult words occurring in a text.

glossator [glos*ay*tor] *n* writer of glosses; a commentator.

glossitis [glos*It*is] *n* inflammation of the tongue.

glossolalia [glosOl*ay*li-a] *n* the utterance of nonsensical syllables, allegedly belonging to a human or non-human language unknown to the speaker.

glossy [*glos*i] *n* having highly polished surface ~ **glossily** *adv* ~ **glossiness** *n.*

glottal [*glot*al] *adj* of, or produced in, the glottis; **g. stop** sound produced by complete closure of the glottis.

glottis [*glot*is] *n* opening between the vocal chords.

glove [*gluv*] *n* covering for a hand, *esp* one with separate compartment for each finger; padded hand-covering used in boxing; **hand in g.** in close friendship or alliance; **throw down the g.** challenge to battle; **with the gloves off** pugnaciously, in deadly earnest ~ **glove** *v/t* provide with gloves, cover with a glove.

glover [*gluv*er] *n* one who makes or sells gloves.

glow [*glO*] *v/i* be luminous from great heat; burn without flame or smoke; give out a steady light; blaze with light; grow red; (*fig*) feel warm, feel elated ~ **glow** *n* light and heat together, incandescence; bright colour; blush; (*fig*) feeling of wellbeing; fervour, enthusiasm.

glower [*glowr*] *v/i* scowl, stare frowningly (at).

glowing [glO-ing] *adj* in a glow; (*fig*) vivid, highly-coloured; ardent; enthusiastic ~ **glowingly** *adv.*

glow-lamp [*glO*-lamp] *n* incandescent lamp.

glow-worm [*glO*-wurm] *n* type of beetle, female of which emits phosphorescence.

gloxinia [gloks*in*i-a] *n* tropical plant with bell-shaped flowers.

gloze [*glOz*] *v/i* **g. over** explain away.

glozing [*glO*zing] *n* flattery, deceit.

glucose [glOOkOs] n (chem) dextrose, grape-sugar > PDB, PDS.

glucoside [glOOkOsId] n (chem) derivative of glucose or any other sugar > PDS.

glue [glOO] n adhesive substance, esp one obtained from animal tissue ~ **glue** v/t join with glue; (fig) concentrate upon; (pass) be constantly associated with.

gluey [glOO-i] adj like glue, sticky ~ **glueyness** n.

glum [glum] adj morose, sullen ~ **glumly** adv ~ **glumness** n.

glut [glut] n excessive amount; greater amount than can be consumed ~ **glut** (pres/part **glutting**, p/t and p/part **glutted**) v/t fill or supply excessively; feed excessively, satiate.

gluten [glOOtin] n protein in wheat flour.

glutinosity [glOOtinositi] n stickiness.

glutinous [glOOtinus] adj like glue, sticky ~ **glutinously** adv ~ **glutinousness** n.

glutton [gluton] n one who overeats habitually; (fig) insatiable enthusiast or addict; (zool) wolverine ~ **gluttonous** adj ~ **gluttonously** adv.

gluttony [glutoni] n excessive eating; greed.

glyceride [gliseRId] n (chem) ester of glycerin with a fatty acid > PDS.

glycerine, glycerin [gliseReen] n thick syrupy sweetish liquid obtained from fats and oils, used in pharmacy, plastics, and explosives > PDS.

glycerol [gliseRol] n (chem) glycerine.

glycogen [glIkojin] n animal starch > PDS.

glycol [glIkol] n viscous liquid used as anti-freeze compound and in the manufacture of certain plasticizers > PDS.

glycosuria [glIkosewrRi-a] n (med) disease causing glucose to be excreted in urine.

glyph [glif] n (archi) ornamental vertical groove; (arch) figure cut in relief.

glyphic [glifik] adj carved.

glyphography [glifogRafi] n electrotype process for printing from a raised surface.

glyptic [gliptik] adj pertaining to carving, esp to engraving on gems, ivory etc ~ **glyptics** n (pl) art of engraving on gems.

glyptography [gliptogRafi] n glyptics.

G-man [jee-man] n (US coll) special (police) agent of the Federal Bureau of Investigation.

gnarl [naarl] n knot in wood or in a tree-trunk.

gnarled [naarld] adj covered with gnarls; (fig) rugged, weather-beaten in appearance.

gnash [nash] v/t grind (teeth) with rage.

gnat [nat] n small winged insect, mosquito.

gnathic [nathik] adj pertaining to the jaw.

gnaw [naw] v/t bite persistently, wear away with teeth; chew; (fig) cause persistent pain to, torment ~ **gnawer** n ~ **gnawing** n and adj.

gneiss [nIs] n (geol) banded, granite-like rock > PDG.

gnome (1) [nOm] n (myth) subterranean dwarf or goblin; (fig) ugly, dwarfish person; (sl) international financier or banker.

gnome (2) n didactic maxim, aphorism.

gnomic [nOmik] adj aphoristic.

gnomish [nOmish] adj like a gnome (1).

gnomon [nOmon] n pin of sundial which by its shadow indicates the time of day; (geom) that part of a parallelogram which remains after one similar is removed from one of its corners.

gnosis [nOsis] n special insight into spiritual mysteries; mystical knowledge.

Gnostic [nostik] n one of an early heretical Christian sect, who blended mystical theology and neo-Platonic philosophy ~ **gnostic** adj.

Gnosticism [nostisizm] n doctrine of Gnostics.

gnotobiotics [nOtObI-otiks] n (pl) (biol) study of organisms grown in sterile or completely specified environments.

gnu [nOO] n large African antelope, wildebeast.

go (p/t went, p/part gone) [gO] v/i travel, move, proceed; move away, leave; disappear; die; (of machines) function, work properly; behave, act; become; be, live; turn out, happen; extend, reach; be sold; be put or kept (in specified place); be passed on by inheritance; **g. about** travel, pay visits; be current; (naut) change tack; **g. against** oppose; **g. ahead** proceed forward; start; progress, g. at tackle; attack; **g. back on** break (promise); withdraw from (undertaking); **be going to** (with inf) be about to (expressing action in near future); **g. by** pass; elapse; calculate, deduce from; be led by; **g. down** sink; (of sun etc) set; (coll) leave a university; be swallowed; (coll) be believed or accepted; (coll) fall ill; be remembered or recorded; **g. for** (coll) attack violently; (coll) try to get; (sl) be attracted by; **g. in for** devote oneself to, have as one's hobby; **g. into** examine closely; undertake; occupy oneself with; **let g.** release; **let oneself g.** behave unrestrainedly; **g. off** explode, fire; go away, esp suddenly; (coll) deteriorate; take place; **g. on** continue; persist; (coll) nag, argue; **g. on for** approach; **g. out** be extinguished; leave one's house; attend social functions; become unfashionable; **g. (all) out for** strive eagerly to obtain; be enthusiastic about; **g. over** examine carefully; study; (coll) make an impression; **g. round** be sufficient to provide shares for all; **g. through** examine; **g. through with** persevere in; **g. under** fail, succumb; sink; **g. up** rise; ascend; increase; **g. with** match, harmonize with; agree with; **g. without** endure a lack of ~ **go** n movement; activity; energy; attempt; (coll) situation; happening, event; bargain; success; **have a g.** try, make an attempt; **no g.** impossible; **on the g.** active, working without rest ~ **go** adj (sl) ready to start, in good working order.

go (2) n (Jap) Japanese board-game.

goad [gOd] n sharp-pointed stick for driving animals forward; (fig) stimulus, incentive ~ **goad** v/t drive forward with a goad; (fig) incite, provoke.

go-ahead [gO-ahed] adj enterprising, pushing ~ **go-ahead** n signal or permission to proceed.

goal [gOl] n that which one wishes to attain; aim, purpose; destination; (games) posts between which the ball must pass to score a point; point so scored; (racing) winning-post.

goalie [gOli] n (coll) goalkeeper.

goalkeeper [gOlkeeper] n player positioned to defend the goal.

goal-line [gOl-lIn] n end boundary of playing-field.

goalmouth [gOlmowth] n space between goal-posts.

goalpost [gOlpOst] *n* one of the two posts between which the ball must pass for a goal to be scored.

goat [gOt] *n* horned ruminant quadruped, the male being bearded; (*fig*) lecher; **act the (giddy) g.** (*coll*) behave foolishly; **get one's g.** (*coll*) annoy.

goatee [gOtee] *n* straggling goat-like beard.

goatherd [gOt-hurd] *n* one who tends goats.

goatish [gOtish] *adj* like a goat; lecherous ~ **goatishly** *adv* ~ **goatishness** *n*.

goatsucker [gOtsuker] *n* the nightjar.

gob [gob] *n* (*sl*) mouth; (*vulg*) globule of saliva; (*US sl*) naval rating.

gobang [gObang] *n* Japanese board-game.

gobbet [gobit] *n* morsel of food; (*coll*) brief portion of a text set for translation or comment in an examination.

gobble (1) [gob'l] *v/t* and *i* eat quickly, noisily, and greedily ~ **gobbler** *n*.

gobble (2) *v/i* (*of turkey*) make a throaty noise ~ **gobble** *n* gobbling noise.

gobbledygook [gob'ldigOOk] *n* (*sl*) pompous nonsense.

Gobelin [gobelin] *n* type of 15th-century French tapestry ~ **gobelin** *adj* of or like gobelin tapestry.

go-between [gO-bitween] *n* intermediary; agent; messenger; pimp.

goblet [goblit] *n* drinking vessel with a base and stem but no handles.

goblin [goblin] *n* evil and mischievous spirit; **g. fish** small Australian fish.

goby [gObi] *n* small fish with ventral fins joined into a sucker.

go-by [gO-bɪ] *n* act of ignoring, avoiding, or rejecting; **give one the g.** avoid; abandon; snub.

go-cart [gO-kaart] *n* frame on wheels in which an infant can learn to walk; light handcart; perambulator; go-kart.

god [god] *n* one who or that which is worshipped; supernatural being ruling over some aspect of the universe or of human life, deity; male deity; (*fig*) object of excessive admiration, love *etc*; person showing abnormally high qualities; **G.** the Almighty Creator; **the gods** deities worshipped in polytheistic religions, *esp* those of ancient Greece and Rome; (*coll*) highest gallery in theatre; **act of G.** (*leg*) uncontrollable natural calamity; **house of G.** church, chapel, or temple; **little tin g.** (*coll*) petty tyrant; **G.'s acre** churchyard.

god-awful [god-*awf*ool] *adj* (*sl*) very unpleasant.

godchild [godchɪld] *n* one who is sponsored at baptism.

goddam, goddamn, goddamned [godam, god-damd] *adj* damned, damnable, accursed.

goddaughter [god-dawter] *n* female godchild.

goddess [godes] *n* female deity; (*fig*) beautiful or much-loved woman.

godfather [godfaaTHer] *n* male godparent; (*sl*) head of a criminal organization.

godfearing [godfeerRing] *adj* pious.

godforsaken [godforsaykin] *adj* desolate, dreary; wicked.

godhead [godhed] *n* quality of being God or a god; divine nature or essence; deity.

godless [godlis] *adj* ungodly, wicked; ɪrreligious; atheistic ~ **godlessly** *adv* ~ **godlessness** *n*.

godly [godli] *adj* devout, pious ~ **godliness** *n*.

godmother [godmuTHer] *n* female godparent; **fairy g.** (*coll*) benefactress.

godparent [godpairRent] *n* sponsor at baptism.

godsend [godsend] *n* unexpected piece of good fortune.

godship [godship] *n* godhead, divinity.

godson [godsun] *n* male godchild.

godspeed [godspeed] *n* parting wish for another's success or good luck.

godwit [godwit] *n* marsh bird like snipe.

goer [gO-er] *n* one who goes; fast horse or vehicle; (*sl*) an adept or expert.

gofer [gOfer] *n* a thin batter-cake.

goffer [gOfer] *v/t* crimp by means of heated irons; emboss on edge of book ~ **goffer** *n* frilled or pleated edging ~ **goffering** *n*.

go-getter [gO-geter] *n* (*coll*) pushing, enterprising person ~ **go-getting** *adj*.

goggle [gog'l] *v/i* stare stupidly; have bulging eyes; roll one's eyes ~ **goggle** *n* open-eyed stare.

goggle-box [gog'l-boks] *n* (*sl*) television set.

goggle-eyed [gog'l-ɪd] *adj* having bulging or staring eyes; looking stupidly amazed.

goggles [gog'lz] *n* (*pl*) spectacles with protective leather side-pieces; (*coll*) spectacles, *esp* with thick lenses.

goglet [goglit] *n* jar for keeping water cool.

go-go [gO-gO] *adj* wild, unrestrained, risky.

going [gO-ing] *n* act of moving; departure; pace of travelling; condition of ground for travelling, racing *etc* ~ **going** *adj* prosperous; in working order; available; **get g.** start working or acting.

going-over [gO-ing-Over] *n* (*coll*) process of examining, correcting, or putting in order; (*sl*) prolonged punching or beating.

goings-on [gO-ingzon] *n* (*pl*) (*coll pej*) behaviour.

goitre [goiter] *n* enlargement of thyroid gland of neck.

goitrous [goitRus] *adj* having a goitre.

go-kart [gO-kaart] *n* low open framework on wheels, driven by a small motor.

gold [gOld] *n* soft, yellow precious metal; objects, *esp* coins, made from this; wealth; (*fig*) noble nature; deep yellow colour; (*archery*) gilt bull's eye of target; **g. standard** currency system under which money is exchangeable for fixed weight of gold > PDPol ~ **gold** *adj* of or like gold; deep yellow.

goldbeater [gOldbeater] *n* one who hammers out gold into gold-leaf.

gold-digger [gOld-diger] *n* prospector for gold; (*coll*) woman who tries to get money or presents from rich men.

gold-dust [gOld-dust] *n* gold in the form of fine powder.

golden [gOlden] *adj* of or like gold; deep yellow; (*fig*) valuable; happy; **g. age** (*myth*) prehistoric era of bliss and innocence; (*fig*) period of highest prosperity, happiness *etc*; **g. balls** pawnshop; **g. calf** false idol; idolization of wealth; **g. number** number used in calculating date of Easter; **g. opportunity** favourable chance; **g. section** line so divided that the smaller part is to the larger as the larger is to the whole; **g. syrup** refined treacle; **g. wedding** fiftieth anniversary of wedding-day.

goldeneye [gOldenɪ] *n* kind of wild duck.

goldenrod [gOldenRod] n plant with spike of golden flowers.

goldfield [gOldfeeld] n area in which gold is found or mined.

goldfinch [gOldfinch] n singing bird with yellow markings.

goldfish [gOldfish] n small reddish fish of carp family.

gold-foil [gOld-foil] n gold beaten into thin sheets.

gold-lace [gOld-lays] n braid made of gold thread, used on uniforms and for ornament.

gold-leaf [gOld-leef] n gold beaten into very thin sheets.

goldmine [gOldmIn] n working from which gold is extracted; (fig) source of great profits.

gold-plate [gOld-playt] n articles made of gold or plated with gold upon another metal.

goldrush [gOldRush] n rush of prospectors to a goldfield.

goldsmith [gOldsmith] n craftsman who works in gold; one who sells articles made of gold.

golem [gOlem] n (Heb) magically animated clay figure in Jewish legends.

golf [golf/gof] n a game in which a small ball is driven into a series of widely spaced holes on an open course, by striking it with various clubs ~ **golf** v/i play golf ~ **golfer** n one who plays golf.

golf-club [golf-klub] n long-shafted club used to strike the ball in golf; association for the purpose of playing golf; premises of such an association.

golf-course [golf-kawrs] n land laid out for golf.

golf-links [golf-links] n (pl) golf-course.

goliard [goli-ard] n medieval writer of satiric Latin verse.

golliwog [goliwog] n grotesque black doll; person with fuzzy hair.

golly [goli] interj (coll) exclamation of surprise.

golosh boot-trade spelling of **galosh**.

gombeen-man [gombeen-man] n (Ir) money-lender.

gonad [gonad] n (biol) organ producing gametes; reproductive gland > PDB.

gondola [gondola] n Venetian canal-boat with high prow and stern; boat-shaped car of airship; hanging framework used for working on walls or windows of high buildings.

gondolier [gondoleer] n boatman who propels a gondola.

gone [gon] p/part of **go** ~ **gone** adj (coll) ruined, lost; doomed; dead; **g. on** (sl) infatuated with.

goner [goner] n (sl) dead man; doomed or ruined man.

gonfalon [gonfalon] n banner with streamers, hanging from a crossbar on a staff.

gong [gong] n suspended metal disc, giving out resonant note when struck; (sl) medal ~ **gong** v/t and i strike on a gong; summon or call to a halt by striking a gong.

gonk [gonk] n comic-looking or fantastic doll in cloth or furry fabric.

gonorrhoea [gonoRee-a] n (med) a venereal disease ~ **gonorrhoeal** adj.

goo [gOO] n (sl) anything sticky; sentimentality.

good (comp **better**, superl **best**) [good] adj having desirable qualities; suited to its purpose; praise-worthy, meritorious; helpful, producing desirable results; health-giving; morally excellent; pious, holy; well-behaved; skilful, efficient; in sound condition; healthy; valid; agreeable, enjoyable; capable; sufficient; ample; **a g. deal** fairly large amount; **g. for** beneficial to; strong enough for (an effort); likely to live (a specified time); able and willing to pay; **make g.** compensate; be successful; demonstrate, prove; **a g. many** fairly large number; **a g. thing** something worth having; a successful speculation; witty saying; **a g. time** life-filled with pleasures; **in g. time** early; punctual; **all in g. time** in due course; **a g. while** a long time ~ **good** n that which is good; virtue; benefit; (collect) virtuous persons; (pl) property, possessions; merchandise; articles (other than livestock) sent by train; **for g. (and all)** permanently, finally; **the goods** (sl) what is most needed; **deliver the goods** (sl) carry out a promise.

goodbye [goodbI] exclam and n farewell.

good-for-nothing [good-for-nuthing] adj and n worthless (fellow).

good-hearted [good-haartid] adj kind, well-meaning.

good-humoured [good-hewmerd] adj cheerful; not easily angered.

goodish [goodish] adj quite good, fair.

good-looking [good-looking] adj handsome.

goodly [goodli] adj comely, handsome; fine, grand; of large size, ample.

goodman [goodman] n (ar Scots) householder; husband.

good-natured [good-naycherd] adj amiable, kindly, easy-going.

goodness [goodnis] n quality of being good; excellence; virtue; kindness; best part; most nourishing part ~ **goodness** interj exclamation of surprise, also **g. gracious! g. me! my g.!**

goods-train [goodz-tRayn] n train for transport of merchandise only.

good-tempered [good-temperd] adj not easily angered.

goodwife [goodwIf] n (ar Scots) housewife.

goodwill [goodwil] n kindness; willingness; upright intention; (leg) value of reputation and popularity of a business, shop etc.

goody (1) [goodi] n small item of tasty food, esp sweet or cake; (ar) old woman.

goody (2) n heroic or faultless character in a film, play or book, esp a thriller.

goody-goody [goodi-goodi] adj and n priggishly or sentimentally pious (person).

gooey [gOO-i] adj (sl) sticky; sickly; sentimental.

goof [gOOf] n (sl) silly, stupid person; **g. balls** (sl) barbiturate drugs ~ **goof** v/i make a fool of oneself, blunder ~ **goofy** adj.

googly [gOOgli] n (cricket) off-break ball bowled with leg-break action.

gook [gOOk] n (US pej sl) Asiatic person.

goon [gOOn] n (coll) grotesque fool.

goosander [goosander] n large diving bird closely allied to the duck.

goose (pl **geese**) [gOOs] n genus of large web-footed birds; domestic bird of this genus; female of this bird; (coll) fool; silly girl; (pl **gooses**) tailor's iron; **cook someone's g.** (coll) ruin, frustrate or kill someone; spoil someone's chances ~ **goose** v/t (vulg coll) prod the anus or sexual organs of.

gooseberry [*goozb*eRi] *n* edible fruit of a thorny bush; (*coll*) chaperon; (*mil coll*) barbed wire.

gooseflesh [*gOO*sflesh] *n* pimply roughness of skin, caused by cold or fear.

goosegog [*gooz*gog] *n* (*coll*) gooseberry.

goosegrass [*gOO*sgRaas] *n* common hedgerow weed; also called cleavers.

gooseneck [*gOO*snek] *n* curved pipe or piece of iron.

goosestep [*gOO*s-step] *n* (*mil*) German stiff-legged parade step.

gopher [*gO*fer] *n* small American burrowing rodent.

Gordian [*gaw*rdi-an] *adj* **cut the G. knot** get out of a difficulty by the shortest and most drastic means.

gore (1) [*gawr*] *n* blood; clotted blood.

gore (2) *n* triangular section of a garment, wider at the lower edge ~ **gore** *v/t* insert a gore in.

gore (3) *v/t* pierce with horns or tusks.

gorge [*gaw*rj] *n* deep, narrow valley with steep walls > PDG; (*ar*) throat; **one's g. rises** one feels sick with disgust ~ **gorge** *v/i* and *t* eat greedily or in excess ~ **gorged** *adj* replete; crammed full.

gorgeous [*gaw*rjus] *adj* showy, magnificent; (*coll*) delightful; glamorous ~ **gorgeously** *adv* ~ **gorgeousness** *n*.

gorget [*gaw*rjit] *n* armour to protect the throat; a necklace; patch of colour on bird's neck.

Gorgon [*gaw*rgon] *n* (*Gk myth*) snake-haired ogress, the sight of whom turned men to stone; fierce and ugly woman.

gorgonian [gawr*gOn*i-an] *adj* like a Gorgon.

Gorgonzola [gawrgon*zO*la] *n* strong-flavoured Italian cheese.

gorilla [go*Ri*la] *n* large African anthropoid ape.

gormand see **gourmand**.

gormandize [*gaw*rmand*I*z] *v/i* eat gluttonously.

gormless [*gaw*rmles] *adj* (*coll*) helplessly stupid, slow-witted.

gorse [*gaw*rs] *n* prickly yellow-flowered shrub.

gorsy [*gaw*rsi] *adj* thickly grown with gorse.

gory [*gaw*rRi] *adj* blood-stained; involving bloodshed; (*fig*) gruesome.

gosh [*gosh*] *interj* (*coll*) exclamation of surprise.

goshawk [*gos*-hawk] *n* large short-winged hawk.

gosling [*goz*ling] *n* young goose.

go-slow [*gO*-*slO*] *adj* and *n* (pertaining to) systematic curtailment of output by workers.

gospel [*go*spel] *n* (*NT*) one of four accounts of Christ's life and teachings; extract from this read during Communion Service or Mass; teachings of Christ; Christian doctrine; (*fig*) principles of conduct, systematic teachings; **g. truth** absolute truth.

gospeller [*go*speler] *n* (*coll*) evangelist preacher.

gossamer [*go*samer] *n* filmy cobweb threads floating in air, or found on grass and bushes; anything very light and filmy; lightweight waterproof cloth ~ **gossamery** *adj*.

gossip [*go*sip] *n* spiteful, ill-founded rumour; frivolous discussion of other people's business; friendly chat; one who spreads spiteful rumours; busybody; chatterer; (*ar*) close friend; old woman ~ **gossip** *v/i* exchange gossip; spread rumours; chat casually and intimately.

gossipy [*go*sipi] *adj* of gossip; fond of gossip.

gossoon [*go*sOOn] *n* (*Ir*) servant boy; lad.

got [*got*] *p/t* and *p/part* of **get**.

Goth [*goth*] *n* member of ancient Germanic tribe; (*fig*) uncivilized person.

Gothic [*goth*ik] *adj* of or like Goths; (*archi*) pertaining to a medieval style with pointed arches *etc* > PDAA; imitating, based on, this style; (*print*) having elaborate pointed characters, as in German type; pertaining to an 18th-century school of sensationalist romantic literature; (*ar*) barbarous; medieval ~ **Gothic** *n* language of the Goths; Gothic architecture.

gothicize [*goth*is*I*z] *v/t* and *i* give Gothic style to; adopt or defend Gothic style; render medieval.

Gothick [*goth*ik] *adj* (*coll*) (*archi*) in 19th-century style imitating medieval Gothic; (*literature*) macabre, full of sensational horrors.

gotten [*go*ten] (*US* and *dial*) *p/part* of **get**.

gouache [g*OO*-ash] *n* opaque watercolour paint mixed with gum; method of painting in gouache > PDAA.

Gouda [*gow*da] *n* kind of Dutch cheese.

gouge [*gow*j] *n* chisel with curved cutting edge for hollowing out wood ~ **gouge** *v/t* and *i* cut with a gouge; **g. out** prise out; force out with thumb.

goulash [g*OO*laash] *n* rich stew of meat and vegetables, flavoured with paprika.

gourd [*goord*/*gawrd*] *n* large fleshy fruit; dried hollowed husk of this fruit used as a vessel.

gourmand [*goor*mand] *n* glutton; gourmet.

gourmet [*goor*may] *n* connoisseur of food and wine; epicure.

gout (1) [*gowt*] *n* painful swelling of the joints ~ **gouty** *adj* ~ **goutiness** *n*.

gout (2) *n* (*ar*) drop, *esp* of blood.

gov [*guv*] *n* (*sl*) master; sir; father.

govern [*guv*ern] *v/t* and *i* rule; control, guide, regulate; (*gramm*) determine mood or case (of).

governable [*guv*ernab'l] *adj* that can be ruled.

governance [*guv*ernans] *n* act of governing; state of being governed.

governess [*guv*ernis] *n* instructress of young children in a private family.

government [*guv*ernment] *n* ruling of a state; system of political administration; persons responsible for ruling a state; the state itself.

governmental [guvern*men*tal] *adj* relating to government or to a government.

governor [*guv*ernor] *n* one who governs, ruler; official governing state, colony *etc*; member of governing body of an institution; (*mech*) device to regulate functioning of a machine, *esp* to limit its speed; (*sl*) father; employer, master; sir.

governor-general [guvernor-*jene*Ral] *n* principal governor of colony or dominion, viceroy.

governorship [*guv*ernorship] *n* office of a governor; exercise or tenure of this office.

gowan [*gow*-an] *n* (*Scots*) daisy.

gowk [*gowk*] *n* (*dial*) cuckoo; (*coll*) simpleton.

gown [*gown*] *n* loose full-length garment; woman's full-length one-piece dress; academic robe; official robe of barrister, mayor, alderman *etc*; (*collect*) members of university; lawyers ~ **gown** *v/t* clothe with a gown; admit to academic status.

gownsman [*gownz*man] *n* one in residence at a university.

goy (*pl* **goyim**) [*goi*] *n* Yiddish name for a Gentile.

grab (*pres/part* **grabbing**, *p/t* and *p/part* **grabbed**) [*gRab*] *v/t* (*coll*) clutch, seize suddenly and roughly; take unjustly ~ **grab** *n* act of grabbing, clutch; hinged and toothed bucket hung from crane and used to excavate and shift soil > PDE; child's card game ~ **grabber** *n* one who or that which grabs.

grabble [*gRab*'l] *v/t* grope about; sprawl.

grace [*gRays*] *n* elegance, beauty; elegance in movement; charm; good manners; kindness, favour; mercy; respite; God's mercy or favour; (*theol*) supernatural power given by God to the soul to enable it to attain virtue and salvation; virtue so attained; state of soul when free from serious sin; prayer before or after meals; (*myth*) one of three goddesses of beauty; **act of g.** official pardon to criminals; **airs and graces** affected manners; **fall from g.** lapse into sin, behave less well than before; **in the good graces of** in favour with; **with good (bad) g.** showing willingness (unwillingness); **Your G.** mode of address to duke, duchess, or archbishop; **year of g.** year of Christian era ~ **grace** *v/t* adorn, give charm to.

grace-cup [*gRays*-kup] *n* last drink at a feast; large goblet from which this is drunk.

graceful [*gRays*fool] *adj* elegant, showing grace; moving beautifully ~ **gracefully** *adv* ~ **gracefulness** *n*.

graceless [*gRays*les] *adj* not in favour with God, ungodly; clumsy ~ **gracelessly** *adv* ~ **gracelessness** *n*.

grace-note [*gRays*-nOt] *n* (*mus*) note added as embellishment, ornament > PDM.

gracile [*gRas*il] *adj* slender.

gracility [*gRas*iliti] *n* slenderness.

gracious [*gRay*shus] *adj* kind, winning; polite to inferiors; elegant, refined; merciful, nobly forgiving; **g.! good g.!** exclamations of surprise; **g. living** expensive display of alleged good taste in housing, food, clothes *etc* ~ **graciously** *adv* ~ **graciousness** *n*.

gradate [*gRadayt*] *v/t* and *i* arrange in grades; merge by degrees.

gradation [*gRadayshon*] *n* transition by degrees or stages; gradual passage from one state to another; act of grading; state of being graded; (*mus*) diatonic succession of chords; (*phil*) change of vowels in series, caused by variation of stress or tone ~ **gradational** *adj*.

grade [*gRayd*] *n* degree of quality, size *etc*; (*phil*) one of series of vowels formed by gradation; (*biol*) animal produced by cross-breeding; (*US*) school form; mark; gradient; **make the g.** achieve standard, succeed ~ **grade** *v/t* classify.

gradely [*gRayd*li] *adj* (*dial*) fine, pleasant ~ **gradely** *adv* (*dial*) thoroughly, satisfactorily.

gradient [*gRayd*i-ent] *n* degree of slope; sloping portion of road, railway, pipe *etc* > PDE.

gradin, gradine [*gRayd*in] *n* one of series of rising steps or seats; shelf behind altar.

gradual (1) [*gRadew*-al] *adj* taking place by degrees; slow; gentle ~ **gradually** *adv* ~ **gradualness** *n*.

gradual (2) *n* antiphon in the Mass, between epistle and gospel; book containing graduals.

graduate [*gRadew*-ayt] *v/t* and *i* classify in grades; mark a scale in degrees; obtain a university degree ~ **graduate** [*gRadew*-at] *n* one who has obtained a university degree; (*US*) one who has completed his schooling ~ **graduated** *adj* marked with graduations.

graduation [*gRadew*-ayshon] *n* act of graduating; act of taking a university degree; mark indicating measure, *esp* on medicine bottle; state of being graded or graduated.

graduator [*gRadew*-ayter] *n* instrument for marking lines into small equal sections.

gradus [*gRaydus*] *n* list of Latin synonyms with quantities marked.

Graecism, Grecism [*gRee*sizm] *n* Greek idiom; imitation of Greek style.

Graecize, Grecize [*gRee*sIz] *v/t* give Greek style to; imitate the Greeks.

graffito (*pl* **graffiti**) [*gRafeet*O] *n* slogan or other inscription surreptitiously written on a wall; (*arch*) drawing or inscription scratched on wall; (*art*) decoration by scratching through glaze, plaster *etc* to reveal contrasting undercoat.

graft [*gRaaft*] *n* shoot from one plant inserted into another to form new growth; (*surg*) living tissue taken from one part of body and applied to another to replace damaged tissue > PDB; (*coll*) illicit profits, *esp* bribes; corruption, *esp* in political life; (*sl*) hard work ~ **graft** *v/t* and *i* induce union between tissues normally separate; join one thing inseparably to another; (*coll*) engage in bribery, jobbery *etc* ~ **grafting** *n*.

grafter [*gRaaft*er] *n* one who grafts; instrument for grafting; (*coll*) corrupt official; swindler.

grail [*gRayl*] *n* mysterious holy vessel mentioned in Arthurian literature.

grain [*gRayn*] *n* seed of cereals, corn; small hard particle; very small quantity; smallest unit in apothecaries' and troy scales of weight; direction of fibres in wood *etc*; pattern of fibres in wood; texture of leather; (*ar*) dye, *esp* red or purple; **against the g.** against one's inclination ~ **grain** *v/t* and *i* rub into fine particles; give granular surface to; paint in imitation of grain of wood; bear grains ~ **graining** *n* ~ **grainy** *adj*.

gralloch [*gRal*ok] *n* guts of a deer ~ **gralloch** *v/t* gut a dead deer.

gram (1), **gramme** [*gRam*] *n* metric unit of mass, one-thousandth of a kilogram.

gram (2) [*gRam*] *n* chickpea used as fodder.

gramarye [*gRam*aRi] *n* (*ar* and *poet*) magic.

gramercy [*gRam*ursi] *interj* (*ar*) thank you.

graminaceous [*gRam*inayshus] *adj* like grass; pertaining to grasses.

gramineous [*gRam*ini-us] *adj* graminaceous.

graminivorous [*gRam*inivoRus] *adj* feeding on grass.

grammalogue [*gRam*alog] *n* word represented by a single sign.

grammar [*gRam*er] *n* study of word-forms, syntax, and relations of words to each other in sentences; rules of correct usage of a language; book on this; (*fig*) elementary rules of any subject; **g. school** secondary day-school teaching pupils selected for intellectual ability.

333

grammarian [gRamaïRi-an] *n* student or teacher of grammar; writer on grammar.

grammatic [gRamatik] *adj* pertaining to grammar, following the rules of grammar ~ **grammatical** *adj* ~ **grammatically** *adv* ~ **grammaticalness** *n*.

gramme see gram.

gram-molecule [gRam-*moli*kewl] *n* (*chem*) molecular weight of a compound expressed in grams.

gramophone [gRamofOn] *n* machine for reproducing recorded sounds by means of the vibration of a needle passing along grooves in revolving disk.

gramophonic [gRamofonik] *adj* of or like a gramophone.

grampus [gRampus] *n* the spouting whale; (*fig*) person who breathes loudly.

gran [gRan] *n* (*coll abbr*) grandmother.

granadilla [gRanadila] *n* fruit of the passion-flower.

granary [gRanaRi] *n* storehouse for threshed grain; (*fig*) region producing grain in abundance.

grand [gRand] *adj* splendid, imposing; large; important; distinguished; haughty, pretentious; chief, main; (*coll*) very good, very pleasant; **g. piano** large harp-shaped piano with horizontal strings ~ **grand** *n* (*coll*) grand piano; (*US sl*) a thousand dollars.

grandam [gRandam] *n* (*ar*) grandmother.

grand-aunt [gRand-aant] *n* sister of a grandparent.

grandchild [gRandchIld] *n* child of one's child.

grand-dad, grandad [gRandad] *n* (*coll*) grandfather.

granddaughter [gRanddawter] *n* female grandchild.

grandee [gRandee] *n* Spanish nobleman; person of high rank or position.

grandeur [gRandyer] *n* quality of being grand; great and imposing size; splendour, magnificence, sublimity.

grandfather [gRandfaaTHer] *n* parent's father; **g. clock** tall standing clock worked by weights and pendulum.

grandiloquence [gRandilokwens] *n* pompous and lofty style of language ~ **grandiloquent** *adj*.

grandiose [gRandi-Os] *adj* grand, imposing; pretentious, bombastic ~ **grandiosely** *adv*.

grandiosity [gRandi-ositi] *n* pretentiousness.

grandly [gRandli] *adv* in a grand way.

grandma [gRanmaa] *n* (*coll*) grandmother.

grandmother [gRandmuTHer] *n* parent's mother.

grand-nephew [gRand-nevew] *n* son of one's nephew or niece.

grandness [gRandnis] *n* quality of being grand.

grand-niece [gRand-nees] *n* daughter of one's nephew or niece.

grandpapa, grandpa [gRanpapaa, gRanpaa] *n* (*coll*) grandfather.

grandparent [gRandpairRent] *n* parent of one's parent.

grandsire [gRandsIr] *n* (*ar*) grandfather; ancestor; one variety of changes rung on bells.

grandson [gRandsun] *n* male grandchild.

grandstand [gRands*t*and] *n* main group of raised seats for spectators at races, sports *etc*.

grand-uncle [gRand-unk'l] *n* brother of a grandparent.

grange [gRaynj] *n* country house with farm buildings nearby; (*ar*) granary.

grangerize [gRaynjeRIz] *v/t* add illustrations to a book by introducing extra prints, paintings *etc*.

graniferous [gRanifeRus] *adj* bearing grain.

granite [gRanit] *n* coarse-grained igneous rock > PDE, PDG ~ **granite** *adj* made of granite; (*fig*) stubborn, hard-hearted.

granny [gRani] *n* (*coll*) grandmother; **g. knot** wrongly made reef-knot tending to slip.

granolithic [gRanolithik] *adj* and *n* (formed of) concrete made from crushed granite, cement, and sand > PDE.

grant [gRaant] *v/t* allow, concede a request; bestow, award; (*leg*) make a legal assignment; admit (a point); concede for sake of argument ~ **grant** *n* something bestowed, gift; sum of money bestowed to further a specified aim, *esp* in scholarship; money given by State or local authority to maintain a student; (*leg*) conveyance of property by deed ~ **grantable** *adj*.

grantee [gRaantee] *n* (*leg*) one to whom a grant is made.

grantor, granter [gRaanter] *n* one who makes a grant.

granular [gRanewlar] *adj* of small grain-like particles; having rough gritty surface.

granulate [gRanewlayt] *v/t* and *i* make into small grain-like particles; roughen surface of; become granular ~ **granulated** *adj* granular.

granulation [gRanew*lay*shon] *n* gritty surface; small hard lump; act of granulating.

granule [gRanewl] *n* small grain-like particle.

granulous [gRanewlus] *n* of or having granules.

grape [gRayp] *n* fruit of the vine; (*poet*) vine; grapeshot; (*pl*) (*vet*) wart-like growth on horse's leg; **g. sugar** glucose, dextrose.

grapefruit [gRaypfROOt] *n* large, pale yellow citrous fruit.

grape-hyacinth [gRayp-hI-asinth] *n* small dark-blue hyacinth.

grapery [gRaypeRi] *n* vinery.

grapeshot [gRayp-shot] *n* cluster of small iron balls fired together from a cannon.

grapevine [gRaypvIn] *n* vine; (*coll*) false rumour; **the g. (telegraph)** (*coll*) means of spreading news, rumours *etc* quickly and untraceably.

graph [gRaf/gRaaf] *n* (*math*) diagram showing relation of one variable quantity to another > PDE.

graphic [gRafik] *adj* expressed by visual symbols; pertaining to writing; pertaining to printing, drawing or painting; (*fig*) vividly descriptive; (*sci*) diagrammatic ~ **graphical** *adj* graphic ~ **graphically** *adv*.

graphics [gRafiks] *n* (*pl*) use of graphs in calculation; use or production of diagrams; decorative printing.

graphite [gRafIt] *n* blacklead, plumbago; a form of carbon, used for pencil leads, in electrical apparatus, and as a lubricant.

graphology [gRafoloji] *n* study of handwriting, *esp* to deduce characteristics of writer > PDP.

graphomania [gRafOmayni-a] *n* obsessive urge to write > PDP.

grapnel [gRapnel] *n* fluked anchor on end of rope thrown to grapple ship or mooring.

grapple [gRap'l] *v/t* and *i* clutch hold of, seize tightly; wrestle; (*fig*) apply one's mind to, cope energetically with; (*naut*) lay hold of with a grapnel ~ **grapple** *n* act of grappling; (*naut*) grapnel.

grappling-iron [gRapling-I-ern] *n* grapnel.

grapy [gRaypi] *adj* of or like grapes.

grasp [gRaasp] *v/t* and *i* seize firmly with hand or arm; clutch; understand; **g. at** try to seize ~ **grasp** *n* act of grasping, grip; power of understanding; control; firm handclasp.

grasper [gRaasper] *n* one who grasps; one who is grasping.

grasping [gRaasping] *adj* eager for gain, power *etc*; rapacious, avaricious ~ **graspingly** *adv*.

grass [gRaas] *n* wild low-growing herbage with blade-like leaves; (*bot*) any plant of the order *Gramineae;* piece of land covered with grass; (*sl*) policeman; informer; (*sl*) marijuana; (*typ*) casual work; **out at g.** at pasture; (*fig*) not working ~ **grass** *v/t* sow grass on; cover with turf; put out to graze; shoot down (quarry); land (fish); (*coll*) knock down, bring to the ground; (*sl*) inform against.

grasscutter [gRaaskuter] *n* lawnmower.

grass-green [gRaas-gReen] *adj* bright green.

grasshopper [gRaas-hoper] *n* small leaping insect, akin to locust.

grassiness [gRaasinis] *n* state of being grassy.

grassland [gRaasland] *n* land used as pasture; region whose natural vegetation is grass > PDG.

grassplot [gRaasplot] *n* patch of grass, lawn.

grassroots [gRaasROOts] *n* (*pl*) (*fig*) ordinary members or adherents of a party or movement; opinions of such people, *esp* if simple or unreasoned; basic elements, fundamentals.

grass-snake [gRaas-snayk] *n* harmless British snake.

grass-widow [gRaas-*wid*O] *n* woman whose husband is temporarily absent.

grass-widower [gRaas-*wid*O-er] *n* man whose wife is temporarily absent.

grassy [gRaasi] *adj* like grass; covered with grass.

grate (1) [gRayt] *n* cast-iron fire bars and frame of fireplace.

grate (2) *v/t* and *i* scrape on or with a rough surface; scrape into small shreds or fragments; make a harsh grinding noise; **g. on** (*fig*) annoy, make unpleasant impression on.

grateful [gRaytfool] *adj* thankful, showing or feeling gratitude; (*ar*) pleasant, cheering ~ **gratefully** *adv* ~ **gratefulness** *n*.

grater [gRayter] *n* implement for grating.

graticule [gRatikewl] *n* fine scale in an optical instrument; network of lines on a map.

gratification [gRatifi*kay*shon] *n* act of gratifying; state of being gratified; that which gratifies; (*ar*) reward, tip.

gratify [gRatifl] *v/t* please, satisfy; comply with, indulge ~ **gratifier** *n* ~ **gratifying** *adj* ~ **gratifyingly** *adv*.

gratin [gRatan(g)] *n* surface produced on cooked dish by sprinkling with grated cheese or breadcrumbs before baking.

grating (1) [gRayting] *n* perforated cover over window, drain *etc*; (*opt*) parallel lines cut on a flat glass plate so as to produce spectra > PDS.

grating (2) *adj* (*of sound*) harsh, rasping; jarring, irritating ~ **gratingly** *adv*.

gratis [gRaatis/gRaytis] *adv* free of charge.

gratitude [gRatitewd] *n* thankfulness and appreciation for kindness or benefits received.

gratuitous [gRatew-itus] *adj* freely given; performed without charge; done without adequate reason, uncalled-for ~ **gratuitously** *adv* ~ **gratuitousness** *n*.

gratuity [gRatew-iti] *n* gift in return for services, tip; sum given to member of armed forces at end of his service.

gravamen [gRavaymen] *n* (*Lat*) most damaging part (of accusation or complaint).

grave (1) [gRayv] *n* hole dug in earth for burial of corpse; place of burial, tomb; (*fig*) death.

grave (2) *adj* serious, important; solemn; ominous; austere; (*phon*) [gRaav] with falling pitch, low-pitched, denoted by symbol (ˋ).

grave (3) *v/t* (*ar*) engrave, carve; (*fig*) impress deeply.

grave (4) *v/t* renovate and tar and pitch (ship's hull).

grave-goods [gRayv-goodz] *n* (*pl*) (*arch*) objects buried with a corpse.

gravel [gRavel] *n* deposit of small pebbles mixed with sand or clay on river-bed or shore > PDG; (*med*) deposit of small limy crystals in bladder; disease characterized by this ~ **gravel** (*pres/part* **gravelling**, *p/t* and *p/part* **gravelled**) *v/t* cover with gravel; (*fig*) disconcert, perplex, floor.

gravelly [gRaveli] *adj* of or like gravel.

gravely [gRayvli] *adj* seriously.

graven [gRayven] *adj* (*ar*) engraved, sculptured.

graver [gRayver] *n* one who engraves; engraving tool.

Graves (1) [gRaav] *n* a white Bordeaux wine.

graves (2) *n* (*pl*) see greaves (2).

gravestone [gRayvstOn] *n* inscribed stone slab marking a grave.

graveyard [gRayvyaard] *n* burial-ground.

gravid [gRavid] *adj* pregnant.

gravimetric [gRavi*met*Rik] *adj* measured by weight; **g. analysis** branch of chemical quantitative analysis depending on measurements made by weighing > PDS.

graving-dock [gRaving-dok] *n* dock where a ship's hull can be cleaned, tarred *etc*.

gravitate [gRavitayt] *v/i* move towards a body under influence of gravity; move towards the earth; (*fig*) be attracted by, tend to go towards.

gravitation [gRavitayshon] *n* act of gravitating; force of gravity > PDS.

gravitational [gRavitayshonal] *adj* of or by gravity.

gravity [gRaviti] *n* quality of being grave, seriousness; solemnity; (*phys*) tendency of every particle in the universe to attract and be attracted by every other particle; force exerted by the earth or by any heavenly body to attract matter to its centre > PDS; **specific g.** ratio of density of a substance to that of water > PDS.

gravure [gRavewr] *n* process of printing from engraved copper plates.

gravy [gRayvi] *n* juices exuded by meat during roasting; sauce made from these.

gravy-boat [gRayvi-bOt] *n* vessel in which gravy is served.

gray see grey.

grayling [gRayling] *n* a freshwater fish.

graze (1) [gRayz] *v/t* touch or scrape lightly in passing ~ **graze** *n* shallow skin wound caused by scraping, abrasion; slight passing contact.

graze (2) *v/i* and *t* feed on grass, go to pasture; put out to pasture.

grazing [gRayzing] *n* pasture; act of grazing.

grease [gRees] *n* animal fat melted down; any semi-solid oily or fatty substance; thick lubricating oil; uncleaned wool; (*coll*) bribe; flattery; (*vet*) inflammation of fetlock; **g. paint** mixture of grease and paint used as make-up by actors ~ **grease** *v/t* apply grease to; (*coll*) bribe; flatter.

greaseproof [gReespROOf] *adj* impervious to grease.

greaser [gReezer] *n* one who lubricates machinery; (*US*) nickname for a Mexican or Spanish American; (*sl*) tough, rowdy youth riding a motorcycle; unpleasant person.

greasy [gReezi/gReesi] *adj* covered in grease; like grease, slippery, slimy; (*naut*) stormy (weather); (*fig*) unctuous, fawning ~ **greasily** *adv* ~ **greasiness** *n*.

great [gRayt] *adj* large in size, amount, area *etc*; important; extreme, intense; excellent, superior; of high rank or position; prominent; noble; (*coll*) very good, amusing, pleasant *etc*; (as *pref*) indicating further step in genealogical relationship; (*ar*) pregnant; **g. at** very clever or skilful at; **g. circle** circle obtained by cutting a sphere by a plane passing through its centre; **G. Dane** large breed of dog, akin to mastiff; **g. on** keenly interested in.

great-aunt [gRayt-aant] *n* grand-aunt.

greatcoat [gRaytkOt] *n* heavy overcoat.

great-grandchild [gRayt-gRandchIld] *n* child of one's grandchild.

great-granddaughter [gRayt-gRand-dawter] *n* female great-grandchild.

great-grandfather [gRayt-gRandfaaTHer] *n* male great-grandparent.

great-grandmother [gRayt-gRandmuTHer] *n* female great-grandparent.

great-grandparent [gRayt-gRandpairRent] *n* parent of one's grandparent.

great-grandson [gRayt-gRandsun] *n* male great-grandchild.

great-hearted [gRayt-haartid] *adj* noble, magnanimous, generous.

greatly [gRaytli] *adv* to a great degree; in a great way.

greatness [gRaytnis] *n* quality of being great.

Greats [gRayts] *n* (*pl*) (*coll*) final Honours School of Literae Humaniores at Oxford University.

greaves (1) [gReevz] *n* (*pl*) armour for lower leg.

greaves (2), **graves** [gReevz, grayvz] *n* (*pl*) sediment of animal fat.

grebe [gReeb] *n* British tailless diving bird with partially webbed feet.

Grecian [gReeshan] *adj* Greek ~ **Grecian** *n* Greek scholar.

Grecism see **Graecism**.

Grecize see **Graecize**.

greed [gReed] *n* excessive desire to obtain and possess; excessive liking for food; gluttony; desire for wealth, power *etc*.

greedy [gReedi] *adj* desiring selfishly and excessively; showing greed ~ **greedily** *adv* ~ **greediness** *n*.

greedy-guts [gReedi-guts] *n* (*sl*) glutton.

Greek [gReek] *n* and *adj* (native) of Greece; (language) of Greece; **all G.** (*coll*) incomprehensible.

green [gReen] *adj* of a colour between blue and yellow; consisting of fresh leaves or vegetables; unripe; not mature; sickly or pale in complexion; (*fig*) envious, jealous; (*coll*) inexperienced; credulous, easily tricked; (*fig*) flourishing, undying; **g. belt** area round a town where building is forbidden; **g. light** permission to advance, proceed, *etc*; **g. paper** (*pol*) document setting out proposals for discussion rather than agreed policy ~ **green** *n* green colour; area or plot of grass; (*golf*) area of mown and level turf; green badge of Irish Nationalism; (*pl*) cooked leaf vegetables, *esp* cabbage ~ **green** *v/t* and *i* make or become green.

greenback [gReenbak] *n* (*coll*) American banknote.

greenery [gReeneRi] *n* green vegetation.

greenfinch [gReenfinch] *n* kind of finch with olive-green plumage.

greenfly [gReenflI] *n* the green aphis.

greengage [gReengayj] *n* sweet green-skinned plum.

greengrocer [gReengROser] *n* retail dealer in vegetables and fruit ~ **greengrocery** *n*.

greenheart [gReenhaart] *n* variety of hard West Indian timber.

greenhorn [gReenhawrn] *n* inexperienced person, beginner; dupe.

greenhouse [gReenhows] *n* building with glass roof and sides, *usu* heated, for cultivation of delicate plants.

greening [gReening] *n* apple which is green when ripe.

greenish [gReenish] *adj* somewhat green.

greenness [gReennis] *n* quality of being green.

greenroom [gReenROOm] *n* waiting-room for actors when not on stage.

greensand [gReensand] *n* (*geol*) variety of sandstone, flecked with green > PDG.

green-sickness [gReen-siknis] *n* (*obs*) chlorosis.

greenstick [gReenstik] *n* (*med*) partial fracture in which one side of the bone is only bent.

greenstuff [gReenstuf] *n* green vegetables; green fodder.

greensward [gReenswawrd] *n* (*ar*) green turf.

greenwood [gReenwood] *n* leafy forest.

greet (1) [gReet] *v/t* receive or encounter with expression of feeling; salute; welcome; send friendly message to.

greet (2) *v/i* (*Scots* and *dial*) weep, lament.

greeting [gReeting] *n* act of one who greets; friendly message.

gregarious [gRigairRi-us] *adj* living in flocks or herds; (*fig*) fond of company or of crowds ~ **gregariously** *adv* ~ **gregariousness** *n*.

Gregorian [gRigawrRi-an] *n* and *adj* (plainsong) introduced by Pope Gregory I > PDM; (calendar) introduced by Pope Gregory XIII.

gremlin [gRemlin] *n* (*sl*) mischievous imp or goblin supposed to be responsible for mechanical faults in aircraft or other pieces of machinery.

grenade [gRinayd] *n* small bomb thrown by hand; small globular fire-extinguisher.

grenadier [gRenadeer] *n* (*orig*) soldier who threw grenades; soldier in Grenadier Guards.

grenadine [gRenadeen] *n* syrup made from pomegranates; type of light loosely woven cloth; type of carnation; larded and glazed fricassee.

grew [gROO] *p/t* of **grow**.

grey, gray [gRay] *adj* of colour between white and black; cloudy; dim; (*fig*) dreary; **g. matter** (*physiol*) tissue of central nervous system > PDB; (*coll*) brain, intelligence ~ **grey, gray** *n* grey colour; grey horse; (*Negro sl*) white man; (*sl*) conventional middle-aged person ~ **grey, gray** *v/t* and *i* make or become grey.

greybeard [gRaybeerd] *n* old man; kind of stoneware jug; kind of straggling lichen.

greycing [gRaysing] *n* (*coll*) greyhound racing.

greyhound [gRayhownd] *n* breed of dog used for hunting and racing.

greyish [gRay-ish] *adj* somewhat grey.

greylag [gRaylag] *n* kind of migrating goose.

greyness [gRaynis] *n* quality of being grey.

grid [gRid] *n* grating, gridiron; (*mot*) luggage carrier; national network of electricity cables or gas-supply pipes; network of squares for map or plan referencing; (*elect*) electrode in a discharge tube; (*eng*) timber framework on which ship can be beached for repair.

griddle, girdle [gRid'l, gird'l] *n* iron plate for baking scones *etc* over a fire.

griddle-cake [gRid'l-kayk] *n* one baked on a griddle.

gride [gRid] *v/i* move with harsh grating noise.

gridiron [gRidI-ern] *n* cooking utensil with iron bars for grilling over a fire; network of railway tracks; (*US*) a football field.

grief [gReef] *n* deep sorrow; mourning; cause of grief; **come to g.** suffer misfortune, injury, disaster *etc*; **good g.!** exclamation of surprise.

grievance [gReevans] *n* that which gives grounds for complaint.

grieve [gReev] *v/t* and *i* cause grief to; feel grief, mourn.

grievous [gReevus] *adj* distressing, severe, painful; deplorable; (*ar*) burdensome, oppressive ~ **grievously** *adv* ~ **grievousness** *n*.

griffin, gryphon [gRifin, gRifon] *n* (*myth, her*) fabulous monster, partly eagle and partly lion.

griffon [gRifon] *n* small rough-haired terrier; griffin; large species of vulture.

grig [gRig] *n* small eel; sand eel; cricket, grasshopper; **merry as a g.** very lively.

grill [gRil] *n* gridiron for cooking; food cooked on a grill; grill-room; grating ~ **grill** *v/t* and *i* cook or be cooked on a grill; expose or be exposed to extreme heat, scorch; (*sl*) interrogate closely and brutally.

grillage [gRilij] *n* foundation made of two layers of steel joists crossing at right angles > PDE.

grille [gRil] *n* framework of metal bars, *esp* covering window or separating one part of a building from another.

grill-room [gRil-ROOm] *n* room in a restaurant in which grilled food is served.

grilse [gRils] *n* young salmon when first returning from sea to river.

grim [gRim] *adj* stern, angry-looking, gloomy; frightening; sinister, ghastly; (*coll*) unpleasant.

grimace [gRimays] *n* ugly or jocular facial contortion ~ **grimace** *v/i* make grimaces.

grimalkin [gRimalkin] *n* old female cat.

grime [gRim] *n* black ingrained dirt; filthiness, squalor ~ **grime** *v/t* coat with dirt.

griminess [gRiminis] *n* dirtiness.

grimly [gRimli] *adv* in a grim way.

grimness [gRimnis] *n* quality of being grim.

grimy [gRimi] *adj* black with dirt, filthy.

grin (*pres/part* **grinning**, *p/t* and *p/part* **grinned**) [gRin] *v/i* and *t* smile broadly, showing the teeth; express by grinning; **g. and bear it** force oneself to be cheerful in face of trouble ~ **grin** *n* broad smile; forced or cruel smile.

grind (*p/t* and *p/part* **ground**) [gRInd] *v/t* and *i* reduce to small pieces or powder by rubbing with pressure; wear down; polish, sharpen, or roughen by friction; rub (one's teeth) hard against one another; (*coll*) toil, drudge; study hard; teach intensively; turn handle of barrel organ; (*fig*) oppress ~ **grind** *n* act of grinding; (*coll*) hard, dull work; strenuous race; (*sl*) steeplechase; (*vulg sl*) sexual intercourse; (*sl*) rotating movement of hips in dancing.

grinder [gRInder] *n* one who or that which grinds; molar tooth.

grindstone [gRIndstOn] *n* revolving disc of sandstone used for grinding; **keep one's nose to the g.** keep one at hard monotonous work.

gringo [gRing-gO] *n* Latin American name for an English-speaking foreigner.

grip (*pres/part* **gripping**, *p/t* and *p/part* **gripped**) [gRip] *v/t* and *i* clutch firmly, grasp; (*fig*) rouse or maintain the interest of; understand ~ **grip** *n* act or manner of gripping, grasp; (*fig*) power of understanding, mastery; control; power of rousing or keeping interest; handle of tool *etc*; travelling-bag, suitcase; influenza, grippe; **get to grips with** tackle.

gripe [gRip] *v/t* and *i* cause, or feel, spasms of pain in the bowels; (*ar*) clutch; (*sl*) complain ~ **gripe** *n* spasm of pain in bowels; (*ar*) clutch.

grippe [gRip] *n* (*Fr*) influenza.

gripping [gRiping] *adj* that grips; thrilling.

grisaille [gRizayl] *n* painting executed wholly in shades of grey > PDAA.

grisette [gRizet] *n* (*Fr*) a working girl.

griskin [gRiskin] *n* lean bacon from loin of pork.

grisly [gRizli] *adj* gruesome, horrible ~ **grisliness** *n*.

grison [gRizun] *n* kind of South American weasel; South American grey monkey.

grist [gRist] *n* corn for grinding; ground malt.

gristle [gRis'l] *n* cartilage, *esp* in cooked meat.

gristly [gRisli] *adj* having much gristle.

grit [gRit] *n* small chips of stone; coarse sand; gritstone; (*coll*) courage, endurance ~ **grit** (*pres/part* **gritting**, *p/t* and *p/part* **gritted**) *v/t* and *i* clench or grind (the teeth); grate.

gritstone [gRitstOn] *n* quartz rock resembling sandstone.

gritty [gRiti] *adj* of, like, or containing grit.

grizzle (1) [gRiz'l] *n* grey colour; grey horse.

grizzle (2) *v/i* (*coll*) whimper, cry fretfully; grouse.

grizzled-groundwork

grizzled [*gRiz'*ld] *adj* partly grey.

grizzly [*gRiz*li] *adj* grey-haired; **g. bear** large fierce North American bear.

groan [*gROn*] *n* deep inarticulate sound expressing pain, grief, or disapproval; (*of wood*) deep creaking sound ~ **groan** *v/i* utter a groan; **g. under** suffer as a result of; be oppressed or weighed down by.

groat [*gROt*] *n* (*hist*) English silver coin worth fourpence.

groats [*gROts*] *n* (*pl*) hulled grain.

grocer [*gROs*er] *n* retail dealer selling dry and tinned foods, household requisites *etc*.

grocery [*gROs*eRi] *n* grocer's trade; (*pl*) goods sold by a grocer.

grog [*gRog*] *n* mixture of spirits and water.

groggy [*gRog*i] *adj* (*coll*) unsteady, tottering; feeling faint; weak, liable to collapse ~ **groggily** *adv* ~ **grogginess** *n*.

grogram [*gRog*Ram] *n* stiff coarse silken fabric.

groin [*gRoin*] *n* meeting-point of belly and thigh; (*archi*) line formed by intersection of two vaults; groyne ~ **groin** *v/t* and *i* (*archi*) form a groin.

grommet see **grummet**.

gromwell [*gRom*wel] *n* plant of borage family.

grook [*gROOk*] *n* short rhyming statement or slogan.

groom [*gROOm*] *n* servant in charge of horses; officer of royal household; bridegroom ~ **groom** *v/t* rub down, brush and comb a horse; (*fig*) prepare (person) for some special occasion or office; keep one's clothes and person smart.

groomsman [*gROOmz*man] *n* friend who attends the bridegroom, best man, or one of a number of attendants.

groove [*gROOv*] *n* long furrow or channel, *esp* cut in metal or wood by a tool; spiral channel in bore of gun; **in the g.** (*sl*) in right mood; exhilarated; in top form; **get into a g.** (*coll*) become fixed in habits ~ **groove** *v/t* cut a groove in.

groover [*gROOv*er] *n* tool for making grooves; one who makes grooves.

groovy [*gROOv*i] *adj* (*sl*) in latest teenage fashion, up-to-date; sexually attractive; in excellent condition, in top form.

grope [*gROp*] *v/i* and *t* search with hands without use of one's sight; seek for or behave hesitantly; advance very cautiously; (*sl*) caress sexually ~ **groping** *n* and *adj* ~ **gropingly** *adv*.

grosbeak [*gRos*beek] *n* the hawfinch.

groschen [*gROsh*en] *n* (*Germ*) small silver coin.

gross (1) (*pl* **gross**) [*gROs*] *n* twelve dozen.

gross (2) *adj* heavily built, fat, coarse; vulgar, obscene; obviously wrong, flagrant; (*leg*) inexcusable; total, inclusive, without deductions ~ **gross** *n* whole; majority, greater part ~ **gross** *v/t* **g. up** state or calculate a gross sum, *esp* by adding tax previously paid to net sum ~ **grossly** *adv* ~ **grossness** *n*.

grot [*gRot*] *n* (*poet*) grotto.

grotesque [*gROtesk*] *adj* incongruous, absurd; fantastic, bizarre; distorted; (*arts*) highly decorated with animal forms, foliage *etc* > PDAA ~ **grotesque** *n* (*art*) grotesque style; work in this style; (*fig*) person of grotesque appearance; (*typ*) square-cut letter without serifs ~ **grotesquely** *adv* ~ **grotesqueness** *n*.

grotesquerie [*gROteskeRi*] *n* a grotesque quality, action, remark; (*pl*) (*collect*) grotesque objects.

grotto (*pl* **grottoes**) [*gRotO*] *n* cave, *esp* in limestone; (*archi*) artificial cavern, decorated with shells *etc*, used as a retreat; miniature shrine made of shells.

grotty [*gRoti*] *adj* (*sl*) bad, unpleasant.

grouch [*gRowch*] *n* (*coll*) grumble; (*US*) grumbler ~ **grouch** *v/i*.

ground (1) [*gROwnd*] *n* soil, surface of land; area of land *esp* if devoted to specified sport or other use; sea-bottom; foundation, basis; first coat of paint; dominant colour against which design stands out; (*pl*) reason(s), motive, pretext; (*pl*) estate round dwelling-house; (*pl*) dregs, sediment; **break new g.** be a pioneer; take first steps; **common g.** points on which agreement exists already; **down to the g.** (*coll*) completely; **g. floor** floor of building level with ground; **gain g.** advance, make progress; **give (lose) g.** be forced to retreat; **g. staff** mechanics *etc* attending to maintenance of aircraft; **g. state** (*phys*) most stable energy state of nucleus, atom or molecule; **g. wave** (*rad*) radio wave propagated close to the Earth's surface without reflection from the ionosphere ~ **ground** *v/t* and *i* place on the ground; give firm basis to; (*naut*) run aground; (*elect*) earth; prevent (aircraft or airman) from flying; give basic education to.

ground (2) *p/t* and *p/part* of **grind** ~ **ground** *adj* reduced to small pieces by grinding; shaped, polished or roughened by grinding.

groundbait [*gROwnd*bayt] *n* bait dropped to bottom of water to attract fish.

ground-bass [*gROwnd*-bays] *n* (*mus*) bass theme persistently repeated while upper parts proceed > PDM.

groundhog [*gROwnd*hog] *n* woodchuck; aardvark.

grounding [*gROwnd*ing] *n* act of placing on the ground; act of preparing a surface as a ground; instruction in basic principles of a subject.

groundless [*gROwnd*lis] *adj* without foundation; unjustified ~ **groundlessly** *adv* ~ **groundlessness** *n*.

groundling [*gROwnd*ling] *n* (*hist*) one who occupied cheap place in pit of Elizabethan theatre; (*fig*) person with little taste; fish keeping close to sea-bottom or river-bed.

groundnut [*gROwnd*nut] *n* peanut, South American earthnut.

groundplan [*gROwnd*plan] *n* (*archi*) horizontal section through a building taken at ground level; (*fig*) essential outline of scheme *etc*.

ground-rent [*gROwnd*-Rent] *n* rent paid to owner of freehold land by leaseholder.

groundsel [*gROwnd*sel] *n* yellow-flowered weed.

groundsheet [*gROwnd*sheet] *n* waterproof sheet used by campers *etc* when sleeping on the ground.

groundsman [*gROwndz*man] *n* one in charge of sports ground.

ground-swell [*gROwnd*-swel] *n* heavy rolling of the sea continuing when wind has dropped.

ground-to-air [gROwnd-tOO-*air*] *adj* (*of missile*) fired from the ground to attack aircraft, orbiting satellite, or missile.

groundwork [*gROwnd*wurk] *n* essential preliminaries, basic part of work; (*arts*) background.

group [grOOp] *n* number of objects or people which can be regarded as collective unit or as sharing certain characteristics; number of people sharing views, social customs, beliefs *etc*; small band of musicians and singers performing pop or jazz; *(arts)* several figures combined in one design; **g. captain** rank in Air Force equivalent to colonel or naval captain; **g. therapy** *(psych)* guided discussion between a group of people suffering from similar psychological or medical problems ~ **group** *adj* characteristic of human beings as members of social groups > PDP ~ **group** *v/t* and *i* form into a group; cluster; classify.

grouping [grOOping] *n* act of forming a group; mode of arrangement within a group.

grouse (1) *(pl* **grouse**) [grOws] *n* gallinaceous gamebird with feathered feet; flesh of this.

grouse (2) *v/i (coll)* grumble, complain ~ **grouse** *n* ~ **grouser** *n*.

grout [grOwt] *n* liquid cement slurry, used to pour into joints of masonry > PDE ~ **grout** *v/t* fill up with grout.

grouts [grOwts] *n (pl)* coarse meal; dregs.

grove [grOv] *n* small wood.

grovel *(pres/part* **grovelling**, *p/t* and *p/part* **grovelled**) [grOvel] *v/i* lie flat on one's face; crawl or squirm on the ground; *(fig)* humble oneself; show abject fear ~ **groveller** *n*.

grovelling [grOveling] *adj* abject; that grovels.

grow *(p/t* **grew**, *p/part* **grown**) [grO] *v/i* and *t* become larger; develop, become more mature; increase; live, flourish; become; cause or allow to grow, cultivate; **g. on** gain influence over; win admiration of; **g. out of** become too big for; become too mature for; **g. up** become mature.

grower [grO-er] *n* one who or that which grows; cultivator; market-gardener.

growl [grOwl] *n* deep rumbling sound made in the throat to express anger or menace; harsh threatening tone of voice; threatening rumble ~ **growl** *v/i* and *t* utter a growl; express by growling; grumble.

growler [grOwler] *n* one who growls; *(obs coll)* four-wheeled cab.

grown [grOn] *p/part* of **grow** ~ **grown** *adj* adult.

grown-up [grOn-up] *adj* and *n* adult.

growth [grOth] *n* act or rate of growing; increase, development; stages of development; that which grows or has grown; *(med)* morbid formation of tissue; excrescence; *(finance)* increase in capital value.

groyne, groin [grOin] *n* low barrier built out into sea to resist shifting of beach or tidal erosion > PDG.

grub (1) [grUb] *n* larva of an insect; drudge; *(coll)* food; *(cricket)* ball that keeps close to ground; *(coll)* dirty child.

grub (2) *(pres/part* **grubbing**, *p/t* and *p/part* **grubbed**) *v/t* and *i* dig; clear (ground) by digging; *(fig)* work arduously, *esp* at dull research work; **g. out**, **g. up** dig up by the roots.

grubber [grUber] *n* one who or that which grubs.

grubby [grUbi] *adj* grimy, dirty; infested with grubs ~ **grubbily** *adv* ~ **grubbiness** *n*.

Grub-street [grUb-stReet] *n (collect)* hack writers ~ **Grub-street** *adj* typical of literary hackwork or hacks.

grudge [grUj] *v/t* be unwilling to give; feel ill-will, envy ~ **grudge** *n* resentment due to some particular cause; cause for quarrel.

grudging [grUjing] *adj* unwillingly given, ungracious; mean ~ **grudgingly** *adv*.

gruel [grOO-il] *n* thin porridge; *(coll)* punishment.

gruelling [grOO-iling] *adj (coll)* exhausting; severe ~ **gruelling** *n (sl)* harsh treatment, a severe beating.

gruesome [grOOsum] *adj* horrifying, macabre ~ **gruesomely** *adv* ~ **gruesomeness** *n*.

gruff [grUf] *adj* rough, surly; unfriendly; *(of voice)* hoarse ~ **gruffly** *adv* ~ **gruffness** *n*.

grumble [grUmb'l] *v/i* express discontent; mutter angrily; rumble ~ **grumble** *n* act of grumbling; complaint ~ **grumbler** *n*.

grumbling [grUmbling] *adj* that grumbles; inclined to grumble; *(of pain)* persistent but not acute ~ **grumblingly** *adv*.

grummet, grommet [grUmit/grOmit] *n (naut)* ring of rope; ring of metal; metal eyelet > PDSa; circular washer of hemp and red lead > PDE; cabin-boy.

grumpy [grUmpi] *adj* sulky, bad-tempered ~ **grumpily** *adv* ~ **grumpiness** *n*.

Grundyism [grUndi-izm] *n* prudery.

grunion [grUnyon] *n* a N. American river fish.

grunt [grUnt] *n* deep nasal snort, *esp* that made by pigs; guttural noise expressing annoyance ~ **grunt** *v/i* and *t* utter a grunt; express by grunting.

Gruyère [grOOyair] *n* kind of Swiss cheese.

gryphon see **griffin**.

g-string [jee-stRing] *n* type of narrow ornamental loincloth worn by female cabaret dancers *etc*.

guana [gwaana] *n* a large lizard.

guanidine [gwaanideen] *n (chem)* basic, soluble, organic compound used in plastics, explosives *etc* > PDS.

guano [gwaanO] *n* deposit of dung of sea-birds; fertilizer made from this.

guarantee [gaRantee] *n* formal undertaking that contract, conditions *etc* will be carried out; pledge, security given in support of this; manufacturer's undertaking to make good defects in his product under certain conditions; *(leg)* one who offers surety; one who accepts a surety ~ **guarantee** *v/t* undertake, promise; give a guarantee or guaranty for.

guarantor [gaRantawr] *n (leg)* one who gives a guaranty or guarantee.

guaranty [gaRanti] *n (leg)* contract accepting responsibility for another's liabilities; undertaking to maintain another's rights; guarantee.

guard [gaard] *n* that which protects; one who protects; sentry; armed escort; official in charge of railway train; state of vigilance against danger, wariness; posture of defence; frame of wires or bars shielding a fireplace, heater, stove *etc*; part of swordhilt protecting hand; small tight fingering to prevent another from slipping ~ **guard** *v/t* and *i* protect, defend; keep watch over; prevent from escaping; restrain; take up defensive position; **g. against** take precautions against, attempt to prevent.

guarded [gaardid] *adj* protected; cautious, non-committal, discreet ~ **guardedly** *adv* ~ **guardedness** *n*.

guardhouse [gaardhows] *n* (*mil*) building for soldiers on guard duty; building where defaulters are detained.

guardian [gaardi-an] *n* one who guards; (*leg*) one who has custody of a child ~ **guardian** *adj* protecting; acting as guardian ~ **guardianship** *n* state of being a guardian.

guard-rail [gaard-Rayl] *n* a third rail on railway curve, check-rail; handrail, banister.

guardroom [gaardROOm] *n* guardhouse.

guardsman [gaardzman] *n* member of one of the household regiments.

guava [gwaava] *n* tropical tree of myrtle family; fruit of this.

gubernatorial [gewbernatawrRi-al] *adj* pertaining to a government or governor.

gubbins [gubinz] *n* (*coll*) any complicated machine or apparatus; simpleton, fool.

gudgeon (1) [gujon] *n* small freshwater fish; (*fig*) someone easily duped.

gudgeon (2) *n* piston pin; metal dowel for locking neighbouring stones together; upstanding pin on which hinge of a gate hangs; socket of rudder.

guelder-rose [gelder-ROz] *n* small tree bearing clusters of white flowers, snowball tree.

guerdon [gurdon] *n* reward ~ **guerdon** *v/t*.

Guernsey [gurnzi] *n* breed of dairy cows; thick woollen sweater.

guerilla, guerrilla [geRila] *n* member of an armed band carrying on warfare by ambushes *etc* from secret bases in wild country; warfare of this type; **urban g.** person who plants bombs or shoots or kidnaps political enemies in cities, for ideological motives ~ **guerilla, guerrilla** *adj*.

guess [ges] *v/t* and *i* form a judgement without sufficient evidence, conjecture; estimate, surmise; (*US* and *sl*) think likely, be almost sure ~ **guess** *n* judgement or opinion reached by guessing; act of guessing.

guesstimate [gestimayt] *n* (*coll*) estimate that involves some guesswork.

guesswork [geswurk] *n* act or process of guessing; judgement *etc* depending on guesses.

guest [gest] *n* person receiving hospitality from another; person entertained at another's expense; person paying for accommodation at hotel *etc*; **paying g.** person paying for board and lodging in private house ~ **guest** *adj* for the use of guests; performing, visiting *etc* by invitation.

guest-house [gest-hows] *n* house where paying guests can lodge.

guest-night [gest-nIt] *n* evening on which guests are entertained at dinner by a society, club, or college.

guff [guf] *n* (*coll*) humbug; nonsense.

guffaw [gufaw] *n* loud vulgar laugh ~ **guffaw** *v/i*.

guidance [gIdans] *n* act of guiding; direction, instruction.

guide [gId] *v/t* show (a person) the way, point out a direction; direct, control; have influence over; assist and direct the movements of ~ **guide** *n* one who or that which guides; one who conducts travellers, sightseers *etc*; book of instructions; guidebook; director, instructor; exemplar; (*pl*) (*mil*) troops trained to reconnoitre; (*mech*) that which controls direction of piece of machinery >

PDE; (*cap*) member of organization to train girls in good citizenship, self-reliance *etc*.

guidebook [gIdbook] *n* book containing information for tourists.

guide-dog [gId-dog] *n* dog trained to guide a blind person.

guided missile [gIdid-misIl] *n* projectile whose course can be controlled after launching and throughout flight.

guidelines [gIdlInz] *n* (*pl*) general advice and guidance for use in future problems.

guidepost [gIdpOst] *n* signpost.

guidon [gIdon] *n* (*mil*) forked or pointed cavalry standard.

guild [gild] *n* (*hist*) association of craftsmen; association formed with some specific aim.

guilder [gilder] *n* Dutch silver coin; (*hist*) Dutch or German gold coin.

guildhall [gildhawl] *n* former meeting-place of a guild; town-hall; **the G.** hall of the Corporation of the City of London.

guile [gIl] *n* cunning, deceitfulness.

guileful [gIlfool] *adj* crafty, deceitful ~ **guilefully** *adv* ~ **guilefulness** *n*.

guileless [gIl-les] *adj* innocent, straightforward ~ **guilelessly** *adv* ~ **guilelessness** *n*.

guillemot [gilimot] *n* a web-footed seabird of the auk family.

guilloche [gilOsh] *n* (*archi*) ornament consisting of two intertwining bands.

guillotine [giloteen] *n* instrument of execution by beheading, having a heavy blade sliding down between two posts; machine for cutting edges of pages of book; (*surg*) type of cutting instrument; (*coll*) resolution to curtail Parliamentary debate by voting at previously fixed time ~ **guillotine** *v/t* behead by means of guillotine; cut with a guillotine; (*coll*) curtail Parliamentary debate.

guilt [gilt] *n* fact of having broken a law; sense of wrong-doing arising out of real or imagined contravention of moral, religious or social standards; responsibility for offences committed, culpability; sinfulness.

guiltily [giltili] *adv* in a guilty way.

guiltiness [giltinis] *n* quality of being guilty.

guiltless [giltles] *adj* innocent ~ **guiltlessly** *adv* ~ **guiltlessness** *n*.

guilty [gilti] *adj* having incurred guilt; pertaining to guilt; revealing guilt; blameworthy.

guinea [gini] *n* (*hist*) English gold coin worth 21 shillings; sum of 21 shillings.

guinea-fowl [gini-fowl] *n* an African gallinaceous bird.

guinea-pig [gini-pig] *n* small domesticated rodent a variety of cavy; (*fig*) person used as test-case in medical, psychological, or sociological experiments and research; (*sl*) person receiving a guinea as fee; **g. director** (*sl*) one who allows his name to appear on a board of directors, in return for a fee, but takes no active part.

guinea-worm [gini-wurm] *n* a parasitic threadworm.

guipure [gipOOr] *n* kind of coarse, large-patterned lace; gimp.

guise [gIz] *n* style of clothes; disguise; false appearance; pretence; (*ar*) behaviour; custom.

guiser [gIzer] *n* masked mummer.

guitar [*gitaar*] *n* plucked six-stringed musical instrument > PDM.

guitarist [*gitaaR*ist] *n* one who plays a guitar.

gulch [*gulsh/gulch*] *n* (*US*) deep narrow ravine.

gules [*gewlz*] *n* and *adj* (*her*) (the colour) red.

gulf [*gulf*] *n* large deep bay > PDG; deep hollow, chasm; whirlpool; (*fig*) impassable gap; **G. Stream** warm current in North Atlantic.

gull (1) [*gul*] *n* one of various kinds of web-footed seabirds.

gull (2) *n* dupe, fool ~ **gull** *v/t* make a dupe of, swindle.

gullet [*gulit*] *n* interior part of throat, passage from mouth to stomach.

gulley see **gully.**

gullibility [*gulibiliti*] *n* stupid credulity.

gullible [*gulib'l*] *adj* easily duped.

gully, gulley [*guli*] *n* channel worn by running water > PDG; pit in gutter of road > PDE; deep drain; (*cricket*) area of field behind slips; fielder stationed there ~ **gully, gulley** *v/t* make a gully.

gulp [*gulp*] *v/t* and *i* swallow noisily or in large mouthfuls; make movement or noise as if swallowing; choke back, repress as if by swallowing ~ **gulp** *n* act of gulping; large mouthful; noise of gulping.

gum (1) [*gum*] *n* flesh around the teeth.

gum (2) *n* sticky substance exuded by certain trees; liquid glue; gelatinous sweetmeat; sticky secretion from the eye; (*coll*) gumtree; **g. arabic** fine gum obtained from acacia; **chewing g.** rubbery substance made from chicle, sweetened and flavoured ~ **gum** (*pres/part* **gumming,** *p/t* and *p/part* **gummed**) *v/t* and *i* coat with gum; stick or stiffen with gum; exude gum; **g. up** (*sl*) put out of working order.

gumbo [*gumbO*] *n* African herb producing edible pods, okra; soup thickened with these.

gumboil [*gumboil*] *n* small abscess on gums of the mouth.

gumboots [*gumbOOts*] *n* (*pl*) rubber boots reaching to knee or thigh; waders.

gumma (*pl* **gummata, gummas**) [*guma*] *n* (*med*) soft syphilitic tumour.

gummy [*gumi*] *adj* of or like gum; sticky ~ **gummily** *adv* ~ **gumminess** *n.*

gumption [*gumpshon*] *n* (*coll*) common sense, shrewdness; initiative, resource.

gumtree [*gumt*Ree] *n* tree that exudes gum; **up a g.** (*sl*) in a predicament.

gun [*gun*] *n* weapon consisting of metal tube from which missiles are fired by gunpowder; similar weapon not discharged by gunpowder; cannon; sporting firearm without rifling; (*coll*) any firearm, including revolver or pistol; discharge of a gun; person carrying a gun; tool for projecting or spraying liquids; **big g.** (*coll*) important person; **blow great guns** blow a gale; **g. dog** trained retriever; **stick to one's guns** stand firm, refuse to retreat ~ **gun** (*pres/part* **gunning,** *p/t* and *p/part* **gunned**) *v/i* and *t* shoot with a gun; go shooting for sport; **g. for** (*sl*) seek out in order to shoot or harm.

gunboat [*gunbOt*] *n* armed light vessel of shallow draught.

gun-carriage [*gun*-kaRij] *n* wheeled platform on which heavy gun is mounted and transported.

guncotton [*gun*koton] *n* powerful explosive formed by the action of nitric acid on cellulose.

gunfire [*gunf*Ir] *n* the discharge of guns.

gunite [*gun*It] *n* type of high-strength concrete formed by ejecting mortar from a compressed-air ejector > PDE.

gunlock [*gun*lok] *n* mechanism which explodes the charge in certain guns.

gunman [*gun*man] *n* armed gangster.

gunmetal [*gun*metal] *n* alloy of copper, tin, lead and zinc; dark shade of grey.

gunnage [*gun*ij] *n* number of guns carried by a warship.

gunner [*gun*er] *n* artilleryman; one who fires a gun; (*naut*) warrant officer in charge of ordnance.

gunnery [*gun*eRi] *n* science of artillery.

gunny [*gun*i] *n* coarse jute sacking.

gunpoint [*gun*point] *n* muzzle of a gun; **at g.** while being threatened with a gun.

gunpowder [*gun*powder] *n* explosive mixture of potassium nitrate, charcoal, and sulphur; **g. tea** green tea with leaves rolled into pellets.

gunroom [*gun*ROOm] *n* room in private house where guns are kept; (*naut*) junior officers' mess.

gunrunner [*gun*Runer] *n* one who smuggles guns and ammunition ~ **gunrunning** *n.*

gunshot [*gun*shot] *n* range of a gun; the shooting of a gun ~ **gunshot** *adj* caused by shot from a gun.

gunshy [*gun*shI] *adj* liable to be frightened by sound of firing.

gunsmith [*gun*smith] *n* maker and repairer of firearms.

gunstock [*gun*stok] *n* piece of wood to which a gun-barrel is fixed.

gunter [*gun*ter] *n* two-foot rule marked with various scales and logarithms; (*naut*) sail, bent to a gaff, and slung from a strop about two-thirds along > PDSa; **Gunter's chain** surveyor's 66 ft chain.

gunwale [*gun'l*] *n* upper edge of boat's side.

gup [*gup*] *n* (*coll*) gossip; chatter; nonsense.

guppy [*gupi*] *n* kind of bright-coloured small tropical fish.

gurgitation [*gurjitay*shon] *n* surging or eddying of a liquid.

gurgle [*gurg'l*] *v/i* make irregular bubbling sound in flowing; make similar sound in the throat ~ **gurgle** *n* gurgling sound.

guru [*goo*ROO] *n* Hindu teacher of meditation; one who teaches esoteric religious wisdom.

gush [*gush*] *v/i* flow out strongly and copiously; emit a copious stream; (*fig*) talk effusively; express stupid enthusiasm or sentimentality ~ **gush** *n* act of gushing; violent flow; (*fig*) excessive or stupid show of emotion; sentimental talk.

gusher [*gush*er] *n* one who or that which gushes; oil-well from which the oil flows without needing to be pumped.

gushing [*gush*ing] *adj* flowing copiously; effusively sentimental ~ **gushingly** *adv.*

gusset [*gusit*] *n* triangular piece of cloth, leather *etc* let into a garment to enlarge or strengthen it; steel bracket > PDE ~ **gusset** *v/t* add a gusset to.

gust [*gust*] *n* sudden strong rush of wind; (*fig*) brief outburst of emotion.

gustation [*gustay*shon] *n* act or faculty of tasting.

gustative [gustativ] *adj* pertaining to the sense or organs of taste.

gustatory [gustateRi] *adj* gustative.

gusto [gustO] *n* relish; zest, enjoyment.

gusty [gusti] *adj* blowing in gusts, blustery; subject to gusts of emotion ~ **gustily** *adv* ~ **gustiness** *n*.

gut [gut] *n* part of alimentary canal from pylorus to anus; (*pl*) bowels; (*pl*) (*coll*) courage, will-power, stamina; fine thread made from animal intestines used in surgery, for stringing musical instruments *etc*; thread drawn from silkworms used to make fishing-casts; narrow channel or passage ~ **gut** (*pres/part* **gutting**, *p/t* and *p/part* **gutted**) *v/t* remove guts of; destroy inner contents of (house *etc*), *esp* by fire; (*coll*) read rapidly so as to get the gist of.

gutsy [gutsi] *adj* (*coll*) full of courage, stamina or outspokenness; greedy.

gutta-percha [guta-*pur*cha] *n* rubbery substance obtained from sap of certain Malayan trees.

guttate [gutayt] *adj* (*zool*, *bot*) in the form of drops.

gutter [guter] *n* small open watercourse; trough under eaves to carry away rainwater; channel between road and pavement to carry away rainwater; (*fig*) squalid poverty; lowest social class; (*typ*) inner margin of a page; **g. press** sensational newspapers ~ **gutter** *v/t* and *i* provide gutters for; make grooves in; (*of candle*) burn quickly and irregularly, with wax dripping down one side.

guttering [guteRing] *n* system of gutters.

guttersnipe [gutersnip] *n* child living in slums.

guttiferous [gutifeRus] *adj* (*bot*) exuding drops, *esp* of gum.

guttiform [gutifawrm] *adj* shaped like a drop.

guttural [guteRal] *adj* pertaining to the throat; (*of voice*) rasping, harsh; (*phon*) produced in the throat; velar, produced between back of tongue and soft palate ~ **guttural** *n* (*phon*) guttural sound.

guy (1) [gI] *n* rope used to guide and steady a hoisted weight; rope, chain *etc* used as a stay; tent rope ~ **guy** *v/t* steady with a guy > PDSa.

guy (2) *n* effigy of Guy Fawkes publicly burnt on 5 November; person in ridiculous or shabby clothes; (*US and coll*) man, fellow ~ **guy** *v/t* mock; mimic scornfully.

guzzle [guz'l] *v/t* and *i* swallow greedily ~ **guzzler** *n*.

gybe [jIb] *v/i* (*of sail or a boom*) swing from side to side; change course > PDSa.

gym [jim] *n* (*coll*) gymnasium; gymnastics.

gymkhana [jim*kaa*na] *n* meeting for a display of athletics, *esp* for racing.

gymnasium (*pl* **gymnasiums**) [jim*nay*zi-um] *n* hall equipped for teaching and practising gymnastics; (*in Germany etc*) boys' high-school.

gymnast [jimnast] *n* one skilled in physical exercises.

gymnastic [jimnastik] *adj* of physical exercise.

gymnastics [jimnastiks] *n* (*pl*) art of training physical health and strength by exercises; non-competitive athletic exercises.

gymslip [jimslip] *n* short tunic worn by girls doing gymnastics.

gynaecological [gInikolojikal] *adj* of, by, or for gynaecology.

gynaecologist [gInikolojist] *n* doctor specializing in women's diseases, pregnancies *etc*.

gynaecology [gInikoloji] *n* (*med*) study of women's diseases, pregnancy and childbirth.

gynandromorph [jInandROmorf] *n* (*biol*) organism of mixed sex > PDB.

gyp (1), **gip** [jip] *n* (*sl*) give (**someone**) g. give pain, hurt.

gyp (2) *n* (*at Cambridge and Durham Universities*) college servant.

gypsophila [jipsofila] *n* garden plant bearing sprays of small white flowers.

gypsum [jipsum] *n* calcium sulphate, from which plaster of Paris is made > PDS.

gypsy see **gipsy**.

gyral [jIRal] *adj* moving in a circle.

gyrate [jIRayt] *v/i* rotate round fixed axis.

gyration [jIRayshon] *n* rotation round fixed axis.

gyratory [jIRayteRi] *adj* gyrating.

gyre [jIr] *n* circular or spiral movement.

gyrocompass [jIROkumpas] *n* non-magnetic compass operating on a gyroscopic principle > PDS.

gyroplane [jIROplayn] *n* aircraft deriving its lift chiefly from rotors freely rotating in a horizontal plane.

gyroscope [gIRoskOp/jIRoskOp] *n* spinning wheel so mounted that it is free to rotate about any axis, used to stabilize ships, aircraft *etc* > PDS.

gyroscopic [gIRoskopik/jIRoskopik] *adj* of, by or containing a gyroscope.

gyrostat [jIRostat] *n* gyroscope fixed in rigid case.

gyrostatic [jIRostatik] *adj* of or by a gyrostat.

gyrostatics [jIRostatiks] *n* (*pl*) branch of dynamics dealing with rotating bodies.

gyve [jIv] *n* fetter, shackle; handcuff ~ **gyve** *v/t* shackle with gyves.

H

h [*aych*] eighth letter of English alphabet.

ha [*ha*] *interj* exclamation of surprise *etc*; **h. h.** written representation of laughter.

hab-dabs [*hab*-dabz] *n* (*pl*) (*coll*) nervous irritability or fear; jitters.

habeas corpus [haybi-as-*kawr*pus] *n* (*Lat*) writ requiring prisoner to be brought before a court to establish whether his detention is lawful.

haberdasher [*haber*dasher] *n* retail dealer in ribbons, thread, tape *etc* ~ **haberdashery** *n* goods sold by a haberdasher.

habergeon [*haber*jon] *n* sleeveless waist-length shirt of mail.

habiliment [ha*bili*ment] *n* dress, clothing.

habit (1) [*habit*] *n* action or practice which has become automatic through repetition; customary tendency; usual behaviour, custom; normal condition; (*med*) constitution; (*psych*) automatic response to specific situations > PDP; (*biol*) characteristic mode of growth.

habit (2) *n* garment, *esp* distinctive clothing of a religious order, profession, class *etc*; **riding h.** wide skirt worn by women riding side-saddle ~ **habit** *v/t* clothe.

habitability [habita*bili*ti] *n* state of being habitable.

habitable [*hab*itab'l] *adj* able or fit to be lived in ~ **habitably** *adv* ~ **habitableness** *n*.

habitant [*hab*itant] *n* an inhabitant.

habitat [*hab*itat] *n* usual natural surroundings and conditions of animals and plants.

habitation [habi*tay*shon] *n* act of inhabiting; dwelling-place.

habitual [ha*bit*ew-al] *adj* formed by habit, customary, usual; addicted to a specified habit ~ **habitually** *adv* ~ **habitualness** *n*.

habituate [ha*bit*ew-ayt] *v/t* accustom, render familiar with; cause to form a habit.

habitude [*hab*itewd] *n* usual way of acting; habit.

habitué [ha*bit*ew-ay] *n* (*Fr*) one who regularly frequents a place.

hachures [hash*OOrz*] *n* (*pl*) hatch lines, fine lines of shading on maps to indicate steepness of slope > PDG.

hacienda [hasi-*enda*] *n* (*Sp*) estate, large plantation; ranch.

hack (1) [*hak*] *v/t* cut, chop, *esp* with axe; gash, cut roughly; kick the shins of; strike clumsily; break up (clods of earth) ~ **hack** *n* act of hacking; rough cut or notch; kick; cut caused by kicking; dry harsh cough; tool used for hacking, mattock.

hack (2) *n* horse let out for hire; overworked horse; poor-quality saddle-horse; (*fig*) drudge, overworked person, *esp* one who does inferior and badly-paid literary work ~ **hack** *adj* fit for a hack; drudging ~ **hack** *v/t* and *i* let out for hire; employ as drudge; work as a hack; jog along on a horse.

hack (3) *n* concrete slab for drying bricks before burning.

hacking [*hak*ing] *adj* (*of cough*) short and dry.

hackle [*hak'l*] *n* long neck-feathers of cock, peacock *etc*; angler's fly made from these; iron comb for dressing flax or hemp; **with hackles up** (*fig*) very angry; on the point of fighting.

hacklet [*hak*lit] *n* the kittiwake.

hackney [*hak*ni] *n* horse let out for hire; horse for general use; (*obs*) hackney-carriage ~ **hackney** *v/t* overwork, use excessively; render commonplace or trite; let out for hire.

hackney-carriage [*hak*ni-ka*rij*] *n* vehicle for public hire.

hackneyed [*hak*nid] *adj* trite, commonplace.

hacksaw [*hak*saw] *n* saw with replaceable blade for cutting metal.

hackwork [*hak*wurk] *n* dull, repetitive work.

hack-writer [*hak*-RIter] *n* one who makes a living by inferior journalism or novels *etc*.

had [*had*] *p/t* and *p/part* of **have**.

haddock [*hadok*] *n* common edible sea-fish.

hade [*hayd*] *n* (*geol*) angle between a fault plane and the vertical.

Hades [*haydeez*] *n* (*class myth*) abode of the dead.

hadji, haji, hajji [*haj*-ee] *n* title of Mohammedan who has made pilgrimage to Mecca.

hadn't [*hadnt*] *abbr* had not.

hadron [*had*Ron] *n* (*phys*) strongly interacting elementary particle ~ **hadronic** [had*Ron*ik] *adj*.

hae [*hay*] *v/t* (*Scots*) have.

haema- *pref* relating to blood.

haemal [*heem*al] *adj* (*med*) pertaining to blood or blood-vessels.

haematic [hee*matik*] *adj* (*med*) pertaining to, containing, acting upon, blood.

haematin, hematin [*heem*atin, *hem*atin] *n* (*chem*) pigment found in haemoglobin.

haematite, hematite [*heem*atIt, *hem*atIt] *n* (*min*) natural ferric oxide.

haemato- *pref* pertaining to blood.

haemo- *pref* pertaining to blood.

haemoglobin [heem*Ogl*Obin] *n* respiratory pigment of red blood-corpuscles > PDB.

haemophilia [heem*Ofi*li-a] *n* (*med*) hereditary human disease in which blood-clotting is defective > PDB ~ **haemophiliac** *adj* and *n*.

haemorrhage, hemorrhage [*heme*Rij] *n* (*med*) rupture of a blood-vessel and spread of blood over the surrounding tissues.

haemorrhoids, hemorrhoids [*heme*Roidz] *n* (*pl*) veins liable to discharge blood, *esp* piles.

haemostatic [heemo*statik*] *n* and *adj* (substance) that stops bleeding.

hafnium [*haf*ni-um] *n* (*chem*) a rare metal used in manufacture of tungsten filaments > PDS.

haft [*haaft*] *n* handle, hilt ~ **haft** *v/t* fit haft to.

hag (1) [*hag*] *n* ugly, malicious old woman; witch.

hag (2) (*pres/part* **hagging**, *p/t* and *p/part* **hagged**) *v/t* fell (timber); hack, cut ~ **hag** *n* act of felling; felled trees; cutting in peat-bog; marshy spot; firm area in marshy ground.

hagfish [*hag*fish] *n* a parasitic fish.

Haggadah, Haggada [ha*gaa*da] *n* legendary or anecdotic part of the Talmud.

haggard (1) [*hag*ard] *adj* looking exhausted, hollow-eyed; gaunt ~ **haggardly** *adv*.

haggard (2) *n* wild hawk, *esp* female.

haggis [*hag*is] *n* Scottish dish of sheep's inner organs mixed with oatmeal, seasoned and boiled in the sheep's stomach-bag.

haggish [*hag*ish] *adj* like a hag ~ **haggishly** *adv* ~ **haggishness** *n*.

haggle [*hag*'l] *v/i* wrangle over price when bargaining ~ **haggler** *n* person who haggles.

hagiarchy [*hag*i-aarki] *n* government by saintly men or priests; hierarchy of saints.

hagio- *pref* holy; pertaining to saints.

hagiocracy [hagi-*ok*Rasi] *n* hagiarchy.

hagiographer [hagi-*og*Rafer] *n* one who writes the biography of saints.

hagiographic [hagi-*og*Rafik] *adj* of saints' lives.

hagiography [hagi-*og*Rafi] *n* biography of a saint; collection of such biographies and legends.

hagiolatry [hagi-*ol*atRi] *n* excessive veneration of saints.

hagiologic, hagiological [hagi-olo*j*ik, hagi-olo*j*ikal] *adj* of or as hagiology.

hagiology [hagi-olo*j*i] *n* literature dealing with the lives of saints; book of saints' lives.

hagioscope [hagi-osk*Op*] *n* (*archi*) narrow opening or oblique squint in the wall of a medieval church through which the altar was visible.

hagridden [*hag*Riden] *adj* afflicted by a nightmare; obsessed.

hah [ha] *interj* exclamation of surprise *etc*.

ha-ha [*ha*-ha] *n* ditch not seen except from close by; sunken fence.

haik [hayk] *n* Arab's large outer cloak.

haiku [*hi*koo] *n* Japanese poem of seventeen syllables in three lines; English imitation of this.

hail (1) [hayl] *n* (*collect*) pellets of ice falling from clouds > PDG; storm of this; anything which falls rapidly, violently and copiously ~ **hail** *v/i* and *t* fall as hail; fall or hurl rapidly, violently or copiously.

hail (2) *interj* (*ar*) respectful exclamation of greeting ~ **hail** *v/t* and *i* greet; (*naut*) call out to, signal to (a ship); (*fig*) accost, call out to; **h. from** (*naut* and *coll*) come from, *esp* as one's home ~ **hail** *n* act of calling out; shout to attract attention; greeting; distance over which a shout can be heard; **within h.** near enough to be shouted to; **h. fellow well met** on very familiar terms.

Hail Mary [hayl-*mair*Ri] *n* name of a prayer to the Virgin Mary.

hailstone [*hayl*stOn] *n* pellet of ice falling from clouds.

hailstorm [*hayl*stawrm] *n* storm of hail.

hair [*hair*] *n* filament growing from animal's skin > PDB; (*collect*) mass of hairs on human head; (*collect*) mass of hairs on animal's body, fur; (*bot*) fine filament or fibre; **hair's breadth** very small distance; **keep one's h. on** (*sl*) keep calm; **let one's h. down** unpin piled-up hair; (*sl*) abandon all restraint, behave without inhibitions; **make one's h. stand on end** horrify; **not turn a h.** show no fear or weariness; **put one's h. up** wear long hair piled up or braided up on crown of head; **split hairs** make too subtle distinctions; **tear one's h.** show great grief or vexation; **to a h.** exactly ~ **hair** *adj* of or for hair.

hairball [*hair*bawl] *n* mass of hair in animal's stomach.

hairbell see **harebell**.

hairbreadth [*hair*bRedth] *n* very small space ~ **hairbreadth** *adj* very narrow.

hairbrush [*hair*bRush] *n* brush for brushing human hair.

haircloth [*hair*kloth] *n* rough cloth woven of horsehair and wool.

hair-crack [hair-kRak] *n* very fine crack.

haircut [*hair*kut] *n* act or process of having one's hair trimmed; style in which this is done.

hair-do [*hair*-dOO] *n* (*coll*) style in which woman's hair is cut or set.

hairdresser [*hair*dReser] *n* one who cuts, sets or tints hair ~ **hairdressing** *n*.

hair-grass [*hair*-gRaas] *n* kind of thin grass.

hairgrip [*hair*gRip] *n* flat tight hairpin.

hairiness [*hair*Rinis] *n* quality of being hairy.

hair-lead [*hair*-led] *n* (*typ*) a very thin lead for spacing out printed matter.

hairline [*hair*lIn] *n* very thin line; thin upstroke in handwriting; rope or fishing line of hair; limit of growth of hair, *esp* round forehead.

hairnet [*hair*net] *n* fine net to keep hair tidy.

hair-pencil [*hair*-pensil] *n* painter's brush of fine camel hair.

hairpiece [*hair*pees] *n* tress of false hair.

hairpin [*hair*pin] *n* two-pronged pin used to keep hair tidy; **h. bend** very sharp U-shaped bend in road.

hair-raising [*hair*-Rayzing] *adj* terrifying; amazing; full of suspense.

hairshirt [*hair*shurt] *n* shirt made of haircloth.

hairslide [*hair*slId] *n* small metal clip, or hinged ornamental clip, for keeping women's hair tidy.

hair-splitting [*hair*-splIting] *n* act of making minute distinctions in argument.

hairspring [*hair*spRing] *n* fine spring which regulates the balance-wheel of a watch.

hairstreak [*hair*stReek] *n* kind of small butterfly.

hairstroke [*hair*stROk] *n* hairline in writing; serif.

hairstyle [*hair*stIl] *n* style in which one's hair is cut or set.

hair-tidy [*hair*-tIdi] *n* small receptacle for hairs combed out.

hair-trigger [*hair*-tRiger] *n* trigger which fires on the slightest pressure.

hairy [*hair*Ri] *adj* covered with hair; of or like hair ~ **hairily** *adv* ~ **hairiness** *n*.

haji, hajji see **hadji**.

hake [hayk] *n* sea fish related to cod.

hakim (1) [*haak*im] *n* Moslem ruler.

hakim (2) [ha*keem*] *n* Moslem doctor.

halation [ha*lay*shon] *n* (*phot*) fogging of a photograph caused by tendency of light to spread and form haloes.

halberd, halbert [*hal*berd, *hal*bert] *n* (*hist*) long-handled battle-axe surmounted by a spike.

halberdier [halber*deer*] *n* soldier armed with halberd.

halcyon [*hal*si-on] *n* kingfisher ~ **halcyon** *adj* calm, peaceful; **h. days** period of calm weather at winter solstice; (*fig*) times of peace and happiness.

hale (1) [hayl] *adj* healthy, robust, vigorous; **h. and hearty** very healthy.

hale (2) *v/t* drag, haul.

half (*pl* **halves**) [*haaf*] *n* one of two exactly
equal parts into which a thing is or can be
divided; one of two shares or portions of roughly
equal amount; (*leg*) one of two parties in transaction; school term; (*coll*) half pint of beer
etc; (*sport*) half-back; **better h.** (*joc*) wife;
by halves incompletely, partly; **go halves**
share equally; **too (clever** *etc*) **by h.** far too
(clever *etc*) ~ **half** *adj* consisting of, equal to a
half; partial, imperfect ~ **half** *adv* to the extent
of a half; partly; imperfectly; nearly; considerably; **not h.!** (*sl*) very much so; **not h. bad**
(*sl*) fairly good; very good.

half-and-half [*haaf*-and-*haaf*] *n* something that
is half one thing and half another; drink consisting of equal parts of two liquors ~ **half-and-
half** *adj* and *adv*.

half-back [*haaf*-bak] *n* player in football or
hockey whose position is between the forwards
and the backs.

halfbaked [*haaf*baykt] *adj* only partly cooked;
(*fig*) not properly thought out; lacking in intelligence.

half-blood [*haaf*-blud] *n* relationship between
two people sharing only one parent; person so
related; halfbreed.

half-bound [*haaf*-bownd] *adj* (*bookbinding*)
bound in leather on back and corners only.

half-bred [*haaf*-bRed] *adj* of or like a halfbreed;
only half educated; showing poor manners.

halfbreed [*haaf*bReed] *n* and *adj* (one) whose
parents are of different races.

half-brother [*haaf*-bRUTHer] *n* brother related
through one parent only.

halfcaste [*haaf*kaast] *n* and *adj* halfbreed.

halfcock [*haaf*kok] *n* position of hammer of a
gun when pulled back halfway; **go off at h.**
explode prematurely; (*fig*) act prematurely, fail.

half-crown [haaf-*kRown*] *n* (*hist*) British silver
coin worth two shillings and sixpence; sum of
money equal to this.

half-deck [*haaf*-dek] *n* deck extending half the
length of a ship.

half-dollar [haaf-*doler*] *n* (*US and Canada*) coin
worth 50 cents; (*coll*) half-crown.

half-hardy [*haaf*-haardi] *adj* (*hort*) able to grow in
the open except in winter.

half-hearted [haaf-*haartid*] *adj* lacking enthusiasm; divided in feelings ~ **half-heartedly**
adv ~ **half-heartedness** *n*.

half-hitch [*haaf*-hich] *n* kind of hitch-knot.

half-holiday [haaf-*holidi*] *n* holiday lasting half a
day, *usu* the afternoon.

half-hour [haaf-*owr*] *n* period of thirty minutes, the
half of one hour ~ **half-hourly** *adj* and *adv* at
intervals of half an hour.

half-landing [haaf-*landing*] *n* (*bui*) area halfway
up a staircase the full width of both flights and
with a depth equal to the width of one flight.

half-length [*haaf*-length] *n* and *adj* (portrait)
showing only upper part of sitter.

half-life [*haaf*-lIf] *n* state of severely reduced
activity *etc*; (*phys*) time needed for radioactivity
of a substance to decrease by half.

half-mast [haaf-*maast*] *n* position of flag lowered
halfway down the staff in sign of mourning.

half-moon [haaf-*mOOn*] *n* moon when half its
disk is illuminated; shape of this.

half-mourning [haaf-*mawrn*ing] *n* mourning
dress of black with white, grey or violet.

half-nelson [haaf-*nelson*] *n* wrestling hold in
which one arm is passed under the opponent's
from behind and the hand pressed against his
neck.

half-note [*haaf*-nOt] *n* (*US*) minim.

half-pace [*haaf*-pays] *n* (*bui*) staircase landing;
raised floor in window bay.

half-pay [haaf-*pay*] *n* (*mil, naut*) reduced pay
given to a retired officer ~ **half-pay** *adj*.

halfpence [*hay*pens] *pl* of halfpenny.

halfpenny (*pl* **halfpence** or **halfpennies**) [*hayp*-
ni] *n* British coin worth half a penny.

half-seas-over [haaf-seez-*Over*] *adj* (*sl*) rather
drunk.

half-sister [*haaf*-sister] *n* sister related through
one parent only.

half-timbered [haaf-*timberd*] *adj* (*bui*) having
walls of timber-framing with brick or plaster
infilling.

half-time [haaf-*tIm*] *n* work and pay for half the
day only; interval between two halves of a
game.

half-title [*haaf*-tIt'l] *n* (*typ*) short title of a book
usually printed on the leaf preceding the title-
page.

halftone [*haaf*tOn] *n* (*mus*) semitone; (*phot*)
process block made by photographing the picture
to be reproduced through a glass screen covered
with a network of fine cross lines ~ **halftone**
adj.

half-truth [*haaf*-tROOth] *n* incomplete or misleading statement of the facts.

half-volley [haaf-*voli*] *n* (*games*) act of striking or
kicking the ball immediately after it bounces.

halfway [*haaf*way] *adj* and *adv* at half the
distance; midway between two points.

halfwit [*haaf*wit] *n* idiot; very foolish person ~
halfwitted *adj*.

halibut [*halibut*] *n* large edible flatfish.

halide [*halId*] *n* (*chem*) binary compound in which
one element is a halogen.

halidom [*halidom*] *n* (*ar*) holy place, chapel; a
holy relic or object.

halieutic [hali-*ewtik*] *adj* of fishing ~ **halieutics**
n (*pl*) art of fishing.

halitosis [halit*Osis*] *n* (*med*) bad breath.

hall [*hawl*] *n* large dining room; large public room;
large municipal building; large private house;
room, passage or lobby into which the main
entrance of a building opens; residential university building, college; (*hist*) large main room of
king's or chieftain's dwelling; (*theat*) **the halls**
vaudeville theatres.

hallelujah, halleluiah, alleluia [hali*lOO*ya,
alil*OO*ya] *interj* (*Heb*) praise the Lord!

halliard see halyard.

hallmark [*hawl*maark] *n* official stamp of the
Goldsmiths' Company, used to mark attested
gold and silver articles; (*fig*) mark of genuineness
or high quality ~ **hallmark** *v/t* stamp with a
hallmark.

hallo, halloa, hello [hal*O*, hel*O*] *interj* word of
informal greeting; exclamation of surprise; call
to attract attention ~ **hallo** *v/i* say or call hallo.

halloo [hal*OO*] *interj* and *n* cry to incite hunting

dogs, or to attract attention ~ **halloo** *v/i* shout halloo.

hallow [*halO*] *v/t* make holy, consecrate; honour as holy ~ **hallow** *n* (*ar*) saint.

Hallowe'en [halO-*een*] *n* 31 October, eve of All Saints' Day.

hall-porter [hawl-*porter*] *n* porter on duty in the entrance hall of a hotel, block of flats *etc*.

Hallstatt [*halstat*] *adj* (*arch*) belonging to the early Iron Age in Europe.

hallucinate [hale*ws*inayt] *v/t* cause hallucinations in.

hallucination [halewsin*ays*hon] *n* experience resembling sense-perception of object, but without such object being really present > PDP; the imaginary object thus perceived; delusion.

hallucinatory [halews*in*ayteRi] *adj* of or like a hallucination; producing hallucinations.

hallucinogen [hal*ew*sinOjen] *n* (*med*) substance causing hallucinations ~ **hallucinogenic** *adj*.

hallucinosis [halewsinOsis] *n* (*psych*) disordered mental condition subject to the occurrence of hallucinations.

hallux (*pl* **halluces**) [*hal*uks, hal*ew*seez] *n* innermost digit of animal's hind-foot > PDB.

hallway [*hawl*way] *n* entrance hall.

halm see **haulm**.

halma [*hal*ma] *n* board game for two or four players.

halo (*pl* **haloes**) [*hay*lo] *n* ring of refracted light round bright object > PDG; gold or silver disk, ring or rays behind or above head of Christ or saints in paintings; (*fig*) sanctity; (*fig*) glamour, romantic glory ~ **halo** *v/t* and *i* form a halo (for) ~ **haloed** *adj* invested with a halo.

halogen [*hal*ojin] *n* (*chem*) one of the non-metallic elements, fluorine, chlorine, bromine and iodine.

halogenate [hal*oj*inayt] *v/t* (*chem*) introduce a halogen into (a compound) ~ **halogenation** *n*.

haloid [*hal*oid] *n* and *adj* (*chem*) (substance) resembling a salt.

halt (1) [*hawlt*] *v/t* and *i* stop; (*mil*) cause to cease marching; cease moving, *esp* cease walking or working; (*mil*) cease marching ~ **halt** *n* act of halting; place where one halts, stopping-place; small railway-station; bus-stop; stoppage.

halt (2) *v/i* (*ar*) be lame, limp; (*fig*) speak hesitatingly; be faulty in metre; be logically faulty ~ **halt** *adj* (*ar*) lame.

halter [*hawl*ter] *n* rope by which a horse is led or tied up; rope with noose for hanging criminals; woman's backless and sleeveless blouse, dresstop or brassiere held up by a strap round the neck ~ **halter** *v/t*.

halting [*hawl*ting] *adj* stumbling; hesitant, uncertain ~ **haltingly** *adv*.

halve [*haav*] *v/t* divide into halves; share equally between two; (*golf*) **h. hole** (**match**) take same number of strokes as opponent.

halves [*haavz*] *pl* of **half**.

halyard, halliard [*hal*yaard] *n* (*naut*) rope used to raise or lower sail, flag *etc*.

ham [*ham*] *n* seasoned and smoked thigh of pig; portion of this; thigh of any animal; back of human thigh; (*coll*) actor who overacts absurdly; amateur actor; (*coll*) amateur radio operator ~

ham (*pres/part* **hamming**, *p/t* and *p/part* **hammed**) *v/t* and *i* (*coll*) overact.

hamadryad [hama*dRI*-ad] *n* (*myth*) wood-nymph; (*zool*) venomous Indian cobra; large baboon of Abyssinia.

Hamburg [*ham*burg] *n* variety of black grape; breed of domestic fowl; hamburger.

hamburger [*ham*burger] *n* bread roll stuffed with minced steak fried and seasoned.

hames [*haymz*] *n* (*pl*) two curved pieces on collar of cart-horse through which the reins pass.

hamfisted [ham*fis*tid] *adj* clumsy with one's hands.

hamhanded [ham*han*did] *adj* hamfisted.

hamite (1) [*haym*It] *n* fossil cephalopod with shell shaped like a hook.

Hamite (2) [*ham*It] *n* member of race including Somalis, Egyptians *etc*.

Hamitic [ha*mit*ik] *adj* relating to the Hamites and the Hamitic family of African languages ~ **Hamitic** *n* one of the Hamitic languages.

hamlet [*ham*lit] *n* small village.

hammer [*ham*er] *n* tool for striking, driving in nails *etc*, with steel head held by wooden handle at right angles to it, fitted into central eye; felted mallet striking strings of piano; auctioneer's mallet; device to strike bell of clock; (*mech*) heavy beating or crushing device; (*firearms*) striker on gunlock; (*fig*) one who crushes resistance, oppressor; **come under the h.** be auctioned; **go at it h. and tongs** set to work vigorously and noisily; quarrel violently; **H. and Sickle** emblem of Soviet Russia or of Communism ~ **hammer** *v/t* and *i* strike with a hammer; strike violently; knock loudly; (*coll*) attack; defeat overwhelmingly; (*Stock Exchange sl*) declare (a member) a defaulter; **h. away at** work energetically and persistently at; **h. in, h. into** drive in by hammering; (*fig*) teach by frequent repetition; **h. out** work out (plan, problem *etc*) by assiduous thought and discussion.

hammer-cloth [*ham*er-kloth] *n* cloth covering driver's seat on horse-drawn coach or carriage.

hammerhead [*ham*erhed] *n* head of a hammer; kind of shark; kind of shellfish; kind of African bird ~ **hammerheaded** *adj*.

hammer-lock [*ham*er-lok] *n* wrestling hold in which opponent's arm is bent back and held behind him.

hammertoe [*ham*ertO] *n* (*med*) deformation of toe with joint permanently bent upwards.

hammock [*ham*ok] *n* bed formed by suspending the ends of a net or piece of cloth by cords; **h. chair** folding chair formed by strip of canvas hanging from wooden frame.

hammy [*ham*i] *adj* having the smell or flavour of ham; (*theat coll*) overacting, exaggerated.

hamose [haymOs] *adj* (*bot*) with hooks, hooked.

hamper (1) [*ham*per] *n* large lidded basket.

hamper (2) *v/t* obstruct, impede, fetter ~ **hamper** *n* (*naut*) cumbrous but necessary gear ~ **hamperer** *n*.

hamster [*ham*ster] *n* large rat with cheek-pouches.

hamstring [*ham*stRing] *n* tendon behind human knee; tendon behind horse's hock ~ **hamstring** *v/t* lame by cutting hamstring of; (*fig*) destroy the power of, prevent from acting.

hand [*hand*] *n* extremity of arm beyond wrist; skill in using one's hands, dexterity, touch; active share; member of ship's crew; workman; performer; handwriting; position or direction to left or right; indicator on dial; unit of measurement, about 4 inches; (*fig*) power; protection; (*cards*) number of cards dealt to one player in one game; one round in game of cards; player at cards; (*fig*) consent to marriage; **at h.** nearby, available; **at first h.** without intermediary; **at second h.** not from original source, but through others; **by h.** without use of machinery; without use of postal services; **bring up (baby *etc*) by h.** rear (baby) by bottle-feeding; **change hands** pass to another owner; **come to h.** be received; **from h. to h.** directly from one person to another; **from h. to mouth** precariously, without foresight; **get one's h. in** acquire skill by practice; **h. in h.** each holding the other's hand; in alliance, united; **h. in glove** closely united; acting as accomplices; **hands off!** leave it alone!; go away!; **h. over h.** (*climbing or swimming*) by using each hand alternately; **h. to h.** at close quarters; **hands up!** surrender!; **have a free h.** be free to act as one chooses; **have a h. in** take part in; **in h.** under control; in reserve; in course of completion; **in the hands of** in the possession of; under the care of; in the power of; **in good hands** well cared for; **keep one's h. in** practise a skill; **lay hands on** seize by force; strike, attack; **laying on of hands** (*eccles*) confirmation; ordination; **lend a h.** help; **off h.** spontaneously, without preparation; casual, flippant; **off one's hands** no longer one's responsibility; **an old h.** an expert; **on h.** available; **on all hands** everywhere; **on the other h.** from another point of view; **out of h.** out of control; at once, unhesitatingly; **play into the hands of** give (opponent) an advantage; **play one's own h.** look after one's interests; **shake hands** greet by clasping and shaking another's hand; strike a bargain; part; **take a h.** play a part; **take in h.** undertake to control, educate *etc*; take charge of; **upper h.** advantage; **wash one's hands of** disclaim responsibility for; **win hands down** win easily ~ **hand** *v/t* give or pass into another's hands; transmit, convey, offer by hand; **h. down** transmit by inheritance or tradition; deliver by hand; send in; **h. on** send or transmit to another; **h. out** distribute; **h. over** give into another's keeping, transfer; **h. round** distribute; **h. it to** (*sl*) give due credit to ~ **hand** *adj* worked by hand, without mechanical means; held in the hands or in one hand.

handbag [*hand*bag] *n* woman's light bag for small personal items.

handbarrow [*hand*baRO] *n* light wheelbarrow; portable framework with handles at each end.

handbell [*hand*bel] *n* bell rung by hand; (*pl*) set of musical bells.

handbill [*hand*bil] *n* small printed notice.

handbook [*hand*book] *n* short treatise; guidebook.

handbrace [*hand*bRays] *n* drilling tool with bit.

handbrake [*hand*bRayk] *n* auxiliary hand-operated brake in a motor vehicle.

handcart [*hand*kaart] *n* small cart pushed or pulled by hand.

handclap [*hand*klap] *n* sound made by clapping hands, *esp* as applause; **slow h.** slow clapping in unison to convey boredom or disapproval.

handclasp [*hand*klaasp] *n* act of greeting or bidding farewell by gripping another's hand.

handcraft see **handicraft**.

handcuff [*hand*kuf] *n* one of a pair of metal rings joined by a short chain, used to fetter a prisoner's wrists ~ **handcuff** *v/t* put handcuffs on.

handed [*hand*id] *adj* having hands; **three h.** (*etc*) played by stated number of players.

handedness [*hand*idnis] *n* preference for using one hand rather than the other.

handfasting [*hand*faasting] *n* (*ar*) betrothal; obsolete form of private marriage.

handful [*hand*fool] *n* as much as a hand may hold; (*fig*) small amount; (*coll*) person, animal, or thing difficult to manage.

handglass [*hand*glaas] *n* small mirror or magnifying glass with handle; (*hort*) small glazed frame.

hand-grenade [*hand*-gRinayd] *n* (*mil*) small bomb thrown by hand.

handgrip [*hand*gRip] *n* grip of a hand, hearty handshake; characteristic method of shaking hands used by members of secret societies.

handhold [*hand*hOld] *n* place to which a hand can cling in climbing.

handicap [*hand*ikap] *n* that which hampers, disadvantage; disability, crippling defect; (*sport*) disadvantage imposed on superior contestants; race or competition in which handicaps are imposed ~ **handicap** (*pres/part* **handicapping**, *p/t* and *p/part* **handicapped**) *v/t* be a handicap to; impose handicaps on; place at disadvantage.

handicraft, handcraft [*hand*ikRaaft, *hand*kRaaft] *n* work requiring individual skill both manual and artistic ~ **handicraftsman, handcraftsman** *n*.

handily [*hand*ili] *adv* in a handy way; conveniently close, at hand ~ **handiness** *n*.

handiwork [*hand*iwurk] *n* work done without mechanical aid; thing made by hand; (*fig*) result of someone's plan or work.

handkerchief [*hang*kerchif] *n* small square of material for wiping the nose.

handle [*hand*'l] *n* part of an object designed to be held in the hand in using or carrying it; **fly off the h.** (*coll*) lose self-control in anger; **give a h. to** provide with an excuse for an attack; provide pretext for; give opportunity of advantage to one's enemy; **have a h. to one's name** have title ~ **handle** *v/t* touch or feel with the hands; move by hand; control; treat, behave towards; treat of, discuss; (*comm*) deal in.

handlebar, handlebars [*hand*'lbaar, *hand*'lbaarz] *n* crossbar controlling steering apparatus of bicycle; **h. moustache** (*coll*) thick moustache extending widely across the face.

handling [*hand*ling] *n* way in which a thing is handled, management, treatment.

handmade [*hand*mayd] *adj* made by hand, not by machinery.

handmaid [*hand*mayd] *n* (*ar*) servant-girl; (*fig*) subordinate, humble helper or servant.

hand-me-down [*hand*-mi-down] *adj* (*US coll*) ready-made; cheap; second-hand.

handmill [*hand*mil] *n* small appliance for grinding coffee *etc* by hand.

handout [*hand*owt] *n* something handed out, *esp* statement prepared for journalists; (*US*) food or clothing given to beggar.

handover [*hand*Over] *n* act of transferring ownership or control of something to another.

hand-picked [*hand*-pikt] *adj* carefully selected.

handrail [*hand*Rayl] *n* rail forming top of a balustrade on a balcony, bridge or stair.

handscrew [*hand*skROO] *n* (*carp*) a screw clamp.

handsel [*hand*sel] *n* (*ar*) gift for luck; New Year gift; part payment to confirm a bargain ~ **handsel** (*pres/part* **handselling**, *p/t* and *p/part* **handselled**) *v/t* (*ar*) pay or give handsel; (*fig*) inaugurate, use for first time.

handset [*hand*set] *n* liftable part of telephone comprising both receiver and mouthpiece.

handshake [*hand*shayk] *n* act of greeting or bidding farewell by grasping and shaking another's right hand; **golden h.** money given to business men *etc* on retirement from a post.

handsome [*hand*sum/*han*sum] *adj* good-looking, having beauty and dignity; having virile beauty; generous; ample; **h. is as h.** [= *handsomely*] does generosity and noble actions are more important than good looks or promises; **come down h.** (*coll*) be generous ~ **handsomely** *adv* ~ **handsomeness** *n*.

handspike [*hand*spIk] *n* iron-tipped wooden lever.

handspring [*hand*spRing] *n* rapid somersault during which the body is supported by the hands.

handstand [*hand*stand] *n* feat of balancing on one's hands, with the body and legs vertically raised.

handwork [*hand*wurk] *n* work done by hand.

handwriting [*hand*RIting] *n* writing by hand; style of writing peculiar to each person.

handy [*hand*i] *adj* within easy reach, accessible; convenient, easily handled; skilful in manual work, dexterous ~ **handy** *adv* close by.

handyman [*hand*iman] *n* man useful for doing odd jobs; skilful workman.

hang (*p/t* and *p/part usu* **hung**; when meaning killed, *p/t* and *p/part* **hanged** or (*coll*) **hung**) [*hang*] *v/t* and *i* suspend from above, attach to higher object; be suspended, dangle; kill or execute by suspending by the neck from a noose; be killed or executed by this method; suspend (paintings *etc*) from hook in wall or picture-rail; exhibit (paintings); fix (wallpaper) to wall; fix (door) on hinges; leave (meat) suspended till fit to eat; drape; be draped, fall in folds; (*coll euph*) damn; **h. about**, **h. around** linger, loiter; lurk in, prowl; **h. back** hesitate, refuse to act or advance; **h. by a thread** be very precariously placed; **h. fire** (*of firearm*) delay in firing; (*fig*) develop slowly, be delayed; **let go h.** not care about; **h. on** cling to, depend on; cling, support oneself by clinging, persevere; (*coll*) wait; **h. oneself** commit suicide by hanging; **h. one's head** show signs of shame; bend the head forwards; **h. out** (*sl*) live, lodge; hang (wet linen *etc*) outside to dry; **h. together** act in unison, be allies, back each other; fit well together; be consistent, be logically connected; **h. up** place on hook, peg *etc*; replace telephone receiver; be hung up be delayed; **h. upon** lean on; listen eagerly to ~ **hang** *n* way a thing hangs or is hung; way a machine *etc* works; significance,

meaning; (*coll euph*) damn; **get the h. of** (*coll*) understand.

hangar *n* [*hang*ar] covered shed, *esp* for aircraft.

hangdog [*hang*dog] *adj* looking guilty; sullen.

hanger [*hang*er] *n* one who or that which hangs; coathanger; support from which something can hang; loop of swordbelt; short broadsword; dagger; S-shaped hook; ∿-shaped stroke in handwriting; wood growing on steep slope.

hanger-on [*hang*er-on] *n* one who constantly associates with another in hope of receiving favours; unwanted follower; miner who hooks tubs on and off an endless-rope haulage.

hanging [*hang*ing] *n* act of one who or that which hangs; execution by hanging; that which is hung; drapery on walls; bed-curtain ~ **hanging** *adj* that hangs; suspended; liable to incur death-penalty; **h. buttress** (*archi*) decorative buttress giving little support; **h. gardens** gardens rising in terraces; **h. judge** (*coll*) judge who frequently imposes the death-penalty.

hang-glider [*hang*-glIder] *n* large stringless kite supporting a framework that can bear a man's weight; person who practises hang-gliding.

hang-gliding [*hang*-glIding] *n* sport of floating on rising air-currents while hanging from a large kite.

hangman [*hang*man] *n* public executioner.

hangnail [*hang*nayl] *n* loose skin near root of fingernail.

hangover [*hang*Over] *n* (*coll*) unpleasant after-effects of getting drunk; (*fig*) unpleasant survival of outdated views, rules *etc*.

hang-out [*hang*-owt] *n* (*sl*) place where one lives.

hang-up [*hang*-up] *n* (*coll*) obsessional problem, *esp* of fear or guilt; delay.

hank [*hangk*] *n* coil of yarn, worsted *etc*, *usu* of specific length.

hanker [*hang*ker] *v/i* **h. after**, **h. for** long for, yearn for ~ **hankering** *n*.

hanky [*hang*ki] *n* (*coll abbr*) handkerchief.

hanky-panky [*hang*ki-*pang*ki] *n* (*coll*) trickery.

Hansard [*han*saard] *n* official printed report of Parliamentary proceedings.

Hanse [*hans*] *n* (*hist*) medieval guild; fee or toll levied by a guild; **the H.** (*hist*) commercial association of various free towns ~ **Hanseatic** [hansi-*at*ik] *adj*.

hansom [*han*sum] *n* light two-wheeled cab formerly much used in London.

hap [*hap*] *n* (*ar*) chance, luck; happening ~ **hap** (*pres/part* **happing**, *p/t* and *p/part* **happed**) *v/i* (*ar*) happen.

ha'penny [*hay*pni] *n* halfpenny.

haphazard [hap*haz*ard] *n* and *adj* (something) which occurs by chance or at random ~ **haphazard** *adv* at random; accidentally, by chance.

hapless [*hap*lis] *adj* unlucky, wretched ~ **haplessly** *adv* ~ **haplessness** *n*.

haplo- *pref* single.

haplography [hap*log*Rafi] *n* scribal error of writing once what should appear twice (e.g. tinnabulation for tintinnabulation).

haploid [*hap*loid] *n* and *adj* (*biol*) (*cell*) having unpaired, single chromosomes > PDB.

haply [*hap*li] *adv* (*ar*) perhaps.

ha'p'orth [*hay*perth] *n* (*abbr*) a halfpennyworth.

happen [*hap*en] *v/i* occur, come to pass; occur

by chance; **h. along** (*coll*) arrive by chance, drop in; **h. on, h. upon** find by chance, come across; **h. to be (do)** be (do) by chance; **h. to (someone)** befall, affect occur to ~ **happen** *adv* (*northern dial* and *coll*) maybe, perhaps.

happening [*hap*ening] *n* that which happens; (*sl*) fantastic or weird event, *esp* one designed as entertainment and involving the audience in unplanned outbursts of feeling or violence; exciting and unpredictable event.

happenstance [*hap*enstans] *n* (*US*) chance event, unpredictable circumstance.

happy [*hap*i] *adj* feeling or expressing joy, glad; pleased, contented; causing joy, gladness or pleasure; lucky, fortunate; successful; apt, appropriate; (*coll*) tipsy ~ **happily** *adv* ~ **happiness** *n*.

happy-go-lucky [hapi-gO-*luk*i] *adj* carefree, thoughtless; easy-going.

hara-kiri [haRa-*kir*Ri] *n* Japanese method of ritual suicide by disembowelment.

harangue [ha*Rang*] *n* loud, angry, or ranting speech, *esp* to a crowd ~ **harangue** *v*/*t* and *i*.

harass [*ha*Ras] *v*/*t* harry, vex by repeated attacks; worry, pester ~ **harassingly** *adv*.

harassment [*ha*Rasment] *n* act of harassing; state of being harassed.

harbinger [*haar*binjer] *n* one who or that which announces the approach of something, forerunner ~ **harbinger** *v*/*t* herald.

harbour [*haar*ber] *n* area of coastal water affording shelter to sea-going ships > PDG, PDE; (*ar*) place of refuge, shelter ~ **harbour** *v*/*t* and *i* shelter, offer a refuge to; conceal, give secret lodgings to; secretly ponder over; take shelter; come into a harbour.

harbourage [*haar*beRij] *n* shelter, refuge.

harbour-bar [*haar*ber-baar] *n* shoal at mouth of harbour.

harbour-master [*haar*ber-maaster] *n* one who has official charge of a harbour.

hard [*haard*] *adj* firm, not easily pierced or compressed; difficult to do; difficult to understand; vigorous, violent; strenuous, energetic; merciless, severe, exacting; bitter, angry; unfair; causing distress, poverty, pain *etc*; toughened by work or exercise; (*of weather*) cold, stormy; (*of sounds*) metallic; (*of lines, colours etc*) too vivid, too clearcut; (*pop phon*) voiceless, plosive; (*of water*) lathering slowly owing to the presence of dissolved calcium > PDS; (*of radiation*) having a short wavelength, penetrating; **h. and fast** strict, inflexible; **be h. on** treat severely; **h. cash** ready money; **h. core** (*bui*) broken brick or rubble; **h. court** tennis court with hard, not grassy, surface; **h. currency** dollars; currency convertible into dollars; **h. drinking** frequent and heavy drinking of alcohol; **h. food** corn fodder; **h. labour** punitive labour imposed on criminals; **h. lines** cruel fate or treatment; **h. luck** very bad luck; **h. of hearing** rather deaf; **h. up** short of money ~ **hard** *adv* in a hard way; to a degree which produces hardness; energetically; violently; severely; excessively; with difficulty; closely; **h. by** close, nearby; **die h.** die out very slowly; **h. hit** badly damaged, deeply affected; **it will go h.** it will cause serious trouble ~ **hard** *n* firm ground of landing-place; causeway; raised path

across marshy land; (*coll*) hard labour; (*sl*) sexual erection.

hardback [*haard*bak] *n* and *adj* (*book*) bound in stiff covers, not paperbacked.

hardbake [*haard*bayk] *n* almond toffee.

hardbaked [*haard*baykt] *adj* baked until hard; (*coll*) callous.

hardbitten [haard*bit*en] *adj* tough in fight; stubborn.

hardboard [*haard*bawrd] *n* (*bui*) fibreboard formed under pressure to a density of 30–50 lb per cubic foot.

hardboiled [*haard*boild] *adj* (*of egg*) boiled until whole interior is solid; (*sl*) shrewd, hard-headed; callous, exacting; not easily shocked.

hard-bound [*haard*-bownd] *adj* (*of books*) bound in stiff covers, not paperbacked.

hardcore [*haard*kawr] *adj* stubbornly resisting change or reform, unrepentant, unwavering; extremely brutal, obscene or vicious.

hard-cover [*haard*-cuver] *adj* hard-bound.

hard-earned [*haard*-urnd] *adj* earned by great toil, *esp* for low pay.

hard-edge [*haard*-ej] *adj* and *n* (of or in) a form of abstract painting using clear-cut flat coloured shapes.

harden (1) [*haar*den] *v*/*t* and *i* make hard, hardy or insensitive; make courageous; become hard; (*comm*) (*of prices*) cease to fluctuate, rise; **h. off** expose seedlings gradually to cold.

harden (2) *n* coarse fabric.

hardened [*haar*dend] *adj* made hard; inveterate, unrepentant.

hardener [*haar*dener] *n* that which hardens; coating, ingredient *etc* added to something to harden it ~ **hardening** *n* and *adj* (process of) making hard or hardy.

hard-favoured [haard-*fay*verd] *adj* plain-looking, with rugged features; having a harsh expression, stern.

hard-featured [haard-*fee*cherd] *adj* hard-favoured.

hard-fisted [haard-*fist*id] *adj* niggardly.

hard-handed [haard-*hand*id] *adj* having hard hands through labour; oppressive, severe.

hard-headed [haard-*hed*id] *adj* shrewd, businesslike; unsentimental.

hard-hearted [haard-*haart*id] *adj* cruel, unfeeling ~ **hard-heartedly** *adv*.

hardihood [*haard*ihood] *n* courage; daring.

hardily [*haard*ili] *adv* boldly, toughly.

hardiness [*haard*inis] *n* quality of being hardy.

hardline [*haard*lIn] *adj* having a tough and inflexible attitude or policy ~ **hardliner** *n*.

hardly [*haard*li] *adv* with difficulty, barely, scarcely; severely, cruelly.

hardness [*haard*nis] *n* quality of being hard.

hardpan [*haard*pan] *n* hardened or cemented layer of soil impervious to drainage > PDE.

hard-pressed [haard-*pRest*] *adj* struggling against great difficulties; short of time, money *etc*.

hards [*haard*z] *n* coarse flax.

hard-sell [*haard*-sel] *n* technique of selling goods by aggressive persistence.

hard-set [haard-*set*] *adj* firmly set, rigid; (*fig*) obstinate.

hardship [*haard*ship] *n* that which is hard to bear, suffering, privation.

hard-standing [haard-*stand*ing] *n* paved or concreted area where a car, boat or caravan is kept.

hard-tack [*haard*-tak] *n* ship's biscuit.

hardtop [*haard*top] *n* (*mot*) automobile with steel top and no sliding roof.

hardware [*haard*wair] *n* ironmongery; (*coll*) machinery; items of equipment; weapons.

hardwood [*haard*wood] *n* tough timber; timber of deciduous trees.

hardy [*haar*di] *adj* tough, resistant under hardships; robust; bold; (*hort*) resistant to frost, able to flourish unprotected in all weathers.

hare [*hair*] *n* wild rodent allied to rabbit; (*sl*) wild, impracticable scheme; (*coll*) person chased in game of paperchase; **h. and hounds** paperchase; **start a h.** raise irrelevant issue in argument ~ **hare** *v/i* (*coll*) run wildly; run fast.

harebell, hairbell [*hair*bel] *n* plant with blue, bell-shaped flowers; Scottish bluebell.

harebrained [*hair*bRaynd] *adj* rash, senseless.

harelip [*hair*lip] *n* congenital deformity causing split upper lip in human beings.

harem, hareem [*hair*Rem, ha*Reem*] *n* (*collect*) wives and concubines of a Muslim; their quarters.

hare's-foot [*hairz*-foot] *n* species of clover; a cosmetician's tool.

haricot [*ha*RikO] *n* French bean; kind of stew made of mutton and vegetables.

hark [*haark*] *v/t* and *i* listen to; hearken; **h. back** retrace one's steps; revert to previous topic.

harken see **hearken**.

harl, harle [*haarl*] *n* fibre of flax; barb of feather; (*Scots*) (*bui*) rough cast.

harlequin [*haar*likwin] *n* traditional comic character in pantomime ~ **harlequin** *adj* multi-coloured; gaily coloured; (*of spectacles*) having oval slanted lenses and coloured frames.

harlequinade [haarlikwin*ayd*] *n* pantomime scene in which harlequin appears.

harlot [*haar*lot] *n* whore, prostitute.

harlotry [*haar*lotRi] *n* prostitution; (*ar*) roguery.

harm [*haarm*] *n* injury, damage ~ **harm** *v/t* injure, hurt, damage.

harmattan [haar*ma*tan] *n* dry Sahara wind on the Guinea coast in winter > PDG.

harmful [*haarm*fool] *adj* causing harm ~ **harmfully** *adv* ~ **harmfulness** *n*.

harmless [*haarm*lis] *adj* causing no harm; incapable of harming, inoffensive ~ **harmlessly** *adv* ~ **harmlessness** *n*.

harmonic [haar*mon*ik] *adj* (*mus*) relating to harmony; relating to the harmonic series; (*math*) having reciprocals in arithmetical progression; **h. series** (*mus*) set of tones produced by a string or air-column vibrating as a unit or in aliquot parts > PDM ~ **harmonic** *n* one tone of the harmonic series; overtone whose frequency is a multiple of the fundamental; (*pl*) (*phys*) waves, superimposed on a fundamental wave, having a frequency which is a whole multiple of the fundamental frequency > PDS ~ **harmonically** *adv*.

harmonica [haar*mon*ika] *n* mouthorgan; musical instrument consisting of tuned glasses or of series of glass or metal plates > PDM.

harmonics [haar*mon*iks] *n* (*pl*) branch of acoustics relating to music; harmonic series.

harmonious [haar*mon*i-us] *adj* in harmony,

having no discords, melodious; (*fig*) agreeing well; agreeably proportioned ~ **harmoniously** *adv* ~ **harmoniousness** *n*.

harmonist [*haar*monist] *n* one skilled in musical harmony; one who collates parallel narratives, *esp* of the Gospels ~ **harmonistic** [haarmon*is*tik] *adj*.

harmonium [haar*mon*i-um] *n* reed organ supplied with wind by means of pedals > PDM.

harmonization [haarmon*i*zayshon] *n* act of harmonizing; state of being harmonized.

harmonize [*haar*moniz] *v/t* and *i* bring into harmony; reconcile; (*mus*) add harmony to (melody); sing or play in harmony; be in harmony (with).

harmony [*haar*moni] *n* pleasing relationship or proportion, concord; (*fig*) agreement, state of happy and peaceful relationship; (*mus*) simultaneous sounding of notes in a way that is musically significant > PDM; art of writing music with a pleasing sequence of chords; rules governing this; (*poet*) music; **h. of the Gospels** arrangement of Gospel texts to form one continuous self-consistent narrative.

harness [*haar*nis] *n* straps and trappings of a horse; straps to confine a baby in cot or pram, or to guide toddler in walking; parachute bodystraps; (*ar*) armour; equipment; **die in h.** continue to work until death ~ **harness** *v/t* put into harness; (*fig*) put to work; control and use.

harp [*haarp*] *n* plucked stringed instrument with open triangular frame > PDM ~ **harp** *v/i* play the harp; **h. on** talk persistently about.

harper [*haar*per] *n* one who plays the harp.

harpist [*haar*pist] *n* professional harper.

harpoon [haarp*OOn*] *n* barbed spear attached to a long rope, used for hunting whales ~ **harpoon** *v/t* spear with harpoon.

harpsichord [*haar*psikawrd] *n* keyboard instrument with strings plucked mechanically > PDM.

harpy [*haar*pi] *n* (*Gk myth*) fierce, filthy and greedy monster, half woman and half bird; (*fig*) cruel and grasping person; **h. eagle** large tropical American eagle.

harquebus, arquebus [(h)*aar*kwibus] *n* earliest type of hand-gun.

harquebusier, arquebusier [(h)aarkwibus*eer*] *n* soldier armed with a harquebus.

harridan [*ha*Ridan] *n* disreputable old hag.

harrier (1) [*ha*Ri-er] *n* one who or that which harries; kind of fierce low-flying hawk.

harrier (2) *n* kind of small hound; cross-country runner.

Harrovian [ha*Rov*i-an] *n* and *adj* (pupil or expupil) of Harrow School.

harrow [*ha*RO] *n* heavy spiked implement dragged across ploughed land to level or break up the soil; **under the h.** (*fig*) in anguish ~ **harrow** *v/t* drag a harrow over; (*fig*) cause anguish or distress to, hurt the feelings of.

harrowing (1) [*ha*RO-ing] *adj* distressing, painful to the feelings ~ **harrowingly** *adv*.

harrowing (2) *n* (*ar*) act of plundering, ravaging; **the H. of Hell** the release of souls from Limbo by Christ immediately after his Resurrection.

harry [*ha*Ri] *v/t* make armed raids on; plunder, ravage; (*fig*) harass, pester.

harsh [*haarsh*] *adj* hard and rough to the touch;

(of sounds) jarring; *(of colours)* glaring; severe, cruel ~ **harshly** *adv* ~ **harshness** *n*.

hart [*haart*] *n* adult male deer.

hartebeest [*haart*ibeest] *n* large South African antelope.

hartshorn [*haarts*-hawrn] *n* solution of ammonia in water; kind of plantain.

hartstongue [*haarts*tung] *n* a common fern.

harum-scarum [hairRum-*skair*Rum] *adj* and *n* rash, scatter-brained (person).

haruspex [haRuspeks] *n* (*Rom hist*) type of augur basing his divinations on study of animal entrails.

harvest [*haar*vist] *n* act of gathering in crops; gathered crops; season of gathering crops; *(fig)* results obtained by work; **h. festival** church service of thanksgiving for the harvest; **h. moon** full moon nearest to autumn equinox ~ **harvest** *v/t* and *i* reap and gather in (crops); store up (crops); *(fig)* obtain as result of work or deeds.

harvester [*haar*vister] *n* one who or that which gathers in crops; reaping-machine; harvest-mite; **h. ant** species of ant that stores seeds; **h. bug** chigoe.

harvest-home [haarvist-*hOm*] *n* completion of a harvest; feast to celebrate this.

harvest-mite [*haar*vist-mIt] *n* small insect infesting grass stalks.

harvest-mouse [*haar*vist-mows] *n* small field-mouse which nests in standing corn.

has [*haz*] *3rd pers sing pres ind* of **have**.

has-been [*haz*-been] *n* (*coll*) one whose fame, powers *etc* are fading away.

hash [*hash*] *n* dish of cooked meat, chopped fine and re-heated; (*coll*) mess, muddle; (*coll*) trite material presented in new form; (*sl*) hashish; **settle one's h.** (*coll*) ruin, spoil the plans of ~ **hash** *v/t* make into a hash, chop up; *(fig)* make a mess of, mismanage.

hashish [*hash*ish] *n* dried leaves or resin of Indian hemp, smoked or chewed as an intoxicant and narcotic.

haslets [*hayz*lits] *n* (*pl*) heart, liver, lungs *etc* of an animal; pig's fry.

hasn't [*haz*nt] *abbr* has not.

hasp [*haasp*] *n* metal clasp; hinged flap used in fastening door, lid, *etc*; skein of thread; spindle for thread ~ **hasp** *v/t* fasten by a hasp.

hassle [*has*'l] *n* and *v/t* and *i* (*coll*) pester by constant demands or requirements; hustle.

hassock [*hasok*] *n* thick tuft of coarse grass; hard cushion used for kneeling.

hast [*hast*] (*ar*) *2nd pers sing pres ind* of **have**.

hastate [*hastayt*] *adj* (*bot*) spear-shaped.

haste [*hayst*] *n* speed, hurry, quickness; rashness due to excessive speed ~ **haste** *v/t* and *i* hasten.

hasten [*hays*'n] *v/t* and *i* make to haste, urge on; hurry, move or do with haste.

hasty [*hays*ti] *adj* done with haste, hurried; showing haste; rash; hot-tempered; swift; **h. pudding** pudding quickly made by stirring flour into boiling milk or water ~ **hastily** *adv* ~ **hastiness** *n*.

hat [*hat*] *n* covering for the head, *usu* fairly stiff and having a brim; **h. in hand** obsequiously; **my h.!** (*coll*) exclamation of surprise; **old h.** (*sl*) old-fashioned; **talk through one's h.** talk nonsense, reveal one's ignorance; **under one's h.** (*coll*) confidential.

hatband [*hat*band] *n* ribbon round crown of hat immediately above brim.

hatch (1) [*hach*] *n* half-door, door with open space above the wicket; trapdoor covering opening in floor or roof; opening in wall between kitchen and dining room; (*naut*) trapdoor covering opening in deck; hatchway; **under hatches** (*naut*) below deck, *esp* imprisoned there as punishment; *(fig)* in bondage; dead and buried; gloomy.

hatch (2) *n* fine line, used for shading in engraving ~ **hatch** *v/t*.

hatch (3) *v/t* and *i* produce (young) from egg; emerge from egg; incubate; *(fig)* plan, think out, *esp* in secret ~ **hatch** *n* act of hatching; that which is hatched, brood.

hatchback [*hach*bak] motorcar with lifting door at the rear.

hatcher [*hach*er] *n* one who or that which hatches eggs; incubator.

hatchery [*hach*eRi] *n* place where fish are hatched.

hatchet [*hach*it] *n* small axe; **bury the h.** bring a quarrel to an end; **h. face** thin narrow face with prominent nose and jaw.

hatchetman [*hach*itman] *n* (*coll*) one who ruthlessly puts into effect the harsh decisions of another.

hatching [*hach*ing] *n* shading carried out in parallel lines > PDAA.

hatchment [*hach*ment] *n* (*her*) coat-of-arms of a recently deceased person painted on a black, lozenge-shaped panel hung cornerwise outside his house.

hatchway [*hach*way] *n* (*naut*) opening in deck giving access to lower deck or hold.

hate [*hayt*] *n* feeling of extreme dislike, ill-will and hostility; object of this feeling ~ **hate** *v/t* and *i* feel hate (towards); dislike strongly.

hateful [*hayt*fool] *adj* arousing hatred; deserving hatred ~ **hatefully** *adv* ~ **hatefulness** *n*.

hater [*hayt*er] *n* one who feels hatred.

hath [*hath*] (*ar*) *3rd pers sing pres ind* of **have**.

hatpin [*hat*pin] *n* long pin with ornamental head, used for fixing woman's hat on her hair.

hatrack [*hat*-Rak] *n* row of pegs to hang hats on.

hatred [*hayt*Rid] *n* hate; lasting and strong ill-will, enmity.

hatstand [*hat*stand] *n* article of furniture on which hats are hung.

hatted [*hatid*] *adj* wearing a hat.

hatter [*hat*er] *n* one who makes or sells hats; **mad as a h.** very eccentric, crazy; (*US*) very angry.

hat-trick [*hat*-tRik] *n* (*cricket*) act of taking three wickets with successive balls; similar feat in any sport.

hauberk [*haw*berk] *n* coat of mail.

haughty [*haw*ti] *adj* proud, arrogant; scornful ~ **haughtily** *adv* ~ **haughtiness** *n*.

haul [*hawl*] *v/t* and *i* drag, tug, pull with effort; transport; (*naut*) alter ship's sailing course; bring (ship) near or into the wind; **h. over the coals** (*coll*) scold ~ **haul** *n* act of hauling; distance hauled; catch of fish; *(fig)* profits of an enterprise, booty.

haulage [*haw*lij] *n* process of hauling; force expended in hauling; charge for hauling;

(*mining*) engine driving rope-operated haulage system; **road h.** long-distance transport of goods by lorry ~ **haulage** *adj*.

haulier [*haw*li-er] *n* man employed in hauling something, *eg* coal in a mine; **road h.** contractor undertaking long-distance transport of goods by road.

haulm, halm [*hawm*] *n* stalks; stubble; straw.

haunch [*hawnsh*] *n* part of body including hip, buttock and upper thigh; (*archi*) shoulder of arch.

haunt [*hawnt*] *v/t* visit habitually, frequent; (*of ghosts*) appear frequently to (person), or in (place); persecute by frequent visitations or appearances; pervade; (*fig*) obsess, fill the mind of ~ **haunt** *n* place to which a person or animal often or habitually goes; habitat.

haunted [*hawntid*] *adj* frequented by ghosts; suffering from constant anxiety, remorse *etc*.

haunting [*hawnting*] *adj* that haunts; hard to forget ~ **hauntingly** *adv*.

hautboy [Oboi] *n* (*ar*) the oboe.

haute couture [Ot-koo*tewr*] *n* (*Fr*) art of designing exclusive fashionable clothes for women; leading designers of such clothes.

hauteur [O*tur*] *n* (*Fr*) haughtiness.

Havana [ha*va*na] *n* cigar made in Cuba.

have (*2nd pers sing pres indic* (*ar*) **hast**; *3rd pers sing pres indic* **has** or (*ar*) **hath**; *p/t* and *p/part* **had**) [*hav*] *v/t* own, possess; possess as a characteristic quality *etc*; keep, hold; experience, feel; enjoy; undergo; take; eat, drink, consume; obtain; bear (offspring); cause to be done; allow, tolerate; (*coll*) outwit, dupe; (*coll*) defeat; *v/aux used with past participles to form compound past tenses*; **h. at** (*ar*) attack; **h. had it** (*coll*) miss one's last chance; die; be ruined; **h. in** (*coll*) invite, offer hospitality to; **h. it in for** be persistently hostile to, persecute; **h. it off with** (*sl*) have sexual intercourse with; **h. on** be wearing; (*sl*) hoax, deceive; **h. it out (with)** settle by open argument; **h. to** be obliged to; **h. to do with** concern; deal with, associate with; **h. up** (*coll*) prosecute in court ~ **have** *n* (*coll*) trick; (*pl*) those who are rich, powerful, or privileged.

havelock [*hav*lok] *n* white cloth covering for the hat, to protect the neck from the sun.

haven [*hay*ven] *n* harbour; (*fig*) refuge.

havener [*hay*vener] *n* a harbour-master.

have-not [*hav*-not] *n* one who is poor or under-privileged.

haven't [*havnt*] *abbr* have not.

haver [*hay*ver] *v/i* (*Scots and northern dial*) talk nonsense; dither ~ **havers** [*hay*verz] *interj* nonsense!

haversack [*hav*ersak] *n* canvas bag carried on the back or over the shoulder.

havoc [*hav*ok] *n* devastation.

haw (1) [*haw*] *n* fruit of the hawthorn.

haw (2) *n* nictitating membrane, 'third eyelid'.

haw (3) *interj* inarticulate sound expressing hesitation, doubt or embarrassment ~ **haw** *v/i* make such a sound; **hum and h.** hesitate in speaking.

hawfinch [*haw*finch] *n* a large-beaked finch.

haw-haw [*haw*-haw] *interj* written representation of loud laughter.

hawk (1) [*hawk*] *n* any short-winged long-tailed falcon; any of the smaller members of the falcon family; (*coll*) one who urges that a war be more

fiercely waged; (*fig*) rapacious person; swindler; fiercely watchful person ~ **hawk** *v/i* and *t* hunt with a hawk, practise falconry; swoop down on (prey).

hawk (2) *v/t* and *i* cough up (phlegm); clear one's throat ~ **hawk** *n* noise made in clearing the throat.

hawk (3) *v/t* and *i* sell (goods) from door to door, *esp* with barrow or cart; cry for sale in streets; **h. about** (*fig*) spread (news *etc*).

hawker [*haw*ker] *n* pedlar, *usu* equipped with barrow or cart.

hawk-eyed [*hawk*-Id] *adj* keen-sighted; (*fig*) very observant.

hawkmoth [*hawk*moth] *n* large hovering moth.

hawk-owl [*hawk*-owl] *n* owl which hunts by day.

hawse [*hawz*] *n* that part of a ship's bows in which the hawseholes are cut; hawseholes.

hawsehole [*hawz*-hOl] *n* hole in ship's bows for anchor cables to pass through.

hawser [*haw*zer] *n* small cable; thick rope.

hawthorn [*haw*thawrn] *n* thorny tree with white, red or pink flowers and red berries.

hay (1) [*hay*] *n* grass mown and dried for fodder; grass grown for mowing; **hit the h.** (*sl*) go to bed; **make h.** dry mown grass by exposure to sun and air; **make h. of** (*fig*) throw into confusion; **make h. while the sun shines** seize an opportunity ~ **hay** *v/t* and *i* turn into hay; supply with hay; make hay.

hay (2), **hey** (2) *n* country dance with winding movement.

haybox [*hay*boks] *n* airtight box padded with hay in which food can be kept at cooking heat.

haycock [*hay*kok] *n* heap of hay ready for carting.

hayfever [*hay*feever] *n* allergic catarrh of nose and throat, caused by inhaling pollen, dust or other irritants.

hayfield [*hay*feeld] *n* field of grass grown for hay; field where hay is being made.

hayfork [*hay*fawrk] *n* long-handled fork, used for turning or loading hay.

hayloft [*hay*loft] *n* loft in which hay is stored.

haymaking [*hay*mayking] *n* process of cutting and drying grass for hay ~ **haymaker** *n*.

hayrick [*hay*Rik] *n* haystack.

hayseed [*hay*seed] *n* seed of grass; (*US sl*) country bumpkin.

haystack [*hay*stak] *n* outdoor pile of hay.

hayward [*hay*ward] *n* (*hist*) official empowered to inspect hedges and fencing and to impound straying cattle.

haywire [*hay*wIr] *adj* (*coll*) wildly excited, crazy; disorganized; tangled.

hazard [*haz*ard] *n* risk, peril; chance; game of dice; (*golf*) obstacle; (*billiards*) shot in which one ball is played into pocket; (*tennis*) winning opening; **losing h.** (*billiards*) in-off shot; **winning h.** (*billiards*) pot ~ **hazard** *v/t* expose to peril, risk; venture.

hazardous [*haz*ardus] *adj* involving risk ~ **hazardously** *adv* ~ **hazardousness** *n*.

haze (1) [*hayz*] *n* light mist slightly reducing visibility > PDG; (*fig*) vagueness, slight mental confusion ~ **haze** *v/i* and *t* become or make hazy.

haze (2) *v/t* bully; jeer at; (*US*) rag; (*naut*) drive too hard, overwork.

hazel [*hay*zel] *n* small tree with edible nuts;

colour of ripe hazelnuts, light brown ~ **hazel**
adj light brown; made of wood of hazel.
hazelnut [*hayze*lnut] *n* nut of the hazel.
hazy [*hayzi*] *adj* dimmed by haze, misty; (*fig*)
vague; mentally muddled ~ **hazily** *adv* ~
haziness *n*.
H-bomb [*aych*-bom] *n* hydrogen bomb.
he [*hee*] *pron 3rd pers sing masc nom* ~ **he** *n* and
adj male.
he! he! [*hee*-hee] *interj* representation of scornful
laughter.

head [*hed*] *n* topmost or foremost part of body,
consisting of skull and brain, face, jaws, ears
etc; (*fig*) intelligence; one individual in a group;
chief, leader, ruler, director, principal; highest
part, top; foremost part, front; projecting part,
promontory; section, subdivision; top of pimple
or boil; froth on beer *etc*; source of river; side
of coin on which ruler's portrait is stamped;
cutting or striking part of tool; (*coll*) headache;
(*racing*) length of a horse's head; (*sl*) one who has
had a psychedelic experience; drug-addict; **above
one's h.** beyond one's understanding; **bring to
a h.** force matters to a crisis; **by a short h.** (*racing*)
by a small margin of distance; **come to a h.**
reach a crisis or decisive stage; (*of pimple etc*)
be about to burst; **give (one) his h.** allow complete freedom to; **go to one's h.** intoxicate,
over-excite; **keep one's h.** remain calm and
sensible; **lose one's h.** panic, become flustered;
not make h. or tail of be quite bewildered by;
off one's h. mad; delirious; wildly excited;
over the h. of despite the prior claims of;
h. over heels upside down; utterly; **put heads
together** consult together; **h. voice** falsetto;
h. of water potential energy per unit weight of
fluid above a certain point > PDE ~ **head** *adj*
chief; senior ~ **head** *v/t* and *i* lead, direct;
provide a head or heading for; strike or touch
with one's head; divert the course of; go in
specified direction; **h. for** go towards; be likely
to encounter (trouble *etc*); **h. off** intercept,
force to change course; divert.
headache [*hed*ayk] *n* continuous pain in the head;
(*coll*) troublesome problem ~ **headachy** *adj*.
headband [*hed*band] *n* band worn round head;
(*bookbinding*) narrow strip of silk fastened inside
back of head and tail of bound book.
headboard [*hed*bawrd] *n* board, *usu* padded, at
the head end of a bed.
head-dress [*hed*-dRes] *n* ornamental covering for
the head.
header [*hed*er] *n* act of falling or diving head first;
(*football*) act of striking the ball with the head;
(*bui*) brick laid across wall to bond it together;
exposed end of brick.
headfirst [*hed*furst] *adv* headlong.
headgear [*hed*geer] *n* any covering for the head.
head-hunting [*hed*-hunting] *n* practice of cutting
off enemies' heads and preserving them as
trophies ~ **head-hunter** *n*.
headiness [*hed*inis] *n* quality of being heady.
heading [*hed*ing] *n* act of one who heads; title
words at top of page or column of words, or at
beginning of chapter; subdivision of treatise,
speech *etc*.
headlamp [*hed*lamp] *n* powerful lamp fixed to
front of car.

headland [*hed*land] *n* steep cliff jutting out to
sea.
headlight [*hed*lIt] *n* headlamp; lantern at masthead of ship.
headline [*hed*lIn] *n* boldly printed heading of
newspaper article; (*rad*) brief summary of news
bulletin; words printed along top of page;
(*naut*) rope securing sail to yard; **hit the head-
lines** (*sl*) become famous.
headlong [*hed*long] *adv* with head foremost;
hastily, rashly ~ **headlong** *adj* rash, impetuous.
headman [*hed*man] *n* chieftain; foreman.
headmaster [hed*maaster*] *n* principal master of
a school.
headmistress [hed*mistRis*] *n* principal mistress
of a school.
head-on [hed-*on*] *adj* and *adv* (colliding) with
direct impact, head to head or front to front.
head-page [*hed*-payj] *n* (*typ*) page beginning a
book, chapter *etc*.
headphones [*hed*fOnz] *n* (*pl*) (*rad*, *tel*) apparatus
with receivers fitting on to the head.
headpiece [*hed*pees] *n* anything fitting closely
over the head; (*coll*) the head, brain(s); (*typ*)
decorative block at top of first page of book,
chapter *etc*; (*ar*) helmet.
headquarters [hed*kwawrterz*] *n* (*mil*) residence of
commander-in-chief; central office of an organization.
headrest [*hed*Rest] *n* that which supports the
head.
headroom [*hed*ROOm] *n* height of ceiling, bridge,
arch, doorway *etc* considered in relation to height
of those passing beneath.
headscarf [*hed*skaarf] *n* square of silk, nylon *etc*
folded and tied round head.
head-set [*hed*-set] *n* headphones and microphone
fitting on to the head.
headship [*hed*ship] *n* position or office of a leader
or headmaster.
headshrinker [*hed*shRinker] *n* headhunter who
shrinks the dried flesh of his victim's head; (*sl*)
psychiatrist.
headsman [*hedz*man] *n* executioner who beheads.
headstall [*hed*stawl] *n* light harness without bit.
headstock [*hed*stok] *n* part of lathe supporting
the spindle.
headstone [*hed*stOn] *n* upright stone at head of
grave; cornerstone; keystone.
headstrong [*hed*stRong] *adj* wilful; rash.
headwaters [*hed*wawterz] *n* (*pl*) stream or streams
forming source of river.
headway [*hed*way] *n* motion forward, *esp* of ship;
progress, *esp* against opposition; rate of progress;
(*archi*) headroom.
headwind [*hed*wind] *n* wind blowing directly
against one's course.
headword [*hed*wurd] *n* word in bold type used as
a heading.
heady [*hed*i] *adj* intoxicating, exciting; rash.
heal [*heel*] *v/t* and *i* cure, make sound or healthy;
(*of wounds*) close up and form new skin; (*fig*)
repair; restore peace of mind to ~ **healer** *n* one
who heals, *esp* by non-medical means ~ **healing**
adj and *n*.
health [*helth*] *n* state of well-being; state of being
vigorous and free from disease; bodily condition,
whether good or bad; hygiene; toast drunk wish-

ing someone health and prosperity; **h. food** food made from pure natural products without chemical additives or processes; **h. physics** study of ill-effects of ionizing radiations on humans and their protection therefrom; **h. store** shop selling herbal remedies and health foods.

healthful [*helth*fool] *adj* conducive to good health.

healthy [*helth*i] *adj* in good health; conducive to good health, salutary; beneficial, wholesome ~ **healthily** *adv* ~ **healthiness** *n*.

heap [*heep*] *n* pile, mass of things lying on top of one another; (*coll*) large quantity or number; (*pl*) (*coll*) plenty; **struck all of a h.** (*coll*) amazed, overwhelmed ~ **heap** *v/t* pile into a heap; amass, accumulate; bestow lavishly ~ **heaps** *adv* (*sl*) very much; plenty.

hear [*heer*] *v/t* and *i* perceive (sound) by **ear**; listen to; obey; grant (request); (*leg*) try as judge; be capable of perceiving sounds; receive news, information *etc*, **h! h!** *exclam* of approval of a speaker's words; **h. from** receive message, letter *etc* from; **h. of** be informed about; **(he) will not h. of it** (he) refuses to consider or allow it; **h. out** listen to until the end ~ **hearer** *n*.

hearing [*heer*Ring] *n* faculty or sense by which sound is perceived; process of listening; opportunity to speak and be listened to; (*leg*) trial of case at law, *esp* before judge without jury; earshot.

hearing-aid [*heer*Ring-ayd] *n* electric amplifier worn by partially deaf people.

hearken, harken [*haar*ken] *v/i* listen attentively.

hearsay [*heer*say] *n* what one hears others say, rumour ~ **hearsay** *adj*.

hearse [*hurs*] *n* vehicle for transporting a coffin to the grave; framework supporting pall.

heart [*haart*] *n* muscular organ whose pulsations keep the blood circulating > PDB; (*fig*) affection, love; humane feelings; courage, spirit, energy; soul, inmost self; central part, core; representation of a heart; object shaped like a heart; (*hort*) firm centre of lettuce, cabbage *etc*; (*pl*) (*cards*) suit marked with red heart-shaped figures; **after my own h.** just as I like; **at h.** fundamentally, in one's deepest feelings; **break one's h.** grieve profoundly; **by h.** from memory, by rote; **eat one's h. out** pine, grieve bitterly; **have at h.** care deeply about; **have the h. to** be callous enough to; **h. and soul** enthusiastically, **h. to h.** intimate; **lose one's h. to** fall in love with; **out of h.** discouraged; **pluck up h.** grow braver or more confident; **set one's h. on** desire fervently, resolve to obtain; **take h.** grow braver; **take to h.** be strongly impressed by; grieve over; **with all one's h.** with deep affection; very willingly; enthusiastically ~ **heart** *v/i* **h. up** (*of vegetables*) form a firm centre.

heartache [*haart*ayk] *n* gnawing grief.

heartbeat [*haart*beet] *n* one pulsation of the heart; sound of this.

heartblock [*haart*blok] *n* (*med*) disease in which the heartbeats are slow or irregular.

heartbreak [*haart*Rayk] *n* bitter disappointment, deep grief ~ **heartbreaking** *adj* causing heartbreak; (*coll*) exhausting, boring.

heartbroken [*haart*bROken] *adj* afflicted by deep sorrow.

heartburn [*haart*burn] *n* burning sensation in stomach or throat, caused by acidity of stomach.

heartburning [*haart*burning] *n* concealed envy or bitterness.

hearten [*haar*ten] *v/t* encourage, embolden.

heartfelt [*haart*felt] *adj* deeply felt, sincere.

hearth [*haarth*] *n* stone or brick surface on which a domestic fire is made; fireplace and surrounding area; (*fig*) home.

hearthrug [*haarth*Rug] *n* small carpet in front of fireplace.

hearthstone [*haarth*stOn] *n* stone slab which forms the hearth; soft stone used for whitening hearths and doorsteps.

heartily [*haar*tili] *adv* in a hearty manner ~ **heartiness** *n*.

heartland [*haart*land] *n* central or vitally important region of a country.

heartless [*haart*lis] *adj* unfeeling, cruel ~ **heartlessly** *adv* ~ **heartlessness** *n*.

heart-rending [*haart*-Rending] *adj* deeply moving, causing great grief.

heart-searching [*haart*-surching] *n* conscientious self-examination.

heartsease [*haart*seez] *n* the wild pansy; peace of mind.

heartsore [*haart*sawr] *adj* grieving.

heart-strings [*haart*-stRingz] *n* (*pl*) deepest feelings.

heart-throb [*haart*-thRob] *n* (*sl*) person one is in love with.

heartwhole [*haart*hOl] *adj* not in love.

hearty [*haar*ti] *adj* vigorous; in sound health; (*of land*) fertile; cordial, affectionate; sincere; cheerful; (*coll*) cheery, loudly jovial; (*coll*) fonder of sport than of intellectual pursuits; philistine; (*of meal*) large, satisfying ~ **hearty** *n* (*sl*) athlete (*opp* aesthete); (*pl*) comrades.

heat [*heet*] *n* state of being hot, warmth; perception of warmth; hot weather; (*fig*) enthusiasm, strong feeling; indignation, ferocity; (*of female mammals*) period of readiness for mating; (*phys*) kinetic energy of molecular movement > PDS; (*sport*) single course in race or contest; eliminating round; (*sl*) fierce interrogation; (*sl*) pressure, physical violence; **h. capacity** (*phys*) heat required to raise the temperature of a body $1°$ C; **h. death** (*astron*) final state of the physical universe, when all energy has become unavailable > PDS; **h. pump** machine for extracting low temperature heat from a fluid to heat a building, *etc* > PDS; **h. shield** the part of a spacecraft which protects it from excessive heating on re-entering the atmosphere; **h. stroke** collapse caused by great heat ~ **heat** *v/t* and *i* make hot; excite, irritate; become hot.

heated [*heet*id] *adj* vehement, passionate ~ **heatedly** *adv*.

heat-engine [*heet*-enjin] *n* engine producing motive power from heat.

heater [*heet*er] *n* device for heating.

heath [*heeth*] *n* open uncultivated ground, covered with shrubs: heather, ling.

heathcock [*heeth*kok] *n* the blackcock.

heathen [*hee*THen] *n* and *adj* (adherent) of a religion neither Christian, Jewish, Muslim, nor Buddhist; (*coll*) (person) without any religion, agnostic; (*fig*) savage.

heathendom [*hee*THendum] *n* heathen areas; heathen civilizations; heathenism.

heathenish [*hee*THenish] *adj* of or like a heathen, pagan; (*fig*) barbarous, outlandish.

heathenism [*hee*THenizm] *n* state of being heathen; doctrine or practice of heathen religion.

heather [*heTH*er] *n* plant of heath family; expanse of land covered with this ~ **heathery** *adj* covered with heather.

heathy [*heethi*] *adj* covered with heath or heather.

heating [*heeting*] *n* means of providing heat; apparatus for making a building warm ~ **heating** *adj* that heats.

heat-proof [*heet*-pROOf] *adj* that can be heated without being damaged.

heatwave [*heet*wayv] *n* unbroken spell of unusually hot weather.

heave (*p/t* and *p/part* **heaved** or (*naut*) **hove**) [*heev*] *v/t* and *i* lift up, swing upwards; haul, drag along; shift with difficulty; throw (something heavy); utter (a sigh, groan *etc*); rise and fall rhythmically; retch; swell, bulge; (*naut*) haul (rope or cable); (*of ship*) move; weigh anchor; (*geol*) displace (stratum); **h. in sight** (*naut*) appear on horizon; **h. to** bring (ship) to standstill ~ **heave** *n* act of heaving.

heaven [*heven*] *n* abode of God or of gods; abode or state of virtuous souls and supernatural beings; place or state of spiritual joy; awareness of God's presence; (*coll*) happiness, intense pleasure; (*ar*) sky; (*ar*) one of various spheres forming the universe; **H. God**; **move h. and earth** do all that can be done.

heavenly [*heven*li] *adj* of, from or like heaven; (*coll*) very delightful ~ **heavenliness** *n*.

heavenward [*heven*ward] *adj* and *adv* towards heaven.

heaver [*heev*er] *n* man who moves heavy goods; (*naut*) bar used for levering rope.

heavily [*hevi*li] *adv* in a heavy way.

heaviness [*hevi*nis] *n* quality of being heavy.

Heaviside layer [hevisId-*lair*] *n* region of the upper atmosphere which reflects the longer wireless waves > PDS.

heavy [*hevi*] *adj* having weight, of high specific gravity; difficult to lift or move; burdensome; serious, ponderous; dull; forceful, violent; distressing; sad, gloomy; lethargic; clumsy; indigestible; doughy; (*of weather*) oppressive, thundery; (*of soil*) muddy, thick with clay; (*mil*) equipped with powerful arms; (*theat coll*) villainous or pompous (role); **h. hydrogen** deuterium or tritium; **h. water** deuterium oxide > PDS ~ **heavy** *adv*.

heavy-duty [hevi-*dewti*] *adj* designed to withstand hard use.

heavy-handed [hevi-*handid*] *adj* clumsy; tactless; brutal, bullying.

heavy-hearted [hevi-*haart*id] *adj* sad, depressed, gloomy.

heavy-laden [hevi-*layden*] *adj* burdened, oppressed.

heavyweight [*hevi*wayt] *n* boxer over 12 st 7 lb; (*fig*) person of importance ~ **heavyweight** *adj*.

hebdomadal [hebd*oma*dal] *adj* weekly.

Hebe [*heebi*] *n* (*Gk myth*) female cupbearer to the gods; (*coll*) waitress, barmaid.

hebephrenia [heebi*fr*eeni-a] *n* (*psych*) form of schizophrenia characterized by silly mannerisms and personal untidiness > PDP.

hebetude [*hebi*tewd] *n* stupidity.

Hebraic [heebRay-ik] *adj* pertaining to the Hebrews.

Hebraism [*hee*bRay-izm] *n* the Hebrew religion, Judaism; Hebrew culture or mentality; Hebrew idiom ~ **Hebraist** *n* scholar of Hebrew.

Hebraistic [heebRay-istik] *adj* Hebrew.

Hebrew [*hee*bROO] *n* Israelite, Jew; ancient language of the Jews ~ **Hebrew** *adj*.

hecatomb [*heka*tOm/*heka*toom] *n* massacre, great slaughter; (*hist*) Greek sacrifice of 100 oxen.

heck [hek] *n* and *interj* (*coll euph*) hell.

heckle [*hek'l*] *v/t* and *i* interrupt public speaker with taunts or hostile questions ~ **heckler** *n*.

hectare [*hek*taar] *n* metric unit of area; 10,000 square metres or 2·471 acres.

hectic [*hek*tik] *adj* feverish, agitated; very active or exciting; rushing; (*med*) consumptive, wasting ~ **hectically** *adv*.

hecto- *pref* hundred.

hectograph [*hekt*Ograaf] *n* machine for duplicating copies from gelatine surface.

hectolitre [*hekt*Oleeter] *n* metric measure of capacity; 100 litres or 26·418 gallons.

hectometre [*hekt*Omeeter] *n* metric measure of length; 100 metres or 328 ft. 1 in.

hector [*hek*ter] *v/t* and *i* bully; swagger.

he'd [*heed*] *abbr* he had; he would; he should.

heddles [*hed'*lz] *n* (*pl*) vertical wires in a loom which separate the warp threads to let the shuttle pass ~ **heddle** *v/t*.

hedge [*hej*] *n* closely planted line of shrubs or small trees forming boundary or fence; (*fig*) barrier; row of persons or things; that which restrains ~ **hedge** *v/t* and *i* surround with a hedge; plant or maintain a hedge; enclose; (*coll*) protect oneself against loss in betting by placing secondary bets; (*coll*) refuse to commit oneself, speak or act ambiguously; **h. in** restrict ~ **hedger** *n*.

hedgehog [*hej*hog] *n* small wild quadruped with prickly back; (*fig*) irritable person; (*mil*) strongpoint offering resistance on all sides.

hedgehop [*hej*hop] *v/i* (*aer coll*) fly extremely low.

hedgerow [*hej*RO] *n* hedge, *esp* of small trees.

hedonic [heed*onik*] *adj* of pleasure; of hedonism.

hedonics [heed*oniks*] *n* (*pl*) the doctrine of hedonism; branch of psychology studying feelings of pleasure and its opposite.

hedonism [*heed*onizm] *n* (*philos*) theory that pleasure is the highest good; (*psych*) theory that human actions are determined primarily by seeking pleasant, and avoiding unpleasant, feelings; (*pop*) pursuit of pleasure ~ **hedonist** *n*.

hedonistic [heedon*istik*] *adj* of hedonism; (*pop*) pleasure-seeking ~ **hedonistically** *adv*.

heebie-jeebies [*hee*bi-jeebiz] *n* (*pl*) (*US sl*) jitters, great nervousness.

heed [*heed*] *v/t* and *i* pay attention (to), note carefully ~ **heed** *n* attention, care; caution; obedience; **take h.** be careful; be attentive.

heedful [*heed*fool] *adj* careful, cautious; attentive ~ **heedfully** *adv* ~ **heedfulness** *n*.

heedless [*heed*lis] *adj* taking no heed, careless; reckless ~ **heedlessly** *adv* ~ **heedlessness** *n*.

hee-haw [*hee*-haw] *n* bray of a donkey; (*fig*) coarse laugh, guffaw ~ **hee-haw** *v/i*.

heel (1) [*heel*] *n* hind part of human foot; corresponding part of animal foot; hock; raised part of shoe beneath heel of foot; part of shoe, stocking *etc* covering heel of foot; lower end; hind end; last part; (*US sl*) cad, despicable fellow; **Achilles' h.** single vulnerable spot; **at (upon) one's heels** close behind one; **down at h.** shabby; **come to h.** (*of dog*) walk close behind its master; (*fig*) submit to discipline, cease to rebel; **cool (kick) one's heels** be kept waiting; **lay by the heels** capture; render powerless; **out at h.** shabby; **show a clean pair of heels** escape; **take to one's heels** run away ~ **heel** *v/t* and *i* provide with a heel; (*Rugby football*) pass (ball) backwards out of scrum by kicking with heel.

heel (2) *v/i* and *t* tilt over to one side, *esp* of ship; cause to tilt over ~ **heel** *n* list of a ship.

heelball [*heel*bawl] *n* ball of cobbler's wax.

heeled [heeld] *adj* (*US sl*) having money; carrying a gun.

heeltap [*heel*tap] *n* drink left in bottom of glass.

heft [heft] *v/t* (*US* and *dial*) lift, test weight of.

hefty [*hef*ti] *adj* (*coll*) weighty; big and strong ~ **heftily** *adv* ~ **heftiness** *n*.

hegemony [hijemoni/higemoni] *n* leadership, control by one state over others.

heifer [*hef*er] *n* cow which has not yet calved.

heigh [hay] *interj* exclamation of encouragement or inquiry.

heigh-ho [hay-*hO*] *interj* exclamation of weariness.

height [hIt] *n* measurement from bottom to top; elevation, altitude; stature; (*fig*) peak, culmination; hill, mountain.

heighten [*hI*ten] *v/t* and *i* make high or higher; increase in size or degree.

heinous [*hay*nus] *adj* hateful, odious ~ **heinously** *adv* ~ **heinousness** *n*.

heir [air] *n* one who succeeds to another's property, rank or rights at the latter's death; one entitled or legally appointed so to succeed; one who has inherited, successor; **h. apparent** one who is certain to be heir unless he himself dies first; **h. at law** natural heir; **h. presumptive** one who will be heir unless there should be born someone of closer kinship to the holder.

heirdom [*air*dum] *n* state of being an heir.

heiress [*air*Res] *n* female heir.

heirloom [*air*lOOm] *n* something inherited from one's forefathers, *esp* chattel descending as inalienable trust.

heist [hIst] *v/t* and *i* (*sl*) steal cars.

held [held] *p/t* and *p/part* of **hold**.

heliacal [hilI-akal] *adj* (*astron*) of or near the sun.

helianthus [heeli-*an*thus] *n* genus of plants including the sunflower.

helical [*hel*ikal] *adj* spiral.

helices [*hel*iseez] *pl* of **helix**.

helicopter [*hel*ikopter] *n* aircraft deriving its lift chiefly from power-driven horizontally rotating rotors.

helio- *pref* pertaining to the sun.

heliocentric [heeli-OsentRik] *adj* considering or having the sun as centre.

heliograph [heeli-OgRaaf] *n* signalling device which reflects sunlight in flashes; instrument for photographing the sun ~ **heliograph** *v/t*

and *i* signal by heliograph; photograph with a heliograph.

heliography [heeli-ogRafi] *n* scientific study of the sun's surface; art of signalling by heliograph; photographic method of engraving.

heliotherapy [heeli-OtheRapi] *n* (*med*) treatment of disease by sunbathing.

heliotrope [heeli-OtrOp] *n* garden plant with fragrant purple flowers; pale purple colour; (*bot*) plant whose flowers turn towards the sun; the bloodstone.

heliotropism [heeli-otRopizm] *n* tendency in plants to turn to face the light.

heliport [*hel*ipawrt] *n* a helicopter airport.

helium [heeli-um] *n* (*chem*) light non-inflammable gaseous element > PDS, PDG.

helix (*pl* **helices**) [*heel*iks] *n* spiral, coil; anything coiled; border of outer ear; (*zool*) genus of spiral-shelled molluscs.

he'll [heel] *abbr* he will; he shall.

hell [hel] *n* abode or state of devils and damned souls; place or state of intense suffering; (*ar*) abode of dead, underworld; (*coll*) place frequented by vicious persons, *esp* gambler's den; **a h. of a** (*coll*) a very intense (large *etc*); **for the h. of it** (*coll*) just for fun; **give h. to** (*coll*) treat roughly or severely; **like h.** (*coll*) very much, very intensely, very badly; (*ironic*) not in the least, certainly not; **ride h. for leather** ride at top speed; **the h.** *coll phr used as intensifier*.

hellbent [*hel*bent] *adj* recklessly determined, dogged.

hellcat [*hel*kat] *n* bad-tempered woman; witch.

hellebore [*hel*ibawr] *n* the Christmas rose; purgative obtained from root of this; poisonous plant of same genus as this.

Hellene [*hel*een] *n* and *adj* Greek.

Hellenic [heleenik/helenik] *adj* Greek ~ **Hellenic** *n* common dialect of later Greek writers.

Hellenism [*hel*inizm] *n* Greek idiom; Greek culture or mentality; Greek nationality.

Hellenist [*hel*inist] *n* student of ancient Greek; one who adopts Greek ways; (*NT*) Greek Jew.

Hellenistic [helinistik] *adj* relating to Greeks of post-Classical period.

hellhound [*hel*hownd] *n* demon in shape of dog; wicked or ferocious person.

hellish [*hel*ish] *adj* of hell; like hell; fit for hell, extremely wicked; (*coll*) very unpleasant ~ **hellish** *adv* (*coll*) very unpleasantly ~ **hellishly** *adv* ~ **hellishness** *n*.

hello see **hallo**.

helm (1) [helm] *n* tiller or steering mechanism of ship; (*fig*) guidance, control.

helm (2) *n* helmet ~ **helmed** *adj*.

helmet [*hel*mit] *n* armour protecting head and face; protective steel headgear; fencing mask; pith hat; (*bot*) curled upper calyx of certain flowers; (*chem*) top of retort ~ **helmeted** *adj* wearing a helmet.

helminth [*hel*minth] *n* parasitic worm.

helmsman [*helm*zman] *n* one who steers.

helot [*hel*ot] *n* serf, *esp* in ancient Sparta.

help [help] *v/t* and *i* aid, work jointly with; be of use (to); conduce towards; serve food to; (*after* **can** *or* **can't**) avoid, refrain from, prevent; **it can't be helped** it is inevitable; **no more**

than you can h. only what you can't avoid;
h. oneself to take; h. out assist, *esp* in a crisis
~ help *n* act of helping, aid, assistance; that
which helps, remedy; one who helps; (*coll*)
part-time servant ~ helper *n* one who helps.
helpful [*help*fool] *adj* that helps; willing to help;
useful ~ helpfully *adv* ~ helpfulness *n*.
helping [*help*ing] *n* portion of food for one person
~ helping *adj* that helps.
helpless [*help*lis] *adj* unable to help oneself;
incompetent; powerless ~ helplessly *adv* ~
helplessness *n*.
helpmate, helpmeet [*help*mayt, *help*meet] *n*
helpful partner, *esp* a wife.
helter-skelter [helter-*skel*ter] *adj* and *adv* in
disordered hurry ~ helter-skelter *n* tower with
external spiral chute.
helve [*helv*] *n* handle of certain tools.
Helvetian [helveeshon] *adj* Swiss.
hem (1) [*hem*] *n* edge of cloth doubled back and
stitched down; border, outer edge of garment ~
hem (*pres*/*part* hemming, *p*/*t* and *p*/*part*
hemmed) *v*/*t* and *i* sew a hem (on); h. in
enclose, encircle.
hem (2), hum (2), h'm *interj* and *n* coughing
sound to express hesitation or sarcastic comment
~ hem *v*/*i* utter this sound, hesitate in speech.
he-man [*hee*-man] *n* (*coll*) a virile fellow.
hemi- *pref* half; on one side.
hemicycle [*hemi*sik'l] *n* a half circle.
hemiplegia [hemi*pleeji*-a] *n* (*med*) paralysis
of one side of body.
hemisphere [*hemi*sfeer] *n* half of a sphere;
half of the earth's surface > PDG ~ hemispherical [hemis*fe*rikal] *adj*.
hemistich [*hemi*stik] *n* (*pros*) half of line of verse.
hem-line [*hem*-lIn] *n* lower edge of skirt, *esp*
considered in relation to height from ground.
hemlock [*hem*lok] *n* umbelliferous plant producing a powerful sedative, from which a poison
can be distilled.
hemp [*hemp*] *n* plant from which a narcotic drug
is obtained; this drug; fibres of this and allied
plants, used in ropes and coarse fabric; (*fig*)
hangman's rope ~ hempen *adj*.
hemstitch [*hem*stich] *n* decorative stitch used to
finish a hem ~ hemstitch *v*/*t*.
hen [*hen*] *n* female of the domestic fowl; any
female bird; (*coll*) fussy person; (*sl*) woman.
henbane [*hen*bayn] *n* poisonous weed with dull
yellow flowers.
hence [*hens*] *adv* therefore, so; from this; from
this time; (*ar*) away from here.
henceforth [hens*fawr*th] *adv* from now on.
henceforward [hens*fawr*ward] *adv* from now
on.
henchman [*hensh*man] *n* faithful attendant;
staunch supporter.
hendeca- *pref* eleven.
hendiadys [hend*I*-adis] *n* (*gramm*) figure of
speech in which a single idea is presented in two
words linked by a conjunction.
henge [*henj*] *n* (*arch*) circular monument with
inner ditch and outer bank, sometimes containing
wooden posts or standing stones.
henna [*hena*] *n* an Asiatic shrub; red dye for hair
or nails, obtained from this.

hennery [*hene*Ri] *n* place where poultry are
reared.
hen-party [*hen*-paarti] *n* (*coll*) party for women
only.
henpeck [*hen*pek] *v*/*t* nag, domineer over (one's
husband) ~ henpecked *adj*.
henry [*hen*Ri] *n* (*elect*) the unit of inductance >
PDS.
hep [*hep*] *adj* (*sl*) appreciative of swing music;
up-to-date; lively; h. to informed about.
hepat-, hepato- *pref* of the liver.
hepatic [hi*pat*ik] *adj* pertaining to the liver;
liver-coloured.
hepatica [hi*pat*ika] *n* European anemone.
hepatitis [hepat*I*tis] *n* (*med*) inflammation of the
liver.
hep-cat [*hep*-kat] *n* (*sl*) person who is hep;
musician who plays swing music.
hepta- *pref* seven.
heptad [*hep*tad] *n* seven; group of seven.
heptagon [*hep*tagon] *n* (*geom*) plane figure with
seven sides ~ heptagonal [hep*tag*onal] *adj*.
heptahedron [hepta*hed*Ron] *n* solid figure with
seven faces ~ heptahedral *adj*.
heptane [*hep*tayn] *n* (*chem*) liquid hydrocarbon
present in petroleum > PDS.
heptarchy [*hep*taarki] *n* government by seven
rulers; country divided into seven kingdoms.
heptateuch [*hep*tatewk] *n* first seven books of the
Bible.
her [*hur*] *possessive adj* of or belonging to a femal
~ her *pron objective case of* she.
herald [*he*Rald] *n* official who makes public
announcements or carries ceremonial messages;
official who grants and regulates armorial
bearings; (*fig*) one who brings news, one who
announces the approach of anything; (*hist*)
official who arranged tourneys ~ herald *v*/*t*
proclaim, announce, usher in.
heraldic [he*Ral*dik] *adj* of heraldry ~ heraldic-
ally *adv*.
heraldry [*he*RaldRi] *n* study and regulation of the
use of armorial bearings; office of herald;
heraldic devices.
herb [*hurb*] *n* plant whose stem dies down
annually; plant used medicinally, or to flavour
food.
herbaceous [hur*bay*shus] *adj* dying down in
winter; pertaining to herbs; (*bot*) resembling
a leaf; h. border garden border planted with
herbaceous flowers.
herbage [*hur*bij] *n* herbs, grass, pasturage; (*leg*)
right of pasturage.
herbal [*hur*bal] *adj* of herbs ~ herbal *n* book on
herbs and their medicinal properties.
herbalist [*hur*balist] *n* (*orig*) botanist; dealer in
herbs, *esp* as medicines.
herbarium [hur*bair*Ri-um] *n* collection of preserved plant specimens; place where this is kept.
herbicide [*hur*bisId] *n* any chemical that kills
plants.
herbiferous [hur*bife*Rus] *adj* producing herbs.
herbivorous [hur*bivo*Rus] *adj* feeding on herbage.
Herculean [hurkew*lee*-an] *adj* of immense size
and strength; (*of task*) difficult to accomplish.
Hercules [*hur*kewleez] *n* (*myth*) Greek hero famous for strength; man of immense physical

strength; Pillars of H. rocks on either side of the Straits of Gibraltar.

herd (1) [*hurd*] *n* numerous group of large animals living and feeding together; group of domestic animals of one breed, *esp* cattle or pigs; (*fig*) crowd of people acting as group rather than as individuals; mob, rabble; **h. instinct** tendency of crowds to be swayed by mass emotion and to turn against idiosyncratic individuals; gregariousness ~ **herd** *v/t* and *i* collect into a herd; drive forward like a herd; tend as a herd; huddle together.

herd (2) *n* (*ar*) herdsman.

herdsman [*hurdz*man] *n* one who tends a domestic herd.

here [*heer*] *adv* in this place; at this point; towards this place; **h. and there** scattered about; **neither h. nor there** irrelevant, of no importance; **h. goes!** now for it!; **here's to here's a health to; h. you are** (*coll*) this is what you want ~ **here** *n* this place.

hereabout, hereabouts [*heer*Rabowt, *heer*Rabowts] *adv* near this place.

hereafter [*heer*Raafter] *adv* after this time, in the future; after death ~ **hereafter** *n* life after death.

hereat [*heer*Rat] *adv* at this; when this happened.

hereby [*heer*bI] *adv* by this means; (*ar*) near here.

hereditable [hi*Red*itab'l] *adj* that may be inherited.

hereditament [he*Rid*itament] *n* (*leg*) property that may be inherited.

hereditary [hi*Red*itaRi] *adj* passing down by inheritance; transmitted by heredity; **h. factor** gene > PDB ~ **hereditarily** *adv* by way of inheritance.

heredity [hi*Red*iti] *n* (*biol*) transmission from parents to offspring of physical and mental characteristics; totality of characteristics so transmitted; process by which this occurs; study of biological laws governing this.

herein [heer*Rin*] *adv* in this.

hereinafter [heer*Rin*aafter] *adv* henceforth, in the rest of this document.

hereof [heer*Rov*] *adv* of this.

heresiarch [hi*Reesi*-aark] *n* founder of a heresy.

heresy [*he*Risi] *n* erroneous religious belief, opinion contrary to official teaching of a Church; (*fig*) any opinion contrary to an officially or generally approved theory.

heretic [*he*Ritik] *n* one who maintains a heresy.

heretical [hi*Reti*kal] *adj* of, like, or believing in, a heresy; of a heretic ~ **heretically** *adv*.

hereto [heert*OO*] *adv* to this; hitherto.

heretofore [heertOO*fawr*] *adv* before this.

hereunder [heer*Rund*er] *adv* below (in document).

hereunto [heer*Runt*OO] *adv* up to this point.

hereupon [heer*Rup*on] *adv* upon this matter; following on this; immediately afterwards.

herewith [heer*wITH*] *adv* with this; now.

heriot [*he*Ri-ot] *n* (*leg hist*) custom of giving the feudal lord the best beast in a tenant's possession at his death.

heritable [*he*Ritab'l] *adj* that can be inherited; who can inherit ~ **heritability** [herita*bili*ti] *n*.

heritage [*he*Ritij] *n* anything to which one

succeeds by birth; characteristics transmitted by heredity; social and intellectual environment into which an individual is born > PDP.

heritor [*he*Ritor] *n* one who inherits.

herm [*hurm*] *n* post or pillar topped by representation of Hermes.

hermaphrodism, hermaphroditism [hur*maf*Rodizm, hur*maf*Roditizm] *n* state of being a hermaphrodite.

hermaphrodite [hur*maf*Rodit] *n* and *adj* (human being or animal) having both male and female sexual organs or characteristics; (person or animal) with indeterminate sexual organs; (*bot*) (plant) having both stamens and carpels in one flower ~ **hermaphroditic** [hurmaf*Rodi*tik] *adj*.

hermeneutic [hurmin*ewt*ik] *adj* pertaining to interpretation, *esp* of the Scriptures.

hermetic [hur*met*ik] *adj* airtight, tightly closed; **H.** (*ar*) pertaining to alchemy; occult ~ **hermetically** *adv* so as to be airtight.

hermit [*hur*mit] *n* one living in solitude in order to pray and meditate; (*fig*) recluse; **h. crab** soft-bodied crab living in discarded mollusc shell.

hermitage [*hur*mitij] *n* dwelling place of hermit.

hern [*hurn*] *n* (*ar*) heron.

hernia [*hur*ni-a] *n* (*med*) protrusion of organ through aperture in its containing wall; rupture, *esp* abdominal ~ **hernial** *adj*.

hero [*heer*RO] *n* man of outstanding courage and endurance; man greatly admired or worthy to be admired, person of outstanding qualities; chief male character in book, play, film, story *etc*; (*myth*) legendary warrior or performer of great feats, *esp* one revered as demigod; **h. worship** exaggerated admiration for some person.

heroic [hi*RO*-ik] *adj* of or like a hero, nobly courageous; on a large scale, larger than life; requiring great courage, strength *etc*; pertaining to epic poetry; (*of language*) magniloquent; **h. age** legendary period when heroes flourished; (*fig*) warlike period; period of greatest glory; **h. couplet** (*pros*) rhymed decasyllabic couplet with five stresses; **mock h.** deliberate application of lofty epic style to trivial subjects; **h. verse** any metre traditionally used in epics.

heroical [hi*RO*-ikal] *adj* heroic ~ **heroically** *adv*.

heroics [hi*RO*-iks] *n* (*pl*) over-dramatic speech.

heroin [*he*RO-in/hi*RO*-in] *n* narcotic and euphoric drug derived from morphine.

heroine [*he*RO-in] *n* female hero; chief female character in book, play *etc*.

heroism [*he*RO-izm] *n* quality of being a hero; noble courage.

heron [*he*Ron] *n* type of long-legged wading bird.

heronry [*he*RonRi] *n* place where herons breed.

herpes [*hur*peez] *n* (*med*) skin disease characterized by small blisters; **h. zoster** shingles.

herpetic [hur*pet*ik] *adj* of or like herpes.

herpetology [hurp*it*oloji] *n* (*zool*) study of reptiles ~ **herpetologist** *n*.

herring [*he*Ring] *n* an edible salt-water fish; **red h.** (*fig*) interesting but irrelevant fact or suggestion introduced to divert attention from main point.

herringbone [*he*RingbOn] *adj* resembling the pattern of a herring's spine and ribs; stitched or woven in this pattern; (*archi*) laid in alternating diagonals ∼ **herringbone** *n*.

hers [*hurz*] *possessive pron* and *adj* belonging to her.

herself [hurself] *pron* *refl* and *emph* that very woman; her usual or normal self.

hertz [*hurts*] *n* unit of frequency of a periodic phenomenon, equal to 1 cycle per second.

Hertzian waves [*hurtz*i-an-wayvz] *n* (*pl*) electromagnetic waves used in radio transmission > PDS.

he's [*heez*] *abbr* he is; he has.

hesitance, hesitancy [*hez*itans, *hez*itansi] *n* act or quality of hesitating; speech impediment ∼ **hesitant** *adj* ∼ **hesitantly** *adv*.

hesitate [*hez*itayt] *v/i* and *t* pause in doubt before deciding, acting or speaking; be unwilling; falter; speak falteringly; speak with stammer or similar defect ∼ **hesitating** *adj* ∼ **hesitatingly** *adv*.

hesitation [hezit*ay*shon] *n* act or state of hesitating; irresolution; reluctance; speech defect.

Hesperian [hesp*eer*Ri-an] *adj* (*poet*) western.

Hesperus [*hes*peRus] *n* the evening star.

hessian [*hes*ian] *n* coarse sackcloth; type of boot.

hest [*hest*] *n* (*ar*) a command.

hetaera (*pl* **hetaerae**) [het*ee*Ra] *n* (*in ancient Greece*) mistress, concubine; courtesan.

heter-, hetero- *pref* other, different; abnormal.

heteroclite [*hete*Rokl1t] *adj* (*gramm*) irregular.

heterocyclic [hete*Ros*Iklik] *adj* (*chem*) containing a ring structure of atoms including atoms of elements other than carbon > PDS.

heterodox [*hete*Rodoks] *adj* unorthodox, conflicting with generally or officially accepted opinion ∼ **heterodoxy** *n*.

heterodyne [*hete*RODIn] *n* (*rad*) beat effect produced by superimposing two waves of different frequency > PDS.

heterogamous [hete*Rog*amus] *adj* (*zool*) alternating in successive generations between two forms of reproduction > PDB ∼ **heterogamy** *n*.

heterogeneity [heteROjin*ee*-iti] *n* condition of being composed of diverse constituents.

heterogeneous [heteROj*eeni*-us] *adj* diverse in kind, varied; dissimilar; (*math*) incommensurable; (*chem*) not of a uniform composition; showing different properties in different portions ∼ **heterogeneously** *adv*.

heterogenesis [heteROj*eni*sis] *n* (*biol*) production of an organism otherwise than from a parent of the same kind; spontaneous generation.

heteronym [*hete*Ronim] *n* word spelt like another, but having different sound and meaning.

heterosexual [heteRos*eks*sew-al] *adj* sexually or emotionally attracted to the opposite sex.

heterosexuality [heteRoseksew-*al*iti] *n* state or quality of being heterosexual > PDP.

hetman [*het*man] *n* Cossack leader.

het-up [het-*up*] *adj* (*coll*) excited, overwrought, worried.

heuristic [hewr*Ris*tik] *n* and *adj* (education) in which the pupil discovers things for himself; (*math*) involving inductive reasoning from past experience when no algorithm exists; (*of computers*) proceeding by trial and error ∼ **heuristics** *n* (*pl*).

hew (*p/t* **hewed**, *p/part* **hewn** or **hewed**) [*hew*] *v/t* and *i* strike with sharp instrument, chop,

hack; fell with axe; shape with axe-cuts; **h. out** carve or hollow out by hewing ∼ **hewer** *n*.

hewn [*hewn*] *adj* made by hewing, shaped by blows of an axe

hex [*heks*] *n* (*coll*) that which brings bad luck ∼ **hex** *v/t* and *i* practise witchcraft, bewitch.

hex-, hexa- *pref* six, sixth, six times.

hexad [*hek*sad] *n* six; group or series of six.

hexagon [*hek*sagon] *n* (*geom*) plane figure with six sides.

hexagonal [heks*ag*onal] *adj* six-sided.

hexahedron [heksah*ed*Ron] *n* solid figure with six faces ∼ **hexahedral** *adj*.

hexameter [heks*am*iter] *n* verse of six feet.

hexametric, hexametrical [heksa*met*Rik, heksa*met*Rikal] *adj* of or in hexameters.

hexane [*hek*sayn] *n* (*chem*) liquid hydrocarbon present in petroleum > PDS.

hexapod [*hek*sapod] *n* and *adj* (*zool*) (insect) having six feet.

hexateuch [*hek*satewk] *n* first six books of Bible.

hexose [*hek*sOz] *n* (*chem*) type of sugar containing six carbon atoms in the molecule > PDS.

hey (1) [*hay*] *interj* exclamation to attract attention.

hey (2) see **hay** (2).

heyday [*hay*day] *n* peak, prime.

hi [*hI*] *interj* exclamation to attract attention or express greeting.

hiatus (*pl* **hiatuses**) [hI-*ay*tus] *n* gap, empty space; break in continuity; (*gramm*) slight pause between two vowels.

hibernal [hI*bur*nal] *adj* of or like winter; appearing in winter.

hibernate [*hI*burnayt] *v/i* pass the winter in state of torpor > PDB.

hibernation [hIbur*nay*shon] *n* act or state of hibernating.

Hibernian [hI*bur*ni-an] *n* and *adj* (native) of Ireland.

hibiscus [hI*bis*kus] *n* rose mallow.

hiccup, hiccough [*hik*up] *n* spasmodic involuntary contraction of diaphragm and closure of glottis; sound produced by this; (*pl*) series of these spasms ∼ **hiccup** *v/i* and *t* utter a series of hiccups; utter with a hiccup.

hick [*hik*] *n* (*US sl*) country bumpkin.

hickory [*hik*oRi] *n* N American hardwood tree; wood of this; walkin -stick of this wood.

hid [*hid*] *p/t* and (*ar*) *p/part* of hide (2).

hidalgo [hi*dal*gO] *n* (*Sp*) Spanish nobleman.

hidden [*hid*en] *p/part* of hide (2).

hide (1) [*hId*] *n* skin of large animal, *esp* when stripped off; skin dressed for leather; (*coll*) human skin; **have a thick h.** (*coll*) be very insensitive to criticism *etc*; be insolent; **tan the h. of** (*coll*) thrash ∼ **hide** *v/t* flay; (*coll*) thrash.

hide (2) (*p/t* **hid**, *p/part* **hidden** or (*ar*) **hid**) *v/t* and *i* prevent from being seen or found, conceal; prevent from being known, keep secret; keep oneself out of sight, go into concealment ∼ **hide** *n* place of concealment; concealed observation post.

hide (3) *n* (*hist*) measure of land, notionally about 120 acres.

hide-and-seek [*hId*-and-seek] *n* children's game in which one player searches for others who have hidden.

hidebound [*híd*bownd] *adj* rigidly conventional, narrow-minded; (*of animals*) having skin adhering too closely to the flesh; (*of trees*) having tight bark which impedes growth.

hideous [*hídi*-us] *adj* very ugly; repulsive, horrible ~ **hideously** *adv* ~ **hideousness** *n.*

hideout [*híd*owt] *n* safe hiding place.

hiding (1) [*híd*ing] *n* concealment; place of concealment.

hiding (2) *n* (*coll*) a thrashing, flogging.

hie [*hí*] *v/i* (*ar*) go quickly.

hier-, hiero- *pref* sacred; priestly.

hierarch [*hí*-eRaark] *n* spiritual ruler, chief priest.

hierarchal [hí-eRaark̄al] *adj* pertaining to a hierarch or a hierarchy.

hierarchic, hierarchical [hí-eRaarkik, hí-eRaarkikal] *adj* pertaining to a hierarch or a hierarchy.

hierarchy [*hí*-eRaarki] *n* organization of persons in graded ranks, each rank controlling that below it; graded system, *esp* of officials; (*eccles*) body of religious rulers; bishops and cardinals collectively; (*theol*) each of three divisions of angels.

hieratic [hí-eRatik] *adj* pertaining to priests; sacred; ritualistic; **h. writing** later form of hieroglyphs.

hieroglyph [*hí*-eROglif] *n* character used in ancient Egyptian writing system; character used in any picture script; symbolic figure; (*fig*) incomprehensible or secret writing.

hieroglyphic [hí-eROglifik] *adj* written in hieroglyphs; of or like a hieroglyph ~ **hieroglyphics** *n* (*pl*) writing in hieroglyphs ~ **hieroglyphically** *adv.*

hierophant [*hí*-eROfant] *n* priest of a mystery cult; interpreter of esoteric doctrines.

hi-fi [hí-fí] *n* and *adj* (equipment) reproducing sound with high fidelity.

higgle [*híg*'l] *v/i* haggle ~ **higgler** *n.*

higgledy-piggledy [híg'ldi-*píg*'ldi] *adv* and *adj* in disorder, jumbled together.

high [*hí*] *adj* extending far upwards, lofty, tall; at a specified altitude; extending a specified distance upwards; of exalted rank, powerful; noble; haughty; most important, main; excellent; of great degree, intense; expensive; shrill; (*of meat*) slightly tainted; (*coll*) drunk; (*sl*) exhilarated by drugs; **h. and dry** stranded; abandoned; helpless; **h. and low** everywhere; **h. colour** ruddy complexion; **H. Court** supreme court of justice; **h. explosive** very powerful explosive; **h. living** expensive way of life, luxury; **h. noon** exactly noon; **H. Priest** chief priest, *esp* in Judaism; **ride the h. horse** behave arrogantly; **H. School** type of grammar school; **h. seas** all sea beyond territorial waters; **h. street** main street; **h. table** table on dais where senior members of college *etc* dine; **h. tea** late tea with meat, fish *etc*; **h. tension** high voltage; **h. tide** maximum height of tide; time when this is reached; (*fig*) climax, greatest extent; **h. time** time when something urgently needs doing; **h. words** angry words ~ **high** *adv* to or at a high level or degree; intensely; at high pitch; for high stakes ~ **high** *n* high degree; high place; (*mot*) high gear; (*meteor*) anticyclone; **on h.** aloft; in Heaven.

highball [*hí*bawl] *n* (*US*) whisky or brandy and soda.

highbinder [*hí*bInder] *n* (*US sl*) gangster.

highborn [*hí*bawrn] *adj* of noble birth.

highbrow [*hí*bRow] *n* and *adj* (*coll, freq cont*) intellectual.

highchair [*hí*chair] *n* baby's chair with tray attached.

High Church [hí-*church*] *adj* of or pertaining to that party in the Church of England which gives great importance to ritual, the sacraments, the episcopacy *etc* ~ **High-Churchman** *n.*

high-class [hí-klaas] *adj* of best quality, excellent.

highday [*hí*day] *n* festival.

highfalutin [hífalOOtin] *adj* (*coll*) ridiculously pompous.

high-fidelity [hí-fídeliti] *adj* achieving approximately exact sound-reproduction by using wide range of sound waves.

high-flier [hí-*flí*-er] *n* one who goes to extremes; ambitious or potentially successful person.

highflown [*hí*flOn] *adj* (*of style*) bombastic.

high-frequency [hí-*free*kwensi] *adj* (*elect*) having a frequency between 3 and 30 megacycles per second.

high-grade [hí-gRayd] *adj* of high quality.

high-handed [hí-*hand*id] *adj* domineering, arbitrary.

high-hat [hí-hat] *adj* and *n* (*US*) snobbish (person) ~ **high-hat** *v/t* treat superciliously, patronize.

high-jump [hí-jump] *n* athletic contest in jumping high; **for the h.** (*sl*) due to be hanged; on trial on capital charge.

highland [*hí*land] *n* mountainous region; **the Highlands** the mountainous part of Scotland ~ **Highland** *adj* pertaining to the Highlands ~ **Highlander** *n* native of the Highlands; soldier in Highland regiment.

high-life [hí-líf] *n* social life of aristocrats and the rich.

highlight [*hí*lIt] *n* best or most conspicuous part; reflection of light on shiny object; part of painting *etc* possessing the most intense light ~ **highlight** *v/t* illuminate brightly; (*fig*) make prominent, emphasize.

highly [*hí*li] *adv* in or to a high degree.

highly-strung [híli-*strung*] *adj* easily upset or over-excited.

highminded [hímíndid] *adj* having fine ideals or principles, noble; (*ar*) proud ~ **high-mindedly** *adv* ~ **high-mindedness** *n.*

highness [*hí*nis] *n* quality of being high; title of honour given to royal persons.

high-pitched [hí-*picht*] *adj* shrill; (*of roof*) steep; (*fig*) lofty, aspiring.

high-powered [hí-powrd] *adj* having great power, abilities, importance, or energy.

high-pressure [hí-*pResh*er] *adj* driven by great pressure of steam, water *etc*; to be used under high-pressure conditions; (*fig*) carried out at great speed or with great energy; forceful.

high-principled [hí-*pRin*sip'ld] *adj* honourable.

high-rise [hí-RIZ] *adj* (*of buildings*) having many storeys ~ **high-riser** *n* skyscraper.

highroad [*hí*ROd] *n* main road; (*fig*) easiest or most direct way.

high-sounding [hɪ-*sownding*] *adj* (*of style*) impressive, pompous.

high-spirited [hɪ-*spɪ*Ritid] *adj* gallant, brave; lively, gay; (*of horse*) mettlesome, frisky.

high-stepper [hɪ-*steper*] *n* horse which lifts its feet high; (*fig*) distinguished, brilliant person.

hight [hɪt] *adj* (*ar*) named.

high-up [hɪ-up] *n* and *adj* (*coll*) (person) of great importance or high rank.

highwater [hɪ*wawter*] *n* high tide; **h. mark** furthest point reached by water at high tide; (*fig*) moment of greatest development, success *etc*.

highway [hɪ*way*] *n* public road; main road; (*fig*) easiest or most direct way.

highwayman [hɪ*wayman*] *n* one who robs travellers by road, *esp* a mounted robber.

hijack [hɪjak] *v/t* (*coll*) steal by force; steal a vehicle or aircraft and its load; force an aircraft pilot to change course and convey the hijacker to the destination he demands; hold an aircraft's passengers or crew to ransom; steal (liquor) from bootlegger; doublecross ~ **hijacker** *n*.

hijinks [hɪjinks] *n* (*pl*) (*US*) high jinks.

hike [hɪk] *n* (*coll*) long country walk; walking tour ~ **hike** *v/i* go on a hike ~ **hiker** *n* ~ **hiking** *adj* and *n*.

hilarious [hɪlair*Ri*-us] *adj* very merry, rowdily cheerful; extremely funny ~ **hilariously** *adv* ~ **hilariousness** *n*.

hilarity [hɪla*Riti*] *n* mirth, cheerfulness.

hill [hɪl] *n* elevated portion of earth's surface which is lower than a mountain; small artificial mound; **old as the hills** immemorial.

hillbilly [hɪl*bili*] *adj* and *n* (*US coll*) (pertaining to) a backwoodsman or mountain farmer; (of or in) a style of song characteristic of these.

hillock [hɪl*ok*] *n* small hill; small heap of earth.

hillside [hɪls*ɪd*] *n* slope of a hill.

hilltop [hɪl*top*] *n* top of a hill.

hilly [hɪli] *adj* having many hills ~ **hilliness** *n*.

hilt [hɪlt] *n* handle of sword or dagger; **up to the h.** as far as possible, completely.

hilum [hɪl*um*] *n* (*bot*) scar on seed coat where it was joined to seed-case; (*physiol*) small opening or depression.

him [him] *personal pron objective case of* **he**.

himself [him*self*] *pron refl* and *emph* that very man; his usual or normal self.

hind (1) [hɪnd] *n* female red deer.

hind (2) *n* (*ar*) farm servant, peasant; (*dial*) skilled farm-workman; bailiff.

hind (3) *adj* in or at the back, posterior.

hinder (1) [hɪnder] *adj* in or at the back, posterior.

hinder (2) [hinder] *v/t* and *i* impede, prevent, obstruct; act as impediment.

Hindi [hɪndi] *n* and *adj* (language) of northern and central India; official language of India.

hindmost [hɪnd*mOst*] *n* and *adj* (one who or that which is) farthest in the rear.

hindquarter [hɪnd*kwawrter*] *n* hind leg and loin of meat carcass; (*pl*) posterior, rump.

hindrance [hind*Rans*] *n* one who or that which hinders, obstruction; act of hindering.

hindsight [hɪnds*ɪt*] *n* ability to judge or understand an event correctly after its results have become known; back sight of gun.

Hindu [hind*OO*] *n* member of an Aryan non-Muslim people in India; one who professes Hinduism ~ **Hindu** *adj*.

Hinduism [hind*OO*-izm] *n* Indian religion based on the Vedas; the cults of Vishnu, Krishna, Siva, Rama, *etc*.

Hindustani [hind*OOstaani*] *n* and *adj* (native) of Hindustan; (language) of Hindustan, being Hindi with an admixture of other languages.

hinge [hinj] *n* joint on which door, lid *etc* hangs and turns; (*fig*) that on which something depends, cardinal point ~ **hinge** *v/t* and *i* provide hinges for; turn on a hinge; (*fig*) depend on.

hinny [hini] *n* offspring of stallion and she-ass.

hint [hint] *n* slight or indirect suggestion; brief and useful advice ~ **hint** *v/t* and *i*.

hinterland [hinterland] *n* district behind coastland or seaport > PDG.

hip (1) [hip] *n* projecting part of body formed by upper thigh-bone and side of pelvis, haunch; (*bui*) junction of two sides of roof; **h. and thigh** mercilessly; **on the h.** at a disadvantage.

hip (2) *n* fruit of rosebush.

hip (3) *interj* signal twice used to introduce a united cheer.

hip (4) *n* (*coll*) melancholy ~ **hip** (*pres/part* **hipping**, *p/t* and *p/part* **hipped**) *v/t* depress, make gloomy ~ **hipped** *adj* depressed, bored.

hip (5) *adj* (*sl*) hep, up-to-date.

hip-bath [hip-baath] *n* portable bath in which one can sit but not lie.

hippidom, hippydom [hipidum] *n* (*sl*) the way of life of a hippy.

hippo [hipO] *n* (*coll*) hippopotamus.

hippo- *pref* horse, horse-like.

hippocampus (*pl* **hippocampi**) [hipo*kampus*] *n* small fish with horse-like head.

hippocras [hipo*kRas*] *n* a cordial; spiced wine.

Hippocratic [hipo*kRatik*] *adj* of Hippocrates; **H. oath** oath to observe medical code of ethics.

hippodrome [hipo*dROm*] *n* variety-theatre; arena for horse-shows, show-jumping *etc*; (*hist*) arena for chariot racing.

hippogriff [hipo*gRif*] *n* fabulous monster, part griffin and part horse.

hippopotamus (*pl* **hippopotami**) [hipo*potamus*] *n* large amphibious African quadruped.

hippy [hipi] *n* one who seeks mystic experience through psychedelic drugs, preaches love and happiness, and avoids conventional work and political involvement; person of unconventional, Bohemian appearance or behaviour ~ **hippy** *adj*.

hipster [hipster] *adj* (*of clothes*) held by a belt round hips, not at waist.

hircine [hurs*ɪn*] *adj* of or like a goat, *esp* in smell.

hire [hɪr] *v/t* engage services of a person for payment; obtain use or temporary possession of something for payment; **h. out** lend in exchange for payment ~ **hire** *n* act of hiring; payment made in hiring; rights acquired by hiring ~ **hirer** *n*.

hireling [hɪr-ling] *n* one who works only for the sake of wages; a mercenary person.

hire-purchase [hɪr-*purchis*] *n* contract to pay for something by instalments with right of use after first payment ~ **hire-purchase** *adj*.

hirsute [hurs*ewt*] *adj* hairy.

his [hiz] *possessive pron* and *adj* belonging to him.

Hispanic [hispanik] *adj* Spanish.

hispid [hispid] *adj* (*bot, zool*) bristly.

hiss [*his*] *v/i* and *t* make prolonged sound similar to that of *s*; express scorn or rage by this sound; express disapproval of (actor *etc*) by hissing ~ **hiss** *n* noise made by hissing ~ **hissing** *n* and *adj*.

hist [*hist*] *interj* (*ar*) listen!; hush!

histamine [*histameen*] *n* (*med*) drug tending to lower the blood-pressure; (*biol*) one of the bases in body tissue.

histo- *pref* of or relating to organic tissue.

histogram [*histOgRam*] *n* (*stat*) diagram which shows a frequency distribution.

histological [*histoloJikal*] *adj* of histology.

histologist [*histolojist*] *n* student of histology.

histology [*histoloji*] *n* branch of anatomy which deals with the structure of tissues.

historian [*histawRi-an*] *n* student of history; writer of a history.

historiated [*histawRi-aytid*] *adj* adorned with figures (*eg* flowers, animals *etc*) having significance; provided with maps, charts, pictures as historical background material.

historic [*histoRik*] *adj* pertaining to history; recorded in history; associated with some notable event; famous; likely to become famous, epoch-making.

historical [*histoRikal*] *adj* true to facts of history, authentic; pertaining to the science of history; based on or suggested by history; tracing or explaining a development; **h. present** (*gramm*) present tense used with reference to past events ~ **historically** *n*.

historicity [*histoRisiti*] *n* fidelity to facts of history, authenticity.

historiographer [*histoRi-ogRafer*] *n* writer of a history; official historian.

history [*histeRi*] *n* chronological record or narrative of past events; series of past events in the existence of a nation, individual, institution *etc*; growth and development of a system of ideas, art, language *etc*; methodical account of this; historical play; story; **make h.** do something important and memorable; establish a precedent; **natural h.** zoology; botany.

histrionic [*histRi-onik*] *adj* pertaining to actors or acting, dramatic; melodramatic, theatrical; insincere ~ **histrionically** *adv*.

histrionics [*histRi-oniks*] *n* (*pl*) technique of acting; insincere display of emotion.

hit (*pres/part* **hitting**, *p/t* and *p/part* **hit**) [*hit*] *v/t* and *i* strike, knock, give a blow to; reach (a target); (*sl*) go to or along (road *etc*); find by chance; injure; be hard h. suffer; **h. it guess** accurately; (*sl*) go away; **h. off** describe briefly and accurately; imitate; sketch rapidly; **h. it off with** suit, get on well with; **h. it up** (*sl*) behave riotously; **h. on** (**upon**) find by chance or unexpectedly; **h. out** strike vigorously, attack strongly; **h. the hay** (*sl*) go to bed; **h. the trail** (*sl*) go away, leave ~ **hit** *n* blow, stroke; act of hitting; sarcastic remark, joke or taunt; (*coll*) popular success; piece of good luck; **make a h. with** impress favourably ~ **hit** *adj* (*coll*) very popular, highly successful.

hitch [*hich*] *v/t* and *i* pull up, lift or move abruptly; fasten by a hook; fasten loosely; harness; become fastened or entangled; (*sl*) fit in with; **get on well with**; (*coll*) ask for a lift in car, lorry *etc* ~ **hitch** *n* act of hitching; slight obstacle

or impediment; kind of temporary knot; jerky movement; limp ~ **hitched** *adj* (*sl*) married.

hitchhike [*hich-hIk*] *v/i* travel by asking for lifts in cars or lorries ~ **hitchhiker** *n*.

hither [*hiTHer*] *adv* to or towards this place; **h. and thither** in various directions ~ **hither** *adj* nearer, on this side.

hitherto [*hiTHertOO*] *adv* up to this time; until now.

hitherward [*hiTHerwerd*] *adv* (*ar*) hither.

hit-or-miss [*hit-awr-mis*] *adj* haphazard, casual.

hitter [*hiter*] *n* person who hits.

hive [*hIv*] *n* receptacle in which bees are kept; colony of bees living in a hive; busy and crowded place ~ **hive** *v/t* and *i* gather (bees) into a hive; store (honey) in a hive; live in or enter a hive; **h. off** (*comm*) allocate production to a subsidiary company; transfer to a sub-unit within an organization.

hives [*hIvz*] *n* (*pl*) rash, skin eruption; croup.

h'm see **hem** (2).

ho [*hO*] *interj* exclamation of surprise; cry to attract attention.

hoar [*hawr*] *adj* covered with hoarfrost; (*ar*) grey-haired; white; venerable ~ **hoar** *n* hoarfrost.

hoard [*hawrd*] *n* accumulated store; secret store; treasure; large amount ~ **hoard** *v/t* and *i* amass large quantities of; gather and keep secretly; (*fig*) cherish secretly ~ **hoarder** *n*.

hoarding (1) [*hawrding*] *n* act of person who hoards; hidden store (of money *etc*).

hoarding (2) *n* high wooden fence; high fence on which posters are displayed.

hoarfrost [*hawrfRost*] *n* deposit of ice crystals on objects near the ground, frozen dew > PDG.

hoarhound see **horehound**.

hoariness [*hawRines*] *n* state of being hoary.

hoarse [*haws*] *adj* husky, raucous ~ **hoarsely** *adv* ~ **hoarseness** *n*.

hoarstone [*hawrstOn*] *n* boundary stone; memorial stone; a standing stone.

hoary [*hawRi*] *adj* grey, *esp* through age; grey- or white-haired; (*fig*) ancient; (*bot*) covered with short white hairs.

hoax [*hOks*] *n* deception meant as a joke; practical joke ~ **hoax** *v/t* trick, play a practical joke upon ~ **hoaxer** *n*.

hob (1) [*hob*] *n* low ledge beside a fireplace on which things may be kept hot.

hob (2) *n* hobgoblin, imp.

hobbit [*hobit*] *n* one of an imaginary race of dwarfs in the novels of J. R. R. Tolkien.

hobble [*hob'l*] *v/i* and *t* limp, walk clumsily; fasten two legs of a horse together to check its movements; (*fig*) be clumsy or inefficient ~ **hobble** *n* clumsy walk, limp; rope used for hobbling horses; **h. skirt** very narrow skirt which impedes movement ~ **hobblingly** *adv*.

hobbledehoy [*hob'ldihoi*] *n* clumsy, bad-mannered youth.

hobby (1) [*hobi*] *n* favourite pastime, spare-time occupation done for pleasure; hobbyhorse.

hobby (2) *n* small kind of falcon.

hobbyhorse [*hobihawrs*] *n* child's toy consisting of a wooden horsehead on a stick; rocking-horse; draped and horse-headed wicker framework worn by a mummer at folk festivals; (*fig*) favourite theme; fixed idea, fad.

hobgoblin [hobgoblin] *n* mischievous imp or fairy; bugbear, bogy.

hobnail [*hob*nayl] *n* large-headed nail used for studding soles of boots; **h. liver** (*med*) form of cirrhosis of the liver ~ **hobnailed** *adj* studded with hobnails; (*fig*) rustic, boorish.

hobnob (*pres/part* **hobnobbing**, *p/t* and *p/part* **hobnobbed**) [*hob*nob] *v/i* be on friendly terms; drink together; chat ~ **hobnob** *n* (*sl*) friendly chat.

hobo [*hO*bO] *n* (*US*) tramp; migratory worker.

Hobson's choice [hobsonz-*chois*] *n* either what is offered, or nothing.

hock (1) [*hok*] *n* joint in the hind leg of a quadruped between knee and fetlock; joint of meat cut immediately above the foot; (*human anat*) back of the knee ~ **hock** *v/t* hamstring.

hock (2) *n* a German white wine.

hock (3) *v/t* (*US sl*) pawn, pledge ~ **hock** *n* (*US sl*) in h. pawned; in prison.

hockey [*hok*i] *n* team-game in which a ball is struck with curved sticks towards opposing goals.

hocus [*hO*kus] *v/t* cheat; drug, stupefy ~ **hocus** *n* drugged drink.

hocus-pocus [*hO*kus-*pO*kus] *n* trickery, deception; mystifying jargon; nonsense.

hod [*hod*] *n* (*bui*) long-handled tray, shaped like a box cut diagonally in two, for carrying bricks *etc* on the shoulder; cylindrical coal-scuttle.

hodden [*hod*en] *n* (*Scots*) coarse undyed woollen cloth; **h. grey** hodden cloth of mixed black and white wool.

hodge-podge see hotchpotch.

hodman [*hod*man] *n* bricklayer's assistant.

hodometer [ho*dom*iter] *n* instrument attached to wheel of vehicle to measure distance covered.

hodoscope [*hod*OskOp] *n* (*phys*) instrument for tracing the path of a charged particle.

hoe [*hO*] *n* (*hort*) tool for breaking up surface soil, destroying weeds, *etc* ~ **hoe** *v/t* and *i* uproot or break up with a hoe; use a hoe.

hoedown [*hO*down] *n* (*US*) party at which there is country dancing.

hog [*hog*] *n* pig raised for slaughter; castrated pig; (*dial*) hogget; (*fig*) greedy, bad-mannered or filthy person; (*mech*) upward bend > PDE, **go the whole h.** do something thoroughly; **road h.** reckless or inconsiderate motorist ~ **hog** (*pres/part* **hogging**, *p/t* and *p/part* **hogged**) *v/t* and *i* behave greedily; (*coll*) take for oneself; **arch** (the back); **h. it** (*sl*) live in rough or dirty surroundings; sleep heavily.

hogback, hogsback [*hog*bak, *hogz*bak] *n* ridge with sharp crest > PDG; (*arch*) ancient stone shaped like a hog's back.

hogg, hogget [*hog*, *hog*et] *n* yearling sheep.

hoggish [*hog*ish] *adj* like a hog; greedy; selfish; dirty ~ **hoggishly** *adv* ~ **hoggishness** *n*.

hogmanay [*hog*manay] *n* (*Scots*) New Year's Eve; festivities held then.

hogshead [*hogz*-hed] *n* large cask; liquid measure equal to 52½ imperial gallons, or 54 gallons in the case of beer and cider.

hogskin [*hog*skin] *n* leather made from hog's skin.

hogwash [*hog*wosh] *n* swill given as food to pigs; (*coll*) cheap talk or writing; (*sl*) bad-quality liquor.

hoick [*hoik*] *v/t* and *i* raise or rise abruptly, jerk up.

hoicks [*hoik*s] *interj* hunting cry to encourage hounds.

hoi polloi [hoi-po*loi*] *n* (*Gk*) (*pej*) the masses.

hoist [*hoist*] *v/t* raise with difficulty, heave; raise by means of tackle ~ **hoist** *n* act of hoisting; device for hoisting, lifting tackle > PDE ~ **hoist** *adj* (*ar*) hoisted; **h. with one's own petard** caught in a trap one had designed to catch others.

hoity-toity [hoiti-*toit*i] *adj* arrogant; irritable; fastidious ~ **hoity-toity** *interj* exclamation of reproof to one showing arrogance, temper, or fastidiousness.

hokey-pokey [hOki-*pO*ki] *n* cheap ice-cream.

hokum [*hO*kum] *n* (*US coll*) crude sentimentality or melodrama.

hold (1) (*p/t* and *p/part* **held**) [*hOld*] *v/t* and *i* grasp or support with the hand; keep in the hand; grip, retain; support, sustain; keep in place; own, have possession of; (*mil*) occupy, maintain against attack; keep in one's charge; contain, enclose; have the capacity to contain; keep in mind; maintain (opinion); consider, regard; believe, think; restrain, control; keep the attention of; organize, cause to take place (a meeting *etc*); withstand strain; remain fixed; continue; be valid, remain in force; **h. back** restrain, hesitate; **h. by** be guided by; maintain, stick to; **h. down** keep (job *etc*) in spite of difficulties; **h. forth** speak at length; proffer; **h. good** be true, be valid; **h. hard!** wait! go slowly!; **h. in** restrain; **h. it!** (*coll*) stay as you are! don't move!; **h. off** keep at a distance; prevent from attacking; delay; remain aloof; **h. on** cling, grip; endure, persist among difficulties; (*tel*) keep the connexion; **h. on!** (*coll*) stop! wait!; **h. one's own** maintain one's position *etc* against attack or competition; **h. one's tongue** (*ar peace*) remain silent; **h. out** offer; maintain resistance, endure; last; **h. out on** (*coll*) keep secrets from; **h. over** postpone; use as threat; **h. to** keep to, abide by; **h. up** exhibit; (*coll*) delay, cause stoppage of; (*coll*) stop by threat of force, in order to rob; rob at gunpoint; **h. them up!** put your hands above your head; **h. water** be consistent, be logically acceptable; **h. with** approve of ~ **hold** *n* act of holding; something to which one can hold; (*fig*) control, authority; influence; understanding; method of holding, *esp* in wrestling; fortress, stronghold; **get h. of** obtain, find, get in touch with; influence unduly; **have a h. over** have means of dominating, blackmailing *etc*; **no holds barred** even unfair methods allowed.

hold (2) *n* (*naut*) space below deck in which cargo is stored.

holdall [*hOld*awl] *n* capacious portable case or bag.

holder [*hOl*der] *n* one who holds; that which holds or contains; protective cloth for handling hot saucepans, kettles *etc*; tenant; possessor.

holderbat [*hol*derbat] *n* (*bui*) a fixing for holding a pipe to a wall or soffit.

holdfast [*hOld*faast] *n* something which one can hold on to; something which holds things together; clamp; (*bot*) sucker.

holding [*hOl*ding] *n* act of one who holds; tenure of land; piece of land or investment held.

hold-up [*hOld*up] *n* delay in traffic; stoppage; robbery at gunpoint.

hole [*hOl*] *n* cavity, empty space or depression in solid body; pit, excavation; gap, opening, perforation; burrow; rent, tear; outlet; inlet; (*coll*) awkward situation, dilemma; (*coll*) small dingy house or room; dull place; (*golf*) small pit into which players must drive ball; point scored by being first to do so; (*elect*) mobile electron vacancy in a semiconductor which acts as a charge carrier; **h. in the heart** an opening in the internal dividing wall of the heart; **make a h. in** (*sl*) consume a large part of; **pick holes in** find faults or flaws in ~ **hole** *v/t* and *i* make a hole or holes in or through; drive into a hole; **h. out** (*golf*) get ball into hole; **h. up** hide oneself, lurk.

hole-and-corner [hOl-and-*kaw*rner] *adj* furtive, underhand.

holey [*hO*li] *adj* (*coll*) full of holes.

holiday [*hol*iday] *n* day or period of rest from work; day or period of recreation and amusement, festival; (*eccles*) festival commemorating important religious event or person; (*pl*) period during which schools are closed; **Bank H.** general statutory holiday throughout England; **H. of Obligation** (*RC*) day on which Catholics are bound to hear Mass and rest from work ~ ~ **holiday** *adj* festive, gay; smart ~ **holiday** *v/i* take a holiday.

holiday-maker [holiday-*may*ker] *n* person taking a holiday elsewhere than at home; tripper.

holily [*hO*lili] *adv* in a holy way.

holiness [*hO*linis] *n* quality of being holy, sanctity; **His H.** title of the Pope; title of Bishop of Eastern Church.

holism [*hO*lizm] *n* (*philos*) theory concerning natural tendency of groups of units to form themselves into wholes.

holistic [hO*lis*tik] *adj* relating to organic and functional relations between parts and a whole.

holla, hollo [*hol*a, hol*O*] *interj* (*obs*) cry to attract attention; exclamation of surprise or greeting.

holland [*hol*and] *n* kind of coarse linen.

hollandaise [holand*ayz*] *n* type of creamy sauce for fish, vegetables *etc*.

Hollander [*hol*ander] *n* Dutchman; Dutch ship.

Hollands [*hol*andz] *n* kind of Dutch gin.

holler [*hol*er] *v/t* and *i* (*coll*) yell.

hollo see **holla.**

hollow [*hol*O] *n* concave place, depression, shallow pit; hole; groove; small valley ~ **hollow** *adj* having the interior empty, not solid; having a depression in it, sunken; (*ac*) echoing; muffled; (*fig*) insincere, false; insubstantial; unreal; (*coll*) hungry ~ **hollow** *adv* in a hollow way; **to beat h.** (*coll*) defeat thoroughly ~ **hollow** *v/t* make hollow, scoop out.

hollow-eyed [*hol*O-Id] *adj* with sunken eyes, haggard.

hollowly [*hol*Oli] *adv* in a hollow way ~ **hollowness** *n.*

hollow-ware [*hot*O-wair] *n* hollow kitchen utensils made of metal.

holly [*hol*i] *n* evergreen shrub with glossy prickly leaves and red berries.

hollyhock [*hol*ihok] *n* tall garden flowering plant.

holm [*hOm*] *n* island in a river; piece of flat land near a river.

holmium [*hol*mi-um] *n* (*chem*) rare lanthanide element > PDS.

holm-oak [*hOm*-Ok] *n* evergreen oak, ilex.

holo- *pref* entire; (*geol*) relating to recent strata.

holocaust [*hol*Okawst] *n* great slaughter, massacre; sacrifice entirely consumed by fire.

hologram [*hol*Ogram] *n* image or pattern produced by holography.

holograph [*hol*Ograaf] *n* and *adj* (document) wholly in the handwriting of the signatory.

holography [holo*gRa*fi] *n* (*phot*) method of producing three-dimensional images from wavefronts of reflected light.

hols [holz] *n* (*pl*) (*coll*) school holidays.

holster [*hOl*ster] *n* leather pistol case.

holt [*hOlt*] *n* (*ar*) small wood, copse.

holy [*hO*li] *adj* sacred, pertaining to God; held in religious awe; saintly, free from sin; pious; connected with religion; **H. Father** the Pope; **H. Ghost** Third Person of the Trinity, the Paraclete; **H. Land** Israel; **h. terror** (*coll*) exasperating person; frightening person; **h. war** war conducted for religious motives; **h. water** water blessed by a priest and used as a sacramental; **H. Week** week immediately preceding Easter Sunday; **H. Writ** the Bible ~ **holy** *n* holy place; **H. of Holies** innermost chamber of Jewish Tabernacle; (*fig*) very sacred place.

holy-day [*hO*li-day] *n* religious festival.

holystone [*hO*listOn] *n* sandstone used for scouring decks of ships ~ **holystone** *v/t.*

homage [*hom*ij] *n* allegiance; respect, reverence; act symbolizing this; (*hist*) ceremony whereby a man declared himself the vassal of another.

homburg [*hom*burg] *n* felt hat for men.

home [*hOm*] *n* house where one lives; house of one's parents; place where one was born; occupants of a house, family; native country; institution caring for the sick, old, poor *etc*; small private hospital; haunt, usual habitat; (*games*) goal; base; **at h.** in one's own house; willing to receive visitors; at ease; **make oneself at h.** act without formality; **nothing to write h. about** not exciting ~ **home** *adj* pertaining to home, domestic; **H. Counties** counties nearest to London; **H. Guard** reserve force of part-time volunteers organized for local defence; **h. help** woman sent by welfare service to do housework or shopping for invalids and old people; **H. Office** Government department dealing with domestic affairs; **H. Rule** self-government; **h. town** town where one was born and brought up; **h. truths** true but unpleasant remarks about one's character or behaviour ~ **home** *adv* towards home; to its right place; as far as it will go; **bring h. to** cause (someone) to realize fully or feel deeply ~ **home** *v/i* find one's way home; **h. on to** (*of missiles*) be automatically guided towards (target) by heat *etc* emitted by the latter.

homebird [*hOm*burd] *n* person who enjoys living at home.

homecoming [*hOm*kuming] *n* arrival home.

homefarm [*hOm*faarm] *n* farm attached to residence of owner of estate.

homeland [*hOm*land] *n* native land; land in which one lives.

homeless [*hOm*les] *adj* having no home of one's own; living in bad temporary accommodation.

homely [*hOm*li] *adj* like home; simple, familiar, unpretentious; (*US, of persons*), plain, not beautiful ~ **homeliness** [*hOm*lines] *n*.

home-made [*hOm*-mayd] *adj* made, cooked *etc* at home; made, cooked *etc* individually or in small batches, not mass-produced.

homeo- *pref* the same, like.

homeopath see **homoeopath**.

homeostasis [hOmi-O*stay*sis] *n* (*biol, psych*) force enabling an individual to maintain physical or psychological stability despite conflicts in the external environment.

homeotherapy see **homoeotherapy**.

homer (1) [*hOm*er] *n* Hebrew measure of capacity, about 80 gallons.

homer (2) *n* homing pigeon.

Homeric [hO*me*Rik] *adj* pertaining to the Greek poet Homer; epic, heroic; loud (laughter).

homesick [*hOm*sik] *adj* filled with longing for home ~ **homesickness** *n*.

homespun [*hOm*spun] *adj* (*of cloth*) handwoven at home; (*fig*) simple, homely, unsophisticated ~ **homespun** *n* handwoven cloth.

homestead [*hOm*sted] *n* large house with outbuildings; home.

homesters [*hOm*sterz] *n* (*games coll*) team playing on their own ground.

homestretch [*hOm*stRech] *n* part of race-track between last bend and finishing post.

home-thrust [*hOm*-thRust] *n* thrust with a weapon which is driven right in; (*fig*) pointed remark that wounds deeply.

homeward(s) [*hOm*werd(z)] *adv* towards home.

homework [*hOm*wurk] *n* work to be done by pupil after school hours; (*fig*) essential research or study in preparation for a discussion *etc*.

homey see **homy**.

homicidal [homis*I*dal] *adj* of or like homicide; murderous; liable to commit homicide ~ **homicidally** *adv*.

homicide [*homis*Id] *n* the killing of one human being by another; one who kills a human being.

homiletic [homi*let*ik] *adj* of or like a homily ~ **homiletics** *n* (*pl*) art of preaching.

homilist [*hom*ilist] *n* writer of homilies.

homily [*hom*ili] *n* sermon, religious or moral discourse; (*fig*) tedious lecture.

homing [*hOm*ing] *n* tendency or ability of certain animals to return home from long distances ~ **homing** *adj* returning home; trained to return home; (*mil, of missile*) having a self-steering device guiding it towards target.

homini- *pref* pertaining to man.

hominid [*hom*inid] *n* (*zool*) member of the family comprising man and man-like fossils; (*coll*) ape-like man; semi-human creature.

hominy [*hom*ini] *n* dish of boiled maize.

homo (1) [*hom*O] *n* (*zool*) member of the genus whose only living representative is man > PDB.

homo (2) *n* and *adj* (*sl, pej*) homosexual.

homo-, homoeo- *pref* the same, of the same kind.

homodont [*hom*Odont] *n* and *adj* (animal) having teeth all of the same kind.

homoeomorphous [hOmi-O*mawr*fus] *adj* of similar structure; of identical crystalline formation.

homoeopath, homeopath [*hOm*i-O*path*] *n* one who treats diseases by minute doses of substances which would produce the disease in healthy persons ~ **homoeopathic** [hOmi-O*path*ik] *adj* ~ **homoeopathy** [hOmi-*o*pathi] *n*.

homoeotherapy, homeotherapy [hOmi-O*the*Rapi] *n* treatment by homoeopathic methods.

homogamous [ho*mog*amus] *adj* (*bot*) having flowers whose male and female parts mature simultaneously.

homogeneity [homoje*nee*-iti] *n* quality or state of being homogeneous.

homogeneous [homO*jeen*i-us] *adj* composed of similar constituents throughout; (*math*) commensurable ~ **homogeneously** *adv* ~ **homogeneousness** *n*.

homogenize [ho*moj*enIz] *v/t* make homogeneous; make more uniform by breaking down and blending the particles of.

homogeny [ho*moj*ini] *n* similarity of organs in different species indicative of common ancestry.

homograph [*hom*OgRaaf] *n* one of two or more words having the same spelling but different meanings.

homographic [homOg*Raf*ik] *adj* of homography.

homography [ho*mog*Rafi] *n* system of spelling in which a separate symbol is used for each sound.

homologous [ho*mol*ogus] *adj* similar, corresponding in structure, position, composition *etc* > PDB, PDS.

homologue [*hom*olog] *n* that which is homologous.

homology [ho*mol*oji] *n* state of being homologous.

homonym [*hom*onim] *n* one of two or more words having the same sound but different meanings; a namesake.

homonymic, homonymous [homo*nim*ik, ho*mon*imus] *adj* having the same name; of or like a homonym.

homophilia [homo*fil*i-a] *n* emotional but non-physical affection for persons of one's own sex.

homophone [*hom*ofOn] *n* homonym; one of two or more letters or symbols expressing the same sound.

homophonic, homophonous [homo*fon*ik, ho*mof*onus] *adj* of or like a homophone; (*mus*) pertaining to homophony.

homophony [ho*mof*oni] *n* (*mus*) having parts that move together, not polyphonic or contrapuntal > PDM.

homosexual [homo*sek*sew-al] *n* and *adj* (one) sexually or emotionally attracted to persons of one's own sex > PDP ~ **homosexually** *adv*.

homosexuality [homoseksew-*al*iti] *n* state or quality of being homosexual.

homuncule [ho*mung*kewl] *n* tiny man, dwarf.

homy, homey [*hOm*i] *adj* of or like home; comfortable; welcoming, friendly.

hone [*hOn*] *n* whetstone ~ **hone** *v/t* sharpen.

honest [*on*est] *adj* trustworthy, not given to lying, stealing, or cheating; frank, sincere; not criminal; fair, impartial; conscientious; (*obs, of women*) chaste; make an h. woman (of) marry one's mistress ∼ **honestly** adv.

honest-to-goodness [onest-tOO-goodnis] adj (coll) genuine.

honesty [onesti] n quality of being honest; garden plant with decorative seedpods.

honey [huni] n sweet sticky fluid made by bees from nectar; (fig) anything soothing; (coll) darling; (coll) anything delightful ∼ **honey** adj of, like, or producing honey.

honeybee [hunibee] n bee which gathers and stores honey.

honeycomb [hunikOm] n structure of hexagonal wax cells made by bees to hold honey or larvae; hexagonal pattern; anything pierced by hexagonal holes ∼ **honeycomb** v/t pierce with many holes, riddle; undermine.

honeydew [huni-dew] n sweet sticky substance secreted by aphides and found on plants; (poet) ambrosia; kind of sweetened tobacco.

honeyed [hunid] adj covered with honey; sweetened with honey; (fig) flattering; coaxing.

honeymoon [hunimOOn] n holiday spent together by a newly-married couple; (fig) period of untroubled happiness ∼ **honeymoon** v/i.

honeysuckle [hunisuk'l] n climbing shrub with fragrant yellow flowers.

honk [honk] n sound made by horn of motor vehicle; cry of wild goose ∼ **honk** v/i.

honky-tonk [honki-tonk] n (US sl) disreputable club or roadhouse; ragtime music.

honorarium [oneRairRi-um] n voluntary payment for professional services.

honorary [oneRiRi] adj conferred as an honour; pertaining to honour; holding office without payment; (of post etc) without payment.

honorific [oneRifik] adj conferring honour.

honour [oner] n good reputation, integrity; standard of ideal qualities admired in a particular social group; quick resentment of insults or offences; nobility of character, high-mindedness; (of women) reputation for chastity; respect, reverence, esteem; high rank; something conferred as mark of esteem; act of courtesy; compliment; (pl) acts expressing esteem; specialized university degree; (whist) court cards of trumps; (bridge) court cards and ten of trumps; **h. bright** (coll) truly, without deceit; **debt of h.** debt contracted by betting or gambling; **do the honours** act as host; **maid of h.** one who attends on royal personage; **on one's h.** pledging one's reputation as sign of veracity, obedience etc; binding oneself to behave well without supervision ∼ **honour** v/t confer honour on; respect, esteem; venerate; pay as agreed on; recognize validity of (cheque etc); keep (promise).

honourable [oneRab'l] adj worthy of honour; honest, upright; a courtesy title ∼ **honourably** adv.

hooch [hOOch] n (US sl) bad whisky.

hood [hood] n soft garment covering head and neck, sometimes attached to coat or cloak and hanging from shoulders when not in use; cowl; loose cowl worn with graduate's gown showing degree and university of wearer; collapsible cover of motorcar, perambulator etc; device to prevent escape of fumes from retorts, stoves etc; chimney cowl; canopy over window or door ∼

hood v/t cover with or as with a hood; provide a hood for ∼ **hooded** adj.

hoodie [hoodi] n grey and black crow.

hoodlum [hOOdlum] n (US sl) young tough.

hoodoo [hOOdOO] n one who or that which brings bad luck; bad luck ∼ **hoodoo** v/t cause bad luck to; lay curse on.

hoodwink [hoodwink] v/t cover the eyes of (a horse); blindfold; (fig) dupe, deceive.

hooey [hOO-i] n and interj (US coll) nonsense.

hoof (pl **hoofs, hooves**) [hOOf] n horny sheath protecting feet of certain animals; (joc) human foot; **on the h.** (of cattle) alive ∼ **hoof** v/i **h. it** (sl) walk; dance; **h. out** (sl) kick out; dismiss abruptly ∼ **hoofed, hooved** adj.

hoo-ha [hOO-ha] n (coll) noise; quarrel; fuss.

hook [hook] n metal rod curved at one end used for hanging, holding or catching hold; curved, barbed, and sharpened wire or rod for catching fish; small bent metal fastening for clothes; curved chopper or cutting implement; curved spit of land > PDG; line curved at tip; (games) sideways stroke; **by h. or by crook** by any available method; **go off the hooks** go mad; behave wildly; die; **let off the h.** allow to escape from dilemma or difficult situation; **on one's own h.** on one's own initiative; **sling one's h.** (sl) go away ∼ **hook** v/t and i catch with a hook; fasten, hang or hold by a hook; crook; be fastened by a hook; (fig) capture the affections, attention etc of; (boxing) strike with bent arm; (golf, cricket) strike to the left; (Rugby football) pass ball back with heel in a scrum; **h. it** (sl) go quickly away; **h. on to** attach oneself to, follow; **get hooked on** (sl) become an addict to ∼ **hooked** adj.

hookah [hooka] n Oriental tobacco pipe in which smoke is drawn by a long tube through water.

hooker (1) [hooker] n one who or that which hooks; (US sl) prostitute.

hooker (2) n Dutch two-masted fishing boat; fishing smack; old ship.

hookey, hooky [hooki] n (US coll) truant; **blind h.** a gambling card-game.

hook-up [hook-up] n (rad) temporary connexion enabling radio programmes to be transmitted from more than one station simultaneously.

hookworm [hookwurm] n tropical intestinal parasite of man > PDB.

hooligan [hOOligan] n noisy and violent young man; destructive ruffian ∼ **hooliganism** n wanton destruction and damage to property; noisy voilence without rational motive.

hoop (1) [hOOp] n circular ring of wood or metal, esp to bind casks; large ring used as child's toy; ring of whalebone or wood formerly used to extend women's skirts; metal arch through which ball is driven in croquet; **go through the h.** (coll) have a bad time; be punished ∼ **hoop** v/t bind with a hoop.

hoop (2) n wheezy or hoarse cry ∼ **hoop** v/i.

hooper [hOOper] n maker and repairer of casks, barrels etc.

hooping-cough see **whooping-cough**.

hoop-la [hOOp-laa] n game in which prizes are won by throwing wooden rings over them; (coll) excitement, bustle.

hoopoe [hOOpOO] n a crested bird.

hoor, hooer [*hoor*] *n* (*sl* and *dial*) whore.

hooray [hoo*Ray*] *interj* and *i* hurrah.

hoosgow [*hOO*sgow] *n* (*US sl*) prison.

hoot [*hOOt*] *v/i* and *t* (*of owls*) utter a hollow wavering cry; (*of persons*) utter similar sound, *usu* as sign of hostility or scorn; laugh loudly with a wavering note; (*of motor-horns, sirens etc*) emit a deep hollow whistling note ~ **hoot** *n* hooting cry or note; (*sl*) something very amusing; **not care a h.** not care at all.

hootenanay [hOO*tenani*] *n* (*Scots*) session of folk-dancing and folk-singing.

hooter [*hOOt*er] *n* one who or that which hoots; siren; steam whistle; horn of motorcar.

hoots [*hoots*] *interj* (*Scots*) cry of impatience or disapproval.

hoove [*hOOv*] *n* disease of cattle causing distension of stomach.

Hoover [*hOO*ver] *n* (*tr*) vacuum cleaner ~ **hoover** *v/t* (*coll*) clean with vacuum cleaner.

hooves [*hOOvz*] *pl* of hoof.

hop (1) (*pres/part* **hopping**, *p/t* and *p/part* **hopped**) [*hop*] *v/i* and *t* jump on one leg; advance by series of such jumps; (*of animals*) advance by short leaps, spring lightly; **h. it** (*sl*) go quickly away; **h. the twig** (*sl*) die; evade one's creditors ~ **hop** *n* act of hopping; (*coll*) informal party and dance; (*aer*) one stage of a long-distance flight; **on the h.** very active, restless; (*coll*) unprepared, off guard.

hop (2) *n* plant bearing cones used to flavour beer; cone of this plant ~ **hop** (*pres/part* **hopping**, *p/t* and *p/part* **hopped**) *v/t* and *i* flavour with hops; gather hops; produce hops.

hop (3) (*pres/part* **hopping**, *p/t* and *p/part* **hopped**) *v/t* **h. up** (*sl*) supercharge (car engine).

hop-bine [*hop*-bIn] *n* twining stem of hop (2).

hope [*hOp*] *n* pleasurable and confident expectation; expectation that something desired will happen; probability that something desired may happen; person or thing from whom or which future good is to be expected; (*sl*) expectation which has little chance of fulfilment ~ **hope** *v/i* and *t* expect and desire, feel hope; **h. against h.** go on hoping for what seems impossible.

hopeful [*hOp*fool] *adj* feeling hope; giving good reason to hope, promising; likely to succeed ~ **hopeful** *n* young h. (*joc*) promising young person.

hopefully [*hOp*fooli] *adv* in a hopeful way; (*coll* and *US*) it is hoped that.

hopeless [*hOp*les] *adj* without hope, despairing; giving no ground for hope, desperate; incurable; (*coll*) very inefficient, quite unable to do (a specific thing) ~ **hopelessly** *adv* ~ **hopelessness** *n*.

hoplite [*hop*lIt] *n* (*Gk hist*) heavily-armed foot soldier.

hop-o'-my-thumb [*hop*omithum] *n* a pygmy, dwarf.

hopper (1) [*hop*er] *n* that which hops; funnel through which grain is fed to a mill, coal to a furnace *etc*; self-discharging dredging barge.

hopper (2) *n* hop-picker.

hop-picker [*hop*-piker] *n* one employed to pick hops; machine for picking hops.

hopple [*hop*'l] *n* rope or thong to tie an animal's legs together ~ **hopple** *v/t* hobble, tie the legs of.

hop-pole [*hop*-pOl] *n* long pole supporting growing hops.

hopscotch [*hop*skoch] *n* children's game in which players kick a stone through a series of squares drawn on the ground, while hopping from square to square.

horal [*haw*Ral] *adj* appertaining to an hour or hours ~ **horally** *adv* hourly.

horary [*haw*ReRi] *adj* relating to an hour or hours, marking the hours; hourly; lasting an hour or a short time.

horde [*hawrd*] *n* large destructive crowd or gang; large herd or pack; band of warlike nomads; (*pl*) great numbers, crowds ~ **horde** *v/i* assemble in hordes.

horehound, hoarhound [*hawr*-hownd] *n* plant the juice of which is used for medicinal purposes.

horizon [ho*RI*zon] *n* line bounding observer's view of earth or sea, apparent meeting-place of sky and earth or sea > PDG; (*fig*) limits of thought, interest *etc*; **soil h.** (*geol*) distinctive layer of soil fairly parallel to surface > PDE; **true h.** (*astron*) celestial circle parallel to the apparent horizon.

horizontal [ho*Ri*zontal] *adj* parallel to the horizon, at right angles to the vertical; parallel to the earth's surface, level, flat; **h. bars** bars fixed above and parallel to the floor, used in gymnastics ~ **horizontally** *adv*.

hormonal [hawr*mOn*al] *adj* of, by, or containing a hormone.

hormone [*hawr*mOn] *n* (*physiol*) substance produced in one part of an organism and transported to another, stimulating growth, activity, *etc* > PDB, PDP.

horn [*hawrn*] *n* one of a pair of hard pointed excrescences on heads of cattle, deer, goats *etc*; bony growth on rhinoceros's nose; any natural growth protruding from an animal's head; substance composing horns of cattle, deer *etc*; vessel made of hollowed ox horn; vessel similar to this in shape; curved point or projection; (*vulg coll*) erected penis, erection; hooter, siren, or other device giving out a harsh and hollow note; (*mus*) one of a group of metal wind-instruments > PDM; **draw in one's horns** reduce one's activities, expenditure *etc*; **English h.** oboe of lower pitch > PDM; **make horns** at gesture of extending index and little finger while clenching the others, used as insult or to avert the evil eye; **h. of plenty** cornucopia, symbol of abundance; **wear the horns** (*ar*) be a cuckold ~ **horn** *adj* made of horn ~ **horn** *v/t* provide with horns; gore with horns; **h. in on** (*sl*) intrude, butt in, interfere with.

hornbeam [*hawrn*beem] *n* deciduous hardwood tree.

hornbill [*hawrn*bil] *n* bird having a horny growth above its bill.

hornblende [*hawrn*blend] *n* rock-forming mineral consisting mainly of silicates of calcium, magnesium and iron.

hornbook [*hawrn*book] *n* sheet of paper mounted on wood and protected by transparent sheet of ·horn, showing the alphabet *etc*, formerly used in infant schools.

horned [*hawrnd*] *adj* having horns; curved and pointed; crescent-shaped.

hornet [*hawrnet*] *n* large species of wasp.

hornpipe [*hawrnpIp*] *n* old type of wind-instrument; lively nautical dance; music for such a dance > PDM.

hornrims [*hawrnRimz*] *n* (*pl*) (*coll*) spectacles with thick dark frames.

hornstone [*hawrnstOn*] *n* (*min*) chert.

hornswoggle [*hawrnswog'l*] *v/t* (*US coll*) cheat, deceive.

horny [*hawrni*] *adj* of or like horn; (*of skin*) calloused; (*vulg coll*) having or about to have an erection; lustful; **Old H.** the Devil.

horologe [*hoRoloj*] *n* timepiece, clock, sundial.

horologer [*hoRolojer*] *n* clock- or watch-maker.

horologist [*hoRolojist*] *n* horologer.

horology [*hoRoloji*] *n* art of measuring time or making timepieces.

horoscope [*hoROskOp*] *n* astrological prediction of a person's luck and future, based on calculation of position of stars and planets at the moment of his birth ~ **horoscopic** [*hoROskopik*] *adj*.

horoscopy [*hoRoskopi*] *n* art of prediction by horoscopes.

horrendous [*hoRendus*] *adj* (*coll*) horrific.

horrible [*hoRib'l*] *adj* causing, or capable of causing, horror; repulsive, terrifying; shocking; (*coll*) very unpleasant or ugly ~ **horribly** *adv* ~ **horribleness** *n*.

horrid [*hoRid*] *adj* repulsive, frightful, horrible; (*coll*) unpleasant, annoying; (*ar*) bristling ~ **horridly** *adv* ~ **horridness** *n*.

horrific [*hoRifik*] *adj* highly gruesome, terrifying or shocking; deliberately stimulating fear, disgust *etc* as form of entertainment.

horrify [*hoRifI*] *v/t* fill with horror, shock.

horror [*hoRer*] *n* intense feeling of repulsion and fear; disgust, loathing; that which rouses such feelings; (*coll*) something ugly and ridiculous; disagreeable person; **the horrors** strong irrational fear, *esp* in delirium tremens; **h. comic strip** magazine exploiting horrific themes, drawings *etc*; **h. film** film treating gruesome, terrifying or supernatural subjects in a sensationalist way.

horror-stricken, horror-struck [*hoRer-stRiken, hoRer-stRuk*] *adj* filled with horror, terrified, shocked.

hors d'œuvre [*awrdu(r)vr*] *n* (*Fr*) light savoury dish served first at a meal.

horse [*hawrs*] *n* common large hoofed quadruped used for riding upon or as beast of burden; stallion; cavalry; frame on which something is supported; apparatus used for vaulting exercises; (*sl*) heroin; **h. of another colour** a different matter; **dark h.** person with hidden merits; **flog a dead h.** try to revive a forgotten controversy *etc*, work for a lost cause; **hold your horses** calm down; don't hurry; **on one's high h.** behaving haughtily, giving oneself airs; **white horses** waves crested with foam; **a willing h.** a keen worker ~ **horse** *adj* of, for, or like a horse ~ **horse** *v/t* provide with a horse or horses.

horseback [*hawrsbak*] *n* **on h.** riding a horse; mounted.

horseblock [*hawrsblok*] *n* block of stone or wood on which to stand to mount a horse.

horsebox [*hawrsboks*] *n* closed waggon or van for transporting horses.

horse-chestnut [hawrs-*chesnut*] *n* large tree bearing shiny nuts in spiny cases; nut of this tree.

horsecloth [*hawrskloth*] *n* specially shaped blanket for covering a horse's back.

horsecoper [*hawrskOper*] *n* dealer in horses, *esp* one of doubtful honesty.

horse-doctor [*hawrs-dokter*] *n* (*coll*) veterinary surgeon.

horseflesh [*hawrsflesh*] *n* edible flesh of a horse; (*collect*) horses.

horsefly [*hawrsflI*] *n* insect which stings horses; gadfly.

Horse Guards [*hawrs-gaardz*] *n* (*pl*) household cavalry, *esp* cavalry brigade of the British Guards; their headquarters in Whitehall, London.

horsehair [*hawrs-hair*] *n* hair from the mane and tail of a horse; fabric made of this and used in upholstery.

horse-laugh [*hawrs-laaf*] *n* a guffaw.

horseleech [*hawrsleech*] *n* large blood-sucking leech; (*fig*) insatiable person.

horseman [*hawrsman*] *n* man who rides well.

horsemanship [*hawrsmanship*] *n* art of riding horses.

horse-marines [*hawrs-maReenz*] *n* (*pl*) (*joc*) imaginary force of naval cavalry; **tell that to the h.** (*coll*) expression of incredulity.

horseplay [*hawrsplay*] *n* rough boisterous behaviour.

horsepower [*hawrspowr*] *n* unit of power, rate of work done in lifting 550 lb. one foot per second.

horseradish [*hawrsRadish*] *n* plant with pungent root used as flavouring.

horse-sense [*hawrs-sens*] *n* common sense, shrewdness.

horseshoe [*hawrs-shOO*] *n* protective strip of metal nailed to underside of horse's hoof and shaped to fit it; anything shaped like this.

horsetail [*hawrstayl*] *n* tail of a horse; genus of flowerless plants > PDB.

horse-trading [*hawrs-tRayding*] *n* crude barter; (*fig*) arrangement whereby people agree to do favours for one another.

horsewhip [*hawrswip*] *n* whip for driving team of horses ~ **horsewhip** (*pres/part* **horsewhipping**, *p/t* and *p/part* **horsewhipped**) *v/t* flog with a horsewhip.

horsewoman [*hawrswooman*] *n* woman who rides well.

horsy [*hawrsi*] *adj* highly interested in horses, horse-racing, riding *etc*; looking or behaving like a person with such interests ~ **horsiness** *n*.

hortative [*hawrtativ*] *adj* exhorting, encouraging.

hortatory [*hawrtateRi*] *adj* hortative.

horticultural [*hawrtikulcheRal*] *adj* of horticulture.

horticulture [*hawrtikulcher*] *n* art of growing flowers, fruit, and vegetables.

horticulturist [*hawrtikulcheRist*] *n* gardener.

hosanna [hOz*ana*] *interj* (*Heb*) shout of adoration.

hose (1) [*hOz*] *n* flexible pipe for conveying and directing a stream of water ~ **hose** *v/t* pour water on from a hose.

hose (2) *n* (*pl*) (*ar*) close-fitting coverings for the legs, stockings.

hosepipe [*hOzpIp*] *n* hose (1).

hosier [*hOzi-er*] *n* one who deals in hosiery.

hosiery [*hOzheRi*] *n* men's underwear, socks, collars *etc*; shop or business dealing in these.

hospice [*hospis*] *n* house where travellers are entertained, *esp* one kept by monks; home for paupers or the sick.

hospitable [*hospi*tab'l] *adj* offering welcome to guests; inviting, generous, kindly ∼ **hospitably** *adv* ∼ **hospitableness** *n*.

hospital [*hospital*] *n* place where the sick and injured are lodged and given medical treatment; charitable foundation for the aged and infirm or for educational purposes.

hospitality [*hospi*taliti] *n* friendly welcome and entertainment given to guests; willingness to entertain guests.

hospitalize [*hospital*Iz] *v/t* send to hospital; admit into hospital.

hospitaller [*hospi*taler] *n* (*hist*) member of a religious order formed to care for the sick or for travellers; member of modern charitable organization providing first aid and ambulance service.

hoss [*hos*] *n* (*coll*) horse.

host (1) [*hOst*] *n* large crowd or army.

host (2) *n* one who entertains a guest; innkeeper, hotelkeeper; (*zool*) animal on which parasites live > PDB; (*med*) person who has received a transplant.

host (3) *n* (*eccles*) the consecrated bread used in the Eucharist.

hostage [*hostij*] *n* person handed over to or seized by the enemy or by bandits as a surety.

hostel [*hostel*] *n* supervised lodging-house for students, young people or workers; residential hall at a university; building providing temporary accommodation for young hikers.

hosteller [*hostiler*] *n* one lodging in a hostel; hiker travelling from hostel to hostel.

hostelry [*hostel*Ri] *n* inn.

hostess [*hOstes*] *n* woman who receives guests; wife of a host; female innkeeper or hotelkeeper; woman employed to attend on travellers in aircraft; woman supervising waitresses in restaurant; paid female dancing-partner in nightclub *etc*; **h. gown** long elegant négligé gown.

hostile [*hostIl*] *adj* characteristic of an enemy; showing enmity, unfriendly ∼ **hostilely** *adv*.

hostility [*hos*tiliti] *n* enmity, hatred; (*pl*) acts of war.

hostler see **ostler**.

hot [*hot*] *adj* having perceptible degree of heat, very warm; producing burning sensation to the taste, pungent; (*fig*) violent, impetuous; passionate; lustful; sexually aroused; (*hunting, of scent*) fresh and strong; (*coll*) eager; excited, flurried; (*jazz coll*) highly syncopated, with strong beat; (*coll, of news etc*) very recent; sensational; (*sl*) clever, expert; (*coll*) indecent; (*sl, of stolen goods*) sought by police, difficult to dispose of; **h. air** meaningless talk, empty promises *etc*; **h. dog** (*US*) hot sausage sandwich; **get h.** be near to discovering something hidden; (*jazz*) be carried away by music; **h. line** direct telephone line linking two heads of governments; **h. news** recent and sensational news; **not so h.** (*coll*) not very good; **h. on** keen on, expert in; **h.**

on the track of pursuing closely; **h. seat** (*sl*) position of unwelcome responsibility or embarrassment; **h. stuff** (*sl*) someone or something of excellent quality; **h. water** (*coll*) trouble ∼ **hot** *adv* in a hot manner, so as to heat; eagerly, vigorously; **blow h. and cold** hesitate, change one's attitude repeatedly ∼ **hot** (*pres/part* **hotting**, *p/t* and *p/part* **hotted**) *v/t* and *i* **h. up** (*coll*) make or become hotter, more exciting, more powerful *etc*.

hotbed [*hotbed*] *n* (*hort*) layer of earth heated by fermenting manure in which plants are forced; (*fig*) place favourable to rapid growth, *esp* of something evil.

hot-blooded [*hot-bl*udid] *adj* passionate.

hotchpot [*hoch*pot] *n* (*leg*) gathering together of properties for purpose of equal division.

hotchpotch, hodge-podge [*hoch*poch, *hoj*-poj] *n* thick mixed stew; (*fig*) confused mixture, jumble.

hotel [*hOtel*] *n* house for commercial accommodation and entertainment of travellers.

hotelier [*hOteli*-er] *n* one who runs a hotel.

hotfoot [*hotfoot*] *adv* eagerly, hastily.

hot-gospeller [*hot-gospeler*] *n* (*coll*) emotional evangelistic preacher.

hothead [*hot*-hed] *n* rash, impetuous person ∼ **hotheaded** *adj*.

hothouse [*hot*-hows] *n* building artificially heated for growing delicate plants.

hotly [*hotli*] *adv* in a hot way; eagerly; angrily; passionately.

hotplate [*hotplayt*] *n* heated metal dish, shelf or cabinet for keeping food hot.

hotpot [*hotpot*] *n* meat and vegetable stew.

hotpress [*hotpres*] *n* device for glazing paper with hot plates ∼ **hotpress** *v/t*.

hot-rod [*hot-rod*] *n* (*sl*) supercharged car.

hot-spot [*hot-spot*] *n* part of the wall surface of the induction manifold of an internal combustion engine on which the fuel mixture is vaporized.

Hottentot [*hotentot*] *n* member of a negroid South African race; language of this race; (*fig*) uncivilized person.

hot-water-bottle [*hot-wawter-bot'l*] *n* rubber or metal container filled with hot water for warming a person in bed.

hough [*hok*] *n* hock of a horse; back of human knee.

hound [*hownd*] *n* dog that hunts by scent; pursuer in paperchase; (*fig*) blackguard ∼ **hound** *v/t* pursue, persecute.

hour [*owr*] *n* sixty minutes, one twenty-fourth part of a day and night; period of time; fixed or appointed moment of time; occasion; destined moment; (*pl*) period regularly appointed for business *etc*; (*pl*) (*eccles*) seven periods of the day appointed for prayer; prayers to be said at these times; **at the eleventh h.** at the last possible moment; **in an evil h.** acting under an unfortunate impulse; bringing bad luck; **keep good (late) hours** go to bed and get up early (late); **the small hours** the hours just after midnight.

hourglass [*owr*glaas] *n* sandglass which takes one hour to run.

hour-hand [*owr*-hand] *n* that hand of a clock or watch which indicates the hour.

houri [*hoor*Ri] *n* nymph in the Mohammedan paradise; voluptuous, seductive woman.

hourly [*owr*li] *adj* occurring every hour; lasting

one hour; continual, frequent ~ **hourly** *adv* every hour; frequently.

house [*hows*] *n* building designed for human habitation, dwelling; hotel, boarding-house, inn; residential hall or college at a university; business firm; boarding-house attached to school; its inmates; subdivision of a school; members of a household, domestic circle; family, lineage; theatre; convent; a legislative body when in session; building used for meetings of such a body; debating society while in session; (*astrol*) one of twelve divisions of the sky; **the H. House of Commons** Parliament; House of Lords; Stock Exchange; Christ Church, Oxford; Peterhouse, Cambridge; **bring the h. down** (*theat*) cause great applause or laughter; **h. charge** basic charge for meals in restaurants in addition to cost of food consumed; **free h.** public house not under contract to one particular brewer; **full h., good h.** (*theat*) large audience; **h. of ill fame** brothel; **keep h.** run a household; **keep open h.** be very hospitable; **like a h. on fire** very fast; **make a h.** have a quorum; **on the h.** at the expense of the inn, firm *etc*; **safe as houses** absolutely safe; **set one's h. in order** correct abuses in one's household, life, conduct *etc* ~ **house** [*howz*] *v/t* and *i* provide a house or shelter for; find room for; lodge and feed; dwell.

house-agent [*hows*-ayjent] *n* person who negotiates the buying, selling and letting of houses.

house-arrest [hows-a*Rest*] *n* legal confinement to one's own house, or to some other building not a prison.

houseboat [*hows*bOt] *n* boat fitted for living in.

housebound [*hows*bownd] *adj* kept indoors by illness, work *etc*.

houseboy [*hows*boi] *n* African or Asian domestic servant in a white man's home.

housebreaker [*hows*bRayker] *n* thief who breaks into a house, *esp* by day; one who demolishes houses ~ **housebreaking** *n*.

housecoat [*hows*kOt] *n* woman's elegant dressing-gown.

housedog [*hows*dog] *n* dog kept in a house; dog trained to guard a house.

housefather [hows*faa*THer] *n* warden of a children's home; older boy responsible for helping a young newcomer at a school.

houseful [*hows*fool] *n* as many or as much as a house can accommodate.

household [*hows*-hOld] *n* persons living together in one house, family and servants; home ~ **household** *adj* domestic; **h. gods** (*Rom myth*) minor gods protecting a household; images of these; (*fig*) treasured family possessions; **H. Troops** regiments appointed to attend the Sovereign; **h. word** familiar and much-used word, phrase *etc*; well-known name.

householder [*hows*-hOlder] *n* occupier of a house; head of a household.

house-hunting [*hows*-hunting] *n* searching for a house to buy or rent.

housekeeper [*hows*keeper] *n* woman hired to run a house and supervise servants.

housekeeping [*hows*keeping] *n* art of running a house, domestic management; **h. money** allowance made by husband to wife to cover domestic expenses.

housel [*howz*el] *n* (*ar*) Eucharist.

houseleek [*hows*leek] *n* plant with rosettes of leaves growing on walls and roofs.

housemaid [*hows*mayd] *n* female servant whose main work is the cleaning of rooms; **h.'s knee** inflammation of kneecap.

housemaster [*hows*maaster] *n* master in charge of a house at a boarding-school.

house-party [*hows*-paarti] *n* party of guests staying for some days in a country house.

house-physician [*hows*-fizishun] *n* senior resident physician in a hospital.

house-plant [*hows*-plaant] *n* pot-plant grown at normal indoor temperature.

houseproud [*hows*pRowd] *adj* priding oneself on the cleanliness of one's home.

houseroom [*hows*ROOm] *n* accommodation.

house-surgeon [*hows*-surjun] *n* senior resident surgeon in a hospital.

house-to-house [*hows*-too-hows] *adj* and *adv* visiting each house in turn.

housetop [*hows*top] *n* roof of house.

house-trained [*hows*-tRaynd] *adj* (*of pet animals*) trained to urinate and defecate in permitted places only; (*fig*) domesticated, well-behaved.

house-warming [*hows*-wawrming] *n* party given to celebrate one's entry into a new home.

housewife [*hows*wIf] *n* mistress of household; woman who runs her own house; [*huzif*] small case holding sewing kit ~ **housewifely** *adj*.

housewifery [*hows*wifRi/*huzi*fRi] *n* housekeeping; domestic economy.

housework [*hows*wurk] *n* regular cleaning, *etc* necessary to the upkeep of a house.

housey-housey [*howz*i-howzi] *n* game of chance resembling lotto.

housing (1) [*howz*ing] *n* act of providing with a house or houses, accommodation; **h. estate** planned area of houses, often owned by a local authority and let to ratepayers.

housing (2) *n* protective covering, *esp* horse's ornamental body-cloth.

hove [*hOv*] (*naut*) *p/t* and *p/part* of **heave**.

hovel [*hovel*/*huvel*] *n* wretched dwelling; hut, shed ~ **hovel** *v/i* dwell in a hovel.

hover [*hover*/*huver*] *v/i* remain suspended in the air above one spot; (*fig*) linger; waver, hesitate.

hovercraft [*hover*kRaaft] *n* (*tr*) type of vehicle moving along about 2 ft above any fairly level surface on a cushion of compressed air.

how (1), **howe** [*how*] *n* hill; burial-mound.

how (2) *adv interrog* and *rel* in what way; by what means or method; to what extent; that; what; (*introducing exclams*) to what a degree, extent or amount; **and h.!** (*US*) *phrase added for emphasis*; **all you know h.** (*sl*) as well as you can; **how's that?** (*cricket*) appeal to umpire to rule whether a batsman is out ~ **how** *n* method, means.

howbeit [how*bee*-it] *adv* (*ar*) nevertheless.

howdah [*how*da] *n* canopied seat on the back of an elephant.

how-do-you-do, how-d'ye-do [how-dyi-*dOO*] *interj* normal formula on being introduced to a stranger ~ **how-do-you-do, how-d'ye-do** [how*did*OO] *n* (*coll*) awkward state of affairs.

howdy (1) [*how*di] *interj* (*coll*) how-do-you-do?

howdy (2) *n* (*dial*) midwife.

howe see how (1).

however [how-*ever*] *adv* and *conj* in whatever way, by whatever means; nevertheless; *interrog* (*coll*) how, by what means whatever?

howitzer [*howitser*] *n* artillery weapon with high trajectory and low muzzle velocity.

howl [*howl*] *v/i* (*of animals*) utter long mournful cry; (*of persons*) cry aloud with pain or rage, wail; laugh loudly; **h. down** prevent (one) from being heard by shouts of rage or mockery ~ **howl** *n* long loud cry, wail; outburst of laughter.

howler [*howler*] *n* one who or that which howls; S. American monkey; (*coll*) ridiculous error; obvious lie.

howling [*howling*] *adj* that howls; (*coll*) extreme. great, obvious; **h. wilderness** wild and remote place ~ **howlingly** *adv*.

howsoever [howsO-*ever*] *adv* however, by whatever means.

hoy (1) [*hoi*] *n* large single-deck boat; small vessel for transportation to and from ship close inshore.

hoy (2) *interj* (*coll*) exclamation of address or summons; hey, hi ~ **hoy** *v/i*.

hoyden [*hoiden*] *n* wild, boisterous girl, tomboy ~ **hoydenish** *adj*.

hub [*hub*] *n* central part of a wheel; (*fig*) centre of interest or activity.

hubbub [*hubub*] *n* confused sound of voices; uproar; riot.

hubby [*hubi*] *n* (*coll dim*) husband.

hubris [*hewb*Ris] *n* arrogance, insolence.

huckaback [*huk*abak] *n* strong rough linen cloth used as towelling.

huckleberry [*huk*'lbeRi] *n* N. American shrub; its fruit which resembles the bilberry.

huckster [*huk*ster] *n* hawker, pedlar; dealer in small wares ~ **huckster** *v/i* haggle.

huddle [*hud*'l] *v/t* and *i* heap up confusedly; gather into a confused mass; crowd together ~ **huddle** *n* crowded mass of things or people; go into a h. (*sl*) discuss something privately.

hue (1) [*hew*] *n* tint, shade; complexion.

hue (2) *n* **h. and cry** angry pursuit; outcry, clamorous disapproval.

huff [*huf*] *v/t* and *i* breathe heavily, blow; bully, insult; take offence, sulk, show anger; (*draughts*) remove an opponent's piece for failing to take when able to; **be huffed** show anger ~ **huff** *n* angry mood, sulkiness; (*draughts*) act of huffing.

huffish [*huf*ish] *adj* sulky, showing anger ~ **huffishly** *adv* ~ **huffishness** *n*.

huffy [*huf*i] *adj* huffish ~ **huffily** *adv* ~ **huffiness** *n*.

hug (*pres/part* **hugging**, *p/t* and *p/part* **hugged**) [*hug*] *v/t* clasp strongly in the arms, embrace warmly; keep close alongside; cherish, be fond of; **h. oneself** be pleased with oneself; **h. the wind** (*naut*) keep close hauled ~ **hug** *n* act of hugging, close embrace; wrestling hold.

huge [*hewj*] *adj* very big, enormous, vast ~ **hugely** *adv* very much ~ **hugeness** *n*.

hugger-mugger [*huger*-muger] *n* secrecy; disorder, confusion ~ **hugger-mugger** *adj* and *adv*.

Huguenot [*hewg*enO] *n* and *adj* French Protestant of the sixteenth and seventeenth centuries.

hula [*hOO*la] *n* Hawaiian women's dance; **h. hoop**

light hoop which can be swung round and round the body by rapid movements of the hips and pelvis; **h. skirt** Hawaiian grass skirt.

hulk [*hulk*] *n* hull of dismantled ship; old unseaworthy ship formerly used as prison; big, ungainly person.

hulking [*hulking*] *adj* big and clumsy, unwieldy.

hull (1) [*hul*] *n* body of a ship ~ **hull** *v/t* pierce the hull of.

hull (2) *n* pod, shell of peas *etc* ~ **hull** *v/t* remove the hull of.

hullabaloo [*hul*abalOO] *n* uproar, din.

hullo [*hul*O] *interj* and *n* hallo.

hum (1) (*pres/part* **humming**, *p/t* and *p/part* **hummed**) [*hum*] *v/i* and *t* produce a low continuous buzzing or droning sound; produce a musical sound through the nose, with lips closed; utter (a tune) in this way; **h. and haw** hesitate in speaking; make inarticulate noises between words; hesitate; **make things h.** cause lively activity ~ **hum** *n* act or sound of humming; continuous low and indistinct noise.

hum (2) *interj* see **hem** (2).

hum (3) *v/i* (*sl*) smell unpleasantly ~ **hum** *n*.

human [*hew*man] *adj* of, like or characteristic of mankind; showing sympathy, kindness or understanding; appealing to the gentler emotions, pathetic; **h. relations** relationships between individual people; **h. rights** basic rights to which all people are entitled ~ **human** *n* member of mankind.

humane [hew*mayn*] *adj* gentle, kind, sympathetic; merciful; cultured, civilized; of humanism; **h. killer** device for slaughtering animals painlessly ~ **humanely** *adv* ~ **humaneness** *n*.

humanism [*hew*manizm] *n* system of thought which sets up ethical but not religious standards; theory of knowledge which gives first place to the study of man; literary culture, *esp* study of Greek and Roman art, thought *etc*.

humanist [*hew*manist] *n* one who adopts the views of humanism; classical scholar, *esp* of the Renaissance period ~ **humanist, humanistic** [hewman*is*-tik] *adjs*.

humanitarian [hewmani*tair*Ri-an] *adj* wishing or tending to reduce suffering and promote welfare of mankind; merciful; benevolent; (*theol*) denying the divinity of Christ ~ **humanitarian** *n* one who follows humanitarian principles.

humanitarianism [hewmani*tair*Ri-anizm] *n* humanitarian behaviour or principles.

humanity [hew*man*iti] *n* state or quality of being human; human race as a whole; quality of being humane; humane act; **the Humanities** classical or literary studies.

humanization [hewman*i*zayshon] *n* act or process of humanizing; state of being humanized.

humanize [*hew*man*iz*] *v/t* and *i* make or become human or humane, civilize; **humanized milk** cow's milk so treated as to resemble woman's milk ~ **humanizer** *n*.

humankind [*hew*man*kind*] *n* mankind.

humanly [*hew*manli] *adv* by human means; from a human point of view; without God's help.

humble [*humb*'l] *adj* not proud, ashamed, abased; having a low opinion of oneself, unassuming; submissive; poor, mean; unimportant ~ **humble** v/t humiliate, put to shame.

humblebee [humb'lbee] n bumblebee.

humble-pie [humb'l-pI] n (ar) pie made from deer's entrails, umble-pie; **eat h.** submit to humiliation, apologize humbly.

humbles see **umbles.**

humbly [humbli] adv in a humble way.

humbug [humbug] n insincerity, hypocrisy; hypocritical words or actions; sham, trickery; hoax; impostor, hypocrite; kind of peppermint sweetmeat ~ **humbug** (pres/part **humbugging,** p/t and p/part **humbugged**) v/t trick by hypocrisy.

humdinger [humdinger] n (US sl) anything fine or remarkable.

humdrum [humdRum] adj commonplace, dull.

humectation [hewmektayshon] n act of moistening.

humeral [hewmeRal] adj (anat) pertaining to the shoulder ~ **humeral** n (eccles) vestment covering the shoulders.

humerus [hewmeRus] n (anat) bone of upper arm.

humid [hewmid] adj moist, damp.

humidifier [hewmidifI-er] n apparatus for maintaining or increasing air humidity.

humidify [hewmidifI] v/t moisten.

humidity [hewmiditi] n moisture, dampness; degree of moisture; measure of water-vapour present in air > PDS, PDG.

humidor [hewmidor] n device for keeping air moist in tobacco-jar etc; tobacco-jar.

humify [hewmifI] v/t moisten.

humiliate [hewmili-ayt] v/t make humble, expose to scorn or ridicule; expose the faults of, put to shame; lower the pride or self-respect of.

humiliation [hewmili-ayshon] n act of humiliating; state of being humiliated; degradation, disgrace; that which humiliates.

humility [hewmiliti] n quality of being humble; clear recognition of one's own faults and shortcomings; meekness.

humming [huming] n sound produced by person or thing that hums; drone, buzz ~ **humming** adj that hums.

humming-bird [huming-burd] n small tropical bird which makes a humming sound by vibrating its wings when hovering; **h. hawk-moth** British moth capable of hovering.

hummock [humok] n hillock; sandhill; ridge of ice in ice-field ~ **hummocky** adj.

humoresque [hewmeResk] n type of light music > PDM.

humorist, humourist [hewmeRist] n person given to making jokes; one skilled in comic writing, drawing or acting.

humoristic [hewmeRistik] adj comic, witty.

humorous [hewmeRus] adj causing laughter, funny; witty; having a sense of humour ~ **humorously** adv ~ **humorousness** n.

humour [hewmer] n capacity for seeing the funny side of things; cheerful and good-tempered amusement; that which causes good-tempered laughter, agreeable absurdity; mood, frame of mind; (ar) temperament; (ar) whim; (med) one of the semi-fluid parts of the eye; (ar med) one of four basic fluids in the body influencing human health and character; **out of h.** annoyed;

depressed ~ **humour** v/t indulge the moods or whims of; manage (a person) tactfully.

humourist see **humorist.**

humoursome [hewmersum] adj (ar) capricious.

hump [hump] n lump, swelling; lump on back of camel etc; abnormal lump on human back, due to spinal deformity; hillock; **get, have the h.** (coll) be in a bad-tempered mood, depression ~ **hump** v/t curve (one's back) into a hump; (sl) carry on one's back; (sl) have sexual intercourse with ~ **humped** adj.

humpback [humpbak] n person with humped back, hunchback; type of whale; type of salmon ~ **humpbacked** adj.

humph [humf] interj an expression of dissatisfaction or doubt.

humpty [humpti] n pouffe, large firm cushion placed on floor and used as seat.

humpy [humpi] adj having humps; like a hump; bad-tempered, surly.

humus [hewmus] n mould, organic matter in soil resulting from decomposition of plant and animal tissue > PDB, PDG.

Hun [hun] n one of a race of Asiatic nomads which devastated Europe in the 4th and 5th centuries; (sl) German; (fig) ruthless destroyer.

hunch [hunsh] n (coll) shrewd guess, intuition; premonition; hump, lump; a hunk ~ **hunch** v/t arch (back) into a hump; draw up (shoulders).

hunchback [hunshbak] n person with humped back ~ **hunchbacked** adj.

hundred [hundRed] n and adj ten times ten, 100; former subdivision of an English county; **long h.** 120; **hundreds** (coll) very many; **hundreds and thousands** type of very small sweetmeats.

hundredfold [hundRedfOld] adj and adv multiplied by a hundred.

hundredth [hundRedth] n and adj (that) which follows ninety-nine others in a series; (that) which is one of a hundred equal parts; **Old H.** metrical paraphrase of the Hundredth Psalm; tune to which this is sung.

hundredweight (abbr **cwt**) [hundRedwayt] n English measure of weight equal to 112 pounds avoirdupois or to one-twentieth of a ton; American measure of weight equal to 100 pounds; **metric h.** fifty kilograms.

hung [hung] p/t and alternative p/part of **hang; h. up** (sl) persistently depressed; frustrated; obsessed.

Hungarian [hung-gairRi-an] n and adj (native) of Hungary; (language) of Hungary.

hunger [hung-ger] n desire for food; physical weakness and discomfort caused by lack of food; famine; (fig) need, craving, appetite; **h. strike** refusal of prisoner to eat ~ **hunger** v/i feel hungry; lack food; **h. after, h. for** crave, desire; need.

hung-over [hung-Over] adj (coll) suffering from a hangover.

hungry [hung-gRi] adj feeling hunger; starving; eager for food; (of land) infertile; (fig) desiring greatly, avid ~ **hungrily** adv.

hunk [hunk] n large lump or slice.

hunkers [hunkerz] n (pl) (Scots and dial) buttocks; **on one's h.** squatting.

hunks [*hunks*] *n* (*coll*) surly old man; miser.

hunky [*hunk*i] *adj* (*US sl*) satisfactory.

hunky-dory [hunki-*dawr*i] *adj* (*US sl*) excellent, satisfactory.

hunt [*hunt*] *v/t* and *i* pursue wild animals in order to kill them; pursue (fox, hare or stag) on horseback and with hounds; pursue in order to capture; search for; follow the chase; act as master or huntsman to pack of hounds; (*mech*) oscillate excessively; **h. down** pursue ruthlessly; capture; **h. out, h. up** search keenly for; find after prolonged search ~ **hunt** *n* act of hunting, pursuit; group of persons who regularly hunt the fox, hare, or stag; such persons together with their horses and hounds; area over which they hunt.

hunter [*hunt*er] *n* one who hunts, huntsman; searcher; horse used in hunting; watch with face protected by metal case; **h.'s moon** full moon in October.

hunting [*hunt*ing] *n* act of one who hunts.

hunting-box [*hunt*ing-boks] *n* small house occupied only in the hunting season.

hunting-crop [*hunt*ing-kRop] *n* type of short whip.

hunting-ground [*hunt*ing-gRownd] *n* tract of country over which hunting is carried on; (*fig*) place where something may be searched for with good hope of success; **happy h.** (*joc*) Heaven; a heaven for dogs or other animals.

hunting-lodge [*hunt*ing-loj] *n* hunting-box.

huntress [*hunt*Res] *n* woman who hunts.

huntsman [*hunts*man] *n* man who hunts; man in charge of hounds during hunt.

hurdle [*hurd*'l] *n* light wooden and osier framework used as temporary fence; fence-like obstacle to be leapt over in certain races; (*fig*) barrier, obstacle ~ **hurdle** *v/i* and *t* leap an obstacle in racing; leap an obstacle with legs outstretched; make hurdles; enclose with hurdles.

hurdler [*hurd*ler] *n* one who runs in hurdle races; one who makes hurdles.

hurdy-gurdy [*hurd*i-gurdi] *n* barrel-organ.

hurl [*hurl*] *v/t* and *i* throw forcefully; utter with violence; hurtle, hurl; play at hurling ~ **hurler** *n* one who hurls or plays at hurling.

hurley [*hurl*i] *n* (*Ir*) hurling.

hurling [*hurl*ing] *n* act of one who hurls; Irish game resembling hockey; Cornish ball-game.

burly-burly [*hurl*i-burli] *n* uproar; bustle.

hurrah, hurray [hoo*Raa*, hoo*Ray*] *interj* shout of joy or acclamation ~ **hurrah, hurray** *v/i*.

hurricane [*hur*ikayn] *n* very violent wind; tropical cyclone occurring in W. Indies; wind of 75 miles an hour or more > PDG.

hurricane-lamp [*hur*ikayn-lamp] *n* oil lamp with well-shielded flame.

hurried [*hur*id] *adj* done or acting with haste ~ **hurriedly** *adv*.

hurry [*hur*i] *n* excessive haste, bustle; need for haste, urgency; **in a h.** impatient; eager; (*coll*) readily, soon ~ **hurry** *v/t* and *i* hasten, move or cause to move quickly; do quickly; show undue haste or eagerness; **h. up** increase the speed of, do or move more quickly.

hurry-scurry [*hur*i-skuRi] *v/i* and *n* rush.

hurst [*hurst*] *n* hillock; sandbank; copse.

hurt (*p/t* and *p/part* hurt) [*hurt*] *v/t* and *i* cause injury or pain (to); damage; give offence or distress (to); give a sensation of pain; come to harm, suffer injury ~ **hurt** *n* wound, injury; pain; harm, damage ~ **hurt** *adj* feeling or showing pain, distress or offence.

hurtful [*hurt*fool] *adj* harmful, causing pain or damage ~ **hurtfully** *adv* ~ **hurtfulness** *n*.

hurtle [*hurt*'l] *v/i* be projected violently through the air.

husband [*huz*band] *n* man married to a woman; (*ar*) manager of an estate, farm *etc*; **ship's h.** agent responsible to a ship's owners for providing equipment, stores *etc* ~ **husband** *v/t* manage carefully, use economically; (*ar*) marry.

husbandman [*huz*bandman] *n* farmer.

husbandry [*huz*bandRi] *n* agriculture, farming; careful management, thrift, saving.

hush [*hush*] *v/t* and *i* make or become silent; make calm, soothe; **h. up** keep secret, suppress information about ~ **hush** *n* silence, peaceful stillness ~ **hush!** *interj* keep silent!

hush-hush [*hush*-hush] *adj* (*coll*) very secret.

hush-money [*hush*-muni] *n* money paid to preserve a secret; money obtained by blackmail.

husk [*husk*] *n* dry outer covering of some seeds and fruits ~ **husk** *v/t* strip the husk from.

husky (1) [*husk*i] *adj* of or like a husk; (*of voice*) hoarse, rasping; (*US*) big and strong, hefty.

husky (2) *adj* and *n* Eskimo (dog).

huss [*hus*] *n* dogfish, rock salmon.

hussar [hoo*zaar*] *n* light-armed cavalryman.

hussif see housewife.

hussy [*huz*i] *n* (*cont*) impertinent girl; woman of doubtful character.

hustings [*hust*ingz] *n* (*pl*) (*hist*) platform from which Parliamentary candidates formerly addressed electors; (*fig*) electioneering, election speeches; City of London court.

hustle [*hus*'l] *v/t* and *i* hurry; jostle violently, urge along roughly; act rapidly and efficiently; (*sl*) earn money illegally, live by prostitution or as a gigolo ~ **hustle** *n* ~ **hustler** *n* energetic person who gets things done; (*sl*) prostitute; pimp; gigolo.

hut [*hut*] *n* small wooden building, shed ~ **hut** (*pres/part* hutting, *p/t* and *p/part* hutted) *v/t* and *i* provide a hut for; live in a hut.

hutch [*huch*] *n* wooden box with wire netting or bars in front for keeping rabbits *etc* in; trough; coal haulage truck; bin, chest, *esp* for flour or grain; (*coll*) cottage ~ **hutch** *v/t* put in a hutch; wash (ore) in a hutch.

hutment [*hut*ment] *n* encampment of huts.

hutting [*hut*ing] *n* material for making army huts.

huzza [huzaa] *interj* (*obs*) hurrah.

hwyl [*hwil*] *n* (*Wel*) passionate eloquence.

hyacinth [*hi*-asinth] *n* bulbous plant with spikes of bell-shaped flowers; kind of garnet; kind of zircon; sapphire.

hyacinthian, hyacinthine [hi-asinthi-an, hi-*asinth*In] *adj* of or like a hyacinth; dark blue.

hyaena see hyena.

hyaline [*hi*-alIn] *n* and *adj* (substance) like glass.

hyalite [*hi*-alIt] *n* (*min*) colourless variety of opal. **hyalo-** *pref* of or like glass.

hyaloid [*hi*-aloid] *adj* like glass, clear, transparent; **h. membrane** transparent membrane which covers the vitreous body of the eye.

hybrid [*hi*bRid] *n* plant or animal resulting from a

cross between parents that are genetically unlike
>PDB, PDP; (*fig*) anything derived from mixed
origins; word containing elements from different
languages ~ **hybrid** *adj*.

hybridism [*h*Ibʀidizm] *n* state of being hybrid.

hybridizable [*h*IbʀidIzab'l] *adj* capable of producing hybrids.

hybridization [hIbʀidIzayshon] *n* process of
interbreeding; hybridism.

hybridize [*h*Ibʀidɪz] *v*/*t* and *i* produce hybrids.

hydatid [*h*Idatid] *n* (*path*) fluid-filled cyst
containing larvae of certain tapeworms > PDB.

hydr- *pref* of or like water.

hydra [*h*IdRa] *n* (*myth*) monstrous snake whose
many heads grew again as fast as they were cut
off; (*fig*) a spreading evil difficult to destroy;
(*zool*) a freshwater polyp.

hydrangea [hIdRaynja] *n* kind of shrub with
large spherical heads of flowers.

hydrant [*h*IdRant] *n* pipe for drawing water from a
watermain.

hydrate [*h*IdRayt] *n* (*chem*) compound of water
with a substance > PDS, PDE ~ **hydrate** *v*/*t*
and *i* make or become a hydrate.

hydration [hIdRayshon] *n* process of hydrating.

hydraulic [hIdRawlik] *adj* relating to the flow
of liquids, pertaining to hydraulics; worked by
flow or pressure of water or other fluids, *esp*
through pipes > PDE; (*of cement*) hardening or
setting under water; containing water ~
hydraulically *adv* by means of water-power.

hydraulics [hIdRawliks] *n* (*pl*) science which
studies the flow of liquids; hydrodynamics as
applied to engineering.

hydric [*h*IdRik] *adj* (*chem*) containing hydrogen.

hydride [*h*IdRId] *n* (*chem*) compound of hydrogen
and another element.

hydro [*h*IdRO] *n* (*coll*) hotel providing facilities for
hydropathic treatment.

hydro- *pref* pertaining to or containing water;
(*chem*) pertaining to hydrogen; (*med*) dropsical.

hydrocarbon [hIdROkaarbon] *n* (*chem*) compound
of hydrogen and carbon only > PDE.

hydrocephalic [hIdROsefalik] *adj* suffering from
hydrocephalus.

hydrocephalus, hydrocephaly [hIdROsefalus,
hIdROsefali] *n* (*path*) excessive amount of fluid
in skull resulting in abnormal enlargement of
head and mental deficiency.

hydrochloric [hIdROklawRik] *adj* (*chem*) containing hydrogen and chlorine > PDS; **h. acid**
strong acid consisting of solution of hydrogen
chloride in water > PDS.

hydrodynamics [hIdROdinamiks] *n* (*pl*) mathematical study of the movement, energy and pressure of liquids in motion ~ **hydrodynamic**
adj.

hydroelectric [hIdRO-*i*lektRik] *adj* generating
electricity by energy of falling water > PDE,
PDG.

hydroelectricity [hIdRO-ilektRisiti] *n* electricity
generated by water-power.

hydrofoil [*h*IdROfoil] *n* a type of vessel whose hull
is lifted above the surface by compressed air when
travelling fast.

hydrogen [*h*IdROjen] *n* an element; a colourless,
odourless, inflammable gas > PDS; **h. ion**
positively charged hydrogen atom, proton >

PDS; **h. peroxide** solution of peroxide of
hydrogen, used as bleaching agent or disinfectant;
sulphuretted h. poisonous gas smelling like
bad eggs; hydrogen sulphide.

hydrogenation [hIdROjenayshon] *n* (*chem*) process
of combination with hydrogen; subjection to
effects of hydrogen action > PDS.

hydrogen-bomb [*h*IdROjen-bom] *n* highly destructive atom bomb operated by nuclear fusion.

hydrogenize [hIdROjenIz] *v*/*t* combine with
hydrogen; charge with hydrogen.

hydrogenous [hIdROjenus] *adj* pertaining to or
containing hydrogen.

hydrograph [*h*IdROgRaaf] *n* graph of level or flow
of water in a channel at every season > PDE.

hydrographer [hIdROgRafer] *n* one who compiles
hydrographs; expert in hydrography.

hydrography [hIdROgRafi] *n* science which
describes the waters of the earth's surface;
surveying and mapping of flowing and navigable
water.

hydrolastic [hIdROlastik] *adj* (*of a motor vehicle
suspension*) using a compressed fluid system in
place of metal springs.

hydrology [hIdROloji] *n* study of water in streams,
lakes, wells *etc* > PDG

hydrolysis [hIdRolisis] *n* (*chem*) decomposition of
a substance by water, the water being also decomposed > PDS.

hydrometer [hIdRomiter] *n* instrument for
measuring the density or specific gravity of liquids
> PDS ~ **hydrometry** [hIdRometRi] *n*.

hydropathic [hIdRopathik] *adj* of or by hydropathy.

hydropathy [hIdRopathi] *n* (*med*) treatment of
diseases by drinking or application of water.

hydrophilic [hIdROfilik] *adj* (*chem*) having an
affinity for water.

hydrophobia [hIdROfObi-a] *n* rabies; difficulty in
swallowing liquids; intense fear of water.

hydrophobic [hIdROfObik] *adj* pertaining to
hydrophobia; (*chem*) having no affinity for water;
water-repellent.

hydrophyte [*h*IdROfIt] *n* aquatic plant > PDB.

hydropic [hIdRopik] *adj* dropsical.

hydroplane [hIdROplayn] *n* motorboat designed
to skim over the surface of the water; board fixed
to motorboat enabling it to skim; seaplane; rudder controlling vertical movement of submarine.

hydroponics [hIdROponiks] *n* (*pl*) cultivation of
plants in solution of nutrient salts > PDB.

hydrosphere [*h*IdROsfeer] *n* collective body of
all waters covering earth's surface > PDG, PDS.

hydrostat [*h*IdROstat] *n* device indicating level
of water in boilers.

hydrostatic [hIdROstatik] *adj* pertaining to
liquids in equilibrium; operated by pressure of
water > PDE ~ **hydrostatics** *n* (*pl*) study of
pressures and forces in liquids at rest.

hydrous [*h*IdRus] *adj* (*chem*) containing water.

hydroxide [hIdRoksId] *n* (*chem*) compound
derived from water by replacement of one of the
hydrogen atoms in the molecule by some other
atom or group > PDS.

hydroxyl [*h*IdRoksil] *n* (*chem*) univalent radical
consisting of one hydrogen and one oxygen atom
in combination > PDS.

hyena, hyaena [hI-*eena*] *n* carnivorous dog-like
quadruped; (*fig*) cruel and rapacious person.

hyeto- *pref* pertaining to rain.

hyetograph [*hI*-etogRaaf] *n* self-recording instrument that registers rainfall > PDG.

hygiene [*hI*jeen] *n* science and practice of maintaining health; sanitary principles; cleanliness.

hygienic [hIjeenik] *adj* of hygiene; sanitary; wholesome, clean ~ **hygienically** *adv*.

hygro- *pref* pertaining to humidity.

hygrograph [*hI*gRogRaaf] *n* self-recording hygrometer > PDG.

hygrometer [hIgRomiter] *n* instrument for measuring the relative humidity of the atmosphere or of gases > PDG, PDE.

hygroscope [*hI*gRoskOp] *n* instrument indicating changes in atmospheric humidity > PDG.

hygroscopic [hIgRoskopik] *adj* absorbing moisture from the air.

hylic [*hI*lik] *adj* (*philos*) material.

hylo- *pref* pertaining to matter.

hylotheism [*hI*lOthee-izm] *n* doctrine identifying God with matter ~ **hylotheist** *n* and *adj*.

hylozoism [*hI*lOzO-izm] *n* theory that all matter has life ~ **hylozoist** *n* and. *adj*.

hymen [*hI*men] *n* marriage; (*Gk myth*) god of marriage; (*anat*) membrane partly closing entrance to the vagina of virgins.

hymeneal [hImenee-al] *adj* pertaining to marriage; pertaining to the hymen.

hymenoptera [hImenopteRa] *n* order of. insects having four membranous wings > PDB.

hymn [him] *n* religious song, *usu* in the vernacular and sung by the congregation; song of praise to divine being > PDM ~ **hymn** *v/t* and *i* sing hymns in honour of.

hymnal [*him*nal] *adj* of or like a hymn ~ **hymnal** *n* hymnbook.

hymnbook [*him*book] *n* book containing hymns.

hymnist [*him*nist] *n* one who composes hymns.

hymnody [*him*nodi] *n* art of singing hymns; hymns collectively; history of hymns.

hymnographer [himnogRafer] *n* one who writes or studies hymns.

hymnography [himnogRafi] *n* art of writing hymns; historical study of hymn-writing.

hymnology [himnoloji] *n* hymnography.

hyoid [*hI*-oid] *n* (*anat*) bone between root of tongue and larynx ~ **hyoidean** [hI-*oidi*-an] *adj*.

hyoscin, hyoscine [*hI*-oseen] *n* (*med*) poisonous alkaloid from henbane used as a nerve depressant and hypnotic.

hyoscyamine [hI-*osI*-amin] *n* (*med*) poisonous alkaloid from henbane.

hyp- *pref* diminished, defective; below.

hype [*hIp*] *n* (*sl abbr*) hypodermic needle, *esp* for injecting drugs; drug addict ~ **hype** *v/t* and *i* inject (oneself) with drugs; **hyped up** stimulated by drugs.

hyper- *pref* excessive; going beyond or above.

hyperbola [hI*pur*bola] *n* (*geom*) curve traced out by a point which moves so that its distance from a fixed point always bears a constant ratio greater than unity to its distance from a fixed straight line.

hyperbole [hI*pur*boli] *n* rhetorical exaggeration designed to emphasize, not to deceive.

hyperbolic [hIper*bol*ik] *adj* (*geom*) pertaining to a hyperbola; (*rhet*) exaggerated ~ **hyperbolical** *adj* ~ **hyperbolically** *adv*.

hyperbolist [hI*pur*bolist] *n* one who uses hyperbole.

hyperborean [hIper*baw*Ri-an] *n* and *adj* (inhabitant) of the extreme north; bitterly cold.

hyperconscious [hIper*kon*shus] *adj* very aware, too much aware.

hypercritical [hIper*kR*itikal] *adj* excessively severe in criticizing ~ **hypercritically** *adv*.

hypercriticism [hIper*kR*itisizm] *n* excessively severe criticism.

hyperdulia [hIper*dew*li-a] *n* (*RC*) especial veneration paid to the Virgin Mary.

hypermarket [*hI*permaarkit] *n* very large self-service store for food and household goods, *usu* outside town.

hypermetrical [hIper*met*Rikal] *adj* (*pros*) metrically redundant.

hypermetropia [hIper*met*ROpi-a] *n* (*opt*) long sight, defect of vision where the subject cannot clearly see nearby objects > PDP, PDS.

hyperon [*hI*peRon] *n* (*phys*) type of elementary particle with a short life and a greater mass than a neutron > PDS.

hyperphysical [hIper*fiz*ikal] *adj* supernatural.

hypersensitive [hIper*sen*sitiv] *adj* abnormally or excessively sensitive.

hypersonic [hIper*son*ik] *adj* (*aer*) pertaining to speeds above Mach 5 (five times speed of sound, *ie* 3,300 m.p.h.).

hypertension [hIper*ten*shon] *n* (*med*) abnormally high blood-pressure in arteries.

hyperthyroidism [hIpur*thyR*oidizm] *n* (*path*) condition caused by excessive activity of the thyroid gland, Graves' disease > PDP.

hypertonic [hIper*ton*ik] *adj* (*chem*) having a higher osmotic pressure than another solution.

hypertrophied [hI*per*tRofid] *adj* overgrown.

hypertrophy [hI*pur*tRofi] *n* (*path*) excessive growth of tissue in an organism > PDB.

hyperventilation [hIperventil*ay*shon] *n* (*med*) abnormally rapid breathing.

hyphen [*hI*fen] *n* short dash linking two parts of a compound word or of a divided word, **or** indicating syllabic divisions in a word ~ **hyphen** *v/t* hyphenate.

hyphenate [*hI*fenayt] *v/t* link by a hyphen; divide by hyphens ~ **hyphenation** *n*.

hypnagogic [hipnag*oj*ik] *adj* inducing sleep; pertaining to a state of drowsiness > PDP; **h. visions** vivid and *usu* weird visual images in the mind of one who is drowsy but not asleep.

hypno- *pref* of or like sleep or hypnosis.

hypnoid, hypnoidal [*hip*noid, hip*noi*dal] *adj* resembling sleep; pertaining to light hypnosis.

hypnosis [hip*nO*sis] *n* artificially induced state of relaxation and concentration and characterized by extreme suggestibility > PDP; art of inducing this state, hypnotism.

hypnotherapy [hipn*O*theRapi] *n* medical treatment using hypnosis.

hypnotic [hip*not*ik] *adj* inducing sleep; pertaining to hypnosis or hypnotism; (*coll*) riveting the attention ~ **hypnotic** *n* substance producing sleep, narcotic; person unusually sensitive to hypnotism.

hypnotism [*hip*notizm] *n* act or art of inducing a state of hypnosis; scientific study of hypnosis;

state of hypnosis; (*fig*) power of dominating another's will by suggestion ~ **hypnotist** *n* one who practises hypnotism.

hypnotize [*hip*notIz] *v/t* induce hypnosis in; (*fig*) dominate by willpower and suggestion; rivet the attention of, fascinate.

hypo- *pref* diminished, defective; below.

hypo (1) [*h*IpO] *n* a salt used for fixing photographs, sodium thiosulphate > PDS.

hypo (2) *n* (*coll abbr*) hypodermic syringe or injection.

hypocaust [*h*IpOkawst] *n* system of heating from beneath the flooring; chamber for heated air below floor of Roman house or bath.

hypochondria [hIp*O*kond*R*i-a] *n* exaggerated or obsessive anxiety about one's health; mistaken belief that one is ill; (*path*) deep depression.

hypochondriac [hIp*O*kond*R*i-ak] *n* person suffering from hypochondria ~ **hypochondriac** *adj* pertaining to hypochondria; (*anat*) pertaining to the body surface in the liver region.

hypochondriacal [hIp*O*kond*RI*-akal] *adj* pertaining to hypochondria.

hypochondriasis [hIp*O*kond*RI*-asis] *n* (*med*) hypochondria.

hypocrisy [hip*ok*Risi] *n* act or habit of pretending to be better than one is; act of disguising one emotion, thought *etc* by falsely displaying another; discrepancy between one's public and private morality; insincere piety or morality.

hypocrite [*hip*Ok*R*it] *n* one who practises hypocrisy.

hypocritical [hip*O*k*R*itikal] *adj* of or like a hypocrite; of hypocrisy ~ **hypocritically** *adv.*

hypodermic [hIp*O*durmik] *adj* injected into tissues under the skin; pertaining to such injections ~ **hypodermic** *n* hypodermic injection; syringe used in giving this; drug administered in this way.

hypodermis [hIp*O*durmis] *n* (*bot*) layer of cells immediately beneath epidermis of plant > PDB; (*anat*) tissues beneath the skin.

hypostasis (*pl* **hypostases**) [hIp*ostasis*] *n* (*philos*) basic reality underlying attributes; (*theol*) one Person of the Trinity; (*med*) excess of blood.

hypostatic [hIp*O*statik] *adj* pertaining to hypostasis; **h. union** (*theol*) union of Three Persons of the Trinity; union of divine and human nature in Christ ~ **hypostatically** *adv.*

hypotenuse [hIp*o*tenewz] *n* (*geom*) the side of a right-angled triangle opposite the right angle.

hypothalamus [hIp*Othal*amus] *n* (*anat*) area of the frontal brain in vertebrates coordinating mechanisms of temperature control, rage *etc* > PDP, PDB.

hypothermia [hIp*O*thurmi-a] *n* (*med*) condition of very low bodily temperature, *esp* among old people.

hypothesis (*pl* **hypotheses**) [hIp*oth*isis] *n* unproved theory, provisional explanation of observed facts; supposition, guess.

hypothesize [hIp*othes*Iz] *v/t* and *i* assume; frame a hypothesis.

hypothetic, hypothetical [hIp*O*thetik, hIp*O*thetikal] *adj* based on hypothesis; assumed as hypothesis, conjectural ~ **hypothetically** *adv.*

hypothyroidism [hIp*Oth*I*R*oidizm] *n* insufficient secretion activity of the thyroid gland ~ PDP.

hypotonic [hIp*O*to*n*ik] *adj* (*chem*) having a lower osmotic pressure than another solution.

hypsometer [hips*o*miter] *n* instrument for calculating altitude by measuring boiling-point of water > PDG, PDS.

hyrax (*pl* **hyraxes, hyraces**) [*h*I*r*Raks] *n* (*zool*) species of small African and Asian mammals.

hyson [*h*Ison] *n* kind of green China tea.

hyssop [*his*op] *n* aromatic mint; (*bibl*) plant whose twigs were used for sprinkling in Jewish religious rites; (*RC*) holy-water sprinkler.

hysterectomy [histe*R*ektomi] *n* (*surg*) excision of the uterus.

hysteresis [histe*R*eesis] *n* (*phys*) lag between releasing of stress and cessation of strain in materials subjected to tension or magnetism > PDS, PDE ~ **hysteretic** [histe*R*etik] *adj.*

hysteria [his*teer*Ri-a] *n* extreme emotional excitement; (*psych*) nervous disorder arising from repression, characterized by dissociation and producing physiological symptoms > PDP; (*coll*) violent outburst of emotion.

hysteric, hysterical [his*te*Rik, histe*R*ikal] *adj* of, like, or suffering from hysteria; (*fig*) overexcited, emotional; uncontrolled ~ **hysterically** *adv.*

hysterics [histe*R*iks] *n* (*pl*) outburst of violent weeping or laughing.

hysteron proteron [histe*R*on-p*R*ote*R*on] *n* (*gramm*) reversal of normal order of words or ideas.

hysterotomy [histe*R*otomi] *n* (*surg*) incision into uterus; Caesarean section.

I

I (1) [*I*] ninth letter of the English alphabet.

I (2) (*pl* **we**) *pron 1st pers sing nom* myself.

iamb [I-*amb*] *n* (*pros*) foot consisting of one unstressed followed by one stressed syllable, or of one short followed by one long syllable.

iambic [I-*ambik*] *n* and *adj* (verse) in iambs.

iambus [I-*ambus*] *n* (*pros*) iamb.

iatrochemistry [I-atRO*kemist*Ri] *n* medieval medical chemistry > PDS.

Iberian [I*beer*Ri-an] *n* and *adj* (inhabitant) of ancient Iberia or of modern Spain and Portugal; (language) of ancient Iberia; (*anthrop*) (member) of the prehistoric neolithic race of West Europe, Britain, and North Africa.

ibex (*pl* **ibexes**) [*I*beks] *n* species of wild goat.

ibidem (*abbr* **ibid.** or **ib.**) [ib*I*dem] *adv* in the same place (in a literary work); from the same author or work.

ibis (*pl* **ibises**) [*I*bis] *n* genus of wading birds.

ice [*Is*] *n* water frozen to a solid state > PDS; ice-cream; **i. age** geological period of widespread glaciation > PDG; **break the i.** overcome formality or reserve; begin some difficult or delicate undertaking; **cut no i.** achieve nothing; fail to impress; **thin i.** risky situation ~ **ice** *v*/*t* and *i* cover with ice; freeze; chill with ice; cover with icing sugar.

ice-axe [*Is*-aks] *n* axe used by mountaineers for cutting steps in ice.

iceberg [*Is*burg] *n* large mass of floating ice > PDG.

iceblink [*Is*blink] *n* glare on horizon caused by reflections from ice-floes > PDG.

ice-boat [*Is*-bOt] *n* boat with runners for travelling on ice; ice-breaker.

icebound [*Is*bownd] *adj* hemmed in by ice; made inaccessible by ice.

icebox [*Is*boks] *n* refrigerator, *esp* one in which food *etc* is cooled by contact with ice; inner compartment of a refrigerator, in which water can be frozen.

ice-breaker [*Is*-bRayker] *n* strongly built boat capable of forcing a way through floating ice.

icecap [*Is*kap] *n* mass of snow and ice covering large land areas round the poles > PDG.

ice-cream [*Is*-k*Reem*] *n* frozen cream or custard, flavoured and sweetened.

icefield [*Is*feeld] *n* large ice-floe > PDG.

ice-floe [*Is*-flO] *n* mass of floating ice > PDG.

ice-foot [*Is*-foot] *n* mass of ice projecting into the sea on an Arctic or Antarctic shore > PDG.

icehouse [*Is*hows] *n* storehouse for ice.

Icelander [*Is*lander] *n* native of Iceland.

Icelandic [*Is*landik] *n* and *adj* (language) of Iceland.

Iceland moss [*Is*land-*mos*] *n* edible Arctic lichen used as medicine.

Iceland spar [*Is*land-*spaar*] *n* very pure calcite.

iceman [*Is*man] *n* (*US*) person who sells or delivers ice.

icepack [*Is*pak] *n* mass of floating broken ice packed tightly together; cold compress with crushed ice.

icerink [*Is*Rink] *n* indoor skating rink of artificial ice.

ichabod [*ik*abod] *interj* (*Heb*) exclamation of grief for lost glories.

I ching [*ee* ching] *n* Chinese system of drawing oracles from permutations of long and short rods.

ichneumon [ik*new*mon] *n* small Egyptian carnivore resembling a weasel; **i. fly** wasp-like insect whose larvae are parasites to the larvae of other insects.

ichnography [ik*nog*Rafi] *n* (*archi*) art of drawing ground-plans.

ichor [*I*kawr] *n* (*Gk myth*) blood of the gods; thin fluid discharged from wound, ulcer *etc*.

ichthy-, ichthyo- *pref* pertaining to fish.

ichthyography [ikthi-*og*Rafi] *n* treatise on fishes.

ichthyoid [*ik*thi-oid] *adj* resembling a fish.

ichthyolite [*ik*thi-olIt] *n* (*geol*) fossil fish.

ichthyology [ikthi-*oloji*] *n* study of fishes.

ichthyophagous [ikthi-*of*agus] *adj* fish-eating.

ichthyosaurus [ikthi-O*sawr*Rus] *n* extinct marine reptile with fish-like tail-fin > PDB.

ichthyosis [ikthi-Osis] *n* (*path*) a skin disease.

ichthys [*ik*this] *n* representation of a fish as emblem of Christ.

icicle [*Isik*'l] *n* slender hanging piece of ice formed by the freezing of dripping water.

icily [*Is*ili] *adv* in an icy way ~ **iciness** *n*.

icing [*Is*ing] *n* formation of ice, *esp* on aeroplane wings; mixture of sugar, egg-white *etc* used as coating for cakes; **i. sugar** sugar capable of hardening into a firm coating.

icon, ikon [*I*kon] *n* representation of Christ or a saint, *usu* in metal and enamel, revered *esp* in the Eastern Orthodox Church; sacred image.

iconic [*I*konik] *adj* pertaining to portraits or figures; following a traditional style in art.

icono- *pref* pertaining to an image.

iconoclasm [*I*konoklazm] *n* act of breaking up religious images or sacred objects; (*hist*) 8th-century movement in Eastern Christian Church to abolish all sacred images, emblems *etc*; (*fig*) attempt to overthrow established customs or generally held beliefs ~ **iconoclast** *n* one who practises iconoclasm.

iconoclastic [Ikono*klastik*] *adj* of, like, or practising iconoclasm.

iconographer [Ikono*g*Rafer] *n* student of iconography.

iconography [Ikono*g*Rafi] *n* study of meanings conventionally attached to pictorial representations; system of emblems; study of portraits of a particular person; art of illustration > PDAA.

iconometer [Ikono*m*iter] *n* (*phot*) viewfinder giving direct view of object; (*sur*) instrument used to find size and distance of an object.

iconostasis [Ikono*stasis*] *n* screen between chancel and nave in Orthodox church, on which icons are hung.

icosahedron–idol

icosahedron [IkOsa*heed*Ron] *n* (*geom*) solid figure with twenty equal faces.

icterus [*ik*teRus] *n* (*path*) jaundice; (*bot*) plant disease in which the leaves turn yellow.

ictus [*ik*tus] *n* (*pros*) rhythmic stress.

icy [*I*si] *adj* of or like ice; frozen; freezing; (*fig*) chilling; distant in manner, indifferent.

id [*id*] *n* (*psych*) impersonal mass of interacting energies or forces constituting the unconscious > PDP.

I'd [*id*] *abbr* I had; I would; I should.

ide [*Id*] *n* freshwater fish allied to carp.

idea [I*dee*-a] *n* mental conception, notion, cognitive process > PDP; thought, opinion; plan; knowledge; (*philos*) immediate object of thought, perception or understanding; subjective notion; absolute truth lying behind the existence of a phenomenon; (*Gk philos*) eternally existing pattern of which material objects are imperfect copies; self-active cause of life.

ideal [I*dee*-al] *adj* finest imaginable, perfect; representing or expressing a mental conception, not an actual object > PDAA; existing only in the mind; relating to an idea ∼ **ideal** *n* standard of excellence conceived in the mind; perfect model which one strives to imitate > PDP; that which exists only in the mind.

idealism [I*dee*-alizm] *n* tendency to guide one's conduct by ideal standards; tendency to idealize; (*fig*) quixotic behaviour; unrealistic aspirations; (*philos*) any system that explains the universe in terms of ideas and maintains that all phenomena are subjective; doctrine that material objects are copies of eternal models > PDP; (*arts*) doctrine that art should represent ideals, not individual persons or objects > PDAA.

idealist [I*dee*-alist] *n* one who tends to live according to ideals; one who believes in idealism.

idealistic [Idee-a*lis*tik] *adj* of or like idealism or idealist, guided by ideals ∼ **idealistically** *adv*.

idealization [Idee-alIz*ay*shon] *n* act of idealizing; idealized view.

idealize [I*dee*-alIz] *v/t* and *i* represent or regard (person or thing) as fulfilling a standard of excellence; allow one's ideals or wishes to affect one's judgement (of); exaggerate the good qualities (of); form ideals; practise idealism.

ideally [I*dee*-ali] *adv* perfectly; as an ideal.

ideation [Idee-*ay*shon] *n* process of learning by forming or connecting ideas > PDP.

idée fixe [eeday-*feeks*] *n* (*Fr*) obsession.

idem [*I*dem] *n* (*Lat*) the same (book, author *etc*); as mentioned before.

identical [I*den*tikal] *adj* the very same; exactly alike; similar in every respect; **i. twins** twins developed from a single ovum ∼ **identically** *adv*.

identifiable [Identif*I*-ab'l] *adj* that can be identified.

identification [Identifik*ay*shon] *n* act of identifying; state of being identified.

identify [I*den*tifI] *v/t* prove or declare the identity of; show who or what (someone or something) is; regard or represent as identical; associate closely with; (*psych*) unconsciously model one's behaviour on that of someone to whom one is emotionally tied > PDP; **i. with** regard oneself as sharing the characteristics of.

identikit [I*den*tikit] *n* composite picture of face of unidentified person, built up from features said by witnesses to resemble his.

identity [I*den*titi] *n* fact or condition of being a specified person or thing; state or quality of persisting unchanged; state of being identical, sameness; (*math*) statement of equality between known or unknown quantities, which holds true for all values of the unknown quantities > PDS; **i. card, i. disk** *etc* official card, disk *etc* carried or worn to prove one's identity.

ideogram [*I*di-Og*ram*] *n* ideograph.

ideograph [*I*di-Og*Raaf*] *n* any character, symbol or figure which suggests the idea of an object without expressing the sounds in its name.

ideological [Idee-o*loji*kal] *adj* of, caused by an ideology.

ideologist [Idee-*oloji*st] *n* believer in an ideology.

ideologue [*idee*-olog] *n* theorist, visionary.

ideology [Idee-*oloji*] *n* body of ideas forming basis for political, economic or social system; (*philos*) theory that all ideas derive from sensations; science of ideas; (*fig*) vague theorizing, impractical views.

ides [*Idz*] *n* (*pl*) (*Rom calendar*) fifteenth of March, May, July or October; thirteenth of the other months.

idio- *pref* peculiar to one person or thing.

idiocy [*idi*-osi] *n* state of being an idiot; foolish behaviour or remark.

idiom [*idi*-om] *n* mode of expression, phrasing *etc* peculiar to one specified language; language or dialect peculiar to specified group of speakers; characteristic feature of a person's written or spoken style.

idiomatic [idi-o*matik*] *adj* of or containing idioms; fluent and colloquial ∼ **idiomatically** *adv*.

idiopathic [idi-o*pathik*] *adj* (*of disease*) primary.

idiopathy [idi-*opathi*] *n* (*med*) primary disease, not produced by another.

idioplasm [*idi*-oplazm] *n* (*biol*) that part of a living substance which is concerned in reproduction.

idiosyncrasy [idi-O*singk*Rasi] *n* individual peculiarity, characteristic personal mannerism or habit or way of speaking *etc*; (*med*) physical constitution of a particular person.

idiosyncratic [idi-Osingk*Rat*ik] *adj* of or as an idiosyncrasy; characteristic.

idiot [*idi*-ot] *n* imbecile; person of lowest grade of mental deficiency > PDP; (*coll*) fool.

idiotic [idi-*otik*] *adj* of or like an idiot; very foolish ∼ **idiotically** *adv*.

idle [*Id*'l] *adj* doing nothing, inactive; lazy; useless, ineffectual; trivial, frivolous; **i. wheel** cogged wheel placed between two others for transferring motion > PDE ∼ **idle** *v/i* and *t* do nothing; waste one's time in doing nothing; (*of engine*) revolve slowly, tick over.

idler [*Id*leR] *n* one who idles; lazy person; loafer, time-waster.

idly [*Id*li] *adv* in an idle way ∼ **idleness** *n*.

Ido [*eed*O] *n* an artificial universal language similar to Esperanto.

idol [*Id*ol] *n* image, effigy or natural object worshipped as a god; heathen god; person or thing excessively admired or loved; (*philos*) widely accepted misconception or fallacy.

idolater [Idolater] *n* worshipper of idols; (*fig*) devoted admirer (of).

idolatress [IdolatRes] *n* female idolater.

idolatrize [IdolatRIz] *v/t* idolize.

idolatrous [IdolatRus] *adj* worshipping idols; of or like idolatry ~ **idolatrously** *adv*.

idolatry [IdolatRi] *n* worship of idols; (*fig*) excessive admiration.

idolization [IdolIzayshon] *n* act of idolizing.

idolize [IdolIz] *v/t* make an idol of, love to excess.

idolum (*pl* **idola**) [IdOlum] *n* mental image; apparition; fallacy.

idyll [Idil/idil] *n* happy, poetic, and romantic incident or scene in rural surroundings; story or episode exemplifying happy youthful love; short poem on homely or pastoral subjects, *usu* happy or romantic in tone.

idyllic [Idilik] *adj* like an idyll; simple and peaceful; picturesque ~ **idyllically** *adv*.

if [*if*] *conj* supposing that, in case that; allowing that; whether.

igloo [iglOO] *n* Eskimo hut built of blocks of frozen snow.

igneous [igni-us] *adj* of or like fire; (*geol*) produced by volcanic action > PDG.

ignescent [ignesent] *adj* giving off sparks when struck.

ignis fatuus [ignis-*fatew*-us] *n* (*Lat*) pale flame seen over marshy ground at night, will-o'-the-wisp > PDS; (*fig*) misleading hope or aspiration.

ignitable [ignItab'l] *adj* that can be ignited.

ignite [ignIt] *v/t* and *i* set on fire, kindle; (*chem*) heat to the temperature at which combustion takes place; take fire.

ignition [ignishon] *n* setting on fire; strong heating; firing of an explosive mixture of gases by means of an electric spark; **i. key** key to operate ignition mechanism in a motor engine.

ignoble [ignOb'l] *adj* despicable, dishonourable; base; (*ar*) plebeian ~ **ignobleness** *n* ~ **ignobly** *adv*.

ignominious [ignomini-us] *adj* involving or deserving disgrace; shameful, despicable; humiliating ~ **ignominiously** *adv*.

ignominy [ignomini] *n* public disgrace; dishonour, shameful behaviour.

ignoramus (*pl* **ignoramuses**) [igneRaymus] *n* ignorant person.

ignorance [igneRans] *n* lack of knowledge or education; inexperience; unawareness.

ignorant [igneRant] *adj* lacking knowledge, uneducated; revealing ignorance ~ **ignorantly** *adv*.

ignore [ignawr] *v/t* take no notice of, disregard; (*leg*) (*of Grand Jury*) reject (indictment).

iguana [igwaana] *n* large S. American tree-lizard.

iguanodon [igwanodon] *n* huge, extinct dinosaur.

ikon see **icon**.

ileum [ili-um] *n* (*anat*) lower part of small intestine.

ilex (*pl* **ilexes**) [Ileks] *n* evergreen oak, holm-oak; (*bot*) genus of shrubs including holly.

iliac, ileac [ili-ak] *adj* (*anat*) of or in the small intestine; of or in the upper part of the hip-bone.

Iliad [ili-ad] *n* Greek epic poem, ascribed to Homer, describing the siege of Troy.

ilium (*pl* **ilia**) [ili-um] *n* (*anat*) upper part of hip-bone > PDB.

ilk [ilk] *adj* (*Scots*) same; **of that i.** of the place or estate or clan which has the same name as the surname of the owner; (*coll*) of that kind.

I'll [Il] *abbr* I shall; I will.

ill (*comp* **worse**, *superl* **worst**) [il] *adj* unwell, sick, diseased; bad; evil, wicked; malicious, hostile; harmful; unfavourable; foreboding misfortune; bad-tempered ~ **ill** *n* harm; misfortune; wickedness ~ **ill** *adv* badly; with difficulty; **i. at ease** uncomfortable; **speak i. of** disparage.

ill-advised [il-advIzd] *adj* unwise; rash.

ill-affected [il-a*fek*tid] *adj* unfavourably disposed.

illation [ilayshon] *n* deduction, inference.

illative [ilaytiv] *adj* of or like or expressing an inference; that may be inferred.

ill-blood [il-blud] *n* resentment; enmity.

ill-bred [il-bRed] *adj* badly brought up; rude, bad-mannered.

ill-breeding [il-bReeding] *n* rudeness, bad manners.

ill-conditioned [il-kondishond] *adj* bad-tempered, surly; inclined towards wickedness; in poor general health.

illegal [ileegal] *adj* unlawful, contrary to law.

illegality [ileegaliti] *n* state of being illegal; illegal act.

illegally [ileegali] *adv* against the law.

illegibility [ilejibiliti] *n* quality of being illegible.

illegible [ilejib'l] *adj* difficult or impossible to decipher; that cannot be read ~ **illegibly** *adv*.

illegitimacy [ilijitimasi] *n* state of being illegitimate.

illegitimate [ilijitimit] *adj* born out of wedlock, bastard; unlawful; illogical, incorrectly deduced ~ **illegitimate** [ilijitimayt] *v/t* render or declare illegitimate ~ **illegitimately** *adv*.

ill-fated [il-*fay*tid] *adj* unfortunate, luckless; bringing bad luck.

ill-favoured [il-*fay*verd] *adj* ugly.

ill-gotten [il-goten] *adj* obtained dishonestly.

ill-humoured [il-*hew*merd] *adj* bad-tempered.

illiberal [ilibeRal] *adj* not generous; petty, narrow-minded; uncultured.

illiberality [ilibeRaliti] *n* quality of being illiberal.

illicit [ilisit] *adj* unlawful; not permitted ~ **illicitly** *adv*.

illimitability [ilimitabiliti] *n* boundlessness.

illimitable [ilimitab'l] *adj* that cannot be limited, boundless ~ **illimitably** *adv*.

illiquid [ilikwid] *adj* (*of assets*) not liquid.

illiteracy [iliteRasi] *n* inability to read or write owing to lack of education > PDP.

illiterate [iliteRit] *adj* unable to read or write; uneducated, very ignorant; uncultured ~ **illiterate** *n* illiterate person ~ **illiterately** *adv*.

ill-judged [il-jujd] *adj* unwise.

ill-mannered [il-*ma*nerd] *adj* rude.

ill-natured [il-*nay*cherd] *adj* malicious; churlish ~ **ill-naturedly** *adv*.

illness [ilnes] *n* state of being ill, sickness; specified disease.

illogical [ilojikal] *adj* contrary to the rules of logic; irrational; ignorant of the rules of logic ~ **illogically** *adv*.

illogicality [iloji*k*aliti] *n* quality of being illogical; illogical statement or idea.

ill-omened [il-Omend] *adj* unlucky; inauspicious.

ill-starred [il-*staard*] *adj* unlucky, disastrous.

ill-tempered [il-*temperd*] *adj* surly, cross.

ill-timed [il-*tImd*] *adj* unwise or inappropriate at a particular time.

ill-treat [il-*tReet*] *v/t* treat badly; treat cruelly, maltreat ∼ **ill-treatment** *n*.

illume [ilewm] *v/t* (*poet*) illuminate.

illuminant [ilewminant] *n* and *adj* (that) which gives light.

illuminate [ilewminayt] *v/t* throw light upon, light up; adorn with lights. *esp* coloured lamps; embellish (manuscript) with coloured miniatures, ornamental initial letters, borders *etc*; (*fig*) make clearer, explain; enlighten.

illuminati [ilOOmi*n*aati/ilewmi*n*aytI] *n* (*pl*) members of any of various religious sects claiming to have direct inspiration from God; (*hist*) members of an 18th-century German deistic and republican secret society; (*fig*) persons claiming to possess special enlightenment.

illumination [ilewmi*n*ayshon] *n* act of illuminating; state of being illuminated; that which illuminates; miniature, coloured decoration, or ornamental initial letter in a manuscript; amount of light falling on a surface; (*pl*) display of ornamental coloured lights, flood-lighting *etc*; (*fig*) divine inspiration; spiritual or intellectual enlightenment.

illuminative [ilewminativ] *adj* giving light.

illuminator [ilewminayter] *n* one who or that which illuminates; one who embellishes manuscripts.

illumine [ilewmin] *v/t* light up; enlighten.

ill-usage [il-yOOzij] *n* harsh treatment.

ill-use [il-yOOz] *v/t* treat badly or unkindly.

illusion [ilewzhon] *n* deceptive appearance, misleading visual impression; anything that gives false impression to the senses; mistaken belief or opinion; subjective falsification of memory > PDP; conjuring trick; delusion, hallucination ∼ **illusional** *adj*.

illusionism [ilewzhonizm] *n* (*arts*) use of technique to make a painted object or scene seem real > PDAA; (*philos*) theory that the external world is an illusion ∼ **illusionist** *n* believer in illusionism; conjurer.

illusive [ilewsiv] *adj* causing illusion; caused by illusion; deceptive.

illusory [ilewzeRi] *adj* of or like an illusion; based on illusion; not real; deceptive.

illustrate [i*l*ustRayt] *v/t* make clear, explain, by means of examples; exemplify; ornament (book) with pictures ∼ **illustrated** *adj*.

illustration [ilust*R*ayshon] *n* drawing or picture in book; that which illustrates, example; act of making clear or evident; exemplification.

illustrative [i*l*ustRativ] *adj* serving to illustrate ∼ **illustratively** *adv*.

illustrator [i*l*ustRayter] *n* one who illustrates, *esp* one who draws illustrations.

illustrious [i*l*ustRi-us] *adj* distinguished, famous, glorious ∼ **illustriously** *adv* ∼ **illustriousness** *n*.

ill-will [il-*wil*] *n* malice, enmity.

im- *neg pref* used before *b*, *m* and *p*.

I'm [*Im*] *abbr* I am.

image [imij] *n* figure carved, painted, engraved *etc* to represent a person or thing; effigy, statue; idol; exact likeness; metaphor, figure of speech; symbol; mental conception, idea; (*psych*) revived sense experience without sensory stimulation > PDP; (*opt*) figure formed by rays of light on retina, lens, or mirror > PDS; (*coll*) person or thing strikingly like another; (*coll*) the public's idea of what a political party, commercial product *etc* is like ∼ **image** *v/t* make an image of; imagine; mirror, reflect; portray; symbolize.

imagery [imijeRi] *n* (*collect*) metaphors, symbols and figurative language as used in a specified work or by a specified writer; recurrent images; statues, effigies.

imaginable [ima*j*inab'l] *adj* that may be imagined.

imaginal [ima*j*inal] *adj* (*ent*) of an imago > PDB.

imaginary [ima*j*ineRi] *adj* existing only in the imagination; not real; **i. number** (*math*) number with a negative square.

imagination [imaji*n*ayshon] *n* act or process of imagining; power of imagining; power of forming mental concepts or images of things not experienced; artistically inventive or creative faculty; power of mentally re-creating past experiences > PDP; mental image; fanciful idea.

imaginative [ima*j*inativ] *adj* having much imagination; creative; formed by the imagination ∼ **imaginatively** *adv* ∼ **imaginativeness** *n*.

imagine [ima*j*in] *v/t* and *i* form an image in the mind; form an idea of; suppose, conjecture.

imagines [imayjineez] *pl* of **imago**.

imagism [ima*j*izm] *n* poetic movement of the early 20th century, advocating use of precise images, contemporary subjects and free verse ∼ **imagist** *n* and *adj*.

imago (*pl* **imagines**) [imaygO] *n* sexually mature insect; (*psych*) idealized memory or phantasy of person beloved in one's childhood > PDP.

imam [imaam] *n* Muslim priest; Muslim prince and religious leader.

imbalance [imb*a*lans] *n* lack of proportion or equilibrium; lack of muscular coordination or balance > PDP.

imbecile [imbeseel/imbesIl] *n* person of second degree of mental deficiency > PDP; feeble-minded person; (*coll*) silly fool ∼ **imbecile** *adj* of or like an imbecile; very stupid.

imbecilic [imbisilik] *adj* very stupid.

imbecility [imbisiliti] *n* state of being an imbecile; extreme stupidity or folly; very stupid act.

imbibe [imb*I*b] *v/t* drink in, draw in; absorb; (*fig*) receive into the mind; (*coll*) drink to excess.

imbrex (*pl* **imbrices**) [imbReks] *n* (*bui*) an overlapping gutter tile.

imbricate [imb*R*ikayt] *v/i* and *t* (*zool*, *bot*) overlap ∼ **imbricate** *adj* overlapping.

imbroglio (*pl* **imbroglios**) [imb*R*Oli-O] *n* complicated or confusing situaion .

imbrue [imb*R*OO] *v/t* drench, soak; stain.

imbue [imbew] *v/t* steep, saturate; dye, tinge; inspire, instil (ideas *etc*) into.

imburse [imburs] *v/t* supply with money.

imitable [imitab'l] *adj* that can or should be imitated ∼ **imitability** *n*.

imitate [*imi*tayt] *v/t* copy closely, take as model; copy the conduct, appearance *etc* of; look very like; counterfeit; mimic

imitation [imit*ay*shon] *n* act of imitating; that which imitates, copy; counterfeit.

imitative [*imi*tativ] *adj* that imitates, tending to imitate; done in imitation, not original ~ **imitatively** *adv* ~ **imitativeness** *n*.

imitator [*imi*taytor] *n* one who or that which imitates.

immaculate [im*ak*ewlit] *adj* sinless, pure; free from stain, very clean and neat; (*zool*) without markings; (*theol*) without original sin ~ **immaculately** *adv*.

immanence [*ima*nens] *n* pervasive presence within something; (*theol*) presence of God throughout universe ~ **immanency** *n* immanence ~ **immanent** *adj*.

immaterial [imat*eer*Ri-al] *adj* not consisting of matter; spiritual; not important.

immaterialism [imat*eer*Ri-alizm] *n* (*philos*) doctrine that matter has no real existence; doctrine that spirit exists independently of matter ~ **immaterialist** *n* and *adj*.

immateriality [imateerRi-*a*liti] *n* quality or state of being immaterial.

immature [ima*tyoor*] *adj* not fully developed or formed, not adult; lacking adult wisdom, self-control or emotional balance; not ripe.

immaturity [ima*tyoor*Riti] *n* state of being immature.

immeasurability [imezheRa*bili*ti] *n* quality of being immeasurable.

immeasurable [im*ezh*eRab'l] *adj* that cannot be measured; vast, enormous ~ **immeasurableness** *n* ~ **immeasurably** *adv*.

immediacy [im*ee*di-asi] *n* state or quality of being immediate.

immediate [im*ee*di-it] *adj* with nothing coming between; at once, instant; direct, without intermediary; next, very near; contiguous ~ **immediately** *adv*.

immemorable [im*eme*Rab'l] *adj* not worth remembering.

immemorial [imem*aw*Ri-al] *adj* very remote; very ancient ~ **immemorially** *adv* since very remote times.

immense [im*ens*] *adj* extremely large, huge; very great; (*sl*) very good, splendid ~ **immensely** *adv* to an immense degree; very much, extremely.

immensity [im*ensi*ti] *n* hugeness; vast space.

immensurable [im*ens*heRab'l] *adj* that cannot be measured.

immerse [im*urs*] *v/t* plunge or dip deeply into; baptize by plunging under water; (*fig*) absorb, engross; (*fig*) involve, entangle.

immersion [im*ur*shon] *n* act of immersing; state of being immersed; baptism by plunging under water; (*astron*) disappearance of a celestial body behind another or in its shadow; **i. heater** electric resistance heater submerged in a water tank.

immesh [im*esh*] *v/t* enmesh, entangle.

immigrant [*imi*gRant] *n* and *adj* (person) coming into a country from abroad to settle there permanently.

immigrate [*imi*gRayt] *v/i* and *t* come or bring into a foreign country to live there permanently.

immigration [imigR*ay*shon] *n* act of immigrating; group of immigrants.

imminence [*imi*nens] *n* state of being imminent.

imminent [*imi*nent] *adj* coming on soon, about to happen, threatening ~ **imminently** *adv*.

immiscible [im*isi*b'l] *adj* that cannot be mixed.

immitigable [im*iti*gab'l] *adj* that cannot be mitigated; unrelenting, unappeasable ~ **immitigably** *adv*.

immixture [im*iks*cher] *n* act of mixing; state of being mixed.

immobile [im*Ob*Il] *adj* not moving; that cannot be moved; fixed.

immobility [imO*bili*ti] *n* state or quality of being immobile.

immobilize [im*Ob*ilIz] *v/t* render immovable; render (troops) incapable of mobilization; keep stationary; (*currency*) remove from circulation and hold as security.

immoderate [im*ode*Rit] *adj* excessive; unreasonable ~ **immoderately** *adv* ~ **immoderateness** *n*.

immoderation [imode*Ray*shon] *n* excess, lack of moderation.

immodest [im*ode*st] *adj* indecent, improper; displaying too much sexual allure; presumptuous, pert ~ **immodestly** *adv*.

immodesty [im*ode*sti] *n* quality of being immodest; immodest behaviour.

immolate [*im*Olayt] *v/t* kill as sacrifice; offer up, sacrifice.

immolation [imO*lay*shon] *n* act of immolating; sacrificial victim; state of being sacrificed ~ **immolator** *n* one who immolates.

immoral [im*o*Ral] *adj* contrary to moral law, wicked; unchaste, sexually lax; obscene; unscrupulous ~ **immorally** *adv*.

immorality [imo*Ra*liti] *n* quality of being immoral; immoral act.

immortal [im*aw*rtal] *adj* that will not die; that will not cease; enjoying imperishable fame ~ **immortal** *n* one who will not die; one whose fame is imperishable ~ **immortally** *adv*.

immortality [imawrt*a*liti] *n* quality or state of being immortal; endless existence; imperishable fame.

immortalize [im*aw*rtalIz] *v/t* make famous for ever; make immortal ~ **immortalization** [imawrtalIz*ay*shon] *n*.

immortelle [imawrt*el*] *n* flower that keeps its colour when dried.

immovability [imOOva*bili*ti] *n* state or quality of being immovable.

immovable [imOO*vab*'l] *adj* that cannot be moved; firmly fixed; steadfast, unalterable; (*leg*) permanent ~ **immovably** *adv*.

immune [im*ewn*] *adj* free or exempt from; secure against; able to resist infection; **i. body** antibody > PDB.

immunity [im*ewn*iti] *n* freedom or exemption from obligation, tax, duty *etc*; ability to resist infection > PDB.

immunization [imyoonIz*ay*shon] *n* act of making immune; state of being immune.

immunize [*im*yoonIz] *v/t* make immune.

immunology [imew*no*loji] *n* science dealing with immunity from disease > PDB.

immuno-suppressive [imewnO-sup*Re*siv] *adj* (*med*) reducing a body's normal tendency to reject alien organisms, *esp* transplanted tissue.

immure [im*ewr*] *v/t* imprison; (*refl*) shut oneself up, live in strict seclusion.

immutability [imewta*bi*liti] *n* unchangingness.

immutable [im*ew*tab'l] *adj* unchangeable, without variation ~ **immutably** *adv*.

imp (1) [*imp*] *n* minor demon; mischievous goblin, sprite *etc*; mischievous child.

imp (2) *v/t* engraft new feathers on to damaged ones; strengthen.

impact [*im*pakt] *n* collision > PDE; force of a collision, shock; strong impression or effect ~ **impact** [im*pakt*] *v/t* press or drive strongly together.

impaction [im*pak*shon] *n* act of impacting; state of being impacted.

impair [im*pair*] *v/t* weaken; lessen the value of, reduce; injure.

impairment [im*pair*ment] *n* that which impairs; state of being impaired; act of impairing.

impale [im*payl*] *v/t* transfix; kill by fixing on an upright sharp stake; (*her*) blazon (two coats of arms) on one vertically divided shield; (*ar*) fence round ~ **impalement** *n* act of impaling; state of being impaled.

impalpable [im*pal*pab'l] *adj* not perceptible to the touch; intangible; (*fig*) not easily understood ~ **impalpably** *adv*.

impanel [im*pan*el] *v/t* empanel.

impar-, impari- *pref* in an uneven number.

imparisyllabic [impa*Ri*si*la*bik] *n* and *adj* (noun) having more syllables in genitive than in nominative case.

impart [im*paart*] *v/t* communicate, transmit; make known; bestow.

impartation [impaar*tay*shon] *n* act of imparting.

impartial [im*paar*shal] *adj* not favouring one side more than another; unprejudiced, fair ~ **impartially** *adv*.

impartiality [impaarshi-*a*liti] *n* quality of being impartial.

impassable [im*paas*ab'l] *adj* that cannot be passed over or traversed ~ **impassably** *adv*.

impasse [im*paas*/am*paas*] *n* blind alley; (*fig*) deadlock; stalemate.

impassibility [impasi*bi*liti] *n* quality of being impassible; unshakable calmness.

impassible [im*pas*ib'l] *adj* not capable of suffering, immune to all injury; incapable of strong feelings; hard-hearted, unfeeling.

impassion [im*pa*shon] *v/t* move the deepest feelings of; rouse to passion ~ **impassioned** *adj* passionate, ardent.

impassive [im*pa*siv] *adj* without emotion, unmoved, calm; without suffering ~ **impassively** *adv* ~ **impassiveness** *n*.

impassivity [impa*si*viti] *n* complete calmness.

impaste [im*payst*] *v/t* lay on (colours) thickly in painting; cover with paste.

impasto [im*pas*tO] *n* (*in painting*) technique of laying colours on thickly, usually with a knife.

impatience [im*pay*shens] *n* lack of patience; eagerness; irritability; intolerance.

impatient [im*pay*shent] *adj* unwilling to endure suffering, restraint, delay *etc*; eager; irritable; intolerant ~ **impatiently** *adv*.

impawn [im*pawn*] *v/t* pawn; pledge.

impeach [im*peech*] *v/t* indict, charge with (crime, *esp* high treason); accuse; discredit; inform against ~ **impeachable** *adj* liable to be impeached.

impeachment [im*peech*ment] *n* act of impeaching, accusation; reproach, discredit.

impeccability [impeka*bi*liti] *n* quality or character of being impeccable.

impeccable [im*pek*ab'l] *adj* faultless, without blame; incapable of sin ~ **impeccably** *adv*.

impecuniosity [impikewni*o*siti] *n* state of being impecunious.

impecunious [impi*kew*ni-us] *adj* without money; chronically poor.

impedance [im*pee*dans] *n* (*elect*) total opposition to an alternating current flowing through a circuit, equal to the square root of the sum of the squares of the resistance and the reactance.

impede [im*peed*] *v/t* hinder; obstruct.

impediment [im*pe*diment] *n* hindrance; obstruction; speech defect, stammer, lisp *etc*.

impedimenta [impedi*men*ta] *n* (*pl*) baggage.

impel (*pres/part* **impelling**, *p/t* and *p/part* **impelled**) [im*pel*] *v/t* drive or urge forward; drive or force into action.

impellent [im*pel*ent] *n* and *adj* (that) which impels.

impeller [im*pe*ler] *n* rotor of jet engine; rotor of any propulsive device.

impend [im*pend*] *v/i* be about to happen, be threateningly close; overhang ~ **impendent** *adj* ~ **impending** *adj*.

impenetrability [impenitRa*bi*liti] *n* quality of being impenetrable.

impenetrable [im*pen*itRab'l] *adj* that cannot be penetrated or pierced; that cannot be seen through; incomprehensible; inscrutable; that will not receive new ideas, impressions *etc*, obtuse; (*philos*) preventing any other substance from occupying the same place at the same time ~ **impenetrably** *adv*.

impenetrate [im*pen*itRayt] *v/t* penetrate deeply.

impenitence [im*pen*itens] *n* incapacity or refusal to repent ~ **impenitent** *adj* and *n* unrepentant (person) ~ **impenitently** *adv*.

imperative [im*pe*Rativ] *adj* peremptory, authoritative; essential, urgent, highly important; obligatory; (*gramm*) expressing command ~ **imperative** *n* order; rule of conduct considered as unconditionally binding > PDP; (*gramm*) mood of verb expressing command; word, sentence *etc* expressing command ~ **imperatively** *adv*.

imperceptibility [impersepti*bi*liti] *n* quality of being imperceptible.

imperceptible [imper*sep*tib'l] *adj* too small, slight or gradual to be perceived; minute, insignificant ~ **imperceptibly** *adv*.

imperceptive [imper*sep*tiv] *adj* impercipient.

impercipient [imper*si*pi-ent] *adj* lacking perception.

imperfect [im*pur*fect] *adj* defective, incomplete,

faulty; **i. tense** (*gramm*) tense denoting continuous action, *usu* in the past ~ **imperfect** *n* (*gramm*) the imperfect tense ~ **imperfectly** *adv*.
imperfection [imper*fek*shon] *n* state of being imperfect; fault, shortcoming; defect.
imperfective [imper*fek*tiv] *n* and *adj* (*gramm*) (tense) denoting continuous or repeated acts.
imperforate, imperforated [im*pur*feRayt, im*pur*feRaytid] *adj* without perforations; (*anat*) lacking a natural opening; wholly closed.
imperial [im*peer*Ri-al] *adj* of or pertaining to an empire or emperor; fitting for an emperor, majestic, lordly; pertaining to the British Empire; fixed as standard throughout Great Britain; **I. Preference** traditional system of preferential trade agreements between Great Britain and Commonwealth countries > PDPol ~ **imperial** *n* small beard or tuft of hair grown on chin; size of paper or slate; former Russian gold coin; (*bui*) dome with point at top ~ **imperially** *adv*.
imperialism [im*peer*Ri-alizm] *n* the founding, development and maintenance of an empire; the practice by a country of acquiring and exploiting dependent territories, colonialism; systematic attempt to dominate weaker countries by political or economic means; support for or approval of such policies > PDPol.
imperialist [im*peer*Ri-alist] *n* and *adj* (supporter) of imperialism; (adherent) of an emperor.
imperialistic [im*peer*Ri-a*list*ik] *adj* of, like, or supporting imperialism.
imperialize [im*peer*Ri-alIz] *v/t* render imperial; bring into an empire; imbue with imperialism.
imperil (*pres*/*part* **imperilling**, *p*/*t* and *p*/*part* **imperilled**) [im*pe*Ril] *v/t* expose to danger.
imperious [im*peer*Ri-us] *adj* dictatorial, overbearing; haughty, arrogant; urgent, imperative ~ **imperiously** *adv* ~ **imperiousness** *n*.
imperishable [im*pe*Rishab'l] *adj* not subject to decay; immortal, eternal.
impermanence [im*pur*manens] *n* transitoriness.
impermanent [im*pur*manent] *adj* not permanent, transitory ~ **impermanently** *adv*.
impermeable [im*pur*mi-ab'l] *adj* not porous; impenetrable, impervious ~ **impermeability** *n*.
impersonal [im*pur*sonal] *adj* without personality, revealing no individual characteristics; showing no feelings, not intimate; automatic, mechanical; (*gramm*) (*of verbs*) used only in *3rd pers sing*, usually with the subject *it* ~ **impersonally** *adv*.
impersonality [impurso*na*liti] *n* quality of being impersonal.
impersonate [im*pur*sonayt] *v/t* pretend to be another, either fraudulently or as entertainment.
impersonation [impurso*nay*shon] *n* act of impersonating; mimicry, dramatic imitation; method of acting a dramatic part; stage representation of a masculine character by a woman, or of a feminine character by a man.
impersonator [im*pur*sonayter] *n* one who impersonates another; **female i.** actor who takes female parts; **male (masculine) i.** actress who takes masculine parts.
impertinence [im*pur*tinens] *n* quality of being impertinent, rudeness, insolence; lack of pertinence, irrelevance; an impertinent act or speech.
impertinent [im*pur*tinent] *adj* rude, impudent;

off the point, irrelevant; inappropriate, inopportune ~ **impertinently** *adv*.
imperturbability [imperturba*bili*ti] *n* quality of being imperturbable; unshaken, calm.
imperturbable [imper*turb*ab'l] *adj* not easily disturbed or excited ~ **imperturbably** *adv*.
impervious [im*pur*vi-us] *adj* that cannot be penetrated; not porous; (*fig*) not influenced by, not receptive towards ~ **imperviously** *adv* ~ **imperviousness** *n*.
impetigo [impi*tIg*O] *n* a skin disease.
impetrate [*im*petRayt] *v/t* (*theol*) obtain by prayer.
impetuosity [impetew-*osi*ti] *n* quality of being impetuous; impetuous act or speech.
impetuous [im*pet*ew-us] *adj* acting too hastily; impulsive; eager; rash; rushing violently ~ **impetuously** *adv* ~ **impetuousness** *n*.
impetus [*im*pitus] *n* driving force; momentum; (*fig*) stimulus, incentive.
impfing [*impf*ing] *n* act of placing small crystal in a liquid to induce crystallization.
impi [*im*pi] *n* body of Zulu warriors.
impiety [im*pI*-iti] *n* lack of piety; ungodliness; impious act; lack of reverence.
impinge [im*pinj*] *v/i* come into contact (with); **i. on** strike, fall (on); encroach, infringe; affect ~ **impingement** *n*.
impious [*im*pi-us] *adj* lacking piety or reverence; profane; wicked ~ **impiously** *adv* ~ **impiousness** *n*.
impish [*imp*ish] *adj* like an imp, mischievous ~ **impishly** *adv* ~ **impishness** *n*.
implacability [implaka*bili*ti] *n* quality of being implacable; ruthlessness.
implacable [im*plak*ab'l] *adj* that cannot be appeased, unrelenting ~ **implacably** *adv*.
implant [im*plaant*] *v/t* insert deeply, fix into; insert into living tissue; (*fig*) instil, impress into the mind ~ **implant** [*im*plaant] *n* (*zool*) material inserted into embryo > PDB; (*med*) tube of radioactive material inserted into tissues.
implantation [implan*tay*shon] *n* act of implanting; that which is implanted.
implausibility [implawzi*bili*ti] *n* quality of being implausible; implausible statement, claim *etc*.
implausible [im*plaw*zib'l] *adj* not appearing to be true, unlikely ~ **implausibly** *adv*.
implement [*im*pliment] *n* article used in carrying out a task; tool, instrument ~ **implement** [im*plim*ent] *v/t* carry into effect, accomplish; complete; (*Scots leg*) fulfil (contract *etc*).
implementation [impliment*ay*shon] *n* act of implementing; state of being implemented.
implicate [*im*plikayt] *v/t* prove (someone) to have shared in or been connected with (a crime *etc*); involve; entangle; (*log*) necessitate a specified inference, imply.
implication [impli*kay*shon] *n* act of implying or implicating; state of being implied or implicated; that which is implied.
implicit [im*plis*it] *adj* implied though not plainly stated; absolute, complete, unquestioning ~ **implicitly** *adv* ~ **implicitness** *n*.
implied [im*plId*] *adj* conveyed without direct statement, intended to be inferred.
implode [im*plOd*] *v/t* and *i* burst inward; collapse violently inwards under pressure, heat *etc*; (*phon*)

abruptly interrupt breath-stream to pronounce plosive consonants.

implore [im*plawr*] *v/t* ask or beg earnestly ~ **imploring** *adj* ~ **imploringly** *adv*.

implosion [im*plO*zhon] *n* act of imploding.

imply [im*plI*] *v/t* suggest a secondary meaning not directly stated; hint at, insinuate; necessitate a certain inference or logical conclusion.

impolicy [im*poli*si] *n* unwise behaviour.

impolite [impo*lIt*] *adj* rude, discourteous, bad-mannered ~ **impolitely** *adv* ~ **impoliteness** *n*.

impolitic [im*politik*] *adj* injudicious, not wise.

imponderability [imponde*Ra*bi*liti*] *n* quality of being imponderable; that which is imponderable.

imponderable [im*ponde*Rab'l] *n* and *adj* (that) which has no sensible weight; very light; (that) which cannot be estimated or calculated ~ **imponderableness** *n* ~ **imponderably** *adv*.

import [im*pawrt*] *v/t* and *i* bring into a country from abroad; introduce; imply, signify; be important to ~ **import** [*imp*awrt] *n* that which is brought into a country from abroad > PDG; that which is implied; signification, meaning; importance, consequence.

importable [im*pawr*tab'l] *adj* that may be imported.

importance [im*pawr*tans] *n* quality or state of being important; reason why something is important.

important [im*pawr*tant] *adj* mattering greatly, very significant or far-reaching in its effects; valuable; occupying an influential position, eminent; officious, pompous; self-satisfied ~ **importantly** *adv*.

importation [impawr*tay*shon] *n* act or practice of importing; that which is imported.

importer [im*pawr*ter] *n* one who imports goods.

importunate [im*pawr*choonit] *adj* pestering, persistent; continually demanding or pleading; insistent ~ **importunately** *adv*.

importune [im*pawr*choon/impawr*chOOn*] *v/t* pester by unceasing demands, requests *etc*.

importunity [impawr*chOO*niti] *n* quality of being importunate; importunate behaviour.

impose [im*pOz*] *v/t* and *i* levy, exact; force to do or accept, lay (a burden, task *etc*) on; foist, trick into accepting; (*typ*) arrange pages of type in a 'forme', so that they will read consecutively when the printed sheet is folded; **i. on, i. upon** deceive, mislead; take unfair advantage of.

imposing [im*pOz*ing] *adj* commanding respect, impressive ~ **imposingly** *adv*.

imposition [impo*zi*shon] *n* act of imposing; that which is imposed; task given as school punishment; unreasonable demand; duty; tax; imposture, fraud; **i. of hands** sacramental gesture of bishop in confirmation or ordination.

impossibility [imposi*bi*liti] *n* state of being impossible; that which is impossible.

impossible [im*posib'l*] *adj* not possible; that cannot be, be done, be thought *etc*; (*coll*) insufferable; socially unacceptable ~ **impossibly** *adv*.

impost (1) [*imp*Ost] *n* tax or duty imposed; weight carried by horse in handicap racing.

impost (2) *n* (*archi*) block of masonry or brickwork on which an arch rests.

impostor [im*poster*] *n* one who impersonates another for fraudulent purposes; one who deceives by pretending to be what he is not; fraud, cheat.

imposture [im*poscher*] *n* deception by false pretences, fraud.

impot [*imp*ot/impO] *n* (*coll abbr*) imposition, task set as punishment.

impotence, impotency [*imp*Otens, *imp*Otensi] *n* state of being impotent.

impotent [*imp*Otent] *adj* powerless to act, helpless; (*of males*) lacking power to perform the sexual act; feeble ~ **impotently** *adv*.

impound [im*pownd*] *v/t* take into custody; confine; take possession of, confiscate; enclose (cattle) in a pound.

impoverish [im*pove*Rish] *v/t* make poor; exhaust the resources or the fertility of; deprive of interest or of charm ~ **impoverishment** *n* act of impoverishing; state of being impoverished.

impracticability [imp*Ra*ktika*bi*liti] *n* quality of being impracticable.

impracticable [imp*Ra*ktikab'l] *adj* that cannot be effected or done; impossible; (*fig*) stubborn; (*of roads*) impassable ~ **impracticably** *adv*.

impractical [imp*Ra*ktikal] *adj* not practical; not useful; inefficient; not realistic; impracticable.

impracticality [imp*Ra*kti*ka*liti] *n* quality of being impractical.

imprecate [*imp*Rikayt] *v/t* call down curses or misfortune on.

imprecation [imp*Rika*yshon] *n* curse.

imprecatory [*imp*Rikayte*Ri*] *adj* of or as a curse.

imprecise [impRis*Is*] *adj* not clearly stated, vague, not defined ~ **imprecision** [impRi*si*zhon] *n*.

impregnability [impregna*bi*liti] *n* state or quality of being impregnable.

impregnable [imp*Reg*nab'l] *adj* that cannot be captured by assault; (*fig*) invincible ~ **impregnably** *adv*.

impregnate [*imp*Regnayt] *v/t* make pregnant; fertilize; saturate, fill; (*fig*) inspire (with).

impregnation [impRe*gna*yshon] *n* act of impregnating; that which impregnates; state of being impregnated.

impresario [impResaa*Ri*-O] *n* manager of an operatic or theatrical company.

imprescriptible [impRis*kRi*ptib'l] *adj* unchallengeable, inviolable; inalienable.

impress (1) [imp*Res*] *v/t* produce a strong and lasting effect on the mind or feelings of, appear remarkable to; fix firmly into the mind of; mark (a surface) by pressure, stamp ~ **impress** [*imp*Res] *n* mark made by pressure, imprint; act of impressing; (*fig*) effect made by powerful personality *etc*; characteristic mark.

impress (2) *v/t* compel to serve in army or navy; commandeer, seize for public use; (*fig*) bring into use; force into service ~ **impressment** *n*.

impressible [imp*Resi*b'l] *adj* capable of being impressed; yielding to pressure; susceptible.

impression [imp*Resh*on] *n* act of impressing; state of being impressed; mark left by pressure, stamp, imprint; effect produced by external stimulus or influence; general idea, notion; indistinct idea, vague feeling; (*typ*) degree of pressure on a sheet in printing press; the imprint of type; a printed copy; number of copies printed at any one time; reprint without alterations; **be under the i.** think, have a vague idea.

impressionability [imp*R*eshona*bi*liti] *n* state or quality of being impressionable.

impressionable [imp*R*esh*o*nab'l] *adj* susceptible, *esp* to emotional or moral impressions.

impressionism [imp*R*esh*o*nizm] *n* style of painting seeking exact analysis of tone, colour, and effects of light in order to record immediate sense-impressions of visual experience > PDAA; artistic or literary attempt to convey a general impression of a vie*w*, object, or experience, rather than to record it in precise detail ~ **impressionist** *n* and *adj*.

impressionistic [imp*R*esh*o*nistik] *adj* conveying a general impression; of or like impressionism; **i.** criticism evaluation of a work of art not related to an accepted standard, but based rather on the individual reaction of the critic.

impressive [imp*R*esiv] *adj* making powerful impression on mind or emotions ~ **impressively** *adv* ~ **impressiveness** *n*.

imprest [imp*R*est] *n* loan to an individual in order that he may perform duties for the State.

imprimatur [impri*may*ter] *n* licence to print a book, *esp* one granted by the Roman Catholic Church;(*fig*) approval, sanction.

imprimis [imp*R*imis] *adv* (*Lat*) in the first place.

imprint [imp*R*int] *v/t* mark by pressure, stamp; make by pressure; print; fix in the mind, impress ~ **imprint** [imp*R*int] *n* that which is printed, stamp, mark made by pressure; distinctive sign; (*print*) publisher's or printer's name, address *etc*, with date of publication, printed at beginning or end of book *etc*.

imprinting [imp*R*inting] *n* (*psych*) process by which a very young animal learns to recognize identifying characteristics of others of its species, or of a substitute parent.

imprison [imp*R*izun] *v/t* put in prison; confine.

imprisonment [imp*R*izunment] *n* act of imprisoning; state of being imprisoned; time spent in prison.

improbability [imp*R*oba*bi*liti] *n* quality of being improbable; that which is improbable.

improbable [imp*R*obab'l] *adj* not likely to be true; not likely to happen ~ **improbably** *adv*.

improbity [imp*R*obiti] *n* dishonesty.

impromptu [imp*R*omptew] *adj* and *adv* (said or done) on the spur of the moment, without preparation ~ **impromptu** *n* short piece of music suggesting improvisation; unprepared spontaneous speech, performance *etc*.

improper [imp*R*oper] *adj* unseemly, not what should be said, done, *etc*; indecent; unsuitable, unfit; **i.** fraction (*math*) fraction whose numerator is greater than its denominator ~ **improperly** *adv*.

impropriate [imp*R*opri-ayt] *v/t* take over as private property, annex for private use; transfer (ecclesiastical property) to a layman ~ **impropriate** *adj* transferred to a layman ~ **impropriation** [imp*R*opri-*ay*shon] *n*.

impropriety [imp*R*o*pR*i-iti] *n* state or quality of being improper; improper act, remark *etc*.

improvable [imp*R*OOvab'l] *adj* that can be improved.

improve [imp*R*OOv] *v/t* and *i* make or become better or more valuable; make good use of; recover from illness; edify; moralize over.

improvement [imp*R*OOvment] *n* act or process of improving; state of being improved; that which improves.

improver [imp*R*OOver] *n* one who or that which improves; an apprentice.

improvidence [imp*R*ovidens] *n* quality of being improvident; improvident act.

improvident [imp*R*ovident] *adj* not looking ahead, not providing for the future; spendthrift ~ **improvidently** *adv*.

improving [imp*R*OOving] *adj* tending to improve; edifying, moralizing ~ **improvingly** *adv*.

improvisation [imp*R*ovi*z*ayshon] *n* act of improvising; that which is improvised.

improvise [imp*R*oviz] *v/t* and *i* make or do on the spur of the moment, *esp* with makeshift materials; compose or perform according to spontaneous fancy without preparation > PDM.

imprudence [imp*R*OOdens] *n* quality of being imprudent; imprudent act.

imprudent [imp*R*OOdent] *adj* rash; indiscreet ~ **imprudently** *adv*.

impudence [im*p*ewdens] *n* quality of being impudent; impudent act.

impudent [im*p*ewdent] *adj* insolent, saucy ~ **impudently** *adv*.

impudicity [impewd*i*siti] *n* lack of modesty; shamelessness.

impugn [im*p*ewn] *v/t* criticize, argue against ~ **impugnment** *n*.

impuissance [im*p*wee*s*ans] *n* feebleness, lack of power ~ **impuissant** *adj*.

impulse [im*p*uls] *n* sudden strong urge to action; stimulus; tendency to act at once without deliberation > PDP; act of impelling, thrust; (*phys*) force acting during very short time > PDS; (*biol*) message conducted along nerve-fibre > PDB.

impulsion [im*p*ulshon] *n* act of impelling; state of being impelled; incitement; emotional urge.

impulsive [im*p*ulsiv] *adj* tending to act on impulse; based on impulse; that can impel ~ **impulsively** *adv* ~ **impulsiveness** *n*.

impunity [im*p*ewniti] *n* exemption from punishment, injury or loss; **with i.** with no risk of unpleasant consequences.

impure [im*p*ewr] *adj* not pure, dirty; mixed with other substances, adulterated; (*fig*) not disinterested; unchaste, sexually immoral.

impurity [im*p*ewr*R*iti] *n* state or quality of being impure; that which is impure; foreign substance in another substance; immoral conduct.

imputable [im*p*ewtab'l] *adj* that may be imputed; attributable.

imputation [impew*t*ayshon] *n* act of imputing; accusation, charge; slur, indirect reproach; (*theol*) attribution of one person's righteousness or guilt to another.

impute [im*p*ewt] *v/t* attribute, ascribe (*usu* in bad sense); lay to the charge of.

imshi [*im*shi] *interj* (*mil sl*) go away!

in [*in*] *prep* contained by, within; surrounded by; covered by; wearing; during; at the end of (period of time); within the scope of; occupied by; as regards, by way of; using, by means of; made of; belonging to; into; being a member of ~ **in** *adv* towards the inside, inwards; inside; indoors, at home; (*of fire*) alight; (*pol*) in office; (*cricket*) batting; (*coll*) in fashion; in favour; **i. for**

certain to receive or experience; committed to; entered for; **i. on** having a share or part in; **i. with** friendly with, associated with ~ **in** *adj* interior; internal; (*coll*) fashionable, sophisticated; **i. patient** resident patient at hospital ~ **in** *n* the **ins** those in office; (*cricket*) side which is batting; **the ins and outs** complex details, intricacies.

in- (1) *pref* not.

in- (2) *pref* into, towards; in, upon.

inability [ina*bili*ti] *n* want of ability; lack of power.

inaccessibility [inaksesi*bili*ti] *n* state or quality of being inaccessible; state of unresponsiveness on the part of an individual > PDP.

inaccessible [inak*ses*ib'l] *adj* that cannot be reached or attained; hard to reach or attain; aloof; unresponsive ~ **inaccessibly** *adv.*

inaccuracy [ina*kyoo*Rasi] *n* lack of accuracy; mistake, error.

inaccurate [ina*kyoor*Rit] *adj* not accurate; erroneous ~ **inaccurately** *adv.*

inaction [ina*k*shon] *n* lack of activity; idleness; inertness.

inactivate [ina*k*tivayt] *v/t* make inactive; put out of action; dissolve, destroy.

inactive [ina*k*tiv] *adj* not active; inert; lazy ~ **inactively** *adv.*

inactivity [inak*tivi*ti] *n* state of being inactive.

inadaptability [inadapta*bili*ti] *n* incapacity to adapt.

inadaptable [inada*p*tab'l] *adj* that cannot be adapted; not adapting oneself easily.

inadaptation [inadap*tay*shon] *n* state of being not adapted or badly adapted.

inadequacy [ina*dik*wasi] *n* state of being inadequate; inability to cope with a situation > PDP.

inadequate [ina*dik*wit] *adj* insufficient, not fulfilling requirements; incompetent ~ **inadequately** *adv.*

inadmissibility [inadmisi*bili*ti] *n* quality of being inadmissible.

inadmissible [inad*mi*sib'l] *adj* that cannot be admitted or allowed.

inadvertence, inadvertency [inad*vurt*ens/ inad*vurt*ensi] *n* quality of being inadvertent; mistake, oversight.

inadvertent [inad*vurt*ent] *adj* not paying attention; careless; unintentional, accidental ~ **inadvertently** *adv.*

inalienable [ina*yli*-enab'l] *adj* that cannot be alienated or transferred ~ **inalienably** *adv.*

inamorata [inamo*Raa*ta] *n* woman who is loved.

inamorato [inamo*Raat*O] *n* man who is loved, lover.

inane [ina*yn*] *adj* very stupid, senseless; empty, void ~ **inane** *n* infinite space ~ **inanely** *adv.*

inanimate [ina*ni*mit] *adj* lifeless, dead; (*fig*) dull, listless.

inanition [ina*nish*on] *n* exhaustion from lack of food.

inanity [ina*ni*ti] *n* senseless remark or act.

inappetence [ina*pit*ens] *n* lack of desire ~ **inappetent** *adj.*

inapplicability [inaplika*bili*ti] *n* quality of being inapplicable.

inapplicable [ina*plik*ab'l] *adj* not applicable; not relevant ~ **inapplicably** *adv.*

inapposite [ina*poz*it] *adj* irrelevant; unsuitable; ill-timed ~ **inappositely** *adv.*

inappreciable [inap*Ree*sh-ab'l] *adj* negligible, insignificant ~ **inappreciably** *adv.*

inapprehensible [inap*Ri*hensib'l] *adj* that cannot be understood.

inapprehension [inap*Ri*henshon] *n* lack of understanding or apprehension ~ **inapprehensive** *adj* not understanding; not noticing any danger.

inapproachable [inap*RO*chab'l] *adj* not to be approached; distant, reserved ~ **inapproachably** *adv.*

inappropriate [inap*RO*pri-it] *adj* not appropriate; unsuitable ~ **inappropriately** *adv* ~ **inappropriateness** *n.*

inapt [ina*pt*] *adj* unskilful; unsuitable ~ **inaptly** *adv* ~ **inaptness** *n.*

inaptitude [ina*pt*itewd] *n* lack of aptitude; unsuitability.

inarch [ina*arch*] *v/t* graft by inserting a shoot or bud unseparated from its parent stem.

inarticulate [inaar*tik*ewlit] *adj* not distinctly spoken; unable to speak clearly; unable to express oneself readily; unexpressed; silent, reticent; (*anat*) not jointed ~ **inarticulately** *adv* ~ **inarticulateness** *n.*

inartistic [inaar*tist*ik] *adj* not done artistically; not skilled in art; without taste for art ~ **inartistically** *adv.*

inasmuch [inaz*much*] *adv* **i. as** seeing that, since; in so far as.

inattention [ina*ten*shon] *n* dispersal of attention, lack of concentration; failure to pay attention; carelessness; negligence.

inattentive [ina*tent*iv] *adj* not paying attention ~ **inattentively** *adv* ~ **inattentiveness** *n.*

inaudibility [inawdi*bili*ti] *n* state or quality of being inaudible.

inaudible [ina*wd*ib'l] *adj* that cannot be heard ~ **inaudibly** *adv.*

inaugural [ina*w*gewRRal] *adj* pertaining to or made at an inauguration.

inaugurate [ina*w*gewRayt] *v/t* induct or install in office with ceremony; formally commence or introduce; ceremonially declare open, ready for use, *etc.*

inauguration [inawgew*Ray*shon] *n* act of inaugurating ~ **inauguratory** *adj.*

inauspicious [inaws*pish*us] *adj* unlucky, ill-omened; unfavourable ~ **inauspiciously** *adv* ~ **inauspiciousness** *n.*

inband [in*band*] *adj* (*of stone or brick*) laid lengthways across a wall.

inbeing [in*bee*-ing] *n* essence; basic nature.

inboard [in*bawrd*] *adj* and *adv* within the ship; near centre on ship, aircraft, or vehicle.

inborn [in*bawrn*] *adj* present in the individual at birth, innate; inherent.

inbreathe [in*bReeTH*] *v/t* and *i* inhale.

inbred [in*bRed*] *adj* inborn, innate; natural; engendered by the mating of closely related individuals; having hereditary defects increased by inbreeding.

inbreed [in*bReed*] *v/t* and *i* breed by mating of closely related individuals > PDB ~ **inbreeding** *n.*

inbuilt [in*-bilt*] *adj* built-in; innate; basic.

Inca [*inka*] *n* member of race which occupied

Peru before the arrival of the Spaniards; king
or prince of this race ~ **Inca** *adj*.

incalculable [in-*kal*kewlab'l] *adj* that cannot be
calculated; not to be relied on, uncertain ~
incalculably *adv*.

incandesce [in-kan*des*] *v/i* and *t* glow or cause
to glow with heat.

incandescence [in-kan*des*ens] *n* state of glowing
at high temperatures; white or bright-red heat
> PDS ~ **incandescent** *adj* luminous, bril-
liant; (*fig*) ardent, fiery.

incantation [in-kan*tay*shon] *n* magical chant or
verbal formula; sorcery.

incapability [inkaypa*bil*iti] *n* inability; helplessness; unfitness.

incapable [in-*kay*pab'l] *adj* not able; not capable; helpless; legally unfit or disqualified ~
incapably *adv*.

incapacitate [in-ka*pas*itayt] *v/t* render incapable
or unfit; disable, *esp* by injuries; disqualify.

incapacitation [in-kapasi*tay*shon] *n* act of
incapacitating; state of being incapacitated.

incapacity [in-ka*pas*iti] *n* lack of capacity;
inability; incompetence; legal disqualification.

incarcerate [in-*kaars*eRayt] *v/t* imprison.

incarceration [in-kaarseRay*shon*] *n* imprisonment.

incarnadine [in-*kaar*nadIn] *adj* flesh-pink.

incarnate [in*kaar*nit] *adj* in flesh and blood,
living in human form; embodied; in tangible
form; personified ~ **incarnate** [in*kaar*nayt/in-
kaarnayt] *v/t* give living human form to; embody,
personify; express in tangible form.

incarnation [in-kaar*nay*shon] *n* act or process of
taking on a human body and personality; act
of personifying or giving tangible form to; **the I.**
(*theol*) the taking on of human body and personality by God.

incautious [in-*kaw*shus] *adj* lacking caution;
rash, unwary ~ **incautiously** *adv* ~ **in-
cautiousness** *n*.

incendiarism [in*send*i-eRizm] *n* act or practice
of maliciously setting fire to property.

incendiary [in*send*i-eRi] *n* and *adj* (person)
who maliciously sets fire to property; (that)
which destroys by fire; (*fig*) (person or thing)
stirring up violence, hatred, or rebellion.

incense (1) [in*sens*] *n* mixture of herbs and spices
etc giving off fragrant smoke when burnt;
smoke of these used in religious ceremonies;
(*fig*) homage; flattery ~ **incense** *v/t* burn incense
in honour of; fumigate with incense, cense.

incense (2) [in*sens*] *v/t* enrage; provoke.

incense-boat [in*sens*-bOt] *n* small vessel for
holding incense.

incensory [in*sens*eRi] *n* vessel in which incense is
burned.

incentive [in*sen*tiv] *n* that which stimulates to
action, motive ~ **incentive** *adj* urging to action,
rousing, stimulating.

incept [in*sept*] *v/t* and *i* absorb (foreign matter)
into the body; be admitted to degree of Master or
Doctor at the University of Cambridge.

inception [in*sep*shon] *n* beginning; ceremony of
incepting at Cambridge University.

inceptive [in*sep*tiv] *adj* beginning, commencing;
(*gramm*) denoting the beginning of an action.

incertitude [in*surt*itewd] *n* uncertainty, doubt;
insecurity

incessancy [in*ses*ansi] *n* state of being incessant.

incessant [in*ses*ant] *adj* constant, unceasing;
uninterrupted ~ **incessantly** *adv*.

incessive [in*ses*iv] *adj* proceeding by stages.

incest [in*sest*] *n* sexual intercourse between those
who are closely related by blood kinship.

incestuous [in*ses*tew-us] *adj* relating to or
guilty of incest ~ **incestuously** *adv*.

inch [*inch*] *n* one-twelfth of a linear foot; amount
sufficient to cover a surface to the depth of one
inch; small amount or degree; (*pl*) height, stature;
i. by i., **by inches** very gradually; **every i.**
entirely ~ **inch** *v/t* and *i* mark in inches;
measure in inches; drive in gradually; advance
by small degrees.

inchmeal [*inch*meel] *adv* very gradually.

inchoate [*in*-kO-ayt] *adj* just begun; undeveloped;
lacking organization ~ **inchoate** *v/t* and *i*
begin; originate ~ **inchoately** *adv*.

inchoation [in-kO-*ay*shon] *n* commencement.

inchoative [in-*kO*-ativ] *adj* beginning; (*gramm*)
expressing the beginning of an action.

inch-tape [*inch*-tayp] *n* tape-measure divided into
inches.

inchworm [*inch*wurm] *n* type of looper caterpillar.

incidence [*in*sidens] *n* fact, act, or manner of
falling on to; manner of affecting; scope,
range, or frequency of occurrence; direction in
which line, ray, moving body *etc* falls upon a
surface; **angle of i.** angle between a ray meeting
a surface and a line perpendicular to that surface.

incident [*in*sident] *n* happening, event, occurrence; minor episode, *esp* in a literary work;
(*leg*) privilege or burden attached to office or
property ~ **incident** *adj* associated with, likely
to happen to; appertaining to; falling or striking
(upon).

incidental [insi*den*tal] *adj* casual, unplanned;
subordinate; occurring in connexion with,
liable to occur in; (*of music*) intermittently
accompanying a spoken play or film; (*of expenses*)
in addition to main expense ~ **incidental** *n*
that which is incidental ~ **incidentally** *adv*.

incinerate [in*sine*Rayt] *v/t* burn to ashes.

incineration [insine*Ray*shon] *n* complete burning.

incinerator [in*sine*Rayter] *n* furnace for burning
refuse.

incipience [in*sipi*-ens] *n* beginning.

incipient [in*sipi*-ent] *adj* beginning, in the first
stages ~ **incipiently** *adv*.

incise [in*sIz*] *v/t* cut in o; engrave, carve.

incision [in*sizh*on] *n* act of incising; cut, gash,
esp in surgery; (*fig*) trenchancy; (*bot, zool*) deep
indentation of a margin.

incisive [in*sIs*iv] *adj* cutting sharply; (*fig*)
vigorous and clear; penetrating, acute ~ **in-
cisively** *adv* ~ **incisiveness** *n*.

incisor [in*sIz*er] *n* cutting front tooth of mammal
> PDB ~ **incisory** *adj* sharp.

incitation [insIta*y*shon] *n* incitement.

incite [in*sIt*] *v/t* stir up; urge; encourage.

incitement [in*sIt*ment] *n* that which incites,
stimulus; act of inciting; state of being incited.

incivility [insi*vil*iti] *n* rudeness; rude act.

incivism [in*siv*izm] *n* bad citizenship; lack of
patriotism.

inclemency [in-*klem*ensi] *n* harshness, severity.

inclement [in-*klement*] *adj* harsh, merciless; (*of weather*) cold, stormy ~ **inclemently** *n*.

inclinable [in-*klIn*ab'l] *adj* tending towards; well-disposed, favourable to.

inclination [in-klin*ay*shon] *n* act of inclining; tendency, disposition; liking, preference; act of bowing or bending; slope, slant; dip of magnetic needle; (*geom*) angle formed by intersection of two lines or planes.

incline [in-*klIn*] *v/i* and *t* slope, slant; stoop, bend; be disposed, tend; cause to slope or bend; influence; **be (feel) inclined** to feel that one wishes to ~ **incline** [*in*-klIn] *n* slope, gradient.

inclinometer [in-klinomiter] *n* instrument for measuring the earth's magnetic force.

inclose [in-*klOz*] *v/t* enclose.

inclosure [in-*klO*zher] *n* enclosure.

include [in-*klOO*d] *v/t* contain, comprise; reckon as part or member of; **i. out** (*sl*) exclude ~ **including** *prep* reckoning in, counting among.

inclusion [in-*klOO*zhon] *n* act of including; state of being included; that which is included.

inclusive [in-*klOO*siv] *adj* and *adv* including both limits stated; containing, comprising; including everything ~ **inclusively** *adv*.

incog [in-*kog*] *abbr* (*coll*) incognito.

incognito [in-*kog*nitO] *adj* and *adv* under a false name ~ **incognito** *n* false name assumed to conceal one's identity; person using a false name.

incognizable, incognoscible [in-*kog*nizab'l, in-kog*nos*ib'l] *adj* that cannot be known.

incoherence, incoherency [in-kO*heer*Rens, in-kO*heer*Rensi] *n* state of being incoherent.

incoherent [in-kO*heer*Rent] *adj* disconnected, rambling; inconsistent ~ **incoherently** *adv*.

incohesive [in-kO*hee*siv] *adj* not cohesive.

incombustibility [in-kombusti*bi*liti] *n* quality of being unburnable.

incombustible [in-kom*bust*ib'l] *adj* that cannot be burnt ~ **incombustibly** *adv*.

income [*in*-kum] *n* total money periodically accruing to a person from wages, profits, interest, rent on property *etc*, *gener* reckoned by the year; **i. tax** tax levied on annual income above a certain level.

incomer [*in*-kumer] *n* one who comes in; intruder; new resident; immigrant.

incoming [*in*-kuming] *adj* coming in; accruing; entering into succession, office *etc*; (*of period of time*) about to start.

incommensurable [in-komen*she*Rab'l] *adj* that cannot be measured or estimated in terms of the same unit, standard, or scale; not comparable with; not worthy to be compared with.

incommensurate [in-komen*she*Rit] *adj* disproportionate, unequal; inadequate; incommensurable ~ **incommensurately** *adv* ~ **incommensurateness** *n*.

incommode [in-kom*Od*] *v/t* cause inconvenience or trouble to; embarrass; disturb.

incommodious [in-kom*Odi*-us] *adj* inconvenient, uncomfortable; too small ~ **incommodiously** *adv*.

incommodity [in-kom*od*iti] *n* inconvenience.

incommunicability [inkomewnika*bi*liti] *n* quality of being incommunicable.

incommunicable [in-kom*ew*nikab'l] *adj* that cannot be communicated or imparted ~ **incommunicably** *adv*.

incommunicado [in-komewnikaa*dO*] *adj* and *adv* prevented from communicating with others; in solitary confinement.

incommunicative [in-kom*ew*nikativ] *adj* unable or unwilling to talk freely; unwilling to give information; reserved, reticent ~ **incommunicatively** *adv* ~ **incommunicativeness** *n*.

incommutable [in-kom*ew*tab'l] *adj* that cannot be changed or exchanged ~ **incommutably** *adv*.

incomparable [in-*kom*peRab'l] *adj* not to be compared (with, to); unequalled; unique, matchless ~ **incomparably** *adv* ~ **incomparableness** *n*.

incompatibility [in-kompati*bi*liti] *n* state or quality of being incompatible; (*biol*) failure to set seed after pollination > PDB.

incompatible [in-kom*pat*ib'l] *adj* unable to agree or get on well (with); inconsistent; unreconcilable, logically opposed (to); (*med*) unable to coexist inside one body ~ **incompatibly** *adv*.

incompetence [in-*kom*pitens] *n* state of being incompetent.

incompetent [in-*kom*pitent] *adj* lacking the necessary skill, knowledge *etc* for a task; very inefficient, useless; legally unqualified ~ **incompetently** *adv*.

incomplete [in-kom*pleet*] *adj* defective, not complete; not perfect ~ **incompletely** *adv* ~ **incompleteness** *n*.

incomprehensibility [in-kompRihensi*bi*liti] *n* quality of being incomprehensible.

incomprehensible [in-kompRi*hens*ib'l] *adj* that cannot be comprehended or understood; (*theol*) infinite ~ **incomprehensibly** *adv*.

incomprehension [in-kompRi*hen*shon] *n* inability or failure to understand.

incompressible [in-kom*pRes*ib'l] *adj* not compressible.

inconceivability [in-konseeva*bi*liti] *n* quality of being inconceivable.

inconceivable [in-kon*seev*ab'l] *adj* that cannot be imagined or thought of; (*coll*) incredible; most unlikely ~ **inconceivably** *adv*.

inconclusive [in-kon-*klOO*siv] *adj* not conclusive; not decisive, leading to no conclusion ~ **inconclusively** *adv* ~ **inconclusiveness** *n*.

incondite [in-*kond*It] *adj* badly-constructed; confused; unfinished, crude.

incongruity [in-kong-g*Roo*-iti] *n* state or quality of being incongruous.

incongruous [in-*kong*-gRoo-us] *adj* not in keeping with its setting, context, or surroundings; unsuitable; absurd ~ **incongruously** *adv*.

inconsecutive [in-kon*sek*ewtiv] *adj* not in continuous regular order.

inconsequence [in-*kon*sikwens] *n* quality of being inconsequent.

inconsequent [in-*kon*sikwent] *adj* disconnected, without logical connexion; irrelevant ~ **inconsequently** *adv*.

inconsequential [in-konsik*wen*shal] *adj* inconsequent; unimportant ~ **inconsequentially** *adv*.

inconsiderable [in-kon*side*Rab'l] *adj* insignificant; trivial.

inconsiderate [in-kon*side*Rit] *adj* with no regard for the feelings of others, thoughtless; hasty, rash ~ **inconsiderately** *adv.*

inconsideration [in-konsider*ay*shon] *n* quality of being inconsiderate; disregard.

inconsistency [in-kon*sis*tensi] *n* quality of being inconsistent; that which is inconsistent.

inconsistent [in-kon*sis*tent] *adj* self-contradictory; changeable in opinions *etc*; not agreeing, incompatible (with); not suitable, incongruous ~ **inconsistently** *adv.*

inconsolable [in-kons*Ola*b'l] *adj* that cannot be consoled ~ **inconsolably** *adv.*

inconsonance [in-*kon*sonans] *n* disagreement; discord.

inconsonant [in-*kon*sonant] *adj* disagreeing, discordant ~ **inconsonantly** *adv.*

inconspicuous [in-kon*spik*ew-us] *adj* not easily seen, not striking in appearance ~ **inconspicuously** *adv* ~ **inconspicuousness** *n.*

inconstancy [in-*kon*stansi] *n* quality of being inconstant.

inconstant [in-*kon*stant] *adj* variable, changeable; fickle; irregular, unsteady ~ **inconstantly** *adv.*

incontestable [in-kon*tes*tab'l] *adj* undeniable, unquestionable ~ **incontestably** *adv* ~ **incontestability** [in-kontesta*bili*ti] *n.*

incontinence [in-*kon*tinens] *n* state of being incontinent.

incontinent (1) [in-*kon*tinent] *adj* unrestrained, lacking self-control, *esp* over sexual passion; unchaste; (*med*) unable to restrain emission of urine or faeces ~ **incontinently** *adv* in an incontinent way; at once, immediately.

incontinent (2) *adv* (*ar*) immediately, at once.

incontrollable [in-kon*tROla*b'l] *adj* not controllable ~ **incontrollably** *adv.*

incontrovertible [in-kontRo*vurti*b'l] *adj* not to be argued against or disproved ~ **incontrovertibly** *adv.*

inconvenience [in-kon*veen*yens] *n* quality or state of being inconvenient; that which is inconvenient; cause of discomfort ~ **inconvenience** *v/t* cause trouble to, embarrass, annoy.

inconvenient [in-kon*veen*yent] *adj* not convenient; troublesome; uncomfortable; difficult, awkward ~ **inconveniently** *adv.*

inconvertibility [in-konvurti*bili*ti] *n* state or quality of being inconvertible.

inconvertible [in-kon*vurti*b'l] *adj* that cannot be changed or exchanged; that cannot be exchanged for coin ~ **inconvertibly** *adv.*

incoordinate [in-kO-*awr*dinit] *adj* not coordinated; (*of muscles*) not cooperating correctly in complex movements.

incoordination [in-kO-awrdi*nay*shon] *n* lack of or defect in coordination.

incorporate [in-*kawr*peRayt] *v/t* and *i* unite into one body or mass; adopt as member of group; form legal corporation; include; blend, mix ~ **incorporate** [in-*kawr*peRit] *adj* united in one body, mass or society; forming legal corporation; closely united.

incorporation [in-kawrpe*Ray*shon] *n* act of incorporating; state of being incorporated.

incorporeal [in-kawr*paw*Ri-al] *adj* having no body; spiritual.

incorrect [in-ko*Rekt*] *adj* not accurate; untrue; wrong in one's conduct or behaviour ~ **incorrectly** *adv* ~ **incorrectness** *n.*

incorrigible [in-*ko*Rijib'l] *adj* incapable of being improved or reformed ~ **incorrigibly** *adv.*

incorruptibility [in-koRupti*bili*ti] *n* state or quality of being incorruptible.

incorruptible [in-ko*Rup*tib'l] *adj* that cannot decay, eternal; that cannot be bribed ~ **incorruptibly** *adv.*

incorruption [in-ko*Rup*shon] *n* freedom from decay; imperishability.

incorruptness [in-ko*Rup*tnes] *n* honesty.

incrassate [in-*kRa*sayt] *adj* (*bot*, *zool*) thick, thickened ~ **incrassation** [in-kRa*say*shon] *n.*

increase [in-*kRees*] *v/i* and *t* grow, become greater; multiply; make greater; add to, enlarge ~ **increase** [*in*-kRees] *n* act, state or process of increasing; growth; increment, that which is added; (*ar*) produce, crops.

increasingly [in-*kRees*ingli] *adv* to an increasing extent; more and more.

incredibility [in-kRedi*bili*ti] *n* quality of being incredible.

incredible [in-*kRed*ib'l] *adj* that cannot be believed; (*coll*) extraordinary ~ **incredibly** *adv.*

incredulity [in-kRed*ew*liti] *n* quality of being incredulous; inability to believe.

incredulous [in-*kRed*ewlus] *adj* not believing; showing disbelief; unwilling to believe, sceptical ~ **incredulously** *adv* ~ **incredulousness** *n.*

increment [*in*-kRiment] *n* act or process of increasing; addition; amount of change or rate of change; (*math*) finite increase of a variable; **unearned i.** increased value of property due to external factors, not to improvements in it.

incremental [in-kRi*men*tal] *adj* of or by increase.

incriminate [in-*kRim*inayt] *v/t* charge with a crime; reveal the guilt of.

incrimination [in-kRimi*nay*shon] *n* act of incriminating; state of being incriminated; that which incriminates.

incriminatory [in-kRimi*nay*teRi] *adj* incriminating.

incrust [in-*kRust*] *v/t* encrust.

incrustation [in-kRus*tay*shon] *n* crust, layer, *esp* of corrosive deposit on wall surface, or of fur in a water pipe; technique of ornamentation wherein one material is inlaid on another.

incubate [*in*-kewbayt] *v/t* and *i* sit on (eggs) to hatch; hatch artificially; (*fig*) plan, brood upon.

incubation [in-kew*bay*shon] *n* act of hatching; (*med*) period between infection and first appearance of symptoms ~ **incubational** *adj.*

incubator [*in*-kewbayter] *n* heated apparatus for hatching eggs artificially, for cultivating bacteria, or for rearing prematurely born children.

incubus [*in*-kewbus] *n* demon supposed to mate with sleeping women; (*fig*) anything weighing on the mind, obsessive anxiety; nightmare.

incudes [inku*deez*] *pl* of incus.

inculcate [*in*-kulkayt] *v/t* teach by frequent repetition; impress on the mind, instil.

inculcation [in-kul*kay*shon] *n* act of inculcating.

inculpate [*in*-kulpayt] *v/t* accuse of crime; incriminate, reveal the guilt of.

inculpation [in-kul*pay*shon] *n* act of inculpating; that which inculpates; state of being inculpated.

inculpatory [in-kulpayteRi] *adj* that inculpates.

incumbency [in-kumbensi] *n* ecclesiastical benefice; tenure of this; fact of holding ecclesiastical benefice.

incumbent [in-kumbent] *adj* morally binding, obligatory; (*ar*) lying or resting (upon) ~ **incumbent** *n* clergyman holding a benefice.

incunabula [in-kewnabewla] *n* (*pl*) books printed before 1500; early stages, beginnings.

incur (*pres/part* **incurring**, *p/t* and *p/part* **incurred**) [in-kur] *v/t* make oneself liable to; bring upon oneself.

incurability [in-kewrRabiliti] *n* quality or state of being incurable.

incurable [in-kewrRab'l] *adj* that cannot be cured ~ **incurable** *n* person suffering from an incurable disease ~ **incurably** *adv*.

incurious [in-kewrRi-us] *adj* devoid of curiosity; without interest ~ **incuriously** *adv*.

incurrable [in-kurRab'l] *adj* that may be incurred.

incurrence [in-kurRens] *n* act of incurring.

incursion [in-kurshon] *n* invasion; raid, attack.

incursive [in-kursiv] *adj* invading; aggressive.

incurvate [in-kurvayt] *v/t* and *i* bend inwards, curve back ~ **incurvate** *adj* curved back or bent inwards.

incurvation [in-kurvayshon] *n* inward bend.

incus (*pl* **incudes**) [inkus, inkewdeez] *n* a small bone of the middle ear.

incuse [in-kewz] *n* and *adj* (impression) hammered or stamped in ~ **incuse** *v/t* impress by stamping; stamp with a device *etc*.

indaba [indaaba] *n* (*S. African*) conference.

indebted [indetid] *adj* owing money (to); under obligation.

indecency [indeesensi] *n* quality of being indecent; indecent act, words *etc*.

indecent [indeesent] *adj* obscene, immodest; unseemly, not fit or proper ~ **indecently** *adv*.

indeciduous [indisidew-us] *adj* evergreen.

indecipherable [indisifeRab'l] *adj* that cannot be deciphered; illegible.

indecision [indisizhon] *n* inability to decide, prolonged hesitation.

indecisive [indisisiv] *adj* not decisive or conclusive; irresolute, hesitating ~ **indecisively** *adv*.

indeclinable [indiklinab'l] *adj* (*gramm*) having no inflexions.

indecorous [indekeRus] *adj* showing bad manners or bad taste ~ **indecorously** *adv* ~ **indecorousness** *n*.

indecorum [indikawRum] *n* indecorousness; indecorous act.

indeed [indeed] *adv* really, in fact; certainly; *also emph* ~ **indeed** *interj* exclam of surprise, *irony, interrogation etc*.

indefatigability [indifatigabiliti] *n* tirelessness.

indefatigable [indifatigab'l] *adj* tireless; unremitting ~ **indefatigably** *adv*.

indefeasible [indifeezib'l] *adj* that cannot be made void or be forfeited ~ **indefeasibly** *adv*.

indefectible [indifektib'l] *adj* without defect, faultless; not liable to become defective, unfailing.

indefensibility [indifensibiliti] *n* quality of being indefensible.

indefensible [indifensib'l] *adj* that cannot be

defended; that cannot be excused or justified ~ **indefensibly** *adv*.

indefinable [indifinab'l] *adj* that cannot be defined; indescribable ~ **indefinably** *adv*.

indefinite [indefinit] *adj* vague, not precise; not accurately defined; not clearly stated; not limited; (*gramm*) not indicating person, number to which it refers; not indicating whether action is completed or still continuing ~ **indefinitely** *adv* ~ **indefiniteness** *n*.

indelibility [indelibiliti] *n* quality of being indelible.

indelible [indelib'l] *adj* that cannot be blotted out or effaced; producing an indelible mark; (*fig*) that cannot be wiped out or forgotten ~ **indelibly** *adv*.

indelicacy [indelikasi] *n* quality of being indelicate; indelicate act, words *etc*.

indelicate [indelikit] *adj* lacking delicacy; coarse, unrefined; indecent ~ **indelicately** *adv*.

indemnification [indemnifikayshon] *n* act of indemnifying; that which indemnifies, sum paid to indemnify; state of being indemnified.

indemnify [indemnifi] *v/t* safeguard against; compensate for (loss *etc*); free from (liability, penalty *etc*).

indemnity [indemniti] *n* protection, insurance against loss *etc*; compensation for loss *etc*.

indent (1) [indent] *v/t* and *i* cut notches along the edge of, make recesses in; (*print*) set further in from margin than rest of paragraph, page *etc*; (*leg*) indenture, draw up in duplicate; make official order for goods, *usu* in duplicate ~ **indent** [indent] *n* notch, dent, marginal cut; indenture; official order for goods.

indent (2) *v/t* make dent in.

indentation [indentayshon] *n* act of indenting; notch, dent; zigzag moulding.

indention [indenshon] *n* (*print*) act of indenting.

indenture [indencher] *n* (*leg*) document in duplicate cut into two parts along zigzag line; contract, agreement, *esp* one binding apprentice to employer; official certificate, deed *etc*; indentation, notch ~ **indenture** *v/t* bind by contract.

independence [indipendens] *n* quality or state of being independent.

independent [indipendent] *adj* not bound or subject to another; not dependent on another; free from control; unwilling to accept favours, help, advice *etc*; resenting authority; not influenced by or related to anything else; (*of income*) enabling one to live without working for pay; (*of persons*) financially self-supporting; not needing to work for a living ~ **independent** *n* one who is not attached to a political party; Congregationalist ~ **independently** *adv*.

indescribability [indiskRibabiliti] *n* quality of being indescribable.

indescribable [indiskRibab'l] *adj* that cannot be described ~ **indescribably** *adv*.

indestructibility [indistRuktibiliti] *n* quality of being indestructible.

indestructible [indistRuktib'l] *adj* that cannot be destroyed ~ **indestructibly** *adv*.

indeterminable [inditurminab'l] *adj* that cannot be ascertained or defined; (*of dispute*) that cannot be settled ~ **indeterminably** *adv*.

indeterminacy [inde*tur*minasi] *n* state of being indeterminate; **i. principle** (*phys*) theory that the mass and speed of particles cannot be simultaneously ascertained.

indeterminate [inde*tur*minit] *adj* not fixed, not definite; vague, uncertain; (*math*) with no fixed value ~ **indeterminately** *adv* ~ **indeterminateness** *n*.

indetermination [inditurmi*nay*shon] *n* lack of determination; vacillation, hesitation.

indeterminism [indi*tur*minizm] *n* (*philos*) theory that human action is not entirely determined by stimuli or motives, buti s to some extent free.

index (*pl* **indexes** or (*math*) **indices**) [indeks] *n* pointer, indicator on dial or other measuring device; alphabetical list of names or subjects *etc* in a book, with page references; (*math*) exponent > PDS; (*anat*) forefinger; (*fig*) indication, sign; **card i.** alphabetical list of items each written on a separate file; **the I.** (*RC*) list of books not to be read without permission ~ **index** *v/t* provide an index for; enter in an index ~ **indexer** *n* one who makes an index.

index-finger [indeks-*fing*-ger] *n* forefinger.

Indian [*in*di-an] *adj* pertaining to India, to the East Indies, or to the aborigines of North or South America; pertaining to an Indian; **I. club** bottle-shaped club swung as gymnastic exercise; **I. corn** maize; **I. file** single file; **I. ink** black pigment made of lampblack and animal glue; **I. summer** warm spell in late autumn > PDG; (*fig*) revival of youthful feelings in old age ~ **Indian** *n* native of India; aboriginal of North or South America; aboriginal of East or West Indies; **Red I.** aboriginal of North America.

india-paper [indi-a-*payper*] *n* a thin, soft paper used for impressions of engravings; a very thin, tough, opaque printing-paper.

india-rubber [indi-a-*Ruber*] *n* soft, elastic substance obtained from the juice of certain tropical trees; small piece of this used for erasing pencil marks.

indicant [*in*dikant] *n* and *adj* (that) which points out or indicates.

indicate [*in*dikayt] *v/t* show, point out; make known, reveal; be a sign of; imply; show a need of; **be indicated** be necessary or advisable.

indication [indi*kay*shon] *n* act of indicating; that which indicates, sign, hint; state of being indicated; (*med*) symptom showing that a certain treatment is advisable.

indicative [in*di*kativ] *n* and *adj* (that) which indicates; (*gramm*) (mood) which states as fact or asks questions of fact ~ **indicatively** *adv*.

indicator [*in*dikayter] *n* one who or that which points out; pointer on dial; recording instrument; (*chem*) substance which by a colour change indicates the completion of a chemical reaction.

indicatory [in*di*kateRi] *adj* that indicates.

indices [*in*diseez] alternative pl of **index**.

indicia [in*di*shi-a] *n* (*pl*) signs; markings.

indict [in*dIt*] *v/t* charge with crime.

indictable [in*dIt*ab'l] *adj* liable to indictment; exposing one to being indicted.

indiction [in*dik*shon] *n* (*hist*) fifteen-year cycle, *esp* that fixed by Roman Emperors for tax valuations.

indictment [in*dIt*ment] *n* act of indicting; formal accusation of a crime; document embodying this.

indifference [in*dife*Rens] *n* the quality or state of being indifferent.

indifferent [in*dife*Rent] *adj* not caring, having no strong feelings; not interested; of poor quality, mediocre; unimportant; (*ar*) impartial; (*elect*) neutral ~ **indifferently** *adv*.

indifferentism [in*dife*Rentizm] *n* theory that all religious systems are equally valuable and valid; habitual indifference, *esp* towards religion ~ **indifferentist** *n* and *adj*.

indigence [*in*dijens] *n* extreme poverty ~ **indigent** *adj* ~ **indigently** *adv*.

indigenous [in*di*jinus] *adj* native, belonging naturally (to), not foreign.

indigested [indi*jes*tid] *adj* confused, chaotic; not well thought out; not digested.

indigestibility [indijesti*bi*liti] *n* quality of being indigestible.

indigestible [indi*jes*tib'l] *adj* not easily digested.

indigestion [indi*jes*chon] *n* difficulty of digestion, dyspepsia; pain or discomfort caused by this; state of being undigested ~ **indigestive** *adj*.

indignant [in*dig*nant] *adj* feeling or expressing anger which one considers justified ~ **indignantly** *adv*.

indignation [indig*nay*shon] *n* justified anger and scorn, *esp* if roused by wickedness, injustice *etc*.

indignity [in*dig*niti] *n* treatment calculated to humiliate; insult.

indigo [*in*digO] *n* deep blue dye obtained from the indigo plant; plant producing this ~ **indigo** *adj* deep blue.

indirect [indi*Rekt*] *adj* not direct, devious, roundabout; not straightforward, dishonest; secondary; not first-hand; (*gramm*) in reported speech; **i. object** (*gramm*) word denoting person or thing secondarily affected 'y the verb; **i. taxation** tax levied on goods ,o that buyer pays both price and tax ~ **indirectly** *adv* ~ **indirectness** *n*.

indirection [indi*Rek*shon] *n* indirect course; dishonest means.

indiscernible [indi*sur*nib'l] *adj* not discernible; not visible ~ **indiscernibly** *adv* ~ **indiscernibleness** *n*.

indiscipline [in*di*siplin] *n* lack of discipline.

indiscreet [indisk*Reet*] *adj* not discreet; foolish, rash; tactless ~ **indiscreetly** *adv*.

indiscrete [indisk*Reet*] *adj* not formed of distinct parts.

indiscretion [indisk*Resh*on] *n* quality of being indiscreet; indiscreet act.

indiscriminate [indisk*Rim*init] *adj* lacking discrimination; making no distinctions; random, confused ~ **indiscriminately** *adv* ~ **indiscriminateness** *n*.

indispensability [indispensa*bi*liti] *n* quality of being indispensable.

indispensable [indis*pen*sab'l] *adj* that cannot be dispensed with; essential; (*of law etc*) not to be set aside ~ **indispensably** *adv*.

indispose [indis*pOz*] *v/t* make unwilling or unfavourable; render unfit; make slightly ill.

indisposition [indispozi*shon] *n* slight illness; unwillingness, dislike.

391

indisputability [indispewt*a*b*i*liti] *n* quality of being indisputable.

indisputable [indis*pew*tab'l] *adj* certain, not open to question ~ **indisputably** *adv*.

indissolubility [indisolyoob*i*liti] *n* quality of being indissoluble.

indissoluble [indis*o*lyoob'l] *adj* that cannot be dissolved; permanent, binding for ever ~ **indissolubly** *adv* ~ **indissolubleness** *n*.

indistinct [indis*tinkt*] *adj* not distinct, not clear; obscure; vague, confused; faint ~ **indistinctly** *adv* ~ **indistinctness** *n*.

indistinguishable [indis*ting*-gwishab'l] *adj* that cannot be distinguished ~ **indistinguishably** *adv*.

indite [ind*I*t] *v/t* put in words, compose; write.

indium [*i*ndi-um] *n* a soft silvery metal > PDS.

indivertible [indiv*u*rtib'l] *adj* that cannot be turned aside ~ **indivertibly** *adv*.

individual [indi*vi*dyoo-al] *adj* single, separate; distinctive, characteristic of a single person or thing; for or pertaining to a single person or thing ~ **individual** *n* one particular member of a class of persons, animals or things; single thing or person; (*coll*) person.

individualism [indi*vi*dyoo-alizm] *n* social theory emphasizing rights of individuals over those of the state; preference for independent thought, action *etc*; selfishness, self-centredness ~ **individualist** *n* and *adj*.

individualistic [individyoo-al*i*stik] *adj* acting or thinking independently; unique, original.

individuality [individyoo-al*i*ti] *n* quality of being an individual; distinguishing characteristics of an individual > PDP; separate existence; (*coll*) distinctive personality; uniqueness.

individualization [individyoo-al*Iz*ayshon] *n* act of individualizing.

individualize [indi*vi*dyoo-al*I*z] *v/t* mark out from other persons, be distinctive mark of, characterize; treat or consider individually.

individually [indi*vi*dyoo-ali] *adv* separately, one by one; distinctively.

individuate [indi*vi*dyoo-ayt] *v/t* and *i* make or become individual.

individuation [individyoo-ayshon] *n* act or process of individuating; emergence of individual structures *etc* from an undifferentiated mass > PDP.

indivisibility [indivizib*i*liti] *n* quality of being indivisible.

indivisible [indi*vi*zib'l] *n* and *adj* (that) which cannot be divided ~ **indivisibly** *adv*.

indocile [ind*O*sil] *adj* rebellious, unwilling to be guided, trained *etc*.

indocility [indO*si*liti] *n* rebelliousness.

indoctrinate [ind*o*ktRinayt] *v/t* imbue with principles, opinions *etc*; teach thoroughly.

indoctrination [indoktRinayshon] *n* act or process of indoctrinating.

Indo-European [indO-yoorRopee-an] *n* large family of languages spoken in many parts of Europe and Western Asia; parent language from which these developed; member of race speaking one of these ~ **Indo-European** *adj*.

Indo-Germanic [indO-*i*urmanik] *n* and *adj* Indo-European.

indolence [*i*ndolens] *n* quality of being indolent.

indolent [*i*ndolent] *adj* idle, lazy; inactive; (*med*) causing no pain ~ **indolently** *adv*.

indomitable [ind*o*mitab'l] *adj* that cannot be mastered; unyielding ~ **indomitably** *adv*.

Indonesian [indOneeshan] *n* and *adj* (native or language) of the East Indian islands.

indoor [*i*ndawr] *adj* done, kept, or existing inside a building; of or for the inside of a building.

indoors [ind*awrz*] *adv* within a house or building.

indorsation [indawrsayshon] *n* endorsement.

indorse [ind*awrs*] *v/t* endorse.

indraught [indRaaft] *n* inward draught or current.

indrawn [*i*ndRawn] *adj* drawn in.

indri [*i*ndRi] *n* large kind of lemur.

indubitable [indew*bi*tab'l] *adj* that cannot be doubted; quite certain ~ **indubitably** *adv*.

induce [ind*ew*s] *v/t* persuade; cause, bring about; (*elect*) produce by induction; (*log*) infer by reasoning from particular cases to general conclusions.

inducement [ind*ew*sment] *n* that which persuades or stimulates to action; motive, incentive; act of inducing.

induct [ind*u*kt] *v/t* install ceremonially in office.

inductance [ind*u*ktans] *n* (*elect*) coefficient of self-induction > PDS.

inductile [ind*u*ktIl] *adj* not ductile, not pliable.

induction [ind*u*kshon] *n* act of inducting, ceremonial installation; (*log*) reasoning from particular cases to general principles; (*psych*) production of effect elsewhere than at original locus of activity > PDP; (*elect*) transference of electric or electro-magnetic force without direct contact > PDS; **i. coil** instrument for producing a high electromotive force from a supply of low electromotive force > PDS; **i. motor** type of electric motor requiring an alternating current supply > PDS.

inductive [ind*u*ktiv] *adj* pertaining to induction; producing or produced by induction ~ **inductively** *adv*.

inductivity [indukt*i*viti] *n* capacity for induction.

inductor [ind*u*kter] *n* one who inducts; piece of electrical apparatus that acts by induction.

indulge [ind*u*lj] *v/t* and *i* yield to the wishes of; give way to (a longing, impulse *etc*); pamper, spoil; gratify, favour; (*coll*) drink too much alcohol; **i. in** allow oneself the pleasure of; treat oneself to.

indulgence [ind*u*ljens] *n* act or practice of indulging; favour, privilege; tolerance; (*RC*) remission of punishment for sins whose guilt has been forgiven ~ **indulgenced** *adj* (*RC*) conferring an indulgence on the user.

indulgent [ind*u*ljent] *adj* yielding to the wishes of others; easily forgiving, not severe ~ **indulgently** *adv*.

indult [ind*u*lt] *n* (*RC*) permission.

indurate [*i*ndewrRayt] *v/t* and *i* harden; make or become callous.

induration [indewrRayshon] *n* act of hardening; hardness; lack of feeling.

indusium [ind*ew*si-um] *n* (*bot*) a hairy cup enclosing a stigma; covering of fruit-cluster in some ferns; (*ent*) insect larva case.

industrial [ind*u*stRi-al] *adj* pertaining to industry; designed for use in industry; **i. action** (*pol*) a strike, go-slow, or work-to-rule; **I. Revolution**

series of social and economic changes in England from late 18th to mid 19th century associated with spread of industries ~ **industrial** n person engaged in industry; (pl) stocks and shares in industry.

industrialism [in*dust*Ri-alizm] n social system based or centred on industrial pursuits.

industrialist [in*dust*Ri-alist] n magnate in industry; supporter of industrialism.

industrialize [in*dust*Ri-alIz] v/t make industrial; devote resources to development of industries.

industrially [in*dust*Ri-ali] adv in an industrial way; as regards industry.

industrious [in*dust*Ri-us] adj hardworking, keen and active in work ~ **industriously** adv.

industry [*in*dustRi] n large-scale mechanized production of goods, manufacture; particular branch of manufacture or trade; quality of being industrious; painstaking work.

inebriate [in*eeb*Ri-ayt] n habitual drunkard ~ **inebriate** v/t make drunk ~ **inebriate** adj drunken.

inebriation [ineebRi-*ay*shon] n drunkenness.

inebriety [ineeb*RI*-eti] n intoxication; habitual drunkenness.

inedible [in*ed*ib'l] adj not suitable to be eaten.

inedited [in*ed*itid] adj not edited; unpublished.

ineffable [in*ef*ab'l] adj more than can be expressed, unutterable ~ **ineffably** adv.

ineffaceable [ini*fay*sab'l] adj that cannot be effaced ~ **ineffaceably** adv.

ineffective [ini*fek*tiv] adj producing no effect; useless; incompetent ~ **ineffectively** adv ~ **ineffectiveness** n.

ineffectual [ini*fek*choo-al] adj producing no effect; powerless; vain. ~ **ineffectually** adv.

ineffectuality [inifekchoo-*al*iti] n quality of being ineffectual.

inefficacious [inefi*kay*shus] adj not producing the desired result.

inefficacy [in*efi*kasi] n inability to produce desired result.

inefficiency [ini*fish*ensi] n quality of being inefficient.

inefficient [ini*fish*ent] adj not efficient; unable to work satisfactorily; wasteful ~ **inefficiently** adv.

inelastic [inil*ast*ik] adj lacking elasticity; rigid, unadaptable.

inelasticity [inila*stis*iti] n rigidity.

inelegance [in*eli*gans] n lack of elegance; clumsiness, roughness; coarseness; that which is inelegant ~ **inelegant** adj ~ **inelegantly** adv.

ineligibility [inelij*ib*iliti] n quality of being ineligible.

ineligible [in*eli*jib'l] adj not qualified or worthy to be chosen ~ **ineligibly** adv.

ineluctable [inil*uk*tab'l] adj not to be escaped; against which struggle is useless.

inept [in*ept*] adj absurdly inappropriate; fatuous ~ **ineptly** adv ~ **ineptness** n.

ineptitude [in*ept*itewd] n quality of being inept; inept remark etc.

inequality [inik*wol*iti] n lack of equality, disparity; variability; unevenness.

inequitable [in*ek*witab'l] adj not just ~ **inequitably** adv.

inequity [in*ek*witi] n injustice; unfairness.

ineradicable [iniRad*ik*ab'l] adj that cannot be eradicated ~ **ineradicably** adv.

inerrable [inu*Rab*'l] adj unerring; infallible.

inert [in*urt*] adj showing no activity; chemically inactive > PDS; motionless; unable to move itself or offer resistance to motion; (fig) sluggish ~ **inertly** adv ~ **inertness** n.

inertia [in*ur*sha] n state of being inert; sluggishness; (phys) tendency of a body to preserve its state of rest or uniform motion in a straight line > PDS; **i. selling** (comm) practice of sending people goods they have not asked for, and demanding payment if they are not promptly returned.

inertial [in*ur*shal] adj pertaining to inertia; **i. control** method of missile guidance depending on forces of inertia.

inescapable [inis*kay*pab'l] adj that cannot be escaped ~ **inescapably** adv.

inessential [inis*en*shal] n and adj (that) which is not essential.

inestimable [in*est*imab'l] adj invaluable, extremely precious ~ **inestimably** adv.

inevitability [inevit*ab*iliti] n quality of being inevitable.

inevitable [in*evi*tab'l] adj that cannot be avoided or prevented, certain to happen ~ **inevitably** adv.

inexact [ineg*zakt*] adj not precise; not accurate ~ **inexactly** adv.

inexactitude [inegz*akt*itewd] n quality of being inexact; inexact statement etc.

inexcusable [ineks*kew*zab'l] adj that cannot be excused or justified ~ **inexcusably** adv.

inexhaustible [inegz*aws*tib'l] adj that cannot be exhausted; unfailing; unceasing ~ **inexhaustibly** adv.

inexorability [ineks*eRa*biliti] n quality of being inexorable.

inexorable [in*ek*seRab'l] adj that cannot be persuaded or moved by entreaty; unbending; relentless ~ **inexorably** adv.

inexpedience, inexpediency [ineks*peedi*-ens, ineks*peedi*-ensi] n quality of being inexpedient.

inexpedient [ineks*peedi*-ent] adj not expedient; not advisable; unprofitable ~ **inexpediently** adv.

inexpensive [ineks*pen*siv] adj not expensive, cheap ~ **inexpensively** adv.

inexperience [ineks*peer*Ri-ens] n lack of experience or of knowledge gained by experience ~ **inexperienced** adj.

inexpert [in*eks*pert] adj not expert; unskilful ~ **inexpertly** adv.

inexpiable [in*eks*pi-ab'l] adj that cannot be expiated or atoned for; (ar) implacable ~ **inexpiably** adv.

inexplicability [ineksplik*ab*iliti] n quality of being inexplicable.

inexplicable [in*eks*plikab'l] adj that cannot be explained, unaccountable ~ **inexplicably** adv.

inexplicit [ineks*plis*it] adj not clearly stated ~ **inexplicitly** adv ~ **inexplicitness** n.

inexpressible [ineks*pRes*ib'l] adj that cannot be expressed or described ~ **inexpressibly** adv.

inexpugnable [ineks*pug*nab'l] adj that cannot be captured; invincible ~ **inexpugnably** adv.

inextinguishable [ineks*ting*-gwishab'l] adj that

cannot be extinguished, unquenchable ~ **inextinguishably** adv.

inextricable [inekstRikab'l] adj that cannot be disentangled or solved ~ **inextricably** adv.

infallibility [infalibiliti] n quality of being unable to err; **Papal I.** doctrine that the Pope is infallible when as head of the Church he pronounces upon a matter of faith or morals.

infallible [infalib'l] adj incapable of erring; always right; unfailing; inevitable ~ **infallibly** adv.

infamous [infamus] adj extremely wicked, vile; scandalous; disgraceful ~ **infamously** adv.

infamy [infami] n quality of being infamous, vileness; public disgrace; infamous act.

infancy [infansi] n state or period of being an infant, babyhood; (leg) minority; (fig) very early stages, beginnings.

infant [infant] n baby, very young child; (leg) one who is under eighteen (formerly twenty-one) years of age ~ **infant** adj young; pertaining to infants.

infanta [infanta] n any royal princess o f Spain or Portugal except the heiress-apparent.

infante [infantay] n any royal prince of Spain or Portugal except the heir-apparent.

infanticide [infantisId] n murder of an infant, esp newborn baby; murderer of an infant.

infantile [infantIl] adj of infants or infancy; babyish; childish; **i. paralysis** poliomyelitis.

infantilism [infantilizm] n abnormal persistence of childish characteristics in adult life.

infantine [infantIn] adj infantile, childish.

infantry [infantRi] n (collect) foot-soldiers.

infantryman [infantRiman] n foot-soldier.

infarction [infaarkshon] n (med) act of cutting off the normal blood-supply (to an organ etc); state of being deprived of blood; **coronary i.** the cutting-off of blood-flow to the heart by occlusion of the coronary artery ~ **infarcted** adj.

infatuate [infatew-ayt] v/t fill with blind love, besot; make foolish ~ **infatuated** adj blinded by unreasonable love, made foolish by passion.

infatuation [infatew-ayshon] n unreasonable love.

infect [infekt] v/t communicate disease to, contaminate; pollute, corrupt; pass on (ideas, moods etc) to, affect by example.

infection [infekshon] n act or process of infecting; that which infects; communication of disease; widespread or subtle influence; transmission.

infectious [infekshus] adj that infects; capable of infecting; likely to communicate disease; easily transmitted, apt to spread ~ **infectiously** adv.

infective [infektiv] adj (med) infectious.

infelicitous [infelisitus] adj not apt; tactless, clumsy; unhappy.

infelicity [infelisiti] n quality of being infelicitous; tactless remark etc.

infer (pres/part **inferring**, p/t and p/part **inferred**) [infur] v/t deduce, conclude from evidence and reasoning; draw conclusions; (pop) imply.

inferable [infurRab'l] adj that can be inferred.

inference [infeRens] n act of inferring; that which is inferred; deduction; implication.

inferential [infeRenshal] adj inferred ~ **inferentially** adv by inference.

inferior [infeerRi-er] adj lower, subordinate;

of less value or quality; of lower rank; of bad quality ~ **inferior** n person of lower rank.

inferiority [infeerRi-oRiti] n state of being inferior; **i. complex** (psych) abnormal mental state due to lack of self-confidence and often resulting in compensatory aggressive behaviour > PDP; (coll) awareness of one's inferiority.

infernal [infurnal] adj of or like hell; deserving hell, diabolical; (coll) extremely unpleasant; (myth) pertaining to the world of the dead; **i. machine** time-bomb; explosive booby-trap ~ **infernally** adv.

inferno [infurnO] n hell; something like hell.

infertile [infurtIl] adj not fertile; barren.

infest [infest] v/t overrun, swarm over; plague.

infestation [infestayshon] n act of infesting; state of being infested.

infibulation [infibewlayshon] n practice of fastening sexual organs with a clasp to prevent intercourse.

infidel [infidel] n and adj (person) not believing in a specified religion; (adherent) of a false religion; pagan; agnostic.

infidelity [infideliti] n unfaithfulness of husband or wife, adultery; state of being an infidel; absence of religious belief; unfaithful or disloyal act.

infield [infeeld] n farm-land nearest to farm-buildings; land regularly cropped; (cricket) area near wicket; (baseball) area within base lines.

infighting [infIting] n fighting or boxing at close quarters; conflict or rivalry between members of a single group.

infilling [infiling] n act of filling in gaps; act of building on empty land between existing built-up areas.

infiltrate [infiltRayt] v/t and i penetrate by stealth; gain access by underhand methods; filter or cause to filter through, permeate; (mil) pass behind enemy's lines in small groups.

infiltration [infiltRayshon] n act of infiltrating; state of being infiltrated; infiltrated substance.

infinite [infinit] adj having no limits, boundless; extremely great; that cannot be counted, measured etc; (gramm) non-finite, not limited by number or person; (math) greater than any assignable quantity ~ **infinite** n that which is infinite; God; infinite space; (math) an infinite quantity ~ **infinitely** adv to an infinite degree; extremely.

infinitesimal [infinitesimal] adj extremely small, minute; infinitely small; (math) smaller than any assignable quantity > PDS; **i. calculus** (math) differential and integral calculus ~ **infinitesimal** n infinitesimal quantity.

infinitive [infinitiv] n and adj (gramm) (verb-form) expressing action only but not person, number etc.

infinitude [infinitewd] n infinity.

infinity [infiniti] n quality of being infinite; that which is infinite; infinite space, time or number; (math) infinite quantity > PDS; (phot) 100 ft or more from the camera.

infirm [infurm] adj feeble, weak; irresolute, uncertain; bed-ridden; crippled.

infirmary [infurmeRi] n hospital; room set aside for the care of the sick or injured.

infirmity [in*fur*miti] *n* state of being infirm; disease, disablement; moral weakness or defect.

infix [in*fiks*] *v/t* fix firmly into; (*gramm*) insert (a formative element) into the body of a word ~ **infix** [*infiks*] *n* (*gramm*) inserted element.

inflame [in*flaym*] *v/t* and *i* set on fire; (*med*) make or become swollen, sore and abnormally hot; (*fig*) rouse passion or violence in; intensify, exacerbate.

inflammability [inflama*bili*ti] *n* quality of being inflammable.

inflammable (1) [in*flam*b'l] *adj* that may be set on fire easily; easily excited ~ **inflammably** *adv*.

inflammable (2) *adj* (*US*) that cannot be set on fire.

inflammation [inflam*ay*shon] *n* act of inflaming; state of being inflamed; (*med*) redness and swelling with heat and pain > PDB.

inflammatory [in*flam*ateRi] *adj* tending to inflame or to excite.

inflate [in*flayt*] *v/t* distend with air or gas; increase amount of money, *esp* paper money, in circulation; raise (prices) artificially; (*fig*) fill with pride, puff up.

inflated [in*flay*tid] *adj* swollen or distended with air; (*of language*) too ornate, florid; (*fig*) haughty, very proud; (*bot*) hollow and distended.

inflation [in*flay*shon] *n* act of inflating; state of being inflated; rise in level of prices due to relative increase of purchasing power > PDPol; fall in value of money; increase in amount of paper money circulating.

inflationary [in*flay*shoneRi] *adj* pertaining to monetary inflation.

inflationism [in*flay*shonizm] *n* systematic monetary inflation; policy advocating this ~ **inflationist** *adj*.

inflect [in*flekt*] *v/t* bend inwards, curve; modulate (voice); (*gramm*) vary some element in a word, *usu* the ending, to express grammatical relationships.

inflection, inflectional see **inflexion**.

inflective [in*flek*tiv] *adj* capable of being inflected.

inflexed [in*flekst*] *adj* (*bot, zool*) bent inwards.

inflexibility [infleksi*bili*ti] *n* quality of being inflexible.

inflexible [in*fleksib*'l] *adj* unbending, unyielding; that cannot be changed or turned aside; ruthless; that cannot be curved, rigid ~ **inflexibly** *adv*.

inflexion, inflection [in*flek*shon] *n* act of inflecting; state of being inflected; (*gramm*) variation within a word to express grammatical relationship, tense, case *etc*; word-ending used to inflect; (*mus*) modulation of voice > PDM ~ **inflexional, inflectional** *adj*.

inflict [in*flikt*] *v/t* cause to suffer or undergo (something unpleasant); impose (penalty) on.

infliction [in*flik*shon] *n* act of inflicting; that which is inflicted; trouble, annoyance.

inflorescence [inflo*Resens*] *n* (*bot*) process of flowering; arrangement of flowers upon a stem > PDB; whole group of flowers on one plant.

inflow [*infl*O] *n* act of flowing in; amount that flows in; rate of inward flow.

influence [*infl*oo-ens] *v/t* have a mental, moral or emotional effect on; affect, modify; guide, control the behaviour or opinions of; persuade ~ **influence** *n* act of influencing; ability to influence; result produced by influence; one who or that which influences; persuasion; power of influencing persons in authority or in important positions; (*astrol*) supposed effect of stars on human character or fate.

influent [*infl*OO-ent] *adj* flowing in ~ **influent** *n* tributary stream.

influential [infloo-*en*shal] *adj* having or exerting influence; powerful ~ **influentially** *adv*.

influenza [infloo-*enza*] *n* contagious virus disease characterized by fever, catarrh and weakness.

influx [*infl*uks] *n* act of flowing in; constant arrival of large quantities of anything, copious flow; junction of tributary to river.

info [*inf*O] *n* (*sl abbr*) information.

inform [in*fawrm*] *v/t* and *i* give knowledge or instruction to, tell (someone) about; give information which causes someone to be arrested or accused; bring a charge against; fill (with a quality), pervade; give life or vigour to.

informal [in*fawr*mal] *adj* without formality; casual, friendly, free and easy; not according to official or customary form; not requiring formal dress ~ **informally** *adv*.

informality [infawr*mali*ti] *n* quality of being informal; informal act or procedure.

informant [in*fawr*mant] *n* one who gives information.

information [infawr*may*shon] *n* act of telling or of imparting knowledge; knowledge acquired from another; facts *etc* communicated or learnt; news; (*leg*) accusation made to magistrate but less formal than an indictment; **i. theory** branch of cybernetics concerned with the amount of information required to control a process.

informative [in*fawr*mativ] *adj* giving information or instruction ~ **informatively** *adv*.

informatory [in*fawr*mateRi] *adj* giving information or knowledge.

informed [in*fawrmd*] *adj* having information; educated; enlightened.

informer [in*fawr*mer] *n* one who informs, *esp* against a criminal or fugitive.

infra [*infr*a] *adv* (*Lat*) below; further down; further on; **i. dig** (*coll*) below one's dignity.

infra- *pref* below; less than; in low degree.

infracostal [infra*kostal*] *adj* (*anat*) below the ribs.

infraction [in*frak*shon] *n* act of breaking; violation, infringement.

infrangible [in*fran*jib'l] *adj* that cannot be broken or violated.

infra-red [infra-*Red*] *adj* (*of invisible heat radiation*) possessing wavelengths between those of visible light and of wireless waves > PDS.

infrastructure [infra*stRuk*cher] *n* lowest part of a building or structure, foundation, base; (*fig*) lower grades within an organization; basic necessities on which more complex activities depend.

infrequency [in*fReek*wensi] *n* state or quality of being infrequent.

infrequent [in*fReek*went] *adj* not frequent; rare, unusual ~ **infrequently** *adv*.

infringe [in*fRinj*] *v/t* break (law, rule, contract *etc*); transgress, disobey ~ **infringement** *n*.

infundibular [infun*dibe*wler] *adj* funnel-shaped.

infuriate [in*fewr*Ri-ayt] *v/t* provoke to fury or rage, madden ~ **infuriating** *adj*.

infuse [in*fewz*] *v/t* pour into; steep in liquid; (*fig*) instil, implant.

infusible [in*fewz*ib'l] *adj* difficult to melt, having very high melting point > PDS.

infusion [in*fewz*hon] *n* act of infusing; liquid obtained by infusing; mixture, blend.

infusoria [infewz*aw*Ri-a] *n* (*pl*) microscopic organisms found in infusions of organic matter > PDB.

infusorial [infewz*aw*Ri-al] *adj* of or containing infusoria; **i. earth** kieselguhr.

ingathering [in-g*aTH*eRing] *n* act of gathering or collecting; harvesting.

ingeminate [in*jem*inayt] *v/t* repeat, reiterate.

ingenious [in*jeen*i-us] *adj* clever at inventing or contriving; skilful and resourceful; cleverly made or contrived ~ **ingeniously** *adv*.

ingenue [an-zhayn*ew*] *n* (*Fr*) innocent or naive girl; actress playing such a girl.

ingenuity [injin*ew*iti] *n* quality of being ingenious.

ingenuous [in*jen*ew-us] *adj* guileless; unsuspecting; frank, candid ~ **ingenuously** *adv* ~ **ingenuousness** *n*.

ingest [in*jest*] *v/t* take (food) into stomach.

ingestion [in*jes*chon] *n* act of ingesting.

ingle [*ing*-g'l] *n* fire burning on the hearth; fireplace.

ingle-nook [*ing*-g'l-nook] *n* chimney corner.

inglorious [in-g*law*Ri-us] *adj* bringing no honour, shameful; little-known, not famous ~ **ingloriously** *adv*.

ingoing [*in*-gO-ing] *n* act of entering; sum paid by new tenant for facilities or fixtures left behind ~ **ingoing** *adj* going in, entering.

ingot [*ing*-got] *n* block of metal cast in mould > PDE; bar of gold or silver.

ingrain [in-g*Rayn*] *adj* dyed in the yarn before being manufactured; (*fig*) inborn; inveterate.

ingrained [in-g*Raynd*] *adj* permeating every part; firmly established, inveterate.

ingrate [*in*-g*Rayt*] *adj* and *n* (*ar*) ungrateful (person).

ingratiate [in-g*Ray*shi-ayt] *v/i* **i. oneself** make oneself agreeable to, try to win favour from.

ingratiating [in-g*Ray*shi-ayting] *adj* seeking to win favour; attractive ~ **ingratiatingly** *adv*.

ingratitude [in-g*Rat*itewd] *n* lack of gratitude.

ingredient [in-g*Reed*i-ent] *n* component, one element in a mixture; one food used with others to make a cooked dish.

ingress [*in*-g*Res*] *n* act of entering; (*leg*) power or right of entry.

in-group [*in*-g*ROO*p] *n* persons closely linked by shared interests.

ingrowing [*in*-g*RO*-ing] *adj* growing inwards.

inguinal [*ing*-gwinal] *adj* of or near the groin.

ingurgitate [in-gurji*tayt*] *v/t* and *i* swallow greedily; (*fig*) engulf.

ingurgitation [in-gurji*tay*shon] *n* swallowing.

inhabit [in-*habit*] *v/t* dwell in; occupy.

inhabitable [in-*habit*ab'l] *adj* fit to live in.

inhabitancy [in-*habit*ansi] *n* residence as an inhabitant, *esp* during a specified period.

inhabitant [in-*habit*ant] *n* one who lives in a particular place.

inhabitation [in-habit*ay*shon] *n* act of inhabiting; state of being inhabited; dwelling-place.

inhalant [in*hay*lant] *n* medicament absorbed by inhaling.

inhalation [inha*lay*shon] *n* act of inhaling; that which is inhaled; medicated vapour.

inhale [in*hayl*] *v/t* breathe in, draw into the lungs; habitually draw tobacco smoke into one's lungs.

inhaler [in*hay*ler] *n* apparatus for inhaling medicated vapour; one who inhales in smoking.

inharmonious [inhaarm*Oni*-us] *adj* not in harmony, discordant; conflicting ~ **inharmoniously** *adv*.

inhere [in*heer*] *v/i* be an essential and natural part; be inseparable; be vested in; be naturally implied.

inherence [in*heer*Rens] *n* quality of inhering.

inherent [in*heer*Rent] *adj* essentially belonging to or existing in ~ **inherently** *adv*.

inherit [in*he*Rit] *v/t* and *i* receive (property *etc*) as an heir; possess as hereditary characteristic; come into possession as an heir.

inheritable [in*he*Ritab'l] *adj* that can be inherited; entitled to inherit.

inheritance [in*he*Ritans] *n* act of inheriting; that which is inherited; (*biol*) characteristics passed on from parents to offspring > PDP.

inheritor [in*he*Riter] *n* one who inherits.

inheritress, inheritrix [in*he*RitRes, in*he*RitRiks] *n* female who inherits.

inhesion [in*heez*hon] *n* inherence.

inhibit [in*hibit*] *v/t* restrain; check the natural impulse or activity of; hinder; (*eccles*) forbid (priest) to exercise ministerial functions; (*psych*) check by inhibition.

inhibited [in*hibit*id] *adj* prevented from acting, developing *etc*; restrained by inhibition; (*coll*) unhealthily self-restrained; morbidly shy or guilt-ridden.

inhibition [inhib*ish*on] *n* act of inhibiting; that which inhibits; state of being inhibited; (*psych*) restraint, *usu* unconscious, preventing manifestation of an impulse, function, activity *etc* > PDP; (*coll*) unhealthy suppression of natural urges; (*biol*) prevention of action of an effector by influence of nerve impulses > PDB; temporary restraint of function; (*leg*) decree forbidding further action; (*eccles*) order forbidding priest to exercise ministerial functions.

inhibitory [in*hibit*eRi] *adj* tending to inhibit; of the nature of an inhibition.

inhospitable [inho*spit*ab'l] *adj* not showing hospitality; giving no shelter, bleak ~ **inhospitably** *adv*.

inhuman [in*hew*man] *adj* cruel, brutal, callous; not of or like the human race ~ **inhumanly** *adv*.

inhumane [inhew*mayn*] *adj* cruel, brutal.

inhumanity [inhew*man*iti] *n* cruelty, brutality.

inhumation [inhew*may*shon] *n* burial in ground.

inhume [in*hewm*] *v/t* bury.

inimical [in*im*ikal] *adj* hostile, unfriendly; harmful; unfavourable ~ **inimically** *adv*.

inimitability [inimita*bil*iti] *n* quality of being inimitable.

inimitable [in*im*itab'l] *adj* that cannot be imitated; unique, unrivalled ~ **inimitably** *adv*.

iniquitous [in*ik*witus] *adj* very wicked; unjust ~ **iniquitously** *adv*.

iniquity [in*ik*witi] *n* quality of being iniquitous; great wickedness; injustice; sinfulness.

initial [inishal] *adj* of or at the beginning, first ∼ **initial** *n* first letter of a word, *esp* of a name or title ∼ **initial** (*pres/part* **initialling**, *p/t* and *p/part* **initialled**) *v/t* write the initial of one's name or names on ∼ **initially** *adv* at the beginning, at first.

initiate [inishi-ayt] *v/t* originate, set in motion; admit to membership of a social group, *usu* with ceremonies; impart secret knowledge to; instruct in the rudiments of ∼ **initiate** [inishi-at] *n* and *adj* (one) who has been initiated.

initiation [inishi-ayshon] *n* act of initiating; state of being initiated; ritual or ceremony of initiating.

initiative [inishi-ativ] *n* first step; act of setting a process in motion; ability or willingness to take the lead; right or duty to make first move; enterprise; capacity for acting independently or showing originality ∼ **initiative** *adj* beginning; initiating.

initiator [inishi-aytor] *n* one who initiates.

initiatory [inishi-ayteRi] *adj* initiating.

inject [injekt] *v/t* drive (liquid) forcefully into (cavity, tissues *etc*), *esp* with hypodermic syringe; fill with liquid under pressure.

injection [injekshon] *n* act of injecting; that which is injected; **i. moulding** method of moulding thermoplastics by heating and injecting them into a mould; article so moulded.

injector [injekter] *n* that which injects.

in-joke [in-jOk] *n* joke which only members of a limited group can appreciate.

injudicial [in-jOOdishal] *adj* not in legal form.

injudicious [injOOdishus] *adj* lacking judgement; rash, unwise ∼ **injudiciously** *adv* ∼ **injudiciousness** *n*.

injunction [injunkshon] *n* instruction, command, order; (*leg*) court order forbidding a person to infringe another's rights.

injure [injer] *v/t* harm, damage; do wrong to.

injured [injerd] *adj* wronged; harmed, hurt; offended; expressing awareness of having been wronged, offended *etc*; reproachful.

injurious [injoorRi-us] *adj* wrongful, iniquitous, unjust; slanderous, insulting; harmful, noxious ∼ **injuriously** *adv* ∼ **injuriousness** *n*.

injury [injeri] *n* harm done: wound, physical hurt; offence, outrage; that which damages or causes harm.

injustice [injustis] *n* unjust act; unfairness.

ink [ink] *n* coloured fluid used in writing or in printing; dark liquid given off by cuttlefish *etc* ∼ **ink** *v/t* mark, cover, or blacken with ink.

ink-bag [ink-bag] *n* bladder containing dark liquid in cuttlefish.

inkhorn [inkhawrn] *n* (*obs*) small container for ink; **i. terms** pedantic language, *esp* in 16th century.

inkling [inkling] *n* vague idea; faint suspicion or awareness.

inkstand [inkstand] *n* stand for holding bottles of ink and pens.

inkwell [inkwel] *n* cup for holding ink which fits into a hole in a desk.

inky [inki] *adj* of ink; like ink; black.

inlaid [inlayd] *p/t* and *p/part* of **inlay**.

inland [inland] *adj* away from the coast, in the inner areas of a country; done, obtained *etc* within a country; not foreign; **i. revenue** revenue from taxes and duties levied inside a country ∼ **inland** *adv* in or towards the inner areas of a country.

inlander [inlander] *n* one dwelling inland.

in-law [in-law] *n* relative, *esp* parent, of one's wife or husband.

inlay (*p/t* and *p/part* **inlaid**) [inlay] *v/t* imbed pieces in contrasting colour or material into a groundwork, so as to produce a pattern but keep a level surface ∼ **inlay** [inlay] *n* inlaid ornamentation; pieces of material to be inlaid.

inlet [inlet] *n* small opening into coastline or bank; creek; something let in or inserted; means of entrance.

inlier [inlI-er] *n* mass of old stratified rocks surrounded by newer strata > PDG.

inly [inli] *adv* inwardly; intimately; sincerely.

inmate [inmayt] *n* one who lives in (an asylum, institution *etc*).

inmost [inmOst] *adj* farthest in; (*fig*) deepest; most secret.

inn [in] *n* house providing lodging and catering for travellers; **Inns of Court** four legal societies through one of which a person may be admitted to the bar; buildings of three societies.

innards [inerdz] *n* (*pl*) (*sl*) stomach; guts.

innate [in-nayt] *adj* inborn, natural, instinctive ∼ **innately** *adv* ∼ **innateness** *n*.

inner [iner] *adj* inside, interior, nearer the centre; **i. man** soul; (*coll*) appetite, stomach ∼ **inner** *n* (*archery*) ring of target next to bullseye; shot hitting this ring.

innermost [inermOst] *adj* inmost.

innervate [inurvayt] *v/t* (*physiol*) supply with nerves; excite (muscle or gland) to activity.

innervation [inurvayshon] *n* nerve supply to an organ; act of innervating > PDP, PDB.

innings [iningz] *n* (*cricket, baseball*) turn for batting by player or side; (*fig*) period; turn; **have a good (long) i.** (*fig*) live long; be lucky.

innkeeper [inkeeper] *n* one who keeps an inn.

innocence [inOsens] *n* quality of being innocent.

innocent [inOsent] *adj* free from guilt, blameless; not guilty of a specific charge; harmless; guileless, ingenuous; ignorant, simple ∼ **innocent** *n* simple, ingenuous child or person; idiot; **i. of** (*fig*) quite without ∼ **innocently** *adv*.

innocuous [inokew-us] *adj* harmless ∼ **innocuously** *adv* ∼ **innocuousness** *n*.

innovate [inOvayt] *v/i* introduce something new.

innovation [inOvayshon] *n* act or process of innovating; new method *etc*; change.

innovator [inOvayter] *n* one who innovates.

innoxious [inokshus] *adj* harmless.

innuendo (*pl* **innuendoes**) [inyoo-endO] *n* indirect and malicious suggestion, insinuation; half-concealed accusation.

innumerable [inewmeRab'l] *adj* that cannot be reckoned, countless.

inobservance [inobzurvans] *n* failure to observe (a rule, custom *etc*); ∼ **inobservant** *adj*.

inoculate [inokewlayt] *v/t* (*bath*) render immune to specific disease by infecting with weakened and controlled form of same disease; inject serum or vaccine into; (*fig*) imbue with; (*hort*) graft buds on to.

inoculation [inokew*lay*shon] *n* act of inoculating.
inoculator [in*oke*wlayter] *n* one who inoculates.
inodorous [in*Ode*Rus] *adj* having no smell.
inoffensive [ino*fe*nsiv] *adj* giving no offence; harmless ~ **inoffensively** *adv.*
inofficious [ino*fi*shus] *adj* without office; (*leg*) negligent of duty.
inoperable [in*ope*Rab'l] *adj* (*surg*) not suitable for treatment by operation.
inoperative [in*ope*Rativ] *adj* not working; invalid (*esp* of laws).
inopportune [in*ope*rtewn] *adj* ill-timed, unseasonable ~ **inopportunely** *adv.*
inordinate [ina*wr*dinit] *adj* immoderate, excessive ~ **inordinately** *adv.*
inorganic [inawr*ga*nik] *adj* not organic; composed of lifeless matter; not a result of natural growth; lacking systematic coordination; (*chem*) of mineral origin; not belonging to the class of carbon compounds.
inorganization [inawrgan*Iza*yshon] *n* lack of organization.
inornate [inawr*nayt*] *adj* simple, plain.
inosculate [in*oske*wlayt] *v/t* and *i* (*of ducts, organs etc*) join end to end; (*of fibres*) intertwine; (*fig*) amalgamate.
inosculation [inoskew*lay*shon] *n* act of inosculating.
in-patient [*in*-payshent] *n* one who resides in hospital while receiving treatment.
input [*in*poot] *n* (*elect*) current put into or received by an apparatus; amount of raw materials *etc* put into a machine, factory *etc*; data supplied to or stored in a computer ~ **input** *v/t* feed (data) into a computer.
inquest [*in*-kwest] *n* judicial inquiry, *esp* into the cause of a death.
inquietude [in-*kwI*-etewd] *n* restlessness, uneasiness.
inquire, enquire [in-*kwIr*] *v/t* and *i* ask questions; seek information; make inquiries; find out; **i. after** ask about someone's health; **i. into** investigate ~ **inquiring** *adj* seeking information, curious; expressing inquiry ~ **inquiringly** *adv.*
inquiry, enquiry [in-*kwI*rRi] *n* act of inquiring; question; search for information or knowledge; investigation, official examination of facts.
inquisition [in-kwi*zi*shon] *n* prolonged and severe investigation, searching examination; (*hist*) medieval ecclesiastical court for the discovery and suppression of heresy; (*RC*) the Holy Office, an organization for the protection of faith and morals, the censorship of books *etc* ~ **inquisitional** *adj.*
inquisitive [in-*kwi*zitiv] *adj* too fond of asking questions, very curious; prying ~ **inquisitively** *adv* ~ **inquisitiveness** *n.*
inquisitor [in-*kwi*ziter] *n* one who holds an official inquiry; member of the Court of Inquisition.
inquisitorial [in-kwizit*aw*Ri-al] *adj* of or like an inquisitor; very searching; prying ~ **inquisitorially** *adv.*
inroad [*in*ROd] *n* hostile advance, sudden attack; encroachment.
inrush [*in*Rush] *n* act of rushing in, irruption.
insalubrious [insa*lew*bRi-us] *adj* not healthy.
insalubrity [insa*lew*bRiti] *n* unhealthiness.
insane [in*sayn*] *adj* so mad as not to be legally

responsible for one's deeds; mad, mentally deranged; crazy, very foolish ~ **insanely** *adv.*
insanitary [in*sa*niteRi] *adj* not sanitary; injurious to health; likely to carry infection.
insanity [in*sa*niti] *n* state of being insane.
insatiable [in*say*shi-ab'l] *adj* that cannot be satisfied or appeased ~ **insatiably** *adv.*
insatiate [in*say*shi-it] *adj* insatiable.
inscape [*in*skayp] *n* formative essence.
inscribe [insk*RIb*] *v/t* write, carve, or engrave on; dedicate; (*geom*) draw (a figure) within another; enter in a book, list, register *etc.*
inscription [insk*Rip*shon] *n* act of inscribing; words inscribed; dedication; lettering on coins and medals ~ **inscriptional** *adj.*
inscriptive [insk*Rip*tiv] *adj* of an inscription.
inscrutability [inskROO*ta*biliti] *n* quality of being inscrutable.
inscrutable [insk*ROO*tab'l] *adj* that cannot be understood; enigmatic, mysterious ~ **inscrutably** *adv.*
insect [*in*sekt] *n* invertebrate animal with six legs and body having three distinct parts > PDB; (*pop*) any small flying or crawling animal.
insectarium [insekt*air*Ri-um] *n* place for keeping or for breeding insects.
insecticide [in*sek*tisId] *n* chemical preparation for destroying insects.
insectifuge [in*sek*tifewj] *n* preparation that drives insects away.
insection [in*sek*shon] *n* incision.
insectivore [in*sek*tivawr] *n* member of a group of insect-eating mammals > PDB.
insectivorous [insek*tivo*Rus] *adj* feeding on insects.
insectology [insek*to*loji] *n* study of insects.
insecure [insi*kewr*] *adj* not secure, not safe; not feeling safe; not well protected; unreliable ~ **insecurely** *adv.*
insecurity [insi*kew*Riti] *n* state or quality of being insecure.
inseminate [in*se*minayt] *v/t* introduce semen into, *esp* artificially; impregnate; sow, implant.
insemination [insemi*nay*shon] *n* act of inseminating.
insensate [in*sen*sayt] *adj* irrational, unreasoning; stupid; incapable of having sensations, not alive ~ **insensately** *adv.*
insensibility [insensi*bi*liti] *n* state or quality of being insensible.
insensible [in*sen*sib'l] *adj* not perceiving, having no sensation; unconscious; unaware, indifferent; callous; that cannot be perceived; imperceptible, very gradual ~ **insensibly** *adv* in an insensible way; gradually, imperceptibly.
insensitive [in*sen*sitiv] *adj* not sensitive, unaffected by certain impressions or emotions ~ **insensitively** *adv* ~ **insensitiveness** *n.*
insentient [in*sen*shi-ent] *adj* not having perception; inanimate.
inseparability [insepe*Ra*biliti] *n* quality or state of being inseparable.
inseparable [in*sepe*Rab'l] *adj* that cannot be separated; constantly in one another's company ~ **inseparably** *adv.*
inseparate [in*sepe*Rit] *adj* not separated.
insert [in*surt*] *v/t* set or place in or among;

introduce into ~ **insert** [*in*surt] *n* that which is inserted or to be inserted.

insertion [in*sur*shon] *n* act of inserting; state of being inserted; that which is inserted, *esp* a word or words into written or printed matter; lace *etc* inserted into piece of needlework.

inset [*in*set] *n* that which is set in; insertion; small map, drawing *etc* printed or drawn within another; extra page or set of pages inserted in a proof or book ~ **inset** *v/t*.

inshore [*in*shawr] *adj* and *adv* near or towards the shore.

inside [ins*Id*/*ins*Id] *n* inner part, surface, side; interior; (*coll*) stomach, bowels (also *pl*) ~ **inside** *adj* internal, in or on the inside; secret, confidential; trustworthy ~ **inside** *adv* into or in the inside; indoors; (*coll*) in prison ~ **inside** *prep* within; into; in less than (a specified time or distance); **i. of** less than (specified time).

insider [ins*Id*er] *n* one who is inside; member of society, group *etc*; one with information, knowledge *etc* not generally available.

insidious [in*sidi*-us] *adj* making stealthy progress; working secretly to destroy or entrap; sly, treacherous ~ **insidiously** *adv* ~ **insidiousness** *n*.

insight [*in*sIt] *n* thorough and wise understanding; discernment; perception; opportunity to observe or understand > PDP.

insignia [in*signi*-a] *n* (*pl*) badges of office or of honour; distinguishing marks.

insignificance [insig*nifi*kans] *n* quality or state of being insignificant.

insignificant [insig*nifi*kant] *adj* not important, trivial; without meaning; unimpressive; contemptible ~ **insignificantly** *adv*.

insincere [insin*seer*] *adj* not sincere; dissembling; false; deceitful ~ **insincerely** *adv*.

insincerity [insin*se*Riti] *n* quality of being insincere.

insinuate [in*sin*ew-ayt] *v/t* and *i* hint at, convey indirectly; cunningly and gradually gain affection, power *etc*; gradually penetrate ~ **insinuating** *adj* ~ **insinuatingly** *adv*.

insinuation [insinew-*ay*shon] *n* act of insinuating; hint, indirect allusion, innuendo.

insipid [in*sip*id] *adj* having no strong taste, lacking flavour; (*fig*) not stimulating, dull ~ **insipidly** *adv*.

insipidity [insi*pid*iti] *n* lack of flavour; dullness.

insist [in*sist*] *v/t* and *i* order or demand emphatically; assert strongly and repeatedly; stress the importance of; persist in.

insistence [in*sis*tens] *n* act of insisting; quality of being insistent ~ **insistency** *n*.

insistent [in*sis*tent] *adj* demanding; urgent; emphatic; persistent ~ **insistently** *adv*.

insobriety [ins*Ob*RI-eti] *n* drunkenness.

insofar [ins*Ofaar*] *adv* to the degree that.

insolation [ins*Olay*shon] *n* radiant energy received from the sun by the earth > PDG; exposure to sunlight; sunstroke.

insole [*in*sOl] *n* inner sole of boot or shoe.

insolence [*in*solens] *n* quality of being insolent.

insolent [*in*solent] *adj* rude; haughty, contemptuous; insulting ~ **insolently** *adv*.

insolubility [insolyoob*ili*ti] *n* quality of being insoluble.

insoluble [in*sol*yoob'l] *adj* that cannot be dissolved; that cannot be explained or solved ~ **insolubly** *adv*.

insolvency [in*sol*vensi] *n* state of being insolvent.

insolvent [in*sol*vent] *n* and *adj* (person) unable to pay debts, bankrupt.

insomnia [in*somni*-a] *n* inability to sleep, *esp* if chronic ~ **insomniac** *n* person suffering from insomnia.

insomuch [ins*Omuch*] *adv* in so far, to such a degree.

insouciance [ins*OO*si-ens] *n* (*Fr*) open indifference, state of not caring ~ **insouciant** *adj*.

inspan (*pres*/*part* inspanning, *p*/*t* and *p*/*part* inspanned) [in*span*] *v/t* yoke (oxen *etc*) to waggon.

inspect [in*spekt*] *v/t* look closely into; examine officially or thoroughly.

inspection [in*spek*shon] *n* act of inspecting; careful examination; official investigation.

inspector [in*spek*ter] *n* one who inspects and reports on; police officer ranking between sergeant and superintendent.

inspectorate [in*spek*toRat] *n* office of inspector; body of inspectors; area supervised by an inspector.

inspectorial [inspek*tawri*-al] *adj* of an inspector; of inspection.

inspectorship [in*spek*tership] *n* office of an inspector; tenure of this.

inspectress [in*spek*tRis] *n* female inspector.

inspiration [inspi*Ray*shon] *n* creative impulse, stimulus to artistic or intellectual activity; one who or that which gives this; sudden brilliant idea; act of inspiring; state of being inspired; divine guidance, *esp* of the authors of the Bible; act of inhaling ~ **inspirational** *adj*.

inspirationism [inspi*Ray*shonizm] *n* belief in divine inspiration of the Bible.

inspiratory [inspi*Ray*teRi/ins*pIr*RateRi] *adj* relating to the drawing in of breath.

inspire [ins*pIr*] *v/t* stimulate to creative or intellectual activity; endow with genius; communicate superhuman power or knowledge to; instil into, fill (the mind) with; rouse, excite ~ **inspiring** *adj*.

inspirit [ins*pi*Rit] *v/t* give vigour, courage or spirit to; put new life into ~ **inspiriting** *adj*.

inspissate [ins*pisa*yt/*in*spisayt] *v/t* thicken render; more dense ~ **inspissation** [inspis*ay*shon] *n*.

inst [*inst*] *n* (*comm abbr*) the current month.

instability [insta*bili*ti] *n* lack of stability; tendency to excessive and variable emotional reactions > PDP; unreliability of character.

install, instal [in*stawl*] *v/t* settle into seat or place; ceremonially place in an office, induct; invest with rank; put into position for use.

installation [insta*lay*shon] *n* act of installing; complete apparatus in position and ready for use.

instalment [in*stawl*ment] *n* one part of something which is produced, supplied *etc* in parts at regular intervals; one part-payment of a sum to be paid off at intervals; one part of book, play *etc* produced as serial; act of installing.

instance [*in*stans] *n* single fact, event *etc* illustrating general statement; example; request, suggestion; (*leg*) stage in legal procedure; **for i** as an example; **in the first i.** as a first step in the beginning ~ **instance** v/t mention as an instance, give as example.

instancy [*in*stansi] n insistence; urgency.

instant [*in*stant] adj immediate; acting, made, happening etc at once; (of foods) partially precooked and sold needing only easy final preparation; (fig) hasty and superficial; (comm) at the present time; of the current month; (ar) constantly active ~ **instant** n precise moment of time; very brief period; **on the i.** immediately.

instantaneous [instan*tay*ni-us] adj acting, happening or done in an instant; immediate ~ **instantaneously** adv.

instanter [in*stan*ter] adv immediately.

instantly [*in*stantli] adv immediately.

instate [in*stayt*] v/t establish, install.

instead [in*sted*] adv in the place of; as a substitute for.

instep [*in*step] n arched upper side of human foot; part of a shoe, stocking etc which covers the instep.

instigate [*in*stigayt] v/t urge on, incite; stir up.

instigation [insti*gay*shon] n act of instigating; that which instigates.

instigator [*in*stigayter] n one who instigates.

instil (pres/part **instilling**, p/t and p/part **instilled**) [in*stil*] v/t teach (ideas) gradually but powerfully; pour in drop by drop.

instillation [insti*lay*shon] n act of instilling.

instilment [in*stil*ment] n act of instilling.

instinct [*in*stinkt] n congenital and unreasoned tendency to specified reactions, behaviour etc; elaborate pattern of actions occurring as a whole in response to stimuli; natural unreasoned impulse or response > PDP; (fig) congenital aptitude ~ **instinct** [in*stinkt*] adj filled with; animated by.

instinctive [in*stink*tiv] adj prompted by instinct; involuntary > PDP ~ **instinctively** adv.

instinctual [in*stink*tew-al] adj relating to instinct.

institute [*in*stitewt] v/t set up, establish; found; start; appoint, install ~ **institute** n society established for some particular object; headquarters of such a society; (pl) established principles, laws etc; (pl) book summarizing basic principles.

institution [insti*tew*shon] n act of instituting; that which is instituted; state of being instituted; institute, established society or organization; headquarters of this; home, school, hospital etc run by such a society or by public authorities; well-known and long-established custom, rule, practice etc; (coll) well-known personality.

institutional [insti*tew*shonal] adj of or like an institution; organized into one institution; (US) designed to enhance prestige.

institutionalism [insti*tew*shonalizm] n characteristics of life in charitable institutions; principles of organized religion.

institutionalize [insti*tew*shonalIz] v/t make into an institution; set up as an institution; (coll) put (a person) into an institution; (psych) cause to become too dependent and apathetic.

instruct [in*struKt*] v/t teach, impart knowledge to, inform; give orders or directions to.

instruction [in*struK*shon] n act of instructing; teaching, training; information; order, direction.

instructional [in*struK*shonal] adj of instruction.

instructive [in*struK*tiv] adj serving as a lesson containing information ~ **instructively** adv.

instructor [in*struK*ter] n teacher, trainer.

instructress [in*struK*tRis] n female instructor.

instrument [*in*stROoment] n anything used as an aid in doing physical work; tool, implement; object used to produce musical sound > PDM; person sent to perform a task for another; agent; (leg) document, deed ~ **instrument** v/t (mus) arrange for performance by instruments.

instrumental [instROo*men*tal] adj serving as an instrument or means; caused by an instrument; produced by or composed for musical instruments ~ **instrumental** n (gramm) case denoting means or agency ~ **instrumentally** adv.

instrumentalist [instROo*men*talist] n one who plays a musical instrument.

instrumentality [instROomen*tal*iti] n agency.

instrumentation [instROomen*tay*shon] n the writing of music for particular instruments > PDM; use of scientific instruments.

insubordinate [insu*bawr*dinayt] adj rebellious, disobedient; resisting discipline.

insubordination [insubawrdi*nay*shon] n rebelliousness; rebellious act.

insubstantial [insub*stan*shal] adj having no substance, not real; flimsy, too light.

insubstantiality [insubstanshi-*al*iti] n unreality.

insufferable [in*suf*eRab'l] adj not to be endured; unbearably conceited ~ **insufferably** adv.

insufficiency [insu*fish*ensi] n state or quality of being insufficient, lack.

insufficient [insu*fish*ent] adj not sufficient; not adequate ~ **insufficiently** adv.

insufflate [in*suf*layt] v/t blow or breathe into, fill with air ~ **insufflation** [insu*flay*shon] n.

insufflator [insu*flay*ter] n respiratory apparatus.

insular [*in*sewler] adj of or like an island; of or like inhabitants of an island; cut off from general currents of thought; narrow-minded, smugly intolerant.

insularism [*in*sewlaRizm] n insularity.

insularity [insewla*Ri*ti] n isolation from general trends of thought; narrow outlook.

insulate [*in*sewlaytl] v/t isolate, cut off; (phys) prevent passage of heat, electricity, or sound to or from anything by isolating it with nonconducting substance; (geog) make into an island.

insulation [insewl*ay*shon] n act of insulating; state of being insulated; that which insulates.

insulator [*in*sewlaytor] n insulating substance or device.

insulin [*in*sewlin] n preparation from the pancreas used in the treatment of diabetes > PDB, PDP, PDS; **i. shock** state of convulsions or coma induced by overdose of insulin.

insult [in*sult*] v/t treat contemptuously; offend the honour or dignity of; abuse ~ **insult** [*in*sult] n act, word or gesture which insults; affront, offence to one's honour ~ **insulting** [in*sult*ing] adj ~ **insultingly** adv.

insuperability [insewpe*Ra*biliti] n quality of being insuperable.

insuperable [in*sew*peRab'l] adj that cannot be overcome or surmounted; invincible ~ **insuperably** adv.

insupportable [insu*pawr*tab'l] adj unbearable, intolerable ~ **insupportably** adv.

insurable [inshoorRab'l] *adj* capable of being insured.

insurance [inshoorRans] *n* act of insuring; state of being insured; contract whereby a company or the State agrees to pay compensation for death, injuries, loss *etc* in return for an agreed premium; premium paid for this; **i.** **policy** written contract of insurance.

insurant [inshoorRant] *n* one who pays premium in insurance contract.

insure [inshoor] *v/t* enter into contract of insurance against loss of (life, health, property *etc*); make sure; make safe.

insurer [inshoorRer] *n* one who contracts to pay insurance for another's loss.

insurgency [insurjensi] *n* state of being insurgent.

insurgent [insurjent] *adj* in revolt, rebelling against government *etc* to overthrow it ~ **insurgent** *n* rebel, one who is in revolt.

insurmountable [insermowntab'l] *adj* that cannot be surmounted or overcome ~ **insurmountably** *adv*.

insurrection [inserRekshon] *n* act of rising against established authority; rebellion, revolt ~ **insurrectional** *adj* ~ **insurrectionary** *adj*.

insurrectionist [inserRekshonist] *n* rebel; one who encourages rebellion.

insusceptibility [insuseptibiliti] *n* quality or state of being insusceptible.

insusceptible [insuseptib'l] *adj* not capable of being moved by feeling; not capable of being affected.

intact [intakt] *adj* untouched; unharmed; entire.

intaglio [intali-O] *n* depth carving; figure cut or engraved in a hard substance; jewel with incised figure or device > PDAA.

intake [intayk] *n* that which is taken in; act of taking in; rate at which something is taken in; point at which a tube narrows; airshaft in a mine; inlet of pipe or channel; valve by which explosive mixture enters cylinder of car engine *etc*; enclosed land; group of persons joining an organization at the same date.

intangibility [intanjibiliti] *n* quality of being intangible.

intangible [in*t*anjib'l] *adj* that cannot be perceived by touch; not material; that cannot be clearly understood; vague ~ **intangibly** *adv*.

integer [intijer] *n* the whole of anything; (*math*) whole number.

integral [intigRal] *adj* whole, complete; essential; (*math*) pertaining to or consisting of integers ~ **integral** *n* integer; function obtained by integration; **i.** **calculus** branch of mathematics concerned with the process of integrating ~ **integrally** *adv*.

integrality [intigRaliti] *n* wholeness.

integrand [intigRand] *n* (*math*) function to be integrated.

integrate [intigRayt] *v/t* and *i* make into a whole, complete; form into a mature and balanced personality; join with other social groups to form a united community; abolish segregation; coordinate; give the total of; (*math*) find the value of a function with a known differential coefficient ~ **integrate** *adj* whole; made of components.

integration [intigRayshon] *n* act or process of integrating; state of being integrated; harmonious combination of elements into a complex whole;

removal of social barriers between previously segregated groups; development and unification of awareness in young children > PDP; (*math*) process of integrating.

integrationist [intigRayshonist] *n* and *adj* (supporter) of integration between Negroes and whites.

integrity [integRiti] *n* completeness, wholeness; (*fig*) moral soundness; uprightness, probity.

integument [integewment] *n* outer covering; skin; (*bot*) outer covering of a seed; rind, shell.

intellect [intelekt] *n* faculty of knowing, perceiving and thinking; reasoning power; intelligence; person outstanding for such power.

intellection [intelekshon] *n* the conceptual and rational processes > PDP.

intellective [intelektiv] *adj* of or by intellection.

intellectual [intelekchoo-al] *adj* pertaining to intellect; appealing to or performed by intellect; having a powerful and trained intelligence; inclined to activities or pleasures of the intellect rather than of the body or emotions ~ **intellectual** *n* intellectual person.

intellectualism [intelekchoo-alizm] *n* tendency to value intellect and reason above other mental or emotional faculties; fondness for intellectual activities; doctrine that all knowledge derives from reason ~ **intellectualist** *n* and *adj*.

intellectuality [intelekchoo-aliti] *n* quality or state of being intellectual.

intellectualize [intelekchoo-alIz] *v/t* and *i* treat intellectually; use the intellect.

intellectually [intelekchoo-ali] *adv* in an intellectual way; as regards intellect.

intelligence [intelijens] *n* ability to understand, reason, and perceive; quickness in learning, mental alertness; ability to grasp relationships > PDP; information, news, *esp* military; act of gathering secret military information; an intelligent being; **i.** **quotient** number indicating level of intelligence > PDP; **i.** **service** government service occupied in gathering secret information; **i.** **test** task designed to test mental development > PDP.

intelligencer [intelijenser] *n* secret agent.

intelligent [intelijent] *adj* having or showing intelligence; clever; capable of reasoning ~ **intelligently** *adv*.

intelligentsia [intelijentsi-a] *n* (*pl*) intellectual persons considered as a class or group.

intelligibility [intelijibiliti] *n* quality of being intelligible.

intelligible [intelijib'l] *adj* that can be understood ~ **intelligibly** *adv*.

intemperance [intempeRans] *n* lack of moderation; excess, over-indulgence; drunkenness.

intemperate [intemperit] *ad* not moderate, violent, excessive; lacking self-restraint; addicted to excessive drinking of alcohol ~ **intemperately** *adv*.

intend [intend] *v/t* have as purpose, mean to achieve or obtain; mean, signify; plan, design.

intended [intendid] *n* (*coll*) one's future husband or wife.

intense [intens] *adj* existing in high degree, extreme; deeply-felt, ardent; violent, excessive; strongly emotional; (*phot*) opaque ~ **intensely** *adv* ~ **intenseness** *n*.

intensification [intensifi*kay*shon] *n* act of intensifying; state of being intensified.

intensifier [intensifi-er] *n* that which intensifies; (*phot*) substance used to increase the density or contrast of a film or plate.

intensify [intensifi] *v/t* and *i* make or become more intense.

intension [intenshon] *n* intensity, intensification; vigorous mental effort; (*log*) connotation.

intensity [intensiti] *n* quality of being intense; quantitative aspect of sensation > PDP; depth, strength *etc*.

intensive [intensiv] *adj* with regard to force or degree; concentrating large efforts *etc* on specific objective; thorough and vigorous; (*gramm*) giving emphasis; **i. care unit** (*med*) hospital department where patients critically ill are constantly watched and treated ~ **intensively** *adv*.

intent (1) [intent] *adj* having the mind fixed on an object; concentrating; earnest ~ **intently** *adv*.

intent (2) *n* design, purpose; motive; **to all intents** in almost all ways, very nearly; virtually.

intention [intenshon] *n* purpose, aim, design; meaning; (*eccles*) purpose to be achieved by prayer; (*philos*) concept; (*surg*) process of healing fractures or wounds.

intentional [intenshonal] *adj* done on purpose ~ **intentionally** *adv*.

inter (*pres/part* **interring**, *p/t* and *p/part* **interred**) [intur] *v/t* bury.

inter- *pref* among; between; mutual, mutually.

interact [inteRakt] *v/t* act upon each other.

interaction [inteRakshon] *n* reciprocal action.

interbreed [interbReed] *v/t* and *i* crossbreed.

intercalary [inturkaleRi] *adj* inserted, interpolated; intervening, lying between; (*of day(s) or month*) inserted in the calendar (to make the calendar year equal to the solar year); (*of a year*) having such additions.

intercalate [inturkalayt] *v/t* insert, interpolate; insert in calendar.

intercalation [interkalayshon] *n* insertion.

intercede [interseed] *v/i* plead or pray on behalf of another; mediate.

intercellular [interselewler] *adj* (*bot*) between cells > PDB.

intercept [intersept] *v/t* prevent from reaching a destination; seize or halt on the way; obstruct the progress of; (*math*) cut off by two points or line; ~ **intercept** *n* (*math*) part intercepted; radio message ~ **interception** *n*.

interceptor [intersepter] *n* one who or that which intercepts; fighter aircraft.

intercession [interseshon] *n* act of interceding; prayer for others ~ **intercessional** *adj*.

intercessor [interseser] *n* one who intercedes; mediator ~ **intercessory** *adj*.

interchange [interchaynj] *v/t* and *i* exchange with each other; give and take mutually; exchange the places of; alternate; ~ **interchange** [interchaynj] *n* reciprocal exchange; alternation; complex road junction with underpass and flyover.

interchangeable [interchaynjab'l] *adj* that can be interchanged ~ **interchangeably** *adv*.

intercollegiate [interkoleeji-it] *adj* shared by different colleges.

intercom [interkom] *n* internal telephone system, *esp* in aircraft.

intercommunicate [interkomewnikayt] *v/i* communicate with each other; (*of rooms*) open one into the other ~ **intercommunication** [interkomewnikayshon] *n*.

intercommunion [interkomewnyon] *n* mutual communion, *esp* between religious bodies.

intercommunity [interkomewniti] *n* quality of being common to several.

interconnect [interkonekt] *v/t* and *i* connect or link together; be connected, be linked.

intercontinental [interkontinental] *adj* existing between or connecting different continents.

intercostal [interkostal] *adj* between the ribs.

intercourse [interkawrs] *n* dealings of people with each other; fellowship, communion; copulation.

intercrop [interkRop] *n* crop grown between the rows of another crop ~ **intercrop** *v/t* and *i*.

interdenominational [interdinominayshonal] *adj* common to different religious denominations.

interdepend [interdipend] *v/i* depend on each other.

interdependence [interdipendens] *n* mutual dependence ~ **interdependent** *adj*.

interdict [interdikt] *n* decree forbidding something; (*RC*) exclusion from sacraments and religious ceremonies ~ **interdict** [interdikt] *v/t* forbid; issue an interdict against.

interdiction [interdikshon] *n* prohibition ~ **interdictory** *adi*.

interdigital [interdijital] *adj* between the fingers or toes.

interdigitate [interdijitayt] *v/t* and *i* interlock.

interest [intRist/inteRest] *n* concentrated attention, pleasurable preoccupation or concern; that which holds one's attention; benefit, advantage; legal or financial share or right; influence, power; sum paid by borrower for use of sum lent; something added; group of persons working towards same aim ~ **interest** *v/t* rouse or hold the attention of; concern; cause to take a share in or to occupy oneself with.

interested [intRistid/inteRestid] *adj* having the interest aroused; biased, personally involved in; taking an interest or a share in; showing interest ~ **interestedly** *adv*.

interesting [intRisting/inteResting] *adj* arousing interest, capturing the attention; **in an i. condition** (*obs coll*) pregnant ~ **interestingly** *adv*.

interface [interfays] *n* surface separating two media or chemical phases; that which mediates; (*fig*) zone of contact, medium of communication ~ **interface** *v/i* and *t* harmonize; **i. with** work harmoniously in conjunction with.

interfacing [interfaysing] *n* layer of stiffer fabric inside a collar, lapel *etc*.

interfere [interfeer] *v/i* meddle, take a part in other people's affairs; intervene; (*phys*) modify each other; (*of horses*) knock feet together in moving; **i. with** prevent, hinder; annoy; molest; assault sexually; tamper with.

interference [interfeerRens] *n* act of interfering; that which interferes; unjustified intervention, meddlesome behaviour; (*phys*) addition or combination of waves > PDS; (*rad*) distortion or interruption of sound caused by signals from other transmitters or electrical disturbance.

interferential [interfeRenshal] *adj* (*phys*, *rad*) of interference.

interfering [interfeerRing] *adj* that interferes; meddlesome.

interferometer [interfeerRomiter] *n* optical instrument for producing interference; **radio i.** type of radio telescope > PDS.

interferon [interfeerRon] *n* (*biol*) protein produced by cells to protect them against attack by viruses.

interfuse [interfewz] *v/i* and *t* blend; pervade; flow into each other ~ **interfusion** *n*.

intergalactic [intergalaktik] *adj* between the galaxies; from galaxy to galaxy.

interglacial [interglaysi-al] *adj* (*geol*) between two glacial periods.

interim [interim] *n* intermediate period, intervening time; interim dividend ~ **interim** *adj* for the meantime, temporary, provisional.

interior [inteerRi-er] *adj* inner; of, on, or in the inside; internal; far from the coast or boundary; domestic, not foreign; pertaining to the inside of a house ~ **interior** *n* inside, inner part; inside of the body, *esp* digestive system; inland or central region; home affairs of a country; department dealing with these; painting of an indoor scene; domestic scene ~ **interiorly** *adv* in or towards the interior; inwardly.

interjacent [interjaysent] *adj* lying between or among.

interject [interjekt] *v/t* remark or exclaim in interruption, say as an aside; insert; interpose.

interjection [interjekshon] *n* exclamation, remark; (*gramm*) word used as an exclamation.

interlace [interlays] *v/t* and *i* twist over and under each other, interweave ~ **interlace** *n*.

interlard [interlaard] *v/t* insert striking or contrasting remarks *etc* into; diversify.

interleaf (*pl* **interleaves**) [interleef] *n* blank leaf inserted in a book *etc*.

interleave [interleev] *v/t* insert and bind up blank pages among others in a book *etc*.

interline [interlin] *v/t* write or print between lines or in alternate lines; insert a special lining between the outer cloth and the lining (of garment).

interlinear [interlini-er] *adj* written or printed between lines.

interlock [interlok] *v/t* and *i* connect firmly together; lock into one another ~ **interlock** [interlok] *n* a clutch in steel-sheet piling.

interlocution [interlokewshon] *n* conversation, discussion, dialogue.

interlocutor [interlokewter] *n* one who takes part in a dialogue.

interlocutory [interlokewteRi] *adj* of dialogue; (*leg*) not final.

interlope [interlOp] *v/i* meddle, intrude.

interloper [interlOper] *n* one who intrudes without right; meddler; unauthorized trader.

interlude [interlewd] *n* episode or period contrasting with what precedes and follows; intervening time, interval; piece of music inserted between other pieces, between stanzas, or between acts of a play *etc*; short entertainment between acts of a more serious play.

interlunar [interlOOner] *adj* (period) when the moon is about to change from old to new.

intermarriage [intermaRij] *n* marriage between persons of different races, religions or nations; marriage between near relations.

intermarry [intermaRi] *v/i* marry one of different race *etc* or of near kindred.

intermediary [intermeedi-eRi] *adj* being or coming between; acting as go-between or agent between two persons or parties ~ **intermediary** *n* one who or that which is intermediary.

intermediate [interme di-at] *adj* existing or occurring between two things, stages, points of time *etc*; in the middle ~ **intermediate** *n* examination to be taken between Matriculation and Finals; intermediate object ~ **intermediate** [intermeedi-ayt] *v/i* be an intermediary ~ **intermediately** *adv*.

interment [inturment] *n* burial.

intermezzo [intermetsO] *n* short musical composition > PDM; interlude between acts of play, opera *etc*.

interminable [inturminab'l] *adj* without end; apparently endless ~ **interminably** *adv*.

intermingle [interming-g'l] *v/t* and *i* mingle together.

intermission [intermishon] *n* temporary cessation; interval, pause; respite; music played during a theatrical interval.

intermit (*pres/part* **intermitting**, *p/t* and *p/part* **intermitted**) [intermit] *v/t* and *i* stop for a while, suspend; cease temporarily or at intervals.

intermittent [intermitent] *adj* ceasing or lessening at intervals ~ **intermittently** *adv*.

intermix [intermiks] *v/t* and *i* mix together ~ **intermixture** *n*.

intern (1) [inturn] *n* (*US*) resident assistant surgeon or physician in a hospital.

intern (2) *v/t* imprison or place under restraint as political prisoner, prisoner of war, or potentially hostile alien in wartime.

internal [inturnal] *adj* inner, in the inside; of, or pertaining to, the inside; intrinsic; domestic, not foreign; inward; **i. combustion engine** engine driven by burning of vaporized liquid fuel (or gas) in cylinder ~ **internally** *adv*.

international [internashonal] *adj* pertaining to or carried on between different nations; **i. date line** meridian where date changes by one day > PDG ~ **international** *n* player taking part in international sport; international sporting contest; (*cap*) international socialist organization ~ **internationally** *adv*.

Internationale [internashonaal] *n* anthem of International Socialist Movement.

internationalism [internashonalizm] *n* advocacy of close cooperation and association between nations; attempt to eliminate or disregard national differences; international socialism ~ **internationalist** *n* believer in internationalism; expert in international law.

internationalize [internashonalIz] *v/t* make international; bring under the control of different nations.

internecine [interneesIn] *adj* deadly; mutually destructive.

internee [internee] *n* one who is or has been interned.

internment [inter*n*ment] *n* act of interning; state of being interned.

interosculate [inte*Ros*kewlayt] *v/i* unite with each other; (*biol*) have some common characteristics.

interpellate [inter*pe*layt/inter*pe*layt] *v/t* demand explanations; interrupt discussion (in foreign legislative bodies) in order to question.

interpellation [inter*pe*layshon] *n* act of interpellating; interpellated question.

interpenetrate [inter*peni*tRayt] *v/t* and *i* penetrate thoroughly; penetrate each other ~ **interpenetration** [interpeni*tRa*yshon] *n*.

interphone [*inter*fOn] *n* (*US*) intercom.

interplanetary [inter*plani*taRi] *adj* between the planets; from planet to planet.

interplay [*in*terplay] *n* reciprocal action or effect.

Interpol [*in*terpol] *n* international police organization.

interpolate [in*tur*polayt] *v/t* corrupt a text; insert (spurious passage) into a text, book *etc*; (*math*) introduce a series.

interpolation [interpo*lay*shon] *n* act of interpolating; interpolated word or passage; state of being interpolated.

interpose [inter*pOz*] *v/t* and *i* put between, insert; intervene with (objection, offer); break in with (remark); interfere, intervene; interrupt.

interposition [interpO*zish*on] *n* intervention; that which is interposed.

interpret [in*tur*pRet] *v/t* and *i* explain the meaning of; give an artistic performance or representation of; translate, *esp* orally; act as interpreter; take to mean, assign a significance to.

interpretable [in*tur*pRetab'l] *adj* that can be interpreted.

interpretation [inturp*Ri*tayshon] *n* act of interpreting; exposition; meaning, significance; artistic performance (of piece of music, character in play *etc*).

interpretative [in*tur*pRitativ] *adj* that interprets.

interpreter [in*tur*pRiter] *n* one who interprets, *esp* one who translates a foreign language orally.

interpretership [in*tur*pRitership] *n* post as interpreter.

interracial [inter*Ray*shal] *adj* between different races.

interregnum [inter*Reg*num] *n* interval between successive reigns, governments, or ministries; (*fig*) pause, break.

interrelated [inter*Ri*laytid] *adj* related to one another.

interrelation [inter*Ri*layshon] *n* mutual relation.

interrogate [inte*Ro*gayt] *v/t* and *i* examine by searching questions.

interrogation [inte*Ro*gayshon] act of interrogating; question, inquiry; **note of i.** question mark.

interrogative [inter*Ro*gativ] *adj* of or denoting a question; inquiring; (*gramm*) indicating a question; expressed in form of a question ~ **interrogative** *n* (*gramm*) word or word-form indicating that a question is being asked ~ **interrogatively** *adv*.

interrogator [inte*Ro*gayter] *n* one who interrogates, questioner; examiner.

interrogatory [inter*Ro*gateRi] *adj* expressing or pertaining to a question ~ **interrogatory** *n*

inquiry; (*leg*) series of formal questions to be answered on oath.

interrupt [inter*Rupt*] *v/t* break in on; cause a break in, disturb the continuity of; obstruct.

interrupted [inter*Rup*tid] *adj* not continuous, broken; disturbed.

interruption [inter*Rup*shon] *n* act of interrupting; state of being interrupted; that which interrupts.

intersect [inter*sekt*] *v/t* and *i* cut or pass across; divide by cutting; cross each other.

intersection [inter*sek*shon] *n* act of intersecting; state of being intersected; place where two or more roads cross; (*geom*) point or line in which two lines or two planes intersect ~ **intersectional** *adj*.

intersex [*in*terseks] *n* (*biol*) abnormal condition of being intermediate between male and female; organism in this condition.

intersexual [inter*sek*shoo-al] *adj* between the sexes; indeterminate in sex.

interspace [*in*terspays] *n* space between two things; interval ~ **interspace** [inter*spays*] *v/t* put a space between.

intersperse [inter*spurs*] *v/t* scatter or place here and there; diversify.

interstate [inter*stayt*] *adj* pertaining to relations between the states of a federal government.

interstellar [inter*ste*ler] *adj* between the stars; from star to star.

interstice [in*tur*stis] *n* small opening, cranny.

interstitial [inter*stish*al] *adj* of or in an interstice ~ **interstitial** *n* additional atom or ion in a crystal lattice causing a defect.

intertribal [intert*RI*bal] *adj* between different tribes.

intertwine [inter*twIn*] *v/t* and *i* twine or twist together ~ **intertwinement** *n*.

interurban [inte*Rur*ban] *adj* between cities and towns.

interval [*in*terval] *n* space between two points or objects, gap; period of time between two events; degree of difference or separation; pause between two acts of play, opera *etc*; (*mus*) difference in pitch between two sounds > PDM.

intervene [inter*veen*] *v/i* take a part in, attempt to influence or modify the course of; come in between; take place between two events or times; (*leg*) come in as third party in an action.

intervenient [inter*veen*i-ent] *adj* intervening.

intervention [inter*ven*shon] *n* act of intervening; mediation; act of taking sides in a dispute between other states; interference in the affairs of another state in violation of that state's independence > PDPol.

interventionist [inter*ven*shonist] *adj* and *n* (person) advocating intervention.

interview [*in*tervew] *n* formal meeting and conversation; meeting to test the suitability of a candidate for a post or for entrance to college *etc*; meeting at which a reporter questions a person about whose views or personality he wishes to write; article based on such a meeting; similar meeting conducted in front of a television or radio audience ~ **interview** *v/t* have an interview with; question, test.

interviewee [intervewee] *n* person questioned at an interview.

interviewer [intervewer] *n* one who conducts an interview.

intervocalic [intervokalik] *adj* (*phon*) preceded by and followed by a vowel.

interwar [interwawr] *adj* of or in the interval between two wars, *esp* of or in the period 1918 to 1939.

interweave (*p/t* interwove, *p/part* interwoven) [interweev] *v/t* and *i* weave together; (*fig*) mix.

interwind [interwind] *v/t* and *i* wind together, wind through each other; intertwine.

intestacy [intestasi] *n* state of dying intestate.

intestate [intestayt] *adj* having made no will; not disposed of by will ~ **intestate** *n* one who dies intestate.

intestinal [intestinal] *adj* of or in the intestines.

intestine [intestin] *n* alimentary canal between stomach and anus; bowel > PDB ~ **intestine** *adj* (*fig*) internal; domestic, not foreign; civil.

intimacy [intimasi] *n* state of being intimate; close friendship; sexual intercourse.

intimate (1) [intimat] *adj* closely linked by friendship; pertaining to one's deepest feelings or thoughts; private, very personal; close, familiar; having a friendly and informal atmosphere; joined in sexual intercourse; having sexual relationship with ~ **intimate** *n* close friend.

intimate (2) [intimayt] *v/t* make known, announce; hint, suggest.

intimation [intimayshon] *n* act of intimating; hint, suggestion; announcement.

intimidate [intimidayt] *v/t* frighten, terrorize; coerce by threats or violence.

intimidation [intimidayshon] *n* act of intimidating ~ **intimidatory** *adj*.

intimity [intimiti] *n* intimacy.

intinction [intinkshon] *n* (*eccles*) act of dipping the Eucharistic bread into the wine.

into [intoo] *prep* from outside to inside; from one state to another; continuing to the midst of (a period of time); (*math*) dividing; (*sl*) enthusiastic about, interested in, taking part in.

intolerable [intoleRab'l] *adj* that cannot be endured or tolerated ~ **intolerably** *adv*.

intolerance [intoleRans] *adj* quality of being intolerant.

intolerant [intoleRant] *adj* unable or unwilling to tolerate; hostile towards differing views, beliefs, or customs; bigoted ~ **intolerantly** *adv*.

intonation [intonayshon] *n* rise and fall of pitch in speaking voice; modulation of voice; (*mus*) manner of sounding notes of scale; opening phrase in plainsong; act of intoning.

intone [intOn] *v/t* and *i* chant with occasional modulations of pitch; recite in a monotone; give a musical tone to.

intoxicant [intoksikant] *n* and *adj* (that) which intoxicates.

intoxicate [intoksikayt] *v/t* make drunk; (*fig*) rouse to enthusiasm or frenzy ~ **intoxicating** *adj* ~ **intoxicatingly** *adv*.

intoxication [intoksikayshon] *n* act of intoxicating; state of being intoxicated.

intra- *pref* within.

intractability [intRaktabiliti] *n* quality of being intractable.

intractable [intRaktab'l] *adj* that cannot be brought under control; stubborn; very hard to deal with ~ **intractably** *adv*.

intrados [intRaydos] *n* (*archi*) lower curve of arch.

intramural [intRamewrRal] *adj* forming part of normal university syllabus; within the walls or boundaries.

intramuscular [intRamuskewlar] *adj* (*med*) into a muscle.

intransigence [intRansijens] *n* refusal to compromise; fixed hostility.

intransigent [intRansijent] *adj* refusing to compromise or come to terms, obstinately hostile ~ **intransigent** *n* intransigent person.

intransitive [intRansitiv] *n* and *adj* (*gramm*) (verb) not governing an object ~ **intransitively** *adv*.

intrant [intRant] *n* one who enters on a duty or office; one who enters a college, society *etc*.

intravenous [intRaveenus] *adj* (*med*) into a vein.

in-tray [in-tRay] *n* container for incoming correspondence and documents requiring attention.

intrepid [intRepid] *adj* fearless ~ **intrepidly** *adv*.

intrepidity [intRepiditi] *n* fearlessness.

intricacy [intRikasi] *n* quality of being intricate.

intricate [intRikit] *adj* entangled; involved, complicated; obscure ~ **intricately** *adv*.

intrigue [intReeg] *v/i* and *t* plot secretly, make sly schemes; have a secret love affair; rouse the curiosity of, fascinate; puzzle, mystify ~ **intrigue** [intReeg/intReeg] *n* secret or illicit love affair; plot, secret scheme.

intrinsic [intRinsik] *adj* pertaining to the real nature or essence of a thing; inherent; real, genuine ~ **intrinsically** *adv*.

intro- *pref* within.

introduce [intROdews] *v/t* bring in, lead in; put in, insert; add; make acquainted, present; give experience or knowledge of; bring into use, make known; bring to notice, present formally before a legislative body; begin, open.

introduction [intROdukshon] *n* act of introducing; formal presentation of one person to another; preface; preliminary remarks; elementary textbook; opening section.

introductory [intROdukteRi] *adj* serving to introduce; preliminary.

introit [intRO-it/intRoyt] *n* (*RC*) psalm verse recited by priest on first reaching the altar during Mass.

intromit (*pres/part* intromitting, *p/t* and *p/part* intromitted) [intROmit] *v/t* allow to enter; insert.

introspect [intROspekt] *v/i* examine one's own mental processes.

introspection [intROspekshon] *n* act of observing one's own feelings and mental processes, self-analysis > PDP.

introversion [intROvurshon] *n* habitual direction of one's interest inwards; preoccupation with one's own thoughts, feelings *etc* > PDP.

introvert [intROvurt] *n* one who habitually tends to introversion or introspection ~ **introvert** [intROvurt] *v/t* turn inwards.

intrude [intROOd] *v/t* and *i* force one's way in; enter without invitation; encroach; thrust in ~ **intruder** *n* one who intrudes; single raiding aircraft.

intrusion [intROOzhon] *n* act of intruding;

encroachment; (*geol*) penetrating of rocks through or among other rocks; (*pl*) rocks of this kind.

intrusive [intROOsiv] *adj* tending to intrude; coming in without invitation or welcome ~ **intrusively** *adv* ~ **intrusiveness** *n*.

intrust [intRust] *v/t* entrust.

intuit [intew-it] *v/t* and *i* know by intuition, perceive instinctively.

intuition [intew-ishon] *n* immediate unreasoned perception; instinctive knowledge > PDP; knowledge or opinion reached in this way.

intuitional [intew-ishonal] *adj* of or by intuition.

intuitionalism [intew-ishonalizm] *n* (*philos*) doctrine that truth is only perceived by intuition ~ **intuitionalist** *n* and *adj*.

intuitionism [intew-ishonizm] *n* theory which stresses the immediacy of knowledge of certain fundamental truths > PDP ~ **intuitionist** *n*.

intuitive [intew-itiv] *adj* perceived by intuition; perceiving by intuition ~ **intuitively** *adv*.

intumesce [intewmes] *v/i* swell, become swollen; expand with heat ~ **intumescence** *n* ~ **intumescent** *adj*.

inunction [inunkshon] *n* act of anointing; act of rubbing ointment or oil into.

inundate [inundayt] *v/t* flood, overflow; swamp, deluge; (*fig*) overwhelm.

inundation [inundayshon] *n* flood.

inurbane [inurbayn] *adj* discourteous, rude; unpolished.

inurbanity [inurbaniti] *n* discourtesy.

inure, enure [inyoor] *v/t* and *i* cause to become accustomed, harden; (*leg*) come into operation or into use ~ **inurement** *n*.

inurn [inurn] *v/t* place in an urn; bury (ashes).

inutility [inewtiliti] *n* uselessness.

invade [invayd] *v/t* enter (country) as enemy to conquer it; (*fig*) crowd into, assail; encroach upon, violate ~ **invader** *n*.

invalid (1) [invalid] *n* and *adj* (person) suffering from prolonged ill-health; used by or for such persons ~ **invalid** [invalid/invalid] *v/t* (*mil*) remove from active service because of wounds or illness; disable, render infirm.

invalid (2) [invalid] *adj* not valid, null and void; having no cogency.

invalidate [invalidayt] *v/t* render null and void.

invalidation [invalidayshon] *n* act of rendering or state of being invalid; that which renders invalid.

invalidism [invalidizm] *n* state of being an invalid; neurotic exaggeration of chronic ill-health.

invalidity [invaliditi] *n* state of being not valid.

invaluable [invalew-ab'l] *adj* that cannot be valued, extremely precious, priceless ~ **invaluably** *adv*.

invar [invaar] *n* alloy of iron, nickel and carbon·

invariability [invairRi-abiliti] *n* uniformity.

invariable [invairRi-ab'l] *adj* not liable to change, uniform, constant ~ **invariably** *adv* unalterably; regularly; always.

invasion [invayzhon] *n* act of invading; state of being invaded.

invective [invektiv] *n* violent and hostile words, abuse.

inveigh [invay] *v/i* attack with violent words, rail against.

inveigle [inveeg'l] *v/t* coax, entice. wheedle; entrap ~ **inveiglement** *n*.

invent [invent] *v/t* devise something new and original; think out, devise in the mind; devise as falsehood or fiction.

invention [invenshon] *n* act of inventing; that which is invented, device, contrivance; creative faculty; fictitious statement, lie; (*mus*) short keyboard composition > PDM; (*ar*) finding.

inventive [inventiv] *adj* quick at inventing or contriving; ingenious ~ **inventively** *adj* ~ **inventiveness** *n*.

inventor [inventer] *n* one who invents.

inventory [inventRi] *n* detailed list of goods and chattels; articles named in such a list ~ **inventory** *v/t* make a detailed list of.

Inverness [invernes] *n* sleeveless cloak with cape over shoulders.

inverse [invurs] *adj* opposite, contrary, inverted; **i. proportion** (*math*) process whereby one quantity increases proportionately as another decreases, their product remaining constant ~ **inverse** *n* that which is inverted or exactly opposite ~ **inversely** *adv*.

inversion [invurshon] *n* act of inverting; state of being inverted; reversal of order, place or relation; reversal of normal sexual role or characteristics > PDP; (*mus*) variation obtained from a melody by reversing the direction of all the latter's intervals > PDM; reversal of position of two counterpointed melodies > PDM; (*chem*) conversion of cane-sugar into glucose and laevulose > PDS; (*gramm*) reversal of normal word-order; **temperature i.** (*meteor*) increase of temperature with height above earth's surface > PDG.

invert [invurt] *v/t* turn upside down; reverse the position or order of; produce inversion in > PDP, PDM, PDS ~ **invert** [invurt] *n* one whose sexual role or instinct is reversed; (*archi*) reversed arch; **i. sugar** equal mixture of glucose and laevulose > PDS.

invertebrate [invurtibRayt] *n* and *adj* (animal) without a backbone > PDB; (*fig*) (person) lacking moral firmness.

inverter [invurter] *n* that which or one who inverts; (*elect*) device for converting direct current into alternating current.

invest [invest] *v/t* lay out (money) in order to obtain returns on it; clothe, array; confer office or dignity on; endue; besiege; **i. in** put money into (shares, a business *etc*); (*coll*) buy; spend money on.

investigate [investigayt] *v/t* try to discover the truth about; examine systematically, enquire carefully into.

investigation [investigayshon] *n* act of investigating; examination, enquiry.

investigator [investigaytor] *n* one who investigates ~ **investigatory** *adj* of or like an investigation.

investiture [investicher] *n* act or ceremony of presenting with an office, rank, decoration *etc*; state of being invested with.

investment [investment] *n* act of laying out money; money invested; that in which money is invested; act of besieging; investiture.

investor [invester] *n* one who invests money.

inveteracy [inveteRasi] *n* state or quality of being inveterate.

inveterate [inveteRit] *adj* long-established; deeply-rooted, obstinate; out-and-out, thoroughgoing; embittered ∼ **inveterately** *adv*.

invidious [invidi-us] *adj* likely to arouse envy or ill-will; offending ∼ **invidiously** *adv* ∼ **invidiousness** *n*.

invigilate [invijilayt] *v/t* keep watch on candidates at an examination ∼ **invigilation** [invijilayshon] *n* ∼ **invigilator** *n*.

invigorate [invigeRayt] *v/t* give vigour or strength to; brace, animate ∼ **invigoration** [invige-Rayshon] *n*.

invincibility [invinsibiliti] *n* quality or state of being invincible.

invincible [invinsib'l] *adj* that cannot be conquered; **i. ignorance** (*theol*) ignorance which one cannot remedy by one's own efforts ∼ **invincibly** *adv*.

inviolability [invI-olabiliti] *n* quality of being inviolable.

inviolable [invI-olab'l] *adj* that cannot or must not be violated, dishonoured, or broken ∼ **inviolably** *adv*.

inviolate [invI-olayt] *adj* not violated or profaned, kept sacred; unbroken, unharmed.

invisibility [invizibiliti] *n* state or quality of being invisible.

invisible [invizib'l] *adj* that cannot be seen; **i. exports** that part of a country's income from overseas which is derived otherwise than by export of goods > PDG, PDPol; **i. ink** ink that only shows when heated ∼ **invisibly** *adv*.

invitation [invitayshon] *n* act of inviting; offer of hospitality; message *etc* that invites.

invite [invIt] *v/t* ask (someone) to come to a social gathering *etc*; courteously request; (*of thing*) attract, allure; ask for encourage; provoke ∼ **invite** [invIt] *n* (*pop coll*) invitation.

inviting [invIting] *adj* attractive; tempting ∼ **invitingly** *adv*.

invocation [invOkayshon] *n* act of invoking, *esp* in prayer; petition for help.

invocatory [invokateRi] *adj* that invokes.

invoice [invois] *n* detailed list of goods despatched ∼ **invoice** *v/t* make out an invoice of.

invoke [invOk] *v/t* address in prayer; appeal for help, vengeance *etc*; call on as a witness; summon by magical means.

involucre [invelewker] *n* (*bot*) whorl of bracts round base of flower; protective cluster of leaves or scales > PDB.

involuntary [involunteRi] *adj* done independently of a person's will; unintentional > PDP; not done from choice ∼ **involuntarily** *adv* ∼ **involuntariness** *n*.

involute [involOOt] *adj* (*bot*) with the edges rolled inwards at each side; (*zool*) closely coiled.

involution [involOOshon] *n* act of involving; state of being involved; complication, entanglement; act of rolling inwards or curling up; (*biol*) decrease in size, retrogression > PDB, PDP; (*gramm*) involved construction; (*math*) the raising of a quantity to any given power.

involve [involv] *v/t* entangle; cause to become associated with; surround inextricably with difficulties; complicate; imply, necessarily entail; (*math*) raise to any given power.

involved [involvd] *adj* complicated, tangled; obscure; causing great difficulty.

involvement [involvment] *n* state of being involved; act of involving.

invulnerability [invulneRabiliti] *n* quality or state of being invulnerable.

invulnerable [invulneRab'l] *adj* that cannot be wounded or injured ∼ **invulnerably** *adv*.

inward [inwerd] *adj* internal; being or placed within; towards the interior; pertaining to mind or soul ∼ **inward, inwards** *adv* towards the interior or the centre; in the mind or soul.

inwardly [inwerdli] *adv* internally; within; towards the centre; mentally; secretly.

inwardness [inwerdnes] *n* inner meaning or quality; spirituality; depth and sincerity of feeling.

inwards (1) [inerdz] *n* (*pl*) (*coll*) entrails.

inwards (2) *adv* see **inward**.

inweave (*p/t* **inwove**, *p/part* **inwoven**) [inweev] *v/t* and *i* weave into; weave together.

inwrought [inRawt] *adj* worked in or among other things; adorned (with pattern *etc*).

iodide [I-odId] *n* binary compound with iodine > PDS.

iodine [I-odeen/I-odIn] *n* a volatile non-metallic element used in medicine and photography > PDS; antiseptic tincture of iodine.

iodism [I-odizm] *n* iodine poisoning.

iodize [I-odIz] *v/t* treat with iodine.

iodoform [I-Odofawrm] *n* antiseptic iodine compound.

iolite [I-olIt] *n* violet-blue silicate of aluminium, iron and magnesium.

ion [I-on] *n* electrically charged particle, atom or group of atoms > PDS.

Ionian [I-Oni-an] *n* member of the subdivision of ancient Greeks inhabiting Attica in Asia Minor ∼ **Ionian** *adj* of Ionia; **I. mode** mode corresponding to scale of C major > PDM.

ionic (1) [I-onik] *adj* pertaining to an ion or ions.

Ionic (2) *adj* Ionian; **I. order** style of Greek architecture with fluted columns and voluted capitals > PDAA.

ionization [I-onIzayshon] *n* act of ionizing; state of being ionized.

ionize [I-onIz] *v/t* and *i* form into ions, charge (particles) with electricity > PDS.

ionosphere [I-onosfeer] *n* ionized region of upper atmosphere reflecting wireless waves > PDS.

iota [I-Ota] *n* the Greek letter *i*; (*fig*) very small quantity, jot.

I.O.U. [I-O-yOO] *n* formal signed acknowledgement of a debt.

ipecacuanha [ipikakew-ana] *n* South American plant whose root is used as an emetic.

I.Q. [I-kew] intelligence quotient.

ir- form of *neg pref* **in-**.

I.R.A. [I-aar-ay] *n* the 'Irish Republican Army', an illegal nationalist movement in Ulster and Eire.

Iranian [IRayni-an] *n* and *adj* (inhabitant) of Persia or Iran; (language) belonging to a subdivision of Indo-European including Zend and Old Persian.

irascibility [irasi*bi*liti] *n* state or quality of being easily angered.

irascible [i*Ra*sib'l] *adj* easily angered, irritable ~ **irascibly** *adv*.

irate [I*Ra*yt] *adj* angry; enraged ~ **irately** *adv*.

ire [I*r*] *n* anger, wrath.

ireful [I*r*fool] *adj* wrathful, angry ~ **irefully** *adv*.

irenic [I*Ree*nik] *adj* of peace-making.

iridescence [i*Ri*desens] *n* quality of changing in colour when reflecting light from various angles; shimmering changeable colour ~ **iridescent** *adj*.

iridium [i*Ri*di-um] *n* rare metallic element resembling platinum > PDS.

iridize [i*Ri*diz] *v/t* tip with iridium.

iris (*pl* **irises** or (*anat*) **irides**) [I*Ri*s] *n* coloured membrane round the pupil of the eye > PDB, PDP; genus of flowering plants with tuberous roots; (*phot*) diaphragm controlling amount of light entering camera; (*Gk myth*) rainbow; a messenger.

iriscope [I*r*RiskOp] *n* instrument for exhibiting prismatic colours.

irised [I*r*Rist] *adj* coloured like the rainbow.

Irish [I*r*Rish] *n* and *adj* (inhabitant or language) of Ireland; **I. stew** mutton boiled with onions and potatoes.

Irishism [I*r*Rishizm] *n* idiom of Irish or Anglo-Irish language.

iritis [I*r*RItis] *n* inflammation of the iris of the eye.

irk [*urk*] *v/t* bore, weary; annoy; (*ar*) tire.

irksome [*urk*sum] *adj* tedious; troublesome, annoying ~ **irksomely** *adv* ~ **irksomeness** *n*.

iron [I*rn*] *n* hard metallic element > PDS, PDE; tool or implement made of this; flat-bottomed implement heated and used to press cloth smooth; stirrup; iron-headed golf club; (*sl*) revolver; (*fig*) strength of character, power; (*pl*) fetters; supports for crippled legs; **have many irons in the fire** have many simultaneous tasks or enterprises; **i. entering the soul** bitter anger or grief; **of i.** severe, harsh; **while the i. is hot** while the opportunity is favourable ~ **iron** *adj* made of iron; like iron, strong; harsh, merciless; **I. Age** (*arch*) cultural phase marked by use of iron for weapons and tools; **i. curtain** frontier separating Communist states from rest of Europe; ideological barrier between Communist and non-Communist countries > PDPol; (*fig*) systematic secrecy; **i. hand** severe control; **i. lung** apparatus maintaining artificial respiration in patient lying within it; **i. rations** emergency rations ~ **iron** *v/t* smooth (cloth) with an iron; cover with iron; provide iron parts for; fetter; **i. out** (*fig*) remove (difficulties, disagreement *etc*).

ironbark [I*rn*baark] *n* an Australian eucalyptus.

ironbound [I*rn*bownd] *adj* bound with or encircled by iron; (*of coast*) rocky; merciless, unbending.

ironclad [I*rn*klad] *n* and *adj* (warship) protected by iron plates.

iron-founder [I*rn*-fownder] *n* one who manufactures cast-iron ~ **iron-foundry** *n* works where cast-iron is made.

iron-grey [I*rn*-g*Ra*y] *adj* and *n* (of) the colour of iron freshly broken.

ironic, ironical [I*r*Ronik, I*r*Ronikal] *adj* of irony; said in irony; using irony ~ **ironically** *adv*.

ironing [I*r*ning] *n* process of smoothing clothes *etc* with a hot iron; clothes *etc* to be ironed.

ironing-board [I*r*ning-bawrd] *n* padded board on which clothes are laid to be ironed.

ironist [I*r*Ronist] *n* one who uses irony.

ironmaster [I*r*nmaaster] *n* iron-founder; one who manufactures iron articles.

ironmonger [I*r*nmunger] *n* one who deals in metal goods ~ **ironmongery** *n*.

ironmould [I*r*nmOld] *n* stain made by iron-rust or ink.

Ironside [I*r*nsId] *n* one of Oliver Cromwell's troopers.

ironstone [I*r*nstOn] *n* impure iron ore.

ironware [I*r*nwair] *n* goods made of iron; hardware.

ironwood [I*r*nwood] *n* a hard, heavy wood.

ironwork [I*r*nwurk] *n* anything made of iron; (*pl*) place where iron is smelted.

irony (1) [I*r*ni] *adj* of, containing, or like iron.

irony (2) [I*r*Roni] *n* subtle mockery or humour; sarcasm; way of speaking in which words mean the opposite of their normal or apparent meaning; situation, turn of events *etc* which frustrates and appears to mock the hopes or aims of human beings; result opposite to what might reasonably be expected; **dramatic i.** device whereby a character in a play or book says something which has one meaning for him and a deeper one only visible to audience or reader; **Socratic i.** apparent ignorance assumed to outwit opponent in argument.

irradiance [i-*Ra*ydi-ans] *n* quality or state of emitting rays of light; brilliant light ~ **irradiancy** *n* ~ **irradiant** *adj*.

irradiate [i-*Ra*ydi-ayt] *v/t* and *i* shed light on, make bright; expose to radiation; treat with therapeutic rays; (*fig*) make clear, illuminate; light up; animate, enliven; emit, pour forth; emit rays of light.

irradiation [i-*Ra*ydi-*ay*shon] *n* process of irradiating; state of being irradiated; ray of light; (*opt*) apparent increase in size or brightness of light objects seen against dark backgrounds > PDP, PDS; (*phys*) exposure to radioactivity or other radiations; (*biol*) spread of a nerve impulse or reflex response to wider area than that originally affected > PDP.

irradiative [i-*Ra*ydi-aytiv] *adj* that irradiates.

irrational [i-*Ra*shonal] *adj* not having the faculty of reasoning; inconsistent with reason or logic; inconsistent with normal behaviour of rational beings; absurd, very foolish; (*math*) not expressible by a whole number or vulgar fraction ~ **irrational** *n* (*math*) irrational number ~ **irrationally** *adv*.

irrationality [i-Rasho*na*liti] *n* state or quality of being irrational.

irrationalize [i-*Ra*shonalIz] *v/t* make irrational.

irrealizable [i-*Ree*-alIzab'l] *adj* that cannot be realized; not convertible into money.

irreclaimable [i-Ri*klay*mab'l] *adj* that cannot be reclaimed; incorrigible.

irrecognizable [i-Rekogn*I*zab'l] *adj* that cannot be recognized ~ **irrecognizably** *adv*.

irreconcilability [i-Rekons*I*la*b*iliti] *n* quality of being irreconcilable.

irreconcilable [i-Rekons*I*lab'l] *adj* that cannot be reconciled; uncompromisingly hostile; conflicting, incompatible ~ **irreconcilable** *n* uncompromising opponent ~ **irreconcilably** *adv*.

irrecoverable [i-R*i*ku*ve*Rab'l] *adj* that cannot be recovered or regained; irretrievable ~ **irrecoverably** *adv*.

irrecusable [i-R*i*k*ewz*ab'l] *adj* not to be rejected; that must be admitted.

irredeemable [i-R*i*deemab'l] *adj* that cannot be redeemed; not convertible into cash ~ **irredeemable** *n* a stock which has no prospect of ever being paid off ~ **irredeemably** *adv*.

irredentism [i-R*i*dentizm] *n* political belief that a state should include all those citizens of other states who speak the same language or belong to the same ethnic group as the majority of its own citizens ~ **irredentist** *n* and *adj*.

irreducibility [i-Ridews*i*b*i*liti] *n* quality of being irreducible.

irreducible [i-R*i*d*ews*ib'l] *adj* not capable of being reduced or lessened; (*math*) not capable of further simplification ~ **irreducibly** *adv*.

irrefragable [i-R*i*f*Rag*ab'l] *adj* beyond dispute, undeniable ~ **irrefragably** *adv*.

irrefrangible [i-R*i*f*Ran*jib'l] *adj* not capable of being broken; (*opt*) not capable of being refracted.

irrefutability [i-R*i*fewt*a*b*i*liti] *n* quality of being irrefutable.

irrefutable [i-R*i*f*ewt*ab'l] *adj* that cannot be disproved ~ **irrefutably** *adv*.

irregular [i-R*e*gewler] *adj* not regular; uneven; not symmetrical; not uniform; not according to rule or general type or custom; disorderly; not according to law; immoral; (*gramm*) with inflexions differing from the normal; (*mil*) not belonging to the regular army ~ **irregular** *n* soldier not belonging to the regular army ~ **irregularly** *adv*.

irregularity [i-Rege*wla*Riti] *n* quality of being irregular; that which is irregular; deviation from order, symmetry normal recurrence *etc*.

irrelative [i-R*e*lativ] *adj* not relative, unconnected; having no relations ~ **irrelatively** *adv*.

irrelevance, irrelevancy [i-R*e*levans, i-R*e*le-vansi] *n* quality of being irrelevant; that which is irrelevant.

irrelevant [i-R*e*levant] *adj* not applicable, not pertinent; not to the point ~ **irrelevantly** *adv*.

irreligion [i-R*i*l*i*jon] *n* indifference to or contempt of religion.

irreligious [i-R*i*l*i*jus] *adj* indifferent to or lacking religion; hostile to religion; impious ~ **irreligiously** *adv*.

irremediable [i-R*i*meedi-ab'l] *adj* that cannot be remedied or corrected; incurable ~ **irremediably** *adv*.

irremissible [i-R*i*mis*i*b'l] *adj* unpardonable; inexcusable ~ **irremissibly** *adv*.

irremovable [i-R*i*mOOvab'l] *adj* that cannot be removed or displaced; permanent ~ **irremovably** *adv*.

irreparable [i-R*e*peRab'l] *adj* that cannot be repaired, recovered, or restored ~ **irreparably** *adv*.

irreplaceable [i-R*i*plays*a*b'l] *adj* that cannot be replaced.

irrepressible [i-R*i*pResib'l] *adj* that cannot be restrained or controlled ~ **irrepressibly** *adv*.

irreproachable [i-R*i*pROch*a*b'l] *adj* blameless, faultless ~ **irreproachably** *adv*.

irresistibility [i-R*i*zisti*b*iliti] *n* quality of being irresistible.

irresistible [i-R*i*z*i*stib'l] *adj* that cannot be resisted; overwhelming, overpowering; very convincing ~ **irresistibly** *adv*.

irresolute [i-R*e*zolewt] *adj* lacking resolution; hesitating, undecided ~ **irresolutely** *adv* ~ **irresoluteness** *n*.

irresolution [i-R*e*zol*ew*shon] *n* hesitancy.

irresolvable [i-R*i*zolv*a*b'l] *adj* that cannot be solved; that cannot be separated into parts.

irrespective [i-R*i*sp*e*ktiv] *adj* and *adv* regardless of; without reference to; not taking into account ~ **irrespectively** *adv*.

irresponsibility [i-R*i*sponsi*b*iliti] *n* freedom from responsibility; unreliableness; recklessness.

irresponsible [i-R*i*sp*o*nsib'l] *adj* lacking a sense of responsibility; incapable of bearing responsibility; unreliable, untrustworthy; unauthorized; reckless ~ **irresponsibly** *adv*.

irresponsive [i-R*i*sp*o*nsiv] *adj* not responsive ~ **irresponsiveness** *n*.

irretrievable [i-R*i*tReev*a*b'l] *adj* not capable of being recovered; irreparable ~ **irretrievably** *adv*.

irreverence [i-R*e*v*e*Rens] *n* state or quality of being irreverent; irreverent conduct or speech.

irreverent [i-R*e*v*e*Rent] *adj* lacking in reverence; disrespectful ~ **irreverently** *adv*.

irreversibility [i-R*i*vursi*b*iliti] *n* quality of being irreversible.

irreversible [i-R*i*v*u*rsib'l] *adj* that cannot be reversed or revoked ~ **irreversibly** *adv*.

irrevocability [i-R*e*voka*b*iliti] *n* quality of being irrevocable.

irrevocable [i-R*e*vokab'l] *adj* that cannot be recalled; unalterable, final ~ **irrevocably** *adv*.

irrigable [*i*-Rigab'l] *adj* that can be irrigated.

irrigate [*i*-Rigayt] *v/t* convey water to (land) by artificial channels, dams, sluices *etc* > PDG, PDE; (*med*) keep moist; inject liquid into; wash out.

irrigation [i-R*i*gayshon] *n* act of irrigating > PDG, PDE; state of being irrigated.

irrigative [*i*-Rigativ] *adj* that irrigates; of or for irrigation.

irrigator [*i*-Rigayter] *n* one who or that which irrigates.

irritability [i-R*i*ta*b*iliti] *n* state or quality of being irritable.

irritable [*i*-Ritab'l] *adj* easily provoked or annoyed; easily made painful, sore; responsive to stimulation > PDB, PDP ~ **irritably** *adv*.

irritant (1) [*i*-Ritant] *n* and *adj* (that) which irritates.

irritant (2) *adj* (*leg*) rendering null and void.

irritate (1) [*i*-Rit*a*yt] *v/t* arouse impatience or bad temper in, annoy; excite, stir up; cause

itching, soreness or discomfort in; stimulate to
activity.

irritate (2) *v/t* (*leg*) render null and void.

irritating [*i*-Ritayting] *adj* that irritates; annoying,
vexing ~ **irritatingly** *adv.*

irritation [i-Ritayshon] *n* act or process of
irritating; state of being irritated; annoyance,
vexation; itching, inflammation; that which
irritates ~ **irritative** [*i*-Ritaytiv] *adj.*

irruption [i-Rupshon] *n* act of bursting in; sudden
invasion ~ **irruptive** *adj.*

is [*iz*] *3rd pers sing pres ind* of **be.**

isabella, isabelle [*iz*abela, *iz*abell] *n* and *adj*
greyish yellow.

isatin, isatine [*I*satin] *n* (*chem*) compound
obtained by oxidizing indigo.

ischial [*i*ski-al] *adj* in the region of the hip.

ischiatic, ischiadic [iski-*a*tik, iski-*a*dik] *adj*
of the hip; of sciatica.

ischium [*i*ski-um] *n* lowest section of hip-bone.

Ishmael, Ishmaelite [*ish*mayl, *ish*maylIt] *n* social
outcast; one who hates society.

isinglass [*I*sing-glaas] *n* gelatinous product
made from fish-bladders > PDS.

Islam [*iz*laam] *n* religion revealed through Mohammed; nations and persons accepting this;
Muslims collectively.

Islamic [iz*lam*ik] *adj* of Islam.

island [*I*land] *n* piece of land surrounded by
water > PDG; anything resembling an island;
group of cells differing from the surrounding
ones ~ **island** *adj* of or like an island; found on
islands ~ **island** *v/t* make into an island;
set with islands; isolate.

islander [*I*lander] *n* one who lives on an island.

isle [*Il*] *n* (*poet*) island.

islet [*I*let] *n* small island.

ism [*izm*] *n* (*freq pej*) doctrine, theory.

isn't [*iz*nt] *abbr* is not.

iso- *pref* equal; same.

isobar [*Is*Obaar] *n* line on map joining places
having equal atmospheric pressure > PDG;
(*phys*) isotopes of different elements having
identical mass numbers > PDS.

isobaric [IsOba*Rik*] *adj* of or in isobars.

isobath [*Is*Obaath] *n* line on map joining points
on seabed of equal depth > PDG.

isochore [*Is*Okawr] *n* line graphically representing
relationship between pressure and temperature
of liquid or gas at constant volume > PDS.

isoclinal [IsO*kl*Irnal] *adj* inclining in the same
direction; (*of places*) having the same magnetic
inclination > PDS.

isodont [*Is*Odont] *n* and *adj* (animal) with the
teeth all alike.

isogonal [Is*o*gonal] *n* (*geom*) having equal angles.

isolate [*Is*Olayt] *v/t* set apart, separate from
others; make lonely; put in quarantine; (*elect*)
insulate; (*chem*) separate (an element) from a
compound; (*biol*) grow a pure culture of.

isolation [IsO*lay*shon] *n* act of isolating; state
of being isolated; state of being alone, loneliness.

isolationism [IsO*lay*shonizm] *n* policy of avoiding involvement in the affairs of foreign countries
> PDPol ~ **isolationist** *n* and *adj.*

isomer [*Is*omer] *n* (*chem*) isomeric substance.

isomeric [IsO*me*Rik] *adj* (*chem*) having the same

molecular formula but having different properties > PDS.

isomerism [Is*o*meRizm] *n* state of being isomeric.

isometric [Iso*met*Rik] *adj* equal in measurement;
(*physiol*) causing tension but not contraction in
muscles; (*of pictures*) projected on the same scale
in three directions ~ **isometrics** *n* (*pl*) exercises
in which muscles exert force against one another
or against fixed objects.

isomorphic [Iso*mawr*fik] *adj* (*chem*) having
similar crystalline form ~ **isomorphism** *n.*

isopod [*Is*Opod] *n* crustacean with seven pairs of
legs almost of the same length.

isoprene [*Is*OpReen] *n* colourless liquid, a polymer
of which is the main constituent of natural rubber.

isosceles [Is*o*sileez] *adj* (*of a triangle*) having
two sides equal.

isoseismal [IsO*sIz*mal] *adj* **i. line** line on map
joining points at which an earthquake shock was
of the same intensity > PDG.

isostasy [Is*o*stasi] *n* state of equilibrium between
highlands and lowlands of earth > PDG.

isostatic [IsO*stat*ik] *adj* of or by isostasy.

isotherm [*Is*Othurm] *n* line on map joining
places of same mean temperature > PDG.

isothermal [IsO*thur*mal] *adj* (*chem*) occurring at a
constant temperature.

isotone [*Is*OtOn] *n* (*phys*) one of several atoms
whose nuclei contain the same number of
neutrons, but one of different atomic number.

isotonic [IsO*ton*ik] *adj* (*chem*) having the same
osmotic pressure > PDB, PDS.

isotope [*Is*OtOp] *n* (*chem*) one of several atoms of
the same element identical in chemical properties
but differing in mass number > PDS.

isotopic [IsO*top*ik] *adj* of or as an isotope.

isotropic [IsO*trop*ik] *adj* exhibiting uniform
properties throughout; transmitting light similarly in all directions > PDS, PDP.

Israeli [iz*Ray*li] *n* and *adj* (citizen) of the state of
modern Israel.

Israelite [*iz*RelIt] *n* Jew of Biblical period;
a Jew, *esp* an orthodox Jew.

issuance [*ish*yoo-ans] *n* act of issuing.

issue [*isy*OO/*ishy*OO] *n* act of emitting or distributing; publication; act of flowing or coming
out; that which is emitted; discharge, outflow;
point at which something flows out, outlet;
river-mouth; number, quantity or set of things
distributed at one time; goods sent to troops by
government; point or subject of argument,
discussion *etc*; important and controversial
matter, problem; result; (*leg*) children; profits
from land or property; **at i.** in dispute, under
discussion; **join i. with** enter into argument with
~ **issue** *v/t* and *i* give out, supply; publish;
distribute; put in circulation; come or go out;
flow or pour out; originate, be derived from; be
descended from; result (in).

issueless [*isy*ooles] *adj* having no children.

isthmian [*ismi*-an/*isth*mi-an] *adj* of an isthmus.

isthmus [*ismus*/*isth*mus] *n* narrow strip of land
connecting two large land areas > PDG;
(*bot, zool*) narrow passage between two larger
parts; (*anat*) narrow part of brain stem > PDP.

istle [*istli*] *n* tough fibre made from American
tropical plants.

it (1) [*it*] *3rd pers sing neut pron* ~ **it** *n* (*coll*) perfection, ideal person or thing; person of importance; (*sl*) sex-appeal; charm; (*in games*) the player who must catch the others.

it (2) *n* (*coll abbr*) Italian vermouth.

Italian [*ital*yan] *n* and *adj* (native) of Italy; (language) of Italy.

Italianate [*ital*yanayt] *adj* Italian in style.

Italianize [*ital*yanɪz] *v/t* and *i* make or become Italianate.

italic [*ital*ik] *adj* (*print*) in sloping type; pertaining to ancient Italy ~ **italics** *n* (*pl*) italic type.

italicize [*ital*isɪz] *v/t* print in sloping type, *usu* for emphasis.

itch [*ich*] *n* sensation of irritation on skin causing desire to scratch, persistent tickle; (*med*) contagious skin disease caused by burrowing insect; (*fig*) restless craving, troublesome urge ~ **itch** *v/i* have an itch; feel irritation of the skin; crave, yearn ~ **itchy** *adj*.

item (1) [*It*em] *n* one article in an account or list; paragraph of news; subsection of programme, agenda *etc*.

item (2) *adv* (*Lat*) likewise, also.

itemize [*It*emɪz] *v/t* set out in detail; account for item by item.

iterance [*ite*Rans] *n* iteration.

iterate [*ite*Rayt] *v/t* repeat; say or do repeatedly.

iteration [*ite*Rayshon] *a* act of repeating; that which is repeated.

iterative [*ite*Rativ] *adj* repeating; (*gramm*) indicating repetition.

ithyphallic [ithi*fal*ik] *adj* (*of statues etc*) having or representing an erect penis.

itinerancy [*itine*Ransi/*Itine*Ransi] *n* state or practice of being itinerant.

itinerant [*itine*Rant/*Itine*Rant] *adj* travelling from place to place; (*of judges, preachers etc*) on circuit; wandering ~ **itinerant** *n* one who travels or wanders about; tramp.

itinerary [*Itine*ReRi/*itine*ReRi] *n* places to be visited in the course of a journey; route from place to place; guidebook; account of travels ~ **itinerary** *adj* pertaining to roads or to travel.

itinerate [*itine*Rayt/*Itine*Rayt] *v/i* travel from place to place.

its [*its*] *possessive pron* and *adj* belonging to it.

it's [*its*] *abbr* it is; it has.

itself [it*self*] *pron, emph or reflex form of* **it**.

I've [*Iv*] *abbr* I have.

ivied [*Ivid*] *adj* covered with ivy.

ivory [*Ive*Ri] *n* hard white bony substance of tusks of elephants, walrus or narwhal; colour of this, creamy white; (*pl*) piano-keys; (*pl sl*) teeth; dice; billiard balls; **i. black** form of carbon obtained from animal charcoal > PDS; black pigment made from this; **black i.** (*coll*) African Negro slaves; **i. tower** (*fig*) place of refuge from society; isolation deliberately sought by artist, writer *etc* ~ **ivory** *adj* of or like ivory; creamy white.

ivy [*Ivi*] *n* n evergreen climbing plant.

ivy-mantl d [*Ivi*-manteld] *adj* covered with ivy.

ixia [*iks*i-a] *n* genus of South African bulbous flowering plants.

ixiolite [*iks*i-Olɪt] *n* mineral resin found in bituminous coal.

izard [*iz*erd] *n* kind of antelope.

J

j [*jay*] tenth letter of English alphabet.

jab (*pres/part* jabbing, *p/t* and *p/part* jabbed) [*jab*] *v/t* poke with sudden force; pierce, stab ~ **jab** *n* sudden piercing; sharp poke; (*coll*) hypodermic injection.

jabber [*jaber*] *v/t* and *i* speak quickly and confusedly, gabble; talk without stopping, chatter ~ **jabber** *n* gabbled speech; chatter.

jabiru [*jabi*ROO] *n* tropical wading bird.

jabot [zhabO] *n* decorative frill on bodice or shirt-front.

jacaranda [jaka*Ra*nda] *n* American tropical tree with fragrant wood.

jacinth [*ja*sinth] *n* reddish-orange variety of zircon used as a gemstone.

jack [*jak*] *n* equipment for raising heavy loads from below, *esp* for lifting wheel of car off ground > PDE; (*cards*) lowest court-card, knave; (*bowls*) small white ball used as mark; (*coll*) sailor device for turning roasting-spit; (*naut*) flagstaff at bow of ship; flag flown from this; (*ar*) fellow; (*ar*) workman; (*hist*) padded leather protective jacket; leather bottle; (*elect*) single prong plug carrying more than one circuit; (*sl*) methylated spirits; **before you can say J. Robinson** at once, very quickly; **every man j.** everybody; **J. Frost** personification of frost; **J. of all trades** one who can do many jobs; **j. tar** sailor; **Union J.** national flag of Great Britain and Northern Ireland ~ **jack** *v/t* **j. up** raise by means of a jack: increase (prices); (*coll*) give up; **j. off** (*vulg sl*) ejaculate semen.

jack- *pref* male; large, strong.

jackal [*ja*kawl] *n* wild scavenging animal of dog family; (*fig*) one who drudges for another.

jackanapes [*jaka*nayps] *n* mischievous boy; conceited person, fop; (*ar*) ape, monkey.

jackaroo [*jaka*ROO] *n* (*Aust coll*) trainee worker on sheep or cattle station.

jackass [*jaka*s] *n* male ass; fool; **laughing j.** (*Aust orni*) giant kingfisher.

jackboot [*jak*bOOt] *n* large boot reaching above knee.

jackdaw [*jak*daw] *n* bird of the crow family.

jacket [*ja*kit] *n* short coat; covering round tank, pipe *etc*; loose decorative wrapper of book; coat of various animals; jockey's blouse; skin of unpeeled cooked potato ~ **jacket** *v/t* provide with jacket; (*coll*) thrash.

jack-fish [*jak*-fish] *n* pike.

jackhammer [*jak*hamer] *n* compressed-air drill held in the hand to drill rocks.

jack-in-office [*jak*-in-ofis] *n* (*coll*) pompous or bullying petty official.

jack-in-the-box [*jak*-in-the-boks] *n* toy consisting of a boxed puppet which springs up when the lid is opened.

jack-in-the-green [*jak*-in-the-gReen] *n* man inside leaf-covered framework at May-day festivities; (*bot*) kind of primrose.

jack-knife [*jak*-nIf] *n* large pocket-knife with folding blade; dive in which diver bends and touches

his feet before reaching water ~ **jack-knife** *v/i* bend sharply in the middle or at the connexion between two sections, double up.

jacko see **jocko**.

jack-o'-lantern [jak-o-*lan*turn] *n* will-o'-the-wisp.

jackpot [*jak*pot] *n* pool in the game of poker; money prize which increases in value until won; (*coll*) **hit the j.** have exceptional luck.

jacks [*jaks*] *n* children's game of tossing and picking up pebbles or metal shapes.

jackstraw [*jak*stRaw] *n* a straw effigy; (*fig*) a nonentity; game of spillikins; a spillikin.

jacob [*jay*kob] *n* (*sl*) ladder.

Jacobean [jako*bee*-an] *adj* of or relating to the period when James I was king of England.

Jacobin (1) [*jak*obin] *n* and *adj* radical, revolutionary; (*hist*) (member) of group of French revolutionaries in 1789; (*ar*) (friar) of Dominican order.

jacobin (2) *n* breed of pigeon with neck-feathers like a cowl.

Jacobinism [*jak*obinizm] *n* advocacy of violent revolution; (*hist*) principles of French Jacobins.

Jacobite [*jak*obIt] *n* (*hist*) follower of the abdicated James II or of his descendants ~ **Jacobite** *adj*.

Jacob's ladder [jaykobz-*lad*er] *n* (*bot*) blue- or white-flowered garden plant; (*naut*) rope ladder with wooden rungs; long steep flight of steps; iron steps and bridge crossing a railway line.

jaconet [*jak*onit] *n* cotton cloth of medium weave.

jactation [jakta*tay*shon] *n* boasting.

jactitation [jakti*tay*shon] *n* (*path*) uneasy tossing of a patient who is seriously ill; twitching of muscle or limb; seed scattering by a high wind; (*leg*) false boastful statement, *usu* actionable pretension of marriage.

jade (1) [*jayd*] *n* worthless or worn-out horse; (*pej* or *joc*) woman; inconstant woman, hussy ~ **jade** *v/t* and *i* exhaust, tire; grow weary, droop.

jade (2) *n* (*min*) hard pale-green gem stone; the colour jade green.

jaded [*jayd*id] *adj* exhausted; wearied by excess.

jaffa [*ja*fa] *n* kind of large orange grown in Israel.

jag (1) [*jag*] *n* pointed projection, tooth; notch; rough tear in cloth *etc*; (*sl*) intoxicated or drugged state; dose of a drug; (*coll*) spree, drinking-bout ~ **jag** (*pres/part* jagging, *p/t* and *p/part* jagged) *v/t* cut or tear leaving rough ragged edge.

jag (2) *n* (*coll abbr*) Jaguar motorcar.

jagged [*jag*id] *adj* with uneven edge; having sharp irregular serrations.

jaguar [*jag*ew-er] *n* large yellowish spotted carnivorous animal of cat family; (*tr*) (*cap*) make of powerful motorcars.

Jah [*jaa*] *n* (*Heb*) Jehovah.

jail, jail-bird, jail-fever, jailer see **gaol**.

jailbreak [*jayl*bRayk] *n* act of escaping from prison.

Jain [*jIn*] *n* member of dissenting Hindu sect ~ **Jainism** *n*.

jakes [*jayks*] *n* (*ar*) latrine, privy.

jalap [*jal*ap] *n* root of Mexican plant used as laxative.

412

jalopy [jalopi] n (coll) old rickety motorcar.

jalousie [zhalOOzee] n (Fr) window-blind with sloping slats.

jam (1) (pres/part jamming, p/t and p/part jammed) [jam] v/t and i press tightly into small space, pack or squeeze tightly; wedge; obstruct by wedging, block; thrust violently; (rad) make (transmission) unintelligible by using same wavelength; become wedged; cease to work through blocking of moving part ∼ jam n tightly-packed mass; dense crowd; blockage; (coll) difficult situation, tight spot.

jam (2) n pulped fruit boiled and preserved with sugar; (sl) something pleasant; money for j. something for nothing; great luck; j. session informal improvised performance by jazz musicians ∼ jam (pres/part jamming, p/t and p/part jammed) v/t and i make into jam; (jazz) improvise.

Jamaican [jamaykan] n and adj (native) of Jamaica.

jamb [jam] n (bui) vertical face inside an opening, to the full thickness of wall; vertical side members of window- or door-frame.

jambok [shambok] n South African whip of hide.

jamboree [jamboRee] n rally of boy scouts; (coll) celebration, spree.

jamming [jaming] n (rad) outside interference with transmission from signals emitted on same wavelength by another transmitter.

jammy [jami] adj of, like, or covered with jam.

jangle [jang'l] v/i and t make harsh or clashing noise; speak harshly; cause (bells etc) to make a harsh sound ∼ jangle n harsh clashing sound; confused din; dispute.

janitor [janitor] n doorkeeper, porter; (US and Scots) caretaker.

janizary, janissary [janizeRi, janiseRi] n Turkish infantry soldier; (hist) member of Sultan's bodyguard.

jankers [jankerz] n (sl) military prison.

jannock [januk] adj (northern dial) genuine, straightforward, excellent.

Jansenism [jansenizm] n 17th-century heresy within Roman Catholic Church, holding the natural human will to be incapable of good ∼ Jansenist n and adj.

January [janew-aRi] n first month of the year.

Janus [jaynus] n (Rom myth) god represented with two faces, one looking forward and the other back.

Jap [jap] n and adj (abbr abbr) Japanese.

japan [japan] n hard black varnish or lacquer used by Japanese to render woodwork lustrous ∼ japan (pres/part japanning, p/t and p/part japanned) v/t coat with japan.

Japanese [japaneez] n and adj (native) of Japan; (language) of Japan.

jape [jayp] v/i joke, jest ∼ jape n.

japonica [japonika] n name for various flowering shrubs of Japanese origin.

jar (1) (pres/part jarring, p/t and p/part jarred) [jaar] v/i and t vibrate harshly; produce discordant effect, grate; disagree (with); dispute; cause to vibrate, shake; cause to make discordant noise; j. on irritate, be unpleasant to ∼ jar n harsh grating noise; vibration from shock of impact; shock; disagreement, dissension.

jar (2) n vessel (usu cylindrical) of earthenware or of glass without a spout; contents of a jar.

jar (3) n on the j. ajar.

jardinière [zhaardinyair] n (Fr) ornamental flowerpot, usu on a stand.

jargon (1) [jaargon] n language peculiar to one art, trade, or branch of learning, too technical to be intelligible to the ordinary public; pompous language full of clichés; gibberish.

jargon (2) n (min) kind of zircon.

jargonelle [jaargonel] n variety of pear ripening early.

jargonize [jaargoniz] v/t and i speak in jargon.

jarl [yaarl] n (hist) Scandinavian nobleman.

jarring [jaarRing] adj harsh, discordant; irritating; causing shock ∼ jarringly adv.

jasmine [jasmin] n (bot) climbing shrub with fragrant white or yellow flowers.

jasper [jasper] n (min) coloured impure form of natural silica.

jato [jaytO] n (aer) take-off assisted by auxiliary jet engine.

jaundice [jawndis] n (med) disease caused by obstruction of bile and characterized by yellow tint of eyes and skin; (fig) embittered feelings; jealousy ∼ jaundiced adj affected by jaundice; (fig) distorted by pessimism, hate, or jealousy.

jaunt [jawnt] n pleasure trip, short and pleasant outing ∼ jaunt v/i go on a jaunt.

jaunting-car [jawnting-kaar] n (Ir) light two-wheeled vehicle with seats set back to back.

jaunty [jawnti] adj self-confident, carefree; sprightly; gay; swaggering ∼ jauntily adv ∼ jauntiness n.

Javanese [jaavaneez] n and adj (native) of Java.

javelin [javlin] n light spear for throwing by hand.

jaw [jaw] n one of two bones forming framework of mouth, in which teeth are set; (pl) mouth; (pl) (mech) gripping or crushing device; (pl) sides of ravine or narrow valley etc; (sl) continual talk; prolonged reproof or sermon; hold your j.! (sl) shut up!; pi j. (sl) pious talk ∼ jaw v/i and t (sl) talk at length; reprove, admonish; preach at.

jawbone [jawbOn] n bone forming part of jaws, esp either of the two constituting the lower jaw.

jaw-breaker [jaw-bRayker] n (coll) word difficult to pronounce; long word.

jay [jay] n noisy, vividly coloured bird of crow family; (sl) fool, dupe; talkative person.

jaywalker [jaywawker] n person who walks across or along roads regardless of traffic.

jazz [jaz] n type of syncopated, strongly rhythmic music of American Negro origin in which improvisation is much used > PDM ∼ jazz adj pertaining to jazz; (of pattern) composed of violently contrasting colours and shapes ∼ jazz v/i and t dance to jazz music, arrange in jazz style; j. up (sl) make lively.

jazzy [jazi] adj of or like jazz; glaringly patterned ∼ jazzily adv ∼ jazziness n.

jealous [jelus] adj feeling hatred, suspicion, and fear towards a rival, esp in love; envious, feeling hatred towards those more fortunate than oneself; vigilant, on guard to protect or preserve ∼ jealously adv ∼ jealousness n.

jealousy [jelusi] n condition of being jealous.

jean [jeen] n strong twilled cotton fabric.

413

jeans [*jeenz*] *n* (*pl*) close-fitting trousers, *usu* of twilled cotton fabric; overalls of this fabric.

jeep [*jeep*] *n* small open high-powered motor truck with four-wheel drive.

jeer [*jeer*] *v/i* and *t* speak mockingly and contemptuously, scoff, sneer; **j. at** mock, taunt, insult ~ **jeer** *n* taunt, scoffing remark ~ **jeering** *adj* ~ **jeeringly** *adv*.

Jehad see Jihad.

Jehovah [*jihOva*] *n* the God of Israel, Jahweh; **J.'s Witnesses** Christian pacifist and fundamentalist sect.

jejune [*jijOOn*] *adj* boring; arousing no emotion; immature, naïve; meagre ~ **jejunely** *adv* ~ **jejuneness** *n*.

jejunum [*jijOOn*um] *n* (*anat*) middle part of small intestine.

jell [*jel*] *v/i* (*of jam etc*) turn to jelly, set; (*coll*) take definite form, crystallize.

jellied [*jelid*] *adj* set or solidified into a jelly; prepared in or with jelly.

jelly [*jeli*] *n* soft resilient semi-transparent foodstuff produced by boiling animal bones and tissue and allowing to cool; food of similar consistency produced by boiling fruit and adding gelatine; any substance of similar consistency; (*sl*) gelignite, gelatine dynamite; **royal j.** concentrated food given by bees to their young, *esp* to immature queen bees ~ **jelly** *v/i* and *t* turn into jelly.

jellyfish [*jelifish*] *n* free-floating polyp or medusa with soft semi-transparent body and hanging tentacles; (*coll*) weak-willed person.

jemmy [*jemi*] *n* burglar's crowbar.

jennet [*jenit*] *n* small Spanish breed of horse; female donkey.

jenneting [*jeniting*] *n* kind of early apple.

jenny [*jeni*] *n* spinning-jenny; travelling crane.

jeopardize [*jepardIz*] *v/t* place in danger, expose to hazard.

jeopardy [*jepardi*] *n* risk, danger.

jerboa [jurbO-a] *n* African desert rat with long hind legs.

jeremiad [jeRimI-ad] *n* lengthy bitter complaint or lament.

jerfalcon see gerfalcon.

jerk (1) [*jurk*] *n* quick sharp movement; sudden tug; spasm; involuntary muscular movement, twitch; **physical jerks** (*coll*) gymnastic exercises ~ **jerk** *v/t* and *i* move with a jerk; **j. off** (*vulg sl*) ejaculate semen.

jerk (2) *v/t* preserve (meat) by cutting into strips and drying.

jerkin [*jurkin*] *n* (*hist*) man's close-fitting leather jacket; short, close-fitting waistcoat.

jerky [*jurki*] *adj* moving in jerks; spasmodic ~ **jerkily** *adv* ~ **jerkiness** *n*.

jeroboam [jeRobO-am] *n* wine-bottle containing 10–12 quarts.

jerrican [*jeRikan*] *n* (*mil*) petrol or water container holding 4½ gallons.

jerry [*jeRi*] *n* (*sl*) chamber-pot; (*mil coll*) German soldier; (*collect*) Germans.

jerry-builder [*jeRi*-bilder] *n* speculator who builds cheap shoddy houses ~ **jerry-built** *adj* hastily built out of bad materials.

jersey [*jurzi*] *n* close-fitting jumper; breed of dairy cow; type of fine woollen fabric.

Jerusalem artichoke [jeROOsalem-*aart*ichOk] *n* edible root of kind of sunflower.

ess [*jes*] *n* (*falconry*) strap round hawk's leg to which leash is attached ~ **jess** *v/t* provide with jesses.

jest [*jest*] *n* saying or action meant to produce laughter, joke; object of ridicule; **in j.** not seriously ~ **jest** *v/i* speak or act frivolously; make jokes ~ **jesting** *adj* ~ **jestingly** *adv*.

jester [*jester*] *n* one who makes or plays jokes; (*hist*) professional fool or buffoon.

Jesuit [*jezew-it*] *n* member of Roman Catholic religious order, the Society of Jesus; (*fig*) cunning intriguer; casuist; **J.'s bark** cinchona.

jesuitic, jesuitical [jezew-*it*ik, jezew-*it*ikal] *adj* of or like Jesuits; (*fig*) crafty; casuistic; dissembling ~ **jesuitically** *adv*.

jesuitry [jezew-itRi] *n* sophistry, casuistry; craftiness.

jet (1) [*jet*] *n* very hard lustrous form of natural carbon, used for beads *etc*; glossy black colour ~ **jet** *adj* of or like jet; deep black.

jet (2) *n* stream of liquid or gas forced from small opening under pressure; nozzle of pipe giving out liquid or gas; aircraft propelled by a jet engine; **j. engine** engine in which an ejected, directed stream of gas provides the thrust ~ **jet** *adj* of or by a jet engine; **j. lag** fatigue and disorientation caused by long journeys in jet aircraft; **j. set** rich cosmopolitan pleasure-seekers who travel by jet aircraft ~ **jet** (*pres/part* **jetting**, *p/t* and *p/part* **jetted**) *v/i* and *t* gush out in a jet; give out in a jet.

jet-black [jet-*blak*] *adj* of deep lustrous black.

jeton see jetton.

jet-propelled [jet-pRo*peld*] *adj* driven by a jet engine.

jet-propulsion [jet-pRO*pu*lshon] *n* propulsion by jet engines.

jetsam [*jet*sam] *n* things jettisoned from ship in distress and cast ashore by the sea; **flotsam and j.** (*fig*) those who are down and out.

jetstream [*jet*stReem] *n* stream of gas ejected by jet engine; (*meteor*) strong wind confined to limited altitudes.

jettison [*jetison*] *v/t* throw (goods, equipment, bombs *etc*) overboard to lighten ship or aircraft; (*fig*) abandon, get rid of ~ **jettison** *n* act of throwing goods *etc* overboard.

jetton, jeton [*jeton*] *n* token used in gambling.

jetty (1) [*jeti*] *n* small landing-pier; groyne, small mole.

jetty (2) *adj* jet-black.

Jew [*jOO*] *n* man born of Hebrew stock; believer in Hebrew religion; (*pej sl*, no *cap*) extortionate moneylender, astute trader, or miser, of any race.

jewel [*jOO*-il] *n* precious stone, gem; ornament set with gems; gem used in watches for pivot-hole; (*fig*) cherished person or thing ~ **jewel** *v/t* adorn with jewels, set jewels in.

jeweller [*jOO*-iler] *n* one who deals with jewels either as craftsman or as trader.

jewellery, jewelry [*jOO*-ilRi] *n* (*collect*) jewels, *esp* as adornment.

Jewess [*jOO*-es] *n* Jewish woman.

Jewish [*jOO*-ish] *adj* pertaining to Jews; like a Jew ~ **Jewishly** *adv* ~ **Jewishness** *n*.

Jewry [*j*OORi] *n* (*collect*) Jews; Jewish religion and civilization; (*hist*) ghetto.

jew's-harp [*j*OOz-haarp] *n* (*mus*) primitive instrument held in mouth, played by vibrating its metal strip with the finger > PDM; (*coll*) haircomb covered in tissue paper, used as child's musical instrument.

Jezebel [*j*ezibel] *n* shameless woman.

jib (1) [*jib*] *n* (*naut*) foremost sail, set between foremasthead and bowsprit > PDSa; **the cut of one's j.** (*naut coll*) one's appearance ~ **jib** (*pres/part* **jibbing**, *p/t* and *p/part* **jibbed**) *v/t* and *i* swing (sail or yard) from one side of vessel to the other.

jib (2) *n* lifting arm of crane or derrick.

jib (3) (*pres/part* **jibbing**, *p/t* and *p/part* **jibbed**) *v/i* (*esp of horse*) refuse to proceed, balk; **j. at** (*fig*) show reluctance, raise objections to.

jib-boom [*jib*-bOOm] *n* (*naut*) spar forming continuation of bowsprit; arm of crane.

jib-door [*jib*-dawr] *n* door whose face is flush with the wall and decorated so as to be as little seen as possible.

jibe see **gibe** (1).

jiffy, jiff [*jif*i, *jif*] *n* (*coll*) brief space of time.

jig [*jig*] *n* type of lively dance > PDM; (*mech*) template guiding cutting tool; machine on which a prototype article is made; type of coal or mineral ore washer; **the j. is up** (*sl*) the game is up, there is no hope left ~ **jig** (*pres/part* **jigging**, *p/t* and *p/part* **jigged**) *v/t* and *i* dance a jig; move jerkily; bounce up and down; (*mech*) sieve (ore) under water.

jigger (1) [*jig*er] *n* one who jigs; sieve for jigging ore; rest for billiard-cue; iron-headed golf-club; (*naut*) kind of small tackle; small lug-sail; smack with jigger sail; woman's short outdoor coat; (*coll*) measure for liquor; (*coll*) gadget.

jigger (2) *n* sandflea, chigoe.

jiggered [*jig*erd] *adj* (*coll*) amazed; **I'm j.!** exclamation of surprise.

jiggery-pokery [*jig*eRi-*p*OkeRi] *n* (*coll*) trickery, underhand dealing.

jiggle [*jig*'l] *v/t* and *i* move by slight jerks.

jigsaw [*jig*saw] *n* machine fretsaw for cutting irregular patterns; **j. puzzle** picture mounted on cardboard or wood and cut into small irregular pieces which when correctly interlocked reconstitute the picture.

Jihad, Jehad [ji*haad*] *n* Mohammedan holy war against infidels; (*fig*) vigorous campaign.

jilt [*jilt*] *v/t* discard, dismiss (a lover) after giving encouragement ~ **jilt** *n* woman who does this.

Jim Crow [jim-*k*RO] *n* (*US*) segregation or discrimination against Negroes; (*obs sl*) a Negro ~ **Jim-Crow** *adj*.

jiminy [*jim*ini] *interj* (*coll*) exclamation of surprise.

jim-jams [*jim*-jamz] *n* (*pl*) (*coll*) nervousness, the creeps; delirium tremens.

jingle [*jing*-g'l] *n* light ringing sound as when small pieces of metal strike together; simple catchy verse with much repetition of sounds ~ **jingle** *v/i* and *t* make or cause to make a jingle ~ **jingling** *adj* ~ **jingly** *adj*.

jingo [*jing*-gO] *n* one who is aggressively patriotic; warmonger; **by j.!** (*coll*) exclamation of surprise or emphasis.

jingoism [*jing*-gO-izm] *n* aggressive patriotism ~ **jingoist** *adj* and *n* ~ **jingoistic** [jing-gO-*i*stik] *adj*.

jink [*jink*] *v/t* and *i* dodge about; (*aer coll*) manoeuvre to elude hostile fire ~ **jink** *n* quick elusive movement; **high jinks** noisy frolics.

jinnee (*pl* **jinn**) [*jinnee*] *n* (*myth*) supernatural being in Muslim demonology.

jinricksha [jin*rik*sha] *n* (*Jap*) rickshaw.

jinx [*jinks*] *n* (*US coll*) bringer of bad luck, hoodoo.

jitney [*jit*ni] *n* (*US sl*) five-cent coin ~ **jitney** *adj* (*US sl*) cheap.

jitter [*jit*er] *v/i* (*coll*) have an attack of nerves.

jitterbug [*jit*erbug] *n* (*coll*) person who dances with convulsive gesticulations to jazz music; type of convulsive dance; highly nervous person, person who panics easily ~ **jitterbug** (*pres/part* **jitterbugging**, *p/t* and *p/part* **jitterbugged**) *v/i*.

jitters [*jit*erz] *n* (*pl*) (*coll*) extreme nervousness; panic; **have the j.** be scared.

jittery [*jit*eRi] *adj* nervy, jumpy.

jiu-jitsu see **ju-jutsu.**

jive [*jiv*] *n* highly emotional swing or jazz music; energetic form of dance to jazz music ~ **jive** *v/i*.

jizz [*jiz*] *n* (*coll*) essence, living quality.

job (1) [*job*] *n* piece of work; something that must be done, task; employment, occupation, post; public duty performed for private profit; matter, affair; (*coll*) criminal act, *esp* theft; **a good j.** task well done; something lucky; **just the j.** exactly what one wants; **j. lot** miscellaneous goods; **on the j.** (*coll*) busy; ready for anything ~ **job** (*pres/part* **jobbing**, *p/t* and *p/part* **jobbed**) *v/i* and *t* do casual work or piecework; use public position for private gain; divide up (work) among several contractors; hire out; act as broker.

job (2) (*pres/part* **jobbing**, *p/t* and *p/part* **jobbed**) *v/t* and *i* jab, prod.

jobber [*job*er] *n* dealer in Stock Exchange securities; one who does piecework; one who betrays public trust for corrupt ends.

jobbery [*job*eRi] *n* corrupt practice in public positions.

jobbing [*job*ing] *n* piecework; jobbery; broking.

jobmaster [*job*maaster] *n* one who hires out horses.

Job's comforter [jObz-*kum*ferter] *n* one whose attempts at comforting only add to one's grief.

jockey [*jok*i] *n* professional rider of racehorses; disc-jockey; **J. Club** group of racehorse owners who regulate racing ~ **jockey** *v/t* and *i* jostle against another in riding; cheat, trick; manoeuvre; drive (a person) to do something by crafty manoeuvres against him; **j. for position** compete in crafty ways; manoeuvre for advantage.

jocko, jacko [*jok*O, *jak*O] *n* chimpanzee.

jock-strap [*jok*-strap] *n* protective covering and support for the external male genitals.

jocose [jo*kO*s] *adj* playful, jesting ~ **jocosely** *adv* ~ **jocoseness** *n*.

jocosity [jo*kos*iti] *n* facetiousness.

jocular [*jok*ewlar] *adj* merry; humorous.

jocularity [jokew*lar*Riti] *n* facetiousness.

jocund [*jok*und] *adj* cheerful, gay ~ **jocundly** *adv*.

jocundity [jo*kund*iti] *n* cheerfulness.

jodhpurs [*jod*purz] *n* (*pl*) riding-breeches close-fitting below knee and reaching to the ankles.

joey [*jO*-i] *n* (*Aust*) young kangaroo.

jog (*pres/part* jogging, *p/t* and *p/part* jogged) [*jog*] *v/t* and *i* push gently, nudge; shake slightly; (*fig*) rouse (memory, attention *etc*); move slowly but steadily; run steadily but not fast, *esp* for exercise; keep moving; j. along continue steadily and uneventfully ∼ **jog** *n* slight push, nudge; slow jolting trot.

jogging [*joging*] *n* sport of running long distances at a moderate pace, *esp* in towns.

joggle (1) [*jog'l*] *v/t* and *i* jerk slightly, jolt.

joggle (2) *n* (*bui*) recess on one block of masonry which fits a projection on another block; (*mech*) slight sharp bending of a steel angle ˃ PDE ∼ **joggle** *v/t* secure with a joggle.

jogtrot [*jogt*Rot] *n* slow steady jolting trot; (*fig*) monotonous but steady advance ∼ **jogtrot** *adj* at a slow steady pace; (*fig*) humdrum.

Johannine [*jOhan*In] *adj* of or written by the apostle John.

Johannisberger [*jOhan*isburger] *n* a Rhine wine.

John [*jon*] *n* a man's name; (*coll*) lavatory; **J. Bull** the typical Englishman; England (*personified*); **J. Collins** drink of gin, lemon and soda; **J. Doe** (*leg*) fictitious plaintiff; **J. Dory** the dory.

Johnny, Johnnie [*joni*] *n* (*coll*) young fellow, chap; dandy.

Johnsonese [*jonson*eez] *n* verbose and over-latinate literary style, remotely resembling that of Dr Samuel Johnson.

join [*join*] *v/t* and *i* connect, fasten together; link; come together, unite, meet; combine; act in concert with; participate; become member of (club *etc*); accompany, associate oneself with; go into the company of; **j. battle** start to fight or quarrel; **j. forces** (*fig*) agree to act together with, ally oneself to; **j. up** enlist ∼ **join** *n* point or line where two things join, junction, seam.

joinder [*joind*er] *n* (*leg*) union.

joiner [*join*er] *n* craftsman in wood, maker of furniture *etc* as distinct from carpenter ∼ **joinery** *n*.

joint [*joint*] *n* point, line, or surface where two or more things join; structure whereby two bones fit together; section of meat carcass as cut ready for cooking; (*bot*) place on stem from which leaf or branch springs; (*geol*) crack formed at weak spot in mass of rock ˃ PDG; (*US coll, pej*) bar, restaurant, place of entertainment; any place; **clip j.** (*coll*) nightclub, bar *etc* charging extortionate prices; **out of j.** dislocated; (*fig*) disorderly; **put one's nose out of j.** supplant, give cause of jealousy to ∼ **joint** *adj* shared by, done by, or involving two or more persons ∼ **joint** *v/t* fasten or fit together by joints; separate into joints; plane edge of (board); fill (interstices in brickwork) with mortar, point ∼ **jointed** *adj* having joints ∼ **jointedly** *adv*.

jointer [*joint*er] *n* (*bui*) bricklayer's tool used in pointing; (*carp*) plane used for smoothing long edges to be joined.

jointly [*joint*li] *adv* together, in conjunction.

jointress, jointuress [*joint*Res] *n* widow holding jointure.

joint-stock [joint-*stok*] *n* capital held in the form of shares; **j. company** company where each shareholder can transfer shares without consent of other holders.

jointure [*join*cher] *n* (*leg*) estate settled on a wife for her lifetime.

jointuress see jointress.

joist [*joist*] *n* wood or rolled-steel beam directly supporting a floor.

joke [*jOk*] *n* anecdote, witticism, or incident which raises a laugh, jest; something not meant to be taken seriously; ridiculous thing or person; **no j.** a serious matter; **practical j.** trick played on a person to raise a laugh at his expense ∼ **joke** *v/i* make jokes; talk jestingly ∼ **jokingly** *adv*.

joker [*jOk*er] *n* one who jokes; odd card in a pack used in some games; (*coll*) fellow; hidden factor which will affect matters in an unforeseen way.

jokey, joky [*jOki*] *adj* (*coll*) fond of joking; intended as a joke.

jollification [jolifi*kay*shon] *n* merrymaking.

jollify [*joli*fI] *v/i* and *t* (*coll*) be jolly; make jolly (*esp* with drink).

jollity [*joli*ti] *n* state of being jolly; merrymaking.

jolly [*joli*] *adj* gay, in high spirits; fond of gaiety; exuberantly cheerful or friendly, hearty; plump and merry-looking; (*coll*) pleasant, amusing; (*coll*) slightly drunk ∼ **jolly** *adv* (*coll*) very ∼ **jolly** *v/t* coax into good humour, cajole; flatter, persuade by flattery ∼ **jolly** *n* (*naut coll*) a Royal Marine.

jollyboat [*roli*bOt] *n* (*naut*) ship's boat.

jolt [*jOlt*] *v/t* and *i* give sudden strong jerk or bump to, jog violently; move along with jerks and bumps ∼ **jolt** *n* strong jerk, heavy bump; (*fig*) shock.

Jonah [*jO*na] *n* one who brings bad luck to others; unlucky person.

Jonathan [*jonathan*] *n* variety of red apple.

jongleur [zhong-*glur*] *n* (*hist*) medieval wandering minstrel.

jonquil [*jong*-kwil] *n* type of scented narcissus.

jordan [*jawr*dan] *n* (*sl*) chamberpot.

jorum, joram [*jawr*Rum] *n* large drinking vessel.

josh [*josh*] *n* and *v/t* (*US coll*) hoax.

joss [*jos*] *n* Chinese idol.

josser [*jos*er] *n* (*coll*) fellow, chap.

joss-stick [*jos*-stik] *n* Chinese incense stick.

jostle [*jos*'l] *v/t* and *i* push roughly, hustle; make one's way by pushing; shove (against) ∼ **jostle** *n* rough push.

jot [*jot*] *n* very small amount ∼ **jot** (*pres/part* jotting, *p/t* and *p/part* jotted) *v/t* **j. down** note briefly in writing.

jota [*jO*ta] *n* traditional Spanish dance.

jotter [*jot*er] *n* book for rough notes.

jotting [*jot*ing] *n* brief written note.

joule [*jOOl*] *n* electrical unit of work ˃ PDS.

jounce [*jowns*] *v/t* and *i* bump, bounce, jolt.

journal [*jurnal*] *n* daily record of events; diary; daily newspaper; magazine or periodical; (*naut*) log book; (*comm*) daily statement of accounts; (*mech*) part of shaft or axle resting on bearings.

journalese [jurna*leez*] *n* (*cont*) slipshod style of writing full of clichés and with syntax distorted by compression.

journalism [*jur*nalizm] *n* profession of producing, managing, editing, or writing for newspapers or periodicals ∼ **journalist** *n* one who is engaged in journalism.

journalistic [jurnalistik] *adj* of or like journalists or newspapers.

journalize [jurnalIz] *v/t* and *i* enter in a journal; keep daily record; work as journalist.

journey [jurni] *n* act of travelling, *esp* to distant place; distance that can be travelled in specified time ∼ **journey** *v/i* travel.

journeyman [jurniman] *n* worker who has finished his apprenticeship; (*fig*) drudge, hack; mediocre workman.

joust [jowst] *v/i* (*hist*) engage in mounted combat with lance, tilt ∼ **joust** *n* act of jousting; tournament.

Jove [jOv] *n* (*Rom myth*) Jupiter; **by J.!** (*coll*) exclamation of surprise or emphasis.

jovial [jOvi-al] *adj* cheerful, hearty ∼ **jovially** *adv*.

joviality [jOvi-aliti] *n* cheerfulness, heartiness.

Jovian [jOvi-an] *adj* of Jove; (*astron*) of the planet Jupiter; (*fig*) majestic.

jowl [jowl] *n* jaw; cheek; flabby fold of flesh round jaws and chin; dewlap of cattle *etc*; **cheek by j.** close together, side by side.

joy [joi] *n* happiness; deep feeling of gladness; one who or that which causes joy ∼ **joy** *v/i* and *i* (*poet*) make or be joyful.

joyful [joifool] *adj* feeling or expressing joy; causing joy ∼ **joyfully** *adv* ∼ **joyfulness** *n*.

joyless [joiles] *adj* affording no joy, dismal, miserable ∼ **joylessly** *adv* ∼ **joylessness** *n*.

joyous [joi-us] *adj* joyful ∼ **joyously** *adv* ∼ **joyousness** *n*.

joyride [joiRId] *n* (*coll*) a ride in car without owner's permission; (*coll*) a ride at great speed; ride taken for pleasure.

joystick [joistik] *n* (*coll*) control column of an aircraft.

juba [jOOba] *n* noisy, rollicking, Negro dance.

jube [jOObi] *n* (*eccles*) a rood-screen.

jubilant [jOObilant] *adj* shouting for joy, elated, triumphant ∼ **jubilantly** *adv*.

jubilate (1) [jOObilayt] *v/i* rejoice, express joy, triumph or exultation.

Jubilate (2) [joobilaati] *n* (*liturg*) hundredth psalm used as canticle.

jubilation [jOObilayshon] *n* act of rejoicing.

jubilee [jOObilee] *n* fiftieth or twenty-fifth anniversary of an important event; occasion for jubilation; (*RC*) year during which special indulgences are granted; (*hist*) Jewish year of emancipation to be celebrated every fifty years; **silver j.** twenty-fifth anniversary; **diamond j.** sixtieth anniversary; **golden j.** fiftieth anniversary.

Judaeo- *pref* Jewish.

Judaic, Judaical [jOOday-ik, jOOday-ik'l] *adj* Jewish.

Judaism [jOOday-izm] *n* the Jewish religion; Jewish custom.

Judaize [jOOday-Iz] *v/t* and make Jewish, convert to Judaism; follow Jewish customs or religious rites ∼ **Judaizer** *n*.

Judas [jOOdas] *n* betrayer, traitor; peep-hole in door; **J.** tree bearing deep purple flowers before the leaves appear.

judder [juder] *v/i* (*of car engine*) fire erratically or jerkily; vibrate unpleasantly.

judge [juj] *n* official appointed to hear and try cases in law court; one nominated to give decision in any dispute; one with special qualifications for giving an opinion; (*Heb hist*) ruler in period between Joshua and the kings; (*pl*) (*cap*) book of Old Testament covering period when Israel was ruled by judges ∼ **judge** *v/t* and *i* try (case) in law court; sentence (person) in law court; form opinion, consider; give opinion or decision (on); estimate worth (of); censure, reprimand; act as a judge; come to a decision.

Judge-Advocate [juj-*adv*Okit] *n* (*leg*) prosecuting officer in court-martial.

judgement, judgment [jujment] *n* sentence or decision of law court; opinion; power of discrimination; criticism, censure; disaster considered as punishment sent by God; **the J., the last J.** judgement-day; **sit in j.** criticize.

judgement-day [jujment-day] *n* final day of the world on which God's judgement will be pronounced, doomsday.

judgement-seat [jujment-seet] *n* (*leg*) judge's seat; tribunal.

judgment see judgement.

judicatory [jOOdikayteRi] *adj* exercising judicial functions ∼ **judicatory** *n* court of justice.

judicature [jOOdikacher] *n* process of administering justice; body of judges of a country; judicial system.

judicial [jOOdishal] *adj* of or befitting a law court or a judge; impartial, fair, unbiased; **j. murder** sentence of death legal but considered to be unjust ∼ **judicially** *adv*.

judiciary [jOOdishi-aRi] *n* body of judges in a state.

judicious [jOOdishus] *adj* exhibiting judgement, sagacious, prudent, sensible, wise ∼ **judiciously** *adv* ∼ **judiciousness** *n*.

judo [jOOdO] *n* Japanese system of unarmed combat by using the adversary's own weight and impetus to throw him.

judy [jOOdi] *n* (*sl*) woman, girl; ridiculous person, *esp* woman; **make a j. of oneself** (*coll*) play the fool.

jug (1) [jug] *n* deep vessel with handle and spout for holding liquids; contents of this; (*sl*) prison ∼ **jug** (*pres/part* jugging, *p/t* and *p/part* jugged) *v/t* boil or stew in a jug; (*coll*) put in prison.

jug (2) *n* representation of nightingale's note.

jugal [jOOgal] *adj* and *n* (of) the cheekbone.

jugate [jOOgayt] *adj* (*bot*) with little leaves in pairs; (*numis*) side by side.

jugful [jugfool] *n* contents of a jug; amount a jug will hold.

Juggernaut [jugernawt] *n* (*Hindu myth*) title of Krishna; image of Krishna drawn in procession on a chariot, under the wheels of which fanatical devotees threw themselves; (*fig*) relentless destructive force.

juggins [juginz] *n* (*coll*) simpleton, fool.

juggle [jug'l] *v/i* and *t* skilfully toss up balls, knives *etc*; perform manual tricks of dexterity; **j. with** deceive; manipulate or misrepresent so as to deceive ∼ **juggle** *n* feat of sleight of hand, dexterous trick; (*fig*) fraud, deception ∼ **juggler** *n* ∼ **jugglery** *n*.

Jugoslav see Yugoslav.

jugular [*jug*ewler] *adj* (*anat*) of or relating to the neck or throat; **j. veins** large veins of the neck ~ **jugular** *n* (*anat*) the jugular vein.

jugulate [*jug*ewlayt] *v/t* kill by cutting the throat; (*fig*) strangle; (*med*) check (disease) by drastic remedy.

juice [*jOOs*] *n* liquid content of fruit or vegetable; moisture in cooked meat; natural fluid, secretion; (*fig*) essence; (*coll*) petrol; (*coll*) electric current; **step on the j.** (*coll*) accelerate a car.

juicy [*jOO*si] *adj* full of juice, succulent; (*sl*) full of interest, spicy, suggestive ~ **juicily** *adv* ~ **juiciness** *n*.

ju-ju [*jOO*-jOO] *n* African fetish; African magical rites or spells; charm; taboo.

jujube [*jOO*jOOb] *n* sweet flavoured jelly-like lozenge; (*bot*) berry of the zizyphus shrub.

ju-jutsu, ju-jitsu, jiu-jitsu [jOO-*jits*OO] *n* judo.

jukebox [*jOOk*boks] *n* automatic record-player operated by inserting a coin.

julep [*jOO*lep] *n* sweet drink to take medicine in; (*US*) sweetened iced drink of spirituous liquor flavoured with mint.

Julian [*jOO*li-an] *adj* relating to Julius Caesar (*esp* of the calendar introduced by him).

julienne [zhOOli-*en*] *n* (*Fr*) clear meat soup with finely chopped vegetables; kind of pear.

juliet-cap [*jOO*li-et-kap] *n* girl's small plain cap worn on back of head.

July [jOO*lI*] *n* seventh month of the year.

jumbal see **jumble** (2).

jumble (1) [*jumb*'l] *v/t* and *i* confuse, mix together without order ~ **jumble** *n* confused state; disordered heap or collection of heterogeneous objects; **j. sale** sale of varied cheap second-hand goods in aid of charity.

jumble (2), **jumbal** *n* kind of thin sweet cake.

jumbo [*jumb*O] *n* pet name for elephant; anybody or anything bigger than usual; **j. jet** jet aircraft seating several hundred passengers.

jump [*jump*] *v/i* and *t* spring, leap; move suddenly and involuntarily, start; leap over or across; cause to jump; omit, skip, ignore; be jerked away from; throb painfully; (*sl*) flee from; **j. at** accept or take eagerly; **j. a claim** take over the land, rights *etc* to which another has a previous claim; **j. on, j. upon** (*coll*) reprimand unhesitatingly; **j. the gun** act prematurely; **j. the queue** obtain service, goods *etc* out of one's turn; push ahead of those already waiting; **j. to it** (*coll*) hurry, be active; **j. to conclusions** form hasty conclusions on too little evidence; **j. with** agree with ~ **jump** *n* act of jumping, leap; height or distance traversed in a leap; contest in jumping; nervous movement, jerk of surprise; obstacle to be jumped over; sudden rise, acceleration or increase; vertical recoil of gun; omission of one or more steps in a series, abrupt transition; sudden change of direction; (*geol*) fault; **the jumps** (*sl*) twitching movement, nervous restlessness; **on the j.** (*coll*) busy, active; **for the high j.** (*mil*) up for trial.

jumped-up [*jumpt*-up] *adj* having recently acquired wealth or position, *esp* without acquiring manners and habits to suit one's new position; conceited, impudent.

jumper (1) [*jump*er] *n* one who or that which jumps; insect that jumps; (*eng*) heavy steel

boring bar > PDE; member of religious sects who leap up and down when praying; (*coll*) ticket-collector on bus, tram, or tube; **counter j.** (*coll*) shop assistant.

jumper (2) *n* woman's loose light-weight pullover; woman's knitted blouse; sailor's hip-length tunic or jacket.

jumping-off [jumping-*of*] *adj* **j. point** starting place.

jump-jet [*jump*-jet] *n* (*aer*) jet aircraft capable of vertical take-off and landing.

jump-suit [*jump*-sewt] *n* one-piece garment consisting of trousers and bloused top.

jumpy [*jump*i] *adj* nervous ~ **jumpily** *adv* ~ **jumpiness** *n*.

junction [*junk*shon] *n* act of joining; condition of being joined; place or point of union; meeting place of railway lines.

juncture [*junk*cher] *n* a joining; place where things join; state of affairs, point of time; crisis, emergency.

June [jOOn] *n* sixth month of the year.

jungle [*jung*-g'l] *n* wild uncultivated land with dense undergrowth; equatorial forest; (*fig*) place or way of life where one is exposed to ruthless competition or exploitation; (*fig*) confused impenetrable mass; **j. fever** pernicious malarial fever ~ **jungly** *adj*.

junior [*jOO*ni-er] *n* younger; less experienced; subordinate, of lower status; (*of a son*) bearing same name as his father ~ **junior** *n* one who is younger, less experienced or subordinate; (*US coll*) son.

juniper [*jOO*niper] *n* (*bot*) one of a genus of evergreen trees the berries of which yield an oil used medicinally and to flavour gin.

junk (1) [*junk*] *n* (*coll*) useless discarded articles, rubbish, lumber; (*fig*) nonsense; (*naut*) old rope-ends re-used; (*naut*) hard salt meat; blubber containing spermaceti in head of sperm-whale; **j. shop** (*sl*) narcotic drug; shop selling inferior second-hand goods.

junk (2) *n* flat-bottomed Chinese sailing vessel.

junker [*yoong*ker] *n* (*Germ*) Prussian aristocrat.

junket [*junk*it] *n* dish of curdled milk; feast, merrymaking ~ **junket** *v/i* make merry.

junketing [*junk*iting] *n* merrymaking; (*US*) banquet, trip *etc* enjoyed at public expense.

junkie, junky [*junk*i] *n* (*sl*) drug addict.

Juno [*jOO*nO] *n* (*Rom myth*) goddess and queen of heaven, wife of Jupiter; (*fig*) woman of majestic stature and beauty; (*astron*) small planetary body whose orbit lies between Jupiter and Mars.

junoesque [jOOnO-*esk*] *adj* of majestic beauty.

junta [*junt*a] *n* (*Sp* and *Ital*) council; junto.

junto [*junt*O] *n* (*pol*) faction; influential clique.

Jupiter [*jOO*piter] *n* (*Rom myth*) Jove, the supreme god; (*astron*) the largest planet > PDS.

jupon [*jOO*pon] *n* (*hist*) doublet worn with armour.

Jurassic [jOO*Ras*ik] *adj* (*geol*) having predominance of oolitic limestone; pertaining to the fourth geological period > PDB.

juridical [joor*id*ikal] *adj* pertaining to administration of law; legal ~ **juridically** *adv*.

jurisconsult [joor*Ris*kon*sult*] *n* one who is an authority on points of law

jurisdiction [joor*Ris*dikshon] *n* authority or

power to administer law; extent of authority; area or sphere where authority can be exercised ~ **jurisdictional** *adj*.

jurisprudence [joorRis*pROO*dens] *n* science and philosophy of law; a legal system.

jurisprudent [joorRis*pROO*dent] *n* and *adj* (person) skilled in jurisprudence.

jurisprudential [joorRis*pROO*den*shal] *adj* of or relating to jurisprudence.

jurist [*joor*Rist] *n* one versed in law; writer on law; law graduate; (*US*) lawyer.

juror [*joor*Rer] *n* member of a jury; person taking an oath.

jury (1) [*joor*Ri] *n* body of persons sworn to return a verdict on evidence in a court of law: judges or umpires in a competition.

jury (2) *adj* (*naut*) used as temporary substitute.

jurybox [*joor*Riboks] *n* enclosed seats in a court for members of a jury.

juryman [*joor*Riman] *n* member of a jury

jurymast [*joor*Rimaast] *n* (*naut*) spar used as temporary replacement for lost or broken mast.

jussive [*ju*siv] *adj* (*gramm*) expressing a command.

just [*just*] *adj* fair, equitable, impartial; upright, virtuous; well-grounded; justified; true, correct; well-deserved ~ **just** *adv* exactly; almost exactly; at the very moment; not long before; barely; (*coll*) absolutely.

justice [*ju*stis] *n* state or quality of being just; fairness; abstract principle deciding the rightness of actions, relationships *etc*; administration of law; imposition of legal or just punishment; rightness, accordance with truth; magistrate, judge; **do j. to oneself** make fullest use of one's capacities; **do j. to appreciate** fully; **J. of the Peace** unpaid local magistrate; **poetic j.** author's manipulation of his plot to ensure happiness for the good characters and failure for the wicked.

justiceship [*ju*stis-ship] *n* rank or position of a justice.

justiciable [jus*tish*i-ab'l] *adj* subject to trial in court of law.

justiciary [jus*tish*i-eRi] *n* one who administers justice.

justifiability [jus̆tifi-a*bi*liti] *n* quality of being justifiable.

justifiable [*ju*stifi-ab'l] *adj* that can be justified ~ **justifiably** *adv*.

justification [justifi*kay*shon] *n* act of justifying; that which justifies; defence, vindication; state of being justified; (*theol*) release of a sinner from sin by faith and through merits of Christ.

justificative [*ju*stifikativ] *adj* that justifies.

justificatory [*ju*stifikayteRi] *adj* that justifies.

justify [*ju*stifi] *v/t* show to be true, right, or reasonable; prove, confirm; exonerate; (*typ*) space out (type); (*theol*) free from sin.

justly [*just*li] *adv* in a just way, fairly; correctly ~ **justness** *n*.

jut (*pres/part* **jutting**, *p/t* and *p/part* **jutted**) [*jut*] *v/i* protrude ~ **jut** *n* protrusion, projection.

Jute (1) [*jOOt*] *n* member of a Germanic tribe which settled in Britain in 5th century.

jute (2) *n* strong vegetable fibre used for making rope, sacking *etc*; Indian plant from the bark of which this is obtained.

juvenescence [jOOvi*ne*sens] *n* youthfulness; process of growing from childhood to youth; immaturity ~ **juvenescent** *adj*.

juvenile [jOOvin*Il*] *adj* youthful; suited to youth; characteristic of youth; (*leg*) below permissible school-leaving age; liable to be tried in special court ~ **juvenile** *n* young person; (*theat coll*) actor playing youthful parts; book, magazine *etc* intended for the young.

juvenilia [jOOv*i*nili-a] *n* (*pl*) productions of an author's or artist's youth.

juvenility [jOOv*i*niliti] *n* state or quality of being youthful.

juxta- *pref* close to, beside.

juxtapose [*juk*stap*Oz*] *v/t* place side by side.

juxtaposition [jukstap*Oz*ishon] *n* the placing of objects side by side; state of being thus placed.

K

k [*kay*] eleventh letter of English alphabet; **K.O.** (*boxing sl*) knock out.

kabbala see cabala.

kabuki [kab*OO*ki] *n* Japanese folk-drama.

kadi see cadi.

kaffir, kafir [*kafer*] *n* Negro of South African branch of Bantu race; language of this race; (*pl*) (*Stock Exchange coll*) South African gold mining shares.

kaftan see caftan.

kail see kale.

kainite [*ki*nIt] *n* double salt of magnesium sulphate and potassium chloride, used as fertilizer > PDS.

kainozoic see cainozoic.

Kaiser [*ki*zer] *n* (*hist*) emperor of Germany; emperor of Holy Roman Empire.

kaka [*kaa*kaa] *n* New Zealand parrot.

kakemono [kakem*OnO*] *n* Japanese painting or inscription on hanging scroll of silk or paper.

kale, kail [*kayl*] *n* type of curly-leaved cabbage; (*Scots*) vegetable soup.

kaleidoscope [kal*I*dosk*O*p] *n* (*opt*) tube containing at one end loose pieces of coloured glass whose reflections form varying patterns as the tube is moved; (*fig*) constantly varying pattern.

kaleidoscopic [kal*I*dos*ko*pik] *adj* of or like a kaleidoscope; ever-changing.

kalends see calends.

kaleyard, kailyard [*kayl*yaard] *n* (*Scots*) kitchen-garden; **k. school** group of authors writing in Lowland dialect on peasant life.

kali [*kaa*li] *n* prickly saltwort.

kalmia, calmia [*kal*mi-a] *n* class of North American evergreen shrub.

Kalmuck [*kal*muk] *n* (member of) Tatar race living on the Caspian Sea.

kame [*kaym*] *n* mound of gravel formed by deposit from glacier > PDG.

kamikaze [kamik*aa*zi] *n* Japanese pilot who deliberately crashes his aircraft filled with explosives on its target; (*fig*) suicidally reckless pilot or driver.

Kanaka [*kan*aka] *n* a Hawaiian.

kangaroo [kang-ga*ROO*] *n* marsupial animal with powerful hindquarters by which it moves in a series of leaps; (*pl*) (*Stock Exchange coll*) Australian land, tobacco, and mining shares; **k. court** non-legal tribunal set up by unauthorized persons to punish offences against them; notoriously unjust tribunal; **k. rat** a small marsupial animal; North American jumping rodent.

Kantian [*kant*i-an] *n* and *adj* (follower) of philosophic system of Kant.

kaolin [*kaa*-olin/*kay*-olin] *n* china clay, used for manufacture of porcelain.

kaon [*kay*-on] *n* (*phys*) short-lived elementary particle; a type of meson > PDS.

kapok [*kay*pok] *n* silky fibres obtained from seeds of silk-cotton tree.

kaput [ka*poot*] *adj* (*coll*) (*Germ*) broken, finished; dead, out of order, not working.

karacul see caracul.

karate [ka*Raa*tay/ka*Raa*ti] *n* Japanese system of unarmed combat by heavy blows of the hand, foot, head or elbow.

karma [*kaa*rma] *n* (*Buddhism*) intentional good or evil acts which will bear fruit in this or future lives; (*non-Buddhist*) fate, destiny.

karoo, karroo [ka*ROO*] *n* dry and barren South African plateau.

karyo- *pref* (*biol*) relating to a nucleus.

kata- *pref* downwards; throughout; against; backwards.

katabatic [katabatik] *adj* (*meteor*) (of local wind) produced by flow of radiation-cooled air down mountain slope or valley > PDG.

katabolism see catabolism.

katydid [*kay*tidid] *n* large North American tree-grasshopper.

kava [*kaa*va] *n* Polynesian intoxicating drink.

kayak [*kI*-ak] *n* canvas-covered non-collapsible canoe.

kea [*kay*-a] *n* New Zealand parrot which kills sheep.

kebab [ki*bab*] *n* Oriental dish of lumps of meat roasted on a spit.

keck [*kek*] *v/i* retch.

keckle [*kek*'l] *v/i* cackle; chuckle, giggle.

kedge [*kej*] *v/t* and *i* (*naut*) move (a ship) by hauling on a hawser fixed to a small anchor ~ **kedge** *n* small anchor for mooring or for kedging.

kedgeree [keje*Ree*] *n* Indian dish of seasoned rice, eggs, onions, beans *etc*; European dish of rice and fish, eggs *etc*.

keek [*keek*] *v/i* and *n* (*Scots* and *dial*) peep.

keel (1) [*keel*] *n* boat's lowest timbers or set of plates running from stem to stern on which the hull is built; vertical fin under aircraft; (*poet*) ship; **false k.** secondary keel added to the original one; **on an even k.** without rolling from side to side; steadily ~ **keel** *v/t* and *i* turn over so as to display the keel of; **k. over** capsize.

keel (2) *n* (*naut*) a lighter, *esp* used on Tyneside and in Yorkshire; amount of coal filling this.

keelhaul [*keel*hawl] *v/t* drag under the keel of a ship as punishment; (*fig*) reprimand severely.

keelman [*keel*man] *n* one working on a keel (2).

keelson see kelson.

keen (1) [*keen*] *adj* sharp, having good cutting edge; acute; very sensitive; intense; eager; penetrating; shrewd; closely contested; **k. on** eager, ambitious for; very fond of ~ **keenly** *adv* ~ **keenness** *n*.

keen (2) *n* (*Ir*) loud wailing lamentation, dirge ~ **keen** *v/i* and *t* lament with a keen, wail over ~ **keener** *n* hired mourner.

keep (*p/t* and *p/part* kept) [*keep*] *v/t* and *i* retain in one's possession, still have; preserve; maintain, cause to remain; maintain at one's own cost; provide necessities of life for; preserve for future use; have in stock; observe, fulfil (promise *etc*); be faithful to; celebrate; manage, run (shop *etc*); defend, guard; make regular entries

420

in; be in a certain condition; continue, go on; remain in sound condition; remain; **k. at** persist in; pursue diligently; force (others) to remain at work; **k. away** remain away; prevent from reaching or coming; put at a distance; **k. back** withhold, hide; restrain; hinder; **k. down** limit; oppress; suppress, restrain; **k. from** prevent, restrain from; withhold, hide; **k. in** confine or remain indoors; detain (schoolchildren) as punishment; restrain; prevent (fire) from dying; **k. in with** remain friendly with; **k. off** avert; hold at a distance; stay away from; refrain from; **k. on** continue; continue to wear; continue to employ; repeat (an action); **k. on at** (*coll*) nag; **k. out** prevent from entering; remain outside; not be involved in; **k. to** fulfil (promise *etc*); limit oneself to; **k. together** remain together; prevent from separating; **k. under** control, repress, oppress; **k. up** maintain, preserve; continue; prevent from falling or failing; show courage and perseverance; **k. up with** advance at the same rate as; (*coll*) prove one is the social equal of ~ **keep** *n* sustenance, that which is needed to maintain a person or animal; cost of sustaining or maintaining; strongly fortified central tower of castle; **for keeps** (*coll*) permanently.

keeper [*keep*er] *n* one who keeps or guards, custodian; person in charge of someone, *esp* a lunatic; person in charge of (some place or thing); gamekeeper; person running a business or shop; ring serving to guard another on the finger; (*mech*) device (of various kinds) for holding something in position; (*elect*) short soft iron bar placed across poles of a magnet to prevent loss of magnetism.

keepership [*keep*ership] *n* office or rank of keeper.

keeping [*keep*ing] *n* act of holding, maintaining, or retaining; custody, charge; fitness, suitability, congruity; **in k.** consistent, in harmony (with).

keepsake [*keep*sayk] *n* gift kept in remembrance of the giver.

keg [*keg*] *n* small barrel; a type of beer.

kelp [*kelp*] *n* kind of seaweed; ashes of this.

kelpie [*kel*pi] *n* (*Scots folklore*) a water-spirit in the form of a horse.

kelson, keelson [*kel*son] *n* (*naut*) inner keel fitted over the floor timbers to bind them to the keel.

Kelt (1), **Keltic** see **Celt, Celtic.**

kelt (2) [*kelt*] *n* (*Scots*) salmon or sea-trout after spawning.

kemp [*kemp*] *n* thick fibre found in poor wools.

ken [*ken*] *n* range of knowledge or perception ~ **ken** (*pres/part* **kenning**, *p/t* and *p/part* **kenned**) *v/t* (*Scots*) know; recognize.

kendo [*ken*dO] *n* Japanese art of swordsmanship.

kennel (1) [*ken*el] *n* small hut or shelter for a dog; fox's lair; (*fig*) hovel; (*pl*) building in which several dogs are housed; pack of dogs ~ **kennel** (*pres/part* **kennelling**, *p/t* and *p/part* **kennelled**) *v/t* and *i* keep or put in a kennel; live in a kennel.

kennel (2) *n* gutter; open drain.

kenning [*ken*ing] *n* type of decorative noun-phrase used in old Germanic poetry.

kenosis [ken*O*sis] *n* (*theol*) Christ's surrender of divine power in the incarnation.

kenotic [ken*o*tik] *adj* of or by kenosis.

Kentish [*ken*tish] *adj* of or relating to the county

of Kent; **K. rag** a sandy limestone; **K. fire** rounds of applause or dissent.

kentledge [*kent*lij] *n* (*naut*) pig-iron carried as permanent ballast; (*eng*) loading used to give stability to crane *etc* > PDE.

kepi, képi [*kep*ee] *n* (*Fr*) type of peaked cap with flat top sloping towards the front.

kept [*kept*] *p/t* and *p/part* of **keep** ~ **kept** *adj* financially supported by one's lover.

keramic see **ceramic.**

keratin [*ke*Ratin] *n* (*biol*) tough fibrous protein forming principal constituent of wool, hair, horns, and hoofs > PDB.

keratitis [keRa*tl*tis] *n* (*path*) inflammation of cornea.

kerato- *pref* horn-like, horny; of the cornea.

keratose [*ke*RatOs] *adj* and *n* horny (substance in skeleton of certain sponges).

kerb [*kurb*] *n* hard stone edging of pavement *etc*; **k. drill** precautionary rules to be followed by children when crossing roads; **on the k.** (*of Stock Exchange business*) transacted in the street outside normal hours ~ **kerb** *v/t* provide with kerb.

kerb-crawling [*kurb*-k*Raw*ling] *n* and *adj* (practice of) driving slowly along in order to accost and pester women pedestrians.

kerbstone [*kurb*stOn] *n* stone forming part of a kerb; **k. broker** broker who is not member of Stock Exchange.

kerchief [*kur*cheef] *n* (*hist*) square piece of cloth folded and worn as head-covering by women.

kerf [*kurf*] *n* a saw-cut in wood or stone; cut end, stump; a cut into coalface by coalcutter.

kerfuffle [ker*fuf*'l] *n* (*sl*) fuss; panic.

kermes [*kur*meez] *n* pregnant female of Mediterranean insect used for making dye; red dye made from these; (*chem*) amorphous trisulphide of antimony.

kermis, kermess [*kur*mis, *kur*mes] *n* Dutch or Flemish annual fair.

kernel [*kur*nel] *n* soft inner part of nut or of fruit-stone; grain of wheat *etc*; (*fig*) core, central part ~ **kernelled** *adj*.

kerosene [*ke*ROseen] *n* paraffin oil > PDS.

kerrie [*ke*Ri] *n* knobkerrie.

Kerry [*ke*Ri] *n* breed of Irish terrier; breed of Irish cattle.

kersey [*kur*zi] *n* coarse ribbed woollen cloth.

kerseymere [*kur*zimeer] *n* kind of cashmere.

kestrel [*kest*Rel] *n* small hawk or falcon.

ketch [*kech*] *n* (*naut*) small two-masted coasting vessel.

ketchup, catsup [*kech*up] *n* sauce made from tomatoes, mushrooms *etc.*

ketone [*keet*On] *n* (*chem*) series of organic compounds which includes acetone > PDS.

kettle [*ket*'l] *n* metal vessel with lid, spout, and handle, used for boiling water; **a nice k. of fish** quandary, muddle, mess.

kettledrum [*ket*'l-dRum] *n* cauldron-shaped brass or copper drum tuned to definite pitch > PDM; (*obs coll*) large teaparty.

kettle-holder [*ket*'l-hOlder] *n* pad of cloth for use when handling a hot kettle.

kevel [*kev*el] *n* (*naut*) cleat; bollard.

key (1) [*kee*] *n* metal instrument to fasten or unfasten a lock; (*fig*) explanation, solution; clue; translation for use with textbook; set of correct answers; dominating position; (mus) classification of notes in scale in relation to one tonic note > PDM; pitch; (arts) average or predominant colour values > PDAA; (fig) tone, style; (mus) lever on instrument > PDM; button or lever on typewriter, telegraphic instrument etc; spanner; (bui) basic coat of wall-plaster adhering to laths; any rough surface which helps adhesion; keystone of arch; instrument for winding a watch; wedge for tightening joints; (pl) (theol) spiritual authority of Pope or priests; **House of Keys** legislative assembly of Isle of Man; **master (skeleton) k.** key made so as to open several locks; **k. money** premium demanded from prospective tenant before he can occupy premises; **k. pattern** a fret pattern; **power of the keys** (theol) authority to forgive sins; **k. signature** indication on musical score of number of sharps and flats in prevailing key > PDM ~ **key** adj essential; in central or dominating position ~ **key** v/t secure or tighten with a wedge; lock; (mus) adjust pitch, tune up; **k. up** (fig) brace up; stimulate, render tense with excitement.

key (2) n reef, small flat island.

key (3) see **quay**.

keyboard [keebawrd] n complete set of keys on piano, organ, typewriter etc > PDM.

keyhole [keehOl] n hole admitting key into a lock.

keynote [keenOt] n (mus) lowest note or tonic in the scale of a particular key; (fig) predominant tone style.

keyring [keeRing] n split ring to hold bunch of keys together.

keystone [keestOn] n (bui) central wedge-shaped stone at crown of an arch, put in last; (fig) fundamental element, essential basis.

khaki [kaaki] n dull brownish-yellow colour; (mil) cloth of this colour used for field-service uniform ~ **khaki** adj.

khalifa, khalifat see **caliph, caliphate.**

khamsin [kamseen] n hot, dry, southerly wind experienced in Egypt from April to June > PDG.

khan [kaan] n (hist) title of medieval Asian emperors; (modern) title of rank in Central Asia.

kibble [kib'l] n large bucket used in shaft sinking for hoisting rock etc > PDE.

kibbutz (pl **kibbutzim**) [kibuts] n Israeli collective farm and commune.

kibe [kIb] n broken chilblain esp on heel.

kibitzer [kibitser] n (coll) interfering busybody who gives unwanted advice.

kibosh [kIbosh] n (sl) rubbish, nonsense; **put the k. on** (sl) put an end to, prevent.

kick (1) [kik] v/t and i hit with foot; drive violently, move by kicking; jerk foot forward; (of gun) recoil; (of cricket ball) rear up sharply; (fig) resist; (coll) give up (a habit); **k. about** lie neglected; **k. against the pricks** do oneself harm in rebelling; **k. off** make first kick in football match; **k. one's heels** be idle; **k. over the traces** rebel against restraint; **k. up** cause (fuss, disturbance) ~ **kick** n act of kicking; jerk; recoil of gun; (sl) thrill, stimulant; (coll) strength, vitality; (sl) sixpence; **the k.** (sl) dismissal; **for kicks** (sl) to get a thrill.

kick (2) n the hollow in the butt of a glass bottle.

kick-off [kik-of] n start of football match.

kickshaw [kikshaw] n a toy, trifle; elaborately cooked dish.

kick-start [kik-staart] n foot-operated lever for starting engine of motorcycle.

kick-up [kikup] n (coll) commotion, row; merry party.

kid [kid] n young goat; flesh of this; leather made of kid's skin; (coll) child; young person; (sl) hoax ~ **kid** adj made of kidskin; (coll) young, younger; childish ~ **kid** (pres/part **kidding**, p/t and p/part **kidded**) v/t and i (of goat) give birth (to kids); (coll) deceive, fool; tease, joke (with); hoax.

Kidderminster [kiderminster] n (tr) kind of carpet of flat weave and two-ply fabric.

kiddie, kiddy [kidi] n (coll) small child.

kiddle [kid'l] n river barrier with nets for catching fish.

kidglove [kidgluv] adj delicate, fastidious, not using severe methods.

kidnap (pres/part **kidnapping**, p/t and p/part **kidnapped**) [kidnap] v/t carry off by force, esp for ransom; steal (child) ~ **kidnapper** n.

kidney [kidni] n one of pair of abdominal glandular organs excreting urine; (fig) kind, class.

kidney-bean [kidni-been] n scarlet runner bean; dwarf French bean.

kidskin [kidskin] n skin of young goat used for gloves, footwear etc.

kieselguhr [keezelgoor] n porous and absorbent powder of hydrated silica > PDS.

kike [kIk] n (pej sl) Jew.

kilderkin [kilderkin] n cask containing 16 or 18 gallons.

kill [kil] v/t cause to die, put to death; destroy vital power of; cause death; (fig) suppress, veto, finish; cause (time) to pass as quickly as possible; (coll) make a deep impression on; render ineffective by contrast; (tennis etc) hit (ball) so that opponent cannot return it; (football) stop (ball) dead; (coll) muffle, make silent; cause to cease; **k. off** remove by killing; **k. with kindness** overwhelm, harm, by excessive kindness ~ **kill** n act of killing esp in hunting; that which is killed; number of animals killed.

killer [kiler] n one who or that which kills; one who is liable to kill, actual or potential murderer; **k. whale** the grampus.

killick, killock [kilik, kilok] n (naut) heavy stone serving as anchor; (naut) small anchor.

killing [kiling] n act of destroying life; (coll) large profit made in financial deal ~ **killing** adj that kills; capable of killing; (coll) very amusing; exhausting; fascinating.

killjoy [kiljoi] n gloomy person.

killock see **killick.**

kiln [kiln] n furnace or large oven used in various manufacturing processes.

kilo- pref a thousand, thousandfold (in metric units).

kilo [keelO] n (abbr) kilogram; kilometre.

kilocycle [kilOsIk'l] n (elect, rad) measure of frequency, 1,000 cycles per second.

kilogram, kilogramme [kilOgRam] n 1,000 grams, 2·2046 lb.

kilolitre [kilOleeter] n 1,000 litres.

kilometer [kilOmeeter/kilomiter] n 1,000 metres; 1,094 yards; 0·6214 mile.

kiloton [*kil*Otun] *n* explosive force equal to that of a thousand tons of TNT.

kilowatt [*kil*Owot] *n* (*elect*) unit of power, 1,000 watts.

kilowatt-hour [*kil*Owot-owr] *n* unit of work; work done by one kilowatt maintained for an hour.

kilt [*kilt*] *v/t* tuck up (skirt) round body; gather (skirt) in vertical pleats ~ **kilt** *n* Highland Scotsman's pleated *usu* tartan knee-length skirt ~ **kilted** *adj* wearing the kilt; vertically pleated.

kilter [*kilter*] *n* proper working order; **out of k.** not working properly.

kimono [ki*mOnO*] *n* long Japanese robe with short wide sleeves; dressing-gown or wrap of similar style.

kin [*kin*] *n* (*collect*) relatives; **next of k.** nearest relation ~ **kin** *adj* related.

kinaesthesis [kines*thee*sis] *n* (*psych*) the sensation of muscular effort > PDP ~ **kinaesthetic** *adj*.

kind (1) [*kind*] *n* sort, variety, class; (*philos*) essential character; (*ar*) breed, race; (*eccles*) bread or wine of Eucharist; **k. of** (*adv phr*) (*coll*) to some extent, partly, somewhat; **of a k.** of the same sort; of indifferent quality; **pay (back) in k.** pay in goods, not money; give someone treatment similar to that one received from him.

kind (2) *adj* affectionate, friendly; considerate; doing good to others; expressing affection, benevolence *etc*.

kindergarten [*kind*ergaarten] *n* infant school.

kind-hearted [kInd-*haar*tid] *adj* having a kind disposition ~ **kind-heartedness** *n*.

kindle [*kind*'l] *v/t* and *i* set light to; start burning, catch light; (*fig*) illuminate; excite, stir up; be or become excited; glow ~ **kindler** *n*.

kindling [*kindling*] *n* fuel for starting a fire.

kindly [*kInd*li] *adj* kind; showing or expressing kindness ~ **kindly** *adv* in a kind way; **take k. to** find congenial ~ **kindliness** *n*.

kindness [*kInd*nis] *n* quality of being kind; kind act, benevolent or obliging action.

kindred [*kind*Red] *n* (*collect*) relatives; blood relationship ~ **kindred** *adj* related by blood, of common stock; (*fig*) similar, allied, congenial.

kine [*kIn*] *n* (*ar pl*) cows.

kinema see **cinema**.

kinematic, kinematical [kini*matik*, kini*matikal*] *adj* relating to kinematics.

kinematics [kini*matiks*] *n* (*pl*) (*phys*) theory of motion without reference to forces or mass.

kinematograph, kinematography see **cinematograph, cinematography**.

kinesic [ki*neezik*] *adj* (*of body movements*) conveying information.

kinetic [ki*netik*] *adj* (*phys*) of, relating to, caused by, motion; **k. art** sculptures or reliefs of which parts are put in motion by machinery, electricity, magnets, or air currents; **k. energy** (*phys*) energy which a body possesses by virtue of its motion > PDS.

kinetics [ki*netiks*] *n* (*pl*) branch of dynamics concerned with the relations between the motions of bodies and the forces acting upon them.

kineto- *pref* moving; relating to motion.

king [*king*] *n* male ruler of nation, tribe *etc*, *usu* by hereditary right; one who is supreme; one who dominates, controls, or leads; (*cards*) card with picture of king; (*chess*) piece which must be defended against checkmate; (*draughts*) piece whose powers are extended after reaching eighth square; **K. of Arms** title of chief heralds; **k. of beasts** the lion; **k. of birds** the eagle; **K. of Kings** God; title of various Oriental monarchs; **k.'s evil** scrofula; **K.'s highway** public road; **uncrowned k.** one who has powers but not rank ~ **king** *v/t* and *i* make king; behave like a king, domineer.

kingbolt [*king*bOlt] *n* (*mech*) chief bolt; bolt connecting front axle of vehicle to body.

kingcraft [*king*kRaaft] *n* art of ruling.

kingcup [*king*kup] *n* buttercup; marsh-marigold.

kingdom [*king*dum] *n* state ruled by a king, monarchy; territory under the rule of a king; the dominion of God here or hereafter; domain, sphere *esp* of nature; **k. come** the next life; the end of the world; death; **United K.** Great Britain and N. Ireland.

kingfish [*king*fish] *n* name given to various fishes remarkable for food-value or size.

kingfisher [*king*fisher] *n* small brilliantly-feathered diving and fish-eating bird.

kinglet [*king*let] *n* petty king; golden-crested wren.

kingly [*king*li] *adj* of or like a king; suitable for a king; noble, splendid ~ **kingly** *adv* (*ar*) ~ **kingliness** *n*.

kingpin [*king*pin] *n* kingbolt; chief or central pin in game of ninepins *etc*; (*fig*) leader; indispensable person or thing.

kingpost [*king*pOst] *n* (*carp*) vertical timber reaching from centre of a horizontal tie-beam to ridge of rafters; (*aer*) strut to which bracing wires are fastened.

kingship [*king*ship] *n* state or office of a king.

kingsize, kingsized [*king*sIz, *king*sIzd] *adj* (*coll*) exceptionally large or good.

kink [*kink*] *n* twist in rope, wire, hair *etc* causing it to bend back; (*fig*) mental twist, peculiarity of character ~ **kink** *v/t* and *i* make a kink (in).

kinkajou [*kink*ajOO] *n* nocturnal animal of racoon family.

kinkle [*kink*'l] *n* small kink ~ **kinkled** *adj*.

kinky [*kink*i] *adj* having kinks; (*coll*) eccentric, queer; weirdly attractive; sophisticated; perverted; mad ~ **kinkily** *adv* ~ **kinkiness** *n*.

kino [*keen*O] *n* an astringent gum.

kinsfolk [*kinz*fOk] *n* (*pl*) relatives.

kinship [*kin*ship] *n* blood relationship; (*fig*) affinity, similarity.

kinsman [*kinz*man] *n* male relative, *esp* one related by blood.

kinswoman [*kinz*woom an] *n* female relative, *esp* one related by blood.

kiosk [*kee*-osk] *n* light open building used as bandstand, refreshment stall, newspaper stall *etc*; telephone booth; Turkish pavilion.

kip (1) [*kip*] *n* (*sl*) bed; lodging-house; sleep ~ **kip** (*pres/part* **kipping**, *p/t* and *p/part* **kipped**) *v/i* (*sl*) go to bed; sleep.

kip (2) *n* untanned hide of young animal.

kip (3) *n* (*eng*) a kilopound, 1,000 lb. weight.

kipper [*kip*er] *n* smoked and salted herring; male salmon at spawning time; (*sl*) fellow ~ **kipper** *v/t* cure (fish) by drying, smoking, and salting.

kirk [*kurk*] *n* (*Scots* and *northern dial*) church; **k. session** the lowest Presbyterian court.

kirsch [*keersh*] *n* (*Germ*) a cherry liqueur.

kirschwasser [*keersh*vaser] *n* kirsch.

kirtle [*kurt'l*] *n* (*ar*) woman's gown or outer petticoat; man's tunic.

kismet [*kiz*met] *n* fate, destiny, *esp* in Islamic belief.

kiss [*kis*] *v/t* and *i* press or touch with lips to show love, reverence or homage; touch gently; (*billiards*) touch lightly or for the second time; (*refl*) kiss one another; **k. the dust** (*fig*) be killed; be humiliated; **k. the rod** accept punishment meekly ∼ **kiss** *n* touch or caress by the lips; light touch; kind of sweetmeat; **k. of death** approval or support that is sure to do harm, not help; **k. of life** method of reviving an unconscious person by breathing into his mouth; (*fig*) renewed vigour, revival; **k. of peace** ceremonial kiss symbolizing religious unity and brotherly love.

kiss-curl [*kis*-kurl] *n* small curl on forehead or temple.

kisser [*kiser*] *n* one who kisses; (*sl*) mouth.

kist [*kist*] *n* (*dial*) box, chest; (*arch*) cist.

kistvaen [*kist*vayn] *n* (*arch*) cist.

kit (1) [*kit*] *n* outfit, equipment; (*mil*) personal equipment other than arms; set of tools; box or bag in which equipment or tools are carried; small round wooden tub ∼ **kit** (*pres/part* **kitting**, *p/t* and *p/part* **kitted**) *v/t* (*mil*) provide with kit.

kit (2) *n* (*ar*) small fiddle.

kit (3) *n* (*abbr*) kitten.

kitbag [*kit*bag] *n* (*mil*) long canvas bag in which a soldier carries his belongings.

kitchen [*kichen*] *n* place where food is cooked; **k. unit** compact combination of kitchen stove, sink, drainer, cabinet *etc*.

kitchener [*kichen*er] *n* a cooking range.

kitchenette [*kichen*et] *n* small compact combined kitchen and pantry.

kitchen-garden [*kichen*-gaarden] *n* vegetable garden.

kitchen-maid [*kichen*-mayd] *n* female servant helping a cook.

kitchen-midden [*kichen*-mid'n] *n* (*arch*) prehistoric refuse heap.

kitchen-sink [*kichen*-sink] *adj* (*of plays etc*) showing sordid aspects of modern life.

kite [*kit*] *n* bird of prey of hawk family; (*fig*) predatory person; light frame covered with paper or cloth which is blown upwards by strong wind and controlled from the ground by long cord; (*sl*) an aircraft; (*comm coll*) bill drawn to raise money on credit; worthless bill; **fly a k.** (*coll*) test public opinion by hints, rumours *etc*; (*comm coll*) try to raise money by worthless bills or other questionable means; **k. balloon** captive observation balloon.

kith [*kith*] *n* (*ar*) friends, acquaintances; **k. and kin** friends and relations; (*freq*) family.

kitsch [*kish*] *n* (*Germ*) (*coll*) pretentious nonsense; tastelessness, vulgarity, *esp* in art or fashions.

kitten [*kiten*] *n* young cat; (*fig*) playful or coquettish girl; **have kittens** (*coll*) be very agitated or frightened ∼ **kitten** *v/t* and *i* give birth to (kittens).

kittenish [*kiten*ish] *adj* playful; like a kitten.

kittiwake [*kiti*wayk] *n* kind of seagull.

kittle [*kit'l*] *adj* (*Scots*) requiring careful handling.

kitty (1) [*kiti*] *n* pool of stakes in card games; jointly-held stock of money; (*bowls*) the jack.

kitty (2) *n* pet name for a kitten.

kiwi [*kee*wee] *n* tailless New Zealand bird with undeveloped wings; (*sl*) New Zealander; (*sl*) member of ground staff of airfield.

klaxon [*klak*son] *n* strident electric hooter.

Kleenex [*klee*neks] *n* (*tr*) small sheet of absorbent paper tissue used as handkerchief *etc*.

kleptomania [kleptOmayni-a] *n* obsessive impulse to steal for no practical motive > PDP ∼ **kleptomaniac** *n* and *adj*.

klystron [*klist*Ron] *n* electron tube converting stream of electrons to high-frequency waves.

knack [*nak*] *n* skill, aptitude for doing something well; talent; clever trick; (*ar*) snapping sound, click, *esp* of fingers.

knacker [*nak*er] *n* person who buys old unfit horses to slaughter them for their carcasses; person who buys old houses or ships to break them up for scrap.

knackered [*nak*erd] *adj* (*sl*) exhausted; worn out, useless.

knackers [*nak*erz] *n* (*pl*) (*sl*) testicles.

knag [*nag*] *n* knot in wood; knob, peg.

knap (*pres/part* **knapping**, *p/t* and *p/part* **knapped**) [*nap*] *v/t* break by sharp blow; shape (flints) by breaking; (*sl*) take; steal.

knapsack [*nap*sak] *n* bag slung from shoulder or back containing supplies, equipment *etc*.

knapweed [*nap*weed] *n* (*bot*) common field-plant with purple flowers.

knar [*naar*] *n* knot in wood *esp* bark-covered knob.

knave [*nayv*] *n* rogue; (*cards*) the jack lowest-ranking court card; (*ar*) boy, servant.

knavery [*nayv*eRi] *n* roguery; dishonest behaviour.

knavish [*nayv*ish] *adj* dishonest, mean ∼ **knavishly** *adv* ∼ **knavishness** *n*.

knead [*need*] *v/t* squeeze and press (clay, moistened flour *etc*) so as to form dough or paste; massage; (*fig*) shape.

kneading-trough [*need*ing-tRof] *n* vessel for kneading dough in.

knee [*nee*] *n* joint between upper and lower part of human leg; similar joint in animal; angular or curved piece of wood or metal; part of clothing covering the knee; **bend (bow) the k.** kneel; submit; **gone at the knees** (*coll*) decrepit ∼ **knee** *v/t* and *i* touch or hit with knee; (*of trousers*) become baggy at the knees.

kneebrace [*neeb*Rays] *n* (*eng*) stiffener from stanchion to roof-truss > PDE.

knee-breeches [*nee*-bRichiz] *n* (*pl*) breeches fastening just below the knee.

kneecap [*nee*kap] *n* bone covering front of knee-joint, the patella; covering to protect knee ∼ **kneecap** *v/t* shoot (person) in the knee.

knee-deep [*nee*-deep] *adj* up to the knee.

knee-high [*nee*-hI] *adj* tall enough to reach the knees.

kneehole [*nee*hOl] *n* space between side-drawers of desk for admitting user's legs.

kneejoint [*nee*joint] *n* knee; (*mech*) movable right-angled joint.

kneel (*p/t* and *p/part* **knelt** or **kneeled**) [*neel*] *v/i* rest one's weight upon one or both bended knees; **k. to** kneel before; pray to; implore.

kneeler [*neeler*] *n* one who kneels; hassock; bench or stool to kneel on.

kneepan [*nee*pan] *n* kneecap.

knell [*nel*] *n* sound of bell tolling *esp* at death or funeral; (*fig*) omen of death ~ **knell** *v/t* and *i* summon by knell; announce or sound solemnly.

knelt [*nelt*] *p/t* and *p/part* of **kneel.**

knew [*new*] *p/t* of **know.**

knickerbockers [*nik*erbokerz] *n* (*pl*) loose breeches fastened below the knee.

knickers [*nik*erz] *n* (*pl*) knickerbockers; woman's undergarment covering from waist to crotch or thighs.

knick-knack [*nik*-nak] *n* trifle: small ornamental article.

knife (*pl* **knives**) [*nIf*] *n* cutting implement *usu* consisting of one-edged blade set in a handle; sharp blade of machine; **war to the k.** war with no quarter asked or given; **get one's k. into** bear a spiteful grudge against, persecute ~ **knife** *v/t* cut with knife, stab.

knife-edge [*nIf*-ej] *n* sharp edge of knife; sharp crest of rock or ice, an arête; wedge-shaped steel support on which pendulum *etc* balances.

knife-rest [*nIf*-Rest] *n* support for carving knife and fork at table.

knight [*nIt*] *n* commoner holding a personal nonhereditary dignity conferred by the sovereign and carrying with it the title *Sir*; title conferred by various societies on distinguished members; (*hist*) man, *usu* of gentle birth, ceremonially admitted to military rank; (*fig*) valiant man; champion or devoted admirer of a lady; (*chess*) piece in form of horse's head; **k. bachelor** lowes' rank among British knights, one belonging to no Order of Knighthood; **k. of the shire** (*hist*) parliamentary representative of a county; **k. of the road** highwayman ~ **knight** *v/t* confer knighthood on.

knightage [*nIt*ij] *n* (*collect*) knights; list of knights.

knight-errant (*pl* **knights-errant**) [*nIt*-eRant] *n* medieval knight travelling in search of adventure; (*fig*) quixotic person ~ **knight-errantry** *n*.

knighthead [*nIt*hed] *n* (*naut*) one of a pair of stout timbers supporting the bowsprit.

knighthood [*nIt*-hood] *n* rank or character of a knight; a company of knights; the collective body of knights.

knightly [*nIt*li] *adj* of or like a knight; chivalrous; valiant; courteous.

knight-service [*nIt*-*sur*vis] *n* (*hist*) tenure of land in return for military service.

knit (*pres/part* **knitting,** *p/t* and *p/part* **knitted, knit**) [*nit*] *v/t* and *i* make (fabric) by looping stitches of wool or thread together into a close pattern; draw (eyebrows) together in a frown; make compact; join closely together; become compact; become well joined; **k. up** become linked up, united ~ **knitter** *n*.

knitting [*nit*ing] *n* act of one who knits; piece of work being made by knitting.

knitting-needle [*nit*ing-need'l] *n* slender rod used in knitting.

knitwear [*nit*wair] *n* clothing made by knitting.

knives [*nIvz*] *pl* of **knife.**

knob [*nob*] *n* small rounded protuberance on a surface or at the end of anything; door handle; smallish lump; **with knobs on** (*coll*) only more so ~ **knobbed** *adj*.

knobble [*nob*'l] *n* little knob.

knobbly, knobby [*nob*li, *nob*i] *adj* having knobs.

knobkerrie [*nob*keRi] *n* stick with heavy rounded end, used as weapon by Africans.

knobstick [*nob*stik] *n* knobkerrie; (*sl*) blackleg.

knock [*nok*] *v/t* and *i* strike, hit, rap; give short sharp blow (*esp* at a door to gain entry); collide, clash; (*of petrol engine*) make a tapping noise; (*mech*) rattle; (*sl*) find fault with, run down; **k. about** handle roughly; (*coll*) lead an unsettled life; wander; **k. against** meet by chance; **k. back** (*sl*) swallow; startle; **k. down** floor with a blow; sell with tap of hammer (to bidder at auction sale); (*comm*) reduce price; **k. off** stop working; (*sl, vulg*) have sexual intercourse with; (*sl*) steal; deduct; kill; (*coll*) finish hurriedly; compose hurriedly; **k. out** (*boxing*) floor (opponent) for the count; stun; (*fig*) overwhelm; **k. together** construct roughly or hastily; **k. up** (*cricket*) score (runs); (*tennis*) practice shots; arouse by knocking; (*esp pass*) exhaust; construct hurriedly; (*sl*) make pregnant; **k. into a cocked hat, k. spots off** defeat, demolish; **k. the bottom out of** demolish (an argument); **k. on the head** make an end of, thwart ~ **knock** *n* short sharp blow, rap; (*cricket*) innings; tapping noise due to over-compression of mixture in petrol engine; **take a k.** (*coll*) suffer financial loss.

knockabout [*nok*abowt] *adj* rough, boisterous; slapstick; (*of clothes*) suitable for rough wear ~ **knockabout** *n* slapstick farce; comedian specializing in such farces; small single-masted yacht.

knockdown [*nok*down] *adj* and *n* stunning (blow); overwhelming (shock); **k. price** reserve price at auction.

knocker [*nok*er] *n* one who knocks; thing which knocks, *esp* a hinged metal striker fixed to a door.

knock-kneed [nok-*need*] *adj* having legs curved inwards so that the knees touch in walking; (*fig*) weak, cowardly.

knock-on [nok-*on*] *n* (*Rugby football*) act of striking the ball forward ~ **knock-on** *adj* (*coll*) cumulative.

knockout [*nok*owt] *n* (*boxing*) blow which incapacitates opponent during the referee's count; auction sale at which goods previously bought cheaply by agreement between dealers are resold; eliminating round in tournament or competition; (*coll*) person or thing excelling others or causing amazement ~ **knockout** *adj*.

knoll [*nOl*] *n* hillock, mound.

knop [*nop*] *n* knob-shaped decoration.

knot (1) [*not*] *n* tightly tied loop of thread, string *etc* made as fastening; ornamental loop of ribbon, braid *etc*; (*fig*) difficulty, complication; (*fig*) bond, link; hard lump in tree-trunk where branch springs; hard cross-grained lump in sawn timber; knob; small group of people, cluster; (*naut*) unit of ship's speed, one nautical mile per hour; **tie oneself in knots** make difficulties for oneself ~ **knot** (*pres/part* **knotting,** *p/t* and *p/part* **knotted**) *v/t* and *i* tie into a knot; make knots in; fasten by a knot; twist and tie up thread to form a loose fringe; become entangled or knotty; **get knotted!** (*sl*) go away! leave me in peace!

knot (2) *n* wading seabird of snipe family.

knotgrass [*notg*Rass] *n* common weed with wiry creeping stem.

knotty [*noti*] *adj* full of knots; (*fig*) complicated, difficult ~ **knottily** *adv* ~ **knottiness** *n*.

knout [*nowt*/k'*noot*] *n* Russian leather-thonged whip ~ **knout** *v/t* flog with a knout.

know (*p/t* **knew**, *p/part* **known**) [*nO*] *v/t* and be aware of or acquainted with; be informed of; have knowledge about; understand, be proficient in; recognize, distinguish; be certain; be on terms of personal acquaintance with; (*leg*, *ar*) have sexual intercourse with; k. about be informed of; k. of have heard about, be informed of; **not that I k. of** (*coll*) not as far as I know; **k. a thing or two, k. what's what** be no fool, have common sense ~ **know** *n* (*coll*) **in the k.** having private information.

knowable [*nO*-ab'l] *adj* that can be known; easy to get on with ~ **knowably** *adv* ~ **knowability** [*nO*-a*bili*ti] *n*.

know-all [*nO*-awl] *n* busybody; person who claims to know everything.

knowhow [*nO*how] *n* technical knowledge, knowledge of how to do a specified task.

knowing [*nO*-ing] *adj* artful, shrewd; intelligent ~ **knowingly** *adv* consciously, deliberately; shrewdly ~ **knowingness** *n*.

knowledge [*noli*j] *n* act or process of knowing, perception, awareness; that which is known; experience, information; learning; body of facts acquired by study; (*leg*) cognizance; **carnal k.** (*leg*) sexual intercourse; **to one's k.** as far as one knows.

knowledgeable [*noli*jab'l] *adj* (*coll*) intelligent, clever; well-informed ~ **knowledgeably** *adv*.

known [*nOn*] *p/part* of **know**.

knuckle [*nuk'l*] *n* joint of a finger, *esp* joint of finger to hand; carpal or tarsal joint of quadruped; joint of meat cut from this area; **near the k.** almost obscene ~ **knuckle** *v/t* and *i* touch, rub or strike with knuckles: **k. down** to work steadily at; submit to; **k. under** admit defeat, submit.

knucklebone [*nuk'l*-bOn] *n* bone of knuckles; joint of meat including knuckle; metacarpal or metatarsal bone of quadruped; (*pl*) boys' game played with sheep's knucklebones.

knuckleduster [*nuk'l*-duster] *n* metal guard protecting the knuckles in fist-fighting and serving to increase damage caused by a blow.

knur, knurr [*nur*] *n* hard knob on tree-trunk; wooden ball used in certain games.

knurl [*nurl*] *n* small hard knob; slight ridge on metal.

koala, koolah [kO-*aa*la, *kO*Ola] *n* (*Aust*) small bear-like marsupial animal living in trees.

koan [*kO*-an] *n* irrational riddle or problem used in Zen Buddhist teaching.

kobold [*kO*bold] *n* (*Germ myth*) house-haunting puck; mine-haunting gnome.

Kodak [*kO*dak] *n* (*tr*) type of portable camera.

koedoe, koodoo, kudu [*kOO*dOO] *n* large white-striped African antelope.

kohl [*kOl*] *n* powdered antimony used as eye-shadow.

kohlrabi [*kOl*Raabi] *n* cabbage with turnip-shaped stem.

kola see **cola**.

kolinsky [ko*lin*ski] *n* Siberian mink.

kolkhoz [kol*koz*] *n* (*Rus*) Soviet collective farm.

koodoo see **koedoe**.

kook [*kOOk*] *n* (*coll*) unconventional or eccentric person.

kookaburra [*kOO*kabuRa] *n* large Australian kingfisher.

kooky [*kOO*ki] *adj* (*coll*) very up-to-date and sophisticated; eccentric or bohemian in fashion, unconventional, easy-going, unpredictable.

koolah see **koala**.

kopeck, kopek, see **copeck**.

kopje [*kopi*] *n* (*South African Dutch*) hillock.

Koran [ko*Raan*] *n* sacred book of Muslims.

kosh see **cosh**.

kosher, cosher [*kO*sher] *adj* (*Heb*) pure, fulfilling requirements of Jewish law; (*coll*) acceptable, genuine.

kotow see **kowtow**.

koumiss, kumis [*kOO*mis] *n* fermented liquor made by Tatars from mares' milk.

kourbash [*koor*bash] *n* Turkish and Egyptian leather-thonged whip.

kowtow, kotow [kow*tow*, kO*tow*] *n* act of kneeling and bowing to the ground, formerly used in China ~ **kowtow, kotow** *v/i* make a kowtow, (*fig*) defer to obsequiously.

kraal [*kRaal*] *n* South African native fenced village of huts surrounding cattle enclosure ~ **kraal** *v/t* confine in a kraal.

krait [*kRIt*] *n* a venomous Indian snake.

kraken [*kRaa*ken] *n* legendary gigantic Scandinavian sea-monster.

Kremlin [*kRem*lin] *n* (*Rus*) town citadel *esp* that in Moscow; (*fig*) government of Soviet Union.

kriegspiel [*kReeg*shpeel] *n* (*Germ*) game in which pieces representing military units are manoeuvred on maps.

krill [*kRil*] *n* plankton.

krimmer [k*Ri*mer] *n* grey lambskin fur.

kris [*kRis*] *n* wavy-bladed Malay dagger.

krone [*kRO*ni] *n* Scandinavian silver coin; former Austrian silver coin; former German gold piece.

kryptol [*kRi*ptol] *n* mixture of graphite, carborundum and clay used as an electrical resistance.

krypton [*kRi*pton] *n* (*chem*) an inert gas which occurs in the atmosphere > PDS.

kudos [*kew*dos] *n* (*coll*) credit, fame, glory.

kudu see **koedoe**.

Ku-Klux-Klan [*kOO*-kluks-klan] *n* secret society periodically active in Southern States of America working to exalt white racial supremacy and terrorize Negroes and Jews.

kukri [*kook*Ri] *n* curved Gurkha knife.

kulak [*kOO*lak] *n* Russian peasant landowner.

kumis see **koumiss**.

kummel [*kim*el] *n* (*Germ*) liqueur flavoured with cumin.

kumquat [*kum*kwot] *n* Chinese citrus fruit used in the making of preserves and confectionery.

kung fu [koong *foo*] *n* Chinese form of karate.

Kuomintang [kwOmin*tang*] *n* Chinese nationalist party; Chinese government driven out by communist revolution of 1949.

kvas, kvass [*kvas*] *n* (*Rus*) rye beer.

kwashiorkor [*kwa*shi-orkor] *n* disease caused by lack of proteins in the diet.

kyloe [*kr*lO] *n* (*Scots*) breed of long-horned Highland cattle.

Kymric see **Cymric.**

kyrie eleison [kiRi-ay-*elay*-ison] *n* (*Gk* = Lord have mercy) (*eccles*) in RC and Eastern Churches the words of a supplication, *esp* as used in the Mass; musical setting of these words.

L

l [el] twelfth letter of the English alphabet;
anything shaped like an L; Roman numeral
= 50; L plates metal plates on which an L is
painted, attached to the front and rear of a motor
vehicle to indicate that the driver is a learner
and has not yet passed the official driving-test.

la (1) [la/laa] exclam (ar) expressing surprise.

la (2), lah [laa] n (mus) sixth note of the octave
in tonic sol-fa; sixth note in the scale of C major,
A.

laager, lager [laager] n (S African Dutch) camp
enclosed by a circle of waggons for defence ~
laager, lager v/i form a laager.

lab [lab] n (coll abbr) laboratory.

label [laybel] n strip of paper or other material for
fixing to an object and inscribing with a name,
address or other information; (fig) descriptive
phrase applied to a person or group; (archi)
dripstone ~ label v/t fix label to; (fig) characterize, classify; (phys) replace a stable atom (in a
compound) with a radioisotope so that its path
may be monitored.

labial [laybi-al] n and adj (phon) (sound) made by
the lips ~ labialize v/t and i modify (sound)
by lip action ~ labially adv.

labile [laybIl] adj unstable; prone to change or
move.

labio- pref pertaining to the lips.

labiodental [laybi-Odental] n and adj (phon)
(sound) produced simultaneously by lips and
teeth.

labiovelar [laybi-Oveelar] n and adj (phon) (sound)
produced simultaneously by lips and throat.

laboratory [laboRatoRi] n building or room
equipped and used for scientific experiments;
language l. set of cubicles equipped with tape-
recorders etc for teaching foreign languages.

laborious [labawRi-us] adj industrious; involving hard work; showing signs of much effort
~ laboriously adv ~ laboriousness n.

labour [layber] n hard work, toil; task; manual
work; those who work as employees for their
living, esp at heavy manual work; the working
classes; (cap) supporters of the Labour Party;
pains of childbirth, parturition; L. Exchange
State-organized agency for finding jobs for unemployed workers; hard l. work imposed on
criminals as penalty; L. of Hercules very
strenuous task; l. leader Trade Union administrator; l. of love task gladly undertaken;
L. Party (pol) political party of moderate Socialist
views in Britain and certain other English-speaking countries. > PDPol ~ labour v/i and t work
hard, exert oneself; strive, toil; be afflicted by;
have difficulty in doing; discuss lengthily or over-
emphatically; be in childbirth; (naut) roll.

laboured [layberd] adj showing signs of great
effort; not spontaneous; clumsy, over-emphatic;
over-elaborate.

labourer [laybeRer] n worker; manual worker;
farm-worker.

labouring [laybeRing] adj that labours; l. man
manual worker.

labourite [laybeRit] n (pol) supporter of the
Labour Party.

labour-saving [layber-sayving] adj designed to
reduce the amount of manual work.

labrador [labRadawr] n a breed of Newfoundland
dog.

laburnum [laburnum] n small tree bearing
drooping clusters of yellow flowers.

labyrinth [labiRinth] n complex network of
winding paths; maze; anything very complex
and intricate ~ labyrinthine [labiRinthIn] adj.

lac (1) [lak] n shellac.

lac (2), lakh n (Indian) a hundred thousand
(rupees).

lace [lays] n fine patterned mesh or net-like
fabric; string or thong used as fastening, esp
for shoes etc; ornamental gold braid; small
quantity of spirits added to coffee etc ~ lace v/t
and i fasten by a lace; ornament with lace; mix
spirit into; make lace; l. into (coll) thrash;
criticize severely.

lacepaper [layspayper] n paper cut or embossed
in lacy pattern.

lacerate [laseRayt] v/t tear; cut, slash; distress
bitterly, wound the feelings of ~ lacerate adj
(biol) jagged ~ laceration [laseRayshon] n.

lace-ups [lays-ups] n (pl) (coll) shoes or boots
fastened by laces.

lacewing [layswing] n insect with large gauzy
wings.

laches [lachiz] n (leg) negligence; unreasonable
delay in making a claim.

lachrymal [lakRimal] adj of or relating to tears;
secreting tears ~ lachrymal n (arch) phial to
contain tears.

lachrymatory [lakRimatoRi] adj relating to or
causing tears ~ lachrymatory n (arch) phial
to contain tears.

lachrymose [lakRimOs] adj very ready to weep;
tearful ~ lachrymosely adv.

lacing [laysing] n act or method of tying; rope
etc used as a fastening; light wooden or metal
bars reinforcing a strut > PDE; (coll) thrashing.

lack [lak] n absence; need; shortage, dearth;
destitution; for l. of due to deficiency of; no l.
of enough of ~ lack v/t and i be without; need;
be wanting.

lackadaisical [lakadayzikal] adj languid, listless;
dreamy ~ lackadaisically adv.

lackaday [lakaday] interj (ar) alas!

lackey [laki] n liveried manservant; (fig) servile
person ~ lackey v/t attend upon as manservant;
(fig) be obsequious to.

lacking [laking] adj (coll) feeble-minded, stupid.

lacklustre [lakluster] adj dull, dim.

laconic, laconical [lakonik, lakonikal] adj using
few words; pithy, terse ~ laconically adv.

lacquer [laker] n hard glossy varnish made of
shellac; one of various resinous Oriental varnishes;

object coated with lacquer ~ **lacquer** *v/t* coat with lacquer ~ **lacquering** *n* act of coating with lacquer; decoration with lacquer.

lacrymator [*lak*Rimayter] *n* tear gas.

lacrosse [la*k*Ros] *n* game in which a small ball is carried and thrown by a stick with a net in its curved end.

lactase [*lak*tayz] *n* (*bioch*) enzyme which catalyses the conversion of lactose into glucose.

lactation [lak*tay*shon] *n* act of secreting milk; act of suckling; period of suckling > PDB.

lacteal [*lak*ti-al] *adj* of or like milk; (*anat*) carrying a milky fluid ~ **lacteals** *n* (*pl*) (*anat*) vessels of the mesentery carrying chyle > PDB.

lactic [*lak*tik] *adj* (*chem*) of or relating to milk; formed from sour milk > PDS, PDB; **l. acid** organic acid formed during the souring of milk.

lactiferous [lak*tife*Rus] *adj* secreting milk; (*bot*) secreting milky juice.

lacto- *pref* relating to milk.

lactose [*lak*tOs] *n* sugary substance occurring in milk > PDS.

lacuna (*pl* **lacunae**) [la*kew*na] *n* gap, empty space, *esp* in book *etc* ~ **lacunal** *adj*.

lacustrine [la*kust*Rin] *adj* of or relating to lakes.

lacy [*lay*si] *adj* of or like lace.

lad [*lad*] *n* boy; young man; (*coll*) man of dashing and (often) wild character.

ladder [*lad*er] *n* device for climbing, consisting of two parallel supports and numerous cross-pieces serving as foot-holds; vertical flaw in fabric of stocking *etc* caused by broken thread; (*fig*) means of achieving success, fame *etc* ~ **ladder** *v/i* and *t* (*of stockings*) develop a vertical flaw.

laddie, laddy [*lad*i] *n* (*Scots dim*) lad.

lade (*p/t* **laded**, *p/part* **laden** or **laded**) [*layd*] *v/t* put cargo or freight into or onto; load; remove with a ladle.

laden [*lay*den] *adj* loaded down; burdened.

la-di-da [*laa*-di-daa] *adj* (*coll*) giving oneself superior airs; high-class; affected in manners, voice *etc*.

ladies [*lay*diz] *n* (*sing*) (*coll*) women's public lavatory.

lading [*lay*ding] *n* cargo, freight.

ladle [*layd*'l] *n* deep long-handled spoon ~ **ladle** *v/t* scoop or serve out with a ladle; **l. out** (*fig*) distribute lavishly.

lady [*lay*di] *n* upper-class woman, gentlewoman; woman having good manners and education and honourable character; (*coll*) any woman; woman with whom a man is in love; housewife; (*coll*) wife; (*pl*) mode of address to the women in a gathering; **L.** title of wives of baronets, knights, and peers below the rank of duke; title of daughters of peers above the rank of viscount; **L. Bountiful** benefactress; patronizing and interfering woman addicted to works of charity; **L. Chapel** chapel dedicated to the Virgin Mary within a larger church; **L. Day** the March quarter-day, March 25; **Our L.** the Virgin Mary; **l.'s maid** female servant whose duty is to attend to a lady's clothes and personal requirements; **l.'s man** man who enjoys courteous flirtation with women ~ **lady** *adj* female.

ladybird [*lay*diburd] *n* small red or yellow black-spotted flying beetle.

lady-help [*lay*di-help] *n* woman who does housework for wages but is not of the working class.

ladyhood [*lay*dihood] *n* status or quality of a lady.

lady-in-waiting [laydi-in-*way*ting] *n* attendant to a lady of royal rank.

ladykiller [*lay*dikiler] *n* (*coll*) man with flair for attracting women.

ladylike [*lay*dilIk] *adj* looking or behaving like a lady; genteel; (*pej*) unmanly.

ladylove [*lay*diluv] *n* darling, sweetheart.

ladyship [*lay*diship] *n* condition or status of lady; **her l., your l., their ladyships** (*respectful and occasionally ironical forms of address and designation*).

ladysmock [*lay*dismok] *n* wild orchis.

laevo-, levo- *pref* towards the left.

laevorotary [layv*OROta*Ri] *adj* (*chem*) rotating to the left, *esp* the plane of polarization of light by certain crystals.

laevulose, levulose [*lee*vewlOs, *lev*ewlOs] *n* (*chem*) fruit-sugar, fructose.

lag (1) (*pres/part* **lagging**, *p/t* and *p/part* **lagged**) [*lag*] *v/i* move more slowly than another, be too slow; loiter, linger ~ **lag** *n* retardation, delay; time between the action of a force and its effect; lapse of time.

lag (2) *n* (*coll*) convict or ex-convict, *esp* one who has been to jail several times ~ **lag** (*pres/part* **lagging**, *p/t* and *p/part* **lagged**) *v/t* (*sl*) put in jail; arrest.

lag (3) (*pres/part* **lagging**, *p/t* and *p/part* **lagged**) *v/t* insulate (boiler, hot-water pipes *etc*) with wrappings, boards *etc* against loss of heat ~ **lag** *n* board used in lagging boiler *etc*; stave of a cask.

lagan [*lag*an] *n* (*leg*) goods or wreckage resting on seabed.

lager (1) [*laa*ger] *n* a type of light beer.

lager (2) see **laager**.

laggard [*lag*ard] *n* and *adj* (person or thing) that moves too slowly.

lagging [*lag*ing] *n* covering material for boiler or pipes *etc*.

lagoon [lag*OOn*] *n* shallow stretch of salt water partly or wholly separated from the sea by a narrow strip of land; sheet of water enclosed by an atoll > PDG.

lah see **la** (2).

lahar [*lay*haar] *n* avalanche of mud.

laic [*lay*-ik] *n* layman ~ **laic** *adj* non-clerical, lay (2) ~ **laical** *adj*.

laicize [*lay*-isIz] *v/t* put under control of or make open to laymen; deprive of priestly status.

laid [*layd*] *p/t* and *p/part* of **lay** (3) ~ **laid** *adj* (*of paper*) having a ribbed appearance; **l. off** dismissed owing to shortage of work, *usu* only temporarily; **l. up** confined to bed by sickness.

lain [*layn*] *p/part* of **lie** (2).

lair [*lair*] *n* resting-place for animals, *esp* wild animals ~ **lair** *v/i* rest in a lair.

laird [*laird*] *n* (*Scots*) landowner ~ **lairdship** *n*.

laissez-aller [laysay-*alay*] *n* (*Fr*) lack of restraint, laxity in manners or morals.

laissez-faire, laisser-faire [laysay-*fair*] *n* (*Fr*) policy of non-interference, absence of governmental controls.

laity [*lay*-iti] *n* persons not in Holy Orders; those not belonging to a particular profession.

lake (1) [*layk*] *n* large sheet of water enclosed by land > PDG; **the L. District** a region of north-west England containing many lakes; **l. dwellings** prehistoric houses built on piles in lakes > PDG; **L. Poets** Wordsworth, Coleridge and their immediate circle.

lake (2) *n* a reddish pigment ~ **laky, lakey** *adj*.

lakeland [*layk*land] *n* the Lake District.

lakh see **lac** (2).

laky [*layki*] *adj* of or like a lake; having many lakes.

Lallans [*lalanz*] *n* and *adj* (speech) of the Lowlands of Scotland.

lalling [*laling*] *n* continuous repetition of a single speech-sound.

lam (*pres/part* **lamming**, *p/t* and *p/part* **lammed**) [*lam*] *v/t* (*sl*) beat, thrash.

lama [*laa*ma] *n* Buddhist priest in Mongolia or Tibet; **Dalai** (or **Grand**) **L.** chief Tibetan Lama.

Lamaism [*laa*ma-izm] *n* Tibetan and Mongolian form of Buddhism.

Lamarckism [*la*maarkizm] *n* (*biol*) view that acquired characteristics are inherited > PDB.

lamasery [*la*maaseRi] *n* monastery of lamas.

lamb [*lam*] *n* young sheep; flesh of this as food; (*coll*) dear child; **the L. (of God)** Christ ~ **lamb** *v/i* and *t* (*of sheep*) give birth (to); tend lambing ewes.

lambaste [*lam*bayst] *v/t* (*coll*) thrash; criticize severely.

lambent [*lam*bent] *adj* (*of flames*) gently flickering, licking but not burning a surface; having soft clear light; (*fig*) light and witty, playful ~ **lambently** *adv*.

lambert [*lam*bert] *n* unit of brightness, the uniform brightness of a perfectly diffusing surface emitting one lumen per square centimetre > PDS.

lambing [*lam*ing] *n* time when lambs are born; birth of lamb.

lambkin [*lam*kin] *n* small lamb.

lamblike [*lam*līk] *adj* gentle.

lambskin [*lam*skin] *n* dressed skin of lamb complete with wool; leather made from lamb's skin.

lambswool [*lamz*wool] *n* soft wool from lambs; hot ale spiced and sweetened and mixed with the pulp of roasted apples.

lame [*laym*] *adj* having leg or foot injured or defective; walking with a limp; (*fig*) inadequate, unconvincing; (*ar*) disabled in any limb; (*pros*) not smooth in movement; **l. duck** (*coll*) helpless person; unprofitable business enterprise; Stock Exchange defaulter; damaged ship; (*US*) one who is finishing a term of office and has not been reelected ~ **lame** *v/t* make lame.

lamé [*laa*may] *n* and *adj* (fabric) interwoven with thread of gold or of silver.

lamella (*pl* **lamellae**) [*la*mela] *n* (*zool*) thin bony plate; scale; layer > PDB ~ **lamellar** *adj* ~ **lamellate** [*la*melayt] *adj*.

lamelliform [*la*melifawrm] *adj* like a thin plate.

lamely [*laym*li] *adv* in a lame way; inadequately.

lameness [*laym*nis] *n* state of being lame.

lament [*la*ment] *v/i* and *t* feel or express deep grief (for or at); bewail, mourn; **the late lamen-ted** a dead person ~ **lament** *n* words, song or cries expressing deep grief; dirge; elegy.

lamentable [*la*mintab'l] *adj* distressing, grievous; wretched, deplorable; (*coll*) inferior, contemptible ~ **lamentably** *adv*.

lamentation [*la*min*tay*shon] *n* act of lamenting; lament.

lamia [*laymi*-a] *n* (*myth*) evil spirit in woman's form; female vampire; witch.

lamina (*pl* **laminae**) [*la*mina] *n* thin layer or plate; scale; leaf-blade ~ **laminal** *adj* ~ **laminar** *adj*.

laminable [*la*minab'l] *adj* (*metal*) suitable for beating or rolling into thin plates.

laminate [*la*minayt] *v/t* and *i* roll or beat into thin layers or plates; cover with thin metal sheets; build up (a material) by placing layer upon layer of material; make (plastic material) by subjecting sheets of material to pressure and heat > PDB1; split into thin sheets ~ **laminate** *n* a laminated structure ~ **laminated** *adj*.

lamination [*la*min*ay*shon] *n* act of laminating.

lamini- *pref* of or relating to thin layers.

Lammas [*la*mas] *n* 1st August.

lammergeyer [*la*mergī-er] *n* the bearded vulture.

lamming [*lam*ing] *n* (*coll*) thrashing.

lamp [*lamp*] *n* any device providing light by electricity or by burning oil or gas; (*fig*) source of knowledge or inspiration; device producing therapeutic rays; **smell of the l.** (*of a written work*) show signs of much toil.

lampblack [*lamp*blak] *n* black pigment made from soot.

lampion [*lamp*i-on] *n* small ornamental oil-lamp, *usu* with coloured glass.

lamplighter [*lamp*līter] *n* one whose job is to light street-lamps.

lampoon [*lampOO*n] *n* violently abusive or scurrilous satire ~ **lampoon** *v/t* write a lampoon about ~ **lampoonist** *n* writer of lampoons.

lamp-post [*lamp*-pOst] *n* strong pillar supporting street-lamp.

lamprey [*lamp*Ri] *n* eel-like fish with sucker mouth.

lampshade [*lamp*shayd] *n* covering to concentrate or diffuse the light from a lamp.

lanate [*lay*nayt] *adj* (*bot, zool*) woolly.

Lancastrian [*lan*kastRi-an] *n* and *adj* (person) born or living in Lancashire; (*hist*) (supporter) of the House of Lancaster in the Wars of the Roses.

lance [*laans*] *n* long-shafted weapon with metal-pointed head; similar weapon for spearing fish; **break a l. with** engage in argument with ~ **lance** *v/t* pierce with lancet; pierce with lance.

lance-corporal [*laans-kawr*poRal] *n* (*mil*) rank between private and corporal.

lanceolar [*laan*si-Oler] *adj* lanceolate.

lanceolate [*laan*si-Olayt] *adj* tapering to a point.

lancer [*laan*ser] *n* (*modern*) soldier belonging to regiment of Lancers; (*hist*) mounted soldier armed with lance; (*pl*) kind of quadrille; music for this.

lance-sergeant [*laans-saar*jant] *n* (*mil*) corporal acting as sergeant.

lancet [*laan*sit] *n* double-edged pointed surgical instrument; **l. arch** narrow arch with sharply pointed top; **l. window** narrow window tapering to sharp arch ~ **lanceted** *adj* having lancet arches or windows.

lanciform [*laan*sifawrm] *adj* narrow and sharp.

lancinating [*laan*sinayting] *adj* (*of pain*) acute.

lancination [laansi*nay*shon] *n* act of cutting with lancet; sharp stabbing pain.

land [*land*] *n* dry solid part of earth's surface; specified region forming geographical or political unit; country, nation; ground, soil; ground owned as property, estate; rural area, countryside; (*fig*) rural or agricultural life; **l. army** body of female farm workers in Britain in the Second World War; **l. hemisphere** northern half of the globe > PDG; **make l.** reach or see the shore; **see how the l. lies** find out the present state of affairs ~ **land** *adj* on, of or for the land ~ **land** *v/t* and *i* put or bring on shore; come to shore; disembark; set (aircraft) down on land or water; deposit from transport vehicle; put or come into difficulties; bring (fish) to shore; (*coll*) win, obtain; (*coll*) arrive; (*coll*) strike (*a blow*); **l. up** find oneself in, eventually arrive at.

land-agent [*land*-ayjent] *n* person employed to manage an estate; person dealing with the sale of land ~ **land-agency** *n*.

landau [*lan*daw] *n* four-wheeled horse-drawn carriage with folding hood; former type of motorcar with similar hood.

landaulet [landaw*let*] *n* former type of motorcar with folding hood at back.

land-breeze [*land*-bReez] *n* wind blowing during the day from the land out to sea > PDG.

land-chain [*land*-chayn] *n* (*sur*) measuring line.

land-crab [*land*-kRab] *n* crab living mainly on land but breeding in the sea.

landed [*land*id] *adj* owning land; consisting of or obtained from land or real estate; disembarked; (*coll*) in difficulties.

landes [*lawn*dz] *n* (*pl*) low sandy plains bordered by dunes.

landfall [*land*fawl] *n* first sighting of land after a voyage or flight over sea.

landfill [*land*fil] *n* (*eng*) material for filling disused pits, quarries *etc*.

land-girl [*land*-gurl] *n* woman employed as farm-worker, *esp* in wartime in Britain; member of the Women's Land Army.

landgrave [*land*-gRayv] *n* (*hist*) German count or prince ruling semi-independent territory.

land-hunger [*land*-hung-ger] *n* keen desire to own land ~ **land-hungry** *adj*.

landing [*land*ing] *n* act of coming or bringing to land; act of going ashore, *esp* by military force; level space between two flights of stairs; passage at top of stairs on to which rooms open; place where one disembarks.

landing-craft [*land*ing-kRaaft] *n* (*mil*) vessel designed to put troops ashore on hostile territory.

landing-net [*land*ing-net] *n* net for bringing large hooked fish to shore.

landing-stage [*land*ing-stayj] *n* platform for disembarkation of passengers or cargo; pier, jetty.

landlady [*land*laydi] *n* woman in charge of boarding-house or inn; woman who lets rooms; woman landlord.

landline [*land*lIn] *n* overland communication cable.

landlocked [*land*lokt] *adj* surrounded by land.

landloper, landlouper [*land*lOper] *n* (*Scots*) tramp, vagrant.

landlord [*land*lawrd] *n* owner of property let to tenants; man in charge of an inn or lodging-house.

landlouper see **landloper**.

landlubber [*land*luber] *n* one not accustomed to seafaring.

landmark [*land*maark] *n* conspicuous feature of landscape, by which one can recognize a locality; boundary-mark; (*fig*) that which marks an important change or new stage, turning-point.

landmass [*land*mas] *n* large area of land.

landmine [*land*mIn] *n* (*mil*) explosive charge hidden on or under the ground and detonated by passage of men or vehicles; (*pop*) bomb dropped by parachute.

landowner [*land*Oner] *n* person owning land.

landrail [*land*Rayl] *n* the corncrake.

landrover [*land*ROver] *n* sturdy motorcar resembling a jeep, used in agriculture *etc*.

landscape [*land*skayp] *n* rural scenery, *esp* as seen from a particular viewpoint; painting or photograph representing this; art of representing scenery; **l. gardening** art of laying out parks, large gardens *etc* in imitation of picturesque natural scenery ~ **landscape** *v/t* embellish by landscape gardening.

landscapist [*land*skaypist] *n* painter of landscapes.

landslide [*land*slId] *n* downward movement of mass of earth or rocks from mountain or cliff > PDG; (*pol*) overwhelming electoral victory.

landslip [*land*slip] *n* small landslide.

landsman (*pl* **landsmen**) [*land*zman] *n* one whose occupation is on land; (*naut*) landlubber.

land-surveying [*land*-survay-ing] *n* art of measuring and mapping tracts of land or buildings > PDE ~ **land-surveyor** *n*.

land-swell [*land*-swel] *n* heaving motion of sea near coast.

land-tax [*land*-taks] *n* tax levied on owners of land and buildings.

landward [*land*werd] *adj* and *adv* facing the land; towards the land ~ **landwards** *adv*.

land-wind [*land*-wind] *n* land-breeze.

lane [*layn*] *n* narrow road bordered by hedges *etc*; narrow street; regular route for ships or aircraft; each of two or more courses designated for vehicles moving abreast on the same road; path marked out for each competitor in a race.

lang syne, langsyne [lang-*sIn*] *n* and *adv* (*Scots*) (days) long ago.

language [*lang*-gwij] *n* system of vocal sounds by which a group of persons can communicate; graphic representation of this; any system of signs, gestures, symbols *etc* used as means of communication; characteristic way of using words, style of speaker or writer; specialized terminology of a science, profession, craft *etc*; **bad l.** swearing, profanity; obscene words; **dead l.** language no longer in spoken use; **strong l.** swearing; words expressing violent feeling.

languid [*lang*-gwid] *adj* lacking vitality, apathetic, listless ~ **languidly** *adv* ~ **languidness** *n*.

languish [*lang*-gwish] *v/i* become languid; be or

431

become unhealthy or weak; droop; pine, endure prolonged sufferings; gaze with sentimental melancholy ~ **languishing** *adj* that languishes; sentimental; yearning; melancholy.

languor [*lang*-ger] *n* mental or physical weariness; sentimental melancholy; lassitude > PDP ~ **languorous** *adj*.

langur [lung-*goor*] *n* Indian long-tailed monkey.

lank [*lank*] *adj* limp, hanging loosely; long and thin; lean; (*of hair*) straight and limp ~ **lankness** *n*.

lanky [*lanki*] *adj* thin and tall; lank ~ **lankily** *adv* ~ **lankiness** *n*.

lanner [*lan*er] *n* kind of Mediterranean falcon, *esp* the female ~ **lanneret** *n* male lanner.

lanolin [*lan*Olin] *n* waxy substance obtained from wool-grease and used in ointments and cosmetics.

lantern [*lan*tern] *n* portable and partly transparent case enclosing candle or oil-burning wick; upper chamber of lighthouse, containing the lights; (*archi*) glazed or open-sided structure on tower or dome *etc* to admit light or air > PDBI; **l. slides** small semi-transparent pictures to be projected on to a screen by a strong beam of light.

lantern-jawed [*lan*tern-jawd] *adj* having long narrow jaws and hollow cheeks.

lanthanide [*lan*thanId] *n* one of fifteen rare metallic elements; rare earth; lanthanon > PDS.

lanthanum [*lan*thanum] *n* (*chem*) rare element, first of the lanthanide series > PDS.

lanthorn [*lan*tern] *n* (*ar*) lantern.

lanyard [*lan*yaard] *n* (*naut*) short rope; cord on which a knife *etc* may be hung round the neck; (*mil*) loop of cord at shoulder of certain uniforms.

lap (1) (*pres/part* lapping, *p/t* and *p/part* lapped) [*lap*] *v/t* and *i* drink by rapid scooping movement of the tongue; make a sound resembling that of this action, splash softly; **l. up** drink by lapping; (*coll*) drink greedily; listen to or accept very eagerly ~ **lap** *n* act of lapping; sound of lapping.

lap (2) (*pres/part* lapping, *p/t* and *p/part* lapped) *v/t* and *i* wrap round, enfold; surround; place (something) so that it covers and projects beyond something else; complete one circuit of a race-track; have a lead of one circuit over ~ **lap** *n* one circuit of a race-track; (*fig*) stage in progress or development: that which overlaps; flap of cloth *etc*.

lap (3) *n* area from knees to waist of seated person; the part of a skirt *etc* covering this; **in the l. of luxury** in very luxurious surroundings.

lap (4) *n* revolving disc for cutting or polishing metal, glass, gems *etc*.

lapdog [*lap*dog] *n* small pet dog.

lapel [*lapel*] *n* part of coat doubled back below the neck on either side towards the shoulders.

lapidary [*lap*ideRi] *adj* inscribed on stone; suitable for inscription on stone; (*fig*) concise, precise; relating to the cutting, polishing or engraving of gems ~ **lapidary** *n* craftsman who cuts, polishes or engraves gems; expert on gems; medieval treatise on the miraculous qualities of stones and gems; **l. bee** wild bee that builds in crevices in stone walls.

lapis lazuli [lapis-*laz*ewlI] *n* a brilliant blue mineral > PDS; colour of this.

Laplander [*lap*lander] *n* member of a Mongoloid race inhabiting northern Scandinavia.

Lapp [*lap*] *n* Laplander ~ **Lapp** *adj*.

lappet [*lap*et] *n* loose fold, flap; loose hanging band on woman's hat.

Lappish [*lap*ish] *n* and *adj* (language) of Lapps.

laprobe [*lap*ROb] *n* (*US*) rug for the knees.

lapsable [*lap*sab'l] *adj* (*leg*) liable to lapse.

lapse [*laps*] *n* unimportant mistake or fault, slip; error; deviation from moral standards; gradual passage, *esp* of time; period of time now past; (*leg*) forfeiture by neglect or disuse ~ **lapse** *v/i* deviate from moral standards, err; pass gradually away; (*leg*) become forfeit by neglect or disuse; revert; cease to exist ~ **lapsed** *adj* fallen into error; no longer practising one's religion; (*leg*) in disuse; reverted.

lapse-rate [*laps*-Rayt] *n* (*meteor*) rate of temperature change with height in atmosphere > PDG.

lapwing [*lap*wing] *n* peewit, bird of the plover family.

lar (*pl* lares) [*laar*] *n* (*Rom myth*) household god; (*pl fig*) home.

larboard [*laar*bawrd] *n* (*naut*) left side of ship looking forward, port ~ **larboard** *adj*.

larceny [*laar*sini] *n* (*leg*) stealing, theft.

larch [*laarch*] *n* a coniferous tree; wood of this tree.

lard [*laard*] *n* refined pig fat used in cookery ~ **lard** *v/t* smear with lard; insert bacon fat into (meat) before cooking; intersperse (speech, style *etc*) with striking phrases ~ **lardy** *adj*.

larder [*laar*der] *n* storeroom for food.

lares [*lair*Reez] *pl* of **lar**.

large [*laarj*] *adj* of considerable size or amount; big; roomy, spacious; copious; far-reaching; generous; liberal ~ **large** *adv* in a large way; impressively ~ **large** *n* (*mus*) longest medieval note > PDM; **at l.** free, in general; amply.

large-handed [laarj-*hand*id] *adj* generous.

large-hearted [laarj-*haar*tid] *adj* sympathetic; generous, charitable; tolerant.

largely [*laarj*li] *adv* to a large extent or degree ~ **largeness** *n*.

largescale [*laarj*skayl] *adj* extensive; over a wide area; of large scope; (*of map*) on a large scale.

largess, largesse [laar*jes*] *n* (*ar*) money given, alms; bounty, generosity.

largish [*laarj*ish] *adj* somewhat large.

largo [*laarg*O] *adv* (*mus*) slowly and in noble style > PDM ~ **largo** *n* piece of music played slowly and nobly.

lariat [*la*Ri-at] *n* long rope with noose; lasso.

lark (1) [*laark*] *n* one of a genus of small birds including the skylark.

lark (2) *n* joke; prank ~ **lark** *v/i* play tricks.

larkspur [*laark*spur] *n* annual delphinium.

larky [*laark*i] *adj* playful, mischievous.

larn [*laarn*] *v/t* (*coll* or *dial*) teach; learn.

larrikin [*la*Rikin] *n* (*Aust sl*) young hooligan.

larrup [*la*Rup] *v/t* thrash; whip.

larva (*pl* larvae) [*laar*va] *n* insect in pre-adult state after emerging from the egg > PDB ~ **larval** *adj*.

laryngeal [la*Rin*ji-al] *adj* of the larynx.

laryngitis [laRin*jI*tis] *n* inflammation of the larynx.

laryngoscope [la*Ring*-gOskOp] *n* instrument consisting of mirrors by which the larynx can be seen.

larynx (*pl* **larynges**) [la*R*ingks] *n* (*anat*) cavity in windpipe containing vocal cords > PDB.

lasagne [laza*n*yi] *n* (*Ital*) ribbon-like pasta served with meat.

lascar [*las*kaar] *n* East Indian sailor.

lascivious [lasi*v*i-us] *adj* lustful, lewd ~ **lasciviousness** *adv* ~ **lasciviousness** *n*.

laser [*lay*zer] *n* optical maser > PDEl.

lash [*lash*] *v/t* and *i* strike violently; beat with a whip, flog; rouse to violence, provoke; twitch violently to and fro; tie with a rope, bind up; (*fig*) attack verbally, pour scorn on; **l. out** at lunge, kick; attack fiercely ~ **lash** *n* thong of a whip; stroke given with whip; eyelash.

lasher [*lash*er] *n* opening in, or pool below, a weir.

lashing [*lash*ing] *n* cord used as fastening; beating, thrashing; (*pl coll*) large quantity.

lash-up [*lash*-up] *n* (*coll*) hasty improvisation.

lass [*las*] *n* girl, sweetheart.

lassie [*las*i] *n* (*dim*) lass.

lassitude [*las*itewd] *n* weariness, weakness.

lasso [lasOO] *n* long rope or thong with running noose ~ **lasso** (*p/t* **lassoed**) *v/t* catch with a lasso.

last (1) [*laast*] *adj* coming at the end of a series in time or place; hindmost; conclusive, final; least in degree or merit; nearest in time preceding the present, most recent; newest, up-to-date; least likely; least desirable; **the L. Day** Doomsday; **l. straw** unbearable climax of many annoyances; **the L. Things** Death, Judgement, Hell and Heaven; **l. word** final conclusive argument; (*coll*) most recent thing; perfection ~ **last** *adv* finally, after all others; most recently ~ **last** *n* that which is last; end; that which is most recent; **see (hear) the l. of** see (hear) for the last time.

last (2) *v/i* continue, endure; remain in good condition; continue undiminished; **l. out** hold out; suffice.

last (3) *n* shoemaker's model of human foot.

last (4) *n* measure of weight or quantity.

last-ditch [*laast*-dich] *adj* stubbornly resisting attack till the last possible moment.

lastex [*las*teks] *n* (*tr*) type of elastic yarn.

lasting [*laas*ting] *adv* durable; permanent ~ **lastingly** *adv*.

lastly [*laast*li] *adv* finally, in the end.

latch [*lach*] *n* simple fastening for door, window or gate; spring lock which can be opened from outside with a key; **on the l.** secured only by latch; **off the l.** ajar ~ **latch** *v/t* and *i* fasten with a latch; be capable of being so fastened.

latchet [*lach*it] *n* (*ar*) leather shoelace.

latch-key [*lach*-kee] *n* key for opening the main door of a house; **l. child** schoolchild whose home is normally empty when he returns.

late [*layt*] *adj* happening or arriving after the expected or right time; happening towards the end of a stated period; recently ended, former; recently dead; recently existing or active ~ **late** *adv* after the expected or right time; towards the end of a period; at or till a late hour of night; **of l.** recently.

latecomer [*layt*kumer] *n* one who has arrived late.

lateen [la*teen*] *n* (*naut*) type of triangular sail for small boats; boat having such a sail.

lately [*layt*li] *adv* recently, not long ago.

latency [*lay*tensi] *n* quality of being latent.

lateness [*layt*nis] *n* state or quality of being late.

latent [*lay*tent] *adj* present but not yet fully active; hidden, dormant; **l. heat** heat required to effect a change of state without change of temperature > PDS; **l. period** (*med*) period of incubation of disease.

lateral [*late*Ral] *adj* of or at the side; towards the side; **l. thinking** ability to solve problems by unorthodox or imaginative ideas ~ **lateral** *n* that which is at the side; side branch or shoot ~ **laterally** *adv*.

latest [*lay*test] *adj* most recent ~ **latest** *n* (*coll*) most recent news or fashion; **at the l.** not later than.

latex [*lay*teks] *n* milky juice secreted by various plants > PDB; milky juice of the rubber tree.

lath [*laath*] *n* thin strip of wood used as base for plaster; slat in venetian blind.

lathe [*lay*TH] *n* machine on which wood or metal is turned to a circular shape.

lather [*la*THer/*laa*THer] *n* foam produced by soap or detergent in water; copious sweat of a horse ~ **lather** *v/i* and *t* form a lather; cover with lather; sweat freely; (*coll*) thrash, beat severely ~ **lathery** *adj*.

lati- *pref* broad.

Latin [*latin*] *n* language of the ancient Romans; member of any people speaking a language derived from this ~ **Latin** *adj* of ancient Rome; in the Latin language; pertaining to the Roman Catholic Church; **L. America** American countries having Spanish or Portuguese as their main language; **L. Quarter** area of Paris mainly inhabited by artists and students; **L. races** people speaking a language derived from Latin.

Latinate [*latin*ayt] *adj* resembling or borrowing from Latin.

Latinism [*latin*izm] *n* Latin idiom.

Latinist [*latin*ist] *n* scholar of Latin.

latinity [*latin*iti] *n* Latin scholarship.

latinize [*latin*Iz] *v/t* and *i* put into Latin; use words or idioms borrowed from Latin; bring into conformity with Roman Catholic practices or beliefs ~ **latinization** [latinIzayshon] *n*.

latitude [*lati*tewd] *n* freedom from restrictions, toleration; scope; angular distance of a place north or south of the equator > PDG; (*pl*) regions ~ **latitudinal** [latitewdinal] *adj*.

latitudinarian [latitewdinai*R*i-an] *n* and *adj* (person) of liberal views in religious matters.

latrine [la*tReen*] *n* privy, *esp* in camp.

latten [*laten*] *n* alloy resembling brass.

latter [*later*] *adj* second; more recently mentioned (of two); (*ar*) latest, final; **L. Day** Doomsday; **L. Day Saints** Mormons; **l. end** death.

latterday [*later*day] *adj* modern; recent.

latterly [*later*li] *adv* recently.

lattice [*latis*] *n* structure of laths or pieces of metal crossed diagonally > PDE; window with glass framed by cross-strips of lead; (*chem*) network of fixed points about which molecules, atoms, or ions vibrate in a crystal; (*phys*) regular structure of fissile material and moderator in a nuclear reactor.

laud [*lawd*] *v/t* praise, approve of ~ **laud** *n* (*eccles*) praise; (*pl*) liturgical prayers recited at dawn.

laudable [*lawd*ab'l] *adj* praiseworthy ~ **laudably** *adv.*

laudanum [*lod*anum] *n* tincture of opium.

laudatory [*lawd*ateRi] *adj* expressing praise.

laugh [*laaf*] *v/i* and *t* utter inarticulate vocal sounds expressing amusement, joy or scorn, *gen* with a smile; express or utter by laughing; (*fig*) give an impression of peace and joy; **l. at** be amused by; make fun of, ridicule; defy, ignore; **l. away** dispel by laughter; **l. in the face of** defy; deride; **l. in one's sleeve** laugh secretly; **l. off** turn (an embarrassing or threatening situation) into a joke ~ **laugh** *n* act of laughing; sound of laughing; **have the l. of** score off.

laughable [*laafab'l*] *adj* ridiculous.

laughing [*laaf*ing] *adj* that laughs; expressing joy or amusement; causing laughter; **l. gas** nitrous oxide, used as mild anaesthetic > PDS; **l. hyena** spotted hyena; **l. jackass** giant Australian kingfisher.

laughing-stock [*laaf*ing-stok] *n* person or thing arousing ridicule.

laughter [*laaf*ter] *n* act of laughing; sound of laughing.

launce [*laans*] *n* the sand-eel.

launch (1) [*lawnch*] *v/t* and *i* set in motion; begin, initiate; set (vessel) afloat, *esp* for the first time; fire (rocket); start (person) in career; set out from shore; **l. into** begin enthusiastically; **l. out** begin some large undertaking ~ **launch** *n* act of launching.

launch (2) *n* large boat used for pleasure or as patrol-boat and *usu* motor-driven; largest boat carried by warship.

launching-pad [*lawn*ching-pad] *n* hard flat surface from which rocket is launched.

launder [*lawn*der] *v/t* and *i* wash and iron linen and clothes; (*of fabrics*) be capable of being washed.

launderette [lawnde*Ret*] *n* place where washing machines can be used on paying a fee.

laundress [*lawnd*Res] *n* woman whose job is to launder linen or clothes.

Laundromat [*lawnd*ROmat] *n* (*tr, US*) automatic clothes-washing machine; launderette.

laundry [*lawnd*Ri] *n* place where clothes and linen are laundered; clothes *etc* requiring washing; clothes *etc* freshly laundered.

laureate [*law*Ri-at/*loRi*-at] *adj* crowned with laurel as a mark of distinction; **Poet L.** poet appointed to the British Royal Household and expected to write poems on state occasions ~ **laureateship** *n* office of Poet Laureate.

laurel [*lo*Rel] *n* bay-tree or any plant of its genus; its foliage as an emblem of victory or distinction; **rest on one's laurels** be satisfied with what one has already achieved ~ **laurelled** *adj* adorned with laurel; distinguished.

laurustinus [loRust*i*nus] *n* an evergreen spring-flowering shrub.

lava [*laa*va] *n* molten rock issuing from volcano and hardening as it cools > PDG.

lavatory [*lav*ateRi] *n* room fitted with washbasins and water-closets; water-closet, privy.

lave [*lay*v] *v/t* (*poet*) wash; (*of river*) flow past.

lavender [*lav*ender] *n* plant with pale purple flowers cultivated for its scent; scent of this;

pale purple colour; **lay up in l.** preserve carefully; **l. water** scent distilled from lavender.

laver (1) [*lay*ver] *n* kind of edible seaweed.

laver (2) *n* (*poet*) basin for washing.

lavish [*lav*ish] *adj* generous, liberal, prodigal ~ **lavish** *v/t* bestow recklessly; squander ~ **lavishly** *adv* ~ **lavishness** *n*.

law [*law*] *n* rule imposed by authority; body of rules enforced by government on a community; one such rule; any custom, rule or principle widely accepted and observed in a community, class, profession *etc*; generalized formulation based on a series of events or processes observed to recur regularly under certain conditions; widely observable tendency; general or instinctive tendency; the legal profession; jurisprudence; legislation; (*sport*) allowance of time or distance, a start; **go to l.** start a lawsuit; **have the l. on** start legal action against, prosecute; **l. Latin** type of debased Latin in legal documents; **lay down the l.** speak with offensive self-assurance, domineer; **L. Lords** peers qualified by judicial experience to deal with legal questions in the House of Lords; **L. Officer** legal adviser to the Government; Attorney or Solicitor General; **the l.** (*coll*) police; a policeman.

law-abiding [*law*-ab*Iding*] *adj* keeping the law; peaceable; respectable.

lawbreaker [*law*bRayker] *n* criminal, one who has broken a law ~ **lawbreaking** *n*.

lawful [*law*fool] *adj* keeping the law; permitted by law; (*of offspring*) legitimate ~ **lawfully** *adv* ~ **lawfulness** *n*.

lawgiver [*law*giver] *n* framer and promulgator of laws.

lawless [*law*les] *adj* without law; not conforming to law; not restrained by law, unruly ~ **lawlessly** *adv* ~ **lawlessness** *n*.

lawn (1) [*lawn*] *n* fine linen; (*fig*) episcopacy.

lawn (2) *n* stretch of flat ground covered with close-mown grass.

lawnmower [*lawn*mO-er] *n* machine for cutting grass of a lawn.

lawn-sprinkler [lawn-*spRing*-kler] *n* hose with revolving nozzle.

lawn-tennis [lawn-*tenis*] *n* form of tennis played in the open air upon grass or hard court.

lawrencium [lawr*Rensi*-um] *n* (*chem*) a transuranic element > PDS.

lawsuit [*law*sewt] *n* case heard in a court of law.

lawyer [*law*yer] *n* member of legal profession, *esp* solicitor.

lax [*laks*] *adj* careless; slack; not strict; (*of bowels*) acting easily ~ **laxly** *adv* ~ **laxness** *n*.

laxative [*laks*ativ] *n* and *adj* (medicine) causing easy action of bowels.

laxity [*laks*iti] *n* slackness; lack of principles; imprecision.

lay (1) [*lay*] *n* short narrative poem; ballad; short lyric; song.

lay (2) *adj* not in holy orders; non-professional; **l. brother** (**sister**) man (woman) who has taken the vows of a religious order, but is employed mostly in manual work; **l. reader** layman licensed to conduct certain religious services.

lay (3) (*p/t* and *p/part* laid) *v/t* and *i* put down, place; cause to lie in a certain position; cause to fall, knock down; cause to subside, settle **or**

disappear; (*of birds*) produce an egg; set in order, arrange (*esp* eating utensils *etc* on a table or firewood and coals in a grate); wager, bet; propose the odds in betting; accuse, make a charge; impose as tax, duty *etc*; assert; (*naut*) place in dock; (*sl, of men*) have intercourse with; **l. aboard** (*naut*) come alongside; **l. about one** fight energetically; **l. aside** store up; set aside; discard; discontinue; **l. before** bring to the notice or judgement of; **l. by** set aside, discard; store up; **l. by the heels** imprison; catch; **l. down** discard, relinquish; sacrifice; declare, assert; decree; plan; **l. eyes on** catch sight of; **l. hands on** seize, take by force; find; (*eccles*) confirm, consecrate, ordain; heal by prayer and touch; **l. in** gather stores of; **l. off** temporarily dismiss from work; (*sl*) cease; keep away from; (*naut*) steer (vessel) further away; **l. on** apply; provide lavishly; strike; supply (water, gas, electricity) to a house; **l. it on** (*coll*) flatter; exaggerate; **l. open** expose; cut open, gash; **l. out** arrange in good order, display; arrange (corpse) for burial; spend (money); plan; knock down, stun; **l. oneself out** exert oneself; **l. to** (*naut*) halt (ship); ascribe to; **l. up** put away; store up; (*pass*) be kept in bed by illness; **l. upon** impose ~ **lay** *n* act of laying eggs; direction in which something is laid or lies; (*coll*) course of action, plan; (*sl*) criminal occupation; (*coll*) wager; (*sl*) sexual partner, *usu* the passive one.

lay (4) *p/t* of **lie** (2).

layabout [*lay*-abowt] *n* tramp, loafer.

layby [*lay*bI] *n* recessed space beside a road in which vehicles may park without hindering traffic; railway siding.

layer [*lay*-er] *n* one who lays odds; hen which lays (many, few) eggs; [*lair*] stratum; thickness of substance spread over a surface; (*hort*) branch of growing shrub pressed into the earth so that it may strike roots ~ **layer** [*lair*] *v/t* (*hort*) bend layer and cover with earth; make a layer of.

layette [lay-*et*] *n* outfit of clothes, blankets *etc* for a newborn baby.

layfigure [*lay*figer] *n* jointed model of the human figure used by artists; (*fig*) nonentity.

laying on [*lay*-ing-on] *n* **l. of hands** (*eccles*) act of ritually touching in order to bless, heal, ordain or confirm.

layman [*lay*man] *n* one not in holy orders; one who is not qualified in a particular science or profession.

lay-off [*lay*-of] *n* temporary dismissal from work.

layout [*lay*owt] *n* planning of land, streets *etc*; design of printed matter; rough draft; drawing showing general plan of construction.

layshaft [*lay*shaaft] *n* secondary shaft of a machine, *esp* in gearbox.

lazar [*laz*er] *n* (*ar*) leper; diseased beggar.

lazaretto [laza*Ret*O] *n* place for quarantine.

laze [layz] *v/i* spend one's time idly, loaf about; do nothing; rest oneself ~ **laze** *n* act of lazing; time spent in lazing.

lazy [*lay*zi] *adj* idle, unwilling to act, slothful ~ **lazily** *adv* ~ **laziness** *n*.

lazybones [*lay*zibOnz] *n* (*coll*) lazy person.

lazy-tongs [*lay*zi-tongz] *n* (*pl*) extensible tongs to lift things at a distance.

lea (1) [*lee*] *n* (*poet*) meadow, grassland.

lea (2) *n* length of yarn.

leach [*leech*] *v/t* wash mineral salts out from (soil, ore *etc*) ~ **leach** *n* brine which drains out when salt is leached.

lead (1) [*led*] *n* a heavy fusible metal element > PDS; lump of this used in sounding at sea; graphite used in pencils; (*typ*) metal strip separating lines; blacklead; (*pl*) sheets of lead covering roofs or parts of roofs; **l. line** weighted sounding line; **red l.** oxide of lead; **swing the l.** (*sl*) find a plausible excuse for malingering; **white l.** lead carbonate ~ **lead** *adj* made of lead ~ **lead** *v/t* cover with lead; insert lead strips in.

lead (2) (*p/t* and *p/part* led) [*leed*] *v/t* and *i* guide, conduct; persuade, influence; act as chief of, play the chief part in; govern, direct; walk at the head of; bring; experience or cause to experience; be ahead, be the first; be the chief; excel; (*of roads*) be the means of reaching, go to; (*cards*) play first card; (*mil*) command; **l. astray** mislead, give bad example to; **l. off** make a start; make first move; **l. on** lead forward; lure; **l. out of** (*of rooms*) communicate directly with; **l. to** have as result; **l. up to** approach (a topic) gradually ~ **lead** *n* act of leading; initiative; hint or example on how to act; capacity to act first; dominating or most active part; front place in a race; distance between the foremost competitor and the next; leash or chain to lead a dog, horse *etc*; electric wire or cable; clue; (*theat*) most important role; actor or actress playing this; (*cards*) right to play first; first card played; artificial watercourse; channel in icefield; (*journalism*) main or opening paragraph; main or first story in newspaper or broadcast news bulletin.

leaded [*led*id] *adj* (*typ*) separated by leads; **l. lights** (*bui*) small panels of glass held in lead cames.

leaden [*led*en] *adj* made of lead; dark grey; heavy, unresponsive, dull ~ **leadenness** *n*.

leader [*leed*er] *n* one who or that which leads; editorial article in newspaper; chief of a political party; leading competitor in a race; (*mus*) principal violin; chief member of an ensemble; (*US*) conductor of orchestra or band; (*leg*) senior counsel; (*hort*) strongest shoot or branch; (*typ*) group of two or three dots across a page.

leaderette [leede*Ret*] *n* short leading article.

leadership [*lee*dership] *n* exercise of authority in a social group; status of being a leader; qualities needed by a leader; group of leaders.

lead-in [*leed*-in] *n* (*rad*) wire connecting aerial to receiver; preliminary remarks.

leading (1) [*leed*ing] *n* authority, guidance; **men of light and l.** influential teachers ~ **leading** *adj* that guides; controlling; foremost; **l. article** newspaper article expressing editor's views, *esp* on political questions; **l. actor** (**actress**) one who plays the chief role; **l. case** (*leg*) case establishing a precedent; **l. lady** leading actress; **l. light** (*coll*) prominent person; **l. note** seventh degree of major scale > PDM; **l. question** question which suggests the required answer; **l. strings** straps supporting a baby when learning to walk; (*fig*) excessive guidance, strict control.

leading (2) [*led*ing] *n* (*bui*) lead glazing.

lead-off [*leed*-of] *n* (*coll*) beginning, start.

leadswinger [*led*swinger] *n* (*sl*) malingerer.

leady [*ledi*] *adj* resembling lead, *esp* in colour.

leaf (*pl* **leaves**) [*leef*] *n* basic organ of photosynthesis in plants, *usu* flat and green; thin sheet of paper; page of book, folio; hinged, retractable or removable flap of a table; very thin sheet of metal; **in l.** having leaves; **take a l. from the book of** imitate; **turn over a new l.** reform one's conduct ~ **leaf** *v/i* and *t* (*of plants*) form leaves; **l. through** turn the pages of, glance quickly through.

leafage [*leefij*] *n* foliage.

leafless [*leefles*] *adj* without leaves.

leaflet [*leeflet*] *n* small pamphlet; (*bot*) small leaf; subdivision of compound leaf; (*zool*) organ resembling small leaf.

leafmould [*leefmOld*] *n* compost formed from rotted leaves.

leafy [*leefi*] *adj* abounding in leaves; of or like a leaf ~ **leafiness** *n*.

league (1) [*leeg*] *n* (*ar*) three miles.

league (2) *n* alliance; compact between states or persons to protect or further their common interests; association, group of persons or clubs *etc* linked by a common aim; group of sports clubs playing each other for a championship; **L. of Nations** international organization 1920–1946 > PDPol ~ **league** *v/t* and *i* join together in a league ~ **leaguer** *n* member of a league.

leak [*leek*] *v/i* (*of liquids or gas*) pass into or out of a vessel through a crack or hole; ooze slowly in or out; **l. out** (*fig*) become illicitly or accidentally known ~ **leak** *n* crack or hole through which gas or liquid leaks; gas or liquid that leaks in or out; amount of this; escape of electric charge through faulty insulation; (*fig*) unauthorized disclosure.

leakage [*leekij*] *n* process of leaking; liquid lost or entering through a leak; allowance for leakage; unaccountable gradual disappearance of something; unauthorized disclosure.

leaky [*leeki*] *adj* having a leak, inclined to leak ~ **leakily** *adv* ~ **leakiness** *n*.

leal [*leel*] *adj* (*Scots*) loyal, true.

lean (1) [*p/t* and *p/part* **leaned** or **leant**) [*leen*] *v/i* and *t* be out of perpendicular, slope; rest against; support oneself on; rely on; cause to lean; be inclined to; **l. over backward** (*coll*) make excessive efforts to counteract or avoid something ~ **lean** *n* act of leaning; degree of slope; inclination.

lean (2) *adj* thin, gaunt; (*of meat*) without fat; (*of plant*) not nutritious; (*of soil*) poor ~ **lean** *n* lean part of cooked meat.

leaning [*leening*] *n* act or condition of one who leans, inclination; predilection, tendency.

leanness [*leen-nis*] *n* quality of being lean (2).

leant [*lent*] *p/t* and *p/part* of **lean** (1).

lean-to [*leen-tOO*] *n* building whose sloping roof leans against wall of another building; penthouse.

leap (*p/t* and *p/part* **leaped** or **leapt**) [*leep*] *v/t* and *i* jump over or across; spring upwards, make a jump or series of jumps; cause (a horse) to leap; copulate; **l. at** accept eagerly ~ **leap** *n* act of leaping, jump; distance leapt; sudden movement up or forwards; **by leaps and bounds** very quickly; **a l. in the dark** action whose consequences cannot be foreseen, risk; **l. year** year when February has twenty-nine days.

leapfrog [*leepfRog*] *n* game in which one player bends down while another leaps over him from behind ~ **leapfrog** *v/t* play at leapfrog; (*fig*) overtake one another in turn.

leapt [*lept*] *p/t* and *p/part* of **leap**.

learn (*p/t* and *p/part* **learned** or **learnt**) [*lurn*] *v/t* and *i* acquire knowledge (of); acquire skill (in); commit to memory; hear, get to know about; experience; try to become or develop by practice; (*sl*) teach ~ **learned** [*lurnid*] *adj* having or showing much knowledge, erudite; relating to study or scholarship ~ **learnedly** *adv* ~ **learner** *n* one who is learning; novice, apprentice.

learning [*lurning*] *n* act or process of acquiring knowledge > PDP; acquired knowledge; extensive knowledge gained by study, erudition.

learnt [*lurnt*] *p/t* and *p/part* of **learn**.

lease [*lees*] *n* contract whereby one party conveys land or tenements to the other for a stipulated time in return for rent; (*fig*) time during which something is granted; **new l. of life** renewal of vitality ~ **lease** *v/t* let out on lease; hold by lease ~ **leasable** *adj*.

leasehold [*lees-hOld*] *n* and *adj* (tenure) by lease ~ **leaseholder** *n*.

lease-lend, lend-lease [*lees-lend*, *lend-lees*] *n* agreement whereby during World War II the USA lent or gave warships, munitions *etc* to her Allies in exchange for the use of military bases; system of mutual aid among the Allies after the war ~ **lease-lend** *v/t*.

leash [*leesh*] *n* strap or chain by which dogs are held; group of three hounds or hares; thong by which hawk is held; **strain at the l.** strive impatiently to be free ~ **leash** *v/t* hold by a leash.

least [*leest*] *adj* smallest ~ **least** *adv* to the smallest degree or extent ~ **least** *n* smallest amount or degree; **at l.** at any rate; **not in the l.** not at all.

leastways [*leestwayz*] *adv* (*dial*, *sl*) leastwise.

leastwise [*leestwIz*] *adv* at least.

leather [*leTHer*] *n* skin of animals prepared by tanning; article made from this; stirrup strap; football; cricket-ball; (*pl*) riding-breeches ~ **leather** *adj* made of leather ~ **leather** *v/t* cover with leather; (*coll*) thrash.

leatherette [*leTHeRet*] *n* cloth and paper imitation of leather.

leather-jacket [*leTHer-jakit*] *n* larva of crane-fly.

leathern [*leTHern*] *adj* of or like leather.

leatherneck [*leTHernek*] *n* (*US sl*) US Marine.

leathery [*leTHeRi*] *adj* like leather; tough; dry.

leave (1) [*leev*] *n* permission; permission to go or remain away; time spent away from work or duty (*esp mil*); holiday; **French l.** absence without permission; **take l.** say goodbye.

leave (2) (*p/t* and *p/part* **left**) *v/t* and *i* go away (from); cease to remain (in); (*obs*) depart; fail to take or bring; allow to remain untaken, unchanged, unused *etc*; abandon, desert; have at the time of one's death; bequeath; entrust (to); deposit; pass beyond; cause to be in (a specified state); (*ar*) cease; (*arith*) yield as remainder; **l. alone** not touch, disturb, or interfere with; **l. behind** not take or bring; **l. (one) cold** rouse no interest (in); **l. go** cease to grip, let go; **l. off**

cease; cease to wear; **l. out** omit; fail to take into account.

leaved [*leevd*] *adj* having a specified number or type of leaves.

leaven [*leven*] *n* substance which makes dough rise, yeast; (*fig*) that which modifies the character, spiritual influence ~ **leaven** *v/t* raise by leaven; mix with leaven; modify, influence.

leaves [*leevz*] *pl* of **leaf**.

leave-taking [*leev*-tayking] *n* act of saying good-bye, *esp* ceremoniously.

leavings [*leev*ingz] *n* (*pl*) what is left; scraps from a meal; cast-off rubbish.

lecher [*lech*er] *n* one who freely indulges his sexual instincts.

lecherous [*lech*eRus] *adj* lustful ~ **lecherously** *adv* ~ **lecherousness** *n*.

lechery [*lech*eRi] *n* habitual sexual indulgence.

lectern [*lek*tern] *n* reading-desk in church.

lectionary [*lek*shoneRi] *n* book containing the lessons read in church throughout the year.

lecture [*lek*cher] *n* informative discourse before an audience; rebuke, admonition; **read one a l.** reprove one ~ **lecture** *v/t* and *i* deliver a lecture or course of lectures (to); reprove, scold.

lecturer [*lek*cheRer] *n* one who delivers lectures, *esp* in college or university ~ **lectureship** *n* office of lecturer.

led [*led*] *p/t* and *p/part* of **lead** (2).

ledge [*lej*] *n* narrow shelf projecting from wall; projection from face of cliff; one of the horizontal timbers on the back of a batten door.

ledger [*lej*er] *n* (*comm*) book containing debit and credit accounts, *esp* of a business or firm; horizontal pole in a scaffolding > PDBl; stone slab covering grave or coffin.

ledger-bait [*lej*er-bayt] *n* fishing bait anchored to one place.

lee [*lee*] *n* (*naut*) shelter, protection; side that is sheltered from the wind ~ **lee** *adj* farthest removed from the wind; **l. shore** shore on to which the wind blows; **l. tide** tide running in the same direction as the wind.

leeboard [*lee*bawrd] *n* wooden framework fixed to side of flat-bottomed vessel to diminish her drift to leeward.

leech (1) [*leech*] *n* (*ar, joc*) physician.

leech (2) *n* blood-sucking worm living in ponds; (*fig*) one who persistently gets profit from another.

leech (3) *n* (*naut*) free edge of a sail.

leek [*leek*] *n* vegetable akin to onion.

leer (1) [*leer*] *n* sidelong furtive smirk or glance; lustful look ~ **leer** *v/i*.

leer (2) *n* place where glass is annealed.

leery [*leer*Ri] *adj* (*sl*) cunning; wary.

lees [*leez*] *n* (*pl*) sediment of wine, dregs.

leeward [*lOO*erd/*lee*werd] *adj* and *adv* on or towards the lee, away from the wind ~ **leeward** *n* lee ~ **leewardly** *adj* (*of ship*) drifting to leeward.

leeway [*lee*way] *n* drift of ship to leeward of her course; (*fig*) loss of progress or time; (*coll*) margin of time *etc*, room for manoeuvre; **make up l.** make up for delay.

left (1) [*left*] *p/t* and *p/part* of **leave** (2).

left (2) *adj* on or of that side of a body where the heart normally is; in the direction of one's left

side; (*pol*) socialist, radical ~ **left** *adv* towards the left ~ **left** *n* left side or direction; left hand; (*pol*) party or group of socialist, liberal, or radical beliefs.

left-hand [*left*-hand] *adj* on the left side; done with the left hand.

left-handed [*left*-*han*did] *adj* habitually using the left hand rather than the right; designed to be used with the left hand or twisted towards the left; **l. compliment** ambiguous compliment implying a reproach; insincere compliment; **l. marriage** morganatic marriage ~ **left-handedly** *adv* ~ **left-handedness** *n*.

left-hander [*left*-*han*der] *n* left-handed person; stroke or blow given with left hand.

leftish [*left*ish] *adj* tending towards left-wing political views.

leftist [*left*ist] *n* and *adj* (supporter) of socialism, radicalism, or liberalism.

leftover [*left*Over] *n* and *adj* (something) remaining unused, uneaten, unsold *etc*.

leftward [*left*werd] *adv* on or towards the left.

left-wing [*left*-*wing*] *adj* socialist, radical, or liberal; tending to more extreme radical views than the rest of a group or party; (*sport*) stationed on the left of the centre-forward ~ **left-winger** *n*.

leg [*leg*] *n* limb on which an animal stands and walks; artificial limb corresponding to this; slender support on which furniture *etc* rests; animal's leg as food; one stage in a journey; part of garment covering human leg; (*cricket*) area of field to batsman's left; (*naut*) tack to windward; **l. before wicket** (*cricket*) the deflection by batsman's legs of a ball which would otherwise have hit the wicket; **get on one's hind legs** (*coll*) stand up, *esp* to speak; **give a l. up** help someone to climb; (*fig*) help; **have no l. to stand on** have no justification or defence; **make a l.** (*ar*) bow; **on one's last legs** very nearly dead or obsolete; exhausted; **pull the l. of** make fun of, tease; **shake a l.** (*sl*) dance; hurry; **l. show** (*theat*) entertainment specializing in nude or semi-nude female participants; **show a l.** (*coll, naut*) get out of bed ~ **leg** (*pres/part* **legging**, *p/t* and *p/part* **legged**) *v/t* and *i* (*coll*) trip up; **l. it** walk; run; run away.

legacy [*leg*asi] *n* money or property bequeathed by will; (*fig*) something handed down; consequence.

legal [*leeg*al] *adj* pertaining to law; permitted by law; required by law ~ **legally** *adv*.

legalism [*leeg*alizm] *n* undue respect for legal forms; (*theol*) doctrine of justification by works ~ **legalist** *n* and *adj* ~ **legalistic** [leeg*alist*ik] *adj*.

legality [lee*gal*iti] *n* lawfulness; quality of being in conformity with law.

legalize [*leeg*aliz] *v/t* make legal, authorize ~ **legalization** [leeg*al*Izayshon] *n*.

legate (1) [*leg*at] *n* envoy who represents the Pope; delegate.

legate (2) [li*gayt*] *v/t* (*leg*) bequeath.

legatee [lega*tee*] *n* one to whom a legacy has been bequeathed.

legation [le*gay*shon] *n* a diplomatic mission below the status of an embassy resident in a foreign capital; the official residence of the minister in charge of the mission; the offices of the mission.

legato [legaatO] *adj* and *adv* (*mus*) (performed) smoothly not staccato.

legend [lejend] *n* unreliable story based on oral tradition but popularly thought to have some factual basis; group of such tales; (*fig*) famous person of whom such tales are told; account of a saint's life; inscription on coin or medal; inscription below a picture; **Golden L.** medieval collection of saints' lives ~ **legendary** *adj* of or like a legend; known only through legends; tending to inspire legends ~ **legendary** *n* collection of legends.

legendry [lejendRi] *n* legends collectively.

legerdemain [lejerdemayn] *n* conjuring trick.

legged [legd/legid] *adj* having a specified type or number of legs.

legging [leging] *n* (*gen pl*) outer covering of cloth or leather to protect the leg from knee to ankle.

leggo [legO] *exclam* (*coll*) let go!

leggy [legi] *adj* long-legged ~ **legginess** *n*.

leghorn [leghawrn/legawrn] *n* straw plaiting for hats; hat made from this; a breed of domestic fowl.

legible [lejib'l] *adj* (*of writing*) clear enough to be read easily ~ **legibly** *adv* ~ **legibility** [lejibiliti] *n*.

legion [leejon] *n* body of troops; vast host, multitude; large organized group; (*hist*) infantry unit in Roman army; **British L.** an ex-service men's association; **Foreign L.** corps of foreign volunteers in French army; **L. of Honour** French order of chivalry and merit ~ **legionary** *n* and *adj* (member) of a legion.

legislate [lejislayt] *v/i* make laws.

legislation [lejislayshon] *n* act of making laws; body of laws enacted.

legislative [lejislativ] *adj* pertaining to legislation; having the duty of law-making; enacted by legislation ~ **legislatively** *adv*.

legislator [lejislayter] *n* maker of laws.

legislature [lejislacher] *n* body of persons who make, repeal or amend laws.

legist [leejist] *n* one versed in law.

legit [lejit] *adj* (*sl*) legitimate, *esp* of plays.

legitimacy [lejitimasi] *n* fact or quality of being legitimate.

legitimate [lejitimit] *adj* lawful, rightful; born of lawfully married parents; justifiable, reasonable; (*of kings*) lawfully inheriting the throne; **l. drama** (*theat*) plays, as contrasted with variety shows, pantomimes, films *etc* ~ **legitimate** [lejitimayt] *v/t* make legitimate; give the status of legitimate child to (a bastard) ~ **legitimately** *adv* ~ **legitimation** [lejitimayshon] *n*.

legitimatize, legitimize [lejitimatIz, lejitimIz] *v/t* make legitimate.

legman [legman] *n* one whose work requires much travelling, *esp* a reporter or salesman.

legpull [legpool] *n* trick, practical joke.

leg-room [leg-ROOm] *n* sufficient space to stretch one's legs out.

legume [legyoom] *n* pod, fruit that liberates its seeds by splitting; plant that bears such fruit; such plants used as fodder, *esp* clover.

legumin [ligewmin] *n* proteid substance in seeds of leguminous plants.

leguminous [ligewminus] *adj* bearing legumes; of or like a legume.

lei [lay] *n* Polynesian garland of flowers.

leister [leester] *n* salmon-spear.

leisure [lezher] *n* freedom from work; free unoccupied time; at one's l. at one's convenience ~ **leisured** *adj* having much leisure.

leisurely [lezherli] *adj* having leisure; calm, without haste ~ **leisurely** *adv* ~ **leisureliness** *n*.

leitmotiv [lIttmOteef] *n* (*Germ*) (*mus*) theme used recurrently to denote a specific person, object, feeling *etc* > PDM; (*fig*) recurrent imagery or association of ideas.

lem [lem] *n* vehicle for landing on the moon from a spacecraft.

lemming [leming] *n* small arctic migratory rodent.

lemon [lemon] *n* pale yellow citrus fruit with acid juice; tree which bears this; pale yellow colour; (*sl*) ugly girl; (*sl*) dishonest trick; **l. drop** boiled sweet with lemon flavour; **l. sole** type of plaice; **l. squash** lemonade, *esp* if highly concentrated ~ **lemon** *adj* made or flavoured with lemons; pale yellow.

lemonade [lemonayd] *n* drink made with sweetened lemon juice and water or synthetic lemon flavouring, soda-water flavoured with lemon and concentrated.

lemur [leemer] *n* (*zool*) nocturnal arborial mammal resembling the monkey ~ **lemuroid** [lemyoorRoid] *adj*.

lemures [lemewReez] *n* (*pl*) (*Rom myth*) ghosts.

lend (*p/t* and *p/part* **lent**) [lend] *v/t* grant someone the temporary possession or use of; let out (money) at interest; contribute, impart; (*refl*) be suitable for; consent to do; **l. a hand** give help ~ **lendable** *adj* that can be lent ~ **lender** *n*.

lending-library [lending-lIbReRi] *n* institution from which books may be borrowed.

lend-lease see **lease-lend**.

length [length] *n* measurement from end to end of a thing; duration of time; extent of distance; range; at l. eventually; in great detail; for a long time; at full l. stretched right out; by a l. (*racing*) by the distance of its own length; go to any l. do anything, however unpleasant or wicked; keep at arm's l. keep at a distance; (*fig*) treat coldly.

lengthen [lengthen] *v/t* and *i* make longer; become longer.

lengthways, lengthwise [lengthwayz, lengthwIz] *adv* in the direction of the length.

lengthy [lengthi] *adj* very long; lasting too long; verbose, diffuse ~ **lengthily** *adv* ~ **lengthiness** *n*.

lenience, leniency [leeni-ens, leeni-ensi] *n* mercifulness, absence of severity; tolerance ~ **lenient** *adj* ~ **leniently** *adv*.

Leninism [leninizm] *n* political and economic principles of Lenin ~ **Leninist** *n* and *adj*.

lenitive [lenitiv] *adj* and *n* soothing (medicine).

lenity [leniti] *n* mildness, mercifulness.

lens [lenz] *n* any device (*usu* a piece of glass) which causes a beam of rays to converge or diverge on passing through it > PDS; (*anat*) transparent structure behind pupil of eye in vertebrates > PDB.

lent (1) [lent] *p/t* and *p/part* of **lend**.

Lent (2) n (eccles) forty-day period of penances and fasting from Ash Wednesday till Easter Saturday inclusive; L. lily daffodil; L. term school or college term ending at Easter.

lenten [lenten] adj pertaining to Lent, used in Lent; (fig) meagre.

lenticular [lentikyooler] adj shaped like a lens or a lentil; pertaining to the lens of the eye.

lentil [lentil] n seed of a leguminous plant, dried and used for food.

lentisk [lentisk] n the mastic tree.

lentoid [lentoid] adj shaped like a lens or lentil.

Leo [lee-O] n (astron) constellation of the Lion, fifth sign of the zodiac.

leonine [lee-onIn] adj of or like a lion.

leopard [leperd] n large spotted carnivorous animal of the cat tribe, the panther; (her) lion portrayed sideways, but looking full-faced out of the shield; American l. the jaguar; snow l. the ounce ~ leopardess n female leopard.

leotard [lee-Otaard] n close-fitting body-garment, usu with long sleeves and attached tights, worn by dancers, acrobats etc.

leper [leper] n one suffering from leprosy.

Lepidoptera [lepidopteRa] n (pl) order of insects including butterflies and moths > PDB ~ lepidopterous adj.

leprechaun [lepRekawn] n (Irish folklore) sprite in form of little old man.

leprosarium [lepRosaarRi-um] n hospital or colony for lepers.

leprosy [lepRosi] n disease forming white scales upon the skin and causing loss of feeling, esp in hands and feet ~ leprous adj.

lepton [lepton] n (phys) collective name for electrons, muons, and neutrinos > PDS.

lesbian [lezbi-an] adj pertaining to homosexuality among women ~ lesbian n female homosexual ~ lesbianism n.

lese-majesty [leez-majesti] n high treason.

lesion [leezhon] n injury, damage; (path) morbid change affecting bodily functions.

less [les] adj smaller; of smaller amount; fewer ~ less adv to a smaller extent ~ less prep minus, except for ~ less n smaller amount; smaller share; inferior or younger person.

lessee [lesee] n one who holds a property on lease.

lessen [lesen] v/t and i make or become less.

lesser [leser] adj less, smaller.

lesson [leson] n something to be learnt by a pupil; instruction given in school; anything taught by experience or observation; warning example; portion of Scripture read at religious service.

lessor [lesawr] n one who grants a lease.

lest [lest] conj in case, for fear that.

let (1) [let] n (ar) impediment; (lawn tennis) service in which ball touches top of net before falling on the other side ~ let (pres/part letting, p/t and p/part let or letted) v/t (ar) prevent, hinder.

let (2) (pres/part letting, p/t and p/part let) v/t permit, allow, cause; cause (blood) to flow; hire out (accommodation) for rent; assume, suppose; imp in 1st and 3rd pers expressing wish or command; l. alone not interfere with; have nothing to do with; (coll) not to mention; l. be leave in peace; l. down lower; lengthen; leave in the lurch, fail; disappoint; l. go cease to

grip; set free, release; pay no more attention to; l. in allow to enter; insert; l. loose set free, unchain; l. off emit; fire (gun); excuse from punishment, treat leniently; (of house etc) let in portions; l. on (coll) reveal; pretend; l. out release; reveal accidentally; make (garment) wider; hit out; (coll) remove suspicion from, exonerate; l. slip release (hounds); miss (opportunity); accidentally reveal; l. up (coll) slacken, cease.

letdown [letdown] n (coll) disappointment; anticlimax.

lethal [leethal] adj that kills or could kill; l. chamber room where persons or animals are killed by gassing.

lethargic [lithaarjik] adj torpid, drowsy.

lethargy [letharji] n state of unnatural drowsiness; inactivity; apathy.

Lethe [leethi] n (Gk myth) river whose waters caused forgetfulness; (fig) the forgetting of one's past life, griefs etc ~ Lethean [leethee-an] adj.

let-out [let-owt] n (coll) opportunity to escape.

lettable [letab'l] adj that may be let, suitable for letting.

letter [leter] n written, printed or engraved symbol representing a sound or sounds of speech; written communication; (pl) literature, authorship, scholarship; (pl) document of authorization, certification etc; (pl) capacity to read; the l. of the law rigidly literal interpretation of the law ~ letter v/t and i mark letters (on); draw letters.

letter-bomb [leter-bom] n explosive package sent to victim by post.

letterbox [leterboks] n receptacle in which letters are posted or delivered.

lettercard [leterkaard] n card that can be folded and sealed by a gummed edge.

letterhead [leterhed] n name, address etc of firm or person printed on sheet of writing paper.

lettering [leteRing] n act of writing, drawing or engraving letters; actual letters so inscribed; style in which this is done.

letterpress [leterpRes] n (typ) printing from type; words as distinguished from illustrations.

lettuce [letis] n plant with soft large leaves much used as salad.

let-up [let-up] n (coll) pause, interruption.

leuc-, leuco- pref white.

leucocyte [lOOkOsIt] n white blood corpuscle.

leucorrhoea [lOOkoRee-a] n (path) mucous discharge from lining membrane of the female genital organs.

leucotomy [lOOkotomi] n (surg) the cutting of white matter between the prefrontal lobe and the thalamus in order to modify behaviour in certain mental cases.

leukaemia [lOOkeemi-a] n (path) disease characterized by excess of white corpuscles in the blood.

Levant (1) [livant] n countries adjoining the eastern Mediterranean ~ levanter n wind blowing from the east through the Straits of Gibraltar > PDG; inhabitant of the Levant.

levant (2) v/i run away, abscond, esp leaving unpaid debts ~ levanter n.

Levantine [livantIn] n and adj (inhabitant) of the Levant; (ship) trading with the Levant.

levee (1) [levi/livee] n natural bank formed during

levee–liberate

flooding by deposition of silt > PDG; (*US*) artificial embankment of river.

levee (2) [*levi*/*levay*] *n* reception held by a king for men only.

level [*level*] *n* horizontal surface, plane; flat ground; gallery in a mine; specified height; normal height; standard, status, *esp* social, moral or intellectual; instrument to test whether a surface is truly horizontal, or to measure differences of altitude > PDE; **on a l. with** (*fig*) equal in status or standards; **on the l.** (*coll*) honest, aboveboard ~ **level** *adj* horizontal; flat, smooth; equal in status or standards; calm, sensible; (*mus*) not varying in pitch; (*phon*) equally stressed on both syllables; **one's l. best** one's utmost; **l. crossing** place where road and railway cross at the same level ~ **level** *adv* so as to be level; in a level way ~ **level** (*p*/*part* **levelling**, *p*/*t* and *p*/*part* **levelled**) *v*/*t* make level; put on the same level; demolish; aim (weapon); (*phon*) reduce distinct sounds to one sound; **l. down** equalize by lowering the higher of two standards, groups *etc*; **l. off** reach and maintain a steady level; cease rising or falling; make or become smooth; **l. up** equalize by raising the lower of two standards, groups *etc* ~ **levelly** *adv*.

level-headed [*level-hedid*] *adj* sensible; calm.

lever [*leever*] *n* rigid bar rotating on a fixed point of support and used to raise or shift a heavy object > PDE, PDS; any device applying force in this way; (*fig*) means of influencing ~ **lever** *v*/*t* and *i* use a lever on; act as a lever.

leverage [*leeveRij*] *n* action of a lever; power of a lever; system of levers; (*fig*) means of influencing.

leveret [*leveRit*] *n* young hare.

leviable [*levi*-ab'l] *adj* (*of tax*) capable of being levied.

leviathan [*livI*-athan] *n* sea-monster; huge ship; anything enormous.

levis [*leevIs*] *n* (*pl*) (*tr*) type of strong denim jeans with metal rivets.

levitate [*levitayt*] *v*/*i* and *t* rise or raise into the air by non-physical means; become or make buoyant > PDP ~ **levitation** [*levitayshon*] *n*.

Levite [*leevIt*] *n* Jew of the tribe of Levi, *esp* one acting as assistant to the priests; (*coll*) Jew; (*coll*) priest.

Leviticus [*levitikus*] *n* third book of the Pentateuch, containing laws relating to Jewish priests.

levity [*leviti*] *n* flippancy, frivolity; instability; inconstancy; (*phys*) lightness, buoyancy.

levy [*levi*] *n* imposition or collection of a tax; tax imposed by decree; military conscription; conscripted troops ~ **levy** *v*/*t* and *i* impose a tax, tribute or fine; conscript (troops); raise money by a levy; **l. war** declare and begin war.

lewd [*lewd*/*lOOd*] *adj* unchaste, licentious; indecent, obscene; (*ar*) ignorant ~ **lewdly** *adv* ~ **lewdness** *n*.

Lewis gun [*lOO*-is-gun] *n* light machine-gun fired from the shoulder.

lewisite [*lOO*-isIt] *n* lethal blistering liquid containing arsenic > PDS.

lexical [*leksikal*] *adj* pertaining to vocabulary; pertaining to dictionaries ~ **lexically** *adv*.

lexicographer [*leksikogRafer*] *n* compiler of a dictionary.

lexicography [*leksikogRafi*] *n* compilation of

dictionaries ~ **lexicographical** [*leksikogRafikal*] *adj*.

lexicon [*leksikon*] *n* dictionary, *esp* of dead languages; round game played with letters.

ley (1) [*lay*] *n* land temporarily sown with grass.

ley (2) *n* imaginary straight line supposedly linking prehistoric landmarks.

Leyden jar [*layden-jaar*] *n* form of electrostatic condenser > PDS.

lez [*lez*] *n* (*sl*) lesbian.

li [*lee*] *n* Chinese measure of length, $\frac{1}{3}$ of a mile.

liability [*lI*-*abiliti*] *n* predisposition, tendency (to); (*leg*) condition of being legally answerable; sum which one is bound to pay; (*coll*) disadvantage, unwelcome responsibility, handicap.

liable [*lI*-ab'l] *adj* apt, inclined; subject to; likely to have or suffer; (*leg*) bound, responsible.

liaise [lee-*ayz*] *v*/*i* (*coll*) **l. with** act as means of communication and coordination between.

liaison [lee-*ayzon*] *n* association, cooperation; illicit sexual relationship; (*mil*) coordination and communication between two units or allied armies, or between higher and lower commands; (*phon*) joining of final consonant of one word to initial vowel of next; **l. officer** officer acting as link between units, armies or commands.

liana, liane [li-*aana*, li-*aan*] *n* tropical climbing plant > PDG.

liar [*lI*-er] *n* one who tells lies.

lias [*lI*-as] *n* (*geol*) blue limestone.

lib [*lib*] *n* and *adj* liberal (in politics); liberation, *esp* from legal or social oppression; **Gay L.** militant movement to liberate homosexuals from legal or social penalties; **Women's L.** movement seeking economic, social and legal equality for women.

libation [lI*bayshon*] *n* act of pouring out wine as religious offering; (*coll*) drink, drinking bout.

libel [*lIbel*] *n* (*leg*) written or printed statement likely to damage a person's reputation; act of publishing such a statement; (*pop*) harmful misrepresentation; untrue and harmful remark ~ **libel** (*pres*/*part* **libelling**, *p*/*t* and *p*/*part* **libelled**) *v*/*t* (*leg*) publish a libel against; (*pop*) misrepresent, untruthfully detract from the merits of.

libellous [*lIbelus*] *adj* constituting a libel ~ **libellously** *adv*.

liberal [*libeRal*] *adj* generous; abundant, ample; broad-minded, tolerant; having wide sympathies; enlightened, advanced in views; favouring political liberty and democratic reforms; **L. Party** (*pol*) progressive but non-Socialist British political party > PDPol ~ **Liberal** *n* member of the Liberal Party; (*no cap*) person of tolerant and progressive views.

liberalism [*libeRalizm*] *n* aims and principles of the Liberal Party; broad-mindedness, tolerance; progressive outlook ~ **liberalist** *adj* and *n* ~ **liberalistic** [*libeRalistik*] *adj*.

liberality [*libeRaliti*] *n* quality of being liberal; generosity; bountifulness.

liberalize [*libeRalIz*] *v*/*t* and   make liberal-minded; become liberal ~ **liberalization** [*libeRalIzayshon*] *n*.

liberally [*libeRali*] *adv* generously; abundantly.

liberate [*libeRayt*] *v*/*t* set free, release; (*chem*) allow (gas) to escape ~ **liberation** [*libeRayshon*] *n* act or process of setting free ~ **liberator** [*libe*Rayter] *n* one who sets free.

libertarian [libert*air*Ri-an] *n* one who holds doctrine of the freedom of the will; advocate of liberty ~ **libertarian** *adj*.

libertine [*liberteen*] *n* person who habitually leads a sexually immoral life, debauchee; (*ar*) freethinker ~ **libertine** *adj*.

libertinism [*libertinizm*] *n* agnosticism, freethinking; debauchery, licentiousness.

liberty [*liberti*] *n* freedom; absence of all undesired compulsion or restraint; opportunity, permission; offensive lack of self-restraint, insulting attitude or behaviour; (*pl*) privileges or rights conferred by grant; **at l.** free; not busy; not in use; **civil l.** liberty of a citizen to act as he chooses without interfering with the liberty of others or infringing the law; **religious l.** freedom to believe and worship as one chooses without interfering with the beliefs and worship of others; **take liberties with** act insultingly towards; tamper with.

libidinal [*libid*inal] *adj* pertaining to libido.

libidinous [*libid*inus] *adj* lustful, lewd.

libido [lib*id*O] *n* (*psych*) sexual desire; total life-energy of the individual > PDP.

Libra [*leeb*Ra] *n* (*astron*) the constellation of the Scales, seventh sign of the zodiac.

librarian [l*ibRair*Ri-an] *n* custodian of a library ~ **librarianship** *n*.

library [*l*I*b*RERi] *n* a collection of books; place where books are kept and can be consulted; establishment containing books which can be borrowed by the public or by members of some association; series of books of similar kind issued by the same publisher.

librate [*l*I*b*Rayt] *v/i* oscillate from side to side; poise or balance.

libration [l*ib*rayshon] *n* (*astron*) an oscillation of the moon.

librettist [lib*Ret*ist] *n* writer of libretti.

libretto (*pl* **libretti/librettos**) [lib*Ret*O] *n* text of an opera or musical play.

lice [*l*Is] *pl* of **louse**.

licence [*l*Isens] *n* permission granted by authority; document granting permission; excessive freedom; lack of discipline; undisciplined conduct, licentiousness; **poetic l.** justifiable deviation by writer from strict accuracy or rules.

license [*l*Isens] *v/t* grant a licence to or for; authorize ~ **licensed** *adj* having a licence, authorized, *esp* to sell liquor; having special privileges; **l. victualler** publican authorized to sell food and drinks.

licensee [lIsen*see*] *n* one to whom a licence is granted, *esp* to sell alcoholic drinks.

licenser [*l*Isenser] *n* one who grants licences, *esp* to publish books or perform plays.

licentiate [lIsen*shi-it*] *n* one authorized by licence to practise a specified profession.

licentious [lIsen*shus*] *adj* lascivious, dissolute ~ **licentiously** *adv*.

lichen [*lich*en/*l*Iken] *n* one of a class of cryptogamous plants formed by symbiotic association of a fungus and an alga > PDB; (*med*) a pustular skin-disease ~ **lichinous** *adj*.

lichgate, lychgate [*lich*ga͞yt] *n* roofed gateway to churchyard.

licit [*l*Isit] *adj* lawful, permitted ~ **licitly** *adv*.

lick [*lik*] *v/t* pass the tongue over; flicker round, touch lightly; (*coll*) defeat thoroughly; thrash; puzzle; **l. the boots of** cringe before, flatter abjectly; **l. the dust** be knocked down; be killed or defeated; **l. into shape** educate, improve the manners or efficiency of ~ **lick** *n* act of licking; area where animals gather to lick the salt in the soil; small amount; (*coll*) spurt of speed or energy; heavy blow; **a l. and a promise** quick superficial wash ~ **licking** *n* and *adj*.

licketysplit [*like*tisplit] *adv* (*US sl*) very fast.

lickspittle [*liks*pit'l] *n* a toady.

licorice see **liquorice**.

lictor [*lik*ter] *n* (*Rom hist*) officer who attended a magistrate.

lid [*lid*] *n* covering for open top of a vessel; one of the movable coverings of the eyeball; (*sl*) helmet; hat, cap; **put the l. on** (*coll*) bring to an end, be the climax to ~ **lidded** *adj* having a lid; having eyelids.

lido [*leed*O/*l*I*d*O] *n* open-air swimming pool, *usu* with terrace, bandstand, *etc*.

lie (1) [*l*I] *n* false statement made deliberately and with evil intentions; deceptive appearance; **give the l. to** openly accuse (someone) of lying; **white l.** justifiable falsehood ~ **lie** *v/i* tell a lie.

lie (2) (*p/t* **lay**, *p/part* **lain**) *v/i* be in or assume a recumbent position; be placed; be; remain; be situated; stretch, extend; remain motionless, *esp* if dead; be buried; (*ar*) pass the night; **as far as in me lies** as well as I can; **l. down** take a recumbent position, *esp* in order to rest; **l. down under** accept without protest; **l. in** stay late in bed; be in childbirth; **l. in state** be honourably displayed to the public; **l. low** be in hiding; **l. off** (*naut*) stand some way from shore; **l. over** be postponed; **l. to** (*naut*) halt; **l. up** keep to one's bed; (*of ship*) go into dock; **l. with** have sexual intercourse with ~ **lie** *n* position or way in which a thing lies; **l. of the land** contours and natural features of an area; (*fig*) state of affairs.

lied (*pl* **lieder**) [*leed*] *n* (*Germ*) German folksong; type of German art-song with piano accompaniment.

lie-detector [*l*I-ditekter] *n* instrument to detect physiological changes due to emotional stress under questioning > PDP.

lie-down [*l*I-down] *n* (*coll*) short rest in bed.

lief (*comp* **leever**) [*leef*] *adv* (*ar*) willingly.

liege [*leej*] *adj* (*of overlord*) entitled to homage; (*of vassal*) bound to do homage ~ **liege** *n* lord to whom homage is due, feudal superior ~ **liegeman** *n* vassal.

lie-in [*l*I-in] *n* (*coll*) act of staying late in bed in the morning.

lien [*lee*-en] *n* (*leg*) right to retain property until a debt due in respect of it is discharged.

lieu [*lew*/lOO] *n* place; **in l.** of instead of.

lieutenancy [leften*ansi*/(*US*) lOOten*ansi*] *n* rank, office or status of a lieutenant; tenure of this office; collective body of lieutenants.

lieutenant [lef*tenant*/(*US*) lOOten*ant*] *n* deputy, substitute; (*mil*) officer of rank next below captain; (*nav*) officer of rank next below lieutenant commander; **l. commander** (*nav*) officer of rank next below commander; **l. colonel** (*mil*) officer of rank between major and colonel; **l. general** (*mil*) officer of rank between major-general and general; general's deputy; **l. governor** assistant governor, subordinate to governor-general.

life (*pl* **lives**) [*lıf*] *n* property of certain forms of matter whereby they are able to grow, feed, and propagate; state or period of existence in which an organism can perform these functions; period between birth and death; living creatures collectively; human existence; human experience; human social activity and relationships; way of living; conduct, career; liveliness, energy, vitality; biography; period during which an organization *etc* will last or flourish; source of energy, inspiration; **l. assurance** (**insurance**) contract for payment of specified sum when a person dies or reaches a specified age, in exchange for payment of premiums; **l. cycle** progressive series of changes in an organism or lineal succession of organisms > PDB; **eternal l.** conscious existence after physical death; **for l.** for the rest of one's life; indefinitely; **for dear l.** urgently, earnestly; **from the l.** drawn or described from a living model; **high l.** aristocratic society; **l. imprisonment** (*leg*) an indeterminate period of imprisonment; **l. interest** (*leg*) claim or interest valid only while one lives; **large as l.** lifesize; unmistakable, real; **l. peer** peer whose title is not inherited by his heir; **see l.** acquire wide experience; **l. story** biography; **to the l.** copying exactly ~ **life** *adj* pertaining to life; for as long as life lasts.

lifebelt [*lıf*belt] *n* belt of buoyant material to support a person in the water.

lifeblood [*lıf*blud] *n* blood necessary to life; (*fig*) vital part.

lifeboat [*lıf*bOt] *n* buoyant and self-righting boat for saving life at sea; small boat carried by ship for use in case of wreck ~ **lifeboatman** *n*.

lifebuoy [*lıf*boy] *n* lifebelt.

lifeguard [*lıf*gaard] *n* bodyguard of soldiers; man trained to rescue and revive drowning persons; protective device; **Life Guards** two cavalry regiments acting as bodyguard to British Sovereign.

lifejacket [*lıf*jakit] *n* inflated jacket to support persons in water.

lifeless [*lıf*les] *adj* dead; having no life, inanimate; not lively, dull, dreary ~ **lifelessly** *adv*.

lifelike [*lıf*lIk] *adj* resembling a living form, realistic.

lifeline [*lıf*lIn] *n* diver's signalling line; rope used in rescue work at sea; (*fig*) anything on which one's life depends.

lifelong [*lıf*long] *adj* lasting all one's life.

lifemanship [*lıf*manship] *n* (*coll*) ability to make oneself seem superior.

life-preserver [lIf-pRIzurver] *n* weighted stick, bludgeon; knuckleduster; life-saving device for use in shipwreck or fire.

lifer [*lıf*er] *n* one sentenced to penal servitude for life; life sentence.

lifesize [*lıf*sIz] *adj* (*arts*) of the same size as the object represented.

lifespan [*lıf*span] *n* (*bid*) average length of life before natural death.

lifestyle [*lıf*stıl] *n* one's chosen way of life; preferred habits, tastes *etc*.

lifetime [*lıf*tIm] *n* duration of one's life.

lift [*lift*] *v/t* and *i* raise from the ground, pick up; raise to a higher level; direct upwards; move into erect position; (*of fog etc*) disperse; (*hort*) dig up; (*surg*) alter the facial appearance by surgery ; (*coll*) steal; (*sport*) cause (ball) to rise; (*coll*) plagiarize ~ **lift** *n* act of lifting; that which lifts; state of being lifted; free transport offered to a walker; transport by air; apparatus for moving persons or goods from one storey to another; upward trend or movement; rising inflexion of voice; upright carriage of head; act or method of raising a ballerina ~ **lifter** *n* one who, that which lifts; (*sl*) thief.

liftboy, liftman [*lift*boi, *lift*man] *n* boy or man operating a lift between storeys of hotel, shop *etc*.

lift-off [*lift*-of] *n* launching of rocket or spacecraft.

ligament [*ligament*] *n* connecting band; (*anat*) strong band of tough fibrous tissue.

ligature [*liga*cher] *n* anything used for binding or tying; act of tying; (*surg*) thread used to tie a severed blood-vessel *etc*; (*mus*) group of notes sung to one syllable > PDM; (*typ*) two or more letters joined together and forming one character or type ~ **ligature** *v/t*.

light (1) [*lıt*] *n* (*phys*) those frequencies of electromagnetic radiation which directly stimulate the organ of vision; brightness, radiance; degree or strength of brightness; that which emits brightness; daylight; lamp, candle, torch *etc*; means of kindling fire, match; window; perpendicular division of a mullioned window; mental or spiritual illumination; explanation, enlightening remark *etc*; knowledge; aspect, way in which one considers something; prominent person; animated facial expression; (*painting*) representation of brightness; bright area of a picture; (*pl, theat*) footlights; (*pl, sl*) eyes; **ancient lights** right of a houseowner to prevent the obstruction of light; **according to one's lights** to the best of one's knowledge and capacities; **come to l.** become known, be found or found out; **in the l.** of considering, taking into account; **throw l. on** explain, make clearer; **see the l.** be born; be made public; undergo religious conversion; **stand in the l. of** obscure; (*fig*) hamper, obstruct; **l. year** distance travelled by light in one year, about 6 million million miles > PDS ~ **light** (*p/t* and *p/p/part* **lighted** or **lit**) *v/t* and *i* kindle; cause to emit light; give light to, illuminate; supply light to or for; **l. up** begin to emit light; begin to burn; (*coll*) begin to smoke a cigarette or pipe; (*of facial expression*) become cheerful and animated ~ **light** *adj* fairly bright; not dark; without shadows; pale.

light (2) *adj* not heavy, of little weight; of less than correct legal weight; without much equipment, baggage or weapons; easy to bear or do; not tiring; easily digested; agile, dexterous; graceful; slight, unimportant, trivial; frivolous; immoral, unchaste; cheerful, carefree: amusing but superficial; dizzy, giddy; (*of sleep*) from which one wakes easily; (*of soil*) sandy, porous; **make l. of** treat as of small importance ~ **light** *adv* in a light way; easily, without encumbrances.

light (3) *v/t* jump down, alight; **l. into** (*sl*) attack; **l. out** (*coll*) go away; **l. upon** find by chance.

lighten (1) [*lIt*en] *v/t* and *i* make brighter, light up; shine, grow bright; emit flashes of lightning.

lighten (2) *v/t* and *i* make or become less heavy; remove a burden from; make or become more cheerful.

lighter (1) [*lit*ter] *n* flat-bottomed boat used for unloading ship away from the wharf-side.

lighter (2) *n* instrument for lighting; device for producing a flame.

light-fingered [lit-*fing*-gerd] *adj* dexterous; thievish.

light-handed [lit-*hand*id] *adj* having a delicate and skilful touch; carrying little in the hand; not over-emphasized.

light-headed [lit-*hed*id] *adj* delirious; frivolous, thoughtless.

light-hearted [lit-*haart*id] *adj* cheerful; free from care.

lighthouse [*lit*-hows] *n* structure, *usu* tower, having a recognizable flashing light to guide ships or warn them of danger.

lighting [*lit*ting] *n* illumination; system of lights and apparatus giving light to a house, street *etc*.

lightly [*lit*li] *adv* with little weight, gently, nimbly; slightly (cooked); in small quantity; without gravity, gaily; without careful consideration; with indifference, slightingly.

light-minded [lit-*mind*id] *adj* frivolous.

lightness [*lit*nes] *n* quality of being light.

lightning [*lit*ning] *n* discharge of electricity between two charged clouds or between a cloud and the earth; flash of light caused by this; **l. conductor** metal rod ending in a sharp point fixed to a high part of a building and connected to earth > PDS; **l. glance** quick piercing glance; **like l.** extremely fast; **l. strike** strike of workers started without warning.

light-o'-love [lit-O-*luv*] *n* wanton woman.

lights [*lits*] *n* (*pl*) lungs of sheep, pigs and bullocks, *esp* as food.

lightship [*lit*ship] *n* vessel anchored in some place of danger and carrying a warning light.

lightweight [*lit*wayt] *n* and *adj* (person or thing) of less than normal weight; (boxer) between 9 st and 9 st 9 lb weight; (person) of little importance.

lightyear [*lit*year] *n* (*astron*) distance travelled by light in one year, approximately 6 million million miles; an astronomical measure of distance.

ligneous [*ligni*-us] *adj* like wood; made of wood.

ligni- *pref* made of or like wood.

lignite [*lign*It] *n* brownish-black natural deposit resembling coal > PDS, PDG.

lignum-vitae [lignum-*vi*tee] *n* South American tree with extremely hard wood; wood of this tree.

like (1) [*lik*] *adj* resembling; same or similar in quality, quantity, degree *etc*; having the expected qualities *etc*; in keeping with, true to; (*ar*) probable ~ **like** *adv* in the same or similar way; in a specified manner; (*sl* or *dial*) so to speak, as it were; (*coll*) probably ~ **l. enough** probably ~ **like** *n* that which is similar; something equal or comparable; **the likes of us** (**them** *etc*) (*coll*) people like us (them *etc*) ~ **like** *conj* (*coll*) in the same way as; (*sl*) as if.

like (2) *v/t* be fond of; be attracted to; (*w inf*) find it agreeable; wish; choose; **not l. to be** unwilling to; **I l. that!** (*coll iron*) exclamation of incredulity and annoyance ~ **like** *n* that which one likes; **likes and dislikes** preferences and prejudices.

likeable [*lik*ab'l] *adj* agreeable, attractive ~ **likeably** *adv* ~ **likeableness** *n*.

likelihood [*lik*lihood] *n* probability.

likely [*lik*li] *adj* probable, to be expected; plausible; promising; suitable ~ **likely** *adv* probably.

like-minded [lik-*mind*id] *adj* similar in temperament or outlook.

liken [*lik*en] *v/t* compare.

likeness [*lik*nes] *n* similarity, resemblance; photograph or painting of a person, portrait; (*ar*) form, appearance.

likewise [*lik*wiz] *adv* in the same manner; also, moreover.

liking [*lik*ing] *n* fondness; inclination; **to one's l.** suiting one's taste.

lilac [*li*lak] *n* shrub with purple, white or mauve flowers; pale pinkish mauve colour ~ **lilac** *adj*.

Lilliputian [lili*pew*shan] *adj* tiny.

lilt [lilt] *n* markedly rhythmic and melodious quality in speech or song; swing; cadence; song with this quality ~ **lilt** *v/t* and *i* sing or speak with a lilt.

lily [*li*li] *n* bulbous plant with large flowers of white, reddish, purple, or orange colour; (*fig*) pallor, symbol of purity; **l. of the valley** plant having two large leaves and spray of scented white flowers.

lily-livered [lili*liverd*] *adj* cowardly.

lily-pad [*lili*pad] *n* (*US*) leaf of waterlily.

lily-white [*lili*wIt] *adj* very white; (*joc*) much loved.

limb (1) [*lim*] *n* leg; arm; wing; large branch; (*coll*) mischievous young person; **l. of the law** any legal functionary; **out on a l.** isolated, in difficulties.

limb (2) *n* edge, border; edge of the disk of sun or moon ~ **limbate** *adj* bordered.

limbeck see **alembic**.

limber (1) [*limber*] *n* (*mil*) wheels and shaft forming detachable front of gun-carriage ~ **limber** *v/i* attach limber to gun.

limber (2) *adj* flexible, supple; lithe ~ **limber** *v/t* make supple; **l. up** make supple by exercise.

limber (3) *n* (*naut*) hole that allows water to drain to the pump-well.

limbless [*lim*lis] *adj* having no limbs; having lost one or more limbs.

limbo [*limb*O] *n* (*theol*) state or region allotted to souls of unbaptized infants; state or region where souls of righteous men who died before Christ awaited His coming; (*fig*) place for unwanted or forgotten people and things.

lime (1) [*lim*] *n* calcium oxide obtained by heating limestone, quicklime > PDS; calcium hydroxide obtained by adding water to quicklime, slaked lime > PDS; limestone; birdlime ~ **lime** *v/t* mix, treat or dress with lime; catch with birdlime; (*fig*) catch, snare.

lime (2) *n* citrus fruit akin to lemon but smaller and more acid; juice of this; tree bearing this.

lime (3) *n* the linden tree.

lime-juice [*lim*-jOos] *n* sweetened juice of lime (2).

limelight [*lim*lIt] *n* bright white light produced by heating lime in oxyhydrogen flame; light used to illuminate stage of theatre; (*fig*) attention, publicity; in the l. on that part of the stage so lit; (*fig*) attracting public interest.

limerick [*lime*Rik] *n* type of 5-lined humorous or nonsensical poem.

limestone [*lIm*stOn] *n* rock consisting essentially of calcium carbonate > PDG.

limetree [*lImt*Ree] *n* linden tree; tree bearing limes (2).

lime-twig [*lIm*-twig] *n* twig smeared with birdlime.

limewater [*lImw*awter] *n* solution of calcium hydroxide in water used as antacid.

limey, limy [*lImi*] *n* (*US* and *Aust sl*) British sailor; Englishman.

limit [*limit*] *n* boundary; point which cannot or must not be passed; (*coll*) someone or something quite intolerable; (*math*) limiting value > PDS; **within limits** (*fig*) moderately ~ **limit** *v/t* confine within bounds or boundaries, restrict ~ **limitable** *adj*.

limitary [*limit*eRi] *adj* limited; confining.

limitation [limit*ay*shon] *n* act of limiting; state of being limited; that which limits; (*leg*) fixed period after which a claim or action can no longer be brought; **know one's limitations** know how much one is capable of doing, reaching *etc*.

limited [*limit*id] *adj* confined within limits; restricted, narrow; **l. liability company** one in which the shareholder's obligation to meet any losses the company may suffer is limited to the unpaid-up portion (if any) of the nominal value of the shares; **l. monarchy** one in which the monarch's power is restricted by the constitution.

limn [*lim*] *v/t* paint or draw, *esp* in miniature; (*fig*) describe ~ **limner** [*lim*ner] *n*.

limousine [*limo*ozeen] *n* car in which driver's seat is enclosed by a glass screen.

limp (1) [*limp*] *v/i* walk lamely, with uneven motion; (*of verse*) scan imperfectly; (*fig*) move slowly because of damage ~ **limp** *n* act of limping; lameness.

limp (2) *adj* lacking stiffness; soft; flabby; (*fig*) weak.

limpet [*limp*et] *n* (*zool*) mollusc that clings tightly to rocks; (*fig*) someone who will not relinquish a position or office; (*mil*) adhesive bomb; (*eng*) adhesive open caisson > PDE.

limpid [*limp*id] *adj* clear, transparent ~ **limpidity** [limp*t*diti] *n* ~ **limpidly** *adv*.

limply [*limp*li] *adv* softly, loosely; flabbily; weakly.

limpness [*limp*nis] *n* quality of being limp.

limy [*lImi*] *adj* smeared with birdlime; containing lime; (*sl*) limey.

linage [*lIn*ij] *n* number of printed lines on page; payment for this.

linchpin [*linch*pin] *n* pin passed through axletree to keep wheel in place; (*fig*) vital part.

lincrusta [lin-*k*Rusta] *n* (*tr*) kind of thick embossed wallpaper.

linctus [*link*tus] *n* syrupy soothing medicine for throat and chest.

linden [*lin*den] *n* tree with yellow scented flowers.

line (1) [*lIn*] *n* string, thin cord; very thin mark, indentation or stroke of pen, pencil *etc*; boundary, limit or starting-point marked by a line; thin furrow on face or hands, wrinkle; telegraph or telephone wire; cord with hooks, used in fishing; row, straight series; row of letters or words on a

page; metrical unit printed as a single row of words; (*pl*) verses, poem; (*coll*) short letter; row of persons side by side or one behind the other; row of soldiers in formation; series of fortifications, trenches *etc*; fortified area closest to enemy's positions; railway track; regular system of transport by road, rail, sea or air; (*math*) that which has length but no breadth; (*geog*) equator; course of action; official policy; method; occupation, career, trade; hobby; field of interest; (*comm*) series of similar goods; lineage, family; (*pl*) (*theat*) words of a role; (*pl*) (*coll*) passage of verse, *usu* classical, to be copied out by schoolchild as punishment; (*pl*) (*coll*) marriage certificate; **the l.** (*mil*) regular infantry troops; **all along the l.** in every part; **l. of battle** troops disposed in readiness to meet enemy; **bring into l.** cause to agree or conform; **draw the l. at** refuse to do or tolerate; **get a l. on** (*sl*) find out something about; **hard lines** (*coll*) bad luck; **l. of least resistance** course of action presenting fewest difficulties; **on the l.** (*of paintings*) hung at eye-level; **read between the lines** discover hidden meaning in; **ship of the l.** battleship; **shoot a l.** (*sl*) boast; **toe the l.** conform, obey ~ **line** *v/t* and *i* mark with a line or lines; mark with furrows or wrinkles; place in a row; place a row of (people, trees *etc*) along; **l. in** draw the outlines of; **l. up** take up position in a row; put (people) in a row.

line (2) *v/t* cover the inside of (garment, box *etc*) with layer of different material; be a lining for; fill; (*of animals*) copulate with; **l. one's pockets** make money; **l. one's stomach** eat.

lineage [*lini*-ij] *n* descent; ancestry.

lineal [*lini*-al] *adj* in direct line of descent ~ **lineally** *adv*.

lineament [*lini*-ament] *n* (*usu pl*) feature of the face; distinctive characteristic.

linear [*lini*-er] *adj* of or in lines; resembling a line or thread; (*arts*) depending chiefly on outlines > PDΛΛ; (*math*) having only first degree terms; **l. accelerator** apparatus for accelerating ions to high energies > PDS; **l. paper** with watermark lines to guide the writing ~ **linearly** *adv*.

lineate (1) [*lini*-ayt] *adj* (*bot*) marked with lines.

lineate (2) *v/t* arrange in lines.

lineation [lini-*ay*shon] *n* act of marking with lines; arrangement of lines; (*verse*) division into lines.

lineman [*lIn*man] *n* man who attends to railway, telegraph or telephone lines.

linen [*linen*] *n* cloth woven of flax; article made from this; garment or article of a type formerly made from linen; underclothes; bedclothes; tablecloths, napkins *etc*; **wash dirty l. in public** discuss private scandals in front of outsiders ~ **linen** *adj* made of linen.

linen-draper [*linen*-dRayper] *n* retailer of linen and cotton goods.

liner [*lIn*er] *n* large vessel belonging to a steamship line; passenger aircraft belonging to an air line; **l. train** permanently coupled fast goods train plying between industrial centres.

linesman [*lInz*man] *n* man who tests safety of railway lines; (*sport*) umpire posted near boundary line; (*mil*) soldier of the line.

line-up [*lIn*-up] *n* arrangement of persons in a line;

444

identity parade; inspection parade; deployment of troops before battle; arrangement of competitors or players before beginning of race or game.

ling (1) [*ling*] *n* a sea-fish like cod.

ling (2) *n* a kind of heather.

lingam [*ling*-gam] *n* (*Hindu*) phallus, representation of male sexual organ used as religious emblem.

linger [*ling*-ger] *v/i* tarry, delay; loiter; continue to live though suffering from disease; be slow to disappear ~ **lingering** *adj* protracted; slow~ **lingeringly** *adv.*

lingerie [*lanzhe*Ree] *n* (*Fr*) women's underwear.

lingo [*ling*-gO] *n* (*pej*) language, *esp* foreign.

lingua-, linguo- *pref* of the tongue.

lingua franca [ling-gwa-f*Ranka*] *n* language used over wide area by people of various races, though not their native tongue > PDG; mixed language of Greek, Arabic, Italian and French used in East Mediterranean areas.

lingual [*ling*-gwal] *adj* pertaining to the tongue; formed by the tongue ~ **lingual** *n* lingual sound.

linguist [*ling*-gwist] *n* one skilled in foreign languages.

linguistic [ling-gwistik] *adj* pertaining to the study of language in general, or of a specified language or languages; pertaining to the meaning of statements or words ~ **linguistical** *adv* ~ **linguistics** *n* (*pl*) scientific study of the nature of language, or of the development and nature of a specific language.

liniment [*lini*ment] *n* an embrocation.

lining [*lI*ning] *n* stuff with which garments are lined; any material used to cover an inner surface.

link (1) [*link*] *n* that which connects two parts, objects or persons; one ring or loop of a chain; one of a pair of buttons joined by a chain and used for fastening shirt-cuffs; (*fig*) person or thing that closes a gap or provides a connexion; (*mech*) short connecting-rod; (*sur*) measure of 7·92 in.; (*US*) measure of 1 ft.; **missing l.** that which is lacking to complete a series; hypothetical creature exactly intermediate in evolution from ape to man ~ **link** *v/t* and *i* join; be joined; connect.

link (2) *n* torch of tow and pitch.

linkage [*link*ij] *n* system of links; (*biol*) tendency for characteristics to be associated in hereditary transmission > PDP, PDB.

linkman [*link*man] *n* one who links items in a TV or radio show, compère; one who provides liaison, intermediary; (*hist*) one who carries a link (2).

links [*links*] *n* golf-course; (*Scots*) undulating sandy ground near seashore.

linn [*lin*] *n* (*Scots*) waterfall; pool.

linnet [*linet*] *n* small brown songbird.

lino [*lI*nO] *n* (*abbr*) linoleum; linocut.

linocut [*lI*nOkut] *n* technique of engraving in relief on a block of linoleum > PDAA; print so produced.

linoleum [linOli-um] *n* detachable floor covering built up from linseed oil and hessian canvas.

linotype [*lI*nOtIp] *n* (*print*) machine that casts a whole line of type in one bar.

linsang [*lin*sang] *n* civet cat of Borneo and Java.

linseed [*lin*seed] *n* seed of flax; **l. cake** crushed flax seeds from which the oil has been extracted;

l. **oil** oil extracted from flax seeds; **l. poultice** poultice made from boiled linseed.

linsey-woolsey [linzi-*woolzi*] *n* fabric of coarse wool and cotton.

lint [*lint*] *n* (*surg*) soft linen prepared to apply to a wound.

lintel [*lin*tel] *n* horizontal stone or beam spanning opening of door or window.

lion [*lI*-on] *n* large carnivorous tawny quadruped of cat-tribe; (*fig*) famous or outstanding person; (*fig*) England; (*astron*) fifth sign of zodiac, the constellation Leo; **like a l.** fiercely; bravely; **the l's share** the largest share.

lioness [*lI*-ones] *n* female lion.

lion-hearted [lI-on-*haar*tid] *adj* very brave.

lion-hunter [*lI*-on-hunter] *n* one who hunts lions; (*fig*) one who seeks the company of celebrities.

lionize [*lI*-onIz] *v/t* treat (person) as a celebrity.

lip [*lip*] *n* either of the fleshy edges of the mouth; edge, rim; (*coll*) impudence; **hang on the lips of** listen eagerly to; **open one's lips** speak; **stiff upper l.** imperturbability, suppression of all signs of feeling ~ **lip** (*pres*/*part* **lipping**, *p/t* and *p/part* **lipped**) *v/t* touch with the lips.

lip-, lipo- (1) *pref* lacking.

lip-, lipo- (2) *pref* of or like fat.

lipid [*lip*id] *n* (*chem*) type of insoluble organic compound, consisting of esters of fatty acids, which includes fats, oils and waxes.

lipread [*lip*Reed] *v/t* and *i* understand spoken words solely by watching the movements of the speaker's lips ~ **lipreading** *n.*

lipsalve [*lip*salv] *n* ointment for the lips.

lipservice [*lip*survis] *n* insincere promises; insincere expression of respect, devotion *etc.*

lipstick [*lip*stik] *n* cosmetic used for colouring the lips.

liquate [li*kwayt*] *v/t* (*metal*) separate components of a mixture or alloy by heating until one constituent melts.

liquefaction [likwi*fak*shon] *n* act or process of liquefying > PDS; state of being liquefied.

liquefy [*lik*wifI] *v/t* and *i* make or become liquid.

liquescent [li*kwe*sent] *adj* in process of becoming liquid; capable of becoming liquid.

liqueur [li*kyoor*/li*kur*] *n* strong alcoholic liquor sweetened and flavoured.

liquid [*lik*wid] *n* matter in a state intermediate between gas and solid, fluid; substance capable of flowing; (*phon*) term applied to the consonants *l, r, m, n* ~ **liquid** *adj* fluid, capable of flowing; watery; clear and moist-looking; (*of assets*) that can readily be converted into cash; (*of sounds*) harmonious.

liquidate [*lik*widayt] *v/t* and *i* pay (debt); (*comm*) wind up the affairs of (a company); estimate assets and debts of; make or become bankrupt; put an end to, destroy; (*coll*) kill ~ **liquidation** [likwi*day*shon] *n* bankruptcy; destruction; assassination ~ **liquidator** *n.*

liquidity [li*kwi*diti] *n* state of being liquid; degree to which a substance is liquid.

liquidize [*lik*widIz] *v/t* crush to a liquid pulp.

liquor [*lik*er] *n* alcoholic drink; water in which meat has been boiled; liquid substance; **in l.** drunk ~ **liquor** *v/i* **l. up** drink alcohol.

liquorice, licorice [*like*Ris/*like*Rish] *n* plant from whose root a sweet black substance is extracted; this substance, used in medicine or as a sweet.

lira (*pl* **lire**) [*leer*Ra] *n* Italian silver coin and monetary unit.

lisle [*l*Il] *n* cotton fabric used for gloves and formerly for stockings.

lisp [*lisp*] *n* defect of speech which substitutes *th* for *s* ~ **lisp** *v/i* and *t* speak or say with a lisp.

lissom [*lis*um] *adj* lithe, supple.

list (1) [*list*] *n* catalogue of names, words *etc*; inventory ~ **list** *v/t* make a list of; write down in a list.

list (2) *n* inclination to one side, *esp* of ship; slope ~ **list** *v/i* slope, lean, *esp* of ship.

list (3) *v/i* (*obs abbr*) enlist as soldier.

list (4) *n* border, edging; selvedge of cloth; cheap coarse cloth.

list (5) *v/i* (*ar*) desire, choose ~ **list** *n* (*ar*) desire.

list (6) *v/i* and *t* (*ar*, *poet*) listen (to).

listen [*lis*en] *v/i* attentively exercise the sense of hearing; **l. for** listen in hope of hearing a specified sound; **l. in** listen to radio programmes; intercept radio or telephone messages; **l. to** direct one's hearing towards; pay aural attention to; obey; take notice of ~ **listener** *n* ~ **listening** *adj*.

listless [*list*les] *adj* lacking interest or desire, apathetic ~ **listlessly** *adv* ~ **listlessness** *n*.

lists [*lists*] *n* (*pl*) (*hist*) barriers surrounding ground for tournaments; **enter the l.** (*fig*) take part in a contest, controversy *etc*.

lit [*lit*] *p/t* and *p/part* of **light** (1); **well l.** (*sl*) quite tipsy; **l. up** (*sl*) slightly drunk.

litany [*litani*] *n* form of prayer consisting of various supplications or invocations each followed by an unvarying response.

litchi [*leechee*] *n* Chinese fruit with brown shell.

literacy [*lite*Rasi] *n* condition or state of being literate.

literal [*lite*Ral] *adj* exact, completely accurate; following the actual words of a text without interpretation *etc*; (*of translation*) word for word; (*theol*) rejecting allegorical or mythological interpretations of scripture; (*of persons*) lacking imagination, matter-of-fact; (*print*) relating to a letter of the alphabet; (*math*) expressed by letters.

literalism [*lite*Ralizm] *n* insistence on following the actual words of a text; rigidity in interpretation ~ **literalist** *n* and *adj*.

literally [*lite*Rali] *adv* word for word; without exaggeration or metaphor; accurately; (*coll*) absolutely, thoroughly ~ **literalness** *n*.

literary [*lite*ReRi] *adj* pertaining to literature; practising literature; expert in or fond of literature; pertaining to the written rather than the spoken forms of language; formal, not colloquial; (*of style in written works*) aesthetically pleasing; **l. property** rights and profits of an author.

literate [*lite*Rit] *adj* able to read and write; cultured, educated ~ **literate** *n*.

literati [*lite*Raati/*lite*RaytI] *n* (*pl*) literary or learned men.

literatim [*lite*Raytim] *adv* (*Lat*) letter for letter, literally.

literature [*lite*Racher] *n* written works that achieve or attempt aesthetic merit; non-scientific and non-technical written works; body of such works

produced by a specified nation, period *etc*; written works on a specified subject; (*coll*) any book, pamphlet *etc*.

litharge [*lith*aarj] *n* (*chem*) lead monoxide > PDS.

lithe [*lITH*] *adj* pliant, flexible ~ **litheness** *n*.

lithium [*lithi*-um] *n* (*chem*) the lightest metallic elemen > PDS.

litho- *pref* pertaining to stone; pertaining to stone in the bladder or kidneys.

lithograph [*lith*OgRaaf] *v/i* and *t* print by lithography ~ **lithograph** *n* design *etc* printed by lithography ~ **lithographic** [*lith*OgRaf ik] *adj*.

lithography [*lith*OgRafi] *n* art of printing copies from designs on a prepared stone or metal slab > PDAA.

lithology [*lith*oloji] *n* scientific study of stones and rocks > PDG; (*path*) study of stones found in the body.

lithosphere [*lith*osfeer] *n* the Earth's outer crust.

litigant [*liti*gant] *n* and *adj* (person) engaged in a lawsuit.

litigate [*liti*gayt] *v/i* and *t* be party to a lawsuit; contest at law ~ **litigation** [*liti*gayshon] *n*.

litigious [*liti*jus] *adj* eager to go to law; contentious; disputable at law.

litmus [*lit*mus] *n* substance of vegetable origin turned red by acids and blue by alkalis; **l. paper** paper impregnated with this and used as an indicator of acids and alkalis.

litotes [*lI*toteez/*leet*oteez] *n* (*rhet*) method of expressing a quality by understatement or by negative phrasing.

litre [*leet*er] *n* metric unit of volume slightly more than 1¾ pints > PDS.

litter [*lit*er] *n* rubbish left lying about untidily, *esp* out of doors; scattered oddments; straw *etc* used as bedding for animals; number of young produced by an animal at one birth; straw *etc* protecting plants from frost; couch furnished with shafts for carrying; framework for carrying wounded or sick persons, stretcher ~ **litter** *v/t* and *i* make untidy by scattering rubbish in or on; lie scattered about; (*of animals*) bring forth young.

litterateur [*lit*eRa*tur*] *n* (*Fr*) a literary man.

litterbin [*lit*erbin] *n* receptacle for litter placed in streets *etc*.

litterlout [*lit*erlowt] *n* (*coll*) one who scatters litter.

little (*comp* **less** or **lesser**, *superl* **least**) [*lit*'l] *adj* small; brief; short; unimportant; young; mean, contemptible; **l. folk** (**people**) elves or fairies; **no l.** a considerable amount of; **l. ones** children; offspring ~ **little** *n* small quantity; short distance; brief time; **l. by l.** gradually; **for a l.** for a short time; **in l.** on a small scale, in miniature ~ **little** *adv* to a small extent or degree, slightly; not at all.

little-ease [*lit*'l-eez] *n* (*hist*) cage or cell in which a prisoner could neither stand up nor lie full length.

little-go [*lit*'l-gO] *n* (*obs coll*) preliminary examination at Cambridge University.

littleness [*lit*'lnis] *n* state or quality of being little.

littler, littlest [*lit*ler, *lit*lest] *adjs* (*coll*) *comp* and *superl* of **little**.

littoral [*lite*Ral] *n* seashore, strip of land along a coast; area between high and low tide levels > PDB, PDG ~ **littoral** *adj* on the seashore.

liturgic, liturgical [litur̄jik, litur̄jikal] *adj* pertaining to, used in a liturgy ~ **liturgically** *adv*.

liturgy [*liter̄ji*] *n* prescribed prayers and rituals used in public worship; the service of the Eucharist; the Mass; the Book of Common Prayer.

livable, liveable [*liv̄ab'l*] *adj* worth living, bearable; suitable for living in; possible to live with.

live (1) [*liv̄*] *adj* alive, living; lively, energetic; *(of coals)* glowing; *(sl)* covered with vermin, grubs *etc*; **l. bait** living worm used as fishing bait; **l. birth** birth of living child; **l. broadcast** programme broadcast or televised during actual performance, not pre-recorded; **l. cartridge** cartridge containing bullet; **l. rail** electrified rail; **l. wire** electrified wire; *(fig)* lively, energetic person ~ **live** *adv* (*rad, tel*) without pre-recording or filming, directly transmitted.

live (2) [*liv̄*] *v/i* and *t* be alive, have life; dwell, reside; subsist; supply one's needs; pass one's life in a specified manner; lead a rich and varied life; be remembered; *(of characters in books etc)* be convincing and memorable; **l. and let l.** be tolerant; **l. by** support oneself by; **l. down** cause (scandal *etc*) to be forgotten, rehabilitate oneself after; **l. in** *(of servant)* lodge in the building where one is employed; **l. on** support oneself by, live at the expense of; **l. through** pass through and survive; **l. it up** *(coll)* pursue a life of hectic pleasure; **l. up to** be worthy of; **l. together, l. with** live in the same house as; have an established sexual relationship with.

liveable see **livable**.

livelihood [*liv̄lihood*] *n* means of earning one's living, means of subsistence.

livelong [*liv̄long/liv̄long*] *adj* (*poet*) lasting; **the l. day** (**night**) all through the day (night).

lively [*liv̄li*] *adj* vigorous, energetic; gay; moving quickly; intense, vivid; alert; lifelike; *(coll)* excitingly dangerous ~ **livelily** *adv* ~ **liveliness** *n*.

liven [*liv̄en*] *v/t* and *i* put life into; **l. up** become more lively; make more lively.

liver (1) [*liv̄er*] *n* one who lives.

liver (2) *n* large glandulous organ which secretes bile and purifies the blood > PDB; flesh of this used as food; *(coll)* liverishness ~ **liver** *adj* dark reddish brown.

liverfluke [*liv̄erflOOk*] *n* fluke infesting bile-ducts of sheep and cattle > PDB.

liveried [*liv̄eRid*] *adj* wearing livery.

liverish [*liv̄eRish*] *adj* (*coll*) suffering from deranged liver, bilious; irritable ~ **liverishness** *n*.

liverwort [*liv̄erwurt*] *n* flowerless plant resembling a moss > PDB.

livery [*liv̄eRi*] *n* distinctive uniform worn by servants of one employer; ceremonial uniform worn by members of certain London City Companies; (*leg*) delivery of property into one's possession; (*ar*) allowance of food for horses or servants; (*fig*) clothing, garb; **at l.** *(of horses)* stabled, groomed and fed at a fixed charge to the owner; **l. company** a City of London Company; **l. man** member of such a Company; **l. stable** stable where owners can board horses out; stable from which horses are hired out.

lives [*liv̄z*] *pl* of **life**.

livestock [*liv̄stok*] *n* animals kept on a farm.

livid [*liv̄id*] *adj* bluish, leaden in colour; very

pale; black and blue; *(coll)* very angry ~ **lividity** [*liv̄iditi*] *n*.

living [*liv̄ing*] *n* financial means whereby one supports oneself; wages, income, salary; trade, craft, profession, business; standard or way of life; (*eccles*) benefice; **the l.** (*pl*) those who are alive ~ **living** *adj* alive, not dead; lifelike; energetic, lively; *(of rock)* in its natural state; *(of water)* flowing; **l. wage** wage adequate to support oneself and one's family; **within l. memory** within the memory of people still living.

living-room [*liv̄ing-ROOm*] *n* room occupied during the day but not used for meals.

living-space [*liv̄ing-spays*] *n* area claimed by a nation as essential to its development.

lizard [*liz̄erd*] *n* reptile with four legs, scaly hide and long tail; skin of this dressed for use on handbags, shoes *etc*.

llama [*laam̄a*] *n* South American ruminant quadruped related to the camel.

lo [*lO*] *interj* (*ar*) look! see!

load [*lOd*] *n* burden; that which is carried, *esp* if bulky or heavy; quantity which a specified vehicle can carry; charge of gun; *(fig)* that which causes anxiety, grief *etc*, mental burden; (*mech*) work being done by dynamo, engine *etc*; weight carried by a structure; **loads of** *(coll)* plenty of ~ **load** *v/t* and *i* put a load on or into; lay a burden on; bestow in great quantities; put charge into (gun); oppress, burden; add weight to one end or side of; adulterate.

loaded [*lOdid*] *adj (of dice)* weighted for advantage in cheating; *(fig)* containing a hidden danger or trap, unfair.

loader [*lOder*] *n* one who or that which loads; mechanical shovel; device for loading a gun.

loadline [*lOdlin*] *n* (*naut*) line on sides of ship marking depth at which she floats when fully loaded; Plimsoll mark.

load-shedding [*lOd-sheding*] *n* temporary break in electricity supply to one area to relieve strain on generating plant.

loadstar see **lodestar**.

loadstone, lodestone [*lOdstOn*] *n* magnetic variety of natural iron oxide; magnet > PDE, PDS.

loaf (1) (*pl* **loaves**) [*lOf*] *n* portion of bread of definite size and weight baked in one mass; small cone of sugar; preparation of food shaped like loaf of bread; (*sl*) head; intelligence; **l. sugar** refined sugar cut into small cones.

loaf (2) *v/i* spend time idly; stroll about aimlessly ~ **loafer** *n*.

loam [*lOm*] *n* rich soil composed of sand, clay, silt and humus; paste of clay, sand and water used in brickmaking ~ **loam** *v/t* cover or smear with loam ~ **loamy** *adj*.

loan [*lOn*] *n* something lent; money lent; act of lending; issue of stock by Government; **have the l. of** borrow; **on l.** lent ~ **loan** *v/t* (*US*) lend.

loanword [*lOnwurd*] *n* word adopted into one language from another.

loath, loth [*lOth*] *adj* unwilling; **nothing l.** quite willing.

loathe [*lOTH*] *v/t* detest, be filled with disgust by ~ **loathing** *n* detestation, disgust.

loathly [*lOTHli*] *adj* disgusting; hideous.

loathsome [*lOTHsum*] *adj* disgusting, hateful ~ **loathsomeness** *n*.

loaves [lOvz] *pl* of **loaf** (1).

lob [lob] *n* (*cricket*) high-pitched slow ball bowled underhand; (*lawn tennis*) ball hit high in the air ~ **lob** (*pres/part* **lobbing**, *p/t* and *p/part* **lobbed**) *v/t* and *i*.

lobar [lObar] *adj* pertaining to a lobe, *esp* of lung.

lobate [lObayt] *adj* (*bot*) divided into lobes.

lobby [lobi] *n* hall; corridor; waiting-room; (*House of Commons*) room where Members and public can meet; corridor where Members vote; group of persons lobbying a Member, Senator *etc*; political pressure-group ~ **lobby** *v/t* try to persuade a Member of Parliament, Senator *etc* to favour a particular group of persons or interests ~ **lobbyist** *n* one who lobbies.

lobe [lOb] *n* lower pendulous part of the external ear; rounded projecting part of an organ; division of lungs or of brain ~ **lobed** *adj* having lobes.

lobelia [lObeelya] *n* genus of herbaceous plants cultivated for their brightly coloured flowers.

loblolly [lobloli] *n* (*naut*) gruel; **l. boy** (**man**) (*naut*) surgeon's assistant.

lobotomy [lObotomi] *n* (*surg*) leucotomy.

lobscouse [lobskows] *n* (*naut*) meat and vegetable hash.

lobster [lobster] *n* large edible marine crustacean.

lobster-pot [lobster-pot] *n* basket in which lobsters are trapped.

lobule [lobyool] *n* a small lobe.

lobworm [lobwurm] *n* large worm used as bait by anglers.

local [lOkal] *adj* of or in a particular place or district; restricted to a particular area; **l. colour** careful representation in literary or artistic work of details characteristic of the area where the story *etc* is set; **l. option** right of a district to regulate the sale of alcohol within its bounds ~ **local** *n* inhabitant of a specified place or district; (*coll*) public house in one's own district.

locale [lOkaal] *n* scene of some specified event.

localism [lOkalizm] *n* attachment to the place where one lives; narrow outlook due to this; provincialism; pronunciation or phrase characteristic of a district.

locality [lOkaliti] *n* position, place, district; **bump of l.** ability to identify a particular locality and find one's way.

localize [lOkaliz] *v/t* restrict to a particular place or area; give local characteristics to; set (story, film *etc*) in a particular district ~ **localization** [lOkalIzayshon] *n*.

locally [lOkali] *adv* in a specified district; nearby, in the neighbourhood.

locate [lOkayt] *v/t* identify the place or area where something is; assign to or set in a particular place or position.

location [lOkayshon] *n* act of locating; position; place, outside a film studio, where scenes of a moving picture are shot; (*S. Africa*) area assigned to Africans to live in.

locative [lokativ] *n* and *adj* (*gramm*) (case) denoting the position of something.

loch [lokh] *n* (*Scots*) lake; arm of the sea > PDG.

loci [lOsI/lOkI] *pl* of **locus**.

lock (1) [lok] *n* tress of hair; tuft of wool; (*pl*) hair.

lock (2) *n* device with springs and levers for

fastening a door, box *etc*; mechanism which explodes charge in firearm; stretch of water on river or canal cut off by watertight gates through which vessels can be moved from one level to another > PDE; wrestler's grip; device to immobilize a wheel; stoppage in machinery, blockage; coupling; (*mot*) extent of turning arc of steering wheel; **l. gate** watertight gates of canal or river lock; **l. hospital** hospital treating venereal diseases; **l., stock and barrel** entirely ~ **lock** *v/t* and *i* fasten or be fastened with a lock; embrace; become rigidly fixed; block, jam; **l. in** confine in room *etc* by locking door; **l. out** exclude from room, house *etc* by locking door; prevent (workmen) from entering factory *etc* to work; **l. up** imprison; confine in lunatic asylum.

locker [loker] *n* one who locks; box or small cupboard with lock; **Davy Jones's l.** the bottom of the sea.

locket [lokit] *n* small metal case containing portrait or keepsake and worn as ornament.

lockjaw [lokjaw] *n* (*med*) a form of tetanus.

lock-out [lok-owt] *n* refusal of employer to let his employees return to work until they accept his conditions.

locksmith [loksmith] *n* maker and repairer of locks.

lock-up [lok-up] *n* time for locking up (building *etc*); prison; place of temporary detention; **l. shop** shop with no living quarters attached.

loco [lOko] *adj* (*sl*) mad.

loco- *pref* in, by, or from a place.

locomotion [lOkOmOshon] *n* act of moving, ability to move, from one place to another.

locomotive [lOkOmOtiv] *adj* moving from place to place by its own power ~ **locomotive** *n* engine that draws railway trains by its own power > PDE ~ **locomotor** *adj* pertaining to locomotion.

locum [lOkum] *n* doctor or clergyman deputizing for another.

locus (*pl* **loci**) [lOkus] *n* place, position; (*math*) line tracing out the path of a point through space > PDS; **l. classicus** (*Lat*) most authoritative passage (of a book *etc*) to illustrate a point or subject; best-known typical instance; **l. standi** (*Lat*) official position; (*leg*) right to intervene in lawsuit.

locust [lOkust] *n* migratory insect allied to grasshopper and destructive to vegetation; **l. bean** fruit of carob tree; **l. tree** carob tree.

locution [lokewshon] *n* phrase, idiom; style of speaking.

lode [lOd] *n* composite vein of metal ore > PDE.

lodestar, loadstar [lOdstaar] *n* polestar; (*fig*) guide, model.

lodestone see **loadstone**.

lodge [loj] *n* small house at entrance to park or to grounds of a mansion; small house for use of huntsmen *etc*; room at gateway of college *etc* for use of porters *etc*; residence of head of Cambridge or Oxford college; local branch of Freemasons; building where these meet; beaver's lair; wigwam ~ **lodge** *v/i* and *t* reside, dwell, *esp* temporarily and for payment of rent; occupy lodgings; be embedded, be firmly fixed (in); offer lodging to, house; place firmly; place safely; lay (statement) before legal authorities.

lodgement see **lodgment.**

lodger [*lo*jer] *n* one who lives in one part of another person's house and pays rent for this.

lodging [*lo*jing] *n* accommodation, *esp* if temporary; (*pl*) rooms hired in private house.

lodging-house [*lo*jing-hows] *n* house where rooms are let by the week or day.

lodgment, lodgement [*lo*jment] *n* accumulation of deposited matter; act of lodging; state of being lodged; stable position won by effort.

loess [*lO*-es] *n* (*geol*) deposit of wind-borne silt or loam > PDG.

loft (1) [*loft*] *n* attic; room over stable; pigeonhouse; flock of pigeons; gallery in church.

loft (2) *v/t* (*golf*) hit (ball) high ~ **loft** *n* stroke which lofts the ball; slope on edge of golf-club which causes this ~ **lofter** *n* golf-club for lofting.

lofty [*lo*fti] *adj* of great height; (*fig*) dignified, exalted; haughty ~ **loftily** *adv* ~ **loftiness** *n*.

log (1) [*log*] *n* rough unhewn mass or length of wood; apparatus for measuring ship's speed; daily record of a ship's voyage, aircraft flight, or car journey ~ **log** (*pres/part* **logging**, *p/t* and *p/part* **logged**) *v/t* record in a logbook; (*of ships etc*) move at (a specified speed); keep official record of; fell and cut up (timber) ~ **log** *adj* built of unhewn timber.

log (2) *n* (*abbr*) a logarithm.

loganberry [*lO*ganbeRi] *n* hybrid of raspberry and blackberry.

logan-stone [*lO*gan-stOn] *n* large stone so poised on that it will rock at a slight touch.

logarithm [*loge*Rithm] *n* (*math*) power to which a given number must be raised to produce another given number > PDS ~ **logarithmic, logarithmical** [*loge*Rithmik, loge*Ri*thmikal] *adj*.

logbook [*log*book] *n* daily record of the journey of a ship, aircraft, or car; document recording age, ownership *etc* of a motor vehicle; daily record of progress, observations, performance *etc*.

loge [*lO*zh] (*Fr*) *n* a theatre box.

loggerhead [*log*erhed] *n* heated metal bell for melting tar; (*ar*) fool; **at loggerheads** persistently quarrelling or disagreeing.

loggia [*lo*ji-a] *n* covered but not enclosed extension to a house; a gallery.

logic [*lo*jik] *n* science of formal deductive and inductive reasoning; process of argument or rational thought; mode of reasoning; (*coll*) reasonable argument or conclusion; (*fig*) necessary sequence of cause and effect.

logical [*lo*jikal] *adj* pertaining to logic; in accordance with rules of logic; capable of thinking logically; consistent; rational ~ **logicality** [loji-*ka*liti] *n* ~ **logically** *adv*.

logician [*lo*jishan] *n* one skilled in logic; student of logic.

logistics [*lo*jistiks] *n* (*pl*) (*mil*) art of moving and quartering troops; (*math*) computation; (*fig*) skill in planning the practical requirements of a journey, gathering, *etc*.

logo [*log*O] *n* (*print*) printed symbol, monogram or pattern used as trademark or as badge of an organization; single piece of type bearing this.

logo- *pref* pertaining to speech or words; pertaining to reason.

logorrhoea [logo*Ree*-a] *n* excessive or incoherent outpouring of words.

logos [*log*os] *n* (*theol*) the Word of God incarnate, Christ.

logroll [*log*ROl] *v/i* (*fig*) systematically praise another's work or assist his aims on condition that he praises or assists one's own ~ **logroller** *n* writer, politician *etc* who logrolls ~ **logrolling** *n* and *adj*.

logwood [*log*wood] *n* heartwood of an American tree used in dyeing.

loin [*loin*] *n* fleshy part of animal or human being just above hip and on either side of spine; flesh of this as food; (*pl fig*) male procreative power; male ancestry; **gird up one's loins** prepare for action.

loincloth [*loin*kloth] *n* strip of cloth tied round the loins to cover the lower part of the body.

loir [*loir*] *n* a large kind of dormouse.

loiter [*loi*ter] *v/i* remain lingering near a place; dawdle, delay ~ **loiterer** *n*.

loll [*lol*] *v/i* and *t* stand or sit in a limp lazy attitude; lounge; let (head or tongue) droop loosely.

Lollard [*lo*lard] *n* (*hist*) follower of John Wyclif.

lollipop [*lo*lipop] *n* (*coll*) large hard boiled sweet on a stick; warning disk on a pole held up to halt traffic while schoolchildren cross road.

lollop [*lo*lop] *v/i* (*coll*) move by clumsy bounds; bob up and down; lounge.

lolly [*lo*li] *n* (*coll*) lollipop; (*sl*) money.

lone [*lO*n] *adj* solitary; isolated, lonely; unfrequented; **play a l. hand** (*fig*) do something without the support of others; **l. wolf** person who chooses to live or work alone.

loneliness [*lO*nlines] *n* quality or state of being lonely.

lonely [*lO*nli] *adj* solitary; unfrequented; depressed for lack of friends.

loner [*lO*ner] *n* person who chooses to live or work alone.

lonesome [*lO*nsum] *adj* feeling lonely; desolate.

long (1) [*long*] *adj* greatly extended in distance or time; extending over a specified space or time; appearing to last a long time, tedious; **l. face** gloomy expression of face; **l. hundred** 120; **in the l. run** eventually, ultimately; **l. nose** gesture of contempt made by placing the thumb against the nose and stretching the fingers out; **l. shot** (*coll*) unlikely but accurate guess; **l. suit** (*fig*) strongest point; **l. wave** (*rad*) band of longest wavelengths used in broadcasting ~ **long** *adv* for a long time; at a remote time; **so l.** (*coll*) goodbye; **so l. as** provided that ~ **long** *n* (*mus*) a time-value in an obsolete system of notation > PDM; **the L. vac** (*coll*) university summer vacation.

long (2) *v/i* desire earnestly, yearn (for).

longarm [*long*aarm] *n* pruning-knife or shears on very long handle.

longboat [*long*bOt] *n* largest boat carried by sailing vessel.

longbow [*long*bO] *n* powerful archery bow; **draw the l.** (*coll*) exaggerate.

longevity [lonj*e*viti] *n* long life.

longhand [*long*hand] *n* ordinary writing as distinguished from shorthand or typing.

long-headed [long-*he*did] *adj* having skull long in proportion to its breadth, dolichocephalic; (*fig*) shrewd.

longing [*longing*] *adj* and *n* (feeling) great desire.

longitude [*lonjitewd/longitewd*] *n* angular distance east or west from standard meridian, *esp* Greenwich > PDG, PDS.

longitudinal [*lonjitewdinal/longitewdinal*] *adj* running lengthwise ~ **longitudinally** *adv*.

long-johns [*long*-jonz] *n* (*pl*) underpants with full-length or knee-length legs.

long-range [*long*-Raynj] *adj* (*of gun*) able to shoot accurately at a long distance; (*of forecast*) referring to a more distant future.

longshoreman [*long*shawrman] *n* one who is employed on the shore and on wharves on various odd jobs.

longshot [*long*shot] *n* (*cin*) photograph taken from far-off.

long-sighted [*long*sItid] *adj* capable of seeing at a great distance; capable of seeing only distant things clearly; (*fig*) prudent, foreseeing.

longstanding [*long*standing] *adj* continuing or existing for a long while.

long-suffering [*long*-*sufe*Ring] *adj* patient.

long-term [*long*-turm] *adj* designed to meet conditions, results *etc* in the distant future; whose effects will only be seen in the distant future.

longways [*long*wayz] *adv* lengthwise.

longwinded [*long*windid] *adj* able to run for a long time without getting out of breath; (*fig*) tediously diffuse in talking or writing.

loo (1) [*lOO*] *n* round card-game played for a pool; forfeit paid to the pool ~ **loo** *v/t* compel to pay forfeit to the pool.

loo (2) *n* (*coll*) water-closet, lavatory.

loofah [*lOO*fa] *n* sponge made from fibrous part of a tropical gourd.

look [*look*] *v/i* and *t* attentively exercise the sense of sight; direct the eyes (at); gaze, stare; convey by the expression of one's eyes; seem, appear; (*fig*) consider; **l. about one** examine one's surroundings or situation; **l. after** take care of; **l. alive** be alert; **l. at** direct the eyes at, gaze at; examine; **l. back** remember; cease to progress; **l. down on** despise; **l. for** seek; expect; **l. forward** to expect with pleasure; **l. in on** pay a casual visit to; **l. into** investigate, examine; **l. on** be a spectator; take no part in; regard, consider; **l. out** be careful; **l. out for** be on the watch for; **l. sharp** be alert or energetic; **l. to** count on, seek help *etc* from; **l. up** consult a book in order to find out about; visit; begin to improve; **l. up to** respect ~ **look** *n* act of looking; glance, *esp* if expressing emotion; expression of eyes or face; appearance; impression produced by appearance; **good looks** handsomeness, beauty ~ **look** *interj* (also **l. here, l. you**) pay attention! consider!

looker [*looker*] *n* one who looks; **good l.** (*coll*) good-looking person.

looker-on [lookeRon] *n* spectator.

look-in [*look*-in] *n* (*coll*) chance to take part; chance of success; hasty glance; short visit.

looking-glass [*looking*-glaas] *n* mirror.

lookout [*look*owt] *n* act of keeping watch; place from which it may be kept; one who keeps watch; prospect; **that's my l.** that concerns only me.

look-see [*look*-see] *n* (*sl*) hasty glance or examination.

loom (1) [*lOO*m] *n* machine for weaving cloth.

loom (2) *v/i* appear indistinctly, *esp* in magnified form; (*fig*) appear important and menacing; **l. large** appear disproportionately important.

loon [*lOO*n] *n* (*Scots* and *coll*) boor, lout; fool; (*dial*) puffin; guillemot.

loony [*lOO*ni] *adj* (*coll*) mad, crazy; **l. bin** (*sl*) lunatic asylum ~ **loony** *n* (*sl*) madman.

loop [*lOO*p] *n* bend made in cord, wire *etc* in such a way that the ends cross; figure produced by curve crossing itself; noose; bend, doubling; (*railway*) loop-line; (*ar*) loophole ~ **loop** *v/t* and *i* form into a loop; fasten with loop; **l. the l.** (*aer*) describe a complete vertical circle in the air~ **looper** *n* caterpillar which advances by repeatedly arching its body into a loop.

loophole [*lOO*phOl] *n* vertical slit in castle wall, for shooting through; (*fig*) means of evading or escaping.

loop-line [*lOO*p-lIn] *n* railway line which branches from the main line but later rejoins it.

loopy [*lOO*pi] *adj* (*sl*) crazy.

loose [*lOO*s] *adj* not fastened or pre-packed; not tied up or confined; able to move freely; not tight, not firmly fixed; not close-fitting; careless, inaccurate, vague; dissolute, immoral; not closely woven; flabby; (*of bowels*) inclined to diarrhoea; **l. box** stable or van in which an animal can move about; **at a l. end** uncertain what to do next; unoccupied ~ **loose** *adv* in a loose way; **play fast and l.** behave rashly or unscrupulously ~ **loose** *n* release; **on the l.** free from restraint; on a spree ~ **loose** *v/t* untie, undo; release from confinement or restraint, set free; detach; fire (gun); shoot (arrow); (*eccles*) absolve.

looseleaf [*lOO*sleef] *adj* (*of notebook etc*) with separately detachable pages.

loosely [*lOO*sli] *adv* in a loose way.

loosen [*lOO*sen] *v/t* and *i* make or become loose or looser; relax; **l. up** make (muscles) supple by exercise; (*fig*) grow less shy or reticent.

looseness [*lOO*snis] *n* quality of being loose.

loosestrife [*lOO*s-stRif] *n* popular name for several species of flowering waterside plants.

loot [*lOO*t] *v/t* and *i* plunder the enemy's goods; seize (goods) by force of arms; sack ~ **loot** *n* booty, plunder; (*coll*) financial gain ~ **looter** *n*.

lop (1) (*pres/part* **lopping**, *p/t* and *p/part* **lopped**) [*lop*] *v/t* chop off; shorten (branches *etc*) by chopping; trim back, prune ~ **lop** *n* that which is lopped from a tree.

lop (2) (*pres/part* **lopping**, *p/t* and *p/part* **lopped**) *v/i* hang loosely, droop (*esp* of animal's ears); move in clumsy jerky leaps.

lope [*lOp*] *v/i* run strongly and smoothly in long strides ~ **lope** *n* loping pace or movement.

lopeared [*lop*eerd] *adj* with long drooping ears.

loppings [*lop*ingz] *n* (*pl*) branches and twigs trimmed from trees.

lopsided [*lop*sIdid] *adj* with one side smaller than the other; unevenly balanced ~ **lopsidedly** *adv*.

loquacious [lokwayshus] *adj* talkative ~ **loquacity** [lokwasiti] *n*.

loquat [*lO*kwat] *n* Chinese and Japanese tree with small red fruit of sharp taste; Mediterranean tree with sweet yellow fruit.

lord [*lawrd*] *n* ruler, master; peer, nobleman; feudal superior; **the L.** God; Jesus Christ; **the (House of) Lords** upper chamber of British

Parliament; **lords and ladies** (*bot*) wild arum; **L. Chancellor** chief judge of England; **the L.'s Day** Sunday; **L., good L., o L.** exclamations of surprise or dismay; **live like a l.** live luxuriously; **L. Mayor** mayor of London or of certain other cities; **my L.** form of address to bishops, peers below a duke, judges in court, *etc*; **Our L.** Jesus Christ; **L. Rector** honorary head of a Scottish university; **the L.'s Supper** the Eucharist ∼ **lord** *v/i* domineer; **l. it over** behave arrogantly to, domineer over.

lordling [*lawrd*ling] *n* young or petty lord.

lordly [*lawrd*li] *adj* dignified; magnificent; haughty ∼ **lordliness** *n*.

lordship [*lawrd*ship] *n* power or jurisdiction of a lord; territory ruled by a lord; control, authority; **your l., his l.** formal mode of addressing or referring to persons with the title 'Lord'.

lore [*lawr*] *n* specialized knowledge; knowledge handed down by tradition, *esp* within a limited group; esoteric knowledge.

lorgnette [lawrn*yet*] *n* pair of eyeglasses on long handle; opera-glass.

lorikeet [*lo*Rikeet/*lo*Ri*keet*] *n* small Malayan parrot.

loris [*lo*Ris] *n* either of two species of lemur found in India, Sri Lanka, and the East Indies.

lorn [*lawrn*] *adj* forlorn; lonely.

lorry [*lo*Ri] *n* large strong open truck or wagon.

lorry-hop [*lo*Ri-hop] *v/i* (*sl*) travel by getting free lifts on lorries.

lorryload [*lo*RilOd] *n* as much as a lorry can carry.

lory [*lo*Ri] *n* small parrot of Australia and Asia.

lose (*p/t* and *p/part* lost) [*lOO*z] *v/t* and *i* no longer have; be deprived of by accident or misfortune; mislay, fail to find; fail to get or win; be too late for; be bereaved of; waste; be defeated or beaten; suffer loss, become worse off; fail to hear, see or understand; cause or allow to perish; (*of clock or watch*) go too slowly; (*refl*) miss the right path; become absorbed in; **l. one's head** become flustered, panic; **l. one's temper** grow angry; **l. one's way** fail to find the right path; **l. out** (*US*) be defeated after a struggle.

loser [*lOO*zer] *n* one who loses; one who is beaten in game, competition *etc*; **bad l.** one who shows annoyance when beaten.

losing [*lOO*zing] *adj* leading to defeat or loss.

loss [*los*] *n* act or process of losing; result of losing; that which is lost; harm, deprivation; waste; bereavement; failure to gain, win, obtain *etc*; (*mil*) men killed, incapacitated or captured; equipment destroyed or captured; **at a l.** making a deficit; perplexed.

loss-leader [*los*-leeder] *n* goods sold at a loss in order to attract customers.

lost [*lost*] *p/t* and *p/part* of **lose** ∼ **lost** *adj* that cannot be found; having lost one's way; ruined, destroyed; wrecked; drowned; wasted; damned; hopelessly immoral; **get l.!** (*coll*) go away!; **l. in** engrossed by; **l. on** having no influence on; wasted on; **l. to** not having, not capable of; wrested from.

lot [*lot*] *n* large quantity; item to be sold by auction; plot of land; (*cin*) studio and surrounding land; that which fate or chance bestows; destiny; luck; one of a set of pebbles, sticks, marked pieces of paper *etc* used to decide something by chance; (*coll*) person, character; **lots of** (*coll*) many, much; **cast (draw) lots** decide by the random throwing or taking of marked objects; **the (whole) l.** the total number or quantity existing or available.

loth see **loath**.

lotion [*lO*shon] *n* liquid preparation used externally to treat skin diseases or to improve the complexion ∼ **lotion** *v/t* apply lotion to.

lotos see **lotus**.

lottery [*lote*Ri] *n* competition in which certain tickets drawn at random win prizes; (*fig*) matter of chance.

lotto [*lot*O] *n* game of chance in which numbers are drawn at random, bingo.

lotus, lotos [*lO*tus] *n* Egyptian waterlily; Indian waterlily; (*archi*) ornamental pattern based on a waterlily; (*Gk myth*) plant whose fruit caused bliss and complete idleness; **l. position** cross-legged posture used in meditation.

lotus-eater [*lO*tus-eeter] *n* (*Gk myth*) member of an imaginary tribe who lived in happy idleness; (*fig*) dreamy and inactive person.

loud [*lowd*] *adj* producing considerable sound, noisy; (*fig*) boisterous; (*fig*) too showy, gaudy, vulgar ∼ **loud** *adv* ∼ **loudly** *adv* ∼ **loudness** *n*.

loudhailer [*lowd*hayler] *n* megaphone.

loudspeaker [*lowd*speeker] *n* (*rad*) amplifier which radiates soundwaves so that they can be heard by a number of persons.

lough [*lokh*] *n* lake; loch.

lounge [*lownj*] *v/i* recline lazily, loll; move lazily, stroll; be idle ∼ **lounge** *n* act of lounging; comfortable sitting-room, *esp* in hotel or club; sofa, couch; best bar in a public house; **l. lizard** idle hanger-on, *esp* one who pays court to rich elderly women; **l. suit** suit for informal daytime wear ∼ **lounger** *n* idler.

lour, lower (2) [*lowr*] *v/i* (*of persons*) frown, scowl; (*of sky, clouds etc*) look dark and threatening ∼ **louring, lowering** *adj*.

louse (*pl* **lice**) [*lows*] *n* parasitic insect infesting hair and skin of human beings and animals; (*sl*) contemptible wretch.

lousy [*lowzi*] *adj* infested with lice; (*coll*) extremely bad, unwell or unpleasant; **l. with** full of; having plenty of ∼ **lousily** *adv* ∼ **lousiness** *n*.

lout [*lowt*] *n* coarse ill-mannered fellow ∼ **loutish** *adj*.

louver, louvre [*lOO*ver] *n* (*hist*) turret-shaped ventilator on a hall roof; (*bui*) window-frame with inclined slats for ventilation > PDBl.

lovable [*luv*ab'l] *adj* that can or should be loved; charming, attractive ∼ **lovably** *adv* ∼ **lovableness** *n*.

lovat [*luv*at] *adj* and *n* grey-green.

love [*luv*] *n* warm affection, strong emotional attachment; sexual passion or desire; charity, benevolence; self-sacrificing goodwill; devotion; one whom or that which one loves; attractive person or thing; term of endearment; (*tennis*) no score; (*myth* and *arts*) the god Cupid, represented as winged child with bow and arrow; **fall in l. (with)** begin to feel passionate attachment (for); **for the l. of** for the sake of; **give (send) one's l. to** convey affectionate greetings to; **make l.** express sexual desire, *usu* physically; **make l. to** have sexual intercourse with; caress, kiss, fondle; (ar) woo; (fig) seek the favour of; **not for l. nor money** not on any terms; **no l. lost** enmity; **play for l.** play without stakes ∼ **love** v/t and i feel love (for); like very much; be very glad (to).

love-affair [luv-afair] n relationship between persons in love with each other; sexual relationship outside marriage.

lovebird [luvburd] n small African parakeet, budgerigar; (sl) lover.

lovechild [luvchild] n illegitimate child.

love-feast [luv-feest] n religious service including a simple meal.

love-hate [luv-hayt] adj (of relationship) containing strong elements of simultaneous love and hate.

love-in [luv-in] n (sl) a gathering of hippies.

loveless [luvles] adj not feeling love; not loved by anyone; without love ∼ **lovelessly** adv ∼ **lovelessness** n.

lovelight [luvlIt] n tender or happy facial expression of one who is in love.

loveliness [luvlinis] n quality of being lovely.

lovelock [luvlok] n curl of hair over temples or brow.

lovelorn [luvlawrn] adj suffering through unrequited or thwarted love; jilted.

lovely [luvli] adj beautiful, attractive; (coll) delightful ∼ **lovely** n (coll) attractive girl.

love-making [luv-mayking] n words or actions expressing sexual desire; sexual acts; courtship.

love-nest [luv-nest] n house, flat etc where two lovers habitually meet, usu in secret.

lover [luver] n one who loves (a specified person or thing); one of a pair of persons who are in love and/or have sexual relationship with each other outside marriage (gen masc when sing); admirer, devotee ∼ **loverlike** adj.

lovesick [luvsik] adj pining away for love.

lovey [luvi] n (sl) darling.

loving [luving] adj feeling love; expressing love; tender, affectionate; dutiful ∼ **lovingly** adv.

loving-cup [luving-kup] n large cup passed round among several persons from which each drinks.

loving-kindness [luving-kIndnis] n tender care; mercy.

low (1) [lO] n sound made by cattle ∼ **low** v/i utter this sound.

low (2) adj not high, not far above a surface; of less than usual height; not intense; (of numbers, sums etc) not large; not high in pitch; inferior; of inferior rank, social class, or status; poor; humble; vulgar; obscene; dishonourable; (biol) primitive; (ethn) uncivilized; (fig) melancholy; **L. Church** evangelical section of Church of England; **l. comedy** farce; burlesque; **L. Countries** Holland, Belgium, and Luxemburg; **l. frequency** (elect, rad) of a frequency less than 1,000 periods per second; **L. Mass** Mass without singing or use of incense; **l. spirits** melancholy, depression; **L. Sunday** first Sunday after Easter; **l. tide**, **l. water** ebb-tide; **in l. water** (fig) short of money ∼ **low** adv in a low position; at a low degree; in low voice or pitch; at little cost; **bring l.** humiliate, degrade; ruin; **lay l.** kill; knock down; **lie l.** remain hidden; **run l.** (of supplies) begin to be short, dwindle ∼ **low** n

low or lowest position, point, price or degree; nadir; (mot) gear used for slowest speeds.

lowborn [lObawrn] adj born of humble parents.

lowbrow [lObRow] n and adj (coll) (person) not intellectual.

low-budget [lO-bujit] adj economical, cheap.

low-class [lO-klaas] adj of inferior quality or rank.

lowdown [lOdown] adj (coll) mean, dishonourable ∼ **lowdown** n (sl) inside information; full information; mean trick.

low-grade [lO-gRayd] adj of inferior quality.

lower (1) [lO-er] adj (comp) less high; **l. animals** all animals except man; **l. case** (typ) letters which are not capitals; **L. Chamber (House)** House of Commons; **l. classes** working classes, proletariat; the poor; **l. deck** (nav) petty officers and men; **l. regions** hell; (coll) basement ∼ **lower** v/t and i cause to descend or decrease; diminish; descend; decrease; humiliate ∼ **lower** adv (comp) less highly.

lower (2) [lowr] see **lour.**

lowering (1) [lO-eRing] adj that lowers; degrading; (of diet) plain, not highly nourishing.

lowering (2) [low-eRing] adj see **louring.**

lowermost [lO-ermOst] adj lowest.

lowest [lO-est] adj and adv superl of **low** (2).

lowing [lO-ing] n sound made by cattle.

low-key [lO-kee] adj (arts) in dark tones of colour; (fig) unemphatic, restrained; (mus) in a low key.

lowland [lOland] n low-lying land of a region; **the Lowlands** south-eastern region of Scotland ∼ **lowland** adj belonging to low-lying land; belonging to the Scottish Lowlands ∼ **lowlander** n inhabitant of the Scottish Lowlands or of a lowland area.

lowly [lOli] adj humble, meek; of low rank, class, or status ∼ **lowly** adv ∼ **lowliness** n.

low-lying [lO-lI-ing] adj (of land) not much above sea-level.

low-necked [lO-nekt] adj (of garment) cut so as to show the neck, upper chest and shoulders bare.

low-pitched [lO-picht] adj low in pitch; (bui) having a low ceiling; (of roof) gentle in slope.

low-powered [lO-powrd] adj having little power or importance.

low-profile [lO-pROfIl] adj unobtrusive, trying not to attract attention.

loyal [loi-al] adj true to one's allegiance, faithful, esp to the Crown, a cause, a person etc; upright, honourable ∼ **loyally** adv.

loyalist [loi-alist] n one who remains loyal to the government in times of revolt or disturbance; **Ulster L.** one who supports the union of Ulster with England.

loyalty [loi-alti] n quality of being loyal.

lozenge [lozenj] n small flat medicinal tablet, usu sweetened, to be dissolved in the mouth; (geom) parallelogram of four equal sides with two obtuse and two acute angles; (archi) diamond-shaped pattern; window-pane of this shape; facet of this shape on gem; (her) shield or figure of this shape.

L-plate [el-playt] n plate displayed on motor vehicle driven by provisionally licensed learner.

LSD [el-es-dee] n (med) lysergic acid diethylamide, a synthetic drug causing hallucinations and emotional disturbance.

lubber [*luber*] *n* clumsy, stupid fellow; (*naut*) untrained seaman ~ **lubberly** *adv* and *adj*.

lube [*lOOb*] *n* (*coll*) lubricating oil.

lubra [*loobRa*] *n* Australian female aboriginal.

lubricant [*lOObRikant*] *n* and *adj* (oil or grease) that lubricates.

lubricate [*lOObRikayt*] *v/t* diminish friction (*esp* in machinery) by applying oil or grease to; make slippery; (*sl*) bribe; (*sl*) ply with drink ~ **lubrication** [*lOObRikayshon*] *n*.

lubricator [*lOObRikayter*] *n* one who lubricates; a lubricant; instrument for applying oil or grease.

lubricity [*lOObRisiti*] *n* slipperiness, smoothness; (*fig*) shiftiness, dishonesty; lewdness, lust, salaciousness ~ **lubricious** *adj* ~ **lubricous** [*lOObRikus*] *adj*.

lucarne [*lOOkaarn*] *n* dormer window in roof or spire.

luce [*lews*] *n* a full-grown pike.

lucent [*lOOsent*] *adj* bright, shining; transparent.

lucerne [*lOOsurn*] *n* plant resembling clover grown for fodder.

lucid [*lewsid/lOOsid*] *adj* clear, easy to understand; thinking and expressing oneself clearly; sane, rational; (*poet*) transparent, bright; (*of star*) visible to naked eye; **l. interval** period of sanity between fits of madness or rage.

lucidity [*lewsiditi/lOOsiditi*] *n* state or quality of being lucid ~ **lucidly** *adv*.

luck [*luk*] *n* good or bad fortune, chance; good fortune; **down on one's l.** unlucky; impoverished; **in l.** fortunate; **out of l.** having bad luck; **worse l.!** unfortunately.

luckily [*lukili*] *adv* fortunately.

luckless [*lukles*] *adj* unlucky ~ **lucklessly** *adv*.

lucky [*luki*] *adj* fortunate; likely to bring good luck; **l. bag, l. dip** tub from which hidden objects can be selected by touch.

lucrative [*lOOkRativ*] *adj* profitable, money-making ~ **lucratively** *adv* ~ **lucrativeness** *n*.

lucre [*lOOker*] *n* (*pej*) money, profit; **filthy l.** ill-gotten gain; (*joc*) money.

lucubrate [*lOOkewbRayt*] *v/i* study, *esp* by night; produce learned and elaborate writings or discourse ~ **lucubration** [*lOOkewbRayshon*] *n*.

Luddite [*ludIt*] *n* one of a band of English workmen who tried in 1811–16 to prevent industrialization by wrecking factories and machinery.

ludicrous [*lOOdikRus*] *adj* ridiculous, absurd ~ **ludicrously** *adv* ~ **ludicrousness** *n*.

ludo [*lOOdO*] *n* game played on a chequered board with counters and dice.

lues [*lOO-eez*] *n* syphilis ~ **luetic** *adj*.

luff [*luf*] *v/t* and *i* (*naut*) bring (head of ship) nearer wind; get on windward side of (other boat) ~ **luff** *n* side of fore-and-aft sail nearest to mast or stay; broadest part of ship's bow.

Luftwaffe [*looftvaafe*] *n* the German Air Force.

lug (1) [*lug*] *n* large marine worm.

lug (2) see **lug-sail**.

lug (3) *n* (*dial*) ear; small flat curved projection used as handle on pot, jar *etc*; loop on harness; projection for holding bolts.

lug (4) (*pres/part* lugging, *p/t* and *p/part* lugged) *v/t* and *i* pull or drag with violent effort; drag along; **l. in** introduce (a subject) irrelevantly ~ **lug** *n* act of lugging.

luge [*lOOzh*] *n* small toboggan for one person.

luggage [*lugij*] *n* baggage of a traveller.

luggage-rack [*lugij-Rak*] *n* shelf for luggage in compartment of railway train.

lugger [*luger*] *n* small vessel with lug-sails.

lug-sail [*lug-sayl*] *n* four-cornered sail bent on an oblique yard.

lugubrious [*lOOgOObRi-us*] *adj* gloomy.

lukewarm [*lOOkwawrm*] *adj* neither hot nor cold, tepid; (*fig*) lacking enthusiasm, indifferent.

lull [*lul*] *v/t* and *i* induce calmness in, soothe; induce (child *etc*) to fall asleep, *esp* by singing and rocking; allay; diminish, subside ~ **lull** *n* brief period of calm between outbreaks of storm, pain, fighting *etc*.

lullaby [*lulabI*] *n* soothing song to induce child to sleep.

lulu [*lOOlOO*] *n* (*US sl*) anything very easy or pleasant.

lumbago [*lumbaygO*] *n* rheumatic pain in the lower back ~ **lumbaginous** [*lumbayjinus*] *adj*.

lumbar [*lumber*] *adj* (*anat*) of or near the loins; **l. region** back of body from ribs to haunch.

lumber (1) [*lumber*] *n* large useless objects; disused furniture; rubbish; timber sawn into rough planks ~ **lumber** *v/t* and *i* clutter up with rubbish, encumber; overcrowd; cut timber for market ~ **lumberer** *n* lumberman.

lumber (2) *v/i* move heavily and clumsily ~ **lumbering** *adj*.

lumber-jack [*lumber-jak*] *n* lumberman.

lumber-jacket [*lumber-jakit*] *n* warm hip-length jacket fastening up to neck.

lumberman [*lumberman*] *n* man who cuts down trees and prepares them for the market.

lumber-room [*lumber-ROOm*] *n* room where unused furniture *etc* is kept.

lumen [*lOOmen*] *n* unit of luminous flux > PDS.

luminary [*lOOmineRi*] *n* a source of light, *esp* one of the heavenly bodies; (*fig*) distinguished and learned person.

luminescent [*lOOminesent*] *adj* emitting light.

luminosity [*lOOminositi*] *n* brightness.

luminous [*lOOminus*] *adj* emitting light; bright, glowing; (*fig*) clear; phosphorescent; **l. flux** amount of light passing through an area per second; **l. paint** paint, containing a phosphorescent compound, which glows after exposure to light ~ **luminously** *adv*.

lumme, lummy [*lumi*] *interj* (*sl*) exclamation of surprise.

lump [*lump*] *n* shapeless mass; clod; a swelling on the body; large piece; (*coll*) slob, stupid person; lout; small cube of sugar; **in the l.** as a whole; **l. in the throat** constriction caused by emotion; **l. sum** sum paid at one time in settlement of several claims ~ **lump** *v/t* and *i* form into lumps; (*coll*) carry; **l. along** walk heavily and clumsily; **l. it** (*coll*) put up with something unpleasant; **l. together** include indiscriminately in one mass.

lumpen [*lumpen*] *adj* (*Ger*) **l. proletariat** the poorest of the lower class; ignorant, shiftless people, *esp* those uninterested in revolutionary politics.

lumpish [*lumpish*] *adj* shapeless; clumsy; stupid.

lumpy [*lumpi*] *adj* full of lumps; shapeless.

lunacy [*lOOnasi*] *n* madness; great foolishness.

lunar [*lOOner*] *adj* pertaining to the moon;

l. month period from one new moon to the next, 29.5305887 days; (*pop*) four weeks.
lunate [*lOO*nayt] *adj* crescent-shaped.
lunatic [*lOO*natik] *adj* insane, mad; foolish; **l. asylum** hospital for the care of the mentally ill; **l. fringe** fanatical minority of extremists ~ **lunatic** *n* madman.
lunation [*lOO*nayshon] *n* period of a lunar month.
lunch [*lunch*/*lunsh*] *n* meal or snack taken between noon and 1 p.m.; workman's mid-morning snack ~ **lunch** *v/i* and *t* entertain to lunch; eat lunch.
luncheon [*lunsh*on/*lunch*on] *n* formal midday meal; lunch; **l. meat** type of processed tinned meat; **l. voucher** voucher to be exchanged for food in restaurant.
lunch-hour [*lunch*-owr] *adj* and *n* (of or in) a midday break from work.
lunette [*lOO*net] *n* (*archi*) curved opening in vault; tympanum; semi-circular space filled with painting or sculpture.
lung [*lung*] *n* organ for breathing air > PDB; (*fig*) large open space in a city.
lunge (1) [*lunj*] *n* long rope for exercising a horse ~ **lunge** *v/t* exercise horse on a lunge.
lunge (2) *n* sudden forward thrust or blow; (*boxing*) blow delivered from the shoulder ~ **lunge** *v/i*.
lungfish [*lung*fish] *n* fish with lungs as well as gills.
lungwort [*lung*wurt] *n* species of lichen; type of plant with spotted leaves.
lunik [*lOO*nik] *n* (*aer*) a lunar sputnik.
lupin [*lOO*pin] *n* garden plant with flowers in long spikes.
lupine [*lOO*pIn] *adj* of or like a wolf.
lupus [*lOO*pus] *n* tuberculous disease of skin of face.
lur, lure (2) [*lOO*r] *n* long curved trumpet used for calling cattle home; type of Bronze Age trumpet.
lurch (1) [*lurch*] *n* **leave in the l.** forsake (a person) in difficulties.
lurch (2) *n* sudden stagger ~ **lurch** *v/i* move in unsteady jerks, stagger.
lurcher [*lurch*er] *n* dog bred from cross between sheepdog and greyhound.
lure (1) [*lewr*/*lOO*r] *n* decoy; bait; (*fig*) enticement, beguiling charm; (*falconry*) bait to recall hawk from hunting ~ **lure** *v/t* attract, entice, *esp* into danger or sin; recall or capture by a lure.
lure (2) see **lur**.
lurid [*lewr*Rid/*loor*Rid] *adj* ghastly, horrifying; sensational, scandalous; (*of colours*) crude, glaring; casting a harsh unnatural light ~ **luridly** *adv* ~ **luridness** *n*.
lurk [*lurk*] *v/i* hide, lie in ambush; (*fig*) exist unknown, be latent ~ **lurker** *n* ~ **lurking** *adj*.
luscious [*lush*us] *adj* pleasing to the taste, delicious; excessively ripe and sweet, cloying; of rich sensuous beauty ~ **lusciously** *adv*.
lush [*lush*] *adj* (*of plants*) growing abundantly; fresh and juicy; (*coll*) ample; delightful; (*sl*) drunk ~ **lush** *n* (*sl*) drinking-bout; alcohol ~ **lush** *v/t* (*sl*) drink; **l. up** ply with drink.
lust [*lust*] *n* sexual desire, *esp* considered as excessive or sinful; (*fig*) intense desire ~ **lust** *v/i* feel strong (*esp* sexual) desire.
lustful [*lust*fool] *adj* feeling or showing lust ~ **lustfully** *adv* ~ **lustfulness** *n*.

lustily [*lust*ili] *adv* vigorously, heartily.
lustral [*lust*Ral] *adj* purificatory.
lustrate [*lust*Rayt] *v/t* purify by ritual cleansing or offerings ~ **lustration** [*lust*Rayshon] *n*.
lustre [*lust*er] *n* sheen, gloss, iridescence > PDP; brilliancy; dazzling beauty; (*fig*) renown, glory; one of circle of glass prisms hung round a vase, candlestick *etc*; **l. ware** pottery with glaze giving metallic effect.
lustrous [*lust*Rus] *adj* shining, radiant.
lusty [*lust*i] *adj* vigorous, healthy; hearty; strong.
lutanist [*lOO*tanist] *n* lute-player.
lute (1) [*lOO*t] *n* fretted stringed musical instrument plucked with the fingers > PDM.
lute (2) *n* clay or cement used to stop up joints, cracks *etc* ~ **lute** *v/t*.
luteous [*lOO*ti-us] *adj* deep orange-yellow.
lutetium [*lOO*teeshi-um] *n* (*chem*) rare lanthanide element > PDS.
Lutheran [*lOO*theRan] *adj* pertaining to Martin Luther, German leader of Protestant Reformation ~ **Lutheran** *n* follower of Luther; member of Lutheran Church ~ **Lutheranism** *n*.
lux [*luks*] *n* unit of illumination, one lumen per square metre.
luxate [*luk*sayt] *v/t* dislocate ~ **luxation** [*luk*sayshon] *n*.
luxe [*lOO*ks/*luks*] *n* richness; **de l.** luxurious, splendid, costly, sumptuous.
luxuriance [lug*zewr*Ri-ans] *n* abundant growth, lushness; fertility; abundance, profusion; extravagance ~ **luxuriant** *adj* ~ **luxuriantly** *adv*.
luxuriate [lug*zewr*Ri-ayt] *v/i* revel (in); live luxuriously; grow profusely.
luxurious [lug*zewr*Ri-us] *adj* providing or provided with luxuries; sumptuous, splendid; lavish; extremely comfortable; fond of luxury ~ **luxuriously** *adv* ~ **luxuriousness** *n*.
luxury [*luk*sheRi] *n* way of life that satisfies all material desires regardless of expense; something agreeable but not necessary; expensive pleasure or comfort; self-indulgence in material pleasures; enjoyment ~ **luxury** *adj* (*coll*) luxurious.
lycanthropy [lIk*anth*Ropi] *n* symptom of mental disorder in which the sufferer thinks he is a wolf or other animal and acts like one; supposed power of a magician to change into a wolf.
lycée [*lee*say] *n* French secondary school maintained by State.
lyceum [lI*see*-um] *n* building housing a literary society, with lecture halls, library *etc*.
lych-gate see **lich-gate**.
lyddite [*lid*It] *n* explosive consisting of picric acid mixed with nitrobenzene and vaseline.
lye [*lI*] *n* alkaline solution of wood-ashes in water used in washing and in soap-making.
lying (1) [*lI*-ing] *adj* deliberately false, untrue; that tells lies ~ **lyingly** *adv*.
lying (2) *adj* recumbent; prostrate.
lying-in [lI-ing-*in*] *n* confinement, childbirth.
lyke-wake [*lIk*-wayk] *n* watch kept at night over dead body.
lyme-grass [*lIm*-gRaas] *n* species of grass planted on sand to bind it together.
lymph [*limf*] *n* colourless fluid formed in tissues of

animal body and drained into the blood-system by lymphatic vessels > PDB; clear fluid exuding from inflamed tissues, *esp* that taken from cowpox vesicles for use as vaccine.

lymphatic [lim*f*atik] *adj* pertaining to lymph; secreting or conveying lymph; (*fig*) sluggish ~ **lymphatics** *n* (*pl*) vessels conveying lymph.

lynch [*linch*] *v/t* attack and put to death (a presumed offender) by mob violence without legal trial ~ **lynch** *adj*; **l. law** execution by a mob without trial ~ **lynching** *n* act of killing by lynch law.

lynchet [*lin*chet] *n* (*arch*) ridge or ledge on hillside caused by ploughing.

lynx [*links*] *n* animal of cat tribe with short thick tail and tufted ears; (*fig*) very sharp-sighted or observant person.

lyre [*lir*] *n* ancient Greek string instrument plucked with a plectrum > PDM; (*fig*) poetic talent; **l. bird** Australian bird with long lyre-shaped tail.

lyric [*li*Rik] *n* words for a song, *esp* a modern popular song; short poem suitable for singing; short stanzaic poem primarily expressing the writer's emotions or thoughts ~ **lyric** *adj* of or like a song; (*of poem*) short, stanzaic, personal and emotional; pertaining to the lyre.

lyrical [*li*Rikal] *adj* lyric; of or like lyric poetry; (*coll*) enthusiastic ~ **lyrically** *adv*.

lyricism [*li*Risizm] *n* lyrical quality or character.

lyrist [*lir*Rist/*li*Rist] *n* player on the lyre; composer of lyrics.

lysergic [lɪ*surj*ik] *adj* **l. acid** crystalline acid obtained from ergot or synthetically made, used in making a hallucinogenic drug.

lysis [*li*sis] *n* (*biol*) disintegration of bacterial cells.

lysol [*li*sol] *n* disinfectant mixture of cresol and soap > PDS.

M

m [*em*] thirteenth letter of the English alphabet; Roman numeral = 1,000; (*abbr*) million.

ma [*maa*] *n* (*coll abbr*) mother.

ma'am [*mam*/*maam*] *n* (*abbr*) madam.

mac (1) [*mak*] *pref* (*Gael*) son of ~ **mac** *n* (*coll*) form of address; Scotsman.

mac (2) *n* (*coll abbr*) mackintosh.

macabre [*makaaber*] *adj* gruesome.

macadam [*makadam*] *n* road-surfacing material of hard stone broken into small pieces > PDE ~ **macadamize** *v/t* make or cover (road) with this.

macaroni [*makaROni*] *n* a wheaten paste made into long thin tubes and dried; (*hist*) 18th-century dandy; (*sl*) an Italian.

macaronic [*makaRonik*] *adj* (*of verse*) written in a mixture or combination of two languages.

macaroon [*makaROOn*] *n* biscuit or cake made chiefly of almonds and sugar.

macassar [*makaser*] *n* type of hair-oil.

macaw [*makaw*] *n* tropical American parrot.

mace (1) [*mays*] *n* staff of office with a metal head; (*hist*) spiked iron club.

mace (2) *n* spice made from dried nutmeg.

mace (3) *n* (*tr*) (*US*) form of teargas used by police, causing choking, vomiting and diarrhoea.

macebearer [*maysbairRer*] *n* one who carries a mace in procession.

macedoine [*masaydwan*] *n* (*Fr*) dish of chopped mixed fruits or vegetables in jelly.

macerate [*maseRayt*] *v/t* soften by steeping; make lean by fasting.

mach [*mach*/*maakh*/*maak*] *n* (*aer*) ratio of speed of aircraft *etc* to the speed of sound, 770 miles an hour; **m. meter** instrument registering speed in maches.

machete [*machayti*] *n* large chopping knife.

machiavellian [*maki-aveli-an*] *adj* cunning; unscrupulous; without political morality.

machinate [*makinayt*] *v/i* plot, intrigue; contrive ~ **machination** [*makinayshon*] *n* plot.

machine [*masheen*] *n* any tool or device for overcoming resistance by applying force, *usu* at another point; any apparatus that applies power so as to perform work or direct movement > PDS, PDE; organization for carrying out a specified function; (*fig*) person who acts without apparent reasoning or emotion; **m. tool** any tool operated by machinery ~ **machine** *v/t* and *i* make, finish or heat by machinery; use a machine ~ **machiner** *n* one who operates a machine.

machine-gun [*masheen-gun*] *n* quick-firing small-arm mechanically operated gun ~ **machine-gun** *v/t*.

machinery [*masheeneRi*] *n* machines; the parts of a machine; contrivances; organized means for achieving some process; (*fig*) devices, *esp* supernatural, aiding development of literary plot.

machinist [*masheenist*] *n* one who invents, makes or operates a machine.

machismo [*machizmO*/*mashizmO*] *n* (*Sp*) urge to

prove one's virility through violent or rash acts or by domineering over others.

mackerel [*makeRel*] *n* an edible sea-fish; (*sl*) pimp; **m. sky** sky streaked with small masses of high cloud > PDG.

mackintosh [*makintosh*] *n* raincoat, *esp* one made of waterproof rubber-coated fabric.

mackle [*mak'l*] *n* (*typ*) an impression blurred from defective printing.

macrame [*makRaami*] *n* decorative fringe *etc* of knotted cord; art of making this.

macro- *pref* large; long.

macrobiotic [*makRObI-otik*] *adj* (*of diet*) consisting of vegetarian foods without chemical fertilizers or additives and containing a balance of acids and alkalis.

macrocephalic [*makROsefalik*] *adj* having an abnormally large head.

macrocosm [*makROkozm*] *n* the whole universe; society taken as a whole.

macron [*makRon*] *n* horizontal mark (-) placed over a vowel to show that the sound is long.

macula [*makewla*] *n* spot, stain; blemish; sunspot ~ **maculate** *v/t* mark with spots.

mad [*mad*] *adj* insane, mentally disordered; frenzied, frantic; wild; foolish, rash; (*coll*) excessively fond of or eager for; (*of dog*) suffering from rabies; **like m.** (*coll*) extremely ~ **mad** (*pres*/*part* **madding**, *p*/*t* and *p*/*part* **madded**) *v/t* and *i* (*ar*) make or become mad; act as if mad.

madam [*madam*] *n* term of formal address to a woman, *esp* one in authority or of high rank; (*coll*) manageress of a brothel.

madame (*pl* **mesdames**) [*madam*] *n* title of a married Frenchwoman.

madcap [*madkap*] *adj* and *n* wild or rash (person).

madden [*maden*] *v/t* make mad; make angry ~ **maddening** *adj* ~ **maddeningly** *adv*.

madder [*mader*] *n* plant whose root gives a red dye.

made [*mayd*] *p*/*t* and *p*/*part* of **make** (1) ~ **made** *adj* artificially produced; (*of a person*) successful; (*of the body*) built, formed.

Madeira [*madeerRa*] *n* a rich white wine; **M. cake** a fruitless cake of spongy texture.

madeleine [*madelayn*] *n* small rich cake.

mademoiselle [*madmwazel*] *n* title of an unmarried Frenchwoman.

madhouse [*madhows*] *n* lunatic asylum; (*coll*) noisy, disorganized assembly of people.

madly [*madli*] *adj* in a mad way.

madman [*madman*] *n* one who is mad.

madness [*madnis*] *n* state of being mad, insanity; mad behaviour; extreme rashness or folly.

Madonna [*madona*] *n* the Virgin Mary; statue or picture of the Virgin Mary; **M. lily** large white lily with several blossoms.

madras [*madRaas*] *n* type of strong cotton or silk fabric, *usu* striped; large square headscarf.

madrigal [*madRigal*] *n* type of contrapuntal part-song for several voices without independent instrumental parts > PDM; short love-lyric.

maecenas [meeseenas] n patron of art or literature.

maelstrom [maylstrom] n large whirlpool; (fig) violent upheaval.

maenad [meenad] n frenzied woman, bacchante.

maestro [mIstRO] n master of an art, esp music; eminent composer or conductor.

Mae West [may-west] n inflatable lifejacket for airmen.

maffick [mafik] v/i celebrate uproariously.

mafia [mafee-a] n Sicilian secret criminal society; international organization of criminals.

mag [mag] n (coll abbr) magazine; magneto; magpie; talkativeness.

magazine [magazeen] n periodical publication containing articles or stories by different authors; storehouse for explosives, ammunition or weapons; cartridge chamber of repeating rifle.

mage [mayj] n (ar) magician.

magenta [majenta] n deep purple-red dye.

maggot [magot] n wormlike larva of flies or of certain moths and beetles; cheese-mite; (coll) whim, odd notion ~ maggoty adj.

Magi [mayjI] n (pl of magus); the M. three 'wise men' who visited Jesus Christ in his infancy.

magic [majik] n primitive system of thought ascribing physical processes to supernatural agencies; any attempt to influence events, objects or persons by supernatural power other than prayer; witchcraft, sorcery; mysterious influence or method; unanalysable charm; conjuring tricks; black m. malevolent magic performed with the aid of demons; white m. beneficial magic ~ magic, magical adj of, caused by, or used in magic; like magic; mysterious; full of strange charm ~ magically adv.

magician [majishan] n one who uses magic; sorcerer; conjuror.

magic-lantern [majik-lantern] n device that throws magnified images of pictures on glass on to a screen.

magisterial [majisteerRi-al] adj pertaining to a magistrate or master; commanding, authoritative; dignified ~ magisterially adv.

magistracy [majistRasi] n office of magistrate; body of magistrates.

magistrate [majistRayt] n public officer who administers the law; Justice of the Peace.

magistrature [majistRacher] n magistracy; tenure of a magistrate's office.

magma (pl magmas) [magma] n (geol) pasty mixture of mineral matter; molten rock below the earth's crust > PDG.

magnanimity [magnanimiti] n quality of being magnanimous.

magnanimous [magnanimus] adj noble in character; incapable of meanness, jealousy or injustice; generous ~ magnanimously adv.

magnate [magnayt] n man of power or wealth, esp in finance or industry.

magnesia [magneeshi-a] n magnesium oxide; white powder obtained from magnesium carbonate used medicinally as an antacid > PDS.

magnesium [magneesi-um] n (chem) a light silvery-white metal > PDS.

magnet [magnet] n piece of iron, cobalt, nickel etc capable of attracting or repelling other pieces of metal > PDS; (fig) anything that attracts.

magnetic [magnetik] adj acting as a magnet; worked by magnetism; (fig) powerfully attractive; hypnotic; m. field field of force exerted by a magnet > PDS; m. mine mine detonated by magnetic force; m. pole one of two points to the North and South to which the ends of a freely-swinging bar magnet point > PDG, PDS; m. storm sudden large disturbance of earth's magnetic field, affecting radio, telegraphy, and compasses > PDG, PDS; m. tape plastic tape coated with a ferromagnetic powder, used to record information in a tape recorder ~ magnetically adv.

magnetism [magnetizm] n magnetic force; phenomena produced by this; scientific study of this; (fig) power of attracting or influencing people; terrestrial m. magnetic properties of the earth > PDG, PDS.

magnetize [magnetIz] v/t make magnetic; (fig) attract ~ magnetization [magnetIzayshon] n.

magneto (1) [magneetO] n small dynamo with permanent magnet, esp one that produces the ignition spark in a petrol internal combustion engine.

magneto- (2) pref using magnetism; produced by magnetism.

magneto-hydrodynamics [magneetO-hIdROdInamiks] n (elect) method of generating electricity directly from a flame or plasma > PDS.

magnetometer [magneetomiter] n instrument for comparing strengths of magnetic fields > PDS.

magnetophone [magneetOfOn] n type of microphone.

magnetosphere [magneetOsfeer] n region of space within earth's magnetic field.

magnetostriction [magneetOstRikshon] n change in the dimensions of a ferromagnetic substance on magnetization.

magnetron [magnetRon] n (rad) vacuum tube in which the flow of ions is magnetically controlled.

Magnificat [magnifikat] n Hymn of the Virgin Mary used as a canticle.

magnification [magnifikayshon] n act of magnifying; extent to which a thing is magnified.

magnificence [magnifisens] n excellence; glory.

magnificent [magnifisent] adj splendid; of outstanding richness, quality, beauty etc; noble; (coll) excellent ~ magnificently adv.

magnifico [magnifikO] n person of high rank or importance.

magnifier [magnifI-er] n one who or that which enlarges.

magnify [magnifI] v/t cause to appear larger, esp by use of a lens; exaggerate; enlarge; (ar) praise.

magniloquence [magnilOkwens] n pompous language or style; boastful eloquence ~ magniloquent adj.

magnitude [magnitewd] n size; greatness, extent; importance; degree of brilliance of a star > PDS.

magnolia [magnOli-a] n genus of flowering trees.

magnum [magnum] n two-quart bottle.

magpie [magpI] n common black-and-white long-tailed bird of crow family; (fig) petty thief; (fig) chatterbox; (shooting) outermost but one of divisions of target.

magus (pl magi) [maygus] n member of Persian priestly caste; astrologer; magician.

Magyar [*magyaar*] *n* member of the dominant race in Hungary; a Hungarian; the Hungarian language ~ **Magyar** *adj* Hungarian.

Maharaja [maha*Raa*ja] *n* title of a major Indian ruling prince.

Maharani [maha*Raa*ni] *n* wife of a Maharajah; Indian ruling princess.

Maharishi [maha*Ri*shi] *n* Hindu sage.

Mahatma [ma*hat*ma] *n* Indian religious adept.

mah-jong [maa-*jong*] *n* Chinese game played with 144 decorated blocks.

mahlstick see **maulstick.**

mahogany [ma*hog*ani] *n* hard, fine-grained reddish wood; South American tree producing this; furniture, *esp* dining table, made of this; reddish-brown colour.

Mahometan see **Mohammedan.**

mahout [ma*howt*] *n* elephant driver and keeper.

maid [*mayd*] *n* female servant; girl; unmarried woman; virgin; **M. of Honour** unmarried lady attending on queen or princess.

maiden [*may*den] *n* virgin, girl; young unmarried woman; (*hist*) type of guillotine; (*cricket*) maiden over ~ **maiden** *adj* virginal; unmarried; of or like a maiden; (*fig*) unused; unblemished; done or experienced for the first time; **m. name** woman's surname before her marriage; **m. over** (*cricket*) over in which no runs are made; **m. speech** first speech in Parliament of a new member.

maidenhair [*may*denhair] *n* type of fern.

maidenhead, maidenhood [*may*denhed, *may*denhood] *n* state of being a maiden, virginity; the hymen.

maidenly [*may*denli] *adj* of or like a maiden; modest.

maidservant [*mayd*survant] *n* female servant.

mail (1) [*mayl*] *n* armour of interlocking steel rings.

mail (2) *n* letters conveyed by post; postal system; vehicle conveying letters, parcels *etc*; postal collection or delivery; mailbag ~ **mail** *adj* pertaining to the postal system; **m. boat (coach, train)** boat (coach, train) carrying letters, parcels *etc* ~ **mail** *v/t* send by post.

mail (3) *n* (*Scots*) tax; rent; tribute.

mailbag [*mayl*bag] *n* strong canvas bag for carrying mail.

mailcart [*mayl*kaart] *n* cart for carrying mails; light pushcart for children.

mailed [*mayld*] *adj* wearing armour; **the m. fist** (*fig*) physical violence.

mail-order [*mayl*-awrder] *adj* pertaining to the system of ordering and buying goods by post ~ **mail-order** *n* an order for goods to be sent by post.

maillot [*mI*-yO] *n* one-piece swimsuit; very close-fitting garment worn by dancers, athletes *etc*.

maim [*maym*] *v/t* cripple; mutilate.

main (1) [*mayn*] *adj* chief, most important; largest; **the m. chance** one's own profit or advantage; **by m. force** by sheer physical strength ~ **main** *n* principal pipe, cable *etc* in water, sewage, gas or electricity system; (*poet*) high sea; (*ar*) physical strength; (*ar*) mainland; **with might and m.** by force; with all one's strength; **in the m.** on the whole.

main (2) *n* a cockfight; (*dicing*) stake; throw.

mainbrace [*mayn*bRays] *n* (*naut*) brace of the main-yard; **splice the m.** (*naut*) serve out double ration of grog.

mainland [*mayn*land] *n* larger part of a continent or country, as distinct from islands nearby.

mainline [*mayn*lIn] *adj* and *n* (of or on) a main railway line; (*sl*) (of or in) a major vein ~ **mainline** *v/i* (*sl*) inject drugs in one's veins.

mainly [*mayn*li] *adv* mostly; chiefly.

mainmast [*mayn*maast] *n* (*naut*) principal mast.

mainprize [*mayn*pRIz] *n* (*leg*) act of standing surety for another.

mainsail [*mayn*s'l/*mayn*sayl] *n* (*naut*) principal sail.

mainsheet [*mayn*sheet] *n* (*naut*) rope to work the mainsail.

mainspring [*mayn*spRing] *n* chief spring in a watch; (*fig*) chief motive for, source of, an action.

mainstay [*mayn*stay] *n* (*naut*) stay for the mainmast; (*fig*) chief support.

mainstream [*mayn*stReem] *adj* belonging to the main or central tradition of an art *etc*; not eccentric, archaic or experimental.

maintain [mayn*tayn*] *v/t* carry on, keep up; preserve, support; retain, keep; defend; affirm; keep in working order, repair.

maintenance [*mayn*tenans] *n* act of maintaining; state of being maintained; that which maintains, means of support; allowance for a person's living expenses; alimony; **cap of m.** ceremonial cap borne before the sovereign.

maisonnette [mayzo*net*] *n* part of a house used as a self-contained dwelling; small house.

maize [*mayz*] *n* edible grain of an American plant; plant producing this.

majestic [ma*jes*tik] *adj* possessing majesty; very stately ~ **majestical** *adj* ~ **majestically** *adv.*

majesty [*maj*esti] *n* sovereign power; stately dignity, grandeur; title of a sovereign.

majolica [mI-*ol*ika/ma*jol*ika] *n* kind of enamelled Italian pottery.

major [*may*jer] *adj* more important; larger; elder; (*surg*) involving possible danger to life; **m. interval** (*mus*) one having a semitone more than the corresponding minor interval > PDM; **m. premiss** (*log*) first statement of syllogism, containing general rule; **m. scale** (*mus*) scale with semitones between 3rd and 4th and between 7th and 8th notes > PDM; **m. term** (*log*) predicate of conclusion of syllogism ~ **major** *n* (*mil*) officer ranking between captain and lieutenant-colonel; (*leg*) person over 18 (formerly 21) years old ~ **major** *v/i* (*US*) graduate.

majordomo [mayjer*dO*mO] *n* manager of a royal or large household.

major-general [mayjer-*jen*eRal] *n* (*mil*) officer ranking next below a lieutenant-general.

majority [ma*jo*Riti] *n* the greater number; greater number of votes; number of votes by which one party leads another in an election; rank of major; (*leg*) age of full legal responsibility.

majuscule [ma*jus*kewl/*maj*ewskewl] *n* a large letter.

make (1) (*p/t* and *p/part* made) [*mayk*] *v/t* and *i* put together, construct; form; cause to be or happen; produce; prepare; cause to be in specified state; compose; enact (law); devise, think out; earn; acquire; appoint; promote; be essential to; cause success of; amount to; do, perform; develop into; prove to be; compel; estimate, reckon; form opinion on, interpret; represent; behave; reach, arrive at; catch (train *etc*); (*coll*) win status, fame, membership *etc*; (*cards*) take (a trick); (*games*) score; (*of tide*) rise; (*sl*) steal; (*sl*) become the lover of; **m. as if** seem about to; **m. at** move quickly towards; **m. away with** kill, destroy; steal; **m. believe** pretend; **m. the best of** use advantageously; not grumble about; **m. do (with)** be content with (something inferior); **m. for** go towards; attack; tend towards; tend to cause; **m. good** succeed despite disadvantages; compensate; restore; **m. it** (*coll*) succeed, achieve; arrive in time; **m. off** run away; **m. off with** steal; **m. out** see or understand after some difficulty; pretend; try to prove, argue; draft, write out; (*coll*) succeed; get on; **m. over** transfer legally; renovate; **m. towards** go towards; **m. up** compose; form; invent; apply cosmetics to; complete; reconcile; set up for printing; **m. it up** be reconciled; **m. up one's mind** decide; **m. up to** try to win the favour of, flatter ~ **make** *n* way in which a thing is made; goods made by a specified manufacturer; style; form; character; **on the m.** (*coll*) pursuing profits or success; (*sl*) trying to find a sexual partner.

make (2) *n* (*ar*) mate; equal, match.

make-believe [*mayk*-bieev] *n* act of behaving as if one believed that which one knows to be false; mild fantasy; pretence > PDP.

maker [*mayker*] *n* one who makes; (*ar*) a poet; **our M.** God the Creator.

makeshift [*mayk*shift] *adj* and *n* (used as) temporary inferior substitute.

make-up [*mayk*-up] *n* cosmetics; act of colouring the face, *esp* for the stage, screen *etc*; materials used for this; way in which a thing is composed; character, temperament; arrangement of type on printed page or poster.

makeweight [*mayk*wayt] *n* something added to make up required weight; (*fig*) person or thing of small value used to fill a gap.

making [*mayking*] *n* act of forming, producing, creating; cause of success, maturity *etc*; (*pl*) earnings; (*pl*) potential qualities.

mal- *pref* bad, wrong.

malacca [*malaka*] *n* walking stick of palm-cane.

malachite [*malakit*] *n* green copper carbonate.

maladjusted [*malajustid*] *adj* unable to adjust oneself to one's environment > PDP; imperfectly adjusted ~ **maladjustment** *n*.

maladministration [*maladministRayshon*] *n* inefficient or dishonest management.

maladroit [*maladRoit*] *adj* awkward, clumsy ~ **maladroitly** *adv* ~ **maladroitness** *n*.

malady [*maladi*] *n* disease, illness.

Malaga [*malaga*] *n* a sweet, white Spanish wine.

malaise [*malayz*] *n* slight bodily discomfort; uneasiness, lassitude.

malapropism [*malapRopizm*] *n* ridiculous misuse of a word through confusion with one of similar sound.

malapropos [*malapRopO*] *adv* inappropriately; awkwardly ~ **malapropos** *adj* inappropriate.

malaria [*malairRi-a*] *n* type of fever transmitted by mosquito-bite ~ **malarial** *adj* of or causing malaria; marshy; unhealthy.

malarkey [*malaarki*] *n* (*sl*) nonsense.

malcontent [*malkontent*] *n* discontented person, rebel against authority; condition of discontent ~ **malcontent** *adj* discontented; rebellious.

male [*mayl*] *adj* belonging to the sex which begets offspring by fertilizing the female; of or appropriate to this sex, virile; comprising men only; (*bot*) with stamens; (*mech*) fitting into a corresponding hollow ~ **male** *n* animal or plant of male sex; man.

malediction [*malidikshon*] *n* a curse.

malefactor [*malifakter*] *n* evil-doer, criminal.

malefic [*malefik*] *adj* having evil influence.

maleficent [*malefisent*] *adj* harmful; criminal.

malevolence [*malevolens*] *n* disposition to wish that another may be harmed or grieved, ill-will, malice ~ **malevolent** *adj* ~ **malevolently** *adv*.

malfeasance [*malfeezans*] *n* (*leg*) wrongdoing.

malformation [*malfawrmayshon*] *n* abnormal formation of an organism or organ.

malfunction [*malfunkshon*] *n* inability of an organ, machine *etc* to function correctly ~ **malfunction** *v/i*.

malice [*malis*] *n* desire to injure or harm another; ill-will; spite; (*leg*) illegal or wicked intention.

malicious [*malishus*] *adj* feeling malice; caused by malice ~ **maliciously** *adv* ~ **maliciousness** *n*.

malign [*malin*] *adj* harmful; sinister; malicious ~ **malign** *v/t* slander, speak evil of.

malignancy [*malignansi*] *n* quality of being malignant.

malignant [*malignant*] *adj* desiring to do harm or to injure; filled with hate; (*med*) virulent, likely to be fatal; cancerous ~ **malignantly** *adv*.

malignity [*maligniti*] *n* intense hatred; great malevolence; (*med*) quality of being malignant.

malinger [*maling*-ger] *v/i* pretend to be ill in order to avoid duty ~ **malingerer** *n*.

mall [*mawl*] *n* broad alley or avenue; (*hist*) mallet; game of pall-mall; **the M.** [*mal*] an alley in St James's Park, London.

mallard [*malaard*] *n* common wild duck; drake of this.

malleable [*mali*-ab'l] *adj* capable of being hammered into a different shape; (*fig*) pliable, amenable ~ **malleability** [*mali-abiliti*] *n*.

mallet [*malit*] *n* wooden-headed hammer; long-handled wooden-headed hammer used as striker in polo, croquet *etc*.

mallow [*malO*] *n* common wild plant with pink or mauve flowers.

malm [*maam*] *n* soft, chalky loam.

malmsey [*maamzi*] *n* a sweet white wine.

malnutrition [*malnewtRishon*] *n* inadequate nourishment.

malocclusion [*maloklooshon*] *n* (*med*) faulty alignment of teeth and jaws.

malodorous [*malOdeRus*] *adj* having an offensive smell.

malpractice [*malpRaktis*] *n* wrongdoing, *esp* dishonest abuse of an official position; (*leg*) negligence in medical care.

malt [*mawlt*] *n* dried fermented grain used in brewing ~ **malt** *v/t* make grain into malt.

Malta [*mawlta*] *n* and *adj* **M. fever** undulant fever.

Maltese [*mawl*teez] *n* and *adj* (inhabitant) of Malta.

maltha [*maltha*] *n* type of cement; type of semi-solid bitumen; one of various hydrocarbon mixtures.

malt-house [*mawlt*-hows] *n* building where malt is made and stored.

Malthusian [mal*thewz*i-an] *adj* advocating control of the growth of population.

maltose [*mawlt*Os] *n* sugar made by the action of malt on starch > PDS.

maltreat [malt*Reet*] *v/t* treat cruelly or roughly.

maltster [*mawlt*ster] *n* one who makes malt.

malversation [malvers*ay*shon] *n* fraud; misuse of public funds.

mam [mam] *n* (*coll abbr*) mother; madam.

mama [ma*maa*] *n* (*coll*) mother.

mamba [*mam*ba] *n* African tree-snake; dance similar to the rhumba.

mamilla [ma*mil*a] *n* nipple ~ **mamillary** *adj* of the nipples or breast.

mamma (1) [ma*maa*/ma*ma*] *n* (*coll*) mother.

mamma (2) [*mamaa*] *n* mammary gland of females; rudimentary mammary gland of males.

mammal [*mam*al] *n* animal which suckles its young > PDB.

mammary [*mam*aRi] *adj* of or in the breast; **m. gland** milk-producing gland in female mammals.

mammon [*mam*on] *n* wealth, *esp* personified.

mammoth [*mam*oth] *n* large extinct species of elephant ~ **mammoth** *adj* (*coll*) huge.

mammy [*mam*i] *n* (*coll*) mother; (*US*) Negro nurse or servant.

man (*pl* **men**) [man] *n* adult human male; human being, person; the human species, mankind; person with manly qualities; male employee; man-servant; husband; lover; (*hist*) vassal; piece used in chess, draughts *etc*; (*coll*) form of address; (*games*) member of team; (*pl*) private soldiers; **m. and boy** since boyhood; **best m.** groomsman at wedding; **m. in the street** typical or average citizen; **m. of the world** man with much social experience; **old m.** (*coll*) father; friendly form of address; husband; **to a m.** without exception ~ **man** (*pres/part* **manning**, *p/t* and *p/part* **manned**) *v/t* provide enough men for work, defence *etc*; strengthen.

mana [*maa*na] *n* awe-inspiring impersonal supernatural force emanating from objects, places, or persons.

manacle [*man*ak'l] *n* and *v/t* handcuff.

manage [*man*ij] *v/t* and *i* control; influence; guide the running of (a business, household *etc*), direct; handle, deal with; contrive; succeed despite difficulties, cope; see to ~ **manageable** *adj* that can be managed or done; docile.

management [*man*ijment] *n* process or act of managing; administration; group of executives directing an industrial undertaking; skill in contriving, handling *etc*.

manager [*man*ijer] *n* one who controls or directs ~ **managerial** [mani*jee*Ri-al] *adj*.

managing [*man*ijing] *adj* controlling; (*coll*) domineering; **m. director** director of a company who administers its operations.

man-at-arms [man-at-*aarmz*] *n* (*hist*) heavily armed mounted soldier.

manatee [mana*tee*] *n* aquatic seacow.

manciple [*man*sip'l] *n* steward of college *etc*.

mandala [*man*dala] *n* Oriental mystical symbol of the universe, combining circle and square.

mandamus [man*daa*mus] *n* (*leg*) writ issued by a higher court to expedite proceedings.

mandarin (1) [*man*deRin] *n* Chinese official; statuette of Chinese man, *usu* with movable head; form of Chinese language used in official documents; (*fig*) pompous official, bureaucrat; **m. duck** species of strikingly marked duck; **m. English** excessively formal style.

mandarin (2) *n* kind of small orange.

mandatary [man*day*teRi] *n* person or state to whom a mandate is entrusted.

mandate [*man*dayt] *n* order; instruction or authorization to pursue a specified policy, *esp* that given by electors to their delegates or representatives; delegation by the League of Nations to a member state to administer a backward territory or one formerly governed by a defeated enemy > PDG; (*RC*) a papal rescript ~ **mandate** *v/t* delegate administrative power to; authorize (a delegate).

mandatory [*man*dateRi] *adj* containing a command; obligatory.

mandible [*man*dib'l] *n* lower jaw; jawbone; biting mouth-part in insects *etc* ~ **mandibular** [man*dib*ewlar] *adj* of a mandible.

mandolin, mandoline [*man*Olin] *n* (*mus*) instrument with metal strings > PDM.

mandorla [man*dawr*la] *n* (*arts*) oval halo enclosing a whole figure.

mandragora [man*dRag*oRa] *n* mandrake.

mandrake [*man*dRayk] *n* plant with forked root used in witchcraft or as a narcotic.

mandrel, mandril [*man*dRil] *n* iron bar supporting articles to be turned on a lathe; light miner's pick; axe of circular saw > PDE.

mandrill [*man*dRil] *n* kind of baboon with brightly coloured face and rump.

mane [mayn] *n* long hair on neck of some animals.

man-eater [*man*-eeter] *n* cannibal; animal which eats men.

manes [*may*neez] *n* (*pl*) (*Rom myth*) benevolent spirits of the dead, *esp* of ancestors.

manful [*man*fool] *adj* brave; vigorous ~ **manfully** *adv* ~ **manfulness** *n*.

manganese [*mang*-ganeez] *n* greyish-white metallic element; black oxide of this > PDS.

mange [maynj] *n* skin disease of hairy animals.

mangel-wurzel, mangold-wurzel [*mang*-g'l-wurz'l] *n* large coarse beet.

manger [*mayn*jer] *n* feeding trough for horses or cattle.

manginess [*mayn*jinis] *n* state of being mangy.

mangle (1) [*mang*-g'l] *v/t* maul, hack; disfigure; misrepresent, garble.

mangle (2) *n* machine with rollers for pressing clothing *etc* ~ **mangle** *v/t* press in a mangle.

mango (*pl* **mangoes**) [*mang*-gO] *n* Indian tree; fruit of this.

mangold-wurzel see **mangel-wurzel**.

mangosteen [*mang*-gusteen] *n* a tropical fruit.

mangrove [*mang*-gROv] *n* tropical tree growing on swampy shores.

mangy [*mayn*ji] *adj* having the mange; scabby; (*fig*) mean; shabby; sordid.

manhandle [*man*hand'l] *v/t* treat or move roughly; move by hand.

manhattan [man*hat*en] *n* cocktail of whisky and vermouth with a dash of bitters.

manhole [*man*hOl] *n* opening through which a man can pass to reach drains, tanks *etc*; inspection chamber in sewer > PDE; **m. cover** cast-iron plate closing a manhole.

manhood [*man*hood] *n* status or age of being a man; virility; courage; men collectively.

man-hour [*man*-owr] *n* unit of work-time, work done by one man in one hour.

manhunt [*man*hunt] *n* pursuit of a fugitive.

mania [*may*ni-a] *n* mental disorder with high uncontrolled excitement > PDP; violent madness; (*fig*) excessive enthusiasm or desire, craze.

maniac [*may*ni-ak] *n* person suffering from mania ~ **maniac** *adj* of or like mania ~ **maniacal** [man*I*-akal] *adj* of or like mania.

manic [*man*ik] *adj* of mania; **m. depressive** (person) suffering from alternate periods of excitement and depression > PDP.

manichean [man*ikee*-an] *adj* of manicheism.

manichee [*man*ikee] *n* believer in manicheism.

manicheism [*man*ikee-izm] *n* (*hist*) religious and philosophic doctrine that the universe is ruled by equal powers of good and evil.

manicure [*man*ikewr] *v/t* shape and polish (fingernails); treat and beautify the hands of ~ **manicure** *n* act of manicuring; state of being manicured; manicurist ~ **manicurist** *n* one whose profession is to manicure.

manifest [*man*ifest] *adj* obvious, clear ~ **manifest** *v/t* and *i* reveal, make evident; become visible, show ~ **manifest** *n* list of ship's cargo.

manifestation [manifest*ay*shon] *n* act of revealing; that which is revealed; display; appearance or occurrence ascribed to a ghost.

manifestly [*man*ifestli] *adv* obviously, clearly.

manifesto [man*if*estO] *n* public declaration of intentions or opinions.

manifold [*man*ifOld] *adj* having many forms, uses *etc*; various; numerous ~ **manifold** *n* chamber with several outlets *esp* for conducting vapour or gas into and away from the cylinders of an internal combustion engine ~ **manifold** *v/t* make carbon copies of.

manikin, mannikin [*man*ikin] *n* little man, dwarf; lay figure; tailor's dummy.

manilla (1) [*man*ila] *n* ring of metal worn by Africans.

manilla (2) *n* fibrous hemp.

manioc [*man*i-ok] *n* cassava flour or bread.

maniple [*man*ip'l] *n* (*hist*) subdivision of Roman cohort; (*eccles*) narrow vestment worn on the left arm during celebration of the Eucharist.

manipulate [man*ip*ewlayt] *v/t* control, mould or work by hand; handle skilfully; influence, manage or use unscrupulously; alter fraudulently.

manipulation [manipewl*ay*shon] *n* act of working by hand; skilful managing ~ **manipulatory** *adj*.

mankind [man*kInd*] *n* the human race.

manlike [*man*lIk] *adj* having the qualities of a man.

manly [*man*li] *adj* brave; virile; befitting a man ~ **manliness** *n*.

man-made [*man*-mayd] *adj* artificial, not occurring naturally; made by chemical processes, not directly derived from natural products.

manna [*man*a] *n* food miraculously supplied to the Israelites in the wilderness; (*fig*) spiritual food; (*fig*) providential help; (*bot*) gum of Arabian tamarisk.

manned [*mand*] *adj* (*of rocket, spacecraft etc*) having human beings on board as crew.

mannequin [*man*ikin] *n* woman who wears new clothes to display them before possible customers; dummy for display of clothes in shop windows.

manner [*man*er] *n* way in which something happens or is done; characteristic style; method; custom; behaviour; mannerism; (*pl*) social behaviour, degree of politeness; (*ar*) kind, sort; **all m.** of all kinds of; **by any m. of means at all; in a m.** to some extent; **to the m. born** naturally well fitted for (an occupation, position *etc*).

mannered [*man*erd] *adj* having specified manners; having mannerisms; affected, unnatural.

mannerism [*man*eRizm] *n* habitual personal trick of expression or behaviour; deliberate affectation in style; (*arts*) Italian 16th-century style characterized by distortion, strain and emotionalism > PDAA ~ **mannerist** *n* and *adj* (*arts*) (person) practising mannerism.

mannerless [*man*erles] *adj* lacking acceptable social manners.

mannerly [*man*erli] *adj* with good social manners.

mannikin see **manikin.**

mannish [*man*ish] *adj* (*of a woman*) like a man in appearance, clothes, or behaviour.

manoeuvre [man*OO*ver] *v/t* and *i* move skilfully amid obstacles or difficulties; show skill in intrigue; exert clever influence (on); move (troops) according to strategical plan; carry out manoeuvres ~ **manoeuvre** *n* act of manoeuvring; stratagem; clever move; strategic movement of troops; (*pl*) mock warfare designed as training in strategy and tactics ~ **manoeuvrable** *adj* that can be easily manoeuvred ~ **manoeuvrability** [man*OO*vRabiliti] *n*.

man-of-war [man-ov-*wawr*] *n* warship.

manometer [man*om*iter] *n* instrument for measuring gaseous pressure or blood-pressure ~ **manometric** [manomet*Rik*] *adj*.

manor [*man*er] *n* estate consisting of house and ancient rights over land possessed by the owner; (*sl*) area supervised by one unit of a police force; **lord of the m.** owner of a manor.

manor-house [*man*er-hows] *n* home of owner of a manor.

manorial [man*awr*Ri-al] *adj* of a manor.

manpower [*man*powr] *n* number of people working or available to work on specified military or industrial task; work done by men without machines; force exerted by a man at work.

manqué [*man*ki] *n* (*roulette*) the numbers 1 to 18 when there is a bet on them.

mansard [*man*saard] *n* roof with two slopes on one face > PDBl; garret.

manse [*mans*] *n* residence of Scottish Presbyterian or Methodist minister.

manservant [*man*survant] *n* male servant.

mansion [*man*shon] *n* an imposing residence, large house; (*pl*) block of flats.

mansion-house [*man*shon-hows] *n* manor-house; mansion; **the M.** residence of Lord Mayor of London.

man-sized [*man*-sIzd] *adj* (*coll*) large or difficult enough to suit a man.

manslaughter [*man*slawter] *n* unlawful but un-intentional killing of a human being ~ **man-slayer** *n* one who commits manslaughter; killer.

mantel [*mantel*] *n* mantelpiece.

mantelpiece [*mantel*pees] *n* ornamental structure over and around a fireplace.

mantelshelf [*mantel*shelf] *n* projecting part of a mantelpiece.

mantic [*mantik*] *adj* relating to divination or pro-phecy.

mantilla [man*tila*] *n* type of woman's ornamental veil or shawl over head and shoulders.

mantis [*mantis*] *n* genus of orthopterous insects.

mantissa [man*tisa*] *n* (*math*) the decimal portion of a common logarithm.

mantle [*mant*'l] *n* sleeveless cloak; mesh covering gas flame and becoming incandescent; (*fig*) cover-ing; (*zool*) lining of mollusc shell ~ **mantle** *v/t* and *i* cover or become covered; suffuse.

mantra, mantrum [*mant*Ra, *mant*Rum] *n* word or sound repeated as an aid to Buddhist or Hindu meditation.

man-trap [*man*-tRap] *n* trap of two steel claws to catch trespassers.

mantrum see **mantra.**

manual (1) [*manew*-al] *adj* of the hand, per-formed by hand ~ **manually** *adv.*

manual (2) *n* small textbook, handbook; organ keyboard.

manufactory [manew*fakt*eRi] *n* a factory.

manufacture [manew*fak*cher] *v/t* produce (articles) by organized manual labour or machin-ery, *esp* in large quantities; concoct, devise (false story *etc*) ~ **manufacture** *n* process or act of manufacturing; method or style of this; that which is manufactured ~ **manufacturer** *n.*

manumission [manew*mish*on] *n* release from slavery.

manumit (*pres/part* **manumitting,** *p/t* and *p/part* **manumitted**) [manew*mit*] *v/t* release from slavery.

manure [ma*newr*] *n* dung used as soil fertilizer; any soil fertilizer ~ **manure** *v/t* apply manure to.

manuscript [*man*ewskRipt] *adj* written by hand ~ **manuscript** *n* document written by hand or typed; author's draft as submitted for printing.

Manx [*manks*] *adj* of or in the Isle of Man; **M. cat** tailless breed of cat ~ **Manx** *n* Celtic language of the Isle of Man.

many [*meni*] *adj* numerous ~ **many** *n* a consider-able number; **a good (great) m.** a large number; **the m.** the majority; the multitude.

many-sided [meni-*std*id] *adj* having many sides; (*fig*) having many talents, interests *etc.*

Maoism [*ma*-O-izm] *n* Chinese Communist system founded by Mao Tse-tung ~ **Maoist** *n* and *adj.*

Maori (*pl* **Maoris**) [*mowr*Ri] *n* aboriginal of New Zealand; his language ~ **Maori** *adj.*

map [*map*] *n* representation on flat surface of all or part of earth's surface > PDG; similar repre-sentation of relative position of stars as seen from earth, or of the surface of other planets; **off the m.** inaccessible; (*coll*) unimportant; **put on the m.** make famous ~ **map** (*pres/part* **mapping,**

p/t and *p/part* **mapped**) *v/t* represent on a map; **m. out** plan in detail.

maple [*mayp*'l] *n* tree or shrub of genus *Acer*; wood of this; sap of this.

maquette [ma*ket*] *n* small model in clay *etc* in preparation for full-sized sculpture.

maquis [ma*kee*] *n* French guerrilla organization during German occupation in World War II; member of this; wild scrub of Mediterranean lands.

mar (*pres/part* **marring,** *p/t* and *p/part* **marred**) [*maar*] *v/t* damage, spoil; ruin.

maraca [ma*Raka*] *n* rattle made from gourd con-taining beads or seeds.

maraschino [maRa*sheen*O/maRa*skeen*O] *n* sweet liqueur made from black Dalmatian cherries.

marathon [*ma*Rathon] *n* long-distance foot-race; (*fig*) prolonged and exhausting contest or achieve-ment.

maraud [ma*Rawd*] *v/i* make raids for plunder ~ **marauder** *n.*

marble [*maarb*'l] *n* hard crystalline limestone capable of being highly polished; sculpture *etc* made of this; small ball of glass *etc* used in child-ren's game; (*pl*) game played with these ~ **marble** *adj* of or like marble; cold, callous; very pale ~ **marble** *v/t* stain with streaks of colour ~ **marbled** *adj* (*bookbinding*) stained like marble ~ **marbling** *n* (*bookbinding*) process of applying imitation marble markings to surfaces.

marcasite [*maar*kasIt] *n* white iron pyrite; small 'brilliant' of polished steel used for costume jewellery.

March (1) [*maarch*] *n* third month of the year.

march (2) *n* boundary, frontier; (*pl*) Welsh **Marches** border of England and Wales ~ **march** *v/i* **m. with** (*ar*) lie alongside, border on.

march (3) *v/i* and *t* walk with regular rhythmic steps, *esp* in military formation; walk in stately manner; advance steadily; cause (troops) to march; force someone to walk; go to war ~ **march** *n* act of marching; distance marched; progress, advance; (*mus*) piece suitable for march-ing to > PDM; **steal a m. on** secretly gain advantage over.

marchioness [maar*shon*es] *n* wife or widow of a marquis.

marchpane [*march*payn] *n* marzipan.

march-past [*maarch*-paast] *n* ceremonial parade past some prominent person who takes the salute.

mare (1) [*mair*] *n* female of the horse; **m.'s nest** supposed discovery which leads to nothing; **Shanks's m.** one's own legs; **m.'s tails** wispy, tufted cirrus clouds.

mare (2), *pl* **maria** [*mair*Ri, *mair*Ri-a] *n* large level area on surface of moon, Mars, *etc.*

margarine [*maar*gaReen/*maar*jaReen] *n* butter substitute made from vegetable and animal fats and oils > PDS.

marge [*maarj*] *n* (*coll abbr*) margarine.

margin [*maar*jin] *n* edge, rim; verge of a road; blank space surrounding printed or written matter; extra amount of space, money, time *etc* beyond strict necessity; (*comm*) difference be-tween selling and buying price of goods; cover deposit for speculative dealings ~ **margin** *v/t* provide margins for; write in the margin.

marginal [*maar*jinal] *adj* of, near or on the margin; near the border, borderline; not central, relatively unimportant; (of electoral seats) held by a narrow majority; (of land) relatively unproductive ~ **marginally** adv. slightly.

marginalia [maarjinayli-a] n (pl) notes written in margins.

margrave [maargRayv] n (hist) hereditary title of certain princes of the Holy Roman Empire.

marguerite [maargeReet] n the ox-eye daisy.

maria [mairRi-a] n (pl) large lunar plains.

Marian [mairRi-an] adj relating to the Virgin Mary; relating to Mary, Queen of England, or to Mary, Queen of Scots.

marigold [maRigOld] n plant with bright yellow composite flowers.

marijuana, marihuana [maRiwaana] n habit-forming narcotic preparation of hemp leaves smoked in cigarettes.

marimba [maRimba] n kind of xylophone.

marina [maReena] n harbour specially designed for sailing boats, sometimes surrounded by hotels etc.

marinade [maRinayd] n fish or meat steeped in mixture of vinegar, wine, spices etc; this mixture ~ **marinade, marinate** v/t and i steep in this.

marine [maReen] adj of the sea; found in the sea; pertaining to sea-trade; **m. store** second-hand junk shop ~ **marine** n naval or merchant fleet; soldier serving on warship; **tell that to the (horse) marines** exclamation of scornful disbelief.

mariner [maRiner] n sailor, seaman.

mariolatry [mairRi-olatRi] n allegedly idolatrous reverence for the Virgin Mary.

marionette [maRi-onet] n puppet moved by strings.

marital [maRital] adj relating to a husband or to marriage ~ **maritally** adv.

maritime [maRitIm] adj of the sea; of navigation; near the sea, seaside; having a navy.

marjoram [maarjeRam] n an aromatic herb.

mark (1) [maark] n visible sign on a surface; impression; spot, stain, blemish; identifying sign; sign indicating ownership, place of manufacture etc; numerical or alphabetical symbol of comparative merit in examinations, competitions etc; target; boundary, limit; (Rugby football) heel-mark made by player who has made a fair catch; **beside the m.** irrelevant; **easy m.** (coll) person easily cheated or persuaded; **make one's m.** become famous or successful; **up to the m.** of required standard ~ **mark** v/t make a mark on or in; stain; award marks of merit to; keep score in certain games; pay attention to, notice; indicate by a mark; be a distinguishing sign of or in; (Stock Exchange) record a transaction for the Official List; **m. down** reduce price of; make a note of; **m. off** put marks of measurement on; divide by boundary marks; **m. out** trace boundary lines on; indicate; destine; **m. time** move feet in marching rhythm but without advancing; (fig) cease to progress; **m. up** keep count of; increase price of; (coll) give credit for.

mark (2) n unit of German currency; (hist) medieval unit of weight for gold or silver.

mark (3) n (mil) particular model of piece of equipment.

marked [maarkt] adj bearing a mark; obvious,

conspicuous; considerable; doomed; suspected, watched ~ **markedly** adv noticeably.

marker [maarker] n one who or that which marks; bookmark; device for keeping the score.

market [maarkit] n open space or public building for buying and selling; assembly of people for buying and selling; the Stock Exchange, or different parts of it specializing in certain types of stock; opportunity for buying and selling; supply-and-demand position governing trading; value of commodities, stocks, shares, in the market; **in the m. for** wanting to buy; **on the m.** for sale; **play the m.** speculate on the Stock Exchange; **m. research** research by manufacturers into consumers' views on their goods ~ **market** v/t send, take (goods) to market; buy or sell in a market ~ **marketable** adj that can be bought or sold.

market-garden [maarkit-gaarden] n garden in which vegetables and fruit are grown for market ~ **market-gardener** n.

marketing [maarkiting] n process of putting goods on the market; trade done at a market.

marketplace [maarkitplays] n open space where a market is held.

market-price [maarkit-pRIs] n price for which a commodity is sold in open market.

marking [maarking] n act of marking, esp the recording of dealings in securities for the Stock Exchange Official List; distinctive pattern on skin or feathers of animal or bird; process of assessing the merits of examination scripts, school work etc; **m. ink** indelible ink for making identifying marks on clothing etc.

marksman [maarksman] n one skilled in shooting at a target, accurate shooter ~ **marksmanship** n.

marl (1) [maarl] n a loam or clay mixed with calcium carbonate > PDG ~ **marl** v/t fertilize with marl.

marl (2) v/t (naut) fasten with a small line; wind marline round (rope).

marline [maarlin] n (naut) thin cord of two strands.

marlinespike [maarlinspIk] n (naut) pointed iron tool for separating the strands of a rope.

marmalade [maarmalayd] n jam made by boiling a pulp of citrus fruit in sugar; **m. cat** cat of deep orange-red colour.

marmite [maarmIt] n proprietary name for a yeast preparation.

marmoreal [maarmawRi-al] adj like marble; like a statue; cold.

marmoset [maarmozet] n small tropical American monkey.

marmot [maarmot] n rodent of squirrel family.

marocain [maROkayn] n dress fabric with a fine cord like a wavy rib.

maroon (1) [maROOn] n a shade of very dark red.

maroon (2) v/t abandon in isolated desolate region; (fig) leave without means of transport; desert.

maroon (3) n loudly detonating signal-rocket.

maroon (4) n West Indian Negro, esp if fugitive from slavery; descendant of such fugitives.

marquee [maarkee] n large tent. esp one containing entertainment or refreshment.

marquess see **marquis**.

463

marquetry [*maar*ketRi] *n* wood inlay patterning on furniture *etc*.

marquis, marquess [*maar*kwis] *n* rank of nobility immediately below that of duke; courtesy title of duke's eldest son ∼ **marquisate** *n* rank of marquis.

marquise [maar*keez*] *n* (*in France*) marchioness; (*bui*) projecting canopy over the entrance to a building; finger-ring set with cluster of stones in the shape of a pointed oval.

marriage [*ma*Rij] *n* legal union sanctioning the cohabitation and sexual intercourse of a man and woman; civil or religious ceremony instituting this, wedding; relationship between husband and wife; (*fig*) close permanent union ∼ **marriageable** *adj* suitable for marriage.

married [*ma*Rid] *adj* united in marriage; of or like marriage or married people.

marrow [*ma*RO] *n* soft, fatty substance in cavities of bones; species of edible gourd; (*fig*) essence.

marrowbone [*ma*RObOn] *n* bone containing much marrow, *esp* one used in cookery; (*pl*) (*coll*) knees.

marrowfat [*ma*ROfat] *n* large kind of pea.

marry (1) [*ma*Ri] *v/t* and *i* join in marriage; give in marriage; take as husband or wife; (*fig*) unite closely.

marry (2) *interj* (*ar*) indeed.

Mars [*maarz*] *n* Roman God of war; planet in orbit between the Earth and Jupiter > PDS.

Marseillaise [maarse*layz*/maar*say*-ayz] *n* the national anthem of France.

marsh [*maarsh*] *n* tract of low-lying boggy land; **m. gas** methane.

marshal (*pres/part* **marshalling**, *p/t* and *p/part* **marshalled**) [*maar*shal] *v/t* arrange in systematic order; guide ceremonially; (*leg*) arrange in order of priority ∼ **marshal** *n* court official in charge of ceremonies; (*mil*) highest-ranking officer in certain countries; (*US*) executive officer of a judicial district, sheriff.

marshalling-yard [*maar*shaling-yaard] *n* area of railway junction where goods wagons are sorted out and reassembled according to destination.

marsh-gas [*maarsh*-gas] *n* methane.

marsh-mallow [maarsh-*ma*lO] *n* herb with large, thick, velvety leaves and pink flowers; sweetmeat made from roots of this.

marsh-marigold [maarsh-*ma*RigOld] *n* plant with heart-shaped glossy leaves and golden-coloured flowers; the kingcup.

marshy [*maar*shi] *adj* of or like a marsh.

marsupial [maar*sew*pi-al] *n* and *adj* (animal) which carries its young in a pouch > PDB.

mart [*maart*] *n* auction room; market.

martello [maar*tel*O] *n* circular protective tower.

marten [*maar*ten] *n* small weasel-like animal valued for its fur.

martial [*maar*shal] *adj* of or pertaining to war; warlike ∼ **martially** *adv*.

martian [*maar*shan] *n* and *adj* (hypothetical inhabitant) of Mars.

martin [*maar*tin] *n* species of swallow.

martinet [maarti*net*] *n* strict disciplinarian.

martingale [*maar*ting-gayl] *n* harness strap linking horse's nose-band to its girth.

martini [maar*teeni*] *n* cocktail of gin, vermouth, and bitters.

Martinmas [*maar*tinmas] *n* feast of St Martin 11 November.

martlet [*maart*let] *n* the swift; the martin.

martyr [*maar*ter] *n* one who suffers death or persecution rather than abandon his faith or principles; one who suffers much ∼ **martyr** *v/t* put to death; torture.

martyrdom [*maar*terdom] *n* state of being a martyr; sufferings or death of a martyr; extreme pain.

martyrology [maarte*Rol*oji] *n* list or history of martyrs.

marvel [*maar*vel] *n* that which or one who causes amazement or admiration ∼ **marvel** (*pres/part* **marvelling**, *p/t* and *p/part* **marvelled**) *v/i* feel amazement or admiration; be puzzled.

marvellous [*maar*velus] *adj* astonishing; surprising; arousing wonder and admiration; supernatural; (*coll*) extremely good, pleasant *etc* ∼ **marvellously** *adv* ∼ **marvellousness** *n*.

Marxism [*maark*sizm] *n* philosophy of history and programme of revolutionary reform expounded by Karl Marx and adopted as basis of Communism > PDPol ∼ **Marxist** *n* follower of Marx ∼ **Marxist** *adj*.

marzipan [*maar*zipan] *n* confectionery made from powdered almonds, eggs, and sugar.

mascara [mask*aar*Ra] *n* cosmetic for colouring eyelashes and eyebrows.

mascon [*mas*kon] *n* area of strong gravity on moon, due to underground concentration of massive material.

mascot [*mas*kot] *n* talisman; person or object that brings good luck.

masculine [*mas*kewlin] *adj* of male sex; like a male, virile; strong; mannish; (*gramm*) (of gender or form) normally denoting males; **m. ending** (*pros*) ending in stressed syllable; **m. rhyme** rhyme formed by words with stressed endings ∼ **masculine** *n* masculine word or gender.

masculinity [maskew*lin*iti] *n* quality of being masculine.

maser [*may*zer] *n* amplifier or oscillator producing very short electromagnetic waves; **optical m.** maser producing intense infra-red radiation; laser > PDEl.

mash [*mash*] *n* mass of ingredients forming a soft pulp; mashed potatoes ∼ **mash** *v/t* crush or beat to pulp; (*brewing*) mix (malt) with hot water.

mashie [*mashi*] *n* golf-club with iron head and lofted face.

mask [*maask*] *n* covering which conceals or protects all or part of the face; representation of stylized or grotesque human face in paper *etc*; elaborate head-covering with grotesque or non-human features worn in religious or magical rituals; respirator worn over nose and mouth; clay or wax impression of face of dead person; head and face of fox; masker; (*fig*) that which conceals, deception ∼ **mask** *v/t* and *i* cover with a mask; wear a mask; disguise, conceal ∼ **masked** *adj* wearing a mask, concealed; **m. ball** ball where guests wear masks ∼ **masker** *n* one who wears a mask; one taking part in masque or masquerade.

masochism [*mas*Okizm] *n* tendency to derive sexual pleasure from suffering physical pain and humiliation > PDP; (*coll*) apparent enjoyment of hardships ~ **masochist** *n* one prone to masochism ~ **masochistic** [masОki*st*ik] *adj*.

mason [*may*son] *n* a stone worker or stone setter; builder in stone; freemason.

masonic [ma*son*ik] *adj* of Freemasonry.

masonry [*may*sonRi] *n* stonework and the craft of stone wall building including the preparation and fixing of the stones; Freemasonry.

masque [*maask*] *n* form of dramatic entertainment consisting originally of tableaux and dancing, later having some dialogue and songs; literary composition intended to be so performed.

masquerade [maa*ske*Ray*d*] *n* ball at which people wear masks; playlet with masked actors; disguise ~ **masquerade** *v/i* disguise oneself.

Mass (1) [*mas*] *n* celebration of the Eucharist, *esp* according to Roman Catholic ritual; (*mus*) setting for words of certain prayers of the Mass > PDM; **black m.** blasphemous and obscene imitation of Mass, a ceremony used in sorcery; **dialogue M.** Mass in which the congregation makes the responses and joins in certain prayers; **high (low) M.** Mass with (without) singing and the use of incense; **Tridentine Mass** Latin text of the Mass as used from 1564 to 1969.

mass (2) *n* coherent body of matter of indefinite shape; large quantity or number; crowd; main part; majority; quantity of matter in a body > PDS; bulk; (*pl*) the proletariat ~ **mass** *v/t* and *i* form into a mass; concentrate ~ **mass** *adj* of or like a mass; of or for large numbers of people; in large quantities; **m. meeting** large public meeting, *esp* political; **m. number** (*phys*) number of nucleons in an atomic nucleus; **m. psychology** study of the behaviour, reactions *etc* of people when associated in large numbers; **m. observation** record of customs, views, preferences *etc* of a representative section of a population.

massacre [*mas*aker] *n* indiscriminate killing; the killing of helpless persons ~ **massacre** *v/t* kill indiscriminately.

massage [ma*saazh*] *n* treatment in which muscles and body are rubbed or kneaded, usually with the hands ~ **massage** *v/t* treat with massage.

masseur [ma*sur*] *n* man who practises massage.

masseuse [ma*surz*] *n* woman who practises massage.

massif [ma*seef*] *n* mountainous mass breaking into peaks > PDG.

massive [*mas*iv] *adj* large; heavy; bulky; very powerful ~ **massively** *adv* ~ **massiveness** *n*.

mass-media [mas-*meed*i-a] *n* (*pl*) means of communication reaching the majority of the public simultaneously.

mass-produce [mas-pRo*dews*] *v/t* manufacture in large quantities to an identical pattern ~ **mass-production** [mas-pRo*duk*shon] *n*.

massy [*mas*i] *adj* weighty; solid; bulky.

mast (1) [*maast*] *n* long upright pole supporting sails, rigging *etc* of ship; flagpole; pole supporting radio aerial ~ **masted** *adj* having a mast.

mast (2) *n* fruit of oak beech *etc*.

mastectomy [mas*tek*tomi] *n* (*surg*) removal of a breast.

master [*maas*ter] *n* one who has authority or control; leader, commander; teacher; religious teacher, prophet; employer; male head of a household; person eminently skilful in some art, craft, or quality; skilled self-employed craftsman; title of heads of certain colleges or of certain religious organizations; official in charge of a specified department; mode of address to young boys; courtesy title of heirs to certain Scottish baronies; captain of merchant ship; **m. copy** that from which other copies are made; **m. hand** expert skill; **m. key** that can open many different locks; **M. of Arts (Science** *etc*) person holding the second (or, in Scottish universities, the first) degree of the specified university faculty; **old m.** any European painter of acknowledged greatness from 13th to 18th century; painting by one of these; **m. switch** electric switch controlling whole installation ~ **master** *v/t* become master of; subdue; defeat; become thoroughly skilled in.

masterful [*maas*terfool] *adj* domineering, able to impose one's will on others; (*US* and *pop*) masterly ~ **masterfully** *adv* ~ **masterfulness** *n*.

masterly [*maas*terli] *adj* showing very high talent or skill ~ **masterliness** *n*.

master-mariner [maaster-*ma*Riner] *n* captain of merchant ship.

mastermind [*maas*termInd] *n* genius; one very skilful at leading others ~ **mastermind** *v/t* (*sl*) plan and organize (an elaborate crime).

masterpiece [*maas*terpees] *n* work of art or skill of supreme excellence; best piece of work of an artist, writer *etc*.

mastership [*maas*tership] *n* office of a master; dominion; mastery.

masterstroke [*maas*terstRОk] *n* plan carried into effect with signal success.

mastertouch [*maas*tertuch] *n* detail that reveals genius.

mastery [*maas*teRi] *n* state of being a master; authority of a master; superiority; victory; thorough knowledge or skill.

masthead [*maast*hed] *n* top of a mast

mastic [*mast*ik] *n* resin of the pistachio tree used as a varnish when dissolved in alcohol; a permanently plastic waterproof material used for sealing joints *etc* > PDE; **m. asphalt** a wearing course to a road or waterproofing to a roof.

masticate [*mast*ikayt] *v/t* and *i* chew with the teeth ~ **mastication** [masti*kay*shon] *n* act of chewing ~ **masticator** *n* that which or one who chews; device for grinding or pulping ~ **masticatory** [masti*kay*teRi] *adj*.

mastiff [*mast*if] *n* large thickset breed of dog.

mastitis [mas*tI*tis] *n* inflammation of the breast.

masto- *pref* of or in the breast.

mastodon [*mast*Odon] *n* genus of extinct mammals related to the elephant.

mastoid [*mast*oid] *adj* shaped like a nipple; **m. process** excrescence of bone behind the ear.

masturbate [*mast*erbayt] *v/i* manipulate one's own sexual organs so as to produce excitation > PDP ~ **masturbation** [masterbayshon] *n*.

mat (1) [*mat*] *n* coarse fabric of fibre, straw *etc* used as floor-covering; piece of this used as protection against damp or dirt, or placed near an entrance to wipe the feet on; piece of rubber *etc* of similar use; fabric used as packing material; small piece of fabric, wood *etc* placed beneath

hot plates on a table; tangled hair; **on the m.**
(coll) in trouble; reprimanded ~ **mat** *(pres/part*
matting, *p/t* and *p/part* **matted)** *v/t* and *i*
cover with mats; tangle; become tangled.

mat (2), **matt** *adj* not glossy, dull ~ **mat, matt**
n dull surface ~ **mat** *(pres/part* **matting,** *p/t*
and *p/part* **matted)** *v/t* remove gloss of.

matador [*mata*dawr] *n* man who finally dispatches
the bull in a bullfight; kind of dominoes.

match (1) [*mach*] *n* that which is exactly like
another in appearance; one of pair or set of objects; person of skill, strength, intelligence *etc*
equal to another's; someone equal or superior
to another; sporting contest; marriage; person
eligible for marriage ~ **match** *v/t* and *i* be identical in appearance (to); be the equal of; find a
match for; pit against each other in contest;
marry; suit; be the same colour as.

match (2) *n* slender strip of wood tipped with
combustible material for producing fire.

matchboard [*mach*bawrd] *n* board with a groove
along one edge and a tongue along the other.

matchbox [*mach*boks] *n* box containing matches.

matchet [*mach*et] *n* a machete.

matchless [*mach*lis] *adj* unequalled.

matchlock [*mach*lok] *n* lock of a musket fired by
a lighted fuse of hemp or tow; a musket so fired.

matchmaker [*mach*mayker] *n* one who schemes to
bring about marriages; one who manufactures
matches.

matchstick [*mach*stik] *n* the wooden part of a
match; anything very thin and straight, *esp* thin
legs or arms.

matchwood [*mach*wood] *n* wood for making
matches; splintered wood.

mate (1) [*mayt*] *n* fellow-worker, companion;
friend; sexual partner, *esp* of animals; spouse;
assistant; *(naut)* officer second in command ~
mate *v/i* take sexual partner *(esp* of animals),
couple; marry.

mate (2) *v/t* and *n* checkmate.

maté [*matay*] *n* Paraguay tea.

mater [*mayter*] *n (anat)* either of two membranes
enclosing the brain and spinal cord; *(sl)* mother.

material [*mateer*Ri-al] *adj* of matter; substantial,
tangible; corporeal; important, essential; relevant; not spiritual; *(leg)* affecting a judicial
decision; affecting the validity of a document *etc*
~ **material** *n* that of which a thing is made;
matter, substance; textile fabric, cloth; factual
knowledge needed for the writing of a work;
human beings regarded as potentially capable of
training, education *etc*; *(pl)* implements, apparatus; **raw m.** unprocessed substances from which
articles are to be manufactured; **writing m.**
paper, pen, ink *etc*.

materialism [*mateer*Ri-alizm] *n (philos)* theory
that matter is the only reality; undue concern
with financial success, physical pleasure *etc*; lack
of moral or religious outlook; rejection of spiritual
or supernatural doctrines and explanations ~
materialist *n* one who believes or practises
materialism ~ **materialist, materialistic** *adj*.

materialization [*mateer*Ri-alIz*ay*shon] *n* act or
process of materializing; a materialized ghost.

materialize [*mateer*Ri-alIz] *v/t* and *i* give material form to; *(of spirits)* assume material form or

bodily shape; become real, be carried into practice.

materially [*mateer*Ri-ali] *adv* in a material way;
in an important or relevant way; essentially.

maternal [*mat*urnal] *adj* of or like a mother or
motherhood; motherly; *(of kinship)* on the mother's
side ~ **maternally** *adv*.

maternity [*mat*urniti] *n* condition of being a
mother; motherhood ~ **maternity** *adj* pertaining to pregnancy or childbirth; **m. clothes** clothes
suitable for pregnant women; **m. hospital**
hospital for women during confinement.

matey [*mayti*] *adj (coll)* friendly, sociable ~
mateyness, matiness *n*.

mathematic [*matha*matik] *adj* of or by mathematics ~ **mathematical** *adj* of or by mathematics; strictly accurate ~ **mathematically** *adv*.

mathematician [*mathamat*ishan] *n* one skilled in
mathematics.

mathematics [*matha*matiks] *n (pl)* the science
of magnitude and number.

maths [*maths*] *n (pl) (coll)* mathematics.

matily [*mayti*li] *adv (coll)* in a friendly way.

matinée [*mat*inay] *n* afternoon theatrical performance; **m. coat** baby's woollen coat.

matins [*mat*inz] *n (RC)* first canonical hour;
non-Eucharistic morning service of Anglican
Church.

matriarch [*mat*Ri-aark/*mayt*Ri-aark] *n* woman in
authority over family or household; domineering
mother; female head of a tribe ~ **matriarchal**
[*mayt*Ri-*aar*kal] *adj*.

matriarchy [*mat*Ri-aarki/*mayt*Ri-aarki] *n* social
system in which the mother is head of the family
and tribe, and in which descent and inheritance
are through the female line.

matric [*mat*Rik] *n (coll)* matriculation.

matrices [*mat*Riseez] *pl* of **matrix.**

matricide [*mayt*RisId] *n* one who murders his
mother; the murder of a mother ~ **matricidal**
[*mayt*Ris*I*dal] *adj*.

matriculate [*mat*Rikewlayt] *v/t* and *i* enrol as
member of university or college; pass examination entitling to university membership.

matriculation [*mat*Rikewl*ay*shon] *n* act of matri-
culating; examination entitling to this.

matrilinear [*mat*Ril*i*ni-ar] *adj* through, or from,
the mother's side of the family.

matrimonial [*mat*Rim*On*i-al] *adj* of or for marriage ~ **matrimonially** *adv*.

matrimony [*mat*Rimoni] *n* marriage.

matrix *(pl* **matrices)** [*mat*Riks/*mayt*Rikz] *n* womb;
cavity in which anything is formed or developed;
casting mould; solid material in which larger
grains, stones, gems *etc* are embedded > PDE.

matron [*mayt*Ron] *n* elderly married woman;
woman in charge of an institution, *esp* of the
nursing and domestic staff of a hospital or
nursing-home; housekeeper or nurse at a
boarding-school.

matronly [*mayt*Ronli] *adj* of or like a matron; *(of
women)* plump and dignified.

matt see **mat** (2).

matted [*mat*id] *adj* tangled.

matter [*mat*er] *n* that of which all physical objects consist; substance; material; content, that
which is said or written *etc*; affair, concern,

business; occasion, cause; thing; importance; cause of pain, anxiety *etc*; trouble; documents; copy to be set in type; pus; **for that m.** as far as that is concerned; **m. of course** natural and inevitable outcome; something to be expected or taken for granted; **m. of opinion** debatable view ~ **matter** *v/i* be important; suppurate.

matter-of-fact [mater-ov-*fakt*] *adj* unimaginative, prosaic; unemotional; concerned only with facts.

matting [*mat*ing] *n* material for mats; coarse fabric.

mattock [*mat*ok] *n* pickaxe with one adze-like and one chisel-edged blade.

mattress [*mat*Res] *n* large soft resilient pad on which one lies in bed, made of a case stuffed with hair, feathers *etc* or with rubbery material; system of springs, wires *etc* fitted to bedstead.

maturation [matewr*Ray*shon] *n* process of maturing > PDP ~ **maturative** [ma*tewr*Rativ] *adj*.

mature [ma*tewr*] *adj* fully developed; ripe; not childish; wise; well thought-out; (*comm*) due for payment ~ **mature** *v/t* and *i* become or cause to become mature, ripen; think out fully; develop fully; (*comm*) become payable.

maturity [ma*tewr*Riti] *n* state of being mature.

matutinal [matewt*I*nal] *adj* of or in the morning.

matzo [*maa*tsO] *n* unleavened bread.

maudlin [*mawd*lin] *adj* drunken and tearful; very sentimental; self-pitying.

maul [*mawl*] *v/t* injure by tearing and bruising; treat savagely; handle roughly or coarsely ~ **maul** *n* large wooden mallet.

maulstick, mahlstick [*mawl*stik] *n* padded knobbed stick used as painter's hand-rest.

maunder [*mawn*der] *v/i* speak vaguely and disconnectedly; mutter; move or act dreamily.

maundy [*mawn*di] *n* ceremonial washing of the feet of inferior clergy by their superiors or of poor persons by the sovereign on the Thursday before Easter; ceremonial royal almsgiving on this day; **M. Thursday** the Thursday before Easter.

Mauresque see Moresque.

mauser [*mowz*er] *n* type of magazine rifle.

mausoleum [mawso*lee*-um] *n* monumental tomb.

mauve [*mOv*] *n* light reddish purple extracted from coal-tar aniline > PDS; the colour of this ~ **mauve** *adj*.

maverick [*mav*eRik] *n* (*US*) unbranded calf or yearling; (*coll*) one who acts independently.

mavis [*may*vis] *n* song-thrush.

maw [*maw*] *n* (*of animals*) stomach, *esp* fourth stomach of ruminant; open jaws; (*of birds*) crop; (*fig*) gulf.

mawkish [*mawk*ish] *adj* over-sentimental, feebly emotional; sickly, insipid ~ **mawkishly** *adv* ~ **mawkishness** *n*.

maxi- *pref* (*coll*) full size, not miniature; (*of skirts*) long.

maxilla (*pl* **maxillae**) [maks*il*a] *n* the jaw.

maxillary [maks*ile*Ri] *adj* of the jaw.

maxim (1) [*maks*im] *n* a generalization on life and conduct; guiding principle, rule of conduct.

Maxim (2) *n* early type of machine-gun.

maximal [*maks*imal] *adj* of the greatest possible size, duration, *etc*.

maximize [*maks*imIz] *v/t* increase to a maximum.

maximum (*pl* **maxima**) [*mak*simum] *n* the greatest possible number, quantity or degree ~ **maximum** *adj* greatest.

May (1) [*may*] *n* fifth month of the year; **M. Day** 1st May, *esp* as traditional folk-festival or modern festival in honour of workers; **M. Queen** girl chosen for beauty to preside at May Day festivities; **M. Week** week in early June when festivities and boat-races are held at Cambridge University.

may (2) *n* hawthorn blossom ~ **may** *v/i* gather may.

may (3) (*p/t* **might**, no *p/part*) *v/i* be able; be possible; be allowed; (*as aux*) expressing doubt, wish or hope.

maya [*mI*-ya] *n* (*Hindu philos*) illusion, *esp* of reality of material universe.

maybe [*may*bee] *adv* perhaps, possibly.

maybug [*may*bug] *n* cockchafer.

maybush [*may*boosh] *n* hawthorn bush.

mayday [*may*day] *n* signal of acute danger or distress used at sea.

mayfly [*may*flI] *n* species of fly; imitation of this used in angling.

mayhem [*may*hem] *n* (*leg*) physical injury, *usu* to a limb, as ground for action for damages; (*coll*) rowdy mischief.

Maying [*may*-ing] *n* celebration of May Day festivities.

mayn't [*maynt*] (*coll abbr*) may not.

mayonnaise [may-o*nayz*] *n* thick sauce of egg yolk beaten up with edible vegetable oil and seasoned, used as salad-dressing; cold dish having this as dressing.

mayor [*mair*] *n* chief officer of city or borough.

mayoralty [*mair*Ralti] *n* office or period of office of mayor.

mayoress [mair*Res*] *n* wife or female relative of a mayor assisting him in social and ceremonial duties; female mayor.

maypole [*may*pOl] *n* high decorated pole round which merrymakers dance on May Day; (*coll*) tall, thin, over-dressed woman.

mayst, mayest [*mayst*] (*ar*) *2nd pers sing pres* of **may** (3).

mazarine [*maze*Rin] *n* and *adj* deep rich blue.

maze [*mayz*] *n* intricate network of paths separated by hedges or walls, designed as a puzzle for those entering or leaving it; (*fig*) bewilderment.

mazer [*may*zer] *n* cup or bowl, *usu* of maplewood.

mazurka [ma*zur*ka] *n* lively Polish dance; the music for this.

mazy [*may*zi] *adj* like a maze; puzzled.

McCarthyism [ma*kaar*thi-izm] *n* (*US*) policy of expelling suspected Communists from all responsible posts; unscrupulous methods of investigation connected with this.

McCoy [ma*koi*] *n* **the real M.** the real or genuine thing or person.

me [*mee*] *pron acc* and *dat* of **I**.

mead (1) [*meed*] *n* alcoholic drink made of fermented honey.

mead (2) *n* (*poet*) meadow.

meadow [*med*O] *n* tract of grassland, grassy field; hayfield; low well-watered land.

meadowsweet [*med*Osweet] *n* plant with white fragrant flowers.

meagre [*meeger*] *adj* lean; scanty; barren.

meal (1) [*meel*] *n* food eaten at one time, repast; occasion of taking food.

meal (2) *n* grain ground to coarse powder.

mealie [*meeli*] *n* maize.

meal-ticket [*meel*-tikit] *n* (*US*) voucher for a free or cheap meal; (*fig*) one who or that which pays one's essential expenses.

mealtime [*meel*tIm] *n* hour at which a meal is normally eaten; time spent in eating a meal.

mealy [*meeli*] *adj* resembling meal; covered with flour; pale; (*of horses*) spotty.

mealybug [*meeli*bug] *n* small insect infesting greenhouse plants.

mealy-mouthed [meeli-*mowTHd*] *adj* unwilling to speak bluntly and frankly, hypocritical.

mean (1) (*p/t* and *p/part* meant) [*meen*] *v/t* and *i* intend, have as one's purpose; signify, convey; be of importance (to a person); indicate; refer to; **m. business** (*coll*) be in earnest; **m. mischief** intend to do something malicious; be a sign of future evil or misfortune.

mean (2) *adj* intermediate, midway; average; in the middle; intervening ~ **mean** *n* midpoint between extremes; moderate course of action; the average; (*math*) mean term or quantity.

mean (3) *adj* miserly; petty, despicable; cowardly and malicious; shabby, dingy; inferior; of low rank, value *etc*; (*US*) bad tempered; (*coll*) ashamed; petty ~ **meanly** *adv* ~ **meanness** *n*.

meander [mee-*an*der] *n* winding course'; one curve in the winding course of a river > PDG ~ **meander** *v/i* flow in a twisting course; move aimlessly, ramble.

meaning [*meen*ing] *n* that which is meant, sense; significance; import ~ **meaning** *adj* significant, expressive ~ **meaningly** *adv* significantly.

meaningful [*meen*ingfool] *adj* having meaning, conveying information; purposeful; significant; expressive ~ **meaningfully** *adv*.

meaningless [*meen*inglis] *adj* without meaning; senseless, purposeless; conveying no information ~ **meaninglessly** *adv* ~ **meaninglessness** *n*.

means [*meenz*] *n* (*pl, occ sing*) method by which a thing is done; agency, instrumentality; wealth; income; **by all m.** certainly; **by no m.** not at all.

means-test [*meenz*-test] *n* inquiry into financial resources of a person seeking unemployment benefit, State assistance *etc* ~ **meanstest** *v/t*.

meant [*ment*] *p/t* and *p/part* of mean (1).

meantime [*meen*tIm] *adv* and *n* (in the) interval between two given times.

meanwhile [*meen*wIl] *adv* and *n* meantime.

measles [*meez'lz*] *n* infectious disease accompanied by a red rash.

measly [*meez*li] *adj* (*coll*) worthless, despicable; stingy; (*med*) suffering from measles.

measurable [*mezhe*Rab'l] *adj* that can be measured; moderate.

measure [*mezher*] *v/t* and *i* find the size or quantity of in terms of specified units; estimate against a standard, judge; test by competition or trial; be of (a specified size, quantity *etc*); **m. one's length** fall flat; **m. out** deal out in specified quantities; **m. swords** fight; **m. up to** conform to, reach (a standard) ~ **measure** *n* size, quantity *etc* expressed in specified units; unit of measurement; method of measuring; any device for measuring; standard, criterion; metre; limit, fixed extent; Parliamentary bill; (*pl*) course of action, procedure; (*math*) number dividing exactly into another; (*mus*) bar > PDM; time in which a tune is written; rhythm; (*ar*) dance; (*pl*) (*geol*) strata; **beyond m.** excessive; **greatest common m.** (*math*) largest number exactly dividing into several given numbers; **made to m.** (*of clothes*) made individually to fit one's measurements.

measured [*mezherd*] *adj* well thought out, careful; deliberate; steady.

measureless [*mezher*liss] *adj* boundless, infinite.

measurement [*mezher*ment] *n* act of measuring; (*pl*) size expressed in specific units, dimensions.

meat [*meet*] *n* flesh of animals taken as food; (*ar*) any food; (*ar*) a meal; (*fig*) intellectual stimulus; (*sl*) human flesh.

meatball [*meet*bawl] *n* rissole.

meat-safe [*meet*-sayf] *n* small cupboard for storing meat.

meaty [*meeti*] *adj* of or like meat; fleshy but not fatty; (*fig*) intellectually stimulating; concentrated, pithy.

Mecca [*meka*] *n* city of pilgrimage for Muslims, birthplace of Mohammed; (*fig*) place visited by devotees; goal of one's ambitions.

meccano [me*kaan*O] *n* (*tr*) toy consisting of miniature parts from which engineering models can be constructed.

mechanic [me*kanik*] *n* man skilled in making, using, or maintaining machinery; skilled workman, artisan ~ **mechanic** *adj* (*ar*) mechanical.

mechanical [me*kani*kal] *adj* of, like, or by machines; produced by machinery; done without thinking, automatic; unoriginal ~ **mechanically** *adv*.

mechanician [mekani*shan*] *n* skilled mechanic.

mechanics [me*kaniks*] *n* (*pl*) branch of physical science dealing with behaviour of matter under the action of force > PDS; (*fig*) way in which something works.

mechanism [*mekanizm*] *n* machinery; machine-like interrelation of parts or of causes and effects; means by which a thing functions; (*psych*) semi-automatic reaction pattern subconsciously directed > PDP.

mechanistic [mekan*istik*] *n* of or like machinery; of mechanisms; **m. theory** view that all features of living beings can be explained as mechanical results of purely physical causes.

mechanize [*mekanIz*] *v/t* equip with machinery; cause to function by machinery; make mechanical, *esp* replace workers with machines; (*mil*) equip with armoured vehicles and mechanical weapons ~ **mechanization** [mekanIz*ay*shon] *n*.

medal [*medal*] *n* small metal disk of metal bearing inscription or device to commemorate an event or to honour a person for some achievement; small disk bearing a saint's image ~ **medalled** *adj* having a medal.

medallic [me*dalik*] *adj* of, on, or like a medal.

medallion [me*dalyon*] *n* large medal; large round ornamental design or portrait.

medallist [*medalist*] *n* one who makes medals; one who has gained a medal.

meddle [*med'l*] *v/i* interfere needlessly or harmfully in what does not concern one ~ **meddlesome** adj.

media [meedi-a] pl of **medium**; (n pl) means of communication to the public; newspapers, TV and radio collectively.

mediaeval see **medieval**.

medial [meedi-al] adj in the middle; mean, average ~ **medially** adv.

median [meedi-an] adj and n in or through the middle; intermediate; (math) line joining a vertex of a triangle to the mid-point of the opposite side.

mediate [meedi-ayt] v/i and t intervene between disputants to reconcile them; cause by intervening; form intermediate link between; be a medium for ~ **mediate** adj in the middle; acting through an intermediary, not direct.

mediation [meedi-ayshon] n act of mediating; intercession ~ **mediative** [meedi-ativ] adj.

mediator [meedi-ayter] n one who mediates; intercessor; peacemaker ~ **mediatory** [meedi-ayteRi] adj.

medical [medikal] adj of or connected with the art of treating and curing diseases; of or by medicine; **m. practitioner** qualified doctor ~ **medical** n (coll) student of medicine; examination in medicine; general examination of one's health ~ **medically** adv.

medicament [medikament/medikament] n medical remedy.

medicate [medikayt] v/t impregnate with anything medicinal; treat medically ~ **medication** [medikayshon] n ~ **medicative** [medikativ] adj.

medicinal [medisinal] adj possessing healing properties; of medicine ~ **medicinally** adv.

medicine [medsin/medisin] n substance taken internally to treat disease; science of preventing, treating and curing disease; (fig) salutary punishment ~ **medicine** v/t treat by medicine.

medicine-man [medsin-man] n magician among primitive peoples, witchdoctor.

medico [medikO] n (sl) doctor; medical student.

medieval, mediaeval [medi-eeval] adj of or in the Middle Ages; imitating the Middle Ages.

medievalism [medi-eevalizm] n medieval outlook or customs; admiration for or imitation of these ~ **medievalist** n one who studies medieval history, literature etc; one who admires or imitates medieval customs etc.

mediocre [meedi-Oker] adj of middling quality, neither good nor bad; second-rate, inferior; insignificant.

mediocrity [meedi-okRiti] n state or quality of being mediocre; mediocre person.

meditate [meditayt] v/i and t think deeply, esp on religious subject; repress normal mental activity so as to gain spiritual insight; muse, ponder; plan; intend.

meditation [meditayshon] n act of meditating; systematic reflection on religious topics.

meditative [meditativ] adj thoughtful, pondering ~ **meditatively** adv.

medium (pl **media**, **mediums**) [meedi-um] n that which is of intermediate size, degree etc; means, agency, channel; substance within which objects exist or through which a force is transmitted; material in which an artist works; liquid used to bind powdered colours into paint >

PDAA; (spiritualism) one who receives and transmits messages from departed spirits > PDP; **the happy m.** wise avoidance of extremes; **mass media** means of communication reaching the majority of the public ~ **medium** adj of intermediate size, degree etc; average, moderate; in the middle; **m. wave** (rad) wave between 100 and 800 metres.

mediumistic [meedi-umistik] adj of or like spiritualist mediums.

mediumship [meedi-umship] n function of being a medium in spiritualism.

medlar [medler] n tree with fruit resembling the crab apple, best eaten half-rotten; fruit of this.

medley [medli] n confused and varied crowd of things or people; heterogeneous group; (mus) piece made up of brief excerpts from other works.

medulla [midula] n (med) spinal cord; marrow; pith of hair; inner part of certain organs; (bot) pith of plants; **m. oblongata** upper part of spinal cord forming hindmost part of brain > PDP ~ **medullary** adj.

meed [meed] n (poet) reward; what one merits.

meek [meek] adj gentle, submissive.

meerschaum [meersham] n white clay used for making bowls of tobacco-pipes.

meet (1) [meet] adj (ar) proper, fitting.

meet (2) (p/t and p/part met) v/t and i come face to face (with), encounter; come in contact (with), touch; converge, join; assemble; encounter socially, be or become personally acquainted (with); come together for negotiation; encounter in conflict, oppose; satisfy; pay, comply with; await arrival of; refute; **m. with** find by chance; undergo, experience ~ **meet** n gathering of huntsmen and hounds for a hunt.

meeting [meeting] n act of coming together, encountering or joining; assembly, esp for specified purpose; persons assembled.

meeting-house [meeting-hows] n building for religious gatherings of Quakers, Dissenters etc.

meetly [meetli] adv (ar) fittingly ~ **meetness** n.

mega- pref large; one million times.

megacycle [megasik'l] n (elect) measure of frequency in alternating current or oscillatory discharge, a million cycles per second > PDS.

megadeath [megadeth] n death of one million people; unit used in reckoning mortality in nuclear war.

megalith [megalith] n huge prehistoric stone monument ~ **megalithic** [megalithik] adj.

megalomania [megalOmayni-a] n (psych) excessive overestimation of one's own importance, abilities etc; form of insanity characterized by this > PDP ~ **megalomaniac** adj and n.

megalopolis [megalopolis] n very large conurbation with interdependent industries.

megaphone [megafOn] n speaking-trumpet for making one's voice sound louder and so carry farther.

megaton [megatun] n explosive force equal to that of a million tons of TNT.

megavolt [megavOlt] n one million volts.

megawatt [megawot] n one million watts.

megrim [meegRim] n migraine; (pl) depression.

meiosis [mI-Osis] n understatement; (biol) two successive cell-divisions starting in a diploid cell, such that the chromosomes are duplicated only once in the whole process > PDB ∼ **meiotic** [mɪ-otik] *adj*.

mekometer [me*kom*eter] *n* (*geol*) instrument for measuring distances by very short radio waves.

melan-, melano- *pref* black.

melancholia [melan*k*Oli-a] *n* type of mental disorder with marked feelings of depression > PDP.

melancholic [melan*k*olik] *adj* gloomy; dedepressed ∼ **melancholic** *n* person suffering from melancholia.

melancholy [*me*lankoli] *n* prolonged dejection and depression of spirits ∼ **melancholy** *adj* sad, gloomy, depressed; dismal, depressing.

melanin [*me*lanin] *n* dark brown pigment in human and animal skin, tissues and hair.

melanism [*me*lanizm] *n* excess of melanin.

meld [meld] *v/t* and *i* (*US*) merge.

mêlée, (*US*) **melee** [*me*lay] *n* (*Fr*) confused general fight; scuffle, skirmish.

meliorate [*mee*li-eRayt] *v/t* and *i* improve.

meliorism [*mee*li-eRizm] *n* doctrine that the world may be made better by persistent effort.

melisma [mi*liz*ma] *n* group of notes sung to one syllable; florid melody > PDM.

mellifluence [me*lif*loo-ens] *adj* quality of being mellifluous ∼ **mellifluent** *adj* mellifluous.

mellifluous [me*lif*loo-us] *adj* (*of words, music, voice*) sweetly or smoothly flowing ∼ **mellifluously** *adv*.

mellow [*mel*O] *adj* mature, well-ripened; soft and sweet; full and rich; smooth; grown wise and gentle through age or experience; (*sl*) jovial; merrily drunk ∼ **mellow** *v/t* and *i* make or become mellow ∼ **mellowly** *adv* ∼ **mellowness** *n*.

melodeon [me*lO*di-on] *n* small keyboard organ; accordion.

melodic [me*lod*ik] *adj* of or in melody; tuneful ∼ **melodically** *adv*.

melodious [me*lO*di-us] *adj* having a melody; tuneful; pleasant-sounding ∼ **melodiously** *adv*.

melodist [*me*lodist] *n* singer; composer of melodies.

melodrama [me*lOd*Raama] *n* play having sensational episodes and crude emotional impact; sensational incident; (*ar*) play with words spoken against a musical background > PDM.

melodramatic [me*lOd*Ramatik] *adj* like a melodrama; sensational, exaggerated ∼ **melodramatically** *adv*.

melody [*me*lodi] *n* succession of notes varying in pitch, tune > PDM; pleasing series of sounds; song, air.

melon [*me*lon] *n* kind of gourd.

melt [melt] *v/t* and *i* make or become liquid, dissolve; blend; fade, vanish; make or become tender, fill with pity ∼ **melt** *n* molten metal.

melting [*mel*ting] *adj* tender; pitying; sentimental; soft, soothing; **m. point** the temperature at which a solid melts ∼ **meltingly** *adv*.

melting-pot [*mel*ting-pot] *n* crucible; (*fig*) place where diverse ideas, characters *etc* meet and assimilate.

member [*mem*ber] *n* part of body, organ, limb; one part of a complex whole; person belonging to a society, group *etc*; (*gramm*) clause; (*math*) group of figures or symbols forming part of an expression; **M. of Parliament** elected representative in House of Commons.

membership [*mem*bership] *n* state of being member of a society, group *etc*; total number of members of a society *etc*; members collectively.

membrane [*mem*bRayn] *n* (*anat*) thin tissue which covers or lines a part or organ; parchment.

membraneous, membranous [mem*bR*ayni-us, *mem*bRanus] *adj* of or like membrane.

memento (*pl* **mementos, mementoes**) [mi*men*tO] *n* souvenir, keepsake; reminder.

memo [*mem*O] *n* (*coll abbr*) memorandum.

memoir [*mem*waar] *n* biography, *esp* one based on personal knowledge; essay on learned topic; (*pl*) published reminiscences; autobiography; collection of learned articles.

memorabilia [memeRa*bil*i-a] *n* (*pl*) things worth remembering.

memorable [*mem*eRab'l] *adj* worthy of being remembered; remarkable ∼ **memorably** *adv*.

memorandum (*pl* **memoranda, memorandums**) [meme*Ran*dum] *n* note made for future reference; brief record of a transaction; summary of terms of contract *etc*; **m. of association** (*leg*) articles of registration of a company.

memorial [mi*maw*Ri-al] *n* object, *esp* monument, commemorating a person or event; custom observed as commemoration; (*leg*) document stating terms of a petition; document informally stating opinions or advice; (*pl*) historical accounts, chronicles ∼ **memorial** *adj* rousing memory, commemorating; in memory of (the dead).

memorize [*mem*eRIZ] *v/t* learn by heart, commit to memory.

memory [*mem*eRi] *n* faculty of mentally retaining impressions of past experience, ability to remember > PDP; that which is remembered; commemoration; period during which something is remembered; posthumous reputation.

memsahib [*mem*saa-ib] *n* (*hist*) Indian form of address to a European woman.

men [men] *pl* of **man**.

menace [*men*as] *n* threat; (*coll*) pest ∼ **menace** *v/t* threaten ∼ **menacing** *ad* ∼ **menacingly** *adv*.

menagerie [mi*naj*eRi] *n* collection of wild animals exhibited in captivity; place where they are kept.

menarche [me*naar*ki] *n* onset of first menstruation.

mend [mend] *v/t* and *i* repair; remove effects of damage to; correct, amend; improve; reform; add fuel to; get better in health ∼ **mend** *n* hole or break which has been mended; patch, darn; **on the m.** recovering from illness *etc*.

mendacious [men*day*shus] *adj* untruthful; lying, *esp* habitually ∼ **mendacity** [men*das*iti] *n*.

mendelevium [mende*lee*vi-um] *n* (*chem*) a transuranic element > PDS.

Mendelian [men*dee*li-an] *adj* of Mendel's theory of heredity > PDB.

mendicancy [*men*dikansi] *n* state of being a beggar, *esp* habitually ∼ **mendicant** *n* beggar ∼ **mendicant** *adj* living solely on alms; begging.

mendicity [men*dis*iti] *n* state of being a beggar.

menfolk [*men*fOk] *n* (*pl*) men; male relatives.

menhir [*men*heer] *n* (*arch*) prehistoric monument consisting of one large upright stone.

menial [*mee*ni-al] *adj* of or suited to a servant; (*of work*) servile; mean ∼ **menial** *n* domestic servant.

meninges [men*in*jeez] *n* (*pl*) (*med*) membranes enclosing the brain and spinal cord.

meningitis [menin*ji*tis] *n* inflammation of membranes enclosing the brain or spinal cord.

meniscus [men*i*skus] *n* curved upper surface formed by a column of liquid in a vessel or tube; a crescent shaped body; (*anat*) a disk of cartilage in a joint.

menopause [*men*Opawz] *n* time of life in women at which menstruation ceases; **male m.** (*coll*) restlessness and discontent in middle-aged men.

menorrhoea [men*O*Ree-a] *n* menses.

menses [*men*seez] *n* (*pl*) monthly discharge of blood from the womb.

menstrual [*men*stRoo-al] *adj* pertaining to the menses; (*astron*) monthly.

menstruate [*men*stRoo-ayt] *v/i* discharge menses ~ **menstruation** [menstRoo-*ay*-shon] *n*.

menstruous [*men*stRoo-us] *adj* of the menses; menstruating.

mensurable [*men*shooRab'l] *adj* capable of being measured; (*mus*) in fixed rhythm.

mensural [*men*shooRal] *adj* pertaining to measure.

mensuration [menshoo*Ray*shon] *n* act of measuring: measurement of lengths, areas and volumes.

menswear [*menz*wair] *n* clothes for men.

mental [*men*tal] *adj* of or in the mind; pertaining to insanity or psychological disorders; (*coll*) crazy; imbecile; **m. arithmetic** sums calculated in the mind, not on paper; **m. defective** any individual unable to profit from schooling or adapt himself to complex environment > PDP.

mentality [men*tal*iti] *n* intellectual capacity; habitual outlook.

mentally [*men*tali] *adv* in, by or as regards the mind.

menthol [*men*thol] *n* substance obtained from oil of peppermint > PDS.

mention [*men*shon] *v/t* speak or write briefly about, refer to; name ~ **mention** *n* act of mentioning; reference, brief remark; **honourable m.** award for good work which has not won a prize.

mentor [*men*tor] *n* wise and reliable adviser.

menu [*men*ew] *n* list of dishes available or to be served; the meal itself.

Mephistophelian [mefisto*feel*i-an] *adj* cunning and malevolent; sinister; fiendish.

mephitic [me*fit*ik] *adj* stinking; noxious.

mercantile [*mur*kantIl] *adj* pertaining to merchants or to trade; commercial.

mercenary [*mur*sinaRi] *adj* influenced only by hope of gain; greedy for wealth; working for payment, hired ~ **mercenary** *n* professional soldier employed by foreign state.

mercer [*mur*ser] *n* dealer in fabrics and cloth.

merchandise [*mur*chandIz] *n* wares, goods or the commodities of commerce.

merchant [*mur*chant] *n* one who trades on a large scale, *esp* with foreign countries ~ **merchant** *adj* relating to trade and merchants; **m. prince** rich and powerful trader; **m. ship** vessel used in trading; **m. service** fleet of merchant ships.

merchantman [*mur*chantman] *n* merchant ship.

merciful [*mur*sifool] *adj* showing mercy, lenient; compassionate; providential ~ **mercifully** *adv*.

merciless [*mur*siles] *adj* pitiless; unrelenting ~ **mercilessly** *adv*.

mercurial [mur*kew*Ri-al] *adj* lively, active; changeable; (*chem*) of mercury; of medical preparations of mercury.

mercury [*mur*kewRi] *n* (*chem*) liquid, silvery, metallic element > PDS, quicksilver; (*astron*) planet nearest to sun > PDS; (*Rom myth*) messenger of the gods; (*coll*) messenger.

mercy [*mur*si] *n* forgiveness and leniency to an offender; forbearance towards those in one's power; pity for human suffering; fortunate event, blessing; kindness, favour; **at the m. of** defenceless against; **m. killing** euthanasia ~ **mercy** *adj* done, brought *etc* to relieve human suffering.

mercy-seat [*mur*si-seet] *n* throne of God; (*bibl*) covering of Ark of Covenant.

mere (1) [*meer*] *n* pool, lake.

mere (2) *adj* nothing more nor less than; simple ~ **merely** *adv* only; purely, simply.

meretricious [me*Rit*Rishus] *adj* falsely attractive; tawdry; (*ar*) of a harlot ~ **meretriciously** *adv*.

merganser [mur*gan*ser] *n* one of a genus of large duck-like birds.

merge [*murj*] *v/i* and *t* become completely absorbed (into); lose identity; absorb, swallow up; fade or vanish (into) very gradually; (*comm*) combine (companies) under one head ~ **merger** *n* process of combining under one head; union, combine, absorption; (*leg*) absorption of estate *etc* into another more valuable.

meridian [me*Rid*i-an] *n* (*geog*, *astron*) line of longitude passing through the poles and cutting the equator at right angles > PDG, PDS; zenith; (*fig*) culmination; noon ~ **meridian** *adj* of noon; culminating.

meridional [mi*Rid*i-onal] *adj* in or of the south, *esp* of Europe; of a meridian.

meringue [me*Rang*] *n* baked mixture of sugar and white of egg; cake of this.

merino [me*Reen*O] *n* breed of sheep with very fine wool; fine woollen dress fabric ~ **merino** *adj*.

merit [*me*Rit] *n* quality deserving praise or reward; worth, ability; (*pl*) intrinsic rightness or wrongness; **Order of M.** British order awarded for distinguished services ~ **merit** *v/t* deserve, have a right to, earn ~ **merited** *adj* deserved, earned.

meritocracy [me*Rit*okRasi] *n* social system giving power to those who show personal abilities and achievements.

meritocrat [*me*RitOkRat] *n* person wielding power because of abilities, not birth or wealth.

meritorious [me*Rit*awRi-us] *adj* deserving reward or praise ~ **meritoriously** *adv*.

merkin [*mur*kin] *n* artificial vagina.

merlin [*mur*lin] *n* very small falcon.

mermaid [*mur*mayd] *n* imaginary creature, half woman and half fish.

merman [*mur*man] *n* male counterpart of mermaid.

Merovingian [meRo*vin*jan] *adj* of the first dynasty of Frankish kings.

merriment [*me*Riment] *n* hilarity; mirth.

merry (1) [*me*Ri] *adj* gay, cheerful; causing mirth; fond of fun; (*sl*) slightly drunk ~ **merrily** *adv* ~ **merriness** *n*.

merry (2) *n* the wild black cherry.

merry-go-round [*me*Ri-gO-Rownd] *n* rotating

structure with seats formed as horses, cars *etc*, and ridden at fairs *etc*.

merrymaking [*me*Rimayking] *n* festivity; gaiety.

mésalliance [mayzali-ahngs] *n* (*Fr*) marriage with a social inferior.

mescal [mes*kal*] *n* intoxicating drink causing hallucinations, made from juice of the agave; cactus yielding mescalin.

mescalin [*mes*kalin] *n* narcotic and strongly hallucinative drug extracted from a Mexican cactus.

meseems [mis*eems*] *v/impers* (*ar*) it seems to me.

mesh [mesh] *n* open spaces or interstices of a net or sieve; netting; woven wire cloth; trap ~ **mesh** *v/t* and *i* ensnare; (*fig*) cooperate; (*mech*) engage, interlock.

mesmeric [mez*me*Rik] *adj* hypnotic.

mesmerism [*mez*meRizm] *n* (*obs*) process of inducing a hypnotic state ~ **mesmerist** *n* (*obs*) hypnotist.

mesmerize [*mez*meRIz] *v/t* (*obs*) hypnotize; (*fig*) render motionless through fear or fascination, hold the entire attention of.

mesne [*meen*] *adj* intermediate, middle.

meso- *pref* middle.

mesoderm [*mez*Odurm] *n* (*biol*) germ-layer of animal embryo > PDB.

mesolithic [mez*Olith*ik] *adj* of the middle Stone Age.

mesomorph [*mez*Omawrf] *n* person of muscular build, neither thin nor fat.

meson [*mee*zon] *n* (*phys*) type of elementary particle with mass between that of electron and proton.

mesotron [*mes*OtRon] *n* (*phys*) meson.

mesozoic [mes*Oz*O-ik] *n* third major geological era > PDG, PDB.

mess [*mes*] *n* muddle, confusion; dirtiness; untidiness; difficult situation, predicament; group of persons habitually eating together, *esp* in armed forces; messroom; animals' food mash; (*ar*) food, *esp* liquid ~ **mess** *v/t* and *i* make dirty or untidy; make a muddle of, bungle; mismanage; take one's meals habitually in a specified group; **m. about** spend time idly, potter; work inefficiently; make untidy; fiddle with; **m. up** make dirty or untidy; spoil.

message [*mes*ij] *n* indirect communication from one person to another; errand; inspired teaching, revelation; moral or social teaching.

messenger [*mes*enjer] *n* one who carries a message.

Messiah [mesI-a] *n* (*Judaism*) the leader or deliverer foretold by various prophets; (*Christianity*) Christ; (*fig*) saviour; deliverer.

messianic [mesI-*an*ik] *adj* of, like or claiming to be the Messiah; expecting the coming of a new Messiah or the second coming of Christ ~ **messianism** *n*.

messily [*mes*ili] *adv* dirtily ~ **messiness** *n*.

messmate [*mes*mayt] *n* one who eats at the same table; comrade.

Messrs [*mes*erz] *abbr pl* of **Mister**.

messuage [*mes*wij] *n* (*leg*) dwelling house with adjoining buildings and lands.

messy [*mes*i] *adj* in or like a mess, dirty, untidy.

mestizo [mes*teez*O] *n* Spanish and American-Indian halfcaste.

met (1) [*met*] *p/t* and *p/part* of **meet** (2).

met (2) *adj* (*coll abbr*) meteorological.

meta- *pref* beyond, after; among; with; *also to express change*.

meta [*meta*] *n* (*abbr*) metaldehyde.

metabolic [*metab*olik] *adj* of metabolism.

metabolism [me*tab*olizm] *n* all chemical processes in a living organism > PDB; **basal m.** rate of energy expenditure in an animal at rest > PDB ~ **metabolize** *v/t* change by metabolism.

metabolite [me*tab*olIt] *n* substance taking part in metabolism; product of a metabolic process > PDB.

metacarpus [metak*aar*pus] *n* (*anat*) palm of hand > PDB ~ **metacarpal** *adj*.

metal [*metal*] *n* any lustrous substance which is malleable, ductile, a good conductor *etc* > PDS; broken stone for road-making; glass in fusion; (*pl*) rails ~ **metal** *adj* made of metal ~ **metal** (*pres/part* **metalling**, *p/t* and *p/part* **metalled**) *v/t* cover with metal; make (road) with broken stones.

metaldehyde [me*tal*dihId] *n* white solid substance used as fuel in small burners > PDS.

metallic [mi*tal*ik] *adj* of, like, containing metal; having a ringing sound; **m. currency** currency using metal coins.

metalling [*metal*ing] *n* making roads with broken stones; stones used for this.

metallize [*metal*Iz] *v/t* form into a metal; render metallic; vulcanize (rubber).

metalloid [*metal*oid] *n* (*chem*) element with properties of both metals and non-metals.

metallurgy [me*tal*urji] *n* science and technology of metals; extraction of metals from their ores ~ **metallurgist** *n* ~ **metallurgic** [metal*urj*ik] *adj*.

metamorphic [metam*awr*fik] *adj* showing or caused by change of form; **m. rock** rock which has changed in character and form > PDG.

metamorphose [metam*awr*fOz] *v/t* and *i* transform.

metamorphosis (*pl* **metamorphoses**) [metam*awr*fOsis] *n* complete or remarkable change, transformation; (*biol*) rapid transformation from larval to adult form.

metaphor [*meta*for] *n* figure of speech implying but not explicitly stating a comparison between two objects or actions.

metaphoric [meta*fo*Rik] *adj* of, like, or containing metaphor; not literal ~ **metaphorical** *adj* ~ **metaphorically** *adv*.

metaphysical [meta*fiz*ikal] *adj* of metaphysics; based on pure reasoning; transcendental; (*of poetry*) in or like a 17th-century style blending intellectual subtlety, wit, passion and directness; (*fig*) excessively subtle; fantastic; supernatural ~ **metaphysical** *n* one of a 17th-century group of poets ~ **metaphysically** *adv*.

metaphysician [metafi*zish*an] *n* one versed in metaphysics.

metaphysics [meta*fiz*iks] *n* (*pl*) branch of philosophy concerned with the ultimate nature of being and knowing; study of ultimate abstract principles.

metastable [metas*tayb'l*] *adj* (*chem*) unstable in certain circumstances but not liable to alter spontaneously; (*phys*) (*of an atom, nucleus or* *system*) having an excited energy level which has an appreciable lifetime.

metatarsus [meta*taar*sus] *n* (*anat*) area of foot between ankle and toes ~ **metatarsal** *adj*.

metathesis [mi*tath*isis] *n* (*phon*) transposition of sounds or letters in a word.

metazoa [meta*zO*-a] *n* animals whose bodies consist of many cells > PDB.

metcast [*met*kaast] *n* meteorological weather forecast.

mete (1) [*meet*] *v*/*t* (*ar*) **m. out** measure out; allot.

mete (2) *n* (*leg*) boundary.

metempsychosis [metempsi*kO*sis] *n* passing of soul after death from one body to another.

meteor [*meeti*-or] *n* solid body which enters the atmosphere from outer space, becoming luminous by incandescence > PDG, PDS; (*fig*) anything dazzling but brief.

meteoric [meeti-o*Rik*] *adj* of meteors; of the atmosphere; (*fig*) swift and dazzling but brief ~ **meteorically** *adv*.

meteorite [*meeti*-o*Rit*] *n* mass of stone or metal that has fallen to earth from outer space > PDG.

meteoroid [*meeti*-o*Roid*] *n* small solid body in outer space.

meteorology [meeti-o*Roloji*] *n* scientific study of the weather and of atmospheric processes > PDG ~ **meteorological** [meeti-o*Rolo*jikal] *adj* ~ **meteorologist** *n* one skilled in meteorology.

meter [*meeter*] *n* that which measures; instrument which automatically records consumption of gas, water, electricity *etc*; parking-meter; taximeter; (*US*) metre.

meterage [*meeteRij*] *n* act of recording by meter; amount thus recorded.

methane [*meth*ayn] *n* inflammable gas formed by decay of organic matter, firedamp > PDE, PDS.

methanol [*meth*anol] *n* (*chem*) methyl alcohol.

methinks [mi*thinks*] *v*/*impers* (*ar*) it seems to me.

method [*meth*od] *n* manner, way of doing; systematic and orderly procedure or arrangement; (*bot*, *zool*) classification.

methodical [mi*thod*ikal] *adj* done or arranged systematically; orderly ~ **methodically** *adv*.

Methodism [*meth*odizm] *n* doctrines and practices of various Nonconformist sects derived from the teachings of John and Charles Wesley ~ **Methodist** *n* member of such a sect ~ **Methodistic** [methodistik] *adj*.

methodize [*method*Iz] *v*/*t* arrange systematically.

methodology [method*oloji*] *n* study of systematic methods of scientific research.

methought [mi*thawt*] *p*/*t* of **methinks**.

meths [*meths*] *n* (*pl*) (*coll*) methylated spirits.

methyl [*meth*il] *n* (*chem*) the univalent organic radical CH_3; **m. alcohol** wood spirit > PDS.

methylate [*meth*ilayt] *v*/*t* replace a hydrogen atom with a methyl group; add methyl alcohol to denature ethyl alcohol; **methylated spirits** denatured ethyl alcohol containing methyl alcohol > PDS ~ **methylate** *n* any compound containing a methyl group.

meticulous [mi*tik*ewlus] *adj* over-exact, punctilious ~ **meticulously** *adv*.

metol [*meet*ol] *n* (*chem*) white, crystalline chemical used as a photographic developer.

metonymy [mi*ton*imi] *n* substitution of one word for another when the objects each refers to are habitually associated.

metre (1) [*meet*er] *n* rhythmic and systematic arrangement of syllables in verse according to stress or length; (*mus*) arrangement of accented and unaccented beats > PDM.

metre (2) *n* unit of length in metric system, 39·37 in.

metric [*met*Rik] *adj* pertaining to system of measurement based on the metre (2), the litre and the gram; **m. ton** one thousand kilograms.

metrical (1) [*met*Rikal] *adj* of or in poetic metre; in verse; regularly rhythmical.

metrical (2) *adj* of measurement.

metrication [metRi*kay*shon] *n* adoption of, or conversion to, metric measurements.

metrician [met*Rish*an] *n* one who is skilled in verse metres.

metrics [*met*Riks] *n* (*pl*) study of versification.

metrist [*met*Rist] *n* one who writes in verse.

metro [*met*RO] *n* underground railway.

metronome [*met*RonOm] *n* (*mus*) instrument for sounding an adjustable number of beats per minute > PDM ~ **metronomic** [metRo*nom*ik] *adj*.

metropolis [met*Rop*olis] *n* capital city; archbishop's see.

metropolitan [metRo*pol*itan] *adj* of or in a capital city; of an archbishop or his see; **m. France** France as opposed to its colonies ~ **metropolitan** *n* bishop with jurisdiction over others of a province, archbishop; inhabitant of a capital.

mettle [*met*'l] *n* courage; vigour, ardour; **on one's m.** eager to excel ~ **mettlesome** *adj* high-spirited, vigorous.

mew (1) [*mew*] *n* type of seagull.

mew (2) *n* and *v*/*i* miaow (softly).

mew (3) *v*/*t* and *i* keep (hawks) in cage; imprison, confine; (*ar*) (*of hawks*) moult ~ **mew** *n* cage for moulting hawks; process of moulting.

mews [*mewz*] *n* group of stables round an open yard or lane; such stables converted to dwelling-places.

mezuza [mez*OO*za] *n* (*Heb*) small scroll of religious texts fixed to doorpost of Jewish house.

mezzanine [*mez*aneen] *n* (*bui*) an intermediate storey; (*theat*) floor beneath stage.

mezzo [*medz*O] *adv* (*Ital*) (*mus*) fairly; midway; **m. voce** with moderate tone; **m. forte** fairly loud; **m. rilievo** sculpture in half relief > PDAA.

mezzo-soprano [medzO-so*Raan*O] *n* female voice between soprano and contralto; singer with such a voice.

mezzotint [*medz*Otint] *n* mode of engraving in which the plate is first covered with a mesh of small blurred dots, and then partially smoothed to form lighter areas > PDAA.

mho [*mO*] *n* (*elect*) reciprocal ohm > PDS.

mi [*mee*] *n* (*mus*) third note of sol-fa scale; third note of C major scale, E.

miaow [mi-*ow*] *n* cry of a cat ~ **miaow** *v*/*i*.

miasma (*pl* **miasmas, miasmata**) [mi-*az*ma] *n* unwholesome mist or vapour ~ **miasmal** *adj*.

mica [*mI*ka] *n* (*min*) group of mineral silicates having easily separable crystalline layers.

mice [*mIs*] *pl* of **mouse**.

Michaelmas [*mik*elmas] *n* feast of St Michael,

29 September; **M. daisy** tall perennial variety of aster; **M. term** autumn term at colleges *etc*.

Mick, Mickey [*mik, miki*] *n* (*sl*) an Irishman; **take the m.** (out of) (*coll*) mock, tease; insult.

mickle [*mik'l*] *adj* (*Scots*) great, large.

micro- *pref* very small; one-millionth of.

microbalance [*mī*krObalans] *n* sensitive balance for weighing quantities down to a millionth of a gram.

microbe [*mī*krOb] *n* microscopic organism, *esp* one causing disease.

microbial [mīkrObi-al] *adj* of microbes; caused by a microbe.

microbic [mīkrObik] *adj* microbial.

microbiology [mīkrObī-*oloji*] *n* study of micro-organisms.

microcard [*mī*krOkaard] *n* filing card bearing a microphotograph.

microcephalic [mīkrOsi*falik*] *adj* having abnormally small head and brain.

microclimate [mīkrO*kli*mat] *n* conditions of temperature, moisture *etc* affecting a very small area.

microcosm [*mī*krOkozm] *n* any community seen as a small self-contained world; man as epitome of the universe; small-scale representation.

microcurie [mīkrO*kewr*Ree] *n* a unit of measurement of radioactivity, one-millionth of a curie.

microdot [*mī*krOdot] *adj* (*phot*) of very fine dots.

microelectronics [mīkrO-ilekt*Ro*niks] *n* (*pl*) design and process of construction of electronic devices using extremely small solid state components.

microfarad [mīkrO*fa*Rad] *n* (*elect*) one-millionth of a farad.

microfiche [*mī*krOfish] *n* piece of film bearing a microphotograph.

microfilm [*mī*krOfilm] *n* film used to photograph documents, books *etc* on very small scale ~ **microfilm** *v/t*.

microhm [*mī*krOm] *n* one-millionth of an ohm.

micromesh [*mī*krOmesh] *adj* (*of stockings*) of very fine mesh.

micrometer [mīk*Ro*miter] *n* instrument for the accurate measurement of small distances.

microminiaturization [mīkrO*mi*natewrRIzay-shon] *n* reduction in size of electronic devices *esp* by using solid state components.

micron [*mī*krOn] *n* one-millionth of a metre.

micro-organism [mīkrO-*awr*ganizm] *n* organism so small as to be visible only under the microscope, unicellular organism.

microphone [*mī*krOfOn] *n* device for converting sound-waves into electrical energy which may then be reconverted into sound after transmission by wire or radio > PDB, PDS.

microphonics [mīkRo*fo*niks] *n* (*pl*) science of electrical transmission or amplification of sound.

microphotograph [mīkrO*fO*togRaaf] *n* photograph reduced to very small scale; photograph taken through a microscope; photograph taken on very small scale for enlargement.

microphotography [mīkrO*fo*tog*R*afi] *n* art of taking microphotographs.

microphyte [*mī*krOfīt] *n* microscopic vegetable organism.

microscope [*mī*krOskOp] *n* optical or electronic instrument which magnifies objects too minute to be seen without it > PDB, PDS.

microscopic [mīkro*sko*pik] *adj* of a microscope; visible only through a microscope; very small ~ **microscopical** *adj* microscopic ~ **microscopically** *adv*.

microscopy [mīk*Ro*skopi] *n* investigation by means of a microscope ~ **microscopist** *n*.

microtome [*mī*krOtOm] *n* instrument for cutting thin sections of a material for microscopic examination.

microwave [*mī*krOwayv] *n* electromagnetic radiation with wavelengths between 1 mm. and 30 cm.

micturate [*mik*tewRayt] *v/i* urinate.

micturition [miktewR*ish*on] *n* act of urinating; abnormally frequent urination.

mid [*mid*] *adj* middle, situated between ~ **mid** *prep* (*poet*) amid.

mid-air [*mid*-air] *adj* in the middle of the air, in the middle of a flight, i.e. not during take-off or landing.

midday [mid-*day*] *adj* and *n* (of or at) noon.

midden [*mid*en] *n* dunghill; pile of refuse.

middle [*mid*'l] *adj* equally distant from two extremes, intermediate; halfway between beginning and end; (*cap*) (*denoting a period in the history of the development of a language*) between the earlier stage and the modern; m. **age** period between the end of youth and onset of old age; **M. Ages** period of history from fall of Western Roman Empire to the Renaissance; m. **class** section of population neither working-class nor aristocrats; m. **ear** tympanum; m. **term** (*log*) term common to both premises of a syllogism; m. **voice** (*gramm*) special verb-form expressing reflexive or intransitive act; m. **watch** (*naut*) watch between midnight and 4 am ~ **middle** *n* point, area or period between extremes, centre; waist ~ **middle** *v/t* place in the middle, centre; (*football*) kick to centre from wings; (*cricket*) hit with full force of bat.

middle-aged [mid'l-*ayjd*] *adj* no longer young; between forty and sixty years old.

middle-bracket [*mid*'l-bRakit] *adj* towards the middle of a series of categories.

middlebrow [*midl*'bRow] *n* and *adj* (person) of tastes intermediate between highbrow and lowbrow.

middle-class [*mid*'l-klaas] *adj* and *n* (of or in) the middle classes. neither aristocratic nor working class; **lower m.** including shopkeepers, self-employed artisans *etc*; **upper m.** including landowners, members of the professions, *etc*.

middleman [*mid*'lman] *n* intermediary; (*comm*) agent or wholesaler who buys from the manufacturers to sell to the retailer.

middlemost [*mid*'lmOst] *adj* nearest the middle.

middleweight [*mid*'lwayt] *n* boxer whose weight is between 10 stone 7 lb and 11 stone 6 lb.

middling [*mid*ling] *adj* mediocre; moderate, fair; of middle size or quality; (*coll*) fairly well in health ~ **middlingly** *adv* ~ **middlings** *n* (*pl*) second-rate grade of goods.

middy [*mid*i] *n* (*coll*) midshipman.

midge [*mij*] *n* small flying insect.

midget [*mij*it] *n* extremely small person ~ **midget** *adj* tiny, miniature.

midi [midi] n and adj (coll) (skirt) of medium length.

midland [midland] adj and n (in) the middle part of a country ~ Midlands n (pl) middle counties of England.

midmost [midmOst] adj and adv in the very middle.

midnight [midnIt] n the middle of the night; twelve o'clock at night ~ midnight adj of or at midnight; completely dark; burn the m. oil do intellectual work late at night.

mid-off [mid-of] n (cricket) (position of) fieldsman in front of the batsman to the left of the bowler.

mid-on [mid-on] n (cricket) (position of) fieldsman in front of the batsman to the right of the bowler.

midriff [midRif] n the diaphragm.

midship [midship] adj and n (of or in) the middle of a ship ~ midships adv.

midshipman [midshipman] n (naut) officer ranking below a sub-lieutenant but above a cadet.

midst [midst] n middle; in the m. of among; occupied in ~ midst prep (ar) among.

midsummer [midsumer] n the summer solstice, about 21 June; M. Day 24 June; m. madness complete folly.

midway [midway] adj and adv halfway.

mid-week [mid-week] adj of or in the middle of a week, not at the weekend.

midwife [midwIf] n woman trained to help women in childbirth.

midwifery [midwifeRi] n science or skill of a midwife; obstetrics.

midwinter [midwinter] n the winter solstice, about 21 December.

mien [meen] n air, manner, demeanour.

miff [mif] n (coll) bad temper; tiff ~ miff v/t and i annoy; show annoyance.

might (1) [mIt] n strength, force, power.

might (2) p/t of may.

mighty [mIti] adj strong, powerful, great ~ mighty adv (coll) extremely ~ mightily adv powerfully; (coll) extremely ~ mightiness n.

mignonette [minyonet] n plant with sweet-scented flowers.

migraine [meegRayn] n severe headache, often on one side only, with nausea and depression.

migrant [mIgRant] n and adj (person or animal) that migrates.

migrate [mIgRayt] v/i move from one region to another, esp at regular seasonal intervals; move to a new district.

migration [mIgRayshon] n act of migrating; group of migrating animals or persons ~ migratory adj that migrates; of migration.

Mikado [mikaadO] n title of the Emperor of Japan.

mike (1) [mIk] n (sl) microphone.

mike (2) [mIk] v/i (sl) be idle.

mil [mil] n one thousandth of an inch.

milady [milaydi] n my lady.

milch [milch] adj giving milk.

mild [mIld] adj gentle, tender; placid; pleasant; moderate; warm; not strong; not bitter ~ mildly adv ~ mildness n.

mildew [mildew] n one of various small destructive whitish fungi growing on plants, food etc ~ mildew v/i be or become covered with mildew ~ mildewy adv.

mile [mIl] n unit of linear measurement equal to 1,760 yards; nautical m. unit of distance equal to 6,080 feet; Roman m. 1,000 paces.

mileage [mIlij] n distance travelled reckoned in miles; rate of travel in miles; number of miles travelled by motor vehicle per gallon of fuel; (fig) effectiveness, useful advantage.

milestone [mIlstOn] n roadside stone marking distance in miles to or from a place; (fig) important event marking beginning or end of an era, stage of development etc.

miliary [mili-aRi] adj (path) having vesicles or nodules shaped like millet seed.

milieu [meelyer] n (Fr) immediate environment, physical and social.

militancy [militansi] n quality of being militant.

militant [militant] adj active in political conflict; pugnacious; at war, fighting ~ militant n one who fights; one active in conflict ~ militantly adv.

militarism [militaRizm] n outlook of an enthusiastic soldier or pugnacious person; admiration for military methods; aggressive patriotism; reliance on armed strength ~ militarist n upholder of militarism; expert on military matters ~ militarist, militaristic adj.

militarize [militaRIz] v/t make fit for war; fill with warlike spirit.

military [militaRi] adj of soldiers or war; warlike; soldierly; engaged in war ~ military n soldiers, army.

militate [militayt] v/i m. against be in conflict with, hinder.

militia [milisha] n military force auxiliary to the regular army, esp one of civilians recruited from each county ~ militiaman n.

milk [milk] n white fluid secreted by female mammals to feed their young; milk of cows; white juice of certain plants ~ milk v/t and i draw milk from; (coll) extort all possible profit from; yield milk.

milk-and-water [milk-and-wawter] adj weak, insipid.

milkbar [milkbaar] n place where milkshakes etc are sold.

milker [milker] n cow yielding milk; one who milks.

milk-float [milk-flOt] n cart on which bottles of milk are carried to customers.

milkiness [milkinis] n quality of being milky.

milking [milking] n act of one who milks ~ milking adj used in milking cows.

milkmaid [milkmayd] n woman who milks cows.

milkman [milkman] n man who sells milk.

milkshake [milkshayk] n drink of whisked and flavoured milk.

milksop [milksop] n effeminate coward.

milk-sugar [milk-shooger] n lactose.

milkteeth [milkteet'] n (pl) teeth of a child or immature animal > PDB.

milky [milki] adj like milk; white and opaque; containing or yielding milk; M. Way band of faint diffuse light visible at night and formed by the concentration of stars in the galaxy.

mill [mil] n machine for grinding grain; building containing such machinery; apparatus for grinding coffee, pepper etc; machinery for processing cotton, paper, wood etc; building containing this, factory; (*sl*) fist-fight; **go through the m.** suffer many misfortunes ~ **mill** *v/t* and *i* grind; serrate the rim of (coin); stamp; cut (steel) into shape; (*sl*) punch heavily, pummel; **m. about** go round and round, move haphazardly about.

millboard [*mil*bawrd] *n* board made from wood pulp *etc* used in bookbinding *etc*.

milldam [*mil*dam] *n* dam across a stream whose water turns a millwheel.

millenarian [mili*nai*ri-an] *n* one who believes in the millennium ~ **millenarian** *adj* relating to the millennium.

millenary [*mili*naRi] *adj* of a thousand; lasting a thousand years, immemorial; of the millennium ~ **millenary** *n* a thousand years; thousandth anniversary or its celebration.

millennium [mi*leni*-um] *n* a thousand years; period of Christ's future reign on earth; future age of peace and prosperity ~ **millennial** *adj* relating to the millennium.

millepede, millipede [*mili*peed] *n* small worm-like animal with numerous legs.

miller [*mil*er] *n* one who owns or works in a flour-mill.

millesimal [mi*lesi*mal] *adj* and *n* thousandth (part).

millet [*mil*it] *n* a cereal grown as food.

mill-hand [*mil*-hand] *n* factory-worker.

milli- *pref* one thousandth.

milliard [*mili*-aard] *n* a thousand millions.

millibar [*mili*baar] *n* unit of atmospheric pressure > PDS, PDG.

milligram, milligramme [*mili*gRam] *n* one thousandth of a gramme.

millimetre [*mili*meeter] *n* one thousandth of a metre.

milliner [*mili*ner] *n* maker or seller of women's hats and of lace, ribbons and trimmings ~ **millinery** *n* articles sold by milliners; milliner's business.

milling [*mili*ng] *n* act of passing through a mill; (*mech*) removing metal shavings from a surface by pushing it on a moving table past a rotating toothed cutter; serrated rim of a coin.

million [*mil*yun] *n* and *adj* a thousand thousands; (*fig*) very large number.

millionaire [milyu*nair*] *n* extremely rich man; man possessing a million pounds, dollars *etc* ~ **millionairess** *n* female millionaire.

millionfold [*mil*yunfOld] *adj* and *adv* a million times.

millionth [*mil*yunth] *n* and *adj* (that) which comes after 999,999 others in a series; (that) which is one of a million equal parts.

millipede see millepede.

millpond [*mil*pond] *n* reservoir of water to drive a mill; (*fig*) absolutely calm water.

millrace [*mil*Rays] *n* current of water which drives a millwheel.

millstone [*mil*stOn] *n* one of two circular stones for grinding corn; (*fig*) encumbrance.

millwheel [*mil*wheel] *n* large water-wheel which drives machinery in a mill.

milometer [mi*lomi*ter] *n* instrument recording number of miles travelled by a motor vehicle.

milt [milt] *n* roe of male fish; (*ar*) spleen ~ **milt** *v/t* (*of fish*) impregnate (the female roe).

mime [mIm] *n* art of theatrical communication

solely by use of gestures and facial expressions; actor using this method; mimic, buffoon; (*Gk* and *Rom*) variety of farce with much mimicry ~ **mime** *v/t* and *i* express by gestures and expression; act in a mime; mimic.

mimeograph [*mimi*-ogRaaf] *n* apparatus for taking copies from typewritten stencil.

mimesis [mi*mee*sis] *n* (*biol*) protective similarity to animal of another species.

mimetic [mi*meti*k] *adj* imitative; (*biol*) mimicking another species.

mimic (*p/t* and *p/part* mimicked) [*mimi*k] *v/t* and *i* copy closely, imitate; copy with exaggeration, burlesque; (*biol*) develop protective similarity to another species or to the environment > PDB ~ **mimic** *adj* imitating, copied from; copied on small scale; unreal, sham ~ **mimic** *n* one who mimics.

mimicry [*mimi*kRi] *n* act or practice of imitating in speech or gesture; (*biol*) protective similarity.

mimosa [mi*mOza*] *n* genus of leguminous shrubs.

minaret [*mina*Ret] *n* tall slender turret on a mosque.

minatory [*mina*toRi] *adj* threatening.

mince [mins] *v/t* and *i* cut or chop into very small pieces; express in softened terms, tone down; talk or move with affected primness; **not to m. matters (words)** to speak plain truth ~ **mince** *n* finely chopped meat.

mincemeat [*mins*meet] *n* mixture of currants, sugar, chopped almonds, suet, peel *etc*; **make m. of** destroy.

mincepie [mins*pI*] *n* pie made with mincemeat.

mincer [*min*ser] *n* one who or that which cuts into small pieces.

mincing [*min*sing] *adj* affectedly dainty.

mincing-machine [*min*sing-masheen] *n* machine which cuts meat *etc* into small pieces.

mind [mInd] *n* consciousness, intelligence, reason; memory; intellectuality; (*fig*) man of outstanding intelligence; opinion, mood, intention; liking, wish; moral and intellectual outlook; **call to m.** remember; **have a m.** intend, desire; **have on one's m.** be worried about; **be in two minds** hesitate; **make up one's m.** decide; **speak one's m.** speak plainly; **take one's m. off** distract ~ **mind** *v/t* and *i* pay attention to; beware of; take care of, look after; be worried or hurt (by), object (to); feel strongly about; (*ar*) remember.

mind-bending [*mInd*-bending] *n* and *adj* (process of) permanently conditioning the mind to accept certain beliefs or views; brainwashing; (*coll*) very impressive or remarkable.

mind-blowing [*mInd*-blO-ing] *n* (*sl*) (*of drugs*) inducing ecstasy; (*coll*) very impressive or remarkable.

minded [*mIn*ded] *adj* inclined.

mindful [*mInd*fool] *adj* attentive; observant.

mindless [*mInd*les] *adj* without mind, unreasoning; stupid; careless.

mine (1) [mIn] *poss pron* belonging to me.

mine (2) *n* deep excavation from which coal or minerals are dug; buildings, machinery *etc* connected with this; (*fig*) rich source of supply; (*mil, eng*) charge of explosives detonated in a container; tunnel under enemy's fortifications; (*fig*) plot ~ **mine** *v/t* and *i* dig, sink a mine;

476

extract from a mine; undermine; lay explosive mines.

minefield [m**ɪ**nfeeld] *n* (*mil*) area of sea or land where mines have been laid.

minelayer [m**ɪ**nlay-er] *n* ship which lays mines.

miner [m**ɪ**ner] *n* one who works in a mine, *esp* in a coalmine.

mineral [mineRal] *n* natural inorganic substance of specific composition found in the earth > PDG, PDS; any substance dug by mining; substance containing a metal; (*pl*) (*coll*) aerated drinks ∼ **mineral** *adj* of, containing or like a mineral; **m. kingdom** all objects neither animal nor vegetable; inorganic matter; **m. oil** kerosene; **m. water** water containing noticeable quantity of mineral matter in solution; (*coll*) non-alcoholic aerated drink.

mineralize [mineRalɪz] *v*/*t* and *i* change into a mineral; impregnate with mineral salts; (*chem*) combine to form an ore; seek specimens of minerals ∼ **mineralization** [mineRalɪzayshon] *n*.

mineralogy [mineRaloji] *n* scientific study of minerals ∼ **mineralogist** *n*.

minestrone [minestROni] *n* thick vegetable soup with vermicelli.

minesweeper [m**ɪ**nsweeper] *n* ship fitted with nets for clearing a minefield.

mingle [ming-g'l] *v*/*t* and *i* mix, blend.

mingy [minji] *adj* (*coll*) miserly; worthless.

mini [mini] *n* (*coll*) miniature object; a type of small car; miniskirt ∼ **mini** *adj* small.

mini- *pref* very small, miniature.

miniature [minatewr] *n* coloured initial letter or picture in an illuminated manuscript; small highly-detailed painting, drawing, or portrait, *esp* on vellum or ivory > PDAA; small reproduction; **in m.** on a small scale ∼ **miniature** *adj* small ∼ **miniaturist** *n* one who produces small-scale paintings or photographs.

minibus [minibus] *n* car seating many passengers.

minicab [minikab] *n* cheap taxi hired by telephone but not plying for hire in the streets.

minim [minim] *n* (*mus*) note equal to two crotchets > PDM; (*fluid measure*) one sixtieth of a drachm; one drop; a down-stroke in writing.

minimal [minimal] *adj* minimum, least.

minimize [minimɪz] *v*/*t* make as small as possible; underestimate.

minimum (*pl* **minima**) [minimum] *adj* and *n* smallest possible (amount or degree).

mining [m**ɪ**nɪng] *n* act of working in a mine.

minion [minyon] *n* beloved favourite; youth with whom a sodomite has sexual relations, catamite; toady; hireling; small printing type.

miniskirt [miniskurt] *n* very short skirt ending several inches above the knee.

minister [minister] *n* person in charge of specified branch of government administration; government representative abroad, of lower rank than ambassador; agent, servant; clergyman, *esp* Nonconformist ∼ **minister** *v*/*i* serve; attend to the needs of; help; act as minister.

ministerial [ministeerRi-al] *adj* of a government minister or ministry; administrative, executive; instrumental, subordinate; of a minister of religion ∼ **ministerially** *adv*.

ministering [ministRing] *adj* serving; helpful.

ministrant [ministRant] *n* and *adj* (person) that ministers.

ministration [ministRayshon] *n* act of giving aid or service; service as a priest.

ministry [ministRi] *n* office of a minister; body of government ministers; the Cabinet; branch of State administration; building housing this; body of clergymen; profession of a clergyman; period of office as minister.

miniver [miniver] *n* ermine fur; white fur.

mink [mink] *n* small animal of the weasel family; fur of this; garment made from this.

minnesinger [minisinger] *n* German medieval troubadour who composed love lyrics.

minnow [minO] *n* small freshwater fish.

Minoan [minO-an] *n* and *adj* (inhabitant or language) of ancient Crete.

minor [m**ɪ**ner] *adj* less; smaller; inferior; unimportant; (*school coll*) younger; (*mus*) less by a semitone than major > PDM; (*surg*) not involving danger to life; **m. canon** clergyman attached to a cathedral but not member of its chapter; **m. key** (*mus*) key whose semitones are between the second and third and fifth and sixth notes of the scale > PDM; **m. order** (*RC*) ecclesiastic office below that of subdeacon ∼ **minor** *n* person not yet legally of age; (*eccles*) Franciscan friar; (*mus*) minor key or scale.

minority [m**ɪ**noRiti] *n* the smaller number, part or group, *esp* of voters; number of votes cast for a losing party; group of persons differing from a larger group in race, religion, language, views, customs *etc*; state or period of being not legally of age.

minster [minster] *n* church of a monastery; cathedral; large and important church.

minstrel [minstRel] *n* itinerant medieval singer, musician or reciter of poetry; (*pl*) group of singers and banjoists with blackened faces ∼ **minstrelsy** *n* art or occupation of a minstrel; songs or poetry of minstrels; poetry, *esp* if close to folk-song.

mint (1) [mint] *n* place where money is legally coined and issued; source, origin; (*fig*) great quantity ∼ **mint** *v*/*t* coin money; (*fig*) invent ∼ **mint** *adj* newly made and unused.

mint (2) *n* plant of pungent aromatic flavour; boiled sweet flavoured with this; **m. chocolate** mint-flavoured paste in chocolate casing; **m. julep** iced whisky or brandy flavoured with mint; **m. sauce** sauce of chopped mint, sugar, vinegar, and water.

mintage [mintij] *n* process of minting; money issued, *esp* from a particular mint at a particular time; duty or charge for minting.

minuet [minew-et] *n* graceful dance in triple time of French rustic origin; music for this > PDM.

minus [m**ɪ**nus] *prep* and *adj* less, with deduction of; deprived of, lacking, without; **m. charge** (*elect*) negative charge ∼ **minus** *n* sign (−) denoting subtraction or negativity.

minuscule [minuskewl] *n* lower-case letter; small letter; a small cursive script.

minute (1) [m**ɪ**newt] *adj* very small; petty, trifling; exact, precise; detailed.

minute (2) [minit] *n* brief time, moment; one sixtieth of an hour; one sixtieth of a degree; brief written comment, note; memorandum ~ **minutes** *n (pl)* official record summarizing business at a meeting ~ **minute** *v/t* and *i* estimate (time) to the minute; record in a minute or in the minutes; keep minutes of.

minute-book [*minit*-book] *n* record of business at meetings.

minute-gun [*minit*-gun] *n* gun fired once a minute as sign of distress or mourning.

minute-hand [*minit*-hand] *n* hand of watch or clock that marks minutes.

minutely [m**I**newtli] *adv* in a minute way; in detail; with precision.

minuteness [m**I**newtnis] *n* quality of being minute.

minutiae [m**I**newshi-ee] *n (pl)* small details.

minx *(pl* **minxes)** [*minks*] *n* pert, impudent woman.

miocene [*mI*-oseen] *adj* and *n (geol)* (pertaining to) the middle division of Tertiary era.

miracle [*mi*Rak'l] *n* event inexplicable by natural laws and so ascribed to divine or supernatural action; marvel, extraordinary event or object; **m. play** form of medieval religious play.

miraculous [mi*Rak*ewlus] *adj* of, like or causing a miracle; supernatural; marvellous, astonishing ~ **miraculously** *adv* ~ **miraculousness** *n.*

mirage [mi*Raazh*] *n* optical illusion in which images of distant objects become visible by refraction of light > PDG; *(fig)* deluding hope.

mire [m**I**r] *n* swampy ground; mud; *(fig)* dirt ~ **mire** *v/t* and *i* defile with mud; sink into mire.

mirk see murk.

mirror [*mi*Rer] *n* polished reflecting surface, *usu* glass backed with metal; *(fig)* pattern, model; true image; **m. image** reflection or copy reversing right and left sides of the original; **m. writing** writing produced in reverse direction > PDP ~ **mirror** *v/i* reflect as in a mirror.

mirth [*murth*] *n* merriment, gaiety; laughter.

mirthful [*murth*fool] *adj* merry, gay ~ **mirthfully** *adv* ~ **mirthfulness** *n.*

mirthless [*murth*lis] *adj* bitter, ironic; sad ~ **mirthlessly** *adv.*

miry [m**I**rRi] *adj* muddy, swampy.

mis- *pref* bad, unfavourable; wrong; wrongly, badly.

misadventure [misadv*encher*] *n* unfortunate accident; bad luck; **by m.** accidentally.

misalliance [misal*I*-ans] *n* marriage with an inferior; unsuitable marriage.

misanthrope [*mi*santhr*Op*] *n* one who hates and shuns contact with human beings; embittered recluse; cynic ~ **misanthropic** [misan*thRop*ik] *adj* ~ **misanthropist** [mis*anth*Ropist] *n* misanthrope.

misanthropy [mis*anth*ropi] *n* bitter hatred of mankind: bitter cynicism.

misapply [misa*plI*] *v/t* apply or use wrongly.

misapprehend [misapRi*hend*] *v/t* misunderstand.

misapprehension [misapRi*hen*shon] *n* act of misunderstanding; mistaken idea or opinion.

misappropriate [misap*ROp*Ri-ayt] *v/t* take and put to a wrong use; use dishonestly as one's own ~ **misappropriation** [misapROpRi-*ay*shon] *n.*

misbegotten [misbi*goten*] *adj* illegitimate; *(fig)* badly planned; dishonest, contemptible.

misbehave [misbi*hayv*] *v/i* behave badly ~ **misbehaviour** *n.*

misbelief [misbi*leef*] *n* mistaken religious belief heresy ~ **misbeliever** *n* heretic; infidel.

miscalculate [mis*kal*kewlayt] *v/t* and *i* judge or calculate wrongly ~ **miscalculation** [miskalkew*lay*shon] *n* error in calculating or judging.

miscall [mis*kawl*] *v/t* call by a wrong or inappropriate name; *(dial)* revile; *(cards)* call incorrectly.

miscarriage [mis*ka*Rij] *n* premature birth of a foetus which dies; failure; error, act of going astray.

miscarry [mis*ka*Ri] *v/i* go astray; fail; err; give birth prematurely to a foetus which dies.

miscast [mis*kaast*] *v/t* give (theatrical part) to unsuitable actor.

miscegenation [misiji*nay*shon] *n* interbreeding of races, *esp* between whites and coloured people.

miscellaneous [misi*layn*i-us] *adj* diverse, consisting of several kinds.

miscellany [mis*el*ani] *n* mixture of various things; collection of writings on different subjects or by different authors.

mischance [mis*chaans*] *n* unfortunate accident.

mischief [*mis*chif] *n* naughtiness, annoying but not seriously wicked behaviour; trouble; damage, harm; injury; destruction; wickedness; *(coll)* naughty child; **make m.** cause quarrels.

mischief-maker [*mis*chif-mayker] *n* one who stirs up quarrels; spiteful gossip.

mischievous [*mis*chivus] *adj* doing or causing mischief; naughty; roguish; harmful ~ **mischievously** *adj* ~ **mischievousness** *n.*

miscible [*mis*ib'l] *adj* that can be mixed.

misconceive [miskon*seev*] *v/t* and *i* form a wrong idea of.

misconception [miskon*sep*shun] *n* mistaken idea.

misconduct [mis*kon*dukt] *n* improper conduct; illicit sexual intercourse ~ **misconduct** [miskon*dukt*] *v/t* and *refl* mismanage; behave badly, *esp* have illicit sexual intercourse.

misconstruction [miskon*stRuk*shun] *n* wrong interpretation.

misconstrue [miskon*stRew*] *v/t* translate or interpret wrongly.

miscount [mis*kownt*] *v/t* and *i* count wrongly ~ **miscount** *n* mistake in counting.

miscreant [*mis*kRi-ant] *adj* and *n* (of or like a) villain, scoundrel; *(ar)* non-Christian, heretic.

misdeal [mis*deel*] *v/t* deal (cards) wrongly ~ **misdeal** *n* wrong deal.

misdeed [mis*deed*] *n* wrong or evil deed, crime.

misdemeanour [misdi*meen*or] *n* misdeed; *(leg)* minor indictable offence.

misdirect [misdi*Rekt*] *v/t* give wrong instructions to; aim wrongly; apply to wrong purpose ~ **misdirection** *n.*

misdoubt [mis*dowt*] *v/t* have forebodings about.

miser [m**I**zer] *n* one who lives stingily so as to amass wealth.

miserable [*mize*Rab'l] *adj* very unhappy, wretched; scanty; squalid; worthless ~ **miserably** *adv.*

miserere [mize*Rair*Ri] *n (Lat)* the fifty-first Psalm; cry for mercy; misericord seat.

misericord [mise*Ri*kawrd] *n* ledge under hinged

seat which, when turned up, gives support to a person standing.

miserly [*mɪ*zerli] *adj* like a miser, avaricious.

misery [*mɪ*zeRi] *n* great unhappiness; extreme pain or discomfort; squalor, wretchedness.

misfire [mis*fɪr*] *v/i* (*of gun*) fail to explode; (*of engine*) fail to ignite in cylinder; (*fig*) fail to produce desired effect ~ **misfire** *n* failure to explode or ignite.

misfit [*mɪs*fit] *n* person who is not suited to his environment or occupation; that which fits badly.

misfortune [misfaw*r*tewn] *n* bad luck; disaster.

misgive (*p/t* **misgave**, *p/part* **misgiven**) [misg*ɪv*] *v/i impers* give rise to fear or suspicion.

misgiving [misg*ɪ*ving] *n* fear; suspicion; anxiety.

misgotten [misg*o*ten] *adj* acquired by wrongful means.

misgovern [misg*u*vern] *v/t* govern unjustly or inefficiently.

misguided [misg*ɪ*d*ɪ*d] *adj* foolish, based on error ~ **misguidedly** *adv*.

mishandle [mish*a*nd'l] *v/t* treat roughly; deal tactlessly with; mismanage.

mishap [*mɪs*hap] *n* unfortunate accident.

mishear [*mɪs*heer] *v/t* and *i* fail to hear accurately misunderstand something heard.

mishmash [*mɪsh*mash] *n* silly medley.

misinform [misinfaw*r*m] *v/t* give incorrect information to.

misinterpret [misint*ur*pRit] *v/t* interpret wrongly; misunderstand.

misjudge [misj*u*j] *v/t* judge incorrectly; fail to appreciate, underestimate ~ **misjudgement** *n*.

mislay (*p/t* and *p/part* **mislaid**) [mis*lay*] *v/t* lose temporarily; forget where one has put (something).

mislead (*p/t* and *p/part* **misled**) [mis*leed*] *v/t* deceive deliberately or accidentally; lead astray.

mislike [mis*lɪk*] *v/t* dislike.

mismanage [mism*a*nij] *v/t* manage badly or carelessly.

misnomer [misn*O*mer] *n* mistaken or unsuitable name; incorrect term.

miso- *pref* hating; hatred.

misogamist [mɪs*o*gamist/mis*o*gamist] *n* one who hates marriage ~ **misogamy** *n* hatred of marriage.

misogynist [mɪs*o*jinist/mis*o*jinist] *n* one who hates women ~ **misogyny** *n* hatred of women.

misplace [mis*plays*] *v/t* put in the wrong place; apply to unsuitable purpose; bestow on unworthy person; mislay.

misprint [mis*pRint*] *v/t* print incorrectly ~ **misprint** [*mɪs*pRint] *n* error in printing.

misprize see **misprize**.

misprision [mis*pRɪ*zhon] *n* a mistake; scorn; underestimation; (*leg*) offence, misdemeanour; concealment of another's offence.

misprize, misprise [mis*pRɪz*] *v/t* undervalue.

mispronounce [mispR*o*n*owns*] *v/t* pronounce incorrectly.

misquote [miskw*Ot*] *v/t* quote incorrectly.

misread [mis*Reed*] *v/t* read incorrectly; misinterpret.

misremember [misR*i*member] *v/t* remember incorrectly.

misrepresent [misRep*Rɪ*zent]´*v/t* represent falsely or incorrectly; convey an inaccurate impression of, *usu* deliberately ~ **misrepresentation** [mis-Rep*Rɪ*zent*ay*shon] *n* deliberately misleading account.

misrule [mis*ROOl*] *n* bad government; riot, disorder ~ **misrule** *v/t*.

Miss (1) (*pl* **Misses**) [*mɪs*] *n* form of address for unmarried woman with no other title; young unmarried woman; (*pej*) girl.

miss (2) *v/t* and *i* fail to reach, hit find or meet; fail to catch or grip; fail to see, hear or understand, fail to achieve; be or do without; notice and regret the absence of; discover the loss of; omit, overlook; escape; **be missing** be absent. fail to appear or return; **m. out** omit; **m. out on** (*coll*) miss an opportunity (of advantage or pleasure) ~ **miss** *n* failure to hit, reach *etc*; **feel the m. of** (*coll*) feel the lack or loss of; **give it a m.** (*coll*) omit, avoid, leave alone; **near m.** shot *etc* which only just misses its objective; narrow escape.

missal [*mɪs*al] *n* (*RC*) book containing the service of the Mass for each day of the year.

missel-thrush, mistle-thrush [*mɪs*el-th*Rush*] *n* largest European thrush.

misshapen [mis-*shayp*'n] *adj* deformed.

missile [*mɪs*ɪl] *n* anything projected or thrown as a weapon; rocket with explosive warhead.

missing [*mɪs*ing] *adj* not present; lost; not accounted for.

mission [*mɪs*hon] *n* act of sending; group of delegates sent abroad for specific purpose; aim one is sent to achieve; vocation, lifelong duty or purpose; body of missionaries; centre for missionary work, or for religious and social work; course of talks and services to revive the religious activity of a group or district.

missionary [*mɪs*honaRi] *adj* pertaining to religious missions ~ **missionary** *n* one who carries on missionary work, *esp* in heathen country; one who tries to make converts or advance some cause.

Missis, Missus [*mɪs*iz] *n* (*coll*) wife; mistress of a household; spoken form of **Mrs.**

missive [*mɪs*iv] *n* letter, *esp* a formal one.

misspell [mis-*spel*] *v/t* spell incorrectly ~ **misspelling** *n*.

misspend [mis-*spend*] *v/t* waste.

Missus see **Missis**.

Missy [*mɪs*i] *n* (*coll*) Miss; little girl.

mist [*mɪst*] *n* droplets of water formed by the condensation of water-vapour on dust particles > PDG; that which blurs the sight; that which dims or darkens ~ **mist** *v/t* and *i* cover as with a mist; be or become misty; blur; darken.

mistakable [mis*tayk*ab'l] *adj* liable to be mistaken or misunderstood.

mistake (*p/t* **mistook**, *p/part* **mistaken**) [mis*tayk*] *v/t* and *i* understand wrongly; identify wrongly; err ~ **mistake** *n* error; misconception, misunderstanding ~ **mistaken** *adj* in error; wrong; misunderstood; ill-judged ~ **mistakenly** *adv*.

Mister [*mɪs*ter] *n* title of address to a man with no other title, written **Mr.**

mistily [*mɪs*tili] *adv* in a misty way.

mistiness [*mɪs*tinis] *n* quality of being misty.

479

mistle-thrush see **missel-thrush.**

mistletoe [*mis*'ltO] *n* parasitic evergreen plant with white berries.

mistral [*mist*Raal] *n* cold, dry, north-west wind of the south of France > PDG.

mistress [*mist*Ris] *n* female head of a household; woman holding authority; female teacher; woman with whom a man regularly has illicit sexual intercourse, concubine; (*poet*) beloved woman; (*ar*) polite mode of address to a woman.

mistrust [mist*Rust*] *v/t* doubt, regard with suspicion ~ **mistrust** *n* suspicion, lack of confidence ~ **mistrustful** *adj* suspicious.

misty [*mi*sti] *adj* covered with mist; (*of eyes*) filled with tears; (*fig*) obscure, vague.

misunderstand (*p/t* and *p/part* **misunderstood**) [misunder*stand*] *v/t* mistake the meaning of; fail to understand ~ **misunderstanding** *n* error, failure to understand; slight quarrel, estrangement.

misuse [mis*ewz*] *v/t* use or treat improperly; use for a wrong purpose; ill-treat ~ **misuse** [mis*ews*] *n* improper use.

mite (1) [m*I*t] *n* anything very small; small child; (*ar*) coin worth half a farthing; (*fig*) small but willing contribution.

mite (2) *n* small parasitic arachnid.

mitigable [*mi*tigab'l] *adj* that can be mitigated.

mitigate [*mi*tigayt] *v/t* make less severe; alleviate; moderate, soften ~ **mitigation** [miti*gay*shon] *n* act of mitigating; that which mitigates; extenuation, excuse ~ **mitigative** [*mi*tigativ] *adj.*

mitochondrion (*pl* **mitochondria**) [m*I*t*O*kon-dRi-on] *n* (*biol*) minute body, many of which occur in the cytoplasms of most cells > PDB.

mitosis [m*I*t*O*sis] *n* (*biol*) process by which a diploid cell reproduces, forming two identical daughter cells > PDB.

mitre (1) [m*I*ter] *n* (*carp*) angle joint between two members of similar cross section > PDBl ~ **mitre** *v/t* join by a mitre.

mitre (2) *n* (*eccles*) episcopal head-dress shaped like a cleft cone ~ **mitre** *v/t* bestow a mitre upon ~ **mitred** *adj* wearing a mitre.

mitt [mit] *n* mitten; (*sl*) hand; (*pl*) (*sl*) boxing gloves.

mitten [*mit*en] *n* glove without fingers; glove enclosing all fingers in one compartment; **give the m. to** (*coll*) jilt.

mix [miks] *v/t* and *i* mingle, combine into a compound; prepare from various ingredients; stir together; unite; meet socially; get on well with; **m. up** confuse, muddle; **m. up** in implicate, involve; **m. with** frequent the company of ~ **mix** *n* proportions of a batch of concrete, mortar or plaster; powdered ingredients already mixed for use in cooking.

mixed [mikst] *adj* blended from different elements; not all alike; muddled; done or used by persons of both sexes; including persons of different classes, races, or groups; **m. blessing** something with both good and bad aspects; **m. marriage** marriage between persons of different religions or races.

mixed-up [mikst-up] *adj* (*coll*) mentally confused; emotionally unstable, maladjusted.

mixer [*mik*ser] *n* one who or that which mixes;

machine for mixing ingredients in cooking; **a good m.** person who is at ease in social relations.

mixture [*miks*cher] *n* act of mixing; process of becoming mixed; that which is mixed; (*chem*) combination of substances which do not lose their properties > PDS.

mix-up [*miks*-up] *n* (*coll*) muddle.

mizen, mizzen [*mi*zen] *n* fore-and-aft sail set on the aftermost mast ~ **mizen-mast** *n* aftermost mast of a three-masted ship.

mizzle [*mi*z'l] *n* and *v/i* drizzle; (*sl*) go away.

mnemonic [ni*mo*nik] *n* and *adj* (verse, formula *etc*) aiding the memory ~ **mnemonics** *n* (*pl*) method or artificial system for aiding or training the memory.

mo [mo] *n* (*coll abbr*) moment.

moan [m*O*n] *n* low sound of pain or grief; (*coll*) complaint ~ **moan** *v/i* and *t* utter a moan; (*poet*) lament; (*coll*) grumble.

moat [m*O*t] *n* ditch round a fortress or castle, *usu* filled with water ~ **moated** *adj.*

mob [mob] *n* lawless and excited crowd; mass of people; (*sl*) gang of criminals; (*Aust*) flock, herd ~ **mob** (*pres/part* **mobbing**, *p/t* and *p/part* **mobbed**) *v/t* crowd wildly round; attack in a wild crowd.

mobcap [*mob*kap] *n* frilled cap formerly worn indoors by women.

mobile [m*O*b*I*l] *adj* easily moving or moved; adaptable; quickly changing ~ **mobile** *n* ornament consisting of light shapes of metal, paper *etc* swinging freely on wires.

mobility [m*O*b*i*liti] *n* quality of being mobile.

mobilization [m*O*bil*I*zayshon] *n* act of mobilizing.

mobilize [m*O*bil*I*z] *v/t* and *i* call up (armed forces) for active service; assemble for warfare; render available; gather forces.

möbius strip [*mer*bi-us-st*Ri*p] *n* (*math*) surface having only one side and one edge, formed by joining the ends of a rectangular band after rotating one end through 180°.

mobster [*mob*ster] *n* (*sl*) gangster.

moccasin [*mo*kasin] *n* one-piece shoe made of soft leather.

mocha [m*O*ka] *n* fine grade of coffee.

mock [mok] *v/t* and *i* laugh scornfully at, ridicule; mimic contemptuously; jeer (at); delude; render useless; **m. up** (*coll*) improvise ~ **mock** *adj* falsely imitating, sham ~ **mock** *n* object of scorn and jeering ~ **mocker** *n.*

mockery [*mo*keRi] *n* ridicule, derision; object of ridicule; travesty.

mock-heroic [mok-he*RO*-ik] *adj* parodying heroic style in literature.

mocking-bird [*mo*king-burd] *n* American bird which mimics songs of other birds.

mock-orange [mok-o*Ri*nj] *n* the syringa.

mock-turtle [mok-*tur*t'l] *n* soup of calf's head made to imitate turtle soup.

mock-up [*mo*k-up] *n* full-scale model, replica; improvisation.

mod [mod] *adj* (*sl*) up-to-date, elegant, *esp* in clothing ~ **mod** *n* (*sl*) dandified youth or girl, *usu* riding motor scooters.

modal [m*O*dal] *adj* in or of a mode; (*gramm*) expressing mood; (*leg*) containing provisions on the method of making a deed *etc* effective; (*log*) containing a statement of limitation.

modality [mOd*ality*] *n* quality of being modal.

mode [*mOd*] *n* method, way of acting or doing; style, convention; fashion; custom; (*mus*) arrangement of notes in a scale, *esp* in Greek and medieval scales > PDM; (*log*) manner in which one proposition qualifies another.

model [*model*] *n* something to be copied, pattern; example; small-scale reproduction; three-dimensional plan; one who poses for an artist or photographer; one who wears and exhibits clothes, mannequin; garment of new and individual design; one of a series of varying designs of the same type of object ~ **model** *adj* reproducing, *esp* on small scale; to be imitated, exemplary ~ **model** (*pres/part* **modelling**, *p/t* and *p/part* **modelled**) *v/t* and *i* form, shape from clay; wax *etc*; make a model of; plan out; mould, imitate, conform to; display (clothes); act as a model, pose ~ **modeller** *n* one who models in clay, wax *etc*.

moderate [*moderit*] *adj* not extreme; reasonable, restrained; mild; mediocre; of medium size *etc* ~ **moderate** *n* one whose opinions are not extreme ~ **moderate** [*moderayt*] *v/t* and *i* keep within bounds, restrain, mitigate; make or become less violent; act as moderator ~ **moderately** *adv*.

moderation [moderayshon] *n* quality of being moderate; act of moderating; self-restraint; (*pl*) first public examination in the University of Oxford, taken only in some subjects.

moderato [moderaatO] *n* (*mus*) at a moderate pace > PDM.

moderator [*moderayter*] *n* one who or that which moderates; president of a Presbyterian assembly; presiding examiner; (*phys*) substance used in nuclear reactors to reduce the speed of fast neutrons > PDS.

modern [*modern*] *adj* of or in present or recent times; not old-fashioned ~ **modern** *n* one with modern ideas; one living in modern times.

modernism [*modernizm*] *n* adherence to up-to-date views, methods or tastes; comparatively new usage, word *etc*; system of biblical study based on recent historical and textual research ~ **modernist** *n* and *adj* (supporter) of modernism.

modernistic [modern*istik*] *adj* of modernism; recent and revolutionary, avant-garde.

modernity [mod*urniti*] *n* quality of being modern.

modernize [*modernIz*] *v/t* make modern; adapt to modern taste ~ **modernization** [modernI-zayshon] *n*.

modest [*modest*] *adj* humble, diffident; reserved, retiring; pure, chaste; moderate, not lavish or expensive; not alluring, not displaying one's body ~ **modestly** *adv*.

modesty [*modesti*] *n* quality of being modest.

modicum [*modikum*] *n* small quantity.

modification [modifi*kayshon*] *n* act of modifying; state of being modified; that which modifies ~ **modificator** *n* one who or that which modifies ~ **modificatory** *adj* modifying.

modify [*modifI*] *v/t* alter slightly, make minor changes in; moderate; (*phon*) change the vowel sound of; (*gramm*) qualify the sense of.

modish [*mOdish*] *adj* fashionable, smart.

modiste [mOd*eest*] *n* dressmaker; milliner.

modular [*modewler*] *adj* of modules.

modulate [*modewlayt*] *v/t* and *i* regulate, adjust; vary in pitch; (*mus*) change from one key to another > PDM; (*phys*) change some characteristic of one wave motion in accordance with some characteristic of another wave motion > PDS; (*fig*) change in mood; change imperceptibly.

modulation [modew*layshon*] *n* act of modulating; inflexion of the voice or tone.

modulator [*modewlayter*] *n* one who or that which modulates; (*mus*) diagram or wall chart showing relationships in tonic sol-fa.

module [*mOdewl*] *n* standardized unit of length in building > PDBl; separable unit in a multi-stage rocket, containing instruments or men; standardized separable unit of furniture, equipment *etc*; unit in a computer programme; unit in a syllabus; (print) box; (*coll*) group, set.

modulus [*modewlus*] *n* (*math*) divisor which leaves the same remainder when dividing all numbers of a set; constant multiplier or co-efficient; constant used to determine a ratio.

modus [*mOdus*] *n* (*Lat*) method, manner; style; **m. operandi** (*Lat*) method of working or operating; **m. vivendi** (*Lat*) way of living; working agreement while a dispute is awaiting settlement.

mog, moggie [*mog, mogi*] *n* (*sl*) cat.

Mogul [*mOgul*] *n* a Mongolian; follower of Baber or of Genghiz Khan.

mohair [*mOhair*] *n* hair of Angora goat; fabric made from this.

Mohammedan, Mahometan [mOh*ami*dan, ma-h*omi*tan] *n* and *adj* (follower) of Mohammed, Muslim ~ **Mohammedanism** *n*.

Mohawk [mO*hawk*] *n* member of tribe of North American Indians; language of these.

Mohican [mO-*ikan*, mO-*eekan*] *n* and *adj* (member or language) of an extinct tribe of North American Indians.

mohole [*mOhOl*] *n* hole drilled through earth's crust to the magma.

moidore [*moidawr*] *n* former Portuguese gold coin.

moiety [*moi-iti*] *n* a half; share, part.

moiré [*mwaa*Ray] *n* type of watered or clouded finish on fabrics or metallic surfaces.

moist [*moist*] *adj* damp; wet; rainy.

moisten [*moisen*] *v/t* wet slightly.

moisture [*moischer*] *n* condensed water vapour; dampness.

moisturize [*moistewrIz*] *v/t* increase or restore the moisture of ~ **moisturizer** *n*.

moke [*mOk*] *n* (*sl*) donkey.

molar (1) [*mOler*] *n* and *adj* (tooth) that grinds.

molar (2) *adj* (*mech*) of mass; in the mass (as contrasted with molecular).

molasses [mO*lasiz*] *n* dark syrup drained from sugar during refining; treacle.

mole (1) [*mOl*] *n* dark spot on human skin.

mole (2) *n* a breakwater, jetty; artificial harbour.

mole (3) *n* small burrowing soft-furred animal.

mole (4) *n* (*phys*) an amount of substance containing the same number of atoms or molecules as two grams of hydrogen.

molecular [mol*ekewler*] *adj* of molecules; **m. biology** study of the structure and function of molecules of biological importance; **m. weight** sum of the atomic weights of all the atoms comprising a molecule.

molecule [*moli*kewl] *n* smallest portion (of a substance) capable of existing independently with all its properties > PDS; small particle.

molehill [*mOl*hil] *n* small heap of earth cast up by a burrowing mole.

moleskin [*mOl*skin] *n* skin of the mole used as fur; strong fustian with shaved pile; (*pl*) trousers of such fustian.

molest [mo*lest*] *v/t* pester, annoy; harm; accost illegally ~ **molestation** [molesta*yshon*] *n*.

moll [*mol*] *n* (*sl*) gangster's mistress; woman.

mollify [*moli*fI] *v/t* soften; appease, pacify.

mollusc [*mol*usk] *n* one of a large group of invertebrates with soft bodies > PDB; shellfish.

mollycoddle [*moli*kod'l] *v/t* pamper.

Moloch [*mOl*ok] *n* Canaanite idol to whom children were sacrificed; (*fig*) cruel power to which sacrifice is made.

molten [*mOl*ten] *adj* of or like melted metal.

molybdenum [moli*bd*enum] *n* (*chem*) hard white metal used in the manufacture of special steels and alloys.

moment [*mO*ment] *n* brief time, instant; importance: (*mech*) measure of the tendency of a force to cause rotation > PDS; **m. of truth** crisis which reveals one's real nature.

momentary [*mO*menteRi] *adj* lasting only a short while; brief and quick ~ **momentarily** *adv*.

momentous [mO*men*tus] *adj* very important.

momentum [mo*men*tum] *n* (*mech*) product of the mass and the velocity of a body; (*pop*) impetus; (*fig*) increase in force and effect.

mon- *pref* single, alone.

monad [*mo*nad] *n* (*chem*) element having a valency of one; (*biol*) a primary organic unit; (*philos*) a simple individual element > PDP ~ **monadic** [mo*nad*ik] *adj*.

monarch [*monerk*] *n* supreme ruler; sovereign; chief of its kind.

monarchic, monarchical [mo*naar*kik, mo*naar*kikal] *adj* of or like a monarch; royal; ruled by a monarch; of or like a monarchy.

monarchism [*moner*kizm] *n* principles of monarchic government ~ **monarchist** *n* supporter of a monarchy or of a king.

monarchy [*moner*ki] *n* State or government where supreme power is in the hands of one person; kingdom; **constitutional m.** monarchy where the king's power is limited by law.

monastery [*mo*nasteRi] *n* community of men living under religious vows; (*rare*) convent.

monastic, monastical [mo*nas*tik, mo*nas*tikal] *adj* of a monastery; of monks, friars, or nuns or their way of life.

monasticism [mo*nas*tisizm] *n* monastic system or way of life.

monatomic [mona*tom*ik] *adj* (*chem*) having one atom in the molecule; containing one replaceable atom.

monaural [mo*nawr*Ral] *adj* (hearing) with one ear only; (*of sound reproduction*) from one direction only, not stereophonic.

Monday [*mun*di] *n* second day of the week ~ **Mondayish** *adj* (*coll*) reluctant to resume work.

monetarism [*muni*taRizm] *n* (*econ*) control of a country's economy by regulating its money supply ~ **monetarist** *adj* and *n*.

monetary [*mo*niteRi/*mu*niteRi] *adj* of money.

money (*pl* **money** or **monies**) [*muni*] *n* coins or banknotes used as a medium of exchange; wealth; property; **in the m.** (*sl*) wealthy; **make m.** grow rich; **put m. into** invest in; **money's worth** full value.

moneybox [*muni*boks] *n* box for storing coins.

moneyed [*muni*d] *adj* wealthy.

money-grubber [*muni*-gRuber] *n* avaricious man; one whose main aim is to get rich.

moneylender [*muni*lender] *n* one who lends money at interest.

money-spinner [*muni*-spiner] *n* very profitable enterprise; type of small red spider.

monger [*mung*-ger] *n* trader, dealer.

mongol [*mong*-gol] *n* type of congenital mental defective; (*cap*) a Mongolian ~ **mongoloid** *adj*.

Mongolian [mong-*gOl*i-an] *n* and *adj* (member or language) of a yellow-skinned race of Central Asia.

mongolism [*mong*-golizm] *n* former term for a congenital chromosome defect causing mental deficiency, Down's syndrome.

mongoose (*pl* **mongooses**) [*mong*-gOOs] *n* (*zool*) small Indian ferret-like mammal, ichneumon.

mongrel [*mung*-gRel] *n* animal, *esp* dog, of mixed and unidentifiable breed ~ **mongrel** *adj* produced by crossing various breeds; mixed.

moniker [*moni*ker] *n* (*sl*) name.

monism [*moni*zm] *n* (*philos*) theory that the universe consists of aspects or modes of a single substance ~ **monist** *n* believer in monism ~ **monistic** [mo*nis*tik] *adj*.

monition [mo*nish*on] *n* official warning, injunction; summons.

monitor [*moni*ter] *n* one who admonishes, warns or advises; school prefect, pupil having special responsibilities; one who listens to and reports on foreign broadcasts; a kind of lizard; (*naut*) a shallow-draught heavy gunboat ~ **monitor** *v/t* listen to and report on (foreign broadcasts); check accuracy of (wavelength) ~ **monitory** *adj* warning, admonishing.

monitress [*moni*tRes] *n* female monitor, *esp* in schools.

monk [*munk*] *n* male member of a religious community vowed to poverty, obedience and chastity.

monkey [*mung*ki] *n* any non-human primate *exc* lemurs, *esp* one with a tail; rogue; mimic; (*eng*) drop-hammer; striker of pile-driver; (*sl*) 500 pounds or dollars; **m. business** (*coll*) trickery, mischief; **get one's m. up** (*sl*) get angry; **have a m. on one's back** (*sl*) be a drug addict; bear a grudge; **make a m. of** make a fool of, use as a dupe; **m. tricks** mischief ~ **monkey** *v/t* and *i* mimic; **m. (about) with** handle mischievously, destructively or carelessly; play tricks on; take liberties with.

monkey-engine [*mung*ki-enjin] *n* piledriver.

monkey-jacket [*mung*ki-jakit] *n* sailor's short tight jacket.

monkey-nut [*mung*ki-nut] *n* peanut.

monkey-puzzle [*mung*ki-puz'l] *n* tree with spiny leaves and branches.

monkey-wrench [*mung*ki-Rench] *n* adjustable spanner.

monkfish [*mungk*-fish] *n* a kind of shark.

monkish [*mung*kish] *adj* like or of a monk.

monkshood [*mungk*shood] *n* aconite.

mono- *pref* single, alone; not stereophonic.

mono [*mon*O] *adj* (*coll*) monaural.

monobasic [monO*bay*sik] *adj* (*chem*) having one atom of acidic hydrogen > PDS.

monochord [monOkawrd] *n* (*mus*) instrument with only one string > PDM.

monochromatic [monOkrO*matik*] *adj* of one colour only.

monochrome [*mon*OkROm] *n* a painting or reproduction in one colour.

monocle [*mon*ok'l] *n* single eyeglass.

monocoque [*mon*Okok] *n* vehicle with chassis and body built as one unit.

monocular [mon*o*kewler] *adj* having, using or for one eye only.

monodrama [*mon*OdRaama] *n* dramatic piece for a single performer.

monody [*mon*odi] *n* lyric ode for a single reciter; mournful song or poem; (*mus*) melody for single voice with accompaniment > PDM.

monogamy [mo*nog*ami] *n* practice of marrying only one partner at a time; (*hist*) practice of marrying only once in one's life; (*zool*) fact of having only one mate at a time ~ **monogamous** *adj* practising monogamy.

monogram [*mon*Ogram] *n* figure consisting of two or more interwoven letters.

monograph [*mon*Ograaf] *n* treatise on a single aspect of a subject

monohull [*mon*Ohul] *n* boat with only one hull.

monolith [*mon*Olith] *n* upright monument of a single stone ~ **monolithic** *adj* of or like a monolith; (*fig*) massive and uniform.

monologue [*mon*Olog] *n* dramatic entertainment by one actor; long uninterrupted speech.

monomania [monO*may*ni-a] *n* obsessive preoccupation with a single idea; mental derangement on one subject only > PDP ~ **monomaniac** *n* and *adj* (person) suffering from monomania.

monomark [*mon*Omaark] *n* letters or figures used as identification mark.

monomer [*mon*Omer] *n* (*chem*) compound consisting of single unpolymerized molecules; molecule which is capable of polymerizing.

monophonic [monO*fonik*] *adj* monaural.

monoplane [*mon*Oplayn] *n* aircraft with one set of wings.

monopole [*mon*OpOl] *n* (*phys*) basic magnetic particle occurring in two forms of opposite polarity.

monopolist [mo*nop*olist] *n* one who holds or favours a monopoly.

monopolize [mo*nop*olIz] *v/t* hold exclusive possession of; enjoy the whole of.

monopoly [mo*nop*oli] *n* exclusive possession of a trading right; exclusive control.

monorail [*mon*ORayl] *n* railway with single rail to the track; single elevated rail along which special vehicles are run > PDE.

monosyllabic [monO*silabik*] *adj* having one

syllable; speaking in monosyllables; curt, uncommunicative.

monosyllable [monO*silab*'l] *n* word of one syllable.

monotheism [*mon*Othee-izm] *n* doctrine that there is only one god ~ **monotheist** *n* believer in monotheism ~ **monotheistic** [monOthee-*istik*] *adj*.

monotint [*mon*Otint] *n* a monochrome.

monotone [*mon*OtOn] *n* single, unvaried tone; succession of sounds at same pitch; (*fig*) monotonous repetition ~ **monotone** *v/t* and *i* sing or speak at one pitch.

monotonous [mo*not*onus] *adj* without variation of pitch; boring and unvaried; dully repetitive ~ **monotony** *n* quality of being monotonous.

monotype [*mon*OtIp] *n* (*print*) machine that sets type by individual letters; (*bot*, *zool*) a species forming a genus by itself; (*arts*) a single print from a copper plate > PDAA.

monovalent [monO*valent*] *n* (*chem*) univalent.

Monseigneur (*pl* **Messeigneurs**) [mons*ay*nyur, *pl* mes*ay*nyur] *n* French title of address to princes and high Roman Catholic dignitaries.

Monsignor [mon*seen*yer] *n* title given to officers of the Pope's court and some RC dignitaries.

monsoon [mons*OOn*] *n* seasonal wind of the Indian Ocean > PDG.

monster [*mon*ster] *n* abnormally huge animal or plant; deformed person or creature, monstrosity; imaginary or mythical creature of impossible biological form; abnormally cruel or wicked person ~ **monster** *adj* huge, extraordinarily big.

monstrance [*mon*stRans] *n* transparent vessel in which the consecrated Host is shown for adoration or carried in procession.

monstrosity [mon*st*Rositi] *n* anything deformed or hideous; quality of being monstrous.

monstrous [*mon*stRus] *adj* unnaturally large; shocking; absurd; hideous; malformed ~ **monstrously** *adv*.

montage [mon*taazh*] *n* the sticking of one layer over another, *esp* as in photomontage > PDAA; final selection and juxtaposition of shots to form a cinema film; art of cutting effectively from one shot to another.

month [*munth*] *n* one of twelve subdivisions of a year; period from new moon to new moon; four weeks.

monthly [*munth*li] *adj* occurring once a month; done in a month ~ **monthly** *n* periodical published once a month; (*pl*) menses ~ **monthly** *adv* once a month, every month.

monument [*mon*ewment] *n* building, tombstone *etc* erected to preserve the memory of a person or event; any building or erection of historic or artistic importance; something of lasting value; (*ar*) record, document.

monumental [monew*mental*] *adj* of or serving as a monument; of lasting importance; massive; vast; (*arts*) more than life-size; **m. mason** carver of tombstones ~ **monumentally** *adv*.

moo [*m*OO] *n* the cry of a cow ~ **moo** *v/i* utter a moo, low.

mooch [*m*OOch] *v/i* and *t* (*coll*) loiter, hang about; saunter idly; (*sl*) cadge.

moo-cow [*m*OO-kow] *n* (*childish coll*) cow.

mood (1) [*m*OOd] *n* temporary state of feeling or

outlook; bad temper, sulkiness; depression; **in the m. for** disposed to, wishing to.

mood (2) *n* (*gramm*) variation in verb form to show how the act or state denoted is to be regarded; (*log*) class or form of a syllogism; (*mus*) mode.

moody [*mOOdi*] *adj* indulging in varying moods; sulky; gloomy; irritable ~ **moodily** *adv* ~ **moodiness** *n*.

moon [*mOOn*] *n* natural satellite of the earth > PDG, PDS; satellite of any other planet; month; (*fig*) unattainable ideal; **cry for the m.** yearn for the impossible; **over the m.** (*coll*) wildly happy ~ **moon** *v/i* wander about dreamily or sadly.

moonbeam [*mOOnbeem*] *n* ray of moonlight.

moonbug [*mOOnbug*] *n* vehicle for landing on the moon from a spacecraft.

moonface [*mOOnfays*] *n* (*med*) abnormally round fattened face.

moonlight [*mOOnlIt*] *n* light reflected from the moon ~ **moonlight** *adj* lit by the moon; happening in moonlight or by night; **m. flit** act of leaving home secretly by night to avoid arrest, claims for debts, *etc* ~ **moonlight** *v/i* (*coll*) to work or act surreptitiously; elope ~ **moonlighter** *n* (*hist*) Irish Land League terrorist.

moonlit [*mOOnlit*] *adj* lit by the moon.

moonscape [*mOOnskayp*] *n* scenery of the moon's surface.

moonshine [*mOOnshIn*] *n* moonlight; nonsense, foolish talk; (*sl*) illicitly distilled whisky, smuggled spirits ~ **moonshiner** *n* (*sl*) smuggler or illicit distiller of whisky, rum *etc*.

moonshot [*mOOnshot*] *n* spacecraft sent from earth to moon; act of launching this.

moonstone [*mOOnstOn*] *n* opalescent feldspar.

moonstrike [*mOOnstRIk*] *n* act of landing an artificial satellite or rocket on the moon's surface.

moonstruck [*mOOnstRuk*] *adj* crazy.

moony [*mOOni*] *adj* dreamy, listless; (*sl*) crazy; like the moon in colour or shape.

moor (1) [*moor*] *v/t* and *i* (*naut*) fasten, secure (ship) with chains or cable and anchor > PDSa; come in to shore and secure ship.

moor (2) *n* wild stretch of open country, usually elevated and covered with heather, coarse grass, bracken *etc*.

Moor (3) *n* member of the mixed Berber and Arab race of Morocco.

moorage [*moorRij*] *n* place to moor a ship.

moorhen [*moorhen*] *n* female red grouse; the waterhen.

mooring [*moorRing*] *n* place where a ship is moored; (*pl*) any layout of anchors, weights and chains to which a vessel may make fast.

Moorish [*moorRish*] *adj* of the Moors; in architectural style introduced by the Moors.

moorland [*moorland*] *n* large tract of moor.

moose [*mOOs*] *n* the North American elk.

moot [*mOOt*] *adj* debatable, not settled ~ **moot** *v/t* raise (a point) for discussion ~ **moot, mote** *n* (*hist*) assembly of freemen of a town.

mop (1) [*mop*] *n* long-handled cleaning tool with a head of soft yarn or cloth; (*coll*) thick untidy hair ~ **mop** (*pres/part* **mopping**, *p/t* and *p/part* **mopped**) *v/t* clean or wipe with a mop; wipe; **m. up** finish off quickly; round up; defeat.

mop (2) *n* and *v/i* (*ar*) grimace.

mope [*mOp*] *v/i* be depressed and listless.

moped [*mOped*] *n* light motor-driven bicycle.

mopedallist [*mOpedalist*] *n* moped rider.

moppet [*mopit*] *n* (*coll*) attractive child.

mopping-up [*moping-up*] *n* (*mil*) act of rounding up and disposing of remnants of opposing army.

moquette [*moket*] *n* a fabric used for carpets and soft furnishings.

moraine [*moRayn*] *n* debris deposited by a glacier.

moral [*moRal*] *adj* relating to the rightness or wrongness of human behaviour, ethical; having or teaching high standards of behaviour, virtuous; chaste; of or in the mind, not physical; based on or appealing to a sense of justice, duty *etc*; influencing the mind; highly probable; showing sympathy and approval; **m. victory** defeat regarded as being in fact a success ~ **moral** *n* ethical significance, moral teaching implied in (a story *etc*); (*pl*) behaviour, habits, *esp* in sexual matters; (*pl*) ethics.

morale [*moRaal*] *n* mental state, *esp* as regards courage, confidence and discipline.

moralist [*moRalist*] *n* one who teaches morals ~ **moralistic** [*moRalistik*] *adj*.

morality [*moRaliti*] *n* principles of conduct, ethics; moral rightness; virtue; chastity; late medieval type of allegorical religious play.

moralize [*moRalIz*] *v/t* and *i* interpret in a moral sense, draw a moral from; write or speak on moral subjects.

morally [*moRali*] *adv* as regards morality; virtually, in effect; very probably.

morass [*moRas*] *n* swamp, bog; (*fig*) difficult situation; moral degradation.

moratorium [*moRatawRi-um*] *n* legally or officially determined period of delay before the fulfilment of an agreement or the paying of debts; (*fig*) respite; agreed delay or pause; (*US*) large-scale interruption of work for public demonstration.

morbid [*mawrbid*] *adj* abnormal, diseased; pathological; gloomy; gruesome ~ **morbidly** *adv*.

morbidity [*mawrbiditi*] *n* unhealthiness; disease.

mordant [*mawrdant*] *adj* biting, caustic; smarting; sarcastic; (*fabric dyeing*) serving to fix colours ~ **mordant** *n* a colour fixative > PDS; etching acid ~ **mordantly** *adv* sarcastically.

more [*mawr*] *adj* greater in quantity, degree, extent *etc*; additional ~ **more** *adv* to a greater degree, extent *etc*; further; again; **m. or less** roughly, approximately ~ **more** *n* larger or additional quantity.

morel [*moRel*] *n* an edible fungus.

morello [*moRelO*] *n* variety of bitter cherry.

moreover [*mawrROver*] *adv* besides, in addition.

mores [*moRez*] *n* customs and conduct considered vital by a specified social group; social behaviour.

Moresque, Mauresque [*mawResk*] *adj* Moorish.

morganatic [*mawrganatik*] *adj* **m. marriage** marriage with a woman of inferior rank, in which neither she nor her children acquire the husband's rank or inherit his possessions.

morgue [*mawrg*] *n* building where corpses are placed for identification.

moribund [*moRibund*] *adj* dying; decaying.

Mormon [*mawrmon*] *n* member of Church of Jesus Christ of Latter-day Saints.

morn [*mawrn*] *n* (*poet*) morning; (*Scots*) tomorrow.

morning [mawrning] n first part of day, from dawn to noon; (fig) early part ~ **morning** adj of or in the morning; m. **coat** tail-coat for formal daytime use; m. **dress** formal clothes for daytime use; m. **room** sitting-room used in the morning; m. **star** planet Venus when seen before dawn; (fig) forerunner.

Morocco [moRokO] n flexible fine leather.

moron [mawrRon/mORon] n feeble-minded person, halfwit ~ **moronic** [mawrRonik] adj.

morose [moROs] adj sullen; gloomy; brooding ~ **morosely** adv ~ **moroseness** n.

morpheme [mawrfeem] n (gramm) any meaningful linguistic unit, whether word or affix, which cannot be divided into smaller meaningful units.

morphia [mawrfi-a] n (pop) morphine.

morphine [mawrfeen] n powerful narcotic and analgesic extracted from opium > PDS.

morphinism [mawrfinizm] n habitual taking of morphine; diseased state caused by this.

morphinomania [mawrfinOmayni-a] n addiction to morphine as a drug ~ **morphinomaniac** n a morphine addict.

morphology [mawrfoloji] n study of the forms of plants and animals; study of the internal forms of words ~ **morphological** [mawrfolojikal] adj.

morris [moRis] n type of English folk dance usu semi-dramatic and using mime; a game played with stones.

morris-dance [moRis-daans] n a morris ~ **morris-dancer** n performer in a morris.

morris-tube [moRis-tewb] n small-bore barrel inserted into a rifle for shooting practice.

morrow [moRO] n (poet) tomorrow, next day; (ar) morning; (fig) immediately subsequent period.

morse (1) [mawrs] n the walrus.

morse (2) n system of signalling in which letters are expressed by dots and dashes.

morsel [mawrsel] n small quantity or piece.

mortal [mawrtal] adj that can die; causing death, fatal; of or like death; lasting till death; punishable by death; very grave; implacable; (coll) long and boring; (coll) extreme; m. **sin** sin entailing damnation ~ **mortal** n creature, usu human being, that can die ~ **mortally** adv.

mortality [mawrtaliti] n state of being mortal; death; deathrate; the human race.

mortar [mawrter] n mixture of cement, lime putty and sand for laying bricks > PDBI; short cannon firing shells at high angles; thick strong bowl in which substances are pounded and ground up ~ **mortar** v/t bind (bricks) with mortar; shell from a mortar; pound in a mortar

mortarboard [mawrterbawrd] n small square board on which building mortar is mixed; (coll) academic cap with flat square top.

mortgage [mawrgij] n (leg) temporary conveyance of an estate as security for money lent until the loan is repaid; deed of such conveyance ~ **mortgage** v/t convey on mortgage; (fig) pledge.

mortgagee [mawrgijee] n one who lends money on mortgage.

mortgagor [mawrgijer] n one who conveys property on mortgage.

mortician [mawrtishan] n undertaker.

mortification [mawrtifikayshon] n act of mortifying; state of being mortified; that which mortifies; humiliation; (med) gangrene.

mortify [mawrtifI] v/t and i inflict penitential austerities on, subdue by self-denial; humiliate; wound the feelings of; (med) become gangrenous, decay ~ **mortifying** adj humiliating.

mortise [mawrtis] n hole cut into stone or timber to receive a projecting tenon ~ **mortise** v/t cut a mortise in; join by a mortise and tenon.

mortmain [mawrtmayn] n (leg) possession of property by a corporation not permitted to transfer it.

mortuary [mawrtew-eRi] n building where corpses are kept awaiting burial or identification ~ **mortuary** adj of death or burial.

mosaic (1) [mOzay-ik] n pattern formed by juxtaposing small pieces of differently coloured marble, glass, stone etc; (fig) intricate pattern of fragments ~ **mosaic** adj in or like mosaic.

Mosaic (2) adj pertaining to Moses or to the Law given through him.

moselle [mOzel] n type of German dry white wine.

mosey [mOzi] v/i (sl) stroll, saunter.

Moslem see **Muslim**.

mosque [mosk] n building where Muslims worship.

mosquito [moskeetO] n gnat that sucks blood.

mosquito-net [moskeetO-net] n netting that excludes mosquitoes.

moss [mos] n low, tufted plant without flowers; ground covered with moss; bog.

mossgrown [mosgROn] adj covered with moss.

moss-rose [mos-ROz] n variety of cabbage rose.

mossy [mosi] adj of, like, or covered with moss.

most [mOst] adj greatest in amount, quality, extent, degree etc ~ **most** adv in the greatest degree ~ **most** n greatest amount, quantity etc; the best; **at m.** not more than; **make the m. of** profit fully from.

mote (1) [mOt] n particle of dust; speck; spot; anything small.

mote (2) see **moot**.

motel [mOtel] n group of bungalows rented to motorists for short periods.

motet [mOtet] n type of church choral composition > PDM; medieval vocal composition with several melodies in counterpoint > PDM.

moth [moth] n lepidopterous insect, usu nocturnal, whose antennae are not club-shaped; one such insect whose larvae feed on wool and fabric.

mothball [mothbawl] n ball of camphor repellent to clothes-moth ~ **mothball** v/t lay up (ship, machine etc) when not in use, after protecting it from deteriorating.

motheaten [motheeten] adj spoilt by clothes-moth; (fig) shabby, worn-out.

mother [muTHer] n female parent; (fig) protectress, female guardian; source; title of respect for nuns, esp the head of a convent; **M. Carey's chicken** the stormy petrel; **M. Carey's goose** the great fulmar; **M. Church** the Christian Church; oldest church of parish; chief church of diocese, cathedral; m. **country** country from which colonies were founded; native country; m. **ship** ship acting as depot and base to others; m. **tongue** native language; m. **wit** common sense, inborn intelligence ~ **mother** v/t act as or like a mother to; cherish, tend affectionately; give birth to; **Mothering Sunday** fourth Sunday in Lent.

mothercraft [*mu*THerkRaaft] *n* science of the care of young children.

motherhood [*mu*THerhood] *n* condition of being a mother; feelings of a mother.

mother-in-law (*pl* **mothers-in-law**) [*mu*THer-in-law] *n* mother of one's husband or wife.

motherly [*mu*THerli] *adj* like a mother; kind, protective ~ **motherliness** *n*.

mother-of-pearl [*mu*THer-ov-*purl*] *n* iridescent, hard lining of some varieties of shell.

mothproof [*moth*pRoof] *adj* proof against damage by clothes-moth ~ **mothproof** *v/t* make mothproof.

motif (*pl* **motifs** or **motives**) [*mOteef*] *n* recurrent theme or feature in a work of art, *esp* in music; ornamental pattern in needlework.

motion [*mO*shon] *n* act or process of moving, movement; gesture; proposal put to a meeting or assembly; (*leg*) application for a ruling; act of emptying the bowels; dung ~ **motion** *v/t* and *i* make a gesture, indicate by gesture; propose a motion.

motionless [*mO*shonlis] *adj* not moving.

motion-picture [*mO*shon-pikcher] *n* cinema film.

motivate [*mO*tivayt] *v/t* provide an inducement; act as an incentive; be the motive of ~ **motivation** [mOtiv*ay*shon] *n*.

motive [*mO*tiv] *n* factor that determines the direction of an individual's behaviour; that which causes or influences an action; incentive; cause > PDP; motif ~ **motive** *adj* causing movement or action ~ **motive** *v/t* motivate.

motley [*mot*li] *adj* in or of different colours; varied, mixed; ill-assorted ~ **motley** *n* particoloured clothes of a jester.

motor [*mO*ter] *n* device for converting other forms of energy into mechanical energy; internal combustion engine giving motion to vehicle or vessel; motorcar; machine converting electric to mechanical power; (*anat*) muscle moving a part of the body; nerve that stimulates such a muscle > PDB ~ **motor** *v/i* and *t* travel in or convey by motorcar ~ **motor** *adj* causing motion; driven by a motor.

motorbike [*mO*terbIk] *n* (*coll*) motorcycle.

motorboat [*mO*terbOt] *n* boat propelled by a motor.

motorcade [*mO*terkayd] *n* (*US*) procession of motorcars.

motorcar [*mO*terkaar] *n* passenger vehicle driven by a motor.

motorcoach [*mO*terkOch] *n* large vehicle for transporting passengers on long-distance road journeys.

motorcycle [*mO*tersIk'l] *n* powerful two-wheeled vehicle driven by a motor ~ **motorcycle** *v/i*.

motoring [*mO*terRing] *n* act or habit of travelling by car, *esp* for pleasure.

motorist [*mO*terRist] *n* one who drives a motorcar; one who travels by motorcar.

motorize [*mO*terRIz] *v/t* equip with motor transport or with motors.

motorman [*mO*terman] *n* driver of electric train or tram.

motor-spirit [*mO*ter-spiRit] *n* petrol.

motorway [*mO*terway] *n* road specially built for fast motor traffic.

mottle [*mot*'l] *v/t* mark with irregular stains of various colours ~ **mottle** *n* blotch, spot; pattern of blotches ~ **mottled** *adj* conspicuously spotted, *esp* with varying colours.

motto (*pl* **mottoes**) [*mot*O] *n* short saying expressing a rule of conduct, maxim; short phrase attached to heraldic crest, or inscribed on anything as appropriate to it.

moue [*mOO*] *n* (*Fr*) a grimace of the lips expressing discontent.

moujik see **mujik.**

mould (1) [*mOld*] *n* fine, rich soil; earth.

mould (2) *n* minute fungus appearing on various substances exposed to damp.

mould (3) *n* hollow receptacle in which soft material can be put to harden to desired shape; something shaped in a mould; blancmange; jelly; shape, style; (*fig*) character ~ **mould** *v/t* shape in a mould; shape by handling or squeezing; (*fig*) form the character of, influence; shape, make.

moulder (1) [*mOl*der] *n* one who moulds.

moulder (2) *v/i* crumble, decay.

moulding [*mOl*ding] *n* process or manner of shaping; that which has been moulded; (*bui*) slender, ornamental, continuous projection to throw shadow or to divert water away from a wall; ornamental strip of patterned wood.

mouldy [*mOl*di] *adj* covered with mould; decaying; (*sl*) worthless.

moult [*mOlt*] *v/i* and *t* shed feathers, fur *etc* seasonally ~ **moult** *n* act or period of moulting.

mound [*mownd*] *n* heap of earth and stones deliberately raised; natural hillock; barrow; defensive bank of earth and stones ~ **mound** *v/t* pile up.

mount (1) [*mownt*] *n* mountain, high hill.

mount (2) *v/t* and *i* climb on to or up; go to the top of; rise; increase; get on to (a horse); fix in position on a base or in a framework; stage, produce (plays); stuff (animal skins *etc*); provide a frame or setting for; provide a horse for; **m. guard** keep watch over, *esp* as sentry ~ **mount** *n* horse for riding; framework, setting; base on which a picture is fixed before framing; gun-carriage; glass slide to which specimens are fixed.

mountain [*mown*ten] *n* mass of land of great altitude; large heap; (*fig*) anything very large ~ **mountain** *adj* of or like a mountain; found on mountains; used among mountains; **m. ash** rowan; **m. dew** whisky.

mountaineer [mownt*eer*] *n* dweller among mountains; expert mountain climber ~ **mountaineer** *v/i* climb mountains, *esp* as sport.

mountainous [*mown*tenus] *adj* with many mountains; extremely large.

mountebank [*mown*tibank] *n* buffoon, clown; impostor, charlatan; quack doctor.

mounted [*mown*tid] *adj* fixed on a mount; on horseback.

mounting (1) [*mown*ting] *adj* increasing.

mounting (2) *n* that which serves as a frame, setting, support *etc.*

Mounty [*mown*ti] *n* (*coll*) member of Canadian Mounted Police.

mourn [*mawrn*] *v/t* and *i* feel or express grief; grieve for the death of; deplore ~ **mourner** *n.*

mournful [*mawrn*fool] *adj* expressing grief; gloomy ~ **mournfully** *adv* ~ **mournfulness** *n.*

mourning [*mawr*ning] *n* grief, *esp* for a death; black clothes worn as sign of grief for a death; period during which such clothes are worn ~ **mourning** *adj* grieving, lamenting; worn or used as sign of mourning.

mouse (*pl* **mice**) [*mows*] *n* common species of small rodent; (*fig*) shy person; (*sl*) black eye ~ **mouse** [*mowz*] *v/i* (*of cat*) hunt for mice.

mouse-colour [*mows*-kuler] *n* dark brownish-grey.

mousetrap [*mows*tRap] *n* spring-trap for mice; (*coll*) stale cheese; cheese of indifferent flavour.

mousse [*mOOs*] *n* dish of whipped flavoured eggs and cream, or creamy substance.

moustache [*moostaash*] *n* hair on upper lip.

mousy [*mows*i] *adj* of or like a mouse; dull brown; timid, shy.

mouth [*mowth*] *n* opening in an animal's head by which it eats and utters sounds; opening, outlet; entrance; **down in the m.** gloomy; **shut one's m.** be silent ~ **mouth** [*mowTH*] *v/t* and *i* speak with emphatic movements of jaws and lips; declaim; chew; hold in the mouth; train (horse) to obey the bit; grimace.

mouthful [*mowth*fool] *n* amount which fills the mouth; small quantity; (*sl*) word or phrase hard to pronounce; useful remark.

mouthorgan [*mowth*awrgan] *n* (*mus*) small metal wind instrument, harmonica > PDM.

mouthpiece [*mowth*pees] *n* that part of a musical instrument, tube, or pipe which is held in the mouth; spokesman, one who expresses the views of a group or of another.

mouthwash [*mowth*wosh] *n* medicated liquid for treating infections of mouth and throat.

movable [*mOO*vab'l] *adj* that can be moved or changed ~ **movables** *n* (*pl*) possessions that can be moved, chattels.

move [*mOOv*] *v/t* and *i* change position (of); transfer, shift; set in motion; be capable of motion; stir the emotions (of); influence; provoke, rouse; go from one place to another; be shifted; develop, change; grow; go to live elsewhere; live in specified social group; take action, *esp* tactical action in games *etc*; make formal proposal at meetings *etc*; **m. in** settle in a new house or district; **m. on** (*of police*) prevent from loitering; progress, advance; **m. out** leave ~ **move** *n* act of moving; action; change of residence; tactical action in games *etc*; right or turn to act; **get a m. on** hurry; **on the m.** constantly moving; migrating.

movement [*mOO*vment] *n* act or process of moving; motion; activity; change, trend, tendency; organized activity to achieve an aim; group of those active for such an aim; moving parts of a mechanism, *esp* of a watch; (*mus*) major division in a large composition > PDM; tempo; (*pl*) activity; comings and goings.

mover [*mOO*ver] *n* one who or that which moves; proposer, instigator.

movie [*mOO*vi] *n* (*sl*) cinema film; cinema ~ **movie** *adj* (*sl*) of or in the cinema.

moving [*mOO*ving] *adj* causing motion; in motion; causing emotion, pathetic; **m. staircase** escalator ~ **movingly** *adv.*

mow (1) (*p/t* **mowed**, *p/part* **mown**) [*mO*] *v/t*

and *i* cut grass *etc* by machine or with a scythe; **m. down** kill in great numbers; fell indiscriminately ~ **mower** *n* one who or that which mows; machine for cutting grass of lawns.

mow (2) *n* stack of hay, sheaves of corn *etc.*

mow (3) *n* and *v/i* (*ar*) grimace.

Mr [*mister*] *n* (*abbr*) mister.

Mrs [*misiz*] *n* (*abbr* of **Mistress**) title of address for married woman with no other title.

Ms [*muz/miz*] *n* title of address for a woman who does not wish to indicate whether she is married or not, or whose marital status one does not know.

much [*much*] *adj* great in amount; long; numerous ~ **much** *adv* to a great degree; almost; **m. of a muchness** not very different ~ **much** *n* great quantity.

mucilage [*mew*silij] *n* gummy substance extracted from plants ~ **mucilaginous** [mewsi*laj*inus] *adj.*

muck [*muk*] *n* filth, dirt; manure; refuse; (*coll*) trash; **make a m. of** (*coll*) bungle; make filthy ~ **muck** *v/t* manure; **m. about** (*coll*) behave idly or mischievously; play the fool; **m. in with** (*coll*) share lodgings, rations *etc* with; **m. out** clean (stables) of dung; **m. up** (*coll*) spoil; mismanage, bungle; make dirty.

muckheap [*muk*heep] *n* manure heap.

muckle [*muk*'l] *n* (*Scots*) large quantity.

muckraker [*muk*Rayker] *n* one who searches out and publicizes hidden scandals ~ **muckraking** *adj* and *n.*

mucksweat [*muk*swet] *n* profuse sweat.

mucky [*muk*i] *adj* (*coll*) dirty, disgusting ~ **muckily** *adv* ~ **muckiness** *n.*

mucous [*mew*kus] *adj* of, like, or covered with mucus; secreting mucus; slimy.

mucus [*mew*kus] *n* slimy secretion of certain membranes > PDB.

mud [*mud*] *n* very wet earth; (*fig*) something despicable; (*sl*) opium; **one's name is m.** one is in disgrace; **m. pack** layer of fuller's earth applied to, then sponged off, the face to beautify it; **m. pie** mud moulded to a shape; **throw m. at** speak ill of.

muddle [*mud*'l] *n* confusion; disorder; bewilderment ~ **muddle** *v/t* and *i* confuse, bewilder; jumble up; **m. along, m. through** survive or succeed despite inefficiency.

muddle-headed [*mud*'l-*hed*id] *adj* stupidly confused.

muddy [*mud*i] *adj* covered with mud; like mud; cloudy; confused ~ **muddy** *v/t* make muddy.

mudfish [*mud*fish] *n* fish which burrows in the mud.

mudflap [*mud*flap] *n* flap hung behind rear wheel of car to prevent mud being thrown up on to following cars.

mudflat [*mud*flat] *n* area of flat, muddy land.

mudguard [*mud*gaard] *n* protective strip over wheel of vehicle to prevent splashes of mud.

mudlark [*mud*laark] *n* one who scavenges articles from gutters and the banks of tidal rivers; one who plays in mud; slum child.

mud-slinging [*mud*-slinging] *n* slander, insult.

mud-wall [*mud*-wawl] *n* wall in which mud has been used instead of mortar.

muesli [*mewz*li] *n* mixture of rolled oats, nuts, sugar, raisins *etc.*

muezzin [moo-*ezin*] *n* Muslim official who announces the hours of prayer.

muff (1) [*muf*] *n* warm soft covering for the hands or feet; cover protecting car radiator from cold.

muff (2) *n* one who is clumsy at sport; fool; milksop; blunderer ~ **muff** *v/t* (*sport*) miss, bungle.

muffin [*muf*in] *n* flat, round, porous cake, eaten hot with butter.

muffineer [mufi*neer*] *n* dish to keep muffins hot; castor for sprinkling sugar or salt on muffins.

muffin-man [*muf*in-man] *n* street vendor of muffins.

muffle [*muf*'l] *v/t* wrap up warmly; wrap up so as to deaden the sound of; make dull.

muffler [*muf*ler] *n* thick warm scarf; (*mot*) silencer; pad of felt interposed between hammers and strings of piano when the soft pedal is depressed.

mufti (1) [*muf*ti] *n* (*mil*) civilian clothes; plain clothes, not a uniform.

mufti (2) *n* expounder of Muslim law.

mug (1) [*mug*] *n* heavy cylindrical drinking cup; contents of this; (*sl*) face.

mug (2) *n* (*sl*) fool, easy dupe.

mug (3) (*pres/part* **mugging**, *p/t* and *p/part* **mugged**) *v/t* (*th eat*) overact; **m. up** (*coll*) study intensively ~ **mug** *n* (*coll*) eager student, swot.

mug (4) (*pres/part* **mugging**, *p/t* and *p/part* **mugged**) *v/t* (*coll*) attack and rob in a public place; attack from behind by gripping the throat; a **mugger** *n* ~ **mugging** *n*.

muggins [*mug*inz] *n* (*sl*) fool.

muggy [*mug*i] *adj* warm and damp, sultry.

mugwump [*mug*wump] *n* (*sl*) one who will not commit himself, *esp* in politics; one who is or thinks himself important.

mujik, moujik, muzhik [*mooz*heek] *n* (*hist*) Russian peasant.

mulatto (*pl* **mulattoes**) [mew*lat*O] *n* offspring of a Negro and a white.

mulberry [*mul*beRi] *n* a tree with edible berries; fruit of this; dark reddish purple.

mulch [*mulch*] *n* half-rotten vegetable matter spread round roots of plants ~ **mulch** *v/t* cover with mulch.

mulct [*mulkt*] *v/t* impose a fine upon ~ **mulct** *n* fine.

mule (1) [*mewl*] *n* offspring of a male ass and a mare; (*fig*) obstinate person; kind of spinning-machine; hybrid.

mule (2) *n* heelless slipper.

muleteer [mewle*teer*] *n* one who drives mules.

mulish [*mew*lish] *adj* like a mule; obstinate.

mull (1) [*mul*] *v/t* warm, sweeten and spice (wine or beer).

mull (2) *v/t* (*sl*) bungle; **m. over** ponder on.

mullet [*mul*et] *n* one of two kinds of edible fish.

mulligatawny [muliga*taw*ni] *n* highly-seasoned curry soup.

mullion [*mul*yon] *n* vertical stone bar between window panes.

multi- *pref* many; more than two.

multicellular [multi*sel*ewler] *adj* (*of an organism*) consisting of more than one cell.

multifarious [multi*fair*Ri-us] *adj* many and varied.

multiform [*multi*fawrm] *adj* having many forms or shapes.

multilateral [multi*late*Ral] *adj* having many sides; by, with or for several nations or parties ~ **multilaterally** *adv*.

multimillionaire [multimilyu*nair*] *n* one who possesses several million pounds, dollars, francs *etc*.

multinational [multi*nash*onal] *n* and *adj* (organization) having commercial interests in several countries.

multiple [*multip*'l] *adj* having many parts; numerous; (*math*) repeated; compound; **m. shop (store)** retail business with branches in many towns; **m. star** group of stars looking like a single one, *esp* if linked by gravitation ~ **multiple** *n* (*math*) number containing another an exact number of times; **common m.** number containing two or more others an exact number of times.

multiplex [*multi*pleks] *adj* with many parts.

multiplication [multipli*kay*shon] *n* act of increasing in number; operation by which any given number is multiplied.

multiplicity [multi*plis*iti] *n* state of being multiplied; great number; great variety; quality of being multiple.

multiply [*multi*plI] *v/t* increase in number; increase many times; breed.

multitude [*multi*tewd] *n* great number; great throng of people; the common people.

multitudinous [multi*tew*dinus] *adj* very numerous.

mum (1) [*mum*] *adj* silent ~ **mum** *interj* silence! **mum's the word** keep this secret.

mum (2) *n* (*coll abbr*) mother.

mum (3) (*pres/part* **mumming**, *p/t* and *p/part* **mummed**) *v/t* and *i* mime, act without words.

mumble [*mumb*'l] *v/t* and *i* speak indistinctly; chew gently or slowly ~ **mumble** *n*.

mumbo-jumbo [mumbO-*jumb*O] *n* foolish religious or superstitious reverence; object of this; meaningless phrases, jargon.

mummer [*mum*er] *n* mimer, *esp* if masked; actor in folk-play; (*coll*) actor ~ **mummery** *n* dumb-show, mime; meaningless ceremony.

mummerset [*mum*erset] *n* (*coll*) inaccurate or jocular imitation of dialect of south-west England, *esp* as used on stage.

mummify [*mum*ifI] *v/t* make into a mummy (2).

mummy (1) [*mum*i] *n* (*coll*) mother.

mummy (2) *n* body preserved by embalming.

mumps [*mumps*] *n* contagious inflammation of parotid and salivary glands.

munch [*munch*] *v/t* and *i* chew vigorously.

mundane [*mun*dayn] *adj* belonging to this world; worldly; earthly; uninspiring, dull.

municipal [mew*nis*ipal] *adj* pertaining to local self-government of a city, town or borough.

municipality [mewnisi*pal*iti] *n* town, city or district possessing local self-government; governing body of such a place.

munificence [mew*nif*isens] *n* lavish generosity, liberality ~ **munificent** *adj* ~ **munificently** *adv*.

muniments [*mew*niments] *n* (*pl*) (*leg*) title-deeds; records upholding a claim; archives.

munitions [mew*nish*onz] *n* (*pl*) military stores, *esp* ammunition, shells *etc* ~ **munition** *v/t* supply, equip with munitions.

muon [*mew*-on] *n* (*phys*) short-lived elementary particle > PDS.

mural [*mewr*Ral] *adj* of, like, or on a wall ~ mural *n* a painting on a wall.

murder [*murder*] *n* unlawful and intentional killing of a human being; unjustifiable action causing loss of life; (*coll*) something very hard or unpleasant; capital m. murder punishable by death ~ murder *v/t* kill deliberately and unlawfully; slay; (*fig*) ruin (music, play *etc*) by bad performance.

murderer [*murderer*] *n* one who has committed murder.

murderess [*murder*Ris] *n* female murderer.

murderous [*murderus*] *adj* of or like murder; intending to murder; fatal; violent.

murex (*pl* murices, murexes) [*mewr*Reks, *pl mewr*Riseez, *mewr*Reksez] *n* type of tropical whelk; purple dye secreted by this.

murine [*mewr*RIn] *adj* like a mouse.

murk, mirk [*murk*] *n* darkness; gloom.

murky [*murki*] *adj* dark; gloomy; dingy; (*coll*) shameful ~ murkily *adv* ~ murkiness *n*.

murmur [*murmer*] *v/t* and *i* speak in soft low voice; produce a low continuous indistinct sound; grumble ~ murmur *n* act of murmuring; low indistinct sound; complaint ~ murmurer *n*.

murrain [*mu*Rin] *n* infectious cattle disease.

muscat [*muskat*] *n* type of grape; wine made from this.

muscatel, muscadel [muska*tel*, muska*del*] *n* rich sweet white wine; grape from which this is made; dessert raisin of this grape; sweet pear.

muscle [*mus*'l] *n* animal tissue consisting of highly contractile cells, through which movement is effected > PDB; (*fig*) strength ~ muscle ' *v/i* m. in on (*coll*) force one's way into; poach on someone's preserves.

muscle-bound [*mus*'l-bownd] *adj* with muscles strained and stiff through over-exercise.

muscleman [*mus*'lman] *n* (*coll*) one who earns his living by displaying his strength; thug, strong ruffian.

Muscovite [*musk*OvIt] *n* and *adj* (native) of Moscow; (*min*) a variety of mica.

muscular [*muskewler*] *adj* of, affecting or done by the muscles; having well-developed muscles; strong; brawny ~ musculature *n* muscular system of a body or limb.

Muse (1) [*mewz*] *n* (*myth*) any one of the nine sister-goddesses, each identified with a particular art or science; (*fig*) poetic inspiration; one who inspires a poet.

muse (2) *v/i* think deeply, ponder ~ muse *n* (*ar*) meditation; reverie.

museum [mewz*ee*-um] *n* institution for the collection, preservation, study and exhibition of objects of scientific, historical or artistic interest; building where these are housed; m. piece object fit for preservation in a museum; (*fig*) old-fashioned person or thing.

mush [*mush*] *n* soft pulpy mass; maize porridge; (*coll*) sentimentality; (*rad*) interference from powerful stations; (*sl*) face.

mushroom [*mush*Room] *n* quick-growing fleshy edible fungus; anything resembling this in shape or in speed of development; cloud produced by nuclear explosion ~ mushroom *adj* of or like a mushroom; developing fast ~ mushroom *v/i* be shaped like a mushroom; spring up rapidly; gather mushrooms.

mushy [*mushi*] *adj* like mush; (*coll*) sentimental.

music [*mewzik*] *n* rhythmic combination of sounds affecting the aesthetic sense or the emotions; art of producing this; example of this; written or printed score of musical composition; (*ar*) band, orchestra; (*fig*) pleasing sound; m. centre combined apparatus for playing records, tapes, cassettes and radio; public building offering facilities for studying and playing music; face the m. accept responsibility for one's conduct; face the consequences of an act.

musical [*mewzikal*] *adj* of, like or producing music; skilled in music; fond of music; performed to music; pleasant to hear; m. box toy in which tunes are played on a metal comb by revolving spikes; m. comedy (play) theatrical or cinema entertainment with many light songs; m. glasses set of glass vessels producing notes when struck or rubbed ~ musical *n* musical comedy or play.

musicality [mewzik*aliti*] *n* quality of being musical.

musically [*mewzikali*] *adv* in a musical way.

music-hall [*mewzik*-hawl] *n* comic variety show; theatre for this.

musician [mewz*ish*an] *n* one skilled in music; one who performs music.

musicianship [mewz*ish*anship] *n* skill in performing or perception in appreciating music.

musicology [mewzik*oloji*] *n* scholarly study of music.

music-stand [*mewzik*-stand] *n* light desk holding music score.

music-stool [*mewzik*-stOOl] *n* piano-stool.

musk [*musk*] *n* strong perfume obtained from the male musk-deer; plant with similar smell.

musk-deer [*musk*-deer] *n* small Asian deer.

musket [*muskit*] *n* early type of smooth-bore hand-gun.

musketeer [muski*teer*] *n* (*hist*) soldier armed with a musket.

musketry [*muskit*Ri] *n* use of small-arms and rifles; rifle-shooting; (*hist*) body of musketeers.

musk-ox [*musk*-oks] *n* ruminant of arctic America.

musk-rat [*musk*-Rat] *n* North American water-rat; fur of this.

musk-rose [*musk*-ROz] *n* rambling rose with a musky smell.

musky [*muski*] *adj* having the smell of musk.

Muslim, Moslem [*muz*lim, *moz*lem] *n* and *adj* (follower) of Mohammed.

muslin [*muz*lin] *n* fine thin cotton fabric ~ muslin *adj*.

musquash [*musk*wosh] *n* the musk-rat.

muss [*mus*] *v/t* and *n* (*US*) mess.

mussel [*mus*'l] *n* a bivalve mollusc.

Mussulman (*pl* Mussulmans) [*mus*ulman] *n* (*ar*) a Muslim.

must (1) [*must*] *v/i* (*aux*) be obliged to, be under a necessity to; be necessary; be very likely, almost certain ~ must *n* (*coll*) something which it is essential to do, see, read *etc*.

must (2) *adj* (*of elephants*) frenzied ~ must *n* frenzy to which male elephants are subject.

must (3) *n* new, unfermented wine.

must (4) *n* mustiness, mould.

mustang [*mustang*] *n* American wild horse.

mustard [*musterd*] *n* plant with a pungent taste; seeds of this ground and used as a condiment; keen as m. enthusiastic.

mustard-gas [*musterd-gas*] *n* type of poisonous irritant gas > PDS.

muster [*muster*] *n* an assembling of troops, *esp* for parade, inspection *etc*; number on parade; muster-roll; a gathering; pass m. be adequate ~ muster *v/t* and *i* bring together, summon; assemble for parade *etc*; m. up gather together.

muster-roll [*muster*-ROl] *n* register of troops *etc*.

mustn't [*musn't*] *abbr* must not.

musty [*musti*] *adj* mouldy; stale; antiquated.

mutable [*mewtab'l*] *adj* liable to change; inconstant, unstable ~ mutability [*mewtabiliti*] *n* changeability.

mutagen [*mewtajen*] *n* (*biol*) substance which causes mutations.

mutant [*mewtant*] *n* (*biol*) creature differing from its parents by mutation, freak caused by mutation.

mutate [mewt*ayt*] *v/t* and *i* cause or undergo mutation.

mutation [mewt*ayshon*] *n* alteration, change, variation; (*biol*) sudden and relatively permanent genetic change, *usu* due to influence of radiation or chemicals > PDB; new type of organism arising from mutation; (*phil, of vowels*) change of quality due to influence of the vowel of the next syllable.

mute [*mewt*] *adj* silent; dumb; speechless; not pronounced ~ mute *n* one who is mute; dumb person; hired mourner at funeral; contrivance to reduce volume of instrument and/or modify its tone > PDM ~ mute *v/t* muffle, reduce the sound of.

mutes [*mewts*] *n* (*pl*) birds' dung.

mutilate [*mewtilayt*] *v/t* maim; cut off; remove an essential part of; render imperfect.

mutilation [mewtil*ayshon*] *n* act of mutilating; disfigurement.

mutineer [mewtin*eer*] *n* one who mutinies.

mutinous [*mewtinus*] *adj* rebellious ~ mutinously *adv*.

mutiny [*mewtini*] *n* concerted revolt against authority, *esp* in armed forces; revolt ~ mutiny *v/i* revolt.

mutism [*mewtizm*] *n* state of being dumb > PDP; persistent refusal to speak.

mutt [*mut*] *n* (*coll*) fool.

mutter [*muter*] *v/t* and *i* speak in a low voice; grumble ~ mutter *n* subdued murmur or sound.

mutton [*muton*] *n* flesh of sheep as food; dead as m. completely dead.

muttonfist [*mutonfist*] *n* large coarse hand.

muttonhead [*mutonhed*] *n* (*sl*) fool.

mutual [*mewtew-al/mewchew-al*] *adj* reciprocal; joint, shared; common ~ mutually *adv*.

mutualism [*mewtew-alizm/mewchew-alizm*] *n* beneficial interdependence.

muzak [*mewzak*] *n* continuous programme of recorded light music relayed throughout a building, train, aircraft *etc*.

muzhik see mujik

muzzle [*muz'l*] *n* projecting nose and mouth of an animal; straps to prevent an animal's biting; mouth of a gun ~ muzzle *v/t* put a muzzle on; restrain; silence.

muzzy [*muzi*] *adj* dazed; vague; tipsy.

my [*mI*] *poss adj* belonging to me ~ my *interj* exclamation of surprise and joy.

Mycenean [mIs*inee*-an] *n* and *adj* (inhabitant or language) of the ancient Greek city of Mycenae, or of the Bronze Age culture of the East Mediterranean area.

mycology [mIk*oloji*] *n* scientific study of fungi ~ mycologist *n* student of mycology.

mycosis [mIk*Osis*] *n* disease caused by fungal infestation.

myelitis [mI-el*Itis*] *n* inflammation of spinal cord.

myo- *pref* of muscle.

myoglobin [mI-Ogl*Obin*] *n* (*bioch*) form of haemoglobin which occurs in muscle fibre.

myopia [mI-*Opi*-a] *n* short-sight ~ myopic *adj*.

myosotis [mI-Os*Otis*] *n* forget-me-not plant.

myriad [*miRi*-ad] *adj* countless ~ myriad *n* ten thousand; a very large number.

myrmidon [*murmidon*] *n* ruthless servant.

myrrh [*mur*] *n* bitter, aromatic gum.

myrtle [*murt'l*] *n* tall shrub with evergreen leaves and fragrant flowers.

myself [mIs*elf*] *pron emph* and *refl* I; me.

mysterious [mist*eer*Ri-us] *adj* not easily understood; secret ~ mysteriously *adv*.

mystery [*misteRi*] *n* something hard to understand; something secret or obscure; secret religious rites; (*eccles*) revealed incomprehensible doctrine; sacrament; (*ar*) handicraft; guild of craftsmen; m. play type of medieval religious drama.

mystic [*mistik*] *adj* of mysticism; of or like a religious mystery; occult; allegorical; mysterious, weird ~ mystic *n* one who practises mysticism.

mystical [*mistikal*] *adj* mystic ~ mystically *adv*.

mysticism [*mistisizm*] *n* belief in the attainment, through contemplation, of truths inaccessible to the understanding; system of prayer *etc* designed to achieve this; (*coll*) vague irrational religious or occult notions.

mystification [mistifik*ayshon*] *n* act of bewildering; bewilderment; perplexity.

mystify [*mistifI*] *v/i* bewilder, baffle.

mystique [mist*eek*] *n* air of mystery surrounding some art, cult, occupation *etc* and deliberately maintained by its devotees; set of beliefs, customs, skills *etc* cherished by such devotees.

myth [*mith*] *n* traditional story embodying ancient religious ideas or supernatural concepts; widespread but false idea; fictitious person or creature.

mythic, mythical [*mith*ik(al)] *adj* of or in a myth; legendary; fictitious ~ mythically *adv*.

mythological [mithOl*oj*ikal/mIthOl*oj*ikal] *adj* of myths or mythology, mythical.

mythologist [mith*oloj*ist] *n* student of mythology.

mythologize [mith*oloj*Iz/mItho*loj*Iz] *v/t* and *i* explain by a myth; invent myths; study myths.

mythology [mith*oloji*/mItho*loji*] *n* system of traditional stories embodying ancient religious ideas; the science of myths.

mythomania [mithO*mayni*-a] *n* obsessive tendency to invent elaborate lies.

myxoedema [mikseed*eema*] *n* disease due to deficiency of thyroid gland > PDP.

myxomatosis [miksomat*Osis*] *n* virus disease of rabbits.

N

n [*en*] fourteenth letter of English alphabet; (*math*) unknown quantity or power.

Naafi [*na*fi] *n* (*abbr*) government institution that runs canteens, shops and entertainment for service personnel.

nab (*pres/part* **nabbing**, *p/t* and *p/part* **nabbed**) [*nab*] *v/t* (*sl*) catch; arrest; steal.

nabob [*nay*bob] *n* very rich man, *esp* one who has made his fortune in India.

nacelle [*na*sel] *n* framework containing engine of aeroplane; car of airship.

nacre [*nay*ker] *n* iridescent lining of certain shells, mother-of-pearl ~ **nacreous** *adj.*

nadir [*nay*der/*nay*deer] *n* (*astron*) point immediately opposite the zenith; (*fig*) lowest point.

nag (1) [*nag*] *n* small horse, pony.

nag (2) (*pres/part* **nagging**, *p/t* and *p/part* **nagged**) *v/t* and *i* persistently find fault or scold; annoy by constant scolding or grumbling; give constant pain ~ **nag** *n* act of nagging ~ **nagger** *n.*

naiad (*pl* **naiads, naiades**) [*nI*-ad] *n* (*class myth*) nymph of lake or river.

nail [*nayl*] *n* horny growth on upper surface of tip of fingers and toes; claw; talon; small flat-headed metal spike, used to fix things together, or as a peg; metal stud on sole of boot; **hard as nails** wiry, tough; stern, harsh; **hit the n. on the head** guess or describe accurately; **on the n.** at once; **tooth and n.** violently ~ **nail** *v/t* fasten with nails; (*fig*) pin down; (*sl*) catch; detect; **n. one's colours to the mast** uphold one's views firmly.

nail-bomb [*nayl*-bom] *n* small hand-thrown bomb packed with gelignite and nails.

nailbrush [*nayl*bRush] *n* brush for cleaning fingernails.

nailfile [*nayl*fIl] *n* metal or emery file for shaping fingernails.

nail-scissors [*nayl*-sizerz] *n* (*pl*) short strong scissors with curved blades for cutting finger- and toenails.

nail-varnish [*nayl*-vaarnish] *n* tinted varnish, *gen* red or pink, for women's fingernails.

nainsook [*nayn*sook] *n* type of cotton fabric.

naïve [nI-*eev*] *adj* simple, artless, innocent; foolishly frank or credulous; immature ~ **naïvely** *adv* ~ **naïveté, naïvety** [na-*eev*ti] *n.*

naked [*nay*kid] *adj* not wearing clothes, nude; bare; hairless; leafless; without normal covering; (*fig*) unconcealed, plain, obvious; without elaboration or decoration; (*of sword*) unsheathed; (*fig*) defenceless; **n. light** unshaded source of light; **with the n. eye** without use of telescope or other optical device; without protection for the eye ~ **nakedly** *adv* ~ **nakedness** *n.*

namby-pamby [nambi-*pam*bi] *adj* and *n* weakly sentimental, childish, effeminate (person or writing).

name [*naym*] *n* word by which a person, thing or idea is denoted, designation; reputation, fame; lineage, ancestry; authority; support; **call names** (*coll*) abuse; insult; **n. day** feast of the saint whose name one bears; **in the n. of** as representative of; appealing to the authority of ~ **name** *v/t* give a name to, call; speak of by name; identify; nominate, appoint; **n. the day** choose date of one's wedding.

nameable, namable [*naym*ab'l] *adj* that can be named.

name-dropping [*naym*-dRoping] *n* talking about famous people as if one knew them well, to impress one's hearers.

nameless [*naym*les] *adj* not known by name; anonymous; vague, undefined; not famous; not fit to be mentioned, abominable.

namely [*naym*li] *adv* that is to say.

nameplate [*naym*playt] *n* plaque on door of house or room bearing name of its occupant.

namesake [*naym*sayk] *n* one having the same name as another.

nan [*nan*] *n* (*coll*) grandmother.

nancy, nancy-boy [*nan*si, *nan*si-boi] *n* (*sl*) effeminate youth, homosexual.

nankeen [nan-*keen*] *n* yellow cotton cloth; (*pl*) trousers made of this.

nanna [*nana*] *n* (*coll*) grandmother.

nanny [*nani*] *n* female servant charged with the care and upbringing of children below school age; (*coll*) grandmother.

nanny-goat [*nani*-gOt] *n* she-goat.

nano- *pref* one thousand millionth.

nap (1) [*nap*] *n* short sleep ~ **nap** (*pres/part* **napping**, *p/t* and *p/part* **napped**) *v/i* doze, sleep for a short while; **be caught napping** be taken unawares.

nap (2) *n* downy surface of cloth ~ **nap** (*pres/part* **napping**, *p/t* and *p/part* **napped**) *v/t* give a nap surface to.

nap (3) *n* a card-game; **go n. on** vouch for the certainty of.

nap (4) (*pres/part* **napping**, *p/t* and *p/part* **napped**) *v/t* (*racing*) tip as winner.

napalm [*nay*paam] *n* jellied petrol used in bombs and flame-throwers.

nape [*nayp*] *n* back of the neck.

naphtha [*naf*tha] *n* general name for mixtures of hydrocarbons obtained by distillation of petroleum, coaltar, *etc* > PDS.

naphthalene [*naf*thaleen] *n* (*chem*) white crystalline solid distilled from coaltar and used in dyeing > PDS.

napkin [*nap*kin] *n* linen square used at meals to wipe fingers and protect clothes; similar square of paper; baby's nappy; **n. ring** ornamental ring to hold rolled-up table-napkin.

napoleon [na*pOl*i-on] *n* French gold coin worth twenty francs; man's topboot; card-game.

napoleonic [napOli-*on*ik] *adj* like Napoleon I; imperious, dominating; very ambitious.

napoo [naa*pOO*] *adj* and *interj* (*sl*) good for nothing, done for, finished.

nappy (1) [*napi*] *n* cloth worn by baby to absorb excreta, diaper.

nappy (2) *adj* (*of ale*) strong, heady.

narc [naark] n (sl abbr) narcotic drug.

narcissism [naarsisizm] n excessive admiration for and interest in oneself; morbid love for one's own body > PDP ~ **narcissist** n ~ **narcissistic** [naarsisistik] adj.

narcissus [naarsisus] n white jonquil; genus comprising jonquils and daffodils.

narcolepsy [naarkOlepsi] n (med) abnormal irrepressible need to sleep ~ **narcoleptic** adj and n.

narcosis [naarkOsis] n deep unconsciousness produced by drugs.

narcotic [naarkotik] n and adj (drug) inducing unconsciousness, sleep, or insensibility to pain; (fig) (that) which dulls awareness or activity.

narcotism [naarkotizm] n condition produced by narcotics; deep stupor; addiction to narcotics.

narcotize [naarkotIz] v/t make insensible by a narcotic.

nard [naard] n aromatic ointment; plant yielding this, the spikenard.

nares [nairReez] n (pl) nostrils and nasal passages.

narghile, nargileh [naargili] n hookah.

nark [naark] n (sl) police spy, informer ~ **nark** v/t (sl) inform against; infuriate; n. it stop it! keep quiet! ~ **narky** adj (sl) bad-tempered, sarcastic.

narrate [naRayt] v/t relate, tell the story of.

narration [naRayshon] n act of narrating; storytelling; story, account.

narrative [naRativ] n story, connected account of events ~ **narrative** adj narrating; in the form of narration.

narrator [naRayter] n one who tells a story; one who provides narratives linking sections of play etc; character in novel etc through whose words the story is presented.

narrow [naRO] adj of little breadth in proportion to length; constricted, limited; restrictive; barely achieved; prejudiced, bigoted, ignorant; miserly; interpreted strictly, literal; (of inquiry) searching, thorough ~ **narrow** v/i and t become or cause to become narrower; lessen.

narrowly [naROli] adv closely, strictly; only just.

narrow-minded [naRO-mIndid] adj incapable of broad views; prejudiced, bigoted ~ **narrow-mindedness** n.

narrows [naROz] n (pl) narrowest part of anything; narrow passage; strait.

narthex [naartheks] n (archi) long arcaded porch across the west end of early Christian churches.

narwhal [naarwal] n tusked arctic whale.

nary [nairRi] adj (sl and dial) never one.

nasal [nayzal] n of or in the nose; (phon) pronounced with breath passing through the nose ~ **nasal** n (phon) nasal sound; (hist) nosepiece of helmet ~ **nasally** adv.

nasalize [nayzalIz] v/t give nasal pronunciation to ~ **nasalization** [nayzalIzayshon] n.

nascent [naysent] adj about to be or in process of being born; beginning to develop or appear ~ **nascency** n birth.

naso- pref of or in the nose.

nasturtium [nasturshum] n garden plant with pungent flavour and flowers of warm shades.

nasty [naasti] adj unpleasant to taste or smell; disgusting, repulsive; disagreeable; dangerous; spiteful; threatening; difficult to deal with; obscene; a n. bit of work very unpleasant person; turn n. become spiteful or vindictive ~ **nastily** adv ~ **nastiness** n.

natal [naytal] adj of or at birth.

natality [naytaliti] n birthrate.

natant [naytant] adj swimming; (of water-plants) floating ~ **natation** [natayshon] n act of swimming or floating.

nation [nayshon] n large group of people sharing the same cultural and racial heritage and usually living in one area under one government.

national [nashonal] adj of, characteristic of, or common to a nation; owned or subsidized by the state; public, general; n. anthem official song of a state; n. debt total debt owed by a state; n. service compulsory period of training in the armed forces; N. Trust British charitable body for preserving buildings or land of outstanding beauty ~ **national** n citizen of a state.

nationalism [nashonalizm] n love of one's country; desire for the political independence of one's nation; policy striving for this ~ **nationalist** n and adj (supporter) of nationalism ~ **nationalistic** [nashonalistik] adj.

nationality [nashonaliti] n status of belonging to a particular nation; separate existence as a nation.

nationalization [nashonalIzayshon] n acquisition by the state of any property.

nationalize [nashonalIz] v/t transfer (property) from private to state ownership > PDPol.

nationally [nashonali] adv in a national way.

native [naytiv] n one born in and usually also living in a specified place; one of the nation, tribe etc originally inhabiting a colonized country; person of non-European race; indigenous animal or plant; oyster artificially bred in British waters ~ **native** adj pertaining to one's birthplace; belonging to one by birth, congenital; natural, inborn; indigenous; pertaining to the original inhabitants of a colonized country or to their culture, language etc; (of metals) pure, uncombined; go n. (of a white person) live among non-whites and adopt their way of life.

nativity [nativiti] n birth, esp of Christ; artistic representation of incidents associated with Christ's birth; play dealing with these; Christmas; (astrol) horoscope.

natter [nater] v/i and n (coll) chatter, gossip; grumble.

natterjack [naterjak] n species of small toad.

natty [nati] adj neat, smart.

natural [nacheRal] adj of, connected with or arising from external physical world; occurring in nature, not artificially prepared; uncultivated, undomesticated, wild; normal, ordinary; to be expected; not supernatural or miraculous; real, lifelike; spontaneous; innate; characteristic; simple, artless: caused by basic or common instincts; (mus) without sharps or flats; n. child a bastard; n. gas mixture of gaseous hydrocarbons, predominantly methane, found in the earth, usually near deposits of oil; n. history elementary botany and zoology; (ar) scientific study of all nature; n. law ethical rules supposedly innate, universal, and reasonable; n.

philosophy physics; **n. religion** religion and ethics based on reason without divine revelation; **n. selection** evolutionary theory of the survival of the fittest > PDB ~ **natural** *n* (*coll*) one who does something very well without previous training; one who or that which is naturally suitable; (*obs coll*) congenital imbecile; (*mus*) sign (♮) showing that a note is to be neither sharp nor flat.

naturalism [*nache*Ralizm] *n* literary or artistic attempt at completely lifelike representation; realism; (*philos*) rejection of the supernatural; view of life based on reason without revelation; theoretic state of human society arising from free play of instincts.

naturalist [*nache*Ralist] *n* botanist; zoologist; one who practises literary or artistic naturalism; believer in naturalism; dealer in animals as pets; taxidermist ~ **naturalist** *adj* ~ **naturalistic** [nache*Ralistik*] *adj*.

naturalize [*nache*Raliz] *v/t* admit to the position of a native-born subject; introduce and adopt from abroad ~ **naturalization** [nache*Raliz*ayshon] *n*.

naturally [*nache*Rali] *adv* by natural tendency; instinctively; of course.

nature [*naycher*] *n* the external physical world and its processes, forces,· and phenomena; (*cap*) a personification of these; landscape, animals and vegetation, as contrasted with man-made objects, and especially as affecting the aesthetic sense; character, personality; instinctive behaviour; total properties; sort, kind; **in a state of n.** not affected by human or social influence; naked; **n. trail** path through countryside planned to display interesting plants, animals *etc*.

nature-study [*naycher*-studi] *n* elementary botany and zoology.

nature-worship [*naycher*-wurship] *n* cult of gods that personify natural phenomena; excessive enthusiasm for natural scenery.

naturism [*naycher*Rizm] *n* primitive belief in sacredness of natural phenomena > PDP; nudism ~ **naturist** *adj* and *n*.

naught [*nawt*] *n* (*ar*) nothing; nought.

naughty [*nawt*i] *adj* (*of children*) disobedient, troublesome; mischievous; (*ar*) improper, lewd ~ **naughtily** *adv* ~ **naughtiness** *n*.

nausea [*nawsi*-a] *n* unpleasant sensation in the stomach, with tendency to vomit; disgust, loathing ~ **nauseant** *n* and *adj* (*med*) (substance) causing nausea.

nauseate [*nawsi*-ayt] *v/t* make sick; disgust ~ **nauseating** *adj* ~ **nauseatingly** *adv*.

nauseous [*nawsi*-us] *adj* causing nausea; very disagreeable to the taste; loathsome.

nautch [*nawch*] *n* Indian professional dancing.

nautical [*nawt*ikal] *adj* associated with seafaring and navigation; **n. mile** 6,080 ft ~ **nautically** *adv*.

nautilus [*nawt*ilus] *n* a small cephalopod.

naval [*nayv*al] *adj* in or of the navy; performed by the navy; consisting of warships.

nave (1) [*nayv*] *n* central part of wheel, hub.

nave (2) *n* central part of church west of chancel.

navel [*nayv*el] *n* rounded pit in the centre of the abdomen; (*fig*) centre; **n. orange** orange, often seedless, with depression in top; **n. string** umbilical cord.

navigable [*navi*gab'l] *adj* through or over which

a ship can be navigated; that can be steered ~ **navigability** [navigabiliti] *n*.

navigate [*navi*gayt] *v/t* steer (ship, aircraft *etc*) on a set course; pass through or over in a vessel; **navigating officer** officer who directs a ship's course.

navigation [navi*gay*shon] *n* science of directing a ship or aircraft by astronomy, geometry *etc*; act of navigating; shipping in transit; act of voyaging.

navigator [*navi*gayter] *n* officer in charge of a ship's or aircraft's navigation; (*ar*) navvy.

navvy [*navi*] *n* labourer employed on manual digging in constructing roads, railways, sewers *etc*; type of mechanical excavator.

navy [*nayv*i] *n* all warships of a state; fleet of warships; fleet; men required to maintain and fight in a navy.

navy-blue [nayvi-*blOO*] *adj* and *n* dark blue.

navy-cut [*nayv*i-kut] *n* finely sliced cake tobacco.

nay [*nay*] *adv* (*ar*) no ~ **nay** *n* (*ar*) a refusal.

Nazarene [naza*Reen*] *n* early name given to Christians; member of early Jewish-Christian sect; the N. Christ.

Nazarite [*naza*Rit] *n* Hebrew ascetic.

naze [*nayz*] *n* cliff, headland.

Nazi [*naat*si] *n* member of a nationalist, militarist and racialist German party led by Adolf Hitler; person of political views akin to those of Nazis ~ **Nazi** *adj* ~ **Nazism** *n*.

Neanderthal [ni-*andertaal*] *adj* N. man extinct type of man of the Pleistocene period > PDB.

neap [*neep*] *n* tide of comparatively small range occurring twice per lunar month > PDG ~ **neap** *adj*.

Neapolitan [nee-a*polit*an] *n* and *adj* (inhabitant) of Naples; N. ice ice-cream made in layers of different colours and flavours.

near [*neer*] *adj* close, not far from; close in time, degree, or relationship; about to happen; cherished, intimate; resembling; stingy; **n. miss** bomb *etc* that damages a target but does not actually hit it; **n. side** left side ~ **near** *adv* not far; almost ~ **near** *v/i* and *t* approach.

nearby [*neerbI*] *adj* close at hand, adjacent.

nearly [*neer*li] *adv* almost; in a near way.

nearness [*neer*nis] *n* quality of being near.

nearsighted [neers*It*id] *adj* shortsighted.

neat (1) [*neet*] *n* (*ar*) ox, cow, or bull.

neat (2) *adj* well arranged, tidy; simple but attractive; clean; deft, skilful; apt, witty; precise; undiluted, without water ~ **neaten** *v/t* make neat, tidy up.

neath [*neeth*] *prep* (*poet*) beneath.

neatly [*neet*li] *adv* in a neat way.

neatness [*neet*nis] *n* state or quality of being neat.

neb [*neb*] *n* beak; nose; tip.

nebula (*pl* **nebulae**) [*nebewla*] *n* (*astron*) galaxy or galactic material visible as cloudy luminous patch in the sky; area of interstellar dust or gas visible as dark patch in the sky; (*anat*) cloudy white speck on the cornea ~ **nebular** *adj*.

nebulizer [*nebew*lIzer] *n* apparatus for turning liquid into fine spray.

nebulosity [nebew*lositi*] *n* cloudy, faintly luminous appearance; (*fig*) vagueness.

nebulous [*nebew*lus] *adj* of or like a nebula; cloudy, indistinct.

necessary [neseseRi] *adj* indispensable, essential; needed; compulsory; inevitable; pre-determined by logic, natural laws, circumstances *etc* ~ **necessary** *n* that which is indispensable or essential ~ **necessarily** *adv* inevitably.

necessitarian [nesesitairRi-an] *n* one who believes that all human actions are determined by laws of causation, and not by free will.

necessitate [nesesitayt] *v/t* compel, force; render necessary.

necessitous [nesesitus] *adj* poor, in want.

necessity [nesesiti] *n* that which is necessary; compulsion, constraint; that which is essential; circumstances compelling something to exist or occur; fate; poverty; **of n.** inevitably.

neck [nek] *n* part of body between head and shoulders; narrow connecting portion; isthmus; narrow mountain pass; narrow channel; (*sl*) impudence; (*racing*) length of a horse's head; **n. and crop** completely; **get it in the n.** suffer severe punishment, scolding or attack; **n. and n.** exactly abreast; **n. or nothing** recklessly; **pain in the n.** annoying or boring person or thing ~ **neck** *v/i* (*coll*) kiss and caress.

neckband [nekband] *n* band to which collar is fixed.

neckcloth [nek-kloth] *n* cravat.

neckerchief [nekercheef] *n* square of material worn round the neck.

necking [neking] *n* prolonged kissing and caressing.

necklace [neklis] *n* ornamental beads, jewels, or metal band worn round the neck.

necklet [neklet] *n* small necklace; small fur collar clasping the neck.

neckline [neklIn] *n* shape of neck opening of dress, blouse *etc*.

necktie [nektI] *n* narrow strip of material worn over or within the collar and tied in front.

neckwear [nekwair] *n* (*collect*) scarves, neckties and collars.

necro- *pref* connected with death.

necromancy [nekROmansi] *n* magical communication with the dead; evil magic, sorcery ~ **necromancer** *n* ~ **necromantic** *adj*.

necrophilic [nekROfilik] *n* and *adj* (person) morbidly attracted by dead bodies.

necrophily [nekROfili] *n* morbid erotic attraction to dead bodies.

necrophobia [nekROfObi-a] *n* horror of the presence of death or of dead bodies.

necropolis [nekRopolis] *n* large cemetery.

necropsy [nekRopsi] *n* postmortem examination.

necrosis [nekROsis] *n* gangrene; death of tissue, *esp* bone, in living body ~ **necrotic** [nekRotik] *adj*.

nectar [nekter] *n* sugary fluid excreted by flowers; (*Gk myth*) drink of the gods; (*fig*) delicious drink; very sweet drink ~ **nectareous** [nektairRi-us] *adj*.

nectarine [nekteRin] *n* smooth-skinned peach.

nectary [nekteRi] *n* (*bot*) organ secreting nectar in flower; (*zool*) tube through which aphides secrete sweet fluid.

née [nay] *adj* (*Fr*) born; indicating married woman's maiden name.

need [need] *v/t* and *i* require; lack; (*ar*) be in poverty; (*aux*) be obliged to ~ **need** *n* that which

is required or desired; necessity; condition in which something important is lacking; poverty; want; distress; emergency.

needful [needfool] *adj* necessary, requisite ~ **needful** *n* (*coll*) money ~ **needfully** *adv*.

needle [need'l] *n* small slender sharp-pointed steel implement used to draw thread through fabric; slender pointed rod used in knitting; short pointed piece of metal, wood *etc* conveying vibrations of gramophone record to diaphragm; magnetized steel in compass; slender pinnacle; obelisk; leaf of fir or pine tree; point of hypodermic syringe; (*coll*) hypodermic injection; anything thin and sharp; **the n.** (*sl*) nervous alarm or excitement ~ **needle** *v/t* prick or pierce with a needle; (*coll*) annoy; goad; heckle; tease.

needle-bath [need'l-baath] *n* showerbath under fine pressurized jets.

needlebook, needlecase [need'lbook, need'lkays] *n* small decorative holder for sewing needles.

needless [needles] *adj* unnecessary, useless ~ **needlessly** *adv* ~ **needlessness** *n*.

needlewoman [need'lwooman] *n* skilful female sewer; professional sempstress or dressmaker.

needlework [need'lwurk] *n* sewing; embroidery.

needs [needz] *adv* necessarily.

needy [needi] *adj* poor, in want ~ **needily** *adv*.

ne'er [nair] *adv* (*poet*) never.

ne'er-do-well [nair-doo-wel] *n* improvident good-for-nothing person.

nef [nef] *n* ornament in the form of a ship.

nefarious [nefairRi-us] *adj* wicked; unlawful.

negate [nigayt] *v/t* deny; nullify.

negation [nigayshon] *n* act of negating; denial, contradiction; antithesis; absence; destruction.

negative [negativ] *adj* expressing negation; nullifying; forbidding; having no well-marked positive qualities; colourless; not helpful or constructive; (*math*) denoting that which is to be subtracted; (*elect*) of or from the cathode; (*phot*) reversing natural light and dark ~ **negative** *n* word or statement expressing denial, refusal or prohibition; (*elect*) cathode; (*phot*) plate or film bearing negative image; **n. pole** south-seeking pole of magnet ~ **negative** *v/t* disprove; reject, refuse; veto; nullify, cancel; destroy ~ **negatively** *adv* ~ **negativeness** *n*.

negativism [negativizm] *n* rejection of positive standards; refusal to accept constructive suggestions ~ **negativistic** [negativistik] *adj*.

neglect [niglekt] *v/t* leave without proper care; omit carelessly; not notice, disregard ~ **neglect** *n* act of neglecting, lack of proper care; state of being neglected ~ **neglectful** *adj* negligent, careless.

négligé, négligée [neglizhay] *n* woman's soft ornamental dressing-gown; state of being incompletely dressed.

negligence [neglijens] *n* lack of attention or care; behaviour caused by this; disordered appearance ~ **negligent** *adj* careless; remiss ~ **negligently** *adv*.

negligible [neglijib'l] *adj* that can be neglected, unimportant.

negotiable [nigOshab'l] *adj* that can be transferred; that can be negotiated; (*of roads*) over which one can pass ~ **negotiability** [nigOshabiliti] *n*.

negotiate [nigOshi-ayt] v/t and i settle by discussion and bargaining; come or try to come to terms; confer, seek agreement; transact business; pass over or through (an obstacle); obtain cash for (a bill etc) ~ negotiation [nigOshi-ayshon] n act of negotiating; conference, discussion.

negotiator [nigOshi-ayter] n one who negotiates.

Negress [neegRes] n female Negro.

negrillo [negRilO] n African Negro pigmy.

negrito (pl negritoes) [negReetO] n Negro pigmy in Malayo-Polynesian region.

negritude see nigritude.

Negro (pl Negroes) [neegRO] n member of dark-skinned race in Africa or of African origin ~ Negro adj of or concerning Negroes; N. Minstrels troupe of singers and dancers made up as Negroes.

negroid [neegRoid] n and adj (person) with some physical Negro characteristics.

negrophil [neegROfIl] n one who sympathizes with Negroes.

negrophobe [neegROfOb] n one who has intense hatred and fear of Negroes.

negus [neegus] n mixture of wine and hot water sweetened and flavoured.

neigh [nay] v/i utter the cry of a horse ~ neigh n.

neighbour [nayber] n one who lives in the next house; one who lives nearby; member of the same community as oneself; one towards whom one must show friendship ~ neighbour v/t adjoin.

neighbourhood [nayberhood] n state of being near; nearby district, surrounding area; region where one lives; local community; in the n. of about, approximately; close to.

neighbouring [naybeRing] adj adjacent; nearby.

neighbourly [nayberli] adj friendly, kindly, helpful ~ neighbourliness n.

neither [nITHer/neeTHer] pron, adj, adv, conj not either.

nelly (1) [neli] n (sl) effeminate youth.

nelly (2) n (sl) not on your n! certainly not!

nelson [nelson] n (wrestling) hold in which the arm is passed under the opponent's from behind, and the hand presses on the back of his neck.

Nemesis [nemisis] n fated punishment, retribution.

nenuphar [nenewfaar] n waterlily.

neo- pref new, modern.

neoclassical [nee-Oklasikal] adj of or in a revival of classical style in art etc.

neocolonialism [nee-OkolOni-alizm] n the use of economic pressure by a powerful country to dominate a less developed one.

neodymium [nee-OdImi-um] n (chem) rare lanthanide element > PDS.

neolithic [nee-Olithik] adj of the later Stone Age; of the stage in development of civilization when polished stone tools were made > PDB.

neologism [nee-olojizm] n innovation in language; word or idiom with a new meaning; new word or idiom coined or introduced; (theol) new, esp rationalist, doctrine ~ neologist n and adj.

neology [nee-oloji] n use of new terms; new word; new meaning; (theol) rationalism ~ neologize v/i.

neon [nee-on] n inert gas occurring in the atmosphere > PDS; n. light electric lamp containing neon gas in a nearly evacuated tube; n. sign advertisement using neon light.

neophyte [nee-OfIt] n (eccles) new convert; beginner.

neoplasm [nee-Oplazm] n (path) new abnormal growth of tissue > PDB.

neoplatonism [nee-Oplaytonizm] n (philos) blend of Platonism with Eastern mysticism ~ neoplatonic [nee-Oplatonik] adj ~ neoplatonist [nee-Oplaytonist] n.

neoprene [nee-OpReen] n synthetic rubber with high heat and ozone resistance.

nephew [nevew] n son of one's brother or sister; (ar euph) bastard son.

nephoscope [nefOskOp] n instrument for finding altitude and velocity of clouds.

nephrite [nefRIt] n (min) jade.

nephritic [nefRitik] adj (med) affecting the kidneys; suffering from disease of kidneys.

nephritis [nefRItis] n (med) inflammation of the kidneys.

nephro- pref of the kidneys.

nepotic [nepotik] adj of or showing nepotism.

nepotism [nepotizm] n favouritism to one's relatives, esp by unjustifiably promoting them to well-paid posts.

Neptune [neptewn] n (myth) Greek sea-god; (astron) large planet between Uranus and Pluto.

neptunium [neptewni-um] n (chem) a transuranic element > PDS.

nereid [neerRi-id] n (class myth) sea-nymph; (zool) sea-centipede.

nervation [nervayshon] n (bot, zool) arrangement of veins in a leaf or in insect's wing.

nerve [nurv] n bundle of fibres transmitting sensory or motor impulses between brain and body > PDB; (fig) courage; strength; sinew; (coll) impudence, audacity; (bot) vein of leaf; (pl) undue emotional sensitiveness; irritability, restlessness; fear; n. gas (mil) any of various deadly gases acting on the nervous system; get on the nerves of annoy; war of nerves campaign of rumour, propaganda etc to demoralize an enemy ~ nerve v/t give courage to; strengthen.

nerve-cell [nurv-sel] n conductive cell in nervous tissue, neuron > PDB.

nerve-centre [nurv-senter] n ganglion > PDB; (fig) centre from which complex activities are controlled.

nerveless [nurvles] adj weak, without vigour; numb; (bot, ent) without nervures; (biol) without nervous system.

nerve-racking [nurv-Raking] adj causing intense anxiety, suspense or irritation.

nerve-strain [nurv-stRayn] n undue strain on nervous system; (coll) emotional tension.

nervine [nurvIn] n and adj (medicine) acting on the nerves.

nervous [nurvus] adj of or affecting the nerves; frightened, timid; tense, on edge; highly strung; muscular; strong; vigorous; n. breakdown (coll) illness characterized by emotional or mental abnormality; n. system mechanism coordinating an animal's activities > PDB ~ nervously adv ~ nervousness n.

nervure [nurvewr] n (bot) vein of leaf; (ent) rib of insect's wing.

nervy [*nurvi*] *adj* easily excited; irritable; frightened.

nescience [*nesi-ens*] *n* lack of knowledge ~ **nescient** *adj* ignorant; agnostic.

ness [*nes*] *n* headland, promontory.

Nessie [*nesi*] *n* (*coll*) an alleged prehistoric monster inhabiting Loch Ness in Scotland.

nest [*nest*] *n* structure built by bird to shelter its eggs and young; shelter built by other egg-laying animals; breeding-place; home; swarm; brood; cluster, group; set of tables or boxes of graded sizes made to fit one into the other ~ **nest** *v/i* make a nest; search for birds' nests.

nest-egg [*nest-eg*] *n* real or dummy egg left in hen's nest to stimulate laying; money saved up.

nestle [*nes'l*] *v/i* settle down cosily; press closely against; lie in sheltered position.

nestling [*nesling*] *n* young bird which cannot yet fly.

Nestorian [*nestawRi-an*] *n* and *adj* (heretic) maintaining that the divine and the human personalities of Christ did not merge.

net (1) [*net*] *n* mesh of knotted cord, thread, wire *etc* with mesh-openings of various sizes; piece of this used to catch fish, birds *etc*; piece of this used as protective covering; strip of this dividing tennis court or ping-pong table, or surrounding goal in certain games ~ **net** (*pres/part* **netting**, *p/t* and *p/part* **netted**) *v/t* and *i* catch in a net, trap, snare; cover with a net; make a net; (*games*) send (ball) into the net.

net (2), **nett** *adj* not subject to deduction; remaining as profit after all deductions have been made; (*of weights*) not including packaging ~ **net** (*pres/part* **netting**, *p/t* and *p/part* **netted**) *v/t* make as clear profit.

netball [*netbawl*] *n* team-game whose aim is to throw a large ball through a round net on a tall pole.

nether [*neTHer*] *adj* lower, underneath; **n. limbs** legs; **n. world** world of the dead; hell.

nethermost [*neTHermost*] *adj* lowest.

netsuke [*netsookay*] *n* Japanese belt-ornament of carved ivory or wood.

nett *see* **net** (2).

netting [*neting*] *n* act of making network; piece of net.

nettle [*net'l*] *n* plant with stinging hairs on leaves and stalk; **grasp the n.** deal promptly and firmly with a difficulty ~ **nettle** *v/t* provoke. irritate.

nettlerash [*net'lRash*] *n* allergic blistering.

network [*netwurk*] *n* net, *esp* of decorative pattern; interlaced lines; system of interlinked streets, canals *etc*; group of interlinked radio stations; (*fig*) group of persons sharing an aim, interest *etc* and frequently communicating with or helping each other.

neum, neume [*newm*] *n* (*mus*) sign in medieval notation showing the note(s) to which a syllable of vocal music was to be sung > PDM.

neural [*newrRal*] *adj* (*anat*) concerned with the nervous system > PDB.

neuralgia [*newRalji-a*] *n* disorder of a nerve causing acute but not usually continuous pain ~ **neuralgic** *adj*.

neurasthenia [*newrRastheeni-a*] *n* excessive fatigue and weakness, both bodily and mental > PDP ~ **neurasthenic** [*newrRasthenik*] *adj*.

neuritis [*newRItis*] *n* inflammation of a nerve.

neuro- *pref* of nerves.

neurology [*newRoloji*] *n* study of the structure and functions of the nervous system > PDP ~ **neurological** [*newROlojikal*] *adj* ~ **neurologist** [*newRolojist*] *n*.

neuron [*newrRon*] *n* nerve-cell > PDB.

neuropath [*newrROpath*] *n* one suffering from nervous disease.

neuropathology [*newrROpatholoji*] *n* study of nervous diseases ~ **neuropathologist** *n*.

neuropathy [*newRopathi*] *n* nervous disease.

neurosis [*newROsis*] *n* (*psych*) any psychic disorder caused by mental abnormality or conflict, *usu* accompanied by fears, obsessions *etc* > PDP; (*med*) functional nervous disorder.

neurotic [*newRotik*] *adj* of neurosis; of the nervous system; (*coll*) abnormally sensitive, morbidly emotional; obsessive ~ **neurotic** *n* one who suffers from neurosis ~ **neurotically** *adv*.

neuter [*newter*] *adj* (*gramm*) neither masculine nor feminine; intransitive; (*biol*) sexless; (*rare*) neutral ~ **neuter** *n* animal deprived of sexual organs; animal with sexual organs undeveloped; (*gramm*) word or form of neuter gender ~ **neuter** *v/t* deprive (animal) of sexual organs; castrate.

neutral [*newtRal*] *adj* taking neither side in a conflict; uninvolved; impartial; without distinguishing characteristics; (*biol*) neuter; asexual; (*of gears*) disengaged; (*chem*) neither acid nor alkali; (*elect*) neither positive nor negative ~ **neutral** *n* one who takes neither side; person, group or nation that takes no part in a war; (*of gears*) state of being disengaged.

neutralism [*newtRalizm*] *n* systematic neutrality in political conflicts.

neutrality [*newtRaliti*] *n* non-participation in a war between other states > PDP.

neutralize [*newtRaliz*] *v/t* render neutral; officially declare (an area) to be neutral territory; render ineffectual, counteract; render inert ~ **neutralization** [*newtRalizayshon*] *n*.

neutrally [*newtRali*] *adv* in a neutral way.

neutrino [*newtReenO*] *n* (*phys*) uncharged elementary particle with zero rest mass > PDS.

neutro- *pref* neuter; neutral.

neutron [*newtRon*] *n* electrically uncharged particle of slightly greater mass than the proton > PDS.

never [*never*] *adv* at no time; not at all; **well I n.!** exclamation of surprise.

nevermore [*nevermawr*] *adv* never again.

never-never [*never-never*] *adj* **N. Land** (*Aust*) North Queensland; (*coll*) an impossible Utopia; **on the n.** (**scheme**) (*coll*) by hire-purchase.

nevertheless [*neverTHeles*] *adv* in spite of that.

new [*new*] *adj* only recently existing, done or made; not known before; just discovered or acquired; inexperienced; fresh; modern; unfamiliar, novel; of the first phase of a cycle; **n. moon** moon in its first quarter; **n. penny** British coin introduced in 1971, worth one hundredth of a pound; **N. Style** reformed calendar introduced in 1582 and adopted in England in 1751; **N. Testament** later and exclusively Christian section of Bible; **n. world** North America; **n. year** first few days of January; day on which a year begins;

N. Year's Day 1st January ~ **new** *adv* lately, afresh.

newblown [new*blОn*] *adj* just blossoming.

newcomer [new*k*umer] *n* person just arrived.

newel [new*el*] *n* (*bui*) post in a flight of stairs carrying the ends of outer string and handrail and supporting them at a corner; (*bui*) stone column carrying the inner ends of the treads of a spiral stone staircase.

newfangled [new*fang*-g'ld] *adj* of extreme and unpleasing modernity.

Newfoundland [new*fundland*/new*fownd*-land] *n* large breed of dog.

new-laid [new-*layd*] *adj* (*of egg*) quite fresh.

newly [new*li*] *adv* recently; afresh, again.

newly-weds [new*li-wedz*] *n* (*pl*) (*coll*) recently married couple.

newmarket [new*maarket*] *n* a card-game.

news [new*z*] *n* recent and interesting events; fresh information; tidings; broadcast information on current events; **n. editor** newspaper editor in charge of news items.

newsagent [new*z*ayjint] *n* shopkeeper who sells newspapers.

newscast [new*z*kaast] *n* radio or TV news bulletin.

newscaster [new*z*kaaster] *n* reader of news bulletins on radio or television.

newsflash [new*z*flash] *n* (*rad, TV*) brief news item interrupting another programme.

newshawk [new*z*hawk] *n* (*coll*) journalist.

newsletter [new*z*leter] *n* pamphlet or sheet giving news to members of a specified group.

newspaper [new*z*payper] *n* daily or weekly publication containing news and articles on current topics.

newspeak [new*speek*] *n* emotionally charged language used in politics to rouse irrational approval or disapproval.

newsprint [new*z*pRint] *n* paper on which newspapers are printed.

newsreel [new*z*Reel] *n* short film showing recent events.

newsroom [new*z*Room] *n* room where newspapers can be read; room in newspaper office where reports are edited.

news-theatre [new*z*-thi-ater] *n* cinema continuously showing newsreels and short films.

news-vendor [new*z*-vender] *n* man who sells newspapers in the street.

newsy [new*zi*] *adj* full of news.

newt [new*t*] *n* small tailed amphibian.

newton [new*ton*] *n* unit of force, that which gives a mass of 1 kilogram an acceleration of 1 metre per second per second.

next [nekst] *adj* nearest in space, relationship or degree; adjoining; following or about to follow immediately after; **the n. man** (*coll*) any average or typical person; **n. to** (*fig*) almost ~ **next** *adv* nearest; immediately after ~ **next** *n* that which is next ~ **next** *prep* nearest to.

next-of-kin [nekst-ov-*kin*] *n* nearest blood relative.

nexus [*nek*sus] *n* interdependence of two elements, items or events; connexion; group of interconnected items; **causal n.** necessary connexion between cause and effect.

nib [nib] *n* point of a pen; split metal pen-point inserted into penholder; (*bui*) downward projecting lug at upper end of a tile; (*pl*) crushed cocoa-beans; **his nibs** (*sl*) smart gentleman.

nibble [nib'l] *v/t* and *i* eat by small bites; bite gently or with hesitation; **n. at** (*fig*) remain undecided over (plan *etc*) though attracted by it ~ **nibble** *n* act of nibbling; small or gentle bite.

niblick [nib*lik*] *n* golf club with lofted head to lift ball out of bunker.

nice [nIs] *adj* pleasant, attractive; socially acceptable, well-bred; kind, friendly; dainty; fastidious, discriminating; needing careful thought ~ **nicely** *adv* ~ **niceness** *n*.

Nicene [nI*seen*] *adj* of or at the church councils held at Nicaea in A.D. 325 and 787; **N. Creed** confession of faith drawn up at first of these.

nicety [nI*siti*] *n* accuracy, precision; exactitude; subtle distinction or detail; **to a n.** with precision.

niche [nich] *n* small recess in a wall to contain a statue; (*fig*) suitable and pleasant career, appointment *etc*.

nick (1) [nik] *n* small notch or gash; favourable throw at dice; **in good n.** (*coll*) in good health or condition; **in the n. of time** only just in time; at the perfect moment ~ **nick** *v/t* and *i* cut a notch in; (*sl*) steal; **n. in** slip quickly into (another's) place.

Nick (2) *n* Old N. the Devil.

nick (3) *n* (*sl*) prison.

nickel [*nik*el] *n* hard silvery-white magnetic metal > PDS; (*US*) five-cent piece.

nickelodeon [nikel*Оdi*-on] *n* (*US coll*) jukebox.

nicker (1) [*nik*er] *v/i* and *n* (*Scots*) neigh.

nicker (2) *n* (*sl*) guinea; pound sterling.

nick-nack se*e* **knick-knack**.

nickname [*nik*naym] *n* extra name given as sign of affection, joke, or mockery ~ **nickname** *v/t* give a nickname to.

nicotine [*nik*Оteen] *n* colourless, intensely poisonous oily alkaloid found in tobacco leaves.

nicotinic [niko*tinik*] *adj* pertaining to nicotine; **n. acid** member of vitamin B complex found in meat > PDB.

nicotinism [*nik*otinizm] *n* diseased condition caused by too much tobacco.

nictitate [*nik*titayt] *v/i* blink; **nictitating membrane** transparent fold of skin forming a third eyelid.

niece [nees] *n* daughter of one's brother or sister.

niello (*pl* **nielli, niellos**) [ni-*elО*] *n* black mixture of lead, sulphur and metals to fill in engraved patterns on gold or silver > PDAA; work inlaid with this ~ **niello** *v/t* inlay with niello.

niff [nif] *v/i* (*sl*) smell nasty ~ **niff** *n*.

nifty [*nifti*] *adj* (*coll*) smart, fine; clever; smelly; swift, agile.

niggard [*niger*d] *n* miser; stingy person ~ **niggard** *adj* ~ **niggardly** *adv*.

nigger [*niger*] *n* (*coll, pej*) Negro; coloured man; very dark brown; **n. in the woodpile** secret malevolent influence; **work like a n.** work very hard ~ **nigger** *adj* of or like a Negro; very dark brown.

nigger-driver [*niger*-dRIver] *n* (*coll*) one who forces others to overwork.

nigger-lover [*niger*-luver] *n* (*coll, pej*) one who favours Negro emancipation or civil rights.

niggle [nig'l] *v/i* be fussy over petty details ~

niggling *adj* too fussy; small but persistent; petty, finicking.

nigh [*nI*] *adj, adv* and *prep* (*ar* and *poet*) near.

night [*nIt*] *n* period of darkness between twilight and dawn; darkness; (*fig*) death; ignorance; despair; adversity; **n. and day** unceasingly; **have a good n.** sleep well; **make a n. of it** spend all night in amusements.

night-blindness [nIt-*blInd*nis] *n* difficulty in seeing things in moderate darkness > PDP.

nightcap [*nIt*kap] *n* cap formerly worn in bed; drink taken just before going to bed.

nightclub [*nIt*klub] *n* club for drinking, dancing, and cabaret shows.

nightdress [*nIt*dRes] *n* woman's loose garment worn in bed.

nightfall [*nIt*fawl] *n* dusk.

nightgown [*nIt*gown]·*n* nightdress.

nightie [*nIt*i] *n* (*coll abbr*) nightdress.

nightingale [*nIt*ing-gayl] *n* a small migratory song-bird; (*fig*) excellent singer.

nightjar [*nIt*jaar] *n* type of nocturnal bird.

night-life [*nIt*-lIf] *n* entertainments available in a town at night.

nightlight [*nIt*lIt] *n* dim light kept burning at night.

nightly [*nIt*li] *adj* and *adv* (happening) every night.

nightmare [*nIt*mair] *n* vivid dream marked by acute anxiety; horrible experience; obsessive fear; (*ar*) demon that oppresses sleepers ~ **nightmarish** *adj* like a nightmare.

nightschool [*nIt*skOOl] *n* institution offering evening educational courses.

nightshade [*nIt*shayd] *n* name of various plants with poisonous berries.

nightshift [*nIt*shift] *n* gang of workmen employed during the night.

nightshirt [*nIt*shurt] *n* long shirt worn by men in bed.

night-soil [*nIt*-soil] *n* sewage, *esp* as manure.

night-time [*nIt*-tIm] *n* night.

nightwalker [*nIt*wawker] *n* prostitute.

nightwatch [*nIt*woch] *n* body of men on guard or look-out duty by night; period of keeping watch by night; hour of changing watch by night; (*pl*) sleepless period of the night ~ **nightwatchman** *n* man employed to stay on guard in a building all night.

nighty [*nIt*i] *n* (*coll*) nightdress.

nignog [*nig*nog] *n* (*pej sl*) Negro or other darkskinned person.

nigrescence [nI*gRes*ens] *n* blackness; process of turning black ~ **nigrescent** *adj*.

nigritude, negritude [*nig*Ritewd] *n* blackness; Negro culture.

nihilism [*nI*-ilizm/*nI*hilizm] *n* complete scepticism; systematic rejection of all beliefs and institutions; anarchic revolutionary movement in Tsarist Russia > PDPol ~ **nihilist** *n* and *adj* ~ **nihilistic** [nI-il*ist*ik/nIhil*ist*ik] *adj*.

nil [*nil*] *n* nothing.

nimble [*nimb*'l] *adj* quick-moving, agile; alert ~ **nimbly** *adv* ~ **nimbleness** *n*.

nimbus [*nimb*us] *n* rain-cloud; halo.

niminy-piminy [nimini-*pim*ini] *adj* too dainty or affected; prudish.

nincompoop [*ning*kumpOOp] *n* fool, simpleton.

nine [*nIn*] *n* and *adj* cardinal number next above

eight; symbol of this, 9; **the N.** the muses; **dressed up to the nines** very smartly dressed; **n. days' wonder** cause of short-lived excitement.

ninefold [*nIn*fOld] *adj* and *adv* nine times as much or as many; nine parts.

ninepins [*nIn*pinz] *n* game in which players bowl a ball at nine wooden skittles.

nineteen [*nIn*teen] *n* and *adj* nine more than ten; **n. to the dozen** very fast and copiously.

nineteenth [*nIn*teenth] *n* and *adj* (that) which follows 18 others in a series; (that) which is one of 19 equal parts; **the n. hole** (*coll*) the bar in a golf club-house.

ninetieth [*nIn*ti-eth] *n* and *adj* (that) which follows 89 others in a series; (that) which is one of ninety equal parts.

ninety [*nIn*ti] *n* and *adj* nine times ten; **the nineties** ninth decade of a life or a century, *esp* of the 19th century.

ninny [*nin*i] *n* simpleton, fool.

ninth [*nInth*] *n* and *adj* (that) which follows eight others in a series; (that) which is one of nine equal parts ~ **ninthly** *adv*.

niobium [nI-*Obi*-um] *n* (*chem*) rare metallic element > PDS ~ **niobic** *adj*.

nip (1) (*pres/part* **nipping**, *p/t* and *p/part* **nipped**) [*nip*] *v/t* pinch or bite sharply; check growth of, *esp* by cold; blight; clip; (*fig*) check; depress; (*sl*) steal; catch in the act; **n. along** go quickly; **n. in** quickly take another's place; interrupt; **n. in the bud** check at an early stage; **n. out of** move quickly from ~ **nip** *n* pinch; bite; sudden frost; coldness in the air.

nip (2) *n* small quantity of spirits; a sip ~ **nip** (*pres/part* **nipping**, *p/t* and *p/part* **nipped**) *v/i* take frequent small drinks of spirits.

nipper [*nip*er] *n* one who or that which nips; large claw of crab or lobster; (*sl*) small boy; (*pl*) small pincers.

nipping [*nip*ing] *adj* (*of wind*) keen and cold.

nipple [*nip*'l] *n* teat of woman's breast; artificial teat of feeding-bottle; small projection, *esp* one through which grease is injected into a machine.

nippy [*nip*i] *adj* quick, swift, active; frosty, cold ~ **nippy** *n* (*sl*) waitress.

nirvana [nur*vaa*na] *n* (*Buddhism*) discovery of deep wisdom by destruction of mental and emotional obstacles; inexpressible state after death; (*non-Buddhist*) absorption of the soul in the divine.

nisi [*nI*sI] *adj* (*leg*) becoming valid after a certain interval unless something intervenes to prevent it.

Nissen [*nis*en] *adj* **N. hut** tunnel-shaped hut of corrugated iron.

nit (1) [*nit*] *n* egg of a louse on human hair.

nit (2) *n* (*sl*) nitwit, fool.

nit-picking [nit-*pik*ing] *n* (*fig, coll*) petty faultfinding, constant criticism of minor details.

nitrate [*nIt*Rayt] *n* salt of nitric acid ~ **nitrate** *v/t* treat with nitric acid or a nitrate ~ **nitration** *n*.

nitre [*nIt*er] *n* potassium nitrate; saltpetre.

nitric [*nIt*Rik] *adj* pertaining to nitre; **n. acid** colourless, corrosive, acid liquid > PDS.

nitrification [nItRif*ikay*shon] *n* conversion, by the action of bacteria, of nitrogen compounds from animal and plant waste into nitrates in the soil.

nitro- *pref* nitric; containing nitrogen.

nitrobenzene [nItRObenzeen] *n* almond-scented oily liquid used in perfumery > PDS.

nitrocellulose [nItROselewlOz] *n* a solid high explosive used with nitroglycerin in gelatin explosives, also a constituent of lacquers, plastic wood and some glues > PDS.

nitrogen [nItrOjen] *n* colourless gaseous element, main constituent of air; **n. cycle** circulation of nitrogen atoms through action of living organisms; **n. fixation** conversion of atmospheric nitrogen into organic nitrogen compounds > PDB, PDS ~ **nitrogenous** [nItROjenus] *adj* of, containing nitrogen.

nitroglycerin [nItROgliseRin] *n* a liquid high explosive > PDS.

nitrous [nItRus] *adj* of or containing nitrogen; **n. oxide** laughing-gas.

nitty-gritty [niti-gRiti] *n* (*coll*) practical details or facts, the core of a problem.

nitwit [nitwit] *n* (*sl*) fool.

nix (1) [niks] *n* (*sl*) nothing; no.

nix (2), **nixie** *n* water-sprite.

no (1) [nO] *adj* not any, not one, none; hardly any; **n. go, n. way** (*coll*) no use, impossible ~ **no** *adv* not at all; not; neither; not in any degree, respect or way; **n. can do** (*sl*) impossible; **n. more** not any more; never again; dead; destroyed ~ **no** *interj* exclamation expressing refusal, denial, or forbidding ~ **no** (*pl* noes) *n* act of saying no; (*pl*) those voting against a motion.

no (2) *n* stylized form of Japanese dance drama.

Noah's ark [nO-az-aark] *n* toy in the form of a small model of the Ark with human and animal figures.

nob [nob] *n* (*sl*) head; fine gentleman; (*cribbage*) knave of same suit as the card turned up ~ **nob** (*pres/part* **nobbing**, *p/t* and *p/part* **nobbed**) *v/t* (*sl*) hit on the head.

no-ball [nO-bawl] *n* (*cricket*) ball not bowled in accordance with the rules.

nobble [nob'l] *v/t* (*sl*) prevent (horse) from winning race by drugging or injuring it, or by bribing its jockey; acquire dishonestly; cheat; kidnap ~ **nobbler** *n*.

nobbut [nobut] *adv* (*dial*) nothing but.

nobby [nobi] *adj* (*sl*) smart, stylish.

nobelium [nObeli-um] *n* (*chem*) a transuranic element > PDS.

nobiliary [nObili-eRi] *adj* indicating noble rank; of the nobility.

nobility [nObiliti] *n* quality of being noble; body of those with hereditary titles.

noble [nOb'l] *adj* having or showing high ideals, courage, selflessness *etc*; famous for courage or virtue; admirable; stately, impressive; of high rank; belonging to a family with a hereditary title; (*chem*) unreactive ~ **noble** *n* one who has a hereditary title, peer; former English gold coin.

nobleman [nOb'lman] *n* peer, noble.

nobleness [nOb'lnis] *n* quality of being noble.

noblesse [nObles] *n* class of nobility; **n. oblige** [nObles-Obleezh] high rank entails obligations.

noblewoman [nOb'l-wooman] *n* woman of noble birth.

nobly [nObli] *adv* in a noble way.

nobody [nObodi] *n* no person at all; person of no importance.

nock [nok] *n* notch in arrow to take the bowstring;

notch at each end of a bow; (*naut*) upper forecorner of boom-sail ~ **nock** *v/t* cut a notch in; adjust (arrow) to bowstring.

nocti- *pref* of or by night.

noctule [noktewl] *n* (*zool*) largest British species of bat.

nocturn [nokturn] *n* (*RC*) office recited at night; (*mus, arts*) nocturne.

nocturnal [nokturnal] *adj* of or at night; active by night.

nocturne [nokturn] *n* (*mus*) short pensive lyrical piece, *esp* for piano > PDM; (*arts*) night-scene.

nod (*pres/part* **nodding**, *p/t* and *p/part* **nodded**) [nod] *v/i* and *t* move the head briskly down as sign of assent or as curt greeting; droop the head when drowsy: be inattentive or off one's guard; make a mistake by inattention; **n. through** accept (proposal) quickly and without discussion; **nodding acquaintance** slight acquaintance ~ **nod** *n* act of nodding; **on the n.** agreed to without discussion; unopposed; unnoticed (*US sl*) on credit.

nodal [nOdal] *adj* of or like a node; **n. point** point of conveyance > PDS; point of rest in vibrating body ~ **nodality** [nOdaliti] *n*.

noddle [nod'l] *n* (*coll*) the head.

node [nOd] *n* joint on plant-stem from which leaves spring; knob on branch or trunk; knobbly swelling; point of intersection; point of rest in vibrating body; (*astron*) point at which the orbit of a planet intersects the ecliptic.

nodical [nOdikal] *adj* (*astron*) of the nodes.

nodose [nOdOz] *adj* (*bot*) full of nodes, knotty.

nodosity [nOdositi] *n* quality of being nodose.

nodular [nodewlar] *adj* of or having nodes; having nodules; like a nodule.

nodule [nodewl] *n* small rounded lump; lump of mineral in another substance; knob on plant stem or root ~ **nodulose** *adj* ~ **nodulous** *adj*.

nodus [nOdus] *n* node; (*fig*) complication.

nog (1) [nog] *n* (*bui*) nailing block for fixing joinery.

nog (2) *n* strong ale egg-flip.

noggin [nogin] *n* mug, cup; small quantity of liquor; (*US*) bucket.

nogging [noging] *n* (*bui*) brickwork infilling.

no-go [nO-gO] *adj* (*of an area*) where entry is prevented by the inhabitants; where outsiders must not or dare not go.

no-good [nO-good] *adj* and *n* useless, worthless (person).

nohow [nOhow] *adv* (*sl*) by no means.

noise [noiz] *n* loud or unpleasant sound; (*ar*) rumour; (*rad*) undesirable extraneous background sounds or signals > PDEl; **big n.** (*sl*) person of importance ~ **noise** *v/t* pass (news) round in talk.

noisome [noisum] *adj* harmful; unhealthy; disgusting; having a bad smell ~ **noisomely** *adv* ~ **noisomeness** *n*.

noisy [noizi] *adj* making a loud noise; clamorous; rowdy ~ **noisily** *adv* ~ **noisiness** *n*.

nomad [nOmad] *n* one who habitually wanders; member of tribe that meanders in search of fresh pasture > PDG ~ **nomad** *adj*.

nomadic [nOmadik] *adj* always wandering.

no-man's-land [nO-manz-land] *n* piece of unowned land; (*mil*) space between front trenches of two opposed armies.

nomenclature [nOmenklacher] *n* system of naming, *esp* for classification; list of names, catalogue.

nominal [*nom*inal] *adj* existing in name only; very slight ~ **nominally** *adv*.

nominalism [*nom*inalizm] *n* doctrine that universal or abstract words have no realities corresponding to them ~ **nominalist** *n* and *adj* ~ **nominalistic** [nominal*i*stik] *adj*.

nominate [*nom*inayt] *v/t* appoint to a certain office; propose as candidate.

nomination [nomin*ay*shon] *n* act of nominating.

nominative [*nom*inativ] *n* and *adj* (*gramm*) (case) indicating the subject of a sentence.

nominator [*nom*inayter] *n* one who nominates.

nominee [nomin*ee*] *n* person nominated.

nomogram [*nO*mogRam] *n* type of graph from which the value of one variable can be read off when the values of two other variables are known.

non- *pref* not, contrary of.

nonage [*nO*nij] *n* state of not being of age, minority; early period, immaturity.

nonagenarian [nonajen*airR*i-an] *n* person between ninety and one hundred years old.

non-aligned [non-al*I*nd] *adj* taking neither side in international political conflict, *esp* that between Communist and capitalist nations ~ **non-alignment** *n*.

nonary [*nO*neRi] *n* group of nine; **n. scale** (*math*) scale of notation based on nine.

nonce [*nons*] *n* **for the n.** temporarily, for once.

nonce-word [*nons*-wurd] *n* word invented for a special context and used only once.

nonchalance [*non*shalans] *n* lack of anxiety or emotion, coolness ~ **nonchalant** *adj* ~ **nonchalantly** *adv*.

non-collegiate [non-kol*ee*jit] *n* and *adj* (university student) not a member of a recognized college.

non-combatant [non-*kom*batant] *adj* and *n* (pertaining to) a member of the armed forces whose duties do not include fighting; a civilian.

non-com [non-*kom*] *n* (*coll*) non-commissioned officer.

non-commissioned [non-kom*ish*ond] *adj* not holding a commission; **n. officer** one having the rank of sergeant or corporal in the armed forces without a commission from the Crown.

non-committal [non-kom*it*al] *adj* concealing one's opinions or allegiance; refusing to take sides, neutral.

non-conductor [non-kon*duk*ter] *n* substance which does not allow the passage of heat or electricity.

Nonconformist [non-kon*fawr*mist] *n* and *adj* (member) of Protestant body separated from Church of England; (one) not conforming to an established church or to accepted opinions *etc*.

nonconformity [non-kon*fawr*miti] *n* refusal to conform.

nondescript [*non*diskRipt] *adj* without distinguishing features; vague; insignificant; not easily classified ~ **nondescript** *n*.

none [*nun*] *pron* no one; not one; not any ~ **none** *adv* not at all, in no way.

non-effective [non-i*fek*tiv] *n* and *adj* (person) not fit for active service.

nonentity [non*en*titi] *n* person of no importance; that which does not exist; state of not existing.

nones [*nOnz*] *n* (*eccles*) daily office said formerly at 3 p.m.

nonesuch, nonsuch [*nun*such] *n* thing or person that has no equal; a species of lucerne.

nonet [*nO*net] *n* musical composition for nine voices or instruments; nine performers for this.

non-event [non-i*vent*] *n* an event publicized beforehand as important, but which proves trivial or fails to occur.

non-flammable [non-*flam*ab'l] *adj* not inflammable.

non-intervention [non-interv*en*shon] *n* policy of not intervening in affairs of other nations.

non-moral [non-*mo*Ral] *adj* not capable of being judged as either moral or immoral; outside the application or applicability of moral standards.

nonpareil [nonpa*Rel*] *adj* having no equal, unrivalled, unique ~ **nonpareil** *n* person or thing with no equal; paragon; kind of apple.

non-party [non-*paar*ti] *adj* not controlled by or committed to a political party.

non-person [non-*pur*son] *n* person deprived of legal rights and of contact with others as political punishment.

nonplus (*pres/part* **nonplussing,** *p/t* and *p/part* **nonplussed**) [non*plus*] *v/t* disconcert, baffle; reduce to perplexed silence ~ **nonplus** *n* state of perplexity; quandary.

non-resident [non-*Re*zident] *n* and *adj* (person) not residing in a particular place.

non-resistance [non-*Ri*zistens] *n* refusal to resist aggression, *usu* for moral reasons ~ **non-resistant** *n* and *adj*.

nonsense [*non*sens] *n* meaningless words; ridiculously unreasonable idea, belief or behaviour; absurdity; **n. verses** intentionally illogical or incomprehensible verses ~ **nonsensical** [non*sen*sikal] *adj*.

non sequitur [non-*sek*witer] *n* (*Lat*) (*log*) a logical fallacy in which the conclusion does not follow from the premises.

non-skid [non-*skid*] *adj* designed to prevent skidding.

non-slip [non-*slip*] *adj* designed to prevent slipping.

nonsmoker [non*smO*ker] *n* person who does not smoke; railway compartment where smoking is prohibited ~ **nonsmoking** *adj*.

nonstarter [non*staar*ter] *n* horse which does not compete in a race it was entered for; person who has no chance of competing successfully.

non-stick [non-stik] *adj* (*of cooking pans*) coated with a substance to which food does not stick.

nonstop [non*stop*] *n* express train not stopping at intermediate stations; journey made without a halt ~ **nonstop** *adj* and *adv* without stopping.

nonsuch see **nonesuch**.

nonsuit [non*sewt*] *n* (*leg*) quashing of a suit when the plaintiff has failed to make out a case ~ **nonsuit** *v/t* stop the plaintiff's suit.

non-U [non-*yew*] *adj* (*coll*) not belonging to or used by the upper class; typical of middle or lower class in words, manners *etc*.

non-union [non-*ewni*-on] *adj* outside a trade union.

non-user [non-*ewzer*] *n* (*leg*) failure to exercise a right, by which it may lapse.

non-violence [non-*vI*-Olens] *n* use of conspicuous but peaceful means of public protest against political or social injustice; refusal to use violence in self-defence ~ **non-violent** *adj*.

noodle (1) [*n*OO*d'l*] *n* fool.

noodle (2) *n* small strip of plain cooked dough served in soup.

nook [*nook*] *n* narrow corner; comfortable sheltered spot; secluded place; recess.

noon [*n*OO*n*] *n* midday; (*fig*) culmination ~ **noon** *adj* of or at noon.

noonday [*n*OO*n*day] *n* and *adj* noon.

noontide [*n*OO*n*tId] *n* noon.

noose [*n*OO*s*] *n* loop with running knot which tightens as the cord is pulled; loop on hangman's rope; (*fig*) execution by hanging ~ **noose** *v/t* catch in a noose.

nopal [*n*O*pal*] *n* a cactus plant; a prickly pear.

nope [*n*O*p*] *interj* (*coll, esp US*) no.

nor (1) [*nawr*] *conj* used *correlatively with* **neither**; *at the beginning of a sentence* and . . . not.

nor' (2) (*abbr*) north (in compounds like *nor'-east*).

Nordic [*nawr*dik] *adj* of or like the tall fair race of Scandinavia.

Norfolk [*nawr*fok] *adj* **N. jacket** loose jacket with pleats and belt.

norland [*nawr*land] *n* northern country.

norm [*nawrm*] *n* what is normal or average; recognized standard; pattern; daily standard of output to be reached by a worker.

normal [*nawr*mal] *adj* conforming to usual standard; average; natural; not diseased, malformed or spoilt; (*math*) perpendicular; (*chem*) (*of a solution*) containing one equivalent weight of solute in a litre of solution; **n. school** (*obs*) institution for training primary teachers ~ **normal** *n* that which is normal; (*math*) perpendicular line.

normalcy [*nawr*malsi] *n* normality in social conditions.

normality [naw*r*maliti] *n* state of being normal; norm; (*chem*) concentration of a solution in terms of a normal solution.

normalize [*nawr*malIz] *v/t* bring into conformity with normal usage; (*metal*) treat steel by heating to relieve internal stresses > PDS.

normally [*nawr*mali] *adv* in a normal way; usually.

Norman [*nawr*man] *n* member of the French-Scandinavian race which conquered England in 1066; inhabitant of Normandy; French dialect spoken by these ~ **Norman** *adj* of the Normans; **N. architecture** 11th- and 12th-century style of English architecture.

normative [*nawr*mativ] *adj* establishing a standard; laying down rules of accepted usage.

norn [*nawrn*] *n* (*Norse myth*) a goddess of fate.

Norse [*nawrs*] *n* and *adj* (language) of medieval Scandinavia, *esp* Norway and Iceland ~ **Norseman** *n* inhabitant of medieval Scandinavia.

north [*nawrth*] *n* compass direction opposite to the midday sun; northern part of a country or of the earth ~ **north** *adj* in, of or from the north; towards the north ~ **north** *adv* towards the north.

north-east [nawrth-*eest*] *n, adj* and *adv* (direction) midway between north and east; **N. Passage** sea route along north coast of Europe and Asia ~ **north-easter** *n* strong wind from north-east ~

north-easterly *adj* ~ **north-eastern** *adj* ~ **north-eastward** *n, adj* and *adv* (direction) towards the north-east.

norther [*nawr*THer] *n* cold violent north wind sometimes experienced in the southern United States > PDG.

northerly [*nawr*THerli] *adj* in the north; (*of wind*) blowing from the north ~ **northerly** *adv* to the north.

northern [*nawr*THern] *adj* in or of the north; **n. lights** aurora borealis ~ **northerner** *n* inhabitant of a northern region.

northernmost [*nawr*THernmOst] *adj* farthest north.

northing [*nawr*thing] *n* distance travelled northwards measured in degrees of latitude.

Northman [*nawr*thman] *n* Norseman.

north-north-east [*nawr*th-nawrth-eest] *n* direction midway between north and north-east.

north-north-west [*nawr*th-nawrth-west] *n* direction midway between north and north-west.

northward [*nawr*thwerd] *n* and *adj* (part) in or towards the north ~ **northward, northwards** *adv* towards the north.

north-west [nawrth-*west*] *n, adj* and *adv* (direction) midway between north and west; **N. Passage** sea route along north coast of America ~ **north-wester** *n* strong wind from north-west ~ **north-westerly** *adj* ~ **north-western** *adj* ~ **north-westward** *n, adj* and *adv* (direction) towards the north-west.

Norwegian [nawr*wee*ji-an] *n* and *adj* (inhabitant or language) of Norway.

nose [*n*O*z*] *n* projecting part of face containing breathing passages and organ of smell; sense of smell; front end of some pointed thing; front part of aircraft; prow; spout; nozzle; (*sl*) spy; **follow one's n.** go straight ahead; **be led by the n.** obey blindly; **pay through the n.** pay too high a price; **poke one's n. in** interfere; **put one's n. out of joint** give cause of jealousy to; **turn up one's n. at** despise; **n. to tail** each placed or following immediately behind another ~ **nose** *v/t* and *i* press the nose against, nuzzle; sniff at or round; move cautiously; **n. on** (*sl*) inform against; **n. out** detect by smelling; (*fig*) discover.

nosebag [*n*O*z*bag] *n* feeding-bag hung from a horse's head.

noseband [*n*O*z*band] *n* lower band of bridle.

nosebleed [*n*O*z*bleed] *n* bleeding from the nose.

nosedive [*n*O*z*dIv] *n* steep plunge of an aircraft ~ **nosedive** *v/i*.

nose-flute [*n*O*z*-flOOt] *n* flute blown by the nostrils.

nosegay [*n*O*z*gay] *n* bunch of flowers.

nosepiece [*n*O*z*pees] *n* part of helmet protecting the nose; lower end of microscope; nozzle.

nose-ring [*n*O*z*-Ring] *n* leading-ring in animal's nose; ornamental ring worn in the nose.

nosey, nosy [*n*O*zi*] *adj* (*coll*) very inquisitive; **n. parker** inquisitive person ~ **nosily** *adv* ~ **nosiness** *n*.

nosh *n* [*nosh*] (*sl*) food ~ **nosh** *v/t* and *i* (*sl*) eat.

nosing [*n*O*zing*] *n* half-round, overhanging edge to a stair tread, flat roof, window sill *etc*.

noso- *pref* of disease.

nosology [noso*loji*] *n* science of diseases;

classification of diseases ~ **nosological** [nosOlojikal] *adj* ~ **nosologist** [nosolojist] *n*.

nostalgia [nostalji-a] *n* yearning for what is past or inaccessible; sentimental evocation of past happiness; homesickness ~ **nostalgic** *adj* ~ **nostalgically** *adv*.

nostril [nostril] *n* one opening of the nose.

nostrum [nostRum] *n* (*cont*) quack medicine; favourite remedy.

nosy see **nosey**.

not [not] *adv* expressing negation, denial or refusal.

notabilia [nOtabili-a] *n* (*pl*) things worth noting.

notability [nOtabiliti] *n* state of being notable; that which is notable.

notable [nOtab'l] *adj* remarkable, eminent; worthy of notice; conspicuous ~ **notable** *n* eminent man ~ **notably** *adv*.

notary [nOtaRi] *n* public official who draws up or attests contracts, protests, bills of exchange *etc*.

notation [nOtayshon] *n* system of representing scientific concepts, numbers or musical notes by signs > PDM.

notch [noch] *n* V-shaped cut, slit or indentation; cut made on tally-stick; score; nock ~ **notch** *v/t* and *i* cut a notch in; mark up (a score); fit (arrow) to bowstring.

note [nOt] *n* brief written comment, summary, memorandum or record; brief informal letter; explanatory comment; diplomatic communication; banknote, paper money; written promise to pay a sum of money; sound of definite pitch > PDM, PDP; written symbol of this; key of a keyboard > PDM; reputation, fame; attention, notice; distinctive feature; punctuation mark; **take n. of** notice carefully ~ **note** *v/t* record in writing; observe, notice.

notebook [nOtbook] *n* book for memoranda.

notecase [nOtkays] *n* wallet for banknotes.

noted [nOtid] *adj* well-known; famous ~ **notedly** *adv* especially.

notelet [nOtlet] *n* ornamental folded sheet of paper for writing brief letters.

notepad [nOtpad] *n* block of small sheets of paper fastened together.

notepaper [nOtpayper] *n* paper for writing letters.

noteworthy [nOtwurTHi] *adj* worthy of notice, remarkable.

nothing [nuthing] *n* complete absence of all entities; absence of the thing sought; something of no importance, trifle; zero, nought; **n. but** only; **come to n.** fail; **n. doing** (*coll*) impossible; **n. for it** (but) inevitable (that); **for n.** gratis; in vain; **n. in it** no truth in it; easy; **make n. of** be unable to understand; dismiss lightly; **mean n. to** be quite unimportant to; convey no meaning to; **next to n.** very little; **n. to** insignificant compared with ~ **nothing** *adv* not at all ~ **nothingness** *n* non-existence; worthlessness.

notice [nOtis] *v/t* observe, pay attention to; show recognition of; refer to; write a review of ~ **notice** *n* advance information, announcement; warning, *esp* of termination of contract; dismissal (of servant); written warning or announcement, *esp* in a public place; review (of book *etc*); act of observing, attention; **at short n.** with little time for preparation.

noticeable [nOtisab'l] *adj* striking, easily seen; remarkable ~ **noticeably** *adv*.

notifiable [nOtifi-ab'l] *adj* that must be notified to authority.

notification [nOtifikayshon] *n* act of notifying; that which notifies; formal notice or announcement.

notify [nOtifi] *v/t* make known, announce; inform, tell officially.

notion [nOshon] *n* idea, conception; opinion; (*log*) general class to which an object belongs.

notional [nOshonal] *adj* expressing an abstract concept; speculative; imaginary ~ **notionally** *adv*.

notoriety [nOtoRI-eti] *n* quality of being notorious; one who or that which is notorious.

notorious [nOtawrRi-us] *adj* having a widespread bad reputation; well known ~ **notoriously** *adv*.

notwithstanding [notwiTHstanding] *prep*, *conj* and *adv* in spite of.

nougat [nOOgaa/nugat] *n* sweet sticky paste containing nuts.

nought [nawt] *n* zero, nothing; figure o representing this; **set at n.** defy, ignore.

noumenon (*pl* **noumenona**) [nOOminon] *n* (*philos*) that which is grasped by the intellect but has no phenomenal attributes.

noun [nown] *n* (*gramm*) word that names a person, thing, action, quality, state *etc*.

nourish [nuRish] *v/t* sustain by feeding; (*fig*) encourage, keep active ~ **nourishing** *adj*.

nourishment [nuRishment] *n* food, sustenance.

nous [nows] *n* (*coll*) intelligence, common sense.

nouveau-riche [nOOvO-Reesh] *n* (*Fr*) one who has grown rich without acquiring good class manners.

nova [nOva] *n* (*astron*) star whose brilliance flares up suddenly for a short while > PDS.

novel [novel] *adj* new; unusual ~ **novel** *n* fairly long fictional prose story *usu* dealing with human relationships and actions.

novelette [novelet] *n* short novel of inferior quality; (*mus*) type of short romantic instrumental piece > PDM ~ **novelettish** *adj* crudely sentimental; trivial.

novelist [novelist] *n* writer of novels.

novelty [novelti] *n* quality of being novel, newness; that which is new; newly marketed ornament, toy *etc*.

November [november] *n* eleventh month of the year.

novena [nOveena] *n* (*RC*) prayer or set of prayers repeated daily for nine days.

novice [novis] *n* inexperienced beginner; one who has joined a religious order but has not yet taken the full vows; recent convert.

novitiate, noviciate [nOvishi-ayt] *n* state or period of being a novice; place where novices live.

novocaine [nOvOkayn] *n* (*tr*) a type of local anaesthetic.

now [now] *adv* at this time, at present; at once; at the time referred to; **n. n.!** *exclam of rebuke*; **n. . . . n.** at one time . . . at another; **n. and then** occasionally; **just n.** a few moments ago ~ **now** *conj* in connexion with this; after this; so; but ~ **now** *n* the present time.

nowadays [now-adayz] *adv* in these times.

noway, noways [nOway(z)] *adv* not at all.

nowhere [nOwair] adv not in any place; **n. near** far from; **be n.**, **get n.** be quite unsuccessful.

nowise [nOwIz] adv not at all.

nowt [nowt] n (dial and coll) nothing.

noxious [nokshus] adj harmful, injurious ~ **noxiously** adv ~ **noxiousness** n.

nozzle [noz'l] n projecting vent or spout.

n-th [enth] adj multiplied by an unknown mathematical quantity; (coll) innumerable, greater or more often than can be said.

nuance [new-aa(n)s] n subtle difference.

nub [nub] n small lump; point of story.

nubbin [nubin] n (US) dwarfed or malformed ear of maize or vegetable.

nubile [newbIl] adj (of a girl) old enough to marry; (coll) attractive ~ **nubility** [newbiliti] n.

nuci- pref of or like a nut.

nuclear [newkli-er] adj of or in a nucleus; of or caused by nuclear fission; pertaining to the structure of atoms; **n. disarmament** renunciation of nuclear weapons; **n. family** family group consisting of parents and children only; **n. fission** the breaking of a heavy atom into two or more atoms of about equal mass, with vast release of energy > PDS; **n. fusion** joining together of two light nuclei to form a heavier one with vast release of energy; **n. physics** study of the atom and its particles; **n. power** country possessing nuclear weapons; electric power generated by atomic fission of uranium, plutonium etc; **n. reactor** structure in which the energy of nuclear fission can be released under control > PDS; **n. test** the testing of a nuclear weapon; **n. weapon** bomb or missile exploding by nuclear fission or fusion.

nucleate [newkli-ayt] v/t and i form into a nucleus; gather about a nucleus.

nuclei [newkli-I] pl of **nucleus**.

nucleic [newkli-ik] adj **n. acid** compound of pentose sugar, phosphoric acid and nitrogen-containing base characteristic of all living things > PDB.

nucleo- pref of a nucleus.

nucleon [newkli-on] n (phys) proton or neutron.

nucleonics [newkli-oniks] n (pl) branch of science dealing with atomic nuclei and their reactions.

nucleo-protein [newkli-O-pROteen] n a compound of nucleic acid and protein of which viruses mostly consist.

nucleus (pl **nuclei**) [newkli-us] n vital central point; central part round which others are grouped; particle of matter acting as a centre; (fig) starting-point; (phys) positively charged body constituting main mass of an atom > PDS; (biol) that part of a cell which contains the chromosomes > PDB; (astron) centre of head of comet; centre of sunspot.

nuclide [newklId] n (phys) atom of an isotope having a defined energy state.

nude [newd] adj naked, esp. deliberately so; bare, uncovered; displaying or representing naked persons; (leg) void unless under seal ~ **nude** n artistic representation of a naked figure; naked person, esp woman; **in the n.** unclothed.

nudge [nuj] v/t push slightly with the elbow ~ **nudge** n.

nudism [newdizm] n practice of going naked for reasons of health or religion ~ **nudist** adj and n.

nudity [newditi] n nakedness.

nuff [nuf] n (coll abbr) enough.

nugatory [newgateRi] adj worthless, unimportant; invalid; ineffectual.

nugget [nugit] n rough lump of native gold.

nuisance [newsans] n that which or one who causes annoyance, inconvenience or injury.

null [nul] adj of no legal force, void; of no value or consequence; futile.

nullify [nulifI] v/t make null and void; make useless; cancel ~ **nullification** [nulifikayshon] n.

nullity [nuliti] n state of being null and void (esp of marriage); anything invalid; nothingness; insignificant person.

numb [num] adj without feeling, stiff through cold ~ **numb** v/t make numb ~ **numbness** n.

number [number] n abstract unit in mathematical system; name or symbol of this; numerical symbol identifying a person or thing; aggregate of a group of persons or things, sum total; large collection or quantity; single issue of serial or periodical; single item in a musical or variety performance; (gramm) form expressing whether a word refers to one or more persons or things; (pl) verse, metre; large quantity; arithmetic; **back n.** previous issue (of periodical); (fig) old-fashioned person; **in n.** amounting (to); **n. one** (coll) oneself; **out of n.**, **without n.** too many to be counted; **one's n. is up** one is dead or ruined ~ **number** v/t assign a number to; count; be of specified sum or quantity; **one's days are numbered** one will soon die; **n. among** include.

numberless [numberlis] adj too many to be counted.

number-plate [number-playt] n metal plate showing index-mark and number of a motor vehicle; metal plate showing number of a house.

numbly [numli] adv in a numb way.

numbness [numnis] n state of being numb.

numeracy [newmeRasi] n understanding of basic scientific concepts.

numeral [newmeRal] n symbol or word denoting a number ~ **numeral** adj of or expressing a number ~ **numerally** adv.

numerate [newmeRat] adj able to understand basic scientific and mathematic concepts.

numeration [newmeRayshon] n system of numbering; act of numbering.

numerator [newmeRayter] n (math) upper number in a vulgar fraction; one who counts; census-taker.

numerical [newmeRikal] adj pertaining to numbers; expressed in numbers ~ **numerically** adv.

numerous [newmeRus] adj very many, abundant; consisting of many units ~ **numerously** adv.

numinous [newminus] adj divine; suggestive of divine presence or power; awe-inspiring.

numismatic [newmizmatik] adj of coins or medals ~ **numismatics** n (pl) study of coins or medals ~ **numismatist** [newmismatist] n.

numskull [numskul] n stupid fool, blockhead.

nun [nun] n member of a women's religious community vowed to poverty, chastity and obedience; (zool) name of certain birds and moths.

nuncio [nunshi-O] n a papal ambassador.

503

nunnery [*nune*Ri] *n* convent for women.

nuptial [*nup*shal] *adj* pertaining to marriage ~ **nuptials** *n* (*pl*) wedding ceremony.

nurse (1) [*nurs*] *n* person, *usu* woman, trained to look after the sick or injured; woman employed to look after children; woman employed to suckle a baby; (*fig*) that which shelters, encourages or tends anything immature ~ **nurse** *v/t* and *i* give skilled care to (sick, injured); look after (child); suckle; cherish; foster, encourage; clasp tenderly; manage carefully and economically; spare the strength (of); act as nurse, *esp* professionally; **n. the fire** (*fig*) sit very close to the fire.

nurse (2) *n* dog-fish; shark.

nurseling see **nursling**.

nursemaid [*nurs*mayd] *n* servant girl who helps to bring up young children.

nursery [*nurse*Ri] *n* room set apart for children's use; place where young plants are reared for transplanting; place where vegetables, fruit, flowers *etc* are grown for sale; **n. garden** nursery for plants; **n. governess** governess to very young children; **n. rhymes** traditional verses for children; **n. school** school for children under five.

nurseryman [*nurse*Riman] *n* man who grows plants *etc* for sale.

nursing [*nurs*ing] *n* act of nursing; profession of nursing ~ **nursing** *adj* (*of mother*) giving breast-milk.

nursing-home [*nurs*ing-hOm] *n* small privately owned institution where patients pay to be nursed.

nursling, nurseling [*nurs*ling] *n* child under the care of a nurse.

nurture [*nur*cher] *n* upbringing, education; fostering care; nourishment ~ **nurture** *v/t* rear, train; feed.

nut [*nut*] *n* dry one-seeded fruit in a hard woody wall > PDB; edible kernel of this; small lump of coal; small metal block, square or hexagonal, with a circular hole threaded to fit a screw and tighten a bolt; knob regulating tension of violin bow; (*sl*) head; (*sl*) crazy person, madman; (*obs sl*) fop; **do one's n.** (*sl*) behave wildly through anger, anxiety *etc*; **hard (tough) n. to crack** difficult problem; difficult person to deal with; **off one's n.** (*sl*) mad ~ **nut** (*pres/part* **nutting**, *p/t* and *p/part* **nutted**) *v/i* gather nuts.

nutation [newt*ay*shon] *n* (*bot*) spiral course of apex of growing plant > PDB; (*astron*) oscillation of earth's axis.

nutbrown [*nut*bRown] *n* and *adj* reddish brown.

nut-butter [nut-*but*er] *n* butter substitute made from nuts.

nutcase [*nut*kays] *n* (*sl*) madman.

nutcracker [*nut*kRaker] *n* bird of crow family feeding on nuts ~ **nutcrackers** *n* (*pl*) pincers for cracking nuts.

nuthatch [nut-*hach*] *n* small bird which feeds on nuts.

nuthouse [*nut*hows] *n* (*sl*) lunatic asylum.

nutmeg [*nut*meg] *n* round aromatic seed of Malayan tree, used as spice.

nutria [*newt*Ri-a] *n* fur of the coypu.

nutrient [*newt*Ri-ent] *n* and *adj* (that) which nourishes.

nutriment [*newt*Riment] *n* nourishment, food.

nutrition [newt*Ri*shon] *n* process of receiving nourishment; food ~ **nutritional** *adj*.

nutritious [newt*Ri*shus] *adj* efficiently sustaining life and growth, nourishing ~ **nutritiously** *adv*.

nutritive [*newt*Ritiv] *adj* nutritious.

nuts [*nuts*] *adj* and *interj* (*sl*) mad, crazy; nonsense; **be n. on** be very fond of; **not for n.** not at all.

nutshell [*nut*shel] *n* hard woody shell of a nut; **in a n.** very concisely.

nutter [*nut*er] *n* (*sl*) madman.

nutty [*nut*i] *adj* having taste like nuts; (*sl*) mad, crazy; **n. about** very fond of ~ **nuttily** *adv* ~ **nuttiness** *n*.

nuzzle [*nuz*'l] *v/t* and *i* push the nose forward against.

nyctalopia [nikta*lOp*i-a] *n* night-blindness; day-blindness.

nycti- *pref* by night.

nylon [*nI*lon] *n* a synthetic plastics material with properties comparable to those of natural silk > PDS; **nylons** (*pl*) stockings made of nylon.

nymph [*nimf*] *n* (*myth*) female guardian spirit inhabiting a tree, river, hill *etc*; (*poet*) beautiful girl; (*biol*) immature form of certain insects > PDB; pupa, chrysalis ~ **nymphal** *adj*.

nymphet [nim*fet*] *n* (*coll*) very young but sexually attractive girl.

nympho [*nimf*O] *n* (*coll abbr*) nymphomaniac.

nymphomania [nimfO*mayn*i-a] *n*· (*path*) exaggerated sexual desire in women ~ **nymphomaniac** *adj* and *n* (woman) suffering from nymphomania.

nystagmus [nist*ag*mus] *n* (*path*) involuntary jerky movements of the eyes > PDP.

nystatin [*nI*statin] *n* antibiotic used for treating fungal diseases.

O

o (1) [O] fifteenth letter of the English alphabet; symbol for nought, zero; anything shaped like an o; (*chem*) oxygen; **o.k.** see **okay.**

o (2) *interj* (*poet*) oh!; exclamation of appeal, invocation or solemn address.

o' (3) *abbr* of.

oaf [*Of*] *n* rough clumsy fool, lout; idiot; (*ar*) misshapen child ~ **oafish** *adj.*

oak [*Ok*] *n* one of a genus of forest trees; timber of this; heavy outer door of oak-wood; **the Oaks** race run at Epsom for three-year-old fillies ~ **oak** *adj* made of oak-wood.

oak-apple [*Ok*-ap'l] *n* fleshy excrescence on oak-tree caused by gall-flies.

oaken [*Ok*en] *adj* made of oak-wood.

oak-gall [*Ok*-gawl] *n* oak-apple.

oakum [*Ok*um] *n* fibre obtained by untwisting old ropes.

oar [*awr*] *n* long pole with flattened blade, used to propel a boat; oarsman; **oars!** order given in a rowing boat to cease pulling; **lie on your oars!** cease pulling; **put one's o. in** interfere; **rest on one's oars** relax; **toss oars** salute with raised oars ~ **oar** *v/i* (*poet*) row ~ **oared** *adj* with oars.

oarlock [*awr*lok] *n* rowlock.

oarsman [*awr*zman] *n* a rower.

oasis (*pl* **oases**) [O-*ay*sis] *n* fertile area in the middle of a desert > PDG.

oast [*Ost*] *n* kiln for drying hops.

oast-house [*Ost*-hows] *n* building containing an oast.

oat [*Ot*] *n* (*usu pl*) cereal plant with edible grain; grains of this; (*poet*) pipe or flute made of oat stalk; **feel one's oats** (*coll*) feel energetic or important; **sow one's wild oats** indulge in dissipation when young.

oatcake [*Ot*kayk] *n* oatmeal biscuit.

oaten [*Ot*en] *adj* made of oats or of oat straw.

oath [*Oth*] *n* solemn assertion or promise with invocation of the power of God or of some sacred person or thing; blasphemous curse or exclamation, profanity; **on o.**, **under o.** (*leg*) having sworn on the Bible to speak the truth.

oatmeal [*Ot*meel] *n* meal made from oats.

ob- *pref* against; down; completely.

obbligato [obligaat*O*] *adj* (*mus*) essential, compulsory > PDM ~ **obbligato** *n* accompaniment by a compulsory additional instrument.

obduracy [*ob*dewRasi] *n* stubbornness; impenitence ~ **obdurate** *adj* stubborn; hard-hearted; impenitent ~ **obdurately** *adv.*

obeah, obi [*Obee*-a, *Ob*i] *n* type of West African witchcraft; amulet or magic object used in this.

obedience [*Obee*di-ens] *n* act of obeying; act of submitting to authority or of complying with rules, orders *etc*; (*eccles*) body of persons submitting to the authority of a specified church; authority, dominion.

obedient [*Obee*di-ent] *adj* willing to obey; submissive; carrying out an order or rule ~ **obediently** *adv.*

obeisance [*Ob*ay*sance] *n* low bow; deep curtsy; homage.

obelisk [*ob*ilisk] *n* four-sided stone pillar tapering to a point; (*typ*) mark (†) denoting reference to a footnote *etc*; obelus ~ **obelize** *v/t* (*typ*) mark with an obelisk.

obelus (*pl* **obeli**) [*ob*ilus] *n* mark (—, ÷, or †) used in ancient manuscripts to mark a corrupt or spurious passage.

obese [*Obee*s] *adj* extremely fat ~ **obesity** [*obee*siti] *n.*

obey [*Ob*ay] *v/t* and *i* carry out the orders or wishes of; follow the rules of; submit to; be obedient.

obfuscate [*ob*fuskayt] *v/t* darken; bewilder.

obi (1) [*Ob*i] *n* broad Japanese sash.

obi (2) see **obeah.**

obit [*obit*] *n* record of the date of a person's death.

obiter [*Obit*er] *adv* (*Lat*) incidentally; **o. dictum** (*pl* **o. dicta**) (*leg*) remark made by the judge which does not form an essential part of his judgement; incidental remark.

obituary [*obit*ew-eRi] *n* newspaper announcement of a person's death, with a short biography; (*eccles*) register of deaths.

object [*objekt*] *n* thing; that which can be seen or touched; aim, purpose; that towards which one's feelings or attention is directed; (*gramm*) word or group of words governed by a verb or preposition; (*coll*) person or thing looking odd or ridiculous; **o. lesson** lesson illustrated by display of objects to be studied; (*fig*) vivid lesson or warning; **no o.** not important ~ **object** [*objekt*] *v/t* and *i* give as reason for disagreement; **o. to** dislike; disapprove of; protest against.

object-finder [*objekt*-finder] *n* device to mark position of object on microscopic slide.

object-glass [*objekt*-glaas] *n* lens of optical instrument nearest to object to be viewed.

objectify [*objekt*ifi] *v/t* represent as material object, express in concrete form.

objection [*objek*shon] *n* reason why something cannot or must not be done; argument or statement expressing this; dislike; disapproval; drawback, flaw.

objectionable [*objek*shonab'l] *adj* unpleasant, offensive; open to objection.

objective [*objekt*iv] *adj* relating to objects; actually existing independently of the perceiver's mind; real; not distorted by personal emotions or prejudice; impartial; clear-sighted; relating to purpose; (*gramm*) (case) of a word governed by a verb or preposition ~ **objective** *n* aim, purpose, goal; (*mil*) position to be attacked or reached; lens of camera; object-glass ~ **objectively** *adv.*

objectivism [*objekt*ivizm] *n* (*philos*) doctrine that knowledge based on sense-perceptions corresponds to reality.

objectivity [objekt*iv*iti] *n* state of being objective; ability to free oneself from personal prejudice; impartial judgement or assessment.

object-lens [*objekt*-lenz] *n* object-glass.

505

objector [ob*jekter*] *n* one who protests against something; **conscientious o.** one who refuses to do military service on moral grounds.

object-staff [*objekt-staaf*] *n* surveyor's levelling staff.

objurgation [objer*gay*shon] *n* scolding, abuse.

oblate (1) [*oblayt*] *n* one dedicated to monastic life.

oblate (2) [*oblayt*] *adj* (*geom*) flattened at the poles.

oblation [*oblay*shon] *n* solemn religious offering, *esp* in the Eucharist; (*pl*) donations for pious uses.

obligate [*obligayt*] *v/t* bind, compel; place under obligation.

obligation [obli*gay*shon] *n* feeling of inner compulsion to act in specified way; moral or legal compulsion; binding agreement; that which one is bound to do; state of indebtedness to another for benefits received from him; **holiday of o.** (*RC*) feast-day other than a Sunday when one is bound to attend Mass.

obligatory [*obliga*teRi] *adj* binding; compulsory.

oblige [*oblīj*] *v/t* bind, compel; necessitate; do a service to; (*coll*) do as a favour to; work for.

obliging [*oblīj*ing] *adj* helpful, courteous.

oblique [*Obleek*] *adj* slanting; neither vertical nor horizontal; indirect; hinting, alluding; not straightforward; indirect; (*gramm*) of any case but the nominative; **o. angle** any angle not of 90° ~ **oblique** *v/i* move in slanting direction; turn aside ~ **obliquely** *adv* ~ **obliqueness** *n*.

obliquity [*oblik*witi] *n* indirectness; dishonesty; crookedness; state of being oblique.

obliterate [*oblite*Rayt] *v/t* blot out, erase; destroy all traces of ~ **obliteration** [oblite*Ray*shon] *n*.

oblivion [obl*ivi*-on] *n* forgetfulness; state of being forgotten.

oblivious [obl*ivi*-us] *adj* no longer aware, forgetful; (*pop*) unconscious, not realizing.

oblong [*oblong*] *n* and *adj* (*geom*) (rectangular figure) longer in one direction than in the other.

obloquy [*oblo*kwi] *n* blame; abuse; disgrace.

obnoxious [ob*nok*shus] *adj* unpleasant, odious; harmful; (*rare*) open or liable to attack or injury ~ **obnoxiously** *adv* ~ **obnoxiousness** *n*.

oboe [ObO] *n* high-pitched double reed woodwind instrument; reed-stop in an organ > PDM.

oboist [ObO-ist] *n* one who plays the oboe.

obol [*obol*] *n* silver coin of ancient Greece.

obscene [ob*seen*] *adj* indecent, lewd; disgusting; referring too frankly or offensively to sex; (*fig*) morally repulsive ~ **obscenely** *adv*.

obscenity [ob*seni*ti] *n* state of being obscene; that which is obscene; obscene language.

obscurantism [obskew*Ran*tizm] *n* opposition to progress or increase of knowledge ~ **obscurantist** *n* and *adj*.

obscuration [obskew*Ray*shon] *n* act of darkening; state of being darkened; eclipse.

obscure [ob*skewr*] *adj* dark, dim; not well lighted; hard to understand; indistinct, vague; not widely known; hidden, secluded; gloomy ~ **obscure** *v/t* darken; hide; confuse, make hard to understand ~ **obscurely** *adv*.

obscurity [ob*skewr*Riti] *n* state of being obscure.

obsequies [*obsik*wiz] *n* (*pl*) funeral rites.

obsequious [ob*seek*wi-us] *adj* fawning, servile; excessively humble or submissive ~ **obsequiously** *adv* ~ **obsequiousness** *n*.

observable [ob*zurv*ab'l] *adj* noteworthy, discernible.

observance [ob*zurv*ans] *n* act of observing (law, custom *etc*); customary ceremony, rite or practice, *esp* religious; commemoration.

observant [ob*zurv*ant] *adj* noticing closely, watchful; strict in observing rules *etc* ~ **observantly** *adv*.

observation [obzer*vay*shon] *n* act of observing, *esp* scientifically; capacity to observe; remark, criticism; (*pl*) facts collected and recorded ~ **observation** *adj* used for observing ~ **observational** *adj*.

observatory [ob*zurv*ateRi] *n* building equipped for making astronomical observations; place commanding an extensive view.

observe [ob*zurv*] *v/t* and *i* keep to, obey, follow; notice carefully; pay attention to; say, remark; be watchful ~ **observer** *n* one who looks at; one who observes; (*mil*) one who keeps watch, *esp* for enemy aircraft; one who attends a conference to report on it, but takes no part in it.

obsess [ob*ses*] *v/t* fill (the mind) excessively.

obsession [ob*seshon*] *n* abnormally persistent idea or urge > PDP; constant preoccupation ~ **obsessional** *adj* liable to have obsessions.

obsessive [ob*ses*iv] *adj* of or like an obsession; abnormally persistent ~ **obsessively** *adv*.

obsidian [ob*sidi*-an] *n* dark-coloured glassy volcanic rock.

obsolescence [obso*les*ens] *n* state of gradually disappearing through disuse; state of becoming obsolete; **planned o.** deliberate designing of products that will soon be useless or outdated ~ **obsolescent** *adj* becoming obsolete; gradually disappearing.

obsolete [*obsoleet*] *adj* no longer used; out of date, old-fashioned ~ **obsoletely** *adv* ~ **obsoleteness** *n*.

obstacle [*obstak'l*] *n* thing causing obstruction; hindrance.

obstetric [ob*stet*Ric] *adj* of or for midwifery or childbirth ~ **obstetrical** *adj* obstetric ~ **obstetrics** *n* (*pl*) science of midwifery.

obstetrician [obstet*Rish*an] *n* one skilled in obstetrics.

obstinacy [*obstinasi*] *n* unshakable persistence; stubbornness ~ **obstinate** *adj* persisting immovably or unreasonably in one's opinions, plans *etc*; stubborn; (*med*) resisting treatment ~ **obstinately** *adv*.

obstreperous [obst*Repe*Rus] *adj* noisy; uncontrollable, turbulent ~ **obstreperously** *adv*.

obstruct [ob*stRukt*] *v/t* hinder, impede; make impassable; block up; oppose.

obstruction [ob*stRuk*shon] *n* act of obstructing; that which obstructs; hindrance.

obstructionism [obst*Ruk*shonizm] *n* systematic attempt to hinder progress or legislation ~ **obstructionist** *n* and *adj*.

obstructive [ob*stRuk*tiv] *n* and *adj* (person or thing) that obstructs ~ **obstructively** *adv*.

obstructor [ob*stRuk*ter] *n* one who or that which obstructs; opponent of progress.

obstruent [*obst*Roo-ent] *n* and *adj* (*med*) (something) causing obstruction.

obtain [ob*tayn*] *v/t* and *i* get, acquire, procure; be usual; be valid or acceptable.

obtainable [ob*tayn*ab'l]] *adj* that can be got, available.

obtention [ob*tens*hon] *n* act of obtaining.

obtrude [ob*tROO*d] *v*/*t* and *i* thrust forward; force into notice; intrude.

obtrusion [ob*tROO*zhon] *n* act of obtruding.

obtrusive [ob*tROO*siv] *adj* demanding excessive notice; thrusting; intruding ~ **obtrusively** *adv*.

obtuse [ob*tews*] *adj* blunt; stupid, slow to understand; **o. angle** (*geom*) angle of more than 90° ~ **obtusely** *adv* ~ **obtuseness** *n*.

obverse [*ob*vurs] *adj* facing the observer; forming a counterpart; (*bot*) broader at apex than at base ~ **obverse** *n* (*of coin*) side bearing the head or main device; (*log*) statement complementary to another; counterpart ~ **obversely** *adv*.

obviate [*ob*vi-ayt] *v*/*t* do away with; prevent; make unnecessary.

obvious [*ob*vi-us] *adj* very easy to perceive; plainly seen or understood; too apparent; too simple ~ **obviously** *adv* ~ **obviousness** *n*.

ocarina [oka*Ree*na] *n* small keyless wind instrument > PDM.

occasion [o*kayzh*on] *n* point of time of an event, *esp* an important one; favourable opportunity, right time; contributory cause; immediate stimulus to events having a more deep-rooted cause; (*pl*) lawful occupation; **on o.** when necessary; **rise to the o.** be equal to an emergency ~ **occasion** *v*/*t* cause; bring about.

occasional [o*kayzh*onal] *adj* happening from time to time, not constant; irregular; rare; designed for some special occasion or use ~ **occasionally** *adv*.

Occident [*ok*sident] *n* western hemisphere; west; Europe and America as contrasted with Asia, India *etc*.

Occidental [oksi*den*tal] *adj* of, in, or like the Occident ~ **Occidentalism** *n* Occidental way of life; preference for this ~ **Occidentalize** *v*/*t* cause (Orientals) to adopt Occidental customs.

occipital [ok*sip*ital] *adj* of the occiput.

occiput [*ok*siput] *n* back part of the head.

occlude [ok*lOO*d] *v*/*t* shut in or out; enclose; (*chem*) absorb (gases) > PDS.

occlusion [ok*lOO*zhon] *n* act of occluding; state of being occluded; (*phon*) momentary closure; normal overlap of upper teeth over lower when jaws are shut; (*meteor*) closing of the cold front of a depression on to the warm front > PDG.

occult [o*kult*] *adj* of or about supernatural beings and forces other than God or gods; of or about magic, astrology, alchemy, theosophy *etc*; secret, esoteric; supernatural ~ **occult** *n* magical or esoteric knowledge or experience ~ **occult** *v*/*t* and *i* (*astron*) eclipse.

occultation [okul*tays*hon] *n* (*astron*) eclipse.

occultism [*ok*ultizm] *n* belief in and practice of occult doctrines and arts; magic ~ **occultist** *n*.

occultly [o*kult*li] *adv* in an occult way.

occultness [o*kult*nis] *n* quality of being occult.

occupancy [*ok*ewpansi] *n* act of taking possession of and residing in a house *etc*; term during which a house *etc* is occupied; (*leg*) act of acquiring that which has no owner.

occupant [*ok*ewpant] *n* one who occupies a house, post *etc*.

occupation [okew*pays*hon] *n* act of taking possess-

ion; period of tenure; (*mil*) act or period of possessing conquered territory; period of residence; regular task, duty or activity; trade, employment.

occupational [okew*pays*honal] *adj* of, for, or by one's trade, employment or habitual work; **o. disease** disease caused by the conditions or nature of one's work; **o. therapy** remedial use of light manual tasks, handicrafts *etc*.

occupier [*ok*ewpI-er] *n* person who resides in a house or estate.

occupy [*ok*ewpI] *v*/*t* get and keep possession of; reside in; hold (post *etc*); settle troops in (conquered territory); sit or lie in; hold the attention of; **o. oneself with, be occupied with** be busy at.

occur (*pres*/*part* occurring, *p*/*t* and *p*/*part* occurred) [o*kur*] *v*/*i* happen; exist, be found; **o. to** come into the mind of.

occurrence [o*ku*Rens] *n* event; act of occurring.

ocean [*Osh*an] *n* sheet of salt water surrounding the land-masses of the earth; a major subdivision of this > PDG; (*fig*) vast quantity ~ **ocean** *adj* of or in the ocean; **o. current** movement of surface water of an ocean > PDG.

Oceania [Oshi-*ayn*i-a] *n* the islands of the Pacific Ocean.

oceanic [Oshi-*an*ik] *adj* of or in the ocean; living in sea-water below 200 metres; (*climate*) influenced by the ocean; (*fig*) vast.

oceanography [Oshanog*Raf*i] *n* study of the ocean ~ **oceanographical** [OshanOg*Raf*ikal] *adj*.

ocellate [O*sel*ayt/o*sel*ayt], **ocellated** [O*sel*aytid/o*sel*aytid] *adj* like an eye or eyes; marked with ocelli.

ocellus (*pl* ocelli) [O*sel*us] *n* (*zool*) small or simple form of eye; eye-like spot on plumage or wings.

ocelot [*O*silot] *n* large South American wildcat; tiger-cat.

ochre (1) [*O*ker] *n* natural form of ferric oxide used as yellow or brown pigment ~ **ochreous**, **ochrous** [*O*kRee-us, *O*kRus] *adj*.

o'clock [*O*klok] *adv* by, according to a clock.

oct-, octa-, octo- *pref* eight.

octad [*ok*tad] *n* (*math*) series of eight; (*chem*) element having combining power of eight hydrogen atoms.

octagon [*ok*tagon] *n* (*geom*) plane figure with eight sides ~ **octagonal** [ok*tag*nal] *adj* eight-sided.

octahedron (*pl* octahedra) [okta*heed*Ron] *n* (*geom*) solid body with eight plane faces ~ **octahedral** *adj*.

octameter [ok*tam*iter] *n* and *adj* (*pros*) (line) containing eight feet.

octane [*ok*tayn] *n* liquid paraffin hydrocarbon present in petroleum; **o. number** measure of the anti-knock characteristics of a fuel > PDS.

octave [*ok*tayv] *n* (*mus*) pitch interval between notes one of which has a frequency twice that of the other > PDM; note eight diatonic degrees from another; (*eccles*) eighth day or period of eight days after a festival; (*pros*) octet.

octavo [ok*tayv*O] *n* book having eight leaves or sixteen pages to the sheet.

octennial [ok*ten*i-al] *adj* occurring every eight years; lasting eight years.

octet [ok*tet*/ok*tet*] *n* (*mus*) composition for eight voices or instruments; (*chem*) group of eight electrons; (*pros*) eight-line stanza; first eight lines of sonnet.

octillion [okt*i*li-on] *n* eighth power of one million; (*US*) ninth power of one thousand.

octo- *pref* see oct-.

October [okt*O*ber] *n* tenth month of the year.

octodecimo [okt*O*des*i*mO] *n* book having eighteen leaves, or thirty-six pages, to the sheet.

octogenarian [okt*O*jen*air*Ri-an] *n* and *adj* (person) aged between eighty and ninety years.

octopod [*o*ktopod] *n* eight-limbed animal, *esp* octopus.

octopus (*pl* **octopodes, octopuses**) [*o*ktopus] *n* (*zool*) cephalopod mollusc having eight arms bearing many suckers; (*fig*) powerful organization with far-reaching branches.

octosyllabic [okt*O*si*lab*ik] *adj* having eight syllables.

octosyllable [okt*O*si*lab*'l] *n* word of eight syllables; (*pros*) line of eight syllables.

octuple [*o*ktewp'l] *adj* eight times as much, eightfold ~ **octuple** *v/t* multiply by eight.

ocular [*o*kewlar] *adj* of the eye; visual ~ **ocular** *n* eye-piece of optical instrument ~ **ocularly** *adv*.

oculate [*o*kewlayt] *adj* having ocelli.

oculist [*o*kewlist] *n* medical specialist in the treatment of the eye.

odal [*O*dal] *n* (*hist*) absolute tenure of land without feudal service.

odalisque [*O*dalisk] *n* female slave or concubine in a harem.

odd [*o*d] *adj* strange, unusual; eccentric; surprising; not regular; unimportant; (*of numbers*) not divisible by two; in the series one, three, five *etc*; identified by an odd number; one of pair of objects if the other is missing; part of incomplete set; surplus; to spare; o. job casual employment, single piece of work.

Oddfellow [*o*dfelO] *n* member of a friendly society resembling the Freemasons.

oddity [*o*diti] *n* unusual, eccentric person or thing; quality of being strange.

oddly [*o*dli] *adv* strangely.

oddment [*o*dment] *n* remnant, something left over; small trifle.

oddness [*o*dnis] *n* strangeness.

odds [*o*dz] *n* (*pl*) inequality; difference; chance in favour of one side in a contest; that which would be needed for equality; allowance made to the weaker player; (*betting*) ratio between money staked and amount payable if the bet is won; **at o.** disagreeing, quarrelling; **o. and ends** remnants, fragments, trifles; **it makes no o.** it doesn't matter; **long o.** heavy probability; **over the o.** too much; **what's the o.?** what difference does it make?

odds-on [*o*dz-*on*] *adj* a better than even (chance).

ode [*O*d] *n* poem in elaborate or irregular lyric form.

odious [*O*di-us] *adj* hateful; disgusting, loathsome ~ **odiously** *adv* ~ **odiousness** *n*.

odium [*O*di-um] *n* state or quality of being odious; hatred; bitter blame.

odometer [*O*dom*i*ter] *n* instrument for measuring mileage of a wheeled vehicle.

odont-, odonto- *pref* of the teeth.

odontoglossum [Odont*O*glo*su*m] *n* tropical American orchid.

odontoid [Odont*o*id] *adj* tooth-shaped.

odontology [odont*o*loji] *n* study of teeth.

odoriferous [Ode*Ri*feRus] *adj* fragrant, sweet-smelling ~ **odoriferousness** *n*.

odorous [Ode*R*us] *adj* sweet-smelling; (*coll*) bad-smelling ~ **odorously** *adv* ~ **odorousness** *n*.

odour [Oder] *n* smell; sweet smell, scent; (*fig*) reputation; **o. of sanctity** obvious holiness.

odyssey [*o*disi] *n* (*fig*) prolonged adventurous journey; account of this.

oecology see ecology.

oecumenical see ecumenical.

oedema, edema [eedee*m*a] *n* swelling of tissue by increase of fluid content; localized dropsy.

oedipal [eedipal] *adj* (*psych*) of, caused by, the Oedipus complex.

Oedipus complex [eedipus-kompleks] *n* unconscious sexual love of a son for his mother, with jealous hate of the father > PDP.

œil-de-bœuf [u-ee-de-*buf*] *n* (*archi*) small round or oval window.

o'er [*awr*] *prep* and *adv* (*poet*) over.

oersted [*u*rsted] *n* unit of magnetic intensity.

oesophagus [ees*o*fagus] *n* gullet, tube leading from mouth to stomach ~ **oesophageal** [eeso-*faji*-al] *adj*.

oestrogen [eest*R*ojin] *n* any of various female sex hormones > PDB.

oestrous [eest*R*us] *adj* pertaining to the female reproductive cycle > PDB.

oestrus [eest*R*us] *n* period of sexual excitement in female animals.

of [*o*v] *prep* belonging to; concerning; having; formed from; coming from; made by; due to, caused by; by; from; containing; distant from; during; at; in.

off [*o*f] *adv* away, to or at a distance; separated from; not on; not functioning; not at work or on duty; **o. and on** from time to time, irregularly; **they're o.!** (*racing*) the race has begun!; **o. with you!** go away! ~ **off** *prep* not on; down from; away from; (*coll*) disliking, averse to ~ **off** *adj* separated; (*of horse, vehicle etc*) on the right side; remote; unlikely; unlucky; not available; cancelled; in bad health; inactive, dull; disappointing; stale; decaying, tainted; (*sl*) unfair, ill-mannered; (*cricket*) to the right of a right-handed batsman ~ **off** *n* (*cricket*) offside.

offal [*o*fal] *n* edible internal organs of animals; discarded rubbish, garbage; waste matter; carrion.

offbeat [*o*fbeet] *adj* (*jazz*) with strong accent on second and fourth beat; (*coll*) unusual.

offchance [*o*fchaans] *n* slight possibility.

off-colour [*o*f-*kuler*] *adj* unwell; (*sl*) indecent.

offcut [*o*fkut] *n* piece of material remaining after a larger item has been cut out; trimming.

off-day [*o*f-day] *n* day when one is unusually unlucky, clumsy, inefficient *etc*.

offence [o*fens*] *n* breach of law or custom; wrongful deed; sin; insult; annoyance, resentment; (*mil*) attack; **take o.** feel offended.

offend [o*fend*] *v/t* and *i* insult; hurt the feelings of, annoy; disgust; outrage; do wrong, break (law or custom); sin ~ **offender** *n* one who offends; lawbreaker, criminal.

offensive [o*fe*nsiv] *adj* displeasing, annoying; disgusting; insulting; indecent; (*mil*) for use in attacking ~ **offensive** *n* act of attacking; effort to achieve a goal *etc*; **take the o.** be the first to attack ~ **offensively** *adv* ~ **offensiveness** *n*.

offer [o*fe*r] *v/t* and *i* present as a gift or for sale; present to be taken or refused; give; give as sacrifice or as sign of worship; hold out towards; show signs of; happen ~ **offer** *n* act of offering; that which is offered; expression of willingness; proposal; bid.

offering [o*fe*Ring] *n* something offered in worship or as alms; money donated; gift.

offertory [o*fe*rtoRi] *n* (*eccles*) act of offering the Eucharistic bread and wine to God before the consecration; prayer said then; alms collected during or after a religious service; music to be played at the offertory.

offhand [o*fh*and] *adj* casual, curt; aloof; extempore ~ **offhand** *adv* without preparation, extempore.

offhanded [o*fh*andid] *adj* offhand ~ **offhandedly** *adv*.

office [o*fis*] *n* duty, task; function; building or room where clerical and administrative work is done; place of business; position entailing responsibility; government department; religious ceremony, rite; (*pl*) kitchen *etc*; lavatory; (*sl*) hint; **good offices** helpful intervention; **last offices** preparation of a corpse for burial; prayers said over a corpse.

office-boy [o*fis*-boi] *n* errand-boy employed in an office.

officer [o*fis*er] *n* one holding a position of authority and responsibility; one holding a commission in the armed forces; master, captain or mate of merchant ship; **o. at (of) arms** herald; **o. of the day** executive officer on duty on a specified day; **police o.** police constable ~ **officer** *v/t* provide officers for; be in command of.

official [o*fish*al] *n* one holding responsible post in a public organization; one holding public office; officer; judge in ecclesiastical court ~ **official** *adj* of or in a position of authority; holding office; by or from persons in authority; authorized; authoritative; formal, ceremonious; lawful.

officialdom [o*fish*aldom] *n* body of public officials; bureaucracy; bureaucratic outlook, manner *etc*; red tape.

officialese [o*fish*a*leez*] *n* jargon characteristic of official documents.

officialism [o*fish*alizm] *n* rules, methods or routine of officials; excessive use of these.

officially [o*fish*ali] *adv* in an official way.

officiant [o*fish*i-ant] *n* one who conducts a religious ceremony.

officiate [o*fish*i-ayt] *v/i* preside; conduct a ceremony, *esp* religious ~ **officiator** *n*.

officinal [o*fis*inal] *adj* (*of drugs etc*) of recognized medical value; stocked by chemists.

officious [o*fish*us] *adj* offering unwelcome advice, help *etc*; meddling, intruding; (*of officials*) overbearing, authoritarian; (*diplomacy*) informal ~ **officiously** *adv* ~ **officiousness** *n*.

offing [o*fing*] *n* area of sea visible from shore and nearer to horizon than to land; **in the o.** (*fig*) likely to come or happen; approaching.

offish [o*fish*] *adj* (*coll*) aloof.

off-key [*of*-kee] *adj* out of tune.

off-licence [*of*-lIsens] *n* licence to sell intoxicants not to be consumed on the premises; shop or public house holding this licence.

offload [o*flOd*] *v/t* unload.

off-peak [*of*-peek] *adj* not during the period of greatest activity or demand.

offprint [*of*pRint] *n* separate reprint of article from magazine *etc*.

off-putting [*of*-*pooting*] *adj* (*coll*) disconcerting, causing dislike or hesitation.

offscourings [*of*skowrRingz] *n* (*pl*) rubbish; worthless part.

offset [*of*set] *n* beginning, start; (*hort*) side-shoot used to propagate new plant; (*naut*) current flowing outwards from shore; (*typ*) transfer of ink from one printed sheet to another; method of printing from rubber roller marked by inked plate; (*bui*) ledge produced when thickness of wall is lessened; (*surveying*) horizontal distance measured at right angles to survey line to locate a point off the line ~ **offset** (*pres/part* **offsetting**, *p/t* and *p/part* **offset**) *v/t* and *i* compensate for; make an offset.

offshoot [*of*shOOt] *n* secondary growth or development; branch; collateral descendant.

offshore [*of*shawr] *adv* and *adj* at a distance from the shore, but within the offing; in a direction away from the shore.

offside [*of*sId] *adj* (*in ball-games*) on the opposite side; debarred from playing in specified position.

offspring [*of*spRing] *n* children; (*fig*) result.

offstage [*of*stayj] *adj* when not acting in front of an audience: not seen or known by the public.

off-the-cuff [of-THe-*kuf*] *adj* spontaneous, not prepared or rehearsed.

off-the-peg [of-THe-*peg*] *adj* (*of clothes*) ready-made, mass-produced.

offward [*of*werd] *adv* (*naut*) away from shore.

off-white [*of*-wIt] *n* and *adj* extremely pale grey or cream, almost pure white.

oft [*of*t] *pref* and *adv* (*poet* and *ar*) often.

often [ofen/*of*ten] *adv* many times; in many cases.

oftentimes [ofentImz] *adv* (*ar*) often.

ogam see **ogham**.

ogee [O*jee*] *n* (*archi*) S-shaped double curve.

ogham, (US) ogam [ogam] *n* ancient Irish alphabet of groups of strokes ~ **oghamic** [ogamik] *adj*.

ogival [O*jI*val] *adj* (*archi*) with ogives; in the shape of an ogive.

ogive [O*jIv*] *n* (*archi*) pointed arch; diagonal vault-rib.

ogle [O*g'l*] *v/t* and *i* cast obviously amorous glances (at) ~ **ogle** *n* ~ **ogling** *adj*.

ogmic [ogmik] *adj* of or in ogham writing.

ogre [O*ger*] *n* evil giant, *esp* if man-eating; (*fig*) bad-tempered man.

ogreish, ogrish [Ogerish, Ogrish] *adj* like an ogre.

ogress (*pl* **ogresses**) [O*gRes*] *n* female ogre.

oh [O] *interj* expressing any emotion.

ohm [O*m*] *n* unit of electric resistance > PDS.

ohmic [Omik] *adj* measured in ohms; of an ohm.

oho [O*hO*] *interj* expressing surprise.

oil [*oil*] *n* one of various fatty organic or mineral substances liquid at 20° C, inflammable, and not soluble in water; one of these used as fuel, lubricant, or in cooking; (*pl*) pigments to be mixed in

509

oil; painting done with these; (*sl*) flattery; bribe; Holy O. blessed oil used sacramentally; **midnight o.** reading or study done late at night; **pour o. on troubled waters** tactfully soothe quarrelling persons; **throw o. on the flames** make a quarrel *etc* worse; **strike o.** find a supply of mineral oil; (*fig*) make a valuable discovery; **grow rich ~ oil** *v/t* lubricate with oil; cover or smear with oil; **o. the palm** of bribe; **o. the wheels** avert difficulties, disagreements *etc*.

oilbox [*oil*boks] *n* receptacle attached to wheel-hub holding supply of lubricant.

oilcake [*oil*kayk] *n* cattle fodder from crushed oil-seeds.

oilcan [*oil*kan] *n* small-nozzled can for lubricating machinery.

oilcloth [*oil*kloth] *n* cotton material waterproofed with oxidized oil; thin linoleum.

oilcolour [*oil*kuler] *n* paint in which the pigment is blended with oil.

oiled [*oild*] *adj* lubricated; smooth-running, efficient; (*sl*) drunk.

oilfield [*oil*feeld] *n* area producing mineral oil.

oil-fired [*oil*-fIrd] *adj* using oil as fuel.

oil-gauge [*oil*-gayj] *n* device to measure density of oils; device to indicate quantity of oil in container.

oiliness [*oil*ines] *n* quality of being oily.

oilless [*oil*-les] *adj* containing no oil, not lubricated; (*of a bearing*) not needing lubrication.

oilmeal [*oil*meel] *n* ground oilcake.

oil-painting [*oil*-paynting] *n* art of painting with oil-colours; picture painted in oils.

oilpaper [*oil*payper] *n* paper made transparent or waterproof by being soaked in oil.

oilpress [*oil*pRes] *n* device to extract oil from seeds *etc*.

oilrig [*oil*Rig] *n* framework supporting machinery for drilling oilwells, *esp* at sea.

oilsilk [*oil*silk] *n* transparent silk fabric impregnated with oxidized oil.

oilskin [*oil*skin] *n* cloth made waterproof by dressing with oil; garment made of this.

oil-slick [*oil*-slik] *n* film of oil floating on water, *esp* at sea.

oilstone [*oil*stOn] *n* (*carp*) a hone.

oil-sump [*oil*-sump] *n* oil reservoir in lower part of engine crankcase.

oil-tanker [*oil*-tanker] *n* vehicle or vessel carrying oil in bulk.

oilwell [*oil*wel] *n* borehole from which petroleum flows or is pumped.

oily [*oili*] *adj* of or like oil; containing oil; covered or stained with oil; (*fig*) flattering; servile; unctuous.

ointment [*oint*ment] *n* oily or fatty substance applied to the skin for medicinal purposes or as a cosmetic.

okapi [*Okaa*pi] *n* an African ruminant mammal.

okay, o.k. [*Okay*] *adj* and *adv* (*coll*) all right, correct; good; agreed; approved of ~ **okay, o.k.** *v/t* (*coll*) agree to, approve of, allow ~ **okay, o.k.** *n* (*coll*) agreement, sanction.

oke [*Ok*] *adj* and *adv* (*sl*) okay.

okra [*ok*Raa/*Ok*Raa] *n* a plant with fibrous stem and edible seeds.

old [*Old*] *adj* having lived long, aged; made or having existed in the distant past; worn out, exhausted; retired, former; obsolete; of specified age; (*coll*) well-known and liked; experienced, wise; **o. age** period of life from 60 or 65 onwards; **O. Age Pension** state pension granted to old persons; **o. boy** former pupil of specified school; (*coll*) friendly form of address between men, now usually jocular; **o. country** mother-country of colonial settlers, *esp* England; **o. guard** long-standing staunch adherents of a movement; **o. hand** person with experience; **o. hat** (*coll*) out of date; **o. maid** middle-aged spinster; (*coll*) fussy or timid man; **o. man** friendly form of address between men; (*coll*) commander; boss; (*sl*) husband; **o. master** any great European painter from 15th to 18th century; painting by one of these; **o. woman** (*sl*) wife; **O. World** Europe, Asia and Africa ~ **old** *n* (*pl*) old people or things; **of o.** in past times.

olden [*Ol*den] *adj* (*ar*) of or in former times.

old-fashioned [Old-*fash*'nd] *adj* out-of-date; following the customs, taste *etc* of a previous generation; (*sl*) suspicious, critical; bad-tempered ~ **old-fashioned** *n* (*US*) type of whisky drink; glass with flared top and false bottom.

oldie [*Ol*di] *n* (*coll*) old person or thing.

old-maidish [Old-*mayd*ish] *adj* prudish, prim; fussy, timid.

oldster [*Old*ster] *n* (*coll*) person no longer young.

oldtime [*Old*tIm] *adj* (*coll*) old-fashioned.

oldtimer [*Old*tImer] *n* person of long experience.

old-world [Old-*werld*] *adj* pleasantly old-fashioned, quaint; not American.

oleaginous [Oli-*aj*inus] *adj* oily, greasy.

oleander [Oli-*an*der] *n* evergreen poisonous shrub with bright red flowers.

oleaster [Oli-*as*ter] *n* shrub with olive-like fruit; wild olive.

olefine, olefin [*ol*ifeen] *n* (*chem*) one of a series of unsaturated, aliphatic hydrocarbons > PDS.

oleic [Olee-ik] *adj* (*chem*) of oil > PDS; **o. acid** unsaturated fatty acid used in the manufacture of soap.

oleiferous [Olee-*ife*Rus] *adj* producing oil.

olein [Olee-in] *n* (*chem*) glyceride of oleic acid.

oleo- *pref* of or like oil.

oleograph [Oli-ogRaaf] *n* print made to resemble an oil painting.

olfactory [ol*fak*teRi] *adj* pertaining to the sense of smell > PDB.

olig-, oligo- *pref* few; small.

oligarch [*ol*igaark] *n* member of an oligarchy.

oligarchic [oli*gaar*kik] *adj* of an oligarchy.

oligarchy [*ol*igaarki] *n* government by a few persons or families; state so governed; body of people so ruling.

oligopoly [oli*gop*oli] *n* (*comm*) a market situation where each of several producers is able to influence the market but not able to ignore his competitors' reactions.

olio [Oli-o] *n* (*Sp*) mixed stew.

oliphant [*ol*ifant] *n* horn of elephant-ivory; (*ar*) elephant.

olivaceous [oli*vay*shus] *adj* olive green.

olivary [*ol*iveRi] *adj* shaped like an olive.

olive [*ol*iv] *n* (*bot*) evergreen Mediterranean tree; oil-bearing fruit of this; yellowish green; rolled and seasoned slice of meat ~ **olive** *adj* dull yellowish green; sallow.

olive-branch [*o*liv-b*R*anch] *n* emblem of peace or reconciliation; (*joc*) child.

olive-green [*o*liv-g*R*een] *n* and *adj* dull yellowish green.

olive-oil [*o*liv-oil] *n* oil pressed from olives, used in cookery and medicine.

olivine [*o*liveen] *n* green chrysolite.

oloroso [Olo*RO*so] *n* sweet heavy sherry.

Olympiad [O*l*impi-ad] *n* (*Gk hist*) period of four years between celebrations of Olympic games.

Olympian [*o*limpi-an] *adj* god-like, mighty; fit for a god; lofty, condescending, self-important ~ **Olympian** *n* (*Gk myth*) one of the major gods.

Olympic [O*l*impik] *adj* O. games international four-yearly athletic meeting; (*Gk hist*) four-yearly games in honour of Zeus.

ombre [*o*mber] *n* 18th-century card game for three.

ombudsman [*o*mboodzman] *n* official empowered to investigate individual complaints of bureaucratic injustice.

omega [O*m*ega] *n* last letter of Greek alphabet; (*fig*) final point, ultimate goal.

omelet, omelette [*o*mlet] *n* eggs beaten, flavoured and fried.

omen [O*m*en] *n* thing or event preternaturally indicating the future, portent.

ominous [*o*minus] *adj* foreboding evil; threatening ~ **ominously** *adv* ~ **ominousness** *n*.

omissible [O*m*isib'l] *adj* that can be omitted.

omission [O*m*ishon] *n* act of leaving out, omitting; thing left out; failure to perform duty.

omit (*pres/part* omitting, *p/t* and *p/part* omitted) [O*m*it] *v/t* leave out; fail to do or include.

omni- *pref* all.

omnibus (*pl* omnibuses) [*o*mnibus] *n* large public vehicle conveying passengers along a fixed route, bus ~ **omnibus** *adj* having many uses; comprising many objects; **o. book, o. volume** book containing several works previously published separately, *usu* by same author.

omnifarious [omni*fair*Ri-us] *adj* of all kinds.

omniparity [omni*pa*Riti] *n* equality in all things; equality for all.

omnipotence [om*nip*Otens] *n* absolute and unlimited power.

omnipotent [om*nip*Otent] *adj* all-powerful, almighty.

omnipresence [omni*pRe*zens] *n* faculty of being present everywhere at once.

omnipresent [omni*pRe*zent] *adj* present everywhere at once.

omniscience [om*n*isi-ens/om*n*ishens] *n* total and unlimited knowledge.

omniscient [om*n*isi-ent/om*n*ishent] *adj* knowing everything.

omnium [*o*mnium] *n* sum total; **o. gatherum** miscellaneous collection.

omnivorous [om*niv*eRus] *adj* eating all kinds of food; (*fig*) reading or enjoying indiscriminately.

omophagous [O*m*ofagus] *adj* eating raw flesh.

omoplate [O*m*Oplayt] *n* the shoulder-blade.

omphalic [om*f*alik] *adj* like or of the navel.

omphalus [*o*mfalus] *n* navel; shield-boss.

on [*o*n] *prep* above and touching; covering; supported by; at the date of; on to; concerning; near to; (*coll*) at the expense of; to the loss of ~ **on**

adv in contact; in position; continuing uninterruptedly or in the same direction; functioning, yielding power, heat, motion *etc*; taking or about to take place, not cancelled; (*coll*) willing; at stake; **o. and off** now and then, intermittently; **o. and o.** without interruption ~ **on** *adj* (*cricket*) to left of the batsman ~ **on** *n* (*cricket*) on-side.

onager (*pl* onagri, onagers) [*o*najer] *n* a wild ass.

onanism [O*n*anizm] *n* the interrupting of coition before the emission of semen; masturbation ~ **onanist** *n*.

once [*wuns*] *adv* on a single occasion, at one time only; in former times; **all at o.** suddenly; **at o.** immediately; **for o.** as an exception; **o. in a way** occasionally; **o. upon a time** long ago ~ **once** *conj* as soon as ~ **once** *n* one occasion.

once-over [*wuns*-Over] *n* (*coll*) short superficial examination, inquiry or treatment.

oncoming [*o*n-kuming] *adj* approaching from in front; (*sl*) friendly, making advances ~ **oncoming** *n* approach.

oncost [*o*n-kost] *n* overhead expenses; **o. man** (*mining*) miner not on piecework.

one [*wun*] *adj* single, being or of unity; forming a single whole, undivided; united; certain; some ~ **one** *n* the first integer; symbol of this; the first object in a numbered series; a particular single person or thing; **o. and all** everyone; **o. another** reciprocally; **o. by o.** singly in succession; **o. up on** (*coll*) at an advantage over ~ **one** *pron* a certain person or thing; someone; anybody, people; **a o.** (*coll*) remarkable person; **a o. for** (*coll*) an enthusiast for.

one-armed [*wun*-aarmd] *adj* having only one arm; **o. bandit** slot gambling machine.

one-eyed [*wun*-Id] *adj* blind in one eye; having only one eye; (*sl*) petty, unimportant; inferior.

one-horse [*wun*-hawrs] *adj* drawn by or made to be drawn by a single horse; (*coll*) on small scale, inferior.

oneiro- *pref* of dreams.

oneirology [onIr*Ro*loji] *n* study of dreams and their interpretation.

oneness [*wun*-nes] *n* being one; uniqueness, singularity; state of being united, concord, unity; changelessness, sameness.

one-off [*wun*-of] *adj* only made or done once, impossible to repeat.

one-piece [*wun*-pees] *adj* made as a single complete item; not made of separate parts.

oner [*wun*er] *n* (*coll*) remarkable person or thing; an expert; knock-out blow.

onerous [*o*neRus] *adj* burdensome, laborious ~ **onerously** *adv* ~ **onerousness** *n*.

oneself [wun*self*] *pron emph* and *refl* form of **one.**

one-sided [wun-s*I*did] *adj* unequally balanced; considering only one side of a question; biased, prejudiced ~ **one-sidedly** *adv* ~ **one-sidedness** *n*.

onestep [*wun*step] *n* simple type of ballroom dance.

onetime [*wun*tIm] *adj* (*coll*) former.

one-track [*wun*-t*R*ak] *adj* (*fig*) interested in one thing only.

one-up [*wun*-up] *adj* having an advantage of one point over an adversary; maintaining psychological superiority.

one-upmanship [wun-*up*manship] *n* (*coll*) art or

practice of maintaining an advantage over others by displaying superior knowledge, possessions *etc.*

one-way [*wun*-way] *adj* (*of streets*) in which traffic is allowed in one direction only.

onfall [*on*fawl] *n* an attack, onset.

ongoing [*ong*O-ing] *adj* still existing or progressing; not completed.

onion [*un*yon] *n* pungent bulb used as vegetable and flavouring; flaming rocket used against aircraft; (*sl*) head; **know one's onions** be clever and experienced; **off one's o.** (*sl*) mad ~ **oniony** *adj.*

onlooker [*on*looker] *n* spectator.

only [*On*li] *adj* alone of its kind, sole, unique; best of its kind ~ **only** *adv* solely, exclusively; merely; **if o.** oh that (*expressing strong wish*); **o. just** barely; **o. too** very ~ **only** *conj* except that.

onomastic [on*O*mastik] *adj* of proper names.

onomatopoeia [onomat*O*pee-a] *n* formation of words by imitation of natural sounds associated with the act or object to be denoted; (*rhet*) choice of words whose sound fits their sense ~ **onomatopoeic** *adj.*

onrush [*on*Rush] *n* impetuous forward rush.

onset [*on*set] *n* attack; beginning.

onshore [*on*shawr] *adj* blowing towards land.

onslaught [*on*slawt] *n* vigorous attack.

onto [*on*too] *prep* to a position upon.

onto- *pref* being, existence.

ontogenesis [ont*O*jenisis] *n* (*biol*) course of development of the individual ~ **ontogenetic** [ont*O*jenetik] *adj.*

ontogeny [on*to*jini] *n* ontogenesis > PDP.

ontological [onto*lo*jikal] *adj* of ontology.

ontology [on*to*loji] *n* (*philos*) part of metaphysics relating to the nature of existence.

onus [*On*us] *n* burden, responsibility; **o. probandi** (*leg*) responsibility of proving one's assertion.

onward [*on*werd] *adv* and *adj* in a forward direction; advancing.

onwards [*on*werdz] *adv* onward.

onyx [*on*iks/*On*iks] *n* variety of agate.

oo- *pref* of an egg.

oocyte [*O*-osIt] *n* cell which forms ovum > PDB.

oodles [*OO*d'lz] *n* (*pl*) (*coll*) a great number.

oof [*OOf*] *n* (*sl*) money.

oogenesis [*O*-ojenisis] *n* (*zool*) formation of ovum > PDB.

ooh [*OO*] *interj* expressing excitement, happy surprise, or pain.

oolite [*O*-olIt] *n* granular form of limestone; (*geol*) rocks of this structure ~ **oolitic** [*O*-o*li*tik] *adj.*

oologist [*O*-*o*lojist] *n* birds'-egg enthusiast.

oomph [*oomf*] *n* (*sl*) energy; sex appeal.

oops [*OO*ps] *interj* expressing dismay at a blunder.

ooze [*OO*z]*n* liquid mud, *esp* on ocean or river bed > PDG; slowly trickling liquid ~ **ooze** *v/i* and *t* trickle slowly; drip; exude; **o. away** (*fig*) gradually disappear; **o. with** exude ~ **oozily** *adv* ~ **oozy** *adj.*

opacity [*O*pasiti] *n* state of being opaque; darkness; (*fig*) inability to understand; obscurity.

opal [*O*pal] *n* iridescent semi-precious siliceous stone.

opalescence [*O*pa*le*sens] *n* iridescence ~ **opalescent** [*O*pa*le*sent] *adj* iridescent.

opaline [*O*palIn] *adj* like opal.

opaque [*O*payk] *adj* not transparent, letting no light through; dark; obscure; stupid ~ **opaquely** *adv* ~ **opaqueness** *n.*

op-art [*op*-aart] *adj* and *n* (of or in) a form of abstract art using geometric patterns, *usu* in black and white, to produce optical illusions of movement.

ope [*Op*] *v/t* and *i* (*poet*) open.

open [*Op*en] *adj* not closed, enclosed or covered in; allowing free passage; unrestricted, free; freely available or accessible; ready to admit customers or the public; ready to do business; unbiased; broad-minded; generous; frank; widely known, obvious; visible; not decided, settled or agreed on; not already occupied; (*of an offer*) neither accepted nor withdrawn; (*of country*) not wooded; (*mil*) undefended, liable to be attacked; (*bot*) with petals expanded; (*phon*) without complete closure of air-passages; (*of syllable*) ending in a vowel; **o. air** out of doors; **o. cheque** uncrossed cheque; **o. court** trial conducted in public; **keep o. house** be always willing to receive guests; **o. letter** letter addressed to one person but published by the writer so as to be public; **o. order** (*mil*) formation of men three or more yards apart; **o. secret** something supposed to be secret but in fact well known; **o. shop** business employing both union and non-union workers; **o. and shut** straightforward; **o. university** educational scheme of university level studies by correspondence and TV and radio tuition, requiring no previous qualifications; **o. verdict** verdict of coroner's jury recording inability to decide the cause of death; **with o. arms** gladly welcoming; **with o. hand** generously ~ **open** *n* the open air; unprotected position; **come into the o.** be frank ~ **open** *v/t* and *i* unfasten; spread out; cut a passage through; make accessible; begin; set up, start; declare to be open to the public; unfold; come into view; **o. the eyes of** undeceive; **o. on to** lead into, give access to; **o. out** unfold, spread; **o. up** explore; begin firing (on); become open; start (an enterprise); (*coll*) speak freely.

open-air [Open-*air*] *adj* done out of doors; fond of out-of-doors activities.

opencast [*Open*kaast] *adj* (*mining*) excavating surface areas only.

open-eared [Open-*eerd*] *adj* listening eagerly.

open-ended [Open-*end*id] *adj* not planned to stop at a fixed time; not guided towards pre-selected conclusions; (*fig*) flexible, adaptable.

opener [*Open*er] *n* one who or that which opens, *esp* implement to open tins or bottles.

open-eyed [Open-*Id*] *adj* vigilant; amazed ~ **open-eyed** *adv* with full awareness; in amazement.

open-field [Open-*feeld*] *adj* (*hist*) **o. system** system by which arable land of village was divided into strips among the villagers.

open-handed [Open-*hand*id] *adj* generous.

open-hearted [Open-*haart*id] *adj* kindly; frank.

opening [*Opening*/*Opn*ing] *n* act of making or becoming open; gap, hole, breach; first part, beginning; opportunity, *esp* for career; **o. time** hour when licensed houses can start to sell liquor ~ **opening** *adj* that opens; (*med*) aperient.

openly [*Open*li] *adv* without concealment; publicly.

open-minded [Open-*mInd*id] *adj* unprejudiced.

open-mouthed [Open-*mowtHd*] *adj* and *adv* gaping in astonishment; greedy, greedily; eager, eagerly.

openness [Open-nes] *n* quality of being open; candour; impartiality.

openplan [Openplan] *adj* with no or few internal walls or partitions.

openwork [Openwurk] *n* and *adj* (embroidery *etc*) showing spaces in the material.

opera [*ope*Ra] *n* drama in which most of the words are set to orchestral music > PDM; company performing this; **o. bouffe** [*ope*Ra-bOOf] comic opera; **grand o.** large-scale opera on tragic theme; **light o.** romantic and amusing opera.

operable [*ope*Rab'l] *adj* (*surg*) that can be operated on.

opera-cloak [*ope*Ra-klOk] *n* woman's long cloak.

opera-glasses [*ope*Ra-glaasiz] *n* (*pl*) binoculars for use in theatres.

opera-hat [*ope*Ra-hat] *n* collapsible top-hat.

opera-house · [*ope*Ra-hows] *n* theatre in which operas are performed.

operate [*ope*Rayt] *v/t* and *i* carry out (a function), work; cause (machinery) to work; perform surgical operation (on); (*mil*) go into action; manoeuvre.

operatic [*ope*Ratik] *adj* pertaining to opera.

operating [*ope*Rayting] *adj* of or used in an operation, *esp* in surgery.

operation [*ope*Rayshon] *n* act of operating; series of acts; military action; plan, project; undertaking, task; surgical procedure carried out on live body, *esp* with instruments.

operational [*ope*Rayshonal] *adj* of or for an operation; fit to take part in, required for, a military operation; in working order.

operative [*ope*Rativ] *adj* working; exerting influence, producing effect; valid ~ **operative** *n* worker, *esp* in a factory ~ **operatively** *adv*.

operator [*ope*Rayter] *n* one who works a machine, *esp* radio transmitter or telephone switchboard; one who performs a surgical operation; one who deals in stocks and shares.

operculum (*pl* **opercula**) [*ope*urkewlum] *n* organ resembling a lid; (*zool*) gill-cover of fishes; flap closing the shell of some molluscs; (*bot*) lid of seed-capsule.

operetta [*ope*Reta] *n* short light opera.

ophicleide [*ofi*klId] *n* obsolete brass instrument with keys > PDM.

ophidian [*ofi*di-an] *adj* and *n* (of or like) a snake.

ophiology [ofi-*olo*ji] *n* study of snakes.

ophthalmia [of*thal*mi-a] *n* inflammation of the eye.

ophthalmic [of*thal*mik] *adj* of the eye.

ophthalmology [of*thal*moloji] *n* scientific study of the eye.

ophthalmoscope [of*thal*mOskOp] *n* instrument for examining the interior of the eye.

opiate [Opi-ayt] *n* and *adj* (medicine) containing opium; soporific; (that) which causes sleep or lethargy, or dulls the feelings.

opine [Op*In*] *v/t* express as one's opinion.

opinion [op*in*yon] *n* considered view, judgement, belief; estimate; point of view ~ **opinionated** *adj* obstinate in one's opinions; dogmatic ~ **opinionative** *adj* opinionated.

opisometer [Opi*som*iter] *n* instrument for measuring distances on a map.

opium [Opi-um] *n* intoxicant and narcotic drug obtained from seed-capsules of the white poppy; **o. den** place where opium can be bought and smoked ~ **opiumism** *n* addiction to opium.

opossum [O*pos*um] *n* small marsupial mammal of America; Australian phalanger.

oppidan [o*pi*dan] *n* (*Eton College*) pupil who boards in the town.

opponent [op*On*ent] *n* enemy; adversary; one who takes the opposite side ~ **opponent** *adj* opposing.

opportune [*ope*rtewn] *adj* suitable, appropriate; well timed ~ **opportunely** *adv* ~ **opportuneness** *n*.

opportunism [*ope*rtewnizm] *n* policy of basing one's conduct on present circumstances not on principles; practice of taking profit from all occasions ~ **opportunist** *n* and *adj*.

opportunity [*ope*rte*w*niti] *n* favourable time for action; favourable chance.

oppose [op*Oz*] *v/t* and *i* resist, strive to defeat; argue against; vote against; pit against ~ **opposer** *n* ~ **opposing** *adj*.

opposite [*opo*zit] *adj* facing, in front of; on the other side of a division; antagonistic, contrary; in reverse direction; corresponding; **o. number** person whose position corresponds to one's own; counterpart ~ **opposite** *n* one who or that which is the contrary of another.

opposition [op*Oz*ishon] *n* act of opposing; that which opposes; opposing party; obstacle; resistance, hostility; position of being opposite ~ **opposition** *adj* of an opposing party, *esp* in Parliament; (*astron*) position of two planets when they are in line with the sun, but on opposite sides of it ~ **oppositionist** *adj* and *n*.

oppress [op*Res*] *v/t* treat cruelly, tyrannize over; crush, keep down; rule tyrannically; depress; make weary.

oppression [op*Res*hon] *n* act of oppressing; tyranny; weariness; depression.

oppressive [op*Res*iv] *adj* that oppresses; tyrannical; exhausting; (*of weather*) sultry ~ **oppressively** *adv* ~ **oppressiveness** *n*.

oppressor [op*Res*er] *n* one who oppresses.

opprobrious [op*RObR*i-us] *adj* insulting; disgraceful; reproachful; scurrilous ~ **opprobriously** *adv*.

opprobrium [op*RObR*i-um] *n* abusive language; reproach; cause of reproach; disgrace, dishonour.

opt [opt] *v/i* choose, decide; **o. out** choose to take no part in.

optant [optant] *n* person who may choose his nationality.

optative [optativ] *n* and *adj* (*gramm*) (mood) expressing desire.

optic [optik] *adj* pertaining to the eyes or sight; **o. art** op-art ~ **optic** *n* (*sl*) eye.

optical [optikal] *adj* of sight; of the eyes; **o. illusion** illusion due to misinterpretation of what is seen ~ **optically** *adv*.

optician [op*tish*an] *n* one who makes and sells spectacles and optical instruments.

optics [optiks] *n* scientific study of light and sight.

optimism [optimizm] *n* cheerful hopefulness; tendency to look on the bright side; doctrine that good outweighs or will conquer evil; (*philos*) doctrine that this world is the best possible.

optimist [optimist] *n* believer in optimism.

optimistic [optimistik] *adj* showing or believing in optimism; hopeful ~ **optimistical** *adj* ~ **optimistically** *adv*.

optimize [optimIz] *v/t* and *i* make the best of; take favourable view.

optimum [optimum] *adj* and *n* best, most favourable (condition, degree *etc*).

option [opshon] *n* right or power to choose; choice; (*comm*) contract to buy or sell at fixed price on fixed date: **keep one's options open** avoid committing oneself.

optional [opshonal] *adj* not compulsory; that can be accepted or refused ~ **optionally** *adv*.

opulence [opewlens] *n* wealth; abundance.

opulent [opewlent] *adj* wealthy; abundant, luxuriant ~ **opulently** *adv*.

opus [Opus] *n* work, composition, *esp* in music > PDM; **magnum o.** chief work of musician, writer *etc*.

opuscule, opusculum (*pl* **opuscula**) [opuskewl, opuskewlum] *n* a minor literary or musical work.

or (1) [awr] *n* (*her*) gold.

or (2) *conj* introducing an alternative; introducing a synonym; otherwise, if not so.

or (3) *conj* (*ar*) ere, before.

oracle [oRak'l] *n* prophecy or advice given by Greek or Roman priest under divine inspiration; place where this was given; (*fig*) remarkably wise person; prophecy or advice, *esp* if obscure; (*OT*) sanctuary of Jewish temple; High Priest's breastplate: **work the o.** obtain one's end by intrigue.

oracular [oRakewler] *adj* of or like an oracle; ambiguous, riddling; prophetic; wise; solemn.

oracy [oRasi] *n* fluency in talking, ability to express ideas well in speech.

oral [awRal] *adj* of, in or by the mouth; spoken, verbal; o. **contraceptive** any of various hormone pills to inhibit ovulation ~ **oral** *n* verbal examination ~ **orally** *adv*.

orange [oRinj] *n* large citrus fruit with red-gold rind; tree producing this; reddish gold colour; **Blenheim o., Cox's o.** types of eating apple ~ **orange** *adj* reddish-golden.

orangeade [oRinjayd] *n* sweet drink made with orange-juice or synthetic orange flavouring.

orange-blossom [oRinj-blosum] *n* white flower of orange-tree, worn by brides.

Orangeman [oRinjman] *n* member of an Irish Protestant political society.

orangepeel [oRinjpeel] *n* rind peeled from an orange.

orangery [oRinjeRi] *n* hothouse or sheltered orchard where oranges are grown in cool climates.

orange-stick [oRinj-stik] *n* small wooden stick for manicure.

orangetip [oRinjtip] *n* a type of butterfly.

orang-outang, orang-utan [awRang-OOtang, awRang-OOtan] *n* a large anthropoid ape.

orate [oRayt] *v/i* (*coll*) make a speech.

oration [oRayshon] *n* formal discourse.

orator [oRater] *n* public speaker; eloquent speaker; **Public O.** the official speaker for a University.

oratorical [oRatoRikal] *adj* of or like an oration or orator ~ **oratorically** *adv*.

oratorio [oRatawRi-O] *n* musical composition for solo voices, chorus and orchestra > PDM.

oratory (1) [oRateRi] *n* art of an orator; rhetoric.

oratory (2) *n* small room or chapel set apart for private prayer; (*RC*) Society of St Philip Neri.

orb [awrb] *n* sphere; globe; small globe surmounted by a cross, symbol of sovereignty ~ **orb** *v/t* (*poet*) encircle ~ **orbed** *adj* spherical; round.

orbicular [awrbikewler] *adj* circular; spherical.

orbit [awrbit] *n* (*astron*) curving track followed by artificial satellite or heavenly body in revolving round another body; single circuit of this track; circular path; (*fig*) range of influence; way of life; (*phys*) path taken by electrons round the nucleus; (*anat*) eye-socket ~ **orbit** *v/i* and *t* (*of satellite*) revolve (round); move in its correct orbit.

orbital [awrbital] *adj* of the eye-socket; of an orbit.

orc [awrk] *n* a grampus.

orchard [awrcherd] *n* plantation of fruit-trees.

orchestra [awrkestRa] *n* numerous body of musicians for playing instrumental music > PDM; space in front of stage for such musicians; (*Gk theat*) space where chorus danced.

orchestral [awrkestRal] *adj* by or for an orchestra; of or like an orchestra.

orchestrate [awrkestRayt] *v/t* score (a work) for orchestral performance > PDM ~ **orchestration** [awrkestRayshon] *n*.

orchid [awrkid] *n* any of a family of three-petalled flowers of striking colour and shape.

orchidaceous [awrkidayshus] *adj* of or like orchids; showy.

orchis [awrkis] *n* orchid, *esp* wild variety.

orchitis [awrkItis] *n* (*path*) inflammation of the testicles ~ **orchitic** [awrkitik] *adj*.

ordain [awrdayn] *v/t* consecrate as priest; admit to Holy Orders; decree, enact ~ **ordainer** *n*.

ordeal [awrdeel] *n* painful test of courage, endurance *etc*; painful experience; (*hist*) trial in which the accused must prove his innocence by successfully undergoing some dangerous and painful test.

order [awrder] *n* relative position in space, time or degree; systematic arrangement, tidiness; logical or natural sequence; plan; discipline, state of being under control; command, instruction; demand that goods *etc* be supplied; authorization; warrant, permit; authorized procedure; proper behaviour, *esp* in Parliament, committees *etc*; healthy condition, soundness; capacity to work as intended; kind, group, type; social class; title of various religious or aristocratic organizations; body of members of these; (*bot, zool*) subdivision of a class; (*archi*) style; (*mil*) formation; (*eccles*) customary formula of a service or sacrament; (*pl*) (*eccles*) status and office of priest, deacon or (*RC*) subdeacon; **in o.** sound, healthy; working correctly; according to correct procedure; **in o. to so as to,** intending to; **out of o.** ill; broken, not working correctly; violating correct procedure; **tall o.** (*coll*) large demand ~ **order** *v/t* command, decree; direct (goods *etc*) to be made, brought *etc*; arrange, put in correct sequence; direct, regulate; **o. arms** (*mil*) place rifle at one's right side with butt resting on ground; **o. about** bully, domineer over.

ordering [awrdeRing] *n* arrangement, disposal.

orderly [awrderli] *adj* arranged in good order; tidy, systematic; law-abiding, well disciplined; well behaved; (*mil*) on duty; concerned with daily administration ~ **orderly** n hospital attendant; soldier in attendance on an officer.

ordinal (1) [awrdinal] n and adj (number) denoting position in a series.

ordinal (2) n book containing form of service used in ordination and episcopal consecration.

ordinance [awrdinans] n that which is ordered by authority; decree, regulation; religious ceremony, esp a sacrament.

ordinand [awrdinand] n candidate for ordination.

ordinary [awrdineRi] adj usual, customary; normal, average; commonplace; dull ~ **ordinary** n officer holding authority in his own right; cleric holding authority in his own area; set-price meal at inn; inn; (eccles) form of a religious service; (her) a simple charge; **in o.** holding regular appointment; **out of the o.** exceptional ~ **ordinarily** adv usually.

ordinate [awrdinayt] n (mâth) distance of a point on a graph from the x-axis.

ordination [awrdinayshon] n act of conferring Holy Orders; reception of Holy Orders.

ordnance [awrdnans] n artillery; military stores and supplies; **o. survey** accurate detailed geographical survey made for the Government.

ordure [awrdewr] n filth; dung; obscenity.

ore [awr] n mineral from which metal can be extracted; any mineral, even non-metal-bearing, except fuels.

orfray see **orphrey**.

organ [awrgan] n part of animal or plant forming structural and functional unit; keyboard instrument in which wind is blown by bellows through pipes > PDM; means of influencing public opinion or expressing the opinion of a group; newspaper.

organdie [awrgandi] n transparent muslin.

organ-grinder [awrgan-gRInder] n one who plays a barrel-organ.

organic [awrganik] adj of, in or affecting bodily organs; having bodily organs; belonging to, or characteristic of, an organized structure; organized, systematic; of or like an organism; basic, essential; **o. chemistry** chemistry of carbon compounds excluding carbonates, oxides, and sulphides; **o. compound** compound found in, or derived from, biological organisms; compound studied in organic chemistry ~ **organically** adv

organism [awrganizm] n (biol) individual capable of growth and reproduction; organized structure of parts working together for the existence of the whole.

organist [awrganist] n player on the organ.

organization [awrganIzayshon] n act of organizing; state of being organized; differentiation of parts and functions, and integration into a systematic interconnected whole; association of persons with a common purpose.

organize [awrganIz] v/t and i group into systematic whole; arrange, prepare; make efficient; cause to cooperate; become an organization ~ **organized** adj having organs or organic life; formed into an organization; well planned or prepared, efficient ~ **organizer** n one who organizes.

organ-loft [awrgan-loft] n raised gallery for an organ.

organo- pref of organisms; of bodily organs, of organic compounds.

organometallic [awrganOmetalik] adj of an organic compound which contains a metal atom or atoms.

organon [awrganon] n a system of rules in logic.

orgasm [awrgazm] n culmination of sexual act; violent excitement, esp erotic.

orgasmic [awrgazmik] adj of, like or producing an orgasm.

orgiastic [awrji-astik] adj of or like orgies.

orgy (pl **orgies**) [awrji] n drunken revelry; uninhibited sexual activity, esp by a group of revellers; period of excessive activity; (hist) religious festivities, esp in honour of Dionysus.

oriel [awRi-el] n recessed or projecting window.

Orient (1) [awR-ient] n eastern part of world, Asia; (poet) eastern sky; lustrous pearl ~ **orient** adj lustrous; (poet) eastern.

orient (2) [awR-ient] v/t and i orientate.

Oriental [awRi-ental] n and adj (native) of Asia, of the Far East ~ **Orientalism** n Oriental characteristic or outlook ~ **Orientalist** n expert on Oriental languages or culture ~ **Orientally** adv.

orientate [awRi-entayt] v/t and i place or be placed in relation to points of compass; face, be directed towards; place (map) on same bearings as oneself; face eastwards; build with long axis running east; (refl) take one's bearings; (fig) take up a mental attitude (towards); become familiar with.

orientation [awRi-entayshon] n direction in relation to points of compass; awareness of spatial relationships; (fig) tendency, inclination.

orienteering [awRi-enteerRing] n (coll) contest in path-finding and cross-country running.

orifice [oRifis] n small opening.

oriflamme [oRiflam] n (hist) sacred French battle-standard.

origami [oRigaami] n Japanese art of folding paper into intricate designs.

origin [oRijin] n beginning, source; initial cause; parentage, ancestry; (math) point from which measurements are taken.

original [oRijinal] adj directly from the origin; earliest; having existed from the beginning; done, made or expressed for the first time; new; capable of producing new ideas or artistic forms; creative, inventive; unconventional, eccentric; **o. sin** inborn sinfulness of human nature; the first human sin ~ **original** n that from which copies are made; first pattern, model; genuine work of art or literature, not a copy; language in which a work was first written; (coll) unconventional or eccentric person; (ar) source, originator.

originality [oRijinaliti] n quality or state of being original; inventiveness; creativity; novelty.

originally [oRijinali] adv in the beginning, at first; in an original way.

originate [oRijinayt] v/t and i give rise to, bring about; come into existence.

origination [oRijinayshon] n act or fact of originating.

originative [oRijinativ] adj creative, inventive.

oriole [awRi-Ol] n black and yellow passerine bird.

orison [oRizon] n (poet) prayer.

Orlon [awrlon] n (tr) synthetic fabric similar to nylon.

orlop [awrlop] n (naut) lowest deck.

ormer [*awr*mer] *n* type of univalve mollusc.

ormolu [*awr*molOO] *n* gold-coloured alloy of copper, zinc and tin; gilded bronze; lacquered brass; furniture ornamented with this.

ornament [*awr*nament] *n* embellishment, that which decorates or adorns; decorative object, *esp* for a room; trinket; article used in church ritual; (*fig*) one who does credit or adds dignity ~ **ornament** [*awr*nament] *v/t* decorate, embellish.

ornamental [awr*nam*ental] *adj* decorative, adding beauty ~ **ornamentally** *adv.*

ornamentation [awrnament*ay*shon] *n* act of ornamenting; style in which a thing is ornamented.

ornate [awr*nayt*] *adj* elaborately ornamented ~ **ornately** *adv* ~ **ornateness** *n.*

ornery [*awr*neRi] *adj* (*US coll*) surly, cross; coarse, cheap, bad.

ornitho- *pref* of birds.

ornithology [awrni*thol*oji] *n* scientific study of birds ~ **ornithological** [awrnitho*loj*ikal] *adj* ~ **ornithologist** *n.*

orotund [o*RO*tund] *adj* pompous, boastful.

orphan [*awr*fan] *n* one who has lost one or both parents ~ **orphan** *v/t* deprive of parent(s) ~ **orphan** *adj.*

orphanage [*awr*fanij] *n* institution for care of orphans; state of being an orphan.

orphanhood [*awr*fanhood] *n* state of being an orphan.

Orphean [awr*fee*-an] *adj* of Orpheus; Orphic, (*poet*) melodious.

Orphic [*awr*fik] *adj* of the mystical doctrines attributed to Orpheus; oracular.

orphrey, orfray [*awr*fRi] *n* band of gold embroidery.

orpiment [*awr*piment] *n* natural arsenic trisulphide, a yellow mineral used as a pigment.

orpin, orpine [*awr*pin] *n* (*bot*) purple stonecrop.

Orpington [*awr*pington] *n* breed of domestic fowl.

orrery [*o*ReRi] *n* mechanism showing movements of the planets.

orris (1) [*o*Ris] *n* embroidery made of gold and silver lace.

orris (2) *n* fragrant root of a species of iris.

ortho- *pref* correct, straight.

orthochromatic [awrthOk*RO*matik] *adj* (*phot*) representing colours truly > PDS.

orthodontics [awrth*Od*ontiks] *n* (*pl*) branch of dentistry that corrects irregularities of the teeth.

orthodox [*awr*thOdoks] *adj* correct in opinions; following generally held beliefs or views; theologically correct; **O. Church** the Greek or Eastern branch of Christendom.

orthodoxy [*awr*thOdoksi] *n* state of being orthodox; orthodox views.

orthogonal [awr*thog*anol] *adj* pertaining to right angles or perpendiculars.

orthographic [awrthog*Raf*ik] *adj* of spelling; **o. projection** (*geog*) map drawn as if viewed from infinity > PDG.

orthography [awr*thog*Rafi] *n* method or rules of spelling; correct spelling; (*drawing*) correct projection of an elevation.

orthopaedic [awrthO*peed*ik] *adj* (*med*) of or practising remedial manipulation and surgery on deformed bones.

orthopaedics, orthopaedy [awrthO*peed*iks, awr-

thO*peed*i] *n* branch of surgery dealing with bone deformities ~ **orthopaedist** *n.*

orthopterous [awr*thop*teRus] *adj* belonging to the order of insects whose wings fold down the back.

ortolan [*awr*tOlan] *n* (*orni*) garden bunting.

oryx [*o*Riks] *n* genus of African antelopes with long straight horns.

Oscar [*os*kar] *n* prize for high achievement in cinema acting, production *etc.*

oscillate [*os*ilayt] *v/i* swing or cause to swing to and fro; vibrate; waver, hesitate; vary between two states; (*rad*) radiate electro-magnetic waves; suffer interference from this.

oscillation [osi*lay*shon] *n* act of oscillating.

oscillator [*os*ilayter] *n* any device exhibiting sustained oscillations; (*elect*) apparatus generating electro-magnetic waves.

oscillograph [o*sil*Ograaf] *n* (*elect*) instrument for recording oscillations.

oscilloscope see **cathode ray oscilloscope.**

osculate [*os*kewlayt] *v/t* and *i* kiss; (*math*) touch at several points ~ **osculation** [oskew*lay*shon] *n* ~ **osculatory** *adj.*

osier [*Oz*i-er] *n* species of willow used in basketmaking; **o. bed** place where many osiers grow.

osmium [*oz*mi-um] *n* a hard and heavy metal of the platinum group.

osmometer [oz*mom*iter] *n* instrument for measuring osmotic pressures ~ **osmometry** *n.*

osmosis [oz*mO*sis] *n* flow of liquid through a semi-permeable membrane.

osmotic [oz*mot*ik] *adj* pertaining to osmosis; **o. pressure** pressure applied to a solution in order to prevent the solvent flowing through a semipermeable membrane.

osprey [*os*pRay] *n* large fish-eating bird of prey; egret plume.

osseous [*osee*-us] *adj* bony; having bones.

ossicle [*os*ik'l] *n* small bone.

ossiferous [o*sif*eRus] *adj* where deposits of bones may be found.

ossification [osifi*kay*shon] *n* process of ossifying; ossified state.

ossify [*os*ifI] *v/i* and *t* develop from tissue into bone; convert into bone; become immovable; (*fig*) cease to progress; harden.

ossuary [*os*ew-eRi] *n* charnel-house; burial-urn.

osteitis [osti-*I*tis] *n* inflammation of bone or bonetissue.

ostensible [os*tens*ib'l] *adj* apparent, pretended; declared but not true ~ **ostensibly** *adv.*

ostensory [os*tens*eRi] *n* (*eccles*) a monstrance.

ostentation [osten*tay*shon] *n* pretentious display; vulgar exhibition of wealth, knowledge *etc.*

ostentatious [osten*tay*shus] *adj* making too obvious a display of wealth, skill, virtue *etc* ~ **ostentatiously** *adv.*

osteo- *pref* of or in bone.

osteo-arthritis [osti-O-aar*thRI*tis] *n* arthritis of one or more of the major joints.

osteology [osti-*ol*oji] *n* the study of bones.

osteopath [*osti*-Opath] *n* one who practises osteopathy; bone-setter.

osteopathy [osti-*op*athi] *n* treatment of disease by bone manipulation.

ostler, hostler [*os*ler] *n* inn-servant who has care of the horses.

ostracism [ostRasizm] *n* deliberate exclusion from a social group; banishment, *esp* in ancient Athens.

ostracize [ostRasIz] *v/t* exclude, refuse to associate with; banish.

ostrich [ostRich] *n* large flightless African bird; (*fig*) one who refuses to face unpleasant truths; one who deludes himself.

other [uTHer] *adj* different, not the one already mentioned; second; additional, more; **the o. day** recently; **every o. day** on alternate days; **o. than** besides ~ **other** *pron* different or additional person or thing; **someone (something)** or **o. an** unknown person or thing ~ **other** *adv* otherwise.

otherness [uTHernis] *n* state of being separate and distinct; quality of being alien; difference.

otherwise [uTHerwIz] *adv* in another way, differently; or else.

otherworld [uTHerwurld] *n* supernatural realm; realm of the dead, or of fairies, spirits *etc*.

otherworldly [uTHerwurldli] *adj* chiefly guided by religious considerations; impractical; spiritual.

otiose [Oti-Os/Oshi-Os] *adj* futile, superfluous.

otitis [Otītis] *n* inflammation of the ear.

otology [Otoloji] *n* study of the ear.

ottava rima [otaava-Reema] *n* (*Ital*) (*pros*) type of eight-line stanza.

otter [oter] *n* web-footed river mammal; weighted board used as fishing tackle; **o. hound** hound used for hunting otters.

Ottoman (1) [otOman] *n* and *adj* Turk.

ottoman (2) *n* settee of various shapes; low upholstered sofa concealing a box.

oubliette [OObli-*et*] *n* hidden dungeon entered by a trapdoor.

ouch (1) [owch] *n* jewelled brooch or buckle.

ouch (2) *interj* exclamation of pain.

ought (1) [awt] *v/aux* have as a duty, be morally bound; be practically certain.

ought (2) see **aught**.

ouija [weeja] *n* (*tr in US*) board marked with letters and signs, used in spiritualistic seances.

ounce (1) [owns] *n* unit of weight, $\frac{1}{16}$ lb. avoirdupois; $\frac{1}{12}$ lb. troy; (*fig*) small amount; **fluid o.** 28·41 cubic centimetres.

ounce (2) *n* lynx; snow-leopard.

our [owr] *adj* of or concerning us; **O. Lady the Virgin Mary; O. Lord** Christ.

ours [owrz] *pron* and *adj* (the one, those) belonging to us.

ourself [owr*self*] *pron* (*used only by sovereigns*) myself.

ourselves [owr*selvz*] *pron refl* and *emph* form of **we** and **us**.

ousel see **ouzel**.

oust [owst] *v/t* drive out; eject, dispossess.

out [owt] *adv* and *adj* away from the interior, from within; not inside; remote; moving away; away from home; excluded; at an end; deviating, incorrect; set free; published, revealed; no longer fashionable; in the open air; on strike; dislocated; mistaken; quarrelling; in bloom; (*of girls*) old enough to mix with adult society, presented at Court; (*boxing*) unable to rise within ten seconds; unconscious; (*games*) beyond the boundary lines; (*cricket*) no longer batting; (*light, fire etc*) extinguished; **o. and o.** complete, thorough; **o. and away** by far; **all o.**, flat o. with utmost speed or strength; **have it o.** make explicit; bring a

quarrel to its crisis; **o. for, o.** to striving to get or do; **o. of** from; because of; beyond; (*of animals*) having as female parent; **o. of it** (*coll*) excluded, isolated; **o. on** (*ar*) shame on; **o. with it !** disclose (a secret) ~ **out** *n* that which or one who is out ~ **out** *v/t* (*coll*) knock out; send away, turn out.

out--*pref* outside; remote; longer; in greater degree; excessively; more successfully.

outback [owtbak] *n* (*Aust*) uncultivated inland area.

outbid (*pres/part* **outbidding**, *p/t* and *p/part* **outbid**) [owtbid] *v/t* bid higher than.

outboard [owtbawrd] *adj* on the outside of a ship or boat; **o. motor** portable engine attached to the outside of the stern.

outbound [owtbownd] *adj* outward bound.

outbrave [owtbRayv] *v/t* defy; excel.

outbreak [owtbRayk] *n* sudden beginning of violence, anger, disease *etc*.

outbreeding [owtbReeding] *n* breeding between unrelated individuals or strains.

outbuilding [owtbilding] *n* building belonging to a house but not attached to it.

outburst [owtburst] *n* a bursting out; sudden violent expression of feelings.

outcast, outcaste [owtkaast] *n* person rejected by a social group; friendless person; criminal, vagabond *etc*; pariah.

outclass [owtklaas] *v/t* be far superior to.

outcome [owtkum] *n* result, effect.

outcrop [owtkRop] *n* portion of rock stratum projecting from the earth's surface; (*fig*) sporadic outbreak; unexpected occurrence.

outcry [owtkRI] *n* widespread protest; indignation, disapproval; uproar.

outdated [owtdaytid] *adj* old-fashioned.

outdistance [owtdistans] *v/t* go farther than, leave behind.

outdo (*p/t* **outdid**, *p/part* **outdone**) [owtdOO] *v/t* surpass, do more than; overcome.

outdoor [owtdawr] *adj* of or in the open air, not in a building ~ **outdoors** *adv*.

outer [owter] *adj* farther out; external; exterior; objective, real; **o. space** region beyond earth's atmosphere, or beyond solar system ~ **outer** *n* outermost circle of target.

outermost [owtermOst] *adj* farthest out.

outface [owtfays] *v/t* stare boldly at; defy successfully.

outfall [owtfawl] *n* outlet of river, drain *etc*.

outfield [owtfeeld] *n* outlying land of a farm; (*cricket*) that part of the field which is farthest from the batsman.

outfit [owtfit] *n* complete set of clothes or equipment needed for specified purpose; (*sl*) group, gang ~ **outfit** *v/t* equip ~ **outfitter** *n* one who provides outfits; one who sells men's clothes.

outflank [owtflank] *v/t* (*mil*) move round the flank of an enemy so as to attack his rear; (*fig*) outwit.

outflow [owtflO] *n* act of flowing out; amount that flows out.

outgeneral [owtjeneRal] *v/t* surpass in military tactics.

outgo (*p/t* **outwent**, *p/part* **outgone**) [owtgO] *v/t* surpass ~ **outgo** [owtgO] *n* expenditure.

outgoing [owtgO-ing] *n* act of going out; (*pl*) expenses, outlay ~ **outgoing** *adj* going out; retiring (from office *etc*); concerned with other people.

outgrow (*p*/*t* **outgrew**, *p*/*part* **outgrown**) [owt*g*ROh] *v*/*t* grow faster than; grow too big for (clothes); become too mature for; discard or lose on growing older.

outgrowth [owt*g*ROth] *n* offshoot; excrescence.

outgun [owt*gun*] *v*/*t* have more or better guns than; be a better gunfighter than.

outhouse [owt-hows] *n* detached shed.

outing [owting] *n* pleasure-trip, excursion.

outlandish [owt*land*ish] *adj* foreign-looking; strange-looking; uncouth; remote.

outlast [owt*laast*] *v*/*t* last longer than.

outlaw [owt*law*] *n* person deprived of all legal rights and protection; banished person; outcast; one who defies or flees from the law ∼ **outlaw** *v*/*t* condemn to outlawry; declare to be illegal; ostracize, expel ∼ **outlawry** *n* state of being an outlaw.

outlay [owt*lay*] *n* money spent on a definite object; expenditure.

outlet [owt*let*] *n* opening through which liquid passes out ; (*fig*) means of expressing or putting into action.

outlier [owt*lI*-er] *n* person or thing detached from a main mass or found outside its usual environment.

outline [owt*lIn*] *n* line or lines defining the apparent outer edge of an object; representation of this in drawing; brief general explanation or summary without detail ∼ **outline** *v*/*t* draw the outlines of; describe without detail, summarize.

outlive [owt*liv*] *v*/*t* live longer than.

outlook [owt*look*] *n* view from a place; foreseeable future, prospect; mental attitude, way of thought.

outlying [owt*lI*-ing] *adj* at some distance.

outmarch [owt*maarch*] *v*/*t* march faster than.

outmatch [owt*mach*] *v*/*t* surpass.

outmoded [owt*mOd*id] *adj* no longer in fashion.

outmost [owt*mOst*] *adj* outermost.

outnumber [owt*number*] *v*/*t* exceed in number.

out-of-date [owt-ov-*dayt*] *adj* obsolete, old-fashioned.

out-of-door [owt-ov-*dawr*] *adj* outdoor.

out-of-the-way [owt-ov-THe-*way*] *adj* not easily accessible; unusual.

out-patient [owt-*payshent*] *n* hospital patient who lives at home and attends for treatment.

outplay [owt*play*] *v*/*t* play much better than; defeat by greater skill.

outpoint [owt*point*] *v*/*t* score more points than.

outpost [owt*pOst*] *n* (*mil*) detachment placed at a distance from an encamped army; (*fig*) settlement far from civilization.

outpouring [owt*pawR*ing] *n* effusive expression of feelings.

output [owt*poot*] *n* production; quantity produced; rate of production.

outrage [owt*R*ayj] *n* violent injury or offence; act of extreme cruelty or indecency; rape ∼ **outrage** [owt*R*ayj] *v*/*t* commit an outrage against; offend violently; rape.

outrageous [owt*R*ayjus] *adj* highly offensive; atrocious, flagrant ∼ **outrageously** *adv* ∼ **outrageousness** *n*.

outré [OOt*R*ay] *adj* (*Fr*) exaggerated, eccentric; in bad taste.

outreach [owt*R*eech] *n* deliberately planned contact between members of an organization and non-members.

outride (*p*/*t* **outrode**, *p*/*part* **outridden**) [owt*R*Id] *v*/*t* ride farther or faster than.

outrider [owt*R*Ider] *n* motorcyclist preceding and guarding a motorcar; mounted attendant accompanying a carriage.

outrigger [owt*R*iger] *n* (*naut*) framework projecting from boat on to a float as stabilizer; boat with rowlocks on outboard supports; mast and lifting tackle; projecting stabilizing beam.

outright [owt*R*It] *adv* thoroughly, entirely; at once; frankly ∼ **outright** *adj* thorough; direct, frank.

outrun (*pres*/*part* **outrunning**, *p*/*t* **outran**, *p*/*part* **outrun**) [owt*R*un] *v*/*t* run or move faster than.

outsail [owt*sayl*] *v*/*t* sail faster than.

outset [owt*set*] *n* beginning, start.

outshine (*p*/*t* and *p*/*part* **outshone**) [owt*sh*In] *v*/*t* shine brighter than; seem finer than.

outside [owt*sId*] *n* external part; outer surface; superficial appearance; extreme limit, utmost; state or quality of being external ∼ **outside** *adj* external; on or of the outer part; out of doors; unconnected; almost; unlikely ∼ **outside** [owt*sId*] *adv* on the outer side; out of doors ∼ **outside** [owt*sId*] *prep* on the outer side of; apart from.

outsider [owt*sId*er] *n* person outside a specified social group; horse that is thought unlikely to win; person with little chance of success; (*coll*) vulgar, ill-bred person.

outsize [owt*sIz*] *n* and *adj* (garment) larger than the standard sizes.

outskirts [owt*skurts*] *n* (*pl*) outer areas.

outsmart [owt*smaart*] *v*/*t* (*coll*) outwit.

outspan [owt*span*] *v*/*t* unyoke (oxen) from wagon ∼ **outspan** *n* act of unyoking; unyoking place.

outspoken [owt*spOken*] *adj* plain-speaking; frank.

outspread (*p*/*t* and *p*/*part* **outspread**) [owt*spR*ed] *v*/*t* and *i* stretch out, expand.

outstanding [owt*standing*] *adj* prominent, remarkable; not yet completed; (*of debt*) unpaid ∼ **outstandings** *n* (*pl*) unsettled debts.

outstare [owt*stair*] *v*/*t* abash by staring.

outstation [owt*stayshon*] *n* station in a remote area.

outstay [owt*stay*] *v*/*t* stay longer than; **o. one's welcome** stay so long that one is no longer welcome.

outstretched [owt*stR*echt] *adj* held forth, extended.

outstrip (*pres*/*part* **outstripping**, *p*/*t* and *p*/*part* **outstripped**) [owt*stR*ip] *v*/*t* run faster than; surpass.

out-talk [owt-*tawk*] *v*/*t* talk louder, faster, or longer than; talk down.

out-tray [owt-*tR*ay] *n* tray holding letters, documents *etc* that have been dealt with and can be removed.

outvote [owt*v*Ot] *v*/*t* defeat by a majority of votes.

outward [owt*werd*] *adj* of or on the outside, external; physical; moving to the outside; **o. bound** travelling from native to foreign land, *esp* across sea ∼ **outward, outwards** *adv* towards the outside ∼ **outwardly** *adv* externally ∼ **outwardness** *n* externality.

outwear (*p*/*t* **outwore**, *p*/*part* **outworn**) [owt*wair*]

518

v/t last longer than; wear out, spoil by constant use.

outweigh [out*way*] v/t be heavier, more important, or more influential than.

outwit (*pres*/*part* **outwitting**, p/t and p/*part* **outwitted**) [owt*wit*] v/t defeat or deceive by superior cleverness.

outwork (1) [owt*wurk*] n fortification well in advance of the main defences; work done outside the shop or factory.

outwork (2) [owt*wurk*] v/t do more work than.

outworn [owt*wawrn*] adj obsolete.

ouzel, ousel [*OO*zel] n variety of thrush.

ouzo [*OO*zO] n Greek alcoholic spirit flavoured with aniseed.

ova [*O*va] pl of **ovum**.

oval [*O*val] n and adj (object or figure) shaped like an egg, elliptical.

ovarian [*O*va*i*Ri-an] adj of an ovary.

ovary [*O*ve*Ri*] n (biol) female reproductive organ producing ova; part of pistil containing seeds > PDB.

ovate [*O*vayt] adj egg-shaped.

ovation [*O*vayshon] n enthusiastic welcome or applause by an audience.

oven [*uv*en] n closed receptacle of brick or metal for baking food; kiln, small furnace.

oven-ready [*uv*en-Redi] adj (of food) partially cooked or prepared before sale so as to need only final cooking in oven.

ovenware [*uv*enwair] n dishes, casseroles etc that can stand the heat of an oven without cracking.

over [*O*ver] prep covering upper surface of; on or on to the top of; above; on opposite side of; spanning, crossing; across; more than; during; superior to; longer than; **be all o.** (someone) show great signs of affection for ~ **over** adv above; away; from side to side; down; upside down; ended; past; remaining after subtraction; excessively; on all its surface; **o. and o.** many times; **o. again** once more ~ **over** n (cricket) six balls bowled in succession from the same end of the pitch.

over- pref excessive, excessively; outer; upper; superior; passing across or beyond.

overact [Over-*akt*] v/t and i (theat) act with exaggerated emphasis.

overall (1) [Ove*Rawl*] adj total; inclusive ~ **overall** adv over the whole area or surface.

overall (2) n loose light outer garment to protect clothes from dirt; (pl) loose protective trousers; officer's dress trousers.

overarm [Over-*aarm*] adj and adv (sport) with arm raised above the shoulder.

overawe [Over-*aw*] v/t inspire fear in, daunt.

overbalance [Over*balans*] v/i and t lose one's balance and fall; upset the balance of; outweigh.

overbear (p/t **overbore**, p/part **overborne**) [over*bair*] v/t impose one's will on, domineer over.

overbearing [Over*bair*Ring] adj domineering, bullying; masterful ~ **overbearingly** adv.

overblown [Over*blOn*] adj past full bloom.

overboard [Over*bawrd*] adv over the side; out of the ship; **go o.** (coll) be enthusiastic; **throw o.** abandon.

overbuild (p/t and p/part **overbuilt**) [Over*bild*] v/t put too many buildings upon ; build in excess

of demand ~ **overbuilt** adj too densely built upon.

overcast [Over*kaast*] adj cloudy; gloomy ~ **overcast** (p/t and p/part **overcast**) v/t make cloudy or gloomy; stitch raw edge of cloth to prevent unravelling.

overcharge [Over*chaarj*] v/t and i demand too high a price (from); overload; fill to excess; charge too heavily with electricity; put too much powder into (gun) ~ **overcharge** [Over*chaarj*] n excessive price or charge.

overcloud [Over*klowd*] v/t cover with clouds.

overcoat [Overk*Ot*] n coat worn outside a suit; topcoat.

overcome (p/t **overcame**, p/part **overcome**) [Over*kum*] v/t and i conquer, master; be victorious; surmount; defeat; exhaust.

overcompensation [Overkompen*say*shon] n exaggerated effort to counteract or compensate for a defect > PDP.

overcrowd [Over*kRowd*] v/t fill with too many people; force to live in too small a space.

overdo (p/t **overdid**, p/part **overdone**) [Over-*dOO*] v/t exaggerate, over-emphasize; cook too long; **o. it** exhaust oneself by being too active; go too far; do too much.

overdone [Over*dun*] adj exaggerated; overcooked.

overdose [Overd*Os*] n too large a dose; harmfully large dose ~ **overdose** v/t.

overdraft [Overd*Raaft*] n (banking) act of overdrawing an account; amount overdrawn.

overdraw (p/t **overdrew**, p/part **overdrawn**) [Overd*Raw*] v/t exaggerate; (banking) draw more out from an account than one has in it.

overdress [Overd*Res*] v/t and i dress too elaborately or formally.

overdrive (p/t **overdrove**, p/part **overdriven**) [Overd*RIv*] v/t exhaust by forcing to work too hard; drive too hard ~ **overdrive** [Overd*RIv*] n (mot) mechanism that reduces engine speed in relation to car speed.

overdue [Over*dew*] adj later than appointed time; not paid when due.

overestimate [Over-*esti*mayt] v/t reckon at too high a value or two large a quantity ~ **overestimate** n excessive valuation.

overfall [Over*fawl*] n rough water caused by conflicting currents or by shoals; outlet at dam or weir.

overflow [Over*flO*] v/t and i flow over; flood, cover with liquid; be too large for its limits, break out of bounds; fill more than allotted space ~ **overflow** [Over*flO*] n that which overflows; excessive amount; outlet for excess water; **o. meeting** secondary meeting for those who found no room in the main one ~ **overflowing** adj amply provided (with).

overfly [Over*flI*] v/t (of aircraft) fly over (a specified place).

overgrow (p/t **overgrew**, p/part **overgrown**) [Over*gRO*] v/t grow over, cover with growth; grow too big ~ **overgrown** adj covered with vegetation; too tall and lanky; too big ~ **overgrowth** [Over*gROth*] n.

overhand [Over*hand*] adj and adv overarm.

overhang (p/t and p/part **overhung**) [Over*hang*] v/t project over; overshadow; impend over, threaten ~ **overhang** [Overhang] *n* projecting part.

overhaul [Over*hawl*] *v/t* examine thoroughly, seek out all faults in; catch up with, pass from behind ~ **overhaul** [Over*hawl*] *n* thorough examination.

overhead [Over*hed*] *adv* above one's head, high up ~ **overhead** *adj* above one's head; high above the ground, in mid-air; (*of expenses*) permanent and stable; relating to rent and upkeep of premises ~ **overheads** [Overhedz] *n* (*pl*) overhead expenses.

overhear (*p/t* and *p/part* **overheard**) [Over*heer*] *v/t* hear without the speaker's knowledge; listen secretly to.

overjoyed [Over*joyd*] *adj* highly delighted.

overkill [Overkil] *n* capacity for causing destruction by nuclear warfare in excess of that needed to exterminate the enemy.

overladen [Over*layden*] *adj* (*of ship*) overloaded; (*arts*) too profusely covered (with ornament).

overland [Overland] *adj* and *adv* by land, not by sea.

overlap (*pres/part* **overlapping**, *p/t* and *p/part* **overlapped**) [Over*lap*] *v/t* and *i* project over, partly cover; coincide in time; be partly alike, correspond partly with ~ **overlap** [Overlap] *n* overlapping part; degree to which something overlaps.

overlay (*p/t* and *p/part* **overlaid**) [Over*lay*] *v/t* cover with layer or coating; cover and conceal ~ **overlay** [Overlay] *n* second coating.

overleaf [Over*leef*] *adv* on the other side of the page or document.

overload [Over*lOd*] *v/t* put too great a weight on; (*elect*) overcharge ~ **overload** [OverlOd] *n*.

overlook [Over*look*] *v/t* look from above on to; have a view of; fail to see, neglect; disregard; not punish, condone; supervise; (*ar*) bewitch.

overlord [Overlawrd] *n* feudal superior; supreme lord.

overlordship [Overlawrdship] *n* authority of an overlord.

overly [Overli] *adv* (*US* and *Scots*) too much.

overman [Over*man*] *v/t* set more men than needed at work in (a factory *etc*).

overmantel [Overmantel] *n* ornamental woodwork over a mantelpiece.

overmuch [Over*much*] *adj* and *adv* too much.

overnight [Over*nIt*] *adv* during a whole night; for one night only; on the evening before; very suddenly.

overpass [Overpaas] *n* bridge crossing a motorway.

overpitch [Over*pich*] *v/t* (*cricket*) bowl (a ball) beyond a good length.

overplay [Over*play*] *v/t* **o. one's hand** take unjustified risks, gamble too highly on.

overplus [Overplus] *n* surplus.

overpower [Over*powr*] *v/t* conquer, subdue ~ **overpowering** *adj* exceedingly strong.

overprint [Over*pRint*] *v/t* print more on a surface already bearing printing; print too many copies of; (*phot*) print too darkly.

overproof [Over*pROOf*] *adj* containing more alcohol than proof spirit.

overrate [Over*Rayt*] *v/t* assess at too high a value.

overreach [Over*Reech*] *v/t* and *i* outwit, defeat by cunning; (*of horses*) cut foreleg with hind hoof; **o. oneself** fail by trying to be too clever.

overreact [Over*Ree-akt*] *v/i* react with exaggerated vigour or violence.

override (*p/t* **overrode**, *p/part* **overridden**) [Over*RId*] *v/t* disregard, *esp* roughly or authoritatively; take precedence over; trample on; exhaust (a horse).

overrule [Over*ROOl*] *v/t* set aside by higher authority; prevail over; (*leg*) annul.

overrun (*pres/part* **overrunning**, *p/t* **overran**, *p/part* **overrun**) [Over*Run*] *v/t* and *i* invade destructively; conquer by rapid advance; infest; go beyond; (*print*) transfer to next line or page; last for longer than the allotted time.

oversea, overseas [Over*see*, Over*seez*] *adj* and *adv* across or beyond a sea; foreign; abroad.

oversee (*p/t* **oversaw**, *p/part* **overseen**) [Over*see*] *v/t* supervise (*esp* workmen) ~ **overseer** *n* superintendent; slave-driver; foreman.

oversell (*p/t* and *p/part* **oversold**) [Over*sel*] *v/t* sell more than one can supply; make exaggerated claims for, praise too highly.

overset [Over*set*] *v/t* upset; overthrow.

oversew (*p/t* **oversewed**, *p/part* **oversewn**) [Over*sO*] *v/t* stitch (two edges) together with needle always entering from same side.

oversexed [Over*sekst*] *adj* having unusually strong sexual urges.

overshadow [Over*shadO*] *v/t* cast a shadow on; loom over; (*fig*) make gloomy; cause to seem relatively unimportant.

overshoe [Over*shOO*] *n* galosh.

overshoot (*p/t* and *p/part* **overshot**) [Over*shOOt*] *v/t* shoot too far beyond or above; fail to stop at right point, go beyond; shoot too much game in (an area) ~ **overshot** [Overshot] *adj* (*of waterwheel*) driven by falling water.

oversight [OversIt] *n* accidental omission; mistake; forgetfulness; failure to observe; supervision.

oversized [Over*sIzd*] *adj* abnormally big.

overslaugh [Overslaw] *n* (*mil*) relief from ordinary duty when detailed for something more urgent; (*US*) obstructive sandbank in a river ~ **overslaugh** [Over*slaw*] *v/t* (*US*) obstruct; pass over (someone) for promotion in favour of another.

oversleep (*p/t* and *p/part* **overslept**) [Over*sleep*] *v/i* sleep longer than one should.

overspend (*p/t* and *p/part* **overspent**) [Over*spend*] *v/t* and *i* spend more than; spend beyond one's means.

overspill [Overspil] *n* excess population of a town *etc* spreading into surrounding areas.

overspread (*p/t* and *p/part* **overspread**) [Over*spRed*] *v/t* extend over; be diffused over.

overstate [Over*stayt*] *v/t* state too strongly; exaggerate ~ **overstatement** *n*.

overstay [Over*stay*] *v/i* and *t* stay too long; stay longer than.

overstep (*p/t* and *p/part* **overstepped**) [Over*step*] *v/t* go beyond (right limits).

overstock [Over*stok*] *v/t* fill up (shop *etc*) with too great a supply of goods.

overstrung [Over*stRung*] *adj* having nerves too highly strung; too sensitive; (*of piano*) with two sets of strings one crossing the other.

oversubscribed [Oversubsk*RIbd*] *adj* (*of share*

issue) with applications to buy in excess of available shares.

overt [Ovurt] *adj* evident; unconcealed.

overtake (*p/t* **overtook**, *p/part* **overtaken**) [Overtayk] *v/t* move faster than and pass from behind; take by surprise; overwhelm; afflict.

overtask [Overtaask] *v/t* overtax.

overtax [Overtaks] *v/t* make too heavy demands on.

overthrow (*p/t* **overthrew**, *p/part* **overthrown**) [OverthRO] *v/t* throw to the ground, knock down; destroy; defeat ~ **overthrow** [OverthRO] *n* defeat, destruction; fall; (*cricket*) ball fielded but thrown beyond wicket; run(s) so made.

overtime [Overtlm] *n* time spent in work beyond normal working hours; wages for this, *esp* at higher rate than normal; (*sport*) extra time for play in a tied match ~ **overtime** *adv* and *adj* beyond normal hours.

overtly [Ovurtli] *adv* openly, evidently.

overtone [OvertOn] *n* harmonic note > PDM; (*fig*) implication; emotional colouring (of words).

overtop (*pres/part* **overtopping**, *p/t* and *p/part* **overtopped**) [Overtop] *v/t* rise above, exceed in height; surpass.

overtrump [OvertRump] *v/t* and *i* take (a trumped trick) with a higher trump.

overture [Overtewr/Overcher] *n* orchestral piece introducing opera or play > PDM; (*pl*) offer to open negotiations; friendly advances.

overturn [Overturn] *v/t* and *i* cause to fall over; turn over, be upset; capsize.

overtype [Overtlp] *v/t* and *i* type a word above deleted words.

overweening [Overweening] *adj* haughty, arrogant; presumptuous, too confident.

overweight [Overwayt] *n* and *adj* more than the weight needed or allowed or normal.

overwhelm [Overwelm] *v/t* sweep over, cover completely; bring to ruin; overpower with emotion; astonish, confuse.

overwinter [Overwinter] *v/i* spend the whole winter (in a place).

overwork [Overwurk] *v/t* and *i* exhaust with work; work too much ~ **overwork** *n*.

overwrought [OverRawt] *adj* too excited, tense with emotion; (*of style*) too elaborate.

ovi- (1) *pref* of an egg.

ovi- (2) *pref* of sheep.

oviduct [Ovidukt] *n* (*zool*) tube carrying ova from ovary.

oviform [Ovifawrm] *adj* egg-shaped.

ovine [Ovln] *adj* of sheep.

ovipositor [Ovipoziter] *n* (*ent*) organ through which a female insect lays eggs > PDB.

ovoid [Ovoid] *adj* and *n* egg-shaped (figure).

ovulate [Ovewlayt] *v/i* produce ova or ovules; discharge ova from ovary ~ **ovulation** *n*.

ovule [Ovewl] *n* (*bot*) rudimentary unfertilized seed > PDB.

ovum (*pl* **ova**) [Ovum] *n* unfertilized egg-cell > PDB.

owe [O] *v/t* and *i* be under obligation to pay; be in debt; be bound to give; be indebted to as origin ~ **owing** *adj* unpaid; **o. to** caused by, as a result of.

owl [owl] *n* large-headed nocturnal bird of prey with mournful cry; (*coll*) stupid person with a serious manner.

owlet, howlet [owlit] *n* young owl; little owl.

owlish [owlish] *adj* stupidly solemn; with a fixed stare ~ **owlishly** *adv*.

owl-light [owl-lit] *n* dusk.

own [On] *adj* belonging to oneself; exclusively possessed; done by oneself ~ **own** *pron* that which one possesses; **come into one's o.** obtain one's rights; **hold one's o.** maintain one's position against attack; **on one's o.** independent; alone ~ **own** *v/t* possess; admit, confess; acknowledge as one's own; **o. up** (*coll*) confess.

owner [Oner] *n* possessor; one who has legal title.

owner-driver [Oner-dRIver] *n* one who drives his own car.

owner-occupier [Oner-okewpl-er] *n* one who owns the house he lives in.

ownership [Onership] *n* state or fact of being an owner, possession; period of possession.

ox (*pl* **oxen**) [oks] *n* castrated adult male of domestic cattle; bovine cattle.

oxalic [oksalik] *adj* **o. acid** white crystalline poisonous soluble solid used in bleaching, metal polishes, *etc* > PDS.

oxbow [oksbO] *n* U-shaped yoke or collar for an ox; (*US*) horseshoe bend in a river; land inside this bend > PDG.

Oxbridge [oksbRij] *adj* and *n* (of) Oxford and Cambridge Universities.

oxen *pl* of **ox**.

ox-eyed [oks-Id] *adj* with large round eyes.

oxhide [oks-hId] *n* leather from ox's skin.

oxidant [oksidant] *n* substance which supplies the oxygen in an oxidation process, *esp* in combustion.

oxidase [oksidayz] *n* enzyme which catalyses an oxidation reaction.

oxidation [oksidayshon] *n* combination with oxygen; addition of oxygen or other electronegative atom or group; removal of hydrogen or other electropositive atom or group.

oxide [oksId] *n* binary compound with oxygen.

oxidization [oksidIzayshon] *n* oxidation.

oxidize [oksidIz] *v/t* and *i* turn into an oxide, unite with oxygen; cover with an oxide; make or become rusty ~ **oxidizer** *n* oxidizing agent.

oxlip [okslip] *n* hybrid between primrose and cowslip.

Oxonian [oksOni-an] *n* and *adj* (inhabitant) of Oxford; (member) of the University of Oxford.

oxy- *pref* of oxygen; of an oxide; sharp.

oxyacetylene [oksi-aseteleen] *adj* of acetylene gas burning in oxygen; cutting or welding with this flame.

oxygen [oksijen] *n* invisible gaseous element in the atmosphere, essential to life > PDS.

oxygenate [oksijenayt] *v/t* mix with oxygen, *esp* the blood in respiration; cause oxygen to combine with (substance); oxidize.

oxygenize [oksijenIz] *v/t* oxygenate.

oxygen-mask [oksijen-maask] *n* breathing apparatus supplying oxygen.

oxygen-tent [oksijen-tent] *n* enclosed structure supplied with oxygen, to assist breathing.

oxymoron [oksimawRon] *n* figure of speech in which contradictory ideas are closely associated.

oyer [oi-er] *n* (*leg*) Assize court trial.

oyez [*Oyes*] *interj* call by a public crier or court officer for silence and attention.

oyster [*oister*] *n* edible bivalve mollusc.

oyster-bed [*oister-bed*] *n* breeding-place for oysters.

oyster-catcher [*oister-kacher*] *n* type of wading seabird.

ozone [*OzOn*] *n* allotropic form of oxygen containing three atoms in the molecule > PDS; (*pop*) bracing air of the sea-coast.

P

p [*pee*] sixteenth letter of English alphabet; (*abbr*) decimal penny, coin worth one hundredth of a pound i.e. one fifth of a shilling; **mind one's p's and q's** behave very politely.

pa [*paa*] *n* (*coll abbr*) father.

pabulum [*pabewlum*] *n* food, nutriment.

pace (1) [*pays*] *n* speed of walking or running; rate of advance; single step in walking; distance covered by this; method of walking or running, *esp* of horse; **put (one) through one's paces** test one's knowledge or skill ~ **pace** *v/i* and *t* walk slowly and with dignity; provide standard of speed for (a runner); test the speed of; **p. out** measure by counting regular steps.

pace (2) [*paysi*] *prep* (*Lat*) in spite of the opposition of; with the consent of.

pacemaker [*pays*mayker] *n* one who accompanies a runner, cyclist *etc*, so as to set the rate of speed required; (*med*) pulsating device implanted in the chest to correct faulty heartbeats.

pachyderm [*pak*idurm] *n* (*zool*) thick-skinned quadruped, such as elephant, rhinoceros *etc*.

pacific [*pasifik*] *adj* peaceable, unwarlike; **P. Ocean** ocean between Asia and America ~ **pacifically** *adv*.

pacification [pasifi*kay*shon] *n* act or process of pacifying; process of subduing resistance ~ **pacificatory** *adj*.

pacifism [*pasi*fizm] *n* belief that violence is evil even in self-defence; refusal to sanction or share in any war.

pacifist [*pasi*fist] *n* and *adj* (upholder) of pacifism.

pacify [*pasi*fI] *v/t* allay anger of, appease; restore to order; subdue resistance in (conquered area).

pack [*pak*] *n* bundle of goods carried by man or beast; haversack; group of animals herding together *esp* for hunting; set of hounds; crowd, mob; (*cont*) large quantity; set of playing cards; cold compress; large area of compressed ice; (*phot*) packet of film placed flat in camera; (*Rugby football*) the forwards of a team, scrum ~ **pack** *v/t* and *i* put in a container for travel or storage; gather (clothes *etc*) for a journey; crowd together, fit tightly into small space; apply wet compress to; choose members of (jury, committee *etc*) so as to ensure specified decision; (*US*) carry; **p. it in** (up) (*sl*) stop, cease, finish; **p. off, send packing** dismiss abruptly; **p. up** (*coll*) stop working, break down; leave, die.

package [*pakij*] *n* small parcel; small bundle; container in which goods are packed; **p. deal** transaction in which the bad has to be taken along with the good; **p. tour** journey made at fixed inclusive price as one of an organized group of travellers.

packaging [*paki*jing] *n* art of packing goods in efficient and attractive containers.

packer [*paker*] *n* one who or that which packs.

packet [*pakit*] *n* parcel, package; packet-boat; (*sl*) large sum of money; (*sl*) heavy blow; heavy punishment; trouble.

packet-boat [*pakit*-bOt] *n* mail-boat.

packhorse [*pak*hawrs] *n* horse for carrying goods.

pack-ice [*pak*-Is] *n* mass of broken floating ice.

packing [*paking*] *n* material used for packing goods to prevent damage; protective material wrapped round waterpipes *etc*; hemp *etc* to make a pump watertight; act or art of putting goods into packs or packages.

packing-case [*paking*-kays] *n* large wooden box.

packing-needle [*paking*-need'l] *n* large curved needle for sewing up packages.

packing-sheet [*paking*-sheet] *n* canvas sheet for packing goods in.

packman [*pakman*] *n* pedlar.

pack-saddle [*pak*-sad'l] *n* saddle for supporting packs.

packthread [*pak*thRed] *n* strong thread for sewing up packages.

pact [*pakt*] *n* agreement, covenant.

pad (1) (*pres/part* **padding**, *p/t* and *p/part* **padded**) [*pad*] *v/i* walk with soft muffled tread; (*of horse*) move at gentle pace; (*sl*) trudge, tramp ~ **pad** *n* (*sl*) road; (*ar*) gentle-paced horse.

pad (2) *n* mass of soft material used to prevent damage or friction, or to alter apparent shape (of the body); (*aer*) rocket-launching platform; fleshy underparts of a paw; pawmark; stuffed leg-guard; large leaf of water-lily; number of sheets of writing or drawing paper fastened together; (*sl*) bed, bedroom ~ **pad** (*pres/part* **padding**, *p/t* and *p/part* **padded**) *v/t* cover or stuff with soft material; protect with a pad; enlarge by surrounding with a pad; enlarge (book, speech *etc*) by adding superfluous verbiage or repetitions.

padding [*pading*] *n* material used for making a pad; space- or time-filling additions to book, speech *etc*.

paddle (1) [*pad'l*] *n* short broad oar used without rowlock; single board of paddle-wheel; short spade; wooden panel in sluice for closing water passage; **double p.** paddle with blade at each end ~ **paddle** *v/t* and *i* propel (boat) with a paddle; row gently; **p. one's own canoe** advance unaided.

paddle (2) *v/i* walk barefoot in shallow water.

paddle-wheel [*pad'l*-wheel] *n* wheel with boards set at right angles to its circumference, used to propel a boat.

paddock (1) [*padok*] *n* small field where horses are exercised or kept; enclosure where racehorses are assembled before a race; (*Aust*) enclosed field.

paddock (2) *n* (*ar*) toad; frog.

paddy (1) [*padi*] *n* growing rice.

paddy (2) *n* (*coll*) burst of anger; (*cap*) Irishman.

paddyfield [*padi*feeld] *n* field of rice.

paddywhack [*padi*wak] *n* (*coll*) burst of anger; smack.

padlock [*padlok*] *n* movable lock which engages with a staple to hold a hasp in position ~ **padlock** *v/t*.

padre [*paad*Ray] *n* naval or military chaplain; (*coll*) clergyman.

paduasoy [*pad*ewasoi] *n* corded silk fabric.

paean [*pee*-an] *n* (*Gk*) hymn of thanksgiving or victory; song of triumph.

paederast see pederast.

paediatric, pediatric [peedi*at*Rik] *adj* relating to paediatrics.

paediatrician, pediatrician [peedi*at*Rishan] *n* specialist in children's diseases.

paediatrics, pediatrics [peedi*at*Riks] *n*(*pl*) science of children's diseases.

paedo-, pedo- *pref* of a child.

paedophile, paedophiliac [*peed*Ofil, peed*O*fili-ak] *n* one who feels sexual desire for young children.

paella [paa-*el*a] *n* (*Sp*) dish of rice and fish or chicken.

paeony see peony.

pagan [*pay*gan] *n* heathen, believer in a polytheistic religion; (*coll*) person without any religion or ethical code; materialist ~ **pagan** *adj*.

paganism [*pay*ganizm] *n* polytheistic religion ~ **paganize** *v*/*t* convert or reduce to paganism.

page (1) [*payj*] *n* boy servant in livery employed as messenger, footman, or personal attendant; boy attendant on a bride; (*hist*) boy of noble birth in first stage of training for knighthood ~ **page** *v*/*t* call aloud for (a person) through the rooms of a building.

page (2) *n* one side of a leaf of a book, letter *etc*; (*fig*) episode ~ **page** *v*/*t* (*print*) mark page-numbers on proof-sheet.

pageant [*paj*ent] *n* series of scenes or tableaux representing historical episodes; richly costumed parade; magnificent display.

pageantry [*paj*entRi] *n* splendid ceremonial, pomp.

pageboy [*payj*boi] *n* page (1); a shoulder-length hairstyle with fringe.

pager [*pay*jer] *n* portable radio device emitting summons signals.

paginal [*paj*inal] *adj* of or like a page of book.

paginate [*paj*inayt] *v*/*t* mark (pages) with consecutive numbers.

pagination [paji*nay*shon] *n* the paging of a book; act of paging a book.

pagoda [pag*O*da] *n* oriental temple built as a tapering tower of several storeys.

pah [*paa*] *interj* exclamation of disgust.

paid [*payd*] *p*/*t* and *p*/*part* of pay (1); **put p. to** (*coll*) put an end to; prevent.

pail [*payl*] *n* bucket, deep conical vessel for carrying liquid, held by hoop across its mouth; pailful.

pailful [*payl*fool] *n* amount that is or can be contained in a pail.

pain [*payn*] *n* sensation of physical suffering or acute discomfort; emotional suffering, grief; penalty; (*pl*) effort, care ~ **pain** *v*/*t* cause pain to, inflict suffering on.

pained [*paynd*] *n* showing pain; distressed; offended.

painful [*payn*fool] *adj* causing pain; distressingly bad; (*ar*) laborious ~ **painfully** *adv* ~ **painfulness** *n*.

pain-killer [*payn*-kiler] *n* drug that removes or reduces pain.

painless [*payn*les] *adj* causing no physical suffering ~ **painlessly** *adv* ~ **painlessness** *n*.

painstaking [*paynz*tayking] *adj* careful, industrious.

paint [*paynt*] *n* colouring matter mixed in liquid for applying to a surface; pigment; coloured cosmetic, rouge ~ **paint** *v*/*t* and *i* apply pigment to, colour with paint; produce (picture) with liquid or viscous pigments; portray; describe vividly; practise the art of painting; use coloured cosmetics; cover, smear; **p. the town red** (*coll*) go on a spree.

paintbox [*paynt*boks] *n* box containing cakes or tubes of pigment and mixed colours.

paintbrush [*paynt*bRush] *n* brush for applying paint.

painted [*payn*tid] *adj* represented in a picture; coated with paint; **P. Lady** an orange butterfly with black and white spots.

painter (1) [*payn*ter] *n* one who paints pictures; workman who applies paint, *esp* to woodwork of houses.

painter (2) *n* mooring-rope at the bow of a small boat; **cut the p.** (*fig*) sever all connexion with.

painting [*payn*ting] *n* coloured picture executed by hand; art of painting pictures; act of colouring surfaces.

pair [*pair*] *n* couple of matching or corresponding things; mated couple of animals; married couple; two persons or things usually used, found, or working, together; two horses harnessed together; object formed of two equal corresponding parts; (*Parliament*) one of two members of opposing parties who agree to be simultaneously absent at a division ~ **pair** *v*/*t* and *i* arrange in couples; mate; marry; **p. off** form into pairs or couples.

Paisley [*payz*li] *adj* **P. pattern** textile pattern of curling cone-like motifs.

pajama [pa*jaama*] *n* (*US*) pyjama.

Pakistani [paaki*staa*ni] *n* inhabitant of Pakistan.

pal [*pal*] *n* (*coll*) close friend ~ **pal** (*pres*/*part* **palling**, *p*/*t* and *p*/*part* **palled**) *v*/*i* **p. up with** become very friendly with.

palace [*pal*is] *n* large and splendid house; residence of monarch or high prelate; large public hall for dancing or entertainment.

paladin [*pal*adin] *n* one of Charlemagne's twelve peers; knightly hero.

palaeo-, (*US*) **paleo-** *pref* ancient, primitive.

palaeographer [pali-*og*Rafer] *n* expert in palaeography.

palaeographic [pali-og*Raf*ik] *adj* of or by palaeography.

palaeography [pali-*og*Rafi] *n* study of ancient inscriptions, scripts, and manuscripts.

palaeolithic [pali-o*lith*ik] *adj* of the earlier Stone Age > PDB.

palaeontology [pali-on*tol*oji] *n* study of fossils.

palaeozoic [pali-Oz*O*-ik] *adj* containing ancient forms of life; **P. Era** second major geological era.

palais [*pal*ay] *n* (*coll*) large dance hall.

palankeen, (*US*) **palanquin** [palan-*keen*] *n* Oriental covered litter.

palatable [*pal*atab'l] *adj* of pleasant flavour; acceptable.

palatal [*pal*atal] *n* and *adj* of the palate; (*phon*) (sound) produced by contact of tongue and hard palate.

palatalize [*pal*atalIz] *v*/*t* (*phon*) pronounce closer to front of mouth.

palate [*pal*at] *n* roof of the mouth; sense of taste; capacity to judge merits of wine or food; **hard p.** bony front area of palate; **soft p.** fleshy back area of palate.

palatial [pa*lay*shal] *adj* like a palace; (*of buildings*) large and splendid.

Palatine (1) [*pal*atIn] *adj* (*of count or earl*) having royal privileges within his own territory.

palatine (2) *adj* pertaining to the palate.

palaver [pa*laa*ver] *n* conference, discussion; gossip, chatter ∼ **palaver** *v/i*.

pale (1) [*payl*] *n* upright wooden stake; fence; boundary; (*her*) vertical stripe; (*hist*) English-controlled area round Dublin; **beyond the p.** socially unacceptable.

pale (2) *adj* whitish, with very little colour; faint, dim ∼ **pale** *v/i* become pale; fade; become comparatively less important *etc*.

paleface [*payl*fays] *n* name applied to white men by North American Indians.

palely [*payl*-li] *adv* in a pale way ∼ **paleness** *n*.

paleo- see palaeo-.

palette [*pal*it] *n* small board on which an artist mixes his colours; range or selection of colours.

palette-knife [*pal*it-nIf] *n* flexible steel knife used for mixing or applying paint.

palfrey [*pawl*fRi] *n* (*ar*) saddle-horse.

Pali [*paa*li] *n* sacred language of Buddhists.

palimpsest [*pal*impsest] *n* twice-used writing material, where partly erased early writing can be seen below more recent writing.

palindrome [*pal*indROm] *n* word or sentence which is unaltered if read backwards.

paling [*pay*ling] *n* fence made of pales.

palingenesis [palin*jen*isis] *n* rebirth; reincarnation; (*biol*) exact reproduction in offspring of ancestral characteristics.

palinode [*pal*inOd] *n* retraction of previous statement, *esp* in poetry.

palisade [*pal*isayd] *n* fence of pointed wooden or metal stakes.

pall (1) [*pawl*] *n* cloth covering a coffin; heavy covering; pallium; coronation robe; cloth covering a chalice.

pall (2) *v/i* become boring.

Palladian [pa*lay*di-an] *adj* (*archi*) in Italian Renaissance style; in English seventeenth-century classic style.

palladium (1) [pa*lay*di-um] *n* protective image, *esp* of a god; safeguard.

palladium (2) *n* (*chem*) silvery white metal of the platinum group > PDS.

pallbearer [*pawl*bairRer] *n* attendant at a funeral.

pallet (1) [*pal*it] *n* straw mattress; hard bed.

pallet (2) *n* palette; (*cer*) flat board with handle attached; organ valve.

palliasse [pal*yas*] *n* a straw mattress.

palliate [*pal*i-ayt] *v/t* partly alleviate; lessen; extenuate, excuse.

palliation [pali-*ay*shon] *n* act of palliating; state of being palliated; that which palliates.

palliative [*pal*i-ativ] *n* and *adj* (that) which palliates.

pallid [*pal*id] *adj* very pale.

pallium [*pal*i-um] *n* (*RC*) white vestment of Pope and archbishops.

pall-mall [*pel*-mel/*pal*-mal] *n* seventeenth-century game resembling croquet.

pallor [*pal*er] *n* extreme paleness.

pally [*pal*i] *adj* (*coll*) very friendly.

palm (1) [*paam*] *n* tree with branchless trunk and tuft of leaves; leaf of this as symbol of victory, martyrdom, or pilgrimage; **P. Sunday** Sunday before Easter.

palm (2) *n* inner surface of hand from wrist to finger-base; breadth of this; **grease (oil) the p. of** bribe; **have an itching p.** be avaricious, *esp* for bribes ∼ **palm** *v/t* hide in the palm; hide or transfer by sleight of hand; **p. off** pass (worthless object) to another by trick or lies.

palmar [*palm*er] *adj* (*anat*) of a palm (2).

palmary [*palm*eRi] *adj* supreme, victorious.

palmate [*palm*ayt] *adj* shaped like a palm (2).

palmer [*paam*er] *n* pilgrim, *esp* one who has been to the Holy Land.

palmette [*palm*et] *n* (*archi*) classical conventionalized ornament resembling a palm leaf.

palmetto [*palm*etO] *n* name of various small palms.

palmiped [*palm*iped] *adj* and *n* web-footed (bird or animal).

palmist [*paam*ist] *n* one who practises palmistry.

palmistry [*paam*istRi] *n* method of deducing a person's character and destiny from wrinkles on his palm.

palm-oil (*US* palm oil) [*paam*-oil] *n* oil obtained from various species of palm tree; (*fig*) a bribe.

palmy [*paam*i] *adj* flourishing, successful; of or having palm trees.

palmyra [palm*IR*Ra] *n* species of Indian palm.

palooka [pa*lOO*ka] *n* (*sl*) incompetent games player.

palp [*palp*] *n* (*zool*) feeler > PDB ∼ **palp** *v/t* touch or feel gently; examine by touching.

palpability [palpa*bil*iti] *n* quality of being palpable.

palpable [*palp*ab'l] *adj* that can be felt by touch; obvious, evident ∼ **palpably** *adv*.

palpate [*palp*ayt] *v/t* (*med*) examine by touch.

palpitate [*palp*itayt] *v/i* (*of heart*) beat irregularly and too fast; throb ∼ **palpitating** *adj* thrilling ∼ **palpitation** [palpi*tay*shon] *n*.

palstave [*pawl*stayv] *n* (*arch*) type of prehistoric bronze cutting implement.

palsy [*pawl*zi] *n* disease causing trembling of limbs; paralysis ∼ **palsy** *v/t* cause to tremble uncontrollably; paralyse.

palter [*pawl*ter] *v/t* deal evasively, equivocate.

paltry [*pawl*tRi] *adj* trifling, insignificant; contemptible ∼ **paltriness** *n*.

paludal [pal*ew*dal] *adj* marshy; malarial.

pampas [*pam*pas] *n* (*pl*) grassy plains of South America; **p. grass** tall ornamental grass.

pamper [*pam*per] *v/t* bring up in too much comfort, coddle; be too indulgent to.

pamphlet [*pam*flit] *n* short printed, but unbound, treatise on a matter of current interest.

pamphleteer [pamfli*teer*] *n* writer of pamphlets.

pan (1) [*pan*] *n* broad, shallow cooking-vessel or container; small hollow; kneecap; upper part of skull; (*sl*) face; (*firelock gun*) container of priming; bowl of water-closet ∼ **pan** (*pres/part* **panning**, *p/t* and *p/part* **panned**) *v/t* wash (sand *etc*) to extract gold; (*coll*) criticize harshly; **p. out** (*coll*) produce money; succeed; turn out.

pan (2) (*pres/part* **panning**, *p/t* and *p/part*

panned) *v/i* (*cin*) (*of camera*) move continuously while shooting so as to secure a panoramic effect.

Pan (3) *n* (*Gk myth*) satyr-god of fields and woods; personification of natural forces and instincts.

pan (4) *n* panchromatic film.

pan- *pref* total, universal; of or for all members of specified group.

panacea [pana*see*-a] *n* remedy for all disorders.

panache [pan*aash*] *n* plume of feathers, *esp* on helmet; (*fig*) ostentation, swagger.

panama [pana*maa*] *n* light hat of undyed straw.

pancake [*pankayk*] *n* thin cake of fried batter; (*aer*) vertical descent with aircraft kept level; **P. Day** Shrove Tuesday; **p. ice** thin cake of floating ice ~ **pancake** *v/t* land abruptly and flatly.

panchromatic [pan-k*RO*matik] *adj* (*phot*) (*of film*) sensitive to light of all colours including red.

pancreas [*pankRi*-as] *n* large intestinal gland secreting insulin and digestive enzymes.

pancreatic [pankRi-*atik*] *adj* of the pancreas.

panda [*pan*da] *n* large black-and-white Chinese and Tibetan bear; small carnivorous Himalayan mammal; **p. car** police car with white stripe; **p. crossing** crossing place marked by white stripes on road.

pandemic [pand*emik*] *n* and *adj* (disease) prevalent everywhere throughout an area or among a population.

pandemonium [pandim*Oni*-um] *n* wild uproar and confusion.

pander [*pan*der] *n* one who procures for another the means of gratifying his sexual desires, pimp; one who assists the evil desires of others~ **pander** *v/i* act as a pander: **p. to** gratify, encourage (evil wishes).

pandit see **pundit**.

pandy [*pan*di] *n* (*school coll*) a stroke of a cane *etc* on the hand.

pandybat [*pan*dibat] *n* thick, stiff leather strap for beating boys' hands.

pane [*payn*] *n* sheet of glass in a window; panel; rectangular figure ~ **paned** *adj* made of contrasting strips of material.

panegyric [pani*ji*Rik] *n* eloquent praise, eulogy.

panel [*pan*el] *n* rectangular piece of fabric, wood *etc* set into and contrasting with a surface; long narrow design, picture *etc*; board or surface containing instruments and controls of car, aircraft *etc*; list of persons called to jury service; list of persons entitled to free medical care under former Health Insurance Act; group of persons answering questions or taking part in a game or quiz before an audience; (*Scots leg*) indicted person ~ **panel** *adj* of or for patients treated under Health Insurance Act ~ **panel** (*pres/part* **panelling**, *p/t* and *p/part* **panelled**) *v/t* divide into or decorate with panels; (*Scots leg*) indict.

panel-game [*pan*el-gaym] *n* entertainment in which a group of persons is asked to solve various puzzles before an audience.

panelist [*pan*elist] *n* one of a group of persons taking part in a quiz, panel-game *etc*.

panelling [*pan*eling] *n* series of panels.

pang [*pang*] *n* sudden spasm of pain.

panhandle [*pan*hand'l] *n* (*US*) narrow projection of land ~ **panhandle** *v/t* and *i* (*coll*) beg, *esp* on the street.

panic [*pan*ik] *n* sudden wild terror, *esp* affecting

many persons ~ **panic** (*pres/part* **panicking**, *p/t* and *p/part* **panicked**) *v/i* and *t* be seized with wild terror, lose self-control through fear; terrify ~ **panic** *adj* caused by terror.

panicky [*pan*iki] *adj* (*coll*) very nervous, liable to panic.

panic-stricken [*pan*ik-st*Ri*ken] *adj* feeling panic, terrified.

panjandrum [panj*and*Rum] *n* pompous man.

panne [*pan*] *n* velvet-like fabric with long nap.

pannier [*pan*i-er] *n* one of two large baskets carried by beast of burden; large basket carried on the back; framework or drapery to enlarge or adorn a dress at the hips.

pannikin [*pan*ikin] *n* small tin bowl or mug.

panoply [*pan*Opli] *n* complete suit of armour; splendid outfit or array ~ **panoplied** *adj*.

panorama [pano*Raa*ma] *n* wide unbroken view of landscape *etc*; general survey; series of scenes showing stages in a historical narrative; realistic picture or series of pictures painted on the inside of a cylinder within which the viewer stands ~ **panoramic** [pano*Ram*ik] *adj*.

pan-pipe [*pan*-pIpl] *n* (*mus*) primitive instrument made of series of pipes fixed side by side to give a scale > PDM; mouth organ.

pansy [*pan*zi] *n* wild and garden flower of violet family; (*sl*, *pej*) homosexual youth, effeminate youth ~ **pansy** *adj* (*sl*) effeminate, homosexual.

pant (1) [*pant*] *v/i* and *t* breathe fast and convulsively; gasp; throb; (*fig*) yearn; utter gaspingly ~ **pant** *n* short harsh breath, gasp.

pant (2) *n* (*dial*) drinking-fountain; pool.

pant- see **panto-**.

pantaloon [*pant*al*OO*n] *n* (*theat*) foolish old man; (*pl*, *obs*) long tight trousers.

pantechnicon [pant*ek*nikon] *n* warehouse for storing furniture; van for removing furniture.

pantheism [*pan*thi-izm] *n* doctrine that God and the universe are identical ~ **pantheist** *n* and *adj*.

pantheon [*pan*thi-on] *n* temple of all the gods; group of gods worshipped by specified nation; building commemorating the illustrious dead of a nation.

panther [*pan*ther] *n* leopard; (*US*) puma.

panties [*pan*tiz] *n* (*pl*) (*coll*) women's short knickers.

pantile [*pan*tIl] *n* roofing tile shaped like an S laid horizontally > PDBl.

panto-, **pant-** *pref* all, universal.

panto [*pan*tO] *n* (*coll*) pantomime.

pantograph [*pan*tOg*Raa*f] *n* instrument for copying a plan or drawing on a different scale; overhead current collector on electric vehicle.

pantomime [*pan*tOmIm] *n* spectacular, farcical and romantic play based on a fairytale and performed during Christmas season; mime; harlequinade; (*hist*) Roman actor in mimes ~ **pantomime** *v/t* and *i* mime.

pantomimic [pant*Omim*ik] *adj* of pantomime; of mime.

pantry [*pan*tRi] *n* small room where plates, cutlery, glasses *etc* are stored; larder.

pants [*pants*] *n* (*pl*) men's drawers; (*US*) trousers; (*coll*) girls' knickers.

panzer [*pant*ser] *n* German tank or armoured car.

pap (1) [*pap*] *n* soft pulpy food, mash.

pap (2) *n* nipple; (*pl*) adjacent conical hill summits.

papa [pa*paa*] *n* (*obs coll*) father.

papacy [*pay*pasi] *n* office of Pope; tenure of this; administrative system based on papal authority.

papain [*pa*payn] *n* enzyme capable of digesting protein, used as a meat tenderizer.

papal [*pay*pal] *adj* of the Pope; of papacy .

papalism [*pay*palizm] *n* the papal system; support of this ~ **papalist** *n* and *adj*.

papaw, pawpaw [pa*paw*, paw*paw*] *n* tropical tree with oblong melon-like edible fruit; North American tree with oblong edible fruit.

paper [*pay*per] *n* substance made from pulped rags or vegetable fibre used in thin sheets for writing, printing, drawing, packaging *etc*; newspaper, magazine; scholarly essay or lecture; set of examination questions; (*pl*) bills of exchange; currency notes; documents, *esp* of identity; (*sl*) free theatre tickets; **commit to p.** write down; **p. money** currency notes; **on p.** judging by written plans or evidence; theoretically; **send in one's papers** resign from office ~ **paper** *adj* made of paper ~ **paper** *v/t* cover (walls) with decorative paper; **p. up** block up (crack *etc*) by covering with paper; **p. the house** (*theat sl*) fill theatre by giving out tickets free.

paperback [*pay*perbak] *n* book bound in paper ~ **paperback** *v/t* republish (hardback book) in paperback format.

paperboy [*pay*perboi] *n* boy who sells or delivers newspapers.

paperchase [*pay*perchays] *n* sport of pursuing two runners who scatter a trail of torn-up paper.

paperclip [*pay*perklip] *n* bent springy wire for holding sheets of paper together.

paperhanger [*pay*perhanger] *n* workman who covers walls with wallpaper.

paperknife [*pay*pernif] *n* blunt blade for slitting pages, opening letters *etc*.

papermill [*pay*permill] *n* factory where paper is made.

paperweight [*pay*perwayt] *n* small heavy ornamental object laid on loose papers to prevent scattering.

paperwork [*pay*perwurk] *n* the keeping of records, filling of forms, *etc*.

papier-mâché [papyay-*ma*shay] *n* light but tough material made by pressing and drying paper-pulp mixed with glue.

papilla (*pl* **papillae**) [pa*pi*la] *n* nipple-like projection, *esp* on tongue or skin > PDB, PDP ~ **papillary** *adj*.

papist [*pay*pist] *n* (*cont*) Roman Catholic ~ **papistic, papistical** [pa*pi*stik, pa*pi*stikal] *adj*.

papoose [pa*pOOs*] *n* Red Indian infant.

paprika [pa*pri*ka] *n* red capsicum pepper.

papyrus (*pl* **papyri**) [pa*pIr*Rus] *n* Egyptian sedge; writing material made from this; document written on this.

par (1) [*paar*] *n* equality of value; (*comm*) value of one currency in terms of that of another; face value nominal value (*esp* of stocks and shares); (*fig*) normal state of health or energy; (*golf*) best score for a hole or course which a first-rate player should achieve.

par (2) *n* (*coll abbr*) paragraph.

para- (1) *pref* beside, beyond; wrong; contrary; abnormal.

para- (2) *pref* as defence against.

parable [*pa*Rab'l] *n* short story with hidden moral or spiritual meaning.

parabola [pa*Ra*bola] *n* (*math*) curve traced by point which moves so that its distance from a fixed point is equal to its distance from a fixed straight line.

parabolic [pa*Ra*bolik] *adj* like or expressed in a parable; of or shaped like a parabola ~ **parabolical** *adj* ~ **parabolically** *adv*.

paraboloid [pa*Ra*boloid] *n* (*math*) solid obtained by rotating a parabola about its axis of symmetry.

paracetamol [pa*Ra*seetamol] *n* an analgesic drug.

parachute [*pa*RashOOt] *n* large umbrella-shaped fabric fastened to persons or objects leaping or dropped from aircraft, to check the speed of fall ~ **parachute** *v/i* and *t* leap or drop from aircraft by parachute.

parachutist [*pa*RashOOtist] *n* one trained to make leaps by parachute.

Paraclete [*pa*Rakleet] *n* the Holy Ghost.

parade [pa*Rayd*] *n* military muster and review; march-past; proud display, ostentation; raised promenade along a seashore; parade-ground ~ **parade** *v/i* and *t* march solemnly past; muster (troops) for inspection; display proudly.

parade-ground [pa*Rayd*-gRownd] *n* area where troops are paraded.

paradigm [*pa*Radim] *n* pattern, example; (*gramm*) full scheme of declension or inflexion.

paradise [*pa*Radis] *n* state or place of perfect happiness; heaven; state or place of happy innocence inhabited by mankind before the first sin; **fool's p.** illusory joy; **bird of p.** New Guinea bird with beautiful plumage.

paradisiac, paradisial [pa*Radi*si-ak, pa*Radi*si-al] *adj* of or like paradise.

parados [*pa*Rados] *n* earthwork to guard against attack from rear.

paradox [*pa*Radoks] *n* statement apparently inconsistent or absurd yet really true; something conflicting with probability.

paradoxical [pa*Rado*ksikal] *adj* of or like a paradox; apparently self-contradictory; using paradoxes ~ **paradoxically** *adv*.

paraffin [*pa*Rafin] *n* one of a series of inflammable hydrocarbons obtained by distilling wood, shale, petroleum *etc* > PDS; **liquid p.** a mild laxative; **p. oil** kerosene, refined petroleum; **p. wax** white solid consisting of higher paraffin hydrocarbons.

paragon [*pa*Ragon] *n* person or thing supremely excellent; diamond weighing more than 100 carats.

paragraph [*pa*RagRaaf] *n* distinct section in a prose writing, marked off by indentation of first line; short independent item in newspaper ~ **paragraph** *v/t* divide into paragraphs; write a newspaper paragraph about.

paragraphic [pa*Ra*gRa*fi*k] *adj* of or in paragraphs.

parakeet, paroquet [*pa*Rakeet/*pa*Raket] *n* small long-tailed tropical parrot.

paraldehyde [pa*Ra*ldihid] *n* a narcotic drug.

parallactic [pa*Rala*ktik] *adj* of a parallax.

parallax [*pa*Ralaks] *n* apparent shift of position of an object due to an actual change in position of the observer > PDP, PDS; (*astron*) difference between a star's position as seen from earth or from the sun.

parallel [*pa*Ralel] *adj* (*of lines*) equidistant for their

527

whole length; markedly similar; (*mus*) preserving the same interval; **in p.** (*elect*) with like poles connected > PDS ~ **parallel** *n* closely similar thing or event; comparison; parallel line; (*geog*) one of a series of imaginary lines parallel to the equator > PDG ~ **parallel** *v/t* be parallel to; be equivalent or closely comparable to; find something equivalent to.

parallelepiped [paRa*lel*ipiped] *n* (*geom*) solid figure with six faces, all of which are parallelograms.

parallelism [*pa*Ralelizm] *n* state of being parallel; close correspondence.

parallelogram [paRa*lel*OgRam] *n* (*geom*) four-sided rectilinear figure whose opposite sides are parallel.

paralyse [*pa*Ralīz] *v/t* affect with paralysis; deprive of power of action; render helpless.

paralysis [pa*Ra*lisis] *n* (*med*) loss or impairment of motion or sensation, due to disorder in the neuromuscular system; (*fig*) interruption of movement or activity; powerlessness.

paralytic [paRa*lit*ik] *n* and *adj* (person) suffering from paralysis; causing paralysis; (*sl*) very drunk.

paramagnetism [paRa*mag*netizm] *n* (*phys*) form of magnetism in which a substance acquires magnetic properties when placed in a magnetic field > PDS ~ **paramagnetic** *adj*.

paramedical [paRa*med*ikal] *adj* assisting or supplementing the work of doctors and surgeons.

parameter [pa*Ra*miter] characteristic or constant factor; (*math*) variable which determines the specific form of a function; (*stat*) a variable sought by means of evidence from samples; (*pl fig*) defining or determining limits, outer limits.

paramilitary [paRa*milit*aRi] *adj* organized to assist armed forces; acting like, or imitating the organization of, an army.

paramount [*pa*Ramownt] *adj* supreme.

paramour [*pa*Ramoor] *n* illicit lover; mistress.

paranoia [paRa*noi*-a] *n* mental disorder with persistent delusions, *esp* of persecution or power.

paranoiac [paRa*noi*-ak] *n* and *adj* (person) suffering from paranoia.

paranoid [*pa*Ranoid] *adj* suffering from paranoia or from some of its symptoms; having delusions of persecution or of power.

paranormal [paRa*nawr*mal] *adj* not explicable by normal scientific laws, but not regarded as supernatural.

parapet [*pa*Rapet] *n* low protective wall along a bridge, balcony *etc*; (*mil*) rampart in front of troops.

paraph [*pa*Raf] *n* flourish at the end of a signature.

paraphernalia [paRafer*nayl*i-a] *n* (*pl*) personal belongings; equipment, accessories.

paraphrase [*pa*RafRayz] *v/t* re-express the meaning of a passage in fuller and clearer wording ~ **paraphrase** *n* new and fuller rendering; free translation; metrical version of scriptural texts.

paraplegia [paRa*pleej*i-a] *n* (*med*) paralysis of lower part of body and both legs ~ **paraplegic** *n* and *adj* (person) suffering from paraplegia.

parapsychology [paRasi*kol*oji] *n* study of telepathy, precognition, extrasensory perception *etc*.

paraquat [*pa*Rakwot] *n* a powerful poisonous weedkiller.

parasite [*pa*Rasīt] *n* useless person who lives on the resources of others; (*biol*) organism living in or

on another from which it obtains food > PDB; flatterer, toady.

parasitic, parasitical [paRa*sit*ik, paRa*sit*ikal] *adj* of or like a parasite ~ **parasitically** *adv*.

parasol [*pa*Rasol] *n* light, gaily-coloured umbrella carried as protection against the sun.

parataxis [paRa*tak*sis] *n* (*gramm*) arrangement of successive clauses without any connecting word.

paratroops [*pa*RatrOOps] *n* (*pl*) airborne soldiers landed by parachute ~ **paratrooper** *n*.

paratyphoid [paRa*tī*foid] *n* form of enteric fever resembling mild typhoid.

parboil [*paar*boil] *v/t* boil partially; (*fig*) overheat.

parbuckle [*paar*buk'l] *n* a purchase obtained by looping a rope round a cask, barrel *etc* to roll it up an incline.

parcel [*paar*sel] *n* small package wrapped in paper; portion of land forming part of a manor; (*ar*) part; **p. post** post-office department transmitting parcels ~ **parcel** (*pres/part* **parcelling,** *p/t* and *p/part* **parcelled**) *v/t* (*naut*) cover (rope) with canvas for protection; **p. out** share out in small portions; **p. up** make into a package, wrap up.

parcelgilt [*paar*selgilt] *adj* partly gilded.

parcener [*paar*siner] *n* (*leg*) co-heir.

parch [*paarch*] *v/t* and *i* dry up with heat or with thirst; roast slightly, toast; become very dry.

parchment [*paarch*ment] *n* animal skin prepared without tanning and used for writing or painting; manuscript written on parchment.

parclose [*paar*klOz] *n* (*archi*) dividing screen round chapel or shrine.

pard [*paard*] *n* (*ar*) leopard.

pardon [*paar*d'n] *n* forgiveness; act of excusing a fault or breach of etiquette; (*eccles*) indulgence; (*leg*) remission of punishment ~ **pardon** *v/t* forgive; excuse; (*leg*) grant a pardon.

pardonable [*paar*donab'l] *adj* excusable, admitting of pardon ~ **pardonably** *adv*.

pardoner [*paar*doner] *n* (*hist*) person licensed to sell or grant indulgences.

pare [*pair*] *v/t* trim, cut edges of; cut away; gradually reduce.

paregoric [paRi*gor*ik] *n* soothing medicine containing opium.

parent [*pair*Rent] *n* father or mother; ancestor; origin, source ~ **parent** *adj*.

parentage [*pair*Rentij] *n* ancestry; origin.

parental [pa*Ren*tal] *adj* of or like a parent ~ **parentally** *adv*.

parenthesis (*pl* **parentheses**) [pa*Ren*thisis] *n* word or words inserted into a sentence which is grammatically complete without it; (*pl*) pair of brackets enclosing a parenthesis; (*fig*) interlude, unconnected episode.

parenthetic, parenthetical [paRin*thet*ik, paRin*thet*ikal] *adj* of or like a parenthesis; in parenthesis ~ **parenthetically** *adv*.

parenthood [*pair*Rent-hOOd] *n* state of being a parent.

paresis [*pa*Resis] *n* partial paralysis; syphilitic paralysis > PDP.

par excellence [paar *eks*elons] *adv* (*Fr*) to a supreme degree, as the best or most typical of its kind.

parget [*paar*jet] *v/t* cover with plaster ~ **parget** *n* plaster on wall or ceiling, *esp* ornamental.

parhelion (*pl* **parhelia**) [paar*heel*i-on] *n* very

bright spot on solar halo, forming image of the sun > PDG.

pariah [pa*RI*-a/pa*Ri*-a] *n* member of very low Hindu caste; (*fig*) social outcast.

pariah-dog [pa*RI*-a-dog/pa*Ri*-a-dog] *n* stray mongrel dog in India.

Parian [*pair*Ri-an] *adj* of or like the white marble of Paros ~ **Parian** *n* fine white porcelain.

parietal [pa*RI*-etal] *n* of the wall of any cavity of the body or of a hollow organ > PDB; **p. bones** bones covering upper surface of brain.

pari mutuel (*pl* **paris mutuels**) [pa*Ri*-*mew*tew-el] *n* (*Fr*) system of betting in which winners divide the money staked by losers.

paring [*pair*Ring] *n* thin portion trimmed off.

pari passu [pa*Ree pas*OO] *adv* (*Lat*) at an equal rate or pace.

parish [*pa*Rish] *n* smallest local unit in civil or ecclesiastical administration; area over which a single clergyman has authority; churchgoers of such an area; churchgoers attending a specified church; **p. council** local administrative body; **on the p.** (*hist*) receiving Poor Relief; **p. pump** (*fig*) topic of purely local interest.

parishioner [pa*Rish*oner] *n* member of an ecclesiastical parish.

parish-register [pa*Rish-Rej*ister] *n* book recording baptisms, marriages and funerals held at a particular church.

Parisian [pa*Riz*yen] *adj* of, from, or like Paris.

parisyllabic [pa*Risi*labik] *adj* (*Gr and Lat gramm*) having an equal number of syllables in nominative and genitive singular.

parity [*pa*Riti] *n* equality; equivalence; similarity of reasoning, analogy; (*comm*) standard rate of exchange; **conservation of p.** (*phys*) principle that no fundamental distinction exists between left and right, space reflection symmetry > PDS.

park [*paark*] *n* public garden in a town; tract of land officially preserved as beauty-spot or as sanctuary for rare animals *etc*; space where motor vehicles may be left; enclosed land surrounding a mansion; (*hist*) royal hunting preserve; (*mil*) artillery encampment ~ **park** *v/t* and *i* leave (motor vehicles) stationary; (*coll*) put, leave in one spot; enclose or put in a park.

parka [*paar*ka] *n* hooded and padded jacket.

parker (1) [*paar*ker] *n* one who parks a car.

parker (2) (*coll*) **nosey p.** one who is persistently curious about others.

parkin [*paar*kin] *n* round cake or biscuit made of oatmeal, ginger and treacle.

parking-meter [*paar*king-*mee*ter] *n* kerbside coin-operated meter beside which cars may be parked for a specified period of time.

Parkinson's disease [*paar*kinsonz di*zeez*] *n* (*med*) chronic progressive disease of the old, marked by tremor, rigidity, peculiar gait and mask-like face.

parky [*paar*ki] *adj* (*sl*) chilly.

parlance [*paar*lans] *n* idiom, vocabulary.

parley [*paar*li] *n* discussion; conference between opponents, *esp* on terms of peace; **sound a p.** invite to a parley ~ **parley** *v/i* and *t* confer, discuss; (*coll*) speak (a foreign language).

parliament [*paar*liment] *n* wholly or partially elected legislative body; (*cap*) supreme legislative body of Great Britain.

parliamentarian [paarlimen*tair*Ri-an] *n* one

skilled in parliamentary procedure; (*hist*) Roundhead.

parliamentary [paarlimen*te*Ri] *adj* of or by Parliament; **p. language** polite language.

parlour [*paar*ler] *n* room for receiving guests, *esp* in monastery or convent; (*obs*) living-room; (*US*) room in certain shops *etc* where customers are received; **p. games** guessing games, competitions *etc* held at parties.

parlourmaid [*paar*lermayd] *n* female servant who waits at table.

parlous [*paar*lus] *adj* difficult; dangerous.

Parmesan [*paar*mizan] *n* type of strong cheese.

Parnassian [paar*nas*i-an] *n* and *adj* (member) of a mid nineteenth-century school of French poets.

parochial [pa*ROk*i-al] *adj* of a parish; of narrow range, narrow-minded ~ **parochially** *adv*.

parochialism [pa*ROk*i-alizm] *n* excessive limitation of interests; narrow outlook.

parodist [*pa*Rodist] *n* writer of parodies.

parody [*pa*Rodi] *n* close but mocking imitation of a writer's style or of a specific literary work; burlesque; bad imitation, travesty ~ **parody** *v/t* imitate mockingly; travesty.

parole [pa*ROl*] *n* word of honour; pledge given by prisoner to return if temporarily released without guard; **on p.** having given such a pledge ~ **parole** *v/t* release (prisoner) on parole.

paroquet see **parakeet**.

parotid [pa*Rot*id] *adj* situated beside the ear; **p. gland** large salivary gland in front of the ear.

parotitis [paRo*tI*tis] *n* mumps.

parousia [pa*Row*zi-a] *n* (*theol*) the second coming of Jesus Christ.

paroxysm [*pa*Roksizm] *n* violent temporary increase of a disease; spasm, fit; climax; crisis of emotion ~ **paroxysmal** [paRok*siz*mal] *adj*.

parquet [*paar*kay/*paar*ki] *n* (*bui*) wooden floor covering of hardwood blocks in geometrical patterns; (*US*) theatre stalls ~ **parquet** *v/t* fit parquet flooring.

parquetry [*paar*ketRi] *n* parquet flooring.

parricidal [pa*Ris*idal] *adj* of or like parricide.

parricide [*pa*Risid] *n* act of murdering one's father; murderer of a father; murder or murderer of a close relative.

parrot [*pa*Rot] *n* one of a genus of tropical birds with hooked beak and fleshy tongue, some of which can imitate human speech; person who repeats words *etc* without understanding them; imitator; **p. fever** psittacosis ~ **parrot** *v/t* imitate or repeat without understanding.

parrot-fish [*pa*Rot-fish] *n* one of various brightly coloured fishes; fish whose mouth resembles a parrot's bill.

parry [*pa*Ri] *v/t* ward off; evade ~ **parry** *n*.

parse [*paarz*] *v/t* (*gramm*) describe (a word) according to its part of speech, inflexion and syntactic connexions.

parsec [*paar*sek] *n* (*astron*) unit of measurement of distance, 3·26 light years.

Parsee [paar*see*] *n* person of Persian descent and Zoroastrian religion living in India.

parsimonious [paarsim*Oni*-us] *adj* sparing of money; niggardly ~ **parsimoniously** *adv* ~ **parsimoniousness** *n*.

parsimony [*paar*simoni] *n* niggardliness.

parsley [*paar*sli] *n* plant with aromatic leaves used

as a garnish and for seasoning; **cow p.** wild chervil.

parsnip [*paar*snip] *n* plant whose root is used as vegetable.

parson [*paar*son] *n* beneficed clergyman of the Church of England; clergyman; **p.'s nose** (*coll*) rump of a cooked fowl ~ **parsonical** *adj*.

parsonage [*paar*sonij] *n* house of a parson.

part [*paart*] *n* section, division; piece, portion; fragment; component, constituent; share; actor's role; words of this; side (in dispute), party; one among several concerted actions; duty; (*mus*) one of the melodies in a harmony; melody assigned to one voice or instrument > PDM; (*pl*) region; (*pl*) talents, ability; (*pl*) genitals; **p. and parcel** inseparable component; **for my p.** as far as I am concerned; **for the most p.** mostly; **p. of speech** category of words classified by function; **play a p.** act deceitfully; **play a p. in** share in (a joint activity); **take p. in** share in; **take in good p.** accept with good humour; **take the p. of** support ~ **part** *v/t* and *i* divide up; separate; open up; leave (a companion); break off a relationship; go in different directions; **p. with** give away or sell; surrender.

partake (*p/t* partook, *p/part* partaken) [paar*tayk*] *v/t* and *i* take a share in; participate; **p. of** eat or drink; be rather akin to.

parterre [paar*tair*] *n* level space containing flower-beds.

parthenogenesis [paarthen*O*je*n*isis] *n* development of ovum without fertilization > PDB; virgin birth.

Parthian [*paar*thi-an] *adj* **P. shot** pointed remark by one who departs without giving time for an answer.

partial [*paar*shal] *adj* comprising only part, incomplete; biased in favour of one side, unfair; **p. to** specially fond of ~ **partially** *adv*.

partiality [paarshi-*al*iti] *n* bias in favour; fondness.

partible [*paar*tib'l] *adj* divisible.

participant [paar*ti*sipant] *n* one who takes a share with others.

participate [paar*ti*sipayt] *v/i* have a share, take part.

participation [paartisi*pay*shon] *n* act of taking part or sharing; share.

participial [paarti*si*pi-al] *adj* of, containing, or formed from a participle.

participle [*paar*tisip'l] *n* type of adjective derived from and having some functions of a verb.

particle [*paar*tik'l] *n* very small part, fragment; (*phys*) any sub-atomic constituent of matter; (*gramm*) short minor part of speech; prefix or suffix with a distinct meaning.

particoloured [*paar*tikulerd] *adj* differently coloured in different parts.

particular [paar*ti*kewler] *adj* of a single person or thing; distinct; special; characteristic; attentive to details; exacting, fussy; remarkable; (*log*) applying only to some of a class ~ **particular** *n* detail; distinct part or item; (*pl*) detailed account; **in p.** especially.

particularity [paartikew*la*riti] *n* characteristic of an individual; precise attention to details.

particularize [paar*ti*kewla*RIz*] *v/t* mention specially; describe in detail.

particularly [paar*ti*kewlerli] *adv* especially; specifically; in detail.

parting [*paar*ting] *n* act of dividing or separating; line along which hair is divided; **p. of the ways** place where road forks and a choice must be made; leave-taking ~ **parting** *adj* done or given at moment of separation.

partisan, partizan (1) [paarti*zan*] *n* zealous supporter of a party; guerrilla fighter, *esp* in a resistance or liberation movement ~ **partisan, partizan** *adj*.

partisan, partizan (2) [*paar*tizan] *n* (*hist*) long-headed pike.

partisanship [*paar*tizanship] *n* zealous or biased support; blind loyalty.

partite [*paar*tIt] *n* divided to the base.

partition [paar*ti*shon] *n* act of dividing; that which divides; interior wall dividing two rooms; one of divided parts, compartment ~ **partition** *v/t* divide up; **p. off** separate by a partition.

partitive [*paar*titiv] *adj* denoting part of a collective whole; **p. genitive** word in the genitive case expressing the whole of which a part is taken.

partizan see partisan.

partly [*paart*li] *adv* to some extent, not entirely.

partner [*paart*ner] *n* sharer in an act or enterprise; one who has a share in the profits or losses of a business and owns part of the capital or stock; one of two persons dancing together; husband or wife; player in the same team or side; (*sl*) friend, associate; (*pl*, *naut*) timbers supporting mast, capstan *etc*; **sleeping p.** partner who does not share in managing a business ~ **partner** *v/t* be partner to; dance with.

partnership [*paart*nership] *n* state of being a partner; joint share in a business *etc*; association.

part-owner [paart-*O*ner] *n* one who owns something jointly.

partridge [*paar*Rij] *n* a small British gamebird.

part-song [*paart*-song] *n* song for two or more voices, each singing a different part > PDM.

part-time [*paart*-tIm] *adj* of or for less than normal number of hours of work ~ **part-timer** *n*.

parturition [paartewRi*shon*] *n* act of bringing forth; childbirth.

party (1) [*paar*ti] *n* group of persons united in opinions and policy, *esp* in politics; faction, side; organized political group; group of persons taking part in specified activity or enjoyment; (*mil*)squad detailed for special duty; social gathering; guests at this; person taking part in an action, accessory; (*leg*) person engaging in a contract, transaction or lawsuit; (*coll*) person; **p. line** policy laid down by head of political party; telephone line shared by several subscribers; **p. wall** common wall of two pieces of property.

party (2) *adj* (*her*) (*of shield*) divided into parts of different tinctures.

parvenu [*paar*venew] *n* (*Fr*) person of low birth who has obtained riches or power; upstart.

parvis [*paar*vis] *n* enclosed area in front of church.

pas [*paa*] *n* (*Fr*) step in dancing; kind of dance; precedence.

paschal [*pas*kal] *adj* of the Jewish Passover; of Easter.

pash (1) [*pash*] *v/t* (*dial*) crush; hurl.

pash (2) *n* (*school sl*) sentimental attachment, hero-worship.

pasha [*paa*sha/pa*shaa*] *n* (*hist*) title of high-ranking Turkish officers or officials.

pasque-flower [*paask*-flowr] *n* species of anemone flowering in April.

pass (1) [*paas*] *v/i* and *t* go; move on; go past, leave behind; cease; change; transfer, transmit; send; say; (*of time*) elapse; cross; excel, exceed; happen; make or become current; reach required standard; be acceptable; (*of laws etc*) give or obtain sanction; consent to; pronounce (judgement); (*cards*) miss a turn; spend time; (*games*) transfer (ball) to another player; **p. away** die; **p. the buck** (*coll*) shift one's responsibility to another; **p. by** go past; ignore; **p. for** be thought to be; **p. off** take place; decrease; cause to be regarded as; **p. out** faint, lose consciousness; successfully complete training; **p. over** overlook; **p. through** experience, endure; travel through; **p. up** (*sl*) refuse.

pass (2) *n* act or process of passing; permit to go through or into; free ticket; standard which satisfies examiners but does not reach credit or honours; crisis, difficult circumstances; gesture of the hands; (*coll*) amorous advances, attempt to kiss, caress *etc*; (*fencing*) lunge; (*games*) transfer of ball; kick; throw; **bring to p.** cause; **come to p.** happen; **a pretty p.** awkward situation.

pass (3) *n* narrow passage; gap between mountains; narrow channel.

passable [*paas*ab'l] *adj* fairly good, tolerable; that can be passed through or over ~ **passably** *adv*.

passage [*paa*sij] *n* act of passing; movement from one place to another; sea-journey; accommodation on a ship; payment for this; means of access; corridor; narrow road or track; channel; specified portion of literary or musical work; **bird of p.** migratory bird; **p. of arms** combat; dispute ~ **passage** *v/t* and *i* (*in horse riding*) move or cause to move sideways.

passant [*pa*sant] *adj* (*her*) walking with dexter forepaw raised.

passbook [*paas*book] *n* book recording customer's transactions with a bank; (*S. Africa*) booklet holding African's identity documents and permits to live or work in certain areas.

passé [*pa*say] *adj* (*Fr*) out of date; faded.

passenger [*pa*sinjer] *n* one who travels in a ship, train, coach *etc*; (*coll*) member of crew, team *etc* who does not work hard enough to justify his presence; **p. pigeon** migratory American pigeon.

passe-partout [paas-paart*OO*] *n* (*Fr*) master-key; adhesive tape for framing pictures *etc*.

passer-by [paaser-*bI*] *n* person who happens to be passing a spot where a specified thing can be seen or event is occurring.

passerine [*pa*seRIn] *n* and *adj* (*orni*) (bird) with large first toe directed back, the other three forward; of or like a sparrow.

passible [*pa*sib'l] *adj* capable of suffering; susceptible.

passim [*pa*sim] *adv* (*Lat*) everywhere; all through (a book); here and there.

passing [*paa*sing] *adj* that passes, transient; brief and casual ~ **passing** *n* act of one who passes; death; **p. bell** bell tolled to mark a death ~ **passing** *adv* (*ar*) very.

passion [*pa*shon] *n* strong emotion; deep love or desire; burst of anger; enthusiasm; (*cap*) sufferings and death of Christ; Gospel account of this; musical setting of this > PDM; **P. Play** medieval drama on the Passion of Christ; modern play of this type; **P. Sunday** fifth Sunday of Lent; **P. Week** Holy Week.

passionate [*pa*shonit] *adj* having easily roused emotions; ardent, intense; easily angered; sexually ardent ~ **passionately** *adv* ~ **passionateness** *n*.

passion-flower [*pa*shon-flowr] *n* a large-flowered climbing plant.

passionless [*pa*shonlis] *adj* feeling or showing no emotion ~ **passionlessly** *adv* ~ **passionlessness** *n*.

passive [*pa*siv] *adj* not active; acted upon but not acting; inert; quietly receptive; (*gramm*) indicating that the subject is acted on by the verb; **p. resistance** resistance without use of force; refusal to cooperate with laws *etc* thought unjust, even under threats ~ **passive** *n* (*gramm*) passive voice ~ **passively** *adv* ~ **passiveness** *n*.

passivity [pa*si*viti] *n* passiveness; inertia.

pass-key [*paas*-kee] *n* master-key.

pass-law [*paas*-law] *n* (*S. Africa*) law controlling the movements and domicile of Africans.

passman [*paas*man] *n* student reading for a pass degree.

Passover [*paas*Over] *n* Jewish feast commemorating the night when Jewish homes in Egypt were spared by the destroying angel; lamb then sacrificed; (*fig*) Christ.

passport [*paas*pawrt] *n* document granted by a government to a citizen to be shown when crossing a frontier.

password [*paas*wurd] *n* secret word authorizing those who know it to pass sentries *etc*.

past [*paast*] *adj* (*of time*) ended, bygone; (*gramm*) expressing past action or state ~ **past** *n* time that has gone by; events of a former time; earlier life; disreputable earlier life ~ **past** *prep* after; beyond; further than; no longer capable of ~ **past** *adv* going up to and beyond.

pasta [*pa*sta] *n* (*Ital*) type of flour paste used for macaroni, ravioli *etc*.

paste [*payst*] *n* soft moist compound; sticky compound of starch or flour and water; soft clay; vitreous compound used for artificial gems; mixture of flour, fat, and water ~ **paste** *v/t* stick with paste; (*coll*) thrash.

pasteboard [*payst*bawrd] *n* stiff substance made by pasting together several sheets of paper; (*sl*) visiting-card; playing-card.

pastel [*pa*stel] *n* powdered pigments mixed with gum > PDAA; crayon made with this; drawing in pastel; **p. colour** soft pale shade of colour.

pastellist [*pa*stelist] *n* one who draws with pastel crayons.

pastern [*pa*stern] *n* part of horse's foot between fetlock and hoof.

pasteurize [*pa*steRIz] *v/t* sterilize (milk *etc*) by heat ~ **pasteurization** [pasteRIz*a*yshon] *n*.

pastiche [pa*steesh*] *n* artistic, musical, or literary work imitating another's style; medley of passages from other works.

pastille [*pa*stil] *n* small sweet, often medicated; aromatic paste burnt as deodorizer or disinfectant.

pastime [*paast*Im] *n* recreation, amusement.

pasting [*paysting*] *n* (*coll*) a severe beating.
pastmaster [*paastmaaster*] *n* great expert.
pastor [*paaster*] *n* clergyman; priest.
pastoral [*paasteRal*] *adj* of or like shepherds and their life; rural; used for pasture; (*arts*) of or about rural life elegantly and conventionally treated; of the clergy *esp* in relation to the congregation; **p. staff** crosier; **p. theology** study of duty of the clergy to the congregation ~ **pastoral** *n* poem on rural life, in an elegant conventional manner; official letter from a bishop to his diocese.
pastorale [*pasteRaali*] *n* musical composition in pastoral style.
pastry [*paystRi*] *n* baked dough of flour and fat; pie, tart *etc* made of this.
pastrycook [*paystRikook*] *n* one who makes and sells pies, tarts *etc*.
pasturage [*paascheRij*] *n* pasture; cattle-grazing.
pasture [*paascher*] *n* piece of land used to graze cattle; grass land ~ **pasture** *v/i* and *t* graze.
pasty (1) [*paysti*] *adj* resembling paste; pale, unhealthy-looking.
pasty (2) [*pasti*] *n* meat pie in pastry and baked without a dish.
pat (1) [*pat*] *n* quick light tap or slap; sound of this; light footstep; small shaped lump of butter ~ **pat** (*pres/part* **patting**, *p/t* and *p/part* **patted**) *v/t* and *i* tap lightly, *esp* as mark of affection; **p. on the back** congratulate, approve of.
pat (2) *adv* just at the right moment; aptly; (*of speech*) fluently.
patball [*patbawl*] *n* (*coll*) tennis badly played.
patch [*pach*] *n* piece of material sewn or stuck to another to mend a hole; cover for an injured eye; small piece of land; contrasting piece or area; small piece of black plaster worn as a facial ornament; **bad p.** (*coll*) period of difficulty or unhappiness; **not a p. on** (*coll*) very inferior to ~ **patch** *v/t* mend by sewing or sticking a patch on; **p. up** mend, *esp* roughly or incompletely.
patchily [*pachili*] *adv* in a patchy way.
patchiness [*pachinis*] *n* quality of being patchy.
patchouli [*pachOOli*] *n* Eastern aromatic plant; perfume obtained from it.
patch-pocket [*pach-pokit*] *n* pocket made by sewing a square of fabric outside a garment.
patchwork [*pachwurk*] *n* work made of small pieces of various cloths sewn together; (*fig*) work of uneven quality; jumble, rough mixture.
patchy [*pachi*] *adj* uneven in quality or quantity.
pate [*payt*] *n* (*coll*) head, brains.
pâté [*patay*] *n* meat pie, pasty; spiced meat paste.
patella (*pl* **patellae**) [*patela*] *n* kneecap.
paten [*paten*] *n* silver or gold plate used to hold the bread at the Eucharist.
patent [*paytent*] *adj* clearly visible, obvious; protected by a patent; (*coll*) new and clever; **p. leather** thin shiny black leather; **letters p.** document from a sovereign granting a privilege, *esp* a patent; **p. medicine** ready-made proprietary medicine ~ **patent** *n* licence granting sole right to make and sell an invention; royal or official grant of privilege; invention protected by patent; (*coll*) clever device; **P. Rolls** annual lists of patents ~ **patent** *v/t* obtain a patent for.
patentee [*paytentee*] *n* one who holds a patent.
patently [*paytentli*] *adv* obviously, clearly.

pater [*payter*] *n* (*schoolboy sl*) father.
paterfamilias (*pl* **patresfamilias**) [*paterfamili-as*] *n* father of a family; master of the house.
paternal [*paturnal*] *adj* fatherly; related to one on the father's side.
paternalism [*paturnalizm*] *n* kind but oppressive rule, benevolent tyranny ~ **paternalist** *adj* and *n*.
paternally [*paturnali*] *adv* as or like a father.
paternity [*paturniti*] *n* fatherhood; descent on the male side.
paternoster [*paternoster*] *n* the Lord's Prayer, *esp* in Latin; eleventh bead of rosary; words of a charm, incantation; **p. line** fishing line with hooks and sinkers at intervals.
path [*paath*] *n* track formed by constant walking; track for pedestrians only; garden footpath; course, line of movement; (*fig*) conduct; duty.
Pathan [*pataan*] *adj* and *n* Afghan (tribesman).
pathetic [*pathetik*] *adj* rousing pity or sympathy; of the emotions; **p. fallacy** fallacy of imputing human feelings to inanimate nature ~ **pathetically** *adv*.
pathfinder [*paathfInder*] *n* explorer; (*mil*) aircraft which marks the target area for a bomber force; (*aer*) navigational radar device.
pathic [*pathik*] *n* catamite, minion.
patho- *pref* of suffering or disease.
pathogen [*pathOjen*] *n* any organism causing disease.
pathogenic [*pathOjenik*] *adj* causing disease ~ **pathogenesis** *n*.
pathological [*patholojikal*] *n* of pathology; of disease; caused by disease, *esp* by mental disorder; abnormal ~ **pathologically** *adv*.
pathologist [*patholojist*] *n* expert on disease.
pathology [*patholoji*] *n* study of disease.
pathos [*paythos*] *n* that which evokes pity.
pathway [*paathway*] *n* track for pedestrians.
patience [*payshens*] *n* ability to bear pain, misfortune *etc* bravely; ability to wait calmly; perseverance; forbearance when provoked; solo card game; **be out of p. with** be exasperated by.
patient [*payshent*] *adj* showing patience; forbearing; persistent in; (*log*) capable of bearing (an interpretation) ~ **patient** *n* person under medical treatment ~ **patiently** *adv*.
patina [*patina*] *n* green coating of oxide on old bronze; glossiness of old woodwork.
patio [*pati-O/paati-O*] *n* roofless inner courtyard.
patois [*patwaa*] *n* (*Fr*) local dialect.
patrial [*paytRi-al*] *n* and *adj* (*leg*) (Commonwealth citizen) whose parent or grandparent was British by birth or naturalization.
patriarch [*patRi-aark/paytRi-aark*] *n* male head of a family or tribe; venerable old man; title of certain bishops and archbishops, *esp* in the Orthodox Church; one of the early leaders of the Jews.
patriarchal [*patRi-aarkal/paytRi-aarkal*] *adj* of or like a patriarch; venerable, majestic.
patriarchate [*patRi-aarkayt/paytRi-aarkayt*] *n* (*eccles*) office of a patriarch.
patriarchy [*patRi-aarki/paytRi-aarki*] *n* primitive form of government where oldest man of tribe *etc* is ruler.
patrician [*patRishan*] *n* Roman noble; person of noble family.
patricide [*patRisId*] *n* (*US*) parricide.

patrilinear [patʀɪlini-ar] *adj* operating through, or derived from, the father's side of the family.

patrimony [patʀimoni] *n* inheritance from one's father; (*eccles*) church endowments.

patriot [paytʀi-ot/patʀi-ot] *n* one who is devoted to his country.

patriotic [patʀi-*otik*] *adj* of or like a patriot; for the sake of one's country ~ **patriotically** *adv*.

patriotism [pɹaytʀi-otizm/patʀi-otizm] *n* devotion to or love of one's country.

patristic [patʀistik] *adj* of the Fathers of the Church; of the writings of these.

patrol (*pres/part* **patrolling**, *p/t* and *p/part* **patrolled**) [patʀol] *v/t* and *i* (*mil*) go through (an area) to prevent disorder in it; go the rounds; walk regularly up and down (in) ~ **patrol** *n* act of patrolling; body of troops, police *etc* sent to patrol; unit of six Scouts; body of troops sent ahead to reconnoitre.

patrolcar [patʀolkaar] *n* car in which police patrol roads.

patrolman [patʀolman] *n* (*US*) policeman.

patron [paytʀon] *n* one who protects or gives financial support; regular customer; one who can bestow a church benefice; (*Rom antiq*) protector and former owner of freed slave; **p. saint** saint invoked as protector and helper of a person, group, or place.

patronage [patʀonij] *n* influential support; patronizing manner; regular custom; right of presenting to a benefice.

patronal [patʀonal] *adj* of a patron saint.

patroness [paytʀones] *n* female patron.

patronize [patʀonɪz] *v/t* treat condescendingly; show one's superiority to; be a regular customer of ~ **patronizing** *adj* ~ **patronizingly** *adv*.

patronymic [patʀonimik] *n* and *adj* (name) derived from a father or ancestor.

patsy [patsi] *n* (*sl*) butt, victim, fall-guy.

patten [paten] *n* wooden shoe raised on iron ring.

patter (1) [pater] *n* rapid speech of comedian, conjurer *etc*; words sung very rapidly ~ **patter** *v/t* and *i* speak at great speed.

patter (2) *n* sound of many quick light taps; sound of light quick footsteps ~ **patter** *v/i*.

pattern [patern] *n* model to be copied; shape to be copied in making something; sample; (*numis*) coin struck for experimental purposes only; design; artistic arrangement of repeated or corresponding parts; (*US*) length of cloth sufficient for garment ~ **pattern** *v/t* put a pattern on; give artistic design or shape to.

patterning [paterning] *n* act of imposing pattern on; design; artistic pattern.

patty [pati] *n* small meat pie.

pauci- *pref* few, little.

paucity [pawsiti] *n* fewness, scarcity.

Pauline [pawlɪn] *adj* of or by St Paul.

paunch [pawnch] *n* belly, stomach, *esp* when large; first stomach of a ruminant; (*naut*) rope matting to prevent chafing ~ **paunchy** *adj* having a large belly.

pauper [pawper] *n* destitute person supported by public funds or charity; very poor person.

pauperize [pawpeʀɪz] *v/t* reduce to extreme poverty; cause to depend on public funds.

pause [pawz] *n* temporary cessation; (*pros*) caesura; (*mus*) lengthening of a note or rest for a period at the discretion of the performer; sign (⌒) marking this ~ **pause** *v/i* stop for a while; linger (over).

pavane, pavan [pavaan, pavan] *n* stately 16th- and 17th-century dance > PDM.

pave [payv] *v/t* cover with pavement; provide pavement for; **p. the way for** facilitate the coming of.

pavement [payvment] *n* footway beside a road; hard road surface of asphalt, wood blocks *etc*; **p. artist** one who draws pictures on pavements to get money from passers-by.

pavilion [pavilyon] *n* large tent; light ornamental building or annex; building attached to a games field ~ **pavilion** *v/t* cover with a pavilion or tent.

paw [paw] *n* foot of an animal without hoofs; (*coll*) hand ~ **paw** *v/t* touch with paw; handle coarsely or unnecessarily; (*of horse*) scrape the ground with a hoof.

pawky [pawki] *adj* shrewd, sly ~ **pawkily** *adv* ~ **pawkiness** *n*.

pawl [pawl] *n* catch or bar to prevent recoil.

pawn (1) [pawn] *n* lowest grade of piece in chess; unimportant subordinate or agent.

pawn (2) *v/t* deposit as security for money lent; (*fig*) risk ~ **pawn** *n* thing pledged; **in p. deposited** as pledge.

pawnbroker [pawnbʀoker] *n* one who lends money on interest on the security of an article.

pawnshop [pawnshop] *n* pawnbroker's place of business.

pawnticket [pawntikit] *n* voucher for object pawned.

pawpaw see **papaw**.

pax [paks] *n* (*sl*) truce, peace; (*eccles*) kiss given in token of peace; object so kissed.

pay (1) (*p/t* and *p/part* **paid**) [pay] *v/t* and *i* give money to in return for work or goods; discharge (debt); give what is deserved or due; render; be profitable or advantageous; give payment; (*naut*) let out (a rope); **p. away** spend; **p. back** repay (loan); reward; retaliate; **p. down** pay at once; **p. in** contribute (money); **p. off** settle wages of and discharge; make final payment of (debt); give a handsome return; attain full effectiveness; (*naut*) fall away to leeward; **p. out** distribute as payment; take revenge on; (*naut*) let (rope) run out; **p. up** pay a debt ~ **pay** *n* wages, salary.

pay (2) *v/t* (*naut*) run pitch into seams that have been caulked.

payable [pay-ab'l] *adj* due to be paid; profitable.

pay-as-you-earn [pay-az-yew-urn] *n* deduction of income-tax at source.

pay-bed [pay-bed] *n* bed reserved for paying patients in a free hospital.

payday [payday] *n* day on which wages are paid.

payee [pay-ee] *n* person to whom payment is made; person to whom a cheque or bill is made payable.

payload [paylod] *n* weight which an aircraft or vehicle is capable of carrying.

paymaster [paymaaster] *n* officer or official who pays troops, workmen *etc*; **P. General** official through whom all Treasury payments are made.

payment [payment] *n* act of paying; sum paid; (*fig*) recompense.

paynim [paynim] *n* (*ar*) heathen; Muslim.

pay-off [pay-of] *n* (*coll*) final settlement of accounts; retribution; climax; unexpected conclusion.

pay-out [*pay*-owt] *n* distribution of payments.

paypacket [*pay*pakit] *n* packet containing one's wages; (*fig*) weekly wage.

payroll [*pay*ROl] *n* list of employees and of their wages.

paysheet [*pay*sheet] *n* payroll.

pea [*pee*] *n* leguminous plant with edible seeds in pods; seed of this as vegetable; **sweet p.** plant allied to this and cultivated for its flowers.

peace [*pees*] *n* absence of war, quarrels, or disturbance; tranquillity, calmness; concord; treaty ending a war; freedom from annoyance or interruption; **at p.** reconciled; calm; dead; **hold one's p.** be silent.

peaceable [*pees*ab'l] *adj* fond of peace, not quarrelsome; at peace ~ **peaceably** *adv* ~ **peaceableness** *n*.

peaceful [*pees*fool] *adj* calm, tranquil ~ **peacefully** *adv* ~ **peacefulness** *n*.

peacemaker [*pees*mayker] *n* one who restores friendship between opponents; (*fac*) lethal weapon.

peace-offering [*pees*-ofeRing] *n* present given to restore friendly relationship.

peacetime [*pees*tIm] *adj* and *n* (of or in) period when there is no war.

peach (1) [*peech*] *n* sweet stone-fruit with velvety rosy-yellow skin; (*sl*) pretty girl; anything very pleasant.

peach (2) *v/i* (*sl*) turn informer.

peach-colour [*peech*-kuler] *n* and *adj* yellowish pink.

peacock [*pee*kok] *n* bird of species whose male has bright plumage and a large fan-like blue-spotted tail; symbol of pride; vain or proud person; **p. blue** bright lustrous blue ~ **peacock** *v/i* give oneself airs; display one's beauty, skill *etc*

peagreen [*pee*gReen] *adj* and *n* light green.

peahen [*pee*hen] *n* female of the peacock.

pea-jacket [*pee*-jakit] *n* short thick overcoat worn by sailors.

peak (1) [*peek*] *n* pointed mountain top; projecting point of a cap's brim; narrowed end of ship's hold; (*fig*) maximum; **p. hour, p. period** period when something is at its maximum ~ **peak** *v/t* and *i* (*naut*) tilt upwards; (*of whale*) raise (tail) upright in air ~ **peaked** *adj* having a peak.

peak (2) *v/i* grow weak or thin, pine away.

peak-load [*peek*-lOd] *n* maximum intensity of traffic, electricity consumption *etc*.

peaky (1) [*pee*ki] *adj* having a peak (1).

peaky (2) *adj* thin and pale.

peal [*peel*] *n* loud ringing of bells; set of bell changes; set of bells tuned to one another; loud burst of sound ~ **peal** *v/i* and *t* ring loudly.

peanut [*pee*nut] *n* plant whose edible two-seeded fruit ripens underground, groundnut; oily edible seed of this; (*pl*) (*coll*) a trifling sum; **p. butter** butter-substitute made from this.

pear [*pair*] *n* sweet juicy oval fruit; tree that bears this.

pearl [*purl*] *n* lustrous white concretion formed inside various molluscs, *esp* oysters; bead imitating this; mother-of-pearl; (*fig*) outstandingly fine person or thing; very precious thing; (*print*) a very small size of type; **cast pearls before swine** offer fine things to those unfit to appreciate them ~ **pearl** *v/t* and *i* decorate with or form

into small glistening drops; fish for pearls; adorn with pearls or pearl-like beads.

pearl-barley [purl-*baar*li] *n* barley rubbed down into small grains.

pearl-diver [*purl*-dIver] *n* one who gathers pearl-oysters by diving for them.

pearlies [*purl*iz] *n* (*pl*) large mother-of-pearl buttons; clothes adorned with these buttons; London costermongers who wear these.

pearl-shell [*purl*-shel] *n* shell with mother-of-pearl lining.

pearly [*purl*i] *adj* like pearl; **p. king** costermonger wearing pearlies.

pearmain [*pair*mayn] *n* a variety of apple.

peasant [*pez*ant] *n* countryman, rural labourer; one who owns and cultivates a small plot of land; (*coll*) uneducated low-class person, boor.

peasantry [*pez*antRi] *n* peasants as a class; group of peasants; rural workers and small farmers.

pease [*peez*] *n* (*obs*) peas; **p. pudding** split peas boiled and mashed.

peasecod [*peez*kod] *n* (*ar*) shell or pod of peas.

peashooter [*pee*shOOter] *n* tube through which dried peas are blown by children; (*sl*) revolver.

pea-soup [pee-sOOp] *n* thick soup made from dried peas; **p. fog** very thick yellow fog.

pea-souper [*pee*-sOOper] *n* thick yellow fog.

peat [*peet*] *n* fibrous substance formed of partly decayed vegetable matter in bogs > PDB, PDE; block of this used as fuel.

peatbog [*peet*bog] *n* bog where peat is dug.

peatmoss [*peet*mos] *n* peatbog.

peaty [*pee*ti] *adj* of or like peat; containing peat.

pebble [*peb*'l] *n* small rounded stone; rock-crystal lens; **not the only p. on the beach** not the only person worth considering.

pebbledash [*peb*'ldash] *n* wall surfacing made by spraying gravel on soft plaster > PDBl.

pebbly [*peb*li] *adj* covered with pebbles.

pecan [*pee*kan] *n* (*US*) species of hickory; richly-flavoured nut of this tree.

peccadillo [pekadil*O*] *n* trivial fault.

peccant [*pek*ant] *adj* committing sin; wicked; (*med*) morbid.

peccary [*pek*eRi] *n* South 'American pig-like mammal.

peccavi [pe*kay*vI] *n* (*Lat*) **cry p.** admit one's guilt.

peck (1) [*pek*] *n* one fourth of a bushel; **p. of troubles** very many troubles.

peck (2) *v/t* and *i* strike with the beak; make (hole) by pecking; **p. at** strike at with the beak; (*fig*) nag at; (*coll*) eat a small amount without appetite ~ **peck** *n* blow of bird's beak; hasty and unfeeling kiss.

pecker [*pek*er] *n* one who pecks; kind of hoe; (*coll*) courage; (*vulg sl*) penis.

peckish [*pek*ish] *adj* (*coll*) hungry.

pecten [*pek*ten] *n* (*zool*) comb-like structure.

pectic [*pek*tik] *adj* of pectin; producing pectin.

pectin [*pek*tin] *n* gelatinous substance found in certain fruits > PDB, PDS.

pectoral [*pek*teRal] *adj* of or in the breast; worn on the breast; (*med*) for the chest; **p. fins** fish's fins just behind the gills ~ **pectoral** *n* ornamented breastplate.

peculate [*pek*ewlayt] *v/t* and *i* embezzle ~ **peculation** [pekew*lay*shon] *n*.

peculiar [pik*ew*li-ar] *adj* unlike others, strange; eccentric; special; belonging to one person or thing only, exclusive; characteristic ~ **peculiar** *n* exclusive possession *etc*; (*eccles*) parish or church not under diocesan control; (*typ*) type specially cast ~ **peculiarly** *adv* specially; strangely.

peculiarity [pikewli-*a*Riti] *n* distinguishing characteristic; oddity, eccentricity.

pecuniary [pik*ew*ni-eRi] *adj* of money.

pedagogic [pedagojik] *adj* of teaching; of teachers ~ **pedagogics** *n* (*pl*) pedagogy.

pedagogue [*ped*agog] *n* schoolmaster; pedant.

pedagogy [*ped*agoji] *n* art and practice of teaching.

pedal [*ped*al] *n* foot-operated lever on machine *etc*; treadle by which a bicycle is propelled; (*mus*) foot-operated lever on organ, piano *etc* > PDM; sustained note > PDM ~ **pedal** (*pres/part* **pedalling**, *p/t* and *p/part* **pedalled**) *v/t* and *i* propel (bicycle *etc*) by working the pedals, cycle; use the pedals of ~ **pedal** *adj* of the feet.

pedalo [*ped*alO] *n* small raft propelled by a foot-operated paddle-wheel.

pedant [*ped*ant] *n* one who makes too much display of knowledge; scholar whose main interest is in minute details; dry, pompous, or dull scholar.

pedantic [ped*a*ntik] *adj* of or like a pedant ~ **pedantically** *adv*.

pedantry [*ped*antRi] *n* state or quality of being a pedant; pedantic behaviour.

peddle [*ped*'l] *v/t* and *i* go from house to house with small goods for sale; carry round for sale; (*cont*) persistently urge or recommend ~ **peddler** *n*.

pederast, paederast [*ped*eRest/*peed*eRast] *n* man who commits sodomy or other homosexual acts with a young boy ~ **pederasty, paederasty** *n*.

pedestal [*ped*estal] *n* base for a column, statue, or ornament; one of the two sets of drawers of a knee-hole writing table; **set on a p.** admire greatly, venerate.

pedestrian [ped*est*Ri-an] *n* person walking along a road or other traffic-route; walker; **p. crossing** marked crossing-place on road *etc* where pedestrians have priority ~ **pedestrian** *adj* of, for, or like a walker; dull, prosaic.

pedi- *pref* of a foot or feet.

pediatric, pediatrician, pediatrics, pediatrist see **paediatric** etc.

pedicel, pedicle [*ped*isel, *ped*ik'l] *n*(*bot*) stalk of an individual flower of an inflorescence; (*zool*) stalk-like structure.

pedicure [*ped*ikewr] *n* chiropody; chiropodist.

pedigree [*ped*igRee] *n* ancestry; genealogical table ~ **pedigree** *adj* (*of animals*) bred from known high-quality stock.

pediment [*ped*iment] *n* (*Gr archi*) triangular gable-end area, often filled with sculpture.

pedlar [*ped*ler] *n* salesman of minor items who goes from house to house.

pedo- see **paedo-**.

pedology [ped*olo*ji] *n* study of soils.

pedometer [ped*om*iter] *n* instrument which records distance travelled by a walker.

peduncle [pid*ung*k'l] *n* (*bot*) stalk of an inflorescence; (*zool*) stalk-like process; (*anat*) band of nerve fibres joining parts of the brain.

pee [*pee*] *v/i* (*coll*) urinate ~ **pee** *n* urine.

peek [*peek*] *n* and *v/i* peep (2).

peel (1) [*peel*] *n* skin of fruit or vegetable, rind; **candied p.** rind of citrus fruit preserved in sugar ~ **peel** *v/t* and *i* cut or tear off the rind or skin of; strip away; shed its rind or skin; come off in shreds; (*sl*) undress; **p. off** veer away from others of a group.

peel (2) *n* small square fortress tower.

peel (3) *n* baker's shovel.

peeler (1) [*peel*er] *n* (*obs coll*) policeman.

peeler (2) *n* one who or that which peels.

peeling [*peel*ing] *n* that which has been peeled off.

peen [*peen*] *n* wedge-shaped end of hammer head.

peep (1) [*peep*] *n* and *v/i* cheep, chirp.

peep (2) *v/i* glance quickly and furtively; look through a small space; look through half-shut eyes; begin to show itself; show itself by slight signs; **Peeping Tom** one who spies furtively on women ~ **peep** *n* act of peeping; quick, furtive glance; **p. of day** dawn.

peeper [*peep*er] *n* one who peeps; (*sl*) eye.

peephole [*peep*hOl] *n* small hole in door *etc*.

peepshow [*peep*shO] *n* lighted box containing small pictures viewed through holes fitted with lenses; (*fig*) spectacle rousing vulgar curiosity.

peeptoe [*peep*tO] *adj* leaving big toe bare.

peer (1) [*peer*] *n* person of equal rank or merit; person of similar age and status as oneself; one entitled to sit in the House of Lords; **life p.** one whose peerage does not pass to his heir; **spiritual p.** bishop entitled to sit in the House of Lords; **temporal p.** any peer not a bishop.

peer (2) *v/i* look closely or intently.

peerage [*peer*Rij] *n* body of peers, rank of peer; book containing list of peers and their families.

peeress [*peer*Res] *n* female peer; wife of peer.

peerless [*peer*les] *adj* unequalled, matchless.

peeve [*peev*] *v/t* (*coll*) annoy ~ **peeve** *n* (*coll*) annoyance, grudge ~ **peeved** *adj*.

peevish [*peev*ish] *adj* irritable ~ **peevishly** *adv*.

peewit see **pewit**.

peg [*peg*] *n* wooden or metal pin projecting from wall *etc* as a support; split or hinged stick to fix clothes to a clothesline; pin fastening something to the ground; small bolt; (*coll*) drink, *esp* of spirits; **off the p.** (*of clothes*) ready-made; **a square p. in a round hole** person doing uncongenial work; **take (one) down a p.** humiliate ~ **peg** (*pres/part* **pegging**, *p/t* and *p/part* **pegged**) *v/t* and *i* fasten or mark with a peg; (*comm*) fix (prices) at stable level; **p. away** work hard and steadily; **p. out** mark with pegs; (*coll*) die; (*croquet, cribbage*) win.

pegboard [*peg*bawrd] *n* thin board studded with small holes suitable for inserting pegs or hooks.

peg-leg [*peg*-leg] *n* (*coll*) wooden leg.

pegtop [*peg*top] *adj* (*of trousers*) broad at the thigh and narrow at the ankle.

pejorative [*pee*jeRativ/pejoRativ] *adj* disparaging, scornful.

pekinese, pekingese [*pee*kineez] *n* breed of small pug-dog.

pekoe [*pek*O/*beek*O] *n* kind of black tea.

Pelagian (1) [pel*ay*ji-an] *n* and *adj* (heretic) who denies the doctrine of original sin.

pelagian (2) *adj* pelagic.

Pelagianism [pel*ay*ji-anizm] *n* heresy denying the doctrine of original sin.

535

pelagic [pel*a*jik] *adj* of or in the main water-mass of sea or lake > PDB.

pelargonium [pelaargOni-um] *n* genus of plants of the geranium order.

pelf [pelf] *n* (*cont*) money.

pelican [*pel*ikan] *n* genus of large fish-eating birds with a long beak and pouch hanging from it.

pelisse [pe*lees*] *n* woman's long cloak with wide sleeves; child's outer coat; military cloak.

pellagra [pe*layg*Ra] *n* a nutritional disease, often involving mental depression.

pellet [*pel*et] *n* small ball of soft substance; pill; small shot; small rounded boss; cylindrical wood plug.

pellicle [*pel*ik'l] *n* thin skin; membrane.

pellitory [*pel*iteRi] *n* bushy plant with green flowers, growing on old walls; plant with a pungent root.

pell-mell [*pel*-mel] *adv* in disorderly haste, confusedly ~ **pell-mell** *n* disorder.

pellucid [pe*lew*sid] *adj* transparent; lucid, clear.

Pelmanism [*pel*manizm] *n* type of memory-training system.

pelmet [*pel*met] *n* strip of cloth or board concealing curtain rods or runners.

pelota [pe*lO*ta] *n* Basque ball-game resembling tennis.

pelt (1) [pelt] *n* animal skin with its fur or wool; skin ready for tanning.

pelt (2) *v*/*t* and *i* throw things at; (*of rain*) pour down violently; run at full speed ~ **pelt** *n* act of pelting; **at full p.** very fast.

pelvic [*pel*vik] *adj* of the pelvis.

pelvis [*pel*vis] *n* bony girdle formed by hip-bones and sacrum; hollow within this; cavity in the kidney.

pemmican [*pem*ikan] *n* form of prepared buffalo flesh or venison; mixture of raisins, coconut, dates, figs, peanuts *etc* ground and compressed.

pen (1) [pen] *n* small enclosure for domestic animals ~ **pen** (*pres*/*part* **penning**, *p*/*t* and *p*/*part* **penned**) *v*/*t* shut in a pen; enclose, imprison.

pen (2) *n* instrument for writing with ink, *usu* a metal nib in a holder; (*fig*) art or profession of writing; (*ar*) quill shaped for writing; **ball point p.** pen having a ball-bearing at the tip and using ink paste; **fountain p.** pen with reservoir of ink ~ **pen** (*pres*/*part* **penning**, *p*/*t* and *p*/*part* **penned**) *v*/*t* write down.

pen (3) *n* female swan.

penal [*pee*nal] *adj* of or as legal punishment; rendering one liable to punishment; **p. servitude** imprisonment with hard labour; **p. settlement** convict settlement.

penalization [peenal*z*ayshon] *n* act of penalizing.

penalize [*pee*naliz] *n* inflict punishment or hardship on; (*sport*) subject to penalty; handicap.

penally [*pee*nali] *adv* as legal punishment.

penalty [*pen*alti] *n* legal punishment; loss or suffering incurred by sin, folly *etc*; (*sport*) disadvantage imposed for a breach of rule; **p. kick** free kick at goal awarded to one team after breach of rules by other team.

penance [*pen*ans] *n* act performed as a proof of repentance; punishment of sin willingly accepted; the sacrament of confession; (*fig*) discomfort.

penannular [pen*anew*lar] *adj* (*of a ring*) in the form of a complete circle except for one break.

penates [pen*ay*teez] *n* (*pl*) Roman household gods.

pence [*pens*] *pl* of penny.

penchant [paw(ng)shaw(ng)] *n* (*Fr*) inclination; fondness, liking.

pencil [*pen*sil] *n* writing and drawing implement in the form of a strip of graphite, coloured chalk or crayon encased in wood and sharpened: cosmetic encased in a thin holder; (*opt*) set of converging or diverging rays; (*geom*) number of lines meeting in one point ~ **pencil** (*pres*/*part* **pencilling**, *p*/*t* and *p*/*part* **pencilled**) *v*/*t* write, draw, or mark with a pencil.

pendant, pendent [*pen*dent] *n* jewel, locket *etc* worn on a chain round the neck; hanging ornament; (*naut*) pennant at masthead; (*archi*) lengthened ceiling boss; (*fig*) counterpart, complement ~ **pendent, pendant** *adj* hanging, suspended; overhanging; pending; incomplete.

pendentive [pendentiv] *n* (*archi*) the spherical triangle formed between the supporting arches where a dome rests upon a square base.

pending [*pend*ing] *adj* not yet decided, unsettled ~ **pending** *prep* until.

pendulous [*pen*dewlus] *adj* hanging downwards; swinging to and fro.

pendulum [*pen*dewlum] *n* body swinging freely from a fixed suspension point > PDS; swinging weight in clock mechanism; **swing of the p.** (*fig*) natural trend towards reversals of public opinion.

penetrable [*pen*itRab'l] *adj* that can be penetrated.

penetrate [*pen*itRayt] *v*/*t* and *i* pass into, enter; pierce; get through; see through; understand; be understood or felt; permeate.

penetrating [*pen*itRayting] *adj* that penetrates; very intelligent or perceptive; piercing; audible from far off; shrill ~ **penetratingly** *adv*.

penetration [penet*Ray*shon] *n* act of penetrating; keen intelligence or perception; **peaceful p.** steady but gradual method of spreading ideas.

penetron [*pen*etRon] *n* (*phys*) meson.

pen-friend [*pen*-fRend] *n* person, *usu* foreigner, with whom one exchanges letters without meeting.

penguin [*pen*-gwin/*peng*-gwin] *n* Antarctic seabird whose wings are modified into scaly flippers; (*tr*) series of paperback books.

penial [*pee*ni-al] *adj* of the penis.

penicillate [penisilayt] *adj* having small tufts of hair, scales *etc*; marked with fine lines.

penicillin [penisilin] *n* (*med*) class of antibiotics capable of destroying several types of disease bacteria.

penicillium (*pl* **penicillia**) [penisili-um] *n* (*bot*) one of a group of fungi growing as mould on stale food *etc*.

peninsula [pen*in*sewla] *n* stretch of land almost surrounded by water; **the P.** Spain and Portugal ~ **peninsular** *adj*.

penis [*pee*nis] *n* male organ of copulation and urination.

penitence [*pen*itens] *n* sorrow for sin.

penitent [*pen*itent] *adj* repentant, sorry for sin ~ **penitent** *n* repentant sinner; one doing penance.

penitential [peni*ten*shal] *adj* of or expressing repentance; of penance ~ **penitential** *n* book of prescribed penances ~ **penitentially** *adv*.

penitentiary [peni*ten*sheRi] *n* reformatory, house of correction; (*US*) state prison; (*RC*) body assigning penances for grave sins ~ **penitentiary** *adj* penitential.

penitently [*penitentli*] *adv* in a penitent way.

penknife [*pen*-nɪf] *n* small folding pocket knife.

penmanship [*pen*manship] *n* skill in writing by hand; style of handwriting.

pen-name [*pen*-naym] *n* author's pseudonym.

pennant [*penant*] *n* long narrow flag of a ship.

penniform [*peni*fawrm] *adj* shaped like a feather.

penniless [*peniles*] *adj* destitute, very poor.

pennill (*pl* **pennillion**) [*penil*] *n* (*Wel*) improvised verse sung to the harp; stanza of this.

pennon [*penon*] *n* long narrow triangular flag; (*naut*) pennant.

penn'orth [*penerth*] *n* (*coll*) pennyworth.

penny (*pl* **pennies** or **pence**) [*peni*] *n* former British bronze coin worth one twelfth of a shilling; **decimal p., new p.** British coin introduced in 1971 worth one hundredth of a pound, i.e. one fifth of a shilling; **a pretty p.** quite a large sum; **turn an honest p.** earn some money.

penny-a-liner [peni-a-*lɪn*er] *n* inferior journalist, hack, *esp* one who pads out his work to earn more.

penny-farthing [peni-*faar*THing] *n* obsolete type of bicycle with one large and one small wheel.

penny-in-the-slot [*peni*-in-THe-slot] *adj* (*of machine*) operated by insertion of a coin; (*fig*) automatic.

penny-pinching [*peni*-pinching] *adj* and *n* niggardly, miserly (behaviour).

pennyroyal [peni*Roi*-al] *n* species of mint yielding a medicinal oil.

pennyweight [*peni*wayt] *n* troy weight equal to 24 grains.

penny-wise [*peni*-wɪz] *adj* economical over trifles.

pennywort [*peni*wurt] *n* name of several plants with small round leaves.

pennyworth [*peni*wurth] *n* amount that can be bought for a penny; very small amount.

penology [peen*oloji*] *n* study of legal punishment and the prevention of crime.

pen-pusher [*pen*-poosher] *n* (*coll*) clerical worker.

pensile [*pensil*] *adj* hanging down.

pension (1) [*penshon*] *n* annuity granted to an employee on retirement; periodic payment made to public servants, or to members of the armed forces on completion of service or disablement, or to their dependants; annual state grant to persons of distinction who need it; **old age** (or **retirement**) **p.** weekly sum paid by the State to elderly people ~ **pension** *v/t* pay a pension to; **p. off** permit or cause to retire with a pension.

pension (2) [*paan*(g)syon(g)] *n* (*Fr*) boarding house; **en p.** paying for board and lodging.

pensionable [*penshonab'l*] *adj* entitled to a pension (1).

pensionary [*penshoneRi*] *n* pensioner ~ **pensionary** *adj* of or maintained by a pension.

pensioner [*penshoner*] *n* one in receipt of a pension, *esp* old-age pension; Cambridge undergraduate paying for his own keep.

pensive [*pensiv*] *adj* thoughtful, serious; melancholy ~ **pensively** *adv* ~ **pensiveness** *n*.

penstock [*pen*stok] *n* rectangular sluice gate which opens by lifting upwards; pressure pipe supplying water to a water turbine.

pent [*pent*] *adj* confined, shut in; repressed.

penta- *pref* five.

pentacle [*pent*ak'l] *n* pentagram.

pentad [*pent*ad] *n* group of five; period of five years.

pentagon [*pent*agon] *n* (*geom*) five-sided figure; (*mil*) fort with five bastions; (*US*) five-sided building on the outskirts of Washington, D.C., occupied by the Department of Defense ~ **pentagonal** [pent*agonal*] *adj*.

pentagram [*pent*agRam] *n* five-pointed star drawn in one line, used in magic.

pentameter [pent*amiter*] *n* (*pros*) five-foot line of verse.

pentane [*pent*ayn] *n* (*chem*) paraffin hydrocarbon occurring in petroleum > PDS.

pentateuch [*pent*atewk] *n* first five books of the Old Testament.

pentathlon [pent*athlon*] *n* athletic contest comprising five different forms of competition.

pentatonic [penta*tonik*] *n* and *adj* (scale) comprising only five notes > PDM.

Pentecost [*penti*kost] *n* Jewish harvest festival; Christian festival in honour of the Holy Ghost, Whitsun ~ **Pentecostal** *adj*.

Pentecostalism [penti*kostalizm*] *n* Christian movement stressing the gifts of the Holy Spirit, *esp* glossolalia and healing powers ~ **Pentecostalist** *n* and *adj*.

penthouse [*pent*-hows] *n* small house or apartment on the flat roof of a building with walking space round it; projecting hood over window or door; **p. roof** roof sloping in one direction only.

pentode [*pent*Od] *n* thermionic valve containing five electrodes > PDEl.

pentose [*pent*Oz] *n* (*chem*) type of sugar containing five carbon atoms in the molecule > PDS.

pentstemon [pent*steemon*] *n* genus of herbaceous plants with brightly-coloured flowers.

pent-up [*pent*-up] *adj* confined; repressed.

penultimate [pen*ultimayt*] *adj* and *n* last (syllable) but one.

penumbra [pen*umbRa*] *n* partly shadowed area round a complete shadow, *esp* in an eclipse > PDG, PDS; lighter border of sunspot; borderline between light and shade ~ **penumbral** *adj*.

penurious [pen*ewRi*-us] *adj* stingy; scanty; impoverished ~ **penuriously** *adv* ~ **penuriousness** *n*.

penury [*pen*ewRi] *n* poverty, destitution.

peon [*pee*-on] *n* (*in Sp America*) debtor working as bondsman for his creditor; convict hired out as labourer; (*in India*) foot-soldier; policeman; manservant.

peonage [*pee*-onij] *n* state of being a peon.

peony, paeony [*pee*-oni] *n* plant with large red, pink, or white globular flowers.

people [*peep*'l] *n* body of persons of specified race, nation, community, class, or place; the masses, proletariat; persons in general; relatives, family; followers, servants; congregation; **the little p.** fairies ~ **people** *v/t* populate.

pep [*pep*] *n* (*coll*) energy, vigour ~ **pep** (*pres/part* **pepping**, *p/t* and *p/part* **pepped**) *v/t* **p. up** (*coll*) stimulate, encourage; make more vigorous, energetic, or lively.

peperino [pepe*Reen*O] *n* (*geol*) porous volcanic rock.

peplum [*pep*lum] *n* short skirt attached to a coat.

pepper [*pep*er] *n* hot pungent condiment obtained from dried berries; plant producing these; fresh fruit of various species of capsicums, *esp* those used in certain savoury dishes; (*coll*) vigour, enthusiasm ~ **pepper** *v/t* flavour with pepper; hit with multiple small shot; beat.

pepper-and-salt [pepper-and-*sawlt*] *adj* and *n* black and grey (cloth).

pepperbox [*pep*erboks] *n* perforated container for holding pepper.

peppercorn [*pep*erkawrn] *n* dried berry of black pepper; nominal rent for leasehold premises.

peppermint [*pep*ermint] *n* aromatic herb of the mint family; sweetmeat flavoured with this.

pepperpot [*pep*erpot] *n* pepperbox; (*fig*) hot-tempered person.

peppery [*pep*eRi] *adj* strongly flavoured with pepper; irritable, quick-tempered.

pep-pill [*pep*-pil] *n* (*coll*) stimulant drug.

peppy [*pep*i] *adj* (*sl*) lively, energetic.

pepsin [*pep*sin] *n* gastric enzyme splitting proteins in acid solution > PDB.

pep-talk [*pep*-tawk] *n* (*coll*) speech urging hearers to courage, activity *etc*.

peptic [*pep*tik] *adj* of or assisting digestion.

peptide [*pep*tId] *n* (*bioch*) compound containing two or more amino-acids linked together > PDS.

per [*pur*] *prep* in or for each; by means of.

per- *pref* through, completely.

peradventure [peRadvencher] *adv* (*ar*) perhaps.

perambulate [peRambewlayt] *v/t* and *i* walk right round or over, *esp* to survey the boundaries of; walk about ~ **perambulation** [peRambewlay-shon] *n*.

perambulator [peRambewlayter] *n* pram, light hand-pushed carriage for a baby.

percale [perkayl] *n* closely woven cotton fabric.

perceive [perseev] *v/t* see, apprehend; understand; observe, become aware of.

percentage [persentij] *n* rate per hundred; proportion; interest paid on every hundred units.

percept [*pur*sept] *n* (*philos*) mental product of the act of perceiving; thing perceived.

perceptibility [perseptibiliti] *n* quality of being perceptible.

perceptible [perseptib'l] *adj* that can be perceived ~ **perceptibly** *adv* to a perceptible degree, visibly.

perception [persepshon] *n* process of becoming immediately aware of something, faculty of perceiving > PDP; insight, understanding ~ **perceptional** *adj*.

perceptive [perseptiv] *adj* capable of perceiving; intelligent; quick to notice ~ **perceptively** *adv* ~ **perceptiveness** *n*.

perceptivity [perseptiviti] *n* power of perceiving.

perch (1) (*pl* perch) [*purch*] *n* an edible freshwater fish.

perch (2) *n* pole or bar for birds to roost on; branch *etc* on which a bird rests; seat, *esp* in high position; secure resting-place; measure of 5½ yards; square **p.** measure of 30½ square yards ~ **perch** *v/i* and *t* (*of bird*) alight; sit down on a high or unusual resting-place; fix in a high spot.

perchance [perch*aans*] *adv* perhaps.

percheron [*pur*sheRon] *n* breed of draught-horses.

percipience [persipi-ens] *n* quality of being perceptive or percipient.

percipient [persipi-ent] *adj* capable of perceiving; perceptive ~ **percipient** *n* one who perceives; one who can receive information by telepathy ~ **percipiently** *adv*.

percolate [*pur*kolayt] *v/t* and *i* filter; drip slowly (through); gradually become known.

percolation [purkolayshon] *n* act of percolating.

percolator [*pur*kolayter] *n* coffee-making apparatus in which water percolates through the coffee-grounds.

percuss [perkus] *v/t* (*med*) strike, tap.

percussion [perkushon] *n* impact, collision; noise produced by striking; (*mus*) instruments played by striking a resonant surface > PDM; **p. bullet** explosive bullet; **p. cap** small cap holding detonating powder, used in firearms ~ **percussive** *adj*.

perdition [perdishon] *n* damnation.

perdu [perdew] *adj* (*Fr*) hidden; **lie p.** (*mil*) lie in ambush; disappear, conceal oneself.

perdurable [perdewrRab'l] *adj* long-lasting, everlasting ~ **perdurably** *adv*.

peregrination [peRigRinayshon] *n* long journey.

peregrine [*pe*RigRin] *adj* a species of falcon.

peremptory [*pe*RempteRi] *adj* admitting no refusal, absolute; dictatorial, imperious ~ **peremptorily** *adv*.

perennial [peReni-al] *adj* continuing from year to year, permanent; (*of plants*) living through a number of years > PDB ~ **perennial** *n* perennial plant; **hardy p.** (*fig*) recurrent problem, dispute *etc*.

perfect [*pur*fekt] *adj* faultless; complete; absolutely correct; absolute, utter; (*gramm*) expressing completed action; (*mus*) (*of intervals*) neither augmented nor diminished > PDM ~ **perfect** [perfekt] *v/t* make perfect, complete; put finishing touches to; bring to highest standard.

perfectible [perfektib'l] *adj* that can be made perfect.

perfection [perfekshon] *n* state of being perfect; that which is perfect; act of perfecting; **to p.** perfectly.

perfectionism [perfekshonizm] *n* wish or attempt to reach perfection; theory that man can become perfect ~ **perfectionist** *n* and *adj*.

perfective [purfektiv] *n* and *adj* (*gramm*) (tense) expressing single or completed acts.

perfectly [*pur*fektli] *adv* completely, absolutely; faultlessly.

perfervid [perfurvid] *adj* very ardent.

perfidious [perfidi-us] *adj* faithless, treacherous ~ **perfidiously** *adv*

perfidy [*pur*fidi] *n* treachery.

perforate [*pur*feRayt] *v/t* and *i* make hole or holes through; make a row of holes in paper so that it can be torn across through them.

perforation [perfeRayshon] *n* hole; act of perforating.

perforce [perfawrs] *adv* by necessity.

perform [perfawrm] *v/t* and *i* do; carry out, complete; enact, render (a play *etc*); display one's artistic or theatrical skill, *esp* as public entertainment; (*of animals*) display tricks *etc*.

performance [perfawrmans] *n* carrying out of an action; performing of a play, music *etc*; entertainment; achievement, feat; (*coll*) silly display.

performer [per*fawr*mer] *n* one who performs; actor, entertainer; musician.

perfume [*pur*fewm] *n* pleasant odour; scented liquid sprinkled on the body ~ **perfume** [per*fewm*] *v/t* apply scent to; impart pleasant odour to ~ **perfumer** *n* one who sells or makes perfume.

perfumery [per*fewm*eRi] *n* (*collect*) scents; place where perfumes are made or sold.

perfunctory [per*fungkt*eRi] *adj* performed merely as a duty; hasty, superficial.

pergola [*pur*gola] *n* structure of intersecting beams carried on posts over which climbing plants are trained.

perhaps [per*haps*] *adv* possibly, maybe.

peri [*peer*Ri] *n* (*myth*) Persian spirit or fairy.

peri- *pref* round about, enclosing.

periagua see piragua.

perianth [*pe*Ri-anth] *n* (*bot*) outer part of flower enclosing stamens and carpels > PDB.

pericarditis [peRikaard*It*is] *n* (*path*) inflammation of the pericardium.

pericardium [peRi*kaar*di-um] *n* membrane surrounding the heart.

pericarp [*pe*Rikaarp] *n* (*bot*) wall of ovary after it has matured into a fruit > PDB.

perigee [*pe*Rijee] *n* (*astron*) point where an orbit is closest to earth.

perihelion [peRi*heel*i-on] *n* (*astron*) point where an orbit is closest to the sun > PDG.

peril [*pe*Ril] *n* danger, risk.

perilous [*pe*Rilus] *adj* dangerous, involving peril ~ **perilously** *adv* ~ **perilousness** *n*.

perimeter [pe*Rim*iter] *n* outer edge, boundary; (*geom*) distance all round a plane figure; its outer boundary line; instrument for measuring a person's field of vision > PDP.

perinatal [peRi*nay*tal] *adj* (*med*) immediately before or after birth.

period [*peer*Ri-od] *n* portion of time; era, epoch; phase, stage; interval between recurrent phases; space of time during which one revolution of a recurrent cycle is completed; phase of menstrual cycle at which bleeding occurs; (*astron*) time taken to complete one revolution; (*gramm*) complete sentence, *esp* if complex; full stop; (*pl*) rhetorical passages; **safe p.** phase of menstrual cycle at which conception is least likely ~ **period** *adj* of a specified historic era.

periodic [peerRi-*odik*] *adj* recurring at regular intervals; pertaining to the revolution of a heavenly body; **p. table** (*chem*) arrangement of the elements showing their periodic relation to atomic weights > PDS.

periodical [peerRi-*odik*al] *adj* periodic ~ **periodical** *n* magazine *etc* published at regular intervals of more than one day ~ **periodically** *adv*.

periodicity [peerRi-*odis*iti] *n* quality of recurring at regular periods.

peripatetic [peRipa*tetik*] *adj* walking from place to place, itinerant; (*philos*) Aristotelian.

peripeteia [peRipe*t*I-a] *n* reversal, abrupt change of fortune, *esp* in drama.

peripheral [pe*Rif*eRal] *adj* of or on the circumference or outer edge; on the outskirts; not central; of minor importance ~ **peripherally** *adv*.

periphery [pe*Rif*eRi] *n* circumference, bounding line; outer edge; outer surface; outskirts.

periphrasis (*pl* **periphrases**) [pe*Rif*Rasis] *n* indirect reference, circumlocution.

periphrastic [peRif*Rast*ik] *adj* using periphrasis.

periscope [*pe*Risk*Op*] *n* device for viewing objects above eye-level and where direct vision is obstructed > PDS.

periscopic [peRi*skop*ik] *adj* of a periscope; **p. lens** lens giving a wide field of view.

perish [*pe*Rish] *v/i* die; be destroyed; end; decay, rot away.

perishable [*pe*Rishab'l] *adj* liable to decay ~ **perishables** *n* (*pl*) goods specially liable to decay.

perished [*pe*Rishd] *adj* (*coll*) exhausted by cold or hunger.

perisher [*pe*Risher] *n* (*sl*) unpleasant person.

perishing [*pe*Rishing] *adj* bitterly cold; extreme; that perishes; (*sl*) objectionable, unpleasant ~ **perishingly** *adv*.

peristalsis [peRi*stal*sis] *n* wave-like contractions of the alimentary canal which propel its contents along ~ **peristaltic** *adj*.

peristyle [*pe*Rist*Il*] *n* (*archi*) range of columns round an open interior court or inside a temple.

peritoneum [peRito*nee*-um] *n* (*anat*) lining of the cavity of the abdomen.

peritonitis [peRiton*It*is] *n* inflammation of the peritoneum.

periwig [*pe*Riwig] *n* wig, *esp* of lawyers.

periwinkle (1) [*pe*Riwingk'l] *n* trailing evergreen plant with blue flowers.

periwinkle (2) small edible marine mollusc with snail-like shell.

perjure [*pur*jer] *v/refl* make an untrue statement on oath; break one's oath ~ **perjured** *adj* ~ **perjurer** *n*.

perjury [*pur*jeRi] *n* deliberate false statement made under oath; crime of making such a statement; grave breach of oath or promise.

perk (1) [*purk*] *v/i* **p. up** look up jauntily; recover from depression or illness; be cheeky; (*refl*) make oneself smart.

perk (2) *n* (*coll*) perquisite.

perk (3) *v/i* (*coll, of coffee*) bubble in percolator.

perky [*purk*i] *adj* cheerful jaunty; impudent ~ **perkily** *adv* ~ **perkiness** *n*.

perlite [*purl*It] *n* small enamel-like globules of obsidian.

perm (1) [*purm*] *n* (*coll*) permanent wave ~ **perm** *v/t* and *i*.

perm (2) *n* (*coll*) permutation (in football pools).

permafrost [*purm*afRost] *n* layer of permanently frozen soil.

permanence [*pur*manens] *n* quality of being permanent.

permanency [*pur*manensi] *n* permanence; that which is permanent; secure tenure (of post *etc*).

permanent [*pur*manent] *adj* long-lasting; unchanging; intended to last for indefinite period; **p. wave** artificially induced and long-lasting waving or curling of the hair; **p. way** track on which railway lines are laid ~ **permanently** *adv*.

permanganate [per*mang*-ganayt] *n* salt of permanganic acid; **potassium p.** deep purple crystalline salt used as a disinfectant when dissolved in water.

permeability [permi-a*bili*ti] *n* porousness; (*phys*)

539

ratio of the magnetic induction in a medium to the field producing it.

permeable [*pur*mi-ab'l] *adj* porous.

permeate [*pur*mi-ayt] *v/t* and *i* spread through, penetrate ~ **permeation** [permi-*ay*shon] *n*.

Permian [*pur*mi-an] *n* (*geol*) uppermost division of Palaeozoic strata.

permissible [per*mis*ib'l] *adj* that can be permitted ~ **permissibly** *adv*.

permission [per*mish*on] *n* act of permitting, consent.

permissive [per*misiv*] *adj* allowing, permitting; allowing but not enforcing; willing to tolerate sexual immorality, lawless behaviour, drug-taking *etc* ~ **permissively** *adv* ~ **permissiveness** *n*.

permit (*pres/part* **permitting**, *p/t* and *p/part* **permitted**)[per*mit*] *v/t* and *i* allow, grant leave; not oppose; tolerate; make possible, admit ~ **permit** [*pur*mit] *n* document giving formal permission; warrant, licence.

permutation [permew*tay*shon] *n* (*math*) change of order of a specified number of objects; each of the different possible arrangements of these.

permute [per*mewt*] *v/t* alter the order of; interchange.

pern [*purn*] *n* the honey-buzzard.

perne [*purn*] *v/i* (*dial*) turn spirally.

pernicious [per*nish*us] *adj* very harmful, destructive ~ **perniciously** *adv* ~ **perniciousness** *n*.

pernickety [per*niki*ti] *adj* (*coll*) fussy, hard to please.

perorate [*pe*RORayt] *v/i* conclude (a speech); speak formally.

peroration [peRO*Ray*shon] *n* conclusion of a speech.

peroxide [pe*Roks*Id] *n* oxide containing more oxygen than a normal oxide; oxide that yields hydrogen peroxide; **hydrogen p.** an antiseptic and bleaching liquid; **p. blonde** (*coll*) girl who has bleached her hair.

perpend (1) [per*pend*] *v/t* (*ar*) consider.

perpend (2) [per*pend*] *n* (*bui*) face joint; vertical line of joints in alternate courses of brickwork.

perpendicular [perpen*dike*wler] *adj* at right angles to the plane of the horizon, upright, vertical; (*geom*) at right angles to any plane or line; very steep; (*archi*) in the late English Gothic style ~ **perpendicular** *n* perpendicular line; vertical position; instrument for finding perpendicular line; plumb-line ~ **perpendicularly** *adv*.

perpetrate [*pur*pitRayt] *v/t* commit (evil) ~ **perpetration** [purpit*Ray*shon] *n*.

perpetual [per*petew*-al] *adj* never ending, eternal; permanent; going on continuously; very frequent; for all one's life ~ **perpetually** *adv*.

perpetuate [per*petew*-ayt] *v/t* prolong indefinitely; preserve from oblivion.

perpetuation [perpetew-*ay*shon] *n* act or process of perpetuating; state of being perpetuated.

perpetuity [perpit*ew*-iti] *n* quality of lasting indefinitely; **in p.** for an unlimited period.

perplex [per*pleks*] *v/t* puzzle, confuse; make intricate.

perplexity [per*plek*siti] *n* state of being confused; hesitation, uncertainty; that which perplexes.

perquisite [*pur*kwizit] *n* any legitimate profit

attached to a post but not included in the regular salary or wage.

perron [*pe*Ron] *n* (*archi*) large flight of outdoor steps.

perry [*pe*Ri] *n* drink of fermented pear-juice.

perse [*purs*] *adj* and *n* greyish blue.

persecute [*pur*sikewt] *v/t* treat cruelly, oppress, *esp* on account of religion or politics; annoy, harass; persistently attack.

persecution [persi*kew*shon] *n* act of persecuting; persistent annoyance, cruelty or attack; **p. complex**, **p. mania** delusion that one is being persecuted > PDP.

persecutor [*pur*sikewter] *n* one who persecutes.

perseverance [perse*veer*Rans] *n* act of persevering; prolonged patient effort ~ **perseverant** *adj* ~ **perseverantly** *adv*.

persevere [persi*veer*] *v/i* continue in spite of obstacles; make prolonged efforts.

Persian [*pur*shan] *n* and *adj* (native or language) of Persia; **P. cat** cat with long silky fur.

persiennes [persi-*enz*] *n* (*pl*) (*Fr*) window shutters made like Venetian blinds.

persiflage [*pur*siflaazh] *n* (*Fr*) light mockery, banter.

persimmon [per*sim*on] *n* American date-plum.

persist [per*sist*] *v/i* continue firmly despite opposition; continue to exist, remain; survive.

persistence, persistency [per*sis*tens, per*sis*tensi] *n* quality of being persistent.

persistent [per*sis*tent] *adj* persisting; continuing, lasting; obstinate; hard to get rid of; continual ~ **persistently** *adv*.

person [*pur*son] *n* human being; (*leg*) a living human body; physical appearance, looks; (*leg*) human being, group, or corporation having rights and duties; (*theol*) one of the three modes of existence of God; (*gramm*) one of three classes of pronouns and verbal endings expressing the speaker, the one spoken to, and the one spoken of; **in p.** physically present or active.

persona [per*so*na] *n* personality as shown in relationship to others; assumed personality; **p. grata** (*Lat*) person approved of or acceptable.

personable [*pur*sonab'l] *adj* of pleasing appearance, good-looking.

personage [*pur*sonij] *n* person of importance; character in a play.

personal [*pur*sonal] *adj* of, by or for a particular person, individual; private, intimate; offensive to an individual, insulting; of relationships between persons; of bodily appearance; (*gramm*) of or expressing one of the three persons; (*leg*) of or concerning all property except land; **p. column** part of newspaper where private messages or advertisements are printed; **p. equation** time interval between perceiving and recording an event for an individual.

personality [perso*nal*iti] *n* fact or state of being a person, identity; well-known person, celebrity; total mental, moral, social, and emotional qualities of an individual; character, *esp* as perceived by others > PDP; (*pl*) offensive remarks aimed at a person; **p. cult** excessive reverence for a political leader; **multiple p.** (*psych*) alternation of markedly different characteristics in one person.

personalize [*pur*sonalIz] *v/t* personify, represent as a person; make personal; adapt to suit one person only.

personally [*pur*sonali] *adv* as or by a person; done, seen *etc* by oneself; as regards oneself.

personalty [*pur*sonalti] *n* (*leg*) property excluding land.

personate [*pur*sonayt] *v/t* act the part of (in a play); pretend to be.

personification [personifi*kay*shon] *n* act of personifying; embodiment.

personify [per*son*ifI] *v/t* attribute personal characteristics and qualities to (inanimate objects); be a typical example of, embody.

personnel [person*el*] *n* body of employees, all members of a staff *etc*; body of persons constituting an armed force, manpower.

perspective [per*spek*tiv] *n* art or system of representing three-dimensional objects in spatial recession on a plane surface > PDAA; apparent relative size, distance *etc* of objects in space > PDP; perception of the relative importance of facts, ideas *etc*; vista, distant view; **in p.** (*fig*) in true relationship or relative importance ~ **perspective** *adj*.

Perspex [*pur*speks] *n* (*tr*) strong transparent plastic used in windscreens *etc*.

perspicacious [perspi*kay*shus] *adj* shrewd, acute, understanding quickly and clearly ~ **perspicaciously** *adv*.

perspicacity [perspi*kas*iti] *n* shrewdness.

perspicuity [perspi*kew*-iti] *n* lucidity.

perspicuous [per*spik*ew-us] *adj* lucid, clearly expressed ~ **perspicuously** *adv*.

perspiration [perspi*Ray*shon] *n* act of sweating; sweat.

perspiratory [per*spIr*RateRi] *adj* of, like, or exuding sweat.

perspire [per*spIr*] *v/i* and *t* sweat, exude moisture through skin pores.

persuade [per*swayd*] *v/t* induce, convince; influence in acts or beliefs by argument or appeal ~ **persuaded** *adj* convinced.

persuasion [per*sway*zhon] *n* act of persuading; state of being persuaded; conviction, strong belief; sect, denomination.

persuasive [per*sway*siv] *adj* that persuades; convincing, effective ~ **persuasive** *n* inducement ~ **persuasively** *adv* ~ **persuasiveness** *n*.

pert [*purt*] *adj* saucy, cheeky.

pertain [per*tayn*] *v/i* **p. to** belong or relate to; be connected with; be suitable for.

pertinacious [perti*nay*shus] *adj* obstinate, persistent ~ **pertinaciously** *adv*.

pertinacity [perti*nas*iti] *n* persistency.

pertinence, pertinency [*pur*tinens, *pur*tinensi] *n* quality of being pertinent.

pertinent [*pur*tinent] *adj* relevant ~ **pertinently** *adv*.

pertly [*purt*li] *adv* in a pert way.

pertness [*purt*nis] *n* quality of being pert.

perturb [per*turb*] *v/t* disturb, alarm, cause anxiety to.

perturbation [pertur*bay*shon] *n* state of being perturbed; disorder, confusion; alarm, agitation; (*astron*) deviation of a planet from its true orbit due to gravitational attraction of other planets.

peruke [pe*ROOk*] *n* a wig.

perusal [pe*ROO*zal] *n* careful reading.

peruse [pe*ROOz*] *v/t* read carefully.

pervade [per*vayd*] *v/t* penetrate all parts of, spread throughout; permeate.

pervasion [per*vay*zhon] *n* act of pervading.

pervasive [per*vay*siv] *adj* that pervades; widespread, not localized; diffuse ~ **pervasively** *adv* ~ **pervasiveness** *n*.

perverse [per*vurs*] *adj* obstinately persisting in evil; contradicting or opposing without good reason; cantankerous; (*leg*) contrary to evidence or judge's direction ~ **perversely** *adv* ~ **perverseness** *n*.

perversion [per*vur*shon] *n* act of perverting; state of being perverted; deviation from normality, *esp* in sexual practice > PDP; distortion, misrepresentation.

pervert [per*vurt*] *v/t* turn away from its proper use or sense; misapply; twist the meaning of; corrupt, deprave; teach wrong opinions or evil practices to ~ **pervert** [*pur*vurt] *n* one whose sexual desires or practices are abnormal; (*cont*) convert to an erroneous religion.

peseta [pe*sayta*] *n* Spanish coin of base metal.

pesky [*pes*ki] *adj* (*US coll*) vexatious.

peso [*pays*O] *n* South American silver coin.

pessary [*pes*eRi] *n* instrument worn in the vagina to remedy displacement of the uterus or as contraceptive; vaginal suppository.

pessimism [*pes*imizm] *n* tendency to expect misfortune; gloominess of outlook; doctrine that evil is more powerful than good or that evil rules the universe ~ **pessimist** *n* and *adj*.

pessimistic [pesi*mis*tik] *adj* of or like pessimism; expecting misfortune; gloomy; melancholy ~ **pessimistically** *adv*.

pest [*pest*] *n* troublesome, harmful thing or person; destructive insect or small animal; (*ar*) plague; (*coll*) nuisance.

pester [*pes*ter] *v/t* annoy; cause slight but repeated vexation to.

pesticide [*pes*tisId] *n* any chemical for destroying animal pests.

pestiferous [pes*tife*Rus] *adj* very harmful.

pestilence [*pes*tilens] *n* fatal infectious disease, *esp* bubonic plague ~ **pestilent** *adj* noxious, deadly; harmful, destructive; (*coll*) annoying.

pestilential [pesti*len*shal] *adj* causing disease; harmful; (*coll*) annoying.

pestle [*pes*'l] *n* implement with a heavy rounded head for pounding substances in a mortar.

pet (1) [*pet*] *n* tame animal kept as companion; dearly loved and pampered person, *esp* child; darling; **p. name** affectionate nickname ~ **pet** *adj* favourite, well loved ~ **pet** (*pres/part* **petting**, *p/t* and *p/part* **petted**) *v/t* and *i* caress, fondle; pamper, spoil; kiss and cuddle.

pet (2) *n* fit of peevish sulkiness.

petal [*pet*al] *n* one section of flower corolla.

petalled, petaled [*pet*ald] *adj* with petals.

peter [*pee*ter] *v/i* **p. out** (*coll*) gradually diminish and cease.

petersham [*pee*tersham] *n* strong corded ribbon

Peter's pence [peeterz-*pens*] *n* (*pl*) voluntary donations to the papal treasury; (*hist*) tax levied by the Pope.

petiole [*pet*i-Ol] *n* leaf-stalk ~ **petiolate** *adj*.

petite–phasic

petite [pe*teet*] *adj* (*of woman*) small and having a good figure.

petition [pe*tishon*] *n* humble request or entreaty; formal request to persons in authority to grant a favour or reform *etc*; prayer; (*leg*) formal written application ~ **petition** *v/t* and *i* make a humble or formal request (to).

petitioner [pe*tishoner*] *n* one who makes a petition; plaintiff in divorce suit.

petrel [*petRel*] *n* small black-and-white seabird; **stormy p.** person whose presence is apt to provoke fierce disputes.

petrifaction [petRi*fakshon*] *n* act of petrifying; state of being petrified.

petrify [*petRifI*] *v/t* and *i* turn into stone; cover with mineral incrustations; (*coll*) horrify; (*fig*) lose sensitivity, alertness *etc*; stony.

petro- *pref* of rock; stony.

petrochemical [petRO*kemikal*] *n* any chemical product obtained from petroleum.

petrol [*petRol*] *n* refined petroleum used as fuel in internal combustion engines; **p. bomb** bottle containing petrol or other inflammable liquid, plugged with a smouldering rag and thrown as a weapon; **p. pump** machine for supplying petrol to cars *etc* in measured quantities; **p. station** garage supplying petrol.

petrolatum [petRO*laytum*] *n* petroleum jelly, a whitish jelly obtained from petroleum and used as lubricant and in medicine.

petroleum [pe*tROli-um*] *n* mineral oil, natural mixture of hydrocarbons and other organic compounds > PDS; **p. ether** mixture of liquid hydrocarbons, distilled from petroleum.

petrology [pet*Roloji*] *n* study of rocks.

petticoat [*petikOt*] *n* women's underskirt, *esp* if starched or flounced; (*sl*) woman, girl; **p. government** women's authority over men.

pettifogger [*petifoger*] *n* lawyer who uses tricks or quibbles, dishonest lawyer ~ **pettifoggery** *n*.

pettifogging [*petifoging*] *adj* using dishonest tricks or quibbles in law.

pettily [*petili*] *adv* in a petty way.

pettiness [*petinis*] *n* quality of being petty.

pettish [*petish*] *adj* easily offended, peevish.

pettitoes [*petitOz*] *n* (*pl*) pig's trotters.

petty [*peti*] *adj* unimportant, trivial; contemptible, ungenerous; spiteful or mean over small matters; minor; on a small scale; **p. cash** small items of expenditure; **p. larceny** theft of articles of little value; **p. officer** non-commissioned naval officer.

petulance [*petewlans*] *n* irritable temper, peevishness ~ **petulant** *adj* ~ **petulantly** *adv*.

petunia [pe*tewni-a*] *n* genus of ornamental plants with white and purple bell-shaped flowers.

petuntse [pe*tuntsi*] *n* (*cer*) white earth used with kaolin in making porcelain.

pew [*pew*] *n* long bench with back and sides, used as seat in church; (*coll*) seat, chair.

pewit, peewit [*peewit*] *n* bird of the plover family, lapwing; cry of this bird.

pewter [*pewter*] *n* alloy of approximately four parts of tin to one of lead; vessel, plate or utensil made of this ~ **pewter** *adj*.

peyote [pay-*yOtay*] *n* Mexican cactus yielding mescalin.

pfennig [*pfenig*] *n* German copper coin, one hundredth of a mark.

phaeton [*fayton*] *n* light open carriage drawn by one or two horses.

phage [*fayj*] *n* (*abbr*) bacteriophage.

phagocyte [*fagOsIt*] *n* white blood-corpuscle capable of destroying harmful bacteria > PDB.

phalanger [fa*lanjer*] *n* genus of small Australian arboreal marsupials.

phalanx (*pl* **phalanges** or **phalanxes**) [*falanks*] *n* body of soldiers drawn up in close formation; solidly massed group; (*fig*) group of militant supporters; (*anat*) bone of finger or toe.

phalarope [*faleROp*] *n* genus of small wading birds.

phallic [*falik*] *adj* of or like a phallus.

phallicism, phallism [*falisizm, falizm*] *n* worship of the phallus.

phallus [*falus*] *n* male sexual organ, *esp* as religious symbol of the fertilizing power in Nature; image, carving, charm *etc* representing this.

phanon see **fanon**.

phantasm [*fantazm*] *n* visual illusion; apparition, phantom; subjective visual impression.

phantasmagoria [fantazmaga*wRi-a*] *n* series of visual illusions; dream-like sequence of figures *etc* indistinctly seen.

phantasmal [fan*tazmal*] *adj* like a phantasm.

phantasy see **fantasy**.

phantom [*fantom*] *n* supernatural apparition; ghost, spectre; imaginary figure; hallucination; visual illusion ~ **phantom** *adj* spectral; imaginary, illusive, unreal.

Pharaoh [*fairRO*] *n* title of the kings of ancient Egypt.

Pharisaic [faRi*say-ik*] *adj* of or like a Pharisee; self-righteous, hypocritical ~ **Pharisaical** *adj* ~ **Pharisaically** *adv*.

Pharisaism [*faRisay-izm*] *n* doctrine, behaviour, or outlook of a Pharisee.

Pharisee [*faRisee*] *n* member of an ancient Jewish sect noted for strictness in points of ritual and law; one who prides himself on being unusually holy; hypocrite; one who over-values outer forms and observances in religion.

pharmaceutical [faarma*sewtikal*/faarma*kewtikal*] *adj* of pharmacy; engaged in pharmacy.

pharmaceutics [faarma*sewtiks*/faarma*kewtiks*] *n* (*pl*) science of pharmacy.

pharmacist [*faarmasist*] *n* one skilled in the preparation of medicines.

pharmacology [faarma*koloji*] *n* study of medicinal drugs.

pharmacopoeia [faarmak*Opee-a*] *n* official list of medicinal drugs and directions for their preparation; collection of drugs.

pharmacy [*faarmasi*] *n* art of mixing and dispensing medicinal drugs; chemist's dispensary.

pharos [*fairRos*] *n* a lighthouse.

pharynx [*faRingks*] *n* cavity behind nose and mouth opening into the larynx.

phase [*fayz*] *n* a stage or form in a cycle of growth or change; transitory stage; aspect; aspect of moon or planet at one stage of its cycle of illumination; (*elect*) stage in cycle of alternating current; (*chem*) separate part of a heterogeneous system ~ **phase** *v/t* separate into phases of activity or operation; **p. out** gradually cease to make, use, do *etc*.

phasic [*fayzik*] *adj* of or like a phase.

542

phatic [*f*atik] *adj* (*gramm*) expressing general politeness or goodwill rather than specific information.

pheasant [*f*ezant] *n* a long-tailed gamebird.

phen-, pheno- *pref* derived from benzine.

phenobarbitone [feenObaarbitOn] *n* a sedative and soporific drug.

phenol [*f*eenol] *n* (*chem*) carbolic acid.

phenomena [fenomina] *pl* of **phenomenon**.

phenomenal [fenominal] *adj* of or like a phenomenon; extraordinary, exceptional ~ **phenomenally** *adv*.

phenomenalism [fenominalizm] *n* (*philos*) doctrine that human knowledge is confined to phenomena, and never attains to the real nature of things ~ **phenomenalist** *n* and *adj*.

phenomenon (*pl* **phenomena**) [fenominon] *n* anything perceived by the senses; anything striking or exceptional; prodigy; (*philos*) a possible datum, or group of data, of experience at any moment.

phenotype [feenOtIp] *n* (*biol*) set of characteristics determined both by heredity and environment.

pheromone [feerROmOn] *n* (*biol*) chemical substance secreted by an animal to attract or influence others of its species.

phew [*f*ew] *interj* exclamation expressing surprise, weariness, or relief.

phial [*f*I-al] *n* small glass bottle.

phil-, philo- *pref* loving; studying.

philander [filander] *v/i* flirt, make love frivolously or insincerely ~ **philanderer** *n*.

philanthrope [*f*ilanthROp] *n* philanthropist.

philanthropic [filanthRopik] *adj* benevolent, motivated by love for humanity ~ **philanthropically** *adv*.

philanthropist [filanthRopist] *n* humane and benevolent person; one who practises philanthropy.

philanthropy [filanthRopi] *n* unselfish benevolence; active generosity in social works; love of mankind.

philatelist [filatelist] *n* stamp-collector.

philately [filateli] *n* stamp-collecting.

philharmonic [filaarmonik] *adj* devoted to music; of or for musical concerts.

Philhellenism [filhelenizm] *n* love of Greece and Greek culture; support for Greek struggle for political independence.

philibeg see **filibeg**.

philippic [filipik] *n* oration of Demosthenes against Philip of Macedon; bitter denunciatory invective.

Philistine [filistIn] *n* self-satisfied uncultured person hostile to art, literature *etc*; aggressive low-brow; (*OT*) non-Semitic Palestinian tribe at war with the Jews ~ **Philistine** *adj*.

Philistinism [filistinizm] *n* outlook of a Philistine, uncultured ignorance.

phillumenism [filOOmenizm] *n* the collecting of matchbox labels.

philo- *pref* fond of, loving, liking.

philodendron [filOdendRon] *n* tropical climbing plant with large leathery leaves.

philologian [filolOji-an] *n* philologist.

philological [filolojikal] *adj* of philology.

philologist [filolojist] *n* student of philology.

philology [filoloji] *n* study of the structure and development of language; linguistics.

philosopher [filosofer] *n* student of philosophy;

person of calmly reasonable outlook; one who bears misfortune well; **p.'s stone** imaginary substance thought to turn any metal to gold.

philosophic, philosophical [filosofik, filosofikal] *adj* of philosophy or philosophers; reasonable; wise; stoical, resigned ~ **philosophically** *adv*.

philosophize [filosofIz] *v/i* reason philosophically.

philosophy [filosofi] *n* the study of the ultimate nature of existence, reality, knowledge and goodness, as discoverable by human reasoning; any specified system of thought on these matters; general mental and moral outlook on life; wisdom; rationality; calmness; resignation, stoicism; (*ar*) science.

philtre (*US* **philter**) [filter] *n* magic drink, love-potion.

phiz, phizog [fiz, fizog] *n* (*sl*) face.

phlebitis [flebItis] *n* inflammation of the walls of a vein.

phlebotomy [flebotomi] *n* operation of opening a vein; blood-letting.

phlegm [*f*lem] *n* viscid fluid secreted by mucous membranes, *esp* in throat and chest; placidity, imperturbability.

phlegmatic [flegmatik] *adj* not easily excited or perturbed, placid; sluggish, stolid ~ **phlegmatically** *adv*.

phlegmy [*f*lemi] *adj* of, like, or producing, phlegm.

phloem [flO-em] *n* (*bot*) soft vascular tissue; bast > PDB.

phlogiston [flOjiston] *n* (*chem*) substance formerly thought to be present in all combustibles.

phlox [floks] *n* cultivated plant with large clusters of white, red or blue flowers.

phobia [fObi-a] *n* persistent or recurrent irrational fear or loathing.

phobic [fObik] *adj* of or like a phobia.

phoenix [feeniks] *n* (*myth*) unique bird fabled to live for 500 years, after which it burnt itself to death and was reincarnated from its own ashes; paragon.

phon [fon] *n* unit of loudness of sounds > PDS.

phonate [fOnayt] *v/i* produce vocal sounds ~ **phonation** [fOnayshon] *n*.

phone (1) [fOn] *n* phoneme.

phone (2) *n*, *v/t* and *i* (*coll*) telephone.

phone-in [fOn-in] *n* (*rad*, *TV*) broadcast programme including questions and comments by telephone from members of the public.

phoneme [fOneem] *n* single speech-sound; group of sounds so similar that the speaker thinks them identical ~ **phonemic** [fOneemik] *adj*.

phonetic [fOnetik] *adj* of or representing the sounds of speech; **p. alphabet** system of spelling representing speech-sounds accurately and consistently.

phonetician [fOnitishan] *n* student of phonetics.

phonetics [fOnetiks] *n* (*pl*) branch of linguistics dealing with the sounds of speech.

phoney, phony [fOni] *adj* (*sl*) sham, bogus; insincere ~ **phoney** *n* (*sl*) insincere person.

phonic [fonik] *adj* acoustic, of sound; of vocal sounds.

phono- *pref* of sound; of voice or speech.

phonogram [fOnOgRam] *n* written symbol for a sound of speech; record made by phonograph.

phonograph [fOnOgRaaf] *n* obsolete instrument

for recording sounds on cylindrical wax records and reproducing them; (*US*) gramophone.

phonology [f*O*n*oloji*] *n* history of sound changes in a language; system of speech-sounds of a particular language or period.

phooey [f*OO*-i] *interj* (*sl*) exclamation of disbelief or scorn.

phosgene [f*ozjeen*] *n* (*chem*) carbonyl chloride, a colourless poisonous gas.

phosphate [f*osfayt*] *n* (*chem*) salt of phosphoric acid; (*pl*) such salts used as agricultural fertilizers ~ **phosphate** *v/t* coat (metal) with hot phosphoric acid > PDBl.

phosphine [f*osfeen*] *n* a colourless inflammable poisonous gas > PDS.

phosphite [f*osfIt*] *n* salt of phosphorous acid.

phosphorate [f*osfeRayt*] *v/t* combine with phosphorus; make phosphorescent.

phosphor-bronze [f*osfer-bRonz*] *n* alloy of phosphorus with bronze.

phosphoresce [f*osfeRes*] *v/i* emit light with very little combustion or heat; shine in the dark.

phosphorescence [f*osfeResens*] *n* act or power of shining in the dark without apparent combustion or heat; (*phys*) property of shining after exposure to light ~ **phosphorescent** *adj*.

phosphoric [f*osfoRik*] *adj* of or containing phosphorus in its higher valency; **p. acid** one of three strong acids derived from phosphorus pentoxide.

phosphorite [f*osfeRIt*] *n* non-crystallized phosphate of lime.

phosphorous [f*osfeRus*] *adj* of or containing phosphorus in its lower valency; phosphorescent.

phosphorus [f*osfeRus*] *n* (*chem*) non-metallic element appearing luminous in the dark > PDS.

phosphuretted [f*osfewRetid*] *adj* (*chem*) combined with phosphorus.

phot [f*Ot*] *n* unit of illumination, one lumen per square centimetre.

phot-, photo- *pref* of light; of photography.

photo [f*OtO*] *n* (*coll*) photograph.

photochemical [f*OtOkemikal*] *adj* **p. reactions** chemical reactions which are caused or accelerated by light.

photochromic [f*OtOkRO*mik] *adj* having the ability of darkening in bright light ~ **photochromism** *n*.

photochromy [f*OtOkRO*mi] *n* photography in colour.

photocopy [f*OtOkopi*] *v/t* and *n* (make) copy of document by photographing it.

photoelectric [f*OtO-ilektRik*] *adj* pertaining to the effect of light on electrons; **p. cell** device for detecting and measuring faint light > PDS; device in which light sets electric apparatus in motion.

photo-finish [f*OtO-finish*] *n* (*racing*) so close a finish that only a photograph can decide the winner.

photogenic [f*OtOjenik/*f*OtOjeenik*] *adj* having features that make a pleasing photograph, pretty when photographed; luminous.

photogram [f*OtOgRam*] *n* aerial survey photograph.

photograph [f*OtOgRaaf*] *n* negative picture produced by action of light on chemically sensitized film or glass plate; positive print obtained from this on sensitized paper ~ **photograph** *v/t* and *i*

take a photograph (of); be suitable for being photographed.

photographer [f*otogRafer*] *n* one who takes photographs.

photographic [f*OtOgRafik*] *adj* of or by photography; reproducing or recording very accurately ~ **photographically** *adv*.

photography [f*OtogRafi*] *n* art or process of taking photographs > PDS.

photogravure [f*OtOgRavewr*] *n* art of producing, by the action of light, an incised metal surface for printing from; picture so produced.

photolithography [f*OtOlithogRafi*] *n* process of reproducing in ink any design on prepared stone or zinc by means of photography.

photolysis [f*OtOlIsis*] *n* the breakdown of a compound as a result of irradiation by light.

photometer [f*Otomiter*] *n* instrument for measuring luminous intensity.

photomontage [f*OtOmontaazh*] *n* composite picture made from several photographs; art or process of making this.

photon [f*Oton*] *n* quantum of radiant energy > PDS; unit of visual effect of light > PDS.

photophobia [f*OtOfObi-a*] *n* morbid dread of light; inability to see in strong light > PDP.

photosphere [f*OtOsfeer*] *n* intensely luminous outer portion of the sun or of a star.

photostat [f*OtOstat*] *n* apparatus which makes direct photographic copies of documents *etc* without using a negative; copy made by this ~ **photostat** *v/t* and *i*.

photosynthesis [f*OtOsinthisis*] *n* process by which green plants form organic compounds from water and carbon dioxide in the presence of sunlight > PDB, PDS ~ **photosynthetic** *adj*.

phototropic [f*OtOtRopik*] *adj* (*biol*) bending or growing towards or away from light.

phrase [f*Rayz*] *n* group of words forming a subdivision of a sentence, *esp* one containing no finite verb; group of words functioning as a single part of speech; idiomatic expression; brief effective expression, striking remark; (*mus*) small group of notes forming subsection of a melody; **p. book** collection of idioms and characteristic phrases of a language ~ **phrase** *v/t* express in fitting words; choose words to express; play (melody) with correct division into phrases.

phraseogram [f*Rayzi-OgRam*] *n* symbol in shorthand representing a whole phrase.

phraseology [f*Rayzi-oloji*] *n* choice of words; literary style.

phrenetic [f*Renetik*] *adj* frantic.

phrenic [f*Renik*] *adj* (*anat*) of the diaphragm.

phrenologist [f*Renolojist*] *n* one who practises phrenology.

phrenology [f*Renoloji*] *n* theory that one can deduce a person's character, intelligence *etc* from the outer appearance and shape of his skull.

phthisis [th*Isis*/t*Isis*] *n* tuberculosis of the lungs; wasting disease.

phut [f*ut*] *adv* go **p.** (*coll*) break, come to nothing.

phyla [f*Ila*] *pl* of phylum.

phylactery [fil*akt*eRi] *n* small leather box containing Old Testament Hebrew texts, worn by orthodox Jews at morning prayer on the arm and forehead.

phyle [*fī*li] *n* (*Gk antiq*) clan of kinsmen.
phyletic [fi*let*ik] *adj* (*biol*) racial.
phyllo- *pref* of a leaf or leaves.
phylloxera [filok*seer*Ra] *n* genus of plant lice very destructive to vines.
phylogenesis [fīlO*jen*isis] *n* origin and evolution of a race or species.
phylum (*pl* **phyla**) [*fī*lum] *n* one of the major subsections of the animal kingdom > PDB.
physic [*fiz*ik] *n* medicine, *esp* purge; medical art or science ~ **physic** *v/t* administer physic to.
physical [*fiz*ikal] *adj* of or in the body; of or connected with material objects and the universe perceived by the senses; of physics; of natural science; connected with natural features of the world; according to the laws of nature ~ **physically** *adv*.
physician [fi*zish*an] *n* doctor legally qualified to treat disease by medicines *etc* but not by surgery.
physicist [*fiz*isist] *n* student of physics.
physico- *pref* of physics; physical.
physics [*fiz*iks] *n* (*pl*) the study of the properties of matter and energy.
physio- *pref* physical; of nature.
physiognomic, physiognomical [fizi-o*nom*ik, fizi-o*nom*ikal] *adj* of, by, or skilled in, physiognomy.
physiognomist [fizi-*on*omist] *n* one who can judge character by facial expression and appearance.
physiognomy [fizi-*on*omi] *n* general appearance and usual expression of the face; art of judging character from this; (*sl*) face; general appearance of a country *etc*.
physiography [fizi-o*gRaf*i] *n* study of the physical features of the earth > PDG.
physiological [fizi-o*loj*ikal] *adj* of physiology; of or affecting bodily functions.
physiologist [fizi-*ol*ojist] *n* student of physiology.
physiology [fizi-*ol*oji] *n* study of the functions of and processes in living beings.
physiotherapist [fizi-Othe*Rap*ist] *n* one skilled in physiotherapy.
physiotherapy [fizi-Othe*Rap*i] *n* treatment of disease by exercise, massage, heat *etc*.
physique [fi*zeek*] *n* bodily appearance and characteristics.
phyto- *pref* of plants.
pi (1) [pI] *n* name of Greek letter π; (*math*) ratio of the circumference of a circle to its diameter.
pi (2) *adj* (*sl*) pious.
pi (3) see **pie** (3).
piacular [pI-*ak*ewler] *adj* expiatory.
pia mater [pI-a-*may*ter] *n* (*anat*) innermost membrane covering brain and spinal cord.
pianissimo [pee-a*nis*imO] *adj* and *n* (*mus*) very soft (note or passage) ~ **pianissimo** *adv* very softly.
pianist [*pee*-anist] *n* player on the piano.
pianistic [pee-a*nis*tik] *adj* of, suitable for, playing on a piano.
piano (1) [pee-a*nO*] *n* keyboard instrument whose strings are struck by hammers > PDM; **grand p.** large piano with horizontal strings; **upright p.** piano with vertical strings ~ **piano** *adj* of or for the piano; including a piano.
piano (2) [pee-*aan*O] *adj* and *n* (*mus*) soft (note or passage) ~ **piano** *adv* softly.
pianoforte [pee-anO*fawr*ti] *n* piano (1).

pianola [pee-a*nO*la] *n* player-piano > PDM.
piano-organ [pee-anO-*awr*gan] *n* mechanical piano resembling a barrel-organ > PDM.
piano-stool [pee-anO-*stOOl*] *n* pianist's stool, *usu* of adjustable height.
piastre (*US* **piaster**) [pee-*as*ter] *n* obsolete Spanish silver coin; small Middle Eastern coin.
piazza (*pl* **piazze**) [pee-*at*sa] *n* (*Ital*) public square, *esp* in Italy; (*US*) veranda.
pibroch [*pee*bRokh] *n* bagpipe tune with variations.
pica [*pī*ka] *n* (*typ*) largest size of type ordinarily used for books.
picador [*pik*adawr] *n* (*Sp*) mounted bullfighter who provokes the bull with a lance.
picamar [*pik*amaar] *n* thick, transparent oil obtained from wood-tar.
picaresque [pika*Resk*] *adj* (*of fiction*) relating in many loosely-linked episodes the adventures and travels of a rogue.
picaroon [pika*ROOn*] *n* rogue, brigand, pirate.
picayune [pikay*OOn*] *adj* (*US*) worthless, petty.
piccalilli [pika*lil*i] *n* pickle of chopped vegetables in mustard and vinegar.
piccaninny [pika*nin*i] *n* small Negro child; any small child.
piccolo [*pik*olO] *n* small flute an octave above the ordinary flute > PDM.
pick (1) [pik] *n* digging tool like an axe with two sharp points used for breaking loose rock or coal, or digging stiff clay or gravel; any sharp instrument used for picking.
pick (2) *v/t* and *i* take hold of and remove with fingers; remove flesh, feathers *etc* from; choose carefully, select; probe at with pointed instrument; separate and pull apart; take up in the beak; break up with a pick; steal; open (a lock) by wires *etc* without using a key; **p.** at eat small quantities of; **p. holes in** find fault with; **p. off** shoot carefully one by one; **p. on** unfairly select as object of blame, inquiry *etc*; seek quarrel with; **p. out** select; recognize; relieve by use of contrasting colour; play (tune) tentatively; **p. up** lift in one's hand; obtain casually; acquire; take in (passengers), call for; (*coll*) casually make acquaintance of; (*rad*) get signals from; accelerate; grow livelier; improve; ~ **pick** *n* that which is chosen first; best thing or person.
pickaback [*pik*abak] *adv* (*of a person carried*) on the back of another.
pickaxe, pickax [*pik*aks] *n* tool for breaking ground, pick (1) ~ **pickaxe, pickax** *v/t* and *i*.
picker [*pik*er] *n* one who picks (fruit, potatoes *etc*); **pickers and stealers** petty thieves.
picket [*pik*et] *n* pointed stake; striker or strikers keeping watch by a place of employment to dissuade other workers from going to work; person or group keeping watch in a public place to express a political or social protest; (*mil*) small body of men sent on patrol or on special duty ~ **picket** *v/t* and *i* surround with pickets; act as a picket in a strike or political dispute.
picking [*pik*ing] *n* petty theft; (*pl*) scraps of food, trifles left over; money or objects won by theft, dishonest profits.
pickle [*pik*'l] *n* solution of brine, vinegar *etc* in which food is preserved; (*pl*) vegetables steeped in pickle and used as condiment; (*coll*) trouble,

awkward difficulty; mischievous child; **have a rod in p.** for keep a punishment ready for ~ **pickle** *v/t* preserve in pickle; clean with weak acid solution ~ **pickled** *adj* (*sl*) drunk.

picklock [*pik*lok] *n* thief who opens doors by picking the locks; instrument for picking locks.

pick-me-up [*pik*-mee-up] *n* tonic, stimulant.

pickpocket [*pik*poket] *n* one who steals from pockets.

pick-up [*pik*-up] *n* microphone of a sound-reproducing system; (*rad*) broadcast relayed from one station to another; receptor; (*mot*) acceleration; (*US*) delivery van; (*coll*) person, *usu* woman, whose acquaintance one casually makes, *usu* in order to make love; (*coll*) recovery; stimulant; passengers collected in transit; (*sl*) free lift in a motor vehicle.

picnic [*pik*nik] *n* casual meal eaten out of doors for pleasure; outing at which this is eaten; (*coll*) something easy or pleasant ~ **picnic** (*pres/part* **picnicking** *p/t* and *p/part* **picnicked**) *v/i* eat or take part in a picnic ~ **picnic** *adj* for use on picnics.

pico- *pref* one million millionth.

picot [*peek*O] *n* small loop of thread used as edging; raised knot in embroidery.

picotee [pikо*tee*] *n* small carnation with white or light petals marked with darker colour.

picquet [*pik*et] *n* (*mil*) picket.

Pict [*pikt*] *n* one of a Celtic people formerly dwelling in parts of north Britain ~ **Pictish** *n* and *adj* (language) of Picts.

pictograph [*pik*tOgRaaf] *n* pictorial symbol; writing consisting of pictorial symbols.

pictorial [pik*taw*Ri-al] *adj* of, having, or expressed by, pictures; illustrated ~ **pictorial** *n* magazine of which pictures form an important part ~ **pictorially** *adv*.

picture [*pik*cher] *n* two-dimensional arrangement of lines and colours intended to have aesthetic value; portrait; embodiment; something very like another; film shown at cinema; vivid description; mental image; general aspect or appearance; (*pl*) cinema; (*coll*) very pretty person or thing; **p. gallery** room or building where paintings are exhibited; **p. hat** woman's wide-brimmed hat; **p. house**, **p. palace** cinema; **in the p.** well informed; knowing the facts; important; relevant; **p. window** large window designed to frame a fine exterior view, *esp* one between two narrower windows ~ **picture** *v/t* make a picture of; describe vividly; imagine, think of.

picture-book [*pik*cher-book] *n* child's book consisting mainly of pictures.

picturesque [pikche*Resk*] *adj* suitable for a picture, of romantic or charming appearance; (*of language*) graphic, vivid; (*fig*) of striking appearance, colourful ~ **picturesquely** *adv*.

picture-writing [*pik*cher-*Ri*ting] *n* writing by pictorial symbols.

piddle [*pid*'l] *v/i* (*coll*) urinate; (*ar*) trifle.

piddling [*pid*ling] *adj* (*coll*) petty.

piddock [*pid*ok] *n* a bivalve mollusc.

pidgin, pigeon [*pij*in] *n* (*coll*) business, concern; **p. English** blend of English with Chinese pronunciations and idioms used in the Far East; similar blend of English and native languages used in various African and Oriental countries.

pie (1) [*pI*] *n* magpie; species of woodpecker.

pie (2) *n* dish made of meat, fish, vegetables or fruit covered with pastry and baked; (*coll*) something very easy; **have a finger in the p.** play a part in some affair; **p. in the sky** (*sl*) a blissful life after death.

pie (3) *n* (*typ*) type indiscriminately mixed.

piebald [*pI*bawld] *n* and *adj* (animal) of light colour with irregular dark markings.

piece [*pees*] *n* detached part, fragment; portion; area marked off; item; firearm; one of a set of chessmen or draughts; specific amount or quantity; coin; single object; article (of furniture); specimen; short musical composition; literary or artistic creation; (*sl*) girl, woman; **by the p.** according to amount done; **p. goods** fabrics woven in standard lengths; **of a p.** of the same kind; consistent; **p. of cake** (*sl*) something easy; **p. of eight** Spanish dollar; **p. of one's mind** outspoken reproach or criticism; **p. of work** thing made or produced; specimen; **say one's p.** say what one planned to say ~ **piece** *v/t* mend, put together again; add a patch to; rejoin (broken threads); **p. out** add a piece or pieces to; eke out; **p. together** make (a whole) from fragments; **p. up** patch.

piecemeal [*pees*meel] *adv* bit by bit; scattered.

piecework [*pees*wurk] *n* work paid for by the amount done, not by the time taken.

piecrust [*pI*kRust] *n* pastry covering of a pie.

pied [*pI*d] *adj* of two or more colours.

pied-à-terre [pee-ayta-*tair*] *n* lodgings kept for casual or temporary use.

pie-eyed [*pI*-Id] *adj* (*coll*) drunk.

pier [*peer*] *n* ornamental sea-front jetty where sideshows and amusements are housed; landing-stage, jetty; breakwater, mole; column supporting a bridge; load-bearing brickwork between windows or doors; pillar supporting an arch; short buttress to increase stability of a wall.

pierce [*peers*] *v/t* and *i* cut a way through, go into or through; stab; make a hole in; penetrate; be seen, heard, or felt through; afflict; understand (a problem); be capable of cutting, stabbing *etc*.

piercing [*peer*sing] *adj* penetrating; (*of wind*) strong and cold; shrewd, perceptive ~ **piercingly** *adv*.

pier-glass [*peer*-glaas] *n* full-length mirror.

pierhead [*peer*hed] *n* seaward end of a pier.

pierrot [*peer*RO] *n* stock character in French pantomime, with whitened face and long white clothes; member of a troupe of singers wearing this dress.

pietà [pee-ay*ta*] *n* (*Ital*) a representation of the Virgin Mary mourning over the dead Christ.

pietism [*pI*-etizm] *n* extreme devoutness, exaggerated emotional approach to religion ~ **pietist** *n* and *adj*.

pietistic [pI-e*tist*ik] *adj* fervently pious, excessively emotional in religious matters.

piety [*pI*-eti] *n* willing observance of religious duties, devotion to God; loving dutifulness to parents.

piezo- *pref* of pressure.

piezo-electricity [pee-*ets*O-ilektRisiti] *n* electricity produced by the effect of pressure on certain crystals ~ **piezo-electric** *adj* > PDS.

piezometer [pee-etsomiter] *n* instrument for measuring pressure.

piffle [*pif'l*] *n* nonsense, rubbish ~ **piffling** *adj* ridiculous, nonsensical; petty.

pig [*pig*] *n* swine; castrated swine, hog; (*metal*) iron or lead casting; coarse, greedy, bad-mannered or grossly selfish person; (*sl*) policeman; **buy a p. in a poke** buy or accept something without a chance to judge its merits; **make a p. of oneself** eat or drink too much ~ **pig** (*pres/part*) **pigging**, *p/t* and *p/part* **pigged**) *v/i* (*of sow*) give birth to piglets; **p. it** (*coll*) live in dirty uncomfortable quarters.

pigbin [*pig*bin] *n* bin in which edible refuse is collected for pigs.

pig-boat [*pig*-bOt] *n* (*naut sl*) submarine.

pigbucket [*pig*buket] *n* pail in which kitchen refuse is collected for pigs.

pigeon (1) [*pijin*] *n* bird of dove family; (*sl*) dupe; **clay p.** disk thrown into the air to be shot at; **homing p.** pigeon trained to return home; **p. post** system of sending messages tied to the legs of homing pigeons.

pigeon (2) see **pidgin**.

pigeon-breasted [pijin-bRestid] *adj* with narrow bulging chest.

pigeonhole [*pij*inhOl] *n* small compartment in a desk *etc* in which papers *etc* can be stored; entrance to a dovecote ~ **pigeonhole** *v/t* put in a pigeonhole; put aside, defer considering; classify, arrange in order.

pigeon's-blood [pijinz-*blud*] *adj* deep ruby red.

pigeon-toed [pijin-tOd] *adj* with toes turned inwards.

piggery [*pig*eRi] *n* place where pigs are kept, sty; dirty untidy room or house.

piggish [*pig*ish] *adj* greedy; obstinate; dirty ~ **piggishly** *adv* ~ **piggishness** *n*.

piggy (1) [*pig*i] *n* (*coll*) pig; small pig.

piggy (2) *adj* resembling a pig.

piggyback [*pig*ibak] *adv* and *n* (*coll*) (act of riding) on the back of another person.

piggy-bank [*pig*ibank] *n* money-box shaped like a pig.

pigheaded [pig*hed*id] *adj* stupidly stubborn ~ **pigheadedly** *adv* ~ **pigheadedness** *n*.

pig-iron [*pig*-Irn] *n* impure form of iron obtained by the blast furnace process; cast iron.

piglet [*pig*let] *n* young pig.

pigling [*pig*ling] *n* young pig.

pigmean see **pygmean**.

pigment [*pig*ment] *n* colouring matter > PDS; paint; natural colouring matter in living tissue.

pigmental [pig*men*tal] *adj* of or producing pigment.

pigmentary [*pig*menteRi] *adj* pigmented.

pigmentation [pigment*ay*shon] *n* (*biol*) natura coloration of tissues.

pigmented [pig*men*tid] *adj* coloured by natural pigment.

pigmy see **pygmy**.

pignut [*pig*nut] *n* earthnut; (*US*) hickory nut.

pigskin [*pig*skin] *n* skin of a pig; leather made from it.

pigsticking [*pig*stiking] *n* sport of spearing wild boar from horseback.

pigsty [*pig*stI] *n* pen and shed in which pigs are kept; very dirty and untidy room or house.

pigtail [*pig*tayl] *n* plait of hair hanging down at the back; twisted tobacco.

pigwash [*pig*wosh] *n* kitchen refuse given to pigs.

pi-jaw [*pI*-jaw] *n* (*sl*) speech on religion or morals.

pike (1) [*pIk*] *n* (*hist*) long-handled spear used by foot-soldiers.

pike (2) *n* (*dial*) peak, pointed mountain-top.

pike (3) *n* large voracious freshwater fish.

pike (4) *n* turnpike; toll paid there.

pike (5) *v/i* (*sl*) walk.

pikelet [*pIk*let] *n* small round teacake.

pikestaff [*pIk*staaf] *n* shaft of a pike (1); **as plain as a p.** perfectly obvious.

pilaff [*pilaaf*] *n* Oriental spiced dish.

pilaster [pil*aster*] *n* (*archi*) shallow pier, sometimes fluted, projecting from the face of a wall.

pilatory [pil*ayte*Ri] *n* and *adj* (substance) stimulating growth of hair.

pilch, pilcher [*pilch*, *pil*cher] *n* infant's triangular wrapper, worn over the nappy.

pilchard [*pil*cherd] *n* small sea-fish like herring.

pile (1) [*pIl*] *n* (*eng*) timber, steel, or reinforced-concrete post driven into the ground > PDE; pointed stake ~ **pile** *v/t* drive piles into; provide piles for.

pile (2) *n* heap of objects; large building; (*coll*) large sum of money, fortune; heap of wood *etc* for burning a corpse, pyre; **atomic p.** nuclear reactor, apparatus for releasing nuclear energy under control > PDS; **voltaic (galvanic) p.** early form of electric battery, formed of sheets of zinc and copper separated by dilute sulphuric acid ~ **pile** *v/t* make into a pile, heap up; **p. in** cram (people or objects) into a confined space; **p. on** intensify; **p. it on** (*coll*) exaggerate; **p. up** accumulate, amass; (*naut*) run aground; (*mot*) crash into another car.

pile (3) *n* fine soft hair; nap on cloth.

pile (4) *n* haemorrhoid in the lower rectum.

piledriver [*pIl*dRIver] *n* hoist or movable frame to drive piles into the ground; (*coll*) powerful kick, blow *etc*.

pile-dwelling [*pIl*-dwelling] *n* dwelling raised on piles, often but not always over water or marsh.

pile-up [*pIl*-up] *n* (*coll*) crash involving several vehicles.

pilfer [*pil*fer] *v/t* and *i* steal petty articles in small quantities.

pilferage [*pil*feRij] *n* petty theft.

pilgrim [*pil*gRim] *n* one who for religious reasons visits sacred places, shrines *etc*; (*ar*) traveller; **P. Fathers** band of Puritans who in 1620 left England and founded a colony in Plymouth, New England.

pilgrimage [*pil*gRimij] *n* journey to a sacred spot, shrine *etc*; journey to a place revered for its associations; (*fig*) human lifetime.

piliferous [pil*ife*Rus] *adj* (*bot*) bearing hairs.

piliform [*pIl*ifawrm] *adj* hair-like.

pill [*pil*] *n* medicine formed into a small ball or disk to be swallowed whole; (*sl*) ball, *esp* billiardball; (*sl*) unpleasant person or thing; **bitter p.** something disagreeable and inevitable; **gild (sugar) the p.** try to make unpleasant things seem acceptable; **the p.** (*coll*) any oral contraceptive.

pillage [*pil*ij] *v/t* and *i* plunder, loot ~ **pillage** *n*.

pillar [*piler*] *n* (*archi*) stone or metal column supporting a structure, or standing alone as a monument; (*fig*) prominent supporter; (*mining*) mass of coal supporting the roof of a working > PDE; **from p. to post** from one place to another ~ **pillar** *v/t* support or adorn with pillars.

pillarbox [*pilerboks*] *n* low, hollow pillar erected in street, in which letters may be posted; **p. red** vivid scarlet.

pillbox [*pilboks*] *n* small round box for holding pills; small cylindrical hat; (*mil*) small round concrete emplacement or shelter.

pillion [*pilyon*] *n* seat for second person on motorcycle, placed behind the driver; seat or cushion for second person on horse's back, behind the rider; **ride p.** ride on this seat.

pillion-passenger [pilyon-*pa*senjer] *n* one riding pillion on a motorcycle.

pillory [*pileRi*] *n* wooden framework in which criminals were formerly held by neck and wrists and exposed to public scorn; (*fig*) public scorn and mockery ~ **pillory** *v/t* punish by putting in the pillory; expose to scorn and mockery.

pillow [*pilO*] *n* soft cushion to support the head while sleeping; padded support ~ **pillow** *v/t* rest one's head on; serve as pillow for.

pillowcase [*pilOkays*] *n* washable linen, nylon or cotton cover to enclose a pillow.

pillowslip [*pilOslip*] *n* pillowcase.

pillwort [*pilwurt*] *n* cryptogamous water-plant with globular spore-capsules.

pilo- *pref* or like hair.

pilose [*pilOs*] *adj* covered with hair.

pilosity [*pilositi*] *n* hairiness.

pilot [*pilot*] *n* person licensed to navigate ships through channels and fairways in or out of port; ship's navigator; one who navigates an aircraft; (*fig*) guide, director ~ **pilot** *v/t* steer, navigate; guide; (*US*) secure passage of (a bill) ~ **pilot** *adj* experimental; exploratory; preliminary; acting as starter to larger apparatus; **p. scheme** small-scale trial as preparation for larger scheme.

pilotage [*pilotij*] *n* act of piloting; fee for a pilot.

pilot-balloon [*pilot-balOOn*] *n* balloon used to discover direction and velocity of wind.

pilotboat [*pilotbOt*] *n* boat which takes a pilot to a ship.

pilotcloth [*pilotkloth*] *n* thick blue woollen material.

pilotfish [*pilotfish*] *n* small fish akin to horsemackerel which often accompanies ships.

pilotlight [*pilotlIt*] *n* small light left burning to ignite a gas appliance; small light showing that current is switched on in an electric machine.

pilot-officer [*pilot*-oficer] *n* Royal Air Force officer of rank equivalent to second lieutenant.

pilous [*pilus*] *adj* pilose.

Pilsener [*pilsner*] *n* a light lager beer.

Piltdown [*piltdown*] *adj* **P. man** supposedly a very early type of man, now proved to be a forgery.

pilular [*pilewler*] *adj* of or like a pill.

pilule [*pilewl*] *n* small pill.

pimelode [*pimelOd*] *n* catfish.

pimento [pimentO] *n* dried berries of a West Indian tree used as spice; wood of this tree; sweet pepper.

pimp [*pimp*] *n* man who organizes and profits

from the trade of a prostitute; one who procures means of sexual pleasure for another, pander ~ **pimp** *v/i* act as a pimp.

pimpernel [*pimpernel*] *n* small annual plant with scarlet, blue, or white flowers.

pimple [*pimp'l*] *n* small rounded boil.

pimply [*pimpli*] *adj* having many pimples.

pin [*pin*] *n* short, stiff, pointed wire with rounded or flattened head used for fastening; skittle; short pointed piece of wood or metal, peg; (*fig*) something worthless; (*pl, coll*) legs; **pins and needles** tingling feeling in a limb that has been numb; **safety p.** bent pin whose point is caught, when fastened, in a protective sheath ~ **pin** (*pres/part* **pinning,** *p/t* and *p/part* **pinned**) *v/t* fasten with a pin; hold firmly *esp* under a weight; confine, enclose; (*fig*) prevent from escaping; **p. down** bind (person) to; **p. on** lay blame on; **p. one's faith on** rely implicitly upon.

pinafore [*pinafawr*] *n* sleeveless protective apron; **p. dress** sleeveless dress worn over blouse.

pinaster [*pinaster*] *n* a species of pine.

pinball [*pinbawl*] *n* pintable.

pince-nez [*pans*-nay] *n* (*pl*) (*Fr*) pair of eyeglasses attached to the nose with a spring clip.

pincers [*pinserz*] *n* (*pl*) tool consisting of two pivoted bars whose shorter ends are shaped to grip; (*biol*) pair of organs for seizing and grasping; **p. movement** (*mil*) attack by two converging forces.

pinch [*pinch*] *v/t* and *i* squeeze tightly and painfully between two hard objects, *esp* finger and thumb; compress, press painfully (on); cause to become thin and pale; distress; (*coll*) steal; (*sl*) arrest, catch; live economically; **p. back** (*hort*) pinch off the tip of ~ **pinch** *n* act of pinching; distress, discomfort; emergency; as much as can be held between finger and thumb; small amount; **at a p.** if absolutely necessary; in emergency.

pinchbeck [*pinch*bek] *n* yellow alloy of five parts copper to one of zinc ~ **pinchbeck** *adj* sham.

pincushion [*pin*-kooshon] *n* small hard cushion to hold pins.

Pindaric [pind*a*Rik] *n* and *adj* (ode) in the style or metre of the Greek poet Pindar.

pine (1) [*pin*] *n* coniferous tree with evergreen, needle-shaped leaves; wood of this tree; pineapple.

pine (2) *v/i* become feeble from sorrow or sickness; long intensely (for).

pineal [*pini*-al] *adj* shaped like a pine-cone; **p. body, p. gland** (*anat*) small glandular body situated in the midbrain > PDB, PDP.

pineapple [*pin*ap'l] *n* large, cone-shaped, edible fruit of the ananas; (*sl*) hand-grenade.

pine-barren [*pin*-ba*Ren*] *n* (*US*) sandy tract sparsely covered with pine-trees.

pinecone [*pin*kOn] *n* woody conical fruit of pinetree.

pineneedle [*pin*need'l] *n* long spiky leaf of pinetree.

pinetum [*pin*eetum] *n* plantation of pines.

pin-feather [*pin*-fe*T*Her] *n* small undeveloped feather.

pinfold [*pin*fOld] *n* pound for stray cattle; pen for sheep.

ping-pong [*ping*-pong] *n* (*coll*) table-tennis.

pinguid [*ping*-gwid] *adj* greasy; (*of soil*) fertile.

pinguin [*ping*-gwin] *n* W. Indian plant or fruit.

pinhead [*pin*hed] *n* rounded top of a pin; small spot; tiny object; (*coll*) very stupid person.

pinhole [*pin*hOl] *n* hole in which a pin fits; hole made by a pin.

pinion (1) [*pin*yon] *n* outermost joint of bird's wing; feather, *esp* flight-feather; (*poet*) wing ~ **pinion** *v/t* bind the arms of; tie up firmly; cut off a bird's wing-tip, to prevent flight.

pinion (2) *n* small toothed wheel engaging with a larger one.

pink (1) [*pingk*] *n* pale red colour; garden plant allied to the carnation but with single flowers; dianthus; perfection, acme; fox-hunter's red coat; **in the p.** (*coll*) in perfect health ~ **pink** *adj* pale red, rosy; (*coll*) mildly socialist.

pink (2) *v/t* cut (an edge) into zigzags or scallops; ornament with punched holes; stab, pierce.

pink (3) *v/i* (*mot*) knock, work unevenly.

pink-eye [*pingk*-I] *n* form of contagious conjunctivitis; potato having pink eyes.

pinkish [*pingk*ish] *adj* fairly or slightly pink.

pinky [*pingk*i] *adj* tinged with pink.

pin-money [*pin*-muni] *n* personal allowance made by husband to wife; money earned by doing extra work for personal use for non-essential items.

pinna [*pin*a] *n* (*biol*) outer ear; lobe of leaf; fin.

pinnace [*pin*as] *n* warship's boat; small boat used as tender for larger vessel > PDSa.

pinnacle [*pin*ak'l] *n* small pointed ornamental turret; slender mountain peak; (*fig*) maximum, highest place or degree ~ **pinnacle** *v/t* adorn with pinnacles.

pinnate [*pin*ayt] *adj* (*biol*) like a feather; branching; arranged on each side of a common axis.

pinni- *pref* of or having a fin or flipper.

pinny [*pin*i] *n* (*coll*) pinafore.

pinochle [*pin*ok'l] *n* (*US*) game resembling bezique.

pinole [pin*Ol*i] *n* (*US*) food made from roasted and ground seeds mixed with cinnamon and sugar.

pinpoint [*pin*point] *n* point of a pin; something very small; precise location marked on map, *esp* of area to be bombed ~ **pinpoint** *v/t* locate or define precisely; bomb very accurately.

pinprick [*pin*prik] *n* hole made by a pin; act of stabbing with a pin; pain caused by this; (*fig*) petty annoyance ~ **pinprick** *v/t* annoy in petty ways.

pinstripe [*pin*strIp] *adj* decorated with many extremely narrow stripes.

pint [pInt] *n* measure of liquid capacity, an eighth of a gallon; this amount of beer.

pinta [*pIn*ta] *n* (*coll*) a pint of milk.

pintable [*pin*tayb'l] *n* game of skill or chance in which a ball is set to roll down a board set with many pins.

pintado [pint*aa*dO] *n* guinea-fowl; species of petrel; long silvery fish of the Caribbean seas.

pintle [*pint*'l] *n* upright pin, *esp* one used as pivot.

pin-up [*pin*-up] *n* (*coll*) picture of attractive girl. *esp* nude or semi-nude, to be displayed on wall of barrack-room *etc*; photograph of film-star, pop singer *etc*, either male or female, for display by his or her admirers; one whose picture is thus displayed.

pinwheel [*pin*weel] *n* kind of small revolving firework.

piny [*pI*ni] *adj* abounding in pine-trees.

piolet [*pee*-Olay] *n* ice-axe.

pion [*pI*-on] *n* (*phys*) short-lived elementary particle > PDS.

pioneer [pI-*oneer*] *n* one who is first to attempt, explain. discover or undertake something; one who takes the lead; discoverer; (*mil*) one of a body of soldiers who clear obstructions, build roads *etc* as the army advances ~ **pioneer** *v/t* and *i* be the first to introduce and work at; take the lead in; act as pioneer ~ **pioneering** *adj*.

pious [*pI*-us] *adj* devout, faithful in religious duties; feeling or showing religious fervour; (*ar*) dutiful to parents or country; **p. fraud** excusable deception prompted by good motives; **p. hope** hope unlikely to be fulfilled ~ **piously** *adv*.

pip (1) [pip] *n* disease of poultry and hawks with mucus in the mouth and a white scale on the tongue; (*sl*) depression; bad temper; boredom ~ **pip** (*pres/part* **pipping**, *p/t* and *p/part* **pipped**) *v/i* and *t* (*sl*) be or cause to be depressed, annoyed, or bored.

pip (2) *n* small seed in fleshy fruits.

pip (3) *n* each of the spots on playing-cards, dominoes, dice; image on radar screen; star on uniform of army officers to indicate rank.

pip (4) (*pres/part* **pipping**, *p/t* and *p/part* **pipped**) *v/t* and *i* (*coll*) fail or cause to fail, *esp* in examination; defeat, outwit; put an end to; thwart; blackball; hit (with bullet *etc*); **p. out** die.

pip (5) *n* signaller's pronunciation of the letter *p* to distinguish it from letters of a similar sound.

pip (6) *n* short shrill note repeated as a time-signal in broadcasting or telephoning.

pipe [pIp] *n* tube; long hollow cylinder conveying water, gas, steam *etc*; tubular canal in the body; short tube ending in a bowl for smoking loose tobacco; (*mus*) simple wind instrument consisting of a tube pierced with holes > PDM; cylinder in which air vibrates, *esp* in organ; (*pl*) bagpipes; bo'sun's whistle; shrill thin voice or vocal note; shrill bird-call; a measure of wine, 105 gallons; (*hist*) Exchequer rolls; **p. of peace** pipe ceremoniously smoked by Red Indians to seal a peace-treaty ~ **pipe** *v/t* and *i* play on a pipe; convey by pipe; provide pipes or piping for; utter shrilly; call by bo'sun's whistle; (*TV*, *rad*) relay continuously; **p. down** (*sl*) make less noise; cease speaking; **p. one's eye** (*coll*) weep; **p. up** (*coll*) begin to speak unexpectedly.

pipeclay [*pIp*klay] *n* fine white clay used for making tobacco-pipes and for whitening military trappings; (*fig*) excessive attention to details of military dress ~ **pipeclay** *v/t* whiten with clay.

pipedream [*pIp*dReem] *n* wishful day-dream; impossible hope or plan.

pipefish [*pIp*fish] *n* fish with long snout and slender body.

pipeful [*pIp*fool] *n* enough tobacco to fill the bowl of a pipe.

pipeline [*pIp*lIn] *n* line of pipes carrying petroleum from an oil-well; means of supply; direct and unobstructed communication line; **in the p.** (*fig*) on the way, not yet ready or arrived.

piper [*pI*per] *n* one who plays a pipe, *esp* bagpipes; name of various fish; **pay the p.** bear the cost;

he who pays the p. calls the tune he who provides the money has the right to say how it is to be spent.

pipe-rack [p**ı**p-Rak] *n* stand to hold tobacco-pipes.

pipestone [p**ı**pstOn] *n* a soft stone; a red clay.

pipette [pi*p*et] *n* glass tube used to transfer small amounts of liquid.

piping [p**ı**ping] *n* act of providing with pipes; apparatus or group of pipes; (*sewing*) cord enclosed in narrow tube of fabric and used to strengthen joins and seams; act of one who pipes; shrill call or voice ~ **piping** *adj* shrill; **p. hot** sizzling; extremely hot.

pipistrel [pipist*Rel*] *n* common British bat.

pipit [p**ı**pit] *n* small bird akin to the wagtail.

pipkin [p**ı**pkin] *n* small earthenware pot.

pippin [p**ı**pin] *n* eating apple.

pipsqueak [p**ı**pskweek] *n* contemptible little person or thing; (*coll*) two-stroke motorcycle.

piquancy [p*ee*kansi] *n* quality of being piquant.

piquant [p*ee*kant] *adj* rousing interest, curiosity, or appetite; lively, racy ~ **piquantly** *adv*.

pique (1) [p*ee*k] *v/t* annoy, irritate, offend; arouse (curiosity, interest); **p. oneself** pride oneself (on) ~ **pique** *n* annoyance, resentment.

pique (2) *n* (*in piquet*) act of scoring 30 points before the opponent has begun to score ~ **pique** *v/t* and *i*.

piqué [p*ee*k*ay*] *n* ribbed cotton fabric.

piquet [pi*k*et] *n* card game for two players.

piracy [p**ı**Rrasi] *n* occupation or act of a pirate.

piragua, periague [piRa*g*wa, peRi-a*g*wa] *n* canoe hollowed out of a tree-trunk; flat-bottomed two-masted boat.

pirate [p**ı**RR*at*] *n* one engaged in plunder and robbery on the high seas; privately owned radio transmitter operating without licence; one who operates this; one who illegally infringes another's copyright or trading rights ~ **pirate** *v/t* illegally reproduce (literary or artistic work); infringe the copyright or trading rights of; rob.

piratical [p**ı**R*at*ikal] *adj* of or like a pirate or piracy; published by piracy ~ **piratically** *adv*.

pirn [p**u**rn] *n* (*Scots*) bobbin, spool; fishing reel.

pirogue [piRO*g*] *n* piragua.

pirouette [piROO-*et*] *n* act of spinning round on tiptoe in dancing ~ **pirouette** *v/i*.

piscatorial [piskataw**R**i-al] *adj* of fishing.

piscatory [p**ı**skate**R**i] *adj* of fishing; employed in fishing.

Pisces [p**ı**seez] *n* (*pl*) (*astron*) constellation of the Fishes, twelfth sign of the zodiac.

pisciculture [p**ı**sikulcher] *n* artificial breeding and rearing of fish.

piscina [pi*see*na] *n* fish-pond; (*eccles*) stone basin with drain in chancel wall to receive water used ritually.

piscine (1) [p**ı**seen] *n* swimming pool.

piscine (2) [p**ı**sin] *adj* of fish.

piscivorous [pisive**R**us] *adj* fish-eating.

pish [p**ı**sh] *interjection* used to convey contempt.

piss [pis] *v/i* (*vulg*) urinate, make water; **p. off** (*vulg*) go away ~ **piss** *n* urine; **p. up** (*vulg*) drinking session ~ **pissed** *adj* (*vulg*) very drunk ~ **pissed off** *adj* (*vulg*) very angry or bored.

pistachio [pistaashi-O] *n* edible nut found in the Near East; tree producing this; pale green.

pistil [p**ı**stil] *n* (*bot*) female organ of a flower > PDB.

pistillary [p**ı**stile**R**i] *adj* of a pistil.

pistillate [p**ı**stilayt] *adj* (*of flowers*) having carpels but not stamens; female.

pistol [p**ı**stol] *n* small firearm held in one hand when fired ~ **pistol** (*pres/part* **pistolling**, *p/t* and *p/part* **pistolled**) *v/t* and *i* shoot with a pistol.

pistole [pistOl] *n* (*hist*) gold coin, *esp* of 17th-century Spain.

piston [p**ı**ston] *n* (*mech*) a short cylinder fitted into and moving in a cylindrical tube, used to generate and apply pressure; (*mus*) valve on brass instruments; button controlling organ-stops; **p. rod** rod connecting a piston to other parts of a machine and setting them in motion.

pit [pit] *n* hole; hollow, sunken area; deep hole in the ground, *esp* one dug to excavate coal, chalk *etc*; (*fig*) Hell; abyss; the grave; natural hollow in the body; indentation on the skin; (*theat*) rear portion of ground-floor of auditorium; area where orchestra plays in opera house, music-hall *etc*; trench from which the underside of a motor vehicle can be seen and repaired; area beside race course where racing cars are repaired and wheels changed; sunken enclosure where animals are ensnared, kept, or set to fight; (*US*) part of an Exchange assigned to specified type of dealings ~ **pit** (*pres/part* **pitting**, *p/t* and *p/part* **pitted**) *v/t* make holes, hollows, or indentations in; **p. against** set to fight against; match in warfare or rivalry.

pit-a-pat [pit-a-pat] *adv* and *n* (sounding like) light quick footsteps; go p. (*of heart*) palpitate.

pitch (1) [pich] *n* name given to numerous hard, dark substances which melt to viscous tarry liquids > PDS ~ **pitch** *v/t* apply pitch to.

pitch (2) *v/t* and *i* throw, hurl; fall violently; place in position, *esp* by fixing to the ground; erect (tent); pave with stones set on edge; (*naut*) plunge and rise alternately, *esp* from bow to stern; (*mus*) set in specific key; (*mil*) draw up in battle order; (*cricket, baseball*) throw ball to batsman; set up wicket; (*fig*) narrate, express; **p. into** attack or scold violently; **p. on** (upon) choose ~ **pitch** *n* usual position chosen by street trader *etc*; act of throwing; distance or height of a throw; degree of light or intensity; degree of slope, degree of a roof; (*mus*) relative shrillness of a note, determined by the frequency of its vibrations > PDM; agreed standard of frequency of a tuning note > PDM, PDP; (*cricket*) area between the wickets; *also* the ground where other games are played (hockey, football *etc*); (*mech*) distance between teeth of a cogwheel or turns of thread of a screw.

pitch-and-toss [pich-an-tos] *n* game in which coins are pitched at a mark and afterwards tossed.

pitch-black [pich-blak] *adj* intensely black.

pitchblende [pichblend] *n* natural ore consisting mainly of uranium oxide, the principal source of radium > PDS.

pitch-dark [pich-*daark*] *adj* intensely dark.

pitched [picht] *adj* (*of battle*) planned beforehand.

pitcher (1) [picher] *n* one who pitches; one who occupies a pitch; (*baseball*) player who bowls to the batter; stone used for paving.

pitcher (2) *n* large earthenware vessel with two ear-shaped handles and a lip.

pitcher-plant [picher-plaant] *n* plant with pitcher-shaped leaves which attract and entrap flies.

pitchfork [*pich*fawrk] *n* long-handled, two-pronged fork for lifting and throwing hay *etc* ~ **pitchfork** *v/t* lift and throw with a pitchfork; hastily or roughly assign work or responsibility for.

pitching [*pich*ing] *n* act of one who or that which pitches; pavement made of cobbles or of stones set on edge; facing of stone on a slope.

pitchpine [*pich*pIn] *n* a softwood much used for carpentry.

pitchpipe [*pich*pIp] *n* small musical pipe used to set correct starting note for singers *etc*.

pitchstone [*pich*stOn] *n* a black lustrous volcanic rock.

pitch-wheel [*pich*-weel] *n* gear-wheel.

pitchy [*pich*i] *adj* full of, covered with, or sticky with pitch; resinous; pitch-dark ~ **pitchiness** *n*.

piteous [*piti*-us] *adj* that rouses or should rouse pity, pathetic; contemptibly inadequate, paltry ~ **piteously** *adv* ~ **piteousness** *n*.

pitfall [*pit*fawl] *n* hidden danger or difficulty; hidden hole to trap an animal.

pith [*pith*] *n* core of spongy tissue in plant stems and branches > PDB; inner skins and stringy fibres of orange; (*anat*) spinal cord; marrow; (*fig*) essence; concentrated meaning; physical strength; (*ar*) importance.

pithead [*pit*-hed] *n* entrance of coalmine.

pithecanthropus [pithi*kanth*ROpus] *n* extinct species of anthropoid ape.

pithecoid [*pithi*koid] *adj* of or like an ape.

pithy [*pithi*] *adj* concise and significant, full of concentrated meaning; of, like, or containing, pith ~ **pithily** *adv* ~ **pithiness** *n*.

pitiable [*piti*-ab'l] *adj* that rouses or should rouse pity; miserable; contemptible ~ **pitiably** *adv*.

pitiful [*piti*fool] *adj* that rouses or should rouse pity; contemptible; merciful ~ **pitifully** *adv* ~ **pitifulness** *n*.

pitiless [*piti*les] *adj* feeling no pity, merciless ~ **pitilessly** *adv* ~ **pitilessness** *n*.

pitman [*pit*man] *n* man who works in coal-pit.

piton [*pee*ton] *n* spike driven into rock to support a climber.

Pitot tube [*pI*tot-tewb] *n* instrument for measuring the velocity of a fluid or the airspeed of an aircraft.

pittance [*pit*ans] *n* meagre allowance.

pitter-patter [*piter*-pater] *n* patter (2).

pitting [*pit*ing] *n* corrosion of metal surfaces; small disfiguring holes in paintwork.

pituitary [pit*ew*-iteRi] *n* and *adj* p. gland (**body**) endocrine gland in the skull of vertebrates secreting and controlling hormones.

pituitrin [pit*ew*-itRin] *n* hormone extracted from pituitary gland > PDB.

pity [*piti*] *n* grief and desire to give help roused by awareness of another's sufferings; mercy, compassion; that which causes disappointment, regret *etc* ~ **pity** *v/t* feel pity for.

pityriasis [piti*RI*-asis] *n* (*med*) disease causing flaking of skin; form of dermatitis; dandruff.

pivot [*pivot*] *n* pin or fixed point on which something turns; (*fig*) that on which all depends; (*mil*) man round whom a body of troops wheels; (*football*) a centre half-back ~ **pivot** *v/i* turn as in a hinge; wheel round; depend.

pivotal [*pivo*tal] *adj* as or like a pivot; central, vital.

pixillated [*piks*ilaytid] *adj* (*US*) slightly crazy; drunk.

pixy, pixie [*pik*si] *n* fairy.

pizza [*peet*sa] *n* (*Ital*) open tart containing savoury cheese mixture.

pizzicato [pitsi*kaat*O] *n*, *adv*, *adj* (passage) played on violin, viola *etc* by plucking the strings.

pizzle [*piz*'l] *n* (*vulg*) penis of bull.

placable [*plak*ab'l] *adj* forgiving, easily appeased ~ **placably** *adv*.

placard [*plak*aard] *n* public notice or advertisement, *esp* one fixed to a billboard or hoarding ~ **placard** *v/t* publicize by placard; fix placard to.

placate [pla*kayt*] *v/t* appease the anger or resentment of.

placatory [pla*kayt*eRi] *adj* that placates; trying to placate, conciliatory.

place [*plays*] *n* specific position in space; definite area of space; area; region; building; home; spot; section; space assigned to a person or thing; usual position; seat; social status, rank; relative merit; position on any scale of value; official post; job; membership; passage of book; (*racing*) position among first three finishers; **give p.** yield; **in p.** in its right or usual position; appropriate, fitting; **know one's p.** know what is fitting to one's class or rank; **out of p.** inappropriate; not in its right or usual position; **take p.** happen; **take the p. of** be a substitute for ~ **place** *v/t* put into place; find suitable work for; recognize, remember; assign a place to; assess relative merits of; fix; arrange; invest; arrange (a commercial transaction); **be placed** (*racing*) be one of the first three to finish.

placebo [pla*seeb*O] *n* (*med*) neutral substance given medically as a control in testing a drug, or for psychological effect; (*eccles*) vespers for the dead.

place-card [*plays*-kaard] *n* card indicating place of a diner at table.

place-kick [*plays*-kik] *n* (*Rugby football*) kick at goal after a try, the ball being set up on the ground.

placement [*plays*ment] *n* act of placing; arrangement; investment.

placenta [pla*sent*a] *n* mass of tissue within the womb by which the foetus is nourished and which is discharged after its birth; (*bot*) part of ovary wall on which ovules are borne > PDB.

placer [*plays*er] *n* gravelly or sandy deposit containing gold or heavy minerals; **p. mining** extraction of gold *etc* from a placer by use of running water > PDE.

placet [*plays*et] *n* (*Lat*) vote of assent.

placid [*plas*id] *adj* calm, unruffled.

placidity [pla*sid*iti] *n* quality or state of being placid.

placidly [*plas*idli] *adv* calmly, quietly.

placing [*plays*ing] *n* the sale of the whole or part of a company's capital, but without the usual prospectus and application form procedure.

placket [*plak*it] *n* opening in a skirt by which it is fastened or leading to a pocket.

plagiarism [*playj*i-eRizm] *n* wrongful attempt to pass off another's literary or musical work as one's own; act of copying without permission or acknowledgement.

plagiarist [*playj*i-eRist] *n* one who plagiarizes.

plagiarize [*playj*i-eRIz] *v/t* take (an idea, phrase *etc*) from another's work and use as one's own.

plagiary [*play*ji-ERi] *n* plagiarist; plagiarism.

plague [*playg*] *n* very grave infectious disease; calamity; harmful abundance, infestation; (*coll*) troublesome or annoying person or thing ~ **plague** *v/t* be a persistent trouble to, annoy continually; infect with plague.

plaguesome [*playg*sum] *adj* (*coll*) annoying.

plaguespot [*playg*spot] *n* centre of contagion; mark on the skin left by bubonic plague; (*fig*) centre of moral evil.

plaguy [*playg*i] *adj* (*coll*) annoying ~ **plaguily** *adv*.

plaice (*pl* plaice) [*plays*] *n* an edible flatfish.

plaid [*plad*/(*Scots*) *playd*] *n* piece of woollen cloth with tartan or chequered pattern worn by Scottish Highlanders.

plain (1) [*playn*] *n* tract of flat land > PDG.

plain (2) *adj* clear, easy to see, hear or understand; simple, not ornate; straightforward, outspoken; honest; neither beautiful nor ugly; not remarkable, average; **p. clothes** any clothes that are not a uniform; **p. clothes man** policeman on duty but not in uniform; **p. dealing** honesty; **p. sailing** (*fig*) absence of difficulties or complications ~ **plain** *adv* clearly; bluntly, frankly ~ **plainly** *adv* ~ **plainness** *n*.

plain (3) *v/i* (*poet*) lament.

plainchant [*playn*chaant] *n* plainsong.

plainsman [*playnz*man] *n* man accustomed to life on the plains.

plainsong [*playn*song] *n* type of medieval church music consisting of a single line of vocal melody in free rhythm > PDM.

plainspoken [playn*sp*Oken] *adj* outspoken, frank, unreserved.

plaint [*playnt*] *n* (*poet*) lamentation; complaint; (*leg*) accusation, statement of grievance.

plaintiff [*playn*tif] *n* (*leg*) person who brings an action in a court of law.

plaintive [*playn*tiv] *adj* mournful; grieving, complaining ~ **plaintively** *adv* ~ **plaintiveness** *n*.

plait [*plat*] *n* rope made of three or more intertwisted strands, *esp* of hair, ribbon *etc*; (*rare*) pleat of material ~ **plait** *v/t*.

plan [*plan*] *n* assessment of what must be done to achieve an aim; project, scheme; large-scale detailed map; diagram of a structure projected on a flat surface; detailed scale-drawing ~ **plan** (*pres*/*part* planning, *p/t* and *p/part* planned) *v/t* and *i* make a plan of or for; devise methods of doing; scheme; regulate by a central authority.

planch [*plaansh*/*plaanch*] *n* flat plate, slab.

planchette [plaan*shet*] *n* board running on castors across a sheet of paper and supporting a pencil, used to obtain automatic writing or record involuntary hand-movements.

plane (1) [*playn*] *n* tree of the genus *Platanus*.

plane (2) *n* carpenter's tool for smoothing and shaping wood ~ **plane** *v/t* pare away or make level with a plane.

plane (3) *n* (*abbr*) aeroplane, aircraft; wing of an aircraft ~ **plane** *v/i* glide in an aircraft without use of engine.

plane (4) *n* a completely smooth surface; standard, level of attainment or development ~ **plane** *adj* having a completely smooth surface without undulations.

planet [*plan*et] *n* large solid body moving in orbit round the sun; one of the nine largest of these; similar body orbiting round another star.

plane-table [*playn*-tayb'l] *n* (*surveying*) adjustable swivelling drawing-board set on a tripod > PDE.

planetarium [plane*tair*Ri-um] *n* model of the solar system in a dome-shaped ceiling; building containing such a model.

planetary [*plane*tERi] *adj* of, like, or caused by a planet.

planetoid [*plan*itoid] *n* asteroid.

plangency [*plan*jensi] *n* quality of being plangent.

plangent [*plan*jent] *adj* resonant, reverberating; loud and mournful ~ **plangently** *adv*.

plani- *pref* flat, level.

planish [*plan*ish] *v/t* smooth or polish by light hammering.

planisphere [*plan*isfeer] *n* adjustable chart showing the stars visible at any time; map showing a sphere projected on a plane surface.

plank [*plangk*] *n* (*in softwoods*) piece of sawn timber 2 to 4 in. thick and 11 or more in. wide; (*fig*) basic political principle ~ **plank** *v/t* cover with planks; **p. down** (*sl*) put roughly down; pay out (cash).

plank-bed [*plangk*-bed] *n* bed with boards instead of a mattress.

planking [*plangk*ing] *n* the planks of a structure; (*naut*) outside and inside casing to the frames of a vessel, made of a series of planks or strakes.

plankton [*plangk*ton] *n* (*biol*) collective term for minute animals or plants drifting in seas or lakes.

plano- *pref* flat, level.

plant [*plaant*] *n* vegetable organism; organism able to feed on substances drawn from the air and soil; (*pop*) such an organism having leaves, flowers *etc*, *usu* excluding trees and shrubs; apparatus, complete set of machines or equipment, *esp* for a factory; (*coll*) trap, swindle; (*sl*) fabrication of false evidence; (*sl*) one who joins a gang *etc* to obtain evidence against it ~ **plant** *v/t* put (a plant, bulb, seed *etc*) into soil so that it may grow; provide plants, seeds *etc* for; set firmly into the ground; set in position, put; colonize; (*coll*) leave in the lurch; (*sl*) hide (stolen goods, incriminating evidence) in another's possession; **p. out** move (seedlings) to open ground.

plantain (1) [*plan*tin] *n* genus of wild plants with broad low-spreading leaves.

plantain (2) *n* tropical tree with fruit like the banana.

plantar [*plan*taar] *adj* (*anat*) of or on the sole of the foot.

plantation [plan*tay*shon] *n* grove of young trees; estate cultivated by slave labour; large estate producing cotton, tobacco, sugarcane *etc*.

planter [*plaan*ter] *n* one who grows crops on a plantation; agricultural colonizer, settler; machine for planting seeds.

plantigrade [*plan*tigRayd] *n* and *adj* (animal) walking on the soles of the feet.

plaque [*plak*] *n* inscribed or ornamental wall-tablet.

plash (1) [*plash*] *n* shallow pool, puddle.

plash (2) *n* gentle splashing sound ~ **plash** *v/t* and *i* splash gently; dabble in water; dab liquid on to.

plash (3) *v/t* and *i* interweave living stick horizontally in a hedge.

plashy [*plash*i] *adj* wet, marshy.

plasm [*plazm*] *n* (*biol*) living matter of a cell.

plasma [*plaz*ma] *n* green variety of quartz; colourless coagulable liquid forming part of blood > PDB; plasm; (*astron*) tenuous gas of ionized hydrogen; (*phys*) very hot ionized gas.

plasmic [*plaz*mik] *adj* of plasma; of plasm; of protoplasm.

plasmin [*plaz*min] *n* proteid substance obtained from blood plasma.

plasmo- *pref* of protoplasm; of plasm.

plaster [*plaas*ter] *n* mixture of lime, sand, and water used to coat walls or ceilings; adhesive tape or dressing for a slight wound; medical dressing applied on a wad of fabric; immobilizing case of plaster of Paris enclosing a broken limb; **p. cast** reproduction of sculpture by casting in plaster of Paris > PDAA; **p. of Paris** powdered, roasted gypsum which sets hard when mixed with water > PDS ~ **plaster** *v/t* apply plaster to; bind (wound) with adhesive tape; apply lavishly; cover all over; bomb heavily ~ **plastered** (*sl*) drunk.

plasterer [*plaas*teRer] *n* tradesman who plasters walls and ceilings.

plastery [*plaas*teRi] *adj* like plaster.

plastic [*plas*tik] *adj* that can be shaped by pressing, squeezing *etc*; (*chem*) made of a synthetic plastic; (*arts*) of modelling, moulding, or carving; apparently three-dimensional > PDAA; (*fig*) adaptable; easily influenced or impressed; (*med*) of or by the grafting of fresh tissue; (*biol*) capable of metabolic change; **p. bomb** bomb containing a soft pasty explosive; **p. surgery** the restoration of damaged tissue or the alteration of appearance by grafting of tissue ~ **plastic** *n* (*pop*) any substance of the plastics group.

Plasticine [*plas*tiseen] *n* (*tr*) a long-lasting substitute for modelling clay.

plasticity [*plas*tisiti] *n* quality of being plastic.

plasticizer [*plas*tisizer] *n* (*chem*) substance used to modify the flow properties of a plastics composition, or to impart increased flexibility and toughness.

plastics [*plas*tiks] *n* (*chem*) man-made substances which can be moulded under heat and pressure but are stable in normal use > PDS, PDBl; the science and technique of the manufacture of plastics ~ **plastics** *adj* of, or made of, plastics or a plastic.

plastid [*plas*tid] *n* (*biol*) individual unit of protoplasm > PDB.

plastron [*plas*tRon] *n* (*hist*) steel breastplate; leather pad worn on the chest by fencers.

plat (1) [*plat*] *n* small patch of ground.

plat (2) (*pres/part* **platting**, *p/t* and *p/part* **platted**) *v/t* plait.

plat (3) *n* (*US*) plan showing land ownership, boundaries *etc*.

platan [*plat*an] *n* Oriental plane tree.

plate [*playt*] *n* flat, shallow, round dish of china or metal, from which food is eaten; amount of food on this; sheet of metal; thin sheet of copper *etc* from which engravings are printed; print made from this; sheet of metal inscribed with a person's name *etc* and fixed to his door; illustration to a book; thin piece of plastic material fitted into the mouth to support false teeth or re-align crooked teeth; denture; objects plated with gold or silver, *esp* electroplated spoons, forks, and other domestic utensils; (*phot*) sensitized glass used as negative; (*racing*) cup given as prize; race for such a prize; race where the winner must be sold for a minimum sum; (*baseball*) home base of batting side; **plates of meat** (*sl*) feet ~ **plate** *v/t* cover (metal object) with coating of silver or gold; cover with protective plates of metal; beat into thin plates.

plate-armour [*playt*-aarmer] *n* thick protective metal plates on warships; (*hist*) body armour made of overlapping plates of metal.

plateau [*plat*O/plat*O*] *n* large level area of high land > PDG.

plate-basket [*playt*-baasket] *n* basket lined with baize in which spoons and forks are kept.

plateglass [*playt*glaas] *n* fine quality glass used for large windows, mirrors *etc*.

platelayer [*playt*lay-er] *n* workman who lays or repairs railway lines.

platelet [*playt*let] *n* small coin-shaped particle, many of which occur in blood and clump together to form clots.

platemark [*playt*maark] *n* hallmark on gold or silver plate; mark left on an engraving by the pressure of the plate.

platen [*plat*en] *n* (*print*) plate which presses paper against the type; roller of typewriter.

plater [*playt*er] *n* one who or that which plates; workman who fits plates in shipbuilding; inferior race-horse.

platform [*plat*fawrm] *n* raised flooring at one end of hall *etc*; persons placed there to address a public meeting; area of railway-station beside which trains halt and on which passengers gather or alight; open space by entrance of certain buses, trains *etc*, reserved for the conductor; (*pol*) declared policy, programme; **p. shoes** shoes raised on very thick soles.

plating [*play*ting] *n* process of coating with a thin metal layer; this layer; plate-racing.

platinize [*plat*iniz] *v/t* coat with platinum.

platinoid [*plat*inoid] *n* white alloy of nickel, zinc, copper, and wolfram.

platinum [*plat*inum] *n* heavy malleable, silvery-white, metal element > PDS ~ **platinum** *adj* made of platinum; silvery-white; **p. blonde** woman with silvery hair.

platinum-black [platinum-*blak*] *n* (*chem*) black powder made from platinum. ·

platitude [*plat*itewd] *n* dull and trite remark.

platitudinous [platit*ew*dinus] *adj* of, like, or containing, platitudes.

Platonic [plat*on*ik] *adj* (*philos*) of or derived from Plato; **P. love** non-sexual love between man and woman, based solely on friendship; (*lit*) male homosexual love ~ **Platonically** *adv*.

Platonism [*play*tonizm] *n* philosophy of Plato and his school ~ **Platonist** *n* and *adj*.

platoon [plat*OOn*] *n* small body of infantry; unit forming one fourth of a company.

platter [*plat*er] *n* plate for food, *usu* of wood.

platy- *pref* broad, flat.

platypus [*plat*ipus] *n* (*zool*) Australian primitive mammal, the duckbill.

plaudit [*plaw*dit] *n* act of applauding, *esp* by clapping; (*fig*) approval, praise.

plausibility [plawzib*il*iti] *n* quality of being plausible.

plausible [*plaw*zib'l] *adj* seeming true, convincing,

honest or trustworthy; deceptively seeming true *etc*, specious ~ **plausibly** *adv*.

play [*play*] *v/t* and *i* do, perform for pleasure or amusement; amuse oneself; take part in, practise (game or sport); pretend to be, act as; act on the stage; be; perform (music); produce sound from (a musical instrument, gramophone record, tape-recorder *etc*); move, cause to move; move fast and irregularly, flicker; bring into action, use; reveal and use (a card); gamble; handle idly, fiddle (with); fondle erotically, perform a sexual act; (*mech*) move freely within limits; aim and discharge (at); (*fishing*) exhaust (hooked fish); (*sport*) strike ball; **p. at** do for pleasure; do half-heartedly; pretend to be; **p. back** play previously recorded music *etc*; **p. ball** (*coll*) cooperate; **p. down** minimize, hide the importance of; **p. fair** play (game) according to the rules; act honourably; **p. false** betray; **p. the game** (*fig*) act honourably; **p. hell with** seriously damage or upset; **p. into the hands of** give advantage to (an opponent); **p. it by ear** (*fig*) adapt one's tactics to unforeseen circumstances; rely on one's intuitive judgement; **p. off** use as foil, contrast; stimulate rivalry between; **p. on** continue to play; try to take advantage of (emotions); **p. out** express by playing; play to the end; (*US*) **played, played out** exhausted, worn out; out of date; trite; **p. up** (*coll*) behave mischievously; play (sport) vigorously; emphasize; **p. up to** cooperate with; (*coll*) flatter; **p. upon** try to rouse or take advantage of (another's emotion); **p. with** use as toy, amuse oneself with; take unscrupulous advantage of; consider lightly ~ **play** *n* any activity done for the pleasure it gives; amusement, relaxation; joke; drama, work written for theatrical performance; performance of a drama; gambling; quick flickering movement, *esp* of light and shade; (*mech*) limited secondary movement; scope, space for movement; (*fig*) freedom of activity; manner or style of playing; sexual act or acts.

playable [*play*-ab'l] *adj* capable of being played; (*of ground*) fit to be played on.

play-act [*play*-akt] *v/i* pretend; behave melodramatically.

playback [*play*bak] *n* device on tape-recorder *etc* by which recorded material can be played on the same machine.

playbill [*play*bil] *n* poster or handbill advertising a theatrical performance.

playboy [*play*boi] *n* (*coll*) gay, irresponsible pleasure-seeker; dissipated man.

player [*play*-er] *n* one who plays a game, sport, or musical instrument; professional cricketer or footballer; stage actor.

player-piano [play-er-pi-*an*O] *n* piano fitted with a mechanism by which the keys are depressed by air-pressure supplied by bellows and pedals or electrically > PDM.

playfellow [*play*felO] *n* child who plays with other children.

playful [*play*fool] *adj* gay, fond of fun; said or done as a joke, not serious; expressing high spirits ~ **playfully** *adv* ~ **playfulness** *n*.

playgoer [*play*gO-er] *n* one who often goes to the theatre.

playground [*play*gRownd] *n* outdoor space for children's games or for school sports.

playgroup [*play*gROOp] *n* supervised group of young children meeting regularly for organized play.

playhouse [*play*hows] *n* theatre.

playing-card [*play*-ing-kaard] *n* one of set of cards used for games.

playing-field [*play*-ing-feeld] *n* field mown and marked out for the playing of games.

playlet [*play*let] *n* short drama.

playmate [*play*mayt] *n* playfellow.

play-off [*play*-of] *n* second game between teams that have drawn a match.

playpen [*play*pen] *n* portable framework within which a small child can be safely left.

play-school [*play*-skOOl] *n* nursery school for children under five where informal teaching is imparted through play.

plaything [*play*thing] *n* toy; (*fig*) person or thing treated heartlessly.

playtime [*play*tIm] *n* time for recreation, *esp* in schools.

playwright, play-writer [*play*RIt, *play*-RIter] *n* writer of plays, dramatist.

plaza [*plaaza*] *n* (*Sp*) public square.

plea [*plee*] *n* entreaty, earnest request; claim; excuse; (*leg*) formal statement made by litigant in support of his case; answer made by defendant.

pleach [*pleech*] *v/t* intertwine (branches or stems) to form a fence.

plead [*pleed*] *v/i* and *t* beg or argue earnestly; put forward as excuse, claim, or defence; (*leg*) act as advocate; present the case (of); put forward a plea; **p. guilty (not guilty)** admit (deny) an accusation ~ **pleader** *n* advocate, barrister; one who pleads.

pleading [*pleed*ing] *n* intercession, earnest petition; (*leg*) the presentation of a case in court; formal statement of a case ~ **pleading** *adj* begging, imploring ~ **pleadingly** *adv*.

pleasance [*plez*ans] *n* (*ar*) pleasure garden.

pleasant [*plez*ant] *adj* pleasing, agreeable ~ **pleasantly** *adv* ~ **pleasantness** *n*.

pleasantry [*plez*antRi] *n* good-natured joke; gay talk *etc*.

please [*pleez*] *v/t* and *i* give pleasure or happiness to; satisfy; choose, be willing ~ **please** *adv* and *interj* expressing polite request ~ **pleased** *adj* feeling pleasure.

pleasing [*pleez*ing] *adj* giving pleasure, attractive ~ **pleasingly** *adv*.

pleasurable [*plezh*eRab'l] *adj* giving pleasure, pleasant ~ **pleasurably** *adv* ~ **pleasurableness** *n*.

pleasure [*plezh*er] *n* feeling of contentment or happiness caused by any welcome physical, intellectual, or emotional experience; enjoyment, satisfaction; that which causes contentment, enjoyment *etc*; sensuous enjoyment, physical self-indulgence ~ **pleasure** *v/t* give pleasure, *esp* sexual satisfaction to ~ **pleasure** *adj* used for recreation or amusement.

pleasure-ground [*plezh*er-gRownd] grounds laid out for recreation.

pleat [*pleet*] *n* a flattened fold in cloth ~ **pleat** *v/t* form into pleats.

pleb [*pleb*] *adj* and *n* (*sl*) common (person).

plebby [*pleb*i] *adj* (*sl*) plebeian, common.

plebeian [pli*bee*-an] *n* and *adj* (member) of the lower classes; vulgar, common.

plebiscite [*plebi*sit/*plebi*sIt] *n* referendum, direct vote of the people on an important question.

plectrum [*plek*tRum] *n* small implement for plucking the strings of some musical instruments > PDM.

pledge [*plej*] *n* something given as security for re-payment of a loan or fulfilment of a contract; promise, solemn undertaking; proof, token; act of drinking a toast; **take (sign) the p.** promise never to drink intoxicants ~ **pledge** *v/t* deposit as security; pawn; drink a toast to; promise.

pledgee [plej*ee*] *n* person with whom a pledge is deposited.

pledget [*plej*et] *n* small lint dressing.

pleio-, pleo-, plio- *pref* more.

Pleistocene [*plIst*Oseen] *n* and *adj* (geol) (formation) overlying the Pliocene and containing the greatest number of fossils.

plenary [*plee*neRi] *adj* complete, unqualified; attended by all members; representing all sections; **p. indulgence** (*RC*) remission of all punishment incurred by sins already forgiven ~ **plenary** *n* book containing the gospels, or the epistles, or homilies ~ **plenarily** *adv*.

plenipotentiary [plenipo*ten*sheRi] *n* and *adj* (envoy) possessing full powers.

plenitude [*pleni*tewd] *n* fullness.

plenteous [*plenti*-us] *adj* plentiful, abundant ~ **plenteously** *adv* ~ **plenteousness** *n*.

plentiful [*plenti*fool] *adj* existing in great quantities, abundant ~ **plentifully** *adv*.

plenty [*plenti*] *n* large quantity, ample supply; abundance; prosperity; wealth ~ **plenty** *adv* (*coll*) quite enough.

plenum [*plee*num] *n* space completely filled with matter (*opp* vacuum); full meeting of a public body.

pleonasm [*plee*-onazm] *n* (*rhet*) use of more words than are necessary to express one's meaning; unnecessarily repetitive expression.

pleonastic [plee-*onas*tik] *adj* of or containing a pleonasm ~ **pleonastically** *adv*.

plesiosaurus [pleesi-O*sawr*Rus] *n* large extinct lizard-like marine reptile.

plethora [*pleth*oRa] *n* superabundance, excessive quantity; (*med*) morbid condition due to excess of red corpuscles.

pleura (*pl* **pleurae**) [*ploor*Ra] *n* (*anat*) serous membrane covering the surface of the lung.

pleurisy [*ploor*Risi] *n* (*med*) inflammation of the pleura.

pleuritic [ploor*Rit*ik] *adj* of or suffering from pleurisy.

pleuro- *pref* on or at the side; of the pleura.

plexus (*pl* **plexuses**) [*plek*sus] *n* network of nerve fibres or blood-vessels; (*fig*) network, complication; **solar p.** network of nerves at pit of stomach.

pliability [plI-a*bili*ti] *n* quality of being pliable.

pliable [*plI*-ab'l] *adj* easily bent; (*fig*) easily influenced.

pliancy [*plI*-ansi] *n* quality of being pliant.

pliant [*plI*-ant] *adj* flexible; easily influenced, *esp* for evil.

plicate [*plI*kayt] *adj* (*bot*, *zool*) folded like a fan.

plied [*plI*d] *p/t* and *p/part* of ply (2).

pliers [*plI*-erz] *n* (*pl*) a gripping tool, pivoted like a pair of scissors, usually with blades for cutting built into its jaws.

plight (1) [*plI*t] *n* difficult or unpleasant position.

plight (2) *v/t* promise, *esp* to marry.

Plimsoll-line, Plimsoll-mark [*plim*sol-lIn, *plim*sol-maark] *n* line painted on ship's side to indicate maximum depth to which it may be loaded.

plimsolls [*plim*solz] *n* (*pl*) rubber-soled canvas shoes.

plinth [*plinth*] *n* (*archi*) lowest square member of the base of a column; projecting moulded base of building, statue *etc*.

plinthite [*plinth*It] *n* type of red clay.

Pliocene [*plI*-Oseen] *n* and *adj* (*geol*) (formation) of the Upper Tertiary period > PDG.

pliosaurus [plI-O*sawr*Rus] *n* large extinct marine reptile.

plod (*pres/part* **plodding,** *p/t* and *p/part* **plodded**) [*plod*] *v/i* walk slowly and heavily, trudge; (*fig*) work steadily, *esp* at a dull occupation ~ **plod** *n* slow, heavy walk; dull, steady work; (*Aust*) story.

plodder [*plod*er] *n* steady, though dull, worker.

plonk (1) [*plonk*] *n* hollow echoing sound ~ **plonk** *v/i* and *t* resound hollowly; put down noisily or roughly.

plonk (2) *n* (*coll*) cheap wine.

plop [*plop*] *n* sound made by a large object falling into water without splashing ~ **plop** (*pres/part* **plopping,** *p/t* and *p/part* **plopped**) *v/i* fall with a plop.

plosive [*plO*siv] *n* and *adj* (*phon*) (sound) made by abrupt release of stopped breath.

plot [*plot*] *n* elaborate secret scheme, *usu* wicked; conspiracy, intrigue; series of linked episodes forming the story of a play, novel, film *etc*; small piece of land; crop grown on this; (*US*) ground-plan, diagram of building or site ~ **plot** (*pres/part* **plotting,** *p/t* and *p/part* **plotted**) *v/t* and *i* conspire, devise a secret scheme; devise a literary plot; trace the course of; calculate (movements) on a chart; make a chart, diagram, graph or map of ~ **plotter** *n*.

plough [*plow*] *n* agricultural implement for breaking up soil into furrows before sowing or planting; implement for driving a way through thick snow; (*coll*) examination failure; **the P.** constellation of seven stars in the northern sky ~ **plough** *v/t* and *i* drive a plough (through); force a way (through); (*coll*) fail or cause to fail in an examination; **p. back** plough (grass, straw) into soil as fertilizer; reinvest (profits) in same business; **p. through** (*fig*) read or work doggedly at (something dull or difficult).

ploughboy [*plow*boi] *n* boy who leads the horses which draw the plough.

ploughman [*plow*man] *n* man who guides or drives a plough.

ploughshare [*plow*shair] *n* blade of a plough which cuts the furrow.

plover [*pluv*er] *n* general name of a large family of wading birds.

plow [*plow*] *n* (*US*) plough.

ploy [*ploi*] *n* (*coll*) a manoeuvre or tactical move in a game or to impress, fascinate *etc*; job, work.

pluck [*pluk*] *v/t* and *i* pick; break off or pull out with a jerk; pull off feathers of; pull and release (string of musical instrument); *(coll)* cheat, obtain money from by trickery; *(coll)* cause to fail in examination; p. **up courage** make an effort to be brave ~ **pluck** *n* act of plucking; *(coll)* courage, endurance; animal offal, *esp* liver, lungs, and heart.

plucky [*pluk*i] *adj* brave, resolute ~ **pluckily** *adv* ~ **pluckiness** *n*.

plug [*plug*] *n* piece of wood, cork, metal *etc* used to close a hole or as a wedge; a fixing for nail, screw *etc*; mechanism releasing flush of water in water-closet; *(elect)* pronged device inserted into a socket to connect electrical apparatus with current; *(mot)* sparking plug; cake of tobacco; piece of this; *(coll)* advertisement, recommendation; *(sl)* bullet ~ **plug** *(pres/part* **plugging**, *p/t* and *p/part* **plugged)** *v/t* and *i* close with a plug; put a plug into; *(coll)* work hard and monotonously; *(coll)* publicize by constant repetition; surreptitiously insert advertisement for; *(sl)* shoot; p. **in** *(elect)* connect with current by inserting plug in socket.

plug-in [*plug*-in] *adj (elect)* connected with current by a plug.

plug-ugly [*plug*-ugli] *n (US)* city hooligan.

plum [*plum*] *n* fruit with flattish stone and sweet flesh; raisin, currant; *(fig)* prize, best thing to be found; *(coll)* easy, well-paid job.

plumage [*plOO*mij] *n* feathers on a bird.

plumb (1) [*plum*] *n* lead weight on a line, used to test perpendicularity or to take soundings; **out of p.** not perpendicular ~ **plumb** *v/t* measure the depth of; test perpendicularity of; get to the bottom of; *(fig)* understand, see deeply into ~ **plumb** *adj* vertical, perpendicular ~ **plumb** *adv* straight down; exactly.

plumb (2) *v/i (coll)* work as plumber.

plumbago [plum*bayg*O] *n* graphite, black-lead; *(bot)* plant with grey-blue flowers.

plumber [*plum*er] *n* tradesman who installs or repairs piping used in buildings for water and gas supplies, drainage *etc*.

plumbic [*plum*bik] *adj (chem)* of or containing lead; *(med)* caused by lead.

plumbing [*plum*ing] *n* a plumber's trade; lead working; system of water- and drainage-pipes in a building; *(sur)* transferring a point at one level to a point vertically below or above it > PDE.

plumbism [*plum*bizm] *n* lead-poisoning.

plumb-line [*plum*-lIn] *n* line with a weight attached to it.

plumbo- *pref* of lead.

plumcake [*plum*kayk] *n* rich cake containing raisins and currants.

plum-duff [*plum*-duf] *n* boiled pudding with raisins and currants.

plume [*plOO*m] *n* large feather or tuft of feathers; feather or feathers worn as ornament; tuft; wisp of smoke ~ **plume** *v/t* and *reflex* fit feathers to; preen (feathers); take pride in, boast of.

plummer-block [*plum*er-blok] *n (eng)* a bearing on which a shaft revolves.

plummet [*plum*et] *n* plumb; weight attached to fishing line ~ **plummet** *v/i* drop or sink suddenly and disastrously.

plummy [*plum*i] *adj* of, or like, a plum; *(coll) (of* jobs *etc)* pleasant and well-paid; *(coll) (of voice)* too deep and vibrant; articulating too strongly.

plumose [*plOO*mOs] *adj* feathery.

plump (1) [*plump*] *v/i* and *t* fall abruptly and heavily; cause to fall; p. **for** choose, express strong preference for ~ **plump** *n* sudden heavy fall; sound of this ~ **plump** *adv* suddenly and heavily; decisively; bluntly ~ **plump** *adj* decisive, blunt.

plump (2) *adj* well covered with flesh; inclined to stoutness ~ **plump** *v/t* and *i* make or become fleshier, swell ~ **plumply** *adv* ~ **plumpness** *n*.

plum-pudding [plum-*pood*ing] *n* boiled pudding of flour, suet, raisins, spices, currants, eggs *etc*, flavoured with brandy; suet pudding with raisins and currants.

plumy [*plOO*mi] *adj* feathery; ornamented with plumes.

plunder [*plun*der] *n* goods acquired by force or dishonesty; goods taken in war, booty; *(US)* baggage, household goods ~ **plunder** *v/t* rob; take by force, *esp* in war ~ **plunderer** *n*.

plunge [*plunj*] *v/t* and *i* dip or dive suddenly into liquid; thrust deep into; cause to enter suddenly into difficulties, danger, or unpleasant state; move violently forward or down; *(coll)* gamble for high stakes; *(of ship)* pitch; *(of horse)* throw its weight suddenly on its forefeet ~ **plunge** *n* act of plunging, dive; **take the p.** do something decisive and dangerous.

plunger [*plun*jer] *n* one who or that which plunges; ram or piston of a pump; simple suction instrument for clearing blocked pipes; *(coll)* reckless gambler; horse that plunges.

plunk [*plungk*] *v/t* twang; throw or fall noisily; *(US sl)* shoot ~ **plunk** *n* twanging sound; *(US* ˙ ̄ ̶rd blow; dollar ~ **plunk** *adv*.

pluperfect [plOO*pur*fekt] *n* and *adj (gramm)* (tense) expressing a past action previous to another which is itself past.

plural [*ploor*Ral] *n* and *adj (gramm)* (form) which denotes more than one; consisting of more than one; p. **society** society tolerating minorities.

pluralism [*ploor*Ralizm] *n* holding of more than one office at a time; *(eccles)* holding of more than one benefice at a time; *(philos)* theory that the ultimate reality of the universe consists of a plurality of entities > PDP ~ **pluralist** *n* and *adj*.

pluralistic [ploorRa*listik*] *adj (of a society)* accepting the existence of varied sets of ethical, religious or social values within itself; pluralist.

plurality [ploor*Ral*iti] *n* state of being plural or numerous; large number; greater part, majority; *(eccles)* pluralism; *(US)* majority (of votes).

pluralize [*ploor*RalIz] *v/t* make plural; express in the plural.

pluri- *pref* many.

pluriform [*ploor*Rifawrm] *adj* existing in several different forms; permitting diverse customs, opinions *etc* ~ **pluriformity** *n*.

plus [*plus*] *n (math, elect)* symbol (+) denoting addition, positive quantity, or positive electric charge; extra quantity ~ **plus** *prep* with the addition of ~ **plus** *adj* additional, extra; *(elect)* positive; *(games)* with adverse handicap.

plusfours [plus*fawrz*] *n (pl)* baggy trousers ending four inches below knee.

556

plush [*plush*] *n* silk or cotton cloth with very long nap ~ **plush** *adj* (*sl*) rich.

plushy [*plushi*] *adj* of or like plush; (*sl*) rich, grand; lavish.

Pluto [*plOOtO*] *n* (*class myth*) god of the dead and of wealth; (*astron*) planet whose orbit lies beyond Neptune > PDS.

plutocracy [plOO*tokRasi*] *n* government by the rich; ruling class of wealthy persons.

plutocrat [*plOOtOkRat*] *n* one whose wealth makes him powerful.

plutocratic [plOO*tokRatik*] *adj* of or like a plutocrat; very rich.

Plutonic [plOO*tonik*] *adj* (*geol*) formed very far below the earth's crust, igneous > PDG; of Pluto, infernal; **P. theory** theory that most geological phenomena are due to heat.

plutonium [plOO*tOni*-um] *n* (*chem*) artificially produced radioactive element derived from neptunium > PDS.

pluvial [*plOOvi*-al] *adj* of or caused by rain.

pluviometer [plOOvi-*omiter*] *n* rain-gauge.

pluvious [*plOOvi*-us] *adj* of rain, rainy.

ply (1) [*plI*] *n* fold of cloth; thickness of wood; strand, twist of rope, wool *etc*; (*bui*) thin sheet of wood; sheet of roofing felt built up in several layers.

ply (2) (*p/t* and *p/part* **plied**) *v/t* and *i* wield energetically, work with; offer persistently or pressingly; urge; travel regularly to and fro; wait regularly at definite place for customers; (*naut*) make way against the wind.

plywood [*plIwood*] *n* structural board of great strength, made of a number of thin sheets of wood glued together with the grain of adjacent sheets at right angles to each other.

pneumatic [new*matik*] *adj* of air or gases; containing, or inflated by, air; worked by compressed air.

pneumatics [new*matiks*] *n* (*pl*) science of mechanical properties of elastic fluids, air, and other gases.

pneumato- *pref* of, or worked by, air; of breath; of the Holy Ghost.

pneumatocyst [*new*mat*Osist*] *n* (*zool*) air-cavity.

pneumatology [newmat*oloji*] *n* (*theol*) study of spirits or of the Holy Ghost.

pneumonia [new*mOni*-a] *n* (*med*) acute inflammation of one or both of the lungs.

pneumonic [new*monik*] *adj* of, or affected with, pneumonia.

po [*pO*] *n* (*coll*) chamberpot.

poa [*pO*-a] *n* meadow-grass.

poach (1) [*pOch*] *v/t* cook (egg) by breaking it into boiling water.

poach (2) *v/t* and *i* steal game on another's land; illegally kill or snare (game, fish *etc*); encroach on another's rights or sphere of action; unfairly obtain; (*tennis*) take one's partner's shot; trample (wet ground) into holes.

poacher [*pOcher*] *n* one who takes game illegally; one who takes unfair advantages.

pochard [*pOcherd*] *n* a diving duck.

pochette [posh*et*] *n* lady's small handleless handbag.

pock [*pok*] *n* pustule of smallpox or chicken-pox; scar left by this; (*sl*) syphilis ~ **pocked** *adj*.

pocket [*pokit*] *n* small pouch forming part of a garment, for carrying small objects; small receptacle, bag or pouch; small hollow; small area or group showing local variation from a standard; (*mil*) isolated group of enemy troops; (*aer*) local variation in air-pressure causing aircraft to drop; (*billiards*) bag into which balls may fall; **be in (out of) p.** make a profit (loss) ~ **pocket** *v/t* put into a pocket; take and mean to keep; take as profit; accept meekly ~ **pocket** *adj* small enough to fit in a pocket; miniature, small; **p. battleship** small, strongly-armoured battleship; **p. edition** book in small format.

pocketbook [*pokitbook*] *n* folding case for banknotes and papers, wallet; small notebook.

pocket-borough [pokit-*buRu*] *n* (*hist*) constituency whose representation was in the control of one family.

pocketknife [*pokitnIf*] *n* small knife with folding blades, penknife.

pocket-money [*pokit*-muni] *n* small weekly allowance of money given by a parent to his child.

pock-marked [*pok*-maarkt] *adj* scarred by smallpox *etc*.

pod (1) [*pod*] *n* long, narrow seed-vessel of pea, bean *etc*; silkworm's cocoon; narrow-necked net for catching eels; (*vulg*) belly; (*sl*) drugged cigarette; **in p.** (*sl*) pregnant ~ **pod** (*pres/part* **podding**, *p/t* and *p/part* **podded**) *v/t* and *i* remove (peas) from pod; swell when ripening; **p. up** (*sl*) swell in pregnancy.

pod (2) *n* small group of whales or seals.

podagra [po*dagRa*] *n* (*med*) gout in the foot.

podgy [*poji*] *adj* short and fat.

podiatry [po*dI*-atRi] *n* (*US*) chiropody.

podium (*pl* **podia**) [*pOdi*-um] *n* (*archi*) continuous low wall supporting pillars; broad low base for a tall building; dwarf wall around arena of amphitheatre; continuous bench round room; orchestra conductor's dais; (*biol*) footlike tube on underside of starfish *etc* > PDB.

podo- *pref* of a foot or stalk.

poë [*pO*-i] *n* a New Zealand bird with tufts under its throat.

poem [*pO*-im] *n* rhythmic pattern of words, often with rhyme, forming a literary whole and having an aesthetic or emotional effect; (*fig*) something beautiful and touching.

poesy [*pO*-izi] *n* (*ar*) poetry; poems.

poet [*pO*-it] *n* writer of poems.

poetaster [*pO*-itaster] *n* writer of bad poems.

poetess [pO-i*tes*] *n* woman poet.

poetic, poetical [pO-*etik*, pO-*etik'l*] *adj* of or like a poem or poet; written in verse; suitable for a poem; powerfully imaginative or emotional; creative; romantic; **p. justice** fitting allotment of rewards or punishments to good and evil characters in a book or play; **p. licence** latitude permissible in imaginative writing as regards factual accuracy and the rules of grammar, metre *etc* ~ **poetically** *adv*.

poeticism [*pO*-etisizm] *n* a word sometimes used in prose but normally in verse.

poeticize [pO-*etisIz*] *v/t* and *i* make poetic; put into verse; write poetically; write poems.

poetics [pO-*etiks*] *n* (*pl*) literary criticism of poetry.

poetism [*pO*-itizm] *n* theory that sound is more important than sense in writing poetry ~ **poetist** *n* and *adj*.

poetize [*pO*-itIz] *v/t* and *i* poeticize.

poetry [*pO*-itRi] *n* poems collectively; art of writing poems; quality of being poetic; intense beauty or emotional power.

po-faced [*pO*-fayst] *adj* (*sl*) looking stupidly solemn.

pogo-stick [*pOgO*-stik] *n* strong pole fitted with a crosspiece for the feet and springs by which jumps are made.

pogrom [*pog*Rom] *n* an organized massacre of a sect or class, *esp* of Jews by Christians.

poignancy [*poin*yansi] *n* quality of being poignant.

poignant [*poin*yant] *adj* causing bitter grief; highly pathetic; bitter; pungent ~ **poignantly** *adv*.

poinsettia [poin*seti*-a] *n* Mexican plant with large, showy, scarlet bracts.

point [*point*] *n* sharp tip, tapering end; dot, small mark; decimal dot; full stop; real or imaginary mark showing position; exact place or time; position; outlook; item, subdivision, detail; essential or striking argument or fact; purpose; use, advantage; meaning, gist; unit of measuring, scoring or value; degree; characteristic; small headland; engraver's needle; lace-maker's needle; rationing unit; (*math*) that which has position but no magnitude; (*usu pl*) hinged, tapered rail which switches a train from one track on to another; (*elect*) junction, *usu* wall socket, where apparatus can be connected to wiring system; (*naut*) one of 32 marks on compass; (*print*) unit of measurement; (*cricket*) a fielding position; (*ar*) tag used to fasten clothes; (*pl*) (*ballet*) tip of the toes; (*her*) subdivision of shield; **at all points** completely; **carry one's p.** convince (an opponent), get one's way; **catch (see) the p.** understand; **give points to** be able to offer advantages to and yet defeat; **in p. of fact** in reality; **make a p. of** think it important; **off the p.** irrelevant; **on the p. of** just about to; **p. of view** outlook, opinion; **p. steak** best rump steak; **stretch a p.** make concessions; **what's the p.?** why bother? ~ **point** *v/t* and *i* sharpen, shape to a point; indicate position, *esp* by stretching out a finger towards; mark with dots; punctuate; (*bui*) fill gaps between bricks or stones with mortar; add emphasis to; indicate pauses in; (*of dogs*) indicate presence of quarry by standing rigid, facing towards it with nose and tail outstretched; **p. at** stretch a finger towards; **p. out** indicate the presence or direction of, call attention to; **p. to** indicate, be evidence of; **p. up** emphasize.

point-blank [point-*blank*] *adj* aimed directly or horizontally at close range; (*fig*) downright, unqualified ~ **point-blank** *adv*.

point-duty [*point*-dewti] *n* duty of policeman stationed at a fixed point to direct traffic *etc*.

pointed [*point*id] *adj* tapering to a point; (*fig*) effective; spiteful, satiric; critical; precise ~ **pointedly** *adv*.

pointer [*point*er] *n* rod used to point out details on a blackboard or screen; indication, hint, clue; indicating hand on machine, *esp* clock; dog trained to point out presence of game; small preliminary advertisement.

pointillism [*pwant*ilizm] *n* technique in oil painting whereby brighter secondary colours are ob-

tained by making use of a series of blobs of both primaries > PDAA.

pointing [*pointing*] *n* punctuation; (*bui*) raking out mortar joints ¾ in. deep and pressing into them a surface mortar with a trowel.

pointless [*point*les] *adj* having a blunt end; meaningless; ineffective; futile; (*of game*) in which no point has been scored ~ **pointlessly** *adv* ~ **pointlessness** *n*.

pointsman [*points*man] *n* one in charge of points on railway; policeman on point-duty.

point-to-point [point-to-*point*] *n* steeplechase not organized under National Hunt Rules, usually by a Hunt.

poise (1) [*poiz*] *n* dignity, self-possession; calmness; equilibrium, balance ~ **poise** *v/t* and *i* put or keep in balance; keep in position; perch lightly; hover.

poise (2) *n* (*chem*) unit of viscosity > PDS.

poison [*poiz*'n] *n* any substance which when absorbed by a living body will kill or gravely harm it; (*fig*) anything very harmful; **p. gas** noxious gas used in warfare; **p. pen** writer of malicious anonymous letters ~ **poison** *v/t* kill or harm by poison; administer poison to; (*fig*) corrupt, infect with evil ~ **poisoner** *n*.

poisonous [*poiz*'nus] *adj* containing poison; morally corrupting; (*coll*) very unpleasant ~ **poisonously** *adv* ~ **poisonousness** *n*.

poke (1) [*pOk*] *n* small sack, bag; **buy a pig in a p.** buy without examining the goods.

poke (2) *v/t* and *i* push or thrust into; jab, nudge; grope; (*vulg, of man*) have intercourse with; (*cricket*) bat slowly and cautiously; **p. about** (*coll*) show curiosity, investigate; **p. fun at** ridicule; **p. one's nose into** (*coll*) interfere, show unjustified curiosity ~ **poke** *n* act of poking, nudge, jab.

poke-bonnet [pOk-*bonet*] *n* bonnet with projecting brim.

poker (1) [*pOk*er] *n* metal rod for stirring a fire; tool for pokerwork; (*sl*) university mace; beadle carrying this; **red-hot p.** plant with long spikes of orange-red flowers.

poker (2) *n* card-game in which players bet on the value or alleged value of the cards they hold.

pokerface [*pOk*erfays] *n* person whose face does not reveal his thoughts; inscrutable face.

pokerwork [*pOk*erwurk] *n* ornamentation of wood with a design burnt in.

poky [*pOk*i] *adj* cramped; shabby.

polacca (1) [pol*ak*a] *n* Polish dance in three-four time, polonaise.

polacca (2) *n* a three-masted, square-rigged sailing-vessel > PDSa.

Polack [*pO*lak] *n* (*der sl*) person of Polish descent, native of Poland.

polar [*pO*ler] *adj* of, at, or near, the poles of the earth; magnetic; opposite; varying between opposites; (*elect*) having positive and negative electricity; **p. bear** large white Arctic bear.

polarimeter [pOla*rim*iter] *n* apparatus for measuring the rotation of the plane of vibration of polarized light > PDS.

polariscope [pO*la*RiskOp] *n* instrument for the examination of objects in polarized light.

polarity [pO*la*Riti] *n* quality of having two opposed characteristics, duality; quality of having magnetically or electrically negative and positive ends; magnetic influence; tendency towards a particular direction.

polarization [pOlerIzayshon] *n* act of polarizing; state of being polarized; **p. of light** limitation of vibrations of light-waves to one plane > PDS.

polarize [pOlerIz] *v/t* (*phys*) limit vibrations of (light-waves) to a single plane; give polarity to; (*fig*) divide into two diametrically opposed groups.

polatouche [polatoosh] *n* flying squirrel.

polder [polder] *n* low-lying land reclaimed from the sea or from a lake and protected by dikes.

pole (1) [pOl] *n* long, slender, rounded piece of wood, used as a support or shaft; measure of length equal to 5½ yd; **up the p.** (*sl*) in trouble; furious; crazy ~ **pole** *v/t* propel (boat, punt) by driving a pole against the river-bed.

pole (2) *n* each of the ends of the earth's axis; each of the ends of a magnetic bar; each of the terminal points of an electric battery; (*geom*) fixed point of reference; (*fig*) an opposite extreme; **poles apart** having nothing in common; **magnetic poles** points on the earth's surface where a magnetic needle is vertical > PDS, PDG.

Pole (3) *n* native of Poland.

poleaxe [pOlaks] *n* butcher's slaughtering axe; (*hist*) battleaxe ~ **poleaxe** *v/t* strike or kill with a poleaxe; (*fig*) fell; stun.

polecat [pOlkat] *n* small stinking quadruped of the weasel family.

pole-jump [pOl-jump] *n* high-jump in which jumper uses a pole to help him gain height ~ **pole-jump** *v/i*.

polemic [polemik] *n* controversy, discussion ~ **polemic, polemical** *adj* ~ **polemically** *adv*.

polemist [polemist] *n* controversialist.

polenta [polenta] *n* (*Ital*) porridge of maize, barley, chestnuts *etc*.

Pole star [pOl-staar] *n* the star which is seen in the zenith at the North Pole > PDG; (*fig*) lodestar, guide; centre of attraction.

pole-vault [pOl-vawlt] *n* and *v/i* pole-jump.

police [polees] *n* body of men organized to maintain civil law and order; government department responsible for this; **p. constable** member of police of lowest rank; **p. court** court of summary jurisdiction under a magistrate; **p. dog** dog trained to track or attack criminals; **p. state** totalitarian state regulated by secret police; **p. station** headquarters of local police; **p. trap** secret ambush from which police can detect motorists exceeding the speed-limit ~ **police** *v/t* keep order in by means of police; patrol by police; (*fig*) keep under control.

policeman [poleesman] *n* member of police force, *esp* constable.

policewoman [poleeswooman] *n* female police constable.

policlinic [poliklinik] *n* out-patients' department in hospital.

policy (1) [polisi] *n* course of action, *esp* one planned by a government, political party *etc*; plan, scheme; practical wisdom, sagacity; (*Scots*) grounds of country-house.

policy (2) *n* document embodying an undertaking, in consideration of an annual sum, to pay an agreed sum in case of a specified contingency; (*US*) gambling by lottery.

polio [pOli-O] *n* (*coll*) poliomyelitis.

poliomyelitis [pOli-OmI-elItis] *n* (*med*) inflammation of the spinal cord; infantile paralysis.

polish [polish] *v/t* and *i* make smooth and glossy by rubbing; (*fig*) refine, make elegant; become smooth, take a polish; **p. off** finish quickly, finish off; (*sl*) kill ~ **polish** *n* glossiness, smoothness; substance used for polishing; (*fig*) refined manners.

Polish (2) [pOlish] *adj* of the Poles or of Poland.

polisher [polisher] *n* one who polishes; appliance for polishing.

Politbureau [politbewRO] *n* controlling committee of a Communist party.

polite [polIt] *adj* having good social manners, courteous; refined ~ **politely** *adv* ~ **politeness** *n*.

politic [politik] *adj* prudent; cunning; opportune, expedient; (*ar*) of the State; **body p.** citizens as forming one State.

political [politikal] *adj* of, for, or by, the government of a State; of, or taking part in, politics; **p. economy** economics, the study of production and distribution of wealth ~ **politically** *adv* in a political or politic manner.

politician [politishan] *n* one engaged in party politics; expert on politics; member of the Government or the Opposition.

politico- *pref* political.

politics [politiks] *n* (*pl*) study and practice of public affairs; science and art of government; political schemes, opinions *etc*; administration, management.

polity [politi] *n* system of civil government; organized society; constitution of a State.

polka [polka] *n* lively dance in two-four time; music for this; **p. dot** pattern of regularly spaced dots on fabric.

poll (1) [pOl] *n* register of electors; act or place of voting at an election; number of those who vote; unofficial estimate of public opinion on specific points by questioning a random selection of persons ~ **poll** *v/t* and *i* vote; receive (a certain number of votes).

poll (2) [pOl] *v/t* remove the top or edges of; remove horns (of cattle, sheep); lop off (branches); (*ar*) trim (hair) off; (*leg*) trim edges of (document) ~ **poll** *n* (*ar*) head.

Poll (3) [pol] *n* (*coll*) parrot; (*sl*) prostitute.

poll (4) [pol] *n* (*sl*) **the P.** Cambridge undergraduates who only take a pass degree; **a p. degree** a pass degree.

pollack [polak] *n* colefish.

pollard [polerd] *n* polled animal or tree; hornless animal; stag that has shed its antlers; mixture of bran and flour ~ **pollard** *v/t* cut off top or branches of (tree).

polled [pOld] *adj* hornless; (*of trees*) pollarded.

pollen [polen] *n* (*bot*) fine dust composed of the microspores of seed plants > PDB; **p. count** amount of pollen in the air.

pollex [poleks] *n* (*anat*) the thumb.

pollinate [polinayt] *v/t* (*bot*) fertilize with pollen.

pollination [polinayshon] *n* transference of pollen from anther to stigma.

pollinic [polinik] *adj* of pollen.

polliniferous [polinifeRus] *adj* producing or carrying pollen.

559

polloi [*poloi*] *n* (*pl*) **hoi p.** (*sl*) the common people.

pollster [*pOl*ster] *n* (*coll*) one who conducts a public opinion poll.

poll-tax [*pOl*-taks] *n* capitation tax.

pollute [*polewt*] *v/t* make dirty, defile; contaminate; render harmful or unpleasant for living organisms; profane; corrupt.

pollution [*polewshon*] *n* act of polluting; state of being polluted; that which pollutes; anything that makes an environment harmful or unpleasant to human beings or living organisms.

polo [*pOlO*] *n* game resembling hockey, played on horseback with a wooden ball; **water p.** game played by swimmers with large floating ball.

polonaise [*polonayz*] *n* dignified Polish dance in three-four time; music for it.

poloneck [*pOl*Onek] *adj* (*of sweater etc*) having a thick rolled collar.

polonium [*pol*Oni-um] *n* (*chem*) a radioactive element > PDS.

polony [*pol*Oni] *n* partly cooked pork sausage.

poltergeist [*polt*ergIst] *n* form of goblin or ghost said to manifest its presence by noisy and mischievous behaviour.

poltroon [*polt*ROOn] *n* coward.

poly- *pref* many; (*chem*) a polymer of.

polyandrous [poli-*and*Rus] *adj* (*bot*) having many stamens; having many husbands.

polyandry [poli-*and*Ri] *n* marriage of one woman to two or more husbands.

polyanthus (*pl* **polyanthuses**) [poli-*anth*us] *n* ornamental primula.

polychromatic [polikROm*atik*] *adj* many-coloured.

polychrome [*poli*kROm] *n* and *adj* (painting or painted object) in many colours.

polyclinic [*poli*klinik] *n* general hospital.

polyester [poli-*ester*] *n* any synthetic polymerized fibre or resin.

polygamist [*poli*gamist] *n* one who has several wives.

polygamous [*poli*gamus] *adj* practising polygamy; (*zool*) having more than one mate; (*bot*) bearing male, female, and hermaphrodite flowers.

polygamy [*poli*gami] *n* custom and practice of having two or more spouses at once; marriage of one man to two or more women; (*zool*) state of having several mates.

polygenesis [poli*jenisis*] *n* (*biol*) derivation from more than one source; origin of a new type at more than one place or time.

polyglot [*poli*glot] *n* and *adj* (person) knowing and speaking many languages; (book) written in many languages.

polygon [*poli*gon] *n* plane figure contained by more than four sides.

polyhedron [poli*heed*Ron] *n* solid figure with polygons for its faces ~ **polyhedral** *adj*.

polymath [*poli*math] *n* man of great skill in many branches of knowledge.

polymer [*poli*mer] *n* product of polymerization; complex molecule built up from a number of simple molecules of the same kind ~ **polymeric** *adj*.

polymerize [*poli*meRIZ] *v/t* form by polymerization.

polymerization [polimeRIz*ayshon*] *n* chemical union of molecules of the same compound to form a new compound of the same empirical formula but of greater molecular weight > PDS.

polymorphism [poli*mawr*fizm] *n* occurrence of several types of individual organism within one species > PDB.

polymorphous [poli*mawr*fus] *adj* having many forms, types, or shapes; changing shapes; undefined; impalpable.

polynomial [polin*Omi*-al] *adj* (*math*) consisting of many terms.

polyp [*polip*] *n* sedentary form of aquatic animal like the sea-anemone, jellyfish *etc* > PDB.

polypeptide [poli*pept*Id] *n* (*chem*) chain of three or more amino acids linked together.

polyphase [*poli*fayz] *adj* (*elect*) having two or more alternating currents of identical frequency but different phase.

polyphonic [poli*fon*ik] *adj* of polyphony.

polyphonist [poli*fon*ist] *n* composer of polyphonic music.

polyphony [poli*foni*] *n* (*mus*) combination of parts, each having its own melody and all harmonizing together; counterpoint > PDM.

polyploid [*poli*ploid] *n* and *adj* (*biol*) (*cell*) having more than twice the normal haploid number of chromosomes in a cell.

polypod [*poli*pod] *n* and *adj* (*zool*) (animal) having many feet.

polypoid [*poli*poid] *adj* like a polyp.

polypore [*poli*pawr] *n* fungus growing on wood.

polypropylene [poli*prOp*ileen] *n* colourless, transparent, flexible thermoplastic material of great strength.

polypus [*poli*pus] *n* soft tumour, *esp* in nose.

polysaccharide [polis*aka*RId] *n* class of carbohydrates, including starch and cellulose, derived from the condensation of sugars.

polystyle [*polist*Il] *adj* (*archi*) having many columns.

polystyrene [polist*Ir*Reen] *n* thermoplastic material with good insulating properties.

polysyllabic [polisil*abik*] *adj* having several syllables, *usu* more than three; using long words.

polysyllable [polis*ilab*'l] *n* word consisting of more than three syllables.

polytechnic [poli*tek*nik] *n* and *adj* (*college*) teaching various crafts and technical sciences.

polytheism [poli*thee*-izm] *n* belief in more than one god ~ **polytheist** *n*.

polytheistic [polithee-*istik*] *adj* of, believing in several gods.

polythene [*poli*theen] *n* a tough, flexible, heat-resistant plastic material > PDS, PDBl; a transparent impermeable plastic material.

polyurethane [poli-*ewr*Rithayn] *n* and *adj* (plastic) consisting of polymerized urethane used in lacquers and varnishes.

polyvinyl [poli*vIn*il] *n* **p. chloride** a rubbery plastic used as electric insulator or as flooring material > PDBl.

pomace [*pum*is] *n* pulp of apples crushed in cider-making; any pulp left after juice, oil *etc* have been extracted.

pomade [*pomaad*] *n* scented hair-ointment.

pomander [*pomand*er] *n* mixture of aromatic substances compressed into a ball.

pomatum [*pom*aytum] *n* pomade.

pome (1) [*pOm*] *n* fleshy fruit with core > PDB

pome (2) *n* (*sl*) poem.

pomegranate [*pom*gRanit/*pom*igRanit] *n* fruit of an African and Asiatic tree, consisting of a pulpy mass of seeds in a reddish-gold rind.

Pomeranian [pome*R*ayni-an] *n* a breed of long-haired dogs.

pommel, pummel [*pum*el] *n* knob of sword-hilt; top of arched front of saddle ~ **pommel, pummel** (*pres*/*part* **pommelling, pummelling**, *p*/*t* and *p*/*part* **pommelled, pummelled**) *v*/*t* beat with the fists, punch repeatedly.

pommy [*pom*i] *adj* and *n* (*Aust sl*) English (man).

pomology [po*mol*oji] *n* science and art of fruit-growing.

pomp [*pomp*] *n* magnificent display, splendour; ostentation; pageantry.

pompadour [*pom*padoor] *n* style of hair-dressing in which the hair is piled high above the fore-head over a pad; a rose-pink colour.

pompano [*pom*panO] *n* edible fish of W. Indies and N. America.

pompom [*pom*pom] *n* automatic quick-firing gun firing one-pound shells; pompon.

pompon [*pom*pon] *n* small round ornamental tuft.

pomposity [pom*pos*iti] *n* quality of being pompous; pompous words or behaviour.

pompous [*pom*pus] *adj* excessively dignified, self-important; arrogant; displaying grandeur; bombastic ~ **pompously** *adv* ~ **pompousness** *n*.

ponce [*pons*] *n* (*sl*) man who protects a prostitute and organizes her trade ~ **ponce** *v*/*i*.

poncho [*pon*chO] *n*. cloak made of a rectangular piece of cloth with a centre hole for the head.

pond [*pond*] *n* small pool of water ~ **pond** *v*/*t* and *i* collect (water) to form a pond.

ponder [*pon*der] *v*/*t* and *i* think deeply (about).

ponderability [ponde*R*a*bil*iti] *n* quality of being ponderable.

ponderable [*pon*de*R*ab'l] *n* and *adj* (substance) which can be weighed.

ponderous [*pon*de*R*us] *adj* very heavy; unwieldy; laborious, clumsy ~ **ponderously** *adv* ~ **ponderousness** *n*.

pone (1) [*pOn*i] *n* (*card-games*) player on the right of the dealer.

pone (2) [*pOn*] *n* American Indian maize bread.

pong [*pong*] *n* and *v*/*i* (*sl*) stink.

pongee [*pon*jee] *n* soft unbleached silk.

pongo [*pong-*gO] *n* (*naval sl*) soldier; marine.

poniard [*pon*yaard] *n* dagger ~ **poniard** *v*/*t*.

pontiff [*pon*tif] *n* the Pope; bishop; (*hist*) Roman or Jewish high-priest.

pontifical [pon*tif*ikal] *adj* episcopal; papal ~ **pontifical** *n* book containing forms for rites performed by a bishop; (*pl*) vestments of a bishop ~ **pontifically** *adv*.

pontificate [pon*tif*ikayt] *n* office or rank of Pope or bishop; period of office of Pope or bishop ~ **pontificate** *v*/*i* perform the functions of Pope or bishop; (*fig*) speak pompously and authoritatively, assume airs of infallibility.

pontify [*pon*tifI] *v*/*i* pontificate.

pontoon [pon*tOOn*] *n* flat-bottomed boat or metal cylinder moored to support a river bridge; flat-bottomed barge; caisson; card-game resembling vingt-et-un; **p. bridge** bridge built on pontoons, *esp* for passage of troops ~ **pontoon** *v*/*t* and *i* bridge with pontoons; cross by pontoon bridge.

pony [*pOn*i] *n* small horse not more than 14 hands high; (*sl*) £25; (*sl*) small glass of liquor.

ponytail [*pOn*itayl] *n* hairstyle in which the hair is drawn back and then hangs long and loose.

pooch [*pOO*ch] *n* (*sl*) pet dog.

poodle [*pOO*d'l] *n* breed of dog with curly hair, usually clipped in a fancy style.

poof [*poof*] *n* (*sl*, *pej*) male homosexual.

pooh-pooh [pOO-*pOO*] *v*/*t* express contempt for.

pool (1) [*pOOl*] *n* small body of still water; small quantity of spilled liquid, puddle; deep place in a river where the current is slow.

pool (2) *n* (*gambling*) stakes to be played for; organized gambling on outcome of football matches; form of billiards where each player has a different-coloured ball; (*comm*) form of amalgamation or combination; trust formed to regulate prices *etc* ~ **pool** *v*/*t* put into a common fund; agree to share; amalgamate.

poop (1) [*pOOp*] *n* raised deck at ship's stern ~ **poop** *v*/*t* (*of wave*) break over the poop of.

poop (2) *n* (*sl*) fool.

poor [*poor*] *adj* having too little money, needy; unfortunate, deserving pity; scanty; unproductive; inferior, of little value; contemptible; cowardly; feeble; **the p.** those who have too little money.

poorbox [*poor*boks] *n* box for collecting alms for the poor.

poorhouse [*poor*hows] *n* workhouse.

Poor Law [*poor-*law] *n* body of laws relating to the support of the destitute poor.

poorly [*poor*li] *adv* scantily, insufficiently; meanly ~ **poorly** *adj* (*coll*) somewhat unwell, indisposed.

poorness [*poor*nis] *n* state or quality of being poor; inadequacy.

poor-rate [*poor*-Rayt] *n* rate levied for the relief of the poor.

poor-spirited [poor-*spi*Ritid] *adj* cowardly.

pootle [*pOOt*'l] *v*/*i* (*coll*) drive or walk slowly and placidly; saunter, stroll.

pop (1) (*pres*/*part* **popping**, *p*/*t* and *p*/*part* **popped**) [*pop*] *v*/*t* and *i* quickly and lightly put on, in or under; act suddenly; burst open with a light sharp sound; come hastily in or out; (*sl*) pawn; **p. in** pay a brief unexpected visit; **p. off** go away suddenly; (*sl*) die; **p. the question** (*coll*) propose marriage ~ **pop** *n* sound of a slight explosion; shot; (*coll*) gingerbeer; champagne ~ **pop** *adv* with a slight explosion; suddenly.

pop (2) *adj* (*coll abbr*) popular; of or like pop music; **pop art** paintings deliberately using techniques and subjects from advertisements, strip-cartoons, commercial posters, *etc* ~ **pop** *n* (*mus*) currently popular light music in a style of US derivation, usually songs set to varied instrumentation, commercially promoted via broadcasting and gramophone records > PDM.

pop (3) *n* (*sl* and *US*) father.

popadum [*pop*adum] *n* thin strip or disk of fried dough.

popcorn [*pop*kawrn] *n* (*US*) maize parched till it bursts open, eaten as a sweetmeat.

Pope (1) [*pOp*] *n* the head of the RC Church; (*fig*) one who assumes that he is infallible; **P. Joan** card-game played without the eight of diamonds.

pope (2) *n* parish priest in the Greek Church.

popery [*pOpe*Ri] *n* (*pej*) Roman Catholicism; Papal system.

pop-eyed [*pop*-Id] *adj* with prominent eyes; agog, staring.

popgun [*pop*gun] *n* toy gun which discharges a pellet by compressed air; (*fig*) inefficient gun.

popinjay [*pop*injay] *n* conceited young dandy; parrot.

popish [*pOp*ish] *adj* (*pej*) Roman Catholic.

poplar [*pop*ler] *n* large slender tree, some species of which have quivering leaves; wood of this.

poplin [*pop*lin] *n* ribbed fabric of silk or cotton and wool.

poppet [*pop*it] *n* (*coll*) little darling; pretty child.

popping-crease [*pop*ing-kRees] *n* (*cricket*) white line drawn four feet in front of and parallel to the wicket.

poppy [*pop*i] *n* plant with bright red, white, pink, or yellow flowers; bright scarlet; (*fig*) opium; forgetfulness; **p. head** seed-case of poppy.

poppycock [*pop*ikok] *n* (*coll*) nonsense.

pop-shop [pop-shop] *n* (*sl*) pawnshop.

pop-singer [*pop*-singer] *n* (*coll*) professional singer of popular songs.

popsy [*pop*si] *n* (*coll*) girl; darling girl.

populace [*pop*ewles] *n* common people, general mass of the population.

popular [*pop*ewler] *adj* of or by the populace; liked by many people; for, suited to, or liked by the average person; **P. Front** coalition of left-wing parties; **p. government** government by elected majority.

popularity [popewl*a*Riti] *n* state or quality of being popular.

popularization [popewleRIz*a*yshon] *n* act or process of popularizing; book *etc* designed to popularize.

popularize [*pop*ewleRIz] *v/t* make attractive to the average person; make easily acceptable or understandable.

popularly [*pop*ewlerli] *adv* in a popular way; by or for many people.

populate [*pop*ewlayt] *v/t* form the population of; supply with inhabitants.

population [popewl*a*yshon] *n* inhabitants; number of persons inhabiting a country, town *etc*.

populist [*pop*ewlist] *n* and *adj* (politician) claiming to represent the views of the people in general, or advocating policies to please them.

populous [*pop*ewlus] *adj* having many inhabitants ~ **populously** *adv* ~ **populousness** *n*.

porcelain [*paw*rselin] *adj* and *n* (made of) fine translucent earthenware; china-ware.

porch [*paw*rch] *n* roofed approach to a doorway.

porcine [*paw*rsIn] *adj* of or like swine.

porcupine [*paw*rkewpIn] *n* rodent mammal covered with sharp protective quills; any machine having numerous spikes; (*fig*) touchy person.

pore (1) [*paw*r] *n* minute opening, *esp* in the skin.

pore (2) *v/i* **p. over** look at earnestly; be absorbed in studying.

porge [*paw*rj] *v/t* (*Jewish ritual*) make (meat) ceremonially clean.

pork [*paw*rk] *n* uncured flesh of pig.

porker [*paw*rker] *n* young fattened hog.

porkpie [*paw*rkpI] *n* pie of chopped pork ~ **pork-**

pie *adj* (*of hat*) with flat crown and narrow up-turned brim.

porky [*paw*rki] *adj* of or like pork; (*coll*) fat.

porn, porno [*paw*rn, *paw*rnO] *n* (*coll abbr*) pornography.

pornographer [pawr*nog*Rafer] *n* one who produces or sells pornographic works.

pornographic [pawr*nog*Rafik] *adj* of, like, or containing pornography; obscene ~ **pornographically** *adv*.

pornography [pawr*nog*Rafi] *n* obscene writings or pictures intended to provoke sexual excitement, *usu* produced commercially; obscenity.

porosity [paw*Ros*iti] *n* quality of being porous; porous part, pore.

porous [*paw*Rus] *adj* having pores; permeable by liquids ~ **porousness** *n*.

porphyria [pawrfi*Ri*-a] *n* (*med*) a rare metabolic disease causing abdominal pain and mental disturbance.

porphyry [*paw*rfiRi] *n* (*geol*) any igneous rock with medium or large sized single crystals in a fine-grained matrix.

porpoise [*paw*rpus] *n* small marine mammal.

porrect [po*Rekt*] *adj* stretched forward ~ **porrect** *v/t* (*eccles law*) hand over, tender.

porridge [*po*Rij] *n* dish of oatmeal boiled in water or milk.

porringer [*po*Rinjer] *n* bowl from which porridge is eaten.

port (1) [*paw*rt] *n* harbour, place where vessels call to load and unload goods; town having a harbour; (*fig*) refuge, place of safety.

port (2) *n* opening in the side of a ship, porthole; (*mech*) opening for the passage of steam *etc*; curved tongue-piece in a bridle-bit.

port (3) *v/t* (*mil*) carry (weapon) diagonally across the body from right to left ~ **port** *n* (*mil*) position of ported weapon; (*ar*) bearing, deportment.

port (4) *n* (*naut*) left side of ship looked at from the stern ~ **port** *v/t* turn (helm) to the left.

port (5) *n* a sweet fortified wine.

portability [pawrtab*il*iti] *n* quality of being portable.

portable [*paw*rtab'l] *adj* capable of being easily carried by hand; movable, not fixed ~ **portable** *n* light-weight typewriter, wireless *etc*.

portage [*paw*rtij] *n* act of carrying; cost of carrying; carrying of boats from one navigable water to another or past a fall; part of a water journey where such carrying is necessary ~ **portage** *v/i* use portage.

portal [*paw*rtal] *n* large door or gateway; (*fig*) entrance; framework carrying overhead electric wires, supported on two sides; (*anat*) fissure leading to the liver; **p. vein** vein passing through this.

portamento [pawrtament*O*] *n* (*mus*) unbroken glide from one note to another > PDM.

portative [*paw*rtativ] *n* (*hist*) portable organ.

portcrayon [pawrt*kRay*-on] *n* metal tube to hold crayon, charcoal *etc*, in drawing.

portcullis [pawrt*kul*is] *n* heavy grating sliding in vertical grooves to close a gateway; (*her*) design of crossed vertical and horizontal strips.

portend [pawr*tend*] *v/t* be a warning or omen of.

portent [*paw*rtent] *n* omen, *esp* of evil; marvel.

portentous [pawr*ten*tus] *adj* of or like a portent,

ominous; impressive, imposing; pompous; grave ~ **portentously** *adv* ~ **portentousness** *n*.

porter (1) [*pawr*ter] *n* doorkeeper of hotel, college, public building *etc*; commissionaire; gatekeeper.

porter (2) *n* one who carries passengers' luggage at railway stations; one who carries loads at markets *etc*; **p.'s knot** shoulder-pad used by market porters.

porter (3) *n* bitter dark-brown beer.

porterage [*pawr*teRij] *n* work of a porter; charge for this work.

porterhouse [*pawr*ter-hows] *n* (*US*) eating-house; **p. steak** steak cut from between the sirloin and tenderloin.

portfolio [pawrt*fO*li-O] *n* large flat case for carrying papers, drawings *etc*; State departmental documents; ministerial office; list of securities owned by a person or financial institution.

porthole [*pawrt*-hOl] *n* opening in a ship's side for light and air.

portico [*pawr*tikO] *n* (*archi*) covered colonnade, usually at entrance to a building; porch with columns.

portion [*pawr*shon] *n* part, share; share of property left by will; amount of food served out, helping; dowry; (*fig*) destiny ~ **portion** *v/t* allot as share to; divide into portions.

portionless [*pawr*shonles] *adj* with no inheritance or dowry.

Portland [*pawrt*land] *n* type of yellowish limestone used in building; **P. cement** yellow cement.

portliness [*pawrt*linis] *n* stoutness.

portly [*pawrt*li] *adj* stout, corpulent.

portmanteau (*pl* **portmanteaux**) [pawrt*man*tO] *n* trunk for clothes, large suitcase; **p. word** word made by combining the forms and meanings of two existing words.

portrait [*pawrt*Rit] *n* picture of a person; vivid description of a person.

portraiture [*pawrt*Richer] *n* art of portraying; portrait.

portray [pawrt*Ray*] *v/t* paint or draw a picture of (a person); describe (a person).

portrayal [pawrt*Ray*-al] *n* act of portraying; portrait.

portress [*pawrt*Res] *n* woman doorkeeper.

Portuguese [pawrtew*geez*] *n* and *adj* (native) of Portugal; (language) of Portugal.

pose [*pOz*] *n* attitude, posture, *esp* when assumed for effect; pretence, deliberate and unnatural outlook, behaviour *etc* ~ **pose** *v/t* and *i* place in specified position or attitude, *esp* as model for painting; assume a position or attitude; work as model for artist, photographer *etc*; adopt unnatural behaviour, outlook *etc* for effect; pretend to be; propound (a question, problem *etc*).

poser [*pO*zer] *n* puzzling question; poseur.

poseur (*fem* **poseuse**) [pO*zur*] *n* (*Fr*) one who adopts affected attitudes, prig.

posh [*posh*] *adj* (*sl*) smart, stylish, high-class ~ **posh** *v/i* **p. up** make oneself smart ~ **poshly** *adv* ~ **poshness** *n*.

posit [*pozit*] *v/t* (*log*) assume as basis of argument.

position [po*zish*on] *n* place, situation; attitude, posture, view; office, job, employment; social rank; mental attitude, opinion ~ **position** *v/t* assign a place to; put into place; find the position of.

positional [po*zish*onal] *adj* of position; determined by position.

positive [*pozitiv*] *adj* explicit, express; definitely laid down; absolutely convinced, certain; dogmatic; unconditional, absolute; actual, real; constructive, helpful; (*math*) of quantity greater than zero; (*elect*) electrical state caused by deficiency of electrons; (*of magnet*) pointing north; (*phot*) showing lights and shades as in nature; (*gramm*) expressing simple degree of adjective or adverb; **p. pole** (*elect*) anode ~ **positive** *n* that which is positive; anode; (*phot*) positive print or film.

positively [*pozitivli*] *adv* certainly, absolutely; in a positive way.

positiveness [*pozitivnis*] *n* quality of being positive; assurance, certainty, confidence.

positivism [*pozitivizm*] *n* any philosophic system based solely on facts of experience, empiricism; a 19th-century rationalist system of ethics; **logical p.** (*philos*) theory that only empirical, mathematical or logical statements have meaning, and that metaphysical statements convey only emotions ~ **positivist** *n* and *adj* (advocate) of positivism.

positivistic [poziti*vistik*] *adj* of positivism.

positivity [pozi*tiviti*] *n* quality of being positive.

positron [*pozit*Ron] *n* (*phys*) positive electron.

posology [po*soloji*] *n* (*med*) study of dosages.

posse [*posi*] *n* body of men a sheriff can call out to aid him; force of armed men.

possess [po*zes*] *v/t* own, have; keep; control, dominate; influence powerfully; **be possessed of** have; **p. oneself of** obtain ~ **possessed** *adj* controlled by a devil; frenzied, mad.

possession [po*zes*hon] *n* act of possessing; state of being possessed, *esp* by a devil; ownership; that which is possessed; (*pl*) wealth, property; colonial territories; (*leg*) occupancy.

possessive [po*zesiv*] *adj* of possession; seeking undue influence on the affections and behaviour of others, selfishly domineering; (*gramm*) denoting possession ~ **possessive** *n* (*gramm*) possessive case or pronoun ~ **possessively** *adv* ~ **possessiveness** *n*.

possessor [po*zeser*] *n* one who possesses; (*leg*) one who has control of something without being its real owner.

posset [*posit*] *n* drink of hot milk with ale, wine, spices *etc*.

possibility [posi*biliti*] *n* state or quality of being possible; that which is possible; possible but unlikely event; chance; (*pl*) prospect of future results.

possible [*posib*'l] *adj* that can exist, happen or be done; that may or may not happen; (*coll*) tolerable, acceptable ~ **possible** *n* possibility; (*coll*) acceptable or suitable person.

possibly [*posibli*] *adv* perhaps.

possum [*posum*] *n* (*coll*) opossum; **play p.** sham illness or death; hide; act very cautiously.

post (1) [*pOst*] *n* stake or strong pole driven into the ground; wooden pillar; upright support of door or gate; starting or finishing point of race ~ **post** *v/t* fix (a notice) to a post; make known by public notice.

post (2) *n* official organization for transport and delivery of letters; building or collection-box where letters are left to be transported; act or time of delivering or collecting letters; letters delivered or to be transmitted; (*hist*) riders stationed along a road to transmit letters *etc* or provide horses for travellers ~ **post** *v/t* and *i* consign letters, parcels *etc* to the post for delivery; keep (person) informed; (*comm*) transfer (entry) to a ledger, bring (ledger) up to date; (*hist*) travel by post stages; travel in haste; **well posted** well informed ~ **post** *adv* (*ar*) in great haste.

post (3) *n* position where a soldier *etc* is stationed; place where it is one's duty to be; appointed place or duty; employment, job; (*mil*) fort, outpost; isolated settlement; (*mil*) bugle-call; **last p.** bugle-call sounded at nightfall and at military funerals ~ **post** *v/t* assign a position or duty to; send or appoint to a duty, command, office *etc*.

post- *pref* after, behind.

postage [pOstij] *n* cost of sending (letter *etc*) by post; **p. stamp** official adhesive label affixed by the sender to a letter or parcel; official stamp embossed on an envelope.

postal [pOstal] *adj* of, by or for the carriage of mails; **p. order** money order which is bought from and cashed at a post office; **p. union** arrangement by which governments regulate international post office business.

postbag [pOstbag] *n* bag of letters delivered to a particular person; correspondence received by one person.

postbox [pOstboks] *n* receptacle in which letters are posted.

postboy [pOstboi] *n* postilion.

postcard [pOstkaard] *n* card on which a message may be written and sent by post; such a card bearing a picture, photograph *etc*.

post-chaise [pOst-shayz] *n* (*hist*) hired travelling carriage, the horses of which are changed at each stage.

postcode [pOstkOd] *n* letters and figures added to an address to facilitate postal sorting.

post-coital [pOst-kO-ital] *adj* after coitus.

post-date [pOst-*dayt*] *v/t* date (document, cheque *etc*) later than the time of writing; assign too late a date to.

post-entry [pOst-entRi] *n* subsequent entry, *esp* in a ledger; (*racing*) late entry ~ **post-entry** *adj* after entering; after a first entry.

poster [pOster] *n* one who sticks up bills; placard posted up as advertisement *etc*; **p. paint** gouache.

poste restante [pOst-Restaant] *n* (*Fr*) department in a post office where letters may be kept till called for.

posterior [posteerRi-er] *adj* later, subsequent; at the back, behind ~ **posterior** *n* buttocks.

posteriority [posteerRi-oRiti] *n* state of being later in time.

posterity [posteRiti] *n* descendants; future generations.

postern [postern] *n* back door or gate.

postero- *pref* at the back.

post-free [pOst-fRee] *adv* with no fee for postage.

postgraduate [pOstgRadew-ayt] *adj* of studies undertaken after graduation ~ **postgraduate** *n* graduate who continues to study within a university.

post-haste [pOst-*hayst*] *adv* as fast as possible.

post-horn [pOst-hawrn] *n* coachman's horn.

posthumous [postewmus] *adj* after death; published after the author's death; (*of child*) born after its father's death ~ **posthumously** *adv*.

postiche [posteesh] *n* wig, false hair.

postilion, postillion [postilyun] *n* one who rides the near horse of a carriage team; post-boy.

Post-Impressionism [pOst-impReshonizm] *n* school of painting and sculpture led by van Gogh, Gauguin and Cézanne > PDAA ~ **Post-Impressionist** *n* and *adj*.

postlude [pOstlewd] *n* concluding piece of music.

postman [pOstman] *n* man who delivers letters *etc*; man who collects from letter-boxes.

postmark [pOstmaark] *n* official mark stamped on letters *etc* to cancel the stamp and record date and place of posting.

postmaster [pOstmaaster] *n* person in charge of a post office; **P. General** minister in charge of the postal department of a State.

postmeridian [pOstmeRidi-an] *adj* after midday; of or in the afternoon.

postmistress [pOstmistRes] *n* woman in charge of a post office.

postmortem [pOstmawrtem] *n* medical examination of a dead body, autopsy; (*fig*) discussion of something after it is ended ~ **postmortem** *adj* and *adv* after death.

postnatal [pOstnaytal] *adj* after birth.

postnuptial [pOstnupshal] *adj* after marriage.

post-obit [pOst-Obit] *n* and *adj* (*leg*) (a bond) taking effect after the death of a specified person.

post office [pOst-ofis] *n* State department dealing with the conveyance of letters and parcels by post, telegrams *etc*; local office dealing with postal work.

postpone [pOstpOn] *v/t* put off till a later time, defer ~ **postponement** *n*.

postprandial [pOstpRandi-al] *adj* after dinner or luncheon.

postscript [pOstskRipt] *n* additional paragraph after the signature of a letter or at the end of a document.

postulant [postewlant] *n* petitioner; candidate for admission into a religious order.

postulate (1) [postewlayt] *n* (*log*) a principle provisionally adopted without any evidence being offered; a presupposition upon which an argument *etc* may depend ~ **postulate** *v/t* demand, claim; assume as basis of argument; stipulate; (*eccles*) nominate under sanction of higher authority.

posture [poscher] *n* manner of holding the body, attitude; pose; (*fig*) state of affairs ~ **posture** *v/i* assume an attitude or pose; behave unnaturally for effect.

post-war [pOst-wawr] *adj* after a war.

postwoman [pOstwooman] *n* female postman.

posy [pOzi] *n* bunch of scented flowers; (*ar*) motto inscribed on a ring.

pot [pot] *n* rounded vessel for holding liquids or soft solids; rounded cooking vessel; jar; earthenware dish, vessel, vase *etc*, *esp* if handmade; mug; coffeepot; teapot; chamberpot; flowerpot; (*coll*) cup won as trophy; deep pit containing water; gunshot at short range; basket used as trap for lobsters; (*sl*) marijuana; (*pl*, *coll*) large quantity;

go to p. (*sl*) be ruined, fail ～ **pot** (*pres/part* **potting** *p/t* and *p/part* **potted**) *v/t* and *i* put into a pot; preserve (food) in sealed jar; set (plant) in pot of earth; (*coll*) make (young child) sit on chamberpot; shoot casually or at short range; (*billiards*) drive (ball) into pocket; (*cer*) make pottery by hand.

potable [*p*Otab'l] *adj* fit to drink.

potage [*p*o*taazh*] *n* (*Fr*) soup.

pot-ale [*pot*-ayl] *n* fermented wash left after distillation of whisky.

potash [*potash*] *n* crude potassium carbonate obtained from wood-ash > PDS; any potassium compound; **caustic p.** potassium hydroxide.

potassium [po*tasi*-um] *n* (*chem*) a metallic alkaline element occurring in various salts used as drugs or fertilizers > PDS.

potation [p*O*tayshon] *n* drinking; drink.

potato (*pl* **potatoes**) [po*tayt*O] *n* edible tuber of a cultivated plant; plant producing this.

potbelly [*pot*beli] *n* swollen or protruding abdomen ～ **potbellied** *adj*.

potboiler [*pot*boiler] *n* low-quality literary or artistic work done simply to earn money.

potbound [*pot*bownd] *adj* (*hort*) lacking adequate space for its roots; (*fig*) constricted, cramped, thwarted.

potboy [*pot*boi] *n* youth employed at a public-house to serve beer.

poteen, potheen [po*teen*] *n* (*Ir*) illicit whisky.

potence, potency [p*O*tens, p*O*tensi] *n* power, strength; vigour; power to intoxicate; male sexual efficacy.

potent [p*O*tent] *adj* powerful, influential; intoxicating; (*of men*) sexually vigorous.

potentate [p*O*tentayt] *n* prince, ruler.

potential [po*ten*shal] *adj* existing in undeveloped form, latent; capable of coming into existence or activity; having inherent but unused powers; (*gramm*) expressing possibility; **p. energy** (*phys*) energy which a body possesses by virtue of its position ～ **potential** *n* that which has latent power; resource; capacity; **electric p.** (*at a point*) work necessary to bring unit positive charge from infinity to that point; **p. difference** difference in electric potential between two points; electromotive force ～ **potentially** *adv*.

potentiality [potenshi-*aliti*] *n* latent power; promise of development.

potentiometer [p*O*tenshi-*omiter*] *n* instrument for measuring potential difference; variable resistance; potential divider.

potently [p*O*tentli] *adv* in a potent way.

pot-head [*pot*-hed] *n* (*sl*) one who smokes marijuana.

potheen see **poteen**.

pother [*poTH*er] *n* (*coll*) fuss, uproar.

pot-herb [*pot*-hurb] *n* herb grown for cooking.

pothole [*pot*-h*O*l] *n* deep hole in rock or in river-bed > PDG; hole in surface of road.

potholer [*pot*-h*O*ler] *n* one who goes potholing.

potholing [*poth*Oling] *n* sport of rock-climbing in potholes and underground caves or passages.

pothook [*pot*-hook] *n* hook for hanging pot or kettle on; stroke ending in hook practised by children learning to write.

pothouse [*pot*-hows] *n* small public-house.

pothunter [*pot*hunter] *n* person who enters contests solely to win a prize.

potion [p*O*shon] *n* medicinal, intoxicating or poisonous drink.

potlatch [*pot*lach] *n* expensive hospitality given as status symbol; lavish tribal feast of N. American Indians.

potluck [*pot*luk] *n* whatever food may happen to be available.

potman [*pot*man] *n* man employed in public-house.

potmetal [*pot*metal] *n* alloy of lead and copper; decorative glass coloured while it is being fused.

pot-pourri [p*O*-poorRee] *n* mixture of dried petals and herbs kept for their scent; medley of tunes.

pot-roast [*pot*-R*O*st] *n* braised meat.

potsherd [*pot*shurd] *n* piece of broken earthenware.

potshot [*pot*shot] *n* chance shot taken without careful aim; (*fig*) haphazard attempt.

pottage [*pot*ij] *n* (*ar*) soup, *esp* thickened with vegetables.

potted [*pot*id] *adj* preserved in sealed pot or jar; (*coll*) briefly and inadequately summarized.

potter (1) [*pot*er] *n* maker of earthenware vessels, *esp* by hand.

potter (2) *v/i* move aimlessly about; lounge; move fussily and ineffectually; work casually at trifling tasks; **p. away** waste (time) in pottering.

pottery [*pot*eRi] *n* earthenware dishes, vessels *etc*, *esp* if made by hand; potter's workshop; factory producing earthenware or china; art of making clay objects by hand; **the Potteries** area of Staffordshire where much pottery is made.

potting [*pot*ing] *n* preserving of foodstuffs in pots; putting of plants into pots; taking of pot-shots; art of making pottery by hand.

potting-shed [*pot*ing-shed] *n* gardener's shed for potting plants.

potto [*pot*O] *n* W. African lemur; the kinkajou.

potty (1) [*pot*i] *adj* (*coll*) easy; mad; small, insignificant.

potty (2) *n* (*coll*) chamberpot, *esp* for child.

pouch [*powch*] *n* small bag or wallet; small pocket; (*zool*) bag in which marsupials carry their young; (*US*) diplomatic bag ～ **pouch** *v/t* put into a pouch or pocket; make into a pouch ～ **pouched** *adj* having or forming a pouch.

pouf, pouffe [p*O*Of/poof] *n* cushion firmly stuffed so as to form a low seat; (*pej*) male homosexual; (*ar*) high puffed-out hairstyle.

poulp [p*O*Olp] *n* octopus.

poult [p*O*lt] *n* young chicken, turkey or pheasant.

poulterer [p*O*lteRer] *n* one who sells poultry and game.

poultice [p*O*ltis] *n* soft mass of hot, wet meal *etc* applied to the skin to allay inflammation or pain ～ **poultice** *v/t* apply a poultice to.

poultry [p*O*ltRi] *n* domestic fowls.

pounce (1) [*powns*] *n* sudden swoop or leap (on prey); sudden movement to take something; front claw of bird of prey ～ **pounce** *v/t* leap or swoop suddenly at; attack suddenly; (*fig*) criticize or intervene suddenly; **p. on** catch by pouncing; detect rapidly.

pounce (2) *v/t* ornament by embossing; ornament (cloth) by punching holes in it or by jagging the edges.

pounce (3) *n* fine pumice powder spread on to greasy drawings to make them take ink more easily; pattern transferred by pricking holes in it and rubbing pounce through ~ **pounce** *v/t* apply pounce to; smooth with pumice.

pounce-box, pouncet-box [*powns*-boks, *pownsit*-boks] *n* small box with perforated lid holding perfumes or pounce powder.

pound (1) [*pownd*] *n* basic English monetary unit; (*fig*) English currency; monetary unit of certain other countries; unit of weight containing 16 ounces avoirdupois > PDS; **p. troy** unit of weight containing 12 ounces troy ~ **pound** *v/t* test the weight of (coins).

pound (2) *n* enclosure in which stray livestock are officially detained till their owner pays a fine; net-trap for fish ~ **pound** *v/t* shut up in a pound.

pound (3) *v/t* and *i* reduce to powder or pulp by beating; strike with heavy blows; thump, batter; bombard heavily; walk, run or ride heavily and noisily ~ **pound** *n* heavy blow: thump.

poundage [*pownd*ij] *n* percentage charged as commission on a monetary transaction; percentage of profits allotted to wages; payment by weight; (*hist*) tax on imports and exports.

poundal [*pownd*al] *n* unit of force; force which will impart to a mass of one pound an acceleration of one foot per second per second > PDS.

pounder (1) [*pownd*er] *n* one who or that which pounds; pestle; vessel for pounding in.

pounder (2) *n* and *adj* (something) weighing one pound; (gun) carrying shot of a specified weight.

pour [*pawr*] *v/t*, *i* and *impers* flow or cause to flow in a stream; (*fig*) emit copiously; rush forward; rain heavily; spend lavishly ~ **pour** *n* act of pouring molten metal into a mould; amount poured.

pourpoint [*poor*point] *n* (*hist*) stuffed or quilted doublet.

pout (1) [*powt*] *v/i* and *t* protrude the lips, *esp* to show discontent or sullenness; say in a discontented tone ~ **pout** *n* act of pouting.

pout (2) *n* catfish; blenny fish.

pouter [*powt*er] *n* one who pouts; breed of pigeon which can inflate its crop in a striking manner.

pouting [*powt*ing] *adj* that pouts; sulky, discontented ~ **poutingly** *adv*.

poverty [*pov*erti] *n* state of being poor.

poverty-stricken [*pov*erti-strIken] *adj* in great want, destitute.

powder [*powd*er] *n* fine loose grains produced by grinding a dry solid substance; tinted cosmetic powder, facepowder; gunpowder; medicine in the form of powder ~ **powder** *v/t* and *i* grind into powder; crumble to dust; sprinkle powder on; use cosmetic powder (on).

powder-blue [*powd*er-blOO] *n* powdered smalt for use in a laundry; deep blue colour obtained from this.

powderbox [*powd*erboks] *n* box for facepowder.

powder-compact [*powd*er-kompakt] *n* flat ornamental container for facepowder.

powder-flask [*powd*er-flaask] *n* case for carrying gunpowder.

powder-magazine [*powd*er-magazeen] *n* place where gunpowder and explosives are stored.

powderpuff [*powd*erpuf] *n* small fluffy pad for applying powder to the skin.

powder-room [*powd*er-ROOm] *n* women's lavatory in public building, shop *etc*.

powdery [*powd*eRI] *adj* of, like or covered with powder.

power [*powr*] *n* ability to do something; strength, force; vigour, energy; ability to control or influence others, ability to impose one's will; effectiveness; authority; nation, State, *esp* if large and influential; person in authority; one who influences or controls; (*pl*) deities; supernatural beings; a type of angel; (*phys*) capacity for doing work, mechanical energy; rate at which this is exerted; (*math*) number of times that a quantity is to be multiplied by itself > PDS; (*leg*) authorization to act on behalf of another; (*coll*) large number or amount; (*opt*) magnifying capacity; (*elect*) current used to drive apparatus, not to give light; **the powers that be** (*coll*) those in authority ~ **power** *adj* operated or driven by electricity, motor or engine; **p. politics** system of furthering national interests by threat of armed force ~ **power** *v/t* supply power to (apparatus); propel mechanically or electrically; supply an engine or motor to.

powerdive [*powr*dIv] *n* (*aer*) dive made with engine working ~ **powerdive** *v/i*.

power-driven [*powr*-drIv'n] *adj* operated by engine, motor, electricity *etc*, not by hand.

powerful [*powr*fool] *adj* having great power; highly influential; capable of using great physical strength; producing much force or energy ~ **powerfully** *adv*.

powerhouse [*powr*hows] *n* building in which electric power is generated; (*coll*) energetic person.

powerless [*powr*les] *adj* without power; helpless ~ **powerlessly** *adv* ~ **powerlessness** *n*.

powerpoint [*powr*point] *n* wall socket through which apparatus can be connected to wiring system.

powerstation [*powr*stayshon] *n* powerhouse.

pow-wow [*pow*-wow] *n* Red Indian council; (*coll*) friendly discussion; feast ~ **pow-wow** *v/i*.

pox [*poks*] *n* name for various diseases characterized by pustules on the skin, *esp* syphilis ~ **poxed, poxy** *adjs*.

practicability [pRaktikab*ili*ti] *n* quality of being practicable.

practicable [*pRak*tikab'l] *adj* that can be done, carried out or used; (*theat*) that can open and shut ~ **practicably** *adv*.

practical [*pRak*tikal] *adj* of or concerning action; functional; efficient, skilful in dealing with actual difficulties *etc*; experienced; not theoretic or speculative; usable, workable; suitable to specific task; (*leg*) virtual; **p. joke** joke involving physical action ~ **practical** *n* (*theat*) stage fitting that can be operated by artistes on stage.

practicality [pRakti*kali*ti] *n* quality of being practical.

practically [*pRak*tikali] *adv* in a practical manner; in practice; virtually; almost.

practice [*pRak*tis] *n* frequently repeated act, habit, custom; repeated exercises done to gain skill; performance, action carrying out a theory; usual method or procedure; ritual, ceremony;

professional activity (of doctor, lawyer *etc*); patients; clients; (*coll*) trickery, deceitful schemes; (*math*) concise method of reckoning prices; **in p.** when actually done; in good training; **make a p. of** do habitually; **out of p.** out of training, having lost the skill or habit ∼ **practice** *adj* done to acquire skill or experience; preliminary; experimental.

practician [pRaktishan] *n* one who works at any profession or occupation; practical man.

practise [pRaktis] *v/t* and *i* do regularly or habitually, *esp* to gain skill or experience; exercise oneself (at); train, accustom; carry out (a theory *etc*) in action; carry on (a profession); take unfair advantage of; trick, delude ∼ **practised** *adj* expert, skilled.

practising [pRaktising] *adj* actively engaged in; carrying out the customs, duties or activities (of a religion or profession).

practitioner [pRaktishoner] *n* one who carries on a profession, *esp* medicine; **general p.** doctor who has not specialized in one branch of medicine.

prae- *pref* before.

praesidium, presidium [pReesidi-um] *n* (*in Soviet Russia*) topmost body of various governing councils and committees, *esp* in Council(s) of Ministers and the Supreme Soviet.

praetor [pReeter] *n* (*Rom hist*) consul as leader of an army; annually elected magistrate ranking next to a consul.

praetorian [pRitawrRi-an] *adj* (*Rom hist*) of the Roman emperor's bodyguard; of a praetor.

pragmatic [pRagmatik] *adj* judged or judging by results, practical; interfering; conceited; of pragmatism; (*hist*) of affairs of State.

pragmatical [pRagmatikal] *adj* pragmatic, practical; conceited; interfering; dogmatic ∼ **pragmatically** *adv.*

pragmatism [pRagmatizm] *n* (*philos*) doctrine which tests the truth of a conception by its results in practice; matter-of-fact treatment of things ∼ **pragmatist** *n* and *adj.*

prairie [pRairRi] *n* flat, treeless grassland > PDG.

prairie-dog [pRairRi-dog] *n* N. American gregarious rodent allied to the squirrel.

prairie-oyster [pRairRi-oister] *n* (*coll*) stimulating drink containing raw egg and pungent sauce.

prairie-wolf [pRairRi-woolf] *n* coyote.

praise [pRayz] *v/t* express approval of, commend highly; declare to be glorious ∼ **praise** *n* expression of approval, act of praising; glorification, worship.

praiseworthy [pRayzwurtHi] *adj* deserving praise, commendable ∼ **praiseworthily** *adv* ∼ **praiseworthiness** *n.*

Prakrit [pRaakRit] *n* any Indian dialect except Sanskrit.

praline [pRaaleen] *n* sweetmeat of nuts, *esp* almonds cooked in boiling sugar.

pram (1) [pRam] *n* (*coll abbr*) perambulator.

pram (2) *n* flat-bottomed Dutch lighter.

prance [pRaans] *v/i* (*of horse*) rise by springing forward from the hind legs; move forward by such bounds; (*of person*) walk in swaggering style ∼ **prance** *n.*

prang [pRang] *n* (*sl*) achievement, feat; bombing air-raid; aircraft crash ∼ **prang** *v/t* (*sl*) bomb; crash.

prank (1) [pRank] *n* mischievous joke.

prank (2) *v/t* and *i* adorn gaudily; dress oneself up.

prankster [pRankster] *n* one who plays pranks.

prase [pRayz] *n* translucent green quartz.

praseodymium [praysi-Odmi-um] *n* (*chem*) rare lanthanide element > PDS.

prat [pRat] *n* (*sl*) buttocks.

prate [pRayt] *v/i* and *t* chatter (about).

pratfall [pRatfawl] *n* (*sl*) heavy fall, *esp* for farcical effect in theatre.

pratie [pRayti] *n* (*Anglo-Irish*) potato.

pratique [pRatik] *n* (*Fr*) permission given to a ship to land passengers and goods after showing a clean bill of health, or after quarantine.

prattle [pRat'l] *v/i* talk in childish way, babble.

prattler [pRatler] *n* chatterer; prattling child.

prawn [pRawn] *n* edible marine crustacean resembling a shrimp, but larger ∼ **prawn** *v/i* fish for prawns.

praxis [pRaksis] *n* practice as contrasted with theory; habit, custom.

pray [pRay] *v/t* and *i* ask earnestly for; address adoration, thanksgiving, requests *etc* to God or to a god; speak or think a prayer; **p. in aid** (*ar*) ask for help from ∼ **pray** *adv* and *interj* if you please.

prayer (1) [pRay-er] *n* one who prays.

prayer (2) [pRair] *n* act of praying to God or to a god; prescribed or customary formula of words used in praying; formal request, petition; fervent wish; **P. Book** book containing the liturgy of the Church of England; any book of prayers; **p. meeting** assembly for public prayer, *usu* extempore; **p. rug** mat on which Muslims kneel to pray; **p. wheel** rotating box containing written prayers used by Tibetan Buddhists.

prayerful [pRairfool] *adj* devout; praying frequently ∼ **prayerfully** *adv* ∼ **prayerfulness** *n.*

praying [pRay-ing] *n* act of prayer; **p. shawl** shawl worn by Jews when at prayer.

pre- *pref* before; in front; prior to; previous.

preach [pReech] *v/t* and *i* give a discourse on a religious subject; explain and publicize (a religion); exhort morally; urge strongly, advocate; (*coll*) give unwelcome or unnecessary moral or religious advice.

preacher [pReecher] *n* one who preaches; minister of religion; (*cap*) author of Ecclesiastes.

preachify [pReechifi] *v/i* (*coll*) preach boringly.

preaching [pReeching] *n* act or art of preaching a sermon; religious service including a sermon ∼ **preaching** *adj* that preaches; **p. friars** Dominicans.

preachy [pReechi] *adj* (*coll*) inclined to moralize and admonish.

preamble [pRee-amb'l] *n* introductory remarks, section or paragraph ∼ **preamble** *v/i* say as introduction.

prearrange [pRee-aRaynj] *v/t* arrange beforehand.

prebend [pRebend] *n* stipend of a canon or member of chapter; land or tithe from which this stipend derives; benefice or living serving as stipend.

prebendal [pRibendal] *adj* of a prebendary or prebend.

prebendary [pRebenderRi] *n* holder of a prebend.

precarious [pRikairRi-us] *adj* uncertain; risky; insecure, perilous ∼ **precariously** *adv* ∼ **precariousness** *n.*

precast [*pReek*aast] *adj* (*of concrete*) cast into blocks before use.

precaution [*pRikaw*shon] *n* step taken beforehand to avoid some evil; prudent foresight.

precautionary [*pRikaw*shoneRi] *adj* of or as a precaution.

precede [*pRee*seed] *v/t* walk in front of; come before in time; be of more importance or higher rank than.

precedence [*pRe*sidens/*pRi*seedens] *n* act of preceding; relative rank or importance; right to a specific position by virtue of birth or office.

precedent (1) [*pRe*sident] *n* previous case (*esp* judicial decision) which is taken as authority for later cases of same kind; **without p.** unheard of till now.

precedent (2) [*pRi*seedent] *adj* preceding.

precedented [*pRe*sidentid] *adj* based on a precedent; for which precedents are known.

precentor [*pRi*senter] *n* director of singing in a cathedral choir.

precept [*pRee*sept] *n* rule of conduct, maxim; election writ; order for collection of rates.

preceptive [*pRi*septiv] *adj* didactic.

preceptor [*pRi*septer] *n* teacher, tutor.

preceptorial [*pRi*sept*awr*Ri-al] *adj* of or by a preceptor; designed for small groups of students capable of independent study and discussion.

preceptress [*pRi*septRes] *n* governess.

precession [*pRi*seshon] *n* forward movement; **p. of the equinoxes** (*astron*) earlier occurrence of the equinoxes in each successive sidereal year.

precinct [*pRee*singkt] *n* enclosed grounds round a cathedral, monastery *etc*; street or paved area from which motor traffic is excluded; (*US*) electoral district; (*pl*) environs, neighbourhood.

preciosity [*pRe*shi-*ositi*] *n* excessive refinement, affectation.

precious [*pRe*shus] *adj* valuable, costly; dearly loved; over-refined, affected; (*coll*) utter, complete ~ **precious** *n* (*coll*) darling ~ **precious** *adv* extremely, very ~ **preciously** *adv* as befits something precious; affectedly ~ **preciousness** *n*.

precipice [*pRe*sipis] *n* high vertical face of a rock, cliff; (*fig*) great danger.

precipitable [*pRi*sipitab'l] *adj* (*chem*) capable of being precipitated.

precipitance, precipitancy [*pRi*sipitans, *pRi*sipitansi] *n* rashness; rash deed; undue haste.

precipitant [*pRi*sipitant] *n* (*chem*) substance causing precipitation.

precipitantly [*pRi*sipitantli] *adv* rashly.

precipitate (1) [*pRi*sipitayt] *v/t* and *i* hurl down from a height; cause to happen too soon; cause (something unwelcome) to happen; (*meteor*) cause (vapour) to fall as rain, snow, dew *etc*; (*chem*) form or cause to form as solid substance from a solution > PDS ~ **precipitate** *n* (*chem*) insoluble substance formed in a solution by chemical reaction.

precipitate (2) *adj* done or occurring too hastily; rash, sudden ~ **precipitately** *adv*.

precipitation [*pRi*sipit*ay*shon] *n* undue haste; rashness; (*chem, meteor*) act or process of precipitating > PDS; that which is precipitated; all liquid reaching earth from the atmosphere.

precipitous [*pRi*sipitus] *ad* very steep ~ **precipitously** *adv* steeply, sheer; (*ar*) rashly.

précis [*pRay*see] *n* short summary of statement, document *etc* ~ **précis** *v/t* make a précis of.

precise [*pRi*sIs] *adj* clearly stated, definite; formal, exact; fastidious, over-scrupulous ~ **precisely** *adv* ~ **preciseness** *n*.

precisian [*pRi*sizhan] *n* one who is extremely precise in observing rules, *esp* in religion.

precision [*pRi*sizhon] *n* exactness, accuracy; **p. tools** tools for very exact work.

precisionist [*pRi*sizhonist] *n* one who considers precision in details very important.

preclude [*pRi*klOOd] *v/t* exclude, debar, prevent, make impossible.

precocious [*pRi*kOshus] *adj* having faculties developed unusually early; (*bot*) flowering or fruiting early ~ **precociously** *adv* ~ **precociousness** *n*.

precocity [*pRi*kositi] *n* condition of being precocious; unusually early development.

precognition [*pRee*kogn*ish*on] *n* foreknowledge, paranormal knowledge of an event before it occurs; (*Scots law*) preliminary examination to establish prima-facie case.

precognitive [*pRee*kognitiv] *adj* of or by foreknowledge.

preconceive [*pRee*kon*seev*] *v/t* and *i* form an opinion beforehand.

preconception [*pRee*kon*sep*shon] *n* theory, opinion *etc* formed before having enough evidence; prejudice.

precondition [*pRee*kond*ish*on] *n* essential condition that must be met before an agreement *etc* can be reached.

precook [*pRee*kook] *v/t* cook (food) in advance; cook (food) before selling it.

precursor [*pRi*kurser] *n* one who goes before; forerunner, harbinger.

precursory [*pRi*kurseRi] *adj* preliminary; announcing, anticipating.

predate [*pRee*dayt] *v/t* antedate.

predatory [*pRe*dateRi] *adj* living by preying on others; seeking prey; living by plundering.

predecease [*pRee*disees] *v/t* die before (another person) ~ **predecease** *n* earlier death (than another's).

predecessor [*pRee*diseser] *n* one who precedes another in office, rank *etc*.

predella [*pRi*dela] *n* platform on which an altar stands; raised shelf behind altar; painting or sculpture on these > PDAA; painting forming lower part of a larger one.

predestinarian [*pRi*destin*air*Ri-an/*pRee*destin*air*Ri-an] *adj* of predestination ~ **predestinarian** *n* believer in predestination.

predestinate [*pRi*destinayt/*pRee*destinayt] *adj* foreordained by God; fated ~ **predestinate** *v/t* predestine.

predestination [*pRi*destin*ay*shon/*pRee*destin*ay*shon] *n* (*theol*) act by which God determines every event beforehand; theory that the salvation or damnation of each soul is determined by God before its creation.

predestine [*pRi*destin/*pRee*destin] *v/t* decree or ordain beforehand.

predetermine [*pRee*dit*urm*in] *v/t* decide beforehand; decree beforehand; persuade in advance.

predicability [pRedika*biliti*] *n* quality of being predicable.

predicable [*pRedi*kab'l] *n* and *adj* (*log*) (*that*) which can be predicated or affirmed.

predicament [pRi*dik*ament] *n* unpleasant or dangerous situation; (*log*) a predicable.

predicant [*pRedi*kant] *adj* of preaching.

predicate [*pRedi*kayt] *n* (*log*) that which is affirmed or denied of something; (*gramm*) that which is stated about the subject of a sentence ~ **predicate** *v*/*t* assert; declare to be an attribute of.

predication [pRedi*kay*shon] *n* that which is asserted or affirmed; act of asserting or affirming.

predicative [pRe*dik*ativ] *adj* of or as a predicate.

predicatory [pRedi*kayte*Ri] *adj* of preaching.

predict [pRi*dikt*] *v*/*t* foretell, prophesy.

predictable [pRi*dik*tab'l] *adj* that can be foretold or foreseen; to be expected; whose behaviour can be foreseen.

prediction [pRi*dik*shon] *n* act of predicting; thing predicted.

predictive [pRi*dik*tiv] *adj* foretelling.

predictor [pRi*dik*ter] *n* instrument used in anti-aircraft ranging.

predigest [pReedi*jest*/pReedI*jest*] *v*/*t* digest beforehand; treat (food) so as to make it easy to digest.

predilection [pReedi*lek*shon] *n* preference.

predispose [pReedis*pOz*] *v*/*t* influence in favour of, make susceptible to.

predisposition [pReedispo*zish*on] *n* state of being already inclined or susceptible (to).

predominance [pRi*domi*nans] *n* state or quality of being predominant.

predominant [pRi*domi*nant] *adj* most numerous or influential, prevailing; dominating, more powerful ~ **predominantly** *adv*.

predominate [pRi*domi*nayt] *v*/*t* have the chief power; be in the majority; be the largest or most noticeable component.

pre-elect [pRee-*ilekt*] *v*/*t* choose beforehand; predestinate to salvation.

pre-eminence [pRee-*eminens*] *n* quality of being pre-eminent.

pre-eminent [pRee-*eminent*] *adj* excelling all others; extremely distinguished ~ **pre-eminently** *adv* in the highest degree.

pre-empt [pRee-*empt*] *v*/*t* claim prior right to purchase; acquire beforehand.

pre-emption [pRee-*emp*shon] *n* purchase by one person or body before an opportunity is offered to others; (*mil*) act of attacking first to forestall enemy attacks ~ **pre-emptive** [pRee-*emp*tiv] *adj*.

preen [*pReen*] *v*/*t* and *refl* (*of a bird*) dress (its feathers) with its bill; (*fig*) show self-satisfaction.

pre-exist [pRee-ig*zist*] *v*/*i* exist earlier (than); exist in a previous life.

pre-existence [pRee-ig*zi*stens] *n* quality or state of existing earlier; previous life; supposed life of the soul before conception as human being.

prefab [*pRee*fab] *n* (*coll*) prefabricated house.

prefabricate [pRee*fab*Rikayt] *v*/*t* construct (house *etc*) in separate sections ready for assembling and erection.

preface [*pRef*is] *n* introduction to a book, play *etc*; introductory part of a speech; (*eccles*) part of the Eucharistic service preceding the Conse-

cration ~ **preface** *v*/*t* introduce by a preface; begin, introduce.

prefatory [*pRefate*Ri] *adj* introductory.

prefect [*pRee*fekt] *n* senior pupil with authority over others in school; head of a French administrative department; head of the Paris police; (*Rom hist*) high-ranking magistrate or officer.

prefectorial [pRifekt*awr*Ri-al/pReefekt*awr*Ri-al] *adj* of or like a prefect or his powers.

prefectship [*pRee*fektship] *n* office of a prefect; tenure of this.

prefecture [*pRee*fekcher] *n* prefectship; district under a prefect or governor; (*in France*) official residence of a prefect.

prefer (*pres*/*part* **preferring**, *p*/*t* and *p*/*part* **preferred**) [pRi*fur*] *v*/*t* like better (than), be willing to choose; promote; bring forward, state.

preferable [*pRefe*Rab'l] *adj* more desirable, fit to be preferred ~ **preferably** *adv*.

preference [*pRefe*Rens] *n* liking for one thing above another; thing thus preferred; prior claim; (*pol*/*ec*) favour given to one country above others in trade tariffs; **p. stock** stock on which dividend is paid before any is paid on ordinary shares.

preferential [pRefe*Ren*shal] *adj* of, like, or showing preference.

preferment [pRi*fur*ment] *n* promotion.

preferred [pri*furd*] *adj* having prior claim to payment; **p. stock** preference stock.

prefiguration [pReefige*Ray*shon] *n* act of prefiguring; prototype.

prefigure [pRee*fig*er] *v*/*t* represent or be a symbol of (a future event); imagine beforehand.

prefix [*pRee*fiks] *n* (*gramm*) particle *etc* forming the first part of a compound word; word placed before another ~ **prefix** [pRee*fiks*] *v*/*t* place before; place as a prefix.

prefrontal [pRee*fRun*tal] *adj* in front of the frontal bone of the skull; in the forepart of the frontal lobe of the brain.

preglacial [pRee*glay*shi-al] *adj* (*geol*) before the glacial period.

pregnancy [*pReg*nansi] *n* state of being pregnant; duration of this state.

pregnant [*pReg*nant] *adj* having conceived a child, having a foetus in the womb; (*fig*) full of ideas; containing much meaning, significant; (*gramm*) implying more than the surface meaning ~ **pregnantly** *adv*.

prehensile [pRee*hen*sIl] *adj* (*zool*) able to grasp and hold.

prehension [pRee*hen*shon] *n* act of taking hold; mental apprehension.

prehistorian [pReehist*awr*Ri-an] *n* one who studies prehistory.

prehistoric [pReehisto*Rik*] *adj* of a period before any written records; (*fig*) very ancient or old-fashioned.

prehistory [pRee*hist*eRi] *n* series of events prior to recorded history; an account or study of these; prehistoric archaeology; (*fig*) history of the earliest stages of a process.

prejudge [pRee*juj*] *v*/*t* pass judgement on prematurely.

prejudice [*pRej*oodis] *n* opinion or emotional attitude (*usu* hostile) reached on inadequate evidence; unreasonable opinion; (*leg*) damage, injury; **without p.** without detracting from one's own claim ~ **prejudice** *v/t* instil prejudice into the mind of; (*leg*) injure.

prejudiced [*pRej*oodist] *adj* feeling prejudice, biased; distorted by prejudice.

prejudicial [pRejoo*dis*hal] *adj* harmful, detrimental ~ **prejudicially** *adv*.

prelacy [*pRe*lasi] *n* office of an archbishop or bishop; order or body of bishops; episcopacy.

prelate [*pRe*lat] *n* bishop, archbishop or cardinal.

prelatical [pRi*lat*ikal] *adj* of a prelate or prelacy.

prelim [*pRe*lim] *n* (*coll*) preliminary examination; (*pl*) (*print*) pages preceding actual text.

preliminary [pRi*limin*eRi] *adj* preparatory, introductory ~ **preliminary** *n* (*coll*) first examination; (*pl*) first steps in any undertaking.

prelude [*pRe*lewd] *n* that which precedes, introduction; (*mus*) first movement of a suite; introductory movement before a fugue; short piano piece > PDM ~ **prelude** *v/t* act as prelude to; foreshadow.

prelusive [pRi*lew*siv] *adj* introductory.

premarital [pReema*Ri*tal] *adj* before marriage.

premature [*pRe*matewr] *adj* occurring before the right or usual time; too early; **p. birth** birth before gestation is complete ~ **prematurely** *adv* too soon.

prematurity [pRemat*ewr*Riti] *n* too early development; undue earliness.

premeditate [pRi*med*itayt/pReem*ed*itayt] *v/t* think over or plan in advance.

premeditated.[pRi*med*itaytid/pReem*ed*itayted] *adj* deliberately planned.

premeditation [pReemedi*tay*shon] *n* deliberate planning beforehand; explicit previous intention.

premenstrual [pReemen*stROO*-al] *adj* just before the onset of menstruation.

premier [*pRem*i-er] *adj* first in importance, leading ~ **premier** *n* Prime Minister.

première [pRemi-*air*] *n* first performance of play, film *etc*.

premiership [*pRem*i-ership] *n* office of Prime Minister.

premise, premiss [*pRem*is] *n* assumption or statement on which an argument is based; (*log*) one of two statements from which a third is inferred; (*leg*) introductory part of document, *esp* of lease ~ **premises** *n* (*pl*) house or other building together with its grounds ~ **premise** *v/t* [pReem*Iz*] state as a premise, assume.

premium [*pRem*i-um] *n* prize, reward; bonus; amount paid periodically for renewal of an insurance policy; fee paid for being taught; (*comm*) excess of the market price over the par or paid-up value of stocks, shares or debentures; **at a p.** (*fig*) highly valued, much in demand; **P. Bonds** Government Bonds yielding no interest but offering a chance of a monthly prize.

premolar [pRee*mOl*er] *n* bicuspid cheek tooth in mammals > PDB.

premonition [pReem*on*ishon/pRem*on*ishon] *n* supernatural forewarning; irrational foreboding of evil.

premonitory [pRi*mon*iteRi] *adj* forewarning.

prenatal [pRee*nay*tal] *adj* existing or occurring before birth.

prentice [*pRen*tis] *n* and *adj* apprentice.

prenubile [pRee*new*bIl] *adj* before marriageable age.

preoccupation [pRee-okew*pay*shon] *n* state of being preoccupied; absorption in deep thought; absent-mindedness; constant engrossing thought, chief consideration.

preoccupied [pRee-*ok*ewpId] *adj* absorbed in one thought to the exclusion of others; worried; absent-minded.

preoccupy [pRee-*ok*ewpI] *v/t* occupy beforehand; fill the mind to the exclusion of other matters; cause absent-mindedness.

pre-option [pRee-*op*shon] *n* right of first choice.

preordain [pRee-awr*dayn*] *v/t* appoint beforehand; predestine.

prep (1) [*pRep*] *n* (*sl*) school homework; period in which this is done.

prep (2) *adj* and *n* (*sl*) preparatory (school).

pre-packed [pRee-*pakt*] *adj* offered for sale in a container or package.

preparation [pRepa*Ray*shon] *n* act of preparing; that which is done to prepare; state of being prepared; medicine, cosmetic *etc* prepared for a specific use; school work to be done after school hours, homework; time when this is done.

preparative [pRi*paR*ativ] *adj* that prepares.

preparatory [pRi*paR*ateRi] *adj* that prepares, introductory; **p. school** school where young boys are prepared for a higher school; **p. to** as preparation for, before.

prepare [pRi*pair*] *v/t* and *i* make or become ready; make fit for use; equip; make, put together; cook; mix; teach, train; learn, study; draw up; plan; accustom; lead up to.

prepared [pRi*paird*] *adj* ready, fit; ready to meet attack ~ **preparedly** *adv* ~ **preparedness** *n*.

prepay [pRee*pay*] *v/t* pay in advance.

prepense [pRi*pens*] *adj* deliberate; **malice p.** (*leg*) premeditated malice.

preponderance [pRi*pon*deRans] *n* quality of being preponderant.

preponderant [pRi*pon*deRant] *adj* greater in number, importance, or weight ~ **preponderantly** *adv*.

preponderate [pRi*pon*deRayt] *v/i* exceed in number; have greater importance.

preposition [pRepo*zi*shon] *n* (*gramm*) indeclinable word preceding a noun or pronoun to indicate relationships of time, place, case *etc*.

prepositional [pRepo*zi*shonal] *adj* of, like or containing a preposition.

prepossess [pRee*pozes*] *v/t* influence for or against something; produce a favourable impression on.

prepossessing [pRee*pozes*ing] *adj* attractive.

prepossession [pRee*pozes*hon] *n* state of being prepossessed; prejudice, *usu* favourable.

preposterous [pRi*pos*teRus] *adj* absurd, nonsensical ~ **preposterously** *adv* ~ **preposterousness** *n*.

prepotence, prepotency [pRi*pO*tens, pRi*pO*tensi] *n* quality of being prepotent.

prepotent [pRi*pO*tent] *adj* having superior power; (*biol*) having superior power of transmitting hereditary qualities.

prepuce [*pRee*pews] *n* (*anat*) loose fold of integument covering the end of the penis.

Pre-Raphaelite [pRee-*Rafel*It] *n* one of a 19th-century English group of painters aiming at precision of detail' and usually treating highly romantic subjects ~ **Pre-Raphaelite** *adj.*

pre-release [pRee-Ri*lees*] *n* and *adj* (film) shown before normal date of public showing.

prerequisite [pRee*Rek*wizit] *n* and *adj* (something) essential as prior condition.

prerogative [pRi*Rog*ativ] *n* exclusive right or privilege; **Royal P.** theoretical right of the Sovereign to act independently of Parliament ~ **prerogative** *adj.*

presage [*pRe*sij] *n* foreboding, presentiment; omen ~ **presage** [pRi*sayj*] *v/t* be an omen of.

presbyopia [pRezbi-*Opi*-a] *n* long-sightedness due to advancing old age > PDP.

presbyter [*pRez*biter] *n* elder in the Presbyterian or early Christian church; (*ar*) priest.

presbyterate [pRez*bite*Rayt] *n* office of presbyter.

presbyterial, presbyteral [pRezbi*teer*Ri-al, prez-*bite*Ral] *adj* of a presbyter or presbytery.

Presbyterian [pRezbi*teer*Ri-an] *n* and *adj* (member) of a church governed by presbyters only.

Presbyterianism [pRezbi*teer*Ri-anism] *n* system of governing a church by a single order of ministers called presbyters.

presbytery [*pRez*bitRi] *n* eastern end of church chancel; (*RC*) dwelling of the parish priest; (*in the Presbyterian Church*) body of ministers of a district.

prescience [*pRe*si-ens/*pRee*shi-ens] *n* knowledge of what will happen ~ **prescient** *adj* ~ **presciently** *adv.*

prescientific [pRee*si*-enti*fik*] *adj* before the rise of modern scientific methods.

prescind [pRi*sind*] *v/t* and *i* separate; leave out of consideration.

prescribe [pRi*skRIb*] *v/t* and *i* enjoin, order (*esp* medical treatment); lay down rules, ordain; (*leg*) claim by prescription.

prescript [*pRee*skRipt] *n* law, ordinance.

prescription [pRi*skRip*shon] *n* act of prescribing; direction given in writing by a physician; medicine prescribed; (*leg*) uninterrupted possession over a long period.

prescriptive [pRi*skRip*tiv] *adj* recognized by long-standing custom; derived from prescription ~ **prescriptively** *adv.*

preselector [pRee*si*lekter] *n* (*mot*) mechanism enabling a motorist to select another gear position before changing into it.

presence [*pRe*zens] *n* fact or state of being present; that which is present; closeness; state of being near (*esp* of kings *etc*); demeanour, bearing; person of impressive appearance; dignity; **p. chamber** room in which a king receives guests; **p. of mind** promptness to act or speak suitably in surprising or dangerous circumstances.

present (1) [*pRe*zent] *adj* being here, being within sight or hearing; being at a specified place and time; existing now, neither past nor future; (*gramm*) expressing an existing state or action ~ **present** *n* the present time, now; (*gramm*) present tense; **for the p.** now and for a short future time.

present (2) *n* something freely given, gift.

present (3) [pRi*zent*] *v/t* give, bestow; introduce formally; exhibit, show publicly; organize (a performance); offer; state; cause; aim (a weapon); raise (weapon) in salute; nominate for appointment; (*refl*) come, visit; offer oneself for exami-

nation; (*v/i*) **p.** as appear at first sight, give impression of being ~ **present** *n* (*mil*) vertical position of weapon in salute; position of aimed weapon.

presentable [pRi*zen*tab'l] *adj* suitable for presentation; having pleasing manners and appearance ~ **presentably** *adv.*

presentation [pRezen*tay*shon] *n* act of presenting; bestowal; formal gift, donation; act or right of presenting to a benefice; way of presenting; formal introduction, *esp* at court; (*med*) position of a child about to be born.

presentee [pRezen*tee*] *n* person to whom something is presented; person who is presented.

presentiment [pRi*zen*timent] *n* foreboding of something about to happen, *esp* of something unpleasant.

presently [*pRe*zentli] *adv* after a short time, soon; (*US*) at present, now.

presentment [pRi*zent*ment] *n* presentation, statement, delineation; presenting of an account for payment; (*leg*) presenting of an indictment by a grand jury.

preservation [pRezer*vay*shon] *n* act of protecting; state of being preserved.

preservative [pRi*zur*vativ] *n* and *adj* (substance) which preserves (food *etc*) from decay.

preserve [pRi*zurv*] *v/t* keep safe or uninjured; prevent (food) from decaying; keep unchanged; prolong; rear and protect (game animals) for hunting; keep (woods *etc*) private for one's own use ~ **preserve** *n* (*usu pl*) preserved food; jam; bottled fruit; woods or river kept private for hunting or fishing; (*fig*) exclusive rights.

preserving-pan [prizur*ving*-pan] *n* large open pan for making jam.

pre-shrink [pRee-*shRink*] *v/t* cause (fabric) to shrink before making into clothes.

preside [pRi*zId*] *v/i* occupy the chair at a formal meeting; take a place of authority.

presidency [*pRe*zidensi] *n* office of president; tenure of this; district administered by a president.

president [*pRe*zident] *n* elected head of a republic; head of a college, university, public corporation, government department *etc*; chairman.

presidential [pRez *den*shal] *adj* of a president.

presidentship [*pR* ident*ship*] *n* presidency.

presidiary [pRi*sidi*-eRi] *adj* of or having a garrison.

presidium see **praesidium.**

press (1) [*pRes*] *v/t* and *i* apply weight or force to, squeeze; crush, flatten; thrust at; extract (oil, juice *etc*) by pressure; grasp, clasp; crowd against; attack strongly in battle; urge strongly, insist on; exert pressure; be urgent; try to persuade or compel; cause distress to, oppress; smooth (cloth) with a hot iron; **p. on** hasten forward; continue despite obstacles ~ **press** *n* machine for printing; (*cap*) newspapers and periodicals collectively; (*cap*) journalists collectively; device or machine for compressing, extracting (juice *etc*) by pressure; cupboard with shelves; crowd, throng; **freedom of the P.** absence of censorship; **good P.** favourable comment in newspapers.

press (2) *v/t* enlist by force; force into service.

press-agency [*pRes*-ayjensi] *n* firm undertaking to procure press-cuttings dealing with any particular subject.

press-agent [*pRes*-ayjent] *n* person employed to

organize publicity for a person or organization.

press-box [*p*Res-boks] *n* place provided for reporters at open-air events.

press-clipping [*p*Res-kliping] *n* press-cutting.

press-cutting [*p*Res-kuting] *n* paragraph or short notice cut from a newspaper.

presser [*p*Reser] *n* one who uses a press; part of machine which presses.

press-gallery [*p*Res-galeRi] *n* gallery for reporters in the House of Commons.

pressgang [*p*Resgang] *n* (*hist*) men employed to press men for the army and navy ∼ **pressgang** *v*/*t* press (2).

pressing (1) [*p*Resing] *adj* importunate ∼ **pressingly** *adv*.

pressing (2) *n* one of a series of gramophone records made from the same matrix; act of one who presses.

pressman [*p*Resman] *n* reporter, journalist; man who works a printing-press.

pressmark [*p*Resmaark] *n* marking on a library book or catalogue entry which shows the place of a book in a library.

press-proof [*p*Res-pROOf] *n* last proof examined before a book is finally printed.

press-release [*p*Res-Rilees] *n* statement issued for publication in newspapers.

press-room [*p*Res-Room] *n* room in a printing office where the printing is done.

press-stud [*p*Res-stud] *n* fastening device consisting of a nipple pressed against and held by a spring.

press-up [*p*Res-up] *n* exercise of raising one's rigid body from a prone position by use of one's arms.

pressure [*p*Resher] *n* act of pressing; that which presses, force exerted in pressing; compulsion, compelling force or influence; burden, cause of difficulty or distress; (*phys*) force per unit of area acting on a surface; **atmospheric p.** pressure of weight of air, about 14¾ lb. per square inch > PDG, PDS; **high p.** pressure greater than this; **at high p.** (*fig*) intensively, very energetically; **p. group** group of persons exerting political influence to further their own interests or a cause; **p. suit** inflatable suit worn when flying at high altitude.

pressure-cooker [*p*Resher-kooker] *n* cooking utensil in which food is cooked under steampressure.

pressure-gauge [*p*Resher-gayj] *n* instrument for measuring the pressure of fluids.

pressurize [*p*Resher-Iz] *v*/*t* maintain normal atmospheric pressure in (high-flying aircraft); try forcefully to persuade, convince or coerce.

presswork [*p*Reswurk] *n* work done by a printing press; operating, adjustment or management of a printing press.

prestige [*p*Resteezh] *n* influence gained by high reputation; power to impress and influence; glamour ∼ **prestige** *adj* designed to impress.

prestigious [*p*Restiji-us] *adj* having great prestige; highly honoured.

prestissimo [*p*RestisimO] *adv* (*mus*) as rapidly as possible.

presto [*p*RestO] *adv* (*mus*) very rapidly; **hey p.** conjurer's ejaculation when performing a trick.

prestressed [*p*Rest*Rest*] *adj* **p. concrete** concrete

in which cracking and tensile forces are eliminated by compressing it.

presumable [*p*Rizewmab'l] *adj* probable; that can be assumed to be true ∼ **presumably** *adv*.

presume [*p*Rizewm] *v*/*t* and *i* take upon oneself; venture; assume to be true until contrary evidence comes to light; be presumptuous, take liberties.

presumed [*p*Rizewmd] *adj* taken for granted, supposed ∼ **presumedly** [*p*Rizewmidli] *adv*.

presuming [*p*Rizewming] *adj* presumptuous.

presumption [*p*Rizumpshon] *n* act of presuming; effrontery, arrogance; excessive self-confidence; act of taking for granted on probable evidence; probability.

presumptive [*p*Rizumptiv] *adj* giving reasonable grounds for belief, probable; **heir p.** one who is now heir but may be superseded by the birth of a child in closer succession.

presumptuous [*p*Rizumptew-us] *adj* arrogant; too self-confident; too forward ∼ **presumptuously** *adv* ∼ **presumptuousness** *n*.

presuppose [*p*Reesup Oz] *v*/*t* assume beforehand, presume; require as necessary prior condition.

presupposition [*p*Reesupozishon] *n* act of presupposing; thing presupposed.

pretence [*p*Ritens] *n* act of pretending; false appearance, claim or display; claim to possess merit; pretext; fraud.

pretend [*p*Ritend] *v*/*t* and *i* make oneself appear to be; lay false claim to; feign; allege falsely; play at being, imagine oneself as; lay claim to; attempt.

pretended [*p*Ritendid] *adj* alleged, feigned, unreal ∼ **pretendedly** *adv*.

pretender [*p*Ritender] *n* one who lays claim, *esp* to a throne or inheritance; one who makes false claims.

pretension [*p*Ritenshon] *n* unfounded allegation; assertion of an unfounded claim; quality of being pretentious.

pretentious [*p*Ritenshus] *adj* assuming appearance of great merit; attempting more than one can do; conceited; snobbish ∼ **pretentiously** *adv* ∼ **pretentiousness** *n*.

preter- *pref* beyond, more than.

preterite [*p*Reterit] *n* and *adj* (*gramm*) (tense) expressing past action.

preternatural [*p*Reeternacheral] *adj* beyond what is natural; supernatural.

pretext [*p*Reetekst] *n* false explanation or motive to disguise the true one; excuse.

prettify [*p*Ritifi] *v*/*t* make pretty.

prettily [*p*Ritili] *adv* in a pretty way.

prettiness [*p*Ritinis] *n* quality of being pretty.

pretty [*p*Riti] *adj* pleasing, charming, attractive *esp* in a minor or superficial way; dainty, neat; good; considerable, large; **a p. penny** a lot of money ∼ **pretty** *adv* fairly; considerably; very; **sitting p.** (*sl*) at an advantage; safe; comfortable ∼ **pretty** *n* fluted part of tumbler; (*golf*) fairway.

pretty-pretty [*p*Riti-*p*Riti] *adj* merely pretty; affectedly or superficially charming.

pretzel [*p*Retsel] *n* (*Ger*) type of salty biscuit.

prevail [*p*Rivayl] *v*/*i* be victorious; predominate; be in general use; **p. on** succeed in inducing, persuade.

prevailing [*p*Rivayling] *adj* generally accepted; usual, current; predominating.

prevalence [pREvalens] *n* quality of being prevalent.

prevalent [pREvalent] *adj* usual, widespread ~ **prevalently** *adv*.

prevaricate [pRivaRikayt] *v/t* avoid speaking the truth; answer evasively.

prevarication [pRivaRikayshon] *n* act of prevaricating; equivocal or evasive reply.

prevaricator [pRivaRikayter] *n* one who prevaricates.

prevent [pRivent] *v/t* render impossible; hinder, thwart; stop; (*ar*) guide, precede.

preventable [pRiventab'l] *adj* that can be prevented.

preventative [pRiventativ] *n* and *adj* preventive.

prevention [pRivenshon] *n* act or process of preventing; that which prevents.

preventive [pRiventiv] *adj* able or designed to prevent an evil before it happens; able to prevent disease ~ **preventive** *n* medicine to prevent disease.

preview [pReevew] *n* private showing of pictures, films *etc* before they are seen by the general public.

previous [pReevi-us] *adj* preceding, earlier; (*coll*) too early, too fast ~ **previous** *adv* before ~ **previously** *adv* at an earlier time.

prevision [pRivizhon] *n* act of foreseeing.

pre-war [pRee-wawr] *adj* of or in the period before a war.

prey [pRay] *n* animal hunted for food by another; helpless victim; **beast** (**bird**) **of p.** beast or bird that kills and eats others ~ **prey** *v/i* **p. on** (**upon**) kill and eat; plunder, rob; oppress, depress; weigh on.

priapism [pRI-apizm] *n* lasciviousness; (*path*) morbid erection of the penis.

price [pRIs] *n* money value paid or asked for goods, services *etc*; cost; value; (*betting*) odds; **starting p.** odds offered just before the race begins; **what p.?** (*coll*) what chance is there for?; **without p.** more valuable than any conceivable price ~ **price** *v/t* set a price on, estimate value of; ask the price of; mark the price of.

price-cutting [pRIs-kuting] *n* sharp lowering of prices, *usu* to undercut competitors.

priceless [pRIsles] *adj* extremely valuable; more valuable than any conceivable price; (*coll*) extremely amusing or absurd ~ **pricelessly** *adv* ~ **pricelessness** *n*.

price-list [pRIs-list] *n* catalogue of goods with prices stated.

price-ring [pRIs-Ring] *n* group of sellers acting in collusion to keep prices high.

price-tag [pRIs-tag] *n* label stating price; (*fig*) cost.

pricey [pRIsi] *adj* (*coll*) expensive.

prick [pRik] *v/t* and *i* pierce slightly with sharp point; puncture; cause sharp mental pain to; feel pain of or like a slight stab; make holes in with pointed object; (*of animals*) raise (the ears) alertly; (*ar*) spur on; ride fast; **p. out** plant (seedlings) in prepared holes; **p. one's ears up** listen alertly ~ **prick** *n* small wound or puncture made by sharp point; pain caused by pricking; slight sharp pain; act of pricking; pointed object; (*vulg*) penis; thorn; goad; small dot or mark; hare's footprint; **kick against the pricks** try to resist the inevitable.

prick-eared [pRik-eerd] *adj* having erect ears.

pricker [pRiker] *n* tool for pricking.

pricket [pRikit] *n* buck in his second year; spike on which to stick a candle.

pricking [pRiking] *n* act of one who pricks; feeling of being pricked; feeling of mental pain.

prickle [pRik'l] *n* small thorn; sharp spine; tingling sensation ~ **prickle** *v/t* and *i* prick with a sharp point; tingle as if pricked.

prickly [pRikli] *adj* furnished with prickles; (*fig*) easily angered; **p. heat** inflammation of the sweat glands, causing rash and irritation; **p. pear** edible fruit of a cactus; plant which bears it.

prick-song [pRik-song] *n* (*mus hist*) written music to a plainsong > PDM.

pride [pRId] *n* excessive valuation of or pleasure in one's merits, rank, wealth *etc*; arrogance, exaggerated self-esteem; justifiable self-respect, true sense of one's merits *etc*; satisfaction at achievements; splendour, radiance; that which causes satisfaction; band of lions; flock of peacocks; **p. of place** position of superiority ~ **pride** *v/refl* take pride (in), congratulate oneself (on).

pried [pRId] *p/t* and *p/part* of **pry**.

prie-dieu [pReedyu(r)] *n* (*Fr*) kneeling-stool.

priest [pReest] *n* one whose office is to perform religious rites and offer sacrifice on behalf of the people; man empowered by ordination to consecrate the Eucharist and administer the sacraments; any Christian cleric ranking above a deacon and below a bishop; fisherman's mallet ~ **priest** *v/t* ordain as priest.

priestcraft [pReestkRaaft] *n* crafty political influence of priests; work of a priest.

priestess [pReestes] *n* woman priest.

priesthood [pReest-hood] *n* office of priest; order of priest; priests collectively.

priestly [pReestli] *adj* of, like or befitting a priest ~ **priestliness** *n*.

priest-ridden [pReest-Riden] *adj* dominated by priests.

prig (1) [pRig] *n* one who is sure of his moral superiority to others and quick to condemn them; conceited pedant.

prig (2) (*pres/part* **prigging**, *p/t* and *p/part* **prigged**) *v/t* and *i* steal, pilfer ~ **prig** *n* thief.

priggery [pRigeRi] *n* priggishness.

priggish [pRigish] *adj* superior, like a prig ~ **priggishly** *adv* ~ **priggishness** *n*.

prim [pRim] *adj* easily shocked; priggish; precise, formal in manner; neat in appearance ~ **prim** (*pres/part* **primming**, *p/t* and *p/part* **primmed**) *v/i* assume a precise look; form (the mouth or lips) into an expression of formality.

primacy [pRImasi] *n* position of being first; pre-eminence; (*eccles*) position of archbishop.

prima donna [pReema-dona] *n* (*Ital*) principal female singer in opera.

primaeval see **primeval**.

primal (1) [pRImal] *adj* primeval, primitive; of first importance ~ **primally** *adv*.

primal (2) *n* and *adj* (*psych*) (process of) re-experiencing a trauma suffered at birth or in early childhood ~ **primal** *v/i*.

primarily [pRImeRili] *adv* originally, in the first place; principally.

primary [pRImeRi] *adj* earliest; chief, most important; not derived from anything else; elementary, rudimentary; (*elect*) producing current;

(*biol*) belonging to first stage of development; (*geol*) palaeozoic; **p. colours** colours that cannot be produced by mixing others, *e* red, yellow, and blue; (*phys*) colours by combining which all others can be obtained, *ie* red, green, and bluish violet; **p. school** school for children up to eleven years old, *esp* such a State school ~ **primary** *n* large flight-feather of bird's wing; (*US*) meeting of party voters to choose election candidates; (*elect*) input winding of a coil or transformer.

primate [*pRI*mat] *n* archbishop; patriarch or exarch of the Eastern Church ~ **primate** [*pRI*mayt] *n* member of the order of mammals including man, monkeys, and lemurs > PDB.

primateship [*pRI*matship] *n* position of primate.

primatial [*pRI*mayshal] *adj* of an archbishop; (*zool*) of the order of primates.

prime [*pRIm*] *adj* most important, chief; initial, earliest; of first-rate quality; essential; **p. meridian** meridian from which longitude is measured; **P. Minister** chief minister of a government; **p. mover** (*mech*) initial source of motive power; (*fig*) initiator; **p. number** number only divisible by itself and unity ~ **prime** *n* period of greatest activity, vigour *etc*; finest period; earliest period; (*eccles*) first of the daytime canonical hours; sunrise ~ **prime** *v/t* put explosive charge into; put liquid into (pump, engine *etc*) to start it working; (*coll*) fill (person) with food or drink; supply information to; put a first layer of paint, size or oil on ~ **primely** *adv*.

primer [*pRI*mer] *n* elementary text-book; book for teaching reading; (*ar*) layman's prayerbook; (*typ*) a size of type; cap or tube holding explosives to detonate main charge of gun *etc*; paint, adhesive, size *etc* applied as an undercoat.

primeval [pRI*mee*val] *adj* of the earliest epoch; primitive; prehistoric; very ancient.

priming [*pRI*ming] *n* first coat of paint or size; gunpowder used to explode main charge of bomb, gun *etc*; act of putting this into gun *etc*.

primitive [*pRim*itiv] *adj* of or at the earliest stage of development or evolution; uncivilized; prehistoric; unsophisticated; simple, rough and ready; wild, savage; (*of colours*) primary; (*arts*) before the Renaissance ~ **primitive** *n* member of a primitive society or race; creature or thing at a low stage of development; painter of pre-Renaissance period; painter using unsophisticated technique ~ **primitively** *adv* ~ **primitiveness** *n*.

primly [*pRim*li] *adv* in a prim way.

primness [*pRim*nis] *n* quality of being prim.

primo- *pref* first.

primogenital [pRImO*jen*ital] *adj* of or by primogeniture.

primogenitary [pRImO*jen*iteRi] *adj* primogenital.

primogenitor [pRImO*jen*iter] *n* earliest ancestor.

primogeniture [pRImO*jen*icher] *n* fact of being the eldest child of one's parents; (*leg*) system by which title and real estate pass at death to the eldest son.

primordial [pRI*mawr*di-al] *adj* existing from the earliest stage or period, most ancient; primeval, original; earliest formed ~ **primordially** *adv*.

primp [*pRimp*] *v/t* and *i* adorn, smarten.

primrose [*pRim*ROz] *n* wild plant with pale yellow flowers; pale yellow; **P. League** an English Conservative society; **p. path** pleasure-loving sinful life.

primula [*pRim*ewla] *n* genus of plants including the primrose and polyanthus.

primus [*pRI*mus] (1) *n* (*tr*) stove burning vaporized paraffin oil.

primus (2) *n* title of presiding bishop of Scottish Episcopal Church.

prince [*pRins*] *n* son or close kinsman of sovereign; ruler of certain small states; title of certain high nobles; (*fig*) very outstanding or successful person; **P. Consort** husband of Queen of England; **p. of darkness** the Devil; **P. of Peace** Christ; **P. of Wales** heir apparent to English throne.

princedom [*pRins*dom] *n* principality; position of a prince.

princely [*pRins*li] *adj* like or befitting a prince; lavish, munificent; splendid.

princess [*pRin*ses] *n* female member of a royal family; wife of a prince; **p. dress** woman's close-fitting gown with the bodice and skirt in one piece.

principal [*pRin*sipal] *adj* most important, chief; of highest rank; **p. boy** woman acting role of hero in pantomime; **p. clause** (*gramm*) main clause; **p. parts** (*gramm*) basic forms of verb from which others are formed ~ **principal** *n* head of college, school *etc*; capital sum on which interest is paid; chief participant in a transaction.

principality [pRin*sip*aliti] *n* sovereignty of a prince of a small state; territory ruled by a prince; (*pl*) one of the nine orders of angels.

principally [*pRin*sipali/*pRin*sipli] *adv* chiefly.

principia [pRin*sip*i-a] *n* (*pl*) (*Lat*) first principles.

principle [*pRin*sip'l] *n* general truth, doctrine or proposition, on which others are based; basic moral rule or conviction; ultimate source; elementary constituent; essence; (*pl*) morality.

prink [*pRingk*] *v/t* and *i* adorn, make smart; dress oneself up.

print [*pRint*] *v/t* and *i* reproduce lettering on paper by stamping with inked type; reproduce a pattern from inked or coloured blocks, plates *etc*; publish (book *etc*) in printed form; mark by pressure, imprint; write in separated lettering, write in block capitals; (*phot*) produce picture from negative by exposure to light; (*fig*) impress, fix in the mind *etc* ~ **print** *n* printed lettering, type; engraving or etching reproduced from metal plate; fabric printed with patterns; mould; die, stamp; footprint; mark made by pressure; (*phot*) positive made from negative; **in p.** published; available from the publisher; **out of p.** (*of books*) sold out, not available from the publisher.

printable [*pRint*ab'l] *adj* suitable to be printed; capable of being printed, or printed from.

printer [*pRint*er] *n* one who prints; compositor, pressman; owner of a printing business; **p.'s devil** errand boy in printing office; **p.'s ink** viscous paste used in printing; **p.'s mark** an imprint.

printing [*pRint*ing] *n* process of printing; art, style in which something is printed; typography;

handwriting with each letter separated, block capitals.

printing-press [*pRi*nting-pRes] *n* machine for printing on paper.

printless [*pRi*ntles] *adj* making, leaving no trace.

printseller [*pRi*ntseler] *n* one who sells pictorial prints and engravings.

prior (1) [*pRi*-er] *n* superior of certain monastic orders and houses; monastic officer ranking next to an abbot.

prior (2) *adj* earlier, preceding; more important ∼ **prior** *adv* before, previous to.

priorate [*pRi*-eRayt] *n* position or term of office of a prior; community ruled by a prior where there is no abbot.

prioress [*pRi*-eRes] *n* nun of rank equivalent to a prior.

priority [pRI-*o*Riti] *n* state of being earlier in time or importance; precedence; degree of urgency or importance; right to earliest consideration; preferential treatment; (*pl*) assessment of the relative importance of various aims or values ∼ **priority** *adj* of, or entitling to, priority.

priory [*pRi*-eRi] *n* religious house governed by a prior or prioress.

prise see **prize** (3).

prism [*pRi*zm] *n* (*geom*) solid figure whose ends are equal and similar parallel plane figures, and whose sides are parallelograms; (*opt*) transparent triangular prism used for refracting light; any refracting medium > PDS, PDP.

prismatic [pRIz*ma*tik] *adj* of or like a prism; refracting; **p. colours** colours formed by breaking up sunlight in a prism ∼ **prismatically** *adv.*

prison [*pRi*z'n] *n* building where criminals, captives, political offenders and persons awaiting trial are confined; place of confinement.

prison-breaking [*pRi*z'n-bRayking] *n* act of escaping from prison.

prison-camp [*pRi*z'n-kamp] *n* guarded encampment where prisoners of war and political prisoners are confined.

prisoner [*pRi*z'ner] *n* one confined or restricted, one deprived of freedom; criminal *etc* kept in prison; accused person kept in custody; **p. of war** one captured in battle; **p.'s base** type of children's team game.

prissy [*pRi*si] *adj* (*coll*) prim, prudish.

pristine [*pRi*stIn/*pRi*steen] *adj* ancient, of the earliest times, former, original; as fresh as if new.

prithee [*pRi*THi] *interj* (*ar*) please.

privacy [*pRi*vasi/*pRi*vasi] *n* seclusion; freedom from observation.

private [*pRi*vit] *adj* secret, confidential; not open to the public; individual, personal; unofficial; secluded; having no public or official position; not organized or controlled by the government; **p. eye** detective working for individual employer; **p. means** unearned income; **p. member** member of Parliament who is not in the government; **p. parts** external sex organs; **p. school** school owned and run by an individual; school not under government control; **p. soldier** soldier not holding officer's or non-commissioned rank ∼ **private** *n* private soldier; (*pl*) external sex organs; **in p.** secretly, confidentially; alone.

privateer [pRIva*teer*] *n* (*hist*) armed vessel owned and commanded by private persons having

government permission to attack merchant shipping of a hostile nation; commander or crew of this vessel ∼ **privateering** *n* and *adj.*

privation [pRIv*ay*shon] *n* want of the necessities and comforts of life; destitution, hardship.

privative [*pRi*vativ] *adj* denoting loss, privation; (*gramm*) expressing deprivation.

privet [*pRi*vit] *n* evergreen shrub much used for garden hedges; **p. hawk-moth** large moth whose caterpillars eat privet leaves.

privilege [*pRi*vilij] *n* right or advantage exclusive to a person, class or group; prerogative; personal benefit or advantage; rights and immunities of a member of Parliament ∼ **privilege** *v/t* grant privilege to, grant special benefit or immunity to ∼ **privileged** *adj* endowed with a privilege; completely confidential.

privily [*pRi*vili] *adv* secretly, stealthily.

privity [*pRi*viti] *n* private knowledge; (*leg*) any relation between two parties that is recognized by law.

privy [*pRi*vi] *adj* having knowledge of a secret or plot; private; **P. Council** council of advisers chosen by the King; **p. parts** external sex organs; **p. purse** allowance for a sovereign's personal expenses ∼ **privy** *n* latrine, water-closet; (*leg*) one having interest in a suit *etc.*

prize (1) [*pRi*z] *n* reward gained by merit, in a competition, or in a game of chance; something of great value ∼ **prize** *adj* won as a prize; deserving or having won a prize; excellent; outstanding; **p. fight** boxing match for a money prize; **p. money** money gained as reward or in competition ∼ **prize** *v/t* cherish, value highly.

prize (2) *n* that which is captured in war, *esp* a vessel; booty; **P. Court** court of Admiralty dealing with prizes; **p. money** share of money arising from the sale of prizes.

prize (3), **prise** *v/t* force open, lift up with a lever.

prize-fighter [*pRi*z-fIter] *n* professional boxer.

prizeman [*pRi*zman] *n* winner of a university prize.

pro- (1) *pref* instead of; in favour of.

pro- (2) *pref* before in time; in front of.

pro (1) [*pRO*] *n* argument in favour of something; **the pros and cons** the arguments for and against.

pro (2) *n* (*coll abbr*) professional actor or games player.

probability [pRoba*bi*liti] *n* fact of being probable, likelihood; that which is probable; (*math*) numerical estimate of the likelihood of an event occurring > PDS.

probable [*pRo*bab'l] *adj* likely to happen; likely to be true ∼ **probable** *n* person likely to do, succeed *etc*; likely event ∼ **probably** *adv* more likely than not.

probang [*pRO*bang] *n* (*surg*) flexible rod for clearing blockages from the throat.

probate [*pRO*bayt] *n* (*leg*) the official proving of a will; certified approved copy of a will.

probation [pRO*bay*shon] *n* state or period of being tested; (*leg*) system of suspending sentence provided that the criminal reports regularly to an official and is of good behaviour; novitiate; **p. officer** official to whom criminals on probation must report.

probational [pRObayshonal] *adj* of or as a probation.

probationary [pRObayshoneRi] *adj* undergoing probation; in the position of a probationer; probational.

probationer [pRObayshoner] *n* nurse during the first part of her training; offender put on probation; novice; candidate for Nonconformist ministry.

probative [*p*RObativ] *adj* serving as proof.

probe [*p*ROb] *v/t* investigate, inquire into; (*surg*) insert an instrument into (a wound) to ascertain its depth *etc* ~ **probe** *n* surgical instrument for probing wounds; (*coll*) investigation, inquiry, missile sent into space carrying instruments or men to investigate moon, planets *etc*.

probity [*p*RObiti] *n* integrity, honesty.

problem [*p*Roblem] *n* difficulty, perplexing question; matter for deep consideration; question to be resolved by calculation ~ **problem** *adj* causing uncertainty; difficult to manage, solve or deal with; discussing or exemplifying a moral or social problem.

problematic, problematical [pRoblimatik, pRoblimatikal] *adj* of or like a problem; doubtful ~ **problematically** *adv*.

proboscis [pRobosis] *n* elongated flexible snout; elephant's trunk; elongated mouth-parts of certain insects; (*sl*) long human nose; **p. monkey** long-nosed monkey of Borneo.

procedural [pROseejeRal] *adj* concerning procedure, *esp* in debates or negotiations.

procedure [pROseejer] *n* manner of conducting business, *esp* parliamentary debates; mode of action, behaviour; technique.

proceed [pROseed] *v/i* go forward; begin to act; continue; go on speaking; issue, result, come forth (from); **p. against** take legal action against.

proceeding [pROseeding] *n* action, behaviour; (*pl*) record of the transactions of a society; legal action.

proceeds [*p*ROseedz] *n* (*pl*) money gained, *esp* by a sale or entertainment.

process (1) [*p*ROses] *n* whole series of continuous actions; method by which something is done; system of manufacture; (*leg*) whole course of a lawsuit; (*biol*) bony protuberance; projecting part; (*print*) any method of reproducing designs *etc* except by engraving; **p. control** control of a complex industrial process by electronic means; **in p.** in course of being done ~ **process** *v/t* preserve (food) by special treatment; make or treat in specified way; (*leg*) prosecute.

process (2) [pROses] *v/i* (*coll*) walk in formal procession.

procession [pROseshon] *n* body of persons advancing in formal order; (*fig*) ignominious defeat in a race; (*theol*) act of proceeding from a source, emanation ~ **procession** *v/i* and *t* walk in procession (round or along).

processional [pROseshonal] *n* and *adj* (*eccles*) (hymn or litany) for use in a procession.

processionary [pROseshoneRi] *adj* moving in procession.

proclaim [pROklaym] *v/t* make official announcement of in public; declare openly.

proclamation [pROklamayshon] *n* act of officially announcing; formal announcement.

proclamatory [pROklamateRi] *adj* of or like a proclamation.

proclitic [pROklitik] *n* and *adj* (word) so closely attached to a following word that it is relatively unstressed.

proclivity [pROkliviti] *n* tendency.

proconsul [pROkonsul] *n* governor of a colony; deputy consul; (*Rom hist*) governor of a province.

proconsular [pROkonsewler] *adj* of a proconsul.

proconsulate [pROkonsewlayt] *n* office of proconsul; district under his rule.

procrastinate [pROkRastinayt] *v/t* and *i* defer action repeatedly, delay from day to day.

procrastination [pROkRastinayshon] *n* act or habit of procrastinating.

procrastinator [pROkRastinayter] *n* one who procrastinates.

procreate [*p*ROkRi-ayt] *v/t* and *i* beget.

procreation [pROkRi-ayshon] *n* act of begetting.

procreator [*p*ROkRi-ayter] *n* father.

Procrustean [pROkRusti-an] *adj* producing uniformity by violent methods.

proctor [*p*Rokter] *n* administrative and disciplinary official at Oxford or Cambridge Universities; (*eccles*) representative of diocesan clergy or chapter at convocation; **Queen's P.** (*leg*) Crown official empowered to interfere in divorce, nullity and probate cases to prevent collusion or suppression of facts.

proctorial [pROktawRi-al] *adj* of a proctor.

proctorize [*p*RoktoRIZ] *v/t* exercise the authority of a proctor on.

procurable [pROkewrRab'l] *adj* obtainable.

procural [pROkewrRal] *n* act of procuring.

procuration [pROkewrRayshon] *n* appointment or function of a procurator, agent or proxy; management of another's affairs; procuring for immoral purposes.

procurator [pROkewrRayter] *n* proxy, agent; (*Rom hist*) treasury official; local administrator; **P. Fiscal** (*Scots law*) public prosecutor.

procure [pROkewr] *v/t* and *i* obtain, acquire; provide means of sexual pleasure for another, act as pimp or pander; (*ar*) cause.

procurement [pROkewrment] *n* act of procuring.

procurer [pROkewrRer] *n* pimp; agent.

procuress [pROkewrRis] *n* female pimp, bawd.

prod (*pres/part* prodding, *p/t* and *p/part* prodded) [*p*Rod] *v/t* poke, jab at; rouse, urge; remind ~ **prod** *n* act of prodding, poke ~ **prodder** *n*.

prodigal [*p*Rodigal] *adj* wasteful of money; lavish, generous ~ **prodigal** *n* spendthrift, squanderer; (*fig*) repentant sinner; reformed rake.

prodigality [pRodigaliti] *n* lavish generosity; wastefulness, extravagance with money.

prodigious [pRodijus] *adj* amazing; huge, vast ~ **prodigiously** *adv* ~ **prodigiousness** *n*.

prodigy [*p*Rodiji] *n* outstanding marvel; monstrosity; individual, *esp* a child, of extraordinary ability; genius.

produce [pROdews] *v/t* and *i* show, bring out; cause, give rise to; yield, bear (crops, fruit *etc*); give birth to; make, manufacture; create; organize a performance of (play, film *etc*); (*geom*) extend (a line) ~ **produce** [*p*Rodews] *n* that which is

576

produced; harvest, crop; yield; that which is made, product.

producer [pROde*ew*ser] *ŋ* one who produces; one who organizes and supervises the performance of a play, or directs the production of a film; **p. gas** fuel gas consisting of carbon monoxide, nitrogen, and hydrogen > PDS.

producible [pROde*ew*sib'l] *adj* that can be produced; suitable for production, presentable.

product [pROd*u*kt] *n* that which is produced by manufacture or growth; result of intellectual work; (*math*) quantity obtained by multiplying two or more quantities together; (*chem*) substance formed by chemical change.

production [pROd*u*kshon] *n* act of producing; thing produced; (*pol/ec*) creation of wealth; method, style or interpretation in producing a play.

productive [pROd*u*ktiv] *adj* producing abundantly, fertile; causing; producing economic wealth ~ **productively** *adv* ~ **productiveness** *n*.

productivity [pROdukt*i*viti] *n* rate at which something is produced, *esp* in manufacture.

proem [*pRO*-im] *n* introduction, preface.

prof, proff [*pRof*] *n* (*sl*) professor.

profanation [pROfan*ay*shon] *n* act of profaning; that which profanes.

profane [pROf*ayn*] *adj* showing contempt for sacred things or persons, blasphemous; not concerned with sacred matters, secular; not initiated, ignorant of sacred things; pagan; wicked; (*coll*) swearing irreverently ~ **profane** *v/t* desecrate, treat (something holy) irreverently; wickedly misuse; intrude coarsely ~ **profanely** *adv* ~ **profaneness** *n*.

profanity [pROf*a*niti] *n* quality of being profane; blasphemous language.

profess [pROf*es*] *v/t* and *i* affirm, declare; claim to have or be; pretend, claim falsely; carry on a profession; teach as professor; practise (a religion); take vows as monk or nun.

professed [pROf*est*] *adj* avowed, self-acknowledged; ostensible, falsely declared; having taken vows as monk or nun ~ **professedly** *adv*.

profession [pROf*e*shon] *n* occupation requiring training and intellectual abilities, practised so as to earn a living; body of persons practising such an occupation; declaration, affirmation; act of taking monastic vows.

professional [pROf*e*shonal] *adj* of or as a profession; earning a living by a profession (not by commerce or manual labour); fully trained, skilled (not amateur); practising a sport or game as a means of livelihood ~ **professional** *n* one who earns a living by practising a specified art, sport or profession.

professionalism [pROf*e*shonalizm] *n* position of a professional as distinct from an amateur.

professionalize [pROf*e*shonalIz] *v/t* make professional; give professional status to.

professionally [pROf*e*shonali] *adv* in a professional manner; as a professional; with expert skill.

professor [pROf*e*ser] *n* university teacher holding a chair of a subject; teacher, *esp* at advanced level; one who publicly declares (a religious belief).

professorial [pROfes*aw*Ri-al] *adj* of or like a professor.

professoriate [pROfes*aw*Ri-ayt] *n* professorship; body of professors.

professorship [pROf*e*sership] *n* position of a professor.

proffer [*pROf*er] *v/t* offer, bring for acceptance ~ **proffer** *n* act of offering; something offered.

proficiency [pROf*i*shensi] *n* degree of a person's acquired knowledge or skill in a particular direction.

proficient [pROf*i*shent] *adj* and *n* expert ~ **proficiently** *adv*.

profile [*pROf*Il/*pRO*feel] *n* side view of a face; outline drawing, *esp* of this; short essay describing a person, journalistic character-sketch; (*archi*) sectional drawing; outline; **keep a low p.** avoid attracting attention, behave tactfully and unobtrusively ~ **profile** *v/t* represent in profile, present a side view of.

profit [*pROf*it] *n* advantage, benefit; financial gain; **gross p.** excess of receipts over expenditure before deducting overhead charges and incidental costs; **net p.** excess of receipts when all deductions have been made ~ **profit** *v/t* and *i* be of advantage to, benefit; be useful; make or obtain profit.

profitability [pROfita*bi*liti] *n* quality of being profitable.

profitable [*pROf*itab'l] *adj* beneficial, advantageous, useful; bringing in money, lucrative ~ **profitableness** *n* ~ **profitably** *adv*.

profiteer [pROfit*eer*] *n* one who makes exorbitant profit by taking advantage of scarcities, *esp* in wartime ~ **profiteer** *v/i* ~ **profiteering** *n*.

profitless [*pROf*itles] *adj* useless; of no profit.

profit-sharing [*pROf*it-shairRing] *n* scheme by which employees receive a proportional share in the profits of a business.

profligacy [*pROf*ligasi] *n* quality of being profligate.

profligate [*pROf*ligat] *adj* and *n* very immoral, dissolute (person); recklessly extravagant (person) ~ **profligately** *adv*.

profound [pROf*ownd*] *adj* very deep; deeply felt; intense; showing or requiring great mental power; abstruse; (*of bow or curtsey*) very low ~ **profoundly** *adv* ~ **profoundness** *n*.

profundity [pROf*u*nditi] *n* state or quality of being profound, depth; intensity; abstruseness; very great intellectual power.

profuse [pROf*ews*] *adj* extravagant, lavish; very abundant, excessive ~ **profusely** *adv* ~ **profuseness** *n*.

profusion [pROf*ew*zhon] *n* abundance, copious amount; lavishness, extravagance.

prog [*pRog*] *n* (*sl*) university proctor; (*sl*) food.

progenitor [pROj*e*niter] *n* ancestor.

progeniture [pROj*e*nicher] *n* act of begetting; progeny, descendants.

progeny [*pRo*jini] *n* children; descendants.

progesterone [pROjest*e*ROn] *n* (*biol*) a steroid hormone that prevents ovulation during pregnancy.

prognathous [*pRog*nathus] *adj* having projecting jaws; (*of jaws*) protruding.

prognosis [pRogn*O*sis] *n* judgement as to the future course and termination of a series of events in process; forecast; (*med*) forecast of the probable course and outcome of a disease or disorder.

prognostic [pROgn*o*stik] *n* warning, indication;

forecast drawn from this; omen; (*med*) symptom upon which a prognosis is based ~ **prognostic** *adj* forecasting; of or by prognosis.

prognosticate [pROgnostikayt] *v/t* forecast from indications; be a sign of.

prognostication [pROgnostik*ay*shon] *n* forecast; sign, omen.

programme, program [*pRO*gRam] *n* list of items or performers in a theatrical show, concert, sports meeting *etc*; an entertainment, concert *etc* of several items; series of items broadcast on a particular wavelength; agenda, list or summary of things to be done; statement of policy or intentions, *esp* political; data for a computer; card on which a list of one's partners at a ball may be entered; **p. music** music suggesting in sound a story, picture *etc* ~ **programme, program** *v/t* prepare a programme of work for; give data to (a computer) ~ **programmer** *n*.

progress [*pRO*gRes] *n* forward or onward movement; advance, improvement, satisfactory development; expansion, increase; natural course or development; (*hist*) official journey or tour ~ **progress** [pRO*gRes*] *v/i* advance, move forward towards a goal; improve; develop, *esp* favourably.

progression [pRO*gRes*hon] *n* act of moving forward, progress; stage-by-stage development or advance; (*mus*) motion from one note or chord to another; (*math*) series of quantities each of which has a regular relation to the next.

progressist [*pRO*gResist] *n* believer in progressive politics.

progressive [pRO*gRes*iv] *adj* advancing by stages; progressing; tending to spread or to improve gradually; advocating or tending towards social and political reform; increasing by a ratio; (*med*) increasing in severity; (*gramm*) indicating continuing action; **p. whist** form of whist where players change partners after each game ~ **progressive** *n* one who advocates political or social reform ~ **progressively** *adv* ~ **progressiveness** *n*.

prohibit [pRO*hibit*] *v/t* forbid, *esp* by law; prevent, make impossible; prevent (a person) from an act ~ **prohibiter** *n*.

prohibition [pROhi*bish*on] *n* act of forbidding; forbidding by law of the manufacture and sale of alcoholic drinks.

prohibitionism [pROhi*bish*onizm] *n* legal prohibition of the making or selling of alcoholic drinks; advocacy of this prohibition ~ **prohibitionist** *n* and *adj* (supporter) of prohibition of alcoholic drinks; (state) where alcohol is banned.

prohibitive [pRO*hibit*iv] *adj* prohibiting; (*of price*) so high as to prevent sale ~ **prohibitively** *adv* ~ **prohibitiveness** *n*.

prohibitory [pRO*hibit*eRi] *adj* that forbids.

project [*pRO*jekt] *n* plan, scheme ~ **project** [pRO*jekt*] *v/t* and *i* throw or thrust forward at a goal; propel; jut out; turn (thoughts) to the distant future; cast (beam of light); cast (image) on a screen by a cinematograph or magic lantern; plan out, devise; (*geom*) represent a figure or solid by drawing lines through every point of it on to a surface; (*psych*) form a projection (of).

projectile [pRO*jekt*il] *n* body projected through the air, missile, gun shell; bullet ~ **projectile** *adj*

that hurls or thrusts forward; suitable for being hurled.

projection [pRO*jek*shon] *n* act of projecting; that which juts out; that which is projected; image projected on a surface; (*geog*) representation of part of the earth's surface on a flat surface; mode of representing this; (*psych*) interpretation of situations and events by reading one's own experiences and feelings into them; attribution of one's own motives, feelings *etc* to others; attribution to others of behaviour which would justify one's own feelings about them > PDP; (*geom*) projected figure.

projectionist [pRO*jek*shonist] *n* operator of a cinema projector.

projective [pRO*jek*tiv] *adj* of or by projection.

projector [pRO*jek*ter] *n* one who plans an enterprise; one who plans impracticable or fraudulent schemes; apparatus for projecting rays of light or for throwing a picture on a screen.

prolapse [*pRO*laps] *n* (*path*) slipping down or forward of an organ, *esp* uterus or rectum ~ **prolapse** *v/i*.

prolate [*pRO*layt] *n* and *adj* (*geom*) (spheroid) made by the revolution of an ellipse about its major axis; extended in width.

prole [*pROl*] *n* (*coll*) member of the proletariat.

prolegomenon ‹*pl* **prolegomena**› [pROli*gominon*] *n* long preface to a learned work.

proletarian [pROli*tair*Ri-an] *n* and *adj* (member) of the working class; (person) owning no capital and living on wages only.

proletariat, proletariate [pROli*tair*Ri-at] *n* the class of wage-earners with little or no property of their own and living by the sale of their labour > PDP; the working class, *esp* manual workers.

proliferate [pRO*life*Rayt] *v/i* (*biol*) grow or reproduce by rapid cell-division; (*fig*) increase rapidly in numbers.

proliferation [pRO*life*Rayshon] *n* formation or development of cells by budding or division; (*fig*) rapid increase.

proliferous [pRO*life*Rus] *adj* of or reproducing by proliferation.

prolific [pRO*lif*ik] *adj* producing many offspring; fertile; producing abundantly; rich in ~ **prolifically** *adv* ~ **prolificness** *n*.

prolix [*pRO*liks/pRO*liks*] *adj* speaking or writing too long; verbose, long-winded ~ **prolixly** *adv*.

prolixity [pRO*liks*iti] *n* quality of being prolix.

prologue [*pRO*log] *n* prefatory speech before a play; prefatory section of poem *etc*; event preliminary to a more important one ~ **prologue** *v/t* furnish with a prologue; introduce.

prolong [pRO*long*] *v/t* cause to last longer; lengthen in space, continue.

prolongation [pROlong-*gay*shon] *n* act of prolonging; that which is prolonged; state of being prolonged.

prom [*pRom*] *n* (*coll abbr*) promenade concert; esplanade, embankment; paved area for walking.

promenade [pROme*naad*] *n* short walk for pleasure or exercise, stroll; area where one may walk about freely; esplanade, broad embankment along a seashore; **p. concert** concert at which some of the audience stand; **p. deck** upper deck of liner ~ **promenade** *v/t* and *i* walk (along or through); stroll, walk about for pleasure ∼ **promenader** *n* one who attends promenade concerts; stroller.

promethium [pROmeethi-um] *n* (*chem*) radioactive lanthanide element > PDS.

prominence [pROminens] *n* condition of being prominent; protuberance, projecting point of land; relative importance; conspicuousness.

prominent [pROminent] *adj* outstanding, distinguished; well-known; jutting out; easy to see ∼ **prominently** *adv*.

promiscuity [pROmiskew-iti] *adj* quality or state of being promiscuous.

promiscuous [pROmiskew-us] *adj* indulging indiscriminately in sexual intercourse; mingled indiscriminately; not selected, haphazard ∼ **promiscuously** *adv*.

promise [pROmis] *v/t* and *i* undertake to do or not do something; undertake to give; assure, guarantee; give reasons to hope; foreshadow, be a sign of; **p. well** show signs of future success ∼ **promise** *n* act of promising; undertaking; assurance; thing promised; sign, grounds for hope; **break a p.** fail to do what one promised; **breach of p.** failure to fulfil an engagement to marry ∼ **promised** *adj* guaranteed by promise; **P. Land** (*OT*) Canaan; (*fig*) heaven; eagerly awaited happiness.

promising [pROmising] *adj* showing signs of future excellence; likely to succeed ∼ **promisingly** *adv*.

promissory [pROmiseRi] *adj* conveying a promise; **p. note** written promise to pay a certain sum of money at a fixed time.

promontory [pROmonteRi] *n* point of high land jutting out to sea; (*anat*) protuberance.

promote [pROmOt] *v/t* raise to higher rank; assist, cause to advance; support, encourage; assist in founding or organizing; originate; (*comm*) publicize, advertise; (*leg*) start (an action).

promoter [pROmOter] *n* one who promotes; supporter; one who takes steps to form a joint-stock company; organizer; originator.

promotion [pROmOshon] *n* act of promoting; advancement in rank; state of having been promoted.

prompt [pROmpt] *v/t* and *i* motivate, incite to action; suggest forgotten word to (speaker, *esp* actor), refresh the memory of; urge, inspire; act as prompter ∼ **prompt** *n* act of prompting an actor; (*comm*) time limit ∼ **prompt** *adj* done quickly or at once; quick to act; at the right time, not late; (*comm*) immediate; **p. note** notice of time limit for payment of account; **p. side** side of stage to actor's left when facing the audience.

prompt-book [pROmpt-book] *n* text of play *etc* used by a prompter.

prompt-box [pROmpt-boks] *n* place where prompter sits.

prompt-copy [pROmpt-kopi] *n* prompt-book.

prompter [pROmpter] *n* person who prompts actors when required; instigator.

promptitude [pROmptitewd] *n* readiness of action.

promptly [pROmptli] *adv* at once, quickly, readily ∼ **promptness** *n*.

promulgate [pROmulgayt] *v/t* announce publicly; proclaim (a new law).

promulgation [pROmulgayshon] *n* official or public declaration; passing of a new law.

prone [pROn] *adj* lying prostrate with face downwards; inclined, disposed; liable.

proneness [pROn-nes] *n* inclination.

prong [pRong] *n* forked tool; each point of a fork; pointed projection; point of antler ∼ **prong** *v/t* pierce with or lift on a prong.

pronged [pRongd] *adj* having prongs.

pronominal [pROnominal] *adj* of, like or acting as a pronoun ∼ **pronominally** *adv*.

pronoun [pROnown] *n* word used in place of a noun.

pronounce [pROnowns] *v/t* and *i* utter (a word, sound) in a specified way; articulate; declare solemnly or with authority; state as expert opinion; **p. on** give one's considered opinion about, pass judgement on.

pronounceable [pROnownsab'l] *adj* that can be articulated.

pronounced [pROnownst] *adj* strongly marked, well defined; emphatic ∼ **pronouncedly** *adv*.

pronouncement [pROnownsment] *n* authoritative statement; solemn declaration.

pronto [pROntO] *adv* (*sl*) quickly, at once.

pronunciamento [pROnunsi-amentO] *n* (*Sp*) political manifesto.

pronunciation [pROnunsi-ayshon] *n* manner of pronouncing a word, *esp* that accepted as normal and correct.

proof [pROOf] *n* act or process of showing that a statement is true; that which shows a statement to be true, conclusive evidence; test of quality or standard; standard of strength of distilled alcoholic drinks; (*print*) preliminary impression from type to be corrected; preliminary impression from an engraving plate; (*leg*) written copy of evidence to be given; record of evidence given ∼ **proof** *adj* of tested standard of strength (*esp* of alcohol and weapons); **p. against** strong enough to resist, invulnerable to; (*fig*) unmoved by ∼ **proof** *v/t* make waterproof; make bullet-proof.

proof-reader [pROOf-Reeder] *n* one who reads and corrects printers' proofs.

prop [pROp] (1) *n* a rigid support to hold up a weight; (*fig*) person who gives support ∼ **prop** (*pres/part* propping, *p/t* and *p/part* propped) *v/t* afford support to; **p. up** prevent from falling.

prop (2) *n* (*coll*) any object or costume to be used in a play, opera *etc*.

prop (3) *n* aircraft propeller.

propaganda [pROpaganda] *n* act or method of spreading specified doctrines > PDP; false or distorted information intended to help to spread doctrines *etc*; misleading publicity; organization for spreading doctrines; doctrines thus spread or publicized; book film *etc* intended to publicize doctrines; (*RC*) committee of cardinals to organize foreign missions.

propagandism [pROpagandizm] *n* practice of propaganda ∼ **propagandist** *n* and *adj* (supporter or user) of propaganda.

propagandize [pROpagandIz] *v/t* and *i* convert by propaganda; disseminate propaganda.

propagate [pROpagayt] *v/t* and *i* multiply by

natural reproduction; reproduce itself, have offspring; disseminate, spread; transmit.

propagation [pROpagayshon] *n* act or process of propagating.

propagator [pROpagayter] *n* one who begets offspring; one who spreads ideas *etc*.

propane [pROpayn] *n* inflammable hydrocarbon gas > PDS.

propel (*pres/part* **propelling,** *p/t* and *p/part* **propelled**) [pROpel] *v/t* drive forward, cause to move onward; impel.

propellant [pROpelant] *n* and *adj* (explosive charge) that propels a missile.

propeller [pROpeler] *n* mechanism for driving something forward, *esp* screw of ship or aircraft.

propensity [pROpensiti] *n* tendency.

proper [pROper] *adj* fit, suitable; customary; correct, considered right; normal; decent, chaste; respectable; prim, priggish; one's own; (*coll*) thorough, utter; (*her*) in natural colours; **p. noun** noun denoting a single person or place ~ **proper** *n* (*RC*) parts of the Mass that vary daily.

properly [pROperli] *adv* fittingly; accurately; decently, respectably; thoroughly.

propertied [pROpertid] *adj* possessing property.

property [pROperti] *n* that which is owned, belongings, possessions; land owned, estate; characteristic attribute; (*leg*) right of ownership; (*theat*) costume or object to be used in a play *etc*; **p. man** man in charge of theatrical properties; **personal p.** goods and chattels; **real p.** land owned.

prophecy [pROfisi] *n* act or power of prophesying; prophetic words; thing prophesied.

prophesier [pROfisi-er] *n* one who prophesies.

prophesy [pROfisi] *v/t* and *i* foretell the future by supernatural inspiration or powers; predict.

prophet [pROfit] *n* one who foretells supernaturally; one inspired by God to proclaim his will; inspired religious teacher or leader; fervent teacher, pioneer; (*pl*) prophetical books of the Old Testament; (*coll*) one who describes the probable future.

prophetess [pROfites] *n* woman prophet.

prophetic, prophetical [pROfetik, pROfetikal] *adj* of or like a prophet or prophecy; prophesying; containing prophecies ~ **prophetically** *adv*.

prophylactic [pROfilaktik] *n* and *adj* (medicine) tending to prevent disease.

prophylaxis [pROfilaksis] *n* (med) preventive treatment of disease.

propinquity [pROping-kwiti] *n* nearness.

propitiate [pROpishi-ayt] *v/t* render favourable; conciliate, appease.

propitiation [pROpishi-ayshon] *n* act of propitiating; atonement.

propitiator [pROpishi-ayter] *n* one who propitiates; reconciler, appeaser.

propitiatory [pROpishi-ayteRi] *adj* tending to propitiate.

propitious [pROpishus] *adj* favourable, welldisposed; presenting a favourable opportunity ~ **propitiously** *adv* ~ **propitiousness** *n*.

proportion [pROpawrshon] *n* comparative relationship in size, number, quality *etc*; ratio; relative size or arrangement of parts in a whole; harmonious or just relationship of parts; symmetry, balance; relative share; (*math*) an equality

between two ratios > PDS; (*pl*) dimensions, shape; **out of p.** (*fig*) exaggerated, unreasonable ~ **proportion** *v/t* put into proportion; share out.

proportionable [pROpawrshonab'l] *adj* in due proportion, proportional ~ **proportionably** *adv*.

proportional [pROpawrshonal] *adj* of or in proportion; **p. representation** electoral system reflecting the strength of the parties in the electorate at large > PDPol ~ **proportional** *n* (*math*) a number in a proportion ratio ~ **proportionally** *adv*.

proportionality [pROpawrshonaliti] *n* quality of being proportional.

proportionate [pROpawrshonit] *adj* in due proportion ~ **proportionate** [pROpawrshonayt] *v/t* put into proportion, adjust.

proportioned [pROpawrshond] *adj* adjusted, divided or formed in proportion.

proposal [pROpOzal] *n* an offer, *esp* of marriage; act of proposing; scheme proposed.

propose [pROpOz] *v/t* and *i* suggest, bring forward for discussion; make an offer of marriage; make plans, intend; name (person *etc*) to be toasted.

proposition [pROpozishon] *n* statement, suggestion; scheme suggested, project; (*math*) statement of a theorem or problem; (*log*) statement which affirms or denies; (*coll*) affair, matter to be dealt with; (*sl*) illegal or immoral proposal; **tough p.** (*coll*) someone or something difficult to manage ~ **proposition** *v/t* (*sl*) suggest a scheme or project to; suggest sexual intercourse to.

propositional [pROpozishonal] *adj* of or like a proposition.

propound [pROpownd] *v/t* put forward (question) to be solved; suggest (plan); explain; (*leg*) produce (a will) for its validity to be established ~ **propounder** *n*.

proprietary [pROpRI-eteRi] *adj* held in private ownership; holding property; patented, sold under trade-mark.

proprietor [pROpRI-eter] *n* owner.

proprietorial [pROpRi-etawRI-al] *adj* of ownership; of a proprietor.

proprietorship [pROpRI-etership] *n* ownership.

proprietress [pROpRI-etRes] *n* female proprietor.

propriety [pROpRI-eti] *n* fitness, appropriateness; correct behaviour, decency; **the proprieties** correct manners.

props [pROps] *n* (*pl*) stage properties; (*coll*) man in charge of these.

propulsion [pROpulshon] *n* act of propelling; apparatus or force that propels; strong motive force.

propulsive [pROpulsiv] *adj* that propels.

propylene [pROpileen] *n* olefine hydrocarbon gas; polymerized form of this used as a plastic.

propylite [pROpilIt] *n* type of volcanic rock.

pro rata [pRO Raata] *adj* and *adv* proportional(ly).

prorogation [pRORogayshon] *n* act of proroguing Parliament; time during which it is prorogued.

prorogue [pROROg] *v/t* and *i* discontinue meetings of (Parliament) until next session; cease to meet until next session.

prosaic [pROzay-ik] *adj* matter-of-fact, unimaginative; prosy; suitable only for prose style, not poetry ~ **prosaically** *adv*.

prosaism [pROzay-izm] *n* style only suitable for prose; prosaic phrase.

proscenium [pROseeni-um] *n* front arch framing theatre stage; area of stage between curtain and orchestra; stage of Greek or Roman theatre.

proscribe [pROskRIb] *v/t* forbid by law; denounce; declare outlaw; banish.

proscription [pROskRIpshon] *n* act of proscribing; fact of being proscribed; outlawry; denunciation.

proscriptive [pROskRIptiv] *adj* of proscription; demanding proscription or seeking to proscribe ~ **proscriptively** *adv*.

prose [pROz] *n* language spoken or written without metre or rhyme; plain matter-of-fact style ~ **prose** *v/i* talk or write in a dull, flat manner ~ **prose** *adj* written in prose; prosaic.

prosecute [pROsikewt] *v/t* and *i* take legal proceedings against; conduct a prosecution; continue to do, carry on.

prosecution [pROsikewshon] *n* the carrying out of some pursuit or plan; (*leg*) the institution of a suit or of criminal proceedings against a person; the party prosecuting a suit or a charge.

prosecutor [pROsikewter] *n* one who prosecutes, *esp* in a criminal court; **Public P.** public law officer who conducts criminal prosecutions on behalf of the Crown.

proselyte [pROsilIt] *n* convert; Gentile converted to Judaism ~ **proselyte** *v/t* proselytize.

proselytize [pROsilItIz] *v/t* and *i* make proselytes; make a proselyte of.

proser [pROzer] *n* dull talker.

prosily [pROzili] *adv* in a prosy way.

prosiness [pROzinis] *n* quality of being prosy.

prosit [pROsit] *interj* (*Lat*) expression of good wishes used in drinking a health, *esp* by Germans.

prosodic, prosodical [pROsodik, pROsodikal] *adj* of prosody; according to rules of metre.

prosodist [pROsodist] *n* one skilled in prosody.

prosody [pROsodi] *n* theory and art of versification; study of speech-rhythms.

prospect [pROspekt] *n* something expected or thought likely; probable train of events; wide view, outlook; fact of facing in specified direction; (*pl*) expectations of success, *esp* financial; (*min*) place where a mineral deposit may probably be; (*coll*) person from whom one hopes to gain some advantage; possible customer *etc* ~ **prospect** [pROspekt] *v/t* and *i* search (area) for deposits of minerals, gold, oil *etc*; explore.

prospective [pROspektiv] *adj* to be expected in the future; of the future; probable, expected ~ **prospectively** *adv*.

prospector [pROspekter] *n* one who explores for minerals *etc*.

prospectus [pROspektus] *n* account of a proposed enterprise or literary work; pamphlet issued by a school, hotel *etc* describing itself.

prosper [pROsper] *v/i* and *t* be fortunate, flourish, succeed; cause to flourish, be favourable to.

prosperity [pROspeRiti] *n* state of prospering; good fortune, wealth.

prosperous [pROspeRus] *adj* successful, flourishing; wealthy; favourable ~ **prosperously** *adv* ~ **prosperousness** *n*

prostaglandin [pROstaglandin] *n* (*med*) type of fatty acid causing contraction of muscles of womb.

prostate [pROstayt] *n* (*anat*) gland accessory to male generative organs.

prosthesis [pROsthesis] *n* (*med*) replacement of a missing limb, tooth *etc* by an artificial one ~ **prosthetic** *adj*.

prostitute [pROstitewt] *n* woman who hires out her body for sexual intercourse, whore; **male p.** man who hires himself for homosexual intercourse ~ **prostitute** *v/t* and *i* put to dishonourable use for the sake of money; live by prostitution.

prostitution [pROstitewshon] *n* fact of being a prostitute; organized system by which women hire themselves out for sexual intercourse; (*fig*) shameful misuse of talent *etc*; act of prostituting.

prostrate [pROstRayt] *adj* lying face downwards on the ground; utterly exhausted, overcome; defeated, helpless; humiliated ~ **prostrate** [pROstRayt] *v/t* and *refl* cast to the ground; overwhelm, exhaust, cause to collapse; throw oneself flat on the ground in reverence or humility; (*fig*) abase oneself, cringe.

prostration [pROstRayshon] *n* act of prostrating oneself; state of being overcome by illness, grief *etc*; complete collapse; powerlessness.

prosy [pROzi] *adj* dull, uninteresting; long-winded.

prot- *pref* first, primitive.

protactinium, protoactinium [pROtaktini-um, pROtO-aktini-um] *n* (*chem*) radioactive element > PDS.

protagonist [pROtagonist] *n* principal character in a play or novel; leader of a movement; (*coll*) leading supporter or advocate (of an idea *etc*).

protean [pROtee-an] *adj* constantly changing.

protect [pROtekt] *v/t* defend from harm, keep safe, shelter; safeguard (industries) against foreign competition by import tariffs.

protection [pROtekshon] *n* act of protecting; that which protects, safeguard; shelter; state of being protected; system of helping home industry by laying tariffs on imports; safe-conduct.

protectionism [pROtekshonizm] *n* economic doctrine of protection ~ **protectionist** *n* and *adj*.

protective [pROtektiv] *adj* that protects; showing a wish to protect; **p. colouring** colouring rendering animals hard to see against their usual surroundings, natural camouflage ~ **protectively** *adv* ~ **protectiveness** *n*.

protector [pROtekter] *n* one who or that which protects; regent; one who maintains a woman as his mistress; (*cap*) official title of Oliver and Richard Cromwell.

protectoral [pROtekteRal] *adj* pertaining to the protector of a kingdom or commonwealth.

protectorate [pROtekteRayt] *n* territory governed but not formally annexed by a stronger State > PDPol; office of regent; (*cap*) period of rule of Oliver and Richard Cromwell.

protectress [pROtektRes] *n* woman protector; patroness.

protégé (*fem* **protégée**) [pROtezhay] *n* (*Fr*) one under the care and protection of another.

proteid [pROteed] *n* protein.

proteiform [pROtee-ifawrm] *adj* (*zool*) changeable in form.

protein [pROteen] *n* very complex organic compound of numerous amino-acids > PDB, PDS ~ **protein** *adj* of, containing proteins.

proteinic, proteinous [pROteenik, pROteenus] *adj* of protein.

proteolytic [pROti-Olítik] *adj* capable of decomposing proteins ~ **proteolysis** *n*.

proter-, protero- *pref* anterior, earlier.

protest [pROtest] *v/t* and *i* express disapproval or objections; declare solemnly, affirm; *(leg)* declare formally that a bill of exchange has been refused or dishonoured ~ **protest** [pROtest] *n* act of protesting; expression of disapproval or objection; **under p.** against one's expressed wish ~ **protest** *adj* expressing indignant disapproval.

Protestant [pROtestant] *n* member of any Christian Church separated from the Roman Catholic Church in the sixteenth century; member of any Western church or Christian body outside the Roman Communion; person of evangelical views ~ **Protestant** *adj* of Protestants or Protestantism; regarding salvation by faith as more important than sacraments; evangelical.

Protestantism [pROtestantizm] *n* doctrines and principles of Protestants.

protestation [pROtestayshon] *n* solemn affirmation.

proto- *pref* first, primitive.

protocol [pROtOkol] *n* rules of diplomatic etiquette or procedure; first draft agreement for a treaty; formula beginning or ending a Papal bull ~ **protocol** *v/t* and *i* record in a protocol; draw up protocols.

protogenic [pROtOjeenik] *adj* *(bot, geol)* formed at an early stage.

proton [pROton] *n* *(phys)* positively charged particle of relatively large mass, forming part of an atomic nucleus > PDB.

protoplasm [pROtoplazm] *n* *(biol)* complex semifluid substance being an essential constituent of every living cell > PDB, PDS.

protoplasmic [pROtoplazmik] *adj* of protoplasm.

prototype [pROtotIp] *n* earliest form of an organism or an organ; model, pattern; earliest form of a machine *etc* from which other models are developed ~ **prototypical** [pROtotipikal] *adj*.

Protozoa [pROtozO-a] *n* *(pl)* group of animals consisting only of one cell with a well-defined nucleus > PDB.

protozoan [pROtozO-an] *n* (one) of the Protozoa.

protract [pROtRakt] *v/t* cause to last longer, prolong; *(sur)* draw to scale; *(zool)* thrust out, lengthen ~ **protracted** *adj* ~ **protractedly** *adv*.

protractile [pROtRaktIL/pROtRaktil] *adj* *(zool)* capable of being lengthened.

protraction [pROtRakshon] *n* act of protracting; state of being protracted; extension (of muscle); *(sur)* scale plan.

protractor [pROtRakter] *n* instrument used for measuring angles; *(anat)* muscle which extends a limb.

protrude [pROtROOd] *v/t* and *i* thrust out, cause to project; stand out.

protrusion [pROtROOzhon] *n* act of protruding; that which juts out.

protuberance [pROtewbeRans] *n* state of bulging outward; that which bulges outward, lump, knob, swelling.

protuberant [pROtewbeRant] *adj* bulging outward; rounded and prominent.

proud [pROwd] *adj* feeling or showing pride; haughty, arrogant; having a just awareness of one's merits or achievements; causing justifiable pride, glorious; magnificent: **p. flesh** growth of

granulated flesh round the edges of a wound ~ **proud** *adv* *(coll)* do (someone) **p.** treat or entertain magnificently ~ **proudly** *adv*.

provable [pROOvab'l] *adj* that can be proved.

prove [pROOv] *v/t* and *i* show to be true or valid, establish beyond doubt; turn out to be; test the quality of; *(math)* test accuracy of; *(ar)* discover by experience; *(leg)* obtain probate of.

proven [pROven/pROOven] *adj* proved; **not p.** *(Scots law)* verdict that evidence is insufficient to prove or disprove a prisoner's guilt.

provenance [pROvinans] *n* place from which a thing comes; place of origin.

provender [pROvinder] *n* fodder; *(joc)* food.

proverb [pROvurb] *n* short traditional saying embodying a common belief or truism; something well-known and often mentioned, byword; *(pl)* Old Testament book of Hebrew maxims.

proverbial [pROvurbi-al] *adj* of or like a proverb; generally known, notorious ~ **proverbially** *adv*.

provide [pROvId] *v/t* and *i* procure and supply for use; furnish, equip; *(leg)* make legal, allow; stipulate; make provision; **p. against** take steps to prevent; *(leg)* prohibit; **p. for** supply what is needed for; make suitable arrangements for; make allowance for; *(leg)* permit by law; **p. that** *(leg)* stipulate, enjoin.

provided [pROvIdid] *conj* on condition that.

providence [pROvidens] *n* foresight; prudent care for the future; economy; God's foreseeing care; a special act of God's care; *(cap)* God considered as benevolent protector.

provident [pROvident] *adj* foreseeing; thrifty, economical; **p. society** society whose members pay a regular contribution, from which to receive benefits in sickness, old age *etc* ~ **providently** *adv*.

providential [pROvidenshal] *adj* ordained by Divine providence; fortunate ~ **providentially** *adv*.

providing [pROvIding] *conj* *(coll)* on condition that.

province [pROvins] *n* large administrative division of a country; large area having distinct local culture, dialect *etc* within a country; region remote from the capital city; sphere of authority, action or interest; branch of knowledge; *(eccles)* area under archbishop's jurisdiction.

provincial [pROvinshal] *adj* of or in a province; not of the capital city; countrified ~ **provincial** *n* inhabitant of a province; archbishop; head of a territorial division of a monastic order.

provincialism [pROvinshalizm] *n* countrified speech or manners; narrowness of mind; attachment to interests of one's own province rather than those of the State; word or phrase peculiar to a certain part of the country.

provinciality [pROvinshi-aliti] *n* provincialism.

provision [pROvizhon] *n* act of providing; that which is provided; arrangements made to meet future need; *(pl)* stock or supply of food; *(leg)* stipulation, condition; **make p. for** provide for ~ **provision** *v/t* supply with stocks of food *etc*.

provisional [pROvizhonal] *adj* of or as a temporary arrangement; not finally settled, conditional ~ **provisionally** *adv*.

proviso [pROvIzO] *n* clause in a legal document making a stipulation; condition.

provisory [pROv/ZeRi] *adj* conditional, subject to proviso ~ **provisorily** *adv*.

provocation [pRovo*kay*shon] *n* act of provoking; that which provokes; behaviour meant to rouse another's anger or lust.

provocative [pRo*vo*kativ] *adj* deliberately provoking another's feelings, *esp* to anger or lust ~ **provocatively** *adv*.

provoke [pRov*Ok*] *v/t* rouse, cause (emotion); incite, urge; deliberately try to rouse another's anger or lust; enrage; annoy.

provoking [pRov*Ok*ing] *adj* annoying, exasperating ~ **provokingly** *adv*.

provost [*pROv*ost] *n* head of certain university colleges; (*Scots*) chief magistrate of a burgh.

provost-marshal [pRovO-*maar*shal] *n* officer commanding the military police; (*naval*) chief petty officer acting as master-at-arms for a court-martial; chief police official in some British colonies.

provost-sergeant [pRovO-*saar*jent] *n* sergeant of the military police.

provostship [*pROv*ostship] *n* office of provost.

prow [pRow] *n* bow of a boat or ship.

prowess [*pRow*-es] *n* courage, valour; skill.

prowl [pRowl] *v/i* and *t* wander about stealthily, *esp* in search of plunder or prey; wander stealthily through ~ **prowl** *n* act of prowling; stealthy menacing gait; **on the p.** engaged in prowling; **p. car** (*coll*) police patrol car.

prowler [*pRow*ler] *n* person who prowls, *usu* intending harm.

proximal [*pROk*simal] *adj* (*anat*) nearest to the central axis, or to the point of attachment.

proximate [*pROk*simit] *adj* nearest, next to; **p. cause** direct immediate cause ~ **proximately** *adv*.

proximity [pROk*sim*iti] *n* nearness.

proximo [*pROk*simO] *adv* in the next month.

proxy [*pROk*si] *n* authority given to a person to act for another; person acting as agent or representative for another.

prude [pROOd] *n* person who makes an exaggerated show of modesty and propriety.

prudence [*pROO*dens] *n* quality of being prudent; circumspect behaviour; sagacity.

prudent [*pROO*dent] *adj* cautious, careful; circumspect, judicious ~ **prudently** *adv*.

prudential [pROO*den*shal] *adj* of or showing prudence ~ **prudentially** *adv*.

prudery [*pROO*deRi] *n* outlook or behaviour of a prude.

prudish [*pROO*dish] *adj* of or like a prude; exaggeratedly or affectedly modest ~ **prudishly** *adv* ~ **prudishness** *n*.

prune (1) [pROOn] *n* dried plum; (*US*) plum suitable for drying; dark reddish purple colour.

prune (2) *v/t* cut branches off (a tree or shrub) to strengthen it; cut (tree *etc*) to a better shape; (*fig*) remove anything superfluous; shorten by omissions.

pruning [*pROO*ning] *n* act of cutting off branches *etc*; shortening; **p. hook (knife)** tool with curved blade for pruning trees.

prunus [*pROO*nus] *n* genus of trees bearing stone-fruit.

prurience, pruriency [*pROor*Ri-ens, *pROor*Ri-ensi] *n* state or quality of being prurient.

prurient [*pROor*Ri-ent] *adj* morbidly interested in obscenity; obsessed by sexual imaginings ~ **pruriently** *adv*.

prurigo [pROor*RIg*O] *n* (*path*) chronic itching accompanied by pimples and thickening of skin.

pruritus [pROor*RI*tus] *n* (*path*) itching, *esp* without pimples.

Prussian [*pRush*an] *n* and *adj* (inhabitant) of Prussia; **p. blue** deep blue pigment derived from potassium ferrocyanide.

prussic [*pRus*ik] *adj* (*chem*) **p. acid** intensely poisonous solution of hydrocyanic acid.

pry (*p/t* and *p/part* pried) [pRI] *v/i* look about inquisitively; spy; **p. into** investigate closely and curiously.

psalm [saam] *n* religious song or poem, *esp* of an ancient Jewish type; hymn; (*pl*) Old Testament collection of psalms.

psalmist [*saam*ist] *n* composer of psalms.

psalmodic [sal*mod*ik] *adj* of psalms or psalmody.

psalmodist [*saam*odist/*sal*modist] *n* one who sets psalms to music; singer or writer of psalms.

psalmody [*saam*odi/*sal*modi] *n* art of singing psalms in public worship; arrangement of psalms for singing > PDM.

psalter [*sawl*ter] *n* (*OT*) the Book of Psalms; musical or metrical version of this.

psaltery [*sawl*teRi] *n* ancient stringed instrument plucked like a lyre but having a sounding-board.

psephology [see*fol*oji] *n* the study of election trends or methods of voting ~ **psephologist** *n*.

pseud [sewd] *n* (*sl*) person who makes spurious claims to wisdom, taste *etc*.

pseudo- *pref* false, spurious.

pseudo [sewd*O*] *adj* (*coll*) insincere; fake.

pseudonym [*sewd*onim] *n* fictitious name, *esp* one used by an author.

pseudonymous [sewd*on*imus] *adj* written or writing under an assumed name.

pseudopodium [sewdO*pO*di-um] *n* (*zool*) temporary protrusion of a cell serving locomotion and feeding > PDB.

pshaw [pshaw/shaw] *interj* rubbish, nonsense.

psi [psI] *n* twenty-third letter of Greek alphabet; symbol for telepathy, telekinesis and other paranormal forces.

psittacosis [sitak*O*sis] *n* contagious influenza of parrots, communicable to human beings.

psoriasis [saw*RI*-asis] *n* (*med*) a chronic skin rash.

psyche [sIki] *n* (*Gk*) soul, mind; mentality, character; (*ent*) a genus of moths.

psychedelic [sIki*del*ik] *adj* inducing ecstatic and mystic experiences by hallucinative drugs or semi-hypnotic devices; (*sl*) like a hallucination, dream or nightmare; surrealist, irrational; dazzling in colour or pattern; hypnotic in rhythm.

psychiatric [sIki-*at*Rik] *adj* of psychiatry; suffering from a mental or nervous disorder.

psychiatrist [sIk*I*-atRist] *n* one who practises psychiatry.

psychiatry [sIk*I*-atRi] *n* study and treatment of mental and nervous disorders.

psychic [sIkik] *adj* having occult powers; capable of telepathy, of seeing ghosts and spirits *etc*; of or studying occult phenomena; (*psych*) mental; **p. force** hypothetical cause of telekinetic phenomena ~ **psychic** *n* person having occult, telepathic or mediumistic powers.

psychical [sɪ**k**ikal] *adj* occult, supernatural; mental; **p. research** scientific investigation of alleged cases of telepathy, haunting, spiritism *etc* ~ **psychically** *adv*.

psycho- *pref* mental.

psycho [sɪ**k**O] *n* (*coll*) psychopath; dangerous madman.

psychoanalyse [sɪk**O**-analɪz] *v/t* treat by psychoanalysis; investigate the subconscious associations, reactions *etc* of.

psychoanalysis [sɪk**O**-analisis] *n* method of treating certain mental and nervous disorders, first elaborated by Freud; psychology of the unconscious mind > PDP.

psychoanalyst [sɪk**O**-analist] *n* one who practises psychoanalysis.

psychodynamics [sɪk**O**dɪnamiks] *n* psychology of the unconscious mind.

psychokinesis [sɪk**O**kɪneesis] *n* alleged power to influence movement of material objects by thinking or willing.

psychological [sɪk**O**lojikal] *adj* of or by psychology; in or of the mind; (*pop*) subconsciously motivated; irrational; **p. moment** moment when something is most likely to impress the mind; very suitable opportunity ~ **psychologically** *adv*.

psychologist [sɪ**k**Olojist] *n* one who studies or practises psychology; specialist in specified branch of psychology; (*coll*) one who well understands people's characters, motives *etc*.

psychology [sɪ**k**Oloji] *n* branch of science studying the processes, motives, reactions and nature of the human mind; mental processes, motives *etc*; character, *esp* as interpreted by modern psychologists > PDP.

psychometrics [sɪk**O**metRiks] *n* (*pl*) scientific measurement of intelligence.

psychomotor [sɪk**O**mOter] *adj* causing motion by mental process.

psychoneurosis [sɪk**O**newrROsis] *n* functional mental or nervous disorder of a less severe type than psychosis.

psychoneurotic [sɪk**O**newrRotik] *n* and *adj* (one) suffering from psychoneurosis; caused by psychoneurosis.

psychopath [sɪ**k**Opath] *n* person having abnormal emotional instability, often with anti-social tendencies, but with no specific mental disease.

psychopathic [sɪk**O**pathik] *adj* of or like a psychopath; suffering from mental disease.

psychopathology [sɪk**O**patholoji] *n* pathology of the mind; study of mental disease or disorder.

psychophysics [sɪk**O**fiziks] *n* (*pl*) science of general relations between mind and body, *esp* between physical stimuli and sensory events > PDP.

psychosis [sɪ**k**Osis] *n* a form of insanity involving grave mental disturbance > PDP.

psychosomatic [sɪk**O**sOmatik] *adj* (*of a physical illness, symptom etc*) caused by psychological disorder, *esp* subconscious ~ **psychosomatics** *n* (*pl*) correlation of mental phenomena with bodily conditions.

psychosurgery [sɪk**O**surjeRi] *n* treatment of mental disorders.

psychotherapy [sɪk**O**theRapi] *n* treatment of disease by psychological methods.

psychotic [sɪ**k**Otik] *n* and *adj* (one) suffering from a psychosis; caused by a psychosis.

psychotropic [sɪk**O**tRopik] *adj* (*of drugs*) changing the personality.

psychrometry [sɪ**k**ROmetRi] *n* measurement of atmospheric humidity.

ptarmigan [*taar*migan] *n* bird of grouse family with black and grey plumage in summer and white in winter.

ptero- *pref* wing, feather.

pterodactyl [teR**O**daktil] *n* extinct order of flying reptiles > PDB.

Ptolemaic [tolemay-ik] *adj* (*astron*) considering the earth as a stationary centre of the universe with sun, planets, stars *etc* revolving round it; (*hist*) of a dynasty of Greek rulers of Egypt.

ptomaine [*t*Omayn] *n* (*chem*) name of a class of poisonous organic compounds formed during the putrefaction of proteins.

ptyalin [*tɪ*-alin] *n* ferment in saliva which converts starch into sugar.

pub [*pub*] *n* (*coll abbr*) public-house, inn.

puberty [*pew*berti] *n* age at which a boy or girl becomes capable of adult sexual functions.

pubes [*pew*beez] *n* hair which appears at puberty; lower part of abdomen.

pubescence [pew*b*esens] *n* arrival at the age of puberty; (*biol*) soft down on plants or insects ~ **pubescent** *adj*.

pubic [*pew*bik] *adj* of or on the pubis; **p. hair** hair appearing at puberty on the lower abdomen.

pubis [*pew*bis] *n* (*anat*) bone which forms the anterior wall of pelvis.

public [*publ*ik] *adj* of, by or for a whole community; of, by or for people in general; known or accessible to all; not secret or private; general; national; notorious; **p. enemy** person thought to be dangerous to a community; outlaw; **p. nuisance** (*leg*) illegal act or omission harmful to the community rather than to an individual; (*coll*) someone causing general annoyance or disturbance; **p. ownership** nationalization; **p. relations** relationship of an organization and the public who know of it, use it *etc*; steps taken to ensure that this will be favourable; favourable publicity; **p. relations officer** person who gives information to press or public about an organization *etc*; **p. school** (*England*) expensive fee-paying boarding-school mainly taking upper-class pupils; (*Scots* and *US*) state-controlled school, *gen* without fees ~ **public** *n* community; nation; any section of a community considered as an audience, as possible customers or as interested in a specified person or activity; **in p. openly.

public-address [publik-ad*R*es] *adj* **p. system** system of loudspeakers *etc* enabling a speaker to be heard throughout a building, arena *etc*.

publican [*publ*ikan] *n* innkeeper, keeper of a public house; (*ar*) Roman taxgatherer.

publication [publi*k*ayshon] *n* act of making known to the public; issue of a book, piece of music *etc* in printed form; published book.

public-house [publik-*hows*] *n* licensed house for the sale of alcoholic liquors to be consumed on the premises.

publicist [*pub*lisist] *n* one who publicizes a commodity *etc*; political journalist; writer on international law.

publicity [*pub*l*i*siti] *n* state of being generally known; process of advertising a cause or person; advertisements; notoriety.

publicize [*pub*lisIz] *v/t* make known to the public, *esp* by advertisements, press reports *etc*.

publicly [*pub*likli] *adv* in public, openly, without concealment.

public-school [public-*skOOl*] *adj* of or in an English upper-class fee-paying boarding-school.

public-spirited [publik-*spi*Ritid] *adj* working for the welfare of the people at large.

publish [*pub*lish] *v/t* make generally known, declare publicly; issue (a book, piece of music *etc*) to the public; write and arrange for the distribution of (a book); (*leg*) (*of libel*) communicate to more than one person.

publishable [*pub*lishab'l] *adj* fit for publication.

publisher [*pub*lisher] *n* one who issues books to the public through booksellers.

puccoon [puk*OOn*] *n* N. American plant yielding a red dye.

puce [*pews*] *adj* and *n* brownish-purple.

puck (1) [*puk*] *n* a mischievous goblin.

puck (2) *n* flat rubber disk used in ice-hockey.

pucka see **pukka**.

pucker [*puk*er] *v/t* and *i* draw into wrinkles, crease; become gathered into wrinkles or creases ~ **pucker** *n* a wrinkle, crease.

puckish [*puk*ish] *adj* mischievous, impish.

pud [*pood*] *n* (*coll*) pudding.

puddening [*pood*ening] *n* (*naut*) pad of rope-yarn used to prevent chafing; bow fender > PDSa.

pudding [*pood*ing] *n* boiled or baked mixture of flour, suet *etc*; boiled sweetened rice or sago; any solid sweet dish; a batter; a type of sausage; (*naut*) puddening; **p. face** (*coll*) fat stupid-looking face; **p. head** (*coll*) fool.

pudding-stone [*pood*ing-stOn] *n* composite rock consisting of rounded pebbles embedded in siliceous matrix.

puddingy [*pood*ingi] *adj* of or like a pudding; (*fig*) dull, stupid; fat.

puddle [*pud*'l] *n* shallow pool of liquid, *esp* rainwater; watertight preparation of clay, sand and water ~ **puddle** *v/t* and *i* paddle, wade through a puddle; apply clay, sand and water to (the bottom of a pond *etc*); stir molten iron to make it wrought-iron ~ **puddler** *n*.

pudenda [pewd*en*da] *n*(*pl*) external sex organs, *esp* of female.

pudgy [*puj*i] *adj* short and fat, podgy.

pudic [*pew*dik] *adj* (*anat*) of the pudenda.

pueblo [*pweb*lO] *n* (*Sp*) Indian village in Mexico.

puerile [*pew*rRIl] *adj* childish; trivial, foolish ~ **puerilely** *adv*.

puerility [pewr*Ril*iti] *n* quality of being puerile, foolish childishness; that which is puerile.

puerperal [pew-ur*per*al] *adj* of or after childbirth; **p. fever** fever caused by septic infection after giving birth.

puff [*puf*] *v/t* and *i* breathe jerkily and with difficulty, pant; emit (smoke, steam *etc*) in short repeated jets; smoke (cigarette *etc*) jerkily; (*coll*) publicize, advertise, praise; (*of trains*) advance emitting jets of steam; **p. out** distend, swell;

cause to be out of breath; emit in puffs; **p. up** swell; be conceited or triumphant ~ **puff** *n* short jet or gust of air, smoke, steam *etc*; (*coll*) laudatory advertisement or review; fluffy ball; small fluffy pad for applying powder to the face; light pastry, *usu* filled with jam; loose billowing drapery; (*sl*) lifetime.

puff-adder [*puf*-ader] *n* African viper.

puffball [*puf*bawl] *n* fungus with a ball-shaped head which bursts when ripe in a cloud of fine powder; mass of dandelion seeds.

puffer [*puf*er] *n* one who or that which puffs; (*childish coll*) steam engine.

puffin [*puf*in] *n* seabird with very large particoloured bill.

puffiness [*puf*ines] *n* shortness of breath; state of being puffy.

puff-paste [*puf*-payst] *n* rich light flaky pastry.

puffy [*puf*i] *adj* inflated, puffed out; blowing in gusts; short of breath; swollen.

pug (1) [*pug*] *n* breed of dog resembling a small bulldog; small shunting engine.

pug (2) *n* clay kneaded up ready for making bricks or pottery; material used for soundproofing walls *etc* ~ **pug** (*pres/part* **pugging**, *p/t* and *p/part* **pugged**) *v/t* knead (clay); pack (walls, floor *etc*) with soundproof material.

pug (3) *n* footprint of a wild animal.

pug (4) *n* (*sl abbr*) pugilist, boxer.

pugilism [*pew*jilizm] *n* art of boxing.

pugilist [*pew*jilist] *n* prize-fighter, boxer.

pugilistic [pewjil*is*tik] *adj* of or by boxing.

pugmill [*pug*mil] *n* machine for kneading clay or mixing mortar.

pugnacious [pug*nay*shus] *adj* quarrelsome, ready to fight ~ **pugnaciously** *adv* ~ **pugnaciousness** *n*.

pugnacity [pug*nas*iti] *n* quality of being pugnacious; combativeness.

pugnose [*pug*nOz] *n* short nose sloping upward, snub-nose ~ **pugnosed** *adj*.

puisne [*pew*ni] *adj* (*leg*) of lower rank, junior.

puissance [*pew*-isans/*pwee*sans] *n* (*ar*) power.

puissant [*pew*-isant/*pwee*sant] *adj* (*ar*) powerful.

puke [*pewk*] *v/i* vomit.

pukka, pucka [*puk*a] *adj* genuine; first-rate; **p. sahib** true gentleman.

pulchritude [*pulk*Ritewd] *n* beauty.

pule [*pewl*] *v/i* whimper peevishly, whine.

pull [*pool*] *v/t* and *i* draw forcefully towards a point, drag; remove by pulling, extract; pluck; cause to follow, attract; row; (*print*) take an impression of; (*racing*) rein in a horse to stop him from winning; (*games*) strike (ball) sharply to the left; (*of* handle roughly; **p. apart** tear to pieces; (*fig*) criticize severely; **p. at** suck air and smoke through (one's pipe); suck up, drink; **p. back** drag backwards; halt, check; retreat; **p. down** weaken in health; **p. in** retract; reduce; tighten; (*of train*) enter a station; bring a motor vehicle to the side of the road and halt; (*sl*) arrest; **p. in** at halt briefly at; **p. off** achieve successfully; **p. one's weight** do a fair share of work; do one's best; **p. one's punches** strike less heavily than one could; (*fig*) restrain one's attack; **p. out** extract; drive nearer towards centre of road; (*of train*) leave the station; **p. round** recover or cause to recover from illness; **p. strings** exert secret influence; **p. through** recover or cause to recover from illness; overcome, endure successfully; **p. to pieces** analyse with hostility, criticize severely; **p. together** cooperate; **p. oneself together** regain self-control; **p. up** halt abruptly; check; rebuke; pause ~ **pull** *n* act of pulling; act of sucking in or drinking; *(coll)* influence; advantage; handle to be pulled; *(print)* rough proof; *(games)* stroke driving ball to the left; *(racing)* tug at the reins, check.

puller [*pooler*] *n* one who pulls; instrument for pulling; horse that habitually pulls.

pullet [*poolet*] *n* young hen.

pulley [*pooli*] *n* mechanism composed of a grooved wheel carrying a cord, used for changing the direction of power; combination of such wheels by which power is increased.

pull-in [*pool*-in] *n* halting-place; roadside café, *esp* for lorry-drivers.

Pullman [*pool*man] *n* *(tr)* specially comfortable railway carriage.

pull-on [*pool*-on] *n* and *adj* (garment, *esp* corset) which is pulled on and has no fastenings.

pullover [*pool*Over] *n* woollen jersey without fastenings pulled on over the head.

pull-through [*pool*-thROO] *n* cord used for cleaning a rifle-barrel.

pullulate [*pul*yoolayt] *v/i* multiply rapidly; grow or sprout rapidly.

pull-up [*pool*-up] *n* pull-in.

pulmo- *pref* of a lung.

pulmonary [*pul*moneRi] *adj* of or in the lungs.

pulmonate [*pul*monayt] *n* and *adj* *(zool)* (animal) having lungs.

pulmonic [pul*mon*ik] *adj* pulmonary.

pulp [*pulp*] *n* soft mass of crushed and wetted fibres; soft fleshy part of fruit; mash; **p. magazine** *(coll)* cheap sensationalist magazine ~ **pulp** *v/t* make into pulp.

pulper [*pul*per] *n* machine for pulping.

pulpiness [*pul*pinis] *n* quality of being pulpy.

pulpit [*pool*pit] *n* raised enclosed platform from which a preacher delivers a sermon; *(fig)* means or medium for expressing a point of view.

pulpy [*pul*pi] *adj* of or like pulp.

pulque [*pool*kay] *n* fermented agave sap.

pulsar [*pul*sar] *n* *(astron)* pulsating star; source of pulsed radio signals, within the Milky Way, of undetermined origin.

pulsate [pul*sayt*/*pul*sayt] *v/i* expand and contract rhythmically, throb; *(elect)* vary in intensity.

pulsation [pul*say*shon] *n* movement of the pulse; beating, throbbing; a beat of the heart; vibration; *(elect)* variation of a current.

pulsatory [*pul*sayteRi] *adj* throbbing.

pulse (1) [*puls*] *n* rhythmical throbbing of an artery; place, *esp* on a wrist, where this can be felt; rate of this; single beat or throb of a series; *(phys)* brief increase in the magnitude of a quantity; *(fig)* vitality, excitement; **feel (take) the p.** of feel and time the wrist pulse of; *(fig)* study the reactions of ~ **pulse** *v/i* pulsate.

pulse (2) *n* edible seeds of leguminous plants.

pulverization [pulveRIzayshon] *n* act of pulverizing; state of being pulverized.

pulverize [*pul*veRIZ] *v/t* and *i* reduce to powder; *(fig)* destroy utterly; divide (a liquid) into minute particles of spray; fall to dust; fall to nothingness.

pulverizer [*pul*veRIzer] *n* one who or that which pulverizes.

puma [*pew*ma] *n* large feline mammal of S. America, cougar.

pumice [*pum*is] *n* a light porous volcanic rock used for polishing and scrubbing ~ **pumice** *v/t* polish with pumice.

pumice-stone [*pum*is-stOn] *n* lump of pumice.

pummel [*pum*el] *v/t* strike repeatedly with the fists, pommel.

pump (1) [*pump*] *n* any mechanism for raising liquid in a pipe, *esp* by a piston; mechanism for compressing or exhausting air or gases by the action of piston and cylinder; anything resembling this ~ **pump** *v/t* and *i* raise or extract with a pump; act as a pump; compress (air *etc*) with a pump; move forcefully up and down; *(coll)* extract information by artful questions; *(fig)* exhaust; instil by effort; **p. out** empty by a pump; exhaust; **p. up** inflate (tyre *etc*) with a pump; raise by a pump; **p. ship** *(sl)* urinate.

pump (2) *n* man's light patent leather shoe.

pumpernickel [*poom*pernikel] *n* rye bread.

pumpkin [*pump*kin] *n*· large fruit resembling vegetable marrow; plant bearing this.

pump-room [*pump*-ROOm] *n* building at a spa where the water is distributed and drunk.

pun [*pun*] *n* deliberate use of a word having several meanings or of two words having the same sound but different meanings, so as to create a startling or humorous effect ~ **pun** *(pres/part* **punning,** *p/t* and *p/part* **punned)** *v/i* make puns; **p. on** use as a pun.

punch (1) [*punch*] *n* instrument for making holes by pressure or for impressing a design; steel die; small instrument for piercing holes in railway or bus tickets *etc* ~ **punch** *v/t* make holes in, pierce with a punch.

punch (2) *n* strong blow with the fist; *(fig)* vigour; effectiveness ~ **punch** *v/t* and *i* strike with the clenched fist.

punch (3) *n* wine or spirits mixed with hot water or milk, sweetened and flavoured.

punch (4) *n* draught horse with thickset body and short legs.

Punch (5) *n* name of the stumpy hump-backed figure in the puppet-show of Punch and Judy; English comic weekly magazine.

punchball [*punch*bawl] *n* stuffed leather ball suspended so that boxers may practise punching at it.

punchbowl [*punch*bOl] *n* bowl in which punch is mixed and served; deep hollow in a hillside.

punchdrunk [*punch*dRunk] *adj* showing signs of concussion from repeated blows.

puncheon (1) [*pun*shon] *n* *(carp)* short post in the middle of a truss; kingpost.

puncheon (2) *n* large cask for liquids.

Punchinello [punchi*nel*O] *n* name of the chief character in a puppet-play deriving from Italy.

punch-ladle [*punch*-layd'l] *n* small long-handled ladle for filling glasses from a punchbowl.

punchline [*punch*lIn] *n* humorous or dramatic climax and conclusion.

punch-up [*punch*-up] *n* *(sl)* fist-fight.

punctate [*punk*tayt] *adj* marked with dots.

punctilio [punk*til*i-O] *n* precise or subtle point

of etiquette; scrupulous attention to etiquette or duty.

punctilious [punk*tili*-us] *adj* careful to observe punctilios; precise, scrupulous over all details of behaviour ~ **punctiliously** *adv* ~ **punctiliousness** *n*.

punctual [*punk*choo-al] *adj* arriving or acting at an appointed time, not late; (*geom*) of a point.

punctuality [punkchoo-*aliti*] *n* quality of being punctual.

punctually [*punk*choo-ali] *adv* at the right time.

punctuate [*punk*choo-ayt] *v/t* insert commas, stops and other punctuation marks in; interrupt repeatedly; diversify; emphasize.

punctuation [punkchoo-*ayshon*] *n* act of punctuating; system of marks indicating pauses or logical and grammatical relationships in written language.

puncture [*punk*cher] *n* act of pricking; mark left after pricking; perforation of a pneumatic tyre ~ **puncture** *v/t* and *i* prick, pierce; receive a puncture.

pundit [*pun*dit] *n* learned person; learned Hindu student of philosophy, law *etc*; (*coll*) one who thinks himself an expert.

punditry [*pun*ditRi] *n* opinions of self-styled experts.

pungency [*pun*jensi] *n* quality of being pungent.

pungent [*pun*jent] *adj* having a strong sharp smell or taste; acrid; (*fig*) sarcastic, bitter; (*bot*, *zool*) sharp-pointed ~ **pungently** *adv*.

punily [*pew*nili] *adv* in a puny way, weakly.

puniness [*pew*ninis] *n* quality of being puny.

punish [*pun*ish] *v/t* cause (an offender) to suffer for his offence; inflict a penalty on or for; inflict physical damage on, treat roughly.

punishable [*pun*ishab'l] *adj* liable to or entailing punishment.

punishment [*pun*ishment] *n* act of punishing; penalty inflicted; (*coll*) rough handling.

punitive [*pew*nitiv] *adj* involving punishment; done in order to punish.

punitory [*pew*niteRi] *adj* punitive.

punk [*punk*] *n* (*coll*) type of youth who cultivates tough, deliberately unpleasant image; lout, bum, idiot; (*obs sl*) prostitute; (*US sl*) homosexual; (*US*) rotten wood; fungus growing on this, touchwood ~ **punk** *adj* worthless, rotten; loutish, deliberately offensive; outrageous, violent.

punnet [*pun*it] *n* small chip basket for fruit.

punster [*pun*ster] *n* one who makes puns.

punt (1) [*punt*] *n* flat-bottomed shallow boat with square ends, propelled by a long pole thrust against the bed of a river or lake ~ **punt** *v/t* and *i* propel a punt; convey in a punt.

punt (2) *n* (*Rugby football*) a kick given to the ball dropped from the hands, before it reaches the ground ~ **punt** *v/i*.

punt (3) *v/i* (*cards*) lay a stake against the bank; bet, *esp* on a racehorse.

punter (1) [*punter*] *n* one who manages a punt.

punter (2) *n* one who backs horses.

punty [*punti*] *n* glass-blower's iron rod.

puny [*pew*ni] *adj* small and weak.

pup [*pup*] *n* young dog, puppy; (*coll*) conceited young man; young seal or otter; **be sold a p.** be swindled over a bargain; **in p.** (*of a bitch*)

pregnant ~ **pup** (*pres/part* pupping, *p/t* and *p/part* pupped) *v/i* give birth to pups.

pupa [*pew*pa] *n* (*ent*) chrysalis of insect.

pupate [*pew*payt] *v/i* become a pupa.

pupil (1) [*pew*pil] *n* one who is being taught; (*leg*) ward under age of puberty; **p. teacher** young person training to be a teacher while at the same time teaching under superintendence.

pupil (2) *n* opening in the iris of the eye.

pupilage, pupillage [*pew*pilij] *n* state of being a ward or minor; period of this state; state of being a pupil under instruction.

pupilary, pupillary [*pew*pileRi] *adj* of or as a pupil or student; of the pupil of the eye.

puppet [*pup*it] *n* inanimate figure moved by human agency, *usu* in some kind of theatrical entertainment; (*fig*) one who seems to act independently but is in fact controlled by others for their own ends; **glove p.** doll with hollow cloth body worn on the hand and moved by the fingers inside it; **p. State** apparently independent government actually controlled by a stronger State ~ **puppetry** *n*.

puppet-show [*pup*it-shO] *n* play acted by puppets.

puppy [*pup*ee] *n* young dog; foolish conceited youth.

puppyfat [*pup*eefat] *n* (*coll*) plumpness of children and adolescents that disappears later.

puppyish [*pup*ee-ish] *adj* like a puppy; conceited; boisterous.

Purbeck [*pur*bek] *n* fine variety of limestone.

purblind [*pur*blInd] *adj* partly blind, very short-sighted; (*fig*) stupid, obtuse.

purchase [*pur*chis] *v/t* buy, acquire by payment; obtain by sacrifice, effort *etc*; (*naut*) raise by tackle or leverage; (*leg*) acquire by any means other than inheritance ~ **purchase** *n* act of buying; thing bought; leverage; position for gripping, pulling *etc*; (*leg*) value reckoned by annual profits or returns ~ **purchaser** *n*.

purdah [*pur*da] *n* system of seclusion of women in the East; curtain shutting off Indian women's quarters; striped cotton cloth for curtains.

pure [*pewr*] *adj* unmixed with other substances; unmixed; clean; not tainted by sin, evil motives *etc*; chaste, virginal; complete, utter; sheer; abstract, not applied to practical purposes; of high standard; not born of a mixture of breeds or races ~ **purely** *adv* ~ **pureness** *n*.

purée [*pew*Ray] *n* (*Fr*) any soft food boiled to a pulp and sieved; soup made from this.

purfle [*pur*f'l] *v/t* (*ar*) embroider with a border; (*archi*) ornament with crockets; inlay.

purgation [pur*gay*shon] *n* cleansing from sin or impurities; (*med*) evacuation of the bowels by means of purgative medicine; ritual purification; (*hist*) act of clearing oneself from an accusation of crime.

purgative [*pur*gativ] *n* and *adj* (medicine) causing evacuation of the bowels; (that) which cleanses.

purgatorial [purga*taw*Ri-al] *adj* of purgatory; purifying.

purgatory [*pur*gateRi] *n* (*theol*) state or place in which souls of those who die in a state of grace expiate past sins and are made fit for Heaven; (*fig*) suffering considered as expiating sin; (*coll*) place or state of temporary suffering.

purge [*purj*] *v/t* cleanse, purify; cause evacuation

587

of (the bowels) by medicines; drive out (guilt *etc*); (*pol*) expel unreliable or unwanted members from (a party), *esp* with arrests, executions *etc*; (*leg*) clear oneself from (accusation); expiate (offence) through punishment ~ **purge** *n* purgative medicine; large-scale expulsions from a political party, *esp* with arrests *etc*.

purification [pewrRifi*kay*shon] *n* act of cleansing; state of being cleansed; ritual cleansing from guilt or from pollution incurred by breaking taboos.

purificatory [pewrRifi*kay*teRi] *adj* that cleanses or purifies, *esp* ritually.

purify [*pewr*Rifi] *v/t* make pure.

purism [*pewr*Rizm] *n* strict observance of correctness in grammar or style; example of this ~ **purist** *n* and *adj*.

Puritan [*pewr*Ritan] *n* one whose religious and moral standards are very severe; (*hist*) member of the extreme Protestant wing of the Church of England in the 16th and 17th centuries, opposing episcopacy and ritualism; opponent of Charles I in the Civil War ~ **puritan** *adj* puritanical.

puritanical [pewrRi*tan*ikal] *adj* of or like a Puritan; narrow and strict in religion and morals.

Puritanism [*pewr*Ritanizm] *n* outlook or principles of a Puritan.

purity [*pewr*Riti] *n* state or quality of being pure; chastity; cleanliness; freedom from admixture.

purl (1) [*purl*] *n* (*knitting*) inverted stitch giving a horizontal wavy effect; (*lace-making*) ornamental edging loop ~ **purl** *v/t* and *i* knit purl stitch; make edging loop.

purl (2) *v/i* flow with gentle rippling sound.

purl (3) *n* mixture of hot beer and gin.

purl (4) *v/i* (*coll*) fall heavily, *esp* from horseback.

purler [*purl*er] *n* (*coll*) heavy fall, *esp* from a horse.

purlieu [*pur*lew] *n* (*leg*) border of a forest; (*pl*) outskirts of any place; slum areas.

purlin [*pur*lin] *n* (*bui*) horizontal beam in a roof, at right angles to the principal rafters.

purloin [pur*loin*] *v/t* steal, pilfer.

purple [*purp*'l] *n* colour combining red and blue; cloth of this colour, *esp* as symbol of royalty; **raised to the p.** made cardinal ~ **purple** *adj* of purple colour; (*poet*) deep red; **p. emperor** large butterfly with purple and yellow wings; **p. heart** (*US*) army medal awarded for wounds received on active service; (*sl*) heart-shaped tablet of stimulant drug; **p. patch** intensely and often ridiculously eloquent passage of writing ~ **purple** *v/t* and *i* make or become purple.

purport [*pur*pawrt] *n* meaning, significance; intention, purpose ~ **purport** [per*pawrt*] *v/t* signify, imply; seem to imply, claim to be.

purpose [*pur*pus] *n* goal, object one intends to attain; resolute application of activity towards attaining a goal; **of set p.** firmly resolved, deliberately; **on p.** deliberately, intentionally; **to the p.** relevant ~ **purpose** *v/t* intend.

purposeful [*pur*pusfool] *adj* intentional; having definite purpose ~ **purposefully** *adv* ~ **purposefulness** *n*.

purposeless [*pur*pusles] *adj* lacking a plan or intention; aimless; meaningless; not resolute ~ **purposelessly** *adv* ~ **purposelessness** *n*.

purposely [*pur*pusli] *adv* on purpose, deliberately.

purposive [*pur*pusiv] *adj* tending to serve some purpose; acting with definite purpose.

purpureal [purpewrR-al] *adj* (*poet*) purple.

purr [*pur*] *n* deep vibrating sound made by a cat when pleased; deep humming sound of a powerful motor-engine ~ **purr** *v/i* and *t* make a purring sound; express by purring; (*fig*) express pleasure as if by purring.

purse [*purs*] *n* small bag or case for carrying cash; wealth, funds; sum of money subscribed as a gift or prize; (*US*) handbag ~ **purse** *v/t* thrust out and pucker up (the lips).

purse-proud [*purs*-pRowd] *adj* ostentatiously proud of one's riches.

purser [*purs*er] *n* officer in a ship who keeps the accounts, and superintends the passengers and their requirements.

purse-strings [*purs*-stRingz] *n* (*pl*) (*fig*) control of expenditure.

pursiness [*pur*sines] *n* state of being pursy; shortness of breath.

purslane [*purs*lin] *n* low fleshy herb cultivated for salad.

pursuance [persew-ans] *n* pursuit (of some end); carrying on, continuance ~ **pursuant** [persew-ant] *adj* following upon, in accordance with.

pursue [persew] *v/t* and *i* follow with intent to overtake and capture or kill; follow closely upon; follow to a desired end; carry on (an occupation); proceed along (a path); (*Scots law*) sue in a court of law; follow in pursuit; continue (speaking) ~ **pursuer** *n*.

pursuit [persewt] *n* act of pursuing; a hunt; that which one does, occupation, business; recreation; (*Scots law*) prosecution.

pursuivant [*pur*swivant] *n* officer of the College of Arms ranking below a Herald; (*poet*) attendant.

pursy [*pur*si] *adj* short-winded; fat.

purulence [*pewr*Roolens] *n* state or quality of being purulent.

purulent [*pewr*Roolent] *adj* forming or discharging pus, festering ~ **purulently** *adv*.

purvey [pervay] *v/t* provide, supply.

purveyance [pervay-ans] *n* providing of victuals.

purveyor [pervay-er] *n* one who supplies provisions for a large household or institution; army supply official; (*hist*) domestic officer who collected provisions for the sovereign.

purview [*pur*vew] *n* range, scope; clause expressing an enactment of a statute.

pus [*pus*] *n* yellowish-white viscid matter produced by inflamed or infected flesh.

push [*poosh*] *v/t* and *i* propel in front of one; drive before one; (*fig*) press hard upon; (*fig*) use one's influence to help (person or scheme) forward; (*coll*) illegally sell (drugs); **p. off** (*in a boat*) push oneself away from the shore; (*coll*) go away; **p. on** make one's way forward with some difficulty; **p. out** (*of a boat*) move away from the shore; **p. up the daisies** (*sl*) be dead and buried ~ **push** *n* act of pushing; self-assertiveness, energetic pursuit of one's ambitions; (*sl*) gang, group; (*mil*) strong onslaught or advance; **at a p.** in an emergency; **get the p.** (*sl*) be dismissed from a job; **make a p.** make a strong effort.

pushball [*poosh*bawl] *n* team game played with a ball six feet in diameter.

push-basket [*poosh*-baaskit] *n* basket on wheels in which shopping can be pushed along.
push-bike [*poosh*-bIk] *n* (*coll*) pedal-bicycle.
pushcart [*poosh*kaart] *n* small low cart in which a child can be pushed along; small barrow.
pushchair [*poosh*chair] *n* collapsible wheeled chair for a small child.
pusher [*poosh*er] *n* one who pushes; one who strives hard to advance himself; (*coll*) one who sells illegal drugs; a part of a machine that thrusts; table-implement used by child too young to have a knife and fork.
pushful [*poosh*fool] *adj* (*coll*) too self-assertive.
pushing [*pooshing*] *adj* thrusting; self-assertive; too ambitious or self-confident; energetic ~ **pushingly** *adv* ~ **pushingness** *n.*
pushover [*poosh*Over] *n* (*coll*) something very easy to do; someone very easy to seduce, outwit *etc.*
pushpin [*poosh*pin] *n* (*US*) drawing-pin.
Pushtu, Pushtoo [*pusht*OO] *n* Afghan language.
pushy [*pooshi*] *adj* (*coll*) too ambitious, interfering, or self-assertive.
pusillanimity [pewsilanimiti] *n* cowardice.
pusillanimous [pewsilanimus] *adj* cowardly, timid ~ **pusillanimously** *adv.*
puss [*poos*] *n* (*coll*) cat; hare; mischievous girl; **p. in the corner** a children's game.
puss-moth [*poos*-moth] *n* large European moth with a downy body.
pussy [*poosi*] *n* (*coll*) cat; (*vulg*) vulva.
pussycat[*poosi*kat] *n* (*coll*) cat; catkin.
pussyfoot [*poosi*foot] *v/i* (*US sl*) walk softly; proceed warily, conceal one's plans; refrain from committing oneself ~ **pussyfoot** *n* (*sl*) prohibitionist.
pussy-willow [*poosi*-wilO] *n* willow-tree bearing woolly catkins.
pustular [*pust*ewler] *adj* of, having pustules.
pustulate[*pust*ewlayt] *v/t* and *i* form into pustules.
pustule [*pust*ewl] *n* pimple containing pus; (*bot*) small excrescence on a leaf; (*zool*) warty swelling.
pustulous [*pust*ewlus] *adj* having pustules.
put (1) (*pres/part* putting, *p/t* and *p/part* put) [*poot*] *v/t* and *i* place, set, lay; cause to be in specified condition; move towards; throw; write down; explain, express; direct; apply; estimate, reckon; assign a rank or value to; arrange, lay out; fix; propose, suggest; (*naut*) steer, turn; **p. about** spread (rumour); (*coll*) vex, worry; (*naut*) steer on different course; **p. across** (*coll*) express or explain effectively, be convincing; **p. it across** (*sl*) outwit; **p. away** lay aside; save up, store; (*sl*) kill; imprison; (*coll*) eat or drink; **p. back** replace; retard, check; (*naut*) return; **p. by** save up, store; **p. down** suppress; write down; reckon; enter in account book, subscription list *etc*; kill (animal); **p. forward** propose, suggest; advance (clock); **p. forth** sprout; extend; exert; (*poet*) set out (to sea), launch; **p. in** insert, interpose; do; present, submit; **p. in at** halt at, make a short stay at; (*naut*) call at (a port); **p. in for** apply for; **p. off** postpone, defer; evade (question); discourage; disgust; hinder, annoy; **p. on** clothe oneself in; assume; increase, add; produce on stage; set to work; bet; **p. on** to give information about; help to find or communicate with; **p. out** extend; exert; extinguish, annoy, disconcert;

invest; dislocate; **p. over** communicate or express successfully; **stay p.** remain in place, not move; **p. through** link (one person) by telephone with another; cause to undergo; do, complete; **p. to** suggest, submit; set to work at; (*naut*) steer for the land; **p. together** construct, make; **p. up** raise; propose; suggest; give food and lodging to; lodge; startle (game); (*ar*) sheathe; **p. them up** (*coll*) raise fists ready for boxing; **p. (one) up to** incite, suggest; **p. up with** endure, tolerate; **p. upon** bully, take advantage of; **p. the weight** see put (2); **p. wise** (*sl*) enlighten.
put (2), **putt** (*pres/part* **putting**, *p/t* and *p/part* **putted**) [*put*] *v/t* (*golf*) strike ball gently so that it rolls along the green; (*athletics*) throw (a weight) by lifting it to the shoulder and then thrusting the arm out ~ **put, putt** *n* act of putting; distance that a ball or weight is putted.
putative [*pewt*ativ] *adj* supposed, commonly thought ~ **putatively** *adv.*
put-down [*poot*-down] *n* crushing reply, snub.
putlog [*poot*log] *n* horizontal support for scaffold boards > PDBl.
putrefaction [pewtRifakshon] *n* process of putrefying; rotting matter.
putrefactive [pewtRifaktiv] *adj* causing rotting.
putrefy [*pewt*Rifi] *v/i* decompose, rot.
putrescence [pewtResens] *n* process of becoming putrid; putrescent matter ~ **putrescent** *adj* rotting, decaying.
putridity [pewtRiditi] *n* condition of being putrid.
putrid[*pewt*Rid] *adj* rotten, decayed; stinking; (*sl*) very unpleasant ~ **putridly** *adv.*
putsch [*pooch*] *n* (*Germ*) revolution, political rising.
putt see put (2).
puttee (*pl* **puttees**) [*put*ee/*put*i] *n* strip of cloth wound round the leg from ankle to knee.
putter [*put*er] *n* (*golf*) club used for putting; (*Scots*) one who throws a heavy weight.
putti see putto.
puttier [*put*i-er] *n* one who applies putty.
putting-green [*put*ing-gReen] *n* (*golf*) level closely-mown turf round the hole into which the ball is putted.
putto (*pl* **putti**) [*poot*-tO] *n* (*Ital*) (*arts*) figure of small naked boy, Cupid.
putty [*put*i] *n* fine cement of clay and linseed oil used by glaziers; fine cement of lime and water; polishing powder of tin and lead ~ **putty** *v/t* fix or fill in with putty; polish with putty.
put-up [*poot*-up] *adj* (*coll*) dishonestly arranged so as to deceive or cheat.
put-upon [*poot*-upon] *adj* bullied, exploited.
puzzle [*puz*'l] *v/t* and *i* perplex, confuse, baffle; be bewildered by, think over; **p. out** solve something perplexing ~ **puzzle** *n* that which puzzles; problem, difficult question; verbal problem, riddle *etc*; mechanism, apparatus or game to test ingenuity.
puzzlement[*puz*'lment] *n* perplexity.
puzzler [*puz*ler] *n* one who puzzles; puzzling question.
pyedog[*pI*dog] *n* stray dog, *esp* in India.
pyelitis [pI-elItis] *n* inflammation of the inner kidney.
pygal [*pI*gal] *adj* (*zool*) of or on the rump.
pygmean, pigmean [*pig*mi-an] *adj* small.

pygmy, pigmy [*pig*mi] *n* and *adj* (one) of the dwarf race; (person) of stunted growth.

pyjamas (*US* **pajamas**) [pij*aa*maz] *n* (*pl*) sleeping suit of jacket and trousers; loose trousers worn by Muslims ∼ **pyjama** *adj*.

pylon [*pyl*on] *n* tall structure, *usu* of steel girders, carrying overhead electric cables; tower set as guiding mark for aircraft; (*archi*) gateway, *esp* of Egyptian temple.

pylorus [pi*law*Rus] *n* (*anat*) the opening from the stomach into the duodenum.

pyo- *pref* of pus.

pyorrhoea [pi-o*Ree*-a] *n* discharge of pus; a disease of the gums.

pyracanth [*pir*Rakanth] *n* evergreen thorny shrub with white flowers and scarlet berries.

pyramid [*pi*Ramid] *n* (*geom*) solid figure having a polygon for its base, the other faces being triangles with a common vertex; Egyptian stone tomb of this shape; anything of this form; (*pl*) a billiard game; **p. selling** form of financial exploitation where agents are induced to buy goods for resale and paid to recruit sub-agents.

pyramidal [pi*Ram*idal] *adj* of or like a pyramid.

pyre [*pir*] *n* pile of wood for burning a corpse.

pyrethrum [pir*Reeth*Rum] *n* genus of composite plants akin to chrysanthemums; feverfew; **p. powder** an insecticide.

pyretic [pir*Ret*ik] *adj* of, causing, or curing fever.

pyrexia [pir*Rek*si-a] *n* (*med*) feverish condition.

pyrites [pir*Ri*teez] *n* (*chem*) natural sulphide of iron, copper, cobalt or nickel > PDS.

pyro- *pref* of fire; (*chem*) obtained by heating.

pyrolysis [pir*Rol*isis] *n* chemical decomposition by heat.

pyromania [pirRO*may*ni-a] *n* kind of insanity with a tendency towards incendiarism.

pyrometer [pir*Rom*iter] *n* instrument for measuring high temperatures > PDS.

pyrope [*pir*ROp] *n* a deep red garnet.

pyrotechnic [pirRO*tek*nik] *adj* of or like fireworks ∼ **pyrotechnics** *n* (*pl*) firework display.

pyrotechny [*pir*ROtekni] *n* the making and displaying of fireworks.

Pyrrhic [*pi*Rik] *adj* **P. victory** victory gained at too great a cost.

python [*pi*thon] *n* large, tropical, non-venomous snake that crushes its prey.

pythoness [*pi*thones] *n* oracular priestess of Apollo; prophetess; sorceress.

pyx [*piks*] *n* case in which the consecrated Host is kept or carried; box at the Royal Mint in which specimen gold and silver coins are kept ∼ **pyx** *v/t* test (coins) for weight and quality.

pyxis [*pik*sis] *n* (*class arch*) small box or casket.

Q

q [*kew*] seventeenth letter of the English alphabet.
qua [*kway*] *adv* in the capacity or character of.
quack (1) [*kwak*] *n* the cry of a duck; an outcry ~
quack *v/i* and *t* cry like a duck; talk in a harsh high-pitched voice; chatter, gabble.
quack (2) *n* one who falsely claims knowledge or skill, *esp* in medicine; charlatan ~ **quack** *adj* of or like a quack or quackery.
quackery [*kwak*eRi] *n* the practice of a quack; charlatanry.
quad (1) [*kwod*] *n* (*coll*) quadrangle; quadruplet; quadraphonic.
quad (2) *n* (*typ*) a quadrat ~ **quad** *v/t* insert quadrats in.
quad (3) see **quod**.
quadragenarian [kwodRajen*air*Ri-an] *n* and *adj* (one who is) forty years old.
Quadragesima [kwodRaj*esi*ma] *n* the first Sunday in Lent.
quadrangle [*kwod*Rang-g'l] *n* (*geom*) plane figure defined by four points; square or rectangular courtyard with buildings round it.
quadrant [*kwod*Rant] *n* (*geom*) quarter of a circle or sphere; (*astron*, *naut*) instrument of this shape for measuring angles.
quadraphonic [kwodRa*fo*nik] *adj* of or in a form of stereophonic sound reproduction using four loudspeakers.
quadrat [*kwod*Rat] *n* (*typ*) piece of metal lower than type, used for spacing.
quadrate [*kwod*Rayt] *n* and *adj* (a) square ~ **quadrate** [kwod*Rayt*] *v/t* and *i* square; correspond, agree.
quadratic [kwod*Rat*ik] *adj* having, of, or like, a square; **q. equation** (*math*) equation involving the square of the unknown quantity > PDS.
quadratics [kwod*Rat*iks] *n* (*pl*) algebra of quadratic equations.
quadrature [*kwod*Racher] *n* (*math*) expressing an area (*esp* that of a circle) in terms of a square; (*astron*) relative position of two heavenly bodies 90° from each other.
quadrennial [kwod*Ren*i-al] *adj* comprising or lasting four years; occurring every four years ~ **quadrennially** *adv*.
quadrennium [kwod*Ren*i-um] *n* four years.
quadri-, quadru- *pref* four.
quadrilateral [kwodRi*late*Ral] *n* and *adj* (figure) having four sides and four angles.
quadrille [kwod*Ril*] *n* dance for four couples; music for this; game played by four persons with forty cards.
quadrillion [kwod*Ril*i-on] *n* the number produced by raising a million (*US*, a thousand) to the fourth power.
quadripartite [kwodRi*paart*It] *adj* having four parts; negotiated or contracted by four parties.
quadriplegia [kwodRi*pleeji*-a] *n* (*med*) paralysis of both arms and both legs.
quadrivalent [kwodRi*val*ent/kwodRi*vayl*ent] *adj* (*chem*) having a valency of four; tetravalent.

quadroon [kwod*ROOn*] *n* offspring of a white person and a mulatto.
quadruped [*kwod*Rooped] *n* and *adj* (animal) having four feet.
quadruple [kwod*Roop*'l] *n* number four times another ~ **quadruple** *adj* fourfold; having four parts; multiplied by four ~ **quadruple** *v/t* multiply by four.
quadruplet [*kwod*ROOplit] *n* one of four children born at one birth; one of a set of four things.
quadruplex [*kwod*ROOpleks] *adj* fourfold.
quadruplicate [kwod*ROO*plikat] *n* one of four copies ~ **quadruplicate** *adj* copied four times; fourfold ~ **quadruplicate** *v/t* make fourfold; make four copies of.
quaff [*kwof*] *v/t* and *i* drink in large draughts.
quag [*kwag/kwog*] *n* marshy ground.
quagga [*kwaga/kwoga*] *n* S. African animal allied to the ass and the zebra.
quaggy [*kwagi/kwogi*] *adj* boggy.
quagmire [*kwag*mIr/*kwog*mIr] *n* marsh; soft boggy ground.
quail (1) [*kwayl*] *v/i* be afraid, cower.
quail (2) *n* a small gamebird.
quaint [*kwaynt*] *adj* attractively unusual, *esp* if old-fashioned; odd, fanciful, whimsical ~ **quaintly** *adv* ~ **quaintness** *n*.
quake [*kwayk*] *v/i* tremble, shiver; rock from side to side ~ **quake** *n* tremor; (*coll*) earthquake.
Quaker [*kway*ker] *n* member of the Society of Friends, a pacifist and undogmatic Christian body.
qualifiable [kwolif*I*-ab'l] *adj* that can be qualified or modified.
qualification [kwolifi*kay*shon] *n* act of qualifying; state of being qualified; that which qualifies; modification; limitation of meaning; suitable ability.
qualificatory [*kwo*lifikayteRi] *adj* that qualifies.
qualified [*kwo*lifId] *adj* capable; having the requisite qualifications or ability, eligible.
qualify [*kwo*lifI] *v/t* and *i* give necessary qualities or powers (to); train for a career *etc*; acquire specified degree of knowledge *etc* to undertake a career or profession; make or become competent or legally empowered; modify; make conditional, limit; lessen, moderate.
qualitative [*kwo*litativ] *adj* of, or pertaining to, quality; dealing only with the nature and not the amounts of substances > PDS ~ **qualitatively** *adv*.
quality [*kwo*liti] *n* essential or distinguishing characteristic; good moral, mental or aesthetic characteristic; virtue; degree of goodness or value; high social rank; (*obs* or *joc*) people of high rank ~ **quality** *adj* (*coll*) of high quality, excellent.
qualm [*kwaam*] *n* feeling of nausea; faintness; scruple; misgiving, uneasiness.
quandary [*kwon*deRi] *n* perplexing difficulty; dilemma.
quango [*kwang*O] *n* (*pol*) any administrative board

or commission or similar public body to which the government appoints members but which is not a departmental committee; (US) any nongovernmental, non-profit-making corporation.

quant [kwont] n flanged punting-pole.

quanta see quantum.

quantifier [kwontifI-er] n word or prefix expressing quantity.

quantify [kwontifI] v/t measure or express the quantity of; (log) indicate the quantity of terms in a proposition.

quantitative [kwontitaytiv] adj of or pertaining to quantity; dealing with quantities as well as the nature of substances > PDS.

quantity [kwontiti] n size; amount; extent; specified amount or number; large amount; property of being measurable; that which can be measured or mathematically computed; (pros, phon) length of a sound or syllable, duration; (mus) duration; **negligible q.** person or thing that can be ignored; **q. surveyor** expert who estimates costs of building; **unknown q.** person or thing whose acts, influence etc cannot be foretold.

quantize [kwontIz] v/t and i restrict to discrete values or quanta.

quantum (pl **quanta**) [kwontum] n quantity; amount; proportion; sufficiency; (phys) definite amount of energy associated with electromagnetic waves > PDS; **q. theory** theory that radiation is emitted through space not continuously but in discrete quanta > PDS.

quarantine [kwoRanteen] n period of isolation imposed on persons, animals or ships that may be carriers of infectious disease; isolation under medical observation; place where persons etc are isolated ~ **quarantine** v/t isolate for medical reasons.

quark [kwaark] n (phys) hypothetical particle, the four forms of which are postulated as the basis of all matter.

quarrel (1) [kwoRel] n angry disagreement; dispute, brawl; cause of this, grievance; breach of friendship ~ **quarrel** (pres/part **quarrelling**, p/t and p/part **quarrelled**) v/i disagree or argue angrily; squabble; be annoyed, find fault.

quarrel (2) n short square-headed arrow; (bui) pane of glass in leaded lights.

quarrelsome [kwoRelsum] adj inclined to quarrel; easily provoked.

quarry (1) [kwoRi] n open pit from which building stone, sand, gravel etc are taken; source of information ~ **quarry** v/t and i dig from a quarry.

quarry (2) n animal being hunted or pursued as prey; one who or that which is eagerly sought.

quarry (3) n diamond-shaped pane of glass in leaded lights; unglazed paving or tile.

quart (1) [kwawrt] n quarter of a gallon, two pints; vessel containing two pints.

quart (2) n four successive cards of the same suit; fourth parrying position in fencing.

quartan [kwawrtan] n and adj (fever) recurring every fourth day.

quarte see **carte** (2).

quarter [kwawrter] n one fourth part of a whole; one of the four points of the compass; direction; area, district of a town; one of four subdivisions; one of four divisions of the financial year; first

or third phase of the moon; act of sparing a surrendered enemy, mercy; (of weight) one fourth of a hundredweight; one fourth of a ton; one fourth of a pound; (naut) the side of a ship between midships and stern; a direction 45° to either side; (pl) lodgings; group of persons; (pl mil) barracks; billets; (naut) station, post ~ **quarter** v/t divide into four equal parts; provide food and lodgings for; cut a corpse or carcass in four.

quarterage [kwawrteRij] n quarterly payment.

quarterday [kwawrterday] n the day which begins each quarter of the year on which payments fall due etc.

quarterdeck [kwawrterdek] n upper deck from stern to main-mast; area of deck restricted to officers.

quartering [kwawrteRing] n act of dividing in four; assignment of lodgings; (her) division of a shield containing many coats of arms.

quarterly [kwawrterli] adv once every three months; at every quarterday ~ **quarterly** adj done, paid, published etc once every three months ~ **quarterly** n magazine published quarterly.

quartermaster [kwawrtermaaster] n (mil) officer who organizes billeting and the issue of provisions, equipment etc; (naval) the seaman in charge of the steering.

quartern [kwawrtern] n a standard-sized large loaf of bread.

quarter-sessions [kwawrter-seshonz] n (pl) court held by Justices of the Peace every three months in every county or borough.

quarterstaff [kwawrterstaaf] n short stout pole used as weapon.

quartet, quartette [kwawrtet] n (mus) composition for four instruments or for four voices; four performers for such music; group of four people or things.

quarto [kwawrtO] n book whose sheets are folded into four leaves or eight pages; size of paper, about 9 × 12 in.

quartz [kwawrts] n natural crystalline silica; **q. clock** clock operated by electric vibration of quartz crystal.

quartzite [kwawrtsIt] n sandstone with a deposit of quartz.

quasar [kwayzaar] n (astron) quasi-stellar radio source; extremely dense star emitting high-energy electromagnetic radiation, of unknown origin.

quash [kwosh] v/t make void, annul, subdue.

quasi- pref apparently; not quite; as if; to some extent; partially resembling.

quassia [kwosha] n an American tropical tree which yields a bitter tonic.

quatercentenary [kwotersenteeneRi] n fourhundredth anniversary.

quaternary [kwoturneRi] adj consisting of four; by fours; (geol) of the era after the Tertiary; **q. number** four; sometimes taken as factorial four, equal to ten.

quaternion [kwoturni-on] n a group of four; (pl) (math) a form of calculus.

quatrain [kwotRayn] n four-line stanza, usu rhyming alternately.

quatrefoil [katRefoil] n leaf or flower with four

divisions; an ornament which has four petals or leaflets radiating from a common centre.

quattrocento [kwatROchentO] *n* (*Ital*) the 15th century; Italian art style of this era > PDAA.

quaver [*kway*ver] *n* shaking of the voice; trill; quiver; (*mus*) note half as long as a crotchet ~ **quaver** *v/i* quiver, vibrate; sing or play with trills; speak in a shaky voice.

quay [*kee*] *n* landing-place, pier, wharf.

quean [*kween*] *n* (*ar*) slut, hussy; (*Scots*) young woman; (*Aust sl*) effeminate boy; homosexual.

queasy [*kwee*zi] *adj* sick, feeling nausea; causing nausea; fastidious, easily disgusted or shocked ~ **queasily** *adv* ~ **queasiness** *n*.

queen [*kween*] *n* wife of a king; female sovereign; large fertile female bee, ant, termite *etc*; dominating or extremely attractive woman; most powerful piece at chess; playing-card bearing image of a queen; unspayed female cat; (*sl*, *pej*) effeminate man, homosexual; **q. dowager** widow of a king; **q. mother** mother of reigning sovereign; **q. of the May** pretty girl chosen to preside at May Day feast ~ **queen** *v/t* and *i* make a queen of; rule as queen; (*chess*) convert pawn into queen on reaching eighth line; **q. it** behave like a queen; dominate.

queen-cake [*kween*-kayk] *n* small soft currant cake.

queening [*kween*ing] *n* a winter apple.

queenly [*kween*li] *adj* of, like or befitting a queen; stately; nobly beautiful ~ **queenliness** *n*.

queer [*kweer*] *adj* odd, strange; unwell, indisposed; rousing suspicion; slightly dishonest; (*coll*, *pej*) homosexual; (*coll*) slightly mad; (*sl*) criminal; **q. street** financial difficulties; dishonest dealings ~ **queer** *n* (*coll*, *pej*) male homosexual; **in q.** (*sl*) in trouble ~ **queer** *v/t* (*sl*) spoil; **q. one's pitch** spoil one's chances of success ~ **queerly** *adv* ~ **queerness** *n*.

quell [*kwel*] *v/t* suppress, subdue; allay.

quench [*kwench*] *v/t* extinguish, put out; slake, allay (thirst); destroy; repress, subdue; (*metal*) harden (steel) by immersing in water to cool rapidly.

querist [*kweer*Rist] *n* inquirer, questioner.

quern [*kwurn*] *n* stone handmill for corn.

querulous [*kwe*Roolus] *adj* complaining; discontented; fretful ~ **querulously** *adv* ~ **querulousness** *n*.

query [*kweer*Ri] *n* question; doubt, objection; question-mark ~ **query** *v/t* question; express doubt about; mark with a query.

quest [*kwest*] *n* act of seeking; search; expedition in search of; (*ar*) inquest ~ **quest** *v/i* go in search (of).

question [*kwes*chon] *n* act of asking or inquiring; that which is asked; sentence requiring a reply; matter to be discussed; that which is doubtful, problem; matter, affair; (*hist*) torture to extract information; **call in q.** express doubt about ~ **question** *v/t* and *i* express doubt about; inquire, ask a question; interrogate; object.

questionable [*kwes*chonab'l] *adj* that can or should be questioned; dubious, suspicious; dishonest; discreditable ~ **questionably** *adv*.

question-begging [kweschon-*beging*] *adj* (*of argument*) assuming the truth of a point still disputed.

questioner [*kwes*choner] *n* one who asks questions.

question-mark [*kwes*chon-maark] *n* punctuation mark (?) indicating the preceding sentence to be a question.

question-master [*kwes*chon-maaster] *n* one who answers questions from competitors in a guessing game or puts questions to a brains-trust team.

questionnaire [kweschon*air*] *n* series of questions, *esp* written on a form.

question-time [*kwes*chon-tIm] *n* period assigned to Members of Parliament for questioning Ministers, or to audience for questioning a lecturer *etc*.

queue [*kew*] *n* line of people or vehicles waiting in order of arrival to obtain something, enter a place *etc*; (*fig*) waiting list; (*hist*) man's pigtail; **q. jumper** (*coll*) one who tries to be served or admitted out of turn ~ **queue** *v/i* wait in a queue, line up; **q. for** queue in order to obtain; **q. up** form a queue.

quibble [*kwib*'l] *n* evasive answer or distinction; trivial argument; play on words, pun ~ **quibble** *v/i* evade the point; make puns ~ **quibbler** *n*.

quibbling [*kwib*ling] *adj* equivocating, avoiding the point by petty arguments or distinctions.

quiche [*keesh*] *n* (*Fr*) savoury open tart.

quick [*kwik*] *adj* rapid, swift; sudden; intelligent; acting or reacting rapidly; not lasting long; (*ar*) alive; (*ar*) pregnant ~ **quick** *n* sensitive flesh below finger- or toe-nail; sensitive wound; (*ar*) (*pl*) living persons; **cut to the q.** gravely hurt the feelings of ~ **quick** *adv* rapidly; soon.

quicken [*kwik*en] *v/t* and *i* move more rapidly; cause to be quick; give or restore life to; inspire, urge on; (*of foetus*) show signs of life; revive.

quick-firing [kwik-*fI*Ring] *adj* (*of gun*) automatically firing many bullets in quick succession.

quickie [*kwik*i] *n* (*coll*) something done unusually fast; something very brief.

quicklime [*kwik*lIm] *n* unslaked lime.

quickly [*kwik*li] *adv* rapidly; soon.

quickness [*kwik*nes] *n* speed; rapidity; alertness; intelligence.

quicksand [*kwik*sand] *n* very soft wet sand.

quickset [*kwik*set] *adj* composed of living plants; **q. hedge** hawthorn hedge.

quicksilver [*kwik*silver] *n* mercury.

quickstep [*kwik*step] *n* a rapid ballroom dance; music for this; (*mil*) pace of quick marching.

quicktime [*kwik*tIm] *n* (*mil*) customary rate of marching, 128 steps a minute.

quick-witted [kwik-*wit*id] *adj* intelligent; reacting quickly and cleverly; witty.

quid (1) [*kwid*] *n* piece of chewing tobacco.

quid (2) *n* (*sl*) a pound (in money).

quiddity [*kwid*iti] *n* essence; quibble.

quiescence, quiescency [kwI-*es*ens, kwI-*es*ensi] *n* state of being quiescent.

quiescent [kwI-*es*ent] *adj* still, tranquil, calm; passive ~ **quiescently** *adv*.

quiet [*kwI*-et] *adj* free from disturbance, peaceful, calm; motionless; silent; subdued, discreet; secluded; monotonous; serene ~ **quiet** *n* state or quality of being quiet; peace; silence ~ **quiet** *v/t* and *i* quieten.

quieten [*kwI*-eten] *v/t* and *i* calm down, make quiet; become quiet.

quietism [*kwI*-etizm] *n* form of mysticism based on passive contemplation; calmness, placidity ~ **quietist** *n* and *adj*.

quietly [*kwI*-etli] *adv* in a quiet way ~ **quietness** *n*.

quietude [*kwI*-etewd] *n* calmness, repose.

quietus [kwI-*ee*tus] *n* finishing stroke; death.

quiff [*kwif*] *n* curl or tuft of hair on forehead; (*sl*) clever trick.

quill [*kwil*] *n* hollow stem of bird's feather; long wing-feather; pen made from a large strong feather; spine of a porcupine; bobbin, spool ~ **quill** *v/t* pleat; wind on a quill.

quilt [*kwilt*] *n* bedcover made of cloth stitched together with a soft warm padding between ~ **quilt** *v/t* stitch two pieces of cloth together with padding between.

quilting [*kwilt*ing] *n* process of making quilts; material for making quilts.

quin [*kwin*] *n* (*coll*) quintuplet.

quinary [*kwI*neRi] *adj* of or in fives.

quince [*kwins*] *n* hard yellowish fruit with sharp flavour.

quincentenary [kwinsen*teen*eRi] *adj* and *n* (connected with) a five-hundredth anniversary.

quincunx (*pl* **quincunxes**) [*kwin*-kungks] *n* an arrangement of five objects in a square or rectangle, with one at each corner and one at the centre.

quinine [kwi*neen*/(*US*) *kwI*nIn] *n* bitter-tasting alkaloid obtained from cinchona bark and used medicinally > PDS.

quinqu-, quinque- *pref* five.

quinqua- *pref* fifty.

quinquagenarian [kwinkwaje*nair*Ri-an] *n* and *adj* (one who is) fifty years old.

Quinquagesima [kwinkwa*jes*ima] *n* the Sunday before Lent.

quinquenniad [kwin-*kwen*i-ad] *n* five years.

quinquennial [kwin-*kwen*i-al] *adj* occurring every fifth year; lasting for five years.

quinquennium (*pl* **quinquennia**) [kwin-*kwen*i-um] *n* a five-year period.

quinquereme [*kwin*-kwiReem] *n* (*hist*) galley having five benches of oars.

quinquevalent [kwin-kwi*vay*lent] *adj* (*chem*) having a valency of five > PDS.

quinsy [*kwin*zi] *n* tonsillitis with suppuration of the tonsils.

quint [*kwint*] *n* sequence of five cards of the same suit; (*mus*) a fifth.

quintain [*kwin*tayn] *n* (*hist*) post or object to be tilted at.

quintal [*kwin*tal] *n* a hundred kilograms.

quintan [*kwin*tan] *n* and *adj* (fever) recurring every fifth day.

quintessence [kwin*tes*ens] *n* fundamental essence; purest type or embodiment.

quintet, quintette [kwin*tet*] *n* (*mus*) composition for five voices or five instruments; five performers for such music; group of five people or things.

quintillion [kwin*til*yon] *n* fifth power of a million; (*US*) fifth power of a thousand.

quintuple [kwin*tew*p'l] *adj* and *n* fivefold (thing or amount) ~ **quintuple** *v/t* and *i* multiply fivefold; increase fivefold.

quintuplet [*kwin*tewplet] *n* one of five children born at one birth.

quip [*kwip*] *n* witty remark; jest ~ **quip** (*pres/part* **quipping**, *p/t* and *p/part* **quipped**) *v/i* make quips; scoff.

quipu [*keep*OO] *n* code of knotted cords used in ancient Peru for records, messages *etc*.

quire (1) [*kwIr*] *n* twenty-four sheets of paper.

quire (2) *n* (*ar*) choir.

quirk [*kwurk*] *n* fantastic oddity; sudden strange behaviour; trick; quibble; fantastic flourish.

quirt [*kwurt*] *n* short-handled riding whip.

quisling [*kwiz*ling] *n* traitor who aids the occupying enemy forces.

quit (*pres/part* **quitting**, *p/t* and *p/part* **quitted**) [*kwit*] *v/t* and *i* abandon, leave; depart from; (*coll*) cease, give up, desist; (*ar*) behave ~ **quit** *adj* released from obligation, free.

quitch [*kwich*] *n* couch-grass.

quitclaim [*kwit*klaym] *n* renunciation of legal right; deed embodying this.

quite [*kwIt*] *adv* entirely, absolutely; very; fairly, to some degree ~ **quite** *interj* certainly, of course.

quits [*kwits*] *n* and *adj* (state of) being on even terms, having reached equality; **cry q.** give up a rivalry or quarrel; **double or q.** act of repeating a wager, the previous loser undertaking to pay double or else be free of debt.

quittance [*kwit*ans] *n* discharge from debt or obligation; recompense; repayment.

quitter [*kwit*er] *n* one who abandons a task when difficulty arises.

quiver (1) [*kwiver*] *n* sheath for arrows.

quiver (2) *n* and *v/i* tremble, shake.

quixotic [kwik*sot*ik] *adj* showing extreme chivalrous generosity, utterly selfless; absurdly idealistic or romantic ~ **quixotically** *adv*.

quixotry [*kwik*sotRi] *n* quixotic behaviour.

quiz [*kwiz*] *n* public competition at answering questions or solving problems, *esp* as entertainment; series of questions; puzzle; (*ar*) hoax; (*ar*) one who teases; (*ar*) eccentric person ~ **quiz** (*pres/part* **quizzing**, *p/t* and *p/part* **quizzed**) *v/t* question closely; (*ar*) look mockingly or enviously at; (*ar*) tease, banter, hoax.

quizmaster [*kwiz*maaster] *n* one who questions the competitors in a quiz.

quizzical [*kwiz*ikal] *adj* mocking, ironic; comic ~ **quizzically** *adv*.

quod [*kwod*] *n* (*sl*) prison.

quoin [*koin*] *n* (*bui*) outer corner of a wall; large stone set in the corner of a wall; recess for a post.

quoit [*koit*] *n* flat ring for throwing round a peg; (*pl*) game of throwing these.

quondam [*kwon*dam] *adj* former.

quorum [*kwaw*Rum] *n* minimum number of members of a body required to transact business.

quota [*kwO*ta] *n* allotted share, allowance; proportional share; limited number of persons allowed to immigrate from any one country in one year; limited quantity of goods to be manufactured, sold *etc* in a stated period.

quotability [kwOta*bil*iti] *n* quality of being quotable.

quotable [*kwO*tab'l] *adj* that can be quoted; effective when quoted.

quotation [kwO*tay*shon] *n* act of quoting; saying

or passage quoted; current price of anything; price offered; **q. marks** punctuation marks (' ' or " ") enclosing quoted words.

quote [*kwOt*] *v/t* and *i* repeat another's words, cite; state current price of; offer a price ~ **quote** *n* (*coll*) quotation; (*print*) quotation mark.

quoth [*kwOth*] *v/i* (*ar, poet*) said, spoke.

quotidian [kw*Otidi*-an] *adj* daily; (*fig*) commonplace ~ **quotidian** *n* fever recurring daily.

quotient [*kwOshent*] *n* number resulting from division of one number by another; **intelligence q.** number indicating level of intelligence.

R

r [*aar*] eighteenth letter of the English alphabet; the three R's elementary reading, writing and arithmetic.

rabbet [*Rabit*] *n* joint in woodwork ~ rabbet *v/t* join by a rabbet.

Rabbi [*Rabī*] *n* Jewish minister of religion or teacher of the Law.

rabbin [*Rabin*] *n* Rabbi, *esp* early medieval.

rabbinic, rabbinical [Ra*bin*ik, Ra*bin*ikal] *adj* of or like a Rabbi; of Jewish ritual and teachings; of later Hebrew language or literature.

rabbit [*Rabit*] *n* a burrowing rodent akin to the hare; fur of this; (*coll*) feeble person; poor performer at a game; Welsh r. toasted cheese ~ rabbit *v/i* hunt or shoot rabbits; (*coll*) work perseveringly; talk persistently.

rabbit-hutch [*Rabit*-huch] *n* cage for tame rabbits.

rabbit-punch [*Rabit*-punch] *n* punch on back of neck.

rabbit-warren [*Rabit*-woRen] *n* piece of ground where rabbits burrow and breed; (*fig*) overcrowded confused mass of houses and streets, or rooms and passages.

rabbity [*Rabiti*] *adj* (*coll*) petty, of little value; full of rabbits; of or like a rabbit.

rabble [*Rab'l*] *n* noisy uncontrolled crowd, mob; (*cont*) common people.

rabble-rousing [*Rab'l*-Rowzing] *adj* crudely and emotionally eloquent; designed to rouse mob passions; inciting to violence or revolution.

Rabelaisian [Rabi*layzi*-an] *adj* of or like Rabelais; coarse, frankly and cheerfully obscene.

rabid [*Rabid*] *adj* raging, violent; mad; fanatical; infected with rabies ~ rabidly *adv* ~ rabidness *n*.

rabies [*Raybeez*] *n* infectious disease of dogs *etc* causing madness, hydrophobia.

raca [*Raaka*] *n* (*NT*) Hebrew word of scorn and condemnation.

raccoon, racoon [Ra*kOOn*] *n* furry N. American climbing carnivore.

race (1) [*Rays*] *n* contest of speed between persons, animals or vehicles; swift current of water; narrow water-channel; stream of air from aircraft propeller or turbine engine; rustling movement; groove, slot; (*pl*) horse-races ~ race *v/i* and *t* move very swiftly, rush; compete in speed (against); enter (horse) for a race; move too fast; (*coll*) gamble on horse-races; (*mot*) run an engine when not engaging with gears.

race (2) *n* one of several subdivisions of mankind distinguished by physical characteristics; (*biol*, *bot*) special breed or variety which will reproduce true to type; group descended from common ancestor; family; tribe, clan; any recognizable group sharing certain characteristics ~ race *adj* racial; concerning or regulating relationships between men of different races.

racecard [*Rays*kaard] *n* the day's programme at a race-meeting.

racecourse [*Rays*kawrs] *n* track on which horse-races are run.

raceginger [*Rays*jinjer] *n* unpulverized ginger.

racehorse [*Rays*hawrs] *n* horse bred for racing.

raceme [Ra*seem*] *n* (*bot*) inflorescence consisting of a number of small flowers on equal stalks springing from a central stalk.

race-meeting [*Rays*-meeting] *n* series of horse-races held at a certain course on a specified date.

racemic [Ra*seemik*] *adj* (*chem*) consisting of an equimolecular mixture of the two optically active forms of a substance > PDS.

racer [*Rayser*] *n* one who or that which competes in a race; racehorse; vessel or machine built for racing purposes.

racetrack [*Rayst*Rack] *n* closed track for horse-racing or motor-races.

rachitic [Ra*kitik*] *adj* of or suffering from rickets.

rachitis [Ra*kītis*] *n* rickets.

rachmanism [*Rak*manizm] *n* systematic intimidation of tenants to extort exorbitant rents.

racial [*Rays*hal] *adj* of race (2); concerning differences between races of men; of or regulating relationships between men of different races; r. discrimination legal or social disadvantages imposed by men of one race on those of another; r. prejudice irrational hatred, fear of, or contempt for, men of another race ~ racially *adv*.

racialism [*Rays*halizm] *n* belief that one race is superior to another; conscious and systematic racial prejudice and discrimination; policy of oppressing or exterminating racial minorities ~ racialist *adj* and *n*.

racily [*Rays*ili] *adv* in a racy way ~ raciness *n*.

racism [*Rays*izm] *n* racialism ~ racist *adj* and *n*.

rack (1) [*Rak*] *n* open framework of bars or slotted supports for holding plates, toast *etc* upright; slotted container for hay; group of pegs for hanging coats or hats on; (*hist*) instrument of torture on which men were stretched and dislocated; (*mech*) toothed bar, ratchet; on the r. in great pain or distress ~ rack *v/t* cause great pain or distress to; torture by stretching on the rack; oppress, make exorbitant demands on; r. one's brains make a painful effort to think.

rack (2) *n* light vaporous clouds; drifting wreckage; destruction ~ rack *v/i* drift in wind.

racket (1) [*Rakit*] *n* broad stringed bat used in tennis and similar games; (*pl*) ball-game played against a wall ~ racket *v/t* strike with a racket.

racket (2) *n* loud confused noise, din; excitement; revelry, dissipation; (*coll*) trick, scheme; fraudulent or illegal business; way of making money, *usu* dishonestly; stand the r. take responsibility; pay costs ~ racket *v/i* r. about live a wild life.

racketeer [Raki*teer*] *n* (*coll*) one who operates an illegal business ~ racketeer *v/i*.

rack-rent [*Rak*-Rent] *n* exorbitant rent.

raconteur [Rakon*tur*] *n* (*Fr*) skilful teller of stories.

racoon see raccoon.

racquet [*Rakit*] *n* tennis racket.

racy [*Rays*i] *adj* having strong characteristic flavour; lively, vigorous; amusing, *usu* daringly;

596

mildly indecent; **r. of the soil** characteristically rural (humour, opinions *etc*).

rad [*Rad*] *n* (*phys*) unit of absorbed dose of ionizing radiation equal to 100 ergs per gram.

radar [*Raydaar*] *n* generic term for electronic systems of direction-finding, navigation, and observation of distant objects; **r. trap** radar device for detecting vehicles breaking a speed-limit.

raddle [*Rad*'l] *v/t* paint (face) with rouge; mark with ruddle ~ **raddle** *n* ruddle ~ **raddled** *adj* looking old, worn-out or battered; crudely rouged.

radial [*Raydi*-al] *adj* of or like a ray or rays; issuing from a centre, radiating; of the radius bone.

radialize [*Raydi*-alIz] *v/t* cause to radiate; arrange in radiating pattern.

radial-ply [*Raydi*-al-plI] *n* and *adj* (tyre) with strong tread and fabric in parallel layers.

radian [*Raydi*-en] *n* the angle subtended at the centre of a circle by an arc equal in length to the radius of the circle > PDS.

radiance, radiancy [*Raydi*-ens, *Raydi*-ensi] *n* brightness issuing in rays; vivid brilliance.

radiant [*Raydi*-ant] *adj* emitting rays; shining, brilliant; showing great joy or obvious healthiness; (*phys*) transmitted by radiation ~ **radiant** *n* piece of refractory material radiating heat from gas or electric fire; (*phys*) focus of radiation; (*geom*) straight line assumed to rotate about a fixed pole; (*astron*) apparent central source of meteor shower ~ **radiantly** *adv*.

radiate [*Raydi*-ayt] *v/t* and *i* emit rays of light or heat, wave motions or streams of particles; extend or send out in all directions from a centre; spread out; diffuse; show plainly ~ **radiate** *adj* having rays.

radiation [*Raydi*-*ayshon*] *n* emission of rays; transmission of heat or of light > PDG; radioactivity; emission of electromagnetic waves; **r. sickness** illness caused by exposure to radioactivity.

radiator [*Raydi*-aytor] *n* that which radiates; heating apparatus through which hot air, water, steam *etc* passes; device for cooling the cylinders of a motor-engine; portable electric heater.

radical [*Radi*kal] *adj* thorough, complete; drastic; effecting or advocating far-reaching reforms; left-wing, progressive; basic, original; (*bot*) of or on a root; (*math*) of roots of numbers ~ **radical** *n* one who holds extreme left-wing views; one who advocates far-reaching reforms; (*chem*) radicle > PDS ~ **radically** *adv* fundamentally; completely, thoroughly.

radicalism [*Radi*kalizm] *n* radical political principles.

radicel [*Radi*sel] *n* small root.

radices [*Raydi*seez] *pl* of **radix**.

radicle [*Radi*k'l] *n* (*bot*) the part of an embryo that develops into a primary root; small root; (*chem*) group of atoms which maintains its identity through chemical changes which affect the rest of the molecule > PDS.

radii [*Raydi*-I] *pl* of **radius**.

radio- *pref* of radiation, of rays; of or by radio.

radio [*Raydi*-O] *n* wireless telephony, communication by electromagnetic waves > PDS; wireless receiving set; programmes transmitted by wireless ~ **radio** *v/t* and *i* send (message) by wireless telegraphy ~ **radio** *adj* of or by wireless; emitting or receiving electromagnetic waves; **r. astronomy** study of heavenly bodies by the radio frequency radiations which they emit or reflect; **r. car** taxi, police car *etc* equipped with two-way radio linking it to its headquarters; **r. frequency** frequencies between 10 kilohertz and 100,000 megahertz; **r. telescope** telescope used in radio astronomy.

radioactive [*Raydi*-O-*aktiv*] *adj* (*phys*) possessing, or pertaining to, radioactivity.

radioactivity [*Raydi*-O-*aktiviti*] *n* spontaneous disintegration of unstable atomic nuclei *usu* accompanied by the emission of charged particles and gamma rays > PDS.

radiobiology [*Raydi*-ObI-*oloji*] *n* branch of biology concerned with the effects of ionizing radiation on living organisms.

radiocarbon [*Raydi*-O*kaar*bon] *n* radioisotope of carbon; carbon 14; **r. dating** (*arch*) process of dating ancient organic matter by measuring radioactivity of carbon contained in it.

radiochemistry [*Raydi*-O*kemistRi*] *n* chemical study of radioactive materials > PDS.

radiogram (1) [*Raydi*-OgRam] *n* apparatus combining wireless receiver and gramophone.

radiogram (2) *n* telegram sent by radio.

radiograph [*Raydi*-OgRaaf] *n* X-ray photograph.

radiography [*Raydi*-*ogRafi*] *n* formation of images on fluorescent screens or photographic material by short-wave radiation, such as X-rays and gamma rays > PDS; science of using X-ray photographs for medical diagnosis ~ **radiographer** *n*.

radioisotope [*Raydi*-OIsOtOp] *n* radioactive isotope of an element.

radiolocation [*Raydi*-OlO*kay*shon] *n* radar.

radiology [*Raydi*-*oloji*] *n* science of X-radiation and radioactivity > PDS.

radio-micrometer [*Raydi*-O-mIk*Romiter*] *n* extremely sensitive instrument for measuring heat-radiations > PDS.

radio-opaque [*Raydi*O-O*payk*] *adj* opaque to radiation, *esp* to X-rays.

radiophonic [*Raydi*-O*fonik*] *adj* (*of sound*) electronically produced, not natural.

radioscopy [*Raydi*-*oskopi*] *n* examination of tissues or objects by X-rays.

radiosonde [*Raydi*-Osond] *n* radio transmitter and meteorological instruments carried to great heights by balloon > PDG, PDS.

radiotherapy [*Raydi*-O*theRapi*] *n* treatment of disease by X-rays or radioactivity > PDS.

radish [*Radish*] *n* plant whose pungent root is used for salad.

radium [*Raydi*-um] *n* rare, naturally occurring, radioactive metallic element > PDS.

radius (*pl* radii) [*Raydi*-us] *n* (*math*) distance from centre to circumference of a circle; spoke; (*coll*) circular area; distance measured from a centre; (*anat*) the shorter forearm bone.

radix (*pl* radices) [*Raydiks*] *n* (*math*) quantity or symbol taken as the base of a system of enumeration, logarithms *etc*.

radon [*Raydon*] *n* rare, naturally occurring, radioactive, gaseous element produced by the disintegration of radium; radium emanation > PDS.

raffia [*Rafi*-a] *n* long-leaved Madagascar palm; fibre of this used for tying plants, *etc.*

raffish [*Raf*ish] *adj* disreputable; dissipated ~ **raffishly** *adv* ~ **raffishness** *n.*

raffle [*Raf'*l] *n* lottery in which a prize is won by one ticket drawn at random from among several ~ **raffle** *v/t* dispose of by raffle.

raft [*Raaf*t] *n* flat floating structure of logs or planks fastened together ~ **raft** *v/t* transport by raft.

rafter [*Raaf*ter] *n* piece of timber supporting a roof ~ **rafter** *v/t* furnish with rafters.

rag (1) [*Rag*] *n* tattered piece of cloth; fragment torn from a garment; scrap, remnant; (*pl*) torn or shabby clothes; (*coll*) cheap ill-written newspaper; (*sl*) tongue; **chew the r.** (*sl*) talk; grumble; **glad rags** (*coll*) fine clothes; **r. trade** (*sl*) designing and selling fashionable clothes.

rag (2) *n* coarse-grained sandstone; large roofing-slate, rough on one side.

rag (3) *n* rowdy but good-natured practical joke, *esp* done by group of students; organized students' procession *etc* accompanied by boisterous horse-play; teasing; rough practical joke ~ **rag** (*pres/part* **ragging**, *p/t* and *p/part* **ragged**) *v/t* and *i* tease roughly, play practical jokes on; indulge in boisterous humour.

raga [*Raa*ga] *n* (*mus*) pattern of notes used as theme for improvised variations in Indian music.

ragamuffin [*Raga*mufin] *n* ragged boy or fellow.

ragbag [*Rag*bag] *n* bag in which scraps of fabric are stored; (*fig*) medley, confused mass.

ragbolt [*Rag*bOlt] *n* bolt with jags on the shank.

ragday [*Rag*day] *n* day on which students annually hold a procession with jokes and rowdiness, *usu* in aid of charity.

rage [*Rayj*] *n* violent anger, fury; frenzy; destructive violence; (*coll*) person or thing temporarily much admired, imitated, or practised; brief intense enthusiasm, craze ~ **rage** *v/i* be violently angry; be intensely violent, destructive, or painful; express bitter anger.

ragged [*Rag*id] *adj* worn or torn into tatters; shaggy; jagged, irregular; dressed in tattered clothes; not well synchronized; **r. robin** a wild flower with tattered red petals ~ **raggedly** *adv* ~ **raggedness** *n.*

raging [*Ray*jing] *n* fury; violence ~ **raging** *adj* furious, angry; violent; frantic ~ **ragingly** *adv.*

raglan [*Rag*lan] *n* garment with no seams on the shoulders.

ragman [*Rag*man] *n* one who collects or who deals in rags.

Ragnarok [*Rag*naRok] *n* (*Norse myth*) final destruction of the gods and this world by powers of evil.

ragoût [*Rag*OO] *n* (*Fr*) highly seasoned stew.

rag-paper [*Rag*-payper] *n* fine variety of paper.

rag-tag [*Rag*-tag] *n* **r. and bobtail** riff-raff, persons of no importance.

ragtime [*Rag*tIm] *n* early type of jazz with much syncopation of a simple tune > PDM.

ragwort [*Rag*wurt] *n* a common yellow-flowered weed.

rah [*Raa*] *interj* (*US and coll*) hurrah.

raid [*Rayd*] *n* sudden expedition for plunder or destruction; attack, invasion; aerial bombing; sudden police search of suspect premises ~

raid *v/t* make a raid against or into; plunder; attack ~ **raider** *n.*

rail (1) [*Rayl*] *n* wooden or metal bar; one of a pair of steel lines on which trains or trams run > PDE; railway; balustrade of staircase; rod or bar for hanging clothes *etc* on; (*pl*) railway line; fence, railings; railway stocks and shares; **off the rails** (*of engine*) derailed; (*fig*) mistaken, in error; eccentric ~ **rail** *v/t* send by railway; provide rails for; **r. in** enclose by railings.

rail (2) *v/t* reproach bitterly ~ **railer** *n.*

railhead [*Rayl*hed] *n* farthest point reached by a railway.

railing (1) [*Rayl*ing] *n* fence made of rails.

railing (2) *n* bitter reproach; abuse ~ **railing** *adj* reproachful; derisive.

raillery [*Rayl*eRi] *n* banter; good-humoured pleasantry.

railroad [*Rayl*ROd] *n* (*US*) railway ~ **railroad** *v/t* (*US sl*) hustle (unwilling person) into action; get rid of on a false charge; force through despite opposition.

railway [*Rayl*way] *n* track laid with steel rails on which trains and vehicles are run; system of tracks, rolling-stock and stations run by one organization ~ **railway** *adj* of, for or by a railway.

raiment [*Ray*ment] *n* clothing, apparel, dress.

rain [*Rayn*] *n* condensed water-drops falling to earth from the clouds > PDG; shower; thick fall of drops or small particles; (*fig*) continuous rapid succession; (*pl*) tropical rainy season ~ **rain** *v/i* and *t* fall as rain; fall or pour down thickly or rapidly; **r. cats and dogs** rain heavily.

rainbow [*Rayn*bO] *n* coloured arc produced by refraction and internal reflection of sunlight on waterdrops in the air > PDG, PDS; **colours of the r.** prismatic colours; (*fig*) many varied colours; **r. trout** a brightly coloured Californian trout.

rainbow-tinted [*Rayn*bO-tintid] *adj* of the seven prismatic colours; having many colours.

raincoat [*Rayn*kOt] *n* waterproof coat worn in wet weather.

rainfall [*Rayn*fawl] *n* total amount of rain which falls on a given area in a given time > PDG.

rain-gauge [*Rayn*-gayj] *n* instrument for measuring rainfall on a particular surface > PDG.

rainproof [*Rayn*pROOf] *adj* not admitting rain.

rainwater [*Rayn*-wawter] *n* rain.

rainy [*Ray*ni] *adj* with much rain, wet, showery; **r. day** (*fig*) time of need or misfortune.

raise [*Rayz*] *v/t* lift, cause to rise; increase the amount or value of; set upright; build; produce, create; evoke; suggest, cause; breed and rear to maturity; collect, levy; promote, increase the rank of; inspire, rouse, stir up; restore to life or health; summon up, cause (spirits) to appear; utter loudly; remove (siege, ban *etc*); **r. Cain** cause trouble, act violently; **r. hell** cause violent disturbance; **r. land** (*naut*) get sight of land; **r. a laugh** cause others to laugh; **r. a point** mention a point for discussion; **r. the wind** (*coll*) obtain a loan ~ **raise** *n* (*coll*) increase in wages.

raisin [*Ray*zin] *n* dried grape.

raj [*Raaj*] *n* rule, dominion.

raja, rajah [*Raa*ja] *n* Indian king, prince, or chief.

rajpoot, rajput [Raajpoot] n aristocratic Hindu; one of an Indian warrior class.

rake (1) [Rayk] n long-handled tool set with teeth used for scraping, dragging or smoothing; heavy toothed bar drawn by tractor or horse; pronged tool for drawing out ashes from a furnace or fireplace ∼ **rake** v/t scrape, smooth over or drag together with a rake; scrape together, gather from all sources; draw out ashes from; spray bullets from end to end of; sweep one's eyes along; **r. out** find by careful search; **r. up** gather with difficulty; revive something forgotten.

rake (2) n dissolute or immoral man.

rake (3) n inclination, slope; forward or backward inclination of a ship's masts or funnels; slope of a bow or stern beyond the keel ends ∼ **rake** v/i slope backwards.

rake-off [Rayk-of] n (sl) share of profits, commission, esp in illegal deal.

rakish (1) [Raykish] adj dissolute, debauched ∼ **rakishly** adv ∼ **rakishness** n.

rakish (2) adj sloping backwards; (naut) with masts sharply inclined; built for speed; smart-looking ∼ **rakishly** adv ∼ **rakishness** n.

rallentando [RalentandO] adv (mus) getting gradually slower.

rally (1) [Rali] v/t and i rouse to further effort; reunite, gather together again; recover health, strength, courage etc; revive; gather again in good order; (comm) command higher price ∼ **rally** n act of recovering health etc; act of reassembling after being scattered; large gathering, mass meeting; gathering of car drivers or motorcyclists for long competitive drive; (tennis) interchange of strokes.

rally (2) v/t (ar) tease, chaff.

ram [Ram] n adult male sheep; any device for delivering repeated heavy blows; steel spike on bows of warship, for piercing another ship's hull; battering-ram; iron weight on a drop-hammer; moving block of hydraulic press; first sign of zodiac, constellation Aries ∼ **ram** (pres/part **ramming**, p/t and p/part **rammed**) v/t and i crush down or drive through by repeated blows; compress heavily; collide violently with, crash into; (fig) instil by repetition; (coll) thrust roughly in or on.

Ramadan [Ramadan] n ninth month of the Muslim year, when there is annual fasting.

ramble [Ramb'l] v/i walk about freely for pleasure, rove; wander in speech or in writing; be delirious ∼ **ramble** n act of roaming about, stroll; leisurely country walk.

rambler [Rambler] n one who rambles; climbing rosebush.

rambling [Rambling] adj wandering about; incoherent, delirious; aimless; irregular in design ∼ **ramblingly** adv.

ramification [Ramifikayshon] n division into branches; subdivision in a complex system; indirect consequence; complication; act of forming branching patterns; (bot) arrangement of branches.

ramify [Ramifi] v/i and t divide or cause to divide into branches or into subdivisions; branch out; give rise to complex consequences; become complicated.

ramjet [Ramjet] n (aer) jet engine in which air taken in through an open duct is compressed by the speed of flight, mixed with fuel, ignited and ejected as exhaust.

rammer [Ramer] n one who or that which rams; punner or tool for ramming, pounding etc.

ramp [Ramp] n slope, inclined plane; sloping stair-rail; slope connecting different levels of road etc; change of level; (sl) fraud, swindle; (coll) rampage ∼ **ramp** v/i and t (of plants) climb and spread vigorously; (of animals) bound wildly about; (her) be rampant; (coll) rage, be furious; make a ramp in or on.

rampage [Rampayj] n boisterous or violent behaviour; excitement ∼ **rampage** v/i behave boisterously or violently; dash about; rage.

rampageous [Rampayjus] adj boisterous, violent; noisy ∼ **rampageously** adv.

rampant [Rampant] adj wild; violent, furious, aggressive; rank in growth; widespread; (her) standing on the hind legs ∼ **rampantly** adv.

rampart [Rampaart] n embankment which fortifies; mound of earth which carries a parapet; (fig) a defence ∼ **rampart** v/t fortify with or as with a rampart.

ramrod [RamRod] n rod for forcing down the charge of a muzzle-loading gun; (fig) person of stern, rigid ways or appearance.

ramshackle [Ramshak'l] adj tumbledown, rickety; badly built.

ran (1) [Ran] p/t of **run**.

ran (2) n a length of twenty yards of twine.

rance [Rans] n variegated marble.

ranch [Raanch] n farm where cattle and/or horses are reared ∼ **ranch** v/i own, manage or work upon a ranch ∼ **rancher** n.

rancid [Ransid] adj having a rank, stale smell or taste; (of fats or oils) not fresh ∼ **rancidly** adv.

rancidity [Ransiditi] n quality of being rancid.

rancorous [RangkeRus] adj feeling or showing rancour ∼ **rancorously** adv.

rancour [Rangker] n deep-seated spite or resentment, enmity, malice.

rand [Rand] n border, edge, margin; thin inner sole; ridge of mountains.

randan (1) [Randan] n boat with a rowing crew of three, the one amidships using two oars.

randan (2) n (sl) spree.

random [Random] n **at r.** haphazard, aimlessly ∼ **random** adj made or done without calculation or method; left to chance ∼ **randomly** adv.

randy [Randi] adj (Scots) rowdy; (coll) lustful.

ranee [Raanee] n woman who rules as a raja; consort of a raja.

rang [Rang] p/t of **ring** (2).

range [Raynj] n row, line; area, extent, scope; group or series of similar objects; accessible area; area prepared for practice shooting of rifles etc; distance that can be reached by specified projectile, weapon, vehicle etc; distance that can be reached by sight or hearing; limits; cooking stove; kitchen fireplace; (US) open grazing land ∼ **range** v/t and i arrange in a row or series, set in order; roam over specified area; pass over or along; frequent; extend, stretch; vary between limits; (of guns) have a certain range; **r. oneself** with take sides with, join.

range-finder [Raynj-fInder] n device for measuring distance of target.

ranger [*Raynjer*] *n* one who ranges; wanderer, rover; forest or park officer; mounted patrolman; **R. Guide** senior Guide.

rangy [*Raynji*] *adj* inclined to wander; lean, slim.

rank (1) [*Rangk*] *n* grade, class; high social class; status; degree of value or excellence; line, row; row of soldiers; **r. and file, the ranks** private soldiers, all who are not officers; (*fig*) average or common people; **break ranks** cease to stand in line; be thrown in confusion; **fall in r.** take one's place in an orderly series; **rise from the ranks** be promoted from private to officer; **take r.** enjoy status of, be classified as ~ **rank** *v/t* and *i* classify; be classified as, have the status of; be considered one among.

rank (2) *adj* luxuriant in growth, over-fertile; coarse; rancid, strong-smelling; flagrant; loathsome.

ranker [*Rangker*] *n* soldier in the ranks; commissioned officer who has risen from the ranks.

rankle [*Rangk'l*] *v/i* be inflamed; fester; (*fig*) cause pain or bitterness; be remembered with anger.

rankly [*Rangkli*] *adv* coarsely; flagrantly.

rankness [*Rangkn*is] *n* quality of being rank (2).

ransack [*Ran*sak] *v/t* search thoroughly; plunder.

ransom [*Ran*sum] *n* price paid to obtain release of prisoner, kidnapped person, captured goods *etc*; release from captivity upon payment; **hold to r.** keep prisoner till ransom is paid; demand money under threat of penalties; **king's r.** (*fig*) huge sum of money ~ **ransom** *v/t* redeem from captivity by payment; exact ransom from; (*theol*) redeem from sin.

rant [*Rant*] *v/i* and *t* talk loudly and emotionally (about); talk highflown nonsense ~ **rant** *n* noisy, emotional and meaningless eloquence ~ **ranter** *n* one who rants; (*obs coll*) Methodist preacher.

ranunculus (*pl* **ranunculuses**) [*Ran*ungkewlus] *n* one of a genus of plants including the buttercup.

rap (1) [*Rap*] *n* slight sharp blow; quick light knocking sound; (*sl*) accusation, charge; **take the r.** (*sl*) be punished; take the blame ~ **rap** (*pres/part* **rapping**, *p/t* and *p/part* **rapped**) *v/t* and *i* strike lightly and sharply (on); make a knocking sound; **r. out** say curtly; express by rapping; **r. over the knuckles** (*fig*) rebuke.

rap (2) *n* (*hist*) counterfeit Irish halfpenny; (*fig*) something of no value; **don't care a r.** don't care at all; **not worth a r.** worthless.

rapacious [*Rapayshus*] *adj* greedy, grasping; seizing by force; plundering; living on prey ~ **rapaciously** *adv*.

rapacity [*Rapasiti*] *n* quality of being rapacious.

rape (1) [*Rayp*] *v/t* force (someone) to have sexual intercourse unwillingly; violate; (*ar*) seize and carry off by force ~ **rape** *n* act of raping; violent abduction; (*fig*) violent destruction or plundering; violation.

rape (2) *n* one of the six divisions of Sussex.

rape (3) *n* plant grown as a food for sheep.

rapecake [*Rayp*kayk] *n* sheep's food made of pressed seeds of rape (3).

rapid [*Rap*id] *adj* very swift, speedy; done in a very short time ~ **rapid** *n* (*usu pl*) a sudden descent in a river where the current is swift.

rapidity [*Rap*iditi] *n* quality of being rapid.

rapidly [*Rap*idli] *adv* very swiftly.

rapier [*Raypi*-er] *n* long, thin sword used only for thrusting.

rapine [*Rap*in] *n* act of plundering; pillage.

rapist [*Rayp*ist] *n* one who commits rape (1).

rapport [*Rap*awr] *n* sympathetic relationship, harmony; relationship between hypnotist and hypnotized person > PDP.

rapprochement [*RapRosh*mon(g)] *n* reconciliation; restoration of good relations, *esp* between States.

rapscallion [*Rap*skalyon] *n* scamp, rascal.

rapt [*Rapt*] *adj* carried away by one's thoughts or feelings; enraptured, completely absorbed ~ **raptly** *adv* ~ **raptness** *n*.

raptor [*Rapt*or] *n* (*orni*) bird of prey.

raptorial [*Raptawr*Ri-al] *adj* of or like a bird of prey.

rapture [*Rap*cher] *n* ecstasy, transport; great delight.

rapturous [*Rap*cheRus] *adj* showing or feeling rapture, intensely happy ~ **rapturously** *adv*.

rare (1) [*Rair*] *adj* exceptional; not frequent, unusual; thinly scattered; not dense, tenuous; (*coll*) singularly good, first-rate; **r. earth** (*chem*) lanthanide.

rare (2) *adj* underdone, nearly raw.

rarebit [*Rair*bit/*Rab*it] *n* Welsh r. toasted cheese.

raree-show [*Rair*Ree-shO] *n* portable peepshow.

rarefaction [*RairRif*akshon] *n* act of rarefying; state of being rarefied; diminishing density.

rarefy [*Rair*Rifi] *v/t* and *i* make thin, porous, or less dense; expand without adding to the substance; (*fig*) purify, refine.

rarely [*Rair*li] *adv* seldom.

rareness [*Rair*nis] *n* quality of being rare.

rarification [*RairRifik*ayshon] *n* rarefaction.

raring [*Rair*Ring] *adj* (*coll*) **r. to go** extremely eager to start.

rarity [*Rair*Riti] *n* state of being rare; that which is rare; tenuity; unusual excellence; infrequency.

rascal [*Raas*kal] *n* scoundrel, rogue; dishonest person; scamp; mischievous child.

rascality [*Raas*kaliti] *n* quality of being a rascal; rascally act.

rascally [*Raas*kali] *adj* of or like a rascal.

rash (1) [*Rash*] *n* a skin eruption.

rash (2) *adj* impetuous, hasty; unwise.

rasher [*Rash*er] *n* thin slice of bacon or ham.

rashly [*Rash*li] *adv* in a rash way.

rashness [*Rash*nis] *n* quality of being rash.

rasp [*Raasp*] *n* coarse file; harsh grating sound ~ **rasp** *v/t* and *i* rub or scrape with a rough, coarse file; (*fig*) irritate; grate; make a grating sound.

raspberry [*Raaz*beRi] *n* red fruit of the *Rubus* plant; plant bearing this; (*sl*) fart ;(*sl*) disapproval; curt dismissal; (*sl*) contemptuous noise made with tongue and lips.

raspberry-cane [*Raaz*beRi-kayn] *n* long, woody shoot of the raspberry plant.

raster [*Rast*er] *n* (*rad*) pattern of lines which scan a television screen.

rat [*Rat*] *n* rodent akin to mouse, but larger; (*fig*) cowardly traitor, one who deserts a cause or party in times of difficulty; **rats!** (*sl*) *exclam* of incredulity and scorn; **smell a r.** be suspicious; **water r.** water vole ~ **rat** (*pres/part* **ratting**, *p/t* and *p/part* **ratted**) *v/i* hunt or kill rats; desert a cause or party; **r. on** (*coll*) betray.

ratable, rateable [Raytab'l] *adj* that may be valued; liable to taxation.

ratafia [Ratafee-a] *n* fruit cordial flavoured with crushed kernels; almond-flavoured biscuit.

ratal [Raytal] *n* the amount on which local rates are assessed ~ **ratal** *adj*.

rat-catcher [Rat-kacher] *n* person employed to trap and destroy rats.

ratch [Rach] *n* a ratchet-wheel.

ratchet [Rachit] *n* set of sloping teeth interlocking with a pawl, to prevent a wheel or bar from moving backwards.

ratchet-wheel [Rachit-weel] *n* wheel with ratchet teeth.

rate (1) [Rayt] *n* proportion or standard by which quantity or value is adjusted; fixed price; valuation; relative speed; municipal tax upon property; class of a ship ~ **rate** *v/t* and *i* estimate value, worth, rank *etc* of; assess for municipal rates; (*coll*) regard as; be rated or ranked (as).

rate (2) *v/t* scold angrily; chide; storm (at).

rateable see **ratable**.

ratepayer [Raytpay-er] *n* one who pays municipal rates.

ratfink [ratfink] *n* (*US sl*) particularly loathsome fink.

rather [RaaTHer] *adv* more willingly or readily; preferably; with more reason, more properly; more accurately; in a greater degree; to some extent; somewhat, slightly ~ **rather** [RaaTHer] *interj* (*coll*) yes, certainly.

ratification [Ratifikayshon] *n* act of ratifying; confirmation.

ratify [RatifI] *v/t* confirm, make valid, establish.

rating (1) [Rayting] *n* act of assessing; amount fixed as a municipal rate; (*naut*) sailor who is not an officer; position of an individual sailor in the ship's crew.

rating (2) *n* scolding, firm reprimand.

ratio [Rayshi-O] *n* the numerical relation one quantity bears to another of the same kind > PDS; proportion; fixed numerical relation.

ratiocinate [Rati-osinayt] *v/i* think or argue logically, reason.

ratiocination [Rati-osinayshon] *n* act of reasoning logically; logical deduction.

ration [Rashon] *n* fixed allowance of food or goods; **r. book** booklet of detachable coupons entitling the holder to claim his rations ~ **ration** *v/t* put on fixed rations; supply with rations; share out in fixed portions.

rational [Rashonal] *adj* capable of reasoning; of reason or reasoning; intelligent; reasonable, sensible; in accordance with or based on reason; (*math*) expressible by finite terms or whole quantities.

rationale [Rashonaali] *n* logical cause; reasoned defence, explanation *etc*.

rationalism [Rashonalizm] *n* refusal to believe anything supernatural, miraculous, or unverifiable by human reason alone; doctrine that reason is sole source of knowledge.

rationalist [Rashonalist] *n* believer in rationalism; one who is guided by reason ~ **rationalist** *adj*.

rationalistic [Rashonalistik] *adj* of, or in accordance with, rationalism ~ **rationalistically** *adv*.

rationality [Rashonaliti] *n* capacity of reasoning; reasonableness.

rationalization [RashonalIzayshon] *n* act of rationalizing; process of justifying or explaining a past act or thought by reasoning.

rationalize [RashonalIz] *v/t* and *i* give rational explanation or justification (of); organize reasonably or economically; (*math*) clear of radical signs; rely on reason or reasoning; (*psych*) find allegedly sound reasons for irrational views or behaviour.

rationally [Rashonali] *adv* in a rational way.

rat-race [Rat-Rays] *n* fierce unscrupulous competition to obtain wealth, power, *etc*, *esp* in one's career.

rat-tail, rat-tailed [Rat-tayl, Rat-tayld] *adj* narrow and tapering; (*of a spoon*) having a tapering strip of metal extending under the bowl.

rattan [Ratan] *n* long, thin stem of various climbing palms; walking-stick made from this.

rat-tat [Rat-tat] *n* rapid knocking sound.

ratter [Rater] *n* man or animal that catches rats; one who deserts a cause or party in a crisis.

rattle [Rat'l] *v/i* and *t* make or cause to make a rapid series of sharp noises; move with noisy clatter; drive (vehicle) rapidly; talk fast and thoughtlessly; (*coll*) alarm, upset; **r. off (through)** say, read or do fast and carelessly ~ **rattle** *n* rapid series of sharp noises; child's toy that makes such noises when shaken: noisy superficial talk or talker; wooden device that makes a loud clatter when whirled; sound of breath passing through a partly blocked windpipe.

rattler [Ratler] *n* one who or that which rattles; (*coll*) rattlesnake; noisy person or thing; (*sl*) first-rate person or thing.

rattlesnake [Rat'lsnayk] *n* venomous American snake which can rattle loose joints in its tail.

rattletrap [Rat'ltRap] *n* rickety object; shaky vehicle; (*sl*) one who talks too much.

rattling [Ratling] *adj* that rattles; (*coll*) brisk, vigorous; (*sl*) excellent.

rat-trap [Rat-tRap] *n* trap for catching rats; toothed bicycle pedal; (*sl*) mouth.

ratty [Rati] *adj* infested with rats; like rats; (*sl*) annoyed, bad-tempered.

raucous [Rawkus] *adj* harsh; hoarse ~ **raucously** *adv* ~ **raucousness** *n*.

raunchy [Rawnchi] *adj* (*US*) lecherous, bawdy.

ravage [Ravij] *n* ruin, havoc, waste ~ **ravage** *v/t* devastate, lay waste; pillage; make havoc.

rave [Rayv] *v/i* talk irrationally or wildly; be delirious; speak furiously; rage; **r. about** speak enthusiastically about, go into raptures over ~ **rave** *n* (*coll*) enthusiastic praise; (*sl*) sentimental affection; (*sl*) party, dance.

ravel (*pres/part* **ravelling**, *p/t* and *p/part* **ravelled**) [Ravel] *v/t* and *i* entangle; confuse; involve; separate into threads, fray; become tangled; become unwoven; **r. out** disentangle.

ravelling [Raveling] *n* frayed thread or rope; (*eng*) loss of aggregate from a road surface.

raven [Rayven] *n* large black British bird of the crow family ~ **raven** *adj* like a raven; black.

ravening [Ravening] *adj* ravenous; hunting for prey.

ravenous [Ravenus] *adj* voracious, famished, hungry; rapacious; eager for pleasure ~ **ravenously** *adv* ~ **ravenousness** *n*.

rave-up [Rayv-up] *n* (*coll*) wild or enthusiastic

gathering; session of pop music; party where such music is played.

ravine [Ra*veen*] *n* long, deep gulley; gorge.

ravioli [Ravi-Oli] *n* (*Ital*) small square cases of pasta holding hashed meat and served in savoury sauce.

ravish [Ravish] *v/t* cause great delight to, enrapture; violate, rape; carry off by force.

ravishing [Ravishing] *adj* very lovely; enchanting, delightful ~ **ravishingly** *adv*.

ravishment [Ravishment] *n* delight, ecstasy.

raw [Raw] *adj* uncooked; natural, unprocessed; not trained, educated *etc*; inexperienced, immature; crude; sore, having the skin rubbed or torn off; cold and damp, bleak; (*coll*) bawdy; (*sl*) unfair, harsh ~ **raw** *n* sore skinless place on body; state of being raw; **in the r.** unprocessed, in its natural state; crude, unrefined; (*sl*) naked; **on the r.** in a sensitive place.

rawboned [RawbOnd] *adj* gaunt, very thin.

rawhide [Raw-hId] *n* untanned leather; whip made from this.

rawly [Rawli] *adv* in a raw way.

rawness [Rawnis] *n* quality of being raw.

ray (1) [Ray] *n* shaft of light; beam, gleam; (*phys*) rectilinear path along which radiation travels; radiation; (*geom*) radius; (*bot*) outer whorl of florets in composite flower; (*zool*) spine in fin *etc* ~ **ray** *adj* (*coll*) using or emitting radiations ~ **ray** *v/i* and *t* send out rays, shine; adorn with rays.

ray (2) *n* any species of cartilaginous fish with flat body and long thin tail.

rayless [Raylis] *adj* without rays; without light.

rayon [Ray-on] *n* man-made textile derived from cellulose > PDS; artificial silk.

raze [Rayz] *v/t* erase, obliterate; lay level with the ground, demolish.

razor [Rayzer] *n* sharp instrument for shaving off hair; **on the r.'s edge** on the verge of danger ~ **razor** *v/t* shave with a razor; wound by slashing with razor.

razorback [Rayzerbak] *n* a sharp back like a razor; finbacked whale ~ **razorbacked** *adj*.

razorbill [Rayzerbil] *n* bird with a sharp curving beak; auk.

razor-edge [Rayzer-ej] *adj* having or being a very sharp edge or crest.

razz [Raz] *v/t* and *i* (*sl*) mock, deride ~ **razz** *n* (*sl*) derisive noise.

razzia [Razi-a] *n* pillaging incursion.

razzle-dazzle [Raz'l-daz'l] *n* (*sl*) a rowdy spree or frolic ~ **razzle-dazzle** *v/t* (*sl*) dazzle.

razzmatazz [Razmataz] *n* (*coll*) noisy or showy behaviour to attract publicity; humbug.

re (1) [Ray] *n* (*mus*) second note of the tonic sol-fa scale; second note in the scale of C major, D.

re (2) [Ree] *prep* (*leg*) in the matter of; (*coll*) with regard to.

re- *pref* again, for the second time; back.

reach (1) [Reech] *v/i* retch.

reach (2) *v/t* and *i* get as far as, arrive at; achieve, attain; be long enough or go far enough to touch, pierce, affect *etc*; stretch, extend; stretch out one's arm; touch, take or hand over with outstretched arm; be extended; **r. after, r. for** try to grasp with outstretched arm; (*fig*) aspire towards, try to attain ~ **reach** *n* extent, range; act or power of reaching; possibility of being easily

reached; ability to affect, influence or understand; uninterrupted stretch of water, *esp* of river.

reach-me-downs [Reech-mi-downz] *n* (*pl*) (*coll*) ready-made clothes.

react [Ree-akt] *v/i* act in response to stimulus; respond to another's acts or influence; exert chemical action; **r. against** act contrary to (a previous influence), tend to the opposite of; **r. on** (upon) influence reciprocally.

reactance [Ree-aktans] *n* component of the impedance of an alternating current circuit > PDS.

reaction [Ree-akshon] *n* reciprocal action; response to stimulus > PDP; exhaustion, depression after strain or excitement; contrary action, *esp* revulsion of feeling against progress or reform; (*chem*) interaction of two or more substances, resulting in chemical changes in them > PDS; (*phys*) equal and opposite force exerted upon the agent by the body acted upon.

reactionary [Ree-akshonaRi] *n* and *adj* (person) seeking to destroy or oppose progress or reform.

reactionist [Ree-akshonist] *n* reactionary.

reactivate [Ree-aktivayt] *v/t* cause to become active again.

reactive [Ree-aktiv] *adj* (*chem*) readily entering into chemical reactions; chemically active > PDS.

reactivity [Ri-aktiviti] *n* quality of being reactive; ability to react readily.

reactor [Ree-akter] *n* (*chem*) vessel in which a chemical reaction takes place; (*phys*) assembly in which a nuclear reaction takes place for the production of energy; (*elect*) device for introducing reactance into a circuit.

read (*p/t* and *p/part* read) [Reed, *p/t* and *p/part Red*] *v/t* and *i* see and understand written or printed words, letters or symbols; understand (foreign words) when written; utter aloud something written or printed; know about by reading; understand by studying or contemplating; find the answer to (a riddle or puzzle); interpret; study (*esp* for university degree); (*of instruments*) record, register, indicate; transfer (data) to or from magnetic tape; read aloud in specified manner; convey specified impression when read; be expressed in writing; **r. between the lines** understand hidden implications; **r. for** study in order to qualify as or obtain; **r. into** ascribe further meanings or implications to, assume as meaning; **r. of** learn by reading; **r. oneself in** (*eccles*) read the Thirty-nine Articles publicly on entering into a benefice; **r. up** study, learn more about by reading ~ **read** *n* act of reading ~ **read** [Red] *adj* and *p/part* having learnt by studying or reading.

readable [Reedab'l] *adj* pleasant and easy to read; worth reading, interesting; legible ~ **readably** *adv*.

readdress [Ree-adRes] *v/t* change address on a letter to forward it.

reader [Reeder] *n* one who reads; one who reads a great deal; one who reads aloud; (*cap*) university teacher ranking between professor and lecturer; one who judges manuscripts for a publisher; corrector of printers' proofs; book containing passages for practice in reading or translating; (*eccles*) person authorized to read Scriptural passages in a service.

readership [Reedership] *n* number of persons who

read a specified newspaper *etc*; post of university Reader.

readily [*Red*ili] *adv* easily; willingly; promptly.

readiness [*Red*inis] *n* state of being ready, preparedness; willingness, promptness; ease; aptitude.

reading [*Reed*ing] *n* act of one who reads; ability to read; interpretation, rendering; form of a word or passage in variant versions of a written text; public recital of passages of literature; performance of a play by persons reading it from the text; readable matter; measurements recorded on and read from an instrument; formal presentation of a bill to a legislative body.

reading-desk [*Reed*ing-desk] *n* tall stand supporting a book while it is being read.

reading-lamp [*Reed*ing-lamp] *n* portable shaded lamp.

reading-room [*Reed*ing-ROOm] *n* room in a library, club *etc* where books or newspapers can be read.

readjust [Ree-a*just*] *v/t* and *i* arrange or put in order again; modify previous outlook or behaviour to fit new circumstances ~ **readjustment** *n*.

readmission [Ree-ad*mish*on] *n* act of admitting again one who or that which has been excluded; state of being readmitted.

readmit (*pres/part* **readmitting**, *p/t* and *p/part* **readmitted**) [Ree-ad*mit*] *v/t* admit again.

ready [*Red*i] *adj* prepared; fit to act or be used at once, immediately available; willing; liable, inclined; on the point of; prompt, apt; near at hand; **get r.**, **make r.** prepare; **r. money** cash; notes and coins; **r. reckoner** book of mathematical tables for rapid calculations in business *etc* ~ **ready** *n* (*sl*) cash; **at the r.** (*mil*) in position for immediate firing.

readymade [*Red*imayd] *adj* already made and fit for immediate use; (*of clothes*) made in stock sizes and sold for immediate use; (*fig*) not spontaneous or original; trite; derived from others' opinions *etc*; (*fig*) perfectly apt.

reafforest (*US* **reforest**) [Ree-a*fo*Rest] *v/t* plant new trees to replace others.

reagent [Ree-*ay*jent] *n* (*chem*) substance used to produce a chemical reaction > PDS.

real (1) [*Ree*-al] *adj* actually existing; factual, actual; not imaginary or theoretical; true, genuine; not fictitious; (*philos*) having absolute and independent existence; (*leg*) consisting of permanent or fixed things; **r. estate (property)** land or houses, freehold landed estate; **R. Presence** (*RC*) doctrine that the Eucharistic bread and wine are transubstantiated into the actual body of Christ; Anglican doctrine that Christ's body is sacramentally present in the Eucharistic bread and wine ~ **real** *n* that which is real; **for r.** (*sl*) in reality, in earnest ~ **real** *adv* (*US coll*) truly, really; very.

real (2) *n* an obsolete Spanish silver coin.

realgar [Ree-*al*gar] *n* natural red disulphide of arsenic.

realign [Ree-a*lIn*] *v/t* and *i* change or restore the alignment of; regroup; form a new alliance.

realism [*Ree*-alizm] *n* ability or willingness to face facts; practical outlook, absence of illusions or theorizings; attempt to describe in literature or art some fact as it actually is, *esp* in its unpleasant aspects; frank outspoken accuracy; (*philos*) theory that objects have real existence independently of any perceiver; theory that general ideas have actual existence.

realist [*Ree*-alist] *n* one who practises or believes in realism; one who claims to be without illusions.

realistic [Ree-a*listik*] *adj* practical, clear-sighted; corresponding to facts; closely resembling the object, situation *etc* represented; actual; of realism or realists ~ **realistically** *adv*.

reality [Ree-*aliti*] *n* state or quality of being real; quality of being true to life or fact; that which is real and not imaginary; totality of existing material objects.

realizable [Ree-al*Iz*ab'l] *adj* that may be realized.

realization [Ree-alI*Zay*shon] *n* act of realizing; act of bringing into being; act of becoming aware; conversion of money into land, or of property into money.

realize [Ree-al*Iz*] *v/t* and *i* perceive as a reality; understand clearly; become aware of; bring into being, cause to become fact; make realistic; convert into money; sell; fetch (sum) by sale.

really [Ree-ali] *adv* in reality; truly; actually ~ **really** *interj* exclamation of surprise.

realm [Relm] *n* kingdom; (*fig*) domain, sphere.

realpolitik [Ray-alpoli*tik*] *n* (*Germ*) policy based on material advantage, not principles or ideals.

realtor [Ree-alter] *n* (*US*) real estate agent.

realty [Ree-alti] *n* (*leg*) real property.

ream (1) [*Reem*] *n* quantity of paper consisting of 480 sheets; (*pl*) (*fig*) large quantities. *esp* of written work.

ream (2) *v/t* enlarge; bevel out; (*naut*) open for caulking ~ **reamer** *n* tool used in reaming.

reanimate [Ree-*ani*mayt] *v/t* restore to life; revive; encourage.

reap [*Reep*] *v/t* and *i* cut (corn) with a scythe, sickle, or reaping machine; gather in; (*fig*) obtain as reward for action or effort.

reaper [*Reep*er] *n* one who reaps; reaping-machine.

reaping-hook [*Reep*ing-hook] *n* sickle.

reappear [Ree-a*peer*] *v/i* appear again after absence ~ **reappearance** *n*.

reappraisal [Ree-ap*Ray*zal] *n* fresh assessment.

rear (1) [*Reer*] *v/t* and *i* raise, lift; set up; bring up, educate; cultivate; stand on the hind legs; rise steeply.

rear (2) *n* hind part, that which is behind; hindermost group in procession, marching troops *etc*; (*mil*) part of forces behind front line; position of being at the back; **bring up the r.** be the last (of procession *etc*), come at the end; **in the r.** behind the others; from behind ~ **rear** *adj* of or at the rear, hind.

rear-admiral [Reer-*ad*miRal] *n* (*British navy*) rank between captain and vice-admiral.

rearguard [*Reer*gaard] *n* body of troops which protect the rear of an army; **r. action** engagement fought by the rearguard to protect the main body of troops in retreat.

rearm [Ree-*aarm*] *v/t* and *i* provide with or acquire new weapons; acquire armaments again after being disarmed ~ **rearmament** *n*.

rearmost [*Reerm*Ost] *o 'j* coming last.

rearrange [Ree-a*Raynj* *v/t* put into a new order ~ **rearrangement** *n*.

rearward [Reerward] *n* and *adj* (position) in the rear ~ **rearward** *adv* towards the rear.

rearwards [Reerwardz] *adv* towards the rear.

reason [Reezon] *n* cause; motive, *esp* logical; that which accounts for something; capacity to think logically, explicitly; intellectual faculties; sanity; common sense; that which is in accordance with logic or common sense; **have neither rhyme nor r.** be utter nonsense; **in r.** reasonably, justifiably; **stand to r.** be obviously true or sensible ~ **reason** *v/i* and *t* think or discuss logically; think coherently and explicitly; analyse; argue (over); persuade by argument.

reasonable [Reezonab'l] *adj* endowed with reason; governed by reason; sensible; not excessive, inexpensive; tolerable; just ~ **reasonably** *adv* ~ **reasonableness** *n*.

reasoning [Reezoning] *n* process of thinking involving inference; act or process of thinking logically.

reassemble [Ree-asemb'l] *v/t* and *i* gather together again; put together again (machine *etc*).

reassign [Ree-asIn] *v/t* transfer to another what has already been assigned.

reassurance [Ree-ashoorRans] *n* act of reassuring; that which reassures.

reassure [Ree-ashoor] *v/t* dispel doubts or fears of, give fresh confidence to.

Réaumur [Ray-Omewr] *adj* of or in a thermometric scale where freezing-point is zero and boiling-point 80°.

rebarbative [Ribaarbativ] *adj* forbidding, unattractive; stern, fearsome.

rebate [Reebayt] *n* discount, reduction, deduction from a price; repayment of part of sum paid as tax ~ **rebate** [Ribayt] *v/t* reduce, deduct; cut a rabbet in; (*her*) cut off the tip of.

rebec, rebeck [Reebek] *n* ancient three-stringed musical instrument played with a bow.

rebel [Rebel] *n* one who tries to overthrow legal government by force; one who defies authority and resists control; one who rejects conventions *etc* ~ **rebel** *adj* of or like a rebel or rebellion ~ **rebel** (*pres/part* **rebelling**, *p/t* and *p/part* **rebelled**) [Ribel] *v/i* revolt, take arms (against); resist; react violently (against), resent openly.

rebellion [Ribelyon] *n* open resistance against established authority; act or state of rebelling.

rebellious [Ribelyus] *adj* defying lawful authority; engaged in rebellion; disposed to resist control or conventions ~ **rebelliously** *adv* ~ **rebelliousness** *n*.

rebirth [Reeburth] *n* second birth; renewal, *esp* spiritual; reincarnation; revival.

rebore [Reebawr] *v/t* provide fresh bore for (cylinder of motor engine); bore through again ~ **rebore** [Reebawr] *n* act or process of reboring or being rebored.

reborn [Reebawrn] *adj* born again; spiritually renewed; reincarnated; revived.

re-bound (1) [Ree-bownd] *adj* (*bookbinding*) provided with new binding.

rebound (2) [Ribownd] *v/i* bounce back after hitting something; react (against), recoil (on); renew energy *etc* after depression ~ **rebound** [Reebownd] *n* act of rebounding, bouncing movement; **on the r.** while bouncing back; (*fig*) while reacting against disappointment etc.

rebuff [Ribuf] *n* refusal, rejection; snub; defeat ~ **rebuff** *v/t* reject the request or advances of; snub.

rebuke [Ribewk] *v/t* reprove, chide; disapprove of, blame ~ **rebuke** *n* reproof, chiding.

rebus (*pl* **rebuses**) [Reebus] *n* type of graphic language where the sounds of words and word-elements are represented by pictures or by pictures and letters > PDP; (*her*) device representing a name or title.

rebut (*pres/part* **rebutting**, *p/t* and *p/part* **rebutted**) [Ribut] *v/t* disprove, refute; (*leg*) oppose by plea, argument, or proof.

rebuttal [Ributal] *n* act of refuting; (*leg*) production of evidence to refute a statement.

rebutter [Ributer] *n* one who rebuts; (*leg*) answer of a defendant to a plaintiff's rejoinder.

recalcitrance [RikalsitRans] *n* refusal to submit to authority, control *etc*; obstinate disobedience.

recalcitrant [RikalsitRant] *adj* obstinately resisting control ~ **recalcitrantly** *adv*.

recall [Rikawl] *v/t* call back, summon to return; remember, revive memory of; renew, revive; annul, revoke ~ **recall** *n* act of calling back; message or signal ordering return; power to remember; ability to revoke; **beyond r.** irrevocably forgotten; **total r.** ability to remember something with alli ts details, associated feelings *etc*.

recant [Rikant] *v/t* and *i* declare one's former opinions to have been wrong; publicly renounce (opinion *etc*).

recantation [Reekantayshon] *n* act of recanting.

recap (1) (*pres/part* **recapping**, *p/t* and *p/part* **recapped**) [Reekap] *v/t* and *i* (*coll*) recapitulate ~ **recap** *n* recapitulation.

recap (2) (*pres/part* **recapping**, *p/t* and *p/part* **recapped**) *v/t* put vulcanized rubber strip on (worn tyre) ~ **recap** *n* a recapped tyre.

recapitulate [Reekapitewlayt] *v/t* and *i* rapidly repeat main points of; summarize (an argument); repeat something already experienced.

recapitulation [Reekapitewlayshon] *n* act of recapitulating; **r. theory** that an individual embryo develops in stages repeating those by which its species evolved > PDB.

recapture [Rikapcher] *v/t* regain something captured from oneself by another; seize again someone or something that has escaped; repeat (an elusive feeling, achievement *etc*) ~ **recapture** *n* act of capturing again; that which is recaptured.

recast [Reekaast] *v/t* mould again or in a new shape; remodel; compute again; find new cast for (a play); find a new part for (an actor).

recce [Reki] *n* (*mil sl*) reconnaissance.

recede [Riseed] *v/i* move backwards; move into the distance; slope backwards or away; decline in value; retreat; fade away.

receipt [Riseet] *n* act of receiving; fact of being received; that which is received; written acknowledgement of money or of goods received; (*ar*) recipe; (*pl*) money received ~ **receipt** *v/t* make out a written receipt for; affix a receipt to.

receive [Riseev] *v/t* and *i* obtain or accept (something given, sent, offered *etc*); be given; be subjected to, undergo; take in, admit as guest or member; allow into one's presence; hold, contain; greet, welcome; accept, acknowledge as true; entertain guests; (*eccles*) partake of (consecrated elements); **be at (on) the receiving end** have to bear (something unpleasant) ~ **received** *adj* generally accepted as correct.

receiver [Ris*eever*] *n* one who or that which receives; earpiece of telephone; apparatus that receives, amplifies and rectifies electromagnetic waves in wireless set; one who receives stolen goods; receptacle; (*leg*) one appointed to administer property under litigation.

recension [Ris*enshon*] *n* critical revision of a text; a revised text.

recent [R*eesent*] *adj* that has lately happened or come into existence; modern ~ **recently** *adv*.

receptacle [Ris*eptak'l*] *n* that which receives, holds or contains; (*bot*) support of a head of flowers > PDB.

reception [Ris*epshon*] *n* act of receiving; state of being received; acceptance, admission; act of greeting, entertaining or accommodating guests; formal party or entertainment of guests; manner of greeting or welcoming; act of receiving newly-arrived clients, patients, hotel visitors *etc* and arranging appointments or accommodation for them; **r. room** any room used for entertaining guests; any room other than bedrooms, kitchen *etc*.

receptionist [Ris*epshonist*] *n* person employed to receive clients, patients, hotel guests *etc* and arrange appointments or accommodation for them.

receptive [Ris*eptiv*] *adj* able to receive; quick to receive new ideas, impressions *etc*; sensitive ~ **receptively** *adv* ~ **receptiveness** *n*.

receptivity [Ris*eptiviti*] *n* quality of being receptive; sensitivity.

recess [Ris*es/Reeses*] *n* alcove; hollow place; secluded place; cessation or suspension of business, *esp* of law court or parliament; (*US*) vacation ~ **recess** *v/t* and *i* make an alcove or hollow in; set at some distance back; indent; cease or suspend business.

recession [Ris*eshon*] *n* act of receding; retirement; act of departing in procession; (*econ*) slackening of trade and industry.

recessional [Ris*eshonal*] *n* and *adj* (hymn) sung as choir and clergy leave the chancel.

recessive [Ris*esiv*] *adj* tending to recede or move back; (*biol*) not dominant > PDB.

recharge [Ree*chaarj*] *v/t* charge again; put a new electric charge into; reload (firearm).

recherché [Resh*airshay*] *adj* (*Fr*) uncommon; choice, rare.

rechristen [Reek*Risen*] *v/t* give a new name to; baptize again.

recidivism [Ris*idivizm*] *n* habitual relapse into crime ~ **recidivist** *n* and *adj*.

recipe [R*esipi*] *n* list of ingredients and instructions for preparing cooked food, drinks, medical prescriptions *etc*; prescribed way of making or achieving something.

recipient [Ris*ipi-ent*] *n* and *adj* person (or thing) that receives.

reciprocal [Ris*ipRokal*] *adj* mutual, done or felt by each of two parties for the other; felt or done in return; complementary; mutually interchangeable; inversely corresponding; (*gramm*) express-

ing mutual action ~ **reciprocal** *n* (*math*) quotient arising from dividing unity by a quantity.

reciprocality [Risip*Rokaliti*] *n* fact or quality of being reciprocal.

reciprocally [Risip*Rokali*] *adv* mutually.

reciprocate [Risip*Rokayt*] *v/i* and *t* give or feel in return, exchange mutually; move straight backwards and forwards; alternate.

reciprocation [Risip*Rokayshon*] *n* act of reciprocating; give and take; motion backwards and forwards; alternation.

reciprocity [Resip*Rositi*] *n* state of being reciprocal; mutual cooperation and exchange; equality of trade privileges.

recital [Ris*Ital*] *n* act of reciting; something recited; enumeration of facts; account, narration; musical performance by a soloist or small group; musical programme devoted to one composer or allied group of composers.

recitation [Resit*ayshon*] *n* act of declaiming poetry or prose to an audience, *usu* by heart; act of repeating by heart.

recitative [Resita*teev*] *n* (*mus*) style of singing comparatively close to speech, used in opera *etc* > PDM ~ **recitative** *adj* narrative; pertaining to recitative.

recite [Ris*It*] *v/t* and *i* repeat aloud from memory, *esp* to an audience; narrate; quote; enumerate ~ **reciter** *n* one who recites; narrator.

reck [R*ek*] *v/t* and *i* (*poet*) care, feel concern or anxiety (over).

reckless [R*eklis*] *adj* careless, heedless; rash; neglectful ~ **recklessly** *adv* ~ **recklessness** *n*.

reckon [R*ekon*] *v/t* and *i* count, add (up); account, esteem; calculate; settle accounts with; (*coll*) think, suppose; **r. on** rely on; **r. with** take into account.

reckoner [R*ekoner*] *n* one who reckons; book of calculations.

reckoning [R*ekoning*] *n* calculation; bill of charges, account; settlement of accounts; (*fig*) payment for sin or folly, retribution; (*naut*) estimation of ship's position from log entries or astronomical observations; **be out in one's r.** miscalculate; **day of r.** day when accounts must be paid up; Judgement Day; day of punishment.

reclaim [Rik*laym*] *v/t* claim back; bring (waste or waterlogged land) into cultivation; reform from error, vice *etc*; tame and train (wild beast) ~ **reclaim** *n* restoration, reform; **beyond r.** that cannot be reformed or saved.

reclamation [Reklam*ayshon*] *n* act of reclaiming; demand; recovery; (*ar*) remonstrance.

recline [Rik*lIn*] *v/i* lean back; lie down; lean on one side.

recluse [Rik*lOOs*] *n* one who voluntarily lives alone, solitary person; hermit; anchorite, anchoress.

recognition [Rekog*nishon*] *n* act of recognizing; state of being recognized; acknowledgement.

recognizable [Rekogn*Izab'l*] *adj* that may be recognized ~ **recognizably** *adv*.

recognizance [Rik*ognizans/Rikonizans*] *n* (*leg*) obligation to fulfil a certain condition or to perform a certain act on pain of forfeiting a stated sum; sum to be so forfeited.

recognize [Rek*ognIz*] *v/t* perceive that something one sees, hears *etc*, one has seen, heard *etc* before;

know again, identify as already known; admit, acknowledge to be true, valid *etc*; show appreciation of; greet as acquaintance; formally acknowledge the status of.

recoil [Rik*oil*] *v/i* jerk backwards, rebound; shrink back; feel horror or disgust; withdraw; **r. on** affect the perpetrator ~ **recoil** *n* act of recoiling; rebound, *esp* of gun when fired; feeling of disgust or horror.

recollect [Reko*lekt*] *v/t* and *i* remember, recall the knowledge of; (*refl*) concentrate one's thoughts; recover one's composure.

recollection [Reko*lek*shon] *n* act or power of recollecting; memory; that which is recollected; concentrated devout thought, meditation.

recommence [Reeko*mens*] *v/t* and *i* begin again.

recommend [Reko*mend*] *v/t* speak favourably of; declare to be suitable; advise use of; advise; make acceptable; entrust to the care of.

recommendable [Reko*mend*ab'l] *adj* that can be, or deserves to be, recommended; praiseworthy; advisable.

recommendation [Rekomen*day*shon] *n* act of recommending; that which recommends; course of action recommended; letter of commendation.

recommendatory [Rekomen*dat*oRi] *adj* that recommends.

recompense [*Rek*ompens] *v/t* make a return for; give equivalent for; requite, repay; reward; compensate ~ **recompense** *n* that which is given as a compensation, reward, satisfaction *etc*; requital.

recompose [Reekomp*Oz*] *v/t* compose again; rearrange; restore composure of.

reconcile [*Rek*onsIl] *v/t* restore friendship between; make content; make compatible, harmonize; settle, adjust; (*refl*) become resigned to.

reconciliation [Rekonsili-*ay*shon] *n* act of reconciling; state of being reconciled.

recondite [Rik*ond*It] *adj* little known, obscure; showing or requiring special knowledge; secret ~ **reconditely** *adv* ~ **reconditeness** *n*.

recondition [Reekon*dish*on] *v/t* repair; put into good condition again.

reconnaissance [Rik*on*isans] *n* act of reconnoitring; preliminary investigation or survey.

reconnoitre [Rekon*oiter*] *v/t* and *i* explore (an area) before beginning military operations in it; make a preliminary survey (of).

reconsider [Reekon*sider*] *v/t* think over again, *esp* in order to reverse or modify former decision or opinion.

reconstitute [Ree*kon*stitewt] *v/t* constitute again; give a new constitution to; reconstruct; add water to (dried food).

reconstruct [Reekon*st*Rukt] *v/t* construct or build again; recreate a lost or damaged original form; deduce from fragmentary evidence.

reconstruction [Reekon*st*Ruk*shon] *n* act of reconstructing; that which is reconstructed.

reconvert [Reekon*vurt*] *v/t* convert again; convert back to original state or form.

record [Rik*awrd*] *v/t* and *i* set down permanent evidence of; write down for future information; register; register (sound vibrations) upon grooves of a gramophone disk; make gramophone records (of) ~ **record** [*Rek*awrd] *n* written factual account; that which preserves evidence of the past; official

contemporary written account; list of a person's previous crimes as known to police; person's previous behaviour, career *etc* as known to others; finest performance yet achieved (*esp* in sport); something never before achieved; flat disk engraved with a groove from which sounds are reproduced when it revolves under gramoph ~ needle; performance of music *etc* engraved on such a disk or on magnetic tapes; **beat the r.** surpass the previous best performance; **on r.** known officially or publicly, *esp* from documents; **off the r.** (*coll*) confidentially, not for public information; **r. player** gramophone ~ **record** [*Rek*awrd] *adj* surpassing all previous achievements, quantities, degree *etc*.

record-breaking [*Rek*awrd-bRayking] *adj* surpassing best performance previously known; uniquely successful.

recorder [Rik*awr*der] *n* one who or that which records; judge who presides over the quarter sessions of a borough; vertical flute > PDM; apparatus for recording sounds.

recording [Rik*awr*ding] *n* act of making gramophone record, tape-recording or film; performance so recorded.

recount (1) [Rik*ownt*] *v/t* narrate, relate.

recount (2) [Ree*kownt*] *n* second count, *esp* of votes ~ **recount** [Ree*kownt*] *v/t* count again.

recoup [Rik*OOp*] *v/t* make good, recover (financial losses); reimburse, compensate; (*leg*) diminish by keeping back a part.

recourse [Rik*awrs*] *n* act of seeking help from someone or something.

re-cover [Ree-*kuv*er] *v/t* cover again; provide with a new cover.

recover [Rik*uv*er] *v/t* and *i* get back again; retrieve; regain health after sickness; regain former balance or position; (*leg*) obtain damages or compensation in a lawsuit.

recovery [Rik*uv*eRi] *n* act of recovering; state of having recovered.

recreant [*Rek*Ri-ant] *adj* cowardly; recanting through fear; apostate ~ **recreant** *n*.

re-create [Ree-kRee-*ayt*] *v/t* create or form again; reproduce exactly.

recreation [RekRi-*ay*shon] *n* act of relaxing and amusing oneself after work; amusement, pastime, sport; free interval between school lessons; **r. ground** area of land set aside for sports; playground.

recreational [RekRi-*ay*shonal] *adj* of or as recreation.

recriminate [Rik*Rim*inayt] *v/i* retort with one accusation against another; express mutual reproach.

recrimination [RikRimin*ay*shon] *n* mutual accusation or reproach; counter-charge.

recriminatory [Rik*Rim*inayteRi] *adj* of or as recrimination.

recrudesce [ReekROO*des*] *v/i* recur.

recrudescence [ReekROO*des*ens] *n* recurrence, *esp* of disease or evil; renewed activity ~ **recrudescent** *adj*.

recruit [Rik*ROO*t] *n* one who is newly-enlisted; one who has newly joined an organization *etc* ~ **recruit** *v/t* and *i* enlist or seek to enlist (new soldiers, members *etc*); supply with new men; replenish; restore to health; gain fresh supplies.

recruiting-officer [Ri*k*ROOting-ofiser] *n* officer engaged in enlisting recruits.

recruitment [Ri*k*ROOtment] *n* act of enlisting new recruits.

rect-, recti- *pref* straight.

rectal [*Re*ktal] *adj* of or in the rectum ∼ **rectally** *adv* through the rectum.

rectangle [*Re*ktang'l] *n* quadrilateral figure with four right angles.

rectangled [*Re*ktang'ld] *adj* having one or more angles of 90 degrees.

rectangular [Rek*tang*-gewlar] *adj* shaped like a rectangle.

rectifiable [Rekti*fi*-ab'l] *adj* that can be corrected or adjusted.

rectification [Rektifi*kay*shon] *n* act or process of rectifying; correction; (*chem*) purification of liquid by distillation; (*math*) process of determining length of curve; (*elect*) conversion of alternating into direct current.

rectifier [*Re*ktifi-er] *n* one who or that which rectifies; (*elect*) device for converting alternating into direct current.

rectify [*Re*ktifi] *v/t* correct, amend; adjust; reform; abolish; (*chem*) refine by distillation; (*math*) determine the length of (curve); (*elect*) convert (alternating current) to direct current.

rectilineal, rectilinear [Rekti*lin*i-al, -ar] *adj* in a straight line; consisting of straight lines.

rectitude [*Re*kti*t*ewd] *n* moral or religious uprightness; integrity, honesty; correctness.

recto [*Re*ktO] *n* right-hand page of an open book.

rector [*Re*ktor] *n* parson of a parish who is enentitled to all its tithes; head of certain religious and educational institutions; head of a German university; **Lord R.** chief elective officer of a Scottish university.

rectorial [Rekta*vr*Ri-al] *adj* of a rector.

rectory [*Re*ktoRi] *n* benefice or house of a rector.

rectum [*Re*ktum] *n* lowest portion of the large intestine.

recumbent [Ri*k*umbent] *adj* and *adv* lying down, reclining ∼ **recumbently** *adv*.

recuperable [Ri*k*ewpeRab'l] *adj* recoverable.

recuperate [Ri*k*ewpeRayt] *v/i* and *t* recover; regain health; restore to health.

recuperation [Ri*k*ewpe*Ray*shon] *n* recovery.

recuperative [Ri*k*ewpeRativ] *adj* of or tending to recovery.

recur (*pres/part* recurring, *p/t* and *p/part* recurred) [Ri*k*ur] *v/i* happen again or several times; come back to mind, be remembered; (*math*) be repeated indefinitely.

recurrence [Ri*k*uRens] *n* act of recurring; state of having recurred.

recurrent [Ri*k*uRent] *adj* returning at intervals; (*anat*) turning in the opposite direction ∼ **recurrently** *adv*.

recusancy [*Re*kewzansi] *n* nonconformity.

recusant [*Re*kewzant] *n* and *adj* (*hist*) (person, *esp* RC) who refuses to attend Church of England services when ordered to by law; (one) who rejects State authority in religious matters.

recycle [Rees*Ik*'l] *v/t* re-use (waste material) after cleansing, melting or breaking it down; return to first stage of (cyclic process).

red [Red] *n* one of a range of colours from the long-wave end of the spectrum > PDP; these colours collectively; pigment producing such a colour; that which is red; red ball in billiards; red square in roulette board; a Communist or extreme left-wing Socialist; symbol of danger; **in the r.** (*coll*) bankrupt; in debt; **see r.** be wildly angry ∼ **red** (*comp* **redder,** *superl* **reddest**) *adj* being of the colour red; scarlet; crimson; blood-red; coppery; (*fig*) Communist; extreme Socialist; revolutionary, left-wing; **r. admiral** a black butterfly with red bands; **r. cent** (*US*) former copper cent; **r. corpuscles** blood cells carrying haemoglobin > PDB; **R. Crescent** Muslim branch of the Red Cross organization; **R. Cross** international society organizing hospital and ambulance service for victims of war or disasters; (*hist*) emblem of crusaders; **r. deer** large brown British deer; **R. Ensign** flag of British merchant navy; **R. Flag** symbol of Communism, revolution, or Socialism; name of a revolutionary Communist song; danger signal consisting of red cloth or flag; **r. giant** (*astron*) reddish star in intermediate stage of evolution > PDS; **r. herring** reddish smoked herring; (*fig*) irrelevant fact, argument *etc* introduced to confuse an issue; misleading clue; **r. hot** heated to glowing-point; (*fig*) enthusiastic; enraged; (*sl*) very recent; sensational; highly syncopated; **R. Indian** one of the aborigines of North America; **r. lamp (light)** light shining through red glass, used as symbol of danger, of a brothel, or as a signal to halt; **r. lead** reddish oxide of lead > PDS; **r. ochre** ruddle; **paint the town r.** behave drunkenly or rowdily in public; indulge in wild amusements; **r. rag** (*fig*) that which infuriates; **r. shift** (*astron*) displacement of spectrum lines towards longer wavelengths; **R. star** symbol of Soviet Russia and other Communist States; **r. tape** pink ribbon used to tie official documents in bundles; (*fig*) troublesome official formalities, bureaucratic methods.

redact [Ri*d*akt] *v/t* arrange in fit form for publication, edit.

redaction [Ri*d*akshon] *n* edition, editing.

redbreast [*Re*dbRest] *n* European robin.

redbrick [*Re*dbRik] *adj* (*of a university*) founded in modern times.

redcap [*Re*dkap] *n* goldfinch; any small bird with a red head; one wearing a red cap; (*coll*) military policeman; (*US coll*) railway porter.

redcoat [*Re*dkOt] *n* (*hist*) British soldier.

redden [*Re*den] *v/t* and *i* make red; become red.

reddish [*Re*dish] *adj* fairly red; tinged with red.

reddle [*Re*d'l] *n* red earthy haematite.

rede [Reed] *n* (*ar*) counsel, advice; plan; story; saying ∼ **rede** *v/t* advise; interpret.

redecorate [Reede*ko*Rayt] *v/t* and *i* decorate anew; repaint or repaper (a house).

redeem [Ri*d*eem] *v/t* buy back (something pawned, mortgaged *etc*); clear by paying a lump sum; buy the freedom of, ransom; regain (something lost) by effort; atone for; make up for, compensate; (*theol*) save from hell by divine self-sacrifice.

redeemable [Ri*d*eemab'l] *adj* that can be redeemed.

redeemer [Ri*d*eemer] *n* one who redeems; (*cap*) Jesus Christ.

redemption [Ri*d*empshon] *n* act of redeeming; state of being redeemed; ransom; release; repurchase; atonement; (*theol*) deliverance from sin and its penalties; **beyond r.** impossible to save or reform.

redeployment [Reedi*ploi*ment] *n* transfer of troops to another sector; transfer of workers to different type of employment.

red-green [Red-gReen] *n* **r. blindness** partial colour-blindness > PDP.

red-gum [Red-gum] *n* a rash on gums of teething babies; one of various species of Australian eucalyptus.

red-handed [Red-*han*did] *adj* and *adv* having hands red with blood; (*fig*) (caught) when actually committing wrong.

redhead [Red*hed*] *n* person with coppery or carroty-coloured hair.

rediffusion [Reedi*fewz*hon] *n* (*rad, TV*) relay of broadcast, *esp* by wire.

redingote [Reding-gOt] *n* long double-breasted coat.

redintegrate [Red*in*tigRayt] *v/t* make whole or perfect again, restore; renew.

redirect [ReedI*Rekt*] *v/t* direct again; re-address; send to a new address.

redistribute [ReedistRibewt] *v/t* distribute again or differently, rearrange the distribution of.

redistribution [ReedistRibewshon] *n* second or different distribution; rearrangement.

red-letter [Red-*leter*] *adj* marked with red letters; auspicious; memorable.

redolence [*Redolens*] *n* sweetness of scent.

redolent [*Redolent*] *adj* giving out a sweet scent; **r. of** (*fig*) evoking, suggesting.

redouble [Ree*dub'l*] *v/t* and *i* double again; repeat often; increase by repeated additions; grow more intense; fold back, refold.

redoubt [Ri*dowt*] *n* small detached fort enclosed by a parapet.

redoubtable [Ri*dowt*ab'l] *adj* worthy to be feared, formidable ∼ **redoubtably** *adv.*

redound [Ri*downd*] *v/i* **r. to** contribute to, lead to; **r. upon** recoil on.

redpoll [Red*pOl*] *n* species of red-headed linnet; breed of red-haired hornless cattle.

redress [Ri*dRes*] *n* act of remedying wrongs or oppression; reparation ∼ **redress** *v/t* set right again; remedy; make reparation for.

redshank [Red*shank*] *n* sandpiper.

redskin [Red*skin*] *n* North American Indian.

redstart [Red*staart*] *n* species of migratory warbler allied to thrush.

reduce [Ri*dews*] *v/t* and *i* lessen, decrease; make lower in rank, degree *etc*; weaken, impair; bring to specified condition; force to undergo something unpleasant; break down to simpler form; try to become slim; cause to grow slim; classify; regulate; subdue; (*chem*) remove oxygen from, or add hydrogen to; (*min*) extract (mineral) from ore; (*math*) convert to another denomination; (*surg*) restore (dislocated joint) to correct position; **reduced circumstances** comparative poverty.

reducer [Ri*dewser*] *n* one who or that which reduces; substance that helps one to grow slim; (*phot*) substance that lessens contrasts or density.

reducible [Ri*dew*sib'l] *adj* that can be reduced.

reduction [Ri*duk*shon] *n* act of reducing; state of being reduced; degree by which something is reduced; smaller copy.

reductionism [Ri*duk*shonizm] *n* analysis aimed

at simplifying a complex idea or phenomenon into its component parts ∼ **reductionist** *adj* and *n*.

reductive [Ri*duk*tiv] *adj* (*chem*) reducing; (*fig*) expressing dismissive or destructive criticism.

redundance, redundancy [Ri*dun*dans, Ri*dun*dansi] *n* state or quality of being redundant.

redundant [Ri*dun*dant] *adj* superfluous, excessive; using more words than are necessary; (*of workers*) dismissed from work as being no longer needed; unemployed through decrease of available work.

reduplicate [Ri*dew*plikayt] *v/t* redouble, repeat something already done or existing; repeat initial sound or syllable; duplicate.

reduplication [Ri*dew*pli*kay*shon] *n* act of reduplicating; state of being reduplicated; repetition.

redwood [Red*wood*] *n* Californian giant sequoia tree; reddish timber of this; any tree yielding reddish timber.

re-echo [Ree-ek*O*] *v/i* and *t* echo again; echo back; resound, reverberate.

reed [Reed] *n* type of long-stemmed aquatic or marsh grass; stem of this; musical pipe made from this; vibrating strip of cane or metal in certain wind instruments > PDM; part of loom that separates warp threads; (*archi*) small convex moulding; (*poet*) arrow; pastoral poetry; **broken r.** one who will fail when needed ∼ **reed** *v/t* thatch with reeds; fit a reed to ∼ **reed** *adj* of or like a reed; found among reeds; containing a reed.

re-edit [Ree-*edit*] *v/t* edit again, prepare a new edition.

reedglass [Reed*glaas*] *n* ribbed glass used in doors *etc.*

reedy [Reedi] *adj* abounding in reeds; like a reed, having a thin, sharp tone.

reef (1) [Reef] *n* ridge of rocks or sand just below surface of sea; mineral lode, vein.

reef (2) *n* one of the horizontal parts of a sail which can be folded or rolled up to shorten the sail ∼ **reef** *v/t* reduce (sail area) by taking up part of it.

reefer (1) [Reefer] *n* short thick double-breasted coat.

reefer (2) *n* (*sl*) marijuana cigarette.

reefknot [Reef*not*] *n* symmetrical double knot.

reek [Reek] *v/i* stink, smell strongly and unpleasantly; emit vapour, steam or smoke; (*fig*) show signs of (something unpleasant) ∼ **reek** *n* unpleasant odour stench; (*Scots*) smoke; steam.

reeky [Reeki] *adj* smoky; dirty.

reel (1) [Reel] *n* any round or cylindrical frame on which thread, wire, cord *etc* is wound; bobbin; spool; unit of length of cinema film, about 1,000 feet; quantity of thread *etc* on one reel; small winch controlling fishing line; **off the r.** without pause ∼ **reel** *v/t* wind on a reel; **r. off** utter rapidly without pausing; unwind from reel.

reel (2) *n* lively Scottish dance; music for this.

reel (3) *v/i* stagger, sway from side to side; lose one's balance when struck or made dizzy; (*fig*) be overwhelmed by shock of sudden emotion.

re-eligible [Ree-*elijib'l*] *adj* capable of being elected again to the same position.

re-enter [Ree-*enter*] *v/t* and *i* enter again; (*leg*) resume possession of (leased property) if lessee fails to observe agreed terms.

reeve (1) [*Reev*] *n* (*hist*) chief officer, magistrate; steward.

reeve (2) (*p/t* **reeved** *or* **rove**, *p/part* **reeved**, **rove** *or* **roven**) *v/t* (*naut*) pass (rope) through ring or hole.

re-export [Ree-eks*pawrt*] *v/t* export again; export something previously imported ~ **re-export** [Ree-eks*pawrt*] *n*.

ref [*Ref*] *n* (*sl*) referee; reference, testimonial ~ **ref** *v/t* and *i* (*sl*) be referee (at).

reface [Ree*fays*] *v/t* put new surface upon.

refashion [Ree*fashon*] *v/t* alter the form of.

refection [Ri*fek*shon] *n* light meal.

refectory [Ri*fek*toRi] *n* room where meals are served, *esp* in school, monastery, college *etc*.

refer (*pres/part* **referring**, *p/t* and *p/part* **referred**) [Ri*fur*] *v/t* and *i* send for information or decision; pass on, hand over; send back; allude, speak briefly (of); concern, relate; indicate; have recourse (to), seek information (from); assign, ascribe; **r. back** defer (decision by delegates) until opinions of more authoritative body have been obtained

referral [Ri*fur*Ral] *n* (*leg*) act of sending (case, question *etc*) to another authority for decision.

referee [Refe*Ree*] *n* one to whom anything is referred; one who settles a dispute; umpire, *esp* in football and boxing ~ **referee** *v/t* and *i* act as referee for (sporting match).

reference [*Refe*Rens] *n* act of referring; one who or that which is referred to; allusion; indication of source of quotation, allusion or information; testimonial, formal statement as to another's abilities, character *etc*; person willing to give testimonial if applied to; connexion, relation; **r. book** book meant to be consulted for specific information but not read straight through; **r. library** library of specialized books to be consulted but not borrowed; **terms of r.** limits of scope of inquiry *etc*; **with r. to** concerning, as regards.

referendum (*pl* **referendums** or **referenda**) [Refe*Ren*dum] *n* act of referring a political question to the electorate by a direct vote.

referential [Refe*Ren*shal] *adj* having reference to.

refill [Ree*fil*] *n* that which is used to fill again ~ **refill** [Ree*fil*] *v/t* fill again.

refine [Ri*fIn*] *v/t* and *i* make or become purer; remove impurities from; make or become more elegant, cultured, or polished in manners; make or become more subtle; **r. upon** add even more elegance or subtlety to.

refined [Ri*fInd*] *adj* free from impurities; polished, elegant.

refinement [Ri*fIn*ment] *n* act of refining; state of being refined; elegance of language or manners; high culture; subtlety.

refinery [Ri*fIn*eRi] *n* apparatus for refining; factory *etc* where something is refined.

refit (*pres/part* **refitting**, *p/t* and *p/part* **refitted**) [Ree*fit*] *v/t* and *i* provide fresh fittings and supplies for; repair, make fit for use again; fit on again; be repaired or re-equipped ~ **refit** [Ree*fit*] *n* process of being refitted ~ **refitment** *n* refit.

reflate [Ree*flayt*] *v/t* and *i* (*econ*) counteract deflation by increasing amount of money in circulation ~ **reflation** *n*.

reflect [Ri*flekt*] *v/t* and *i* throw back (light, heat, sound *etc*) from a surface; produce image (of) on polished surface, mirror; reproduce accurately; express; think carefully, consider; **r. on** (**upon**) bring discredit on, cast doubt on; disparage; consider, ponder.

reflectible [Ri*flek*tib'l] *adj* that may be reflected.

reflection, reflexion [Ri*flek*shon] *n* act of reflecting > PDS, PDP; state of being reflected; that which is reflected; thoughtful consideration, meditation; thought; reproach; (*pl*) comments made after thinking on a subject.

reflective [Ri*flek*tiv] *adj* that reflects; thoughtful; reflexive ~ **reflectively** *adv*.

reflector [Ri*flek*tor] *n* one who or that which reflects; polished surface which reflects rays of light, heat or sound in a particular direction.

reflex [*Ree*fleks] *adj* directed backwards; reflected; **r. action** (*physiol*) involuntary action of muscle or nerve in response to external stimulus > PDB, PDS; (*coll*) involuntary or automatic reaction; **r. angle** (*geom*) angle greater than 180° and less than 360° ~ **reflex** *n* a reflex action; reflection, reflected image; external manifestation.

reflexed [Ree*flekst*] *adj* curved or bent back.

reflexion see **reflection**.

reflexive [Ri*flek*siv] *n* and *adj* (*gramm*) (word) denoting action on or referring back to the subject; (verb form) implying action by the subject upon itself.

refloat [Ree*flOt*] *v/t* cause (sunken or stranded vessel) to float again.

reflux [*Ree*fluks] *n* act of flowing back; ebb.

re-form [Ree-*fawrm*] *v/t* and *i* form again.

reform [Ri*fawrm*] *v/t* and *i* change for the better; abandon or cause to abandon habits of sin, crime *etc*; remove social or political injustices, abuses *etc* ~ **reform** *n* act of reforming, improvement; removal of social or political abuses; measure or campaign aimed at effecting this.

reformation [Refawr*may*shon] *n* act of reforming; state of being reformed; amendment; **the R.** 16th-century religious revolt which resulted in formation of Protestant churches.

reformative [Ri*fawr*mativ] *adj* producing a reformation; improving.

reformatory [Ri*fawr*matoRi] *n* former type of institution for the reformation of young criminals, prostitutes *etc* ~ **reformatory** *adj* · producing improvement.

reformed [Ri*fawrmd*] *adj* corrected, amended; cured of former vices or criminal habits; (*theol*) Protestant.

reformer [Ri*fawr*mer] *n* one who brings about a reformation; one who is in favour of reform.

refract [Ri*frakt*] *v/t* and *i* (*of rays and waves*) turn from direct course; bend at an angle when passing from one medium to another of different density > PDS, PDP.

refracting [Ri*frak*ting] *adj* that refracts; **r. angle** angle of two faces of triangular prism; **r. telescope** telescope with object-glass that causes light-rays to converge.

refraction [Ri*frak*shon] *n* act of refracting; state of being refracted; **angle of r.** angle made by a ray of light and a line perpendicular to the surface of the medium it passes through > PDS.

refractive [Ri*frak*tiv] *adj* refracting; of refraction.

refractor [Ri*f*Raktor] *n* a telescope.

refractory [Ri*f*Rakto*R*i] *adj* stubbornly resisting; obstinate, disobedient; (*chem*) not damaged by high temperatures > PDS ~ **refractory** *n* (*chem*) material undamaged by intense heat.

refrain (1) [Ri*f*Rayn] *n* phrase or line repeated in or after each verse of a song or poem.

refrain (2) *v/i* and *t* abstain, forbear; check oneself from acting; (*ar*) curb, restrain.

reframe [Ree*f*Raym] *v/t* frame again; draft afresh.

refrangible [Ri*f*Ranjib'l] *adj* that may be refracted.

refresh [Ri*f*Resh] *v/t* make fresh again; give new strength to; revive; restore; repair; stimulate; (*coll*) give a drink to; (*refl*) take food, drink or sleep.

refresher [Ri*f*Resher] *n* one who or that which refreshes; additional daily fee paid to a counsel; (*coll*) drink; **r. course** course of instruction to persons already once instructed, to bring their knowledge up to date.

refreshing [Ri*f*Reshing] *adj* pleasantly different or new; that refreshes ~ **refreshingly** *adv*.

refreshment [Ri*f*Reshment] *n* act of refreshing; state of being refreshed; that which refreshes, *esp* food or drink; (*pl*) light meal, snack.

refrigerant [Ri*f*Rije*R*ant] *n* and *adj* (substance) that refrigerates; (medicine) that reduces fever.

refrigerate [Ri*f*Rije*R*ayt] *v/t* make cold or cool; keep at a very low temperature.

refrigeration [Ri*f*Rije*R*ayshon] *n* act of cooling or freezing; state of being cooled; preservation of food at low temperatures.

refrigerator [Ri*f*Rije*R*aytor] *n* cabinet in which food is kept at a low, but not freezing, temperature to preserve it; refrigerating machine.

reft [*R*eft] *adj* bereft, deprived.

refuel [Ree*f*ew-el] *v/t* and *i* provide or obtain fresh supplies of fuel.

refuge [*R*efewj] *n* protection from danger or from distress; one who or that which protects; place of shelter, stronghold; raised pavement in the middle of a busy street for use by pedestrians; line of action taken to avoid trouble or difficulty.

refugee [Refew*jee*] *n* one who flees, *esp* to another country, to find safety from persecution or war, or for political reasons.

refulgence [Ri*f*uljens] *n* blaze of light.

refulgent [Ri*f*uljent] *adj* giving a bright light; radiant, brilliant; splendid ~ **refulgently** *adv*.

refund [Ree*f*und] *v/t* pay back, reimburse; restore ~ **refund** [*R*eefund] *n* repayment; sum repaid.

refurbish [Ree*f*urbish] *v/t* renovate, restore to former good condition; polish up again.

refusal [Ri*f*ewzal] *n* act of refusing; choice of taking or refusing.

refuse (1) [Ri*f*ewz] *v/t* and *i* reject (something offered), not take; decline to give or grant (something asked for); withhold, deny; (*of horse*) be unwilling to jump; (*cards*) be unable to follow suit in.

refuse (2) [*R*efews] *n* that which is rejected as useless; waste matter; rubbish, garbage ~ **refuse** *adj* rejected; worthless.

refutation [Refew*t*ayshon] *n* act of refuting; that which disproves.

refute [Ri*f*ewt] *v/t* prove to be false; disprove.

regain [Ree*g*ayn] *v/t* win back, recover possession of; reach again.

regal (1) [Ree*g*al] *adj* of or like a king; fit for a king.

regal (2) *n* small portable 16th- or 17th-century organ > PDM.

regale [Ri*g*ayl] *v/t* entertain or feast lavishly; give great delight to.

regalia [Ri*g*ayli-a] *n* (*pl*) insignia of royalty; symbols or emblems of a society or of civic office; (*hist*) privileges of royalty.

regalism [Ree*g*alizm] *n* doctrine of royal supremacy in church affairs; undue exercise of royal authority ~ **regalist** *adj* and *n*.

regality [Ri*g*aliti] *n* royalty, kingship.

regally [Ree*g*ali] *adv* as befits a king.

regard [Ri*g*aard] *v/t* consider, think, judge; look steadily at; pay attention to, observe; esteem, value; have a bearing on, concern; **as regards** concerning, with reference to ~ **regard** *n* esteem, (good) opinion; care, attention; steady gaze; (*pl*) expressions of kindly feelings; **with r. to** concerning.

regarding [Ri*g*aarding] *prep* concerning.

regardless [Ri*g*aard*l*is] *adj* and *adv* heedless, careless; (*coll*) disregarding expense or consequences ~ **regardlessly** *adv*.

regatta [Ri*g*ata] *n* race-meeting for boats.

regelation [Reeje*l*ayshon] *n* melting and refreezing of water by the application of pressure at constant temperature.

regency [Ree*j*ensi] *n* government by a regent; authority of a regent; duration of government by a regent; (*cap*) period of rule of George, Prince of Wales, as regent of England (1811-20) ~ **Regency** *adj* in the style popular in 1811-20.

regenerate [Ri*j*ene*R*ayt] *v/t* and *i* bring new life to; reform morally; be or cause to be spiritually reborn, recharge (battery); reproduce (lost tissues) by new growth > PDB ~ **regenerate** [Ri*j*ene*R*at] *adj* reformed; reborn.

regeneration [Ri*j*ene*R*ayshon] *n* act of regenerating; state of being regenerated.

regenerator [Ri*j*ene*R*aytor] *n* one who or that which regenerates; device in furnaces for obtaining a high temperature.

regent [Ree*j*ent] *n* one who governs during the illness, absence or minority of a sovereign ~ **regent** *adj* governing as regent.

reggae [Re*g*ay] *n* West Indian type of heavily syncopated rock music.

regicidal [Reji*s*Idal] *adj* of or like regicide.

regicide [Reji*s*Id] *n* act of killing a king; one who kills a king.

régime [Ray*zh*eem] *n* mode of government; prevailing social system; course of treatment, regimen.

regimen [Re*j*imen] *n* regulation of diet and exercise for reasons of health.

regiment [Re*j*iment] *n* the largest military unit, commanded by a colonel; (*fig*) large quantity ~ **regiment** *v/t* form into a regiment; organize into disciplined groups.

regimental [Reji*m*ental] *adj* of a regiment ~ **regimentally** *adv* ~ **regimentals** *n* (*pl*) ceremonial uniform worn by a particular regiment.

regimentation [Rejiment*ay*shon] *n* act or process of organizing in disciplined groups; rigid control, excessive regulation.

610

Regina [Rij*I*na] *n* official title of a reigning queen.

region [*Ree*jon] *n* large area of indefinite extent; district; part of the body; (*fig*) sphere; **in the r. of** approximately, roughly.

regional [*Ree*jonal] *adj* of or in a region; of, in or as a specified district ~ **regionally** *adv*.

register [*Rej*ister] *n* written official record; book in which this is kept; official list of names; apparatus for regulating admission of air or heat; gauge; range of voice or instrument > PDM; stop in an organ ~ **register** *v/t* and *i* enter in a register; record; fit, adjust exactly; enter one's name in a register; be noticed and understood, make an impression; show (feeling) by expression of face; insure against loss or damage in postal delivery; report for registration.

registrar [*Rej*istRar] *n* official keeper of a register.

registration [Rejist*Ray*shon] *n* act of registering; entry in a register.

registry [*Rej*istRi] *n* act of recording in a register; place where a register is kept.

registry-office [Rejistri-*of*is] *n* office of the registrar of births, marriages, and deaths; (*obs*) employment exchange for servants.

regius [*Ree*ji-us] *adj* (*Lat*) royal; appointed or founded by a king.

regnal [*Reg*nal] *adj* of a reign; **r. year** year counted from accession of a king.

regnant [*Reg*nant] *adj* reigning; ruling; predominant, prevailing.

regress [Rig*Res*] *v/i* move backwards; revert to more primitive form; return to former worse state; relapse ~ **regress** [*Reeg*Res] *n* backward movement; relapse; return, re-entry; **infinite r.** endless chain of reasoning leading backwards by interposing a third entity between two others.

regression [Rig*Res*hon] *n* act of going or of turning back; relapse; tendency to revert to a worse or more primitive stage or form > PDP; (*math*) backward flexion of a curve.

regressive [Rig*Res*iv] *adj* moving backwards, tending to regress ~ **regressively** *adv*.

regret (*pres/part* regretting, *p/t* and *p/part* regretted) [Rig*Ret*] *v/t* grieve at, feel sorrow for; grieve over the loss of; remember with sorrow or remorse; deplore ~ **regret** *n* grief, *esp* over a past loss; remorse, repentance.

regretful [Rig*Ret*fool] *adj* feeling regret ~ **regretfully** *adv*.

regrettable [Rig*Ret*ab'l] *adj* to be regretted; unwelcome ~ **regrettably** *adv*.

regroup [Reeg*ROO*p] *v/t* and *i* form again into groups; form into different groups.

regular [*Reg*ewlar] *adj* orderly; conforming to a rule, principle, law or type; symmetrical; normal; unvarying; properly qualified; correct; steady; recurring at set periods; habitual; (*coll*) typical, thorough; (*eccles*) bound by monastic rule; (*gramm*) inflected in the normal way; (*math*) with equal sides and angles; (*mil*) of a permanent army ~ **regular** *n* soldier of a permanent army; one who is permanently in a particular employment; one who habitually visits a particular place; member of an ecclesiastical order.

regularity [Regewla*Ri*ti] *n* quality of being regular.

regularize [*Reg*ewlaRIz] *v/t* make regular.

regularly [*Reg*ewlarli] *adv* in a regular way; at

regular intervals; habitually; constantly; (*coll*) completely.

regulate [*Reg*ewlayt] *v/t* govern by rule; put in order; control by law; cause to function accurately; cause to conform to standard.

regulation [Regew*lay*shon] *n* act of regulating; state of being regulated; prescribed rule, order ~ **regulation** *adj* conforming to rule or imposed standard; prescribed by rule or law.

regulator [*Reg*ewlaytor] *n* one who or that which regulates; lever of a watch.

regurgitate [Ree*gur*jitayt] *v/t* and *i* vomit; bring up again (swallowed food *etc*) to the mouth; throw or pour back; throw or pour out again; flow back.

regurgitation [Reegurji*tay*shon] *n* act of regurgitating.

rehabilitate [Reeha*bil*itayt] *v/t* restore normal capacities of (disabled person, criminal *etc*) by treatment and training; restore to former position, post, rank *etc*; re-establish good reputation of; regain esteem for.

rehabilitation [Reehabili*tay*shon] *n* act or process of rehabilitating; restoration of former capacities, rank, reputation *etc*.

rehandle [Ree*hand*'l] *v/t* handle again; rearrange; treat differently or again.

rehash [Ree*hash*] *v/t* rearrange (material already used) and present in slightly altered form; hash up again ~ **rehash** [Reehash] *n* something rehashed.

rehearsal [Ri*hur*sal] *n* act of rehearsing; act of practising a play or music before its public performance.

rehearse [Ri*hurs*] *v/t* and *i* privately practise (a play music *etc*) before its public performance; repeat; give account of.

Reich [R*Ikh*] *n* (*Germ*) the German State.

reify [*Ree*-ifI] *v/t* (*philos*) regard (abstract concept) as having material reality ~ **reification** *n*.

reign [Rayn] *n* period during which a monarch rules; sovereignty, supreme power; rule; dominance; period of control or influence; **r. of terror** period of political tyranny and violence; authority maintained by bloodshed and threats ~ **reign** *v/i* rule as monarch; prevail, predominate.

reimburse [Ree-im*burs*] *v/t* repay, refund.

reimport [Ree-im*pawrt*] *v/t* import that which has been previously exported ~ **reimport** *n* (*usu pl*) goods which have been reimported.

rein [Rayn] *n* long strap attached to horse's bit, by which to control or lead it; (*fig*) that which restrains; **draw r.** slow down, halt; **give the r. to** allow freedom to, indulge; **tight r.** severe discipline or control ~ **rein** *v/t* put a rein on; **r. in** check or control by reins; (*fig*) restrain, curb.

reincarnate [Ree-in-*kaar*nayt] *v/t* and *i* cause to be born again in another form; appear for a second time in bodily form ~ **reincarnate** *adj*.

reincarnation [Ree-in-kaar*nay*shon] *n* belief that the soul returns to earth after death in a fresh body; act of reincarnating; state of being reincarnate; second or subsequent bodily form taken by a soul.

reindeer [*Rayn*deer] *n* species of large domesticated deer of sub-arctic regions; **r. moss** arctic lichen.

reinforce [Ree-in*fawrs*] *v/t* add strength to;

strengthen by further men or supplies; send additional men *etc* to; **reinforced concrete** concrete strengthened by iron or steel bars embedded in it > PDE ~ **reinforce** *n* stronger or thicker part, *esp* of gun.

reinforcement [Ree-in*fawr*sment] *n* act of reinforcing; state of being reinforced; (*usu pl*) additional men, ships *etc*.

reins [Raynz] *n* (*pl*) (*ar*) kidneys; loins.

reinstate [Ree-in*stayt*] *v/t* restore, re-establish; replace in a former position; repair ~ **reinstatement**.

reinsure [Ree-in*shoor*] *v/t* and *i* insure again; insure against loss by the granter of a policy of insurance.

reissue [Ree-*i*sew] *n* a republication at a different price, or in a different form, of a book already published ~ **reissue** *v/t*.

reiterate [Ree-*ite*Rayt] *v/t* repeat again and again.

reiteration [Ree-ite*Ray*shon] *n* act of repeating several times.

reiterative [Ree-*ite*Rativ] *adj* characterized by repetition ~ **reiterative** *n* (*gramm*) word or part of word repeated to form a reduplicated word.

reject [Ri*jekt*] *v/t* refuse to accept or keep; refuse to grant; discard as useless or below standard; (*of stomach*) throw up, vomit ~ **reject** [Ree*jekt*] *n* that which has been rejected.

rejection [Ri*jek*shon] *n* act of rejecting; refusal to accept or grant.

rejoice [Ri*jois*] *v/t* and *i* make joyful, gladden; feel joy; delight (in); express joy.

rejoicing [Ri*jois*ing] *n* (*usu pl*) joyfulness; outward expression of joy; festivities, celebrations.

rejoin [Ri*join*] *v/t* and *i* join again; reunite; come together again; retort; (*leg*) answer a charge or pleading.

rejoinder [Ri*join*der] *n* an answer to a reply, retort; (*leg*) defendant's answer to plaintiff's replication.

rejuvenate [Ri*jOO*vinayt] *v/t* and *i* make or become young again; renew vigour or freshness.

rejuvenation [RijOO*vi*nayshon] *n* act or process of rejuvenating.

rejuvenescence [RijOOvi*ne*sens] *n* state of becoming or of being made young again; (*biol*) replacement of old cells by new.

rekindle [Ree*kind*'l] *v/t* and *i* kindle again; (*fig*) rouse again.

relaid [Ree*layd*] *p/t* and *p/part* of **relay**.

relapse [Ri*laps*] *v/i* fall back into former worse state; become ill again; revert to former wickedness or bad habit; sink; depreciate ~ **relapse** *n* act of relapsing; renewed attack of illness; backsliding.

relate [Ri*layt*] *v/t* and *i* tell, narrate; associate; establish or perceive connexion between; have connexion with; refer (to); **be related to** belong to same family as; be connected by blood, marriage, or features derived from a common source.

relation [Ri*lay*shon] *n* act of relating; that which is related; state of being connected; connexion between things; kinship, connexion by blood or marriage; kinsman, kinswoman; analogy; (*pl*) way in which people affect each other, feelings aroused in mutual dealings; degree or kind of acquaintance or intimacy.

relational [Ri*lay*shonal] *adj* of, as or showing relation; having kinship.

relationship [Ri*lay*shonship] *n* state of being related; connexion; way in which two people affect each other; mutual dealings, feelings or ties.

relative [Ri*lativ*] *adj* of, having or implying relation; estimated by comparison with something else, not absolute; proportionate; mutual, reciprocal; referring to, connected with; relevant; (*gramm*) referring back to a previous word or words ~ **relative** *n* kinsman, kinswoman; one belonging to same family; (*gramm*) relative word.

relatively [Ri*lativ*li] *adv* in relation to something else; comparatively.

relativism [Ri*lativ*izm] *n* theory that absolute truth, certainty or standards of judgement cannot be reached ~ **relativist** *adj* and *n*.

relativistic [Relativ*ist*ik] *adj* of relativity; of relativism; **r. mass** (*phys*) mass of a body taking into account its velocity > PDS.

relativity [Relat*iv*iti] *n* state or quality of being relative; (*phys*) theory which recognizes the impossibility of determining absolute motion and leads to the concept of a four-dimensional space-time continuum > PDS; (*fig*) theory that it is impossible to establish absolute standards of moral or aesthetic judgement; theory that absolute truth or certainty is unattainable.

relax [Ri*laks*] *v/t* and *i* loosen; slacken; reduce tension (of); make or become less rigid, harsh or intense; cease working, worrying *etc*; rest and enjoy oneself; allow muscles to become limp; make languid; relieve from constipation; **relaxed throat** sore throat.

relaxant [Ri*laks*ant] *n* and *adj* (*med*) (drug) causing muscles to relax.

relaxation [Reelaks*ay*shon/Relaks*ay*shon] *n* act of relaxing; state of being relaxed; slackening of tension, strain, severity or attention; amusement; recreation.

relaxing [Ri*laks*ing] *adj* (*of place*) not bracing, enervating.

relay [*Ree*lay] *n* fresh group of workmen, horses, dogs *etc* to take the place of others tired by work; one of a team that works or runs in stages; (*rad*) broadcast sent from one station to another which rediffuses it to listeners; (*elect*) device by which current of one circuit can control that of another > PDS; **r. race** race between teams whose members each run to a specified point and there hand a token to the next member; **r. station** broadcasting station rediffusing programmes received from another ~ **relay** (*p/t* and *p/part* **relaid**) *v/t* and *i* transmit from relay station; pass on (information received); supply relays.

release [Ri*lees*] *v/t* set free; allow to move or escape; discharge; set free from duties; relieve from pain *etc*; allow to be publicly used, seen, bought, known *etc* for the first time or on certain date; (*leg*) give up, surrender; transmit ~ **release** *n* act of setting free or discharging; state of being set free from confinement, duties, pain *etc*; discharge; act of offering for public use, purchase, inspection *etc* for the first time or on a certain date; film, book *etc* thus offered; (*mech*) catch that releases a mechanism; (*leg*) document of discharge or transfer.

relegate [*Re*ligayt] *v/t* transfer to inferior position or grade; transfer or refer to others; (*football*) transfer (lowest scoring team) to lower division of League table.

relent [*Ri*lent] *v/i* become less severe or harsh.

relentless [*Ri*lentlis] *adj* pitiless; inflexible, inexorable ~ **relentlessly** *adv* ~ **relentlessness** *n*.

re-let [Ree-*let*] *v/t* let again; sublet.

relevance, relevancy [*Re*livans, *Re*livansi] *n* quality of being relevant.

relevant [*Re*livant] *adj* having a bearing on the point discussed, pertinent ~ **relevantly** *adv*.

reliable [Ri*Li*-ab'l] *adj* that may be trusted, dependable ~ **reliably** *adv*.

reliance [Ri*Li*-ans] *n* trust, confident dependence.

reliant [Ri*Li*-ant] *adj* trusting, relying.

relic [*Re*lik] *n* object once belonging to or associated with a saint, *esp* part of his body, preserved and revered as holy; object treasured in memory of the past; something kept or surviving from long ago.

relict [*Re*likt] *n* (*ar*) widow.

relief (I) [Ri*leef*] *n* that which removes or lessens anxiety, pain, grief *etc*; state of feeling less anxiety *etc*; money given to those in great need; help, aid; act of raising a siege; reinforcements and supplies sent to troops in danger; release from a post or duty: that which breaks monotony; contrast; (*leg*) exemption, remission ~ **r. bus** extra bus supplementing normal service; **r. road** road built to ease traffic congestion, bypass.

relief (2) *n* method of carving figures so as to project from a flat background surface > PDAA; degree of projection in such carving; apparent three-dimensional effect in painting *etc* due to contrasts of shading *etc*; (*fig*) distinctness, striking contrast; (*geog*) differences in elevation of part of earth's surface; **r. map** map depicting these by corrugations of its surface, or by light and shade effects > PDG.

relieve [Ri*leev*] *v/t* lessen, mitigate (anxiety, pain, poverty *etc*); raise a siege; break monotony of, provide contrast to; deprive; assist, succour; release from duty *etc*; take over the duties of; **r. oneself** evacuate bowels or bladder; **r. one's feelings** express feelings.

religion [Ri*li*jon] *n* belief in and worship of God or gods; specified system of theology, ritual and morality based on this; outlook and way of life based on this; (*fig*) something revered and sought after; (*eccles*) monastic life.

religiosity [Reliji-*o*siti] *n* excessive devotion to religion; morbidly emotional religious attitude.

religious [Ri*li*jus] *adj* of religion; devout, practising a religion; guided or caused by the principles of a religion; monastic; (*fig*) conscientious, exact ~ **religious** *n* (*eccles*) monk; nun ~ **religiously** *adv* ~ **religiousness** *n*.

reline [Ree*lIn*] *v/t* give a new lining to.

relinquish [Ri*lingk*wish] *v/t* let go; give up, abandon; resign; surrender.

reliquary [*Re*likwaRi] *n* casket for relics.

relish [*Re*lish] *v/t* and *i* enjoy, appreciate; have a taste or trace (of); give flavour to ~ **relish** *n* keen enjoyment, zest; appetite; appetizing taste,

pleasing flavour; that which stimulates enjoyment or interest; spice; trace.

relive [Ree*liv*] *v/i* and *t* live again; experience again by memory or imagination.

reluctance [Ri*luk*tans] *n* unwillingness; (*elect*) resistance to magnetic flux offered by a magnetic circuit > PDS.

reluctant [Ri*luk*tant] *adj* unwilling; disinclined; done or granted unwillingly ~ **reluctantly** *adv*.

rely (*p/t* and *p/part* relied) [Ri*lI*] *v/i* trust; have confidence (in).

rem [*Rem*] *n* unit dose of ionizing radiation; roentgen equivalent mass > PDS.

remain [Ri*mayn*] *v/i* stay behind; be left behind or over; survive; continue unchanged or unmoved; persist.

remainder [Ri*mayn*der] *n* that which is left, the rest; (*arith*) quantity left after subtraction or division; (*comm*) unsold book offered at reduced price ~ **remainder** *v/t* offer at reduced price.

remains [Ri*maynz*] *n* (*pl*) remaining fragments; ruins; things or persons still left; survivors; works left unpublished at author's death; corpse.

remake (*p/t* and *p/part* remade) [Ree*mayk*] *v/t* make again; make differently ~ **remake** [*Ree*mayk] *n* remade version (*esp* of film).

remand [Ri*maand*] *v/t* order (accused person) to be sent back to prison while further inquiries are made ~ **remand** *n* state of being remanded; **r. home** institution for juvenile offenders.

remark [Ri*maark*] *v/t* and *i* observe, notice; say; write; make a comment or observation (on) ~ **remark** *n* comment spoken or written; act of noticing.

remarkable [Ri*maar*kab'l] *adj* striking; worthy of notice; unusual ~ **remarkably** *adv*.

remarriage [Ree*ma*Rij] *n* act of marrying again after death or divorce of previous spouse.

remarry [Ree*ma*Ri] *v/i* and *t* marry again.

remediable [Ri*mee*di-ab'l] *adj* curable.

remedial [Ri*mee*di-al] *adj* of or as a remedy; intended or helping to cure.

remedy [*Re*midi] *n* that which cures disease, trouble or evil; reparation; legal redress ~ **remedy** *v/t* cure; repair; redress.

remember [Ri*mem*ber] *v/t* and *i* keep in mind; recall (past experience) with full recognition; know by heart; (*coll*) give a greeting from; give a present or legacy to; possess, exercise, the faculty of memory.

remembrance [Ri*memb*Rans] *n* act of remembering; memory; state of being remembered; that which assists memory; keepsake; memorial; **R. Day (R. Sunday)** Sunday nearest to November 11, commemorating those who died in the Wars of 1914–18 and 1939–45.

remembrancer [Ri*memb*Ranser] *n* one who or that which reminds; official who collects debts owed to the sovereign.

remind [Ri*mInd*] *v/t* cause to remember; bring to notice of ~ **reminder** *n*.

reminisce [Remi*nis*] *v/i* talk of one's memories.

reminiscence [Remi*ni*sens] *n* something remembered, memory; account of this; anecdote; (*pl*) memoirs; similarity that reminds one of something else.

reminiscent [Remi*ni*sent] *adj* talking of or remem-

bering past events; reminding; resembling ~
reminiscently adv.

remiss [Rimis] adj careless, negligent ~ **remiss-
ly** adv ~ **remissness** n.

remissible [Rimisib'l] adj that can be remitted.

remission [Rimishon] n act of remitting; discharge
of debt or penalty; forgiveness, pardon; abatement.

remit (pres/part **remitting**, p/t and p/part **remitted**) [Rimit] v/t and i refrain from exacting,
forgo; forgive, pardon; lessen, abate; pay, esp
by post; send, transmit; postpone; send to lower
court; refer back.

remitment [Rimitment] n act of remitting money;
forgiveness, pardon.

remittal [Rimital] n act of remitting.

remittance [Rimitans] n act of sending money or
bills in payment for goods; sum of money sent
as payment or as an allowance; **r. man** one who
lives abroad on an allowance sent from home.

remittent [Rimitent] adj alternately increasing and
decreasing in intensity.

remitter [Rimiter] n one who remits; one who
pardons; (leg) remittal to lower court.

remnant [Remnant] n that which is left after removal, loss, destruction etc of a larger part;
scrap, fragment; unsold goods, esp short length
of fabric, offered at reduced price.

remonstrance [RimonstRans] n act of remonstrat-
ing; protest; earnest reproof.

remonstrant [RimonstRant] n and adj (one) who
protests.

remonstrate [RemonstRayt] v/i protest; urge
strong reasons against; reprove.

remonstrator [RemonstRayter] n one who remon-
strates.

remora [RemoRa] n species of fish that attaches
itself to others by a sucker.

remorse [Rimawrs] n pain caused by a sense of
guilt; repentance; regret; **without r.** ruthlessly,
unscrupulously.

remorseful [Rimawrsfool] adj feeling or showing
remorse ~ **remorsefully** adv.

remorseless [Rimawrslis] adj having no pity;
relentless ~ **remorselessly** adv.

remote [RimOt] adj far off, distant in space or
time; not closely connected; slight; vague;
unlikely; **r. control** device for controlling a
machine, weapon etc from a distance by radio
waves ~ **remotely** adv ~ **remoteness** n.

remould [ReemOld] v/t recast, shape afresh ~
remould n (mot) old tyre which has been recast.

remount [Reemownt] v/t and i mount again;
set up again; supply with fresh horses; go back
to, be traceable to ~ **remount** [Reemownt] n
horse to replace one put out of action in war.

removable [RimOOvab'l] adj that can be taken off
or away; who can be dismissed from office.

removal [RimOOval] n act of removing; state of
being removed; change of place; dismissal; act
of doing away with, abolishing; act of shifting
one's possessions to a new house.

remove [RimOOv] v/t and i take away; shift to
another place; get rid of, abolish; go away,
change place of residence; dismiss, expel ~
remove n degree of distance from one object to
another; one step in a scale of distances; degree

of kinship; (in some schools) form between upper
fourth and lower fifth ~ **remover** n.

remunerate [RimewneRayt] v/t repay, reward;
pay for a service.

remuneration [RimewneRáyshon] n act of re-
munerating; that which remunerates; wages, pay,
salary.

remunerative [RimewneRativ] adj affording due
payment; profitable.

renaissance [Rinaysans] n cultural or artistic
revival; **the R.** revival of interest in ancient
Greek art and learning in 15th and 16th centuries;
period characterized by this.

renal [Reenal] adj of or in the kidneys.

rend (p/t and p/part **rent**) [Rend] v/t and i tear,
pull, or wrench (apart, away etc); split; (fig)
cause anguish to; be torn apart.

render [Render] v/t pay back, give in return; tender, proffer, submit; represent, reproduce;
translate; perform, interpret; give up; make,
cause to be; melt and clarify (fat); boil down;
give first coat of plaster or cement to; (naut)
slacken, pay out (rope) ~ **render** n (bui) first
coat of plaster or cement.

rendering [RendeRing] n version, interpretation;
translation; (bui) first coat of plaster.

rendezvous [RondayvOO] n appointed meeting-
place ~ **rendezvous** v/i meet by appointment;
assemble.

rendition [Rendishon] n translation; interpretation;
performance.

reneague, renege [Rineeg] v/i refuse to fulfil one's
undertakings.

renegade [Renigayd] n apostate, deserter.

renew [Rinew] v/t and i restore original freshness,
strength etc of; replace by something new, renovate; make or become as good as new; repeat,
begin again; grow again; prolong validity of;
revive.

renewable [Rinew-ab'l] adj that can be renewed.

renewal [Rinew-al] n act of renewing; state of
being renewed; renovation; revival, restoration.

rennet (1) [Renit] n substance extracted from
membrane of a calf's stomach and used to curdle
milk.

rennet (2) n a kind of apple.

renounce [Rinowns] v/t and i formally and explicitly abandon, disclaim; cast off, repudiate;
give up; withdraw from; (cards) fail to follow
suit.

renovate [RenOvayt] v/t make as good as new;
repair, restore to a sound state.

renovation [RenOvayshon] n act of renovating;
state of being renovated.

renovator [RenOvayter] n one who renovates; re-
decorator of houses, furnishings etc.

renown [Rinown] n fame, celebrity.

renowned [Rinownd] adj celebrated, famous.

rent (1) [Rent] p/t and p/part of **rend**.

rent (2) n hole, tear, slit; cleft.

rent (3) n money to be paid by tenant to landlord
for period of use of a house, rooms, land etc;
payment for temporary use of anything ~ **rent**
v/t and i occupy (land, house etc) for payment of
agreed sum; let out, lease to tenant in exchange
for rent; hire out; be rented; borrow in exchange
for fee.

rental [*Re*ntal] *n* total income from rents; amount paid as rent; rent-roll.

renter [*Re*nter] *n* one who leases an estate or who holds premises by paying rent.

rent-free [*Re*nt-fRee] *adj* and *adv* (occupied) without payment of rent.

rentier [*Raa*(ng)ti-ay/*Re*nti-er] *n* (*Fr*) one whose income is derived from investments.

rent-roll [*Re*nt-ROl] *n* account of rents; total income from rents.

renunciation [Rinunsi-*ay*shon] *n* act of renouncing; repudiation; self-denial.

reopen [Ree-*O*pen] *v/t* and *i* open again; resume.

reorganization [Ree-awrganIz*ay*shon] *n* altered method of organizing; act of reorganizing.

reorganize [Ree-*awr*ganIz] *v/t* and *refl* organize again; change method of organization.

reorientation [Ree-awrRi-ent*ay*shon] *n* altered outlook; new adjustment.

rep (1), **repp** [*Re*p] *n* fabric with close-corded surface.

rep (2) *n* and *adj* (*coll*) repertory (theatre); representative (of a firm), travelling salesman.

repaid [Ri*pay*d] *p/t* and *p/part* of **repay**.

repair (1) [Ri*pair*] *v/i* go.

repair (2) *v/t* restore to a good or sound state; mend, renovate; make amends for ∼ **repair** *n* restoration to a good condition; work carried out in order to repair; condition of soundness; **in good r.** in sound condition; **under r.** being repaired.

repaper [Ree*pay*per] *v/t* put fresh paper on (walls).

reparable [*Re*paRab'l] *adj* that may be made good, repaired or recovered.

reparation [Repa*Ray*shon] *n* act of repairing; state of being repaired; satisfaction, amends; compensation; (*pl*) sum paid by conquered nation to victors in compensation for war damage.

repartee [Repaar*tee*] *n* quick witty retort.

repartition [Reepaar*ti*shon] *n* act of distributing or dividing up again.

repast [Ri*paast*] *n* feast, meal.

repatriate [Ree*pa*tRi-ayt] *v/t* send back to native country.

repatriation [ReepatRi-*ay*shon] *n* act of repatriating.

repay (*p/t* and *p/part* **repaid**) [Ri*pay*] *v/t* pay back; give or do in return; reward.

repayable [Ri*pay*-ab'l] *adj* that can or must be repaid.

repayment [Ri*pay*ment] *n* act of repaying; sum repaid; recompense, requital.

repeal [Ri*peel*] *v/t* revoke, rescind; annul ∼ **repeal** *n* revocation; abrogation.

repeat [Ri*peet*] *v/t* and *i* do, make, or say again; say or do what others have said or done; cause to happen again, reproduce; spread (news *etc*); recur; (*of clock*) strike the hour again; (*vulg, of food*) continue to be tasted long after swallowing; **r. oneself** say the same thing again ∼ **repeat** *n* repetition; pattern which repeats itself; something repeated; (*mus*) passage to be repeated; sign indicating this > PDM ∼ **repeat** *adj* (*coll*) performed a second time.

repeatedly [Ri*peet*idli] *adv* again and again; frequently.

repeater [Ri*peet*er] *n* one who or that which repeats; watch or clock which strikes hours or parts of hours when required; repeating firearm; (*math*) decimal in which the same figures continually recur in the same order.

repeating [Ri*peet*ing] *adj* (*of rifle*) which will fire several shots without reloading.

repel (*pres/part* repelling, *p/t* and *p/part* repelled) [Ri*pel*] *v/t* drive back or away; rouse horror, disgust or dislike in; reject, refuse; repulse.

repellant [Ri*pel*ent] *n* substance for repelling animal pests.

repellent [Ri*pel*ent] *adj* that repels; repulsive, loathsome ∼ **repellently** *adv*.

repent [Ri*pent*] *v/t* and *i* feel sorrow or regret for (one's acts or words); feel sorrow for sin and resolve to amend.

repentance [Ri*pent*ans] *n* grief for one's acts or words and a resolve to change one's conduct or to make amends.

repentant [Ri*pent*ant] *adj* feeling penitent, sorry for past sins or faults; expressing repentance ∼ **repentantly** *adv*.

repeople [Ree*peep*'l] *v/t* provide new population for (under-populated area).

repercussion [Reeper*kush*on] *n* (*usu pl*) indirect effect, consequence or influence; reverberation; recoil.

repertoire [*Re*pertwaar] *n* stock of songs, tricks, plays *etc* that person or company is always ready to perform.

repertory [*Re*pertoRi] *n* repertoire; stock; theatre in which many plays are performed successively, each for a short run, *usu* by a permanent company; company of actors of such a theatre; storehouse ∼ **repertory** *adj*.

repetition [Repi*ti*shon] *n* act of repeating; that which is repeated; recital, recitation.

repetitious [Repi*ti*shus] *adj* repetitive.

repetitive [Re*pe*titiv] *adj* repeating, *usu* too often; unvaried ∼ **repetitively** *adv*.

repine [Ri*pIn*] *v/i* be discontented; complain.

replace [Ri*plays*] *v/t* put again in a former place; supplant, take the place of; supply an equivalent or substitute for; put in a new place; repay.

replacement [Ri*plays*ment] *n* act of replacing; one who or that which replaces, substitute.

replant [Ree*plaant*] *v/t* plant again; plant a second or different crop in.

replay [Ree*play*] *v/t* (*sport*) play (a second match between same teams) when the first was abandoned or drawn ∼ **replay** [Ree*play*] *n* replayed match.

replenish [Ri*plen*ish] *v/t* fill again; stock abundantly; find fresh stocks of.

replenishment [Ri*plen*ishment] *n* act of replenishing; that which replenishes; state of being replenished.

replete [Ri*pleet*] *adj* completely filled; filled to excess, sated.

repletion [Ri*plee*shon] *n* state of being completely filled; act of eating and drinking as much as possible.

replica [*Re*plika] *n* copy of a work of art, *esp* by the artist of the original; exact copy.

replication [Repli*kay*shon] *n* (*leg*) reply of plaintiff to defendant's plea.

reply (*p/t* and *p/part* **replied**) [Ri*plI*] *v/t* and *i* answer; say, write or do in response; (*leg*) answer defendant's plea ~ **reply** *n* act of replying or responding, answer.

repoint [Ree*point*] *v/t* renew edges of (mortar in brickwork).

report [Ri*pawrt*] *v/t* and *i* give account of, describe; write account of for publication; state as a fact; announce officially; transmit, repeat (something said by another); make a report; denounce to those in authority; present oneself for duty, *etc* ~ **report** *n* formal statement of the result of an inquiry; written account of a speech, meeting *etc*; statement about pupil's work and conduct at school; popular talk, rumour; fame, repute; explosive noise, bang.

reportage [Repawr*taazh*/Repawr*taaj*] *n* journalist's report on and interpretation of an event, problem *etc*.

reporter [Ri*pawr*ter] *n* one who writes accounts of events for newspapers; one who reports; one who writes official accounts of legal cases.

repose (1) [Ri*pOz*] *v/t* and *i* lay down, place in restful position; rest; lean (on), be supported (on) ~ **repose** *n* act of resting, rest; sleep; calmness, peace; serenity.

repose (2) *v/t* place, put in.

reposeful [Ri*pOz*fool] *adj* restful.

repository [Ri*pozi*toRi] *n* place where things are placed for safety or for preservation; warehouse, store; person to whom secret *etc* are entrusted.

repossess [Reepo*zes*] *v/t* regain possession of, take back (*esp* goods not paid for).

repot (*pres/part* **repotting**, *p/t* and *p/part* **potted**) [Ree*pot*] *v/t* transfer to a different, *usu* larger, pot.

repoussé [Ri*pOO*say] *adj* embossed by hammering from behind.

repp see **rep** (1).

reprehend [Repri*hend*] *v/t* find fault with; reprove; blame.

reprehensible [Repri*hen*sib'l] *adj* deserving reproof ~ **reprehensibly** *adv*.

represent [Repri*zent*] *v/t* describe; draw, depict; make clear to the mind; symbolize, stand for; be an example of; signify, mean; be spokesman or delegate for; be Member of Parliament for; act on behalf of; state clearly; play the part of; (*refl*) claim to be.

representation [Reprizen*tay*shon] *n* act or fact of representing; fact of being represented; that which represents; picture; dramatic performance; protest; statement of arguments.

representational [Reprizen*tay*shonal] *adj* that represents; (*arts*) aiming at recognizable depiction of objects, figures *etc*; not abstract.

representative [Repri*zen*tativ] *adj* that represents or symbolizes; typical; acting for others; consisting of delegates ~ **representative** *n* one who or that which represents; example; deputy, delegate, substitute; one chosen by a body of electors; (*leg*) one who stands in another's place.

repress [Ri*pRes*] *v/t* crush, curb; forcibly restrain; refuse to allow (instincts, wishes, fears *etc*) to exist in one's conscious mind, thrust into unconsciousness > PDP; (*pop*) subject to unnatural and harmful restraint of emotions, urges *etc*.

repressed [Ri*pRest*] *adj* of, showing, or suffering from repression.

repression [Ri*pResh*on] *n* act of repressing; state of

being repressed; suppression, restraint; (*psych*) act of driving out unwelcome impulses, fears *etc* from consciousness to the unconscious > PDP; neurotic behaviour resulting from this.

repressive [Ri*pRes*iv] *adj* that represses; restraining; tyrannical, autocratic ~ **repressively** *adv*.

reprieve [Ri*pReev*] *v/t* cancel or delay the execution of death sentence or other punishment upon; save from death or destruction, *usu* temporarily; grant respite to ~ **reprieve** *n* act of reprieving, *esp* from death sentence; document authorizing this.

reprimand [*Rep*Rimaand] *n* severe reproof, rebuke ~ **reprimand** *v/t* reprove severely.

reprint [Ree*pRint*] *v/t* print again; produce a new edition or impression of (printed work) ~ **reprint** [*Ree*pRint] *n* a new impression without alterations.

reprisal [Ri*pRI*zal] *n* retaliation, *esp* in war.

reprise [Rep*Reez*] *n* (*mus*) repeated passage.

reproach [Ri*pROch*] *v/t* blame, express grieved disapproval of; **r. with** accuse of ~ **reproach** *n* rebuke, sorrowful or scornful blame; disgrace; one who is disgraced.

reproachful [Ri*pROch*fool] *adj* expressing or containing rebuke ~ **reproachfully** *adv*.

reprobate [*Rep*Robayt] *v/t* condemn strongly, censure; (*theol*) (*of God*) exclude from salvation ~ **reprobate** *adj* and *n* depraved (person); (one) entirely given up to sin.

reproduce [Reep*Ro*dews] *v/t* and *i* copy exactly; imitate; revive, repeat; procreate, produce offspring; produce again; make or grow again.

reproduction [Reep*Ro*dukshon] *n* act or process of reproducing; that which is reproduced; copy; generation of offspring.

reproductive [Reep*Ro*duktiv] *adj* concerned with, used in, reproduction; tending to reproduction, fertile.

reproof (1) [Ri*pROOf*] *n* an expression of blame.

reproof (2) [Reep*ROOf*] *v/t* make waterproof again.

reprove [Ri*pROOv*] *v/t* blame, censure, rebuke.

reptile [*Rep*tIl] *n* one of a class of cold-blooded airbreathing scaly or horny vertebrates, crawling on very short legs or on the belly; (*fig*) sly, mean, base or treacherous person ~ **reptile** *adj* of, being or like a reptile; (*fig*) base; sly, treacherous.

reptilian [Rep*tili*-an] *adj* and *n* (like) a reptile.

republic [Ri*pub*lik] *n* form of government in which supreme power is vested in representatives elected by the people; State which has this form of government.

republican [Ri*pub*likan] *adj* of, as, like or favouring a republic; (*US*) of Republicans ~ **Republican** *n* one who supports or favours a republican State; member of one of the two chief political parties of the United States of America.

republicanism [Ri*pub*likanizm] *n* theory or principles of republican government; advocacy of this; desire for a republican State.

republish [Ree*pub*lish] *v/t* publish again; print a new edition of.

repudiate [Ri*pew*di-ayt] *v/t* disown, disclaim; reject; refuse to admit (debt or obligation); divorce.

repudiation [Ripewdi-*ay*shon] *n* act of repudiating.

repugnance, repugnancy [Ri*pug*nans, Ri*pug*-

nansi] *n* extreme dislike, aversion; incompatibility.

repugnant [Ri*pug*nant] *adj* rousing disgust or hostility, loathsome; contradictory, inconsistent; resistant, opposing ~ **repugnantly** *adv*.

repulse [Ri*puls*] *v/t* repel, drive back; (*fig*) reject; rebuff, snub ~ **repulse** *n* act of repulsing; state of being repulsed; rebuff; refusal.

repulsion [Ri*pul*shon] *n* strong dislike, aversion; act of repulsing; state of being repulsed; (*phys*) tendency of bodies or forces to be driven apart by each other.

repulsive [Ri*pul*siv] *adj* loathsome, disgusting; repelling ~ **repulsively** *adv* ~ **repulsiveness** *n*.

repurchase [Ree*purch*is] *v/t* buy back or again.

reputable [*Rep*ewtab'l] *adj* considered good and trustworthy; esteemed; honourable ~ **reputably** *adv*.

reputation [Repew*tay*shon] *n* judgement or opinion commonly applied to a person or thing, estimation; character generally ascribed to one; fame, celebrity; good name, honour.

repute [Ri*pewt*] *n* reputation; common public valuation of person or thing; fame; good name ~ **repute** *v/t* (*ar*) consider; (*pass*) be generally considered or said to be.

reputed [Ri*pewt*id] *adj* generally regarded as being, said to be ~ **reputedly** *adv*.

request [Ri*kwest*] *n* act of asking for something to be done or granted; petition; that which is asked for; **in r.** frequently asked for ~ **request** *v/t* and *i* express desire for, ask for; make a request.

requicken [Ree*kwik*en] *v/t* and *i* bring to life again; come to life again.

requiem [*Rek*wi-em] *n* (*RC*) Mass for the dead; musical setting of parts of this > PDM; (*fig*) dirge, funerary poem.

requiescat [Rekwi-*eskat*] *n* (*Lat*) a prayer for the repose of the dead.

require [Ri*kwIr*] *v/t* and *i* claim by right or authority; order; demand; need; be necessary.

requirement [Ri*kwIr*ment] *n* that which is required; demand; necessary condition; need.

requisite [*Rek*wizit] *n* and *adj* (something) necessary or indispensable.

requisition [Rekwi*zish*on] *v/t* demand supplies of or right to use, *esp* for military use; commandeer, take possession of by right of authority ~ **requisition** *n* formal official demand; act of requiring or commandeering; state of being demanded.

requital [Ri*kwI*tal] *n* act of requiting; compensation, recompense; vengeance, retaliation.

requite [Ri*kwIt*] *v/t* do or give in return; repay; recompense, reward; avenge; punish.

reredos [*Reer*Redos] *n* ornamental screen behind an altar.

reroute [Ree*ROOt*] *v/t* direct (traffic *etc*) on to a different route; send by a different route.

resale [*Ree*sayl] *n* selling goods one had previously bought.

rescind [Ri*sind*] *v/t* annul, revoke, cancel.

rescript [*Rees*kRipt] *n* official answer of Roman emperor to questions on legal problems; written reply of a Pope to a question officially submitted to him.

rescue [*Res*kew] *v/t* save, set free from danger, destruction, imprisonment *etc*; recover by force; (*leg*) release unlawfully ~ **rescue** *n* act of saving

or setting free from danger *etc*; (*leg*) unlawful removal of prisoner from custody; forceful recapture; **come (go) to the r.** give urgently needed help; **r. work** welfare work among the destitute, *esp* those likely to become criminals, prostitutes *etc*.

research [Ri*surch*] *n* scholarly investigation and study aiming at adding to the sum of knowledge on some specific branch; diligent and careful search ~ **research** *v/i* search or examine with care ~ **researcher** *n*.

reseat [Ree*seet*] *v/t* seat again; replace in a seat; provide with new seat or seats.

resemblance [Ri*zemb*lans] *n* state of being like; similarity.

resemble [Ri*zemb*'l] *v/t* be like; have attributes in common with.

resent [Ri*zent*] *v/t* regard as an insult or affront; feel or express displeasure at; feel indignant at.

resentful [Ri*zent*fool] *adj* feeling resentment; inclined to take offence ~ **resentfully** *adv*.

resentment [Ri*zent*ment] *n* act of resenting; anger at insult or injury; angry indignation.

reservation [Rezur*vay*shon] *n* act of reserving; that which is reserved; unexpressed doubt; tacit withholding of consent or approval; condition, proviso; concealment (of thought); seat, accommodation *etc* booked for one's use; (*leg*) retention of privilege; (*US*) area of land set aside for use of native Indians, for preservation of wild animals, or for public use; (*eccles*) act of keeping consecrated Host for later use.

reserve [Ri*zurv*] *v/t* keep in store for later use, keep as spares; set aside for use of specific person or group; order in advance, book; postpone; (*mil*) exempt from service; have in store for; (*leg*) retain (rights) in conveyed property ~ **reserve** *n* that which is reserved; store, spare supply; state of being reserved; reticence, aloofness; self-restraint; act of withholding approval or consent; cautiousness, suspicion; suppression of truth; limitation; price below which an article must not be sold; area of land enclosed and protected for some specified purpose; (*sport*) spare man or team; (*mil*, *pl*) defensive forces only to be called on in war or emergency; armed forces kept out of action until needed; **gold r.** store of gold kept to cover note issue; **in r.** kept ready for possible future use; **without r.** frankly; without restrictions.

reserved [Ri*zurvd*] *adj* reticent, shy, undemonstrative; kept for a particular person or purpose; booked; exempt from military service; (*mil*) retired but liable to be called on in emergency.

reservist [Ri*zur*vist] *n* (*mil*) member of reserved forces.

reservoir [*Rez*ervwaar] *n* large storage tank holding water supply of a town *etc*; receptacle for storing liquid; (*fig*) reserve supply.

reset (*pres/part* **resetting,** *p/t* and *p/part* **reset**) [Ree*set*] *v/t* set again; sharpen, put a fresh edge on; fix (jewels) in a different setting; set up (printed matter) again ~ **reset** *n* matter set up again in printing.

reshuffle [Ree*shuf*'l] *v/t* arrange again in different order; shuffle (cards) again ~ **reshuffle** *n* rearrangement.

reside [Ri*zId*] *v/i* dwell permanently or for a long time; inhere, be present.

residence [*Rez*idens] *n* act or state of dwelling in a place; act of residing in a specified place to carry out some duty or obtain some qualification; place where one dwells, abode; large, imposing house.

residency [Rezidensi] *n* official residence of the representative of the British government at the court of an Indian prince.

resident [Rezident] *adj* dwelling permanently or for a long time in a place ~ **resident** *n* one who dwells permanently or for some time in a place; minister residing at a foreign court.

residential [Rezidenshal] *adj* of, containing or suitable for residents; of residence; consisting of dwelling-houses, not of shops, offices, factories *etc*.

residentiary [RezidenshaRi] *adj* keeping or bound to an official residence ~ **residentiary** *n* ecclesiastic who keeps an official residence.

residua [Rizidew-a] *pl* of **residuum**.

residual [Rizidew-al] *adj* remaining, left over; remaining unexplained, uncured *etc*; (*math*) remaining after subtraction ~ **residual** *n* residuum; residue.

residuary [Rizidew-aRi] *adj* of or as a residue, remaining; **r. legatee** (*leg*) person to whom the residue of an estate is bequeathed.

residue [Rezidew] *n* that which is left over; rest, remainder; (*leg*) that part of an estate which remains over after all debts, charges, and specific legacies have been deducted; (*chem*) residuum.

residuum (*pl* **residua**) [Rizidew-um] *n* that which is left after combustion, separation, purification *etc*; waste product.

resign [RizIn] *v/t* and *i* give up or back; retire from post *etc*; hand over; abandon; yield; (*refl*) reconcile oneself to, accept calmly.

resignation [Rezignayshon] *n* act of resigning; document announcing this; patience, submission to one's fate.

resigned [RizInd] *adj* patiently accepting, submissive, uncomplaining ~ **resignedly** *adv*.

resile [RizIl] *v/i* resume original shape; rebound.

resilience, resiliency [Rizili-ens(i)] *n* act or power of returning to original shape or condition; recuperative power ~ **resilient** *adj* ~ **resiliently** *adv*.

resin [Rezin] *n* amorphous substance secreted by certain plants and insects; synthetic material with properties resembling natural resins ~ **resin** *v/t* apply resin to.

resiniferous [RezinifeRus] *adj* yielding resin.

resinous [Rezinus] *adj* of, containing, or like resin; obtained from resin.

resist [Rizist] *v/t* and *i* oppose, strive against; withstand, thwart; remain unharmed or uninfluenced by; disobey; repel; refuse to succumb to; show resistance ~ **resist** *n* that which is unaffected by a chemical action, *esp* of a dye or glaze.

resistance [Rizistans] *n* act or capacity of resisting; opposition; hostility; that which hinders or retards; (*phys*) extent to which a conductor resists the flow of electricity > PDS; (*mil*) organized armed opposition by civilians in occupied country; **line of least r.** easiest course of action; **passive r.** any non-violent act done as protest against political abuse *etc*; refusal to cooperate.

resistance-coil [Rizistans-koil] *n* (*elect*) insulated wire coil to offer resistance to current.

resistant [Rizistant] *adj* offering resistance.

resistibility [Rizistibiliti] *n* quality of resisting; quality of being resistible.

resistible [Rizistib'l] *adj* that can be resisted.

resistive [Rizistiv] *adj* able to resist ~ **resistivity** *n* power of electrical resistance of material.

resistless [Rizistlis] *adj* that cannot be resisted ~ **resistlessly** *adv*.

resistor [Rizistor] *n* (*elect*) device to produce resistance.

resite [ReesIt] *v/t* transfer to a new site.

resoluble [Rizolewb'l] *adj* that may be resolved; analysable.

resolute [Rezolewt] *adj* determined, unwavering in purpose; bold ~ **resolutely** *adv* ~ **resoluteness** *n*.

resolution [Rezolewshon] *n* act or process of resolving; firm intention, determination, *esp* to act well; firmness, constancy; formal statement of intentions or views by public assembly or legislative body; solution of problem; quality of being resolute, boldness; analysis, separation into parts; transformation; (*pros*) use of two short syllables for one long; (*med*) reabsorption of inflammation; (*mus*) progression from discord to concord.

resolvable [Rizolvab'l] *adj* that may be resolved.

resolve [Rizolv] *v/t* and *i* decide, firmly intend; separate into component parts; dissolve; analyse; solve, explain; (*mus*) convert into concord; disperse; be analysed ~ **resolve** *n* fixed purpose; determination.

resolved [Rizolvd] *adj* fixed in purpose, determined; solved ~ **resolvedly** *adv*.

resolvent [Rizolvent] *n* and *adj* (substance) that can disperse or dissolve.

resonance [Rezonans] *n* act of resounding; sonority, ringing sound; vibration of one body in response to that of another > PDP; (*elect*) state of equality in frequency of an oscillating system and a force applied to it; (*fig*) overtones.

resonant [Rezonant] *adj* resounding, sonorous; producing or showing resonance ~ **resonantly** *adv*.

resonator [Rezonaytor] *n* device for detecting a particular note in a complex sound; apparatus for detecting Hertzian waves.

resorb [Rizawrb] *v/t* absorb again.

resorcinol [Rezawrsinol] *n* crystalline compound used in medicine or as a dye.

resorption [Risawrpshon] *n* act of resorbing; state of being absorbed again.

resort [Rizawrt] *v/i* **r. to** frequently visit or use; use as means, have recourse to ~ **resort** *n* act of resorting; recourse; place that is frequently visited, *esp* for holidays or cures; person or thing to which one has recourse; means, expedient; **in the last r.** when all else has failed.

resound [Rizownd] *v/i* and *t* send back sound, echo; reverberate; be filled with sound; be repeated; be widely known.

resounding [Rizownding] *adj* echoing, ringing; noisy; hearty.

resource [Risawrs] *n* means of aid or support; source of recreation or distraction; device; (*pl*) means of support, money, property; ingenuity, inventiveness.

resourceful [Risawrsfool] *adj* ingenious, clever at finding expedients ~ **resourcefully** *adv* ~ **resourcefulness** *n*.

respect [Ri*spekt*] *v/t* regard with deference and admiration, look up to; esteem, honour; pay due regard to; observe, obey ~ **respect** *n* deferential esteem and admiration; due obedience, consideration or appreciation; reference, application; specific aspect or feature; (*pl*) greetings; **in r. of, with r.** to as regards; **pay one's respects to** visit or greet as mark of polite esteem.

respectability [Ri*spekta*b*i*liti] *n* quality of being respectable; respectable conduct or person.

respectable [Ri*spekt*ab'l] *adj* worthy of respect; honest, decent; obeying social and moral conventions, *esp* too rigidly; quite good, tolerable; better than average ~ **respectably** *adv*.

respecter [Ri*spekt*er] *n* one who respects; **r. of persons** one who is unduly impressed by wealth and rank; snob.

respectful [Ri*spekt*fool] *adj* showing respect ~ **respectfully** *adv*.

respecting [Ri*spekt*ing] *prep* concerning.

respective [Ri*spekt*iv] *adj* relating to each of several; comparative ~ **respectively** *adv*.

respirable [Re*spi*Rab'l] *adj* that is fit to be breathed.

respiration [Re*spi*Rayshon] *n* act or process of breathing > PDB; absorption of oxygen and emission of carbon dioxide; single breath.

respirator [Re*spi*Raytor] *n* gasmask; any apparatus worn over nose and mouth to protect lungs from fumes, smoke, gases, or cold air; (*med*) apparatus for maintaining artificial respiration.

respiratory [Re*spi*RaytoRi/Re*spi*RatoRi/Re*spi*rRatoRi] *adj* of or connected with breathing > PDB.

respire [Ri*spi*r] *v/i* and *t* breathe; breathe out; (*fig*) feel relief; enjoy a respite.

respite [Re*spi*t/Re*spi*t] *n* temporary rest from labour, effort, pain *etc*; reprieve; delay ~ **respite** *v/t* relieve by interval of rest; reprieve; postpone.

resplendence, resplendency [Ri*splen*dens, Ri*splen*densi] *n* brilliance, vivid brightness; (*fig*) glory.

resplendent [Ri*splen*dent] *adj* brilliant; extremely bright; very glorious ~ **resplendently** *adv*.

respond [Ri*spond*] *v/i* react, *usu* favourably; answer, reply; show sympathy (to); correspond ~ **respond** *n* form of plainsong > PDM.

respondent [Ri*spond*ent] *n* one who answers, *esp* to a lawsuit for divorce ~ **respondent** *adj* answering.

response [Ri*spons*] *n* act of answering; answer, reply; reaction to stimulus > PDP; answering feeling or act; versicle said or sung in answer to a priest > PDM.

responsibility [Ri*sponsi*b*i*liti] *n* state of being or feeling responsible; that for which one is responsible; duty; position involving duties.

responsible [Ri*spons*ib'l] *adj* answerable, liable, accountable (to or for); morally accountable; morally bound to fulfil specified duties *esp* towards others; fit to undertake obligations *etc*, trustworthy; involving responsibility ~ **responsibly** *adv*.

responsions [Ri*spon*shonz] *n* (*pl*) first of three examinations for the degree of Bachelor of Arts at Oxford University.

responsive [Ri*spons*iv] *adj* reacting readily and favourably; answering; sympathetic ~ **responsively** *adv* ~ **responsiveness** *n*.

responsory [Ri*spon*soRi] *n* anthem said or sung alternately by soloist and choir.

rest (1) [*Rest*] *n* cessation of motion or activity; pause, short interval; repose, sleep, quietness; peace, freedom from care *etc*; (*fig*) death; place where something rests; support, prop; lodginghouse; (*mus*) interval of silence; (*ar*) support for butt of lance ~ **rest** *v/i* and *t* cease moving or acting; lie still, sleep; be at peace; be dead; cause to be still; lean (on), be supported (by); place in leaning or lying position; prop up; remain; rely; settle; **r. up** (*US*) take a long rest.

rest (2) *n* remainder, what is left ~ **rest** *v/i* remain; **r. with** be the responsibility of.

restate [Ree*stayt*] *v/t* state again or differently.

restaurant [*Reste*Rong] *n* place where meals can be bought and eaten.

restaurateur [*Resto*Ra*tur*] *n* one who keeps a restaurant.

rest-cure [*Rest*-kewr] *n* period of complete quiet as a treatment for nervous disorders.

restful [*Rest*fool] *adj* giving an impression of peace and quiet, soothing ~ **restfully** *adv* ~ **restfulness** *n*.

rest-home [*Rest*-hOm] *n* home where chronic invalids and elderly people are looked after.

resting-place [*Rest*ing-plays] *n* place where something lies or rests; (*fig*) grave.

restitution [Resti*tew*shon] *n* act of restoring that which has been taken away or lost; reparation.

restive [*Rest*iv] *adj* unwilling to go forward; stubborn, unruly; restless, fidgety; impatient of control ~ **restively** *adv* ~ **restiveness** *n*.

restless [*Rest*lis] *adj* continually moving, fidgety; uneasy; unsettled; sleepless ~ **restlessly** *adv* ~ **restlessness** *n*.

restorable [Ri*stawr*Rab'l] *adj* that may be restored.

restoration [Resto*Ray*shon] *n* act of restoring; renewal; model or drawing of extinct animal in its supposed original form; building *etc* repaired to its supposed original form; reconstruction; reconstructed object; (*cap*) return of Charles II to English throne in 1660; period immediately after this.

restorative [Ri*stawr*Rativ] *n* and *adj* (medicine or treatment) restoring health, strength *etc* ~ **restoratively** *adv*.

restore [Ri*stawr*] *v/t* bring back to a former state, repair; replace; give back; rebuild; heal; bring into existence again; renew.

restrain [Ri*stRayn*] *v/t* hold back, check; repress; confine.

restrained [Ri*stRaynd*] *adj* under control; moderate, without open emotion, exaggeration *etc* ~ **restrainedly** *adv*.

restraint [Ri*stRaynt*] *n* act of restraining; state of being restrained; check, repression, control; limitation; confinement.

restrict [Ri*stRikt*] *v/t* limit, confine; keep within bounds; limit by law; **restricted area** area where a speed limit (*usu* 30 mph) is imposed on vehicles.

restriction [Ri*stRik*shon] *n* act of restricting; that which restricts; law or regulation that restricts; state of being restricted.

restrictive [Ri*stRikt*iv] *adj* imposing restrictions; limiting ~ **restrictively** *adv*.

rest-room [Rest-ROOm] *n* (*euph*) lavatory, *esp* in shop, theatre, *etc*.

restructure [ReestRukcher] *v/t* change or renew the structure of.

result [Rizult] *v/i* follow as a consequence, ensue; end (in) ~ **result** *n* consequence, outcome; conclusion.

resultant [Rizultant] *adj* following as a result; resulting from combination of forces, agents *etc*.

resume [Rizewm] *v/t* and *i* take back, take again; sum up; begin again, continue after interruption.

résumé [Rayzewmay] *n* (*Fr*) summary, précis; condensed statement.

resumption [Rizumpshon] *n* act of resuming.

resurgence [Risurjens] *n* revival; renewal.

resurgent [Risurjent] *adj* reviving; renewed.

resurrect [RezuRekt] *v/t* and *i* bring back to life, revive; bring into use again; rise from the dead.

resurrection [RezuRekshon] *n* act of reviving after death; state of being revived; renewed existence or vigour; (*theol*) the rising of Christ from his grave; the rising of all men from death at the Last Day; **r. man** (*hist*) one who dug up corpses to sell to anatomists; **r. pie** (*coll*) dish of re-heated meat.

resurrectionist [RezuRekshonist] *n* (*hist*) resurrection man.

resuscitate [Risusitayt] *v/t* and *i* revive; restore to vigour; restore from apparent death.

resuscitation [Risusitayshon] *n* act of resuscitating; state of being resuscitated.

retail [Reetayl] *adj* and *adv* (sold) in small quantities to the actual consumer ~ **retail** *v/t* sell (goods) retail; repeat, tell in detail ~ **retail** *n* act of selling goods retail.

retailer [Reetayler] *n* one who sells goods retail.

retain [Ritayn] *v/t* keep, continue to have or hold; hold up or back; remember; engage services of, *esp* by advance fee; **retaining fee** fee paid in advance to barrister or adviser to engage his services; **retaining wall** wall built to hold back earth or water.

retainer [Ritayner] *n* one who or that which retains; attendant, follower; dependant; (*leg*) preliminary fee; agreement by which a barrister acts in a case.

retake (*p/t* **retook**, *p/part* **retaken**) [Reetayk] *v/t* take again; capture again; photograph again ~ **retake** [Reetayk] *n* (*cin*) act of photographing a shot or sequence again.

retaliate [Ritali-ayt] *v/i* return like for like, *esp* evil for evil; take vengeance.

retaliation [Ritali-ayshon] *n* act of retaliating; reprisals, requital.

retaliatory [Ritali-ayteRi] *adj* of or as retaliation; that retaliates.

retard [Ritaard] *v/t* reduce the speed or rate of development of; make slow or late; delay; hamper ~ **retard** *n* delay ~ **retarded** *adj* mentally or educationally backward.

retardation [Ritaardayshon] *n* act of retarding; degree to which something is retarded; backwardness, *esp* mental or educational > PDP; (*phys*) rate of decrease of velocity.

retch [Reech/Rech] *v/i* make an effort to vomit ~ **retch** *n* attempt at vomiting; sound of this.

retention [Ritenshon] *n* act of retaining; state of being retained; power of retaining, *esp* in the mind > PDP; (*path*) failure to get rid of matters normally excreted from the body.

retentive [Ritentiv] *adj* able to retain; having a good memory ~ **retentively** *adv* ~ **retentiveness** *n*.

rethink [Reethink] *v/t* thoroughly re-examine and alter (opinions, plans *etc*) ~ **rethink** [Reethink] *n*.

retiary [ReesheRi] *adj* weaving nets or webs.

reticence [Retisens] *n* quality of being reticent.

reticent [Retisent] *adj* reserved in speech; silent; secretive ~ **reticently** *adv*.

reticle [Retik'l] *n* fine network.

reticular [Ritikewlar] *adj* like a net; formed with interstices ~ **reticularly** *adv*.

reticulate [Ritikewlayt] *adj* of or like network ~ **reticulate** *v/t* make into network.

reticule [Retikewl] *n* obsolete type of small handbag or pouch.

retina (*pl* **retinae**) [Retina] *n* layer of nerve fibres sensitive to light forming lining of eyeball of vertebrates > PDB.

retinitis [Retinitis] *n* inflammation of the retina.

retinue [Retinew] *n* suite of attendants.

retire [Ritir] *v/i* and *t* go away into privacy; give up a business, office *etc*, *esp* on growing old; resign; go to bed; retreat; cause to resign, retreat or withdraw; withdraw (bill) from circulation.

retired [Ritird] *adj* private; withdrawn from society; having given up business or active service, *esp* from age; secluded.

retirement [Ritirment] *n* act of retiring; state of being retired; withdrawal from business or from active service; privacy; secluded place.

retiring [RitirRing] *adj* shy, reserved; unobtrusive ~ **retiringly** *adv*.

retort (1) [Ritawrt] *n* (*chem*) glass vessel consisting of large bulb with a long narrowing neck > PDS; large receptacle used for production of coal-gas ~ **retort** *v/t* purify in a retort.

retort (2) *v/t* and *i* answer angrily or sharply; return a charge or an argument; pay back in kind; make a quick reply ~ **retort** *n* quick reply; sharp rejoinder.

retouch [Reetuch] *v/t* improve (photograph *etc*) by touching up; touch again.

retrace [RitRays] *v/t* go over (same course) again, go back by same path; trace back; renew outlines of (a tracing); look back on, recall; trace to its origins.

retract [RitRakt] *v/t* and *i* draw back or in; take back, revoke, recant, disavow.

retractible [RitRaktib'l] *adj* that may be retracted.

retractile [RitRaktil] *adj* that can be drawn in.

retraction [RitRakshon] *adj* act of retracting; recantation.

retractive [RitRaktiv] *adj* drawing back or in.

retractor [RitRaktor] *n* (*anat*) muscle which draws back; (*surg*) instrument for holding back.

retrain [ReetRayn] *v/t* train again; give new or different training to.

retranslate [ReetRanslayt] *v/t* translate again; translate back into the original language.

retread (1) [ReetRed] *v/t* put new tread on (a tyre) ~ **retread** [ReetRed] *n* new tread for tyre.

retread (2) (*p/t* **retrod**, *p/part* **retrodden**) *v/t* walk over (same track *etc*) again.

retreat [RitReet] *n* act of withdrawing, *esp* before an enemy; secluded place, quiet private spot;

lair; period of seclusion and prayer, *usu* while staying in a religious institution; signal to troops to retreat or retire to night quarters ~ **retreat** *v/i* and *t* move backwards or away; withdraw when attacked or threatened; abandon one's position; cause to move backwards.

retrench [Rit*Rench*] *v/t* and *i* curtail, lessen; abridge; make economies.

retrenchment [Rit*Rench*ment] *n* act of retrenching; defence position constructed within another.

retribution [Retri*bew*shon] *n* punishment, requital for evil done; fitting recompense; distribution of rewards and punishments.

retributive [Rit*Rib*ewtiv] *adj* of or as retribution.

retrievable [Rit*Reev*ab'l] *adj* that may be retrieved.

retrieval [Rit*Reev*al] *n* act of retrieving; process of finding information stored in computer *etc*.

retrieve [Rit*Reev*] *v/t* and *i* find and bring in; recover by searching; regain; rescue; remedy; compensate; (*of dogs*) fetch shot game.

retriever [Rit*Reev*er] *n* dog trained to fetch in game that has been shot; breed of dog derived from the Labrador.

retro- *pref* backwards in space or time.

retroaction [Retro*ak*shon] *n* backward or reversed action; retrospective action.

retroactive [Retro*ak*tiv] *adj* retrospective; working backwards.

retrocede [Retro*seed*] *v/t* and *i* move backwards; move inwards; restore, cede back.

retrocession [Retro*ses*hon] *n* act of retroceding.

retrochoir [*Ret*rokwIr] *n* area behind high altar of cathedral or large church.

retrogradation [Retrogra*day*shon] *n* act of moving backward; deterioration; (*astron*) apparent westward motion of a planet in the zodiac.

retrograde [*Ret*rogRayd] *adj* going or bending backwards; reversed; reverting to more or more primitive stage; deteriorating ~ **retrograde** *v/i* move backwards; decline; revert.

retrogress [Retro*gRes*] *v/i* go backward; degenerate.

retrogression [Retro*gResh*on] *n* act of going backward; degeneration.

retrogressive [Retro*gRes*iv] *adj* going or moving backward; degenerating ~ **retrogressively** *adv*.

retropulsion [Retro*pul*shon] *n* (*path*) spreading of a disease from an external to an internal part.

retro-rocket [*Ret*RO-Rokit] *n* supplementary rocket jet fired to check or alter the course of a missile, spacecraft *etc*.

retrospect [*Ret*Rospekt] *n* act of looking back on past things; review of past events.

retrospection [Retro*spek*shon] *n* act of looking back on past experience > PDP.

retrospective [Retro*spek*tiv] *adj* looking back on the past; applying to or affecting past actions ~ **retrospectively** *adv*.

retroussé [Ret*ROO*say] *adj* (*Fr*) (*of the nose*) turned up at the end.

retroversion [RetRO*vur*shon] *n* state of being bent or turned backwards; backwards displacement.

retrovert [Retro*vurt*] *v/i* and *t* turn or bend back; be displaced to the back.

retry (*p/t* and *p/part* **retried**) [Reet*RI*] *v/t* give fresh judicial trial to.

retsina [Ret*seen*a] *n* Greek wine flavoured with resin.

return [Ri*turn*] *v/t* and *i* give, send, or bring back; come or go back; happen or come again; revert; answer, respond, retort; give as equivalent (for), repay; report officially; elect; produce as profit ~ **return** *n* act of giving or sending back; act of coming or going back; that which is sent back; recurrence, reappearance; official account; act of electing; state of being elected; profits, proceeds; repayment; return-ticket; (*pl*) articles to be sent back to wholesaler ~ **return** *adj* of, as or for a return; done or given in repayment; of or for travel to and back from specified place.

returnable [Ri*turn*ab'l] *adj* that can or should be sent back to sender or supplier.

returning-officer [Ri*turn*ing-ofiser] *n* officer who presides at an election.

return-ticket [Ri*turn*-tikit] *n* ticket for a journey to a place and back again.

reunion [Ree-y*OO*nyon] *n* act of reuniting; state of being reunited; union after separation; a gathering of friends, colleagues *etc*.

reunionism [Ree-y*OO*nyonizm] *n* movement for reunion of Anglican and RC Churches ~ **reunionist** *adj* and *n*.

reunite [Ree-y*OO*nIt] *v/t* and *i* join together after a separation; reconcile; be united again.

rev [*Rev*] (1) (*pres/part* **revving**, *p/t* and *p/part* **revved**) *v/t* and *i* **r. up** (*mot*) increase number of revolutions per minute of (an engine) ~ **rev** *n* (*mot*) revolution of engine.

rev (2) *n* (*coll*) clergyman; priest; Reverend Mother of a convent.

revalue [Ree*valew*] *v/t* increase the value of (currency) ~ **revaluation** *n*.

revamp [Ree*vamp*] *v/t* (*sl*) make better or more efficient; renovate.

revanchism [Ri*vaanch*izm] *n* (*pol*) policy aimed at recovering lost territory by force ~ **revanchist** *adj* and *n*.

reveal (1) [Ri*veel*] *v/t* make visible or known; divulge; allow to appear; make known by supernatural agency.

reveal (2) *n* (*archi*) side of opening for window or doorway.

reveille [Ri*vali*] *n* (*mil*) morning signal for rising.

revel (*pres/part* **revelling**, *p/t* and *p/part* **revelled**) [*Rev*el] *v/i* make merry, feast, carouse; **r. in** enjoy intensely ~ **revel** *n* carousal, merrymaking.

revelation [Revi*lay*shon] *n* act of revealing; that which is revealed; disclosure of something unknown; that which first introduces new impressive knowledge or experience; religious doctrine claiming to be directly taught by God to man; (*cap*) last book of *NT*, Apocalypse.

revelational [Revi*lay*shonal] *adj* of or by revelation.

reveller [*Rev*iler] *n* one who revels.

revelry [*Rev*ilRi] *n* merry-making; noisy festivity.

revenant [*Rev*enant] *n* spirit returned from the dead, ghost.

revendication [Reevendi*kay*shon] *n* formal claim for the surrender of rights.

revenge [Ri*venj*] *n* act of injuring one by whom one was injured, angry or malicious retaliation; injury so inflicted, vengeance; desire to inflict such injury, vindictiveness ~ **revenge** *v/t* inflict injury in return for; take revenge on behalf of, avenge.

revengeful [Ri*venj*fool] *adj* desiring to take revenge ~ **revengefully** *adv* ~ **revengefulness** *n*.

revenue [*Revi*new] *n* income; the annual income of a State; government department concerned with collecting the national revenue.

reverberant [Ri*vurbe*Rant] *adj* resounding.

reverberate [Ri*vurbe*Rayt] *v/t* and *i* send back sound, re-echo; resound; throw back, reflect; rebound.

reverberation [Ri*vurbe*Rayshon] *n* act of reverberating; sound echoed back.

reverberator [Ri*vurbe*Raytor] *n* reflector; reflecting lamp.

reverberatory [Ri*vurbe*RaytoRi] *adj* producing reverberation; throwing back heat.

revere [Ri*veer*] *v/t* regard with respect and admiration; regard as holy, venerate.

reverence [*Reve*Rens] *n* act of revering; feeling of awe and admiration; veneration; **your R.** mode of address to priest, *esp* in Ireland ~ **reverence** *v/t* venerate; regard with awe and admiration.

reverend [*Reve*Rend] *adj* worthy of reverence; entitled to respect; title of respect given to clergy; **R. Mother** Mother Superior of a convent.

reverent [*Reve*Rent] *adj* feeling or expressing reverence; humble ~ **reverently** *adv*.

reverential [Reve*Ren*shal] *adj* feeling, showing or caused by reverence.

reverie [*Reve*Ri] *n* dreaminess, day-dreaming; vague train of thought; piece of music supposed to express this state of mind.

revers [Ri*veer*] *n* (*freq* as *pl* [Ri*veerz*]) lapel; any part of a garment turned back to show the lining.

reversal [Ri*vursal*] *n* act or process of reversing or being reversed; cancellation; total change.

reverse [Ri*vurs*] *v/t* and *i* turn upside down or back to front; move or cause to move backwards; annul, cancel; transpose the positions of; put in or take up a position opposite to the present or normal one; **r. arms** (*mil*) hold rifle with barrel downwards ~ **reverse** *n* what is contrary or opposite; change of circumstances for the worse; setback; defeat; financial loss; back or secondary side; underside; design on this; backward motion; mechanism causing this ~ **reverse** *adj* contrary; opposite; backward.

reversed [Ri*vurst*] *adj* turned backwards or upside down; changed to the contrary; cancelled, revoked ~ **reversedly** *adv*.

reversely [Ri*vursli*] *adv* in a reverse manner.

reversible [Ri*vursib*'l] *adj* that can be reversed.

reversion [Ri*vurshon*] *n* return to former state, habit *etc*; (*leg*) return of an estate to the grantor or his heirs after a particular grant is ended; right of succession; (*biol*) tendency to revert to ancestral type; atavism > PDP; sum payable at a special time.

reversional, reversionary [Ri*vurshonal*, Ri*vurshonaRi*] *adj* of, as or like a reversion.

reverso [Ri*vurs*O] *n* left-hand page of an open book.

revert [Ri*vurt*] *v/i* return to former state; regress; go back again; (*leg*) return to former owner or to his heirs upon death of present user or expiry of grant.

revertible [Ri*vurtib*'l] *adj* that may revert.

revet (*pres/part* **revetting**, *p/t* and *p/part* re-

vetted) [Ri*vet*] *v/t* face (a wall or surface) with harder material.

revetment [Ri*vetment*] *n* protective covering on bank, rock surface *etc* to prevent erosion.

review [Ri*vew*] *n* written evaluation of a recent book, play, film *etc* for publication in journal or newspaper; periodical containing critical articles *etc*; (*mil*) formal inspection and parade of forces; retrospective survey; re-examination; revision ~ **review** *v/t* write review of; inspect (troops); survey again, look back on.

reviewer [Ri*vew*-er] *n* one who writes reviews.

revile [Ri*vIl*] *v/t* and *i* abuse, bitterly reproach; be abusive.

revilement [Ri*vIlment*] *n* reproach; abuse; contemptuous language.

revisal [Ri*vIzal*] *n* revision, correction.

revise [Ri*vIz*] *v/t* study again in preparation for examination; look through in detail to correct or amend; change (views *etc*) after consideration ~ **revise** *n* proof-sheet taken from earlier corrected proof.

revision [Ri*vizhon*] *n* act of studying same material once more; act of re-examining or of looking over; that which has been revised, corrected version.

revisionism [Ri*vizhonizm*] *n* (*pol*) policy seeking to change the basic tenets of a political creed, *esp* of Marxism ~ **revisionist** *adj* and *n*.

revisory [Ri*vIzoRi*] *adj* having the power to revise.

re-vitalize [Ree*vItalIz*] *v/t* bring back vitality to.

revival [Ri*vIval*] *n* act of reviving; state of being revived; return of life, vigour, popularity *etc*; new presentation, production *etc*; intensive campaign of sermons and prayer-meetings to rouse new religious fervour in a district; **R. of Learning** the Renaissance.

revivalism [Ri*vIvalizm*] *n* campaign to reawaken religious fervour by means of special services *etc*; support or advocacy of this.

revivalist [Ri*vIvalist*] *n* one who organizes meetings or preaches in a religious revival ~ **revivalist** *adj*.

revive [Ri*vIv*] *v/i* and *t* return to life; return to health, consciousness, activity *etc*; flourish again; recover from neglect, depression, obscurity *etc*.; reawaken; bring back to life, popularity, activity *etc*; rouse; renew; produce again (play *etc* that has not recently been acted); (*chem*) restore to its natural or metallic state.

reviver [Ri*vIver*] *n* one who or that which revives; preparation for renovating; (*sl*) stimulant; drink.

revivify [Ri*vivifI*] *v/t* restore to life; reanimate; (*chem*) revive.

revocable [*Revo*kab'l] *adj* that can be revoked.

revocation [Revo*kay*shon] *n* act of revoking; state of being revoked; repeal; reversal of a decree.

revoke [Ri*vOk*] *v/t* and *i* annul, repeal; cancel; take back; fail to follow suit at cards although it is possible ~ **revoke** *n* act of revoking at cards.

revolt [Ri*vOlt*] *v/i* and *t* rebel; seek to overthrow those in authority; refuse to obey; feel disgust (at); repel; disgust ~ **revolt** *n* rebellion.

revolting [Ri*vOlting*] *adj* causing disgust; rebellious, conducting a revolt ~ **revoltingly** *adv*.

revolution [Revo*lew*shon] *n* state of revolving; rotation, circular motion of a body on its axis or round a centre; period of rotation; cycle; continued course; radical change of circumstances, attitudes, conditions *etc*; forcible overthrow of political system; attempt at this.

revolutionary [Revol*ew*shonaRi] *adj* of or tending to produce a revolution in government; causing a radical change of outlook, methods *etc* ~ **revolutionary** *n* one in favour of, or taking part in, a revolution.

revolutionize [Revolewshonɪz] *v/t* alter fundamentally and drastically.

revolve [Ri*volv*] *v/i* and *t* turn round; move round a centre; move in a circle; cause to rotate; think over carefully, ponder.

revolver [Ri*volv*er] *n* one who or that which revolves; pistol with revolving cylinder which can be fired several times without reloading.

revue [Ri*vew*] *n* theatrical entertainment with songs, dances and sketches.

revulsion [Ri*vul*shon] *n* sudden violent change of feeling, *usu* to hostility or disgust; (*med*) reduction of a disease in one part of the body by treatment of another part.

revulsive [Ri*vul*siv] *adj* (*med*) causing revulsion; counter-irritating.

reward [Ri*wawrd*] *n* that which is given in return, *usu* for good; recompense; requital; money offered for returning something lost or for detecting a criminal ~ **reward** *v/t* give as return to, repay.

rewire [ReewIr] *v/t* insert new or different electric wiring into.

reword [Reewurd] *v/t* put into different words.

rewrite (*p/t* **rewrote**, *p/part* **rewritten**) [ReeRIt] *v/t* write over again; write in a different way, revise ~ **rewrite** [ReeRIt] *n* rewritten version.

Rex [Reks] *n* title of reigning king; a breed of curly-coated cat.

rexine [Rekseen] *n* a linen-bound plastic substitute for leather.

Reynard [Raynard] *n* traditional name for a fox.

rhabdomancy [Rabdomansi] *n* dowsing.

rhadamanthine [Radamanthɪn] *adj* rigorously just, inflexible.

rhapsodic [Rapsodik] *adj* of or like rhapsody; incoherently enthusiastic.

rhapsodist [Rapsodist] *n* one who composes or writes rhapsodies; one who expresses incoherent delight.

rhapsodize [Rapsodɪz] *v/i* compose or recite a rhapsody; **r. over** express enthusiasm or delight about.

rhapsody [Rapsodi] *n* incoherent and enthusiastic expression of feeling; wild delight; (*mus*) irregular and emotional composition > PDM; ancient Greek epic; section of this for recitation.

rhenium [Reeni-um] *n* a hard heavy grey metallic element > PDS.

rheo- *pref* of electric current; of a current.

rheology [Ree-oloji] *n* study of the deformation and flow of matter.

rheometry [Ree-omitRi] *n* measurement of force and velocity of currents.

rheostan [Ree-ostan] *n* alloy used for electrical resistance wire > PDS.

rheostat [Ree-ostat] *n* (*elect*) instrument for regulating electric current > PDP; variable electric resistance.

rhesus [Reezus] *n* a small Indian monkey; **R. factor** an antigen found in the blood of many human beings > PDB; **R. negative** having no Rhesus factor; **R. positive** having the Rhesus factor.

rhetoric [Retorik] *n* use of language, *usu* elaborate, to persuade or impress; self-consciously elaborate style in speech or writing; style that aims at rousing emotion.

rhetorical [Retorikal] *adj* of or like rhetoric; consciously effective; ornate, showy; playing on the emotions; **r. question** question put for the sake of effect and not expecting or needing an answer.

rheum [ROOm] *n* (*ar*) mucous discharge from membranes of nose, throat or mouth.

rheumatic [ROOmatik] *adj* of, suffering from, or caused by rheumatism; **r. fever** a severe streptococcal contagious infection ~ **rheumatic** *n* one suffering from rheumatism; (*pl*, *coll*) rheumatic pain.

rheumaticky [ROOmatiki] *adj* (*coll*) suffering from rheumatism; like rheumatism.

rheumatism [ROOmatizm] *n* name of various diseases causing pain and stiffness in muscles or joints.

rheumatoid [ROOmatoid] *adj* of or like rheumatism; **r. arthritis** disease causing thickening and distortion of the joints.

rheumy [ROOmi] *adj* (*ar*) of or full of rheum.

rhin- *pref* of the nose.

rhinal [RInal] *adj* of nose or nostrils.

rhinestone [RInstOn] *n* type of rock crystal; colourless artificial gem.

rhino- *pref* of the nose.

rhino (1) [RInO] *n* (*coll abbr*) rhinoceros.

rhino (2) *n* (*sl*) money.

rhinoceros [RInoseRos] *n* large tropical quadruped with one or two horns on the nose.

rhinoscope [RInoskOp] *n* instrument for inspecting the nasal passages.

rhizic [RIzik] *adj* (*math*) of a root.

rhizo- *pref* (*bot*) of a root.

rhizoid [RIzoid] *adj* root-like ~ **rhizoid** *n* hair-like structure serving as a root > PDB.

rhizome [RIzOm] *n* (*bot*) thick underground stem which sends out roots downwards and shoots upwards > PDB.

rhodium [ROdi-um] *n* white metallic element resembling platinum > PDS.

rhodo- *pref* rosy red; of or like roses.

rhododendron [ROdodendRon] *n* genus of evergreen shrubs with brilliant flowers.

rhodolite [ROdolIt] *n* rosy variety of garnet.

rhodopsin [ROdopsin] *n* complex organic compound found in the retina > PDS.

rhomb [Rom/Romb] *n* rhombus.

rhombic [Rombik] *adj* of or like a rhombus.

rhombohedron [RomboheedRon] *n* solid figure contained by six rhombic planes.

rhomboid [Romboid] *n* a rhombus with only its opposite sides equal ~ **rhomboid** *adj* like a rhombus.

rhombus [Rombus] *n* quadrilateral with oblique angles and having all its sides equal.

rhubarb [ROObaarb] *n* herbaceous plant whose fleshy stalks are cooked and eaten as a dessert; genus of plants including this; (*theat coll*) confused noise of many speakers; (*sl*) nonsense; noisy argument.

rhumb [Rum] n (naut) line on the earth's surface cutting all the meridians at the same angle > PDG; a point of the compass.

rhumba see rumba.

rhyme, rime (1) [RIm] n identity or close similarity of sound in words or final syllables, esp at the ends of lines of verse; rhymed verse; poem, poetry; **without r. or reason** nonsensical, inexplicable ~ **rhyme** v/t and i use as a rhyme (to); be a rhyme for; write in rhymed verse; write poetry ~ **rhymed** adj having rhymes.

rhymer [RImer] n one who makes rhymes, versifier; inferior poet.

rhymester [RImster] n rhymer.

rhythm [RiTH'm] n regular occurrence and cessation, or regular increase and decrease, of any activity; pattern formed by alternations of long and short, or of strong and weak stress, esp in sounds; periodic recurrence, cycle; (mus) accentuation and distribution of notes in time > PDM; particular example of this; **r. method** birth-control by restricting intercourse to the infertile phase of the menstrual cycle.

rhythmic [RiTHmik] adj rhythmical.

rhythmical [RiTHmikal] adj of or in a rhythm; showing rhythm ~ **rhythmically** adv.

rib [Rib] n curved bone extending from the spine to enclose the thorax; long narrow ridge along a surface; any thin curved beam, rod etc acting as a support or framework; leaf vein; moulding on vaulted roof, groin; curved timber of ship's frame; vertical row of raised stitches in knitting; **floating r.** rib not attached to breastbone ~ **rib** (pres/part **ribbing**, p/t and p/part **ribbed**) v/t furnish with ribs; form into ribs; (sl) tease.

ribald [Ribald] adj making coarse jokes; indecent in humour; mocking coarsely.

ribaldry [RibaldRi] n coarse joking.

riband [Riband] n (ar) ribbon.

ribbed [Ribd] adj furnished with ribs; ridged.

ribbing [Ribing] n arrangement in ribs; series of ribs, esp in knitting.

ribbon [Ribon] n narrow band of fine fabric; length of this worn as decoration on clothes or in hair; short piece of this used as military decoration, as the badge of a club, team, order of knighthood etc; (fig) long narrow strip; (pl, coll) driving-reins; **r. development** act of building a single row of houses along each side of a road ~ **ribbon** v/t and i form into ribbons; extend in long narrow strips.

riboflavin [RibOflayvin] n (bioch) yellow crystalline compound which is member of vitamin B complex > PDS.

ribose [RibOz] n pentose, a gum-acid non-fermenting sugar; a monosaccharide.

ribosome [RibOsOm] n granule present in all cells on which proteins are synthesized > PDB.

rice [RIs] n cereal plant grown on marshy land in hot countries; white seeds of this used as food.

rice-paper [RIs-payper] n edible paper used for packing sweets, cakes etc; fine paper made from pith of a Chinese tree.

rice-pudding [RIs-pooding] n baked pudding of rice in sweetened milk.

rich [Rich] adj having much money or many possessions, wealthy; abundantly supplied with; plentiful, copious; producing plentifully, fertile; valuable, sumptuous; (of colours, sounds) intense, deep; (of food) very fatty; highly seasoned; indigestible; (coll) highly amusing; ridiculous; (sl) indecent ~ **rich** n a rich person; (collect) rich people; (pl) wealth, abundant possessions; abundance; great value.

richly [Richli] adv in a rich manner; abundantly, thoroughly.

richness [Richnis] n wealth, opulence; splendour; fertility; abundance.

rick [Rik] (1) n stack of corn, hay etc built regularly and thatched ~ **rick** v/t make into ricks.

rick (2) n wrench, sprain ~ **rick** v/t wrench.

rickets [Rikits] n deficiency disease in children, causing softening of the bones.

rickety [Rikiti] adj shaky, tottering; fragile; suffering from rickets.

rickshaw [Rikshaw] n light two-wheeled hand-drawn carriage formerly used in Japan.

ricochet (pres/part **ricochetting**, p/t and p/part **ricochetted**) [Rikoshay/Rikoshet] v/i and t rebound or cause to rebound from flat surface ~ **ricochet** n act of rebounding.

rictus [Riktus] n involuntary grin; vertical width of open mouth, gape.

rid (pres/part **ridding**, p/t and p/part rid) [Rid] v/t clear away, drive away; free (from), disencumber ~ **rid** adj free from; **get r. of** discard; drive away; free oneself from.

ridable [RIdab'l] adj that can be ridden.

riddance [Ridans] n act of ridding; state of being rid of something; **good r.** exclamation welcoming removal of something or someone unwanted.

ridden [Riden] p/part of ride.

riddle (1) [Rid'l] n a deliberately puzzling question, esp one with a verbal trick, pun etc; mysterious or puzzling person, fact or thing ~ **riddle** v/i and t speak in riddles; explain, solve.

riddle (2) v/t pierce with many holes; sift through a large sieve; **be riddled with** be seriously damaged by ~ **riddle** n large-meshed sieve.

ride (p/t **rode**, p/part **ridden**) [Rid] v/t and i sit on and be carried along by (bicycle, horse etc); practise horsemanship; float (on), be borne up (by); shift from proper position while in use; (US coll) exasperate by perpetual criticisms, demands etc; **r. down** trample under horse's hooves; overtake on horseback; **r. easy** (naut) put little strain on the anchors; **r. for a fall** behave recklessly, court disaster; **r. hard** ride far or fast; **r. in** sit in and be carried along by (any vehicle); **let r.** (coll) leave undisturbed, take no action on; **r. out** keep afloat during; **r. to death** kill by riding too hard; make dull or irritating by constant repetition; **r. up** shift upwards when worn or used ~ **ride** n act of riding; journey on horse, bicycle etc; journey in any vehicle; track for riding on; **take for a r.** (sl) kidnap and murder; (sl) make a fool of.

rider [RIder] n one who rides, esp on a horse; additional clause; part of machine working above and upon another part; recommendation added to a verdict; corollary.

riderless [RIderles] adj (of a horse) having lost its rider, without a rider.

ridge [Rij] n long raised strip; long crest; long narrow range of hills or mountains; raised line where two slopes meet; raised part between two grooves, furrows *etc* ~ **ridge** *v/t* and *i* form into ridges; extend in ridges.

ridgepole [*Rij*pOl] *n* upright timber supporting rafters; horizontal tent-pole.

ridgeway [*Rij*way] *n* road along a hill's ridge.

ridicule [*Ridi*kewl] *n* contemptuous laughter, words or actions, mockery ~ **ridicule** *v/t* mock, show contemptuous amusement at.

ridiculous [*Ridik*ewlus] *adj* arousing contemptuous laughter ~ **ridiculously** *adv* ~ **ridiculousness** *n.*

riding (1) [*RId*ing] *n* one of the former three administrative divisions of Yorkshire.

riding (2) *n* act of riding, *esp* on a horse; track for riding along on horseback ~ **riding** *adj* to be used or worn when riding a horse.

riding-habit [*RId*ing-habit] *n* costume formerly worn by women when riding on horseback.

riding-light [*RId*ing-lIt] *n* white light hung in the rigging of a ship at anchor.

riesling [*Reez*ling] *n* a dry white wine.

rife [*Rif*] *adj* prevalent, common, abundant.

riff [*Rif*] *n* repeated background phrase in jazz or pop music.

riffle (1) [*Rif*'l] *n* (*mining*) groove, slab, or cleat set in a sluice > PDE; obstruction in a stream; shallow broken water.

riffle (2) *v/t* flick over rapidly, cause to flutter.

riffler [*Rif*ler] *n* file with curved ends.

riff-raff [*Rif*Raf] *n* rabble; worthless people.

rifle (1) [*Rif*'l] *n* gun with a spirally grooved barrel; (*pl*) troops armed with rifles ~ **rifle** *v/t* furnish (a gun) with spiral grooves.

rifle (2) *v/t* search and rob, plunder.

rifleman [*Rif*'lman] *n* soldier armed with a rifle; soldier in the Rifle Brigade.

rifler [*Rif*ler] *n* robber, plunderer.

rifle-range [*Rif*'l-Raynj] *n* area for practising rifleshooting; distance a shot from a rifle will travel.

rifleshot [*Rif*'l-shot] *n* one who shoots well with a rifle; distance a shot from a rifle will travel; shot fired from a rifle.

rifling [*Rif*ling] *n* act of furnishing a gun with spiral grooves; grooves in gun barrel.

rift [*Rift*] *n* narrow opening; split, cleft; fissure; **r. in the lute** (*fig*) that which gradually spoils harmony or happiness; **r. valley** valley formed by sinking of land between two faults > PDG ~ **rift** *v/t* and *i* split open.

rig (1) (*pres/part* **rigging**, *p/t* and *p/part* **rigged**) [*Rig*] *v/t* equip with tackle and rigging; fit out, equip with clothes; **r. out** equip; **r. up** erect or arrange hastily from makeshift materials ~ **rig** *n* (*coll*) outfit, clothing; (*naut*) arrangement of masts and sails; (*mech*) assembly of mechanical parts.

rig (2) (*pres/part* **rigging**, *p/t* and *p/part* **rigged**) *v/t* arrange or manipulate dishonestly to obtain benefit to oneself ~ **rig** *n* dishonest dealing.

rigging [*Rig*ing] *n* system of wires, ropes *etc* controlling masts and sails.

right [*RIt*] *adj* correct; best, most appropriate or useful; true; just, fair; not mistaken; morally good or desirable; on the side of the body where the heart normally is not; straight, most direct; rectangular; healthy, sound; comfortable; (*cap*) Conservative; reactionary; (*sl*) utter, complete; **all r.** safe, unharmed; very good; **a bit of all r.**

(*sl*) something or someone very pleasant; **r. angle** angle of 90 degrees; **r. in the head** sane; **one's r. mind** sanity; normal state of mind; **put r.** correct mistake or fault in; repair; cure; **r. side** side meant to be seen, top or outer side; **get on the r. side of** (*coll*) win the favour of; **r. sort** (*coll*) pleasant or socially acceptable person ~ **right** *adv* straight, directly; completely, thoroughly; all the way; exactly; correctly, well; on or towards the right; (*dial*, *sl* or *ar*) very; **all r.** correctly; safely; (*sl*) very much so; **r. away** (*coll*) at once; **r. here** (*now*) (*coll*) at this very place (time); **r. in** all the way in; straight in ~ **right** *n* side of the body where the heart normally is not; area or direction corresponding to this; what is legally right; justice; just claim; thing justly claimed, thing to which one is entitled; truth, correctness; that which is correct, good; (*cap*) Conservative or reactionary party; **by r. of** justified by, in consequence of; **in one's own r.** in or as oneself; independently; **put to rights** correct, repair, put into good condition ~ **right** *v/t* put right, correct; counteract (an evil); win justice for; set upright; set in correct position or condition ~ **right** *interj* (*also* **r. oh!**, **r. you are!**) *coll exclam* expressing agreement or consent.

right-about [*RIt*-abowt] *n* opposite direction; reverse; **send to the right-about(s)** dismiss summarily ~ **right-about** *adj* and *adv* in or towards the opposite direction.

right-angled [*RIt*-ang-g'ld] *adj* having or forming an angle of 90 degrees.

righteous [*RIt*chus] *adj* just, morally good; self-consciously and intolerantly virtuous; merited ~ **righteously** *adv* ~ **righteousness** *n.*

rightful [*RItfool*] *adj* just, fair, equitable; having a legitimate claim ~ **rightfully** *adv.*

right-hand [*RIt*-hand] *adj* on or towards the right side (of the body); **r. man** indispensable helper.

right-handed [*RIt*-handid] *adj* using the right hand more easily than the left; done, delivered *etc* by the right hand; turned to the right; made to be used by the right hand.

rightist [*RIt*ist] *adj* and *n* politically Conservative or reactionary (person).

rightly [*RIt*li] *adv* justly, fairly; honestly, uprightly; correctly.

right-minded [*RIt*-mIndid] *adj* just, upright; having orthodox opinions.

rightness [*RIt*nis] *n* quality of being right.

right-of-way [*RIt*-ov-*way*] *n* public right to pass over private property; path open to the public through private property.

right-wing [*RIt*-wing] *adj* politically Conservative or reactionary.

rigid [*Rij*id] *adj* stiff, not easily bent, unyielding; strict, harsh, austere ~ **rigidly** *adv.*

rigidity [*Riji*diti] *n* stiffness, want of pliability; strictness.

rigmarole [*Rig*maROl] *n* long, confused, rambling story; silly, disjointed talk.

rigor [*Riger*] *n* stiffness, *esp* in death; (*in fevers*) shivering and stiffness; **r. mortis** stiffening of a corpse soon after death.

rigorism [*Rige*Rizm] *n* harshness, severity.

rigorist [*Rige*Rist] *n* one who is very strict.

rigorous [*Rige*Rus] *adj* strict, severe; exact, accurate; inclement, harsh ~ **rigorously** *adv* ~ **rigorousness** *n.*

rigour [Riger] *n* strictness, *esp* of opinion, doctrine *etc*; severity; hardship; thoroughness.

Rig-Veda [Rig-vayda] *n* the principal and the oldest of the four Hindu books of Scripture.

rile [Ril] *v/t* (*coll*) make angry, irritate.

rill [Ril] *n* small stream.

rille [Ril] *n* narrow channel in moon's surface.

rim [Rim] *n* border, margin; raised outer edge; frame, brim; outer part of a wheel on which the tyre is fitted; (*naut*) surface (of the water) ~ **rim** (*pres/part* **rimming**, *p/t* and *p/part* **rimmed**) *v/t* form a rim round; edge.

rime (1) [Rim] *n* rhyme.

rime (2) *n* hoarfrost > PDG ~ **rime** *v/i* congeal into or cover with hoarfrost.

rimose, rimous [RImOs, RImus] *adj* full of cracks.

rimy [Rimi] *adj* covered with hoarfrost.

rind [Rind] *n* tough outer layer on bacon, cheese *etc*; outer skin of certain plants, fruits *etc*; bark of trees; peel; husk.

rinderpest [Rinderpest] *n* contagious disease of cattle.

ring [Ring] (1) *n* any circular line, mark, or object; circular object with large hole in the centre; hoop, circlet; circlet of gold or other metal, often set with jewels, worn as ornament round a finger or hanging from ear or nose; group of persons or things forming a circle; enclosed area for boxing match; circus arena; enclosure for bookmakers on racecourse; (*collect*) boxing; bookmakers; (*coll*) group of firms or persons combining to win profits or power for themselves; **make rings round** (*coll*) defeat easily ~ **ring** *v/t* and *i* encircle, surround; put a ring on or round; (*orni*) put stamped dated identification band on (bird's leg); cut groove round (tree-trunk); rise in spirals; (*sl*) transform appearance of (stolen car) for re-sale.

ring (2) (*p/t* **rang**, *p/part* **rung**) *v/i* and *t* make a clear vibrant sound when struck; resound clearly; cause (bell, coin *etc*) to ring; produce or express by ringing bells; **r. a bell** (*coll*) sound familiar, be well known; **r. changes on use**, discuss *etc* a few items repeatedly in varying order; **r. down the curtain** give signal to lower theatre curtain at end of play; (*fig*) declare something to be ended; **r. false** appear insincere, untrue; **r. for** summon by ringing a bell; **r. in** announce (arrival of) by ringing bells; **r. off** end telephone call; **r. out** make a loud, clear, ringing sound; announce (departure of) by ringing bells; **r. true** appear sincere or true; (*of coin*) prove genuine by the quality of sound when struck; **r. up** telephone to; summon by ringing; give signal by bell for raising (curtain of theatre *etc*); record on cash register ~ **ring** *n* act of ringing; sound of bell, gong, struck metal or glass *etc*; telephone call; resonance; (*fig*) convincing effect; set of tuned bells.

ring-bark [Ring-baark] *v/t* cut a ring of bark from.

ringbone [RingbOn] *n* bony growth on horse's pastern.

ringdove [Ringduv] *n* woodpigeon.

ringed [Ringd] *adj* having, marked with, or encircled by a ring or rings.

ringer (1) [Ringer] *n* one who rings birds; quoit which falls round the peg; person or thing that looks exactly like another, double.

ringer (2) *n* one who rings, *esp* church bells; bell-pull.

ring-finger [Ring-fing-ger] *n* third finger of left hand.

ringing [Ringing] *adj* clear, resonant.

ringleader [Ringleeder] *n* leader of revolt, riot, mutiny *etc*.

ringlet [Ringlit] *n* long curly lock of hair; small ring or circle ~ **ringleted** *adj*.

ringmail [Ringmayl] *n* armour made of small rings sewn on leather.

ringmaster [Ringmaaster] *n* manager of a circus arena.

ring-road [Ring-ROd] *n* road skirting a town *etc* used to relieve congestion in the centre.

ringside [Ringsid] *adj* (*of seats*) nearest to a boxing or circus ring; affording the closest view.

ringworm [Ringwurm] *n* contagious skin disease caused by a fungus.

rink [Rink] *n* sheet of artificial ice for skating on; prepared floor for skating with rollerskates; building where one may skate; space on ice marked off for the game of curling ~ **rink** *v/i* skate on a rink.

rinse [Rins] *v/t* wash out soapy water from by passing through clean water; wash in clean water; colour with dilute dye ~ **rinse** *n* act of rinsing; dilute impermanent dye for the hair; liquid used for rinsing.

riot [RI-ot] *n* violent disturbance of public peace by three or more persons; outbreak of lawlessness; uproar, disturbance; rowdy behaviour; (*coll*) noisy amusement or enthusiasm; something causing this; (*fig*) over-abundance; luxuriant growth; **read the R. Act** (*leg*) warn rioters to disperse; (*coll*) warn rowdy or disobedient persons to behave better; **run r.** behave, develop or grow without proper restraint ~ **riot** *v/i* raise an uproar; join in a riot; (*fig*) behave with no restraint; over-indulge oneself (in).

rioter [RI-oter] *n* one who disturbs the peace.

riotous [RI-otus] *adj* behaving lawlessly; rowdy; unrestrained, *esp* in amusement or enthusiasm; wild and noisy; dissipated; luxuriant, over-abundant ~ **riotously** *adv* ~ **riotousness** *n*.

rip (1) (*pres/part* **ripping**, *p/t* and *p/part* **ripped**) [Rip] *v/t* and *i* tear open or apart with violence; move very fast, rush; be easily torn; **let it r.** (*coll*) let (engine *etc*) go as fast as possible; refrain from controlling; **let r.** allow (violent anger *etc*) to appear unchecked; **r. off** tear violently off; (*sl*) steal; defraud; exploit, make excessive profits from; plagiarize; mock, parody ~ **rip** *n* rent, tear.

rip (2) *n* worn-out horse; profligate, rake.

rip (3) *n* eddy, broken water.

riparian [RIpairRi-an] *adj* of or on the banks of a river ~ **riparian** *n* one who owns property on the banks of a river.

ripcord [Ripkawrd] *n* cord to release a parachute if its does not open automatically; cord to open gas bag of balloon.

ripe [Rip] *adj* mature, fully developed; mellow; ready; resembling ripe fruit; (*sl*) remarkably amusing; indecent; drunk.

ripely [Ripli] *adv* in a ripe way.

ripen [Ripen] *v/i* and *t* grow ripe, mature; make ripe.

ripeness [Ripnis] *n* state or quality of being ripe.

rip-off [*Rip*-of] *n* (*sl*) excessive profit; fraud, swindle; theft; parody, hostile imitation; plagiarism.

riposte [Ri*post*] *n* quick return lunge or thrust in fencing; (*fig*) quick retort; repartee ~ **riposte** *v/i*.

ripping [Ri*p*ıng] *adj* (*sl*) excellent, first-rate.

ripple [Rip'l] *n* slight gentle wave; light soft sound; slight wavy mark or movement ~ **ripple** *v/t* and *i* move or cause to move in slight waves; sound like rippling water.

ripply [Ripli] *adj* of, having or like a ripple.

rip-roaring [Rip-*Rawr*Ring] *adj* (*coll*) boisterous.

ripsaw [Ripsaw] *n* saw which saws along the grain.

riptide [RiptId] *n* tide causing violent currents and rough water.

rise (*p/t* rose, *p/part* risen) [RIz] *v/i* move upwards, ascend; stand up, get to one's feet; get out of bed; increase, swell; increase in rank, power, cost or value; increase in intensity; increase in pitch; (*of sun, moon etc*) appear above horizon; (*of fish*) come to surface of water, *esp* to take bait; arise, come to be; rebel, revolt; slope upwards; resurrect; **r. to** be lured or goaded to action by; prove oneself able to cope with ~ **rise** *n* act of rising; ground sloping upwards; increase in amount, intensity, pitch, value *etc*; degree or rate of this; increase in price; increase in wages or salary; amount of this; process of beginning or developing; origin, starting-point; **give r. to** cause; **take a r. out of** provoke by teasing; **take its r. in** originate in.

risen [Rizen] *p/part* of **rise.**

riser [RIzer] *n* one who or that which rises; vertical part of arch, step *etc.*

risibility [Rizibiliti] *n* quality of being risible.

risible [Rizib'l] *adj* inclined to laugh; connected with laughing; laughable.

rising [RIzing] *adj* ascending, sloping upward; growing in strength or intensity; increasing in importance, wealth *etc*; approaching a certain age or amount ~ **rising** *n* act of one who rises, upward movement; revolt, rebellion; resurrection.

risk [Risk] *n* hazard, chance of injury, harm, loss *etc*; sum insured; insured person ~ **risk** *v/t* expose to risk; hazard; take the chances of.

risky [Riski] *adj* hazardous, dangerous; daring; slightly or nearly indecent ~ **riskily** *adv* ~ **riskiness** *n*.

risotto [Riz*ot*O] *n* (*Ital*) rice cooked with onions, cheese, butter *etc.*

risqué [Reeskay] *adj* (*Fr*) bordering on indecency.

rissole [RisOl] *n* fried ball or cake of minced meat or fish.

ritardando [Reetaard*and*O] *adv* (*mus*) slower.

rite [Rıt] *n* act solemnly and devoutly carried out, *usu* as religious ceremony; solemn act established by law or custom; liturgy; branch of Christian Church distinguished by characteristic liturgy.

ritornello [Ritawr*nel*O] *n* (*mus*) refrain; interlude; brief introduction > PDM.

ritual [Ritew-al] *n* system of religious or magical ceremonies; any word, act *etc* forming part of this; solemn customary act; book of prescribed ceremonies ~ **ritual** *adj* of rites; of or as a ritual.

ritualism [Ritew-alizm] *n* system of ritual; observance of ritual, *esp* if unusually elaborate; belief in the importance of ritual.

ritualist [Ritew-alist] *n* and *adj* (person) attaching much importance to ritual.

ritualistic [Ritew-a*list*ik] *adj* of or like ritual ~ **ritualistically** *adv.*

ritually [Ritew-ali] *adv* in a ritual manner.

ritzy [Ritsi] *adj* (*sl*) elegant, luxurious.

rival [RIval] *n* one who competes against another, *esp* to gain something both desire; equal competitor ~ **rival** *adj* of or as a rival, competing ~ ~ **rival** (*pres/part* **rivalling,** *p/t* and *p/part* **rivalled**) *v/t* compete against, try to equal or surpass.

rivalry [RIvalRi] *n* act of competing; state of being rivals; competitive similarity in quality, status *etc.*

rive (*p/t* rived, *p/part* riven) [RIv] *v/t* and *i* split apart, tear.

riven [Riven] *p/part* of **rive.**

river [River] *n* large stream of fresh water flowing into sea, lake or other river > PDG; (*fig*) copious flow; **sell down the r.** (*sl*) betray.

river-basin [River-baysin] *n* land drained by a river and its tributaries.

river-bed [River-bed] *n* ground over which a river flows.

riverine [RiveRIn] *adj* of or like a river; living on or near a river.

rivet [Rivit] *n* short bolt with one end flattened out and used for fastening ~ **rivet** *v/t* join with a rivet; (*fig*) fasten firmly; hold the attention of.

riveter [Riviter] *n* one who or that which rivets.

rivière [Rivi-air] *n* (*Fr*) necklace of precious stones, *usu* of several strings.

rivulet [Rivewlit] *n* small stream.

rixdollar [Riksdoler] *n* name given to several Continental coins of the 16th–19th centuries.

roach (1) [ROch] *n* freshwater fish allied to the carp.

roach (2) *n* (*naut*) concave curve in the foot of a square sail.

road [ROd] *n* broad track with artificial hard surface for travelling; way, route; place for ships to lie at anchor; **on the r.** touring about on business; **on the r. to** progressing towards; **r. sense** ability to use roads safely; **one for the r.** (*coll*) final drink before leaving; **rule of the r.** law or custom regulating behaviour of vehicles, ships *etc* when meeting or passing; **r. show** touring theatrical performance.

roadblock [ROdblok] *n* barricade set up by army, police *etc* to halt or slow down traffic for inspection *etc.*

roadbook [ROdbook] *n* guidebook for travellers by road.

roadhog [ROdhog] *n* motorist or cyclist who disregards the safety or convenience of others using the road.

roadhouse [ROdhows] *n* country inn or restaurant on a main road.

roadman [ROdman] *n* one who keeps a road in repair.

roadmanship [ROdmanship] *n* skill in driving correctly on public roads.

road-map [ROd-map] *n* map classifying roads according to condition and grade.

road-metal [ROd-metal] *n* broken stones used for road-making.

roadside [*RO*dsɪd] *n* border of a road ∼ **roadside** *adj* of, at, or on the border of a road.

roadstead [*RO*dsted] *n* place where ships may ride at anchor.

roadster [*RO*dster] *n* horse accustomed to using a road; cycle or motorcar for use on long journeys; open-topped car; tramp.

roadway [*RO*dway] *n* the part of a road, bridge *etc* to be used by vehicles.

roadworthy [*RO*dwurTHi] *adj* fit for use on a road.

roam [*RO*m] *v/i* and *t* wander aimlessly (over).

roamer [*RO*mer] *n* one who wanders about aimlessly.

roan (1) [*RO*n] *n* and *adj* (horse) of bay or dark colour with grey or white spots; of a mixed reddish colour.

roan (2) *n* soft leather made of sheepskin.

roar [*Rawr*] *v/i* and *t* make a loud, deep, continuous sound; make a confused noise; move fast and noisily; cry loudly; bellow; resound ∼ **roar** *n* loud, deep, continuous sound; confused noise; loud cry; burst of laughter.

roarer [*Rawr*Rer] *n* one who roars; horse with inflammation of breathing-passages.

roaring [*Rawr*Ring] *adj* that roars; noisy, boisterous; very vigorous or brisk ∼ **roaring** *n* sound of one who roars; loud confused sound; grating sound made by horses with diseased breathing-passages.

roast [*RO*st] *v/t* and *i* cook by exposure to direct heat; dry by exposure to heat; heat highly; be roasted; be very hot ∼ **roast** *n* act of roasting; that which is roasted ∼ **roast** *adj* roasted.

roaster [*RO*ster] *n* one who or that which roasts; furnace or an oven for roasting; animal or bird suitable for roasting.

roasting-jack [*RO*sting-jak] *n* contrivance for turning a spit.

rob (*pres//part* **robbing**, *p/t* and *p/part* **robbed**) [*Rob*] *v/t* and *i* steal, often by violence; plunder; unjustly deprive (of).

robber [*Rob*er] *n* one who takes goods or money by force; thief.

robbery [*Rob*eRi] *n* act or practice of robbing.

robe [*RO*b] *n* long loose outer garment; elegant gown; ceremonial garment ∼ **robe** *v/t* and *i* dress with a robe or robes.

robin [*Ro*bin] *n* small warbling bird with a red breast.

robing-room [*RO*bing-ROOm] *n* room in which participants in a ceremony put on their robes.

roborant [*RO*boRant] *n* and *adj* (*med*) tonic.

robot [*RO*bot] *n* machine capable of performing certain human tasks and functions; fictional type of machine in semi-human form; (*fig*) one who works with mechanical and unintelligent efficiency ∼ **robot** *adj* automatically controlled.

roburite [*RO*beRit] *n* a powerful explosive.

robust [*RO*bust] *adj* strong, vigorous, hardy; in excellent health; muscular, sturdy; invigorating; (*fig*) self-reliant ∼ **robustly** *adv* ∼ **robustness** *n*.

robustious [*RO*buschus] *adj* boisterous, noisy.

roc [*Rok*] *n* a huge legendary bird.

rochet [*Ro*chit] *n* linen vestment resembling a surplice open at the sides.

rock (1) [*Rok*] *n* mass of hard mineral matter in earth's crust > PDG; large stone, boulder; crag;

projecting crag in or at the edge of the sea; (*US* and *coll*) a stone of any size; (*fig*) cause of disaster; (*fig*) secure foundation or refuge; type of hard boiled sweet; (*sl*) jewel, *esp* diamond; **on the rocks** wrecked; (*coll*) very short of money; (*of drinks*) poured neat over lumps of ice.

rock (2) *v/t* and *i* swing steadily to and fro; sway; lull to sleep by swinging; shake violently; reel, cause to reel; (*sl*) startle, shock; (*mus*) work up a strong repeated rhythm; dance energetically to rock'n'roll music, jive; **r. the boat** (*coll*) cause trouble ∼ **rock** *n* act of rocking; (*mus*) type of popular music originating from rock'n'roll, usually played on electric instruments and held to be more substantial and original than pop > PDM.

rockbottom [*Rok*bottom] *adj* and *n* (at, on or down to) the lowest point or level.

rockbound [*Rok*bownd] *adj* hemmed in by rocks.

rock-cake [*Rok*-kayk] *n* small cake with rough, hard surface.

rock-crystal [*Rok*-kRistal] *n* pure natural crystalline form of silica > PDS.

rockdrill [*Rok*dRil] *n* machine for boring through hard rock > PDE.

rocker (1) [*Rok*er] *n* one who or that which rocks; curved piece of wood on which cradle, chair *etc* rocks; gold-miner's cradle; **off one's r.** (*sl*) mad.

rocker (2) *n* tough, rowdy youth, *usu* dressed in leather jacket and riding a motorcycle.

rockery [*Rok*eRi] *n* artificial bank of rocks and earth where alpine plants are grown.

rocket [*Rok*it] *n* projectile driven through air or space by the recoil of explosions produced within it; large jet-powered projectile used as missile in war or to place spacecraft *etc* on course; explosive firework that shoots high into the air, used as signal, for display, or to carry a lifeline; (*coll*) severe reprimand ∼ **rocket** *v/i* and *t* rush upwards, rise steeply and rapidly; (*fig*) increase sharply; fire rockets at.

rocket-base [*Rok*it-bays] *n* military base where rocket missiles are kept.

rocketeer [Rokit*eer*] *n* expert on use of rocket missiles.

rocketer [*Rok*iter] *n* gamebird that flies straight up when flushed.

rocket-range [*Rok*it-Raynj] *n* area from which rocket missiles are fired.

rocketry [*Rok*itRi] *n* reliance on or use of rockets as weapons.

rockface [*Rok*fays] *n* surface, *usu* vertical, of rock.

rock-garden [*Rok*-gaarden] *n* large rockery.

rock-hewn [*Rok*-hewn] *adj* carved or quarried from rock.

rockily [*Ro*kili] *adv* in a rocky way.

rockiness [*Ro*kinis] *n* quality of being rocky.

rocking [*Ro*king] *adj* swaying to and fro or backwards and forwards.

rocking-chair [*Ro*king-chair] *n* chair mounted on rockers.

rocking-horse [*Ro*king-hawrs] *n* wooden horse on rockers.

rock-'n'-roll [*Rok*-n-ROl] *n* type of popular music of American 1950s origin, being simple, energetic, and strongly rhythmic; lively acrobatic form of jiving to this music ∼ **rock-'n'-roll** *v/i*.

rockplant [*Rok*plaant] *n* any small plant suitable for growing in rockeries; alpine plant.

628

rockrose [RokRROz] *n* a wild flowering plant.

rock-salmon [Rok-*sam*on] *n* dogfish.

rocksalt [*Rok*sawlt] *n* natural crystalline sodium chloride > PDS.

rocky (1) [*Rok*i] *adj* covered with or formed of rocks; having many rocks; like a rock; (*fig*) firm; hard; stony.

rocky (2) *adj* (*coll*) shaky, unsteady, tottering.

rococo [RokOkO] *n* lavish 17th- and 18th-century ornamental style in interior decoration, based on asymmetrical curves > PDAA; florid ornamentation in any art ~ **rococo** *adj*.

rod [Rod] *n* slender stick or piece of wood; slender stick used for beating, cane; (*fig*) corporal punishment; punitive discipline; thin twig; wand; baton; fishing rod; thin metal bar; measure of length, 5½ yards; (*sl*) revolver; (*sl*) penis.

rode [ROd] *p/t* of ride.

rodent [ROdent] *n* any animal with two or four incisor and no canine teeth > PDB ~ **rodent** *adj* gnawing.

rodeo [ROday-O] *n* display of skill in rounding up cattle, riding unbroken horses, *etc*; act of rounding up cattle on a ranch.

rodomontade [Rodomon*tayd*] *n* bragging, boastful words.

roe (1) [RO] *n* small species of deer; female hart.

roe (2) *n* mass of fish eggs or fish sperm.

roebuck [RObuk] *n* male roe deer.

roentgen [*Runt*gen] *n* unit of measurement of X-rays or gamma-rays > PDS; **R. rays** X-rays.

Rogation [ROgayshon] *n* (*eccles*) litany; **R. days** three days preceding Ascension Day.

Rogational [ROgayshonal] *adj* of Rogation Days.

roger (1) [*Roje*r] *v/t* (*sl*, *of males*) copulate with ~ **roger** *n* (*sl*) copulation.

roger (2) *interj* (*coll*) I agree; I hear and understand (a message).

rogue [ROg] *n* dishonest person; criminal; rascal, scamp (*often joc*); savage solitary male animal of a species usually gregarious; (*fig*) morose or unpredictably savage man; (*hort*) single unwanted seedling of different type or species > PDB; (*ar*) wandering beggar ~ **rogue** *adj* solitary and savage; dangerous ~ **rogue** *v/t* remove unwanted seedlings.

roguery [ROgeRi] *n* dishonesty, fraud; mischievousness.

roguish [ROgish] *adj* mischievous; arch; dishonest ~ **roguishly** *adv* ~ **roguishness** *n*.

roister [Roister] *v/i* behave boisterously; swagger.

roisterer [RoisteRer] *n* swaggering, noisy person.

role [ROl] *n* part or character played by an actor; function, part one plays in any event or process.

roll [ROl] *v/i* and *t* move along by turning over and over; move round and round; revolve, rotate; move on wheels or rollers; pass a roller over something to flatten or spread it; form into a ball or cylinder; coil up; produce a long reverberating sound; utter vibrantly, trill; envelop, wrap up; sway, rock; flow in waves; undulate; flow unceasingly; waddle; wallow; sweep round; **r. along** advance by rolling; (*coll*) advance steadily; **r. in** arrive in large quantities; **be rolling in** have vast quantities of; **r. off** print on a rotary machine or duplicator; **r. on** put on by rolling or unrolling; (*of time*) pass steadily; come soon; **r. out** flatten

with a roller; **r. up** form into a ball, coil or cylinder; wrap up; (*coll*) arrive ~ **roll** *n* act of rolling; that which is rolled; small rounded bun, loaf, or rissole; cylindrical mass; coiled cylindrical cake; long reverberating sound; long coiled strip of parchment, paper, film *etc*; official register or record; list of names; swaying motion, *esp* of ship; roller; **be struck off the rolls** be disqualified from practising as solicitor; **Master of the Rolls** the principal judge of appeal.

rollcall [ROlkawl] *n* act of calling out a list of names of people who should be present.

rolled [ROld] *adj* plated by rolling.

roller [ROler] *n* that which turns on its own axis; long broad bandage; long swelling wave; rolling cylinder on, over or round which something moves.

roller-bearing [ROler-bairRing] *n* friction-reducing bearing containing small cylindrical rollers.

roller-coaster [ROler-kOster] *n* switchback railway.

rollerskate [ROlerskayt] *n* skate mounted on wheels ~ **rollerskate** *v/i*.

roller-towel [ROler-tow-el] *n* long towel with ends joined and hung on a roller.

rollicking [Roliking] *adj* boisterously gay.

rolling [ROling] *adj* that rolls; moving by rotating or on wheels; having broad, rounded slopes; (*sl*) very rich; **r. stone** (*fig*) restless wanderer, good-for-nothing.

rolling-mill [ROling-mil] *n* factory in which heated metal is rolled out into plates.

rolling-pin [ROling-pin] *n* round bar for rolling out dough, pastry *etc*.

rolling-stock [ROling-stok] *n* railway locomotives, carriages, vans *etc*.

rollmop [ROlmop] *n* rolled pickled herring fillet.

rollneck [ROlnek] *n* and *adj* (sweater) with close-fitting high neck folded over.

roll-on [ROl-on] *adj* applied by a rotating ball in nozzle of container ~ **roll-on** *n* type of corset without fastenings.

rolltop [ROltop] *adj* having a sliding top made of flexible slats.

roly-poly [ROli-pOli] *n* boiled pudding made of dough covered with jam and rolled up; (*fig*) plump person.

Roman [ROman] *adj* of or derived from Rome, *esp* ancient Rome; of or like the Roman Catholic Church; **R. alphabet** European alphabet derived from ancient Rome; **R. candle** type of firework; **R. Catholic** member of a branch of the Christian Church of which the Pope is the head; **R. numerals** capital letters used as numerals; **R. nose** nose with high arched bridge; **r. type** ordinary upright type used in printing.

romance [ROmans/ROmans] *n* pleasing and idealized love-story; tender and *usu* happy love-affair; novel, film *etc* mainly describing colourful adventures and idealized love; non-realistic fiction; actual event resembling such fiction; medieval tale of chivalry, *esp* in verse; glamour, mysterious charm, picturesque or sentimental atmosphere; (*phil*) Old French; (*mus*) short emotional composition > PDM ~ **romance** *adj* of or like romance; **R. language** one of a group of languages derived from Latin ~ **romance** *v/i* invent or tell improbable fictions; exaggerate, add fictitious details; tell lies; (*coll*) woo.

romancer [ROmanser] *n* one who composes romances; one who exaggerates or lies.

Romanesque [ROmanesk] *n* (*archi*) European style of architecture from 5th to 12th century, with round arches and thick walls ~ **Romanesque** *adj*.

Romanic [ROmanik] *adj* derived from Latin; pertaining to Romance languages.

Romanist [ROmanist] *n* a Roman Catholic; Anglican who adopts Roman Catholic doctrines or practices.

Romanize [ROmanIz] *v/t* and *i* make Roman; Latinize; convert to Roman Catholicism; adopt Roman Catholic doctrines or practices; use Latin words or phrases.

romantic [ROmantik/Romantik] *adj* of or like romance; of, like, dealing with or fit for idealized love or pleasing adventures; picturesquely strange; having mysterious charm, glamorous; emotional, sentimental; passionate; colourful and improbable; (*of literature, art or music*) showing romanticism ~ **romantic** *n* one whose outlook or behaviour is romantic; writer, artist or musician showing romanticism ~ **romantically** *adv*.

romanticism [ROmantisizm] *n* state or quality of being romantic; the production of romantic effects in any art; literary, artistic or musical movement that directly and unrestrainedly expresses or seeks to rouse personal emotions, or exploits the emotive power of exotic, mysterious, sentimental or sensational subjects; literary movement of the late 18th and early 19th centuries having these characteristics and claiming affinity with medieval literature; anti-classicism.

Romany [Romani] *n* gipsy; the gipsy language.

Romish [ROmish] *adj* (*cont*) of or like the Roman Catholic Church.

romp [Romp] *v/i* play boisterously and noisily; move fast and easily; **r. home** (*coll*) win a race easily ~ **romp** *n* wild, noisy game; child, *esp* girl, who romps.

rompers [Romperz] *n* (*pl*) loose protective trousers for very young child at play.

rondeau [RondO] *n* poem of ten or thirteen lines with two rhymes only and with part of first line repeated as refrain; (*mus*) rondo.

rondo [RondO] *n* musical composition with principal theme repeated after each subordinate theme.

roneo [ROni-O] *n* (*tr*) machine for duplicating typescript ~ **roneo** *v/t* duplicate (typescript).

rood [ROOd] *n* crucifix, *esp* a large one set over the junction of nave and choir; a measure of land, a quarter of an acre.

roodbeam [ROOdbeem] *n* beam across the arch leading to the choir in a church.

roodscreen [ROOdskreen] *n* carved wooden or stone screen dividing the choir from the nave in a church.

roof [ROOf] *n* covering over top of a building; top of a vehicle; (*fig*) house, shelter; **r. of the mouth** palate; **raise the r.** (*coll*) be very noisy ~ **roof** *v/t* cover with or as if with a roof.

roof-garden [ROOf-gaardin] *n* garden grown on soil laid on the flat roof of a building.

roofing [ROOfing] *n* material used to make a roof.

roofless [ROOflis] *adj* having no roof; unsheltered; (*fig*) homeless.

roofrack [ROOfRak] *n* detachable luggage rack on roof of car.

rooftop [ROOftop] *n* outer surface of roof.

rooftree [ROOftRee] *n* ridge-pole of a roof.

rook (1) [Rook] *n* gregarious British bird of crow family; (*fig*) cheat, swindler ~ **rook** *v/t* (*coll*) cheat, swindle; overcharge.

rook (2) *n* the castle at chess.

rookery [RookeRi] *n* group of trees where rooks nest; breeding-place for seabirds; colony of seals; (*fig*) overcrowded slum house.

rookie [Rooki] *n* (*sl*) a raw recruit.

rook-rifle [Rook-RIfl] *n* type of small-bore rifle.

rooky [Rooki] *adj* inhabited by rooks.

room [ROOm] *n* walled-off area within a house or other building; people in a room; unoccupied space; area in which something can fit; opportunity, scope; (*pl*) lodgings ~ **room** *v/i* (*coll*) share a room or lodgings (with).

roomful [ROOmfool] *adj* as many or as much as a room can contain.

roominess [ROOminis] *n* spaciousness.

room-mate [ROOm-mayt] *n* person with whom one shares a room, *esp* in lodgings, hostel or college.

roomy [ROOmi] *adj* spacious; having ample room.

roop [ROOp] *n* hoarseness.

roost (1) [ROOst] *n* pole upon which fowls rest at night; (*fig*) resting-place; **rule the r.** be the leader, rule ~ **roost** *v/i* sleep on a roost; (*fig*) be lodged for the night.

roost (2) *n* powerful tidal current.

rooster [ROOster] *n* domestic cock.

root [ROOt] *n* that part of a plant that absorbs water and nutrients from the soil > PDB; young plant; embedded base; (*fig*) origin, basic cause; essential element; (*math*) one of the equal factors of a number or quantity > PDS; (*mus*) lowest note of a chord in its basic position > PDM; (*phil*) basic element of a word; **take r.** become firmly established ~ **root** *v/t* and *i* fix firmly in the ground or in a base; form roots; be or become firmly established; (*fig*) impress firmly on the mind; have basis or origin (in); uproot; dig out, *esp* with the snout; turn over, rummage about in; **r. about (around)** rummage, search; **r. for** (*US*) encourage by cheering; **r. out, r. up** remove completely, destroy.

rootage [ROOtij] *n* manner of rooting; system of roots.

root-crop [ROOt-kRop] *n* crop of plants with edible roots.

rooted [ROOtid] *adj* having its roots fixed in the earth; firmly implanted; immovable.

rootle [ROOt'l] *v/i* dig about, burrow.

rootstock [ROOtstok] *n* rhizome; (*fig*) original source.

rope [ROp] *n* thick twisted cord, cord more than one inch in circumference > PDSa; row of things strung together; plait; slimy thread-like formation in beer, bread *etc*; (*fig*) hanging; **give one r.** give one free scope; **know the ropes** know the right or usual rules, customs *etc*; know how to get things done ~ **rope** *v/t* tie or join with rope; **r. in** obtain (unwilling) cooperation from.

rope-dancer [ROp-daanser] n one who performs on a tightrope.

rope-end [ROp-end] n short piece of rope used for flogging.

rope-ladder [ROp-lader] n ladder made of ropes.

ropewalk [ROpwawk] n long shed where ropes are made.

ropey [ROpi] adj (coll) worn-out; old-fashioned; inferior.

ropy [ROpi] adj resembling a rope; stringy; glutinous.

Roquefort [Rokfawr] n (Fr) cheese made from milk of goats and ewes.

roquet [ROki] v/t and i make one's ball strike another in croquet.

roral [RawRal] adj of or like dew.

roric [RawRik] adj of or like dew.

rorqual [Rawrkwal] n genus of whales with dorsal fins.

rorty [Rawrti] adj (sl) in good spirits, cheerful.

rosaceous [ROzayshus] adj rose-like; (bot) of the rose family.

rosary [ROzaRi] n string of beads used by Roman Catholics to count prayers; set of prayers so counted; rose-garden.

rose (1) [ROz] n any of a genus of shrubs with prickly stems and white, pink, red or yellow flowers; flower of this; deep pink; perforated nozzle; rosette; rounded ornamental cluster; (fig) beautiful woman; **bed of roses** (fig) uninterrupted pleasure; **under the r.** secretly; in confidence ∼ **rose** adj pink.

rose (2) p/t of rise.

roseate [ROzi-it] adj rose-coloured; (fig) smiling.

rosebud [ROzbud] n bud of rose; (fig) beautiful young girl.

rose-colour [ROz-kuler] n deep pink; (fig) optimistic outlook; **rose-coloured spectacles** unjustified optimism.

rosecut [ROzkut] adj cut into twenty-four triangular planes.

rose-diamond [ROz-dI-amond] n rosecut diamond.

rosemary [ROzmaRi] n an evergreen aromatic shrub.

rose-noble [ROz-nOb'l] n old English gold coin.

roseola [ROzee-ola] n reddish skin-rash; disease, esp German measles, causing this.

rose-red [ROz-Red] n and adj crimson.

rose-tinted [ROz-tinted] adj deep pink; **r. spectacles** unjustified optimism.

rosette [ROzet] n bunch of ribbons arranged in the shape of a rose, esp one worn as a badge.

rosewater [ROzwawter] n perfume made from rose leaves.

rose-window [ROz-windO] n circular window containing tracery branching from the centre.

rosewood [ROzwood] n fragrant ornamental wood; one of various trees producing this.

Rosicrucian [ROzikROOshan] n and adj (member) of a fraternity which studies the occult.

rosily [ROzili] adv in a rosy way.

rosin [Rozin] n resin; residue after oil has been distilled from turpentine ∼ **rosin** v/t rub with rosin.

rosiness [ROziness] n pinkness; cheerfulness.

roster [Roster] n list showing order in which persons take their turn at certain duties.

rostra [RostRa] pl of rostrum.

rostral [RostRal] adj of, on, or like a rostrum or beak.

rostrum (pl rostra) [RostRum] n orator's platform, esp in ancient Rome; prow of war-galley; bird's beak.

rosy [ROzi] adj like a rose; covered with roses; of a warm pink colour; healthily pink; favourable, promising success; cheerful, optimistic.

rot (pres/part **rotting**, p/t and p/part **rotted**) [Rot] v/i and t decompose; cause to decay; become or cause to become corrupt; become diseased; waste away; (sl) tease, make fun of; joke ∼ **rot** n decay, process of rotting; fungus disease of timber, plants etc; liver disease of sheep; (fig) corruption, moral disintegration; (coll) nonsense.

rota [ROta] n list showing the order in which persons take turns at certain duties; (RC) the ecclesiastical court.

Rotarian [ROtairRi-an] n and adj (member) of a Rotary Club.

rotary [ROtaRi] adj turning on an axis; **R. Club** social and charitable organization of professional and business men in a district.

rotate [ROtayt] v/i and t revolve round an axis; act in rotation; cause to revolve ∼ **rotate** [ROtayt] adj wheel-shaped.

rotation [ROtayshon] n act of rotating; rotating motion; alternation; regular succession; **r. of crops** system by which different crops are repeatedly grown on the same land in a specific order.

rotative [ROtaytiv] adj turning on an axis; of or causing rotation.

rotator [ROtaytor] n that which rotates or causes rotation; (anat) muscle which gives rotatory action.

rotatory [ROtaytoRi] adj turning on an axis; following in succession.

rote [ROt] n (ar) repetition; **by r.** repeating (words) mechanically without understanding; by heart.

rot-gut [Rot-gut] n (sl) bad-quality alcohol.

rotifera [ROtifeRa] n (pl) wheel animalcules, a group of minute aquatic animals > PDB

rotograph [ROtogRaaf] n photograph of a page of manuscript.

rotogravure [ROtogRavewr] n photogravure printing on a rotary press.

rotor [ROtor] n rotating part in a machine; blade of a helicopter propellor; rotating electric coil; machine driven by revolving fans.

rotten [Roten] adj decaying; decomposed, putrid; unsound; morally corrupt; untrustworthy; (coll) annoying; of bad quality; unpleasant; unwell; unhappy ∼ **rottenly** adv ∼ **rottenness** n.

rottenstone [RotenstOn] n soft limestone used for polishing.

rotter [Roter] n (sl) untrustworthy or worthless person, cad.

rotula [Rotewla] n (anat) kneecap.

rotund [Rotund] adj round; plump; spherical; (of voice) sonorous.

rotunda [Rotunda] n circular building with domed roof.

rotundity [Rotunditi] n roundness.

rouble [ROOb'l] n Russian silver coin.

roué [ROO-ay] n (Fr) rake, debauchee.

rouge (1) [ROOzh] n red cosmetic used to colour the cheeks; red oxide of iron used for polishing ∼ **rouge** v/t and i colour with rouge.

rouge (2) [*ROOj*] *n* scrimmage in Eton football.

rouge-et-noir [*ROOzh*-ay-nwar] *n* (*Fr*) a gambling card-game.

rough [*Ruf*] *adj* having uneven surface; shaggy; hilly, rocky; corrugated, lumpy; stormy, full of waves; prickly; harsh, discordant; cruel; clumsy; violent, boisterous; coarse, unpolished, unrefined; unfinished, half-made; approximate, inexact; (*sl*) unpleasant; unfair; unwell; **be r. on** be unpleasant or unlucky for; **r. diamond** uneducated, ill-mannered, but good-natured person; **~ rough** *n* rough ground; uncut grass; rough part of any surface or object; unpleasantness, difficulty; hardship; hooligan, noisy and violent fellow; **in the r.** half-made, not finished or polished **~ rough** *adv* roughly, harshly; **cut up r.** (*sl*) show anger **~ rough** *v/t* make rough; **r. in** make a first rough sketch of; **r. it** live in harsh uncomfortable circumstances; **r. out** make a rough plan of, sketch roughly; **r. up** (*sl*) beat up.

roughage [*Ruf*ij] *n* coarse bulky food that stimulates bowel action.

rough-and-ready [Ruf-and-*Red*i] *adj* hastily prepared.

rough-and-tumble [Ruf-and-*tumb*'l] *adj* and *n* confused and boisterous (fight).

roughcast [*Ruf*kaast] *n* coarse plastering for outside walls.

roughdry [*Ruf*dRI] *v/t* dry without ironing.

roughen [*Ruf*en] *v/t* and *i* make rough; become rough.

rough-hewn [*Ruf*-hewn] *adj* rugged; unpolished.

rough-house [*Ruf*-hows] *n* boisterous fight.

roughly [*Ruf*li] *adv* in a rough way; approximately.

roughneck [*Ruf*nek] *n* (*US sl*) hooligan.

roughness [*Ruf*nis] *n* state or quality of being rough.

roughrider [*Ruf*RIder] *n* one who breaks in horses.

roughshod [*Ruf*shod] *adj* (*of horse*) shod with roughened shoes; **ride r. over** treat harshly and inconsiderately, disregard contemptuously.

rough-spoken [*Ruf*-spOken] *adj* using coarse, harsh or ungrammatical language.

rough-up [*Ruf*-up] *n* (*sl*) violent fight.

roulade [ROO*laad*] *n* (*mus*) series of rapid short notes.

roulette [ROO*let*] *n* game of chance played with a revolving disk and a ball; wheeled instrument with points for making a dotted line; **Russian r.** sport of shooting at oneself with a revolver only one chamber of which is loaded; **Vatican r.** (*coll*) use of 'safe period' as contraceptive method.

round (1) [*Rownd*] *adj* circular; spherical, ball-shaped; cylindrical; moving in a circle; curved out, convex; plump; outspoken, blunt; approximately calculated; considerable; whole, complete; mellow; (*phon*) pronounced with protruded lips; **r. dance** dance where dancers form a circle; dance with revolving movements; **r. game** game for indefinite number of players; **r. hand** handwriting with unsloped rounded letters; **r. number** number ending in a zero; approximate number; whole number; **r. pace** rapid pace; **r. robin** petition *etc* with signatures written in a circle so that none heads the list; **r. trip** trip that returns to the starting-point by a different route **~**

round *n* circle; sphere; globe; circular slice; circular course or route; circuit; regular course of patrolling, visiting *etc*; completed series of acts, events *etc*; single bout, game or heat in a series; single distribution of drinks to all members of a group; volley of shots; outburst of applause; (*mus*) short canon with all voices singing in turn at same pitch > PDM; **go the rounds** visit successively; patrol, inspect; (*of news*) be circulated widely; **in the r.** (*arts*) so sculptured as to be viewable from any angle; (*theat*) in an arena or apron theatre; (*fig*) realistically **~ round** *adv* in a circle, circuit or cycle; in repeated circles *etc*; in a curved path; on all sides; in circumference; in or to a different direction; by indirect route; from end to end of (a period); to (a place); around **~ round** *prep* encircling; on all sides of; near; to all parts of; curving to the other side of; **r. the bend** (*sl*) mad; **r. the clock** all day and all night; **get r.** persuade; evade; overcome (difficulty) **~ round** *v/t* and *i* make round; form into a circle, sphere *etc*; become plump or curved; curve (around); turn in a curved path (round); (*phon*) pronounce with protruded lips; **r. off** complete satisfactorily, give pleasing polish or conclusion to; **r. on** attack suddenly, turn against; **r. up** gather from various places; gather by force; increase (prices *etc*) to the nearest round figure.

roundabout [*Rownd*abowt] *n* circular obstacle at crossroads round which traffic may go in one direction only; merry-go-round; circuitous course **~ roundabout** *adj* indirect.

roundel [*Rownd*el] *n* round shape; rondeau.

roundelay [*Rownd*ilay] *n* simple song with a refrain.

rounders [*Rownd*erz] *n* (*pl*) team-game played with bat and ball in which players try to run a round of four bases after hitting the ball.

Roundhead [*Rownd*hed] *n* nickname of Parliamentarians during the English Civil War.

round-house [*Rownd*-hows] *n* (*hist*) prison; (*naut*) cabin on the quarter-deck; officers' latrines.

roundly [*Rownd*li] *adv* in a round form; straightforwardly; bluntly, emphatically.

roundness [*Rownd*nis] *n* quality of being round.

roundshot [*Rownd*shot] *n* cannonball.

roundsman [*Rownd*zman] *n* tradesman's assistant who delivers goods or who collects orders from door to door; (*US*) policeman on a round of inspection.

roundtable [Rownd*tayb*'l] *adj* (*of conference*) held in a friendly spirit between parties of equal power.

round-up [*Rownd*-up] *n* act of gathering cattle for branding; act of forcibly gathering people from various places for questioning *etc*; anthology.

roup [ROO*p*] *n* a disease in poultry.

rouse (1) [*Rowz*] *v/t* and *i* waken; stir into activity, stimulate; startle (game) into breaking cover; awaken, be stirred to action or interest.

rouse (2) *n* draught of liquor; carouse.

rouser [*Rowz*er] *n* one who or that which rouses; (*sl*) something startling; bold lie.

rousing [*Rowz*ing] *adj* that can waken or excite; stirring.

roust [*Rowst*] *v/t* rouse; rout out.

roustabout [*Rowst*abowt] *n* (*US*) dock labourer.

rout (1) [*Rowt*] *v/t* defeat utterly, put to flight **~ rout** *n* utter defeat; confused retreat of defeated army; disorderly or panic-stricken crowd; mob; (leg) group of three or more persons bent on illegal violence; (ar) party.

rout (2) v/t dig up with snout, root up; **r. out** find and force into activity, fetch or drive out by force.

route [ROOt] n course chosen in travelling; (mil) order to march ~ **route** v/t plan a route for; direct along specified road etc.

routine [ROOteen] n regular course of procedure, duties etc; regular habit; boringly automatic procedure; (theat) frequently-repeated formula ~ **routine** adj regularly or unvaryingly done.

roux [ROO] n a preparation of fat and flour used for thickening and for sauces.

rove (1) [ROv] p/t of reave.

rove (2) v/i and t wander; roam (through).

rove (3) adj (naut, of ropes) passed through a hole, loop etc.

rover [ROver] n wanderer; fickle person; (ar) pirate; (archery) mark chosen at random.

roving [ROving] adj and n rambling, wandering.

row (1) [RO] n series of persons or things in a straight line.

row (2) v/i and t propel (boat) by oars; transport by rowing ~ **row** n a spell at rowing, excursion in a rowing-boat.

row (3) [Row] n (coll) noisy disturbance; brawl, quarrel ~ **row** v/t and i (coll) reprimand; quarrel.

rowan [RO-an] n the mountain ash.

rowdy [Rowdi] adj noisy, rough ~ **rowdy** n one who causes noisy brawling; hooligan, ruffian ~ **rowdily** adv ~ **rowdiness** n.

rowdyism [Rowdi-izm] n rowdy behaviour.

rowel [Row-il] n spiked disk of a spur ~ **rowel** v/t insert a rowel in.

row-house [RO-hows] n (US) terrace house.

rowing-boat [RO-ing-bOt] n boat propelled by oars.

rowlock [Ruluk] n forked support in which an oar works.

royal [Roi-al] adj of, like or befitting a king or queen; regal; noble, majestic; very fine ~ **royal** n stag with a head of twelve or more points; (naut) the sail immediately above the topgallant sail; a size of paper; (coll) a member of the royal family.

royalism [Roi-alizm] n loyal adherence to a king or queen; belief in kingship as government.

royalist [Roi-alist] n supporter of kingly government; a supporter of King Charles in the English Civil War ~ **royalist** adj.

royalistic [Roi-alistik] adj of royalism or royalists.

royally [Roi-ali] adv in a royal way; superbly.

royalty [Roi-alti] n rank or office of king or queen; state of being royal, kingship; royal person or persons; percentage of profit paid to an author on each copy sold or performance given of his work; share of profits paid to owner of a patent, owner of land being mined etc.

rozzer [Rozer] n (sl) policeman.

rub (pres/part **rubbing**, p/t and p/part **rubbed**) [Rub] v/t and i move something with pressure over the surface of, apply friction to; dry, clean or polish by rubbing; massage; cause soreness by friction; grate or chafe (against); **r. along** (coll) manage fairly well despite difficulties; **r. down** clean or dry (the body) by rubbing; **r. in** (fig) in-

sistently mention (an unwelcome truth); **r. off** clean off by rubbing; **r. out** erase; (sl) get rid of, kill; **r. up** polish by rubbing; (fig) renew one's knowledge of, revise; **r. up the wrong way** tactlessly irritate ~ **rub** n act of rubbing; friction; massage; obstacle, hindrance.

rubato [ROObaatO] n (mus) slight variation of notes from their strict value > PDM.

rubber (1) [Ruber] n one who or that which rubs; something used for rubbing or cleaning; whetstone; rough file.

rubber (2) n elastic solid obtained from coagulated latex > PDS; piece of this, esp one used to erase pencil-marks; something made of this; (pl) rubber overshoes; **r. goods** (euph) type of contraceptives; **r. solution** acetone-based adhesive for joining rubber ~ **rubber** adj.

rubber (3) n (cards and games) series of three games won by two games out of three.

rubberize [RubeRIz] v/t coat with rubber (2).

rubberneck [Rubernek] n (US sl) person who peers, esp sightseer ~ **rubberneck** v/i go sightseeing.

rubber-stamp [Ruber-stamp] v/t cancel or endorse (document) by stamping; (fig) give automatic and unthinking approval to ~ **rubber-stamp** n and adj.

rubbery [RubeRi] adj of or like rubber (2); tough and resilient.

rubbing [Rubing] n impression of something made by rubbing chalk and graphite on paper placed over it.

rubbish [Rubish] n waste matter, refuse; anything worthless; (coll) nonsense.

rubbishing [Rubishing] adj rubbishy.

rubbishy [Rubishi] adj worthless, useless; (coll) nonsensical.

rubble [Rub'l] n debris of demolished building; rough fragments of stone.

rubdown [Rubdown] n massage.

rube [ROOb] n (US sl) country bumpkin.

rubefacient [ROObifayshent] n and adj (substance) which causes redness of the skin.

rubella [ROObela] n (med) German measles.

rubeola [ROObee-ola] n (med) measles.

rubescent [ROObesent] adj growing red.

Rubicon [ROObikon] n a frontier stream in Italy; **cross the R.** take a decisive step.

rubicund [ROObikund] adj ruddy, red-faced.

rubicundity [ROObikunditi] n redness, esp of face.

rubidium [ROObidi-um] n a soft white metallic element > PDS.

rubiginous [ROObijinus] adj rusty, reddish-brown.

rubric [ROObRik] n instruction, direction or chapter-heading printed or written distinctively, esp in red; liturgical direction or instruction ~ **rubric** adj.

rubrical [ROObRikal] adj marked with or printed in red; of or obeying a rubric ~ **rubrically** adv.

ruby [ROObi] n a deep red transparent gem, a form of corundum; intense redness; small-sized printing type; **r. wedding** fortieth anniversary of wedding ~ **ruby** adj of a deep intense red.

ruche [ROOsh] n pleat, ruffle.

ruck (1) [Ruk] n and v/t and i wrinkle, crease.

ruck (2) n pile; multitude, crowd; horses left behind by the winners in a race.

rucksack [*Rook*sak] *n* knapsack strapped to the back.

ruckus [*Ruk*us] *n* (*coll*) row, quarrel.

ruction [*Ruk*shon] *n* (*coll*) (*usu pl*) row, disturbance, uproar.

rudder [*Rud*er] *n* flat piece of wood or metal at stern of ship or aircraft by which it is steered; (*fig*) anything which guides.

rudderless [*Rud*erlis] *adj* having no means of steering; (*fig*) without direction or guidance.

ruddily [*Rud*ili] *adv* in a ruddy way.

ruddiness [*Rud*inis] *n* state of being ruddy.

ruddle, raddle [*Rud*'l] *n* form of red ochre ~ **ruddle** *v/t* mark (sheep) with ruddle.

ruddy [*Rud*i] *adj* glowing red; (*of face*) very pink; (*sl*) unpleasant, extreme (*euph for* **bloody**) ~ **ruddy** *v/t* and *i* redden.

rude [*ROOd*] *adj* impolite, insolent; showing bad manners; coarse, vulgar; indecent; uneducated, uncivilized; unskilled, primitive; simple; violent, harsh; robust, vigorous ~ **rudely** *adv* ~ **rudeness** *n* ~ **rudery** *n*.

rudiment [*ROO*diment] *n* elementary principle; undeveloped form; partially developed organ, structure *etc*; slight trace, vestige.

rudimentary [ROOdi*men*taRi] *adj* of, like, or containing elementary principles; in an undeveloped or an unformed state.

rue (1) [*ROO*] *n* strong-smelling evergreen shrub.

rue (2) *v/t* and *i* grieve, lament; regret, be sorry for ~ **rue** *n* repentance, regret.

rueful [*ROO*fool] *adj* expressing regret, repentance or disappointment ~ **ruefully** *adv* ~ **ruefulness** *n*.

rufescent [ROO*fes*ent] *adj* reddish.

ruff (1) [*Ruf*] *n* broad pleated linen collar or frill; frilly growth of feathers round the necks of some birds; species of sandpiper; species of pigeon.

ruff (2) *n* (*cards*) act of trumping when one cannot follow suit ~ **ruff** *v/t* and *i* trump.

ruffian [*Ruf*i-an] *n* violent, brutal person tending towards crime.

ruffianly [*Ruf*i-anli] *adj* violent, brutal.

ruffle [*Ruf*'l] *n* pleated strip of fine cloth at neck or wrist of a garment; fluted collar; ripple; subdued beat of the drum ~ **ruffle** *v/t* and *i* disturb the calm of; annoy, discompose; grow rough; be discomposed.

rufous [*ROO*fus] *adj* of brownish-red colour.

rug [*Rug*] *n* piece of thick warm cloth used as coverlet for feet or on a bed; small thick carpet.

Rugby [*Rug*bi] *n* one form of football in which the ball may be handled.

rugged [*Rug*id] *adj* rough, irregular, uneven; rocky; strongly marked; powerful but unrefined; (*coll*) uncomfortable, harsh ~ **ruggedly** *adv* ~ **ruggedness** *n*.

rugger [*Rug*er] *n* (*coll*) Rugby football.

ruin [*ROO*-in] *n* disaster, destruction; downfall; that which destroys; bankruptcy; remains of a partly destroyed city, building *etc* ~ **ruin** *v/t* and *i* bring to ruin; destroy; (*fig*) seduce; fall into ruins; come to ruin.

ruination [ROO-in*ay*shon] *n* downfall, destruction; that which ruins; state of being ruined.

ruinous [*ROO*-inus] *adj* fallen into ruin; decayed; causing ruin; (*coll*) too expensive ~ **ruinously** *adv* ~ **ruinousness** *n*.

rule [*ROOl*] *v/t* and *i* govern; control, dominate; settle or establish by authority; give legal ruling; have supreme power, reign; draw straight lines; (*comm*) maintain a price-level; **r. out** exclude ~ **rule** *n* established principle of guidance and control, regulation; law; authority or power to govern or control; principle; custom, routine; body of precepts for members of a religious order; accepted conventions to be followed in games, grammar, mathematical procedures *etc*; order made by a court of law, ruling; graduated bar of metal or wood for measuring; **as a r.** usually; **golden r.** valuable principle; **r. of thumb** method based on practical experience; **slide r.** ruler equipped with sliding scales for calculation; **work to r.** scrupulously observe all rules on safety, division of labour *etc*, in order to slow up rate of production.

ruler [*ROO*ler] *n* one who governs; one who makes laws; instrument of wood *etc* by which straight lines are drawn.

ruling [*ROO*ling] *n* authoritative legal decision ~ **ruling** *adj* that rules; prevailing; dominating.

rum (1) [*Rum*] *n* alcoholic spirit distilled from molasses or sugarcane.

rum (2) *adj* (*coll*) strange, queer, odd.

rumba, rhumba [*Rum*ba] *n* type of ballroom dance based on Caribbean folk-dancing.

rumbaba [*Rum*baba] *n* rich spongecake soaked in rum syrup.

rumble [*Rumb*'l] *v/i* and *t* make a low, continuous, rolling sound; (*sl*) see through, comprehend ~ **rumble** *n* rumbling sound; seat behind a carriage; (*sl*) pre-arranged gang-fight.

rumbling [*Rumb*ling] *adj* and *n* (making) a low, continuous, rolling sound.

rumbustious [Rum*bus*chus] *adj* boisterous.

ruminant [*ROO*minant] *n* animal with a complex stomach for chewing the cud > PDB ~ **ruminant** *adj* chewing the cud; (*fig*) thoughtful.

ruminate [*ROO*minayt] *v/i* and *t* chew the cud; (*fig*) think deeply, brood (over).

rumination [ROOmi*nay*shon] *n* act of chewing the cud; (*fig*) deep thought.

ruminative [*ROO*minativ] *adj* chewing the cud; (*fig*) meditative ~ **ruminatively** *adv*.

rumly [*Rum*li] *adv* (*coll*) queerly, oddly.

rummage [*Rum*ij] *v/t* and *i* turn over roughly in searching (through), poke about (in); **r. out** find after searching for ~ **rummage** *n* act of searching roughly, ransacking; jumble, heap of articles of small value.

rummage-sale [*Rum*ij-sayl] *n* sale of miscellaneous articles given by the owners, *usu* in aid of charity.

rummy [*Rum*i] *adj* (*coll*) queer, odd ~ **rummy** *n* card-game for two or more players ~ **rummily** *adv* ~ **rumminess** *n*.

rumness [*Rum*nis] *n* (*coll*) oddness.

rumour [*ROO*mer] *n* story or assertion circulating without firm basis in facts; gossip, hearsay.

rumoured [*ROO*merd] *adj* circulating as rumour, stated without factual knowledge.

rump [*Rump*] *n* buttocks; (*fig*) last and worst part.

rumple [*Rump*'l] *v/t* wrinkle, crease; make untidy.

rumpsteak [*Rump*stayk] *n* beefsteak cut from near the rump.

rumpus [*Rump*us] *n* (*coll*) disturbance, quarrel.

run (*pres/part* **running**, *p/t* **ran**, *p/part* **run**) [Run] *v/i* and *t* move swiftly over the ground by using feet alternately; take part in a race; flee, escape by running; move rapidly; pass, proceed, go; flow; melt, drip; be wet; revolve; be in action, work, move; extend, continue; elapse; be current; cause to run; cause to move, drive; chase; thrust; manage, organize; operate; perform; incur; smuggle; discharge; emit as liquid; (*theat*) be continuously performed; **r. across** meet accidentally; **r. after** pursue, chase; persistently try to obtain or seduce; **r. against** collide with, strike against; meet accidentally; **r. at** hurl oneself at; attack; **r. away** flee; **r. away with** elope with; steal; (*of horses*) gallop uncontrollably while carrying a rider or drawing a vehicle; (*fig*) overpower, destroy the self-control of; **r. (one) close** be almost equal to; **r. down** collide with and sink or squash; pursue and catch; speak ill of, disparage; cease working from loss of motive power; **be r. down** be weakened by illness or fatigue; **r. high** be intense; **r. in** (*mot*) drive at moderate speed when new; (*sl*) arrest; **r. into** collide with; meet by chance; encounter; **r. off** print copies of; drain away; **r. off with** elope with; steal; **r. on** continue without pause or break; talk continuously; **r. out (of)** have no more supplies (of); **r. out on** (*sl*) abandon, desert; **r. over** knock down and injure with vehicle; collide with and squash; read, examine or repeat hastily; overflow; **r. through** pierce; read or repeat hastily; spend, waste; **r. up** hoist rapidly; make or build hastily; increase (expenses); **r. up against** encounter (*esp* an obstacle) ~ **run** *n* act of running; trip; distance or time of uninterrupted running; unbroken succession of similar events; trend, course; area where animals habitually pass; grazing ground; burrow; enclosure for fowls; path; batch, flock *etc*; average type; eager demand, rush to buy or obtain; right of access or use; long hole caused by dropped stitch, ladder; (*cricket*) act of batsmen in running between wickets without being put out; point scored for this; (*mus*) roulade; (*theat*) unbroken series of performances; **have a r. for one's money** win something by one's efforts; **have the r. of** be allowed to use or go anywhere in; **in the long r.** eventually; on average, on the whole; **on the r.** fleeing or hiding from enemies, police *etc*; continuously busy.

runabout [Runabowt] *n* small light motorcar or aircraft; rover, gadabout.

run-around [Run-aRownd] *n* (*sl*) series of evasions.

runaway [Runaway] *n* one who runs away from danger or from restraint; deserter; fugitive; bolting horse ~ **runaway** *adj* fleeing from danger or from restraint; rushing uncontrolled; eloping; outstripping all rivals; highly successful.

runback [Runbak] *n* (*tennis*) space behind baseline.

rundown [Rundown] *n* process of deliberately reducing to a lower amount, level *etc*; brief but thorough account or explanation; statistical analysis ~ **rundown** *adj* exhausted, weakened.

rune [ROOn] *n* a letter of the early Germanic alphabet; written or carved magical symbol; incomprehensible writing; Finnish poem; (*fig*) song, *esp* magical.

rung (1) [Rung] *n* bar forming a step in a ladder; spoke; crossbar of chair.

rung (2) *p/t* and *p/part* of **ring**.

runic [ROOnik] *adj* of, like, inscribed with or consisting of runes; of the ancient Scandinavians ~ **runic** *n* (*printing*) kind of display lettering.

run-in [Run-in] *n* (*coll*) gradual approach.

runnable [Runab'l] *adj* in fit state to be hunted.

runnel [Runel] *n* rivulet; small brook; gutter.

runner [Runer] *n* one who runs; one who takes part in a running race; horse that runs in a race; smuggler; (*hist*) police-officer; that upon which anything runs or slides; blade of skate; revolving millstone; creeping stem from a plant; twining or climbing plant; cursorial bird; strip of cloth for covering furniture.

runner-up [RuneR-*up*] *n* one who comes second in a race or competition.

running [Runing] *n* act or motion of one who runs; chance of winning a race; racing; smuggling; discharge of pus *etc*; **in (out of) the r.** having (not having) a chance of success; **make the r.** set the pace ~ **running** *adj* that runs; that flows; unbroken, continuous; following in succession; suppurating; **r. board** board used as step into a motorcar; locomotive footboard; **r. commentary** series of comments upon events as they occur; **r. fire** continuous shooting; **r. fight** battle between one pursuing and one pursued; **r. hand** cursive handwriting; **r. title** title of book printed on each page throughout.

running-jump [Runing-*jump*] *n* jump made after a preliminary run.

running-rigging [Runing-Riging] *n* (*naut*) all rigging except fixed ropes.

runny [Runi] *adj* liquid or semiliquid; melting.

runt [Runt] *n* animal stunted in growth; undersized person; small breed of ox or bullock; large variety of pigeon.

runway [Runway] *n* prepared concrete track for aircraft to take off from or land on; pathway, channel, track.

rupee [ROOpee] *n* Indian standard silver coin.

ruption [Rupshon] *n* rupture.

rupture [Rupcher] *n* act of breaking or bursting open; state of being broken or part'd violently; hernia; quarrel that causes a partin ~ **rupture** *v/t* and *i* burst, break; separate violently, sever; affect with hernia.

rural [RooRal] *adj* of, in or like the country; pastoral, agricultural; suiting the country; **r. dean** clergyman ranking below archdeacon, who supervises the churches of a district.

ruridecanal [RooRidikaynal] *adj* of a rural dean or his office.

Ruritanian [ROORitayni-an] *adj* (*of politics, or of a State*) full of melodramatic adventures, plots, intrigues *etc*.

ruse [ROOz] *n* trick, stratagem; artifice.

rush (1) [Rush] *n* tall plant which grows in wet ground; stem of this used for making mats, baskets *etc*; (*fig*) anything of little or no value.

rush (2) *v/i* and *t* move with violent speed; act hastily; flow or blow violently; hurry along; bring or send in great haste; surmount by speed; force into hasty action; do at high speed; take by storm, capture by violence and speed; enter hastily; **be rushed** be overwhelmed by pressure of work ~

rush *n* rapid or violent movement, *esp* of advance; hasty restless activity, bustle; sudden increase in work, activity, demand *etc*; flow, gush; **gold r.** eager expedition of many prospectors to new-found gold-field; **r. hour** time of day when traffic, business *etc* is heaviest ~ **rush** *adj* (*coll*) done in great haste; urgent; crowded.

rush-candle [*Rush*-kand'l] *n* narrow candle made of rush pith dipped in tallow.

rushen [*Rush*en] *adj* made of rushes.

rush-hour [*Rush*-owr] *adj* of or at the time of day when traffic is heaviest.

rushlight [*Rush*lIt] *n* rush-candle; light from this; small feeble light.

rushline [*Rush*lIn] *n* (*US football*) forward line of attack or defence.

rushy [*Rush*i] *adj* abounding in rushes; made of rushes.

rusk [*Rusk*] *n* light crusty sweet biscuit; piece of crisp-baked bread.

russet [*Rus*it] *n* reddish-brown colour; rough-skinned brownish apple; coarse reddish-brown homespun cloth ~ **russet** *adj* reddish-brown; of russet cloth; (*fig*) homely, simple.

russia [*Rush*a] *n* soft kind of leather used in book-binding.

Russian [*Rush*an] *n* and *adj* (native) of Russia; (language) of Russia.

russianize [*Rush*anIz] *v/t* make Russian; russify.

russification [*Rusifikay*shon] *n* act of impregnating with Russian ideals.

russify [*Rus*ifI] *v/t* impregnate with Russian ideals.

Russo- *pref* of Russia; of the Russians.

Russophil(e) [*Rus*ofil/*Rus*ofIl] *n* uncritical admirer of Russia or the Russians.

Russophobe [*Rus*ofOb] *n* and *adj* (person) who hates or fears Russia intensely or irrationally.

russophobia [*Rus*of*Ob*i-a] *n* intense or irrational dislike or fear of Russia.

rust [*Rust*] *n* hydrated oxide of iron formed by exposure to moisture and air > PDS; reddish colour of this; (*bot*) fungus disease of plants causing reddish spots; (*fig*) inactivity, loss of power through disuse ~ **rust** *v/i* and *t* be affected by rust; lose power through disuse or idleness; corrode; affect with rust.

rustic [*Rus*tik] *adj* of, in or like the country; unsophisticated, simple; unpolished; awkward, uncouth; coarse; plain; (*of woodwork*) of rough untrimmed branches ~ **rustic** *n* countryman ~ **rustically** *adv*.

rusticate [*Rus*tikayt] *v/i* and *t* dwell in or retire to the country; suspend for a time from a university; give a rough surface to (masonry).

rustication [*Rus*ti*kay*shon] *n* residence in the country; temporary suspension from a university.

rusticity [*Rus*ti*si*ti] *n* country manners; simplicity.

rustily [*Rus*tili] *adv* in a rusty way ~ **rustiness** *n*.

rustle [*Rus*'l] *v/i* and *t* make a low crisp whispering sound when moved; cause to make such a sound; (*US sl*) steal, *esp* cattle or horses; **r. up** (*coll*) procure hastily ~ **rustle** *n* low, crisp whispering sound.

rustler [*Rus*ler] *n* (*US sl*) cattle-thief; horse-thief.

rustless [*Rus*tles] *adj* incapable of rusting; not rusty.

rustproof [*Rust*pROOf] *adj* incapable of rusting.

rusty [*Rus*ti] *adj* covered with or affected by rust; as if covered with rust; reddish-brown; discoloured by age; (*fig*) out of practice; impaired by disuse, inaction *etc*; **turn r.** (*sl*) become angry or difficult to manage.

rut (1) [*Rut*] *n* sexual heat of male deer or other animal ~ **rut** (*pres/part* **rutting**, *p/t* and *p/part* **rutted**) *v/t* and *i* cover in copulation; be in rut.

rut (2) *n* sunken groove made by wheels; (*fig*) constant habit; dreary routine ~ **rut** (*pres/part* **rutting**, *p/t* and *p/part* **rutted**) *v/t* make ruts in.

ruth [*ROOth*] *n* (*ar*) mercy, pity.

ruthenium [*ROOthee*ni-um] *n* a hard metallic element > PDS.

ruthless [*ROOth*lis] *adj* without pity, merciless, cruel ~ **ruthlessly** *adv* ~ **ruthlessness** *n*.

rutile [*ROO*tIl] *n* crystalline form of natural titanium dioxide > PDS.

ruttish [*Rut*ish] *adj* in rut (1); lustful.

rutty [*Rut*i] *adj* cut into ruts.

rye (1) [*RI*] *n* a cereal plant; grain of this used as fodder; coarse flour made from this; **r. whisky** whisky distilled from rye grains.

rye (2) *n* (*Romany*) young man.

rye-grass [*RI*-gRaas] *n* kind of grass cultivated for fodder.

S

s [*es*] nineteenth letter of the English alphabet.

Sabaoth [*sa*bay-oth] *n* (*pl*) (*Heb*) armies, hosts.

Sabbatarian [sabatairi-an] *adj* of the Sabbath ~ **Sabbatarian** *n* one who applies to Sundays all the rules of the Jewish Sabbath; one who allows no recreations, travelling *etc* on Sundays.

Sabbatarianism [sabatairi-anizm] *n* principles and observances of Sabbatarians.

Sabbath [*sa*bath] *n* day of the week set apart for rest and divine worship; Sunday; the Jewish Saturday; (*no cap*) a nocturnal meeting of a witches' coven.

sabbatic [sa*ba*tik] *adj* of or like the Sabbath.

sabbatical [sa*ba*tikal] *adj* of or like the Sabbath; **s. year** (*OT*) every seventh year, in which land lay fallow; (*fig*) year's vacation allowed to certain university teachers usually once in seven years.

sable [*sa*yb'l] *n* small arctic carnivore with valuable dark brown fur; fur of this; paintbrush made of this; black; (*pl*) black mourning clothes ~ **sable** *adj* black; dark; made of fur of sable.

sabot [*sa*bO] *n* wooden shoe; wooden-soled shoe.

sabotage [*sa*botaazh] *n* deliberate damage to machinery, industrial plant *etc*, *usu* in industrial disputes or by guerrillas, resistance fighters *etc*; clandestine damage by enemies ~ **sabotage** *v*/*t* deliberately damage.

saboteur [sabo*tur*] *n* one who performs acts of sabotage.

sabra [*sa*bRa] *n* Jew born in modern Israel.

sabre [*sa*yber] *n* cavalry sword with curved blade; **s. rattling** (*fig*) intimidation by threatening war.

sabretache [*sa*bertash] *n* leather case suspended from swordbelt of cavalry officer.

sac (1) [*sak*] *n* (*leg*) right of a lord of a manor to try cases in his own court.

sac (2) *n* (*biol*) pouch, cavity, receptacle.

saccate [*sa*kayt] *adj* (*biol*) shaped like a bag.

sacchar-, saccharo- *pref* of, like, or containing sugar.

saccharimeter [saka*Ri*meter] *n* apparatus for determining the concentration of a sugar solution by means of polarized light > PDS.

saccharin [*sa*kaRin] *n* very sweet chemical compound derived from coal-tar used for sweetening food > PDS; tablet of this; (*fig*) excessively sentimental sweetness ~ **saccharin** *adj* of or like saccharin; (*fig*) too sweet, sentimental.

saccharine [*sa*kaReen] *n* and *adj* saccharin.

saccharoid [*sa*kaRoid] *adj* of or like saccharin; of or like cube sugar.

saccharometer [saka*Ro*miter] *n* type of hydrometer used for finding the concentration of sugar solutions by determining their density > PDS.

saccharose [*sa*kaROs] *n* cane-sugar, beet-sugar.

saccule [*sa*kewl] *n* (*biol*) small sac, cyst.

sacerdocy [saserd*O*si] *n* priesthood.

sacerdotal [saserd*O*tal] *adj* of or like priests or priesthood; priestly.

sacerdotalism [saserd*O*talizm] *n* priestly principles or practice; religious system ascribing great importance to priests; excessive domination by or reverence for priests ~ **sacerdotalist** *n* and *adj*.

sachet [*sa*shay] *n* small soft bag for holding lavender, handkerchiefs *etc*.

sack (1) [*sak*] *n* large strong bag of coarse cloth; amount contained in a sack; (*coll*) dismissal from employment; loose waistless dress or coat; **s. race** race in which competitors' legs are enclosed in a sack ~ **sack** *v*/*t* (*coll*) dismiss from employment; put into a sack.

sack (2) *v*/*t* plunder, loot (captured town) ~ **sack** *n* act of looting.

sack (3) *n* a dry white wine.

sackbut [*sa*kbut] *n* bass wind instrument resembling a trombone; (*bibl*) a Babylonian harp.

sackcloth [*sa*k-kloth] *n* coarse cloth, formerly worn as sign of mourning or of penitence.

sacking [*sa*king] *n* coarse cloth.

sacral [*sa*ykRal] *adj* of the sacrum.

sacrament [*sa*kRament] *n* religious ritual that symbolizes and transmits grace, *esp* one of the seven major Christian rites; (*cap*) the Eucharist; the consecrated Eucharistic Host; (*fig*) any act considered as of symbolic spiritual value; **the Blessed S.** the Eucharist.

sacramental [sakRa*men*tal] *adj* of, like, or as a sacrament; consecrated ~ **sacramental** *n* (*RC*) minor act or rite that may transmit and symbolize grace.

sacramentalism [sakRa*men*talizm] *n* doctrine of the spiritual value of sacraments.

sacramentally [sakRa*men*tali] *adv* by or as a sacrament.

sacramentarian [sakRamentair*i*-an] *n* one who holds extreme views regarding the efficacy of the sacraments ~ **sacramentarian** *adj*.

sacred [*sa*ykRid] *adj* connected with or dedicated to God, a god, or a spiritual purpose; of religion; holy; deeply revered or cherished; inviolable; **s. cow** (*coll*) something too holy to be criticized.

sacredness [*sa*ykRidnis] *n* quality of being sacred.

sacrifice [*sa*kRifIs] *n* act of destroying or giving up something valued for the sake of another, of duty, or of a higher purpose; act of offering or dedicating something to a deity; act of killing or destroying something as an offering to a deity; creature or object thus offered; victim; act of selling at a loss ~ **sacrifice** *v*/*t* and *i* destroy or give up for the sake of another, of duty *etc*; kill or destroy in honour of a deity; offer to a deity; offer a sacrifice.

sacrificial [sakRi*fish*al] *adj* of, for, or performing sacrifices ~ **sacrificially** *adv*.

sacrilege [*sa*kRilij] *n* act of misusing, insulting, or harming anything sacred; (*leg*) breaking into and stealing from a church.

sacrilegious [sakRi*li*jus] *adj* of, like, or committing sacrilege; impious, profane; irreverent ~ **sacrilegiously** *adv*.

sacring [*sa*ykRing] *n* consecration; **s. bell** bell rung at the elevation of the Host and Chalice.

sacrist [*sa*kRist] *n* sacristan.

sacristan [*sa*kRistan] *n* keeper of sacred vessels, vestments *etc* in a church; sexton.

sacristy [*sak*Risti] *n* room in a church where the sacred vessels, books and vestments are kept.

sacrosanct [*sak*ROsankt] *adj* sacred; inviolable.

sacrum [*say*kRum] *n* a composite bone at the base of the spinal column which unites with the vertebrae to form the pelvis.

sad [*sad*] *adj* sorrowful, gloomy, downcast; unfortunate; causing sorrow, lamentable; (*of bread etc*) not having risen.

sadden [*sad*en] *v/t* and *i* make sad; become sad.

saddle [*sad*'l] *n* rider's seat fastened to a horse's back or on a bicycle, motorcycle *etc*; part of animal's back from shoulders to loins; mutton joint cut from this part; mountain ridge joining two peaks; **in the s.** on horseback; in control, dominating ~ **saddle** *v/t* put a saddle on; (*coll*) impose a burden or task on.

saddleback [*sad*'lbak] *n* a roof with a gable at each end; long ridge with a similar slope on each side; the black-backed gull.

saddlebacked [*sad*'lbakt] *adj* having a low back and raised neck and head.

saddlebag [*sad*'lbag] *n* one of two bags slung across an animal from the saddle; tool-bag on a bicycle; heavy fabric for upholstery or rugs.

saddlebow [*sad*'lbO] *n* pommel.

saddler [*sad*ler] *n* one who makes or trades in saddles and harness.

saddlery [*sad*leRi] *n* trade or shop of a saddler; saddles and harness collectively; room where these are kept.

Sadducee [*sad*ewsee] *n* one of a sect among the Jews who kept to the written word of the Law and excluded tradition, and who denied the doctrine of resurrection from the dead.

sadism [*say*dizm] *n* sexual perversion involving cruelty > PDP; delight in inflicting or watching suffering; extreme cruelty.

sadist [*say*dist] *n* one who practises sadism; person delighting in cruelty.

sadistic [*sa*distik] *adj* of or like sadism or sadists; delighting in cruelty ~ **sadistically** *adv.*

sadly [*sad*li] *adv* in a sad way.

sadness [*sad*nis] *n* state or quality of being sad.

sado-masochism [*say*dO-*mas*Okism] *n* combination of sadistic and masochistic traits in the same person.

safari [*sa*faa*Ri*] *n* expedition for hunting, photographing or viewing wild animals; **s. park** area where wild animals are kept for viewing under semi-natural conditions.

safe [*sayf*] *adj* unharmed; not exposed to danger or injury; not dangerous, unlikely to cause harm; secure; cautious; reliable, trusty; certain to win ~ **safe** *n* strong steel cupboard or box for keeping valuables secure; cool store-cupboard or container for food; **s. deposit** building containing safes and strongrooms to be let.

safe-blowing [*sayf*-blO-ing] *n* use of explosives for breaking safes open to rob them.

safe-conduct [sayf-*kon*dukt] *n* document or escort which ensures a safe passage through hostile areas.

safeguard [*sayf*gaard] *n* that which protects; precaution ~ **safeguard** *v/t* protect.

safekeeping [sayf*keep*ing] *n* act of keeping in safety; custody.

safely [*sayf*li] *adv* in a safe way.

safety [*sayf*ti] *n* state or quality of being safe; security; custody ~ **safety** *adj* making safe; minimizing risk or injury; **s. belt** belt holding a person to the seat of a car or aircraft, to minimize injuries in crashing, jolting *etc*; **s. catch** device to prevent accidental firing of gun; device preventing injury from faulty machine; **s. curtain** fireproof curtain between stage and auditorium; **s. glass** unsplintering glass; **s. lock** lock that can be opened only by its own key.

safety-lamp [*sayf*ti-lamp] *n* oil-lamp which will not ignite inflammable gases > PDS.

safety-match [*sayf*ti-mach] *n* match which ignites only on the special surface on the box.

safety-pin [*sayf*ti-pin] *n* brooch-shaped pin with a protected point.

safety-razor [*sayf*ti-Rayzer] *n* razor mounted on a handle with guard.

safety-valve [*sayf*ti-valv] *n* valve which opens automatically to release surplus steam > PDE; (*fig*) outlet for suppressed emotion, high spirits *etc.*

saffron [*saf*Ron] *adj* bright orange yellow ~ **saffron** *n* type of crocus; flavouring matter obtained from this; orange-yellow dye obtained from this.

sag (*pres/part* **sagging,** *p/t* and *p/part* **sagged**) [*sag*] *v/i* droop, bend limply; become limp; become depressed; (*comm*) fall in price; (*naut*) drift off course ~ **sag** *n* act of sagging; degree to which something sags.

saga [*saaga*] *n* medieval Icelandic prose narrative; long novel or series of novels about members of one family or group; heroic or adventurous story.

sagacious [*sa*gay*shus*] *adj* intelligent; shrewd; wise; sensible ~ **sagaciously** *adv* ~ **sagaciousness** *n.*

sagacity [*sa*gasiti] *n* quality of being sagacious.

sage (1) [*sayj*] *n* aromatic herb used in cooking.

sage (2) *adj* wise; grave; solemn ~ **sage** *n* man of great wisdom ~ **sagely** *adv* ~ **sageness** *n.*

sage-green [*sayj*-gReen] *n* greyish green.

saggar [*sager*] *n* fireproof case in which porcelain is enclosed while baking.

Sagittarius [sajit*air*R-us] *n* (*astron*) constellation of the Archer, ninth sign of the zodiac.

sagittary [*saj*iteRi] *n* a centaur.

sago [*say*gO] *n* edible starch obtained from the pith of several palms.

sahib [*saa*-ib/*saab*] *n* Indian title of rank; title of address formerly used by Indians to Europeans in India; member of the former British ruling class in India; (*coll*, now *usu joc*) gentleman.

said [*sed*] *p/t* and *p/part* of **say.**

sail [*sayl*] *n* piece of canvas spread to catch the wind to drive a boat or ship; ship, *esp* one with sails; excursion in a sailing ship; arm of windmill; anything like a sail in shape or function; **set s.** unfurl the sails; set out on voyage; **shorten s.** decrease amount of sail spread; **strike s.** lower the sails; **under s.** moving by use of sails ~ **sail** *v/t* and *i* navigate a sailing ship or boat; be driven by action of wind on sails; move across water; begin a sea voyage; embark; glide, move smoothly; **s. near the wind** (*fig*) act in a way that is almost, but not quite, illegal, immoral, or dangerous.

sail-arm [*sayl*-aarm] *n* arm of windmill.

sailcloth [*sayl*kloth] *n* canvas or other coarse material for making sails.

sailer [*sayl*er] *n* sailing ship.

sailing [*sayl*ing] *n* act or art of navigating a ship, *esp* one with sails; act of moving by sails; departure on a voyage; **plain s.** simple, uncomplicated task; (*naut*) navigation by plane chart ~ **sailing** *adj* moved by sails; of or connected with ships or navigation.

sailor [*sayl*er] *n* seaman, mariner; one of the crew; one who sails; **bad (good) s.** person liable (not liable) to be seasick; **s. hat** flat-topped hat with brim.

sailoring [*sayl*ering] *n* life or activities of a sailor.

sailplane [*sayl*playn] *n* glider.

sailyard [*sayl*yaard] *n* spar on which sails are extended.

sainfoin [*sayn*foin] *n* leguminous herb grown for fodder.

saint [*saynt*] *n* person of great virtue and holiness, *esp* one venerated and invoked after his death; person whose holiness is officially recognized by the Church after his death; any of the dead in heaven; **S. Anthony's fire** ergotism; erysipelas; **S. Bernard** type of very large dog; **S. John's wort** yellow-flowered creeping plant; **S. Vitus' dance** nervous disorder causing convulsive movements ~ **saint** *v/t* (*rare*) canonize ~ **saint** [*sint*/*saynt*] *adj* title of a canonized person.

sainted [*saynt*id] *adj* in heaven; holy.

saintly [*saynt*li] *adj* like a saint; pious ~ **saintliness** *n*.

sake (1) [*sayk*] *n* end, purpose; account, cause, behalf; **for the s. of** in order to please, benefit, or obtain.

sake (2) [*saa*ki] *n* Japanese alcoholic drink made from rice.

saker [*sayk*er] *n* type of falcon; small piece of 17th-century artillery.

sal [*sal*] *n* (*chem*) salt; salts; **s. volatile** [vol*ati*li] pungent alcoholic solution of ammonium carbonate > PDS.

salaam [*salaam*] *n* ceremonial Oriental salutation; a deep bow ~ **salaam** *v/i*.

salable [*sayl*ab'l] *adj* (*US*) saleable.

salacious [*sala*yshus] *adj* lustful, lecherous; concerned with lewd subjects ~ **salaciously** *adv* ~ **salaciousness** *n*.

salacity [*sala*siti] *n* quality of being salacious.

salad [*salad*] *n* dish of raw or cold vegetables prepared with a dressing of oil and vinegar or mayonnaise; lettuce; **fruit s.** dish of mixed sliced fruits ~ **salad** *adj* of or for salads; **s. cream** bottled mayonnaise; **s. days** youthful immaturity; **s. dressing** any sauce *etc* served with salads; mayonnaise; oil and vinegar.

salamander [*sala*mander] *n* lizard-like amphibian once believed to live in fire; (*fig*) one who can bear great heat.

salami [*salaa*mi] *n* (*Ital*) large highly-seasoned sausage.

salaried [*sala*rid] *adj* paid by salary.

salary [*sala*ri] *n* fixed payment for work made at regular intervals, *usu* of a month or more.

sale [*sayl*] *n* act of selling; exchange of an article for money; auction; market; demand; period in which retail goods are offered for sale at reduced prices; event at which goods are sold for charity.

saleable [*sayl*ab'l] *adj* capable of being sold; in demand; marketable.

salep [*salep*] *n* meal made of the dried tubers of various orchids.

sale-price [*sayl*-pris] *n* reduced price of goods offered in a sale.

saleroom [*sayl*ROOm] *n* room where auctions are held; room where goods are displayed for sale.

salesman (*pl* **salesmen**) [*sayl*zman] *n* person employed to sell goods, *esp* by travelling round to potential customers; person clever at persuading customers to buy.

salesmanship [*sayl*zmanship] *n* skill, device, or technique of persuading people to buy one's goods.

sales-resistance [*sayl*z-Rizistens] *n* unwillingness of potential customers to buy; resistance to salesmanship.

sales-talk [*sayl*z-tawk] *n* arguments to persuade someone to buy something.

saleswoman (*pl* **saleswomen**) [*sayl*zwooman] *n* female salesman.

Salic [*salik*/*sayl*ik] *adj* (*hist*) of a tribe of Franks on the lower Rhine; **S. Law** law forbidding succession of women to the crown.

salicin [*sal*isin] *n* a bitter compound obtained from the bark of certain willows.

salicylate [*sal*isilayt] *n* a salt of salicylic acid ~ **salicylate** *v/t* impregnate with salicylic acid.

salicylic [*sal*isilik] *adj* of or obtained from salicin; **s. acid** white crystalline solid used in the manufacture of aspirin > PDS.

salience [*sayl*i-ens] *n* state of being salient.

salient [*sayl*i-ent] *adj* projecting, jutting out; prominent; conspicuous, striking ~ **salient** *n* that which juts out; body of troops projecting from the main line ~ **saliently** *adv*.

saliferous [*sali*feRus] *adj* yielding salt.

saline [*sayl*in] *adj* containing salt; consisting of salt ~ **saline** *n* deposit of salt; saltmarsh.

salinity [*salin*iti] *n* saltiness; proportion or amount of salt in something, *esp* sea-water > PDG.

salinometer [*salin*omiter] *n* type of hydrometer used for measuring concentration of salt solutions.

saliva [*saliv*a] *n* fluid secreted into the mouth to soften and partially digest food; spittle.

salivary [*saliv*eRi] *adj* of, in, or secreting saliva.

salivate [*saliv*ayt] *v/i* secrete an excessive amount of saliva.

salivation [*saliv*ayshon] *n* act of salivating.

salix [*sal*iks] *n* genus of trees which includes willow and osier.

sallow (1) [*sal*O] *n* willow.

sallow (2) *adj* (*of skin*) having a sickly yellow colour.

sally [*sal*i] *n* outburst, sudden rush; unexpectedly rapid and witty remark; (*mil*) sortie of besieged troops ~ **sally** *v/i* **s. forth** rush out; set out; make a sortie.

sally-lunn [*sali*-*lun*] *n* hot buttered teacake.

salmagundi [*salma*gundi] *n* dish of chopped meat *etc* seasoned with anchovies.

salmi [*sal*mee] *n* ragout, *esp* of gamebirds.

salmon [*sam*on] *n* large edible pink-fleshed fish ~ **salmon** *adj* of the colour of salmon.

salmonella [*salmo*nela] *n* (*biol*) type of bacterium causing food-poisoning.

salmon-trout [*sam*on-tRowt] *n* sea-trout.

salon [*salon*(g)] *n* (*Fr*) reception-room; circle of people prominent in the arts; exhibition of pictures.

saloon [sa*lOOn*] *n* large room used for receptions or for public entertainments; large cabin in passenger ship or aircraft; first-class accommodation in a liner; large luxurious railway carriage without compartments; more expensive bar of public house; (*US*) public house; motorcar with closed body and no partition between driver and passengers.

Salopian [sa*lOpi*-an] *n* and *adj* (native) of Shropshire

salse [*sals*] *n* mud-volcano.

salsify [*salsifi*] *n* biennial plant with edible root.

salt [*sawlt*] *n* sodium chloride used to season or preserve food; (*fig*) piquancy, relish; wit; (*chem*) compound formed when the hydrogen of an acid has been replaced by a metal > PDS; (*pl*) any of various effervescent purgative powders; **the s. of the earth** excellent or virtuous people; **old s.** (*coll*) sailor; **with a pinch of s.** sceptically, with some reserve or disbelief; **not worth one's s.** useless, worthless ~ **salt** *v/t* add salt to; flavour with salt; preserve with salt; (*coll*) put precious metal in a mine to make it seem valuable; falsify profits; **s. down** (*coll*) store away ~ **salt** *adj* containing salt; tasting of salt; preserved in salt; **s. lake** lake where evaporation is more rapid than intake of water > PDG.

saltation [sal*tayshon*] *n* act of bounding.

saltatory [sal*tayte*Ri] *adj* bounding; leaping; dancing; advancing in irregular spasms.

saltcellar [*sawlt*seler] *n* small bowl or sprinkler containing salt for use at meals; (*coll*) hollow between collarbone and base of neck.

salter [*sawlt*er] *n* one who makes or sells salt.

saltern [*sawlt*ern] *n* series of pools where salt is extracted from sea-water.

saltglaze [*sawlt*glayz] *n* glaze on stoneware produced by adding salt during firing.

saltiness [*sawlt*inis] *n* quality of being salty.

salting [*sawlt*ing] *n* application of salt; salt-marsh.

saltire [*salt*Ir] *n* (*her*) diagonal cross.

saltlick [*sawlt*lik] *n* rock or soil impregnated with salt, which animals come to lick.

saltmarsh [*sawlt*maarsh] *n* land liable to be overflowed by the sea or by streams of salt water.

saltmine [*sawlt*mIn] *n* mine for rocksalt.

saltpan [*sawlt*pan] *n* basin or pool in which sea-water is evaporated to give salt.

saltpetre [sawlt*peeter*] *n* nitre; potassium nitrate.

saltwater [*sawlt*wawter] *adj* of, in or living in the sea.

salty [*sawlt*i] *adj* tasting of salt; pungent; bawdily witty.

salubrious [sa*lOO*bRi-us] *adj* promoting health ~ **salubriously** *adv* ~ **salubriousness** *n*.

salubrity [sa*lOO*bRiti] *n* quality of being salubrious.

saluki [sa*lOO*ki] *n* a breed of fast, silky-coated Persian hunting-dogs.

salutary [*salewte*Ri] *adj* beneficial, wholesome; having good effects.

salutation [salew*tay*shon] *n* act of saluting or greeting; words or gestures of greeting.

salute [sa*lOOt*] *v/t* and *i* greet or show respect to, by some customary act, gesture or form of words;

(*mil*) make prescribed gesture of respect or acknowledgement (to); honour by firing guns, dipping flags, raising swords *etc*; bow to; touch the hat to; kiss ~ **salute** *n* any customary act, gesture or form of words expressing welcome, respect or homage; ceremonial discharge of guns.

salvable [*salv*ab'l] *adj* that can be salvaged, saved or salved.

salvage [*salv*ij] *n* that which is saved from shipwreck, fire *etc*; waste materials put aside for collection and re-use in manufacture; reward for saving ship or cargo from destruction; act of raising a sunken ship; (*fig*) act of rescuing or redeeming ~ **salvage** *v/t* save from shipwreck, fire, capture or destruction.

salvarsan [*salv*aarsan] *n* arsenical compound used in treatment of syphilis.

salvation [salv*ay*shon] *n* act of saving from destruction, *esp* from sin or damnation; redemption; deliverance from great danger; that which saves or delivers; **S. Army** evangelical and missionary Christian organization giving social and religious aid to the destitute.

Salvationist [salv*ay*shonist] *n* member of the Salvation Army.

salve (1) [*salv/saav*] *n* healing ointment; anything which soothes; remedy ~ **salve** *v/t* soothe, ease; vindicate; reconcile.

salve (2) [*salv*] *v/t* salvage.

salve (3) [*salvee*] *n* (*Lat*) antiphon addressed to the Virgin Mary.

salver [*salv*er] *n* tray on which visiting cards, letters *etc* are presented.

salvia [*salv*i-a] *n* a genus of plants including sage; cultivated species of this with brightly coloured flowers.

salvo (1) [*salv*O] *n* discharge of guns; volley.

salvo (2) *n* (*leg*) conditional clause, reservation; evasion.

salvor [*salv*er] *n* one who saves a ship from loss at sea or from destruction by fire.

sam [*sam*] *n* (*coll*) soul.

Samaritan [sama*Ri*tan] *n* inhabitant of Samaria; helpful and charitable person; member of organization to counsel and comfort potential suicides ~ **Samaritan** *adj* of Samaria.

samarium [sa*mair*Ri-um] *n* (*chem*) rare lanthanide element > PDS.

samba [*samb*a] *n* ballroom dance of Brazilian origin.

sambo [*samb*O] *n* child of a Negro and a mulatto; (*pej coll*) Negro.

Sam Browne [sam–b*Rown*] *n* leather belt worn as part of officers' uniform in the British Army.

same [*saym*] *adj* identical; not different; just mentioned; unchanged; corresponding; monotonous; **all the s.** in spite of this ~ **same** *pron* that which has just been mentioned.

sameness [*saym*nis] *n* state of being the same; monotony.

samisen [*sam*isen] *n* Japanese three-stringed instrument played with a plectrum.

samite [*saym*It] *n* (*ar*) rich silk fabric.

samovar [*sam*Ovaar] *n* Russian tea-urn.

Samoyed [samo-*yed*] *n* one of a Mongolian race inhabiting the extreme north of Asia; kind of dog bred by this race.

sampan [*sam*pan] *n* Chinese river boat with flat bottom.

samphire [*sam*fIr] *n* edible herb which grows on cliffs.

sample [*saam*p'l] *n* single specimen, example or portion showing the qualities and characteristics of a group or whole; representative specimen, *esp* of goods for sale ~ **sample** *adj* representative, typical; of or as a sample ~ **sample** *v/t* and *i* choose representative specimen (of a group), *usu* at random; test quality of by choosing a sample; taste, eat, drink.

sampler [*saam*pler] *n* piece of embroidery or needlework displaying varied stitches.

samurai (*pl* samurai) [*sam*ooRI] *n* (*hist*) member of Japanese feudal military class.

sanative [*san*ativ] *adj* healing, curative.

sanatorium (*pl* sanatoria) [sana*tawr*Ri-um] *n* establishment where tuberculosis is treated; hospital of a school.

sanatory [*san*ateRi] *adj* curative, health-giving.

sanctification [sangtifi*kay*shon] *n* act of sanctifying; state of being sanctified.

sanctify [*sangk*tifI] *v/t* make holy, consecrate; purify from sin; justify as right or holy.

sanctimonious [sangk*tim*Oni-us] *adj* making an unpleasant or unjustified display of piety and virtue; pretending to be holy; hypocritically pious ~ **sanctimoniously** *adv* ~ **sanctimoniousness** *n*.

sanctimony [*sangk*timoni] *n* quality of being sanctimonious.

sanction [*sangk*shon] *n* anything that enforces specified course of conduct; justification; penalty imposed for law-breaking; measure taken to compel a nation to conform to an agreement; ratification, authorization given by a superior; approval, permission ~ **sanction** *v/t* authorize; permit, approve.

sanctity [*sangk*titi] *n* state of being holy; saintliness; inviolability.

sanctuary [*sangk*choo-eRi] *n* holy place; consecrated building, *esp* the inner shrine of a church; place of safety and protection; (*hist*) consecrated place where no arrests could be made; place where birds or animals are left undisturbed; place of peaceful privacy.

sanctum [*sangk*tum] *n* sacred place; place of privacy; inviolable refuge.

Sanctus [*sangk*tus] *n* prayer beginning 'Holy, holy, holy'; music to which this is sung; **s. bell** bell rung when this is said or sung at Mass.

sand [*sand*] *n* hard granular powder, *usu* of impure silica; mass of this found on seashore, in deserts *etc* > PDG; (*pl*) stretches of sand; (*pl, fig*) time; (*US coll*) courage ~ **sand** *v/t* sprinkle or cover with sand; put sand in.

sandal (1) [*san*dal] *n* open shoe consisting of a sole secured by straps ~ **sandalled** *adj* wearing sandals.

sandal (2) *n* a yellowish fragrant wood of various E. Indian trees.

sandalwood [*san*dalwood] *n* sandal (2).

sandbag [*sand*bag] *n* sack filled with sand ~ **sandbag** (*pres/part* sandbagging, *p/t* and *p/part* sandbagged) *v/t* stun by hitting with a sandbag.

sandbank [*sand*bank] *n* submerged ridge of sand.

sandbar [*sand*baar] *n* ridge of sand formed across mouth of river or bay > PDG.

sandblast [*sand*blaast] *n* jet of sand driven against metal or glass to cut or engrave it.

sand-blind [*sand*-blInd] *adj* (*ar*) half-blind.

sandboy [*sand*boi] *n* **as happy as a s.** very happy and carefree.

sandcastle [*sand*kaas'l] *n* miniature castle built by children from damp sand.

sand-dune [*sand*-dewn] *n* ridge of drifted sand.

sanded [*sand*id] *adj* sprinkled, filled or covered with sand.

sandfly [*sand*flI] *n* species of biting midge.

sandglass [*sand*glaas] *n* device for measuring time, formed of two glass bulbs joined by narrow neck through which sand trickles from one bulb to the other in a stated length of time.

sandiness [*sand*inis] *n* state or quality of being sandy.

sandman [*sand*man] *n* imaginary person who makes children sleepy by sprinkling sand in their eyes.

sandmartin [*sand*maartin] *n* small swallow which nests in sandy cliffs or banks.

sandpaper [*sand*payper] *n* paper encrusted with sand for smoothing wood ~ **sandpaper** *v/t* smooth or polish by rubbing with sandpaper.

sandpiper [*sand*pIper] *n* name of several species of plover.

sandpit [*sand*pit] *n* area filled with sand for children to play in.

sandshoe [*sand*shOO] *n* light shoe of canvas or rubber, for use on beaches.

sandstone [*sand*stOn] *n* porous rock formed by sand bound together by calcium carbonate, silica *etc* > PDG.

sandstorm [*sand*stawrm] *n* violent wind carrying masses of sand with it > PDG.

sandwich [*sand*wich] *n* two pieces of buttered bread with jam, paste, meat, cheese or other filling between them; cake formed of two layers of sponge with jam *etc* between them; **s. board** one of two boards joined by straps and worn over back and chest by a man who carries them about to display notices, advertisements *etc*; **s. course** course of studies integrated with fulltime employment; **open s.** single piece of bread on which jam *etc* is spread or some savoury food piled ~ **sandwich** *v/t* place tightly between two other things, squeeze in.

sandwichman [*sand*wichman] *n* one who carries sandwich boards.

sandy [*sand*i] *adj* full of sand; covered with sand; like sand; yellowish-red.

sane [*sayn*] *adj* mentally normal, not suffering from any grave psychological disorder; rational; sensible ~ **sanely** *adv* ~ **saneness** *n*.

sang [*sang*] *p/t* of sing.

sangfroid [saa(ng)f*Rwaa*] *n* (*Fr*) imperturbable calmness in difficult or dangerous circumstances.

Sangraal, Sangrail [sang-*gRayl*] *n* the Holy Grail.

sangui- *pref* of blood.

sanguinary [*sang*-gwineRi] *adj* of or causing bloodshed; bloodthirsty; bloody ~ **sanguinarily** *adv* ~ **sanguinariness** *n*.

sanguine [*sang*-gwin] *adj* hopeful, confident, optimistic; blood-red; red-faced, ruddy ~ **sanguinely** *adv* ~ **sanguineness** *n*.

sanguineous [sang-*gwi*ni-us] *adj* of or like blood; blood-red; containing much blood.

Sanhedrin [*san*idRin] *n* (*hist*) supreme court of justice and council of the Jews.

sanitarian [sanit*air*Ri-an] *n* expert on or advocate of public sanitation.

sanitary [*san*iteRi] *adj* hygienic, preventing infection through dirt and contagion: of or by sanitation; clean; having proper drainage; disinfected; **s. inspector** official appointed by local authority to inspect drainage systems *etc*; **s. towel** absorbent pad worn during menstruation ∼ **sanitarily** *adv* ∼ **sanitariness** *n*.

sanitation [sanit*ay*shon] *n* system of drainage and disposal of sewage; public hygiene.

sanity [*san*iti] *n* state or quality of being sane.

sank [*sank*] *p*/*t* of **sink**.

sans [*sanz*] *prep* (*obs*) without.

sansculotte [saa(ng)kew*lot*] *n* (*cont*) republican party in French Revolution; revolutionary.

sanserif [*san*seRif] *n* and *adj* (*print*) type without serifs.

Sanskrit [*san*skRit] *n* ancient language of the Hindus.

Santa Claus [*san*ta-klawz] *n* legendary figure who is supposed to distribute presents to children at Christmas.

sap (1) [*sap*] *n* circulating juice of living plants; strength, vigour ∼ **sap** (*pres*/*part* **sapping**, *p*/*t* and *p*/*part* **sapped**) *v*/*t* draw off sap from; exhaust, weaken.

sap (2) *n* (*mil*) deep covered trench for approaching and undermining enemy fortifications ∼ **sap** (*pres*/*part* **sapping**, *p*/*t* and *p*/*part* **sapped**) *v*/*t* undermine; weaken, exhaust.

sap (3) *n* (*coll*) fool.

saphead [*sap*hed] *n* (*sl*) fool.

sapid [*sap*id] *adj* savoury; having flavour; interesting.

sapience [*sayp*i-ens] *n* wisdom (*often ironical*).

sapient [*sayp*i-ent] *adj* giving oneself airs of wisdom; wise ∼ **sapiently** *adv*.

sapless [*sap*lis] *adj* having no sap (1); dry, withered; lifeless.

sapling [*sap*ling] *n* young tree; (*fig*) a youth.

saponaceous [sapon*ay*shus] *adj* soapy.

saponification [saponifik*ay*shon] *n* conversion into soap; hydrolysis of an ester > PDS.

saponify [sa*pon*ifI] *v*/*t* convert into soap.

sapper [*sap*er] *n* (*mil*) private in the Royal Engineers; (*fig*) one who undermines.

sapphic [*saf*ik] *adj* of the Greek poetess Sappho; (*pros*) having three rhyming lines and a shorter fourth line unrhymed; (*fig*) lesbian.

sapphire [*saf*Ir] *n* natural crystalline form of blue transparent corundum > PDS; azure ∼ **sapphire** *adj* of light bright blue; of, like or containing sapphires.

sapphism [*saf*izm] *n* erotic attachment between women; lesbianism.

sappiness [*sap*inis] *n* juiciness; succulence.

sappy [*sap*i] *adj* full of sap; juicy; vigorous; (*sl*) foolish, weak.

sap-rot [*sap*-Rot] *n* dry-rot.

sapsago [saps*ayg*O] *n* a hard greenish cheese.

sapwood [*sap*wood] *n* soft wood newly formed under bark > PDB.

saraband [*sa*Raband] *n* slow stately Spanish dance; music for this > PDM.

Saracen [*sa*Rasen] *n* a Muslim, *esp* at the time of the Crusades.

saratoga [saRat*Og*a] *n* large travelling trunk.

sarcasm [*saar*kazm] *n* bitterly ironic remark, sneer; scornful mockery; outlook that expresses itself in sneering.

sarcastic [saar*kas*tik] *adj* bitterly ironical, sneering; prone to sarcasm; contemptuously mocking ∼ **sarcastically** *adj*.

sarcenet see **sarsenet**.

sarco- *pref* fleshy; of flesh.

sarcode [*saar*kOd] *n* jellyish protoplasm forming the bodies of protozoa.

sarcoma [saar*kO*ma] *n* malignant tumour of the connective cells.

sarcophagus [saar*kof*agus] *n* (*arch*) large stone coffin of ancient Egypt, Greece or Rome; stone of which these were made.

sard [*saard*] *n* a deep red semi-precious stone.

sardelle [saar*del*] *n* a small Mediterranean fish like a sardine.

sardine [saar*deen*] *n* immature pilchard or similar small fish, preserved in oil for food; **packed like sardines** closely pressed together.

sardonic [saar*don*ik] *adj* sneering; insincere; bitter, cynical; malicious ∼ **sardonically** *adv*.

sardonyx [*saar*doniks] *n* variety of onyx banded with layers of sard.

sargasso [saar*gas*O] *n* floating gulf-weed.

sari, saree [*saa*Ri] *n* robe worn by Hindu women wound round the body with one end thrown over the head.

sark [*saark*] *n* (*Scots* or *ar*) shirt.

sarking [*saar*king] *n* thin boards for lining a roof under the slates.

sarky [*saar*ki] *adj* (*sl*) sarcastic.

sarong [sa*Rong*] *n* cloth wrapped around the waist to form a knee-length garment, worn in the East Indies.

sarsaparilla [saarsapa*Ri*la] *n* species of climbing shrub; dried root of this used medicinally.

sarsen [*saar*sen] *n* large sandstone boulder.

sarsenet [*saar*senet] *n* thin fine woven silk fabric.

sartorial [saart*awr*i-al] *adj* of a tailor or tailoring; of tailor-made clothes.

sash (1) [*sash*] *n* band or scarf worn over the shoulder or round the waist.

sash (2) *n* wooden or metal frame holding glass of a window and opening by sliding up or down; **s. cord (line)** cord attaching a sash to counterweights, so that it may be easily raised or lowered.

sash-window [sash-*wind*O] *n* window that opens by sliding sashes up or down.

sasquatch [*sas*kwach] *n* name of unidentified animal supposed to inhabit N. American forests.

sassafras [*sas*afRas] *n* small North American laurel; tonic extracted from oil of this.

Sassenach [*sas*enak] *n* Scots name for an Englishman or a Lowland Scot ∼ **Sassenach** *adj*.

sat [*sat*] *p*/*t* and *p*/*part* of **sit**.

Satan [*say*tan] *n* the devil, the chief of the evil spirits in Christian theology.

satanic [sa*tan*ik] *adj* of or like Satan; devilish; fiendishly wicked, cruel or selfish ∼ **satanically** *adv*.

Satanism [*say*tanizm] *n* worship of Satan with

prayers and rituals blasphemously or obscenely parodying Christianity; devilish wickedness ~ **Satanist** *n* and *adj*.

satchel [*sach*el] *n* small bag for books *etc* slung from the shoulder by a strap.

sate (1) [*sayt*] *v/t* satisfy; glut, satiate.

sate (2) *ar p/t* of **sit**.

sateen [sa*teen*] *n* glossy cotton imitating satin.

satellite [*sat*elIt] *n* natural body rotating in orbit round a planet, moon > PDS; projectile or apparatus fired into space to such a distance from the earth that it remains in orbit round it; (*fig*) dependant; obsequious follower; **s. State** State that depends upon and obeys the policies of a more powerful State; **s. town** small town economically dependent on a larger one. ~ **satellite** *adj*.

satiate [*say*shi-ayt] *v/t* fully satisfy appetite or desires of; cause to be weary or oppressed by over-fulfilment, glut ~ **satiate** *adj* (*poet*) glutted.

satiation [sayshi-*ay*shon] *n* act of satiating; satiety.

satiety [sa*tI*-eti] *n* state of being fully satisfied; repletion; state of having had too much of some pleasure, food *etc*; weariness caused by over-fullness.

satin [*satin*] *n* a glossy silken fabric ~ **satin** *adj* made of satin; like satin; smooth and glossy.

satinette [satin*et*] *n* thin glossy fabric imitating satin.

satin-flower [*satin*-flowr] *n* the greater stitchwort; honesty.

satin-paper [*satin*-payper] *n* glossy writing-paper.

satinstitch [*satin*stich] *n* embroidery stitch in parallel lines, giving a glossy surface.

satinwood [*satin*wood] *n* hard lemon-coloured wood used in cabinet-work.

satire [*satIr*] *n* act of attacking any wickedness, folly or abuse by mockery, sarcasm *etc*; poem, novel, play *etc* that does this; lampoon; that which reveals the faults, pretensions *etc* of a person as ridiculous.

satiric, satirical [sati*Rik*, sati*Rik*al] *adj* of, like, as, or by satire ~ **satirically** *adv*.

satirist [*satiRist*] *n* one who writes or uses satire.

satirize [*satiRIz*] *v/t* show to be ridiculous; mock harshly; parody; compose satire against.

satisfaction [satis*fak*shon] *n* act of satisfying; state of being satisfied; contentment, pleasure; compensation; amends, atonement.

satisfactory [satis*fak*teRi] *adj* satisfying the needs or wishes of; sufficient, adequate; pleasing; good; atoning ~ **satisfactorily** *adv*.

satisfy [*satisf*I] *v/t* and *i* completely fulfil the needs or desires of; supply fully; be enough for; content, please; fulfil, observe, comply with; pay off; convince, persuade; allay, relieve; be satisfactory.

satori [sa*toRi*] (*Jap*) (*Buddhism*) sudden enlightenment.

satrap [*satRap*] *n* governor of a province in the ancient Persian Empire; viceroy; despot.

satsuma [sats*OO*ma] *n* (*Jap*) type of mandarin orange; **s. ware** cream-coloured Japanese pottery.

saturant [*sache*Rant] *n* (*chem*) substance that saturates; neutralizer.

saturate [*sache*Rayt] *v/t* soak thoroughly, cause (liquid) to penetrate wholly into; (*fig*) influence

deeply, pervade; be filled with; (*chem*) combine with or dissolve in to the maximum; (*mil*) destroy completely by bombing.

saturated [*sache*Rayted] *adj* (*chem*) (*of a solution*) containing as much solute as can be dissolved; (*of a compound*) containing no double or triple bonds.

saturation [sache*Ray*shon] *n* act of saturating; state of being saturated; **s. bombing** bombing that destroys a whole area completely; **s. point** point at which the greatest possible amount of something has been absorbed.

Saturday [*saterday*] *n* seventh day of the week.

Saturn [*satern*] *n* ancient Italian god of agriculture; (*astron*) a large planet surrounded by characteristic rings > PDS.

saturnalia [satern*ay*li-a] *n* cheerful orgy, occasion of great revelry; (*hist*) Roman festival of Saturn ~ **saturnalian** *adj*.

Saturnian [sa*tern*i-an] *adj* of Saturn; of or like the golden age; happy; virtuous.

saturnine [*saternIn*] *adj* gloomy, morose; having a sombre, frowning expression; phlegmatic, dull.

saturnism [*saternizm*] *n* lead-poisoning.

satyr [*sater*] *n* (*Gk myth*) minor woodland god, of part human and part animal form; grossly lustful man, lecher.

satyriasis [saterRI-asis] *n* morbidly exaggerated sexual desire in men.

satyric [sati*Rik*] *adj* of or like satyrs.

sauce [*saws*] *n* liquid preparation used as a flavouring; gravy; that which gives piquancy; (*coll*) impudence ~ **sauce** *v/t* flavour with a sauce; (*coll*) be impudent to.

sauceboat [*saws*bOt] *n* vessel to hold sauce at table.

saucepan [*saws*pan] *n* deep metal cooking pan with a long handle.

saucer [*saws*er] *n* shallow curved piece of china in which a cup is set; shallow rounded hollow in the ground; **s. eyes** round, staring eyes; **flying s.** mysterious unexplained appearance resembling a glowing disk flying rapidly at great heights, sometimes believed to be a spaceship from other planets.

saucy [*saws*i] *adj* cheeky, pert, impudent; (*sl*) smart, stylish ~ **saucily** *adv* ~ **sauciness** *n*.

sauerkraut [*sowr*kRowt] *n* (*Ger*) chopped cabbage pickled and fermented in salt.

sauna [*sawna/sowna*] *n* Finnish type of steam bath.

saunter [*sawn*ter] *n* leisurely walk; slow gait ~ **saunter** *v/i* stroll leisurely ~ **saunterer** *n*.

saurian [*saw*Ri-an] *n* member of a group of extinct reptiles ~ **saurian** *adj*.

sausage [*sosij*] *n* roll of minced and seasoned meat packed into a skin; any long soft cylindrical object; **s. dog** (*coll*) dachshund.

sausage-meat [*sosij*-meet] *n* minced seasoned meat, *usu* pork or beef.

sausage-roll [sosij-*ROl*] *n* oblong piece of baked pastry containing sausage-meat.

sauté [*sOtay*] *adj* (*Fr*) lightly fried.

sauterne [sO*tairn*] *n* a light white wine.

savable [*sayv*ab'l] *adj* capable of being saved.

savage [*savij*] *adj* uncivilized, primitive; wild; fierce, violent, cruel, brutal ~ **savage** *n* member of a human group considered to be comparatively primitive in social and cultural development;

uncivilized person; fierce, brutal or cruel person ~ **savage** v/t bite or scratch violently, maul; treat brutally ~ **savagely** adv ~ **savageness** n.

savagery [savijeRi] n state or quality of being savage; savage behaviour; cruelty, violence.

savanna, savannah [savana] n extensive grass-covered plain with no trees > PDG.

savant [savant, savon(g)] n learned man, eminent scholar.

savate [savaat] n French method of boxing using feet, head, and hands.

save [sayv] v/t and i make safe, rescue or preserve from danger, harm, loss, destruction etc; store up for future use, hoard; economize, refrain from spending; keep safe, guard, protect; prevent, avoid; dispense with; (theol) redeem, deliver from sin; **s. up** accumulate by saving ~ **save** prep. conj or adv except ~ **save** n (sport) act of preventing opponent from scoring.

saveloy [saviloi] n dried sausage, highly seasoned.

saver [sayver] n one who or that which economizes; one who or that which saves from danger etc.

saving [sayving] adj that saves; economical, frugal; redeeming; **s. grace** that which compensates for faults ~ **saving** n act of one who saves; act of economizing or hoarding; that which is saved by economizing; (pl) money accumulated by economizing ~ **saving** prep and conj except.

savings-bank [sayvingz-bank] n bank which receives small deposits and pays out interest.

saviour [sayvyer] n one who saves, rescues, or redeems; (cap) Jesus Christ.

savory [sayveRi] n aromatic herb used in cooking.

savour [sayver] n flavour, taste; distinctive quality; character ~ **savour** v/i and t have a particular flavour; consume with pleasure, enjoy the taste of; appreciate; **s. of** (fig) show signs of.

savoury [sayveRi] adj having a pleasant flavour; flavoured with salt, herbs, cheese etc, not sweetened; tasty; agreeable, attractive; wholesome; of good reputation ~ **savoury** n any light, tasty dish flavoured with salt, cheese etc ~ **savourily** adv ~ **savouriness** n.

savoy [savoi] n curly-leaved winter cabbage.

savvy [savi] v/t and i (sl) know; be intelligent ~ **savvy** n (sl) common sense.

saw (1) [saw] n cutting tool with a toothed edge ~ **saw** (p/part **sawn** or **sawed**) v/t and i cut with a saw; use a saw; admit of being cut by a saw.

saw (2) n (ar) proverb, saying.

saw (3) p/t of **see**.

sawbill [sawbil] n goosander.

sawbones [sawbOnz] n (obs sl) surgeon.

sawdust [sawdust] n dust formed when wood is sawn.

sawfish [sawfish] n fish with a long saw-like snout.

sawfly [sawflI] n insect whose female has a saw-like ovipositor.

sawmill [sawmil] n factory where timber is sawn up by machine.

sawn [sawn] alternative p/part of **saw** (1).

sawney [sawni] n Scotsman; (sl) fool, simpleton.

sawpit [sawpit] n pit over which timber is sawed.

sawyer [sawyer] n one who saws timber into planks; wood-boring beetle.

sax (1) [saks] n slater's knife with pointed spike attached; (hist) short one-edged sword or dagger.

sax (2) n (coll abbr) saxophone.

sax-, saxi- pref of or in rocks.

saxatile [saksatIl] adj (bot, zool) living among rocks.

Saxe [saks] adj made in Saxony; **s. blue** light, bright blue dye; **s. paper** photographic paper.

saxhorn [saks-hawrn] n brass wind instrument with several valves > PDM.

saxifrage [saksifRij] n a small rock plant.

Saxon [sakson] n one of a Teutonic people from North Germany who conquered England in the 5th and 6th centuries, native of Saxony; language of Saxony ~ **Saxon** adj.

saxony [saksoni] n a fine woollen material.

saxophone [saksofOn] n brass wind instrument with one reed > PDM.

say (p/t and p/part **said**) [say] v/t and i utter, speak, express in audible words; repeat, recite; tell; report; allege, assert; be of opinion; **I s.!** exclamation of surprise, or used to call listener's attention; **says you!** (coll) exclamation of disbelief ~ **say** n right or opportunity to express one's views or wishes; one's expressed opinion ~ **say** interj (coll) exclamation of surprise, or used to call listener's attention.

saying [say-ing] n that which is said; well-known proverb, maxim, or precept.

say-so [say-sO] n (coll) arbitrary decision or order; unsupported assertion.

'sblood [zblud] n (obs) an oath, 'God's blood.'

scab [skab] n incrustation which forms over a sore in healing; contagious skin disease among sheep or cattle; (coll) worker who works after a strike has been called, blackleg ~ **scab** (pres/part **scabbing**, p/t and p/part **scabbed**) v/i form a scab; (coll) work despite a call to strike.

scabbard [skaberd] n sheath of sword, dagger, or bayonet.

scabbed [skabd] adj diseased with scabs; paltry, worthless.

scabby [skabi] adj affected with scabs; rough; itchy; (coll) mean, worthless ~ **scabbily** adv ~ **scabbiness** n.

scabies [skaybeez] n a contagious itching skin-disease.

scabious [skaybi-us] n herbaceous plant with blue, pink, or white flowers.

scabrous [skaybRus] adj likely to cause shock or anger; controversial; indecent; (bot, zool) bristly, rough-surfaced ~ **scabrously** adv ~ **scabrousness** n.

scads [skadz] n (pl, coll) large quantities.

scaffold [skafOld] n temporary structure of poles and platforms to support workmen when erecting or repairing buildings; raised platform for the execution of criminals; (fig) capital punishment; temporary stage ~ **scaffold** v/t furnish with a scaffold.

scaffolding [skafOlding] n builder's scaffold; poles, planks etc used in building this.

scalable [skaylab'l] adj that can be scaled.

scalar [skaylar] adj and n (math) (quantity) possessing only magnitude.

scald (1) [skawld] v/t burn (skin and flesh) by contact with hot liquid or vapour; sterilize with boiling water; plunge in boiling water; heat almost to boiling point ~ **scald** n burn caused by hot liquid or vapour.

scald (2) see **skald**.

644

scaldic see **skaldic.**

scalding [*skawlding*] *adj* boiling hot; (*fig*) bitter and painful.

scale (1) [*skayl*] *n* one of many hard thin flakes forming protective skin of fish or reptile; similar flaky structure on insect's wings, or on certain leaf-buds, pinecones *etc*; flake of dry dead skin; flaky crust forming on metals or stone; film forming over the eye; (*fig*) blindness, illusion ~ **scale** *v/t* and *i* remove scales from; form into scales; peel off, flake off.

scale (2) *n* one of two pans of a balance; (*pl*) balance; any form of weighing machine; **hold the scales even** judge impartially; **turn the s.** be the decisive factor; **turn the s. at** weigh (specified amount) ~ **scale** *v/t* and *i* weigh; have one's weight recorded.

scale (3) *n* system of grading by size, quantity, quality, degree *etc*; relative size, extent *etc*; proportion, ratio; rank; system of precise proportional reproduction, enlargement, or diminution > PDE; graduated markings; ruler; (*mus*) series of notes graduated in pitch according to conventional intervals, *esp* a series of eight such notes > PDP, PDM; (*math*) system of numerical notation based on a specified constant; **on a large s.** amply; extensively; grandly; **out of s.** too large or too small for its surroundings, disproportionate ~ **scale** *v/t* climb up; reach highest point of; fix the relative size *etc* of; **s. up** (**down**) increase (decrease) according to specified ratio.

scalene [*skayleen*] *adj* (*geom*) having no sides or angles equal.

scaliness [*skaylinis*] *n* state or quality of being scaly.

scaling-ladder [*skayling-lader*] *n* ladder for climbing high walls.

scallion [*skalyon*] *n* kind of onion.

scallop [*skolop/skalop*] *n* fan-shaped grooved shell whose edge forms series of convex curves; bivalve mollusc producing these shells; (*pl*) series of convex curves used as ornamental edging; shell worn as pilgrim's badge ~ **scallop** *v/t* ornament with scallop edging; cook in a scallop shell.

scallywag [*skaliwag*] *n* rogue, scamp.

scalp [*skalp*] *n* hairy skin of the top of the head; this torn off as a trophy by North American Indians ~ **scalp** *v/t* tear the scalp from.

scalpel [*skalpel*] *n* small surgical knife.

scalper [*skalper*] *n* surgical instrument for scraping bones.

scaly [*skayli*] *adj* of, like, or covered in scales (1).

scamp (1) [*skamp*] *n* rascal, rogue.

scamp (2) *v/t* make or do carelessly; leave halffinished; make from inferior materials.

scamper [*skamper*] *v/i* run gaily and briskly; run off hastily; flee in confusion ~ **scamper** *n* act of running about gaily, romp; hasty flight.

scampi [*skampi*] *n* (*Ital*) dish of prawns, *usu* fried.

scan (*pres/part* **scanning**, *p/t* and *p/part* **scanned**) [*skan*] *v/t* and *i* examine carefully, scrutinize; survey a distant expanse; glance briefly at; analyse the metre of; read with full emphasis on metrical features; be written correctly by metrical rules; (*rad*) traverse a camera mosaic or cathode ray tube (with an electron beam) in order to form an image or picture; sweep an airspace with a radar beam > PDEl.

scandal [*skandal*] *n* that which shocks, that which incurs widespread blame; disgrace; immoral conduct; gossip alleging something disgraceful, malicious rumour; (*leg*) defamation of character; (*theol*) sin of corrupting the innocent.

scandalize (1) [*skandalIz*] *v/t* offend by improper behaviour; horrify, disgust, shock; (*theol*) corrupt, lead into sin.

scandalize (2) *v/t* (*naut*) haul up the tack of (a gaff-sail) > PDSa.

scandalmonger [*skandalmung-ger*] *n* one who spreads harmful gossip.

scandalous [*skandalus*] *adj* shocking; disgraceful, shameful; harmful to the reputation; defamatory ~ **scandalously** *adv* ~ **scandalousness** *n*.

Scandinavian [*skandinayvi-an*] *n* and *adj* (native) of Scandinavia; (language) of Scandinavia.

scandium [*skandi-um*] *n* (*chem*) rare metallic element > PDS.

scanner [*skaner*] *n* (*TV*) electronic device for picking up and transmitting visual images.

scansion [*skanshon*] *n* metrical system; method of scanning; process of scanning.

scant [*skant*] *adj* too few, too little; inadequate ~ **scant** *v/t* (*ar*) skimp.

scantle [*skant'l*] *n* gauge for cutting slates.

scantling [*skantling*] *n* rough draft; small portion; timber less than 5″ in breadth and thickness.

scanty [*skanti*] *adj* not ample; sparing; hardly sufficient ~ **scantily** *adv* ~ **scantiness** *n*.

scape (1) [*skayp*] *n* shaft; stem; stalk.

scape (2) *v/t* and *i* (*poet*) escape.

scapegoat [*skaypgOt*] *n* one who is blamed or punished for the faults of others; (*OT*) goat to which the sins of the Jews were ceremonially transferred, and which was then driven away.

scapegrace [*skaypgRays*] *n* rascal, ne'er-do-well.

scapement [*skaypment*] *n* escapement.

scapho- *pref* of a boat; shaped like a boat.

scapula [*skapewla*] *n* (*anat*) shoulderblade.

scapular [*skapewler*] *n* (*eccles*) monastic garment made from two strips of cloth joined at the shoulders and hanging down in front and behind; two small squares of cloth worn on chest and back and joined by strings over the shoulders; (*zool*) feather springing from the shoulder of the wing ~ **scapular** *adj* of or on the shoulder.

scapulary [*skapewleRi*] *n* scapular.

scar (1) [*skaar*] *n* mark left by a wound, burn or sore after healing; (*bot*) mark left by fall of leaf *etc*; (*fig*) permanent trace of past suffering; cut, groove ~ **scar** (*pres/part* **scarring**, *p/t* and *p/part* **scarred**) *v/t* and *i* mark with a scar; form a scar.

scar (2) *n* crag, cliff.

scarab [*skaRab*] *n* sacred ancient Egyptian dung-beetle; seal or gem shaped like a beetle.

scarce [*skairs*] *adj* not plentiful; rare; infrequent; **make oneself s.** (*coll*) go away ~ **scarce** *adv* hardly; with difficulty ~ **scarcely** *adv* hardly, only just; with difficulty ~ **scarceness** *n*.

scarcity [*skairsiti*] *n* state or quality of being scarce, rareness; dearth, famine.

scare [*skair*] *v/t* terrify, cause great fear to; drive away by terrifying ~ **scare** *n* panic, intense or contagious fear; state of widespread fear caused by rumours of danger.

scarecrow [*skairkRO*] *n* figure set up to frighten

birds from crops; person whose clothes are ugly and untidy; person of ridiculous appearance, guy.

scaremonger [*skair*mung-ger] *n* one who causes panic by spreading rumours of danger.

scarf (1) (*pl* **scarves** or **scarfs**) [*skaarf*] *n* long strip of material worn round neck or shoulders; muffler; light, loose neckerchief.

scarf (2) *n* joint for two pieces of timber ~ **scarf** *v/t* join the ends of (timber).

scarifier [*ska*RIfI-er] *n* one who scarifies; implement for loosening soil.

scarify [*ska*RIfI] *v/t* scratch, lacerate; (*surg*) make superficial incisions in the skin; (*fig*) lacerate the feelings by criticism; criticize severely.

scarious [*skair*Ri-us] *adj* (*bot*) shrivelled, dry.

scarlatina [skaarla*teena*] *n* scarlet fever.

scarlet [*skaar*let] *adj* brilliant red tinged with orange; **s. fever** infectious disease accompanied by a rash and inflamed tonsils; **s. hat** cardinal's hat; **s. runner** runner bean with scarlet flower; **s. woman** whore; (*cap, pej*) Roman Catholicism; Papacy ~ **scarlet** *n* brilliant red colour; cloth of this; robes of this.

scarp [*skaarp*] *n* steep slope of hill, rocks *etc* ~ **scarp** *v/t* cut steeply.

scarper [*skaar*per] *v/i* (*sl*) run away.

scarred [*skaard*] *adj* marked with scars.

scat (1), **scatt** [*skat*] *n* tribute; rent paid to the Crown in Orkney and Shetland by an odal tenant.

scat (2) *interj* (*coll*) go away! go quickly!

scat (3) *n* (*jazz*) act of singing a rapid sequence of meaningless syllables ~ **scat** *adj* ~ **scat** (*pres/part* **scatting**, *p/t* and *p/part* **scatted**) *v/t* and *i* sing scat.

scathe [*skayTH*] *n* (*ar*) harm, injury ~ **scathe** *v/t* (*ar*) injure; destroy.

scatheless [*skayTH*les] *adj* (*ar*) uninjured.

scathing [*skayTH*ing] *adj* very damaging; bitterly scornful or hostile ~ **scathingly** *adv*.

scatological [skato*loj*ikal] *adj* grossly obscene; of scatology.

scatology [ska*tol*oji] *n* frequent reference to excretory processes in literature; gross obscenity; study of fossil excrement.

scatt see **scat** (1).

scatter [*ska*ter] *v/t* and *i* throw about in all directions; disperse; be dispersed, be routed ~ **scatter** *n* act of scattering, dispersal; that which is scattered, sprinkling.

scatterbrain [*ska*terbRayn] *n* one who is incapable of concentrating; thoughtless, flighty person ~ **scatterbrained** *adj*.

scattered [*ska*terd] *adj* placed far apart, widely dispersed.

scattering [*ska*teRing] *n* that which is scattered; small, widely dispersed amount; act of one who scatters; (*phys*) dispersal or deflection of beam of radiation when traversing a material medium.

scatty [*ska*ti] *adj* (*coll*) crazy; cheerfully scatterbrained ~ **scattily** *adv* ~ **scattiness** *n*.

scavenge [*ska*vinj] *v/t* and *i* gather refuse from the streets; act as a scavenger.

scavenger [*ska*vinjer] *n* one who gathers refuse from houses and streets; animal which feeds on carrion; device for expelling exhaust gases.

scena [*shay*naa] *n* long solo or scene in an opera.

scenario [seenaa*Ri*-O/sinair*Ri*-O] *n* outline of the

scenes and story of a play or film; outline of possible future events.

scene [*seen*] *n* place considered as background to an event, place where something takes place; background for fictional events; striking event or episode, *esp* as seen or visually remembered; (*coll*) outburst of anger, grief *etc*; (*theat*) subdivision of a play; screen or curtain representing scenery for a play; stage with backcloth and props; **behind the scenes** out of sight of an audience, backstage; (*fig*) not known by the public, wielding secret influence; **on the s.** present.

scene-painter [*seen*-paynter] *n* one who paints theatrical scenery; one who is skilled in descriptive writing.

scenery [*seen*eRi] *n* landscape; hills, woods, rivers *etc* considered as forming a beautiful view; painted screens and backcloth of stage-setting.

scenic [*seen*ik/*sen*ik] *adj* of the stage; dramatic, theatrical; pertaining to natural scenery; **s. railway** miniature railway at fun fairs *etc*, carrying passengers through artificial scenery.

scenography [see*nog*Rafi] *n* representation of an object in perspective.

scent [*sent*] *n* odour, smell; pleasant smell; artificial substance used for giving a pleasing smell, perfume; odour left by an animal where it has passed; power of smelling; **on the s.** tracking down an animal by its odour; (*fig*) closely pursuing ~ **scent** *v/t* perceive odour of; find or pursue by sense of smell; track down; suspect the presence of; make fragrant; impregnate with perfume.

scented [*sent*id] *adj* fragrant, sweet-smelling; perfumed.

scentless [*sent*les] *adj* having no scent; leaving no scent.

scepsis [*skep*sis] *n* scepticism; attitude of philosophical doubt.

sceptic [*skep*tik] *n* one who will not accept any statement without rigorous proof; one who doubts a specified religion, philosophy or theory; agnostic; (*philos*) one who holds the doctrines of scepticism.

sceptical [*skep*tikal] *adj* inclined to disbelieve or doubt; incredulous; of or like a sceptic or scepticism ~ **sceptically** *adv*.

scepticism [*skep*tisizm] *n* attitude of mind of a sceptic; disbelief, doubt, *esp* if habitual; refusal to believe without rigorous proof; (*philos*) doctrine that only empirical or tautological statements are meaningful; doctrine that nothing can be known with certainty, even the evidence of the senses being unprovable.

sceptre [*sep*ter] *n* ornamental staff borne as symbol of royal authority; (*fig*) sovereignty.

sceptred [*sep*terd] *adj* having a sceptre; wielding power.

schadenfreude [*shaa*denfRoide] *n* (*Ger*) mischievous joy at misfortunes of others.

schedule [*shed*ewl/*sked*ewl] *n* detailed list of things to be done and times at which to do them, programme of work; timetable; catalogue, inventory; written or printed list; **behind s.** not completed by the stipulated time; **up to s.** completed by the stipulated time, following the timetable ~ **schedule** *v/t* lay down a schedule for, plan in detail to a timetable; write out a schedule of, tabulate.

schema [*skee*ma] *n* scheme; outline; diagram.

schematic [skee*ma*tik] *adj* diagrammatic; described in outline only; systematized ∼ **schematically** *adv*.

schematize [*skee*matIz] *v/t* arrange or represent schematically, systematize.

scheme [*skeem*] *n* plan, systematic project for future activities; systematic organized design; plot, cunning device; synopsis, summary; classification ∼ **scheme** *v/t* and *i* plot, contrive secretly; plan out, design.

schemer [*skeem*er] *n* one who plots; intriguer.

scheming [*skeem*ing] *n* act of plotting or planning ∼ **scheming** *adj* making plots, crafty ∼ **schemingly** *adv*.

scherzo (*pl* **scherzi**) [*skairts*O] *n* (*Ital*) a rapid lively movement in music > PDM.

schism [*sizm*] *n* division caused by grave disagreement within a church or other organization; (*theol*) sin of causing such division.

schismatic [siz*ma*tik] *adj* of or like schism; guilty of schism; split off from the majority section of an originally united body ∼ **schismatic** *n* one who belongs to the minority section of a body split by schism ∼ **schismatically** *adv*.

schist [*shist*] *n* (*geol*) rock which has a foliated structure > PDG.

schizo- *pref* split.

schizo [*skidz*O] *n* and *adj* (*coll abbr*) schizophrenic (person).

schizoid [*skidz*oid] *adj* tending towards schizophrenia > PDP.

schizophrenia [skidzOf*reen*i-a] *n* (*psych*) mental disorder with dissociation between intellectual and affective processes > PDP; (*pop*) mental disorder characterized by alternation between violently contrasting behaviour patterns; multiple personality.

schizophrenic [skidzOf*ren*ik] *adj* of, like or suffering from schizophrenia.

schmaltz [*shmavlts*] *n* (*sl*) stupid sentimentality.

schnapps [*shnaps*] *n* name for various spirits, *esp* Hollands gin.

schnauzer [*shnow*tser] *n* (*Germ*) breed of wire-haired dog with thick eyebrows.

schnizel [*shnit*sel] *n* (*Germ*) veal cutlet.

schnorkel [*shnawr*k'l] *n* tube by which a submerged submarine or swimmer can take in air.

scholar [*skol*er] *n* pupil; learned person; person learned in some special branch of knowledge; member of a school or college who, after examination, is on the foundation and is entitled to an annual sum of money towards his fees; student who has earned by examination an annual grant towards the cost of his education.

scholarly [*skol*erli] *adj* learned, showing erudition; of or befitting a scholar.

scholarship [*skol*ership] *n* high standard of achievements in learning; erudition; humane studies; annual grant for a scholar; status of a scholar.

scholastic [sko*las*tik] *adj* of scholarship, scholarly; of education, *esp* at advanced levels; of scholasticism, of or like medieval philosophy and theology; pedantic ∼ **scholastic** *n* medieval Christian philosopher or theologian ∼ **scholastically** *adv*.

scholasticism [sko*las*tisizm] *n* medieval Christian theology and philosophy based on Aristotle and emphasizing the rational basis for Christian beliefs; very subtle and precise reasoning; quibbling.

scholiast [*skOl*i-ast] *n* commentator, *esp* of the classics; annotator.

school (1) [*skOOl*] *n* shoal of whales or porpoises; large shoal of fish.

school (2) *n* institution where the young are educated; pupils of this collectively; buildings and grounds of this; hours during which teaching is given; specialized educational institution for adults; university faculty; group of philosophers, writers or artists of similar principles, *esp* if following the teachings of a leader; group of persons holding similar opinions; body of opinions, outlook; (*fig*) anything that teaches or forms the character; (*pl*) Oxford degree examination; (*pl*) scholasticism; **comprehensive s.** non-selective large school providing all types of secondary education; **elementary s.** former name for combined primary and secondary modern school; **grammar s.** selective secondary school providing teaching at least to General Certificate of Education standard; (*obs*) school teaching Latin; **high s.** form of grammar school; **of the old s.** old-fashioned; **primary s.** school for children younger than 11; **secondary s.** school for children over 11; **secondary modern s.** selective secondary school providing less academic and specialized teaching than a grammar school ∼ **school** *v/t* train, discipline, teach.

schoolbook [*skOOl*book] *n* textbook for use in schools.

schoolboy [*skOOl*boi] *n* boy who attends school.

schooldays [*skOOl*dayz] *n* (*pl*) period of childhood and adolescence during which one attends school.

schoolfellow [*skOOl*felO] *n* one who attends or attended the same school as another.

schoolgirl [*skOOl*gurl] *n* girl who attends school.

schoolhouse [*skOOl*hows] *n* building used for a school; dwelling of schoolmaster or schoolmistress.

schooling [*skOOl*ing] *n* education, instruction in school; exercising of a horse in a riding-school or in the hunting-field.

schoolman (*pl* **schoolmen**) [*skOOl*man] *n* lecturer or professor in a medieval university.

schoolmarm [*skOOl*maam] *n* priggish, pedantic or bullying schoolmistress.

schoolmaster [*skOOl*maaster] *n* male schoolteacher.

schoolmastering [*skOOl*masteRing] *n* profession of being a male schoolteacher.

schoolmate [*skOOl*mayt] *n* schoolfellow.

schoolmistress [*skOOl*mistRes] *n* female schoolteacher.

schoolroom [*skOOl*Room] *n* room in which instruction is given.

schoolteacher [*skOOl*teecher] *n* one who teaches in a school.

schoolteaching [*skOOl*teeching] *n* art or profession of teaching children and adolescents.

schooner [*skOOn*er] *n* fore-and-aft vessel with two or three masts > PDSa; a measure of beer; **prairie s.** (*US*) large covered wagon.

schottische [shoteesh] *n* a dance like a polka; music for this > PDM.

schwa, shva, sheva [shva, shiva] *n* (phon) indistinct vowel-sound in unstressed syllables.

sciatic [sɪ-atik] *adj* of, in or affecting the hip.

sciatica [sɪ-atika] *n* neuralgia of the sciatic nerve, causing pain in hip and thigh.

science [sɪ-ens] *n* any systematized branch of knowledge dealing with objects, forces and phenomena of the physical universe; any branch of knowledge based on systematic observations of facts and seeking to formulate general explanatory laws and hypotheses that could be verified empirically; knowledge or skill based on study, experience and practice; (ar) learning, knowledge; **applied s.** scientific knowledge adapted for use in industry *etc*; **s. fiction** novel, play or film dealing with fantastic adventures in other planets or in the future, and presupposing that certain scientific or pseudo-scientific inventions or processes, at present unrealized, have been made.

sciential [sɪ-enshal] *adj* pertaining to, having, knowledge.

scientific [sɪ-entifik] *adj* of science; based on principles or methods of science; used in a science; skilled in science; expert, very skilful; systematic, precise; accurate and objective ~ **scientifically** *adv*.

scientist [sɪ-entist] *n* student of any science; person trained in natural science.

Scientology [sɪ-entoloji] *n* (tr) a system of religio-scientific beliefs that claims to release the potential of those who submit to its training method ~ **scientologist** *n*.

sci-fi [sɪ-fɪ] *n* (coll abbr) science fiction.

scilicet [sɪliset] *adv* (Lat) namely.

scimitar [simiter] *n* short curved Oriental sword.

scintilla [sintila] *n* minute particle; gleam.

scintillate [sintilayt] *v/i* sparkle; (fig) talk very wittily or intelligently.

scintillation [sintilayshon] *n* act of sparkling; twinkling of stars.

sciolism [sɪ-olizm] *n* superficial knowledge.

sciolist [sɪ-olist] *n* one who has only superficial knowledge; quack.

scion [sɪ-on] *n* young shoot used as graft; young member of a family, descendant.

scirrhus [sɪRus] *n* (path) hard tumour.

scissile [sisɪl] *adj* that can be cut.

scission [sizhon] *n* act of cutting; split, separation.

scissor [sizer] *v/t* (coll) cut with scissors.

scissors [sizerz] *n* (pl) two-bladed cutting instrument, the blades moving upon a central pivot.

scissure [sishoor] *n* longitudinal cut.

scler-, sclero- *pref* hard, dry; hardening.

scleroma [skleROma] *n* (path) sclerosis.

cieroproteins [skleerROpROteenz] *n* (pl) class of complex proteins forming the framework of many animal tissues > PDS.

sclerosis [skleROsis] *n* (path) morbid hardening of a cell-wall; thickening of a tissue; **disseminated (multiple) s.** a progressive disease of the central nervous system, causing paralysis, tremors, blindness *etc*.

sclerotic [skleRotik] *adj* hard, indurated ~ **sclerotic** *n* firm white outer coat of the eye; medicine which causes hardening.

sclerous [skleerRus] *adj* hardened; bony.

scobs [skobz] *n* sawdust; shavings; filings.

scoff (1) [skof] *n* expression of contempt; derision; taunt ~ **scoff** *v/t* and *i* mock. jeer (at).

scoff (2) *v/t* and *i* (sl) eat greedily; get rid of; snatch ~ **scoff** *n* (sl) food.

scold [skOld] *v/t* and *i* rebuke angrily, noisily find fault (with); express loud angry blame ~ **scold** *n* noisy, nagging woman; shrew.

scollop [skolop] *n* scallop.

sconce [skons] *n* socket of candlestick; ornamental lamp or candlestick fixed to a wall; (ar and sl) head; (Oxford university) tankard of beer as forfeit for breach of convention in a college hall ~ **sconce** *v/t* impose forfeit of beer on.

scone [skon/skOn] *n* small soft cake, usu cooked on a griddle; (sl) head.

scoop [skOOp] *n* large ladle or shovel for lifting and moving liquids or loose substances; act of using a scoop; as much as is lifted by a scoop; (coll) unexpected and profitable piece of luck; exclusive and striking news item for publication; act of obtaining something more quickly than one's rivals ~ **scoop** *v/t* lift or shift by a scoop; shovel up; make a hollow in; scrape out; (coll) obtain exclusive or earliest right to publish; obtain by superior speed; outwit.

scoot [skOOt] *v/i* (coll) rush away; hurry off.

scooter [skOOter] *n* child's vehicle consisting of a narrow board on two wheels and a steering-rod, propelled by thrusts of one foot; light motorcycle ~ **scooterist** *n*.

scope [skOp] *n* range, area, extent; opportunity for activity; (ar) aim, intention; (naut) cable-length.

scorbutic [skawrbewtik] *adj* of or affected with scurvy.

scorch [skawrch] *v/t* and *i* burn the outside of; singe; parch; be singed; (sl) drive or ride at breakneck speed; **scorched earth** policy of destroying everything that might help an advancing enemy ~ **scorch** *n* mark made by scorching; (sl) very fast ride.

scorcher [skawrcher] *n* one who or that which scorches; (sl) something very startling.

scorching [skawrching] *adj* extremely hot ~ **scorchingly** *adv*.

score [skawr] *n* number of points gained by a competitor or team in a game or test; record kept of these; point gained at another's expense; success, advantage; mark made by scratching, notch, cut; such a notch made to mark a tally; sum due, debt; grudge; (mus) music copy showing all different parts allotted to various performers > PDM; (pl **score**) twenty ~ **score** *v/t* and *i* obtain (specified number of points) in a game or test; mark with notches, scratches or grooves; draw heavy lines on; enter in a reckoning; gain an advantage (over); (mus) write down a score for; orchestrate; **s. off** gain an advantage over; outwit; humiliate.

scorer [skawRer] *n* one who keeps a score.

scoria (pl **scoriae**) [skawRi-a] *n* dross; ashes; type of lava > PDG.

scorify [skawRifɪ] *v/t* reduce to dross.

scorn [skawrn] *n* contempt, disdain; attitude or treatment revealing this ~ **scorn** *v/t* feel or show contempt of; reject as inferior or disgraceful.

scornful [skawrnfool] *adj* full of contempt ~ **scornfully** *adv* ~ **scornfulness** *n*.

Scorpio [*skawr*pi-O] *n* (*astron*) constellation of the Scorpion, eighth sign of the zodiac.

scorpion [*skawr*pi-on] *n* arachnid animal with a curving tail containing a sting and having claws like a lobster; six-pointed whip.

scot (1) [*skot*] *n* (*hist*) tax; payment.

Scot (2) *n* native of Scotland.

Scotch (1) [*skoch*] *adj* of or from Scotland; S. broth mutton broth with pearl barley; S. fir pine; S. mist dense mist with drizzling rain; S. terrier breed of short-legged, short-tailed, rough-coated terrier; S. woodcock scrambled eggs and anchovies on toast ∼ Scotch *n* whisky from Scotland; people of Scotland; dialect of Lowlands of Scotland.

scotch (2) *v/t* suppress harshly; thwart, frustrate; crush; (*obs*) gash ∼ scotch *n* slight cut, gash.

scotch (3) *n* block for a wheel ∼ scotch *v/t* wedge with a scotch.

Scotchman (*pl* Scotchmen) [*skoch*man] *n* Scot.

scoter [*skOter*] *n* a large sea-duck.

scotfree [skot*fRee*] *adj* free from penalty or payment; unhurt.

scotodinia [skotO*dIni*-a] *n* dizziness.

scotograph [*skot*Ograaf] *n* instrument for writing in the dark or when blind.

scotoma (*pl* scotomata) [skotOma] *n* blind or partly blind area of the retina.

scotopic [skot*Opik*] *adj* adapted for vision in darkness > PDP.

Scots [*skots*] *adj* of or from Scotland ∼ Scots *n* dialect of Lowlands of Scotland.

Scotsman [*skots*man] *n* a Scot.

Scotticism [*skot*isizm] *n* Scottish phrase or idiom.

Scottie [*skoti*] *n* (*coll*) Scotch terrier; Scotsman.

Scottish [*skot*ish] *adj* of or from Scotland.

scoundrel [*skownd*Rel] *n* rogue, rascal; blackguard ∼ scoundrelly *adv*.

scour [*skowr*] *v/t* and *i* clean by rubbing with some rough substance; clean by flushing with strongly running water; rush through or over; search thoroughly; pursue; rove about in; purge ∼ scour *n* deep, swift current; act of scouring; abrasive powder; bank of silt; diarrhoea in cattle (*also pl*).

scourer [*skowr*Rer] *n* any abrasive powder; pad of abrasive material used for cleaning.

scourge [*skurj*] *n* whip with thongs; (*fig*) pest, severe affliction ∼ scourge *v/t* whip.

scouse [*skows*] *n* thick meat and vegetable broth, typical of Liverpool; (*sl*) Liverpool dialect.

scout (1) [*skowt*] *n* one sent out to discover information about an enemy; (*coll*) helpful, good-natured fellow; male servant in an Oxford college; S. member of an organization to train boys in good citizenship, self-reliance *etc* (formerly called Boy Scout) ∼ scout *v/i* act as a scout; s. about, s. round prowl about in search (of).

scout (2) *v/t* dismiss scornfully.

scoutmaster [*skowt*maaster] *n* leader of a troop of Scouts.

scow [*skow*] *n* large flat-bottomed boat.

scowl [*skowl*] *v/i* frown heavily; look angry or sullen ∼ scowl *n* heavy frown; look of anger.

scrabble [*skrab*'l] *v/i* scratch or scrape with rapid movements of hands or paws; scribble.

scrag [*skRag*] *n* bony end of neck of mutton; anything thin and bony; (*coll*) thin neck ∼ scrag

(*pres/part* scragging, *p/t* and *p/part* scragged) *v/t* seize round the neck; throttle.

scraggy [*skRagi*] *adj* thin and bony ∼ scraggily *adv* ∼ scragginess *n* ∼ scraggly *adj*.

scram (*pres/part* scramming, *p/t* and *p/part* scrammed) [*skRam*] *v/i* (*coll*) rush away, flee.

scramble [*skRamb*'l] *v/t* and *i* mix thoroughly; cook (eggs) by beating up with butter while heating; climb using arms and legs, climb over rough ground; (*rad*, *tel*) change frequency of (message) to make it unintelligible without special receivers; (*of aircraft*) take off hurriedly in emergency ∼ scramble *n* act of scrambling; act of clambering over rocks or rough ground; motorcycle race over rough ground; struggle, tussle.

scrambler [*skRamb*ler] *n* device for scrambling telegraphic messages.

scran [*skRan*] *n* (*coll*) leftover scraps, *esp* of food.

scrannel [*skRan*el] *adj* thin; feeble; reedy.

scrap [*skRap*] *n* fragment, bit, small piece; anything broken or worn-out but capable of being processed for re-use, *esp* old metal objects; newspaper cutting; (*coll*) fight, quarrel; not a s. not at all ∼ scrap (*pres/part* scrapping, *p/t* and *p/part* scrapped) *v/t* and *i* discard as broken or worn out; destroy; throw away; (*coll*) fight.

scrapbook [*skRap*book] *n* album in which newspaper cuttings and pictures are pasted; (*fig*) medley of reminiscences.

scrape [*skRayp*] *v/t* and *i* rub or scratch with something rough or sharp; clean, remove, roughen, or smooth by scraping; make a harsh grating sound; barely manage; s. acquaintance with force another to become acquainted with oneself against his wishes; bow and s. act obsequiously or too ceremoniously; s. together, s. up gather by scraping; gather with great difficulty; s. through barely succeed; barely escape or extricate oneself ∼ scrape *n* act or sound of scraping; graze, abrasion; (*coll*) difficult situation, trouble, caused by one's bad behaviour or folly; (*coll*) thin layer of butter or margarine on bread.

scrapheap [*skRap*heep] *n* pile of scrap metal; rubbish heap; throw on the s. discard as useless.

scrapie [*skRay*pi] *n* virus disease of sheep causing itching.

scrap-iron [*skRap*-I-ern] *n* old iron objects collected for re-working.

scrap-merchant [*skRap*-murchant] *n* one who trades in scrap metal.

scrappy [*skRapi*] *adj* fragmentary ∼ scrappily *adv* ∼ scrappiness *n*.

scrapyard [*skRap*yaard] *n* place where scrap metal is stored.

scratch [*skRach*] *v/t* and *i* mark a surface, *esp* skin, by drawing something sharp across it; wound with claws or fingernails; wound slightly; scrape with fingernails; withdraw from race or contest; s. out obliterate, erase ∼ scratch *n* mark made by scratching; sound of scratching; slight wound; mark from which a race is started; start from s. start at the beginning; (*fig*) start with no advantages or preliminary work done; come up to s. be ready to start; (*fig*) fulfil an obligation or promise; be as good as expected ∼ scratch *adj* gathered hastily from varying sources; of uneven standard; improvised; (*sport*) without handicap.

scratcher [*skRach*er] *n* one who or that which scratches; bird which scratches for its food.

scratch-race [*skRach*-Rays] *n* race where all competitors start without handicap.

scratchy [*skRach*i] *adj* consisting of scratches; irregular; making the noise of scratching; causing itch ~ **scratchily** *adv* ~ **scratchiness** *n*.

scrawl [*skRawl*] *v/t* and *i* draw or write hastily and badly, scribble ~ **scrawl** *n* hasty writing; something illegibly written.

scrawny [*skRaw*ni] *adj* lean and bony, scraggy.

scream [*skReem*] *n* sudden loud shrill cry of pain or fear; sudden shrill laugh; (*coll*) something intensely funny ~ **scream** *v/t* and *i* utter a scream; utter shrilly and violently; (*coll*) laugh wildly and shrilly.

screamer [*skReem*er] *n* one who or that which screams; bird which screams; (*print*) exclamation mark; (*sl*) something remarkably funny, thrilling *etc*.

screaming [*skReem*ing] *adj* that screams; (*coll*) that causes wild laughter ~ **screamingly** *adv*.

scree [*skRee*] *n* steep slope covered with loose fragments of rock.

screech [*skReech*] *v/i* and *t* give a shrill harsh cry; scream; utter harshly ~ **screech** *n* shrill harsh cry; brief scream; harsh shrill laugh.

screech-owl [*skReech*-owl] *n* owl which utters a screech, barn-owl or tawny owl.

screed [*skReed*] *n* long letter or passage from a book.

screen [*skReen*] *n* any light, temporary or removable structure giving shelter from heat, cold or wind, or concealing something; partition between nave and choir of church; hinged and covered portable framework used to protect from draughts; windscreen; large smooth white surface on to which images of cinema films, photographic slides *etc* are projected; (*fig*) the profession of cinema acting; coarse sieve > PDE; (*phot*) device that breaks a photograph into small dots for reproduction; (*mil*) advance party of troops *etc* protecting or concealing main body; system of guards, watchposts *etc* to detect or intercept approaching enemy; (*fig*) system designed to detect and intercept dangerous persons ~ **screen** *v/t* shelter, protect by a screen; act as a shield for; protect; conceal; project (film *etc*) on to a screen; make a film of; examine (group of persons) to identify those who may be dangerous; sieve, sift; **s. off** shut off, conceal behind a screen.

screen-grid [*skReen*-gRid] *n* (*elect*) third electrode in pentode valve.

screenings [*skReen*ingz] *n* (*pl*) what is left after sieving.

screenplay [*skReen*play] *n* script of cinema film.

screenwriter [*skReen*RIter] *n* writer of film scripts.

screw [*skROO*] *n* cylindrical shaft with spiral groove, used as fastening, and inserted by being twisted round and round; screw-propeller; act of screwing; something twisted into a spiral; half-ounce of tobacco; (*coll*) wages, salary; miser; broken-down or diseased horse; (*sl*) prison warder; (*sl*) sexual act, copulation; **have a s. loose** (*coll*) be slightly mad or feeble-minded; **put the s. on** intimate, put pressure on; **turn of the s.** (*fig*) increase of agony, of demands *etc* ~ **screw** *v/t* and *i* fasten with a screw; twist repeatedly; twist as far as possible; distort; squeeze, extract by pressure; admit of being screwed; swerve; (*vulg*) have sexual intercourse with; bugger; **have one's head well screwed on** be sensible, be shrewd; **s. up** tighten by screwing; (*fig*) intensify, bring to a peak.

screwball [*skROO*bawl] *adj* and *n* (*US coll*) crazy (person).

screwdriver [*skROO*dRIver] *n* chisel-shaped tool for turning screws.

screwed [*skrOOd*] *adj* (*sl*) drunk.

screw-propeller [*skROO*-pRopeler] *n* revolving shaft fitted with blades set like the thread of a screw, used for driving ships and aircraft.

screw-top [*skROO*-top] *adj* closed by a lid that screws on to a threaded neck.

screwy [*skROO*-i] *adj* (*US coll*) crazy.

scribal [*skRIb*al] *adj* of or by a scribe; of or in the copying of a manuscript.

scribble (1) [*skRib*'l] *v/t* and *i* write in hasty, badly-formed writing; draw meaningless lines (on); compose carelessly in poor style ~ **scribble** *n* hasty, illegible or careless writing; something scribbled.

scribble (2) *v/t* card wool or cotton roughly.

scribbler (1) [*skRib*ler] *n* one who writes hastily or carelessly; author with little talent.

scribbler (2) *n* carding-machine.

scribe [*skRib*] *n* writer, author; (*hist*) clerk, secretary; copyist of manuscripts; (*bibl*) Jewish keeper of records and commentator on the law; scriber ~ **scribe** *v/t* mark with a scriber.

scriber [*skRib*er] *n* tool for marking lines *etc*.

scrim [*skRim*] *n* strong plainly-woven material.

scrimmage [*skRim*ij] *n* tussle; confused struggle; scrummage ~ **scrimmage** *v/i* tussle, fight confusedly.

scrimp [*skRimp*] *v/t* and *i* make small; stint; be niggardly.

scrimshanker [*skRim*shanker] *n* one who avoids doing his duty; malingerer.

scrimshaw [*skRim*shaw] *n* small ornamental object made by sailors in their spare time ~ **scrimshaw** *v/t* and *i* make ornaments *etc* as a hobby.

scrip (1) [*skRip*] *n* certificate of stock or shares; shares in lieu of dividend; schedule, certificate; temporary paper currency.

scrip (2) *n* (*ar*) small bag, wallet.

script [*skRipt*] *n* handwriting; something handwritten; text of play, film, radio programme *etc*; typescript; set of written answers to an examination; (*print*) type imitating cursive handwriting; (*leg*) original document ~ **script** *v/t* write a script for (play, film *etc*).

scriptorium [skRipt*aw*Ri-um] *n* writing-room in a monastery.

scriptural [*skRip*cheRal] *adj* of, based on, or in Scripture ~ **scripturally** *adv*.

Scripture [*skRip*cher] *n* the Bible; sacred writings forming basis of any religion; biblical text ~ **scripture** *adj*.

scriptwriter [*skRipt*RIter] *n* one who composes plays *etc* for production as films, on radio or on television.

scrivener [*skRiv*ener] *n* (*hist*) one who drew up contracts; notary; moneylender; broker.

scrofula [skRofewla] *n* (*path*) tuberculosis of lymphatic glands ~ **scrofulous** *adj*.

scroll [skROl] *n* roll of parchment or paper; ancient book on such a roll; spiral ornament; curved head of a violin ~ **scroll** *v/i* and *t* roll up like a scroll; decorate with scrolls.

Scrooge [skROOj] *n* miser.

scrotal [skROtal] *adj* of or on the scrotum.

scrotum (*pl* **scrota**) [skROtum] *n* (*anat*) pouch containing the testicles.

scrounge [skRownj] *v/i* and *t* (*sl*) cadge; pilfer.

scrounger [skROwnjer] *n* one who cadges or who pilfers.

scrub (1) [skRub] *n* brushwood, stunted bush or tree; undersized person.

scrub (2) (*pres/part* **scrubbing**, *p/t* and *p/part* **scrubbed**) *v/t* and *i* clean by rubbing hard with a brush, soap and water; rub vigorously; (*sl*) cancel, delete; overtake (car); **s. round it** (*coll*) agree to forget or ignore ~ **scrub** *n* act of scrubbing.

scrubbing-brush [skRubing-bRush] *n* hard stiff brush for scrubbing floors *etc*.

scrubby [skRubi] *adj* small, stunted; covered with brushwood ~ **scrubbily** *adv* ~ **scrubbiness** *n*.

scruff [skRuf] *n* nape of the neck.

scruffy [skRufi] *adj* scurfy; looking dirty or shabby ~ **scruffily** *adv* ~ **scruffiness** *n*.

scrum [skRum] *n* (*Rugby football*) struggle between the forwards of both teams with the ball on the ground between them; (*coll*) milling crowd ~ **scrum** (*pres/part* **scrumming**, *p/t* and *p/part* **scrummed**) *v/i* form a scrum.

scrum-half [skRum-haaf] *n* the half-back who puts the ball into the scrum.

scrummage [skRumij] *n* scrum.

scrump [skRump] *v/t* and *i* pilfer apples.

scrumptious [skRumpshus] *adj* (*coll*) delightful; delicious ~ **scrumptiously** *adv* ~ **scrumptiousness** *n*.

scrumpy [skRumpi] *n* rough cider.

scrunch [skRunch] *v/t* and *i* crunch ~ **scrunch** *n*.

scruple [skROOp'l] *n* doubt arising from difficulty of judging what is right; hesitation or reluctance from religious or ethical motives; $\frac{1}{24}$ ounce Troy weight > PDS; (*obs*) tiny particle ~ **scruple** *v/i* feel conscientious hesitation or reluctance.

scrupulosity [skROOpewlositi] *n* state of being scrupulous, *esp* to an exaggerated degree.

scrupulous [skROOpewlus] *adj* conscientious, careful to act correctly; exact, painstaking; strictly honest; having many scruples ~ **scrupulously** *adv* ~ **scrupulousness** *n*.

scrutineer [skROOtineer] *n* one who scrutinizes election votes.

scrutinize [skROOtinIz] *v/t* examine thoroughly.

scrutiny [skROOtini] *n* close examination; careful investigation; examination of the votes given at an election.

scry [skRI] *v/t* and *i* perceive by crystal-gazing.

scuba [skewba] *n* self-contained breathing apparatus for underwater swimmers.

scud (*pres/part* **scudding**, *p/t* and *p/part* **scudded**) [skud] *v/i* move quickly and smoothly, *esp* driven by wind ~ **scud** *n* act of scudding; mass of wind-driven clouds; brief shower of rain *etc*.

scuff [skuf] *v/t* and *i* scratch (shoes) by dragging the feet when walking; scrape with the feet; walk with dragging feet.

scuffle [skuf'l] *v/i* fight or struggle confusedly ~ **scuffle** *n* confused fight or struggle.

scull [skul] *n* short, light, one-handed oar ~ **scull** *v/t* and *i* propel a boat with sculls.

sculler [skuler] *n* one who sculls; light boat propelled by sculls.

scullery [skuleRi] *n* room where dishes *etc* are washed up and rough household work done.

scullion [skulyon] *n* (*ar*) boy who washes dishes *etc*.

sculp [skulp] *v/i* and *t* (*coll*) make sculpture.

sculpt [skulpt] *v/i* and *t* make sculpture (of); be a sculptor.

sculptor [skulpter] *n* one who carves stone, wood or other material, and models in clay.

sculptress [skulptRes] *n* woman sculptor.

sculpture [skulpcher] *n* art of creating an aesthetically pleasing three-dimensional object, either by carving or chiselling stone, wood *etc*, or by building up a form from clay or other plastic substance > PDAA; work of art so produced ~ **sculpture** *v/t* and *i* produce a sculpture (of); practise the art of a sculptor.

scum [skum] *n* impurities which rise to the top of a liquid when it is boiled or fermented; froth, foam; that which is least valuable, rubbish; (*coll*) person(s) of dirty, vicious or criminal habits; worthless person(s) ~ **scum** (*pres/part* **scumming**, *p/t* and *p/part* **scummed**) *v/t* and *i* remove scum from; form a scum; become covered with scum.

scumble [skumb'l] *v/t* cover (a painting) with a semi-opaque colour > PDAA.

scummy [skumi] *adj* of, like or covered in scum ~ **scummily** *adv* ~ **scumminess** *n*.

scunner [skuner] *n* (*coll*) strong dislike.

scupper [skuper] *n* (*naut*) channel through ship's side to carry off water from the deck ~ **scupper** *v/t* (*coll*) disable, ruin.

scurf [skurf] *n* flakes of dead skin; dandruff; flaky surface.

scurfy [skurfi] *adj* covered in scurf; flaky ~ **scurfily** *adv* ~ **scurfiness** *n*.

scurrility [skuRiliti] *n* quality of being scurrilous; scurrilous language.

scurrilous [skuRilus] *adj* using vulgar or indecent language; coarsely abusive ~ **scurrilously** *adv* ~ **scurrilousness** *n*.

scurry [skuRi] *v/i* run with quick short steps; show undignified haste ~ **scurry** *n* act or noise of scurrying.

scurvy [skurvi] *n* a disease of malnutrition caused by a deficiency of fresh vegetables and fruit ~ **scurvy** *adj* low, contemptible; mean ~ **scurvily** *adv* ~ **scurviness** *n*.

scut [skut] *n* short tail, *esp* that of a rabbit.

scutage [skewtij] *n* (*hist*) tax paid by a feudal tenant in place of military service.

scutcheon [skuchon] *n* escutcheon; plate hung over a keyhole; nameplate.

scutellum [skewtelum] *n* (*bot, zool*) small plate or scale.

scutter [skuter] *v/i* scamper.

scuttle (1) [skut'l] *n* receptacle for small quantity of coal.

scuttle (2) *v/t* sink (a ship) by cutting holes through it; deliberately sink (ships) to prevent capture by enemy; (*fig*) destroy one's own work ∼ **scuttle** *n* act of scuttling; (*naut*) hatchway, lidded opening in deck or side of ship.

scuttle (3) *v/i* scurry, hurry off, bolt ∼ **scuttle** *n* hasty flight; wobbling walk taking short quick steps.

scythe [*sITH*] *n* implement with long curved blade for mowing or reaping ∼ **scythe** *v/t* and *i* cut with a scythe.

sea [*see*] *n* one of the smaller divisions of the ocean >PDG; large expanse of salt water; large wave; flat plain on the moon's surface; (*fig*) vast quantity or expanse; **at s.** in a boat or ship on the sea; (*fig*) bewildered; **go to s.** become a sailor; **put to s.** set sail ∼ **sea** *adj* of, in or on the sea.

sea-anchor [*see*-anker] *n* floating anchor, *usu* of canvas, to prevent drifting.

sea-anemone [see-*anemoni*] *n* a flower-like polyp.

seabank [*seebank*] *n* shore; wall or bank built to keep the sea out.

seabed [*seebed*] *n* ground under the sea.

seabird [*seeburd*] *n* any bird inhabiting the coast and living chiefly on fish.

seaboard [*seebawrd*] *n* seacoast.

seaborne [*seebawrn*] *adj* carried by the sea.

sea-breeze [*see*-bReez] *n* breeze blowing from the sea by day > PDG.

sea-captain [*see*-kaptin] *n* captain of a seagoing ship.

sea-change [*see*-chaynj] *n* transformation brought about by the sea; complete transformation.

seacoal [*seekOl*] *n* coal washed ashore or uncovered by coastal erosion; coal, *orig* brought by sea.

seacoast [*seekOst*] *n* shore of the sea.

seacow [*seekow*] *n* walrus; manatee, dugong.

seadog [*seedog*] *n* old or experienced sailor; seal; dogfish.

seafarer [*seefairRer*] *n* sailor.

seafaring [*seefairRing*] *n* occupation of a sailor ∼ **seafaring** *adj* living as a sailor; habitually travelling by sea.

sea-fennel [*see*-fenel] *n* samphire.

seafood [*seefOOd*] *n* edible shellfish and fish.

sea-front [*see*-fRunt] *n* buildings or parade facing the sea.

sea-girt [*see*-gurt] *adj* surrounded by the sea.

seagoing [*seegOing*] *adj* making voyages out to sea.

sea-green [*see*-gReen] *n* and *adj* bluish-green.

seagull [*seegul*] *n* any gull.

seahorse [*seehawrs*] *n* a small warm-water fish with a horse-like head; fabulous creature, half horse and half fish.

sea-kale [*see*-kayl] *n* colewort.

seal (1) [*seel*] *n* amphibious carnivorous marine mammal with flippers; fur of this ∼ **seal** *v/i* hunt seal.

seal (2) *n* stamp or die engraved with a device; piece of stamped wax attached to a document; (*fig*) proof of genuineness; guarantee of truth or secrecy ∼ **seal** *v/t* affix a seal to; stamp with a seal; close, shut closely; decide upon; confirm, ratify.

sea-lawyer [see-*law*-yer] *n* argumentative sailor; one who is always asserting his rights or complaining of injustice.

sea-legs [*see*-legz] *n* (*pl*) ability to walk steadily on a ship's deck despite its rolling; ability to resist seasickness.

sealer [*seeler*] *n* man or ship hunting seals.

sea-letter [*see*-leter] *n* passport of neutral ship in wartime.

sea-level [*see*-level] *n* level of the sea's surface at mean tide > PDG.

sea-line [*see*-lIn] *n* horizon at sea.

sealing-wax [*seeling*-waks] *n* resinous composition used for sealing letters *etc*.

sea-lion [*see*-lI-on] *n* species of large seal.

seal-ring [*seel*-Ring] *n* finger ring with flat metal or stone surface engraved with a seal.

sealskin [*seelskin*] *n* under-fur of a seal.

sealyham [*seeli*-am] *n* breed of wire-haired terrier.

seam [*seem*] *n* sewn join between two parts of cloth; junction of two planks fitted edge to edge; suture; long wrinkle or scar; (*min*) vein, stratum; (*geol*) thin layer separating two strata ∼ **seam** *v/t* and *i* join together with a seam; form a seam.

seaman (*pl* **seamen**) [*seeman*] *n* sailor; skilled sailor; (*naval*) sailor below the rank of officer.

seamanship [*seemanship*] *n* skill of a good sailor; art of rigging and sailing a ship.

seamark [*seemaark*] *n* lighthouse, beacon *etc* guiding vessels at sea.

seamew [*seemew*] *n* seagull.

sea-mile [*see*-mIl] *n* nautical mile, 6,080 ft.

seaminess [*seeminis*] *n* quality of being seamy.

seamless [*seemles*] *adj* (of garments) made in one piece, without joins.

seamstress, sempstress [*semstRes*] *n* woman who makes her living by sewing; dressmaker.

seamy [*seemi*] *adj* revealing what is unpleasant, disreputable *etc*; having or showing seams.

séance [*say*-aans] *n* a meeting of spiritualists, *usu* with a medium, to obtain messages from the dead; meeting of a society, session.

sea-piece [*see*-pees] *n* seascape.

sea-pink [*see*-pink] *n* thrift.

seaplane [*seeplayn*] *n* aeroplane with floats to enable it to land on and take off from water.

seaport [*seepawrt*] *n* town with a harbour for ocean-going ships.

sea-power [*see*-powr] *n* a country's resources in warships and trading vessels; country whose power is based on a strong fleet.

seaquake [*seekwayk*] *n* earthquake of the sea's floor.

sear, sere [*seer*] *adj* dried up; withered ∼ **sear** *v/t* scorch, burn the surface of; brand; wither up; make callous.

search [*surch*] *v/t* and *i* examine thoroughly the contents of, ransack; scrutinize; investigate; penetrate thoroughly; try to find, seek; examine the garments and body of; **s. for** seek in many places for, try hard to find; **s. me** (*coll*) I have no idea; **s. out** find after searching ∼ **search** *n* act of examining thoroughly or seeking in many places; prolonged attempt to find something lost or hidden; quest, pursuit.

searcher [*surcher*] *n* one who searches.

searching [*surching*] *adj* examining keenly; making a search; minute, thorough ∼ **searchingly** *adv*.

searchlight [*surchlIt*] *n* electric lamp projecting a

powerful movable beam of light over a long distance.

search-party [*surch*-paarti] *n* group of persons who make a search for a lost person or thing.

search-warrant [*surch*-woRant] *n* magistrate's warrant authorizing entry into private premises to search for stolen property, suspected persons *etc*.

seared [*seerd*] *adj* withered, shrivelled; hardened, callous.

sea-room [*see*-Room] *n* ample room for a ship to move in.

sea-rover [*see*-Rover] *n* pirate; piratical ship.

sea-salt [*see*-sawlt] *n* salt obtained by evaporation from seawater.

seascape [*see*skayp] *n* picture of a sea scene.

sea-serpent [*see*-surpent] *n* sea-snake; huge serpent-like monster believed to live in the ocean depths.

seashell [*see*shel] *n* shell of a marine mollusc.

seashore [*see*shawr] *n* coast along the sea; space between high-water and low-water mark.

seasick [*see*sik] *adj* suffering from seasickness.

seasickness [*see*siknis] *n* nausea and vomiting caused by the motion of a ship in rough water.

seaside [*see*sId] *n* land bordering on the sea; holiday resort by the sea.

sea-snail [*see*-snayl] *n* snail-like marine gasteropod; a slimy fish.

season [*see*zon] *n* a subdivision of a year as characterized by special climatic conditions > PDG; one of the four subdivisions of the year in temperate climates; part of the year when certain natural processes occur; time of year when specified human activities, sports, entertainments *etc* customarily occur; time of year when specified animals are fit to be hunted or foods fit for eating; fitting time, suitable opportunity; season-ticket; (*ar*) period ~ **season** *v/t* and *i* make or become mature by exposure to weather or natural processes; add spice, salt or flavourings to; add zest to; (*ar*) moderate.

seasonable [*see*zonab'l] *adj* suitable to the season of year; happening or done at the proper time ~ **seasonably** *adv* ~ **seasonableness** *n*.

seasonal [*see*zonal] *adj* happening or done only at certain seasons of the year ~ **seasonally** *adv*.

seasoned [*see*zend] *adj* hardened by or used to certain conditions, *esp* of hardship; experienced; spiced, flavoured.

seasoning [*see*zoning] *n* anything added to food to give it relish or piquancy; anything which increases enjoyment.

season-ticket [*see*zon-tikit] *n* transport ticket entitling holder to make as many journeys as he wishes during a specified period over a specified route; ticket entitling holder to entry to a series of entertainments *etc* more cheaply than to each individually.

seat [*seet*] *n* that which is or can be sat on; chair, bench, stool; part of chair *etc* on which the buttocks rest; buttocks; that part of a garment which covers the buttocks; right to sit in specified place on specified occasion; membership of a body; membership of Parliament; parliamentary constituency; place where something always or usually is, location; large country residence; manner of sitting on horseback ~ **seat** *v/t* and *i* cause to sit down; provide seats for (specified

number of persons); (*of clothes*) become creased or baggy over the buttocks; put a new seat in or on; be located in; be settled in.

seatbelt [*seet*belt] *n* safety belt fastening person in car or aircraft to his seat.

seated [*seet*id] *adj* sitting.

seating [*see*ting] *n* act of settling into a seat or seats; provision of seats.

sea-to-air [see-tOO-*air*] *adj* (*of missile*) fired from a submarine or other vessel.

sea-trout [*see*-tRowt] *n* salmon-trout.

sea-urchin [*see*-urchin] *n* echinus.

sea-wall [*see*-wawl] *n* wall or embankment to keep out the sea.

seaward [*see*werd] *adj* and *adv* towards the sea.

seaway [*see*way] *n* headway, progress of a ship; a clear way for a ship.

seaweed [*see*weed] *n* any plant growing in the sea.

seawolf [*see*woolf] *n* viking, pirate; large voracious fish.

seaworthiness [*see*wurTHines] *n* state of being seaworthy.

seaworthy [*see*wurTHi] *adj* fit to go to sea.

seawrack [*see*Rak] *n* coarse seaweed; seaweed cast ashore in large masses.

sebaceous [*se*bayshus] *adj* (*physiol*) fatty; containing or secreting fat > PDB.

sebum [*see*bum] *n* fatty matter secreted by skin glands.

sec [*sek*] *adj* (*of wines*) (*Fr*) dry.

secant [*see*kant] *n* (*math*) straight line cutting circle or curve; reciprocal of cosine of an angle > PDS ~ **secant** *adj* cutting; dividing into two parts.

secateurs [*sek*aterz] *n* (*pl*) pair of strong pruning scissors.

secede [*si*seed] *v/i* withdraw from association with a State or group.

secession [*si*seshon] *n* act of seceding.

seclude [*si*klOOd] *v/t* keep apart or away from society.

secluded [*si*klOOdid] *adj* apart from society; private; solitary and quiet.

seclusion [*si*klOOzhon] *n* state of being secluded; retirement, privacy.

second [*se*kond] *adj* ordinal number of two, next after the first; occurring again, additional; repeating or closely resembling something that has once occurred; inferior; of or marking one sixtieth of a minute; **S. Chamber** upper house in a legislative body; **s. childhood** senility, feebleness of body and mind due to old age; **S. Coming** the prophesied return of Christ to earth at the end of the world; **s. cousin** child of one's parent's first cousin; **s. nature** habit so ingrained as to be almost instinctive; **s. sight** faculty of seeing supernatural beings or portents invisible to others, or of seeing events of the future or at a great distance ~ **second** *n* one who or that which comes or ranks next after the first; one who assists and supports another, *esp* a boxer or duellist; one sixtieth of a minute; very brief time, instant; (*mus*) interval covering two degrees of the scale > PDM; (*mus*) alto; (*pl*) inferior goods ~ **second** *v/t* support, encourage; speak in support of a motion immediately after the proposer; (*mil*) [se*kond*] withdraw (officer) from regimental service for temporary special duty ~ **second** *adv* in the second place.

secondary [*sek*onde*R*i] *adj* second in rank, importance *etc*; minor, inferior; second in time or stage of development; (*astron*) revolving round a primary planet; (*geol*) mesozoic; **s. sexual characteristics** (*biol*) differences between male and female that play no part in reproduction; **s. school** school for children over eleven ~ **secondarily** *adv* ~ **secondariness** *n*.

second-best [*sek*ond-best] *adj* of inferior quality, value, rank *etc*; comparatively unattractive or unimportant ~ **second-best** *n* that which is of inferior quality.

second-class [*sek*ond-klaas] *adj* of second or inferior rank, value, quality *etc*; of a class or grade second to the first; having fewer rights or privileges; less well treated ~ **second-class** *adv*.

seconder [*sek*onder] *n* one who supports the mover of a motion.

second-hand (1) [second-*hand*] *adj* not new, bought from a previous owner or user; derived from another, not original; not personally known or experienced, based on hearsay ~ **second-hand** *adv*.

second-hand (2) [*sek*ond-hand] *n* pointer on dial of clock or watch to mark the seconds.

second-rate [sekond-*R*ayt] *adj* of inferior quality, size *etc*.

secrecy [*seek*Resi] *n* state of being kept secret; concealment; privacy, seclusion; act of keeping a secret; reticence.

secret [*seek*Rit] *adj* deliberately concealed; hidden from general knowledge, known only to one or few persons; mysterious; reserved; furtive, clandestine; remote, secluded; **s. service** State organization of spies and counter-spies ~ **secret** *n* something known only to one or few persons; state of being secret; mystery, puzzle; true explanation of or clue to a mystery.

secretaire [sek*Ri*tair] *n* (*Fr*) bureau, writing-desk.

secretarial [sek*Ri*tair*R*i-al] *adj* of, relating to, a secretary.

secretariat [sek*Ri*tair*R*i-at] *n* secretarial staff of a large organization.

secretary [*sek*Rete*R*i/*sek*RitRi] *n* person employed to write correspondence, keep written records *etc* for a firm, person, or society; one who assists another with the routine organization of his business, literary work, social life *etc*; minister in charge of a government department; chief assistant of a minister or ambassador; writing-desk.

secrete [sik*Reet*] *v/t* conceal; (*physiol*) separate from the blood.

secretion [sik*Ree*shun] *n* process of separating materials from the blood either for the use of the body or for expulsion as excreta; secreted matter > PDB; act of concealing.

secretive [*seek*Ritiv/sik*Ree*tiv] *adj* tending to conceal one's doings or thoughts, extremely reticent ~ **secretively** *adv* ~ **secretiveness** *n*.

secretly [*seek*Ritli] *adv* without the knowledge of others, in a secret way.

secretory [sik*Ree*te*R*i] *adj* forming secretions.

sect [sekt] *n* organized group of persons holding minority views in religion, *esp* one that has seceded from a larger body; religious denomination.

sectarian [sek*tair*Ri-an] *adj* of, characteristic of

a sect; tending to form sects, disruptive of unity; bigoted, exclusive ~ **sectarian** *n* member of a sect.

sectary [*sek*te*R*i] *n* member of a sect.

section [*sek*shon] *n* act of cutting or separating; that which is cut off, slice; portion; division, subdivision; one of various separable parts meant to form a whole; distinct group within a community; very thin slice of anything prepared for examination under a microscope; representation of an object cut vertically ~ **section** *v/t* cut into sections; represent in sections.

sectional [*sek*shonal] *adj* of or for a section; made up of sections ~ **sectionally** *adv*.

sectionalism [*sek*shonalizm] *n* tendency to set the interests of one section above those of a whole community.

sector [*sek*ter] *n* (*mil*) section of fortified front or position; (*fig*) area, sphere of activity; (*geom*) portion of circle between two radii and an arc; measuring instrument.

secular [*sek*ewler] *adj* worldly; temporal; not spiritual; not ecclesiastical; continuing over vast periods of time; (*RC*) ordained but not bound by monastic vows.

secularism [*sek*ewle*R*izm] *n* tendency to exclude religious standards from public life; theory that Church and State should be separate; ethical system divorced from religious traditions; state of being secular.

secularist [*sek*ewle*R*ist] *n* believer in secularism ~ **secularist** *adj*.

secularize [*sek*ewle*R*iz] *v/t* make secular; reject religious standards in make worldly; transfer from Church to State; (*RC*) absolve from monastic vows.

secure [sik*ewr*] *adj* free from danger, fear, or attack; firmly fixed, stable; confident; in safe keeping; unable to escape ~ **secure** *v/t* make secure; fasten; guarantee payment of; gain, get full possession of ~ **securely** *adv*.

security [sik*ewr*Riti] *n* state of being or of feeling secure; safety; safety of the State from spying and other hostile activities; assurance; guarantee; pledge for payment of a loan; one who becomes surety for another; (*pl*) shares, bonds *etc*; **s. officer** (*mil*) officer responsible for defeating enemy spying; **s. police** military police; **s. risk** person whose views or character make it likely that he may become a spy against his own country.

sedan [si*dan*] *n* (*hist*) covered chair carried on two projecting poles; (*US*) large closed motorcar.

sedate [si*dayt*] *adj* serious-minded, habitually calm; staid, decorous ~ **sedate** *v/t* administer sedative to ~ **sedately** *adv* ~ **sedateness** *n*.

sedation [si*day*shon] *n* (*med*) act of administering a sedative.

sedative [*sed*ativ] *adj* soothing; allaying anxiety or excessive excitability ~ **sedative** *n* (*med*) sedative drug.

sedentary [*sed*ente*R*i] *adj* habitually sitting still for long periods; requiring little bodily exertion; requiring or caused by sitting; (*zool*) not migratory.

sedge [sej] *n* coarse grasslike plant, *usu* growing beside water.

sedilia [se*dili*-a] *n (pl) (eccles)* three recessed seats within the altar rails.

sediment [*sedi*ment] *n* matter which sinks to the bottom of a liquid; dregs.

sedimentary [sedi*mente*Ri] *adj* of or containing sediment; **s. rocks** rocks which have been deposited as beds, often by water > PDG.

sedimentation [sediment*ay*shon] *n* process or rate of depositing sediment.

sedition [si*dish*on] *n* offence against the authority of the State, not amounting to treason; public commotion, disorder, riot.

seditious [si*dish*us] *adj* of, like or guilty of sedition; rebellious ~ **seditiously** *adv* ~ **seditiousness** *n*.

seduce [si*dews*] *v/t* induce (someone) to agree to an illicit sexual relationship; persuade to commit any evil deed; charm, entice, allure (*usu* to evil).

seducer [si*dews*er] *n* one who has seduced a specified woman; one who habitually seduces women.

seduction [si*duk*shon] *n* act of seducing; state of being seduced; enticement; tempting quality, allurement.

seductive [si*duk*tiv] *adj* alluring, enticing, very attractive; persuasive ~ **seductively** *adv* ~ **seductiveness** *n*.

seductress [si*duk*tRis] *n* seductive woman.

sedulity [se*dewl*iti] *n* quality of being sedulous.

sedulous [*sedew*lus] *adj* assiduous, persistent; painstaking, industrious ~ **sedulously** *adv* ~ **sedulousness** *n*.

see (1) (*p/t* saw, *p/part* seen) [*see*] *v/t* and *i* perceive by the eye, have visual impressions (of); understand, perceive by intelligence or imagination; watch, look at; inspect, examine; visit; escort; consult, have an interview with; ensure, take care that; reflect, think over; **s. about** deal with, attend to; **s. after** deal with; look after; **s. off** accompany (a person) to his point of departure on a journey; **s. out** accompany (a person) till he has left the premises; wait or endure till the end of; **s. over** examine thoroughly; **s. things** (*coll*) have hallucinations; **s. through** understand despite attempted deception; **s. (something) through** remain to ensure the success, or see the outcome, of; **s. to** arrange, deal with, attend to; **be seeing you!** (*coll*) goodbye.

see (2) *n* diocese or jurisdiction of an archbishop or bishop.

seed [*seed*] *n* fertilized ovule of flowering plant > PDB; number of these, *esp* used in sowing; sperm, semen; (*fig*) offspring, descendants; source, origin; (*tennis*) seeded player; **the good s.** religious or moral influence; the Gospels; **run to s.** produce seeds and cease producing flowers or shoots; (*fig*) lose freshness or energy ~ **seed** *v/t* and *i* sow seed (in); form seed; remove seeds from; (*tennis*) arrange competitors in a tournament in categories, so that the best players, or players of a particular nation, do not meet in the early rounds.

seedbed [*seed*bed] *n* ground prepared for the sowing of seeds; (*fig*) favourable environment for development.

seedcake [*seed*kayk] *n* cake containing caraway seeds.

seedcorn [*seed*kawrn] *n* corn kept aside for sowing.

seedily [*seed*ili] *adv* in a seedy way.

seediness [*seed*inis] *n* quality or state of being seedy.

seedling [*seed*ling] *n* young plant raised from seed.

seedpearl [*seed*purl] *n* very small pearl.

seedsman [*seed*zman] *n* one who sells seeds of flowers and vegetables, seedlings, garden tools *etc*.

seedtime [*seed*tIm] *n* season for sowing.

seed-vessel [*seed*-vesel] *n* pod or capsule which contains seeds.

seedy [*seed*i] *adj* full of seeds; (*coll*) shabby; (*coll*) out of sorts, slightly unwell.

seeing [*see*-ing] *conj* considering (that); since.

seek (*p/t* and *p/part* sought) [*seek*] *v/t* and *i* go in search of; look for; try to gain or do.

seeker [*seek*er] *n* one who seeks; inquirer.

seel [*seel*] *v/t* (*ar*) close the eyes of (hawk); hoodwink.

seem [*seem*] *v/t* appear to be; have the appearance of; give or have an impression.

seeming [*seem*ing] *adj* apparent, but perhaps not real ~ **seemingly** *adv*.

seemly [*seem*li] *adj* proper, decent; suited to the occasion *etc* ~ **seemliness** *n*.

seen [*seen*] *p/part* of see (1).

seep [*seep*] *v/i* ooze; drain away, leak.

seepage [*seep*ij] *n* liquid that has seeped.

seer [*seer*] *n* one who sees visions; prophet.

seersucker [*seer*suker] *n* thin puckered fabric of linen or cotton.

seesaw [*see*saw] *n* game in which children seated on each end of a board supported in the middle move alternately up and down; board used in this game; alternate motion ~ **seesaw** *v/i*.

seethe [*seeTH*] *v/i* and *t* bubble violently in boiling; be violently agitated; swirl; (*ar*) soften or cook by boiling.

see-through [*see*-thROO] *adj* transparent or partly transparent.

segment [*seg*ment] *n* (*geom*) portion of a circle cut off by a chord; portion cut or marked off; one of several similar portions forming the body of an animal ~ **segment** *v/t* and *i* divide into segments; be divided into segments.

segmental [seg*ment*al] *adj* segmentary.

segmentary [*seg*mentaRi] *adj* of, like or divided into segments.

segmentation [segment*ay*shon] *n* act of dividing into fragments; (*biol*) formation of cells by cleavage > PDB; formation of a body or limb by repetition of similar units > PDB.

segregate [*seg*Rigayt] *v/t* and *i* separate from others, isolate; divide into separate groups; become isolated or separated.

segregation [segRi*gay*shon] *n* act of segregating; state of being segregated; (*biol*) separation of allelomorphs into different gametes > PDB; (*pol*) system of laws forbidding persons of different races to use the same schools, hotels, public transport, churches or other public facilities; policy or custom preventing persons of different races from meeting as social equals.

segregationist [segRi*gay*shonist] *n* (person) believing in or enforcing racial segregation.

seigneur [*sayn*yer] *n* (*hist*) feudal lord.

seigniorage [*sayn*yeRij] *n* claim of the sovereign to a percentage of all bullion brought to the Mint for coinage; profit gained by issuing coins at a rate above their intrinsic value.

seigniory [*sayny*eRi] *n* feudal lordship; territory of a feudal lord.

seine [*sayn*] *n* large vertical fishing-net with floats and weights.

seise [*seez*] *v/t* (*leg*) put in possession of.

seisin, seizin [*seezin*] *n*(*leg*) act of taking possession.

seismal [*sIz*mal] *adj* seismic.

seismic [*sIz*mik] *adj* of or produced by an earthquake; **s. focus** area of origin of an earthquake.

seismo- *pref* of earthquakes.

seismogram [*sIz*mogRam] *n* record given by a seismograph.

seismograph [*sIz*mogRaaf] *n* instrument that records earth tremors caused by earthquakes or atomic explosions *etc* > PDG.

seismological [sIzmo*loj*ikal] *adj* of seismology.

seismology [sIz*moloji*] *n* science of earthquakes.

seismometer [sIz*mom*iter] *n* instrument for measuring direction and intensity of earthquakes.

seizable [*seez*ab'l] *adj* liable to be taken.

seize [*seez*] *v/t* and *i* grasp suddenly, snatch; take possession of forcibly; comprehend; affect or attack suddenly; (*leg*) seise; confiscate; (*naut*) tie up, lash; **s. up** become jammed or stuck.

seizin see **seisin**.

seizure [*seez*her] *n* act of seizing; sudden attack of illness, *esp* stroke or fit; that which is seized.

selah [*seelaa*] *n* apparently meaningless word occurring in the Psalms, perhaps to mark a pause.

seldom [*seldom*] *adv* rarely, not often.

select [si*lekt*] *v/t* choose carefully, choose as best or fittest; pick out ~ **select** *adj* carefully chosen; finest, fittest, best; accepting or admitting only a few outstanding persons, exclusive; **s. committee** parliamentary committee of inquiry with members from all parties.

selection [si*lek*shon] *n* act of selecting; something selected; number of objects from which one or more can be chosen; collection of samples; anthology; medley of tunes *etc*; **natural s.** Darwinian theory of evolution by propagation of the best-adapted individuals > PDB.

selective [si*lek*tiv] *adj* of, by or using selection; choosing or admitting only a few; responding only to certain stimuli ~ **selectivity** *n*.

selector [si*lek*tor] *n* person or mechanical device that selects.

selenium [se*leeni*-um] *n* a non-metallic element resembling sulphur > PDS; **s. cell** type of photo-electric cell > PDS.

seleno- *pref* of the moon.

selenography [sele*nog*Rafi] *n* scientific description of the moon's surface features.

selenology [sele*noloji*] *n* study of the moon.

selenotropic [seleen*Otropik*] *adj* turning towards the moon.

self (*pl* **selves**) [*self*] *n* a person's own individual identity and character; personality; ego; exclusive interest in what concerns oneself, selfishness; essential character; (*comm*) myself.

self- *pref expressing reflexive action* to, by or for oneself; automatic, due to no exterior propulsion or agency; pure, unmixed.

self-absorbed [self-ab*sawrbd*] *adj* excessively concerned with one's own affairs and interests, egoistic.

self-abuse [self-a*bews*] *n* masturbation.

self-acting [self-*akting*] *adj* automatic.

self-adjusting [self-a*justing*] *adj* adjusting itself automatically.

self-assertion [self-a*surshon*] *n* forceful or inconsiderate assertion of oneself or of one's claims.

self-assertive [self-a*surtiv*] *adj* showing self-assertion.

self-assurance [self-a*shoor*Rans] *n* confidence in oneself ~ **self-assured** *adj*.

self-binder [*self*-bInder] *n* reaping-machine with automatic binding device.

self-centred [self-*senterd*] *adj* interested only in oneself and one's own affairs.

self-coloured [self-*kul*erd] *adj* in its natural colour; of uniform colour.

self-complacent [self-kom*play*sent] *adj* unduly pleased with oneself.

self-conceit [self-kon*seet*] *n* too high an opinion of oneself.

self-confidence [self-*kon*fidens] *n* reliance on oneself and one's powers ~ **self-confident** *adj*.

self-conscious [self-*kon*shus] *adj* conscious of oneself and one's actions as seen by others, embarrassed, shy.

self-contained [self-kon*taynd*] *adj* not needing the help, companionship *etc* of others; reserved; complete in itself; (*of flats, houses etc*) not sharing access or rooms with other premises.

self-control [self-kon*tROl*] *n* power of controlling one's feelings, actions *etc*.

self-deception [self-dise*p*shon] *n* act of deluding oneself as to one's true motives, situation, prospects *etc*; state of being so deluded.

self-defeating [self-di*feeting*] *adj* causing the defeat of one's own aims.

self-defence [self-di*fens*] *n* act or art of defending oneself; **the art of s.** boxing.

self-denial [self-di*nI*-al] *n* refusal to gratify one's own desires ~ **self-denying** *adj*.

self-determination [self-diturmi*nay*shon] *n* right of a nation to determine its own form of government; act of deciding for oneself.

self-educated [self-*edew*kaytid] *adj* educated by one's own efforts, without teachers or without financial help.

self-effacement [self-e*fays*ment] *n* act of avoiding being noticed; willingness to give first place to others.

self-employed [self-em*ploid*] *adj* working in one's own shop, firm *etc*.

self-esteem [self-es*teem*] *n* favourable estimation of one's own qualities.

self-evident [self-*evident*] *adj* obvious; not requiring proof.

self-examination [self-egzami*nay*shon] *n* conscientious analysis of one's motives, character *etc*.

self-existent [self-eg*zistent*] *adj* not owing its existence to any cause but itself.

self-explanatory [self-eks*plan*ateRi] *adj* containing its own explanation.

self-expression [self-eks*pReshon*] *n* free expression of one's personality through one's behaviour, artistic creations, hobbies *etc*.

self-feeder [self-*feeder*] *n* machine refuelling itself.

self-forgetful [self-*fergetfool*] *adj* unselfish.

self-governing [self-*guverning*] *adj* having full political independence, autonomous.

self-government [self-*guv*ernment] *n* government of a people by its own rulers or representatives, political independence.

self-help [self-*help*] *n* unaided effort; the attaining of one's purpose without help from others.

selfhood [*self*hood] *n* individual identity.

self-importance [self-im*pawr*tans] *n* conceited manner; pompousness; exaggerated idea of one's own importance ∼ **self-important** *adj*.

self-induction [self-in*duk*shon] *n* (*elect*) change of magnetic field when the electric current associated with it is changed > PDS.

self-indulgence [self-in*dul*jens] *adj* act of gratifying one's own inclinations and desires ∼ **self-indulgent** *adj*.

self-interest [self-*int*eRest] *n* one's personal advantage; absorption in one's own desires.

selfish [*self*ish] *adj* caring only for one's own profit or pleasure, regardless of the feelings of others ∼ **selfishly** *adv* ∼ **selfishness** *n*.

selfless [*self*les] *adj* not selfish, disregarding or sacrificing one's own interests ∼ **selflessly** *adv* ∼ **selflessness** *n*.

self-love [self-*luv*] *n* excessive interest in oneself; selfishness; instinct to protect one's interests; narcissism.

self-made [self-*mayd*] *adj* successful by one's own efforts; **s. man** one who has risen from poverty to wealth and power by his own efforts only.

self-murder [self-*murd*er] *n* suicide.

self-opinionated [self-o*pin*yonaytid] *adj* obstinately or conceitedly sure that one is right.

self-pity [self-*piti*] *n* emotionally exaggerated awareness of one's troubles.

self-portrait [self-*pawrt*Rit] *n* portrait by an artist of himself.

self-possessed [self-po*sest*] *adj* calm, composed; having presence of mind.

self-raising [self-*Ray*zing] *adj* (*of flour*) containing a proportion of baking-powder.

self-realization [self-ree-al*zay*shon] *n* full development of one's faculties and abilities.

self-registering [self-*Rej*isteRing] *adj* recording automatically.

self-reliant [self-Ri*lI*-ant] *adj* not depending on others for help.

self-respect [self-Ri*spekt*] *n* proper regard for one's own character, reputation, position *etc*.

self-righteous [self-*RI*chus] *adj* convinced of one's own virtuousness, pharisaical ∼ **self-righteously** *adv* ∼ **self-righteousness** *n*.

self-sacrifice [self-*sak*Rifis] *n* surrender of oneself or of one's own interests for the sake of others.

selfsame [*self*saym] *adj* exactly the same.

self-satisfied [self-*satis*fId] *adj* conceited.

self-seeker [self-*seek*er] *n* one who pursues his own advantage regardless of others ∼ **self-seeking** *adj*.

self-service [self-*surv*is] *adj* (*of stores, restaurants etc*) setting out goods on shelves from which customers serve themselves, paying at the exit.

self-sown [self-*sOn*] *adj* growing from seed sown naturally by the parent plant.

self-starter [self-*staart*er] *n* automatic electric device for starting a motorcar.

self-styled [self-*stIld*] *adj* unjustifiably assuming a name or a title; pretended.

self-sufficiency [self-su*fish*ensi] *n* state or quality of being self-sufficient.

self-sufficient [self-su*fish*ent] *adj* needing no companionship from others; able to carry out one's desires without aid; economically independent.

self-supporting [self-su*pawr*ting] *adj* maintaining oneself, itself, without aid.

self-willed [self-*wild*] *adj* obstinate; unwilling to listen to the advice of others.

self-winding [self-*wInd*ing] *adj* winding itself automatically.

sell (*p/t* and *p/part* **sold**) [*sel*] *v/t* and *i* transfer property to another in exchange for its value in money; deal in; give up for a price; betray; (*sl*) deceive, play a trick upon; (*coll*) persuade people of the merits of, publicize attractively; (*of goods*) find buyers; **s. off** sell cheaply so as to get rid of; **s. out** sell one's whole stock; **s. up** sell a debtor's goods to pay his debts ∼ **sell** *n* (*sl*) fraud, hoax, disappointment.

seller [*sel*er] *n* one who sells.

sellotape [*sel*Otayp] *n* (*tr*) transparent adhesive cellulose tape ∼ **sellotape** *v/t*.

seltzer [*selt*ser] *n* mildly stimulant effervescing mineral water.

selvedge [*selv*ij] *n* the edge of cloth where it is woven so that it will not unravel; edge-plate of a lock.

selves [*selvz*] *pl* of self.

semantic [se*ma*ntik] *adj* concerned with the meaning of words ∼ **semantically** *adv*.

semantics [se*ma*ntiks] *n* (*pl*) study of the meanings of words; study of meaning.

semaphore [*sema*fawr] *n* signalling apparatus consisting of arms or flags worked by levers ∼ **semaphore** *v/t* and *i* send message by semaphore.

semblance [*sem*blans] *n* resemblance; appearance, show.

semblant [*sem*blant] *adj* seeming.

semeiography [semeI-o*gRaf*i] *n* (*med*) description of symptoms.

semeiology [semeI-o*loji*] *n* (*med*) study of symptoms.

semen [*see*men] *n* sperm-bearing fluid of male reproductive organs > PDB.

semester [se*mest*er] *n* (*US*) university term.

semi- *pref* half; partly.

semi [*semi*] *n* (*coll abbr*) semidetached house.

semibreve [*semi*bReev] *n* (*mus*) note equal to two minims.

semicircle [*semi*surk'l] *n* half circle; group of persons or things forming a half circle.

semicircular [semi*surk*ewler] *adj* of or in a semicircle; **s. canal** canal of the inner ear containing fluid affected by changes of direction.

semicolon [semi*kOl*on] *n* punctuation mark (;) intermediate in value between comma and period.

semiconductor [semikon*duk*ter] *n* (*elect*) conductor, whose resistance decreases when temperature rises or impurities are present > PDS.

semiconscious [semi*kon*shus] *adj* partially conscious.

semidetached [semidi*tacht*] *adj* (*of a house*) having another built on to it on one side.

semi-final [*semi*-fInal] *adj* and *n* last (match) before the final (of a contest).

semifluid [semiflOO-id] *adj* imperfectly fluid.

seminal [semInal] *adj* of semen; of reproduction; (*fig*) productive, giving rise to many developments; primary ~ **seminally** *adv*.

seminar [seminaar] *n* discussion class for a group of students guided by a tutor; group of advanced students working together under guidance.

seminarist [semineRist] *n* student in a seminary.

seminary [semineRi] *n* (*obs*) school, college; (*RC*) training college for priests.

semi-official [semi-ofishal] *adj* having partial official authority; not fully authorized.

semiotic [semi-otik] *adj* concerning spoken or written signs and symbols ~ **semiotics** *n* (*pl*) the study of the relation of these to their referents.

semi-permeable [semi-purmi-ab'l] *adj* (*of a membrane*) allowing the passage of some substances but not others.

semi-precious [semi-pReshus] *adj* (*of stones*) valuable but not precious.

semi-skilled [semi-skild] *adj* having or requiring a moderate amount of skill in working.

semiquaver [semikwayver *n*] (*mus*) note with half the duration of a quaver.

Semite [seemIt/semIt] *n* member of a racial group including Jews, Arabs, Assyrians *etc*; Jew.

Semitic [semitik] *adj* of or like the Semites; of a group of languages including Hebrew, Arabic *etc*.

semitone [semitOn] *n* (*mus*) an interval equal to half a tone > PDM.

semitropical [semitRopikal] *adj* partly within or bordering on the tropics.

semivowel [semivow-el] *n* sound which has the character of both vowel and consonant.

semolina [semoleena] *n* hard coarsely-ground grains of wheat, used in making macaroni.

sempiternal [sempiturnal] *adj* eternal.

sempstress see **seamstress**.

senate [senat] *n* name of certain upper legislative houses; academic governing body of a university; (*hist*) legislative council of ancient Rome.

senate-house [senat-hows] *n* building in which a senate meets.

senator [s-nater] *n* member of a senate.

senatorial [senatawR-al] *adj* of a senate or senator.

senatus [sinaytus] *n* governing body in a Scottish university.

send (*p*/*t* and *p*/*part* sent) [send] *v*/*t* and *i* cause to go; order or force to go; cause to be carried or conveyed, dispatch; throw; grant, bestow; cause to be or become; compel; dispatch a message; (*sl*) rouse to ecstasy, delight intensely; (*naut*) pitch into trough of sea; **s. down** expel from university; **s. for** summon, ask or order to come; ask or order to be brought; **s. forth** emit; sprout; **s. in** present (report *etc*) for consideration; **s. off** dispatch; escort to point of departure; **s. on** dispatch in advance; re-address and re-post; **s. out** emit; send as messenger *etc*; cause to be distributed, *esp* by post; send (message) by radio; **s. packing** dismiss roughly, get rid of; **s. up** (*sl*) show as ridiculous or false; blow up.

sendal [sendal] *n* medieval type of thin silk fabric.

sender [sender] *n* one who sends.

send-off [send-of] *n* good wishes expressed to one about to start a journey; (*fig*) auspicious beginning to a new undertaking.

send-up [send-up] *n* (*coll*) mocking imitation, parody.

senescence [sinesens] *n* process of degenerative change in growing old ~ **senescent** *adj*.

seneschal [seneshal] *n* (*hist*) steward of a large medieval household.

senile [seenIl] *adj* of, like or caused by old age; feeble-minded through old age > PDP ~ **senilely** *adv*.

senility [seniliti] *n* quality of being senile.

senior [seeni-er] *adj* older; of higher rank or status; having belonged to a society *etc* longer than another; more advanced in education; **the s. service** the Navy ~ **senior** *n* one who is older, of higher rank *etc*.

seniority [seeni-oRiti] *n* priority in age or office.

senna [sena] *n* leaves of various species of cassia, used as purgative.

sennight [senIt] *n* (*ar*) week.

señor [senyawr] *n* Spanish form of address to a man.

señora [senyawrRa] *n* Spanish form of address to a married woman.

señorita [senyawrReeta] *n* Spanish form of address to an unmarried woman.

sensation [sensayshon] *n* perception through the senses, power of feeling; impression perceived through a sense organ > PDP; awareness, feeling; strong excitement caused by news of some event; event or person producing widespread strong excitement, curiosity *etc*.

sensational [sensayshonal] *adj* rousing great excitement, curiosity *etc*; amazing; wonderful; rousing strong emotions, *esp* of horror.

sensationalism [sensayshonalizm] *n* undue exploitation of excitement and curiosity in journalism *etc*; crude presentation of violence, horror, sex *etc* as means of excitement in books, plays, films *etc*; (*philos*) theory that all knowledge is derived solely from sense perceptions > PDP ~ **sensationalist** *n* and *adj*.

sensationally [sensayshonali] *adv* in a sensational way.

sense [sens] *n* feeling, physical perception; one of the five bodily faculties by which the material universe is perceived; awareness; capacity to perceive and respond to anything; emotional awareness, feeling; intelligence and good judgement, *esp* in practical matters; intuition; significance, meaning; (*pl*) bodily desires and pleasures, sensuousness, sensuality; (*pl*) sanity; normal consciousness; sound judgement; **make s. of** find a meaning in; **common s.** practical intelligence, wisdom applied to a particular situation; **sixth s.** intuitive awareness, *esp* of danger ~ **sense** *v*/*t* perceive intuitively, indirectly or half-consciously; understand; perceive through the senses.

sense-datum [sens-daytum] *n* an immediate unanalysable private object of sensation.

senseless [sensles] *adj* meaningless; purposeless; irrational, very foolish; unconscious, stunned ~ **senselessly** *adv* ~ **senselessness** *n*.

sensibility [sensibiliti] *n* sensitiveness; capacity of being stimulated by physical stimuli; capacity to respond strongly and with discrimination to emotional, aesthetic, or spiritual experiences; delicacy, refinement; oversensitiveness, *esp* emotional; (pl) refined awareness of what is right or tasteful.

sensible [sensib'l] adj having or showing common sense, reasonable; of practical intelligence; prudent, wise; aware, conscious; capable of being perceived by the senses; noticeable, clearly perceptible ~ **sensibleness** n.

sensibly [sensibli] adv reasonably, with common sense; prudently, wisely; noticeably.

sensitive [sensitiv] adj reacting quickly to stimuli; easily roused to strong feeling; easily distressed, angered etc; painful when touched, sore; keenly perceptive; having delicate and discriminating taste; delicately adjusted; capable of reacting to (a specified stimulus); (psych) susceptible to occult influences; **s. plant** mimosa ~ **sensitive** n one who is sensitive, esp to telepathy or occult forces ~ **sensitively** adv ~ **sensitiveness** n.

sensitivity [sensitiviti] n state of being sensitive; degree of sensitiveness.

sensitize [sensitIz] v/t (phot) render sensitive to light; (med) render sensitive to foreign protein.

sensor [senser] n (sci) any of various devices for detecting or measuring a specified physical property; metal-detector.

sensorial [sensawRi-al] adj sensory; of the sensorium.

sensorium [sensawRi-um] n grey matter of the brain; nervous system.

sensory [senseRi] adj of or by the senses or sensation; of or by the sense organs and nervous system > PDP.

sensual [sensew-al] adj of physical pleasures, esp those of sex and of food and drink; unduly fond of such pleasures; lustful; voluptuous; (ar) of or perceived by the senses.

sensualism [sensew-alizm] n habitual indulgence in sensual pleasures; (philos) sensationalism.

sensualist [sensew-alist] n one who indulges in sensual or sexual pleasures.

sensuality [sensew-aliti] n quality of being sensual; proneness to sexual indulgence.

sensually [sensew-ali] adv in a sensual way.

sensuous [sensew-us] adj of, by or through the senses; pleasing to the senses, physically beautiful; easily responsive to pleasures of the senses; (coll euph) sensual, sexual ~ **sensuously** adv ~ **sensuousness** n.

sent [sent] p/t and p/part of send.

sentence [sentens] n penalty imposed by a criminal court; judgement imposing this; (gramm) a group of words joined by grammatical devices (or one word only) that does not form part of any larger grammatical group, that usually contains a finite verb, and can convey a complete meaning if it occurs alone; group of words beginning with a capital letter and ending in a period, question mark or exclamation mark; (ar) opinion ~ **sentence** v/t impose a legal penalty on.

sententious [sentenshus] adj of or uttering pompous or trite opinions ~ **sententiously** adv ~ **sententiousness** n.

sentient [senshi-ent] adj capable of sense perception; having sense or feeling.

sentiment [sentiment] n mental attitude determined by an emotion; tendency to be ruled more by emotions than by rationality; delicate feelings,

sensibility; tender emotion; sentimentality; stupid pathos; opinion, view.

sentimental [sentimental] adj of, like or caused by sentiment; of tender emotions; expressing or tending to rouse foolish or exaggerated feelings of tenderness, pity etc.

sentimentalism [sentimentalizm] n sentimental attitude ~ **sentimentalist** n and adj.

sentimentality [sentimentaliti] n quality of being sentimental.

sentimentalize [sentimentalIz] v/i and t behave in a sentimental way; make sentimental, express or explain sentimentally.

sentimentally [sentimentali] adv in a sentimental way.

sentinel [sentinel] n one who keeps watch; sentry.

sentry [sentRi] n soldier on guard, sentinel.

sentrybox [sentRiboks] n small doorless hut to shelter a sentry.

sentry-go [sentRi-gO] n duty of a sentry in pacing to and fro while on guard.

sepal [sepal] n (bot) segment of a calyx.

separability [separabiliti] n quality of being separable.

separable [separab'l] adj that can be separated ~ **separably** adv.

separate [separayt] v/t and i cause to part, disunite; part, be or become divided; be or cause to be apart; break up the relationship between; cease to live together; cause disagreement between; form a barrier or division between; secede; sift; distinguish between ~ **separate** [separit] adj divided, disconnected; not forming part of one whole; distinct, individual; independent; isolated ~ **separately** adv ~ **separateness** n ~ **separates** n (pl) articles of clothing that can be worn either together or with different articles.

separation [separRayshon] n act of separating; state of being separated; disunion; (leg) formal arrangement by which a married couple cease to live together but are not divorced; **s. allowance** State allowance received by the wife of a soldier etc on active service.

separationist [separRayshonist] n and adj separatist.

separatist [separRatist] n one who wishes to secede from a federation etc; one who wishes to leave a political or religious organization; dissenter ~ **separatist** adj.

separative [separRativ] adj causing separation.

separator [separRayter] n one who or that which separates; machine which separates cream from milk.

Sephardi [sefaardi] n Jew from Portugal or Spain ~ **Sephardic** adj.

sepia [seepi-a] n dark brown pigment; cuttlefish producing this.

sepoy [seepoi] n European-trained Indian soldier.

sepsis [sepsis] n infection of the blood by microorganisms, blood-poisoning; putrefaction.

sept [sept] n Irish or Highland clan or family.

sept- pref seven.

septal [septal] adj of a septum; of a sept.

septate [septayt] adj (anat) divided by a septum.

September [september] n ninth month of the year.

septenary [septeeneRi] adj consisting of seven; by sevens; lasting seven years.

septennium [sep*teni*-um] *n* period of seven years.
septentrional [sep*tent*Ri-onal] *adj* northern.
septet [sep*tet*] *n* group of seven; musical composition for seven performers > PDM.
septic [*se*ptik] *adj* producing or infected by sepsis; (*sl*) very unpleasant; **s. tank** outdoor tank in which sewage is broken down by bacteria.
septicaemia [septi*seemi*-a] *n* morbid state of the blood caused by absorption of putrid matter.
septuagenarian [septew-aji*nair*Ri-an] *n* and *adj* (person) seventy years old; (person) between seventy and eighty.
Septuagesima [septew-a*jesi*ma] *n* third Sunday before Lent.
Septuagint [*se*ptew-ajint] *n* Greek version of the Old Testament and Apocrypha.
septum [*se*ptum] *n* (*anat*, *bot*) partition.
sepulchral [si*pulk*Ral] *adj* of a tomb; gloomy, dismal ∼ **sepulchrally** *adv*.
sepulchre [*se*pulker] *n* tomb; burial vault; **whited s.** hypocrite ∼ **sepulchre** *v/t* place in a sepulchre.
sepulture [*se*pulcher] *n* burial, interment.
sequacious [sik*way*shus] *adj* logically following, following as effect from cause; pliant ∼ **sequaciously** *adv* ∼ **sequaciousness** *n*.
sequel [*seek*wel] *n* that which follows, *esp* as a consequence; result, effect; literary work whose story is a continuation of that of a previous work.
sequence [*seek*wens] *n* order in which events or objects follow each other, succession; series; series of cards in order of value; (*mus*) succession of similar harmonious chords > PDM; (*cin*) continuous series of shots ending in a dissolve.
sequent [*seek*went] *adj* following; resulting.
sequential [sik*wen*shal] *adj* in succession; following in consequence ∼ **sequentially** *adv*.
sequester [sik*wes*ter] *v/t* set apart, isolate; (*leg*) sequestrate.
sequestered [sik*wes*terd] *adj* secluded; retired.
sequestrate [sik*wes*tRayt] *v/t* and *i* (*leg*) take and hold (property) pending satisfaction of claims; confiscate.
sequestration [seekwest*Ray*shon] *n* act of sequestrating.
sequestrator [*see*kwest*Ray*ter] *n* one who sequestrates property.
sequin [*seek*win] *n* thin metal disk used as a trimming, spangle; medieval Venetian gold coin.
sequined [*seek*wind] *adj* trimmed with sequins.
sequoia [se*kwoi*-a] *n* either of two species of Californian gigantic conifers.
sérac [say*Rak*] *n* (*Fr*) pinnacle of ice formed by a glacier > PDG.
seraglio [se*Raaly*O] *n* harem; group of women kept as concubines; (*hist*) Sultan's palace.
serai [se*RI*] *n* Oriental inn.
serape [se*Raa*pay] *n* Mexican blanket worn as cloak.
seraph (*pl* **seraphim**) [*se*Raf] *n* angel with six wings, of the highest angelic order.
seraphic [se*Ra*fik] *adj* of or like a seraph; angelic; ecstatic; rapturous; pure.
sere see **sear**.
serenade [se*Renayd*] *n* music played or sung in the open air at night, *esp* by a lover under his lady's window; nocturne > PDM ∼ **serenade** *v/t* and *i* sing a serenade (to).

serendipity [se*Ren*d*ipi*ti] *n* gift of finding valuable things in unexpected places by sheer luck.
serene [si*Reen*] *adj* calm, undisturbed; clear; placid; (*coll*) safe ∼ **serenely** *adv*.
serenity [si*Reni*ti] *n* calmness; stillness.
serf [*surf*] *n* feudal worker belonging either to his master or to the soil of an estate; slave; (*fig*) drudge.
serge [*surj*] *n* strong twilled woollen cloth.
sergeant [*saar*jant] *n* (*mil*) non-commissioned officer next in rank above a corporal; police officer next in rank above a constable.
sergeant-at-arms [saarjant-at-*aarmz*] *n* ceremonial official of Parliament or of a royal household.
sergeant-major [saarjant-*may*jer] *n* (*mil*) chief sergeant of a regiment, squadron or battery.
serial [*seer*Ri-al] *adj* of, like, or forming a series; published, broadcast, filmed *etc* in sections at regular intervals; in instalments; (*mus*) of or in a twelve-note chromatic or atonic scale, without reference to key ∼ **serial** *n* story, novel, play *etc* published, broadcast or televised in instalments; film released in instalments.
serialism [*seer*Ri-alizm] *n* art of serial composition in music ∼ **serialist** *n* and *adj*.
serialize [*seer*Ri-al*Iz*] *v/t* publish or produce as a serial; adapt for serial publication or production.
serially [*seer*Ri-ali] *adv* as a serial.
seriate [*seer*Ri-ayt] *adj* arranged in series.
seriatim [seerRi-*ay*tim] *adv* in regular order.
sericeous [si*Rish*us] *adj* of silk, silky; downy.
sericulture [*se*Rikulcher] *n* the breeding of silkworms for production of raw silk.
series (*pl* **series**) [*seer*Reez] *n* number of similar or related things or events occurring or arranged in an order or succession; sequence; set; row; number of books published successively by one firm in similar format and of similar type; (*math*) succession of numbers or expressions arranged according to a common law > PDS; (*mus*) set of notes forming basic material of a composition > PDM.
serif, ceriph [*se*Rif] *n* (*print*) short line at the top or bottom of letters.
serio-comic [seerRi-O-*komik*] *adj* mixing serious and comic elements.
serious [*seer*Ri-us] *adj* grave, thoughtful, not frivolous; in earnest, not meant as a joke; important; dangerous; thorough, careful; requiring careful thought or attention; concerned with intellectual or spiritual problems ∼ **seriously** *adv* ∼ **seriousness** *n*.
serjeant [*saar*jant] *n* sergeant.
sermon [*sur*mon] *n* religious or moral address forming part of a church service; similar address published in book form; (*fig*) long series of moral reproaches or warnings.
sermonize [*sur*monIz] *v/t* and *i* preach, *esp* boringly; deliver tedious moral rebukes *etc* (to).
serology [seer*Rolo*ji] *n* scientific study of serums, *esp* of the blood ∼ **serologist** *n*.
serosity [seer*Rosi*ti] *n* state of being serous; serous fluid.
serous [*seer*Rus] *adj* of or like serum; secreting serum; thin, watery.
serpent [*sur*pent] *n* reptile with long scaly body and no limbs, snake; (*fig*) treacherous deceiver or

tempter; obsolete S-shaped large wind instrument > PDM.

serpentine [*surp*entIn] *adj* twisting, winding; of or like a snake; (*fig*) treacherous, wily ~ **serpentine** *n* green or red mottled ornamental stone, a hydrated silicate of magnesium.

serrate [*se*Rayt] *adj* notched on the edge ~ **serrate** *v/t* notch the edges of.

serrated [*se*Raytid] *adj* having a saw-like edge.

serration [*se*Rayshon] *n* formation like the edge of a saw.

serried [*se*Rid] *adj* closely-packed; crowded; in compact order.

serum [*seer*Rum] *n* liquid which remains after the clotting and removal of blood corpuscles and fibrin from the blood; any similar body fluid > PDS; such a fluid prepared by culture for use in inoculation.

servant [*surv*ant] *n* employee paid to do household work for or give personal attendance to another; one who serves; one who is in the service of the State; hard-working supporter or adherent; that which serves; **civil s.** member of the Civil Service.

servant-girl [*surv*ant-gurl] *n* female domestic servant.

serve [*surv*] *v/t* and *i* act as a servant (to); work for; wait on; submit to, give allegiance to; satisfy; be of use to; present (food) at table, hand round; suffice, be adequate; undergo (a prison sentence); deliver (a writ *etc*); (*of male animals*) mate with; be a member of, carry out duties in, one of the armed forces; suit, be favourable; be what is needed or useful; lead off in certain games by striking a ball; **s. as** act as substitute for; **it serves him right** he has got what he deserves; **s. time** undergo a prison sentence ~ **serve** *n* (*games*) act of striking the first ball; turn to do this.

server [*surv*er] *n* one who serves; one who assists the priest at Mass.

servery [*surv*eRi] *n* counter or hatch from which food is served.

service [*surv*is] *n* act of serving; work done for another; employment as domestic servant; act that helps another, benefit; organization regularly providing public transport, means of communication, or other public utility; regular public transport on a specified route; department of State; Army, Navy, or Air Force; state of being a member of one of these; duty, *esp* fighting, performed as soldier, sailor, or airman; religious worship performed according to a ritual, liturgical worship; musical setting for liturgical prayers > PDM; act of supplying a customer's needs; act of serving meals, *esp* in a hotel or restaurant; set of matching crockery, cutlery *etc*; (*leg*) the serving of a writ *etc*; (*games*) act of striking the ball to begin play; style of doing this; **active s.** service in the armed forces involving actual fighting; **Civil S.** administrative department of a State ~ **service** *v/t* provide upkeep for, overhaul (machinery); (*of male animals*) mate with ~ **service** *adj* of, in or for the armed forces; supplying a service; **s. area** roadside area where petrol, refreshments *etc* are available; **s. flat** apartment where meals, cleaning *etc* are supplied by the management; **s. hatch** opening in a wall through which food can be passed from kitchen to dining room; **s.**

road small road parallel to a main road, giving access to houses.

serviceable [*surv*isab'l] *adj* capable of or ready for service; useful; fit for use ~ **serviceably** *adv*.

service-book [*surv*is-book] *n* book containing the order of a religious service.

servicing [*surv*ising] *n* regular maintenance work for upkeep of car, machinery *etc*.

serviceman [*surv*isman] *n* man in the Army, Navy or Air Force.

serviette [*surv*i-et] *n* table-napkin, *esp* a paper one.

servile [*surv*Il] *adj* of or like a slave; slavish, cringing, abject; **s. work** (*RC*) manual work ~ **servilely** *adv*.

servility [*surv*Iliti] *n* quality of being servile; servile behaviour.

serving-man [*surv*ing-man] *n* (*ar*) male servant.

servitor [*surv*iter] *n* (*ar*) male servant; type of Oxford undergraduate having a partial college grant.

servitude [*surv*itewd] *n* state of being a slave; bondage, subjection; **penal s.** imprisonment with hard labour for three years or more.

servocontrol [*surv*OkontROl] *n* control operated by a servomechanism ~ **servocontrol** *v/t* and *i*.

servomechanism [survO*mek*anizm] *n* any mechanism which converts a low-powered motion into one requiring much greater power.

sesame [*ses*ami] *n* East Indian herb with oily edible seeds; **open s.** magic formula used to unlock a door; (*fig*) key to a mystery; way out of a difficulty.

sesquipedalian [seskwipi*dayl*i-an] *adj* and *n* many-syllabled (word).

session [*sesh*on] *n* formal meeting of a legislative body, council, court *etc*; period of such a meeting; period during which Parliament regularly meets; university year; (*pl*) meetings of certain courts of law; (*coll*) long period of discussions, business *etc*.

sessional [*sesh*onal] *adj* of a session or sessions.

sesterce [*ses*turs] *n* ancient Roman coin.

sestet [*ses*tet] *n* musical composition for six performers > PDM; group of six musicians; last six lines of a sonnet.

sestina [ses*teen*a] *n* poem of six six-lined stanzas and triplet, the lines of each stanza ending in the same six words but in varying order.

set (*pres/part* **setting**, *p/t* and *p/part* **set**) [set] *v/t* and *i* put, place in specified position; turn, move towards; adjust, prepare for use, put in working order; arrange; fix in a mount, place against a background; harden, solidify, congeal; make or become rigid and unchanging; fix (hair) in waves; cause to do or undertake; impose (a task) on; devise (examination, test *etc*); arrange (type) for printing; compose music for (extant words); evaluate; exhibit as model; (*of sun, moon etc*) sink below horizon; (*naut*) hoist; (*hort*) develop into fruit; (*of jam*) jell; **s. about** begin to do; (*coll*) attack, hit; **s. aside** save up; disregard; **s. back** check, hinder; place farther back; (*sl*) cost money to; **s. down** deposit; write down, record in writing; attribute, reckon; **s. eyes on** see; **s. forth** expound; start on a journey; exhibit; **s. in** appear and gradually increase; flow; become settled; **s. off** begin a journey; cause to begin; enhance, intensify; counterbalance (by); cause to explode; **s. on** incite, egg on; attack; enable (one) to find or trace, give information about; **s. out** state, explain; begin a journey; begin or intend to do; **s. right** correct; **s. to** begin vigorously, *esp* to eat or fight; **s. up** erect, raise upright; establish, found; set in motion, cause; equip; stimulate, invigorate; **s. upon** attack ~ **set** *adj* fixed, immovable; rigid, resolute; established, regular; in working order and ready for use ~ **set** *n* group of similar or related things meant to be used or possessed as a whole; group of closely associated persons, group of friends; act of setting; way something is placed or arranged; arrangement of the hair, *esp* if permed; position, posture; direction of movement, flow; tendency; way that clothes fit; clutch of eggs; number of games played at one time; series of figures forming a dance; (*theat, cin*) scenery, furnishings *etc* forming the setting for a part of the play or film; (*hort*) cutting, slip; (*math*) any collection of objects defined by having a common property; **make a dead s. at** try hard to attract the notice or love of; attack vigorously.

setaceous [*sitayshus*] *adj* bristly.

setback [*setbak*] *n* interruption of progress, check; rebuff; relapse; indentation; recess.

set-down [*set-*down] *n* rebuke, snub.

set-fair [set-*fair*] *adj* (*of weather*) fine and settled.

set-off [set-*of*] *n* thing set off against another; counter-claim; decoration; accidental mark from a printed sheet before it is dry.

set-out [set-*owt*] *n* beginning, start; preparation; display.

set-piece [set-*pees*] *n* large firework built on a scaffolding; elaborate display prepared in advance; elaborate piece of writing.

set-square [set-*skwair*] *n* right-angled triangular instrument used for mechanical drawing > PDE.

sett [*set*] *n* small paving-stone or wooden block; timber frame.

settee (1) [se*tee*] *n* long upholstered seat with a back.

settee (2) *n* single-decked Mediterranean vessel with two or three masts with lateen sails.

setter [*seter*] *n* one who or that which sets; large dog trained to point at game.

setting [*seting*] *n* act of one who sets; direction of a current; hardening; mounting for a jewel; surroundings, background; stage-scenery; music to which words are fitted; process of solidifying or fixing; **s. lotion** lotion sprayed on the hair to fix it in waves.

settle (1) [*set'l*] *n* long wooden high-backed seat.

settle (2) *v/t* and *i* place firmly in position; make one's home (in), live permanently (in); colonize; determine, decide, fix; make or become permanent; establish; become stable; soothe, pacify; make up one's mind (about); conclude, arrange or deal with conclusively; get rid of; pay (bills *etc*); bestow legally, bestow in one's will; sit down, alight; sink to the bottom; subside; become calm; **s. down** cease moving; adapt oneself to new surroundings; grow calm; adopt a regular, conventional way of life; **s. for** agree to accept; **s. in** adapt to new surroundings; start living in new house *etc*; **s. up** complete a transaction; pay bills; **s. with** pay one's debts to; come to agreement with, make a deal with; deal conclusively with.

settlement [*set'*lment] *n* act of settling; state of being settled; agreement reached over a dispute or claim; newly-settled region, colony; group of persons living together; mission centre; (*leg*) conveyance of property; (*mech*) downward movement of a structure due to compression of the soil below it > PDE.

settler [*setler*] *n* one who settles in an undeveloped country, colonist.

settling-day [*setling-*day] *n* day for settling accounts, *esp* on the Stock Exchange.

settlor [*setler*] *n* (*leg*) one who makes a settlement.

set-to [set-t*OO*] *n* fight; vigorous argument.

set-up [set-up] *n* (*coll*) arrangement; organization; situation.

seven [*seven*] *n* and *adj* cardinal number next above six; symbol of this, 7; set of seven persons or things.

sevenfold [sevenf*Old*] *adj* and *adv* repeated seven times.

seventeen [seven*teen*] *n* and *adj* seven more than ten; symbol of this, 17.

seventeenth [seven*teenth*] *n* and *adj* (that) which follows sixteen others in a series; (one) of seventeen equal parts.

seventh [*seventh*] *n* and *adj* (that) which follows six others in a series; (that) which is one of seven equal parts; **s. heaven** extreme bliss ~ **seventhly** *adv*.

seventieth [*seventi-*eth] *n* and *adj* (that) which follows sixty-nine others; (that) which is one of seventy equal parts.

seventy [*seventi*] *n* and *adj* seven times ten.

sever [*sever*] *v/t* and *i* part, separate; divide, cleave; cut off; keep apart.

several [*seveRal*] *adj* more than two, but not very many; separate, distinct; various; (*leg*) capable of being treated separately ~ **several** *n* a few; small number of persons or things.

severally [*seveRali*] *adv* individually, distinctly.

severalty [*seveRalti*] *n* (*leg*) exclusive ownership or tenure.

severance [*seveRans*] *n* act of severing; separation; **s. pay** lump sum paid to an employee when his job ends.

severe [si*veer*] *adj* strict, stern; harsh, merciless; painful, bitter; violent; grave, serious; austere, plain ~ **severely** *adv* ~ **severeness** *n*.

severity [si*veRiti*] *n* quality of being severe.

sew (*p/t* sewed, *p/part* sewn or sewed) [s*O*] *v/t* and *i* fasten together with a needle and thread; join with stitches; work with needle and thread.

sewage [*sew-*ij] *n* waste matter, excreta *etc*, carried away by sewers; **s. farm** place where sewage is processed into manure; **s. works** place where sewage is purified and discharged into sea or river.

sewer (1) [*sew-*er] *n* large underground drain carrying away the sewage of a town ~ **sewer** *v/t* provide sewers for ~ **sewer** *adj* of or in sewers.

sewer (2) [s*O*-er] *n* one who sews.

sewerage [sew-e*Rij*] *n* system of draining by sewers; sewers, drains *etc* collectively.

sewing [s*O*-ing] *n* act or craft of using a needle and thread; that which is sewn, piece of needlework.

sewing-machine [s*O*-ing-masheen] *n* machine used for sewing.

sewn [s*On*] *p/part* of **sew.**

sex [*seks*] *n* organic and functional distinction between male and female; all emotions and cravings arising from this and directly or indirectly connected with reproduction > PDP; love in its physical aspect; acts, *esp* copulation, expressing this; men or women collectively ∼ **sex** *v/t* ascertain the sex of ∼ **sex** *adj* sexual.

sex- *pref* six.

sexagenarian [seksaje*nair*Ri-an] *adj* and *n* (person) sixty years old; (person) between sixty and seventy.

Sexagesima [seksa*jes*ima] *n* second Sunday before Lent.

sex-appeal [*seks*-apeel] *n* power of exciting sexual desire in others; strong sexual attractiveness.

sexed [*sekst*] *adj* having sexual desires or capacities to a specified degree.

sexennial [sekse*n*i-al] *adj* happening once every six years; lasting six years.

sexily [*seks*ili] *adv* in a sexy way.

sexiness [*seks*inis] *n* quality of being sexy.

sexism [*seks*izm] *n* belief that men are superior to women; systematic discrimination against women in law, social position, wages *etc* ∼ **sexist** *n* and *adj*.

sex-kitten [*seks*-kiten] *n* (*coll*) young, sexually provocative, girl.

sexless [*seks*les] *adj* having no sex; lacking the characteristic feelings of sex, frigid; impotent ∼ **sexlessly** *adv* ∼ **sexlessness** *n*.

sex-linked [*seks*-linkt] *adj* (*biol*) genetically dependent on or linked with the sex chromosomes.

sexology [seks*oloji*] *n* scientific study of sexual relationships, impulses *etc*.

sexpartite [seks*part*It] *adj* consisting of six parts.

sexploitation [*seks*ploytayshon] *n* (*joc coll*) commercial exploitation of sexual themes or images.

sexpot [*seks*pot] *n* (*coll*) very sexy woman or girl.

sext [*sekst*] *n* (*eccles*) canonical office for noon.

sextain [*seks*tayn] *n* stanza of six lines.

sextant [*seks*tant] *n* instrument for determining the angle between two objects > PDS, PDE; one sixth of a circle.

sextet [seks*tet*] *n* (*mus*) a composition for six singers or six instruments > PDM; group of six performers.

sexto [*seks*tO] *n* book made by folding each sheet into six leaves.

sextodecimo [sekst*Odes*imO] *n* book made by folding each sheet into sixteen leaves; sheet of paper folded four times.

sexton [*seks*ton] *n* man employed by a church as caretaker, gravedigger, bellringer *etc*.

sextuple [*seks*tewp'l] *adj* six times, sixfold.

sextuplet [*seks*tewplet] *n* one of six children born at one birth.

sexual [*seks*ew-al] *adj* of, associated with, arising from, or based on sex > PDP; of, associated with, copulation; (*biol*) reproducing by union of male and female cells > PDB.

sexuality [seksew-*al*iti] *n* quality of being sexual; emotions, attitudes *etc* as determined by sexual impulses; sexual desire > PDP.

sexually [*seks*ew-ali] *adv* in a sexual way; as regards sex.

sexy [*seks*i] *adj* having and displaying great sexual attractiveness, deliberately alluring; of or about

sex; designed to stimulate sexual instincts, pornographic.

sez [*sez*] (*sl spelling*) says; **s. you** (*sl*) exclamation of disbelief or irony.

sforzando [sfawrts*and*O] *adv* (*Ital, mus*) with special emphasis.

shabby [*shab*i] *adj* showing signs of hard wear, threadbare; dirty, squalid; wearing old, threadbare or dirty clothes; drab, mean-looking; pettily dishonest, mean, shameful ∼ **shabbily** *adv* ∼ **shabbiness** *n*.

shabby-genteel [*shab*i-jenteel] *adj* living in poverty but struggling to conceal the fact.

shack [*shak*] *n* roughly built cabin; log-hut ∼ **shack** *v/i* **s. up with** share house or lodgings with; live together though unmarried.

shackle [*shak*'l] *n* fetter, handcuff; coupling link; (*fig*) restraint ∼ **shackle** *v/t* chain, fetter; (*fig*) restrain, hamper.

shade [*shayd*] *n* area of partial darkness formed by a body that obstructs rays of light, shadow > PDS; area sheltered from direct sunlight; slight difference in colour, brightness, intensity *etc*; tiny amount, degree or difference; faint tinge; shield to protect the eyes from strong light; covering or partial covering for a lamp; presentation of darkness or shadow in a painting *etc*; ghost; (*pl, poet*) spirits of the dead; world of the dead; **in the s.** (*fig*) forgotten, overlooked because of another's achievements ∼ **shade** *v/t* and *i* shield from light, cast a shadow on; darken; indicate relative brightness and darkness on (a painting *etc*); change or merge very gradually; **s. away** (*off*) disappear or change very gradually; **s. into** change imperceptibly into.

shadily [*shayd*ili] *adv* in a shady way.

shadiness [*shayd*inis] *n* quality of being shady.

shading [*shayd*ing] *n* representation of, and contrast between, light and shade in a picture.

shadow [*shad*O] *n* dark patch formed by a body which obstructs rays of light > PDS; such a patch reproducing the shape of the object that forms it; area of comparative darkness, shade; (*pl*) darkness, gloom; anxiety, depression, fear; (*fig*) one who closely and persistently follows another; ghost, phantom; faint, ineffectual representation or copy; imperfect image; very slight difference, amount or degree; premonition; **s. boxing** boxing against an imaginary opponent; **s. cabinet** (*pol*) leaders of an opposition party who will be expected to form the cabinet when they return to power; **reduced to a s.** extremely thin ∼ **shadow** *v/t* follow closely, persistently and secretly, *esp* as spy or bodyguard; cast shadow on, shade; foreshadow, symbolize ∼ **shadow** *adj* ready to function if required but not now in use.

shadowing [*shad*O-ing] *n* gradation of light and colour; shading; act of keeping under close watch.

shadowy [*shad*O-i] *adj* full of shade; dark; insubstantial; dim, vague; mysterious.

shady [*shayd*i] *adj* sheltered from the sun; casting shade; not honest or legal, underhand; of bad reputation, semi-criminal.

shaft [*shaaft*] *n* long straight handle or stem of certain tools and weapons; long thin column; part of column between base and capital; ray of

light, beam; narrow vertical opening of a mine >
PDE; vertical air-vent; bar; stalk, stem; arrow,
spear; (*fig*) jibe, cutting jest; (*pl*) poles between
which a horse is harnessed to pull a vehicle.
shafting [shaa*f*ting] *n* system of shafts by which
power is transmitted.
shag (1) [shag] *n* crested cormorant.
shag (2) *n* cloth with a long coarse nap; strong
fine-cut tobacco; rough mass of hair.
shag (3) (*pres/part* **shagging**, *p/t* and *p/part*
shagged) *v/t* (*vulg sl*) copulate with.
shagged [shag*d*] *adj* shaggy; (*coll*) tired out.
shaggy [shag*i*] *adj* rough-haired; having long untidy hair or wool; unkempt ~ **shaggily** *adv* ~
shagginess *n*.
shagreen [shag*Reen*] *n* strong untanned leather
with granulated surface, made from horsehide,
sharkskin *etc*.
shah [shaa] *n* king of Iran.
shake (*p/t* **shook**, *p/part* **shaken**) [shay*k*] *v/t* and *i*
move quickly up and down or from side to side;
cause to sway or vibrate; jar; render weaker, less
stable or less firm; (*fig*) upset, disconcert, destroy
the confidence of; wave; flap; rock, sway;
tremble, quiver; trill; **s. down** cause to fall, settle
or become compact by shaking; settle in a makeshift bed; (*coll*) go to bed; **s. hands** grasp one
another's hand in greeting, parting, or sign of
agreement; **s. off** get rid of, free oneself from;
s. up stir by shaking; rouse from apathy or idleness ~ **shake** *n* act of shaking; single movement
of shaking; quiver, tremor; drink made by shaking up various ingredients together; (*mus*) trill;
(*coll*) very brief time; (*pl, coll*) alcoholic tremor;
no great shakes (*coll*) not particularly impressive.
shakedown [shay*k*down] *n* makeshift bed.
shaken [shay*k*en] *adj* upset, alarmed, disturbed;
suffering from shock.
shaker [shay*k*er] *n* one who or that which shakes;
container in which to mix drinks by shaking.
shake-up [shay*k*-up] *n* upheaval; complete rearrangement.
shakily [shay*k*ili] *adv* in a shaky way.
shakiness [shay*k*inis] *n* quality of being shaky.
shako [shak*O*] *n* cylindrical military hat with a
peak.
shaky [shay*k*i] *adj* liable to shake; unsteady, tottering; (*fig*) unreliable.
shale [shay*l*] *n* flaky rock of compressed clay >
PDG, PDE; oil extracted from bituminous shale.
shall (*p/t* **should**, no *p/part*) [shal] *v/aux* used to
denote futurity, promise, obligation, intention or
command.
shallop [shal*op*] *n* light open boat.
shallot [shal*ot*] *n* species of small onion.
shallow [shal*O*] *adj* not deep; (*fig*) trivial, superficial; slight ~ **shallow** *n* (*usu pl*) area of shallow
water, shoal ~ **shallow** *v/i* become shallow.
shallow-brained [shal*O*-bRaynd] *adj* weak-
minded; foolish; superficial, frivolous.
shallowly [shal*O*li] *adv* in a shallow way.
shallowness [shal*O*nis] *n* quality of being shallow.
shalom [shal*Om*] *interj* (*Heb*) peace be with you!
shaly [shay*l*i] *adj* of, like or containing shale.
sham (*pres/part* **shamming**, *p/t* and *p/part*
shammed) [sham] *v/t* and *i* feign, simulate;
make a pretence of ~ **sham** *n* false pretence,

imposture; faked article; counterfeit; impostor ~
sham *adj* pretended, feigned; faked, spurious.
shaman [sham*an*] *n* priest-magician in primitive
cultures, *esp* Eskimos, Lapps *etc*.
Shamanism [sham*anizm*] *n* form of religion aimed
at influencing good and evil by the magic of a
shaman; beliefs, rituals and magical techniques of
shamans ~ **Shamanist** *n* and *adj*.
shamble [shamb'l] *v/i* walk in an awkward shuffling way ~ **shamble** *n* shuffling walk.
shambles [shamb'lz] *n* (*pl*) slaughter-house;
butcher's stall; place of slaughter and bloodshed;
place or state of utter confusion.
shambolic [shambol*ik*] *adj* (*coll*) chaotic.
shame [shay*m*] *n* painful awareness of guilt,
humiliation, dishonour *etc*; sense of modesty,
decorum; disgrace; that which causes shame;
(*coll*) unfair happening, hard luck ~ **shame** *v/t*
make ashamed, disgrace; **s. into** cause to do by
making refusal shameful.
shamefaced [shay*m*fayst] *adj* ashamed of oneself;
self-conscious, shy.
shameful [shay*m*fool] *adj* causing shame; disgraceful, outrageous ~ **shamefully** *adv* ~
shamefulness *n*.
shameless [shay*m*les] *adj* not ashamed of one's
faults; hardened, brazen; immodest, boldly
indecent ~ **shamelessly** *adv* ~ **shamelessness** *n*.
shammy [sham*i*] *n* (*coll*) chamois leather.
shampoo [sham*pOO*] *n* special fluid or powder for
washing the hair; act of washing the hair ~
shampoo *v/t* wash (the hair) with shampoo; wash
(carpets, upholstery *etc*) with special soap; (*obs*)
massage (limbs) after a Turkish bath.
shamrock [sham*Rok*] *n* species of trefoil, the
national emblem of Ireland.
shandrydan [shand*Ridan*] *n* a rickety vehicle.
shandy [shand*i*] *n* shandygaff.
shandygaff [shand*igaf*] *n* mixture of beer and
ginger-beer.
shanghai [shangh*I*] *v/t* (*sl*) kidnap (a drugged,
drunk or stunned man) to work as a sailor; trick
or force into unwelcome work.
shank [shank] *n* shin, leg from knee to ankle; (*pl,
coll*) legs; handle of certain tools, shaft; long
middle part of anchor; **S.'s pony** (*joc*) walking
as a compulsory alternative transport.
shank-painter [shank-paynter] *n* (*naut*) rope or
chain fastening anchor to the ship's side.
shan't [shaant] *abbr* shall not.
shantung [shant*ung*] *n* coarse silk fabric, tussore.
shanty (1) [shant*i*] *n* small, crudely-built hut.
shanty (2), **chanty** *n* sailors' work-song, with
solo and chorus > PDM.
shantyman [shant*iman*] *n* leading singer in a
shanty.
shantytown [shant*itown*] *n* town or district of
dilapidated, crudely-built huts.
shape [shay*p*] *n* outward form, outline, figure;
something seen only as an outline; vague form;
apparition; embodiment; mould; that which has
been shaped in a mould; pattern; **in good (poor)
s.** in good (bad) condition; **take s.** become clearer,
more definite *etc*; find practical expression ~
shape *v/t* and *i* form, mould, give shape to;
make, create; become formed; grow clearer *etc*;

develop, turn out; **s. up to** advance against in boxing attitude; (*fig*) defy, challenge.

shape-changer [*shayp*-chaynger] *n* shape-shifter.

shaped [*shaypt*] *adj* having a specified shape.

shapeless [*shayp*les] *adj* having no regular form; without symmetry; loose, floppy; vague ∼ **shapelessly** *adv* ∼ **shapelessness** *n*.

shapely [*shayp*li] *adj* well-formed; well-proportioned.

shape-shifter [*shayp*-shifter] *n* wizard or witch who can turn into an animal at will.

shard [*shaard*] *n* broken piece of pottery; wing-case of a beetle.

share (1) [*shair*] *n* allotted portion of something owned by or distributed among several people; contribution towards joint expenses, common fund *etc*; part-ownership; contributory role; (*comm*) one of the equal portions into which the capital of a joint-stock company is divided; (*pl*) stock; **lion's s.** largest part ∼ **share** *v/t* and *i* divide into portions among several, distribute equally or justly; give away part of; use, incur or experience jointly; participate, play a part (in).

share (2) *n* blade of a plough.

shareholder [*shair*hOlder] *n* one who holds a share or shares in a joint-stock company.

share-pusher [*shair*-poosher] *n* one who offers shares, *esp* in unsound companies.

shark [*shaark*] *n* any of a large group of fierce voracious sea-fish; (*fig*) swindler, grasping and dishonest rogue ∼ **shark** *v/t* swindle.

sharkskin [*shaark*skin] *n* form of sleek heavy rayon; shagreen; skin of a shark.

sharp [*shaarp*] *adj* that can cut or pierce; pointed; having a cutting edge; steep; sudden, abrupt; intense; keen, piercing; harsh, severe; clearly outlined, distinct; eager; rapid; intelligent, alert; unscrupulous, dishonest; shrill; sour, acrid; sarcastic, snubbing, impatient; (*mus*) raised by one semitone ∼ **sharp** *n* (*mus*) sharp note; sign indicating that a note is to be played sharp > PDM; (*sl*) swindler, shark ∼ **sharp** *adv* quickly; punctually; alertly ∼ **sharp** *v/t* (*sl*) swindle.

sharp-cut [*shaarp*-kut] *adj* clearly-outlined.

sharpen [*shaarp*en] *v/t* and *i* make sharp; become sharp; intensify.

sharpener [*shaarp*ner] *n* device for sharpening pencil points; that which or one who sharpens.

sharper [*shaarp*er] *n* one who or that which sharpens; (*coll*) swindler, cheat, *esp* at cards.

sharp-eyed [*shaarp*-Id] *adj* having keen sight; quick to notice.

sharp-set [shaarp-*set*] *adj* having a keen appetite.

sharpshooter [*shaarp*shOOter] *n* skilled marksman; sniper.

sharpshooting [*shaarp*shOOting] *n* sniping.

sharp-witted [shaarp-*wit*id] *adj* having quick, keen intelligence.

shatter [*shat*er] *v/t* and *i* break at once into pieces; smash; (*fig*) destroy, ruin; weaken disastrously.

shave (*p/t* **shaved**, *p/part* **shaved** or **shaven**) [*shayv*] *v/t* and *i* cut hair from with a razor; remove with a razor; pare off in thin slices; graze, touch lightly or just miss touching; perform the act of shaving ∼ **shave** *n* act of shaving; process of being shaved; knife for shaving; thin slice; (*fig*) narrow escape.

shaver [*shayv*er] *n* one who, that which, shaves; (*coll*) youngster.

Shavian [*shayv*i-an] *adj* of or like Bernard Shaw.

shaving [*shayv*ing] *n* thin slice, *esp* of wood; paring; act of one who shaves.

shaving-brush [*shayv*ing-bRush] *n* brush for applying soap to the face before shaving.

shawl [*shawl*] *n* large square of fabric folded and draped over head or shoulders; square of knitted fabric for wrapping babies in.

shawm [*shawm*] *n* obsolete double-reed wind instrument > PDM.

shay [*shay*] *n* chaise.

she [*shee*] *pron* 3rd pers sing fem nom ∼ **she** *adj* female ∼ **she** *n* female; woman.

sheaf (*pl* **sheaves**) [*sheef*] *n* bundle of newly reaped corn, tied and set upright; bundle of papers *etc* tied together; enough arrows to fill a quiver.

shealing see **shieling**.

shear (1) [*sheer*] *n* stress applied to a body in the plane of one of its faces > PDS, PDE ∼ **shear** *v/i* be broken off by sideways pressure.

shear (2) (*p/t* **sheared** or **shore**, *p/part* **sheared** or **shorn**) *v/t* cut or clip off; remove nap or wool from; cut (hair *etc*) closely; cut off by one stroke.

shearing [*sheer*Ring] *n* act of removing with shears; that which is sheared off.

shearlegs [*sheer*legz] *n* apparatus for hoisting heavy weights, *esp* in dock-yards > PDE.

shears [*sheerz*] *n* (*pl*) double-bladed cutting instrument; large strong scissors.

shearwater [*sheer*wawter] *n* a seabird allied to the petrels.

sheath [*sheeth*] *n* long case for a sharp weapon or tool; scabbard; (*biol* and *bot*) enveloping membrane; wing-case; form of contraceptive device.

sheathe [*sheeTH*] *v/t* put into a sheath or scabbard; cover, protect with a case.

sheaves [*sheevz*] *pl* of **sheaf**.

shebang [*shibang*] *n* (*sl*) affair, matter, business; hut, house; shop; brothel.

shebeen [*shibeen*] *n* small sordid pub; place where illicit liquor is sold.

shed (1) (*pres/part* **shedding**, *p/t* and *p/part* **shed**) [*shed*] *v/t* let fall, drop; lose by moulting; cast off, rid oneself of; emit, pour forth; cause (blood) to flow; **s. blood** (*fig*) kill ∼ **shed** *n* parting, dividing line.

shed (2) *n* wooden hut; outhouse; small one-storey building for storage, animals *etc*.

she'd [*sheed*] *abbr* she had; she would.

shedding [*shed*ing] *n* that which has been shed; act of casting off, dropping *etc*.

sheen [*sheen*] *n* gloss, lustre.

sheeny (1) [*sheen*i] *adj* bright, glossy.

sheeny (2) *n* (*coll, pej*) Jew.

sheep (*pl* **sheep**) [*sheep*] *n* ovine ruminant with woolly coat and edible flesh; sheepskin; (*fig*) timid person; one who blindly follows a leader; member of a congregation; **black s.** disreputable person, unsatisfactory member (of family *etc*); **s.'s eyes** bashfully amorous glances; **s. and goats** saints and sinners, good people and bad; **lost s.** (*fig*) sinner.

sheepcote [*sheep*kOt] *n* small enclosure for sheep.

sheep-dip [*sheep*-dip] *n* liquid disinfectant for preserving the wool or killing vermin on sheep.

sheepdog [*sheep*dog] *n* dog trained to guard sheep; collie.

sheepfold [*sheep*fOld] *n* sheepcote.

sheep-hook [*sheep*-hook] *n* shepherd's crook.

sheepish [*sheep*ish] *adj* bashful, timid ~ **sheepishly** *adv* ~ **sheepishness** *n*.

sheep-run [*sheep*-Run] *n* large tract of land for sheep pasture.

sheepshank [*sheep*shank] *n* (*naut*) combination of two hitches for shortening a rope > PDSa.

sheep-shearing [*sheep*-sheerRing] *n* act of shearing sheep; time of year when sheep are sheared.

sheepskin [*sheep*skin] *n* skin and fleece of a sheep, *esp* when used as coat or rug; leather prepared from this; parchment made from this ~ **sheepskin** *adj*.

sheep-track [*sheep*-tRak] *n* path trodden by sheep.

sheep-walk [*sheep*-wawk] *n* tract of land for pasturing sheep.

sheer (1) [*sheer*] *adj* complete, unmixed, absolute; perpendicular, precipitous; (*of fabric*) transparent, very thin ~ **sheer** *adv* vertically, straight down; entirely.

sheer (2) *v/i* swerve aside; **s. off** (*coll*) turn aside, go away ~ **sheer** *n* (*naut*) deviation, swerve; upward curve.

sheer-hulk [*sheer*-hulk] *n* dismantled hull of a vessel fitted with shearlegs.

sheers [*sheerz*] *n* (*pl*) shearlegs.

sheet [*sheet*] *n* large piece of cotton, linen or nylon fabric spread on a bed; piece of paper; thin broad piece of any material; smooth flat expanse or surface; thin flattened piece of metal; (*coll*) newspaper; pamphlet; (*naut*) rope or chain controlling a sail; **blank s.** (*fig*) fresh mind open to receive impressions; **clean s.** record unspoilt by misconduct, unbroken record of good character; **dust s.** piece of cloth spread over furniture *etc* to keep dust off; **three sheets in the wind** (*coll*) visibly drunk; **winding s.** shroud ~ **sheet** *v/t* cover with a sheet ~ **sheet** *adj* (*of metals*) rolled out flat.

sheet-anchor [*sheet*-anker] *n* large emergency anchor; (*fig*) chief support; last refuge.

sheeting [*sheet*ing] *n* material for sheets; metal *etc* in sheet form; timber lining of banks *etc*.

sheet-lightning [*sheet*-lItning] *n* lightning in wide flashes.

sheikh [*sheek/shayk*] *n* Arab chieftain or headsman; Muslim title of respect.

sheila [*sheela*] *n* (*Aust coll*) girl, woman.

shekel [*shek*el] *n* old Hebrew weight; old Hebrew coin; (*pl*) (*coll*) cash, money.

Shekinah [*shek*Ina] *n* radiance denoting the presence of God, *esp* in Solomon's temple.

sheldrake [*sheld*Rayk] *n* a large wild sea-duck.

shelf (*pl* **shelves**) [*shelf*] *n* horizontal board fixed to a wall or forming one of a series in a cupboard, bookcase *etc*; projecting ledge; sandbank; reef; **on the s.** (*coll*) neglected, *esp* unmarried and unwooed.

shelf-life [*shelf*-lIf] *n* length of time stored food *etc* remains usable.

shelf-mark [*shelf*-maark] *n* code-mark on book showing its place in library.

shell [*shel*] *n* firm, hollow outer covering; hard exterior of bird's egg; husk, pod; outer casing of a nut; hard protective outer coat of molluscs, crabs, tortoises *etc*; such a coat, casing *etc* emptied of its contents; animal shell polished for ornamental use; anything whose contents have been lost or destroyed; ruined building with only walls intact; framework; (*mil*) cylindrical projectile with explosive charge, fired from large gun; cartridge; cartridge-case; (*naut*) hull; light racing skiff; (*phys*) orbit, or energy level, occupied by a group of electrons round a nucleus > PDS; (*fig*) shyness, reticence, unwillingness to communicate socially; (*poet*) lyre ~ **shell** *v/t* and *i* remove the shell from; bombard with shells, fire shells at; cast off a shell; **s. out** (*sl*) pay out, hand over (money).

she'll [*sheel*] *abbr* she will; she shall.

shellac [*shel*ak/*shel*ak] *n* coloured resin produced on tree bark by insects > PDS; varnish made from this ~ **shellac** *v/t* varnish with shellac; (*sl*) beat, defeat; abuse.

shellback [*shel*bak] *n* (*naut sl*) old sailor.

shellfish [*shel*fish] *n* any edible aquatic mollusc or crustacean.

shellshock [*shel*shok] *n* former name of various functional nervous disorders caused by experience of warfare > PDP ~ **shellshock** *v/t*.

shelta [*shelta*] *n* secret language of Irish and Welsh tinkers and gipsies.

shelter [*shelter*] *v/t* protect from harm, danger, hardship *etc*; shield; take refuge, seek protection; offer a place of safety, rest *etc* to ~ **shelter** *n* place or state of safety from harm, hardship *etc*; any structure, building, dug-out *etc* designed as protection against bombing; hut, shed *etc* offering protection from bad weather.

sheltie, shelty [*shelti*] *n* Shetland pony.

shelve (1) [*shelv*] *v/t* place on a shelf; defer, postpone indefinitely; fit with shelves.

shelve (2) *v/i* slope gradually.

shelves [*shelvz*] *pl* of **shelf**.

shelving (1) [*shelv*ing] *n* set of shelves; way or process of arranging books, goods *etc* on shelves.

shelving (2) [*shelv*ing] *adj* sloping gently.

shemozzle [*shimoz'l*] *n* (*sl*) uproar, row; trouble.

shenanigan [*shinan*igan] *n* (*coll*) uproar.

Sheol [*shee*-Ol] *n* (*bibl*) abode of the dead.

shepherd [*sheperd*] *n* one who tends sheep; (*fig*) priest, pastor, minister of religion; **the Good S.** Christ; **s.'s pie** meat and onions baked under a layer of mashed potato; **s.'s plaid** black and white checked cloth; **s.'s purse** a cruciferous annual wild plant ~ **shepherd** *v/t* gently drive or guide forward; tend; tend (sheep).

shepherdess [*sheperdes*] *n* female shepherd.

sherardize [*she*RaardIz] *v/t* coat iron or steel with zinc by a special process > PDS.

Sheraton [*she*Raton] *adj* (*of furniture*) designed by, or in the style of, the 18th-century cabinet-maker Sheraton.

sherbet [*shurbet*] *n* cooling Oriental drink of water and fruit juices; type of effervescing drink; effervescent powder.

sherd see **shard**.

shereef, sherif [*sheReef*] *n* title of honour given to descendants of Mohammed through Fatima.

sheriff [*sheRif*] *n* (*US*) elected county officer empowered to enforce law and order; (*hist*) judicial representative of the king in various shires and counties; **s. depute** (*Scots leg*) judge of certain courts; **High S.** honorary administrative and judicial official in certain cities and counties.

sherry [*she*Ri] *n* type of fortified brown wine from southern Spain; **s. cobbler** iced sherry with lemon and sugar.

she's [*sheez*] *abbr* she is; she has.

Shetland pony [shetland-*p*Oni] *n* very small variety of horse with flowing mane and tail.

sheva see **schwa**.

shew see **show**.

shewbread [*sh*Ob*R*ed] *n* showbread.

shibboleth [*shi*boleth] *n* petty or arbitrary test of social correctness; formula, tenet, attitude, custom *etc* enforced on all members of a group.

shied [*shi*d] *p/t* and *p/part* of **shy**.

shield [*sheeld*] *n* piece of defensive armour carried on the left arm to protect the body; protective covering, pad, screen, guard *etc*; (*fig*) defence, protection; protector; escutcheon; sports trophy shaped like a shield ~ **shield** *v/t* protect; protect (criminal or suspect) from the police; shelter.

shieling, shealing [*shee*ling] *n* mountain hut used by shepherds, sportsmen *etc*; small cottage, grazing ground.

shift [*shift*] *v/t* and *i* move from one place into another, alter position or direction (of); **move away**; get rid of; transfer; veer, change; (*coll*) go away; (*coll*) move fast; **s. for oneself** manage one's own affairs with no help from others ~ **shift** *n* change in position; alteration, variation; one of several groups of workmen taking turns at the same task; number of hours at work by one such group; rotation of crops; (*coll*) expedient, device; plan; woman's narrow waistless dress; (*ar*) woman's undergarment, chemise; **get a s. on** (*coll*) start working briskly; **make s. (to)** contrive, manage despite difficulties.

shifter [*shift*er] *n* one who shifts stage scenery.

shift-key [*shift*-kee] *n* device on typewriter to raise the platen for typing capitals *etc*.

shiftless [*shift*les] *adj* lacking in resource; feckless, incapable ~ **shiftlessly** *adv* ~ **shiftlessness** *n*.

shiftwork [*shift*wurk] *n* work in factory *etc* done at abnormally late or early hours, *esp* by night.

shifty [*shift*i] *adj* cunningly deceitful; evasive, unreliable; furtive ~ **shiftily** *adv* ~ **shiftiness** *n*.

shiksa [*shik*sa] *n* (*US sl*) Jewish term for a non-Jewish girl (*usu pej*).

shillelagh [*shi*layla] *n* cudgel made of oak or blackthorn.

shilling [*shi*ling] *n* British silver coin worth twelve old pence or five decimal pence, one twentieth of a pound sterling.

shilly-shally [*shi*li-shali] *n* indecision, hesitation ~ **shilly-shally** *v/i* hesitate.

shimmer [*shim*er] *v/i* give out a faint quivering light ~ **shimmer** *n* faint quivering light.

shimmery [*shim*eRi] *adj* that shimmers.

shimmy (1) [*shim*i] *n* (*coll*) chemise.

shimmy (2) *v/i* (*coll*) wobble, oscillate.

shin [*shin*] *n* front part of human leg between ankle and knee ~ **shin** (*pres/part* **shinning**, *p/t* and *p/part* **shinned**) *v/i* and *t* climb (up) by means of hands and legs; knock or kick the shin of.

shinbone [*shin*bOn] *n* tibia.

shindig [*shin*dig] *n* (*coll*) noisy party, dance *etc*; noisy quarrel, row.

shindy [*shin*di] *n* (*coll*) row, brawl disturbance.

shine (1) (*p/t* and *p/part* shone) [*shI*n] *v/i* and *t* give out or reflect bright light; glow; cause to shine, polish; look very happy; show great intelligence, wit *etc*; excel; be conspicuous for beauty, excellence *etc*; **s. at** be excellent at ~ **shine** *n* glossiness, polish; brilliance; sunshine; (*sl*) row; **take the s. out of** spoil the newness or brilliance of; (*fig*) humiliate.

shine (2) *n* (*US coll*) liking, fancy.

shiner [*shI*ner] *n* one who or that which shines; (*sl*) new coin; (*sl*) black eye.

shingle (1) [*shing*-g'l] *n* thin piece of wood used as a roofing tile; woman's short hairstyle set in regular waves ~ **shingle** *v/t* roof with shingles; set (woman's hair) in shingle waves.

shingle (2) *n* coarse loose pebbles on the seashore.

shingles [*shing*-g'lz] *n* (*pl*) acute inflammatory disease which spreads round the body.

shinny [*shin*i] *v/i* (*US coll*) **s. up** climb.

shinto [*shin*tO] *n* pre-Buddhist religion of Japan, blending nature- and ancestor-worship.

shiny [*shI*ni] *adj* bright, luminous; glossy ~ **shinily** *adv* ~ **shininess** *n*.

ship [*ship*] *n* large sea-going vessel; sailing vessel with at least three square-rigged masts; **s. of the desert** camel; **s. of the line** (*hist*) sailing ship carrying at least 74 guns; **take s.** embark; **when my s. comes home** when I grow rich ~ **ship** (*pres/part* **shipping**, *p/t* and *p/part* **shipped**) *v/t* and *i* transport or send by ship; enrol or accept as crew; embark; take into a ship or boat.

ship-biscuit [*ship*-biskit] *n* coarse hard biscuit.

shipboard [*ship*bawrd] *n* deck of a ship.

ship-breaker [*ship*-b*R*ayker] *n* contractor who breaks up old ships for the materials.

ship-broker [*ship*-b*R*Oker] *n* one who procures cargoes for, or insurance on, ships.

shipbuilder [*ship*bilder] *n* one who builds ships; naval architect.

ship-chandler [*ship*-chaandler] *n* one who sells stores and fittings for ships.

shipload [*ship*lOd] *n* amount of cargo, number of passengers *etc* that a ship carries.

shipmaster [*ship*maaster] *n* captain of a merchant vessel.

shipmate [*ship*mayt] *n* one who serves in the same ship with another; messmate.

shipment [*ship*ment] *n* act of putting anything on board ship for transport; goods shipped.

ship-money [*ship*-muni] *n* (*hist*) tax formerly charged on ports, towns *etc*.

shippen, shippon [*shi*pen] *n* cowhouse.

shipper [*shi*per] *n* one who sends goods by ship.

shipping [*shi*ping] *n* ships collectively, group of ships; act of transporting goods *etc* by ship.

shippon see **shippen**.

shipshape [*ship*shayp] *adj* well-arranged, neat ~ **shipshape** *adv* in good order; tidily.

ship's-husband [*ship*s-huzband] *n* shipowner's agent who attends to repairs, provisioning *etc*.

shipway [*ship*way] *n* wooden ramp from which ships are launched.

shipwreck [*ship*Rek] *n* destruction or great damage to a ship by storm, collision, running aground *etc*; wrecked hulk of a ship, *esp* if left stranded; (*fig*) ruin, loss, calamity ~ **shipwreck** *v/t* and *i* cause or suffer shipwreck; (*fig*) ruin; destroy or be destroyed.

shipwright [*ship*Rit] *n* shipbuilder; ship's carpenter.

shipyard [*ship*yaard] *n* yard where ships are built.

shire [*shIr*] *n* county, territorial division of the British Isles.

shire-horse [*shIr*-hawrs] *n* large breed of draught-horse.

shirk [*shurk*] *v/t* and *i* evade one's duty; unfairly avoid (danger, difficulty *etc*) ~ **shirker** *n*.

shirr [*shur*] *n* elastic thread sewn in a cloth to make it elastic; gathering, pucker ~ **shirr** *v/t* draw into gathers.

shirt [*shurt*] *n* loose thigh-length undergarment for men, with sleeves and fitted collar and cuffs; woman's blouse resembling this; **boiled s.** (*US*) stiffened shirt for formal wear; (*sl*) pompous fool; **have one's s. out** (*sl*) be in a bad temper; **in one's s. sleeves** wearing no jacket; **put one's s. on** (*coll*) bet very heavily on; **lose one's s.** lose heavily at gambling or betting.

shirt-front [*shurt*-fRunt] *n* starched front of a shirt; dickey.

shirting [*shurt*ing] *n* material for shirts.

shirt-tails [*shurt*-tayls] *n* (*pl*) lower part of shirt.

shirtwaist [*shurt*wayst] *n* type of blouse worn tucked under the belt of the skirt.

shirty [*shurt*i] *adj* (*sl*) bad-tempered.

shit [*shit*] *n* (*vulg*) dung; contemptible or unpleasant person ~ **shit** (*p/part* **shitting**, *p/t* **shat**, *p/part* **shat** or **shitten**) *v/t* and *i* (*vulg*) excrete dung.

shiv [*shiv*] *n* and *v/t* (*sl*) knife.

shiver (1) [*shiv*er] *v/i* tremble, quiver; shake with cold, fear *etc* ~ **shiver** *n* involuntary tremor; quiver; (*pl*, *coll*) continual shivering; irrational fear or horror.

shiver (2) *v/i* break into many small fragments, shatter ~ **shiver** *n* splinter, fragment.

shivery [*shiv*eRi] *adj* inclined to shiver; slightly feverish.

shoal (1) [*shOl*] *n* shallow place, submerged sandbank ~ **shoal** *v/i* become shallower.

shoal (2) *n* large number of fishes swimming together; (*fig*) large number, crowd; large quantity ~ **shoal** *v/i* form a shoal.

shock (1) [*shok*] *n* sudden violent impact; collision; jolt, jar; strong reaction of horror, disgust, agitation *etc* at an unpleasant experience; experience causing this; strong unpleasant surprise; nervous and physical collapse caused by violent emotion, physical injury *etc*; strong moral disapproval accompanied by disgust; violent disturbance of the nervous system caused by electric discharge through the body; **s. tactics** (*mil*) violent attack by a massed body of troops; (*fig*) action whose effectiveness depends on surprise; **s. treatment** treatment of certain mental disorders by electric shocks through the brain; **s. troops** troops trained for use in violent massed assaults; **s. wave** (*phys*) narrow region of high pressure and temperature in which air flow changes from subsonic to supersonic ~ **shock** *v/t* and *i* outrage the moral feelings of, scandalize; horrify, disgust; cause violent surprise to, overwhelm with agitation; give an electric shock to; jolt, shake by impact; meet with an impact.

shock (2) *n* pile of sheaves of grain ~ **shock** *v/t* collect sheaves into shocks.

shock (3) *n* thick mass of hair ~ **shock** *adj* shaggy.

shock-absorber [*shok*-absawrber] *n* device attached to the springs of a vehicle to lessen the effects of jolting over uneven ground.

shocker [*shok*er] *n* one who or that which shocks; sensationalist story or magazine; (*coll*) unpleasant person or thing; something of poor quality.

shock-headed [*shok*-hedid] *adj* having a thick mass of hair.

shocking [*shok*ing] *adj* morally offensive; scandalous; horrifying, disgusting; of poor quality, very bad ~ **shockingly** *adv*.

shockproof [*shok*pROOf] *adj* proof against violent jolts *etc* or against electric shocks; unlikely to be morally shocked.

shod [*shod*] *p/t* and *p/part* of shoe.

shoddy [*shodi*] *adj* made of cheap inferior material; petty, mean; worthless; sham ~ **shoddy** *n* coarse cloth made of old woollens unravelled; anything made of cheap inferior materials ~ **shoddily** *adv* ~ **shoddiness** *n*.

shoe [*shOO*] *n* outer covering for the foot, *usu* made of leather; metallic rim or plate nailed to the hoof of a horse, ass *etc* to protect it from injury; the part of a brake which touches the wheel; anything which resembles a shoe in shape or function; **another pair of shoes** quite another matter; **know where the s. pinches** know the meaning of trouble, sorrow *etc* from personal experience; **shake in one's shoes** be apprehensive, nervous ~ **shoe** (*p/t* and *p/part* **shod**) *v/t* furnish with shoes; cover at the bottom or at the tip with iron.

shoeblack [*shOO*blak] *n* one who cleans boots and shoes for a living; black shoepolish.

shoehorn [*shOO*hawrn] *n* appliance to assist one in putting on a shoe.

shoelace [*shOO*lays] *n* thong used as fastening for certain types of shoe.

shoemaker [*shOO*mayker] *n* one who makes or who deals in boots and shoes.

shoestring [*shOO*stRing] *n* shoelace; (*fig*) very inadequate allowance of money; **on a s.** very cheaply.

shoetree [*shOO*tRee] *n* piece of wood *etc* put in a shoe to keep it in shape when not worn.

shog (*pres/part* **shogging**, *p/t* and *p/part* **shogged**) [*shog*] *v/i* (*sl*) **s. off** go away.

shone [*shon*] *p/t* and *p/part* of shine.

shoo [*shOO*] *interj* be off! ~ **shoo** *v/t* drive away by crying 'shoo'.

shook [*shook*] *p/t* and *p/part* of shake.

shoon [*shOOn*] *n* (*pl*) (*ar*) shoes.

shoot (*p/t* and *p/part* **shot**) [*shOOt*] *v/t* and *i* hurl violently forward; project (a missile) from a weapon, *esp* arrow from bow, or bullet, shell *etc* from gun; kill or injure by shooting; thrust out rapidly; rush, dart quickly; flash, emit as darts; cause sharp throbbing pain; practise shooting of game as a sport; grow, *esp* rapidly; (*games*) send the ball directly at the goal; (*cricket*) increase in speed after hitting the ground; (*cin*) photograph, film; **s.!** (*coll*) speak out! begin!; **s. ahead** quickly outdistance others; **s. down** kill by gunfire; bring down (aircraft) by gunfire; **s. home** hit one's target; **s. a line** (*coll*) boast; **s. the moon** (*sl*) decamp by night to avoid paying rent; **s. off** discharge (gun); rush away; **s. one's bolt** make one's utmost effort; **s. up** grow very fast; rise rapidly; try to kill or injure by shooting ∼ **shoot** *n* act of shooting; new growth on plant, sprout; area of land where game is shot; shooting party; chute; **the whole s.** (*coll*) everything; **be shot of** (*coll*) be rid of.

shooter [*shOO*ter] *n* one who or that which shoots; (*cricket*) ball which shoots along the ground without bouncing; (*games*) player who aims the ball at the goal.

shooting [*shOO*ting] *n* act of one who shoots; act of firing guns or discharging arrows; game preserve; right to shoot game over an estate *etc* ∼ **shooting** *adj* that shoots; of or for shooting.

shooting-box [*shOO*ting-boks] *n* small house for use during the shooting season.

shooting-brake [*shOO*ting-bRayk] (*US*) *n* estate car.

shooting-gallery [*shOO*ting-galeRi] *n* small indoor firing-range.

shooting-range [*shOO*ting-Raynj] *n* place for practising shooting.

shooting-star [*shOO*ting-staar] *n* meteorite which has become incandescent by friction on entering earth's atmosphere > PDS.

shooting-stick [*shOO*ting-stik] *n* spiked walking-stick whose handle unfolds to form a seat.

shoot-out [*shOO*t-owt] *n* (*coll*) exchange of shots, *esp* between police and criminals.

shop [*shop*] *n* building in which goods are sold by retail; building in which manufacturing, repairs *etc* are carried out, workshop; (*fig*) one's business, profession *etc*; **all over the s.** scattered everywhere, in disorder; **talk s.** talk about one's business, profession or special interest ∼ **shop** (*pres/part* shopping, *p/t* and *p/part* shopped) *v/t* and *i* visit shops to purchase goods; (*sl*) inform against, betray to police; **s. around** compare merits of goods and terms offered in various shops before buying.

shop-assistant [*shop*-asistant] *n* one employed to sell goods in a retail shop.

shop-bell [*shop*-bel] *n* automatic bell which rings when the door of a shop is opened.

shopgirl [*shop*gurl] *n* girl employed as shop assistant.

shopkeeper [*shop*keeper] *n* owner of a shop; retailer of goods in a shop.

shopkeeping [*shop*keeping] *n* trade of selling retail goods.

shoplifter [*shop*lifter] *n* one who steals from a shop while pretending to purchase ∼ **shoplifting** *n*.

shopman (*pl* shopmen) [*shop*man] *n* shopkeeper; one employed in a shop; mechanic in a workshop.

shopper [*shop*er] *n* one who visits shops to buy goods.

shopping [*shop*ing] *n* act of visiting shops to purchase goods; goods purchased from shops; **s. bag (basket)** bag (basket) in which purchased goods are carried.

shop-soiled [*shop*-soild] *adj* damaged, dirtied, faded *etc* by handling or display in a shop.

shop-steward [*shop*-stew-ard] *n* trade union official in a workshop, factory *etc*.

shopwalker [*shop*wawker] *n* one employed in a large shop to supervise assistants, detect shoplifters *etc*.

shopworn [*shop*wawrn] *adj* shop-soiled.

shore (1) [*shawr*] *n* coast, land bordering on a large extent of water.

shore (2) *v/t* **s. up** prop up, support ∼ **shore** *n* thick beam used as a prop.

shoreward [*shawr*werd] *adj* and *adv* (moving) towards the shore.

shorn [*shawrn*] *p/part* of **shear**.

short [*shawrt*] *adj* not long, brief; not tall; not long or high enough; scanty, deficient; reduced; not well supplied; lasting only a brief while; concise; abrupt; curt; (*of clay, dough etc*) brittle; (*of spirits*) undiluted; (*comm*) maturing early; (*coll*) lacking money; (*phon, pros*) of comparatively brief duration; unstressed; (*cricket*) pitching further than normal from the wicket; **s. circuit** undesired path taken by electric current when brought in contact with a conductor of low resistance > PDS; **s. commons** low rations; **s. cut** unusual route that leads to one's destination more quickly than the normal one; **s. head** distance less than a head's length by which a horse *etc* wins a race; (*fig*) narrow victory; **s. list** list of candidates picked as suitable, from among whom a final choice will be made; **make s. work of** remove, defeat *etc* rapidly; **s. measure** less than had been bought, stipulated *etc*; **nothing s. of** no less than; **s. of** lacking, not having enough of; not reaching; **s. sight** myopia; **s. story** piece of fiction complete in itself but much briefer than a novel; **s. wave** (*rad*) wavelength less than 100 metres ∼ **short** *adv* abruptly, suddenly; in a short manner; **cut s.** curtail; interrupt; **fall s. be** inadequate, fail; **fall s. of** fail to reach; **s. of** except; **run s.** use up one's supplies (of); **stop s.** stop abruptly; **be taken s.** (*sl*) need to defecate with unexpected urgency ∼ **short** *n* that which is brief or short; brevity; short film; short circuit; **for s.** as an abbreviation; **the long and the s. of it** the whole thing briefly expressed ∼ **short** *v/t* and *i* cause or develop a short circuit.

shortage [*shawr*tij] *n* deficiency; lack; the amount lacking.

shortbread [*shawrt*bred] *n* brittle flat cake made with much butter and sugar.

shortcake [*shawrt*kayk] *n* shortbread.

short-circuit [shawrt-*surk*it] *v/t* and *i* (*elect*) cause shortening of electric circuit's path by accidental contact > PDS; develop or take a short circuit; (*fig*) by-pass, follow unusually direct procedure.

shortcoming [shawrt*kum*ing] *n* failure to reach a standard; defect, imperfection.

short-dated [shawrt-*day*tid] *adj* (*comm*) having little time to run.

shorten [*shawr*ten] *v/t* and *i* make or become short or shorter, curtail; reduce; contract.

shortfall [*shawrt*fawl] *n* deficit, amount by which something falls short of a target.

shorthand [*shawrt*-hand] *n* system of rapid writing using symbols and contractions to represent words or word groups; stenography.

shorthanded [shawrt-*hand*id] *adj* short of workmen, assistants *etc*, understaffed.

shorthorn [*shawrt*-hawrn] *n* breed of cattle with short horns.

short-leg [*shawrt*-leg] *n* (*cricket*) one who fields to leg, close in.

shortlist [*shawrt*list] *v/t* include in a selected list of candidates.

shortlived [*shawrt*livd] *adj* not lasting long.

shortly [*shawrt*li] *adv* before long, soon; briefly; curtly, abruptly.

shortness [*shawrt*nis] *n* state or quality of being short.

shorts [*shawrts*] *n* (*pl*) short trousers.

short-sighted [shawrt-*sI*tid] *adj* unable to see objects at a distance clearly, myopic; (*fig*) lacking foresight, unprepared for future developments ~ **short-sightedly** *adv* ~ **short-sightedness** *n*.

short-spoken [shawrt-*spO*ken] *adj* curt, abrupt.

short-tempered [shawrt-*temp*erd] *adj* quick-tempered, easily annoyed.

short-term [*shawrt*-turm] *adj* of or for a short period.

short-waisted [shawrt-*wayst*id] *adj* short in the waist; (*of clothes*) designed to make the wearer appear short in the waist.

short-winded [shawrt-*wind*id] *adj* easily out of breath.

shot (1) [*shot*] *p/t* and *p/part* of **shoot**.

shot (2) *n* act of shooting a firearm; noise of this; bullet; cannonball; lead pellet; range; attempt to shoot, throw, kick *etc* a missile at a target, goal *etc*; (*fig*) attempt; guess; (*coll*) injection; injected dose, *esp* of a stimulant drug; marksman; (*cin*) photograph; act of photographing; (*min*) blasting charge; **big s.** (*sl*) important person; **dead s.** one who never misses in shooting; **s. in the arm** (*coll*) anything that stimulates or gives energy; **s. in the dark** random guess; **have a s.** at try, attempt; **like a s.** very fast; gladly, willingly; **a long s.** remote possibility; unlikely guess; **out of s.** too far to be shot at.

shot (3) *adj* (*of fabrics*) woven so as to change colour when seen from different angles; iridescent; variegated.

shot (4) *n* share of expenses *etc*, contribution.

shotgun [*shotgun*] *n* light sporting gun firing lead pellets; **s. wedding** forced marriage of a man to a woman he has seduced, *esp* if she is pregnant.

should [*shood*] *p/t* of **shall**.

shoulder [*shOl*der] *n* joint where the arm, foreleg or wing joins the body; upper foreleg of an animal as cut for meat; strip of land bordering a road; anything shaped like a shoulder; (*pl*) upper part of the back; **s. to s.** closely side by side; (*fig*) united; **give the cold s. to** avoid, treat coldly, snub; **put one's s. to the wheel** work hard ~ **shoulder** *v/t* push with one's shoulder; thrust aside; lift on to the shoulder and carry; (*fig*) undertake responsibility for; **s. arms** (*mil*) carry (rifle) vertically in front of one shoulder.

shoulderbag [*shOl*derbag] *n* woman's handbag or shopping bag slung by a strap from the shoulder.

shoulderblade [*shOl*derblayd] *n* bone of the shoulder, scapula.

shoulder-bone [*shOl*der-bOn] *n* scapula.

shoulder-knot [*shOl*der-not] *n* ornamental knot of ribbon worn on the shoulders.

shoulder-strap [*shOl*der-stRap] *n* strap or ribbon suspending a garment, handbag *etc* from the shoulder; (*mil*) strap worn from collar to shoulder.

shouldn't [*shood*ent] *abbr* should not.

shout [*showt*] *n* loud call or cry ~ **shout** *v/i* and *t* call out loudly; speak extremely loudly; **s. down** drown another's words by talking loudly or shouting.

shove [*shuv*] *v/t* and *i* push roughly; jostle; (*coll*) put, place; **s. off** push (boat) from the shore; (*coll*) go away ~ **shove** *n* a strong push.

shove-halfpenny [shuv-*hayp*ni] *n* shovelboard played with coins.

shovel [*shuv*el] *n* broad blunt spade with slightly hollowed blade, used for lifting loose earth, snow, coal *etc*; scoop ~ **shovel** (*pres/part* **shovelling**, *p/t* and *p/part* **shovelled**) *v/t* and *i* lift or move with a shovel; use a shovel ~ **shovel** *adj* of or like a shovel; **s. hat** flat clerical hat.

shovelboard [*shuv*elbawrd] *n* game in which wooden discs are pushed along a board to a mark.

show, shew (*p/t* **showed, shewed,** *p/part* **shown, shewn, showed**) [*shO*] *v/t* and *i* cause to be seen, reveal, disclose; exhibit, display; make clear, demonstrate; bestow; guide, conduct; become visible, appear; **s. fight** prove ready to fight or resist; **s. off** exhibit ostentatiously; try to win admiration; boast; **s. out** accompany or guide to an exit; **s. up** expose the real (*usu* unpleasant) nature of, unmask; be clearly visible against contrasting background; (*coll*) be present, appear ~ **show** *n* that which is shown; act of showing; outward or false appearance; exhibition, display; spectacle; theatrical performance; pageant; (*coll*) any organization, performance, arrangement *etc*; **give the s.** away reveal hidden faults of; **s. of hands** vote taken by counting raised hands; **steal the s.** attract most attention ~ **show** *adj* (*coll*) fit for display; put on display, exhibited; excellent; of or in the theatrical profession; **s. piece** something well worth displaying; **s. place** beautiful place, *esp* one much visited by tourists.

showboat [*shO*bOt] *n* (*US*) river steamboat in which theatrical entertainments were given.

showbiz [*shO*biz] *n* (*coll abbr*) show business, the profession of theatrical entertainers.

showbread, shewbread [*shO*bRed] *n* (*OT*) twelve loaves of bread displayed in the Jewish Temple.

showcase [*shO*kays] *n* glass-topped or glass-fronted case containing articles displayed for sale or in a museum *etc*; (*fig*) place where the advantages of a social system *etc* can be observed.

showdown [*shO*down] *n* (*coll*) open trial of strength; open revelation of enmity; unmasking; final reckoning; (*cards*) moment when the cards of all hands are revealed.

shower (1) [*shO*-er] *n* one who or that which shows or exhibits.

shower (2) [*showr*] *n* brief fall of rain, hail or snow; sprinkling; heavy discharge of missiles; abundant flow, outpouring; showerbath ~ **shower** *v/t* and *i* cast or pour out in a shower; fall as a shower; give out abundantly and constantly.

showerbath [*showr*baath] *n* bath in which water is sprayed through a perforated tap overhead; act of washing in such a bath.

showery [*showr*Ri] *adj* with frequent showers of rain.

showgirl [*shO*gurl] *n* attractive girl employed as singer, dancer *etc* in music hall, nightclub *etc.*

showily [*shO*-ili] *adv* in a showy way.

showiness [*shO*-inis] *n* quality of being showy.

showing [*shO*-ing] *n* act of one who shows, display, presentation; declaration, affirmation; single presentation of a film.

show-jumping [*shO*-jumping] *n* display of skill in riding horses over or between obstacles.

showman (*pl* showmen) [*shO*man] *n* one who organizes and presents items in an entertainment, *esp* a circus; one skilled in attracting attention.

showmanship [*shO*manship] *n* skill or technique of a showman.

shown [*shOn*] *p/part* of show.

show-off [*shO*-of] *n* (*coll*) one who seeks admiration.

showpiece [*shO*pees] *n* excellent product or example publicly displayed.

showplace [*shO*plays] *n* beautiful place, house *etc* which people go to see.

showroom [*shOROOm*] *n* large room where goods are displayed for sale.

showy [*shO*-i] *adj* making a show; ostentatious, showing off; gaudy.

shrank [*shRank*] *p/t* of shrink.

shrapnel [*shRap*nel] *n* shell which scatters bullets or pieces of metal when it bursts; pieces scattered by this.

shred [*shRed*] *n* small piece cut or torn off; fragment; tiny particle ∼ **shred** (*pres/part* **shredding**, *p/t* and *p/part* **shredded**) *v/t* cut or tear into shreds; flake off in shreds.

shrew (1) [*shROO*] *n* bad-tempered woman.

shrew (2), *n* small burrowing mammal.

shrewd [*shROOd*] *adj* cunning, clever; piercing ∼ **shrewdly** *adv* ∼ **shrewdness** *n*.

shrewish [*shROO*-ish] *adj* (*of women*) sharp-tempered, inclined to scold and nag ∼ **shrewishly** *adv* ∼ **shrewishness** *n*.

shriek [*shReek*] *v/t* and *i* scream, utter a sharp, shrill cry; laugh wildly ∼ **shriek** *n* shrill cry.

shrievalty [*shReevalti*] *n* office or jurisdiction of a sheriff.

shrift [*shRift*] *n* (*ar*) confession to a priest and absolution; **short s.** (*fig*) summary treatment; lack of toleration.

shrike [*shRik*] *n* bird which preys on insects and impales them on thorns to be eaten later.

shrill [*shRil*] *adj* very high-pitched, piercing in tone; noisy; (*fig*) petulant ∼ **shrill** *v/t* and *i* utter a piercing sound; make a shrill noise ∼ **shrilly** *adv* ∼ **shrillness** *n*.

shrimp [*shRimp*] *n* small edible long-tailed crustacean; (*fig*) tiny person; pale pink colour ∼ **shrimp** *v/i* fish for shrimps.

shrine [*shRin*] *n* casket or chest for holy relics; church, chapel *etc* specially associated with a saint, holy statue, relic *etc*; ornamental structure round a holy statue; sacred place, place of pilgrimage.

shrink (*p/t* shrank, *p/part* shrunk) [*shRink*] *v/i* and *t* grow or cause to grow smaller; contract; shrivel; draw back, flinch; **s. from** retreat in fear or disgust from; be most unwilling to.

shrinkage [*shRink*ij] *n* reduction in size.

shrinking [*shRink*ing] *adj* timid; retiring ∼ **shrinkingly** *adv*.

shrive (*p/t* shrove, *p/part* shriven) [*shRiv*] *v/t* (*ar*) hear the confession of and absolve.

shrivel [*shRiv*el] *v/i* and *t* contract into wrinkles, wither.

shroud [*shRowd*] *n* cloth wrapped round corpse before burial; (*fig*) anything which covers or conceals; (*pl, naut*) ropes from masthead to sides of ship ∼ **shroud** *v/t* wrap in a shroud; (*fig*) conceal.

Shrovetide [*shROvtid*] *n* four days immediately before Lent.

Shrove Tuesday [*shROv-tewz*di] *n* the day before Ash Wednesday.

shrub (1) [*shRub*] *n* drink of sweetened lemon or other juices with rum.

shrub (2) *n* plant with woody stems branching from the root.

shrubbery [*shRub*eRi] *n* shrub plantation.

shrubby [*shRub*i] *adj* of or like a shrub.

shrug [*shRug*] *n* act of drawing up the shoulders to show dislike, doubt, indifference *etc* ∼ **shrug** (*pres/part* **shrugging**, *p/t* and *p/part* **shrugged**) *v/t* and *i* make this gesture; **s. off** contemptuously refuse to consider, make light of.

shrunk [*shRunk*] *p/part* of shrink.

shuck [*shuk*] *n* shell, pod ∼ **shuck** *v/t* remove shell, pod *etc* from ∼ **shucks** *interj* (*US*) nonsense!

shudder [*shud*er] *v/i* shiver suddenly; quake, tremble violently ∼ **shudder** *n* a shaking with horror or disgust.

shuffle [*shuf*'l] *v/t* and *i* change the positions of; move (cards) over each other to mix them up; throw into disorder; speak evasively; move with a dragging, irregular walk; **s. off** get rid of ∼ **shuffle** *n* act of shuffling; act of mixing up cards; a step in ballroom-dancing; evasion; trick.

shun (1) (*pres/part* **shunning**, *p/t* and *p/part* **shunned**) [*shun*] *v/t* avoid, keep away from.

'shun (2) *abbr* (*mil*) attention!

shunt [*shunt*] *v/t* turn (trains) on to a side line; (*fig*) get rid of; push out of the way ∼ **shunt** *n* act of shunting; device for altering the amount of electric current flowing through an apparatus; (*surg*) alternative route for circulation of blood.

shush [*shush*] *interj* and *v/t* and *i* (*coll*) hush.

shut (*pres/part* **shutting**, *p/t* and *p/part* **shut**) [*shut*] *v/t* and *i* close, fasten; block the opening of; fold up; lock up; confine, imprison; exclude; become closed; be capable of closing; close of its own accord; **s. away** keep confined or hidden; **s. down** cease working; stop the working of (factory, business *etc*); **s. in** imprison; enclose; limit access to; **s. off** stop the flow of, *esp* by a switch, valve *etc*; keep separate; **s. one's eyes to** refuse to notice; **s. one's mouth** keep silent, keep a secret; **s. out** exclude, keep out; hide from view; **s. up** close firmly; keep under lock and key; leave (house *etc*) locked up and empty; (*coll*) stop talking; force to stop talking ∼ **shut** *adj* closed.

shutdown [*shut*down] *n* stoppage, *esp* of work in factory.

shut-eye [*shut*-I] *n* (*sl*) nap, short sleep.

shut-out [*shut*-owt] *n* lockout.

shutter [*shut*er] *n* that which shuts; wooden outer cover for a window; device for screening the lens in a camera ∼ **shutter** *v/t* close or fit with a shutter.

shuttle [*shut*'l] *n* weaver's instrument for passing the thread of the weft through the warp; sliding thread-holder in a sewing-machine; **s. service**

train or bus service going to and fro along one fairly short line ~ **shuttle** *v/i* move backwards and forwards regularly between two places.

shuttlecock [*shut*'l-kok] *n* feathered ball used in game of badminton; (*fig*) something continually tossed to and fro.

shva see **schwa**.

shy (1) [*shI*] *adj* timid, *esp* of social contacts; bashful; reserved; wary, suspicious; careful; elusive; **fight s. of** avoid ~ **shy** (*p/t* and *p/part* **shied**) *v/i* swerve suddenly in fear; **s. at** be unwilling to face or do.

shy (2) (*p/t* and *p/part* **shied**) *v/t* (*coll*) throw, fling ~ **shy** (*pl* **shies**) *n* (*coll*) act of throwing; attempt; target at which things are thrown for sport.

shyly [*shI*li] *adv* timidly.

shyness [*shI*nis] *n* timidity.

shyster [*shI*ster] *n* (*US*) unscrupulous lawyer.

si [*see*] *n* (*mus*) seventh note of the sol-fa scale; seventh note in the scale of C major, B.

Siamese [*sI*-ameez] *n* native of Siam; language of Siam ~ **Siamese** *adj* of or from Siam; S. **cat** slender cream-coloured brown-faced cat; S. **twins** twins linked to each other at birth by a fleshy ligament.

sib [*sib*] *adj* (*ar*) related by blood (to).

sibilant [*sibi*lant] *n* and *adj* (consonant) uttered with a hissing sound.

sibilation [sibi*lay*shon] *n* act of hissing.

sibling [*sib*ling] *n* brother or sister.

sibyl [*sibi*l] *n* (*Rom myth*) prophetess; (*fig*) witch; fortune-teller; old hag.

sibylline [*sibi*lIn] *adj* of or uttered by a sibyl; prophetic; cryptic, mysterious.

sic [*sik*] *adv* (*Lat*) thus, so.

siccative [*sik*ativ] *n* and *adj* (substance) causing drying.

sick [*sik*] *adj* ill, suffering from some disease; of or for those who are ill; vomiting; nauseated, wishing to vomit; disgusted; (*coll*) furious; disappointed; weary; (*of jokes*) sinister, macabre, disgusting; **s. at heart** very sad; **s. for** (*poet*) longing for; **s. of** tired of, bored by, exasperated by ~ **sick** *n* (*pl*) those who are ill ~ **sick** *v/t* **s. up** (*coll*) vomit.

sickbay [*sik*bay] *n* infirmary, *esp* on board ship.

sickbed [*sik*bed] *n* bed occupied by a sick person.

sick-call [*sik*-kawl] *n* summons to doctor *etc* to visit a sick person.

sicken [*sik*en] *v/i* and *t* grow ill; show early symptoms of illness; make sick; disgust; **s. of** grow tired of.

sickening [*sik*ening] *adj* showing first symptoms of illness; (*coll*) disgusting; very disappointing or annoying ~ **sickeningly** *adv*.

sickle [*sik*'l] *n* reaping implement with curved blade and short handle.

sickle-feather [*sik*'l-feTHer] *n* long curved feather in a cock's tail.

sick-leave [*sik*-leev] *n* leave of absence because of illness.

sickliness [*sik*linis] *n* state of being sickly.

sicklist [*sik*list] *n* list of sick persons.

sickly [*sik*li] *adj* often ill, weak in health; unhealthy, causing sickness; faint, weak-looking; mawkish, sentimental ~ **sickly** *adv* in a sick manner.

sickness [*sik*nes] *n* state of being sick: illness;

disease; **s. benefit** insurance allowance paid to those out of work through illness.

sick-pay [*sik*-pay] *n* pay given by employer to employee during absence due to illness.

side [*sId*] *n* external surface, *esp* that which lies to the left or right of the longest axis of an object; either surface of a thin flat object; area, space or bulk lying to the left or right of a dividing line; edge, margin; one of two opposing groups, parties, points of view *etc*; (*fig*) aspect, point of view; area between ribs and hip of human body; bank of river, lake *etc*; shore; slope of hill or mountain; line of descent through one parent; (*sl*) boastful, proud or patronizing attitude; (*billiards*) sideways rotation of cue ball; **take sides** form hostile groups (in a dispute); **take sides with** join the party of, support ~ **side** *adj* on one side; lateral; oblique; indirect; minor, subordinate.

sidearms [*sId*aarmz] *n* (*pl*) light firearms carried on the person.

sideband [*sId*band] *n* (*rad*) group of waves of frequencies just below or above that of a transmitter.

sideboard [*sId*bawrd] *n* piece of furniture used in dining-rooms and serving as both cupboard and table; (*pl, coll*) short whiskers.

sideburns [*sId*burnz] *n* (*pl*) (*coll*) short whiskers.

sidecar [*sId*kaar] *n* small carriage for one person attached to the side of a motor-bicycle.

side-dish [*sId*-dish] *n* extra course at a meal.

side-drum [*sId*-dRum] *n* small drum.

side-effect [*sId*-i*fekt*] *n* unintended effect that accompanies the intended effect, *esp* unpleasant effect of a drug.

side-issue [*sId*-ishOO] *n* minor or irrelevant matter.

sidekick [*sId*kik] *n* (*US sl*) subordinate; junior partner.

sidelight [*sId*lIt] *n* light shining from one side; lamp placed on the side of (vehicle, ship *etc*); incidental, indirect or unusual information adding to one's knowledge of a subject.

sideline [*sId*lIn] *n* activity, business *etc* pursued as a secondary occupation; goods sold in addition to one's main type of stock; rope attached to the side of anything; (*pl*) area immediately outside the boundary lines of tennis-court, football-pitch *etc*; area for spectators at sport.

sidelong [*sId*long] *adj* sideways, to one side, oblique ~ **sidelong** *adv*.

sidereal [sI*deer*Ri-al] *adj* of the stars; measured by the apparent movement of the stars.

siderite [*side*RIt] *n* natural ferrous carbonate > PDS; iron meteorite; blue quartz.

siderod [*sId*Rod] *n* coupling rod of railway engine.

sidesaddle [*sId*sad'l] *n* horse's saddle so made that both legs of the rider are on the same side of the horse ~ **sidesaddle** *adv* riding on a sidesaddle.

sideshow [*sId*shO] *n* display, exhibition *etc* of minor importance; sideline; activity of secondary importance; entertainment at a fair.

sideslip [sɪdslip] n skid, act of slipping sideways ~ **sideslip** v/i.

sidesman (pl **sidesmen**) [sɪdzman] n assistant churchwarden.

side-splitting [sɪd-spliting] adj extremely laughable.

sidestep [sɪdstep] n act of stepping sideways, esp to avoid something ~ **sidestep** v/t and i avoid (blow etc) by stepping sideways; (fig) evade.

sidestroke [sɪdstROk] n overhand stroke at swimming; any stroke made sideways.

sidetrack [sɪdtRak] n railway siding ~ **sidetrack** v/t shunt on to a siding; (coll) divert the attention of, confuse with irrelevancies; divert from intended action, investigation etc.

sideview [sɪdvew] n profile, view from one side.

sidewalk [sɪdwawk] n (US) pavement along a road.

sideways [sɪdwayz] adv and adj towards or on one side.

sidewind [sɪdwind] n a wind from the side; an indirect influence.

siding [sɪding] n act of taking sides; short line of rails beside a main railway line used for shunting.

sidle [sɪd'l] v/i move sideways; move in a cringing, fawning manner.

siege [seej] n (mil) act of encamping round a fortified town etc with an army to force it to surrender; duration of this; state of being besieged; (fig) persistent efforts to win favour, love etc; (ar) throne, seat.

siege-gun [seej-gun] n heavy gun used for battering fortifications.

sienna [si-ena] n brownish-yellow pigment composed of clay coloured with iron and manganese.

sierra [see-eRa] n (Sp) long jagged chain of mountains.

siesta [see-esta] n (Sp) short sleep during the early afternoon.

sieve [siv] n framework containing a taut mesh or network for separating solids from liquids or large particles from small; (fig) one who cannot keep secrets; **have a head like a s.** be very forgetful ~ **sieve** v/t pass through a sieve, sift.

sift [sift] v/t and i separate by passing through a sieve; sprinkle in fine particles; examine very carefully.

sifter [sifter] n perforated container for sprinkling sugar, pepper etc on food.

sigh [sɪ] v/i take in a deep breath and let it out slowly and audibly; express grief, fatigue, relief etc by this act; make a sound like this; **s. for** long for, yearn for; grieve over ~ **sigh** n act or sound of sighing.

sight [sɪt] n ability to see, vision; act of seeing, perception by eye; that which is seen; spectacle, view; that which is worth seeing; (coll) something odd or ridiculous to look at; (coll) large amount; device or apparatus fixed to a gun so that it can be exactly aimed; range of vision; (fig) judgement, point of view; (pl) places etc of unusual interest and worth visiting; **at (first) s.**, **on s.** as soon as seen; according to a first impression; **in s.** near enough to be seen, visible; approaching; **keep s. of** keep near enough to see; watch; bear in mind; **know by s.** be able to recognize, but have no personal acquaintance with; **lose s. of** no longer see; forget; **out of s.** too far

to be seen; hidden ~ **sight** v/t and i see, esp for the first time; get near enough to see; aim by using the sight of (a gun etc).

sighted [sɪtid] adj not blind; (of gun) equipped with a sight.

sightless [sɪtles] adj unable to see, blind; (poet) invisible ~ **sightlessly** adv ~ **sightlessness** n.

sightly [sɪtli] adj pleasant to look at.

sight-reader [sɪt-Reeder] n one who reads music, languages etc at sight.

sightseeing [sɪtsee-ing] n act of visiting and inspecting places, objects etc of notable interest.

sightseer [sɪtsee-er] n one who goes sightseeing.

sign [sɪn] n that which conveys meaning, indication; gesture conveying meaning; any written or inscribed mark, other than words, conveying a specific meaning; token, symbol; evidence; portent, omen; miracle; roadside post or board carrying information, warnings etc for traffic; signpost; pictorial board, device etc outside an inn or shop as advertisement; password; (astron) one of twelve divisions of the zodiac; constellation in this; (math) mark indicating a mathematical process > PDS; **s. of the cross** gesture of the hand tracing the shape of a cross, used as Christian gesture of blessing or prayer ~ **sign** v/t and i write one's name (on) as signature; indicate by sign or gesture; mark with a sign, esp the sign of the cross; **s. away** transfer, resign etc by formal document; **s. off** (coll) conclude; depart; (rad) cease transmitting; **s. on** enter into contract of employment; **s. up** enlist; hire, appoint or employ under contract.

signal [signal] n any act, word etc agreed on as marking the moment when some action is to be done; device for communicating at a distance; lights, flags, indicator boards etc for regulating movements of traffic, trains etc; message conveyed by objects or actions; message, esp nonverbal, transmitted by radio; (astron) emission of radio waves ~ **signal** (pres/part **signalling**, p/t and p/part **signalled**) v/t and i express by a signal; make a signal (to) ~ **signal** adj noteworthy, remarkable; conspicuous.

signalbox [signalboks] n raised hut from which railway signals, points etc are worked.

signalize [signalIz] v/t make remarkable; indicate the remarkableness of.

signaller [signaler] n one who signals, esp soldier.

signally [signali] adv remarkably.

signalman (pl **signalmen**) [signalman] n one who works railway signals.

signatory [signateRi] n one who signs a document, esp as representative of a State ~ **signatory** adj.

signature [signacher] n name, initials or mark of a person written by himself; (print) sign indicating order of sheets of a book; (mus) sign that shows the key; **s. tune** tune regularly used to introduce a broadcast serial, variety performer etc.

signboard [sɪnbawrd] n board displaying the name or pictorial device of an inn, shop etc.

signet [signit] n small seal; **Writer to the S.** Scottish law officer.

signet-ring [signit-Ring] n finger-ring set with a signet.

significance [signifikans] n quality of being significant; meaning; importance.

significant [signifikant] adj expressive of something; suggesting a deeper meaning; indicating something important ~ **significantly** adv.

signification [signifi*k*ayshon] n act of signifying; that which is signified; exact meaning or implication.

signify [*signif*I] v/t and i make known, communicate; represent by signs or symbols; mean, denote; matter, be of importance.

sign-manual [sIn-*man*ew-al] n royal signature; autograph signature.

signor [seen*yawr*] n Italian form of address to a man.

signora [seen*yaw*Ra] n Italian form of address to a married woman.

signorina [seenyaw*Ree*na] n Italian form of address to an unmarried woman.

signpost [*sIn*pOst] n post erected at crossroads indicating directions and distances to nearby places; post bearing a traffic sign; (fig) guiding indication ~ **signpost** v/t provide (roads) with signposts; provide indications of direction (for).

Sikh [seek] n member of a Hindu monotheistic, casteless and military community of the Punjab.

silage [*sI*lij] n cattle-fodder partly fermented and stored in a silo > PDS.

silence [*sI*lens] n absence of noise, state of being silent; act of refraining from speech, absence of speech; act of not speaking about a particular subject; secrecy; absence of mention or communication ~ **silence** v/t cause to be silent; prevent from speaking; defeat in argument; (fig) repress, prevent from being expressed.

silencer [*sI*lenser] n one who or that which silences; device for reducing the noise of exhaust fumes from motor engines; device to muffle the report of a gun.

silent [*sI*lent] adj not speaking; not making any sound, noiseless; still, peaceful; not mentioning a particular subject; taciturn, reticent; (phon) not pronounced ~ **silently** adv.

silex [*sI*leks] n flint; silica.

silhouette [silOO-*et*] n profile, outline, esp of an object seen as dark against a bright background; portrait in profile done in solid black against a white background ~ **silhouette** v/t depict in silhouette.

silica [*sil*ika] n hard white or colourless mineral with a high melting point > PDS.

silicate [*sil*ikayt] n salt of silicic acid > PDS; rock chiefly composed of the silicate of a metal.

siliceous [*silish*-us] adj of silica; flinty.

silicic [*silis*ik] adj pertaining to silica.

silicon [*sil*ikon] n non-metallic element similar to carbon > PDS.

silicone [*sil*ikOn] n (chem) one of various polymerized compounds of silicon and hydrocarbon radicals used in lubricants, polishes, lacquers etc.

silicosis [sili*k*Osis] n (path) lung disease caused by inhaling gritty dust.

silk [silk] n fine lustrous thread produced by the pupae of certain moths; soft lustrous fabric made from this; garment made of this, esp robe of a Queen's Counsel; **artificial s.** rayon; **s. hat** top hat covered with silk plush; **take s.** become a Queen's Counsel ~ **silk** adj made of silk.

silken [*silk*en] adj made of silk; like silk; soft; delicate.

silkily [*silk*ili] adv in a silky way.

silkiness [*silk*inis] n quality of being silky.

silkscreen [*silk*skreen] n method of stencil printing through a piece of silk fabric.

silkworm [*silk*wurm] n caterpillar of the moth which produces silk.

silky [*silk*i] adj like silk; glossy, soft; suave.

sill [sil] n block of timber or stone at the base of a door or of a window; (geol) sheet of igneous rock between two layers of sedimentary rock > PDG.

sillabub, syllabub [*sil*abub] n mixture of wine or cider and cream or milk.

silly [*sil*i] adj foolish, lacking intelligence; frivolous, superficial, trivial; stupidly weak or trusting; imbecilic; (ar) innocent, simple ~ **silly** n (coll) silly person ~ **sillily** adv ~ **silliness** n.

silo [*sI*lO] n airtight tower or pit in which green fodder is pressed and preserved; deep pit in which a rocket is stored ready for firing.

silt [silt] n deposit of fine sediment in water ~ **silt** v/t and i fill (up) with silt.

silurian [sil*ewr*Ri-an] adj (of Paleozoic rocks) immediately below the Devonian.

silvan see **sylvan**.

silver [*silv*er] n a white precious metal element > PDS; objects made of or plated with this; coin containing silver alloy; cupro-nickel coin; lustrous white or pale grey colour; **s. gilt** silver article plated with gold ~ **silver** adj made of silver; of a cold lustrous white or pale grey; having a clear, high-pitched ringing sound; (fig) eloquent; **S. Age** (myth) second and inferior age in the world's history; (fig) period comparatively inferior; **s. jubilee** twenty-fifth anniversary of a coronation; **s. lining** sunlit edge of a dark cloud; (fig) prospect of future happiness after present grief; consolation; **s. paper** thin glossy white tinfoil; **s. sand** fine white sand; **s. screen** cinema screen; **s. wedding** twenty-fifth anniversary of wedding ~ **silver** v/t coat with silver; give silvery colour or gloss to.

silver-bath [*silv*er-baath] n solution of silver nitrate in which photographic plates are sensitized.

silverfish [*silv*erfish] n species of silvery-coloured wingless insect.

silver-fox [*silv*er-foks] n variety of fox with white-tipped black fur.

silver-grey [*silv*er-gRay] adj and n lustrous grey.

silver-haired [*silv*er-haird] adj having grey or white hair.

silvering [*silv*eRing] n art or process of coating with silver; silver coating.

silver-plating [silver-*play*ting] n process of depositing a layer of silver, generally by electrolysis.

silverpoint [*silv*erpoint] n technique of drawing on specially prepared paper with silver wire > PDAA; drawing so made.

silverside [*silv*ersId] n top side of a round of beef.

silversmith [*silv*ersmith] n one who makes or sells articles of silver.

silverware [*silv*erwair] n articles of silver.

silverweed [*silv*erweed] n any of various plants with silvery leaves.

silvery [*silv*eRi] adj like silver; lustrous; covered with silver; (of sounds) sweet and clear.

simian [*sim*i-an] adj of anthropoid apes; looking like an ape.

similar [*sim*iler] adj like, resembling, alike; (geom) having corresponding angles equal.

similarity [simila̱Riti] *n* state of being similar, likeness.

similarly [si̱milerli] *adv* in a similar way.

simile [si̱mili] *n* figure of speech in which one thing is explicitly compared to another.

similitude [simi̱litewd] *n* likeness, resemblance; comparison; counterpart.

simmer [si̱mer] *v/t* and *i* boil gently; be just below boiling-point; (*coll*) be filled with barely controlled anger or excitement; s. down (*coll*) calm down ~ simmer *n* state of simmering.

simnel [si̱mnel] *n* type of rich fruit cake covered with almond paste.

simoniac [simO̱ni-ak] *n* one who is guilty of simony.

simony [si̱moni] *n* crime of buying or selling church preferment; sin of making money out of religious privileges.

simoom [simO̱Om] *n* hot, dry desert wind.

simp [simp] *n* (*sl*) simpleton.

simper [si̱mper] *v/i* smile coyly, self-consciously or insincerely ~ simper *n* simpering smile.

simple [si̱mp'l] *adj* easy to do or understand; not elaborate, rich or highly decorated; plain, austere; sincere, honest, frank; unsophisticated; easily deceived; foolish, feeble-minded; of low birth, plebeian; thorough, absolute; mere; unmixed, not compound or complex; pure and s. absolute ~ simple *n* (*ar*) uncompounded herbal medicine.

simple-minded [simp'l-mI̱ndid] *adj* frank; unsuspecting, credulous; feeble-minded, mentally defective.

simpleness [si̱mpelnis] *n* simplicity.

simpleton [si̱mp'lton] *n* imbecile; credulous fool.

simplicity [simpli̱siti] *n* quality or state of being simple.

simplify [si̱mplifI] *v/t* make easy or easier; (*math*) reduce to its simplest terms.

simplistic [simpli̱stik] *adj* over-simplified, naive.

simply [si̱mpli] *adv* in a simple manner; easily; without ostentation; without adornment; merely; (*coll*) absolutely.

simulacrum ʲ[simewla̱ykRum] *n* deceptive representation, sham; image.

simulate [si̱mewlayt] *v/t* mimic, imitate; pretend to be.

simulation [simewla̱yshon] *n* act of simulating.

simultaneity [simultane̱e-iti] *n* quality of being simultaneous.

simultaneous [simulta̱yni-us] *adj* happening at the same time ~ simultaneously *adv* ~ simultaneousness *n*.

sin [sin] *n* violation of a God-given, religious or moral rule; wickedness; immorality; tendency to commit sins; offence; (*coll*) something foolish and regrettable; besetting s. sin one habitually commits; live in s. cohabit though unmarried; original s. inherent human tendency to commit sins; the first human sin, Adam's sin ~ sin (*pres/part* sinning, *p/t* and *p/part* sinned) *v/i* commit sin.

since [sins] *adv* from a certain time until now; before this; ago ~ since *prep* from the time of; during the time after ~ since *conj* from the time when; because.

sincere [sinse̱er] *adj* frank, honest; genuine; not feigned, true ~ sincerely *adv* ~ sincereness *n*.

sincerity [sinse̱Riti] *n* quality of being sincere; honesty; truth, genuineness.

sine [sIn] *n* (*math*) ratio of the side opposite a given angle in a right angle triangle to the hypotenuse; straight line drawn from one extremity of an arc perpendicular to the diameter drawn through the other extremity; s. wave periodic oscillation having the same geometric representation as a graph of a sine function.

sinecure [sI̱nikewr] *n* paid job involving little or no work; (*eccles*) benefice without cure of souls.

sinew [si̱new] *n* tendon, tissue which unites muscle to bone; (*pl*) muscles; (*fig*) anything which gives strength.

sinewy [si̱newi] *adj* having sinews; muscular; strong, vigorous.

sinful [si̱nfool] *adj* committing or having committed sin; being a sin, involving sin ~ sinfully *adv* ~ sinfulness *n*.

sing (*p/t* sang, *p/part* sung) [sing] *v/t* and *i* utter with musical pitch and inflexions of voice; utter tuneful notes; make a shrill buzz or ringing sound; speak with strong changes of intonation; (*fig*) rejoice; (*poet*) compose poetry (about); s. a different tune behave or speak very differently; s. out (*coll*) shout; s. praises of praise highly; s. small (*coll*) behave humbly.

singe [sinj] *n* slight superficial burn ~ singe *v/t* and *i* burn slightly; scorch.

singer [si̱nger] *n* one who sings, *esp* as a profession.

Singhalese, Cingalese, Sinhalese [sing-gale̱ez, sinale̱ez] *n* and *adj* (person or language) of an Aryan people inhabiting Sri Lanka (formerly Ceylon).

single [si̱ng-g'l] *adj* one only; by, of, or for one person only; of or by one pair of persons only; unmarried; sincere, wholehearted; not double, complex or compound; separate, individual ~ single *v/t* s. out select as best, pick out (one person *etc*) ~ single *n* (*sport*) game between one pair only.

single-breasted [si̱ng-g'l-bre̱stid] *adj* (*of clothes*) with only one thickness of material covering the breast.

single-entry [si̱ng-g'l-e̱ntRi] *n* (*comm*) method of book-keeping in which a transaction is entered under one account only.

single-handed [si̱ng-g'l-ha̱ndid] *adj* working alone; unaided; using only one hand.

single-hearted [si̱ng-g'l-haa̱rtid] *adj* honest, sincere; wholehearted, devoted.

single-minded [si̱ng-g'l-mI̱ndid] *adj* intent on one purpose.

singleness [si̱ng-g'lnis] *n* state of being one only; sincerity.

singlestick [si̱ng-g'lstik] *n* long stick used for sword-exercise.

singlet [si̱ng-glit] *n* man's vest.

singleton [si̱ng-g'lton] *n* a single card of a suit in a hand; (*fig*) one isolated specimen or instance.

singly [si̱ng-gli] *adv* one by one, one at a time; without helper, by oneself; unmarried.

singsong [si̱ngsong] *n* session of cheerful unrehearsed singing by a group, *usu* of amateurs; drawling tone of voice with monotonous or exaggerated intonations ~ singsong *adj* speaking in a monotonous drawl.

singular [si̱ng-gewlar] *adj* remarkable, unusual;

odd, strange; relating to or denoting a single person or thing; (*leg*) separate, individual ~ **singular** *n* (*gramm*) form indicating that a word refers only to one person or thing.

singularity [sing-gewlaRiti] *n* peculiarity; strangeness.

singularize [sing-gewlaRIz] *v/t* make singular.

singularly [sing-gewlerli] *adv* remarkably; oddly; particularly, outstandingly.

Sinhalese see **Singhalese**.

sinister [sinister] *adj* indicating or threatening future evil, ominous; mysteriously wicked; treacherous, dangerous; (*ar*) on the left ~ **sinisterly** *adv* ~ **sinisterness** *n*.

sinistral [sinistRal] *adj* turning to the left; left-handed.

sink (*p/t* sank or sunk, *p/part* sunk) [sink] *v/t* and *i* move gradually down, descend slowly; place on lower level; fall or cause to fall below surface of a liquid; fall or cause to fall to the bottom of sea, river *etc*; subside; slope down; slide down; dwindle; droop; fall lower in moral or social scale, be degraded; penetrate deeply; invest; suppress, conceal; lose, *esp* through investment; lose vitality; excavate; **one's heart sinks** one feels foreboding, fear or despair; **s. in** (*coll*) be understood fully ~ **sink** *n* kitchen basin with water taps and outlet for use in washing up *etc*; drain to carry off dirty water; (*fig*) place of sordid evil; (*geol*) area where water percolates away underground.

sinker [sinker] *n* one who or that which sinks; weight fixed to anything to make it sink; **hook, line and s.** thoroughly.

sinkhole [sinkhOl] *n* drainage hole in sink.

sinking [sinking] *adj* that sinks; losing strength; dying; **s. feeling** (*coll*) feeling of faintness due to hunger; feeling of foreboding, fear *etc*; **s. fund** fund set aside annually to pay off debts of a government, company *etc*.

sinless [sinlis] *adj* free from sin, pure, innocent ~ **sinlessly** *adv* ~ **sinlessness** *n*.

sinner [siner] *n* one who sins or has sinned; offender; criminal.

Sinn Fein [shin-*fayn*] *n* Irish nationalist and republican movement.

sino- *pref* Chinese.

sin-offering [sin-ofRing] *n* sacrifice to atone for sin.

sinologist [sInolojist] *n* expert on China, its culture *etc*.

sinology [sInoloji] *n* study of Chinese language, culture, history *etc*.

sinter [sinter] *n* chalky or siliceous deposit from mineral springs ~ **sinter** *v/t* compress metal, glass, or ceramic particles into a coherent solid.

sinuosity [sinew-ositi] *n* quality of being sinuous.

sinuous [sinew-us] *adj* wavy, bending in and out; winding; supple ~ **sinuously** *adv*.

sinus [sInus] *n* cavity in tissue or bone > PDB; cavity of facial bone communicating with the nose; (*path*) fistula, cavity forming pus.

sinusitis [sInusItis] *n* inflammation and blockage of the nasal sinus.

sinusoidal [sInewsoidal] *adj* having the characteristics of a sine wave.

Sioux [sOO] *n* and *adj* (member) of a tribe of North American Indians.

sip (*pres/part* sipping, *p/t* and *p/part* sipped) [sip] *v/t* and *i* drink in repeated small quantities ~ **sip** *n* act of sipping; liquid sipped.

siphon [sIfon] *n* bent tube used for transferring liquid from one level to a lower level via a third level higher than either > PDS; bottle with lever and tube through which aerated water is discharged by pressure of gas ~ **siphon** *v/t* draw off by a siphon.

siphonage [sIfonij] *n* action of a siphon.

sippet [sipit] *n* small piece of toast or fried bread used as a garnish.

sir [sur] *n* term of formal address to a man; title of knight or baronet.

sire [sIr] *n* title of address to a king; (*poet*) father; male parent, *esp* of horse, dog *etc* ~ **sire** *v/t* beget.

siren [sIrRen] *n* apparatus for emitting a loud hooting sound, *esp* as fire or air-raid warning, or as factory signal; (*myth*) sea-nymph whose song lured sailors to destruction; (*fig*) dangerously alluring woman; (*zool*) genus of tailed batrachians with no hind legs; **s. suit** warm one-piece garment like a boilersuit, worn *esp* during air-raids.

Sirius [sIRi-us] *n* the Dog Star.

sirloin [surloin] *n* upper part of loin of beef.

sirocco [siRokO] *n* hot southerly wind blowing from North Africa > PDG.

sirrah [siRa] *n* (*ar*) fellow.

sis [sis] *n* (*coll abbr*) sister.

sisal [sIsal] *n* fibre of the American aloe, used for ropes ~ **sisal** *adj*.

siskin [siskin] *n* small migratory songbird.

sissy see **cissy**.

sister [sister] *n* girl or woman born of the same parents as another person; senior nurse in charge of hospital ward; nun; woman belonging to a religious or charitable community ~ **sister** *adj*.

sisterhood [sisterhood] *n* community of women living under religious vows; state of being a sister; relationship between sisters.

sister-in-law [sister-in-law] *n* sister of one's husband or wife; wife of one's brother.

sisterly [sisterli] *adj* of, like, or befitting a sister.

sistrum [sistRum] *n* ancient Egyptian percussion instrument with jingling rings > PDM.

sit (*pres/part* sitting, *p/t* and *p/part* sat) [sit] *v/i* and *t* rest upon the buttocks on the ground or on some object; rest on the haunches; perch; press down, be a burden (on); (*of clothes*) fit; ride; be in session; be a member of (committee, law court *etc*); remain; (*of birds*) remain covering eggs to hatch them; attempt to pass an examination; pose for one's photograph or portrait; **s. back** relax, remain inactive; **s. down** place oneself on a seat; settle; **s. down under** submit meekly to; **s. for** be Member of Parliament for; **s. in** act as baby sitter; **s. in for** temporarily take the place of; **s. on** (**upon**) be member of (committee *etc*); (*coll*) repress, snub; (*of coroners*) investigate cause of death of; **s. out** remain seated during (something dull); not join in a dance; **be sitting pretty** (*coll*) be safe and at an advantage; **s. tight** remain unmoving, unchanging *etc* despite danger; **s. under** attend the sermons of; **s. up** not go to bed; raise oneself from lying to sitting position; (*coll*) be startled; become suddenly alert ~ **sit** *n* way in which something fits; period of sitting.

sitar, sittar [si*tar*/si*tar*] *n* Indian long-necked plucked string instrument.

sit-down [*sit*-down] *n* and *adj* (strike) in which workmen refuse to leave the factory *etc* but do no work; (demonstration) in which persons picket a building *etc* by sitting down at its entrance.

site [*sIt*] *n* area of ground where something is to be found; area on which a building is to be erected; area of archaeological excavation; position, situation ~ **site** *v/t* locate, find the position of; place or erect in a particular area; plan the relative positions of (buildings).

sited [*sIt*ed] *adj* (of buildings) placed.

sit-in [*sit*-in] *n* form of protest against social or political injustice, in which demonstrators sit in some public building till thrown out by force.

siting [*sIt*ing] *n* way in which a building is placed relative to other buildings *etc*; act of planning the positions of buildings.

sittar see **sitar**.

sitter [*sit*er] *n* one who sits, *esp* for a portrait; hen that incubates; **s. in, baby s.** person employed to remain in a house to see to the safety and needs of a baby while its parents are out.

sitting [*sit*ing] *n* act of one who sits; session, meeting for business; time during which one sits; clutch of eggs.

sitting-room [*sit*ing-ROOm] *n* living-room; reception room.

situate [*sit*ew-ayt] *v/t* place in specified area, position, or circumstances ~ **situate** *adj* situated.

situated [*sit*ew-aytid] *adj* placed in specified circumstances; placed, built *etc* on specified site.

situation [sitew-*ay*shon] *n* position, locality; circumstances; employment, job; moment of crisis or particular interest in a relationship; relationship of persons and circumstances at a particular moment, *esp* in a play *etc*.

sit-upon [*sit*-upon] *n* (*coll euph*) buttocks.

six [*siks*] *n* and *adj* cardinal number next above five; symbol of this, 6; **at sixes and sevens** in a muddle, in confusion.

sixfold [*siks*fOld] *adj* six times as much; repeated six times.

sixfooter [siks*footer*] *n* (*coll*) one who is six feet tall; something six feet long or high.

sixpence [*siks*pens] *n* English silver coin worth six old pennies.

sixpenny [*siks*peni] *adj* worth sixpence.

sixshooter [siks-*shooter*] *n* (*coll*) revolver with six chambers.

sixteen [*siks*teen] *n* and *adj* six more than ten; symbol of this, 16.

sixteenth [siks*teenth*] *n* and *adj* (that) which follows fifteen others in a series; (that) which is one of sixteen equal parts.

sixth [*siksth*] *n* that which follows five others in a series; one of six equal parts; (*mus*) the interval covering six degrees of the scale > PDM ~ **sixth** *adj* next after the fifth; **s. form** highest form in secondary school.

sixty [*siksti*] *n* and *adj* (product of) ten times six; **s. four thousand dollar question** (*coll*) question whose correct answer brings a prize; vitally important question.

sizable [*sIz*ab'l] *adj* of considerable size.

sizar [*sIz*ar] *n* type of Cambridge or Dublin undergraduate having a partial college grant.

size (1) [*sIz*] *n* bulk, degree of bigness or smallness; standardized dimension of clothes, gloves, shoes *etc*; (*hist*) allowance of food to sizars ~ **size** *v/t* arrange or sort out according to size; **s. up** make a judgement on, assess.

size (2) *n* thin liquid glue for glazing, *etc* ~ **size** *v/t* coat with size.

sizzle [*siz*'l] *n* hissing noise, *esp* in frying ~ **sizzle** *v/i* make a hissing noise; be extremely hot.

sjambok [*sham*bok] *n* whip of rhinoceros hide.

skald, scald (2) [*skaald*] *n* Norse poet, writer of skaldic verse.

skaldic, scaldic [*skaald*ik] *adj* of or in a medieval Norse verse-form with elaborate rules of assonance, alliteration *etc*.

skate (1) [*skayt*] *n* an edible cartilaginous flatfish.

skate (2) *n* frame holding a steel blade and strapped to the shoe, used for gliding over ice; rollerskate ~ **skate** *v/i* move on skates or rollerskates; **s. on thin ice** deal cleverly and tactfully with an awkward subject or situation; **s. over, s. round** (*fig*) skilfully avoid mention of.

skateboard [*skayt*bawrd] *n* short plank fitted with rollerskate wheels, used in sport of racing, balancing *etc* ~ **skateboard** *v/i*.

skating-rink [*skay*ting-rink] *n* floor coated with artificial ice for skating.

skedaddle [skid*ad*'l] *v/i* (*coll*) rush away, flee.

skein [*skayn*] *n* yarn, silk, wool *etc* wound in a coil; flock of wild geese in flight.

skeletal [*skel*ital] *adj* of or like a skeleton.

skeleton [*skel*iton] *n* all the bones of a human or animal body; these bones preserved in their natural posture without the flesh; supporting framework; basic essentials; bare summary; (*fig*) very thin person; **s. in the cupboard** shameful secret ~ **skeleton** *adj* of or like a skeleton; consisting of, reduced to the basic minimum needed to keep an enterprise, ship *etc* working.

skeletonize [*skel*itonIz] *v/t* and *i* make a skeleton of; make an abstract of; become a skeleton.

skeleton-key [*skel*iton-kee] *n* thin light key used for picking locks; master-key.

skelp [*skelp*] *v/i* (*coll*) strike, slap.

skep [*skep*] *n* wicker or straw basket; beehive.

skeptic [*skep*tik] *n* (*US*) sceptic.

skepticism [*skep*tisizm] *n* (*US*) scepticism.

skerry [*skeRi*] *n* rocky isle; reef.

sketch [*skech*] *n* rough draft for a painting > PDAA; rapid drawing or painting of some transitory effect of light, movement *etc*; short literary description or character-study; short play depicting character or social relationships; preliminary plan, outline; (*coll*) ridiculous person ~ **sketch** *v/t* and *i* make a sketch (of).

sketchblock [*skech*blok] *n* pad of drawing paper for sketching on.

sketchbook [*skech*book] *n* book for sketching in.

sketchy [*skech*i] *adj* in outline; incomplete ~ **sketchily** *adv* ~ **sketchiness** *n*.

skew [*skew*] *adj* oblique; distorted ~ **skew** *n* (*archi*) sloping coping; oblique movement, position or course; **on the s.** aslant ~ **skew** *v/i* move sideways, turn aside; squint.

skewbald [*skew*bawld] *adj* (*of horse*) marked irregularly with two or three colours.

677

skewer [*skew*-er] *n* metal or wooden pin for keeping meat together; (*fac*) sword ~ **skewer** *v/t* fasten with a skewer; pierce right through.

skew-whiff [skew-*wif*] *adj* and *adv* (*coll*) crooked, askew.

ski [*skee/shee*] *n* long flat strip of wood, metal *etc* curved up at the front end and strapped to the foot, used for sliding over snow ~ **ski** *v/i* slide over snow on skis, *esp* as sport.

skid (*pres/part* **skidding**, *p/t* and *p/part* **skidded**) [*skid*] *v/i* (*of vehicles*) slide sideways out of control; (*fig*) slip and fall, *esp* sideways ~ **skid** *n* act of skidding; drag fastened to vehicle wheel; brake; roller, runner; timber hung over ship's side as buffer.

skidding [*skid*ing] *n* (*of vehicles*) uncontrolled sideways movement.

skidlid [*skid*lid] *n* (*coll*) motorcyclist's crash-helmet.

skidpan [*skid*pan] *n* area of slippery ground where motorists may practise how to control a skidding car.

skid-row [*skid*-ROH] *n* (*US coll*) area where tramps, drop-outs *etc* congregate.

skier [*skee*-er/*shee*-er] *n* one who skis.

skiff [*skif*] *n* any small light boat; light sculling boat.

skiffle [*skif*'l] *n* jazz based on folksong and played by a skiffle-group.

skiffle-group [*skif*'l-gROOp] *n* small group of musicians using guitar and improvised percussion instruments.

skiing [*skee*-ing/*shee*-ing] *n* act or sport of gliding, jumping *etc* on skis; **water s.** sport of remaining upright on water on skis while towed by a motorboat.

skijoring [skee*yur*Ring] *n* sport of skiing while towed by a horse.

skijump [*skee*jump/*shee*jump] *n* act of leaping on skis from the top of an artificial cliff to the slope below; cliff and slope prepared for this.

skilful [*skil*fool] *adj* having or showing skill, expert; clever; dexterous ~ **skilfully** *adv*.

skilift [*skee*lift/*shee*lift] *n* cable-railway or similar device for hauling skiers to the top of a mountain.

skill [*skil*] *n* knowledge of any art or science and dexterity in the practice of it; expertness.

skilled [*skild*] *adj* having skill; requiring skill.

skillet [*skil*it] *n* small metal vessel with a long handle.

skilly [*skil*i] *n* thin broth or gruel.

skim (*pres/part* **skimming**, *p/t* and *p/part* **skimmed**) [*skim*] *v/t* and *i* pass rapidly along or just above the surface (of); remove cream, fat *etc* from the surface of; remove scum from; (*fig*) read or examine quickly and superficially.

skimmer [*skim*er] *n* one who or that which skims; perforated scoop; a seabird.

skim-milk [*skim*-milk] *n* milk from which cream has been skimmed.

skimp [*skimp*] *v/t* and *i* stint; use an insufficient quantity of; be mean.

skimpy [*skim*pi] *adj* meagre, scanty; fitting too tightly; made of too little material ~ **skimpily** *adv* ~ **skimpiness** *n*.

skin [*skin*] *n* natural outer covering of animal body; outermost layer; rind; animal's skin stripped and preserved with its fur or feathers *etc*; semi-solid film forming on surface of a liquid; vessel made of animal skin; **by the s. of one's teeth** narrowly, only just; **s. game** (*coll*) swindle; **have a thick** (**thin**) **s.** be insensitive (sensitive) to criticism; **save one's s.** save one's life ~ **skin** (*pres/part* **skinning**, *p/t* and *p/part* **skinned**) *v/t* and *i* strip the skin from; flay; graze some skin off; become covered with skin; (*coll*) trick out of money, take all the money of; **keep one's eyes skinned** (*coll*) be very watchful and alert.

skindeep [*skin*deep] *adj* superficial.

skin-diving [*skin*-dIVing] *n* act or sport of underwater swimming with oxygen cylinders and mask but no diving suit ~ **skin-diver** *n*.

skin-flick [*skin*-flik] *n* (*coll*) cinema film with nude actors, pornographic film.

skinflint [*skin*flint] *n* miser.

skinful [*skin*fool] *adj* as much as a skin will hold; (*sl*) as much (drink) as the stomach will hold.

skin-grafting [*skin*-gRAafting] *n* transfer of healthy skin to a diseased or injured part.

skinhead [*skin*hed] *n* violent young hooligan with close-cropped hair.

skinny [*skin*i] *adj* consisting of skin only; very thin ~ **skinnily** *adv* ~ **skinniness** *n*.

skint [*skint*] *adj* (*sl*) penniless.

skintight [*skin*tIt] *adj* (*of garments*) fitted very closely to the body.

skip (1) [*skip*] *n* skep; bucket or box for hoisting coal *etc* > PDE; large metal container for transporting builders' rubbish.

skip (2) (*pres/part* **skipping**, *p/t* and *p/part* **skipped**) *v/i* and *t* leap about, frisk; make repeated slight jumps on one spot while swinging a rope under one's feet at each jump; read hastily and with omissions; omit; travel hurriedly; (*coll*) decamp, bolt ~ **skip** *n* slight jump or leap; leap from one foot to the other; (*coll*) informal dance.

skip (3) *n* team captain in bowls or curling.

skipper (1) [*skip*er] *n* captain of a ship, *esp* a merchant ship; (*coll*) captain of a team ~ **skipper** *v/t* and *i* be skipper (of).

skipper (2) *n* one who or that which skips.

skipper (3) *v/i* (*sl*) sleep in the open air.

skipping-rope [*skip*ing-ROp] *n* rope with wooden handles, used in the game of skipping.

skirl [*skurl*] *v/i* (*of bagpipes*) emit a shrill sound ~ **skirl** *n* a shrill sound.

skirmish [*skur*mish] *n* brief or unimportant fight between small groups of soldiers; (*fig*) brief or light-hearted argument, battle of wits *etc* ~ **skirmish** *v/i* engage in a skirmish.

skirt [*skurt*] *n* woman's outer garment fitting round the waist and covering part or all of the legs; corresponding part of woman's frock; loose lower part of coat, cloak *etc*; flank (of beef); (*sl*) woman; (*pl*) edge, border ~ **skirt** *v/t* and *i* form the edge of; be on or move along the border of.

skirting-board [*skurt*ing-bawrd] *n* board which runs round a wall at the bottom.

skit [*skit*] *n* light satirical play about or parody of some person or thing ~ **skit** (*pres/part* **skitting**, *p/t* and *p/part* **skitted**) *v/t* and *i* satirize, write a skit (about).

skitter [*skit*er] *v/i* skim over the surface of water; run quickly and lightly, scurry; (*fishing*) draw the hook rapidly over the water ~ **skitter** *n*.

skittish [*skit*ish] *adj* playful, sprightly; excitable; frivolous ~ **skittishly** *adv* ~ **skittishness** *n*.

skittle [*skit*'l] *v/t* and *i* play ninepins; (*coll*) squander; **s. out** (*cricket*) bowl out easily ~ **skittles** *n* (*pl*) ninepins; game played with these; (*coll*) nonsense.

skive [*skiv*] *v/i* and *t* avoid work, shirk.

skivvy [*skivi*] *n* (*sl*) domestic maid, *esp* maid of all work.

skivy [*skivi*] *adj* (*sl*) dishonest; shirking.

skua [*skew*-a] *n* species of large gull.

skulduggery [skul*duge*Ri] *n* (*coll*) underhand villainy; secret dishonest activities.

skulk [*skulk*] *v/i* lurk; sneak away; move furtively.

skull [*skul*] *n* bony case which encloses the brain; representation of human skull as symbol of death; **s. and crossbones** pirate's flag.

skullcap [*skul*kap] *n* brimless close-fitting cap.

skunk [*skunk*] *n* species of mammal allied to the weasel which emits stinking secretion when attacked; (*coll*) despicable person.

sky [*ski*] *n* upper part of the earth's atmosphere; this as seen from the ground; (*fig*) heaven; climate; prospect, outlook; **the s. is the limit** (*coll*) there is no limit; **s. wave** (*rad*) radio wave propagated by reflection from the ionosphere ~ **sky** *v/t* throw or hit high into the air; hang high up.

sky-blue [*ski*-blOO] *adj* bright light blue.

sky-diving [*ski*-dIving] *n* sport of jumping from aircraft in free fall, using parachute only at last safe moment.

Skye-terrier [ski-*te*Ri-er] *n* small rough-haired Scotch terrier.

sky-high [*ski*-hI] *adj* and *adv* as high as the sky, very high.

skyjack [*ski*jak] *v/t* hijack (aircraft during flight) ~ **skyjacker** *n*.

skylark [*ski*laark] *n* the common lark ~ **skylark** *v/i* (*sl*) romp, frolic; play jokes.

skylight [*ski*lIt] *n* window in roof or ceiling.

skyline [*ski*lIn] *n* horizon; outline of something seen against the sky.

skypilot [*ski*pIlot] *n* (*sl*) clergyman.

skyrocket [*ski*Rokit] *n* rocket fired high ~ **skyrocket** *v/i* rise very fast and high.

skysail [*ski*sayl] *n* square sail set above the royal.

skyscape [*ski*skayp] *n* picture or view consisting mainly of sky.

skyscraper [*ski*skRayper] *n* extremely tall many-storeyed building.

skyward [*ski*werd] *adj* and *adv* towards the sky.

skyway [*ski*way] *n* regular route assigned to aircraft.

slab [*slab*] *n* flat piece of stone; large, heavy piece, chunk; thick piece of bread, cake, pudding *etc*; outer piece sawn off timber log in making planks; (*sl*) operating table; mortuary table.

slabstone [*slab*stOn] *n* flagstone; stone that splits easily in slabs.

slack [*slak*] *adj* limp, sagging, loose; negligent, lazy; inactive, dull; tired; (*of water*) with no current or tide; **s. water** period between tides when water does not move ~ **slack** *n* loose part of rope, garment *etc*; slack water; small fragments or dust of coal > PDE; period of inactivity; ~ **slack** *v/t* and *i* slacken; work slackly; be idle or negligent ~ **slack** *adv* in a slack way.

slacken [*slak*en] *v/t* and *i* make slack; relax; become slack; become slower, less intense *etc*.

slacker [*slak*er] *n* one who does not work thoroughly; lazy person.

slackly [*slak*li] *adv* in a slack way.

slackness [*slak*nis] *n* quality of being slack.

slacks [*slaks*] *n* (*pl*) loose trousers for casual wear; women's trousers.

slag [*slag*] *n* non-metallic material obtained from smelting ores > PDS, PDE; volcanic ash.

slain [*slayn*] *p/part* of slay.

slake [*slayk*] *v/t* quench; satisfy, appease; mix (lime) with water.

slalom [*slay*lom]/[*slaa*lom] *n* ski race between obstacles on zigzag course.

slam (*pres/part* **slamming**, *p/t* and *p/part* **slammed**) [*slam*] *v/t* and *i* shut violently; put down violently; hit, beat; (*of doors*) close noisily; win all tricks at bridge *etc*; (*sl*) blame or criticize harshly ~ **slam** *n* violent shutting of a door; noise made by this; the winning of all tricks at bridge.

slander [*slaan*der] *n* false report made maliciously to injure anyone, *esp* if spoken, not written; calumny ~ **slander** *v/t* make false reports (about).

slanderous [*slaan*deRus] *adj* uttering malicious falsehoods ~ **slanderously** *adv*.

slang [*slang*] *n* very informal colloquial word, phrase *etc* felt to be unacceptable in serious usage; jargon, cant; **back s.** idiom in which words are pronounced as if spelt backwards; **rhyming s.** slang in which a word is represented by another word or phrase that rhymes with it ~ **slang** *v/t* scold or insult roughly, abuse; **slanging match** exchange of insults, violent verbal quarrel.

slangy [*slang*i] *adj* of, like or using slang ~ **slangily** *adv* ~ **slanginess** *n*.

slant [*slaant*] *v/t* and *i* slope; cause to slope; hold or turn obliquely; (*coll*) present (news *etc*) from an unusual point of view; present unfairly so as to prove a point ~ **slant** *n* slope; (*coll*) unusual, prejudiced or unfair presentation or point of view.

slantwise [*slaant*wIz] *adv* obliquely.

slap (*pres/part* **slapping**, *p/t* and *p/part* **slapped**) [*slap*] *v/t* strike with the palm of the hand or with something flat and flexible; **s. down** throw roughly or rudely down; (*sl*) rebuke ~ **slap** *n* blow of the open hand; noise of this; (*fig*) snub, rebuff ~ **slap** *adv* (*coll*) directly, straight; roughly.

slapbang [*slap*bang] *adv* (*coll*) suddenly; roughly.

slapdash [*slap*dash] *adv* carelessly; rashly, impetuously ~ **slapdash** *adj* careless, slipshod.

slap-happy [slap-*hap*i] *adj* (*coll*) jovial, noisily cheerful; cheerfully reckless; punch-drunk.

slapstick [*slap*stik] *n* boisterous farce depending on physical misadventures for its humour, knockabout comedy; wooden board with noisily flapping ends ~ **slapstick** *adj* of, like or performing in boisterous farce.

slap-up [*slap*-up] *adj* (*coll*) lavish, first-class.

slash [*slash*] *v/t* and *i* make long cuts in; wound by cutting, *esp* with razor; strike fiercely with edged weapon or whip; reduce or shorten drastically; reduce (prices) abruptly; criticize harshly; make slashes in (garments) ~ **slash** *n* long cut, gash;

slit made in a garment to show contrasting lining; act of slashing.

slashing [*slash*ing] *adj* criticizing harshly; bitter, cruel; that slashes; (*coll*) excellent.

slat [*slat*] *n* thin narrow strip of wood.

slate (1) [*slayt*] *n* dense greyish rock easily splitting into thin plates > PDG, PDS; piece of this shaped for use as roof covering; piece of this framed and used as writing tablet; dark grey-blue colour; **clean s.** (*fig*) unblemished record ~ **slate** *v/t* cover (roof) with slates.

slate (2) *v/t* (*coll*) abuse; criticize harshly, find fault with; thrash.

slate-pencil [*slayt*-pensil] *n* soft piece of slate for writing on slates.

slater [*slay*ter] *n* one who makes slates; one who slates roofs; woodlouse; (*coll*) harsh critic.

slating (1) [*slay*ting] *n* act of covering with slates; material for slating.

slating (2) *n* (*coll*) severe reprimand or criticism.

slatted [*slat*id] *adj* having slats.

slattern [*slat*ern] *n* untidy, slovenly woman.

slatternly [*slat*ernli] *adj* and *adv* like a slattern.

slaty [*slay*ti] *adj* of, like or containing slate.

slaughter [*slaw*ter] *v/t* kill (animals) for meat, butcher; kill in large numbers, cruelly or needlessly ~ **slaughter** *n* act of slaughtering; massacre, carnage; needless or cruel killing.

slaughterer [*slaw*teRer] *n* one who slaughters cattle.

slaughterhouse [*slaw*terhows] *n* building where beasts are killed for market; (*fig*) scene of great carnage.

slaughterous [*slaw*teRus] *adj* murderous; ruthlessly destructive ~ **slaughterously** *adv*.

Slav [*slaav*] *n* one of an Aryan race inhabiting Eastern Europe ~ **Slav** *adj* Slavonic.

slave [*slayv*] *n* person legally owned by another, bondman; person forced to work for and obey another against his will; one who works in harsh conditions for low pay; one who is dominated or controlled, one who has no freedom ~ **slave** *v/i* work excessively hard or in bad conditions ~ **slave** *adj* of, like or by slaves.

slavedriver [*slayv*dRIver] *n* overseer of slaves; one who forces others to work too hard; bullying master ~ **slavedrive** *v/t*.

slave-labour [slayv-*lay*ber] *n* work done by slaves; work done by ill-treated and underpaid workmen.

slaver (1) [*slay*ver] *n* one who buys and sells slaves; ship on which slaves are transported.

slaver (2) [*slav*er] *n* saliva dribbling from the mouth ~ **slaver** *v/i* slobber; foam at the mouth; (*fig*) be crazy with rage or lust.

slavery [*slay*veRi] *n* condition of a slave; bondage; drudgery; custom of owning slaves.

slave-trade [slayv-tRayd] *n* trade of procuring, buying and selling slaves.

slave-traffic [slayv-tRafic] *n* slave-trade; **white s.** the tricking or forcing of women into prostitution.

slavey [*slay*vi] *n* (*coll*) servant-girl.

Slavic [*slaav*ik] *adj* Slavonic.

slavish [*slay*vish] *adj* of or like a slave; servile, base; entailing drudgery; lacking originality ~ **slavishly** *adv* ~ **slavishness** *n*.

Slavonic [sla*von*ik] *adj* of the Slav race or the Slav language.

slaw [*slaw*] *n* (*US*) salad of cabbage.

slay (*p/t* slew, *p/part* slain) [*slay*] *v/t* kill.

slayer [*slay*-er] *n* one who kills or has killed.

sleazy, sleezy [*slee*zi] *adj* flimsy; (*coll*) sordid.

sled [*sled*] *n* small sledge ~ **sled** (*pres/part* sledding, *p/t* and *p/part* sledded) *v/t* and *i* carry on a sled; travel by sled.

sledge [*slej*] *n* vehicle moved on runners to slide over snow; sledge-hammer ~ **sledge** *v/t* and *i* carry on a sledge; travel by sledge.

sledge-hammer [*slej*-hamer] *n* heavy hammer wielded with both hands.

sleek [*sleek*] *adj* smooth, glossy; (*fig*) well-fed, prosperous; well-groomed, neat; smug, unctuous ~ **sleek** *v/t* make smooth ~ **sleekly** *adv* ~ **sleekness** *n*.

sleep [*sleep*] *n* natural state of relative unconsciousness and immobility recurring in man and animals at least once a day; time this state lasts; (*fig*) lethargy, apathy; death; **put to s.** (*euph*) kill painlessly ~ **sleep** *v/i* and *t* be in or pass into state of sleep; pass the night; (*coll*) provide beds for; (*fig*) lie dormant, be inactive; be dead; (*of a top*) spin so fast as to seem motionless; **s. around** (*coll*) have sexual relations with many people, be promiscuous; **s. in** oversleep; **s. off** recover from (drunkenness *etc*) by sleeping; **s. on it** postpone decision till next day; **s. with** have sexual relations with.

sleeper [*sleep*er] *n* one who sleeps; wooden beam supporting rails of railway; sleeping-car.

sleepily [*sleep*ili] *adv* in a sleepy way.

sleepiness [*sleep*inis] *n* state of being sleepy.

sleeping [*sleep*ing] *adj* asleep; inactive; of or for sleep; **s. partner** partner who supplies capital to a firm *etc* but does not share in running it; **s. pill** pill containing a narcotic drug; **s. sickness** tropical disease, *usu* fatal, characterized by constant sleepiness; sleepy sickness; **s. tablet** sleeping pill.

sleeping-bag [*sleep*ing-bag] *n* warm padded waterproof bag in which campers, soldiers *etc* can sleep on the ground.

sleeping-car [*sleep*ing-kaar] *n* railway coach fitted with berths.

sleeping-draught [*sleep*ing-dRaaft] *n* narcotic medicine, opiate.

sleepless [*sleep*lis] *adj* unable to sleep; not spent in sleeping; always watchful, alert; restless ~ **sleeplessly** *adv* ~ **sleeplessness** *n*.

sleepwalker [*sleep*wawker] *n* one who walks or carries out other activities while asleep, somnambulist.

sleepwalking [*sleep*wawking] *n* somnambulism.

sleepy [*sleep*i] *adj* inclined to sleep, drowsy; lazy; inducing sleep; (*of fruit*) over-ripe; **s. sickness** inflammation of the brain causing much drowsiness and mental deterioration; sleeping sickness.

sleepyhead [*sleep*ihed] *n* (*coll*) person, *esp* child, who looks half asleep.

sleet [*sleet*] *n* fine snow mingled with rain; (*US*) hail, small ice pellets ~ **sleet** *v/i* snow with a mixture of rain; (*US*) hail.

sleeve [*sleev*] *n* that part of a garment that covers all or part of the arm; decorative outer case for a gramophone record; canvas tube hung from a pole to show direction and force of wind; tube enclosing a smaller tube; tubular case or cover; **have up one's s.** keep secretly ready for use; **laugh in one's s.** mock secretly; **wear one's heart on one's s.** display feelings openly.

sleeved [*sleevd*] *adj* having sleeves.

sleevelink [*sleev*link] *n* cufflink, stud.

sleigh [*slay*] *n* vehicle mounted on runners for driving over snow ~ **sleigh** *v/t* and *i* convey by sleigh; travel by sleigh.

sleigh-bell [*slay*-bel] *n* small bell hanging on a sleigh or on its harness.

sleight [*slīt*] *n* dexterous trick.

sleight-of-hand [*slīt*-ov-hand] *n* conjuring trick; clever deception, *esp* by substitution.

slender [*slender*] *adj* having little width compared with length; thin; slight, scanty; feeble ~ **slenderly** *adv* ~ **slenderness** *n*.

sleuth [*slOOth*] *n* detective; (*ar*) trail of scent left by hunted beast ~ **sleuth** *v/t* and *i* hunt down by scent; pursue or investigate as detective.

sleuth-hound [*slOOth*-hound] *n* bloodhound.

slew (1) [*slOO*] *p/t* of **slay**.

slew (2), **slue** *v/t* and *i* swing sideways.

slewed [*slOOd*] *adj* (*sl*) drunk.

slice [*slīs*] *n* thin, broad piece; share, part; representative sample, cross-section; implement for slicing; broad knife for serving fish; slicing stroke ~ **slice** *v/t* cut into thin, broad pieces; cut slices from; divide; hit a ball so that it veers to the right.

slicer [*slīs*er] *n* machine for cutting bread, meat *etc* into slices; slicing stroke.

slick [*slik*] *adj* smooth, sleek; (*coll*) dexterous, clever; superficially clever but unsatisfactory, glib; (*sl*) sexually attractive ~ **slick** *n* film of oil covering a surface ~ **slick** *v/t* make smooth and glossy, *esp* with brilliantine ~ **slick** *adv* straight, head on ~ **slickly** *adv* ~ **slickness** *n*.

slid [*slid*] *p/t* and *p/part* of **slide**.

slide (*p/t* and *p/part* **slid**) [*slīd*] *v/i* and *t* move in one smooth movement along a surface; glide; slip; move smoothly and gradually; cause to slide; **let things s.** take no action while things deteriorate ~ **slide** *n* act of sliding; track of slippery ice; slope down which things are slid, chute; semi-transparent photograph or picture on glass *etc* for projection on to a screen; glass mount for microscopic specimens; clip for holding hair in place; landslide; device to change length of tube of brass instruments > PDM; rapid chromatic run; **s. fastener** zip.

sliderule [*slīd*ROOl] *n* device consisting of two graduated rulers attached to each other, used for quick mathematical calculations > PDS.

sliding-scale [*slīd*ing-skayl] *n* scale of wages, prices *etc* fluctuating according to market prices, cost-of-living index *etc*.

slight [*slīt*] *adj* of small degree, extent or intensity; slender, slim; frail, delicate; not severe, mild; trivial, petty, of little importance ~ **slight** *v/t* treat as unimportant; snub; insult ~ **slight** *n* contemptuous disregard; insult, snub.

slighting [*slīt*ing] *adj* showing contempt, expressing a slight ~ **slightingly** *adv*.

slightly [*slīt*li] *adv* only a little.

slightness [*slīt*nis] *n* quality of being slight.

slily see **slyly**.

slim [*slim*] *adj* slender, thin; having a pleasingly slender body; slight in degree; (*sl*) sly ~ **slim**

(*pres/part* **slimming**, *p/t* and *p/part* **slimmed**) *v/t* and *i* make slim; reduce one's fatness by diets, exercise *etc*.

slime [*slīm*] *n* liquid mud; any soft wet form of dirt; moisture secreted by snails *etc*; bitumen ~ **slime** *v/t* smear or cover with slime.

sliminess [*slīm*inis] *n* quality of being slimy.

slimly [*slim*li] *adv* in a slim way.

slimming [*slim*ing] *n* process of reducing fatness by diets, exercise *etc* ~ **slimming** *adj* reducing or appearing to reduce fatness.

slimness [*slim*nis] *n* quality or state of being slim.

slimy [*slīm*i] *adj* of, like or smeared with slime; secreting slime; (*fig*) fawning, servile.

sling (1) [*sling*] *n* loop of leather and cord by which a stone is swung and thrown; rope *etc* looped round something to hoist or support it; strip of cloth supporting an injured arm ~ **sling** (*p/t* and *p/part* **slung**) *v/t* and *i* hurl, throw with swinging arm; throw from a sling; support in or hoist by a sling; hang and leave swinging; **s. one's hook** (*coll*) go away; **s. out** forcibly drive out.

sling (2) *n* drink made of equal parts of rum or gin and sweetened water.

slink (*p/t* and *p/part* **slunk**) [*slink*] *v/i* and *t* move stealthily, prowl about; glide alluringly; (*of animals*) miscarry.

slinky [*slink*i] *adj* (*coll*) slim; moving smoothly and alluringly; (*of clothes*) close-fitting, *esp* round the hips ~ **slinkily** *adv* ~ **slinkiness** *n*.

slip (*pres/part* **slipping**, *p/t* and *p/part* **slipped**) [*slip*] *v/i* and *t* slide involuntarily, lose balance and fall; move out of place; fall suddenly from the hand; slide, glide, move smoothly; cause to slide into or out of place; move rapidly or stealthily; pass unnoticed; escape; put on, in, away *etc* rapidly or stealthily; pass quickly by; let loose, release; (*coll*) hand over, give; (*of animals*) miscarry, give premature birth (to); **be slipping** (*coll*) lose one's skill, abilities *etc*; **let s.** accidentally reveal; allow to escape or fall; **s. up** (*coll*) make a mistake ~ **slip** *n* act of slipping; sliding fall; mistake, error, *esp* if slight; woman's underskirt, petticoat; pillowcase; dog's leash; narrow strip of paper, thin wood *etc*; footpath between houses; (*pl*) sloping plane on which ships are built or repaired; cutting of a plant; young boy or girl; thin paste of clay, water, and pigment; (*pl*) bathing trunks; (*cricket*) offside ground behind the wicket; **give the s.** to escape cleverly from.

slipknot [*slip*not] *n* knot which slips along its own string to form a running noose.

slip-on [*slip*-on] *n* (*coll*) garment, *esp* corset, that is easily put on.

slipover [*slip*Over] *n* (*coll*) light sleeveless sweater.

slipper [*slip*er] *n* loose shoe of soft material worn indoors; lady's light evening shoe; one who or that which slips ~ **slipper** *v/t* (*coll*) beat with a slipper.

slippered [*slip*erd] *adj* wearing slippers.

slipperiness [*slip*eRinis] *n* state or quality of being slippery.

slipper-slopper [*slip*er-sloper] *adj* sentimental.

slippery [*slip*eRi] *adj* that causes slipping; too smooth, greasy, wet *etc* for safety; difficult to grip; unreliable, changeable; (*fig*) artful, cunning.

slippy [*slip*i] *adj* (*coll*) slippery; quick.

sliproad–slug

sliproad [*slip*ROd] *n* minor bypass road; road giving access to or exit from a motorway.

slipshod [*slip*shod] *adj* carelessly or dirtily dressed, slovenly; careless in working, inaccurate.

slipslop [*slip*slop] *adj* and *n* weak (liquor); sloppy, feeble (talk or writing).

slipstream [*slip*stReem] *n* current of air flung backwards by propeller or jets of an aircraft.

slip-up [*slip*-up] *n* (*coll*) mistake.

slipware [*slip*wair] *n* pottery decorated with contrasting clay paste.

slipway [*slip*way] *n* launching slope; slope where ships are laid up or repaired.

slit (*pres/part* **slitting**, *p/t* and *p/part* **slit**) [*slit*] *v/t* and *i* make a long clean cut or tear (in); split open ∼ **slit** *n* long, narrow, clean-cut opening.

slither [*sliTH*er] *v/i* slip repeatedly; slide unsteadily.

slithery [*sliTH*eRi] *adj* slippery.

slit-trench [*slit*-tRench] (*mil*) narrow protective trench for one soldier.

sliver [*sliv*er] *n* long strip cut, torn, or chopped from something; splinter; long strand of fibre ∼ **sliver** *v/t* and *i* divide into long thin pieces; splinter.

slivovitz [*sliv*ovits] *n* Balkan spirituous liquor made from plums.

slob (1) [*slob*] *n* muddy ground.

slob (2) *n* (*sl*) fool; lout.

slobber [*slob*er] *n* saliva running from the mouth; (*fig*) sentimentality ∼ **slobber** *v/i* let saliva run from the mouth, drivel; **s. over** (*fig*) show sentimental affection for.

sloe [*slO*] *n* wild fruit of blackthorn; **s. gin** liqueur of gin in which sloes have steeped.

slog (*pres/part* **slogging**, *p/t* and *p/part* **slogged**) [*slog*] *v/t* and *i* hit violently and with little art; work hard and persistently; work at a dull task ∼ **slog** *n* hard dull work; violent blow.

slogan [*slO*gan] *n* phrase or word designed to stimulate public interest in a political party, commercial product *etc*; rallying-cry, battlecry.

slogger [*slog*er] *n* one who hits hard; hard worker.

sloop [*slOOp*] *n* sailing vessel with one mast, fixed bowsprit, and jibbed stay > PDSa; type of small warship.

slop (1) (*pres/part* **slopping**, *p/t* and *p/part* **slopped**) [*slop*] *v/t* and *i* spill; overflow, be split; **s. out** remove one's own slops from prison cell ∼ **slop** *n* act of slopping; pool of spilt liquid; (*pl*) liquid food for invalids; dirty water, liquid waste, *esp* urine.

slop (2) *n* (*sl*) policeman.

slop-basin [*slop*-baysin] *n* bowl into which dregs of teacups are emptied.

slope [*slOp*] *n* inclined direction, line or surface; ground rising or falling gradually from the horizontal; degree of this rise or fall, steepness; (*mil*) position of sloped rifle ∼ **slope** *v/t* and *i* place in obliquely inclined position; be in inclined position, have inclined surface; (*sl*) go away, run away; (*mil*) hold (rifle) resting obliquely on shoulder.

sloping [*slOp*ing] *adj* oblique; slanting.

slop-pail [*slop*-payl] *n* bucket for urine and dirty water.

sloppy [*slop*i] *adj* soaking wet; splashed, muddy; (*fig*) maudlin, stupidly sentimental; carelessly

made, done *etc*; slipshod; **s. joe** (*coll*) loose baggy sweater ∼ **sloppily** *adv* ∼ **sloppiness** *n*.

slops (1) [*slops*] *n* (*pl*) liquid food for invalids; dirty water; liquid refuse, *esp* urine.

slops (2) *n* (*pl*) loose working clothes; readymade clothes, bedding *etc* for sailors.

slosh (1) [*slosh*] *n* (*sl*) foolish sentimentality.

slosh (2) *v/t* (*sl*) hit violently; apply lavishly.

sloshed [*sloshd*] *adj* (*sl*) drunk.

slot (1) [*slot*] *n* slit; groove; narrow opening, *esp* one in which a coin is inserted; (*rad*, *TV*) moment at which an item regularly recurs ∼ **slot** (*pres/part* **slotting**, *p/t* and *p/part* **slotted**) *v/t* make a slot in.

slot (2) *n* spoor, track of a deer.

slot (3) *n* door bolt; metal rod.

sloth (1) [*slOth*] *n* laziness, indolence.

sloth (2) [*slOth/sloth*] *n* S. American slow-moving arboreal mammal.

slothful [*slOth*fool] *adj* lazy, inactive, sluggish ∼ **slothfully** *adv* ∼ **slothfulness** *n*.

slot-machine [*slot*-masheen] *n* machine which automatically delivers articles when coins are put into a slot.

slouch [*slowch*] *n* clumsily hunched position of shoulders, heavy stoop; clumsy shuffling gait; **slouch-hat** ∼ **slouch** *v/i* stand or move with a slouch; walk heavily or clumsily.

slouch-hat [*slowch*-hat] *n* hat with brim bent down at one side.

slough (1) [*slow*] *n* marsh, swamp.

slough (2) [*sluf*] *n* cast-off skin of snake or other animal; dead tissue from a wound ∼ **slough** *v/t* and *i* cast off; peel and come off.

sloven [*sluv*en] *n* one who is lazy, dirty, and badly dressed.

slovenly [*sluv*enli] *adj* carelessly and dirtily dressed; untidy ∼ **slovenly** *adv* in a careless, untidy manner.

slow [*slO*] *adj* not quick; taking a long time to develop, complete *etc*; moving at low speed; late; stupid, not understanding readily; boring; not easily excited or angered; inactive ∼ **slow** *v/t* and *i* cause to move slowly; move slowly; **s. down** make or become gradually slower ∼ **slow** *adv* slowly; **go s.** be cautious; (*of workers*) deliberately reduce output.

slowcoach [*slO*kOch] *n* one who is always slow; dull, old-fashioned person.

slowly [*slO*li] *adv* at a slow speed.

slow-match [*slO*-mach] *n* fuse which burns slowly to ignite explosives.

slowmotion [*slO*mOshon] *adj* (*of a filmed sequence*) projected well below normal speed, or filmed at high speed and projected normally; (*fig*) done extremely slowly.

slowness [*slO*nis] *n* quality of being slow.

slow-worm [*slO*-wurm] *n* small limbless lizard.

slubbed [*slubd*] *adj* (*of cotton fabric*) showing thicker strands of twisted fibre.

sludge [*sluj*] *n* muddy deposit of sewage; thick sticky mud; melting snow, slush.

slue see **slew** (2).

slug [*slug*] *n* shell-less gastropod mollusc akin to snail; bullet, *esp* for airgun; (*mining*) large pieces of crude ore; (*print*) strip of type-metal used for spacing; (*ar*) sluggard ∼ **slug** (*pres/part* **slugging**, *p/t* and *p/part* **slugged**) *v/t* and *i* (*coll*) hit violently, knock unconscious; shoot, hit with bullet; lie lazily in bed.

sluggard [*slug*ard] *n* habitually lazy person.

sluggish [*slug*ish] *adj* lazy, inactive; moving too slowly; not functioning actively ~ **sluggishly** *adv* ~ **sluggishness** *n*.

sluice [*sl*OOs] *n* sliding gate, valve *etc* for controlling flow and level of water in a channel; floodgate; trough for washing gold *etc* from gravel > PDE; (*coll*) brisk wash in plenty of water ~ **sluice** *v/t* and *i* allow water to gush over or through; flush; wash down; flow copiously.

slum [*slum*] *n* street or district of dilapidated, dirty, overcrowded houses; squalid, tumbledown house ~ **slum** (*pres/part* **slumming**, *p/t* and *p/part* **slummed**) *v/i* visit slums to give out charity or go sightseeing.

slumber [*slum*ber] *n* sleep ~ **slumber** *v/i* sleep; be dormant.

slumberous, slumbrous [*slum*bRus] *adj* drowsy.

slumberwear [*slum*berwair] *n* pyjamas or nightdress.

slum-clearance [slum-*kleer*Rans] *n* policy of demolishing slum areas and replacing with new, sound houses.

slummy [*slum*i] *adj* of or like a slum.

slump [*slump*] *n* (*econ*) fall in prices or demand, *esp* if prolonged; financial depression; (*fig*) loss of popularity or value; collapse ~ **slump** *v/i* collapse in a heap; sit down heavily and wearily; (*of prices etc*) come down suddenly.

slung [*slung*] *p/t* and *p/part* of **sling**.

slunk [*slunk*] *p/t* and *p/part* of **slink**.

slur (*pres/part* **slurring**, *p/t* and *p/part* **slurred**) [*slur*] *v/t* and *i* pronounce indistinctly by running syllables together; pass over lightly; (*mus*) sing or play legato; (*ar*) calumniate, disparage ~ **slur** *n* reproach; disgrace; stain, stigma; blurred impression in printing; (*mus*) curved line > PDM.

slurp [*slurp*] *v/t* suck up noisily.

slurry [*slu*Ri] *n* thick paste of clay and water; effluent from mine.

slush [*slush*] *n* half-melted snow, *esp* mixed with mud; soft mud, sludge; (*coll*) stupid sentimentality; trash, nonsense.

slushy [*slush*i] *adj* covered with slush; of or like slush; (*coll*) sentimental; trashy.

slut [*slut*] *n* untidy, slovenly woman; woman of bad reputation.

sluttish [*slut*ish] *adj* slatternly; idle and untidy.

sly [*slI*] *adj* cunning, artful, crafty; underhand; with half-concealed humour ~ **sly** *n* **on the s.** secretly; illicitly ~ **slyly, slily** *adv* ~ **slyness** *n*.

slyboots [*slI*boots] *n* (*coll*) artful person; rascal.

slype [*slIp*] *n* roofed passage between two walls, *esp* from cathedral transept to any building within the precincts.

smack (1) [*smak*] *n* slight flavour; tinge, trace ~ **smack** *v/i* have the flavour (of); be suggestive (of).

smack (2) *n* small fishing vessel.

smack (3) *n* blow of the open hand, slap; sharp retort; loud kiss; **have a s. at** (*coll*) try; **s. in the eye** (*coll*) rebuff, snub ~ **smack** *v/t* and *i* make a sound by compressing the lips and then parting them quickly; strike with the flat of the hand; make a sharp noise; crack (a whip) ~ **smack** *adv* (*coll*) suddenly; directly.

smacker [*smak*er] *n* (*coll*) noisy blow; loud kiss.

small [*smawl*] *adj* little; of less than normal size; not full grown, very young; of little importance; paltry, petty; narrow-minded; **s. beer** weak beer; (*fig*) something trivial; **feel s.** feel humiliated; **s. fry** young fish; (*fig*) children; **s. hours** hours between midnight and dawn; **look s.** appear stupid; **sing s.** behave humbly ~ **small** *n* slender part; something, *esp* coal, in small pieces; middle part of the back; (*pl*) underclothes; (*Oxford coll*) responsions.

small-arms [*smawl*aarmz] *n* rifles and revolvers.

smallholding [*smawl*hOlding] *n* small plot of agricultural land let out by a county council; very small farm ~ **smallholder** *n*.

smallpox [*smawl*poks] *n* an acute infectious disease accompanied by eruptions on the skin.

small-screen [*smawl*-skReen] *adj* (*coll*) of, on or for television.

smallsword [*smawl*sawrd] *n* rapier.

smalltalk [*smawl*tawk] *n* light social conversation on trivial subjects.

smalltime [*smawl*tIm] *adj* (*coll*) amateurish, inefficient.

small-town [*smawl*-town] *adj* of, in or like a small town; petty, narrow-minded, provincial.

smalt [*smawlt*] *n* blue glass; dark blue pigment.

smarmy [*smaarm*i] *adj* (*coll*) flattering, insincerely polite.

smart [*smaart*] *v/i* feel sharp, tingling pain; be the cause of sharp pain; feel resentful; rankle ~ **smart** *n* sharp pain, stinging sensation; distress; irritation ~ **smart** *adj* stinging, pungent, keen; vigorous, brisk; clever, intelligent; impertinent; shrewd; witty; spruce, neat, gay; fashionable.

smart-aleck [*smaart*-alik] *n* (*coll*) one who thinks himself clever and witty.

smarten [*smaart*en] *v/t* make neater, more fashionable, brighter *etc*.

smartly [*smaart*li] *adv* in a smart way.

smartness [*smaart*nis] *n* quality of being smart.

smash [*smash*] *v/t* and *i* break to pieces, shatter; crash; collide violently and harmfully (with); hit violently; crush, defeat utterly; ruin, *esp* financially; go bankrupt; be ruined or destroyed ~ **smash** *n* act or sound of smashing; violent collision of vehicles, trains *etc*; disaster; bankruptcy, ruin; **s. and grab** raid robbery by breaking a shop window and seizing goods displayed.

smasher [*smash*er] *n* one who or that which smashes; (*coll*) violent blow; (*coll*) excellent or very remarkable person or thing.

smash-hit [*smash*-hit] *n* (*coll*) highly popular book, film, actor, song *etc*.

smashing [*smash*ing] *adj* devastating, crushing; (*coll*) excellent, outstanding, delightful ~ **smashingly** *adv*.

smash-up [*smash*-up] *n* crash, collision of cars, trains *etc*; bankruptcy, ruin; destruction.

smattering [*smate*Ring] *n* slight or superficial knowledge.

smear [*smeer*] *n* stain, mark caused by contact with something greasy or dirty; (*coll*) attempt to ruin somebody by spreading malicious rumours about him; rumour thus spread ~ **smear** *v/t* and *i* spread grease, dirt *etc* on; stain, daub; make dirty; blur by rubbing; spread malicious rumours about.

smear-word [*smeer*-wurd] *n* epithet implying a scandalous accusation, innuendo.

smell [*smel*] *n* odour; unpleasant odour, stink; sense by which odours are perceived; act of smelling ~ **smell** (*p/t* and *p/part* **smelt**) *v/t* and *i* perceive the odour of; inhale the odour of, sniff at; emit an odour; emit unpleasant odour, stink; (*coll*) appear unpleasant, dishonest *etc*; **s. out** track by scent; detect; **s. a rat** suspect dishonesty, trickery *etc*.

smelliness [*smelinis*] *n* state or quality of being smelly.

smelling-bottle [*smeling*-bot'l] *n* flask of smelling-salts.

smelling-salts [*smeling*-sawlts] *n* (*pl*) perfumed ammonium carbonate used to ward off faintness.

smelly [*smeli*] *adj* having an unpleasant odour.

smelt (1) [*smelt*] *v/t* extract (metal) from ores by heat.

smelt (2) *n* small fish of the salmon family.

smelt (3) *p/t* and *p/part* of **smell**.

smidgin [*smijin*] *n* (*coll*) small amount.

smile [*smIl*] *n* act of drawing the closed lips sideways and up; facial expression showing joy, affection, amusement *etc*; (*fig*) cheerfulness; (*pl*, *fig*) favour ~ **smile** *v/i* and *t* express joy, affection, amusement *etc* by a smile; (*fig*) look cheerful, favourable or prosperous.

smiling [*smIling*] *adj* showing a smile; cheerful; favourable; peaceful ~ **smilingly** *adv*.

smirch [*smurch*] *v/t* and *i* soil, smear, stain ~ **smirch** *n*.

smirk [*smurk*] *n* self-satisfied or unpleasantly knowing smile ~ **smirk** *v/i* give an unpleasant smile, look self-satisfied.

smite [*p/t* smote, *p/part* **smitten**) [*smIt*] *v/t* and *i* (*ar, poet*) strike powerfully; wound; affect strongly; **be smitten by** (*joc*) fall in love with, be deeply moved by.

smith [*smith*] *n* metal worker; one who forges iron.

smithereens [smiTHe*Reenz*] *n* (*pl*) (*coll*) tiny fragments.

smithy [*smiTHi*] *n* smith's workshop, forge.

smitten [*smiten*] *p/part* of **smite**.

smock [*smok*] *n* loose hip-length protective garment of linen or cotton, worn by painters *etc* and formerly by farm workers; similar garment worn by children; (*ar*) chemise, shift ~ **smock** *v/t* and *i* adorn with smocking.

smocking [*smoking*] *n* closely pleated honeycomb needlework.

smog [*smog*] *n* dense fog mixed with much smoke, exhaust-fumes *etc*.

smokable [*smOkab*'l] *adj* fit to be smoked.

smoke [*smOk*] *n* fine solid particles suspended in gas, *esp* carbon particles emitted by burning matter > PDS; thick steam, vapour *etc*; act of smoking tobacco; (*coll*) cigarette, pipe of tobacco, or cigar; **go up in s.** be wasted ~ **smoke** *v/t* and *i* emit smoke; emit steam, vapour *etc*; inhale fumes of burning tobacco from cigarette, pipe *etc* held in the mouth; do this habitually; cure (meat, fish *etc*) by exposing to smoke; fumigate; flavour with smoke; (*obs coll*) tease; hoax; **s. out** drive out by smoke; force to come into the open.

smokeblack [*smOk*blak] *n* amorphous carbon produced by imperfect combustion of resin or oil.

smokebomb [*smOk*bom] *n* bomb that gives out clouds of smoke.

smoke-dried [*smOk*-dRId] *adj* cured with smoke.

smokeless [*smOk*lis] *adj* emitting no smoke when burnt; **s. zone** area where only smokeless fuel is allowed.

smoker [*smOk*er] *n* one who smokes tobacco, *esp* habitually; (*coll*) railway carriage in which smoking is allowed.

smokescreen [*smOk*skReen] *n* (*mil*) cloud of dense smoke to conceal movements of troops, warships *etc*; (*fig*) misleading explanations *etc* to distract attention from the truth.

smokestack [*smOk*stak] *n* tall chimney; ship's funnel.

smokily [*smOk*ili] *adv* in a smoky way.

smokiness [*smOk*inis] *n* quality or state of being smoky.

smoking [*smOk*ing] *n* act of emitting smoke; act of inhaling tobacco smoke, *esp* habitually; process of curing in smoke ~ **smoking** *adj* emitting smoke; of or for smoking tobacco; where smoking tobacco is allowed.

smoking-jacket [*smOk*ing-jakit] *n* loose ornamented jacket, formerly worn by men when smoking at leisure.

smoky [*smOk*i] *adj* emitting much smoke; full of smoke; darkened by smoke; tasting of, cured by smoke.

smooch [*smOOch*] *v/i* (*US*) dawdle, hang about; (*sl*) flirt, caress and kiss.

smoochy [*smOOchi*] *adj* (*US*) smudgy, blurred.

smooth [*smOOTH*] *adj* having an even surface; not rough, hairy, jagged *etc*; moving easily and evenly; without obstacles; calm; polite; suave, flattering ~ **smooth** *n* anything smooth; smooth part; level ground; (*fig*) what is easy and free from trouble ~ **smooth** *v/t* and *i* make smooth; remove lumps, wrinkles *etc*; make easy, remove difficulties; **s. down** make smooth; make or become calmer; **s. over** minimize, gloss over.

smoothbore [*smOOTH*bawr] *n* gun with unrifled barrel.

smooth-faced [*smOOTH*-fayst] *adj* without a beard; having a mild or flattering expression; insincere, glib.

smoothing-iron [*smOOTH*ing-I-ern] *n* flat-iron for pressing clothes.

smoothly [*smOOTH*li] *adv* in a smooth way.

smoothness [*smOOTH*nis] *n* state or quality of being smooth.

smooth-tongued [*smOOTH*-tungd] *adj* polite; flattering, plausible.

smorbrod [*smurb*Ra] *n* (*Danish*) cold savoury food served on slices of bread.

smote [*smOt*] *p/t* of **smite**.

smother [*smuTH*er] *v/t* and *i* stifle, suffocate; suppress; cover thickly with; feel stifled, be suffocated ~ **smother** *n* a stifling cloud; thick dust; **s. love** (*coll*) oppressively protective and possessive love, *esp* of mother for children.

smoulder [*smOld*er] *v/i* burn slowly without flame; exist in a suppressed condition.

smudge [*smuj*] *v/t* and *i* smear, blur; stain; become smeared ~ **smudge** *n* smear, blur, dirty mark.

smudgy [smuji] adj smeared with dirty marks ~ smudgily adv ~ smudginess n.

smug [smug] adj too self-satisfied, rejoicing in one's superiority, safety etc; prudish, prim.

smuggle [smug'l] v/t and i import or export (goods) secretly without paying customs duties; convey secretly.

smuggler [smugler] n one who smuggles, esp habitually and for gain.

smuggling [smugling] n act or practice of one who smuggles.

smugly [smugli] adv in a smug way.

smugness [smugnis] n quality of being smug.

smut [smut] n particle of soot, coal, dirt etc; mark made by this; parasitic fungus on corn and grasses; bawdy jokes, obscene books etc ~ smut (pres/part smutting, p/t and p/part smutted) v/t and i stain with smut; (fig) blacken, tarnish; be affected with smut (of corn).

smutch [smuch] v/t stain with smut ~ smutch n smut.

smutty [smuti] adj soiled with smut; obscene ~ smuttily adv ~ smuttiness n.

snack [snak] n light meal or dish quick to prepare and eat.

snackbar [snakbaar] n small restaurant, or bar in a public-house, where snacks can be obtained.

snaffle [snaf'l] n slender, jointed bridle-bit ~ snaffle v/t put a snaffle on; (coll) steal, purloin.

snafu [snafOO] adj (mil sl) in a hopeless muddle as usual.

snag [snag] n unexpected obstacle, drawback; jagged tree-stump, esp in river-bed; damage to stocking etc caused by jagged object ~ snag (pres/part snagging, p/t and p/part snagged) v/t and i (of stocking etc) tear by catching on jagged object; (of boat) collide with a snag.

snail [snayl] n shell-bearing, slow-moving, slimy mollusc; (fig) slow-moving person; spiral cam.

snake [snayk] n long limbless serpent; (fig) deceitful and malicious person; **s. in the grass** cunningly hidden enemy; **see snakes** have delirium tremens ~ snake v/i move swiftly and smoothly between obstacles; move in series of twists or glides.

snake-charmer [snayk-chaarmer] n one who trains drugged, hypnotized, or tame snakes to perform tricks.

snaky [snayki] adj of or like a snake; full of snakes; twisting, winding; cunning, treacherous, malicious ~ snakily adv ~ snakiness n.

snap (pres/part snapping, p/t and p/part snapped) [snap] v/t and i bite quickly; snatch suddenly; close abruptly and with a click; break suddenly and sharply; make a sharp cracking noise; take a snapshot (of); (coll) speak sharply or angrily; **s. at** try to bite suddenly; seize suddenly or eagerly; speak angrily to; **s. one's fingers at** defy; disregard scornfully; **s. out of it** (coll) recover rapidly from (angry or gloomy mood etc); **s. (someone's) head off** speak curtly and angrily to; interrupt rudely; **s. up** seize eagerly ~ snap n act or sound of snapping; sudden bite; short spell of cold weather; snapshot, informal photograph; spring-catch or clasp; gingerbread biscuit; form of simple card-game; (coll) vigour ~ snap adj unexpected, sudden; unprepared, on the spur of

the moment ~ snap interj exclamation on seeing an object exactly like another.

snapdragon [snapdRagon] n antirrhinum, a flowering plant; Christmas game in which raisins are snatched from a dish of burning brandy.

snap-judgement [snap-juJment] n opinion formed or decision taken in very short time.

snappish [snapish] adj giving sharp replies; irritable; inclined or eager to bite ~ snappishly adv.

snappy [snapi] n irritable; inclined to answer curtly and angrily; lively; brisk, rapid; (coll) smart; **look s., make it s.** (coll) hurry up ~ snappily adv ~ snappiness n.

snapshot [snapshot] n photograph taken with a hand camera, usu without posing ~ snapshot (pres/part snapshotting, p/t and p/part snapshotted) v/t and i take a snapshot (of).

snap-vote [snap-vOt] n vote taken suddenly.

snare [snair] n trap for catching animals; (fig) allurement, temptation; trick ~ snare v/t catch in a snare; trap, inveigle.

snark [snaark] n imaginary indefinable monster.

snarky [snaarki] adj (coll) bad-tempered.

snarl (1) [snaarl] n threatening growl; act of showing the teeth in anger ~ snarl v/i growl threateningly; show the teeth in anger; speak harshly.

snarl (2) n knotty tangle; traffic jam; difficulty ~ snarl v/t and i entangle; complicate; become entangled; **snarled up** (coll, of traffic etc) entangled, jammed.

snatch [snach] v/t and i seize hastily, grab; steal by seizing violently; remove by sudden force; (sl) kidnap; **s. at** try to seize hastily ~ snatch n act of snatching; grabbing or clutching movement; brief period of activity; fragment, disconnected portion; (coll) robbery by seizing goods hastily; (obs coll) female pudenda.

snatchy [snachi] adj scrappy; interrupted, broken.

snazzy [snazi] adj (sl) showy; attractive.

sneak [sneek] v/i and t move furtively, creep; (coll) steal furtively, pilfer; (sl) denounce to authority, inform against; act in a cowardly, underhand way ~ sneak n mean, cowardly person; (sl) telltale, informer; (cricket) ball that keeps close to the ground.

sneakers [sneekerz] n (pl) (coll) rubber-soled canvas shoes.

sneaking [sneeking] adj not openly admitted, private, secret; pettily dishonest or cowardly.

sneak-thief [sneek-theef] n pilferer; one who steals small articles from houses without breaking in.

sneer [sneer] v/i show contempt by mocking looks or remarks; smile scornfully; **s. at** show contempt for ~ sneer n act of sneering; smile, facial expression or verbal remark showing contempt.

sneeze [sneez] v/i eject air through the nostrils convulsively and loudly because of irritation of the nose; **not to be sneezed at** not to be despised or disregarded ~ sneeze n act of sneezing; sound of this.

snell [snel] n short length of catgut or horsehair by which fish-hooks are attached to a line.

snib [snib] n catch, latch, bolt.

snick [snik] v/t and i cut slightly, nick; (cricket) hit ball with glancing stroke ~ snick n slight cut, notch.

snicker [sniker] v/i snigger; neigh ~ snicker n.

snide [snɪd] adj (sl) sneering, pettily critical; hinting maliciously, conveying innuendo; sham, bogus.

snidy [*snɪdi*] *adj* (*sl*) crafty; knowing.

sniff [*snif*] *v/t* and *i* breathe in noisily through the nose, *esp* to check flow of moisture down it; breathe in strongly, inhale (*esp* smells); s. at quickly smell the odour of; express scorn, disapproval or suspicion by sniffing ~ **sniff** *n* act of sniffing; sound of this; that which is sniffed.

sniffle [*snif'l*] *v/i* sniff slightly, *esp* because of tears or mucus in the nose ~ **sniffle** *n* slight sniff.

sniffy [*snifi*] *adj* (*coll*) contemptuous, disdainful; smelly ~ **sniffily** *adv* ~ **sniffiness** *n*.

snifter [*snifter*] *n* (*sl*) short strong drink.

snigger [*sniger*] *v/i* give a half-suppressed laugh, laugh secretly; giggle, titter ~ **snigger** *n* furtive or giggling laugh.

snip (*pres/part* **snipping**, *p/t* and *p/part* **snipped**) [*snip*] *v/t* and *i* clip by repeated short cuts with scissors, pincers *etc* ~ **snip** *n* act of cutting; single short cut with scissors; (*coll*) profitable bargain; certainty of success or profit; tailor; fragment of cloth.

snipe (1) [*snip*] *n* marshland gamebird with long straight bill ~ **snipe** *v/i* shoot snipe.

snipe (2) *v/t* and *i* shoot at and kill (enemy troops) one by one from ambush ~ **sniper** *n*.

snippet [*snipit*] *n* small piece, fragment snipped off.

snitch [*snich*] *v/i* (*sl*) inform; pilfer.

snivel (*pres/part* **snivelling**, *p/t* and *p/part* **snivelled**) [*sniv'l*] *v/i* weep quietly but continuously; grieve or complain fretfully; have mucus running from the nose; sniff repeatedly ~ **snivel** *n* act of snivelling.

snob [*snob*] *n* one who attributes great importance to differences of social class; one who imitates, flatters, or associates with those of higher class than himself, while despising those equal to or below him.

snobbery [*snobeRi*] *n* outlook or behaviour of a snob.

snobbily [*snobili*] *adv* in a snobby way.

snobbiness [*snobinis*] *n* quality of being snobby.

snobbish [*snobish*] *adj* of or like a snob ~ **snobbishly** *adv* ~ **snobbishness** *n*.

snobby [*snobi*] *adj* of or like a snob.

snog (*pres/part* **snogging** *p/t* and *p/part* **snogged**) [*snog*] *v/i* (*sl*) kiss and caress, pet ~ **snog** *n* (*sl*) neck; flirtation; petting session.

snood [*snOOd*] *n* thick ornamental hairnet.

snook [*snook*] *n* gesture of contempt made by placing thumb against nose and extending fingers.

snooker [*snOOker*] *n* variety of pool or pyramids played on billiard-table.

snoop [*snOOp*] *v/i* (*coll*) pry, investigate, or watch by stealth.

snooper [*snOOper*] *n* one who pries; (*sl*) government inspector or investigator.

snooty [*snOOti*] *adj* (*coll*) haughty, conceited ~ **snootily** *adv* ~ **snootiness** *n*.

snooze [*snOOz*] *v/i* take a short sleep ~ **snooze** *n* a short sleep.

snore [*snawr*] *v/i* breathe noisily through the mouth when asleep ~ **snore** *n* act or sound of snoring.

snorkel [*snawrkel*] *n* tube through which a submarine or underwater swimmer can get air.

snort [*snawrt*] *v/i* breathe out noisily and violently through the nostrils ~ **snort** *n* act or sound of snorting.

snorter [*snawrter*] *n* one who snorts; (*coll*) anything unusually large, difficult *etc*; strong wind; harsh reproof, *esp* by letter; (*sl*) snifter.

snorty [*snawrti*] *adj* (*coll*) annoyed, disapproving.

snot [*snot*] *n* (*sl*) mucus from the nose.

snotty [*snoti*] *adj* (*sl*) having nose blocked with mucus; mean; dirty ~ **snotty** *n* (*sl*) midshipman.

snout [*snowt*] *n* animal's projecting nose; large nose; nozzle; projecting front of anything.

snow [*snO*] *n* large feathery flakes of ice-crystals formed by freezing of water-vapour in the air > PDG; expanse of this lying on the ground; (*sl*) powdered cocaine ~ **snow** *v/i* and *t* fall as snow; cause to fall in large quantities; **snowed under** (*fig*) overwhelmed by vast amounts; **snowed up** blocked or immobilized by snow.

snowball [*snObawl*] *n* mass of snow rolled or pressed into a ball; something that grows constantly larger; s. tree variety of guelder rose ~ **snowball** *v/t* and *i* throw snowballs (at); accumulate, grow larger by constant additions from new sources; increase or spread rapidly.

snowblind [*snOblind*] *adj* temporarily and partially blinded by the glaring reflection from snow ~ **snowblindness** *n*.

snowblink [*snOblink*] *n* light in sky reflected from snow or ice.

snowbound [*snObownd*] *adj* kept indoors or cut off from other towns *etc* by heavy snow.

snowcapped [*snOkapt*] *adj* topped with snow.

snowdrift [*snOdRift*] *n* snow blown by the wind to form a bank or heap.

snowdrop [*snOdRop*] *n* bulbous white-flowered plant of early spring.

snowfall [*snOfawl*] *n* amount of snow falling in a given time.

snowfield [*snOfeeld*] *n* region of permanent snow > PDG.

snowflake [*snOflayk*] *n* feathery flake formed of mass of ice-crystals.

snowily [*snO-ili*] *adv* in a snowy way.

snowiness [*snO-inis*] *n* quality of being snowy.

snowline [*snOlin*] *n* lowest limit of perpetual snow.

snowman [*snOman*] *n* human figure made of compressed snow; the **Abominable S.** (*coll*) the yeti.

snowplough [*snOplow*] *n* implement for clearing snow from roads or railways.

snowshoe [*snOshOO*] *n* racket-like frame fixed to shoes to prevent sinking into snow.

snowslip [*snOslip*] *n* avalanche.

snowstorm [*snOstawrm*] *n* heavy fall of snow with high wind.

snowy [*snO-i*] *adj* snowing frequently or heavily; covered in snow; pure white; pure; s. **owl** large arctic owl with white plumage mottled with black.

snub (1) (*pres/part* **snubbing**, *p/t* and *p/part* **snubbed**) [*snub*] *v/t* rebuke or humiliate by sneering or by scornful aloofness; (*naut*) check by sudden jerk ~ **snub** *n* act of snubbing; humiliating rebuke or rebuff.

snub (2) *adj* (*of nose*) short, flat, and with tip turned up.

snub-nosed [*snub-nOzd*] *adj* having a snub nose.

snuff (1) [*snuf*] *n* fine tobacco or other powder to be sniffed up the nose; sniff; **up to s.** (*sl*) clever, knowing; good enough ∼ **snuff** *v/t* and *i* inhale through nose, sniff up; take snuff.

snuff (2) *n* charred candle wick ∼ **snuff** *v/t* and *i* trim (wick) by cutting off snuff; **s. out** extinguish; (*fig*) suppress, destroy; (*coll*) die; kill.

snuffbox [*snuf*boks] *n* small ornamental container for snuff (1).

snuffers [*snuf*erz] *n* (*pl*) implement for cutting snuff off a wick.

snuffle [*snuf*'l] *v/i* breathe noisily through nose partly blocked by mucus; sniff repeatedly and loudly; talk nasally ∼ **snuffle** *n* act or sound of snuffling; moist nasal catarrh.

snug [*snug*] *adj* lying close or comfortable; warm, cosy; compact, trim; well fastened; concealed ∼ **snug** (*pres/part* **snugging**, *p/t* and *p/part* **snugged**) *v/i* be comfortable and close, nestle ∼ **snug** *n* snuggery.

snuggery [*snuge*Ri] *n* small, warm, comfortable room.

snuggle [*snug*'l] *v/i* and *t* lie close for comfort and warmth; cuddle.

snugly [*snug*li] *adv* in a snug way.

snugness [*snug*nis] *n* quality of being snug.

so [*sO*] *adv* and *conj* in such a manner (that); to the extent, degree *etc* (that); with the result (that); very much; in the same way (as), to the same extent, degree *etc* (as); for this reason, therefore; thus; also, too; in order (that); **s. forth** etcetera; **s. long as** on condition that; **s. long!** (*coll*) good-bye; **s. much** an unspecified amount; **s. much for** there is no more to do (say) about; **s. on** etcetera; **or s.** roughly, more or less; **s. what?** (*sl*) what is the point or consequence of that? ∼ **so** *pron* that which has just been mentioned.

soak [*sOk*] *v/t* and *i* wet thoroughly, drench; steep; lie steeped in liquid; permeate; (*coll*) drink excessively and habitually; (*sl*) tax very heavily; charge excessively ∼ **soak** *n* act of soaking; heavy downpour; (*coll*) heavy and habitual drinker; long period of hard drinking.

soakage [*sOk*ij] *n* liquid that has soaked into or through something.

soakaway [*sOk*away] *n* (*bui*) drainage pit.

soaker [*sOk*er] *n* one who or that which soaks; heavy shower; habitual heavy drinker.

soaking [*sOk*ing] *adj* wet through, very wet; capable of wetting thoroughly.

so-and-so [*sO*-and-sO] *n* name used in referring to a person whose name is forgotten, unknown or suppressed; name implying unexpressed term of abuse.

soap [*sOp*] *n* any of various solid or liquid cleansers that form a lather with water; cleansing compound of fatty acid and base > PDS; (*sl*) flattery; **s. opera** (*sl*) commercially sponsored radio or television serial, *esp* if sentimental ∼ **soap** *v/t* rub or wash with soap; (*sl*) flatter.

soapbox [*sOp*boks] *n* crate for holding bars of soap; (*fig*) box or rough platform used by street orators.

soap-bubble [*sOp*-bub'l] *n* thin inflated filmy sphere of soapy water.

soapflakes [*sOp*flayks] *n* (*pl*) thin flakes of readily soluble soap.

soapily [*sOp*ili] *adv* in a soapy way.

soapiness [*sOp*inis] *n* quality or state of being soapy.

soapstone [*sOp*stOn] *n* steatite; French chalk.

soapsuds [*sOp*sudz] *n* (*pl*) foamy lather of soap and water.

soapy [*sOp*i] *adj* of or like soap; covered with or full of soap; smooth, soft, greasy; (*fig*) flattering, servile; unctuous.

soar [*sawr*] *v/i* fly or float at very great height; rise very high ∼ **soar** *n* very high flight.

sob (*pres/part* **sobbing**, *p/t* and *p/part* **sobbed**) [*sob*] *v/i* and *t* catch the breath convulsively; weep noisily ∼ **sob** *n* convulsive catch of the breath, *usu* accompanied by tears.

sober [*sOber*] *adj* not drunk; temperate in the use of alcohol; moderate, well-balanced; self-possessed; serious, sedate; quiet ∼ **sober** *v/t* and *i* make sober; become sober ∼ **soberly** *adv*.

soberness [*sOber*nis] *n* quality of being sober.

sobersides [*sOber*sIdz] *n* (*coll*) serious, sedate person.

sobriety [*sob*RI-iti] *n* state or quality of being sober.

sobriquet [*sOb*Rikay] *n* nickname; assumed name.

sob-sister [*sob*-sister] *n* (*coll*) female journalist specializing in sentimental articles or advice on readers' problems.

sob-story [*sob*-stawRi] *n* (*sl*) deliberately pathetic story, *usu* false.

sob-stuff [*sob*-stuf] *n* (*sl*) exaggerated pathos or sentimentality.

soc [*sok*] *n* (*hist*) power or privilege of holding a local court.

socage [*sokij*] *n* (*hist*) feudal tenure of lands by any certain and determinate service.

so-called [*sO*-kawld] *adj* called thus; called thus, but not entitled to the name.

soccer [*soker*] *n* (*coll*) Association football, played with a round ball.

sociability [*sOsha*biliti] *n* quality of being sociable.

sociable [*sOshab*'l] *adj* willing to be friendly; fond of being with other people; friendly and informal ∼ **sociable** *n* (*coll*) informal party, meeting *etc*; (*hist*) two-seated tricycle; four-seated carriage ∼ **sociably** *adv*.

social [*sOshal*] *adj* of, for, in or forming a society; pertaining to the relations of an individual to the community > PDP; forming a group of mutually dependent members; of or for the welfare of a group or community; of, for, or indicating distinctions of class, status, wealth *etc* within a society; of good manners; friendly, sociable; of amusement, parties *etc*; gregarious; **s. credit** doctrine that industrial profits should be partly transferred to the community > PDPol; **s. science** sociology; **s. security** system by which a community supports its needy members; national insurance; **s. service** welfare work for members of a community; **s. worker** one who is trained to assist or advise people in need, unemployed, criminals *etc* ∼ **social** *n* (*coll*) party, friendly gathering or meeting.

socialism [*sOsha*lizm] *n* political and economic theory that the means of production, distribution and exchange should be owned by the nation, that wealth should be equitably distributed, and that opportunity and security should be available to all.

socialist [*sO*shalist] *adj* of, by or like socialism or socialists ~ **socialist** *n* advocate of socialism; member of a socialist party.

socialistic [sOsha*lis*tik] *adj* of, like, or tending towards socialism ~ **socialistically** *adv*.

socialite [*sO*shalIt] *n* high-class or rich person leading a gay life.

sociality [sOshi-*ali*ti] *n* quality of being social.

socialize [*sO*shalIz] *v*/*t* and *i* govern or organize on socialist principles; nationalize; (*psych*) adapt to social environment; (*coll*) behave in a polite and friendly way, *esp* at parties.

socially [*sO*shali] *adv* in a social way.

society [so*sI*-iti] *n* communal group of mutually dependent individuals; group whose members cooperate for a specified purpose or activity and share certain rules, customs *etc*; group of human beings characterized by specified customs, laws, behaviour *etc*; companionship, friendship; rich, aristocratic and exclusive social group, the upper class ~ **society** *adj* of, in or like the upper class; aristocratic; fashionable; **s. column** section of newspaper reporting activities of fashionable people; **s. life** fashionable pleasures, entertainments, parties *etc*.

socio- *pref* of society, social, of sociology.

sociological [sOsi-o*loji*kal] *adj* of or by sociology; pertaining to the behaviour, customs *etc* of human groups and societies.

sociologist [sOsi-*olo*jist] *n* student of sociology.

sociology [sOsi-*olo*ji] *n* science which studies the behaviour, customs *etc* of groups of human beings; science which studies the organization, growth *etc* of human societies.

sock (1) [sok] *n* short stocking; removable inner sole of shoe; **pull up one's socks** (*coll*) make greater efforts.

sock (2) *v*/*t* (*sl*) punch, hit ~ **sock** *n* (*sl*) blow.

socket [*sok*it] *n* natural or artificial hollow into which something fits.

socle [*sok*'l] *n* (*archi*) plain rectangular block plinth.

Socratic [sO*kRa*tik] *adj* of or like the Greek philosopher Socrates; **S. irony** pretence of ignorance designed to entrap an opponent in argument; **S. method** teaching method based on questioning the pupil.

sod (1) [sod] *n* surface soil held together by roots of grass *etc*; a piece of turf.

sod (2) *n* (*vulg sl*) sodomite; unpleasant, vindictive or ill-tempered person; (*joc*) fellow, person, chap ~ **sod** *v*/*t* bugger.

soda [*sO*da] *n* term applied to various sodium compounds > PDS; (*coll*) sodawater; **bicarbonate of s.** powder used medicinally or in baking; **s. fountain** (*US*) shop selling ice-cream, soft drinks *etc*; **washing s.** sodium carbonate used as a cleanser.

sodality [sO*dali*ti] *n* religious fellowship, fraternity.

sodawater [*sO*da-wawter] *n* water containing carbon dioxide which effervesces when released from pressure > PDS.

sodden [*so*den] *adj* soaked, saturated; not properly baked; stupid with drink ~ **soddenness** *n*.

sodium [*sO*di-um] *n* a metallic element > PDS.

sodomite [*sodo*mIt] *n* one who practises sodomy.

sodomitic [sodo*mi*tik] *adj* of or practising sodomy.

sodomy [*sodo*mi] *n* anal sexual intercourse.

sofa [*sO*fa] *n* long stuffed couch with a raised back and arms.

soffit [*so*fit] *n* (*archi*) under-surface of arch, balcony *etc*.

soft [soft] *adj* giving little resistance to pressure; easily cut, pressed or moulded; smooth to the touch; gentle, not rough, coarse or violent; lenient, tolerant; tender, loving; sympathetic; weak; effeminate; (*coll*) credulous, sentimental; feeble-minded, stupid; cowardly; (*of sound*) low; (*of colour*) not very bright; blurred, indistinct; (*of water*) easily lathered; (*of drinks*) non-alcoholic; (*of drug*) non-addictive; (*of currency*) not convertible into dollars; (*coll*) needing little effort, easy and well-paid; (*of radiation*) having a long wavelength, unpenetrating; **s. goods** textiles; **s. option** choice entailing the least painful consequences; **s. pedal** piano pedal that muffles the tone ~ **soft** *adv* gently, quietly ~ **soft** *interj* (*ar*) quiet! silence!

soft-core [*soft*-kawr] *adj* comparatively harmless, less offensive or vicious than others.

soften [*so*fen] *v*/*t* and *i* make soft or softer; palliate; relent; become soft or softer; **s. up** wear down the resistance of; bully or persuade into submission, acceptance *etc*.

softener [*so*fener] *n* chemical substance that softens hard water.

softening [*so*fening] *n* act of making or becoming softer; **s. of the brain** degeneration of brain tissues; (*fig*) increasing senility or stupidity.

soft-hearted [soft-*haart*id] *adj* easily moved to pity.

softly [*soft*li] *adv* in a soft way; quietly.

softness [*soft*nis] *n* quality of being soft.

softpedal [soft*ped*'l] *v*/*t* (*coll*) under-emphasize, tone down, disguise the extent or importance of.

soft-sell [*soft*-sel] *n* technique of selling goods by friendly persuasion.

softshoe [*soft*shOO] *adj* **s. dancing** form of tap-dancing without the metal shoe-rims.

softsoap [*soft*-sOp] *n* liquid soap made with potash; (*fig*) flattery ~ **softsoap** *v*/*t* flatter.

soft-spoken [soft-*spO*ken] *adj* speaking pleasantly and mildly; conciliatory.

software [*soft*wair] *n* program for computer; disposable or non-material items needed in planning a project.

softwood [*soft*wood] *n* coniferous timber.

softy [*soft*i] *n* (*coll*) silly sentimental person; effeminate man; imbecile; coward.

soggy [*sogi*] *adj* soaked; wet through; marshy; filled with water ~ **soggily** *adv* ~ **sogginess** *n*.

soil (1) [soil] *n* ground, layer of earth whence plants obtain nourishment > PDG, PDS; land, country.

soil (2) *v*/*t* and *i* make or become dirty; pollute, stain ~ **soil** *n* dirt, dirty stain; pollution; sewage; manure.

soirée [swaa*Ray*] *n* (*Fr*) evening party, *usu* with music and refreshments.

soixante-neuf [swasont-nu(r)f] *n* (*Fr*) (*sl*) simultaneous cunnilingus and fellatio.

sojourn [*so*jern/*su*jern] *v*/*i* stay or reside temporarily ~ **sojourn** *n* temporary residence.

soke [sOk] *n* soc.

sol (1) [*sol*] *n* (*mus*) fifth note of the sol-fa scale; fifth note of the scale of C major, G.

sol (2) *n* (*chem*) a colloidal solution.

solace [*sol*is] *n* that which comforts in grief or trouble; consolation ~ **solace** *v/t* comfort.

solar [*sO*lar] *adj* of or from the sun; caused by the sun; measured by the movement of earth relative to the sun; **s. cell** cell which converts sunlight into electrical energy, used as a source of power in space vehicles; **s. day** interval of time between two successive occasions when the sun is at the meridian > PDG, PDS; **s. heating** system for converting the heat of sunlight to heat buildings; **s. myth** myth interpreted as account of the sun's behaviour, effects *etc*; **s. panel** device for receiving the heat of sunlight in solar heating system; **s. plexus** network of nerves in the abdomen; **s. system** group of planets, asteroids, satellites *etc* revolving round the sun > PDG, PDS ~ **solar** *n* solarium.

solarium [*solairRi*-um] *n* room or building constructed for enjoyment of sunshine.

solarize [*sO*laRIz] *v/t* and *i* (*phot*) expose too long; reverse positives and negatives of a film or print.

sold [*sO*ld] *p/t* and *p/part* of sell; **s. on** (*coll*) convinced of the merits of.

soldan [*sol*dan] *n* (*ar*) sultan.

solder [*solder*/*sO*lder] *n* alloy for joining metals > PDS; (*fig*) anything which unites > **solder** *v/t* unite with or as with solder.

soldering-iron [*sO*ldeRing-I-ern] *n* tool for applying solder.

soldier [*sO*ljer/*sO*ldi-er] *n* member of a country's armed forces trained for fighting on land; one who is not an officer; man of military experience or skill; one who fights or struggles for a cause > **soldier** *v/i* serve as a soldier; **s. on** persevere despite great difficulties.

soldiering [*sO*ljeRing] *n* activity or profession of a soldier.

soldierly [*sO*ljerli] *adj* of or like a soldier; befitting a soldier; bold, resolute; with upright bearing.

soldiery [*sO*ljeRi] *n* body of soldiers; soldiers collectively.

sole (1) [*sO*l] *n* flat underside of foot; bottom of shoe or boot; lower part ~ **sole** *v/t* put a sole on.

sole (2) *n* an edible flatfish.

sole (3) *adj* single, only; unique; (*leg*) unmarried.

solecism [*sol*isizm] *n* incorrect grammar or idiom; breach of good manners; instance of ill-breeding.

solely [*sO*l-li] *adv* singly; only; for one reason only.

solemn [*sol*em] *adj* grave, serious; formal; performed or celebrated with formal ceremonies; impressive, dignified; rousing awe and reverence; pompous.

solemnity [*sol*emniti] *n* state or quality of being solemn; ceremony performed with religious reverence; impressiveness; gravity; formality; seriousness.

solemnize [*sol*emnIz] *v/t* perform with ceremonies or with formality; make solemn.

solemnly [*sol*emli] *adv* in a solemn way.

solenoid [*sol*enoid] *n* magnet formed by a coil of electrified wire > PDS.

sol-fa [sol-*faa*] *n* (*mus*) system of denoting notes of a major scale by vocal syllables in a fixed order, regardless of pitch > PDM ~ **sol-fa** *v/i* sing a scale with these syllables.

solicit [*sol*isit] *v/t* and *i* accost and make immoral sexual request or offer to; request earnestly and persistently; pester by begging.

solicitation [*sol*isit*a*yshon] *n* act of soliciting in the streets for immoral purposes; earnest request or invitation.

solicitor [*sol*isitor] *n* lawyer who advises clients and prepares cases for barristers.

solicitous [*sol*isitus] *adj* anxious, concerned; eager ~ **solicitously** *adv* ~ **solicitousness** *n*.

solicitude [*sol*isitewd] *n* anxiety.

solid [*sol*id] *adj* retaining its shape under moderate pressure; neither liquid nor gas; firm, compact; not hollow; of the same substance all through; heavy; indigestible; strongly built; reliable, steady; unanimous; logical, well reasoned; (*math*) three-dimensional ~ **solid** *n* (*phys*) body that is neither liquid nor gas; (*math*) three-dimensional figure; (*US sl*) favour; (*pl*) food that is not chiefly liquid ~ **solid** *adv* unanimously.

solidarity [*sol*idaRiti] *n* unanimous action or attitude based on shared interests; fellow-feeling, practical sympathy.

solidify [*sol*idIfı] *v/t* and *i* make solid; become solid.

solidity [*sol*iditi] *n* state or quality of being solid; firmness; strength; validity.

solidly [*sol*idli] *adv* in a solid way.

solid-state [solid-*stayt*] *adj* pertaining to electronic devices which are all in the solid state, *esp* semiconductors and superconductivity.

soliloquize [*sol*ilokwIz] *v/i* talk to oneself; utter a soliloquy on stage *etc*.

soliloquy [*sol*ilokwi] *n* act of talking to oneself; speech uttered by an actor alone on stage *etc*, supposedly expressing his private thoughts; monologue.

solipsism [*sol*ipsizm] *n* (*philos*) theory that the only possible knowledge is that of oneself.

solipsist [*sol*ipsist] *n* and *adj* (adherent) of solipsism ~ **solipsistic** [solipsistik] *adj*.

solitaire [solitair] *n* single gem in a setting; game played by one person with board and marbles; card game for one person.

solitary [*sol*itaRi] *adj* alone, placed, living, or acting apart from others; lonely; not living in a community; secluded, remote; uninhabited; single ~ **solitary** *n* one who lives alone, recluse; (*coll*) solitary confinement in prison ~ **solitarily** *adv* ~ **solitariness** *n*.

solitude [*sol*itewd] *n* condition of being alone; loneliness; seclusion; solitary place; uninhabited place, desert.

solleret [*sol*eRet] *n* (*hist*) steel shoe.

solmization [solmiz*a*yshon] *n* (*mus*) sol-fa system.

solo (*pl* **solos**, **soli**) [*sO*lO] *n* (*mus*) composition or passage for a single instrument or voice; (*fig*) display, performance *etc* by one person only; variety of whist in which solo play is possible ~ **solo** *adj* alone; single ~ **solo** *adv* alone; unaccompanied.

soloist [*sO*lO-ist] *n* performer of a solo.

so-long [sO-*long*] *interj* (*coll*) goodbye.

solstice [*sol*stis] *n* time of year when the sun reaches its point of furthest distance north or south of the equator > PDG, PDS.

solubility [solew*b*iliti] *n* extent to which a solute will dissolve in a solvent > PDS; state or quality of being soluble.

soluble [solew*b*'l] *adj* that can be dissolved in fluid, *esp* water; that can be solved.

solute [solewt] *n* substance dissolved in a solvent.

solution [solew*sh*on] *n* act, process, or method of solving a problem; explanation, answer to a puzzle, problem *etc*; liquid containing a dissolved solid; (*chem*) homogeneous mixture of substances of dissimilar molecular structure, *esp* of solids in liquids > PDS.

solve [solv] *v/t* find correct answer to (problem, puzzle *etc*); find method of overcoming (difficulties); explain.

solvency [solvensi] *n* ability to pay all debts.

solvent [solvent] *adj* having enough money to pay all debts; able to dissolve; able to relieve, soften *etc* ~ **solvent** *n* substance, *esp* liquid, that can dissolve other substances > PDS; that which relieves, softens, explains *etc*.

somatic [so*m*atik] *adj* of or affecting the body; physical; **s. cells** (*biol*) cells of an organism excluding the germ-cells; tissues excluding the internal organs; **s. death** death of whole body.

somato- *pref* of the body.

sombre [somber] *adj* dark; dismal, gloomy ~ **sombrely** *adv* ~ **sombreness** *n*.

sombrero [som*b*rair*RO*] *n* wide-brimmed soft felt or straw hat.

some [sum] *adj* an unspecified person or thing; an unspecified number or amount of; approximately; (*coll*) large amount of, high degree of; (*sl*) remarkable, great, excellent ~ **some** *pron* unspecified persons or things; an unspecified number or amount ~ **some** *adv* (*sl*) to a certain extent, considerably; for a while.

somebody [sum*b*odi] *n* an unspecified or unknown person; person of importance.

somehow [sum*h*ow] *adv* in a way still unknown or unspecified.

someone [sum*w*un] *n* somebody.

someplace [sum*p*lays] *adv* (*US*) somewhere.

somersault [sumersawlt] *n* leap in which one turns heels over head and lands on one's feet; (*fig*) sudden complete change of opinion, attitude *etc* ~ **somersault** *v/i* make a somersault.

something [sum*th*ing] *n* an unspecified thing, event *etc*; thing or event of importance ~ **something** *adv* in some degree; (*sl*) very; **s. like** approximately; vaguely resembling; (*coll*) considerable, excellent.

sometime [sumtIm] *adv* at a future but unspecified time; at one time, formerly ~ **sometime** *adj* former.

sometimes [sumtImz] *adv* at certain times but not others; at intervals; occasionally, not often.

somewhat [sum*w*ot] *adv* to some extent, fairly; slightly.

somewhere [sum*w*air] *adv* in some unknown or unspecified place.

somnambulism [som*n*ambewlizm] *n* act of walking or of performing actions in sleep.

somnambulist [som*n*ambewlist] *n* sleepwalker.

somni-, somno- *pref* of or during sleep.

somnolence [som*n*olens] *n* tendency to fall asleep; drowsiness, sleepiness.

somnolent [som*n*olent] *adj* sleepy, drowsy; inducing sleep ~ **somnolently** *adv*.

son [sun] *n* male child of specified parent; man seen as formed by or dependent on a country, school, organization *etc*; affectionate form of address to a boy; form of address used by priest to layman.

sonant [sOnant] *adj* and *n* voiced (letter or sound).

sonar [sOnaar] *n* apparatus emitting high-frequency sounds used in locating objects under water; echo-sounder ~ **sonar** *adj* activated by soundwaves; emitting high-pitched sounds.

sonata [so*n*aata] *n* musical composition for one or two players, *usu* in three or four movements of contrasting rhythms > PDM; **s. form** division of a movement into three parts > PDM.

sonatina [so*n*ateena] *n* short and simple sonata.

sonde [sond] *n* radio transmitter or other device sent up into atmosphere by balloon.

son-et-lumière [son-ay-loo*m*yair] *n* (*Fr*) nocturnal entertainment displaying history of famous castle, church *etc* by means of tape-recordings and lighting effects.

song [song] *n* that which is sung, series of melodious utterances of the human voice or of birds; short vocal composition > PDM; poem written to be sung; lyric poem; (*poet*) any poem; (*fig*) melodious sound; (*coll*) trifle; **make a s. about** (*coll*) make a fuss about.

songbird [song*b*urd] *n* any bird that sings.

songster [song*s*ter] *n* one who is skilled in singing; bird that sings.

sonic [so*n*ik] *adj* of sound; **s. bang** strong sound- and shock-waves set up by aircraft flying faster than the speed of sound; **s. barrier** sound-barrier.

son-in-law [sun-in-law] *n* husband of one's daughter.

sonnet [sonit] *n* short poem of fourteen pentameter lines, with a set rhyme scheme.

sonneteer [soni*t*eer] *n* one who writes sonnets.

sonny [suni] *n* friendly form of address to a boy.

sonority [so*n*oRiti] *n* quality of being sonorous.

sonorous [so*n*o*R*us/sona*w*r*R*us] *adj* giving out a resonant, deep or loud sound; rhetorical; melodious ~ **sonorously** *adv* ~ **sonorousness** *n*.

sonship [sun*sh*ip] *n* state of being a son.

sonsy [sonsi] *adj* (*Scots*) good-looking; buxom; good-natured.

soon [sOOn] *adv* in a short time, early; quickly; easily; willingly.

soot [soot] *n* black flaky substance given off from burning matter ~ **soot** *v/t* cover with soot.

sooth [sOO*th*] *n* (*ar*) truth, reality.

soothe [sOO*TH*] *v/t* make calm, reduce anxiety, fear, sorrow *etc* of; reduce pain of.

soothing [sOO*TH*ing] *adj* able to soothe; calming; relieving ~ **soothingly** *adv*.

soothsayer [sOO*th*say-er] *n* one who foretells magically; prophet.

sooty [sooti] *adj* consisting of soot; producing soot; covered with soot; like soot ~ **sootily** *adv* ~ **sootiness** *n*.

sop [sop] *n* food softened by dipping in liquid; (*fig*) small concession or gift to pacify an opponent; (*coll*) fool, weakling, coward ~ **sop** (*pres/part* **sopping**, *p/t* and *p/part* **sopped**) *v/t* dip or steep in liquid; soak; **s. up** absorb (liquid) with sponge *etc*.

690

sophism [*sofi*zm] *n* clever but false argument, plausible fallacy.

sophist [*sofi*st] *n* one whose arguments are clever but false; one who deliberately uses false arguments to persuade others; quibbler; (*Gk hist*) professional philosopher.

sophistic, sophistical [sofi*stik, sofi*stikal] *adj* containing sophisms; of or like a sophist ~ **sophistically** *adv*.

sophisticate [sofi*stikayt*] *v/t* and *i* deprive of simplicity or of naturalness; adulterate (food); corrupt; confuse by sophistic arguments.

sophisticated [sofi*stikaytid*] *adj* no longer having or liking simplicity in pleasures, art, social behaviour *etc*; refined, subtle; critical, cynical, blasé; artificial in behaviour, tastes *etc*; corrupt; sophistic; (*of machines*) complex, having the latest refinements.

sophistication [sofistika*yshon*] *n* state of being sophisticated; act or process of sophisticating.

sophistry [*sofi*stRi] *n* plausible but fallacious reasoning.

sophomore [*sofo*mawr] *n* second-year student at American university.

soporific [sopo*Rifi*k] *n* and *adj* (drug) causing or tending to cause sleep.

sopping [*sopi*ng] *adj* very wet, drenched.

soppy [*sopi*] *adj* thoroughly wet; (*coll*) silly; sentimental ~ **soppily** *adv* ~ **soppiness** *n*.

soprano [so*Raa*nO] *n* highest kind of female or boy's voice > PDM; singer who has this voice; musical part written for such voices.

sorbet [*saw*rbit] *n* sherbet.

sorcerer [*saw*rseRer] *n* magician, wizard.

sorceress [*saw*rseRis] *n* witch, female sorcerer.

sorcery [*saw*rseRi] *n* acts or words aiming at magically affecting persons or things or at knowing the future, *esp* if done by evoking evil spirits and for evil purposes; black magic, witchcraft; enchantment.

sordid [*saw*rdid] *adj* contemptibly evil; ignoble, mean; filthy, squalid; of or about disgusting aspects of poverty, misery, sin *etc*; obscene; having ignoble motives, *esp* desire for money ~ **sordidly** *adv* ~ **sordidness** *n*.

sordine [*saw*rdeen] *n* device to muffle a musical instrument.

sore [*saw*r] *adj* painfully inflamed, painful when touched; grieved; offended, resentful, bitter; causing annoyance or offence; (*ar*) causing great suffering; **s. point** topic that grieves, offends, or causes angry argument ~ **sore** *n* sore place on the body; ulcer, boil; (*fig*) painful memory ~ **sore** *adv* (*ar*) grievously.

sorehead [*saw*rhed] *n* (*sl*) one who is bitterly resentful or chronically bad-tempered.

sorely [*saw*rli] *adv* severely; very much, greatly.

soreness [*saw*rnis] *n* state of being sore.

sorghum [*saw*rgum] *n* genus of grasses including Indian millet.

soroptimist [so*Ropt*imist] *n* member of a women's Rotary club.

sororic [so*RORi*k] *adj* of or like a sister ~ **sororically** *adv*.

sorority [so*RORi*ti] *n* sisterhood; (*US*) female student association.

sorrel (1) [*so*Rel] *n* herb with acrid-tasting leaves.

sorrel (2) *n* yellowish-brown colour; horse of this colour ~ **sorrel** *adj*.

sorrow [*so*RO] *n* deep mental distress caused by loss or misfortune; grief, sadness; regret; that which causes grief, misfortune; mourning ~ **sorrow** *v/i* grieve, mourn.

sorrowful [*so*ROfool] *adj* feeling sorrow; grieved; causing sorrow ~ **sorrowfully** *adv* ~ **sorrowfulness** *n*.

sorry [*so*Ri] *adj* regretful, contrite; grieved; feeling pity; (*ar*) rousing pity, miserable; contemptible, worthless ~ **sorry** *interj* an expression of apology.

sort [*saw*rt] *n* a class, order, species; kind, degree; manner; (*printing*) piece of type considered as part of a fount; **s. of** (*coll*) to some extent, in some way; more or less; **good s.** (*coll*) kind, likeable person; **out of sorts** not very well ~ **sort** *v/t* and *i* separate into classes; select from a number; agree with.

sortable [*saw*rtab'l] *adj* capable of being sorted.

sorter [*saw*rter] *n* one who sorts, *esp* one employed by the Post Office to sort letters.

sortie [*saw*rtee] *n* (*mil*) sally of besieged troops; military flight by aircraft, *esp* bombing raid.

sortilege [*saw*rtilij] *n* divination by drawing lots.

S.O.S. [es-O-es] *n* urgent appeal for help; Morse signal appealing for help in emergency; message, *esp* broadcast, summoning relatives of someone dangerously ill.

so-so [*sO*-sO] *adj* (*coll*) not very good, mediocre ~ **so-so** *adv*.

sostenuto [soste*newt*O] *adv* (*mus*) with the notes held.

sot [*sot*] *n* habitual drunkard; fuddled person.

sottish [*soti*sh] *adj* of or like a sot.

sotto voce [sotO-*vO*chay] *adv* (*Ital*) in an undertone.

sou [*sOO*] *n* French coin, worth five centimes.

soubrette [sOO*bRet*] *n* (*theat*) pert, coquettish girl, *esp* a maid, in a comedy.

souchong [sOO*shong*] *n* kind of China tea.

soufflé [sOO*flay*] *n* light dish made chiefly of beaten whites of eggs.

sough [*suf/sow/sOOkh*] *n* low sighing sound, *esp* of wind in foliage ~ **sough** *v/i* make such a sound.

sought [*sawt*] *p/t* and *p/part* of **seek**.

soul [*sOl*] *n* (*theol*) immortal spiritual component in human beings, regarded as distinct from intellect and body; this surviving after death, separated from the body; (*fig*) that which keeps living creatures alive; the nobler feelings and capacities of the human mind; religious, moral, or artistic sensitivity; conscience; essence; source of vigour or gaiety; (*coll*) person, human being; (*jazz*) emotional power; (*Negro coll*) Negro culture and traditions; pride in these.

soulful [*sOl*fool] *adj* possessing or appealing to lofty religious, spiritual or artistic feelings; sentimental, emotional ~ **soulfully** *adv* ~ **soulfulness** *n*.

soulless [*sOl*-lis] *adj* without a soul; inhuman, impersonal; mechanical; cruel; lacking emotion ~ **soullessly** *adv* ~ **soullessness** *n*.

soulmate [*sOl*mayt] *n* person ideally suited to be another's friend or lover.

soul-searching [*sOl*-surching] *n* anxious self-examination regarding one's beliefs, motives, moral qualities *etc*.

sound (1) [*sownd*] *adj* in good physical condition; healthy, wholesome; normal; undamaged; based on good reasons, logical, justifiable; prudent; correct; reliable; valid; financially safe or reliable; complete, thorough; strong, sturdy; (*of sleep*) deep and unbroken ~ **sound** *adv* in a sound way; (*of sleeping*) deeply.

sound (2) *n* noise, that which can be heard; variations of pressure waves in air *etc* set up by a vibrating source and perceived by the ear > PDP, PDS; impression received by hearing; distance within which something can be heard ~ **sound** *v/t* and *i* cause to produce sound; express by sound; emit a sound; give a specified impression by sound; seem, give an impression; express, celebrate, spread the news of; **s. off** (*coll*) express anger or disapproval ~ **sound** *adj* of by or for wireless broadcasting (not television).

sound (3) *n* narrow passage of waters, strait; airbladder of fish.

sound (4) *v/t* measure the depth of; plunge to the bottom of; (*fig*) test, examine; tactfully ascertain the views, intentions *etc* of; (*med*) probe; test with stethoscope; (*meteor*) examine (atmosphere) by sending up balloons; **s. out** make tactful inquiries ~ **sound** *n* (*med*) surgical probe.

sound-barrier [*sownd*-baRi-er] *n* (*aer*) moment at which an aircraft's speed equals that of soundwaves; **break the s.** fly faster than the speed of sound, 760 m.p.h.; set up strong sound- and shock-waves in doing so.

soundbox [*sownd*boks] *n* box containing stylus and diaphragm of gramophone.

sound-broadcasting [*sownd*-bRawdkaasting] *n* wireless programmes transmitted as sounds only, as distinct from television.

sound-effects [*sownd*-ifekts] *n* (*pl*) all sounds other than words or music that form part of a broadcast or televised programme or of a film.

sounding (1) [*sownding*] *adj* making or giving out sound; noisy; resonant; eloquent but of little value.

sounding (2) *n* process of measuring the depth of water > PDG; process of examining the atmosphere by sending up instruments attached to balloons > PDG; act of exploring, probing or ascertaining.

sounding-board [*sownding*-bawrd] *n* structure placed over a pulpit to reflect the speaker's voice towards the listeners; (*mus*) board which enhances the sound in various instruments > PDM; (*fig*) means of publicizing opinions.

sounding-post [*sownding*-pOst] *n* piece of wood in a violin which transmits the sound > PDM.

soundless [*sownd*lis] *adj* silent ~ **soundlessly** *adv*.

soundly [*sownd*li] *adv* thoroughly; healthily; firmly; well.

soundness [*sownd*nis] *n* quality or state of being sound.

soundproof [*sownd*pROof] *adj* constructed of materials that shut out or deaden external noises; impervious to sound ~ **soundproof** *v/t* render soundproof by use of special materials.

soundtrack [*sownd*tRak] *n* (*cin*) margin on film on which synchronized sound is recorded; words, music, sound-effects *etc* of a film.

soundwave [*sownd*wayv] *n* wave set up in air *etc* by vibrating objects and perceived by the ear.

soup [*sOOp*] *n* liquid food made from water in which meat or vegetables have been boiled; (*sl*) horsepower of engine; **in the s.** (*sl*) in difficulties, in trouble ~ **soup** *v/t* **s. up** (*sl*) supercharge (motor engine).

soupçon [*sOOp*sawn(g)] *n* (*Fr*) slight trace or taste.

souped-up [*sOOp*t-up] *adj* (*mot*)' supercharged; (*fig*) artificially increased or enhanced.

soup-kitchen [*sOOp*-kichen] *n* military mobile kitchen; (*hist*) public establishment supplying free soup to the poor.

soup-plate [*sOOp*-playt] *n* deep plate in which soup is served.

soupspoon [*sOOp*spOOn] *n* large spoon with deep bowl.

soupy [*sOOp*i] *adj* of or like soup; (*coll*) sentimental; (*of voice*) throbbing with emotion.

sour [*sowr*] *adj* sharp to the taste, acid, tart; embittered, peevish, morose; (*of soil*) impoverished; **s. grapes** something one pretends to despise because one cannot have it ~ **sour** *v/t* and *i* make sour; become sour ~ **sour** *n* that which is sour; that which embitters, cruel misfortune.

source [*sawrs*] *n* starting-point, origin; primary cause; document or authority from which information is derived; literary or artistic work from which others derive ideas, themes *etc*; spring, fountain from which a stream flows.

source-book [*sawrs*-book] *n* collection of historical documents.

souring [*sowr*Ring] *n* process of bleaching with acid; anything used to make acid.

sourly [*sowr*li] *adv* in a sour way.

sourness [*sowr*nis] *n* quality of being sour.

sourpuss [*sowr*poos] *n* (*coll*) grumbler; bitter and gloomy person.

souse [*sows*] *n* salt pickle; anything preserved in this; plunge into water ~ **souse** *v/t* pickle; plunge into water.

soused [*sowst*] *adj* pickled; (*coll*) very drunk.

soutane [*sOO*taan] *n* (*Fr*) cassock.

souterraine [*sOO*teRayn] *n* (*arch*) underground passage or chamber.

south [*sowth*] *n* cardinal compass point opposite to the north; region in this direction ~ **south** *adj* in, towards or facing the south; (*of wind*) coming from the south ~ **south** *adv* towards the south ~ **south** *v/i* move southwards.

Southdown [*sowth*down] *n* and *adj* (breed of sheep) from the South Downs of England.

south-east [sowth-*eest*] *n* compass direction between south and east; region in this direction ~ **south-east** *adj* and *adv* in, towards or from the south-east.

southeaster [sowth*eester*] *n* wind from the south-east.

south-easterly [sowth-*eesterli*] *adj* and *adv* coming from the south-east; towards the south-east.

south-eastern [sowth-*eestern*] *adj* in, towards or coming from the south-east.

southerly [*suTH*erli] *adj* in, from, or towards the south.

southern [*suTH*ern] *adj* of or in the south; coming from the south; **S. Cross** cross-shaped constella-

692

tion of the southern hemisphere, pointing to the South Pole > PDG.

southerner [su*TH*erner] *n* inhabitant of a southern region.

southernmost [su*TH*ernmOst] *adj* farthest south.

southing [*sowth*ing] *n* act of going south; time when a heavenly body passes the meridian; (*naut*) difference of latitude towards the south.

southron [su*TH*Ron] *adj* and *n* (*Scots*) (of) an Englishman.

southward [*sowth*wood] *adj* and *adv* towards the south.

southwards [*sowth*woodz] *adv* towards the south.

south-west [sowth-*west*] *n* compass direction between south and west; region in this direction ∼

south-west *adj* and *adv* in, towards, or coming from the south-west.

southwester [southwester] *n* wind from the south-west; sou'wester.

south-westerly [sowth-*west*erli] *adj* and *adv* coming from the south-west; towards the south-west.

south-western [sowth-*west*ern] *adj* in, towards, or from the south-west.

souvenir [sOOveneer/sOOveneer] *n* keepsake, memento.

sou'wester [sow-*west*er] *n* waterproof peaked hat with brim covering the neck; south-westerly gale.

sovereign [*sov*Rin] *n* supreme ruler, monarch (male or female); British gold coin nominally worth one pound ∼ **sovereign** *adj* having supreme independent power; royal; very effective or powerful; excellent.

sovereignty [*sov*Rinti] *n* supreme power or rule; absolute independent power of a State.

Soviet [sOvi-et/sovi-et] *n* elected regional or national governing council in Russia > PDPol; S. Union modern name of the state consisting of the Socialist Republics of Russia, Georgia, the Ukraine *etc* ∼ **Soviet** *adj* governed by councils; of or in the Soviet Union.

Sovietize [sOvi-etIz] *v/t* administer by Soviet councils; incorporate in the Soviet Union; convert to Communism.

sow (1) [*pres/part* sowed, *p/t* and *p/part* sown) [sO] *v/t* and *i* place (seed) in or on soil so that it may grow; scatter seed over; scatter, cause to spread; implant, suggest; teach; disseminate.

sow (2) [sow] *n* adult female pig.

sower [sO-er] *n* one who or that which scatters seed.

sown [sOn] *p/part* of **sow** (1).

sowthistle [*sow*this'l] *n* species of thistle with toothed leaves and milky juice.

soy [soi] *n* Oriental sauce made from pickled soya beans.

soya [*soi*-a] *n* species of Asiatic bean yielding oil; **s. flour** flour made from pressed soya beans.

sozzled [*soz*'ld] *adj* (*coll*) drunk, befuddled.

spa [spaa] *n* health-resort where there is a spring of mineral water.

space [spays] *n* interval of distance between two or more objects, lines or points; area, distance; period of time; adequate area, room; (*math*) infinite extension; (*astron*) total area of the universe; (*pop astron*) region beyond the solar system; region beyond the earth's atmosphere; (*typ*) blank interval between words; thin piece of metal used to make this; (*mus*) interval between lines on

a score; **outer s.** (*pop astron*) region beyond the solar system ∼ **space** *v/t* arrange (objects, lines, points) leaving spaces between them; arrange at intervals; **s. out** cause to be further apart; cause to occur more rarely ∼ **space** *adj* of or in space, *esp* astronomical space; of or for spaceflight.

spacebar [spaysbaar] *n* typewriter bar pressed down to make blank space between words.

spacecraft [spayskRaaft] *n* spaceship.

spaceman (*pl* spacemen) [spaysman] *n* astronaut; one who travels in a spaceship.

spacer [spayser] *n* spacebar; device for reversing telegraphic current.

spaceflight [spaysflIt] *n* flight of a human being or animal in a rocket beyond earth's atmosphere.

spaceprobe [spayspROb] *n* rocket-propelled missile for making measurements in space or studying the moon or planets > PDS.

space-saving [spays-sayving] *adj* designed to be small and compact.

spaceship [spays-ship] *n* rocket or other vehicle capable of passing beyond earth's atmosphere, of orbiting round the earth, or of reaching the moon or the planets.

spacesuit [spays-sewt] *n* protective garment and helmet worn by astronauts.

space-time [spays-tIm] *n* blending of time with three-dimensional space to form a single four-dimensional reality > PDS.

space-travel [spays-tRav'l] *n* spaceflight, *esp* if prolonged; act of journeying to the moon, planets *etc* in a spaceship ∼ **space-traveller** *n*.

spackle [spak'l] *v/t* and *i* fill in defects (in woodwork) with plastic.

spacing [spaysing] *n* way in which or degree to which objects *etc* are spaced out.

spacious [spayshus] *adj* having ample room; extensive, wide ∼ **spaciously** *adv* ∼ **spaciousness** *n*.

spade (1) [spayd] *n* digging tool with broad, flat blade; tool or instrument of similar shape; (*cards*) one of suit of cards marked with a black figure like a pointed heart on a stalk; (*sl*) Negro, West Indian; **call a s. a s.** speak frankly and bluntly ∼ **spade** *v/t* dig with a spade.

spade (2) [spayd] *n* gelding.

spadework [spaydwurk] *n* dull hard work necessary to a larger project.

spado [spaydO] *n* castrated man, eunuch; impotent man.

spaewife [spaywIf] *n* (*Scots*) woman with prophetic powers.

spaghetti [spa*get*i] *n* thin macaroni.

spahi, spahee [spaahee] *n* member of Algerian cavalry corps in French army; (*hist*) Turkish cavalryman.

spake [spayk] *ar p/t* of **speak**.

spallation [spalayshon] *n* (*phys*) nuclear reaction in which an incident particle causes the target nucleus to emit several particles > PDS.

spam [spam] *n* (*tr*) a proprietary word for a brand of spicy tinned pork.

span (1) [span] *p/t* of **spin**.

span (2) *n* extent of something stretched out; full extent in space or time; space between pillars of an arch, supports of a bridge *etc*; length from end to end; extreme breadth, *esp* of bird or aircraft across the wings; team of oxen, mules or plough-horses; breadth across extended hand from thumb-tip to tip of little finger; nine inches ~ **span** (*pres/part* **spanning**, *p/t* and *p/part* **spanned**) *v/t* extend from end to end of, extend right round or across; cross; measure with extended hand.

spancel [*span*s'l] *n* rope for tying hind legs of cow, horse *etc* ~ **spancel** *v/t* tie hind legs of.

spandrel [*spand*Ril] *n* (*archi*) space between curve of arch and rectangle enclosing it.

spangle [*spang*-g'l] *n* small, thin disk of glittering metal; small glittering object ~ **spangle** *v/t* decorate with spangles; cover with small glittering objects.

Spaniard [*span*yard] *adj* a native of Spain.

spaniel [*span*yel] *n* breed of dogs with long drooping ears and silky hair.

Spanish [*span*ish] *n* language of Spain; (*collect*) natives of Spain ~ **Spanish** *adj* of or from Spain; **S. black** pigment from burnt oak; **S. chestnut** edible chestnut; **S. fly** species of beetle, cantharis; **S. grass** esparto grass; **S. Main** Caribbean Sea.

spank [*spank*] *v/t* and *i* strike with the open hand, *esp* on the buttocks; **s. along** move briskly ~ **spank** *n* blow with the open hand, slap.

spanker [*spank*er] *n* one who spanks; fast horse; (*coll*) fine specimen; (*naut*) fore-and-aft sail on mizzen mast.

spanking (1) [*spank*ing] *adj* (*coll*) brisk, quick-moving; large; fine ~ **spankingly** *adv*.

spanking (2) *n* a beating.

spanner [*span*er] *n* wrench for tightening or loosening nuts on screws; connecting-rod of bridge, steam-engine *etc*; **a s. in the works** (*coll*) deliberate hindrance, sabotage.

span-roof [*span*-ROOf] *n* roof with two slopes.

spar (1) [*spaar*] *n* (*naut*) pole used as mast, yard, boom, gaff *etc*.

spar (2) *n* a lustrous crystalline mineral.

spar (3) (*pres/part* **sparring**, *p/t* and *p/part* **sparred**) *v/i* practise boxing, *esp* without hurting one's opponent; (*fig*) have a friendly argument or contest (against) ~ **spar** *n* boxing-match, *esp* for practice; friendly dispute; cockfight.

spare [*spair*] *adj* kept in reserve for use in emergency or as a replacement; extra; freely available; left over, not used or needed; lean, thin; scanty, meagre; (*coll*) angry, curt; **s. part** extra part kept as replacement for a part of a machine; **s. room** room not normally used; guest-room; **s. time** leisure, time left free after work is done ~ **spare** *n* spare part for machine, *esp* motor vehicle ~ **spare** *v/t* and *i* be merciful to, refrain from killing, punishing *etc*; refrain from using; use economically; give away, give in charity; be able to do without ~ **sparely** *adv* ~ **spareness** *n*.

sparerib [*spair*Rib] *n* piece of pork consisting of ribs with little meat.

sparing [*spair*Ring] *adj* scarce, scanty; economical, frugal ~ **sparingly** *adv*.

spark (1) [*spaark*] *n* glowing particle thrown out by burning substance; small flash of light accompanying electric discharge; (*fig*) liveliness; vitality, life; intelligence; slight trace; ignition of motor engine ~ **spark** *v/i* and *t* give out sparks; ignite by producing electric sparks; **s. off** set alight or explode by a spark; (*fig*) cause, precipitate, set in motion.

spark (2) *n* gay young fellow.

sparking-plug [*spaark*ing-plug] *n* device in internal combustion engine by which explosive gas is electrically ignited.

sparkle [*spaark*'l] *v/i* glitter, twinkle; emit sparks; be gay and clever; (*of drinks*) give off bubbles of carbon dioxide, effervesce ~ **sparkle** *n* act of glittering; brilliance; gaiety, wit, lively intelligence.

sparkler [*spaark*ler] *n* one who or that which sparkles; (*sl*) diamond.

sparklet [*spaark*lit] *n* a small sparkle; (*tr*) metal capsule containing carbonic acid gas used in a special type of sodawater siphon.

sparkling [*spaark*ling] *adj* glittering; witty; intelligent; effervescent ~ **sparklingly** *adv*.

sparks [*spaark*s] *n* (*sl*) radio operator, *esp* on ship or aircraft.

sparring [*spaar*Ring] *n* harmless boxing, *esp* for practice; friendly argument or contest; **s. partner** one against whom a boxer practises; opponent in friendly disputes.

sparrow [*spa*RO] *n* small brownish bird of the genus *Passer*.

sparrowhawk [*spa*ROhawk] *n* species of short-winged hawk.

sparse [*spaars*] *adj* thinly scattered; scanty, rare ~ **sparsely** *adv* ~ **sparseness** *n*.

spartan [*spaar*tan] *adj* enduring hardship or pain without complaint, unflinching; harsh, austere, ascetic ~ **Spartan** *n* inhabitant of Sparta; one who endures unflinchingly; one who practises austerity.

spasm [*spazm*] *n* sudden involuntary muscular contraction; sudden convulsive movement; strong but short-lived burst of energy, interest *etc*.

spasmodic [spazmodik] *adj* of or like a spasm; convulsive; showing strong but short-lived energy; intermittent ~ **spasmodically** *adv*.

spastic [*spas*tik] *adj* (*med*) suffering from lack of muscular control because of damage, *esp* congenital, to the brain ~ **spastic** *n* person suffering from such damage.

spat (1) [*spat*] *n* spawn of shellfish, *esp* of oyster.

spat (2) *n* short gaiter covering upper part of shoe.

spat (3) *p/t* and *p/part* of **spit** (2).

spatchcock [*spach*kok] *n* quickly cooked fowl ~ **spatchcock** *v/t* (*coll*) insert as an afterthought.

spate [*spayt*] *n* heavy flood, *esp* of river.

spatial [*spa*ysh'l] *adj* of, in, or concerning space or relations of objects in space ~ **spatially** *adv*.

spatter [*spat*er] *v/t* and *i* splash with drops of liquid, sprinkle ~ **spatter** *n* a shower, sprinkling.

spatula [*spat*ewla] *n* broad-bladed blunt knife for mixing paints, plaster *etc*; (*med*) instrument for flattening the tongue.

spatulate [*spat*ewlit] *adj* shaped like a spatula.

spavin [*spav*in] *n* disease of horses characterized by swelling of joints ~ **spavined** *adj*.

spawn [*spawn*] *n* eggs of fish, frogs, molluscs *etc*; mycelium of fungi; (*cont*) children, offspring ~ **spawn** *v/t* and *i* deposit eggs; give birth to.

spay [*spay*] *v/t* sterilize (female animal) by removing the ovaries.

speak (*p/t* **spoke**, *p/part* **spoken**) [*speek*] *v/t* and *i* utter words, talk; convey meaning; address an audience, give a speech, lecture, sermon *etc*; express, *esp* by words; converse; **s. for oneself** express one's own views only; **nothing to s. of** nothing worth mentioning; **s. out** speak plainly and fearlessly; **s. up** speak loudly and clearly.

speakeasy [*speek*eezi] *n* (*US coll*) place where alcoholic drinks are illegally sold.

speaker [*speek*er] *n* one who speaks; one who delivers a speech, lecture *etc*; (*cap*) one who presides over a deliberative assembly, *esp* the House of Commons.

speaking [*speek*ing] *adj* articulate; vivid, lifelike; **on s. terms** sufficiently well acquainted to talk together; friendly.

speaking-trumpet [*speek*ing-tRumpit] *n* megaphone.

speaking-tube [*speek*ing-tewb] *n* pipe through which the sound of a voice is conveyed.

spear [*speer*] *n* weapon with sharp pointed head on long shaft ~ **spear** *v/t* and *i* kill or pierce with spear; (*of plants*) form a long stem.

spearhead [*speer*hed] *n* pointed head of a spear; (*fig*) vanguard of an attack; leaders of a movement ~ **spearhead** *v/t* be the leader of.

spearmint [*speer*mint] *n* aromatic species of mint; chewing-gum flavoured with this.

spec [*spek*] *n* (*coll abbr*) speculation; **on s. as a** guess or gamble.

special [*spesh*'l] *adj* distinctive, peculiar; for a particular purpose; not ordinary; specific; intensively studied; detailed; of or for one person; (*coll*) unusually good; **s. constable** person temporarily enrolled as policeman in emergency; **s. pleading** (*coll*) quibbling, unfair argument; (*leg*) argument applicable only to the case at issue ~ **special** *n* person or thing appointed or designed for particular purpose; special constable; extra edition of newspaper.

specialist [*spesh*alist] *n* one who devotes himself to one particular branch of a science, art, or profession; authority on one particular subject, *esp* in medicine.

speciality [speshi-*al*iti] *n* something which one knows, does, or makes particularly well; characteristic feature.

specialization [speshalIz*ay*shon] *n* act or process of specializing; state of being specialized.

specialize [*spesh*alIz] *v/i* and *t* limit oneself to studying intensively one or a few branches of knowledge or skill, be or become a specialist; adapt to a specific function, use *etc*.

specially [*spesh*ali] *adv* in a special way.

specialness [*spesh*alnis] *n* quality of being special.

specialty [*spesh*alti] *n* contract under seal; distinctive feature; something made, known, studied *etc* by specialists.

speciation [speesi-*ay*shon] *n* (*biol*) evolution of a new species.

specie [*spee*shee] *n* coin money.

species (*pl* species) [*spee*sheez] *n* (*biol*) group of similar animals or plants able to breed with each other but not with others > PDB; (*coll*) kind, sort, type; (*theol*) appearance as perceived by the senses.

specific [spi*sif*ik] *adv* of one definite sort or kind; explicit, precise; having a defined and limited meaning; of a biological species; of or for a particular disease; **s. gravity** ratio of density of a substance to that of water > PDS; **s. heat** quantity of heat required to raise the temperature of 1 gm. of a substance by 1° C; **s. impulse** ratio of the thrust produced by a rocket engine to the rate of fuel consumption > PDS ~ **specific** *n* remedy for a particular disease; unfailing remedy ~ **specifically** *adv*.

specification [spesifik*ay*shon] *n* act of specifying; detailed statement of work to be done; detailed list of orders, points in a contract *etc*.

specificity [spesi*fis*iti] *n* quality of being specific.

specify [*spes*ifI] *v/t* mention specifically, indicate in precise detail.

specimen [*spes*imen] *n* individual regarded as typical member of a group; natural object preserved, classified, exhibited or studied as typical of its kind; something characteristic, sample; (*coll*) odd person.

speciology [speeshi-*ol*oji] *n* branch of biology dealing with the nature and origin of species.

speciosity [speeshi-*os*iti] *n* speciousness.

specious [*spee*shus] *adj* superficially attractive; apparently right or fair but actually false ~ **speciously** *adv* ~ **speciousness** *n*.

speck [*spek*] *n* small spot, stain or blemish; minute particle ~ **speck** *v/t* mark with a speck or with specks.

speckle [*spek*'l] *n* small spot or stain; patch of light or colour ~ **speckle** *v/t* cover with speckles.

specs [*speks*] *n* (*pl*) (*coll*) spectacles.

spectacle [*spek*tak'l] *n* something displayed or exhibited; impressive or unusual sight; ridiculous sight; film or theatrical show full of spectacular visual effects; pageant; (*pl*) framed optical lenses worn in front of the eyes to correct defects of vision, glasses.

spectacled [*spek*tak'ld] *adj* wearing spectacles; having marks like spectacles.

spectacular [spekt*ak*ewlar] *adj* visually impressive; showy, flamboyant; amazing ~ **spectacular** *n* film or theatrical show with lavish visual effects ~ **spectacularly** *adv*.

spectator [spekt*ay*tor] *n* observer, onlooker.

spectra [*spek*tRa] *pl* of spectrum.

spectral [*spek*tRal] *adj* of or like ghosts; of, on, or like the spectrum > PDS.

spectre [*spek*ter] *n* ghost, spirit appearing visibly; terrifying non-material danger.

spectro- *pref* of the spectrum.

spectrograph [*spek*tRogRaaf] *n* instrument by which spectra may be photographed; photograph taken by this > PDS.

spectrometer [spekt*Rom*iter] *n* instrument to measure angular deviation of light through a prism; instrument to detect isotopes.

spectroscope [*spek*tRoskOp] *n* instrument for observing or analysing a spectrum.

spectroscopic [spektRo*skop*ik] *adj* of or by a spectroscope.

spectrum (*pl* spectra) [*spek*tRum] *n* series of bands of coloured light obtained by refracting white light through a prism > PDP, PDS; characteristic pattern of wavelengths in light emitted by or transmitted through a specified substance > PDS; (*fig*) wide range, graduated series; (*opt*) image persisting on the retina after the stimulus causing it has ceased; **s. analysis** analysis of the chemical nature of a substance by its spectrum > PDS; **s. colours** the colours of the rainbow.

specula [*spek*ewla] *pl* of **speculum**.

specular [*spek*ewlar] *adj* of or like a speculum; like a mirror; **s. reflection** perfectly regular reflection of electromagnetic waves > PDS.

speculate [*spek*ewlayt] *v/i* theorize, make conjectures, wonder; invest money in something that may bring either gain or loss; invest in stocks and shares.

speculation [spekewlayshon] *n* act or process of speculating; unproved theory, conjecture; investment that may bring either gain or loss; investment in stocks and shares.

speculative [*spek*ewlativ] *adj* involving financial risk; given to speculation; theoretical; not verified by fact ~ **speculatively** *adv*.

speculator [*spek*ewlaytor] *n* one who speculates, *esp* in finance.

speculum (*pl* **specula**) [*spek*ewlum] *n* reflector, metal mirror; mirror of telescope; (*med*) instrument to dilate a cavity so that it can be examined; (*orni*) lustrous spot on bird's wing.

sped [*sped*] *p/t* and *p/part* of **speed**.

speech [*speech*] *n* act or faculty of expressing meaning by uttering words; manner of speaking; language; discourse addressed to the public.

speech-day [*speech*-day] *n* annual prize-giving day at a school.

speechify [*speech*ifI] *v/i* make a long public speech.

speechless [*speech*lis] *adj* temporarily unable to speak, *esp* through strong emotion; dumb; silent; (*coll*) amazed ~ **speechlessly** *adv* ~ **speechlessness** *n*.

speech-reading [*speech*-Reeding] *n* lip-reading.

speech-therapy [*speech*-theRapi] *n* treatment, exercises *etc* designed to correct defects of articulation caused by psychological or physical disorders.

speech-training [*speech*-tRayning] *n* training in the art of public speaking; training in correct pronunciation.

speed (1) [*speed*] *n* quickness of movement, rapidity; rate of movement, ratio of distance covered to time taken by moving body; (*sl*) amphetamine; **at full s.** as fast as possible ~ **speed** (*p/t* and *p/part* **sped**, (*mot*) **speeded**) *v/i* and *t* move rapidly; (*mot*) drive unusually fast; exceed a speed-limit; **s. up** accelerate, increase speed.

speed (2) *n* (*ar*) success, prosperity ~ **speed** *v/i* and *t* (*ar*) prosper, succeed; grant success to.

speedball [*speed*bawl] *n* (*sl*) combination of cocaine with heroin or other opiates.

speedboat [*speed*bOt] *n* fast motorboat.

speedcop [*speed*kop] *n* (*sl*) policeman whose duty is to enforce observation of speed-limits.

speeder [*speed*er] *n* one who, that which speeds; device regulating speed.

speedily [*speed*ili] *adv* swiftly, promptly.

speediness [*speed*inis] *n* rapidity; promptness.

speeding [*speed*ing] *n* and *adj* (act of) exceeding a speed-limit.

speed-limit [*speed*-limit] *n* regulation forbidding motor vehicles to exceed a specified speed.

speed-merchant [*speed*-murchant] *n* (*sl*) one who drives a car or motorcycle extremely fast.

speedometer [*speed*omiter] *n* device measuring and indicating speed of a motor vehicle.

speedster [*speed*ster] *n* (*sl*) speed-merchant.

speed-up [*speed*-up] *n* (*coll*) increase of speed, *esp* in production or performance.

speedway [*speed*way] *n* motorcycle racing track; sport of racing motorcycles; road built for fast traffic.

speedwell [*speed*wel] *n* a flowering herb.

speedy [*speed*i] *adj* quick, swift; nimble; prompt.

speleologist [speelee-*olo*jist] *n* one who studies and explores caves *etc*.

speleology [speelee-*olo*ji] *n* scientific study and exploration of caves, underground watercourses *etc*; pot-holing.

spell (1) [*spel*] *n* magical formula of words, incantation; compelling magical power; (*fig*) irresistible attraction.

spell (2) (*p/t* and *p/part* **spelled** or **spelt**) *v/t* and *i* say or write in correct order the letters that form a word; be capable of spelling most words correctly; (*of letters*) form a word; (*fig*) mean, indicate; **s. out** read with difficulty; utter the letters of a word one by one; (*coll*) express or explain in very simple terms.

spell (3) *n* short period, *esp* of activity; (*Aust*) period of inactivity, rest.

spellbinder [*spel*bInder] *n* (*coll*) one who can fascinate an audience.

spellbound [*spel*bownd] *adj* fascinated, held captive by charm or persuasiveness; bewitched.

speller [*spel*er] *n* one who spells; spelling-book.

spelling [*spel*ing] *n* act of saying or writing the letters of a word; way in which a word is spelt; ability to spell.

spelling-bee [*spel*ing-bee] *n* competition in spelling.

spelling-book [*spel*ing-book] *n* book which teaches children to spell.

spelt [*spelt*] *p/t* and *p/part* of **spell** (2).

spelter [*spel*ter] *n* commercial zinc.

spencer (1) [*spen*ser] *n* short woollen jacket.

spencer (2) *n* (*naut*) fore-and-aft sail set abaft the fore- or main-mast.

spend (*p/t* and *p/part* **spent**) [*spend*] *v/t* and *i* pay (money) in exchange for goods, services *etc*; use up, consume gradually; pass (time); exhaust; (*naut*) lose.

spender [*spend*er] *n* one who spends freely.

spendthrift [*spend*thRift] *n* and *adj* (one) who wastes money.

spent [*spent*] *p/t* and *p/part* of **spend** ~ **spent** *adj* exhausted (*of match*) used.

sperm (1) [*spurm*] *n* male seminal fluid > PDB.

sperm (2) *n* whale which yields spermaceti.

spermaceti [spurma*set*i] *n* white waxy substance found in the head of the sperm-whale > PDS.

spermary [*spurm*aRi] *n* male spermatic gland.

spermatic [spur*mat*ik] *adj* of, secreting, or conveying sperm (1); of the spermary.

spermato- *pref* of sperm (1); of spermatozoa.

spermatozoon (*pl* **spermatozoa**) [spurmatoz*O*on] *n* small mobile male gamete > PDB.

spermicide [*spurm*isId] *n* substance that can kill spermatozoa.

spermo- *pref* of seeds.

sperm-whale [*spurm*-wayl] *n* whale that secretes spermaceti.

spew [*spew*] *n* and *v/t* and *i* vomit.

sphagnum [*sfagnum*] *n* bog-moss.

sphenoid [*sfeenoid*] *adj* wedge-shaped; **s. bone** large bone at base of skull.

sphere [*sfeer*] *n* globe, ball; figure whose surface is everywhere equidistant from its centre > PDS; extent of activity, influence, knowledge *etc*; scope, range; (*obs astron*) one of nine transparent globes enclosing and revolving round the earth and supporting the moon, planets, sun and stars.

spheric [*sfeRik*] *adj* spherical.

spherical [*sfeRikal*] *adj* shaped like a sphere, globular; relating to spheres ~ **spherically** *adv*.

spheroid [*sfeerRoid*] *n* and *adj* (figure) which is nearly spherical > PDS.

spherometer [sfiRomiter] *n* instrument for the accurate measurement of small thicknesses, or curvature of spherical surfaces > PDS.

spherule [*sfeRewl*] *n* small sphere.

sphincter [*sfinkter*] *n* circular muscle which contracts or shuts an opening > PDB.

sphinx [*sfinks*] *n* (*Gk myth*) fabulous human-headed lion that asked riddles and killed those who could not solve them; Egyptian statue of such a creature; (*fig*) mysterious, inscrutable person.

sphygmic [*sfigmik*] *adj* of the pulse.

sphygmograph [*sfigmogRaaf*] *n* instrument for recording the movements of the pulse.

sphygmomanometer [sfigmOmanomiter] *n* instrument for measuring blood pressure.

spice [*spIs*] *n* any strong piquant seasoning of vegetable origin; (*fig*) that which adds excitement or interest; trace ~ **spice** *v/t* season with spice.

spicily [*spIsili*] *adv* in a spicy way.

spiciness [*spIsinis*] *n* quality of being spicy.

spick-and-span [spik-and-*span*] *adj* spotlessly clean; smart.

spicy [*spIsi*] *adj* flavoured with spice; pungent; rousing keen interest, *esp* by hints of wickedness, indecency *etc*.

spider [*spIder*] *n* eight-legged arachnid animal, *esp* one which makes webs to capture prey.

spidery [*spIdeRi*] *adj* having thin angular lines; shaped or moving like a spider.

spied [*spId*] *p/t* and *p/part* of **spy**.

spiel [*speel*] *v/t* and *i* (*sl*) say, talk glibly ~ **spiel** *n* long, persuasive speech or story.

spieler [*speeler*] *n* (*sl*) card-sharper; swindler; gambling den; plausible crook.

spiffing [*spifing*] *adj* (*sl*) fine, delightful.

spifflicate [*spif*likayt] *v/t* (*sl*) smash, crush.

spigot [*spigot*] *n* peg or plug closing a cask; faucet.

spike [*spIk*] *n* sharp-pointed rod or bar, *esp* of metal; large nail; pointed stud on sole of boot; ear of corn; inflorescence of small sessile flowers on an axis ~ **spike** *v/t* pierce or fasten with a spike; fix spikes to; block vent of (cannon) with a spike; **s. the guns of** put out of action, thwart.

spikenard [*spIk*naard] *n* fragrant Indian herb; perfumed ointment prepared from this.

spiky [*spIki*] *adj* of, like or having a spike; studded with spikes; (*fig*) quick to take offence; (*sl*) holding High Church views ~ **spikily** *adv* ~ **spikiness** *n*.

spill (1) [*spil*] *n* thin slip of paper or wood to light a fire *etc*.

spill (2) (*p/t* and *p/part* spilt or spilled) *v/t* and *i* let (liquid) fall from a vessel, *esp* by accident; (*of liquids*) fall from a vessel; (*of persons*) fall from vehicle or horse; (*naut*) empty (sail) of wind; **s. the beans** (*coll*) reveal a secret ~ **spill** *n* fall from vehicle or horse.

spillage [*spilij*] *n* act of spilling; amount of liquid spilt.

spillikin [*spili*kin] *n* small carved rod of wood or ivory; (*pl*) game in which one spillikin must be drawn from a pile without moving the others.

spilt [*spilt*] *p/t* and *p/part* of **spill** (2).

spin (*pres/part* spinning, *p/t* span, *p/part* spun) [*spin*] *v/t* and *i* turn rapidly round and round, whirl; draw out and twist (wool, yarn *etc*) to make thread; (*of insects, spiders etc*) form cocoon or web by exuding a filament; cause (ball) to rotate when thrown; (*coll*) move rapidly; **s. out** (*coll*) to make (story, joke *etc*) much longer than necessary. **s. a yarn** (*coll*) tell a long story ~ **spin** *n* act or speed of whirling; twist given to a missile in flight; (*coll*) brief pleasure-outing in a car; (*aer*) dive in which aircraft rotates as it falls; **flat s.** (*coll*) panic.

spina [*speena*] *n* (*Lat*) spine; **s. bifida** (*med*) severe congenital disability caused by imperfect union of spinal canal.

spinach [*spinij*] *n* plant with edible leaves.

spinal [*spInal*] *adj* of or on the spine; **s. column** spine; **s. cord** structure of nerves in the spine.

spindle [*spind'l*] *n* rod used in spinning for twisting the thread; rod bearing bobbin in spinning-machine; shaft or axis upon which anything revolves.

spindleshanks [*spind'*lshanks] *n* person with long thin legs.

spindletree [*spind'*l-tRee] *n* type of small white-flowered tree with hard wood.

spindly [*spind*li] *adj* too thin.

spindrier [*spind*RI-er] *n* machine that dries washed clothes by whirling them round.

spindrift [*spind*Rift] *n* fine spray blown by the wind.

spine [*spIn*] *n* backbone; thin, sharply pointed growth on animal body or plant; thorn; spike; back of a book.

spineless [*spInlis*] *adj* without a spine; (*fig*) cowardly, irresolute; submissive ~ **spinelessly** *adv* ~ **spinelessness** *n*.

spinet [spin*et*] *n* musical instrument like a small harpsichord > PDM.

spinifex [*spIni*feks] *n* type of Australian grass with spiky leaves.

spininess [*spIni*nis] *n* quality of being spiny.

spinnaker [*spinaker*] *n* (*naut*) large jib set on opposite side to mainsail when running > PDSa.

spinner [*spiner*] *n* one who spins; machine for spinning thread; an artificial bait.

spinney, spinny [*spini*] *n* small wood, copse.

spinning [*spining*] *n* act or process of one who spins; act of making a web ~ **spinning** *adj* used in spinning.

spinning-jenny [*spining*-jeni] *n* machine for spinning several threads at once.

spinning-wheel [*spining*-wheel] *n* wheel, driven by foot or hand, for spinning wool, cotton *etc*.

spinny see spinney.

spin-off [*spin*-of] *n* profitable by-product.

spinous [*spi*nus] *adj* spiky, thorny.

spinster [*spin*ster] *n* unmarried woman, *esp* if elderly.

spiny [*spi*ni] *adj* covered with, full of spines; thorny; (*fig*) perplexing, difficult.

spiracle [*spi*rak'l] *n* breathing-hole; blow-hole of whale; opening of trachea of insect.

spiral [*spi*ral] *adj* forming a curved line that passes repeatedly round a central point while moving progressively farther from it; forming a curved slope that rises or falls while circling repeatedly round a central axis ~ spiral *n* coil; spiral curve or slope; objects arranged in spiral pattern; act of rising or falling in spiral motion ~ spiral (*pres/part* spiralling, *p/t* and *p/part* spiralled) *v/t* and *i* arrange in a spiral; rise, fall, or encircle with spiral motion; rise or fall rapidly.

spirality [spi*ral*iti] *n* the quality of being spiral.

spirally [*spi*rali] *adv* in a spiral.

spirant [*spi*rant] *n* and *adj* (consonant) in uttering which the breath is not completely stopped.

spire (1) [*spir*] *n* tapering tower, pinnacle; steeple; tapering flower or stalk ~ spire *v/i* and *t* shoot up like a spire; furnish with a spire.

spire (2) *n* spiral, coil; whorl, twist; single turn in a spiral.

spirillum [spi*ril*um] *n* spiral shaped bacterium.

spirit [*spi*rit] *n* any bodiless living being having intelligence and will; soul; soul of a dead person, ghost; vitality, life; vigour, energy; courage; vivacity; mood, outlook, or attitude; underlying meaning, true inner significance or intention; alcohol; (*pl*) mood; strong distilled alcoholic drink; high spirits gaiety, vivacity; the Holy S. the third person of the Trinity; low spirits gloom, depression; spirits of salts hydrochloric acid ~ spirit *v/t* inspirit; s. away, s. off cause to disappear mysteriously.

spirited [*spi*ritid] *adj* brave and vigorous; lively ~ spiritedly *adv* ~ spiritedness *n*.

spirit-gum [*spi*rit-gum] *n* gum dissolved in alcohol.

spiritism [*spi*ritizm] *n* spiritualism.

spirit-lamp [*spi*rit-lamp] *n* lamp which burns methylated spirit.

spiritless [*spi*ritlis] *adj* lacking vigour, courage, vivacity *etc*; listless; depressed ~ spiritlessly *adv* ~ spiritlessness *n*.

spirit-level [*spi*rit-level] *n* instrument which determines the horizontal line by an air-bubble in alcohol.

spirit-rapping [*spi*rit-raping] *n* noises of rapping, knocking *etc* produced in spiritualist seances and supposed to be code messages from the dead.

spiritual [*spi*ritew-al] *adj* of or like a spirit; having life, intelligence and will but no body; concerned with the needs and faculties of the soul, not materialistic; religious; given or inspired by God; holy ~ spiritual *n* type of religious folksong of American Negroes.

spiritualism [*spi*ritew-alizm] *n* belief that the souls of the dead communicate with the living through persons having special powers; semi-religious cult and practices based on this belief; (*philos*) theory that ultimate reality is spiritual; theory that matter is unreal.

spiritualist [*spi*ritew-alist] *n* one who believes in spiritualism ~ spiritualist *adj*.

spiritualistic [spi*ritew*-alistik] *adj* of or like spiritualism; supposedly caused by spirits of the dead.

spirituality [spi*ritew-al*iti] *n* state or quality of being spiritual; religious outlook.

spiritualize [*spi*ritew-aliz] *v/t* render spiritual; interpret spiritually.

spiritually [*spi*ritew-ali] *adv* in a spiritual way; religiously.

spirituel (*fem* spirituelle) [spi*ritew-el*] *adj* (*Fr*) delicate, refined; witty.

spirituous [*spi*ritew-us] *adj* containing distilled alcohol.

spiro- (1) *pref* coiled, forming a spiral.

spiro- (2) *pref* of breath or breathing.

spirometer [spi*rom*iter] *n* instrument for measuring how much air lungs can contain.

spirt [spurt] *n* and *v/t* and *i* spurt, squirt.

spiry [*spi*ri] *adj* like a spire.

spit (1) [*spit*] *n* long rod on which meat is roasted at a fire; low-lying land jutting out to sea > PDG ~ spit (*pres/part* spitting, *p/t* and *p/part* spitted) *v/t* fix (meat) on a spit; pierce.

spit (2) (*pres/part* spitting, *p/t* and *p/part* spat) *v/t* and *i* eject (saliva) from the mouth; eject small drops or sparks; utter spitefully; (*fig*) drizzle; s. out (*sl*) tell, say ~ spit *n* act of spitting; saliva; drizzle; dead s. of (someone) one who resembles him exactly; s. and polish very careful cleaning and polishing, *esp* of military equipment.

spit (3) *n* depth of earth equal to that of a spade's blade.

spite [spit] *n* petty and malicious hatred, desire to injure; cause of this, grudge; in s. of notwithstanding, in disregard or defiance of ~ spite *v/t* injure or grieve maliciously, act spitefully towards.

spiteful [*spit*fool] *adj* malicious; desiring to injure ~ spitefully *adv* ~ spitefulness *n*.

spitfire [*spit*fir] *n* hot-tempered person.

spittle [*spit*'l] *n* saliva, *esp* if spat out.

spittoon [spit*OOn*] *n* receptacle for spitting into.

spiv [spiv] *n* (*coll*) one who makes his living by shady and dishonest, but not criminal, means.

splash [splash] *v/t* and *i* cause (liquid) to scatter in jets or drops; wet or stain with scattered liquid; be scattered, fly in drops; move roughly in or through liquid; dabble; (*coll*) announce or advertise prominently (in newspaper), print conspicuously ~ splash *n* act or sound of splashing; liquid splashed about; mark, stain caused by splashed liquid; (*coll*) prominent display; (*coll*) sodawater squirted from a siphon; make a s. cause a sensation, *esp* by lavish spending.

splashboard [*splash*bawrd] *n* screen on front of vehicle to prevent passengers being splashed.

splashdown [*splash*down] *n* controlled landing of spacecraft or artificial satellite in the sea.

splashy [*splash*i] *adj* wet and muddy; full of muddy water.

splat [splat] *n* horizontal bar in chair-back.

splatter [*splat*er] *v/t* and *i* spatter.

splay [splay] *v/t* (*archi*) form with oblique sides; slant; (*surg*) dislocate ~ splay *n* oblique surface, side *etc* ~ splay *adj* turned outwards.

splay-footed [splay-*foot*id] *adj* having a broad, flat, out-turned foot.

spleen [*spleen*] *n* soft vascular organ to the left of the stomach > PDB; (*fig*) melancholy; ill-humour, spitefulness.

splendid [*splen*did] *adj* magnificent, gorgeous; glorious; brilliant, dazzling; (*coll*) fine, excellent ~ **splendidly** *adv*.

splendiferous [splendi*feRus*] *adj* (*sl*) splendid.

splendour [*splen*der] *n* magnificence; pomp; great brilliance; glory.

splenetic [spli*net*ik] *adj* bad-tempered, peevish; of the spleen.

splenic [*splen*ik] *adj* of or affecting the spleen.

splice [spl*i*s] *v/t* join (ropes) by interweaving the strands; join two pieces of wood lengthways; (*coll*) marry ~ **splice** *n* union of two ropes by interweaving the strands.

spline [spl*i*n] *n* flexible ruler used in drawing large curves; loose tongue, *usu* of metal, fitting in slots on axle and wheel *etc* allowing one to rotate the other.

splint [*splint*] *n* rigid piece of wood *etc* tied to a broken limb to keep the bone in place; thin strip of wood used in basket-making; callous tumour on leg-bones of horses ~ **splint** *v/t* support with splints.

splinter [*splint*er] *n* small, sharp, broken piece of wood, glass *etc*; **s. group** group of dissidents who separate themselves from a political party, organization *etc* ~ **splinter** *v/t* and *i* break up into splinters.

splinterless [*splint*erlis] *adj* (*of glass*) made so as not to splinter when broken.

splinter-proof [*splint*er-pROOf] *adj* able to resist the splinters of bursting shells.

splintery [*splint*eRi] *adj* full of splinters; liable to splinter easily.

split (*pres/part* **splitting**, *p/t* and *p/part* **split**) [*split*] *v/t* and *i* break or tear apart, *esp* lengthways; be or become disunited; cause separation or grave disagreement between; (*sl*) reveal a secret; (*coll*) share out; **s. the difference** settle a dispute by taking the mean between two extremes; **s. up** separate, part ~ **split** *n* act or process of splitting; result of splitting, crack, tear, fissure; division, disunity, grave disagreement; that which is split; roll or bun sliced open and filled with cream or jam; (*coll*) half-size bottle of sodawater; half-glass of liquor; (*pl*) acrobatic feat of sitting with legs stretched out sideways at right angles to the body ~ **split** *adj* divided, separated; **s. infinitive** (*gramm*) act of inserting an adverb between *to* and the infinitive verb; **s. personality** (*pop psych*) multiple personality; **s. second** (*coll*) extremely brief space of time.

split-level [*split*-level] *adj* (*of houses*) divided vertically so that the floor level of one part is midway between successive storeys of an adjoining part.

split-peas(e) [*split*-peez] *n* dried peas split in half.

split-ring [*split*-Ring] *n* ring whose ends do not join but are tightly overlapped.

split-second [split-*sek*ond] *adj* accurately calculated to minute fractions of time; extremely rapid.

splitter [*split*er] *n* one who or that which splits.

splodge [*sploj*] *n* splotch.

splotch [*sploch*] *n* irregular stain or patch of colour.

splurge [*splurj*] *n* (*coll*) showy display, *esp* of wealth ~ **splurge** *v/t* and *i* show off.

splutter [*splut*er] *v/i* make a series of rapid, light, explosive noises; spit slightly while speaking; speak incoherently; spatter ink from a pen ~ **splutter** *n* spluttering noise.

Spode [*spOd*] *n* type of porcelain.

spoil [*spoil*] *v/t* and *i* damage, destroy or decrease the beauty, usefulness, value *etc* of; deteriorate; cause to become selfish, conceited *etc* by excessive kindness, praise, indulgence *etc*; (*ar*) plunder; **be spoiling for** be eagerly seeking ~ **spoil** *n* (*usu pl*) booty, pillage; profits, benefits won in contest.

spoiled [*spoilt*] *adj* grown selfish, discontented, conceited or unruly through being indulged and flattered.

spoiler [*spoil*er] *n* vane on aircraft or aerodynamic vehicle to deflect or reduce wind pressure.

spoilsport [*spoils*pawrt] *n* person who by interference or disapproval spoils the enjoyment of others.

spoke (1) [*spOk*] *p/t* of **speak**.

spoke (2) *n* one of the bars joining hub and rim of a wheel; rung of a ladder; (*naut*) radial handle of steering wheel; bar used as brake on wheel; **put a s. in one's wheel** frustrate one's plans.

spoken [*spOk*en] *p/part* of **speak**.

spokeshave [*spOk*shayv] *n* plane w th handle at both ends.

spokesman [*spOk*sman] *n* one who is authorized to express the views, demands *etc* of a group.

spoliate [*spOli*-ayt] *v/t* plunder, rob.

spoliation [spOli-*ay*shon] *n* act of plundering, robbery; (*leg*) destruction, alteration, or mutilation of a document.

spondaic [spon*day*-ik] *adj* of spondees.

spondee [*spon*di] *n* (*pros*) metrical foot consisting of two long syllables.

spondyl, spondyle [*spon*dil] *n* vertebra.

sponge [*spunj*] *n* pad of any porous and elastic substance used for applying or removing water *etc* in cleansing; marine animal whose fibrous skeleton can be thus used > PDB; act of washing with a sponge; sponge-cake; unkneaded dough; (*coll*) cadger; **throw up the s.** admit defeat, give in ~ **sponge** *v/t* and *i* clean or wipe with a sponge; absorb; wipe out; **s. on** live at the expense of, cadge from.

sponge-cake [*spunj*-kayk] *n* very light plain cake.

sponger [*spunj*er] *n* one who or that which sponges; one who lives at the expense of others.

sponge-rubber [*spunj*-Ruber] *n* rubber so prepared as to have a spongy texture.

spongily [*spunj*ili] *adv* in a spongy way.

sponginess [*spunj*inis] *n* state of being spongy.

sponging-house [*spunj*ing-hows] *n* house where debtors were formerly placed temporarily before being sent to prison.

spongy [*spunj*i] *adj* like a sponge; elastic, soft and absorbent; soaked through with water.

sponsion [*spon*shon] *n* act of becoming surety; (*leg*) international engagement pending ratification.

sponsor [*spon*ser] *n* one who vouches for the good character of another; one who makes himself responsible for another's acts, surety; godparent; advertiser who finances a radio or television programme ~ **sponsor** *v/t* vouch for;

give one's help or authority to; act as surety for; pay expenses of (radio or television programme) in exchange for right to advertise before or after it; act as godparent to; **sponsored walk** form of charitable fund-raising in which each participant is backed by sponsors who promise to donate money in proportion to the distance he walks.
sponsorial [spon*sawr*Ri-al] *adj* of a sponsor.
sponsorship [*spon*sership] *n* state of being a sponsor.
spontaneity [spontan*ee*-iti] *n* quality of being spontaneous; spontaneous action.
spontaneous [spont*ayni*-us] *adj* without external cause; of one's own free will; self-originated; uninhibited, acting on impulse ~ **spontaneously** *adv* ~ **spontaneousness** *n*.
spoof [*spOOf*] *n* hoax, humorous deception ~ **spoof** *v/t* hoax ~ **spoof** *adj* sham, false.
spook [*spOOk*] *n* (*coll*) ghost, apparition.
spooky [sp*OO*ki] *adj* (*coll*) eerie, uncanny; haunted ~ **spookily** *adv* ~ **spookiness** *n*.
spool [*spOOl*] *n* small cylinder for winding yarn on; central bar of angler's reel; cylinder on which photographic film or magnetic tape is wound ~ **spool** *v/t* wind on a spool.
spoon (1) [sp*OO*n] *n* utensil consisting of a shallow bowl on a handle used for stirring or conveying liquids; wooden-headed golf-club ~ **spoon** *v/t* and *i* take up with a spoon; (*cricket*) hit too gently; (*golf*) hit with wooden club.
spoon (2) *v/i* (*sl*) show sentimental love.
spoon-bait [sp*OO*n-bayt] *n* spoon-shaped piece of metal used as lure in fishing.
spoonbill [sp*OO*nbil] *n* bird with broad, flat bill.
Spoonerism [sp*OO*neRizm] *n* accidental transposition of sounds in adjacent words.
spooney see spoony.
spoonfeed [sp*OO*nfeed] *v/t* feed (baby *etc*) with a spoon; give over-simplified teaching to, expect no active participation from (pupil).
spoonful [sp*OO*nfool] *n* as much as a spoon contains.
spoony, spooney [sp*OO*ni] *adj* (*sl*) stupidly amorous, sentimental ~ **spoony, spooney** *n* fool; sentimental fool.
spoor [*spoor*] *n* track of a wild animal.
sporadic [spo*Radik*] *adj* occasional, occurring at irregular intervals; occurring in isolated instances, scattered ~ **sporadically** *adv*.
sporangium [spo*Ranj*i-um] *n* (*bot*) organ within which spores are produced > PDB.
spore [*spawr*] *n* (*biol*) microscopic reproductive body that becomes detached from the parent and gives rise to a new individual > PDB.
sporran [spo*Ran*] *n* Highlander's pouch worn in front of a kilt.
sport [*spawrt*] *n* any outdoor activity engaged in for pleasure, *esp* by several persons; outdoor team-games; athletics; hunting, shooting, fishing; amusement, fun; joke; amusing thing or person; plaything, victim of a joke *etc*; (*coll*) good-humoured person, *esp* one who does not mind being teased or inconvenienced, or losing a game; (*biol*) freak; plant or animal deviating from normal type > PDB; (*pl*) meeting for athletic contests ~ **sport** *v/t* and *i* wear or display conspicuously; play; joke; amuse oneself; **s. one's oak** (*university sl*) shut one's outer door.

sportily [*spawr*tili] *adv* in a sporty way.
sportiness [*spawr*tinis] *n* quality of being sporty.
sporting [*spawr*ting] *adj* of or for sports; fond of sports; (*coll*) good-humoured when defeated, teased *etc*; willing to take risks; **s. chance** chance in which success is possible but not certain ~ **sportingly** *adv*.
sportive [*spawr*tiv] *adj* merry, playful ~ **sportively** *adv* ~ **sportiveness** *n*.
sportscar [*spawr*tskaar] *n* two-seater car with powerful engine.
sportscoat [*spawr*tskOt] *n* loose informal coat of strong fabric.
sports-day [*spawr*ts-day] *n* day on which a school holds races, athletic contests *etc*.
sports-jacket [*spawr*ts-jakit] *n* man's loosely-fitting jacket, *usu* of tweed, worn on informal occasions.
sportsman (*pl* **sportsmen**) [*spawr*tsman] *n* one who is fond of sport; one who regularly competes in sporting events; one who makes a sport his career; fair-minded, brave, good-humoured person; one who bears defeat, inconvenience *etc* cheerfully.
sportsmanship [*spawr*tsmanship] *n* skill in sports; qualities of a sportsman.
sportswoman (*pl* **sportswomen**) [*spawr*tswooman] *n* woman who is fond of sports, or competes regularly in sporting events, or makes a career in sport.
sporty [*spawr*ti] *adj* (*coll*) fond of sports.
spot [*spot*] *n* small mark or patch of colour on a surface, *esp* if round; pimple; place, small area; small quantity, *esp* of food or drink; (*billiards*) mark on which ball is placed; (*fig*) moral blemish; disgrace; **s. cash** (*comm*) payment on delivery; **in a s.** (*coll*) in difficulties, faced with a problem; **on the s.** at once, there and then; at the place where something is happening; (*coll*) alert, wide-awake; (*sl*) in danger, *esp* of death; **soft s.** (*coll*) liking, fondness ~ **spot** (*pres/part* **spotting**, *p/t* and *p/part* **spotted**) *v/t* and *i* mark with spots; see, catch sight of (something one was on the watch for); notice, detect; be or become marked with spots.
spot-ball [*spot*-bawl] *n* (*billiards*) white ball marked with black spot.
spot-check [*spot*-chek] *n* random inspection or search of potential wrongdoers ~ **spot-check** *v/t* and *i*.
spotless [*spot*lis] *adj* perfectly clean; without blemish ~ **spotlessly** *adv* ~ **spotlessness** *n*.
spotlight [*spot*lit] *n* strong beam of light that can be focused on one spot, *esp* of a stage; electric light casting such a beam ~ **spotlight** *v/t* illuminate in strong concentrated light; (*coll*) draw attention to, reveal or emphasize dramatically.
spot-on [*spot*-on] *adj* (*coll*) perfectly aimed, done *etc*.
spotted [*spot*id] *adj* marked with spots; **s. dog** Dalmatian dog; suet pudding with currants.
spotter [*spot*er] *n* one who spots; one who keeps a look-out for enemy aircraft; one whose hobby is to notice as many different trains, cars *etc* as possible.
spotty [*spot*i] *adj* marked with spots; having pimples; of or like spots ~ **spottily** *adv* ~ **spottiness** *n*.

spouse [*spowz*] *n* husband; wife.

spout [*spowt*] *n* narrow projecting tube on a vessel through which its contents are poured out; projecting pipe conveying water from a roof; strong jet of liquid, gushing stream; jet of water cast up by whale *etc* in breathing; **down the s.** (*sl*) lost, ruined; **up the s.** (*sl*) pawned; (*sl*) pregnant ~ **spout** *v/t* and *i* pour out copiously and strongly; gush; (*coll*) talk copiously; declaim.

spout-hole [*spowt*-hOl] *n* hole through which whale *etc* spouts water in breathing.

sprag [*spRag*] *n* stout piece of wood used as support or brake > PDE ~ **sprag** (*pres/part* **spragging**, *p/t* and *p/part* **spragged**) *v/t* support with sprags; check with a sprag.

sprain [*spRayn*] *v/t* twist or wrench (muscles or ligaments of a joint) without dislocation ~ **sprain** *n* act of spraining muscles or ligaments; swelling and pain caused by this.

sprang [*spRang*] *p/t* of **spring** (1).

sprat [*spRat*] *n* small sea-fish allied to herring.

sprawl [*spRawl*] *v/i* lie or sit with limbs stretched out casually and inelegantly; be spread untidily over a wide area ~ **sprawl** *n* act or position of sprawling; wide untidy expanse, *esp* of buildings.

spray (1) [*spRay*] *n* fine particles of liquid blown or squirted through the air; wind-blown droplets of seawater; apparatus for squirting liquid as spray, atomizer ~ **spray** *v/t* and *i* squirt spray on to; paint, disinfect, treat *etc* with a spray; throw out as spray; become spray.

spray (2) *n* small shoot or branch; ornament, jewel *etc* in the shape of a small branch.

sprayer [*spRay*-er] *n* one who, that which, sprays; apparatus for spraying.

spray-gun [*spRay*-gun] *n* apparatus for spraying paint, varnish *etc* on to a surface.

spread (*p/t* and *p/part* spread) [*spRed*] *v/t* and *i* cause to cover wider area by pressing out thinly; cover (with); extend in space or time; make or become wider or longer; stretch out; unfold, open out widely; be or become widely diffused or circulated; cause to circulate widely, disseminate ~ **spread** *n* act of spreading; extent, increase in space or time; increasing prevalence, diffusion or circulation; range; (*coll*) ample meal, feast; soft tasty paste for sandwiches; **double s.** advertisement taking up two pages; **middle-aged s.** (*coll*) increased plumpness of middle-aged people.

spreadeagle [*spRed*eeg'l] *n* (*her*) eagle with wings and legs outstretched; fowl split open ~ **spread-eagle** *v/t* and *i* tie up with arms and legs stretched fully out; fall or lie with limbs wide apart ~ **spreadeagle** *adj* (*US*) boastfully patriotic; bombastic.

spreader [*spRed*er] *n* one who or that which spreads.

spree [*spRee*] *n* bout of reckless amusement, *esp* drinking and debauchery; amusing enterprise; **spending s.** outburst of extravagant buying.

sprig [*spRig*] *n* small shoot or twig; ornament in the shape of a twig; small nail with no head; offshoot; young fellow ~ **sprig** (*pres/part* **sprigging**, *p/t* and *p/part* **sprigged**) *v/t* ornament with sprigs; drive sprigs into.

sprightly [*spRIt*li] *adj* gay, lively, brisk ~ **sprightliness** *n*.

spring (1) (*p/t* **sprang**, *p/part* **sprung**) [*spRing*] *v/i* and *t* leap up or forwards; move suddenly and rapidly; pounce; appear or emerge unexpectedly; appear from the ground; flow from a source, well, fountain *etc*; arise; become warped, work loose; develop a leak; equip with springs; cause to move rapidly; discharge; (*coll*) disclose suddenly, announce or reveal without warning; (*sl*) rescue (criminal) from prison ~ **spring** *n* leap, bound, pounce; elasticity, ability to recoil or bounce; object, *esp* coiled or bent metal, that returns forcefully to its first shape or position after being compressed; coil of metal *etc* used to supply motive power; coil of metal *etc* used to give elasticity to a seat, absorb effects of jolting *etc*; source of water, fountain > PDG; (*pl, fig*) origin, primary cause; (*archi*) starting-point of a curve.

spring (2) *n* first season of the year, season of renewed growth after winter; (*fig*) youth ~ **spring** *adj* of or in spring.

springback [*spRing*bak] *n* looseleaf paperholder holding pages by a spring.

spring-balance [spRing-*ba*lans] *n* balance that weighs objects by the tension of a spring.

springboard [*spRing*bawrd] *n* resilient board to jump or dive from; (*fig*) vantage-point from which to go into action.

springbok [*spRing*bok] *n* an African antelope.

springclean [*spRing*kleen] *v/t* clean (house, room *etc*) with unusual thoroughness, *esp* annually in spring ~ **springcleaning** *n*.

springe [*spRinj*] *n* (*ar*) snare, noose.

springer [*spRing*er] *n* one who or that which springs; one who rouses game; a variety of spaniel; springbok; (*archi*) point where curve of arch begins; lowest stone of gable-coping; rib of groined roof.

spring-gun [*spRing*-gun] *n* gun automatically discharged by touching a wire which pulls its trigger.

springily [*spRing*ili] *adv* in a springy way.

springiness [*spRing*inis] *n* elasticity.

springload [*spRing*lOd] *v/t* apply force to or load by tension or compression of a spring.

spring-tide [*spRing*-tId] *n* very high tide at new and full moon > PDG.

springtime [*spRing*tIm] *n* spring season.

springy [*spRing*i] *adj* elastic; resilient; able to leap or recoil.

sprinkle [*spRink*'l] *v/t* and *i* scatter in small drops ~ **sprinkle** *n* light shower; small quantity scattered.

sprinkler [*spRink*ler] *n* one who or that which sprinkles; device for watering gardens; device for fighting fire.

sprinkling [*spRink*ling] *n* act of scattering in small drops; small quantity scattered about.

sprint [*spRint*] *v/i* race or run fast for a short distance ~ **sprint** *n* short fast run.

sprinter [*spRint*er] *n* one who runs very fast for short distances.

sprit [*spRit*] *n* (*naut*) small spar crossing diagonally from mast to peak > PDSa.

sprite [*spRIt*] *n* elf, fairy.

sprocket [*spRok*it] *n* (*eng*) tooth on wheel engaging with links of a chain; wheel having such teeth.

sprout [*spRowt*] *v/i* and *t* develop shoots, buds *etc*;

begin to grow; send forth like a bud or shoot ~
sprout *n* young bud or shoot; (*pl*) vegetables like
small cabbages, brussels sprouts.

spruce (1) [*spROOs*] *adj* neat, smart ~ **spruce** *v/t*
and *i* **s. up** smarten (oneself) ~ **sprucely** *adv*.

spruce (2) *n* a type of coniferous tree.

sprue [*spROO*] *n* deficiency disease due to malfunction of small intestine.

sprung [*spRung*] *p/t* of **spring** (1).

spry [*spRI*] *adj* active, lively; vigorous; sharp.

spud [*spud*] *n* short narrow spade; (*coll*) potato;
(*sl*) friend.

spud-bashing [*spud*-bashing] *n* (*sl*) act of peeling
potatoes.

spume [*spewm*] *n* and *v/i* froth, foam.

spumescent [spewm*esent*] *adj* foaming.

spumy [*spewm*i] *adj* frothy, consisting of scum.

spun [*spun*] *p/t* and *p/part* of **spin**.

spunk [*spunk*] *n* tinder, touchwood; (*coll*) courage,
pluck; hot temper; (*vulg*) semen.

spur [*spur*] *n* spiked wheel fixed to horseman's
shoe for goading horse; incentive, stimulus;
pointed projection, *esp* spike on cock's leg; ridge
projecting from mountain range; **on the s. of the
moment** suddenly, spontaneously; **win one's
spurs** prove one's merit; attain honour ~ **spur**
(*pres/part* **spurring**, *p/t* and *p/part* **spurred**) *v/t*
and *i* prick with spurs; incite, urge; equip with
spurs; ride (horse) very fast.

spurge [*spurj*] *n* genus of plants with acrid juice.

spurious [*spewr*Ri-us] *adj* not genuine; counterfeit, false; not legitimate ~ **spuriously** *adv* ~
spuriousness *n*.

spurn [*spurn*] *v/t* reject disdainfully; show contempt for; thrust or kick away.

spurred [*spurd*] *adj* wearing spurs; having shoots
shaped like spurs.

spurt [*spurt*] *v/i* and *t* make a vigorous but brief
effort, *esp* sudden increase in speed; gush out
strongly and suddenly ~ **spurt** *n* sudden vigorous
effort or increase, *esp* of speed; sudden gush.

spur-wheel [*spur*-wheel] *n* gear-wheel with cogs.

sputnik [*spootnik*] *n* an unmanned artificial satellite, *esp* that launched by the Soviet Union in
1957.

sputter [*sputer*] *n* and *v/t* and *i* splutter.

sputtering [*spute*Ring] *n* process for depositing a
film of metal on a surface > PDS.

sputum [*spewtum*] *n* saliva, phlegm *etc* coughed up
and spat out.

spy [*spI*] *n* agent who gathers secret information
about the affairs of one nation to benefit another,
hostile nation; one who keeps watch on others to
discover secrets ~ **spy** (*p/t* and *p/part* **spied**) *v/t*
and *i* seek to discover national secrets on behalf of
an enemy; keep watch, observe (secret acts *etc*);
pry; perceive, detect; **s. out** explore or discover
secretly.

spyglass [*spI*glaas] *n* small telescope.

spyhole [*spI*hOl] *n* peephole.

squab [*skwob*] *n* short plump person; young
pigeon; stuffed cushion; padded sofa ~ **squab**
adj short and fat.

squabble [*skwob*'l] *n* petty quarrel, wrangle ~
squabble *v/i* and *t* wrangle, quarrel over petty
points; (*printing*) disarrange (type).

squab-pie [*skwob*-pI] *n* pigeon-pie; mutton-pie
with onions and apples.

squad [*skwod*] *n* (*mil*) small number of men; small
party or group.

squadron [*skwod*Ron] *n* (*mil*) group of fighter or
bomber aircraft; group of warships commanded
by a flag-officer; body of cavalry equal to two
troops; (*fig*) organized group.

squadron-leader [*skwod*Ron-leeder] *n* R.A.F.
rank equivalent to that of major.

squails [*skwaylz*] *n* game in which disks are
flicked towards a mark in the centre of a board.

squalid [*skwo*lid] *adj* dirty, sordid; disgusting,
despicable; mean, petty; poverty-stricken ~
squalidly *adv* ~ **squalidness** *n*.

squall [*skwawl*] *n* loud harsh wail or scream;
sudden gust of wind; brief and violent storm;
(*fig*) quarrel; unexpected trouble ~ **squall** *v/i*
cry out discordantly.

squally [*skwawl*i] *adj* abounding in squalls.

squaloid [*skway*loid] *adj* of or like a shark.

squalor [*skwo*ler] *n* state or quality of being
squalid; repulsive dirtiness.

squama [*skway*ma] *n* scale; scale-like structure.

squamous [*skway*mus] *adj* scaly.

squander [*skwon*der] *v/t* spend or use up wastefully.

square [*skwair*] *n* figure having four equal sides
and four right angles; anything of this shape;
four-sided open area, paved or laid out as a garden,
and surrounded by buildings; square subdivision
on a games-board; (*math*) product of a quantity
multiplied by itself; (*bui*) area of 100 square
feet; (*geom*) instrument having one straight edge
at right angles to another; (*mil*) body of troops in
square formation; (*sl*) old-fashioned person;
(*sl*) honest person; **back to s. one** (*coll*) back to
starting-point; **on the s.** (*coll*) honest, genuine
~ **square** *adj* having four equal sides and four
right angles; at right angles (to); having firm
straight edges or shape, not drooping or hunched;
clear, outspoken, direct, straight; (*coll*) honest,
fair, aboveboard; (*sl*) old-fashioned, stupidly
prejudiced against or ignorant of new ideas,
amusements *etc*; (*math*) of or being a quantity
multiplied by itself; having two equal factors;
all s. (*games*) with both sides having equal score;
(*coll*) honest, fair; **get s. with** (*coll*) be revenged
on, achieve equality with; **s. meal** good substantial meal; **s. measure** (*math*) square of
linear measure; **s. number** product of a number
multiplied by itself; **s. root** one of two equal
factors of a number ~ **square** *v/t* and *i* make or
become square; draw up, straighten; put or be at
right angles; harmonize, bring into agreement;
persuade, convince; settle, pay; (*coll*) persuade
dishonestly, bribe; obtain connivance of; (*math*)
multiply (number) by itself; **s. up** (*boxing*) adopt
preliminary attitude of arms and fists; (*fig*) prepare to fight; put at right angles; (*coll*) face boldly;
consider realistically; **s. the circle** (*math*) attempt to construct a square exactly equal to a
given circle > PDS; (*fig*) attempt the impossible
~ **square** *adv* forming a right angle.

square-bashing [*skwair*-bashing] *n* (*sl*) military
drill.

square-built [*skwair*-bilt] *adj* straight-edged and
relatively broad.

square-dancing [*skwair*-daansing] *n* form of folk-dancing in which dancers line up in stra ght formations.

square-leg [skwair-leg] n (cricket) fielder at right angles to the wicket on the on-side.

squarely [skwairli] adv at a right angle; directly opposite; plainly, unambiguously; realistically, honestly.

squareness [skwairnis] n quality of being square.

square-rigged [skwair-Rigd] adj (naut) having principal sails set crosswise > PDSa.

squaresail [skwairsayl] n four-cornered sail extended on a yard.

square-shouldered [skwair-shOlderd] adj having shoulders held well up and back.

square-toed [skwair-tOd] adj (of shoes) having a straight-edged tip.

squash (1) [skwosh] v/t and i crush or squeeze to a pulp; compress, press too tightly; crowd tightly; (coll) snub, rebuke, reduce to silence; repress; become crushed to pulp ~ **squash** n drink made of crushed fruit; state of being crushed; tight-packed crowd; pulpy mass; (coll) crowded party or meeting.

squash (2) n game for two persons, played in a walled court with rackets and a soft rubber ball.

squash (3) n fleshy edible fruit of a species of gourd.

squash-court [skwosh-kawrt] n walled court for playing squash (2).

squash-rackets [skwosh-Rakits] n squash (2).

squashy [skwoshi] adj pulpy, crushed to a soft wet mass ~ **squashily** adv ~ **squashiness** n.

squat (pres/part **squatting**, p/t and p/part **squatted**) [skwot] v/i sit on the ground with knees drawn up; kneel and sit back on one's heels; settle in unoccupied buildings or land without permission; take possession of unowned land, be a settler ~ **squat** adj short and thick; thickset.

squatter [skwoter] n one who illegally settles in unoccupied buildings or land; settler who takes unowned land; (Aust) sheep-farmer.

squaw [skwaw] n North American Indian married woman.

squawk [skwawk] v/i utter a loud, harsh cry ~ **squawk** n loud, harsh cry.

squeak [skweek] v/i and t emit a shrill grating noise; utter in a shrill but weak voice; utter shrill brief cries, esp of excitement; (sl) inform, betray ~ **squeak** n shrill weak cry; shrill grating noise; **narrow s.** narrow escape.

squeaker [skweeker] n one who or that which squeaks; device for making shrill noises; (sl) informer.

squeaky [skweeki] adj shrill but faint; emitting squeaks ~ **squeakily** adv ~ **squeakiness** n.

squeal [skweel] v/i and t utter a long shrill cry, esp in pain or excitement; (sl) betray secrets, turn informer; complain at suffering ~ **squeal** n long shrill cry.

squealer [skweeler] n one who squeals.

squeamish [skweemish] adj easily disgusted or distressed, too sensitive ~ **squeamishly** adv ~ **squeamishness** n.

squeegee [skweejee] n strip of rubber fixed to a handle for cleaning wet floors.

squeezable [skweezab'l] adj that may be squeezed.

squeeze [skweez] v/t and i grip and press tightly; press moisture out of, press till dry; pack tightly,

cram; extort by threats; force one's way through or into a narrow space; take impression of on plastic surface ~ **squeeze** n act of squeezing; state of being squeezed; state of being tightly packed; tight-packed crowd; restrictions imposed by a government on financial and commercial activities.

squeezer [skweezer] n one who or that which squeezes; playing-card marked with its value in top left-hand corner.

squelch [skwelch] v/i and t make a splashing and sucking noise by walking through mud, slush etc; (coll) crush, snub, disconcert ~ **squelch** n act or noise of squelching.

squib [skwib] n small explosive firework which emits sparks; (fig) topical political satire; tube of gunpowder for igniting a blasting-charge; **damp s.** joke, pointed remark etc that fails to have much effect.

squid [skwid] n cuttlefish; artificial bait resembling this.

squidge [skwij] v/t squeeze, squash.

squiffy [skwifi] adj (coll) tipsy; askew, crooked; silly.

squiggle [skwig'l] v/i wriggle, writhe; form a squiggle ~ **squiggle** n wavy, twisting line or shape; twisty, illegible handwriting.

squiggly [skwigli] adj twisted, wriggly.

squill [skwil] n bulbous plant resembling a bluebell.

squinch [skwinsh] n (archi) arch across angle of square tower to support octagon.

squint [skwint] n defect of the eyes such that both cannot look in the same direction at once; act of deliberately making the eyes converge or diverge; sidelong or stealthy glance; narrow opening giving a sideways view of something; (coll) glance, look ~ **squint** v/i have a squint; look obliquely; (coll) look, glance.

squint-eyed [skwint-Id] adj squinting.

squire [skwIr] n country landowner, chief landowner in a parish; (hist) attendant upon a knight; (fig) one who escorts or pays court to a lady ~ **squire** v/t attend upon; escort (a lady).

squirearchy [skwIrRaarki] n country landowners as a class; political power of these.

squireen [skwIrReen] n petty squire, esp in Ireland.

squirm [skwurm] v/i wriggle, writhe; (fig) feel embarrassed or humiliated ~ **squirm** n wriggling movement; (naut) twist in a rope.

squirrel [skwiRel] n small bushy-tailed tree-living rodent; (fig) one who hoards objects of small value.

squirt [skwurt] v/t and i eject in a stream; be ejected ~ **squirt** n syringe; jet; (sl) insignificant but bumptious person; mean or untrustworthy person.

squish [skwish] v/t and i (coll) squash (something very moist) ~ **squish** n (coll) act or noise of squishing; moist pulp, soft mud etc.

squit [skwit] n (sl) unimportant person; mean or untrustworthy person; worthless rubbish.

squitters [skwiterz] n (sl) diarrhoea.

stab (pres/part **stabbing**, p/t and p/part **stabbed**) [stab] v/t and i pierce or wound with pointed weapon; make jabbing movement with pointed object; give sharp, throbbing, intermittent pain; roughen (wall) by chipping; **s. in the back** attack or injure treacherously ~ **stab** *n* act of stabbing; blow or wound from pointed weapon; sharp throbbing pain; **a s. at** (*coll*) an attempt at.

stability [sta*biliti*] *n* quality or state of being stable.

stabilization [staybilizayshon] *n* act of making stable; prevention of chemical decomposition of a substance > PDS.

stabilize [stay*biliz*] *v/t* make stable or steady; keep in equilibrium.

stabilizer [stay*bilizer*] *n* that which obtains stability; device for keeping a ship or aircraft *etc* in equilibrium.

stable (1) [stayb'l] *adj* firmly established, steady; not easily overturned or shaken; not liable to change suddenly; not easily upset; resolute, unwavering; (*chem*) not readily decomposed; not tending to decompose spontaneously.

stable (2) *n* building where horses are kept; cattleshed; group of racehorses of a particular owner or trainer ~ **stable** *v/t* and *i* lodge in a stable; put into a stable.

stableboy [stayb'l-boi] *n* boy employed to tend horses in a stable.

stabling [staybling] *n* act of putting into a stable; stable accommodation.

stably [staybli] *adv* in a stable way.

staccato [sta*kaat*O] *adj* and *adv* (*mus*) with each note distinct and detached > PDM.

stack [stak] *n* deliberately-built regular pile, *esp* of hay, straw, corn, or wood; tall chimney; group of chimneys; funnel of ship or steam-engine; large pile; (*coll*) large amount ~ **stack** *v/t* build up into a stack; pile up; **s. the cards** dishonestly arrange playing-cards in a particular order before dealing; arrange secretly and unfairly.

stackpipe [stak*pIp*] *n* (*bui*) vertical pipe carrying bathroom or lavatory wastes to drain.

stackyard [stak*yaard*] *n* enclosure for haystacks.

stacte [stak*tee*] *n* (*OT*) odoriferous spice.

stadium [stay*di*-um] *n* track for athletics, *esp* footraces; sports arena.

staff [staaf] *n* group of persons employed by any single organization, school, hospital, factory *etc*; servants of one employer; (*mil*) administrative personnel; tall pole, long slender stick; rod of office; (*ar*) long walking-stick; (*fig*) prop, support; (*mus*) set of five lines and spaces on which notes are written ~ **staff** *v/t* find a staff of employees for; be the staff of ~ **staff** *adj* of, by, or for a staff.

staff-officer [staaf-*ofiser*] *n* an officer serving on a military general staff.

staffwork [staaf*work*] *n* organizational and administrative work.

stag [stag] *n* male of the red deer; (*comm sl*) one who buys shares in a new issue in order to sell them at a profit immediately on allotment; **s. film** erotic film considered suitable for men only; **s. party** social gathering of men only.

stag-beetle [stag-*beet'l*] *n* beetle, the male of which has antler-like mandibles.

stage [stayj] *n* raised floor or platform in theatre *etc* on which performance takes place; (*fig*) theatrical profession; drama; place where something happens, scene; particular level or period in a developing process; fixed stopping place of a bus, coach or other public vehicle; distance between two stopping places; platform raised by scaffolding or slung from ropes; **go on the s.** become a professional actor or actress; **open s.** projecting or arena stage ~ **stage** *v/t* produce (play *etc*) before an audience; arrange; perform or present with dramatic effect; do for effect ~ **stage** *adj* of, for, or in the theatre or drama.

stagecoach [stayj*kOch*] *n* horsedrawn coach conveying passengers along a regular route.

stagecraft [stayj*kRaaft*] *n* art of writing, acting in, or producing plays.

stage-direction [stayj-d*IRekshon*] *n* instruction in text of play *etc* telling actors what movements to perform on stage, when to enter or leave *etc*.

stagedoor [stayj*dawr*] *n* back door to a theatre, used by actors *etc*.

stage-effect [stayj-*ifekt*] *n* any noise, music, change of lighting *etc* used in producing a play.

stagefright [stayj*fRIt*] *n* nervousness in facing audiences.

stage-hand [stayj-hand] *n* person employed to move scenery, adjust lights *etc* in a theatre.

stagemanage [stayj*manij*] *v/t* act as stagemanager for; cause to appear impressive, ensure the public effectiveness of.

stage-manager [stayj-*manijer*] *n* one who directs actors in rehearsal and is responsible for scenery, staging *etc*.

stager [stayjer] *n* **old s.** one who has acted long; one who has long experience of anything.

stagestruck [stayj*stRuk*] *adj* desiring intensely to become a professional actor or actress; keenly interested in theatrical art.

stage-whisper [stayj-wisper] *n* deliberately loud whisper meant to be heard by others than the person addressed.

stagger [stager] *v/i* and *t* stand or walk unsteadily; reel, totter; startle, shock, surprise unpleasantly; prevent from coinciding, arrange at intervals of time or space ~ **stagger** *n* unsteady movement, tottering gait.

staggers [stagerz] *n* disease of horses and cattle that makes them stagger.

staghound [staghownd] *n* breed of large swift hounds.

stagily [stayjili] *adv* in a stagy way.

staginess [stayjinis] *n* quality of being stagy.

staging [stayjing] *n* platform of boards and scaffolding; act or method of putting a play *etc* on stage; theatrical production.

staging-post [stayjing-pOst] *n* regular stopping place on route of coach, airline service *etc*.

stagnant [stagnant] *adj* not flowing; failing to develop, sluggish, inert ~ **stagnantly** *adv*.

stagnate [stagnayt] *v/i* cease to flow; be motionless; (*fig*) become sluggish, fail to develop.

stagnation [stagnayshon] *n* state of being stagnant.

stagy [stayji] *adj* consciously dramatic, overemphatic; artificial, seeming insincere.

staid [stayd] *adj* sober, sedate, grave ~ **staidly** *adv* ~ **staidness** *n*.

stain [stayn] *v/t* and *i* discolour, soil; blemish; colour with a dye; impregnate with colouring matter; cause discoloration ~ **stain** *n* discoloration; spot of distinct colour; spot, blemish.

stained-glass [staynd-glaas] *n* glass coloured by metallic pigments.

stainless [stay*nlis*] *adj* free from stains; incapable of becoming stained; free from sin; **s. steel** type of steel which contains chromium and which does not rust > PDS.

stair [*stair*] *n* one of a series of steps; (*pl*) series of steps, *usu* inside a building; **below stairs in the basement, in the servants' quarters; foot (head) of the stairs** bottom (top) of a flight of stairs.

staircarpet [*stair*kaarpit] *n* strip of narrow carpet to cover stairs.

staircase [*stair*kays] *n* flight of stairs with banisters, framework *etc*.

stair-rod [*stair*-ROd] *n* metal or wooden rod to keep a staircarpet in place.

stairway [*stair*way] *n* staircase.

staith, staithe [*stay*TH] *n* landing-stage where coal may be loaded and unloaded.

stake [*stayk*] *n* money risked in betting or gambling; that which may be won or lost according to the outcome of an event; pointed wooden post fixed in the ground; post to which persons were tied to be burnt to death; execution by burning; (*fig*) martyrdom; small anvil; **at s.** risked, in danger of being lost; dependent on an outcome ~ **stake** *v/t* wager, risk; support by tying to a stake or stick; mark out or surround with stakes; **s. a claim** mark out boundaries of land one is claiming; claim, declare one's right to.

stakeboat [*stayk*bOt] *n* boat used as starting-point or winning-post in a boat race.

stakeholder [*stayk*hOlder] *n* one who holds the stakes of a wager.

Stakhanovite [sta*kaan*OvIt] *n* workman in Communist country who exceeds the quota of work allotted to him > PDPol.

stalactic [*stal*aktik] *adj* of, like, or containing stalactites.

stalactite [*stal*aktIt] *n* hanging column of calcium carbonate formed from roof of cave by water containing calcium compounds > PDG, PDS.

stalactitic [stalak*titik*] *adj* stalactic.

stalagmite [*stalag*mIt] *n* rising column of calcium carbonate formed from floor of cave by water containing calcium compounds.

stalagmitic [stalag*mitik*] *adj* of or shaped like a stalagmite.

stalagmometry [stalag*mom*itRi] *n* method of measuring surface tension of liquids > PDS.

stale (1) [*stayl*] *adj* not fresh; too long kept; dry, musty; (*fig*) trite; tired by too much work; no longer in good condition; out of practice ~ **stale** *v/t* and *i* make or become stale.

stale (2) *n* urine of horses and cattle ~ **stale** *v/i*.

stalemate [*stayl*mayt] *n* (*chess*) position when the king cannot move without placing himself in check; (*fig*) deadlock, position where neither adversary can move without defeat ~ **stalemate** *v/t* place in stalemate; (*fig*) bring to standstill.

staleness [*stayl*nis] *n* quality of being stale.

stalk (1) [*stawk*] *n* stem of plant; slender support; stem of wineglass; tall chimney; peduncle.

stalk (2) *v/t* and *i* walk stealthily in pursuit of (prey, game *etc*); follow stealthily; stride, walk with stiffly dignified steps; (*fig*) advance relentlessly and silently ~ **stalk** *n* stiffly striding gait; act of stalking game.

stalked [*stawkt*] *adj* having a stem or stalk.

stalker [*stawker*] *n* one who stalks game.

stalking-horse [*stawk*ing-hawrs] *n* that which conceals one's hostile intentions; camouflage, misleading appearance; horse behind which a huntsman hides himself when stalking game.

stall (1) [*stawl*] *n* booth, table, barrow *etc* displaying goods for sale; theatre seat at front of ground floor of auditorium; compartment for one animal in a stable; recessed seat in the choir of a church; protective sheath for finger or toe ~ **stall** *v/t* put or keep in a stall.

stall (2) *v/i* and *t* (*of motor engines*) cease working through loss of energy; (*aer*) go out of control by losing speed; cause to cease working or lose control thus; come to a standstill; delay deliberately; avoid acting, speaking *etc* as long as possible; gain time by excuses.

stall (3) *n* accomplice of a thief who diverts attention while the theft is taking place.

stallage [*stawl*ij] *n* right to erect a stall at a fair; rent for this.

staller [*stawler*] *n* one who or that which stalls.

stallion [*stal*yon] *n* uncastrated male horse.

stalwart [*stawl*wert] *adj* sturdy, muscular; unfailingly reliable, loyal *etc*; undaunted ~ **stalwart** *n* one who is stalwart ~ **stalwartly** *adv*.

stamen [*stay*men] *n* (*bot*) pollen-bearing male organ of flower.

stamina [*stamina*] *n* vigour, vitality, power of endurance.

stammer [*stamer*] *n* speech defect in which speech sounds are involuntarily repeated or can only be uttered with great effort > PDP ~ **stammer** *v/i* and *t* speak with a stammer; utter confusedly and brokenly.

stammering [*stame*Ring] *adj* spoken with a stammer; suffering from a stammer ~ **stammeringly** *adv*.

stamp [*stamp*] *v/t* and *i* make a mark or impression on; affix a stamp to; (*fig*) impress deeply; bring the foot down heavily; strike the foot heavily on the ground; **s. out** put out or crush by bringing the foot down heavily; (*fig*) destroy utterly or brutally ~ **stamp** *n* act of stamping; instrument which makes an impression or which cuts out a pattern; imprinted mark; official mark showing that a tax or duty has been paid; stamped label showing the payment of postage; label or mark certifying ownership, genuineness *etc*; (*fig*) distinguishing mark; downward blow with the foot; blow with a stamping machine; (*fig*) character, type; **trading s.** low-value gift voucher given to customers and collected to be later exchanged for goods.

stamp-collector [*stamp*-kolektor] *n* one who collects postage stamps.

stamp-duty [*stamp*-dewti] *n* tax on certain legal documents.

stampede [stam*peed*] *n* sudden panic causing horses or cattle to scatter and run; sudden unreasoning flight ~ **stampede** *v/i* and *t* flee in panic; cause to stampede; hustle or terrify (someone) into rash action.

stamper [*stamper*] *n* one who or that which stamps.

stamping-ground [*stamp*ing-gRownd] *n* (*coll*) favourite haunt, usual place where specified persons or animals can be found.

stance [*staans*] *n* attitude in standing, *esp* when about to strike a golf or cricket ball; (*fig*) mental attitude, opinion, view.

stanch, staunch [*staanch*] *v/t* stop the flowing of (blood) ~ **stanch** *adj* staunch.

stanchion [*staan*shon] *n* upright prop; upright bar or pair of bars for confining cattle in a stall ~ **stanchion** *v/t* fasten with a stanchion.

stand (*p/t* and *p/part* **stood**) [*stand*] *v/i* and *t* hold oneself upright on one's feet; remain upright on a base; remain upright without moving; be in a specified place, position or state; remain, be; rise to one's feet; move into specified position; put, place, set upright; bear, endure, tolerate; pay for (drink, food *etc*) for another; (*naut*) steer; **s. alone** have no equal; have no friends, supporters *etc*; **s. aside** move to one side; remain inactive, take no part; **s. back** move backwards, get out of the way; **s. by** remain loyal to, help, stay with; remain alert and waiting; **s. down** withdraw from contest, election *etc*; (*mil*) go off duty; release from active service without disbanding; **s. for** represent, symbolize; be candidate for election; (*coll*) bear, tolerate; **s. in** take a share in; **s. in for** (*coll*) act as substitute for; **s. in good stead** be of valuable help; **s. off** keep at a distance; be aloof; (*naut*) keep away; (*coll*) dismiss temporarily from employment; **s. out** be clearly visible, be conspicuous; refuse obstinately, refuse to yield; **s. to** assemble in readiness; **s. up** stand upright, rise to one's feet; (*sl*) keep waiting; jilt; deceive; **s. up for** defend; **s. up to** face or oppose bravely; **s. upon** insist on; **s. with** support, ally oneself with ~ **stand** *n* act of stopping or taking up a position; act of remaining unmoved despite attack, opposition *etc*; structure, framework *etc* on which something is raised, displayed *etc*; stall; raised platform, *esp* for spectators at outdoor sports, processions *etc*; area where taxis and public vehicles may wait; (*cricket*) long period without loss of wicket; (*fig*) resolute resistance; (*US*) witness-box; (*coll*) place at which a theatrical company on tour gives a performance; **make a s.** resist stubbornly; **take one's s. on** take up position on; (*fig*) base one's views, arguments *etc* on.

standard [*stand*ard] *n* that which authority, custom or public opinion lays down as a good model; approved pattern of behaviour, desirable level of efficiency or value *etc*; criterion, test, grade of merit; upright shaft or pole used as support; shrub or tree growing on a single stem; flag, banner, ensign; (*fig*) rallying-point; leadership; **s. of living** level of comfort in food, housing, possessions and material comforts enjoyed by a person or group ~ **standard** *adj* in accordance with a recognized standard; of recognized authority or value; accepted; average, usual.

standard-bearer [*stand*ard-bairRer] *n* soldier who carries a regimental flag; (*fig*) leader.

standardization [standardIzayshon] *n* act of standardizing; state of being standardized.

standardize [*stand*ardIz] *v/t* cause to conform to a standard; make uniform, remove variations, irregularities *etc* from; cause to be all alike.

standard-lamp [*stand*ard-lamp] *n* lamp on a tall upright stand.

standby [*stand*bI] *n* that which may be relied upon in emergency; that which is kept ready for emergency use.

stand-down [*stand*-down] *n* **on s.** temporarily released from active service.

standee [stan*dee*] *n* (*coll*) one who stands instead of sitting.

stand-in [*stand*-in] *n* one who acts as substitute for another; one who deputizes for a cinema actor or actress during preparations for lighting *etc*, or when dangerous stunts are needed.

standing [*stand*ing] *n* status, rank; reputation; duration, continuance ~ **standing** *adj* erect, upright; long-lasting, always in existence; permanently in force; stagnant; (*mil*) permanently kept under arms; **s. jump** jump made without preliminary run; **s. room** only room enough to stand, not sit; **s. stone** upright monolith.

stand-offish [stand-*of*ish] *adj* aloof, haughty, not friendly.

standpipe [*stand*pIp] *n* upright pipe serving as hydrant.

standpoint [*stand*point] *n* point of view.

standstill [*stand*stil] *n* stoppage, cessation of movement or progress.

stand-up [*stand*-up] *adj* erect, upright; (*of meal*) eaten while standing; (*of fight*) openly violent.

stank [*stank*] *p/t* of **stink**.

stannary [*stana*Ri] *n* tin-mine; tin-mining district.

stannate [*stana*yt] *n* salt of stannic acid.

stannel, staniel [*stan*'l, *stan*yel] *n* the kestrel.

stannic [*stan*ik] *adj* of or from tin, *esp* in the quadrivalent state.

stanniferous [stan*ife*Rus] *adj* containing tin.

stannous [*stan*us] *adj* of or from tin, *esp* in the bivalent state.

stannum [*stan*um] *n* tin.

stanza [*stan*za] *n* group of three or more lines of poetry forming a formal unit in a poem.

stanzaic [stan*zay*-ik] *adj* of or in stanzas.

stapes [*stay*peez] *n* (*anat*) innermost bone of middle ear.

staphylitis [stafil*lI*tis] *n* inflammation of the uvula.

staphylococcus [stafilo*kok*us] *n* (*path*) form of bacteria made up of cocci grouped in irregular masses.

staple (1) [*stayp*'l] *n* U-shaped loop of metal, wire *etc* driven into something to fasten or support something; socket for a bolt; socket holding reeds of certain wind-instruments; (*mining*) shaft between seams ~ **staple** *v/t* fasten with staples; hold (papers) together by driving bent wires through them.

staple (2) *n* basic essential food, raw material *etc*; chief produce; unprocessed material; grade of fibre in wool, flax *etc* ~ **staple** *adj* basic, indispensable; chief; standard ~ **staple** *v/t* grade (wool, flax *etc*).

stapler [*stay*pler] *n* one who grades wool; device for fastening papers together with wire.

stapling-machine [*stay*pling-masheen] *n* machine for wire-stitching of paper.

star [*staar*] *n* large incandescent body situated far in outer space, *esp* one visible from earth as a point of light in the night sky > PDS; five- or six-pointed pattern conventionally representing one of these; badge of this pattern as emblem, insignia, award of merit *etc*; highly popular actor or actress, singer *etc*; leading performer in a particular film, play *etc*; (*fig*) luck, fate; success; (*print*) asterisk; **Stars and Stripes** national flag of U.S.A.; **S. Chamber** (*hist*) English civil and criminal court abolished in 1641; **s. in the ascen-**

dant increasing luck and success: **S. of Bethlehem** a white-flowered lily; **S. of David** six-pointed star, emblem of Judaism; yellow cloth badge representing this, which all Jews were forced to wear by the Nazis; **S. of Jerusalem** salsify; **see stars** see flashes of light when concussed; be knocked unconscious; **Yellow S.** Star of David ∼ **star** (*pres/part* **starring**, *p/t* and *p/part* **starred**) *v/t* and *i* mark with an asterisk; award a star to, as sign of merit; decorate with stars; have the leading part in a film, play *etc*; present as leading actor, actress, singer *etc*; present, display or publicize as outstandingly good ∼ **star** *adj* of or for a leading actor, actress, singer *etc*; brilliant, outstanding.

starboard [*staar*bawrd] *adj* and *n* (of or on) the right side of a ship as one looks forward.

starch [*staarch*] *n* carbohydrate stored in plants as granules > PDS; white soluble powder used to stiffen certain fabrics after laundering; carbohydrates in food; (*fig*) rigid manner or outlook ∼ **starch** *v/t* stiffen (fabrics) with starch.

starch-reduced [*staarch*-Ridewst] *adj* (*of bread etc*) containing less than normal amount of starch.

starchy [*staarchi*] *adj* of or containing starch; stiff, formal ∼ **starchily** *adv* ∼ **starchiness** *n*.

star-crossed [*staar*-kRost] *adj* ill-fated.

stardom [*staardum*] *n* status of being a star actor or actress.

stare [*stair*] *v/i* look with eyes fixed and wide open; be obvious ∼ **stare** *n* fixed look with eyes open wide.

starfish [*staarfish*] *n* flat echinoderm with five or more rays.

star-gazer [*staar*-gayzer] *n* (*cont*) astronomer, astrologer; dreamy, impractical person.

star-gazing [*staar*-gayzing] *n* (*cont*) astrology; astronomy; dreaminess.

staring [*stairRing*] *adj* that stares; (*of colours*) too vivid ∼ **staringly** *adv*.

stark [*staark*] *adj* stiff; bleak, grim; complete, absolute; **stark-naked** ∼ **stark** *adv* completely; **s. mad** absolutely mad ∼ **starkly** *adv*.

starkers [*staarkerz*] *adj* (*sl*) stark-naked.

stark-naked [*staark*-naykid] *adj* completely naked.

starkness [*staark*nis] *n* quality of being stark.

starless [*staar*lis] *adj* with no stars visible.

starlet [*staar*lit] *n* young film-actress who considers herself to be, or is unjustifiably publicized as, of outstanding merit.

starlight [*staar*lit] *n* light from the stars.

starling [*staar*ling] *n* small gregarious bird with glossy black feathers.

starlit [*staar*lit] *adj* lighted by stars.

starred [*staard*] *adj* set with stars; influenced by the stars; marked with a star.

starry [*staar*Ri] *adj* covered or adorned with stars; consisting of stars; shining like stars; like a star ∼ **starrily** *adv* ∼ **starriness** *n*.

starry-eyed [*staar*Ri-Id] *adj* with eyes sparkling with love or enthusiasm; (*coll*) naïvely enthusiastic, inexperienced.

star-spangled [*staar*-spang-g'ld] *adj* set with stars; **S. Banner** national flag and anthem of the U.S.A.

start [*staart*] *v/t* and *i* begin; set in motion; begin to move, act, or exist; begin a journey; warp,

distort; dislocate; make a sudden involuntary movement; move in a jerk; wince; cause (hunted animal) to break cover; **s. in** (*coll*) begin; **s. out** begin to act with specified aim; begin a journey; begin a career; **s. up** jump up; appear suddenly; put (engine) in motion ∼ **start** *n* beginning; act of setting out, setting in motion, coming into existence *etc*; place where a race starts from; lead of one competitor over another in a race; advantage in contest; involuntary jerky movement; slight shock; (*coll*) odd occurrence; **by fits and starts** jerkily, spasmodically.

starter [*staar*ter] *n* one who or that which starts; one who gives the signal for a race to start; self-starter; light first course to a meal.

starting-point [*staar*ting-point] *n* point of departure.

starting-post [*staar*ting-pOst] *n* barrier or post from which competitors start in a race.

startle [*staart*'l] *v/t* and *i* give a shock to, alarm; feel sudden alarm.

startling [*staart*ling] *adj* surprising; alarming.

starvation [staarvayshon] *n* act of starving; state of being starved; **s. diet** so low an amount of food as to cause slow starvation.

starve [*staarv*] *v/i* and *t* die of hunger; suffer severely from hunger; (*dial*) suffer from cold; cause to die of or to suffer from hunger.

starveling [*staarv*ling] *n* and *adj* (person, animal or plant) thin and weak from want of food.

stash [*stash*] *v/t* and *i* (*sl*) keep stored away in a hiding-place; stop, cease.

stasis [*stay*sis] *n* (*med*) stagnation of blood or of other body fluids.

state [*stayt*] *n* condition, situation; (*coll*) condition of anxiety, distress *etc*; (*cap*) political community organized under a government, nation, civil government; subdivision of a federation; social status, rank; splendour; **lie in s.** (*of corpse*) be honourably displayed before burial ∼ **State** *adj* of, for or by a State; of or for ceremonial use; of or for persons of high rank ∼ **state** *v/t* declare plainly or in detail; specify; affirm; expound.

state-carriage [stayt-*ka*Rij] *n* carriage used on ceremonial occasions.

state-coach [stayt-kOch] *n* state-carriage.

statecraft [*stayt*kRaaft] *n* art of politics.

stated [*stayt*id] *adj* appointed; explicitly announced; stipulated or agreed on; fixed.

stateless [*stayt*lis] *adj* having no nationality.

stately [*stayt*li] *adj* imposing, magnificent, dignified ∼ **stateliness** *n*.

statement [*stayt*ment] *n* act of stating; that which is stated; formal account, narration *etc*; (*comm*) financial account in detail.

state-paper [stayt-*pa*yper] *n* document relating to affairs of a government.

stateroom [*stayt*rOOm] *n* magnificent room used on ceremonial occasions; private sleeping apartment on board ship or on a train.

States-General [stayts-*jene*Ral] *n* (*hist*) legislative assembly in France before the Revolution.

statesman (*pl* **statesmen**) [*stayts*man] *n* wise, patriotic and skilful politician; member of a government; (*dial*) small landowner.

statesmanship [*stayts*manship] *n* skill and abilities of a statesman.

State-trial [stayt-*tri*-al] *n* trial for offence against the State.

static [*stat*ik] *adj* at rest, not moving; unchanging; **s. electricity** electricity at rest; electric charge acquired by being near to, but not touching, a charged body > PDS, PDEl; **s. pressure** pressure caused by weight without motion ~ **static** *n* atmospheric static electricity, *esp* as causing noise in wireless receivers.

statice [*stat*is] *n* genus of herbaceous plants which includes the sea-lavender.

statics [*stat*iks] *n* (*pl*) wireless interference caused by static electricity; branch of mechanics dealing with bodies at rest and forces in equilibrium.

station [*stay*shon] *n* place where someone or something must stand or stop; buildings, platforms *etc* at which a railway train halts to pick up or set down passengers or goods; local headquarters of police, fire-brigade or other public service; administrative centre; military post; naval base; social position, status, rank; occupation, employment; (*Aust*) cattle farm; **Stations of the Cross** fourteen pictures of the sufferings and death of Christ set up on walls of churches; prayers associated with these ~ **station** *v/t* assign a place or post to; assign to a particular military or naval base.

stationary [*stay*shonaRi] *adj* not moving, remaining in one place; unchanging; neither increasing nor decreasing.

stationer [*stay*shoner] *n* one who sells all kinds of writing materials.

stationery [*stay*shoneRi] *n* pens, paper and writing materials generally; notepaper.

stationmaster [*stay*shonmaaster] *n* official in charge of a railway-station.

station-wagon [*stay*shon-wagon] *n* motor vehicle with square wooden body, removable back seats, and doors in the rear.

statism [*stay*tism] *n* theory that economic and political power should be concentrated in a central government ~ **statist** *adj* and *n*.

statistic [sta*tist*ik] *adj* of or by statistics.

statistical [sta*tist*ikal] *adj* of or by statistics ~ **statistically** *adv*.

statistician [statisti*sh*an] *n* one skilled in dealing with statistics.

statistics [sta*tist*iks] *n* (*pl*) scientific collection and study of numerical facts and data; collection of numerical data concerning births, deaths, health, economic and social conditions of a population; numerical data relevant to any problem or study; **vital s.** statistics of births and deaths; (*coll*) bust, waist, and hip measurements of a woman.

stator [*stay*tor] *n* fixed part of an electric motor or generator which contains the magnetic circuits; assembly of fixed blades in a turbine.

statuary [*stat*ew-aRi] *n* statues collectively; art of sculpture; sculptor ~ **statuary** *adj* of or for making statues; like a statue.

statue [*stat*ew] *n* sculptured or moulded figure, *usu* representing a person or animal at or exceeding life-size.

statuesque [statew-*esk*] *adj* like a statue; having the proportions and dignity of a statue; motionless and impressive ~ **statuesquely** *adv* ~ **statuesqueness** *n*.

statuette [statew-*et*] *n* little statue.

stature [*stat*yer] *n* the natural height of the body; (*fig*) mental or moral greatness.

status [*stay*tus] *n* relative position in society, *esp* as measured by wealth; prestige; rank, standing; (*leg*) legal position; **s. quo** (*Lat*) previously existing condition, unaltered position; **s. symbol** object the possession of which is considered proof of wealth, rank or prestige.

statute [*stat*ewt] *n* law made by a legislative authority; permanent rule made by an institution or its founder; written law; Act of Parliament.

statute-book [*stat*ewt-book] *n* register of statutes.

statutory [*stat*ewtoRi] *adj* of, as or by statute; deriving authority from a statute.

staunch, stanch [*stawnch*] *adj* firm, reliable, trustworthy ~ **staunch** *v/t* stanch ~ **staunchly** *adv* ~ **staunchness** *n*.

stave [*stay*v] *n* side timber of a cask; strip of wood; rung of ladder; verse, stanza; (*mus*) staff ~ **stave** (*p/t* and *p/part* **stove** or **staved**) break a hole in; burst; fit with staves; **s. off** avert temporarily, ward off.

stay (1) [*stay*] *v/i* and *t* remain in a place or state; live as guest or visitor; last out, endure to the end of; pause; hinder, check; (*leg*) postpone; **come to s.** (*coll*) become permanent, established *etc*; be unlikely to cease or change ~ **stay** *n* act of staying; period of being a guest or visitor; restraint, check; (*leg*) suspension of proceedings.

stay (2) *n* prop, support; (*naut*) fore-and-aft rope supporting mast or spar; (*pl*) whalebone corset ~ **stay** *v/t* prop up; satisfy, sustain.

stay-at-home [*stay*-at-hOm] *adj* and *n* unadventurous, unenterprising (person).

stayer [*stay*-er] *n* one who stays; one who can endure long hard effort.

staying-power [*stay*-ing-powr] *n* ability to endure long hard effort.

stay-lace [*stay*-lays] *n* thin cord used in lacing a corset.

staymaker [*stay*mayker] *n* one who makes corsets.

staysail [*stay*sayl] *n* (*naut*) sail extended by a stay.

stead [*sted*] *n* position or place which another had or might have had; **stand in good s.** do good service to.

steadfast [*sted*fast] *adj* firm, unchanging, resolute ~ **steadfastly** *adv* ~ **steadfastness** *n*.

steadily [*sted*ili] *adj* in a steady way.

steadiness [*sted*inis] *n* quality of being steady.

steading [*sted*ing] *n* farmstead.

steady [*sted*i] *adj* firmly fixed; not liable to shake or fall; unwavering; constant, uniform; not fickle or unreliable ~ **steady** *v/t* and *i* make steady; become steady ~ **steady** *adv* steadily; **go s.** (*coll*) be in love with and go about regularly with the same person, though not yet engaged ~ **steady** *n* (*coll*) regular boy-friend or girl-friend.

steak [*stayk*] *n* thick slice of meat or of fish, *esp* of beef.

steal (*p/t* **stole**, *p/part* **stolen**) [*steel*] *v/t* and *i* take (another's property) unlawfully; obtain by stealth or cunning, take without permission; move silently and gradually; **s. a march on** cunningly win an advantage over.

stealth [*stelth*] *n* furtive act or behaviour; secrecy; underhand procedure.

stealthy [*stelthi*] *adj* done cautiously and secretly, furtive ~ **stealthily** *adv* ~ **stealthiness** *n*.

steam [*steem*] *n* vapour into which water turns above its boiling point > PDS; misty film of condensed water vapour; any vapour; **get up s.** (*coll*) collect one's energy; become excited; **let off s.** release pent-up emotion ~ **steam** *v/t* and *i* cook or clean by exposure to steam; emit steam or vapour; move by steam-produced energy; **s. up** become filmed over with condensation; **get steamed up** (*coll*) become excited or angry ~ **steam** *adj* driven by energy of expanding steam; **s. radio** (*coll*) radio as opposed to television.

steamboat [*steembOt*] *n* vessel driven by steam.

steamchest [*steemchest*] *n* chamber in a steam-engine from which steam is conveyed from the boiler to the cylinder.

steamed-up [*steemd-up*] *adj* (*coll*) angry; over-excited.

steam-engine [*steem*-enjin] *n* engine worked by steam pressure > PDS; railway engine so worked.

steamer [*steemer*] *n* ship driven by steam; utensil in which food is steamed; **s. lane** ocean route used by steamers.

steam-gauge [*steem*-gayj] *n* instrument to indicate the pressure of steam.

steam-hammer [*steem*-hamer] *n* powerful hammer worked by steam.

steamily [*steemili*] *adv* in a steamy way.

steaminess [*steeminis*] *n* quality of being steamy.

steam-jacket [*steem*-jakit] *n* hollow casing round a cylinder *etc* into which steam is driven to heat the cylinder.

steam-navvy [*steem*-navi] *n* excavating machine driven by steam.

steampower [*steempow*-er] *n* force applied to machinery driven by steam.

steamroller [*steemROler*] *n* heavy steam-driven roller for levelling roads; (*fig*) massive, irresistible force ~ **steamroller** *v/t* crush; force through.

steamship [*steemship*] *n* ship propelled by steam.

steamtug [*steemtug*] *n* small vessel propelled by steam and used for towing ships.

steamy [*steemi*] *adj* full of steam, misty.

stearic [stee-aRik] *adj* of or from stearin; **s. acid** a fatty acid > PDS.

stearin [*stee*-aRin] *n* the solid portion of any fixed oil or fat.

steatite [*stee*-atIt] *n* soapstone.

steato- *pref* fatty.

steatosis [stee-atOsis] *n* fatty degeneration.

steed [*steed*] *n* (*poet*) horse.

steel [*steel*] *n* iron containing carbon > PDS, PDE; bar of this for sharpening knives; piece of this for striking sparks from flint; weapon or instrument of steel; sword; (*fig*) great hardness; **s. band** West Indian band playing home-made metal instruments; **s. engraving** engraving on a steel plate; **s. wool** mass of shredded steel used for scouring ~ **steel** *v/t* cover with steel; sharpen on steel; harden, make cruel or obstinate ~ **steel** *adj* of, containing, or like steel.

steel-clad [*steel*-klad] *adj* clad in armour.

steel-plated [*steel*-*playtid*] *adj* plated with steel.

steely [*steeli*] *adj* of, like, or made of steel; hard, merciless; glittering with a cold light.

steelyard [*steely*aard] *n* weighing-machine with arms of unequal length > PDS.

steen [*steen*] *v/t* line (a well) with stones.

steenbok [*steenbok*] *n* small South African antelope.

steep (1) [*steep*] *adj* sharply inclined, precipitous, sloping at a high angle; (*coll*) too expensive; outrageous, incredible ~ **steep** *n* (*poet*) precipice.

steep (2) *v/t* and *i* soak in liquid ~ **steep** *n* process of soaking in liquid.

steepen [*steepen*] *v/t* and *i* make steep; become steep.

steeper [*steeper*] *n* vessel used in steeping.

steeple [*steep*'l] *n* tall tapering structure on roof of a church *etc*; spire.

steeplechase [*steep*'lchays] *n* cross-country horse-race in which various obstacles must be jumped over.

steeplejack [*steep*'ljak] *n* one who climbs steeples, tall chimneys, high monuments *etc* to clean or repair them.

steer (1) [*steer*] *v/t* and *i* direct the course of (ship, motorcar *etc*); guide, direct the acts or choices of; be steered; aim one's course; **s. clear of** avoid; **s. for** head towards.

steer (2) *n* young bullock, *esp* castrated one.

steerable [*steer*Rab'l] *adj* that can be steered.

steerage [*steer*Rij] *n* act or method of steering; (*naut*) stern of a ship; cheap accommodation in the stern; effect of a rudder on a ship.

steerage-way [*steer*Rij-way] *n* (*naut*) motion sufficient for effective steering.

steerer [*steer*Rer] *n* one who steers.

steering [*steer*Ring] *adj* that steers; guiding; **s. committee** committee to arrange procedure at a conference.

steering-wheel [*steer*Ring-wheel] *n* wheel that controls the steering of a motorcar, ship *etc*.

steersman [*steer*zman] *n* helmsman, one who steers.

Steinberger [*stIn*burger] *n* a Rhenish white wine.

steinbok [*stIn*bok] *n* steenbok.

stele [*steel*] *n* (*Gk arch*) upright slab bearing inscriptions or sculpture.

stellar [*stelar*] *adj* of or connected with stars; set with stars.

stellular [*stelewlar*] *adj* shaped like a small star.

stem (1) [*stem*] *n* stalk of plant, shrub, leaf, or flower > PDB; slender upright support; narrow part of tobacco-pipe; (*gramm*) unchanging part of word to which inflexional endings are added; (*naut*) curved upright timber to which planks are joined at the bow; (*ar*) family, branch of family ~ **stem** (*pres*/*part* **stemming**, *p*/*t* and *p*/*part* **stemmed**) *v/t* and *i* remove the stem of; **s. from** be derived from, originate from.

stem (2) (*pres*/*part* **stemming**, *p*/*t* and *p*/*part* **stemmed**) *v/t* check the flow of; advance against the resistance of, make headway; (*fig*) face resolutely.

stench [*stench*] *n* strong unpleasant smell.

stencil [*stensil*] *n* piece of thin metal or other material in which patterns have been cut; similar device used for reproducing typescript; decoration made by painting through the spaces in a stencil ~ **stencil** *v/t* decorate, make a copy of, using a stencil.

Sten-gun [*sten*-gun] *n* type of machine-gun.

steno- *pref* narrow; constricted.

stenochromy [stenokRomi] *n* art of printing in several colours at the same time.

stenograph [stenogRaaf] *n* character used in shorthand writing; shorthand typewriting machine.

stenographer [stenogRafer] *n* one who writes shorthand.

stenography [stenogRafi] *n* art of writing in shorthand.

stentorian [stentawRi-an] *adj* (*of voice*) extremely loud.

step [step] *n* act of placing one foot before the other in walking or running; sound of this, footfall; distance between feet in walking, pace, stride; short distance; degree, stage of progress; act aimed at producing specified result; procedure; ledge, stair, rung, plank *etc* on which one treads to climb up or down something; (*pl*) stepladder; staircase; (*fig*) grade; (*mus*) interval between notes of scale; (*naut*) socket of mast; (*dancing*) one of series of characteristic foot movements in a dance; **false s.** mistaken action; **in (out of) s.** walking exactly (not exactly) at the same pace and gait as another; (*fig*) (not) conforming with others; **take steps** adopt measures ~ **step** (*pres/part* **stepping**, *p/t* and *p/part* **stepped**) *v/i* and *t* move and set down the foot; walk, go; tread; perform steps of (a dance); (*naut*) insert (foot of mast) in socket; **s. aside** (*fig*) get out of another's way, retire; **s. in** enter, *esp* a house; intervene; **s. on it** (*coll*) hurry up; **s. out** walk briskly; (*coll*) have a good time, lead a gay social life; (*sl*) be unfaithful; (*sl*) die; **s. up** (*coll*) accelerate, increase.

step- *pref* related not by blood but by remarriage of one parent.

stepbrother [stepbRuTHer] *n* son, by a former marriage, of one's stepmother or stepfather.

stepchild [stepchIld] *n* child of one's husband or wife by a former marriage.

stepdaughter [stepdawter] *n* female stepchild.

stepfather [stepfaaTHer] *n* man who has married one's mother after the death or divorce of one's own father.

stephanotis [stefanOtis] *n* tropical climbing plant with fragrant flowers.

step-ins [step-inz] *n* (*pl*) garments or shoes that can be easily put on and are held by elasticity, not fastenings.

stepladder [steplader] *n* ladder with flat treads instead of rungs, and a hinged support to hold it upright.

stepmother [stepmuTHer] *n* woman who has married one's father after the death or divorce of one's own mother.

step-parent [step-pairRent] *n* later husband or wife of one's parent.

steppe [step] *n* vast treeless plain > PDG.

stepping-stone [steping-stOn] *n* raised stone in stream or swampy place to facilitate crossing; (*fig*) aid to advancement or progress.

stepsister [stepsister] *n* daughter, by a former marriage, of one's stepmother or stepfather.

stepson [stepsun] *n* male stepchild.

steradian [steRaydi-an] *n* unit of solid angle, equal to the angle which encloses a surface on a sphere equal to the square of the radius.

stercoraceous [sturkoRayshus] *adj* of dung.

stercoral [sturkoRal] *adj* of or growing on dung.

stere [steer] *n* metric unit of volume equal to 1 cubic metre.

stereo [steRi-O/steerRi-O] *abbr* stereoscopic; stereophonic; stereotype.

stereo- *pref* three-dimensional; firm, solid.

stereochemistry [steRi-OkemistRi] *n* study of the arrangement in space of the atoms in a molecule.

stereography [steRi-ogRafi] *n* art of representing solid forms on a plane.

stereoisomerism [steRi-O-isOmeRizm] *n* (*chem*) isomerism of optically active compounds due to different three-dimensional arrangement of atoms within the molecules ~ **stereoisomeric** *adj*.

stereophonic [steRi-Ofonik] *adj* (*of sound*) recorded through separated groups of microphones and reproduced through separated loudspeakers, to give an impression of realistic variation in direction of instruments, singers *etc* > PDEl ~ **stereophonically** *adv*.

stereophony [steRi-ofoni] *n* art of stereophonic recording.

stereoscope [steRi-OskOp] *n* optical device that produces the illusion of distance and relief by presenting two images of the same picture, one to each eye > PDS, PDP.

stereoscopic [steRi-Oskopik] *adj* apparently three-dimensional; by or of a stereoscope; **s. vision** binocular visual perception of distance and distance ~ **stereoscopically** *adv*.

stereotype [steRi-OtIp] *n* something reproduced without variations; unchanging conventionalized idea, presentation *etc*; (*print*) metallic plate cast from mould taken from movable type ~ **stereotype** *v/t* repeat without variations, reproduce with dull uniformity; conventionalize, present always in the same way; print in stereotype.

sterile [steRIl] *adj* barren, incapable of producing offspring; producing no crop; containing no live micro-organisms; (*fig*) lacking imagination, emotional power *etc*; producing no results.

sterility [steRiliti] *n* state of being sterile.

sterilization [steRilIzayshon] *n* act or process of sterilizing; state of being sterilized.

sterilize [steRilIz] *v/t* destroy bacteria in or on; wash with antiseptic; make barren, render incapable of reproduction.

sterling [sturling] *adj* in British money; of standard value; genuine, pure; (*fig*) having good moral qualities ~ **sterling** *n* British money; **S. Area** group of countries whose currencies are tied to British monetary standards > PDPol.

stern (1) [sturn] *adj* severe, austere, grim; harsh, strict; ruthless; resolute.

stern (2) *n* hind part of ship or aircraft; rump of an animal.

sternal [sturnal] *adj* of or on the breastbone.

sternfast [sturnfast] *n* rope or chain to moor a ship's stern.

sternly [sturnli] *adv* severely, harshly.

sternness [sturn-nis] *n* quality of being stern.

sternpost [sturnpOst] *n* post in the stern of a ship on which the rudder hangs.

stern-sheets [sturn-sheets] *n* space and benches at rear end of boat.

sternum [sturnum] *n* breastbone.

steroid [steerRoid] *n* (*bioch*) one of a class of derived lipids including sterols and certain hormones > PDB ~ **steroid** *adj*.

sterols [steRolz] *n* (*pl*) class of complex organic alcohols > PDS, PDB.

stertorous [sturtoRus] *adj* snoring; breathing loudly ~ **stertorously** *adv*.

stet [stet] *v/imp* and *t* (*direction to printer*) let it stand; cancel (deletion) by putting dots below what had been deleted and writing 'stet' in margin.

stethoscope [stethoskOp] *n* instrument fo r distinguishing the sounds of heart, lungs and other internal organs.

stethoscopic [stethoskopik] *adj* of or by a stethoscope.

stetson [stetsun] *n* broad-brimmed hat for men.

stevedore [steevedawr] *n* one who loads and unloads ships.

stevengraph [steevengRaaf] *n* picture made of woven silks.

stew (1) [stew] *v/t* and *i* cook slowly in a closed vessel; be cooked slowly and gently; **s. in one's own juice** bear one's troubles without help ~ **stew** *n* meat, vegetables *etc* cooked by stewing; (*sl*) agitated condition; (*ar, usu pl*) brothel.

stew (2) *n* fish pond or tank; artificial oyster bed.

steward [stew-ard] *n* catering manager of college, club *etc*; catering officer of a ship; waiter and cabin attendant on passenger ship; official helping to organize a race-meeting, public entertainment or meeting *etc*; paid manager of a large estate or household.

stewardess [stew-ardes] *n* female attendant on board a ship or airliner.

stewardship [stew-ardship] *n* office of steward of an estate; (*fig*) responsibilities, duties.

stewed [stewd] *adj* (*of tea*) unpleasantly strong through long infusion; (*sl*) drunk.

stewpot [stewpot] *n* earthenware pot for cooking stew in oven.

stich [stik] *n* metrical line, verse; one of the rhythmic lines of the Bible.

stichomythia [stikomithi-a] *n* (*Gr drama*) dialogue in alternate single lines.

stick (1) [stik] *n* thin stiff shoot of wood, thin branch; rod of wood or metal to help balance in walking; any long slender rod used as tool *etc*; slender rounded bar; compositor's tool; group of bombs dropped together from one aircraft; (*coll*) stiffly reserved or dull person; **in a cleft s.** in a dilemma; **wrong end of the s.** misunderstanding of the facts or meaning ~ **stick** (*p/t* and *p/part* sticked) *v/t* fasten to, support with a stick; compose (type).

stick (2) (*p/t* and *p/part* stuck) *v/t* and *i* thrust firmly in; insert (pointed object) forcefully; stab; fix with an adhesive; become firmly fixed, inserted or jammed; remain attached, adhere; (*coll*) put, place; come to a standstill; (*coll*) bear bravely; tolerate, endure; **s. around** (*sl*) stay nearby; **s. at** work hard at; hesitate over; **s. at nothing** be quite unscrupulous; **s. in one's throat** (*fig*) be very hard to accept; **s. it** put up with it, bear to the end; **s. out** protrude; thrust out; be very obvious; persist; **s. out for** persist in asking for; **s. to** refuse to abandon; **s. together** be friends, allies *etc*; remain loyal to each other; **s. up** project upwards; fix in a high place; (*sl*) threaten or rob at gunpoint; **s. up to** (*coll*) face boldly; **s. up for** speak or act in defence of; **s. with** (*coll*) remain loyally with.

sticker [stiker] *n* one who or that which sticks; label *etc* stuck on; butcher's knife; (*cricket*) batsman who stays in for a long time making few runs; (*coll*) perseverant worker.

stickily [stikili] *adv* in a sticky way.

stickiness [stikinis] *n* quality of being sticky.

sticking-place, -point [stiking-plays, -point] *n* place where anything stops and holds firm.

sticking-plaster [stiking-plaaster] *n* adhesive plaster for covering superficial wounds.

stick-insect [stik-insekt] *n* insect closely resembling a twig.

stick-in-the-mud [stik-in-THi-mud] *n* and *adj* (*coll*) (person) stupidly rejecting novelty and progress; (person) incapable of initiative, adventurousness *etc*.

stickjaw [stikjaw] *adj* (*sl*) glutinous toffee, chewing-gum *etc*.

stickleback [stik'lbak] *n* small spiny-backed fish.

stickler [stikler] *n* one who fussily insists on trivial points.

stick-up [stik-up] *n* (*sl*) robbery at gunpoint.

sticky [stiki] *adj* tending to stick to surfaces, adhesive; glutinous; (*coll*) difficult to manage, troublesome; awkward; inclined to raise objections; (*sl*) unpleasant, painful.

stiff [stif] *adj* not easily bent, rigid; not moving easily; firm; formal, not friendly or at ease; stubborn; difficult, needing effort; (*of wind*) strong; (*of muscles*) painful when moved, through overstraining, rheumatism *etc*; (*of drinks*) having high proportion of alcohol; (*coll*) excessive; outrageous; **s. upper lip** impassiveness in facing pain or trouble ~ **stiff** *n* (*sl*) corpse; racehorse that will certainly lose; **big s.** (*sl*) utter fool ~ **stiff** *adv* (*coll*) to death; extremely.

stiffen [stifen] *v/t* and *i* make stiff; become stiff.

stiffener [stifener] *n* one who or that which stiffens; (*coll*) strong drink; pick-me-up.

stiffening [stifening] *n* material used to stiffen something.

stiffly [stifli] *adv* in a stiff way.

stiff-necked [stif-nekt] *adj* (*fig*) stubborn, self-willed.

stiffness [stifnis] *n* state or quality of being stiff.

stifle (1) [stīf'l] *v/t* and *i* suffocate, choke; suppress, quench; smother; feel suffocated.

stifle (2) *n* horse's kneepan; joint of horse's hind-leg between femur and tibia; disease in this joint.

stigma (*pl* **stigmas** or **stigmata**) [stigma] *n* mark of disgrace, infamy; (*ar*) mark made with branding-iron on slave, criminal *etc*; (*zool*) pore, spiracle; (*bot*) surface of carpel that receives pollen; (*path*) small mark or scar; recurrently bleeding wound.

stigmata [stigmata] *n* (*pl*) marks corresponding to Christ's wounds appearing without physical cause on a person's body; (*path*) physical peculiarities indicating disease or degeneracy.

stigmatic [stigmatik] *n* person who has stigmata.

stigmatize [stigmatIz] *v/t* denounce publicly as criminal *etc*, brand; disgrace; cause stigmata to appear upon.

stilboestrol [stilbeestRol] *n* (*bioch*) solid organic compound used as a synthetic oestrogen.

stile [stīl] *n* steps, rails *etc* permanently set up at a fence or hedge to enable people to climb over it; turnstile.

stiletto [stil*et*O] *n* dagger with long, thin blade; pointed instrument for making eyelet holes; **s. heels** high, thin metal heels of ladies' shoes.

still (1) [*stil*] *adj* motionless; calm; quiet, silent; not effervescent ~ **still** *n* (cin) single photograph from the series that form a film ~ **still** *v/t* quieten, cause to grow calmer.

still (2) *adv* up to and including specified time; yet; nevertheless; even more.

still (3) *n* apparatus used in distilling liquors ~ **still** *v/t* distil.

stillborn [*stil*bawrn] *adj* born lifeless; abortive.

still-life [*stil*-lIf] *n* painting representing only inanimate things > PDAA.

stillness [*stil*nis] *n* state or quality of being still.

stillroom [*stil*ROOm] *n* distilling room; storeroom for liquors, preserves *etc*.

stilly [*stil*i] *adj* (*poet*) still, quiet, calm ~ **stilly** *adv* quietly, silently.

stilt [*stilt*] *n* one of a pair of poles with a support for the foot used to raise a person above the ground in walking; long-legged shore-bird allied to the plover.

stilted [*stil*tid] *adj* stiff and pompous in style, pretentious; **s. arch** arch springing from courses of masonry above an impost.

Stilton [*stil*ton] *n* a variety of rich cheese.

stimulant [*stim*ewlant] *n* and *adj* (drink, drug *etc*) that temporarily increases energy or activity; (that) which incites to action.

stimulate [*stim*ewlayt] *v/t* rouse to action, interest or effort; spur on, incite; enliven, excite; increase the energy or activity of.

stimulation [stimewl*ay*shon] *n* act of stimulating; that which stimulates; state of being stimulated.

stimulative [*stim*ewlativ] *adj* having the power of stimulating.

stimulus (*pl* **stimuli**) [*stim*ewlus] *n* that which rouses any organism, organ or other receptor to activity > PDB, PDP; incentive, motive or influence that stirs to action, thought or feeling.

stimy see **stymie.**

sting (*p/t* and *p/part* **stung**) [*sting*] *v/t* and *i* cause sharp, tingling pain to; pierce with a sting; cause sharp suffering to; be capable of stinging; feel sharp tingling pain; (*sl*) get money from (someone) ~ **sting** *n* sharp organ used as weapon by animal, *esp* if bearing poisonous or inflammatory liquid; sharp, poison-bearing hair of plant; wound, pain or inflammation caused by these; (*fig*) acute pain; capacity for causing pain; point of an ironic or malicious joke.

sting-ray [*sting*-Ray] *n* tropical fish with venomous spines on its tail.

stingy [*stin*ji] *adj* mean with money, niggardly ~ **stingily** *adv* ~ **stinginess** *n*.

stink (*p/t* **stank**, *p/part* **stunk**) [*stink*] *v/i* and *t* emit strongly unpleasant smell; (*coll*) be highly offensive; (*sl*) be extremely bad, unpleasant *etc*; **s. out** fill (a place) with stinks; drive out with stinks ~ **stink** *n* strongly unpleasant smell; **raise a s.** cause trouble by complaining.

stinkbomb [*stink*bom] *n* small bomb emitting stinking fumes when exploded.

stinker [*stink*er] *n* one who or that which has an offensive smell; (*sl*) very unpleasant person or thing; very difficult task or problem.

stinking [*stink*ing] *adj* emitting a strong offensive smell; (*coll*) repulsive; (*sl*) very unpleasant; (*sl*) drunk ~ **stinkingly** *adv*.

stinkpot [*stink*pot] *n* device which emitted suffocating fumes, formerly used in naval warfare; (*sl*) very unpleasant person.

stinks [*stinks*] *n* (*pl*) (*school sl*) chemistry.

stint [*stint*] *v/t* give grudgingly in small amounts, dole out meanly ~ **stint** *n* allotted amount of work, *esp* of coal to be mined; limit; species of sandpiper, dunlin; **without s.** lavishly, ungrudgingly.

stipend [*stI*pend] *n* salary, *esp* of clergyman.

stipendiary [stI*pen*di-aRi] *adj* receiving a stipend; paid by salary; **s. magistrate** State-appointed salaried magistrate.

stipple [*stip*'l] *v/t* and *i* paint, draw or engrave by dots instead of lines > PDAA.

stippling [*stip*ling] *n* painting or engraving by means of dots instead of lines.

stipulate [*stip*ewlayt] *v/i* and *t* demand as essential condition to an agreement.

stipulation [stipewl*ay*shon] *n* act of stipulating; contract; condition of an agreement.

stir (*pres/part* **stirring**, *p/t* and *p/part* **stirred**) [*stur*] *v/t* and *i* cause something, *esp* liquid, to move round in a container by moving a spoon, stick *etc* in it; set in movement; change position, move; rouse the emotions of, excite, disturb ~ **stir** *n* act of stirring; movement; excitement; agitation; public interest, sensation; (*sl*) prison.

stirabout [*stur*Rabowt] *n* kind of porridge.

stirk [*sturk*] *n* bull or heifer a year old.

stirring [*stur*Ring] *adj* moving; rousing, exciting ~ **stirringly** *adv*.

stirrup [*sti*Rup] *n* iron hoop suspended from a strap serving as a horseman's footrest; (*naut*) rope support to carry a footrope.

stirrup-cup [*sti*Rup-kup] *n* cup of wine *etc* drunk on horseback before departure.

stirrup-pump [*sti*Rup-pump] *n* fire-fighting apparatus consisting of a hose and pump held steady in a bucket by a foot-plate.

stitch [*stich*] *n* one complete movement of a threaded needle into and out of material in sewing; amount of thread placed by one such movement; single turn of the wool round the needle and off in knitting; method of forming a stitch; (*surg*) loop of thread, wire *etc* to close a wound, suture; sharp stabbing pain in the side; **in stitches** (*coll*) laughing uncontrollably ~ **stitch** *n* sew, fasten with stitches; embroider.

stitchwort [*stich*wurt] *n* herbaceous plant with white starry flowers.

stithy [*sti*THi] *n* (*ar*) smithy.

stiver [*stI*ver] *n* small coin; trifling sum.

stoat [*stOt*] *n* weasel, ferret or allied animal; name given to the ermine when in its summer coat.

stochastic [sto*kas*tik] *adj* having an element of probability or chance.

stock [*stok*] *n* supply of material ready for use; supply of goods ready for sale; store, provision; stump, tree-trunk; strong piece of wood used as support, handle *etc*; plant from which cuttings are taken; family, ancestry; group of animals used for breeding; farm animals, livestock, *esp* cattle;

(comm) money lent to a government at fixed interest; capital of a company divided into shares; *(pl)* framework in which petty criminals were formerly confined by the ankles; *(pl)* framework supporting a ship while it is built; *(hort)* species of shrubby plants with scented flowers; *(ar)* neckcloth; *(cooking)* liquid in which bones, vegetables *etc* are stewed, used for soups, gravy *etc*; **on the stocks** in preparation but not finished; **take s.** make an inventory; assess one's position, prospects *etc*; **watered s.** *(comm)* issue of new shares on which existing shareholders have first option ~ **stock** *adj* kept in stock; habitually used or produced; commonplace, trite ~ **stock** *v/t* supply with stock; keep supplies of, have in stock; store up; supply animals to; put (criminal) in the stocks.

stockade [stok*ayd*] *n* line of stakes set up as fence or barrier ~ **stockade** *v/t* surround with a stockade.

stockbook [stok*book*] *n* *(comm)* ledger recording amount of goods bought and sold.

stock-breeder [stok-bReeder] *n* one who breeds cattle.

stockbroker [stokbROker] *n* one who buys and sells stocks and shares for a commission.

stockdove [stok*duv*] *n* European wild pigeon.

Stock Exchange [stok-ikschaynj] *n* the place where stocks and shares are bought and sold.

stockfish [stok*fish*] *n* fish cut open and dried in the sun without salt.

stockily [stok*ili*] *adv* in a stocky way.

stockiness [stok*inis*] *n* quality of being stocky.

stockinet [stok*inet*] *n* type of elastic knitted fabric.

stocking [stok*ing*] *n* close-fitting knitted or woven covering for the foot and leg.

stockinged [stok*ingd*] *adj* wearing stockings; **in one's s. feet** wearing no shoes or boots.

stock-in-trade [stok-in-tRayd] *n* stock, appliances, assets for carrying on one's business; *(fig)* habitual devices.

stockist [stok*ist*] *n* one who keeps goods in stock.

stockjobber [stok*jober*] *n* member of the Stock Exchange who buys and sells stocks and shares for a broker.

stocklist [stok*list*] *n* publication giving current prices of stocks and shares.

stockman *(pl* **stockmen)** [stok*man*] *n* *(Aust)* herdsman, man in charge of cattle.

stock-market [stok-maarkit] *n* Stock Exchange; market in stocks and shares.

stockpile [stok*pIl*] *n* reserve supply of essential materials ~ **stockpile** *v/t* and *i* accumulate reserve supplies (of).

stockpot [stok*pot*] *n* pot for storing stock for soup-making.

stockrider [stok*RIder*] *n* *(Aust)* horseman in charge of cattle.

stock-still [stok-*stil*] *adv* motionless.

stock-taking [stok-tayking] *n* the making of a list of assets and goods in a shop, business *etc*; *(fig)* re-assessment of one's position and prospects.

stock-whip [stok-wip] *n* short-handled whip with a long lash for herding cattle.

stocky [stok*i*] *adj* short and stout, thickset; sturdy.

stockyard [stok*yaard*] *n* enclosure for cattle or sheep.

stodge [stoj] *n* *(coll)* heavy and unappetizing food;

anything boring and difficult to learn, listen to *etc* ~ **stodge** *v/i* *(sl)* cram oneself with food.

stodgily [stoj*ili*] *adv* in a stodgy way.

stodginess [stoj*ines*] *n* state of being stodgy.

stodgy [stoj*i*] *adj* heavy, thick, indigestible; lumpy; *(fig)* uninteresting.

stoep [stOOp] *n* *(South Africa)* verandah.

stoic [stO-ik] *n* one who bears suffering impassively; one who keeps his feelings rigidly controlled; *(cap)* member of a group of ancient Greek philosophers who sought virtue by subduing all emotions ~ **stoic** *adj*.

stoical [stO-ikal] *adj* of or like a stoic; practising stoicism ~ **stoically** *adv*.

stoichiometry [stoiki-*omit*Ri] *n* branch of chemistry dealing with determination of combining proportions or chemical equivalents > PDS.

stoicism [stO-isizm] *n* attitude and behaviour of a stoic; philosophy of Stoics; impassive courage; indifference to pleasure or to pain.

stoke [stOk] *v/t* and *i* put fuel into a furnace, boiler *etc*; **s. up** *(sl)* feed heartily.

stokehold [stOk-hOld] *n* compartment of a ship's hold where the furnaces are.

stokehole [stOk-hOl] *n* mouth of a furnace.

stoker [stOker] *n* one who tends a furnace.

stole (1) [stOl] *p/t* of **steal**.

stole (2) *n* long strip of material, fur *etc* worn round shoulders or neck by women; long silk band worn round neck by priests.

stolen [stOlen] *p/part* of **steal**.

stolid [stolid] *adj* showing no interest or emotion, stupidly impassive ~ **stolidly** *adv* ~ **stolidness** *n*.

stolidity [stoliditi] *n* quality of being stolid.

stoma *(pl* **stomata)** [stOma] *n* pore of a plant.

stomach [stumak] *n* membranous sac in the abdomen in which food is digested > PDB; belly, abdomen; *(fig)* appetite; liking, wish; *(ar)* temperament; haughtiness ~ **stomach** *v/t* digest; eat with relish; put up with, tolerate.

stomacher [stumaker] *n* *(hist)* triangular panel in a woman's dress, *usu* ornamented and covering breast and upper abdomen.

stomachic [stumakik] *adj* of or in the stomach; aiding digestion.

stomach-pump [stumak-pump] *n* small pump for withdrawing liquids from, or injecting them into, the stomach.

stomatitis [stOmat*I*tis] *n* inflammation of the mouth.

stomato- *pref* of the mouth.

stomatoscope [stOmat*Osk*Op] *n* instrument for examining the mouth.

stomp [stomp] *v/i* *(coll)* tread heavily.

stone [stOn] *n* fairly small piece of rock; block or slab of rock cut to shape for use in building *etc*; solid mineral matter, rock; anything made of stone; gem, jewel; hard seed-case inside certain fruits; calculus, hard concretion forming in bladder or kidneys; *(pl* **stone)** measure of weight equal to 14 lb; *(ar)* testicle ~ **stone** *adj* made of stone; **S. Age** stage of cultural development when a race, tribe *etc* used only stone weapons and tools ~ **stone** *v/t* throw stones at; remove stones from (fruit); pave, face *etc* with stone slabs.

stone-axe [stOn-aks] *n* axe with two blunt edges for cutting stone.

stone-blind [stOn-blInd] *adj* completely blind.

stonechat [stOnchat] n type of small songbird.

stone-cold [stOn-kOld] adj absolutely cold.

stonecrop [stOn-kROp] n species of small succulent plant.

stonecutter [stOnkuter] n one who shapes stones for building.

stoned [stOnd] adj (sl) very drunk; exhilarated by drugs.

stone-dead [stOn-ded] adj absolutely dead.

stone-deaf [stOn-def] adj completely deaf.

stone-fruit [stOn-fROOt] n fruit with seeds which are covered by a hard shell enveloped in the pulp.

stonemason [stOnmayson] n one who builds in stone; one who cuts and shapes stone for building.

stone's-cast [stOnz-kaast] n distance which a stone can be thrown by hand; (fig) short distance.

stone's-throw [stOnz-thRO] n stone's-cast.

stonewall [stOnwawl] v/i (cricket) bat defensively, without trying for runs; (fig) obstruct debate, negotiation, business etc; return persistently noncommittal answers ~ stonewaller n.

stoneware [stOnwair] n high-fired pottery containing high proportion of flint.

stonework [stOnwurk] n masonry.

stony [stOni] adj covered with many stones; of or like stone; (fig) cruel, harsh, unrelenting; (of glances) fixed and hostile; (sl) penniless ~ stonily adv ~ stoniness n.

stony-hearted [stOni-haartid] adj pitiless.

stood [stood] p/t and p/part of stand.

stooge [stOOj] n (theat) subordinate partner in a comic act, who asks the main comedian leading questions, is the butt of his jokes etc; (coll) one who blindly carries out another's wishes; ill-used helper or subordinate; dupe, butt ~ stooge v/i act as stooge.

stook [stook] n bundle of piled-up sheaves ~ stook v/t set up in stooks.

stool [stOOl] n backless seat; footstool; low padded bench to kneel on; chair containing a chamber-pot, commode; act of evacuating the bowels; matter evacuated, faeces; (hort) sucker.

stool-pigeon [stOOl-pijin] n pigeon used as a decoy; (fig) decoy.

stoop (1) [stOOp] v/i and t curve the head and upper body forwards and down; be round-shouldered; lose dignity by one's own fault, demean oneself; (of hawk) swoop down on prey ~ stoop n act of stooping; habitually stooping posture.

stoop (2) see stoup.

stoop (3) n (US) verandah.

stop (pres/part stopping, p/t and p/part stopped) [stop] v/t and i cause (action or process) to cease; put an end to; check, prevent; block, close by obstructing, stuff up; intercept; staunch; fill cavity in (tooth); discontinue; cease, come to an end; pause; halt; stay as guest, visitor etc; (mus) place finger on or in (string or mouth of instrument) to alter pitch > PDM; (gramm) punctuate; s. off, s. over break journey at an intermediate stopping place ~ stop n act of stopping; state of having stopped; place where a public vehicle regularly stops; punctuation mark; (mus) key or lever regulating pitch; row of organ-pipes worked by one lever > PDM; diaphragm of camera; signal, notice etc instructing one to stop;

(phon) sound produced by closure of the mouth or glottis; full s. punctuation mark indicating end of sentence; (fig) sudden and complete stoppage.

stopcock [stopkok] n valve or tap for regulating flow.

stopgap [stopgap] n temporary substitute.

stop-go [stop-gO] n process of alternately stopping and allowing traffic to advance, or economic activity to increase.

stop-light [stop-lIt] n red traffic light as signal to stop; light, usu red, at rear of vehicle, to indicate that the brakes are being applied.

stopoff [stopof] n stopover.

stopover [stopOver] n intermediate stopping-place on journey.

stoppage [stopij] n act of stopping; act of ceasing to work; state of being stopped; deduction from pay.

stopper [stoper] n one who or that which stops; plug, esp for a bottle; put the s. on (coll) suppress, check ~ stopper v/t close with a stopper.

stopping [stoping] n that which stops; a filling for a tooth; act of stopping; act of shortening the vibrating portion of string in a stringed instrument > PDM ~ stopping adj (of trains) that stop at intermediate stations.

stopple [stop'l] n stopper, plug, bung ~ stopple v/t close with a stopple.

stop-press [stop-pRes] n late news printed in a special column of a newspaper after printing has begun.

stopwatch [stopwoch] n watch which can be stopped or started at any moment to measure the exact time taken by any action or event.

storage [stawRij] n act of storing; price paid for storing; space reserved for storing; system of storing electricity; cold s. the keeping of goods in refrigerating chambers; (fig) postponement; s. heater electric device accumulating heat during off-peak hours for later use.

store [stawr] n stock, supply kept for future need; place where things are kept for future use; warehouse, depot; large shop; accumulated quantity; (mil, pl) ammunition, equipment and provisions; in s. kept in reserve; destined to happen in the future; set s. by consider important ~ store v/t lay in a supply of, hoard and preserve; fill with supplies; put away for future use; put in a warehouse; (elect) accumulate.

storehouse [stawrhows] n place where things are stored; warehouse.

storekeeper [stawrkeeper] n one in charge of stores; shopkeeper.

storeroom [stawrROOm] n room in which articles are stored.

storey [stawRi] n one floor of a building; set of rooms on one floor.

storeyed [stawRid] adj built in stories.

storiated [stawRi-aytid] adj ornamented with elaborate designs which tell stories.

storied [stawRid] adj ornamented with designs which tell stories; made famous in story.

stork [stawrk] n a long-necked, long-legged wading bird.

storm [stawrm] n the blowing of a violent wind, usu with rain, thunder etc; violent burst of emotion; tumult, loud clamour; uproar; dense shower of missiles; violent assault on a fortress; **s. in a teacup** great fuss over very little; **take by s.** capture by assault; (*fig*) captivate completely and at once ∼ **storm** *v/t* and *i* capture by assault; blow violently; show violent rage; **s. at** scold violently.

stormbelt [*stawrm*belt] *n* zone where storms are frequent.

stormbound [*stawrm*bownd] *adj* stopped or delayed by storms.

stormcentre [*stawrm*senter] *n* place of lowest pressure in a cyclonic storm; (*fig*) one who causes or leads rebellion, discontent *etc*.

stormcock [*stawrm*kok] *n* fieldfare; mistle-thrush.

stormcone [*stawrm*kOn] *n* canvas cone of a storm-signal.

stormily [*stawrm*ili] *adv* in a stormy way.

storminess [*stawrm*inis] *n* quality of being stormy.

storming-party [*stawrm*ing-paarti] *n* group that leads an assault on a fortified place.

storm-lantern [*stawrm*-lantern] *n* oil lamp whose flame is protected against wind.

stormproof [*stawrm*pROOf] *adj* able to withstand high winds and rain.

stormsignal [*stawrm*signal] *n* hollow cone and drum of canvas hoisted to give warning of approaching storm; (*fig*) warning of danger.

storm-tossed [*stawrm*-tost] *adj* driven to and fro and damaged by storms; (*fig*) having endured much distress, agitation *etc*.

stormy [*stawrm*i] *adj* of or like a storm, tempestuous; violent, passionate; portending the arrival of a storm; **s. petrel** type of petrel believed to portend storms; (*fig*) one whose arrival is likely to mean trouble.

story (1) [*stawR*i] *n* narrative of real or of fictitious events, tale; myth, legend; plot of novel, film or play; (*coll*) falsehood.

story (2) *n* storey.

storyteller [*stawR*iteler] *n* one who tells stories; (*coll*) liar.

stoup, stoop [*stOO*p] *n* flagon; basin for holy water.

stout (1) [*stowt*] *adj* too fat, corpulent; strong, sturdy; vigorous; brave.

stout (2) *n* a strong dark beer.

stout-hearted [stowt-*haart*id] *adj* brave, resolute.

stoutly [*stowt*li] *adv* bravely, resolutely.

stoutness [*stowt*nis] *n* quality of being stout.

stove (1) [*stOv*] *n* apparatus for cooking by gas or electricity; apparatus for cooking or heating by coal, coke, wood, paraffin *etc* in which the flame is enclosed in a container.

stove (2) *p/t* and *p/part* of **stave.**

stovepipe [*stOv*pIp] *n* pipe carrying away smoke from a stove; (*coll*) top-hat.

stow [*stO*] *v/t* put away; pack; lay up; **s. away** hide oneself on board ship; **s. it!** (*sl*) shut up!

stowage [*stO*-ij] *n* act of stowing; state of being stowed; room for stowing articles; price paid for stowing articles.

stowaway [*stO*-away] *n* one who hides on board ship to get a free passage.

strabismus [stRa*biz*mus] *n* squint.

strabotomy [stRa*bot*omi] *n* (*surg*) operation of cutting the muscles which cause squinting.

straddle [*stRad*'l] *v/t* and *i* stand or sit with one leg on each side of, bestride; sit, stand or walk with legs wide apart; (*mil*) fire shots beyond and short of (a target) to fix its range ∼ **straddle** *n* act of straddling; (*Stock Exchange*) contract securing right to deliver or call for stock.

strafe [stRaa*f*] *v/t* shell or bomb severely; (*coll*) punish severely ∼ **strafe** *n* heavy bombardment.

straggle [*stRag*'l] *v/i* wander away from or loiter behind a main group; ramble in small groups; grow or lie untidily; be scattered irregularly along a road *etc* ∼ **straggle** *n* untidy grouping.

straggler [*stRag*ler] *n* one who or that which loiters behind; that which grows untidily.

straggling [*stRag*ling] *adj* irregularly scattered; drooping or growing untidily; sprawling.

straight [*stRayt*] *adj* not bent or curved; upright; correct; level, even; unobstructed; tidy; frank, honest; outspoken; undiluted; **s. face** serious un-smiling expression; **s. fight** (*pol*) contest between two candidates only ∼ **straight** *n* straight part, piece *etc*; final straight stretch of racecourse ∼ **straight** *adv* in a straight line; directly; honestly; bluntly, openly; **s. away, s. off**. immediately; **go s.** (*coll*) abandon criminal or dishonest habits.

straighten [*stRayt*en] *v/t* and *i* make or become straight.

straightforward [stRaytfawr*werd*] *adj* honest; frank, open ∼ **straightforwardly** *adv*.

straightway [*stRayt*way] *adv* (*ar*) immediately.

strain (1) [*stRayn*] *v/t* and *i* stretch tight; exert to the utmost; injure or weaken by over-exertion; make violent efforts; wrench, sprain; press closely; embrace; constrain; pass through sieve, colander *etc* ∼ **strain** *n* act of straining; violent effort, pull; tension; injury or distortion caused by violent effort or tension > PDS; tune, melody; (*fig*) tone, manner, style.

strain (2) *n* race, stock, breed; natural tendency.

strained [*stRaynd*] *adj* produced by or showing too much effort; showing nervous tension, irritability or fatigue; unnatural, forced; unfriendly, verging on a quarrel.

strainer [*stRayn*er] *n* sieve; colander; filter.

strait [*stRayt*] *n* narrow passage of water between two seas; (*pl*) difficult position, distress ∼ **strait** *adj* (*ar*) narrow; strict; difficult.

straitened [*stRayt*end] *adj* suffering financial difficulties; impoverished.

straitjacket [*stRayt*jakit] *n* garment for restraining the arms of violent lunatics; (*fig*) that which prevents free development.

strait-laced [stRayt-*layst*] *adj* (*fig*) extremely strict in moral views.

strait-waistcoat [stRayt-*wayskOt*] *n* straitjacket.

strake [*stRayk*] *n* (*naut*) single breadth of a boat's planking from stem to stern.

strand (1) [*stRand*] *n* shore, beach ∼ **strand** *v/t* and *i* run aground; leave helpless, *esp* without means of transport.

strand (2) *n* single twisted thread of wool, fibre, rope *etc*; lock of hair ∼ **strand** *v/t* make (rope *etc*) by twisting strands.

stranded [*stRand*id] *adj* left without means of transport; left helpless, left without resources.

strange [*stRaynj*] *adj* unusual, unfamiliar; extra-ordinary, odd; hard to explain; previously unknown; foreign; inexperienced; (*phys*) having unpredicted properties, *esp* of certain elementary particles > PDS ~ **strangely** *adv* ~ **strangeness** *n*.

stranger [st*Ray*njer] *n* one from another country or place; unknown person; *(leg)* one not privy or party to an act.

strangle [st*Rang*-g'l] *v/t* kill by compressing the windpipe, throttle; *(fig)* suppress.

stranglehold [st*Rang*-g'l-hOld] *n* grip that could kill by strangling; *(fig)* power to suppress, prevent from free development *etc*; power to blackmail.

strangler [st*Rang*-gler] *n* one who strangles.

strangles [st*Rang*-g'lz] *n (pl)* infectious respiratory disease in horses.

strangulate [st*Rang*-gewlayt] *v/t* strangle; *(med)* compress (blood-vessel, intestine *etc*) so as to arrest circulation.

strangulated [st*Rang*-gewlaytid] *adj* having circulation stopped by compression.

strangulation [st*Rang*-gewl*ay*shon] *n* act of strangling or strangulating; state of being strangulated.

strangury [st*Rang*-gewRi] *n (path)* painful and slow discharge of urine.

strap [st*Rap*] *n* long strip of leather, used as fastening, belt *etc*; act of beating with this; strip of adhesive tape; strop; metal plate for fastening ~ **strap** *(pres/part* **strapping,** *p/t* and *p/part* **strapped)** *v/t* bind or fasten with a strap; beat with a strap; strop.

straphanger [st*Rap*hanger] *n* standing passenger on train, bus *etc* who holds on to a strap to steady himself.

strappado [st*Rapaad*O] *n (hist)* torture or punishment by drawing victim up on a rope and letting him fall with a jerk to the length of the rope.

strapping [st*Rap*ing] *adj* tall, strong, muscular.

strata [st*Raata*/st*Ray*ta] *pl* of **stratum**.

stratagem [st*Rat*ajem] *n* trick to outwit an enemy.

strategic [st*Rat*eejik] *adj* of, for or done by strategy; *(of bombing)* aimed at destroying enemy morale ~ **strategically** *adv*.

strategist [st*Rat*ijist] *n* one skilled in strategy.

strategy [st*Rat*iji] *n (mil)* art of manoeuvring an army effectively; *(fig)* large-scale plan or method for winning a war, battle of wits, contest, game *etc*.

strath [st*Rath*] *n (Scots)* broad river-valley.

strathspey [st*Rath*spay] *n* a Scottish dance; music for this.

stratification [st*Rat*ifi*kay*shon] *n* arrangement in layers; relative position of several layers; act or process of stratifying.

stratiform [st*Rat*ifawrm] *adj* in the form of strata.

stratify [st*Rat*ifI] *v/i* and *t* form into, deposit or arrange in strata; arrange in distinctly separated layers.

stratigraphy [st*Rat*igRafi] *n* study of rock strata.

strato- *pref* of or like stratus cloud; of or in layers.

stratocruiser [st*Rat*OkR*OO*zer] *n* airliner flying in the stratosphere.

stratosphere [st*Rat*osfeer] *n* upper atmospheric layer beginning approximately six miles above earth's surface > PDG.

stratum *(pl* **strata)** [st*Raa*tum/st*Ray*tum] *n* one of a series of distinct layers of rock, *usu* horizontal > PDG; distinct layer or level; social class.

stratus [st*Ray*tus] *n* horizontal layer of cloud.

straw [st*Raw*] *n* dry stalk of wheat, oats *etc*; *(fig)* anything worthless; **a s. in the wind** slight sign foreshadowing a future trend; **last s.** final addition to one's troubles that makes them unbearable; **man of s.** person having no solid financial or moral resources; imaginary representative of a point of view; **s. poll** opinion poll.

strawberry [st*Raw*beRi] *n* creeping plant which bears a fleshy red fruit; fruit of this; **s. pink** dull pinkish crimson ~ **strawberry** *adj* of or containing strawberries; faintly pink; reddish.

strawberry-mark [st*Raw*beRi-maark] *n* reddish birthmark.

strawboard [st*Raw*bawrd] *n* thick paper or cardboard made from straw.

straw-coloured [st*Raw*-kulerd] *adj* pale whitish yellow.

strawy [st*Raw*-i] *adj* of, like or covered with straw.

stray [st*Ray*] *v/i* wander away, lose one's way; *(fig)* abandon one's duty, fall from virtue; *(of thoughts)* not be concentrated on one subject ~ **stray** *n* domestic animal that wanders at large or is lost; waif; lost child; straggler; isolated specimen ~ **stray** *adj* gone astray; lost; sporadic.

streak [st*Reek*] *n* line or stripe of contrasting colour; *(fig)* slight tendency, *esp* in contrast with general character; *(of lightning)* flash ~ **streak** *v/t* and *i* mark with streaks; *(coll)* rush past, dart; run naked in public ~ **streaker** *n*.

streaky [st*Reek*i] *adj* having streaks; *(of bacon)* having layers of fat and lean meat ~ **streakily** *adv* ~ **streakiness** *n*.

stream [st*Reem*] *n* flow of water or other liquid; small river, brook; current; continuous crowd or series of things all moving the same way; *(fig)* trend; group of pupils segregated from others of same age according to ability; **s. of consciousness** unbroken flow of thoughts, feelings and perceptions through the mind; attempt to render this in literature ~ **stream** *v/i* and *t* flow copiously; pour out; move in an unbroken mass or series; float on air; segregate (pupils) by ability.

streamer [st*Reem*er] *n* long strip of coloured paper or ribbon used as decoration *etc*; pennant, long narrow banner; ray of light shooting across the sky.

streamlet [st*Reem*lit] *n* small stream.

streamline [st*Reem*lIn] *n* sleekly curved shape that offers minimum resistance to air or water ~ **streamline** *v/t* build (aircraft, ship, car *etc*) in sleek curves; give a smooth surface to; *(fig)* make more efficient by simplifying.

street [st*Reet*] *n* metalled road with houses on one or on both sides; **on the streets** living as a prostitute; **not in the same s. with** not to be compared with, much inferior to; **streets ahead of** *(fig)* very far ahead of; **up one's s.** *(coll)* within one's competence or sphere of interest.

streetcar [st*Reet*kaar] *n (US)* tram; bus.

street-door [st*Reet*-dawr] *n* main door of a building, front door.

streetwalker [st*Reet*wawker] *n* prostitute.

strength [st*Reng*th] *n* quality of being strong; muscular force; firmness, toughness; vigour; power of resistance; potency, intensity; amount of (naval or military) force; **on the s.** *(mil)* listed as belonging to a regiment *etc*; **on the s. of** relying on; having regard to.

strengthen [st*Reng*then] *v/t* and *i* make or become strong or stronger.

strenuous [stRenew-us] *adj* energetic, vigorous; persistent, zealous; needing effort ~ **strenuously** *adv* ~ **strenuousness** *n*.

streptococcus (*pl* **streptococci**) [stReptOkokus] *n* type of disease bacteria forming chain-like structures.

streptomycin [stReptOmIsin] *n* antibiotic substance effective against certain disease bacteria.

stress [stRes] *n* intense pressure or tension; force on a body expressed per unit area > PDE, PDS; constraining or impelling force; importance; relative force with which a word or part of a word is uttered; accentuation, emphasis; **lay s. on** emphasize ~ **stress** *v/t* emphasize, accentuate; assert the importance of; subject to stress.

stressful [stResfool] *adj* causing emotional or mental stress ~ **stressfully** *adv*.

stretch [stRech] *v/t* and *i* pull or push out so as to increase length or breadth of; extend as far as possible; be fully spread out; become broader or longer through pressure, use *etc*; be elastic; extend, last; extend one's limbs fully; **be stretched** (*sl*) be hanged; **s. one's legs** walk about, *esp* to dispel stiffness; **s. a point** go beyond what is strictly permissible; make concessions ~ **stretch** *n* act of stretching; utmost extent; expanse of level land, water *etc*; uninterrupted period spent in one activity; effort, strain; (*sl*) period of imprisonment; (*naut*) distance covered in one tack; **at a s.** without a break ~ **stretch** *adj* (*coll*) elastic, capable of stretching.

stretcher [stRecher] *n* one who or that which stretches; covered framework on which an injured person can be carried lying flat; (*bui*) brick or stone laid lengthways; (*naut*) crosspiece for a rower to brace his feet on; (*pl, coll*) stockings of elastic nylon.

stretcher-bearer [stRecher-bairRer] *n* one of two people who carry an injured person on a stretcher.

stretcher-party [stRecher-paarti] *n* group sent with stretchers to rescue casualties.

stretchy [stRechi] *adj* apt to stretch.

strew (*p/t* **strewed**, *p/part* **strewn** or **strewed**) [stROO] *v/t* scatter, sprinkle thinly.

strewth see **struth**.

stria (*pl* **striae**) [stRI-a] *n* thin line, stripe, groove, ridge *etc*.

striate, striated [stRI-it, stRI-aytid] *adj* marked with striae ~ **striately** *adv*.

striation [stRI-ayshon] *n* stripe, marking consisting of thin lines, grooves or ridges.

stricken [stRiken] *adj* afflicted, much distressed; (*ar*) wounded ~ **stricken** (*ar*) *p/part* of **strike**.

strict [stRikt] *adj* exact; not lax; punctilious; rigorous, severe; accurate ~ **strictly** *adv* ~ **strictness** *n*.

stricture [stRikcher] *n* sharp criticism, rebuke; (*med*) contraction of duct or channel.

stridden [stRiden] *p/part* of **stride**.

stride (*p/t* **strode**, *p/part* **stridden**) [stRId] *v/i* and *t* walk with long steps; cross over with one long step; bestride ~ **stride** *n* long walking step; **make great strides** progress fast; **take in one's s.** do easily and effortlessly.

stridency [stRIdensi] *n* quality of being strident.

strident [stRIdent] *adj* harsh, shrill, grating; noisy ~ **stridently** *adv*.

stridulant [stRidyoolant] *adj* making a shrill creaking noise.

stridulate [stRidewlayt] *v/i* make a shrill creaking noise, *esp* by rubbing certain parts of the body together > PDB.

stridulation [stRidewlayshon] *n* act of stridulating; noise produced by stridulating.

strife [stRIf] *n* conflict, struggle, discord.

strike (*p/t* **struck**, *p/part* **struck**, **stricken**) [stRIk] *v/t* and *i* hit, deliver blows upon; deal, deliver; inflict; afflict suddenly; overwhelm; come into violent contact with; produce by a stroke; cause (a sound) by striking; impress; affect; occur suddenly in the mind; cause to take root; cease work in demand for higher wages *etc*; reach; level grain in a measure; be driven ashore; lower (sails, flag *etc*); take up (attitude, pose *etc*); (*geol*) extend in a particular direction; **s. oil** (*fig*) have good luck, make a fortune; **s. off** remove, cancel; print; **s. out** hit out; make a stroke in swimming or skating; (*fig*) make a beginning, originate; erase, cancel; **s. up** begin; begin to play or sing ~ **strike** *n* act of refusing to work until granted higher wages *etc*; attack, raid, *esp* by aircraft from an aircraft-carrier; **lucky s.** luçky discovery.

strikebound [stRIkbownd] *adj* immobilized by an industrial strike.

strike-breaker [stRIk-bRayker] *n* worker who agrees to work when the rest are on strike, blackleg.

strike-pay [stRIk-pay] *n* allowance paid by trade union to men on strike.

striker [stRIker] *n* one who or that which strikes; workman on strike; (*soccer*) player whose chief function is to score goals.

striking [stRIking] *adj* that strikes; impressive, powerfully affecting the mind; memorable; remarkable ~ **strikingly** *adv*.

Strine [stRIn] *n* (*coll*) Australian English.

string [stRing] *n* thin cord, twine *etc*, *esp* if used for tying; ribbon; fibre; tendon; cord of catgut, wire *etc* that produces a musical note when stretched tight and made to vibrate > PDM; series of objects linked together; series of things in close succession; (*pl*) stringed instruments in an orchestra; (*pl, coll*) stipulations, unwelcome conditions; **have on a s.** keep (someone) at one's beck and call; **pull strings** obtain preferment, favours *etc* by secret influence ~ **string** (*p/t* and *p/part* **strung**) *v/t* furnish with a string or strings; thread on to string; **s. along** (*coll*) keep in expectation by insincere promises *etc*; go along (with); **s. out** spread singly in a long line; **s. up** tauten the strings of; (*fig*) key up, brace; (*coll*) hang.

string-band [stRing-band] *n* band of stringed musical instruments.

stringboard [stRingbawrd] *n* board supporting ends of steps in staircase.

stringcourse [stRingkawrs] *n* (*archi*) projecting horizontal line of mouldings.

stringed [stRingd] *adj* having strings.

stringency [stRinjensi] *n* state of being stringent.

stringent [stRinjent] *adj* rigidly enforced, strict, severe ~ **stringently** *adv*.

stringer [stRinger] *n* one who strings; one who makes strings; stringboard.

stringy [stRingi] *adj* of, like, or containing strings, fibrous; ropy, viscous ~ **stringily** *adv* ~ **stringiness** *n*.

717

strip (*pres/part* **stripping**, *p/t* and *p/part* **stripped**) [*stRip*] *v/t* and *i* remove outer part or covering of; despoil (of wealth *etc*), plunder; remove clothes from; undress; pull or tear off ~ **strip** *n* long narrow piece; comic s. strip-cartoon.

strip-artist [*stRip*-aartist] *n* striptease performer.

strip-cartoon [*strip*-kaartOOn] *n* serial newspaper cartoon telling a story in a series of small pictures.

stripe [*stRip*] *n* long, narrow band of distinctive colour; band worn on sleeve of uniform as a sign of rank *etc*; stroke with a whip ~ **stripe** *v/t* mark with stripes.

striped [*stRipt*] *adj* marked with stripes of different colours.

strip-lighting [*stRip*-liting] *n* electric lighting by neon tubes.

stripling [*stRipling*] *n* youth, lad.

stripper [*stRiper*] *n* one who strips; strip-artist.

strip-poker [*stRip*-pOker] *n* form of poker in which the loser of each hand must remove one garment.

striptease [*stRipteez*] *n* cabaret or theatrical entertainment in which a performer slowly removes all his or her clothes.

stripy [*stRipi*] *adj* having or resembling stripes.

strive (*p/t* **strove**, *p/part* **striven**) [*stRiv*] *v/i* make great efforts, struggle earnestly; (*ar*) fight.

striven [*stRiven*] *p/part* of **strive**.

strobe-light [*stROb*-lit] *n* rapid flashing light.

stroboscope [*stRobOskOp*] *n* instrument by which to view objects in rapid periodic motion as if they were at rest; lamp emitting strong rapid flashes ~ **stroboscopic** *adj*.

strode [*stROd*] *p/t* of **stride**.

stroke (1) [*stROk*] *n* act of striking, blow; noise of blow; apoplectic attack, *esp* one causing partial paralysis; hostile act; calamity; single movement in a series, *esp* of arms in rowing or swimming, of wing in flying *etc*; act or way of striking ball in games; line made by single movement of brush, pen *etc*; written or printed line, dash; single movement of a piston; rower at stroke-oar; ringing sound made by a clock to mark the hour *etc* ~ **stroke** *v/t* row at stroke-oar of.

stroke (2) *v/t* pass the hand over gently; smooth ~ **stroke** *n* act of stroking.

stroke-oar [*stROk*-awr] *n* oarsman seated nearest to boat's stern who sets the pace for the rest.

stroll [*stROl*] *v/i* walk leisurely, saunter ~ **stroll** *n* leisurely walk.

strolling [*stROling*] *adj* touring from place to place to earn one's living, itinerant.

stroma [*stROma*] *n* (*biol*) framework of tissue of cell or organ.

strong [*stRong*] *adj* physically powerful; forcible; well able to bear or resist, tough; vigorous, energetic; having a powerful effect; intense; healthy, robust; well fortified; violent; convincing, sound; not highly diluted; (*comm*) rising; **s. drink** alcoholic drink, *esp* spirits; **s. language** swearing; **s. point** something one excels at; **s. verb** verb inflected by internal vowel-change ~ **strong** *adv* (*coll*) strongly; **going s.** still flourishing; running vigorously.

strongarm [*stRong*aarm] *adj* (*coll*) bullying, fond of using violence ~ **strongarm** *v/t* beat up.

strongbox [*stRong*boks] *n* safe or iron chest for valuables.

stronghold [*stRong*hOld] *n* fortress; (*fig*) place where something flourishes undisturbed.

strongly [*stRongli*] *adv* powerfully; intensely; vigorously.

strong-minded [stRong-mindid] *adj* having a resolute and vigorous mind.

strongroom [*stRong*ROOm] *n* fire-proof and burglar-proof room where valuables are kept.

strontium [*stRon*shum/*stRonti*-um] *n* a metallic element > PDS; **s. 90** radioactive isotope of strontium.

strop [*stRop*] *n* strip of leather for sharpening razors on; thong, band; loop or noose of leather *etc* ~ **strop** (*pres/part* **stropping**, *p/t* and *p/part* **stropped**) *v/t* sharpen on or with a strop.

strophe [*stROfi*] *n* the first of two corresponding stanzas in an ode; group of lines in a poem, stanza.

strophic [*stROfik*] *adj* of or in strophes.

stroppy [*stRopi*] *adj* (*coll*) bad-tempered; aggressive.

strove [*stROv*] *p/t* of **strive**.

struck [*stRuk*] *p/t* and *p/part* of **strike** ~ **struck** *adj* impressed; (*coll*) charmed, bewitched.

structural [*stRuk*cheRal] *adj* of or pertaining to structure; **s. linguistics** study of the interrelated components of language; **s. psychology** study of the interrelationship of mental experiences ~ **structurally** *adv*.

structuralism [*stRuk*cheRalizm] *n* study of structure rather than function; structural linguistics or psychology ~ **structuralist** *n* and *adj*.

structure [*stRuk*cher] *n* way in which the component parts of a complex whole are interrelated; that which is made up of many component parts; building, *esp* a large one ~ **structured** *adj*.

strudel [*stROO*d'l] *n* type of pastry rolled round a filling.

struggle [*stRug*'l] *v/i* make violent movements or efforts; fight vigorously; tussle, grapple ~ **struggle** *n* strenuous effort; vigorous fight or tussle; violent physical effort.

strum (*pres/part* **strumming**, *p/t* and *p/part* **strummed**) [*stRum*] *v/i* play noisily or badly upon a stringed instrument.

strumpet [*stRum*pit] *n* prostitute, harlot.

strung [*stRung*] *p/t* and *p/part* of **string**.

strut (1) (*pres/part* **strutting**, *p/t* and *p/part* **strutted**) [*stRut*] *v/i* walk with a proud, pompous gait ~ **strut** *n* pompous, self-important gait.

strut (2) *n* timber or piece of iron supporting a rafter; prop.

struth, strewth [*stROOth*] *interj* (*coll*) exclamation of amazement.

strychnine [*stRik*neen] *n* poisonous alkaloid used in medicine in minute doses > PDS.

stub [*stub*] *n* short piece of cigarette or cigar left when rest has been smoked; worn-down piece of pencil; piece of ticket, cheque *etc* kept when rest has been torn off; tree stump ~ **stub** (*pres/part* **stubbing**, *p/t* and *p/part* **stubbed**) *v/t* hit one's foot accidentally on some object; grub up; remove tree stumps, roots *etc* from; **s. out** extinguish (cigarette) by pressing its lighted end against something.

stubble [*stub*'l] *n* short stalks of wheat, barley *etc* left in the ground after harvesting; (*fig*) unshaven bristly hair.

stubbly [*stub*li] *adj* covered with stubble; bristly.

stubborn [*stub*ern] *adj* unreasonably obstinate; very hard to move or influence; resisting strongly ~ **stubbornly** *adv* ~ **stubbornness** *n.*

stubby [*stub*i] *adj* short and thick; short and strong.

stucco [*stuk*O] *n* fine plaster for coating walls and making decorations in relief ~ **stucco** *v/t* coat with fine plaster.

stuck [*stuk*] *p/t* and *p/part* of stick ~ **stuck** *adj* (*coll*) unable to advance or continue; brought to a halt by difficulties; (*sl*) in love; **s. with** (*coll*) unable to get rid of.

stuck-up [*stuk*-up] *adj* (*coll*) conceited, putting on airs. .

stud (1) [*stud*] *n* kind of button with base and head joined by short neck, used in collars *etc*; nail or peg with large flattened head, *esp* as ornament or to mark out lines in the street; small supporting timber ~ **stud** (*pres/part* **studding**, *p/t* and *p/part* **studded**) *v/t* stick studs into; ornament thickly with shining objects; encrust.

stud (2) *n* number of horses kept for breeding, riding, or racing; number of pedigree animals kept for breeding.

studbook [*stud*book] *n* register of pedigrees of thoroughbred animals, *esp* horses.

studding-sail [*stuns*'l/*stun*sayl] *n* (*naut*) narrow sail set at outer edges of square sails > PDSa.

student [*stew*dent] *n* one engaged in study, *esp* at a college, university or other place of instruction; studious person; one receiving an annual grant for study.

studentship [*stew*dentship] *n* state of being a student; grant for study, scholarship.

studfarm [*stud*faarm] *n* farm where horses are bred.

studhorse [*stud*hawrs] *n* horse kept for breeding purposes.

studied [*stud*id] *adj* carefully thought out, well considered; deliberate; elaborate ~ **studiedly** *adv.*

studio [*stew*di-O] *n* workroom of artist, photographer *etc*; room from which broadcasts or recordings are made; room or premises in which cinema films are made; **s. couch** sofa that can be turned into a bed.

studious [*stew*di-us] *adj* keen on studying, devoted to study; zealous, eager; deliberate, studied ~ **studiously** *adv* ~ **studiousness** *n.*

studmare [*stud*mair] *n* mare kept for breeding purposes.

study [*stud*i] *v/t* and *i* apply one's mind to learning, *esp* from books; learn systematically; analyse, examine carefully; learn by heart; show careful concern for ~ **study** *n* act or process of studying; systematic pursuit of knowledge; subject studied; literary essay or exercise on a special subject; room set apart for studying in; drawing or painting of a detail for practice or for use in a larger composition > PDAA; instrumental piece for practice in technique > PDM; reverie.

stuff [*stuf*] *n* material, matter of which something is made; textile fabric, *esp* woollen; (*fig*) rubbish, worthless things; nonsense; **do one's s.** do what is expected of one, play one's part (*esp* in an entertainment); **that's the s.** (*coll*) that's what is needed ~ **stuff** *v/t* and *i* fill tightly, cram; fill with stuffing; preserve and fill out the skin of (dead bird, animal *etc*); (*coll*) over-eat; (*vulg sl*) copulate with; **s. up** block, fill up entirely; **stuffed shirt** (*sl*) pretentious fool.

stuffily [*stuf*ili] *adv* in a stuffy way.

stuffiness [*stuf*inis] *n* quality of being stuffy.

stuffing [*stuf*ing] *n* that which is used for filling; seasoning used inside a bird or meat; **knock the s. out of** (*coll*) defeat utterly; unnerve.

stuffy [*stuf*i] *adj* badly ventilated, lacking fresh air; (*coll*) narrow-minded, easily shocked.

stultification [stultifi*kay*shon] *n* act of stultifying; state of being stultified.

stultify [*stul*tifI] *v/t* cause to become stupid, dull the brain of; cause to seem meaningless, absurd or foolish.

stum [*stum*] *n* unfermented grapejuice.

stumble [*stumb*'l] *v/i* lose balance in walking or running, trip up; speak or read aloud with hesitations and mistakes; (*fig*) make a mistake; commit sin; **s. across (upon)** find by chance; **s. at** hesitate over ~ **stumble** *n* act of stumbling; fall; mistake.

stumbling-block [*stum*bling-blok] *n* obstacle, impediment; that which causes hesitation, doubt, moral offence *etc*. .

stumer [*stew*mer] *n* (*sl*) worthless cheque; forged note; counterfeit coin; anything worthless; ruin, bankruptcy.

stump [*stump*] *n* base of tree-trunk left in ground after the rest has been felled; remaining base of amputated limb; stub of pencil; (*cricket*) one of the three upright sticks of the wicket; (*arts*) roll of paper for rubbing charcoal drawings > PDAA; **draw stumps** (*cricket*) cease play for the day; **stir one's stumps** (*coll*) hurry, become more active ~ **stump** *v/i* and *t* walk heavily; tour a region making political speeches; (*cricket*) put out by knocking down a stump while the batsman is outside his ground; (*coll*) outwit, puzzle, present an unanswerable problem to; **s. up** (*coll*) pay up.

stumper [*stump*er] *n* (*coll*) puzzling question.

stump-orator [*stump*-o*Rat*er] *n* one who travels about making open-air political speeches; rabblerouser.

stumpy [*stump*i] *adj* short and thickset.

stun (*pres/part* **stunning**, *p/t* and *p/part* **stunned**) [*stun*] *v/t* knock unconscious; render helpless with shock or amazement; make dizzy by a blow or by loud noise; (*sl*) overwhelm with delight, love *etc*.

stung [*stung*] *p/t* and *p/part* of sting.

stunk [*stunk*] *p/t* and *p/part* of stink.

stunner [*stun*er] *n* one who or that which stuns; (*coll*) one who is extraordinarily attractive.

stunning [*stun*ing] *adj* that stuns; overwhelming; amazing; (*coll*) delightful, excellent; very beautiful ~ **stunningly** *adv.*

stunsail [*stuns*'l/*stun*sayl] *n* (*naut*) studding-sail.

stunt (1) [*stunt*] *v/t* check the growth of.

stunt (2) *n* remarkable feat of physical skill, *esp* entailing danger; anything sensational done to gain publicity; acrobatic trick; aerobatic trick; sensational newspaper article or campaign ~ **stunt** *v/i* perform stunts ~ **stunt** *adj* of or as a stunt.

stunted [*stunt*id] *adj* dwarfish, having never reached full size; retarded, under-developed.

stuntman [*stunt*man] *n* person paid to perform dangerous acrobatic tricks, feats of strength *etc*, *esp* as stand-in for a cinema actor.

stupa [*stOO*pa] *n* round domed Buddhist shrine.

stupe [*stewp*] *n* compress of flannel used in fomentations.

stupefaction [stewpi*fak*shon] *n* act of stupefying; state of being stupefied; amazement.

stupefy [*stew*pifı] *v/t* make stupid, *esp* by drink, drugs, fatigue *etc*; stun with amazement, astonish.

stupendous [stew*pen*dus] *adj* amazingly great; astonishing; wonderful ~ **stupendously** *adv* ~ **stupendousness** *n*.

stupid [*stew*pid] *adj* lacking intelligence; foolish, *esp* habitually or by nature; having one's intelligence or faculties dulled ~ **stupid** *n* (*coll*) stupid person, fool.

stupidity [stew*pid*iti] *n* state or quality of being stupid.

stupidly [*stew*pidli] *adv* in a stupid way.

stupor [*stew*per] *n* dazed condition; partial unconsciousness; torpor.

sturdy [*stur*di] *adj* hardy, strong; vigorous, robust ~ **sturdily** *adv* ~ **sturdiness** *n*.

sturgeon [*stur*jon] *n* large fish from which caviare and isinglass are obtained.

stutter [*stut*er] *n* and *v/t* and *i* stammer > PDP.

sty (1) (*pl* **sties**) [*stı*] *n* enclosure or pen for pigs; (*fig*) filthy place.

sty, (2) **stye** (*pl* **sties**, **styes**) *n* inflamed swelling on edge of eyelid.

Stygian [*stiji*-an] *adj* (*class myth*) of or like the underworld river Styx; (*fig*) dark, gloomy.

style [*stıl*] *n* characteristic choice and arrangement of words of a particular author or speaker; general characteristics and manner of an individual, group or period in practising any art, craft, skill, or sport; elegance of manner; fashion; manners, deportment; sort, type; title, correct mode of address; mode of reckoning dates; (*hist*) pointed instrument for writing on wax *etc*, stylus; engraving or etching tool; gnomon; (*bot*, *zool*) bristle, pointed growth; (*bot*) support of stigma; **in s.** grandly, lavishly ~ **style** *v/t* call by the title of.

stylish [*stı*lish] *adj* fashionable; smart, showy ~ **stylishly** *adv* ~ **stylishness** *n*.

stylist [*stı*list] *n* writer who cultivates a good style.

stylistic [stı*lis*tik] *adj* of literary or artistic style ~ **stylistically** *adv*.

stylite [*stı*lıt] *n* early Christian recluse who led an ascetic life on top of a pillar.

stylization [stılız*ay*shon] *n* act of stylizing; state of being stylized; stylized representation.

stylize [*stı*lız] *v/t* (*arts*) represent non-naturalistically but according to a recognized convention; cause to conform to a style.

stylograph [*stı*lOg*raaf*] *n* variety of fountain-pen with needle instead of nib.

stylus [*stı*lus] *n* pointed writing-instrument; pointed sapphire, diamond *etc* used as needle for gramophone.

stymie, **stimy** [*stı*mi] *n* (*golf*) position when the opponent's ball lies between that of the player and the hole ~ **stymie** *v/t* hinder by a stymie; (*fig*) check, hinder.

styptic [*stip*tik] *n* and *adj* (preparation) which stops bleeding.

styrene [*stı*Reen] *n* (*chem*) colourless liquid used in the manufacture of plastics and synthetic rubber > PDS.

Styx [*stiks*] *n* (*class myth*) underworld river over which souls of the dead were ferried.

suasion [*sway*zhon] *n* persuasion.

suasive [*sway*ziv] *adj* persuasive.

suave [*swaav*] *adj* courteous, gracious, having pleasing manners; exaggeratedly or insincerely polite; (*of wine*) smooth ~ **suavely** *adv*.

suavity [*swaa*viti] *n* quality of being suave.

sub (1) [*sub*] *n* (*coll abbr*) subscription; sub-editor; subaltern; submarine; substitute.

sub (2) *prep* (*Lat*) under; **s. judice** under consideration; **s. rosa** in secret; privately.

sub- *pref* under, beneath; almost; near; about, towards; inferior; smaller; approximately; almost.

subacid [sub*as*id] *adj* slightly acid.

subagent [sub*ay*jent] *n* one employed by an agent.

subalpine [sub*alp*ın] *adj* of or in regions immediately below Alpine.

subaltern [*sub*altern] *n* (*mil*) officer below rank of captain; (*fig*) subordinate ~ **subaltern** *adj* subordinate; of inferior rank.

subaquatic [subak*wat*ik] *adj* partially aquatic; formed or being under water.

subaqueous [sub*ayk*wi-us] *adj* formed or being under water.

subarctic [sub*aark*tik] *adj* of or in the region bordering on the Arctic; almost as cold as the Arctic.

subatomic [suba*tom*ik] *adj* (*of particles*) smaller than, or forming part of, an atom > PDS.

subaudition [subaw*dish*on] *n* act of understanding what is only implied.

subaxillary [subaks*ile*Ri] *adj* beneath the armpit or wing-cavity; (*bot*) under the axil.

subcaudal [sub*kawd*al] *adj* beneath the tail.

subcentral [subsent*Ral*] *adj* situated under the centre; nearly central.

subclass [*sub*klaas] *n* subdivision of a class.

subcommittee [*sub*komiti] *n* committee formed from a larger committee to deal with some specific matter.

subconscious [sub*kon*shus] *adj* (*of thoughts and feelings*) not fully realized or noticed by the mind in which they are present; wholly or partly unconscious ~ **subconscious** *n* mental processes outside the personal awareness of the individual; unconscious dynamic elements in a personality > PDP ~ **subconsciously** *adv* ~ **subconsciousness** *n*.

subcontinent [sub*kont*inent] *n* very large landmass that is not classed as one of the five continents.

subcontract [sub*kont*Rakt] *n* contract hired out from one contractor to another; contract forming part of another ~ **subcontract** [subkon*tRakt*] *v/t* and *i*.

subcritical [sub*kRit*ikal] *adj* (*of a nuclear reactor*) incapable of maintaining a self-sustaining chain reaction.

subculture [sub*kul*cher] *n* cultural group within a larger culture; (*biol*) culture (of bacteria *etc*) formed from previous culture.

subcutaneous [subkew*tay*ni-us] *adj* just under the skin > PDB ~ **subcutaneously** *adv*.

subdeacon [subdeekon] n minister ranking just below a deacon; assistant to a deacon.

subdean [subdeen] n assistant or deputy of a dean.

subdiaconate [subdI-akonayt] n office of a sub-deacon.

subdivide [subdivId] v/t and i divide (a part) into smaller divisions; split up repeatedly.

subdivision [subdivizhon] n act of subdividing; part or section formed by dividing a larger part or section.

subdominant [subdominant] n (mus) fourth tone of the scale > PDM.

subduable [subdew-ab'l] adj that may be subdued.

subdual [subdew-al] n act of subduing.

subdue [subdew] v/t conquer, overcome; make quieter or softer; make gentler, tame.

subdued [subdewd] adj quiet, gentle; soft, not vivid or harsh; shy; cowed.

sub-edit [sub-edit] v/t act as an assistant editor of.

sub-editor [sub-editer] n assistant editor.

subereous [sewbeRi-us] adj of, like, or derived from cork.

suberic [sewbeRik] adj subereous.

suberin [sewbeRin] n impervious substance found in cork > PDB.

subfamily [subfamili] n (biol) division of a family consisting of one or more genera.

subfusc [subfusk] adj somewhat dark in colour; (sl) insignificant, unimpressive ~ **subfusc** n clothes of dark colour.

subgeneric [subjeneRik] adj of a subgenus.

subgenus [subjeenus] n subdivision of a genus, including one or more species.

subglacial [subglaysi-al] adj (of climate) almost glacial.

subgroup [subgROOp] n subordinate group in a classification.

subheading [subheding] n heading of a subsection of a chapter, essay, treatise etc.

subhuman [subhewman] adj not quite human; considerably below normal human standards of intelligence or behaviour; almost bestial.

subirrigation [subiRigayshon] n irrigation below the surface; partial irrigation.

subjacent [subjaysent] adj underlying; lower in position; lying immediately below.

subject [subjekt] n one owing allegiance to a ruler or under the authority of a State; that which is discussed, described or represented; topic, theme; that which is submitted to examination, treatment, analysis etc; occasion; (mus) group of notes forming basic element in a composition > PDM; (med) person or animal on whom an experiment is performed; corpse for dissection; person having or prone to a particular disease; (philos) the experiencing self, ego; substance; (gramm) word or group of words denoting the person or thing about which something is predicated; noun or pronoun associated by form or word-order with a verb in a sentence or clause, and indicating the person or thing of whom that verb is used ~ **subject** adj owing obedience to; ruled by; liable, prone to; conditional on ~ **subject** adv **s.** to conditionally on ~ **subject** [subjekt] v/t subdue, cause to submit; cause to undergo, expose to.

subject-heading [subjekt-heding] n heading in catalogue, index etc under which references are given.

subjection [subjekshon] n act of subduing; state of being subjected; dependence, submission.

subjective [subjektiv] adj arising from one's own mind and feelings and not corresponding to or caused by external reality; revealing or influenced by personal feeling and views, not objective; (gramm) of the subject; nominative ~ **subjective** n (gramm) nominative case ~ **subjectively** adv.

subjectivism [subjektivizm] n doctrine that human knowledge is relative.

subjectivist [subjektivist] n and adj (adherent) of subjectivism.

subjectivity [subjektiviti] n state or quality of being subjective; doctrine that religious belief should be based on subjective experience; subjectivism.

subject-matter [subjekt-mater] n that which is discussed, described, represented etc; topic, theme.

subjoin [subjoin] v/t add (statement) to a previous statement.

subjugate [subjoogayt] v/t conquer, enslave, dominate.

subjugation [subjoogayshon] n act of subjugating; state of being subjugated.

subjunctive [subjunktiv] n and adj (mood of verb) expressing a wish, condition, hypothesis or contingency.

sublease [sublees] n lease granted by one who is himself tenant of the property leased ~ **sublease** [sublees] v/t sublet.

sublessee [sublesee] n one holding a sublease.

sublessor [sublesawr] n one who sublets.

sublet (pres/part **subletting**, p/t and p/part **sublet**) [sublet] v/t let to another (property of which one is a tenant).

sublethal [subleethal] adj not enough to be lethal.

sublieutenant [subleftenant] n rank between midshipman and lieutenant.

sublimate [sublimayt] v/t (psych) unconsciously transform a sexual impulse into some non-sexual and socially permitted activity > PDP; substitute a nobler satisfaction for a base one; (chem) transform directly from solid state to vapour and back to solid; (fig) refine, purify ~ **sublimate** n (chem) solid obtained by direct condensation of vaporized solid > PDS.

sublimation [sublimayshon] n act or process of sublimating > PDP, PDS; state of being sublimated.

sublime [sublIm] adj noble, grandiose, majestic; awe-inspiring; lofty, haughty; supreme, excelling; (coll) extreme ~ **sublime** n that which inspires awed admiration ~ **sublime** v/t refine; sublimate ~ **sublimely** adv.

subliminal [subliminal] adj below the threshold of consciousness; only subconsciously perceived > PDP; **s. advertising** the presentation of advertisement slogans on cinema or television too rapidly to be consciously seen.

sublimity [sublimiti] n state or quality of being sublime.

sublunary [sublOOneRi] adj beneath the moon; terrestrial, of or in this world.

sub-machine-gun [sub-mas*heen*-gun] *n* type of light machine gun.

submarine [sub*ma*Reen] *n* warship designed to remain under water for long periods ~ **submarine** [subma*Reen*] *adj* growing, living or moving about under the surface of the sea.

submaxillary [submaks*ile*Ri] *adj* under the jaw.

submerge [sub*murj*] *v/t* and *i* plunge, dip or cause to dip below the surface of a liquid; cover with liquid, flood; (*fig*) overwhelm; **the submerged tenth** proportion of a population living in extreme poverty.

submersible [sub*mur*sib'l] *adj* capable of submerging.

submission [sub*mish*on] *n* act of submitting; state of being submitted; obedience, compliance; humility, meekness; that which is submitted.

submissive [sub*mis*iv] *adj* willing to submit; obedient; meek, humble ~ **submissively** *adv* ~ **submissiveness** *n*.

submit (*pres/part* **submitting**, *p/t* and *p/part* **submitted**) [sub*mit*] *v/t* and *i* yield, surrender, agree to obey; present for consideration; suggest, urge.

submultiple [sub*multip*'l] *n* number or quantity contained in another an exact number of times.

subnormal [sub*nawr*mal] *adj* below normal; of markedly less than average intelligence.

suborder [sub*awr*der] *n* (*biol*) subdivision of an order.

subordinancy [sub*awr*dinansi] *n* the state of being subordinate.

subordinate [sub*awr*dinit] *adj* inferior in rank or importance; subsidiary; minor; dependent; **s. clause (phrase)** (*gramm*) clause (or phrase) functionally dependent on another ~ **subordinate** *n* one who works under another; inferior ~ **subordinate** [sub*awr*dinayt] *v/t* assign an inferior rank or position to; consider of minor importance ~ **subordinately** *adv*.

subordination [subawrdi*nay*shon] *n* act of subordinating; state of being subordinate; inferiority; subjection.

suborn [sub*awrn*] *v/t* bribe or induce to commit a crime, *esp* perjury.

subornation [subawr*nay*shon] *n* act of suborning.

subplot [*sub*plot] *n* secondary plot within a play, novel *etc*, partly interwoven with but less important than the main plot.

subpoena [sub*pee*na] *n* writ commanding a person's presence in court under penalty ~ **subpoena** *v/t* serve with a subpoena.

subpolar [sub*pO*ler] *adj* near one of the poles > PDG; (*astron*) under a celestial pole.

subprefect [sub*Ree*fekt] *n* officer under a prefect.

subsaline [sub*sayl*In] *adj* moderately salty.

subscribe [subs*kRIb*] *v/t* and *i* pay regularly to a charity, fund *etc*; make a gift of money to; undertake to buy (magazine *etc*) regularly; indicate consent or agreement, *esp* by signing one's name; agree, approve.

subscriber [subs*kRIb*er] *n* one who subscribes; one who contributes money; one who undertakes to buy a magazine *etc* regularly.

subscript [*subs*kRipt] *adj* written underneath.

subscription [subs*kRip*shon] *n* act of subscribing; signature; sum subscribed; contribution of money for a specific purpose.

subsection [*sub*sekshon] *n* subdivision of a section.

subsequence [*sub*sikwens] *n* state of being subsequent.

subsequent [*sub*sikwent] *adj* later; coming immediately after; following as a result ~ **subsequently** *adv*.

subserve [subs*urv*] *v/t* be helpful, assist, promote.

subservience [subs*urvi*-ens] *n* state or quality of being subservient.

subservient [subs*urvi*-ent] *adj* willing or tending to adapt oneself to the wishes of others; obsequious; useful as a means or subordinate helper ~ **subserviently** *adv*.

subside [subs*Id*] *v/i* sink gradually; cave in, collapse; abate, grow less.

subsidence [subs*Id*ens] *n* act or process of subsiding; downward movement of ground surface, *usu* due to mining > PDE, PDG.

subsidiary [subs*idi*-eRi] *adj* acting as a secondary help; supplementary; subordinate; of or as a subsidy; **s. company** company most of whose shares are held by a larger company ~ **subsidiary** *n* one who or that which is subsidiary.

subsidize [*subs*idIz] *v/t* pay a subsidy to.

subsidy [*subs*idi] *n* grant paid by the State from public funds to help to support an industry, cultural undertaking *etc* for the public benefit; (*hist*) grant paid by Parliament to the Sovereign.

subsist [subs*ist*] *v/i* remain alive or in existence; have the means of living.

subsistence [subs*ist*ens] *n* existence; means of supporting life; livelihood; **s. level** standard of living just high enough to keep one alive.

subsoil [*subs*oil] *n* layer of soil lying immediately beneath the surface soil > PDE, PDG.

subsonic [subs*on*ik] *adj* (*aer*) at less than the speed of sound.

subspecies [*subs*peesheez] *n* subordinate species; subdivision of a species > PDB.

substance [*subs*tans] *n* matter, material, stuff; essential part, quality or meaning; purport, meaning; solidity; wealth; (*philos*) essence.

substandard [subs*tand*erd] *adj* of lower than average standard, inferior; deviating from standard usage.

substantial [subs*tan*shal] *adj* solid, strongly made; ample, satisfying; considerable, important; as regards the essential part, meaning *etc*; wealthy; having substance, material, real.

substantiality [substanshi-*al*iti] *n* state or quality of being substantial.

substantially [subs*tan*shali] *adv* to a considerable degree; as regards essentials.

substantiate [subs*tan*shi-ayt] *v/t* demonstrate the truth of, prove; make real.

substantiation [substanshi-*ay*shon] *n* proof.

substantival [substant*Iv*al] *adj* (*gramm*) of or as a substantive.

substantive [*subs*tantiv] *n* (*gramm*) noun; pronoun; group of words used as noun ~ **substantive** *adj* existing as a real and distinct being; (*gramm*) expressing existence; naming a specific entity; **s. rank** (*mil*) actual paid rank.

substation [*subs*tayshon] *n* subsidiary station.

substitute [*subs*titewt] *v/t* and *i* put (person or thing) in the place of another; use instead of; act as substitute ~ **substitute** *n* person or thing used instead of or acting as deputy for another.

substitution [substi*tew*shon] *n* act of substituting; state of being substituted.

substrate [*sub*stRayt] *n* (*bioch*) substance whose reactivity is increased by a specific enzyme.

substratum [sub*stRaat*um/sub*stRay*tum] *n* that which underlies anything; stratum lying beneath another; underlying basis.

substructure [sub*stRuk*cher] *n* underground structure, foundation.

subsume [sub*sewm*] *v/t* include in a particular category.

subtangent [sub*tan*jent] *n* (*geom*) part of axis contained between ordinate and tangent drawn to same point in curve.

subtemperate [sub*tem*peRit] *adj* bordering on the temperate zone; slightly colder than temperate.

subtenant [sub*ten*ant] *n* tenant holding property under a tenant.

subtend [sub*tend*] *v/t* (*geom*) extend under; be opposite to.

subterfuge [*sub*terfewj] *n* trickery, dishonest way of gaining one's end; concealment of true aims or meaning; equivocation.

subterranean [subte*Ray*ni-an] *adj* underground.

subterraneous [subte*Ray*ni-us] *adj* underground.

subtitle [*sub*tIt'l] *n* one of a series of captions added to a foreign-language film translating and summarizing its dialogue; additional subsidiary title of a book *etc* ~ **subtitle** *v/t* add subtitles to.

subtle [*sut*'l] *adj* delicate, not obvious, elusive; keenly intelligent or perceptive; ingenious; clever; cunning, artful.

subtlety [*sut*'lti] *n* quality or condition of being subtle; that which is subtle.

subtly [*sut*li] *adv* in a subtle way.

subtonic [sub*ton*ik] *n* (*mus*) note next below the tonic.

subtopia [sub*tOp*i-a] *n* (*usu pej*) suburban area, regarded as an ideal place to live in.

subtract [sub*tRakt*] *v/t* take away (a part or quantity) from the rest; deduct; lessen, remove part of.

subtraction [sub*tRak*shon] *n* act or process of subtracting.

subtropical [sub*tRop*ikal] *adj* of, in or from regions near the tropics; having features common to both temperate and tropical zones > PDG.

suburb [*sub*urb] *n* district, *usu* residential, lying on the outskirts of town or city.

suburban [sub*ur*ban] *adj* of, in or like a suburb; living in a suburb; (*fig*) conventional, narrowminded, petty ~ **suburban** *n* suburbanite.

suburbanite [sub*ur*banIt] *n* one who lives in a suburb.

suburbanize [sub*ur*banIz] *v/t* transform into a suburb; make like a suburb.

suburbia [sub*ur*bi-a] *n* suburb, area of suburbs; characteristic outlook of people living in suburbs.

subvariety [*sub*vaRI-iti] *n* subdivision of a variety; subordinate variety.

subvention [sub*ven*shon] *n* subsidy, grant.

subversion [sub*vur*shon] *n* act of subverting; state of being subverted.

subversive [sub*vur*siv] *adj* tending or attempting to undermine authority, established ideas *etc* ~ **subversively** *adv* ~ **subversiveness** *n*.

subvert [sub*vurt*] *v/t* undermine by propaganda *etc*, seek to destroy the authority of; undermine the loyalty, faith *etc* of.

subway [*sub*way] *n* tunnel, underground passage by which pedestrians can cross beneath a railway, road *etc*; (*US*) underground railway, tube.

subzero [sub*zeer*RO] *adj* less than zero in temperature.

succade [su*kayd*] *n* crystallized fruit.

succeed [suk*seed*] *v/t* and *i* follow, come next after; be heir to; be next to take the office, rank, functions *etc* of; accomplish one's purpose, attain a desired aim; prosper, be successful; achieve popularity, acclaim *etc*.

succentor [suk*sen*ter] *n* deputy precentor; leading bass in a choir.

success [suk*ses*] *n* act of succeeding; favourable result; attainment of what is desired; one who or that which succeeds; triumph.

successful [suk*ses*fool] *adj* having succeeded, accomplishing what is intended; prosperous, fortunate ~ **successfully** *adv*.

succession [suk*ses*hon] *n* number of persons, things, events *etc* following one another in space or time, series; act or right of succeeding to an office, rank *etc*; inheritance: **Apostolic S.** spiritual power inherited by bishops from the Apostles or by a Pope from St Peter.

successional [suk*ses*honal] *adj* in regular succession.

successive [suk*ses*iv] *adj* following in order, consecutive ~ **successively** *adv*.

successor [suk*ses*er] *n* one who takes office, rank *etc* after another; heir; one who or that which follows another.

succinct [suk*singkt*] *adj* compressed into few words, brief, concise ~ **succinctly** *adv* ~ **succinctness** *n*.

succinic [suk*sin*ik] *adj* derived from amber; derived from succinic acid; **s. acid** white crystalline organic acid used in the manufacture of dyes, lacquers *etc*.

succose [su*kOs*] *adj* sappy, juicy.

succotash [*suk*otash] *n* (*US*) dish of beans and green corn boiled together.

succour [*suk*er] *n* assistance in difficulty or distress ~ **succour** *v/t* aid; help or relieve in difficulty or distress.

succubus [*suk*ewbus] *n* demon supposed to mate with sleeping men.

succulence [*suk*ewlens] *n* juiciness.

succulent [*suk*ewlent] *adj* juicy; (*bot*) thick and fleshy; able to store water in its tissues ~ **succulent** *n* succulent plant ~ **succulently** *adv*.

succumb [su*kum*] *v/i* submit, yield; give way; die.

succursal [su*kur*sal] *adj* auxiliary.

such [*such*] *adj* of the same or similar kind; of that kind, of the kind stated or implied; so great; so very (good, bad *etc*) ~ **such** *pron* such person, persons, or things (as); (*coll*) these, those, it.

such-and-such [*such*-and-such] *adj* certain, some.

suchlike [*such*lIk] *adj* of such a kind ~ **suchlike** *pron* (*coll*) things of that sort.

suck [*suk*] *v/t* and *i* draw (liquid) into the mouth by action of lips and breathing; imbibe, absorb; hold and lick in the mouth, dissolve by so licking; take milk from (breast, udder); draw in by suction; absorb; **s. in** (*sl*) cheat, swindle; **s. up to** (*sl*) flatter, seek to please ~ **suck** *n* act of sucking; force of suction; small drink; **give s. to** suckle.

sucker [*suk*er] *n* one who or that which sucks;

flexible disk that adheres to a surface by suction; plunger, piston; organ by which an animal adheres to a surface; tube acting by suction; (*bot*) shoot rising from roots or lower stem; (*coll*) easy dupe, gullible fool.

sucking [*suk*ing] *adj* not yet weaned; (*fig*) young and inexperienced.

sucking-pig [*suk*ing-pig] *n* piglet not yet weaned.

suckle [*suk'*l] *v/t* feed (baby, young animal) with milk from breast or udder.

suckling [*suk*ling] *n* baby or young animal not yet weaned.

sucrose [*sewk*ROs/*sOOk*ROs] *n* cane-sugar > PDB, PDS.

suction [*suk*shon] *n* act or process of sucking; creation of a partial vacuum causing a fluid to enter, or a body to adhere to, something under atmospheric pressure.

suction-pump [*suk*shon-pump] *n* pump in which a vacuum is produced and liquid forced up by atmospheric pressure.

suctorial [suk*taw*Ri-al] *adj* sucking; adapted for sucking; capable of adhering by suction.

sudation [sew*day*shon] *n* sweating.

sudatorium [sewda*taw*Ri-um] *n* hot-air bath.

sudd [*sud*] *n* floating mass of vegetable matter.

sudden [*sud*en] *adj* happening unexpectedly; instantaneous, abrupt; **all of a s.** suddenly ~ **suddenly** *adv* ~ **suddenness** *n*.

sudorific [sewdo*Ri*fik] *n* and *adj* (medicine) causing perspiration.

suds [*sudz*] *n* (*pl*) mass of froth and bubbles made by dissolving soap or detergents; soapy water.

sue (*pres/part* suing, *p/t* and *p/part* sued) [*sew*] *v/t* and *i* take legal proceedings (against), prosecute; plead, make a petition.

suède [*swayd*] *n* undressed kid skin or leather.

suet [*sew*-it/*sOO*-it] *n* hard fat around loins and kidneys of an animal; **s. pudding** type of boiled pudding with suet.

suety [*sew*-iti/*sOO*-iti] *adj* of, like or full of suet.

suffer [*suf*er] *v/t* and *i* undergo, experience (something painful or unpleasant); feel pain, grief *etc*; tolerate; unwillingly allow; be damaged or injured; **s. from** be liable to.

sufferable [*suf*eRab'l] *adj* that may be tolerated; that may be endured ~ **sufferably** *adv*.

sufferance [*suf*eRans] *n* tacit permission or toleration, consent implied only by failure to forbid; (*ar*) endurance; **on s.** barely tolerated.

sufferer [*suf*eRer] *n* one who suffers, *esp* chronically.

suffering [*suf*eRing] *n* experience of pain or loss; pain, loss or grief endured ~ **suffering** *adj*.

suffice [*suf*is] *v/i* and *t* be enough, be adequate; content, satisfy.

sufficiency [su*fish*ensi] *n* state of being sufficient; adequate supply.

sufficient [su*fish*ent] *adj* enough, adequate; (*ar*) fit, qualified, competent ~ **sufficiently** *adv*.

suffix [*suf*iks] *n* letter or syllable added to the end of a word ~ **suffix** *v/t* add (letter or syllable) to a word.

suffocate [*suf*okayt] *v/t* and *i* kill or die by lack of air, smother, choke; be or feel choking.

suffocating [*suf*okayting] *adj* feeling or causing suffocation: extremely hot and airless.

suffocation [sufo*kay*shon] *n* act or process of suffocating; state of being suffocated.

suffragan [*suf*Rajan/*suf*Ragan] *n* and *adj* (bishop) assisting another bishop or archbishop.

suffrage [*suf*Rij] *n* vote; right to vote; approval.

suffragette [suf*Raj*et] *n* woman who campaigned for women being enabled to vote in political elections.

suffuse [su*fewz*] *v/t* overspread (with light, fluid or colour); cover with or as with a liquid.

suffusion [su*fewzh*on] *n* act of suffusing; state of being suffused; that which is suffused.

Sufi [*sOO*fi] *n* Muslim ascetic mystic.

sugar [*shoog*er] *n* sweet white crystalline substance, sucrose > PDS; (*chem*) one of various sweet carbohydrates resembling this > PDS; (*coll*) lovely girl; (*fig*) flattery; (*sl*) money ~ **sugar** *v/t* sweeten with sugar; **s. the pill** (*fig*) disguise the unpleasantness of.

sugarbasin [*shoog*erbaysin] *n* small bowl for holding sugar at table.

sugarbeet [*shoog*erbeet] *n* variety of beet from whose root sugar is obtained.

sugarcandy [*shoog*erkandi] *n* sugar clarified and crystallized.

sugarcane [*shoog*erkayn] *n* very tall grass from whose stems sugar is obtained.

sugar-coated [*shoog*er-kOtid] *adj* covered in sugar or icing; (*fig*) having its unpleasantness disguised; sentimentalized; euphemized.

sugardaddy [*shoog*erdadi] *n* (*sl*) rich old man who gives presents to young women.

sugariness [*shoog*eRines] *n* state of being sugary.

sugarloaf [*shoog*erlOf] *n* conical mass of refined sugar; high cone.

sugarplum [*shoog*erplum] *n* sweetmeat of boiled sugar formed into a ball.

sugar-soap [*shoog*er-sOp] *n* chemical abrasive for removing old paint.

sugary [*shoog*eRi] *adj* like sugar; containing sugar; sweetened with sugar; (*fig*) excessively sweet; flattering.

suggest [su*jest*] *v/t* cause to arise in the mind, *esp* by association of ideas; propose for consideration; hint; imply.

suggester [su*jest*er] *n* one who suggests.

suggestibility [sujesti*bili*ti] *n* readiness to accept suggestion, state of being suggestible > PDP.

suggestible [su*jest*ib'l] *adj* easily influenced by suggestion > PDP.

suggestion [su*jes*chun] *n* act of suggesting; that which is suggested; hint, insinuation; proposal; indecent proposal; (*psych*) process of inducing someone to accept an idea or belief uncritically, *usu* by non-logical means; mental process resulting in uncritical acceptance > PDP.

suggestive [su*jest*iv] *adj* evoking an association of ideas; suggesting more than is apparent; provoking thoughts of something indecent ~ **suggestively** *adv* ~ **suggestiveness** *n*.

suicidal [sew-is*I*dal] *adj* of or tending to suicide; wishing to kill oneself; (*fig*) leading to certain death or ruin ~ **suicidally** *adv*.

suicide [*sew*-isId] *n* act of intentionally killing oneself; one who intentionally kills himself; (*fig*) any self-inflicted disastrous action.

suit [*sewt*] *n* lawsuit, act of suing; request; act of asking a woman in marriage; set of outer clothes made of the same material, *esp* man's coat and trousers or woman's short coat and skirt; complete set of armour; one of the four sets of cards in a pack; **follow s.** imitate another's acts ~ **suit** *v/t* and *i* satisfy, please, meet the needs or wishes of; be appropriate to; match; fit; be good for the health of; make appropriate, adapt; be convenient; be becoming to; **s. oneself** do whatever one chooses.

suitability [sewta*biliti*] *n* state or quality of being suitable.

suitable [*sew*tab'l] *adj* fitting, proper, convenient; becoming; adequate ~ **suitably** *adv*.

suitcase [*sew*tkays] *n* small portable trunk or travelling-bag for carrying clothes *etc*.

suite [*sweet*] *n* set of matching furniture for one room; set of rooms; retinue, band of followers; (*mus*) instrumental piece in several loosely connected movements > PDM.

suiting [*sew*ting] *n* cloth to be made into suits.

suitor [*sew*ter] *n* wooer, one wishing to marry a woman; petitioner, applicant.

sulfa, sulpha [*sul*fa] *adj* (*med*) of sulphonamide.

sulk [*sulk*] *v/i* show sullen resentment, be sulky.

sulkily [*sulk*ili] *adv* in a sulky way.

sulkiness [*sulk*inis] quality of being sulky.

sulks [*sulks*] *n* (*pl*) mood of sullenness and ill-humour.

sulky [*sul*ki] *adj* showing anger by silence and withdrawal; gloomy and bad-tempered.

sullen [*sulen*] *adj* persistently and gloomily resentful, morose; dismal; forbidding, baleful ~ **sullenly** *adv* ~ **sullenness** *n*.

sully [*sul*i] *v/t* tarnish; defile, soil; disgrace.

sulph-, sulpho- *pref* of or containing sulphur.

sulpha see **sulfa**.

sulphate [*sul*fayt] *n* a salt of sulphuric acid.

sulphide [*sul*fId] *n* a binary compound of an element or group with sulphur; salt of hydrogen sulphide > PDS.

sulphite [*sul*fIt] *n* salt of sulphurous acid > PDS.

sulphonal [*sul*fonal] *n* crystalline compound used as hypnotic and anaesthetic drug.

sulphonamide [sul*fon*amId] *n* one of a group of organic compounds used in treating various bacterial diseases > PDS.

sulphur [*sul*fer] *n* a pale yellow inflammable non-metallic element > PDS; species of yellow butterfly; **s. dioxide** colourless gas with a choking smell > PDS ~ **sulphur** *adj* pale yellow.

sulphurate [*sul*feRayt] *v/t* combine or impregnate with sulphur; bleach by exposure to fumes of sulphur.

sulphuration [sulfe*Ray*shon] *n* act or process of sulphurating.

sulphureous [sul*fewr*Ri-us] *adj* of or like sulphur; smelling of burning sulphur; pale yellow.

sulphuretted [*sul*fewRetid] *adj* saturated, impregnated or combined with sulphur; **s. hydrogen** colourless poisonous gas smelling like bad eggs > PDS.

sulphuric [sul*fewr*Rik] *adj* derived from or containing sulphur; **s. acid** very corrosive acid, oil of vitriol > PDS; **s. ether** colourless sweetish-smelling liquid used as anaesthetic > PDS.

sulphurize [*sul*feRIz] *v/t* combine with sulphur; subject to the action of sulphur.

sulphurous [*sul*feRus] *adj* containing sulphur; like

sulphur; (*fig*) like the flames of hell; diabolic; menacing, dangerously passionate.

sulphury [*sul*feRi] *adj* resembling sulphur.

sultan [*sul*tan] *n* Muslim sovereign, *esp* former ruler of Turkey; variety of water-hen; variety of domestic fowl.

sultana [sul*taa*na] *n* wife, mother, or daughter of a sultan; kind of raisin grown in Izmir.

sultry [*sul*tRi] *adj* very hot and airless; (*fig*) having powerful sexual allure; lurid, violent ~ **sultrily** *adv* ~ **sultriness** *n*.

sum [*sum*] *n* total produced by adding two or more numbers, things or quantities; particular amount of money; arithmetical problem; totality, comprehensive summary ~ **sum** (*pres/part* **summing**, *p/t* and *p/part* **summed**) *v/t* and *i* **s. up** add up to form a total; summarize, express in few words; (*of judge*) recapitulate and comment on (evidence); (*fig*) form a judgement on.

sumach [*sOO*mak] *n* type of ornamental shrub.

summarily [*sum*eRili] *adv* in a summary way.

summarize [*sum*eRIz] *v/t* and *i* make or be a summary of.

summary [*sum*eRi] *n* brief statement of the main points of a book, speech, argument *etc*; précis, digest ~ **summary** *adj* done briefly and without formalities; briefly expressed, giving the main points only.

summat [*sum*at] *n* (*coll* and *dial*) something.

summation [su*may*shon] *n* process of adding; total reached by adding; cumulative effect of repeated stimuli > PDB, PDP.

summer (1) [*sum*er] *n* warmest season of the year; (*fig*) year of one's age; prime, period of flourishing ~ **summer** *adj* of, occurring or used in summer ~ **summer** *v/i* spend the summer.

summer (2) *n* heavy horizontal beam or girder; large stone laid on column as base of an arch.

summer-house [*sum*er-hows] *n* small open building in a garden used in summer.

summersault [*sum*ersawlt] *n* somersault.

summer-school [*sum*er-skOOl] *n* course of lectures *etc* given at a university, college or similar institution during the summer vacation.

summer-time [*sum*er-tIm] *n* system whereby clocks are put one hour ahead in summer; summer.

summing-up [suming-*up*] *n* summary, *esp* that of a judge on the evidence in a case.

summit [*sum*it] *n* highest point, top; highest peak of mountain; (*fig*) utmost degree, maximum; (*coll*) conference of heads of States.

summit-level [*sum*it-level] *n* highest level; highest point (of road, railway *etc*); **at s.** (*coll*) by discussion between heads of States.

summit-meeting [*sum*it-meeting] *n* (*coll*) political conference between heads of States.

summon [*sum*on] *v/t* call authoritatively, order to come; (*leg*) require the attendance of in court.

summons (*pl* **summonses**) [*sum*onz] *n* act of summoning; authoritative demand to appear, *esp* in court ~ **summons** *v/t* serve with a summons.

sump [*sump*] *n* reservoir for lubricating oil in a motor-vehicle; pit or pool in which water collects.

sumptuary [*sump*choo-eRi] *adj* of or limiting expenditure.

sumptuosity [sumpchoo-*o*siti] *n* sumptuousness.

sumptuous [*sump*choo-us] *adj* costly, luxurious; splendid, magnificent ~ **sumptuously** *adv* ~ **sumptuousness** *n*.

sun [*sun*] *n* incandescent heavenly body round which the planets rotate > PDS, PDG; light or warmth of this; sunlit place; any star round which planets rotate; (*fig*) glorious hero or patron; **a place in the s.** (*fig*) prosperity, opportunity to become prosperous ~ **sun** (*pres/part* **sunning**, *p/t* and *p/part* **sunned**) *v/t* and *i* expose to sunlight; bask in the sun, sunbathe.

sunbathe [*sun*bayTH] *v/i* expose one's body to the warmth of the sun.

sunbathing [*sun*bayTHing] *n* act of one who sunbathes.

sunbeam [*sun*beem] *n* ray of sunlight.

sunblind [*sun*blInd] *n* shade for a window to keep out the sun.

sunbonnet [*sun*bonit] *n* large-brimmed bonnet with a flap to protect the neck from the sun.

sunburn [*sun*burn] *n* reddening or browning of skin by exposure to the sun ~ **sunburn** (*p/t* and *p/part* **sunburned, sunburnt**) *v/t* and *i* turn (skin) red or brown by exposing to the sun.

sunburst [*sun*burst] *n* sudden, strong burst of sunlight; gem representing a rayed sun.

sundae [*sun*day] *n* icecream served with fruit and syrup.

Sunday [*sun*di] *n* first day of the week.

Sunday-school [*sun*di-skOOl] *n* meeting for religious instruction of children on Sundays.

sunder [*sun*der] *v/t* and *i* part, separate.

sundew [*sun*dew] *n* low-growing hairy bog-plant.

sundial [*sun*dI-al] *n* instrument which shows time by the shadow of a pointer on a marked plate.

sundown [*sun*down] *n* sunset.

sundowner [*sun*downer] *n* (*coll*) alcoholic drink taken at sunset; (*Aust*) tramp, *esp* one seeking shelter for the night.

sundries [*sun*dRiz] *n* (*pl*) various unspecified items or matters; odds and ends, petty articles.

sundry [*sun*dRi] *adj* several, various; **all and s.** everyone indiscriminately.

sunflower [*sun*flowr] *n* tall plant with yellow flowers which turn towards the sun.

sung [*sung*] *p/t* and *p/part* of **sing**.

sunglasses [*sun*glaasiz] *n* (*pl*) dark tinted spectacles.

sun-god [*sun*-god] *n* a god considered as ruling or personifying the sun.

sun-hat [*sun*-hat] *n* broad-brimmed hat worn as protection from the sun.

sun-helmet [*sun*-helmit] *n* topee.

sunk [*sunk*] *p/part* of **sink** ~ **sunk** *adj* (*coll*) ruined, lost, doomed.

sunken [*sun*ken] *adj* submerged, lying below water; deep-set, hollow; below ground-level.

sunlamp [*sun*lamp] *n* apparatus emitting ultraviolet rays.

sunless [*sun*les] *adj* receiving little or no sunlight.

sunlight [*sun*lIt] *n* direct light of the sun, sunshine.

sunlit [*sun*lit] *adj* lighted by the sun.

sun-lounge [*sun*-lownj] *n* large-windowed room designed to admit much sunlight.

sunny [*sun*i] *adj* lit or warmed by the sun; cloudless; (*fig*) cheerful; **s. side** (*fig*) comparatively cheerful point of view ~ **sunnily** *adv* ~ **sunniness** *n*.

sunpower [*sun*powr] *n* power obtained by concentrating heat from the sun's rays.

sunproof [*sun*pROOf] *adj* impervious to the rays of the sun.

sunrise [*sun*RIz] *n* first appearance of the sun above the horizon, dawn > PDG.

sun-roof [*sun*-ROOf] *n* sunshine roof of car.

sunset [*sun*set] *n* descent of the sun below the horizon; time of this > PDG; spectacle of this; (*fig*) decline of vigour *etc*; end, last period.

sunshade [*sun*shayd] *n* light umbrella for protection against the sun; eye-shield used in strong sunlight; sunblind.

sunshine [*sun*shIn] *n* direct light of the sun > PDG; place on which this shines; (*fig*) brightness, cheerfulness; **s. roof** car roof that can be slipped open.

sunshiny [*sun*shIni] *adj* bright with sunlight.

sunspot [*sun*spot] *n* dark patch on the sun's surface > PDG, PDS.

sunstroke [*sun*stROk] *n* feverish collapse caused by excessive exposure to sunshine.

suntan [*sun*tan] *n* browning of the skin by exposure to sunlight ~ **suntanned** *adj*.

suntrap [*sun*tRap] *n* unusually sunny place.

sun-up [*sun*-up] *n* (*US*) sunrise.

sunward [*sun*ward] *adj* and *adv* towards the sun.

sunwise [*sun*wIz] *adj* and *adv* clockwise.

sup (*pres/part* **supping**, *p/t* and *p/part* **supped**) [*sup*] *v/t* and *i* take up (liquid) in sips; eat supper ~ **sup** *n* small mouthful of liquid.

super (1) [*sOO*per] *n* (*coll abbr*) supernumerary, actor appearing only in crowd-scenes or in small non-speaking parts; police superintendent.

super (2) *adj* (*coll*) marvellous, superb.

super- *pref* above; higher than; more than normal; superior; secondary.

superable [*sOO*peRab'l] *adj* that may be overcome.

superabundance [sOOpeRa*bun*dens] *n* excessive amount, superfluity.

superabundant [sOOpeRa*bun*dent] *adj* being more than enough; copious; excessive ~ **superabundantly** *adv*.

superadd [sOOpeRad] *v/t* add as further addition.

superaddition [sOOpeRa*dish*on] *n* act of superadding; that which is superadded.

superannuate [sOOpeRanew-ayt] *v/t* dismiss or pension off on account of old age.

superannuated [sOOpeRanew-aytid] *adj* incapacitated or disqualified by age; obsolete, out-of-date.

superannuation [sOOpeRanew-*ay*shon] *n* state of being superannuated; act of superannuating; payment or pension given on retirement.

superb [soo*purb*] *adj* grand, majestic; magnificent, splendid; excellent ~ **superbly** *adv* ~ **superbness** *n*.

supercargo [*sOO*perkaargO] *n* agent who superintends sales of cargo in a merchant ship.

supercharge [*sOO*perchaarj] *v/t* put a supercharger in; surcharge; *(her)* place (one charge) on another.

supercharger [*sOO*perchaarjer] *n* device to increase pressure of petrol mixture to cylinders in motor engine.

supercilious [sOOper*si*li-us] *adj* contemptuous, disdainful; haughty ~ **superciliously** *adv* ~ **superciliousness** *n*.

superconductivity [sOOperkonduk*ti*viti] *n* phenomenon of almost zero resistance exhibited by certain metals at temperatures near to the absolute zero > PDS ~ **superconducting** *adj*.

supercool [*sOO*perkOOl] *v/t* cool below freezing point without solidification > PDS.

supercritical [sOOper*kri*tikal] *adj (of a nuclear reactor)* capable of maintaining a self-sustaining chain reaction.

superdominant [sOOper*do*minant] *n (mus)* sixth note of diatonic scale.

super-duper [sOOper-*dOO*per] *adj (sl)* excellent, outstanding.

super-ego [*sOO*per-egO] *n (psych)* unconscious moral ideal governing behaviour > PDP.

supereminent [sOOpe*re*minent] *adj* surpassingly excellent ~ **supereminently** *adv*.

supererogation [sOOpeReRO*gay*shon] *n* performance of more than duty requires; **works of s.** *(theol)* acts more virtuous than strictly necessary to salvation; *(RC)* such acts performed by saints, the merit of which is transferable to others.

supererogatory [sOOpeRe*Ro*gateRi] *adj* being more than is required by duty.

superfatted [*s*OOper*fat*id] *adj* containing unusually large proportion of fat.

superficial [sOOper*fish*al] *adj* of or on the surface; *(of feelings, knowledge etc)* not deep, not thorough; frivolous.

superficiality [sOOperfishi-*ali*ti] *n* state or quality of being superficial.

superficially [sOOper*fish*ali] *adv* in a superficial way.

superficies [sOOper*fish*i-eez] *n* surface; exterior part.

superfine [*sOO*per*fIn*] *adj* surpassingly fine; of extra quality; over-refined.

superfluity [sOOper*flOO*-iti] *n* greater quantity than is necessary or sufficient.

superfluous [sOO*pur*flOO-us] *adj* more than is necessary or sufficient, excessive, redundant ~ **superfluously** *adv* ~ **superfluousness** *n*.

superflux [*sOO*perfluks] *n* that which is more than is wanted.

superheat [sOOper*heet*] *v/t* heat (liquid) above its boiling point > PDS.

superhet [*sOO*perhet] *n* supersonic heterodyne receiver > PDS, PDEl.

superheterodyne [sOOper*het*eROdIn] *n* supersonic heterodyne > PDS, PDEl.

superhuman [sOOper*hew*man] *adj* above or beyond what is human; of more than human power ~ **superhumanly** *adv*.

superimpose [sOOpeRim*pOz*] *v/t* put or lay on top of something else.

superincumbent [sOOpeRin*kum*bent] *adj* lying or resting on something else.

superinduce [sOOpeRin*dews*] *v/t* bring about as an addition.

superinduction [sOOpeRin*duk*shon] *n* act of superinducing; state of being superinduced.

superintend [sOOpeRin*tend*] *v/t* and *i* have the management of; direct, control.

superintendent [sOOpeRin*tend*ent] *n* one who has charge of some organization, department *etc*; overseer; police officer ranking above chief inspector.

superior [sOO*peer*Ri-er] *adj* of higher rank, degree, grade *etc*; finer, better, nobler; of good quality; upper, higher; high-class; haughty, disdainful; conceited, self-satisfied; **s. to** calmly unaffected by ~ **superior** *n* one who is of higher rank, or finer character *etc* than another; *(cap)* head of a monastic or other religious community.

superiority [sOO*peer*Ri-*o*Riti] *n* state or quality of being superior; **s. complex** *(pop psych)* aggressively self-satisfied or domineering attitude.

superjacent [sOOper*jay*sent] *adj* lying upon or above.

superlative [sOO*pur*lativ] *adj* supremely good, most excellent; **s. degree** *(gramm)* highest degree of comparison of adjective or adverb ~ **superlative** *n (gramm)* (word in) the superlative degree; *(fig)* term of utmost praise ~ **superlatively** *adv*.

superman *(pl* **supermen)** [*sOO*perman] *n* hypothetical human being whose physical and mental powers are extraordinarily highly developed; *(coll)* man of amazing intelligence, efficiency, strength *etc*.

supermarket [*sOO*permaarkit] *n* large self-service shop selling various foods and household articles.

supernational [sOOper*nash*onal]*adj* supranational.

supernatural [sOOper*nache*Ral] *adj* not explicable by the known laws of nature; existing by, due to or exercising powers beyond the laws of nature; of or by God, spirits, demons, ghosts, fairies *etc*.

supernaturalism [sOOper*nache*Ralizm] *n* belief in the supernatural; state of being supernatural ~ **supernaturalist** *n* and *adj*.

supernaturally [sOOper*nache*Rali] *adj* by supernatural power; in a supernatural way.

supernova [sOOper*n*Ova] *n (astron)* exploding star that increases suddenly in brightness.

supernumerary [sOOper*new*meReRi] *n* and *adj* (person or thing) additional to the necessary or normal number; (person) having a non-speaking part in a play or film.

superphosphate [sOOper*fos*fayt] *n (chem)* phosphate containing maximum quantity of phosphoric acid; artificial fertilizer containing superphosphate of lime > PDS.

superpose [sOOper*pOz*] *v/t* lay over or on something.

superposition [sOOperp*O*zishon] *n* act of superposing; state of being superposed.

superpower [*sOO*perpowr] *n* outstandingly powerful nation.

supersaturation [sOOpersache*Ra*yshon] *n* solution holding more dissolved solute than is required to saturate it > PDS.

superscribe [*sOO*perskRIb] *v/t* write or engrave on the top or outside of.

superscription [sOOper*skRip*shon] *n* act of superscribing; that which is superscribed.

supersede [sOOper*seed*] *v/t* replace; take the place of, supplant; render out-of-date.

supersensible [sOOpersensib'l] *adj* beyond the reach of the senses.

supersensitive [sOOpersensitiv] *adj* too highly sensitive.

supersensual [sOOpersensew-al] *adj* beyond the reach of the senses.

supersession [sOOperseshon] *n* act of superseding; state of being superseded.

supersonic [sOOpersonik] *adj* moving faster than the speed of sound; (*of waves*) similar to sound-waves but of too high frequency to be audible to human ears > PDS; ultrasonic; **s. bang** violent audible pressure-wave set up by aircraft flying faster than sound ~ **supersonically** *adv.*

supersonics [sOOpersoniks] *n* (*pl*) study of aeronautical problems in aircraft flying faster than sound; ultrasonics, study of waves of higher frequency than soundwaves > PDS.

superstate [sOOperstayt] *n* very powerful nation having authority over satellite States.

superstition [sOOperstishon] *n* irrational belief in omens, charms, supernatural forces and beings *etc*; irrational belief based on ignorance.

superstitious [sOOperstishus] *adj* of, like or addicted to superstition ~ **superstitiously** *adv* ~ **superstitiousness** *n.*

superstructure [sOOperstRukcher] *n* structure built up on another; upper part of a complex structure; part of building above ground.

supersubtle [sOOpersut'l] *adj* too subtle.

supertanker [sOOpertanker] *n* extremely large ship transporting oil.

supertax [sOOpertaks] *n* additional income tax for those with large incomes.

superterrestrial [sOOperteRestRi-al] *adj* above the earth; above earthly things; celestial.

supertonic [sOOpertonik] *n* (*mus*) note next above tonic in diatonic scale.

supervene [sOOperveen] *v/i* happen or come into existence as an addition or consequence.

supervise [sOOpervIz] *v/t* and *i* keep authoritative watch over; superintend, direct the work of.

supervision [sOOpervizhon] *n* act of supervising; state of being supervised.

supervisor [sOOpervIzer] *n* one who supervises; inspector, overseer ~ **supervisory** *adj.*

supine (1) [sOOpIn] *adj* lying on the back with face upward; taking no action, lacking energy or will-power.

supine (2) [sOOpIn] *n* (*Lat gramm*) verbal noun formed from stem of past participle.

supinely [sOOpInli] *adv* in supine position; in a supine way.

supineness [sOOpIn-nis] *n* state or quality of being supine.

supper [super] *n* light evening meal.

supperless [superlis] *adj* having had no supper.

supplant [suplaant] *v/t* take the place of, displace, *esp* by craft or treachery.

supple [sup'l] *adj* easily bent, pliable; yielding, submissive; sly; obsequious ~ **supple** *v/t* and *i* make pliant; make compliant; become pliant.

supplement [supliment] *n* something added to fill a need; additional part of a book or periodical giving further detailed information; appendix; separable section of newspaper or magazine; (*math*) one of two angles equal to sum of two right angles ~ **supplement** [supliment] *v/t* make

necessary additions to; give additional help, strength *etc* to.

supplemental [supplimental] *adj* additional.

supplementary [supplimenteRi] *adj* additional; (*of angles*) totalling two right angles.

suppleness [sup'lnis] *n* quality of being supple.

supplial [suplI-al] *n* act of supplying.

suppliance [supli-ans] *n* supplication.

suppliant [supli-ant] *adj* humbly beseeching, supplicating ~ **suppliant** *n* one who humbly begs a favour ~ **suppliantly** *adv.*

supplicant [suplikant] *n* and *adj* (*ar*) suppliant.

supplicate [suplikayt] *v/t* ask for earnestly and humbly; pray for; beseech.

supplication [suplikayshon] *n* humble and earnest prayer; entreaty, petition.

supplier [suplI-er] *n* one who supplies.

supply (1) [suplI] *v/t* provide with what is needed, give for use; provide for, satisfy (a need); **s. the place of** replace ~ **supply** *n* store, stock, that which is supplied; amount available; rate or quantity by which something is provided; necessary stores of food, clothing *etc*, *esp* for an army or population; temporary substitute, *esp* for a teacher, servant or clergyman ~ **supply** *adj* of or for the providing of supplies; acting as temporary substitute.

supply (2) [supli] *adv* in a supple way.

support [supawrt] *v/t* prevent from falling, hold or prop up the weight of; regularly provide for the needs of; maintain, provide money for; help; approve of, encourage; advocate; provide arguments in favour of; bear, endure; sustain; **supporting programme** shorter films shown with a main one ~ **support** *n* one who or that which supports; act of supporting; means of maintaining or providing; prop; assistance, backing.

supportable [supawrtab'l] *adj* that may be endured.

supporter [supawrter] *n* one who or that which supports or maintains; defender, partisan, adherent; (*her*) figure on each side of a shield.

supposal [supOzal] *n* supposition.

suppose [supOz] *v/t* assume, consider probable but unproved; imagine, believe; surmise; involve logically, imply; (*pass*) be expected or required by law, morality, duty, custom *etc* (to do something).

supposed [supOzd] *adj* believed to be true, genuine, *etc* ~ **supposedly** [supOzedli] *adv.*

supposing [supOzing] *conj* if.

supposition [supOzishon] *n* act of supposing; that which is supposed; assumption; conjecture; hypothesis ~ **suppositional** *adj.*

supposititious [supozitishus] *adj* falsely substituted, not genuine ~ **supposititiously** *adv.*

suppository [supoziteRi] *n* capsule of medicinal substance introduced into rectum or vagina and left to dissolve.

suppress [supRes] *v/t* crush by force, overpower subdue; keep back, check; withhold, conceal, forbid or prevent publication of; ban; (*psych*) prevent from becoming conscious, repress.

suppressible [supResib'l] *adj* capable of being suppressed.

suppression [supReshon] *n* act of suppressing; state of being suppressed.

suppressor [supReser] *n* one who or that which

suppresses; device on electrical apparatus to prevent interference with radio or television receivers; device on radio and television receivers to suppress interference from nearby electrical apparatus.

suppurate [*supe*wRayt] *v/i* generate or discharge pus, fester.

suppuration [supew*Ray*shon] *n* production of pus.

supra- *pref* above, higher than; beyond.

supranational [sOOp*Ra*nashonal] *adj* having power over or incorporating several nations.

supremacy [sOO*pRe*masi] *n* state of being supreme; highest authority or power.

supreme [sOO*pReem*] *adj* highest in authority or power; highest in degree or importance; greatest possible; utmost; S. Being God; s. sacrifice act of sacrificing one's life; S. Soviet parliament of Soviet Union ~ **supremely** *adv*.

supremo [sOO*pReem*O] *n* (*mil coll*) commander-in-chief; military dictator.

sur- *pref* above, over; beyond.

surcease [sur*sees*] *n* (*ar*) cessation ~ **surcease** *v/i* (*ar*) cease.

surcharge [*sur*chaarj] *n* excessive or additional charge; another valuation or words printed on a postage stamp ~ **surcharge** *v/t* overload; overfill; overcharge; put an extra charge on.

surcingle [sur*sing*-g'l] *n* strap to fasten saddle, blanket *etc* on horse's back; girdle of cassock.

surcoat [*sur*kOt] *n* (*ar*) outer coat; loose coat worn over armour.

surd [*surd*] *n* and *adj* (*math*) (quantity, *esp* root) not expressible in rational numbers > PDS.

sure [*shoor*] *adj* certain to be efficient; reliable, safe; certain to happen; feeling no doubt, quite confident or convinced; true; **make s. (of)** remove all doubt or uncertainty (about); prove; secure possession, support *etc* (of); **to be s.** (*coll*) certainly; indeed; admittedly ~ **sure** *adv* and *interj* (*coll*) certainly; willingly.

surefire [*shoor*fIr] *adj* (*coll*) infallible, certain to succeed.

surefooted [shoor*foot*id] *adj* not liable to fall or stumble.

surely [*shoor*li] *adv* securely, safely; certainly.

sureness [*shoor*nis] *n* state or quality of being sûre.

surety [*shoor*ti] *n* certainty; security; one who makes himself responsible for another's behaviour; one who lays down money as pledge that another will appear in court; money so laid down.

surf [*surf*] *n* waves breaking in foam on shore ~ **surf** *v/i* practise surf-riding.

surface [*sur*fis] *n* outer part, exterior, outside; top of a body of liquid; (*fig*) that which is immediately obvious; that which is only external; (*geom*) that which has length and breadth but no thickness ~ **surface** *v/t* and *i* polish or dress the surface of; come up to the surface of water ~ **surface** *adj* of or on the surface; superficial; travelling or transported by land or sea; **s. noise** noise produced by friction of needle on gramophone record; **s. tension** elastic force in the surface of a liquid which tends to minimize the area of the surface > PDS.

surfaceman [*sur*fisman] *n* railway worker who maintains the lines; one who works above ground at a mine.

surfactant [sur*fak*tant] *n* surface active agent; substance added to a liquid to alter those of its properties which depend on its surface tension.

surfboard [*surf*bawrd] *n* oblong board used in surf-riding.

surfboat [*surf*bOt] *n* buoyant boat for use in surf.

surfeit [*sur*fit] *n* excess, *esp* in eating or drinking; satiety ~ **surfeit** *v/t* and *i* feed to excess; cloy.

surfing [*surf*ing] *n* surf-riding.

surf-riding [*surf*-RIding] *n* sport of riding on surf balanced on an oblong board.

surge [*surj*] *n* large rolling wave, billow; (*fig*) onrush; gush; strong access of emotion ~ **surge** *v/i* swell; rise powerfully; move powerfully forward in a heaving mass.

surgeon [*sur*jun] *n* medical practitioner who treats by surgery; medical officer in the armed forces.

surgery [*sur*jeRi] *n* treatment of injuries or diseases by operations or manipulations; doctor's consulting-room or dispensary; hours at which a doctor can be visited at his surgery by patients.

surgical [*sur*jikal] *adj* of, for or by surgery or surgeons; **s. boot** boot or shoe designed to correct deformity of the foot; **s. spirit** alcohol used as cleanser or disinfectant in surgery ~ **surgically** *adv*.

surlily [*sur*lili] *adv* in a surly way.

surliness [*sur*lines] *n* quality of being surly.

surloin [*sur*loin] *n* sirloin.

surly [*sur*li] *adj* sullen, angry and ill-mannered; morose; churlish, rude.

surmise [*sur*mIz/ser*mIz*] *n* guess, reasonable but unproved supposition ~ **surmise** *v/t* and *i* form a reasonable guess (about).

surmount [ser*mownt*] *v/t* overcome, vanquish; rise above; surpass.

surname [*sur*naym] *n* hereditary family name transmitted in male line; (*ar*) nickname ~ **surname** *v/t* call by surname; give surname or nickname to.

surpass [ser*paas*] *v/t* excel, exceed, go beyond.

surpassing [ser*paas*ing] *adj* excelling all others ~ **surpassingly** *adv*.

surplice [*sur*plis] *n* (*eccles*) loose white linen vestment.

surplus [*sur*plus] *n* excess, that which remains beyond what is used or needed; balance in hand after payment of all liabilities ~ **surplus** *adj* in excess of requirements; redundant, superfluous.

surprise [ser*pRIz*] *n* emotion caused by an unexpected event; that which is unexpected; act of capturing, attacking or gaining an advantage by taking unawares ~ **surprise** *v/t* catch unawares, come unexpectedly against; capture by unexpected attack; cause surprise to, astonish; shock, startle ~ **surprise** *adj* unexpected, done without warning.

surprising [ser*pRIz*ing] *adj* causing surprise; extraordinary; astounding ~ **surprisingly** *adv*.

surrealism [sur*Ree*-alizm] *n* school of art or literature that aims at producing irrational fantasies or hallucinatory and dream-like effects > PDAA ~ **surrealist** *n* and *adj*.

surrealistic [surRi-a*listik*] *adj* of or like surrealism; of or like a horrifying dream or hallucination.

surrender [su*Ren*der] *v/t* and *i* yield to the power or control of another; submit after defeat; give up

729

possession of; yield oneself to; give oneself up (to) ~ **surrender** *n* act of surrendering; state of being surrendered.

surreptitious [suReptish*u*s] *adj* done or obtained stealthily, *esp* dishonestly ~ **surreptitiously** *adv* ~ **surreptitiousness** *n*.

surrogate [*su*ROgayt] *n* one who acts as substitute or deputy; one sacrificially killed as substitute for another; (*psych*) substituted dream-figure > PDP; (*eccles*) deputy bishop.

surround [su*Rownd*] *v/t* enclose on all sides, lie or be all around; be easily available to ~ **surround** *n* that which surrounds; uncovered flooring or linoleum between carpet and walls of room.

surroundings [su*Rownd*ingz] *n* (*pl*) nearby things or areas; neighbourhood; environment, circumstances.

surtax [*sur*taks] *n* additional tax on high incomes ~ **surtax** *v/t* put additional tax on.

surveillance [serv*ay*lans] *n* close watch, supervision, *esp* of a prisoner or suspect.

survey [serv*ay*] *v/t* take a general view of, look at as a whole; examine the condition and value of, inspect and assess; measure the extent and features of (an area of land) by trigonometry *etc* ~ **survey** [*sur*vay] *n* act or process of surveying; general view or consideration; map or drawing showing topography of an area > PDE.

surveyor [serv*ay*-er] *n* one who surveys, *esp* one who measures land; inspector.

survival [serv*I*val] *n* act of surviving; that which has survived from an earlier age; **s. of the fittest** (*biol*) theory that organisms that best adapt to their environment are likeliest to survive and breed; **s. kit** emergency supplies carried by airmen; **s. value** degree to which a characteristic, achievement *etc* can help an individual or species to survive.

survive [serv*Iv*] *v/t* and *i* live longer than; be alive after and in spite of (a danger); continue to live.

survivor [serv*Iv*er] *n* one who lives longer than another; one who remains alive after experiencing some danger, calamity *etc*.

susceptibility [suseptib*il*iti] *n* quality or state of being susceptible; (*pl*) emotional feelings.

susceptible [sus*ep*tib'l] *adj* easily affected by emotion; easily influenced; very sensitive; **s. of** capable of undergoing; **s. to** easily affected by; liable to ~ **susceptibly** *adv*.

susceptive [sus*ep*tiv] *adj* of or by receiving emotional stimuli; susceptible.

suspect [sus*pekt*] *v/t* and *i* believe or imagine to exist or be true, though without proof; believe (person) to be guilty; distrust, have little faith in; think likely; suppose ~ **suspect** [*sus*pekt] *n* one who is suspected of being guilty ~ **suspect** *adj* rousing suspicion, suspected.

suspend [sus*pend*] *v/t* hang up; hang from above; cause to cease for a time, defer; debar temporarily.

suspender-belt [sus*pend*er-belt] *n* woman's undergarment with suspenders for stockings.

suspenders [sus*pend*erz] *n* (*pl*) attachments which hold up socks or stockings; (*US*) braces.

suspense [sus*pens*] *n* state of anxious uncertainty and expectation; (*leg*) temporary cessation of a right.

suspenseful [sus*pens*fool] *adj* (*sl*) deliberately creating and maintaining suspense.

suspension [sus*pen*shon] *n* act of suspending; state of being suspended; (*chem*) mixture consisting of small solid particles dispersed in a liquid; **s. bridge** bridge hung from cables carried by towers > PDE.

suspensory [sus*pen*seRi] *adj* holding up.

suspicion [sus*pish*on] *n* act or feeling of suspecting; mistrust; belief in the guilt of another without proof; (*fig*) very small trace.

suspicious [sus*pish*us] *adj* inclined to suspect; mistrustful; arousing suspicion ~ **suspiciously** *adv* ~ **suspiciousness** *n*.

suspire [sus*pIr*] *v/i* (*poet*) sigh.

suss [*sus*] *v/t* (*sl*) suspect; **s. out** detect, discover; work out; reconnoitre.

sustain [sus*tayn*] *v/t* hold up, bear the weight of; be able to bear (strain, suffering *etc*) without collapse; experience, suffer; enable to bear, strengthen; uphold, maintain; establish by evidence, confirm.

sustenance [*sus*tinans] *n* that which sustains; nourishment, food.

sustentation [susten*tay*shon] *n* support, maintenance; food.

sutler [*sut*ler] *n* (*hist*) one who follows an army to sell food or liquor to the troops.

suttee [*sutee*] *n* (*hist*) former custom whereby a Hindu widow burnt herself to death on her husband's funeral pyre; widow who did this.

sutural [*sew*cheRal] *adj* of or by a suture.

suture [*sew*cher] *n* (*med*) act of stitching the edges of a wound together; thread or stitch used for this; (*anat*) junction of bones of skull ~ **suture** *v/t* unite by a suture.

suzerain [*sew*zeRain] *n* feudal lord; State with sovereignty over another.

suzerainty [*sew*zeRainti] *n* state of being a suzerain.

svelte [*svelt*] *adj* slender, willowy.

swab [*swob*] *n* absorbent mop or pad for wiping floors, decks *etc*; (*med*) absorbent pad; specimen of liquid absorbed by this; (*sl*) clumsy or dirty fool ~ **swab** (*pres/part* **swabbing**, *p/t* and *p/part* **swabbed**) *v/t* mop up, clean or absorb with a swab ~ **swabber** *n*.

swaddle [*swod*'l] *v/t* wind a cloth tightly round; wrap up in much clothing.

swaddling-bands [*swod*ling-bandz] *n* (*pl*) strip of cloth formerly wrapped closely round a baby.

swaddling-clothes [*swod*ling-klOTHz] *n* (*pl*) swaddling-bands.

swag [*swag*] *n* (*sl*) booty obtained by robbery; (*Aust*) pack, bundle; (*US*) draped curtain.

swag-bellied [swag-belid] *adj* having a large floppy belly.

swagger [*swag*er] *v/i* walk haughtily or self-confidently; talk boastingly or hectoringly ~ **swagger** *n* swaggering walk; dashing talk or behaviour; bluster; self-conceit ~ **swagger** *adj* (*coll*) smart, fashionable.

swagger-cane [*swag*er-kayn] *n* soldier's short walking-stick.

swagger-coat [*swag*er-kOt] *n* woman's loose three-quarter-length coat.

swagman (*pl* **swagmen**) [*swag*man] *n* (*Aust*) vagrant, tramp; itinerant labourer; pedlar.

swain [swayn] n (poet or joc) young countryman; lover, admirer.

swallow (1) [swolO] n small migratory bird with pointed wings and forked tail.

swallow (2) v/t and i make (food, drink etc) pass from mouth through throat to stomach; put up with, accept patiently; accept credulously, believe implicitly; **s. up** engulf; overwhelm; consume utterly ~ **swallow** n act of swallowing; amount swallowed at one go; gullet.

swallow-dive [swolO-dIv] n and v/i dive with arms outstretched sideways.

swallow-hole [swolO-hOl] n hole through which a river runs down into the ground.

swallow-tail [swolO-tayl] n deeply-forked tail; butterfly or humming bird with deeply forked tail; dress-coat.

swam [swam] p/t of **swim**.

swami [swaami] n Hindu teacher of meditation and esoteric wisdom.

swamp [swomp] n wet boggy land, marsh > PDG ~ **swamp** v/t cause to fill with water and sink; sink into a bog; (fig) overwhelm with work or difficulties.

swampy [swompi] adj of or like a swamp, marshy.

swan [swon] n species of large, long-necked aquatic bird; constellation Cygnus; (fig) poet ~ **swan** (pres/part **swanning**, p/t and p/part **swanned**) v/i **s. about, s. around** (coll) move slowly and majestically; wander about, travel aimlessly.

swanee-whistle [swonee-wis'l] n crude woodwind instrument with sliding valve > PDM.

swanherd [swonhurd] n official in charge of swans.

swank [swank] v/i (coll) boast, show off, make a show of superiority ~ **swank** n act of swanking.

swanky [swanki] adj (coll) boastful, conceited; worth boasting about, very smart or expensive ~ **swankily** adv ~ **swankiness** n.

swan-maiden [swon-mayden] n (myth) girl who can turn into a swan.

swan-neck [swon-nek] n tube, pipe etc curved like the neck of a swan.

swannery [swoneRi] n place where swans are kept.

swansdown [swonzdown] n soft under-feathers of a swan; fine, soft, thick cloth.

swan-shot [swon-shot] n large size of shot.

swanskin [swonskin] n very soft flannel.

swansong [swonsong] n song traditionally believed to be sung by a dying swan; (fig) last utterance, performance, or work of an artist, writer, actor etc.

swan-upping [swon-uping] n annual inspection and marking of royal swans.

swap, swop (pres/part **swapping, swopping**, p/t and p/part **swapped, swopped**) [swop] v/t and i (coll) barter, exchange as bargain ~ **swap, swop** n (coll) act of swapping; object that has been swapped.

sward [swawrd] n ground covered with short, thick grass; turf.

swarf [swawrf] n metal filings from lathe; wax or wood filings; machine grease.

swarm (1) [swawrm] n large mass of insects moving or working as a group, esp cluster of bees with a queen leaving one hive to found another; crowd, throng; moving mass of small objects or animals ~ **swarm** v/i form a swarm, move in a crowded mass; (of bees) leave a hive in a swarm; (fig) assemble in large numbers, crowd; **be swarming with** (coll) be covered or filled with.

swarm (2) v/t and i climb (rope, pole, etc) by clinging round it with arms and legs and scrambling up.

swarthy [swawrTHi] adj dark-coloured.

swash [swosh] v/i and t (of liquids) swirl, splash about; make a splashing noise ~ **swash** n splash.

swashbuckler [swoshbukler] n swaggering boaster or bully.

swastika [swostika] n cross with four equal arms, each bent back at a right-angle; symbol of the Nazi Party; archaic sun-symbol.

swat (pres/part **swatting**, p/t and p/part **swatted**) [swot] v/t kill (insect) by slapping it with the hand or with something flexible ~ **swat** n flexible instrument for swatting flies etc.

swatch [swotch] n sample of fabric for dressmaking.

swath [swawth] n amount or line of grass, corn etc cut by a mowing machine in a single course; amount cut by a scythe in a single sweep.

swathe [swayTH] v/t wrap or bind with a bandage; wrap up tightly in cloth etc ~ **swathe** n bandage; wrapping; swath.

swatter [swoter] n flexible device for swatting insects.

sway [sway] v/i and t swing or rock to and fro; swing or lean over to one side; influence; have power or authority over; rule ~ **sway** n act of swaying; influence, power, domination.

swear (p/t **swore**, p/part **sworn**) [swair] v/t and i promise, assert or bind oneself by a solemn oath; vow; utter curses or blasphemous words; cause to make a legal oath; impose a promise by oath on; (of animals) growl, make any sound expressing anger; **s. at** speak to with curses and blasphemies; **s. by** invoke as witness to an oath; (coll) have complete confidence in; **s. in** administer legal oath to; **s. off** solemnly renounce; **s. to** affirm or assert with an oath ~ **swear** n (coll) act of cursing or blaspheming.

swearer [swairRer] n one who swears, esp habitually.

swearing [swairRing] n act of taking an oath; act of uttering curses, blasphemies or profane oaths.

swear-word [swair-wurd] n (coll) blasphemous or obscene word used in swearing.

sweat [swet] n moisture exuded from the skin; moisture exuded from or condensing on a surface; process of sweating; state of fear, heat, fever etc accompanied by sweating; (coll) drudgery, laborious work; **cold s.** state of acute fear or anxiety ~ **sweat** v/i and t exude sweat, perspire; exude moisture; cause to sweat; force to work hard for very low wages; work hard, drudge.

sweatband [swetband] n band of leather etc lining a man's hat.

sweated [swetid] adj forced to work excessively long hours for very low pay; produced, made by underpaid workers.

sweater [sweter] n thick woollen jersey; one who or that which sweats or causes to sweat; employer who underpays workmen.

sweat-gland [swet-gland] n (anat) small gland beneath the skin which secretes sweat > PDB.

sweatshop [*swet*shop] *n* factory or shop employing sweated labour.

sweaty [*sweti*] *adj* sweating; covered in sweat; smelling of sweat ~ **sweatily** *adv* ~ **sweatiness** *n*.

swede [*sweed*] *n* Swedish turnip; (*cap*) native of Sweden.

Swedish [*sweed*ish] *n* and *adj* (language) of Sweden.

sweeny [*sweeni*] *n* atrophy of a muscle in horses.

sweep (*p/t* and *p/part* swept) [*sweep*] *v/t* and *i* clean with a broom or brush; brush away; move strongly and smoothly, pass by with strong steady speed, rush; move proudly and steadily; form a large graceful curve; make a broad swinging gesture; drive violently away; obliterate, destroy; carry violently away; **s. the board** win all stakes in gambling; win overwhelmingly ~ **sweep** *n* act of sweeping with a broom; man who cleans soot from chimneys; broad swinging movement or gesture, *esp* in a curve; large graceful curve; strong steady onrush, flow, advance *etc*; long heavy oar; sail of windmill; crossing-sweeper; (*sl*) rogue, scoundrel; (*coll*) sweepstake; **make a clean s. of** get rid of entirely and at once.

sweeping [*sweep*ing] *adj* covering a wide range; comprehending a great deal or great many; disregarding accuracy of detail; making vigorous changes, radical ~ **sweepingly** *adv*.

sweepings [*sweep*ingz] *n* (*pl*) rubbish, fragments collected by sweeping.

sweepnet [*sweep*net] *n* large fishing-net; butterfly-net.

sweepstake [*sweep*stayk] *n* form of gambling on a race *etc*, in which each gambler buys a ticket entitling him to draw the name of one competitor and win all or a proportion of the stakes if this competitor wins the race.

sweet [*sweet*] *adj* tasting like sugar; having a pleasant taste or smell; pleasing, delightful; melodious; having a charming character; tender, gentle, kind; very pretty or pleasing; **be s. on** (*coll*) be in love with; **have a s. tooth** be fond of very sweet food ~ **sweet** *n* one of various small confectioneries made mainly from sugar or chocolate; any sweetened dish of fruit, pudding *etc* served at the end of a meal; darling, beloved person; (*pl*) pleasures.

sweet-and-sour [*sweet*-and-sowr] *adj* (*of sauce*) combining sweet and acid ingredients.

sweetbread [*sweet*bRed] *n* pancreas of sheep or calf, used as food.

sweetbrier [*sweet*bRIr] *n* shrubby plant with a delicate fragrance, wild rose.

sweetcorn [*sweet*kawrn] *n* variety of maize with sweet taste.

sweeten [*sweet*en] *v/t* and *i* make sweet; make pleasing or kind; make less unpleasant, alleviate; become sweet; (*sl*) bribe.

sweetener [*sweet*ner] *n* one who or that which sweetens; (*sl*) bribe, tip.

sweetening [*sweet*ning] *n* substance that sweetens something; act of one who sweetens.

sweetheart [*sweet*-haart] *n* person whom one is in love with and is loved by; beloved, darling.

sweetie [*sweet*i] *n* (*coll*) darling (*esp* used of woman); (*coll*) confectionery, sweet.

sweeting [*sweet*ing] *n* sweet apple; (*ar*) sweetheart.

sweetly [*sweet*li] *adv* in a sweet way.

sweetmeat [*sweet*meet] *n* article of confectionery made mainly from sugar or chocolate.

sweetness [*sweet*nis] *n* state or quality of being sweet.

sweet-oil [*sweet*-oil] *n* olive oil; salad oil.

sweetpea [*sweet*pea] *n* annual climbing plant of the pea family, with scented flowers.

sweet-potato [*sweet*-pOtaytO] *n* tropical climbing plant with edible root.

sweet-william [*sweet*-wilyum] *n* species of dianthus with flowers in clusters.

sweety [*sweet*i] *n* sweetie.

swell (*p/t* swelled, *p/part* swollen or swelled) [*swel*] *v/i* and *t* increase in bulk or extent; bulge; be elated; be filled with pride; be inflated; increase the size of; **swelled head** (*coll*) conceit, pride ~ **swell** *n* act of swelling; extension of bulk; increase of sound; succession of unbroken waves; bulge; (*mus*) combined crescendo and diminuendo; (*coll*) wealthy and fashionable person; person of importance ~ **swell** *adj* (*coll*) smart, showy; excellent, fine.

swell-head [*swel*-hed] *n* (*sl*) conceited person.

swelling [*swel*ing] *n* act of expanding; state of being swollen; unnatural enlargement of a part of the body; boil, inflammation; tumour ~ **swelling** *adj* that swells, bulging; curving; (*of style*) self-consciously noble, lofty.

swell-organ [*swel*-awrgan] *n* organ with pipes enclosed so that the volume of sound can be regulated > PDM.

swelter [*swel*ter] *v/i* be oppressively hot; grow faint with heat; sweat profusely.

swept [*swept*] *p/t* and *p/part* of **sweep.**

swerve [*swurv*] *v/i* and *t* turn abruptly to one side, suddenly diverge from direct course; deflect ~ **swerve** *n* act of swerving, sudden divergence.

swift (1) [*swift*] *adj* speedy, rapid; ready; prompt; brief; sudden ~ **swift** *adv*.

swift (2) *n* small, long-winged, insectivorous bird; common newt.

swifter [*swift*er] *n* (*naut*) rope used to hold capstan bars when shipped > PDSa.

swift-footed [*swift*-footid] *adj* running with speed.

swiftly [*swift*li] *adv* rapidly, fast.

swiftness [*swift*nis] *n* quality of being swift.

swig [*swig*] *n* long drink taken without breathing; large gulp, *esp* of alcoholic drink ~ **swig** (*pres/part* swigging, *p/t* and *p/part* swigged) *v/t* and *i* drink in large gulps; drink without taking breath.

swill [*swil*] *v/t* and *i* wash with copious water; drink in large quantities ~ **swill** *n* act of swilling; liquid pig-food, hogwash; (*coll*) large drink.

swiller [*swil*er] *n* (*coll*) one who habitually drinks too much.

swillings [*swil*ingz] *n* (*pl*) hogwash; refuse *etc* swilled out.

swim (*pres/part* swimming, *p/t* swam, *p/part* swum) [*swim*] *v/i* and *t* float or be supported on water or other fluid; move through water by moving hands and feet, or fins and tail; be drenched; feel dizzy; cause to swim; traverse, cover a distance, by swimming; overflow ~ **swim** *n* act of swimming; spell of swimming; swimming movement; pool frequented by fish in a river; swimming-bladder; **in the s.** up to date, knowing what is going on.

swim-bladder [*swim*-blader] *n* air-bladder of a fish > PDB.

swimmer [*swim*er] *n* one who swims.

swimming [*swim*ing] *n* art of moving through water by means of the limbs; dizziness.

swimming-bath [*swim*ing-baath] *n* large tank of water for swimming in, *usu* in a building.

swimming-belt [*swim*ing-belt] *n* air-filled belt which supports a learner when swimming.

swimmingly [*swim*ingli] *adv* smoothly, easily.

swimming-pool [*swim*ing-pOOl] *n* open-air artificial pool for swimming in.

swimsuit [*swim*sewt] *n* close-fitting garment worn when swimming.

swindle [*swind*'l] *v/t* cheat, defraud grossly ~ **swindle** *n* gross fraud; something fraudulently alleged to be valuable; method of cheating or deceiving for gain.

swindler [*swind*ler] *n* one who swindles.

swine (*pl* **swine**) [*swin*] *n* pig; (*fig*) highly unpleasant, immoral, or dishonest person.

swinefever [*swin*feever] *n* infectious fever affecting pigs.

swineherd [*swin*hurd] *n* one who looks after swine.

swing (*p/t* and *p/part* **swung**) [*swing*] *v/i* and *t* move to and fro, sway, oscillate, rock; cause to sway or rock; cause to move round; rock on a swing; brandish; whirl round; (*coll*) be hanged; lift or throw with a sweeping movement; fluctuate; (*mus*) play liltingly; play swing jazz; (*sl*) enjoy and understand; (*sl*) influence, alter by persuasion; **s. the lead** avoid work by false excuses ~ **swing** *n* act of swinging; loose swaying motion; movement to and fro; arc through which a body swings; seat suspended by ropes in which one can rock backwards and forwards as amusement; rhythm; lilting rhythm; (*mus*) type of jazz for larger bands; **in full s.** fully active.

swingboat [*swing*bOt] *n* boat-shaped seat for swinging in at a fair.

swingeing [*swinj*ing] *adj* forcible, strong; (*coll*) huge.

swinging [*swing*ing] *adj* done with a swing; vigorous; buoyant; (*coll*) leading a gay, sophisticated life; pursuing advanced fashions; daring, wild, immoral ~ **swingingly** *adv*.

swinging-post [*swing*ing-post] *n* post on which door or gate is hung.

swingle [*swing*-g'l] *n* wooden instrument used to beat flax clean ~ **swingle** *v/t* clean flax by beating it.

swinglebar [*swing*-g'l-baar] *n* crossbar to which a horse's traces are attached.

swingwing [*swing*wing] *n* and *adj* (aircraft) the angle of whose wings to the fuselage can be altered in flight.

swinish [*swin*ish] *adj* like swine; coarse, gross ~ **swinishly** *adv* ~ **swinishness** *n*.

swipe [*swip*] *v/t* and *i* hit violently with swinging arm; (*coll*) snatch away, steal ~ **swipe** *n* violent but inaccurately aimed blow; (*pl, coll*) weak beer.

swirl [*swurl*] *v/i* and *t* form eddies, whirl about; carry with an eddying motion; feel dizzy ~ **swirl** *n* whirling motion; eddy.

swish [*swish*] *v/t* and *i* make a whistling sound by

cutting through the air; (*coll*) thrash with birch, cane *etc*; pass through the air with a swish ~ **swish.** *n* whistling sound or movement; stroke with a birch ~ **swish** *adj* (*coll*) smart.

Swiss [*swis*] *n* and *adj* (inhabitant) of Switzerland; **S. bun** iced bun; **S. roll** sponge cake rolled with jam filling.

switch [*swich*] *n* device to make or break electric contact, device to turn electric apparatus on or off; device for transferring a railway train on to another line; complete and unexpected change; small flexible twig or rod; tress of false hair ~ **switch** *v/t* and *i* transfer railway train to another line; divert, transfer; change unexpectedly; change activities or opinions; turn (electric apparatus) on or off; twitch, flick; exchange; **switched on** (*coll*) up-to-date, trendy; stimulated by drugs.

switchback [*swich*bak] *n* railway track rising and falling in steep artificial slopes, as amusement in fairs *etc*; (*fig*) series of violent changes of pace or direction; zigzag railway for steep slopes.

switchboard [*swich*bawrd] *n* board with many electrical switches controlling various circuits, *esp* of telephones.

switchman [*swich*man] *n* railway pointsman.

switch-over [*swich*-Over] *n* act of changing completely from one activity, function, opinion *etc* to another.

swivel [*swiv*'l] *n* link consisting of ring and pivot to allow two parts to revolve independently ~ **swivel** (*pres/part* **swivelling**, *p/t* and *p/part* **swivelled**) *v/t* and *i* move on a pivot; revolve easily.

swivel-eye [*swiv*'l-I] *n* eye that rolls in its socket; squinting eye.

swivel-gun [*swiv*'l-gun] *n* gun mounted on a pivot.

swiz [*swiz*] *n* (*coll*) bitter disappointment; deception, fraud.

swizzle [*swiz*'l] *n* (*coll*) swindle; disappointment; mixed drink.

swizzle-stick [*swiz*'l-stik] *n* stick or glass rod for mixing drinks.

swollen [*swOl*en] *p/part* of **swell**.

swollen-headed [*swOl*en-hedid] *adj* conceited, proud of oneself.

swoon [*swOOn*] *v/i* lose consciousness, faint ~ **swoon** *n* fainting fit.

swoop [*swOOp*] *v/i* descend steeply and powerfully through the air, *esp* to attack or seize; attack suddenly, raid ~ **swoop** *n* act of swooping; sudden attack or raid; pounce; **at one fell s.** in one destructive onslaught, all at once.

swop see **swap**.

sword [*sawrd*] *n* weapon consisting of a long keen-edged blade fixed in a hilt; (*fig*) military power; war; **cross swords** engage in hostilities, be at enmity; **put to the s.** slaughter.

swordarm [*sawrd*aarm] *n* right arm.

swordbelt [*sawrd*belt] *n* belt from which a sword is hung at the side.

sword-dance [*sawrd*-daans] *n* Highland dance performed over two swords laid crosswise on the floor; dance in which swords or sticks are clashed together or interwoven.

swordfish [*sawrd*fish] *n* fish with a long sharp upper jaw.

sword-guard [*sawrd*-gaard] *n* part of hilt which protects the hand.

sword-knot [*sawrd*-not] *n* tassel or loop on hilt of sword.

swordplay [*sawrd*play] *n* fencing.

swordsman (*pl* **swordsmen**) [*sawrdz*man] *n* one skilled in fighting with a sword.

swordsmanship [*sawrdz*manship] *n* skill in use of the sword.

swordstick [*sawrd*stick] *n* thin sword enclosed in a walking-stick.

swore [*swawr*] *p/t* of **swear**.

sworn [*swawrn*] *p/part* of **swear** ~ **sworn** *adj* bound or joined by solemn promise.

swot (*pres/part* **swotting**, *p/t* and *p/part* **swotted**) [*swot*] *v/i* and *t* (*coll*) study hard; **s. up** make great efforts to learn or memorize ~ **swot** *n* (*coll*) one who studies hard; one who prefers studying to sport.

swound [*swownd*] *n* (*ar*) swoon.

swum [*swum*] *p/part* of **swim**.

swung [*swung*] *p/p* and *p/part* of **swing**.

sybarite [*siba*Rlt] *n* one who is too fond of luxurious comfort; one who lives in expensive luxury ~ **sybarite** *adj* effeminately luxurious.

sybaritic [*siba*Ritik] *adj* of or like a sybarite ~ **sybaritically** *adv*.

sybaritism [*siba*Ritism] *n* sybaritic habits.

sycamore [*sika*mawr] *n* species of maple; Egyptian species of fig-tree.

syce [*sIs*] *n* native groom in India.

sycee [*sIsee*] *n* pure silver in small ingots.

sycomore [*siko*mawr] *n* Egyptian species of fig-tree; sycamore.

sycophant [*sikO*fant] *n* obsequious flatterer.

sycophantic [*sikO*fantik] *adj* of or like a sycophant.

syllabary [*sila*beRi] *n* list of symbols representing syllables.

syllabic [*sila*bik] *adj* of, in, having or forming a syllable or syllables; with each syllable distinctly articulated ~ **syllabically** *adv*.

syllabicate [*sila*bikayt] *v/t* form into syllables.

syllabify [*sila*bifI] *v/t* pronounce as a separate syllable.

syllable [*sila*b'l] *n* speech-sound or group of sounds containing one vowel pronounced as a unit and forming a word or part of a word; (*fig*) word ~ **syllable** *v/t* pronounce by syllables.

syllabub [*sila*bub] *n* sillabub.

syllabus (*pl* **syllabuses**) [*sila*bus] *n* summary or outline of a course of studies; subjects to be studied in a particular course; (*RC*) list of heresies and condemned beliefs.

syllogism [*silo*jizm] *n* (*log*) form of argument in which a conclusion is deduced from two propositions.

syllogistic [*silo*jistik] *adj* of, by or like a syllogism ~ **syllogistically** *adv*.

syllogize [*silo*jIz] *v/i* and *t* reason by syllogisms; express as a syllogism.

sylph [*silf*] *n* (*myth*) spirit of the air; (*fig*) slim graceful woman; type of humming bird.

sylvan, silvan [*silvan*] *adj* of or in woods; rustic.

sylviculture [*silvi*kulcher] *n* forestry.

sylvine [*silvIn*] *n* natural potassium chloride.

sym- *pref* together.

symbion [*simbI*-on] *n* (*biol*) organism living in symbiosis.

symbiosis [*simbI*-Osis] *n* (*biol*) association of dissimilar organisms to their mutual advantage > PDB; (*fig*) helpful interdependence.

symbiotic [*simbI*-otik] *adj* living in symbiosis.

symbol [*simbol*] *n* any object, design, sign, act *etc* conventionally accepted as representing some person, abstract idea or quality *etc*; letter, figure, sign *etc* used to express a sound, a mathematical quantity or process, a chemical element *etc*; (*psych*) indirect representation of unconscious material > PDP.

symbolic [*simbolik*] *adj* of, as or using a symbol; representative.

symbolical [*simbolikal*] *adj* of, as or using a symbol; representative ~ **symbolically** *adv*.

symbolism [*simbolizm*] *n* representation by symbols; system of symbols; act of symbolizing; French literary movement aiming to suggest rather than depict reality ~ **symbolist** *adj* and *n*.

symbolization [*simbol*Iz*ay*shon] *n* act of symbolizing; state of being symbolized.

symbolize [*simbol*Iz] *v/t* be a symbol of; typify; represent by symbols; treat as symbolic; use symbols.

symmetric [*simet*Rik] *adj* symmetrical.

symmetrical [*simet*Rikal] *adj* having symmetry; having both sides exactly alike; harmoniously proportioned ~ **symmetrically** *adv*.

symmetrize [*simet*RIz] *v/t* make or arrange in symmetry.

symmetry [*simet*Ri] *n* exact correspondence of size, shape *etc* between opposite sides of a structure or object; harmony of proportion; balance, regularity between parts.

sympathetic [*simpa*thetik] *adj* of, feeling or showing sympathy; sharing similar feelings, outlook *etc*, congenial; due to indirectly transmitted stimulus; **s. ink** ink that only becomes visible when exposed to heat; **s. magic** magic based on similarity between the object or process used and the aim to be achieved; **s. nervous system** chain of ganglions > PDB, PDP ~ **sympathetically** *adv*.

sympathize [*simpath*Iz] *v/i* feel or express sympathy with another; have the same or similar feelings, outlook *etc*.

sympathizer [*simpath*Izer] *n* one who sympathizes; one who supports the aims of a political or social movement without being a member of it.

sympathy [*simpathi*] *n* capacity for sharing the feelings of another; pity, compassion; agreement in feelings, ideas *etc* between two or more persons; expression of condolence or consolation; effect of stimulus on one part, organ, body *etc* transmitted to another.

symphonic [*simfonik*] *adj* of or like a symphony; **s. poem** orchestral work of similar length to a symphony but interpreting some non-musical subject ~ **symphonically** *adv*.

symphony [*simfoni*] *n* large-scale composition in several movements for an orchestra > PDM; (*ar*) harmony of sounds; (*fig*) harmony; **s. orchestra** orchestra numerous enough to play symphonies.

symphysis [*simfisis*] *n* close union between two bones or between bone and cartilage > PDB.

symposium [*simp*Ozi-um] *n* philosophic, scholarly, or scientific discussion between several speakers; book of essays presenting opinions of various writers on a topic; (*Gk hist*) drinking-party, feast.

symptom [*simp*tom] *n* any change or abnormality in physical or mental condition due to and revealing the presence of a disease or disorder; outward sign, token, indication..

symptomatic [simptOmatik] *adj* of or as a symptom; indicating disease, disorder, abnormality *etc* ~ **symptomatically** *adv*.

symptomatology [simptomatoloji] *n* study of symptoms of diseases.

syn- *pref* together; joined, combined.

synaeresis [sineerRisis] *n* (*gramm*) contraction of two vowels or syllables into one.

synaesthesia [sinestheesi-a] *n* (*med*) sensation in one part of body caused by stimulus elsewhere.

synagogue [sinagog] *n* building or meeting-place for Jewish religious ceremonies and instruction; religious gathering of Jews.

synalgia [sinalji-a] *n* (*med*) sympathetic pain.

synapse [sinaps] *n* point of contact between two nerve-cells > PDB.

syncarp [sinkaarp] *n* (*bot*) compound fruit.

synchroflash [*sing*-kROflash] *n* device on a camera to fire a flashlight and open the shutter simultaneously.

synchromesh [*sing*-kROmesh] *n* (*mot*) device ensuring that gears are rotating at the same speed when brought into contact.

synchronism [*sing*-kRonizm] *n* simultaneousness; table of historical events showing which occurred simultaneously.

synchronistic [sing-kRonistik] *adj* synchronous.

synchronization [sing-kROnIzayshon] *n* simultaneous occurrence; act of synchronizing; state of being synchronized.

synchronize [*sing*-kRonIz] *v/t* and *i* cause to happen at the same pace; keep time or cause to keep time (with); regulate (clocks) so as all to show the same time; occur at the same pace; occur or exist at the same time; (*cin*) cause recorded sound-effects to coincide with filmed actions.

synchronous [*sing*-kRonus] *adj* happening at the same pace; existing at the same time ~ **synchronously** *adv*.

synchrotron [*sing*-kRotRon] *n* apparatus for accelerating electrons > PDS, PDEl.

syncopate [*sing*-kOpayt] *v/t* and *i* (*mus*) transfer the accent to a normally unaccented beat > PDM; play in syncopated rhythm; (*gramm*) contract by omitting a medial letter or syllable.

syncopation [sing-kOpayshon] *n* act of syncopating; state of being syncopated.

syncope [*sing*-kOpi] *n* (*med*) fainting-fit; (*gramm*) syncopation.

syncretic [sing-kReetik] *adj* of syncretism.

syncretism [*sing*-kRetizm] *n* an attempt to blend different philosophic or religious schools of thought into one; process of thinking in which ideas are connected by accidental association, not by logic.

syncretize [*sing*-kRetIz] *v/t* and *i* try to reconcile and harmonize (differing schools of thought).

syndetic [sindetik] *adj* (*gramm*) of or as a conjunction.

syndic [*sin*dik] *n* administrative official, *esp* chief magistrate; member of a special committee of the senate in Cambridge University.

syndicalism [*sin*dikalizm] *n* economic theory that industries should be owned and controlled by the workers > PDPol; militant trade unionism.

syndicate [*sin*dikat] *n* group of business associates combining to finance a commercial project, *esp* the formation of a limited liability company; organization that sells articles *etc* for simultaneous publication in various newspapers; group of syndics; council, senate ~ **syndicate** [*sin*dikayt] *v/t* and *i* form into a syndicate; publish simultaneously in various papers.

syndrome [*sin*drOm] *n* (*med*) combination of various symptoms of a disease; (*fig*) patterns of behaviour, opinions *etc* regarded as typical of a particular type of person.

syne [sIn] *adv* (*Scots*) since; long ago.

synecdoche [sinekdoki] *n* (*rhet*) figure of speech in which a whole is put for a part, or a part for a whole.

synergic [sinurjik] *adj* acting together, co-operating.

synergism [sinerjizm] *n* (*theol*) doctrine that human will cooperates with divine grace; (*biol*) combined activity of separate agencies such that the total effect is greater than the sum of effects of each agency alone > PDB.

synergy [sinerji] *n* combined action; cooperation; (*comm*) merger of companies such that their combined assets are worth more than their sum when separate.

synod [sinod] *n* ecclesiastical council; meeting for discussion; **General S.** governing body of the Church of England.

synodal [sinodal] *adj* of, by or as a synod.

synodic [sinodik] *adj* of, by or as a synod.

synodical [sinodikal] *adj* synodic ~ **synodically** *adv*.

synonym [sinonim] *n* word having exactly the same meaning as another in the same language; word denoting the same object or concept as another but having different connotations or implications.

synonymity [sinonimiti] *n* state of being synonymous.

synonymous [sinonimus] *adj* having the same or similar meaning; being a synonym ~ **synonymously** *adv*.

synonymy [sinonimi] *n* state of being synonymous.

synopsis (*pl* synopses) [sinopsis] *n* general view; summary; outline of plot of book, play, film *etc*.

synoptic [sinoptik] *adj* of, being or containing a synopsis; of the synoptic gospels; **s. gospels** (*NT*) the gospels of Matthew, Mark and Luke ~ **synoptic** *n* author of a synoptic gospel ~ **synoptically** *adv*.

synoptist [sinoptist] *n* one of the writers of the synoptic gospels.

synovia [sinOvi-a] *n* albuminous fluid secreted into joints to lubricate them.

synovial [sinOvi-al] *adj* of or secreting synovia.

synovitis [sInOvItis] *n* inflammation of a synovial membrane.

syntactic [sintaktik] *adj* of or according to syntax ~ **syntactically** *adv*.

syntax [*sin*taks] *n* (*gramm*) rules and conventions regulating the order and relationships of words in a sentence; branch of grammar concerning this.

synthesis (*pl* **syntheses**) [*sin*thesis] *n* combination of separate things or concepts to form a complex whole; process of re-combining what has been analysed; (*chem*) formation of a compound from elements or simpler compounds; (*surg*) re-union of dissected parts; (*gramm*) inflexional formation of words.

synthesize [*sin*thesIz] *v/t* and *i* combine, put together; produce imitations of natural products by chemical means.

synthetic [sin*thet*ik] *adj* of or by synthesis; produced by chemical synthesis, not by natural processes; of or as artificial substitute for a natural product; (*coll*) insincere, unreal, bogus ~ **synthetic** *n* synthetic substance.

synthetical [sin*thet*ikal] *adj* synthetic ~ **synthetically** *adv*.

synthetize [*sin*thetIz] *v/t* and *i* synthesize.

syntonic [sin*ton*ik] *adj* (*rad*) tuned to the same wavelength.

syntonize [*sin*tonIz] *v/t* tune (a wireless set).

syphilis [*sif*ilis] *n* an infectious venereal disease.

syphilitic [sifi*lit*ik] *adj* of, caused by, or infected with, syphilis ~ **syphilitic** *n* person suffering from syphilis.

syphiloid [*sif*iloid] *adj* resembling syphilis.

syphon [*sI*fon] *n* siphon.

syringa [si*Ring*-ga] *n* a sweet-scented flowering tree, mock-orange; (*bot*) genus of plants containing the lilacs.

syringe [si*Rinj*] *n* pipe with piston or bulb to draw in liquid by suction and eject it in a stream or spray; **hypodermic s.** small syringe with needle for giving injections ~ **syringe** *v/t* spray or cleanse with a syringe.

syringitis [siRinj*I*tis] *n* inflammation of the eustachian tube.

syrinx [*si*Rinks] *n* panpipe; organ of song in birds; (*anat*) eustachian tube; lower part of larynx; (*surg*) fistula.

syrup [*si*Rup] *n* strong solution of sugar and water or of sugar and fruit-juice; treacle; (*coll*) cloying sentimental sweetness; **golden s.** yellow syrup extracted from sugarcane.

syrupy [*si*Rupi] *adj* of, like or containing syrup; (*coll*) cloying, sentimentally sweet.

systaltic [sis*tal*tik] *adj* alternately contracting and dilating.

system [*sis*tem] *n* group of objects related or interacting so as to form a unity; methodically arranged set of ideas, principles, methods, procedures *etc*; classification; plan; the body as a healthily functioning organism; health.

systematic [siste*mat*ik] *adj* of, having or based on a system; methodical; formed or done according to a regular plan ~ **systematically** *adv*.

systematization [sistematIz*ay*shon] *n* act or process of systematizing; state of being systematized.

systematize [*sis*tematIz] *v/t* arrange according to system or regular method.

systemization [sistemIz*ay*shon] *n* act or process of systematizing; state of being systematized.

systole [*sis*tOli] *n* periodic contraction of heart and arteries to pump the blood outwards.

systolic [sis*tol*ik] *adj* of the systole.

systyle [*sis*tIl] *n* and *adj* (*archi*) (building) with columns placed with a distance of two diameters between them.

syzygy [*si*ziji] *n* (*astron*) conjunction or opposition of two heavenly bodies > PDG.

T

t [*tee*] twentieth letter of the English alphabet; **to a t.** exactly; **T.B.** tuberculosis; **T.N.T.** a powerful high explosive, trinitrotoluene > PDS; **t.t.** teetotal; **T.V.** television.

ta [*taa*] *interj* (*coll*) thank you.

taal [*taal*] *n* Dutch dialect spoken in South Africa.

tab [*tab*] *n* small tag, flap, strap, or strip of cloth; **keep tabs on** keep track of, keep close watch on ~ **tab** (*pres/part* **tabbing,** *p/t* and *p/part* **tabbed**) *v/t* fix a tab to.

tabard [*tabard*] *n* sleeveless coat worn by heralds; (*hist*) sleeveless military tunic.

tabasco [*tabaskO*] *n* a type of peppery sauce.

tabby [*tabi*] *n* grey or brownish cat with darker markings; female cat; spiteful gossiping woman; coarse watered silk ~ **tabby** *adj* with dark stripes and markings brindled.

tabefaction [*tabifakshon*] *n* wasting away from disease.

tabernacle [*tabernak'l*] *n* (*OT*) tent or movable shelter used as temple by the Israelites in their nomadic period; (*eccles*) small cupboard or chest placed on an altar to contain the Eucharistic hosts; (*fig*) shrine, temple; chapel, place of worship; (*archi*) canopied niche; **t. work** (*archi*) series of ornamental canopies.

tabernacular [*tabernakewlar*] *adj* of or like a tabernacle; (*archi*) having light tracery.

tabes [*taybeez*] *n* (*path*) wasting away of tissues due to disease; **t. dorsalis** locomotor ataxia.

tabetic [*tabetik*] *n* and *adj* (person) suffering from tabes.

table [*tayb'l*] *n* piece of furniture with flat top supported on legs at a convenient height for use by a seated person; tablet, inscribed slab; systematic list of figures, names *etc*; index, catalogue; (*math*) list of numbers to be learnt as aids to calculation; list of weights, measures *etc*; (*geog*) plateau; group of persons seated round a table, *esp* to eat; meal, food; (*pl*) backgammon; **at t.** during meals; eating a meal; **lay on the t.** propose, submit for discussion; postpone indefinitely; **the Lord's T.** the Eucharist; **the Round T.** legendary society of knights supposed to be founded by King Arthur; **turn the tables on** retaliate, regain advantage over ~ **table** *v/t* submit for discussion, propose; postpone indefinitely; tabulate; enter into a list, catalogue *etc*.

tableau [*tablO*] *n* group of persons in costume posed motionlessly to represent a well-known historical scene, picture *etc*; dramatically effective grouping of actors *etc*.

tablebook [*tayb'l-book*] *n* book of mathematical tables.

tablecloth [*tayb'l-kloth*] *n* cloth spread over a table, *esp* at meals.

tablecut [*tayb'lkut*] *adj* (*of diamond etc*) cut with a flat face.

table-d'hôte [*taabl'-dOt*] *n* (*Fr*) restaurant meal served at a fixed price.

tableland [*tayb'l-land*] *n* (*geog*) plateau.

table-manners [*tayb'l-manerz*] *n* (*pl*) social manners as shown in behaviour at meals.

tablemat [*tayb'lmat*] *n* mat of cork, thick cloth, wood *etc* placed under hot dishes on a table.

table-napkin [*tayb'l-napkin*] *n* small square of linen or paper for wiping fingers or mouth after eating.

tablespoon [*tayb'l-spOOn*] *n* largest size of spoon used in eating or as cooking measure.

tablespoonful [*tayb'l-spOOnfool*] *n* as much as a tablespoon can hold.

tablet [*tablit*] *n* small flat piece of hard material for writing on; small slab bearing an inscription; small flat medical pill; small flat sweet.

tabletalk [*tayb'l-tawk*] *n* talk during meals; familiar conversation.

table-tennis [*tayb'l-tenis*] *n* a form of tennis played indoors on a table with wooden bats and a celluloid ball.

table-turning [*tayb'l-turning*] *n* movement of tables attributed to spiritualistic power.

tableware [*tayb'l-wair*] *n* crockery used at table for meals.

tabloid [*tabloid*] *n* (*tr*) medicinal tablet;(*fig*) newspaper presenting facts in concentrated simplified form; **in t. form** concentrated ~ **tabloid** *adj* of or like tabloids; compressed; concentrated and simplified.

taboo, tabu [*tabOO*] *n* religious or magical rule forbidding any mention of, or contact with, a person or object considered either as sacred or as accursed, unclean *etc*; strong social custom forbidding an act or the mention of certain topics > PDP ~ **taboo** *adj* too sacred or too accursed or evil to be touched, mentioned, or used; forbidden by strong social convention; banned, prohibited; (*coll*) never to be mentioned or done ~ **taboo** *v/t* forbid by taboo.

tabor [*taybor*] *n* small drum beaten with hand.

tabouret [*taboRit*] *n* small stool; embroidery frame.

tabu see **taboo.**

tabular [*tabewlar*] *adj* arranged in a systematic list; having a broad, flat surface ~ **tabularly** *adv*.

tabulate [*tabewlayt*] *v/t* arrange in lists or tables; give a flat surface to.

tachisme [*tashizm*] *n* technique of producing abstract paintings by splashing or dribbling paint on canvas > PDAA ~ **tachiste** *n* and *adj*.

tachograph [*takOgRaaf*] *n* instrument in a motor vehicle that automatically records its speed and time spent in motion.

tachometer [*takomiter*] *n* instrument which measures velocity; instrument for measuring rate of revolution of an engine or shaft.

tachycardia [*takikaardi-a*] *n* (*med*) too rapid beating of the heart.

tacit [*tasit*] *adj* implied but not openly expressed, expressed only through silence ~ **tacitly** *adv*.

taciturn [*tasiturn*] *adj* speaking little; habitually silent or reserved.

taciturnity [*tasiturniti*] *n* quality of being taciturn.

taciturnly [*tas*iturnli] *adv* in a taciturn way.

tack [*tak*] *n* small broad-headed nail; long loose stitch for temporary fastening in sewing; (*naut*) ship's course, *esp* in relation to wind direction; lower fore-corner of sail; rope fastening this; (*fig*) course of action; (*sl*) food; **hard t.** ship's biscuits. **get down to brass tacks** (*coll*) face basic facts or tasks ~ **tack** *v/t* and *i* fasten with tacks; sew with long loose stitches; (*of ship*) change course obliquely through the wind > PDSa; (*fig*) change course; **t. on** fix loosely; (*fig*) add as an afterthought, append.

tackily [*tak*ili] *adv* stickily.

tackiness [*tak*inis] *n* stickiness.

tacking [*tak*ing] *n* act of one who tacks; series of long loose stitches; **t. thread** soft cotton used in tacking.

tackle [*tak'l*] *v/t* and *i* attempt to deal with, accomplish or solve; set to work at; confront boldly, challenge; grip, grasp; grapple with; (*football*) seize (opponent) so as to get the ball away from him ~ **tackle** *n* gear, equipment; system of ropes and pulleys > PDSa; rigging; act or method of tackling at football.

tackling [*tak*ling] *n* act of one who tackles; rigging of a ship.

tacky [*tak*i] *adj* sticky.

tact [*takt*] *n* skill in dealing with painful or embarrassing topics and situations without offending or hurting others; quick, instinctive ability to say or do the right thing, *esp* in social relationships.

tactful [*takt*fool] *adj* having tact; showing tact ~ **tactfully** *adv* ~ **tactfulness** *n*.

tactical [*takt*ikal] *adj* of, by or for tactics; skilful ~ **tactically** *adv*.

tactician [*takt*ishan] *n* one who is skilled in tactics.

tactics [*takt*iks] *n* (*pl*) art of manoeuvring military forces in battle; method of outwitting an opponent or rival, or of tackling a difficult situation.

tactile [*takt*Il] *adj* of, by or affecting the sense of touch; tangible.

tactility [takt*ili*ti] *n* quality of being tactile.

tactless [*takt*lis] *adj* having no tact; accidentally offensive ~ **tactlessly** *adv* ~ **tactlessness** *n*.

tactual [*takt*ew-al] *adj* tactile.

tadpole [*tad*pOl] *n* young frog, toad *etc*, still having gills and tail.

ta'en [*tayn*] *contr* (*poet* and *dial*) taken.

taffeta [*taf*ita] *n* silk fabric with wavy lustre.

taffrail [*taf*kil] *n* rail round stern of ship.

Taffy (1) [*taf*i] *n* (*coll*) Welshman.

taffy (2) *n* (*US*) toffee.

tag [*tag*] *n* small metal tip on shoelace *etc*; loop or flap at back of boot; hanging flap or shred; hackneyed quotation, cliché; short refrain; catchword; children's game of chasing and touching others; tip of animal's tail ~ **tag** (*pres/part* **tagging**, *p/t* and *p/part* **tagged**) *v/t* fix a tag to; (*coll*) follow closely; **t. along** (*coll*) go with, follow; **t. around with** (*coll*) be constant companion of; **t. on** add as afterthought; append, affix.

taiga [*tI*ga] *n* northern coniferous forest belt.

tail (1) [*tayl*] *n* any bony structure, feathers, fins *etc* forming a distinct part projecting beyond the rear of an animal's body; anything resembling this; rear end of anything; hindmost or lowest part; any long trailing object; (*vulg coll*) penis;

female pudenda; (*coll*) one who tails another; (*pl*) reverse side of coin; (*pl*, *coll*) tailcoat; **turn t.** run away ~ **tail** *v/t* and *i* follow (a person) closely to keep watch on him; remove a tail from; fix a tail to; **t. away, t. off** dwindle, gradually decrease; straggle; deteriorate gradually.

tail (2) *n* (*leg*) limitation of an estate to certain heirs.

tailboard [*tayl*bawrd] *n* board at back of wagon or cart; hinged board closing back of lorry.

tailcoat [*tayl*kOt] *n* man's formal jacket with long divided hanging panel behind.

tailed [*tayl*d] *adj* having a tail.

tail-end [*tayl*-end] *n* hindmost or last part.

tailing [*tay*ling] *n* act of one who tails; part of brick or stone which is put into a wall.

tail-lamp [tayl-lamp] *n* tail-light.

tail-light [*tayl*-lIt] *n* red warning light at rear end of vehicle.

tailor [*tay*ler] *n* one who makes outer clothing, *esp* for men; one who sells men's suits, coats *etc* ~ **tailor** *v/t* and *i* make (cloth) into outer clothing; make clothes for; work as tailor; (*fig*) cause to fit exactly, adapt to the personal needs of.

tailor-bird [*tay*ler-burd] *n* Asiatic bird which sews leaves together to make a nest.

tailoring [*tay*leRing] *n* work of a tailor; style in which a garment is tailored.

tailormade [*tay*lermayd] *adj* individually made, not ready made; (*of women's clothes*) in plain semi-masculine style; (*fig*) precisely adapted to suit a particular need.

tailpiece [*tayl*pees] *n* design placed at end of section in book; (*fig*) postscript, final remark or item.

tailpipe [*tayl*pIp] *n* suction-pipe of pump; exhaust pipe.

tailrace [*tayl*Rays] *n* channel of water below a water-wheel.

tails [*tayl*z] *n* (*pl*) (*coll*) tailcoat; dress-suit.

tailspin [*tayl*spin] *n* (*aer*) type of spinning dive; (*fig*) panic.

taint [*taynt*] *n* trace of dirt, infection, or decay; moral degeneration, disgrace ~ **taint** *v/t* and *i* infect with decay; pollute, corrupt; become infected or polluted.

take (*p/t* **took**, *p/part* **taken**) [*tayk*] *v/t* and *i* catch hold of, seize; remove; carry; win, capture; obtain, gain; earn; use, consume; eat, drink; inhale; be infected by, catch; choose; need; assume; be big enough to contain; understand; experience; rent; engage, hire; be effective; be popular; succeed; photograph; record; (*coll*) endure, accept, tolerate; (*gramm*) be followed by; be inflected with; **t. aback** disconcert, startle; **t. after** resemble, *esp* by heredity; **t. back** retract; **t. care** be cautious; **t. down** write down from dictation; remove by lifting down; lower, let down; **t. for** believe to be; **t. for granted** assume unquestioningly; **t. from** reduce; **t. hold** grasp; acquire power over; **t. in** comprise, include; admit to one's home, welcome; understand; receive, subscribe to; deceive, trick, impose on; make narrower; **t. into one's head** suddenly think or decide; **t. off** remove, *esp* from the body; imitate mockingly, mimic; (*of aircraft*) leave the ground; fly or leap up from the ground; subtract; **t. on** undertake; accept as opponent, challenge; hire, employ; (*coll*) show agitation or distress; **t. oneself off** go away; **t. out** extract; escort to entertainments; accompany; obtain (licence, insurance *etc*); (*mil sl*) destroy by bombing; **t. it out of** exhaust, tire out; **t. it out on** vent (anger *etc*) on, relieve one's anger by attacking; **t. over** assume control of; **t. place** happen; **t. to** be attracted by; form habit (of); **t. to heart** feel deeply; **t. up** pick up, raise; occupy, absorb; return to, resume; engage in as occupation, hobby *etc*; arrest; turn attention to; patronize; **t. up with** associate with; **t. upon oneself** assume responsibility for; undertake ∼ **take** *n* amount taken; (*cin*) the photographing of one scene; (*print*) portion of copy allotted to a compositor.

take-away [*tayk*-away] *n* and *adj* (*coll*) (shop) selling hot foods in containers to be taken away and eaten elsewhere.

take-in [*tayk*-in] *n* fraud, deception.

taken [*tayk*'n] *p*/*part* of **take**.

take-off [*tayk*-of] *n* mocking imitation, mimicry, caricature; act of leaving the ground, *esp* of aircraft; way of disposing the feet when leaving the ground in jumping.

take-over [*tayk*-Over] *n* act of assuming control, *esp* of a commercial company.

taker [*tayk*er] *n* one who or that which takes; one who accepts a bet.

take-up [*tayk*-up] *n* action of drawing together or gathering material.

taking (1) [*tayk*ing] *n* capture; (*coll*) fuss, distress; (*pl*) that which is taken, receipts, gains.

taking (2) *adj* attractive, captivating ∼ **takingly** *adv*.

talc [*talk*] *n* hydrated magnesium silicate > PDS; powder of this, talcum; mica.

talcum [*talk*um] *n* powdered talc, French chalk.

tale [*tayl*] *n* account, story, narrative; fable; rumour, report; (*ar*) total, reckoning; **tell tales** report maliciously; give away a secret.

talebearer [*tayl*bairRer] *n* one who maliciously reports another's misdeeds or secrets.

talent [*tal*ent] *n* special skill, faculty, or aptitude; high mental or artistic ability; (*hist*) ancient weight and monetary unit.

talented [*tal*entid] *adj* possessing high ability.

taleteller [*tayl*teler] *n* talebearer; storyteller.

talion [*tal*i-on] *n* principle or law of punishing an injury by inflicting a similar injury.

taliped [*tal*iped] *adj* club-footed.

talipes [*tal*ipeez] *n* club-foot; club-footedness.

talisman [*tal*izman] *n* any object believed to have magic protective power, lucky charm.

talismanic [taliz*man*ik] *adj* of or like a talisman.

talk [*tawk*] *v*/*i* and *t* speak, express in speech; converse; discuss; gossip; disclose information; **t. at** aim remarks at; **t. back** reply defiantly; **t. big** boast; **t. down** silence by loud or eloquent talk; give (aircraft) instructions for landing; **t. down to** address in condescendingly simple language; **t. into** persuade, convince; **t. of** discuss; suggest, propose; **t. over** discuss; persuade to agree; **t. round** discuss without reaching the point; persuade to agree; **t. to** scold, reprove ∼ **talk** *n* act of talking; conversation; discussion; informal lecture, *esp* broadcast; rumour, gossip.

talkative [*tawk*ativ] *adj* chatty, inclined to talk ∼ **talkatively** *adv* ∼ **talkativeness** *n*.

talker [*tawk*er] *n* one who talks; one who is inclined to talk a great deal; lecturer, speaker; conversationalist.

talkie [*tawk*i] *n* (*coll*) cinema film synchronized with sound.

talking [*tawk*ing] *n* act of speaking ∼ **talking** *adj* that talks; expressive.

talking-point [*tawk*ing-point] *n* topic likely to rouse discussion; topic or argument likely to convince or persuade.

talking-to [*tawk*ing-tOO] *n* (*coll*) scolding, reprimand.

tall [*tawl*] *adj* high in stature; lofty; of a particular height; (*coll*) extravagant, unlikely; very large or great; **t. order** task hard to accomplish; **t. story** very unlikely story ∼ **tall** *adv* (*sl*) boastfully.

tallboy [*tawl*boi] *n* tall chest of drawers.

tallness [*tawl*nis] *n* quality of being tall.

tallow [*tal*O] *n* melted animal fat, used for candles or lubrication ∼ **tallow** *v*/*t* grease with tallow; fatten.

tallow-chandler [tal*O*-*chaand*ler] *n* one who makes or sells tallow candles.

tallow-faced [*tal*O-fayst] *adj* having a pale, yellowish face.

tally [*tal*i] *n* piece of wood marked with notches to indicate sums of money owed *etc*; reckoning, account; score; act of keeping count or reckoning; duplicated account; tag, label ∼ **tally** *v*/*i* and *t* correspond exactly, agree in number; conform, agree; record or reckon on a tally.

tally-ho [tali-*hO*] *n* cry of huntsman when fox is seen.

tallyman (*pl* **tallymen**) [*tal*iman] *n* salesman who sells goods, *usu* of poor quality, on hire-purchase; one who keeps a tally-shop.

tally-shop [*tal*i-shop] *n* shop where goods are sold on hire-purchase.

talmi-gold [*tal*mi-gOld] *n* brass alloy plated with gold.

Talmud [*tal*mud] *n* code of Jewish civil and religious law.

Talmudist [*tal*mudist] *n* one of the authors of the Talmud; one learned in the Talmud; one who follows the Talmud.

talon [*tal*on] *n* claw of bird of prey; long fingernail; (*archi*) ogee moulding.

taloned [*tal*ond] *adj* having talons.

talus [*tayl*us] *n* (*anat*) anklebone; (*geol*) scree.

tamable [*taym*ab'l] *adj* capable of being tamed.

tamarack [*tam*aRak] *n* American larch.

tamarisk [*tam*aRisk] *n* Mediterranean evergreen shrub or tree.

tambour [*tam*boor] *n* drum, *esp* bass drum; circular embroidery frame; (*archi*) cylindrical stone of a column.

tambourine [tambo*Reen*] *n* very small shallow drum with tinkling disks attached > PDM.

tame [*taym*] *adj* brought under control so that wildness is overcome; domesticated; submissive, gentle; spiritless, dull ∼ **tame** *v*/*t* make tame, domesticate; curb.

tameless [*taym*les] *adj* (*poet*) wild, untamable.

tamely [*taym*li] *adv* in a tame way; passively, submissively.

tameness [*taym*nis] *n* quality of being tame.

Tamil [*tam*il] *n* a Dravidian language spoken in South India and Ceylon.

tamis [*tami*] *n* cloth sieve.

tammy [*tami*] *n* (*coll*) tam-o'-shanter.

tam-o'-shanter [tam-o-*shanter*] *n* broad woollen bonnet.

tamp [*tamp*] *v/t* block up with clay or sand; ram down.

tamper [*tamper*] *v/i* **t. with** interfere with, alter fraudulently or harmfully.

tamping [*tamping*] *n* act of ramming down a charge of explosive; plug used for this.

tampion [*tampi*-on] *n* stopper for mouth of gun.

tampon [*tampon*] *n* plug of lint to stop bleeding; absorbent plug worn during menstruation.

tamponade [*tamponayd*] *n* (*surg*) use of a tampon.

tan (1) [*tan*] *n* brownish colour given to the skin by sunburning; golden brown; bark used in tanning ~ **tan** (*pres/part* **tanning**, *p/t* and *p/part* **tanned**) *v/t* and *i* change (hides) to leather by steeping in tannic acid; make or become brown, *esp* by sunburn; (*sl*) flog, beat ~ **tan** *adj* golden-brown.

tan (2) *n* (*abbr*) tangent.

tanagra [*tanagra*] *n* type of ancient Greek terracotta statuettes.

tandem [*tandem*] *n* bicycle for two riders, one in front of the other; vehicle with two horses, one harnessed in front of the other ~ **tandem** *adv*.

tang (1) [*tang*] *n* strong flavour or smell.

tang (2) *n* point, projecting piece; spike by which blade of knife *etc* is fixed to handle ~ **tang** *v/t* provide or fix with a tang.

tangency [*tanjensi*] *n* state of being a tangent; contact.

tangent [*tanjent*] *n* straight line touching a curve at one point > PDS; (*of an angle*) ratio of the side opposite a given angle in a right angle triangle to the base; **go off at a t.** pursue an irrelevant topic or thought ~ **tangent** *adj*.

tangential [tan*jensh*al] *adj* of or like a tangent.

tangerine [tanje*Reen*] *n* species of small tasty orange.

tangibility [tanji*biliti*] *n* quality of being tangible.

tangible [*tanjib*'l] *adj* that can be touched; (*fig*) that can be defined or realized; clear, not vague ~ **tangibly** *adv*.

tangle [*tang*-g'l] *n* confused interwoven knot or mass of threads, branches *etc*; intricate muddle, confusion; kind of seaweed ~ **tangle** *v/t* form into a tangle; complicate; trap, ensnare; **t. with** (*sl*) come into conflict with; embrace.

tangly [*tang*-gli] *adj* full of tangles; in a tangle.

tango [*tang*-gO] *n* type of South American dance > PDM; music for this ~ **tango** *v/i* dance a tango.

tangy [*tangi*] *adj* possessing a strong flavour.

tanist [*tanist*] *n* elected heir to a Celtic chief.

tank [*tank*] *n* large cistern for holding liquids; container for petrol in motor vehicle, or for water in steam-engine; reservoir; (*mil*) heavily armoured vehicle with caterpillar-tracks and mounted with guns ~ **tank** *v/i*; **t. up** fill the tank of.

tankage [*tankij*] *n* storage in tanks; capacity of a tank; charge for storage in tanks.

tankard [*tankard*] *n* large metal or wooden drinking vessel.

tank-engine [*tank*-enjin] *n* locomotive that carries a water-tank.

tanker [*tanker*] *n* ship which transports oil; lorry adapted for transporting petrol, oil *etc* in bulk.

tank-top [*tank*-top] *n* sleeveless pullover with low scooped neckline.

tan-liquor [*tan*-liker] *n* infusion of bark used for tanning.

tannage [*tanij*] *n* process of tanning hides.

tannate [*tanayt*] *n* a salt of tannic acid.

tanner (1) [*taner*] *n* one who tans hides.

tanner (2) *n* (*coll*) sixpence in pre-decimal currency.

tannery [*taneRi*] *n* place where leather is tanned; process of tanning hides.

tannic [*tanik*] *adj* of or made from tree bark, *esp* of oak; **t. acid** astringent soluble solid used in making leather, ink *etc* > PDS.

tanniferous [tani*feRus*] *adj* yielding tannin.

tannin [*tanin*] *n* tannic acid; any similar astringent substance obtained from vegetable matter.

tanning [*taning*] *n* process of turning animal hides into leather by chemical action of tannin.

Tannoy [*tanoi*] *n* (*tr*) a type of loudspeaker system.

tansy [*tanzi*] *n* perennial herb with small yellow flowers and bitter, aromatic leaves.

tantalization [tantal*Izayshon*] *n* act of tantalizing; state of being tantalized.

tantalize [*tantalIz*] *v/t* torment by displaying some desirable but unattainable object; torment by alternate promises and disappointments.

tantalizing [*tantalIzing*] *adj* that tantalizes ~ **tantalizingly** *adv*.

tantalum [*tantalum*] *n* rare metallic element, used for electric lamp filaments > PDS.

tantalus [*tantalus*] *n* decanter-stand with a locking device; species of ibis.

tantamount [*tantamownt*] *adj* equal in value or in effect, equivalent.

tantrum [*tantRum*] *n* ridiculous outburst of bad temper.

tanyard [*tanyaard*] *n* tannery.

Taoism [*taa*-O-izm] *n* Chinese system of religion founded by Lâo-tze ~ **Taoist** *n* and *adj*.

tap (1) (*pres/part* **tapping**, *p/t* and *p/part* **tapped**) [*tap*] *v/t* and *i* strike lightly and rapidly; touch briefly ~ **tap** *n* light blow; sound of this; gentle touch; small piece of leather for mending shoe soles or heels; (*pl*, *mil*) signal for lights-out.

tap (2) *n* device fitted with screw and valve for checking or releasing flow of liquid from a pipe *etc*; taproom; instrument for cutting internal screw-threads; **on t.** (*of drink*) kept ready stored in a cask; (*coll*) constantly and freely available ~ **tap** (*pres/part* **tapping**, *p/t* and *p/part* **tapped**) *v/t* open up (a cask); pierce and draw liquid from; fit a tap to; (*elect*) connect an external conductor to an existing circuit; (*coll*) draw on unused resources, supplies, potentialities *etc* of; (*sl*) extract money from; **t. a line** (**wire**) fix a receiver to a telephone wire so as secretly to overhear conversations on it.

tapdance [*tap*daans] *n* dance in which heel and toe are tapped in rhythm to syncopated music ~ **tapdance** *v/i* ~ **tapdancer** *n*.

tape [*tayp*] *n* strong strip of woven fabric used for fastening; strip of magnetic material on which sounds can be recorded > PDEl; roll or strip of paper on which messages are recorded by telegraph; band or cord stretched across a racetrack at the finishing line; **red t.** legalistic or bureaucratic formalism, **exaggerated** insistence on routine formalities ~ **tape** v/t bind or fasten with tape; record on magnetic tape; **have (something) taped** (coll) understand thoroughly.

tape-line [tayp-lIn] n tape-measure.

tape-machine [tayp-masheen] n receiving instrument of recording telegraph system.

tape-measure [tayp-mezher] n strip of cloth or flexible metal marked with measures of length.

taper [tayper] v/i and t become or cause to become gradually smaller at one end; **t. off** gradually diminish ~ **taper** n small thin candle; small light; that which tapers.

tape-recorder [tayp-Rikawrder] n apparatus for recording sounds on magnetic tape and for reproducing them > PDEl.

tape-recording [tayp-Rikawrding] n recording made on magnetic tape; process of making this.

tapering [taypeRing] adj growing gradually smaller and thinner at one end.

tapestried [tapistRid] adj hung with tapestry.

tapestry [tapistRi] n textile fabric on to which designs are worked by hand; woven fabric with designs imitating this.

tapeworm [taypwurm] n parasitic flatworm that lives in intestines of vertebrates > PDB.

tapioca [tapi-Oka] n edible starchy substance prepared from cassava roots.

tapir [tayper] n South American mammal with short flexible proboscis.

tapis [tapee] n (Fr) carpet; **on the t.** under discussion.

tappet [tapit] n (mech) projecting arm or lever transmitting motion intermittently.

tapping [taping] n act of one who taps; noise of repeated taps; (surg) act of draining fluid from body.

taproom [tapROOm] n room in public house where barrels are stored and where cheaper drinks are sold.

taproot [tapRoot] n enlarged main root of a plant > PDB.

tapster [tapster] n one who draws liquor from barrels.

tar (1) [taar] n thick black sticky liquid obtained by destructive distillation of coal > PDB, PDE; similar liquid obtained from wood ~ **tar** (pres/ part **tarring**, p/t and p/part **tarred**) v/t cover or smear with tar; **tarred with the same brush** having similar faults.

tar (2) n (coll) sailor.

taradiddle, tarradiddle [taRadid'l] n lie, prevarication.

tarantella [taRantela] n lively Neapolitan dance; music for this > PDM.

tarantism [taRantizm] n (med) hysterical disease causing involuntary dancing.

tarantula [taRantewla] n species of large venomous spider.

taraxacin [taRaksasin] n bitter substance obtained from dandelion root.

tarboosh [taarbOOsh] n Muslim brimless tasselled cap, fez.

tarbrush [taarbRush] n brush for applying tar; **touch of the t.** (coll) slight sign of Negro ancestry.

tardo [taardO] adj and adv (mus) slow.

tardy [taardi] adj moving slowly, slow; late; reluctant ~ **tardily** adv ~ **tardiness** n.

tare (1) [tair] n kind of vetch growing in cornfields.

tare (2) n weight of wrappings in which goods are packed; weight of an unladen goods-vehicle; allowance made for this.

targe [taarj] n (ar) small shield.

target [taargit] n object, person or area at which shots, missiles etc are aimed; object or person being attacked; area to be bombed; objective to be achieved; amount etc to be obtained or produced; round board marked with concentric circles set up to be shot at; (hist) small round shield; **t. area** area in which a target is.

target-practice [taargit-pRaktis] n act of shooting at a target for practice in accurate aiming.

tariff [taRif] n list of duties on imports and exports; rate of duty on imports and exports; list of prices and charges, esp of a hotel ~ **tariff** v/t place on a list of tariffs.

tariff-wall [taRif-wawl] n act of setting high duties on imports to discourage them.

tarlatan [taarlatan] n fine transparent muslin.

tarmac [taarmak] n mixture of tar and macadam used as road surfacing material > PDE; airfield runway made of this ~ **tarmac** v/t.

tar-macadam [taarmakadam] n tarmac.

tarn [taarn] n small lake on moor or among mountains.

tarnish [taarnish] v/t and i diminish the lustre of; spoil by exposure to air; (fig) stain, sully; lose lustre ~ **tarnish** n loss of lustre; stain formed on metal exposed to air.

tarot [taRO/taRot] n pack of 78 cards including 22 trumps, used for fortune-telling; trump of this pack; game played with these.

tarpan [taarpan] n small wild Russian horse.

tarpaulin [taarpawlin] n waterproof cloth or canvas coated with tar; (pl) clothes, hat etc made of this.

tarradiddle see taradiddle.

tarragon [taRagon] n an aromatic herb.

tarry (1) [taRi] v/i (ar) loiter, delay; be late.

tarry (2) [taarRi] adj covered with tar.

tarsal [taarsal] adj of or on the tarsus.

tarsia [taarsi-a] n mosaic of inlaid woodwork.

tarsus [taarsus] n bones of human heel and ankle; shank of bird's leg.

tart (1) [taart] adj bitter, sharp, sour; (fig) sarcastic, sharp-tongued.

tart (2) n small pie containing fruit or jam.

tart (3) n (sl) prostitute; woman of loose morals ~ **tart** v/t (sl) **t. up** adorn with cheap, gaudy finery.

tartan [taartan] n woollen fabric with various coloured checks forming patterns belonging to each Highland clan; garment made of this ~ **tartan** adj.

tartar (1) [taartar] n brown crystalline deposit of potassium hydrogen tartrate, forming in winevats > PDS; incrustation of calcium phosphate on teeth; **cream of t.** potassium bitartrate.

tartar (2) n native of Tartary; (fig) person of violent temper ~ **tartar** adj; **t. sauce** mayonnaise flavoured with gherkins.

tartaric [taartaRik] adj of or derived from tartar; derived from tartaric acid; **t. acid** white crystalline organic acid used in dyeing and in baking powder > PDS.

tartarous [taartaRus] *adj* of, like, or containing tartar (1).

Tartarus [taartaRus] *n* (*Gk myth*) hell; the underworld.

tartlet [taartlit] *n* small tart (2).

tartly [taartli] *adv* sharply, acidly; sarcastically.

tartness [taartnis] *n* quality of being tart (1).

tartrate [taartRayt] *n* a salt of tartaric acid.

tartuffe [taartoof] *n* religious hypocrite.

tarty [taarti] *adj* (*sl*) of or like a prostitute.

tasimeter [tasimiter] *n* electrical apparatus for detecting minute variations of pressure or temperature.

task [taask] *n* work that must be done, *esp* if hard or unpleasant; piece or amount of work or study imposed by authority; **take to t.** reprove, find fault with ~ **task** *v/t* impose a task on; impose strain on, overtax.

task-force [taask-fawrs] *n* military force sent to carry out a specific operation; (*fig*) organized group trained for a specified task.

taskmaster [taask-maaster] *n* one who imposes hard work on others.

tassel [tasel] *n* ornamental hanging bunch of threads, silk or other materials; silk marker for a book ~ **tassel** (*pres/part* **tasselling**, *p/t* and *p/part* **tasselled**) *v/t* ornament with tassels.

tassie [tasi] *n* goblet, beaker.

tastable [taystab'l] *adj* that can be tasted.

taste [tayst] *v/t* and *i* perceive the flavour of; eat or drink a small amount, *esp* to judge the flavour of; experience, feel; have the flavour of ~ **taste** *n* sense by which flavours are perceived by the tongue and palate; flavour; sensitive and well-trained appreciation of what is aesthetically pleasing; refinement, delicacy of feeling or judgement; tact; preference, liking; small quantity, sample, *esp* of food or drink; slight trace, tinge.

tastebud [taystbud] *n* papilla, receptor organ for taste > PDB.

tasteful [taystfool] *adj* having or showing aesthetic sensitivity, refinement, good manners *etc* ~ **tastefully** *adv* ~ **tastefulness** *n*.

tasteless [taystlis] *adj* lacking aesthetic sensitiveness, refinement, good manners *etc*; having no flavour ~ **tastelessly** *adv* ~ **tastelessness** *n*.

taster [tayster] *n* one trained to test quality of teas, liquors *etc* by tasting them; instrument for cutting a small sample of cheese; (*coll*) publisher's reader.

tasty [taysti] *adj* pleasant to the taste; savoury; (*sl*) tasteful ~ **tastily** *adv* ~ **tastiness** *n*.

tat (1) (*pres/part* **tatting**, *p/t* and *p/part* **tatted**) [tat] *v/t* and *i* make lace-like fabric of knotted threads.

tat (2) *n* coarse canvas used as sacking.

tat (3) see **tit**.

tat (4) *n* bricabrac; old clothes, ornaments *etc* of little real value.

ta-ta [tataa] *interj* (*childish coll*) goodbye.

tater [tayter] *n* (*sl*) potato.

tatter [tater] *n* rag, torn piece ~ **tatter** *v/t* tear into pieces.

tatterdemalion [taterdimayli-on] *n* person dressed in rags.

tattered [taterd] *adj* torn to shreds, ragged; dressed in rags.

tattily [tatili] *adv* in a tatty way.

tattiness [tatinis] *n* quality of being tatty.

tatting [tating] *n* kind of knotted lace; process of making this.

tattle [tat'l] *n* gossip, trifling chat ~ **tattle** *v/i* prattle, gossip.

tattler [tatler] *n* one who gossips.

tattoo (1) [tatOO] *n* military pageant and parade, *esp* performed by night as entertainment; drum-roll or bugle-call recalling soldiers to barracks; sound resembling a drum-roll; **the devil's t.** act of drumming fingers on hard surface.

tattoo (2) *v/t* mark the skin by pricking and inserting indelible pigments ~ **tattoo** *n* marks or designs made by tattooing.

tatty [tati] *adj* untidy, scrappy, shabby.

tau [tav/tow] *n* Greek letter T; cross shaped like a T; American toad-fish with T-shaped marking.

taught [tawt] *p/t* and *p/part* of **teach**.

taunt [tawnt] *n* bitter jeer or blame; sarcastic or insulting speech ~ **taunt** *v/t* jeer at, reproach sarcastically or contemptuously.

taurine [tawrRIn] *adj* of or like a bull.

tauromachy [tawrRomaki] *n* bull-fighting.

Taurus [tavuRus] *n* (*astron*) constellation of the Bull, the second sign of the zodiac.

taut [tawt] *adj* stretched tight, tightly drawn ~ **tautly** *adv* ~ **tautness** *n*.

tauten [tawten] *v/t* and *i* make or become taut.

tauto- *pref* the same.

tautog [tawtog] *n* American edible sea-fish.

tautological [tawtolojikal] *adj* of or using tautology ~ **tautologically** *adv*.

tautologist [tawtolojist] *n* one who uses tautology.

tautology [tawtoloji] *n* unnecessary repetition of the same idea in different words.

tautomerism [tawtomeRizm] *n* (*chem*) existence of two isomers of a compound in equilibrium > PDS.

tavern [tavern] *n* inn, public-house.

taw (1) [taw] *v/t* turn (skins) into leather, *esp* with mineral agents.

taw (2) *n* a marble; a game at marbles.

tawdry [tawdRi] *adj* cheaply showy, gaudy; lacking taste ~ **tawdrily** *adv* ~ **tawdriness** *n*.

tawny [tawni] *adj* rich yellow tinged with brown ~ ~ **tawnily** *adv* ~ **tawniness** *n*.

tawse [tawz] *n* (*Scots*) leather strap.

tax [taks] *n* compulsory monetary contribution assessed on property, income, goods purchased *etc* for the benefit of the State; strain; burdensome duty ~ **tax** *v/t* impose a tax on; lay heavy burden on; make heavy demands on; **t. with** accuse of.

taxability [taksabiliti] *n* position of being liable to taxation.

taxable [taksab'l] *adj* liable to be taxed.

taxation [taksayshon] *n* act of imposing a tax or taxes; body of taxes raised at a given time.

tax-collector [taks-kolektor] *n* official who collects taxes.

tax-free [taks-fREe] *adj* free from taxation.

taxi [taksi] *n* motorcar for public hire, *esp* one fitted with a taximeter ~ **taxi** *v/i* travel by taxi; (*of aircraft*) run along the ground before taking off or after landing.

taxicab [*tak*sikab] *n* taxi.

taxidermist [*tak*sidurmist] *n* one who practises taxidermy.

taxidermy [*tak*sidurmi] *n* art of preparing and stuffing animal skins to resemble the living creatures.

taximan [*tak*siman] *n* driver of a taxi.

taximeter [taksi*mi*ter] *n* instrument fitted to taxis to show the fare due for mileage covered.

taxin [*tak*sin] *n* resinous substance extracted from yew leaves.

taxi-rank [*tak*si-Rank] *n* place where taxis wait to be hired.

taxis [*tak*sis] *n* (*biol*) movement oriented in relation to its stimulus > PDB; (*surg*) replacement of dislocated parts by pressure; (*zool*) classification; (*gramm*) word-order; (*Gk hist*) division of army.

taxology [taks*olo*ji] *n* science of classification of living things.

taxonomy [taks*ono*mi] *n* taxology.

taxpayer [*taks*pay-er] *n* one who pays tax or taxes; one who is liable to taxation.

te [*tee*] *n* (*mus*) si in tonic sol-fa.

tea [*tee*] *n* dried leaves of an evergreen shrub, prepared for making a drink; drink made by infusing these in boiling water; light afternoon meal; any vegetable infusion; (*sl*) marijuana; **not my cup of t.** not the kind of thing I like.

teabag [*tee*bag] *n* small porous paper or cloth bag holding enough tealeaves to make a single cup of tea.

tea-break [*tee*-bRayk] *n* interruption of work allowed for drinking tea.

tea-caddy [*tee*-kadi] *n* airtight container for tea.

teacake [*tee*kayk] *n* type of light scone.

teach (*p/t* and *p/part* **taught**) [*teech*] *v/t* and *i* systematically impart knowledge or skill to; instruct; train; give systematic instruction about; be a professional teacher.

teachability [teech*abili*ti] *n* quality of being teachable.

teachable [*teech*ab'l] *adj* that can be taught; capable of receiving teaching or training.

teacher [*teech*er] *n* one who teaches; schoolmaster; schoolmistress.

tea-chest [*tee*-chest] *n* large wooden case in which tea is packed.

teach-in [*teech*-in] *n* lengthy public debate on a controversial political issue, *usu* held in a university.

teaching [*teech*ing] *n* art or act of giving knowledge; occupation of a teacher; that which is taught; body of precepts, doctrine *etc* taught by a specific person; **t. hospital** hospital that trains students in medicine and surgery.

teacloth [*tee*kloth] *n* cloth for wiping crockery; cloth for a tea-table.

teacosy [*tee*kOzi] *n* thick cover for keeping a teapot warm.

teacup [*tee*kup] *n* cup used in drinking tea; **storm in a t.** fuss over nothing.

tea-garden [*tee*-gaarden] *n* open-air restaurant where teas are sold; plantation where tea is grown.

teahouse [*tee*hows] *n* house in China or Japan where tea is served.

teak [*teek*] *n* large East Indian tree with very hard wood; wood of this ~ **teak** *adj*.

tea-kettle [*tee*-ket'l] *n* kettle in which water is boiled to make tea.

teal [*teel*] *n* small freshwater web-footed bird.

tealeaf (*pl* **tealeaves**) [*tee*leef] *n* broken fragment of leaf of tea-plant used for making tea, *esp* when swollen by infusion.

team [*teem*] *n* number of animals harnessed together; number of persons working together or making a side in a game ~ **team** *v/t* and *i* join together as a team; **t. up with** (*coll*) collaborate with; work in harmony with; match.

teamster [*teem*ster] *n* driver of a team of animals; (*US*) lorry driver.

teamwork [*teem*wurk] *n* work performed by several persons in collaboration; ability of a group to collaborate harmoniously.

teaparty [*tee*paarti] *n* afternoon party at which tea is served.

teapot [*tee*pot] *n* vessel in which tea is made.

teapoy [*tee*poi] *n* small three-legged table.

tear (1) [*teer*] *n* drop of salty liquid secreted by a gland near the eye, *esp* in response to grief or pain; clear drop of liquid; transparent drop-like particle; **crocodile tears** insincere pretence of grief; **in tears** weeping.

tear (2) (*p/t* **tore**, *p/part* **torn**) [*tair*] *v/t* and *i* pull to pieces, rip up; pull violently away; move very hastily, rush; tug roughly at; be capable of being torn; lacerate; (*fig*) cause grief to; cause dissension, bitterness *etc*; **t. from** take away from by violence; **t. one's hair** pull one's hair violently in grief or rage; be violently grieved or angered; **t. oneself away** depart unwillingly; **t. up** destroy by tearing, tear to shreds; pull violently up; (*fig*) callously destroy; **torn between** painfully unable to choose between conflicting demands, desires *etc* ~ **tear** *n* split or hole caused by tearing; act of tearing.

tearaway [*tair*Raway] *n* (*sl*) violent young hooligan.

teardrop [*teer*dRop] *n* single tear.

tearduct [*teer*dukt] *n* duct leading from lachrymal gland to nasal passage.

tearful [*teer*fool] *adj* shedding tears; easily inclined to weep ~ **tearfully** *adv* ~ **tearfulness** *n*.

teargas [*teer*gas] *n* chemical vapour producing an irritating effect on the eyes > PDS.

tearing [*tair*Ring] *adj* (*coll*) furious, rushing.

tearjerker [*teer*jurker] *n* (*coll*) very sentimental and pathetic book, play, or film.

tea-room [*tee*-ROOm] *n* room or restaurant where teas are sold.

tea-rose [*tee*-ROz] *n* type of Chinese rose.

tease [*teez*] *v/t* and *i* make fun of, either playfully or maliciously; pester with petty annoyances; annoy, exasperate; engage in taunting; scratch or comb out with teasels ~ **tease** *n* one who enjoys teasing others.

teasel, teazel [*teez*'l] *n* plant with large burrs; hooked brush used for combing, carding, raising nap on cloth *etc* ~ **teasel** *v/t* raise a nap on (cloth) with teasels.

teaser [*teez*er] *n* one who or that which teases; (*coll*) difficult problem, poser.

tea-service [*tee*-survis] *n* teaset.

teaset [*tee*set] *n* set of teapot, teacups, plates *etc* for use in serving tea.

teashop [*tee*shop] *n* small restaurant where teas are sold.

teaspoon [*tee*spOOn] *n* small spoon used for stirring tea; smallest size of spoon used as cooking measure or for measuring medicines.

teaspoonful [*tee*spOOfool] *n* as much as a teaspoon will hold.

teat [*teet*] *n* nipple of the female breast through which milk is sucked; nipple of baby's feeding-bottle.

tea-table [*tee*-tayb'l] *n* table at which tea is drunk.

tea-things [*tee*-thingz] *n* (*pl*) crockery, china or silverware for serving tea.

teatime [*tee*tIm] *adj* and *n* (of or at) the usual time for afternoon tea.

teatowel [*tea*towil] *n* towel for wiping china *etc* after washing.

teatray [*tee*Ray] *n* tray on which tea-things are placed.

tea-urn [*tee*-urn] *n* large metal container in which tea is made and from which it is poured by a tap.

teazel see **teasel**.

tec [*tek*] *n* (*sl abbr*) detective; technical college.

technetium [tek*nee*shi-um] *n* (*chem*) rare radioactive element > PDS.

technic [*tek*nik] *adj* technical ~ **technic** *n* technique.

technical [*tek*nikal] *adj* of technique; of, by or for industrial and mechanical arts and skills; peculiar to some specific branch of knowledge, art, industry, *etc*; precisely accurate in description; not understandable by laymen; **t. college** institution teaching engineering and other technical skills.

technicality [tek*nikal*iti] *n* quality of being technical; technical term; detail of procedure; formality.

technically [*tek*nikali] *adv* in a technical way; as regards technique.

technician [tek*nish*an] *n* one skilled in a mechanical skill.

technicist [*tek*nisist] *n* technician.

Technicolor [*tek*nikuler] *n* (*tr*) process for producing cinema films in colour photography.

technicoloured [*tek*nikulerd] *adj* (*coll*) of highly vivid colour; (*fig*) exaggerated in style, emotion *etc*.

techniphone [*tek*nifOn] *n* silent piano for fingering exercises.

technique [tek*neek*] *n* method of performance or execution; skill in an art or in some specialized activity.

technocracy [tek*nok*Rasi] *n* control of industry by skilled technicians; group of skilled technicians wielding authority.

technocrat [*tek*nokRat] *n* member of a technocracy.

technological [tekno*loj*ikal] *adj* of or by technology ~ **technologically** *adv*.

technologist [tek*nol*ojist] *n* one skilled in technology.

technology [tek*nol*oji] *n* science of industrial and mechanical arts; terms employed in an art or science.

techy see **tetchy**.

tectonic [tek*ton*ik] *adj* of structure or building; (*geog*) of processes that build up the earth's crust > PDG ~ **tectonics** *n* (*pl*) art of functional designing and making; (*geog*) the study of the evolution of the earth's crust.

tectorial [tek*tawr*Ri-al] *adj* forming a covering.

ted (1) (*pres/part* **tedding**, *p/t* and *p/part* **tedded**) [*ted*] *v/t* toss and spread (grass) for drying into hay.

Ted (2) *n* (*sl*) Teddy-boy.

tedder [*ted*er] *n* one who or machine which spreads hay.

teddybear [*ted*ibair] *n* soft toy shaped like a stuffed bear; (*Aust*) koala bear.

Teddy-boy [*ted*i-boi] *n* type of tough English youth with fastidious taste in Edwardian-style clothes; **T. suit** black suit with narrow trousers reminiscent of Edwardian fashions.

Te Deum [tee-*dee*-um] *n* (*Lat*) hymn of praise sung as thanksgiving.

tedious [*tee*di-us] *adj* long and boring; wearyingly dull ~ **tediously** *adv* ~ **tediousness** *n*.

tedium [*tee*di-um] *n* quality of being tedious.

tee (1) [*tee*] *n* the letter T; anything shaped like this.

tee (2) *n* (*golf*) tiny heap of sand, or small wooden or plastic support, from which ball is first played at each hole; (*quoits etc*) mark aimed at ~ **tee** *v/t* place (golf ball) on tee; **t. off** play (ball) from tee; **t. up** place on tee; (*fig*) get ready to act.

teem (1) [*teem*] *v/t* and *i* be full of; be prolific; (*ar*) be fertile; produce abundantly.

teem (2) *v/t* pour out, discharge.

teenage [*teen*ayj] *adj* of, for or like a teenager.

teenager [*teen*ayjer] *n* adolescent aged between thirteen and twenty.

teens [*teenz*] *n* (*pl*) period of life between thirteen and twenty years old; adolescence.

teeny [*teen*i] *adj* (*coll*) tiny.

teeny-bopper [*teen*i-boper] *n* (*sl*) young teenager.

teeshirt [*tee*shurt] *n* short-sleeved collarless shirt.

teeter [*tee*ter] *v/i* stand or walk unsteadily.

teeth [*teeth*] *pl* of **tooth**.

teething [*tee*THing] *n* process of growing teeth; **t. troubles** difficulties in early stages of a new undertaking or when first using a new machine.

teetotal [*tee*tOtal] *adj* of or observing total abstinence from intoxicating drinks.

teetotalism [*tee*tOtalizm] *n* total abstention from intoxicating drinks.

teetotaller [*tee*tOtaler] *n* one who practises teetotalism.

teetotum [*tee*tOtum] *n* type of spinning top with flattened sides.

tegument [*teg*ewment] *n* skin, membranous envelope.

tehee [tee*hee*] *n* sound made in giggling, titter.

tektite [tektIt] *n* small glassy body believed to be associated with meteorites > PDS.

telary [*tee*leRi] *adj* of webs; spinning a web.

tele- *pref* at or over a distance; by television.

tele-archics [teli-*aar*kiks] *n* (*pl*) remote control of aircraft by radio.

telecamera [*tel*ikameRa] *n* device used in television to convert optical images into electric signals > PDEl.

telecast [*tel*ikaast] *n* (*US*) televised programme

telecommunication [telikomewni*kay*shon] *n* any method of emitting, transmitting or receiving signals by an electromagnetic system > PDEl.

teledu [*tel*edOO] *n* stinking badger of Java.

telefilm [*tel*ifilm] *n* cinema film shown on television.

telegenic [teli*jen*ik] *adj* looking pleasing or impressive when seen on television.

telegram [*teli*gRam] *n* message sent by telegraph; piece of paper on which this is recorded for transmission or delivery.

telegraph [*teli*gRaaf] *n* method of transmitting messages by electric impulses through wires > PDS, PDEl; **bush t.** method of conveying messages over a long distance by drum-beats, smoke signals *etc*; (*fig*) mysteriously rapid communication of news; **t. line (wire)** wire through which telegrams are sent; **t. pole** pole supporting telegraph wires ~ **telegraph** *v/t* and *i* send telegram (to); (*fig*) convey meaning silently by gestures, grimaces *etc*.

telegraphese [teligRa*feez*] *n* concise language in which telegrams are worded; style of sentence-construction omitting as many words as possible.

telegraphic [teligRa*fik*] *adj* by telegraph; of, for or like a telegram; of or in telegraphese ~ **telegraphically** *adv*.

telegraphist [te*leg*Rafist] *n* telegraph operator.

telegraphy [te*leg*Rafi] *n* process of communicating by telegraph; art of constructing and operating telegraphic apparatus.

telekinesis [teliki*nee*sis] *n* (*psychic research*) alleged movement of a body at a distance without material cause ~ **telekinetic** [teliki*net*ik] *adj*.

telemark [*teli*maark] *n* a kind of turn in skiing.

telemechanics [telime*kan*iks] *n* (*pl*) art of transmitting power to a distance.

telemeter [te*lem*iter] *n* any instrument that measures a physical quantity and conveys its measurement to a distance by a signal.

teleological [teli-o*loj*ikal] *adj* of teleology.

teleology [teli-o*loj*i] *n* doctrine or theory that all things or processes were designed to fulfil a purpose > PDP.

telepathic [teli*path*ik] *adj* of, by, like, or capable of telepathy ~ **telepathically** *adv*.

telepathist [te*lep*athist] *n* one who practises or believes in telepathy.

telepathy [te*lep*athi] *n* alleged non-physical communication of ideas, feelings *etc* from one mind to another at a distance; (*fig*) instantaneous awareness of another's thoughts or feelings.

telephone [*teli*fOn] *n* electric system for transmitting conversation over a distance, *usu* through wires > PDS, PDEl; transmitting and receiving apparatus for this; message or conversation transmitted by telephone ~ **telephone** *v/t* and *i* transmit by telephone; talk by telephone.

telephonic [teli*fon*ik] *adj* of or by telephone ~ **telephonically** *adv*.

telephonist [ti*lef*onist] *n* one who operates a telephone or telephone switchboard.

telephony [ti*lef*oni] *n* method, process, of communicating by telephone.

telephoto [*teli*fOtO] *n* (*coll*) telephotograph; **t. lens** magnifying camera lens > PDS.

telephotograph [teli*fOtog*Raaf] *n* photograph of distant object taken through a highly magnifying lens > PDS.

telephotography [telifotog*Rafi*] *n* process of using a telephoto lens.

teleport [*teli*pawrt] *v/t* transport by telekinesis.

teleprint [*teli*pRint] *v/t* and *i* send (message) by teleprinter; operate a teleprinter.

teleprinter [*teli*pRinter] *n* electrically-operated typewriter by which messages sent by telegraph are reproduced.

teleprompter [*teli*pRompter] *n* (*tr*) concealed device by which a speaker on television can read his script line by line while seeming to speak spontaneously.

telerecord [*teli*Rikawrd] *v/t* record and film for television.

telescope [*teli*skOp] *n* optical device for viewing magnified images of distant objects ~ **telescope** *v/t* and *i* make (an object) shorter or smaller by sliding or folding its sections one inside the other; compress forcibly; amalgamate and compress.

telescopic [teli*skop*ik] *adj* of, like or seen by a telescope; having sections fitting into one another ~ **telescopically** *adv*.

telescopy [ti*les*kopi] *n* practice of using or making telescopes.

telesthesia [telis*theez*i-a] *n* (*zool*) sensibility to events at a distance; (*fig*) second-sight.

teletype [*teli*tIp] *v/t* and *i* transmit by teleprinter.

teletypewriter [telit*Ip*Riter] *n* (*US*) teleprinter.

teleview [*teli*vew] *v/t* and *i* (*US*) watch television ~ **televiewer** *n*.

televise [*teli*vIz] *v/t* transmit by television.

television [*teli*vizhon] *n* transmission of visible moving images by electromagnetic wireless waves, *usu* with synchronized sound signals > PDS, PDEl; apparatus on which these are received; televised programme ~ **television** *adj*.

telex [*tel*eks] *n* teleprinter; system of communications using teleprinters ~ **telex** *v/t* send a message by teleprinter.

telfer see **telpher**.

tell (*p/t* and *p/part* told) [*tel*] *v/t* and *i* relate, recount; make known, inform; express; make out, distinguish; order, command; (*ar*) count; divulge; produce an effect; **t. off** (*coll*) rebuke; **t. on** wear out, exhaust; (*coll*) inform against; **all told** altogether, in all.

tellable [*tel*ab'l] *adj* that can be told.

teller [*tel*er] *n* one who tells; one who counts, *esp* votes; bank-clerk who receives or pays out money.

telling [*tel*ing] *adj* very effective, impressive ~ **tellingly** *adv*.

telltale [*tel*tayl] *n* one who gives away secrets; gossip; informer ~ **telltale** *adj* tending to reveal a secret.

telluric [te*lewr*Rik] *adj* pertaining to the planet Earth; derived from or containing tellurium.

tellurium [te*lewr*Ri-um] *n* silvery-white, brittle, non-metallic element resembling sulphur > PDS.

telly [*tel*i] *n* and *adj* (*coll abbr*) television.

telpher, telfer [*tel*fer] *n* electrically driven hoist hanging from an overhead rail or cable, used for transport > PDE ~ **telpher, telfer** *adj*.

temerarious [teme*Rair*Ri-us] *adj* rash, reckless.

temerity [ti*me*Riti] *n* rashness, great boldness.

temper [*tem*per] *n* temperament, state of mind, *esp* as regards irritability or gentleness; irritable nature, proneness to anger; angry mood; passing mood; right mixture, desired consistency; **keep one's t.** remain calm despite provocation; **lose one's t.** grow suddenly angry ~ **temper** *v/t* and *i* harden (metal or glass) by heating, sudden cooling, and reheating; blend in right proportion;

moderate, tone down, modify; knead and moisten.

tempera [*tempe*Ra] *n* mixture of egg, water *etc* used as medium for powdered pigments > PDAA; distemper used in frescoes.

temperament [*tempe*Rament] *n* natural emotional and moral disposition, constitution of mind > PDP; moderation; proportionate mixture; (*mus*) adjustment of intervals on keyboard instrument so that it can be played in all keys > PDM; (*ar*) one of four physical types of qualities regarded as determining character.

temperamental [*tempe*Ramental] *adj* of temperament; liable to strong changes of mood; unreliable; unstable; having a passionate character ~ **temperamentally** *adv*.

temperance [*tempe*Rans] *n* moderation; abstention from intoxicating drinks.

temperate [*tempe*Rit] *adj* moderate; not extreme; self-restrained; (*of climate*) neither arctic nor tropical; having well-marked seasonal variations > PDG ~ **temperately** *adv* ~ **temperateness** *n*.

temperature [*temp*Racher] *n* degree of heat or cold in atmosphere or in a body > PDS; excessive bodily heat due to fever; **have a t.** be feverish; **take one's t.** measure one's bodily heat by thermometer.

tempered [*temperd*] *adj* moderated; mixed in due proportion; (*of steel*) subjected to tempering; (*mus*) adjusted according to a temperament.

tempest [*tempist*] *n* violent storm of wind, rain *etc*; (*fig*) violent agitation.

tempestuous [tem*pest*ew-us] *adj* of or like a tempest, stormy; violently excited, agitated ~ **tempestuously** *adv* ~ **tempestuousness** *n*.

templar [*templar*] *n* member of a medieval religious and military Order; lawyer living in the Temple, London; member of an order of modern Freemasonry.

template, templet [*templit*] *n* wooden or metal mould used as guide in shaping; piece of wood placed under end of girder *etc* to distribute weight.

temple (1) [*temp'll*] *n* building or place dedicated to a deity; church, place of worship; (*cap*) one of two Inns of Court in London.

temple (2) *n* flat region on either side of the forehead.

temple (3) *n* attachment for keeping cloth stretched on a loom.

templet see **template**.

tempo [*temp*O] *n* degree of speed, rate, pace.

temporal (1) [*tempo*Ral] *adj* of the temples of the head.

temporal (2) *adj* of or in time; not eternal; earthly; secular, not spiritual or ecclesiastic; (*gramm*) of tense.

temporality [*tempo*Raliti] *n* secular possession or power of a religious body.

temporally [*tempo*Rali] *adv* in a temporal way.

temporarily [*tempo*RaRili/*tempo*RairRili] *adv* only for a time.

temporariness [*tempo*RaRinis/*tempo*RairRinis] *n* quality of being temporary.

temporary [*tempo*RaRi] *adj* lasting only for a limited time, transient ~ **temporary** *n* person doing a specified job for a short time only.

temporization [tempoRIz*ay*shon] *n* act of temporizing.

temporize [*tempo*RIz] *v/i* postpone or try to avoid making a decision, act non-committally; do what is merely expedient.

tempt [*temt*] *v/t* try to allure or persuade (someone) to act wrongly, urge to evil acts; induce, persuade; attract, rouse desire in; (*ar*) test.

temptation [temp*tay*shon] *n* act of tempting; state of being tempted; that which tempts; (*ar*) test.

tempter [*tempter*] *n* one who tempts; (*cap*) the devil.

tempting [*tempting*] *adj* enticing to evil; attractive, inviting ~ **temptingly** *adv* ~ **temptingness** *n*.

temptress [*tempt*Ris] *n* woman who tempts.

ten [*ten*] *n* and *adj* one more than nine; symbol of this; **t. times** (*coll*) very much more, larger *etc*.

tenability [tena*biliti*] *n* quality of being tenable.

tenable [tenab'l/teenab'l] *adj* (*of opinions etc*) logical, reasonable; defendable; (*mil*) that can be maintained against attack ~ **tenably** *adv*.

tenacious [tin*ay*shus] *adj* holding firmly; obstinate, unyielding; retentive; sticky ~ **tenaciously** *adv* ~ **tenaciousness** *n*.

tenacity [tin*a*siti] *n* quality of being tenacious.

tenancy [ten*ansi*] *n* act of holding property as a tenant; period during which property is held.

tenant [ten*ant*] *n* one who holds land, house, rooms *etc* from another for payment of rent occupant ~ **tenant** *v/t* hold (land *etc*) under another.

tenanted [ten*antid*] *adj* occupied by a tenant; inhabited.

tenantry [ten*ant*Ri] *n* (*collect*) tenants.

tench [*tench*] *n* a freshwater fish.

tend (1) [*tend*] *v/i* develop or lead in a certain direction; be liable or inclined to; have the effect of.

tend (2) *v/t* take care of, look after.

tendencious see **tendentious**.

tendency [ten*densi*] *n* inclination; process of developing or being likely to develop in a certain way.

tendentious, tendencious [ten*den*shus] *adj* not impartial; described or presented unfairly so as to influence others in a desired direction ~ **tendentiously** *adv* ~ **tendentiousness** *n*.

tender (1) [tend*er*] *n* railway truck carrying fuel and water for a locomotive; small vessel attending a larger one; one who attends to or looks after.

tender (2) *v/t* and *i* offer for acceptance; offer to supply (goods or facilities) at a fixed rate ~ **tender** *n* an offer to do certain work or supply certain goods at a fixed rate; money offered in settlement of a debt or claim; **legal t.** currency recognized legally as acceptable.

tender (3) *adj* affectionate, loving; kind, sympathetic; gentle, soft; easily chewed; painful when touched; frail, delicate; sensitive; youthfully innocent or vulnerable.

tenderfoot (*pl* **tenderfoots**) [tend*er*foot] *n* newcomer to a hard life, novice.

tender-hearted [tender-*haart*id] *adj* gentle, loving; easily moved to pity.

tenderize [tende*RIz*] *v/t* make (meat) tender by bruising it or by chemical means.

tenderloin [tend*er*loin] *n* tenderest part of sirloin; (*US coll*) city area where illegal amusements, vice *etc* are rampant.

tenderly [*tenderli*] *adv* affectionately; gently; delicately.

tenderness [*tendernis*] *n* quality of being tender.

tendon [*tendon*] *n* (*anat*) cord of strong fibrous tissue by which a muscle is attached to a bone.

tendril [*tendRil*] *n* slender thread-like shoot of a plant by which it clings to a support > PDB.

tenebrae [*tenibRay*] *n* (*eccles*) matins and lauds of the last three days of Holy Week.

tenebrous [*tenibRus*] *adj* dark, gloomy.

tenement [*teniment*] *n* one of several sets of rooms in a building, each rented by one family; house, dwelling; (*leg*) property held by a tenant; **t. house** building divided into tenements.

tenet [*tenet*] *n* opinion or belief firmly held as true, dogma, principle.

tenfold [*tenfOld*] *adj* and *adv* ten times (as much or as great).

tennis [*tenis*] *n* game for two or four persons played by striking a ball with rackets over a net; (*hist*) similar game played in a walled court.

tennis-ball [*tenis-bawl*] *n* ball used in tennis.

tennis-court [*tenis-kawrt*] *n* marked area of grass or asphalt on which tennis is played.

tennis-elbow [*tenis-elbO*] *n* inflammation of elbow *usu* caused by strain in playing tennis.

tennis-racket [*tenis-Raket*] *n* stringed bat used in playing tennis.

tenon [*tenon*] *n* projection on timber to be inserted into a mortise ~ **tenon** *v/t* join with tenons.

tenor [*tenor*] *n* general meaning; general direction; (*mus*) highest normal male voice; one who possesses this voice > PDM ~ **tenor** *adj*.

tenpins [*tenpinz*] *n* American version of ninepins.

tense (1) [*tens*] *n* (*gramm*) verb form indicating time in which the action takes place.

tense (2) *adj* stretched tight, strained, taut; (*fig*) strained by strong suppressed emotion; anxious, in suspense; keyed up, overwrought; alert; (*phon*) uttered with tongue in taut position ~ **tense** *v/t* make tense ~ **tensely** *adv* ~ **tenseness** *n*.

tensible [*tensib'l*] *adj* that can be stretched.

tensile [*tensIl*] *adj* of or by tension; that can be stretched.

tension [*tenshon*] *n* act of stretching; condition of being stretched; strain, effort; excitement, anxiety, suspense; uneasiness caused by strong suppressed emotion > PDP; (*elect*) voltage.

tensional [*tenshonal*] *adj* of tension.

tent (1) [*tent*] *n* portable shelter made of canvas supported by poles and ropes; protective covering resembling this; **oxygen t.** airtight shelter placed over bed of a patient being given oxygen ~ **tent** *v/i* encamp in a tent.

tent (2) *n* (*surg*) absorbent plug inserted in a wound ~ **tent** *v/t* insert a tent in.

tent (3) *n* a sweet red Spanish wine.

tent (4) *n* (*Scots*) care, heed.

tentacle [*tentak'l*] *n* long, flexible, slender organ of feeling or motion; feeler.

tentacular [*tentakewlar*] *adj* of or like tentacles.

tentative [*tentativ*] *adj* proposed or done merely as suggestion or experiment; provisional; cautious, diffident ~ **tentatively** *adv* ~ **tentativeness** *n*.

tent-bed [*tent-*bed] *n* small low bed to be used in a tent; bed with canopy.

tenter (1) [*tenter*] *n* one who looks after machinery.

tenter (2) *n* frame or machine for stretching cloth.

tenterhook [*tenterhook*] *n* hooked nail used in stretching cloth; **on tenterhooks** in suspense, anxious, expectant.

tenth [*tenth*] *n* and *adj* (that) which follows nine others in a series; (that) which is one of ten equal parts.

tenthly [*tenthli*] *adv* in the tenth place.

tenth-rate [*tenth-Rayt*] *adj* of very poor quality.

tent-peg [*tent-*peg] *n* peg driven into the ground by which a tent's guy-rope is held firm.

tent-pegging [*tent-*peging] *n* cavalry sport of trying to carry off on a lance a tent-peg in the ground.

tenuity [*tinew-iti*] *n* thinness, slenderness; rarity.

tenuous [*tenew-us*] *adj* thin, slender; rarefied; subtle; slight, flimsy ~ **tenuously** *adv* ~ **tenuousness** *n*.

tenure [*tenyer*] *n* act or right of holding land or office; conditions on which this is held; period of holding this.

tenuto [*tenewtO*] *adj* (*mus*) to be fully sustained.

tepee [*teepee*] *n* wigwam.

tephrite [*tefRit*] *n* a volcanic rock related to basalt.

tepid [*tepid*] *adj* lukewarm, only slightly warm; (*fig*) showing very little enthusiasm, interest *etc*.

tepidity [*tipiditi*] *n* state or quality of being tepid.

tepidly [*tepidli*] *adv* in a tepid way.

tequila [*tekeela*] *n* Mexican alcoholic drink made from the agave.

ter [*tur*] *adv* (*mus*) three times.

tera- *pref* one million million.

teraphim [*teRafim*] *n* (*pl*) (*OT*) images of household gods.

teratogenic [*teRatOjenik*] *n* and *adj* (*med*) (substance) causing malformation of a foetus.

teratology [*teRatoloji*] *n* scientific study of malformations and freaks in animals or plants.

terbium [*turbi-um*] *n* a rare metallic element.

tercel see **tiercel**.

tercentenary [*tursinteenaRi*] *n* three hundredth anniversary.

tercet [*tursit*] *n* (*mus*, *pros*) triplet.

terebene [*teRibeen*] *n* a liquid hydrocarbon used as a disinfectant.

terebinth [*teRibinth*] *n* turpentine-tree.

teredo [*teReedO*] *n* mollusc which bores into underwater timbers of ships.

tergal [*turgal*] *adj* of the back; dorsal.

tergiversate [*turjivursayt*] *v/i* act evasively; change sides; vacillate.

tergiversation [*turjivursayshon*] *n* evasive behaviour; vacillation.

term [*turm*] *n* period of consecutive weeks during which teaching is given in a school, university *etc*; period during which law-courts are in session; limited period; limit, boundary; word conveying a specialized concept used in an art, science, profession *etc*; (*pl*) conditions of an agreement, contract, treaty *etc*; (*pl*) personal relationship; (*pl*) way of speaking, language; (*pl*) money demanded as payment; (*log*) one of the parts of a proposition; (*med*) end of period of pregnancy; menstruation; (*leg*) day fixed for payment; **come to terms** reach agreement; **contradiction in terms** self-contradictory statement; **terms of reference**

limits set to the scope of an investigation ~ term
v/t name, call.

termagant [*tur*magant] *adj* and *n* (of or like) a
shrewish, violent woman.

terminability [turmina*biliti*] *n* quality of being
terminable.

terminable [*turm*inab'l] *adj* that can be brought
to an end.

terminal [*turm*inal] *adj* of, at or near an end or
limit; forming an end, final; of or in the last stage
of a fatal illness; happening once a term; of or
during a school or university term ~ **terminal** *n*
railway terminus; (*archi*) finial, ornament forming an end; (*elect*) either end of a circuit; metal
device attaching these to a plug *etc*.

terminally [*turm*inali] *adv* at the end; once a term.

terminate [*turm*inayt] *v/t* and *i* put an end to;
come to an end; set a limit to.

termination [turmin*ay*shon] *n* act of terminating;
end; conclusion, final part; limit.

terminative [*turm*inativ] *adj* that terminates; of
or at the end ~ **terminatively** *adv*.

terminator [*turm*inaytor] *n* one who or that which
terminates; (*astron*) dividing line between lit and
unlit areas of a moon, planet *etc*.

terminological [turminolo*jikal*] *adj* of terminology; **t. inexactitude** (*joc*) lie.

terminology [turmin*oloji*] *n* technical or specialized terms used in any art or science.

terminus [*turm*inus] *n* station forming the end of a
railway line, bus route *etc*; final point reached,
goal; **t. ad quem** (*Lat*) point which an argument
is intended to reach; **t. a quo** (*Lat*) starting-
point of an argument.

termitary [*turm*iteRi] *n* mound raised by termites
as a nest.

termite [*turm*It] *n* one of an order of destructive
insects living in communities > PDB.

tern (1) [*turn*] *n* one of various long-winged seabirds.

tern (2) *n* set of three.

ternary [*turn*aRi] *adj* threefold, in threes.

terpene [*turp*een] *n* one of a class of isomeric oily
hydrocarbons > PDS.

Terpsichorean [turpsiko*Ri*-an] *adj* of dancing.

terra [*teR*a] *n* (*Lat*) earth; **t. firma** dry land; **t.
incognita** unexplored country.

terrace [*teR*is] *n* high bank whose flat top forms a
pathway in garden or park; flat level area cut
from a slope; row of similar houses built end-to-
end; **t. cultivation** system of cultivating mountain slopes by cutting terraces in them > PDG ~
terrace *v/t* form into terraces.

terracotta [teRa*kota*] *n* hard reddish-brown unglazed pottery.

terrain [teR*ayn*] *n* tract of land, *esp* as regards
features making it suitable as a battlefield.

terramycin [teRam*tsin*] *n* an antibiotic drug.

terrapin [*teR*apin] *n* freshwater turtle.

terraza [teR*atsa*] *n* (*Ital*) floor surface of stone
chips set in concrete.

terrene [teR*een*] *adj* earthly.

terrestrial [teR*estR*i-al] *adj* of or on earth, earthly;
living on dry land; of this world, not celestial;
representing the globe of earth.

terrible [*teR*ib'l] *adj* terrifying, appalling; (*coll*)
excessive; very bad ~ **terribly** *adv* in a terrible
way; (*coll*) extremely.

terrier [*teR*i-er] *n* one of several breeds of small
dogs used for hunting and as pets; (*sl*) member of
the Territorial Army.

terrific [teR*if*ik] *adj* terrifyingly large or powerful;
(*coll*) amazing; amazingly good, enjoyable, admirable *etc* ~ **terrifically** *adv*.

terrify [*teR*ifI] *v/t* fill with terror.

terrine [teR*een*] *n* earthenware vessel containing a
particular food, delicacy *etc*.

territorial [teRit*awr*al] *adj* of territory; of or
limited to a district; **T. Army** military force of
volunteers grouped by regions and serving for
home defence; **t. waters** coastal waters over
which a nation has sovereignty ~ **Territorial** *n*
member of the Territorial Army ~ **territorially**
adv.

territory [*teR*iteRi] *n* land ruled by a single State
or ruler; district dominated by or belonging to a
single social group; area from which an animal
will try to exclude all members of its species
except its mate and offspring > PDB; area
assigned to one member of a group to work in;
dependency, non-self-governing country.

terror [*teR*or] *n* very great fear; object causing this;
(*coll*) nuisance, troublesome, unmanageable
person; **reign of t.** period of rule by one who
crushes opposition by constant violence or
threats.

terrorism [*teR*oRizm] *n* policy of using violence
and intimidation to obtain political demands or
enforce political authority.

terrorist [*teR*oRist] *n* one who seeks political ends
by terrorism; partisan, member of a resistance
organization or guerrilla force using acts of violence ~ **terrorist** *adj*.

terrorization [teRoRIz*ay*shon] *n* act of terrorizing.

terrorize [*teR*oRIz] *v/t* deliberately fill with terror;
rule or dominate by inspiring terror.

terry [*teR*i] *n* piled fabric with uncut loops, used
for towels.

terse [*turs*] *adj* using few words, concise; curt,
abrupt in speech ~ **tersely** *adv* ~ **terseness** *n*.

tertian [*tur*shan] *n* and *adj* (*med*) (fever) recurring
every third day.

tertiary [*tur*shaRi] *adj* of the third rank or order
(*geol*) of the era following the mesozoic > PDG
~ **tertiary** *n* a flight-feather; layman or laywoman
affiliated to a religious order.

tertium quid [tershum-*kwid*] *n* (*Lat*) some unknown thing related to two known things, but
distinct from each.

tervalent [*tur*valent] *adj* (*chem*) having a valency
of three.

Terylene [*teR*ileen] *n* (*tr*) brand of polyester
fibre, filament, yarn, or staple fibre; fabric made
from this.

terza rima [turtsa-*Reem*a] *n* (*pros*) three-line
stanza with second line of each stanza rhyming
with first and third line of the next.

tessellate [*tes*elayt] *v/t* pave with small blocks of
stone forming a pattern.

tessellation [tesel*ay*shon] *n* mosaic, *esp* as paving.

tessera (*pl* **tesserae**) [*tes*eRa] *n* one of many small
blocks of stone, glass *etc* used to make a mosaic.

test (1) [*test*] *n* that which is designed to ascertain
the merits of something; standardized examination or trial; minor or preliminary examination;
the experimental exploding of a nuclear weapon;

circumstances which bring out the true character or quality of a person or thing; (*chem*) analysis; container in which metals are refined; **t. case** (*leg*) case which will establish a precedent; **t. flight** flight in which an aircraft's performance is tested; **t. match** one of a series of cricket matches played between elevens representing their countries ~ **test** *v/t* try by experiment or examination to ascertain the merits, knowledge, truth *etc* of; subject to a test; (*chem*) analyse.

test (2) *n* (*zool*) hard shell.

testable [*test*ab'l] *adj* capable of being tested.

testaceous [*test*ayshus] *adj* (*zool*) having a shell.

testacy [*test*asi] *n* state of being testate.

testament [*test*ament] *n* (*cap*) one of the two major divisions of the Bible; (*coll*) the New Testament; (*leg*) will; **last will and t.** document declaring a person's wishes concerning the disposal of his property after his death.

testamentary [testam*ent*aRi] *adj* (*leg*) of or by a will.

testate [*test*ayt] *n* and *adj* (*leg*) (person) who has left a valid will at death.

testator [test*ay*tor] *n* one who has made or has left a will.

testatrix [test*ay*tRiks] *n* female testator.

test-ban [*test*-ban] *n* agreement between nations to stop testing nuclear weapons.

tester (1) [*test*er] *n* one who or that which tests.

tester (2) *n* canopy over a bed.

tester (3) *n* (*hist*) shilling of Henry VIII.

testes [*test*eez] *pl* of **testis**.

testicle [*test*ik'l] *n* gland which secretes sperm in male animals.

testify [*test*ifI] *v/t* and *i* give evidence, *esp* from first-hand knowledge; **t. to** (*fig*) be evidence of, tend to prove.

testily [*test*ili] *adv* irritably.

testimonial [testim*Oni*-al] *n* document or formal statement declaring knowledge of a person's character, qualifications or abilities; gift presented in token of appreciation and esteem.

testimony [*test*imoni] *n* statement made under oath; evidence; solemn declaration.

testiness [*test*inis] *n* irritability.

testis (*pl* **testes**) [*test*is] *n* (*Lat*) testicle.

test-pilot [*test*-pIlot] *n* one who pilots newly-designed aircraft on experimental flights.

test-tube [*test*-tewb] *n* tube of thin glass closed at one end, used in chemical experiments; **t. baby** (*coll*) baby conceived by artificial insemination, *esp* on an ovum removed from the mother's body and re-implanted after fertilization.

testudo [test*ew*dO] *n* (*Rom hist*) protective cover made by Roman soldiers by holding overlapping shields over their heads; land-tortoise.

testy [*test*i] *adj* irritable, peevish, petulant.

tetanic [ti*tan*ik] *adj* of or causing tetanus.

tetanus [*tet*anus] *n* bacterial disease in which muscles contract in spasms > PDP; lockjaw.

tetany [*tet*ani] *n* disease with muscular spasms caused by calcium deficiency.

tetchy, techy [*tech*i] *adj* easily irritated, touchy ~ **tetchily** *adv* ~ **tetchiness** *n*.

tête-à-tête [tayt-a-*tayt*] *adj*, *adv* and *n* (*Fr*) (in) private interview, close conversation.

tether [*teTH*er] *n* rope or chain by which an animal is linked to a post or peg yet allowed some free movement; **at the end of one's t.** at the end of one's strength, patience, resources *etc* ~ **tether** *v/t* fasten with a tether.

tetra- *pref* fourfold; having four parts.

tetrachord [*tet*Rakawrd] *n* (*mus*) scale series of four sounds > PDM.

tetrad [*tet*Rad] *n* group or set of four; (*chem*) element having a valency of four; (*biol*) paired and duplicated chromosomes of meiosis > PDB.

tetragram [*tet*Ragram] *n* word of four letters.

tetragrammaton [tet*Rag*Ramaton] *n* the Hebrew name of God as written with four consonants only, JHVH.

tetrahedron [tetRa*heed*Ron] *n* four-faced solid figure contained by four triangles > PDS.

tetralogy [tet*Ral*oji] *n* series of four related plays.

tetrameter [tet*Ram*iter] *n* (*pros*) line of verse containing four feet.

tetraplegic [tetRa*plee*jik] *n* and *adj* (*med*) (person) paralysed in all four limbs.

tetrapod [*tet*Rapod] *n* and *adj* (*ent*, *zool*) (animal) having four feet.

tetrarch [*tet*Raark] *n* (*Rom hist*) governor of one quarter of a province; governor of a small territory.

tetrarchy [*tet*Raarki] *n* district ruled by a tetrarch; period of office of a tetrarch.

tetravalent [tetRa*val*ent] *adj* (*chem*) quadrivalent.

tetrode [*tet*ROd] *n* thermionic valve with four electrodes > PDS.

tetter [*tet*er] *n* any of various eruptive skin diseases.

Teuton [*tew*ton] *n* member of any Germanic tribe or nation; (*coll*) German.

Teutonic [tew*ton*ik] *adj* Germanic; German; of the ancient Germanic tribes or language ~ **Teutonic** *n* primitive Germanic.

text [tekst] *n* written or printed words forming a literary work; original words of an author, as opposed to preface, commentaries, notes, translations *etc*; topic, theme for discussion; quotation, proverb, saying *etc* used as authority to support an argument; short passage from the Bible, *esp* used as starting-point for a sermon; **set t.** book or passage set for detailed study for an examination.

textbook [*tekst*book] *n* standard book from which a particular branch of knowledge can be studied; manual ~ **textbook** *adj* behaving or proceeding exactly as theoretical studies predict; proceeding exactly as planned.

text-hand [*tekst*-hand] *n* large style of handwriting.

textile [*tekst*Il] *n* any woven fabric ~ **textile** *adj* of or by weaving; woven; of textiles.

textual [*tekst*ew-al] *adj* of, for or in a text or texts; word for word; of or for ascertaining the original form of a text ~ **textually** *adv*.

textural [*tekst*ewRal] *adj* of texture.

texture [*tekst*cher] *n* degree of roughness or smoothness, coarseness or fineness of some material object, *esp* as felt by touch; way in which a fabric has been woven, *esp* as regards roughness or smoothness; structure, constitution; (*fig*) characteristic quality, nature.

thalamus [*thal*amus] *n* (*bot*) receptacle of a flower; **optic t.** (*anat*) part of brain in which optic nerve is rooted.

thaler [*taa*ler] *n* obsolete German silver coin.

thalidomide [tha*lid*omId] *n* a tranquillizing drug

causing malformation in unborn babies; **t. baby** baby born with deformities caused by thalidomide taken by its mother.

thallium [*thal*i-um] *n* white malleable metal resembling lead > PDS.

than [THan] *conj* used after a comparative to express inequality.

thanat-, thanato- *pref* of death.

thane, thegn [*thayn*] *n* (*hist*) member of an Anglo-Saxon class of landowning nobles.

thank [*thank*] *v/t* express gratitude to; (*fig*) be indebted to; **t. you** I am grateful to you.

thankee [*thankee*] *interj* (*coll*) thank you.

thankful [*thank*fool] *adj* grateful, feeling or expressing thanks ~ **thankfully** *adv* ~ **thankfulness** *n*.

thankless [*thank*lis] *n* ungrateful; not gaining thanks, rousing no gratitude ~ **thanklessly** *adv* ~ **thanklessness** *n*.

thank-offering [*thank*-ofeRing] *n* offering made to express gratitude.

thanks [*thanks*] *n* (*pl*) words expressing gratitude; gratitude; **t. to** owing to, because of ~ **thanks** *interj* thank you.

thanksgiving [*thanks*giving] *n* act of expressing thanks, *esp* to God; form of words expressing thanks; **T. Day** (*US*) annual day of holiday in thanksgiving for the harvest, *usu* fourth Thursday of November.

that (*pl* **those**) [THat] *dem pron* the person or thing just mentioned or pointed out; the person or thing over there; **and all t.** so on and so forth; **after t.** when that had happened; **at t.** even so; as well, in addition; anyway; **like t.** thus; in such a way; **t. is** in other words; **t.'s t.** that settles the matter; that is the end of it; **with t.** thereupon, after that ~ **that** (*pl* **those**) *dem adj* being the one just mentioned or pointed out; being the more remote; well-known; notorious, disapproved of ~ **that** *adv* (*coll*) so much, to such a degree, distance *etc* ~ **that** *rel pron* who; which ~ **that** *conj* introducing a noun clause, or an adverbial clause of result, purpose or reason; introducing exclamations of wish or surprise.

thatch [*thach*] *n* straw or reeds used for covering a roof; (*fig*) thick matted hair ~ **thatch** *v/t* cover (roof) with straw or reeds.

thatching [*thaching*] *n* act of covering with thatch; materials used for thatching.

thaumaturge [*thaw*maturj] *n* one who works miracles; magician; conjurer.

thaumaturgy [*thaw*maturji] *n* act of working miracles or magical tricks.

thaw [*thaw*] *v/i* and *t* (*of snow, ice*) melt; cause (something frozen) to melt; return to normal warmth after being very cold; (*of weather*) grow warm enough for snow and ice to melt; (*fig*) grow friendly after being hostile or aloof ~ **thaw** *n* act of thawing; weather such that snow and ice melt; (*fig*) renewed friendship; detente.

the [THi/THe] *def art* indicating a particular person, thing, class etc; used before certain titles; used before adjectives to make them nouns; **the wife, the boss** *etc* (*coll*) my wife, my boss *etc*; [THee] (*coll*) unique; oustanding, excellent; fashionable ~ **the** *adv* by that amount; to that extent.

theatre [*thee*-ater] *n* building where dramatic performances are held; room in a hospital where operations are performed; dramatic literature, drama; scene where some action takes place; skill in producing dramatic effects; **t. of the absurd** plays using irrational situations or dialogue; **t. of cruelty** plays using physical violence for shock effects; **t. in the round** theatre whose stage is almost completely surrounded by spectators.

theatrical [thee-*at*Rikal] *adj* of the theatre; by or for dramatic performance; dramatic; melodramatic; superficially impressive; showy, insincere.

theatricality [thee-atRi*kali*ti] *n* quality of being theatrical.

theatrically [thee-*at*Rikali] *adv* in a theatrical way.

theatricals [thee-*at*Rikalz] *n* (*pl*) dramatic performances, *esp* by amateurs.

theca [*thee*ka] *n* (*bot, zool*) case, sheath.

thee [THee] *pron* (*ar* and *poet*) 2nd *pers sing acc* you.

theft [*theft*] *n* act of stealing.

thegn see thane.

theine [*thee*-in] *n* caffeine, an organic compound found in tea > PDS.

their [THair] *poss adj* belonging to or connected with them.

theirs [THairz] *poss pron* and *adj* (that, those) belonging to them.

theism [*thee*-izm] *n* belief that a personal God exists, but not that He has given any revelation.

theist [*thee*-ist] *n* one who believes in theism.

theistic [thee-*istik*] *adj* of or like theism.

them [THem] *personal pron objective case of* **they**; (*dial, sl*) those.

thematic [thee*mati*k] *adj* of a theme.

theme [*theem*] *n* chief or recurrent subject of talk or writing; recurrent or important idea or topic in a book *etc, usu* less obvious and more abstract than a subject; (*mus*) melody developed with variations > PDM; (*gramm*) stem; **t. tune** tune recurring several times in a play, film *etc*; signature tune.

themselves [THem*selvz*] *pron* (*pl*) (*emph* and *refl*) them.

then [THen] *adv* at that time; afterwards, next ~ **then** *conj* therefore; accordingly ~ **then** *adj* existing at that time ~ **then** *n* that time.

thence [THens] *adv* from that place; from that time; for that reason.

thenceforth [THens*fawrth*] *adv* from that time onward.

thenceforward [THens*fawr*ward] *adv* from that time onward.

theo- *pref* of God; of a god or gods.

theocentric [thee-O*sent*Rik] *adj* centred in God; having God as centre.

theocracy [thee-*ok*Rasi] *n* government by rulers who claim divine inspiration and authority.

theocratic [thee-O*krat*ik] *adj* of a theocracy.

theodolite [thee-*od*Olit] *n* surveying instrument for measuring angles > PDE.

theologian [thee-ol*O*ji-an] *n* one who studies theology.

theological [thee-ol*o*jikal] *adj* of or by theology ~ **theologically** *adv*.

theologist [thee-*ol*ojist] *n* theologian.

theologize [thee-*ol*ojiz] *v/i* study theology; form or express theological arguments.

theology [thee-*ol*oji] *n* formation of systematic theories on the nature of God and His relation to man and the universe; theological system of a particular religious group or writer; systematic study of religion.

theophany [thee-*ofani*] *n* act by which God or a god manifests his presence or power to men.

theorem [*thee*-ORem] *n* (*math*) proposition to be proved by logical reasoning.

theoretic [thee-o*Retik*] *adj* theoretical.

theoretical [thee-o*Retik*al] *adj* of, by, based on theory; according to theory but not yet proved by practical experience or experiment; speculative ~ **theoretically** *adv*.

theorist [*thee*-oRist] *n* one who theorizes.

theorize [*thee*-oRIz] *v/i* form theories; form arguments or lay down principles without practical experience.

theory [*thee*-oRi] *n* principle suggested to explain observed facts or phenomena; idea, doctrine or system not yet tested by practical experience; hypothesis; underlying doctrines and principles of an art, branch of knowledge, craft *etc*; (*coll*) idea, notion.

theosophical [thee-o*sofik*al] *adj* of theosophy.

theosophist [thi-*osofist*] *n* believer in theosophy.

theosophy [thi-*osofi*] *n* mystical religious system founded in the late 19th century aiming at direct communication between the soul and God.

therapeutic [theRa*pewtik*] *adj* of or for healing.

therapeutical [theRa*pewtik*al] *adj* therapeutic ~ **therapeutically** *adv*.

therapeutics [theRa*pewtiks*] *n* (*pl*) branch of medicine concerning treatment and cure of diseases; therapy.

therapy [*the*Rapi] *n* any treatment aimed at curing a physical or mental disorder; therapeutics.

there [*THair*] *adv* in or towards that place; at that point or stage (of argument, story *etc*); **all t.** (*coll*) shrewd, quick-witted; sane; **get t.** reach an aim, attain an object; **not all t.** mentally deficient; mad; **t. you are**! here is what you wanted; I told you so; **t. you go** you are doing the same thing again ~ **there** *impers pron* used as subject of verb (*esp* be) to introduce a sentence.

thereabouts [THair*Rabouts*] *adv* near that place; near that number, degree *etc*; approximately.

thereafter [THair*Raafter*] *adv* after that.

thereat [*THair*Rat] *adv* at or because of that.

thereby [THair*bI*] *adv* by that means.

there'd [*THaird*] *abbr* there had; there would.

therefore [*THair*for] *adv* for that reason; accordingly.

therein [*THair*Rin] *adv* in this or that place; in this or that time, respect *etc*.

thereinafter [THair*Rinaafter*] *adv* later in the same document.

there'll [*THairl*] *abbr* there will; there shall.

thereof [THair*Rof*] *adv* (*ar*) of this or that.

thereon [THair*Ron*] *adv* (*ar*) on this or that.

there's [*THairz*] *abbr* there is; there has.

thereto [THair*too*] *adv* (*ar*) to this or that; besides.

thereupon [THair*Rupon*] *adv* in consequence of this or that: immediately.

therewith [THair*with*] *adv* with this or that; at once.

theriomorphic [theerRi-o*mawrfik*] *adj* having the form of an animal.

therm [*thurm*] *n* unit of heat equal to 100,000

British thermal units, used in measuring consumption of coal-gas.

therm- *pref* of or by heat.

thermaesthesia [thurmes*theezi*-a] *n* sensitiveness to heat.

thermal [*thurm*al] *adj* of or by heat; (*of springs of water*) naturally hot; **British t. unit** quantity of heat needed to raise one lb. of water one degree Fahrenheit ~ **thermal** *n* vertical rising current of warm air.

thermic [*thurm*ik] *adj* of or by heat.

thermion [*thurm*i-on] *n* (*phys*) ion emitted by incandescent body.

thermionic [thurmi-*onik*] *adj* relating to thermionics; **t. valve** system of electrodes arranged in an evacuated glass or metal envelope.

thermionics [thurmi-*oniks*] *n* (*pl*) branch of physics concerning emission of electrons under the action of heat.

thermistor [*thurm*istor] *n* substance whose electrical resistance decreases in ratio to increasing heat.

thermo- *pref* of or by heat.

thermochemistry [thurm*OkemistRi*] *n* branch of chemistry dealing with the absorptions and evolutions of heat during reactions.

thermocouple [*thurm*Okup'l] *n* thermometer based on thermoelectricity.

thermodynamics [thurmOd*Inamiks*] *n* (*pl*) scientific study of processes involving heat changes.

thermoelectricity [thurmO-e)ektRi*siti*] *n* electricity produced by direct conversion of heat energy into electrical energy.

thermogenesis [thurmO*jenisis*] *n* production of heat in an animal body.

thermograph [*thurm*OgRaaf] *n* self-registering thermometer for recording temperature variations.

thermometer [thur*momiter*] *n* instrument for measuring temperature, *esp* one depending on expansion of mercury with rising heat > PDS; **clinical t.** mercury thermometer for measuring temperature of human body.

thermometry [thur*momitRi*] *n* measurement of temperature.

thermonuclear [thurmO-*newkli*-ar] *adj* of, using, or caused by heat released in nuclear fusion; **t. bomb** hydrogen bomb.

thermopile [*thurm*OpIl] *n* instrument, for detecting and measuring heat radiations, based on thermoelectricity.

thermoplastic [thurmO*plastik*] *n* and *adj* (substance) which becomes soft and plastic when heated.

Thermos [*thurm*os] *n* (*tr*) vacuum flask, closed vessel with double walls enclosing a vacuum, used for keeping liquids hot or cold by insulation.

thermosetting [thurm*oseting*] *adj* becoming permanently hard when once heated.

thermosiphon [thurmO*sifon*] *n* system by which water circulates in a motor engine to cool it.

thermosphere [*thurm*Osfeer] *n* region of the Earth's upper atmosphere in which the temperature increases with altitude.

thermostat [*thurm*Ostat] *n* device for maintaining something at constant temperature by automatically cutting and restoring heat supply as needed.

thermostatic [thurmOstatik] *adj* of or by a thermostat ~ **thermostatically** *adv*.

thermostatics [thurmOstatiks] *n* (*pl*) theory of equilibrium of heat.

thesaurus (*pl* thesauri) [thisawrRus] *n* lexicon of words and phrases grouped by meaning, not alphabetically; dictionary; encyclopaedia.

these [THeez] *pl* of this.

thesis (*pl* theses) [theesis] *n* essay or treatise written by candidate for university degree and *usu* embodying results of research; proposition, theory submitted for discussion or proof; (*pros*) stressed part of a metrical foot.

theurgy [thee-urji] *n* marvel produced by supernatural power; miracle, sorcery.

thewed [thewd] *adj* having muscles.

thews [thewz] *n* (*pl*) sinews, muscles; strength.

thewy [thew-i] *adj* muscular.

they [THay] *pron* 3rd *pers pl nom*.

they'd [THayd] *abbr* they had; they would; they should.

they'll [THayl] *abbr* they will; they shall.

they're [THayr] *abbr* they are.

they've [THayv] *abbr* they have.

thiamin, thiamine [thI-amin, thI-ameen] *n* (*bioch*) white crystalline powder required for carbohydrate metabolism; vitamin B_1; aneurin.

thick [thik] *adj* having relatively great depth or breadth; dense, crowded; compact, closely packed or arranged; frequent; numerous; (*of liquids*) muddy; not flowing easily; relatively dense; (*of air*) full of smoke or dust; (*of voice*) indistinct, blurred; muffled; (*of intellect*) obtuse, dull; (*coll*) very friendly; **a bit t.** too much to put up with; **t. ear** bruised and swollen ear ~ **thick** *n* thickest part; **in the t. of** in the midst of; **through t. and thin** despite all difficulties ~ **thick** *adv* thickly; **lay it on t.** (*coll*) make a fuss about, exaggerate.

thicken [thik'n] *v/t* and *i* make thick; become thick.

thickening [thikening] *n* something which makes a liquid thicker; process of making or becoming thicker; thickest part of something.

thicket [thikIt] *n* dense growth of shrubs or trees ~ **thicketed** *adj* covered by thickets.

thickhead [thikhed] *n* (*coll*) stupid person.

thickish [thikish] *adj* rather thick.

thickly [thikli] *adv* in a thick way.

thickness [thiknis] *n* state or quality of being thick; the third dimension; single layer.

thickset [thikset] *adj* closely planted; short and broad, stocky.

thick-skinned [thik-*skind*] *adj* not sensitive, not easily upset or annoyed; not perceptive.

thick-skulled [thik-*skuld*] *adj* stupid.

thief (*pl* thieves) [theef] *n* one who steals; robber.

thieve [theev] *v/t* and *i* steal.

thievery [theeveRi] *n* act of stealing.

thieves [theevz] *pl* of thief.

thievish [theevish] *adj* of or like a thief; in the habit of stealing; dishonest; stealthy ~ **thievishly** *adv* ~ **thievishness** *n*.

thigh [thI] *n* uppermost part of leg from hip to knee; bone of this, femur.

thighbone [thIbOn] *n* femur, bone between hipjoint and knee.

thimble [thimb'l] *n* small hard cover to protect finger in sewing; short metal tube.

thimbleful [thimb'lfool] *n* as much as a thimble can contain; very small quantity.

thimblerigging [thimb'lRiging] *n* swindling game in which a pea is supposed to be concealed under one of three thimbles, the player betting that he will guess which thimble is covering it; (*fig*) trickery, cheating, dishonest dealing.

thin [thin] *adj* having relatively little depth or breadth, not thick; slender, lean; sparse, scanty; flimsy, transparent; meagre; (*of liquids*) of low density; **t. on the ground** rare, not easily available; **t. on top** (*coll*) going bald; **a t. time** (*coll*) an unpleasant, miserable time ~ **thin** (*pres/part* **thinning,** *p/t* and *p/part* **thinned**) *v/t* and *i* make thin; become thinner.

thine [THIn] *poss pron* and *adj* (*ar* and *poet*) belonging to you.

thing [thing] *n* any object, material or immaterial, existing or thought of; fact; thought, idea; topic, subject; circumstance, event; (*pl*) personal possessions; luggage, clothes, parcels *etc*; (*pl*) affairs, business; (*coll*) what is right, fitting, wanted, useful *etc*; (*sl*) irrational liking or dislike; obsessive idea; (*coll*) what one is good at or enjoys doing; **the t. is** the main point, problem, factor *etc* is; **do one's (own) thing** (*coll*) act naturally, express one's true self; **for one t.** as one consideration; **just the t.** just what was wanted; **just one of those things** something that can't be helped; something overpowering and inexplicable; **know a t. or two** be no fool, be experienced; **no such t.** not at all, certainly not; **not the t.** socially incorrect; **see things** (*coll*) have hallucinations.

thingummy [thingumi] *n* (*coll*) person or thing, *esp* one whose name one has forgotten.

think (*p/t* and *p/part* thought) [think] *v/t* and *i* examine in the mind, reflect; use one's reason; consider, ponder; believe, be of opinion that; surmise; expect; suppose; imagine; **t. about** reflect, ponder on; set mind to consider, remember or imagine; **t. aloud** speak one's thoughts as they come; **t. back** recall, think of the past; **t. big** have ambitious plans; **t. better of** reconsider, reverse (a decision or judgement); **I don't t.!** (*sl*) I certainly do not think so; **t. much of** have a high opinion of; **t. nothing of** have a low opinion of; disregard, not worry over; **t. of** think about; invent, discover; **be thinking of** be inclined but not decided to do; **not t. of** have no intention of; **t. out** plan, solve or decide by careful thought; **t. over** consider carefully, ponder; reconsider; **t. up** (*coll*) invent, discover; **t. well of** approve of, have high opinion of ~ **think** *n* (*coll*) act or process of thinking, *esp* on a problem or difficulty.

thinkable [thinkab'l] *adj* capable of being thought.

thinker [thinker] *n* one who thinks; philosopher.

thinking [thinking] *adj* capable of thought, rational; thoughtful ~ **thinking** *n* act of one who thinks; thought, reflection, *esp* on a problem or difficulty.

thinking-cap [thinking-kap] *n* **put one's t. on** (*coll*) settle down to think something over.

think-piece [think-pees] *n* (*coll*) article or essay seriously analysing a problem.

think-tank [*think*-tank] *n* group of experts supplying new ideas or solutions.

thinly [*thin*li] *adv* with little depth; in a thin way.

thinness [*thin*-nis] *n* state or quality of being thin.

thin-skinned [thin-*skind*] *adj* sensitive, easily upset or annoyed.

thio- *pref* containing sulphur.

third [*thurd*] *n* and *adj* (that) which follows two others in a series; (that) which is one of three equal parts; (*mus*) (interval) taking three steps in a scale > PDM; **t. dimension** distance, depth; **T. World** (*pol*) nations not committed either to Communist or to anti-Communist alliances; nations without advanced industrial technology, economically underdeveloped nations, *esp* of tropical or semi-tropical regions.

third-degree [thurd-di*gree*] *n* harsh treatment of a prisoner in order to obtain a confession.

thirdly [*thurd*li] *adv* in the third place.

third-party [thurd-*paa*rti] *n* (*leg*) person in a law case besides the two chiefly concerned; **t. risks** liability of an insurer towards a person not mentioned in the policy.

third-rate [thurd-*rayt*] *adj* of very poor quality.

thirst [*thurst*] *n* sensation caused by want of drink; desire for drink; (*fig*) strong desire, longing ～ **thirst** *v/i* suffer thirst; **t. for** long, crave for.

thirsty [*thurs*ti] *adj* desiring drink; parched; (*fig*) eagerly desiring, craving; (*coll*) causing thirst ～ **thirstily** *adv* ～ **thirstiness** *n*.

thirteen [thur*teen*] *n* and *adj* one more than twelve; symbol of this, 13.

thirteenth [thur*teenth*] *n* and *adj* (that) which follows twelve others in a series; (that) which is one of thirteen equal parts.

thirtieth [*thurt*i-eth] *n* and *adj* (that) which follows twenty-nine others in a series; (that) which is one of thirty equal parts.

thirty [*thurt*i] *n* cardinal number equal to three times ten; symbol of this, 30; (*pl*) fourth decade of a century or of a person's life.

thirtyfold [*thurt*if*Old*] *adj* and *adv* multiplied by thirty; amounting to thirty.

this (*pl* **these**) [*THis*] *dem adj* and *pron* (being) the person or thing just mentioned or pointed out; (being) the person or thing near at hand; **like t.** thus; in such a way; **what's all t.?** what is the trouble, disturbance *etc* here? ～ **this** *adv* (*coll*) to such a degree, distance *etc*; so much but no more.

thisness [*THis*nis] *n* (*philos*) individuality; quiddity.

thistle [*this*'l] *n* one of various prickly-leaved flowering plants; national emblem of Scotland.

thistledown [*this*'ldown] *n* feathery bristles of thistle seeds.

thistly [*this*li] *adj* overgrown with thistles.

thither [*THiTH*er] *adv* to that place; to that degree, stage *etc*.

thixotropic [thiks*Ot*R*o*pik] *adj* able to become liquid on shaking or stirring and to become more viscous on standing ～ **thixotropy** *n*.

tho' [*THO*] *abbr* though.

thole [th*Ol*] *n* peg fixed in gunwale to keep oar in place.

Thomism [*tOm*izm] *n* scholastic doctrine of St Thomas Aquinas.

thong [*thong*] *n* leather strap or lash.

thoracic [tho*Ras*ik] *adj* of the thorax.

thorax [*thaw*Raks] *n* part of body between neck

and abdomen in mammals; middle region of body of insects > PDB.

thoride [*thaw*Rid] *n* natural radioisotope containing thorium.

thorium [*thaw*Ri-um] *n* a dark grey radioactive metal > PDS.

thorn [*thawrn*] *n* prickle growing on certain trees and bushes; thorny bush; Old English name for the letter þ; (*fig*) annoyance, secret affliction.

thorny [*thawr*ni] *adj* full of thorns; prickly; (*fig*) troublesome, causing difficulty or dispute.

thorough [*thu*Ro] *adj* complete; entire; careful ～ **thorough** *prep* (*ar*) through.

thorough-bass [*thu*Ro-bays] *n* (*mus*) bass part with figures to indicate the harmony.

thoroughbred [*thu*RobRed] *n* and *adj* (animal, *esp* horse) bred solely from known ancestors of good genetic quality; having a known pedigree; (*fig*) (person) of aristocratic ancestry.

thoroughfare [*thu*Rofair] *n* unobstructed road; road for public traffic.

thorough-going [*thu*Ro-gO-ing] *adj* uncompromising, going to any length; thorough.

thoroughly [*thu*Roli] *adv* in all respects; completely, entirely, perfectly.

thoroughness [*thu*Ronis] *n* quality of doing things thoroughly; completeness.

thorough-paced [*thu*Ro-payst] *adj* (*of horse*) perfectly trained; out-and-out, thorough.

thorp, thorpe [*thawrp*] *n* small village.

those [*THOz*] *pl* of **that**.

thou [*THow*] *pron* (*ar* and *poet*) 2*nd pers sing nom* you.

though [*THO*] *conj* in spite of the fact that; even if; granting that; **as t.** as if.

thought (1) [*thawt*] *n* act or process of thinking; reflection; meditation; belief, idea or conclusion reached by thinking; point of view, opinion; body of opinions and conclusions typical of the outlook of an individual, group or period; care, concern; small amount or degree; **have thoughts of** be inclined but not decided to do.

thought (2) *p/t* and *p/part* of **think**.

thoughtful [*thawt*fool] *adj* inclined to think seriously; pensive; kind, considerate; expressing serious thought ～ **thoughtfully** *adv* ～ **thoughtfulness** *n*.

thoughtless [*thawt*lis] *adj* stupidly careless of consequences; inconsiderate ～ **thoughtlessly** *adv* ～ **thoughtlessness** *n*.

thought-reader [*thawt*-Reeder] *n* one capable of thought-reading.

thought-reading [*thawt*-Reeding] *n* intuitive perception of what is passing in another's mind; telepathy.

thought-transference [*thawt*-tRansferenz] *n* telepathy.

thought-wave [*thawt*-wayv] *n* hypothetical telepathic vibration.

thousand [*thowz*and] *n* ten hundred; (*coll*, often *pl*) large number; **one in a t.** exceptionally good, unrivalled ～ **thousand** *adj* being ten times one hundred.

thousandfold [*thowz*andf*Old*] *adj* and *adv* one thousand times as many or as much.

thousandth [*thowz*andth] *n* and *adj* (that) which is last of a thousand; (that) which is one of a thousand equal parts.

thraldom [*thRawl*dom] *n* condition of being a thrall; bondage; captivity.

thrall [*thRawl*] *n* slave, serf; slavery, servitude.

thrash [*thRash*] *v/t* and *i* beat violently; flog; defeat thoroughly; beat grain from chaff, thresh; **t. about** move limbs violently and in disorder; **t. out** clear up (problem *etc*) by thorough discussion.

thrasher [*thRash*er] *n* one who or that which thrashes; kind of large shark; American bird resembling a thrush; threshing-machine.

thrasonical [*thRa*so*ni*kal] *adj* boastful.

thread [*thRed*] *n* very fine cord; filament; logical connexion, sequence; spiral of a screw; **hang by a t.** be in a precarious state ~ **thread** *v/t* pass thread through the eye of; string on to a thread; pass cautiously through.

threadbare [*thRed*bair] *adj* rubbed by long use till the nap is worn away; hackneyed, trite; dressed in old shabby clothes.

threadlike [*thRed*lIk] *adj* like a thread; very slender.

threadworm [*thRed*wurm] *n* threadlike worm, *esp* one infesting human intestines.

threat [*thRet*] *n* act of declaring an intention to inflict pain, punishment *etc*; indication that something unpleasant is likely to happen.

threaten [*thRet*en] *v/t* and *i* declare one's intention to inflict pain; use threats; look as if something unpleasant is likely to happen.

threatening [*thRet*ening] *adj* indicating a threat; menacing ~ **threateningly** *adv*.

three [*thRee*] *n* and *adj* one more than two; symbol of this, 3.

three-cornered [thRee-*kawr*nerd] *adj* having three corners or angles, triangular; **t. fight** contest engaging three competitors.

three-decker [*thRee*-deker] *n* old type of sailing ship with three decks; old type of pulpit with three tiers; sandwich made with three slices of bread and two layers of filling; three-volume novel.

three-dimensional [thRee-dI*men*shonal] *adj* having length, breadth, and height; stereoscopic, producing illusion of depth; (*fig*) realistic.

three-figure [*thRee*-figer] *adj* (*of sums*) between one hundred and a thousand.

threefold [*thReef*Old] *adj* three times as great; having three parts ~ **threefold** *adv* multiplied by three, triply.

three-halfpence [thRee-*hay*pens] *n* sum of one penny and a halfpenny; obsolete silver coin of this value.

three-legged [thRee-*leg*id] *adj* having three legs; **t. race** race run by pairs of competitors, the left leg of one being tied to the right leg of the other.

threepence [*thRep*ens/*thRip*ens/*thRup*ens] *n* three pennies; former coin of this value.

threepenny [*thRep*eni/*thRip*eni/*thRup*eni] *adj* costing threepence; **t. bit** former coin of the value of three old pennies.

threepiece [*thRee*pees] *n* and *adj* (woman's outfit) consisting of jacket, skirt and coat, or of jacket, blouse and skirt.

threeply [*thRee*plI] *adj* (*of wool, thread*) having three strands; (*of wood*) having three layers.

three-quarter [thRee-*kwawr*ter] *adj* being or of three fourths of the whole ~ **three-quarter** *n* (*Rugby football*) one playing between the full-backs and the half-backs.

threescore [thRee*skawr*] *n* sixty.

threesome [*thRee*sum] *n* game of golf played by three persons; group of three companions.

threnody [*thRen*Odi] *n* dirge, lament.

thresh [*thResh*] *v/t* and *i* beat (corn) so as to separate grain from chaff; thrash.

thresher [*thResh*er] *n* one who threshes; threshing-machine; thrasher.

threshold [*thResh*-hOld] *n* piece of wood or stone under a door; entrance, doorway; (*fig*) beginning; (*biol, psych*) lowest intensity at which a stimulus becomes perceptible > PDP; (*phys*) lowest value of a signal which will produce a desired effect.

threw [*thROO*] *p/t* of **throw**.

thrice [*thRIs*] *adv* three times.

thrift [*thRift*] *n* frugality, economy; (*bot*) sea-pink.

thrifty [*thRif*ti] *adj* frugal, economical; careful over spending money ~ **thriftily** *adv* ~ **thriftiness** *n*.

thrill [*thRil*] *v/t* and *i* cause intense excitement to; stir the emotions of; be deeply excited, enthusiastic or stirred; vibrate, tingle ~ **thrill** *n* feeling of intense excitement or enthusiasm; intensely pleasurable emotion; that which causes such a feeling; exciting event.

thriller [*thRil*er] *n* book, play or film dealing with crime, detection, mysteries *etc* so as to rouse strong excitement; sensational book, play or film.

thrilling [*thRil*ing] *adj* intensely exciting; vibrant ~ **thrillingly** *adv*.

thrips [*thRips*] *n* minute insect which sucks sap of plants.

thrive (*p/t* **throve** or **thrived**, *p/part* **thriven** or **thrived**) [*thRIv*] *v/i* prosper; be fortunate; grow well; develop healthily; increase vigorously.

thriven [*thRiv*'n] *p/part* of **thrive**.

thriving [*thRIv*ing] *adj* prosperous, flourishing; growing or developing well and vigorously.

throat [*thROt*] *n* front part of the neck; passage in the neck connecting mouth and nose with stomach and lungs; gullet; windpipe; (*fig*) narrow opening; **jump down someone's t.** rebuke or attack strongly and unexpectedly; **ram (something) down one's t.** force one to accept unwillingly.

throaty [*thROt*i] *adj* hoarse, speaking as if with a sore throat; guttural ~ **throatily** *adv* ~ **throatiness** *n*.

throb (*pres/part* **throbbing**, *p/t* and *p/part* **throbbed**) [*thRob*] *v/i* pulsate, beat strongly or rapidly; quiver ~ **throb** *n* a strong beat, pulsation.

throe [*thRO*] *n* violent pain, brief agony; pang; **in the throes of** struggling with (some difficulty).

thrombin [*thRom*bin] *n* (*bioch*) blood enzyme which is essential to the process of clotting.

thrombosis [thRom*bO*sis] *n* (*med*) clotting of blood in heart or blood-vessel, causing stoppage of circulation.

thrombus [*thRom*bus] *n* (*med*) blood clot.

throne [*thROn*] *n* ceremonial chair for king, bishop *etc*; (*fig*) sovereign power; (*coll*) lavatory, commode; (*pl, theol*) third order of angels ~ **throne** *v/t* and *i* enthrone.

throng [*thRong*] *n* large number of people gathered close together, crowd ~ **throng** *v/i* and *t* form a throng; fill with a throng.

throstle [*thRos*'l] *n* thrush (1); kind of spinning-machine.

throttle [thRot'l] *n* valve in engine to regulate supply of gas, steam *etc*; throat ~ **throttle** *v/t* choke, strangle; (*fig*) suppress; shut off power (of engine) and so lessen speed.

through [thROO] *prep* from end to end or side to side of; in the midst of; by means of; on account of; across; to the end of ~ **through** *adv* from end to end or side to side; to the very end; completely, from beginning to end; **t. and t.** completely, utterly; **be t. with** have finished with; refuse to have any more to do with ~ **through** *adj* unobstructed, passing right through; travelling the whole way without changes.

throughout [thROO-owt] *prep* and *adv* right through; from beginning to end.

through-put [thROO-poot] *n* amount of materials passing through a factory *etc*.

throughway [thROOway] *n* road on which halting is forbidden, motorway.

throve [thROv] *p/t* of **thrive**.

throw (*p/t* **threw**, *p/part* **thrown**) [thRO] *v/t* and *i* hurl, fling, send flying through the air; cast off; dislodge from the saddle; cast to the ground; form (pottery) on a wheel; twist (threads); venture at dice; put roughly or hastily in specified place or state; **t. about** toss; wave violently; scatter; **t. away** waste, squander; give away stupidly or recklessly; utter very casually; **t. back** show characteristics inherited from remote ancestor; **t. in** give as an extra in a bargain; add unexpectedly; **t. in one's hand** give up a plan or undertaking; surrender; **t. in the towel** admit defeat; **t. off** remove hurriedly; recover from; get rid of; utter, write *etc* without effort; **t. oneself at** rush violently towards; make undignified attempts to win the love of; **t. oneself into** work enthusiastically at; **t. oneself on** trust oneself to; **t. open** open wide; allow general access to; **t. out** eject; emit; say casually; reject; **t. over (overboard)** give up, abandon; desert, jilt; reject; **t. a party** (*coll*) give a party; **t. up** give up; lose interest in; (*coll*) vomit; **t. up the sponge** surrender, give in; ~ **throw** *n* act of throwing; distance to which something is thrown; cast of dice; act or manner of throwing an opponent to the ground in wrestling; (*geol*) fault; **stone's t.** very short distance.

throwaway [thRO-away] *adj* spoken with assumed carelessness, with apparent disregard for effect; designed to be thrown away after one use ~ **throwaway** *n* (*coll*) handbill, small pamphlet.

throwback [thRObak] *n* one who reverts to ancestral characteristics not visible in recent generations; act of so reverting.

thrower [thRO-er] *n* one who or that which throws; one who twists silk into thread; potter.

thrown [thROn] *p/part* of **throw**.

throw-out [thRO-owt] *n* one who or that which has been rejected.

thru [thROO] *prep*, *adj*, and *adv* (*US*) through.

thrum (1) (*pres/part* **thrumming**, *p/t* and *p/part* **thrummed**) [thRum] *v/t* and *i* strum.

thrum (2) *n* fringe, loose thread; end of a weaver's thread.

thrush (1) [thRush] *n* any of several species of song-birds with brown plumage and freckled belly.

thrush (2) *n* inflammatory disease of mouth and throat or of vagina.

thrust [thRust] *v/t* and *i* push forcefully; push at; exert strong, steady pressure on; squeeze in; stab; **t. oneself forward** draw attention to oneself ~ **thrust** *n* violent push; act of thrusting; (*archi*, *eng*) stress, lateral or oblique force; forward-moving power of an engine; (*coll*) unscrupulous energy and determination to succeed; **cut and t.** exchange of sword blows; exchange of repartee, rapid argument; **t. fault** (*geol*) fault in which upper strata are pushed over lower ones.

thruster [thRuster] *n* one who or that which thrusts; one who ruthlessly and energetically sets out to succeed in business *etc*; one who rides too close to the hounds in hunting.

thrusting [thRusting] *n* act of one who thrusts ~ **thrusting** *adj* self-assertive; aggressive; ruthless; bumptious ~ **thrustingly** *adv*.

thud [thud] *n* dull sound caused by heavy impact ~ **thud** (*pres/part* **thudding**, *p/t* and *p/part* **thudded**) *v/i* make the sound of a thud; fall or hit with a thud.

thug [thug] *n* murderous ruffian, gangster; robber who brutally attacks his victims; (*hist*) Indian professional assassin.

thuggery [thugeRi] *n* brutal violence.

thulium [thOOli-um] *n* (*chem*) rare lanthanide element > PDS.

thumb [thum] *n* short thick inner digit of the human hand; part of glove covering this; corresponding digit in animals; **rule of t.** empirical method; **under the t. of** dominated by, completely obedient to; **thumbs up!** exclamation of triumph or approval ~ **thumb** *v/t* mark with the thumb; touch with the thumb; dirty the pages of (book *etc*) by constant use; **t. a lift (ride)** ask passing motorists for a lift by holding out a hand with fingers clenched and thumb extended.

thumbed [thumd] *adj* soiled by handling.

thumb-index [thum-indeks] *n* system of indentations at outer edge of pages of a book, enabling sections to be identified when the book is shut.

thumbnail [thumnayl] *n* hard growth on upper tip of human thumb ~ **thumbnail** *adj* miniature; concise.

thumbnut [thumnut] *n* nut with wings to be screwed up by the thumb.

thumbscrew [thumskROO] *n* instrument of torture in which the thumb was compressed.

thumbstall [thumstawl] *n* sheath to protect injured thumb.

thumbtack [thumtak] *n* (*US*) drawing-pin.

thump [thump] *n* heavy blow ~ **thump** *v/t* and *i* strike with a dull, heavy blow; beat.

thumping [thumping] *adj* that thumps; (*coll*) very big or remarkable ~ **thumpingly** *adv*.

thunder [thunder] *n* loud noise due to disturbance of air by electric discharge of lightning; thunderbolt; loud noise; **steal someone's t.** spoil someone's impressive effect by using it oneself before him ~ **thunder** *v/i* emit thunder; utter or emit a loud, deep, roaring sound; speak wrathfully; move very noisily.

thunderbolt [thunderbOlt] *n* flash of lightning striking the ground; hypothetical solid body formerly thought to fall in flash of lightning; (*fig*) overwhelming surprise, *usu* unpleasant; something moving very fast and noisily.

thunderclap [*thun*derklap] *n* loud crash of thunder.

thundercloud [*thun*derklowd] *n* storm cloud which discharges thunder and lightning; (*fig*) look of menacing anger.

thunderer [*thun*deRer] *n* one who causes thunder; Jupiter; Thor; powerful orator.

thunderflash [*thun*derflash] *n* (*mil*) explosive designed to distract attention.

thundering [*thun*deRing] *adj* making a sound like thunder; (*coll*) excessive, violent, very big ∼ **thunderingly** *adv*.

thunderous [*thun*deRus] *adj* of or like thunder; as loud as thunder; violent, destructive ∼ **thunderously** *adv*.

thunderstorm [*thun*derstawrm] *n* storm with thunder and lightning > PDG.

thunderstruck [*thun*derstRuk] *adj* struck by lightning; amazed, astonished; terrified.

thundery [*thun*deRi] *adj* of or like thunder; likely to produce thunderstorms; (*fig*) menacingly angry.

thurible [*thewr*Rib'l] *n* vessel in which incense is burnt.

Thursday [*thurz*di] *n* fifth day of the week.

thus [*THus*] *adv* in this manner; to this extent; accordingly.

thwack [*thwak*] *v/t* strike vigorously with stick *etc* ∼ **thwack** *n* vigorous blow.

thwart (1) [*thwawrt*] *v/t* prevent the plans or wishes of (someone) from being fulfilled; maliciously and successfully obstruct, frustrate.

thwart (2) *n* seat for oarsman in rowing-boat.

thy [*THI*] *pron* and *adj* (*ar* and *poet*) your.

thyme [*tIm*] *n* fragrant herb used in cooking.

thymol [*thI*mol] *n* a phenol obtained from oil of thyme.

thyratron [*thI*Ratron] *n* gas-filled thermionic valve used as a relay > PDEl.

thyroid [*thI*Roid] *n* a large endocrine gland in neck of vertebrates > PDB, PDP ∼ **thyroid** *adj* of the thyroid; **t. cartilage** Adam's apple.

thyroxin [thI*Rok*sin] *n* hormone secreted by thyroid gland.

thyrsus [*thur*sus] *n* (*myth*) staff carried by Bacchus.

thyself [THI*self*] *pron* (*refl* or *emph*) thou.

tiara [ti-*aar*Ra] *n* jewelled coronet worn by women; triple crown worn by a pope.

tibia [*tibi*-a] *n* (*anat*) shinbone.

tic [*tik*] *n* involuntary muscular twitching, *esp* of the face; **t. douloureux** facial neuralgia.

tich [*tich*] *n* (*sl*) (nickname for) a small man.

tick (1) [*tik*] *n* any of various small blood-sucking parasites > PDB; (*sl*) contemptible fellow.

tick (2) *n* cover containing filling to form pillows, mattresses *etc*; strong cloth used to make these covers.

tick (3) *n* (*coll*) credit.

tick (4) *n* light tapping noise of watch, clock, or similar mechanism; mark (√) indicating that something is approved of, correct, or noted; **on the t.** punctually ∼ **tick** *v/i* and *t* make the noise of a tick; mark with a tick; (*sl*) grumble; **t. off** (*sl*) rebuke sharply, scold; **t. over** (*of motor engine*) run quietly when out of gear; (*fig*) be comparatively inactive.

ticker [*tik*er] *n* telegraphic tape-machine; (*sl*) watch; heart.

tickertape [*tik*ertayp] *n* used tape from a telegraphic tape-machine; **t. welcome** (*US*) triumphal parade through streets festooned with this.

ticket [*tik*it] *n* marked card or paper showing holder's right to some privilege, service *etc*; card entitling holder to travel a specified distance by public transport, to have a seat at an entertainment *etc*; price-label; pawnbroker's receipt; document notifying motorist of a fine for illegal parking; (*coll*) principles or membership of a political party; (*US*) list of party candidates; (*sl*) the right thing to do; what is wanted; **t. of leave** document formerly given to prisoners released on restricted conditional discharge ∼ **ticket** *v/t* put a ticket on, label.

ticking [*tik*ing] *n* tick (2).

tickle [*tik*'l] *v/t* and *i* touch lightly so as to produce slight irritation and usually laughter; amuse, cause to laugh; please; itch, tingle; **t. pink** (*sl*) please or amuse greatly ∼ **tickle** *n* sensation of being tickled.

tickler [*tik*ler] *n* one who or that which tickles; difficult problem.

ticklish [*tik*lish] *adj* easily tickled; difficult to deal with, needing skill ∼ **ticklishly** *adv* ∼ **ticklishness** *n*.

tick-tack [*tik*-tak] *n* system of gestures by which bookmakers signal changes in betting odds; **t. man** bookmaker's assistant.

tidal [*tI*dal] *adj* of or affected by tides.

tiddler [*tid*ler] *n* very small fish; stickleback.

tiddley [*tid*li] *adj* (*sl*) slightly drunk, tipsy; (*naut coll*) trim, spruce.

tiddleywinks [*tid*liwinks] *n* children's game in which small disks are snapped into a container.

tide [*tId*] *n* alternate rise and fall of the sea caused by gravitational pull of moon and sun > PDG, PDS; (*fig*) trend, tendency; (*ar*) time, season ∼ **tide** *v/i* **t. over** barely surmount a period of difficulty; manage to cope until help comes.

tidemark [*tId*maark] *n* highest point reached by a tide; (*joc*) dirty smear left by inefficient washing.

tide-waiter [*tId*-wayter] *n* customs officer who boards ships to enforce regulations.

tide-water [*tId*-wawter] *n* tidal flow.

tideway [*tId*way] *n* channel through which tidal waters flow; ebb or flow of tide through a channel.

tidily [*tId*ili] *adv* in a tidy manner; neatly; suitably.

tidiness [*tId*inis] *n* state or quality of being tidy.

tidings [*tId*ingz] *n* (*pl*) news.

tidy [*tId*i] *adj* arranged neatly and in good order; habitually keeping things neatly ordered; trim; (*coll*) fairly large ∼ **tidy** *v/t* and *i* put in order, arrange or put away neatly; **t. up** make neat or orderly; clear up; make oneself neat, clean *etc* ∼ **tidy** *n* small box, bag *etc* in which odds and ends may be kept.

tie [*tI*] *v/t* and *i* fasten or secure with rope, string *etc*; make into a knot; bind, unite; hamper, restrict freedom of; (*of competitors*) make an equal score; reach end of race simultaneously; do equally well; **t. down** tie so as to prevent from rising; bind firmly by obligations, conditions *etc*; **t. in with** link closely with; **t. up** fasten with rope or string; bandage; bind; restrict freedom of; restrict use of (money *etc*) by legal conditions; **t. up with** link or associate closely with; be connected with ∼ **tie** *n* strip of cloth worn round neck and knotted in front; bond, connecting piece, link; emotional relationship considered as binding; that which restricts freedom, obligation; equality of achievement by two or more competitors in sport, elections, examinations *etc*; (*mus*) curved line joining two notes of same pitch > PDM; (*archi, bui etc*) connecting and supporting piece.

tiebeam [*tɪ*beem] *n* lowest horizontal beam of a roof truss.

tied-house [*tɪd*-hows] *n* a public house bound to obtain its supplies from one firm.

tiepin [*tɪ*pin] *n* ornamental pin for necktie.

tier (1) [*tɪ*-er] *n* one who ties.

tier (2) [*teer*] *n* row, rank; several rows placed one above the other.

tierce [*teers*] *n* (*eccles*) third canonical hour; (*fencing*) position with point of weapon raised to eye-level.

tiercel [*teer*sel] *n* male falcon.

tiercet [*teer*set] *n* (*mus, pros*) triplet.

tie-up [*tɪ*-up] *n* link, bond; association, connexion.

tiff [*tif*] *n* slight quarrel.

tiffany [*tif*ani] *n* thin silky gauze.

tiffin [*tif*in] *n* (*Anglo-Indian*) light lunch.

tig [*tig*] *n* children's pursuing game, tag.

tiger [*tɪ*ger] *n* fierce Asiatic feline mammal, tawny in colour, with black stripes; (*fig*) cruel man: skilful and ruthless adversary; (*US*) extra yell after three cheers; **paper t.** enemy whose apparent strength is all sham.

tigercat [*tɪ*gerkat] *n* species of large striped wildcat; ocelot; margay.

tigerish [*tɪ*geRish] *adj* like a tiger; fierce, cruel.

tigerlily [*tɪ*gerlili] *n* lily with orange-spotted flowers.

tigerwood [*tɪ*gerwood] *n* a streaked black and brown wood.

tight [*tɪt*] *adj* knotted closely; fitting very closely; firmly packed, compact, entirely filled; taut, tense; not leaking; strict; (*coll*) stingy, miserly; (*of money*) scarce; (*sl*) drunk; **t. corner** (spot) very dangerous or difficult situation ∼ **tight** *adv* tightly, firmly, closely; **sit t.** stay where one is; stick to one's views, rights *etc*.

tighten [*tɪt*en] *v/t* and *i* make or become tight or tighter; **t. up** make or become stricter.

tight-fisted [*tɪt*-fistid] *adj* miserly.

tight-lipped [*tɪt*-lipt] *adj* having lips closed tightly; stern-looking; secretive.

tightly [*tɪt*li] *adv* in a tight way.

tightness [*tɪt*nis] *n* state or quality of being tight.

tightrope [*tɪt*Rop] *n* tightly stretched rope or cable on which acrobats perform.

tights [*tɪts*] *n* (*pl*) very close-fitting garments covering legs and lower part of body.

tightwad [*tɪt*wod] *n* (*sl*) miser.

tigress [*tɪ*gRes] *n* female tiger.

tike, tyke [*tɪk*] *n* dog, cur; ill-bred person, boor; Yorkshireman.

tiki [*tɪki*] *n* small greenstone Maori amulet.

tilde [*tilde*] *n* diacritical sign (∼) placed above letter *n* in Spanish.

tile [*tɪl*] *n* thin, flat clay brick used for covering roofs, walls, floors *etc*; (*coll*) hat; top-hat; **a t. loose** (*coll*) slightly mad ∼ **tile** *v/t* cover with tiles.

till (1) [*til*] *v/t* cultivate (the ground).

till (2) *prep* and *conj* up to the time of; up to the time when.

till (3) *n* box or drawer into which cash paid in a shop is put.

tillage [*tilij*] *n* agriculture; cultivated land.

tiller (1) [*tiler*] *n* one who cultivates land.

tiller (2) *n* lever on end of rudder for turning it.

tilt (1) [*tilt*] *n* canvas hood or cover, awning.

tilt (2) *v/t* and *i* cause to slope, tip up; slope ∼ **tilt** *n* sloping position.

tilt (3) *v/i* charge on horseback with lance; joust; **t. at** (*fig*) attack, criticize ∼ **tilt** *n* thrust in tilting; tournament; **at full t.** with great speed or force.

tilth [*tilth*] *n* tillage; cultivated soil.

tilt-hammer [*tilt*-hamer] *n* large hammer used in iron-works.

tilt-yard [*tilt*-yaard] *n* place for jousting.

timbal, tymbal [*tim*bal] *n* kettledrum.

timber [*timber*] *n* wood cut up for building purposes; large piece of wood used in structure of ship, building *etc*; trees; **t. line** height on mountain *etc* above which no trees grow ∼ **timber** *v/t* furnish with timber; cover with trees.

timbered [*timberd*] *adj* made of or partly of wood; wooded.

timbre [*tamber/tam*bRe] *n* (*Fr*) quality which distinguishes sounds of same pitch when produced by different musical instruments or voices > PDP, PDM.

timbrel [*tim*bRel] *n* tambourine.

time [*tɪm*] *n* concept based on experience of sequence and change; concept of past, present, and future; duration; point in this at which an event takes place; portion of time, period, epoch; normal or pre-arranged moment for something to happen; interval; date; season; (*mus*) tempo, rhythm > PDM; (*pl*) era, period; **against t.** hurrying to finish by a certain time; **all in good t.** soon enough, no need for haste; **at one t.** formerly; **at the same t.** nevertheless; **behind t.** late; **behind the times** old-fashioned; **do t.** serve a term of imprisonment; **have a good t.** enjoy oneself; **have no t. for** (*coll*) detest, despise; **in good t.** punctual, early; **in no t.** very quickly; **take your t.** do not hurry; **t. after t.** repeatedly; **beat t.** (*mus*) indicate tempo by movements of a baton; **mark t.** make movements of marching without going forward; (*fig*) make no progress; delay, linger; **on t.** punctually ∼ **time** *v/t* ascertain duration or rate of; do or say at the best moment; calculate or regulate the time of ∼ **time** *adj* of or by time; designed to act at a fixed time.

timebomb [*tɪm*bom] *n* bomb designed to explode at a pre-arranged time.

timecard [*tɪm*kaard] *n* card recording workman's hours at work.

time-expired [*tɪm*-ekspɪrd] *adj* having completed term of service.

timefuse [*tɪm*fewz] *n* fuse of timebomb or similar device.

time-honoured [*tɪm*-onerd] *adj* honoured because old; long respected or observed.

timekeeper [*tɪm*keeper] *n* clock, watch; one who records time spent by workmen at work; one who observes time taken by competitors in races, sports *etc*.

timelag [*tɪm*lag] *n* interval between an act and its effect, delay.

timeless [tImlis] adj not limited by time, eternal; not more characteristic of one period than of another ~ **timelessly** adv ~ **timelessness** n.

timely [tImli] adj done or said at the right moment, opportune; early.

timepiece [tImpees] n clock, watch.

timer [tImer] n one who or that which measures or records time.

timesaving [tImsayving] adj more efficient and quicker.

timeserver [tImsurver] n one who unscrupulously varies his opinions to please those having power at the time.

timesheet [tImsheet] n document recording hours spent in working.

time-signal [tIm-signal] n signal indicating time, esp by radio.

time-switch [tIm-swich] n automatic switch set to work at pre-arranged time.

timetable [tIm-tayb'l] n schedule, list of times at which certain things are due to happen or be done; list of times of arrivals and departures of trains, ships, buses etc; list of tasks, lessons etc to be done at specified times.

timework [tImwurk] n work paid for by time taken in doing it.

timeworn [tImwawrn] adj showing signs of decay or damage by age.

timid [timid] adj easily frightened or shy, lacking courage ~ **timidly** adv ~ **timidness** n.

timidity [timiditi] n quality of being timid.

timing [tIming] n act of determining when one event should occur relatively to others; accuracy and good judgement in this; relative arrangement or occurrence of events.

timorous [timeRus] adj fearful, timid ~ **timorously** adv ~ **timorousness** n.

timpano (pl **timpani**) [timpanO] n orchestral kettledrum.

tin [tin] n a soft, silvery, malleable metal > PDS; container made of iron coated with tin, an airtight; contents of a tin; (sl) money; **t. hat** (lid) (coll) steel helmet; **put the t. hat** (lid) **on it** bring to an abrupt end or unpleasant climax; **little t. god** pompous, pampered or self-satisfied man of no real importance ~ **tin** (pres/part **tinning**, p/t and p/part **tinned**) v/t coat or cover with tin; preserve in airtight tin container; (sl) make a record of ~ **tin** adj of tin.

tincan [tinkan] n airtight tin container.

tinct [tinkt] n colour, dye; tinge.

tincture [tinkcher] n tinge of colour; medicinal solution; slight flavour; (her) colour used for the field on emblazoned shields ~ **tincture** v/t tinge.

tinder [tinder] n anything used to kindle fire from a spark; linen impregnated with saltpetre.

tinderbox [tinderboks] n box to hold tinder, flint, and steel.

tine [tIn] n spike, prong, point; branch of a stag's antler.

tinfoil [tinfoil] n alloy of lead and tin beaten to a thin sheet used for wrapping.

ting [ting] n sharp, tinkling sound ~ **ting** v/t and i.

tinge [tinj] v/t colour slightly; modify slightly, add some slight but perceptible quality to ~ **tinge** n faint colour, tint; slight degree of some quality.

tingle [ting-g'l] n prickling or stinging sensation ~ **tingle** v/t and i feel a tingle; smart; vibrate.

tinily [tInili] adv in a tiny way.

tininess [tIninis] n quality of being tiny.

tinker [tinker] v/t and i mend roughly, patch up; **t. with** try inefficiently to mend, improve or alter ~ **tinker** n one who mends pots, pans etc, esp as itinerant workman; act of tinkering; one who tinkers; (dial) gypsy, tramp.

tinkle [tink'l] v/t and i make repeated sharp high-pitched sounds; ring ~ **tinkle** n.

tinned [tind] adj coated with tin; (of food etc) preserved in a tin; (sl, of music etc) recorded.

tinnily [tinili] adv in a tinny way.

tinniness [tininis] n quality of being tinny.

tinning [tining] n process or trade of preserving food etc in tins; process of coating with tin or tinfoil.

tinnitus [tinItus] n (med) sensation of hearing a ringing noise without external cause.

tinny [tini] adj of, like or covered with tin; (of sound) shrill, thin and metallic; (of food) revealing by flavour that it is tinned.

tin-opener [tin-Opener] n tool for opening tins.

tinpan [tinpan] adj and n **t. alley** (of or like) producers of inferior popular music.

tinplate [tinplayt] n iron coated with tin > PDS.

tinpot [tinpot] adj made of inferior materials; petty, worthless.

tinsel [tinsel] n glittering metallic sheets cut in strips etc for decoration; anything gaudy but of little value ~ **tinsel** adj of or like tinsel; gaudy but valueless; cheap and showy ~ **tinsel** v/t decorate with tinsel.

tint [tint] n hue, shade of colour; variation of a colour due to admixture with white ~ **tint** v/t give tints to; colour, dye.

tintack [tintak] n short nail of tinned iron.

tintinnabulation [tintinabewlayshon] n the sound of the ringing of bells.

tintometer [tintomiter] n (tr) instrument which determines tints.

tinware [tinwair] n articles of tinplate.

tiny [tIni] adj minute, very small.

tip [tip] n end, tapering extremity, point; slight touch, pat; useful hint or advice; piece of private profitable information; small sum of money given to servant etc for services done, and not counted as regular wage; small present of money given to child; place where rubbish is dumped ~ **tip** (pres/part **tipping**, p/t and p/part **tipped**) v/t and i cover the tip of; put a tip on; give a tip to; cause to lean or slant, tilt; cause to fall by tilting the container of; pour out; upset; give tips; **t. off** (coll) give private warning or information to; **t. up** cause one end to rise; cause to fall over, upset; fall backwards; **t. the wink to** inform privately, give a hint to; **t. a winner** give hint of which horse etc is likely to win a race; (fig) foresee the success of someone.

tip-and-run [tip-and-Run] n form of cricket in which a run must be made whenever ball has touched bat ~ **tip-and-run** adj attacking briefly and then escaping.

tipcart [tipkaart] n cart which can be emptied by being tipped up.

tipcat [tipkat] n game in which piece of wood is hit with a stick.

tip-off [tip-of] n (sl) private warning, hint or information.

tippet [*tip*it] *n* fur worn over neck and shoulders; short cape.

tipple [*tip*'l] *v/i* habitually take many small drinks of intoxicating liquor ~ **tipple** *n* (*coll*) strong drink ~ **tippler** *n*.

tipsily [*tip*sili] *adv* drunkenly, as if drunk.

tipsiness [*tip*sinis] *n* slight drunkenness.

tipstaff [*tip*staaf] *n* sheriff's officer.

tipster [*tip*ster] *n* one who provides confidential information on likely results in racing.

tipsy [*tip*si] *adj* slightly drunk.

tipsy-cake [*tip*si-kayk] *n* sponge-cake soaked in wine and served with custard.

tiptoe [*tip*tO] *adv* and *adj* (standing or walking) on the toes with heels raised from the ground; on the tips of the toes; (*fig*) eager, excited ~ **tiptoe** *v/i* walk on tiptoe.

tiptop [*tip*top] *adj* (*coll*) of the very best, first-rate.

tirade [t*i*Rayd] *n* long speech of reproof or abuse.

tire (1) [t*i*r] *v/t* and *i* make or become weary; fatigue, exhaust; t. of become bored by; **t. out** exhaust completely.

tire (2) *v/t* (*ar*) adorn ~ **tire** *n* (*ar*) headdress.

tire (3) see **tyre**.

tired [t*i*rd] *adj* wearied, fatigued; **t. of** bored or exasperated by; no longer willing to endure.

tiredness [t*i*rdnis] *n* state of being tired.

tireless [t*i*rlis] *adj* not easily tired; very energetic or persevering ~ **tirelessly** *adv* ~ **tirelessness** *n*.

tiresome [t*i*rsum] *adj* irritating, annoying; boring, tedious ~ **tiresomely** *adv* ~ **tiresomeness** *n*.

tiring [t*i*rRing] *adj* causing fatigue.

tiro see **tyro**.

'tis [tiz] *abbr* (*ar* and *poet*) it is.

tisane [ti*zan*] *n* herbal tea.

tissue [*tis*yew/*tish*OO] *n* soft gauzy paper; small sheet of this for use as handkerchief or in applying cosmetics; fine or transparent fabric; fine fabric interwoven with gold or silver thread; (*fig*) interwoven series, web; (*biol*) fabric of cells and their products > PDB.

tissued [*tis*yewd] *adj* woven with gold or silver.

tissue-paper [tisyew-*pay*per] *n* thin soft gauze-like paper.

tissue-typing [tisyew-t*i*ping] *n* (*med*) matching types of organic tissue to ensure compatibility in transplants.

tit (1) [tit] *n* a kind of small bird, titmouse.

tit (2) *n* **t. for tat** retaliation.

tit (3), **titty** *n* (*sl*) breast, teat.

tit (4) *n* (*sl*) ineffectual fool, weakling.

Titan [t*i*tan] *n* (*Gk myth*) one of a race of gigantic primeval gods; person of great strength or mental stature.

titanic [t*i*tanik] *adj* enormous, gigantic; (*chem*) containing titanium.

titanium [ti*tay*ni-um] *n* (*chem*) metallic element used in alloys and paints > PDS.

titbit [*tit*bit] *n* small piece of particularly tasty food; (*fig*) interesting piece of news or gossip.

titch [tich] *n* (*coll*) small person ~ **titchy** *adj* tiny, contemptibly small.

titfer [*tit*fer] *n* (*sl*) hat.

tithe [t*i*TH] *n* a tenth part; (*hist*) tax of one tenth of annual profit or income, paid to a church ~ **tithe** *v/t* impose tithes upon.

tithe-barn [t*i*TH-baarn] *n* barn for holding corn formerly paid as tithe.

titillate [*tit*ilayt] *v/t* stimulate to pleasing excitement, curiosity *etc*; tickle.

titillation [titi*lay*shon] *n* act of titillating; that which titillates.

titivate [*tit*ivayt] *v/t* and *i* dress up, adorn; put finishing touches to; make oneself smart.

titlark [*tit*laark] *n* (*orni*) meadow-pipit.

title [t*i*t'l] *n* the inscription by which a thing, *esp* a book, is known; name; title-page; appellation of honour or distinction; right of ownership; admitted right or claim; (*eccles*) agreement by which a benefice is held.

titled [t*i*t'ld] *adj* having a title of nobility.

title-deed [t*i*t'l-deed] *n* legal document giving evidence of ownership of property.

title-page [t*i*t'l-payj] *n* page of book giving title, author's name *etc*.

title-role [t*i*t'l-ROl] *n* part in a play which gives its name to the whole.

titling [t*i*tling] *n* act of giving or printing a title.

titmouse [*tit*mows] *n* small insect-eating bird.

titrate [t*i*tRayt] *v/t* (*chem*) determine quantity of (constituent in a compound) by adding a definite amount of a reagent > PDS.

titration [tit*Ray*shon] *n* process of titrating, volumetric analysis > PDS.

titter [*tit*er] *v/i* laugh very quietly, giggle ~ **titter** *n* a smothered laugh, giggle.

tittle [*tit*'l] *n* jot, very small particle.

tittle-tattle [*tit*'l-tat'l] *n* gossip.

tittup [*tit*up] *v/i* behave in a lively way, frisk.

titty see **tit** (3).

titular [*tit*ewlar] *adj* nominal, existing in name only; holding a title without the duties of office; of or pertaining to a title ~ **titular** *n* titular holder of an office.

tizzy [*tiz*i] *n* (*coll*) state of confusion; fuss, panic.

T-junction [tee-junkshon] *n* junction of two roads, pipes *etc* forming the shape of the letter T.

to [too] *prep* in the direction towards; as far as; in comparison with; regarding; expressing degree or end; in contrast with; preceding the unaltered form of a verb to make the infinitive; denoting the indirect object; **t. and fro** backwards and forwards ~ **to** *adv* toward; to its place; so as to join or close.

toad [tOd] *n* a tailless amphibian resembling the frog.

toad-in-the-hole [tOd-in-THi-*hOl*] *n* meat, *usu* sausage-meat, cooked in batter.

toadstool [*tOd*stOOl] *n* any fleshy-topped fungus other than the mushroom, *esp* if poisonous.

toady [*tOd*i] *n* fawning flatterer ~ **toady** *v/t* fawn upon.

toast [tOst] *n* slice of bread browned at a fire or other source of heat; proposal to drink the health of a person, institution *etc*; person, *esp* woman, whose health is drunk ~ **toast** *v/t* and *i* make (bread) brown by exposure to heat; warm at a fire; drink the health of.

toaster [*tOs*ter] *n* one who or that which toasts; device for toasting bread electrically.

toasting-fork [*tOs*ting-fawrk] *n* long-handled fork for toasting bread before a fire.

toastmaster [*tO*stmaaster] *n* announcer of toasts at public dinners *etc*.

toastrack [*tO*strak] *n* stand which holds slices of toast separately.

tobacco [to*bak*O] *n* a plant with narcotic leaves; leaves of this dried and prepared for smoking, chewing, or as snuff.

tobacconist [to*bak*onist] *n* one who sells tobacco.

tobacco-pipe [to*bak*O-pip] *n* pipe used for smoking tobacco.

tobacco-pouch [to*bak*O-powch] *n* pouch for holding a small amount of tobacco.

toboggan [to*bog*an] *n* small sledge for sliding down snowy slopes ~ **toboggan** *v/i*.

toby-jug [*tO*bi-jug] *n* mug shaped like an old man wearing a three-cornered hat.

toccata [to*kaa*ta] *n* (*mus*) composition intended to display the performer's touch > PDM.

tocopherol [to*kof*eRol] *n* (*bioch*) group of alcohols occurring in wheat-germ, egg yolk, *etc*; vitamin E.

tocsin [*tok*sin] *n* alarm-bell; act of ringing this.

tod [*tod*] *n* (*sl*) **on one's t.** alone.

today [too*day*] *adv* on or at this day ~ **today** *n* this day.

toddle [*tod*'l] *v/i* walk unsteadily with short steps; (*coll*) stroll, saunter ~ **toddle** *n* short unsteady walk; saunter.

toddler [*tod*ler] *n* child who has just learnt to walk.

toddy [*tod*i] *n* mixture of whisky and hot water sweetened; palm-tree juice; palm-wine.

to-do [too-*dOO*] *n* fuss, commotion.

toe [*tO*] *n* one of five digits of foot; corresponding part of animal's foot; covering for the toes; **on one's toes** alert; **tread on the toes of** offend, hurt the feelings of ~ **toe** *v/t* touch with the toes; furnish with toes; place tip of foot on; **t. the line** (*fig*) conform to custom; obey orders.

toecap [*tO*kap] *n* leather cap at toe of shoe.

toehold [*tO*hOld] *n* (*coll*) very small foothold.

toenail [*tO*nayl] *n* nail growing on a toe.

toff [*tof*] *n* (*sl*) rich, upper-class, or well-dressed man.

toffee [*tof*i] *n* sweet made of boiled sugar and butter; **t. apple** apple dipped in toffee and eaten from a stick.

tog (*pres/part* **togging**, *p/t* and *p/part* **togged**) [*tog*] *v/t* and *i* (*coll*) dress up.

toga [*tO*ga] *n* loose flowing garment of a Roman citizen.

together [to*geTH*er] *adv* in company; in union; in contest; in the same place; at the same time; as well as.

togetherness [to*geTH*ernis] *n* deliberate fostering of feelings of unity, friendliness *etc*.

toggle [*tog*'l] *n* short tapered bar of wood put through a loop of rope to secure it; small wooden bar used instead of button as fastening.

togs [*togz*] *n* (*pl*) (*coll*) clothes; best clothes.

toil [*toil*] *v/i* work hard; move laboriously ~ **toil** *n* hard work, labour, drudgery.

toiler [*toil*er] *n* one who labours.

toilet [*toil*it] *n* process of dressing, applying cosmetics *etc*; style of dressing, woman's costume; water-closet, lavatory; (*ar*) dressing-table.

toilet-paper [*toil*it-payper] *n* thin paper for use in the lavatory.

toilet-powder [*toil*it-powder] *n* talcum powder.

toilet-roll [*toil*it-ROl] *n* roll of toilet-paper.

toilet-set [*toil*it-set] *n* set of brushes, combs *etc* for a dressing-table.

toilet-table [*toil*it-tayb'l] *n* dressing-table with mirror.

toilette [twa*let*] *n* (*Fr*) process or style of dressing, toilet; elaborate costume.

toils [*toilz*] *n* (*pl*) net, snare; **in the t.** ensnared.

toilsome [*toil*sum] *adj* involving toil; laborious; tiring.

tokay [to*kay*] *n* kind of sweet rich wine from Hungary.

token [*tO*ken] *n* sign, symbol; that which represents or is a substitute for something else; keepsake, gift given as sign of affection; voucher sold by a shop *etc* and exchangeable for specified type of goods ~ **token** *adj* serving as minor substitute; nominal; slight, inadequate; **t. payment** small formal payment, nominal payment.

tolbooth, tollbooth [*tolb*OOth] *n* stall at which tolls, duties, or customs were collected; (*Scots*) town jail.

told [*tOld*] *p/t* and *p/part* of **tell**.

tolerability [toleRa*bili*ti] *n* state or quality of being tolerable.

tolerable [*tole*Rab'l] *adj* not too bad to bear, endurable; fairly good ~ **tolerably** *adv*.

tolerance [*tole*Rans] *n* act or power of tolerating; quality of being tolerant; (*med*) capacity to bear continued use of a drug; (*eng*) permissible deviation from a specified standard or dimension.

tolerant [*tole*Rant] *adj* permitting free expression of views one does not share, not inclined to condemn or persecute others; broad-minded; forbearing, lenient ~ **tolerantly** *adv*.

tolerate [*tole*Rayt] *v/t* allow to exist without interference; not try to prevent or suppress (views, behaviour *etc* which one does not agree with); put up with, bear; be patient towards.

toleration [toleR*ay*shon] *n* act of tolerating; spirit of tolerance.

toll (1) [*tOl*] *n* tax paid for right to use a road, bridge *etc*; tax; telephone call to a fairly distant place; portion of grain kept by miller in payment for grinding; **take t. of** exact payment from; (*fig*) inflict losses on.

toll (2) *v/t* and *i* ring (bell) with slow, deep sound ~ **toll** *n* single stroke of a deep bell.

tollage [*tOl*ij] *n* payment of toll.

tollbooth see **tolbooth**.

toll-call [*tOl*-kawl] *n* telephone call costing more than a local call but less than a trunk call.

tollgate [*tOl*gayt] *n* turnpike, gate barring a road for use of which a toll is charged.

tollhouse [*tOl*hows] *n* house by a turnpike, at which toll is paid.

toluene [*tol*ew-een] *n* colourless liquid occurring in coal-tar > PDS.

tom [*tom*] *n* male animal, *esp* male cat.

Tom [*tom*] *n* a masculine proper name; **T., Dick and Harry** any ordinary or randomly chosen persons; **T. Thumb** dwarf, tiny person; **T. Tiddler's Ground** place where money is lying about.

tomahawk [*tom*ahawk] *n* light hatchet used by Red Indians in war or hunting.

tomato [to*maat*O] *n* red pulpy edible fruit; trailing plant bearing this.

tomb [*tOOm*] *n* grave; vault; (*fig*) death.

tombola [tombOla] *n* type of lottery.
tomboy [tomboi] *n* girl who behaves like a boy.
tombstone [tOOmstOn] *n* stone placed over grave as memorial.
tomcat [tomkat] *n* male cat.
tome [tOm] *n* large book; single volume of a book.
tomfool [tomfOOl] *adj* extremely foolish.
tomfoolery [tomfOOleRi] *n* foolish behaviour; silliness.
tommy [tomi] *n* (*coll*) private in the British Army; (*sl*) bread, provisions.
tommy-gun [tomi-gun] *n* sub-machine-gun with short barrel.
tommyrot [tomiRot] *n* (*coll*) complete nonsense.
tomnoddy [tomnodi] *n* (*coll*) fool.
tomorrow [tomoRO] *adv* on or during the day after this ~ **tomorrow** *n* the day after this.
tompion [tompi-on] *n* inking-pad used in lithography; tampon.
tomtit [tomtit] *n* blue tit.
tomtom [tomtom] *n* African or Oriental type of drum > PDM.
ton [tun] *n* British measure of weight 2,240 lb; American measure of weight, 2,000 lb; metric measure of weight, 1,000 kg; one of various measures of capacity; (*coll*) heavy weight; (*sl*) speed of 100 mph attained by car or motorcycle; (*pl*, *coll*) large quantities.
tonal [tOnal] *adj* of tone; of tonality.
tonality [tonaliti] *n* (*mus*) quality of a tone > PDP; system of tones, key; fact or effect of being written in a single key > PDM.
tone [tOn] *n* a musical sound, sound having pitch, resonance *etc*; modulation of voice, intonation; line, shade of colour; atmosphere, prevailing mood; (*mus*) pure note > PDP; interval of two semitones > PDM; (*med*) healthy functioning, vigour; continuous moderate activity of an organ > PDB; (*arts*) one of a series of gradations in colour from light to dark > PDAA; harmonious relation of these; **t. poem** (*mus*) symphonic poem ~ **tone** *v/t* and *i* give tone to; blend (colours) agreeably by gentle gradations; (*phot*) modify colour of; **t. down** reduce the intensity of; lessen the violence, offensiveness *etc* of; **t. in with** blend harmoniously with; **t. up** intensify, strengthen.
tone-colour [tOn-kuler] *n* timbre > PDM.
tone-deaf [tOn-def] *adj* unable to distinguish differences of pitch.
toneless [tOnles] *adj* without tone; dull, lifeless; unmusical ~ **tonelessly** *adv*.
tongs [tongz] *n* (*pl*) implement consisting of two rods connected at one end by a pivot, used for grasping and lifting.
tongue [tung] *n* fleshy muscular organ in the mouth; language; power or method of speaking; tongue of animal as food; anything narrow, flat and pointed; pointed flap, strap *etc*; clapper of bell; flexible strip of metal in certain musical instruments; pin of a buckle; narrow strip of land; projection to fit into a groove; **gift of tongues** glossolalia; (*fig*) skill in speaking foreign languages; **give t.** speak loudly, cry out; bark; **hold one's t.** be silent; **with t. in cheek** ironically, insincerely ~ **tongue** *v/t* modify (notes) by movement of tongue > PDM.

tongue-tied [tung-tId] *adj* unable to speak freely, *esp* through shyness; having a speech-defect.
tongue-twister [tung-twister] *n* word or phrase difficult to say quickly and correctly.
tonic [tonik] *adj* invigorating, bracing, strengthening; (*mus*) of tones or sounds > PDM; stressed ~ **tonic** *n* invigorating medicine; anything that renews energy or cheerfulness; (*mus*) keynote; **t. sol-fa** system of musical notation in which notes are identified by letters regardless of pitch > PDM.
tonically [tonikali] *adv* in a tonic manner; as a tonic.
tonicity [tonisiti] *n* tone; healthy muscular tension.
tonight [tonIt] *adv* on or during this night ~ **tonight** *n* this present night; the night after today.
tonite [tOnIt] *n* explosive made from gun-cotton.
tonnage [tunij] *n* capacity of a ship expressed in tons > PDSa; duty on ships.
tonne [ton] *n* metric ton, 1000 kilos, 2,205 lb.
tonometer [tonomiter] *n* instrument for measuring pitch or for producing notes of known pitch.
tonsil [tonsil] *n* one of two masses of lymphoid tissue at junction of mouth and throat > PDB.
tonsillitis [tonsilItis] *n* inflammation of the tonsils.
tonsorial [tonsawrRi-al] *adj* of shaving.
tonsure [tonsher] *n* act of shaving all or part of the head; (*RC*) admission into Holy Orders; part of the head which has been shaved ~ **tonsure** *v/t*.
tontine [tonteen] *n* form of annuity, increasing for each subscriber as other subscribers die.
ton-up [tun-up] *adj* (*coll*) fond of travelling at 100 mph by motorcycle.
tonus [tOnus] *n* state of moderate permanent muscular contraction > PDB PDP.
too [tOO] *adv* excessively; more than enough; as well as; moreover.
took [took] *p/t* of take.
tool [tOOl] *n* implement used by workmen; instrument; apparatus; (*fig*) person merely used as an instrument; stamp or design used in bookbinding ~ **tool** *v/t* and *i* shape or mark with a tool; **t. along** (*coll*) drive along in a smooth, leisurely way; **t. up** equip with machine-tools.
toolbox [tOOlboks] *n* box in which tools are kept.
tooler [tOOler] *n* type of chisel.
tooling [tOOling] *n* workmanship done with a tool; ornamentation on bindings of books.
toolshed [tOOlshed] *n* shed where garden tools are kept.
toot [tOOt] *v/i* make a sound like that of a horn ~ **toot** *n* a sound like that of a horn; a blast.
tooth (*pl* teeth) [tOOth] *n* one of the hard growths inside jaws of animals and used in biting; anything shaped like this; prong of a comb; cog; sharp projection; **t. and nail** savagely; **armed to the teeth** fully armed; **cast (something) in one's teeth** blame one for something; **in the teeth of** despite, defying; **long in the t.** growing elderly; **set teeth on edge** displease violently, *esp* by harsh noises; **sweet t.** fondness for sweet food ~ **tooth** *v/t* and *i* furnish with teeth; indent; interlock.
toothache [tOOthayk] *n* pain in nerves of teeth.
toothbrush [tOOthbRush] *n* brush for cleaning the teeth; **t. moustache** narrow, short, stiff moustache.

761

toothcomb [*tOOth*kOm] *n* comb with teeth set very close together; **go through with a t.** (*fig*) search or examine closely and critically.

toothpaste [*tOOth*payst] *n* paste for cleaning the teeth.

toothpick [*tOOth*pik] *n* pointed instrument for removing anything from between the teeth.

toothsome [*tOOth*sum] *adj* pleasant to the taste.

toothy [*tOOth*i] *adj* having large or prominent teeth; displaying one's teeth.

tootle [*tOOt'*l] *v/t* and *i* toot continuously and quietly ∼ **tootle** *n*.

toots, tootsy [*tOOts, tOOtsi*] *n* (*US coll*) darling.

top (1) [*top*] *n* highest point, summit; upper part or surface; highest rank, degree, status *etc*; greatest intensity; (*naut*) small platform at head of lower mast > PDSa; **big t.** circus tent; **blow one's t.** (*coll*) lose one's temper violently; **from t. to toe** entirely, from head to foot; **go over the t.** go into battle; take the plunge; **the tops** (*sl*) the very best ∼ **top** *adj* of, on or at the top; highest; utmost, most intense; best; **t. dog** dog that is winning a fight; (*fig*) person in power, master; **t. drawer** uppermost drawer; (*fig*) high social class ∼ **top** (*pres/part* **topping**, *p/t* and *p/part* **topped**) *v/t* remove the top of; put a top on; be at the top of; cover the top of; excel, exceed, surpass; (*sl*) hang; **t. up** add liquid to (a partly emptied container).

top (2) *n* small pear-shaped toy made to rotate by a whip or mechanically; **sleep like a t.** sleep deeply.

topaz [*tOpaz*] *n* a transparent mineral, *usu* yellowish > PDS; light brownish yellow.

topboot [*top*bOOt] *n* knee-length riding-boot with broad pale band round the top.

topcoat [*top*kOt] *n* overcoat; final coat of paint.

top-dressing [*top-dRe*sing] *n* manure placed on surface of soil; application of this; final coat of paint, polish *etc*.

tope (1) [*tOp*] *v/i* drink hard or excessively.

tope (2) *n* species of small shark, dogfish.

topee, topi [*tOpi*] *n* pith-helmet.

toper [*tOper*] *n* hard drinker, drunkard.

topflight [*top*flIt] *adj* (*coll*) first-rate; of highest rank in achievements.

topgallant [to(p)*galant*] *adj* (*naut*) (*of mast, rigging and sail*) above the topmast > PDSa.

top-hamper [*top*-hamper] *n* (*naut*) gear and fittings above upper deck > PDSa.

top-hat [top-*hat*] *n* man's tall silk hat.

top-heavy [top-*hevi*] *adj* with upper part too heavy for the lower; unstable.

top-hole [top-*hOl*] *adj* (*sl*) excellent.

topi see **topee**.

topiary [*tOpi*-aRi] *n* art of clipping trees and shrubs into ornamental shapes.

topic [*top*ik] *n* subject of conversation, discussion, literary work *etc*.

topical [*top*ikal] *adj* of or being a subject of contemporary interest; current, up-to-date; (*med*) of a particular part of the body.

topicality [topi*kal*iti] *n* quality of being topical.

topically [*top*ikali] *adv* in a topical way.

topknot [*top*not] *n* ribbon worn on top of head; tuft of hair on crown of head; (*sl*) head.

topless [*top*les] *adj* having no top; (*of women's clothes*) leaving the breasts naked.

topmast [*top*maast] *n* (*naut*) mast between lower and topgallant mast.

topmost [*top*mOst] *adj* at the very top, highest.

top-notch [*top*-noch] *adj* (*coll*) first-rate; of highest rank ∼ **top-notcher** *n*.

topo- *pref* of place.

topographer [to*pog*Rafer] *n* one skilled in topography; one who describes a particular place.

topographical [topo*gRaf*ikal] *adj* of topography.

topography [to*pog*Rafi] *n* science of describing or representing the features of a particular place in detail; detailed features of a district > PDG.

topology [to*pol*oji] *n* branch of geometry concerned with the factors which remain unchanged when an object undergoes a continuous deformation.

toponymy [to*pon*imi] *n* study of place-names.

topper [*tOper*] *n* (*sl*) one who or that which is excellent; top-hat.

topping [*tOping*] *adj* (*sl*) excellent ∼ **toppingly** *adv*.

topping-out [*tOping*-owt] *n* builders' celebration of the completion of a building; act of putting the highest stone or brick in place.

topple [*top'*l] *v/i* and *t* tumble forward; cause to totter or fall, throw down.

topsail [*tops*'l] *n* square sail across topmast.

top-secret [top-*seek*Rit] *adj* (*of information*) to be kept extremely secret, *usu* because of military value.

topside [*tops*Id] *n* upper side; joint of beef from between leg and aitchbone; (*pl*) ship's sides above waterline.

topsoil [*top*soil] *n* upper layer of soil.

topsy-turvy [topsi-*turvi*] *adj* and *adv* upside down; in disorder.

toque [*tOk*] *n* woman's round, close-fitting, brimless hat.

tor [*tawr*] *n* isolated mass of rock forming a peak.

Torah [*tawr*Ra] *n* (*Heb*) the Pentateuch.

toran [*tawr*Ran] *n* gateway of Buddhist temple.

torch [*tawrch*] *n* bundle of burning material tied to a stick and carried by hand; small electric battery light carried by hand; (*fig*) something giving spiritual or intellectual light; **carry a t. for** (*US coll*) feel unrequited love or admiration for.

torchbearer [*tawrch*bairRer] *n* (*hist*) one who carried a lighted torch; (*fig*) one who leads or inspires.

torchlight [*tawrch*lIt] *n* illumination by torches ∼ **torchlight** *adj* lit by flaming torches.

torchsong [*tawrch*song] *n* (*US coll*) love song, *esp* of unrequited love.

tore [*tawr*] *p/t* of tear.

toreador [*toRi*-adawr] *n* mounted bullfighter.

torero [to*Rair*RO] *n* bullfighter on foot.

torment [*tawr*ment] *n* extreme pain; great anguish; source of pain or of anguish ∼ **torment** [tawr*ment*] *v/t* cause extreme pain to; torture; harass, tease.

tormentil [*tawr*mentil] *n* low growing herb with yellow flowers and medicinal root.

tormentor [tawr*ment*or] *n* one who or that which torments.

torn [*tawrn*] *p/part* of tear.

tornado [tawr*nayd*O] *n* very violent whirlwind;

extremely violent and destructive storm > PDG; (*fig*) loud, violent outburst.

toroidal [to*R*oidal] *adj* having the shape of a torus.

torpedo [tawr*peed*O] *n* self-propelled underwater missile designed to blow up shipping; similar weapon discharged by aircraft at shipping; species of fish emitting electric discharge; detonating fog-signal ~ **torpedo** *v/t* destroy or damage by a ·torpedo; (*fig*) destroy by a surprise attack.

torpedo-boat [tawr*peed*O-bOt] *n* small swift boat from which torpedoes are discharged.

torpedo-net [tawr*peed*O-net] *n* net of wire hung round a ship to intercept torpedoes.

torpedo-tube [tawr*peed*O-tewb] *n* tube through which a torpedo is discharged.

torpid [*tawr*pid] *adj* numb; sluggish, lethargic; inactive ~ **torpid** *n* clinker-built eight-oared racing-boat at Oxford; (*pl*) races in these boats held in the Hilary term.

torpidity [tawr*pid*iti] *n* state of being torpid.

torpidly [*tawr*pidli] *adv* in a torpid way.

torpor [*tawr*por] *n* numbness; dullness, indifference.

torquate [*tawr*kwayt] *adj* (*zool*) having a ring-like marking round the neck.

torque [*tawr*k] *n* necklace of twisted strands of gold or silver; (*mech*) movement causing rotation.

torrent [*to*Rent] *n* violently rushing stream; (*fig*) rush of words; outburst of tears *etc*.

torrential [to*R*enshal] *adj* of or like a torrent.

torrid [*to*Rid] *adj* dried up; parching; scorching; **t. zone** zone between the tropics > PDG.

torsion [*tawr*shon] *n* act of twisting; state of being twisted; (*mech*) twisting effect of a force on a shaft; force with which a rod, wire *etc* tends to return to its original shape after being twisted; (*surg*) twisting of cut end of artery to avoid haemorrhage ~ **torsional** *adj*.

torso [*tawr*sO] *n* upper part of human body, excluding head and arms; headless and limbless statue.

tort [*tawr*t] *n* (*leg*) injury, harmful act for which a civil action can be brought.

tortilla [tawr*tee*ya] *n* Mexican flat cake of baked maize; type of Spanish omelette.

tortious [*tawr*shus] *adj* (*leg*) of or as a tort.

tortoise [*tawr*tus] *n* reptile encased in a shell from which its head and legs can protrude; (*Rom hist*) testudo.

tortoiseshell [*tawr*teshel] *n* mottled horny plate of the shell of a tortoise; butterfly with wing-markings resembling this; cat with brown, black and tawny markings ~ **tortoiseshell** *adj* made of tortoiseshell; mottled in shades of brown.

tortuosity [tawrtew-*os*iti] *n* quality or state of being tortuous.

tortuous [*tawr*tew-us] *adj* twisting, winding, crooked; devious, not straightforward or simple ~ **tortuously** *adv*.

torture [*tawr*cher] *n* deliberate infliction of extreme pain, *esp* to extort a confession or as a punishment; extreme pain, anguish ~ **torture** *v/t* inflict torture upon; cause extreme pain to; treat very cruelly; (*fig*) distort violently.

torturer [*tawr*cherer] *n* one who or that which tortures.

torus [*tawr*Rus] *n* doughnut-shaped solid of circular or elliptical cross-section.

Tory [*tawr*Ri] *n* and *adj* (member) of the British Conservative party > PDPol.

tosh [*tosh*] *n* (*sl*) nonsense, rubbish.

toss [*tos*] *v/t* and *i* throw lightly up by hand; fling, jerk; pitch; cause to rise and fall violently; jerk (head) up and back; (*of bull*) gore and fling up with the horns; be flung about; fling oneself about; twist and jerk in agitation; spin a coin up to determine a choice by whether it falls head up or not; **t. (up) for** decide by tossing a coin **t. off** say or do casually; (*sl*) masturbate ~ **toss** *n* act of tossing; state of being tossed; act of tossing a coin to determine something; **take a t.** fall from horse.

tosspot [*tos*pot] *n* (*sl*) drunkard.

toss-up [*tos*-up] *n* act of tossing a coin to settle a wager; even chance; situation whose outcome is quite uncertain.

tot (1) [*tot*] *n* tiny child; dram of liquor; small quantity.

tot (2) (*pres/part* **totting**, *p/t* and *p/part* **totted**) *v/t* and *i* **t. up** add up.

tot (3) (*pres/part* **totting**, *p/t* and *p/part* **totted**) *v/i* (*sl*) pick out valuable articles from among refuse ~ **tot** *n* article found thus.

total [*tO*tal] *adj* complete, entire, whole; absolute, utter; **t. war** war in which civilians are attacked ~ **total** *n* full sum or amount; amount reached by addition ~ **total** (*pres/part* **totalling**, *p/t* and *p/part* **totalled**) *v/t* and *i* amount to as total; reach and *i* **t. up** add up.

totalisator see **totalizator**.

totalitarian [tOtali*tair*Ri-an] *adj* (*of a State*) run by a dictator or a single political organization that suppresses all opposition and many rights and freedoms, and demands total allegiance of each citizen > PDPol.

totalitarianism [tOtali*tair*Ri-anizm] *n* practice and principles of a totalitarian State.

totality [tO*tal*iti] *n* entirety; total amount.

totalization [tOtal*Iz*ayshon] *n* act of totalizing; state of being totalized.

totalizator, totalisator [tOtal*Iz*aytor] *r* machine automatically indicating number of b ts made through it on each horse, money due to each winner *etc*.

totalize [*tO*talIz] *v/t* and *i* reckon the total of; use a totalizator.

totally [*tO*tali] *adv* wholly, completely, entirely.

tote (1) [*tOt*] *abbr* (*coll*) totalizator.

tote (2) *v/t* (*US coll*) carry, haul.

totebag [*tO*tbag] *n* (*coll*) very large handbag.

totem [*tO*tem] *n* animal, plant, or object venerated by a primitive tribe or group as symbol of their corporate identity and as protector > PDP; representation of this; **t. pole** large carved post supporting a representation of a totem.

totemic [tO*tem*ik] *adj* of a totem; having totems.

totemism [*tO*temizm] *n* cult of totems; system of social relationships and customs associated with cult of totems.

totemistic [tOtem*ist*ik] *adj* of totemism.

tother [*tuT*Her] *adj* and *pron* (*coll* or *obs*) the other.

totter [*tot*er] *v/i* be unsteady, stagger; be about to fall; be near ruin.

tottery [*tot*eRi] *adj* unsteady; shaky; tottering.

totting see tot (3).

toucan [tOOkan] *n* brightly coloured tropical American bird with an immense beak.

touch [tuch] *v/t* and *i* make physical contact with; be in contact; reach; handle, lay hands on; disturb; interfere with, molest; rouse the emotions of; move to pity or affection; impress; be as good as; achieve, attain; obtain as payment or income; concern; discuss, mention; (*coll*) try to borrow money from; **t. at** call at (a port); **t. down** (*of aircraft*) land, come into contact with the ground; (*Rugby football*) score by touching ball to ground in area behind goalposts; **t. for** (*coll*) try to borrow (specified sum) from; **t. off** ignite, cause to explode; **t. on** (**upon**) mention briefly; **t. up** improve or repair, *esp* by minor applications of paint *etc*; improve, enhance; put finishing touches to; excite; **t. wood** avert bad luck by touching any wooden object and saying 'touch wood' ~ **touch** *n* act or method of touching; sense of feeling; slight amount, trace; characteristic method of using the fingers in playing the piano or other instrument; characteristic technique of an individual in some art, skill, or performance; mild attack of illness; test; children's game of pursuing and touching; (*football*) non-playing area; **in t. with** in communication with; having a social relation with; **put to the t.** test.

touch-and-go [tuch-and-gO] *adj* extremely uncertain; risky.

touchdown [tuchdown] *n* (*football*) act of touching the ground behind the opponents' goal; (*aer*) first contact of aircraft with ground on landing.

touché [tOOshay] *interj* (*Fr*) exclamation acknowledging the aptness of an argument, retort or taunt.

touched [tucht] *adj* emotionally moved; (*coll*) slightly insane; **t. in the wind** easily out of breath.

touchily [tuchili] *adv* irritably, testily.

touchiness [tuchinis] *n* irritability.

touching (1) [tuching] *adj* pathetic, affecting the emotions ~ **touchingly** *adv* ~ **touchingness** *n*.

touching (2) *prep* concerning, as regards.

touch-line [tuch-lIn] *n* (*football*) one of the two longer boundary lines.

touchstone [tuchstOn] *n* dark slate used to test purity of gold and silver; (*fig*) standard, criterion.

touch-type [tuch-tIp] *v/t* and *i* type without looking at the typewriter keys.

touch-typist [tuch-tIpist] *n* one who touch-types.

touchwood [tuchwood] *n* decayed wood or fungus used as tinder.

touchy [tuchi] *adj* easily angered; irritable.

tough [tuf] *adj* not easily damaged; strong, firm; not easily cut or broken; too hard for easy chewing; difficult, involving hard work; (*of persons*) well able to endure suffering or hardship; stubborn; robust; ruthless, unscrupulous; bullying, violent, semi-criminal; **t. luck** (*coll*) bad luck ~ **tough** *n* (*coll*) hooligan; bullying, violent and semi-criminal fellow; gangster, criminal.

toughen [tufen] *v/t* and *i* make or become tough.

toughly [tufli] *adv* in a tough way.

toughness [tufnis] *n* quality of being tough.

toupee [tOOpee/tOOpay] *n* artificial tuft or front of hair.

tour [toor] *n* journey round a district; excursion,

ramble; journey undertaken for pleasure, interest or relaxation. (*mil*) spell of duty ~ **tour** *v/t* and *i* make a tour (round); visit as tourist.

tour-de-force [toor-de-fawrs] *n* (*Fr*) feat of strength or of great skill.

tourer [toorRer] *n* type of open-topped car.

tourism [toorRizm] *n* practice of travelling on pleasure tours.

tourist [toorRist] *n* one who travels on a tour; one who visits a place for interest and pleasure ~ **tourist** *adj* of or for tourists.

tourmaline [toormalin] *n* a class of crystalline minerals > PDS.

tournament [toornament] *n* medieval contest between mounted knights armed with lances; (*games*) contest of skill, *usu* for a championship.

tourney [toorni] *n* medieval tournament.

tourniquet [toornikay] *n* bandage or instrument for compressing an artery to stop a flow of blood.

tousle [towz'l] *v/t* make untidy, rumple, dishevel.

tout [towt] *v/t* and *i* persistently seek customers for one's goods, make importunate attempts to sell; cadge; **t. round** try secretly to pick up tips on race winners and sell these tips to racegoers ~ **tout** *n* one who touts; tipster.

tow (1) [tO] *n* coarse part of hemp or flax.

tow (2) *v/t* and *i* pull (vessel or vehicle) along with a rope; pull behind one ~ **tow** *n* act of towing; state of being towed; **have (taken) in t.** (*fig*) have in attendance; have in one's care; guide.

towage [tO-ij] *n* act of towing; charge for towing.

toward (1) [toowawrd/twawrd] *prep* towards.

toward (2) [tO-ard] *adj* (*ar*) about to happen; in preparation.

towards [toowawrdz/twawrdz] *prep* in the direction of; as regards; near, round about.

towel [tow-il] *n* cloth or absorbent paper for drying (skin, crockery *etc*) after washing; **throw in the t.** admit defeat ~ **towel** (*pres/part* **towelling**, *p/t* and *p/part* **towelled**) *v/t* rub or wipe with a towel; (*sl*) thrash.

towelhorse [tow-ilhawrs] *n* frame for hanging towels on.

towelling [tow-iling] *n* absorbent cloth for making towels; (*sl*) thrashing.

tower [tow-er] *n* very tall building or structure forming part of a building, *usu* square or round and flat-topped; fortress, fortified castle; **t. of strength** person who can be relied on completely ~ **tower** *v/i* rise high up, reach a great height; **t. above** (**over**) be much taller or higher than; (*fig*) be far nobler, more intelligent *etc* than.

towerblock [tow-erblok] *n* very tall block of flats.

towering [tow-eRing] *adj* very high; violent.

towheaded [tOhedid] *adj* with pale yellow hair.

towline [tOlIn] *n* rope used for towing.

town [town] *n* large group of houses and other buildings, larger than a village but not known as a city; inhabitants of this; (*cap*) London; West End of London; **go to t.** (*coll*) go on a spree; become cheerfully excited; spend lavishly.

town-clerk [town-klaark] *n* official who keeps records for a municipality and helps in its administration.

town-council [town-kownsil] *n* elected governing body of a town or city.

town-councillor [town-kownsiler] *n* person elected to a town-council.

764

town-crier [town-*k*RI-er] *n* officer employed by a municipality to make public proclamations.

townee [*town*ee] *n* (*pej*) townsman; (*in university towns*) not a member of the university.

town-hall [town-*hawl*] *n* large public building used for town-council meetings, local administration *etc*.

townified [*town*ifId] *adj* (*coll*) typical of towns and their inhabitants.

town-planning [town-*plan*ing] *n* act or science of planning the building or rebuilding of town areas to make them efficient, convenient, pleasant, healthy *etc*.

townscape [*town*skayp] *n* urban scenery; picture or photograph of this; art of laying out town buildings harmoniously.

townsfolk [*town*zfOk] *n* (*pl*) inhabitants of towns or of a particular town.

township [*town*ship] *n* town and surrounding area forming a municipality; (*S. Africa*) dormitory suburb for Africans only.

townsman [*town*zman] *n* inhabitant of a town.

townspeople [*town*zpeep'l] *n* (*pl*) inhabitants of a town or towns.

towpath [*tO*paath] *n* path beside a river or canal for horses towing barges.

towrope [*tO*ROp] *n* rope used in towing.

toxaemia [toks*eem*i-a] *n* blood-poisoning.

toxic [*tok*sik] *adj* of poison; poisonous; caused by poison ~ **toxically** *adv*.

toxicant [*tok*sikant] *adj* and *n* poisonous (substance).

toxicity [toks*i*siti] *n* degree of poisonousness.

toxico- *pref* of poison.

toxicological [toksiko*lo*jikal] *adj* of toxicology.

toxicologist [toksi*ko*lojist] *n* one who studies poisons.

toxicology [toksi*ko*loji] *n* scientific study of poisons and their effects and antidotes.

toxin [*tok*sin] *n* any of various poisonous substances produced by bacteria and causing disease.

toxophily [toks*of*ili] *n* archery.

toy [*toi*] *n* anything used by, or designed for, a child to play with; plaything; amusing trifle; something of no importance; **t. dog** small pet dog, lapdog ~ **toy** *v/i* **t. with** handle caressingly, fondle; handle absentmindedly; treat as of no value or importance, trifle with.

toyshop [*toi*shop] *n* shop where toys are sold.

trabeated [*tRab*i-aytid] *adj* (*archi*) constructed with beams; covered with a beam or entablature.

trace (1) [*tRay*s] *n* one of two straps by which a vehicle is drawn by horses; **kick over the traces** behave rebelliously, break discipline.

trace (2) *v/t* follow the track of; walk along; follow exactly; find, discover or reason out by following clues; study or explain stage by stage; find out the whereabouts of (a lost person or thing); copy exactly (drawing *etc*) by marking a thin transparent sheet laid on the original; draw, sketch; describe ~ **trace** *n* mark or sign revealing that something is or has been present; track, trail; vestige; token; very small amount, just perceptible amount; **t. element** element essential, though only in minute amounts, to the health of an organism > PDB.

traceability [tRaysa*bi*liti] *n* quality of being traceable.

traceable [*tRays*ab'l] *adj* capable of being traced.

tracer [*tRay*ser] *n* one who or that which traces; radioactive isotope used to trace the course of an element through an organism > PDB, PDS; **t. bullet (shell)** bullet (shell) which leaves a trail of smoke behind it.

tracery [*tRay*seRi] *n* decorative pattern of lines; ornamental stonework between arches of Gothic windows to support the glass.

trachea [tRak*i*-a] *n* windpipe; breathing-tube of insect ~ **tracheal** *adj*.

tracheotomy [tRaki-*ot*omi] *n* (*surg*) operation of making an opening in the windpipe.

trachoma [tRa*kO*ma] *n* contagious disease of the eyelid and eye.

trachyte [*tRak*It] *n* a crystalline volcanic rock.

tracing [*tRay*sing] *n* process of copying through a transparent sheet; copy thus made; track.

tracing-paper [*tRay*sing-payper] *n* thin transparent paper for copying an original by tracing.

track [*tRak*] *n* mark or series of marks left by something that has passed by, trail; footprint; path; rough road; course along which something is moving; course for racing; railway line; metal belt surrounding wheels of tank or similar vehicle; transverse distance between wheels of vehicle; groove in gramophone record; one among several items on a record; (*cin*) soundtrack; **the beaten t.** conventional method; routine *etc*; **off the beaten t.** unusual, original; not widely known, visited *etc*; **in the tracks of** following; **in one's tracks** (*coll*) just where one is standing; **make tracks** (*sl*) go hastily away; **make tracks for** (*coll*) set out towards; **off the t.** following the wrong course; **on the t. of** pursuing closely ~ **track** *v/t* and *i* follow the track of; follow; trace; tow; **t. down** discover or capture after long search; **t. up** measure and adjust the track of vehicle wheels.

tracked [*tRak*t] *adj* (*of tanks etc*) having a metal belt round the wheels instead of tyres.

tracker [*tRak*er] *n* one who or that which tracks; one who tows; **t. dog** bloodhound or other dog used for tracking fugitives.

trackless [*tRak*lis] *adj* pathless; untrodden; leaving no track.

tracksuit [*tRak*sewt] *n* soft garment worn by athletes when training.

trackway [*tRak*way] *n* ancient unpaved road.

tract (1) [*tRak*t] *n* wide area of land, expanse; lengthy period; (*anat*) system of related organs.

tract (2) *n* short pamphlet, *usu* on religion.

tractability [tRakta*bi*liti] *n* quality of being tractable.

tractable [*tRak*tab'l] *adj* easily led, persuaded, or controlled; docile.

tractate [*tRak*tayt] *n* treatise; tract (2).

traction [*tRak*shon] *n* act of dragging; state of being dragged along; method by which power for transport is obtained.

traction-engine [*tRak*shon-enjin] *n* steam-engine for drawing heavy loads along a road.

tractive [*tRak*tiv] *adj* capable of dragging.

tractor [*tRak*tor] *n* that which drags a load; motor vehicle for drawing ploughs *etc*; traction-engine.

trad [*tRad*] *adj* (*sl*) traditional; (*of jazz*) in a style originating in New Orleans *c*. 1920, with well-defined melody and simple rhythms.

trade [tRayd] *n* act or business of buying, selling or bartering goods, commerce; retail business; skilled craft; occupation, employment, *esp* on manual work; persons engaged in the same craft, employment, or work; **the trades** trade-winds ~ **trade** *v/t* and *i* buy and sell; barter, exchange; carry on a commercial business; carry merchandise; **t. in** give as part-payment for a new article; **t. off** barter; **t. on (upon)** exploit, extract unfair advantage from.

trade-board [tRayd-bawrd] *n* committee of employers, employees and experts to regulate conditions of employment in certain trades.

trade-in [tRayd-in] *n* (*coll*) used article offered in part payment for new one.

trademark [tRaydmaark] *n* registered name or symbol used by a manufacturer to identify his goods.

trade-name [tRayd-naym] *n* name by which an article is known among traders; name under which a firm or individual carries on trade.

trade-price [tRayd-pRis] *n* price paid by retailer to wholesaler.

trader [tRayder] *n* one engaged in trade; merchant; trading ship.

tradesman (*pl* **tradesmen**) [tRaydzman] *n* retail shopkeeper.

trade-union [tRayd-yOOni-on] *n* organized body of workmen of any trade to represent their interests > PDPol; **Trades Union Congress** an association of British trade-unions > PDPol.

trade-unionism [tRayd-yOOni-onizm] *n* principles and practice of trade-unions.

trade-unionist [tRayd-yOOni-onist] *n* one who belongs to a trade-union.

trade-wind [tRayd-wind] *n* wind that blows regularly towards the equator from north or south.

trading-estate [tRayding-estayt] *n* area containing houses and light-industrial plants.

tradition [tRadishon] *n* belief, custom, story, law *etc* orally transmitted from one generation to another; process of such transmission; body of principles and experience handed down from past to present; continuity of development, similarity and influence linking writers, artists, thinkers *etc* of one period to those of another.

traditional [tRadishonal] *adj* orally transmitted from the past, handed down by tradition; in accordance with past custom, practice *etc*; not influenced by modern fashions, inventions *etc*.

traditionalism [tRadishonalizm] *n* reverence for tradition; quality of being traditional.

traditionalist [tRadishonalist] *n* one who reveres traditions, *esp* in religious matters ~ **traditionalist** *adj*.

traditionally [tRadishonali] *adv* in a traditional way; according to tradition.

traduce [tRadews] *v/t* deliberately misrepresent; calumniate, slander; abuse, disparage.

traffic [tRafik] *n* movement of vehicles along a road; number of vehicles using a road *etc*; transport, transportation; commerce, trade; illegal trade; **t. jam** congestion of road traffic forcing vehicles to slow down or stop ~ **traffic** (*pres/part* **trafficking**, *p/t* and *p/part* **trafficked**) *v/t* and *i* buy and sell, *esp* illegally; **t. on** take unscrupulous advantage of.

trafficator [tRafikayter] *n* light or other device on a motor vehicle to signal intention to change course.

trafficker [tRafiker] *n* one who carries on an illegal trade; (*ar*) merchant, dealer.

traffic-lights [tRafik-lits] *n* (*pl*) automatic electric lights set up as signals to regulate movement of traffic at crossroads *etc*.

tragacanth [tRagakanth] *n* kind of Asiatic gum used medicinally.

tragedian [tRajeedi-an] *n* writer of tragedies; actor of tragedy.

tragedienne [tRajeedi-*en*] *n* actress of tragedy.

tragedy [tRajidi] *n* play or story describing human misfortunes and errors, ending in disaster or death for the chief character(s); very sad event, calamity, *esp* one causing death or destruction; that which causes extreme grief.

tragic [tRajik] *adj* of or like tragedy; connected with death; fatal; disastrous; expressing, feeling or causing extreme grief.

tragically [tRajikali] *adv* in a tragic manner; with tragic feeling; with tragic results.

tragi-comedy [tRaji-*kom*idi] *n* play or story containing both tragic and comic scenes, *usu* in about equal proportions; play or story in which a potentially tragic situation is given a happy ending; series of events mingling tragic and comic elements.

tragi-comic [tRaji-*komik*] *adj* of the nature of tragi-comedy.

trail [tRayl] *v/t* and *i* drag along the ground or other surface; hang loosely so as to drag along the ground; follow the track of; follow closely and secretly, shadow; grow in long shoots, straggle; tread down (grass); (*coll*) walk slowly and wearily; (*mil*) carry (arms) with butt near the ground and muzzle obliquely forwards; **t. one's coat** act so as to provoke attack ~ **trail** *n* track, marks showing that something has passed; scent or spoor left by a passing animal, *esp* when hunted; indistinct pathway in wild country, track; (*mil*) end of guncarriage that rests on the ground.

trailer [tRayler] *n* one who or that which trails; vehicle designed to be towed by another; caravan; excerpts from a film shown in advance as advertisement.

trail-net [tRayl-net] *n* dragnet, trawl.

train (1) [tRayn] *v/t* and *i* instil good habits or skills into; educate or instruct by systematic discipline and practice; drill; tame, make docile; teach tricks to (animals); prepare oneself for a contest, sport *etc* by systematic practice, dieting, exercise *etc*; (*hort*) cause to grow in a certain direction by tying, pruning *etc*; (*mil*) aim.

train (2) *n* series of railway carriages or trucks drawn by an engine; series of connected thoughts or acts; that which trails; lengthened skirt of dress, cloak *etc* that trails behind; procession; retinue, body of attendants; line of gunpowder to lead fire to an explosive charge; course of action; **in t.** in preparation for action.

train-bearer [tRayn-bairRer] *n* attendant bearing the train of a robe.

trainee [tRaynee] *n* one who is being trained; one whose course of training is shorter than an apprentice's.

trainer [tRayner] *n* one who trains men, horses *etc* for sporting events.

766

train-ferry [tRayn-feRi] n ferry which conveys trains over water from one railway to another.

training [tRayning] n process by which one is trained; process of acquiring skill, qualifications etc; process of fitting oneself for a sport, contest etc by practice, exercise, diet etc; **in t.** physically fit and ready for a sport, feat of endurance etc; undergoing training.

training-college [tRayning-kolij] n college for training school-teachers.

training-ship [tRayning-ship] n ship on which boys are trained for naval service.

training-stable [tRayning-stayb'l] n stable where racehorses are trained.

train-oil [tRayn-oil] n oil obtained from whale blubber.

trainsick [tRaynsik] adj feeling nausea caused by motion in a train ~ **trainsickness** n.

trainspotting [tRaynspoting] n hobby of collecting locomotive numbers.

traipse see trapse.

trait [tRay/tRayt] n characteristic feature.

traitor [tRaytor] n one who is guilty of disloyalty, treason, or treachery; one who betrays a trust.

traitorous [tRaytoRus] adj like a traitor; treacherous ~ **traitorously** adv ~ **traitorousness** n.

traitress [tRaytRes] n female traitor.

trajectory [tRajektoRi] n path of a missile fired or thrown through the air.

tram (1) [tRam] n public vehicle propelled by electricity or steam, or drawn by horses, along rails in a road; truck used in coal mines ~ **tram** (pres/part **tramming**, p/t and p/part **trammed**) v/i travel by tram.

tram (2) n silk thread consisting of two or more strands twisted together.

tramcar [tRamkaar] n tram (1).

tramline [tRamlin] n railway along which tram runs; route of a tram.

trammel [tRamel] v/t confine, restrict; hamper; catch or tie with a trammel ~ **trammel** n shackle; long fish-net; pot-hook; instrument for drawing ellipses; that which confines.

tramp [tRamp] v/i and t tread heavily; travel on foot; travel as or like a vagabond; travel over by tramping; trample ~ **tramp** n act or sound of tramping; long walk; vagabond, homeless wanderer who lives by begging and odd jobs; cargo vessel not attached to a regular line; (US) immoral woman, whore.

trample [tRamp'l] v/t and i tread under foot; crush by treading on; (fig) treat with contempt; perform the action of trampling ~ **trample** n act of trampling.

trampoline [tRampOlin] n strong elastic framework on which acrobats perform trick leaps.

tramway [tRamway] n track on which tramcars run.

trance [tRaans] n condition of unawareness of external things in which visions, hallucinations etc are experienced and any acts performed are unconscious > PDP; mystic rapture, ecstasy; (med) condition of unconsciousness resembling deep sleep.

tranquil [tRankwil] adj calm, peaceful, serene.

tranquillity [tRankwiliti] n state or quality of being tranquil.

tranquillize [tRankwiliz] v/t and i make or become calmer, soothe.

tranquillizer [tRankwilizer] n drug used to calm anxiety, agitation etc.

trans- pref across, over; beyond, on the far side of; through.

transact [tRanzakt] v/t and i perform, do, carry out; do business.

transaction [tRanzakshon] n the carrying out of business; that which is transacted; business, affair; proceeding; (pl) records of proceedings of a learned society.

transalpine [tRanzalpin] adj north of the Alps.

transatlantic [tRanzatlantik] adj beyond the Atlantic; crossing the Atlantic.

transceiver [tRansseever] n portable equipment for transmitting and receiving radio messages, walkie-talkie set.

transcend [tRansend] v/t rise above, surpass, exceed; pass beyond the range of.

transcendence [tRansendens] n state or quality of being transcendent.

transcendent [tRansendent] adj supreme, excelling, surpassing; beyond the sphere of knowledge; outside the material universe, not limited by physical laws ~ **transcendently** adv.

transcendental [tRansendental] adj (philos) intuitive; beyond the sphere of experience; (fig) speculative, obscure; **t. meditation** Oriental technique of meditation aiming at tranquillity and detachment.

transcendentalism [tRansendentalizm] n (philos) system that ascribes more importance to intuitive than to empirical knowledge ~ **transcendentalist** n and adj.

transcontinental [tRanskontinental] adj extending across or crossing a continent.

transcribe [tRanskRib] v/t copy out; write out (notes etc) in full; reproduce in another alphabet; (mus) arrange for performance by a different instrument than the original > PDM.

transcript [tRanskRipt] n written copy.

transcription [tRanskRipshon] n act of transcribing; that which is transcribed, copy.

transducer [tRansdewser] n (phys) device which receives energy in one form and converts it to another form > PDS.

transect [tRansekt] v/t cut across.

transept [tRansept] n (archi) portion of a cruciform church crossing the main axis at right angles.

transfer (pres/part **transferring**, p/t and p/part **transferred**) [transfur] v/t and i send, move or convey from one person or place to another; give, hand over to the possession of another; print from one surface to another ~ **transfer** [tRansfur] n act of transferring; that which is transferred; conveyance; picture or pattern which can be printed by heat or pressure from one surface to another; (mil) soldier etc moved from one troop to another.

transferability [tRansfeRabiliti] n quality of being transferable.

transferable [tRansfurRab'l] adj that can be transferred.

transferee [tRansfeRee] n one to whom a transfer is made; one who is transferred.

transference [tRansfeRens] n act or process of transferring; the transferring of an emotional attitude from one person or object to another associated with it; development of emotional attitude in a patient towards a psychiatrist.

transfiguration [tRansfigew*Ray*shon] *n* striking change of appearance, *usu* for the better; (*cap*) miraculous change in the appearance of Jesus Christ on the Mountain; church festival held on 6 August to commemorate this.

transfigure [tRans*figer*] *v/t* suddenly and strikingly change and improve the appearance of; make more glorious.

transfix [tRans*fiks*] *v/t* pierce through; (*fig*) render immobile; amaze, stun.

transform [tRans*fawrm*] *v/t* and *i* change form or appearance of; change type or character of; change disposition or nature of; be changed in form, character, appearance *etc*.

transformation [tRansfawr*may*shon] *n* act of transforming; state of being transformed; change; **t. scene** (*theat*) scene in which scenery gradually and elaborately changes in view of the audience; (*coll*) amazing change of appearance of a place.

transformer [tRans*fawr*mer] *n* one who or that which transforms; device to change alternating current of one voltage to another voltage, without alteration in frequency > PDS, PDEl.

transfuse [tRans*fewz*] *v/t* pour from one vessel into another; (*med*) transfer (blood) from veins of one person or animal into another; inject into a vein; (*fig*) instil, imbue.

transfusion [tRans*few*zhon] *n* act of transfusing; the transferring of blood taken from the veins of one person into those of another; blood so transfused.

transgress [tRans*gRes*] *v/t* and *i* overstep bounds, exceed; break, violate (a law); offend by breaking a law or convention; sin.

transgression [tRans*gRes*hon] *n* act of transgressing; sin; crime.

transgressor [tRans*gRes*or] *n* one who transgresses.

tranship, trans-ship [tRan*ship*/tRans-*ship*] *v/t* and *i* transfer from one ship to another.

transhipment, trans-shipment [tRan*ship*ment/ tRans-*ship*ment] *n* process of transhipping.

transhumance [trans-*hew*mans] *n* seasonal movement of tribe or of livestock between summer and winter hunting-grounds or pastures.

transience [*tRan*zi-ens] *n* quality or state of being transient.

transient [*tRan*zi-ent] *adj* soon passing; not lasting; transitory; brief ~ **transiently** *adv*.

transire [tRan*zee*Ri] *n* warrant issued by customhouse permitting removal of goods.

transistor [tRan*zis*tor] *n* (*elect*) very small device consisting of three semiconducting layers, widely used in electronic circuits in place of thermionic valves > PDEl, PDS; small portable radio containing this.

transistorize [tRan*zis*toRIz] *v/t* replace thermionic valves with transistors; use transistors in.

transit [*tRan*zit] *n* act of passing or being conveyed from one place to another; (*astron*) the passing of a planet across the sun's disk, or of a moon across a planet's disk; the passing of a heavenly body over a meridian; **in t.** (*of goods*) despatched by sender but not yet received by those to whom they are sent ~ **transit** *v/t* (*astron*) pass across.

transition [tRan*zish*on] *n* passage, change, alteration from one place, state, period *etc* to another; (*mus*) change from one key to another; **t. elements** (*chem*) elements whose properties resemble those of their horizontal neighbours in the periodic table > PDS.

transitional [tRan*zish*onal] *adj* of, forming, occurring during or involving transition; intermediate; in process of changing ~ **transitionally** *adv*.

transitive [*tRan*zitiv] *adj* (*gramm*) having a direct object; able to pass from one person or thing to another ~ **transitively** *adv* ~ **transitiveness** *n*.

transitory [*tRan*zitoRi] *adj* not lasting, fleeting; momentary, brief ~ **transitoriness** *n*.

translatable [tRans*lay*tab'l] *adj* capable of being translated.

translate [tRans*layt*] *v/t* and *i* render into another language; express in clearer terms; be translatable; put into action; remove from one office to another; (*theol*) convey to heaven without death; (*eccles*) transfer the body or relics of (saint *etc*) elsewhere.

translation [tRans*lay*shon] *n* action of translating; that which is translated; version in one language of something spoken or written in another; removal to another place.

translator [tRans*lay*tor] *n* one who translates from one language to another.

transliterate [tRanz*lite*Rayt] *v/t* represent (words of one language) in the alphabet of another.

translucence [tRanz*lOO*sens] *n* condition of being translucent.

translucent [tRanz*lOO*sent] *adj* permitting partial passage of light > PDS; not completely transparent; (*poet*) transparent.

transmigrate [*tRanz*mIgRayt] *v/i* migrate, go to live in another country; (*of the soul*) pass into another body after death.

transmigration [tRanzmIg*Ray*shon] *n* act of passing from one place to another; passing of the soul at death from one body into another, metempsychosis ~ **transmigratory** *adj*.

transmissible [tRanz*mis*ib'l] *adj* capable of being transmitted.

transmission [tRanz*mish*on] *n* act of transmitting; state of being transmitted; that which is transmitted.

transmit (*pres/part* **transmitting**, *p/t* and *p/part* **transmitted**) [tRanz*mit*] *v/t* and *i* pass on, hand over; serve as medium for the passage of; hand down by heredity or inheritance; communicate; pass or convey through a medium; send (message) by radio, telegraphy *etc*.

transmitter [tRanz*mit*er] *n* one who or that which transmits; apparatus for sending messages over telegraph wires; apparatus for sending out wireless waves.

transmogrification [tRanzmogRifi*kay*shon] *n* (*coll*) complete transformation.

transmogrify [tRanz*mog*Rifi] *v/t* (*coll*) transform; completely change appearance or character of.

transmutable [tRanz*mew*tab'l] *adj* that can be transmuted.

transmutation [tRanzmew*tay*shon] *n* act or process of transmuting; state of being transmuted; (*chem*) the changing of one element into another > PDS; (*biol*) mutation.

transmute [tRanz*mewt*] *v/t* change completely in

nature or appearance; change (one substance) into another, *esp* (other metals) into gold.

transom [tRansom] *n* horizontal crossbar of window; window divided by a crossbar; lintel; (*naut*) beam across sternpost > PDSa.

transom-window [tRansom-windO] *n* window divided by a transom; window above lintel of a door.

transparence [tRanspairRens/tRanspaRens] *n* quality of being transparent.

transparency [tRanspairRensi/tRanspaRensi] *n* quality of being transparent; that which is transparent; picture on semi-transparent material visible when lit from behind.

transparent [tRanspairRent/tRanspaRent] *adj* allowing light rays to pass through; allowing objects to be seen clearly through it; (*fig*) clear, obvious; easily detected or understood; sincere ~ **transparently** *adv*.

transpierce [tRanspeers] *v/t* pierce through.

transpiration [tRanspiRayshon] *n* exhalation of vapour through skin or surface; loss of water-vapour by land plants > PDB.

transpire [tRanspIr] *v/t* and *i* exhale as vapour through somata, skin *etc*; become known; (*pop*) happen.

transplant [tRansplaant] *v/t* and *i* dig up (plant) from one place and replant elsewhere; remove from one dwelling place to another; remove to different surroundings; (*surg*) remove (healthy organ or tissue) and graft elsewhere; be capable of being transplanted ~ **transplant** *n* act of transplanting tissue, *esp* from one individual to another; organ or tissue transplanted.

transplantation [tRansplaantayshon] *n* act of transplanting.

transpolar [transpOlar] *adj* (*of air route*) passing near the North Pole.

transport [tRanspawrt] *v/t* convey from one place to another; (*hist*) deport (criminal) to penal settlement; (*fig*) carry away by powerful emotion, enrapture ~ **transport** *n* act or method of conveying persons or goods; vehicles used for this; ship or aircraft for carrying troops; (*fig*) rush of emotion, rapture, ecstasy.

transportable [tRanspawrtab'l] *adj* capable of being transported.

transportation [tRanspawrtayshon] *n* act of transporting, conveyance; penal deportation; (*US*) means of transport.

transporter [tRanspawrter] *n* one who or that which transports; travelling crane; conveyor-belt.

transposal [tRanspOzal] *n* act of transposing.

transpose [tRanspOz] *v/t* and *i* change the order or position of; cause to change places; (*mus*) write or play in a different key > PDM.

transposition [tRanspOzishon] *n* act of transposing; state of being transposed; piece of transposed music.

transsexual [tRans-seksewal] *adj* (*psych*) having the physical features of one sex but the psychological attitudes of the other.

trans-ship see **tranship**.

transubstantiate [tRansubstanshi-ayt] *v/t* change into another substance.

transubstantiation [tRansubstanshi-ayshon] *n* change of substance or essence; (*theol*) doctrine

that the Eucharistic bread and wine are changed in essence, though not in appearance, into Christ's body and blood.

transuranic [tRanzewRanik] *adj* (*chem*) (*of an element*) having an atomic number greater than that of uranium > PDS.

transversal [tRanzvursal] *adj* lying or running across ~ **transversal** *n* line cutting two or more lines ~ **transversally** *adv*.

transverse [tRanzvurs] *adj* crosswise, at right angles to the longest axis or main direction ~ **transverse** *n* that which lies or acts transversely ~ **transversely** *adv*.

transvestism [tRanzvestizm] *n* propensity or tendency to dress in clothes of the other sex ~ **transvestist** *adj*.

transvestite [tRanzvestIt] *n* one who practises transvestism.

trap [tRap] *n* a snare, any contrivance for catching animals, birds or men that enter or touch it; cunning device or plan to deceive, detect, capture *etc*; ambush; box *etc* from which an animal or object can be suddenly released; device to prevent foul air from escaping from drain; trapdoor; light horsedrawn carriage, *usu* with only two wheels; (*sl*) mouth; policeman ~ **trap** (*pres/part* **trapping**, *p/t* and *p/part* **trapped**) *v/t* and *i* catch in a trap; capture or deceive by a trick, ensnare; prevent from escaping; set traps.

trapdoor [tRapdawr] *n* hinged door in roof, ceiling or floor, or in theatre stage.

trapes see **trapse**.

trapeze [tRapeez] *n* swinging horizontal bar for gymnastic and acrobatic feats.

trapezium [tRapeezi-um] *n* (*geom*) quadrilateral having only two sides parallel > PDS.

trapezoid [tRapizoid] *n* and *adj* (*geom*) (quadrilateral) having no two sides parallel.

trapper [tRaper] *n* one who traps wild animals.

trappings [tRapingz] *n* (*pl*) decorations; ornamental harness; finery.

Trappist [tRapist] *n* Cistercian monk bound by vows of perpetual silence and strict austerity.

traps [tRaps] *n* (*pl*) (*coll*) clothes; belongings.

trapse, traipse, trapes [tRayps] *v/i* gad about; walk aimlessly or needlessly.

trash [tRash] *n* useless matter, rubbish; worthless person; shoddy goods; book, play, music *etc* of no merit or interest; (*US*) beggar, destitute person.

trashy [tRashi] *adj* of, like or full of trash; worthless; shoddy ~ **trashily** *adv* ~ **trashiness** *n*.

trauma [tRawma] *n* emotional or psychological injury caused by some shock or unpleasant experience > PDP; (*med*) wound, damage caused by wounding.

traumatic [tRawmatik] *adj* of, caused by, or likely to cause trauma; deeply and unforgettably distressing, shocking *etc* ~ **traumatically** *adv*.

travail [tRavayl] *n* pains of childbirth ~ **travail** *v/i* suffer pains of childbirth; (*fig*) toil painfully, *esp* to create something.

travel (*pres/part* **travelling**, *p/t* and *p/part* **travelled**) [tRavel] *v/i* and *t* make a journey, *esp* to distant places; move in a certain direction; go; go from place to place to obtain business orders; journey over or through ~ **travel** *n* act of travelling; (*pl*) journeys; a tour, *esp* abroad.

travel-agency [tRavel-ayjensi] *n* agency supplying information, booking tickets *etc* for travellers.

travelator [tRavelaytor] *n* moving pavement for pedestrians, formed by endless conveyor belt.

travel-bureau [tRavel-bewRO] *n* office of a travel-agency.

travelled [tRaveld] *adj* having visited many foreign lands.

traveller [tRavler] *n* one who travels; one who travels to obtain orders for goods; **t.'s cheque** cheque issued by a bank for clients travelling abroad, payable at any branch or agent of the bank that issued it; **t.'s joy** wild clematis.

travelogue [tRavelog] *n* (*coll*) film, newspaper article *etc* describing a journey or places to be seen when travelling.

traversable [tRavursab'l] *adj* capable of being crossed.

traverse [tRavurs/tRavurs] *v/t* and *i* travel across or through; lie across; examine carefully; frustrate, thwart; turn and point in another direction, swivel; (*leg*) deny a plea; (*carp*) plane across grain ~ **traverse** *n* that which crosses something else; ledge *etc* crossing a rock-face horizontally; gallery across a building; (*mil*) earthwork crossing a trench *etc* at right angles; movement of traversing; (*leg*) denial of a plea; (*fig*) hindrance ~ **traverse** *adj* and *adv* crosswise.

traverse-table [tRavurs-tayb'l] *n* table reckoning differences of latitude and departure.

travertine [tRaverteen] *n* porous rock formed of lime deposits.

travesty [tRavisti] *n* ridiculous distortion or misrepresentation; parody, absurd caricature ~ **travesty** *v/t* make or be a travesty of; render ridiculous by parody.

trawl [tRawl] *n* open-mouthed fishing-net drawn along sea-bottom ~ **trawl** *v/t* and *i* fish with a trawl.

trawler [tRawler] *n* fishing vessel that uses a trawl; one who trawls.

tray [tRay] *n* flat object of metal, wood, plastic *etc* surrounded by a low rim and used for carrying crockery, food *etc*.

treacherous [tRecheRus] *adj* of or inclined to treachery; disloyal; deceptively attractive- or safe-looking ~ **treacherously** *adv* ~ **treacherousness** *n*.

treachery [tRecheRi] *n* betrayal of trust; faithlessness; treason; deceit.

treacle [tReek'l] *n* dark syrup obtained in refining sugar; molasses.

treacly [tReekli] *adj* thick and sticky like treacle; covered with treacle; (*fig*) over-sweet, too affable.

tread (*p/t* trod, *p/part* trodden, *ar* trod) [tRed] *v/t* and *i* walk on; trample; oppress, subdue; go, step; (*of male birds*) copulate with; **t. on air** (*coll*) be very happy; **t. water** remain upright with head above water by moving one's legs ~ **tread** *n* act or manner of walking; sound of a footstep; part of a tyre that is in contact with the ground; something designed for treading on; top surface of a step; piece of rubber *etc* covering this; sole of shoe.

treadle, treddle [tRed'l] *n* lever, pedal *etc* on which the foot presses to work a machine.

treadmill [tRedmil] *n* wheel turned by weight of persons treading on steps fixed to its rim; (*fig*) monotonous labour, dreary routine.

treason [tReez'n] *n* an attempt to betray or illegally overthrow a sovereign or government; treachery; **high t.** treason directly affecting the monarchy.

treasonable [tReezonab'l] *adj* of or involving treason ~ **treasonably** *adv*. .

treasure [tRezher] *n* hoard of valuable objects, jewels, or money; very valuable object; person or object highly valued or dearly loved; invaluably useful person ~ **treasure** *v/t* keep as valuable; cherish, regard as precious; remember fondly; hoard up.

treasure-house [tRezher-hows] *n* building in which articles of great value are kept.

treasurer [tRezheRer] *n* person in charge of funds of a club, institution *etc*; keeper of a treasury.

treasure-trove [tRezher-tROv] *n* money or gold and silver articles of unknown ownership, found hidden in the ground *etc*.

treasury [tRezheRi] *n* building in which treasure is kept; (*cap*) place where public revenues are kept; government department in charge of public finance; **T. Bench** Parliamentary front bench occupied by chief members of the government; **T. bill** form of government security issued on short-term loans; **T. note** form of paper currency issued by the Treasury.

treat [tReet] *v/t* and *i* behave towards, use or handle in specified way; consider, regard; apply specified process to; attempt to cure of disease, apply remedies to or for; discuss; negotiate, discuss terms; pay costs of (another's meal, pleasures, entertainment *etc*); **t. of** speak or write about; **t. (someone) to** pay for ôn someone's behalf; **t. oneself to** indulge in ~ **treat** *n* great and unusual pleasure, entertainment *etc*; expedition or entertainment planned for pleasure; **stand t.** pay for another's pleasure.

treatise [tReetiz] *n* book or article giving full scholarly account of a particular subject.

treatment [tReetment] *n* act or manner of treating; behaviour towards; any process or method of curing or alleviating disease; chemical or industrial process applied to a substance.

treaty [tReeti] *n* formal league, agreement between States or sovereigns; negotiation.

treble [tReb'l] *adj* triple, threefold; high-pitched ~ **treble** *n* (*mus*) child's high-pitched voice; part written for this; upper range of musical pitch > PDM ~ **treble** *v/t* and *i* multiply by three; become three times as many or as much.

trecento [tRaychentO] *n* the 14th century as a period in Italian art, literature *etc*.

treddle see **treadle**.

tree [tRee] *n* perennial plant of considerable size, having woody trunk and branches; anything resembling this; cobbler's last; shoetree; gallows; (*ar*) the cross of Christ; **family (genealogical) t.** diagram showing descent from a common ancestor; **top of the t.** (*fig*) highest attainable rank, office, status *etc*; **up a t.** (*coll*) in difficulties ~ **tree** *v/t* and *i* force to take refuge in a tree; climb a tree for refuge; (*coll*) put in difficulties.

tree-creeper [tRee-kReeper] *n* any bird which creeps on trunks and branches of trees.

tree-cricket [tRee-kRikit] *n* cicada.

tree-fern [tRee-furn] n fern with tall upright stem.

treen [tReen] n (collect) small domestic objects made of wood.

tree-peony [tRee-pee-oni] n Chinese peony growing as a shrub.

trefoil [tRefoil] n plant whose leaf has three lobes; pattern resembling a clover leaf; (archi) three-lobed carved ornament or tracery.

trek (pres/part **trekking**, p/t and p/part **trekked**) [tRek] v/i make a long journey in search of new home, esp by ox-wagon; (fig) travel far and laboriously, esp on foot ~ **trek** n act of trekking; long hard journey.

trellis [tRelis] n light structure of strips of wood crossing each other; lattice.

tremble [tRemb'l] v/i shake involuntarily with fear, cold, or excitement; feel great fear; quiver, shake ~ **tremble** n act or state of trembling; tremor.

trembler [tRembler] n one who trembles; vibrator for making or breaking an electrical circuit.

trembly [tRembli] adj trembling, inclined to tremble.

tremendous [tRimendus] adj amazing, very impressive; vast, huge; awe-inspiring; (coll) very important; very exciting ~ **tremendously** adv immensely; (coll) very, very much ~ **tremendousness** n.

tremolo [tRemolO] n (mus) rapid alternation of volume or pitch giving a tremulous effect to a note > PDM; vibrato; organ-stop producing vibrato effect.

tremor [tRemer] n fit of trembling or quivering; slight earthquake; feeling of fear.

tremulous [tRemewlus] adj trembling, quivering; timid; wavering ~ **tremulously** adv ~ **tremulousness** n.

trench [tRench] n long narrow hole cut in the earth, ditch; deep ditch used as cover for troops; (pl, fig) frontline fighting ~ **trench** v/t dig a trench in; cut a groove in; encroach.

trenchancy [tRenchansi] n quality of being trenchant.

trenchant [tRenchant] adj sharp, cutting well; (fig) sharply critical or ironic; concisely and strongly expressed ~ **trenchantly** adv.

trench-coat [tRench-kOt] n belted waterproof coat of military type.

trencher [tRencher] n wooden plate upon which bread or meat is cut.

trencherman [tRencherman] n good (poor) t. person with a hearty (small) appetite.

trench-fever [tRench-feever] n kind of fever transmitted by lice, suffered by troops in the war of 1914–18.

trench-plough [tRench-plow] n powerful plough used for deep ploughing.

trend [tRend] n tendency, general direction of development, change or fashion; general purport, main purpose or effect ~ **trend** v/i tend.

trend-setting [tRend-seting] adj starting or popularizing the latest fashion.

trendy [tRendi] adj adopting or popularizing the latest trends in fashion.

trepan (pres/part **trepanning**, p/t and p/part **trepanned**) [tRipan] v/t (surg) cut away an area of bone from the skull, perforate (the skull) ~ **trepan** n small cylindrical saw for trepanning.

trepang [tRipang] n the sea-slug.

trephine [tRifeen] n (surg) trepan with centre-pin.

trepidation [tRepidayshon] n state of alarm, anxiety, or excitement; trembling of limbs.

trespass [tRespas] v/i intrude illegally on another's land; (ar) commit an offence, sin; encroach ~ **trespass** n act of trespassing; offence to another; (ar) sin, misdeed.

trespasser [tRespaser] n one who trespasses on the property of another.

tress [tRes] n lock of hair, plait; (pl) hair of the head ~ **tressed** adj braided, having tresses.

trestle [tRes'l] n framework of wooden legs and bar used as removable support for table, platform etc.

trestle-table [tRes'l-tayb'l] n table made of boards laid on trestles.

tret [tRet] n (comm) allowance made to purchasers for waste or deterioration.

trews [tROOz] n (pl) tartan trousers.

trey [tRay] n a three at cards or dice.

tri- pref three.

triable [tRI-ab'l] adj capable of being tried or tested.

triad [tRI-ad] n group of three; form of poem in which subjects or lines are grouped in threes; (chem) element having a valency of three; (mus) chord of a note with its third and fifth > PDM.

triage [tRI-aj] n (mil) sorting-out, arrangement in order of priority.

trial [tRI-al] n act or process of trying or testing; test, examination, experiment; that which tries or tests; adversity, suffering; annoyance, cause of irritation; (leg) judicial examination in a court of law; **by t. and error** by trying several methods etc before choosing the best; **t. marriage** period of cohabitation without marriage, to test compatibility of persons intending to marry; **on t.** undergoing a trial at law; being tested; on approval; **t. run** act of driving a vehicle to test its efficiency; (fig) period of preliminary testing, rehearsing etc ~ **trial** adj of or as a test.

triangle [tRI-ang-g'l] n plane figure bounded by three straight lines > PDS; drawing implement of this shape; (mus) triangular steel rod used as percussion instrument > PDM; **eternal t.** tense emotional situation arising from the relationship of two men and a woman or of two women and a man.

triangular [tRI-ang-gewlar] adj having three sides or angles; involving three people, groups etc.

triangularity [tRI-ang-gewlaRiti] n quality of being triangular.

triangulate [tRI-ang-gewlit] v/t and i mark into triangles; measure by triangulation.

triangulation [tRI-ang-gewlayshon] n measurement of land by a network of triangles calculated by trigonometry > PDE.

Triassic [tRI-asik] n and adj (geological period) immediately preceding the Jurassic > PDB.

tribal [tRIbal] adj of a tribe.

tribalism [tRIbalizm] n organization of a social group as a tribe or into several tribes.

tribally [tRIbali] adv as a tribe; into tribes.

tribasic [tRIbaysik] adj (chem) having three atoms of hydrogen > PDS.

tribe [tRIb] n social group linked by kinship and having the same beliefs, customs etc, but usu of fairly low culture > PDP; (fig, cont) class, group;

(*biol*) groups of closely related genera within a family.

tribesman (*pl* **tribesmen**) [tRIbzman] *n* member of a tribe.

tribo-electricity [tRIbO-ilektRIsiti] *n* frictional electricity.

tribology [tRIboloji] *n* the study of friction forces and lubrication.

tribulation [tRIbewlayshon] *n* affliction, distress, suffering.

tribunal [tRIbewnal] *n* court of justice; special court of inquiry with judicial powers set up by a government to investigate a specific matter.

tribune (1) [tRIbewn] *n* (*Rom hist*) representative elected by the people to protect their rights; (*fig*) one who champions popular rights.

tribune (2) *n* raised platform for public speakers; bishop's throne; pulpit.

tributary [tRIbewteRi] *adj* paying tribute; contributory; subsidiary; (*of rivers*) flowing into a larger river > PDG ~ **tributary** *n* person or State paying tribute; tributary stream.

tribute [tRIbewt] *n* fixed amount paid by one nation to another for peace or protection; contribution; acknowledgement in words or action of gratitude, admiration or respect.

tricar [tRIkaar] *n* three-wheeled motorcar.

trice (1) [tRIs] *v/t* (*naut*) haul up (a sail) and make secure.

trice (2) *n* instant, moment.

tricel [tRIsel] *n* (*tr*) type of fabric of synthetic fibres resembling silk.

triceps [tRIseps] *n* (*anat*) extensor muscle of upper arm.

trich-, tricho- of the hair; like a hair.

trichina (*pl* **trichinae**) [tRIkIna] *n* very small threadlike worm living as intestinal parasite.

trichinosis [tRIkinOsis] *n* disease caused by presence of trichinae in the body.

trichotomy [tRIkotomi] *n* division into three.

trick [tRIk] *n* cunning act or device used to deceive or cheat another; deception; practical joke, prank; act or device used to amuse by surprising or puzzling; illusion, that which causes an illusion; mannerism; personal and curious habit; eccentricity; knack; conjurer's artifice; round of cards; (*naut*) steersman's turn of duty; **dirty t.** (*coll*) mean, deceitful, unfair act; **do the t.** do just what was needed ~ **trick** *v/t* and *i* cheat or deceive by cunning; **t. out** dress or adorn elaborately ~ **trick** *adj* of or as a trick; designed to startle, entrap or deceive; creating a visual illusion.

trick-cyclist [tRIk-sIklist] *n* (*sl*) psychiatrist.

trickery [tRIkeRi] *n* act or practice of playing tricks; fraud, cheating; stratagem.

trickily [tRIkili] *adv* in a tricky way.

trickiness [tRIkinis] *n* quality of being tricky.

trickle [tRIk'l] *v/i* and *t* flow or cause to flow in a small stream; arrive slowly and in small quantities ~ **trickle** *n* small flow; slow and inadequate supply; **t. charger** (*elect*) slow accumulator charger.

trickster [tRIkster] *n* one who practises trickery, cheating rogue.

tricksy [tRIksi] *adj* mischievous; deceptive.

tricky [tRIki] *adj* difficult to understand or deal with, needing careful handling; complicated;

potentially dangerous; inclined to play tricks; deceitful, crafty.

tricolour [tRIkuler] *n* national flag with three stripes of different colours, *esp* that of France.

tricot [tReekO] *n* (*Fr*) style of knitting done by hand with large stitches; sweater made of this.

tric-trac [tRIk-tRak] *n* form of backgammon.

tricycle [tRIsik'l] *n* cycle with three wheels; three-wheeled motorcar for disabled drivers.

tricyclist [tRIsiklist] *n* one who rides a tricycle.

trident [tRIdent] *n* three-pronged fishing spear, *esp* that of Neptune; symbol of sea-power.

tridentate [tRIdentayt] *adj* three-pronged.

Tridentine [tRIdentIn] *adj* (*RC*) of, established by, the Council of Trent; **T. Mass** Latin text of the Mass as used from 1564 to 1969.

tried [tRId] *p/t* and *p/part* of **try** ~ **tried** *adj* reliable, thoroughly tested.

triennial [tRI-eni-al] *adj* lasting for three years, happening every three years.

trier [tRI-er] *n* one who perseveres; one who tests or examines.

trifid [tRIfid] *adj* (*bot*) divided in three lobes.

trifle [tRIf'l] *n* something of little value or importance; (*coll*) slight amount or degree; sweet dish of custard, sponge cake, jam *etc* ~ **trifle** *v/i* behave frivolously or insincerely; joke, play the fool; waste time; **t. with** thoughtlessly cause pain to; refuse to take seriously; toy with.

trifler [tRIfler] *n* one who wastes time on trivialities; frivolous, insincere person.

trifling [tRIfling] *adj* unimportant, of little value ~ **triflingly** *adv*.

trifoliate [tRIfOli-it] *adj* having three leaflets.

triforium [tRIfawRi-um] *n* (*archi*) arcade in wall of church over arches of nave or choir.

triform [tRIfawrm] *adj* having three shapes, or three divisions.

trig (1) [tRIg] *n* block to check a wheel.

trig (2) *adj* neat, trim.

trig (3) *n* (*coll abbr*) trigonometry.

trigger [tRIger] *n* catch for releasing hammer of gun in firing; catch for releasing a spring; **have one's finger on the t.** (*fig*) have power to order outbreak of war ~ **trigger** *v/i* **t. off** initiate a large-scale, violent or destructive process by a comparatively small act.

trigger-happy [tRIger-hapi] *adj* (*coll*) recklessly eager to start a war or fight.

triglot [tRIglot] *adj* in three languages.

trigonometrical [tRIgonometRIkal] *adj* of or by trigonometry.

trigonometry [tRIgonomitRi] *n* branch of mathematics dealing with measurement of triangles and problems based on this > PDS.

trigraph [tRIgRaaf] *n* group of three letters representing a single sound.

trike [tRIk] *n* (*coll*) tricycle; three-wheeled motorcar for disabled drivers.

trilateral [tRIlateRal] *adj* having three sides.

trilby [tRIlbi] *n* type of man's soft felt hat.

trilingual [tRIling-gwal] *adj* of, in or knowing three languages.

trilith, trilithon [tRIlith, tRIlithon] *n* megalithic monument consisting of two upright stones supporting a third.

trill [tRIl] *n* quavering sound or note, *usu* high-pitched; warble, quavering bird-song; (*mus*) rapid alternation of the written note and that above > PDM ~ **trill** *v/i* sing quaveringly; utter a trill.

trillion [tRilyon] *n* one million cubed; (*US* and *French*) one million squared.

trilobate [tRilObayt] *adj* having three lobes.

trilogy [tRiloji] *n* group of three plays, novels, films *etc* connected by their theme though each complete in itself.

trim (*pres/part* **trimming**, *p/t* and *p/part* **trimmed**) [tRim] *v/t* and *i* put in good order; decorate (hat, garment *etc*); clip; arrange (sails of boat); adjust equilibrium of (boat or aircraft); adjust one's principles, policy *etc* to suit changing circumstances ~ **trim** *adj* neat, tidy; in good order ~ **trim** *n* state of being ready and in good order.

trimaran [tRimaRan] *n* sailing boat with three parallel hulls.

trimester [tRimester] *n* term of three months.

trimly [tRimli] *adv* in a trim way.

trimmer [tRimer] *n* one who or that which trims; timeserver, opportunist; machine for clipping timber.

trimming [tRiming] *n* ornament; accessories.

trimness [tRimnis] *n* state or quality of being trim.

trine [tRIn] *adj* threefold, triple ~ **trine** *n* a set of three ~ **trinal** *adj*.

tringle [tRing-g'l] *n* curtain-rod; (*archi*) small square moulding.

Trinitarian [tRinitairRi-an] *adj* of the Trinity; of Trinitarianism ~ **Trinitarian** *n* believer in Trinitarianism.

Trinitarianism [tRinitairRi-anizm] *n* belief that God is three persons in one God.

trinitrotoluene [tRinitROtolew-een] *n* a type of high explosive, TNT > PDS.

trinity [tRiniti] *n* group of three persons or objects forming a unity or acting as one; **the T.** the three divine persons, Father, Son and Holy Ghost, whose unity forms the Christian God; **T. House** British association for licensing pilots of ships, maintaining lighthouses *etc*; **T. Sunday** the Sunday next after Whitsun.

trinket [tRinkit] *n* small ornament or piece of jewellery of little value.

trinomial [tRinOmi-al] *adj* having three names; (*math*) having three algebraic terms.

trio [tRee-O] *n* set of three; group of three persons associated or acting together; (*mus*) composition for three voices or instruments; set of three singers or players; second part of a march *etc*.

triode [tRI-Od] *n* valve with three electrodes.

triolet [tRI-olit] *n* poem of eight lines with the 1st, 4th, and 7th, and the 2nd and 8th identical, rhyming abaaabab.

trip (*pres/part* **tripping**, *p/t* and *p/part* **tripped**) [tRip] *v/i* and *t* stumble, catch one's foot on an obstacle and fall or nearly fall; cause to stumble or fall; make a mistake, behave indiscreetly; hesitate in speaking; (*poet*) walk or run lightly; (*naut*) release anchor by cable; **t. up** catch out in an error, untruth *etc* ~ **trip** *n* short journey, *usu* for pleasure; journey taken as holiday; excursion, jaunt; act of stumbling; act of causing another to stumble; error, slip, lapse; (*sl*) visionary experience caused by drugs.

tripartite [tRIpaartIt] *adj* of or in three parts.

tripartition [tRIpaartishon] *n* division into three.

tripe [tRIp] *n* stomach of ox, cow, or pig used as food; (*coll*) nonsense, rubbish.

trip-hammer [tRip-hamer] *n* large hammer on pivoted lever.

triphthong [tRifthong] *n* combination of three vowels forming one sound.

triple [tRip'l] *adj* having three parts, threefold; multiplied by three ~ **triple** *v/t* and *i* multiply by three; be three times as many or as large.

triplet [tRiplit] *n* each of three children born at one birth; (*pros*) three lines rhyming together; (*mus*) three notes performed in the time of two.

triplex [tRipleks] *adj* threefold; (*mus*) in triple time; **T. glass** (*tr*) amalgam of glass and mica in three layers.

triplicate [tRiplikit] *adj* threefold; made in three identical copies ~ **triplicate** *n* third copy corresponding to two others ~ **triplicate** [tRiplikayt] *v/t* make three identical copies of; treble.

triplicity [tRiplisiti] *n* state of being triple.

tripod [tRIpod] *n* three-legged support, table, stool *etc*.

tripos [tRIpos] *n* examination for honours degree at Cambridge University.

tripper [tRiper] *n* one who makes a holiday excursion, *esp* for one day only; tourist.

tripperish [tRipeRish] *adj* (*coll*) much visited by trippers.

tripping [tRiping] *adj* walking, running or dancing lightly; fluently spoken ~ **trippingly** *adv*.

triptych [tRiptik] *n* picture on three panels, the side ones hinged to fold over the central one.

tripwire [tRipwIr] *n* wire that will cause a trap to work if an enemy, animal *etc* stumbles against it.

trireme [tRIReem] *n* (*Gk* and *Rom hist*) war-galley with three rows of oars.

trisect [tRIsekt] *v/t* divide into three equal parts.

triskele [tRIskeel] *n* heraldic device of three bent legs joined at the thigh.

tristful [tRistfool] *adj* (*ar*) sad.

trisyllabic [tRisilabik] *adj* having three syllables.

trisyllable [tRisilab'l] *n* word of three syllables.

trite [tRIt] *adj* too often repeated to be effective, hackneyed, commonplace ~ **tritely** *adv* ~ **triteness** *n*.

tritiate [tRIti-ayt] *v/t* and *i* (*phys*) replace a hydrogen atom with a tritium atom.

tritium [tRiti-um] *n* radioisotope of hydrogen with mass number 3.

Triton [tRIton] *n* (*myth*) a minor sea-god, half man and half fish.

triturate [tRitewRayt] *v/t* grind to fine powder.

trituration [tRitewRayshon] *n* act of rubbing to fine powder.

triumph [tRI-umf] *n* great joy at victory or success, exultation; victory, great success or achievement; (*Rom hist*) processional entry of a victorious general into Rome ~ **triumph** *v/i* express joy in victory, exult; gain a victory; be successful.

triumphal [tRI-umfal] *adj* of or celebrating a triumph.

triumphant [tRI-umfant] *adj* exulting in victory; victorious ~ **triumphantly** *adv*.

triumvir [tRI-umver] *n* (*Rom hist*) one of three men sharing supreme power in Rome; (*fig*) one of three men sharing a position of power.

triumvirate [tRI-umveRayt] *n* group of three

triumvirs; group of three men equally sharing power or authority.

triune [tRI-yOOn] *adj* three in one.

trivalent [tRIv*a*lent/tRIvay*l*ent] *adj* (*chem*) having a valency of three; tervalent.

trivet [tRiv*i*t] *n* three-legged stand for holding a vessel over a fire; **right as a t.** perfectly all right.

trivia [tRiv*i*-a] *n* (*pl*) trivial matters, trifles.

trivial [tRiv*i*-al] *adj* of little importance or value; insignificant; superficial, shallow; slight.

triviality [tRiv*i*-*a*lit*i*] *n* state of being trivial; that which is trivial.

trivialize [tRiv*i*-alIz] *v/t* reduce to triviality.

trivially [tRiv*i*-al*i*] *adv* in a trivial way.

trivium [tRiv*i*-um] *n* medieval course of studies comprising grammar, rhetoric and logic.

trochaic [tRo*k*ay-ik] *adj* of or in trochees.

trochee [tROki] *n* (*pros*) metrical foot with two syllables, one long and one short.

trod [tRod] *p/t* of **tread.**

trodden [tRod'n] *p/part* of **tread.**

troglodyte [tRoglodIt] *n* cave-dweller; (*fig*) recluse.

trogon [tROgon] *n* one of a family of tropical birds with brilliant colouring.

troika [tROika] *n* Russian vehicle drawn by three horses harnessed abreast; (*fig*) triumvirate.

Trojan [tROjan] *n* and *adj* (inhabitant) of ancient Troy; (person) of courage or endurance; **work like a T.** work hard and indefatigably.

troll (1) [tROl] *n* (*Scandinavian myth*) malevolent giant or mischievous dwarf; friendly goblin.

troll (2) *v/t* and *i* sing cheerfully; fish with trailing bait.

trolley [tRoli] *n* light low cart or other wheeled structure pushed by hand; light wheeled table for conveying dishes *etc*; truck running on rails; metal arm linking vehicle to electrified overhead rail or cable supplying power to it.

trolleybus [tRolibus] *n* bus powered by electricity from an overhead cable.

trollop [tRolop] *n* immoral and slovenly woman.

trombone [tRombOn] *n* wind instrument with sliding tube > PDM.

trommel [tRomel] *n* revolving cylindrical sieve.

tronc [tRonk] *n* fund in which tips given to waiters *etc* are pooled and later shared out among the staff of a hotel *etc*.

troop [tROop] *n* group of people moving in an orderly way; company, band; crowd; troupe; (*mil*) subdivision of cavalry squadron; (*pl*) soldiers ~ **troop** *adj* of or for soldiers ~ **troop** *v/i* and *t* move as a troop; flock, crowd; **t. the colour** (*mil*) ceremonially escort regimental flag through regiment on parade.

troopcarrier [tROopkaRi-er] *n* large aircraft for transporting soldiers.

trooper [tROoper] *n* cavalry soldier; troopship; **swear like a t.** swear hard and fluently.

troopship [tROopship] *n* ship for transporting soldiers.

trope [tROp] *n* metaphorical expression, figure of speech; (*mus*) musical interpolation in plainsong.

trophy [tROfi] *n* anything captured and kept as memorial of victory or success; prize for a contest; pile of spoils of battle.

tropic [tRopik] *n* one of two parallels of latitude 23° 28′ north and south of the equator > PDG;

the tropics hottest area of the earth, lying between these latitudes ~ **tropic** *adj* tropical.

tropical [tRopikal] *adj* of, within or like the tropics; exceedingly hot; growing or living only in extreme heat ~ **tropically** *adv*.

tropism [tRopism] *n* response of a plant or sedentary animal to a stimulus, shown by growing towards or away from it > PDB, PDP.

tropological [tRopolojikal] *adj* of tropology.

tropology [tRopoloji] *n* use of figurative language; interpretation of biblical passages as metaphors or symbols.

tropopause [tRopOpawz] *n* upper boundary of the troposphere > PDS.

troposphere [tRopOsfeer] *n* lower part of the Earth's atmosphere in which the temperature decreases with height > PDS.

troppo [tRopO] *adv* (*mus*) excessively.

trot (*pres/part* **trotting,** *p/t* and *p/part* **trotted**) [tRot]*v/i* and *t* (*of horse*) move rapidly but not at a gallop; (*of persons*) walk very fast with short steps; run jerkily; cause (horse) to trot; **t. along** (*coll*)go quickly; **t. out** produce for inspection and approval; bring to notice, bring forward (something well known already) ~ **trot** *n* act of trotting; pace of a trotting horse; (*sl*) whore; **on the t.** continually busy; non-stop.

troth [tROth] *n* (*ar*) pledged word; fidelity.

Trotskyist [tRotski-ist] *n* and *adj* (person) following the Communist teachings of Trotsky.

trotter [tRoter] *n* one who or that which trots; horse trained specially for trotting; pig's or sheep's foot used as food.

troubadour [tROObadawr] *n* medieval wandering composer of love poems and songs, *esp* in Provence and southern France.

trouble [tRub'l] *n* difficulty; that which causes worry, distress or annoyance; effort, painstaking work; chronic ailment, disease; danger, risk; unrest, disturbance, upheaval; disagreement, discord; **ask for t.** behave so as to cause difficulty, danger *etc* for oneself; **in t.** having incurred punishment or disapproval by one's behaviour; liable to be punished; in difficulties; **take t.** do something carefully and well, be painstaking ~ **trouble** *v/t* and *i* distress, disturb; worry; bother, annoy, pester; make an effort, take pains; feel distressed; stir up, ruffle; **troubled waters** (*fig*) state of confusion, unrest *etc*.

troublemaker [tRub'lmayker] *n* one who incites others to discontent, rebellion *etc*; one who habitually causes trouble for others.

troubleshooter [tRub'lshOOter] *n* (*US*) one who discovers and removes the source of trouble in a machine, organization *etc*; a public relations officer.

troublesome [tRub'lsum] *adj* annoying; disobedient, unruly; persistent and painful ~ **troublesomely** *adv*.

troublespot [tRub'lspot] *n* place where trouble often occurs.

troublous [tRublus] *adj* agitated, disturbed.

trough [tRof] *n* long narrow container holding food or water for animals; wooden vessel in which dough is kneaded; lower area of water between two waves.

trounce [tRowns] *v/t* beat; punish; defeat; scold, censure.

troupe [tROOp] *n* group of actors, performers *etc* forming a theatrical company; touring company.

trouper [tROOper] *n* member of a troupe; experienced actor or theatrical performer.

trousered [tROwzerd] *adj* wearing trousers.

trousers [tROwzerz] *n* (*pl*) outer garment covering the body below the waist and encasing each leg to the ankle; **wear the t.** (*of a wife*) domineer over a husband.

trousersuit [tROwzersewt] *n* woman's suit of matching jacket and trousers.

trousseau [tROOsO] *n* outfit of clothes and personal belongings for a bride at marriage.

trout [tROwt] *n* edible freshwater fish; (*sl*) stupid, ugly old woman.

trouvère [tROOvair] *n* medieval narrative poet of northern France.

trover [tROver] *n* (*leg*) action for recovery of goods from one to whom they do not belong.

trow [trO] *v/i* (*ar*) think; believe.

trowel [tROwel] *n* small tool with flat blade for spreading mortar; small tool with curved blade for scooping, digging up plants *etc*; **lay it on with a t.** express with gross exaggeration or emphasis.

troy [tROi] *n* British system of weights for gold, silver and precious gems > PDS.

truancy [tROO-ansi] *n* act of playing truant.

truant [tROO-ant] *n* one who selfishly abandons his duties; child who stays away from school for his own pleasure; **play t.** stay away from school or from one's duties ~ **truant** *adj*.

truce [tROOs] *n* agreement to cease fighting for a while; period of this; cessation, respite.

truck (1) [tRuk] *n* open railway-wagon; small strong vehicle for conveying goods; lorry; porter's two-wheeled framework for moving luggage; (*naut*) wooden cap topping a mast > PDSa ~ **truck** *v/t* and *i* transport by truck.

truck (2) *n* goods used in barter; payment made in kind; **have no t. with** have nothing to do with ~ **truck** *v/t* and *i* barter.

truckle [tRuk'l] *v/i* cringe, be servile; **t. to** submit abjectly to, fawn on.

trucklebed [tRuk'lbed] *n* low bed on wheels that can be pushed beneath another bed.

truculence [tRukewlens] *n* state or quality of being truculent.

truculent [tRukewlent] *adj* bullying, aggressive; fierce, violent ~ **truculently** *adv*.

trudge [tRuj] *v/i* walk slowly and with effort ~ **trudge** *n* laborious walk.

true [tROO] *adj* in accordance with fact; accurate; genuine, real; loyal, faithful; honest; **t. bill** bill of indictment endorsed by grand jury; **come t.** happen as had been wished or prophesied; **t. love** faithful and exclusive love; one who loves or is loved thus; **t. to type** being or acting just as one expects from a person or thing of that type; reproducing hereditary characteristics accurately ~ **true** *adv* truly ~ **true** *v/t* make accurate, adjust correctly.

true-blue [tROO-blOO] *adj* utterly honest or faithful; genuine; very orthodox or conservative.

trueborn [tROObawrn] *adj* legitimate.

truebred [tROObRred] *adj* pure-bred.

true-hearted [tROO-haartid] *adj* loyal; sincere.

truelove [tROOluv] *n* one who loves truly; one who is truly loved.

trueness [tROOnis] *n* quality of being true.

truffle [tRuf'l] *n* fleshy edible fungus used as flavouring.

trug [tRug] *n* broad shallow gardening basket, *usu* of wood strips.

truism [tROO-izm] *n* trite statement of something obviously true.

trull [tRul] *n* trollop, strumpet.

truly [tROOli] *adv* accurately; sincerely, genuinely; faithfully; really, indeed.

trump (1) [tRump] *n* card of a suit which ranks above others in a particular game; (*coll*) good-natured, reliable person; **turn up trumps** (*coll*) unexpectedly prove helpful, friendly *etc* ~ **trump** *v/t* and *i* take with a trump card; play a trump card; **t. up** invent falsely as accusation, excuse or explanation.

trump (2) *n* (*ar, poet*) trumpet.

trump-card [tRump-kaard] *n* last card dealt to himself by the dealer, the suit of which determines trumps; **play one's t.** (*fig*) use the fact or argument most likely to succeed.

trumpery [tRumpeRi] *adj* worthless; rubbishy.

trumpet [tRumpit] *n* one of various metal wind instruments with flared opening > PDM; sound of or like this; something shaped like this, funnel; **blow one's own t.** praise oneself, boast ~ **trumpet** *v/t* and *i* sound on a trumpet; make a loud blaring sound; proclaim loudly and publicly.

trumpet-call [tRumpit-kawl] *n* a call sounded on the trumpet; call to action.

trumpeter [tRumpiter] *n* one who plays a trumpet; one who sounds signals on a trumpet; a North American swan.

trumpet-major [tRumpit-mayjer] *n* chief trumpeter in a regiment.

truncate [tRunkayt] *v/t* cut off the top or tip of; cut short; abridge drastically and clumsily; mutilate ~ **truncate** [tRunkayt] *adj* cut short.

truncheon [tRunsh'n] *n* short thick stick used by police as weapon; baton, staff of office.

trundle [tRund'l] *v/t* and *i* roll heavily along; move on wheels; move heavily forward; (*coll*) bowl ~ **trundle** *n* castor, small wheel.

trundle-bed [tRund'l-bed] *n* low bed on wheels.

trunk [tRunk] *n* stem of a tree; body of man or animal excluding head, limbs and tail; long flexible snout of elephant; large suitcase or lidded box for carrying traveller's possessions; main line of communication.

trunk-call [tRunk-kawl] *n* long-distance telephone call.

trunk-hose [tRunk-hOz] *n* (*pl*) (*hist*) short, puffed-out breeches ending at mid-thigh.

trunkline [tRunklIn] *n* the main line of railway, telephone *etc*.

trunkroad [tRunkROd] *n* long-distance main road joining large towns or cities.

trunks [tRunks] *n* (*pl*) shorts worn by swimmers, athletes *etc*; (*ar*) trunk-hose.

trunnion [tRunyon] *n* one of two bars serving as pivots for a cannon, cylindrical machine *etc*.

truss [tRus] *n* framework of beams or girders supporting a roof, bridge *etc* > PDE; surgical appliance worn to support a ruptured organ; tied bundle of hay or straw ~ **truss** *v/t* support with a truss; tie up (carcass of a bird) ready for cooking; (*fig*) tie up tightly with limbs pressed to the body.

trust [*tRust*] *n* belief in, reliance on, a person or thing; belief in another's sincerity, loyalty, honesty *etc*; duty, responsibility one feels bound to fulfil; something entrusted; (*leg*) act of holding property for another's benefit; group of persons administering a fund for the benefit of others; fund or property thus held or administered; (*comm*) group of firms combining to pursue a common interest; **take on t.** accept trustfully without investigation ~ **trust** *v/t* and *i* place confidence in, believe to be honest, loyal *etc*; rely on; confidently expect, believe or hope; entrust; commit to the care of.

trustee [tRus*tee*] *n* one to whom property is committed for the benefit of others; one of a body of men which manages the affairs of an institution.

trusteeship [tRus*tee*ship] *n* office of a trustee; administration of a territory under supervision of the League of Nations or the United Nations.

trustful [*tRust*fool] *adj* that trusts; easily trusting ~ **trustfully** *adv* ~ **trustfulness** *n*.

trustily [*tRust*ili] *adv* in a trusty way.

trustiness [*tRust*inis] *n* quality of being trusty.

trustworthy [*tRust*wurTHi] *adj* worthy of being trusted or believed; reliable; honest, honourable; accurate ~ **trustworthily** *adv* ~ **trustworthiness** *n*.

trusty [*tRust*i] *adj* trustworthy; reliable; faithful.

truth [tROO*th*] *n* quality or state of being true; that which is true; conformity to fact; honesty, sincerity; genuineness; accuracy; principle, doctrine, law *etc* accepted by many as true.

truthful [tROO*th*fool] *adj* habitually speaking the truth; in accordance with the truth ~ **truthfully** *adv* ~ **truthfulness** *n*.

try (*pres/part* trying, *p/t* and *p/part* tried) [tRI] *v/t* and *i* make an effort to do, attempt, endeavour; do as experiment; test; put a strain on, make heavy demands on; examine in court of law, conduct a trial of; annoy; cause suffering to; refine, purify; **t. on** put (clothes) on to see if they fit or suit well; **t. it on** do something risky to see if one can succeed unharmed; **t. out** test the efficiency of ~ **try** *n* attempt; (*Rugby football*) scoring of three points for a touchdown, giving right to try to kick a goal.

trying [*tRI*-ing] *adj* putting strain on one's patience; irritating, vexing; distressing; wearisome.

try-on [*tRI*-on] *n* (*coll*) something done to see how far one will be allowed to act in a certain way.

try-out [*tRI*-owt] *n* (*coll*) preliminary testing, trial.

trypsin [*tRIp*sin] *n* (*bioch*) enzyme, produced by the pancreas, required in the digestion of proteins.

trysail [*tRI*s'l] *n* small sail for use in storms; small fore-and-aft sail.

tryst [*tRIst*] *n* appointment, rendezvous; appointed meeting-place ~ **tryst** *v/i* agree to meet.

tsar, czar [*zaar*] *n* title of the former emperor of Russia.

tsarevich, czarevich [*zaar*Rayvich] *n* title of a reigning tsar's eldest son.

tsarina, czarina [zaar*Ree*na] *n* title of a tsar's wife.

tsetse-fly [*tsetsi*-flI] *n* African fly which conveys the parasite of sleeping sickness.

T-shirt [*tee*-shurt] *n* short-sleeved, tight-fitting, collarless shirt.

T-square [*tee*-skwair] *n* ruler shaped like the letter T.

tsunami [tsOO*naa*mi] *n* (*Jap*) series of large waves caused by earthquake.

tub [tub] *n* deep, round, open-topped wooden vessel, *esp* for holding water; (*coll*) bath; (*coll*) clumsy boat, boat used for rowing practice; (*mining*) wagon carrying coal, ore *etc* from workings to shaft ~ **tub** (*pres/part* **tubbing**, *p/t* and *p/part* **tubbed**) *v/i* and *t* (*coll*) take a bath; practise rowing; put in a tub; (*mining*) line sides of (shaft) with watertight material.

tuba [*tewb*a] *n* brass wind-instrument with a low pitch > PDM.

tubal [*tewb*al] *adj* of or like a tube.

tubby [*tub*i] *adj* short and fat; (*of stringed instrument*) giving a dull sound ~ **tubbily** *adv* ~ **tubbiness** *n*.

tube [tewb] *n* long hollow cylinder; pipe; underground electric railway; (*anat*) long hollow organ; **inner t.** inflatable rubber tube inside pneumatic tyre.

tuber [*tewb*er] *n* (*bot*) swollen end of underground stem containing buds > PDB.

tubercle [*tewb*urk'l] *n* a small swelling; small morbid growth on an organ of the body; small tuber.

tubercular [tewb*urk*ewlar] *adj* of, like, having or caused by tubercles; suffering from tuberculosis.

tuberculosis [tewburkewl*Os*is] *n* infectious disease characterized by presence of tubercles in tissues.

tuberculous [tewb*urk*ewlus] *adj* of or caused by tubercles; suffering from tuberculosis.

tuberose [*tewb*ROz] *n* bulbous plant with fragrant white flowers.

tuberous [*tewb*eRus] *adj* of, like, or from a tuber.

tube-train [*tewb*-tRayn] *n* train of underground railway.

tubing [*tewb*ing] *n* piece of tube; set of tubes.

tub-thumper [*tub*-thumper] *n* tub-thumping preacher or public speaker.

tub-thumping [*tub*-thumping] *adj* and *n* (using) crudely emotional and noisy oratory.

tubular [*tewb*ewlar] *adj* shaped like a tube; having a tube or tubes.

tuck [tuk] *v/t* and *i* press together; fold; gather up; be folded up; **t. in, into** (*coll*) eat heartily ~ **tuck** *n* fold sewn in a garment; (*schoolboy coll*) food, *esp* cakes, jam, and other delicacies.

tuckbox [*tuk*box] *n* wooden box in which schoolboys keep their tuck.

tucker (1) [*tuk*er] *n* (*obs*) lace or muslin trimming of bodice; (*Aust*) food, provisions; **best bib and t.** smartest clothes.

tucker (2) *v/t* (*US*) exhaust, tire out.

tucket [*tuk*it] *n* flourish on a trumpet.

tuck-in [*tuk*-in] *n* (*coll*) large and appetizing meal.

tuckshop [*tuk*shop] *n* confectioner's shop at or near a school.

Tudor [*tewd*er] *adj* of the dynasty that ruled England from 1485 to 1603; in 16th-century English style.

Tuesday [*tewz*di] *n* third day of the week.

tufa [*tewf*a] *n* calcareous rock deposited from springs; type of porous volcanic rock.

tuffet [*tuf*it] *n* small, stiffly padded cushion used as a stool; (*ar*) grassy hillock.

tuft [tuft] *n* light, loose bunch, *esp* of grass, stalks, hair *etc* ~ **tuft** *v/t* and *i* separate into tufts; decorate with tufts; grow in tufts.

tufted [*tuft*id] *adj* having a tuft or tufts.

tuft-hunter [*tuft*-hunter] *n* (*ar*) one who seeks company of wealthy and important people.

tug (*pres/part* **tugging,** *p/t* and *p/part* **tugged**) [*tug*] *v/t* and *i* pull sharply and roughly; haul, pull hard ~ **tug** *n* act of tugging; small steamboat used for towing.

tugboat [*tug*bOt] *n* small powerful steamboat for towing others.

tug-of-war [tug-ov-*wawr*] *n* contest between two teams who pull at a rope from opposite ends across a line marked on the ground; (*fig*) prolonged, fluctuating contest.

tuition [tew-*ish*on] *n* teaching, instruction.

tulip [*tew*lip] *n* bulbous plant with bell-shaped flowers.

tulip-root [*tew*lip-ROOt] *n* disease of oats characterized by swelling of stem.

tulip-tree [*tew*lip-tRee] *n* American tree with tulip-shaped flowers.

tulle [*tewl*] *n* fine silk muslin.

tum [*tum*] *n* (*coll*) stomach; abdomen.

tumble [*tumb*'l] *v/i* and *t* fall; stumble; fall rapidly; collapse completely; move hastily; roll about; turn somersaults; throw down, upset; rumple; **t. to** (*coll*) grasp, realize ~ **tumble** *n* act of falling; somersault.

tumbledown [*tumb*'ldown] *adj* falling into ruin, dilapidated.

tumble-drier [*tumb*'l-dRI-er] *n* machine for drying washing in a horizontally rotating heated drum.

tumbler [*tumb*ler] *n* one who or that which tumbles; acrobatic clown; cylindrical drinking glass with no stem or foot; kind of pigeon; part of a lock.

tumbrel, tumbril [*tumb*Ril] *n* cart in which condemned persons were taken to the guillotine during the French Revolution; dung-cart; (*mil*) two-wheeled cart for carrying ammunition.

tumefaction [tewmi*fak*shon] *n* swelling.

tumefy [*tew*mifI] *v/t* and *i* cause to swell; swell up.

tumescence [tew*mes*ens] *n* swelling, *esp* of sex organs in response to stimulation ~ **tumescent** *adj.*

tumid [*tew*mid] *adj* swollen, bulging.

tummy [*tum*i] *n* (*coll*) stomach; belly, abdomen.

tummy-ache [*tum*i-ayk] *n* (*coll*) pain in stomach or bowels.

tumour [*tew*mer] *n* swelling of or on some part of the body, caused by abnormal growth of tissues.

tump [*tump*] *n* mound.

tumult [*tew*mult] *n* confused noise, uproar, *esp* of a crowd; excitement; confusion.

tumultuous [tew*mul*tew-us] *adj* in confused uproar; disorderly; agitated ~ **tumultuously** *adv* ~ **tumultuousness** *n.*

tumulus [*tew*mewlus] *n* artificial mound of earth; prehistoric burial-mound.

tun [*tun*] *n* large cask for wine or beer; 252 gallons of wine or beer.

tuna [*tew*na] *n* the tunny of the Californian coast.

tunable [*tew*nab'l] *adj* melodious, sweet-sounding ~ **tunably** *adv.*

tundish [*tun*dish] *n* wooden funnel.

tundra [*tund*Ra] *n* subarctic plain producing only mosses, lichens and grass > PDG.

tune [*tewn*] *n* melody, succession of notes pleasingly combined in pitch and rhythm; correctness of pitch; **change one's t.** speak or act very differently; **in t.** at correct pitch; **in t. with** (*fig*) agreeing harmoniously with, congenial to; **out of t.** not at correct pitch; **to the t. of** to the price of ~ **tune** *v/t* and *i* adjust to correct pitch; adjust (motor engine) to condition of best efficiency; **t. in** adjust wireless set to receive programmes on a certain wavelength; **t. oneself to** adjust one's behaviour to fit in with; **t. up** adjust pitch of orchestral instruments before playing; raise to maximum degree of efficiency, health *etc.*

tuneful [*tewn*fool] *adj* having a pleasant tune, melodious ~ **tunefully** *adv* ~ **tunefulness** *n.*

tuneless [*tewn*lis] *adj* having no clearly perceptible tune; out of tune; unmelodious ~ **tunelessly** *adv* ~ **tunelessness** *n.*

tuner [*tew*ner] *n* one who tunes musical instruments.

tungsten [*tung*sten] *n* hard metallic element used in alloys and for electric lamp filaments, wolfram.

tunic [*tew*nik] *n* loose, short-sleeved garment reaching nearly to the knees; military surcoat; loose belted; jacket or coat; (*biol*) covering membrane; husk.

tuning [*tew*ning] *n* (*mus*) adjustment of an instrument to recognized scale > PDM; (*rad*) adjustment of circuit to a desired frequency > PDS, PDEl; (*mot*) adjustment of motor to maximum efficiency.

tuning-fork [*tew*ning-fawrk] *n* two-pronged steel instrument which gives a sound of precise pitch when struck > PDM.

tunnel [*tun*el] *n* underground passage, *esp* one cut for a railway or road to pass under a hill, river *etc*; burrow ~ **tunnel** (*pres/part* **tunnelling,** *p/t* and *p/part* **tunnelled**) *v/t* and *i* dig a tunnel (through).

tunnel-net [*tun*el-net] *n* net with wide mouth and narrow end.

tunny [*tun*i] *n* large edible fish of mackerel family.

tup [*tup*] *n* ram; striking part of a steam hammer ~ **tup** *v/t* (*ar*) mate with (ewe).

tuppence, tuppenny see **twopence, twopenny.**

tu quoque [tew-*kwO*kwi] *n* (*Lat*) argument in which a charge is retorted upon the accuser.

turban [*tur*ban] *n* man's Oriental head-covering consisting of a long sash wound round the head; woman's headdress resembling this.

turbid [*tur*bid] *adj* muddy, opaque with sediment; (*fig*) confused, muddled ~ **turbidly** *adv.*

turbidity [tur*bid*iti] *n* state of being turbid.

turbine [*tur*bIn] *n* motor whose shaft is rotated by jets of steam, water, air *etc* directed on the blades of a wheel > PDS, PDE.

turbo- *pref* driven by a turbine.

turbojet [*turb*Ojet] *n* and *adj* (engine) using exhaust gas to turn a turbine to work the air-compressor; (aircraft) powered by such an engine.

turboprop [*turb*OpRop] *n* (engine) using exhaust gas to turn a turbine to work a propeller; (aircraft) powered by such an engine.

turbot [*tur*bot] *n* large edible flatfish.

turbotrain [*turb*OtRayn] *n* railway train powered by turbine engine.

turbulence [*tur*bewlens] *n* state or quality of being turbulent.

turbulent [*tur*bewlent] *adj* violently disturbed; agitated; disorderly; (*of currents or wind*) disturbed by eddies ∼ **turbulently** *adv*.

turd [*turd*] *n* lump of dung.

tureen [tew*Reen*/tu*Reen*] *n* deep lidded dish for soup.

turf (*pl* **turves, turfs**) [*turf*] *n* area of ground covered with short grass; piece of grass cut from ground with soil adhering to its roots; peat; top layer of soil and leaf mould *etc*; **the t.** horse-racing ∼ **turf** *v/t* cover with turf; **t. out** (*coll*) dismiss or throw out roughly.

turf-accountant [*turf*-akowntant] *n* bookmaker.

turfing [*turf*ing] *n* process of covering with turf; process of digging up turf or peat.

turfing-iron [*turf*ing-ı-ern] *n* tool for cutting strips of turf or blocks of peat from the ground.

turfy [*turf*i] *adj* covered with turf; of or like turf.

turgid [*tur*jid] *adj* swollen, bloated; pompous, bombastic ∼ **turgidly** *adv*.

turgidity [tur*jid*iti] *n* state or quality of being turgid.

Turk [*turk*] *n* member of the Turkish race; (*coll*) troublesome child; **T.'s head** long-handled soft broom or feather-brush, for cleaning ceilings.

turkey (1) [*turk*i] *n* large domestic fowl used as food; **cold t.** painful physical symptoms caused by ceasing to take an addictive drug; **talk t.** talk of serious matters, talk business.

Turkey (2) *adj* and *n* (of or from) the country of the Turks; **T. carpet** thick woollen carpet brightly dyed; **T. red** an orange-red dye.

turkey-buzzard [*turk*i-buzerd] *n* kind of South American vulture.

turkeycock [*turk*ikok] *n* male turkey; (*fig*) conceited person.

Turkish [*turk*ish] *n* and *adj* (language) of the Turks; **T. bath** steam bath followed by massage *etc*; **T. delight** lumps of flavoured gelatine coated in sugar; **T. towelling** rough absorbent cloth used for bathtowels.

turmeric [*tur*meRik] *n* aromatic Indian plant akin to ginger; spice or dye made from this; **t. paper** paper impregnated with turmeric and used as test for alkalis.

turmoil [*tur*moil] *n* commotion, disturbance, confusion.

turn [*turn*] *v/t* and *i* change direction; cause to change direction; revolve, spin; reverse, place in opposite position or direction; change position; transform, change; cause to be in specified condition; become; translate; adapt; convert; use; depend on; shape on a lathe, cut to shape on a revolving wheel; give elegant form to; direct one's eyes or thoughts to; adopt new views, profession *etc*; (*of food*) become sour, go bad; (*mil*) get behind the line of battle of; (*of tide*) change from ebb to flow or vice versa; (*of time*) have just reached and passed a specific hour, age *etc*; **t. against** become hostile to; **t. away** refuse admission to; rebuff; turn oneself so as not to face; **t. back** return; force to return; **t. down** fold downwards; point downwards; moderate, lessen the intensity of; reject, refuse; **t. in** point inwards; (*coll*) go to bed; (*coll*) hand over to those in

authority; **t. off** stop the flow, supply or action of; dismiss; branch off from (a road); **t. on** start the flow, supply or action of; turn upon; (*sl*) alter one's mental or emotional state by psychedelic drugs; excite sexually; **t. out** drive out; prove to be; become; happen; equip; dress; leave one's quarters and appear on duty, parade *etc*; summon to duty, parade *etc*; **t. over** reverse position of; hand over, transfer; think carefully about; **t. to** set oneself to work; ask for help from; rely on; **t. up** arrive casually, appear; happen unexpectedly; be found by chance; plough, dig up; (*coll*) discover; **t. (one) up** (*sl*) make (one) feel sick; **t. it up!** (*sl*) stop it! shut up!; **t. upon** suddenly grow hostile to and attack ∼ **turn** *n* act of turning; bend; rotatory movement; change of direction or position; change, new development; spell of activity, work or enjoyment done by one person in regular alternation with another or others; right, opportunity or obligation to do or enjoy something alternately with others; short stage-performance; special aptitude; short walk, stroll; (*coll*) shock; nausea or faintness on receiving a shock; **t. and t. about** (alternately); **at every t.** constantly; **bad t.** disservice, injury; **done to a t.** perfectly cooked; **good t.** kind, helpful action; **serve one's t.** fulfil one's need; **take turns** do in regular succession; **t. up for the book** (*coll*) unexpected occurrence.

turnabout [*turn*abowt] *n* reversal of direction.

turncoat [*turn*kOt] *n* one who abandons his party or principles.

turncock [*turn*kok] *n* valve which regulates flow of water from the mains.

turndown [*turn*down] *adj* having upper part folded down.

turner [*turn*er] *n* one who or that which turns; one who fashions objects on a lathe.

turnery [*turn*eRi] *n* craft of fashioning objects with a lathe; place where turning is done.

turning [*turn*ing] *n* act of one who turns; bend; place where a road branches off from another; process or craft of forming objects on a lathe.

turning-circle [*turn*ing-sirk'l] *n* smallest circle in which a vehicle can turn round without reversing.

turning-point [*turn*ing-point] *n* decisive moment at which a new course of events or development begins; crisis after which things are altered.

turnip [*turn*ip] *n* plant with round fleshy root used as vegetable.

turnip-fly [*turn*ip-flı] *n* insect whose maggots destroy turnips.

turnip-tops [*turn*ip-tops] *n* (*pl*) leaves of turnip used as vegetable.

turnkey [*turn*kee] *n* warder having keys of prison cells.

turn-out [*turn*-owt] *n* group of persons assembling for a special purpose, *usu* for duty; appearance of equipment or outfit; equipage; set of clothes and accessories worn together; output.

turnover [*turn*Over] *n* amount of money changing hands in business within a specified period; rate at which old members leave and new members join a society, staff, institution *etc*; rate at which stocks of anything are used up and replaced; pie with crust folded over.

turnpike [*turn*pık] *n* gate barring a road to stop

vehicles passing before toll is paid; **t. road** roads on which turnpikes were set up.

turnround [*turn*Rownd] *n* process of unloading a ship and reloading it for its return voyage.

turnspit [*turn*spit] *n* dog or servant formerly employed to turn a roasting-spit.

turnstile [*turn*stīl] *n* revolving gate with four arms allowing only one person to pass at a time, *esp* one at which admission fees are to be paid.

turntable [*turn*tayb'l] *n* revolving platform of gramophone or record-player, on which records are placed for playing; large revolving platform on which railway engines are turned round; any revolving platform or horizontal disk.

turn-up [*turn*-up] *n* narrow band at bottom edge of each trouser-leg, worn turned upwards; (*coll*) disturbance, row.

turpentine [*turp*entīn] *n* liquid used as solvent, distilled from resin of pine trees > PDS; oily resin secreted by pine trees; **t. tree** terebinth.

turpitude [*turp*itewd] *n* base wickedness.

turps [*turps*] *n* (*coll abbr*) turpentine.

turquoise [*turk*oiz] *n* opaque bluish-green precious stone; colour of this ~ **turquoise** *adj*.

turret [*tu*Rit] *n* small tower; revolving armoured gun-emplacement on warship, tank or aeroplane.

turreted [*tu*Ritid] *adj* having a turret.

turret-gun [*tu*Rit-gun] *n* gun mounted in revolving turret.

turtle (1) [*turt*'l] *n* (*ar*) turtledove.

turtle (2) *n* marine tortoise; edible species of this used for soup; **turn t.** capsize.

turtledove [*turt*'lduv] *n* wild dove with a cooing note; (*coll*) lover.

turtleneck [*turt*'lnek] *n* high close-fitting neck of sweater.

turves [*turvz*] *pl* of **turf**.

tush (1) [*tush*] *interj* (*ar*) exclamation of contempt or impatience.

tush (2) *n* horse's long pointed tooth.

tusk [*tusk*] *n* extremely long pointed tooth in certain animals, projecting beyond the mouth.

tusked [*tuskt*] *adj* having tusks.

tusker [*tusk*er] *n* animal with tusks.

tussle [*tus*'l] *v/i* wrestle roughly, fight without weapons ~ **tussle** *n* rough struggle or scuffle.

tussock [*tus*ok] *n* thick clump of grass; **t. grass** type of grass growing in marshy soil; species of tall grass from Patagonia; **t. moth** moth whose caterpillars have tufts of hairs.

tussore [*tus*awr] *n* strong beige or light-brown Indian silk.

tut [*tut*] *interj* exclamation of impatience or disapproval ~ **tut** (*pres/part* **tutting**, *p/t* and *p/part* **tutted**) *v/i* exclaim tut; express disapproval.

tutelage [*tew*tilij] *n* guardianship; state or period of being under a guardian.

tutelar [*tew*tilar] *adj* acting as protector or guardian.

tutelary [*tew*tilaRi] *adj* tutelar.

tutor [*tew*tor] *n* private teacher; university teacher who directs the studies of undergraduates; (*leg*) guardian ~ **tutor** *v/t* and *i* act as a tutor (to).

tutorial [tewt*awr*Ri-al] *adj* of or by a tutor ~ **tutorial** *n* period of instruction and discussion between tutor and undergraduate ~ **tutorially** *adv*.

tutorship [*tew*torship] *n* office of a tutor; appointment as a tutor.

tutti-frutti [tOOti-*f*ROOti] *n* fruit salad; icecream flavoured with different fruits; compote of preserved fruit.

tut-tutting [tut-*tut*ing] *n* and *adj* (act of) expressing disapproval by saying tut.

tutty [*tut*i] *n* impure oxide of zinc.

tutu [tOOtOO/tootoo] *n* short frilled skirt worn by female dancers in classical ballet.

tu-whit, tu-whoo [tOO-*wit*, tOO-*wOO*] *n* conventional imitation of an owl's call.

tuxedo [tuks*eed*O] *n* (*US*) dinner-jacket.

twaddle [*twod*'l] *n* silly talk, nonsense ~ **twaddle** *v/i* talk twaddle.

twain [*twayn*] *adj* (*poet* and *ar*) two ~ **twain** *n* pair, couple.

twang [*twang*] *n* sharp ringing sound made by plucking a taut string; nasal tone in speaking ~ **twang** *v/t* and *i* produce a twang from.

'twas [*twoz*] *abbr* (*ar* and *poet*) it was.

twat [*twot*] *n* (*vulg*) cunt; woman; (*sl*) fool.

twayblade [*tway*blayd] *n* species of orchid with two broad leaves.

tweak [*tweek*] *v/t* pinch or pull suddenly or sharply ~ **tweak** *n* sharp pinch; quick pull.

twee [*twee*] *adj* (*coll, usu cont*) sweet, pretty-pretty.

tweed [*tweed*] *adj* and *n* (made from) Scottish woollen cloth, *usu* woven from yarns of different colour.

Tweedledum [tweed'l*dum*] *n* **T. and Tweedledee** two persons alike in every way; two things equally good (or bad).

'tween [*tween*] *adj* and *prep* (*naut, poet*) between.

tweeny [*twee*ni] *n* (*obs coll*) young servant girl who helps senior maids.

tweet [*tweet*] *n* shrill chirping bird-cry.

tweezers [*twee*zerz] *n* (*pl*) small pincers ~ **tweezer** *v/t* pluck out with tweezers.

twelfth [*twelfth*] *n* and *adj* (that) which follows eleven others in a series; (that) which is one of twelve equal parts; **the t.** 12th August, day on which grouse-shooting season begins; **t. man** reserve player of cricket team; **T. Night** evening of 6th January, feast of the Epiphany.

twelve [*twelv*] *n* and *adj* cardinal number next above eleven; symbol of this, 12.

twelvemonth [*twelv*munth] *n* year.

twelve-note [*twelv*-nOt] *adj* (*mus*) of or in an atonal technique in which a whole composition is derived from a series of twelve notes in a particular order > PDM.

twentieth [*twen*ti-eth] *n* and *adj* (that) which comes after nineteen others in a series; (that) which is one of twenty equal parts.

twenty [*twen*ti] *n* and *adj* cardinal number next after nineteen, twice ten; symbol of this, 20.

'twere [*twur*] *abbr* (*ar* and *poet*) it would be.

twerp, twirp [*twurp*] *n* (*sl*) silly person; unimportant person.

twice [*twīs*] *adv* two times.

twice-told [*twīs*-tOld] *adj* related twice; frequently related, well-known.

twiddle [*twid*'l] *v/t* twirl (fingers or thumbs); fiddle with; **t. one's thumbs** waste time.

twig (1) [*twig*] *n* small shoot from branch of tree.

twig (2) (*pres/part* **twigging**, *p/t* and *p/part* **twigged**) *v/t* and *i* (*coll*) understand.

twiggy [*twigi*] *adj* covered in twigs; as thin as a twig, extremely slim.

twilight [*twi*lit] *n* faint diffused light visible after sunset or before dawn > PDG; partial darkness; (*fig*) gradual decay or destruction of something once glorious ~ **twilight** *adj* of or like twilight; half darkened; **t. sleep** state of semi-unconsciousness induced by drugs, *esp* to reduce pains of childbirth; **t. state** hysterical state of unawareness of external realities > PDP.

twilit [*twi*lit] *adj* dimly lit.

'twill [*twil*] *abbr* (*ar* and *poet*) it will.

twill [*twil*] *n* woven fabric with diagonal ribs.

twilled [*twild*] *adj* woven with diagonal ribs.

twin [*twin*] *n* one of two children or animals born at one birth; one of a pair of exactly similar objects; **identical twins** twins formed by splitting of one fertilized ovum > PDP; **non-identical (fraternal) twins** twins formed from two ova simultaneously fertilized; **Siamese twins** twins linked to each other by a fleshy ligament ~ **twin** *adj* being one of a pair of twins; exactly similar; closely matched or linked ~ **twin** (*pres/part* **twinning**, *p/t* and *p/part* **twinned**) *v/t* and *i* link or match closely, pair up.

twine [*twin*] *n* strong string made of two or three strands twisted together ~ **twine** *v/t* and *i* twist together; wind round; interweave; be interwoven; meander.

twinge [*twinj*] *n* sharp sudden pain; pang ~ **twinge** *v/i* experience a sharp sudden pain.

twinkle [*twink*'l] *v/i* emit rapid flashes of light; glitter; move so rapidly as to be only intermittently visible; (*of eyes*) show sudden amusement ~ **twinkle** *n* twinkling light; look of amusement in the eyes; rapid movement; extremely short period of time.

twinkling [*twink*ling] *n* scintillation; extremely brief moment.

twinning [*twin*ing] *n* act of bearing twins.

twinset [*twin*set] *n* woman's jumper with matching cardigan.

twirl [*twurl*] *n* quick circular movement; twist; curling line ~ **twirl** *v/t* and *i* revolve or cause to revolve quickly; spin, whirl.

twirp see **twerp**.

twist [*twist*] *v/t* and *i* cause to turn, wind, interweave; coil up; turn, bend; writhe; form repeated curves; wrench, sprain; distort, falsify, misinterpret; render abnormal in outlook, emotions *etc*; (*coll*) dance the twist; (*sl*) act dishonestly, cheat ~ **twist** *n* act of twisting; state of being twisted; curve, bend, kink; hank of twisted thread, wool *etc*; spinning motion; deviation from normal course; (*fig*) mental or emotional abnormality; distortion, misrepresentation, false interpretation; (*coll*) dance in which dancer slowly sinks to and rises from a squatting position while constantly twisting body and limbs; **round the t.** (*sl*) mad, crazy.

twister [*twister*] *n* one who or that which twists; (*coll*) insincere or dishonest person; (*cricket*) ball sent with a twist.

twisty [*twisti*] *adj* full of turns, winding; (*coll*) dishonest ~ **twistily** *adv* ~ **twistiness** *n*.

twit (1) (*pres/part* **twitting**, *p/t* and *p/part* **twitted**) [*twit*] *v/t* reproach, taunt, *usu* in jest.

twit (2) *n* (*sl*) fool, twerp.

twitch [*twich*] *n* sudden, *usu* involuntary, contraction of a muscle; sudden jerky movement ~ **twitch** *v/t* and *i* move or pull jerkily; suffer or show a muscular twitch.

twitter [*twiter*] *v/i* (*of birds*) chirp continuously; (*of human beings*) chatter feebly and excitedly ~ **twitter** *n* chirping sound; excited chatter; **all of a t., in a t.** in a state of nervous excitement.

twitty [*twiti*] *adj* (*sl*) silly, daft.

'twixt [*twikst*] *prep* (*poet*) between.

two [*tOO*] *n* cardinal number next above one; pair, couple; **one or t. a few; put t. and t. together** make an obvious deduction ~ **two** *adj* one more than one.

two-edged [*tOO*-ejd] *adj* having an edge on two sides; (*fig*) ambiguous, capable of two opposite uses or effects.

two-faced [*tOO*-fayst] *adj* hypocritical, deceitful.

two-fisted [*tOO*-fistid] *adj* (*coll*) clumsy; vigorous.

twofold [*tOO*fOld] *adj* and *adv* double, doubly.

two-handed [*tOO*-handid] *adj* needing both hands to lift or use.

twopence [*tupens*] *n* sum of two pennies.

twopenny [*tup'ni*] *adj* worth twopence; cheap; unimportant, petty; **t. piece** coin worth two decimal pennies.

twopenny-halfpenny [tup'ni-*hayp'*ni] *adj* worth twopence halfpenny; insignificant, petty.

twopiece [*tOO*pees] *n* woman's bathing costume consisting of separate briefs and brassiere; jacket and skirt or jacket and dress of same material.

twoply [*tOO*pli] *adj* having two strands.

twoseater [*tOO*seeter] *n* motorcar or aircraft with seats for two people only.

twosome [*tOO*sum] *n* game played by two players only; pair of friends or associates.

two-step [*tOO*-step] *n* a ballroom dance in 2/4 time; music for this.

two-stroke [*tOO*-strOk] *adj* (*of engine*) driven by a single explosion to each revolution.

twotime [*tOO*tIm] *v/t* (*US sl*) be unfaithful to, deceive; doublecross.

'twould [*twood*] *abbr* (*ar* and *poet*) it would.

two-way [*tOO*-way] *adj* communicating, moving, flowing or exerting force in two directions; reciprocal, mutual; (*of radio equipment etc*) able both to emit and receive signals.

tycoon [tik*OOn*] *n* (*coll*) powerful businessman.

tyke see **tike**.

tympanitis [timpan*I*tis] *n* inflammation of membrane of middle ear.

tympanum [*timpanum*] *n* membrane of middle ear; (*mus*) drum; (*archi*) semicircular or triangular space of wall enclosed by a pediment, gable, or arch.

type [*tIp*] *n* kind, species, variety; class or group sharing certain characteristics; representative specimen of such a group; (*coll*) fellow; example, model; symbol; block of metal or wood bearing a letter or sign from which an impression is made in printing; size or style of lettering in print; **in t.** set up ready for printing ~ **type** *v/t* and *i* write with a typewriter, be able to use a typewriter; classify according to species, group *etc*.

typecast (*p/t* and *p/part* **typecast**) [*tIp*kaast] *v/t* choose an actor for a part resembling others he has often played, or akin to his own personality.

typeface [*tɪp*fays] *n* inked area of type block; set of type blocks in a particular size or style.

type-founder [*tɪp*-fownder] *n* one who casts printing type.

typescript [*tɪp*skRipt] *n* typewritten document, *esp* typewritten draft of book, article *etc* prepared for printing.

typesetter [*tɪp*seter] *n* compositor, person or machine that sets up type for printing.

typewriter [*tɪp*RIter] *n* small machine with keys tapped by the fingers to print letters *etc* through inked ribbon on to paper ∼ **typewriting** *n*.

typewritten [*tɪp*Riten] *adj* having been printed by a typewriter.

typhoid [*tɪ*foid] *adj* resembling typhus; **t. fever** infectious enteric fever caused by bacillus transmitted in water or food ∼ **typhoid** *n* typhoid fever.

typhoon [tɪ*fOOn*] *n* violent hurricane, *esp* in the China Sea > PDG.

typhous [*tɪ*fus] *adj* of or like typhus.

typhus [*tɪ*fus] *n* acute contagious fever caused by a bacillus carried by parasites.

typical [*tɪp*ikal] *adj* being a perfect specimen of a class, group *etc*; characteristic, illustrating the usual attitude, behaviour *etc* of ∼ **typically** *adv*.

typify [*tɪp*ifI] *v/t* symbolize; be typical of.

typing [*tɪp*ing] *n* act or method of using a typewriter.

typing-paper [*tɪp*ing-payper] *n* sheet of thin paper for use in a typewriter.

typist [*tɪp*ist] *n* one who is skilled ın using a typewriter; secretary employed chiefly for typing correspondence *etc*.

typographer [tɪp*og*Rafer] *n* one who is skilled in typography; printer.

typographical [tɪp*og*Rafikal] *adj* of or by typography or printing.

typography [tɪp*og*Rafi] *n* art of printing; choice, style and arrangement of print to produce a pleasing visual effect.

typological [tɪp*olo*jikal] *adj* of or by typology.

typology [tɪp*olo*ji] *n* classification of objects according to type; (*theol*) interpretation of the Old Testament as symbolic of the New.

tyrannical [ti*Ra*nikal] *adj* of or like a tyrant; oppressive; cruel ∼ **tyrannically** *adv*.

tyrannicide [ti*Ra*nisId] *n* one who kills a tyrant; act of killing a tyrant.

tyrannize [ti*Ra*nIz] *v/i* behave like a tyrant; exercise power oppressively or cruelly; **t. over** rule or control harshly, cruelly *etc*.

tyrannous [ti*Ra*nus] *adj* tyrannical ∼ **tyrannously** *adv* ∼ **tyrannousness** *n*.

tyranny [ti*Ra*ni] *n* harsh, unjust, and oppressive use of power, *esp* by a ruler or government; behaviour of a tyrant.

tyrant [*tIr*Rant] *n* one who maintains power by terrorism; cruel, oppressive, and unjust ruler or master; one who bullies subordinates; oppressor, despot; (*Gk hist*) absolute non-hereditary ruler.

tyre, tire [*tIr*] *n* thick rubber band, either solid or containing inflatable tube, encircling rim of wheel; metal rim of wooden wheel.

Tyrian [*ti*Ri-an] *n* and *adj* rich purple.

tyro, tiro [*tIr*RO] *n* beginner, novice.

Tyrolean [tɪ*Ro*lee-an] *adj* of or from the Tyrol in Austria; **T. hat** man's small green high-crowned hat, *usu* ornamented with small feather.

tzar see **tsar.**

tzigane [tsi*gaan*] *n* Hungarian gypsy.

U

u [*yOO*] twenty-first letter of the English alphabet; **U** (*coll*) characteristic of the upper class; (*of films*) suitable for all ages; **U.N., U.N.O.** the United Nations (Organization); **U.S., U.S.A.** the United States (of America).

ubiquitous [yOO*bik*witus] *adj* appearing or existing everywhere ~ **ubiquitously** *adv*.

ubiquity [yOO*bik*witi] *n* state of being ubiquitous; omnipresence.

U-boat [*yOO*-bOt] *n* German submarine.

udder [*uder*] *n* hanging external organ from which milk of cows, ewes and goats is secreted.

ufo, U.F.O. [*yOO*fO, *yOO*-ef-O] *n* unidentified object or light reported as flying at abnormal speeds or heights.

ugh [*ooh*] *interj* sound like a dry cough, expressing disgust.

uglify [*ugli*fI] *v/t* make ugly, disfigure.

ugliness [*ugli*nis] *n* state or quality of being ugly.

ugly [*ugli*] *adj* repulsive to the sight; hideous, horrible; (*fig*) unpleasant, ill-tempered, offensive; threatening; **u. customer** dangerous, threatening person or animal; **u. duckling** child who at first seems ugly, stupid or clumsy but grows up to be attractive, clever *etc*.

uh-huh [*u*-hu] *interj* grunting exclamation expressing agreement.

uhlan [*yOO*lan] *n* (*hist*) Prussian mounted lancer.

ukase [yOO*kayz*] *n* (*Rus*) decree; any arbitrary order.

Ukrainian [yOO*kRay*ni-an] *n* and *adj* (inhabitant or language) of the Ukraine.

ukulele [yOO*ku*layli] *n* (*mus*) small guitar-like four-stringed instrument > PDM.

ulcer [*ulser*] *n* open sore on skin or mucous membrane discharging pus; (*fig*) corrupting influence.

ulcerate [*ulse*Rayt] *v/i* and *t* break out into ulcers; cause ulcers in.

ulceration [*ulse*Rayshon] *n* ulcerated condition; process of ulcer formation; an ulcer or ulcers.

ulcerous [*ulse*Rus] *adj* like an ulcer; suffering from ulcers; (*fig*) corrupting.

ullage [*uli*j] *n* amount by which bottle, cask or tank falls short of being full ~ **ullage** *v/t* reckon or create ullage in; fill up ullage in.

ulna (*pl* ulnae) [*ulna*] *n* (*anat*) inner bone of forearm; corresponding bone in animals.

ulnar [*ulner*] *adj* of, on, or on same side as the ulna.

ulster [*ulster*] *n* long belted overcoat.

Ulsterman [*ulster*man] *n* native or inhabitant of the political state of Northern Ireland; (*hist*) native or inhabitant of the Irish province of Ulster.

ult [*ult*] *adv* (*abbr*) ultimo.

ulterior [ul*teer*Ri-or] *adj* later in time; more distant in space; (*of motive etc*) undisclosed and frequently unworthy ~ **ulteriorly** *adv*.

ultima [*ultima*] *adj* final, last; **u. Thule** distant, unknown region.

ultimate [*ultimit*] *adj* furthest, utmost; final, last; basic; decisive ~ **ultimate** *n* that which is basic or fundamental; last step, final stage of analysis ~ **ultimately** *adv* finally, in the end.

ultimatum (*pl* ultimatums) [ulti*may*tum] *n* final terms to which one power, party or person demands that another shall agree, *usu* under threat of war, penalties *etc*.

ultimo [*ultim*O] *adv* (*comm*) in the preceding month.

ultra [*ult*Ra] *adj* holding extreme views; excessive ~ **ultra** *n* an extremist ~ **ultra** *adv* extremely, excessively.

ultra- *pref* beyond in space; beyond what is customary, reasonable *etc*; extremely.

ultramarine [ultRama*Reen*] *adj* from overseas; of bright blue colour ~ **ultramarine** *n* bright blue colouring matter > PDS.

ultramicroscope [ultra*mI*kROskOp] *n* high-powered microscope based on the phenomenon of scattering > PDS.

ultramontane [ultRa*mon*tayn] *n* and *adj* (person) holding extreme views in favour of papal power.

ultrashort [ultRa*shawrt*] *adj* extremely short.

ultrasonic [ultRa*son*ik] *adj* (*of vibrations*) beyond the range of normal audibility > PDEl.

ultrasonics [ultRa*son*iks] *n* (*pl*) high-frequency pressure waves above the limit of audibility > PDS; branch of science dealing with these.

ultraviolet [ultRa*vI*-olit] *adj* (*phys*) pertaining to electromagnetic waves in the wavelength between visible light waves and X-rays > PDS.

ululate [*uly*OOlayt] *v/i* howl; wail loudly.

ululation [ulyOO*lay*shon] *n* howling; lamentation.

umbel [*umbel*] *n* (*bot*) flattened flower-head whose stalks radiate from one point.

umber [*umber*] *n* brown earth used as pigment; colour obtained from it; **burnt u.** reddish brown pigment ~ **umber** *v/t* colour with umber; stain brown, darken.

umbilical [um*bili*kal] *adj* (*anat*) of or near the navel; **u. cord** structure joining foetus to placenta > PDB; (*aer*) tube and cable linking an astronaut to his spacecraft when he is outside it.

umbles, humbles [*umb*'lz] *n* (*pl*) edible inward parts of deer.

umbo [*umb*O] *n* boss, knob, *esp* of shield.

umbra (*pl* umbrae) [*umb*Ra] *n* region of complete shadow, *esp* in an eclipse; darkest part of sunspot.

umbrage [*umb*Rij] *n* (*ar*) shade; **take u.** feel offended, be annoyed.

umbrageous [um*bRay*jus] *adj* giving shade; apt to take umbrage, suspicious, resentful.

umbral [*umb*Ral] *adj* (*astron*) of or in the umbra.

umbrella [um*bRel*a] *n* folding framework of ribs covered with cloth and opening from a central stick for use as protection against rain or sun; Oriental portable ceremonial canopy; (*mil*) protective force of fighter aircraft.

umbrella-tree [um*bRel*a-tRee] *n* type of magnolia.

umiak [*OO*mi-ak] *n* large Eskimo canoe.

umlaut [*oom*lowt] *n* (*phil*) change in a vowel

caused by the influence of another vowel in the following syllable; sign (¨) indicating this.

umpire [*ump*Ir] *n* arbitrator whose decision is final; (*sport*) one who sees that rules are not broken, and who decides all doubtful points ~ **umpire** *v/t* and *i* supervise (game); be umpire.

umpteen [*ump*teen] *adj* (*sl*) a large number of ~ **umpteenth** *adj*.

'un [*un*] *pron* (*coll*) one, fellow.

un- *pref* expressing negation before adjectives, adverbs and abstract nouns; expressing reversal of action before verbs.

unabashed [una*basht*] *adj* not disconcerted, irrepressible.

unabated [una*bay*tid] *adj* without loss of force.

unabbreviated [unab*ree*vi-aytid] *adj* not shortened, given in full.

unable [un*ayb'l*] *adj* not able (to do something).

unabridged [unab*rijd*] *adj* reproduced or repeated in full.

unacceptable [unak*sep*tab'l] *adj* that cannot be accepted; not desirable or welcome; disapproved of ~ **unacceptably** *adv*.

unaccompanied [una*kum*panid] *adj* without a companion, alone; (*mus*) without accompaniment.

unaccountable [una*kown*tab'l] *adj* that cannot be explained ~ **unaccountably** *adv*.

unaccustomed [una*kus*tomd] *adj* not accustomed; not customary, unusual.

unacknowledged [unak*nolejd*] *adj* (*of faults*) not confessed; (*of letters etc*) not answered.

unacquainted [unak*wayn*tid] *adj* not acquainted (with), ignorant (of); (*of persons*) having no personal knowledge of each other.

unacted [un*ak*tid] *adj* not performed on the stage; not carried into action.

unactuated [un*ak*tew-aytid] *adj* not influenced to action.

unadaptable [unada*p*tab'l] *adj* not amenable to changed circumstances; impossible to modify.

unadapted [unada*p*tid] *adj* not modified for a specific purpose.

unadmitted [unad*mit*id] *adj* kept secret, not acknowledged; refused admittance.

unadopted [unad*op*tid] *adj* not adopted; (*of roads*) not surfaced, repaired *etc* by the Local Authority.

unadulterated [unad*ulte*Raytid] *adj* not mixed with inferior ingredients; pure, genuine.

unadvised [unad*vIzd*] *adj* not done on advice; imprudent, rash.

unaffected [una*fek*tid] *adj* sincere, spontaneous, natural in manner; undisturbed (by).

unafraid [una*fRayd*] *adj* not afraid, bold.

unaided [un*ay*did] *adj* not helped, without assistance.

unaired [un*atrd*] *adj* not ventilated; not exposed to fresh air in order to remove damp.

unalloyed [una*loyd*] *adj* unmixed, pure; not spoiled by any unpleasant feelings.

unambiguous [unam*big*ew-us] *adj* clear, impossible to misinterpret ~ **unambiguously** *adv*.

un-American [un-ame*Ri*kan] *adj* unfavourable to the U.S.A. or its interests; contrary to usual American habits, outlook, taste *etc*.

unamiable [un*ay*mi-ab'l] *adj* unlovable, disagreeable in manner.

unanimity [yOOna*nim*iti] *n* state or fact of being unanimous.

unanimous [yOO*nan*imus] *adj* (*of persons*) all of one opinion; (*of statements*) backed by general consent ~ **unanimously** *adv*.

unanswerable [un*aan*serab'l] *adj* incapable of being answered or refuted; conclusive ~ **unanswerably** *adv*.

unappealable [unap*eel*ab'l] *adj* (*leg*) (*of a judgement*) incapable of being appealed against; (*of a case*) incapable of being taken to a higher court.

unappeased [unap*eezd*] *adj* not appeased.

unappetizing [un*ap*itIzing] *adj* seeming unwholesome, unattractive.

unappreciated [unap*Ree*shi-aytid] *adj* not sufficiently valued.

unapprehended [unap*Ri*hendid] *adj* not understood; not taken into custody.

unapprehensible [unap*Ri*hensib'l] *adj* that cannot be understood.

unapprehensive [unap*Ri*hensiv] *adj* slow to understand; not suspecting (danger *etc*).

unapproachable [unap*RO*chab'l] *adj* inaccessible, aloof; beyond compare, matchless ~ **unapproachably** *adv*.

unapt [un*apt*] *adj* not apt, unsuitable, inappropriate; not ready, slow, unskilful.

unarguable [un*aar*gew-ab'l] *adj* that cannot be supported by argument; that cannot be refuted by argument.

unarm [un*aarm*] *v/t* and *i* lay aside weapons and armour, disarm.

unarmed [un*aarmd*] *adj* having no weapons; using no weapons; disarmed; (*bot, zool*) not provided with thorns, teeth *etc*.

unarmoured [un*aar*merd] *adj* not protected by defensive armour; (*of cables*) without outer casing of steel wire.

unartistic [unaar*tis*tik] *adj* not artistic, not interested in art.

unashamed [una*shaymd*] *adj* not ashamed, brazen.

unasked [un*aaskt*] *adj* without having been asked; not asked for; not invited.

unassuming [una*sew*ming] *adj* unpretentious, modest ~ **unassumingly** *adv*.

unassured [una*shewrd*] *adj* not assured, insecure, uncertain; not insured against loss.

unattached [una*tacht*] *adj* not attached (to); (*of students*) non-collegiate; not engaged or married.

unattainable [una*tay*nab'l] *adj* that cannot be attained, out of reach.

unattended [una*ten*did] *adj* not escorted or waited upon; with no one in charge; receiving no attention; not followed by or associated with.

unattractive [una*tRak*tiv] *adj* not attracting attention or admiration; plain, ugly.

unauthorized [un*aw*thoRIzd] *adj* without official permission.

unavailable [una*vay*lab'l] *adj* not obtainable; not within reach; not available for consultation *etc*.

unavailing [una*vay*ling] *adj* ineffectual, vain, futile.

unavoidable [una*voi*dab'l] *adj* inevitable.

unawakened [una*way*kend] *adj* still asleep; (*fig*) dormant, latent.

unaware [una*wair*] *adj* not aware (of), ignorant (of) ~ **unaware** *adv* unawares.

unawares [una*wairz*] *adv* unintentionally, in-advertently; without warning, by surprise; with-out being noticed.

unbacked [un*bakt*] *adj* not backed; without a back; (*of horse*) not broken in to the saddle; having no bets placed on it; (*of proposal etc*) not supported.

unbalance [un*balans*] *v/t* throw out of balance; upset physically or mentally.

unbalanced [un*balanst*] *adj* not stable, not steady; mentally unstable, unreasonable; (*comm, of ac-counts*) not brought to a balance, *esp* showing a deficit.

unbar *pres/part* **unbarring**, *p/t* and *p/part* **un-barred**) [un*baar*] *v/t* remove bar from (door *etc*); (*fig*) throw open.

unbearable [un*bair*Rab'l] *adj* intolerable, un-endurable ~ **unbearably** *adv*.

unbeaten [un*beeten*] *adj* unconquered; not sur-passed; (*of path*) untrodden.

unbecoming [unbi*kuming*] *adj* not suitable to; im-proper, indecent; (*of clothing*) detracting from the wearer's appearance.

unbefitting [unbi*fiting*] *adj* not suitable to.

unbeknown, (*coll*) **unbeknownst** [unbin*On*, un-bin*Onst*] *adj* and *adv* not known; **u. to** without the knowledge of.

unbelief [unbi*leef*] *n* disbelief, lack of faith.

unbeliever [unbi*leever*] *n* one who does not be-lieve; pagan; atheist, agnostic, sceptic.

unbelieving [unbi*leeving*] *adj* unable to believe; rejecting belief; incredulous, sceptical ~ **un-believingly** *adv*.

unbend (*p/t* and *p/part* **unbent**) [un*bend*] *v/t* and *i* undo (knot or bend); cast loose (soil); (*fig*) relax one's formality, behave with affability.

unbending [un*bending*] *adj* stiff, rigid; (*fig*) in-flexible; that unbends, relaxing.

unbent [un*bent*] *adj* not bent, straight; unsub-dued; (*of a bow*) relaxed.

unbiased [un*bI*-ast] *adj* not biased, unprejudiced.

unbidden [un*biden*] *adj* not ordered, spontaneous; uninvited.

unbind (*p/t* and *p/part* **unbound**) [un*bInd*] *v/t* free from binding or bonds; loosen, release.

unblemished [un*blemisht*] *adj* not blemished, without disfiguring mark; (*fig*) morally without fault.

unblown [un*blOn*] *adj* (*of flower*) still in bud; (*of runner*) not out of breath; (*of wind instrument*) not sounded.

unblushing [un*blushing*] *adj* impudent, shameless, barefaced ~ **unblushingly** *adv*.

unbolt [un*bOlt*] *v/t* release the bolt of.

unbolted (1) [un*bOltid*] *adj* not fastened by a bolt.

unbolted (2) *adj* (*of flour*) not sifted.

unborn [un*bawrn*] *adj* not yet born; future.

unbosom [un*boozom*] *v/refl* disclose one's secrets, feelings *etc*.

unbounded [un*bowndid*] *adj* boundless; infinite, limitless.

unbowed [un*bowd*] *adj* not bowed; unsubdued, still resisting.

unbrace [un*bRays*] *v/t* unfasten; loosen, relax; en-feeble.

unbreech [un*bReech*] *v/t* take off the trousers from; remove breech from (gun).

unbreeched [un*bReecht*] *adj* (*of young boy*) not yet wearing trousers, still a toddler.

unbridled [un*bRId'l*] *adj* unrestrained, violent.

unbroken [un*bROken*] *adj* uninterrupted, continu-ous; not fractured or shattered, intact; not sub-dued; (*mil*) not thrown into confusion; (*of horse*) untrained; (*of record*) not improved on.

unbuckle [un*buk'l*] *v/t* unfasten buckle of.

unbuilt [un*bilt*] *adj* not yet built; not yet built upon.

unburden [un*burden*] *v/t* relieve of a burden; (*fig*) relieve (the mind) by confession, by speaking of a trouble or anxiety *etc* ~ **unburdened** *adj*.

unbusinesslike [unbi*znislIk*] *adj* not systematic or efficient.

unbutton [un*buton*] *v/t* and *i* undo buttons of; (*fig*) relax, unbend.

uncalculated [un*kalkewlaytid*] *adj* not deter-mined by calculation, indefinite; (*fig*) unexpected, accidental.

uncalled [un*kawld*] *adj* not summoned, not called.

uncalled-for [un*kawld*-fawr] *adj* unnecessary, not requested; unprovoked; impertinent.

uncanny [un*kani*] *adj* weird, mysterious, ap-parently supernatural ~ **uncannily** *adv* ~ **un-canniness** *n*.

uncanonical [un-kan*onikal*] *adj* not in accordance with ecclesiastical canons; not in the canon of Scripture; not suitable for a clergyman.

uncanonized [un*kanonIzd*] *adj* not admitted into the canon of Scripture; not formally declared a saint.

uncap (*p/t* and *p/part* **uncapped**) [un*kap*] *v/t* and *i* remove the cap, closure or cover from; remove one's cap as a mark of respect.

uncared-for [un*kaird*-for] *adj* neglected, not looked after.

uncase [un*kays*] *v/t* take out of a case.

uncatalogued [un*katologd*] *adj* not to be found in a catalogue.

uncate [*ung*kayt] *adj* hooked, hook-shaped.

unceasing [un*seesing*] *adj* continuous ~ **un-ceasingly** *adv*.

uncensored [un*sensord*] *adj* not altered by or not submitted to a censor.

unceremonious [unseRim*Oni*-us] *adj* informal; discourteous, rude, abrupt ~ **unceremoniously** *adv*.

uncertain [un*surten*] *adj* not certain, doubtful; undecided, irresolute; variable, precarious, capri-cious; **in no u. terms** unmistakably, clearly ~ **uncertainly** *adv*.

uncertainty [un*surtenti*] *n* state or quality of being uncertain; lack of certainty; vagueness, unde-pendableness; **u. principle** (*phys*) principle that it is impossible accurately to determine both position and momentum of a particle simultane-ously > PDS.

unchain [un*chayn*] *v/t* let loose from a chain; (*fig*) set free.

unchallengeable [un*chalenjab'l*] *adj* not to be challenged or disputed.

unchancy [un*chaamsi*] *adj* bringing bad luck; ill-omened; ill-judged, clumsy.

unchangeable [un*chaynjab'l*] *adj* not capable of change; immutable ~ **unchangeableness** *n* ~ **unchangeably** *adv*.

unchanging [un*chaynj*ing] *adj* not liable to change.

uncharged [un*chaarjd*] *adj* not charged with electricity; (*leg*) not formally accused; (*of gun*) not loaded.

uncharitable [uncha*Ritab*'l] *adj* lacking charity; unkind, spiteful; harsh in judging others; unwilling to help others, selfish; miserly ∼ **uncharitably** *adv*.

uncharted [un*chaar*tid] *adj* not marked on the map, unexplored, unknown.

unchartered [un*chaar*terd] *adj* not authorized by a charter; (*fig*) unrestrained, lawless.

unchaste [un*chayst*] *adj* having or having had an illicit sexual relationship; offending against sexual morality; lewd, lascivious; immodest ∼ **unchastely** *adv* ∼ **unchasteness** *n*.

unchastity [un*chastiti*] *n* quality of being unchaste.

unchecked [un*chekt*] *adj* proceeding, flowing or developing freely; not disciplined; not tested for accuracy; not reduced in speed.

unchurch [un*church*] *v/t* excommunicate.

uncial [*unsi*-al/*um*shal] *adj* written in large rounded letters, as of Greek and Latin manuscripts from the 1st to 9th centuries A.D. ∼ **uncial** *n* uncial letter, script or manuscript; (*loosely*) capital letter.

unciform [*un*sifawrm] *adj* (*anat, zool*) hook-shaped.

uncinate [*un*sinit] *adj* (*anat, zool, bot*) hooked at the tip; hook-shaped.

uncircumcised [un*sur*kumsIzd] *adj* not circumcised; non-Jewish, Gentile; (*fig*) heathen.

uncivil [un*sivil*] *adj* impolite, rude.

uncivilized [un*sivil*Izd] *adj* not civilized, barbarous.

uncivilly [un*sivili*] *adv* rudely, impolitely.

unclasp [un*klaasp*] *v/t* undo the clasp of; cease clasping.

unclassed [un*klaasd*] *adj* not put into a class; not in one of the first three places in a race or competition.

unclassified [un*klasif*Id] *adj* not arranged in accordance with a classification; not included in any of a series of classes; not regarded as a military or state secret.

uncle [*unk*'l] *n* brother of one's father or mother; husband of one's aunt; (*sl*) pawnbroker; **U. Sam** the government or people of the U.S.A.; **talk like a Dutch u.** reprimand kindly but firmly; **U. Tom** Negro who looks up to and willingly serves white men.

unclean [un*kleen*] *adj* not clean, dirty; not ritually clean, forbidden by taboo; unchaste.

uncloak [un*klOk*] *v/t* and *i* take off a cloak from; (*fig*) uncover, reveal; take off one's cloak.

unclose [un*klOz*] *v/t* and *i* make open; become open.

unclothe [un*klOTH*] *v/t* take the clothes from, strip.

unclouded [un*klowd*id] *adj* free from clouds; (*fig*) untroubled, unspoilt; calm.

unclubbable [un*klubab*'l] *adj* unwilling or unable to fit in with the customs of a club; unsociable.

unco [*unk*O] *adv* (*Scots*) extremely; **the u. guid** self-righteously virtuous people.

uncoil [un*koil*] *v/t* and *i* unwind coils of; become uncoiled.

uncoloured [un*kuler*d] *adj* having no colour, in black and white; not coloured by something; (*fig*) in plain, unaffected style; not exaggerated.

un-come-at-able [un-kum-*at*-ab'l] *adj* (*coll*) inaccessible, not procurable.

uncomfortable [un*kum*fortab'l] *adj* not comfortable; shy, embarrassed; not at ease, uneasy; causing discomfort; awkward, unpleasant, embarrassing ∼ **uncomfortably** *adv*.

uncommercial [un-kom*mur*shal] *adj* not engaged in commerce; not in accordance with commercial usage; not profit-seeking.

uncommitted [un-kom*it*id] *adj* not bound by promise, not pledged (to some course of action); impartial; not done, not perpetrated; not referred to a committee; not sent to prison.

uncommon [un*kom*on] *adj* not common, rare, unusual ∼ **uncommon** *adv* (*coll*) very, remarkably ∼ **uncommonly** *adv* unusually; remarkably.

uncommunicative [unkom*mew*nikativ] *adj* unwilling to talk or give information.

uncompanionable [un-kom*pan*yonab'l] *adj* not sociable, not a good companion.

uncomplaining [un-kom*playn*ing] *adj* patient.

uncompromising [un*komp*ROmIzing] *adj* admitting of no compromise; unyielding, stubborn ∼ **uncompromisingly** *adv*.

unconcern [un-kon*surn*] *n* lack of anxiety or concern, indifference.

unconcerned [un-kon*surnd*] *adj* feeling no anxiety (about); indifferent, unmoved; not interested (in); taking no part (in) ∼ **unconcernedly** *adv*.

unconditional [un-kon*dish*onal] *adj* not limited by any conditions, absolute ∼ **unconditionally** *adv*.

unconditioned [un-kon*dish*ond] *adj* unconditional; out of condition, not in good health; (*met*) infinite, absolute; (*psych*) innate, instinctive.

unconfessed [un-kon*fest*] *adj* not confessed, not admitted.

unconfined [un-kon*fInd*] *adj* free, unrestricted.

unconfirmed [un-kon*furmd*] *adj* not corroborated, not supported by further evidence; not having received confirmation.

unconformable [un-kon*fawr*mab'l] *adj* not conformable; (*geol*) irregular in formation.

unconformity [un-kon*fawr*miti] *n* unwillingness to conform to social customs *etc*; (*geol*) irregularity in formation.

uncongenial [un-kon*jeen*i-al] *adj* not congenial, unsuited; distasteful, repellent.

unconscionable [un*kon*shonab'l] *adj* excessively great; unreasonable, outrageous.

unconscious [un*kon*shus] *adj* not realizing, unaware; having lost consciousness, in a swoon, coma *etc*; done without realizing; unintentional, involuntary; (*psych*) unknown to the person having or experiencing (it); of or in the unconscious ∼ **unconscious** *n* the u. (*psych*) aggregate of dynamic elements forming a personality, some of which the person is unaware of; the subconscious.

unconsciously [un*kon*shusly] *adv* without being aware of it.

unconsciousness [un*kon*shusnis] *n* state or quality of being unconscious; coma, swoon *etc*; unawareness.

unconsidered [un-kon*si*derd] *adj* not taken into consideration, disregarded; negligible.

unconstitutional [un-konsti*tew*shonal] *adj* not in accordance with a political constitution.

unconstrained [un-kon*st*Raynd] *adj* free from constraint, done voluntarily; not self-conscious ~ **unconstrainedly** *adv*.

uncontrollable [un-kont*ROl*ab'l] *adj* not to be controlled, unmanageable.

uncontrolled [un-kont*ROl*d] *adj* unchecked, free.

unconventional [un-konven*shonal] *adj* not conventional, free and easy; not in accordance with usual custom.

unconventionality [un-konvenshona*l*iti] *n* state or quality of being unconventional.

unconventionally [un-konven*shonali] *adv* in an unconventional way.

uncooperative [un-kO-ope*Rativ] *adj* unwilling to cooperate ~ **uncooperatively** *adv*.

uncoordinated [un-kO-*awr*dinaytid] *adj* not coordinated.

uncork [un*kawrk*] *v/t* remove the cork from.

uncorrected [unko*Rek*tid] *adj* not corrected, not revised; not rebuked or punished.

uncouple [un*kup*'l] *v/t* release (railway carriages, hounds *etc*) from being coupled together; disengage.

uncouth [un*kOOth*] *adj* lacking good manners, boorish, awkward in manner; (*ar*) unfamiliar, unknown ~ **uncouthly** *adv* ~ **uncouthness** *n*.

uncovenanted [un*kuv*inantid] *adj* not promised or agreed to.

uncover [un*kuv*er] *v/t* and *i* remove a cover from; lay open; leave unprotected; (*ar*) take off one's hat.

uncreated [un-kRee-*ay*tid] *adj* not produced by creation; self-existent, eternal; not yet made or existing; unborn.

uncritical [un*kRi*tikal] *adj* lacking in discrimination and judgement; not in accordance with the principles of criticism ~ **uncritically** *adv*.

uncropped [un*kRop*t] *adj* not cropped, not eaten by cattle *etc*; (*of land*) not planted with crops; (*of crops*) not reaped; (*of hair*) not cut short.

uncrowned [un*kRow*nd] *adj* not crowned; **u. king** man of undisputed influence and authority.

uncrushable [un*kRu*shab'l] *adj* that cannot be crushed; irrepressible; that shows no creases when crumpled.

unction [un*k*shon] *n* anointing with oil; (*fig*) that which soothes; (*fig*) gusto, relish; fervour, *esp* religious; (*fig*) exaggerated or insincere display of gusto or fervour; suavity, gush; **Extreme U.** sacrament of anointing the dying or those gravely ill with holy oil.

unctuous [un*k*tew-us] *adj* oily, greasy; (*fig*) smug, gushing; with an exaggerated affectation of sincerity, earnestness, or enthusiasm ~ **unctuously** *adv* ~ **unctuousness** *n*.

uncultivated [un-*k*ulti*vay*tid] *adj* (*of plants*) not cultivated; (*of land*) not tilled; (*fig*) not civilized, rude; not improved or developed; not educated or trained.

uncultured [un-*k*ul*cherd*] *adj* without culture, not improved by education; (*of land*) uncultivated.

uncurtained [un*kur*tind] *adj* having no curtains; with curtains drawn back.

uncut [un-*kut*] *adj* not cut; not abbreviated; (*of*

books) with pages not slit open, with margins not cut down; (*of gems*) not cut and polished.

undaunted [un*dawn*tid] *adj* not frightened by danger or difficulty, bold, intrepid ~ **undauntedly** *adv*.

undeceive [undi*seev*] *v/t* reveal truth to (one who was deceived), disillusion.

undecennial [undi*sen*i-al] *adj* occurring every eleventh year.

undecided [undi*sI*did] *adj* not decided; hesitant, in doubt; uncertain.

undecked [un*dekt*] *adj* not decked, without ornaments; (*naut*) without a deck.

undeclared [undi*klaird*] *adj* not declared, not announced; kept secret; (*of goods subject to customs duty*) not shown.

undefended [undi*fend*id] *adj* not defended; unprotected, without defence; (*leg*) not defended by counsel; (*of charge, action at law etc*) having no defence put forward.

undemonstrative [undi*mons*trativ] *adj* not readily showing feeling, reserved, aloof.

undeniable [undi*nI*-ab'l] *adj* not capable of denial, incontestable; unquestionable; unmistakable ~ **undeniably** *adv*.

undenominational [undinomi*nay*shonal] *adj* not restricted to any particular religious sect.

under [*un*der] *prep* below, beneath, lower than; beneath the surface or outer layer of; protected, ruled or educated by; serving, subordinate to; during the reign of; less than; (*of land*) bearing as crop; **u. age** too young to be granted some legal right, privilege *etc*; **u. arms** equipped and ready for warfare; **u. cover** in protected position; concealed; **u. cover of** concealed by; **u. way** (*naut*) beginning to move through water ~ **under** *adj* lower; of lower rank; inner; inferior ~ **under** *adv* in or into a lower position; in or into an inferior or subordinate condition; **down u.** in Australia or New Zealand; **go u.** sink, fail; be defeated; **keep u.** repress, suppress, oppress.

under- *pref* lower, inferior; insufficiently; beneath, below.

underact [unde*Rakt*] *v/t* and *i* (*theat*) act with a lack of dramatic emphasis or with deliberate restraint.

underarm (1) [*u*nde*Raarm*] *adj* and *adv* with the arm kept lower than the shoulder.

underarm (2) *adj* of the armpit; (*of seam*) running from armpit to waist.

underbelly [*u*nderbeli] *n* lower part of the belly; (*fig*) vulnerable area.

underbid (*pres/part* **underbidding**, *p/t* and *p/part* **underbid**) [under*bid*] *v/t* and *i* offer to sell (goods or services) more cheaply than (a competitor); (*bridge*) make a deceptively low bid.

underbrush [*u*nderbRush] *n* undergrowth in forest.

undercarriage [*u*nderkaRij] *n* wheels on which an aircraft lands; framework supporting these.

undercharge [under*chaarj*] *v/t* charge too little; load (gun) insufficiently ~ **undercharge** *n* [*u*nderchaarj] *n*.

underclay [*u*nderklay] *n* thin bed of clay under a coal seam.

undercliff [*u*nderklif] *n* terrace formed under a cliff by falls of rock.

underclothes [*u*nderklOTHz] *n* (*pl*) garments

worn next to or almost next to the skin and under outer clothing.

underclothing [underklOTHing] *n* underclothes.

undercoat [underkOt] *n* layer of paint beneath final coat; under layer of fur, feathers *etc*; coat worn beneath another.

undercopy [underkopi] *n* carbon copy of typewritten document.

undercover [underkuver] *adj* acting as secret agent, making secret inquiries *etc*.

undercroft [underkRoft] *n* vaulted underground chamber; crypt.

undercurrent [underkuRent] *n* current flowing below surface of water; (*fig*) concealed but powerful emotion or tendency.

undercut (*pres/part* **undercutting**, *p/t* and *p/part* **undercut**) [underkut] *v/t* cut away from below; offer to sell more cheaply or work for less wages than (competitors); (*games*) strike (ball) so as to impart backspin ~ **undercut** [underkut] *n* underside of sirloin; (*boxing*) blow delivered with upward arm-movement.

underdevelop [underdivelop] *v/t* (*phot*) develop insufficiently.

underdeveloped [underdivelopd] *adj* not fully developed; with economic resources inadequately used; physically or mentally backward; (*phot*) insufficiently developed.

underdog [underdog] *n* person habitually bullied, exploited or ill-used by others; loser in a contest.

underdone [underdun] *adj* insufficiently cooked.

underdress [underdRes] *v/i* dress too simply or informally for the occasion.

underestimate [underRestimayt] *v/t* set too low a value on; reckon as being less than it really is ~ **underestimate** [undeRestimat] *n* an estimate which is too low.

underexpose [under-ekspOz] *v/t* (*phot*) expose for too short a time.

underfed [underfed] *adj* given too little food.

underfelt [underfelt] *n* felt or rubberized material for laying under a carpet.

underfoot [underfoot] *adv* beneath one's feet; (*fig*) in one's way.

undergarment [undergaarment] *n* single item of underclothing.

underglaze [underglayz] *n* (*cer*) decoration painted on pottery before applying glaze ~ **underglaze** *adj* (*of pigments, colours*) suitable for underglaze.

undergo (*p/t* **underwent**, *p/part* **undergone**) [undergO] *v/t* suffer, endure; submit oneself to.

undergrad [undergRad] *n* (*coll abbr*) undergraduate.

undergraduate [undergRadew-it] *n* university student who has not yet taken his degree.

underground [undergRownd] *adj* below the surface of the earth; secret; **u. movement** political or military resistance movement carrying on secret activities ~ **underground** *n* underground railway; secret resistance movement against dictatorship; group of persons regarding social or artistic orthodoxy as evil, and seeking to undermine it; ~ **underground** *adv* below earth's surface; secretly.

undergrowth [undergROth] *n* mass of shrubs and plants growing under trees.

underhand [underhand] *adj* secretly dishonest,

---

underclothing–underset

sly ~ **underhand** *adv* secretly, furtively; (*of bowling*) with the hand below the elbow, underarm.

underhung [underhung] *adj* (*of lower jaw*) projecting beyond upper jaw; with a projecting lower jaw; (*mech*) supported from below.

underlay [underlay] *n* fabric laid under mattress or carpet; (*typ*) paper to make type, cuts *etc* typehigh ~ **underlay** (*p/t* and *p/part* **underlaid**) *v/t* support by placing something below; (*typ*) make type, cuts *etc* type-high.

underlie (*pres/part* **underlying**, *p/t* **underlay**, *p/part* **underlain**) [underlI] *v/t* lie beneath; be a basis for; be a basic explanation of.

underline [underlIn] *v/t* mark (word or words) with line drawn underneath to express emphasis or indicate italics to a printer; (*fig*) emphasize; (*theat*) announce forthcoming performance at the foot of an advertisement ~ **underline** [underlIn] *n.*

underlinen [underlinen] *n* underwear.

underling [underling] *n* subordinate, servant *etc* of very minor rank.

underlip [underlip] *n* lower lip.

undermanned [undermand] *adj* having too few workers, staff, or crew.

undermentioned [undermenshond] *adj* to be mentioned later in a document.

undermine [undermIn] *v/t* cut or wash away supporting earth from beneath; (*fig*) weaken or destroy secretly and gradually.

undermost [undermOst] *adj* lowest of all.

underneath [underneeth] *prep* and *adv* below; on the under side (of) ~ **underneath** *n* bottom part of anything.

undernourished [undernuRishd] *adj* not sufficiently nourished, underfed.

underpaid [underpayd] *adj* inadequately paid.

underpass [underpaas] *n* road junction where one road passes under the other; (*US*) subway.

underpay [underpay] *v/t* pay inadequately.

underpin (*pres/part* **underpinning**, *p/t* and *p/part* **underpinned**) [underpin] *v/t* provide new permanent support beneath (wall *etc*) without removing superstructure; (*fig*) strengthen, support.

underplot [underplot] *n* subplot.

underprivileged [underpRivilejd] *adj* suffering from social or economic disadvantages, poor.

underproduction [underpRodukshon] *n* production of too few goods *etc*.

underproof [underprOOf] *adj* containing less alcohol than proof spirit.

underquote [underkwOt] *v/t* (*comm*) underbid.

underrate [underRayt] *v/t* place too low an estimate on.

underrun (*p/t* **underran**, *p/part* **underrun**) [underRun] *v/t* and *i* (*naut*) work back along (accessible rope) to recover or clear anything; haul (boat) along a line in the water; last for less than the allotted time.

underscore [underskawr] *v/t* underline.

underseal [underseel] *n* protective coating applied to the under side of cars.

Under-Secretary [under-sekReteRi] *n* assistant Secretary, *esp* in Government department.

undersell (*p/t* and *p/part* **undersold**) [undersel] *v/t* sell at a lower price than (a competitor).

underset [underset] *v/t* (*bui*) strengthen by brick-

787

work, underpin; sublet ~ **underset** *n* (*naut*) undertow.

undersexed [*under*sekst] *adj* having abnormally low degree of sexual desire.

undershot [undershot] *adj* (*of mill-wheel*) driven by water passing under it; (*of jaw*) underhung.

undersign [unders*ı*n] *v*/*t* sign (a letter *etc*) at the foot; **the undersigned** person or persons signing this document.

undersized [*under*sızd] *adj* of less than normal size.

undersold [unders*Old*] *p*/*t* and *p*/*part* of **undersell**.

understand (*p*/*t* and *p*/*part* **understood**) [*under*stand] *v*/*t* and *i* comprehend; have thorough knowledge of; assume, infer, take for granted; learn, be given to understand; have understanding, comprehension; **u. one another, u. each other** be clear as to each other's aims and opinions; **make oneself understood** make one's meaning clear.

understandable [*under*standab'l] *adj* able to be understood; intelligible ~ **understandably** *adv*.

understanding [*under*standing] *n* intelligence; comprehension; mutual informal agreement; sympathy; **on the u. that** on condition that ~ **understanding** *adj* sympathetic; sensible ~ **understandingly** *adv*.

understate [*under*stayt] *v*/*t* minimize the importance of, express by understatement.

understatement [*under*staytment] *n* statement which deliberately minimizes the importance of something, *usu* so as to impress by moderation or irony.

understeer [*under*steer] *v*/*i* (*of motor vehicle*) turn less sharply than expected.

understood [*under*stood] *adj* (*gramm*) supplied mentally, but not expressed; (*fig*) agreed on or known, but not explicitly.

understudy [*under*studi] *n* actor or actress who studies another's part so as to be able to take it if required ~ **understudy** *v*/*t* act as understudy to; study and rehearse (a role).

undertake (*p*/*t* **undertook**, *p*/*part* **undertaken**) [*under*tayk] *v*/*t* and *i* take up, take in hand, embark upon; promise, pledge oneself (to); [*under*tayk] (*coll*) act as funeral undertaker.

undertaken [*under*tayken] *p*/*part* of **undertake**.

undertaker [*under*tayker] *n* one whose business it is to arrange funerals; one who undertakes some task or project.

undertaking [*under*tayking] *n* something undertaken, an enterprise; the business of arranging funerals.

under-the-counter [under-THe-*kovn*ter] *adj* (*coll*) that can only be bought illegally or by bribery.

undertone [*under*tOn] *n* low voice; (*fig*) subordinate element; half-hidden feeling; underlying significance; (*Stock Exchange*) market sentiment regarding the current values of securities.

undertook [*under*took] *p*/*t* of **undertake**.

undertow [*under*tO] *n* returning undercurrent from a wave breaking on the seashore.

underwater [*under*wawter] *adj* below the surface of water; (*naut*) below the waterline.

underwear [*under*wair] *n* underclothes.

underweight [*under*wayt] *adj* weighing less than is normal or correct or wanted ~ **underweight** *n*.

underwent [under*went*] *p*/*t* of **undergo**.

underwood [*under*wood] *n* undergrowth.

underwork [under*wurk*] *v*/*t* and *i* allot too little work to; work for less wages than; do too little work.

underworld [*under*wurld] *n* section of society living by crime and immorality; criminals as a social group; (*myth*) region inhabited by spirits of the dead, *esp* if underground.

underwrite (*p*/*t* **underwrote**, *p*/*part* **underwritten**) [under*RIt*] *v*/*t* (*comm*) undertake to buy (all shares not bought by the public); insure (shipping); do business as underwriter; (*fig*) guarantee, vouch for.

underwriter [*under*RIter] *n* one who insures ships and cargoes against loss or damage; one who undertakes to buy such part of a company's new issue as is not bought by the public.

undescended [undis*end*ed] *adj* (*med, of testicle*) remaining in abdomen instead of entering the scrotum.

undesigned [undiz*Ind*] *adj* not planned; not intentional or deliberate ~ **undesignedly** [undi-z*I*nidli] *adv*.

undesigning [undiz*I*ning] *adj* with no selfish or ulterior motives.

undesirable [undiz*Ir*Rab'l] *adj* not inspiring a wish to possess; objectionable, unpleasant ~ **undesirable** *n* disreputable or unwanted person ~ **undesirably** *adv*.

undetermined [undi*turm*ind] *adj* not decisively settled; indefinite; irresolute.

undeveloped [undi*velopt*] *adj* not fully grown; not put to full use; (*of land*) not built upon.

undeviating [un*dee*vi-ayting] *adj* not turning aside; steady, not varying.

undid [un*did*] *p*/*t* of **undo**.

undies [*und*iz] *n* (*pl*) (*coll*) women's underclothes.

undifferentiated [undife*Ren*shi-aytid] *adj* without characteristics showing, or seeming to show, differences.

undignified [un*dig*nifId] *adj* not befitting one's dignity; too informal or emotional; ridiculous, silly.

undine [*un*deen/*oon*deen] *n* female water-spirit.

undischarged [undis*chaar*jd] *adj* not discharged; not carried out or done; not released; (*of an account or claim*) not paid; (*of gun*) not fired; (*of cargo*) not unloaded.

undisciplined [un*dis*iplind] *adj* untrained, *esp* in military discipline; unruly, disobedient.

undisclosed [undisk*lOzd*] *adj* kept secret.

undiscovered [undis*kuv*erd] *adj* not found; unknown.

undisguised [undis*gIzd*] *adj* not disguised, not concealed; open, avowed.

undistinguished [undis*ting*-gwisht] *adj* commonplace, mediocre.

undivided [undi*vI*did] *adj* not separated into parts; whole; not shared.

undo (*p*/*t* **undid**, *p*/*part* **undone**) [un*dOO*] *v*/*t* unfasten, untie, unwrap; cancel out (something done), counteract or destroy effect of; ruin.

undoing [un*dOO*-ing] *n* cause of a person's downfall or ruin; act of unfastening.

undone [un*dun*] *p/part* of **undo** ~ **undone** *adj* not done, neglected; ruined; destroyed; unfastened.

undoubted [un*dowt*id] *adj* known for certain, undisputable ~ **undoubtedly** *adv*.

undoubting [un*dowt*ing] *adj* believing or trusting without doubts.

undramatic [undRa*mat*ik] *adj* not effective as drama; not suitable for the plot of play; quiet, restrained; understated ~ **undramatically** *adv*.

undraped [und*Rapt*] *adj* naked, nude.

undreamed [und*Reem*d] *adj* not imagined or thought (of).

undreamt [und*Remt*] *adj* undreamed.

undress [und*Res*] *v/t* and *i* take off the clothes of; take one's clothes off ~ **undress** [und*Res*] *adj* and *n* informal (attire), non-ceremonial (uniform).

undressed [und*Resd*] *adj* not clothed, nude; having removed day clothing; (*of game etc*) not prepared for the table; (*of wounds*) not treated and bandaged.

undue [un*dew*] *adj* unreasonable; excessive; not fit, seemly or becoming.

undulant [un*dew*lant] *adj* undulating; **u. fever** brucellosis in human beings.

undulate (1) [un*dew*layt] *v/i* move with wave-like motion; have a wave-like surface.

undulate (2) *adj* having wave-like markings; (*bot zool*) having wave-like surface.

undulation [undew*lay*shon] *n* wave-like motion or surface; wave.

undulatory [undew*lay*teRi] *adj* having a wave-like movement; having a wave-like surface.

unduly [un*dew*li] *adv* unjustly, unreasonably; excessively.

undutiful [un*dew*tifool] *adj* not dutiful; disobedient, rebellious ~ **undutifully** *adv* ~ **undutifulness** *n*.

undying [un*dI*-ing] *adj* everlasting, immortal; unceasing.

unearned [un*urnd*] *adj* not earned; undeserved; not worked for; **u. income** income derived from investments; **u. increment** increase in value of landed property not due to owner's expenditure.

unearth [un*urth*] *v/t* dig up; drive (animal) from burrow; (*fig*) discover (something remote or hidden).

unearthly [un*urth*li] *adj* supernatural; eerie, uncanny; (*coll*) extraordinary; **u. hour (time)** preposterously early or inconvenient hour (or time).

unease [un*eez*] *n* anxious or restless mood.

uneasy [un*eez*i] *adj* not comfortable, restless; worried, apprehensive; not graceful, self-conscious ~ **uneasily** *adv* ~ **uneasiness** *n*.

uneatable [un*eet*ab'l] *adj* too unpleasant, stale or badly cooked to be eaten.

uneconomic, uneconomical [uneeko*nom*ik, uneeko*nom*ikal] *adj* not in accordance with principles of economics; wasteful ~ **uneconomically** *adv*.

unedifying [un*edi*fI-ing] *adj* morally harmful; degrading, vulgar.

unedited [un*edi*tid] *adj* not edited; not hitherto published.

uneducated [un*edew*kaytid] *adj* not educated, illiterate.

unemotional [unim*Osh*onal] *adj* calm, imperturbable ~ **unemotionally** *adv*.

unemployable [unim*ploi*-ab'l] *adj* not fit to be employed, not capable of holding a job; not suitable for use.

unemployed [unim*ploid*] *adj* not having a regular job, out of work; without occupation; not used, not put to use or profit ~ **unemployed** *n* number of persons out of work at a given time.

unemployment [unim*ploi*ment] *n* condition of being without regular work; the existence of large numbers of people without regular work; **u. benefit** regular payments made to unemployed persons.

unenclosed [unin-*klOzd*] *adj* not enclosed; (*of religious orders*) not confined to the cloister.

unending [un*end*ing] *adj* everlasting; ceaseless; interminably boring ~ **unendingly** *adv* ceaselessly, interminably.

unendurable [unin*dewr*Rab'l] *adj* insufferable, intolerable ~ **unendurably** *adv*.

un-English [un-*ing*-glish] *adj* contrary to usual English habits, outlook, taste *etc*.

unenlightened [unin*lI*tend] *adj* not well-informed; bound by prejudice, superstition *etc*; uneducated, ignorant.

unenterprising [un*ent*erpRIzing] *adj* not adventurous, with no initiative.

unenviable [un*envi*-ab'l] *adj* not to be desired or coveted ~ **unenviably** *adv*.

unenvious [un*envi*-us] *adj* not envious.

unequable [un*ekwab*'l] *adj* unsteady, irregular; of variable temperament.

unequal [un*eek*wal] *adj* not equal; not of same size *etc*; uneven; not uniform; **u. to** not able to cope with ~ **unequally** *adv* not equally; irregularly.

unequalled [un*eek*wald] *adj* not equalled, unmatched.

unequivocal [uni*kwiv*okal] *adj* having only one possible meaning; plain, clear ~ **unequivocally** *adv*.

unerring [un*ur*Ring] *adj* not making any error, certain, unfailing ~ **unerringly** *adv*.

unethical [un*eth*ikal] *adj* not morally right; dishonest; immoral ~ **unethically** *adv*.

uneven [un*eeven*] *adj* not smooth or even; irregular, jerky; rough; (*of numbers*) odd; (*fig*) changeable ~ **unevenly** *adv* ~ **unevenness** *n*.

uneventful [un*ivent*fool] *adj* devoid of noteworthy incidents ~ **uneventfully** *adv*.

unexampled [unig*zamp*'ld] *adj* without precedent; exceptional.

unexceptionable [uneks*ep*shonab'l] *adj* not open to criticism, beyond reproach; satisfactory, excellent.

unexceptional [uneks*ep*shonal] *adj* ordinary, not remarkable; admitting of no exceptions.

unexecuted [un*eks*ikewtid] *adj* not carried out; (*of legal document*) not signed and witnessed.

unexpected [uniks*pek*tid] *adj* not expected, unforeseen ~ **unexpectedly** *adv* ~ **unexpectedness** *n*.

unexpressed [uniks*pRest*] *adj* not put into words.

unexpurgated [un*eks*pergaytid] *adj* printed, repeated or told in full without omission of any offensive passages.

unfading [un*fay*ding] *adj* imperishable, eternal.

unfailing [un*fay*ling] *adj* never ceasing, continuous; reliable ~ **unfailingly** *adv*.

unfair [un*fair*] *adj* not fair, unjust ~ **unfairly** *adv* ~ **unfairness** *n*.

unfaithful [un*fayth*fool] *adj* not faithful, *esp* to marriage vows; not accurate ~ **unfaithfully** *adv* ~ **unfaithfulness** *n*.

unfamiliar [unfa*mi*lyer] *adj* strange, not well known; having little knowledge of, inexperienced in.

unfamiliarity [unfamili-*a*Riti] *n* quality of being unfamiliar.

unfashionable [un*fa*shonab'l] *adj* not in fashion; not following the fashion ~ **unfashionably** *adv*.

unfashioned [un*fa*shond] *adj* not shaped.

unfasten [un*faa*sen] *v/t* undo the fastening of, untie.

unfathered [un*faa*THerd] *adj* without legal father, illegitimate; (*fig*) unauthenticated.

unfathomable [un*fa*THomab'l] *adj* impossible to reach the bottom of; vast; (*fig*) obscure, insoluble; inscrutable ~ **unfathomably** *adv*.

unfathomed [un*fa*THomd] *adj* of unknown depth; (*fig*) not fully explored.

unfavourable [un*fay*veRab'l] *adj* adverse; not propitious ~ **unfavourably** *adv*.

unfeeling [un*feel*ing] *adj* incapable of emotions, *esp* of sympathy or love; hard-hearted; insensitive ~ **unfeelingly** *adv*.

unfeigned [un*faynd*] *adj* not pretended, genuine.

unfeminine [un*fem*inin] *adj* unlike a woman; not suitable for a woman.

unfetter [un*fet*er] *v/t* set free.

unfettered [un*fet*erd] *adj* set free; (*fig*) freely expressed, unrestrained; independent.

unfilmed [un*filmd*] *adj* (*of book*) not yet made into a motion picture.

unfinished [un*fin*isht] *adj* incomplete; lacking skilled workmanship, rough, clumsy; lacking polish in style.

unfit [un*fit*] *adj* not fit, unsuitable; in bad health ~ **unfit** (*pres/part* **unfitting**, *p/t* and *p/part* **unfitted**) *v/t* make unsuitable (for), disqualify.

unfitting [un*fit*ing] *adj* unbecoming, improper.

unfix [un*fiks*] *v/t* unfasten; (*fig*) unsettle.

unfixed [un*fikst*] *adj* unfastened; not yet fastened.

unflagging [un*flag*ing] *adj* not interrupted or decreasing through weariness.

unflappable [un*flap*ab'l] *adj* (*coll*) never frightened or upset.

unflattering [un*flat*eRing] *adj* not disguising unpleasing facts; unpleasantly truthful.

unfledged [un*flejd*] *adj* (*of bird*) not yet fully feathered; (*fig*) young and inexperienced.

unflinching [un*flinch*ing] *adj* fearless, resolute.

unfold [un*fOld*] *v/t* and *i* open out of folds; (*fig*) reveal, relate; (*of buds*) become open.

unforced [un*fawrst*] *adj* not done under compulsion; natural, spontaneous; fluent.

unforeseen [unfawr*seen*] *adj* unexpected.

unforgettable [unfor*get*ab'l] *adj* that cannot be forgotten, memorable; vivid.

unforgivable [unfor*givab'l*] *adj* that cannot be forgiven ~ **unforgivably** *adv*.

unforgiving [unfor*giv*ing] *adj* refusing or unwilling to forgive; obdurate; hard-hearted ~ **unforgivingly** *adv* ~ **unforgivingness** *n*.

unformed [un*fawrmd*] *adj* not given full or regular form; undeveloped; untrained; vague, not fully conceived or expressed.

unfortunate [un*fawr*tewnit] *adj* not fortunate, unlucky; afflicted by bad luck, misfortunes *etc*; unsuccessful; likely to bring undesirable results; regrettable ~ **unfortunate** *n* an unfortunate person; (*obs euph*) prostitute ~ **unfortunately** *adv*.

unfounded [un*fownd*id] *adj* not founded on fact, baseless.

unfreeze (*p/t* **unfroze**, *p/part* **unfrozen**) [un*freez*] *v/t* thaw; cause to thaw; discontinue fixing of (prices or wages); lift controls from use, manufacture, or sale of.

unfrequented [unfRik*went*id] *adj* seldom visited, lonely.

unfriended [un*frend*id] *adj* without friends.

unfriendliness [un*frend*lines] *n* absence of goodwill; unkind act.

unfriendly [un*frend*li] *adj* not friendly; hostile.

unfrock [un*frok*] *v/t* deprive (priest) of his religious status.

unfroze [un*frOz*] *p/t* of **unfreeze**.

unfrozen [un*frOz*en] *adj* not frozen; thawed.

unfruitful [un*frOOt*fool] *adj* not bearing fruit; barren; unprofitable.

unfunny [un*fun*i] *adj* failing to amuse.

unfurl [un*furl*] *v/t* and *i* unroll, spread out (flag, sail *etc*); (*of flag etc*) become unrolled, spread out.

unfurnished [un*furn*isht] *adj* not furnished; (*of house, flat etc*) not provided by the landlord with furniture.

ungainly [un*gayn*li] *adj* clumsy, awkward.

ungallant [un-*gal*ant] *adj* not chivalrous, discourteous, *esp* to women ~ **ungallantly** *adv*.

ungarbled [un-*gaarb*'ld] *adj* not distorted or misrepresented.

ungenerous [un*jene*Rus] *adj* not generous; selfish; unfair, mean ~ **ungenerously** *adv*.

ungentlemanly [un*jent*'lmanli] *adj* unbefitting a gentleman.

un-get-at-able [un-get-*at*-ab'l] *adj* inaccessible.

ungifted [un-*gif*tid] *adj* with no natural ability.

ungird (*p/t* and *p/part* **ungirded** or **ungirt**) [un-*gurd*] *v/t* remove the girdle from; take off by undoing girdle or band.

ungirt [un-*gurt*] *adj* with girdle removed; (*fig*) unprepared.

ungloved [un-*gluvd*] *adj* not wearing a glove or gloves.

ungodly [un-*god*li] *adj* wicked; (*coll*) outrageous; **the u.** evil persons.

ungovernable [un-*guvern*ab'l] *adj* impossible to control; licentious; wild ~ **ungovernably** *adv*.

ungoverned [un-*guvernd*] *adj* out of control; wild; licentious.

ungracious [un-*gRay*shus] *adj* discourteous; unkind ~ **ungraciously** *adv*.

ungrateful [un-*gRayt*fool] *adj* feeling or showing no gratitude; (*of soil*) not repaying cultivation; (*of task*) unpleasant; thankless ~ **ungratefully** *adv* ~ **ungratefulness** *n*.

ungrounded [un-*gRownd*id] *adj* without foundation in fact; false, unjustified.

ungrudging [un-*gRuj*ing] *adj* done or given willingly and graciously; unstinted, unsparing ~ **ungrudgingly** *adv*.

ungual [*ung*-gwal] *adj* (*anat*) of a nail or claw.

790

unguarded [un-*gaar*did] *adj* without defence; incautious; **in an u. moment** when off one's guard.

unguent [*ung*-gwent] *n* ointment.

unguiform [*ung*-gwifawrm] *adj* claw-shaped.

ungula [*ung*-gewla] *n* (*geom*) part of a cylinder or cone cut off by a plane which is oblique to the base; (*zool*) hoof; claw, talon.

ungulate [*ung*-gewlayt] *n* and *adj* (animal) which has hoofs > PDB.

unhallowed [un*hal*Od] *adj* not holy, not consecrated; evil, godless.

unhampered [un*ham*perd] *adj* not hindered, free.

unhand [un*hand*] *v/t* release from one's grip, take one's hands off.

unhandled [un*hand*'ld] *adj* not touched by hand; (*fig*) not discussed.

unhandy [un*han*di] *adj* not within easy reach; not convenient to handle; not clever with the hands; awkward, clumsy.

unhappily [un*ha*pili] *adv* unfortunately; miserably.

unhappiness [un*ha*pines] *n* misery.

unhappy [un*ha*pi] *adj* miserable; unlucky, illfated; infelicitous, tactless.

unharmed [un*haarmd*] *adj* not damaged or injured ~ **unharmed** *adv* safely.

unharnessed [un*haar*nist] *adj* released from harness or armour; not brought under control for industrial purposes.

unhasp [un*haasp*] *v/t* unfasten the hasp of.

unhatched [un*hacht*] *adj* not out of the egg; (*fig*) (*of plot etc*) not fully worked out or brought to fruition.

unhealthy [un*hel*thi] *adj* unwholesome, harmful to bodily or mental health; diseased, morbid; symptomatic of disease or abnormality; (*sl*) dangerous ~ **unhealthily** *adv* ~ **unhealthiness** *n*.

unheard [un*hurd*] *adj* not heard; not allowed a hearing; never heard of, strange.

unheard-of [un*hurd*-ov] *adj* unprecedented, outrageous; extraordinary.

unheeded [un*heed*id] *adj* not noticed; disregarded.

unheeding [un*heed*ing] *adj* inattentive; careless.

unhelpful [un*help*fool] *adj* not helpful, giving no help ~ **unhelpfully** *adv*.

unhewn [un*hewn*] *adj* not shaped, unpolished.

unhinge [un*hinj*] *v/t* remove (door *etc*) from hinges; (*fig*) cause to become mentally unbalanced, drive mad ~ **unhinged** *adj*.

unhistorical [unhisto*Ri*kal] *adj* not agreeing with facts of history; not found in history, legendary ~ **unhistorically** *adv*.

unhitch [un*hich*] *v/t* detach (horse) from vehicle; untie, set loose.

unholy [un*hO*li] *adj* wicked, evil; (*coll*) outrageous.

unhook [un*hook*] *v/t* loose from a hook; undo the hooks of.

unhoped [un*hOpt*] *adj* not expected.

unhorse [un*hawrs*] *v/t* cause to fall from a horse.

unhurt [un*hurt*] *adj* not hurt, uninjured.

uni- *pref* one, single.

Uniat, Uniate [*yOO*ni-at] *n* member of an Eastern church which retains Greek liturgy, but acknowledges papal authority.

uniaxial [*yOO*ni-*ak*si-al] *adj* (*opt*) having only one optic axis > PDS.

unicameral [*yOO*ni*kame*Ral] *adj* consisting of a single legislative chamber.

unicellular [*yOO*ni*sele*wlar] *adj* (*biol*) composed of a single cell > PDB.

unicorn [*yOO*nikawrn] *n* fabulous animal like a horse with a single twisted horn in its forehead.

unicycle [*yOO*nisIk'l] *n* one-wheeled cycle used for acrobatic displays.

unification [*yOO*nifi*kay*shon] *n* process or result of unifying.

uniform [*yOO*nifawrm] *adj* similar in every way; unvarying, consistent; of a uniform ~ **uniform** *n* distinctive dress worn by all members of a military or police force, of a school, of a particular organization or group *etc*.

uniformed [*yOO*nifawrmd] *adj* wearing uniform.

uniformity [*yOO*ni*fawr*miti] *n* state of being exactly alike or unvarying; conformity to one standard.

uniformly [*uni*fawrmli] *adv* consistently, without variation.

unify [*yOO*nifI] *v/t* make into one, unite.

unilateral [*yOO*ni*late*Ral] *adj* one-sided; done by or affecting only one side in an agreement or dispute; of, on, or affecting one side only; **u. disarmament** disarmament by one nation without guarantee that its potential enemies will also disarm.

unilateralism [*yOO*ni*late*Ralizm] *n* advocacy of unilateral disarmament ~ **unilateralist** *adj* and *n*.

unilaterally [*yOO*ni*late*Rali] *adv* in a unilateral way; disregarding the actions or wishes of other interested parties.

unimaginable [uni*maj*inab'l] *adj* that cannot be imagined, inconceivable ~ **unimaginably** *adv*.

unimaginative [uni*maj*inativ] *adj* lacking imagination ~ **unimaginatively** *adv* ~ **unimaginativeness** *n*.

unimodal [*yOO*nim*Od*al] *adj* (*of frequency curve*) having only one high point.

unimpaired [unim*paird*] *adj* not weakened; not damaged.

unimpassioned [unim*pa*shond] *adj* without passionate feeling.

unimpeachable [unim*peech*ab'l] *adj* blameless.

unimportance [unim*paw*rtans] *n* quality of being unimportant.

unimportant [unim*paw*rtant] *adj* not important, insignificant.

unimposing [unim*pO*zing] *adj* not impressive in appearance.

unimpressed [unim*pRest*] *adj* not deeply moved or stirred, not impressed.

unimpressive [unim*pResiv*] *adj* not convincing, not striking or commanding.

unimproved [unim*pROOvd*] *adj* not improved; (*of land*) not turned to use, not developed.

uninformed [unin*fawrmd*] *adj* lacking knowledge or information, ignorant.

uninhabitable [unin*habit*ab'l] *adj* not fit to be lived in.

uninhabited [unin*habitid*] *adj* not inhabited; deserted.

uninspired [unin*spIrd*] *adj* lacking inspiration, humdrum.

uninsured [unin*shewrd*] *adj* not covered by insurance.

unintelligent [unin*teli*jent] *adj* not intelligent, stupid ∼ **unintelligently** *adv*.

unintelligible [unin*teli*jib'l] *adj* incapable of being understood ∼ **unintelligibly** *adv*.

unintended [unin*tendid*] *adj* not deliberate.

unintentional [unin*ten*shonal] *adj* not deliberate, involuntary, unintended ∼ **unintentionally** *adv*.

uninterested [un*inte*Restid] *adj* feeling no interest, indifferent, bored.

uninteresting [un*inte*Risting] *adj* not arousing interest ∼ **uninterestingly** *adv*.

uninterrupted [un*inte*Ruptid] *adj* not interrupted, continuous ∼ **uninterruptedly** *adv*.

uninucleate [yOOnine*w*kli-ayt/yOOnine*w*kli-at] *adj* having a single nucleus.

uninvited [unin*vi*tid] *adj* not invited; not asked for.

uninviting [unin*vi*ting] *adj* unattractive, displeasing, repellent ∼ **uninvitingly** *adv*.

union [yOOnyon] *n* act of joining things, parties, countries *etc* into one; condition of being so joined; state of being united in marriage; marriage; association of workers for the promotion of their common interests, trade union; university club and debating society, and its premises; confederation of States; formerly, the linking together of several parishes under a Board of Guardians for the administration of Poor Law relief; workhouse; (*bui*) connexion for pipes; **U. Jack** national flag of Great Britain.

unionism [yOOnyonizm] *n* (*hist*) policy opposing self-government for territories of the British Empire, *esp* Ireland; trade-unionism ∼ **unionist** *n* and *adj*.

uniparous [yOO*nipa*Rus] *adj* (*zool*) producing only one at a birth; (*bot*) with one axis at each branching.

unipartite [yOO*nipaa*rtIt] *adj* not divided into parts.

uniped [yOOniped] *n* legendary man-like creature with only one leg.

unipolar [yOO*nip*Oler] *adj* (*of nerve-cell*) having only one pole.

unique [yOO*neek*] *adj* single, sole; unrivalled; (*coll*) remarkable, singular ∼ **uniquely** *adv* ∼ **uniqueness** *n*.

unisex [yOOni*seks*] *adj* (*of clothes etc*) equally suitable for men or women; tending to eliminate differences between men and women.

unisexual [yOOni*sek*sew-al] *adj* (*bot, zool*) distinctly male or female > PDB.

unison [yOOnison] *n* simultaneous sounding of notes of the same pitch > PDM; (*fig*) perfect agreement.

unit [yOOnit] *n* a thing complete in itself; group of things or persons forming a whole complete in itself; the least whole number, the numeral one; quantity or dimension adopted as standard of measurement; **U. Trust** company formed under the terms of a trust deed to spread investments over a wide variety of securities.

Unitarian [yOOni*tair*Ri-an] *n* and *adj* (member) of a Christian sect which rejects the doctrine of the Trinity and the Divinity of Christ; (member) of a group of deists, humanists and agnostics seeking religious experience and ethical standards without defined dogmas.

Unitarianism [yOOni*tair*Ri-anizm] *n* doctrines of Unitarians.

unitary [yOOni*ta*Ri] *adj* of a unit or units; not divided, integrated.

unite [yOO*ni*t] *v/t* and *i* join into one body; form one body; act together for common purpose; join together; join in marriage; be a connecting link between; come to agreement; form an alliance.

united [yOO*ni*tid] *adj* joined together, brought together; joined in marriage; in agreement; in alliance, associated together for purposes of common action; **U. Nations** international organization of peace-loving states for the maintenance of peace and security > PDPol; **U. States (of America)** Federal Republic of North America > PDPol ∼ **unitedly** *adv* ∼ **unitedness** *n*.

unitive [yOOnitiv] *adj* causing (things or persons) to unite, promoting unity.

unity [yOOniti] *n* state of being a unit; condition of being united; oneness; harmonious cooperation; agreement of aims, interests *etc*; amity, concord; (*math*) the number one; **the unities** (*theat*) principles limiting the action of a drama to one place in the space of one day, and forbidding sub-plots.

univalent [yOOni*va*ylent] *adj* (*chem*) able to combine with or replace one atom of hydrogen.

univalve [yOOnivalv] *n* and *adj* (mollusc) with shell in one piece.

universal [yOOni*vu*rsal] *adj* applicable to or involving all members of a specified category or group; widespread; whole, entire; usable for all purposes; **u. joint** joint which permits movement in any direction; **u. language** language designed to be spoken by everyone; **u. suffrage** right of voting extended to all members of a community ∼ **universal** *n* (*log*) proposition that holds true for all members of a specified class.

universality [yOOni*ver*saliti] *n* quality of being universal, *esp* of a work of art the significance of which exceeds the limits of its period.

universalize [yOOni*vu*rsalIz] *v/t* render universal, regard as universal.

universally [yOOni*vu*rsali] *adv* everywhere; always; by everyone.

universe [yOOnivurs] *n* the whole system of extant material objects and physical forces and the space in which these exist; world; (*fig*) field of knowledge.

university [yOOni*vu*rsiti] *n* corporate institution giving instruction in advanced learning and empowered to confer degrees; (*collect*) members of a university; governing body of such an institution; (*sport*) team, crew, *etc* representing a university.

univocal [yOOniv*O*kal] *adj* having only one possible meaning ∼ **univocally** *adv*.

unjust [un*just*] *adj* not just, not acting fairly; contrary to justice ∼ **unjustly** *adv*.

unkempt [un-*kempt*] *adj* uncombed, having untidy hair; badly dressed, slovenly.

unkennel [un-*kenel*] *v/t* dislodge (fox) from its hole; let (hounds) out of a kennel; (*fig*) bring to light.

unkind [un-*ki*nd] *adj* not kind, liable to hurt the feelings of others; inconsiderate; harsh, cruel.

unkindly [un-*ki*ndli] *adv* in an unkind way ∼ **unkindly** *adj* harsh, unkind; (*of weather*) inclement.

unkindness [un-*ki*ndnis] *n* quality of being unkind; unkind behaviour.

unkingly [un-*king*li] *adj* not like a king; unworthy of a king.

unknightly [un-*nīt*li] *adj* unworthy of a knight.

unknit (*pres/part* **unknitting**, *p/t* and *p/part* **unknitted**) [un-*nit*] *v/t* unfasten, untie; weaken.

unknowable [un-*nO*-ab'l] *adj* which no human mind can know.

unknowing [un-*nO*-ing] *adj* not knowing, unaware ~ **unknowingly** *adv* in ignorance, unawares.

unknown [un-*nOn*] *n* and *adj* (person or thing) not known or identified.

unlade (*p/t* **unladed**, *p/part* **unladen**, **unladed**) [un*layd*] *v/t* unload (cargo) from (a ship).

unlaid [un*layd*] *adj* not laid; (*of table*) not set for a meal; (*of ghost*) still walking; (*of paper*) not showing parallel lines when held up to the light.

unlash [un*lash*] *v/t* let loose the lashings of; untie.

unlawful [un*law*fool] *adj* contrary to the law; contrary to a moral or religious rule ~ **unlawfully** *adv*.

unlearn (*p/t* and *p/part* **unlearned**, **unlearnt**) [un*lurn*] *v/t* rid one's mind of all one has been taught (about).

unlearned (1), **unlearnt** (1) [un*lurnd*, un*lurnt*] *adj* (*of lesson etc*) not learnt.

unlearned (2) [un*lurnid*] *adj* lacking learning, ignorant ~ **unlearnedly** *adv*.

unlearnt (2) [un*lurnt*] *p/t* and *p/part* of **unlearn**.

unleash [un*leesh*] *v/t* release (hounds) from leash to chase prey; (*fig*) let loose (destructive force); release from restraint, give free vent to.

unleavened [un*lev*end] *adj* (*of bread*) made without yeast; (*fig*) not modified or invigorated by fresh influences.

unless [un*les*] *adv* if . . . not; except that.

unlettered [un*let*erd] *adj* not well educated, ignorant; illiterate.

unlicked [un*likt*] *adj* immature, with manners or training still incomplete.

unlike [un*līk*] *adj* and *prep* not like, different from; dissimilar.

unlikelihood [un*līk*lihood] *n* improbability.

unlikeliness [un*līk*linis] *n* improbability.

unlikely [un*līk*li] *adj* improbable, not likely to happen or to be true ~ **unlikely** *adv* not u. not improbably.

unlisted [un*list*id] *adj* (*of stocks*) not quoted on a recognized Stock Exchange.

unload [un*lOd*] *v/t* and *i* remove transported goods, cargo *etc* from (vehicle or ship); remove charge from (gun); get rid of (a burden); give vent to, express freely; (*comm*) sell out (shares).

unlock [un*lok*] *v/t* unfasten the lock of; (*fig*) reveal, disclose (feelings).

unlooked-for [un*lookt*-for] *adj* unexpected.

unloose, **unloosen** [un*lOOs*, un*lOO*sen] *v/t* let loose, set free; loosen.

unlovable [un*luv*ab'l] *adj* not easy to love; unattractive, repellent.

unlovely [un*huv*li] *adj* ugly, unattractive.

unloving [un*luv*ing] *adj* not affectionate, cold.

unluckily [un*luk*ili] *adv* unfortunately, unhappily; badly.

unlucky [un*luk*i] *adj* not lucky; never winning; unfortunate; ill-omened; badly timed.

unmade (1) [un*mayd*] *adj* not yet made; uncreated.

unmade (2) *p/t* and *p/part* of **unmake**.

unmaidenly [un*may*denli] *adj* immodest, not seemly for a girl.

unmake (*p/t* and *p/part* **unmade**) [un*mayk*] *v/t* take apart; depose (from rank or position); destroy, ruin.

unman (*pres/part* **unmanning**, *p/t* and *p/part* **unmanned**) [un*man*] *v/t* deprive of manly courage; unnerve; castrate.

unmanageable [un*man*ijab'l] *adj* that cannot be controlled; impossible to handle conveniently ~ **unmanageably** *adv*.

unmanly [un*man*li] *adj* cowardly; effeminate.

unmanned [un*mand*] *adj* deprived of manly courage, unnerved; not provided with a crew; controlled automatically, not by pilot *etc*; (*of hawk*) untrained.

unmannerly [un*man*erli] *adj* bad-mannered.

unmarked [un*maarkt*] *adj* bearing no mark or impression; having no marks or stains; not noticed; not awarded marks; not corrected by a teacher.

unmarketable [un*maar*kitab'l] *adj* unsaleable.

unmarred [un*maard*] *adj* not damaged; not disfigured; without blemish.

unmarriageable [un*ma*Rijab'l] *adj* too young to marry; very unlikely to find a husband or wife.

unmask [un*maask*] *v/t* and *i* remove mask from; bring to light, expose; take off one's own mask; show one's true character; (*mil*) reveal position of (batteries) by opening fire.

unmeaning [un*mee*ning] *adj* conveying no sense; meaningless.

unmeant [un*ment*] *adj* not deliberate, unintended.

unmeasured [un*mezh*erd] *adj* not admitting of measurement, boundless; unrestrained, unstinted; immoderate, excessive.

unmeet [un*meet*] *adj* (*ar*) unsuitable (for).

unmentionable [un*men*shonab'l] *adj* too unpleasant, horrifying, or obscene to speak of.

unmentionables [un*men*shonab'lz] *n* (*pl*) (*obs joc*) trousers, underclothes.

unmerciful [un*mur*sifool] *adj* showing no mercy, cruel-hearted ~ **unmercifully** *adv*.

unmerited [un*me*Ritid] *adj* not merited, undeserved.

unmetrical [un*met*Rikal] *adj* against the rules of prosody; not written in metre.

unminded [un*mīn*did] *adj* not intending (to); unheeded; not looked after.

unmindful [un*mīnd*fool] *adj* forgetful (of); heedless.

unmistakable [unmis*tay*kab'l] *adj* not to be mistaken or misunderstood; easily recognizable ~ **unmistakably** *adv*.

unmitigated [un*mit*igaytid] *adj* not mitigated; absolute, downright.

unmolested [un*mo*lestid] *adj* left unattacked or undisturbed.

unmoor [un*moor*] *v/t* (*naut*) weigh and hoist one anchor > PDSa.

unmoral [un*mo*Ral] *adj* not moral; not concerned with moral considerations.

unmounted [un*moun*tid] *adj* not mounted, not on horseback; (*of cannon*) not placed on a carriage; (*of picture*) not provided with a mount.

unmoved [un*mOO*vd] *adj* not moved; feeling no emotion; calm, unshaken.

unmurmuring [un*mur*meRing] *adj* uncomplaining, long-suffering.

unmusical [un*mew*zikal] *adj* not musical; not having a good musical ear; harsh-sounding, not harmonious.

unmuzzle [un*muz*'l] *v/t* remove muzzle from (animal); allow to speak freely.

unnamable [un-*naym*ab'l] *adj* not to be named; too horrible to specify.

unnamed [un-*naymd*] *adj* not named, not previously mentioned; nameless.

unnatural [un-*nach*eRal] *adj* not natural, artificial, out of the ordinary, unusual; not in accordance with the ordinary course of nature, abnormal, monstrous; supernatural; contrary to, or without, normal basic instincts; heinous, vile ~ **unnaturally** *adv*.

unnecessary [un-*nes*esaRi] *adj* not necessary; superfluous, needless ~ **unnecessarily** *adv*.

unneighbourly [un-*nay*berli] *adj* not friendly, unbecoming in a neighbour.

unnerve [un-*murv*] *v/t* make weak with terror, deprive of courage.

unnoticed [un-*nOt*ist] *adj* not taken notice of.

unnumbered [un-*numb*erd] *adj* too many to be counted, innumerable; not identified or marked by a number.

unobservant [unobz*urv*ant] *adj* not observant; having little power of observation.

unobserved [unobz*urv*d] *adj* not noticed.

unobtainable [unobt*ayn*ab'l] *adj* not obtainable; out of reach.

unobtrusive [unobt*ROO*siv] *adj* not disposed to intrude, modest; not too obvious, discreet ~ **unobtrusively** *adv*.

unoccupied [un*oke*wpId] *adj* (*of person*) not engaged in any work; (*of house*) empty; (*of territory*) not under military occupation.

unoffending [uno*fend*ing] *adj* not causing offence, inoffensive; having committed no offence.

unofficial [uno*fish*al] *adj* not official, informal; (*of news*) not officially confirmed.

unorganized [un*awr*ganIzd] *adj* not organized; (*biol*) lacking organic structure; (*fig*) lacking structure and unity.

unoriginal [uno*Rij*inal] *adj* copied from another's work; incapable of original work, uninventive.

unorthodox [un*awr*thodoks] *adj* not according to orthodox beliefs, methods *etc*.

unostentatious [unosten*tay*shus] *adj* not attempting to attract attention.

unpack [un*pak*] *v/t* and *i* unfasten (suitcase, parcel *etc*) and remove its contents; remove and put away contents of one's luggage.

unpacked [un*pakt*] *adj* removed from suitcase *etc*; emptied of its contents; not pre-packed.

unparalleled [un*pa*Raleld] *adj* unequalled, incomparable: unprecedented.

unpardonable [un*paar*donab'l] *adj* that cannot be pardoned, inexcusable ~ **unpardonably** *adv*.

unparliamentary [unpaarli*ment*eRi] *adj* not befitting Parliament; **u. language** obscene language, swearing.

unpeg (*pres/part* **unpegging**, *p/t* and *p/part* **unpegged**) [un*peg*] *v/t* unfasten by removing pegs; permit (wages, prices *etc*) to be increased.

unpen (*pres/part* **unpenning**, *p/t* and *p/part* **un-**

penned) [un*pen*] *v/t* release (sheep) from pen; let loose, release.

unpeople [un*peep*'l] *v/t* depopulate.

unpeopled [un*peep*'ld] *adj* not populated.

unperson [un*purson*] *n* person whose existence is officially ignored or whose rights are systematically disregarded.

unpick [un*pik*] *v/t* undo stitches of (piece of sewing or knitting).

unpicked [un*pikt*] *adj* not picked, not selected; (*of sewing etc*) undone; (*of flowers etc*) ungathered.

unpin (*pres/part* **unpinning**, *p/t* and *p/part* **unpinned**) [un*pin*] *v/t* unfasten by removing pins.

unplaced [un*playst*] *adj* not placed; not one of the first three in a race or competition.

unplanned [un*pland*] *adj* not planned; accidental; haphazard, random.

unplayable [un*play*-ab'l] *adj* (*of ball*) incapable of being played; (*of ground*) not fit to play on.

unpleasant [un*plez*ant] *adj* disagreeable ~ **unpleasantly** *adv*.

unpleasantness [un*plez*antnes] *n* disagreeableness; disagreeable incident; hostility, resentment; quarrel.

unpleasing [un*pleez*ing] *adj* disagreeable.

unplug (*pres/part* **unplugging**, *p/t* and *p/part* **unplugged**) [un*plug*] *v/t* open by removing plug from; remove plug of (electric apparatus) from socket.

unplumbed [un*plumd*] *adj* unfathomed.

unpopular [un*pope*wlar] *adj* not popular, not appealing to most people.

unpopularity [unpopewla*Ri*ti] *n* state of being unpopular.

unpractical [un*pRak*tikal] *adj* not capable of practical action, inefficient; that cannot be put into practice ~ **unpractically** *adv*.

unprecedented [un*pRes*identid] *adj* without a precedent, unparalleled, novel.

unprejudiced [un*pRej*oodist] *adj* free from prejudice, impartial.

unprepared [unpRi*paird*] *adj* not prepared; taken by surprise; unready ~ **unpreparedness** [un-pRi*pair*(i)dnis] *n*.

unpresentable [unpRiz*ent*ab'l] *adj* without pleasing manners and appearance.

unpretending [unpRi*tend*ing] *adj* modest, unassuming, making no claims to importance.

unpriced [un*pRIst*] *adj* not having been priced; not marked with a price.

unprincipled [un*pRin*sip'ld] *adj* having no moral principles, unscrupulous.

unprintable [un*pRint*ab'l] *adj* too obscene to print ~ **unprintably** *adv*.

unprized [un*pRIzd*] *adj* not prized; not highly valued.

unprocurable [unpRo*kewr*Rab'l] *adj* not to be procured, unobtainable.

unproductive [unpRo*duk*tiv] *adj* not producing abundantly; not producing economic wealth.

unprofessional [unpRo*fesh*onal] *adj* not professional; unbecoming to one's profession ~ **unprofessionally** *adv* in an unprofessional manner; not from a professional point of view.

unprofitable [un*pRo*fitab'l] *adj* bringing no profit, disadvantageous, useless ~ **unprofitably** *adv*.

unpromising [un*p*Romising] *adj* not showing signs of future excellence; unlikely to succeed.

unpronounceable [unpRo*nown*sab'l] *adj* difficult or impossible to pronounce.

unprovable [un*p*ROOvab'l] *adj* incapable of proof.

unproved [un*p*ROOvd] *adj* not proved, untested.

unprovided [un*p*RovIdid] *adj* not furnished (with); not ready (for).

unprovoked [un*p*RovOkt] *adj* without provocation.

unpublished [un*p*ublisht] *adj* not made generally known; (*of a book etc*) not printed or sold.

unputdownable [unpoot*down*ab'l] *adj* (*coll, of book*) so interesting that the reader cannot put it down.

unqualified [un-*kwo*lifId] *adj* without requisite qualifications; not limited or restricted; (*coll*) downright.

unquenchable [un-*kwench*ab'l] *adj* that cannot be quenched, enduring persistently.

unquestionable [un-*kwes*chonab'l] *adj* not to be questioned; certain, indisputable ∼ **unquestionably** *adv.*

unquestioned [un-*kwes*chond] *adj* undisputed, undoubted.

unquestioning [un-*kwes*choning] *adj* unhesitating, not feeling any doubts ∼ **unquestioningly** *adv* unhesitatingly.

unquiet [un-*kwI*-et] *adj* not quiet, not at peace; restless, anxious ∼ **unquiet** *n* disquiet.

unquotable [un-*kwO*tab'l] *adj* not suitable for quotation; not fit to be repeated.

unquote [un-*kwO*t] *v/t* (*imp*) (*in dictation*) end a quotation.

unravel (*pres/part* **unravelling**, *p/t* and *p/part* **unravelled**) [un*Ravel*] *v/t* and *i* disentangle, undo threads of; (*fig*) make clear, solve; become disentangled.

unreachable [un*Reech*ab'l] *adj* impossible to reach, unattainable.

unread [un*Red*] *adj* not read; illiterate.

unreadable [un*Reed*ab'l] *adj* not easy or pleasant to read; not fit to be read; illegible.

unready [un*Red*i] *adj* not ready or prepared; irresolute.

unreal [un*Ree*-al] *adj* not real, imaginary.

unreality [un*Ree*-aliti] *n* quality of being unreal.

unreasonable [un*Reez*onab'l] *adj* (*of person*) not amenable to reason; making demands for which there is no justification; (*of claim, prices etc*) unjustifiable, exorbitant ∼ **unreasonableness** *n* ∼ **unreasonably** *adv.*

unreasoning [un*Reez*oning] *adj* not influenced by or involving reasoning, irrational ∼ **unreasoningly** *adv.*

unreclaimed [un*Rik*laymd] *adj* not reformed; (*of land*) uncultivated.

unrecognized [un*Rek*ognIzd] *adj* not recognized; not having received adequate appreciation.

unreel [un*Reel*] *v/t* and *i* unwind from a reel.

unrefined [un*Ri*fInd] *adj* not freed from impurities; rude, vulgar.

unreflecting [un*Ri*flekting] *adj* not reflecting light; not thinking, thoughtless.

unregarded [un*Ri*gaardid] *adj* not regarded, unnoticed, not taken into account.

unrehearsed [un*Ri*hurst] *adj* not rehearsed, spontaneous, not meant to happen

unreliability [un*R*ilI-*abi*liti] *n* state of being unreliable.

unreliable [un*R*ilI-ab'l] *adj* not reliable; untrustworthy ∼ **unreliably** *adv.*

unrelieved [un*Ri*leevd] *adj* not relieved; not varied; not given assistance.

unremarkable [un*Ri*maarkab'l] *adj* not remarkable, not worthy of notice.

unremarked [un*Ri*maarkt] *adj* not observed or noticed.

unremitting [un*Ri*miting] *adj* never stopping, incessant ∼ **unremittingly** *adv* unceasingly.

unrequited [un*Ri*kwItid] *adj* not recompensed; not reciprocated; unavenged; **u. exports (imports)** those not paid for in money or goods.

unreserved [un*Ri*zurvd] *adj* without restrictions; not booked in advance; frank, outspoken ∼ **unreservedly** *adv.*

unresolved [un*Ri*zolvd] *adj* not separated into component parts; not analysed, unsolved; undecided; (*mus*) not converted into a concord.

unresponsive [un*Ri*sponsiv] *adj* not reacting readily or sympathetically.

unrest [un*Rest*] *n* restlessness; agitation, disturbance; anxiety.

unrestful [un*Rest*fool] *adj* not giving an impression of peace and quiet; not soothing; fidgety.

unresting [un*Res*ting] *adj* not resting, untiring.

unriddle [un*Rid*'l] *v/t* solve the mystery of.

unrig (*pres/part* **unrigging**, *p/t* and *p/part* **unrigged**) [un*Rig*] *v/t* (*naut*) dismantle (rigging of).

unrighteous [un*RI*chus] *adj* not morally good, wicked; not merited, unjust ∼ **unrighteously** *adv* ∼ **unrighteousness** *n.*

unrip (*pres/part* **unripping**, *p/t* and *p/part* **unripped**) [un*Rip*] *v/t* tear open; rip out stitches from.

unripe [un*Rip*] *adj* not yet ripe, immature.

unrisen [un*Riz*en] *adj* not yet risen.

unrivalled [un*Ri*vald] *adj* without a rival, unequalled, unsurpassed.

unrobe [un*ROb*] *v/t* and *i* remove clothes or robes (of).

unroll [un*ROl*] *v/t* and *i* roll out; uncoil.

unromantic [un*Ro*mantik] *adj* not romantic, commonplace, matter-of-fact.

unruffled [un*Ruf*'ld] *adj* not ruffled; calm, unmoved.

unruliness [un*ROO*lines] *n* state of being unruly.

unruly [un*ROO*li] *adj* disobedient, uncontrolled, disorderly.

unsaddle [un*sad*'l] *v/t* and *i* tal.e the saddle off (a horse); dislodge (a rider) from the saddle.

unsafe [un*sayf*] *adj* not safe, dangerous.

unsaid [un*sed*] *adj* not said, unspoken.

unsaleable, unsalable [un*say*lab'l] *adj* not suitable for sale; unlikely ever to be bought.

unsalaried [un*sala*Rid] *adj* not paid by salary; honorary, unpaid.

unsanctified [un*sankt*ifId] *adj* not consecrated or holy; (*fig*) wicked.

unsanctioned [un*sank*shond] *adj* not authorized.

unsanitary [un*sani*taRi] *adj* not hygienic, unhealthy.

unsaturated [un*satewr*Raytid] *adj* not saturated; (*chem*) (*of a solution*) able to dissolve more of a solute; (*of a compound*) containing a double or triple bond; capable of forming additional compounds.

unsavoury [un*sayve*Ri] *adj* unpleasant to taste or smell; (*fig*) disgusting, immoral.

unsay (*p/t* and *p/part* unsaid) [un*say*] *v/t* retract (something said or written).

unscathed [un*skay*THd] *adj* not injured in mind or body.

unscholarly [un*skol*arli] *adj* not learned, devoid of scholarship; inaccurate; not written as befits a scholar.

unschooled [un*skOOld*] *adj* not educated, untrained, inexperienced.

unscientific [uns*I*-en*tif*ik] *adj* not in accordance with or understanding scientific methods ~ **unscientifically** *adv*.

unscramble [un*skRamb*'l] *v/t* (*of signals*) render intelligible by decoding.

unscratched [un*skRacht*] *adj* not scratched; quite unhurt.

unscreened [un*skReend*] *adj* not screened, not protected by a screen; not sifted through a screen; not made into a motion picture; (*fig*) not investigated for reasons of security.

unscrew [un*skROO*] *v/t* and *i* remove (screw) by turning; unfasten by removing screw(s); become unscrewed.

unscripted [un*skRip*tid] *adj* (*of broadcasts*) not delivered from a prepared script, spontaneous.

unscrupulous [un*skROO*pewlus] *adj* without scruples; sticking at nothing to attain one's object ~ **unscrupulously** *adv* ~ **unscrupulousness** *n*.

unseal [un*seel*] *v/t* remove the seal from; open.

unsealed [un*seeld*] *adj* not closed with a seal; opened.

unsearchable [un*surch*ab'l] *adj* inscrutable, impossible to explain.

unseasonable [un*seezon*ab'l] *adj* not suitable to the season of the year; ill-timed.

unseasoned [un*seezend*] *adj* (*of food*) not spiced or flavoured; (*of timber*) not matured.

unseat [un*seet*] *v/t* throw from the saddle; deprive of position, *esp* of a seat in House of Commons.

unsecured [un*sike*werd] *adj* (*of Loan Stock, promissory notes*) issued without specifically charging all or any of a company's assets.

unseeing [un*see*-ing] *adj* unobservant, unsuspecting; blind.

unseemly [un*seem*li] *adj* not proper or decent; not suited to the occasion ~ **unseemliness** *n*.

unselfish [un*self*ish] *adj* not caring only for one's own profit or pleasure; self-sacrificing, generous ~ **unselfishly** *adv* ~ **unselfishness** *n*.

unserviceable [un*survi*sab'l] *adj* not capable of or ready for service; useless, not fit for use.

unsettle [un*set*'l] *v/t* deprive of peace of mind and security; upset, disturb.

unsettled [un*set*'ld] *adj* changeable; unpaid; not finally decided; restless; not populated.

unsettling [un*set*ling] *adj* disturbing, disquieting.

unsex [un*seks*] *v/t* deprive of sexual potency; deprive of characteristics usual in one's sex, *esp* make unfeminine.

unsexed [un*sekst*] *adj* (*of chicks*) not separated according to sex; having become sexually im-

potent; having discarded the usual social attitudes of one's sex.

unshackle [un*shak*'l] *v/t* release from fetters.

unshaded [un*shay*did] *adj* not sheltered from the sun; (*of light*) not provided with a covering; (*of drawing*) not marked with shading.

unshadowed [un*shad*Od] *adj* not darkened by a shadow; (*fig*) not made sad or gloomy.

unshakable, unshakeable [un*shay*kab'l] *adj* unable to be shaken; (*fig*) firm, resolute ~ **unshakably** *adv*.

unshapely [un*shay*pli] *adj* badly proportioned.

unshaven [un*shay*ven] *adj* not shaved; with a beard.

unsheathe [un*sheeth*] *v/t* draw (weapon) from its sheath.

unsheltered [un*shel*tered] *adj* exposed, not protected.

unship (*pres/part* unshipping, *p/t* and *p/part* unshipped) [un*ship*] *v/t* unload (cargo); (*naut*) remove anything from its place of use.

unshod [un*shod*] *adj* barefooted; (*of horse*) not provided with shoes.

unshrinkable [un*shrink*ab'l] *adj* (*of fabrics*) incapable of shrinking when washed.

unshriven [un*shRi*ven] *adj* not having made confession of sin and been absolved.

unsifted [un*sif*tid] *adj* not separated by passing through a sieve; (*fig*) not carefully examined.

unsighted [un*sIt*tid] *adj* not yet in sight; with one's view obscured; (*of gun*) not provided with sights; (*of shot*) aimed without looking through the sights.

unsightly [un*sIt*li] *adj* not pleasant to look at, ugly.

unsisterly [un*sister*li] *adj* without sisterly love.

unskilful [un*skil*fool] *adj* clumsy ~ **unskilfully** *adv*.

unskilled [un*skild*] *adj* without special training; not requiring skill.

unsleeping [un*sleep*ing] *adj* not sleeping; (*fig*) untiring, constantly alert.

unsling (*p/t* and *p/part* unslung) [un*sling*] *v/t* (*naut*) detach from a sling.

unsociability [uns*O*sha*bili*ti] *n* quality of being unsociable.

unsociable [uns*O*shab'l] *adj* not willing to be friendly; tending to avoid company of others, reserved ~ **unsociably** *adv*.

unsocial [uns*O*shal] *adj* not in accordance with social usage; unsociable.

unsocialized [uns*O*sha*l*Izd] *adj* lacking in social training, social feeling, or social habits; not financed from public funds.

unsoldierly [uns*O*ljerli] *adj* not befitting a soldier.

unsolicited [uns*oli*sitid] *adj* not requested, gratuitous.

unsolvable [un*solv*ab'l] *adj* incapable of being solved.

unsolved [un*solvd*] *adj* not solved; unexplained.

unsophisticated [uns*ofistik*aytid] *adj* inexperienced, simple-minded, naive; unadulterated; (*of machines*) comparatively simple, without complex refinements.

unsought [un*sawt*] *adj* not sought, not asked for.

unsound [un*sownd*] *adj* in bad physical or mental condition; damaged, weakened; rotten; based on error; (*of sleep*) not deep, not unbroken; **of u.**

mind (*leg*) mad, not responsible through mental disturbance ~ **unsoundly** *adv* ~ **unsoundness** *n*.

unsparing [un*spair*Ring] *adj* showing no mercy; lavish, profuse ~ **unsparingly** *adv*.

unspeakable [un*speek*ab'l] *adj* impossible to express in words; indescribable (*usu* in bad sense) ~ **unspeakably** *adv*.

unspecialized [un*spesh*alIzd] *adj* not specialized; general; (*biol*) not specially adapted to a particular habitat or mode of life.

unspecified [un*spesi*fId] *adj* not definitely mentioned or indicated.

unspent [un*spent*] *adj* not spent or used up; unexhausted.

unspoilt [un*spoilt*] *adj* not spoilt, undamaged; (*of a child*) not over-indulged.

unsporting [un*spawr*ting] *adj* unsportsmanlike, not fair.

unsportsmanlike [un*spawrts*manlIk] *adj* not behaving as a sportsman should; unchivalrous.

unspotted [un*spot*id] *adj* unstained; (*fig*) blameless, honourable, pure.

unsprung [un*spR*ung] *adj* without springs; (*of a trap*) still set.

unstable [un*stayb*'l] *adj* not stable, not steady; fickle, unreliable; easily losing mental or emotional balance; (*chem*) easily decomposed.

unsteady [un*stedi*] *adj* not steady; (*fig*) unreliable; profligate ~ **unsteadily** *adv* ~ **unsteadiness** *n*.

unstick (*p/t* and *p/part* **unstuck**) [un*stik*] *v/t* and *i* release or separate what is stuck; cease to adhere; (*sl, of aircraft*) take off.

unstinted [un*stint*id] *adj* lavish, unrestricted.

unstinting [un*stin*ting] *adj* lavishly given; unqualified.

unstop (*pres/part* **unstopping**, *p/t* and *p/part* **unstopped**) [un*stop*] *v/t* take out stopper from; free from obstruction.

unstopped [un*stopt*] *adj* not stopped or blocked; (*phon*) formed with air-passage partly open; (*pros*) with no marked break in syntax at end of line.

unstoppered [un*stop*erd] *adj* without a stopper.

unstrap (*pres/part* **unstrapping**, *p/t* and *p/part* **unstrapped**) [un*stR*ap] *v/t* undo or remove straps from.

unstring (*p/t* and *p/part* **unstrung**) [un*stR*ing] *v/t* loosen or remove strings of; remove (beads *etc*) from a string.

unstrung [un*stR*ung] *adj* with the strings slack or removed; (*fig*) dismayed, with nerves on edge.

unstuck [un*stuk*] *p/t* and *p/part* of **unstick** ~ **unstuck** *adj* not stuck or gummed together; **come u.** go amiss, fail, break down.

unstudied [un*stud*id] *adj* spontaneous, natural; unversed (in).

unsubsidized [un*sub*sidIzd] *adj* not supported by money grants.

unsubstantial [unsub*stan*shal] *adj* lacking substance; not solid or firm; (*of meal*) light; (*fig*) with no trustworthy base, unreal.

unsubstantiated [unsub*stan*shi-aytid] *adj* not supported or confirmed by evidence.

unsuccessful [unsuk*ses*fool] *adj* not successful ~ **unsuccessfully** *adv*.

unsuitability [unsewta*bili*ti] *n* condition of being unsuitable.

unsuitable [un*sew*tab'l] *adj* not meeting requirements; unbecoming ~ **unsuitably** *adv*.

unsuited [un*sew*tid] *adj* not adapted (for); incompatible; having no cards of a particular suit.

unsullied [un*sul*id] *adj* not tarnished or stained; (*fig*) pure, blameless.

unsung [un*sung*] *adj* not sung; not celebrated in poetry; not as famous as one deserves to be.

unsure [un*shoor*] *adj* insecure, uncertain; unreliable; doubtful.

unsuspected [unsus*pek*tid] *adj* not thought guilty; not believed to exist.

unsuspecting [unsus*pek*ting] *adj* feeling no suspicion ~ **unsuspectingly** *adv*.

unsuspicious [unsus*pish*us] *adj* feeling no suspicion; arousing no suspicion ~ **unsuspiciously** *adv* ~ **unsuspiciousness** *n*.

unswayed [un*swayd*] *adj* not influenced (by); unprejudiced.

unswerving [un*swur*ving] *adj* not deviating; (*fig*) firm, loyal ~ **unswervingly** *adv*.

unsympathetic [unsimpa*thet*ik] *adj* feeling or expressing no sympathy, hard-hearted; rousing dislike, antipathetic ~ **unsympathetically** *adv*.

unsystematic [unsiste*mat*ik] *adj* not according to a system or plan; haphazard ~ **unsystematically** *adv*.

untack [un*tak*] *v/t* unfasten by taking out tacking threads or tacks.

untamed [un*taymd*] *adj* still wild, unsubdued, uncontrolled.

untangle [un*tang*-g'l] *v/t* disentangle.

untanned [un*tand*] *adj* (*of hides*) not dressed; (*of skin*) not sunburnt.

untapped [un*tapt*] *adj* not yet used or drawn upon.

untaught [un*tawt*] *adj* uneducated, ignorant; not acquired from teaching, spontaneous.

untaxed [un*takst*] *adj* not taxed; (*fig*) not overburdened.

unteachable [un*teech*ab'l] *adj* that cannot be taught.

untenable [un*ten*ab'l/un*teen*ab'll] *adj* that cannot be defended successfully against attack; (*of argument*) impossible to maintain.

untended [un*tend*id] *adj* neglected.

untether [un*teTH*er] *v/t* set free (tethered animals).

unthink (*p/t* and *p/part* **unthought**) [un*think*] *v/t* rid one's mind of (opinions previously held).

unthinkable [un*think*ab'l] *adj* incredible, impracticable, out of the question; too horrible to think about; (*log*) that cannot be either affirmed or denied.

unthinking [un*think*ing] *adj* thoughtless, inconsiderate ~ **unthinkingly** *adv*.

unthought-of [un*thawt*-of] *adj* not thought of; not imagined; entirely unexpected.

unthread [un*thRed*] *v/t* remove thread from (a needle); (*fig*) find the way through, unravel.

untidily [un*tId*ili] *adv* in an untidy way.

untidiness [un*tId*inis] *n* condition of being untidy.

untidy [un*tId*i] *adj* (*of room etc*) in disorder; (*of person*) slovenly.

untie [un*tI*] *v/t* undo (knot or something tied).

until [un*til*] *prep* up to the time of ~ **until** *conj* up to the time that.

untimely [un*tI*mli] *adj* before the proper time,

premature; at the wrong time, inopportune ~ **untimely** *adv* prematurely; inopportunely.

untinged [un*tinjd*] *adj* not tinged; (*fig*) unaffected; **not u. with** slightly modified by.

untiring [un*tIr*Ring] *adj* tireless, unflagging ~ **untiringly** *adv.*

unto [*un*too] *prep* (*poet* and *ar*) to.

untold [un*tOld*] *adj* not narrated or revealed; not possible to count, unlimited.

untouchable [un*tuch*ab'l] *adj* not possible to touch; not to be touched; not fit to touch ~ **untouchable** *n* member of the lowest group in the Hindu caste system; (*fig*) despised outcast.

untouched [un*tucht*] *adj* not touched; not equalled; intact; not emotionally moved.

untoward [un*tO*-erd/untoo*wawrd*] *adj* inconvenient, regrettable; (*ar*) unseemly; stubborn.

untraceable [un*tRays*ab'l] *adj* that cannot be discovered.

untrained [un*tRaynd*] *adj* without training; uninstructed.

untrammelled [un*tRam*eld] *adj* not restricted, free.

untravelled [un*tRav*eld] *adj* without experience of foreign travel; not visited by travellers.

untried [un*tRId*] *adj* not tested; not tried in court.

untrodden [un*tRod*'n] *adj* unfrequented, remote.

untroubled [un*tRub*'ld] *adj* unperturbed, calm.

untrue [un*tROO*] *adj* not true; erroneous; unfaithful; not in strict accordance with a certain standard or type ~ **untruly** *adv.*

untruss [un*tRus*] *v/t* undo, unfasten.

untrustworthy [un*tRust*wur*THi*] *adj* not to be relied upon; dishonest.

untruth [un*tROOth*] *n* falsehood, a lie.

untruthful [un*tROOth*fool] *adj* not speaking the truth; not true, false; apt to tell lies ~ **untruthfully** *adv* ~ **untruthfulness** *n.*

untutored [un*tew*terd] *adj* not educated or trained; uncultivated; barbarous.

untwine [un*twIn*] *v/t* and *i* unwind, unravel.

untwist [un*twist*] *v/t* and *i* twist backwards and so slacken; become untwisted.

unused (1) [un*yOOzd*] *adj* not made use of.

unused (2) [un*yOOst*] *adj* not accustomed (to).

unusual [un*yOO*zhoo-al] *adj* not usual, rare; exceptional ~ **unusually** *adv* in an unusual way; (*coll*) extremely, very.

unutterable [un*ute*Rab'l] *adj* indescribable; (*coll*) thoroughgoing, complete.

unvalued [un*valewd*] *adj* not submitted to valuation; considered of no value.

unvaried [un*vair*Rid] *adj* unchanging; tedious.

unvarnished [un*vaar*nisht] *adj* not varnished; (*fig*) plain, unadorned.

unvarying [un*vair*Ri-ing] *adj* unchanging; invariable ~ **unvaryingly** *adv.*

unveil [un*vayl*] *v/t* and *i* remove veil from; make visible; take off one's veil; (*fig*) reveal oneself.

unverifiable [un*ve*Rif1-ab'l] *adj* that cannot be verified.

unverified [un*ve*Rif1d] *adj* not confirmed as true.

unversed [un*vurst*] *adj* unskilled, uninstructed.

unvoiced [un*voist*] *adj* unspoken; (*phon*) uttered without vibration of vocal chords.

unwanted [un*wont*id] *adj* not wanted.

unwarily [un*wair*Rili] *adv* in an unwary way.

unwariness [un*wair*Rines] *n* state of being unwary.

unwarlike [un*wawr*lik] *adj* not warlike, unmilitary; peaceable.

unwarrantable [un*wo*Rantab'l] *adj* unjustifiable, indefensible ~ **unwarrantably** *adv.*

unwarranted [un*wo*Rantid] *adj* not justified, unauthorized.

unwary [un*wair*Ri] *adj* not on the alert; rash, incautious.

unwashed [un*wosht*] *adj* not washed; not touched by water (of river *etc*); not in the habit of washing; **the great u.** (*obs coll*) the mob.

unwavering [un*wayve*Ring] *adj* steadfast, firm ~ **unwaveringly** *adv.*

unweaned [un*weend*] *adj* still fed on breast-milk; (*of animals*) not yet separated from the dam.

unwearable [un*wair*Rab'l] *adj* not fit to be worn; not likely to wear out.

unwearied [un*weer*Rid] *adj* not tired; indefatigable.

unwearying [un*weer*Ri-ing] *adj* untiring, indefatigable; persistent.

unwed [un*wed*] *adj* not married.

unwedded [un*wed*id] *adj* not married.

unwelcome [un*vel*kum] *adj* not welcome, not received with pleasure.

unwell [un*wel*] *adj* not well, ill; menstruous.

unwept [un*wept*] *adj* not wept for, unlamented.

unwholesome [un*hOl*sum] *adj* harmful to health; harmful to morals; symptomatic of unhealthiness, morbid ~ **unwholesomely** *adv* ~ **unwholesomeness** *n.*

unwieldy [un*weel*di] *adj* moving with difficulty, clumsy; difficult to use because of weight, shape *etc*; unmanageable, cumbersome.

unwifely [un*wIf*li] *adj* unworthy of a wife.

unwilling [un*wil*ing] *adj* not willing, reluctant ~ **unwillingly** *adv* ~ **unwillingness** *n.*

unwind (*p/t* and *p/part* **unwound**) [un*wInd*] *v/t* and *i* wind off (what has been wound up); become unwound; (*sl*) relax, calm down.

unwinking [un*wink*ing] *adj* with wide-open eyes; (*fig*) vigilant.

unwise [un*wIz*] *adj* not wise, foolish ~ **unwisely** *adv.*

unwitting [un*wit*ing] *adj* unaware; unintentional ~ **unwittingly** *adv* inadvertently.

unwomanly [un*woo*manli] *adj* not womanly, unbecoming to a woman.

unwonted [un*wOnt*id] *adj* unaccustomed, unusual.

unworkable [un*wurk*ab'l] *adj* impossible or difficult to carry out or manage.

unworldly [un*wurld*li] *adj* not worldly, not materialistic, spiritually-minded.

unworn [un*wawrn*] *adj* not showing signs of wear; never having been worn.

unworthy [un*wur*THi] *adj* not worthy, not deserving respect; worthless; undeserving (of) ~ **unworthily** *adv* ~ **unworthiness** *n.*

unwound [un*wownd*] *p/t* and *p/part* of **unwind**.

unwounded [un*wOOnd*id] *adj* not wounded.

unwrap (*pres/part* **unwrapping**, *p/t* and *p/part* **unwrapped**) [un*Rap*] *v/t* remove wrapping from.

unwritten [un*Rit*en] *adj* not written down; unrecorded; **the u. law** assumption that murder done in revenge for an attack on the virtue of one's wife or daughter is justifiable.

unwrought [unRawt] *adj* left unfinished; not elaborated.

unwrung [unRung] *adj* not subjected to wringing; (*fig*) not agonized by worry or pain.

unyielding [unyeelding] *adj* firm, resolute.

unyoke [unyOk] *v/t* free (a draught animal) from the yoke; disconnect (plough).

unzip (*pres/part* **unzipping**, *p/t* and *p/part* **unzipped**) [unzip] *v/t* undo by opening the zip-fastener of.

up [up] *adv* to a higher position than before, upward; on horseback; on to one's feet from a recumbent position; into prominence, vogue; before a judge, court *etc*; (*of assembly*) risen, ended; in residence at school or university; **u. against** confronted with; **well u. in** expert in; **u. to** capable of, equal to, expert in; **be u. to something** be secretly active; **it's all u.** (*coll*) there is no more hope; **what's u.?** (*coll*) what is the matter?; **u. with** (*interj*) hurrah for ~ **up** *prep* upwards towards the top of; along (river) to its source; against the current; **u. stage** at the back of the stage ~ **up** *n* an upward movement; **ups and downs** good and bad luck; **on the u. and u.** (*coll*) getting on, improving; honest, on the level ~ **up** *adj* placed in or moving towards a higher or better position; **on the u. grade** tending to improve; **u. train** train going to the city ~ **up** (*pres/part* **upping**, *p/t* and *p/part* **upped**) *v/i* (*coll*) rise abruptly; begin suddenly or boldly (to do something); **u. with** raise, brandish.

up- *pref* upward, in a higher position.

up-and-coming [up-and-kuming] *adj* making rapid progress in career *etc*, seeming likely to be a success.

Upanishad [oopanishad] *n* one of several Sanskrit philosophical treatises.

upas [yOOpas] *n* fabulous tree said to poison the air around it; (*bot*) a Javanese tree which yields a poisonous juice; (*fig*) poisonous or destructive influence.

upbeat [upbeet] *n* (*mus*) unaccented beat, *esp* the last of a bar ~ **upbeat** *adj* cheerful, optimistic.

upbraid [up-bRayd] *v/t* reproach.

upbringing [upbRinging] *n* rearing and education of the young.

upcast [upkaast] *n* (*geol*) upward dislocation of a seam; ventilating shaft of a mine > PDE ~ **upcast** [upkaast] *adj* turned upwards.

up-country [up-kuntRi] *adj* and *n* (in or from) the interior parts of a country; ignorant, naive.

upcurrent [upkuRent] *n* upward trend.

update [updayt] *v/t* (*coll*) bring into line with latest developments, bring up-to-date.

upend [upend] *v/t* cause to stand up on end.

upgrade [upgRayd] *n* upward slope; **on the u.** ascending; (*fig*) improving ~ **upgrade** [up-gRayd] *v/t* advance (employee) to work of greater responsibility; raise the status of; put higher price on ~ **upgrade** *adv* uphill.

upheaval [up-heeval] *n* sudden far-reaching change or disturbance; commotion; earthquake; eruption.

upheave [up-heev] *v/t* lift up, *esp* with violence.

upheld [up-held] *p/t* and *p/part* of **uphold**.

uphill [up-hil] *adj* ascending; (*fig*) difficult, strenuous ~ **uphill** [up-hil] *adv* towards the top of a hill.

uphold (*p/t* and *p/part* **upheld**) [up-hOld] *v/t* hold up, support; countenance; maintain.

upholster [up-hOlster] *v/t* furnish (room) with carpets, curtains *etc*; stuff and cover (chair *etc*); **well upholstered** (*coll*) plump.

upholsterer [up-hOlsteReR] *n* one whose trade is to stuff and cover chairs *etc*; one who sells upholstery goods.

upholstery [up-hOlsteRi] *n* carpets, curtains, padded and sprung furniture *etc*; trade of an upholsterer.

upkeep [upkeep] *n* maintenance and good repair; cost of this.

upland [upland] *n* (*freq pl*) higher land of a region ~ **upland** *adj* situated, living, growing on high ground.

uplift [uplift] *v/t* raise; hold high; raise the spirits of, cheer; edify, improve the moral or spiritual condition of ~ **uplift** [uplift] *n* momentary joy, enthusiasm *etc*; (*iron*) moral edification, pious talk; (*eng*) upward force on a structure > PDE; (*geol*) upheaval of earth's surface.

upmost [upmOst] *adj* uppermost, highest.

upon [upon] *prep* on.

upper [uper] *adj* higher, above, more elevated; further up or inland; forming the higher part of a building; superior in rank or position; **u. case** (*typ*) case containing capital letters; **u. dog** the victor; **u. hand** mastery, advantage; **U. House** House of Lords; **u. storey** any storey of a house other than the ground floor; (*sl*) head, brains; **u. ten** (*coll*) the aristocracy ~ **upper** *n* part of boot or shoe above the sole; (**down**) **on one's uppers** (*sl*) desperately poor.

upper-bracket [uper-bRakit] *adj* (*coll*) near the top of a graded list.

upper-class [uper-klaas] *adj* of, belonging to or characteristic of the highest social class.

upper-crust [uper-kRust] *adj* (*sl*) upper-class.

uppercut [uperkut] *n* (*boxing*) upward blow to the chin.

uppermost [upermOst] *adj* highest; (*fig*) predominant ~ **uppermost** *adv* in the highest position.

upperworks [uperwurks] *n* (*naut*) superstructure above upper deck.

uppish [upish] *adj* (*coll*) conceited, arrogant; impudent; snobbish ~ **uppishly** *adj* ~ **uppishness** *n*.

uppity [upiti] *adj* (*US coll*) impudently claiming one's freedom, rights *etc*; conceited, uppish.

upright [upRit] *adj* erect, perpendicular; (*fig*) righteous, honest, just, honourable; **u. piano** one with vertical strings ~ **upright** *n* upright beam, pillar *etc*; upright piano.

uprising [upRIzing] *n* revolt, insurrection; (*ar*) act of getting up.

uproar [upRawr] *n* confused noise of shouting, tumult.

uproarious [upRawr-Ri-us] *adj* noisy, boisterous; jovial ~ **uproariously** *adv* ~ **uproariousness** *n*.

uproot [upROOt] *v/t* tear up by the roots; (*fig*) destroy.

uprush [upRush] *n* sudden strong upward flow or movement; upward surge.

upset (*pres/part* **upsetting**, *p/t* and *p/part* **upset**) [up*set*] *v/t* and *i* knock over, turn over; capsize; disturb the calm of, distress; annoy; make ill; put out of order; be overthrown or knocked over ~ **upset** *n* act of upsetting; state of disorder; trouble, annoyance, cause of distress; (*coll*) quarrel; (*carp*) defect in timber ~ **upset** *adj* distressed, grieved; annoyed; **u. price** (*at auction*) lowest price at which a property will be sold.

upsetting [up*set*ing] *adj* causing distress or unwelcome disturbance.

upshot [*up*shot] *n* final result, conclusion.

upside [*up*sīd] *n* upper side or surface.

upside-down [upsīd-*down*] *adv* so that the upper part becomes the lower; **turn u.** throw into confusion.

upsides [up*sīdz*] *adv* **u. with** (*coll*) even with, quits with; alongside of.

upstage [up*stayj*] *adv* (*theat*) away from the footlights, towards back of stage ~ **upstage** *adj* (*sl*) supercilious, snobbish ~ **upstage** *v/t* (*theat*) divert attention from (someone) to oneself.

upstairs [up*stairz*] *n* upper part of a house ~ **upstairs** *adv* towards or in the upper part of a house ~ **upstairs, upstair** [up*stairz*, *up*stair] *adj* in or belonging to the upper part of a house.

upstanding [up*stand*ing] *adj* standing upright, tall and strong; (*fig*) honest, straightforward.

upstart [*up*staart] *n* one who has suddenly risen in importance, *esp* one who therefore acts presumptuously and arrogantly ~ **upstart** *adj*.

upstream [upst*Reem*] *adv* against the current, towards the source ~ **upstream** *adj* situated higher up a stream; moving against the current.

upstroke [*up*stROk] *n* mark made by upward stroke of pen.

upsurge [*up*surj] *n* an upward surge; uprising; a sudden increase.

upswept [up*swept*] *adj* brushed, curved, or sloped upward.

upsy-daisy [*up*si-dayzi] *interj* (*coll*) exclamation used in picking up something, *esp* a child.

upswing [*up*swing] *n* new upward movement, upsurge; upward swing.

uptake [*up*tayk] *n* amount taken up by machine *etc*; intake; understanding, perception; **quick on the u.** (*coll*) intelligent.

upthrow [*up*thRO] *n* (*geol*) upward dislocation of seam.

upthrust [*up*thRust] *n* (*geol*) upheaval of part of the earth's crust.

uptight [up*tīt*] *adj* (*sl*) very tense or nervous.

up-to-date [*up*-to-dayt] *adj* having or informed of all the latest improvements, knowledge, fashions, developments *etc*.

uptown [*up*town] *adj* (*US*) of or in the residential areas of a town.

upturn [up*turn*] *v/t* and *i* turn up or over; turn upside-down; turn upward ~ **upturn** [*up*turn] *n* an upward turn, improvement.

upvalue [up*valew*] *v/t* (*comm*) increase nominal value of.

upward [*up*ward] *adv* in or towards a higher position; towards a higher price; up the course of a stream; along the course of one's life ~ **upward** *adj* ascending.

upwards [*up*wardz] *adv* upward; **u. of** more than; **and u.** and more.

upwind [*up*wind] *adj* and *adv* in the direction opposite to that of the wind.

ur- *pref* primitive, original.

uraemia [yOO*Reem*i-a] *n* (*path*) unhealthy condition of blood caused by presence of urine in it.

uraemic [yOO*Reem*ik] *adj* of or suffering from uraemia.

uraeus [yOO*Ree*-us] *n* figure of the sacred asp or serpent, symbol of royalty in ancient Egypt.

uranian [yOO*Rayn*i-an] *adj* (*poet*) celestial, spiritual; of non-sexual love, platonic; (*psych*) homosexual; (*astron*) of Uranus.

uranism [yOO*Rayn*izm] *n* homosexuality involving also aversion from the opposite sex.

uranium [yOO*Rayn*i-um] *n* metallic element with many radioactive and unstable isotopes, used as source of nuclear energy.

uranous [yOO*Ran*us] *adj* containing or pertaining to uranium.

Uranus [yOO*Rayn*us] *n* planet between Saturn and Neptune > PDS.

urban [*ur*ban] *adj* of or like a town or city; **u. guerrilla** political terrorist who plants bombs and kills or kidnaps in towns; **u. sprawl** uncontrolled spreading of a town.

urbane [ur*bayn*] *adj* having imperturbable good manners, suave; courteous ~ **urbanely** *adv*.

urbanity [ur*ban*iti] *n* quality of being urbane.

urbanization [urbanīza*yshon*] *n* process of urbanizing.

urbanize [*urb*anīz] *v/t* make urban; change (a place) in character from rural to urban.

urchin [*urch*in] *n* mischievous small boy; (*dial*) hedgehog.

Urdu [oord*OO*] *n* form of Hindustani, spoken principally by the Muslims of Pakistan.

urea [yOO*Ree*-a] *n* (*chem*) white crystalline organic compound found in urine > PDS; **u. formaldehyde** plastic material made from urea and formalin, used to make buttons, cups *etc*.

ureter [yOO*Ree*ter] *n* duct conveying urine from kidney to bladder > PDB.

urethane [*y*OO*Rith*ayn] *n* (*chem*) ethyl carbonate; white powder derived from urea, used as a solvent, fungicide and in lacquers.

urethra [yOO*Reeth*Ra] *n* duct discharging urine from bladder.

urethritis [yewReeth*Rī*tis] *n* (*med*) inflammation of urethra.

uretic [yOO*Ret*ik] *adj* pertaining to urine.

urge [urj] *v/t* drive or force forward; earnestly exhort; advocate earnestly; entreat (person) to take some step ~ **urge** *n* drive from within, inner compulsion; strong tendency towards performing some act, *esp* sexual.

urgency [*ur*jensi] *n* quality of being urgent.

urgent [*ur*jent] *adj* requiring speedy action; making pressing demands; highly important ~ **urgently** *adv*.

urging [*ur*jing] *adj* pressing, importunate.

uric [*y*OO*Rik*] *adj* of urine; **u. acid** main nitrogenous constituent of urine > PDB.

urinal [yOO*Rīn*al/yOO*Rī*nal] *n* vessel used as receptacle for urine; building or enclosure for urinating.

urinary [yOO*Rīn*eRi] *adj* pertaining to urine.

urinate [yOO*Rīn*ayt] *v/i* discharge urine.

urination [yOORin*ay*shon] *n* discharge of urine.

urine [*yOO*Rin] *n* yellow liquid secreted by kidneys.

urinous [*yOO*Rinus] *adj* of, like, or derived from urine.

urn [*urn*] *n* large lidded metal vessel with tap, in which water, tea *etc* may be heated and kept; (*arch*) large earthenware or metal vase, *esp* for ashes of the dead; casket for cremated ashes.

uro- *pref* of urine; of urination.

uroscopy [yOORos*kopi*] *n* (*med*) examination of urine to diagnose disease.

ursine [*urs*In] *adj* of or like a bear.

urticaria [urtikair*Ri*-a] *n* (*med*) nettlerash.

us [*us*] *pers pron objective case of* we.

usable [*yOO*zab'l] *adj* that can be used.

usage [*yOO*sij] *n* manner of use; habitual practice creating a standard; customary procedure.

usance [*yOO*zans] *n* custom, usage; (*comm*) time allowed for payment of foreign bills of exchange.

use [*yOOs*] *n* act of using something for a purpose; ability, power or right to use; need, purpose or reason for using or doing; usefulness, advantage, purpose served; wont, custom, familiarity; (*eccles*) distinctive ceremonial or liturgy; (*leg*) profit or benefit from a trust; **have no u. for** (*coll*) think tedious, dislike; **in u.** not obsolete; **of u.** useful; **of no u.** useless; **out of u.** no longer used ~ **use** [*yOOz*] *v/t* and *i* make use of, put to use; employ, handle properly; consume entirely; treat (well or badly); (*p/t only*) be wont or accustomed (to do something); **u. up** consume entirely.

used (1) [*yOOzd*] *adj* that has been used; worn, secondhand; **u. up** (*coll*) utterly exhausted.

used (2) [*yOOst*] *adj* accustomed (to); experienced (in).

useful [*yOOs*fool] *adj* that is effective when used, serviceable; helpful; (*sl*) very capable, effective; **u. life** period during which something is serviceable ~ **usefully** *adv* ~ **usefulness** *n*.

useless [*yOO*slis] *adj* that gives no help or service, not useful; inefficient, incompetent; that cannot succeed, hopeless, in vain ~ **uselessly** *adv* ~ **uselessness** *n*.

user (1) [*yOO*zer] *n* one who uses.

user (2) *n* (*leg*) the enjoyment of a right; **right of u.** right based on continual use.

usher [*usher*] *n* official who shows people to their seats in a public hall *etc*; one who walks before a dignitary in procession; (*obs*) junior master in a boys' school ~ **usher** *v/t* act as usher to (a person); announce, show (in); (*of things*) precede, herald; **u. in** bring in (a banquet); inaugurate, initiate.

usherette [ushe*Ret*] *n* female attendant in a theatre or cinema who shows patrons to their seats.

usual [*yOO*zhoo-al] *adj* customary; normal, prevalent; commonplace; **as u.** as is customary ~ **usual** *n* (*coll*) normal health; habitual drink.

usually [*yOO*zhoo-ali] *adv* as a matter of use or custom; habitually, generally.

usufruct [*yOO*zhoofRukt] *n* (*leg*) right of temporary possession and use of property belonging to another without causing damage to it.

usurer [*yOO*zhuRer] *n* one who lends money at interest, *esp* at exorbitant interest.

usurious [yOO*zhoo*Ri-us] *adj* of, like, or involving usury; exorbitant; practising usury, extortionate; characteristic of a usurer.

usurp [yOO*zurp*] *v/t* appropriate wrongfully; seize forcibly.

usurpation [yOOzurp*ay*shon] *n* act of usurping, *esp* of sovereign power.

usurpatory [yOO*zurp*ateRi] *adj* characterized by usurpation.

usurper [yOO*zurp*er] *n* one who usurps, *esp* one who wrongfully seizes the throne and sovereign power.

usury [*yOO*zhuRi] *n* act of lending money at exorbitant interest; (*fig*) interest on money.

utensil [yOO*ten*sil] *n* any implement or tool used for a particular purpose; vessel or container used for domestic purposes.

uterine [*yOO*teRIn] *adj* (*med*) of or in the uterus; having the same mother, but a different father.

uterus [*yOO*teRus] *n* (*med*) womb > PDB.

utilitarian [yOOtili*tair*Ri-an] *adj* practical, devised for or aiming at usefulness; functional; working for material ends only; of or believing in utilitarianism ~ **utilitarian** *n* believer in utilitarianism.

utilitarianism [yOOtili*tair*Ri-anizm] *n* ethical doctrine that an act is good in so far as it leads to the greatest good of the greatest number of people; practice of judging an act by the degree of its practical usefulness.

utility [yOO*til*iti] *n* serviceableness, usefulness; (*pl*) useful things; any useful service provided for the public ~ **utility** *adj* standardized and severely practical; **u. room** room for storing household equipment.

utilizable [yOOtil*Iz*ab'l] *adj* capable of being used.

utilize [*yOO*tilIz] *v/t* make profitable use of.

utmost [*utm*Ost] *adj* farthest, outermost; of the greatest degree, most extreme ~ **utmost** *n* the most that can be done.

utopia [yOO*tO*pi-a] *n* ideally well organized social community, place where everything is perfect; (*cap*) a fictional island enjoying perfect government.

utopian [yOO*tO*pi-an] *adj* of or like Utopia; ideally perfect but unpractical ~ **Utopian** *n* inhabitant of Utopia.

utricle [*yOO*tRik'l] *n* (*anat*) a sac-like expansion in the vestibule of the inner ear.

utter (1) [*uter*] *adj* complete, extreme.

utter (2) *v/t* produce audibly with the voice; put (false coin, notes) into circulation; publish (a libel).

utterance [*ute*Rans] *n* act of speaking; manner of speaking, delivery; speech.

utterly [*uter*li] *adv* entirely, totally.

uttermost [*uterm*Ost] *adj* outermost, farthest away; utmost ~ **uttermost** *n* the utmost.

U-turn [*yOO*-turn] *n* (*mot*) act of turning a car round to face in direction from which it came; (*pol*) reversal of previous policy.

uvula (*pl* **uvulae**) [*yOO*vyOOla] *n* (*anat*) fleshy appendage, hanging from the soft palate, at the back of the mouth cavity.

uvular [*yOO*vyOOlar] *adj* (*phon*) pronounced with vibration of the uvula.

uxorious [uks*awr*Ri-us] *adj* excessively devoted to and fond of one's wife ~ **uxoriously** *adv* ~ **uxoriousness** *n*.

V

v [*vee*] twenty-second letter of English alphabet; the Roman numeral 5; (*abbr*) (*Lat*) versus (against).

V.C. Victoria Cross; **V.D.** venereal disease; **V.I.P.** (*coll abbr*) very important person; **V neck** the top front part of dress cut in shape of a V; **V sign** derisive obscene gesture made by forming a V with two fingers pointed upwards.

vac [*vak*] *n* (*coll abbr*) vacation.

vacancy [*vayk*ansi] *n* vacant post; empty space, gap, deficiency; state of being empty or unoccupied; (*fig*) lack of intelligence.

vacant [*vayk*ant] *adj* not occupied, not in use; waiting to be filled; empty; having no tenant; blankly stupid ~ **vacantly** *adv.*

vacate [*vak*ayt] *v/t* leave place or post vacant.

vacation [*vak*ayshon] *n* act of leaving vacant; fixed holiday period between law and university terms.

vaccinate [*vaks*inayt] *v/t* inoculate with a vaccine.

vaccination [*vaks*inayshon] *n* inoculation with a vaccine, *esp* that of cowpox as protection against smallpox.

vaccinationist [*vaks*inayshonist] *n* one who advocates vaccination.

vaccinator [*vaks*inayter] *n* one who vaccinates.

vaccine [*vaks*een] *n* a preparation of a virus (*orig* that of cowpox) used for inoculation.

vacillate [*vas*ilayt] *v/i* hesitate, be undecided.

vacillation [*vas*ilayshon] *n* hesitation, indecision.

vacuity [*vak*ewiti] *n* emptiness; lack of intelligence.

vacuole [*vak*ew-Ol] *n* (*biol*) fluid-filled space within the plasma-membrane of a cell > PDB.

vacuous [*vak*ew-us] *adj* empty; stupid; expressionless ~ **vacuously** *adj.*

vacuum [*vak*ew-um] *n* empty space, void, blank; a space in which there are no molecules or atoms > PDS; (*pop*) space containing air or other gas at very low pressure; **v. brake** continuous brake system used on passenger trains; **v. cleaner** apparatus that removes dust from carpets *etc* by suction; **v. flask** bottle-shaped vessel with two walls separated by a vacuum, used to keep liquids at a constant temperature; **v. pump** pump that extracts steam or air from a space to maintain a pressure below atmospheric; **v. tube** (*elect*) evacuated glass or metal envelope through which an electric current is passed.

vagabond [*vag*abond] *n* vagrant with no fixed abode, tramp; (*coll*) rascal ~ **vagabond** *adj* wandering, unsettled, irregular ~ **vagabond** *v/i* wander about like a vagabond.

vagary [*vayg*eRi/*vag*airRi] *n* eccentric, whimsical notion o~ action.

vagina [*vaj*Ina] *n* duct of female mammal connecting uterus with exterior > PDB; (*bot*) sheath-like portion of leaf-base.

vaginal [*vaj*Inal] *adj* sheath-like; of, for, or through the vagina.

vagrancy [*vayg*Ransi] *n* condition of living as a vagrant.

vagrant [*vayg*Rant] *n* beggar with no fixed abode ~ **vagrant** *adj* wandering like a tramp; (*fig*) wayward.

vague [*vayg*] *adj* not distinct or definite; mentally inexact, hazy ~ **vaguely** *adv* ~ **vagueness** *n.*

vain [*vayn*] *adj* useless, unavailing; lacking real worth, trivial, empty; conceited; **in v.** uselessly; to no purpose; **take God's name in v.** invoke Him without due respect, profanely.

vainglorious [*vayng*lawrRi-us] *adj* ostentatiously boastful.

vainglory [*vayng*lawrRi] *n* ostentatious vanity, excessive boastfulness.

vainly [*vayn*li] *adv* uselessly; conceitedly.

valance [*val*ans] *n* short curtain above a window or concealing space underneath a bed ~ **valanced** *adj.*

vale [*vayl*] *n* (*poet*) valley.

valediction [*val*idikshon] *n* a farewell; word or words of farewell.

valedictory [*val*idikteRi] *n* (*US*) farewell oration delivered by senior scholar at graduation ~ **valedictory** *adj* relating to, of the nature of, a valediction.

valence [*vay*lens] *n* (*chem*) valency; (*biol*) ability of a substance to combine with or affect an organism *etc.*

valency [*vay*lensi] *n* (*chem*) combining power of an atom; number of hydrogen atoms which an atom will combine with or replace; **v. bond** link holding atoms together in a molecule > PDS.

valentine [*val*entIn] *n* sweetheart; greeting card decorated with emblems and amorous messages sent anonymously on St Valentine's Day, 14 February.

valerian [*val*eerRian] *n* perennial herb with clusters of pink or white flowers; medicinal root of this.

valet [*val*it/*val*ay] *n* manservant employed to attend to a man's clothes *etc* ~ **valet** *v/t* and *i* clean, mend, brush *etc* (clothes); act as valet (to).

valetudinarian [*val*itewdinairRi-an] *n* and *adj* (person) in poor health; (person) unduly concerned about his health.

Valhalla [*val*hala] *n* (*Norse myth*) Odin's hall in which slain heroes are feasted.

valiant [*val*yant] *adj* brave, courageous ~ **valiantly** *adv.*

valid [*val*id] *n* (*of argument*) soundly based (*leg*) having legal force and authority.

validate [*val*idayt] *v/t* make valid; confirm.

validity [*val*iditi] *n* quality of being valid.

validly [*val*idli] *adv* in a valid manner.

valise [*val*eez] *n* travelling bag; (*mil*) kitbag.

valkyrie [*valk*iRi, valk*I*rRi] *n* (*Norse myth*) type of minor goddess of battle who protected certain warriors, chose which should be slain, led the dead to Valhalla *etc.*

valley [*val*i] *n* long, narrow depression in the earth's surface with a fairly regular downward slope > PDG; (*bui*) intersection between two sloping surfaces of a roof.

vallum [*val*um] *n* (*Lat mil*) defensive rampart.

valorous [*vale*Rus] *adj* exhibiting valour; requiring valour, performed with valour ∼ **valorously** *adv*.

valour [*vale*r] *n* courage, bravery in battle.

valuable [*vale*w-ab'l] *adj* worth much money, costly; very useful; of great worth ∼ **valuable** *n* (*usu pl*) article of value, jewellery *etc* ∼ **valuably** *adv*.

valuation [valew-*ay*shon] *n* estimation of a thing's value or of a person's merit; the value so arrived at.

valuator [valew-*ay*ter] *n* one who gives a valuation; valuer.

value [*vale*w] *n* worth; worth reckoned in money, marketable price; fair equivalent; usefulness; estimation, valuation; desirability, importance; (*arts*) gradation of tone from light to dark > PDAA; (*of word, syllable*) precise meaning or force; (*pl*) ethical standards; **v. judgement** assessment of moral or artistic worth ∼ **value** *v/t* assess value of; esteem, think highly of.

value-added [*vale*w-adid] *adj* **v. tax** tax levied on the increase in value of a product at each stage of its manufacture and marketing.

valued [*vale*wd] *adj* highly esteemed or prized.

valueless [*vale*wlis] *adj* of no value or use.

valuer [*vale*w-er] *n* expert who assesses the monetary value of anything.

valuta [val*OO*ta] *n* value of one currency in terms of another.

valve [*valv*] *n* device to open, close, or regulate a flow; (*anat*) structure which permits flow in one direction only; (*bot*) one of several parts into which capsule separates after dehiscence; (*rad*) system of electrodes arranged in an evacuated glass or metal envelope > PDS; (*mus*) mechanism on brass instruments to divert current of air round an additional length of tubing; (*zool*) a mollusc shell ∼ **valved** *adj*.

valvular [*valv*ewlar] *adj* (*of disease*) affecting a valve; made up of valves; equipped with, working as, a valve.

vamoose, vamose [vam*OOs*, vam*Os*] *v/i* (*sl*) go away quickly.

vamp (1) [*vamp*] *n* woman who uses her charms to captivate men ∼ **vamp** *v/t* allure (a man).

vamp (2) *n* front upper of footwear; patch on footwear; something patched up, *esp* improvised musical accompaniment ∼ **vamp** *v/t* and *i* patch (footwear); improvise (accompaniment); improvise; **v. up** patch up to look like new; renovate.

vampire [*vamp*Ir] *n* reanimated corpse that leaves its grave to suck the blood of sleepers; evil creature that lives by sucking human blood; (*fig*) one who makes unscrupulous demands on others; bloodsucking American bat; (*theat*) stage trapdoor.

vampirism [*vamp*IrRizm] *n* state of being or resembling a vampire; habit of preying on others, financially or emotionally; belief in vampires.

van (1) [*van*] *n* covered motor vehicle for carrying goods; closed railway goods truck.

van (2) *n* vanguard; (*fig*) leaders.

van (3) *n* (*lawn tennis*) advantage, the first point after deuce.

van (4) *n* (*ar*) wing.

vanadium [van*ay*di-um] *n* (*chem*) hard white metallic element used in alloys > PDS.

vandal [*van*dal] *n* one who wilfully or from ignorance destroys or spoils works of art, the countryside *etc*; hooligan who wantonly smashes public property; (*hist*) (*cap*) member of a predatory Teutonic tribe of fifth century A.D. ∼ **vandal** *adj*.

vandalism [*van*dalism] *n* wanton destruction; ignorant or malicious hostility to works of art *etc*.

vandalistic [vandal*i*stik] *adj* characteristic of a vandal or the Vandals.

vandalize [*van*dalIz] *v/t* wantonly destroy or damage.

Vandyke [van*dIk*] *n* a painting by Van Dyck; broad lace collar with deeply cut points; one or more deeply cut points on a border of material; zigzag border; **v. beard** close-cut pointed beard ∼ **vandyke** *v/t* cut (material) with vandykes.

vane [*vayn*] *n* weathercock; sail of windmill; blade of fan or propeller; sight of quadrant or surveying instrument; web of feather.

vanguard [*van*gaard] *n* foremost part of advancing force; forefront.

vanilla [van*i*la] *n* kind of orchid; flavouring extracted from its pods.

vanish [*van*ish] *v/i* pass out of sight, become invisible; disappear, come to an end; (*math*) become zero; **vanishing cream** quickly-absorbed cosmetic ointment.

vanity [*van*iti] *n* excessive, and usually unjustified, self-satisfaction; futility, worthlessness, emptiness; that which is futile or worthless; **v. bag** lady's handbag for cosmetics *etc*.

vanning [*van*ing] *n* (*min*) quick method of assaying sands used in Cornwall > PDE.

vanquish [*van*kwish] *v/t* utterly defeat, subdue.

vantage [*vaan*tij] *n* advantage, superiori y; (*tennis*) first point after deuce; **v. ground, point of v.** (*mil*) favourable position.

vanward [*van*ward] *adj* in the front ∼ **vanward** *adv* forward.

vapid [*vap*id] *adj* without vigour or interest, dully stupid ∼ **vapidly** *adv*.

vapidity [vap*i*diti] *n* quality of being vapid.

vaporization [vaypoRIz*ay*shon] *n* process of converting into or becoming vapour.

vaporize [*vay*poRIz] *v/t* and *i* turn into vapour; become vaporous.

vaporizer [*vay*poRIzer] *n* apparatus for converting a liquid into a fine spray; atomizer.

vaporous [*vay*poRus] *adj* filled with vapour, misty; resembling vapour; (*fig*) fanciful.

vapour [*vay*per] *n* mist, moisture in the air; (*phys*) substance in the gaseous state; a gas below its critical temperature > PDS; (*fig*) something unsubstantial; an idle fancy; (*pl*) (*ar*) nervous depression, hysteria.

vapourings [*vay*peRingz] *n* (*pl*) meaningless talk.

vapoury [*vay*peRi] *adj* like vapour; misty, cloudy.

vaquero [vak*air*RO] *n* (*Sp America and Mexico*) cowboy.

Varangian [va*Ran*ji-an] *n* Scandinavian Russian of ninth and tenth centuries; **V. guard** (*hist*) bodyguard of the Byzantine emperors.

varec [*va*Rek] *n* kelp; seaweed ash from which iodine is extracted.

variability [vairRi-ab*i*liti] *n* state or quality of being variable.

variable [*vair*Ri-ab'l] *adj* that can change; liable to

change; unreliable; (*biol*) not true to type ~
variable *n* that which can change; (*math*) symbol
or term which assumes, or to which may be
assigned, different numerical values ~ **variably**
adv ~ **variableness** *n*.

variance [*vair*Ri-ans] *n* difference; difference of
opinion, dispute; (*leg*) discrepancy between two
statements; (*stat*) the square of the standard
deviation > PDP; **at v.** in a state of enmity or
disagreement.

variant [*vair*Ri-ant] *adj* showing variation, discrepant ~ **variant** *n* something differing from
other forms of the same thing; alternative reading;
different version or modification of an original
text, story *etc*.

variation [vairRi-*ay*shon] *n* process of departure
or change from a standard, type, or norm; extent
or degree of this departure or change; the modified
standard, type *etc* after change; (*astron*) change in
the mean motion or mean orbit of a heavenly body;
(*biol*) change in organism or species > PDB;
(*mus*) development and ornamentation of a
theme; (*naut*) declination of magnetic needle
from true North > PDG; (*stat*) deviation from
the mean of a series ~ **variational** *adj*.

varicated [*va*Rikaytid] *adj* having varices.

varices [*va*Riseez] *pl of* **varix**.

varicoloured [*vair*Rikulerd] *adj* of various colours;
(*fig*) diversified.

varicose [*va*RikOs] *adj* of, for, or affected by,
swollen veins.

varied [*vair*Rid] *adj* of different or various kinds;
changed, altered; changing from time to time;
(*zool*) varicoloured.

variegate [*vair*Rigayt] *v/t* diversify; mark with
different colours.

variegation [vairRi*gay*shon] *n* irregular variation
of colour, *esp* in plants > PDB.

variety [va*RI*-iti] *n* diversity, state of being
varied; varied assortment of things; specimen *etc*
differing from others of its kind or class; (*biol*)
subdivision of a species; (*theat*) light entertainment consisting of a series of short comic items,
songs *etc* ~ **variety** *adj* (*theat*) of, for, or in a
variety entertainment.

variform [*vair*Rifawrm] *adj* having various forms.

variola [va*RI*-ola] *n* (*med*) smallpox ~ **variolar** *adj*.

variometer [vairRi-*omiter*] *n* instrument to show
or measure variations in a physical quantity;
(*rad*) tuning coil which consists of a variable inductance.

variorum [vairRi-*awr*Rum] *adj* with notes by
various commentators.

various [*vair*Ri-us] *adj* exhibiting variety; of
different kinds; (*coll*) several, many ~ **variously**
adv.

varix (*pl* **varices**) [*vair*Riks] *n* (*med*) swollen or
varicose vein; ridge on surface of shell.

varlet [*vaar*lit] *n* (*hist*) attendant, page; (*ar*) rascal.

varmint [*vaar*mint] *n* (*coll*) rascal, scamp; **the v.**
(*coll*) the fox.

varnish [*vaar*nish] *n* a resin, asphalt, or pitch dissolved in oil or spirit which dries to a continuous,
thin, transparent, protective film; glaze, glossy
surface; (*fig*) superficial attractiveness, *esp* in
manners ~ **varnish** *v/t* coat with varnish; (*fig*)
gloss over, conceal.

varsity [*vaar*siti] *n* (*coll*) university.

vary [*vair*Ri] *v/t* and *i* make different, change,
modify; diversify; become different; be of different kinds.

vas (*pl* **vasa**) [*vas*, *pl* *vaysa*] *n* (*anat*) duct; **v.
deferens** duct conveying sperm from testicle.

vasal [*vay*sal] *adj* of or in a duct.

vascular [*va*skewlar] *n* (*bot*, *biol*) containing or
concerning vessels which conduct fluid in plants
and animals > PDB.

vasculum (*pl* **vascula**) [*va*skewlum] *n* (*bot*)
specimen case.

vase [*vaaz*, *US vays/vayz*] *n* decorative container
of glass, metalware, or ceramics.

vasectomy [va*sek*tomi] *n* (*med*) operation to
sterilize men by removing part of each vas
deferens.

Vaseline [*va*seleen] *n* (*tr*) ointment of petroleum
jelly.

vaso- *pref* of blood-vessels; of a duct.

vasodilator [vaysOd*i*laytor] *n* and *adj* (*med*) (substance) which dilates blood-vessels.

vasomotor [vasOm*O*ter] *adj* affecting the diameter
of blood-vessels.

vassal [*va*sal] *n* subordinate; (*hist*) feudal tenant.

vassalage [*va*salij] *n* servitude.

vast [*vaast*] *adj* great in size or bulk; (*coll*) great ~
vastly *adv* immensely; very ~ **vastness** *n*.

vasty [*vaas*ti] *adj* (*poet*) vast, immense.

vat [*vat*] *n* large cask or tub; **v. dyes** class of insoluble dyes > PDS.

vatic [*va*tik] *adj* of a prophet; of prophecy.

Vatican [*va*tikan] *n* palace of the Pope in Rome;
(*fig*) the papacy; officials and administrators
serving the Pope; **First V. Council** General
Council of the *R.C.* Church, 1869-70; **Second
V. Council** General Council of the *R.C.* Church,
1962-5.

vaticinate [vat*i*sinayt] *v/t* and *i* prophesy.

vaudeville [*vO*devil/*vawde*vil] *n* (*theat*) variety
show.

vault (1) [*vawlt*] *n* underground chamber, *esp*
burial chamber; arched roof; strongroom for
valuables; the sky ~ **vault** *v/t*.

vault (2) *v/i* and *t* leap or spring, *esp* with help of
hand or pole; leap over ~ **vault** *n* leap, spring.

vaulted [*vawl*tid] *adj* arched; covered by a vault.

vaulter [*vawl*ter] *n* one who leaps or springs.

vaulting (1) [*vawl*ting] *n* building of a vault or
vaults; a vaulted building; vaults of a roof.

vaulting (2) *n* act of leaping or springing with help
of hand or pole ~ **vaulting** *adj* leaping; (*fig*)
over-confident.

vaunt [*vawnt*] *n* boast ~ **vaunt** *v/t* and *i* praise,
boast about; boast, brag ~ **vaunter** *n*.

veal [*veel*] *n* calf's flesh prepared for food.

vector [*vek*tor] *n* (*biol*) animal that transmits parasites > PDB; (*aer*) course of aircraft; (*math*)
magnitude having direction > PDP, PDS ~
vector *v/t* (*aer*) direct (aircraft) on course by
radio waves.

vectorial [vekta*wr*Ri-al] *adj* of a vector.

Veda [*vay*da] *n* book of Hindu scripture.

Vedanta [vay*dan*ta] *n* Hindu philosophy based on
the Vedas.

vedette [vi*det*] *n* mounted sentry; patrol boat;
film star.

Vedic [*vay*dik] *adj* of or in the Vedas.

veer (1) [*veer*] *v/t* (*naut*) pay out rope or cable.

veer (2) *v/i* and *t* (*of wind*) change direction gradually; (*of ship*) change course; (*fig*) change, alter; cause (ship) to go about.

veering [*veer*Ring] *n* change of direction of a wind.

veg [*vej*] *n* (*coll abbr*) vegetable.

vegan [*vee*gan] *n* vegetarian who also refuses eggs and dairy-products.

vegetable [*vej*itab'l] *n* plant cultivated for food ~ **vegetable** *adj* of, consisting of, obtained from, plants or vegetables; **v. marrow** gourd used as vegetable.

vegetal [*vej*ital] *adj* characteristic of plants; (*physiol*) relating to growth; vegetative.

vegetarian [veji*tair*Ri-an] *n* one who lives on vegetable foods or on a diet excluding meat ~ **vegetarian** *adj*.

vegetarianism [veji*tair*Ri-anizm] *n* systematic refusal to eat any form of animal flesh, for reasons of health, conviction, or religion.

vegetate [*vej*itayt] *v/i* live an empty, secluded life.

vegetation [veji*tay*shon] *n* plants collectively; process of vegetating.

vegetative [*vej*itativ] *adj* able to grow; (*of functions*) concerned in growth and nutrition; asexual > PDB; (*fig*) vegetating.

vehemence [*vee*-imens] *n* impetuosity of action or feeling.

vehement [*vee*-iment] *adj* violent, impetuous; very forceful; passionate ~ **vehemently** *adv*.

vehicle [*vee*-ik'l] *n* wheeled conveyance; means or medium of communication; liquid added to pigment, drug *etc* as a medium.

vehicular [vi*hee*kewlar] *adj* of or by a vehicle.

veil [*vayl*] *n* transparent fabric worn to conceal or protect head or face; (*fig*) that which conceals or obscures; (*eccles*) curtain; **beyond the v.** world after death; **take the v.** become a nun ~ **veil** *v/t* cover with a veil; conceal.

veiled [*vayld*] *adj* covered with a veil; hidden, obscure, indistinct; (*fig*) disguised, hinted at.

veiling [*vayl*ing] *n* soft, gauzy material used for veils.

vein [*vayn*] *n* blood-vessel of small diameter carrying blood from the capillaries to the heart > PDB; anything resembling a vein; vascular bundle of a leaf; framework of insect wing; marking on stone or marble; (*min*) crack, fissure or layer containing metallic ore; (*fig*) recurrent characteristic of character, conduct, style *etc*; mood, disposition ~ **veined** *adj*.

veining [*vayn*ing] *n* vein-like markings; system of veins.

velar [*vee*lar] *adj* (*zool*) of a velum; (*phon*) produced by contact with the velum or soft palate ~ **velar** *n* a velar guttural.

veld, veldt [*felt*] *n* the elevated open country of the Transvaal > PDG.

veleta [ve*lee*ta] *n* ballroom dance in waltz time.

velleity [ve*lee*-iti] *n* (*psych*) slight desire; incomplete or feeble volition.

vellum [*vel*um] *n* fine calfskin used as writing material or for bookbinding; manuscript written on vellum.

velocipede [vi*losi*peed] *n* early type of vehicle propelled by the feet; child's tricycle.

velocity [vi*losi*ti] *n* speed; rate of motion in a given direction.

velours, velour, velure [vel*OO*r] *n* soft fabric with thick, erect pile.

velum [*vee*lum] *n* (*zool*) veil-like membrane or structure; (*anat*) the soft palate.

velure see **velours**.

velvet [*vel*vit] *n* silk fabric with short thick pile on one surface; (*fig*) soft downy surface; **be on v.** have best of a bet or match, be sure to win; live luxuriously; **v. glove** appearance of gentleness concealing strength ~ **velvet** *adj* of or like velvet.

velveteen [velvi*teen*] *n* fabric imitating velvet made from cotton.

velveting [*vel*viting] *n* velvet goods or material.

velvety [*vel*viti] *adj* like velvet.

venal (1) [*vee*nal] *adj* bribable, corruptible; mercenary, sordid ~ **venally** *adv*.

venal (2) *adj* of a vein.

venality [vee*nali*ti] *n* quality of being venal (1); mercenary motive or act.

venation [vi*nay*shon] *n* arrangement of veins in a leaf; system of veins in wing of insect.

vend [*vend*] *v/t* sell; peddle (wares).

vendace [*ven*days] *n* a small freshwater fish.

vendee [ven*dee*] *n* (*leg*) person to whom a thing is sold.

vender (*leg* **vendor**) [*ven*der] *n* person who sells.

vendetta [ven*deta*] *n* hereditary blood feud; (*fig*) persistent savage enmity.

vendible [*vendib*'l] *adj* saleable.

vending [*vend*ing] *n* act of selling; **v. machine** automatic machine for selling goods, slot-machine.

vendor see **vender**.

veneer [vi*neer*] *n* thin layer of fine wood used as facing for stronger but less attractive wood; (*bui*) layer of facing outside a well; (*cer*) thin decorative coating; (*fig*) superficially favourable appearance hiding defects ~ **veneer** *v/t* cover with a veneer.

veneering [vi*neer*Ring] *n* act of placing a veneer on; material used as veneer.

venerability [vene*Ra*biliti] *n* quality of being venerable.

venerable [*vene*Rab'l] *adj* worthy of respect and honour, *esp* because of age; (*coll*) old, antique; (*eccles*) title of archdeacon; (*RC*) title of one who has attained first degree of canonization ~ **venerably** *adv*.

venerate [*vene*Rayt] *v/t* have a profound respect for, revere; worship.

veneration [vene*Ray*shon] *n* act of venerating; profound respect.

venereal [vi*neer*Ri-al] *adj* pertaining to, transmitted by, sexual intercourse; infected with venereal disease ~ **venereally** *adv*.

venesection [veni*sek*shon] *n* (*med*) phlebotomy.

Venetian [vi*nee*shan] *n* and *adj* (citizen) of Venice; **V. blind** window-blind of slats on adjustable tapes.

vengeance [*ven*jans] *n* act aimed at injuring someone who has injured oneself or one's friends, revenge; **with a v.** very thoroughly.

vengeful [*venj*fool] *adj* seeking revenge, vindictive ~ **vengefully** *adv* ~ **vengefulness** *n*.

venial [*vee*ni-al] *adj* (*of sins or faults*) minor, comparatively unimportant; excusable, pardonable; (*theol*) not mortal ~ **venially** *adv*.

veniality [veeni-*al*iti] *n* quality of being venial.

venison [*ven*zun/*veni*zun] *n* deer's flesh as food.

venom [*ven*em] *n* poison secreted by dragon, snake *etc*; (*fig*) spite, rancour; bitter words ~ **venomed** *adj* equipped or charged with venom; poisonous; (*fig*) harmful, noxious.

venomous [*ven*emus] *adj* poisonous; (*fig*) spiteful ~ **venomously** *adv* ~ **venomousness** *n*.

venose [*veen*Os] *adj* (*bot*) with many prominent veins.

venous [*vee*nus] *adj* of or in the veins; (*of blood*) returning to the heart after circulation in the body.

vent [*vent*] *n* narrow opening for passage of liquid or gas; hole, passage, aperture; slit at back of a coat; means of escape, outlet; (*bui*) ventilating duct; flue of chimney; (*anat*) anus; **give v. to** (*fig*) give free expression to ~ **vent** *v/t* and *i* make vent in; let out at a vent; (*fig*) give free expression to; (*of otter*) rise to surface to breathe.

ventage [*vent*ij] *n* vent; finger-hole of wind instrument.

vent-hole [*vent*-hOl] *n* hole for passage of light, air, smoke *etc*.

ventilate [*vent*ilayt] *v/t* introduce free current of fresh air into; oxygenate (blood); (*fig*) discuss freely; bring to public attention.

ventilation [venti*lay*shon] *n* free circulation of fresh air; the air-conditioning of the place ventilated; apparatus used for ventilating; (*fig*) free discussion.

ventilator [*vent*ilaytor] *n* one who or that which ventilates.

ventral [*vent*Ral] *adj* of or on the lower or abdominal surface; (*bot*) facing the centre or axis of a flower > PDB.

ventri- *pref* relating to the belly.

ventricle [*vent*Rik'l] *n* (*anat*) small cavity; main pumping chamber of heart; cavity within brain.

ventricular [ven*tRik*ewlar] *adj* of or affecting a ventricle.

ventriloquial [ventRil*Ok*wi-al] *adj* of, by, or like ventriloquism ~ **ventriloquially** *adv*.

ventriloquism [ven*tRil*okwizm] *n* speech without movement of the lips, giving the illusion that it comes from another person or object ~ **ventriloquist** *n*.

ventro- *pref* of or on the belly.

venture [*ven*cher] *n* course of action attended by risk; (*comm*) a speculation; **at a v.** at random; **V. Scout** senior Scout ~ **venture** *v/t* and *i* expose to danger; to risk; take the risk of; presume to put forward; risk one's safety by going.

venturesome [*ven*chersum] *adj* involving risk; bold, daring ~ **venturesomeness** *n*.

venue [*ven*ew] *n* (*leg*) place fixed for a trial; (*fig*) meeting place; scene, site.

Venus (*pl* **Venuses**) [*vee*nus] *n* (*myth*) Roman goddess of beauty and love; (*fig*) beautiful woman; (*astron*) planet second nearest to the sun.

venusian [ven*ew*zi-an] *n* and *adj* (hypothetical inhabitant) of the planet Venus.

veracious [ve*Ray*shus] *adj* truthful; accurate ~ **veraciously** *adv* ~ **veraciousness** *n*.

veracity [ve*Ras*iti] *n* truthfulness; accuracy.

veranda [ve*Ran*da] *n* covered platform, usually at ground floor level outside a house.

verb [*vurb*] *n* (*gramm*) word which states that a person or thing exists, acts or undergoes an action in the present, past or future.

verbal [*vur*bal] *adj* expressed in, concerned with, words; finding expression in words not deeds; word for word, literal; spoken, not written; (*gramm*) relating to, derived from, a verb.

verbalism [*vur*balizm] *n* expression, *esp* verbose, in words; uncritical acceptance of verbal definitions, as if they were real explanations.

verbalization [vurbalIzay*shon*] *n* act of verbalizing; state of being verbalized.

verbalize [*vur*balIz] *v/t* and *i* make into a verb; put into words.

verbally [*vur*bali] *adv* orally; in actual words.

verbatim [ver*bay*tim] *adv* and *adj* word for word.

verbena [ver*bee*na] *n* genus of herbaceous plants including the vervains.

verbiage [*vur*bi-ij] *n* use of unnecessary words; piece of verbose writing.

verbose [ver*bOs*] *adj* using or expressed in unnecessarily many words ~ **verbosely** *adv* ~ **verboseness** *n*.

verbosity [ver*bos*iti] *n* quality of being verbose.

verdancy [*vur*dansi] *n* quality of being green; (*fig*) inexperience, simplicity.

verdant [*vur*dant] *adj* green; covered with an abundance of vegetation; (*fig*) immature, gullible ~ **verdantly** *adv*.

verdict [*vur*dikt] *n* (*leg*) finding or decision of a jury; decision, judgement, opinion.

verdigris [*vur*digRees] *n* green deposit formed upon copper; green rust on copper or brass.

verdure [*vur*dyer] *n* green vegetation; fresh green colour of vegetation; (*fig*) freshness.

verdurous [*vur*dyeRus] *adj* covered with verdure; of a rich green colour ~ **verdurousness** *n*.

verge [*vurj*] *n* edge, margin, brink; grass border, *esp* of a road; spindle of watch; staff of office; edge of sloping roof which overhangs a gable; (*leg*) sphere of jurisdiction of King's Court ~ **verge** *v/i* incline, descend; **v. on** approach, border on.

verger [*vur*jer] *n* church caretaker; official who carries a verge or staff of office before dignitaries.

veridical [ve*Rid*ikal] *adj* (*of prophetic dreams or visions*) corresponding to events occurring at the time or later.

veriest [*ve*Ri-ist] *adj* greatest, absolute.

verifiable [*ve*Rifi-ab'l] *adj* capable of being verified.

verification [veRifi*kay*shon] *n* act of verifying; search for, or the obtaining of, evidence confirming truth of a theory or hypothesis.

verify [*ve*Rifi] *v/t* show to be true, check; fulfil, confirm; (*leg*) authenticate.

verily [*ve*Rili] *adv* (*ar*) truly, in fact, really.

verisimilitude [veRisi*mil*itewd] *n* likeness to reality or fact; quality of appearing true.

verismo [ve*Riz*mO] *n* (*Ital*) realism in art and literature.

veritable [*ve*Ritab'l] *adj* real, genuine ~ **veritably** *adv*.

verity [*ve*Riti] *n* quality of being true; truth, truthfulness; statement, doctrine *etc* accepted as true; essential truth, established fact.

verjuice [*vur*jOOs] *n* acid juice of sour fruit.

vermeil [*vur*mil] *adj* (*poet*) colour a shade lighter than scarlet; gilding over silver.

vermi- *pref* of or like a worm.

vermicelli [vermi*seli*] *n* very thin macaroni.

vermicide [*vur*mIsId] *n* (*med*) chemical for killing worms; (*med*) medicine for purging the body of worms.

vermicular [ver*mike*wlar] *adj* like a worm in shape, markings, or movement; (*archi*) incised as if by worm-tracks.

vermiculation [vermike*wlay*shon] *n* (*path*) worm-like or peristaltic movement.

vermiculite [*vur*mikewlIt] *n* a mica which expands into threads when heated, used as heat insulator.

vermiform [*vur*mifawrm] *adj* shaped like a worm.

vermifugal [vermi*few*gal] *adj* of or as a vermifuge.

vermifuge [*vur*mifewj] *n* drug for purging the body of worms.

vermilion [ver*mil*yon] *n* brilliant red colour; scarlet; scarlet form of mercuric sulphide, used as a pigment ∼ **vermilion** *adj* of a scarlet colour.

vermin [*vur*min] *n* (*collect*) destructive or harmful animals, usually small; loathsome parasitic insects; (*fig*) rascally parasites; scum of society.

verminous [*vur*minus] *adj* of, like or covered with vermin.

vermouth [*vur*meth/vurm*OOth*] *n* liqueur made from white wine flavoured with wormwood.

vernacular [ver*nake*wlar] *n* native speech or dialect of a people, as opposed to a literary, learned or obsolete language; technical jargon of a particular occupation; (*joc*) strong language, profanity ∼ **vernacular** *adj* native, indigenous; written or spoken in normal current language.

vernal [*vur*nal] *adj* of or like spring; fresh, young.

vernier [*vur*ni-er] *n* short movable scale for measuring subdivisions of a graduated scale > PDS.

veronal [*ve*Ronal] *n* a barbiturate sedative drug.

veronica [ve*Roni*ka] *n* genus of flowering herbs or shrubs with leafy stem.

verricule [*ve*Rikewl] *n* (*ent*) tuft of hairs.

verruca [ve*ROO*ka] *n* wart; contagious wart-like infection of the foot.

verrucose [ve*ROO*kOz] *adj* warty.

versatile [*vur*satIl] *adj* having many different skills; adapting readily to varied activities; changeable; (*bot*, *zool*) able to turn freely in various directions ∼ **versatilely** *adv*.

versatility [versa*tili*ti] *n* quality of being versatile.

verse [*vurs*] *n* one of several similar subsections of a poem, stanza; metre, metrical pattern of a line of poetry; poetry; inferior, *esp* unimaginative or frivolous, poetry; short subsection of chapter of Bible; **free v.** verses of irregular length and loose rhythmic pattern ∼ **verse** *v/t* and *i* versify.

versed (1) [*vurst*] *adj* skilled, experienced.

versed (2) *adj* (*math*, *of a sine*) reversed.

verset [*vur*sit] *n* short verse; (*mus*) short interlude for the organ.

versicle [*vur*sik'l] *n* short Biblical verse or phrase recited in a liturgy.

versification [vursifi*kay*shon] *n* act of composing verse; metrical pattern.

versificator [vursifi*kay*ter] *n* one who versifies; one skilled in metre.

versify [*vur*sifI] *v/i* and *t* compose poetry; convert into verse; relate in verse.

version [*vur*shon] *n* account presenting facts from a particular point of view; translation; rendering, interpretation.

vers libre [vair-*leebR*] *n* (*Fr*) free verse.

verso [*vur*sO] *n* left-hand page; reverse side of medal or coin.

verst [*vurst*] *n* Russian measure of length equivalent to 3,500 feet.

versus [*vur*sus] *prep* (*Lat*) against.

vert (1) [*vurt*] *n* (*hist*) green vegetation in a forest; (*leg*) right to cut green trees; (*her*) green.

vert (2) *v/i* (*sl*) be converted, change religion.

vert (3) *v/i* (*anat*) be turned or twisted.

vertebra (*pl* **vertebrae**) [*vur*tibRa] *n* single joint of the spine; (*pl*) spine, backbone > PDB.

vertebral [*vur*tibRal] *adj* of, on or composed of vertebrae.

vertebrate [*vur*tibRayt] *n* and *adj* (*animal*) having a backbone > PDB.

vertebration [vurtib*Ray*shon] *n* division into vertebrae.

vertex (*pl* **vertices**) [*vur*teks] *n* topmost point, apex; (*astron*) zenith; (*geom*) angle opposite to base of figure; (*anat*) crown of head.

vertical [*vur*tikal] *adj* upright; at right angles to the horizon or to the level ground; perpendicular; of or at the zenith; directly overhead; **v. take-off** (*of aircraft*) act of rising directly into the air without preliminary run ∼ **vertically** *adv*.

verticality [vurti*kali*ti] *n* quality of being vertical.

vertices [*vur*tiseez] *pl* of vertex.

vertiginous [vurti*jin*us] *adj* giddy, dizzy; causing giddiness; whirling, revolving ∼ **vertiginously** *adv* ∼ **vertiginousness** *n*.

vertigo [vurti*gO*/vurt*I*gO] *n* giddiness > PDP.

vertu see **virtu**.

vervain [*vur*vayn] *n* wild verbena.

verve [*vurv*] *n* imaginative vivacity; vigour.

vervet [*vur*vit] *n* small African monkey.

very (1) [*ve*Ri] *adv* in a high degree, to a great extent; extremely; exactly; absolutely ∼ **very** *adj* identical; precise; absolute, exact; (*ar*) true, real; **the v. thing** exactly what is needed.

Very (2) *adj* **V. light** coloured flare fired as signal or temporary lighting.

vesica [ves*I*ka] *n* (*anat*, *bot*) bladder, sac; (*arts*) oval halo, aureole.

vesicant [*ves*ikant] *n* and *adj* (*gas*) producing blisters.

vesicle [*ves*ik'l] *n* small cavity filled with air or liquid; blister; small bladder; sac; bubble; (*geol*) hollow formed by bubble in volcanic rock.

vesico- *pref* of the bladder.

vesicular [ves*ike*wlar] *adj* of or like a vesicle; **v. disease** swinefever.

vespers [*ve*sperz] *n* (*pl*) (*eccles*) evensong, the sixth hour of canonical prayer.

vespertine [*ve*spertIn] *adj* of or during the evening; visible or active in the evening.

vespiary [*ve*spi-aRi] *n* wasps' nest.

vespid [*ve*spid] *n* wasp or hornet.

vessel [*ve*sel] *n* hollow utensil for food or drink; ship, large boat; duct, tube of body or plant; (*bibl*) person regarded as having or receiving some spiritual quality.

vest (1) [*vest*] *n* undergarment worn next to the skin and covering the trunk; waistcoat; (*ar*) robe, gown ∼ **vest** *v/i* and *t* clothe in ceremonial robes.

vest (2) *v/t* and *i* confer a right, power, property *etc* (on); endow; invest.

vesta [*vesta*] *n* type of short match; wax match; **V.** (*Rom myth*) goddess of the household hearth.

vestal [*vestal*] *adj* of Vesta; chaste; **V. virgin** priestess of Vesta; (*fig*) chaste woman ~ **vestal** *n* Vestal virgin; (*fig*) chaste woman; nun.

vested [*vestid*] *adj* legally established in possession; securely possessed; (*fig*) unshakable; **v. interest** financial, social or professional benefit derived from the continued existence of some institution, custom *etc*; group of people enjoying such a benefit.

vestibule [*vestibewl*] *n* entrance hall, lobby; (*anat*) part of the inner ear between the cochlea and the semicircular canals.

vestige [*vestij*] *n* trace of what no longer exists; last remnant; (*biol*) functionless remnant of an organ that has diminished and simplified during evolution > PDB, PDP.

vestigial [*vestiji-al*] *adj* of a vestige; surviving in degenerate form.

vestigiary [*vestiji-aRi*] *adj* vestigial.

vestment [*vestment*] *n* ceremonial garment worn by clergy during religious service or on solemn occasions.

vest-pocket [vest-*pokit*] *adj* small enough to fit into a waistcoat pocket.

vestry [*vestRi*] *n* part of church where vestments and records are kept; administrative meeting of ratepayers of a parish.

vestry-book [*vestRi*-book] *n* book in which the minutes of the parish vestry are kept; a record of the births, marriages and deaths of parishioners.

vestryman [*vestRiman*] *n* member of the parish vestry.

vesture [*vescher*] *n* (*poet*) clothing.

vet [*vet*] *n* (*coll*) veterinary surgeon ~ **vet** (*pres/part* vetting, *p/t* and *p/part* vetted) *v/t* treat (animal) medically; (*coll*) examine or treat (person) medically; examine closely and critically.

vetch [*vech*] *n* plants of the bean family used for forage.

veteran [*veteRan*] *n* person with long experience, *esp* of soldiering; old and experienced person ~ **veteran** *adj* old and experienced; **v. car** car built before 1916.

veterinarian [veteRi*nairRi*-an] *n* veterinary surgeon.

veterinary [*veteRinaRi*] *adj* of or practising medical treatment of animals; **v. surgeon** one trained to treat sick animals.

veto [*veetO*] *n* constitutional right to forbid the passing of a law, political measure *etc* > PDPol; act of exercising this right; absolute prohibition ~ **veto** *v/t* forbid absolutely; block or reject by right of veto.

vex [*veks*] *v/t* annoy, irritate, make unhappy.

vexation [veks*ayshon*] *n* act of vexing; state of being vexed; (*leg*) malicious or trivial harassment.

vexatious [veks*ayshus*] *adj* causing annoyance, irritating ~ **vexatiously** *adv* ~ **vexatiousness** *n*.

vexed [*vekst*] *adj* much disputed, frequently discussed; annoyed.

vexing [*veksing*] *adj* that vexes.

via [*vI-a*] *prep* travelling or sent through.

viability [vI-*abiliti*] *n* quality of being viable.

viable [*vI*-ab'l] *adj* (*biol*) capable of maintaining a separate existence; able to live in particular circumstances; (*fig*) capable of functioning successfully, practicable.

viaduct [*vI*-adukt] *n* long tall bridge carrying a railway, canal *etc* across a valley *etc*.

vial [*vI*-al] *n* small glass bottle.

viands [*vI*-andz] *n* (*pl*) provisions, food.

viaticum [vI-*atikum*] *n* (*eccles*) Eucharist administered to a dying person.

vibes [*vIbz*] *n* (*pl*) (*sl abbr*) vibrations, *esp* psychic.

vibrancy [*vIbRansi*] *n* quality of being vibrant.

vibrant [*vIbRant*] *adj* vibrating, quivering; resonant ~ **vibrantly** *adv*.

vibraphone [*vIbRafOn*] *n* (*mus*) percussion instrument with tuned metal bars over resonators.

vibrate [vI*bRayt*] *v/i* and *t* move rapidly to and fro, quiver; cause to quiver; oscillate; (*fig*) feel a thrill of emotion; resound; give a tremulous sound.

vibration [vI*bRayshon*] *n* rapid to-and-fro motion of a particle or body; quivering or tremulous motion; (*coll*, *usu pl*) wave of alleged psychic force emitted by persons or places, indicating personality or mood.

vibrational [vI*bRayshonal*] *adj* of or like vibration.

vibrato [veeb*RaatO*] *n* (*mus*) rapid regular fluctuation in pitch > PDM ~ **vibrato** *adv*.

vic [*vik*] *n* formation of aircraft in V shape.

vicar [*viker*] *n* incumbent of a parish receiving a stipend but not tithes; **V. of Christ** (*RC*) the Pope; **lay v.** cathedral officer who sings parts of the services.

vicarage [*vikaRij*] *n* house or benefice of a vicar.

vicar-apostolic [vikar-apost*olik*] *n* (*RC*) missionary or titular bishop.

vicar-choral [vikar-*kawRal*] *n* lay vicar.

vicar-general [vikar-*jeneRal*] *n* assistant or deputy of a bishop.

vicarial [vi*kairRi*-al] *adj* of a vicar; vicarious.

vicarious [vi*kairRi*-us] *adj* acting as substitute; done or felt on behalf of another; deputed ~ **vicariously** *adv* ~ **vicariousness** *n*.

vice (1) [*vIs*] *n* wickedness; depravity, evil practices; serious moral fault; fault, defect; **the V.** buffoon in medieval plays.

vice (2) (*US* **vise**) *n* tool that holds an object gripped between adjustable jaws.

vice (3) *n* (*coll abbr*) vice-president; vice-chancellor; deputy.

vice (4) [*vIsi*] *prep* (*Lat*) in place of.

vice- *pref* acting as deputy for.

vice-admiral [vIs-*admiRal*] *n* naval officer ranking next below admiral.

vice-chairman [vIs-*chair*man] *n* assistant or deputy of chairman.

vice-chancellor [vIs-*chaan*selor] *n* chief administrative official of a university; (*leg*) judge in the old Court of Chancery; (*RC*) cardinal in charge of the Papal Chancery.

vice-consul [vIs-*konsul*] *n* deputy of a consul; subordinate consul; proconsul.

vicennial [vi*seni*-al] *adj* lasting 20 years; occurring every 20 years.

vice-president [vIs-*pRezi*dent] *n* deputy of a president.

viceregal [vIs*Reegal*] *adj* of a viceroy.

viceroy [*vIsRoi*] *n* one who rules a territory as deputy for, and with the authority of, a sovereign.

viceroyalty [vɪsRoi-alti] *n* office of a viceroy; period of tenure of this.

viceroyship [vɪsRoiship] *n* viceroyalty.

vice versa [vɪsi-*vur*sa] *adv* (*Lat*) conversely, reversing the relationship.

vicinal [*visi*nal] *adj* neighbouring.

vicinity [*visi*niti] *n* closeness; nearby area, neighbourhood; **in the v. of** close to.

vicious [*vish*us] *adj* of a vice; having vice, very wicked; spiteful; faulty, defective; ill-tempered, uncontrollable; likely to bite, kick *etc*; **v. circle** series of difficulties each of which aggravates the others; (*log*) fallacy of using a conclusion to prove the premiss on which it rests, circular argument ~ **viciously** *adv* ~ **viciousness** *n*.

vicissitude [*visi*sitewd] *n* alternation, change, *esp* in fortune.

victim [*vik*tim] *n* one who suffers through no fault of his own; one who is made to suffer by persons or forces beyond his control; living creature killed as sacrificial offering.

victimization [viktimɪz*ay*shon] *n* act of victimizing; state of being victimized.

victimize [*vik*timɪz] *v/t* make a victim of, make to suffer; penalize, *esp* unjustly.

victor [*vik*ter] *n* one who defeats an enemy or rival; one who wins a contest.

victoria [vik*tawr*Ri-a] *n* type of light low four-wheeled carriage for two; species of very large waterlily; juicy sweet-flavoured kind of red plum; **V. Cross** highest British military decoration for valour.

Victorian [vik*tawr*Ri-an] *adj* living in or typical of the reign of Queen Victoria (1837–1901); prudish ~ **Victorian** *n* one who lived in the reign of Queen Victoria.

Victoriana [viktawrRi-*aa*na] *n* (*pl*) objects, ideas *etc* typical of Queen Victoria's reign.

victorious [vik*tawr*Ri-us] *adj* successful in a contest, conquering ~ **victoriously** *adv* ~ **victoriousness** *n*.

victory [*vik*teRi] *n* defeat of an enemy in battle or of an adversary in a contest; success in a struggle or contest of any kind; **Pyrrhic v.** victory gained at great cost; **moral v.** indecisive result considered as a victory because of its moral effect.

victress [*vik*tRis] *n* female victor.

victual [*vit*'l] *v/t* and *i* furnish with victuals; eat; obtain supply of victuals.

victualler [*vit*'ler] *n* one who supplies provisions; **licensed v.** innkeeper, one licensed to sell food and drink to be consumed on the premises.

victualling [*vit*'ling] *n* act of supplying victuals, *esp* in the navy.

victuals [*vit*'lz] *n* (*pl*) food, provisions.

vicuña [vik*OO*nya] *n* (*Sp Amer*) llama-like animal; cloth made from the wool of this animal; fine wool and cotton mixture.

vide [*vɪ*di] *v/imp* (*Lat*) see, consult.

videlicet [vi*dee*liset] *adv* (*Lat*) namely.

video [*vi*di-O] *adj* and *n* of or by videotape; (*US*) (of, by) television.

videotape [*vi*di-Otayp] *n* magnetic tape on which visual images are recorded for television transmission ~ **videotape** *v/t*.

vidual [*vi*dew-al] *adj* widowed; of a widow.

viduity [vi*dew*-iti] *n* widowhood.

vie [*vɪ*] *v/i* compete, enter into rivalry.

view [*vew*] *n* act of seeing; opportunity to see; state of being seen or visible; that which is seen; scenery, buildings *etc* as seen from a particular place; picture or photograph of this; completeness or distinctness with which something can be seen; opinion, mental attitude; plan, intention; survey; inspection; the sighting of a quarry; **dim v.** (*coll*) unfavourable opinion; **in v.** visible from a particular place; under observation; as an aim or prospect; **in v. of** considering; in anticipation of; **on v.** displayed, exhibited; **with a v. to, with the v. of** intending; foreseeing, considering ~ **view** *v/t* and *i* examine, inspect; consider, judge; estimate; watch on television.

viewer [*vew*er] *n* one who views; one who watches television; apparatus to assist viewing; viewfinder.

viewfinder [*vew*fɪnder] *n* part of camera which shows the area to be photographed.

view-halloo [*vew*-halOO] *n* (*hunting*) cry raised when the fox is seen to break cover.

viewless [*vew*lis] *adj* from which no attractive view can be seen; (*poet*) invisible; blind.

viewpoint [*vew*point] *n* point of view, opinion; place from which something can be seen.

vigil [*vij*il] *n* act of deliberately staying awake at night to pray or keep watch; period thus spent; (*eccles*) eve of a feast-day.

vigilance [*vij*ilans] *n* alertness, watchfulness, caution; (*path*) insomnia; **v. committee** (*US*) self-appointed organization for maintenance of law or morality in corrupt or lawless community; **v. man** member of such an organization.

vigilant [*vij*ilant] *adj* watchful, alert ~ **vigilantly** *adv*.

vigilante [vij*ilan*ti] *n* (*US*) member of a vigilance committee.

vignette [veen*yet*] *n* small ornamental design or illustration in a book, *esp* at head or foot of page; picture whose main subject is merged into its background; (*fig*) brief pen-portrait, word-sketch ~ **vignette** *v/t* depict by a vignette.

vigorous [*vig*eRus] *adj* physically strong and active; sturdy, healthy; forcible, energetic; growing well ~ **vigorously** *adv* ~ **vigorousness** *n*.

vigour [*vig*er] *n* physical strength; energy; good health, vitality; healthy growth; forcefulness, power.

viking [*vɪ*king] *n* (*hist*) Scandinavian trader and sea-raider of the 8th to 11th centuries.

vile [*vɪ*l] *adj* extremely bad; disgusting, shameful; worthless ~ **vilely** *adv* ~ **vileness** *n*.

vilification [vilifik*ay*shon] *n* act of vilifying.

vilify [*vil*ifɪ] *v/t* speak ill of, slander; abuse.

villa [*vil*a] *n* smallish detached or semi-detached house with garden, *usu* in a suburb; country house with large grounds, *esp* in Italy or southern France.

village [*vil*ij] *n* group of houses smaller than a town but larger than a hamlet; small rural community.

villager [*vil*ijer] *n* person, *esp* workman, living in a village.

villain [*vil*an] *n* scoundrel; one whose wickedness harms others; character in a book, play *etc* whose wickedness is a chief element in the plot; (*ar*) villein; (*joc*) rascal.

villainess [*vil*anes] *n* female villain.

809

villainous [*vi*lanus] *adj* of or like a villain; (*coll*) extremely bad ~ villainously *adv* ~ villainousness *n*.

villainy [*vi*lani] *n* conduct of a villain; harmful wickedness.

villanelle [vila*nel*] *n* poem having five 3-lined stanzas and final quatrain, using only two rhymes.

villein [*vi*lin] *n* (*hist*) feudal serf.

villeinage [*vi*linij] *n* status of a villein.

villi [*vi*lI] *pl* of villus.

villous [*vi*lus] *adj* (*zool, bot*) thickly covered with villi.

villus (*pl* villi) [*vi*lus] *n* (*bot*) long slim soft hair; (*anat*) thin hair-like projection, *esp* in intestine.

vim [*vi*m] *n* (*coll*) energy, vigour.

vinaigrette [vinay*gR*et] *n* container for aromatic salts or vinegar, smelling bottle.

vinculum [*vi*nkewlum] *n* (*math*) straight line drawn over two or more terms in a compound quantity.

vindicate [*vi*ndikayt] *v/t* prove the justice, truth, or innocence of; defend successfully against accusations.

vindication [vindi*kay*shon] *n* act of vindicating; that which vindicates.

vindicative [*vi*ndikativ] *adj* that vindicates.

vindicator [*vi*ndikayter] *n* one who vindicates.

vindicatory [*vi*ndikayteRi] *adj* that vindicates; (*of laws*) retributive.

vindictive [vin*di*ktiv] *adj* of, like or as vengeance; revengeful; punitive; v. damages (*leg*) damages awarded not only to compensate the plaintiff but also to punish the defendant ~ vindictively *adv* ~ vindictiveness *n*.

vine [*vi*n] *n* grape-bearing climbing plant with a woody stem; any slender-stemmed plant that trails or climbs.

vineborer [*vi*nbawrRer] *n* weevil which destroys vines.

vine-dresser [*vi*n-dReser] *n* one whose job is to cultivate vines.

vinegar [*vi*niger] *n* dilute acetic acid produced by fermentation of certain liquors > PDS.

vinegar-plant [*vi*niger-plaant] *n* microscopic mould which grows on fermenting liquids.

vinegar-tree [*vi*niger-tRee] *n* Virginian sumach.

vinegary [*vi*nigeRi/*vi*nigRi] *adj* tasting of vinegar; sour; (*fig*) embittered, spiteful.

vinery [*vi*neRi] *n* hot-house in which grape-vines are grown.

vineyard [*vi*nyaard] *n* vine plantation.

vingt-et-un [[van-tay-urn] *n* (*Fr*) card game in which the object is to score 21.

vinic [*vi*nik] *adj* (*chem*) derived from wine or from alcohol.

viniculture [*vi*nikulcher] *n* cultivation of grapes for wine.

vinous [*vi*nus] *adj* of or like wine; addicted to wine; due to use of wine ~ vinously *adv* ~ vinousness *n*.

vintage [*vi*ntij] *n* harvesting of grapes for wine; season of this; wine made from grapes of specified year; quality of this; (*fig*) date, as a criterion of quality ~ vintage *adj* (*of wine*) made from high-quality grapes harvested in specified year; (*fig*) old and of high quality; v. car car built in the period 1917–1930; racing car more than 30 years

old; v. year (*fig*) year whose products are particularly good ~ vintager *n* one who gathers grapes.

vintner [*vi*ntner] *n* wine merchant.

vinyl [*vi*nil] *n* and *adj* (resin) containing the polymerized vinyl radical; v. radical unsaturated radical derived from ethylene; v. chloride substance which polymerizes into a widely used plastic and fibre.

viol [*vi*-ol] *n* obsolete musical instrument with five or more strings played with a bow > PDM; v. da gamba bass viol.

viola (1) [vI-*O*la] *n* large class of herbaceous plants including violet and pansy.

viola (2) [vee-*O*la/vi-*O*la] *n* four-stringed musical instrument played with a bow and slightly larger than a violin > PDM.

violable [*vi*-olab'l] *adj* capable of being violated ~ violableness *n*.

violaceous [vi-o*lay*shus] *adj* violet-coloured.

violate [*vi*-olayt] *v/t* brutally destroy or disturb; treat (something holy) with disrespect; wrongfully disregard or break (an oath, obligation *etc*); rape.

violation [vi-o*lay*shon] *n* act of violating; state of being violated; that which violates.

violator [vi-o*lay*ter] *n* one who violates.

violence [*vi*-olens] *n* great force, intensity; excessive force; harmful or unlawful use of strength; roughness, brute force; physical assault; violation; do v. to (*fig*) insult; cause suffering to; grossly misinterpret.

violent [*vi*-olent] *adj* extremely forceful; very intense, passionate; showing or needing great physical strength; using excessive force; of or caused by a physical assault ~ violently *adv*.

violet [*vi*-olet] *n* a common plant of the viola genus; purplish-blue colour ~ violet *adj* purplish-blue.

violin [vi-o*lin*] *n* musical instrument with four strings played with a bow > PDM; violinist.

violinist [vi-o*lin*ist] *n* one who plays the violin.

violist [*vi*-olist] *n* one who plays the viol or the viola.

violoncellist [vee-olon*chel*ist] *n* one who plays the violoncello.

violoncello [vee-olon*chel*O] *n* large four-stringed musical instrument held between the knees and played with a bow > PDM.

viper [*vi*per] *n* small poisonous European snake, adder; (*fig*) treacherous or spiteful person.

viperine [*vi*peRin] *adj* of or like a viper.

viperish [*vi*peRish] *adj* spiteful; treacherous.

virago [vi*Ray*gO] *n* shrew, bad-tempered, violent woman; masculine type of woman, female warrior.

virelay [*vi*Rilay] *n* (*Fr*) lyric poem with stanzas linked by recurrent rhymes.

virgate (1) [*vu*rgayt] *n* (*hist*) early English measure of land.

virgate (2) [*vu*rgayt] *adj* (*bot, zool*) rod-like.

virgin [*vu*rjin] *n* woman who has never known sexual intercourse; chaste woman; woman or man without any sexual experience; (*ent*) female insect that lays eggs without impregnation; the V. Mary the mother of Christ; V. Birth (*theol*) doctrine that Christ was miraculously born of a virgin ~ virgin *adj* of or like a virgin; chaste;

never yet used, cultivated, conquered *etc*; undefiled; untouched.

virginal (1) [*vur*jinal] *adj* of, like or befitting a virgin; **v. generation** parthenogenesis ~ **virginally** *adv*.

virginal (2) *n* (*often pl*) keyboard instrument of harpsichord type > PDM.

Virginia [vur*jin*i-a] *n* a State in U.S.A.; tobacco grown here; **V. creeper** common climbing plant.

virginity [vur*jin*iti] *n* state, *esp* physical, of being a virgin; chastity; the maidenhead; (*fig*) quality of being untouched, undefiled *etc*.

Virgo [*vur*gO] *n* (*astron*) constellation of the Virgin, the sixth sign of the zodiac; a constellation; **v. intacta** (*leg*) virgin woman with unbroken hymen.

virgule [*vur*gewl] *n* comma.

viridescence [viRi*des*ens] *n* greenness; (*fig*) freshness, youthful vigour.

viridescent [viRi*des*ent] *adj* greenish.

viridian [viRi*di*-an] *n* a bright green pigment.

viridity [viRi*di*ti] *n* greenness.

virile [*vi*RIl] *adj* masculine, manly; displaying masculine strength, not effeminate; sexually potent.

virility [vi*Ri*liti] *n* masculinity, manly vigour; sexual capacity in men.

virology [vIR*Ro*loji] *n* scientific study of viruses and virus diseases ~ **virologist** *n*.

virtu, vertu [vert*OO*] *n* object of v. rare and exquisitely made object of artistic merit.

virtual [*vur*tew-al] *adj* being or acting as such though not so called or defined; for all practical purposes; (*opt*) of or at the point where rays would meet if produced backwards ~ **virtually** *adv* in effect, to all intents and purposes.

virtue [*vur*tew] *n* moral goodness; a specific moral quality; chastity, *esp* of a woman; virginity; beneficial quality or power; excellence, merit; (*theol*) one of the nine orders of angelic beings; **by (in) v. of** because of, through the power of; **make a v. of** claim credit for; **of easy v.** sexually lax.

virtuosity [vurtew-*os*iti] *n* high skill in technique in an art; taste for the fine arts.

virtuoso [vurtew-*Os*O] *n* person who shows great technical skill in an art, *esp* in music; one possessing taste for the fine arts; connoisseur; dilettante.

virtuous [*vur*tew-us] *adj* having or showing virtue; morally good; chaste ~ **virtuously** *adv* ~ **virtuousness** *n*.

virulence [*vi*Rewlens] *n* quality of being virulent; degree of this.

virulent [*vi*Rewlent] *adj* very harmful to health, highly toxic; (*fig*) very bitter ~ **virulently** *adv*.

virus (*pl* **viruses**) [*vIr*Rus] *n* one of various parasitic agents, smaller than bacteria, causing infectious disease in plants and animals > PDB; (*fig*) subtle and harmful influence ~ **virus** *adj* caused by a virus.

visa [*vee*za] *n* endorsement on a passport to allow its holder to enter certain territories ~ **visa** *v/t* endorse (passport).

visage [*vi*zij] *n* human face; expression of face.

visagiste [*vee*zajist] *n* expert in application of theatrical make-up.

visard, vizard [*vi*zaard] *n* (*ar*) mask; visor.

vis-à-vis [*vee*z-a-vee] *prep* and *adv* opposite,

facing; in relationship to ~ **vis-à-vis** *n* person placed opposite; person corresponding in status or function, opposite number.

viscera [*vise*Ra] *n* (*pl*) intestines, liver, lungs and other internal organs of the body.

visceral [*vise*Ral] *adj* of, in or like viscera.

visceri-, viscero- *pref* of or in the viscera.

viscid [*vi*sid] *adj* sticky, glutinous.

viscometer [vis*kom*iter] *n* instrument for measuring viscosity.

viscose [*vis*kOs] *n* viscous solution of cellulose used in making artificial silk > PDS ~ **viscose** *adj* viscous.

viscosity [vis*kos*iti] *n* property of a fluid which resists the forces tending to make it flow; a measure of this property; stickiness > PDS.

viscount [*vi*kownt] *n* member of British peerage ranking between earl and baron.

viscountcy [*vi*kowntsi] *n* viscounty.

viscountess [*vi*kown*tes*] *n* wife of a viscount.

viscounty [*vi*kownti] *n* rank of viscount; (*hist*) territory administered by a viscount.

viscous [*vis*kus] *adj* sticky, gluey, glutinous; (*phys*) soft and adhesive, semi-fluid ~ **viscously** *adv* ~ **viscousness** *n*.

visé [*vee*zay] *n* and *v/t* (*US*) visa.

vise [*vI*s] *n* and *v/t* (*US*) vice (2).

visibility [vizi*bil*iti] *n* range of vision in varying weather conditions; fact of being visible.

visible [*vi*zib'l] *adj* that can be seen; that can be easily understood, obvious ~ **visibly** *adv* ~ **visibleness** *n*.

vision [*vi*zhon] *n* act or power of seeing, sight > PDP; that which is seen; range of sight; something seen in a dream, prophetic trance, mystical experience *etc*; imaginative wisdom, *esp* concerning the future; foresight, insight; description of the future.

visionary [*vi*zhonaRi] *adj* of, like, or seen in a vision; unreal, imaginary; apt to have visions or to form wildly impractical schemes; idealistic, unpractical; fanciful ~ **visionary** *n* one who sees visions; impractical idealist.

visit [*vi*zit] *v/t* and *i* go to see (person or place); go and stay (with or at); pay a social or business call (on); inspect; (*ar*) afflict, come as punishment ~ **visit** *n* act of visiting; social, professional or business call; temporary stay.

visitant [*vi*zitant] *n* one who pays a visit; migratory bird; ghost, apparition.

visitation [vizi*tay*shon] *n* official inspection by a superior; calamity regarded as a punishment sent by God; (*coll*) prolonged visit unpleasant to those being visited; **the V.** (*eccles*) the visit of the Virgin to St Elizabeth.

visitatorial [vizi*tatawr*Ri-al] *adj* of or having the power of official visitation.

visiting [*vi*ziting] *n* act of paying visits; **v. card** small card printed with name and address left by one paying a call.

visitor [*vi*zitor] *n* one who pays a visit; one who stays temporarily with someone; sightseer, tourist; **visitors' book** record of names and addresses of visitors.

visor, vizor [*vI*zor] *n* movable front of helmet covering the face; peak of a cap; movable flap inside vehicle windscreen, to shield eyes from sunlight; (*ar*) mask.

vista [*vi*sta] *n* distant view seen through a long narrow opening; mental survey of distant times or long series of events.

visual [*vi*zew-al] *adj* of or by sight; as or like something seen; **v. aids** maps, diagrams *etc* used in teaching; **v. purple** rhodopsin.

visualization [vizew-al*i*z*ay*shon] *n* act of visualizing.

visualize [*vi*zew-alIz] *v/t* and *i* imagine or remember as if actually seeing; form a clear mental picture of.

visually [*vi*zew-ali] *adv* by sight; so as to affect the sight; by visualizing.

Vita glass [*vi*ta-glaas] *n* (*tr*) glass which does not exclude ultraviolet rays.

vital [*vi*tal] *adj* necessary to the continuance of life; of, having or affecting life; essential, very important; (*fig*) lively, vigorous; **v. statistics** statistics of births and deaths; (*coll*) size of bust, waist, and hips of a woman.

vitalism [*vi*talizm] *n* doctrine that life derives from a non-material principle ~ **vitalist** *n* ~ **vitalistic** *adj*.

vitality [vi*ta*liti] *n* power of remaining alive and vigorous; (*fig*) liveliness, energy; durability.

vitalize [*vi*talIz] *v/t* make living or lively.

vitally [*vi*tali] *adv* to a vital degree.

vitals [*vi*talz] *n* (*pl*) bodily organs necessary to life; (*fig*) essential parts.

vitamin [*vi*tamin/*vi*tamin] *n* one of various organic substances found in foods and essential for the prevention of deficiency diseases.

vitaminize [*vi*taminIz] *v/t* add vitamins to.

vitiate [*vi*shi-ayt] *v/t* spoil, impair; debase, corrupt; (*leg*) invalidate.

vitiation [vishi-*ay*shon] *n* act of vitiating; state of being vitiated.

viticulture [*vi*tikulcher] *n* vine growing.

vitiosity [viti-*o*siti] *n* viciousness; (*Scots leg*) invalidation.

vitreo- *pref* of or like glass.

vitreosity [vitRi-*o*siti] *n* quality of being vitreous.

vitreous [*vi*tRi-us] *adj* glassy; jelly-like, transparent; **v. humour, v. body** jelly-like substance in the eyeball; **v. electricity** positive electricity got by rubbing glass ~ **vitreously** *adv* ~ **vitreousness** *n*.

vitrescence [vitRe*se*ns] *n* glassiness; quality of being vitrescent.

vitrescent [vitRe*se*nt] *adj* capable of becoming glass; glassy.

vitri- *pref* of or like glass.

vitrifaction [vitRi*fak*shon] *n* act or process of making into glass; state of being vitrified.

vitrification [vitRifi*kay*shon] *n* vitrifaction.

vitrify [*vi*tRifI] *v/t* and *i* make into glass by fusing in great heat; become glass or glassy.

vitriol [*vi*tRi-ol] *n* sulphuric acid; (*fig*) sarcasm; (*chem*) a sulphate; **blue v.** copper sulphate; **green v.** ferrous sulphate; **white v.** zinc sulphate.

vitriolic [vitRi-*o*lik] *adj* of, like or obtained from vitriol; (*fig*) intensely sarcastic or condemning.

vitriolize [*vi*tRi-olIz] *v/t* and *i* turn into vitriol; throw vitriol at; become vitriolic.

vitro- *pref* of or like glass.

vituperate [vI*tew*peRayt] *v/t* and *i* scold violently, abuse.

vituperation [vItewpe*Ray*shon] *n* violent abuse.

vituperative [vI*tew*peRativ] *adj* abusive.

viva (1) [*vee*va] *interj* 'long live . . .', a cry of applause.

viva (2) [*vI*va] *n* (*coll*) oral examination.

vivace [veev*aa*chay] *adv* (*mus*) briskly.

vivacious [viv*ay*shus] *adj* brisk, lively; (*bot*) perennial ~ **vivaciously** *adv* ~ **vivaciousness** *n*.

vivacity [viv*a*siti] *n* vigour, liveliness; brilliance.

vivarium [vI*vair*Ri-um] *n* place artificially constructed for keeping animals in their natural surroundings; place where living animals are kept for food.

viva voce [vIva-*vO*si] *adv phr* orally ~ **viva voce** *adj* oral, spoken.

vivi- *pref* living; alive.

vivid [*vi*vid] *adj* vigorous, energetic; strongly or strikingly expressed; clearly or strongly perceived; (*of colour or light*) brilliant, intense ~ **vividly** *adv* ~ **vividness** *n*.

vivification [vivifi*kay*shon] *n* act of vivifying.

vivify [*vi*vifI] *v/t* give life to; revive; enliven, make more striking.

viviparous [viv*i*paRus] *adj* bearing young which develop directly in the womb, without interposed egg-tissues; (*bot*) having seeds that germinate within the parent plant ~ **viviparously** *adv*.

vivisect [vivi*sekt*] *v/t* and *i* practise vivisection (on).

vivisection [vivi*sek*shon] *n* act of operating or experimenting on living animals for medical or scientific research.

vivisectionist [vivi*sek*shonist] *n* one who practises or defends vivisection.

vixen [*vik*sen] *n* female fox; (*fig*) spiteful ill-tempered woman.

vixenish [*vik*senish] *adj* like a vixen.

viz [*viz*] *adv* namely, that is.

vizard see **visard**.

vizcacha [vis*ka*cha] *n* a burrowing rodent.

Vizier [vi*zeer*] *n* title of minister, *esp* Prime Minister, in Ottoman Turkey.

vizor see **visor**.

vocab [v*O*kab] *n* (*coll abbr*) vocabulary.

vocable [v*O*kab'l] *n* word.

vocabulary [v*O*kabewlaRi] *n* total number of words known or used by a person; words characteristic of a person, group, trade *etc*; list of words used in a textbook *etc*, with explanations or translations.

vocal [v*O*kal] *adj* of the voice; produced by voice; spoken; sung; (*mus*) composed for singing; (*fig*) ready or able to express opinions; **v. cords** vibrating membranes of the larynx.

vocalic [v*O*kalik] *adj* of or like a vowel.

vocalism [v*O*kalizm] *n* use of voice; use of vowels; vowel sound.

vocalist [v*O*kalist] *n* (*mus*) singer.

vocality [v*O*kaliti] *n* quality of being vocal.

vocalization [v*O*kalI*z*ayshon] *n* act or method of vocalizing.

vocalize [v*O*kalIz] *v/t* and *i* utter with vibration of vocal cords; convert into a vowel; add vowels or vowel points to; (*mus*) sing vowel sounds; exercise the voice.

vocally [v*O*kali] *adv* in a vocal way; by voice.

vocation [v*O*k*ay*shon] *n* natural ability and liking for some particular work; work undertaken as a moral or religious duty; trade, profession, occupation; divine guidance towards a career (*esp* religious).

vocational [vOkayshonal] *adj* of or for a career, occupation *etc*.

vocative [vokativ] *n* and *adj* (*gramm*) (case) expressing invocation or address.

vociferate [vOsifeRayt] *v/i* and *t* shout, bawl; speak noisily.

vociferation [vOsifeRayshon] *n* shouting.

vociferous [vOsifeRus] *adj* noisy, bawling ∼ **vociferously** *adv* ∼ **vociferousness** *n*.

vodka [vodka] *n* strong Russian alcoholic spirit distilled from rye.

voe [vO] *n* small bay, inlet.

vogue [vOg] *n* current fashion; fashionable habit; popularity; **v. word** word much in fashion.

voice [vois] *n* natural sounds produced in the throat and mouth, *esp* in speaking or singing; characteristic pitch *etc* of these in a particular person; expressed opinion, *esp* in politics; vote; (*fig*) that which expresses a message or meaning; (*phon*) sound produced by vibrating vocal cords; (*mus*) single strand in harmony or counterpoint > PDM; singer; (*gramm*) verb form indicating relation between subject and verb; **give v. to** express; **have a v. in** have the right to express opinion on; **in v.** physically fit to sing or speak well; **lose one's v.** be unable to use one's vocal cords ∼ **voice** *v/t* express in speech, utter; (*phon*) pronounce with vibrating vocal cords; adjust pitch and tone of (wind-instrument).

voiced [voist] *adj* having voice; having tone; (*phon*) uttered with vibrating vocal cords.

voiceless [voislis] *adj* dumb, silent; unspoken; (*phon*) uttered without voice ∼ **voicelessly** *adv* ∼ **voicelessness** *n*.

voice-over [vois-Over] *n* (*cin*, *TV*) spoken commentary or narration by unseen speaker.

voiceprint [voispRint] *n* (*phon*) visual recording of the pitch, stress, speed *etc* of speech.

void [void] *adj* empty; vacant, unoccupied; (*leg*) invalid, of no effect; **v. of** lacking ∼ **void** *n* empty space, vacuum; painful awareness of loss or deficiency; blank space; (*fig*) interstellar space ∼ **void** *v/t* discharge from the body; excrete; vomit; remove; (*leg*) annul.

voidable [voidab'l] *adj* (*leg*) that can be annulled.

voile [vwaal/voil] *n* thin cotton or woollen material.

volatile [volatIl] *adj* changeable, fickle; lively but unstable; (*chem*) tending to evaporate at normal temperatures.

volatility [volatiliti] *n* state or quality of being volatile.

volatilizable [volatilIzab'l] *adj* that can be volatilized.

volatilization [volatilIzayshon] *n* act of volatilizing; state of being volatilized.

volatilize [volatilIz] *v/t* and *i* cause to evaporate; (*fig*) make unsubstantial; evaporate.

vol-au-vent [vol-O-von(g)] *n* (*Fr*) light raised pie filled with meat or fish *etc*.

volcanic [volkanik] *adj* of or like a volcano; (*fig*) tending to act with sudden violence; **v. glass** obsidian ∼ **volcanically** *adv*.

volcano [volkaynO] *n* mountain or hill built up by the eruption of molten rock, ash *etc* from the earth's interior > PDG; **extinct v.** volcano no longer capable of eruption.

vole (1) [vOl] *n* small mouse-like rodent.

vole (2) *n* (*cards*) the winning of all the tricks in the hand ∼ **vole** *v/i* win all the tricks in the hand.

volet [volay] *n* side panel of a triptych.

volition [vOlishon] *n* act of willing; power of conscious decision and intention > PDP.

volitional [vOlishonal] *adj* of or by the will.

volkslied [folksleet] *n* (*Germ*) folksong.

volley [voli] *n* number of missiles thrown or shot at once at one target; rapid series of aggressive words or acts; (*cricket*, *tennis*) act of striking a ball before it has touched ground ∼ **volley** *v/t* and *i*.

volleyball [volibawl] *n* game in which a large ball is struck by hand to and fro across a high net.

volt (1) [vOlt] *n* and *v/i* volte.

volt (2) *n* (*elect*) electromotive force needed to carry one ampere of current against a resistance of one ohm > PDS.

voltage [vOltij] *n* electromotive force measured in volts.

voltaic [voltay-ik] *adj* (*elect*) producing electricity by chemical action > PDS.

volte [volt] *n* (*fencing*) a nimble movement to avoid a thrust; circular movement made by a horse ∼ **volte** *v/i* make a volte.

volte-face [volt-faas] *n* (*Fr*) act of turning to face the opposite direction; (*fig*) complete change of attitude.

voltmeter [vOltmeeter] *n* (*elect*) instrument for measuring electromotive force > PDS.

volubility [volewbiliti] *n* quality of being voluble.

voluble [volewb'l] *adj* talkative, talking fast and copiously ∼ **volubleness** *n* ∼ **volubly** *adv*.

volume [volewm] *n* book; book that is part of a series forming one work; large amount, bulk; intensity of sound, loudness; size measured in cubic units.

volume-control [volewm-kontROl] *n* knob that regulates loudness on a radio, record player *etc* by varying the resistance.

volumetric [volewmetRik] *adj* of or by measurement of volume; **v. analysis** branch of chemical quantitative analysis depending on measurements of volume > PDS.

voluminosity [volewminositi] *n* state or quality of being voluminous.

voluminous [volewminus] *adj* occupying much space, bulky; copious, extensive; enough to fill many volumes ∼ **voluminously** *adv* ∼ **voluminousness** *n*.

voluntarily [voluntaRili] *adv* freely; without payment; spontaneously, willingly.

voluntary [voluntaRi] *adj* done freely and willingly, not compelled; acting freely and willingly; offering services *etc* for no payment; controlled by the will, deliberate; (*of institutions*) supported by private charity ∼ **voluntary** *n* (*mus*) organ music played before or after a church service.

volunteer [volunteer] *v/i* and *t* freely and willingly offer to do or give something; offer oneself spontaneously for military service ∼ **volunteer** *n* one who offers to do a task, *esp* to do military service or undertake dangerous or arduous work ∼ **volunteer** *adj* of or like a volunteer; composed of volunteers; (*bot*) growing spontaneously.

voluptuary [vo*lu*ptew-aRi] *n* and *adj* (person) addicted to luxurious sensual pleasures; sensualist.

voluptuous [vo*lu*ptew-us] *adj* fond of costly and refined sensual pleasures; promoting or suggesting such pleasures, luxurious; showing or arousing sexual desire; expressing physical pleasure; plump and sexually attractive ~ **voluptuously** *adv* ~ **voluptuousness** *n*.

volute [vo*lewt*] *n* (*archi*) spiral scroll on capitals; twist, spiral, convolution; kind of gasteropod or its shell ~ **voluted** *adj*.

vomit [*vomit*] *v/t* and *i* spew, eject (contents of stomach) through the mouth; (*fig*) pour out violently or continuously; cast out with disgust ~ **vomit** *n* that which is or has been vomited; act of vomiting; emetic drug.

vomitive [*vomit*iv] *n* and *adj* (substance) causing vomiting, emetic.

vomitory [*vomit*eRi] *n* and *adj* vomitive.

voodoo [v*OO*d*OO*] *n* system of magical beliefs and practices among Negroes of West Indies and America ~ **voodoo** *v/t* bewitch.

voodooism [v*OO*d*OO*-izm] *n* voodoo.

voracious [vo*Ra*yshus] *adj* ravenous, devouring food copiously; (*fig*) greedy, insatiable; eager ~ **voraciously** *adv* ~ **voraciousness** *n*.

voracity [vo*Ra*siti] *n* voraciousness.

vortex (*pl* **vortices**) [*vaw*rteks] *n* whirlpool; whirling mass; (*fig*) anything which engulfs or absorbs.

vortical [*vaw*rtikal] *adj* whirling; of or like a vortex ~ **vortically** *adv*.

vorticism [*vaw*rtisizm] *n* (*arts*) an English variety of cubism > PDAA ~ **vorticist** *n* and *adj*.

votaress [v*O*taRis] *n* female votary.

votary [v*O*taRi] *n* one who has dedicated himself to a religion; ardent supporter or advocate of; enthusiast.

vote [v*O*t] *v/i* and *t* formally indicate one's preference in a choice between candidates, laws, policies *etc*; appoint, establish or accept by voting; elect; (*coll*) judge by common consent; (*coll*) suggest, propose; **v. down** defeat or reject by voting; **v. in** elect ~ **vote** *n* act of voting; right to vote; decision reached by voting.

voter [v*O*ter] *n* person entitled to vote; elector; one who votes.

voting-paper [v*O*ting-payper] *n* ballot-paper.

votive [v*O*tiv] *adj* given, done or offered *etc* to fulfil a vow.

vouch [v*owch*] *v/i* **v. for** guarantee, confirm; bear witness to the truth, honesty *etc* of.

voucher [v*owch*er] *n* one who vouches; ticket acting as substitute for cash; document confirming some fact, bearing witness to authenticity *etc*.

vouchsafe [vowch*sayf*] *v/t* grant condescendingly, deign to give.

voussoir [v*OO*swaar] *n* (*archi*) wedge-shaped stone in an arch or vault.

vow [v*ow*] *n* solemn promise or pledge, *esp* one made to God or in the name of something holy; what one has promised or sworn to do ~ **vow** *v/t* and *i* bind oneself by a vow (to do, give *etc*); promise solemnly; dedicate, consecrate; (*ar*) assert, declare.

vowel [v*ow*-il] *n* speech-sound formed by vibrating the vocal cords and allowing air to pass through the mouth without audible friction or stoppage; letter representing such a sound ~ **vowel** *adj* of a vowel.

voyage [v*oi*-ij] *n* journey by water, *usu* of some distance; (*fig*) progress ~ **voyage** *v/i* and *t* make a journey by water ~ **voyager** *n*.

voyeur [vwa-*yur*] *n* one who finds sexual pleasure in seeing sexual objects or acts > PDP.

voyeurism [*vwa*-yur*Rizm*] *n* outlook and habits of a voyeur ~ **voyeuristic** *adj*.

vulcanite [*vul*kanIt] *n* hard substance made by treating rubber with sulphur.

vulcanize [*vul*kanIz] *v/t* and *i* heat rubber with sulphur, either to make it hard, or to make it more elastic and durable.

vulgar [*vul*ger] *adj* coarse, unrefined, violating the conventions of polite society; (*ar*) of the common people; **v. fraction** fraction with numerator above denominator; **v. tongue** vernacular.

vulgarian [vul*gair*Ri-an] *n* vulgar person, *esp* one who is rich.

vulgarism [*vul*gaRizm] *n* vulgarity; vulgar word or expression; fault of grammar, pronunciation *etc* typical of uneducated speech.

vulgarity [vul*ga*Riti] *n* coarseness, crudity; lack of good manners and delicacy of feeling; bad taste.

vulgarization [vulgaRIza*y*shon] *n* act of vulgarizing; state of being vulgarized.

vulgarize [*vul*gaRIz] *v/t* make vulgar; cause to be too commonly known, visited *etc*.

vulgarly [*vul*gerli] *adv* in a vulgar way, coarsely; among the common people.

Vulgate [*vul*gayt] *n* fourth-century Latin version of the Bible used by Roman Catholics.

vulnerability [vulne*Ra*biliti] *n* state or quality of being vulnerable.

vulnerable [*vul*neRab'l] *adj* that can be wounded; open to attack, criticism *etc*; sensitive, easily hurt; (*contract bridge*) having won one game towards the rubber ~ **vulnerably** *adv*.

vulpicide [*vul*pisId] *n* act of killing a fox by other method than hunting it with hounds; one who thus kills a fox.

vulpine [*vul*pIn] *adj* of or like a fox; crafty.

vulture [*vul*cher] *n* large bird of prey which feeds mainly on carrion; (*fig*) ruthless extortioner, one who preys on others.

vulturine [*vul*cheRIn] *adj* of or like a vulture.

vulva [*vul*va] *n* (*anat*) the opening of the female genitals.

vulvar [*vul*var] *adj* of or in the vulva.

vulvo- *pref* of or in the vulva.

vying [v*I*-ing] *n* and *adj* (act of) competing.

W

w [*dub*'l-yOO] twenty-third letter of English alphabet; **w.c.** watercloset, lavatory.

wabble see wobble.

wacky [*waki*] *adj* (*coll*) crazy, happily mad.

wad [*wod*] *n* compact mass of soft material used in packing, bandaging *etc*; compact pile of sheets of paper, *esp* of banknotes ~ **wad** (*pres/part* **wadding**, *p/t* and *p/part* **wadded**) *v/t* press into a wad; pack, pad, stuff with a wad; line (garment) with wadding.

wadable, wadeable [*wayd*ab'l] *adj* that can be waded.

wadding [*wod*ing] *n* soft fibrous material for padding, stuffing, quilting *etc*; pad of cotton wool.

waddle [*wod*'l] *v/i* walk heavily with a swaying motion like a duck ~ **waddle** *n* a heavy, ungainly walk.

waddy [*wod*i] *n* war club of Australian aborigines.

wade [*wayd*] *v/t* and *i* cross (shallow stretch of water) on foot; step forward through shallow water, mud, snow *etc*; (*fig*) work laboriously (through); **w. in** step forward into shallow water; (*fig*) intervene, participate vigorously in.

wader [*wayd*er] *n* one who wades; angler's long waterproof boot; long-legged bird frequenting shallow water.

wadi [*wod*i] *n* desert watercourse > PDG.

wafer [*wayf*er] *n* very thin sweet biscuit eaten with ices; thin disk of bread used in Holy Communion; small disk of dried paste used as a seal ~ **wafer** *v/t* seal with a wafer.

waffle (1) [*wof*'l] *n* crisp kind of battercake cooked in an iron mould and eaten with honey or syrup.

waffle (2) *v/i* (*coll*) talk or write too vaguely; talk nonsense; talk incessantly ~ **waffle** *n* twaddle, nonsense.

waft [*woft/waaft*] *v/t* cause to move gently and smoothly through air or over water ~ **waft** *n* movement of bird's wing; faint odour, whiff.

wag (1) [*wag*] *n* one fond of making jokes.

wag (2) (*pres/part* **wagging**, *p/t* and *p/part* **wagged**) *v/t* and *i* move or shake up and down or from side to side ~ **wag** *n* act of wagging.

wage (1) [*wayj*] *n* rate of pay for manual or mechanical work; (*pl*) pay at regular intervals.

wage (2) *v/t* carry on, engage in.

wage-earner [*wayj*-urner] *n* one who works for wages.

wage-freeze [*wayj*-fReez] *n* period during which any increase in wages is forbidden.

wager [*wayj*er] *n* a bet; **w. of battle** (*hist*) trial by combat ~ **wager** *v/t* and *i* bet, stake; make a bet.

waggery [*wag*eRi] *n* comic remarks or conduct; jest, practical joke.

waggish [*wag*ish] *adj* comic, droll, mischievous ~ **waggishly** *adv* ~ **waggishness** *n*.

waggle [*wag*'l] *v/t* and *i* move (finger, hips *etc*) from side to side; shake to and fro ~ **waggle** *n* act of waggling.

waggon, waggoner, waggonette see wagon, wagoner, wagonette.

wagon, waggon [*wag*on] *n* four-wheeled vehicle for carrying heavy loads; railway truck; automobile with removable rear seats and hinged doors in rear to admit luggage ~ **wagoner, waggoner** *n* driver of a wagon.

wagonette, waggonette [wagon*et*] *n* horsedrawn four-wheeled open carriage, with facing seats along the sides; small automobile wagon.

wagon-lit [vagaa(ng)-*lee*] *n* (*Fr*) sleeping-car forming part of a train.

wagtail [*wag*tayl] *n* small bird that moves its long tail feathers up and down.

waif [*wayf*] *n* stray person or animal; (*fig*) abandoned or neglected child; (*leg*) lost property unclaimed; **waifs and strays** homeless persons, *esp* children.

wail [*wayl*] *v/t* and *i* utter long plaintive cries of grief; make mournful sound, lament ~ **wail** *n* cry of grief.

wainscot, wainscoting [*waynz*kot, *waynz*-koting] *n* wood panelling covering part of the height of the walls of a room.

wainwright [*wayn*Rit] *n* builder of wagons.

waist [*wayst*] *n* narrowest part of human trunk between ribs and hip-bones; part of garment that covers this; waistline; narrowed middle of some objects, *eg* violin; (*naut*) middle part of ship's upper deck; (*bui*) least thickness of a reinforced concrete stair slab.

waistband [*wayst*band] *n* band or sash at the waist.

waistcoat [*wayst*kOt] *n* close-fitting sleeveless male garment reaching to the waist, worn above the shirt and under the jacket.

waisted [*wayst*id] *adj* shaped to form a waist.

waist-high [*wayst*-hI] *adj* reaching as high as the waist.

waistline [*wayst*lIn] *n* narrowest part of woman's dress, coat *etc* at or close to the waist; measurement of a person's waist.

wait (1) [*wayt*] *v/t* and *i* watch for, await; postpone (meal) until someone arrives; defer action or remain in readiness until something expected happens; act as waiter or attendant; **w. for** remain in expectation of, await; **w. on, upon** fetch and carry for; (*fig*) attend, accompany; (*ar*) eagerly await; **w. up** not go to bed but remain waiting (for person) ~ **wait** *n* act or period of waiting; **lie in w., lay w.** prepare ambush (for).

wait (2) *n* (*usu pl*) one of group of persons going from door to door at Christmas singing carols > PDM.

waiter [*wayt*er] *n* one who waits; male servant who waits at table in hotel or restaurant; tray, salver.

waiting [*wayt*ing] *n* act of remaining in expectation; attendance (on superior); work of a waiter at table; **in w.** in attendance; **w. list** list of applicants waiting their turn for a vacancy ~ **waiting** *adj* serving.

waiting-room [*wayt*ing-ROOm] *n* room provided for those obliged to wait.

waitress [*wayt*Ris] *n* female servant who serves meals in café, restaurant or hotel.

waive [*wayv*] *v/t* relinquish (claim, right); refrain

815

from insisting upon; dispense with (ceremony); put aside for the present ~ **waiver** *n* (*leg*) act of relinquishing claim or right; document setting this forth.

wake (1) [*wayk*] *n* disturbed pattern of water left by moving ship; **in the w. of** immediately behind.

wake (2) (*p/t* woke, waked, *p/part* waked, woke, woken) *v/t* and *i* cease to sleep; rouse from sleep; stir up, excite; be awake, stay awake; return to consciousness from swoon *etc*.

wake (3) *n* (*hist*) annual festival commemorating dedication of church; vigil beside corpse throughout night before funeral; lamentation, feasting during a wake; (*usu pl*) annual holiday in the north of England ~ **wake** *v/t* hold a wake over (corpse).

wakeful [*wayk*fool] *adj* unable to sleep; vigilant, alert ~ **wakefully** *adv* ~ **wakefulness** *n*.

waken [*wayk*en] *v/t* and *i* cause to wake, rouse, stir up; become awake, recover consciousness.

wakey [*wayk*i] *interj* (*sl*) wake up!

waking [*wayk*ing] *adj* keeping watch; experienced while awake.

wale [*wayl*] *n* flesh mark, weal; rib or heavy twill in a fabric; (*pl*) (*naut*) thickest strakes.

waling [*wayl*ing] *n* horizontal board used in excavation to support sides from collapse >PDE.

walk [*wawk*] *v/i* and *t* advance by placing one foot before the other alternately; advance on foot at slow or moderate pace; traverse (specified distance) by walking; cause to walk; accompany or lead in walking; exercise; (*of ghost*) haunt; manifest its presence; **w. away from** outstrip easily; **w. away with** win easily; **w. into** (*coll*) attack, scold; devour; **w. off with** steal; win easily; **w. on** (*theat*) have a non-speaking part; **w. out** go on strike; leave angrily; **w. out on** desert; leave angrily; **w. out with** court, woo; **w. over** win easily or unopposed; **w. tall** look proud ~ **walk** *n* act of walking; manner of walking, gait; journey or excursion on foot, *esp* for pleasure or exercise; place prepared for walking, path, promenade; **cock of the w.** unrivalled leader; **w. of life** social position or occupation.

walkabout [*wawk*abowt] *n* a royal or important person's informal stroll among crowds; (*Aust*) aborigine's period of wandering in the bush for religious reasons or to relieve psychological stress.

walkaway [*wawk*away] *n* easily won contest.

walker [*wawk*er] *n* one who walks or is fond of walking; trainer of young hounds.

walkie-talkie [wawki-*tawk*i] *n* (*coll*) portable two-way radio-telephone set.

walking [*wawk*ing] *n* act or motion of one who walks; act or habit of going for excursions on foot, *usu* in the country.

walking-stick [*wawk*ing-stik] *n* thick wooden cane or metal stick used as support when walking or carried for fashion.

walkout [*wawk*owt] *n* industrial strike.

walkover [*wawk*Over] *n* easy victory won against no or negligible competition.

walkway [*wawk*way] *n* connecting passage between buildings; covered pavement; planned route for walkers leading to places of particular interest or beauty.

wall [*wawl*] *n* upright structure, usually of uniform thickness, forming part of a room or building or a boundary to land; (*fig*) barrier, rampart; inside surface of cavity or vessel; **walls have ears** beware eavesdroppers; **with one's back to the w.** fighting against odds; **go to the w.** succumb, become bankrupt; **w. box** cast iron box (*esp* letterbox) built into brickwork ~ **wall** *v/t* surround, defend with a wall; **w. up** close aperture with a wall; immure.

walla, wallah [*wol*a] *n* (*Anglo-Indian*) employee, servant; (*coll*) man, fellow.

wallaby [*wol*abi] *n* small kangaroo; (*coll*) **an** Australian.

wallet [*wol*it] *n* pocket-book for banknotes *etc*; (*ar*) pilgrim's knapsack; pedlar's pack.

wall-eye [*wawl*-1] *n* eye with whitish iris; eye with a squint ~ **wall-eyed** *adj*.

wallflower [*wawl*flowr] *n* perennial cruciferous plant with clusters of fragrant flowers; (*coll*) girl who sits out dances for lack of partners.

wall-game [*wawl*-gaym] *n* variety of football played at Eton.

Walloon [wol*OOn*] *n* a dialect of French spoken in south-east Belgium; native of areas where this is spoken; Belgian whose native language is French or Walloon ~ **Walloon** *adj*.

wallop [*wol*op] *v/t* and *i* (*coll*) beat, thrash ~ **wallop** *n* (*coll*) heavy blow, whack; strength to deliver such a blow; (*sl*) beer ~ **wallop** *adv* (*coll*) heavily ~ **walloping** *n* (*coll*) a thrashing, licking ~ **walloping** *adj* (*coll*) of large size.

wallow [*wol*O] *v/i* roll about delightedly, *esp* in mud; (*fig*) indulge to excess, take inordinate delight (in sensual pleasures); **wallowing in money** very rich ~ **wallow** *n* act of wallowing; place where animals wallow.

wallpaper [*wawl*payper] *n* decorated printed paper sold in rolls for pasting on walls.

walnut [*wawl*nut] *n* hard spherical nut with edible kernel; tree that bears this; decorative timber from this tree.

walrus [*wawl*Rus] *n* large, amphibious, arctic mammal with long drooping tusks; **w. moustache** (*coll*) thick drooping moustache.

waltz [*wawls*] *n* dance performed by couples to music in triple time; music to accompany this dance > PDM ~ **waltz** *v/i* and *t* dance a waltz; whirl (partner) round in a waltz ~ **waltzer** *n*.

wampum [*womp*um] *n* Amerindian beads made from shells, *esp* when used as money.

wan [*won*] *adj* pale, colourless, sickly; (*ar*) dark.

wand [*wond*] *n* slim straight stick, *esp* as symbol of authority or magic power; conductor's baton.

wander [*wond*er] *v/i* rove without purpose or planned route, ramble; (*fig*) stray from the point (in discussion *etc*); lose control of one's mind, talk incoherently ~ **wanderer** *n*.

wandering [*wond*eRing] *adj* moving about without purpose or direction; (*fig*) out of one's mind, incoherent, rambling ~ **wandering** *n* (*usu pl*) aimless travel; delirium.

wanderlust [*wond*erlust] *n* urge to travel.

wanderplug [*wond*erplug] *n* (*elect*) plug that can fit any of various sockets.

wane [*wayn*] *v/i* decrease in size, *esp* of illuminated surface of the moon > PDG; decrease in strength or importance ~ **wane** *n* act or process of waning; **on the w.** decreasing.

wangle [*wang*-g'l] *v/t* and *i* (*sl*) arrange (report *etc*) to suit oneself, fake; obtain by guile and trickery; use irregular means to accomplish a purpose ~ **wangle** *n* (*sl*) act of wangling; something dishonestly contrived or manipulated ~ **wangler** *n*.

wank, whank [*wank*] *v/t* and *i* (*vulg*) masturbate.

wanly [*won*li] *adv* in a pale or sickly way.

wanness [*won*-nis] *n* quality of being wan.

want [*wont*] *v/t* and *i* need, require the use, service, presence *etc* of; desire, long for; lack; be lacking, fall short of; be destitute; **be wanted** (*coll*) be sought by police as suspected of a crime; **w. for** lack ~ **want** *n* lack, deficiency; something needed or desired; **be in w.** be extremely poor.

wanting [*won*ting] *adj* needful; insufficient, defective; (*coll*) mentally deficient ~ **wanting** *prep* without, lacking.

wanton [*won*ton] *adj* undisciplined, unrestrained; malicious, unprovoked; irresponsible; capricious, frolicsome; extravagant, lavish; unchaste, licentious ~ **wanton** *n* wanton person, *esp* an unchaste woman ~ **wanton** *v/i* behave wantonly; frolic; run riot ~ **wantonly** *adv* ~ **wantonness** *n*.

wapentake [*wap*entayk] *n* (*hist*) one of the local administrative divisions in the territory of the Five Boroughs in the Danelaw.

wapiti [*waa*piti] *n* species of N. American deer.

war [*wawr*] *n* conflict carried on by physical violence between nations, tribes or other large groups of persons; bitter conflict, rivalry or hostility; **civil w.** war between two parties within one State; **cold w.** antagonism between States without actual fighting; **w. crime** breach of laws or customs of war; **in the wars** showing injuries; **holy w.** war to defend or propagate a religion, crusade; **w. to the knife** merciless hostility; **make w.** fight, engage in warfare; **w. of nerves** systematic attempt to destroy enemy's morale; **open w.** undisguised hostility; **sinews of w.** money and munitions needed for warfare; **w. widow** woman whose husband has been killed at war; **w. work** any work helping a country's ability to make war ~ **war** (*pres/part* **warring**, *p/t* and *p/part* **warred**) *v/i* make war; conflict, contend ~ **war** *adj* of or for war.

warble (1) [*wawrb*'l] *v/i* and *t* sing with a tremolo effect, sing with trills; sing ~ **warble** *n* act or sound of warbling.

warble (2) *n* hard skin tumour in horses, cattle *etc*.

warbler [*wawrb*ler] *n* genus of singing birds.

warbling [*wawrb*ling] *n* a trill; sweet singing, song ~ **warbling** *adj*.

warcry [*wawr*kRI] *n* slogan, formalized cheer *etc* used as encouragement before or during battle; slogan epitomizing aims or loyalties.

ward [*wawrd*] *n* action of watching or guarding; minor under care of a guardian; section or room of hospital, prison *etc*; division of a borough for administrative purposes; (*fencing*) defensive stance or parry; mechanism of a lock that prevents the use of any other key but the right one ~ **ward** *v/t* defend, protect, act as guardian to; **w. off** avert, fend off repel.

wardance [*wawr*daans] *n* ritual dance of savages before battle.

warden [*wawr*den] *n* one who guards; governor; churchwarden; title of head of certain Oxford colleges and some schools; civil defence officer in wartime; (*ar*) gatekeeper, guard; **traffic w.** official authorized to control the parking of vehicles.

warder [*wawr*der] *n* prison officer, jailer; (*ar*) staff of authority.

wardress [*wawr*dRis] *n* female prison officer.

wardrobe [*wawr*dROb] *n* cupboard or piece of furniture in which clothes are kept; stock of clothes.

wardroom [*wawr*dROOm] *n* mess-room of naval officers above rank of lieutenant.

ware (1) [*wair*] *v/t* be on guard against.

ware (2) *n* (*collect*) articles for sale; manufactured articles, *esp* pottery; (*pl*) things offered for sale.

warehouse [*wair*hows] *n* building used for the storage of merchandise ~ **warehouse** *v/t* store in a warehouse.

warfare [*wawr*fair] *n* act of waging war, military operations; (*fig*) conflict, strife.

wargame [*wawr*gaym] *n* game in which players demonstrate tactical skill by moving pieces symbolizing troops, weapons *etc* on maps; reenactment of historical battle with toy soldiers.

warhead [*wawr*hed] *n* explosive charge of guided missile.

warhorse [*wawr*hawrs] *n* (*ar*) a charger; (*fig*) war veteran; elderly and pugnacious person.

warily [*wair*Rili] *adv* in a wary way.

wariness [*wair*Rinis] *n* state or quality of being wary.

warlike [*wawr*lIk] *adj* of, like, or for war; disposed to warfare, bellicose, hostile; skilled in war, martial, valiant.

warlock [*wawr*lok] *n* (*ar*) wizard, sorcerer.

warlord [*wawr*lawrd] *n* military leader, *esp* one who relishes warfare.

warm [*wawr*m] *adj* moderately hot, having a pleasant degree of heat; uncomfortably hot; preventing coldness; affectionate, sympathetic; enthusiastic, ardent; excited; hot-tempered; showing annoyance or hostility; (*of work etc*) strenuous; (*fig*) dangerous; (*of a trail, clue etc*) freshly made; (*coll*) close to truth or to something hidden, on the right track; (*of colour*) with red, yellow or orange predominating; (*coll*) wealthy ~ **warm** *v/t* and *i* make warm or warmer; become warm or warmer; make happy, cheer; **w. up** reheat; become livelier ~ **warm** *n* act of warming; **British w.** short thick overcoat worn by British army officers.

warm-blooded [wawrm-*blud*id] *adj* (*of birds, mammals*) having warm blood; (*fig*) emotional.

warm-hearted [wawrm-*haart*id] *adj* sympathetic, generous.

warming-pan [*wawr*ming-pan] *n* long-handled metal pan holding live coals, formerly used to warm beds.

warmly [*wawr*mli] *adv* with warmth, cordially.

war-minded [wawr-*mInd*ed] *adj* mentally ready for war, eager to fight.

warmonger [*wawr*mung-ger] *n* one who foments war.

warmth [*wawr*mth] *n* sensation below the level of heat; state or degree of being warm; (*fig*) state of excitement, vehemence; anger; enthusiasm, cordiality; glow of colour of certain hues of red.

warn [*wawrn*] *v/t* give information of approaching danger; caution, admonish.

warning [*wawrn*ing] *n* act of one who warns; notice of possible danger; admonition; something that warns, premonition; notice to quit or of the termination of a business relation ~ **warning** *adj* that warns.

warp [*wawrp*] *v/t* and *i* twist out of shape, distort; pervert; (*naut*) move (ship) by hauling on rope attached to fixed object; fertilize (land) by periodic flooding; become twisted or bent ~ **warp** *n* threads running lengthwise in the loom and crossed by the woof; any distortion of timber caused in seasoning; (*naut*) rope used in moving a ship; silty clay formed by flooding low-lying alluvial land.

warpaint [*wawr*paynt] *n* paint applied by savages to face and body; (*fig*) ceremonial dress; finery; (*theat sl*) make-up.

warpath [*wawr*path] *n* route taken by Red Indians on warlike expedition; **on the w.** (*fig*) belligerent.

warped [*wawrpd*] *adj* twisted, bent; perverted.

warplane [*wawr*playn] *n* military aircraft.

warrant [*wo*Rant] *n* justification, foundation, authority; document that authorizes, *esp* arrest or police search; (*leg*) writ; certificate of appointment of officer below commissioned rank; **dividend w.** document authorizing payment of money; **w. officer** highest rank of non-commissioned officer ~ **warrant** *v/t* justify, authorize; vouch for, guarantee; (*coll*) declare, assert.

warranty [*wo*Ranti] *n* authorization, justification; guarantee; (*leg*) vendor's guarantee that property sold is up to standard and his to sell.

warren [*wo*Ren] *n* area of land full of rabbits' burrows; (*fig*) overcrowded confused mass of houses and streets, or rooms and passages.

warrior [*wo*Ri-er] *n* soldier, fighting-man.

warship [*wawr*ship] *n* battleship, man-of-war.

wart [*wawrt*] *n* hard excrescence on the skin; (*bot*) glandular protuberance.

warthog [*wawr*thog] *n* tusked wild hog.

wartime [*wawr*tIm] *adj* and *n* (in) a period of war.

warty [*wawr*ti] *adj* of, or covered with, warts.

war-weary [*wawr*-weerRi] *adj* depressed or exhausted by prolonged war.

wary [*wair*Ri] *adj* cautious; circumspect.

was [*woz*] *1st and 3rd pers pret sing* of **be.**

wash [*wosh*] *v/t* and *i* make clean by the use of water or other liquid; (*fig*) purify; exert a force of water; flow past, lave; cover with thin coat of paint or metal; cleanse oneself; wash clothes *etc*; undergo washing without deterioration; (*coll*) bear investigation, be convincing; **w. away** obliterate; **w. down** clean by pouring water over; **w. (food) down** swallow liquid after eating; **w. one's hands of** disclaim responsibility for; **w. dirty linen in public** conduct personal quarrels in presence of others; **w. out** soak, rinse and squeeze; remove by washing; (*coll*) cancel; **washed out** weary, exhausted; pale; **w. up** clean crockery, cutlery *etc* used at a meal; **washed up** (*coll*) ruined, finished ~ **wash** *n* act of cleansing with liquid, *esp* water; articles needing to be laundered; articles just laundered; rough waves set up behind vessel moving through water; application of thin paint or distemper;

medicinal or cosmetic lotion; thin weak drink; liquid refuse; thin metal plating.

washable [*wosh*ab'l] *adj* that can be washed without damage.

washbasin [*wosh*baysun] *n* vessel for washing in, *esp* fixed bowl with taps and outlet pipe.

washboard [*wosh*bawrd] *n* corrugated board for rubbing clothes on while washing them.

wash-day [*wosh*-day] *n* day for doing the laundry.

washer [*wosher*] *n* one who does the washing; washing-machine; flattened rubber or fibre or steel ring under a bolt head or nut to distribute pressure and form a seal.

wash-house [*wosh*-hows] *n* outhouse laundry.

washily [*wosh*ili] *adv* in a washy manner.

washiness [*wosh*ines] *n* quality of being washy.

washing [*wosh*ing] *n* process of cleansing by water; clothes to be washed; clothes washed; rinsing dust, mud *etc* from ore, coal *etc* ~ **washing** *adj* that can be washed without damage; used for washing; that washes.

washing-day [*wosh*ing-day] *n* wash-day.

washing-machine [*wosh*ing-masheen] *n* machine in which clothes, linen *etc* are automatically washed and rinsed.

washing-soda [*wosh*ing-sOda] *n* crystalline sodium carbonate.

washing-up [*wosh*ing-up] *n* the cleansing of table utensils after a meal; utensils so washed.

washleather [*wosh*leTHer] *n* piece of chamois leather.

wash-out [*wosh*-owt] *n* earth erosion by flood; (*fig*) complete failure; useless person.

washroom [*wosh*ROOm] *n* (*US*) lavatory.

washstand [*wosh*stand] *n* flat-topped piece of bedroom furniture for washbasin *etc*; apparatus of bowl, taps, outlet pipes *etc* fixed to wall of bathroom *etc*.

washy [*wosh*i] *adj* watery; feeble; weak in colour.

wasn't [*wozn't*] *abbr* was not.

wasp [*wosp*] *n* winged insect with yellow markings and powerful sting; (*US*) white Anglo-Saxon Protestant person; **w. waisted** slender at the waist.

waspish [*wosp*ish] *adj* bad-tempered, spiteful.

wassail [*wos*'l/*wosayl/wasayl*] *n* (*ar*) (*as toast*) 'your good health!'; festive occasion, drinking-bout; (*ar*) spiced ale ~ **wassail** *v/t* and *i* drink a health to, toast; drink healths, carouse ~ **wassailer** *n*.

wassailing [*wosayl*ing] *n* act of going from house to house singing Christmas carols.

wast [*wost*] *p/t* (*ar*) *2nd pers sing* of **be.**

wastage [*wayst*ij] *n* amount lost by waste; loss.

waste [*wayst*] *adj* uncultivated, desolate; superfluous, useless; **lay w.** ravage ~ **waste** *n* desolate expanse of land or water; refuse; dirty water; act of wasting, extravagant use; unnecessary expenditure; **go to w.** be squandered; **w. pipe** pipe for carrying off water from basin or sink ~ **waste** *v/t* and *i* use extravagantly, squander; ravage, devastate; (*leg*) let (property) deteriorate through neglect; dwindle; **w. away** lose weight; lose vitality.

wasteful [*wayst*fool] *adj* causing waste, extravagant ~ **wastefully** *adv* ~ **wastefulness** *n*.

waster [*wayst*er] *n* spendthrift, ne'er-do-well.

wasting [*wayst*ing] *adj* that wastes; (*med*) causing loss of weight and strength.

wastrel [*wayst*Rel] *n* ne'er-do-well.

watch [*woch*] *v/t* and *i* observe, be a spectator of; keep under close observation; guard carefully; note carefully; keep vigil, stay deliberately awake; be alert; be on the look-out; **w. for** await alertly; **w. out** be on one's guard; **w. over** guard, protect ∼ **watch** *n* observation, act of watching; alertness, vigilance; vigil; small timepiece worn or carried on the person; (*naut*) period of duty on deck; (*ar*) man or men employed to preserve public order.

watchdog [*woch*dog] *n* dog trained to guard premises.

watcher [*woch*er] *n* one who watches.

watchful [*woch*fool] *adj* vigilant, alert ∼ **watchfully** *adv* ∼ **watchfulness** *n*.

watchguard [*woch*gaard] *n* protective metal grid over watch-glass; chain or strap to attach watch to clothing.

watchkey [*woch*kee] *n* key for winding up a watch.

watchmaker [*woch*mayker] *n* man who makes or repairs watches.

watchman [*woch*man] *n* man who guards premises at night.

watchtower [*woch*tower] *n* lofty tower commanding countryside.

watchword [*woch*wurd] *n* slogan, motto or rallying-cry of party or cause.

water [*wawt*er] *n* transparent colourless liquid, the normal oxide of hydrogen, *usu* containing dissolved substances > PDS; any large expanse of this; sea, river, lake *etc*; urine; any liquid secretion in the body; (*of diamonds*) brilliance; (*naut*) state of the tide; (*pl*) body of water; **deep w.** (*fig*) difficulty; mystery; **hold w.** be watertight; be convincing; **in hot w.** in trouble; **in low w.** short of money; **keep one's head above w.** hold one's own; remain solvent; **make (pass) w.** urinate; **of the first w.** of finest quality; **throw cold w. on** discourage ∼ **water** *v/t* and *i* make wet with water; irrigate; dilute; provide (animals) with water; obtain water to drink; take in water; secrete liquid; (*of mouth*) salivate; (*of eyes*) fill with tears; **w. down** dilute; **make one's mouth w.** be very appetizing or desirable.

waterage [*wawt*eRij] *n* conveyance by water; charge for this.

water-bailiff [*wawt*er-baylif] *n* custom-house official inspecting ships entering or leaving port.

waterbed [*wawt*erbed] *n* rubber mattress filled with water.

water-biscuit [*wawt*er-biskit] *n* thin, plain hard biscuit.

waterborne [*wawt*erbawrn] *n* carried or disseminated by water.

waterbuck [*wawt*erbuk] *n* large South African antelope.

waterbus [*wawt*erbus] *n* boat carrying passengers along a lake or river route.

waterbutt [*wawt*erbut] *n* cask for collecting rain.

water-cannon [*wawt*er-kanon] *n* apparatus that discharges violent jets of water.

water-chute [*wawt*er-shOOt] *n* sloping channel for sliding into water.

water-closet [*wawt*er-kloset] *n* lavatory flushed by cistern.

watercolour [*wawt*erkuler] *n* pigment whose solvent is water; picture painted on paper in this medium; technique of such painting.

watercourse [*wawt*erkawrs] *n* stream; channel made by or for stream.

watercress [*wawt*erkRes] *n* creeping herb growing in water, used in salads.

water-diviner [wawter-div*I*ner] *n* one who uses dowsing rod to detect water underground.

watered [*wawt*erd] *adj* supplied with water; with wavy pattern; (*of capital*) diluted by the issue of stock without increased profits or growth.

waterfall [*wawt*erfawl] *n* precipitous descent of a body of water from a bed of hard rock in river course > PDG.

waterfront [*wawt*erfRunt] *n* (*US*) city buildings or land facing sea or lake.

water-gas [*wawt*er-gas] *n* fuel gas, made by the action of steam on red-hot coke, consisting mainly of carbon monoxide and hydrogen.

waterglass [*wawt*erglaas] *n* sodium silicate, used for egg preserving.

water-hammer [*wawt*er-hamer] *n* knocking noise in water pipe.

water-ice [*wawt*er-*Is*] *n* confection of frozen flavoured water.

wateriness [*wawt*eRines] *n* state or quality of being watery.

watering [*wawt*eRing] *n* act of supplying or sprinkling with water; (*of mouth*) filling with saliva; (*of eye*) running with tears; (*fig*) dilution of company's capital.

watering-can [*wawt*eRing-kan] *n* vessel with long spout for watering plants by hand.

watering-place [*wawt*eRing-plays] *n* pool *etc* where animals drink; health resort with medicinal waters; seaside resort.

waterish [*wawt*eRish] *adj* resembling water; dilute, weak.

waterlevel [*wawt*erlevel] *n* flat surface of still water; height reached by accumulated water; concentration or proportion of water in a substance.

waterlily [*wawt*erlili] *n* aquatic plant with flat floating leaves and large flowers.

waterline [*wawt*erlIn] *n* (*naut*) line where the bottom colour paint meets the topside colour; line to which water rises.

waterlogged [*wawt*erlogd] *adj* made unmanageable by flooding; scarcely afloat.

watermain [*wawt*ermayn] *n* underground pipe carrying water supply.

watermark [*wawt*ermaark] *n* (*typ*) a design manufactured into paper; (*naut*) fore-and-aft set of figures denoting draught marks.

water-melon [*wawt*er-melon] *n* large, yellow edible fruit with juicy pulp.

watermill [*wawt*ermill] *n* mill driven by water.

waterproof [*wawt*erpROOf] *adj* not letting water through ∼ **waterproof** *n* material or garment to keep rain out ∼ **waterproof** *v/t* render waterproof ∼ **waterproofing** process of rendering (material) waterproof.

water-rat [*wawt*er-Rat] *n* semi-aquatic vole.

water-rate [*wawt*er-Rayt] *n* water company's charge for water supply.

watershed [*wawt*ershed] *n* high ground separating the headstreams which are tributary to different water systems or basins > PDG; (*fig*) moment of decisive change.

waterside [*wawt*ersId] *n* edge of sea, lake *etc*.

waterskiing [*wawt*erskee-ing] *n* sport of standing

on skis while being towed by a motorboat ~ **waterskier** n.

water-softener [wawter-sofner] n device for removing the causes of hardness of water > PDS.

watersplash [wawtersplash] n ford across shallow stream.

waterspout [wawterspowt] n tornado occurring at sea > PDG.

water-supply [wawter-suplI] n system of pipes, storage tanks etc supplying water to a town, house etc; amount of water thus supplied; available water.

watertable [wawtertayb'l] n level below which ground is saturated with water.

watertight [wawtertIt] adj so close-fitting that no water can get in or out; (fig) entirely separate; (fig) irrefutable, flawless.

waterwagon [wawterwagon] n mobile tank carrying supplies of water; **on the w.** (coll) abstaining from alcohol.

waterwheel [wawterweel] n wheel turned by flow of water.

waterwings [wawterwingz] n (pl) inflated bladders to support swimmer.

waterworks [wawterwurks] n (pl) buildings housing plant supplying water; (coll) urinary system; **turn on the w.** (sl) weep.

watery [wawteRi] adj of or like water; full of water; containing too much water; indicating rain; (fig) weak, pale, washed out; insipid.

watt [wot] n unit of electrical power > PDS. ˙

wattage [wotij] n power expressed in watts. ˛

wattle (1) [wot'l] n fence of poles and twigs plaited together; fleshy growth at neck of turkey etc; barbel of fish ~ **wattled** adj.

wattle (2) n mimosa.

wave [wayv] v/t and i move (something) to and fro in the air with a sweeping motion, brandish; express (greeting, farewell etc) by raising and moving the hand; make undulations in the hair; raise and move the hand as a signal; sway to and fro, flutter; lie in a series of undulations ~ **wave** n undulation on surface of sea or any large body of water, billow; undulation upon any surface, esp in the hair; one of a series; upsurge; (fig) expression of emotion rapidly communicated from person to person; (phys) periodic disturbance in a medium, or in space, which transmits energy; **w. mechanics** branch of quantum mechanics concerned with the wave-like properties of particles.

waveband [wayvband] n (rad) one particular range of wavelengths.

waved [wayvd] adj (of hair) artificially set in waves.

wavelength [wayvlength] n distance between successive points of equal phase of a wavemotion > PDS; **on the same w.** (fig) sharing similar tastes or opinions; able to understand one another.

wavelet [wayvlet] n a small wave.

wavepower [wayvpowr] n mechanical energy of sea waves, esp if used to generate electricity.

waver [wayver] v/i be unsteady; fluctuate; (fig) vacillate, be irresolute, falter ~ **waverer** n.

wavy [wayvi] adj full of waves; swaying to and fro; with a succession of curves.

wax (1) [waks] n a solid insoluble non-greasy substance which softens and melts at low temperature (eg paraffin wax); (chem) esterified higher fatty acid (eg beeswax) > PDS ~ **wax** v/t treat with wax.

wax (2) n (sl) fit of temper, rage.

wax (3) v/i increase in size; (ar) become.

waxbill [waksbil] n small bird of the weaver family with a bill of waxy appearance.

waxcloth [wakskloth] n impregnated floorcloth.

waxen [waksen] adj made of wax; resembling wax; smooth, pale.

waxpaper [wakspayper] n paper impregnated with wax.

waxwing [wakswing] n bird with red-tipped wings.

waxwork [wakswurk] n technique of making wax figures; statuary in wax; (pl) wax effigies of famous people dressed for exhibition.

waxy [waksi] adj like wax; (sl) angry.

way [way] n road, path; route; direction; distance travelled or to be travelled; progress, headway; condition, state; manner, method; characteristic behaviour; (naut) movement through the water; (pl) habits, idiosyncrasies; (pl) slipway for launching ship; **by the w.** incidentally; **by w. of** as substitute for; with intention of; **get one's own w.** get what one wants; **give w.** weaken, yield; **go out of one's w. for** give oneself trouble for; **have a w. with one** be charmingly persuasive; **in a bad w.** seriously sick in mind or body; **in the family w.** pregnant; **in the w.** obstructing; **no w.!** (coll) certainly not!; it is impossible!; **out of the w.** unusual; inaccessible; **(put someone) out of the w.** kill him; **right of w.** legal right to traverse; **put (someone) in the w. of** provide him with an opportunity; **under w.** moving; (fig) making progress; **ways and means** devices, resources ~ **way** adv (coll) far out; **w. back** (coll) long ago.

waybill [waybil] n list of passengers and goods.

wayfarer [wayfairReR] n traveller on foot.

waylay (p/t and p/part **waylaid**) [waylay] v/t intercept to speak to or to attack.

way-out [way-owt] adj (sl) very unusual or advanced, eccentric.

wayside [waysId] n edge of road or path ~ **wayside** adj.

wayward [waywerd] adj wilful, perverse; inconsiderate; capricious ~ **waywardly** adv ~ **waywardness** n.

we [wee] pron 1st pers pl of **I**; (used by sovereigns, princes and editors) **I**.

weak [week] adj lacking in strength, feeble; frail, delicate; irresolute, not forceful; below the normal standard; insipid, watery; (of a verb) forming its past tense by the addition of -d or -t; **a w. brother (sister)** (US) an unreliable person.

weaken [weeken] v/t and i make weaker; fail in strength; become less determined.

weak-headed [week-hedid] adj mentally deficient.

weak-kneed [week-need] adj (fig) timid, lacking resolution.

weakling [weekling] n person or animal lacking strength; person lacking strength of character or ability.

weakly (1) [weekli] adj poor in health.

weakly (2) adv in a feeble manner.

weak-minded [week-*mI*ndid] *adj* mentally deficient.

weakness [*week*nes] *n* feebleness of body or mind; least efficient part; defect of character, failing; fondness, irrational liking (for); inadequacy.

weak-spirited [week-*spi*Ritid] *adj* lacking courage and independence.

weal (1), **wale** [*weel, wayl*] *n* ridge raised on the flesh by a blow from a lash.

weal (2) *n* happiness, good fortune, wellbeing; **in w. and woe** in good times and bad; **the public w.** the good of society as a whole.

weald [*weeld*] *n* stretch of open country once wooded; **the W.** those parts of Kent, Surrey, and Sussex between the N and S Downs ~ **wealden** *adj.*

wealth [*welth*] *n* plentiful supply, abundance; aggregate (*usu* abundance) of worldly possessions; affluence ~ **wealthy** *adj* rich, affluent.

wean [*ween*] *v/t* accustom (baby) to food other than the mother's milk; (*fig*) cause to break away from an attachment or interest > PDP.

weapon [*wepon*] *n* any object used or designed for attack or defence.

weaponry [*wepon*Ri] *n* military weapons, armaments.

wear (1) (*p/t* **wore**, *p/part* **worn**) [*wair*] *v/t* and *i* have on the body as clothing or ornament; dress oneself in; do (hair) in a certain way; present, exhibit (look, expression); reduce or cause to diminish by use; be so reduced; tire, exhaust; withstand usage, be unimpaired by long usage; (*sl*) accept, tolerate; **w. away** efface; pass slowly; **w. down** gradually reduce; break down (resistance); **w. off** gradually disappear; **w. out** make or become threadbare; tire out, exhaust; **w. well** show little sign of age; long use *etc* ~ **wear** *n* act of wearing; clothes suitable to wear; usage; damage from usage; lasting quality; (**fair**) **w. and tear** damage caused by (reasonable) usage.

wear (2) (*p/t* and *p/part* **wore**) *v/t* and *i* (*naut*) put (ship) about; (*of ship*) change course by turning prow away from the wind.

wearable [*wair*Rab'l] *adj* fit to be worn.

wearily [*weer*Rili] *adj* in a weary manner.

weariness [*weer*Rines] *n* fatigue, tiredness.

wearing [*wair*Ring] *adj* undergoing wear by use; fatiguing.

wearisome [*weer*Risum] *adj* tiring; boring.

weary [*weer*Ri] *adj* exhausted; causing exhaustion, tedious ~ **weary** *v/t* and *i* tire; exhaust the patience of someone; become tired.

weasel [*wee*zel] *n* small carnivorous animal with sharp features and long thin body.

weather [*weTH*er] *n* condition of atmosphere at certain time or over a period > PDG; **keep one's w. eye open** be on the alert; **make heavy w. of** have undue difficulty with; **under the w.** indisposed; depressed ~ **weather** *v/t* and *i* expose to the air, season; show change from exposure to air *etc*; get safely through (storm); (*fig*) survive; (*naut*) pass on windward side of ~ **weather** *adj* (*naut*) facing the wind > PDSa.

weather-beaten [*weTH*er-beeten] *adj* damaged by exposure to the weather; (*of face*) tanned, bronzed, roughened.

weather-boarding [*weTH*er-bawrding] *n* (*bui*)

overlapping boards as protection against bad weather.

weatherbound [*weTH*erbownd] *adj* delayed by adverse winds; kept indoors by bad weather.

weathercock [*weTH*erkok] *n* elaborately-shaped metal device which pivots to indicate wind direction; (*fig*) changeable person.

weathered [*weTH*erd] *adj* (*geol*) worn away by exposure; made to slope to throw off rainwater.

weather-forecast [*weTH*er-fawrkaast] *n* description of weather conditions and prospects based on meteorological observation.

weathering [*weTH*eRing] *n* (*archi*) slope on coping, buttress *etc* to throw off rainwater; (*min*) any chemical or mechanical change in minerals caused by exposure > PDG, PGE.

weatherman [*weTH*erman] *n* (*rad, TV*) expert who describes and forecasts weather conditions.

weatherproof [*weTH*erpROOf] *adj* capable of keeping out wind and rain.

weather-prophet [*weTH*er-pRofit] *n* amateur weather predictor.

weatherside [*weTH*ersId] *n* side on which the wind blows.

weather-station [*weTH*er-stayshon] *n* meteorological observation post.

weatherstrip [*weTH*erstRip] *n* draught excluder around door or window.

weathervane [*weTH*ervayn] *n* weathercock.

weave (*p/t* **wove**, *p/part* **woven**) *v/t* and *i* form (threads) into a fabric by intertwining; plait, twist; wind in and out; change direction frequently, dodge; (*fig*) introduce (details) into story; fabricate (tale); devise, contrive (plot); practise weaving; **get weaving** (*sl*) make an active start, begin energetically ~ **weave** *n* particular pattern of a fabric.

weaver [*weev*er] *n* one who weaves, *esp* cloth.

weaving [*weev*ing] *n* act or process of making fabric from intertwined threads; fabric so made.

weazen see **wizen**.

weazened see **wizened**.

web [*web*] *n* something woven; filmy net spun by spiders *etc*, cobweb; membrane between digits of bat, waterfowl *etc*; large roll of printing-paper; (*archi*) infilling between ribs of a vault; (*bui*) vertical plate joining flanges of joist, girder or beam; **w. of deceit** succession of ingenious falsehoods.

web- *pref* webbed, having membrane between.

webbed [*web*'d] *adj* with membrane between the digits.

webbing [*web*ing] *n* strong wide tape used in upholstery; (*archi*) infilling between ribs of vault.

wed (*pres/part* **wedding**, *p/t* and *p/part* **wedded**) [*wed*] *v/t* and *i* marry, join in marriage; (*fig*) unite.

we'd [*weed*] *abbr* we had; we would.

wedded [*wed*id] *adj* married; of marriage; (*fig*) devoted (to), committed (to).

wedding [*wed*ing] *n* marriage ceremony.

wedding-breakfast [*wed*ing-bRekfast] *n* reception held after a wedding.

wedding-dress [*wed*ing-dRes] *n* elaborate white dress worn by bride at wedding.

wedding-ring [*wed*ing-Ring] *n* ring that bridegroom places on bride's finger during marriage service; similar ring for bridegroom.

wedge [*wej*] *n* V-shaped piece of wood or metal

used for splitting or for fixing firmly; anything of this shape; **thin end of the w.** apparently insignificant event or step that will lead to important results ∼ **wedge** *v/t* and *i* make or become immovably fixed; fix firmly; split with a wedge; (*cer*) knead or roll out clay by hand.

Wedgwood [*wej*wood] *n* (*cer*) variety of fine pottery; **w. blue** a soft powdery blue.

wedlock [*wed*lok] *n* condition of being married, matrimony.

Wednesday [*wenz*di/*wednz*di] *n* the fourth day of the week.

wee (1) [*wee*] *adj* very small ∼ **wee** *n* (*Scots*) a short time.

wee (2), **wee-wee** *n* (*sl*) urine ∼ **wee** *v/i* (*sl*) urinate.

weed [*weed*] *n* wild prolific plant, *esp* one which tends to choke others; (*sl*) cigar; tobacco; cannabis; (*fig*) lanky person in poor physical condition ∼ **weed** *v/t* and *i* clear (ground) of weeds; pull out weeds; **w. out** remove, eliminate.

weedkiller [*weed*kiler] *n* any chemical preparation for killing weeds.

weeds [*weedz*] *n* (*pl*) mourning garments worn by widow.

weedy [*weed*i] *adj* full of weeds; lacking stamina, lanky.

week [*week*] *n* a period of seven days, *esp* that from Sunday to Saturday; (*pop*) the working days of a week; **a w.** every week; **this day w.** a week from today; **w. in w. out** without a break; **Holy W.** the week preceding Easter Sunday.

weekday [*week*day] *n* any day of the week except Sunday ∼ **weekday** *adj*.

weekend [*week*end] *n* from Friday or Saturday to the end of Sunday night ∼ **weekend** *adj* for the weekend ∼ **weekend** *v/i* spend a weekend (at place).

weekly [*week*li] *adj* and *adv* (done, appearing *etc*) once a week ∼ **weekly** *n* periodical published once a week.

ween [*ween*] *v/t* (*ar*) suppose, believe.

weeny [*ween*i] *adj* (*coll*) tiny.

weep (*p/t* and *p/part* **wept**) [*weep*] *v/t* and *i* shed (tears); shed tears for, lament; drip (moisture); shed tears; exude moisture; (*of trees*) droop down.

weeper [*weepe*r] *n* hired mourner; crape worn by a mourner; (*pl*) (*sl*) side-whiskers.

weepie [*weep*i] *n* (*coll*) film, book *etc* full of sentimental pathos.

weeping [*weep*ing] *n* act of shedding tears or of dripping or oozing; lamentation ∼ **weeping** *adj* (*of trees*) drooping.

weepy [*weep*i] *adj* (*coll*) inclined to weep easily, tearful ∼ **weepy** *n* weepie.

weevil [*weev*il] *n* any long-snouted beetle.

wee-wee see **wee** (2).

weft [*weft*] *n* thread shuttled crosswise through the fabric between the warp.

weigh [*way*] *v/t* and *i* ascertain the weight of; have a certain weight; (*naut*) raise (anchor); (*fig*) consider carefully; have importance; **w. down** press down, depress; **w. in** (*of boxer*) test weight before fight; (*of jockey*) test weight after race; **w. in with** introduce (something new or unexpected); **w. out** measure out, allot portions of; (*of jockey*) test weight before race; **w. up** ap-

praise; **w. with** influence ∼ **weigh** *n* process of weighing.

weighbridge [*way*brij] *n* weighing machine with platform on to which laden vehicles are driven to be weighed.

weigh-in [*way*-in] *n* testing of jockey's weight after a race, or boxer's before a fight.

weight [*wayt*] *n* heaviness of anything, *esp* as expressed numerically in units of a recognized system; (*sci*) force of attraction of the Earth on a given mass; one of a number of standardized pieces of metal used to ascertain the exact heaviness of anything; system of weights used for this; heavy lump of metal used to hold something in place or as part of a mechanism; (*fig*) burden; value; influence; significance; **throw one's w. about** domineer, bully ∼ **weight** *v/t* load with a weight, make heavy; increase heaviness of; overload, burden.

weighting [*wayt*ing] *n* extra pay to compensate for higher cost of living.

weightless [*wayt*les] *adj* unaffected by gravity, floating freely in space ∼ **weightlessness** *n*.

weight-watcher [*wayt*-wocher] *n* one who takes care not to become too fat.

weighty [*wayt*i] *n* heavy, ponderous; carefully considered and not to be disregarded ∼ **weightily** *adv* ∼ **weightiness** *n*.

weir [*weer*] *n* small dam across river; fence of stakes across a stream to trap fish.

weird [*weerd*] *adj* eerie, uncanny; odd; (*coll*) mad, eccentric ∼ **weird** *n* (*Scots* and *ar*) fate ∼ **weirdly** *adv*.

weirdie [*weerd*i] *n* (*sl*) eccentric person; hippy; homosexual, pervert.

welch see **welsh** (1 and 2).

welcome [*wel*kum] *n* hospitable reception of stranger or guest; cordial greeting to person on arrival; reception (not necessarily pleasant) ∼ **welcome** *adj* most agreeable to entertain; giving pleasure, pleasing; willingly permitted (to), at liberty (to); **make w.** receive hospitably ∼ **welcome** *v/t* greet (visitor, guest) cordially; receive (guest) gladly and hospitably; be glad of (suggestion *etc*); **welcomed by** greeted with (something not necessarily pleasant).

weld [*weld*] *v/t* and *i* join (two surfaces) by fusion or pressure or both > PDE; (*fig*) unite; undergo jointing by welding.

welder [*weld*er] *n* skilled operator who can weld by gas and electricity.

welfare [*wel*fair] *n* wellbeing, happiness; freedom from want, sickness *etc*; **W. State** State that makes itself responsible for the social security and welfare of its citizens; **w. work** any activity designed to improve social conditions of an individual or group ∼ **welfare** *adj*.

welkin [*wel*kin] *n* (*poet*) sky.

well (1) [*wel*] *n* underground source of water; shaft or borehole sunk in ground to obtain water or oil; (*bui*) deep enclosed space; liftshaft; space between outer edges of two flights of stairs; space in court before judge ∼ **well** *v/i* pour forth, flow; **w. over** overflow.

well (2) *adv* satisfactorily; skilfully, effectively, thoroughly; intimately; fully, quite; fittingly, in proper fashion; with friendliness or consideration; justly; much, considerably; with good reason; easily; **as w.** besides, in addition; with equal justification; **as w. as** in addition to; **doing w.** making good recovery; prospering, thriving; **w. away** making good progress; (*sl*) tipsy; **just as w.** with no loss of advantage; **well set-up** (*of person*) sturdy ~ **well** *interj* expressing surprise, doubt, resignation *etc* ~ **well** *n* that which is thought good ~ **well** *adj* in good health; right; advisable; favourable, satisfactory; **w. enough** fairly good; **w. off** fortunate; wealthy.

we'll [*weel*] *abbr* we will; we shall.

well-appointed [wel-a*poi*ntid] *adj* equipped with everything necessary; elegantly furnished.

well-balanced [wel-*balanst*] *adj* judicious, sensible; of good proportions.

well-behaved [wel-bi*hayvd*] *adj* (*of person*) having good manners; (*of animal*) properly trained.

wellbeing [wel*bee*-ing] *n* bodily satisfaction; welfare.

wellbred [wel*bRed*] *adj* of good stock; with good manners.

well-connected [wel-ko*nektid*] *adj* from a good (upper class) family.

welldeck [*weldek*] *n* deck area not roofed by another deck.

well-disposed [wel-dis*pOzd*] *adj* friendly.

well-favoured [wel-*fayverd*] *adj* good-looking.

wellhead [*welhed*] *n* source of a spring; (*fig*) fountain-head.

well-heeled [wel-*heeld*] *adj* (*coll*) rich.

wellhole [*welhOl*] *n* open space for stair or lift; large borehole.

well-informed [wel-in*fawrmd*] *adj* equipped with a great variety of knowledge.

wellingtonia [welingt*Oni*-a] *n* sequoia.

Wellingtons [*welingtonz*] *n* (*pl*) waterproof boots up to the knee.

wellknit [wel*nit*] *adj* compact and strongly built.

wellknown [wel*nOn*] *adj* widely known.

well-lined [wel-*lInd*] *adj* (*of purse*) full of money.

well-meaning [wel-*meening*] *adj* with good intentions.

wellmeant [wel*ment*] *adj* said or done with the best intentions.

wellnigh [*welnI*] *adv* very nearly.

well-off [wel-*of*] *adj* fortunate; wealthy.

well-oiled [wel-*oild*] *adj* (*sl*) tipsy; (*fig*) flattering.

well-read [wel-*Red*] *adj* with a wide and scholarly knowledge of literature and books.

well-spoken [wel-*spOken*] *adj* pertinently said; courteous; speaking with a cultured accent.

wellspring [*welspRing*] *n* source of a spring; (*fig*) never-failing supply.

well-timed [wel-*tImd*] *adj* opportune.

well-to-do [wel-to-*dOO*] *adj* prosperous, wealthy.

well-turned [wel-*turnd*] *adj* elegantly phrased.

wellwisher [*welwisher*] *n* one friendly to another.

wellworn [*welwawrn*] *adj* (*fig*) hackneyed, trite.

Welsh (1), **Welch** [*welsh*] *n* and *adj* (people) of Wales; (native Celtic language) of Welsh people; **w. rabbit** (**rarebit**) toasted cheese.

welsh (2), **welch** [*welsh*] *v/i* and *t* (*of bookmaker*) decamp without paying winners of bets ~ **welsher** *n*.

welt [*welt*] *n* strip of leather projecting beyond upper sole of boot or shoe to which sole is attached; strip of material forming border, binding or hem;

ridge or scar raised on skin by lash; weal ~ **welt** *v/t* provide with welt; (*coll*) thrash.

weltanschauung [velt*anshowung*] *n* (*Germ*) general philosophical outlook upon life; philosophic view of the meaning of the universe.

welter [*welter*] *v/i* tumble about (in), wallow (in); (*of waves*) toss, surge ~ **welter** *n* confused mass; tumult.

welterweight [*welter*wayt] *n* boxer weighing between 135 and 147 lb., wrestler of similar weight; extra weight carried by a racehorse.

wen [*wen*] *n* lump or sebaceous cyst on the skin.

wench [*wench*] *n* (*joc*) girl, young woman; (*ar*) prostitute ~ **wench** *v/i* indulge in promiscuous sexual intercourse with women.

wend [*wend*] *v/i* **w. one's way** journey slowly.

went [*went*] *p/t* of go.

wept [*wept*] *p/t* and *p/part* of weep.

were [*wur/wair*] *pret p/* and *pret subj pl* and 1st and 3rd *pers pret subj sing* of be.

we're [*weer*] *abbr* we are.

weren't [*wurnt/wairnt*] *abbr* were not.

werewolf, werwolf [*weer*woolf, *wair*woolf] *n* (*myth*) person supposed to assume shape and habits of a wolf.

wert [*wurt*] (*ar*) 2nd *pers sing pret ind* and *subj* of be.

Wesleyan [*wez*li-an] *n* and *adj* (member) of the Methodist Church founded by John Wesley.

west [*west*] *n* the direction of the setting sun; one of the four points of the compass; Europe and America as contrasted with Asia; capitalist as contrasted with Communist countries ~ **west** *adj* in the west; towards or facing the west; (*of wind*) coming from the west; **the W. End** fashionable district of London ~ **west** *adv* towards the west; **go west** (*coll*) be finished, die.

West-End [*west*-end] *adj* of, from, or like the fashionable district of London.

westerly [*westerli*] *adj* relating to the west, western; facing or situated towards the west; (*of wind*) coming from the west ~ **westerly** *adv* towards the west, westward ~ **westerlies** *n* (*pl*) winds from the west > PDG.

western [*western*] *adj* of, in, coming from or characteristic of, the west ~ **western** *n* story or film dealing with cowboy or frontier life in the American West.

westernize [*western*Iz] *v/t* introduce western ideas, institutions *etc* into.

westernmost [*western*mOst] *adj* farthest to the west.

westing [*westing*] *n* (*naut*) distance to the west; direction westwards.

westward [*westwerd*] *adj* and *adv* towards the west ~ **westward** *n* a region or direction to the west.

westwards [*westwerdz*] *adv* towards the west.

wet [*wet*] *adj* covered or saturated with liquid; rainy; (*sl*) sentimental; weak, spiritless; (*US coll*) allowing sale of alcohol; **w. blanket** (*coll*) spoilsport; **w. dock** dock with water kept at high-tide level; **w. dream** erotic dream causing involuntary emission of semen ~ **wet** (*pres/part* **wetting**, *p/t* and *p/part* **wetted**) *v/t* make wet; drench; **w. one's whistle** drink ~ **wet** *n* moisture; water; rain; (*sl*) person lacking spirit; sentimental person; (*sl*) a drink.

wether [weTHer] *n* castrated ram.

wetly [wetli] *adv* in a wet way.

wetness [wetnes] *n* condition of being wet.

wetnurse [wetnurs] *n* woman employed to suckle another's child ~ **wetnurse** *v/t* act as wetnurse to; (*fig*) coddle.

wetting [weting] *n* process of becoming or being made wet; a soaking.

we've [weev] *abbr* we have.

wey [way] *n* a measure of weight for dry goods.

whack [wak] *v/t* and *i* strike, *esp* noisily; (*coll*) defeat; (*coll*) share out; **w. up** (*sl*) accelerate ~ **whack** *n* resounding blow; sound of this; (*coll*) share, fair share; **have a w. at** attempt; attack.

whacked [wakt] *adj* (*coll*) exhausted.

whacker [waker] *n* (*sl*) anything very large; bold lie.

whacking [waking] *n* a thrashing ~ **whacking** *adj* (*coll*) huge.

whacko [wakO] *interj* (*sl*) splendid!

whacky [waki] *adj* (*sl*) crazy.

whale [wayl] *n* huge warm-blooded air-breathing marine mammal; (*coll*) **a w.** at expert at; **a w. for** keen on ; **a w.** of no end of ~ **whale** *v/i* hunt whales.

whalebone [waylbOn] *n* horny substance growing in the upper jaw of certain whales.

whaler [wayler] *n* ship equipped for whaling; man employed in whaling; long narrow double-ended boat.

whaling [wayling] *n* the business of catching whales and processing them while at sea ~ **whaling** *adj* for the purpose of catching whales.

whank see wank.

wharf (*pl* **wharves**) [wawrf] *n* berth where a ship can tie up and load or unload > PDE ~ **wharf** *v/t* and *i* berth (ship); discharge (cargo); (*of ship*) anchor at a berth.

wharfage [wawrfij] *n* dues for use of a wharf; berth at a wharf.

wharfinger [wawrfinjer] *n* person in charge of a wharf.

what [wot] *adj* (*inter*) which? of which kind, degree *etc*?; (*exclam*) how much; how great; how strange ~ **what** *pron* (*rel*) that which; those which; (*inter*) which thing or things? how much?; **know w.'s w.** be experienced; be sensible ~ **what** *interj* expressing surprise; (*inter*) what did you say?; **w. ho!** *interj* of greeting or surprise ~ **what** *adj* (*rel*) (*vulg*) which; who.

whate'er [wotair] *pron* and *adj* (*poet*) whatever.

whatever [wotever] *pron* and *adj* anything at all; any, no matter what; **or w.** (*coll*) or anything similar; etcetera.

whatnot [wotnot] *n* shelved cabinet for display of ornaments *etc*; some unspecified thing.

whatsoever [wotsO-ever] *pron* and *adj* whatever.

whaup [wawp/whawp] *n* (*Scots*) the curlew.

wheat [weet] *n* cereal plant; its grain ground into flour.

wheatear [weeteer] *n* small migratory bird.

wheaten [weeten] *adj* made from wheat.

wheedle [weed'l] *v/t* influence or deceive person by smooth words; **w. out of** get from by flattery.

wheel [weel] *n* circular frame with radiating spokes or solid disk of metal or wood which revolves around central axis, *esp* one shod with iron or inflated rubber tyre on which vehicle rests or moves, or one by which a vehicle or ship is steered; (*mech*) such a device to transmit or regulate motion; rotation in a wide arc; set of short lines of verse concluding stanza; refrain or chorus to song; (*US*) a dollar; (*hist*) instrument of torture; (*fig*) controlling power; **put a spoke in someone's w.** frustrate his designs; **wheels within wheels** complex hidden motives and influences; **grease the wheels** (*coll*) advance money for particular purpose ~ **wheel** *v/t* and *i* make (vehicle) move; move on wheels; cause (line of troops) to swing round in wide arc; (*of troops*) change direction; (*of bird*) fly in circles.

wheelbarrow [weelbarO] *n* wood, steel or plastic container with a single wheel in front and two handholds behind by which it is lifted and moved.

wheelbase [weelbays] *n* distance between front and rear axles of a vehicle.

wheelchair [weelchair] *n* invalid's chair on wheels.

wheeled [weeld] *adj* fitted with a wheel or wheels.

wheelhouse [weelhows] *n* (*naut*) enclosed space sheltering the helmsman, the wheel, compass *etc*.

wheel-window [weel-windO] *n* (*archi*) circular window with mullions radiating from its centre.

wheelwright [weelRit] *n* craftsman who makes and repairs wheels and wheeled vehicles.

wheeze [weez] *v/i* make whistling or rattling sound when breathing ~ **wheeze** *n* wheezing sound; sound of difficult breathing; (*coll*) music-hall gag; trick, dodge.

wheezy [weezi] *adj* that wheezes; short of breath ~ **wheezily** *adv* ~ **wheeziness** *n*.

whelk [welk] *n* an edible shellfish.

whelp [welp] *n* puppy; lion or tiger cub; (*der*) callow youth ~ **whelp** *v/t* and *i* (*of animals*) give birth to; bear young.

when [wen] *adv* (*inter*) at what time? on which day?; how soon? ~ **when** *conj* at the moment that; at, during or after the time at which; on the occasion that, whenever; in spite of the fact that, although; considering that, if ~ **when** *pron* what time; which time.

whence [wens] *adv* (*inter*) from where? from what place?; **w. comes it that?** how is it that? ~ **whence** *pron* (*rel*) from which; to the place from which.

whene'er [wenair] *adv* (*poet*) whenever.

whenever [wenever] *adv* and *conj* at every time when.

whensoever [wensO-ever] *adv* and *conj* at any time when.

where [wair] *adv* at what place? to what place? in what particular? ~ **where** *conj* in the place at which ~ **where** *pron* what place? which place?; at which, to which, in which; in the circumstances in which.

whereabouts [wairRabowts] *adv* (*inter*) where? in what place? ~ **whereabouts** *n* place where a person or thing is probably to be found.

whereas [wairRaz] *conj* (*leg preamble*) in view of the fact that; in contrast with the fact that; but on the contrary, while.

whereat [wairRat] *adv* at which.

whereby [wairbI] *adv* (*inter*) by what means, how?; (*rel*) by means of which.

where'er [wairRair] *adv* (*poet*) wherever.

wherefore [*wair*fawr] *adv* (*inter*) for what purpose or reason? why?; (*rel*) in consequence of which, for which reason ~ **wherefore** *n* reason, cause.

wherein [wair*Rin*] *adv* (*inter*) in what respect?; (*rel*) in which.

whereof [wair*Rov*] *adv* of which; of what.

whereon [wair*Ron*] *adv* (*inter*) on what; (*rel*) upon which.

wheresoever [wairsO-*ever*] *adv* and *conj* to or in whatever place; wherever.

whereto [wair*tOO*] *adv* (*inter*) for what? to what end? in what direction?; (*rel*) to which.

whereunder [wair*Runder*] *adv* under which.

whereunto [wair*Runtoo*] *adv* whereto.

whereupon [wairRu*pon*] *adv* (*inter*) on what?; (*rel*) upon which, as a result of which; immediately after which.

wherever [wair*Rever*] *adv* at, in or to whatever place; anywhere, no matter where.

wherewith [wair*wiTH*] *adv* (*inter*) with what?; (*rel*) with which.

wherewithal [*wair*wiTHawl] *adv* wherewith ~ **wherewithal** *n* the means, the money needed.

wherry [*we*Ri] *n* heavy barge; light rowing-boat.

whet (*pres/part* **whetting**; *p/t* and *p/part* **whetted**) [*wet*/whet] *v/t* make sharp by rubbing, strop; stimulate; **w. one's whistle** have a drink ~ **whet** *n* act of whetting; (*coll*) appetizer, dram.

whether (1) [*we*THer] *conj* expressing alternative possibilities, doubt; **w. or no** in either case.

whether (2) *pron* (*ar*) which of two.

whetstone [*wet*stOn] *n* stone used to sharpen cutting tools.

whew [hew] *interj* expressing relief, wonder *etc*.

whey [way] *n* watery part of curdled milk.

whey-faced [*way*-fayst] *adj* sallow, pallid.

which [*wich*] *adj* (*inter*) what person or thing? ~ **which** *pron* (*rel*) the thing or things that; (*inter*) what person or thing?

whichever [wich*ever*] *pron* and *adj* any one of several, any that.

whichsoever [wichsO-*ever*] *pron* and *adj* whichever.

whiff (1) [*wif*] *n* slight puff of air; slight smell; breath; (*coll*) small cheroot ~ **whiff** *v/i* puff; emit a slight smell, smell unpleasant.

whiff (2) *n* light sculling-boat with outriggers.

whiff (3) *n* flatfish resembling the turbot.

whiffle [*wif*'l] *v/t* and *i* cause to move as if driven by gust; (*of wind*) veer about; (*of ship*) drift.

whiffy [*wif*i] *adj* smelly.

Whig [*wig*] *n* and *adj* (*hist*) (member) of an English political group aiming at giving more power to Parliament, which after 1868 became the Liberal Party ~ **Whiggish** *adj*.

while [*wil*] *adv* and *conj* as long as, during the time that, at the same time that; although, where-as ~ **while** *n* space of time; **worth (one's) w.** worth doing, advantageous ~ **while** *v/t* cause (time) to pass (away) without boredom.

whilst [*wilst*] *conj* while.

whim [*wim*] *n* capricious fancy; (*mining*) horse-drawn hoist.

whimbrel [*wim*bRel] *n* species of curlew.

whimper [*wim*per] *v/i* cry weakly; utter plaintive cries ~ **whimper** *n* feeble cry.

whimsy, whimsy [*wim*zi] *n* whim, freak, caprice; self-conscious semi-humorous sentimentality.

whimsical [*wim*zikal] *adj* capricious, fanciful, odd, eccentric, queer ~ **whimsically** *adv*.

whimsy see **whimsey**.

whin [*win*] *n* furze, gorse.

whinchat [*win*chat] *n* small brown singing-bird.

whine [*wIn*] *v/i* utter peevish high-pitched cries; complain peevishly and without good reason ~ **whine** *n* wailing cry; fretful complaint; (*mot*) high-pitched note ~ **whining** *n, adv* and *adj*.

whinny (*pres/part* **whinnying**; *p/t* and *p/part* **whinnied**) [*win*i] *v/i* (*of horse etc*) make a sound through the nostrils of pleasurable excitement ~ **whinny** *n* this kind of noise.

whinstone [*win*stOn] *n* hard dark-coloured rock.

whip (*pres/part* **whipping**; *p/t* and *p/part* **whipped**) [*wip*] *v/t* and *i* beat with a lash, thrash; whisk into a froth; bind (rope); sew over seam; fish (stream) with a fly; (*fig*) vanquish, defeat decisively; move fast or nimbly, act quickly; **w. in** move quickly; keep (hounds) from scattering; **w. off** snatch away suddenly; carry off; drink quickly, toss off; **w. out** draw (weapon *etc*) quickly; make hasty exit; utter sharply, rap out; **w. up** stimulate into activity; gather, collect; seize, snatch; beat into froth; prepare hasty (meal) ~ **whip** *n* lash attached to handle; blow of lash; Member of Parliament responsible for ensuring presence of his party members at voting time; whipper-in; pulley for hoisting; confection of beaten eggs, cream *etc*.

whipcord [*wip*kawrd] *n* tough hempen string; firm fabric with diagonal rib.

whiphand [*wip*hand] *n* upper hand, advantage, mastery.

whiplash [*wip*lash] *n* lash of a whip; sudden violent movement; **w. injury** injury (*esp* to neck) caused by sudden backward jerk.

whipper [*wip*er] *n* one who or that which whips ~ **whipper-in** (*pl* **whippers-in**) *n* hunt official who keeps the hounds from scattering; competitor finishing or running last.

whipper-snapper [*wip*er-snaper] *n* pert, impudent child; insignificant yet officious person.

whippet [*wip*et] *n* slender, long-legged dog bred for coursing and racing; (*mil*) speedy light tank.

whipping [*wip*ing] *n* act of beating with a lash; decisive defeat; overseaming.

whipping-boy [*wip*ing-boi] *n* scapegoat.

whipping-top [*wip*ing-top] *n* child's toy set spinning by whipping.

whip-poor-will [*wip*erwil] *n* nocturnal N. American bird with an insistent call resembling its name.

whippy [*wip*i] *adj* slender; flexible; (*coll*) nimble.

whipround [*wip*Rownd] *n* appeal circulated to associates for contributions to some cause *etc*.

whipstock [*wip*stok] *n* handle of whip.

whir see **whirr**.

whirl [*wurl*] *v/i* and *t* spin or cause to spin round very fast; move rapidly, *esp* in a circle; hurry away; be giddy or confused ~ **whirl** *n* rapid rotation; swift movement; rush; agitation; bewilderment.

whirligig [*wurl*igig] *n* spinning toy; a merry-go-round.

whirlpool [*wurl*pOOl] *n* circular eddy in river or sea > PDG.

whirlwind [*wurl*wind] *n* a column of air rotating

825

rapidly with low atmospheric pressure at its centre; (*fig*) very rapid or violent process.

whirlybird [*wurliburd*] *n* (*sl*) helicopter.

whirr, whir (*pres/part* **whirring,** *p/t* and *p/part* **whirred**) [*wur*] *v/i* spin or vibrate rapidly; make a buzzing sound by such vibrations ∼ **whirr, whir** *n* such a buzzing sound.

whisht see whist (2).

whisk [*wisk*] *v/t* and *i* remove swiftly and lightly; move about, swing, toss; beat (eggs *etc*) lightly; move briskly ∼ **whisk** *n* rapid sweeping motion; light, stiff brush; utensil for beating eggs *etc*.

whisker [*wisker*] *n* long stiff hair at side of an animal's mouth; (*pl*) moustache; beard on side of man's face; **by a w.** by a very narrow margin; **within a w. of** almost, very nearly ∼ **whiskery** *adj* having long or thick whiskers.

whiskey [*wiski*] *n* Irish whisky.

whisky [*wiski*] *n* alcoholic liquor distilled from malted barley and other grains.

whisper [*wisper*] *v/t* and *i* speak very quietly; make murmuring, rustling sound; converse secretly; (*fig*) circulate (insinuations *etc*) secretly ∼ **whisper** *n* quiet, murmuring sound; words spoken very quietly; (*fig*) insinuation, hint; rumour, *esp* malicious ∼ **whisperer** *n.*

whist (1) [*wist*] *n* card-game for two pairs of players.

whist (2), **whisht** *interj* be quiet.

whistle [*wis'l*] *v/i* and *t* produce a piping note or succession of such notes through pursed-up lips or from a wind instrument; (*of bird, missile etc*) make shrill sound; render (tune) by whistling; **w. up** summon by whistling; send for ∼ **whistle** *n* simple form of wind instrument; shrill, piping sound; steam-operated device to produce such a sound; (*sl*) throat.

whistler [*wisler*] *n* one who, or that which, whistles; (*rad*) atmospheric whistle of descending pitch picked up by radios, caused by radiation from lightning.

whistle-stop [*wis'l-stop*] *n* (*US coll*) small railway station where only slow trains stop; small town; politician's brief pause for speech-making during electioneering tour.

Whit (1) [*wit*] *adj* of or at Whitsun; **W. Sunday** the seventh Sunday after Easter, Pentecost.

whit (2) *n* (*ar*) minute quantity; **not a w., no w.** not at all.

white [*wIt*] *n* the appearance of light reflected from a surface without any one colour predominating; colour without hue; anything of this colour; pigment producing this; person whose natural skin colour is a pale yellowish-white or pink; (*typ*) area of paper not printed; (*pl*) white sports clothes; (*pl*) leucorrhœa; **w. of egg** albumen surrounding yolk; **w. of the eye** white part of cornea ∼ **white** *adj* of the colour of fresh snow; reflecting light but having no predominant colour; pale; colourless; having a naturally pale skin, not belonging to the negroid or Asiatic races; (*fig*) benevolent; honest, honourable; pure; **w. ant** termite; **w. bear** Polar bear; **w. coat** (*plastering*) final coat; **w. damp** (*mining*) carbon monoxide; **w. dwarf** (*astron*) small whitish star in final stages of evolution; **w. elephant** (*fig*) something large or expensive but useless; **w. ensign** flag flown by ships of British Navy;

w. feather symbol of cowardice; **W. Friar** Carmelite monk; **w. frost** hoarfrost; **w. heat** degree of heat which makes metal glow white; (*fig*) intense passion; **w. horses** waves with foamy crests; **W. House** official residence of President of United States in Washington; **W. Lady** cocktail of gin and lemon; **w. lead** basic lead carbonate; **w. lie** harmless or justifiable lie; **w. man** member of the light-skinned race; (*fig*) upright honourable man; **w. meat** flesh of poultry, veal, rabbit or pork; **w. metal** a tin-based alloy; **w. paper** official pamphlet, report *etc* published by British government; **w. sale** sale of linen goods at bargain prices; **w. slave** girl forced or trapped into prostitution; **w. spirit** mixture of petroleum hydrocarbons used as a paint solvent; **w. witch** woman using alleged supernatural powers for good only.

whitebait [*wItbait*] *n* the young of various small fishes eaten as a delicacy.

whitecollar [*wItkoler*] *adj* engaged in non-manual work.

Whitehall [*wIt-hawl*] *n* London street in and near which government departments are situated; (*fig*) the British government; bureaucracy.

white-headed [*wIt-hedid*] *adj* (*coll*) favourite.

whiteheart [*wIt-haart*] *n* juicy, light-coloured cherry.

whiten [*wItten*] *v/t* and *i* make white, whitewash, bleach; (*fig*) make appear guiltless; grow white.

whitener [*wItener*] *n* ingredient in a washing powder that whitens.

whiteness [*wItnes*] *n* state or quality of being white.

whitening [*wItning*] *n* whiting (2); process of making or becoming white; substance used to make things white.

white-out [*wIt-owt*] *n* condition of much reduced visibility caused by snowstorm.

whitethorn [*wItthawrn*] *n* hawthorn.

whitethroat [*wItthrOt*] *n* species of warbler bird.

whitewash [*wItwosh*] *n* liquid formed by soaking quicklime in excess water, limewash; (*fig*) explanation which covers up mistakes or faults ∼ **whitewash** *v/t* paint over with whitewash; (*fig*) gloss over, cover up (faults *etc*); cause to seem innocent; clear of blame.

whitey [*wIti*] *n* (*pej sl*) white man.

whither [*wiTHer*] *adv* (*inter*) to what place, which way?; (*rel*) to any place that ∼ **whither** *pron* (*rel*) to or towards which.

whithersoever [*wiTHersO-ever*] *adv* (*ar*) to whatever place.

whiting (1) [*wIting*] *n* edible sea fish.

whiting (2) *n* crushed chalk used for making whitewash, distemper.

whitish [*wItish*] *adj* fairly white.

whitlow [*witlO*] *n* tumour near a fingernail.

Whitsun [*witsun*] *n* the weekend including Whit Sunday; the week beginning with Whit Sunday ∼ **Whitsun** *adj*.

Whitsuntide [*witsuntId*] *n* and *adj* Whitsun.

whittle [*wit'l*] *v/t* and *i* cut off shavings from, shape (piece of wood) with a knife; (*fig*) reduce gradually; cut or shape wood by shaving it with a knife.

whiz, whizz [*wiz*] *n* buzzing sound ∼ **whiz**

(*pres/part* **whizzing**, *p/t* and *p/part* **whizzed**)
v/i move very quickly; make a buzzing sound.

whizzbang [*wiz*bang] *n* (*sl*) high-velocity shell;
firework.

whizzkid [*wiz*kid] *n* (*coll*) brilliantly clever and
ambitious young man; self-confident person who
seeks quick results.

who [*hOO*] *pron* (*inter*) what or which person?; (*rel*)
that person who; **W.'s W.** annual publication
giving brief biographies of prominent living persons.

whoa, wo [*wO*] *interj* (*to horses*) stop!

whodunnit [*hOOdunit*] *n* (*coll*) detective story.

whoever [hOO-*ever*] *pron* anyone who.

whole [*hOl*] *adj* complete in all parts, entire; unbroken, undamaged; uninjured; (*ar*) healthy; **go
the w. hog** do something thoroughly; **w. number** integer ~ **whole** *n* total amount; sum of all
parts; thing complete in itself.

wholehearted [hOl*haart*id] *adj* single-minded,
sincere.

whole-hogger [hOl-*hog*er] *n* (*pol*) enthusiastic,
out-and-out supporter; person who does things
thoroughly ~ **whole-hogging** *adj*.

wholemeal [hOl*meel*] *n* and *adj* (flour) containing husk as well as grain of cereal.

wholeness [hOl*nes*] *n* state of being whole, completeness.

wholesale [hOl*sayl*] *n* (*opp* retail) sale of goods in
bulk or quantity ~ **wholesale** *adj* relating to
bulk sales of goods; (*fig*) unlimited, indiscriminate ~ **wholesale** *adv* in bulk, in large quantities; indiscriminately ~ **wholesaler** *n* wholesale
trader.

wholesome [hOl*sum*] *adj* (*of food etc*) rich in food
value; in good condition; good for one's health;
(*fig*) beneficial, salutary; morally sound.

wholetime [hOl*tIm*] *adj* fulltime, occupying all
normal working hours; unceasing, constant.

who'll [*hOOl*] *abbr* who will; who shall.

wholly [hOl-li] *adv* entirely, completely, altogether.

whom [*hOOm*] *pron* (*inter* and *rel*) *objective case of*
who.

whomsoever [hOOmsO-*ever*] *pron* (*inter* and *rel*)
objective case of whosoever.

whoop [*hOOp*] *v/i* utter loud cry or yell; make the
noise peculiar to whooping cough ~ **whoop** *n*.

whoopee [*w*OO*pee/w*OO*pee*] *interj* (*US*) yell of
joy; **make w.** have a hilarious time, go on the
spree.

whooping-cough, hooping-cough [hOO*ping*-
kof] *n* infectious ailment with periodic spasms of
coughing followed by long, hollow, breathing-in
noises.

whoosh [*wOOsh*] *v/i* move quickly with a rushing
sound.

whop (*pres/part* **whopping**, *p/t* and *p/part*
whopped) [*wop*] *v/t* (*sl*) thrash; defeat, *esp* in
boxing.

whopper [*wop*er] *n* (*coll*) something huge, *esp* a lie.

whopping [*wop*ing] *adj* (*coll*) huge.

who're [*hOOr*] *abbr* who are.

whore [*hawr*] *n* woman who has sexual relations
for gain, prostitute ~ **whore** *v/i* keep company
with whores, indulge in lechery.

whorehouse [*hawr*hows] *n* brothel.

whoring [*hawr*Ring] *n* lechery, prostitution; keeping company with whores.

whorl [*wurl*] *n* single coil of a spiral; (*bot*) leaves,
flowers *etc* encircling the stem; (*zool*) single coil
of spiral shell.

whortleberry [*wurt*'l-beRi] *n* bilberry.

who's [*hOOz*] *abbr* who is; who has.

whose [*hOOz*] *pron* (*inter* and *rel*) *possessive case of*
who *and* which; of whom; of which.

whosesoever [hOOz-sO-*ever*] *pron* (*inter* and *rel*)
possessive case of whosoever.

whoso [*hOO*sO] *pron* (*inter* and *rel*) whosoever.

whosoever [hOOsO-*ever*] *pron* (*inter* and *rel*)
whoever; anyone at all who.

why [*wI*] *adv* (*inter*) for what reason?; (*rel*) because of which ~ **why** *interj* an expression of
surprise ~ **why** *n* reason for or cause of something.

wick [*wik*] *n* length of twisted thread in candle or
oil lamp, which when ignited burns slowly and
steadily; **get on one's w.** (*sl*) irritate one.

wicked [*wik*id] *adj* sinful; vicious; extremely bad;
(*coll*) mischievous, roguish ~ **wickedly** *adv* ~
wickedness *n*.

wicker [*wik*er] *n* thin flexible twig ~ **wicker** *adj*
made of plaited wickers.

wickerwork [*wik*erwurk] *adj* and *n* (made of)
plaited wickers; wicker basket, stool *etc*.

wicket [*wik*it] *n* small gate or door forming part of
a larger one; sluice in a lock gate; (*cricket*) set of
three upright stumps on which two bails rest;
cricket pitch; condition of this; batsman's innings.

wicket-keeper [*wik*it-keeper] *n* (*cricket*) fieldsman
standing immediately behind the batsman's
wicket.

widdershins [*wid*ershinz] *adv* anti-clockwise.

widdle [*wid*'l] *v/i* (*coll*) urinate.

wide [*wId*] *adj* extending relatively far from side
to side, broad; far-reaching; sp cious; all-embracing; (*sl*) cunning, unscrupul us; lacking in
moral sense ~ **wide** *adv* widely; to the full
extent; far; **w. of** far from ~ **wide** *n* (*cricket*)
ball bowled beyond a stated limit outside the
wicket; **to the w.** utterly.

wide-angle [*wId*-ang-g'l] *adj* (*of a lens*) having a
wide angle of view and a short focal length.

wide-awake [*wId*-a*wayk*] *adj* alert, sharp-witted
~**wideawake** *n* (*coll*) wide-brimmed felt hat.

wide-eyed [*wId*-Id] *adj* and *adv* with naive surprise or admiration.

widely [*wId*li] *adv* over a wide area; over a wide
range; at a wide interval; considerably.

widen [*wId*en] *v/t* and *i* increase in width.

widespread [*wId*spRed] *adj* found in many places;
extending far.

widgeon [*wij*un] *n* migratory freshwater duck.

widow [*wid*O] *n* a woman who has not remarried
after the death of her husband; **grass w.** wife
separated temporarily from her husband ~ **widow** *v/t* make (someone) a widow; (*fig*) deprive of
something valued.

widower [*wid*O-er] *n* man whose wife has died
and who has not remarried.

widowhood [*wid*Ohood] *n* state of being a widow.

width [*width*] *n* measurement from side to side;
state of being wide; piece of material of the full
width as woven.

wield [*weeld*] *v/t* grasp and direct the movement of, handle; use ably; control.

wife (*pl* **wives**) [*wīf*] *n* the woman to whom one is married; married woman; (*ar*) woman; **take to w.** marry; **old wives' tale** foolish, superstitious belief.

wifely [*wīf*li] *adj* of, like or befitting a wife.

wig [*wig*] *n* artificial hair worn to hide baldness or as disguise or adornment.

wigging [*wig*ing] *n* (*sl*) a scolding.

wiggle [*wig*'l] *v/t* and *i* move to and fro with short jerky movements ~ **wiggle** *n* wavy line, squiggle; short jerky movement.

wight [*wīt*] *n* (*ar*) person, creature.

wigwam [*wig*wam] *n* light conical tent of N. American Indians.

wild [*wīld*] *adj* not domesticated; not cultivated; savage, uncivilized; undisciplined, unrestrained, dissipated; disordered (appearance); boisterous, stormy (weather *etc*); intensely excited; demented; (*coll*) angry; badly aimed, erratic; rash, visionary (scheme *etc*) ~ **wild** *n* remote uninhabited region ~ **wild** *adv* wildly.

wildcat [*wīld*kat] *n* large undomesticated cat ~ **wildcat** *adj* (*of scheme*) unsound, speculative, risky; (*of strike*) unauthorized by union officials.

wildebeest [*wild*ebeest/*vild*ebayst] *n* the gnu.

wilderness [*wild*ernes] *n* uncultivated region; any large desolate area; **in the w.** (*fig*) out of political office; in exile or disgrace.

wild-eyed [wīld-*īd*] *adj* staring in horror *etc*.

wildfire [*wīld*fīr] *n* destructive fire; summer lightning; highly inflammable substance; Greek fire; **like w.** very rapidly.

wildfowl [*wīld*fowl] *n* gamebird(s).

wildlife [*wīld*līf] *n* wild animals collectively.

wildly [*wīld*li] *adv* in a wild way.

wildness [*wīld*nis] *n* state or quality of being wild.

wile [*wīl*] *n* trick, ruse; (*pl*) cajolery ~ **wile** *v/t* entice, trick; (*used for* while) **w. away time** pass time pleasantly.

wilful [*wīl*fool] *adj* obstinately self-willed, headstrong; done on purpose, premeditated ~ **wilfully** *adv* ~ **wilfulness** *n*.

wilily [*wīl*ili] *adv* in a wily manner.

wiliness [*wīl*inis] *n* cunning, guile.

will (1) [*wil*] *n* impulse to act, conscious adoption of a line of action, volition; power of willing; strength of mind and moral fibre; intention, choice, determination; wish, desire; legal document in which a person gives instructions for the disposal of his property after death ~ **will** *v/t* and *i* bequeath in a will; ordain, decree; influence (person) by the exercise of the will; intend.

will (2) (*p/t* **would**) *v/aux* expressing future tense; expressing insistence, resolve, habit, or intention.

willies [*wiliz*] *n* (*pl*) (*sl*) feeling of nervousness or discomfort.

willing [*wil*ing] *adj* eager; eager to help; cooperative; performed or offered ungrudgingly ~ **willingly** *adv* ~ **willingness** *n*.

will-o'-the-wisp [wil-o-THe-*wisp*] *n* phosphorescent light seen over marshy ground; (*fig*) something unreliable; elusive person or thing.

willow [*wil*O] *n* tree of genus *Salix*; wood of this; (*coll*) cricket bat.

willow-pattern [*wil*O-patern] *n* (*cer*) type of oriental design in blue, frequently copied on English chinaware.

willowy [*wil*Owi] *adj* slender and drooping.

willpower [*wil*powr] *n* strength of will.

willy-nilly [wili-*nili*] *adv* willingly or unwillingly, compulsorily.

wilt (1) [*wilt*] (*ar*) 2nd pers sing pres of **will**.

wilt (2) *v/t* and *i* (*of plants*) cause to droop; droop, fade.

wily [*wīl*i] *adj* crafty; guileful.

wimple [*wimp*'l] *n* linen veil covering the head, sides of face and neck ~ **wimpled** *adj* wearing a wimple.

win (*pres/part* **winning**, *p/t* and *p/part* **won**) [*win*] *v/t* and *i* achieve or gain by effort, *esp* in contest; gain, reach with an effort; be victorious, prevail; obtain as a prize; obtain by betting or gambling; (*sl*) steal; **w. hands down** win decisively; **w. over** persuade; **w. through**, (*US*) **w. out** overcome one difficulty after another ~ **win** *n* victory, success in a contest.

wince [*wins*] *v/i* make an involuntary movement, *esp* in pain; shrink back, flinch ~ **wince** *n* involuntary movement.

winceyette [winsi-*et*] *n* plain cotton cloth of light weight.

winch [*winch*] *n* hand-operated winding drum; small engine-driven haulage or hoist.

winchester [*win*chester] *n* (*tr*) breech-loading repeating rifle; large bottle.

wind (1) [*wind*/(poet) *wīnd*] *n* current of air moving with speed > PDG; breath; ease or regularity of breathing; flatulence; wind instruments; (*fig*) meaningless words; (*sl*) stomach; **break w.** fart; **in the w.** in preparation, *esp* secretly; likely to happen or be done; **get w. of** hear a hint or rumour; **get w. up** (*sl*) grow frightened; **like the w.** very fast; **put the w. up** (*sl*) frighten; **raise the w.** (*sl*) raise urgently needed money; **sail close to the w.** verge on indecency or dishonesty; **second w.** steady breathing regained after initial breathlessness from effort; (*fig*) ability to renew one's effort ~ **wind** *v/t* cause to become breathless, *esp* by a blow; allow (horse) to recover breath; (*hunting*) detect scent of; [*wīnd*] (*p/t* **winded** or **wound**) blow a note on (horn, bugle *etc*) ~ **wind** *adj* (*mus, of instruments*) sounded by blowing into > PDM.

wind (2) (*p/t* and *p/part* **wound**) [*wīnd*] *v/t* and *i* turn; raise by turning; tighten spring of watch by turning a key; make into a coil or ball; wrap (round); move along constantly changing direction; turn and twist; **w. up** sum up; finish, conclude; tighten spring of (watch *etc*) by winding; (*comm*) liquidate (company); **wound up** (*fig*) emotionally excited; likely to go on talking for a very long time ~ **wind** *n* bend, single turn.

windbag [*wind*bag] *n* wordy orator or talker.

windbound [*wind*bownd] *adj* unable to sail because of contrary winds.

windbreak [*wind*bRayk] *n* fence, hedge *etc* breaking force of wind.

windcheater [*wind*cheeter] *n* hooded waterproof reaching to the knees.

winder [*wīn*der] *n* (*bui*) triangular or wedge-shaped tread which changes the direction of a stair; (*mining*) engine which pulls cage or skip up mine shaft; key for winding up spring.

windfall [*wind*fawl] *n* fruit blown down; (*fig*) unexpected good fortune; legacy.

windgauge [*wind*gayj] *n* instrument to measure force of wind.

windhover [*wind*hover] *n* the kestrel.

windiness [*wind*inis] *n* quality of being windy.

winding [*wind*ing] *adj* full of twists and bends.

winding-sheet [*wind*ing-sheet] *n* shroud.

windings [*wind*ingz] *n* (*pl*) bends, curves.

windjammer [*wind*jamer] *n* large sailing vessel; windcheater.

windlass [*wind*las] *n* hand winch for hauling or hoisting > PDSa.

windmill [*wind*mil] *n* mill or water-pump driven by sails rotated by the wind.

window [*wind*O] *n* opening in wall, roof, vehicle *etc* to admit light and air, *usu* filled by glass panes often in a movable frame.

windowbox [*wind*Oboks] *n* box fixed to window-sill in which to grow plants.

window-dressing [*wind*O-dREsing] *n* art of displaying goods attractively in a shop window; (*fig*) skill in making the best impression.

windowed [*wind*Od] *adj* with windows.

window-shopping [*wind*O-shoping] *n* habit of gazing at shop windows without buying anything.

windowsill [*wind*Osil] *n* horizontal ledge under a window.

windpipe [*wind*pIp] *n* trachea, the passage between mouth and lungs.

windpower [*wind*powr] *n* mechanical energy of the wind, *esp* when used to turn windmills, generate electricity *etc*.

windrow [*wind*RO] *n* line of hay *etc* laid out to dry.

windsail [*wind*sayl] *n* (*naut*) widemouthed canvas shute to ventilate lower decks.

windscreen [*wind*skREen] *n* front window of motor vehicle; **w. wiper** automatic rubber blade to wipe raindrops from windscreen.

windsock [*wind*sok] *n* canvas tube flown from aerodrome mast to indicate wind direction.

windswept [*wind*swept] *adj* exposed to, swept by, winds.

wind-tunnel [*wind*-tunel] *n* conical or cylindrical structure through which air is blown at measured speeds to test its effect on models of aircraft, bridges *etc*.

wind-up [*wind*-up] *n* the finish; final settlement.

windvane [*wind*vayn] *n* instrument to indicate wind direction > PDG.

windward [*wind*werd/*wind*erd] *n* (*naut*) direction or side from which the wind blows ~ **windward** *adj* towards or on the side from which the wind blows ~ **windward** *adv* towards the wind.

windy [*wind*i] *adj* exposed to the wind; where the wind rarely stops blowing; (*fig*) wordy, boastful; (*coll*) frightened, apprehensive; causing flatulence.

wine [*wIn*] *n* fermented juice of fruit, *esp* grapes; a bright deep red ~ **wine** *v/t* and *i* to entertain (person) to wine; drink wine.

wineberry [*wIn*beRi] *n* edible sweet berry resembling raspberry.

winebibber [*wIn*biber] *n* habitual drinker of wine.

wineglass [*wIn*glaas] *n* glass for drinking wine.

wineglassful [*wIn*glaasfool] *n* liquid capacity of a wineglass.

winepress [*wIn*pREs] *n* vat or machine in which grapes are crushed to make wine.

wineskin [*wIn*skin] *n* skin container for wine.

wing [*wing*] *n* limb by which bird, insect *etc* flies; projecting area of an aeroplane's structure by which it is supported in the air; any projection from the side of something; side, flank; (*mil*) unit placed to guard a flank; (*RAF*) group of three squadrons; (*pl*) pilot's badge; (*games*) player at extreme right or left of forward line; (*fig, pol*) group holding more extreme views than the majority of the party they belong to; (*pl*) sides of stage; (*archi*) lateral extension of a building; **in the wings** (*coll*) present but not visible; waiting, in reserve; **on the w.** flying; **under one's w.** under one's protection ~ **wing** *v/t* and *i* fly (over or through); send flying; wound in the wing; (*fig*) wound in arm or leg; fit wings to.

wingcase [*wing*kays] *n* horny covering over insect's wing.

wing-commander [*wing*-kumaander] *n* (*RAF*) officer corresponding in rank to a commander in the navy or a lieutenant-colonel in the army.

winged [*wing*d] *adj* equipped with wings; swift; wounded; (*fig*) lofty, sublime.

wingsheath [*wing*sheeth] *n* wingcase.

wingspan [*wing*span] *n* wingspread.

wingspread [*wing*spREd] *n* width from tip to tip of extended wings; surface or area of aircraft's wings.

wink [*wink*] *v/i* and *t* rapidly shut and open one or both eyes; blink; flash intermittently; (*ar*) close one's eyes; **w. at** make a signal to by winking; pretend not to see, connive at ~ **wink** *n* act of winking; signal of complicity or amusement given by winking; **forty winks** (*coll*) a short nap; **tip the w. to** (*sl*) give a hint to.

winkers [*wink*erz] *n* (*pl*) (*coll*) flashing signal lights on a car.

winking [*wink*ing] *n* act of one who winks; **as easy as w.** (*coll*) very easy; **like w.** (*coll*) very fast, very vigorously.

winkle (1) [*wink*'l] *n* an edible shellfish.

winkle (2) *v/t* **w. out** extract, prise out.

winkle-pickers [*wink*'l-pikerz] *n* (*pl*) (*coll*) shoes with sharp-pointed toes.

winner [*win*er] *n* one who wins; (*sl*) someone or something certain to succeed.

winning [*win*ing] *n* victory; (*pl*) money won at games of chance; (*mining*) extracting coal or ore from the ground ~ **winning** *adj* victorious; (*of stroke*) that clinches the victory; attractive, captivating ~ **winningly** *adv* engagingly.

winning-post [*win*ing-pOst] *n* post which marks finish of a race.

winnow [*win*O] *v/t* fan (grain *etc*) free of husks and chaff; (*fig*) separate, sift good from bad.

wino [*wIn*O] *n* (*sl*) alcoholic addicted to wine.

winsome [*win*sum] *adj* charming, sweet ~ **winsomely** *adv* ~ **winsomeness** *n*.

winter [*win*ter] *n* coldest season, between autumn and spring ~ **winter** *adj* of, like, happening or used in winter; **w. garden** conservatory with plants; park or garden with evergreens; **w. quarters** billets for troops during winter; place of lodging during winter; **w. sports** skating, skiing and other open-air sports requiring wintry conditions ~ **winter** *v/i* and *t* spend a winter; give food and shelter in winter to (animals).

wintergreen [*win*tergREen] *n* N. American evergreen shrub producing an aromatic medicinal oil.

winter-weight [*win*terwayt] *adj* (*of clothes*) thick enough to be warm in winter.

wintry [*win*tRi] *adj* characteristic of winter, cold, stormy, icy; (*fig*) cheerless, unfriendly.

winy [*win*i] *adj* with the colour or taste of wine.

wipe [*wip*] *v/t* clean or dry by rubbing with a cloth *etc*; (*sl*) strike; **w. away, off, up** get rid of by wiping; **w. away, out** clean by wiping, get rid of by wiping; (*fig*) obliterate, cancel; **w. the floor with** (*sl*) vanquish in argument; utterly defeat; rebuke severely ~ **wipe** *n* action of wiping; (*sl*) blow, swipe.

wirable [*wir*Rab'l] *adj* that can be wired.

wire [*wir*] *n* strong thin metal thread; flex of such threads twisted together; (*coll*) telegram; **w. drawing** process of making steel wire by drawing it through holes > PDE; **w. gauge** scale of diameters of wires; **live w.** electrified wire; (*coll*) lively, energetic person; **pull wires** exert secret influence; **w. tapping** act of listening in to private telephone conversations ~ **wire** *v/t* join, fasten, strengthen *etc* with wires; equip with electrical wiring system; (*coll*) telegraph; **w. in (to)** get to work vigorously.

wiredrawn [*wir*dRawn] *adj* drawn out to a fine thread; (*fig*) presented with unnecessary subtlety and fine distinctions.

wirehaired [*wir*haird] *adj* with short, rough, stiff hair.

wireless [*wir*les] *n* transmission of sound by means of electromagnetic waves; radio; (*pop*) radio receiving set; programmes transmitted by radio; wireless telephony ~ **wireless** *adj* having no wires; of radio or broadcasting; transmitted by radio ~ **wireless** *v/t* and *i* transmit by radio.

wire-netting [*wir*-*net*ing] *n* mesh of galvanized wire.

wirepuller [*wir*pooler] *n* intriguer who uses his influence secretly to further his own interests or those of his friends.

wiretapping [*wir*taping] *n* eavesdropping on telephone calls by secretly fixing a receiver to the wire.

wirewool [*wir*wool] *n* pad of fine wire used for scouring utensils.

wireworm [*wir*wurm] *n* larva of the click-beetle.

wirewove [*wir*wOv] *adj* (*of paper*) of fine quality.

wirily [*wir*Rili] *adv* in a wiry manner.

wiriness [*wir*Rines] *n* quality of being wiry.

wiring [*wir*Ring] *n* system of wires for an electrical installation.

wiry [*wir*Ri] *adj* like wire; (*of persons*) lean yet strong, capable of endurance.

wisdom [*wiz*dom] *n* mature intelligence, perception and discretion; sagacity, common sense, sound judgement.

wisdom-tooth [*wiz*dum-tOOth] *n* one of four back molar teeth which appear only in adults.

wise (1) [*wiz*] *n* having or showing wisdom; perceptive, prudent, discreet; well informed; (*sl*) knowing all about, well warned against; **w. guy** (*sl*) one who thinks himself cleverer than he is; **w. man (woman)** benevolent wizard (witch); **none the wiser** no better informed; **put w. to** (*sl*) make aware of; warn against ~ **wise** *v/t* (*sl*) **w. up** inform, make aware, warn.

wise (2) *n* way, manner.

wiseacre [*wiz*ayker] *n* person who thinks he knows everything.

wisecrack [*wiz*kRak] *n* (*coll*) smart witticism or retort ~ **wisecrack** *v/i* and *t*.

wisely [*wiz*li] *adv* in a wise way.

wish [*wish*] *n* ideal representation of something, accompanied by a felt impulse towards its realization > PDP; a desire, longing; a desire put into words; that which one desires ~ **wish** *v/t* and *i* desire, long for; express a desire in words; be anxious that; **w. (person or thing) on one** (*coll*) recommend, send or transfer to one; foist or palm off on one.

wishbone [*wish*bOn] *n* forked breastbone of a fowl.

wishful [*wish*fool] *adj* desiring, hoping; **w. thinking** acceptance of the thought that conditions are as one would wish them to be > PDP ~ **wishfully** *adv*.

wishy-washy [*wishi*-woshi] *adj* feeble, insipid.

wisp [*wisp*] *n* small bunch of straw or hay; thin strand of hair, material *etc* ~ **wispy** *adj*.

wist [*wist*] (*ar*) *p/t* and *p/part of* **wit** (2).

wistaria, wisteria [wis*tair*Ri-a, wis*teer*Ri-a] *n* flowering climbing plant.

wistful [*wist*fool] *adj* yearning with little hope of satisfaction; thoughtful ~ **wistfully** *adv*.

wit (1) [*wit*] *n* ability to say clever and amusing things, intelligent humour; ability to perceive unexpected connexions or contrasts and express them cleverly; person having this ability; mental alertness, intelligence; (*pl*) mental powers; (*ar*) mind; **at one's wits' end** not knowing what to do next; **live by one's wits** gain one's living by ingenuity rather than by work.

wit (2) (*pres/t* **wot, wottest**, *p/t* and *p/part* **wist**) *v/t* and *i* (*ar*) know; **to w.** that is to say.

witch [*wich*] *n* woman believed to have supernatural (*usu* evil) powers, sorceress; ugly malevolent old woman; member of a nature-worshipping cult alleged to be derived from pre-Christian religions; (*fig*) fascinating woman ~ **witch** *v/t* bewitch.

witchcraft [*wich*kRaaft] *n* magical power; magical practices, *esp* for evil purposes.

witchdoctor [*wich*dokter] *n* magician of primitive tribe, *esp* one who counteracts witchcraft.

witch-elm see **wych-elm.**

witchery [*wich*eRi] *n* fascination; witchcraft.

witch-hazel see **wych-hazel.**

witchhunt [*wich*hunt] *n* act of seeking out witches to kill them; act of seeking out people suspected of unpopular political views to drive them out of public or influential positions.

witchhunting [*wich*hunting] *n* witchhunt.

witching [*wich*ing] *adj* of, like or suited to witchcraft; fascinating, charming.

with [*wiTH*] *prep* in the company of, beside, in physical proximity to; against, in opposition to, in contrast to, in spite of, from; compared to, equal to; at the same time as, in the same direction as; possessed of, characterized by; by means of *etc*; **be w.** it be up-to-date; understand (something new); **in w.** on friendly terms with; in league with; **w. that** thereupon.

with- *pref* against, in opposition; moving away, back.

withal [wiTHawl] adv (ar) besides; thereupon; in spite of all ~ withal prep (ar) with.

withdraw (p/t withdrew, p/part withdrawn) [wiTHdRaw] v/t and i draw aside or back; take away, remove; take back, retract (statement etc); move back, recede; retire from; refuse to participate.

withdrawal [wiTHdRaw-al] n process of withdrawing; w. symptoms painful symptoms experienced after ceasing to take alcohol or other addictive drug.

withdrawn [wiTHdRawn] adj unsociable; introvert; abstracted, absent-minded.

withe [with/wiTH/wIth], withy [wiTHi] n flexible stick cut from willow tree, used for basket making.

wither [wiTHer] v/i and t shrivel up, fade; grow feebler or fainter; cause to fade, blight; (fig) snub, reduce to embarrassed silence.

withered [wiTHerd] adj shrivelled; wizened.

withering [wiTHeRing] adj that withers; crushingly scornful, snubbing ~ witheringly adv.

withers [wiTHerz] n (pl) ridge between shoulderblades of horse.

withershins [wiTHershinz] adv anti-clockwise.

withhold (p/t and p/part withheld) [wiTH-hOld] v/t keep back; refuse to grant.

within [wiTHin] adv inside, indoors, internally; in the heart or soul, inwardly ~ within prep inside, in the interior of; within the limit of, not beyond, not exceeding ~ within n the interior.

without [wiTHowt] adv outside, externally; (ar) out of doors ~ without prep not having, devoid of, lacking; free from; in the absence of; (ar) outside; (followed by pres/part or v/n) and not ~ without conj (coll) unless, but ~ without n the exterior.

withstand (p/t and p/part withstood) [wiTHstand] v/t resist, oppose successfully; be capable of enduring or keeping out.

withy see withe.

witless [witles] adj lacking intelligence; foolish.

witness [witnis] n an observer of a fact or event; one who gives testimony, esp one who gives evidence in a court of law; person who attests another's signature to a document; evidence, testimony ~ witness v/t and i observe personally; give evidence of; act as witness to the signing of (document); give evidence, bear witness, testify.

witness-box [witnis-boks] n stand in law-court from which witnesses give evidence.

witticism [witisizm] n witty remark.

wittily [witili] adv in a witty manner.

witting [witing] adj deliberate, intentional.

wittingly [witingli] adv consciously; intentionally.

witty [witi] adj sparkling with wit; cleverly amusing.

wive [wIv] v/t and i marry; get married.

wivern see wyvern.

wives [wIvz] pl of wife.

wizard [wizerd] n man who practises magic; (fig) ingenious person; expert ~ wizard adj (sl) firstrate, marvellous.

wizardry [wizerdRi] n spells and charms of a wizard; (fig) remarkable skill or expertness.

wizen, weazen [wizen, weezen] adj dried up, wrinkled.

wizened, weazened [wizend, weezend] adj wizen.

wo see whoa.

woad [wOd] n plant yielding blue dye; this dye.

wobble, wabble [wob'l] v/i move unsteadily without sure direction, shake, rock; (fig) be uncertain in one's opinions ~ wobble n unsteady movement; act of wobbling ~ wobbly adj.

wodge [woj] n (coll) chunk, lump.

woe [wO] n sorrow, grief, misfortune, trouble; w. is me alas; cursed am I.

woebegone [wObigon] adj miserable; of mournful appearance.

woeful [wOfool] adj wretched; full of misery ~ woefully adv.

wog [wog] n (sl, pej) an Arab; an Indian; a Negro; any person of darkish or olive-coloured skin.

woke [wOk] p/t and p/part of wake (2).

woken [wOken] p/part of wake (2).

wold [wOld] n expanse of open country.

wolf (pl wolves) [woolf] n rapacious, gregarious animal of dog family; (fig) person of rapacious, greedy disposition; (sl) man who pesters women with his attentions; (mus) jarring sound on stringed instrument > PDM; cry w. raise a false alarm ~ wolf v/t eat rapidly and greedily.

wolfcub [woolfkub] n young wolf; junior Scout.

wolfdog [woolfdog] n dog for hunting wolves; hybrid between dog and wolf.

wolfhound [woolfhownd] n dog for hunting wolves.

wolfish [woolfish] adj fierce, cruel, rapacious; (sl) lustful ~ wolfishly adv ~ wolfishness n.

wolfram [woolfRam] n tungsten.

wolf-whistle [woolf-wis'l] n (coll) two-note whistle expressing admiration of a woman's physical charms.

wolverine [woolveReen] n North American carnivore; its fur; (US) native or resident of Michigan.

wolves [woolvz] pl of wolf.

woman (pl women) [wooman] n adult human being of female sex; women in general; lady-inwaiting; feminine nature or character; women's lib. (coll) militant movement seeking to liberate women from legal, economic and social disadvantages ~ woman adj female.

womanhood [woomanhood] n state of being a grown woman; feminine nature or character.

womanish [woomanish] adj effeminate, weak.

womanize [woomanIz] v/t and i make womanish; (coll) indulge in casual sexual intercourse with women.

womankind [woomankInd] n women in general.

womanly [woomanli] adj with the qualities usually associated with the female sex; characteristic of a grown woman.

womb [wOOm] n organ in mammals in which the embryo develops, uterus > PDB.

wombat [wombat] n a burrowing marsupial mammal.

Womble [womb'l] n (tr) type of soft toy representing a rodent-like animal, based on a television children's cartoon.

women [wimin] pl of woman.

womenfolk [wiminfOk] n (pl) women; one's female relatives.

womenkind [wiminkInd] n (pl) women; one's female relatives.

won [wun] p/t and p/part of win.

wonder [wunder] n an emotion excited by strange,

novel, or impressive objects or occurrences; anything or anyone that excites this emotion; miracle, marvel; prodigy ~ **wonder** *v/i* and *t* feel awed surprise, marvel; marvel (at); seek to know, be curious; **I w.** (*coll*) I doubt it; **I shouldn't w.** (*coll*) I should not be surprised (if).

wonderful [*wun*derfool] *adj* marvellous, amazing; (*coll*) very good ~ **wonderfully** *adv*.

wondering [*wun*deRing] *adj* feeling wonder or doubt ~ **wonderingly** *adv*.

wonderland [*wun*derland] *n* land of marvels and unusual happenings, fairyland; place of amazing beauty, luxury *etc*.

wonderment [*wun*derment] *n* surprise, astonishment, wonder.

wondrous [*wund*Rus] *adj* wonderful ~ **wondrous** *adv* (*ar*) wonderfully ~ **wondrously** *adv*.

wonky [*won*ki] *adj* (*sl*) unsteady, wobbly; hesitant, wavering; not well.

won't [*wOnt*] *abbr* will not.

wont [*wOnt*] *adj* accustomed ~ **wont** *n* usual custom, practice ~ **wonted** *adj* customary, usual.

woo [*wOO*] *v/t* seek to marry or win the love of; (*fig*) attempt to win.

wood [*wood*] *n* extensive group of growing trees; fibrous substance forming trunk and branches of tree; square sawn timber; firewood; wooden part of spear *etc*; (*collect*) woodwind instruments of an orchestra; cask or barrel; heavy wooden ball used in game of bowls; **cannot see the w. for the trees** unable to recognize essentials because of too much incidental detail; **out of the w.** free from danger, out of difficulty.

wood-alcohol [*wood*-alkOhol] *n* methyl alcohol.

wood-anemone [*wood*-anemoni] *n* white, bell-like, wild flower.

woodbine [*wood*bIn] *n* honeysuckle.

woodblock [*wood*blok] *n* a die cut from wood; wooden block used for flooring or in road surfacing.

woodchuck [*wood*chuk] *n* North American marmot.

woodcock [*wood*kok] *n* bird resembling the snipe.

woodcraft [*wood*kRaaft] *n* knowledge of forestry; ability to find one's way through woods and forests.

woodcut [*wood*kut] *n* wooden block upon which a picture, design, lettering *etc* has been incised for reproduction; print made from this.

woodcutter [*wood*kuter] *n* forester; wood-engraver.

wooded [*wood*id] *adj* covered with trees.

wooden [*wood*en] *adj* made of wood; (*fig*) stupid, awkward, lacking sensitivity; showing no emotion; stiff; (*of sound*) dull.

wood-engraving [*wood*-ingRayving] *n* art of cutting designs in relief on a polished block of wood; print from such a block.

wooden-headed [*wood*en-hedid] *adj* (*fig*) stupid.

woodenly [*wood*enli] *adv* in a wooden manner.

woodland [*wood*land] *n* wooded country ~ **woodland** *adj* pertaining to woods.

woodlark [*wood*laark] *n* short-tailed lark with spotted breast.

woodlice [*wood*lIs] *pl* of **woodlouse**.

woodlouse (*pl* **woodlice**) [*wood*lows] *n* small crustacean found under wood, stones *etc*.

woodman [*wood*man] *n* one employed to fell, or look after, trees.

woodnote [*wood*nOt] *n* bird song; (*fig*) artless spontaneous verse.

woodpecker [*wood*peker] *n* bird with elongated bill and tongue which extracts insects from the bark of trees.

woodpigeon [*wood*pijin] *n* wild pigeon. *esp* the ringdove.

woodpile [*wood*pIl] *n* stack of wood.

woodpulp [*wood*pulp] *n* broken-up wood fibres used in manufacture of cardboard, paper *etc*.

woodshed [*wood*shed] *n* shed where wood for fuel is kept; **something nasty in the w.** (*sl*) shocking secret.

woodsman [*wood*zman] *n* forester; one skilled in woodcraft.

wood-spirit [*wood*-spiRit] *n* methyl alcohol.

woodwind [*wood*wind] *n* (*collect*) types of wind instrument generally made of wood > PDM.

woodwork [*wood*wurk] *n* structure made wholly or partly of wood; carpentry.

woodworking [*wood*wurking] *n* art of making usable articles out of timber ~ **woodworking** *adj* shaping things in wood.

woodworm [*wood*wurm] *n* wood-eating larva of certain beetles.

woody [*wood*i] *adj* covered with woods; of wood or woods; made of wood; like wood; **w. nightshade** hedgerow climbing plant, bittersweet.

wooer [*wOO*-er] *n* one who woos.

woof (1) [*wOOf*] *n* cross threads in woven fabric.

woof (2) [*woof*] *n* and *v/i* (give) a gruff bark.

wooing [*wOO*ing] *n* courtship.

wool [*wool*] *n* short thick hair of sheep or other animal; yarn spun from this; cloth woven from this yarn; (*joc*) a person's hair; **dyed in the w.** dyed before spinning; (*fig*) thoroughgoing; **lose one's w.** (*sl*) get angry; **keep your w. on** don't get angry; **pull the w. over someone's eyes** hoodwink him.

woolfat [*wool*fat] *n* lanolin.

woolgathering [*wool*gaTHering] *n* absentmindedness ~ **woolgathering** *adj*.

woolgrower [*wool*gRO-er] *n* one who raises sheep for their wool.

woollen (1) [*wool*en] *adj* made of wool.

woollen (2) *n* cloth made of wool; (*pl*) woollen garments.

woolliness [*wool*ines] *n* state or quality of being woolly.

woolly (1) [*wool*i] *adj* made of, covered with, resembling, wool; (*fig*) lacking clarity or precision; (*coll*) rude, untutored.

woolly (2) *n* woollen garment; jersey.

woolly-bear [*wool*i-bair] *n* hairy caterpillar of the tiger-moth.

woolly-headed [*wool*i-hedid] *adj* with thick woolly hair; (*fig*) muddled, vague.

woolpack [*wool*pak] *n* wool packed in canvas *etc*; a bale of wool; (*meteor*) rounded cumulus cloud.

woolsack [*wool*sak] *n* bale of wool; cushion stuffed with wool on which the Lord Chancellor sits in House of Lords; (*fig*) position and dignity of Lord Chancellor.

woolstapler [*wool*staypler] *n* wool merchant.

wop [*wop*] *n* (*sl*) (*pej*) Italian or Spaniard.

word [*wurd*] *n* unit of language expressive of some object, idea or relation; written or printed representation of this; what is said; short speech or conversation; message, news; password; affirmation, promise; recommendation; (*pl*) lyric set to music; quarrelsome talk; (*theol*) Second Person of the Trinity; the Holy Scriptures; the Gospel; **as good as one's w.** fulfilling one's promise; **big words** arrogant speech; **eat one's words** take back what one has said; **have a w. with** speak briefly to; **last w.** most up-to-date of its kind; (*coll*) the limit; **my w.!** exclamation of surprise; **say a good w. for** recommend; defend; **w. for w.** literally, exactly ~ **word** *v/t* express in speech or writing.

wordblind [*wurd*blind] *adj* pathologically unable to spell, suffering from dyslexia.

wordbook [*wurd*book] *n* dictionary; (*mus*) libretto.

worded [*wurd*id] *adj* expressed in words, phrased.

word-formation [*wurd*-fawrmayshon] *n* making new words by the addition of prefixes, suffixes *etc*.

wordily [*wurd*ili] *adv* in a verbose style.

wordiness [*wurd*ines] *n* verbosity.

wording [*wurd*ing] *n* choice of words and phrasing.

wordless [*wurd*les] *adj* without words; speechless.

word-painting [*wurd*-paynting] *n* vivid verbal description.

word-perfect [*wurd*-purfekt] *adj* (*of speech*) accurately memorized; (*of person*) accurate in memorizing.

word-picture [*wurd*-pikcher] *n* a vivid description in words.

wordplay [*wurd*play] *n* repartee; puns.

wordy [*wurd*i] *adj* verbose, diffuse.

wore [*wawr*] *p/t* of **wear**.

work [*wurk*] *n* serious purposeful activity, mental or physical, *usu* costing effort; labour; occupation, employment; task, duty; that at which one is working; product of labour; needlework; product of artistic activity; (*mech*) product of a force and the distance it travels through > PDS; (*pl*) mechanism, engine *etc*; factory; good deeds done with Christian motives; excavations; engineering or building structure; **at w.** engaged in a task; present at one's place of employment; **give (one) the works** (*sl*) shoot at, kill; beat up; **go to w.** start a task; **have one's w.** cut out face a difficult task; **in w.** employed, having a job; **make short w. of** finish or destroy quickly ~ **work** *v/i* and *t* labour; be occupied or employed; act as was planned, operate successfully, have the desired effect; (*coll*) arrange; obtain cunningly; progress, make way (through); reach a new position or state by repeated small movements; move with agitation; operate; manipulate, control; accomplish; cause to work; hammer out, shape by pressure; spread or take effect gradually; **w. at** apply one's energy to; **w. in** find room for; gradually mix into; (*of workers*) remain at work in defiance of dismissal or closure of factory; **w. in with** combine well with; **w. off** find an outlet for; get rid of; **w. on** influence; be busy at; **w. out** calculate, solve; be capable of being solved; reach solution or fulfilment; plan in detail; exhaust; amount to; **w. up** stir up, excite; elaborate, develop; study thoroughly.

workable [*wurk*ab'l] *adj* that can be done, practicable; that will operate or go; (*of substances*) that can be manipulated or worked upon.

workaday [*wurk*aday] *adj* typical of, usual on, an ordinary working day; dull, ordinary, humdrum.

workbag [*wurk*bag] *n* bag to hold tools, needlework *etc*.

workbasket [*wurk*baaskit] *n* basket for needlework and for needles, cottons *etc*.

workbox [*wurk*boks] *n* workbasket.

workday [*wurk*day] *n* day on which most people are at work.

worker [*wurk*er] *n* one who or that which works; wage-earner; neuter bee, ant *etc*.

workforce [*wurk*fawrs] *n* workers in a particular factory or industry.

workhouse [*wurk*hows] *n* public institution for paupers.

work-in [*wurk*-in] *n* refusal by workers to leave a factory *etc* or cease production, in protest at planned closure or dismissals.

working [*wurk*ing] *n* operation, activity, functioning; manner in which a mechanism or process takes place; (*carp*) swelling or shrinkage of timber; (*mining*) sections where excavation is or has been in progress; (*tel*) technique of routing calls ~ **working** *adj* of, at or for work; engaging in manual labour; occupied by, spent in, work; used when at work; usable as basis to work from; **w. capital** (*comm*) surplus of current assets over current liabilities; **w. class** wage-earning section of a community, *esp* those in manual labour; proletariat; **w. drawing** detailed architectural plan for contractor to work from; **w. load** safe maximum load in normal conditions; **w. man** member of the working class; wage-earner; **w. party** investigatory committee of experts; **w. profit** (*mining*) proceeds of sale of product minus cost of production.

working-day [*wurk*ing-day] *n* a workday; number of hours constituting a normal day's work.

working-out [*wurk*ing-owt] *n* calculation; development; elaboration; outcome.

workman (*pl* **workmen**) [*wurk*man] *n* man employed in manual work; (good or bad) craftsman (judged by his skill).

workmanlike [*wurk*manlik] *adj* characteristic of a skilled workman; efficient, competent.

workmanship [*wurk*manship] *n* skill in making, craftsmanship; article produced by work.

work-out [*wurk*-out] *n* (*coll*) trial run; boxing bout.

workshop [*wurk*shop] *n* space fitted up for light engineering in factory or house; group of people meeting for discussion and joint experimental projects.

workshy [*wurk*shi] *adj* unwilling to take a job; lazy.

work-to-rule [*wurk*-too-ROOl] *n* curtailment of output by workers by observing safety rules *etc* with exaggerated care.

world [*wurld*] *n* the earth; the universe; a planet, star *etc*; mankind; human life and experience; human society; a subsection of this; sphere of interest or activity; any area considered as an environment for creatures within it; materialistic standards, aims *etc* as opposed to spiritual; materialistic persons or society; (*fig*) vast quantity or number; **for all the w. (as if)** just as if; **dead to**

the w. (*sl*) helplessly drunk; very deeply asleep; **man of the w.** experienced, sophisticated person; **New W.** the Americas; the Western Hemisphere; **the next w.** life after death; **not for the w.** not on any consideration; **Old W.** Europe, Asia and Africa; **out of this w.** (*coll*) sublime, magnificent; **w.** power nation having world-wide influence; **think the w. of** esteem very highly; **w. without end** eternally.

worldliness [*wurld*linis] *n* quality of being worldly.

worldling [*wurld*ling] *n* one devoted to material things.

worldly [*wurld*li] *adj* not spiritual or idealistic; materialistic; social; of or by the standards of secular society.

worldly-minded [*wurld*li-mIndid] *adj* intent on gain and worldly pleasure.

worldlywise [wurldliwIz] *adj* experienced in the ways of society.

worldwide [*wurld*wId] *adj* extending over the whole world, universal.

worm [wurm] *n* any long invertebrate, *esp* the earthworm; (*fig*) obsequious contemptible person; maggot, grub; thread of screw; ligament in dog's tongue ~ **worm** *v/i* and *t* wriggle along like a worm; edge along slowly and with difficulty; insinuate (oneself into); extract (information *etc*) by persistent but indirect questioning; rid of parasitic worms.

wormcast [*wurm*kaast] *n* small heap of earth excreted by earthworm.

wormeaten [*wurm*eeten] *adj* full of wormholes; (*fig*) antiquated.

wormhole [*wurm*hOl] *n* hole in ground made by worm; hole in wood made by grub.

worm-powder [*wurm*-powder] *n* preparation to rid the intestines of worms.

wormwood [*wurm*wood] *n* plant used to flavour absinthe; (*fig*) bitterness, mortification.

wormy [*wurm*i] *adj* of or like a worm; full of worms; (*fig*) earthy; wormeaten.

worn (1) [wawrn] *p/part* of **wear**.

worn (2) *adj* showing signs of usage; showing fatigue, anxiety *etc*.

worn-out [wawrn-owt] *adj* made useless by usage; exhausted; (*fig*) trite, out-of-date.

worried [*wu*Rid] *adj* troubled, anxious, uneasy.

worrier [*wu*Ri-er] *n* one who worries much.

worrit [*wu*Rit] *v/t* and *i* (*dial*) worry.

worry [*wu*Ri] *v/t* and *i* make anxious; be anxious; (*of dog*) shake and tear with the teeth; harass, pester; obtain by persistence ~ **worry** *n* anxiety; a cause of perturbation; **w. beads** string of movable beads used to relieve tension by fiddling.

worrying [*wu*Ri-ing] *adj* causing worry: that worries ~ **worryingly** *adv*.

worse [wurs] *adj* (*comp* of **bad**) bad to a greater degree; less good; poorer in condition, circumstances, health; **the w. for** damaged or impaired by; **none the w. for** not harmed by; (*coll*) improved by; **w. and w.** progressively worse ~ **worse** *comp adv* in a worse way, more severely; **w. off** in less fortunate circumstances ~ **worse** *n* that which is worse; **go from bad to w.** deteriorate.

worsen [*wur*sen] *v/t* and *i* make or become worse.

worsening [*wur*sening] *n* deterioration.

worship [*wur*ship] *n* reverence, veneration, *esp* that paid to a deity > PDP; practice, ritual or act expressing this; communal religious service; **His W.** title of a mayor; **Your W.** mode of address to magistrate ~ **worship** (*pres/part* **worshipping,** *p/t* and *p/part* **worshipped**) *v/t* and *i* revere; idolize; offer adoring prayer to; participate in religious service.

worshipful [*wur*shipfool] *adj* (*as form of address to show respect*) worthy of honour.

worst [wurst] *adj* (*superl* of **bad**) bad in the greatest degree ~ **worst** *adv* in the worst way ~ **worst** *n* that which is worst ~ **worst** *v/t* defeat.

worsted [*woos*tid] *n* cloth woven from closely twisted woollen yarn ~ **worsted** *adj*.

worth [wurth] *adj* valued at; deserving of, meriting; repaying; having possessions amounting to; **for all one is w.** to the limit of one's powers; **be w. while,** (*coll*) w. it repaying the time, trouble *etc* spent on it ~ **worth** *n* value, intrinsic excellence; merit, *esp* of moral qualities; amount that can be bought for a given sum of money; (specified sum's) equivalent (in coins of lesser value).

worthily [*wur*THili] *adv* in a worthy manner.

worthiness [*wur*THines] *n* quality of being worthy.

worthless [*wurth*les] *adj* of no value, useless; (*of person*) shiftless, of bad character.

worthwhile [wurth*wI*l] *adj* worth the effort, trouble *etc*.

worthy [*wur*THi] *adj* deserving, praiseworthy, estimable ~ **worthy** *n* eminent person, notable; (*joc*) person.

wot [wot] *v/i* (*ar*) I know; he knows.

wotcher [*wo*cher] *interj* (*sl*) what cheer! (*used as a greeting*).

would [wood] *p/t* of **will**.

would-be [*wood*-bee] *adj* aspiring or attempting, *usu* unsuccessfully.

wouldn't [*wood*'nt] *abbr* would not.

wound (1) [wOOnd] *n* injury in form of cut, rent, or hole made in skin or tissues of the body; (*fig*) injury to person's feelings, affront ~ **wound** *v/t* hurt, injure body or feelings.

wound (2) [wownd] *p/t* and *p/part* of **wind** (2) and **wind** (3).

wove (1) [wOv] *p/t* and *p/part* of **weave**.

wove (2) *adj* **w. paper** paper not showing wire marks.

woven [wOven] *p/part* of **weave**.

wow [wow] *n* (*theat sl*) a tremendous success ~ **wow** *interj* (*sl*) exclamation expressing admiration.

wrack [Rak] *n* seaweed washed ashore; (*ar*) destruction.

wraith [Rayth] *n* apparition, *esp* of person just before his death; ghost; (*fig*) very thin, pale person.

wrangle [Rang-g'l] *v/i* argue, dispute angrily ~ **wrangle** *n* angry dispute.

wrangler [*Rang*-gler] *n* one who disputes; (*at Cambridge University*) candidate placed in the first class of the mathematical tripos.

wrap (*pres/part* **wrapping,** *p/t* and *p/part* **wrapped**) [Rap] *v/t* fold round; cover; (*fig*) conceal; **w. up** enfold thoroughly in a covering; wear several layers of warm clothing; (*fig*) conceal by verbose or obscure language; **wrapped up in**

(*fig*) absorbed by; devoted to ~ **wrap** *n* outer covering; shawl. scarf; rug, blanket.

wrapper [*Ra*per] *n* one who or that which wraps; loose outer garment; loose paper cover for book; gummed strip of paper wrapped round newspaper *etc* for mailing.

wrapping [*Ra*ping] *n* material in which to wrap something.

wrap-up [*Ra*p-up] *n* (*coll*) elaborate concealment of truth.

wrath [*Ro*th] *n* fierce indignation, violent anger.

wrathful [*Ro*thfool] *adj* angry, enraged ~ **wrathfully** *adv*.

wrathy [*Ro*thi] *adj* (*coll*) wrathful.

wreak [*Ree*k] *v*/*t* give vent to (wrath), exact (vengeance).

wreath [*Ree*th] *n* arrangement of intertwined leaves or flowers, *esp* one given in memory of deceased person; chaplet, garland; wisp of smoke or mist.

wreathe [*Ree*TH] *v*/*t* and *i* twist, entwine, encircle; move in coils.

wreck [*Re*k] *n* ship abandoned at sea or fast on rocks; ruin, destruction; broken remains of structure after a disaster; person enfeebled by sickness *etc* ~ **wreck** *v*/*t* and *i* sail (ship) to destruction; sabotage; demolish (structure); be wrecked.

wreckage [*Re*kij] *n* broken remains, *esp* of ship or structure after a disaster; act of wrecking.

wrecker [*Re*ker] *n* one who purposely destroys, *esp* person on land who lures ship to destruction in order to plunder the wreckage; person whose duty it is to recover cargo from a wrecked ship; (*US*) van equipped to remove disabled motor vehicles.

wren (1) [*Re*n] *n* species of small songbird.

Wren (2) *n* (*coll*) member of the Women's Royal Naval Service.

wrench [*Re*nch] *n* sharp violent twist; injury by twisting; sprain; adjustable spanner to turn nuts; (*fig*) grief at separation ~ **wrench** *v*/*t* twist, turn sharply; (*fig*) distort.

wrest [*Re*st] *v*/*t* tug violently; obtain by force; (*fig*) extract by effort and toil; distort, misinterpret ~ **wrest** *n* action of wresting; key for tuning a wire-stringed instrument.

wrestle [*Re*s'l] *v*/*i* and *t* struggle to overthrow (opponent) by grappling, tripping or applying arm or foot lock; contend in this way in an organized contest; **w. with** fight against in this way; (*fig*) contend against (temptations *etc*); make effort to overcome (difficulty) ~ **wrestle** *n* bout of wrestling; (*fig*) struggle.

wrestler [*Re*sler] *n* one who wrestles, *esp* for a living.

wretch [*Re*ch] *n* poor, unfortunate person; contemptible creature.

wretched [*Re*chid] *adj* miserable; dismal, squalid; contemptible, of poor quality ~ **wretchedly** *adv* ~ **wretchedness** *n*.

wrick, rick [*Ri*k] *v*/*t* twist, sprain slightly ~ **wrick** *n* a twist or sprain.

wriggle [*Ri*g'l] *v*/*i* and *t* make twisting movements, squirm; (*fig*) dodge, evade; **w. out of** escape from a difficult situation by cunning ~ **wriggle** *n* act of wriggling; squirming movement.

wriggler [*Ri*gler] *n* one who wriggles; one who equivocates.

wring (*p*/*t* and *p*/*part* **wrung**) [*Ri*ng] *v*/*t* twist; force out moisture; squeeze; **w. from** extort ~ **wring** *n* act of wringing; a press for cheese, cider *etc*.

wringer [*Ri*nger] *n* that which wrings; machine with rollers for forcing moisture from clothes after washing.

wringing [*Ri*nging] *adj* and *adv* wet enough to wring water from.

wrinkle [*Ri*nk'l] *n* crease, fold, *esp* of skin; (*coll*) useful tip or hint ~ **wrinkle** *v*/*t* and *i* crease into wrinkles; become creased.

wrist [*Ri*st] *n* joint between hand and forearm; part of garment covering this joint.

wristband [*Ri*stband] *n* tight part of sleeve at wrist, cuff.

wristlet [*Ri*stlit] *n* band or strap worn round the wrist; **w. watch** wristwatch.

wristwatch [*Ri*stwoch] *n* watch worn on strap or bracelet fastened round the wrist.

writ (1) [*Ri*t] *ar p*/*t* and *p*/*part* of **write**.

writ (2) *n* (*leg*) document giving royal instructions to person to do, or to refrain from doing, something; Holy W. the Bible.

write (*p*/*t* **wrote**, *p*/*part* **written**) [*Ri*t] *v*/*i* and *t* set down on paper a succession of conventional signs expressive of some object, idea, or relation; communicate in writing; be an author; produce (book *etc*); **w. in for** apply by letter for; **w. off** cancel; consider as cancelled; **w. out** copy out in writing; write in full; **w. up** bring up to date in writing; praise in writing; exaggerate in writing.

write-off [*Ri*t-of] *n* a complete loss, *esp* car so badly damaged that repairs are not worth while.

writer [*Ri*ter] *n* one who writes; author; (*nav*) clerk; W. to the Signet (*Scots*) solicitor.

write-up [*Ri*t-up] *n* flattering advertisement or press notice.

writhe [*Ri*TH] *v*/*i* twist the body as if suffering pain; (*fig*) squirm, agonize.

writing [*Ri*ting] *n* act of one who writes; style of handwriting; anything written; (*pl*) an author's literary works.

writing-case [*Ri*ting-kays] *n* portable receptacle containing writing materials.

writing-desk [*Ri*ting-desk] *n* desk or folding box for writing at.

writing-paper [*Ri*ting-payper] *n* highly glazed paper of good quality cut to a size suitable for letter writing.

writing-table [*Ri*ting-tayb'l] *n* table or desk designed for writing at.

written (1) *p*/*part* of **write**.

written (2) *adj* set down in writing; not typed, printed, or spoken.

wrong [*Ro*ng] *adj* incorrect, erroneous; not just; evil, sinful; not suitable; **get hold of the w. end of the stick** misunderstand; **get on the w. side of** rouse hostility in; **w. side** (*of fabric*) inner side; **w. 'un** (*coll*) dishonest person, rogue; (*cricket*) googly ~ **wrong** *adv* in a wrong way; **go w.** make a mistake; end badly; lapse into sin; cease functioning, function badly; **get it w.** calculate badly; misunderstand; **get (one) in w. with** (*US*) bring one into disfavour with ~ **wrong** *n* injustice; sin; that which is wrong ~ **wrong** *v*/*t* be unjust or cruel to; injure; think ill of without cause.

wrongdoing [*Rong*dOO-ing] *n* sin, evil conduct.

wrongful [*Rong*fool] *adj* unjust; unlawful ~ **wrongfully** *adv*.

wrong-headed [*Rong*-hedid] *adj* wilfully perverse.

wrongly [*Rong*li] *adv* in a wrong way.

wrote [*ROt*] *p/t* of **write**.

wroth [*ROth/Roth*] *adj* (*ar* and *poet*) very angry.

wrought (1) [*Rawt*] *ar p/t* and *p/part* of **work**.

wrought (2) *adj* hammered, beaten into shape; **w. iron** malleable, fibrous, pure iron.

wrought-up [*Rawt*-up] *adj* overwrought.

wrung [*Rung*] *p/t* and *p/part* of **wring**.

wry [*RI*] *adj* twisted; (*fig*) embittered; ironical; expressing distaste ~ **wryly** *adv*.

wryneck [*RI*nek] *n* bird related to the woodpecker.

wrynecked [*RI*nekt] *adj* with twisted neck.

wryness [*RI*nis] *n* quality of being wry.

wychelm, witchelm [*wich*elm] *n* wild elm.

wychhazel, witchhazel [*wich*hayzel] *n* North American shrub whose bark yields a liquid popular as a remedy for bruises.

Wykhamist [*wIk*amist/*wik*amist] *n* past or present pupil of Winchester College.

wyvern, wivern [*wI*vern] *n* legendary and heraldic creature resembling a two-legged dragon.

X

x [*eks*] twenty-fourth letter of English alphabet; (*Rom num*) ten; (*math*) unknown quantity; (*fig*) anything or anyone unknown; **X** (*of films*) not suitable for persons under 18.

xanth-, xantho- *pref* yellow.

xanthene [*zan*theen] *n* (*chem*) an oxide used in manufacture of dyestuffs.

xanthophyll [*zan*thOfil] *n* (*chem*) yellow pigment in withering leaves > PDB.

xanthopsia [zan*thops*i-a] *n* (*path*) jaundiced condition in which all objects appear yellow > PDP.

xanthous [*zan*thus] *adj* yellow-skinned, *esp* Mongolian.

xebec [*zee*bek] *n* small Mediterranean sailing vessel, usually three-masted.

xeme [*zeem*] *n* (*orni*) fork-tailed gull.

xen-, xeno- *pref* relating to foreigners; external, foreign, strange.

xenia [*zee*ni-a] *n* (*bot*) changes of endosperm due to effect of foreign pollen > PDB.

xenoglossia [zen*O*g*losi*-a] *n* (*psychical research*) alleged ability to use and understand a language one has never learnt.

xenolith [*zen*Olith] *n* (*geol*) piece of rock of one kind in a rock of another kind.

xenon [*zen*on] *n* (*chem*) inert gas occurring in the air > PDS.

xenophobe [*zen*Of*O*b] *n* (person) hating foreigners or strangers.

xenophobia [zen*OfO*bi-a] *n* irrational hate or fear of foreigners or strangers.

xer-, xero- *pref* dry.

xerasia [zeer*Rayz*i-a] *n* (*path*) morbid dryness of the hair.

xeroderma, xerodermia [zeerRO*dur*ma, zeerRO*durmi*-a] *n* (*path*) morbid dryness of the skin.

Xerography [ze*Rog*Rafi] *n* (*tr*) a photographic copying process using dry powder.

xerophilous [zee*Ro*filus] *adj* (*bot*, *zool*) able to thrive in conditions of long drought.

xerophyte [*zeer*ROfIt] *n* (*bot*) plant able to endure prolonged drought > PDB, PDG.

xiphoid [*zif*oid] *adj* (*anat*) sword-shaped.

Xerox [*ze*Roks/*zeer*Roks] *n* and *v/t* (*tr*) (reproduce by) a certain type of xerography; reproduction thus produced.

Xmas *n* written abbreviation of **Christmas.**

X-ray [*eks*-Ray] *n* electromagnetic radiation similar to light but of shorter wavelength, which is capable of penetrating matter > PDS; photograph taken by X-rays ∼**X-ray** *v/t* photograph (an organ, bone *etc*) by X-rays, *usu* to diagnose injury or disease ∼**X-ray** *adj* of or by X-rays.

xyl-, xylo- *pref* wood, pertaining to wood.

xylem [*zI*lem] *n* (*bot*) woody vascular tissue > PDB.

xylene [*zI*leen] *n* (*chem*) oily liquid, consisting of three isomers, obtained from coal-tar, used in the manufacture of dyes.

xylo- *pref* of, like, or on wood.

xylocarp [*zI*lOkaarp] *n* hard, woody fruit; tree bearing such fruit.

xylograph [*zI*lOgRaaf] *n* engraved picture or pattern on wood; woodblock painting.

xylographic [zIlo*Ra*fik] *n* of or by xylography.

xylography [zI*log*Rafi] *n* technique of wood-engraving in white lines on black ground > PDAA; technique of patterning that reproduces the effect of wood grain.

xyloid [*zI*loid] *adj* of or like wood.

xyloidine [zI*loi*din] *n* (*chem*) explosive substance made by treating vegetable fibre with nitric acid.

Xylonite [*zI*lonIt] *n* (*tr*) (*chem*) thermoplastic material of the cellulose nitrate type.

xylophone [*zI*lOfOn] *n* (*mus*) percussion instrument consisting of graduated strips of hard wood which vibrate when struck > PDM.

xylose [*zI*lOs] *n* (*chem*) wood-sugar > PDS.

xyster [*zis*ter] *n* (*surg*) instrument for scraping bones.

Y

y [*wı*] twenty-fifth letter of English alphabet.

y- (*ar*) *pref* denoting p/part of certain verbs.

yabber [*yaber*] *n* and *v/i* (*Aust coll*) chatter.

yacht [*yot*] *n* light sailing vessel for racing; private vessel for pleasure trips ∼ yacht *v/i* sail a yacht.

yachtclub [*yotklub*] *n* club for yachtsmen.

yachting [*yoting*] *n* act or sport of sailing a yacht.

yachtsman [*yots*man] *n* one who sails or owns a yacht.

yachtsmanship [*yots*manship] *n* skill in sailing a yacht.

yack [*yak*] *v/i* and *n* yak (2).

yaffle [*yaf'l*] *n* green woodpecker.

yah [*yaa*] *interj* exclamation of derision or defiance.

yahoo [yaa*hOO*] *n* brutish, bestial person.

Yahweh [*yaavay*] *n* the God of Israel, Jehovah.

yak (1) [*yak*] *n* long-haired Asiatic ox.

yak (2) (*pres/part* yakking, *p/t* and *p/part* yakked) *v/i* (*coll*) chatter idly or spitefully, gossip; talk quickly ∼ yak *n*.

yale (1) [*yayl*] *n* (*her*) fabulous beast with tusks and horns.

Yale (2) *n* (*tr*) type of cylinder lock.

yam [*yam*] *n* a tropical climbing plant; its edible root; (*US*) sweet potato.

yammer [*yamer*] *v/i* (*dial*) yelp; whine; (*coll*) jabber, talk nonsense.

yang [*yang*] *n* active principle of the cosmos in Chinese philosophy, opposite of yin.

yank (1) [*yank*] *v/t* and *i* (*coll*) pull sharply ∼ yank *n* jerk, sharp tug.

Yank (2) *n* and *adj* (*sl*) Yankee.

Yankee [*yankee*] *n* an American; (*US*) a New Englander; inhabitant of the northern States ∼ Yankee *adj* American.

yap (*pres/part* yapping, *p/t* and *p/part* yapped) [*yap*] *v/i* (*of dog*) yelp, bark snappishly; (*coll*) talk noisily, chatter ∼ yap *n* excited bark or yelp; (*coll*) stupid noisy talk; (*sl*) mouth.

yapon, yaupon [*yaw*pon] *n* kind of holly found in the southern States of America; tea brewed from its leaves.

yapp [*yap*] *n* style of limp leather bookbinding with overlapping cover.

yard (1) [*yaard*] *n* British unit of length, 36 inches or 3 feet long, defined as 0·9144 metres; piece of fabric *etc* one yard long; (*naut*) spar supporting sail; (*bui*) measure of lime, mortar, stone *etc*.

yard (2) *n* enclosed area, usually paved, adjoining a building; enclosure for some specific purpose, *eg* churchyard, brickyard, railway marshalling yard; the Y. Scotland Yard, headquarters of the London Metropolitan Police ∼ yard *v/t* enclose, keep in a yard.

yardage (1) [*yaardij*] *n* length in yards; area in square yards; (*bui*) volume of earth in cubic yards.

yardage (2) *n* use of a yard for cattle *etc*; charge for this.

yardangs [*yaar*dangs] *n* steep overhanging ridges of rock found in the deserts of Central Asia.

yardarm [*yaard*aarm] *n* (*naut*) outer extremity of a yard.

yardmaster [*yaard*maaster] *n* official in charge of a railway marshalling yard.

yard-measure [*yaard*-mezher] *n* tape or rod one yard long with subdivisions of a yard marked on it.

yardstick [*yaard*stik] *n* yard-measure; (*fig*) standard of comparison.

yarmulka [*yaar*mulka] *n* Jewish man's skullcap.

yarn [*yaarn*] *n* continuous thread of synthetic fibrous material or of twisted fibres of wool, cotton *etc*; (*coll*) anecdote, *esp* long rambling tale; spin a y. tell a story ∼ yarn *v/i* (*coll*) tell stories; have a long comfortable chat.

yarrow [*ya*RO] *n* common weed with flat-topped clusters of small flower-heads.

yashmak [*yash*mak] *n* Muslim woman's veil.

yataghan [*yata*gan] *n* curved Muslim sword with decorated pommel but no hilt.

yaw [*yaw*] *v/i* (*of ship or aircraft*) steer out of course, deviate from line of flight ∼ yaw *n* ∼ yawing *n*.

yawl [*yawl*] *n* two-masted vessel whose mainmast is tall and carries several sails; a small ship's boat or fishing boat.

yawn [*yawn*] *v/i* breathe in involuntarily through a wide-opened mouth; (*fig*) open wide, gape; (*fig*) be bored or sleepy ∼ yawn *n* act of yawning.

yawning [*yawn*ing] *adj* having or forming a wide gap; that yawns.

yawp [*yawp*] *v/i* (*US coll*) yawn; yap; chatter.

yaws [*yawz*] *n* framboesia, a tropical skin disease.

ye (1) [*yee*] *pron* (*pl*) (*ar or poet*) you.

ye (2) [yee/THee] *art* (*pseudo ar corruption*) the.

yea [*yay*] *interj* and *n* (*ar*) yes.

yeah [*ye/yair*] *adv* and *interj* (*coll*) yes.

year [yur/yeer] *n* unit of time (365 days, or 366 days in a leap year) from 1 January to 31 December; period of 365 days reckoned from a certain date; cycle of the seasons; period of time taken by the earth to complete its orbit round the sun > PDS, PDG; (*pl*) age, time of life; bissextile y. year of 366 days; calendar, civil, or legal y. 1 January to 31 December; fiscal y. financial year ending on 5 April; leap y. year of 366 days; lunar y. year of 354 days, divided into 12 lunar months; y. of grace, y. of our Lord particular year of the Christian era; a y. per annum; every year; y. in y. out occurring year after year; with dull, unfailing regularity.

yearbook [*yur*book/*yeer*book] *n* reference book published annually.

yearling [*yur*ling/*yeer*ling] *n* animal, *esp* colt, in its second year ∼ yearling *adj* a year old.

yearlong [*yur*long/*yeer*long] *adj* persisting for a whole year.

yearly [*yur*li/*yeer*li] *adj* once a year or every year ∼ yearly *adv* annually; every year.

yearn [*yurn*] *v/i* feel longing, desire, pity (for *or* after); feel tenderly towards.

yearning [*yurn*ing] *n* longing, desire; tender feeling.

yeast [*yeest*] *n* fungoid substance used in brewing, breadmaking *etc* which causes alcoholic fermentation by enzyme action > PDS.

yeasty [*yeest*i] *adj* of or like yeast; containing yeast; frothy; restless; frivolous, wordy.

yell [*yel*] *v/t* and *i* utter in a loud voice; cry out loudly, scream, howl; laugh boisterously ~ **yell** *n* loud, piercing cry; (*coll*) something intensely funny.

yellow [*yel*O] *adj* having the colour of gold, lemons *etc*; yellow-skinned, Mongolian; (*sl*) cowardly, mean-spirited; **y. fever, y. jack** infectious tropical fever; **y. flag, y. jack** flag displayed to indicate a contagious disease; **y. pages** section of telephone directory reserved for business subscribers, printed on yellow paper; **y. peril** supposed danger that the Asiatic peoples may overwhelm the white; **y. press** newspapers unscrupulously sensational; **y. streak** cowardly flaw in person's character ~ **yellow** *n* one of the primary colours having a bright, clear, golden hue > PDP; pigment of this colour; object of this colour, yolk of egg; (*fig*) cowardice, meanness ~ **yellow** *v/t* and *i* paint yellow; become yellow.

yellowback [*yel*Obak] *n* cheap sensational novel in yellow covers.

yellowbelly [*yel*Obeli] *n* (*sl*) coward.

yellowhammer [*yel*Ohamer] *n* (*orni*) yellow-feathered bunting.

yellowish [*yel*O-ish] *adj* somewhat yellow.

yellowy [*yel*O-i] *adj* somewhat yellow in colour.

yelp [*yelp*] *n* short, sharp bark of pain or excitement ~ **yelp** *v/i* utter a yelp.

yen (1) (*pl* yen) [*yen*] *n* the currency of Japan.

yen (2) *n* (*US sl*) intense desire, yearning, urge ~ **yen** (*pres/part* yenning, *p/t* and *p/part* yenned) *v/i* yearn; feel a longing or urge.

yeoman (*pl* yeomen) [*yO*man] *n* (*hist*) attendant of some importance in royal or noble household; (*hist*) attendant on knight or official; (*hist*) small landowner serving as footsoldier; landowning countryman; (*mil*) member of the Yeomanry; **y. service** effective aid in time of need; **Yeomen of the Guard** bodyguard of the sovereign of England, now warders or beefeaters at Tower of London.

yeomanly [*yO*manli] *adj* of or like a yeoman.

Yeomanry [*yO*manRi] *n* (*hist*) company of yeomen; (*mil*) British territorial volunteer cavalry force recruited from landowning countrymen; landowning countrymen in general.

yep [*yep*] *interj* (*US sl*) yes.

yes [*yes*] *adv* and *interj* an expression of affirmation or of assent; (*inter*) indeed? is that so? ~ **yes** (*pl* yeses) *n* affirmative reply.

yes-man [*yes*-man] *n* (*coll*) one who docilely agrees with every opinion of his employer, leader *etc*.

yester- *pref* pertaining to yesterday; preceding, last before this.

yesterday [*yes*terdi] *n* the day before today; (*pl*) former times ~ **yesterday** *adv* on the day before today; not long ago.

yet [*yet*] *adv* up till now; up till then; at this moment, now; some future day, eventually; in addition, besides, further; (*to comp*) even, still; as **y.** up to now; **nor y.** and also not, and not

even ~ **yet** *conj* but still, nevertheless, however.

yeti [*yay*ti] *n* name of unidentified ape-like animal supposed to inhabit Himalaya mountains.

yew [*yOO*] *n* dark-leaved evergreen coniferous tree; wood of this.

Yggdrasil [*igd*Razil] *n* (*Norse myth*) gigantic ash-tree whose branches reach to the sky and cover the earth.

Yid [*yid*] *n* (*pej*, *sl*) a Jew.

yiddish [*yid*ish] *n* mixed dialect of High German, Hebrew and Slavonic, used by Jews in Europe and America.

yield [*yeeld*] *v/t* and *i* produce, bear (crops *etc*); bring in (as financial return); furnish; give as favour, grant, concede; give up, surrender; provide produce; give a return; give way under physical pressure; be amenable (to treatment) ~ **yield** *n* produce, crop; profit, return; (*min*) weight of valuable metal obtained per ton of ore.

yielding [*yeeld*ing] *adj* about to surrender; compliant; flexible.

yin [*yin*] *n* passive principle of the cosmos in Chinese philosophy, opposite of yang.

yippee [*yip*ee] *interj* (*coll*) exclamation of delight.

yippie [*yip*i] *n* (*US coll*) one who adopts a hippy life-style but is politically committed.

yob [*yob*] *n* (*pej sl*) boy; fellow; lout.

yod [*yod*] *n* name of the tenth letter in the Hebrew alphabet; (*phil*) consonantal *i* (= y).

yodel (*pres/part* yodelling, *p/t* and *p/part* yodelled) [*yO*d'l] *v/t* and *i* sing with rapid alternations between natural voice and falsetto, as in Swiss and Tyrolean style > PDM ~ **yodel** *n* wordless song or cry in this style.

yoga [*yO*ga] *n* Hindu system of meditation and asceticism ending in a trance, interpreted as union with God.

yogh [*yog*/*yok*] *n* the Middle English letter ȝ.

yoghurt, yogurt, yaourt [*yO*gurt/yogurt, ya-awrt] *n* thickly clotted and fermented milk, *esp* goat's milk.

yogi [*yO*gi] *n* one who practises yoga.

yogs [*yogz*] *n* (*pl*) (*sl*) ages, years.

yo-heave-ho [yO-heev-*hO*] *interj* (*naut*) chant of sailors while heaving at a rope or capstan.

yoicks [*yoiks*] *interj* foxhunting cry.

yoke [*yOk*] *n* shaped wooden harness across necks of draught oxen; frame of similar shape for carrying couple of pails; part of garment fitting the shoulders and upper chest; pair (of oxen); (*fig*) authority, dominion; (*bui*) a spreader beam; (*eng*) stiff, steel angle sections on timbers ~ **yoke** *v/t* put yoke upon; (*fig*) join together.

yokefellow [*yOk*felO] *n* partner in some task; husband; wife.

yokel [*yO*kel] *n* (*pej*) countryman, bumpkin.

yolk (1) [*yOk*] *n* the yellow part of egg > PDB.

yolk (2) *n* greasy secretion in the skin of sheep which keeps wool soft; **in the y.** (*of wool*) in its natural state.

yolky (1) [*yO*ki] *adj* of or like egg-yolk; having a large yolk.

yolky (2) *adj* (*of wool*) greasy.

yon [*yon*] *adj* and *adv* (*ar* and *poet*) (that) over there ~ **yon** *pron* that (those) over there; that, those.

yonder [*yon*der] *adj* and *adv* over there; distant but within sight; in that direction.

yoni [*yO*ni] *n* (*Hindu*) representation of female sexual organ used as religious symbol.

yore [*yawr*] *n* long ago; times past; **of y.** formerly.

york [*yawrk*] *v/t* (*cricket*) bowl out with a yorker.

yorker [*yawr*ker] *n* (*cricket*) ball which pitches directly underneath the bat.

Yorkist [*yawr*kist] *n* and *adj* (*hist*) (adherent) of the House of York in Wars of the Roses.

Yorkshire [*yawrk*sher] *adj* belonging to Yorkshire; **Y. pudding** light batter pudding baked in beef fat; **Y. terrier** small long-haired variety of terrier; **come (put) Y. on** (*coll*) cheat, be too smart for.

you [*yOO*] *pron* (*2nd pers sing or pl*) the person or persons addressed; (*indef pron*) one, anyone.

you'd [*yOOd*] *abbr* you would; you had.

you'll [*yOOl*] *abbr* you will; you shall.

young [*yung*] *adj* newly born, not old; in early stages of growth; juvenile; fresh, vigorous; inexperienced, immature; (*coll joc*) small, diminutive ~ **young** *n* offspring; **the y.** young people.

youngish [*yung*ish] *adj* fairly young.

youngling [*yung*ling] *n* (*poet*) young child or animal.

youngster [*yung*ster] *n* lad, boy; child.

your [*yawr*] *poss adj* belonging to or connected with you; (*ar, impers or cont*) that you know of; average; typical.

you're [*yawr*] *abbr* you are.

yours [*yawrz*] *poss pron* and *adj* (that, those) belonging to you or connected with you; **y. truly** (*vulg coll*) I; me.

yourself [*pl* **yourselves**] [yawr*self*] *pron* (*emph* and *refl*) you.

youth [*yOOth*] *n* state of being young, early life; young man; young people collectively; **Y. Hostel** building where hikers can put up for the night at little expense ~ **youth** *adj* for, of or by young people.

youthful [*yOOth*fool] *adj* like youth; young; juvenile ~ **youthfully** *adv* ~ **youthfulness** *n*.

you've [*yOOv*] *abbr* you have.

yowl [*yowl*] *n* long and loud cry of distress or pain (*esp* of animals) ~ **yowl** *v/i*.

Yo-yo [*yO*-yO] *n* (*tr*) grooved spherical top made to run up and down a string.

ytterbium [i*turb*i-um] *n* (*chem*) a rare metallic element > PDS.

yttrium [*it*Ri-um] *n* (*chem*) a rare metallic element > PDS.

yucca [*yuk*a] *n* genus of American tropical flowering plants of lily family.

Yugoslav, Jugoslav [*yoog*Oslaav] *n* and *adj* (citizen) of Yugoslavia.

yuk [*yuk*] *interj* (*coll*) exclamation of disgust.

Yule [*yOOl*] *n* festival of Christmas.

Yule-log [*yOOl*-log] *n* log burnt as part of Christmas festivities.

Yuletide [*yOOl*tId] *n* Christmas time.

yummy [*yum*i] *adj* (*coll*) delicious.

yum-yum [*yum*-yum] *interj* (*coll*) exclamation of appreciation, *esp* of food or girls.

yurt [*yoort*] *n* skin-tent used by Asiatic nomads.

Z

z [*zed*, *(US)* *zee*] twenty-sixth and last letter of English alphabet.

zabaglione [zabali-Oni] *n* (*Ital*) sweet dish of whipped egg-yolks, sugar and wine.

zaffre, zaffer [*zafer*] *n* a cobalt oxide, used as blue pigment in stained glass *etc*.

zany [*zayni*] *n* clown, buffoon; idiot, fool; comedian's stooge; (*hist*) servant-clown in 16th-century Italian drama ~ **zany** *adj* (*coll*) clownish; idiotic; crazy.

zap (*pres/part* **zapping**, *p/t* and *p/part* **zapped**) [*zap*] *v/t* (*coll*) hit, knock; attack; kill.

zapateado [zapati-*aa*dO] *n* vigorous Spanish dance for a single performer, with much stamping with the heels.

Zarathustrian [zaRa*th*OOstRi-an] *n* and *adj* Zoroastrian.

zaratite [za*Rat*It] *n* (*min*) emerald nickel.

zariba, zareba [za*Ree*ba] *n* stockade; fortified camp.

zax [*zaks*] *n* sax (1).

zeal [*zeel*] *n* fervent and unremitting enthusiasm; fervour, ardour.

zealot [*zelot*] *n* religious fanatic; fanatical supporter.

zealous [*zel*us] *adj* full of zeal; earnest, actively enthusiastic ~ **zealously** *adv* ~ **zealousness** *n*.

zebra [*zeeb*Ra/*zeb*Ra] *n* elegant African quadruped with striped coat; **z. crossing** pedestrian crossing painted with broad white stripes.

zebra-wood [*zeeb*Ra-wood] *n* straight-grained, light-brown, figured timber from South America.

zebrine [*zeeb*RIn/*zeb*RIn] *adj* like the zebra.

zebu [*zeeb*OO] *n* Oriental domestic humped ox.

zed [*zed*] *n* name of letter z.

zedoary [*zed*O-eRi] *n* aromatic medicinal East Indian root.

zee [*zee*] *n* (*US*) name of letter z.

Zeitgeist [ts*Itg*Ist] *n* (*Germ*) cultural trends and taste of a particular period.

zel [*zel*] *n* (*mus*) kind of cymbal.

zeme, zemi [*zee*mi] *n* West Indian fetish or guardian spirit.

Zen [*zen*] *n* a form of Buddhism emphasizing sudden intuitive enlightenment.

zenana [*zenaa*na] *n* the women's apartments in an Indian or Persian house.

Zend [*zend*] *n* ancient Indo-European language related to Old Persian.

Zend-Avesta [zend-a*vesta*] *n* (*orig*) the Zoroastrian scriptures with commentary; sacred writings of the Parsees preserved in the Zend language.

Zener [*zee*ner] *adj* (*tr*) **Z. cards** set of 25 cards each bearing one of five different designs, used in psychical research.

zenith [*zen*ith] *n* (*astron*) point on the celestial sphere directly overhead; (*fig*) highest point (in career *etc*), acme.

zenithal [*zen*ithal] *adj* of or at the zenith > PDG.

zeolite [*zee*-Olit] *n* mineral hydrated silicate of

aluminium and calcium; artificial substance used to soften water by the base-exchange method.

zephyr [*zefer*] *n* light westerly wind; (*poet*) gentle breeze; (*obs*) light woollen fabric; garment made from this.

Zeppelin (*abbr* **Zep**) [*zep*elin] *n* German dirigible airship used during the First World War.

zero (*pl* **zeros**) [*zeer*RO] *n* nought, nothing, nil; the symbol o ('nought'); lowest point; starting point of any scale of measurement; freezing-point of water on Centigrade thermometer; (*meteor*) limited visibility; (*fig*) a cipher, a nonentity; Japanese fighter aircraft; **at z.** (*aer*) below 500ft.; **z. hour** (*mil*) precise moment fixed for attack; (*fig*) moment of crisis.

zest [*zest*] *n* enjoyment, gusto; relish, piquancy.

zestful [*zest*fool] *adj* with great enjoyment.

zeugma [*zewg*ma] *n* (*gramm*) use of one adjective or verb with two nouns when, in fact, it is applicable only to one, not both.

Zeus [*zews*] *n* supreme god of the ancient Greeks.

zibeline [*zibel*In] *n* sable; beaver cloth.

zibet [*zibit*] *n* Asiatic civet-cat.

ziggurat [*zigoo*Rat] *n* pyramidal Sumerian temple with terraced storeys.

zigzag [*zigzag*] *n* line which forms repeated sharp angles or bends in alternate directions; (*archi*) chevron moulding ~ **zigzag** *adj* like a zigzag ~ **zigzag** *adv* by a zigzag course ~ **zigzag** (*pres/part* **zigzagging**, *p/t* and *p/part* **zigzagged**) *v/t* and *i* cause to move in a zigzag direction; move in a zigzag; **z. rule** folding ruler in 6-inch sections pivoted together at each end.

zimmer [*zim*er] *n* (*tr*) metal framework supporting cripples when walking or standing.

zinc [*zink*] *n* hard bluish-white metal, used in alloys and for galvanizing iron > PDS.

zincograph [*zink*OgRaaf] *n* zinc plate for use in engraving; design or print made by zincography.

zincography [zink*og*Rafi] *n* art of engraving and printing from zinc plates.

zing [*zing*] *n* (*coll*) energy, gusto.

zinnia [*zin*i-a] *n* annual plant of aster family with bright composite flowers.

Zion [*zI*-on] *n* hill in Jerusalem; (*fig*) city of Jerusalem; religious system of the Jews; the Christian Church, Christianity; the heavenly Jerusalem, Heaven, Paradise; place of worship, Nonconformist chapel.

Zionism [*zI*-onizm] *n* political and military movement which established the independent Jewish State of Israel ~ **Zionist** *adj* and *n* > PDPol.

zip [*zip*] *n* device for fastening openings in clothes *etc*, consisting of two rows of small teeth that interlock when a Y-shaped frame is pulled up them; whizzing sound; (*coll*) energy vigour ~ **zip** (*pres/part* **zipping**, *p/t* and *p/part* **zipped**) *v/t* and *i* fasten with a zip; whizz; dart, move swiftly.

zip-fastener [zip-*faas*ner] *n* zip.

zipper [*zip*er] *n* zip.

zippy [*zip*i] *adj* (*coll*) lively; energetic.

zircon [zurkon] n (min) crystalline substance of various colours used in imitation gems.

zirconia [zurkOni-a] n (chem) zirconium oxide.

zirconium [zurkOni-um] n (chem) metallic element used in alloys, refractories and paints.

zither [ziTHer] n (mus) stringed instrument laid on the knees or table, and plucked with a plectrum.

zodiac [zOdi-ak] n zone of the heavens (divided into twelve sections or signs) in which lie the paths of the sun, moon and chief planets >PDG.

zodiacal [zOdI-ak'l] adj of or in the zodiac.

zoetrope [zO-itrOp] n device for producing an illusion of movement; stroboscope > PDP.

zoic [zO-ik] adj showing traces of life; (geol) containing fossils.

zollverein [tsolferIn] n a customs union between States agreeing to impose a uniform rate of duties on imports from other countries while preserving free trade among themselves.

zombi, zombie (pl **zombis, zombies**) [zombi] n (W. Indian and African voodoo) corpse revived and controlled by witchcraft or a spirit; supernatural being or force that enters, reanimates and controls a corpse; python god; (coll) one who lives and acts mechanically, without intelligence or enjoyment; one who seems more dead than alive.

zonal [zOnal] adj of or as a zone; marked out into zones ~ **zonally** adv.

zonary [zOneRi] adj (zool) arranged in a band or girdle.

zonate [zOnayt] adj (zool, bot) marked with rings.

zone [zOn] n region, subdivision of an area of land, town etc; area distinguished by specified characteristics; (geog) one of five regions of the earth characterized by major differences of climate > PDG; belt, stripe; (ar) girdle; (math) portion of surface of sphere cut off by two parallel planes ~ **zone** v/t divide into zones; mark with zones; subdivide (town, district, country), to organize distribution of goods, transport, development etc.

zoning [zOning] n designation of areas of a town for various types of development (residential, shopping etc).

zoo-, zo- pref of animals or animal life.

zoo [zOO] n place where wild animals are kept and shown to the public.

zooblast [zO-Oblast] n an animal cell.

zoogamy [zO-ogami] n sexual reproduction in animals.

zoogeography [zO-ojee-ogRafi] n study of the distribution of animals on the earth's surface.

zooid [zO-oid] n (biol) member of a colony of animals which are joined together.

zoological [zO-olojikal/zoolojikal] adj of or for zoology; **z. gardens** place where wild animals are kept and shown, zoo.

zoologist [zO-oloji/zoo-oloji/st] n one who studies zoology.

zoology [zO-oloji/zoo-oloji] n scientific study of animals.

zoom [zOOm] v/t and i move with a loud buzzing noise; (aer) make (aircraft) rise from a level course by sudden upward flight; ascend sharply and steeply; (fig) rise sharply in price ~ **zoom** n sudden upward flight; **z. lens** lens with variable focal length capable of quick alteration between long shots and close-ups.

zoomorphic [zO-omawrfik] adj conceived as having animal shape and represented thus in design etc; with animal motifs.

zoomorphism [zO-omawrfizm] n conception and representation of deities and superhuman beings in the shape of animals.

zoophyte [zO-OfIt] n (zool) animal of plant-like form.

zoospore [zO-Ospawr] n (bot, zool) spore capable of spontaneous movement.

zoot [zOOt] adj (sl) gaudy; very fashionable; **z. suit** (sl) man's suit with long coat and very tight trousers.

zootomy [zO-otomi] n dissection of animals.

zoril [zoRil] n small African animal like the skunk.

Zoroastrian [zoRO-astRi-an] adj of Zoroaster or his religion ~ **Zoroastrian** n follower of Zoroaster; Parsee.

Zoroastrianism [zoRO-astRi-anizm] n religious system taught by Zoroaster and his followers; fire-worship.

Zouave [zOO-aav] n light infantryman belonging to a crack French regiment originally recruited from Algerians and wearing colourful Oriental uniform.

zounds [zowndz] interj (ar) mild oath, shortened form of **by God's wounds**.

Zulu [zOOlOO] n S. African native of the Bantu nation of Natal; their language; angler's artificial fly.

zygo- pref shaped like a yoke; in pairs.

zygoma (pl **zygomata**) [zIgOma/zigOma] n (anat) cheek bone.

zygomorphic [zIgOmawrfik] adj (bot) bilaterally symmetrical > PDB.

zygospore [zIgO-spawr] n (bot) thick-walled resting spore, product of sexual fusion of two similar cells > PDB.

zygote [zIgOt] n (biol) cell formed by union of two gametes; fertilized ovum before it develops further > PDB.

zymase [zImays] n (chem) enzyme present in yeast > PDS.

zymology [zImoloji] n study of fermentation.

zymolysis [zImOlIsis] n (bioch) fermentation produced by an enzyme.

zymotic [zImotik] adj (of diseases) induced by infection and the fermentation of germs.

zymurgy [zImurji] n commercial application of zymology in brewing, distilling, and wine-making.

MORE ABOUT PENGUINS
AND PELICANS

For further information about books available from Penguins please write to Dept EP, Penguin Books Ltd, Harmondsworth, Middlesex UB7 ODA.

In the U.S.A.: For a complete list of books available from Penguins in the United States write to Dept DG, Penguin Books, 299 Murray Hill Parkway, East Rutherford, New Jersey 07073.

In Canada: For a complete list of books available from Penguins in Canada write to Penguin Books Canada Ltd, 2801 John Street, Markham, Ontario L3R 1B4.

In Australia: For a complete list of books available from Penguins in Australia write to the Marketing Department, Penguin Books Australia Ltd, P.O. Box 257, Ringwood, Victoria 3134.

In New Zealand: For a complete list of books available from Penguins in New Zealand write to the Marketing Department, Penguin Books (N.Z.) Ltd, P.O. Box 4019, Auckland 10.

In India: For a complete list of books available from Penguins in India write to Penguin Overseas Ltd, 706 Eros Apartments, 56 Nehru Place, New Delhi 110019.

In the beginning was the Word – preserved in

PENGUIN REFERENCE BOOKS

THE PENGUIN DICTIONARY OF HISTORICAL SLANG

Eric Partridge

abridged by Jacqueline Simpson

This volume has been the standard work on the subject for years – now Penguin have extracted the most valuable parts of it, including all the expressions coined or used before 1914, to make up the present 50,000 entries.

Often wry and flippant, occasionally 'blue', and sometimes uproariously funny, they recapture the rich idiom of English life and language through the ages, recalling the vigour of Elizabethan phrase, the ribald tongue of dockside and pub, the richer coinages of messdeck and barracks, the euphemisms and witticisms of the nineteenth-century drawing room, and the irrepressible wit of errand boys and costermongers.

THE PENGUIN DICTIONARY OF SURNAMES

SECOND EDITION
Basil Cottle

An analysis of British surnames, including the 100 commonest in the United Kingdom, the British Commonwealth and the United States. In this second edition Basil Cottle has added 4,000 new entries, concentrating on the rare and the complicated.

Entries are assigned to the four broad classes of surname, i.e. those based on:

First names: e.g. Jackson, Rhys, McAdam, O'Brien
Localities: e.g. Baldock, Bewley, Kirk, Shaw
Occupations: e.g. Caird, Fuller, Provost, Smith
Nicknames: e.g. Moneypenny, Kellogg, Gotobed, Wellbeloved

Mangled by centuries of mispronunciation, misunderstanding and mis-spelling, the surnames we have inherited are explained here by a philologist with an alert sense of humour.

Many a true word is spoken in . . .

PENGUIN REFERENCE BOOKS

'Penguin Reference books are becoming indispensable; they are easy to travel with and, if they wear out, cheap to replace' – Cyril Connolly in the *Sunday Times*

ROGET'S THESAURUS

New edition completely revised, modernized and abridged by
Robert A. Dutch

'This must surely be the most indispensable publication ever compiled. In its revised form it is even more invaluable' – *John O'London's*

USAGE AND ABUSAGE

Eric Partridge

Language is everybody's business and enters into almost every sphere of human life. This book wittily attacks linguistic abuse of all kinds, and at the same time offers constructive advice on the proper use of English.

THE PENGUIN DICTIONARY OF QUOTATIONS

J. M. and M. J. Cohen

The reader, the writer, the after-dinner speaker, the crossword-solver and the browser will find what they want among the 12,000 or so quotations which include immortal lines from Shakespeare, the Bible or *Paradise Lost* side by side with remarks and stray lines by almost unknown writers.

THE PENGUIN DICTIONARY OF MODERN QUOTATIONS

J. M. and M. J. Cohen

This companion to *The Penguin Dictionary of Quotations* ranges from the wit of the Goon Show to the declarations of statesmen and the most memorable sayings of the famous and infamous.

'Proper words in proper places' – *or not* – *in*

WORDPOWER

AN ILLUSTRATED DICTIONARY OF VITAL WORDS

Edward de Bono

Could you make an *educated guess* at the *downside-risk* of a *marketing strategy*? Are you in the right *ball-game*, and faced with a *crisis* could you find an *ad hoc* solution? Would you recognize a *Catch-22* situation?

These are just a few of the 265 specialized words that Dr de Bono defines here. Most of them are partly familiar, some are borrowed from business, technology and the sciences because of their usefulness. All of them are powerful tools of expression if used precisely; and, with the help of apt cartoons and illustrations, Dr de Bono defines them in terms of their usage so that the reader *can* use them precisely.

So the next time an economic adviser talks about cash-cows, or the local councillor starts a campaign about ecology, you know what to do. Reach for *Wordpower* and add a 'thinking chunk' to your vocabulary.

TANGRAM

THE ANCIENT CHINESE SHAPES GAME

Joost Elffers

Tangram, the 1,000-year-old Chinese puzzle, is an exciting game which stimulates creativity and fantasy and which can be played either by one person or by a group.

The game consists of seven pieces, formed by cutting a square in a certain way, with which you can copy the examples given in the book. This may sound easy enough, but as soon as one starts playing it becomes obvious that Tangram presents a real and pleasurable challenge to one's skill and imagination.

Over 1,600 examples, with solutions.

THE NEW PELICAN GUIDE TO ENGLISH LITERATURE

Edited by Boris Ford

Authoritative, stimulating and accessible, the original seven-volume *Pelican Guide to English Literature* has earned itself a distinguished reputation. Now enlarged to nine titles, this popular series has been wholly revised and updated.

What this work sets out to offer is a guide to the history and traditions of English literature, a contour-map of the literary scene. Each volume includes these standard features:

 (i) An account of the social context of literature in each period.

 (ii) A general survey of the literature itself.

 (iii) A series of critical essays on individual writers and their works – each written by an authority in their field.

 (iv) Full appendices including short author biographies, listings of standard editions of authors' works, critical commentaries and titles for further study and reference.

The *Guide* consists of the following volumes:

A time for such a word? Try

PENGUIN CROSSWORD BOOKS

A fix for the addicts among our readers – a selection of crosswords varying in type and difficulty, guaranteed to have you cross-eyed or cheating for hours on end . . .

THE DAILY TELEGRAPH CROSSWORD BOOKS

There are fourteen of them – and, as an added bonus, *The Daily Telegraph 50th Anniversary Crossword Book.*

THE PENGUIN BOOKS OF SUN CROSSWORDS

Four recollections of puzzles that have the same answers for two sets of clues – 'coffee-time' or 'cryptic', depending on your mood.

THE PENGUIN BOOKS OF TIMES CROSSWORDS

A trilogy from the bottom left-hand corner of the back page.

THE PENGUIN BOOKS OF SUNDAY TELEGRAPH CROSSWORDS

Four more leisurely occupations for those who couldn't get at the paper when it came – or couldn't get the answers.

THE PENGUIN BOOKS OF SUNDAY TIMES CROSSWORDS

Three books that may make you cross, but will certainly teach you some words . .

and

THE EVENING STANDARD JUMBO CROSSWORD BOOK

THE PENGUIN BOOK OF FINANCIAL TIMES CROSSWORDS

THE SUNDAY EXPRESS BOOK OF SKELETON CROSSWORDS